The Dictionary of Art · volume eight

The Dictionary of Art

8

Cossiers

TO

Diotti

GROVE

The Dictionary of Art

edited by JANE TURNER, in thirty-four volumes, 1996

Reprinted with minor corrections, 1998

This edition is distributed within the United Kingdom and Europe
by Macmillan Publishers Limited, London, and within the United States and Canada by
Grove's Dictionaries Inc., New York.

Text keyboarded by Wearset Limited, Sunderland, England
Database management by Pindar plc, York, England
Imagesetting by William Clowes Limited, Suffolk, England
Printed and bound by China Translation and Printing Services Ltd, Hong Kong

British Library Cataloguing in Publication Data

The dictionary of art
  1. Art - Dictionaries 2. Art - History -
    Dictionaries
I. Turner, Jane
703

ISBN 1-884446-00-0

Library of Congress Cataloging in Publication Data

The dictionary of art / editor, Jane Turner.
  p. cm.
  Includes bibliographical references and index.
  Contents: 1. A to Anckerman
  ISBN 1-884446-00-0 (alk. paper)
  1. Art—Encyclopedias.
  I. Turner, Jane, 1956–
N31.D5 1996   96–13628
703—dc20   CIP

Contents

General Abbreviations

The abbreviations employed throughout this dictionary, most of which are listed below, do not vary, except for capitalization, regardless of the context in which they are used, including bibliographical citations and for locations of works of art. The principle used to arrive at these abbreviations is that their full form should be easily deducible, and for this reason acronyms have generally been avoided (e.g. Los Angeles Co. Mus. A. instead of LACMA). The same abbreviation is adopted for cognate forms in foreign languages and in most cases for plural and adjectival forms (e.g. A.= Art, Arts, Arte, Arti etc). Not all related forms are listed below. Occasionally, if a name, for instance of an artists' group or exhibiting society, is repeated within the text of one article, it is cited in an abbreviated form after its first mention in full (e.g. The Pre-Raphaelite Brotherhood (PRB) was founded...); the same is true of archaeological periods and eras, which are abbreviated to initial letters in small capitals (e.g. In the Early Minoan (EM) period...). Such abbreviations do not appear in this list. For the reader's convenience, separate full lists of abbreviations for locations, periodical titles and standard reference books and series are included as Appendices A–C in vol. 33.

A.	Art, Arts	Anthropol.	Anthropology	Azerbaij.	Azerbaijani
A.C.	Arts Council	Antiqua.	Antiquarian, Antiquaries	B.	Bartsch [catalogue of Old Master prints]
Acad.	Academy	app.	appendix		
AD	Anno Domini	approx.	approximately	b	born
Add.	Additional, Addendum	AR	Arkansas (USA)	BA	Bachelor of Arts
addn	addition	ARA	Associate of the Royal Academy	Balt.	Baltic
Admin.	Administration			bapt	baptized
Adv.	Advances, Advanced	Arab.	Arabic	BArch	Bachelor of Architecture
Aesth.	Aesthetic(s)	Archaeol.	Archaeology	Bart	Baronet
Afr.	African	Archit.	Architecture, Architectural	Bask.	Basketry
Afrik.	Afrikaans, Afrikaner	Archv, Archvs	Archive(s)	BBC	British Broadcasting Corporation
A.G.	Art Gallery	Arg.	Argentine	BC	Before Christ
Agrar.	Agrarian	ARHA	Associate of the Royal Hibernian Academy	BC	British Columbia (Canada)
Agric.	Agriculture			BE	Buddhist era
Agron.	Agronomy	ARIBA	Associate of the Royal Institute of British Architects	Beds	Bedfordshire (GB)
Agy	Agency			Behav.	Behavioural
AH	Anno Hegirae	Armen.	Armenian	Belarus.	Belarusian
A. Inst.	Art Institute	ARSA	Associate of the Royal Scottish Academy	Belg.	Belgian
AK	Alaska (USA)			Berks	Berkshire (GB)
AL	Alabama (USA)	Asiat.	Asiatic	Berwicks	Berwickshire (GB; old)
Alb.	Albanian	Assist.	Assistance	BFA	Bachelor of Fine Arts
Alg.	Algerian	Assoc.	Association	Bibl.	Bible, Biblical
Alta	Alberta (Canada)	Astron.	Astronomy	Bibliog.	Bibliography, Bibliographical
Altern.	Alternative	AT&T	American Telephone & Telegraph Company	Biblioph.	Bibliophile
a.m.	ante meridiem [before noon]			Biog.	Biography, Biographical
Amat.	Amateur	attrib.	attribution, attributed to	Biol.	Biology, Biological
Amer.	American	Aug	August	bk, bks	book(s)
An.	Annals	Aust.	Austrian	Bkbinder	Bookbinder
Anatol.	Anatolian	Austral.	Australian	Bklore	Booklore
Anc.	Ancient	Auth.	Author(s)	Bkshop	Bookshop
Annu.	Annual	Auton.	Autonomous	BL	British Library
Anon.	Anonymous(ly)	Aux.	Auxiliary	Bld	Build
Ant.	Antique	Ave.	Avenue	Bldg	Building
Anthol.	Anthology	AZ	Arizona (USA)		

Bldr	Builder
BLitt	Bachelor of Letters/Literature
BM	British Museum
Boh.	Bohemian
Boliv.	Bolivian
Botan.	Botany, Botanical
BP	Before present (1950)
Braz.	Brazilian
BRD	Bundesrepublik Deutschland [Federal Republic of Germany (West Germany)]
Brecons	Breconshire (GB; old)
Brez.	Brezonek [lang. of Brittany]
Brit.	British
Bros	Brothers
BSc	Bachelor of Science
Bucks	Buckinghamshire (GB)
Bulg.	Bulgarian
Bull.	Bulletin
bur	buried
Burm.	Burmese
Byz.	Byzantine
C	Celsius
C.	Century
c.	*circa* [about]
CA	California
Cab.	Cabinet
Caerns	Caernarvonshire (GB; old)
C.A.G.	City Art Gallery
Cal.	Calendar
Callig.	Calligraphy
Cam.	Camera
Cambs	Cambridgeshire (GB)
can	canonized
Can.	Canadian
Cant.	Canton(s), Cantonal
Capt.	Captain
Cards	Cardiganshire (GB; old)
Carib.	Caribbean
Carms	Carmarthenshire (GB; old)
Cartog.	Cartography
Cat.	Catalan
cat.	catalogue
Cath.	Catholic
CBE	Commander of the Order of the British Empire
Celeb.	Celebration
Celt.	Celtic
Cent.	Centre, Central
Centen.	Centennial
Cer.	Ceramic
cf.	confer [compare]
Chap., Chaps	Chapter(s)
Chem.	Chemistry
Ches	Cheshire (GB)
Chil.	Chilean

Chin.	Chinese
Christ.	Christian, Christianity
Chron.	Chronicle
Cie	Compagnie [French]
Cinema.	Cinematography
Circ.	Circle
Civ.	Civil, Civic
Civiliz.	Civilization(s)
Class.	Classic, Classical
Clin.	Clinical
CO	Colorado (USA)
Co.	Company; County
Cod.	Codex, Codices
Col., Cols	Collection(s); Column(s)
Coll.	College
collab.	in collaboration with, collaborated, collaborative
Collct.	Collecting
Colloq.	Colloquies
Colomb.	Colombian
Colon.	Colonies, Colonial
Colr	Collector
Comm.	Commission; Community
Commerc.	Commercial
Communic.	Communications
Comp.	Comparative; compiled by, compiler
Concent.	Concentration
Concr.	Concrete
Confed.	Confederation
Confer.	Conference
Congol.	Congolese
Congr.	Congress
Conserv.	Conservation; Conservatory
Constr.	Construction(al)
cont.	continued
Contemp.	Contemporary
Contrib.	Contributions, Contributor(s)
Convalesc.	Convalescence
Convent.	Convention
Coop.	Cooperation
Coord.	Coordination
Copt.	Coptic
Corp.	Corporation, Corpus
Corr.	Correspondence
Cors.	Corsican
Cost.	Costume
Cret.	Cretan
Crim.	Criminal
Crit.	Critical, Criticism
Croat.	Croatian
CT	Connecticut (USA)
Cttee	Committee
Cub.	Cuban
Cult.	Cultural, Culture
Cumb.	Cumberland (GB; old)

Cur.	Curator, Curatorial, Curatorship
Curr.	Current(s)
CVO	Commander of the [Royal] Victorian Order
Cyclad.	Cycladic
Cyp.	Cypriot
Czech.	Czechoslovak
$	dollars
d	died
d.	denarius, denarii [penny, pence]
Dalmat.	Dalmatian
Dan.	Danish
DBE	Dame Commander of the Order of the British Empire
DC	District of Columbia (USA)
DDR	Deutsche Demokratische Republik [German Democratic Republic (East Germany)]
DE	Delaware (USA)
Dec	December
Dec.	Decorative
ded.	dedication, dedicated to
Democ.	Democracy, Democratic
Demog.	Demography, Demographic
Denbs	Denbighshire (GB; old)
dep.	deposited at
Dept	Department
Dept.	Departmental, Departments
Derbys	Derbyshire (GB)
Des.	Design
destr.	destroyed
Dev.	Development
Devon	Devonshire (GB)
Dial.	Dialogue
diam.	diameter
Diff.	Diffusion
Dig.	Digest
Dip. Eng.	Diploma in Engineering
Dir.	Direction, Directed
Directrt	Directorate
Disc.	Discussion
diss.	dissertation
Distr.	District
Div.	Division
DLitt	Doctor of Letters/Literature
DM	Deutsche Mark
Doc.	Document(s)
Doss.	Dossier
DPhil	Doctor of Philosophy
Dr	Doctor
Drg, Drgs	Drawing(s)
DSc	Doctor of Science/Historical Sciences
Dut.	Dutch
Dwell.	Dwelling
E.	East(ern)

EC	European (Economic) Community
Eccles.	Ecclesiastical
Econ.	Economic, Economies
Ecuad.	Ecuadorean
ed.	editor, edited (by)
edn	edition
eds	editors
Educ.	Education
e.g.	*exempli gratia* [for example]
Egyp.	Egyptian
Elem.	Element(s), Elementary
Emp.	Empirical
Emul.	Emulation
Enc.	Encyclopedia
Encour.	Encouragement
Eng.	English
Engin.	Engineer, Engineering
Engr., Engrs	Engraving(s)
Envmt	Environment
Epig.	Epigraphy
Episc.	Episcopal
Esp.	Especially
Ess.	Essays
est.	established
etc	*etcetera* [and so on]
Ethnog.	Ethnography
Ethnol.	Ethnology
Etrus.	Etruscan
Eur.	European
Evangel.	Evangelical
Exam.	Examination
Excav.	Excavation, Excavated
Exch.	Exchange
Excurs.	Excursion
exh.	exhibition
Exp.	Exposition
Expermntl	Experimental
Explor.	Exploration
Expn	Expansion
Ext.	External
Extn	Extension
f, ff	following page, following pages
F.A.	Fine Art(s)
Fac.	Faculty
facs.	facsimile
Fam.	Family
fasc.	fascicle
fd	feastday (of a saint)
Feb	February
Fed.	Federation, Federal
Fem.	Feminist
Fest.	Festival
fig.	figure (illustration)
Fig.	Figurative
figs	figures
Filip.	Filipina(s), Filipino(s)
Fin.	Finnish
FL	Florida (USA)
fl	*floruit* [he/she flourished]
Flem.	Flemish
Flints	Flintshire (GB; old)
Flk	Folk
Flklore	Folklore
fol., fols	folio(s)
Found.	Foundation
Fr.	French
frag.	fragment
Fri.	Friday
FRIBA	Fellow of the Royal Institute of British Architects
FRS	Fellow of the Royal Society, London
ft	foot, feet
Furn.	Furniture
Futur.	Futurist, Futurism
g	gram(s)
GA	Georgia (USA)
Gael.	Gaelic
Gal., Gals	Gallery, Galleries
Gaz.	Gazette
GB	Great Britain
Gdn, Gdns	Garden(s)
Gdnr(s)	Gardener(s)
Gen.	General
Geneal.	Genealogy, Genealogist
Gent.	Gentleman, Gentlemen
Geog.	Geography
Geol.	Geology
Geom.	Geometry
Georg.	Georgian
Geosci.	Geoscience
Ger.	German, Germanic
G.I.	Government/General Issue (USA)
Glams	Glamorganshire (GB; old)
Glos	Gloucestershire (GB)
Govt	Government
Gr.	Greek
Grad.	Graduate
Graph.	Graphic
Green.	Greenlandic
Gr.-Roman	Greco-Roman
Gt	Great
Gtr	Greater
Guat.	Guatemalan
Gym.	Gymnasium
h.	height
ha	hectare
Hait.	Haitian
Hants	Hampshire (GB)
Hb.	Handbook
Heb.	Hebrew
Hell.	Hellenic
Her.	Heritage
Herald.	Heraldry, Heraldic
Hereford & Worcs	Hereford & Worcester (GB)
Herts	Hertfordshire (GB)
HI	Hawaii (USA)
Hib.	Hibernia
Hisp.	Hispanic
Hist.	History, Historical
HMS	His/Her Majesty's Ship
Hon.	Honorary, Honourable
Horiz.	Horizon
Hort.	Horticulture
Hosp.	Hospital(s)
HRH	His/Her Royal Highness
Human.	Humanities, Humanism
Hung.	Hungarian
Hunts	Huntingdonshire (GB; old)
IA	Iowa
ibid.	*ibidem* [in the same place]
ICA	Institute of Contemporary Arts
Ice.	Icelandic
Iconog.	Iconography
Iconol.	Iconology
ID	Idaho (USA)
i.e.	*id est* [that is]
IL	Illinois (USA)
Illum.	Illumination
illus.	illustrated, illustration
Imp.	Imperial
IN	Indiana (USA)
in., ins	inch(es)
Inc.	Incorporated
inc.	incomplete
incl.	includes, including, inclusive
Incorp.	Incorporation
Ind.	Indian
Indep.	Independent
Indig.	Indigenous
Indol.	Indology
Indon.	Indonesian
Indust.	Industrial
Inf.	Information
Inq.	Inquiry
Inscr.	Inscribed, Inscription
Inst.	Institute(s)
Inst. A.	Institute of Art
Instr.	Instrument, Instrumental
Int.	International
Intell.	Intelligence
Inter.	Interior(s), Internal
Interdiscip.	Interdisciplinary
intro.	introduced by, introduction
inv.	inventory

Inven.	Invention
Invest.	Investigation(s)
Iran.	Iranian
irreg.	irregular(ly)
Islam.	Islamic
Isr.	Israeli
It.	Italian
J.	Journal
Jam.	Jamaican
Jan	January
Jap.	Japanese
Jav.	Javanese
Jew.	Jewish
Jewel.	Jewellery
Jord.	Jordanian
jr	junior
Juris.	Jurisdiction
KBE	Knight Commander of the Order of the British Empire
KCVO	Knight Commander of the Royal Victorian Order
kg	kilogram(s)
kHz	kilohertz
km	kilometre(s)
Knowl.	Knowledge
Kor.	Korean
KS	Kansas (USA)
KY	Kentucky (USA)
Kyrgyz.	Kyrgyzstani
£	libra, librae [pound, pounds sterling]
l.	length
LA	Louisiana (USA)
Lab.	Laboratory
Lancs	Lancashire (GB)
Lang.	Language(s)
Lat.	Latin
Latv.	Latvian
lb, lbs	pound(s) weight
Leb.	Lebanese
Lect.	Lecture
Legis.	Legislative
Leics	Leicestershire (GB)
Lex.	Lexicon
Lg.	Large
Lib., Libs	Library, Libraries
Liber.	Liberian
Libsp	Librarianship
Lincs	Lincolnshire (GB)
Lit.	Literature
Lith.	Lithuanian
Liturg.	Liturgical
LLB	Bachelor of Laws
LLD	Doctor of Laws
Lt	Lieutenant
Lt-Col.	Lieutenant-Colonel
Ltd	Limited

m	metre(s)
m.	married
M.	Monsieur
MA	Master of Arts; Massachusetts (USA)
Mag.	Magazine
Maint.	Maintenance
Malay.	Malaysian
Man.	Manitoba (Canada); Manual
Manuf.	Manufactures
Mar.	Marine, Maritime
Mason.	Masonic
Mat.	Material(s)
Math.	Mathematic
MBE	Member of the Order of the British Empire
MD	Doctor of Medicine; Maryland (USA)
ME	Maine (USA)
Mech.	Mechanical
Med.	Medieval; Medium, Media
Medic.	Medical, Medicine
Medit.	Mediterranean
Mem.	Memorial(s); Memoir(s)
Merions	Merionethshire (GB; old)
Meso-Amer.	Meso-American
Mesop.	Mesopotamian
Met.	Metropolitan
Metal.	Metallurgy
Mex.	Mexican
MFA	Master of Fine Arts
mg	milligram(s)
Mgmt	Management
Mgr	Monsignor
MI	Michigan
Micrones.	Micronesian
Mid. Amer.	Middle American
Middx	Middlesex (GB; old)
Mid. E.	Middle Eastern
Mid. Eng.	Middle English
Mid Glam.	Mid Glamorgan (GB)
Mil.	Military
Mill.	Millennium
Min.	Ministry; Minutes
Misc.	Miscellaneous
Miss.	Mission(s)
Mlle	Mademoiselle
mm	millimetre(s)
Mme	Madame
MN	Minnesota
Mnmt, Mnmts	Monument(s)
Mnmtl	Monumental
MO	Missouri (USA)
Mod.	Modern, Modernist
Moldav.	Moldavian

Moldov.	Moldovan
MOMA	Museum of Modern Art
Mon.	Monday
Mongol.	Mongolian
Mons	Monmouthshire (GB; old)
Montgoms	Montgomeryshire (GB; old)
Mor.	Moral
Morav.	Moravian
Moroc.	Moroccan
Movt	Movement
MP	Member of Parliament
MPhil	Master of Philosophy
MS	Mississippi (USA)
MS., MSS	manuscript(s)
MSc	Master of Science
MT	Montana (USA)
Mt	Mount
Mthly	Monthly
Mun.	Municipal
Mus.	Museum(s)
Mus. A.	Museum of Art
Mus. F.A.	Museum of Fine Art(s)
Music.	Musicology
N.	North(ern); National
n	refractive index of a medium
n.	note
N.A.G.	National Art Gallery
Nat.	Natural, Nature
Naut.	Nautical
NB	New Brunswick (Canada)
NC	North Carolina (USA)
ND	North Dakota (USA)
n.d.	no date
NE	Nebraska; Northeast(ern)
Neth.	Netherlandish
Newslett.	Newsletter
Nfld	Newfoundland (Canada)
N.G.	National Gallery
N.G.A.	National Gallery of Art
NH	New Hampshire (USA)
Niger.	Nigerian
NJ	New Jersey (USA)
NM	New Mexico (USA)
nm	nanometre (10^{-9} metre)
nn.	notes
no., nos	number(s)
Nord.	Nordic
Norm.	Normal
Northants	Northamptonshire (GB)
Northumb.	Northumberland (GB)
Norw.	Norwegian
Notts	Nottinghamshire (GB)
Nov	November
n.p.	no place (of publication)
N.P.G.	National Portrait Gallery
nr	near

Nr E.	Near Eastern	Per.	Period	Ptg(s)	Painting(s)
NS	New Style; Nova Scotia (Canada)	Percep.	Perceptions	Pub.	Public
		Perf.	Performance, Performing, Performed	pubd	published
n. s.	new series			Publ.	Publicity
NSW	New South Wales (Australia)	Period.	Periodical(s)	pubn(s)	publication(s)
NT	National Trust	Pers.	Persian	PVA	polyvinyl acetate
Ntbk	Notebook	Persp.	Perspectives	PVC	polyvinyl chloride
Numi.	Numismatic(s)	Peru.	Peruvian	Q.	quarterly
NV	Nevada (USA)	PhD	Doctor of Philosophy	4to	quarto
NW	Northwest(ern)	Philol.	Philology	Qué.	Québec (Canada)
NWT	Northwest Territories (Canada)	Philos.	Philosophy	*R*	reprint
		Phoen.	Phoenician	*r*	*recto*
NY	New York (USA)	Phot.	Photograph, Photography, Photographic	RA	Royal Academician
NZ	New Zealand			Radnors	Radnorshire (GB; old)
OBE	Officer of the Order of the British Empire	Phys.	Physician(s), Physics, Physique, Physical	RAF	Royal Air Force
				Rec.	Record(s)
Obj.	Object(s), Objective	Physiog.	Physiognomy	red.	reduction, reduced for
Occas.	Occasional	Physiol.	Physiology	Ref.	Reference
Occident.	Occidental	Pict.	Picture(s), Pictorial	Refurb.	Refurbishment
Ocean.	Oceania	pl.	plate; plural	*reg*	*regit* [ruled]
Oct	October	Plan.	Planning	Reg.	Regional
8vo	octavo	Planet.	Planetarium	Relig.	Religion, Religious
OFM	Order of Friars Minor	Plast.	Plastic	remod.	remodelled
OH	Ohio (USA)	pls	plates	Ren.	Renaissance
OK	Oklahoma (USA)	p.m.	post meridiem [after noon]	Rep.	Report(s)
Olymp.	Olympic	Polit.	Political	repr.	reprint(ed); reproduced, reproduction
OM	Order of Merit	Poly.	Polytechnic		
Ont.	Ontario (Canada)	Polynes.	Polynesian	Represent.	Representation, Representative
op.	opus	Pop.	Popular	Res.	Research
opp.	opposite; opera [pl. of opus]	Port.	Portuguese	rest.	restored, restoration
OR	Oregon (USA)	Port.	Portfolio	Retro.	Retrospective
Org.	Organization	Posth.	Posthumous(ly)	rev.	revision, revised (by/for)
Orient.	Oriental	Pott.	Pottery	Rev.	Reverend; Review
Orthdx	Orthodox	POW	prisoner of war	RHA	Royal Hibernian Academician
OSB	Order of St Benedict	PRA	President of the Royal Academy	RI	Rhode Island (USA)
Ott.	Ottoman			RIBA	Royal Institute of British Architects
Oxon	Oxfordshire (GB)	Pract.	Practical		
oz.	ounce(s)	Prefect.	Prefecture, Prefectural	RJ	Rio de Janeiro State
p	pence	Preserv.	Preservation	Rlwy	Railway
p., pp.	page(s)	prev.	previous(ly)	RSA	Royal Scottish Academy
PA	Pennsylvania (USA)	priv.	private	RSFSR	Russian Soviet Federated Socialist Republic
p.a.	per annum	PRO	Public Record Office		
Pak.	Pakistani	Prob.	Problem(s)	Rt Hon.	Right Honourable
Palaeontol.	Palaeontology, Palaeontological	Proc.	Proceedings	Rur.	Rural
		Prod.	Production	Rus.	Russian
Palest.	Palestinian	Prog.	Progress	S	San, Santa, Santo, Sant', São [Saint]
Pap.	Paper(s)	Proj.	Project(s)		
para.	paragraph	Promot.	Promotion	S.	South(ern)
Parag.	Paraguayan	Prop.	Property, Properties	s.	solidus, solidi [shilling(s)]
Parl.	Parliament	Prov.	Province(s), Provincial	Sask.	Saskatchewan (Canada)
Paroch.	Parochial	Proven.	Provenance	Sat.	Saturday
Patriarch.	Patriarchate	Prt, Prts	Print(s)	SC	South Carolina (USA)
Patriot.	Patriotic	Prtg	Printing	Scand.	Scandinavian
Patrm.	Patrimony	pseud.	pseudonym	Sch.	School
Pav.	Pavilion	Psych.	Psychiatry, Psychiatric	Sci.	Science(s), Scientific
PEI	Prince Edward Island (Canada)	Psychol.	Psychology, Psychological	Scot.	Scottish
Pembs	Pembrokeshire (GB; old)	pt	part	Sculp.	Sculpture

SD	South Dakota (USA)	suppl., suppls	supplement(s), supplementary	Urb.	Urban
SE	Southeast(ern)	Surv.	Survey	Urug.	Uruguayan
Sect.	Section	SW	Southwest(ern)	US	United States
Sel.	Selected	Swed.	Swedish	USA	United States of America
Semin.	Seminar(s), Seminary	Swi.	Swiss	USSR	Union of Soviet Socialist Republics
Semiot.	Semiotic	Symp.	Symposium		
Semit.	Semitic	Syr.	Syrian	UT	Utah
Sept	September	Tap.	Tapestry	*v*	*verso*
Ser.	Series	Tas.	Tasmanian	VA	Virginia (USA)
Serb.	Serbian	Tech.	Technical, Technique	V&A	Victoria and Albert Museum
Serv.	Service(s)	Technol.	Technology	Var.	Various
Sess.	Session, Sessional	Territ.	Territory	Venez.	Venezuelan
Settmt(s)	Settlement(s)	Theat.	Theatre	Vern.	Vernacular
S. Glam.	South Glamorgan (GB)	Theol.	Theology, Theological	Vict.	Victorian
Siber.	Siberian	Theor.	Theory, Theoretical	Vid.	Video
Sig.	Signature	Thurs.	Thursday	Viet.	Vietnamese
Sil.	Silesian	Tib.	Tibetan	viz.	*videlicet* [namely]
Sin.	Singhala	TN	Tennessee (USA)	vol., vols	volume(s)
sing.	singular	Top.	Topography	vs.	versus
SJ	Societas Jesu [Society of Jesus]	Trad.	Tradition(s), Traditional	VT	Vermont (USA)
Skt	Sanskrit	trans.	translation, translated by; transactions	Vulg.	Vulgarisation
Slav.	Slavic, Slavonic			W.	West(ern)
Slov.	Slovene, Slovenian	Transafr.	Transafrican	w.	width
Soc.	Society	Transatlant.	Transatlantic	WA	Washington (USA)
Social.	Socialism, Socialist	Transcarpath.	Transcarpathian	Warwicks	Warwickshire (GB)
Sociol.	Sociology	transcr.	transcribed by/for	Wed.	Wednesday
Sov.	Soviet	Triq.	Triquarterly	W. Glam.	West Glamorgan (GB)
SP	São Paulo State	Tropic.	Tropical	WI	Wisconsin (USA)
Sp.	Spanish	Tues.	Tuesday	Wilts	Wiltshire (GB)
sq.	square	Turk.	Turkish	Wkly	Weekly
sr	senior	Turkmen.	Turkmenistani	W. Midlands	West Midlands (GB)
Sri L.	Sri Lankan	TV	Television		
SS	Saints, Santi, Santissima, Santissimo, Santissimi; Steam ship	TX	Texas (USA)	Worcs	Worcestershire (GB; old)
		U.	University	Wtrcol.	Watercolour
		UK	United Kingdom of Great Britain and Northern Ireland	WV	West Virginia (USA)
SSR	Soviet Socialist Republic			WY	Wyoming (USA)
St	Saint, Sankt, Sint, Szent	Ukrain.	Ukrainian	Yb., Y.-b.	Yearbook, Year-book
Staffs	Staffordshire (GB)	Un.	Union	Yem.	Yemeni
Ste	Sainte	Underwtr	Underwater	Yorks	Yorkshire (GB; old)
Stud.	Study, Studies	UNESCO	United Nations Educational, Scientific and Cultural Organization	Yug.	Yugoslavian
Subalp.	Subalpine			Zamb.	Zambian
Sum.	Sumerian			Zimb.	Zimbabwean
Sun.	Sunday	Univl	Universal		
Sup.	Superior	unpubd	unpublished		

A Note on the Use of the Dictionary

This note is intended as a short guide to the basic editorial conventions adopted in this dictionary. For a fuller explanation, please refer to the Introduction, vol. 1, pp. xiii–xx.

Abbreviations in general use in the dictionary are listed on pp. vi–xi; those used in bibliographies and for locations of works of art or exhibition venues are listed in the Appendices in vol. 33.

Alphabetization of headings, which are distinguished in bold typeface, is letter by letter up to the first comma (ignoring spaces, hyphens, accents and any parenthesized or bracketed matter); the same principle applies thereafter. Abbreviations of 'Saint' and its foreign equivalents are alphabetized as if spelt out, and headings with the prefix 'Mc' appear under 'Mac'.

Authors' signatures appear at the end of the article or sequence of articles that the authors have contributed; in multipartite articles, any section that is unsigned is by the author of the next signed section. Where the article was compiled by the editors or in the few cases where an author has wished to remain anonymous, this is indicated by a square box (□) instead of a signature.

Bibliographies are arranged chronologically (within section, where divided) by order of year of first publication and, within years, alphabetically by authors' names. Abbreviations have been used for some standard reference books; these are cited in full in Appendix C in vol. 33, as are abbreviations of periodical titles (Appendix B). Abbreviated references to alphabetically arranged dictionaries and encyclopedias appear at the beginning of the bibliography (or section).

Biographical dates when cited in parentheses in running text at the first mention of a personal name indicate that the individual does not have an entry in the dictionary. The presence of parenthesized regnal dates for rulers and popes, however, does not necessarily indicate the lack of a biography of that person. Where no dates are provided for an artist or patron, the reader may assume that there is a biography of that individual in the dictionary (or, more rarely, that the person is so obscure that dates are not readily available).

Cross-references are distinguished by the use of small capital letters, with a large capital to indicate the initial letter of the entry to which the reader is directed; for example, 'He commissioned Leonardo da Vinci . . .' means that the entry is alphabetized under 'L'.

C

[continued]

Cossiers, Jan (*b* Antwerp, 15 July 1600; *d* Antwerp, 4 July 1671). Flemish painter and draughtsman. After serving an apprenticeship with his father, Anton Cossiers (*fl* 1604– *c.* 1646), and then with Cornelis de Vos, he went first to Aix-en-Provence, where he stayed with the painter Abraham de Vries (1590–1650/62), and then to Rome, where he is mentioned in October 1624. By 1626 he had returned to Aix and had contact with, among others, Nicolas-Claude Fabri de Peiresc, the famous humanist, who recommended him to Rubens. By November 1627 Cossiers had settled back in Antwerp. The following year he became a master in the Guild of St Luke, and in 1630 he married for the first time; he married a second time in 1640.

Cossiers's earliest works, which are difficult to date more precisely than the 1630s, consist of genre scenes, mostly life-size representations of fortune-tellers, gypsies, smokers and the like (e.g. *The Fortune-teller*, Valenciennes, Mus. B.-A.). In the choice of subject-matter and the unusual use of chiaroscuro, these works are related to similar paintings by the Utrecht, Antwerp and Roman Caravaggisti, but Cossiers had a freer style.

Although Peiresc wrote to Cossiers's teacher de Vries in 1629, saying that Rubens had considered taking Cossiers along to Spain as a journeyman, apparently this never happened. Rubens did, however, involve Cossiers in the execution of the various large series of paintings he was commissioned to make in the 1630s. Thus in 1635 Cossiers contributed to the decorations for the Triumphal Entry into Antwerp of Cardinal-Infante Ferdinand, and between 1636 and 1638 he painted a number of the mythological scenes designed by Rubens for Philip IV's hunting-lodge, the Torre de la Parada near Madrid. For this cycle Cossiers painted the following compositions after designs by Rubens: *Jupiter and Lycaon* and *Narcissus* (both Madrid, Prado), as well as *Deucalion and Pyrrha*, *Polyphemus* and the *Death of Hyacinthus* (all untraced).

After Rubens's death in 1640, Cossiers executed numerous history pieces with religious themes for churches in the southern Netherlands as well as for the open market in Antwerp. Among his most important commissions outside Antwerp were the *Adoration of the Shepherds* for the former 'secret' church of the Amsterdam Jesuits, De Krÿlberg (The Chalk Hill) (1657; now Minneapolis, MN, Inst. A.), and the enormous *Passion* series (1655–6) for the choir of the Béguinage church in Mechelen. In his later work, especially after *c.* 1650, religious themes predominate, mainly those related to the Counter-Reformation. Through such commissions, Cossiers became one of Antwerp's most prominent artists during the second half of the 17th century. Stylistically, the later works are characterized by an even freer application of paint and the use of rather subdued colour, qualities apparently quite unusual among contemporary Antwerp painters. Cossiers's compositions are striking, moreover, for the emphatic rendering of pathos, both in the figures' exaggerated

Jan Cossiers: *The Artist's Son, Guilliellemus*, red and black chalk with touches of white chalk, 268×183 mm, ?1658 (New York, Pierpont Morgan Library)

emotional expressions and their lively gestures. Little is known about Cossiers's workshop practice. He must nevertheless have been a fluent and accomplished draughtsman, as can be seen, for instance, in the drawn portraits of his children, striking and sensitive characterizations that reveal sharp psychological insight (e.g. *The Artist's Son, Guilliellemus*, New York, Pierpont Morgan Lib.; see fig.).

BIBLIOGRAPHY

Thieme–Becker

M. L. Hairs: *Dans le sillage de Rubens: Les Peintres d'histoire anversois au XVIIe siècle* (Liège, 1977), pp. 31–2

B. Nicolson: *The International Caravaggesque Movement* (Oxford, 1979), pp. 43–4

J. Stoffels: *Jan Cossiers (c. 1600–1671): Een monografische benadering* (thesis, Ghent, Rijksuniv., 1986)

The Age of Rubens (exh. cat., ed. P. C. Sutton; Boston, MA, Mus. F.A.; Toledo, OH, Mus. A.; 1993–4), pp. 402–5

Flemish Drawings in the Age of Rubens (exh. cat. by A.-M. Logan, Wellesley Coll., MA, Davis Mus. & Cult. Cent., 1993–4), pp. 138–9

HANS VLIEGHE

Cossington Smith, Grace (*b* Sydney, 22 April 1892; *d* 1984). Australian painter. From 1910 to 1912 she attended drawing classes at the studio of the Australian painter Anthony Dattilo Rubbo (1871–1955) in Sydney. Early in 1912 she travelled to England, where she attended drawing classes at Winchester School of Art, returning to Sydney in 1914. She then worked again at Rubbo's studio and began to paint. Cossington Smith was quick to absorb the principles of Post-Impressionism, which she learnt from Rubbo. In 1915 she exhibited the *Sock Knitter* (1915; Sydney, A.G. NSW), the first fully Post-Impressionist work to be exhibited in Australia, at the Royal Art Society of New South Wales annual show. She continued to attend Rubbo's studio until 1926 and *c.* 1920 her painting became darker as she concentrated on tone and perspective. In 1925 she returned to colour and modernism in her painting and associated with Roy de Maistre and Roland Wakelin after their return from Europe. She also exhibited with the Contemporary Group, founded by George W. Lambert and the Australian painter Thea Proctor (1879–1966) in 1926, and so was at the centre of modernism in Australia. In 1928 she had her first one-woman show at the Grosvenor Galleries in Sydney, marking the beginning of her public recognition.

Throughout the 1930s and 1940s Cossington Smith devoted herself mainly to landscape and still-lifes, again under the influence of Post-Impressionism, as shown in *Wildflowers in Jug* (1936; Sydney, A.G. NSW). After the 1950s she concentrated increasingly on interiors, as well as still-lifes, using lighter, larger brushstrokes in a manner reminiscent of Bonnard, as in *Interior in Yellow* (1962–4; Canberra, N.G.). It was only in the 1960s that her reputation as a pioneer Australian modernist was acknowledged.

BIBLIOGRAPHY

B. Smith: *Australian Painting, 1788–1970* (Melbourne, 1971)

Grace Cossington Smith (exh. cat. by D. Thomas, Sydney, A.G. NSW, 1973)

Cossio, Pancho [Francisco] **Gutierrez** (*b* Pinar del Río, Cuba, 20 Oct 1884; *d* Alicante, 16 Jan 1970). Spanish painter of Cuban birth. He was self-taught and began to draw as a child, copying illustrations from magazines. In 1914, when he was already in Madrid, he attended the studio of the Valencian painter Cecilio Plá (1860–1934), where he took his first steps towards mastering colour and painting technique and used impasto to execute a wide variety of experimental works. In 1920 he moved to Santander, where he had previously lived, which affected him because of its people and seaside position. Among the few surviving works up to the time of his first one-man exhibition in 1921 (Santander, Ateneo), the human figure predominated; these included scenes of villagers and seamen (e.g. *Cantabria, People of the Land*, 1919; Santander, Mus. Mun. B.A.), which he executed with great sobriety of gesture and intense colour, and other paintings in which traditional and avant-garde elements are harmoniously blended, such as *Bullfighter* (1920; Santander, Mus. Mun. B.A.) and *Small Fishing Boats* (1921; Santander, Mus. Mun. B.A.).

Encouraged by the poet Gerardo Diego and the sculptor Daniel Alegre (1887–1944), Cossio moved in 1923 to Paris, where he received favourable notices for nudes shown at the Salon des Indépendants in 1923 and 1924. He became a close friend of Georges Braque, whom he met in 1925, and in 1926 met Christian Zervos, subsequently contributing to his review *Cahiers d'art*. During his stay in Paris until 1932, when he returned to Santander, he developed his characteristic mature themes of the sea, still-lifes (e.g. *Gloves*, 1929; Madrid, Mus. A. Contemp.) and portraits in a curvilinear post-Cubist style, uniting colour and subject-matter as interdependent elements. From 1932 to 1940 he abandoned all artistic activity, marginalized (like other avant-garde artists) because of the Spanish Civil War (1936–9), devoting himself to politics and football. When he began painting again in 1940, he returned to the concerns of his Parisian period in such works as *The Melon* (1941; Buenos Aires, Mus. N. B.A.) and two splendid versions of *Portrait of the Artist's Mother* (1942, e.g. Madrid; Mus. A. Contemp.). During this period he began to superimpose a white speckling over the image, giving it an enchanting atmospheric depth; this became part of his characteristic technique.

During the 1950s Cossio enjoyed growing success and gradually purified his technique, applying the paint with a palette knife. His use of transparent veils of colour and white helped create a misty atmosphere and a sensation of timelessness. His paintings of this period include *Window Facing the Sea* (1955; Santander, Mus. Mun. B.A.) and the *Big Table* (1960; Madrid, Mus. A. Contemp.). After his move to Alicante in the early 1960s his paintings became more overtly figurative, with more clearly defined, rounded forms and more diaphanous colours, without the characteristic white flecks. He also began to use gouache and collage.

BIBLIOGRAPHY

Pintores montañeses, 1856–1956 (exh. cat. by J. Simón Cabarga, Santander, Casa Cult., 1956), pp. 31–3, 44

J. A. Gaya Nuño: *Vida y obra de Pancho Cossio* (Madrid, 1973)

L. Rodríguez Alcalde: *Cossio* (Madrid, 1973)

A. Martínez Cerezo: *La pintura montañesa* (Madrid, 1975), pp. 96–107

Pancho Cossio y las vanguardias (1898–1942) and *Pancho Cossio y la posguerra (1942–1970)* (exh. cat. in 2 vols by F. Calvo-Serraller and L. Navarro, Madrid, Cent. Cult. Conde Duque, 1986)

PILAR BENITO

Cossutius (, Decimus) (*fl c.* 170 BC). First known Roman architect. Though a Roman citizen, he probably came from wealthy, Hellenized Campania (annexed by Rome). The pro-Roman King Antiochus IV Epiphanes of Syria (*reg* 175–163 BC) commissioned him to work on the Temple of Olympian Zeus at Athens (*see* ATHENS, §II, 4). Vitruvius (*On Architecture* VII, Preface 15 and 17) noted the temple's huge cella and double Corinthian colonnade, which showed architectural learning and were admired by connoisseurs for their magnificence; he regretted that Cossutius left no annotated specification, as Greek architects had done. Surviving material, if datable to his time, is Greek and advanced in style, unlike contemporary building in Rome. The name Cossutius (in Latin letters) is also twice scratched inside a 2nd-century BC aqueduct near Antioch in Syria, suggesting that the architect worked on Antiochus' building programme there. He may have travelled with his own workforce (as was common in the Greek world), probably chiefly his slaves and freedmen: the inscription could record a freedman, properly bearing his patron's name. He may also have worked on the new Temple of Jupiter Capitolinus at Antioch and on buildings presented by Antiochus to various Greek cities.

Descendants or connections of Cossutius remained in the East, profitably providing sculpture for Rome, as attested by inscriptions at Delos, Athens and Paros, as well as at Pisa, near the Carrara quarries. Two neo-Attic statues of *Pan* (London, BM) found near Rome are signed by the freedman M. Cossutius Cerdo; other freedmen sculptors of the family are known, one sometimes identified with the Menelaus who carved the classicizing Ludovisi group (Rome, Mus. N. Romano) of a young man and woman, perhaps *Orestes and Electra*.

BIBLIOGRAPHY

E. Rawson: 'Architecture and Sculpture: The Activities of the Cossutii', *Pap. Brit. Sch. Rome*, xliii (1975), pp. 34–47

M. Torelli: 'Industria estrattiva, lavoro artigianale, interessi economici: Qualche appunto', *Mem. Amer. Acad. Rome*, xxxvi (1980), pp. 312–33

ELIZABETH RAWSON

Costa. Italian family of painters. (1) Lorenzo Costa (i) was one of the leading artists of the school of Ferrara. His work is a link between the Late Gothic style of Cosimo Tura and that of the High Renaissance. His son (2) Ippolito Costa spent ten years as an artist at the Gonzaga court in Mantua. (3) Lorenzo Costa (ii) was probably the son of Ippolito and, except for a period in Rome, spent most of his career in Mantua, particularly working on decorations in the Palazzo Ducale.

(1) Lorenzo (di Ottavio) Costa (i) (*b* Ferrara, *c.* 1460; *d* Mantua, 5 March 1535). He was the son of a painter, Giovanni Battista (?)Costa, and he received his early training in the studio of Ercole de' Roberti in Ferrara. Probably in the early 1480s he moved to Bologna, where he became the favoured artist of Giovanni II Bentivoglio (*see* BENTIVOGLIO, (2)). Major commissions for Bolognese churches suggest that at one time he was the most sought-after artist in Bologna.

Costa's early works were identified only in the 20th century, mainly by Roberto Longhi. Tracing his early activity is difficult, as there are no surviving signed or documented works before 1488, the date of the *Family of*

Giovanni II Bentivoglio Kneeling before the Virgin (Bologna, S Giacomo Maggiore). On the basis of this altarpiece Longhi attributed to Costa a group of paintings in a style similarly strongly linked to Ercole, including the paintings depicting *Scenes of the Argonauts* (dispersed) and the beautiful altarpiece of the *Virgin and Child with Saints* (ex-Berlin, Kaiser-Friedrich Mus., destr.) from S Maria delle Rondini, Bologna. Longhi's reconstruction showed strong links between Costa's early paintings and his later documented works. It also confirmed his attention to classical sources, particularly evident in the *St Jerome* altarpiece in the Castelli Chapel, S Petronio, Bologna. This painting was probably executed some time after 1484, the date of Baldassare Castelli's will. Its attribution to Costa dates from Vasari, but other artists have been proposed, including Ercole. The resemblance of the *St Jerome* to the style of Ercole is, rather, an indication of Costa's increasing skill in this period. Following the example of Ercole, Francesco del Cossa and Cosimo Tura, Costa's adherence to the restrained form of classicism practised locally gained him the patronage of Giovanni II Bentivoglio. For Giovanni he provided decorations (from 1483) for the new palace (destr. 1502) and tempera paintings (1488; destr.) in the Bentivoglio Chapel of S Giacomo Maggiore, Bologna. Ercole's influence is still apparent in Costa's frescoes depicting the *Triumph of Death* and the *Triumph of Glory* (1488–90), also for the Bentivoglio Chapel. Giovanni subsequently invited him to participate in the decoration of the oratory of S Cecilia, S Giacomo Maggiore, Bologna, for which he painted frescoes of the *Conversion of St Valerian* and the *Charity of St Cecilia* in 1505–6.

Other works were undertaken by Costa in that fruitful period at the end of the century; for the Gozzadini family he designed the window of *St John on Patmos* (*c.* 1490; Bologna, S Giovanni in Monte). From 1491 he worked with Francesco Francia in the Vaselli Chapel in S Petronio, Bologna, where he painted 12 *Apostles* and the *Annunciation*. His last work for S Petronio was the great altarpiece (1492) in the Rossi Chapel depicting the *Virgin and Child Enthroned with SS Sebastian, James, Jerome and George* (see fig.) with, in the lunette, three *Angelic Musicians*. Also from 1492 is the *Concert* (London, N.G.). This depicts three singers in a style close to that of the Bentivoglio altarpiece and antedates similar Venetian scenes. The signed altarpiece the *Virgin and Child with SS Petronius and Tella* (Bologna, Pin. N.) is dated 1496, and the altarpiece *Virgin and Child Enthroned with Saints* for the Ghedini family (Bologna, S Giovanni in Monte) is from 1497. The pronounced formality of the Ghedini altarpiece may be a result of Costa's exposure to Tuscan and Umbrian art, particularly that of Perugino and Filippino Lippi, during a journey to Florence in the 1490s (Longhi). In 1499 Costa was in Ferrara painting decorations (destr.) in the choir of the cathedral, and this may be the date of the Pala Strozzi, the *Virgin and Child with SS William of Aquitaine and John the Baptist* (London, N.G.). The *Nativity* (London, N.G.), also painted about this time, is close in style to the signed and dated predella of the *Epiphany* (1499; Milan, Brera).

Costa's works from between 1502 and 1505 include *St Peter Enthroned with SS Francis and Domenic* (Bologna, Pin. N.), *Pietà* (Berlin, Bodemus. Gemäldegal.) and the

Lorenzo Costa (i): *Virgin and Child Enthroned with SS Sebastian, James, Jerome and George*, 1492 (Bologna, S Petronio)

Virgin and Child with SS Peter, Philip, John the Evangelist and John the Baptist (London, N.G.). In 1504 Isabella d'Este, Marchioness of Mantua, commissioned Costa to paint the *Allegory* (1504–6; Paris, Louvre) for her *studiolo*. With the end of Bentivoglio rule in Bologna in 1506, Costa moved to Mantua, where he succeeded Andrea Mantegna as court painter to the Gonzagas. Subsequently, probably in 1511, he completed the *Reign of Comus* (Paris, Louvre), begun by Mantegna for the *studiolo* but left unfinished at his death (1506). From 1507 to 1512 Costa worked with Francesco Bonsignori on the decorations of the palace of S Sebastiano (destr. 1630), Mantua. He painted numerous portraits, in both Bologna and Mantua; surviving examples include the *Woman with a Lap Dog* (London, Hampton Court, Royal Col.), sometimes identified with untraced, documented portraits (1508) of Isabella d'Este and her daughter, Eleonora, and *Battista Fiera* (London, N.G.), the Mantuan poet and physician.

Among Costa's late works are the *Venus* (*c*. 1518; Budapest, N.G.), probably painted for Francis I, King of France, the signed altarpiece *St Anthony of Padua with SS Ursula and Catherine* (*c*. 1518; New York, Met.), painted for S Nicolò, Carpi, and the *Investiture of Federico Gonzaga as a Captain of the Church* (1522; Prague, N. Mus.). His last known work, the *Virgin Enthroned with Saints* (Mantua, S Andrea), is signed and dated 1525.

BIBLIOGRAPHY

Bolaffi; *DBI*

G. Vasari: *Vite* (1550, rev. 2/1568); ed. G. Milanesi (1878–85), iii, p. 131

E. Cabassi: *Notizie degli artisti carpigiani con le aggiunte . . . d'altri artisti dello stato di Modena* (1784); ed. A. Gariuti (Modena, 1986)

G. Campori: *Gli artisti italiani e stranieri negli stati estensi* (Modena, 1855)

R. Longhi: *Officina ferrarese* (Florence, 1956)

R. Varese: *Lorenzo Costa* (Milan, 1967)

C. Volpe, ed.: *Il Tempio di San Giacomo in Bologna: Studi sulla storia e le opere d'arte* (Bologna, 1967), pp. 117–31, 136–46

B. Berenson: *Central and North Italian Schools* (1968)

P. Venturoli: 'Lorenzo Costa', *Stor. A.*, i–ii (1969), pp. 161–8

B. B. Frederiksen and F. Zeri: *Census of Pre-19th Century Italian Paintings in North American Public Collections* (Cambridge, MA, 1972)

D. Benati: 'Da Lorenzo Costa a Francesco Francia', *La Basilica di San Petronio in Bologna* (Bologna, 1983), pp. 174–94

M. Lucco: 'Lorenzo Costa', *La pittura in Italia: Il quattrocento*, 2 vols, ed. F. Zeri (Milan, 1986, rev. 2/1987), i, pp. 604–5

E. Landi: 'Lorenzo Costa', *Arte emiliana: Dalle raccolte storiche al nuovo collezionismo*, ed. G. Manni, E. Negro and M. Pirondini (Modena, 1989), p. 32

E. Negro: 'Lorenzo Costa', *Arte emiliana: Dalle raccolte storiche al nuovo collezionismo*, ed. G. Manni, E. Negro and M. Pirondini (Modena, 1989), p. 32

(2) Ippolito Costa (*b* Bologna or Mantua, 1506; *d* Mantua, 8 Nov 1561). Son of (1) Lorenzo Costa. From 1529 to 1539 he is documented among the artists of the Gonzaga court in Mantua. The style of his earliest known work, the *Virgin and Child with Three Saints* (1531; Milan, Mus. Poldi Pezzoli), painted for a member of the Gonzaga family, recalls works by his father and Girolamo da Carpi, who may have been his teachers. A similar approach is evident in the *Virgin and Child Enthroned with SS Benedict and John the Evangelist* (Gonzaga, S Benedetto), while his mature works are clearly influenced by Giulio Romano and Tuscan-Roman Mannerism. These include *St Agatha* (1552; Mantua Cathedral) and the *Deposition* (Mantua, S Gervasio), which are comparable to contemporary examples by his pupil Bernardino Campi. His documented portrait of Bishop Ippolito Capilupi and Margherita Paleologa, wife of Federico II Gonzaga, are untraced.

BIBLIOGRAPHY

DBI; Thieme–Becker

F. Russoli: *La Pinacoteca Poldi Pezzoli* (Milan, 1955)

Mantova: Le arti, iii (Mantua, 1965) [entries by E. Marani, C. Perina]

La pittura in Italia: Il cinquecento, ed. G. Briganti, ii (Milan, 1988), pp. 687–8 [entry by C. Tellini Perina]

(3) Lorenzo Costa (ii) (*b* Mantua, 1537; *d* Mantua, 1583). Probably the son of (2) Ippolito Costa. It is likely that his early training was with his father in Mantua in the period after the death (1546) of Giulio Romano, when the architect Giovanni Battista Bertani was a major influence. Three of Lorenzo's paintings are mentioned in a document dated 1560; in 1561 he was paid for a banner (untraced) for the chapter house of Mantua Cathedral. From 1561 to 1564 he was in Rome, where he worked at the Vatican with Federico Zuccaro on decorations for the Borgia tower, the tribunal of the Ruota, the Belvedere and the Casino of Pius IV. In 1564 he was still in Rome, painting a series of papal portraits for Alfonso Gonzaga of Novellara. In this period he became acquainted with Bertani, with whom he worked on altarpieces for S Barbara in Mantua; he received payments between 1569 and 1572 for the *Baptism of Constantine* and the *Martyrdom of St Adrian*, based on drawings by Bertani.

Lorenzo's work in the apartments of Guglielmo Gonzaga, Duke of Mantua, in the Corte Nuova and Corte Vecchia of the Palazzo Ducale, Mantua, is documented from 1569 to 1581. In the Corte Nuova, Aldrovandi (*c.* 1575) mentioned the Camera di Nettuno, decorated with fish by Costa. Other works in the Corte Nuova included decorations (mainly destr.) in the Camera di Giove, the Camera di Apollo, the Loggie dei Frutti and the Sala di Manto (1574), decorated with episodes from the mythical history of the city. He may also have painted battle scenes for the Sala dei Capitani, which probably correspond to two drawings in London (BM). The lunettes (badly damaged) in the Camera delle Virtù, and a few fragments in a small chapel, can be convincingly attributed to Costa (Bazzotti and Berzaghi). Guglielmo's apartment in the Corte Vecchia was largely redecorated in the 18th century, but the ceiling decorations in the Sala dello Zodiaco (formerly Stanza dei Cani) survive; its frieze is now in the Sala del Crogiuolo (Berzaghi).

While Lorenzo was in Rome he learnt from the paintings of Federico Zuccaro, Taddeo Zuccaro and Federico Barocci, whose influence is apparent in the works done after his return to Mantua. In addition to the documented altarpieces for the basilica of S Barbara are wall paintings in the Capella della Preziosissima Sangue in S Andrea in Mantua; the altarpiece of *St Helena and the Cross* in SS Fabiano e Sebastiano, San Martino dell'Argine; the *Supper in the House of the Pharisees* in the parish church of Boccadiganda, Mantua; the *Preaching of St John the Baptist* in S Leonardo; the *Martyrdom of St Laurence* in S Maria delle Grazie, Mantua; and the *Miracle of the Multiplication of the Loaves* in S Barnaba, Mantua.

BIBLIOGRAPHY
DBI [full bibliog.]
U. Aldrovandi: *Itineraria Mantuae* (*c.* 1575)
R. Berzaghi: 'La Corte Vecchia del duca Guglielmo, tracce e memorie', *Quad. Pal. Te*, iii (1985), pp. 43–64
U. Bazzotti and R. Berzaghi: 'Degli Dei la memoria, e degli Heroi, Palazzo Ducale, l'appartamento di Guglielmo Gonzaga', *Corte Nuova* (Mantua, 1986)
P. Carpeggiani and C. Tellini Perina: *S Andrea in Mantova: Un tempio per la città del principe* (Mantua, 1987), pp. 40, 42, 130
C. P. Tellini: 'L. Costa il Giovane ad vocem', *La pittura del cinquecento: Dizionario biografico degli artisti* (Milan, 1989), p. 688

MARIA CRISTINA CHIUSA

Costa, Giovanni [Nino] (*b* Rome, 15 Oct 1826; *d* Pisa, 31 Jan 1903). Italian painter and critic. He was taught by one of the leading Neo-classical painters in Rome, Vincenzo Camuccini, from 1843 to 1847. He also studied under Francesco Podesti and Francesco Coghetti at the Accademia di S Luca, Rome. These painters instilled in Costa the basic academic techniques, in particular that of painting a scene or figure in *mezza macchia*, or half-tones, which he was to apply to great effect in his landscape paintings. In 1848 Costa joined Giuseppe Garibaldi's Legione Romane; after the fall of the Roman Republic in 1849 he took refuge from the papal police in the Campagna, outside Rome. Between 1849 and 1859 Costa lived and worked in this region and met several foreign artists, including the Swiss painter Emile François David (1824–91) and the English painter Charles Coleman (1807–74), who encouraged his interest in landscape painting; the latter introduced him to Frederic Leighton and George Heming Mason, and they became lifelong friends. Costa recalled these years and described his working practices in his memoirs, *Quel che vidi e quel che intesi* (published posthumously in 1927): his first *bozzetto* was the basis for all subsequent ideas, being inspired 'by the love for eternal truth' (p. 120). His emphasis on working directly from nature and his clear uncluttered style owe as much to the *vedutisti* tradition as to the Roman Puristi and the Nazarenes. Contact with Coleman and Leighton, among others, developed his inclination towards a romanticism and lyricism that is evident in his early work and was to dominate his later work. Costa's most important painting of his early years, *Women Loading Wood at Porto d'Anzio* (1850–52; Rome, G.N.A. Mod.; see fig.), combines these influences. As late as 1861 his impressionistic technique was described derisively as 'primitive' in *Il mondo illustrato*

Giovanni Costa: *Women Loading Wood at Porto d'Anzio*, oil on canvas, 730×1470 mm, 1850–52 (Rome, Galleria Nazionale d'Arte Moderna)

when the work was exhibited at the Società Promotrice di Belle Arti in Florence. This was the type of criticism that was made of the MACCHIAIOLI.

Costa first met the Macchiaioli painters in 1859 as he returned from fighting in the Piedmontese army in the north of Italy. He knew Serafino da Tivoli (1826–92) from the Roman campaign and through him was introduced to the group of artists who gathered at the Caffè Michelangiolo in Florence. The subtle modulation of colour in Costa's landscape studies particularly impressed Giovanni Fattori. Costa's tonal approach to landscape painting, his use of suffused light and tendency to evoke rather than describe a scene are evident in such works as the *Dead River* (*c.* 1859; untraced, see Broude, p. 87). In 1861 Costa travelled to Paris in connection with the exhibition of *Women Loading Wood* at the Salon and to acquaint himself with the work of Corot and the painters of the Fontainebleau school. Contact with French artists served to enhance these characteristics. Costa also visited London and through Leighton was introduced to the Pre-Raphaelites, reinforcing the move towards romanticism in his landscapes. This is revealed in a painting that he reworked during the course of several years, *The Nymph* (1863–95; Rome, G.N.A. Mod.), in which the idealized female form is set among foliage shimmering in the evening light. The only Italian painter to approach nature in a similar way was Antonio Fontanesi, whom Costa had met briefly in Piedmont in 1859. Costa's work greatly appealed to the English, no doubt helped by an endorsement from Leighton. One of his most notable patrons was George James Howard, 9th Earl of Carlisle, who may have suggested the subject of *The Nymph*.

Costa fought at Mentana in 1867 and took part in the liberation of Rome in 1870. In that year he was elected Professore di Pittura at the Accademia di Belle Arti in Florence. In 1875 he founded the Gold Club, an association of artists living in Rome who painted from nature. From 1877 he exhibited at the Grosvenor Gallery in London with a group of Italian and English painters who were to be the founder-members of the ETRUSCAN SCHOOL in Rome; Costa was their recognized leader. In 1885 Costa's belief that progressive artists needed a forum where commercialism and vulgar taste (specifically the fashion for the work of Mariano José Bernardo Fortuny y Marsal) would be ignored led to the foundation of In Arte Libertas. The first exhibition of this association, members of which included Vincenzo Cabianca (1827–1902), who had been part of the Macchiaioli group, Alessandro Castelli (1809–1902), Onorato Carlandi (*b* 1848) and Enrico Coleman (1846–1911), was held in Rome in 1886. Edward Burne-Jones, Dante Gabriel Rossetti and Leighton were among the English artists who exhibited in 1890 with In Arte Libertas.

Costa continued to paint around Porto d'Anzio and also along the coast near Livorno. From the late 1870s his paintings became even more subtle in tone, and the shimmering light that he depicted gives to his pictures an ethereal quality. His late works include *S Giovanni in Laterano from the Villa Mattei* (*c.* 1884; Castle Howard, N. Yorks) and the *Tiber at Castel Fusano* (untraced, see 1989 exh. cat., no. 80), which display his ability to capture the most delicate gradations of light with the use of translucent tones.

WRITINGS
G. Guerazzi, ed.: *Quel che vidi e quel che intesi* (Milan, 1927/*R* 1983)

BIBLIOGRAPHY
C. Demo: article in *Il mondo illustrato*, iv/20 (18 May 1861), pp. 317–18
Collection of Pictures by Professor G. Costa (exh. cat., London, F.A. Soc., 1882)
O. R. Agresti: *Giovanni Costa: His Life, Work and Times* (London, 1904)
D. Durbé: *I Macchiaioli* (Rome, 1978)
N. Broude: *The Macchiaioli* (New Haven and London, 1987)
The Etruscans: Painters of the Italian Landscape, 1850–1920 (exh. cat. by C. Newall, York, C.A.G.; Stoke-on-Trent, City Mus. & A.G.; London, Leighton House A.G. & Mus.; 1989)

□

Costa, Joseph Mendes da. *See* MENDES DA COSTA, JOSEPH.

Costa, Lúcio (*b* Toulon, 27 Feb 1902). Brazilian architect, urban planner, architectural historian and writer of French birth. His parents were Brazilian, and he returned to Brazil in 1917 and entered the Escola Nacional de Belas Artes, Rio de Janeiro, graduating as an architect in 1923. From 1922 he worked with Fernando Valentim, adopting the style favoured by the Traditionalist movement, which took its inspiration from 18th-century Brazilian colonial architecture in an attempt to develop a national style. He designed several houses and won two important competitions, both with neo-colonial designs: the Brazilian Pavilion at the International Exhibition (1925) in Philadelphia, and the headquarters of the Argentine Embassy (1928), Rio de Janeiro (neither of which was built).

In 1930, following the installation of the new revolutionary government, Costa was appointed to direct the Escola Nacional de Belas Artes in Rio and to reform its teaching system. At first his nomination was seen as a victory for the supporters of the neo-colonial style over the academics, but Costa broke with both and created a course, given by specially invited Modernist teachers including Gregori Warchavchik, which introduced the principles of avant-garde European architecture to Brazil. His actions were denounced by the teaching staff and the Traditionalist leader, and Costa subsequently lost his government support. In 1931 he joined Warchavchik, who had just completed his first modern houses in Rio de Janeiro; working together until 1933, they carried out several early Modern Movement projects, including the Alfredo Schwartz House (1932) and the low-cost housing complex (1933) in Gambôa. During this period Costa became the leading proponent of avant-garde architecture in Rio de Janeiro and was increasingly inspired by the Rationalism of Le Corbusier who, he considered, gave due importance to the plastic and artistic dimension of architecture, whereas Functionalism implied a reduction of the architect's work to the mere resolution of technical problems.

In 1935 Costa began his involvement with the most influential modern building in Brazil when a competition was held for the headquarters of the Ministry of Education and Health (now the Palácio da Cultura; *see* BRAZIL, fig. 5), Rio de Janeiro. First prize was awarded to a project, with decorative motifs inspired by ceramics from the Ilha de

Marajó, by Archimedes Memória (1893–1960), the academic architect who had taken over the directorship of the Escola Nacional de Belas Artes from Costa in 1931, and his associate Francisque Cuchet. Under pressure from Modernist intellectuals on his staff, the Minister awarded the prize to the winning team but then made Costa, whose entry had not been placed, responsible for developing a new design. Costa assembled a team of architects from his immediate circle: Carlos Leão (*b* 1906), Jorge Moreira, Affonso Eduardo Reidy and, later, two new graduates, Ernani Vasconcellos (*b* 1912) and Oscar Niemeyer, and he persuaded the Minister to invite Le Corbusier to come to Rio as consultant on the project (*see* BRAZIL, §IV, 2(ii) and fig. 5). It was not finished until 1943, but it achieved immediate success among architects in Rio and guaranteed the predominance of the style and of Le Corbusier's influence in official buildings thereafter.

In 1937 Costa joined the Serviço do Patrimônio Histórico e Artístico Nacional (SPHAN), a federal body for the preservation of art and architecture, where he worked until his retirement in 1972; he carried out a series of studies on the history of Brazilian architecture, the most important being 'Arquitetura Jesuítica no Brasil' (1941). After joining SPHAN he produced relatively few buildings, as he no longer maintained an office, but in 1938 he won the competition for the Brazilian Pavilion at the World's Fair in New York; Niemeyer came second but Costa, believing Niemeyer's design to be better, shared the prize with him and invited him to participate in the development of the project (with Paul Lester Weiner in New York; *see* BRAZIL, fig. 6). In several of his essays Costa expressed his admiration for Niemeyer's inventive forms and defended his sculptural approach as coming direct from Le Corbusier. In other works of the period, Costa developed a new language; paradoxically, in those projects where monumental considerations were secondary, he developed a synthesis of modern and colonial styles, using such traditional features as verandahs, bay windows and tiled

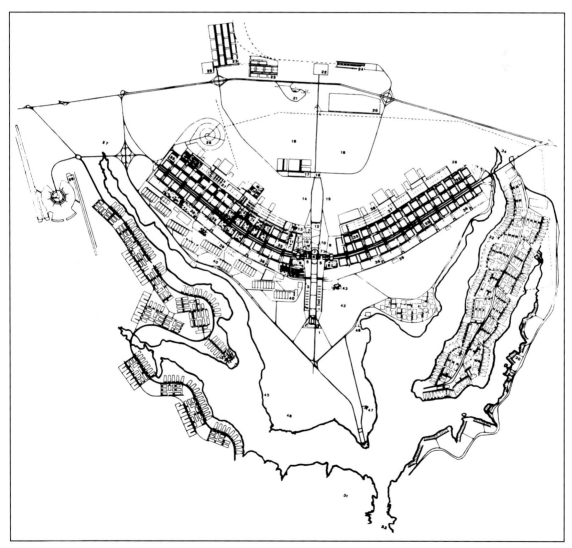

Lúcio Costa: master-plan for Brasília, 1957

roofs with overhanging eaves. This can be seen in his few house designs, such as the Argemiro Hungria Machado house (1942), in the country houses of Mrs Roberto Marinho (1942) and Barão de Saavedra (1942–4), both in Petrópolis, and in his design for the Hotel do Parque S Clemente (1944), Nova Friburgo, partly inspired by Niemeyer's plan for the Hotel de Ouro Preto (1942). Between 1948 and 1950 Costa worked on a group of three blocks of flats in Guinle Park, Rio de Janeiro, which foreshadowed the superblock solution he was to adopt in Brasília. He then participated in the Commission of Five who were asked to assess designs for the UNESCO headquarters in Paris (1952–3); the others were Walter Gropius, Le Corbusier, Sven Markelius and Ernesto Nathan Rogers. During this period he produced an initial design for the Casa do Brasil at the Cité Universitaire in Paris, which was the basis for Le Corbusier's definitive design. In 1956 he designed buildings for the Jockey Club Brasileiro and the Banco Aliança, both in Rio de Janeiro.

In 1957 Costa won the competition for the master-plan for the new capital of the country, BRASÍLIA (see fig.). In this plan he departed from the usual grid system of roads and designed a linear traffic axis, where the main residential areas are located; at right angles to this is a monumental axis where institutional, government and major public buildings are located. The resulting cross-shaped plan, which Costa likened to the human gesture of possession, clearly expressed the urban planning principles contained in the Athens Charter (1933) of CIAM calling for the separation of different urban activities into zones and the use of isolated, single-function buildings. Low-rent accommodation was provided in rows of single-storey houses and medium- and high-rent accommodation was provided in superblocks, i.e. areas 350 m square in which blocks of flats, usually six storeys high and built on pilotis, were placed at right angles to each other. These superblocks were built along the traffic axis, on either side of the monumental axis, and local commerce was provided in small streets between them. Costa's plan, dominated by the juxtaposition of motorway technology and urbanism, fulfilled the explicit intention of President Juscelino Kubitschek of building a city for the car; its clarity provided an appropriate framework for the public buildings later designed by Niemeyer. Costa also designed some buildings at Brasília, including the bus station (1959), the television tower (1959) and a superblock (1961).

Later urban plans prepared by Costa included that for the Barra da Tijuca (1969), an area extending nearly 20 km along the coast south of Rio de Janeiro. He applied the same principles of zoning as in Brasília but included small, separate residential areas or 'urban nuclei' with various types of accommodation including houses and flats, as well as parks and nature reserves to preserve the local ecology. Because of its costs, this plan was never fully implemented. In 1987 he produced a plan for the extension of Brasília, proposing the construction of two new wings for low-cost housing. The proposal was faithful to the plan of 1957 in its functional zoning and segregation of the people in low-cost accommodation into satellite cities, but it was widely criticized, a reflection of changing views on urban planning. Nevertheless, Costa's pivotal role in the introduction and development of modern architecture in Brazil, not only in his buildings but also in his teaching and support of others, was unassailable, and he received many honours and awards during his career.

WRITINGS
'Arquitetura jesuítica no Brasil', *Rev. SPHAN*, 5 (1941)
Arquitetura brasileira (Rio de Janeiro, 1952)
Scientific and Technological Humanism (Cambridge, MA, 1961)
Sôbre arquitetura (Porto Alegre, 1962)
Brasília revisitada (Rio de Janeiro, 1987)

BIBLIOGRAPHY
H. R. Hitchcock: *Latin American Architecture since 1945* (New York, 1955)
H. E. Mindlin: *Modern Architecture in Brazil* (Amsterdam and Rio de Janeiro, 1956)
J. O. Gazaneo and M. M. Scarone: *Lúcio Costa* (Buenos Aires, 1959)
A. Magalhães and E. Feldman: *Doorway to Brasília* (Philadelphia, 1959)
F. Bullrich: *New Directions in Latin American Architecture* (London and New York, 1969)
P. F. Santos: *Quatro séculos de arquitetura* (Barra do Piraí, 1977)
E. D. Harris: *Le Corbusier and the Headquarters of the Brazilian Ministry of Education and Health, 1936–1945* (diss., U. Chicago, IL, 1984)

SYLVIA FICHER

Costa, Olga (*b* Leipzig, 1913; *d* Guanajuato, 28 June 1993). Mexican painter of Russian descent. She went to Mexico in 1925 and attended the Academia de San Carlos, Mexico City (1933–6), where she met the painter JOSÉ CHÁVEZ MORADO, whom she married. In 1941 she co-founded the Galería Espiral and in 1943 she founded the Sociedad de Arte Moderno, one of the first galleries to promote foreign artists in Mexico. From 1945 she exhibited regularly at the Galería de Arte Mexicano, Mexico City. Costa painted *costumbrista* subjects, depicting regional customs, as well as still-lifes, portraits and landscapes. Her style was traditionalist, without being folkloric in a popular manner. Her best-known work is perhaps the *Fruit Seller* (1951; Mexico City, Mus. A. Mod.). From 1966 she lived in Guanajuato, where she played an active role in local artistic activities. In April 1993 the Museo-Casa Olga Costa-José Chávez Morado was opened in León, Guanajuato.

BIBLIOGRAPHY
Frida Kahlo acompañada de siete pintoras: María Izquierdo, Cordelia Urueta, Olga Costa, Remedios Varo, Alice Rahon, Leonora Carrington y Soffía Bassi (exh. cat. by J. O'Gorman and others, Mexico City, Mus. A. Mod., 1967)
La vida a cuadros (exh. cat., Mexico City, Gal. Tonalli, 1988)
La mujer en México (exh. cat., Mexico City, Cent. Cult. A. Contemp., 1990) [entries by L. Nochlin and E. Sullivan]

JULIETA ORTIZ GAITÁN

Costa, Ottavio (*b* Albenga, 1554; *d* Rome, 13 Jan 1639). Italian banker and patron. He was from a rich, mercantile family from Albenga on the Ligurian coast. From 1547 the family held rights over the neighbouring fiefdom of Conscente. His brothers, Pier Francesco Costa (1545–1625) and Alessandro Costa (1555–1624), obtained important ecclesiastical positions, while Ottavio remained responsible for the family business affairs and built up a significant art collection. He moved to Rome some time before 1576, purchased a number of properties in the city and established an important banking business with Giovanni Enriquez de Herrera (*d* 1610). By the end of the 16th century he was a major banker, holding financial contracts with the Curia. Under Pope Gregory XIV he became Depositor General. An energetic collector of painting and sculpture, it appears that Costa most valued his Roman collection of contemporary paintings (for the 1639 inventory, see Spezzaferro, 1975, p. 118). Caravaggio, d'Arpino and Reni were his stated favourites, with Caravaggio heading the list. He may have owned up to five or more works by the artist. *Judith and Holofernes* (Rome, Pal. Barberini) was evidently his most prized possession. He sent paintings and sculpture from Rome to the family palace in Albenga. Together with his brothers, he had a church built at Conscente (begun 1596). Furnishings included Reni's *Martyrdom of St Catherine* (*in situ*) and a copy of *St John the Baptist* (Kansas City, MO, Nelson–Atkins Mus. A.) by Caravaggio, the original of which he kept in Rome. Costa's connections through marriage with the Knights of Malta possibly helped in furthering Caravaggio's career in Malta, and his partnership with Herrera may well have influenced the latter to employ contemporary painters (Carracci and pupils) to decorate his family chapel in S Giacomo degli Spagnoli (now known as the church of the Madonna del Sacro Cuore), Rome.

BIBLIOGRAPHY

J. Delumeau: *Vie économique et sociale de Rome dans la seconde moitié du XVIe siècle*, 2 vols (Paris, 1957–9), i, pp. 482–3; ii, pp. 856, 881

J. Hess: 'Caravaggio's Paintings in Malta: Some Notes', *Connoisseur*, cxlii (Nov 1958), pp. 142–7

P. Matthiesen and S. Pepper: 'Guido Reni: An Early Masterpiece Discovered in Liguria', *Apollo*, xci (1970), pp. 452–62

L. Spezzaferro: 'Detroit's *Conversion of the Magdalene* (the Alzaga Caravaggio): 4. The Documentary Findings: Ottavio Costa as a Patron of Caravaggio', *Burl. Mag.*, cxvi (1974), pp. 579–86

——: 'Ottavio Costa e Caravaggio: Certezze e problemi', *Novità sul Caravaggio: Saggi e contributi*, ed. M. Cinotti (Regione Lombardia, 1975), pp. 103–18

PETER HIGGINSON

Costa, Pereira da. *See* PEREIRA DA COSTA.

Costa Andrade, Manuel (*d* Oporto, 31 July 1756). Portuguese wood-carver. He was a leading member of the school in Oporto responsible technically for interpreting the designs of the JOANINE style. He also worked throughout northern Portugal and was one of those whose carvings led to the wide diffusion of Joanine *talha* (carved and gilded wood). His first recorded work is the high altar (1731) of the chapel at Arnelas, Vila Nova da Gaia, when his guarantor was the painter and gilder Manuel Pinto Monteiro (*fl* 1709–36). In the same year Pinto Monteiro was again guarantor, together with the sculptor Manuel Carneiro Adão (*fl* 1719–47), when Costa Andrade signed a contract for carving the retable and other work (all *c.* 1731) in the chapel of Nossa Senhora da Conceição in the convent church at Monchique, Oporto.

In a period of intense activity that extended into the 1750s, Costa Andrade produced some magnificent works. These include the commission in 1733 to carve the high altar in the chapel of Senhor Jesus at Carvalhinho, Oporto, a work that has a stylistic affinity with the high altar (*c.* 1730) of the church of the Franciscan convent of S Clara, Oporto, designed by Miguel Francisco da Silva. In 1734 he contracted, with Manuel da Rocha, to carve the high altar in the church at S João da Foz, Oporto, also after the design of Miguel Francisco da Silva. In 1737 he carved the retable in the chapel of Santos Passos in the church at Leça da Palmeira after the design of the architect Francisco do Couto e Azevedo. Costa Andrade executed

two fine retables in the convent church of S Francisco, Oporto: Nossa Senhora do Rosário dos Escravos (also known as Nossa Senhora do Socorro, 1740) and Nossa Senhora da Graça (also known as Nossa Senhora da Rosa, 1743), both to the design of Francisco do Couto e Azevedo. In 1743 Costa Andrade also carved the altar and tribune of the chancel in the convent church of S Francisco, Guimarães, after the designs of Miguel Francisco da Silva. In 1750 he undertook two important works, the retable for the Third Order of St Francis at S Cosme, Gondomar, and the superb high altar and tribune in the church at Nevogilde, Oporto.

BIBLIOGRAPHY

D. de P. Brandão: 'Alguns retábulos e painéis de igrejas e capelas do Porto', *Doc. & Mem. Hist. Porto*, xxxiii (1963)

A. de M. Basto: *Apontamentos para um dicionário de artistas e artífices que trabalharam no Porto do século XV ao século XVIII* (Oporto, 1964)

N. M. Ferreira Alves: *A arte da talha no Porto na época barroca: Artistas e clientela. Materiais e técnica, Doc. & Mem. Hist. Porto*, xlvii (1989)

NATÁLIA MARINHO FERREIRA ALVES

Costa Ataíde, Manoel da. *See* ATAÍDE, MANOEL DA COSTA.

Costa e Silva, José da (*b* Povos, nr Lisbon, 25 July 1747; *d* Rio de Janeiro, 21 March 1819). Portuguese architect, active also in Brazil. He studied in Italy under royal patronage, a pattern of artistic education established in Portugal at the beginning of the 18th century. He went first to Bologna, in 1769, becoming a member of the Academia in 1775. He spent a few months in Rome and made an extensive tour of Italy before returning to Lisbon in 1779. In 1781 he was invited to run the school of architecture at the new Academia do Nu in Lisbon, founded under Mary I. He also became an honorary member of the Accademia di S Luca, Rome. In 1785 he completed the sanctuary of the Italian church of Nossa Senhora do Loreto, Lisbon, the rebuilding of which was started by Manuel Caetano de Sousa.

Costa e Silva's first major work was the opera house, the Teatro S Carlos (1792–3), Lisbon, which was built in six months for a group of wealthy citizens anxious to follow the latest fashions in Italian opera. The design was consciously Neo-classical: the three-bay arcaded *porte-cochère* and severe pilastered façade on a rusticated base were modelled on Giuseppe Piermarini's Teatro della Scala (1776–8), Milan, which Costa e Silva had probably seen in 1779. The interior, a horse-shoe plan with four tiers, was sumptuously decorated with gilt. Also in 1792 Costa e Silva started work on the Royal Palace of Runa, near Lisbon, which incorporated a military hospital and a church. Work was suspended in 1807 owing to the Napoleonic invasion, although parts of the hospital remain.

From 1795 Costa e Silva was occupied with designs for the new royal palace of Ajuda (also called Nossa Senhora da Ajuda), Lisbon, to replace the one destroyed by the earthquake of 1755. The Italian Francesco Saverio Fabri also presented plans, and work started in 1802 jointly under Fabri and Costa e Silva. The design has been linked to the former royal palace (begun 1752), Caserta, by Luigi Vanvitelli, but the scale is much more intimate and the detailing Neo-classical; the prominent corner towers, however, are essentially Portuguese.

In 1812 Costa e Silva emigrated to Brazil, following the king, John VI, who, fleeing the Napoleonic invasion, had established the court in Rio de Janeiro in 1807. Costa e Silva was the major exponent of Neo-classicism in Brazil until the arrival in 1816 of the French Mission, headed by Auguste-Henri Grandjean de Montigny. The opera house in Rio de Janeiro, the Real Teatro S João (1811–13; destr.), also with a three-bay arcaded *porte-cochère* and pilastered façade, although with a pediment on the central pavilion, resembled Costa e Silva's Teatro S Carlos so closely that he is believed to have been involved in its final design. In 1813 he was appointed Royal Master of Works, advising on the many improvements necessary to various palaces in Rio de Janeiro and Salvador in order to establish the royal court in the somewhat backward conditions then found in Brazil. The large collection of drawings and books on architecture that Costa e Silva brought with him were sold in 1818 to the Royal Library (now the National Library), Rio de Janeiro.

BIBLIOGRAPHY

Viterbo

J. A. França: *Lisboa Pombalina* (Lisbon, 1965)

R. dos Santos: *Oito séculos de arte portuguesa*, ii (Lisbon, 1966)

P. F. Santos: *Quatro séculos de arquitetura* (Rio de Janeiro, 1981)

Costa Faro, António da. *See* FARO, ANTÓNIO DA COSTA.

Costakis, George [Kostaki, Georgy (Dionisovich)] (*b* Moscow, 3 July 1912; *d* Athens, 9 March 1990). Greek collector and embassy official of Russian birth. He grew up in a family of Russo-Greek merchants (his father emigrated to Russia in 1907), and from the age of 19 he was an employee in various diplomatic legations in Moscow. He worked as an administrator in the Canadian embassy until 1976; his contacts there and his Greek nationality proved useful for his collecting activities. Costakis first became interested in collecting at the beginning of the 1930s when the Soviet government embarked on a massive sale of antiques and art works to buyers in foreign currency. He began by acquiring Dutch Old Master paintings, carpets and antiques; from 1940 he started collecting Russian icons, gradually assembling an important collection of 15th- to 17th-century icon paintings. After 1947 he started acquiring works by Russian modernist painters at a time when such work was out of official favour, beginning with works by Chagall and Kandinsky, already famous in the West; he then decided to research and record, through his collection, the history of the Russian avant-garde, the modernist movements in Russian art of the first three decades of the 20th century, and he played a leading role in the rediscovery and recognition of many avant-garde artists.

By the early 1960s Popova and Klyun were already the highlights of Costakis's collection, and they were consistently and comprehensively represented in it. Among the works by Malevich in the collection, one of the most important was the portrait of *Matyushin* (1913; now Moscow, Tret'yakov Gal.). The collection also included notable examples of works by Malevich's followers, Il'ya Chashnik (1902–29), Nikolay Suyetin (1897–1954), Lev

Yudin (1903–41), Ivan Kudryashov (1896–1972) and others connected with Suprematism in the second decade of the 20th century, such as El Lissitzky (e.g. *Proun 1C*, 1919; see Rudenstine, p. 245) and Klucis (e.g. *Dynamic City*, 1919–21, and a series of artistic projects, including a number of street agitprop sets, 1922; see Rudenstine, pp. 207, 209–18). Also in the collection was a unique group of works illustrating the discussions that took place at INKHUK (the Institute of Artistic Culture) in Moscow, which played such a significant part in the history of Russian art in the 1920s (see Rudenstine, pp. 110–27). Tatlin was represented by a number of works, among them some stage designs (e.g. Glinka's *Ivan Susanin*, 1912–14; now Moscow, Tret'yakov Gal., see Rudenstine, p. 476), paintings such as the still-life *Meat* (1947; now Moscow, Tret'yakov Gal., see Rudenstine, p. 481) and material connected with Tatlin's model of the flying bicycle *Letatlin* (see Rudenstine, p. 482).

Costakis collected the works of abstract artists working in Moscow at the beginning of the 1920s carefully and systematically. Kandinsky's pupil Konstantin Vyalov (1900–76), Kliment Red'ko (1897–1956), Mikhail Plaksin (1898–1965) and Solomon Nikritin (1898–1965) were all represented. Constructivism was represented by some important works by Rodchenko and Stepanova, and there were works by avant-garde artists such as Pougny, Exter, Yakulov, Vera Pestel' (1886–1952), Udal'tsova, Antonina Sofronova (1892–1966), Rozanova, Miturich, Lentulov, Vladimir Burlyuk, artists such as A. Yavlensky and Poliakoff, who worked in the West, and the important innovative artists Larionov and Goncharova. The collection revealed the complex and intense artistic climate of Leningrad in the 1920s (Matyushin, the artistic dynasty of Enders, Filonov and his analytical school). Costakis was noted for his courage and integrity in selecting and promoting new artists.

From the 1950s Costakis also started collecting works by the new generation of modernists who came into their own in the post-Stalinist era, in particular the subtle metaphysical painter Dmitri Krasnopevtsev (*b* 1925) and the Abstract Expressionist Anatoly Zverev (*b* 1931). Costakis again strove for a broad and objective demonstration of the history of contemporary movements in the USSR, and acquired for his collection the works of M. Shvartsman, Il'ya Kabakov, Ernst Neizvestny, Oleg Tselkov (*b* 1934), Vladimir Weisberg (*b* 1924), Dmitry Plavinsky (*b* 1937), Edward Steinberg (*b* 1937), Vladimir Yankilevsky (*b c.* 1935), Oscar Rabin, Boris Sveshnikov (*b* 1927), Vladimir Nemukhin (*b* 1925) and others, whose works characterized the artistic tendencies of the time.

The existence of Costakis's collection in Moscow was a partial compensation for the lack of exhibited avant-garde works in Soviet museums. In its sheer scope the collection not only surpassed all other collections in the USSR that also contained the works of the avant-garde of the 1910s and 1920s, but also stood comparison with the largest state collections, such as that of the Tret'yakov Gallery in Moscow and the Russian Museum in Leningrad. The importance to Russian cultural life of Costakis's activity as a collector was comparable to that of Sergey Shchukin earlier in the century. When Costakis left the USSR for Greece in 1978, he presented the Tret'yakov Gallery in

Moscow with *c.* 80% of his collection. The first public exhibition of the works brought out of the USSR took place in the Kunstmuseum, Düsseldorf, in 1977. This collection was later studied and documented at the Solomon R. Guggenheim Museum, New York, where it was exhibited in 1981.

BIBLIOGRAPHY
Werke aus der Sammlung Costakis: Russische Avantgarde, 1910–1930 (exh. cat., ed. S. V. Wiese; Düsseldorf, Kstmus., 1977)
A. Z. Rudenstine, ed.: *Russian Avant-garde Art: The George Costakis Collection* (London, 1981)
Art of the Avant-garde in Russia: Selections from the George Costakis Collection (exh. cat. by M. Rowell and A. Z. Rudenstine, New York, Guggenheim, 1981)
P. Roberts: *Costakis* (Markham, Ont., 1991)

V. RAKITIN

Costa Meesen, Félix da (*b* Lisbon, 19 July 1639; *d* Lisbon, 1712). Portuguese painter and theorist. He belonged to a family concerned with theoretical ideas at a time when there was little interest in artistic theory in Portugal, and he described himself as 'pintor teorico e practico' (*A antiguidade da arte da pintura*). His father, the painter Luis da Costa, translated the work of Albrecht Dürer and Paulus Galarius Saludianus, and his brother, Brás de Almeida, was the author of two treatises on geometry. Félix da Costa wrote the most important theoretical work on painting in Portuguese of the second half of the 17th century, *A antiguidade da arte da pintura* (1696; MS., New Haven, CT, Yale U. Lib.), which is a valuable source for the study of Portuguese painting of the late 16th and the 17th centuries.

Da Costa also wrote *O Profeta Esidras e o Império Otomano, que há-de destruir o Rei Encoberto no seu regresso de África*, which may correspond to a manuscript by him in the Library of the Palace of Ajuda, Lisbon, entitled *Thezoiro descoberto: Discurso em que se mostram por razois claras e evidentes quem he o Rey encuberto que ha-de restaurar a Santa Cidade de Hyerusalem do poder dos Infieis* (1685). This work places da Costa among the group of Portuguese thinkers for whom the political circumstances of the annexation of Portugal to the Spanish crown between 1580 and 1640 gave a nationalistic meaning to the Messianic beliefs in the myth of the return of the dead King Sebastian (*reg* 1557–78). Da Costa reveals a strong strain of religious mysticism in his testimony to the Inquisition in the trial of Pedro Serrão in 1676 and by the deeply religious tone of his own will.

Little is known of da Costa's work as a painter, although according to his own account he served his apprenticeship in London, where he painted a portrait of *Catherine of Braganza* (untraced). Engravings made after originals by da Costa include the portrait of *Dr Curvo Semedo*, which serves as frontispiece to Semedo's *Polyanthea medicinalis* (Lisbon, 1697), and the portrait of *António Galvam de Andrade* in his *A arte da Cavallaria da Gineta* (Lisbon, 1678), which contains illustrations by da Costa. He also designed a jewelled altar (1693) for the Capela de S Vicente in Lisbon Cathedral (destr. 1755).

The importance and significance of da Costa lies in *A antiguidade da arte da pintura*, which was probably written in connection with his attempt to revive the Irmandade de S Lucas and to found an official academy of painting.

This objective led him to give preference to Mannerist painters, who had done much to obtain recognition of the noble and liberal nature of their art, to the detriment of his own contemporaries, some of whom, such as Bento Coelho da Silveira, he ignores. The way in which he exalts the Italianizing artists of the 16th century contrasts with the bleak picture he gives of the 'decline of painting' in his own time. His theoretical arguments were strongly influenced by 17th-century Spanish treatises, of which he reveals a profound knowledge possibly on account of the long residence in Spain of his brother, Brás de Almeida. In particular da Costa quotes at length from *Diálogos sobre la pintura* (1633) by Vicente Carducho, and the apocryphal *Memorial informatorio* and the *Notícia general para la estimación de las artes* (Madrid, 1600), both by Gaspar Gutiérrez de los Rios.

BIBLIOGRAPHY
R. dos Santos: *Personagens portuguesas do seculo XVII* (Lisbon, 1942)
G. Kubler: *The Antiquity of the Art of Painting by Félix da Costa* (New Haven, 1967)

JOAQUIM OLIVEIRA CAETANO

Costa Mota, António Augusto da (*b* Coimbra, 1862; *d* Lisbon, 1930). Portuguese sculptor. He studied at the Escola de Belas-Artes, Lisbon, and was a pupil of Vítor Bastos and José Simões de Almeida. In 1893 he gained recognition by winning the Afonso de Albuquerque competition in which António Teixeira Lopes and Simões de Almeida also competed. His work is always naturalistic in character, though at times rather scenographic with a tendency to over-embellish. In Lisbon he made the monuments to *Pinheiro Chagas* (bronze, 1908; Avenida da Liberdade), *Sousa Martins* (bronze, 1907; Campo de Sant' Ana) and *Eduardo Coelho* (bronze, 1904; S Pedro de Alcântara). He made a bust of *King Charles* (undated) and a statue of *Jurisprudence* (marble, 1921; both Lisbon, Assembl. N.). Among his many statues throughout Portugal are *Joaquim Augusto de Aguiar* (bronze, 1912; Coimbra, Largo da Portagem).

Costa Mota could model expressive heads, but in comparison with Teixeira Lopes and other sculptors of the Naturalist generation his work is of lesser quality. His finest sculpture, *Bernardim Ribeiro* (1907; Lisbon, Mus. N. A. Contemp.), is a classical and lyrical work inspired by *Florentine Page* by Paul Dubois (1865; Troyes, Mus. A. Mod.). Costa Mota exhibited in 1891 and 1892 at the Grémio Artístico (Artistic Guild), winning a second-class medal, and from 1901 at the Sociedade Nacional de Belas-Artes (medal of honour). In 1908 he exhibited at the Exposicão Internacional do Rio de Janeiro. His nephew, the sculptor António Augusto da Costa Mota (1877–1956), was a pupil.

BIBLIOGRAPHY
R. Arthur: *Arte e artistas contemporâneos* (Lisbon, 1898), pp. 19–28; (Lisbon, 1903), pp. 117–24
J.-A. França: *A arte em Portugal no século XIX*, ii (Lisbon, 1966), pp. 221–2

LUCÍLIA VERDELHO DA COSTA

Costa Noronha, Manuel Pereira da. *See* PEREIRA DA COSTA, (2).

Costanzi [Costansi]. Italian family of artists. Giovanni Costanzi (?1674–1754) was active in Rome as a gem-engraver. His engraved diamond showing the *Head of Nero* was noted by Stosch (1724) and Mariette (1750). Among other commissions, he executed a chalcedony intaglio of the *Head of Gordian* for Frederick II, King of Prussia. Of his three sons, (1) Placido Costanzi was a painter; Tommaso Costanzi (?1700–1747) was a gem-engraver, highly esteemed by Mariette and Giovanni Pichler, although none of his works is known; and (2) Carlo Costanzi had an ambitious and successful career as a gem-engraver.

LUCIA PIRZIO BIROLI STEFANELLI

(1) Placido Costanzi (*b* Rome, 1702; *d* Rome, 3 Oct 1759). Painter. He studied for five years with Francesco Trevisani and then with Benedetto Luti (1666–1724). From the latter he acquired the basic stylistic components of his artistic language with elements derived from Sebastiano Conca and the decorative works of Sebastiano Ricci, Giovanni Odazzi and Giovanni Battista Gaulli. At the same time he inclined towards a moderate form of classicism, which led him to study the works of Raphael, Annibale Carracci and Domenichino.

Costanzi had early success, with commissions from both Italian and foreign clients. He painted the decorations (untraced; documented by a sketch in Piacenza, Coll. Alberoni) for the villa of Cardinal Alberoni (1664–1752) outside Porta Pia, while for Cardinal Tolomei (*d* 1726) he produced the altarpiece of the *Conception with God the Father, St John the Baptist and an Angel* (destr.) for the church of the Maddalena in Pistoia. Together with other famous artists of the time, including Conca, Pietro Bianchi (ii) and Odazzi, he painted parts of the series illustrating the *Life of Alexander VII*, commissioned by Cardinal Chigi Zondadari (1665–1737). Costanzi himself contributed the scenes of *Fabio Chigi, later Alexander VII, Arriving at the Congress of Munster* and *Cardinal Zondadari Taking Leave of the Spanish Officials* (the latter is signed and dated 1727; both Rome, G.N.A. Ant.); and *Cardinal Zondadari Blessing the People near Rome* (signed and dated 1728; Minneapolis, MN, Inst. A.). These paintings are rather Rococo in tone, reminiscent of the work of Costanzi's teachers, Trevisani and Luti; at the same time they already show significant differences in the darker palette, the more traditional manner as well as a special sensitivity to nature, all derived from his study of Raphael and Annibale Carracci.

For the Palazzo Reale in Turin Costanzi painted two classical subjects for overdoor panels, *Clelia before Porsenna* (signed and dated 1749) and the *Continence of Scipio* (both Turin, Pal. Reale). *Mercury Leading the Arts towards Eternal Fame* (signed and dated 1750; see 1987 exh. cat.) was probably painted for Marchese Andrea Gerini of Florence. He also produced paintings for Cardinal Orsini (1719–89), including the *Allegory of the Treaty of Aquileia* (1752; Livorno, Leonardini priv. col., see Clark, fig. 71).

Among Costanzi's prestigious foreign commissions were the *Founding of Alexandria* for the Spanish court (signed and dated 1737; La Granja, S Ildefonso, Pal. Riofrío), part of the decoration of the throne-room at La Granja, in which other Roman artists—Trevisani, Conca and Imperiali—also participated. For Ernst Guido, Count of Harrach, he made two paintings of biblical subjects (1750–51; Rohrau, Schloss); and for George, Lord Keith, a sketch of the *Battle of Bannockburn* (1751) and a portrait (1752; London, N.P.G.).

Costanzi also took part in some important projects of church decoration both in Rome and in the Lazio region. In 1727 he produced the fresco of the *Apotheosis of SS Gregory and Romuald* (Rome, S Gregorio Magno al Celio), where, amid echoes of Ricci (in the figure of God the Father), Gaulli and Odazzi, there is a calm classicism deriving from Maratti. This figurative tendency was consolidated in the later decoration (1730) of S Maria in Campo Marzio, Rome, and in that of the church of Castel S Pietro (1732), near Palestrina. In the modello (1730; Malibu, CA, Getty Mus.; see fig.) for the frescoed vault in S Maria in Campo Marzio, Rome, a Rococo gaiety envelops the main figures, which are also inspired by early 17th-century classicism. The fresco in Castel S Pietro, of *St Peter Triumphant over Paganism*, is characterized by a frontality and a lack of depth, along with echoes, in the figures, of works by Raphael and the frescoed pendentives by Domenichino in S Andrea della Valle, Rome.

Among Costanzi's vast output of religious paintings, Pio mentions altarpieces sent to Aquila, to Gerona in Spain and to Lima, Peru (for the Dominicans), as well as four pictures sent to France. The *Redeemer Blessing*, which, together with the *Immaculate Conception* (both Rome, Gal. Accad. N. S Luca), was probably the reception piece for the artist's admission to the academy in 1741, shows a search for formal perfection and compositional equilibrium anticipating the canons later formulated by Winckelmann. This made Costanzi one of the most significant forerunners of the Neo-classical movement (Faldi).

The *Miracle of St Joseph of Copertino* (1750; Rome, G.N.A. Ant.) foreshadows the Romantic taste in the use of figures in costume—a constant motif in so much 18th-century painting from Giuseppe Passeri to Giuseppe Cades. The *Resurrection of Tabitha* (Rome, S Maria degli Angeli), painted for the basilica of St Peter, shows the accentuated classicism of Costanzi's stylistic language in its full maturity. Payment for this altarpiece was made from 1736 to 1740, but it was probably modified by the artist in 1757–8 (as is shown by the date added to the painting). A *bozzetto* (Bremen, Ksthalle) shows the changes he made.

For the French Benedictine abbey of Beaume les Dames (near Besançon), commissioned by the Abbess Henriette de Crux de Dames, he painted three canvases. These represent the *Presentation of the Virgin at the Temple* (signed and dated 1758; Besançon, Chapelle du Lycée), the *Flight into Egypt* and *Christ among the Doctors* (signed and dated 1759; both Besançon, St François Xavier). These are among Costanzi's last works and again use classical schemes. The *Martyrdom of St Torpes*, commissioned by the deputies of S Ranieri for Pisa Cathedral, was left unfinished (model; Pisa, Mus. N. S Matteo) on Costanzi's death and completed by his pupil Giovanni Battista Tempesti.

Costanzi collaborated with such landscape artists as Giovanni Battista Busiri and Jan Frans van Bloemen, painting the figures for their landscapes. Among these

Placido Costanzi: modello for the frescoed vault in S Maria in Campo Marzio, Rome, oil on canvas, 654×813 mm, 1730 (Malibu, CA, J. Paul Getty Museum)

were the *View of the Colosseum from the Vialone della Navicella* (1737; Rome, Gal. Accad. N. S Luca) and the decoration (1741–2; *in situ*) of the coffee-house at the Palazzo del Quirinale in Rome (1741–2). Costanzi was a member of the Accademia dei Virtuosi at the Pantheon and of the Accademia di San Luca (1741), of which he was elected Principe in 1758–9.

BIBLIOGRAPHY

DBI

N. Pio: *Vite* (1724); ed. C. Enggass and R. Enggass (1977), pp. 194–5, 297–9

I. Faldi: 'Gli inizi del neoclassicismo in pittura nella prima metà del settecento', *Nuove idee e nuova arte nel '700 italiano. Atti del Convegno dei Lincei: Roma, 1977*, pp. 495–523

A. M. Clark: 'An Introduction to Placido Costanzi', *Studies in Roman Eighteenth Century Painting* (Washington, DC, 1981), pp. 54–67

A. Brejon de Lavergnée: 'Un Ensemble de tableaux romains peints pour les églises de Franche-Comté: Costanzi, Pietri, Mazzanti, Conca, Trevisani', *'Il se rendit en Italie': Etudes offertes à André Chastel* (Rome, 1987), pp. 537–50

The Settecento Italian Rococo and Early Neo-classical Paintings, 1700–1800 (exh. cat., London, Matthiesen F.A., 1987)

A. M. Rybko: 'Costanzi, Placido', *La pittura in Italia: Il settecento*, ii (Milan, 1989), pp. 681–2

Settecento pisano: Pitture e sculture a Pisa nel secolo XVIII (exh. cat. by R. P. Ciardi, Pisa, Cassa di Risparmio, 1990)

G. Sestieri: 'Aggiunte a Placido Costanzi', *Paragone*, xlii/25 (1991), pp. 66–77

ANA MARIA RYBKO

(2) Carlo Costanzi (*b* Naples, 1705; *d* Rome, 1781). Gem-engraver, brother of (1) Placido Costanzi. He had a flamboyant character and was criticized for his quarrelsome temperament and great avidity for honours and glory. His unbridled ambition is documented by a letter (dated 15 June 1753) to Ridolfino Venuti (see Giulianelli, 1753), in which he lists his various honours for inclusion in the second edition of Mariette's book. He was, however, a very skilful engraver; Mariette (1750) thought him the best one in Rome, and he obtained commissions from the major European courts. His gem-engraved portraits include *James Stuart, the Old Pretender*; *Empress Maria-Teresa*; *Cardinal Renato Imperiali*; *Catherine II, Empress of Russia* (all untraced); *Benedict XIII* (sardonyx; Florence, Pitti); and *Baron Philipp von Stosch* (sapphire; Florence, Pitti). An emerald (untraced), engraved by Costanzi on one side with a portrait of *Benedict XIV* and on the other with *SS Peter and Paul*, was sent by the Pope to the Treasury of S Petronio in Bologna.

Costanzi's repertory also included portraits of figures from antiquity (e.g. Otto, Plato) and reproductions of ancient sculptures (e.g. *Antinous* from the marble at the Museo Capitolini, Rome), as well as reproductions of famous antique gems (*Aesculapius, Massinissa*; both untraced). A particularly noted work is the copy in chalcedony, for Cardinal Melchior de Polignac, of the famous antique intaglio of the *Head of Medusa*, then in the Strozzi collection; because of its perfect adherence to the model, it was long thought to be the original stone. Carlo's works, unlike those of his father and brother Tommaso, are often signed with *Cavalier Carlo Costanzi, Cavalier C. Costanzi f.* or *Eques Costansi f.*.

BIBLIOGRAPHY

DBI [with complete bibliog. and list of works]
P. von Stosch: *Gemmae antiquae caelatae* (Amsterdam, 1724)
P.-J. Mariette: *Traité des pierres gravées* (Paris, 1750)
P. Giulianelli: *Memorie degli intagliatori moderni in pietre dure, cammei e gioie* (Livorno, 1753)

LUCIA PIRZIO BIROLI STEFANELLI

Costanzo, Marco (di) (*fl c.* 1450–1500). Italian painter. A Syracusan whose identity was established by an inscription and date (no longer legible) on a panel of *St Jerome* (Syracuse Cathedral, Sacristy), painted for S Girolamo fuori le Mura. His relationship with his fellow Sicilian Antonello da Messina is not clear; it has been suggested that they were students together in Naples, but it seems more likely that Costanzo was influenced by Antonello in the 1470s than that they shared a common background in the 1440s. The *St Jerome* is strongly Netherlandish in character, ultimately reflecting a prototype by Jan van Eyck. Di Marzo read the date as 1468 and considered the painting to be an advanced work for a provincial artist, both in its use of perspective and its subtle lighting effect. Longhi suggested that the date had been mistranscribed, and a date of *c.* 1480 is generally accepted. If dated *c.* 1480, it is possible for some details, such as the carved prie-dieu, oriental rug and illusionistic corbel, to be credited to the influence of Antonello's *Annunciation* (1474; Syracuse, Pal. Bellomo).

A group of small panels of the Apostles and *Christ the Redeemer* (originally numbering 13) (Syracuse Cathedral, Sacristy) have been associated with Costanzo. The fluidity and sense of atmosphere recall Antonello, and there are also echoes of central Italian art (Melozzo da Forlì, Luca Signorelli and the Spaniard Pedro Berruguete, who worked at Urbino). At least two of the panels in the series (*St John the Evangelist* and the *Redeemer*) are by other hands and have been reasonably attributed to Salvo d'Antonio and Jacobello d'Antonio respectively. This would suggest that Costanzo was directly associated with Antonello's workshop in Messina in the decade after the master's death in 1479, when first Jacobello d'Antonio, Antonello's son, then probably Salvo d'Antonio, his nephew, ran the bottega.

In 1500 Costanzo was commissioned by the Confraternità di Santo Spirito to paint a *Crucifixion* and a *Pietà* (both untraced) and to renovate their *gonfalone* (untraced). A *Trinity between SS James and Stephen* dated 1495 (Syracuse, Pal. Bellomo), painted for Santo Spirito, is attributed to him and, although retouched, probably preserves the original composition. Bottari noted a Spanish influence in this work and described Costanzo as a Sicilian Berruguete.

BIBLIOGRAPHY

G. Di Marzo: *Delle belle arti in Sicilia*, iii (Palermo, 1862), p. 107
S. Bottari: 'Un pittore siciliano del quattrocento, Marco Costanzo', *Boll. A.*, xxxvi (1951), pp. 124–9
Antonello e la pittura del '400 in Sicilia (exh. cat., ed. G. Vigni and G. Carandente; Messina, Pal. Comunale, 1953), pp. 75–7
R. Longhi: 'Frammento siciliano', *Paragone*, iv/43 (1953), pp. 31–44 (38)
S. Bottari: *La pittura del quattrocento in Sicilia* (Messina and Florence, 1954), pp. 44–6, 62–83
Antonello da Messina (exh. cat., ed. A. Marabottini and F. Sricchia Santoro; Messina, Mus. Reg., 1981), pp. 219–22
F. Sricchia Santoro: *Antonello e l'Europa* (Milan, 1986), pp. 143–8

JOANNE WRIGHT

Costanzo da Ferrara [Costanzo de Moysis; Costanzo Lombardo] (*b* Venice, *c.* 1450; *d* ?Naples, after 1524). Italian medallist and painter. It is generally believed that he is the painter also known as Costanzo Lombardo, recorded in Naples *c.* 1484, and Costanzo de Moysis, described as a painter from Venice and recorded painting in Naples in 1483 and frescoing the *Story of the Prince of Rossano* (destr.) in the Villa Duchesca in 1488 (Strazzullo). Most of the information about him comes from a letter dated 24 August 1485 from Battista Bendidio, the Ferrarese envoy in Naples, to Ercole d'Este, Duke of Ferrara. Bendidio mentioned that Costanzo had lived for a considerable time in Ferrara and married a Ferrarese woman. He also reported that when Sultan Mehmed II of Turkey had requested that a painter be sent to Istanbul to paint his portrait, King Ferdinand I of Naples had dispatched Costanzo, who stayed there several years and was knighted by the Sultan. Babinger (1967) suggested that he could have left Naples for Istanbul in spring 1478, about a year before Gentile Bellini went to the Turkish court.

No painted portrait of Mehmed II by Costanzo has been positively identified, but two medals of the Sultan are by his hand; both are signed and one is dated 1481. The undated medal (unique copy, Washington, DC, N.G.A.) is far more refined in technique than the dated medal and probably the earlier of the two, dating from about 1478–9 (Hill and Pollard). Vasari believed the medals were by Pisanello, and the powerful profile portraits, by far the best that survive of the Turkish conqueror, and the spirited equestrian portraits on the reverses owe much to Pisanello. After the Sultan's death on 3 May 1481, Costanzo returned to Naples, and in 1485, on the commission of Bendidio, he painted a portrait of *Ferrante d'Este* (untraced), son of Ercole d'Este. He was recorded again at the Neapolitan court in 1492, and Pietro Summonte, in a letter of 1524 from Naples to Marcantonio Michiel in Venice, reported that Costanzo was still alive. Raby (1987) attributed three watercolour drawings to Costanzo that were previously given to Gentile Bellini: a *Seated Scribe* (Boston, MA, Isabella Stewart Gardner Mus.), a *Seated Solak* and a *Seated Turkish Woman* (both London, BM).

BIBLIOGRAPHY

DBI; Thieme–Becker: 'Costanzo'; 'Moysis, Costanzo de'
A. Armand: *Les Médailleurs italiens*, i (Paris, 2/1883–7), pp. 78–9
G. Gruyer: *L'Art ferrarais*, i (Paris, 1897), p. 651
C. von Fabriczy: 'Summontes Brief an M. A. Michiel', *Rep. Kstwiss.*, xxx (1907), pp. 149–59
J. von Karabacek: *Abendländische Künstler zu Konstantinopel im XV. und XVI. Jhdt, I: Italienische Künstler am Hofe Muhammeds II des Eroberers, 1451–1481* (Vienna, 1918)
G. Habich: *Die Medaillen der italienischen Renaissance* (Stuttgart and Berlin, 1922), p. 52

G. F. Hill: *Corpus*, i (1930), p. 80

B. Gray: 'Two Portraits of Mehmet II', *Burl. Mag.*, lxi (1932), pp. 4–6

F. Babinger: *Mehmed der Eroberer und seine Zeit* (Munich, 1953; rev. Eng. trans., Princeton, NJ, 1978), pp. 380–81, 388, 505–6

F. Babinger: 'Un ritratto ignorato di *Maometto II*, opera di Gentile Bellini', *A. Veneta*, xv (1961), pp. 25–32

G. F. Hill and G. Pollard: *Renaissance Medals from the Samuel H. Kress Collection at the National Gallery of Art* (London, 1967), no. 102

F. Strazzullo: 'Lavori eseguiti in Castelcapuano nell'anno 1488', *Napoli Nob.*, xiv (1975), pp. 143–9

M. Andaloro: 'Costanzo da Ferrara: Gli anni a Costantinopoli alla corte di Maometto II', *Stor. A.*, xii (1980), pp. 185–212

G. Pollard: *Medaglie italiane del rinascimento: Museo Nazionale del Bargello*, i (Florence, 1985), p. 183

J. Raby: 'Pride and Prejudice: Mehmed the Conqueror and the Italian Portrait Medal', *Stud. Hist. A.*, xxi (1987), pp. 171–94

——: 'Constanzo da Ferrara', *The Currency of Fame: Portrait Medals of the Renaissance*, ed. S. K. Scher (New York, 1994), pp. 87–90

MARK M. SALTON

Costa Pinheiro(, António Agostinho) (*b* Moura, 8 Jan 1932). Portuguese painter and printmaker. In 1957 the artist emigrated to Munich where he studied at the Akademie der Bildenden Künste. On a scholarship in Paris (1960–62), he collaborated with his compatriots René Bertholo and Lourdes Castro in the magazine and exhibitions of the KWY group of Portuguese emigré artists. The crispness of his painting technique demonstrates his predilection for drawing and graphics. His early works were gestural and calligraphic, but in the 1960s he adopted a playful figuration, paralleling the work of Bertholo and Joaquim Rodrigo, in which caricatural figures combine with imaginary objects to relate absurd and humorous narratives. In the series of paintings of Portuguese kings (mid-1960s), for example *Peter I* (1966; Mannheim, Kurt Egger priv. col.), and in the series dealing obsessively with the poet Fernando Pessoa (1970s to 1980s) the artist investigated his cultural roots. He also made theatre sets and masks and illustrated several books.

BIBLIOGRAPHY

Costa Pinheiro: Die Könige (exh. cat., Munich, Gal. Leonhart, 1966)

Costa Pinheiro (exh. cat., Lisbon, Gal. 111, 1987)

RUTH ROSENGARTEN

Costa Rica, Republic of [Sp. República de Costa Rica]. Central American country, bordered by Nicaragua to the north, by Panama to the south-east, by the Caribbean Sea to the east and by the Pacific Ocean to the south and west (see fig. 1). The capital is San José. The Sierra Madre cuts across the country from north-west to south-east, forming a central plateau that is the main centre of population.

1. Introduction. 2. Architecture. 3. Painting, graphic arts and sculpture. 4. Patronage and institutions.

1. INTRODUCTION. Columbus arrived at the town of Cariari (Puerto Limón) on 18 September 1502, during his fourth voyage. His brother Bartolomé explored the interior of the region but left no settlements. In 1509 the territory of Costa Rica became part of Castilla de Oro and was governed from Panama by Diego de Nicuesa. It was incorporated in the Audiencia de Guatemala, established *c*. 1521. During the government of Pedrarias Dávila, Gaspar Espinosa led an expedition to the Gulf of Nicoya, where the first Spaniards settled. Francisco Fernández de Córdoba, who had founded the town of Bruselas (1524)

1. Map of Costa Rica

on the Nicoya Peninsula, was impressed by the wealth of flora and fauna and in 1539 gave the region the name of Costa Rica (rich coast). It was not until 1560 that Juan de Cavallón penetrated into the interior and founded first the city of Castillo de Garcimuñoz (1561) and later Ciudad de los Reyes and the port of Landecho. Juan Vásquez de Coronado, the first Governor of Costa Rica, founded the city of Cartago in 1564 and introduced cattle farming and European plants. The central plateau began to be populated, but the depredations of pirates, attacks by Mosquito Indians and commercial restrictions imposed by Spain made economic progress difficult.

After the kingdom of Guatemala proclaimed independence, without bloodshed, in September 1821, Costa Rica declared its independence. With the other provinces of the former kingdom, in 1822 Costa Rica joined the Mexican Empire of Iturbide; when this broke up in 1823, it joined the Central American Federation. Despite its separation from the Central American Federation in November 1838, Costa Rica did not proclaim absolute independence until August 1848.

In 1948 the Costa Rican Congress declared fraudulent the elections in which the opposition candidate Otilio Ulate Blanco had defeated the official candidate, Rafael Angel Calderón Guardia, and this led to civil war. A rebellion, led by José Figueres, set up a Government junta, and a Constituent Assembly declared the election of Ulate valid. He governed until 1953, when he was succeeded by Figueres. Power then alternated between the National Liberation Party and the opposition Social Christian United Party.

This article covers the arts produced in Costa Rica from the colonial period onwards. For a discussion of the arts of Pre-Columbian Costa Rica, *see* SOUTH AMERICA, PRE-COLUMBIAN, §II.

BIBLIOGRAPHY

M. A. Jiménez: *Desarrollo constitucional de Costa Rica* (San José, 1979)
C. Melendez: *Conquistadores y pobladores: Origenes histórico-sociales de los costarricenses* (San José, 1982)
E. Fonseca: *Costa Rica colonial: La tierra y el hombre* (San José, 1984, 3/1986)
C. F. Echeverría: *Historia crítica del arte costarricense* (San José, 1986)

C. GUILLERMO MONTERO

2. ARCHITECTURE. Although Spanish explorations date from 1539, it was not until the early 1560s that the settlements of Real de Ceniza, Garcimuñoz and the colonial capital Cartago (formerly Ciudad del Lodo) were established. The first settlements were mainly on the central plateau, although incursions from the sea and frequent earthquakes led to underpopulation, and few buildings survive from the 16th to 18th centuries. The ruined church at Ujarrás may date from the early 17th century (Marco Dorta) and shows 16th-century Mexican influence. Only part of the three-storey façade remains: it has a wide entrance arch with squat pilasters rising from its springing line to the first horizontal division, and the remains of scrolls rise to a modest bell gable with twin bell arches. The Franciscan sanctuary of Orosi (1766) reflects the Baroque of the first half of the 18th century, perhaps indirectly by way of León, Nicaragua, the seat of the bishopric that controlled the church in Costa Rica, and its cathedral. It is a low, rectangular church with a shallow-pitched overhanging tile roof, similar in design to the Franciscan churches in Paraguay but without a surrounding colonnade gallery. A sturdy attached two-storey tower is set back slightly from a barely adorned gable and girdled by a balcony with a blind balustrade (as in León Cathedral) overlooking the monastery patio; there are unique, centrally placed pilasters on each exposed face of its lower storey.

Colonial traditions carried over into the 19th century and are evident in churches built in its early decades. The design of the church of Guadalupe (completed 1810, under the direction of Mariano Ormuza y Matute), Cartago, is derived from the *Mudéjar* style. Its three round-arched entrances are set in rectangular architrave frames. The bell gable is divided between two storeys, the upper part of which is roofed and can almost be classed as a central tower. The early 19th-century parish church at Heredia is an example of the use of low, broad-based towers as buttresses in 'earthquake Baroque', though by this date the design is more Neo-classical in feeling. Twin three-storey towers with modest pyramidal cupolas are set back behind the façade, which itself projects either side of a barnlike church. The façade, also buttress-like, is a two-storey, tripartite composition with simple arched entrances on the lower storey and coupled pilasters supporting a pediment above; the pilasters are repeated on the end bays, which themselves have miniature cupolas giving the appearance of secondary towers.

Buildings constructed soon after independence continued the trend towards Neo-classicism. They include the Comandancia (military headquarters) by the Mexican Miguel Velázquez and the Palacio Nacional by the German engineer Franz Kurtze, both in San José; colonial features based on local skills reappeared in such buildings as the barracks and the Universidad de S Tomás (both San José). New French and German immigrants helped induce changes: the Caribbean bungalow style began to replace Hispanic domestic models, and *fin-de-siècle* eclecticism ran alongside the established styles. As elsewhere in Latin America, prefabricated iron buildings were imported from Europe, including the Edificio Metálico (mid-1870s), San José, imported from Belgium. The Neo-classical Teatro Nacional (1897), San José, is a small and charming replica of the Paris Opéra. It is among many academicist buildings designed by the engineer Lesmes Jiménez Bonnefill, who studied in Belgium. Jiménez also worked in a neo-Gothic style, as in his church of La Merced (1903–5), San José, an elegant composition finished in stucco though with classical undertones, especially in the central tower, which carries a simple hexagonal spire.

Anti-academicism brought a flowering of *modernismo* *c*. 1900, for example in the work of Francesco Tenca (*d* 1908), especially in private houses such as that for Jiménez la Guardia (1900), San José. Eclecticism continued during the 20th century. Luis Llach Logostera (*fl* 1900–15; trained in Barcelona) ranged from a mix of Byzantine, Classical and *Mudéjar* elements in the Basílica Nuestra Señora de Los Angeles (1912), Cartago, to a stripped-down classical style in the Edificio Correos y Telegráficos (1914), San José. The Neo-classical and neo-Baroque continued after World War I: José Francisco Salazar Quesada (1892–1968) designed the Club Unión (1921; destr.), San José, and the Basílica S Domingo (1924; with Teodorico Quirós), Heredia. José María Barrantes Monge (1890–1966) produced a number of churches in the 1930s and 1940s, including Nuestra Señora de Desamparados (1935), San José, its portico supported on unique coupled Tuscan columns. On the other hand, Quirós's church S Isidro de Coronado (1935), San José, is a fine late example of Gothic Revival with pinnacled buttresses and a crocketted spire. Art Deco appears in Barrantes's three-storey apartments (1935) on Avenida 6, Calle 1, San José, almost concurrently with Neo-Colonial in a number of houses and La Sabema national airport, San José (1935; now the Museo de Arte Costarricense). The advent of the Modern Movement took place in the 1930s, much influenced by the work of German immigrant Paul Ehrenberg Brinkman (1900–65). His flat-roofed, single-storey dwelling for Dr Gonzala Cubero (1933), and the Almacén Borbón (1935), both San José, are reminiscent of the dynamism of German Expressionism of the mid-1920s; with a series of cinemas (built well into the 1940s), they retain some Art Deco detailing. The same is true for some of Salazar's buildings of this period, but his three-storey Hospital S Juan de Dios (1934), San José, is a plain-surfaced building with only a touch of Art Deco in the entrance details; the Secretaría de Salubridad Pública (1936–40), San José, is a Rationalist building reminiscent of the Perret brothers' work. The Perrets' influence also seems evident in some of Barrantes's later churches, such as Nuestra Señora del Carmen, Cartago (1945). Ehrenberg continued to lead the way, however: his Trejos González building (1954) has fully glazed infill between projecting concrete floors, although there is still an echo of Erich

Mendelsohn in the Schyfter building (1954), San José; his pitched-roof houses, such as the Puci Poli dwellings (1950), San José, and Jane Davidson de Salazar (1956), San José, have elements of the Neo-Colonial style.

Stronger American influence in the 1960s produced many International Style urban developments, followed by a return to deeper consideration for context by such locally trained architects as Jorge Borbón (*b* 1933), Edgar Vargas (*b* 1922) and Hernan Jiménez (*b* 1942). The Chilean Bruno Stagno (*b* 1943) is perhaps the best known of the later generation of architects: his houses in San José (1976) are expressive of the new mood of social and environmental relevance, and his later work, such as the building for Escuela 'Country Day', San Antonio (1983), Escazú, has been labelled *arquitectura mestiza*, reflecting the serious attempts to define a contextual image.

BIBLIOGRAPHY
E. A. de Varona: *Orosi* (San José, 1949)
P. Kelemen: *Baroque and Rococo in Latin America* (New York, 1951), pp. 70–71
D. Angulo Iñiguez and others: *Historia del arte hispano-americano*, iii (Barcelona, 1956), pp. 80–81, 90–92
E. Marco Dorta: *Arte en América y Filipinas*, Ars Hispaniae, xxi (Madrid, 1973), p. 211
C. Altezor Fuentes: *Arquitectura urbana en Costa Rica: Exploración histórica* (San José, 1986)
'Casas en Iberoamerica', *Summa A.*, 235 (March 1987), pp. 51–71
R. Segre: 'Bruno Stagno, arquitecto', *Proa*, 407 (Nov 1991), pp. 11–29

JUAN BERNAL PONCE

3. PAINTING, GRAPHIC ARTS AND SCULPTURE. In the period between colonization and independence painting and sculpture in Costa Rica were generally imported from Ecuador, Guatemala and Mexico. In the second half of the 19th century a local sculptural tradition emerged in the work of Fadrique Gutiérrez (1841–97), who created monumental pieces in stone, and Juan Mora González (1862–95), who created a series of portraits and polychrome wood statues. Artistic activity in Costa Rica became more eclectic only in the early 20th century. During the 1920s and 1930s regular exhibitions, including the Salones Anuales de Artes Plásticas, were held in San José. In 1928 the painter and architectural engineer TEODORICO QUIRÓS and the painter and sculptor MAX JIMÉNEZ founded the Círculo de Amigos del Arte; the group, whose members typically depicted rural scenes in an academic manner, held regular exhibitions sponsored by the *Diario de Costa Rica* at Las Arcadas, San José, stimulating artistic production at a national level. In 1935 the Monument to Motherhood competition fuelled the debate between academicists and modernists. Controversy focused on Francisco Zúñiga's sculpture of a woman, for it was deemed that the uneducated masses could understand only realism, not modern art; Zúñiga left for Mexico in 1936. A growing division between academic and more modern styles was embodied in the work of one member of the Círculo de Amigos del Arte, FRANCISCO AMIGHETTI, whose wood-engravings and drawings, although regionalist in subject, were more expressionistic than other members' work; Amighetti was also influential in his creation of mural paintings, a form he had studied in Mexico and on which he collaborated with such artists as Margarita Bertheau (1913–75).

2. Rafael Fernández: *Flying Figure*, acrylic on hardboard, 500×760 mm, 1972 (Washington, DC, Museum of Modern Art of Latin America)

The painter MANUEL DE LA CRUZ GONZÁLEZ was exiled following the revolution of 1948; in Venezuela his style developed towards geometric abstraction (e.g. *Space-Colour*, *c.* 1962–5; artist's col., see Ulloa, p. 108), and on his return his work was considered avant-garde. González was a member of Grupo Ocho, one of a number of groups that existed throughout the 1960s, whose members were interested in experimenting with non-figurative art while trying to gain popular acceptance for it; they held exhibitions at Las Arcadas, San José, in 1961–2, and organized festivals, increasing contact between Costa Rican artists and the international art world. Other groups included Grupo Taller and Grupo Totem. González himself was included in the first Bienal Centroamericana de Pintura in 1971. The engraver JUAN LUIS RODRÍGUEZ was an important figure in graphic arts, stimulating interest in printmaking by setting up an engraving workshop within the fine arts faculty of the Universidad de Costa Rica, San José, in 1972–3. A number of artists turned to Surrealism in the late 20th century, including Rafael Fernández (*b* 1935). His paintings are somewhat reminiscent of Chagall (see fig. 2).

BIBLIOGRAPHY

El arte religioso en Costa Rica (exh. cat. by F. Amighetti, San José, Mus. N. Costa Rica, 1955)

Modern Artists of Costa Rica: An Exhibition of Paintings and Sculptures Assembled by the Group 8 of San José (exh. cat., Washington, DC, Pan Amer. Un., 1964)

L. Ferrero: *La escultura en Costa Rica* (San José, 1973)

R. Ulloa Barrenechea: *Pintores de Costa Rica* (San José, 1975)

C. F. Echeverría: *Ocho artistas costarricenses y una tradición* (San José, 1977)

L. Ferrero: *Cinco artistas costarricenses: Pintores y escultores* (San José, 1985)

——: *Sociedad y arte en la Costa Rica del siglo 19* (San José, 1986)

4. PATRONAGE AND INSTITUTIONS. The Escuela Nacional de Bellas Artes, San José, was founded in 1897 under the directorship of the Spanish painter Tomás Povedano, whose own academic paintings of rural scenes influenced TEODORICO QUIRÓS and others of his generation who attended the school. The newspaper *Diario de Costa Rica* sponsored exhibitions held regularly between 1928 and 1937 at Las Arcadas, San José, by the group Círculo de Amigos del Arte. In 1940 the Escuela de Bellas Artes was incorporated into the Universidad de Costa Rica, San José, as a faculty of fine arts under Angela Castro Quesada. Quirós was Dean of the faculty from 1942 to 1945, encouraging a revival of the academic style on which it was founded. The Casa del Artista, San José, was founded in 1948 to provide artistic training to poorer students. Also in San José, the Escuela de Arte y Decoración Esempi was founded in 1955 under Francisco Alvarado Abella. At a government level, the Dirección General de Artes y Letras was set up in 1963 to stimulate artistic activity in the country; it initiated the collection that later became the basis of the permanent collection of the Museo de Arte Costarricense, San José. In 1970 the Ministerio de Cultura, Juventud y Deportes was created to promote cultural activities; the Museo de Arte was later attached. The engraver JUAN LUIS RODRÍGUEZ set up an engraving workshop within the fine arts faculty of the university in 1972–3, and this initiative was followed up in 1977 by the foundation of another engraving studio at the Universidad Nacional de Heredia. Upon the conception of the Museo de Arte in 1977 the Dirección General de Artes y Letras

ceased to exist. The museum's aim was to preserve, disseminate and stimulate artistic activity and the national artistic heritage and identity. It opened in May 1978 in the former airport building of La Sabema.

BIBLIOGRAPHY

S. Rovinski: *Cultural Policy in Costa Rica* (Paris, 1977)

C. Kandler: *National Museum of Costa Rica: One Hundred Years of History* (San José, 1987)

C. GUILLERMO MONTERO

Costa Sequeira, José da. *See* SEQUEIRA, (2).

Coste, Pascal(-Xavier) (*b* Marseille, 26 Nov 1787; *d* Marseille, 8 Feb 1879). French architect and writer. The designer of many of the principal public buildings of Marseille, he also published the first accurate records of the Islamic monuments of Cairo, North Africa and the Middle East—a central interest of mid-19th-century architectural theorists and ornamentalists.

After studying both engineering and drawing in Marseille, Coste began his career in 1804 as site inspector and draughtsman for the Neo-classicist Michel-Robert Penchaud, a municipal and departmental architect, for whom he worked for a decade. In 1814, on the recommendation of Percier & Fontaine, he entered the Ecole des Beaux-Arts in Paris and the ateliers of Antoine-Laurent-Thomas Vaudoyer and Jean-Baptiste Labadye (1777–1850). An encounter in Paris with the geographer Jombert, who had been a member of the scientific mission that accompanied Napoleon's invasion of Egypt in 1798, was to influence his subsequent career. In 1817 Jombert recommended Coste to Muhammad 'Ali, Khedive of Egypt, to plan and supervise construction of a saltpetre factory. Coste spent most of the next decade in Egypt, becoming architect to the Khedive, entrusted with the design of a palace and bath complex for Muhammad 'Ali, two mosques and large-scale engineering works. In 1820 he became chief engineer for Lower Egypt, designing 19 telegraph towers to connect Alexandria and Cairo and digging the first of an important network of canals. He became a passionate student of ancient Egyptian and Islamic architecture. His delicately detailed and rendered drawings, which recorded at once the colourful and picturesque aspects and the structural framework of buildings, were much admired when exhibited in the Paris Salon and were promoted by Jean Nicolas Huyot, whom Coste had met in Egypt in 1821 and who helped obtain state support for the publication of Coste's luxurious book *Architecture arabe ou monuments du Kaire* (1839). It was the first publication of Cairene Islamic monuments and marked the beginning of Coste's lifelong interest in the various manifestations of the style throughout the Mediterranean. The forms and principles of Islamic architecture made available by Coste's plates were to influence French architects, but Coste himself did not exploit Islamic motifs in any of his non-Egyptian buildings until the very end of his career, when he produced the richly polychromatic mausoleum for Camille Olive in the St Pierre Cemetery at Marseille (1872). Bitten by a yellow serpent in 1827, Coste returned to Marseille, where in 1829 he was named Professor of Architecture at the Ecole des Beaux-Arts.

In 1830 Coste won the competition for the new parish church of St Lazare in Marseille (1833–9), the first of a series of churches in which he enriched the model of the Early Christian basilica first introduced in Paris by Lebas's Notre Dame de Lorette (1824). He also built the churches of St Joseph (1833–43) and St Barnabus (1845–7) and the parish church at Mazargues (1846–9); none of these was completed according to his plans until much later owing to lack of funds. Named Municipal Architect in 1844, he designed many utilitarian structures for the city including a series of fountains, the slaughterhouse (1846–51) and the prison (1851), though all these were overshadowed by his masterpiece, the new Bourse (1852) at the foot of the Canebière, a monument to the port city's commercial flowering at mid-century. A great commercial palazzo with columnar loggia enriched by trophies and decoration that celebrated Marseille's long history of commercial and navigational successes, it confirmed Coste's belief, put to the local academy in the 1840s, that only a continuation of the inherited system of Renaissance composition could represent progress in art.

Coste remained an indefatigable traveller into his 80s and was rarely in Marseille for more than six months of the year; he travelled as far as Moscow and Andalusia, visiting nearly every French province and European country and recording historical and contemporary architecture in the hundreds of sketches he left to the city of Marseille on his death (Marseille, Bib. Mun.). In 1839 he was selected to accompany Félix-Edouard, Comte de Sercey, and the painter Eugène Flandin (1809–76) on a two-year royal mission to Persia, which resulted in *Voyage en Perse* (1843–54), the huge folio volumes of engravings in collaboration with Flandin, and his own publication *Monuments modernes de la Perse, mesurés, dessinés et décrits* (1867), which consolidated Coste's reputation as an expert on the language and evolution of Islamic ornament.

UNPUBLISHED SOURCES
Marseille, Bib. Mun. [bound portfolios containing Coste's sketches]

WRITINGS
Architecture arabe ou monuments du Kaire (Paris, 1839, dated 1837–9)
'Y a-t-il possibilité de créer une architecture nationale en France?', *Mém. Acad. Sci., B.-Lett. & A. Marseille* (1848), pp. 209–27
with E. Flandin: *Voyage en Perse* (Paris, 1853)
Monuments modernes de la Perse, mesurés, dessinés et décrits (Paris, 1867)
Mémoires d'un artiste, 2 vols (Marseille, 1878)

BIBLIOGRAPHY
J. Richaud: 'Pascal Coste', *Rev. Gén. Archit.*, xxxvi (1879), pp. 40–43
E. Parrocel: 'Pascal Coste, étudié comme dessinateur, ingénieur, architecte et écrivain', *Réun. Soc. B.-A. Dépts* (1881), pp. 227–44
F. Rebuffat: 'Le Palais de la Bourse et son histoire', *Marseille sous le Seconde Empire* (Marseille, 1960)
R. Guiral: 'L'Architecte marseillais Pascal Coste et son oeuvre en Egypte, sous Méhemet-Ali', *Provence Hist.*, xix/76 (1969), pp. 133–42
——: 'Un Architecte français en Afrique du Nord dans la première moitié du XIXe siècle', *Rev. Occident Musulman & Médit.*, vi (1969), pp. 103–9
R. Bertrand: 'Une Oeuvre "mauresque" de Pascal Coste: Le Tombeau de Camille Olive au cimetière Saint-Pierre', *Rev. Marseille*, cxvi (1979), pp. 73–8
D. Jasmin: 'Le Travail d'un architecte marseillais en Orient (1817–1841)', *Persp. Médit.*, xiv (1983), pp. 3–9
——: 'Pascal Coste et l'Egypte', *Mnmts Hist.*, cxxv (1983), pp. 29–33
D. Armogathe and S. Leprun, eds: *Pascal Coste, ou l'architecture cosmopolite* (Paris, 1990)
R. Bertrand: 'Le Tombeau de Camille Olive', *Marseille: La Passion des contrastes*, eds M. Culot and D. Droucourt (Liège, 1991), pp. 258–65
D. Jasmin: 'Architecture et urbanisme', *Marseille au XIXe siècle: Rêves et triomphes* (exh. cat., ed. E. Temime and others; Marseille, 1991–2), pp. 127–55
B. Bergdoll: 'Pascal Coste: Du classicisme à l'historicisme', *Marseille au XIXe siècle: Rêves et triomphes* (exh. cat., ed. E. Temime and others; Marseille, 1991–2), pp. 187–93

BARRY BERGDOLL

Costoli, Aristodemo (*b* Florence, 6 Sept 1803; *d* Florence, ?22 June 1871). Italian sculptor and painter. At the age of 12 he entered the Accademia di Belle Arti e Liceo Artistico in Florence to study painting under Giuseppe Bezzuoli, Pietro Benvenuti and Pietro Ermini (*fl* 1800–15) and sculpture under Stefano Ricci (1765–1837). A *Self-portrait* (1828; Florence, Pitti) in oil on canvas demonstrates a Romantic style learnt from Bezzuoli and anticipates Costoli's abilities to render portraiture in sculpture. In 1828 he won a four-year stipendium, enabling him to travel to Rome. While there he produced the over life-size gesso *Meneceus* (1830; Florence, Pitti; marble version, 1853), which was praised for its classically rendered, idealized body when exhibited at the Esposizione di Roma in 1830. He returned to Florence and, his reputation increasing, was appointed Assistant Master of Sculpture under Lorenzo Bartolini at the Accademia in 1839. In 1842 he executed a statue of *Galileo Galilei* for the city's Museo della Specola (now the Museo Zoologico 'La Specola'; *in situ*) and a second version for the exterior loggia of the Uffizi (*in situ*). In 1846 he sculpted a marble portrait bust of his patron *Leopold II, Grand Duke of Tuscany* (Lucca, Villa Guinigi). In that year he also participated in a competition for a monument to Christopher Columbus, but the commission was given to Bartolini, who died before completing the full-size work; Costoli, Pietro Freccia (1814–56) and others finished it by 1862 (Genoa, Piazza Acquaverde; *in situ*), Costoli's contribution being a figure of Prudence for the base and a low relief of *Columbus Planting the Cross on the Beach*. Another sculpture with this theme is the *Discovery of America* (1848; Florence, Pitti), a bronze group 860 mm high on an ebony base. Its rather small dimensions and elegant decorative qualities inspired many copies. Despite their artistic differences, in 1850 Costoli succeeded Bartolini as Professor of Sculpture at the Accademia. His last work was the monument to the singer *Angelica Catalani* (1867; Pisa, Camposanto), an ambitious, multi-figured work that includes figures of Charity, St Cecilia and an angel, as well as that of the deceased in her family's arms. Critics admired Costoli's flawless technique and his Neo-classical style that also bore signs of a restrained naturalism, but they faulted his sculptures for a certain coldness.

BIBLIOGRAPHY
P. Emiliani Giudici: 'Correspondance particulière', *Gaz. B.-A.*, iii (1859), pp. 238–43
A. De Gubernatis: *Dizionario degli artisti italiani viventi: Pittori, scultori, e architetti* (Florence, 1892)
Cultura neoclassica e romantica nella Toscana granducale (exh. cat., ed. S. Pinto; Florence, Pitti, 1972)

□

Costume book. *See* FASHION PLATE AND COSTUME BOOK.

Cosway. English artists. (1) Richard Cosway and his wife, (2) Maria Cosway, were successful artists who established a fashionable salon in their London home in the 1780s and 1790s. Richard Cosway is best known for his 'stained' drawings, while Maria's oeuvre, and her life, developed a somewhat broader range than those of her husband.

(1) Richard Cosway (*bapt* Okeford, nr Tiverton, Devon, 5 Nov 1742; *d* London, 4 July 1821). Painter, draughtsman, dealer and collector. Probably the son of a schoolmaster, he showed a precocious talent for drawing and studied at Shipley's Drawing School in the Strand, where he won several prizes. He attended the Richmond House academy, set up by Charles Lennox, 3rd Duke of Richmond, where he met Giovanni Battista Cipriani. He first exhibited at the Society of Artists in 1760, showing there again between 1767 and 1779. He also showed at the Free Society of Artists between 1761 and 1766. In 1769 he entered the Royal Academy Schools, becoming an ARA in 1770, when he began to exhibit at the Academy, and RA the following year. In 1781 Cosway married the Anglo-Florentine artist (2) Maria Cosway, née Hadfield, and they moved in 1784 to Schomberg House, Pall Mall, which became a centre for fashionable London society. In 1786 he made a brief visit to Paris and in 1791 he moved to a larger house in Stratford Place, London.

Cosway, who from 1785 signed many works *Primarius Pictor Serenissimi Walliae Principis* ('Principal painter of his most serene Prince of Wales'), painted miniatures and produced 'stained' drawings in prodigious numbers; he painted rather fewer full-scale oil portraits. For the miniatures, as with his other work, he relied heavily on his brilliant use of line. Such miniatures as the *Portrait of an Unknown Lady* (1798; London, V&A) are characterized by his delight in delineating the curly grey hair and tilted heads of his sitters; colour is restricted to hints of red for the flesh tones and blue in the background sky. The 'stained' drawings epitomize elegance and bear comparison with Sir Thomas Lawrence's sketches. Cosway's studies are made with consummate ease and minimal colour, for example the graphite and watercolour full-length portrait of *The Hon. Peter Robert Burrell (later 2nd Lord Gwydyr and 19th Lord Willoughby de Eresby)* (1807; Drummond Castle, Tayside; see fig.); the enlarged eyes, the colouring of the face and hair and the delicately drawn figure are all typical.

Although his oil paintings are less successful, these do not deserve the low regard in which they are generally held. He painted some religious and historical subjects, for instance his altarpiece of the *Liberation of St Peter* (1784; Tiverton, St Peter's), the style of which betrays Cosway's affiliation with Cipriani. He also painted portraits, most notably for the Courtenay, Pleydell-Bouverie and Spencer-Churchill families. *Lucy, Harriet and Caroline Courtenay* (1798; Powderham Castle, Devon) is a fine example, combining stylistic traits of Matthew William Peters and John Hoppner. Cosway supplemented his income by dealing, and the Prince Regent, later George IV, appears to have been one of his principal clients. He built up a fine collection of Old Master paintings, drawings and prints, sculpture, furniture, *objets d'art* and curiosities and an extensive library, all of which was sold by Maria Cosway at five auctions held in 1821 and 1822 by George Stanley.

Richard Cosway: *The Hon. Peter Robert Burrell (later 2nd Lord Gwydyr and 19th Lord Willoughby de Eresby)*, graphite with watercolour on paper mounted on card, 279×216 mm, 1807 (Drummond Castle, Tayside)

BIBLIOGRAPHY

Waterhouse: *18th C.*
G. C. Williamson: *Richard Cosway RA and his Wife and Pupils: Miniaturists of the Eighteenth Century* (London, 1897, rev. 1905)
F. Lugt: *Marques* (1921), p. 111
G. Reynolds: *English Portrait Miniatures* (London, 1952/*R* Cambridge, 1988), pp. 124–30
J. Murdoch and others: *The English Miniature* (London, 1981), pp. 184–8
S. Lloyd: 'Richard Cosway RA: The Artist as Collector, Connoisseur and Virtuoso', *Apollo*, cxxxiii (1991), pp. 398–405
Richard and Maria Cosway: Regency Artists of Taste and Fashion (exh. cat by S. Lloyd, London, N.P.G., 1995)

HUGH BELSEY

(2) Maria (Louisa Caterina Cecilia) Cosway [née Hadfield] (*b* Florence, 1759; *d* Lodi, nr Milan, 5 Jan 1838). Painter and etcher, wife of (1) Richard Cosway. Her parents managed three inns in Florence that were popular with the English on the Grand Tour. Her brother was the architect George Hadfield. As a pupil of Violante Cerroti and Johan Zoffany, Maria copied at the Uffizi from 1773 to 1778, in which year she was elected to the Florentine Accademia del Disegno. In the following year she travelled to London, where on 18 January 1781 she married (1) Richard Cosway. Between 1781 and 1801 she exhibited at the Royal Academy, London, showing some portraits but mainly history paintings; she took her subjects from such literary sources as the Old Testament, Homer, Virgil, Petrarch, Tasso and Shakespeare. Her two main stylistic influences, serving respectively the decorative and the visionary aspects of her work, were Angelica Kauffman and Henry Fuseli. The full-length portrait of *Georgiana, Duchess of Devonshire, as Cynthia* (exh. RA 1782; Chatsworth, Derbys), which was engraved by Valentine Green in 1783, won her the most attention, but more striking was the *Self-portrait* (untraced; probably exh. RA 1787) showing her with arms crossed; Green engraved it in 1787. During the 1780s Maria Cosway was hostess at some of the most fashionable musical evenings in London. Visits to Paris in 1786 and 1787 were the setting for a love affair with Thomas Jefferson. After a period in Italy (1790–94) she worked in London on a series of projects published by Rudolph Ackermann, which included her etchings of Richard Cosway's drawings (1800) and her original designs illustrating two moral tales for women (both 1800), as well as more successful illustrations (1803) to a poem by Mary Robinson (1758–1800).

In Paris, from 1801–3, Maria Cosway made copies and hand-coloured etchings of Old Masters in the Louvre; three subscription numbers of these were published in 1802. In 1803, under the patronage of Joseph Fesch, then Archbishop of Lyon, she founded a school for girls in that city. From 1812, with the support of Duca Francesco Melzi d'Eril (1753–1816), she established a Collegio delle Dame Inglesi in Lodi. Returning to London (1817–22) to nurse her husband, she organized five major sales of his collections. After his death she exhibited his drawings of 'sacred, historical and poetical subjects' at George Stanley's auction rooms in Old Bond Street; failing to find an appropriate buyer in England, she transferred the collection to Italy, where she promoted it vigorously. Most of Richard Cosway's drawings, together with many of Maria Cosway's papers and relics, are preserved in the Fondazione Cosway, Lodi. The Collegio became one of the most prestigious in Lombardy, and in 1834 Maria was made a baroness by Francis I, Emperor of Austria. She was a prolific letter writer, and there exist several collections of her correspondence: with the antiquary Baron d'Hancarville (Lodi, Bib. Laudense); with the collector Francis Douce (Oxford, Bodleian Lib.); with the engraver Francesco Rosaspina (1762–1841; Forlì, Bib. Com. Saffi); and with the architect John Soane (London, Soane Mus.).

UNPUBLISHED SOURCES
London, V&A, MS (Eng.) L. 961-1953 [autobiographical letter of Maria Cosway to Sir William Cosway (24 May 1830)]

PRINTS
Imitations in Chalk, Etched by Mrs Cosway from Original Drawings by Richard Cosway (London, 1800)
Gallery of the Louvre, Represented by Etchings Executed Solely by Mrs Maria Cosway, with an Historical and Critical Description of all the Pictures. . .by J. Griffiths (Paris, 1802)

BIBLIOGRAPHY
G. C. Williamson: *Richard Cosway, RA and his Wife and Pupils: Miniaturists of the Eighteenth Century* (London, 1897, rev. 1905)
H. D. Bullock: *My Head and My Heart: A Little History of Thomas Jefferson and Maria Cosway* (New York, 1945)
J. Walker: 'Maria Cosway: An Undervalued Artist', *Apollo*, cxxiii (1986), pp. 318–24
E. Cazzulani and A. Stroppa: *Maria Hadfield Cosway: Biografia, diari e scritti della fondatrice del Collegio delle Dame Inglesi in Lodi* (Orio Litta, 1989)
S. Lloyd: 'The Accomplished Maria Cosway: Anglo-Italian Artist, Musician, Salon Hostess and Educationalist (1759–1838)', *J. Angl.-It. Stud.*, ii (1992), pp. 108–39

STEPHEN LLOYD

Cosyns [Cosijn], **Jan** (*b* ?Brussels, 1647; *d* ?Brussels, 1708). Flemish sculptor and architect. He became a master sculptor in Brussels in 1678. Under the direction of Lucas Faydherbe he collaborated on the decoration (1678) of the right-hand choir chapel in Onze-Lieve-Vrouw van de Zavelkerk, Brussels, which was being fitted out as a funerary chapel for Graf Lamoral of Thurn and Taxis. Cosyns was responsible for the marble statues, which he executed to a design by MATTHEUS VAN BEVEREN. A small ivory of an *Infants' Bacchanalia* (Munich, Bayer. Nmus.) in the style of Lucas Faydherbe and Peter Scheemakers is also by his hand. After the bombardment of Brussels by the French (Aug 1695) during the War of the Grand Alliance, Cosyns worked on the restoration of the guild houses on the Grand-Place under the supervision of the municipal architect, Willem de Bruyn (1649–1719). Designs possibly by Cosyns include those for the gable (1697) of the guild house of the tallow merchants (Maison de la Brouette) and those (1696–7) for the adjacent house of the bakers (Maison du Roi d'Espagne). The sculptural work on the latter is certainly by his hand. In 1697 Cosyns built Bellona House for Prince Eugene of Savoy-Carignan. The façade, with a colossal order of Ionic pilasters, is in Louis XIV style. In general, Cosyns's architectural style reflects the transition from late Baroque exuberance to severe Classicism.

BIBLIOGRAPHY
Thieme–Becker
P. Fierens: *De Groote Markt van Brussel* (Brussels, 1941)
E. V. Philippowich: *Elfenbein: Ein Handbuch für Sammler und Liebhaber* (Brunswick, 1961)
J. van Ackere: *Barok en classicisme in België* (Brussels, 1974)

J.-P. ESTHER

Côte d'Ivoire, République de [Ivory Coast]. Country in West Africa on the Gulf of Guinea, bordered by Liberia and Guinea to the west, Mali and Burkina Faso to the north and Ghana to the east. Côte d'Ivoire, formerly a descriptive name for part of the Western African coast known as a source of ivory, was a French colony from 1893 until its independence in 1960. Since 1983 its capital has been Yamoussoukro, though the former capital Abidjan continues to be the country's most important city. This entry covers the art produced in Côte d'Ivoire since colonial times. For art of the region in earlier periods *see* AFRICA, §VII, 4. *See also* AKAN, AKYE, BAULE, DAN, GURO, LOBI and SENUFO.

1. GEOGRAPHY AND CULTURAL HISTORY. With an area of some 322,463 sq. km, the southern region of the country is forest, and the northern region is open savannah. Between the two is an area of wooded savannah, which in its central part descends nearly to the coast—the so-called Baule V, between the Bandama and Comoé rivers. The population (*c.* 11,613,000; UN estimate, 1988) comprises groups belonging to four major language families: Akan (the Baule, Anyi, Akye and Lagoon groups in the central and south-eastern regions), Kru (We, Bete, and Dida in the south-west), Mande (Northern Mande or Malinke in the north-west and such Southern Mande groups as the Guro and Dan in the west and west-central regions) and Gur (Senufo, Lobi, and Kulango in the north-east).

2. CONTINUING TRADITIONS. The traditional arts of Côte d'Ivoire are rich and varied. Sculpture in wood has been created by artists in virtually every part of the country. The Baule, Guro, Bete, Dan, Senufo, Kulango and Lobi have all produced different styles of figurative sculpture. The use of masks—for political, ritual or celebratory purposes—is also common. Wood has been carved into such utilitarian forms as architectural elements (especially decorated doors), furniture (beds, chairs and stools), utensils (bowls, spoons and paddles), tools (handles of axes and adzes, bellows and paddles and boards for modelling wax in metal casting) and musical instruments. Ivory has also been carved for side-blown trumpets, combs, pendants, hair combs and picks and large bulbous bangles.

Copper alloys have been cast and worked in various ways. Using the lost-wax process, artists have created metal masks, helmets, small figurative sculptures, geometric and figurative goldweights and an incredible variety of bracelets, anklets, rings and pendants (Blandin, 1988). Gold has been cast or hammered to create pendants, hair ornaments and other items of jewellery; it has also been beaten into foil and used to cover items of regalia for the Baule and other Akan groups. Iron has been worked principally for utilitarian tools but has also been forged into figurative forms.

Clay, mainly used for the production of various types of utilitarian pottery—bowls, jars, lamps and pipes—has been employed by the Anyi and such different Lagoon groups as the Akye and Abe for figurative vessels. The Anyi, like their neighbours in Ghana, have also produced funerary sculptures.

Male weavers have used cotton to produce textiles on narrow-looms, most often using the natural colours of cotton (white or a light ochre) or combining them with indigo. Ikat dyeing technique characterizes the cloth of the Baule and the Dyula. Raffia was woven by women among the Dida near the coastal lagoons in a most original manner and tied and dyed in black, red and yellow.

All of these arts continued to be practised into the colonial period, and many of them have continued into the late 20th century. Modern materials and techniques have been used increasingly, and styles have changed over time. Lost-wax casting has come to include, for example, the use of recycled aluminium. On sculpture, industrial paints have often been substituted for traditional dyes, and industrial colour-fast dyes have expanded the range of colours used in textile production.

3. ARCHITECTURE. Since the beginning of the 20th century European culture and technology have had a profound impact on architecture. Early colonial architecture survives in, for example, the coastal town of Grand Bassam, Côte d'Ivoire's first capital, and in some administrative buildings in regional urban centres. Architecture also became a symbol of the state's modernity in the 1960s and 1970s, when the government financed new infrastructures in those towns selected to host Independence Day activities. The historic town of Bondoukou, for example, with its once classic Sudanese-style architecture, lost its regional identity and was transformed into a town hardly distinguishable from any other. By the late 20th century modern architecture was in an international, modernist style, with European or European-trained architects designing schools, hotels, office buildings and churches. Yamoussoukro boasts a number of new higher-education campuses and a basilica inspired by St Peter's, Rome.

4. PAINTING AND OTHER ARTS. Although wall painting was practised traditionally by such peoples as the Dan and We, and cloth was painted in geometric patterns by the Senufo and Dyula, painting really only developed following colonization. As elsewhere in West Africa, commercial sign painting has produced vibrant visual imagery, and some commercial artists have also produced commemorative portraits based on photographs. Painting has also been produced by a large number of artists trained in Western traditions at the Institut National des Arts, Abidjan (see §8 below). These artists trace their artistic genealogy to the first internationally recognized, modern Ivorian artist, Christian Lattier (1925–77; see §5 below).

The most important Ivorian artists of the 1960s and 1970s include Célestin Dogo Yao (b 1939), Michel Kodjo (b 1935) and Emile Gérard Santoni (b 1943). Célestin Dogo Yao, who trained with the French artist Jean Lérat at the Ecole Nationale des Arts Appliqués à l'Industrie at Bourges, France, is a specialist in architectural ceramics and has incorporated motifs from Baule ceramics into his work. Michel Kodjo trained at the Ecole Nationale des Arts Décoratifs in Nice, France, as well as the Ecole des Beaux-Arts de Clermont-Ferrand, and has created paintings, engravings and sculptures. Emile Gérard Santoni also trained at the Ecole Nationale des Arts Décoratifs, Nice, and has worked on film set decoration in addition to abstract paintings and tapestries. Subsequent developments in academic art only began to be discussed critically in the late 1980s and early 1990s, when such artists as Youssouf Bath (b 1949) gained international recognition. Commercial artists, painters of barbers' and shops' signs, have produced thousands of signs on plywood panels that have become collectable. Such 'naive' artists as Zéphérin Makre (1964–93), famous for his cityscapes of Abidjan, have also attracted the interest of foreigners, and his works have been exhibited abroad. Frédéric Bruly Bouabré (b 1923), another self-taught artist, has recorded his individual interpretation of the world in more than a thousand ballpoint and crayon drawings on small pieces of cardboard. He gained an international reputation through his inclusion in the *Magiciens de la terre* exhibition (1989 exh. cat.; see also 1991–2 exh. cat.). Some artists have been trained through apprenticeships with established commercial artists. Joël Ola Wouwou Odumann (b 1958), known as Joël, for example, was a student of B. P. Konan (b 1940) and went on to equal him in popularity (Lerat, 1992).

5. SCULPTURE. Sculpture has not been widely practised by modern Ivorian artists. Mention must be made, however, of the sculptures produced under the direction of the French artist Charles Alphonse Combes (1891–1968), who lived in Côte d'Ivoire from 1925 and established a studio of painting and sculpture in which his students replicated his Africanist vision of demure 'negresses' and stylized 'masks'. Côte d'Ivoire's most famous sculptor, indeed its most famous visual artist, was Christian Lattier

important has been Roger Bédiat. With a keenly discerning eye he collected thousands of works of traditional art. Following the sale of his collection in 1966, many of these works went into private collections, but hundreds of other works in his collection were sold to the Musée d'Abidjan in the 1950s. From the 1960s to the 1980s resident expatriates collected and dealt in traditional African art, the local art market flourished, and such hitherto neglected arts as those of the Lobi were 'discovered'. In addition, traditional chiefs in the central and eastern regions have maintained state treasuries of gold-covered regalia, and President Félix Houphouet-Boigny (1905–93) amassed a significant collection of Baule art in gold. The collecting of modern works of art has been undertaken largely by expatriates, and most of these works have been exported.

7. MUSEUMS AND EXHIBITIONS. The dominant institution promoting the traditional arts of Côte d'Ivoire from the 1940s has been the Musée National (formerly Musée d'Abidjan). It was initially part of the Institut Français d'Afrique Noire (IFAN, the French colonial research institute based in Dakar, Senegal). The museum's collecting and exhibition activities were dominated from the late 1940s to the late 1970s by the ethnographer Bohumil Holas, a naturalized Frenchman born in Czechoslovakia.

In the late 20th century the Ministère des Affaires Culturelles, Abidjan, attempted to decentralize Côte d'Ivoire's museums and create museums of traditional art and culture in such regional centres as Korhogo and Bondoukou. Local initiatives have also created small museums in such villages and smaller towns as Zaranou, Bonoua and Boundiali, and individual initiatives have led to the creation of two private museums. The collector Don Bosco created a small museum of traditional art in the town of Duékoué, and the prophet Djouman Mihin created a museum in Vavoua for the 'fetishes' given to him by his followers (Ravenhill, 1981).

Contemporary art was never a focus of the Musée National for either collecting or exhibitions; instead, the Centre Culturel of the French Embassy became the popular venue for one-person and group shows. There, Ivorian artists have found a steady market for their work in the expatriate community. The Association des Plasticiens Ivoiriens has organized annual exhibitions, usually in hotel exhibition halls.

8. ART EDUCATION. In addition to the Institut National des Arts, Abidjan, the government of Côte d'Ivoire has promoted the teaching of art in secondary schools and in specialized schools in Bingerville and Abengourou. Art was also a significant component of the 'Programme d'éducation télévisuelle' transmitted to primary schools in the 1970s. Commercial artists often provide instruction to paying apprentices.

BIBLIOGRAPHY

R. Bonneau: *Ecrivains, cinéastes et artistes ivoiriens: Aperçu bio-bibliographique* (Abidjan, n.d.) [1973]

J. Castel: *Inventaire des formes de représentation graphique en Côte d'Ivoire et propositions d'exploitation* (Abidjan, n.d.) [?1973]

P. L. Ravenhill: 'Le Musée du prophète Djouman Mihin, Vavaoua, Côte d'Ivoire', *Godo-godo*, 6 (1981), pp. 129–43

Ministère des Affaires Culturelles: *Architecture coloniale en Côte d'Ivoire* (Abidjan, 1985)

——: *L'Art des enseignes* (Abidjan, 1985)

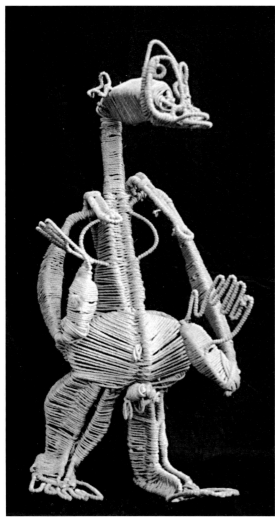

Christian Lattier: *Les Premiers Jours d'Etienne*, string and iron, 1.26×0.50×0.36 m, 1963–4 (Abidjan, Musée National de la Côte d'Ivoire)

(1925–77). Lattier studied sculpture and architecture at the Ecole des Beaux-Arts, Paris, from 1953 to 1957; he continued to live in France, working at one time on the restoration of Chartres Cathedral, before returning to Côte d'Ivoire in 1962 to take up the position of professor of sculpture at the Ecole National Supérieure des Beaux Arts d'Abidjan. His best-known works are public sculptures combining rope and other fibres with metalwork and basketry, at such venues as the city hall and the international airport at Abidjan; a number of smaller works are in public and private collections (see fig.). Ceramic sculpture is not widely practised, although the work of Célestin Dogo Yao has achieved some success in architectural decoration. The cement sculptures of Koffi Mourouffie have also received attention and were exhibited at the Centre Georges Pompidou, Paris, in 1977.

6. PATRONAGE, COLLECTING AND DEALING. Of collectors resident in Côte d'Ivoire, undoubtedly the most

J.-M. Lerat: *Chez bonne idée: Images du petit commerce en Afrique de l'Ouest* (Paris, 1986/*R* 1990)

A. Blandin: *Bronzes et autres alliages: Afrique de l'Ouest* (Narignane, 1988)

Magiciens de la terre (exh. cat. by H. Martin and others, Paris, Pompidou, 1989), pp. 108–9

G. Stanislas: *Contemporary African Artists: Changing Tradition* (exh. cat., New York, 1990)

P. Gaudibert: *L'Art africain contemporain* (Paris, 1991), p. 91

'Frédéric Bruly Bouabré', *Africa Now* (exh. cat., Las Palmas de Gran Canaria, Cent. Atlantic. A. Mod.; Groningen, Groniger Mus.; Mexico City, Cent. Cult. A. Contemp.; 1991–2), pp. 179–83

J. Kennedy: *New Currents, Ancient Rivers: Contemporary African Artists in a Generation of Change* (Washington, DC, and London, 1992), pp. 92–3

J.-M. Lerat: *Ici bon coiffeur: Les Enseignes de coiffeurs en Afrique* (Paris, 1992)

P. L. Ravenhill: 'The Passive Object and the Tribal Paradigm: Colonial Museography in French West Africa', *How To Do Things with Objects* (exh. cat., ed. M.-J. Arnoldi, C. Geary and K. Hardin; Washington, DC, N. Mus. Afr. A.; Bloomington, IN, U. A. Mus., 1993)

PHILIP L. RAVENHILL

Cotelle, Jean, II (*b* Paris, 1642; *d* Villiers-sur-Marne, 24 Sept 1708). French painter, draughtsman, miniature painter and engraver. He studied drawing with his father Jean Cotelle I (1607–76), an ornamental painter at the court of Louis XIII. He went on to learn miniature painting with Elisabeth Sophie Chéron and portraiture with Claude Lefèbvre. He spent the years 1662–70 in Rome under the protection of Anne, Princesse de Rohan-Guéménée, and in 1672 was received (*reçu*) by the Académie Royale as a miniature painter on presentation of the *Entry of the King and Queen into Paris* (untraced). In 1681 he painted the *Marriage at Cana* (untraced) as that year's 'May' (the picture commissioned annually by the Paris Goldsmiths' Corporation for the Cathedral of Notre-Dame). His portraits are now known only through engravings, such as that of the *Princesse de Rohan-Guéménée* made by François de Poilly I. His reputation rests, however, on the series of 21 views of the château of Versailles, its gardens and fountains that he painted for the gallery of the Grand Trianon (Trianon de Marbre). This series, completed by three further views by Etienne Allegrain and Jean-Baptiste Martin I, was finished in 1691 and remains *in situ*. Although the landscapes are in the Flemish realist tradition that informs much 17th-century French topographical painting, the perspective is distorted in a way reminiscent of theatre designs, and the foregrounds are populated with representations of the loves of the gods in a style close to that of Alessandro Albani. The strange effect of this combination of the realistic and the mythological is less obvious in the surviving gouache modelli (Versailles, Château, and Paris, Mus. A. Déc.). These remarkable paintings, with their original sense of colour, are works of some quality, which makes the loss of the greater part of Cotelle's oeuvre all the more regrettable. A few engravings from his hand survive, including a suite of decorative designs for fire-dogs.

BIBLIOGRAPHY

Mariette

T. Lhuillier: 'Notes pour servir à la biographie des deux Cotelle peintres du Roi', *Réun. Soc. B.-A. Dépt.*, xvii (1893), pp. 625ff

A. Schnapper: *Tableaux pour le Trianon de Marbre 1688–1714* (Paris, 1967)

LAURENCE GUILMARD GEDDES

Coter, Colijn [Colin; Collin; Colyn] **de** (*fl c.* 1480–1525). South Netherlandish painter. Contracts survive for two lost works by this artist: one of 1493, in the ledgers of the Guild of St Luke in Antwerp, names a 'Colyn van Brusele' as a master of the Guild, commissioned by the Confraternity of St Luke to decorate the vault of its chapel in Onze Lieve Vrouw (later the cathedral); the other, in the accounts of the Confraternity of St Eligius, Brussels, reveals that Coter undertook in 1509–10 to paint the doors of a tabernacle, which was completed in 1511. The dates of these documents mark the known boundaries of Coter's artistic activity, but his surviving work suggests these may be extended from 1480 to 1525. Three signed paintings are known: *St Luke Painting the Virgin* in the parish church of Vieure, Cosne d'Allier, the altarpiece of the *Trinity* (Paris, Louvre) and the *Virgin Crowned by Angels* (Düsseldorf, priv. col.; see Friedländer, 1969, pl. 90). Inscriptions stating that Coter painted the works in Brussels appear on the borders of the robes. These works serve as reference points for other attributions and illustrate the essential phases of Coter's stylistic and technical evolution.

Coter's sources of inspiration were varied, resulting in work that was both eclectic and archaic (with the compositions focused on a few monumental figures), but his borrowings were always recast in his own personal style. He derived compositions, decorative motifs and the form of his figures from Rogier van der Weyden but his sense of mass and volume from the work of the Master of Flémalle. Coter's interest in the description of three-dimensional form became a constant concern, evident as much in the underdrawing as in the painting of most of his pictures. These two contrary stylistic tendencies marked all of his work. To a lesser extent, Coter was also influenced by artists of his own generation. In his late work, this led to a softening of style, the appearance of new morphological types, an interest in the realistic treatment of the nude and the exploration of perspective effects and foreshortening.

On the basis of these various influences and Coter's transition from the more traditional technique of his early Netherlandish predecessors to a simplified technique developed for the more rapid building up of form, his work may be classified into five groups and a new chronology proposed. The earliest works, associated with the signed *St Luke Painting the Virgin* (see fig.), are closest to the tradition of early Netherlandish painters and the followers of van der Weyden in Brussels. This group includes two panels of the *Legend of St Rombaut* in Mechelen Cathedral, the *Man of Sorrows* (Bourg-en-Bresse, Mus. Ain), and the painted wings of the earliest carved altarpiece of the *Passion* in Strängnäs Cathedral, a key work that is now attributed to the painter (Périer-D'Ierteren, 1984); others in this group are *Christ Interceding* and the *Virgin Interceding* (both Paris, Louvre); *Donor with St John the Baptist and St Barbara* (Bratislava, Slovak N. Mus.); *Mary Magdalene Afflicted* and *St John the Baptist Weeping* (both Budapest, Mus. F.A.). A second group, characterized by a concern for volume inspired by the Master of Flémalle, includes the signed *Trinity* altarpiece, the *Virgin Crowned by Angels* (Chicago, IL, A. Inst.), the *Adoration of the Magi* (Ghent, Mus. S. Kst.) and the *St*

Colijn de Coter: *St Luke Painting the Virgin*, oil on canvas, 1.30×1.05 m, 15th century (Cosne d'Allier, parish church of Vieure)

Alban altarpiece (Brussels, Mus. A. Anc.; Cologne, Wallraf-Richartz-Mus.). Coter then began to produce works of a more personal, expressive nature, such as the painted wings of a carved altarpiece in St Nicolas, Orsoy, the *Descent from the Cross* (Berlin, ex-Wetzel col.) and *Ecce homo* from the Forest wing (Brussels, ex-Charlent col.). The signed *Virgin Crowned by Angels* forms part of a group of works showing contemporary influences, which includes the Bernatsky Triptych (Madison, U. WI, Elvehjem A. Cent.) and versions of the *Descent from the Cross* (Brussels, Mus. A. Anc.; Messina, Mus. Reg.; Stuttgart, Staatsgal.). Finally, two archaizing works, reviving the spirit of van der Weyden, constitute a group apart: the *Pietà* (Amsterdam, Rijksmus.) and the *Lamentation* (The Hague, Dienst Rijksverspr. Kstvoorwerpen).

A primary characteristic of Coter's work is the exploration of pictorial effects: the monumentality of crowded compositions giving an impression of *horror vacui* and a broadening of forms; three-dimensional effects created by chiaroscuro, which emphasizes the bulk of the figures and the sculptural quality of the drapery; decorative effects in the imitation of, for example, brocades and in the distribution of blocks of colour; and expressive effects using twisted figures, angular drapery and faces overladen with graphic detail, similar to the minor Brussels masters.

The underdrawing shows that contours, often modified, were drawn rapidly and confidently with vigorous strokes, while shadows are indicated by areas of broad, spirited hatching, providing the basis for the stark chiaroscuro with dense shadow contrasted with thickly painted highlights. Generally Coter simplified the paint structure,

loading the base tones with lead white and reducing the coloured glazes to a single, saturated layer or eliminating them altogether. The transparency and luminosity of the modelling is thus sacrificed to surface effects.

Coter's art influenced virtually all Brussels painting from 1480 to 1515 and also that of Antwerp and Mechelen. He did not create a uniform style so much as invent figure types and compositions. His reliance on earlier masters may have assured his success, but that also depended on his innovative approach and technique. His simplification of the modelling, while still preserving the outward appearance of the early Netherlandish painters, paved the way for the mass production of pictures. Coter's artistic personality was undoubtedly an important factor in the spread of his influence. As head of his own workshop, he may also have been the artist in charge of certain collaborative projects such as the panels in Mechelen Cathedral, the first Strängnäs altarpiece or the altarpiece in St Nicolas, Orsoy. These influenced the workshop products, particularly the production of painted wings for carved altarpieces intended for export from Brabant. Coter is also said to have produced cartoons for the Brussels tapestry workshops.

BIBLIOGRAPHY

BNB; Thieme–Becker

A. Dinaux: 'Collin de Coter, peintre bruxellois', *Archvs Hist. & Litt. N. France & Midi Belgique*, 3rd ser., v (1855), pp. 539–41

M. J. Friedländer: 'Bernaert van Orley und die Brüsseler Schule', *Jb. Kön.-Preuss. Kstsamml.*, xxix (1908), pp. 225–46

——: 'Die Brüsseler Tafelmalerei gegen den Ausgang des 15. Jahrhunderts', *Belgische Kunstdenkmäler*, i (Munich, 1923), pp. 309–20

E. Hensler: 'Eine neuentdeckte Madonna von Colijn de Coter', *Jb. Preuss. Kstsamml.*, xlv (1924), pp. 117–120

F. Winkler: *Altniederländische Malerei: Die Malerei in Belgien und Holland von 1400–1600* (Berlin, 1924), pp. 194, 371–2

M. J. Friedländer: *Die alterniederländische Malerei* (Berlin, 1924–37); Eng. trans. as *Early Netherlandish Painting*, 16 vols (Leiden, 1967–76), iv (1969), p. 67; xiv (1976), p. 13

G. Weyde and O. Benesch: 'Zwei niederländische Altarflügel in der Pressburger Tiefenwegkapelle', *Pantheon*, i (1928), pp. 68–70

J. Duverger: *Brussel als kunstcentrum in de XIVe en de XVe eeuw*, Bouwstoffen tot de Niederlandsche kunstgeschiedenis, iii (Antwerp, 1935), p. 68

J. Maquet-Tombu: *Colyn de Coter, peintre bruxellois*, Bibliothèque du XVe siècle (Brussels, 1937)

E. Pelinck: 'Cornelis Engebrechtz, de herkomst van zijn Kunst', *Ned. Ksthist. Jb.*, ii (1948–9), pp. 40–43

E. Panofsky: *Early Nederlandish Painting: Its Origins and Character*, 2 vols (New York, 1953, rev. 1971), pp. 175, 352

H. Adhémar: *Les Primitifs flamands: Corpus de la peinture des anciens Pays-Bas méridionaux au quinzième siècle*, Paris, Louvre (Brussels, 1962), pp. 73–100

J. Folie: 'Les Oeuvres authentifiées des Primitifs flamands', *BIRPA*, vi (1963), pp. 183–255

S. Ringbom: 'Icon to Narrative: The Rise of the Dramatic Close-up in Fifteenth Century Devotional Painting', *Acta Acad. Abo.: Human.*, xxxi/2 (1965), pp. 131–4

P. Philippot: *Pittura fiamminga e rinascimento italiano* (Turin, 1970)

J. Giesen: 'Colyn de Coter: Ein Maler im Schatten grosser Zeitgenossen', *Kst & S. Heim*, lxxxiii/8 (1971), pp. 467–71

P. Hibbs-Decoteau: *Colin de Coter and the Bernatsky Triptych* (Madison, 1975)

C. Périer-D'Ieteren: 'Le Dessin sous-jacent dans l'oeuvre de Colyn de Coter', *Actes du 4e colloque sur le dessin sous-jacent dans la peinture: Louvain-la-Neuve, 1981*, pp. 131–6

——: 'Aspects récents de l'étude des volets de Colyn de Coter: Marie-Madeleine affligée et Saint Jean pleurant du Musée de Budapest', *Bull. Mus. Hong. B.-A.*, lviii–lix (1982), pp. 107–22

——: *Les Volets peints des retables bruxellois conservés en Suède et le rayonnement de Colyn de Coter* (Stockholm, 1984)

—: *Colyn de Coter et la technique picturale des peintres flamands du XVe siècle* (Brussels, 1985)

E. De Vos: 'Ein neues Fragment des jüngsten Gerichtes von Colijn de Coter', *Pantheon* (in preparation)

C. PÉRIER-D'IETEREN

Cotes, Francis (*b* London, 20 May 1726; *d* London, 19 July 1770). English painter and pastellist. He was the son of an apothecary and the elder brother of Samuel Cotes (1734–1818), a painter in miniature. Around 1741 he was apprenticed to George Knapton, who taught him to paint in oil and to draw in crayon, at which he became very accomplished. Rosalba Carriera had popularized crayon portraiture among Grand Tourists in Venice, and her example no doubt helped Cotes in his early work. Nevertheless, he did not imitate her soft modelling and delicate colour in such portraits as *Elizabeth, Lady Carysfoot* (1751; Ann Arbor, U. MI, Mus. A.), in which he used bold tones, strong lines and an almost universal portrait format, established in the 1740s and 1750s. He was fortunate in making crayon portraits of *Maria Gunning* and *Elizabeth Gunning* (1751; versions in Edinburgh, N.G.; London, N.P.G.; and elsewhere), as his work reached a wide public through engravings made after them. Between 1753 and 1756 the Swiss pastellist Jean Etienne Liotard was in

Francis Cotes: *The Hon. Lady Stanhope and the Countess of Effingham as Diana and her Companion*, oil on canvas, 2.40×1.53 m, 1765 (York, City Art Gallery)

England, and his realistic approach to portraiture persuaded Cotes to abandon the Rococo portrait type. In *Taylor White* (1758; London, Foundling Hosp.) he adopted a very naturalistic pose, in which the sitter is seen to be engaged in checking ledgers—an appropriate pose for the Treasurer of Thomas Coram's hospital for abandoned children.

Although Cotes never gave up working in pastel, especially for his more intimate subjects, he had pushed crayon to the limits of the medium and therefore turned to oil painting as a means of developing his style in larger-scale works. In this he sometimes overworked his colours, but in his most successful pictures the oil paint is thinly applied, in imitation of his unsurpassed pastel technique. Cotes's work of the early 1760s can be compared with that of Joshua Reynolds and Allan Ramsay. Although he retained much of the charm of his earlier work, Cotes did not achieve the kind of psychological insight that characterizes Reynolds's work. His portrait of *Francis Burdett* (1764; Hull, Ferens A.G.) has a clarity and warmth that Reynolds's contemporaneous portraits lack, but Cotes expended his attention on the costume rather than the character. This emphasis did, however, make Cotes's portraits of children particularly successful.

Around 1764 Cotes began employing the drapery painter Peter Toms, and this greatly increased his output. In 1765 he married and became a director of the Society of Artists, with whom he had exhibited since 1760; he also took on the pastellist John Russell as a pupil. By this time Cotes had become an important figure in the London art world, and he was instrumental in setting up the Royal Academy in 1768. He was able to present the case for an academy to George III, having undertaken two exceptional double portraits for the royal family in 1767, the more interesting of which is *Princess Louisa and Queen Carolina Matilda of Denmark* (London, Buckingham Pal., Royal Col.). He became especially adventurous in the double-portrait form: *The Hon. Lady Stanhope and the Countess of Effingham as Diana and her Companion* (1765; York, C.A.G.; see fig.) admirably balances informality and tradition but maintains an equal interest in each of the figures.

BIBLIOGRAPHY

Introducing Francis Cotes RA (exh. cat., ed. A. Smart; U. Nottingham, A.G., 1971)

E. M. Johnson: *Francis Cotes* (Oxford, 1976)

HUGH BELSEY

Cothem, Jacob van (*fl c.* 1513). Netherlandish sculptor or dealer. His name appears in the records of the Abbey of Averbode in connection with the acquisition of three carved and polychromed wooden altarpieces for the abbey church in 1513 and 1514. He is not referred to specifically as a painter or carver in the Averbode accounts, and it is possible that he acted in the capacity of dealer in altarpieces to be sold on the open market.

The third altarpiece mentioned in the Averbode records has been tentatively identified with a small *Lamentation* altarpiece (1.61×1.70 m; Antwerp, Mus. Vleeshuis) that is stamped with the Antwerp carvers' mark of quality and bears the arms and device of Gerard van der Scaeft, abbot of Averbode in the early 16th century; it also has a painted figure of a donor, identified in an inscription as Nicolaas Huybs, the porter of the abbey. The painted wings and

the costumes of the carved figures show the impact of
ANTWERP MANNERISM, but the dignity, simplicity and
monumentality of the *Lamentation* are less typical of
Antwerp carving of the period.

BIBLIOGRAPHY

P. Lefèvre: 'Textes concernant l'histoire artistique de l'abbaye d'Aver-
bode', *Rev. Belg. Archéol. & Hist. A.*, v (1935), pp. 51–2
A. D. Jansen and C. van Herck: *Kerkelijke kunstschatten* (Antwerp, 1949),
p. 61, no. 83
R. Marijnissen: 'Het retabel uit de verzamelingen van het museum
Vleeshuis', *Antwerpen*, vii (1961), pp. 6–15
I. Vandevivere and C. Dumortier: 'Deux bergers du retable sculpté
anversois d'Aldenhoven conservés au Musée de Louvain-La Neuve',
Rev. Archéologues & Historiens A. Louvain, xx (1987), pp. 223–33

K. W. WOODS

Cotignola, Francesco da. *See* ZAGANELLI, FRANCESCO.

Cotman, John Sell (*b* Norwich, 16 May 1782; *d* London,
24 July 1842). English painter and etcher.

1. Life and work. 2. Working methods and technique.

1. LIFE AND WORK. Cotman was born in the parish of
St Mary Coslany, Norwich, the son of Edmund Cotman,
a hairdresser, later a haberdasher, and Ann Sell. In 1793
he entered Norwich Grammar School as a 'freeplacer'. In
1798 he moved to London, where he worked as an
assistant to the publisher Rudolph Ackermann. Following
in the footsteps of Turner and Thomas Girtin he joined
Dr Monro's 'Academy' in 1799 and became a member of
the sketching society that had developed around the
personality and talent of Girtin. He exhibited at the Royal
Academy for the first time in 1800, when he was awarded
the large silver palette by the Society of Arts.

Between 1800 and 1805 Cotman embarked on a number
of sketching tours that were to have a dramatic effect on
his artistic development. In 1800 and 1802 he travelled to
Wales in search of the picturesque and saw the castles and
mountainous terrain that were to fire his imagination for
the rest of his life. On his second trip Cotman was
probably accompanied by Paul Sandby Munn (1773–
1845), who was also with him during the early stages of
his first trip to Yorkshire in 1803. The influence of
Yorkshire on Cotman was as significant as it was to both
Girtin and Turner. Cotman was introduced to the Cholmeley family of Brandsby Hall, north of York, through a
lifelong patron, Sir Henry Englefield. He also stayed with
the Cholmeleys in 1804 and 1805, and it was with Francis
Cholmeley jr that he was invited to visit Rokeby Hall to
stay with the Morritts in 1805. This visit resulted in some
of the finest and most delicate watercolours in the history
of European watercolour painting. Cotman made a number of trips along the River Greta to Barnard Castle,
gathering material for at least 17 watercolours such as *On
the River Greta, Yorkshire* (*c.* 1806–7; Norwich, Castle
Mus.; see fig. 1), six of which he exhibited at the Royal
Academy and in Norwich.

In 1806 Cotman was disappointed not to be elected a
member of the recently founded (1804) Society of Painters
in Water-Colours. He exhibited for the last time at the
Royal Academy and returned to Norwich that winter
where he set up a 'School for Drawing and Design'. He
held a retrospective exhibition of several hundred works

1. John Sell Cotman: *On the River Greta, Yorkshire*, pencil and
watercolour on buff laid paper, 326×229 mm, *c.* 1806–7 (Norwich,
Castle Museum)

in his new premises, made some first experiments in oil
painting and also advertised as a portrait painter. These
ventures were not as successful as he had hoped and,
despite his prolific output in watercolour and oil at this
period, the local public was slow to purchase his work. As
a watercolourist of original vision Cotman was at his peak;
Kett's Castle (1809–10; Norwich, Castle Mus.) is an
example of the way in which he was able to translate the
patterns of nature into exquisite two-dimensional designs.

In 1809 Cotman married Ann Miles of Felbrigg. Shortly
afterwards he opened a circulating library of drawings for
pupils to copy, by which to teach the 'Cotman style'. He
was competing with his fellow artists, including John
Crome, who also advertised as drawing-masters. In 1810
he was elected vice-president of the Norwich Society of
Artists and also exhibited in London at the Associated
Artists in Water-Colours and at the British Institution. At
this time a number of his exhibited works were almost
certainly in oils. The following year Cotman became
president of the Norwich Society of Artists, exhibited for
the second and last time at the Associated Artists in Water-
Colours and published his *Miscellaneous Etchings*. This was
the first of a series of published etchings, and he held high
hopes for this aspect of his career. In 1812 Dawson
Turner, one of Cotman's patrons, encouraged him to
move to Yarmouth where he began the enormous task of
executing over 400 etched plates to be published in six

volumes (*Architectural Antiquities of Norfolk*; 1812–8). Although he regarded this work as 'A Herculean Labor' it also held out 'the distant view of reputation' and the possibility of a secure livelihood. His expectations, however, were not fully realized.

Cotman's *Architectural Antiquities of Normandy* (1822) probably brought him his widest acclaim. It was the product of three separate trips to Normandy. His first tour, in 1817, he made alone; but the following year he was joined by members of Dawson Turner's family, for whom he was both friend and drawing-master. The same year he contributed monochrome drawings to be engraved as illustrations in the two volumes of *Excursions in the County of Norfolk* (1818–19). During his last tour in 1820 he reached the southernmost region where he found 'everything a painter could wish for. . .the Wales of France' (Cotman to his wife, 26 Aug 1820). He also executed a series of monochrome watercolours in preparation for a 'picturesque tour of Normandy', which was never published.

Cotman returned to Norwich in December 1823 and opened a school of drawing in his grand residence at St Martin at Palace Plain. He exhibited at the British Institution that year and again, for the last time, in 1827. On 1 May 1824 a sale of a large number of his drawings, mostly of Normandy subjects, was held at Christie's, London. This period of Cotman's life coincided with technical and visual innovations in his work that were not always appreciated. He was an ambitious man and laboured hard for reputation, but his frequent professional disappointments could cast him into deepest melancholy, often leading to depressive illness. In 1826, the year when he suffered his worst fit of depression, he informed the Rev. Charles Parr Burney that his state of mind was 'one chaos of agony'. Burney was just one of Cotman's patrons who was kept waiting for his commissions.

In 1825 Cotman was elected a member of the Old Water-Colour Society without having to submit the usual drawings for approval. During the early 1830s his reputation grew, and in 1833, after a vice-presidency of two years, he was elected president of the Norwich Society of Artists for the second time. That year the Society (since 1828 called the Norfolk and Suffolk Institution for the Promotion of the Fine Arts) was disbanded at a meeting in his house. In 1834 Cotman moved to London to take up the post of drawing-master at King's College School. In 1838 Henry Bohn published Cotman's *Liber studiorum* and his collected etchings (excluding the *Normandy* series), *Specimens of Architectural Remains in Various Counties in England, but Especially in Norfolk*. That year Cotman exhibited for the first and only time with the Society of British Artists. In the autumn of 1841 he went on a last sketching tour of Norfolk. The visit resulted in a magnificent series of on-the-spot sketches of 'rare and beautiful Norfolk', as well as the unfinished oil, *From my Father's House at Thorpe* (*c*. 1841–2; Norwich, Castle Mus.). His collection was sold at Christie's, London, on 17–18 May and 6 June 1843.

Of Cotman's five children, three became artists. From 1834 his daughter Ann Cotman (1812–62) and his eldest son Miles Edmund Cotman (1810–58), whose style had been close to his own since 1829, helped Cotman to produce drawing copies for his pupils to which he would add his signature. The derivative student copies in the 'Cotman style' of this period should not be mistaken for the work of John Sell Cotman himself. His second son, John Joseph Cotman (1814–78), continued the family drawing practice in Norwich. John Joseph's own work achieved a heightened sense of colour, which often extended the emotive force of his landscapes beyond simply topographical representation.

A fourth member of the Cotman family to achieve success as an artist was Frederic George Cotman (1850–1920). Born in Ipswich, he was the youngest son of Henry Edmund Cotman (1802–71), a silk mercer of Norwich and younger brother of John Sell Cotman. His main reputation was for portraits of London society, homely genre scenes and highly finished narrative pictures. His later impressionistic oils and watercolours of his native East Anglia are among his most successful work.

2. WORKING METHODS AND TECHNIQUE.

(i) Pencil. Cotman's use of pencil *c*. 1800–02 consisted of quite heavy parallel strokes of hatching within the outline of the subject, to indicate light and shade. By 1804 his use of pencil had become lighter and daintier, with idiosyncratic dashes, particularly to indicate foliate forms in the foreground. The drawings of 1805–7 develop tone by using a softer pencil. From 1808 to 1810 his use of line took on a more chunky rhythm which paralleled the development of his watercolour technique. The drawings executed while at Yarmouth, particularly his on-the-spot sketches of antiquities, are spare, but in them Cotman captured intricacies of detail while retaining a rhythmic flow, usually with a soft pencil. His monochrome drawings of Normandy were the product of meticulous on-the-spot studies, often made with the help of a *camera lucida*. He would also make rapid sketches of architectural details and his later drawing developed a more flamboyant flourish. By 1829 his pencilwork combined the use of the point of the pencil to outline essential structure with the use of the softer side of the pencil to create foliate or shadowed areas with rapid hatching. His vigorous yet apparently languid drawing reached its climax in his late chalk drawings, which are characterized by loose and rapid hatching. Throughout his career he made colour notes for reference in the studio.

(ii) Watercolour. Cotman's watercolours of *c*. 1800–03 are either reddish or grey in tone, the former being the unintended result of fading indigo. This early work shows the influence of Thomas Girtin, particularly in the use of dot and dash accents applied with the brush. At this stage he allowed his colour to gather in pools to achieve a patchwork effect. The Greta watercolours achieve a sense of perfect control during the years 1805–6. It has been suggested that these were the product of the artist painting *en plein air*, a point of view apparently substantiated by Cotman's own statement to Dawson Turner on 30 November 1805 that he had been 'colouring from nature'. The discovery of a portfolio of Yorkshire colour studies almost certainly executed in the studio by Cotman (London, Sotheby's, 11 July 1986) was the first real evidence

(although not universally accepted by experts on water-colours) of his painstaking preparatory work during this period before tackling the final synthesis of his subject on large and fragile sheets. Cotman's use of wash c. 1807–8 became purer, utilizing solid blocks of brighter colour. By about 1810 his control of colour and form was at its most abstract. During his Yarmouth years Cotman's watercolours were almost entirely monochrome, often allied with his printing projects. In the mid-1820s his command of colour became increasingly flamboyant. This new sense of colour was matched by a new technique in which Cotman would add a flour or rice paste to his watercolour to form a semi-opaque medium that intensified colour, also causing it to remain moist on the paper for longer than pure wash. This enabled Cotman to wipe, drag or otherwise manipulate the colour in a manner that echoed the possibilities of oil. An example of this technique is *Storm on Yarmouth Beach* (1831; Norwich, Castle Mus.; see fig. 2). In the late 1830s he returned to a monochromatic scale, using the paste technique to create a velvety softness even in the deepest blacks.

(iii) Oil and etching. Cotman's achievement as an oil painter has always been underrated. Although he painted in oil throughout his life, his oils are difficult to date, due to lack of documentary evidence. He always used a loaded brush and was at his most innovative in the mid-1820s, two of his finest oils being *The Baggage Wagon* and *The Mishap* (both c. 1824–8; Norwich, Castle Mus.). By 1836 he had

developed a more liquid technique, and a number of unfinished canvases reveal his later use of an ochre-coloured ground over which he sketched his design in black chalk.

In his etchings Cotman always sought accuracy in the depiction of archaeological subjects. Apprentices helped him to produce the etchings, while he himself 'only finished the works and sketched abroad' for some two or three years (1814–17). There remains a visionary quality to his etchings that recalls the grandeur of scale exemplified in the work of Piranesi, whom Cotman himself admitted was a strong influence.

BIBLIOGRAPHY

L. Binyon: *John Crome and John Sell Cotman* (London, 1897)
——: 'Life and Work of John Sell Cotman: Masters of English Landscape Painting, J. S. Cotman, David Cox, Peter de Wint', *The Studio* (1903) [special no.]
J. Reeve: *Memoir of John Sell Cotman* (Norwich, 1911)
A. E. Popham: 'The Etchings of John Sell Cotman', *Print Colr Q.* (Oct 1922), pp. 236–73
A. P. Oppé: 'The Watercolour Drawings of John Sell Cotman', *The Studio* (1923) [special no.]
H. Isherwood Kay: 'John Sell Cotman's Letters from Normandy 1817–1820', *Walpole Soc.*, xiv–xv (1926–7)
S. D. Kitson: *The Life of John Sell Cotman* (London, 1937/R 1982)
Burl. Mag., lxxxi (1942) [issue ded. to Cotman]
V. Rienaecker: *John Sell Cotman, 1782–1842* (Leigh-on-Sea, 1953)
M. Rajnai and M. Allthorpe-Guyton: *John Sell Cotman, 1782–1842: Drawings of Normandy in Norwich Castle Museum* (Norwich, 1975) [fully illus.]
A. Hemingway: 'Cotman's "Architectural Antiquities of Normandy": Some Amendments to Kitson's Account', *Walpole Soc.*, xcvi (1976–8)

2. John Sell Cotman: *Storm on Yarmouth Beach*, watercolour and pen and ink, with some scraping out, 366×536 mm, 1831 (Norwich, Castle Museum)

A. M. Holcomb: *John Sell Cotman* (London, 1978) [good illus.]

M. Rajnai and M. Allthorpe-Guyton: *John Sell Cotman, 1782–1842: Early Drawings (1798–1812) in Norwich Castle Museum* (Norwich, 1979) [fully illus.]

A. M. Holcomb and M. Y. Ashcroft: *John Sell Cotman in the Cholmeley Archive*, N. Yorks Co. Rec. Office Pub. (Northallerton, 1980)

A. Hemingway: ' "The English Piranesi": Cotman's Architectural Prints', *Walpole Soc.*, xcviii (1982)

John Sell Cotman 1782–1842 (exh. cat. by A. Moore, Norwich, Castle Mus., 1982) [fully illus.]

John Sell Cotman, 1782–1842 (exh. cat., ed. M. Rajnai; ACGB, 1982)

A. Hemingway: 'Meaning in Cotman's Norfolk Subjects', *A. Hist.*, vii/1 (1984), pp. 57–77

For further bibliography *see* NORWICH, §2.

ANDREW W. MOORE

Cottage orné. Ornamental cottage associated with the Picturesque movement in late 18th-century and early 19th-century Britain, fashionable among wealthy landowners indulging in make-believe by idealizing selected aspects of rural life. Early examples (1748–56) are by Thomas Wright (1711–86) in the grounds of Badminton House, Glos, while the most celebrated are the nine that form the village of Blaise Hamlet, Henbury, Bristol, built by JOHN NASH (i) in 1810–11.

The typical *cottage orné* was made up of features from traditional vernacular buildings. It tended to be overtly rustic and asymmetrical in design, often with an undulating thatched roof, latticed windows, verandahs (sometimes supported by tree trunks), ornate, oversized chimney-stacks and bargeboards. Along with the hermitage and grotto, the *cottage orné* was part of the garden furniture of the period. It varied in size according to function, from the garden building, lodge or workman's home to the large villa or royal residence (e.g. John Nash's building, 1813–16, at the nucleus of the Royal Lodge at Windsor, Berks). Pattern books by J. B. Papworth, Peter Frederick Robinson (1776–1858) and John Plaw proliferated with examples of the *cottage orné* and helped to popularize the type. The Lodge (*c.* 1810; see fig.) at Gaunt's House, Hinton Martell, Dorset, is a good example of a small pattern-book version of a *cottage orné*, with latticed windows, a porch and an umbrella-like thatched roof. Cahir (1814), Co. Tipperary, Ireland, possibly by John Nash, is a large country house with an undulating thatched roof, trelliswork and typical asymmetrical design.

Not all examples of the *cottage orné* were specially built as such; sometimes existing buildings were given rustic features, for example the Queen's Cottage, Kew, Surrey, which was built as a pavilion for Queen Charlotte in 1770 and embellished with a half-timbered upper storey and a thatched roof around 1805. The English fashion for idealizing country life spread to Europe, and *cottages ornés* are found at the Petit Hameau (1773), Chantilly, by Jean-François Leroy and at Liselund (1793), Island of Mon, Denmark. During the 1820s and 1830s many examples of the *cottage orné* were built in Britain as substantial villas, and thereafter the term 'villa' was more generally used; they still retained many of the picturesque ideals, however, and the typical asymmetric design.

BIBLIOGRAPHY

J. Plaw: *Rural Architecture: Designs from the Simple Cottage to the Decorative Villa* (London, 1785)

——: *Ferme ornée: Rural Improvements* (London, 1795)

J. B. Papworth: *Rural Residences* (London, 1818)

P. F. Robinson: *Rural Architecture: A Series of Designs for Ornamental Cottages* (London, 1823)

G. Darley: *Villages of Vision* (London, 1975)

N. Temple: *John Nash and the Village Picturesque* (Gloucester, 1979)

D. Watkin: *The English Vision* (London, 1982)

VICTORIA MERRILL

The Lodge, Gaunt's House, Hinton Martell, Dorset, *c.* 1810

Cottancin, Paul (*b* Reims, 12 Jan 1865; *d* 1928). French engineer. The son of an industrialist, he graduated in 1886 from the Ecole Centrale, Paris. Shortly after, he became the director of a public works company and soon became interested in reinforced concrete, in common with many builders of the period, some of whom filed their own patent applications. He took out his first patent for composite framework in 1890, but his system of reinforcement (patented 1896) was probably perfected during the building of the Lycée Victor Hugo (1894–6) and the church of St Jean de Montmartre (1897–1904), both in Paris and designed by ANATOLE DE BAUDOT. Cottancin used a fine metal mesh, which made it possible to use thin slabs, as little as 70 mm thick for the floor of St Jean, which also formed the ceiling to the crypt (*see* CONCRETE, §II, 1(iii)). A cement mortar was used, and in the vertical parts bricks were set around the armatures, both to economise on shuttering and to form the wall. This system required careful construction and was soon supplanted by that of François Hennebique, which was far simpler in practice and also had the advantage of an efficient commercial organization behind it. Cottancin nevertheless continued to construct industrial and commercial buildings, for example mills near Reims, as well as private projects, including the Château de Joeuf for Henri de Wendel and residential properties designed by Jules Lavirotte (e.g. 29 Avenue Raffi, Paris, 1901). Cottancin was also interested in the harnessing and distribution of water, and he took out several patents on these subjects.

BIBLIOGRAPHY
F. Boudon: 'Recherche sur la pensée et l'oeuvre d'Anatole de Baudot, 1834–1915', *Archit., Movt, Cont.* (March 1973) [supernumerary issue with mention of Cottancin and reinforced concrete]

BERNARD MARREY

Cottart [Cottard], **Pierre** (*b ?c.* 1630; *d* 1701). French architect and engraver. Although his name appears in the accounts of the king's works between 1670 and 1674, and he received a royal pension from 1697, his career is relatively obscure. His first engravings date from 1649, and his *Recueil de plusieurs pièces d'architecture*, consisting of 12 plates and dedicated to Charles de Rostaing, was reprinted in 1660. It included the chapel of the Fathers of Mercy (destr.) in the Rue des Archives, for which Cottart had proposed an elevation incorporating in the lower part the ground floor erected by Charles Chamois. Germain Boffrand completed the building 40 years later.

Cottart's major work, however, which was the subject of nine engravings and which still survives, is the mansion of the Maître des Requêtes, Amelot de Bisseuil, at 47 Rue Vieille-du-Temple, Paris, now known as the Hôtel des Ambassadeurs de Hollande. Here, between 1657 and 1660, Cottart restored some old buildings on very restricted sites, transforming them into fashionable residences comprising two courtyards linked by a carriage arch beneath the centre of the main block. Perspective effects and skilful planning were combined to create the illusion of more extensive space. In 1665 Cottart worked on the completion of the town hall at Troyes (begun 1624), building the first floor and decorating it with black marble columns. The Château de Villacerf, near Troyes, which he built for Edouard Colbert in 1675, is known only from eight engravings. Preceded by a vast forecourt, it rose among wide moats filled from the Seine. A large, square drawing-room occupied the centre of the single main block, which terminated in twin pavilions.

Cottart also supplied drawings (1665) for the east façade of the Louvre as well as designs for a grand staircase (five plates) and other designs for 'a German prince'. He had a special interest in interior decoration and left three collections of engravings on this subject, including the *Recueil de plusieurs morceaux d'ornements*. An edition of his collected works, engraved by him in 1686, confirms the superiority of his draughtsmanship over his skill as a builder. He remained faithful to the style of the 1660s, as represented by Louis Le Vau and François Le Vau: a style with a taste for the monumental and for sculptural ornament, high pitched roofs, very wide bays and, in the interior decoration, Italianate rooms, heavy, rich mouldings and an architectural treatment of the wall surface.

PRINTS
Recueil de plusieurs pièces d'architecture (Paris, 1650); repr. as *Recueil des plus beaux portails de plusieurs églises de Paris* (1660)
Recueil de plusieurs morceaux d'ornements (Paris, 1685)

BIBLIOGRAPHY
L. Hautecoeur: *Architecture classique* (1948), ii, pp. 133–8
E. J. Ciprut: 'Les Architectes de l'ancienne église de la Merci', *Bull. Soc. Hist. A. Fr.* (1954), pp. 203–9
R. A. Weigert: *Département des estampes: Inventaire du fonds français: Graveurs du XVIIe siècle*, Paris, Bib. N. cat., iii (Paris, 1954)

JEAN-PIERRE BABELON

Cotte, Robert de (*b* Paris, 1656–7; *d* Passy, Paris, 15 July 1735). French architect and urban planner. The most influential French Baroque architect during the Régence, he was Premier Architecte du Roi between 1708 and 1734. Financial constraints limited his work for the Crown, but he built many hôtels for the nobility, involved himself in numerous urban planning schemes and was frequently consulted by patrons abroad, particularly in Germany.

1. EARLY YEARS. By 1676 de Cotte was working for Jules Hardouin Mansart, whose brother-in-law he later became. In 1681 Hardouin Mansart was appointed Premier Architecte du Roi to Louis XIV, and during his absence from court in 1687 de Cotte first attracted the attention of the King with his own drawings for the colonnade of the Grand Trianon at Versailles. Destined to play an important role in the Service des Bâtiments du Roi, in 1689 de Cotte embarked on a trip to Italy lasting six months in order to complete his architectural education.

Although the King's costly wars brought a temporary halt to royal projects in the 1690s, the Treaty of Ryswick of 1697 initiated a new phase of activity that culminated in the reorganization of the Service des Bâtiments. De Cotte was named supervisor of the central design office in Paris and was also promoted to the position of Architecte Ordinaire, second in command to Hardouin Mansart, whom he succeeded as Director of the Académie Royale d'Architecture in 1699. That year he was also made head of the Manufacture des Gobelins, and in 1702 he was ennobled. His first independent commission was in 1699 for Saint-Denis Abbey, where he replaced the irregular grouping of medieval buildings with a classical design of four wings surrounding a large cloister. Following Hardouin Mansart's death in 1708, de Cotte became Premier Architecte du Roi, a position he maintained for the next 26 years. As head of a government agency, he employed the combined talents of numerous architects, draughtsmen, sculptors and engravers. An able draughtsman himself, he worked out his initial ideas in rough sketches, brushed almost entirely freehand and shaded to give a striking impression of depth. Like his contemporaries, he respected the rule of decorum (*bienséance*) in these designs: in a society governed by hierarchy and public display it was considered appropriate that all elements of a building should conform to the status and needs of its patron. De Cotte's chief strength lay in a capacity to synthesize and update the manner of his great 17th-century predecessors François Mansart, Hardouin Mansart and Louis Le Vau.

2. PALACES AND HÔTELS. In the second decade of the 18th century, many European princes turned to de Cotte for designs for palaces and villas in the style associated with Louis XIV. For Maximilian II Emmanuel, Elector of Bavaria (1662–1726), de Cotte drew up plans in 1714–15 for the palace of Schleissheim near Munich, which included a scheme (unexecuted) with three wings that was based on the layout of Versailles. De Cotte also carried on a lengthy correspondence with Joseph-Clemen, Elector of Cologne, concerning projects for the palace of Bonn and the châteaux of Poppelsdorf, Brühl and Godesberg, even though in the end budgetary constraints limited

the work to modifications of Enrico Zuccalli's half-completed Residenz at Bonn and the construction of Schloss Clemensruhe near by. In the middle of this *maison de plaisance* was a circular court and gallery, and its external elevations, modelled after Hardouin Mansart's façades for the Château de Clagny, Versailles, were modified in execution to suit German taste. In 1715 he put forward two proposals (unexecuted) for the Buen Retiro, the retreat of Philip V outside Madrid, offering either a plan with three wings or a cross in a square. Typical of the 18th-century concern with commodious living-quarters, both schemes complied with the royal couple's request for doubled pairs of *appartements* facing north and south, to be inhabited alternately in summer and winter. The external elevations (see fig. 1) were deliberate quotations of the Louvre and Versailles. So widespread was de Cotte's fame as a consultant for court architecture that in 1723 the Prince-Bishop of Würzburg, Johann Philipp Franz von Schönborn, sent his architect Balthasar Neumann on a mission to Paris for an assessment by de Cotte (and Germain Boffrand) of plans for the Würzburg Residenz.

As a fashionable court architect, de Cotte also devoted much time during the second decade of the century to designing new hôtels in Paris for public officials and the nobility. Through his arrangement of major and minor rooms, de Cotte sought to satisfy both the public and private needs of his clients. At the Hôtel du Lude (1710; destr. 1861) he gave an unusual precedence to pomp and display by providing a magnificent suite of four rooms in succession down the length of the garden façade. The sober elevations of this astylar hôtel reflect his quest for a simple, understated beauty through the harmonious inter-weaving of its parts. Several hôtel exteriors betray de Cotte's love for the Palladian-style villa. The *corps de logis* of the Hôtel d'Estrées (1711–13), Rue de Grenelle, does not fill the entire width of the site, as is common in Parisian hôtels, but consists of a free-standing block. The court elevation is also Palladian, with its richly articulated central pavilion carrying orders and a crowning pediment and flanked on either side by astylar walls. In general, the originality of de Cotte's hôtel elevations lies in the flatness and delicacy of the ornamental quoins and mouldings, and in the simple, unifying shape of the roofs, from which he usually omitted dormers. One, the Hôtel du Maine (begun

1716; destr.), was originally commissioned by Marie-Thérèse de Bourbon-Condé, Princesse de Conti (1666–1732), but was sold to the Duc de Maine, the legitimized son of Louis XIV, at which time it was completed and decorated by Armand-Claude Mollet.

3. URBAN PLANNING, ECCLESIASTICAL SCHEMES AND LATE WORKS. The eastern side of Paris had provided the most fashionable places for strolling in the 17th century, but by 1700 the focus had shifted to the west, partly as a result of the magnetic pull of Versailles. Between 1715 and 1719 de Cotte and his assistant Jean Beausire (1658–1743) drew up plans for refashioning the principal western entrances into the city: the Place du Pont-Tournant (Place de la Concorde) and the Place du Dôme des Invalides. De Cotte envisioned a new Porte de la Conférence opening on to the Quai des Tuileries, and his design (1717–19; unexecuted), which employed both rustication and the orders, fused the concept of the Roman triumphal arch with that of the Italianate city gate. To facilitate the piping of water from the Seine to neighbour-hoods on the Right Bank, he erected a new hydraulic machine surmounted by a pump-house, the Pompe de la Samaritaine (1714–15; destr. 1813), on the Pont-Neuf. Water from the pump was directed to the Château d'Eau du Palais-Royal (constructed by de Cotte in 1719; destr. 1848). The heavily channelled and vermiculated rustication of this somewhat palace-like façade proclaimed neverthe-less its utilitarian function. Between 1711 and 1714 de Cotte also submitted over a dozen proposals for the Place Bellecour, Lyon. However, the site was both immense and awkwardly shaped; the solution, modified in execution, suffers from the extreme distance between de Cotte's Italianate elevations, which face each other across the square.

De Cotte's first independent ecclesiastical commission came in 1710 with the rebuilding of the church and forecourt of the convent of the Visitation in the Rue St Jacques, Paris. His scheme for a centrally planned church with attached nuns' choir was closely modelled on François Mansart's church of the convent of the same Visitandine order in the Rue St Antoine, but it was not taken up. Two other unexecuted projects were for church portals: St

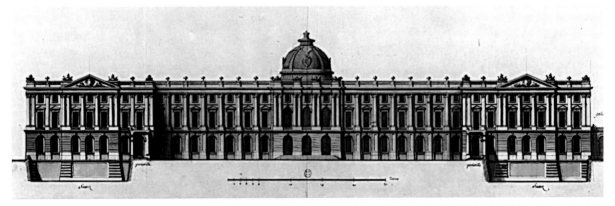

1. Robert de Cotte: first project (1715; unexecuted) for the courtyard elevation of the Palace of Buen Retiro, Madrid (Paris, Bibliothèque Nationale)

2. Robert de Cotte: Palais Rohan, Strasbourg, 1731–42

Etienne (1718), Dijon, and Notre-Dame-de-Bonne-Nouvelle (1724), Orléans; both borrow from the Baroque format of the two-storey basilican façade. De Cotte's sole commission for a large-scale basilica was his project of 1724 for St Louis de Versailles; yet even here only the Maison des Pères de la Mission and the Chapelle Provisoire de St Louis (destr. 1760) were built. His plan rejected the Italianate basilican ideal, which places its emphasis on the nave, in favour of a more traditional, essentially medieval ground-plan with an elaborate ambulatory and Lady chapel. For its façade, de Cotte devised several alternatives, including a traditional two-towered portal and a highly sculptural solution of the Gesù type that, in its massing of columns, recalls the Roman High Baroque. With his façade for St Roch (designed c. 1728; built 1736–8), de Cotte completed one of the major basilicas in Paris. His emphasis on vigorous plasticity and vertical unity was managed by means of superimposed columns rising through broken entablatures to support a crowning pediment. He also became involved in remodelling two smaller Parisian façades: for the church of the Capucines (1721–2) and the chapel of the Hôpital de la Charité (1732).

In response to the desire of several French bishops to be housed in buildings of a strongly secular style, de Cotte designed the palaces of Châlons-sur-Marne (1719–20; not completed), Verdun (1724–35; altered in execution) and Strasbourg (Palais Rohan, planned 1727–8, built 1731–42). Although based on the hôtel type, these buildings were differentiated by de Cotte's incorporation of ceremonial chambers within, and the use of emblematic motifs on the exterior (for example the giant order and square dome at the Palais Rohan; see fig. 2). In the palace of Thurn und Taxis, Frankfurt (designed 1727; built 1731–6; partly destr. 1944), de Cotte similarly exploited the form of the hôtel for Prince Anselm von Thurn und Taxis, Postmaster of the Holy Roman Empire.

De Cotte's interest in urban planning and palace design continued into his late years. In 1728 his design for a civic building of extreme length for the Place Royale, Bordeaux, was submitted, but only its general disposition was retained in the executed scheme begun several years later by Jacques Gabriel V. A late project of 1729–32 was one of the few commissions de Cotte received from Louis XV: unfortunately never built, his proposal for a *maison de plaisance* in the forest of Compiègne featured an X-shaped villa at the centre of a vast, symmetrically organized complex of gardens and stables. As usual, de Cotte adapted to current use several prestigious solutions of the previous period, using elements from Hardouin Mansart's château of Marly, Versailles, and Boffrand's hunting pavilion of Bouchefort, near Brussels, built for the Elector of Bavaria.

De Cotte's contribution to the development of the Rococo interior was slight, since he left the major decisions concerning design to the craftsmen who carried out the decorative work. However, as chief representative and disseminator of a national style he influenced the next generation of architects, especially those who worked on palaces and ecclesiastical buildings. On his retirement in 1734, the post of Premier Architecte du Roi passed to the Gabriel dynasty, first to Jacques V, then in 1742 to Ange-Jacques. Through them the style of the Grand Siècle, which de Cotte had perpetuated, was eventually eclipsed by Neo-classicism.

BIBLIOGRAPHY

P. Marcel: *Inventaire des papiers manuscrits du cabinet de Robert de Cotte* (Paris, 1906)
L. Hautecoeur: *Architecture classique* (Paris, 1943–57), iii
W. Graf Kalnein: *Das kurfürstliche Schloss Clemensruhe in Poppelsdorf* (Düsseldorf, 1956)
B. Jestaz: *Le Voyage d'Italie de Robert de Cotte* (Paris, 1966)
J.-L. d'Iberbille-Moreau: *Robert de Cotte: His Career as an Architect and the Organization of the Service des Bâtiments* (diss., U. London, 1972)
W. G. Kalnein and M. Levey: *Art and Architecture of the Eighteenth Century in France*, Pelican Hist. A. (Harmondsworth, 1972)
J.-D. Ludmann: *Le Palais Rohan de Strasbourg* (Strasbourg, 1979)
R. Neuman: *Robert de Cotte and the Perfection of Architecture in Eighteenth-century France* (Chicago, 1994)

ROBERT NEUMAN

Cottet, Charles (*b* Le Puy, 12 July 1863; *d* Paris, Sept 1925). French painter and printmaker. He studied at the Académie Julian in Paris and trained under Alfred Roll and Pierre Puvis de Chavannes. In 1885 he went to Brittany and until 1913 spent several months there each year, often in winter, staying at Camaret where he accompanied fishermen to the islands of Sein and Ouessant and attended religious festivals in the area. Brittany is the subject of most of his work, in particular the Breton harbours at twilight (e.g. *Evening Light: The Port of Camaret*, 1893; Paris, Mus. d'Orsay), stormy seascapes and scenes of bereavement. Combining symbolism and the ordinary lives of the Breton people, he attempted to address fundamental human issues in such paintings as *Grief by the Sea* (1908; Paris, Mus. d'Orsay), *Marine Bereavement* (Antwerp, Kon. Mus. S. Kst.) and *The People of Ouessant Watching over a Dead Child* (1899; Paris, Petit Pal.). The same sombre vision persists in the landscapes and genre scenes from his travels in Spain (1904) and Iceland (1907). Although Cottet was an admirer of Puvis de Chavannes and was associated with the Nabis painters, the dark tones and strong values of his work belong to the tradition of Realism. He was considered the leader of the BANDE NOIRE, a group that formed after he met Lucien Simon and André Dauchez (1870–1943) in 1895. After exhibiting with his friends Edouard Vuillard, Pierre Bonnard and Félix Vallotton in the galleries of Ambroise Vollard and of Louis Le Barc de Boutteville in Paris, Cottet embarked on a successful and prolific career, marked by his forceful personality and the originality of his work. He made 60 etchings between 1905 and 1910, but gradually stopped painting around 1913 after an illness.

BIBLIOGRAPHY

J. Chantavoine: 'Charles Cottet', *Gaz. B.-A.*, n.s. 4, vi (1911), pp. 103–20
Charles Cottet (exh. cat., preface L. Bénédite; Paris, Gal. Petit, 1911)
L. Aubert: *Peintures de Charles Cottet* (Paris, 1928)
Charles Cottet (exh. cat. by A. Cariou, Quimper, Mus. B.-A., 1984)

ANDRÉ CARIOU

Cottingham, Lewis Nockalls (*b* Laxfield, Suffolk, 24 Oct 1787; *d* London, 13 Oct 1847). British architect, designer, writer and collector. He trained as a builder and from 1814 worked independently as an architect in London, his practice consisting mainly of church restorations. He published many books on design and architecture: his designs for ornamental metalwork appeared as *Ornamental Metal Worker's Director* (1823), and his lithographs of Gothic mouldings, finials and other details, published as *Working Drawings of Gothic Ornaments* ([1824]), provided architects with models for Gothic capitals and carvings; his publications on architecture include *Westminster Hall* (1822) and *Plans. . .of the Chapel of King Henry the Seventh* (1822–9).

During the 1840s Cottingham designed a variety of pieces of Gothic furniture for his friend, John Harrison of Snelston Hall, Derbys, some of which incorporated fragments of authentic Gothic carving. His design (London, V&A) for a drawing-room cabinet for Snelston Hall, although not strictly archaeological, was based on existing examples of Gothic detailing. Cottingham's discovery of a series of medieval tiles in the Chapter House at Westminster Abbey stimulated a revival of encaustic tiles, subsequently produced by such firms as Minton; he designed such tiles for St John, Barr & Co. of Worcester.

As a collector Cottingham amassed numerous Gothic architectural fragments and carvings, as well as a substantial number of casts and drawings. In 1852 his collection was given to the Architectural Museum in Canon Row, Westminster, which contained plaster casts and architectural fragments drawn from private and public sources; the museum was taken over in 1904 by the Architectural Association, which in 1916 donated its collection to the Victoria and Albert Museum. Cottingham's practice was continued by his son, Nockalls Johnson Cottingham (1823–54), who also designed stained glass, notably at Hereford Cathedral.

WRITINGS

Westminster Hall (London, 1822)
Plans, Elevations, Sections, Details and Views of the Magnificent Chapel of King Henry the Seventh at Westminster Abbey Church, 2 vols (London, 1822–9)
Ornamental Metal Worker's Director (London, 1823); rev. as *The Smith and Founder's Director, Containing a Series of Designs and Patterns for Ornamental Iron and Brasswork* (London, 1824); rev. as *The Smith's, Founder's and Ornamental Metal Worker's Director* (London, 1845)
Working Drawings of Gothic Ornaments, etc., with a Design for a Gothic Mansion (London, [1824])

BIBLIOGRAPHY

High Victorian Design (exh. cat., ed. S. Jervis; Ottawa, N.G., 1974–5)

E. A. CHRISTENSEN

Cotton. Fibre made from the long, soft hairs (lint) surrounding the seeds of the cotton plant (*Gossypium*). In the right climate (temperate to hot), cotton is easy to grow; it is also cheap to harvest and easily packed into compact bales for transport and export. Indigenous to India (*see* INDIAN SUBCONTINENT, §VII, 2(i)), the Sudan and Ethiopia, it was later grown in Egypt, China (*see* CHINA, §XII, 1(i)), western Central Asia (*see* CENTRAL ASIA, §I, 6(i)(b)), North America and elsewhere. Cotton is a very versatile fibre: used alone it can produce very fine, light and quite strong textiles (lawn and muslin), and used alone or in combination with other fibres it can make extremely durable and heavy fabrics (e.g. for use in bedspreads, rugs and carpets). It takes dyestuffs very well and can be painted or printed with designs. The first mention of cotton is in the *Annals* of Sennacherib of Assyria (*reg* 705–681 BC), although it became important there only after the introduction of Islam in the mid-7th century AD (*see* ANCIENT NEAR EAST, §II, 6 and ISLAMIC ART, §VI, 1). It was imported into the Middle East and North Africa in the 1st century AD and from there was traded throughout Spain and gradually through the rest of Europe. This article is concerned with the production and use of cotton in the Western world. (For a discussion of the properties, manufacture and conservation of cotton *see* TEXTILE, §I.) Further information on cotton is given within the relevant country and civilization surveys in the sections on textiles.

1. IMPORTS AND EUROPEAN MANUFACTURE. In England in the 16th century the term 'cotton' appears to have been applied to cheap, thick woollens, but almost simultaneously real cotton was also being made. Through the establishment of the East India companies in the Netherlands (1597), England (1600) and France (1664), raw cotton and painted cottons were imported into Europe from India. They were known first as calicos, as they were imported from the port of Calicut in south-west India. Despite the distances involved in importing cotton, by the end of the 17th century it was displacing the cheaper types of linen. The popularity of cheap, lightweight Indian fabrics and especially of the painted cottons alarmed manufacturers in Europe. Textiles from the 'Indies' were accordingly prohibited for sale in England in 1699 and in France in 1717. They could, however, be re-exported both

2. Cotton handkerchief, plate-printed with the *Brentford By-election* by Joseph Ware of Crayford, 1768 (London, Victoria and Albert Museum)

to other contries in Europe that did not have indigenous industries and to the American colonies. Lightweight, mixed fabrics of silk and cotton or pure cotton were very suitable for the American summer climate. Imported Indian textiles—including those for which the patterns were sent from Europe to be made in India—were, with such other 'luxury' items as porcelain and silk, hugely influential on the decorative arts in Europe and contributed to the rise of chinoiserie.

The huge popularity of the imported cotton led to imitation, and the ease with which cotton could be grown in a suitable climate inspired English colonists to set up plantations in the southern American colonies. A rearguard action was fought in England against the production of such cottons, and an act of 1736 allowed that it was legal in England to produce 'fustian', a fabric with a linen warp and a cotton weft; this was to prove very important to textile printing in the United Kingdom (*see* §2 below).

From its introduction into Europe, cotton was woven into cheap materials for underwear and stockings, and by the mid-18th century it was used for cotton velveteen and corduroy; an English corduroy waistcoat (London, V&A; see fig. 1) is so decorative that it is comparable with contemporary silks. Also in the 18th century there was a steadily growing quilt-making industry in Bolton, Lancs: production was based on two types, one with a looped pile (caddy), and the other flat-woven in double cloth, imitating hand-quilted covers made in Marseille and hence called 'Marseille' or 'Marcella' quilts (*see* QUILTING). The second technique was also used for men's summer waist-coats and for ladies' pockets, of which there are a few examples from the 18th century and many from the 19th,

1. Cotton corduroy waistcoat, English, mid-18th century (London, Victoria and Albert Museum)

woven on power looms with jacquard control (*see* TEX-TILE, §II, 1(ii)).

Although the finest Indian painted cottons continued to be imported throughout the 18th century into Europe despite the restrictions, there was an increasing emphasis on the import of the raw fibre. Large factories were established in Lancashire for the production of cotton fabrics. Robert Peel, grandfather of the 19th-century prime minister, was a Lancashire cotton manufacturer who controlled spinning mills, weaving and cotton-printing factories. Lancashire cottons of all kinds dominated the European market for most of the 19th century. Cotton was also combined with worsted wool to make furnishings and men's waistcoats, thus meeting a new demand in the 19th century from a burgeoning middle class. Most of these fabrics were made on the borders of Lancashire and Yorkshire, and some made in Halifax were exhibited at the Great Exhibition of 1851 in London. Cotton was also used to make enormous shawls (*see* SHAWL) in the 1850s and 1860s. The designs originated in the *shāls* woven from delicate goat's wool in Kashmir in the late 18th century. By the late 19th century jacquard-woven cottons manufactured on power looms were also creating serious competition for the Irish table-linen industry. The growth of the Lancashire cotton industry was reflected in a decline in the Indian cotton industry. The export of American cotton to newly established cotton industries in other parts of Europe hastened this decline still further. The collapse, however, of virtually all the European cotton industries in the second half of the 20th century led to a revival in India

3. Cotton fabric from a dress, block-printed with dark ground, made by William Kilburn, English, 1790–91 (London, Victoria and Albert Museum)

of both hand- and machine-woven fabrics. Good cotton and the use of traditional patterns and cheaper modern dyestuffs are favourable to the Indian manufacturer.

2. PRINTED COTTONS. Not until the import of painted cottons from India in the 17th century was there any real attempt in Europe to create a pattern by printing instead of by weaving (*see* INDIAN SUBCONTINENT, §VII, 3(ii)). There had been some linens printed in the 15th and 16th centuries with printer's ink, but the colours were not fast. The impact of Indian painted cottons was huge: the fabric itself seemed impossibly fine to the European customer, and the use of vibrant colours encouraged competition (*see* TEXTILE, §III, 1(ii)(f)). By the late 17th century both the Dutch and the English were printing rather hesitantly in madder colours. The cottons produced have a naive charm but do not compare in quality with the cottons from India. By using different mordants, however, colours ranging from nearly black to pale pink could be achieved; it took another half century to achieve indigo printing. Despite the difficulties of using it, indigo yielded a crisp, fast blue that was particularly good for the large-scale, monochrome, copperplate-printed textiles made from the 1750s. English printers led Europe in these developments, and some of the finest furnishing copperplate textiles printed by Robert Jones at Old Ford or the Bromley Hall factory have never been equalled and were even imitated later by French factories (*see* ENGLAND, §XI, (iv)). From the late 17th century a large number of snuff handkerchiefs were produced in Europe, the majority of which were copperplate-printed. Some printers concentrated specifically on the production of handkerchiefs, while others produced them as part of their range. Although many 18th-century handkerchiefs depicted such topical or political subjects as the *Trial of Dr Sacheverell* or the *Brentford By-election* (see fig. 2), by the 19th century they were being produced for a much wider market. By the mid-18th century English block-printed textiles were printed in a full range of colours, which could copy both the patterns and the colouring of contemporary dress silks. Block-printing of cotton was used to great effect by William Morris in the 19th century (*see* MORRIS, WILLIAM, fig. 3).

By the 1730s English printed fustians were being exported to the American colonies and, from the 1770s, pure cottons. A parliamentary act of 1774 permitted the use of British all-cotton cloths for printing, provided that they had three blue threads woven into their selvages to distinguish them from French and Indian cottons. This act was not repealed until 1812. The raw cotton, however, might have originally come from the southern American colonies. Even after American Independence (1776), English traders continued to export their cottons, thus discouraging the Americans from setting up their own cotton-printing industries. Only in the later 19th century were American cotton printers sufficiently skilled to compete with the English.

In France it became legal to print cottons in 1759 (*see* FRANCE, §XI, 4). A number of factories were set up in various regions, notably in Rouen, Nantes and Jouy-en-Josas. Significantly, there is evidence that CHRISTOPHE-PHILIPPE OBERKAMPF, founder of the Jouy factory, bought his cottons for printing from the East India

4. Cotton block-printed *mezzara*, Italian, 19th century (London, Victoria and Albert Museum)

Company sales in London because French cottons were not fine enough. It is not always easy to identify a cotton printed in Mulhouse in France in the late 18th century from one printed in Lancashire, especially if it has a dark ground (very fashionable at the time), which would make it impossible to see the obligatory three blue threads of an English cotton dating from between 1774 and 1812 (see fig. 3).

Factories for printing cottons were also set up in other parts of Europe, especially in Germany, Switzerland and Bohemia. Most of their products were made to be sold locally or in nearby states. In Italy the factories produced printed cottons for local use, and the *mezzara* of Genoa, large shawls with patterns inspired by those of contemporary imported Indian painted bedspreads, became particularly well known throughout Europe (see fig. 4). Another development, of the mid- and late 19th century, was the production of cottons printed for overseas markets. Turkey red printed cottons were produced in Scotland for the African market (*see* SCOTLAND, §XI) and in Moscow for the Central Asian and Swiss markets. Printed

cottons were traded in both Europe and America through the use of pattern cards, which were sent by an agent to his counterpart abroad; the recipient then ordered the required fabric by number. Nathan Meyer Rothschild (1777–1836) from Frankfurt am Main was a particularly successful cotton printer: he traded Lancashire printed cottons all over Europe and established his family's fortune in Britain.

BIBLIOGRAPHY

J. Taylor: *A Descriptive and Historical Account of the Cotton Manufacture of Dacca, in Bengal* (London, 1851)
D. King: 'Textiles and the Origins of Printing in Europe', *Pantheon*, xx (1962), pp. 23–30
M. Edwards: *The Growth of the British Cotton Trade, 1780–1815* (Manchester, 1969)
J. Irwin and K. B. Brett: *Origins of Chintz* (London, 1970)
F. Montgomery: *Printed Textiles: English and American Cottons and Linens, 1700–1850* (London, 1970)
A. L. Eno, ed.: *Cotton was King: A History of Lowell, Massachusetts* (Lowell, 1976)
S. D. Chapman and S. Chassagne: *European Textile Printers of the Eighteenth Century* (London, 1981)
Colour and the Calico Printer (exh. cat., Farnham, W. Surrey Coll. A. & Des., 1982)

J. Brédif: *Toiles de Jouy: Classic Printed Textiles from France, 1760–1843* (London, 1989)

W. Hefford: *The Victoria and Albert Museum's Textile Collection: Design for Printed Textiles in England, 1750–1850* (London, 1992)

NATALIE ROTHSTEIN

Cotton, Sir **Robert Bruce** (*b* Denton, Cambs, 22 Jan 1571; *d* London, 6 May 1631). English antiquarian, politician, collector and patron. He began his career in antiquarian studies as a protégé of William Camden; in *c.* 1586 this pair joined two other enthusiasts in order to found the Society of Antiquaries. (This society terminated *c.* 1607 and was not revived until 1757.) In 1599–1600 Cotton and Camden made a visit to the 'Picts Wall' (Hadrian's Wall), where they saw artefacts that were to have a significant influence on antiquarian scholarship. The historian and cartographer John Speed made use of Cotton's cabinet of coins in his *Historie of Great Britaine* (1610). The first English translation of Camden's *Britannia* (1610) by Philemon Holland contains an engraving after a drawing by Cotton of a Roman military altar at Alauna near Maryport, Cumbria (1600; London, BM). On Camden's death in 1623 Cotton inherited his manuscripts and is thought to have supervised the erection of Camden's monument, attributed to Nicholas Stone (i), in Westminster Abbey, London.

Cotton was a collector of antiquities and a patron of sculptors. He built two octagonal summer-houses at his country house, Conington Castle, Cambs (largely destr.), near Peterborough, to contain a collection of inscriptions, the remnant of which is now in the Museum of Archaeology and Anthropology, Cambridge University. About 1613 Cotton erected a series of cenotaphs and grave altars to members of his family at All Saints, Conington. Among them is one to Prince Henry of Scotland (*d* 1152), with whom Cotton claimed consanguinity through his descent from Robert the Bruce: this monument is based on the Alauna military altar referred to earlier. About the same time, Cotton composed the Latin epitaph for the tomb of *Mary, Queen of Scots* in Westminster Abbey.

Cotton's library, originally in his house at Blackfriars, London, was moved, probably in 1622, to his new house at Westminster, next to the Houses of Parliament. The room in which it was housed was described in 1692 as a rectangle 6 ft×26 ft (l. 83×7.92 m), with fourteen *scrinia* (cylindrical cases) labelled with the names of the first twelve Roman Emperors, Cleopatra and Faustina, 'their heads . . . in brass statues'. The arrangement, it has since been conjectured, began with *Julius Caesar* opposite the door and proceeded in an anticlockwise direction chronologically up to *Domitian*, which was an overdoor. Among the greatest manuscript treasures still in the Cotton collection, now housed in the British Library, London, are the Lindisfarne Gospels of *c.* 698–721 (Nero D IV), the Cotton Genesis (Otho B VI) and the Saxon Pentateuch (Claudius B IV). Cotton also owned the Utrecht Psalter (now Utrecht, Bib. Rijksuniv.).

Cotton's library at Westminster held the most valuable collection of manuscripts in England and was renowned throughout Europe. By a statute of 1700 the library became the property of the nation and survived unscathed until shortly after it had been moved to Ashburnham House in Westminster, where in 1731 some of the most important manuscripts were destroyed by fire. Of the original 958 manuscripts, 97 were lost; 105 of the 861 remaining were reduced to bundles of damaged notes. In 1753 the Cotton manuscripts joined the Hans Sloane collection of natural and artificial curiosities bought by Parliament in that year, and with these deposits, the British Museum began.

BIBLIOGRAPHY

T. Smith, ed.: *Catalogus librorum manuscriptorum bibliothecae Cottonianae* (Oxford, 1696)

J. Planta: *A Catalogue of the Manuscripts in the Cottonian Library* (London, 1802) [the most recent cat.]

H. Mirrlees: *A Fly in Amber: Being an Extravagant Biography of the Romantic Antiquary Sir Robert Bruce Cotton* (London, 1962)

K. Sharpe: *Sir Robert Cotton, 1586–1631: History and Politics in Early Modern England* (Oxford, 1979)

D. Howarth: 'Sir Robert Cotton and the Commemoration of Famous Men', *BL J.* (1992), i, pp. 1–28

DAVID HOWARTH

Cotton Genesis. Byzantine illuminated manuscript (London, BL, Cotton MS. Otho B. VI), probably of the late 5th century AD. It consists of the fragments of 129 folios, shrunken and charred by a fire in 1731, which are all that remain of one of the most profusely illustrated and magnificent books of the period. The manuscript has long been the focus of scholarly attention, and work on a facsimile was begun in 1621–2 by Nicolas-Claude Fabri de Peiresc, although it probably did not advance far.

All discussion of the Cotton Genesis starts from the ingenious reconstruction by Weitzmann and Kessler, according to whom the manuscript originally comprised some 221 folios (*c.* 330×250 mm) and contained the text of Genesis, illustrated by some 339 illuminations distributed throughout the book, most half-page or larger (including perhaps 36 full-page). These adopted a literal approach to the text, but some contained extra-biblical details derived from written commentaries (Christian or Jewish) or possibly from more informal, oral traditions. They were framed scenes with fully painted illusionistic settings, and they used a full range of pigments, including gold leaf for some details. Although Weitzmann and Kessler argued for an origin in Egypt, the evidence for this has been questioned by Wenzel.

The manuscript is also remarkable for the later use to which it was put. The cycle of 113 Genesis scenes in the mosaics of the narthex of S Marco, Venice, set up in the second and third quarters of the 13th century, were based, according to Weitzmann, on a careful study of the Cotton Genesis (*see* VENICE, §IV, 1(iii)). Since this connection was first observed by Tikkanen, it has played a central role (too important, according to Lowden) in conceptions of how medieval monumental cycles were developed from models in manuscripts.

BIBLIOGRAPHY

J.-J. Tikkanen: *Die Genesismosaiken von S Marco und ihr Verhältnis zu den Miniaturen der Cottonbibel* (Helsingfors, 1889)

K. Weitzmann: 'The Genesis Mosaics of San Marco and the Cotton Genesis Miniatures', *The Mosaics of San Marco*, ed. O. Demus (Chicago, 1984), ii, pp. 105–42, 253–7

K. Weitzmann and H. Kessler: *The Cotton Genesis: British Library Codex Cotton Otho B. VI* (Princeton, 1986)

M. Wenzel: 'Deciphering the Cotton Genesis Miniatures: Preliminary Observations Concerning the Use of Colour', *BL J.*, xiii (1987), pp. 79–100

J. Lowden: 'Concerning the Cotton Genesis and other Illustrated Manuscripts of Genesis', *Gesta*, xxxi (1992), pp.40–53

JOHN LOWDEN

Cotzumalhuapa. *See* SANTA LUCÍA COTZUMALHUAPA.

Coubillier, Frédéric [Friederich Wilhelm] (*b* Longeville, nr Metz, 1 Nov 1869; *d* Düsseldorf, 17 March 1953). German sculptor. He received his first training in the studio of his father, Joseph Coubillier (1836–88) in Trier. After his father's death he had to work in the Kunstanstalt Schülter in Cologne and then in the studio of Wilhelm Albermann in Düsseldorf, before he could begin studying in the sculptors' class at the Königlich Preussische Kunstakademie in Düsseldorf in 1895 under Karl Janssen. While still a student he won the competition held by the Düsseldorf *Verschönerungsverein* to design the fountain in the Königsallee. He completed his Triton fountain, designed in Neubarock style with Jugendstil elements, in 1902. In the same year he was commissioned to make the statue of Graf Adolf I von Berg at the Schloss Burg an der Wupper (nr Solingen).

From 1903 to 1910 Coubillier lived in Rome, where in 1903 he made the bronze group *Reunion* for the monument in the Nordfriedhof, Düsseldorf, to the industrial family from Düsseldorf, the Pfeiffer–Schiess: in this the mother is seen reunited with her son above the clouds. In 1913 Coubillier completed another fountain project, the *Industry Fountain*, on the Fürstenplatz in Düsseldorf. The figures, 3.75 m high, of the god Vulcan and his assistants, a smelter and a miner, were interpreted as allegories for the town of Düsseldorf as the capital of the steel industry. Later in his career Coubillier turned towards religious art. When his studio was bombed in 1943 he lost many of his works of art and models. His last work consisted of the 14 stations of the cross for the castle chapel of the Grafen von Spee in Heltorf bei Angermund.

BIBLIOGRAPHY
A. Dahm: 'Friedrich Wilhelm Coubillier', *Düsseldorf. Kultkal.*, xx (1950), pp. 489–93
I. Zacher: *Düsseldorfer Friedhöfe und Grabmäler* (Düsseldorf, 1982), pp. 210–11

INGE ZACHER

Coubine, Othon. *See* KUBÍN, OTOKAR.

Couch. *See under* SOFA.

Coucy-le-Château. Castle complex in Aisne, northern France. The castle was built between 1225 and 1242 on a spur overlooking the valley of the River Ailette between Soissons and Laon, which cuts the road to St Quentin. A colossal feudal fortress, strongly fortified by the lords of Coucy, who were rich enough in territory and alliances to erect an extraordinary building (see fig.), it commands the lines of approach from *c.* 10 km in every direction.

The site was mentioned as early as the 9th century, and in the 10th century it was already one of the most important feudal bases of the French kings; however, the complex visible today—castle, outer bailey and walled town—was built by Enguerrand III, Lord of Coucy, between 1225 and 1242. This great baron joined a revolt against Louis IX during the regency of Blanche of Castile, and it was at

Coucy-le-Château, *c.* 1225–42

this time that he erected the fortifications as a direct challenge to royal power.

The castle, at the extremity of the spur, is an irregular quadrilateral defended by four circular towers each nearly 20 m in diameter, far larger than those of the royal donjons built all over France in the first quarter of the 13th century. These towers contain hexagonal rib-vaulted chambers defended by arrow loops. In the middle of the south-east curtain wall facing the plateau, Enguerrand built an impressive donjon 31.25 m in diameter and 54 m high from the bottom of the moat, with walls 7.5 m thick at their base. It was surrounded on two-thirds of its circumference by a revetment wall. The donjon was entirely destroyed in 1918. The enormous tower had only three storeys, each rib-vaulted and nearly 15 m high, equivalent to five floors of a modern block of flats. At the top was a parapet with pointed crenellations, which once gave access to wooden hoardings supported on stone corbels.

Inside the castle enclosure are the ruins of a 13th-century chapel. The residential buildings along the south-west and north-west walls were entirely renovated and redecorated before 1386 by Enguerrand VII of Coucy. Above lofty cellars, the state rooms with large traceried windows were adorned with stained glass and statues of the Nine Heroes and Heroines, historical and mythological figures celebrated in chivalric literature. Impressive remnants survive today, testimony to the desire for ostentation and luxury shown by builders in the late 14th century at the height of the Hundred Years War.

The outer bailey was sufficiently large to house a village: it had twelve mural towers, two of which made up the entrance portal. This enclosure was built at the same time as the castle; the towers have vaulted chambers with long arrow loops, some of which were enlarged at the bottom for firing. In the centre of the outer bailey was a 12th-century Romanesque chapel; all around it were once located ancillary services, kitchens, stables, forges and tennis courts. The curtain wall of the outer bailey is mostly extant, and it is the clearest evidence of the power acquired by the Coucy lords in the first half of the 13th century, being comparable in size to many contemporary urban enclosures, but with flanking towers that were much more powerful owing to their greater diameter.

The fortification of the site also includes the wall of the town itself, with the Porte de Laon, its most prestigious feature. This magnificent structure was built in the 1240s and is remarkably well preserved. It is flanked by two circular towers with long arrow loops, and the entrance passage is defended by two portcullises and a murder hole, with guard rooms above and a long, vaulted corridor underneath leading to a barbican, which was entirely rebuilt in the 16th century. The rest of the wall was defended by round towers, 12 of them dating from the 13th century; it has been renovated many times, as can be seen, for example, in the cannon loops visible at the Porte de Chauny.

Inside the wall, a fine Gothic church and medieval houses help to make Coucy one of the most representative sites of medieval architecture. Even without the donjon, it is architecturally and historically an incomparable fortified site. As military architecture, Coucy is a clear example of principles defined by the royal architects in the first third of the 13th century, while the Porte de Laon, probably the latest building, represents a more advanced current, linked with such examples of Louis IX's fortifications as the castles of Carcassonne and Angers.

BIBLIOGRAPHY

E. Viollet-le-Duc: *Description du château de Coucy* (Paris, n.d.)
——: *Dictionnaire raisonné de l'architecture française du XIe au XVIe siècle*, 10 vols (Paris, 1858–68)
L. Broche: 'Notes sur d'anciens comptes de la châtellenie de Coucy', *Bull. Soc. Acad. Laon*, xxxii (1908), p. 339
E. Lefèvre-Pontalis: *Le Château du Coucy*, Petites Monographies Grands Edifices France (Paris, 1909, 2/1928)
F. Enaud: *Le Château de Coucy* (Paris, 1961)
J. Mesqui and C. Ribéra-Pervillé: 'Les Châteaux de Louis d'Orléans et leurs architectes (1391–1407)', *Bull. Mnmtl*, cxxxviii (1980), p. 294

JEAN MESQUI

Couder, (Louis-Charles-)Auguste (*b* London, 1 April 1789; *d* Paris, 21 July 1873). French painter. A pupil of Jean-Baptiste Regnault and David, he exhibited for the first time in the Salon of 1814 with *The Death of General Moreau* (Brest, Mus. Mun.). In 1817 *The Levite of Ephraïm* (Arras, Abbaye St Vaast, Mus. B.-A.) was widely praised by the critics. In 1818 he received his first official commission, for the decoration of the vaulted ceiling of the vestibule to the Galerie d'Apollon in the Louvre (*in situ*). Couder's reputation as a history painter was based on the commissions he executed for the Musée Historique in Versailles. In addition to many portraits, he produced large paintings, in which rich colouring was combined with precise academic drawing: for example, *The Battle of Lawfeld* (exh. Salon, 1836) and *The Siege of Yorktown* (exh. Salon, 1837; sketch in Blérancourt, Château, Mus. N. Coop. Fr.–Amér.), both painted for the Galerie des Batailles (*in situ*); *The Federation of 14 July 1790* (exh. Salon, 1844; Versailles, Château); and the *Oath Taken in the Jeu de Paume* (exh. Salon, 1848; Versailles, Château), which was inspired very directly by David. *The Opening of the States General at Versailles on 5 May 1789* (exh. Salon, 1840; Versailles, Château) is a good illustration of his ability to present a historical reconstruction containing a large number of figures without monotony, thanks to his talent for portraiture and the skilful disposition of light.

Religious easel painting and church decoration were also important elements in Couder's oeuvre. In 1819 he painted an *Adoration of the Magi* for the Chapelle des Missions Etrangères, Paris (*in situ*). In 1832 he went to Munich in order to acquire a deeper understanding of fresco technique and there collaborated with Peter Cornelius on the decoration of the Alte Pinakothek. On his return to Paris in 1833 he painted a fresco of *The Stoning of St Stephen* for a chapel in Notre-Dame-de-Lorette (*in situ*). Between 1838 and 1841 he was involved with Jules-Claude Ziegler, Victor Schnetz, François Bouchot (1800–42), Léon Cogniet, Alexandre Abel de Pujol and Emile Signol in the decoration of the church of La Madeleine, where he painted *The Meal in the House of Simon* (fresco, *in situ*) for one of the lunettes in the nave. The composition, restricted to a few figures, the rigorously classical forms and sober colours reveal the influence of German religious painting and were in distinct contrast to the academicism of his historical commissions. Couder became a member of the Institut in 1839. In 1844 he painted in St Germain l'Auxerrois, Paris, *The Ascension of Christ* (fresco, chapel of the tomb of St Germain l'Auxerrois). His knowledge of fresco procedures gained him the task of restoring the Galerie François Ier in the château of Fontainebleau in the late 1840s.

Couder also produced anecdotal genre paintings in a classical style: for example, *The Death of Masaccio* (exh. Salon, 1817; Quimper, Mus. B.-A.) and *The Death of Vert-Vert*, inspired by a poem by Gresset (1829, according to Breton; Beauvais, Mus. Dépt. Oise). He took inspiration from Ossianic and Romantic literature, evolving a more personal and freer style in such works as *Despair of Cuchulin* (Dijon, Mus. Magnin) and *Scenes from Notre-Dame de Paris* (polyptych in Neo-Gothic frame; exh. Salon, 1833; Paris, Mus. Victor Hugo).

WRITINGS
Considérations sur le but moral des arts (Paris, 1867)

BIBLIOGRAPHY
E. Breton: *Notice sur la vie et les ouvrages de A. Couder* (Meulan, 1874)
M.-M. Aubrun: 'La Genèse d'une oeuvre d'Auguste Couder: Le *Repas chez Simon le Pharisien*', *Bull. Soc. Hist. A. Fr.* (1980), pp. 247–56
T. W. Gaehtgens: *Versailles: De la résidence royale au Musée Historique* (Paris, 1984), pp. 211–17
B. Foucart: *Le Renouveau de la peinture religieuse en France (1800–1860)* (Paris, 1987), pp. 186–7

PASCALE MÉKER

Coudray, Clemens Wenzeslaus [Wenzel] (*b* Ehrenbreitstein, 23 Nov 1775; *d* Weimar, 4 Oct 1845). German architect. He worked under Christian Friedrich Schuricht in Dresden in the 1790s before studying in Paris at the Ecole Polytechnique (1800–04) under Jean-Nicolas-Louis Durand; he visited Rome in 1804–5. Most of his life was spent in Weimar, where he was appointed Oberbaudirektor (1816) to the Grand Duchy of Saxe-Weimar-Eisenach, one of the smaller and poorer of the German states, for which most of his work was undertaken. This included the Erfurter Tor (1822–4), the Bürgerschule (1822–5), the Wagenremise (1823) and the Hoftheater (1825–9; destr. 1905), plain buildings strongly influenced by Durand. Coudray also founded a school for building workers, the Freie Gewerkschule (1829). Weimar's most eminent citizen, Johann Wolfgang von Goethe, took a close interest in Coudray's work, including his only major Greek Revival building, the Fürstengruft (1823–7). This mausoleum was commissioned by Grand Duke Charles Augustus (*reg* 1758–1828) and has a Doric portico and a centrally planned interior with an octagonal domed lantern. As both Friedrich Schiller (1827) and Goethe (1832) are also buried there, it is now known as the Goethe und Schiller Gruft. Coudray's last major work was the west wing of the Schloss (1830–45), remarkable for its frescoed interiors dedicated to Weimar's intellectual geniuses, including Goethe and Schiller. The rooms dedicated to these two were painted by Bernhard Neher (1806–86); the Goethe-zimmer was based on a design by Schinkel. Coudray also had an extensive private practice, and surviving houses by him stand on Heinrich Heine Strasse (1817 and 1821) and at nos 2–8 Steubenstrasse (1827). The latter are united behind a single palatial façade reminiscent of John Nash's terraces around Regent's Park, London.

BIBLIOGRAPHY

W. Schneemann: *C. W. Coudray: Goethes Baumeister* (Weimar, 1943) [includes extracts from Coudray's writings]
D. Dolgner: 'C. W. Coudray: Studienarbeiten aus der Pariser Zeit', *Wiss. Z. Hochsch. Archit. & Bauwsn, Weimar*, v–vi (1975), pp. 485–500
A. Jericke and D. Dolgner: *Der Klassizismus in der Baugeschichte Weimars* (Weimar, 1975)
D. Watkin and T. Mellinghoff: *German Architecture and the Classical Ideal, 1740–1840* (London, 1987)

STEFAN MUTHESIUS

Coudray, Marie-Alexandre-Lucien (*b* Paris, 21 Feb 1865; *d* 1932). French medallist. He trained in Paris at the Ecole des Beaux-Arts under Augustin-Alexandre Dumont, Gabriel-Jules Thomas, Henri-Emile Allouard (1844–1929) and Hubert Ponscarme, winning the Prix de Rome for medal engraving in 1893. His *Orpheus at the Entrance to the Underworld*, struck for the Exposition Universelle of 1900, was immensely popular and is to this day one of the best known of French Art Nouveau medals. Coudray's other works included a series of highly sentimental plaquettes, such as *Agriculture* (1905), *Flora* (1905) and the *Charmer* (1906); his *Gallia Tutrix* (1904) was a medal celebrating the beneficent effects of French colonial rule.

BIBLIOGRAPHY

Forrer

MARK JONES

Coughtry, Graham (*b* St Lambert, Quebec, 8 June 1931). Canadian painter. He studied in Arthur Lismer's children's classes at the Montreal Museum of Fine Art, at that Museum's School of Art and Design with Goodridge Roberts and Jacques de Tonnancour and at the Ontario College of Art (1949–53), where he met Michael Snow. Taking inspiration from Pierre Bonnard, Alberto Giacometti and from Abstract Expressionism, Coughtry established his dual interest in the human figure in motion and in expressively brushed surfaces in works such as *Emerging Figure* (1959; Montreal, Mus. F.A.), developing these themes in series such as the *Two Figure* paintings of the 1960s and the *Water Figure* paintings of the 1970s. Concerned above all with colour relationships and with the act of painting, Coughtry's works characteristically show generalized figures as emerging within the fabric of

the painting as the result of the process rather than as a depiction of a particular person. He exhibited widely, for example representing Canada at the São Paulo Biennale in 1959 and at the Venice Biennale in 1960, and was an influential teacher of painting at various Canadian institutions including the Ontario College of Art and York University, both in Toronto.

BIBLIOGRAPHY

Graham Coughtry Retrospective (exh. cat. by B. Hale, Oshawa, Ont., McLaughlin Gal., 1976)

KEN CARPENTER

Coulisse [Fr.: 'wing']. Element at the side of an image, especially in panoramic landscapes, which directs the spectator's eye towards the central view in the distance. The term derives from those pieces of stage scenery that mask the wings of the theatre and create an illusion of recession (*see also* REPOUSSOIR).

☐

Coulte, Maximilian. *See* COLT, MAXIMILIAN.

Counihan, (Jack) Noel (*b* Melbourne, 4 Oct 1913; *d* Melbourne, 5 July 1986). Australian painter, printmaker, draughtsman, sculptor, cartoonist and illustrator. Largely self-taught, he began printmaking in 1931 and worked as a caricaturist, cartoonist and illustrator for the weekly and left-wing press, his outlook influenced by experience on the dole and political struggle during the Depression. In 1941 he began oil painting, his first pictures being mainly a celebration of Australian working-class tenacity during the 1930s: for example *At the Start of the March* (1944; Sydney, A.G. NSW). A founder-member of the Contemporary Art Society in 1938, he initiated its 1942 anti-Fascist exhibition and helped organize an Artists' Unity Congress, receiving awards for his paintings of miners in the ensuing *Australia at War* exhibition in 1945. From 1939 to 1940 he was in New Zealand and from 1949 to 1952 in Europe, mostly London. Later he made frequent trips to Britain and France, as well as visiting the USSR and Mexico.

Counihan's imaginative and creative versatility enabled him to produce extended pictorial metaphors for inherent contemporary crises, embodying potent artistic responses to specific conditions of oppression and discrimination, the nuclear threat and attendant social alienation. From the late 1960s he created images in numerous interrelated series challenging Australia's involvement in the Vietnam War, for example *Boy in Helmet IV* (1967, Morwell, Latrobe Valley A. Cent.). He also made portraits, monumental figure studies, grotesque terracotta figures (1974–5) and, from 1981, works in various media allegorizing Catalan peasant life in France.

BIBLIOGRAPHY

M. Dimmack: *Noel Counihan* (Melbourne, 1974)
R. Smith: *Noel Counihan Prints, 1931–1981: A Catalogue Raisonné* (Sydney, 1981)
V. Lindesay: *Noel Counihan Caricatures* (Melbourne, 1985)
R. Smith: 'The Art of Commitment: The Place of Noel Counihan', *Arena*, 77 (1986), pp. 36–51
B. Smith: *Noel Counihan: Artist and Revolutionary* (Melbourne, 1993)

ROBERT SMITH

Counterproof [Fr. *contre preuve*; offset]. Reversed image of a print or drawing. It is made by pressing a blank sheet

Guercino: *Hebrew Priest*, red chalk, 185×181 mm, *c.* 1646 (left) and (right) a counterproof of the drawing, retouched by an anonymous later (?18th-century) hand, red chalk, 205×180 mm, *c.* 1646 (both Windsor, Windsor Castle, Royal Library)

of paper against the original, both being dampened slightly and then run through a rolling press together. The counterproof image, usually fainter than the original, is transferred on to the second sheet in reverse (see fig.). A counterproof is often made as part of the working process: after gauging the effects of the reversal, the printmaker or draughtsman is able to revise, correct or introduce new elements to the original as seems appropriate.

The process of pulling a counterproof is especially useful in between states of a print, since the counterproof is in the same direction as the printing-plate on which the artist is working. Such a counterproof can only be made from a newly printed proof that still has wet ink. The proof itself is damaged by the process: the intense pressure used to transfer the image removes ink from the original print and smooths out the impression marks.

For draughtsmen, pulling a counterproof is a simple method of reversing a design, for example for an engraving, book illustration or tapestry. It also enables a designer to reproduce a motif or series of motifs around two or four axes without further effort, as in the design for a damask napkin.

Some artists, including Thomas Rowlandson, have used counterproofing as a measure of reproducing their own work for sale; counterproofs of Old Master drawings have also been produced by forgers, especially in the 18th century. In both cases, the counterproof drawing is often gone over by hand to increase its veracity. Unless retouched, a counterproof drawing has a pale, rather monotonous and flat appearance. It is also sometimes recognizable from the shading, which appears left-handed, and from any inscription, heraldic motif or collector's mark, which is similarly reversed. As with prints, the process is harmful to the original drawing, because it lifts and thins the original medium, causing the surface to become flatter in texture and fainter in hue. The actual

colour of the original may also change as a result of being moistened; red chalk, for instance, assumes an orange-red cast.

BIBLIOGRAPHY
J. Hankwitz: *An Essay on Engraving and Copper-plate Printing* (London, 1732)
C. Klackner: *Proofs and Prints, Engravings and Etchings* (New York, 1884)
J. Watrous: *The Craft of Old Master Drawings* (Madison, WI, 1957)
SHIRLEY MILLIDGE

Country house. Large and prestigious residence in a rural area. Usually set off by gardens and surrounded by extensive parkland and agricultural estates, it remained one of the most prominent cultural forms in England for more than five centuries. The owners of these houses were not only the source of most political, economic and social influence but were also arbiters of taste. As patrons and collectors they influenced the whole field of artistic endeavour, and their collections and furnishings, interior decorations and gardens combined with the architectural fabric of their houses to create ensembles rivalling in artistic importance the French CHÂTEAU and the Italian VILLA.

1. 14th and 15th centuries. 2. 16th century. 3. 17th century. 4. 18th century. 5. 19th and 20th centuries.

1. 14TH AND 15TH CENTURIES. The genesis of the country house can be found in the lightly fortified residences of feudal magnates of the Middle Ages. These were generally arranged in a courtyard form, with a hall, kitchen, service rooms and family apartments in the main court, and an outer or base court containing lodgings and storage buildings. The entrance was protected by a gate-house, and the principal fenestration was concentrated on the internal elevations of the courts. In the early Middle Ages, the essential elements of hall, kitchen, chapel and lodgings were often separate structures or groups of buildings isolated within a defensive enclosure (e.g. Penshurst Place,

Kent, built *c.* 1340 for Sir John de Pulteney), but these tended gradually to coalesce to form a tighter plan in which the rooms themselves defined the extent of the house. A hall and service range would be extended by flanking projecting wings, and the courtyard might be enclosed by a gate-house range. This sort of evolutionary development can be seen at Haddon Hall, Derbys, where a new hall was added *c.* 1370 to an earlier house, and the building was gradually expanded into a double-courtyard house over the next two centuries. The irregular relationship of the various ranges—an inevitable result of such an extended building programme—was of little consequence. Indeed, exactly the same informality was present in those houses built in a single campaign: for example, any attempt at symmetry in the outer court at Wingfield Manor House, Derbys, built for Ralph, Lord Cromwell, over a period of less than 15 years from 1440, was deliberately abandoned in the main courtyard, where the hall, state apartments and great tower were given unmistakable emphasis.

Such a programme reflected precisely the role of the great medieval house as the symbol of the power wielded by its owner. The HALL was the formal architectural focus of this symbolism, and its form changed very little throughout the medieval period. It was entered at one end through a screens passage that divided it from the service rooms. At the far end was the high table reserved for the head of the family, raised up on a dais and dramatically lit by a large window or a projecting bay. Private apartments were usually off the dais end of the hall; by the end of the Middle Ages they included an informal parlour and a great chamber, which, in preference to the hall, was increasingly used as the main room of state. The importance of these

rooms was marked by the richness of their carved decoration. Visitors and the remainder of the household were accommodated in the courtyard ranges.

The architectural treatment of the various elements of the great house reflected very closely their relative importance in maintaining the owner's dignity and status. Certain key features such as the hall, the chamber and the chapel were emphasized by means of their size and decoration, while the more utilitarian structures (essential for the functioning of the household) were plainly finished. Towers and decorative crenellations played an important role in this visual scheme, since they were symbolic of the military strength that was the ultimate measure of real power during this period. Not all medieval houses adopted the courtyard form, although it clearly represented the most socially prestigious plan. Where a large band of permanent retainers was not essential, the ranges of lodgings that justified and defined the courts were omitted, but all the other facilities of the great household had to be contrived within a smaller compass. For example, at Great Chalfield Manor (*c.* 1470–80), Wilts, the moat was used to form an invisible courtyard within which the gate-house and chapel (in this case the parish church) were isolated structures completely detached from the house itself. The hall, with its higher roof-line, gabled porch and bay window, and tall chimney-stack, dominates the composition, but the decorated oriels in both flanking wings indicate the presence of chambers of some importance on the first floor and supply an architectural balance that is subtly and deliberately asymmetrical.

2. 16TH CENTURY. The shift from casual balance to determined symmetry is one of the more significant

1. Compton Wynyates, Warwickshire, completed *c.* 1520

2. Robert Smythson: Hardwick Hall, Derbyshire, west front, 1590–98

developments of the 16th century and is illustrated by two courtyard houses of the 1520s: Compton Wynyates, Warwicks, and Hengrave Hall, Suffolk. Compton Wynyates, built for Sir William Compton, courtier and close companion of Henry VIII, represents a continuation of medieval traditions. The ranges that form the principal courtyard are of differing heights, united only by an irregular battlement (see fig. 1). The gate-house is asymmetrically placed, so that it leads directly across the court to the screens passage at the far end of the traditional hall in the opposite range. The hall occupies the full height of this range, and the position of its high table is marked by the tall projecting bay window, which forms the courtyard's principal architectural feature. There was no attempt at symmetry on any of the elevations at Compton Wynyates, and all openings and projections are entirely determined by the function and importance of the rooms they serve. At Hengrave Hall (1524–40), built for Sir Thomas Kytson, a conscious effort to contrive a visual balance is apparent on the entrance front of the inner courtyard, where the elevation is elongated by a wing extending to the east. This was designed to create the illusion of uniformity and to give the entrance a central position.

Although the early date once claimed for Barrington Court, Somerset, is no longer tenable, and the rigorous symmetry of the courtyard elevations of Sutton Place, Surrey, begun shortly before Hengrave for Sir Richard Weston, has been ascribed to an 18th-century remodelling, nevertheless from the late 1530s onwards, in the wake of Henry VIII's hunting lodge at Nonsuch, Surrey, the traditional functional hierarchy of the late Middle Ages was largely replaced by an architectural aesthetic firmly based on the harmony of symmetry. The external elevations of Sutton Place were comparatively plain and irreg-

ular, but during the 16th century houses became more outward-looking, and architecture became more a matter for public show as the need for security diminished.

Courtyard houses continued to be built for those who needed to entertain Elizabeth I on her annual Progress, but they exhibited a much greater unity than their medieval prototypes. The architectural effect was as much a product of ordered discipline and lavish decoration as it was of sheer size. Parallel with these prodigy houses, other builders were erecting smaller and more compact dwellings, often consciously based on geometrical proportions or dressed up to reflect courtly preoccupations with chivalry and allegory. Both Sir Francis Willoughby's fantasy castle (1580–88) at Wollaton, Notts, and John Thynne's classical Longleat (1572–80), Wilts, demonstrate, in their radically different ways, the need to display in a most single-minded fashion the taste of those who commissioned them. The E-plan houses that predominated in the latter part of Elizabeth's reign and the early decades of the 17th century illustrate this public pride in a quieter vein. These were basically single courtyard houses with the gate-house range removed, so that all the architecture and embellishment of the principal elevations were open to view. The emphasis formerly reserved for the gate-house was transferred to the main entry of the house, usually centrally positioned in the main range, and the projecting wings to either side were used to frame the symmetrical composition, which by then had become thoroughly absorbed into the conventions of such designs.

Applied decoration was generally confined to the frontispiece and the ends of the wings, leaving the plain walls and the regularity of the large windows to point up the contrast and to provide their own architectural effect. The essence of these houses was a delight in the dramatic effects of massing and the manipulation of the planes of the walls, rather than an ostentatious display of decoration. Only at roof level did the discipline often seem to break down, but the lively skylines with their gables and turrets and crowded rows of tall chimney-stacks were an integral part of the design and were consciously emphasized in order to draw the eye upwards and so increase the impression of height. Just as the important domestic rooms had moved off the ground floor to the upper storeys, so the roof became for a brief period a significant social area, used for evening banquets and as a viewing gallery from which to enjoy the surrounding park or countryside. What appeared as crowded, spiky decoration from the ground was also meant to be seen at close quarters as a series of architectural vignettes that would amuse and entertain (*see also* BANQUETING HOUSE).

The organization of Hardwick Hall (1590–98), Derbys, powerfully illustrates the new arrangement (see fig. 2). Externally, the glittering windows grow in height as they ascend the building, culminating in tall roof-top pavilions adorned with the builder's initials. Internally, the ground-floor hall is little more than a grand entrance foyer and passage to the spacious staircase, which takes the visitor up beyond the family apartments on the first floor to the principal rooms of state on the floor above. Here the sequence of richly decorated antechambers, chambers and withdrawing chambers flanked by a full-length gallery define a marked change in domestic life from the medieval period. Each room is heated by a grand fireplace and flooded with natural light from vast glazed windows. Bare walls are hidden by wooden panelling and opulent plaster-work in heavy relief, and the long gallery is decorated with rich tapestries and rows of portraits. The Elizabethans chose to indulge their taste for the excesses of Flemish Mannerism on their interior decoration rather than on their exterior elevations. The strapwork and lush foliage of their plasterwork and the grotesque figures supporting their chimney-pieces were often in stark contrast to the more disciplined qualities of the architecture that contained them.

3. 17TH CENTURY. Large courtyard houses, such as Audley End (1603–16), Essex, for the Earl of Suffolk, and Blickling Hall (1619–23), Norfolk, for the Lord Chief Justice, Sir Henry Hobart, continued to be built in the early years of the 17th century by ambitious men, but their cost and the changing relationship between sovereign and subject under the Stuarts soon rendered them anachronistic. Significantly, when Robert Cecil, 1st Earl of Salisbury, built his new country house at Hatfield, Herts, in 1607–12, he adopted the more economical solution of an open E-plan, but with the accommodation in ranges two rooms deep instead of the traditional single-room width (*see* CECIL, (2)). The more compact house that resulted was still able to provide separate suites of state apartments for James I and his queen, Anne of Denmark. The trend towards more compact houses with the accommodation in the main range in 'double-pile' form had been apparent among lesser courtiers for some years. It signalled the end of any lingering significance that the medieval hall might still have had. Once it was no longer possible to light such a hall from two sides, its decline into the entrance hall had begun. At Charlton House (1607–12), Greenwich, built

for Sir Adam Newton, tutor to Henry, Prince of Wales, the hall was placed at right-angles to the alignment of the main range, creating a double-pile central block with short single-pile wings to either side. This effectively produced an H-plan, which allowed for more convenient circulation than the E-plan.

Charlton, with its emphatic frontispiece, dramatic roof-line and plain walling was still in the Elizabethan tradition, but the H-plan was adopted in the 1630s for a fashionable group of houses built in the style sometimes described as ARTISAN MANNERISM. Most of these houses seem to have been designed by skilled craftsmen, such as bricklayers and carpenters, and their clients were often merchants connected with the City of London, where the style flourished in the newly erected halls of the livery companies (*see* LIVERY HALL). Swakeleys, Middx, built in 1638 for Sir Edmund Wright, a Cheshire merchant who became Lord Mayor of London, is one of the most distinctive examples. They were invariably built of brick and are characterized by windows in large rectangular openings, a pronounced stress on the horizontal lines of the façades, a surface emphasis on the decorative qualities of classical features such as segmental and triangular pediments and pilasters and, above all else, an enthusiastic delight in shaped gables.

The classical elements featured in these houses were never more than decorative motifs borrowed from an eclectic repertory, but at Court a much more serious attempt was undertaken by INIGO JONES to introduce the principles of Italian Renaissance classicism into architectural design. Jones was exclusively the Court's architect, and the Palladian influence of such buildings as the Queen's House at Greenwich (begun 1616; *see* GREENWICH, §1) and the Banqueting House, Whitehall (1619–22; *see* LONDON, §V, 5), found only a faint echo in the designs by others for country houses. The Great Chamber portico at Raynham Hall (1620s), Norfolk, the entrance screen at Castle Ashby (*c.* 1630), Northants, and the south front of Wilton House, Wilts (1630s; for illustration *see* WILTON), were isolated examples outside the mainstream of contemporary architecture. This was symptomatic of the Court's growing political alienation, which culminated in the Civil War of the 1640s and effectively brought domestic building to a halt for a decade or more.

After the establishment of the Protectorate in 1649, John Webb (*see* WEBB, JOHN (i)) attempted to consolidate the Palladian tradition, but his discredited Royalist connections largely frustrated him. In 1649 he recast the interior of Wilton House in a sequence of cube and double-cube rooms that were to be highly influential on interior decoration in the 18th century, but the chaste classicism of his other commissions—Gunnersbury House (1658–63; destr.), Middx; Amesbury House (1661; destr.), Wilts; and Lamport Hall (1650s), Northants—were out of tune with the spirit of the age. Of greater importance was the distinctive new house-type evolved by a gentleman architect, ROGER PRATT. His attractive designs established the classical country house as the English archetype in a way that was much more akin to the native temperament than the stark discipline of Jones's Palladianism.

About 1650, shortly after returning from a six-year tour on the Continent, Pratt designed Coleshill House, Berks (see fig. 3), for his relative Sir George Pratt. Coleshill incorporated all the elements that were to be so influential both in England and its American colonies for a century or more. It had an exceedingly compact plan contrived within a double-pile rectangle. The kitchen and other services were placed in a semi-basement, which had the effect of raising the principal rooms above ground level and allowed for a grand flight of entrance steps. The main rooms were in the centre of the house on an axis leading through from the front door and consisted of a magnificent staircase hall with a great parlour looking out over the garden front and a great dining-room above. The four corners of the house on both principal floors were divided into suites of apartments, each containing a chamber with two smaller closets leading off. Communication was by an axial spine corridor, with back stairs at either end to allow servants access from the basement service rooms without them mingling with guests using the main staircase. The decoration, including pedimented doorcases and chimney-pieces and heavily moulded ceilings divided up into rectangular compartments, was derived from Jones, who had provided advice in the early stages of construction. The elevations were given a strong horizontal emphasis with a rusticated podium and a deep overhanging cornice. The hipped roof was capped with a balustraded viewing platform, a central lantern and tall chimney-stacks.

The basic theme that Pratt established was immensely popular, and large numbers of houses based on the Coleshill arrangement were constructed during the later 17th century. In some cases further accommodation was introduced in flanking wings, in the manner of Clarendon House (1664–7; destr. 1683), Piccadilly, London, the extended version that Pratt designed for Edward Hyde, 1st Earl of Clarendon. Reduced in size, this type was suitable for housing the minor gentry or, as at Hathaways (1685), South Littleton, Worcs, and the Parsonage (1675), Stanton Harcourt, Oxon, for the wealthy clergy. Pratt's influence led to a growing formality in the planning of the house. A central public reception room, often two full storeys in height (and increasingly called the saloon), led into sequences of antechambers, bedchambers and closets that were symmetrically disposed and had their own social hierarchy in terms of rank and privacy. The further a guest was able to penetrate, the higher was his or her standing, with the bedchamber the ultimate destination in which privileged visitors were received, and the closet alone reserved for privacy. The sequence can be clearly perceived in the plan of Ragley Hall, Warwicks, designed c. 1678 by Robert Hooke for the 1st Earl of Conway. Externally the arrangements were neatly advertised by the elevational device of having a central emphasis for the public rooms and symmetrical pavilions marking the bedchambers that terminated the façades. At Ragley the layout was contrived within a rectangular block, but the sequence lent itself equally to a linear form, with single suites flanking a central saloon as at Petworth (1688–93), W. Sussex. The formality of the country house plan during this period was complemented by the axial layouts to be found in the landscaped parks in which these houses were built. The great avenues that radiate from Badminton House, Glos, and from others to be seen in the contemporary engravings of JOHANNES KIP, capture perfectly the desired effect.

3. Roger Pratt: Coleshill House, Berkshire, east front, 1658–62 (destroyed by fire 1952)

Towards the end of the 17th century, the more sophisticated builders reacted against the understated style associated with Pratt and moved towards something altogether more lively and exciting, a style usually identified as English Baroque. This was dramatic architecture on a large scale, with profuse decoration and deliberately distorted classical features creating a bold, almost shocking impact. These qualities are present in the monumental south range that William Talman (*see* TALMAN, (1)) added to CHATSWORTH HOUSE, Derbys, in 1687–9. Twelve bays long, it has a six-bay recessed centre and end pavilions made emphatic by their fluted giant pilasters. These pilasters, the enormous key-stone above each window, the heavy cornice and a roof-top balustrade crowned with urns were all part of Talman's intention to provide a sense of drama and movement. The massiveness that characterizes Chatsworth is a key-note of English Baroque architecture and is also visible in the buildings of NICHOLAS HAWKSMOOR and JOHN VANBRUGH. At Easton Neston, Northants, designed *c.* 1690 by Hawksmoor for Sir William Fermor, the smooth ashlar of the elevations contrasts with the complicated articulation, to give an air of monumentality to what is a comparatively small house.

4. 18TH CENTURY. Vanbaugh's first building, CASTLE HOWARD (1701–24; *see* VANBRUGH, JOHN, fig. 1), N. Yorks, was designed with essential assistance by Hawksmoor, as was Vanbrugh's next commission, BLENHEIM PALACE (1705–16; *see* VANBRUGH, JOHN, fig. 2). The sheer bravado of the architectural invention and the confident manipulation of the different elements of the complicated plans seem to be entirely Vanbrugh's work. Blenheim was a palace provided by a grateful nation for a military hero, but similar characteristics appear on a more domestic scale at Vanbrugh's other country houses, for example at Seaton Deleval, Northumb. (1718–28; *see* VANBRUGH, JOHN, fig. 4). Vanbrugh's interior planning exploited the possibilities of the formal relationships of state rooms and apartments in an equally dramatic manner; his elaborate patterns of symmetry and extended vistas embraced not only a house and its service buildings but also the gardens and landscape park beyond.

The liveliness of the Baroque continued to appeal to many discerning patrons in the early decades of the 18th century, and their demands were met from two sources. For those unable to afford designs of the first rank, the emerging professional class of building contractors was able to produce original plans as one of their services and provided a perfectly satisfactory solution in the provinces. Indeed, the houses built by such families of builders as the Smiths of Warwick or the Bastards of Blandford are among the most competent and pleasing creations of the period. Higher up the social spectrum such architects as JAMES GIBBS and THOMAS ARCHER (both of whom had travelled and lived abroad) offered their sophisticated clients options that were altogether more cosmopolitan. The characteristic designs of both groups were less flamboyant than the powerful schemes of Vanbrugh. Often they placed the cornice below a full attic storey and relied on giant pilasters and emphatic window surrounds for their decorative effects.

The Hanoverian succession in 1714 and the consequent consolidation of political power by a Whig aristocracy antithetical to the associations of the Baroque style with Rome and Catholicism brought about a reaction in architectural style that rapidly took on the fervour of a moral crusade. Palladio and Inigo Jones were set up as the two modern masters to be followed, in pursuit of the harmony and proportion of Italian classicism prior to its deterioration into the Mannerism of the 17th century (*see* PALLADIANISM). In about 1725–9 Richard Boyle, 3rd Earl of Burlington (*see* BOYLE, (2)), designed and built a wing in the form of a villa, attached to his family house at Chiswick. Burlington's villa ranks as one of the most influential buildings in English domestic architecture (for illustrations *see* CHISWICK HOUSE and BOYLE, (2), fig. 3). Built on a square plan, with the principal rooms in a *piano nobile* above a rustic podium, it is characterized by the 1-3-1 bay rhythm balanced by a central hexastyle portico, ashlar walls devoid of surface decoration and prominent Diocletian windows lighting the rotunda that rises from the centre of the roof. Henry Herbert, 9th Earl of Pembroke, was another architect earl designing in the same style (*see* HERBERT, (3)), and bolstered by auspicious aristocratic patronage, Palladianism reigned supreme in country house architecture for the rest of the 18th century (e.g. Harleyford Manor, Bucks, *c.* 1755, by ROBERT TAYLOR).

The early Palladian architects continued to employ for their house plans the formal arrangement of state rooms flanked by apartments. The dominant feature—a central pedimented portico—gave a logical impetus to axial planning, and the linear form of interconnecting rooms enabled extended elevations to be designed in the appropriate form on the huge scale of Wanstead House (from 1713; destr. 1824), Essex, by COLEN CAMPBELL, or Wentworth Woodhouse (1737–64), Yorks, by HENRY FLITCROFT. Principal rooms were inevitably on the *piano nobile*, while the rusticated podium housed service rooms and informal living-rooms. The mixture of uses at this lower level indicates a loosening of formal social conventions that gained greater momentum as the century progressed. With growing improvements in transportation, the 18th century saw an increase in country house visiting and the institution of house parties in which entertainment played an important role. The plan of the house as a symbolic celebration of a rigid hierarchy of status and power slowly declined, to be replaced by a circuit of reception rooms designed for more sociable uses and often set around a staircase of considerable grandeur or striking design, as at Berrington Hall, Hereford & Worcs, by Henry Holland (see fig. 4), built in 1778–81. With more rooms required for public resort on the principal floor, apartments began to shrink in size, and the bedchambers were removed elsewhere. The circular planning to be found in houses was repeated in the park, where the straight lines and axial vistas of the 17th century were replaced by more subtle and romantic landscapes; contrived views and architectural features were designed to provide a series of incidents enjoyed on a circuit of the grounds (*see* GARDEN, §VIII, 4(iv)).

From the mid-18th century, architects began to seek inspiration in the architecture of ancient Greece and pre-Imperial Rome. The language of contemporary classical architecture was expanded, and the eclectic archaeological

4. Henry Holland: Berrington Hall, Hereford & Worcester, staircase, looking south, c. 1780

approach that it fostered made possible a consciously modern style for which intuitive feeling became an important part of aesthetic appreciation. Pre-eminent among this generation was Robert Adam (*see* ADAM (i), (3)), who together with the more restrained classicist WILLIAM CHAMBERS dominated the architectural profession in the late 18th century, introducing a whole new vocabulary of Greek and Etruscan decorative motifs. Adam's greatest contribution was probably to interior design, where he dramatically juxtaposed rooms of different shapes and proportions and decorated them with pastel colours and delicate plasterwork, as for example at Osterley Park (1763–80; for illustration *see* ETRUSCAN STYLE) and Syon House (1762–9), both in Middlesex.

In the late 18th century, this liberation from the rigid rule of Palladianism stimulated a remarkable flowering of invention that encompassed a whole range of variations on antique architecture and design. This extended from the sombre massiveness of such Neo-classical houses as Dodington Park (1798–1813), Glos, by James Wyatt (*see* WYATT, (2)), to the academic achievement of the GREEK REVIVAL, so evocatively expressed in the remodelling of the Grange (1805–9), Northington, Hants, by WILLIAM WILKINS.

The creation of more natural-looking country house landscapes in the late 18th century by such designers as 'Capability' Brown and Humphry Repton was undertaken at a time when architectural symmetry was becoming far less important than it had been at any time since the 16th century. The principal rooms in the house began to move down from the *piano nobile* to the ground floor and were increasingly integrated with the gardens that surrounded them. Abandoning a rustic podium meant that alternative

arrangements had to be made for the service rooms. The solution often provided by such architects as John Nash (i) was to attach a separate servants' wing to the house, with no attempt undertaken to create a matching balance. In the same spirit there was also a much more eclectic approach to the architecture itself, whereby the elements of historic precedent were freely borrowed and mixed in a picturesque and often asymmetrical manner. Such an approach ultimately led to a more insular examination of England's historic past and the revival of medieval Gothic forms. The light-hearted GOTHICK of such 18th-century buildings as Strawberry Hill (from 1753) by Horace Walpole (*see* WALPOLE, (2)) and the remodelled Great Hall at Lacock Abbey (1753–6; *see* ENGLAND, fig. 7), Wilts, by SANDERSON MILLER was essentially an aspect of the PICTURESQUE, and such architecture was merely an incident in a romantically contrived landscape.

5. 19TH AND 20TH CENTURIES. By the second quarter of the 19th century, inspired by the Anglo-Catholic religious revival, the Gothic Revival had become a far more serious matter, and its adoption as an architectural style was seen as a moral imperative. The polemics of A. W. N. Pugin in seeking to revive the architectural and spiritual qualities of the Middle Ages, and historical research by various bodies, created a vigorous new movement that almost totally superseded the classical principles that had been dominant since the mid-17th century. During the early Victorian period the importance of the country house as a social and cultural phenomenon increased, as country house ownership spread through a broader spectrum of society to embrace financiers and manufacturers as well as the established aristocracy. However, despite a great increase in building as a result of the new wealth generated by the Industrial Revolution, the country house was no longer in the vanguard of architectural innovation. This was partly a result of the difficulties encountered in the 1840s in translating the forms of an idealized 14th-century house into a suitably comfortable abode for a 19th-century gentleman. Pugin's designs, such as that for Scarisbrick Hall (1837–45), Lancs, epitomized his uncompromising moral approach, but they required a client (in this case Charles Scarisbrick) as austerely dedicated to the same spiritual principles. Such clients were comparatively rare, and by the mid-19th century country house design had become more eclectic. Inspiration was increasingly drawn from later—and more comfortable—periods of architectural history, particularly the Elizabethan and Jacobean. Just as Palladianism had developed, the second generation of Gothic Revival architects liberated themselves from the self-imposed archaeological restraints of their predecessors, and the confident creations of such architects as WILLIAM BURGES and J. L. PEARSON, while still retaining a Gothic idiom, were wholly original.

The writings of John Ruskin further expanded design sources and increased interest in the polychrome effects of contrasting brickwork and stone. Polychromy is a characteristic of many Victorian country houses, such as Elvetham Hall (1859–62), Hants, by S. S. TEULON. Other continental influences included the Italianate villas of Charles Barry (*see* BARRY, (1)) and, later in the century, the exaggerated French-style châteaux that seem to have been particularly favoured by those, such as the ROTHS-CHILD family, who had made their fortunes in commerce. Changing social attitudes, coupled with a greater freedom in architectural taste, also led to a marked increase in the size of the country house in the 19th century. Asymmetrical plans extended in an informal manner to accommodate the proliferation of specialized rooms demanded by a plethora of social activities. Separate quarters were necessary to segregate the unmarried sexes among both servants and household; even children tended to be isolated within their own areas of the house. Chapels and baronial halls were reinstated as important elements of the great house as their owners once again began to take a serious interest in the spiritual needs of the household and the welfare of their tenants. The multitude of named rooms in the published plans of Bear Wood, Berks (1865–8; see fig. 5), designed by ROBERT KERR for John Walter, the owner of *The Times*, vividly illustrates the needs of a wealthy household of the time. The opulent furnishings of the rooms were arranged in crowded groupings, a reaction to the sparse furniture lined up against the walls in the public rooms of 18th-century houses.

The most successful country house architect of the late 19th century was RICHARD NORMAN SHAW. By marrying the romantic outlines of a mythical old England, full of half-timbered gables and steeply pitched roofs (*see* OLD ENGLISH STYLE), with up-to-date plumbing and other conveniences (e.g. Cragside, Northumb., 1869–85), he created a truly original style that owed little to the historical rectitude of Pugin but greatly appealed to his patrons, who demanded domestic comfort. At the turn of the century, his successor was EDWARD LUTYENS, whose vast practice dominated the declining years of the country house. Some of Lutyens's most charming houses, such as Folly Farm (1912), Sulhamstead, Berks, were little more than extended farmhouses, but in his more monumental works he ushered in an appreciation for the understated qualities of

English architecture of the time of Wren, which for many of his clients represented an ideal of effortless good taste. In effect, after an interlude of less than a century, the country house had returned to the disciplines of symmetry and restraint. Lutyens was the last architect to found a substantial practice based largely on country house building. The effects of two world wars, with a global financial slump between them, increased taxation, and the disappearance of cheap labour (essential for maintaining such vast establishments) combined to destroy the country house way of life. Despite much uncertainty over the future of the country house and its contents, its survival into the second half of the 20th century is a tribute to the conservation movement and a public recognition of its importance to English culture.

BIBLIOGRAPHY
J. Summerson: *Architecture in Britain: 1530–1830*, Pelican Hist. A. (Harmondsworth, 1953, rev. 7/1983)
C. Hussey: *English Country Houses: Early Georgian, 1715–1760* (London, 1955/*R* 1986)
——: *English Country Houses: Mid-Georgian, 1760–1800* (London, 1956/*R* 1986)
——: *English Country Houses: Late Georgian, 1800–1840* (London, 1958/*R* 1986)
M. Wood: *The English Mediaeval House* (London, 1965/*R* 1981)
M. Girouard: *Robert Smythson and the Architecture of the Elizabethan Era* (London, 1966, rev. as *Robert Smythson and the Elizabethan Country House*, 2/1983)
O. Hill and J. Cornforth: *English Country Houses: Caroline, 1625–1685* (London, 1966/*R* 1985)
J. Lees-Milne: *English Country Houses: Baroque, 1685–1715* (London, 1970)
M. Girouard: *The Victorian Country House* (Oxford, 1971; rev. London, 2/1979)
O. Cook: *The English Country House: An Art and a Way of Life* (London, 1974/*R* 1984)
J. Fowler and J. Cornforth: *English Decoration in the 18th Century* (London, 1974, rev. 1978)
M. Airs: *The Making of the English Country House, 1500–1640* (London, 1975)
J. Cornforth: *English Interiors 1790–1848: The Quest for Comfort* (London, 1978)

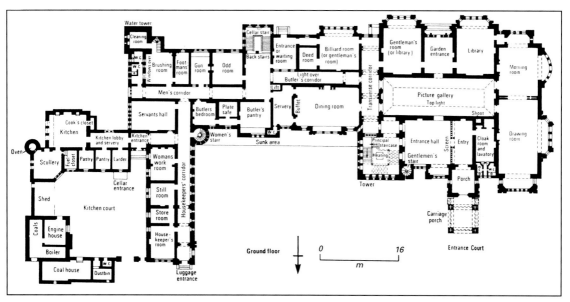

5. Robert Kerr: Bear Wood, Berkshire, ground-plan, 1865–74

M. Girouard: *Life in the English Country House: A Social and Architectural History* (London, 1978)

P. Thornton: *Seventeenth-Century Interior Decoration in England, France and Holland* (London, 1978)

J. Harris: *The Artist and the Country House* (London, 1979, rev. 2/1985)

C. Aslet: *The Last Country Houses* (London, 1982)

J. M. Robinson: *The Latest Country Houses* (London, 1984)

J. Harris: *The Design of the English Country House, 1620–1920* (London, 1985)

M. Howard: *The Early Tudor Country House: Architecture and Politics, 1490–1550* (London, 1987)

G. Stamp: *The English House, 1860–1914: The Flowering of English Domestic Architecture* (London, 1987)

MALCOLM AIRS

Courajod, Louis(-Charles-Léon) (*b* Paris, 22 Feb 1841; *d* Paris, 26 June 1896). French art historian and collector. After studying at the Ecole des Chartes in Paris (1864–7), he worked at the Cabinet des Estampes of the Bibliothèque Nationale and then at the Louvre (1874), becoming curator of the newly formed department of medieval and modern sculpture in 1893. Courajod's initial interests were in local history, but his work at the Bibliothèque Nationale kindled an enthusiasm for art history, and he became noted for his study of documents and precocious attention to the social context of art. Sculpture was his particular interest. He collected Italian plaquettes, and, as curator at the Louvre, he secured the acquisition of such prestigious Italian works as the *Virgin and Child* by Jacopo della Quercia. He bequeathed to the museum the Courajod *Christ*, one of the finest examples of Burgundian Romanesque wood sculpture, which the Louvre committee had refused to acquire.

Courajod was professor of the history of sculpture at the Ecole du Louvre (1887–94), teaching courses on the 15th-century Renaissance in northern Europe, the origins of Gothic and the contrasting relationship between Gothic and Renaissance art. He communicated to his students, among them André Michel and Paul Vitry, his concern that the study of objects should be complemented by documentary research. An enthusiastic admirer of French, medieval and realist art, he was an opponent of academicism, which he considered decadent.

Courajod published numerous works on objets d'art and on individual sculptures in the Louvre collection. He produced a major study of Alexandre Lenoir (*see* LENOIR, (1)) and his museum of French sculpture, compiling an inventory of its contents, then divided between the Louvre, Versailles and the Ecole des Beaux Arts. He was also one of the earliest historians of the Italian Renaissance, publishing documents on the art and artists of Cremona in the 15th and 16th centuries (1885).

WRITINGS

Le Livre-Journal de Lazare Duvaux: Marchand bijoutier ordinaire du roi (1748–1758), 2 vols (Paris, 1873)

L'Ecole royale des élèves protégés (Paris, 1874)

Alexandre Lenoir, son journal et le musée des monuments français, 3 vols (Paris, 1878–87)

'Documents sur l'histoire des arts et des artistes à Crémone aux XVe et XVIe siècles', *Mém. Soc. N. Antiqua. France*, xlv (1885)'La Polychromie dans la statuaire du Moyen Age et de la Renaissance', *Mém. Soc. N. Antiqua. France*, xlviii (1888)

L'Imitation et la contrefaçon des objets d'arts antiques aux XVe et XVIe siècles (Paris, 1889)

H. Lemonnier and A. Michel, eds: *Louis Courajod, leçons professées à l'Ecole du Louvre*, 3 vols (Paris, 1899–1903) [with bibliog.]

Regular contributions to *Gaz. B.-A.* (1874–89)

BIBLIOGRAPHY

'Louis Courajod (1841–1896)', *Rev. Champagne & Brie* (1896)

A. Michel: Obituary, *Gaz. B.-A.*, xvi (1896), pp. 202–17

GENEVIEVE BRESC-BAUTIER

Courbes, Jean [Juan de(s)] (*b* Paris, 1592; *d c.* 1641). French engraver, active in Spain. He worked first for publishing companies in Paris, executing portraits of *Mary Sidney* and *Philip Sidney* for the French translation of Philip Sidney's *Arcadia of the Countess of Pembroke* (Paris, 1624). Courbes worked in Spain between 1620 and 1640, mainly in Madrid but also for clients in other parts of the country. He engraved numerous portraits, including that of *Lope de Vega* (1562–1635), for whose work he produced many title pages and illustrations. He also portrayed *Luis Góngora* (1561–1627), *Henry III of Castille* (*d* 1406), *Philip IV* and nine members of the Hurtado de Mendoza family for *Historia de Cuenca* (Madrid, 1629). He engraved a large number of frontispieces with portraits and plates for books, among which his allegories, executed in collaboration with Melchor Prieto (*d* 1648) for his *Psalmodia Eucharistica* (Madrid, 1622), are outstanding.

BIBLIOGRAPHY

J. Caveda: *El grabado en España hasta los primeros anos del siglo XVII* (Madrid, 1865)

E. Lafuente Ferrari: *Los retratos de Lope de Vega* (Madrid, 1935), p. 69

J. Ainaud Lasarte: *Grabado*, A. Hisp., xviii (Madrid, 1962)

E. Páez Ríos: *Iconografía hispana* (Madrid, 1966)

M. Agulló: 'Más documentos sobre impresores y libreros madrileños de los siglos XVI y XVII', *An. Inst. Estud. Madril.*, ix (1973), p. 156

E. Vetter: *Die Kupferstiche zur Psalmodia Eucharistica des Melchor Prieto von 1622* (Münster, 1973)

A. Gallego: *Historia del grabado en España* (Madrid, 1979)

E. Páez Ríos: *Repertorio* (Madrid, 1981–3)

B. García Vega: *El grabado del libro español: Siglos XV–XVI–XVII* (Valladolid, 1984)

J. M. Matilla: *La estampa en el libro barocco: Juan de Courbes* (Madrid, 1991)

BLANCA GARCÍA VEGA

Courbet, (Jean-Désiré-)Gustave (*b* Ornans, Franche-Comté, 10 June 1819; *d* La Tour-de-Peilz, nr Vevey, Switzerland, 31 Dec 1877). French painter and writer. Courbet's glory is based essentially on his works of the late 1840s and early 1850s depicting peasants and labourers, which were motivated by strong political views and formed a paradigm of Realism (*see* REALISM). From the mid-1850s into the 1860s he applied the same style and spirit to less overtly political subjects, concentrating on landscapes and hunting and still-life subjects. Social commitment, including a violent anticlericalism, re-emerged in various works of the 1860s and continued until his brief imprisonment after the Commune of 1871. From 1873 he lived in exile in Switzerland where he employed mediocre artists, but also realized a couple of outstanding pictures with an extremely fresh and free handling. The image Courbet presented of himself in his paintings and writings has persisted, making him an artist who is assessed as much by his personality as by his work. This feature and also his hostility to the academic system, state patronage and the notion of aesthetic ideals have made him highly influential in the development of modernism.

I. Life and work. II. Working methods and technique. III. Writings. IV. Critical reception and posthumous reputation.

I. Life and work.

1. Training and early works, to *c*. 1849. 2. The Realist debate: peasant and modern 'history' pictures, 1849–55. 3. Leisure and private life as subject-matter: landscapes, hunting scenes, still-lifes and portraits, late 1850s and the 1860s. 4. Renewed political awareness in the 1860s. 5. The Commune, exile in Switzerland and collaboration: late works, 1871–7.

1. TRAINING AND EARLY WORKS, TO *c*. 1849. Courbet came from a well-to-do family of large-scale farmers in Franche-Comté, the area of France that is the most strongly influenced by neighbouring Switzerland. Ornans is a picturesque small country town on the River Loue, surrounded by the high limestone rocks of the Jura; its population in Courbet's day was barely 3000. This social and geographical background was of great importance to Courbet. He remained attached to Franche-Comté and its peasants throughout his life, portraying rural life in many pictures. In 1831 Courbet started attending the Petit Séminaire in Ornans, where his art teacher from 1833 was Père Baud (or Beau), a former pupil of Antoine-Jean Gros. While there he also met his cousin, the Romantic poet Max Buchon (1818–69), who had a determining influence on his later choice of direction. In the autumn of 1837 he went to the Collège Royal at Besançon and also attended courses at the Académie there under Charles-Antoine Flageoulot (1774–1840), a former pupil of Jacques-Louis David. Except for a few early paintings and drawings (Ornans, Mus. Maison Natale Gustave Courbet), Courbet's first public works were the four figural lithographs of 1838 illustrating Buchon's *Essais poétiques* (Besançon, 1839). He went to Paris in the autumn of 1839 to embark on a conventional training as a painter. Like many other young artists of his period he was not impressed by the traditional academic teaching at the Ecole des Beaux-Arts in Paris; instead, after receiving a few months' teaching from Charles de Steuben (1788–1856), he attended the independent private academies run

by Père Suisse and Père Lapin and also received advice from Nicolas-Auguste Hesse. At the same time he copied works by the Old Masters at the Louvre.

Like Rembrandt and van Gogh, Courbet painted a large number of self-portraits, especially in the 1840s. These quite often show the artist in a particular role or state of mind. The *Self-Portrait as a Sculptor* (*c*. 1844; New York, priv. col., see 1977–8 exh. cat., pl. 9) and *Self-portrait with a Leather Belt* (1845; Paris, Mus. d'Orsay) belong in the first category, and the *Self-portrait as a Desperate Man* (two versions, *c*. 1843; e.g. Luxeuil, priv. col., see 1977–8 exh. cat., pl. 5), *The Lovers* (1844; Lille, Mus. B.-A.), *Self-portrait as a Wounded Man* (two versions; e.g. *c*. 1844–54; Paris, Mus. d'Orsay) and *Self-portrait with a Pipe* (*c*. 1847–8; Montpellier, Mus. Fabre) belong in the second. Courbet seems to have painted himself so often for two main reasons: because of lack of models and because of a protracted crisis of artistic identity. This introspectiveness lasted until the Commune (1871) and shows that he was still influenced by the self-centredness (*égotisme*) typical of the Romantics and that, despite his extrovert image, he felt lonely in Paris for a long time.

In 1846 Courbet visited the Netherlands, where he painted mainly portraits, the most outstanding of which is the portrait of the art dealer *H. J. van Wisselingh* (1846; Fort Worth, TX, Kimbell A. Mus.). He also stayed briefly in Belgium in 1846 and 1847, and travel sketches made in both countries have been preserved (Marseille, priv. col., see 1984 exh. cat.). In the museums in The Hague and Amsterdam he was interested by Rembrandt's chiaroscuro and the expressive, free brushwork of Frans Hals, qualities that subsequently influenced his own painting technique. These experiences had a beneficial effect on *After Dinner at Ornans* (1849; Lille, Mus. B.-A.), a dark, silent group portrait that won him the esteem of Ingres and Delacroix in 1849. It is not clear whether Courbet ever visited England or whether a passage in a letter of 1854 relating to such a visit (see 1977–8 exh. cat., app.) should be interpreted as an imaginary journey. In this he alludes to

1. Gustave Courbet: *A Burial at Ornans*, oil on canvas, 3.15×6.68 m, 1849–50 (Paris, Musée d'Orsay)

Hogarth and, though he did paint some satirical pictures, a mention of Constable would have been more illuminating regarding his painting technique.

2. THE REALIST DEBATE: PEASANT AND MODERN 'HISTORY' PICTURES, 1849–55. Courbet achieved his real breakthrough with three works that were exhibited in Paris at the Salon of 1851 (postponed from 1850). Two of these, *The Stone-breakers* (1849; ex-Gemäldegal. Neue Meister, Dresden, untraced; *see* REALISM, fig. 1) and *A Burial at Ornans* (1849–50; Paris, Mus. d'Orsay; see fig. 1), had already attracted attention in Besançon and Dijon, while the third, the *Peasants of Flagey Returning from the Fair* (1850, revised 1855; Besançon, Mus. B.-A. & Archéol.; *see* GENRE, fig. 4), was exhibited in Paris only. (*The Stone-breakers* was thought to have been destroyed in 1945, but in 1987 the Gemäldegalerie Neue Meister in Dresden catalogued it as missing.) Although all three pictures were influenced by the Dutch Old Masters, they are distinguished by their austerity and directness. Courbet's friends, CHAMPFLEURY and Buchon, saw them as breaking away

from academic idealism and spoke approvingly of Courbet's 'realism'.

Many visitors to the Salon were shocked, however, both because the paintings depicted ordinary people (moreover on a scale normally reserved for portraits of the famous) and because the peasants and workers, based on real people, seemed particularly ugly. In these pictures Courbet was trying to blend large-scale French history painting with Dutch portrait and genre painting, thereby achieving an art peculiar to his own period that would introduce the common man as an equally worthy subject. The pictures also reveal unusual characteristics of social commitment. The labourers in *The Stone-breakers*, with their averted faces and ragged clothing, symbolize all those workers who toiled on the edge of subsistence. It was this picture that attracted most attacks from the caricaturists and critics in 1851. The group of country mourners in a *Burial at Ornans*, a scene possibly based on the burial of Courbet's great-uncle Claude-Etienne Teste (1765–1848), stirred the townspeople's fear of being swamped by the rural population. Buchon saw the grave-digger in this picture as

2. Gustave Courbet: *The Meeting*, also known as *Bonjour Monsieur Courbet*, oil on canvas, 1.29×1.49 m, 1854 (Montpellier, Musée Fabre)

3. Gustave Courbet: *Painter's Studio: A Real Allegory Determining a Phase of Seven Years of my Artistic Life*, oil on canvas, 3.59×5.98 m, 1854–5 (Paris, Musée d'Orsay)

representing the avenger of the stone-breakers. Some years later Pierre-Joseph Proudhon noted the proud superiority of the rugged peasants from Franche-Comté in the *Peasants of Flagey Returning from the Fair*. All three paintings deal with the demographic movements between town and country. At the time this was an acute social issue, which greatly concerned the staunchly regionalist Courbet. The last of these peasant 'history pictures' was *The Grain-sifters* (1855; Nantes, Mus. B.-A.), a quiet, simple picture of people at work, which has even been interpreted as having a feminist message (Fried, 1990).

The Bathers (1853; Montpellier, Mus. Fabre) and *The Wrestlers* (1853; Budapest, Mus. F.A.) are among those provocative pictures that attacked the prevailing aesthetic norms and, as 'modern history pictures', also represented a challenge to society. These pictures show fat, naked women and toil-worn naked men, thus rejecting the academic concept of nude painting and rousing the ire of middle-class Salon critics and caricaturists who considered the pictures un-French. Courbet was able to launch such attacks in the early days of the authoritarian Second Empire only because he had a powerful protector in Charles, Duc de Morny. *The Bathers* won praise from Delacroix and was regarded by Alfred Bruyas, a banker's son from Montpellier, as marking the beginning of an independent, modern form of art. Courbet confirmed this perception a year later with *The Meeting*, also known as *Bonjour Monsieur Courbet* (1854; Montpellier, Mus. Fabre; see fig. 2), which was painted for Bruyas entirely in light colours, with the landscape executed in a concise, free style. Above all, this picture, which includes a self-portrait, reveals something of the identity crisis referred to above, with Courbet fluctuating between underestimating and overestimating

himself. Borrowing from the image of the Wandering Jew, he represented himself as a spurned outsider and at the same time as a superior 'wise man', greeting Bruyas and his servant from a somewhat higher plane. He thus shows, albeit defensively, how an artist without state or church patronage becomes precariously dependent on a private patron.

The culmination of the series featuring Courbet's relation to society is the *Painter's Studio* (1854–5; Paris, Mus. d'Orsay; see fig. 3), which he painted for the Exposition Universelle held in Paris in 1855. Though he had 11 other works accepted, the *Painter's Studio* was rejected. So Courbet showed it at the independent exhibition he funded and held in the Pavillon du Réalisme on a site close to that of the official exhibition. This large picture has been called a triptych because it consists of three clearly distinguished parts: at the centre Courbet portrayed himself painting a landscape next to a woman or 'Muse', a cat and a peasant boy. On the left he depicted the 'external' or political world, and on the right the 'internal' or aesthetic world. Courbet himself holds the place of the redeemer. He modelled many of the figures on friends and various political and other personalities, including Napoleon III. With this composition, he brought the dispute about the politically and aesthetically disruptive effects of Realist art to a conclusion. The full title of the work is the *Painter's Studio: A Real Allegory Determining a Phase of Seven Years of my Artistic Life*, which suggests that Courbet saw the work as summing up his development since the Revolution of 1848. But at the same time it contains a vision of the future: Courbet sits at his easel, which shows not his surrounding society but a landscape in Franche-Comté. This indicates that he saw nature, rather than politics or industry, as having the power for the renewal and recon-ciliation needed by contemporary society—still a Romantic concept.

3. LEISURE AND PRIVATE LIFE AS SUBJECT-MATTER: LANDSCAPES, HUNTING SCENES, STILL-LIFES AND PORTRAITS, LATE 1850S AND THE 1860S. In the *Painter's Studio* Courbet had provocatively placed landscape on a higher level than history painting. He had, of course, painted landscapes before this, but now he gave this genre pride of place. While he combined landscape and figure painting in the *Painter's Studio* and also in the *Young Ladies on the Banks of the Seine (Summer)* (1856–7; Paris, Petit Pal.; see fig. 4), in most of his pictures of the late 1850s and 1860s landscape predominates.

'To be in Paris, but not of it: that was what Courbet wanted' (Clark, 1973, p. 31). He did not produce a single townscape of Paris, and his landscapes confronted Pari-sians with the image of a different world. The meaning of these landscapes is complex: they reflect an increasing need for recreation areas for leisure and holiday activities, a theme that was to become dominant among the Impres-sionists in the 1870s and 1880s. Courbet had even wanted

to decorate railway stations with pictures of holiday destinations, a project that would have greatly promoted tourism, though it was never realized. However, many of his landscapes are not idyllic but rather enclosed and fortress-like (according to Champfleury). They represent a kind of regional defence force and thus stress the autonomy of the provinces with regard to the centralist power of the State. Regionalism is emphasized in numer-ous depictions of hidden forest ravines and grottoes, which give the effect of being places of refuge or even of representing the search for concealment in a womb (1978–9 exh. cat.). In particular, the various versions of the *Puits noir* (e.g. 1865; Toulouse, Mus. Augustins) and the *Source of the Loue* (e.g. 1864; Zurich, Ksthaus) can be cited as examples of this.

Hunting scenes by Courbet such as *Stag Taking to the Water* (1865; Marseille, Mus. B.-A.) or *The Kill: Episode during a Deer Hunt in a Snowy Terrain* (1867; Besançon, Mus. B.-A. & Archéol.) are similarly ambivalent. They illustrate the artist's passion for hunting, which was enhanced by trips to German hunting reserves around Baden-Baden and Bad Homburg. He often chose the

4. Gustave Courbet: *Young Ladies on the Banks of the Seine (Summer)*, oil on canvas, 1.74×2.06 m, 1856–7 (Paris, Musée du Petit Palais)

peace after the hunt, as in *The Quarry* (1857; Boston, MA, Mus. F.A.) and the *Hunt Breakfast* (*c.* 1858–9; Cologne, Wallraf-Richartz-Mus.), but at the same time used hunting to suggest political persecution. The latent social and political messages in the hunting pictures did not prevent them from generally satisfying a non-political clientele. After the success at the Salon of 1866 of *Covert of Roe-deer by the Stream of Plaisir-Fontaine* (1866; Paris, Mus. d'Orsay) Courbet had even hoped for an imperial distinction, though this was not forthcoming.

From 1859 Courbet often stayed on the Normandy coast. While there he painted a large number of seascapes (several versions of the *Cliff at Etretat*, e.g. the *Cliff at Etretat after the Storm*, 1869; Paris, Mus. d'Orsay) and beach and wave pictures, which mark a new peak in his creative achievement. The style of these pictures is very varied: some are block-like and self-contained compositions, which appeared to many critics to have been built by a mason or made from marble (e.g. the two versions of *The Wave*, 1870; Paris, Mus. d'Orsay; Berlin, Alte N.G.), and in the same works Courbet completely dissolved the surface of objects, so moving away from naturalistic representation. The tendency towards abstraction and surface colour increased steadily from about 1864; in this respect Courbet was an important forerunner of Cézanne.

In his paintings of nudes Courbet seems to have taken a different path. He attempted to beat the Salon tradition by painting completely naturalistically and choosing garishly brilliant colours. This is particularly true of *The Sleepers* (1866; Paris, Petit Pal.). Here it was far less the form than the subject-matter that was shocking. Lesbian women had hitherto been a theme treated only in small-scale graphic work, whereas Courbet presented it in a format that was larger even than that used for genre painting. The female nude entitled the *Origin of the World* (1866; Japan, priv. col., see 1988–9 exh. cat., p. 178) is also extremely provocative (though like the previous picture it was painted for a private client, the Turkish diplomat Khalil-Bey). *Lady with a Parrot* (1866; New York, Met.) again has slightly ironic links with Salon painting, with the parrot symbolizing a magic bird as in the writings of Gustave Flaubert. *Venus and Psyche* (1864 version, destr.; 1866 version, Basle, Kstmus.) is a fourth important picture in this category.

The still-lifes form another theme in Courbet's art. They reached their first peak as early as the mid-1850s when Courbet painted *Bunch of Flowers* (1855; Hamburg, Ksthalle) in which it is unclear whether the pictoral space is limited by a wall or the sky. This deliberate lack of definition links interior and exterior space in an extremely modern manner. Courbet painted some superb still-lifes during his stay in the Saintonge area in 1862–3 where he worked for a time with Corot. Important examples of his

5. Gustave Courbet: *Pierre-Joseph Proudhon and his Children in 1853*, oil on canvas, 1.47×1.98 m, 1865–7 (Paris, Musée du Petit Palais)

still-lifes are the heavy, assembled blooms in *Magnolias* (1862; Bremen, Ksthalle) and *Flowers in a Basket* (1863; Glasgow, A.G. & Mus.). In *The Trellis* (1862; Toledo, OH, Mus. A.) Courbet combined a still-life of flowers in the open air with a portrait of a woman, producing an asymmetric composition similar to that in works by Degas. Courbet did not produce still-life works of equal stature again until after the Commune.

Turning to themes relating to leisure and private life was a move forced on painters by the political situation in the Second Empire—a withdrawal as happened with Honoré Daumier. The *Painter's Studio*, with its reference to Napoleon III, represents an exception to this tendency; it did not attract unpleasant consequences simply because Courbet composed the picture as a group portrait without any offensive intentions. Individual portraits were another category that flourished in this period. The *Sleeping Spinner* (1853; Montpellier, Mus. Fabre), however, shows that Courbet often depicted types rather than individuals, in this case a peasant girl lost in reverie. Of the portraits he painted in Saintonge, *Dreaming: Portrait of Gabrielle Borreau* (1862; Chicago, IL, A. Inst.) combines a dreamy expression with a very free use of colour in the natural background. The four versions of *Jo: The Beautiful Irish Girl* (*c.* 1865; e.g. Stockholm, Nmus.), depicting Whistler's mistress Joanna Heffernan, stand halfway between Romanticism and Symbolism, showing links with Whistler and the Pre-Raphaelites. The model's sensuous red hair also conjures up the idea of the *femme fatale*. Among the portraits of men, that of *Pierre-Joseph Proudhon and his Children in 1853* (1865–7; Paris, Petit Pal.; see fig. 5) deserves a special mention. Courbet had been a close friend of Proudhon's since the philosopher's arrival in Paris in 1847 and painted the work after his death as a memorial. In a second phase of painting he eradicated Proudhon's wife, leaving only his two small daughters. As a result, the solitariness and monumentality of the philosopher are considerably enhanced. As in *Gabrielle Borreau*, the figures in *Pierre-Joseph Proudhon* are painted carefully, while the background is intentionally rendered in a free, slapdash manner, which excited both criticism and admiration.

4. RENEWED POLITICAL AWARENESS IN THE 1860s. Two works, *Priests Returning from the Conference* (1862–3; destr.; oil sketch, Basle, Kstmus.) and *Pierre-Joseph Proudhon*, were precursors to a more open use of pictures as a political weapon. Though Courbet's potential for satirical criticism was repressed during the reign of Napoleon III, it was not extinguished, and, like Daumier, Courbet reverted to explicitly political subjects towards the end of the Second Empire. At the beginning of the decade he had painted a portrait of his friend *Jules Vallès* (*c.* 1861; Paris, Carnavalet), an anarchist writer and later Communard. In 1868 Courbet published in Brussels the anticlerical pamphlets *Les Curés en goguette* and *La Mort de Jeannot* to accompany works on this theme. Champfleury, wary of this development, feared a whole series of anticlerical frescoes. The same year Courbet painted *Charity of a Beggar at Ornans* (1868; Glasgow, A.G. & Mus.; see fig. 6), which made a clear reference to the ragged proletariat. Courbet announced that other 'socialist' pictures would follow, a move that was obviously encouraged by the electoral success of the Left in the towns. For the Salon of 1868 he planned a portrait of *Martin Bidouré*, a peasant who was executed after having fought against the coup d'état of 1851. It was clearly intended that Courbet's political urge would be discouraged by the offer in 1870 of the Cross of the Légion d'honneur, an award he, like Daumier, refused.

5. THE COMMUNE, EXILE IN SWITZERLAND AND COLLABORATION: LATE WORKS, 1871–7. During the Commune in Paris (18 March–29 May 1871) Courbet did little drawing or painting. He was, however, very active in art politics and, as president of the commission for the protection of the artistic monuments of Paris and delegate for the fine arts, he even saved the Louvre. As he was accused of having been behind the demolition of the Vendôme Column, he was put on trial and gaoled after the Commune's overthrow. He painted a few still-lifes while in prison, but his best pictures—*Still-life with Apples and Pomegranate* (London, N.G.), *Still-life: Fruit* (Shelburne, VT, Mus.), *Still-life: Apples, Pears and Primroses on a Table* (Pasadena, CA, Norton Simon Mus.), *Self-portrait in Prison* (Ornans, Mus. Maison Natale Gustave Courbet) and both versions of *The Trout* (Zurich, Ksthaus; Paris, Mus. d'Orsay)—were not painted until after his release, perhaps not until 1872–3, though some are signed *in vinculis faciebat* or 'Ste-Pélagie' (the name of one of the prisons).

On 23 July 1873 Courbet crossed the frontier into Switzerland as he had been judged responsible for the cost of re-erecting the Vendôme Column and was afraid that he might be arrested. The four and a half years of his exile in Switzerland are often regarded as a period of decline. It

6. Gustave Courbet: *Charity of a Beggar at Ornans*, oil on canvas, 2.10×1.75 m, 1868 (Glasgow, Art Gallery and Museum)

is true that in this period Courbet definitely painted with an eye to the market: he was in fact hoping to raise the money to pay for the column so that he could return to France, an aim prompted by the great success of an exhibition at the Galerie Durand-Ruel in Paris in 1872. He therefore engaged a number of journeymen painters whom he instructed in his style: first and foremost Marcel Ordinaire (1848–96), Chérubino Pata (1827–99) and André Slomcynski (1844–1909), but also Auguste Baud-Bovy, François Bocion, Ernest-Paul Brigot (1836–1910), Jean-Jean Cornu (1819–76), Hector Hanoteau (1823–90), Auguste Morel and Alphonse Rapin (1839–89). This collaboration was a disaster, particularly as Courbet apparently signed the works produced by his assistants to augment their value; other works known as 'mixed' pictures must have been only started by him or touched up at the end. Moreover, in his despair Courbet drank a lot as well as suffering from dropsy so that he was only rarely capable of painting well. This makes it all the more remarkable that in these last years he achieved some superb landscapes and portraits. Having experimented with sculpture (1862–4), he turned once more to this medium, creating, for example, a monumental *Bust of Liberty* (1875) for La Tour-de-Peilz, near Vevey.

The first notable painting done by Courbet in Switzerland is a portrait of his father *Régis Courbet* (1873; Paris, Petit Pal.), a picture that once again exercised his full powers. The most noteworthy of his landscapes are the many brilliant versions of Lake Geneva (e.g. *Lake Geneva at Sunset*, 1874; Vevey, Mus. Jenisch) and of the castle of Chillon that stands on its shore (e.g. 1874; Ornans, Mus. Maison Natale Gustave Courbet). Many of these pictures demonstrate marvellous atmospheric effects: *Winter Landscape: The Dents du Midi* (1876; Hamburg, Ksthalle) and *Grand Panorama of the Alps* (1877; Cleveland, OH, Mus. A.) are outstanding among his late works. The former conveys a gloomy mood with heavy, thickly applied colours, while the latter, which used to be wrongly described as unfinished, is in some ways an answer to the Impressionists (even though Courbet was not able to see the First Impressionist Exhibition of 1874). While retaining his use of dark colouring in this work, Courbet broke the objects up into flecks or spots in a technique similar to that of the Impressionists. A basic incoherence between the objects and a consequent independent existence of the painterly means are apparent, anticipating the 20th century.

II. Working methods and technique.

1. PAINTING. Courbet's painting technique is not easy to describe because of its variety and disregard for the academic rules governing composition. He often inserted his figures as if they were removable set pieces (Berger). In spite of this 'collage' technique, many of his pictures look as if they had been painted at a single sitting because of their unity of colour. They were in fact often produced very quickly. Courbet prided himself on being able to paint a picture in two hours as well as produce several versions of equal quality. As every object was in theory of equal importance to him, quite often there is an egalitarian structure in his work. On the other hand Courbet's pictures frequently form a closed world: landscapes can give the

impression of being locked away, and, though they are at close quarters, people may turn away from the viewer (*The Stone-breakers*, *The Bathers*, *The Wrestlers* and *The Grain-sifters*). Thus a 'wooden' composition is often found in conjunction with a fluid use of colour.

The special quality of Courbet's work is really achieved by means of colour. Courbet initially imitated 17th-century Dutch and Spanish painters (Rembrandt, Hals, Velázquez, Ribera) from whom he derived the use of black as the starting-point. He employed a dark ground throughout his life, but the treatment of surfaces changed. Courbet resorted more and more to using broad brushes: he rejected detailed academic painting and seems never to have used a mahlstick. By working increasingly with a spatula and palette knife—implements that he used to apply and scrape off colour 'like a mason'—he gave colour a special, substantial quality, which influenced van Gogh and Cézanne.

In figure works Courbet used a variety of procedures and often maintained clear, compact boundaries between objects, though in *A Burial at Ornans*, for example, he merged the figures together in a single dark mass. In the portrait of *Adolphe Marlet* (1851; Dublin, N.G.) the flesh tones were applied on top of parts of the clothing, so disregarding naturalism in favour of an emphasis on the formal qualities of colour. In his final portrait, of his father, the colour does not seem to have been applied spontaneously and freely, but in an even-handed, distanced, almost icy manner—as if Courbet had withdrawn from the outside world.

Colour was applied in a perfunctory, almost careless way in the landscapes, as, for example, in the background of *The Meeting*. In *Rocky Landscape near Ornans* (1855; Paris, Mus. d'Orsay) spots of white were dabbed on to trees to create the effect of blossom. By the 'spontaneous' use of colour, Courbet suggested the effect of instantaneous movement in his landscapes, conveying the impression of light flickering over the rocks, of the surface of the water rippling and of leaves trembling in the wind. By 1864 Courbet's interest in the interaction of colour predominated. In the *Source of the Lison* (1864; Berlin, Alte N.G.) or in the many versions of the *Source of the Loue* Courbet spread colour, dissociated from any object, over the entire surface.

2. DRAWING. Unlike Delacroix or Jean-François Millet, Courbet is not one of the foremost French draughtsmen of the mid-19th century. He had taught himself to draw, but his opposition to the classical primacy of drawing led him to work directly with colour. He produced drawings of exceptional expressive power (including two self-portraits; 1847, Cambridge, MA, Fogg; *c.* 1846–8, Hartford, CT, Wadsworth Atheneum) as well as of great penetration (e.g. *Juliette Courbet, Sleeping*, 1840–41; Paris, Louvre). Courbet emerges as a draughtsman essentially in two ways: firstly he produced large single sheets (in chalk or charcoal) with portrait drawings made as pictures, and secondly numerous sketches (mainly drawn with pencil or chalk, occasionally with a wash), which have been preserved either in sketchbooks or singly. The large picture-like drawings, some of them signed like paintings, were sometimes exhibited, even alongside paintings in the Salon,

and are now held in a small number of large museums. For a long time many of the sketches remained in the possession of the Courbet family. In 1907 one sketchbook was acquired by the Louvre, followed by two others in 1939, and many loose sketches were still in private hands in the late 20th century (*c.* 30 collections). The drawings in the three sketchbooks (with two exceptions) are regarded as being in the artist's own hand, but there is controversy over the date and authenticity of many of the loose sketches, which are very uneven in quality.

A painterly treatment of the surface, using broad layers of strokes and smudging, is typical of the picture-like drawings, while the sketches, varied as they are, are characteristically composed of broken, often stiff lines. In both, however, Courbet's aversion to an academically smooth and beautiful use of line is discernible. In the sketches from his Swiss journey (see 1984 exh. cat.) the material structure of objects is clearly apparent; other travel sketches (e.g. *Tree on Rock near Spa*, *c.* 1849; Marseille, priv. col., see 1984 exh. cat., no 48) show, in a very similar way to Courbet's landscape paintings, how changeable and fragile the substance of objects is in light.

III. Writings.

Courbet was not a theorist, but his manifestos, letters and aphorisms, even though influenced by Buchon, Champfleury, Baudelaire and Jules-Antoine Castagnary, are extremely important in considering the debate over Realism, the concept of the independent artist and the ties between art and politics. Courbet also talked in great detail about his pictures in his letters.

1. THE REALIST DEBATE. In 1849 at the end of a letter about *The Stone-breakers* Courbet enunciated a principle that he later elevated to be the basis of Realism. Writing to the Director of the Ecole des Beaux-Arts, he said: 'Yes, M. Peisse, art must be dragged in the gutter!' (Riat, p. 74). This one sentence and its logical conversion into practice brought personal enmities and negative criticisms to Courbet for nearly 30 years.

Courbet had adopted the concept of 'Realism', which he first used in the *Journal des faits* in 1851, from Champfleury. It can therefore be supposed that the following statement (usually described as the 'Manifesto of Realism') was also influenced by Champfleury. It served as the foreword to the catalogue of the special exhibition of Courbet's work that opened on 28 July 1855 in the purpose-built Pavillon du Réalisme in Paris. His insistence on depicting scenes from his own era reflected a demand that had prevailed in France since the Revolution to replace classical imagery with that drawn from contemporary subjects (Courthion, ii, pp. 60–61):

> The name 'Realist' has been imposed on me just as the name 'Romantic' was imposed on the men of 1830. . . . Working outside any system and with no previous prejudice I have studied the art of the Old Masters and the art of the Modern Masters. I no more want to imitate the former than copy the latter; nor have I pursued the futile goal of art for art's sake. No! I simply wanted to draw from a complete knowledge of tradition a reasoned and independent sense of my own individuality. I sought knowledge in order to acquire skill, that was my idea. To be capable of conveying the customs,

the ideas and the look of my period as I saw them; to be not just a painter, but a man as well; in short, to produce living art, that is my aim.

The idea of 'living art' greatly exercised Courbet's mind thereafter and had a self-liberating effect, for, in contrast to the protagonists of the French Revolution, Courbet did not believe that man was born free, rather that he became free only through work. Work, including art, could lead to freedom only if it also improved the condition of society. He spoke of this at a conference of artists in Antwerp in 1861 (Riat, pp. 191–2):

> The basis of realism is the denial of the ideal . . . *Burial at Ornans* was really the burial of Romanticism. . . . We must be rational, even in art, and never allow logic to be overcome by feeling. . . . By reaching the conclusion that the ideal and all that it entails should be denied, I can completely bring about the emancipation of the individual, and finally achieve democracy. Realism is essentially democratic art.

Courbet's missionary mentality led to the rapid dissemination of a 'doctrine' of Realism, which inevitably attracted pupils to Courbet. Yet he did not want to be a teacher as he intended to encourage the artistic expression of each individual. He gave the following explanation of this apparent dichotomy at the opening of his studio (Castagnary, pp. 180–83):

> I do not and cannot have pupils . . . I cannot teach my art or the art of any school, since I deny that art can be taught, or to put it another way I claim that art is completely individual and for each artist it is only the talent that results from his own inspiration and his own study of tradition. . . . In particular it would be impossible for art in painting to consist of any other things than the representation of objects which the artist can see and touch. . . . There can be no schools. . . . Unless it becomes abstract, painting cannot allow a partial aspect of art to dominate, be it drawing, colour or composition.

2. POLITICAL VIEWS. Courbet's political aphorisms cover his whole working period and had a far-reaching influence into the 20th century. However he was politically committed in a strict sense for only short periods (1848–51, 1855, 1863–4, 1868–71), and even then it is only rarely possible to discern a directly political iconography in his pictures. In February 1848 he made a chalk drawing of a man on a barricade waving a gun and flag for the periodical *Le Salut public* edited by Baudelaire (printed in the second issue of the journal), yet in letters (Courthion, ii, p. 74) he denied any participation in the political events of that year. Nor did he take part in the competition to produce an allegory for the Republic, though he encouraged Daumier to do so. He wrote that, instead, he was 'going to enter the competition open to musicians for a popular song' (Riat, p. 53). It is all the more probable that he took part as he did himself write poetry (Herding, 1988).

Throughout his life Courbet was strongly opposed to state power, an attitude that brought him into conflict with the government of the Second Empire. His ideas on this issue emerge in the discussion he had in 1854 with the Comte de Nieuwerkerke, Intendant des Beaux-Arts de la

Maison de l'Empereur. The administration wanted to ensnare the recalcitrant artist by offering him an official commission for a large painting for the Exposition Universelle to be held in Paris in 1855. Courbet rejected the invitation with anti-authoritarian arguments (Courthion, ii, p. 81):

> Firstly because he [Nieuwerkerke] maintained to me that there was a government and I did not in any way feel included in that government, I myself was a government, and . . . if he liked my pictures he was free to buy them from me, and I asked only one thing of him, that he should allow the art of his exhibition to be free.

This request met with only partial success; the *Painter's Studio* was not admitted into the official exhibition. In this, Courbet, driven by his need for independence, anticipated the later Salon des Refusés and secessionist movements.

In declining the honour of becoming a Chevalier of the Légion d'honneur in 1870, Courbet reiterated his liberal and individualistic principles (Courthion, ii, p. 124):

> The State has no competence in matters relating to art. . . . When it leaves us free, it will have fulfilled its duties towards us. . . . when I am dead people must say of me: he never belonged to any school, any church, any institution, any academy and above all to any régime, except for the rule of freedom.

This stance as an outsider and individualist did not prevent Courbet from perceiving himself as a socialist and being seen as one. On 15 November 1851 Courbet was described in the *Journal des faits* as a 'socialist painter', and he immediately accepted this designation as his letter of 19 November 1851 to the editor demonstrates; the letter appeared on 21 November, thus just two weeks before Louis-Napoléon Bonaparte's coup d'état (*Bull. Amis Gustave Courbet*, lii (1974), p. 12):

> I am strong enough to act alone . . . M. Garcin calls me the socialist painter; I gladly accept that description; I am not only a socialist, but also a democrat and republican, in short a supporter of all that the revolution stands for, and first and foremost I am a realist.

Courbet's individualism extended to the wider demand for decentralization. This idea was first expressed in a letter Courbet wrote to Proudhon in 1863 for Proudhon's essay on his art (published in Paris in 1865 under the title 'Du principe de l'art et de sa destination sociale') in which he linked decentralization with his principle that 'independence leads to everything' (*Bull. Amis Gustave Courbet*, xxii (1958), p. 7). In a letter written to Jules Vallès during the Commune in 1871, Courbet stated that he regarded the USA and Switzerland as models for the future form of the French State; he felt France should be decentralized and divided into cantons (Courthion, ii, pp. 47–9). Courbet returned to the theme of decentralization in two further letters (Courthion, ii, pp. 49–59). However, these ideas should not be seen as forming a purely political manifesto. Courbet's painting provided an analogy for decentralization: firstly in its subject-matter, in his preference for the provinces over Paris, and secondly in its form, since for him each object had the same weight.

3. CHARACTER AND PERSONALITY. Courbet was regarded as a remarkable figure by his contemporaries: a sturdy man with a look of the people, far removed from Parisian taste, an artist without restraint, someone who saw himself as an anarchist and socialist but who made more of a fuss about it than his knowledge of the subject warranted. Presenting a noisy, obstreperous, extrovert image, he apparently found companionship only in bohemian circles (e.g. at the famous Brasserie Andler where he met Baudelaire, Proudhon, Corot and, later on, Monet). This idea of an 'uncivilized' and 'independent' Bohemian formed an important feature of Courbet's self-image. He first expressed this Romantic notion in a letter to his friend Francis Wey in 1850: 'In our so very civilized society I have to live like a savage; I have to free myself even of governments. To accomplish this I have therefore just embarked on the great independent, vagabond life of the Bohemian.' (Riat, pp. 80–81). Later too Courbet was repeatedly described by himself and others as 'sauvage' (Courthion, i, pp. 98, 102, 105, 120, 216; ii, p. 93).

In his writings, including his autobiography of 1866 (Courthion, ii, pp. 25–33), Courbet often appears as a lively man who, though fond of laughter and singing, suffered from bouts of depression and a fear of persecution. These qualities are also evident in his extensive correspondence with his patron Bruyas, to whom he wrote at the end of 1854: 'Behind the laughing mask that you see I conceal inside me suffering, bitterness and a sadness that clings to my heart like a vampire.' (Courthion, ii, p. 84). Courbet's last important letter, of 1 March 1873, was again addressed to Bruyas; in it he links his personal suffering with that of society: 'The devotion I have always had for those who suffer has paralyzed the well-being which I could have achieved for myself in life. I have no regrets; I dread only one thing, ending up like Don Quixote, for lying and self-centredness are inseparable.' (Courthion, ii, p. 152).

IV. Critical reception and posthumous reputation.

Courbet rapidly achieved a high and controversial profile in his lifetime through his character, life style and political views. Art critics (such as Théophile Gautier, Charles Perrier (*fl*1850s), Maxime Du Camp, Prosper Mérimée (1803–70) and Alexandre Dumas *fils* (1824–95)) and caricaturists (such as Bertall, Cham, Paul Hadol (1835–75) and Quillenbois (*b*1821)) reproached him not only for 'democratizing art' (prompted by *The Stone-breakers*) but also for extolling the world of peasants, labourers or wrestlers and for his coarse painting style. Courbet's defenders (such as Buchon, Champfleury, Castagnary and Théophile Thoré), who pointed to his social commitment, his honest concern with the present and his modernity, were barely able to dent the prevailing academic concepts until the mid-1860s. Only Castagnary eventually succeeded in doing so, but only by a conformist strategy, which sacrificed the content of Courbet's painting. Castagnary was the first to point out the colourful charm, dreamy depths and lively atmosphere of Courbet's pictures; he even maintained that Courbet had never basically been a Realist. Conversely, Champfleury gradually parted company with Courbet for political reasons, and when he learnt in 1882 that Courbet was to be honoured with a large retrospective exhibition in the Ecole des Beaux-Arts, he criticized him as an annoying example of folksiness and spoke of his equivocations and lack of character. Even before that, in 1866, Zola had played Courbet the painter off against Courbet the politician; he particularly hated the sociological interpretation of Courbet's pictures by Proudhon (Picon and Bouillon, pp. 36–56). On the other hand, the socialist writer Thoré thought that Courbet had become depoliticized as he was now 'accepted, bemedalled, decorated, glorified, embalmed' (Thoré, ii, p. 276).

A rehabilitation of Courbet's reputation began in the 1880s when France remembered its republican traditions. Thenceforward Courbet was perceived both as a politically committed artist and as a modernist (see Sanchez), though the polemics against him continued (see Champfleury). In Germany Courbet had been highly regarded by the avantgarde from the time of the exhibitions of his work in Munich (1851, 1869) and Frankfurt am Main (1852, 1854, 1858). Julius Meier-Graefe put this admiration on a scholarly level as early as 1905, emphasizing Courbet's role as a pioneer of modernism, at the same time, moreover, that Cézanne (in conversations recorded by Joachim Gasquet (1873–1921) in *Cézanne* (Paris, 1926)) expressed his reverence for Courbet. The situation in England was similar after pictures by Courbet were exhibited there (in 1856 and 1862).

The position has not altered much since then. Even in France the reproach of 'lowness' levelled at Courbet and the hatred of the Communards gradually disappeared, and Apollinaire's description of Courbet as the father of modernism has prevailed. In 1946 a small museum devoted to Courbet was opened in Ornans, and in 1971 this was expanded and moved into the house where he was born. The Musée Maison Natale de Gustave Courbet contains works by Courbet and his friends as well as photographs, letters and other material relating to the artist. (For illustration of a photograph of Courbet by Etienne Carjat *see* PHOTOGRAPHY, fig. 9.)

Since the 1970s the attitudes of Zola and Thoré have been reiterated and even intensified. A resolution of the sterile dispute over Courbet the artist and Courbet the politician can be achieved only by looking at the multiple meanings in Courbet's work from a different perspective (Hofmann in 1978–9 exh. cat.); by considering new aspects (e.g. the 'gender aspect', see 1988–9 exh. cat.); and by trying to understand Courbet's anti-normative method and rejection of naturalism (which has been so liberating to modernism) as analogies for his anarchic social utopias. Courbet's enduring achievement was unquestionably to free art from the strait-jacket of the academic 'ideal'. Therefore in a special sense he has become 'the artists' artist' (Sedgwick), while some art historians still approach him with reserve.

WRITINGS

P. Courthion, ed.: *Courbet raconté par lui-même et par ses amis*, 2 vols (Geneva, 1948–50)
P. Borel, ed.: *Lettres de Gustave Courbet à Alfred Bruyas* (Geneva, 1951)
P. ten-Doesschate Chu, ed.: *Courbet's Letters* (Chicago, 1992)

BIBLIOGRAPHY

EARLY SOURCES

Champfleury: 'Du réalisme: Lettre à Madame Sand', *L'Artiste*, n. s. 5, xvi (1855), pp. 1–5
J.-A. Castagnary: *Les Libres Propos* (Paris, 1864), pp. 174–201
T. Thoré: *Salon de W. Bürger*, 2 vols (Paris, 1870)
P. Mantz: 'Gustave Courbet', *Gaz. B.-A.*, xvii (1878), pp. 514–27; xviii (1878), pp. 17–29, 371–84
J.-A. Castagnary: *Salons (1857–1870)*, 2 vols (Paris, 1892)
——: 'Fragments d'un livre sur Courbet', *Gaz. B.-A.*, n. s. 2, v (1911), pp. 5–20; vi (1912), pp. 488–97; vii (1912), pp. 19–30

GENERAL

L. Nochlin, ed.: *Realism and Tradition in Art, 1848–1900* (Englewood Cliffs, 1966)
L. Nochlin: *Realism* (Harmondsworth, 1971)
T. J. Clark: *The Absolute Bourgeois: Artists and Politics in France, 1848–1851* (London, 1973)
G. Lacambre and J. Lacambre, eds: *Champfleury: Le Réalisme* (Paris, 1973)
G. Picon and J.-P. Bouillon: *Emile Zola: Le Bon Combat: De Courbet aux Impressionnistes* (Paris, 1974)
G. Lacambre and J. Lacambre, eds: *Champfleury: Son regard et celui de Baudelaire: Textes choisis et présentés, accompagnés de 'L'Amitié de Baudelaire et de Champfleury' par Claude Pichois* (Paris, 1990)

MONOGRAPHS AND SYMPOSIA

G. Riat: *Gustave Courbet: Peintre* (Paris, 1906)
C. Léger: *Courbet selon les caricatures et les images* (Paris, 1920)
J. Meier-Graefe: *Courbet* (Munich, 1921)
C. Léger: *Courbet et son temps* (Paris, 1949)
G. Mack: *Gustave Courbet* (London, 1951)
L. Aragon: *L'Exemple de Courbet* (Paris, 1952)
R. Fernier: *Gustave Courbet* (Paris, 1969)
A. Fermigier: *Courbet* (Geneva, 1971)
T. J. Clark: *Image of the People: Gustave Courbet and the 1848 Revolution* (London, 1973)
R. Lindsay: *Gustave Courbet: His Life and Art* (New York, 1973)
L. Nochlin: *Gustave Courbet: A Study in Style and Society* (New York, 1976)
B. Foucart: *Courbet* (Paris, 1977)
P. ten-Doesschate Chu, ed.: *Courbet in Perspective* (Englewood Cliffs, 1977)
Malerei und Theorie: Das Courbet Colloquium: Frankfurt am Main, 1979
A. Callen: *Courbet* (London, 1980)
M. Fried: *Courbet's Realism* (Chicago and London, 1990); review by K. Herding in *Burl. Mag.*, cxxxiii (1991), pp. 723–4
K. Herding: *Courbet: To Venture Independence* (New Haven and London, 1991)
J.-H. Rubin: *Gustave Courbet: Realist and Visionary* (in preparation)

CATALOGUES

R. Fernier: *La Vie et l'oeuvre de Gustave Courbet: Catalogue raisonné*, 2 vols (Lausanne and Paris, 1977–8); review by K. Herding in *Pantheon*, xxxix (1981), pp. 282–6
Gustave Courbet, 1819–1877 (exh. cat. by H. Toussaint and M.-T. de Forges, Paris, Petit Pal.; London, RA; 1977–8)
Courbet und Deutschland (exh. cat. by W. Hofmann in collaboration with K. Herding, Hamburg, Ksthalle; Frankfurt am Main, Städel. Kstinst. & Städt. Gal.; 1978–9)
Courbet et la Suisse (exh. cat., ed. P. Chessex; La Tour-de-Peilz, Château, 1982)
Les Voyages secrets de Monsieur Courbet: Unbekannte Reiseskizzen aus Baden, Spa und Biarritz (exh. cat., ed. K. Herding and K. Schmidt; Baden-Baden, Staatl. Ksthalle; Zurich, Ksthaus; 1984)
Courbet à Montpellier (exh. cat., ed. P. Bordes; Montpellier, Mus. Fabre, 1985)
Courbet Reconsidered (exh. cat., ed. S. Faunce and L. Nochlin; New York, Brooklyn Mus.; Minneapolis, Inst. A.; 1988–9)

SPECIALIST STUDIES

Studies of particular works

R. Huyghe, G. Bazin and others: *Courbet: 'L'Atelier du peintre: Allégorie réelle', 1855* (Paris, 1944)
M. Winner: 'Gemalte Kunsttheorie: Zu Gustave Courbets *Allégorie réelle* und der Tradition', *Jb. Berlin. Mus.*, iv (1962), pp. 150–85
L. Nochlin: 'Gustave Courbet's *Meeting*: A Portrait of the Artist as a Wandering Jew', *A. Bull.*, xlix (1967), pp. 209–22
B. Farwell: 'Courbet's *Baigneuses* and the Rhetorical Feminine Image', *Women as Sex Objects: Studies in Erotic Art, 1730–1970*, ed. T. Hess and L. Nochlin (New York, 1972), pp. 65–79
B. Nicolson: *Courbet: 'The Studio of the Painter'* (New York, 1973)
A. Seltzer: 'Courbet: All the World's a Studio', *Artforum*, xvi (1977), pp. 44–50

J.-L. Fernier: *Courbet: 'Un Enterrement à Ornans', anatomie d'un chef d'oeuvre* (Paris, 1980)

M. Fried: 'The Structure of Beholding in Courbet's *Burial at Ornans*', *Crit. Inq.*, ix (1983), pp. 635–83

——: 'Courbet's Metaphysics: A Reading of *The Quarry*', *Reconstructing Individualism: Autonomy, Individuality and the Self in Western Thought*, ed. T. C. Heller and others (Stanford, 1986), pp. 75–105

L. Nochlin: 'Courbet's *L'Origine du monde*: The Origin without an Original', *October*, xxxvii (1986), pp. 76–86

Other

J. Meier-Graefe: *Corot und Courbet* (Leipzig, 1905)

G. Boas: *Courbet and the Naturalistic Movement* (Baltimore, 1938)

M. Schapiro: 'Courbet and Popular Imagery: An Essay of Realism and Naiveté', *J. Warb. & Court. Inst.*, iv (1941), pp. 164–91

K. Berger: 'Courbet in his Century', *Gaz. B.-A.*, n. s. 6, xxiv (1943), pp. 19–40

Bull. Amis Gustave Courbet (1947–)

J. P. Sedgwick: 'The Artist's Artist', *ARTnews*, lviii (1960), pp. 40–44, 65–6

T. J. Clark: 'A Bourgeois Dance of Death: Max Buchon on Courbet', *Burl. Mag.*, cxi (1969), pp. 208–12, 286–90

L. Dittmann: *Courbet und die Theorie des Realismus: Beiträge zur Theorie der Künste im 19. Jahrhundert* (Frankfurt am Main, 1971), pp. 215–39

R. Bonniot: *Courbet en Saintonge* (Paris, 1973)

A. Bowness: 'Courbet and Baudelaire', *Gaz. B.-A.*, n. s. 6, xc (1977), pp. 189–99

K. Herding: 'Gustave Courbet (1819–1877): Zum Forschungsstand', *Kunstchronik*, xxx (1977), pp. 438–56, 486–96

A. Bowness: 'Courbet's Proudhon', *Burl. Mag.*, cxx (1978), pp. 123–8

K. Herding, ed.: *Realismus als Widerspruch: Die Wirklichkeit in Courbets Malerei* (Frankfurt am Main, 1978, rev. 1984)

J.-P. Sanchez: 'La Critique de Courbet et la critique du réalisme entre 1880 et 1890', *Hist. & Crit. A.*, iv–v (1978), pp. 76–83

T. Reff: 'Courbet and Manet', *A. Mag.*, liv (1980), pp. 98–103

J.-H. Rubin: *Realism and Social Vision in Courbet and Proudhon* (Princeton, 1980)

A. M. Wagner: 'Courbet's Landscapes and their Market', *A. Hist.*, iv (1981), pp. 410–31

L. Nochlin: 'The De-politicization of Gustave: Transformation and Rehabilitation under the Third Republic', *October*, xxii (1982), pp. 65–77

N. McWilliams: 'Un Enterrement à Paris: Courbet's Political Contacts in 1845', *Burl. Mag.*, cxxv (1983), pp. 155–6

K. Herding: 'Lautmalereien: Zu einigen unbekannten Gedichten und Briefen Courbets', *Kunst um 1800 und die Folgen: Werner Hofmann zu Ehren*, ed. C. Beutler (Munich, 1988), pp. 233–43

P. ten-Doesschate Chu: *Courbet and the 19th Century Media Culture* (in preparation)

KLAUS HERDING

Courde de Montaiglon, Anatole de. *See* MONTAIGLON, ANATOLE DE COURDE, COMTE DE.

Courret, Eugenio (*b* France; *d* ?France). French photographer. He moved to Lima, Peru, in about 1861. There he formed a partnership with the French photographer Eugenio Maunoury. By 1864 he had his own studio, which became the most successful photographic centre in Lima. He was the leading Peruvian portrait photographer of the 19th century and at the Exposition Universelle in Paris in 1900 he won a gold medal. As well as carrying out commissions he took photographs of Lima, leaving valuable documentary records not only of its architecture but also of historical events.

BIBLIOGRAPHY
D. McElzoy: *The History of Photography in Peru in the Nineteenth Century, 1836–1876* (diss., Albuquerque, U. NM, 1977)

ERIKA BILLETER

Court, Joseph-Désiré (*b* Rouen, 14 Sept 1797; *d* Paris, 23 Jan 1865). French painter and museum director. In 1817 he entered the Académie des Beaux-Arts in Paris, where he studied under Antoine-Jean Gros. In 1821 he won the Prix de Rome with *Samson Handed over to the Philistines by Delilah* (1821; Paris, Ecole N. Sup. B.-A.). He began exhibiting at the Salon in 1824 and in 1827 showed *Scene from the Deluge* (1827; Lyon, Mus. B.-A.), painted while he was in Rome, and the *Death of Caesar* (Paris, Louvre). The latter proved a sensational success: it was initially bought by the Musée du Luxembourg, Paris, and was re-exhibited in 1855 before being sent to the Louvre. The subject derives from Plutarch and shows Antony stirring the Roman citizens to avenge the murder of Caesar. It was praised chiefly for its dramatic composition.

In 1830 and 1831 Court took part in the competitions set up to provide paintings for the Salon de Séances in the Chambre de Députés, Paris. His three works, on the required subjects, were the *Oath of Louis-Philippe* (1830; Saint-Germain-en-Laye, Mus. Mun.), *Mirabeau and Dreux-Brézé* and *Boissy d'Anglas Saluting the Head of Féraud* (both 1831; Rouen, Mus. B.-A.). None of Court's entries was successful, but their reception reflects contemporary debates about the requirements of official art: although it conformed largely to traditional modes of representation, *Mirabeau and Dreux-Brézé* was criticized as being too theatrical and was perceived as lacking the historical literalness required of official art. As a protest against the decision of the competition jury, Court exhibited *Boissy d'Anglas* at the Salon of 1833.

At the Salon of 1836 Court exhibited two further examples of official art: the *Duc d'Orléans Signs the Act Proclaiming a Lieutenance-générale of the Kingdom, 31 July 1830* and the *King Distributing Battalion Standards to the National Guard, 29 August 1830* (both Versailles, Château). The latter was hung in the Salle de 1830 in the south wing of the château of Versailles, a room designed to celebrate the Revolution of 1830 that brought Louis-Philippe to power. In order to create the sense of recording a first-hand experience, Court depicted a close-up view of the event, rather than a panoramic scene. As with other official works, however, the appearance of historical truth disguised the propagandist intent. The picture professed the physical strength of the monarchy and reflected the importance of the National Guard to its security, though in August 1830 the Marquis de Lafayette was in fact Commander-in-Chief of the National Guard.

Court increasingly devoted himself to painting portraits, such as that of *Marshal Vallée* (1839; Versailles, Château). He also painted a number of religious works, such as the *Embarkation of St Paul for Jerusalem* (1835; Paris, SS Gervais & Protais). After his early successes and critical acclaim, Court's later work was rather mediocre, though his portraits are of historical interest. He continued to exhibit regularly at the Salon, and in 1853 he was appointed director of the Musée des Beaux-Arts in Rouen, a post he held until his death.

BIBLIOGRAPHY
Bénézit; *DBF*

H. Marcel: *La Peinture française au XIXe siècle* (Paris, 1905), pp. 128–31

P. Grunchec: *Le Grand Prix de peinture* (Paris, 1983)

M. Marrinan: *Painting Politics for Louis-Philippe: Art and Ideology in Orléanist France, 1830–1848* (New Haven and London, 1988)

Court, Juste le. *See* CORTE, JOSSE DE.

Court, Suzanne de (*fl c.* 1600). French enameller. She was the daughter of Jean de Court, from whom she learnt the art of enamelling. Instead of using the *grisaille* technique (*see* ENAMEL, §2(vii)), she developed a unique enamelling style noted for its vivid colours. An example of her work is *The Annunciation* (Limoges enamel plaques, 190×135 mm, *c.* 1600; Baltimore, MD, Walters A.G.).

For illustration of her work *see* LIMOGES.

BIBLIOGRAPHY
K. Petersen and J. J. Wilson: *Women Artists* (New York and London, 1976)
C. Petteys and others: *Dictionary of Women Artists* (Boston, 1985)

Courtauld. English family of silversmiths, industrialists, collectors and patrons, of French origin. The family originated from the town of St Pierre on the Ile d'Oléron off La Rochelle. They arrived in London a few years after the Revocation of the Edict of Nantes in 1685, and between 1708 and 1780 three generations of Courtauld silversmiths were registered at the Goldsmiths' Company. Augustine Courtauld (*c.* 1686–*c.* 1751) was apprenticed to SIMON PANTIN in 1701 and, after becoming a freeman of the Goldsmiths' Company in 1708, he started a business as a plateworker in Church Court, off St Martin's Lane in London. The majority of his work is of high quality, for example a silver tea-table (1742; St Petersburg, Hermitage) and the state salt of the Corporation of the City of London (1730; London, Mansion House). Augustine's brother Pierre Courtauld (1690–1729) registered a mark in 1721, but none of his works has been identified. Samuel Courtauld I (1720–65) was apprenticed to his father, Augustine, in 1734 but did not enter his own mark until 1746. Like his father he produced many pieces in the fashionable Rococo style of the mid-18th century, for example a large two-handled soup tureen and cover (1751; Courtaulds plc, on loan to U. London, Courtauld Inst. Gals) and an oval shaving basin (1757; St Petersburg, Hermitage). In 1749 he married Louisa Perina Ogier (*c.* 1730–1807), and on Samuel's death she continued the business. In 1765 Louisa Courtauld registered her own mark, which appears on a silver table bell of 1766–7 (Oxford, Ashmolean; *see* BELL, fig. 2). Three years later she took into partnership George Cowles (*d* 1811), and their joint mark appears on articles in the Neo-classical style made between 1768 and 1777. At the demise of this partnership Louisa entered a joint mark with her son Samuel Courtauld II (1752–1821), but the partnership continued for only a further three years until he emigrated to the USA to pursue a career as a merchant. Louisa's other son, George Courtauld (*b* 1761), became a silk-weaver, thus initiating the family's connection with the textile industry. The exact relationship of the collector (1) Samuel Courtauld to the earlier generations is unclear.

BIBLIOGRAPHY
J. F. Hayward: *Huguenot Silver in England, 1688–1727* (London, 1959)
——: *The Courtauld Silver* (London and New York, 1975)
A. G. Grimwade: *London Goldsmiths, 1697–1837: Their Marks & Lives* (London, 1976, rev. 3/1990)

STEPHEN T. CLARKE

(1) Samuel Courtauld (*b* Braintree, Essex, 7 May 1876; *d* London, 1 Dec 1947). Industrialist, collector and patron. He was born at Bocking Place, Braintree, where his grandfather, George Courtauld (1802–61), had become established as a silk-weaver by 1816. After being educated at Rugby School, at the age of 20 he travelled to Krefeld and Paris to study textile manufacture and returned to the rapidly developing and internationally expanding family textile firm, which entered the field of synthetic fibres. By 1908 he had become general manager of the mills, and he was promoted to the Board of Directors in 1915. He became Chairman in 1921, a post he held for 25 years. His marriage in 1901 and his visits to Florence and Rome and to many Paris exhibitions stimulated his interest in music and art. It was not until 1922, however, that he began collecting art, and he kept the works at his house at 20 Portman Square, London, designed by Robert Adam. Initially inspired by Hugh Lane's collection of modern art, his predominant (but not exclusive) taste was for French Impressionism and Post-Impressionism, and his aim was to enrich weak national holdings. He rapidly became the supreme collector in the United Kingdom of paintings by all the major masters of these schools. Most spectacularly he owned works by Monet, Renoir, Degas, Manet (including his exceptional *Bar at the Folies-Bergère*; U. London, Courtauld Inst. Gals), Seurat, van Gogh and Gauguin and later developed a passion for Cézanne. In 1923 he gave £50,000 to the Tate Gallery in London for the purchase of French paintings by selected artists, from which masterpieces by such artists as van Gogh and Seurat, including Seurat's *Bathers at Asnières* (now London, N.G.), were acquired. After his wife's death in 1931 he gave the lease of his house in Portman Square and a capital endowment to the University of London in order to found the pioneering Courtauld Institute of Art. In addition he presented many of his pictures to the University of London together with £70,000 to house them in the Courtauld Institute Galleries in Bloomsbury, London. Courtauld was also largely responsible for the importation of the Warburg Institute from Hamburg to London and acted as a Trustee of the Tate Gallery as well as twice being the Chairman of the National Gallery in London. In 1989–90 the Courtauld Institute of Art and the Courtauld Institute Galleries were moved to Somerset House in London.

DNB
BIBLIOGRAPHY
D. Cooper: *The Courtauld Collection* (London, 1954)

HARLEY PRESTON

Courtens. Belgian family of artists. The landscape painter (1) Franz Courtens was an influential figure in late 19th-century Belgian painting. His eldest son, Herman Courtens (1884–1956), a portrait and still-life painter, executed a portrait of his father (Antwerp, Kon. Mus. S. Kst.). Alfred Courtens (1889–1967) became an academic sculptor, and the youngest son, (2) Antoine Courtens, was a modernist architect.

(1) Franz Courtens (*b* Dendermonde, nr Ghent, 14 Feb 1854; *d* Brussels, 2 Jan 1943). Painter. Until 1870 he studied at the Académie in Dendermonde under Jacob Rosseels (1828–1912), Isidore Meyers (1836–1917) and Frans Vinck (1827–1903). In 1873 he left for Antwerp and in 1874 settled in Brussels, where he joined the open studio of the circle of progressive artists established by Henry Stacquet (1838–1906), Victor Uytterschaut (1847–1917) and Périclès Pantazis; they shared Courtens's admiration for the painters of the Barbizon school, reflected in his work from this time, for example *Hyacinth Field* (1883; Munich, Neue Pin.).

In the early 1880s Courtens worked in Brabant with Guillaume Vogels and Isidore Verheyden. Their influence may be seen in *Mussel Boat* (1883; Stuttgart, Staatsgal.), Courtens's first significant success, hailed by the journal *L'Art moderne* (9 Sept 1883) for its innovative treatment of light and atmosphere. Subsequently his style changed little: *Golden Rain* (Budapest, Mus. F.A.), for example, which had great success at the Exposition Universelle in Paris in 1889, shows a similar approach to the subject. Courtens continued to be successful for the rest of his life, receiving commissions from Leopold II, and in 1932 a large retrospective was held in his honour at the Palais des Beaux-Arts, Brussels. Courtens was the most important figure in the transition from Realism to Impressionism in Belgian landscape painting, and his work became an important model for the painters of the Dendermonde school such as Valerius De Saedeleer.

BIBLIOGRAPHY
Thieme–Becker
G. Vanzype: *Franz Courtens* (Brussels, 1950)
Het landschap in de Belgische Kunst, 1830–1914 (exh. cat., ed. R. Hoozee; Ghent, Mus. S. Kst., 1980), p. 188

RICHARD KERREMANS

(2) Antoine Courtens (*b* Brussels, 13 March 1899; *d* Brussels, 21 June 1969). Architect, son of (1) Franz Courtens. He studied architecture at the Ecole Saint-Luc, Brussels, and the National Hoger Instituut voor Schone Kunsten in Antwerp, graduating in 1924 and becoming a Rome scholar. After making several student trips, he worked in Victor Horta's studio on the project for the Palais des Beaux-Arts in Brussels. He then worked with the Mercier brothers' decorating company in Paris and spent a brief period first in Lyon with Tony Garnier and then in Düsseldorf (1927). Upon his return he became an important figure in the modernist movement in Belgium, constructing several buildings in the late 1920s that are among the best examples of Art Deco architecture in Brussels. The Haerens House (1928), Uccle, and the Palais de la Folle Chanson (1928), Ixelles, for example, were built in an Art Deco style inspired by Horta's Palais des Beaux-Arts. Courtens was then commissioned by the Louis Empain group to carry out several projects overseas, the most important of which was the building of the Domaine de l'Esterel (1935–8), a vast sports and residential complex on Mason Lake in the Laurentians, Quebec, Canada. This unusual project, which ranged from small log cabins to aerodynamic-looking hotels and clubhouse, gave him the opportunity to display his ability to manipulate architectural language. He was also responsible for several kiosks (1931–3) built on the Belgian coast for the Société Nationale des Chemins de Fer Vicinaux, the façade of the church of Jesus (1937–9), Rue Royale, Brussels, and the post office building (1951) in Léopoldville (now Kinshasa).

BIBLIOGRAPHY
Musée des Archives d'Architecture Moderne: Collections, Brussels, Mus. Archvs Archit. Mod. cat. (Brussels, 1986)

ANNE VAN LOO

Courtin, Pierre (Louis Maurice) (*b* Rebréchieu, Loiret, 20 Jan 1921). French printmaker and painter. From 1939 to 1942 he studied at the Ecole des Beaux-Arts in Orléans with the French illustrator Louis-Joseph Soulas (*b* 1905), and in 1941 he exhibited at the Salon de l'Imagerie, Musée Galleria in Orléans. In 1942 he entered the Ecole des Beaux-Arts in Paris and the following year the Ecole des Arts Décoratifs, where he remained for only two weeks. He then studied at the Académie Julian and in the studio of André Lhote and was at the Académie Ranson in 1944. He had his first exhibition of prints at the Galerie Guiot in Paris in 1944 and the following year exhibited with the group Jeune Gravure Contemporaine, of which he was a member from 1946 to 1956. In 1945 he illustrated William Faulkner's *As I Lay Dying*. From 1947 to 1951 he worked as an engraver for the printer Georges Leblanc and in the same capacity for Jacques Villon.

Courtin's early works, dating from 1944–5, were largely of the female figure and showed the influence of Cubism. Nevertheless he had produced his first abstract work in 1944 and from 1947 his engravings are entirely abstract, such as *Castle of Zinc* (1956; Chicago, IL, A. Inst.). The works up to *c.* 1950 are often rigidly geometrical and thereafter become softer and more informal. In 1949 Courtin, with Raoul Ubac and the French painters Gérard Vulliamy (*b* 1909) and Roger Chastel (*b* 1897), was one of the co-founders of the group Graphies, which exhibited at the Galerie des Deux Iles in Paris. Courtin's engravings are most characteristic for the bas-relief effect produced by cutting the plates, often zinc, very deeply. Though mainly known for his engravings he also painted in gouache and oils, as in *My Mother is Black* (1978; see 1989 exh. cat., pl. 9), and he produced colour lithographs.

BIBLIOGRAPHY
J. Putman and D. Meiller: *Pierre Courtin: L'Oeuvre gravé 1944–1972* (Annecy, 1973)
Pierre Courtin: Gouaches et peintures (exh. cat. by J. Demougin, Paris, Pompidou, 1976)
Pierre Courtin: Huiles et gouaches (exh. cat. by L. Pons, Paris, Gal. Claude Bernard, 1989)

□

Courtois. *See* CORTESE.

Courtonne, Jean (*b* Paris, 1671; *d* Paris, 1739). French architect. He was the most important member of a family of architects active in Paris. His early work included adding a storey to the Hôtel de Sillery (1712) and additions to the Hôtel de Vendôme (1715) in the Rue d'Enfer, but his most significant contribution was the design of two *hôtels particuliers* in the Faubourg Saint-Germain, the fashionable neighbourhood on the west bank of the Seine. About 1720 he drew up plans for the first of these, the Hôtel de Matignon (in the Rue de Varenne), built 1722–4 for Christian-Louis de Montmorency-Luxembourg, Prince of Tingry. In his initial project Courtonne organized the plan of this 'hôtel-entre-cour-et-jardin' around a single longitudinal axis, thus conforming to current practice. However, in his definitive plan the axes of the court and garden façades were made discontinuous, and although the circulatory path through the building lacked symmetry, this arrangement allowed both the court façade and the stable court to gain in breadth and prominence. His plan also placed an unusual emphasis on the public rooms, apparently as a means of accommodating the collections of the owner. In 1723, before it was finished, the Prince sold it to Jacques III de Goyen-Matignon, Comte de Thorigny, who dismissed Courtonne and brought in his own designer, Jean Mazin. Courtonne's own designs included drawings for the sculpted ornamentation of the court façade, the oval vestibule and several cornices in the main rooms, and his overall project was followed throughout, except for minor modifications in the plan of the lesser private rooms and the elimination of a pediment to crown the street portal. Despite the lack of Classical orders on the exterior elevations of the *corps de logis*, the overwhelming effect of the Hôtel de Matignon, as observers at the time noted, was closer to that of a palace than an hôtel particulier. The central projection of the court façade, decorated with flat channelled rustication, wrought iron and sculpted keystones and brackets, was adapted from the type of garden front found in contemporary châteaux, while the façade facing the garden appeared to be a free-standing block, comparable with that of a *maison de plaisance*. This impression was further aided by the low pitch of the roofs, barely rising above the horizontal cornice supporting a balustrade.

During the same period Courtonne also worked on the smaller Hôtel de Noirmoutiers (1722–3) in the Rue de Grenelle, built for Antoine-François de La Trémoille, Duc de Noirmoutiers. Here he organized the rooms around a single central axis. The tripartite arrangement of the garden façade is highly original, with its gentle crescendo of layered surfaces towards the central bay. In 1725 he published the *Traité de la perspective pratique*. This consisted of an illustrated manual of perspective intended for architects; a discussion of the new trends in Parisian architecture recently put into practice by such contemporaries as Pierre Lassurance I, Germain Boffrand and Robert de Cotte; and plates of his own hôtels, with a discussion of his designs. In 1728 Courtonne became a member of the Académie Royale d'Architecture, lecturing there from 1730. A second treatise, *Nouveau essai sur le bon goust en architecture*, read before the Académie in 1733, remains in manuscript form. His son, Jean-Baptiste Courtonne (d 1781), was a painter and architect and built the château of Villarceaux (Val-d'Oise) in 1758.

WRITINGS

Traité de la perspective pratique, avec les remarques sur l'architecture, suivies de quelques édifices considérables mis en perspective, & de l'invention de l'auteur (Paris, 1725)
Nouveau essai sur le bon goust en architecture (MS. treatise, 1733)

BIBLIOGRAPHY

W. Kalnein and M. Levey: *Art and Architecture of the Eighteenth Century in France*, Pelican Hist. A. (Harmondsworth, 1972)
Le Faubourg Saint-Germain: La Rue de Grenelle (exh. cat., Paris, Mus. S.E.I.T.A., 1980)
Le Faubourg Saint-Germain: La Rue de Varenne (exh. cat., Paris, Mus. Rodin, 1981)
D. Wiebenson, ed.: *Architectural Theory and Practice from Alberti to Ledoux* (Chicago, 1982)

ROBERT NEUMAN

Courtyard. Open area, partially or fully enclosed, adjacent to or within a building. The concept of the courtyard, which provides sheltered, secluded and secure exterior space, is fundamental to the traditions of both sacred and domestic architecture in many parts of the world. It developed particularly in hot, arid climates, as in North Africa and the Near East, where it offers a cool outdoor space protected from sun and hot winds.

Courtyards have been found in the earliest houses and palaces of the Near East, such as UR in Mesopotamia (early 2nd millennium BC), where excavations have revealed private housing consisting of a courtyard surrounded by a range of rooms, including a reception hall. In ancient Greece, courtyards—often with a peristyle—usually featured as a part of domestic planning as well as in buildings for public entertainments such as the palaestra (wrestling ground) and in *katagogeia* (hotels), where rooms were arranged around a peristyle (*see* GREECE, ANCIENT, §II, 1(i)(c) and (e)). Roman domestic practice also featured courtyards in buildings both public (e.g. Sanctuary of Bel, ded. 32 AD; *see* PALMYRA, fig. 1c) and domestic (e.g. numerous dwellings at Pompeii, before 79 AD). The characteristic form of the Roman *domus* or private house consisted of rooms opening off a courtyard or atrium, which was partly roofed with a central opening (*compluvium*) over an *impluvium* or rain basin that collected water from the roof. A passage then led to a second courtyard, usually with a peristyle surrounding a garden (*see* ROME, ANCIENT, §II, 1(i)(c) and fig. 8; *see also* GARDEN, fig. 7). The peristyle court was suitable for use in both hot and moderate climates and it therefore appeared in buildings all over the Roman Empire.

Early Christian churches, which were modelled on basilicas or baths rather than pagan temple forms, often included courtyards, usually enlarged atria with a central fountain for purification, built at their entrances (Old St Peter's, Rome, after 324 AD; destr.). In the Middle Ages, courtyards in the form of cloisters formed an essential part of monastic life as places for reading, study and seclusion from the increasing numbers of lay employees, as well as for growing herbs for medicinal purposes (*see* CLOISTER, §1). By association with monasteries, courtyards were incorporated into hospitals (*see* HOSPITAL, §I), for example in the Ospedale Maggiore (1457), Milan (*see* FILARETE, §2), and Thomas Dance's Guy's Hospital (1721–4), London, but their use was discontinued in the 19th century as changing perceptions of hygiene affected hospital design.

Courtyards were common in nearly all forms of Islamic architecture (*see* ISLAMIC ART, §II, 1(iii)) as they were suited to the hot and dry climate of most of the traditional Islamic lands. Many mosques open on to an arcaded courtyard with a central fountain (*see* MOSQUE), two examples being the Patio de los Naranjos in the Great Mosque in Córdoba, Spain (785–987; for plan *see* ISLAMIC ART, fig. 26) and the Masjid-i Shah (1612–30) in Isfahan. Similar forms were used in domestic accommodation, and in the Alhambra at Granada, for example, there are several courtyards with gardens and fountains, which are fully integrated into the design of the living space and are of increasing intimacy, notably the Patio de los Arrayanes (see fig.) and the Patio de los Leones (*see* GRANADA, fig. 3xii).

A central courtyard, or cortile, was a characteristic feature of palazzo design in Renaissance Italy. Outstanding examples include those in the Palazzo Medici-Riccardi (begun 1444), Florence, by Michelozzo di Bartolomeo; the Palazzo Ducale (begun 1464), Urbino (for illustration *see* LAURANA, LUCIANO); and the Palazzo della Cancelleria (begun 1495) and Palazzo Venezia (begun 1455), both in Rome (*see* ITALY, figs 10 and 11). Bramante's Cortile del Belvedere (begun 1505) at the Vatican was a monumental example linking two buildings 300 m apart, on a sloping site and containing a complex arrangement of ramps, staircases and terraces (*see* ROME, fig. 40, and BRAMANTE, DONATO, §I, 3(ii)(a)); it was later cut in two by the Vatican Library (1585–90) by Domenico Fontana (iii).

As the Renaissance spread to France in the early 16th century, courtyards became a principal feature in the planning of *hôtels particuliers*, such as the Cour Carrée in the Palais du Louvre (begun 1546; for illustration *see* LESCOT, PIERRE) and the Hôtel de Sully (1624–9), by Jean Androuet Du Cerceau, both Paris. They often became the major external feature on densely occupied urban sites (e.g. the Hôtel de Beauvais, 1654–60, Paris, by Antoine Le Pautre) or developed into a forecourt closed off from the street by a range containing stable and servants' quarters. They were adopted also in Spain, most magnificently in the circular courtyard (foundations laid 1540) of Charles V's palace at Granada (for illustration *see* MACHUCA, PEDRO) and in the grandly architectural courts, such as the Patio de los Evangelistas, of the Escorial (1563–82),

Patio de los Arrayanes (Court of the Myrtles), Alhambra, Granada, mid-14th century

Madrid, by JUAN BAUTISTA DE TOLEDO and JUAN DE HERRERA. Comparable arcaded courtyards built in England at this time include university quadrangles, for example Tom Quad (begun 1525), Christ Church, and Canterbury Quad (1631–6), St John's College, both at Oxford University (*see* OXFORD, figs 2 and 3); the two successive buildings for the Royal Exchange (1566–70; 1667–9; destr. 1838), London; and the Fountain Court (early 1690s) at Hampton Court by Christopher Wren.

During the early 19th century the fashion developed for roofing existing courtyards with cast iron and glass. An early example of this was the covering in of the Halle au Blé, Paris, with an iron roof (1808–13; later rebuilt) by François-Joseph Bélanger, replacing an earlier timber roof that covered the originally open, circular courtyard of the building (1763–9) by NICOLAS LE CAMUS DE MÉZIÈRES. One of the first examples of a building designed with a covered courtyard was Charles Barry's Reform Club (1838–40), London, built in the form of a 16th-century Roman palazzo with a central cortile. A similar later example is Fenway Court (completed 1899; now the Isabella Stewart Gardner Museum), Boston, which incorporates architectural elements from European buildings into its central covered courtyard and is laid out as a garden.

The courtyard form has been used in a variety of ways by 20th-century architects, for example in museums, as in the Fondation Maeght (1959–64), Saint-Paul-de-Vence (for illustration *see* SERT, JOSEP LLUÍS), and the Museo Nacional de Antropología (1964), Mexico City, by Pedro Ramírez Vázquez (*see* MEXICO, fig. 6), but more particularly in courtyard housing projects. In Mexico, Luis Barragán used courtyards derived in part from Mexican vernacular architecture in both domestic and sacred buildings, such as the Barragán house (1947), Tacubaya, and the Capillo de las Capuchinas (1952–5), Tlalpan. In Berlin, the form was continued by the Office for Metropolitan Architecture in their projects (1980; unexecuted) for housing in Kochstrasse, which drew on the traditional arrangement of domestic accommodation in Berlin after the late 19th century.

BIBLIOGRAPHY
A. Blunt: *Art and Architecture in France, 1500–1700*, Pelican Hist. A. (Harmondsworth, 1957)
A. Rossi: *The Architecture of the City* (Padua, 1966; Eng. trans., Cambridge, MA, 1982)
J. B. Ward-Perkins: *Roman Imperial Architecture*, Pelican Hist. A. (Harmondsworth, 1970, 2nd edn 1981)
G. Goodwin: *A History of Ottoman Architecture* (London, 1971)
L. H. Heydenreich and W. Lotz: *Architecture in Italy, 1400–1600*, Pelican Hist. A. (Harmondsworth, 1974)
A. Purves: 'The Persistence of Formal Patterns', *Perspecta*, xix (1982), pp. 138–63
W. Blaser: *Atrium: Five Thousand Years of Open Courtyards* (Basle, 1985)
C. Zucchi: *L'architettura dei cortile milanesi, 1535–1706* (Milan, 1989)
L. Pellecchia: 'Architects Read Vitruvius: Renaissance Interpretations of the Atrium of the Ancient House', *J. Soc. Archit. Historians*, li (Dec 1992), pp. 377–416
□

Cousen. English family of engravers.

(1) John Cousen (*b* nr Bradford, 19 Feb 1804; *d* London, 26 Dec 1880). He was apprenticed to the animal engraver John Scott (1774–1828) in London and possibly was a pupil of William Finden and Edward Finden. He engraved for J. M. W. Turner's *Turner's Annual Tours* (London, 1833–5), W. Brockedon's *Illustrations of the Passes of the Alps* (London, 1828–9), volumes of *Keepsake* (London, 1828–56), *Heath's Picturesque Annual* (London, 1833–5), R. Jennings's *Landscape Annual* (London, 1830–39) and the *Oriental Annual* (London, 1834–40). Many of the topographical volumes published by H. Fisher and G. Virtue contain his work, a number after William Henry Bartlett. Bartlett's own publications also carry plates engraved by Cousen, as does John Ruskin's *Modern Painters* (London, 1843–60). Thirty-two plates appeared in the *Art Journal* between 1849 and 1866. He exhibited at the Royal Academy, London, in 1863–4 and engraved three large plates, *Mercury and Herse* (1842; priv. col.) after Turner and two after Clarkson Stanfield (e.g. *Morning after the Wreck*, 1844; Sheffield, Graves A.G.).

(2) Charles Cousen (*b* Bradford, *c.* 1813; *d* ?London, Nov 1889). Brother of (1) John Cousen. He was taught engraving by his elder brother John and may also have been a pupil of the Findens. The majority of his book illustration was done after William Henry Bartlett, frequently as attractive vignettes that appeared in many of the same volumes as his brother's work. Dr William Beattie's *Switzerland Illustrated* (London, 1836), *Scotland Illustrated* (London, 1838) and *The Waldenses* (London, 1838) contain his earliest work; they were followed by plates in Nathaniel Parker Willis's *American Scenery* (London, 1840) and *Canadian Scenery* (London, 1842), Julia Pardoe's *Beauties of the Bosphorus* (London, 1840), Henry Stebbing's *Christian in Palestine* (London, [1847]) and Bartlett's own books between 1844 and 1854. Fifty-nine plates appeared in the *Art Journal* between 1850 and 1888. He painted in his younger days and exhibited at the Society of British Artists in London in 1848.

BIBLIOGRAPHY
DNB
A. J. [London] (1881), p. 63; (1889), p. 364
Bradford Antiqua., ii (1895), pp. 203–5
B. Hunnisett: *An Illustrated Dictionary of British Steel Engravers* (Aldershot, 1989)

BASIL HUNNISETT

Cousin. French family of painters, draughtsmen and designers. From the 17th century, when André Félibien (in his *Entretiens*) wrote the first important critical appraisal of Jean Cousin, until the 20th century, historians had fused two artists, father and son, into one personality that had become almost entirely mythical, with a career that spanned virtually the entire 16th century. The archival researches of Roy demonstrated that there had been an elder Jean Cousin, born probably no earlier than 1490 and surely not much after 1505, who died in 1560 or possibly 1561, and a younger Jean Cousin, his son, also an artist, who was a student at the University of Paris in 1542 and died around 1595. A seemingly unrelated sculptor of the same name was active in Paris in the 1540s but was dead by 1549. No work by him has been identified, but he was commissioned in 1541 to execute six statues for the cloisters of the convent of the Célestins in Paris. Although few paintings can be securely attributed to (1) Jean Cousin (i), he was a major figure in the classicizing trend of French art in the 1540s and 1550s. (2) Jean Cousin (ii) is

1. Jean Cousin (i): *Eva Prima Pandora*, panel, 0.98×1.50 m, *c.* late 1540s (Paris, Musée du Louvre)

a more shadowy figure, who carried on his father's workshop and style into the second half of the 16th century.

(1) Jean Cousin (i) [*le père*] (*b* ?Souci, nr Sens, *c.* 1500; *d* ?Paris *c.* 1560). He was from the region of Sens and started his career in that city. He is first documented in 1526 doing a land survey and again in 1530 designing fortifications for a village, fixing a clock and repairing and painting a statue for Sens Cathedral. By the later 1530s he must have been well established and affluent, since he was buying property. Before 1540 he moved to Paris, where he was employed at the end of 1539 on the decorations for the visit of Charles V. He was active there until his death but retained close ties with Sens, where he owned property and where he still worked periodically, as would his son.

One painting, *Eva Prima Pandora* (see fig. 1), remained in the family of the artist in Sens until the early 20th century. Its traditional attribution to Cousin seems totally sound, but a date is harder to assign. It is unlikely to have been painted before the move to Paris, since the artist seems to have known Benvenuto Cellini's bronze relief the *Nymph of Fontainebleau* (Paris, Louvre), with its similar pose and elongated anatomical characteristics. It is more likely, therefore, to be a work of the later 1540s. It is a large and impressive panel on which the painter has fully assimilated the classicizing style of the court of Francis I. It also shows a strong affinity with northern Romanist art, especially that of Jan van Scorel and his circle; this is apparent especially in the expansive landscape background with ancient ruins. The sophisticated subject, which invites the combination of a Christian theme with Classical motifs, shows Cousin as an artist deeply involved in the new culture of Renaissance France.

A number of works have survived that make it possible to form an idea of Cousin's work in the mid-1540s. The most important is a commission from the powerful Cardinal de Givry, Bishop of Langres, for cartoons for a set of tapestries woven in Paris and given to his cathedral. Three of the set of eight hangings representing the *Life of St Mamas*, the patron saint of the cathedral, remain, two in the cathedral itself and the third in the Louvre, Paris (see fig. 2). Here again, Cousin showed himself an adept of the most current classicizing trends. Motifs were borrowed from Italian prints and from Sebastiano Serlio's architectural treatise, but in a fully informed way. The borders show Cousin to have been conversant with and capable of original variations on the ornamental strapwork invented by the artists working at the royal château of Fontainebleau. A drawing (Paris, Bib. N.) showing episodes from the *Martyrdom of St Mamas* is clearly related to the tapestries and gives a more direct idea of Cousin's style than the weavings. The figures are elongated and very individual. There is the same kind of extensive landscape enriched with Classical motifs as in the *Eva Prima Pandora*.

The same taste for classicizing landscapes also appears in two signed engravings, an *Annunciation* and a *Deposition*, which must date from about the same time. Finally, several etchings in the manner of the FONTAINEBLEAU SCHOOL were designed by Cousin, some of which even bear his

2. Tapestry after cartoons by Jean Cousin (i): *Life of St Mamas*, mid-1540s (Paris, Musée du Louvre)

monogram. One of these, a curious kind of mausoleum etched in 1545 by one Master N. H. (*fl* first half 16th century), shows Cousin as a brilliant inventor of ornament, and it is noteworthy that he had not only assimilated the manner elaborated at Fontainebleau but was also familiar with the style of ornament named after Cornelis Floris that was invented in Flanders around 1542. Its particular feeling for space seems to have been congenial to Cousin, which confirms his affinity with Netherlandish art apparent in the *Eva*.

The last known work of Jean Cousin (i) is a perspective treatise, the *Livre de perspective*, published in Paris in 1560 but apparently ready by 1556. Cousin was involved with geometry from the beginning of his career, since he did land surveying. His method of construction is complex, and, it may be assumed, in the tradition of Jean Pelerin as much as that of the Italian perspectivists. Cousin himself drew the illustrations on the woodblocks (*see* PERSPEC-TIVE, fig. 3), which were cut by Aubin Olivier (*d* 1581). It is one of the most beautiful books of its time. The frontispiece is a *tour de force* of fantastical spacial inventiveness, although its immediate kinship to the designs of Floris is obvious.

Very few paintings have been attributed to the elder Cousin, *Charity* (Montpellier, Mus. Fabre) being the only one in addition to *Eva* that is generally accepted. Nor is there documentary evidence for work in that medium. On the other hand, he was traditionally considered the designer of many stained-glass windows. It seems improbable that he was a glass painter himself, but he must have made drawings for windows. His contribution to this crucial domain of French Renaissance art needs serious investigation. Documentary evidence shows that a significant part of his activity was devoted to cartoons for tapestries and embroideries, as well as 'toiles peintes'—painted hangings that were a less expensive substitute for tapestries. He also participated in the design of ephemeral festival decorations, including those for the famous entry of Henry II into Paris in 1549, which has been described justly as the great manifesto of the new art in France. It seems very probable that Cousin also participated in the reform of book illustration in Paris; the designs for the 1543 edition of *Horus Apollon* have been attributed to him.

From an early date Cousin was considered a sculptor and the creator of the important alabaster funerary monument of *Admiral Philippe Chabot* (Paris, Louvre) for the Orléans Chapel at the church of the Célestins in Paris. Various hypotheses have been proposed to fit the known evidence, the most widespread being that Bontemps, Pierre carved the magnificent reclining statue of the deceased to designs by Cousin and that Jean Cousin (ii) designed or even carved the surrounding monument after 1565 (for this view *see* BONTEMPS, PIERRE). This seems untenable: it is much more likely that the elder Cousin designed the whole monument, probably around 1545, and that it was slowly executed by professionals and put into place in 1565. There is no reason to believe that either Jean Cousin *père* or *fils* was a sculptor, but the problem has been complicated by the archival evidence of a sculptor of the same name active in Paris in the 1540s.

Jean Cousin (i)'s importance lies less in his activity as a painter than in his work as a designer who furnished the practitioners of traditional artistic techniques (weavers, wood-engravers, stone-carvers, embroiderers, glass painters) with models in the new Renaissance style. The fact that he was removed from the final execution makes his work particularly difficult to study and to assess.

(2) Jean Cousin (ii) [*le fils*] (*b* ?Sens, *c.* 1525; *d* ?Paris, *c.* 1595). Son of (1) Jean Cousin (i). He was a student at the University of Paris in 1542, an interesting index of his father's social and cultural ambitions. He must have learnt and practised art in his father's studio until the latter's death and continued very much in the same vein. Although he is mentioned by a number of contemporary writers, his artistic personality is even more elusive than his father's. One painting can be definitely ascribed to him and shows his style in later life: the *Last Judgement* (Paris, Louvre), which shows innumerable figures in a vast space but on a small canvas. It is painted with great finesse but little energy and displays a sophisticated sense of colour. A book of emblems of Fortune (Paris, Bib. Inst. France), which bears a date of 1568, was certainly drawn by him. On the basis of this work Otto Benesch attributed a whole corpus of drawings to him, but recent studies have shown that the style of some of these drawings is so close to the manner of his father that the distinction between the two is by no means easy. In addition, two very interesting compositions engraved by Etienne Delaune with the name of Cousin as designer, the *Brazen Serpent* and the *Conversion of St Paul*, are generally considered the work of Jean Cousin (ii), but they are undated and the chronology of Delaune's work does not make it possible to assign them a date; they might be no later than 1560 and designed by Jean Cousin (i).

In 1589 Jean Cousin (ii) contracted for the publication of a drawing book, the *Livre de pourtraicture*, which appeared in 1595 and remained extremely popular until the 19th century. The elder Cousin had already announced the publication of such a work in his *Livre de perspective* of 1560, and it is not impossible that the son was still using work by his father at this late date.

BIBLIOGRAPHY
A. Firmin Didot: *Etude sur Jean Cousin* (Paris, 1872)
M. Roy: *Artistes et monuments de la Renaissance en France* (Paris, 1929), pp. 1–120
O. Benesch: 'Jean Cousin le fils, dessinateur', *Prométhée*, 20 (1939–40), pp. 271–80
L'Ecole de Fontainebleau (exh. cat., Paris, Grand Pal., 1972)
M. Beaulieu: 'Pierre Bontemps et les Cousin père et fils, artistes sénonais de la Renaissance', *Mél Stiennon* (1983), pp. 35–48
C. Grodecki: *Documents du minutier central: Histoire de l'art au XVIe siècle*, 2 vols (Paris, 1985–6)
The French Renaissance in Prints from the Bibliothèque Nationale de France (exh. cat., New York, Met., 1995)

HENRI ZERNER

Cousin, Louis. *See* PRIMO, LUIGI.

Cousinet. French family of silversmiths. René Cousinet (*c.* 1626–92) was made a master in 1652 or 1654. An *Orfèvre du Roi*, he received payment between 1666 and 1684 for silver furniture (destr. 1689) made for Louis XIV, including mirror-frames, large repoussé chargers, containers for orange trees and chandeliers.

Two of René Cousinet's sons were associated with the Swedish court of Karl XII (*reg* 1697–1718). Jean-François Cousinet (*fl* 1686–*c.* 1711) became a master in Paris in 1686, but lived in Stockholm from 1694 to 1711. While there he executed a silver baptismal font (1696–1707; Stockholm, Kun. Slottet), designed as three caryatid putti emerging from a triangular pedestal and supporting a large shell-form basin. His brother, Nicolas-Ambroise Cousinet (*fl* 1696–*c.* 1715), became a master in Paris in 1696, but no silver by him is known. In 1703 he moved to Versailles, having been employed the previous year by Daniel Crönstrom, the Swedish envoy to the French court, to make drawings (Stockholm, Nmus.) of the French royal silver to be sent to Stockholm. These drawings are the single record of French royal domestic plate of the period. Henri-Nicolas Cousinet (*fl* 1724–68), son of Nicolas-Ambroise, made a travelling set (1729–30; Paris, Louvre) for Queen Maria Leczynska (1703–68). He is also recorded as a sculptor to the Prince de Condé. Ambroise-Nicolas Cousinet (*fl* 1745–*c.* 1765), brother of Henri-Nicolas, became a master in 1745. His only recorded work is a set of 16 large statuettes (Lisbon, Mus. N. A. Ant.) executed in 1757 for José Mascarenhas, Duke of Aveiro (1708–59). The figures, representing dancing couples of eight different nationalities, are the only such set of French silver sculpture for the dining-table from this period. The models for the figures may have been supplied by Henri-Nicolas Cousinet.

BIBLIOGRAPHY
H. Nocq: *Le Poinçon de Paris*, 4 vols (Paris, 1926–31), i, pp. 309–10
C. Hernmarck: *The Art of the European Silversmith, 1430–1830* (London and New York, 1977), i, pp. 216, 222; ii, figs 551, 971

Versailles: The View from Sweden (exh. cat. by E. Evans Dee and G. Walton, New York, Cooper-Hewitt Mus., 1988)

Versailles et les tables royales en Europe (exh. cat., ed. P. L. Pizzi; Versailles, Château, 1993), pp. 179–83

CLARE LE CORBEILLER

Cousinet, Catherine-Elisabeth. *See under* LEMPEREUR, LOUIS-SIMON.

Cousins, Samuel (*b* Exeter, Devon, 9 May 1801; *d* London, 7 May 1887). English engraver. He was the son of an Exeter tailor. Cousins's talent for drawing came to the notice of the Society of Arts, and as a result he worked as an apprentice (1814–21), then as assistant (1821–5), to S. W. Reynolds. His early career as an independent engraver was associated with 33 successful plates after Thomas Lawrence, who himself published *Master Lambton* (1826; London, BM) in 1827. In 1835 he was elected Associate Engraver of the Royal Academy. In 1837 he engraved *Bolton Abbey in the Olden Time* (London, BM), the first of seven popular subject plates after Edwin Henry Landseer; most of his plates were after contemporary portraits. Cousins became the first engraver academician in 1855 and a full R.A. in 1867. He retired, but the Old Masters exhibition at Burlington House, London, in 1870 aroused such interest in the work of Joshua Reynolds that he was persuaded to engrave 14 popular plates after Reynolds between 1873 and 1879.

BIBLIOGRAPHY
DNB
G. Pycroft: *Memoir of Samuel Cousins* (Exeter, 1887)
A. C. Whitman: *Samuel Cousins* (London, 1904)

DAVID ALEXANDER

Coussin, Jean-Antoine (*b* Paris, 1770; *d* Paris, 26 March 1849). French architect and writer. He studied at the Ecole des Beaux-Arts, Paris, where in 1797 he won first prize in the competition for the Prix de Rome. One of his projects as a *pensionnaire* in Rome was a proposed restoration of the Temple of Vesta (published posthumously). His career after his return to France was lacklustre, but commissions included restorations of the Hôtel de Bouillon, Paris, the Hôtel d'Arenberg, Brussels, where he installed a new library, an abattoir at Ménilmontant and several country houses, including one for M. Pepin at Villette-aux-Aulnes. Coussin is best known for *Du génie de l'architecture* (1822), published to great contemporary acclaim but now forgotten. In a text that ranged in content from the primitive hut to the latest Paris sewers, Coussin appealed for a return to a basic approach to architecture, attacking speculators for their commercial approach to design and architects for pandering to them. He hoped to convince the public of the value of design based on theory, rather than as a mere fashionable appliqué for standard building types. In high-flown language he contrasted the speculators' materialism with the true 'genius' of architecture, and found the mathematical basis for each style, constructing a system for their acceptable use based on 'sentiment, genius and taste'. His analysis was similar to that of Julien-David Le Roy in the 1760s and his language was sympathetic to such ascendant elements of Romanticism as Eclecticism and the Néo-Grec.

WRITINGS
Du génie de l'architecture (Paris, 1822)
Le Temple de Vesta (Rome): Restauration exécutée en 1802 (Paris, 1879)
BIBLIOGRAPHY
Bellier de La Chavignerie-Auvray; Thieme-Becker

JUANITA M. ELLIAS

Coustain, Pierre (*b* ?Burgundy, *c.* 1420; *d* Bruges, before 1502). Franco-Flemish painter and designer. He is first documented painting stained glass in Philip the Good's Burgundian castle of Argilly in 1448 and 1452. He was appointed a painter to the Duke in January 1454, just before he worked with Colard le Voleur, Master of the Entertainments at Hesdin, on fountains and other machines for the Banquet of the Pheasant in Lille. During the next years, Coustain was responsible for painting the banners and heralds' tabards for several court festivities and funerals. He coloured statues of *St Philip* and *St Elizabeth* on the ducal palace in Brussels in 1462 and painted a *Crucifixion* and a *Virgin and Child* on the panels placed at the head and foot of the Duke's catafalque in 1467.

Coustain was most active under Charles the Bold. In 1468 he and the Duke's other painter, Jean Hennecart, were in Bruges, supervising 166 painters and sculptors in the production of the decorations for the meeting of the Order of the Golden Fleece as well as decorations, mechanical devices, props and sets for *tableaux vivants* for Charles's subsequent wedding to Margaret of York. In 1472, having won a ruling allowing him, as a ducal servant, to practise in Bruges independently of the painters' guild, he and Hennecart painted there a large number of standards and banners for the Duke's current military expeditions. During 1473 he also occupied the now nominal post of Master of the Hesdin Devices. After Charles's death in 1477, Coustain served the new Duchess, Mary, in making the decorations for her entry into Bruges that year, for the meeting of the Fleece in 1479 and the funeral of her infant son in 1481. He spent his last years as the custodian of the ducal residence in Bruges.

No extant work by Coustain is known. It is possible, but unproven, that he painted figures of saints on some of the banners captured by the Swiss at Grandson and Mürten in 1476 (Saint-Gallen, Hist. Mus.; Solothurn, Mus. Altes Zeughaus; Dijon, Mus. B.-A.).

BIBLIOGRAPHY
L. de Laborde: *Preuves*, ii of *Les Ducs de Bourgogne* (Paris, 1849–52)
[W. H. J. Weale]: 'Inventaire des chartes et documents appartenant aux archives de la corporation de St Luc et St Eloi à Bruges', *Beffroi*, i (1863), pp. 204–6
J. Duverger and A. de Groote: 'Werk van Hugo van der Goes en van Antoon van Dijk te Brugge', *Miscellanea J. Gessler*, i (Deurne, 1948), p. 141
A. Chatelet: 'Résurrection de Pierre Coustain', *Bull. Soc. Hist. A. Fr.* (1962), pp. 7–13
F. Deuchler: *Die Burgunderbeute: Inventar der Beutestücke aus den Schlachten von Grandson, Mürten und Nancy, 1476–7* (Berne, 1963), pp. 371–4
Die Burgunderbeute und Werke burgundischer Hofkunst (exh. cat., ed. F. Deuchler and others; Berne, Hist. Mus., 1969), pp. 153–4
A. de Schryver: 'Les Peintres en titre à la cour de Bourgogne: Pierre Coustain et Jean Hennequart', *Dictionnaire des artistes et ouvriers d'art de la France*, i (in preparation)

ANNE HAGOPIAN VAN BUREN

Coustou. French family of sculptors. François Coustou (*d* 1690), a wood-carver and brother-in-law of the sculptor

Antoine Coyzevox, had two sons who became sculptors, (1) Nicolas Coustou and (2) Guillaume Coustou (i), and a daughter, Eléonore, whose son was the sculptor Claude Francin. The brothers moved from their native Lyon to train with Coyzevox in Paris, where they spent the greater part of their careers. They worked on royal projects, notably at the château of Marly, Yvelines, which was the original location of Guillaume Coustou's celebrated Marly *Horses* now in the Louvre, Paris. Of Guillaume's sons, Charles Pierre Coustou (1721–97) was active as an architect, and (3) Guillaume Coustou (ii) became a sculptor, like his uncle and father spending his early career in Rome and returning to work in France but also contributing to the statuary for Sanssouci, Potsdam.

(1) Nicolas Coustou [*l'aîné*] (*b* Lyon, *bapt* 9 Jan 1658; *d* Paris, 1 May 1733). In 1676 he went to Paris to study under his maternal uncle, Antoine Coyzevox. In 1682 he won the Prix de Rome, and from 1683 until 1686 he was at the Académie de France in Rome, where among other works he made a copy with variations (marble; Versailles, Château, Parterre de Latone) of the antique statue of *Commodus as Hercules*. On his return to France he was approved (*agréé*) by the Académie Royale in 1687 and received (*reçu*) as a full member in 1693 on presentation of an allegorical relief representing the *Recovery of Louis XIV from Illness* (marble; Paris, Louvre). He had a very

successful academic career there, being appointed a professor in 1702, rector in 1720 and chancellor in the year of his death. In 1690 he married Suzanne Houasse, daughter of the painter René-Antoine Houasse.

From 1691 Nicolas Coustou was one of the busiest sculptors employed by the Bâtiments du Roi, carving numerous stone reliefs for the interior of the Dôme des Invalides, Paris (1691–9; *in situ*), and for the façade a colossal marble statue of *St Louis* (1701–6; *in situ*), after a model by François Girardon, while for Versailles he produced a large marble statue of *Julius Caesar* (1696–1713; installed Paris, Jard. Tuileries, 1722; now Paris, Louvre). At this time he also worked on private commissions, including the monument to the *Maréchal de Créqui* in the church of the Jacobins, Paris (marble and bronze, in collaboration with Coyzevox, 1695; destr.), and statues of *St Joseph* and *St Augustine* for the Order of the Visitandines at Moulins, Allier (stone, 1696; Moulins, Lycée Banville, chapel). However, most of his energies were devoted to the decoration for Louis XIV of the park at the château of Marly, Yvelines, where from 1697 he was responsible for numerous vases, sphinxes, groups of children and tritons (destr. or dispersed). On a more ambitious scale he also executed for Marly the great group of *The Seine and the Marne* (marble, 1699–1712; now Paris, Jard. Tuileries; see fig.) and the dynamic Baroque groups

Nicolas Coustou: *The Seine and the Marne*, marble, 2.70×2.44×2.20 m, 1699–1712 (Paris, Jardins des Tuileries)

Meleager Slaying a Stag and *Meleager Slaying a Boar* (marble, 1703–6; *in situ*), as well as the seated figures of *Adonis*, the *Nymph with a Quiver* and the *Nymph with a Dove* (all marble, 1708–10; Paris, Louvre). The works for Marly all have the bucolic charm that epitomizes the informal spirit of the park.

In 1709–10 Nicolas contributed minor works to the decoration of the chapel of the château of Versailles, but in his affecting *Pietà*, part of the ensemble of the *Vow of Louis XIII* for the choir of Notre-Dame, Paris (marble, 1712–28; *in situ*), he created one of the masterpieces of French 18th-century religious sculpture. Equally masterful in another vein is his bronze reclining female nude representing the river *Saône*, designed as one of a pair with his brother's *Rhône* to adorn the pedestal of Martin Desjardins's equestrian statue of *Louis XIV* (1714–20; destr.) in the Place Bellecour, Lyon. A decline in quality may be detected in such later works as the large allegorical relief of the *Crossing of the Rhine* (marble, 1715–18; Versailles, Château) and the statue of *Louis XV as Jupiter* (marble, 1726–31; Paris, Louvre). It may be argued, however, that the former was completed by his brother and the latter was designed as a pendant to Guillaume's *Marie Leczinska as Juno*. Nonetheless, the statue of the *Maréchal de Villars* in Roman military costume (marble, 1719–33; Aix-en-Provence, Hôtel de Ville), which was also finished by his brother, exemplifies the magisterial quality of his work.

Nicolas Coustou was the most gifted exponent of the developing ROCOCO style in sculpture, creating works in which animated grace predominates but never at the expense of structure and harmony. He was aided in his achievement by his remarkable facility in the working of marble. Through such pupils as Claude Lamoureux (*fl* 1686–99), who worked in Denmark, Jacques Bousseau, who was active at the Spanish court, and Louis-François Roubiliac, who worked in England, he exerted considerable influence on the evolution of European sculpture.

(2) Guillaume Coustou (i) [*le jeune*] (*b* Lyon, 29 Nov 1677; *d* Paris, 22 Feb 1746). Brother of (1) Nicolas Coustou. He trained with his brother and their maternal uncle Antoine Coyzevox in Paris. In 1697 he won the Prix de Rome, but he was not awarded a place at the Académie de France in Rome. Instead he went to Italy at his own expense and worked in Rome for Pierre Legros (ii), by whose lively Baroque style he was influenced. Around 1700 he returned to France to assist Coyzevox with the execution of his two monumental equestrian statues of *Fame* and *Mercury*, intended for the ornamental horse pond in the park at the château of Marly, Yvelines (marble, 1701–2; Paris, Louvre). In 1704 he was received (*reçu*) as a member of the Académie Royale, presenting a statuette of *Hercules on the Funeral Pyre* (marble; Paris, Louvre), a work that reveals his virtuosity as a marble-carver and his predisposition for dynamic composition. He had a successful career within the Académie: in 1706 he was appointed assistant professor, in 1715 professor, in 1726 assistant rector and in 1733 rector.

Like both his uncle and his brother, Guillaume worked mainly for the crown, receiving numerous commissions from the Bâtiments du Roi. His first important work was the decorative bronze sculpture executed in collaboration with Corneille van Clève for the baldacchino of the high altar of the Dôme des Invalides, Paris (1702; destr. 1790s). From 1707 he made important contributions to the sculptural decoration of the chapel of the château of Versailles, including lead and stone statues for the exterior and stone bas-reliefs for the interior. With van Clève he appears to have been responsible for the introduction in the sphere of religious sculpture of the new, elegant and animated sculptural style that was to supersede the classicism prevailing at Versailles. For the more light-hearted context of the park at Marly, he carved running statues of *Hippomenes* and *Daphne* (marble, 1711–14; Paris, Louvre) as companions to the statue of *Atalanta* by Pierre Le Pautre and that of *Apollo* by Nicolas Coustou. With Coyzevox and Nicolas, he worked on the last great official project of Louis XIV's reign, carving the magnificent kneeling statue of *Louis XIII* (1712–15) for the ensemble of the *Vow of Louis XIII* in the choir of Notre-Dame, Paris. He collaborated again with his brother when he modelled the powerful reclining river god representing the *Rhône*, while Nicolas worked on *Saône*, for the pedestal of Desjardins's equestrian statue of *Louis XIV* (bronze, 1714–20; destr.) in the Place Bellecour, Lyon.

Guillaume Coustou continued to be in demand in the years after Louis XIV's death, when he executed a number of important private commissions, including funerary monuments such as those to *Maréchal d'Estrées and his Wife* (marble, *c*. 1720; Versailles, Château) and *Cardinal Dubois* (marble, 1725; fragment, Paris, St Roch). He carved the decorations for the bridges at Blois, Loir-et-Cher (1724; *in situ*), Juvisy-sur-Orge, Essonne (1728; dismantled 1972), and Compiègne, Oise (1730; destr. World War I). He also decorated the façade of the Palais-Bourbon (*c*. 1724–30; destr.) and produced portrait busts,

Guillaume Coustou (i): one of the Marly *Horses*, 1739–45 (shown in the Place de la Concorde, Paris; now Paris, Musée du Louvre)

such as those of the *Marquis d'Argenson* (marble, *c.* 1721; Versailles, Château) and *Samuel Bernard* (marble, 1727; New York, Met.), as well as religious sculpture, including a statue of *St Francis Xavier* (marble, 1722; Paris, St Germain-des-Prés). In 1725 the Duc d'Antin, Surintendant des Bâtiments du Roi, commissioned the elegant and light-hearted statue of *Marie Leczinska as Juno* (marble, 1726–31; Paris, Louvre) as a pendant to Nicolas Coustou's *Louis XV as Jupiter*. Guillaume's ornamental carving for the façade of the Hôtel des Invalides, Paris—for example his two monumental groups of *Mars* and *Minerva* (1733–4)—have all the grandeur and authority of the art of Louis XIV's reign. By the 1730s he was the most prominent sculptor in royal employment, and this status was acknowledged when he was given the commission for what have become his most famous works, two magnificent monumental horses restrained by grooms, intended to replace the less energetic horses by Coyzevox at the horse pond at Marly. The Marly *Horses* (marble, 1739–45; ex-Place de la Concorde, Paris; now Paris, Louvre; see fig.) are among the sculptural masterpieces of the 18th century and have been widely reproduced, in a variety of materials. Among Guillaume's pupils were his son (3) Guillaume (ii), his nephew Claude Francin and Edme Bouchardon.

(3) Guillaume Coustou (ii) (*b* Paris, 19 March 1716; *d* Paris, 13 July 1777). Son of (2) Guillaume Coustou (i). Having studied with his father, he won the Prix de Rome in 1735 and was at the Académie de France in Rome in 1736–40. In 1742 he was received (*reçu*) as a member of the Académie Royale, presenting a seated statue of *Vulcan* (marble; Paris, Louvre), and he went on to pursue a successful official career. His eclectic style mirrored the evolution of French sculpture in the mid-18th century, ranging from the Baroque of the *Apotheosis of St Francis Xavier* (marble, *c.* 1743; Bordeaux, St Paul) to the cold classicism of his statue of *Apollo* commissioned by Mme de Pompadour for the park at the château of Bellevue, Hautes-de-Seine (marble, 1753; Versailles, Château). He worked fluently but without great originality in various sculptural forms, producing portrait busts and religious and mythological works. Among his most important sculptures are the statues of *Mars* and *Venus*, commissioned by Frederick II of Prussia (marble, 1769; Potsdam, Schloss Sanssouci); the pedimental reliefs executed in conjunction with Michel-Ange Slodtz for Ange-Jacques Gabriel's buildings (from 1753) on the Place de la Concorde (originally Place Louis XV), Paris; and the monument in Sens Cathedral to the Dauphin (son of Louis XV), *Louis de Bourbon and his Wife* (marble and bronze, 1766–77). Although its allegorical programme, devised by Charles-Nicolas Cochin II, has been criticized as overcomplex, this free-standing tomb, an early masterpiece of sentimental Neo-classicism, is one of the most important pieces of funerary sculpture of the 18th century in France.

BIBLIOGRAPHY

Mariette; Lami; Souchal; Thieme-Becker
C. de Contamine: *Eloge historique de M. Coustou l'aîné* (Paris, 1737)
A.-N. Dézallier d'Argenville: *Vies des fameux architectes et sculpteurs* (1788), p. 276
L. Gougenot: *Vie de Coustou le jeune* (Paris, 1903)
M. Audin and E. Vial: *Dictionnaire des artistes lyonnais* (Paris, 1918)
F. Souchal: *Les Frères Coustou* (Paris, 1980)

——: 'Guillaume II Coustou (1716–1777): Notes biographiques sur un sculpteur de Louis XV', *Thèmes et figures du siècle des lumières*, ed. R. Trousson (Geneva, 1980), pp. 259–70
——: 'L'Apothéose de Saint François Xavier de Guillaume II Coustou', *Gaz. B.-A.*, n. s. 6, cxi (1988), pp. 43–8

FRANÇOIS SOUCHAL

Coutan, Jules-Félix (*b* Paris, 22 Sept 1848; *d* Paris, 23 Feb 1939). French sculptor and designer. He was a pupil of Pierre-Jules Cavelier at the Ecole des Beaux-Arts, Paris, and in 1872 won the Prix de Rome for his statue *Ajax Struck down while Defying the Gods*, spending the years 1872–6 at the Académie de France in Rome. In 1876 he sent his first submission to the Paris Salon, and from 1880 he was involved in many projects for the sculptural decoration of public buildings in Paris, including the Palais de Justice, the Hôtel de Ville (herald in 14th-century dress, bronze, 1885), the Bibliothèque Nationale (*Calligraphy*, marble, 1893) and the Opéra-Comique (caryatids, 1899). His bronze relief of *Eagle Hunters* for the Muséum National d'Histoire Naturelle, Paris (plaster version, 1900; Paris, Mus. d'Orsay), is an example of the *fin-de-siècle* neo-Baroque style.

Coutan executed a pediment at Grand Central Station, New York (1907–13), and the monument to *Carlos Pellegrini* in Buenos Aires (1914; Avenue Libertator). He was also interested in the applied arts and occasionally collaborated with the jewellers and founders Christofle. From *c.* 1893 he was Director of Design at the Sèvres porcelain manufactory, producing for the Exposition Universelle of 1900 in Paris the monumental portico for the Sèvres Pavillon de la Manufacture Nationale.

BIBLIOGRAPHY

Sculptures des XIXe et XXe siècles (exh. cat., ed. B. Chavanne and B. Gaudichon; Poitiers, Mus. Ste Croix, 1983)
La Sculpture française au XIXe siècle (exh. cat., ed. A. Pingeot; Paris, Grand Pal., 1986)

LAURE DE MARGERIE

Coutan, Louis-Joseph-Auguste (*b c.* 1772; *d* Paris, *bur* 24 Feb 1830). French merchant, collector and amateur painter. He was a wholesale fabric dealer who made his fortune in Paris during the Bourbon Restoration. He invested it in a collection of paintings and drawings containing works by virtually all the contemporary French artists, from Jacques-Louis David to Paul Delaroche; its highly personal nature reflected his broad and avant-garde artistic taste. Coutan took particular pride in assembling a representative selection of works of the modern school. Prominent in the collection were studies for important works in the form of drawings and oil sketches; to Coutan these mattered as much as highly finished paintings. He was a friend of many of the artists whose works he collected, especially Antoine-Jean Gros, Nicolas-Toussaint Charlet and Théodore Gericault, and preferred to make purchases directly from the artists, rather than from sales of other collections. Opinions differ as to the extent of Coutan's activities as a painter. It is possible that he studied painting with Ary Scheffer; the Bibliothèque Doucet in Paris classified him as a history painter, and in the introduction to the catalogue of the sale of his collection in 1830 he is said to have devoted the last ten years of his life to painting, but no history paintings by him are known, and he seems to have been merely an assiduous amateur.

A part of Coutan's collection, comprising 85 paintings and 21 drawings was sold in 1829 (Paris, Henry, 9–10 March). After Coutan's death, a second sale in 1830 disposed of 97 paintings and 240 drawings (Paris, Schroth, 19 April). In each sale the emphasis was on anecdotal history, genre and figure studies, as well as landscapes, and more traditional history paintings that reflected contemporary taste. Among the paintings that fetched the highest prices at the posthumous sale were three in the Troubadour style: Ingres's *Henry IV Playing with his Children* (1828; untraced); a painting of the same subject by Richard Parkes Bonington; and François-Marius Granet's *The Painter Sodoma Carried to the Hospital* (Paris, Louvre). Jacques-Louis David's *Belisarius Receiving Alms* (oil sketch, sold London, Christie's, 15 April 1992) and Paulin Guérin's *Marcus Sextus* represent Coutan's more traditional interests.

A sizeable portion of Coutan's collection was left to his wife and by her to her brother, Ferdinand Hauguet (who in the early 1830s managed Ingres's studio in Paris). In due course it passed to Hauguet's son, to the son's wife, née Marie-Thérèse Schubert, and finally to her sister, Mme Milliet. In 1883 the collection was offered to the Louvre, Paris, which selected ten paintings: Pierre-Paul Prud'hon's *Christ on the Cross with the Virgin and Mary Magdalene*, an oil sketch for Prud'hon's painting (Paris, Louvre) of the same subject and the *Marriage of Hebe and Hercules*; Gros's *Bonaparte on the Pont d'Arcole*; Ingres's *Pius VII in the Sistine Chapel*; four horse subjects by Gericault; and *Anne of Austria and Mazarin* and a *View of Venice* by Bonington. The drawings that the Louvre accepted from the Coutan collection included 12 finely finished wash drawings by Ingres, and the selection as a whole is known as the Collection Coutan, donation Hauguet-Schubert-Milliet. The works not accepted by the Louvre were sold in 1898 (Paris, Haro, 16–17 Dec).

BIBLIOGRAPHY
Notice of death, *J. Artistes & Amateurs* (28 Feb 1830), p. 176
H. de Chennevières: 'Les Donations et les acquisitions du Louvre depuis 1880', *Gaz. B.-A.*, n.s. 1, xxviii (1883), pp. 346, 355–60
F. Lugt: *Marques* (1921), p. 84
——: *Ventes* (1938–64), nos 11957, 12321, 48644
H. Naef: *Die Bildniszeichnungen des J.-A.-D. Ingres* (Berne and Berlin, 1977), iii, pp. 413–6; v, pp. 312–3
Richard Parkes Bonington: 'On the Pleasure of Painting' (exh. cat. by P. Noon, New Haven, Yale Cent. Brit. A.; Paris, Petit Pal.; 1991–2), pp. 41–3

PATRICIA CONDON

Coutances Cathedral. Cathedral dedicated to Notre-Dame in Manche, Normandy, France. The see of Coutances is first mentioned in 511, but in 836 Viking invasions forced the bishop to abandon his cathedral, and the see was not re-established until 1024. A new cathedral was begun by Bishop Geoffrey de Mountbray after his election in 1048, with financial help from Robert Guiscard, Duca d'Apulia, Calabria and Sicily. It was consecrated in 1056, though it is possible that work continued after this date. The earliest work in the present building dates from this campaign, all trace of previous cathedral churches on the site having disappeared.

The *Livre noir* of Coutances, containing a chronicle of the cathedral from 836 to 1093, reveals that there was a lantern tower over the crossing of the Romanesque building, though the arrangement of the east end is unclear. Substantial remains of the western parts of the Romanesque cathedral survive, with the west towers almost intact within their taller Gothic casings; they are square at the base and octagonal at the top, like the west towers of Jumièges Abbey. The Gothic nave seems to have been built on a Romanesque skeleton: the exterior and interior walls of the gallery are essentially 11th century, so that more 11th-century work must be encased in the arcade and aisle walls below. The unvaulted gallery of the Romanesque cathedral was lit by windows beneath arches of alternate dark and light stone reminiscent of the 11th-century work at the Le Mans Cathedral. It seems likely that some sections of the present clerestory are also Romanesque (though this view has recently been challenged) and that Coutances should be considered one of the earliest Norman buildings with a clerestory passage extended beyond the transept. All the Romanesque work is in the local granite.

About 1180 there was an attempt to redesign the west bay of the nave, apparent in the richly foliated early crocket capitals on the piers that support the west towers and in the simple vault rib profile of the tower bay. Shortly thereafter the entire nave was refashioned: the resemblance of foliage on capitals and the triforium tympana to that in the nave of Bayeux Cathedral (1180s) and the introduction of moulding types from the choir of St Etienne, Caen (1180s), suggest that the campaign began before 1200. The Gothic nave is 21.4 m high to the vaults and has a three-storey elevation: an arcade of cruciform composite piers, an unvaulted gallery with an imposing gallery arcade and a clerestory with a passage running in front of simple lancet windows. The quadripartite vault is supported by solid shaft groups that divide the interior firmly into bays, and most rib or arch mouldings are composed of triple rolls. This type of design is derived from Early Gothic buildings in Upper Normandy, notably La Trinité, Fécamp (begun 1168), and St Laurent, Eu (begun 1186).

The next major phase in construction comprised the choir, the transepts and the crossing tower, with another remodelling of the west end. The latter can probably be dated, since sculptors from the cloister at Le Mont-Saint-Michel worked on the side porches, presumably shortly after the cloister was finished in 1228. Cumulative evidence suggests that the Gothic choir was begun *c.* 1220 and finished when Bishop Hugh de Morville was buried in it in 1238.

The east end of Coutances is 21.4 m high, built of limestone from near Valognes. Although not large, it appears spacious and luminous. Its expansive plan has double ambulatories and shallow radiating chapels. The double elevations are stepped in section. The main elevation has two storeys: a tall arcade with composite piers in the straight bays and double columns in the apse and a clerestory with a passage screened by an arcade and balustrade (see fig.). The elevation of the inner aisle has three storeys: a columnar arcade, arcaded blank wall and

Coutances Cathedral, choir and inner south choir aisle, *c.* 1220–38

a clerestory with wall passage. Both elevations are thick-walled, and a false passage of a type derived from Laon Cathedral runs behind detached shafts in front of the ambulatory windows. Vault patterns are relatively complex, with quinquepartite vaults in the ambulatory and, most unusually, a ridge rib linking the bosses of the high vault. Many windows, including those in both clerestories and in the south transept chapel, are of plate tracery with twin lancets beneath a down-turned trefoil. The exterior is distinguished by slender flying buttresses, by stair-towers marking the junction of apse and straight bays and by the single sweep of roof catching the cornice of the undulating ambulatory chapels. A magnificent lantern tower, an octagon surrounded by octagonal stair-turrets, crowns the east end, which is solidly built to support its massive weight. The lantern is 57.45 m high to the vaults.

The sources of the choir design are twofold. The architect must have trained at the late 12th-century choir of St Etienne at Caen, the seminal work in the development of the mature Norman Gothic style. This is apparent in many features, including the continuous cornice above the undulating chapels and the ribs springing from small corbels attached to capitals. Important aspects of the design, such as the double ambulatories of stepped elevation, belong to a tradition deriving from Bourges Cathedral, specifically from the choir of Le Mans Cathedral (1217–54). Details such as the nibbed bosses at Coutances, a feature otherwise unknown in Normandy, suggest that the architect of Coutances had first-hand knowledge of Le Mans. However, he could only have seen drawings of the proposed designs of Le Mans, since Coutances was finished before the main two-storey elevation of Le Mans

was begun. Subsequent alterations to the Cathedral included the building of a series of elegant interconnecting nave aisle chapels *c.* 1300 and the expansion of the axial chapel of the choir in the 14th century. The Cathedral, which is *c.* 80 m long, was restored after World War II by Y. Froidevaux.

BIBLIOGRAPHY

Toustain de Billy: *Histoire ecclésiastique du diocèse de Coutances* (1706); ed. F. Dolbet, 3 vols (Rouen, 1874–86)
E. A. Pigeon: *Histoire de la cathédrale de Coutances* (Coutances, 1876)
E. Lefèvre-Pontalis: 'Coutances: Cathédrale', *Congr. Archéol. France*, lxxv (1908), pp. 247–77
P. Colmet-Daage: *La Cathédrale de Coutances* (Paris, 1933)
A. Mussat: 'La Cathédrale Notre-Dame de Coutances', *Congr. Archéol. France*, ccxxiv (1966), pp. 9–50
J. Herschman: 'The Norman Ambulatory of Le Mans Cathedral and the Chevet of the Cathedral of Coutances', *Gesta*, xx (1981), pp. 323–32
L. Grant: *Gothic Architecture in Normandy, 1150–1250* (diss., U. London, 1986)

LINDY GRANT

Couto, António (*b* Barcarena, Oeiras, 8 April 1874; *d* Lisbon, 3 July 1946). Portuguese architect. He trained at the Escola de Belas Artes in Lisbon and began his career in 1899, working for the royal court under the direction of Ventura Terra. This was an important stage in Couto's training and, like other Portuguese architects of his generation, he became strictly academic in outlook and out of touch with international developments. In 1910 Couto joined the Ministry of Public Works, where he continued the restoration of Lisbon Cathedral begun by A. Fuschini. He also became a skilful designer of single-family houses; an example is 77 Avenida Duque de Loulé, Lisbon, which won the Valmor Prize in 1907 and is notable for its decorative composition, derived from 16th-century French models. He also won a prize for his Portuguese Pavilion at the Panama Pacific International Exposition held in San Francisco in 1915, which was in a neo-Manueline style appropriate in its conservatism to the new republican regime. In the same year, in collaboration with the architect Adães Bermudes and the sculptor Francisco Franco (*b* 1885), he won first prize in the competition for a monument to the *Marquês de Pombal*, Praça do Marquês de Pombal, Lisbon, installed in a symbolic position in the city. This was another eclectic design in the triumphant spirit of French Second Empire sculpture, which guaranteed the required ideological effect. This project concluded the most important period of Couto's work. In the 1920s and 1930s he was unable or unwilling to move on to the Modernist aesthetic when it finally reached Lisbon. In 1940, still faithful to academicism, he executed in collaboration with the sculptor Simões Almeida Sobrinho (1880–1950) an equestrian monument to *Mouzinho de Albuquerque* for the city of Lourenço Marques (now Maputo, Mozambique), attempting to prolong within the Portuguese empire a conventional image of heroism that had become outmoded in Europe.

BIBLIOGRAPHY

J.-A. França: *A arte em Portugal no século XIX*, ii (Lisbon, 1966)

RAQUEL HENRIQUES DA SILVA

Couto dos Santos Leal, José do (*b* Lisbon, *c.* 1750; *d* Coimbra, 5 Sept 1829). Portuguese architect. He was trained in Lisbon during the period of large-scale rebuilding that followed the 1755 earthquake. About 1780 he went to Coimbra, where he saw William Elsden's Neo-classical university buildings and where he became involved with and accepted this new style and aesthetic. He was mainly active in Coimbra, where for about 20 years (1780–1800) he was architect and in charge of works (*mestre de obras*) at the monastery of Santa Cruz. The great triumphal arch (*c.* 1800) in late Baroque style in front of the entrance of the church of Santa Cruz and the remodelling of part of the old monastery cellars can be attributed to him. In Coimbra in the first quarter of the 19th century he also made plans and studies for completing the Jardim Botânico, begun by Elsden in 1773; here he was responsible for the design of the main entrance gate (built 1843). He drew up the plans for the Colégio dos Militares (plans early 19th century; destr.) and for the University Gaols (plan 1819; destr.) and City Gaols (plans early 19th century, never built) in Coimbra, as well as for the elevation of the palace and estate (*quinta*) of the Inquisition.

During the first quarter of the 19th century Couto dos Santos Leal also worked in the central and northern regions of Portugal, including at the church of Midões and at Nogueira do Cravo, Coimbra, on the extensive rebuilding (*c.* 1805–20), incorporating earlier parts, such as the principal and side portals. He also worked at the palace of Francisco de Paula Vieira da Silva Tovar, Folhadosa, where he rebuilt the palace and façade in a provincial Neoclassical style. Leal was active during a period of great building work and renovation, and among his numerous other projects were those for the chapel of the palace of Pais do Amaral, Mangualde, also in a provincial Neoclassical style, for the monastery hospices at the Serra do Pilar, Oporto, and his work at the monastery of Refoios de Lima, Minho.

BIBLIOGRAPHY
P. Dias: *Coimbra: Arte e história* (Coimbra, 1983), pp. 46, 125, 169
LURDES CRAVEIRO

Coutouzis, Nikolaos. *See* KOUTOUZIS, NIKOLAOS.

Couture, Guillaume-Martin (*b* Rouen, 1732; *d* Paris, 29 Dec 1799). French architect. He studied under Jacques-François Blondel at the Académie Royale d'Architecture, Paris, and then entered the practice of Antoine-Mathieu Le Carpentier, where he worked on the latter's scheme for a new town hall (1758) in Rouen. He travelled to Italy but returned to Paris in 1760. He built an extension to La Bouexière's house in Montmartre, town houses for La Guiche (at 15, Rue du Regard), de Saxe (*c.* 1770; destr.) and de Coislin, the house for Le Normant d'Etoiles in the Rue du Sentier and the Bellevue Pavilion at Sèvres. He rebuilt (1776) the part of the hall in the Palais de Justice that had been destroyed by fire. On the death of Pierre Contant d'Ivry, under whom he had directed works, Couture was selected by the Conseil on 31 December 1777 to take up the building of the church of La Madeleine. He modified the plans, opting for a Greek cross with a dome, rather than Contant's Latin cross. He removed the pinnacles, added two bays and proposed adding a section that projected the whole width of the façade and was decorated with an eight-columned peristyle. The work was abandoned in 1790 and was completed after 1807 to plans by Alexandre-Pierre Vignon. Couture travelled around Italy in 1790 and assembled a collection of mouldings of capitals and ornaments. He also prepared plans for the town halls in Caen and Rouen.

PRINTS
Recueil de vases (Paris, n.d.) [set of 6 engraved designs]
BIBLIOGRAPHY
J. Soreau: Obituary, *Mag. Enc.* (1800), pp. 505–11
H. Ottomeyer: 'Autobiographies d'architectes parisiens, 1759–1811', *Bull. Soc. Hist. Paris & Ile-de-France*, 98 (1971), pp. 164–6
M. N. BAUDOUIN-MATUSZEK

Couture, Thomas (*b* Senlis, 21 Dec 1815; *d* Villiers-le-Bel, 3 March 1879). French painter and teacher. A student of Antoine-Jean Gros in 1830–38 and Paul Delaroche in 1838–9, he demonstrated precocious ability in drawing and was expected to win the Prix de Rome. He tried at least six times between 1834 and 1839, but achieved only second prize in 1837 (entry untraced). Disgusted with the politics of the academic system, Couture withdrew and took an independent path. He later attacked the stultified curriculum of the Ecole des Beaux-Arts and discouraged his own students from entering this institution. He first attained public notoriety at the Paris Salon with *Young Venetians after an Orgy* (1840; Montrouge, priv. col., see Boime, p. 85), the *Prodigal Son* (1841; Le Havre, Mus. B.-A.) and the *Love of Gold* (1844; Toulouse, Mus. Augustins). These early canvases are treated in a moralizing and anecdotal mode; the forms and compositional structures, like the debauched and corrupt protagonists, are sluggish and dull. Yet what made his work seem fresh to the Salon audience was his use of bright colour and surface texture derived from such painters as Alexandre-Gabriel Decamps and Eugène Delacroix, while his literary bent and methodical drawing demonstrated his mastery of academic tradition. The critics Théophile Gautier and Paul Mantz (1821–95) proclaimed him as the leader of a new school that mediated between the old and the new, and looked to him for a revitalization of Salon painting. The air of compromise his works projected made him appear a cultural representative of the *juste milieu* policies of Louis-Philippe.

However Couture was far from happy in this role. Longing to make a statement worthy of the grand tradition of David and Gros, he started to work in the mid-1840s on the monumental *Romans of the Decadence* (completed 1847; Paris, Mus. d'Orsay). It was the triumph of the Salon of 1847 and destined to become his best-known picture. An extension of the moralizing themes of his first Salon exhibits, it represents the waning moments of an all-night orgy in the vestibule of a vast Corinthian hall. The exhausted and drunken revellers are contrasted with the solemn tutelary statues of the great Roman republicans in the niches around the hall; the heroes' descendants have fallen into venality and corruption. The work was interpreted as a satire on the July Monarchy (1840–48) and a wide range of government critics—aristocratic, radical and bourgeois—perceived it as a forecast of the regime's impending doom. The picture also had its admirers in government circles: François Guizot, the king's chief minister, was instrumental in its purchase by the state.

The collapse of the July Monarchy in 1848 seemed to confirm a prophetic interpretation of the picture, and

Thomas Couture: *Enrolment of the Volunteers of 1792*, oil on canvas, 4.80×9.75 m, begun 1847 (Beauvais, Musée Départemental de l'Oise)

Couture was encouraged to produce a new monumental painting celebrating the Revolution for the Salle des Séances in the Assemblée Nationale. He had already begun his *Enrolment of the Volunteers of 1792* (incomplete; Beauvais, Mus. Dépt. Oise; see fig.) near the end of 1847, inspired by a series of lectures given by Jules Michelet at the Collège de France, which aimed to regenerate French society through the invigorating impulses of its youth. Michelet invoked 1789 as an exemplary model, and similarly in the *Enrolment* Couture depicted all classes in society forging a new national unity in the face of external threat. The exhilaration of the picture, its energetic sweep and movement, contrasts sharply with the *Romans* and attests to the sense of revitalization sparked by the 1848 revolution. But the work was never completed: with the counter-revolution in June 1848 and the installation of Louis-Napoléon as emperor the political climate altered so drastically that the *Enrolment* lost its raison d'être. The canvas has some figures almost complete but mainly only underdrawing.

Couture managed to maintain close ties with the various governments of Napoleon III. He received a number of major commissions, but completed only the wall paintings in the chapel of the Virgin, St Eustache, Paris. His *Baptism of the Prince Imperial* (Compiègne, Château), celebrating the dynastic heir of the Second Empire, was commissioned in 1856 with the *Return of the Troops from the Crimea* (Le Havre, Mus. B.-A.) but remained unfinished. A combination of jealous intrigues and his own unstable temperament led to a falling out with the imperial family, and by the end of the 1850s he had nothing to show for his labours except innumerable sketches (e.g. Senlis, Mus. A. & Archéol.).

Couture returned to Senlis in 1859 and devoted the rest of his life to satisfying the tastes of private patrons, many of them Americans. He embarked on a series of pictures based on the characters of the *commedia dell'arte*. His satirical *Realist* (1865; Cork, Crawford Mun. A.G.) shows a bohemian art student seated on the head of the Olympian Jupiter painting the head of a pig. His misanthropic disposition is revealed in his *Courtesan's Chariot or Love Leading the World* (several versions, 1870s; e.g. Philadelphia, PA, Mus. A.), which shows a bare-breasted female pulled in a carriage by four men representing Youth, Riches, Courage and Poetry. The courtesan drives them with a whip, transforming them into beasts of burden. He was a particularly fine portrait painter, as can be seen in the *Young Italian Girl* (1877; Senlis, Mus. A. & Archéol.).

Couture's posthumous reputation rests mainly on his pedagogic skills. In 1847 he announced that he was opening an atelier in Paris independent of both classical and Romantic schools. He soon became a popular teacher. His distrust of academic education and honours, his innovative technical procedures and obsession with the pure colour and fresh brushwork of the sketch, which he encouraged his students to retain into the finished picture, exercised a profound influence. Among his pupils were Edouard Manet, Pierre Puvis de Chavannes, Anselm Feuerbach and many American artists—who preferred his teaching to the more rigid discipline of the Ecole and the Düsseldorf school—notably John La Farge, William Morris Hunt and Eastman Johnson.

Many of Couture's paintings and drawings were destroyed in 1870 during the Franco-Prussian War. The Musée d'Art et Archéologie, Senlis, has a collection of his portraits and oil sketches.

WRITINGS
Méthodes et entretiens d'atelier (Paris, 1867)
Entretiens d'atelier: Paysage (Paris, 1869)

BIBLIOGRAPHY
Catalogue des oeuvres de Thomas Couture (exh. cat. by R. Ballu, Paris, Pal. Indust., 1880)

G. Bertauts-Couture: *Thomas Couture (1815–1879): Sa vie, son oeuvre, son caractère, ses idées, sa méthode, par lui-même et par son petit-fils* (Paris, 1932)

American Pupils of Thomas Couture (exh. cat. by M. E. Landgren, College Park, U. MD A.G., 1970)

Thomas Couture, 1815–79 (exh. cat. by M. J. Salmon, Beauvais, Mus. Dépt Oise, 1972)

P. Vaisse: 'Couture et le Second Empire', *Rev. A.* [Paris], xxxvii (1977), pp. 43–68

——: 'Thomas Couture ou le bourgeois malgré lui', *Romanticisme*, xvii–xviii (1977), pp. 103–22

A. Boime: *Thomas Couture and the Eclectic Vision* (New York, 1979)

ALBERT BOIME

Couturier, Robert (*b* Angoulême, Charente, 2 May 1905). French sculptor. In 1918 he went to the Ecole Estienne in Paris to learn lithography, but the death of his father in 1922 forced him to interrupt his studies and earn a living. He began to sculpt in 1924 when he was working as a model for the French sculptor Armand Bloch (1866–1932). In 1928 he competed unsuccessfully for the Blumenthal prize, although he won it two years later. Through the competition in 1928 he met Aristide Maillol, who was a member of the jury and who was to have a great influence on Couturier's early work. Over the next few years Couturier participated in various group exhibitions, including the Salon des Tuileries, Salon du Temps Présent and the Salon de la Jeune Génération. In 1936 he was commissioned to produce *The Gardener* for the esplanade of the Palais de Chaillot in Paris. The following year he made 200 plaster figures and 500 m of bas-relief work (destr.) for the Pavillon de l'Elégance at the Exposition Internationale des Arts et Techniques dans la Vie Moderne in Paris. He was also commissioned to design a bas-relief for the Palais Ariana in Geneva in 1938. He claimed that he finally broke from the influence of Maillol with his sculpture *Leda* (1944; Pau, Jacques de Laprade priv. col., see Jianou, pl. 4).

In 1945 Couturier was appointed professor of sculpture at the Ecole des Arts Décoratifs in Paris and in the same year he co-founded the Salon de Mai. Through the 1940s and 1950s he began to develop his more characteristic, open style of sculpture as shown in *Girl Skipping* (1950; Antwerp, Openluchtmus. Beeldhouwkst Middelheim). Some of his works such as *Woman Drying her Leg* (1952; Paris, Pompidou) clearly display the impoverished materials from which they were made. In 1960 he created stone reliefs entitled *The Arts* for the French Embassy in Tokyo.

BIBLIOGRAPHY

I. Jianou: *Couturier* (Paris, 1969)

Robert Couturier (exh. cat. by G. Diehl, Paris, Mus. Rodin, 1970)

Couvay, Jean (*b* Arles, *c.* 1622; *d* Paris, *c.* 1675–80). French engraver. He travelled to Italy and was a friend of the print-publisher François Langlois de Chartres and the painter Claude Vignon. Basically a reproductive engraver, his line engraving showed strength and precision. Although he reproduced the works of some Italian artists, such as Annibale Carracci (the *Virgin Suckling the Child*, see Weigert, no. 5), Guercino and Guido Reni (*St Jerome*, w 28), he chiefly made prints after French masters, in particular Vignon, Simon Vouet and Grégoire Huret.

About 150 prints by him are known, including *St Peter* after Vignon [w 36] and a *Virgin* after Vouet [w 16].

BIBLIOGRAPHY

R.-A. Weigert: *Inventaire du fonds français: Graveurs du dix-septième siècle*, Paris, Bib. N., Cab. Est. cat., iii (Paris, 1954), pp. 199–219 [w]

MAXIME PRÉAUD

Couven, Johann Joseph (*b* Aachen, 10 Nov 1701; *d* Aachen, 12 Sept 1763). German architect. He may originally have studied engineering and was also well versed in the literature relating to Classical architecture, being influenced by Johann Conrad Schlaun, with his knowledge of Italian and south German architecture, and later by Jacques-François Blondel, especially the latter's designs for Rococo gardens. Couven's first public commission (1724; Aachen, Mus. Burg Frankenberg) was to draw up a plan of the city of Aachen. From 1727 to 1731 he worked on alterations to the façade of the Rathaus in Aachen, becoming Aachen's first city architect in 1739. He carried out several commissions for merchant and patrician houses in Aachen and Eupen. Examples of his work as a church architect include the abbey church of St John (1735–54) in Burtscheid, the parish church of St Michael (1747–51), Burtscheid, the chapel of the Nispert family in Eupen and the Annakirche in Aachen (both 1748). Couven also built such castles as Schloss Jägerhof (1752–63) in Düsseldorf, Gut Kalkofen (1750–53), near Aachen, Schloss Maaseyck (1752; destr.) and Schloss Breill (1754; destr.), near Geilenkirchen. Surviving church interiors by Couven include the Lutheran church (1737) in Vaals, St Nicholas (1740) in Eupen and the Theresienkirche (1746–51) in Aachen. Some of his domestic interiors have been transferred to museums (Aachen, Couven-Mus.; Nuremberg, Ger. Nmus.; San Francisco, CA, Mus. A.).

Couven's churches of St John and St Michael in Burtscheid are west German late Baroque buildings with more than regional significance. They are notable for their use of brick and bluestone, for the combining of features from longitudinal and centralized buildings and for the introduction of his Teutonic, or German, order. Couven excelled, however, in designing houses and pavilions, conveying grandeur to smaller-scale, bourgeois dimensions, typically articulated vertically into three or five bays with a sharp contrast between the brick walls and the bluestone decorative work. Carved oak wainscoting with elegant Rococo ornamentation in conjunction with tapestries are indicative of his search for architectural unity even in small spaces. After his death his work was continued by his son Jakob Couven (1735–1812).

UNPUBLISHED SOURCES

Aachen, Suermondt-Ludwig-Mus. [drgs for buildings in Aachen, Eupen and Düsseldorf]

BIBLIOGRAPHY

P. J. Schoenen: *Johann Joseph Couven* (Düsseldorf, 1964)

K. Köver: *Johann Joseph Couven: Ein Architekt des 18. Jahrhunderts zwischen Rhein und Maas* (exh. cat., Aachen, Suermondt-Ludwig-Mus., 1983)

ULRICH SCHNEIDER

Couvillon, Louis. *See* QUÉVILLON, LOUIS.

Couzijn, Wessel (*b* Amsterdam, 17 June 1912; *d* Amsterdam, 16 May 1984). Dutch sculptor. He took sculpture classes at the Rijksakademie van Beeldende Kunsten,

Amsterdam, and in 1936 won the Prix de Rome with his statue of *Orpheus with the Lyre* (Amsterdam, Rijksakad. Beeld. Kst.). After periods in Rome and Paris he spent World War II in the USA. On his return, towards the end of 1946, he found the Netherlands devastated, and during the years following the war there was a growing demand for monuments and memorials celebrating the liberation. One such memorial commission led to his *Design for a Merchant Marine Monument* of 1951, a plaster cast consisting of four irregular-shaped surfaces piled on top of each other and joined together by three vertical 'masts'. The design was rejected, and the same fate awaited a number of other bronze sculptures for which Couzijn submitted designs. Neither totally abstract nor figurative, these sculptures were eventually thought inappropriate for public monuments. In 1960, however, Couzijn's work dominated the Dutch pavilion at the Venice Biennale and he was commissioned to make *Corporate Entity* (bronze, 14×6×8 m, 1960–63). It is made up of three components. Since 1963 it has dominated the space in front of the Unilever Building in Rotterdam.

In his wax models Couzijn used *objets trouvés*, including pieces of tubing, tree bark and bottle tops, to give the bronze cast a rough surface. In 1966 he used a combination of traditional bronze and everyday objects to macabre effect in *Auschwitz* (The Hague, Rijksdienst Beeld. Kst, on loan to Otterlo, Kröller-Müller), a work made up of anthropomorphic bronze fragments jammed into firescreens. In 1967 Couzijn began to work with stainless steel, although the structure of his works remained basically unchanged. During the 1970s Couzijn began making pencil drawings, using a subtle crosshatching technique. These tended to have mystical overtones, as in *Portrait of an Artist* (pencil and collage, 1980; Otterlo, Kröller-Müller).

BIBLIOGRAPHY

K. E. Schurman: *Wessel Couzijn* (Amsterdam, 1967)

Couzijn: Beelden (exh. cat. by R. W. O. Oxenaar, Amsterdam, Stedel. Mus., 1968)

Couzijn: Beeldhouwer (exh. cat., ed. I. Boelema and A. Overbeek; Otterlo, Kröller-Müller, 1986)

HANS EBBINK

Cova, Jacobus. *See* COENE, JACQUES.

Covarrubias, Alonso de (*b* Torrijos, Toledo, 1488; *d* Toledo, 11 May 1570). Spanish architect and sculptor. Recognized as an innovator by his contemporaries, he was one of the most important members of the first generation of Spanish Renaissance architects, who proved able to develop from the Gothic and plateresque styles prevalent in the first decades of the 16th century to the purest unornamented style ultimately inspired by Sebastiano Serlio. His artistic evolution was not the result of a direct knowledge of Italian art but was acquired from the treatise literature and from the suggestions of other Spanish architects who, unlike him, had travelled to Italy.

1. Early work, before *c.* 1540. 2. Later work, after *c.* 1540.

1. EARLY WORK, BEFORE *c.* 1540. He probably trained in Torrijos with Antón Egas, to whose niece he was married; he was first documented with Egas in Salamanca in 1510. Later, as a master mason, Covarrubias

attended, as did Egas, the Expertise in Salamanca (1512) to plan the new cathedral. He collaborated on the execution of tombs for Toledo Cathedral and for the church of S Andrés, Toledo (1513–14). At Sigüenza Cathedral he worked with others on the retable of St Librada (Wilgefortis) and the sepulchre–retable of Bishop Fadrique of Portugal (1514–18). Between 1517 and 1524 he worked in Toledo under the direction of the Egas brothers at the Hospital de Santa Cruz and the Capilla de la Trinidad (1521) in the cathedral, which may have been his first, modest, architectural design. The Pharmacy Cloister (1525; destr.) in the monastery of Nuestra Señora de Guadalupe, Cáceres, executed in collaboration with Antón Egas and Juan Torollo, was his first important project. The convent church of Nuestra Señora de la Piedad (1526), Guadalajara, built entirely to his design, is of Gothic construction with a stylistically correct Renaissance decoration. He began to employ this genre with increasing confidence, as shown by his contribution to the planning of the columned church at Meco (Madrid; 1527–8), and by his reports and partial designs for the cathedrals of Segovia and Salamanca and the Colegio Fonseca in Salamanca (1529). In the same year he established contact with Diego de Siloé during the competition for the decoration of the Capilla de Reyes Nuevos in Toledo Cathedral; Covarrubias was to work on this project until 1534.

Although such works as the monastery of Nuestra Señora de la Concepción (1530), Guadalajara, SS Justa y Rufina (1530), Toledo, the parish church of Algete (1533), Madrid, and the sanctuary of the collegiate church of S Máximo (1533), Baza (Granada), reflect the traditional training of Covarrubias, others that he executed during the 1530s reveal his incipient skill in incorporating features of Renaissance design. Thus his scheme for the sacristy (1532) of Sigüenza Cathedral features a wall articulation that displays three-quarter columns rising against arch piers to support an entablature, from which springs a barrel vault, its soffit covered with rosettes and decorative heads. At the columned church at Yepes (1534), Toledo, he created a complete Renaissance-style building, introducing scalloped semi-domes and replacing the traditional Gothic piers with clusters of elongated columns of classical appearance. This simplification of the decoration is also evident in his façade for S Clemente el Real (1534), Toledo, and in his remodelling of the staircase by Egas in the Hospital de Santa Cruz, where Covarrubias used ashlar walling with a decorative surface treatment. He employed the same motif in his major work of this period, the Archbishop's Palace in Alcalá de Henares (*c.* 1535–46; destr.), where he was responsible for the façade, a courtyard with an imposing, square turning staircase and the Ave Maria gallery, and where he introduced a method of integrating structure and plateresque decoration in a completely new way. The palace was commissioned by JUAN PARDO DE TAVERA, who was appointed Archbishop of Toledo in 1534 and became one of Covarrubias's principal patrons. Covarrubias's interest in proportion, symmetry and coherence of form is also apparent in his courtyard of the Hieronymite monastery of S Bartolomé at Lupiana (Guadalajara; 1535), where he continued to suppress plateresque decoration.

In 1534 Covarrubias was appointed surveyor to the fabric of Toledo Cathedral, a position he retained until 1566. His work here included the façade of the chapel of S Juan Bautista (1536). The most important of his widely spread, minor projects was the planning, in collaboration with Diego de Siloé, of the upper level of the choir-stalls (from 1537), which was sculpted by Alonso Berruguete and Felipe Bigarny (*c.* 1475–1542).

Covarrubias readily accepted commissions in other cities in spite of his duties at Toledo Cathedral. In 1537, together with Luis de Vega, he was chosen by Charles V, Holy Roman Emperor, to be surveyor to the fabric of the Alcázares (palaces) at Madrid, Toledo and Seville, a post he was to hold until 1569. He had already started work on remodelling the Alcázar of Madrid (1536–52; destr. 1734), where he built the Patio del Rey and equipped it with a new type of double square turning staircase (1536–41), the Patio de la Reina (1540–52), the chapel, the south front and the façade (1541–7). While respecting the *mudéjar* style of some of the rooms, he simplified their traditional décor and began to introduce Renaissance forms derived from Serlio, employing rustication and the superimposition of orders. Nevertheless, in the courtyard he still used a system of brackets supporting a lintel and cornice, as he did at the patio of the Dominican convent at Ocaña (Madrid; *c.* 1540), the Archbishop's Palace in Toledo (1540) and the palace of the Marquis of Villena at Cadalso de los Vidrios (Madrid). His designs from the end of the 1530s show an increasing tendency to shed ornamentation and aim for greater symmetry and formal coherence in the Spanish Renaissance manner.

2. LATER WORK, AFTER *c.* 1540. Covarrubias's designs from the early 1540s unmistakably reveal the decisive influence of Serlio and Vitruvius, for example in the Cloister of the Generals (1541) at the monastery of S Pedro Mártir, Toledo. A particularly fine response to their theories is the Hospital de S Juan Bautista, Toledo (1541–50; see fig. 1), also known as the Tavera Hospital. Here the role of his fellow architect Bartolomé Bustamante was limited in scope: Covarrubias alone was responsible for the layout, which is a synthesis of his experiments in Madrid and the traditions of hospital building as adhered to by his father-in-law, Enrique Egas. The adoption of a double square turning staircase in the passageway separating the two courtyards, as shown on the plan of 1541 (Toledo, Hosp. Tavera), and the articulation of the façades, without orders but with an intricate interrelationship between windows with bossed frames and rusticated wall surfaces, reveal a stylistic continuity going back to the Alcázar of Madrid. They are also evidence of his preoccupation with the formal composition of the wall, full of Serlian features and no longer characterized by the loose composition typical of the plateresque. The twin cloisters, separated by a diaphanous fifth walkway in the form of a gallery rather than by a massive passageway, provide an interplay of space and perspective new in Spain. The cloisters exhibit the first use of groin vaults in Castile, the correct superimposition of orders of columns with arches supporting orthodox entablatures, and a new angle solution that was to prove very influential. Despite some solecisms, the cloisters' classicism, lack of ornamentation

1. Alonso de Covarrubias: Hospital de S Juan Bautista, Toledo, courtyard, 1541–50

and use of rustication marked a radical change in Castilian architecture.

In 1543 Covarrubias began to remodel the medieval Alcázar of Toledo in a Renaissance style. In the façade (1545–52; see fig. 2) he introduced a classic order, albeit only on the two end elevations, as an element in the vertical articulation: royal taste, however, required the inclusion of certain emblematic and decorative features alongside the classic elements, although the grotesque ornamentation of the plateresque is absent. The sobriety of the rectangular courtyard with two storeys of Corinthian cloisters is complete, while the tripartite opening of the entrance hall is another innovation. A sense of strict axial symmetry is promoted by the location of the stairway at the rear of the courtyard, rather than its usual placement near the entrance. In Covarrubias's previous designs this feature had always been placed in a central, visible position as a double square turning staircase for the use of two symmetrical courtyards. In Toledo, while retaining the characteristic, Spanish open stairwell, he opened the staircase on to the courtyard through galleries. Planned in 1550 and begun in 1553, it was the first example of the imperial type of five (E-shaped) flights to be built in Europe, although as early as 1546 he had designed a perfect imperial staircase of three parallel flights (not executed) for the monastery of S Miguel de los Reyes in Valencia. His interest in the symmetrical variations of the open-welled staircase made him the creator of this type, which was later adopted throughout Europe.

In his plan for S Miguel de los Reyes, Covarrubias introduced a personal variant of the Classical orders inside a church. This involved the superimposition of orders for the first time in Spain, rather than the previous solutions of an oversize column pier or a pier with half columns resting against it. He adopted the new arrangement in the Hieronymite church of S Catalina at Talavera de la Reina (Toledo; 1549) and in the church of the Concepción Francisca in La Puebla de Montalbán (*c.* 1553); in neither

2. Alonso de Covarrubias: Alcázar, Toledo, north façade, 1545–52

scheme, however, was he able to give external expression to this solution. In the latter, abandoning his attempt to unify the interior and exterior, he introduced an 'order' of herms as a second order.

During this period Covarrubias confidently used two distinct options within his Renaissance style. To the sobriety of the last two works he again added decoration, but it was now subordinate to the architectural framework. The sanctuary (1552) of the parish church of S Román, with its dome, and the remodelling of both the staircase of S Juan de los Reyes and the chapels of the community house of S María la Blanca (1554), also with various dome shapes, are characteristic examples of this decorated style in Toledo. By contrast, other buildings there are completely austere in form, such as the monastery of S Agustín (1552); the plan for the Plaza de Bisagra (1553), which is absolutely modular, its internal façades treated as one unit; or the U-shaped villa of Diego López de Ayala (1552) nearby at Casasbuenas. This severity extends even to the design of the palace of the Prince of Eboli at Pastrana (Guadalajara; *c.* 1552) and reaches its full development in the Puerta Nueva de Bisagra at Toledo (1559). In the latter, Covarrubias played exclusively with the rustication and the banded pilasters of a gateway framed by two large circular towers and surmounted by a gigantic imperial coat of arms crowned by an orthodox pediment, thereby demonstrating his mastery of huge, bare forms and of the heightened contrast between plane and volume in a perfect assimilation of Serlio's rules.

In 1562 Covarrubias planned the restoration of the sanctuary of the monastery church of S Clemente el Real, Toledo, which he had previously remodelled in 1534, retaining the Gothic rib vaults supported by caryatids. In 1565 he designed the Puerta de la Presentación for Toledo Cathedral, a gateway leading from the cloister to the church. In order to ensure that this harmonized with the existing Gothic areas on either side, he produced for the two façades a simple, classic design that is covered with grotesques, as if he were returning to traditions of his training or wished to incorporate his work into an over-decorated medieval frame. The following year he was retired by the Cathedral chapter with full honours and distinctions. His last work, probably in collaboration with Giovanni Battista Castello, was a design for the lower gallery of the rear elevation of the Alcázar at Toledo (1568); either this soon disappeared or it was never built. In 1569 he also retired from the Royal Works. His death in the following year ended an era in the history of 16th-century Castilian architecture. His Spanish-Renaissance style was replaced, even in Toledo itself, by the new classic forms imported directly from Italy and by the ESTILO DESORNAMENTADO, which was promoted in the court of Philip II and represented by Juan Bautista de Toledo and Juan de Herrera.

BIBLIOGRAPHY
E. Llaguno y Amirola: *Noticias* (1829)
F. Pérez Sedano: *Notas del archivo de la catedral de Toledo*, Datos Documentales Inéditos para la Historia del Arte Español (Madrid, 1914)
M. R. Zarco del Valle: *Documentos de la catedral de Toledo*, 2 vols, Datos Documentales Inéditos para la Historia del Arte Español (Madrid, 1916)
A. Rodríguez y Rodríguez: *El Hospital de San Juan Bautista, extramuros de Toledo* (Toledo, 1921)
V. García Rey: 'El famoso arquitecto Alonso de Covarrubias: Datos inéditos de su vida y obras', *La Arquitectura*, ix (1927), pp. 167–75, 207–12, 311–19, 375–80, 415–20; x (1928), pp. 3–7, 95–9, 236–7, 268–9, 297–9, 331
F. Layna Serrano: 'Alonso de Covarrubias y la iglesia de la Piedad de Guadalajara', *Bol. Soc. Esp. Excurs.*, xlv (1941), pp. 31–48
——: *Los conventos antiguos de Guadalajara* (Madrid, 1943)
J. Camón Aznar: *La arquitectura plateresca*, 2 vols (Madrid, 1945)
F. Chueca Goitia: *Arquitectura del siglo XVI*, A. Hisp., xi (Madrid, 1953)
J. Camón Aznar: *La arquitectura y la orfebrería españolas del siglo XVI*, Summa A., xvii (Madrid, 1959)
A. Rodríguez G. de Ceballos: *Bartolomé de Bustamante (1501–1570) y los orígenes de la arquitectura jesuítica en España* (Rome, 1967)
C. Wilkinson: *The Hospital of Cardinal Tavera in Toledo: A Documentary and Stylistic Study of Spanish Architecture in the Mid-sixteenth Century* (New York and London, 1976)
F. Marías: 'La escalera imperial en España', *L'Escalier dans l'architecture de la Renaissance: Actes du colloque: Tours, 1979*, pp. 165–70
——: *La arquitectura del Renacimiento en Toledo, 1541–1631*, 4 vols (Toledo, 1983–6)
V. Gerard: *De castillo a palacio: El Alcázar de Madrid en el siglo XVI* (Madrid, 1984)
F. Marías: 'L'ospedale del Cardinal Tavera a Toledo: Da *hospitium pauperum* a *domus infirmorum*', *Ric. Stor. A*, 32 (1987), pp. 27–44
——: *El largo siglo XVI: Los usos artísticos del Renacimiento español* (Madrid, 1989)
FERNANDO MARÍAS

Covarrubias, Miguel (*b* Mexico City, 22 Nov 1904; *d* Mexico City, 4 Feb 1957). Mexican illustrator and writer. He worked as a draughtsman on maps and street plans in the Secretaría de Comunicaciones, Mexico City, *c.* 1919, and in 1920 he made a series of caricatures for a student magazine, *Policromías*. He soon established himself as an illustrator, publishing his work from 1921 to 1923 in large circulation newspapers such as *El Heraldo*, *El Mundo* and the *Universal Ilustrado*.

In 1923 Covarrubias settled in New York, where he began writing about the theatre, writing and drawing for the magazine *Vanity Fair* (1924–36) and drawing for the *New Yorker* (1925–50). In 1925 he published *The Prince of Wales and other Famous Americans*, a shrewd, witty chronicle of his contemporaries. He was particularly interested in non-Western societies and their cultural traditions, about which he wrote extensively with the aim of presenting the history of a region as a continuous process. On his return to Mexico in 1942 he broadened his interests to include museology and dance. He painted in the manner of his caricatures, executing various murals in Mexico City that explored his ethnographic interests.

WRITINGS
The Prince of Wales and other Famous Americans (New York, 1925)
Negro Drawings (New York, 1927)
Island of Bali (New York, 1937)
Mexico South: The Isthmus of Tehuantepec (New York, 1946)
The Eagle, the Jaguar and the Serpent (New York, 1954)
The Indigenous Art of Mexico and Central America (New York, 1957)

BIBLIOGRAPHY
L. García Noriega: *Miguel Covarrubias* (Mexico City, 1987)
ESTHER ACEVEDO

Coverdale, William Hugh (*b* Kingston, Ont., 27 Jan 1871; *d* New York, 10 Aug 1949). Canadian engineer, businessman and collector. His interest in Canadian colonial history prompted him to begin collecting Canadiana in the 1920s. He amassed some 500 paintings, watercolours and drawings and nearly 2000 prints. The most intriguing works in the collection are six watercolours (Ottawa, N. Archv) by Robert Hood (*c.* 1797–1821), recording his journey as a midshipman on an Arctic expedition (1819–21). Other artists represented in the collection include George Heriot, James Pattison Cockburn (1778–1847) and James Duncan (1806–81). Although Coverdale assembled these works, they were the property of the Canada Steamships Line, of which he was president and director (1922–49). The collection was displayed at the Manoir Richelieu, a grand summer hotel at Murray Bay (now Pointe-au-Pic), Quebec, owned by the Canada Steamships Line. Coverdale supervised the hanging of the collection, which remained there until the hotel was sold in 1969. The following year most of the collection was sold to the Canadian Government; 62 works were placed in the National Gallery of Canada, Ottawa, and the larger portion went to the National Archives of Canada, Ottawa.

Coverdale also assembled a collection of early Quebec furniture and Native North American artefacts that were installed in another Canada Steamships Line resort, the Hotel Tadoussac, Tadoussac, Quebec. The collection was sold in 1968 to the Government of Quebec and placed in the Musée du Québec, Quebec City. Coverdale was instrumental in assembling a marine collection for the Canada Steamships Line that includes works of art, maps and artefacts. Coverdale's personal collection of Canadian furniture and artefacts was housed at his summer home near Kingston, Ontario, and it remains in the care of his family.

BIBLIOGRAPHY
Who's Who in Canada, 1945–46 (Toronto, 1946)
Who Was Who in America (Chicago, 1950)
W. M. E. Cooke: *W. H. Coverdale Collection of Canadiana: Paintings, Watercolours and Drawings (Manoir Richelieu Collection)* (Ottawa, 1983)
LYDIA FOY

Covo, Battista da (*b* ?Mantua, *c.* 1486; *d* Mantua, 17 Nov 1546). Italian architect and designer. He is first recorded in Mantua in 1522, when he was working on the new apartments in the Reggia dei Gonzaga (Palazzo Ducale) of Isabella d'Este, Marchesa of Mantua. Her rooms, located on the ground-floor of the Corte Vecchia, look out over a small secret garden with walls articulated by Ionic half columns. This garden has traditionally been attributed to Covo, but modern historians have expressed doubt. Nevertheless, Covo's presence on the site during the building of Isabella's apartments, as well as the trust repeatedly expressed in him by the Marchesa, are well documented. In 1524 he presented a project (unrealized) for the abbey church of S Benedetto in Polirone. After 1524, following the transfer of Giulio Romano to the court of Federico II Gonzaga, 5th Marchese (later 1st Duke) of Mantua, Covo was put in charge of the construction of the buildings designed by Giulio, including the Palazzo del Te and Mantua Cathedral. In the early 1530s Covo worked for Isabella d'Este on the remodelling of the castle of Solarolo (destr.) in Romagna. In 1546, after Giulio's death, Covo received the prestigious title of Prefect of the Ducal Buildings, but his untimely death only a few days later prevented him from taking up his new post. Ducal decrees, an elegant inscription (Mantua, S Andrea) and the praise of Bernardo Cles, Bishop of Trent, all compliment Covo on his ability as a designer. It is unlikely, however, that he had many opportunities for the practical application of his talent. The lack of firm examples for comparison makes it difficult to support the hypothesis of an attribution to Covo of a variety of projects, including the restoration of the church of S Maria del Gradaro (rest. and remod., 20th century), Mantua, or the remodelling of the rustic sanctuary of the church of the Madonna della Comuna at Ostiglia, near Mantua.

BIBLIOGRAPHY

DBI

L. Negri: 'Giovanni Battista Covo, l'architetto di Isabella d'Este', *Riv. A.*, xxix (1954), pp. 55–96

E. Marani: *Mantova: Le arti*, ii (Mantua, 1960–65), pp. 179–84

H. Burns: 'The Gonzaga and Renaissance Architecture', *Splendours of the Gonzaga* (exh. cat., ed. D. Chambers and J. Martineau; London, V&A, 1981) pp. 27–38

A. Belluzzi: 'Battista Covo, Giulio Romano e Gerolamo Mazzola Bedoli a San Benedetto in Polirone', *Dal Correggio a Giulio Romano: La committenza di Gregorio Cortese* (exh. cat., ed. P. Piva and E. Del Canto; San Benedetto Po, 1989), pp. 119–31

AMEDEO BELLUZZI

Covocle. *See* PAPHOS, OLD.

Cowan, R(eginald) Guy (*b* East Liverpool, OH, 1 Aug 1884; *d* 1957). American potter and designer. Born into an Ohio pottery family, he studied ceramics under Charles Fergus Binns at Alfred University, Alfred, NY. In 1913 he opened his first pottery in Cleveland, OH, and in 1917 received his earliest public recognition when awarded the first prize for pottery at the Art Institute of Chicago. After World War I, he chose Rocky River, a suburb of Cleveland, as the site for a pottery where he produced limited edition vases and figurines. His Cowan Pottery Studio exclusively produced his award-winning designs until 1927, when he brought in the sculptor, Paul Manship, to work with him, as well as other young potters and designers including Waylande Gregory (1905–71), Viktor Schreckengost (*b* 1906) and Edris Eckhardt (*b* 1910). Unable to overcome the economic obstacles of the Depression, the operation closed in 1931, and Cowan went to Syracuse, NY, where he became art director for the Onondaga Pottery Co. and a leading force for the Ceramic National Exhibitions.

BIBLIOGRAPHY

G. W. Scherma: 'R. Guy Cowan and his Associates', *Transactions of the Ceramics Symposium: Syracuse, 1979*, pp. 66–72

ELLEN PAUL DENKER

Cowie, James (*b* Cuminestown, nr Turriff, Aberdeenshire [now Grampian], 16 May 1886; *d* Edinburgh, 18 April 1956). Scottish painter. He studied English at Aberdeen University (1906–9) and trained as a teacher at the United Free Church Training College in Aberdeen. In 1909 he became an art master at the Fraserburgh Academy and he held various teaching posts until 1948. From 1912 to 1914 he studied at the Glasgow School of Art, but it was not until 1935 that he had his first one-man show at the

McLellan Galleries in Glasgow. His work was characterized by a cool objectivity and restrained palette, as in *In the Classroom* (1922; Aberdeen, A.G.). Of all painters he was most influenced by Paul Nash, whose work he probably discovered in the mid-1920s, in particular by his use of spatial ambiguity and multiple-point perspective as in *Composition* (1947; Edinburgh, N.G. Mod. A.).

See also SCOTLAND, §III, 3.

BIBLIOGRAPHY

R. Calvocoressi: *James Cowie* (Edinburgh, 1979)

C. Oliver: *James Cowie* (Edinburgh, 1980)

Cowin, Douglass M(aurice) (*b c.* 1910). South African architect. He studied architecture at Liverpool University, England, graduating in 1933. His father was the architect Norris Tynwald Cowin (*c.* 1875–1942). On his return to South Africa in October 1933, he joined his father's architectural firm, Cowin, Powers & Ellis (later Cowin & Ellis), in Johannesburg. In 1925 he became an Associate of the RIBA and a practising member of the South African Institute of Architects in 1926. On the whole he stood somewhat apart from Rex Martienssen and the homogeneous Transvaal Group. He differed from them in background by not being a graduate of the University of the Witwatersrand as they were; in his refusal to acknowledge Martienssen's leadership, although he respected him; and in his approach to architecture, seeking a regional idiom appropriate to South Africa's climate and culture, rather than the endorsement of the International style. This found expression particularly in his domestic architecture.

After briefly experimenting with the flat roof, Cowin developed a domestic style of architecture that was a unique symbiosis of the pristine geometry of the Modern Movement and the spreading low-pitched roof. In this synthesis of European sophistication and indigenous romanticism he laid the foundation of what a South African newspaper (*The Star*, 28 Dec 1937) was to call the 'South African style', a vernacular domestic architecture based on a somewhat degraded model of his elegant houses. Early examples of his work include his own house, the lyrical Casa Bedo (1936), with its Miesian glass walls, screen walls and steel columns capped by a hovering Wrightian low-pitched roof; Casa Neathbed (1937); and Stainbank (1937), all in Johannesburg. The climax of this style is the bravura Epping Lodge, Morningside (1938; with George Abbott), with its spectacular external staircase hovering over the swimming-pool.

Of Cowin's larger buildings in Johannesburg, the finest is the 20th Century Cinema and office block (1940), the felicitous outcome of a collaboration with Norman Hanson. His Wispeco building (1946) is a restrained experiment in curtain walling; and his later Ingrams building (*c.* 1950) for the medical profession combines bold massing of three prisms with a pastiche of surface materials. In these projects there is evident competence, but it is in the design of the private house that Cowin's mastery is revealed. In 1944 he became President of the Transvaal Provincial Institute (TPI); having moved to White River, Eastern Transvaal, to farm (1950), in 1963 he resigned from the TPI, and he later emigrated to Canada.

WRITINGS

'The Flat Roof in Domestic Architecture', *Archit. S. Africa*, 2 (1934), pp. 101–2

'The Ideal Home', *S. Afr. Archit. Rec.* (Oct 1934), pp. 250–56

BIBLIOGRAPHY

G. Herbert: *Martienssen and the International Style: The Modern Movement in South African Architecture* (Cape Town, 1975)

GILBERT HERBERT

Cowper, George Nassau Clavering, 3rd Earl Cowper [Viscount Fordwich until 1764] (*b* London, 26 Aug 1738; *d* Florence, 23 Dec 1789). English patron, active in Italy. He left England in 1757 on the Grand Tour and three years later, after an infatuation with the Marchesa Corsi, he settled in Florence. As a leader of the Anglo-Florentine community he patronized literary figures, scientists and musicians as well as artists; he showed his collection of paintings to artists and fellow connoisseurs and formed an important collection of scientific instruments (*see* SCIENTIFIC INSTRUMENTS). He particularly admired the highly finished work of Anton Raphael Mengs and acquired his *Holy Family with St John the Baptist* (priv. col.; Roettgen, p. 33) in 1762. Other commissions were, however, less distinguished: Joseph Macpherson (1726–*c*. 1786) made miniature copies (Windsor Castle, Royal Col.) of the self-portrait collection in Florence (Uffizi) which were eventually presented to George III; and, after he became 3rd Earl in 1764, Cowper commissioned Francis Harwood (*fl* 1748–83) to carve an elaborate tomb for the 2nd Earl in St Mary's, Hertingfordbury, Herts. On his succession Cowper inherited a fortune from his maternal grandfather Henry, 1st Earl of Grantham, and he was able to commission paintings from Mengs and landscapes by artists working in the tradition of Claude Lorrain. These included John Parker (*fl* 1762–85), Hugh Primrose Dean (*c*. 1745–*c*. 1784), Philipp Hackert (Frankfurt am Main, Goethemus.), Francesco Zuccarelli (Firle Place, E. Sussex) and Jacob More.

Johan Zoffany contacted Cowper soon after arriving in Florence in 1772. Apart from painting portraits of the Earl and his fiancée, Hannah Gore (Firle Place, E. Sussex), Zoffany became Cowper's agent. He acquired Raphael's *Virgin and Child* (the 'Large Cowper *Madonna*'; Washington, DC, N.G.A.) for Cowper around 1775. In 1778 Fra Bartolommeo's *Holy Family with St John the Baptist* (Firle Place, E. Sussex) was added to the collection and by 1779, the date of the first inventory (see Sutton), he had acquired another painting by Raphael, the *Virgin and Child* (the 'Small Cowper *Madonna*'; Washington, DC, N.G.A.), and Pontormo's *Joseph's Brethren Beg for his Help, Joseph Sold to Potiphar* and *Pharaoh with his Butler and Baker* (all London, N.G.). Cowper's enthusiasm for collecting waned after Zoffany's departure from Florence in 1778 and Mengs's death the following year. Cowper's interest was transferred to Mengs's mediocre pupil Giuseppe Antonio Fabrini (1740–95).

Among other honours Cowper had been created a Prince of the Holy Roman Empire in 1777 and he became increasingly embittered that no further British honours were bestowed on him. As part of an ultimately unsuccessful bid to influence George III on Cowper's behalf, Zoffany had negotiated royal acceptance of Raphael's *Self-portrait* (London, Hampton Court, Royal Col.). Finally

Cowper returned to London in 1786 to make a personal appeal. He failed to gain preferment, but he did have the opportunity to sit to John Flaxman for a relief portrait which Wedgwood used for a ceramic medallion. Disillusioned, Cowper returned to Florence, where his last act of patronage was Innocenzo Spinazzi's monument to *Machiavelli* (completed 1787) at Santa Croce.

Cowper's Old Master paintings and portraits were sent to England in 1790, but most of the contemporary landscapes were not thought to be worth shipping. The former pictures remained at Panshanger, Hertford, descending eventually to Lady Desborough. After her death in 1952 the largest group of paintings passed to her daughter Viscountess Gage at Firle Place, E. Sussex, where they remain.

UNPUBLISHED SOURCES

Hertford, Herts Record Office [Panshanger pap.]

BIBLIOGRAPHY

D. Sutton: 'Paintings at Firle Place', *Connoisseur*, cxxvii (1956), pp. 78–84

B. Moloney: *Florence and England: Essays on Cultural Relations in the Second Half of the Eighteenth Century* (Florence, 1969)

S. Roettgen: *Anton Raphael Mengs (1728–1779) and his British Patrons* (London, 1993)

HUGH BELSEY

Cox, Anthony. *See under* ARCHITECTS' CO-PARTNERSHIP.

Cox, David (*b* Birmingham, 29 April 1783; *d* Harborne, 7 June 1859). English painter. After taking drawing lessons from Joseph Barber (1757/8–1811) in Birmingham, Cox worked briefly as an apprentice to a painter of lockets and snuff-boxes named Fieldler. This was followed about 1800 by a longer period painting scenery for the New Theatre, Birmingham. On the promise of similar employment at Astley's Amphitheatre in Lambeth, Cox travelled to London in 1804, but when this came to nothing he decided to make his name as a watercolour painter. He began exhibiting at the Royal Academy in 1805 and from 1809 until its demise in 1812 with the Associated Artists in Water-Colours, of which he became both member and president in 1810. He was elected an Associate of the Society of Painters in Water-Colours in 1812 and within a month had advanced to full membership. He remained a loyal supporter of the Society and a regular contributor to its exhibitions for the rest of his life.

During his first years in London, Cox sought instruction from John Varley. While it appears that he had no more than a few lessons, Varley's broad wash technique, deep, clear colour and solidly structured compositions were predominant influences on Cox's early style. The works of his first decade in London were picturesque rural subjects and occasional imitations and pastiches of classical landscapes, such as *In Windsor Park* (1807; London, V&A), based loosely on a model by Gaspard Dughet.

Cox relied largely on teaching to support himself and his family. By 1808 he was taking pupils, and in 1813 the first of his drawing-manuals began coming out in parts. Following a brief and unsatisfactory period as drawing-master at Farnham Military Staff College, Cox accepted a teaching position at Miss Croucher's School for Young Ladies in Hereford and moved there in 1814.

David Cox: *Beeston Castle, Cheshire*, watercolour and gouache with scratching out, 604×859 mm, 1849 (London, British Museum)

During the 1820s Cox produced several ambitious large-scale exhibition watercolours, notably *George IV Embarking for Scotland from Greenwich* (Liverpool, Walker A.G.), which was exhibited at the Society of Painters in Water-Colours in 1823. In these works he tackled new subjects or sought to give definite form to the types of classical–pastoral composition that had always formed part of his output. Under the influence of Turner and Richard Parkes Bonington, his colours became brighter and his handling more varied, with broad washes in the manner of Varley giving way to masses of individual brushstrokes. Three visits to the Continent—to the Low Countries in 1826, to Calais, Amiens and Paris in 1829, and to coastal France in 1832—resulted in vibrant pencil and wash sketches, but, with the exception of his numerous treatments of the coastal scenery of Calais and Dieppe, he made little use of them in his exhibition watercolours.

At the beginning of 1827 Cox and his family moved back to London. In the 1830s he contributed to the genre of the historical costume piece with a series of watercolours set mostly in Haddon Hall and Hardwick Hall. He also developed what would become his most popular and frequently repeated motifs: market people crossing Lancaster Sands and a mounted figure entering a hayfield. Having made many sketching excursions to Wales, he provided illustrations for Thomas Roscoe's *Wanderings and Excursions in North Wales* (1836) and a later companion volume on South Wales. Cox drew much of his later subject-matter from the mountainous landscape of North

Wales in the vicinity of Bettws-y-Coed, which he visited yearly between 1844 and 1856.

Cox seldom painted in oils but in the later 1830s began experimenting with the medium, taking lessons from William James Müller. In order to devote more time to his new pursuit, Cox retired from his teaching practice in June 1841 and moved to Harborne, outside Birmingham. While his oils often achieve the freshness and immediacy of his watercolours, he had difficulty in getting his oil paintings accepted in London, and they were exhibited only in the provinces.

Cox's watercolours of the 1840s reveal a bolder technique. Although he maintained the distinction between sketches and finished watercolours, the distance between the two narrowed considerably. The finished works were frequently painted on a rough Scottish wrapping paper, and his compositions became simpler and more schematic. Effects of storm and wind predominated, as in the large and impressive *Beeston Castle, Cheshire* (1849; London, BM; see fig.). While frequently deploring the looseness and sketchiness of his handling, critics admired his depth and power.

In June 1853 a stroke left his vision and coordination impaired, seriously limiting the amount of new work he could undertake; his final works show increasing suppression of detail. *On the Moors, Near Bettws-y-Coed*, also known as *The Challenge* (London, V&A), exhibited in 1856, shows his late watercolour style at its most concentrated and powerful.

Cox's son, David Cox the younger (1809–85), also a landscape painter in watercolours, modelled his style on that of his father, as well as assisting with his teaching and taking over his father's pupils at the time of his retirement to Harborne. After being with the New Society of Painters in Water-Colours between 1841 and 1846, he became an Associate of the Society of Painters in Water-Colours in 1848.

WRITINGS
A Treatise on Landscape Painting and Effect in Water Colours (London, 1813–14, rev. 2/1840–41)
Progressive Lessons on Landscape for Young Beginners (London, 1816)
The Young Artist's Companion (London, 1819–20, rev. 2/1825)

BIBLIOGRAPHY
N. N. Solly: *Memoir of the Life of David Cox* (London, 1873/R 1973)
W. Hall: *A Biography of David Cox* (London, 1881)
David Cox, 1783–1859 (exh. cat., ed. S. Wildman; Birmingham, Mus. & A.G., 1983) [with bibliog. based on Margaret Rooker's unpubd *Bibliography on David Cox* (1955)]
S. Wilcox: *David Cox: His Development as a Painter in Watercolors* (diss., Yale U., 1984)
SCOTT WILCOX

Cox, Gonzales. *See* COQUES, GONZALES.

Cox, Kenyon (*b* Warren, OH, 27 Oct 1856; *d* New York, 17 March 1919). American painter, illustrator and writer. He was a member of a prominent Ohio family who fostered in him a strong sense of moral responsibility. From an early age he wished to be a painter and despite severe illnesses studied at the McMicken School in Cincinnati, OH, and at the Pennsylvania Academy of Fine Arts, Philadelphia (1876–7). From 1877 to 1882 he was in Paris, where he worked first with Carolus-Duran, then with Alexandre Cabanel and Jean-Léon Gérôme at the Ecole des Beaux-Arts. He considered Gérôme his master, though he did not adopt his style or subject-matter. In the autumn of 1878 Cox travelled to northern Italy, where he imbibed the spirit of the Italian Renaissance. As a student he gravitated steadily toward the reigning academic ideal of draughtsmanship, especially of the figure, that was to persist throughout his career (e.g. *An Eclogue*, 1890; Washington, DC, N. Col. F.A.). He did paint outdoors, both landscapes and genre, and attained a sense of spontaneity and charm in many such works, but he always insisted on careful composition and interpreted form. He exhibited at the Salon in Paris between 1879 and 1882.

Cox returned to Ohio in the autumn of 1882 and moved to New York a year later. He made a living illustrating magazines and books and writing occasional art criticism. In 1892 he began his career as a mural painter with four mural decorations for the Manufactures and Liberal Arts Building at the World's Columbian Exposition in Chicago, IL. He painted a lunette, *Venice* (1894), at Bowdoin College, Brunswick, ME, and in 1896 finished two large lunettes for a gallery in the Library of Congress, Washington, DC. A steady flow of commissions for public buildings followed, providing what he called 'a precarious living'. Among these were a mural for the Public Library, Winona, MN (the *Light of Learning*, 1910; *in situ*), and the sculpture *Greek Science* for the Brooklyn Institute of Arts and Sciences, NY (1907–9).

Cox believed that works of art should speak a universal language based on Classical and Renaissance precedents and promote in the viewer a unified experience of expanded imagination and attachment to tradition. He ardently believed that art is a unifying force in society. Thus in his murals he used idealized, usually female, figures to symbolize abstract ideas such as Truth or Beauty. He was a skilful academic draughtsman and a strong colourist, and he adopted elements of the simplified, decorative style of Pierre Puvis de Chavannes and of the Italian Renaissance masters. However formal, at their best Cox's works are beautifully crafted and impressive. They represent his conception of the artist as a special person with unusual perception who should express ideals in a lofty but comprehensible way.

In his later years, Cox, while not opposed to change, was an outspoken opponent of modernism. Though sceptical of the claims of Impressionism, which dissolved the palpable form and design he thought necessary for artistic expression, he nonetheless approved of the new emphasis on colour and, to a lesser extent, on light in painting. He viewed the most radical aspects of modern art that tended towards abstraction as divisive and particularly disliked the new emphasis on self-conscious individual expression, or 'egotism', because he feared that the artist would ultimately communicate only to a handful of devotees rather than act as a unifying social force. He taught at the Art Students League in New York from 1884 until 1909. In 1892 he married a pupil, Louise King (1865–1945), who also attained some reputation as a painter.

UNPUBLISHED SOURCES
New York, Columbia U., Avery Archit. Mem. Lib. [Cox's pap.]

WRITINGS
Old Masters and New: Essays in Art Criticism (New York, 1905)
Painters and Sculptors (New York, 1907)
The Classic Point of View (New York, 1911)
Artist and Public (New York, 1913)
Concerning Painting: Considerations Theoretical and Historical (New York, 1917)
H. W. Morgan, ed.: *An American Art Student in Paris: The Letters of Kenyon Cox, 1877–1882* (Kent, OH, 1986)
——: *An Artist of the American Renaissance: The Letters of Kenyon Cox, 1883–1919* (Kent, OH, 1995)

BIBLIOGRAPHY
M. C. Smith: 'The Works of Kenyon Cox', *Int. Studio*, xxxii (1907), pp. i–xiii
H. W. Morgan: *Keepers of Culture: The Art-thought of Kenyon Cox, Royal Cortissoz and Frank Jewett Mather, Jr.* (Kent, OH, 1989)
——: *Kenyon Cox, 1856–1919: A Life in American Art* (Kent, OH, 1994)
H. WAYNE MORGAN

Cox, Philip (Sutton) (*b* Sydney, 10 Sept 1939). Australian architect and writer. He graduated in architecture at the University of Sydney in 1962, began a private practice with Ian McKay (1963–6) and won a number of major awards. The firm of Philip Cox & Associates was established in 1967, and Cox developed a substantial interest in conservation and in Australian architectural history, with publications from 1968. These reflected his interest in the Australian vernacular, although they sometimes resorted to nostalgic stereotyping in the manner of his first co-author, Professor J. M. Freeland.

Cox's early executed designs, for example the C. B. Alexander Agricultural College (1964), Tocal, New South Wales, combined the natural materials, earthy colours and textures of the Sydney 'nuts and berries' school (*see* SYDNEY SCHOOL) with vernacular elements such as verandahs. He rebuilt Cadman's Cottage (1972), Sydney, a work criticized by specialist conservationists, and he was involved in a major restoration programme on the early 19th-century buildings of Norfolk Island from 1970. The National Sports Stadium (1974), Canberra, with upward sweeping awning suspended above the grandstand by clusters of cables attached to five steel masts, illustrates his interest in structural virtuosity, marking a shift towards the tradition of the Melbourne 'nuts and bolts' school. His infill housing (1977 and 1979) in Forbes and Brougham Streets, Woolloomooloo, Sydney, used shapes evocative of the terraced-house context such as the Edwardian bullnose verandah roof profile, as well as new motifs, including the quadrant awning (or 'Woolloomooloo hood'), and were later regarded by some as essays in Postmodernism. In the Markets Three Campus of the New South Wales Institute of Technology (1980), Sydney, he retained sections of the old fruit market façades, again attracting criticism for his departure from mainstream Australian conservation philosophy. Yulara Tourist Village (1982), Ayers Rock, Northern Territory, with its dramatic suspended awnings of translucent polyester/polyvinyl chloride fabric, brought great popularity. His Exhibition Building (1986), Darling Harbour, Sydney, is another more formal exercise in structural virtuosity, in which a network of slender steel members is used to suspend roofing over the large spans of the exhibition halls. In 1987 his practice became Philip Cox Richardson Taylor & Partners Pty Ltd.

WRITINGS

with J. M. Freeland: *Rude Timber Buildings in Australia* (Sydney, 1970)
with C. Lucas: *Australian Colonial Architecture* (Melbourne, 1978)

BIBLIOGRAPHY

R. Pegrum and others: *Australian Architects: Philip Cox* (Canberra, 1984)
'Philip Cox: RAIA Gold Medal, 1984', *Archit. Australia*, lxx/6 (1985), pp. 45–76

MILES LEWIS

Coxcie [Coxie; Coxcyen], **Michiel**, the elder (*b* Mechelen, 1499; *d* Mechelen, 10 March 1592). Flemish painter. He was instrumental in replacing the dominant Netherlandish linear tradition, still apparent in the work of Pieter Coecke van Aelst and Bernard van Orley. Influenced by Italian art and the work of Gerard David, Adriaen Isenbrandt and other Bruges painters, Coxcie developed a more volumetric conception of the human form and initiated a large-scale figural mode and a heroic ideal.

Before his departure for Italy, Coxcie seems to have emulated the work of Isenbrandt in particular, as in his signed *Annunciation* (ex-Christie's, London, 21 July 1950, lot 31). He seems to have arrived in Rome in 1529, nine years after the death of Raphael, his primary inspiration. He became a member of the Accademia di S Luca in 1534 and is known to have been associated with the della Valle household. He also had personal contact with Vasari. Coxcie's most prominent Italian patron was Cardinal Enkevooirt, who in 1531 commissioned frescoes from him of the *Life of St Barbara* for the chapel of St Barbara, S Maria dell'Anima, Rome. He also painted frescoes in Old St Peter's (destr.) and made designs for engravings of the *Story of Cupid and Psyche*. A copy after a drawing by

Perino del Vaga (both London, BM) shows that he also admired Raphael's followers.

By 1539 Coxcie had returned to Brabant and entered the painters' guild in Mechelen. In 1543 he became a citizen of Brussels and also lived in Mechelen, Antwerp and Ghent, amassing a certain wealth. He was a versatile artist working in different media. In the 1540s he completed glass paintings, begun earlier by Bernard van Orley, for the chapel of the Blessed Sacrament, Brussels Cathedral, commemorating the wedding of Emperor Charles V. His designs were used by Brussels tapestry manufacturers. A payment made to him for the decoration of rooms belonging to the association of lawyers in Brussels in 1546 refers to sculptures that he seems to have designed but might have included work in other media as well. Although many engravings were made after his paintings, only one autograph print, the *Brazen Serpent*, is known.

The finest panel painting from the period immediately after his return from Italy is the triptych of the *Holy Kinship* (Kremsmünster, Stiftsgal.; see fig.), signed and dated 1540. It is probably identical with the altarpiece that Coxcie is known to have painted for the Guild of Stocking Weavers. According to tradition, this work, from Antwerp Cathedral, was admired and studied by Rubens. Some of the poses and architectural framework allude overtly to the work of Raphael. In contrast to the earlier *Holy Kinship* altarpiece by Quinten Metsys (Brussels, Mus. A. Anc.), Coxcie reduced the hieratic potential of the scene in favour of greater intimacy, using monumental figures and local colour. The composition is balanced, and the primary

Michiel Coxcie: triptych of the *Holy Kinship*, oil on panel, 2.45×1.91 m, 1540 (Kremsmünster, Stiftsgalerie)

colours appear saturated in a manner almost unknown in the southern Netherlands at that date.

In the *Last Supper* from Brussels Cathedral (1567; Brussels, Mus. A. Anc.), Coxcie adopted the symbolic gestures common in Classical sculpture. In his later work the human form itself often assumes a pale, stonelike complexion, evident in the two large triptychs of the *Martyrdom of St Sebastian* (Antwerp, Kon. Mus. S. Kst., and Mechelen Cathedral). These paintings were commissioned by the Guild of Archers, both in Brussels and in Mechelen, in 1575 and 1587 for Ste Gudule, Brussels, and Mechelen Cathedral respectively, and are based on a composition of the same subject by Hans Memling (Brussels, Mus. A. Anc.) or on a common source. The saint is seen isolated in full-length, his spiral pose and facial contortion creating an expressive effect. Dramatic contrasts of light and shadow and sombre colour are far removed from the unsullied yellow and green highlights of the *Holy Kinship* of 1540. Coxcie seems to have been influential in the later 16th-century trend in Flemish painting in suppressing the local colour he had earlier used with such novelty and relying more exclusively on darker hues and the effects of shadows.

Coxcie also produced secular works of a more festive nature. *St Cecilia Playing the Organ* (Madrid, Prado) recalls the prominence of Flemings in the musical life of the period. Rubens owned one of the many versions of the work and it inspired him to produce his own painting of the subject (Berlin, Gemäldegal.). Drawings exist by Coxcie for a series of *Triumphs* and a series of the *Loves of Jupiter*, the latter an unusual theme for Netherlandish artists. Tapestries made after his designs reveal further secular subject-matter.

Ducal inventories show that Coxcie was favoured as a portrait painter by the nobility. He painted an epitaph (Leuven, Mus. Vander Kelen-Mertens) to *Gui de Morillon* (*d* 1548), who was one of the highest imperial functionaries in the southern Netherlands, and a large triptych of the *Death of the Virgin* for Notre-Dame du Sablon, Brussels (Brussels, Mus. A. Anc.), which was commissioned by the humanist politician Gillis van Busleyden and Leonard von Thurn und Taxis and includes their portraits. His *Portrait of ?Christina of Denmark* (Oberlin Coll., OH, Allen Mem. A. Mus.) shows the influence of Pieter Pourbus.

In 1592 Coxcie signed himself 'Painter to the King' on his triptych of scenes from the *Life of St Gudule* (Brussels Cathedral), but as early as 1557 Philip II of Spain commissioned him to make a copy (Madrid, Prado) of the Ghent Altarpiece by Jan van Eyck (Ghent, St Bavo). The King collected other examples of his work. A monogrammed devotional panel of *Christ Carrying the Cross* (Madrid, Prado) has been identified with one listed among the effects of Philip's father, Emperor Charles V. In Charles's cloister retirement at Yuste, it formed a diptych with a picture of the *Virgin* by Titian. A second monogrammed version survives (Vaduz, Samml. Liechtenstein). Coxcie's monumental half-length composition seems to have inspired numerous other paintings of the theme, produced in Brussels, Antwerp and Cologne.

Guild records and the orthodox beliefs of Coxcie's patrons suggest that, even during the zenith of Calvinism in Antwerp, Coxcie remained faithful to the Catholic church. His religious paintings were influential for Marten de Vos, Hendrik de Clerck and Rubens. Opinion of his work has been mixed: Charles V and later Rubens admired it, while Cardinal Antoine Perrenot de Granvelle and van Mander were less enthusiastic. Dubbed in his own day 'the Flemish Raphael', Coxcie was later sometimes condemned as an eclectic, but he has become upheld as an important figure in the introduction of Italian art in the north.

Coxcie's son Michiel the younger (*d* 1616) was also a painter, and his documented triptych the *Temptation of St Anthony* (Mechelen, Onze-Lieve-Vrouw-over-de-Dijle) shows that he perpetuated his father's style.

BIBLIOGRAPHY

Thieme–Becker

G. Vasari: *Vite* (1550, rev. 2/1568); ed. G. Milanesi (1878–85), v, pp. 435–6, 573; vii, p. 582

K. van Mander: *Schilder-boeck* ([1603]–1604), fols 258b–9a

E. Neeffs: *Histoire de la peinture et de la sculpture à Malines*, i (Ghent, 1876), pp. 146–73

H. E. van Gelder and J. Duverger, eds: *Kunstgeschiedenis der Nederlanden*, i (Antwerp, 1954), pp. 415–18, 527–8

L. van Puyvelde: *La Peinture flamande au siècle de Bosch et Breughel* (Paris, 1962)

R. C. van den Boogert: 'Habsburgs imperialisme en de verspreiding van renaissancevormen in de Nederlanden: De vensters van Michiel Coxcie in de Sint-Goedele te Brussel', *Oud-Holland*, cvi (1992), no. 2, pp. 57–80

Hand. Kon. Kring Oudhdknd., Lett. & Kst Mechelen/Bull. Cerc. Archéol., Litt. & A. Malines, xcvi (1992) [issue dedicated to Coxcie]

K. Johns: 'Peter Paul Rubens, Michael Coxcie und der Antwerpener Strumpfwirker-Altar', *Die Malerei Antwerpens: Gattungen, Meister, Wirkungen: Studien zur flämischen Kunst des 16. und 17. Jahrhunderts. Internationales Kolloquium: Wien, 1993*

KARL T. JOHNS

Coxe, Peter (*b* 1752 or 1753; *d* London, 22 Jan 1844). English auctioneer. One of the new breed of professional auctioneers that sprang up in the late 18th century, he was the son of a royal physician in the court of George II. Educated briefly at Charterhouse, he left school at the age of 13 and in 1794 formed the auctioneering company Coxe, Burrell & Foster. This was one of a number of new firms that opened in London in the wake of the French Revolution, dealing in works of art from the collections of displaced European nobility. In May 1802 Coxe sold off the remainder of the collection of Louis-Philippe-Joseph, Duc d'Orléans, the most prestigious array of Italian art, including Titian's *Noli me tangere* (London, N.G.), to come on to the British market and one that opened connoisseurs' eyes to the possibility of collecting quality Italian paintings. Among other important collections sold by Coxe around the turn of the 18th century were those of the English dealer Michael Bryan and Greffiers Fagel, the latter containing many significant Dutch and Flemish works. Coxe continued to run his business in the early 19th century, organizing, for example, the posthumous studio sale of Philippe Jacques de Loutherbourg. He also began to write artistic and political tracts, including two poems written under the pseudonym of Fabricia Nunnez entitled *Architectural Hints in Lines to those Royal Academicians who are Painters . . .* (London, 1806). His final piece of verse was *To Sir John Soane, Royal Academician* (London, 1832).

BIBLIOGRAPHY

DNB

W. Buchanan: *Memoirs of Painting*, 2 vols (London, 1824)

W. T. Whitley: *Art in England, 1800–1820* (Cambridge, 1928), pp. 124, 129, 194

MARTIN POSTLE

Coxe-DeWilde Pottery. American pottery in Burlington, NJ. It was founded in 1688 by Dr Daniel Coxe (*b* ?Stoke Newington, England, 1640/41; *d* ?London, 19 Jan 1730) and John DeWilde (*b c.* 1665; *d* Doctor's Creek, NJ, 1708). A Cambridge-trained physician, Dr Coxe had extensive interests in the American colonies and was Governor of East and West Jersey from 1688 to 1692. His contract with DeWilde for a pottery 'for white and Chiney ware' was only one of the many ways in which he profited from his colonial holdings. From 1675 DeWilde had trained in London delftware potteries and by the time of his association with Coxe was a master potter and maker of delftware. Documents show that tin-glazed earthenwares were sold in the Delaware River valley, Barbados and Jamaica, although no pieces from this pottery survive. The pottery was probably disbanded when Coxe sold his Jersey holdings to the West Jersey Society in 1692.

BIBLIOGRAPHY
B. L. Springsted: 'A Delftware Center in Seventeenth-century New Jersey', *Amer. Cer. Circ. Bull.*, iv (1985), pp. 9–46

ELLEN PAUL DENKER

Coxhead, Ernest (Albert) (*b* Eastbourne, Sussex, 1863; *d* Berkeley, CA, 27 March 1933). English architect, active in the USA. He was trained in the offices of several English architects and attended the Royal Academy Schools, London. In 1886 he moved with his older brother, Almeric Coxhead (1862–1928), to Los Angeles where he established an independent practice. The Coxheads moved to San Francisco four years later and soon formed a partnership that lasted until Almeric's death. Ernest Coxhead appears to have retained charge of designing. Until the early 1890s the firm specialized in churches; thereafter, most executed projects were for houses in San Francisco and its suburbs. Coxhead's building schemes of the 1890s were highly inventive, sometimes eccentric, drawing on both the classical tradition in England and contemporary English Arts and Crafts work. He was adept at developing complex, dramatic spatial sequences and creating mannerist plays with form, scale and historical allusions. Like his friend Willis Jefferson Polk, Coxhead excelled in the design both of modest, informal dwellings such as his own house (1893) in San Francisco and of large, elaborate ones such as the Earl House (*c.* 1895–8, destr. 1957), Los Angeles. Among his most original designs was an unsuccessful entry to the Phoebe Hearst architectural competition for the University of California, Berkeley (1898). Here, grand classical elements are interspersed among others more suggestive of a northern Italian hill town, to form an intricate collage that is a pronounced departure from most planning projects of the period.

After 1900 Coxhead's career declined, the reasons for which are difficult to pinpoint. He continued to practise for another 30 years; however, most of this work fails to match the vital, ingenious spirit that marked earlier efforts.

BIBLIOGRAPHY
A. Coxhead: 'The Telephone Exchange', *Architect & Engin. CA*, xviii/1 (1909), pp. 34–46
'An Echo of the Phoebe Hearst Architectural Competition for the University of California', *Architect & Engin. CA*, xxx/2 (1912), pp. 97–101
J. Beach: 'The Bay Area Tradition, 1890–1918', *Bay Area Houses*, ed. S. Woodbridge (New York, 1976), pp. 23–98
R. Longstreth: *On the Edge of the World: Four Architects in San Francisco at the Turn of the Century* (New York, 1983)

RICHARD LONGSTRETH

Coypel. French family of painters. Their work, over three successive generations, maps the progress of history painting in late 17th-century and early 18th-century France. The family's founder, (1) Noël Coypel, was a follower of Poussin, painting in a similar academic, classicizing style. Noël's elder son, (2) Antoine Coypel, was the most distinguished artist of the family, who achieved the highest honours: stylistically, he was drawn away from the influence of his father and Charles Le Brun by the attractions of the style of Rubens and the theories of Roger de Piles. The work of (3) Noël-Nicolas Coypel, his younger brother and frequent imitator, is distinguished by its decorative quality. Antoine's son, (4) Charles-Antoine Coypel, tended to revert to the classicizing style of the 17th century; his history and other paintings reflect his lifelong interest in the theatre in their strongly dramatic manner.

BIBLIOGRAPHY
Mariette
D. Wildenstein: 'L'Oeuvre gravée des Coypel', *Gaz. B.-A.*, n. s. 5, lxiii (1964), pp. 141–52; lxiv (1964), pp. 261–74

(1) Noël Coypel (*b* Paris, 25 Dec 1628; *d* Paris, 24 Dec 1707). He trained with an unknown painter in Orléans and in the studio of Noël Quillerier (1594–1669) in Paris. From the age of 18 Coypel collaborated with Charles Errard le fils, who was considered the most important designer of decorative schemes in Paris, until Errard was appointed director of the Académie de France in Rome in 1666. Collaboration with him gave Coypel the opportunity to take part in large projects. His first commission, a contribution to the stage scenery for Luigi Rossi's opera *Orfeo*, has not survived, but his second work, carried out under Errard's direction, gives an idea of the nature of his style. This is the ceiling painting in the Grande Chambre of the Palais du Parlement in Rennes (now the Palais de Justice), which was executed in 1663. As was his usual practice, Errard designed the general structure and individual decorative forms, entrusting Coypel with the task of painting. The detailed iconography of the nine painted compartments of the ceiling, which vary in dimension, is not clear in every case: most of the problematic figures are probably personifications of political virtues, which Coypel, in his distinctive way, represented without fore-shortening or change in proportion. The figures, extremely plastic in conception and classicizing in the manner of Poussin, appear parallel to the picture plane, with no concession to the spectator's viewpoint. Two small panels contemporary with the ceiling in Rennes, a *Visitation* and an *Adoration of the Shepherds* (both Paris, Hôp. Laënnec, Chapel), likewise demonstrate why Coypel was justly called 'Coypel le Poussin' by connoisseurs of his time. Both representations have a friezelike composition; the classically modelled figures have moderate, albeit differentiated expressions. An earlier painting of *St James the Greater Led to Execution* (1661; Paris, Louvre), commissioned from Coypel for Notre-Dame de Paris by the Goldsmiths' Corporation, shows Poussin's influence in the overall composition and background architecture, as well as in the types of the individual figures.

In 1663 Coypel was approved (*agréé*) as a history painter by the Académie Royale de Peinture et de Sculpture. For his *morceau de réception* he painted *God Reproving Cain after the Death of Abel* (Paris, Louvre). This tondo composition displays more drama than Coypel's previous works: the compositional structure is diagonal rather than friezelike, and the gestures of the figures are highly animated. After only one year's membership of the Académie, Coypel was promoted to the rank of professor, an index of his growing popularity. In the years 1667–8 he, like most of the important painters of his generation, worked on the decoration of the Tuileries palace in Paris, being entrusted with the wall and ceiling paintings in the Appartement du Roi, on the upper floor of the palace. Several of these are extant. For the ceiling of the anteroom he painted a *Personification of the Earth* (Lyon, Mus. B.-A.); of the wall paintings, representing scenes from the life of Hercules, there survive *Hercules Wrestling with Achelous* (tondo; Lille, Mus. B.-A.) and *Hercules and the Hydra* (Avignon, Mus. Calvet), a scene that incorporates an extensive landscape. *Hercules Wrestling with Achelous* shows a reddish tonality until then unusual for Coypel, but the academic treatment of the naked body is still entirely consistent with his style, as is shown particularly by a comparison with his *morceau de réception*. Of the rest of the decorations there remain two representations of *Justice* and *Vigilance* (both Fontainebleau, Château); these robust female figures are painted on wood, so were probably part of the wall panelling. Part of the same decorative scheme were paintings of *Apollo and Marsyas* (Marseille, Mus. B.-A.), a scene that includes a sweeping landscape, and *Apollo Crowned by Victory* and *Apollo Crowned by Minerva* (both Paris, Louvre). These last two pictures again show Coypel's typical classicizing, academic treatment of the body and face. The personifications of *March* and *September* (Washington, DC, Fr. Embassy) from the Tuileries also show this style, although they were altered in the 19th century by the addition of an ornamental border. Coypel's most beautiful painting for the Tuileries, and altogether one of his most important works, is the *Adoration of the Shepherds* (Nancy, Mus. B.-A.), created as a free-standing panel painting for the oratory: the depiction of light, the treatment of colour and the serene, restrained composition of the work produce a particularly harmonious effect.

Before the work in the Tuileries was completed, many of the artists working there were called away to the château of Versailles. Coypel also received commissions for that new palace; however, he executed them in Rome, where from 1672 he held the post of Director of the Académie de France. The large-format ceiling paintings (Versailles, Château), which were published as engravings, show scenes from Roman history: their friezelike composition and the dignified bearing of the figures were again inspired by Poussin. In 1674 Coypel returned to Paris. In 1675 he painted a *Visitation* (now Lyon, Cathedral). The large, vertical-format painting is monumental in effect, especially in comparison with the small *Visitation* of 1663. The

figures express extreme agitation; they are raised up on two steps and framed by a cloud saturated with light. Coypel was Rector of the Académie Royale from 1690 and its director from 1695 to 1699, the crowning achievement of his official career. However, towards the end of his life Coypel's career suffered a reversal when Jules Hardouin Mansart, Surintendant des Bâtiments du Roi, replaced him as director of the Académie; he did not, however, succeed in preventing Coypel from participating to a modest extent in the decoration of the church of Les Invalides, the main building project in Paris at the beginning of the 18th century.

BIBLIOGRAPHY

P.-M. Auzas: 'Précisions nouvelles sur les "Mays" de Notre-Dame de Paris', *Bull. Soc. Hist. A. Fr.* (1953), pp. 40–44

J. Wilhelm: 'Les Tableaux de l'Hôtel de Ville de Paris et de l'Abbaye Sainte Geneviève: Tableau de Noël Coypel, commémorant la victoire de Senef en 1674', *Bull. Soc. Hist. A. Fr.* (1956), pp. 26, 27

B. de Montgolfier: 'Les Peintres de l'Académie royale à la Chartreuse de Paris', *Gaz. B.-A.*, n. s. 5, lxiv (1964), pp. 199–216

N. Sainte-Fare-Carnot: 'La Décoration de la chapelle de l'Hôpital des Incurables (Hôpital Laënnec, rue de Sèvres)', *Bull. Soc. Hist. A. Fr.* (1974), pp. 55–61

A. Schnapper: *Jean Jouvenet (1644–1717) et la peinture d'histoire à Paris* (Paris, 1974), pp. 35, 109–11

A. Schnapper and D. Ternois: 'Une Vente de tableaux provenant des églises parisiennes en 1810', *Bull. Soc. Hist. A. Fr.* (1976), pp. 115–62

A. Schnapper: 'Noël Coypel et le grand décor peint des années 1660', *Antol. B.A.*, i (1977), pp. 7–17

N. Sainte-Fare-Carnot: 'Le Décor des Tuileries sous le règne de Louis XIV', *Notes & Doc. Mus. France*, xx (1988), nos 55–65

CATHRIN KLINGSÖHR-LE ROY

(2) Antoine Coypel (*b* Paris, 12 April 1661; *d* Paris, 7 Jan 1722). Son of (1) Noël Coypel.

1. TRAINING AND EARLY WORK, TO *c.* 1688. Antoine studied at the Collège d'Harcourt and then trained in his father's studio and at the Académie Royale. In 1672 Noël Coypel was made Director of the Académie de France in Rome, and Antoine, who accompanied his father to Italy, benefited from the education given to the students there. He also joined in their long sessions spent copying Raphael's frescoes in the Vatican Loggie and the works of the Carracci and Domenichino in the Palazzo Farnese. He met Giovanni Lorenzo Bernini and Carlo Maratti and was awarded a drawing prize by the Accademia di S Luca. During his return journey Antoine stopped in northern Italy to study the works of Correggio—which were to have a decisive influence on him—as well as those of Titian and Veronese. On reaching Paris in April 1676 he resumed his place as a student at the Académie Royale, where he was awarded second prize for painting in November of that year.

In 1680 Antoine made a name for himself when he received the prestigious commission for the May of Notre-Dame (untraced), an altarpiece ordered each year by the Goldsmiths' Corporation for the cathedral of Paris. In 1681 he painted three scenes (untraced) from the *Life of the Virgin* for the church of the Convent of the Assumption in the Rue Saint-Honoré. The same year he was received (*reçu*) as a member of the Académie Royale with an *Allegory of the Victories of Louis XIV* (Montpellier, Mus. Fabre). In 1684 he was made an assistant professor at the Académie, and in 1685–6 he decorated the Pavillon de l'Aurore (destr.) at the château of Choisy, near Paris, for Anne-Marie-Louise d'Orléans, Duchesse de Montpensier (1627–93), the King's cousin. In 1685 he was awarded the title of Peintre Ordinaire by Monsieur (Philippe I, Duc d'Orléans), the King's brother; this marked the beginning of the patronage extended to him by the Orléans family. In 1688 he was commissioned to undertake eight pictures on the theme of Apollo for the Grand Trianon at Versailles, but he only executed one, *Apollo and Daphne* (*in situ*), as the project was abandoned for financial reasons. Up to this point in his career Antoine's work was dominated by two major influences, those of his father and of the Premier Peintre du Roi, Charles Le Brun; but these were gradually to diminish.

2. PRIVATE COMMISSIONS, 1689–99. During this ten-year period Antoine received no official commissions from the Bâtiments du Roi. At the time France was involved in the War of the League of Augsburg, and the budget of the royal works had been reduced. Antoine was obliged to find private patrons, and he altered his style to suit them. Having grown up in Le Brun's shadow, he had until then striven to establish himself as a painter in the Grand Style and had worked on large-scale decorative works—especially on religious, mythological and regal themes. The dearth of official commissions made him a painter of cabinet pictures, and he orientated his style

towards a freer mythology peopled with smiling nymphs, such as the *Bacchus and Ariadne* (1693; Philadelphia, PA, Mus. A.) for Monsieur. Flattering the taste of an aristocratic clientele by producing small-scale paintings of lightweight subjects, his artistic development was influenced by the theorist Roger de Piles, whom Antoine had met in Rome. He also met Richelieu, who collected works by Rubens, and took part in the current debate between the Rubénistes and the Poussinistes on the relative importance of colour and line (*see* RUBÉNISME). Antoine's pictures during this period were very close to those by Rubens in style; indeed, his renowned *Democritus* (1692; Paris, Louvre) was so powerful an evocation of Rubens's manner that it was for a long time attributed to him. From 1695–6 Antoine executed a series of seven paintings on Old Testament themes, in which he gave free rein to his taste for expressing the passions. They include *Esther Swooning before Ahasuerus* (1696; Paris, Louvre; see fig.) and the *Sacrifice of Jephthah* (Dijon, Mus. B.-A.).

In 1695 Antoine was appointed draughtsman to the Académie des Inscriptions et Belles-Lettres in succession to the engraver Sébastien Leclerc (i), and he made a number of designs for the Histoire métallique du Roi, the series of medals illustrating the events of the reign of Louis XIV.

Antoine Coypel: *Esther Swooning before Ahasuerus*, oil on canvas, 1.5×1.37 m, 1696 (Paris, Musée du Louvre)

3. MAJOR COMMISSIONS, 1699–1709. The initial years of the 18th century were a time of official commissions for Antoine, often executed in collaboration with painters such as Jean Jouvenet, Charles de La Fosse, Bon Boullogne and Louis Boullogne (ii). In 1699 he contributed *Zephyrus and Flora* (Paris, Louvre), representing Spring, to a cycle of four seasons painted by these artists for the royal château of Marly. In 1700–02 they decorated the château of Meudon for Louis de Bourbon, the Grand Dauphin: Antoine was commissioned to execute seven paintings, among them such unusual subjects as *Silenus Smeared with Berries by the Nymph Aeglë* (Reims, Mus. St Rémi), drawn from Virgil's *Eclogues*, and *Hercules Bringing Alcestis back from Hades* (Cholet, Mus. A.), from *Alcestis* by Euripides. In 1701 he painted a *Triumph of Venus* (Paris, Louvre) for the Ménagerie at the château of Versailles and a *Zephyrus and Flora* for the Grand Trianon (*in situ*). The same year he painted *Eliezer and Rebecca* (Paris, Louvre) for the King.

This was also a period of large-scale decorations. Antoine's patron since 1701, Philippe II, Duc d'Orléans, the future Regent, commissioned him to decorate the Grande Galerie of the Palais Royal, Paris. Antoine chose the *Story of Aeneas*, executing the sketches in 1702. He carried out the ceiling decorations, representing the *Assembly of the Gods*, in 1703, and the entire ceiling, with its six additional paintings placed in the springing of the vault, was completed in 1705. This ambitious decorative scheme no longer exists but is known through engravings, Coypel's preparatory drawings (Paris, Louvre) and an oil sketch (Angers, Mus. B.-A.). In it Coypel revealed his interest in the Roman Baroque, particularly Pietro da Cortona's great illusionistic ceilings open to the heavens, such as that in the Gran Salone of the Palazzo Barberini, Rome, of which Antoine owned a reduced copy. The mocking nymphs and satyrs that animated his own work were, however, in the light-hearted style of their day. In 1709 he completed his other important decorative work, the vault of the chapel at the château of Versailles (*in situ*). This is a large religious decoration organized around a *trompe l'oeil* opening through which cloud-borne heavenly figures appear to enter.

Antoine was at this time at the height of his career and received commissions from abroad. In 1699-1700 he was approached by Daniel Cronström, the Swedish envoy in Paris, to execute a painting for his king, Charles XII; but the Great Northern War, which broke out in 1700 between Sweden and a coalition of north European states, put an end to the project. In 1701 he nevertheless executed some designs for medals for Sweden. In 1708–9 he was commissioned to execute a painting of *St Peter Delivered by an Angel* (untraced) for Cardinal Pietro Ottoboni in Rome.

4. LATE WORK, FROM 1710. During the last phase of his career Antoine accumulated official appointments and honours: he was made Garde des Tableaux et Dessins de la Couronne in 1710, Director of the Académie Royale in 1714 and Premier Peintre du Roi the following year. He was weakened by illness, however, and either painted little or repeated previous compositions; from 1710, for example, he reproduced his Old Testament series in the form of tapestry cartoons (e.g. the *Judgement of Solomon*;

Angoulême, Mus. Mun.) for the Gobelins. In 1715 he completed the Galerie d'Enée at the Palais Royal; this consisted of seven wall canvases on martial or otherwise dramatic themes from the *Story of Aeneas* (Paris, Louvre; Arras, Mus. B.-A.; Montpellier, Mus. Fabre), rendered in a spirit quite different from his earlier work. Towards 1717 he executed two paintings for the choir of Notre-Dame: an *Assumption* (untraced) and *Jesus among the Doctors* (Villeneuve-sur-Lot, chapel of the Pénitents-Blancs). By this time, clearly seeing himself as the guardian of traditional values in painting, he accentuated the severity of his compositions and returned to the Grand Style. In 1721 he published a collection of theoretical texts on art that he had worked on during the previous decade. Far from being a 'colourist' manifesto, this collection promoted eclecticism and, at the end of his life, established Antoine on middle ground in the debates then agitating French artistic circles.

Some historians have seen in Antoine's art a prefiguration of Rococo painting of the 18th century, but this view requires some modification. Brought up by a father close to Le Brun and trained in Italy, Antoine grew up with classicism; like many other artists of his generation, he was nevertheless attracted to the arguments of the colourists. Jouvenet, La Fosse and the Boullogne brothers also made room for Rubens-inspired colour on their palettes, foreshadowing the 18th-century development towards a smaller scale and a more graceful and lighter style. The new century was full of optimism, styles were changing, and Antoine was part of this development; his own style hardened towards the end of his career, however, and he returned to subjects of greater pathos. The Louvre has an outstanding collection of his drawings, many in the three crayon technique, while his small output of original engravings has been discussed by Wildenstein.

WRITINGS

Epître en vers d'un père à son fils sur la peinture (Paris, 1708)
Discours prononcés dans les conférences de l'Académie royale de peinture et de sculpture (Paris, 1721); reprinted in *Conférences de l'Academie royale de peinture et de sculpture*, ed. H. Jouin (Paris, 1883), pp. 215–366

BIBLIOGRAPHY

C.-A. Coypel: 'Vie d'Antoine Coypel', *Vies des Premiers Peintres du Roi depuis M. Le Brun jusqu'à présent*, ed. B. Lépicié, ii (Paris, 1742), pp. 1–41
A.-J. Dézallier D'Argenville: *Abrégé de la vie des plus fameux peintres* (1745–52, 2/1762), iv, pp. 339–45
L. Dimier: 'Antoine Coypel', *Les Peintres français du XVIIIe siècle* (Paris, 1928), i, pp. 93–154
D. Wildenstein: 'L'oeuvre gravé des Coypel', *Gaz. B.-A.*, n.s. 5, lxiii (1964), pp. 141–52; lxiv (1964), pp. 261–74
A. Schnapper: 'Le Grand Dauphin et les tableaux de Meudon', *Rev. A.* [Paris], i–ii (1968), pp. 57–64
——: 'Antoine Coypel: La Galerie d'Enée au Palais-Royal', *Rev. A.* [Paris], v (1969), pp. 33–42
——: 'The *Moses* of Antoine Coypel', *Bull. Allen Mem. A. Mus.*, xxxvii/2 (1979), pp. 58–70
N. Garnier: *Antoine Coypel, 1661–1722* (Paris, 1989) [monograph covering paintings, drawings and engravings]

NICOLE GARNIER

(3) Noël-Nicolas Coypel (*b* Paris, 17 Nov 1690; *d* Paris, 14 Dec 1734). Son of (1) Noël Coypel by his second marriage. Trained by his father and at the Académie Royale, Noël-Nicolas was at first overshadowed by his very successful older half-brother, (2) Antoine Coypel. His unremarkable earliest known works, *Manna from*

Heaven and the *Sacrifice of Melchizedek* (both 1713; Paris, St Nicolas-du-Chardonnet), were painted the year before his marriage to Françoise Legendre. He was approved (*agréé*) by the Académie on 31 December 1716 and was received (*reçu*) as a full member in 1720 with *Neptune Rescuing Amymone* (Valenciennes, Mus. B.-A.). This work owes a great debt to the lively and colourful art of Louis Boullogne (ii), as did its predecessor, the *Adoration of the Shepherds* (*c.* 1715; Paris, St Nicolas-des-Champs). Often lacking in compositional imagination, Noël-Nicolas successfully based a number of his pictures on reworkings of paintings by other artists. These include a very polished and attractive *Sacrifice of Isaac* (1721; Tourcoing, Mus. Mun. B.-A.), inspired by Antoine's version of the same theme (1707), and *Arion and the Dolphin* (1724; Versailles, Hôtel de Ville), based on a composition by Louis de Silvestre of 1701 (Compiègne, Château). A dynamic, well-organized work, *Arion and the Dolphin* is the only example of an official commission from the Bâtiments du Roi in Noël-Nicolas's oeuvre.

In the 1720s Noël-Nicolas produced several mythological pieces based on works by Antoine. His *Venus, Bacchus and the Three Graces* (1726; Geneva, Mus. A. & Hist.) takes the figure of Venus and the gestures of her suitor from a lost painting by his half-brother, while Noël-Nicolas's voluptuous *Rape of Europa* (1727; priv. col., see 1975–6 exh. cat., pl. v) is closely related to a complex compositional drawing by Antoine (Paris, Louvre). Both works, however, show Noël-Nicolas's individual style, the grace and harmony of his carefully planned and well-lit compositions and an engaging use of his favourite female types. The *Rape of Europa* in particular foreshadows the seductive mythological compositions of François Boucher. Noël-Nicolas entered this painting for the competition of 1727 organized by the Directeur des Bâtiments, Louis-Antoine de Pardaillon de Gondrin, Duc d'Antin, to encourage the Académie's painters. Although many contemporary critics held it to be the finest work in the competition, first prize was shared by Jean-François de Troy and François Lemoyne. To redress this injustice one of the secretaries of state, the Comte de Morville, bought the *Rape of Europa* for 1500 livres, which was equivalent to the prize offered by Louis XV. Noël-Nicolas's graceful and luminous style was developed further in the *Judgement of Paris* (1728; Stockholm, Nmus.) and the *Bath of Diana* (1728; St Petersburg, Hermitage). Both are original compositions and both make full use of a dramatic, hidden source of light—the sun spilling its rays into a grotto or cavern to animate the scene within and to highlight the delicate eroticism of the nymphs. The sure, diagonal composition and the charm of its characters make the *Judgement of Paris* in particular one of Noël-Nicolas's most attractive paintings.

The biennial Salon exhibitions were in abeyance between 1704 and 1737, and Noël-Nicolas had few opportunities to show his work in public, apart from the religious works he painted for churches. Many of these have been destroyed, but three works from the mid-1720s are known: the *Rest on the Flight into Egypt* (1724; New York, Mr & Mrs A. Frankel priv. col.), *St James Healing the Sick* (1726; Cleveland, OH, Mus. A.) and *St Francis of Paola Crossing the Straits of Messina* (Lyon, Cathedral). They are linked by their common use of the same male figure types, gestures, expressions, putti and dramatic lighting. *St James Healing the Sick* possesses a monumentality reminiscent of works by Jean Jouvenet. The *St Francis* is Noël-Nicolas's one extant large-scale religious painting: only an oil sketch (Nancy, Mus. Hist. Lorrain) and a drawing (Paris, Louvre) are known of the scheme generally considered to have been his masterpiece—the ceiling and altarpiece of the Chapel of the Virgin in St Sauveur, Paris (destr. 1778). Begun in 1731, this scheme was exceptional both for its illusionism—very rare in the French decorative tradition—and for its use of stucco figures by the sculptor Jean-Baptiste Lemoyne (ii) as an integral element in the design. Despite difficulties over payment, the work was a great success, and Noël-Nicolas's career advanced accordingly; by 1733 he was a professor at the Académie Royale. He died prematurely the next year, following a domestic accident.

BIBLIOGRAPHY

J. Messelet: 'Noël-Nicolas Coypel', *Les Peintres français du XVIIIe siècle*, ed. L. Dimier (Paris, 1930), ii, pp. 217–27

The Age of Louis XV: French Painting, 1710–1774 (exh. cat., ed. P. Rosenberg; Toledo, OH, Mus. A.; Chicago, IL, A. Inst.; Ottawa, N.G.; 1975–6), p. 31, pls 37, v

D. Lomax: 'Noël-Nicolas Coypel (1690–1734)', *Rev. A.* [Paris], 57 (1982), pp. 29–48

JOSHUA DRAPKIN

(4) Charles-Antoine Coypel (*b* Paris, 11 July 1694; *d* Paris, 14 June 1752). Son of (2) Antoine Coypel. His father remained a decisive influence on Charles-Antoine's painting and theory throughout his life. A precociously successful artist, Charles-Antoine did not travel to Italy, as was customary for history painters, but became a member of the Académie Royale in 1715, with *Medea and Jason* (Berlin, Schloss Charlottenburg) as his *morceau de réception*. In 1716 he undertook his first major commission, a series of tapestry cartoons (Compiègne, Mus. Mun. Vivenel) illustrating episodes from Cervantes's *Don Quixote*. He also embarked on a career in 1718 as a dramatist, but though he wrote numerous plays in the 1720s, few were performed. Discouraged, he abandoned the theatre; this decision is commemorated in *Painting Ejecting Thalia* (1732; Norfolk, VA, Chrysler Mus.). In contrast, Charles-Antoine's artistic career was extremely successful. In 1722 he inherited from his father the position of painter to Philippe II, Duc d'Orléans, and he later became the favourite painter of Louis XV's queen, Maria Leczinska. In 1727 he took part in the competition organized by the Duc d'Antin, Surintendant des Bâtiments du Roi, to encourage history painting; Charles-Antoine's entry, *Perseus and Andromeda* (Paris, Louvre), did not win but was much admired by some critics and was purchased for Louis XV. It is a grandiose, operatic work in which figures in exaggerated poses of grief and fear are bound together by the swirling movement of the composition.

The theatrical character of Charles-Antoine's pictures became more pronounced with time; his many portraits of actors, such as the pastel of *Adrienne Lecouvreur* (1730; ex-A. Seligman priv. col., Paris), demonstrate his continued contact with the stage. His genre scenes, such as *Children's Games* (1731; exh. London, Owen Edgar, 1984; untraced), which are among his most original works, often reflect the same moralizing concerns as his comedies.

Charles-Antoine's dramatic ambitions for painting are most evident in his tapestry cartoons for the Gobelins. Between 1733 and 1741 he painted four large cartoons, inspired by the operas of Jean-Baptiste-Maurice Quinault; these include the *Sleep of Rinaldo* (Nantes, Mus. B.-A.), which, in its landscape setting and decorative character, follows pictorial traditions of representing this subject. His second series of history paintings, mostly based on earlier pictures, which he began *c.* 1747, represent a new departure. The emphasis on the exaggerated gestures of a few figures in an elaborate architectural setting in his painting of *Athaliah Recognizing Joaz* (1741; Brest, Mus. Mun.) is highly dramatic. His originality in the depiction of expression in painting has been contested; certainly these later works bear an evident debt to Poussin and Charles Le Brun.

Charles-Antoine's theoretic statements, especially *Le Parallèle de l'éloquence et de la peinture* (1751), are also closely related to Le Brun's writings. The distinctive character of his art lies not only in the specifically theatrical interpretation he gave to the academic doctrine of *ut pictura poesis*, but also in its function as a bulwark against the blandness of the Rococo, as represented in the works of François Boucher. After his steady ascent through the academic hierarchy, which culminated in his appointment in 1747 as Premier Peintre du Roi, Charles-Antoine was closely associated with Charles-François-Paul Lenormand de Tournehem's efforts as Directeur des Bâtiments to revive history painting; he played a major role in the foundation of a special school for young artists, the Ecole des Elèves Protégés, which was a vital part of the reforms. Charles-Antoine's style is invariably artificial; Pierre-Jean Mariette complained that his too early success had led him to avoid all study of nature in his work. But his position as an intermediary between the age of Le Brun and that of Jacques-Louis David gives his work a historical importance that should not be underestimated.

WRITINGS
C.-A. Coyel:'Vie d'Antoine Coypel', *Vies des Premiers Peintres du Roi depuis M. Le Brun jusqu'à présent*, ed. B. Lépicié, ii (Paris, 1742), pp. 1–41
Le Parallèle de l'éloquence et de la peinture (Paris, 1751)

BIBLIOGRAPHY
Mariette
F. Ingersoll-Smouse: 'Charles-Antoine Coypel', *Rev. A. Anc. & Mod.*, xxxvii (1920), pp. 143–54, 285–92
A. Schnapper: ' "Le Chef-d'oeuvre d'un muet" ou la tentative de Charles Coypel', *Rev. Louvre* (1968), pp. 253–64
The First Painters of the King (exh. cat., ed. C. B. Bailey; New York, Stair Sainty Matthiesen, 1985)
T. Lefrançois: *Charles Coypel (1694–1752)* (Paris, 1994)

EMMA BARKER

Coyzevox [Coysevox], **Antoine** (*b* Lyon, 29 Sept 1640; *d* Paris, 10 Oct 1720). French sculptor. He was the son of Pierre Coyzevox (*fl* 1636–40), a joiner, and was one of the most accomplished sculptors of the reign of Louis XIV. He went to Paris in 1657 and entered the studio of Louis Lerambert, whose niece he married in 1666. (In 1679 he married his second wife, Claude Bourdy, the sister of a Lyon sculptor.) Also in 1666 he was accorded the title Sculpteur du Roi, and from 1667 to 1671 he worked at Saverne in the service of Cardinal François-Egon de Furstemberg, Prince-Bishop of Strasbourg, on the decoration of his new palace (destr.). He returned to Paris in 1671, but in 1675–7 he was in Lyon, where he carved his first religious work, a free-standing group of the *Virgin and Child* (marble, 1675–6; Lyon, St Nizier); in 1677 he was appointed a professor at the Lyon Académie. He planned to settle in Lyon and to set up a school attached to the Académie, but the success of his busts of the leading figures of the court of Louis XIV, such as *Charles Le Brun* (terracotta, 1676; London, Wallace), *Jean-Baptiste Colbert* (marble, 1677; Lignières, Cher, Château) and *Michel Le Tellier* (marble, *c.* 1677; Paris, Bib. Ste Geneviève), encouraged him to pursue his career in the capital. He soon became the principal portrait sculptor at court and one of the leading sculptors in France, working both for the Bâtiments du Roi and for private patrons. He settled in Paris in 1678 and was appointed a professor at the Académie Royale; in 1684 he was living at the Gobelins manufactory, though he also had a studio at the château of Versailles, and in 1698 he was granted an apartment in the Louvre, Paris.

Coyzevox's official career did not prevent him from accepting private commissions, especially for funerary sculpture. In 1677–8, in collaboration with Gaspard Collignon (*d* 1702), he executed the tomb of *Nicolas Bautru, Marquis de Vaubrun, and his Wife* (marble and gilt lead; chapel of the Château de Serrant, Maine-et-Loire), and later, in collaboration with Jean-Baptiste Tuby, that of *Jean-Baptiste Colbert* (marble, 1685–93; Paris, St Eustache). With Tuby and Etienne Le Hongre he made the tomb of *Cardinal Mazarin* (marble and bronze, 1689–93; Paris, Chapel of the Inst. France; see fig.); among his other notable tombs are those of *Charles Le Brun* (marble, *c.* 1692; Paris, St Nicolas-du-Chardonnet), *Henri de Lorraine, Comte d'Harcourt* (marble, 1704–11; Royaumont Abbey, Val d'Oise) and *Jules Hardouin Mansart* (marble, 1712; destr.; portrait medallion in Versailles, Château). All these have particularly fine portrait effigies of the deceased.

In his official capacity, Coyzevox worked extensively at the château of Versailles, producing sculptural embellishment for the Escalier des Ambassadeurs (1678–81, destr. 1750), including a magnificent bust of *Louis XIV* (marble; Versailles, Château) portrayed in Roman armour and full-bottomed wig; this was the first of a series of busts depicting the Sun King at various phases of his life. In 1679–82 Coyzevox took part in the decoration of the Grande Galerie, producing models for decorative sculpture in stucco and bronze (*in situ*), and the façade of the Cour de Marbre, including stone seated statues of *Might* and *Justice* (*in situ*). His most prominent work at Versailles is a large oval stucco relief in the Salon de la Guerre, which represents the King on horseback in classical armour, trampling an enemy. The *Triumph of Louis XIV* (*c.* 1681–3; *see* VERSAILLES, fig. 2) is one of the best examples of Coyzevox's vigorous, yet restrained and controlled style.

Coyzevox also produced sculpture for the gardens at Versailles (*see* VERSAILLES, §2). In 1682–3 he collaborated with Tuby on works for the *bosquet* of the Arc de Triomphe and later produced a number of sensitive marble copies of antique sculptures, including the *Nymph with a Shell* (1683–5; Paris, Louvre), the Medici *Venus* (1683–5; untraced), the *Crouching Venus* (1684–6; Paris, Louvre) and

Antoine Coyzevox, Jean-Baptiste Tuby and Etienne Le Hongre: tomb of *Cardinal Mazarin*, marble and bronze, 1689–93 (Paris, Chapel of the Institut de France)

Castor and Pollux (1685–1712; originally Galerie des Antiques, since 1712 in the Allée Royale, Versailles). The splendid marble *Vase of War*, decorated with an elaborate relief, dates from 1684, forming a pair with Tuby's *Vase of Peace* on the Parterre d'Eau. The bas-relief sculptures of the Colonnade date from 1685–7, as do the colossal bronze reclining river gods of the Parterre d'Eau by Coyzevox, Thomas Regnaudin, Le Hongre and Tuby. Coyzevox's *Garonne* and *Dordogne* (*in situ*), cast by the Keller brothers, are among the most successful of these groups.

In 1686 Coyzevox was entrusted with the large bronze equestrian statue of *Louis XIV* for the Place Royale at Rennes (erected 1726, destr. 1790s; bas-reliefs from the pedestal, *France Triumphing over the Seas* and *Louis XIV Receiving the Ambassadors from Siam*, Rennes, Mus. B.-A. & Archéol.). In 1687 the City of Paris commissioned from him a bronze statue of *Louis XIV in Triumph* for the Hôtel de Ville (Paris, Carnavalet). At the end of the century he was involved in the decoration of the Dôme

des Invalides (*see* PARIS, §V, 7), producing most notably the colossal marble statue of *Charlemagne* (1695–1706), which stands in the portal of the church. This was the period of Coyzevox's highest academic honours. He was elected Rector of the Académie Royale in 1694 and Director in 1702, the year in which the King granted him the unusually high pension of 4000 livres. Backed by Hardouin Mansart, he promoted the careers of his nephews from Lyon, Nicolas Coustou and Guillaume Coustou (i), who in turn became the leading sculptors of their generation. With them he played a part in the sculptural decoration of the park of the château of Marly, Yvelines. Coyzevox's four large free-standing groups for the park, *Neptune, Amphitrite, The Seine* and *The Marne* (marble, 1698–1707; Paris, Louvre), are the masterpieces of his old age and demonstrate the flexibility of a talent that was able to adapt the classicizing art of Versailles to the more delicate and elegant atmosphere at Marly. His large equestrian groups of *Mercury* and *Fame* (marble, 1701–2; Paris, Louvre) were intended for the ornamental horse pond at Marly and were moved to the entrance to the Tuileries gardens, Paris, in 1719; their lively spirit belongs to the art of the Rococo though they retain the dignity of the Grand Siècle. These characteristics of grace and charm became more pronounced in his marble statues of *Flora* and a *Hamadryad* (1709; Paris, Louvre) and of the Duchesse de Bourgogne as *Diana the Huntress* (1710; Paris, Louvre).

During his long career Coyzevox evolved from an early indebtedness to classical sources towards a more lively and graceful style, always balanced and faithful to nature. The kneeling marble effigy of *Louis XIV* for the group known as the *Vow of Louis XIV* (1713–15; Paris, Notre-Dame) is especially vivid and lifelike. Coyzevox owed much of his contemporary reputation to his talent for capturing the personalities of his models. This gift made him one of the great portraitists in the history of sculpture and enabled him to leave, in addition to his decorative and monumental works, a gallery of busts of the leading figures of his time, all of rare psychological penetration.

BIBLIOGRAPHY

Souchal; Thieme-Becker

L. Dussieux and others, eds: *Mémoires inédits*, ii (1854), pp. 33–9 ['Eloge funèbre' by J.-B. Fermelhuis (1721)]

A.-N. Dézallier d'Argenville: *Vies des fameux architectes et sculpteurs*, ii (1787), pp. 234–46

G. Keller-Dorian: *Antoine Coysevox: Catalogue raisonné de son oeuvre*, 2 vols (Paris, 1920)

L. Benoist: *Coysevox* (Paris, 1930)

U. Scheuerle: *Antoine Coysevox: Park Figuren, Studien zum Stil und Stilwandel* (diss., Munich, Ludwig-Maximilians U., 1969)

FRANÇOIS SOUCHAL

Cozad, Robert Henry. *See* HENRI, ROBERT.

Cozens. English family of artists. (1) Alexander Cozens was best known for drawings of imaginary mountain landscapes, in which the motifs were suggested by ink blots loosely sketched on the paper; these works played a large part in popularizing the 18th-century concept of the Sublime. His son and greatest pupil, (2) John Robert Cozens, transferred his father's landscapes of imagination into landscapes from nature, using his knowledge of the emotive powers of landscape to produce some of the most poetic and evocative watercolours of the British school.

(1) Alexander Cozens (*b* Russia, 1717; *d* London, 23 April 1786). Painter, drawing-master and theorist. His early years were spent in St Petersburg, where his father, Richard, originally from Deptford, was a master ship-builder to Peter the Great. Educated in England from 1727, Cozens was studying painting in London in 1735, but in the early 1740s he appears to have returned to Russia, where he worked on improving his topographical skills. In 1746 he sailed from St Petersburg to Livorno and studied in Italy for two years. His work there consisted mainly of pencil sketches of landscape, detailed pen-and-ink drawings and washed views made around Rome and along the Ligurian coast. In Rome he studied oil painting in the studio of Claude-Joseph Vernet, whose influence can be seen not only in Cozens's later oils but also in some of the landscapes drawn from nature during his time there. A surviving Roman sketchbook (New Haven, CT, Yale Cent. Brit. A.) shows the first evidence of his passion for devising and listing methods for drawing landscapes in various media. In January 1750 Cozens was appointed drawing-master to Christ's Hospital (a London charity school that educated orphans for apprenticeship). He taught there for four years, using as models his own drawings and the *New and Compleat Drawing Book* (1750), attributed to Edward Lens and Bernard Lens (iii), and incorporating engravings made after drawings by Bernard Lens (ii).

Cozens's earliest-known private pupils were George Simon, Viscount Nuneham (later 2nd Earl Harcourt), and his sister Elizabeth. He taught them landscape drawing by having them copy from his own work and later taught Elizabeth to compose landscapes using ink blots. This method was first set out by Cozens in 1759 in his *Essay to Facilitate the Inventing of Landskips* (copy in St Petersburg, Hermitage). In this two-page essay, Cozens noted that his method of inventing landscapes from blots improved upon that of Leonardo, who had recommended looking at cracks in walls and patterns in stones for inspiration. The only materials required by Cozens's method were a large brush fully loaded with Indian ink and two sheets of paper, one of them thin, for tracing the blot: 'With the swiftest hand make all possible variety of shapes and strokes upon your paper, confining the disposition of the whole to the general form in the example which you choose for your style of composition.' At the end of the *Essay*, an example of a blot and finished outline landscape was provided for each of the eight compositional styles.

In the 1760s Cozens's work as a private drawing-master increased, and his pupils included Amabel, Lady Grey (later Lady Polwarth, and then Marchioness de Grey), and members of the Grimston family of Yorkshire. William Mason and William and Sawrey Gilpin corresponded with Cozens, and they and Joseph Wright experimented with his methods. Around 1763 he began giving drawing lessons at Eton College. The sketchbook of one of his pupils, Sir George Beaumont, indicates that Cozens taught by traditional methods—copying from drawing manuals and from simple drawings by him and etchings after his own work. He used his blot method with more advanced pupils at Eton and with private pupils such as William Beckford,

who, taught by Cozens from the mid-1770s, became a lifelong friend and patron.

From 1760 Cozens was a member of the Society of Arts and the Free Society of Artists. He exhibited historical landscapes in oils (all untraced), views of Rome in water-colour and imaginary landscapes based on blots, in brown and black monochrome, which were heavily varnished and are now often very dark. Because of the vague titles under which he exhibited—*A Landscape* and *Its Companion*, for example—it is impossible to match them with the dozens of surviving landscapes from this period.

In the late 1760s and early 1770s Cozens was working on an elaboration of his 1759 *Essay*, to be entitled *The Various Species of Landscape Composition in Nature*. A printed list and 16 outline landscape etchings survive (London, BM and Tate), but the project appears not to have been completed. He exhibited several virtually monochrome landscapes at the Royal Academy in the 1770s, such as *Landscape in Chiaroscuro*, shown in 1773. Surviving landscape compositions from this period, such as the *Coastal Landscape* (New York, Met.), fall into the 16 types listed in the *Various Species*, although mountainous and sublime landscapes predominate (e.g. *High Hills*, Leeds, C.A.G.). Manuscript lists by students of Cozens's theories (London, Tate; New Haven, CT, Yale Cent. Brit. A.) reveal how Cozens indicated to the viewer the appropriate reaction to each of the 16 compositions in *Various Species*. The second composition, for example, of mountain tops, was intended to arouse such feelings as surprise, terror, silence, power and strength. These manuscript notes, along with comments on his system by contemporaries, indicate that Cozens intended his landscapes to have a moral effect on those who viewed them.

The 300 or so subscribers to Cozens's *Principles of Beauty, Relative to the Human Head* (1778) included George III, Edmund Burke, numerous aristocrats, several artists and pupils from Eton. A large folio, with an essay in English and French, it included tables of noses, eyes and mouths as well as profile outlines of the 16 kinds of beauty ('sensible', 'spirited', 'haughty' etc). Hairstyles after

Alexander Cozens: *Landscape with a Waterfall*, brown ink and grey wash, 227×301 mm, probably mid-1780s (London, British Museum)

the Antique, on tissue paper, could be placed over these different profiles, and Cozens intended the work for use both by professional and by amateur artists.

Cozens's later years were devoted to teaching the British royal family and working on his final and best-known publication, *A New Method of Assisting the Invention in Drawing Original Compositions of Landscape* (1786), the most detailed explanation of his blot system, with 16 aquatint plates of blots. The wash drawings produced by Cozens in preparation and as explanatory examples for this system are his most beautiful works, such as the *Landscape with a Waterfall* (London, BM; see fig.).

Cozens's landscape systems were greatly admired by his contemporaries. He was a deeply intellectual and ambitious artist who devised systems for amateur and professional artists that had not only intrinsic artistic value but an additional purpose of providing moral improvement through the study of spiritually uplifting landscape compositions.

WRITINGS

An Essay to Facilitate the Inventing of Landskips, Intended for Students in the Art (London, 1759)

The Shape, Skeleton and Foliage of Thirty-two Species of Trees (London, 1771)

Principles of Beauty, Relative to the Human Head (London, 1778)

A New Method of Assisting the Invention in Drawing Original Compositions of Landscape (London, 1786)

BIBLIOGRAPHY

K. Sloan: 'A New Chronology for Alexander Cozens', *Burl. Mag.*, cxxvii/983 (1985), pp. 70–75; cxxvii/987 (1985), pp. 355–63

For further bibliography, *see* §2 below.

(2) John Robert Cozens (*b* London, 1752; *d* London, *bur* 1 Jan 1798). Painter, draughtsman and printmaker, son of (1) Alexander Cozens.

1. LIFE AND WORK. He was taught by his father, and an album by John Robert (Aberystwyth, N. Lib. Wales) indicates that he also learnt to sketch landscape directly from nature. The album contains drawings that record sketching tours to Nacton, near Ipswich, Suffolk (Aug 1768); day trips to the outskirts of London: Greenwich and Blackheath (1768, 1771), Epsom (1768) and Hampstead (1770–71); and a trip to Matlock, Derbys (June 1772). The earliest of these sketches are careful pencil drawings, some later reworked in pen, ink and wash, and there is at least one attempt at added colour. Later drawings are freer, either noting an idea for a composition or recording light and shade with rapid washes of ink over pencil. His father worked mainly in monochrome brown or grey washes, and John Robert's earliest exhibits (he exhibited at the Society of Artists every year from 1767 to 1771) were also in this medium.

Around 1772 Cozens seems to have followed his uncle, Robert Edge Pine, to Bath, where in November 1773 he published *Eight Views of Bath* that he had drawn, etched and washed himself. He was still there the following March when he advertised these topographical views, enlivened with staffage, in the *Bath Chronicle*. In 1776 he exhibited his first oil painting at the Royal Academy; this, a *Landscape with Hannibal in his March over the Alps, Showing to his Army the Fertile Plains of Italy* (untraced), was greatly admired. A blot drawing of this subject (London, V&A; attrib. Alexander Cozens and John Robert Cozens) indicates that this large history painting in oils was composed according to his father's blot method for inventing landscapes.

In late summer 1776 Cozens accompanied Richard Payne Knight, the scholar, antiquarian and connoisseur, to the Swiss Alps. Together they visited, among other places, the pass between Chamonix and Martigny, the Rhône glacier and the Reichenbach falls, which were almost inaccessible and had seldom before been approached by British tourists. Cozens depicted the sublimity of the Alps in 57 pen, ink and wash drawings made for Payne Knight as a record of his tour, stimulated, perhaps, by Edmund Burke's *Philosophical Inquiry into our Ideas of the Beautiful and Sublime* (1757) and other literature on the subject.

During the next 18 months, often in the company of Thomas Jones, Cozens travelled around the Italian countryside, visiting Tivoli and Naples as well as the volcanic lakes of the Alban Hills. His choice of subject-matter—as shown in *Lake Nemi* and *Lake Albano* (versions in Toronto, A.G. Ont.; London, V&A, and elsewhere)—often reflected those Classical sites popular with Grand Tourists. His depictions utilized the classical compositional formulae of Claude Lorrain, Nicolas Poussin and Gaspard Dughet. Sometimes his choice of subject-matter, however, also reflected his own familiarity with Classical authors and his profound understanding of the Sublime: the dark caverns Cozens painted in the Campagna (examples in Birmingham, Mus. & A.G.; London, V&A) are redolent of Hades in Virgil's *Aeneid*.

Cozens made larger, more finished and more colourful versions of some of the Payne Knight watercolours for other British patrons, while still in Rome and following his return to England. In Rome, Payne Knight had commissioned Cozens also to make large watercolours from drawings by Charles Gore (1729–1807) and J. P. Hackert, done in 1777 on their expedition under the leadership of Payne Knight to investigate the ancient remains and modern manners of Sicily. One of the most evocative and Sublime of these is the view of *Mount Etna from the Grotto del Capro* (London, BM), which depicts the expedition's members huddled around a fire before their midnight ascent of the volcano.

Cozens left Rome for England on 8 April 1779, living in Bath until 1782. There he worked up finished watercolours from his Continental sketches and drawings; his many patrons included Sir Richard Colt Hoare, Joseph Windham, Thomas Sunderland, Dr Chelsum and, most particularly, the young, wealthy William Beckford, who lived not far from Bath at Fonthill, Somerset, and who was also a pupil and close friend of Cozens's father, Alexander.

In May 1782, as one among a large entourage of tutors, doctors, musicians and servants, Cozens left for Italy with Beckford. They travelled swiftly through the Tyrol to Padua, Venice and Rome, finally arriving at Sir William Hamilton's villa in Naples. The route and Cozens's subsequent activities in and around Naples are documented in seven sketchbooks (pencil and grey wash; U. Manchester, Whitworth A.G.). Beckford left for Geneva that September, while Cozens remained in Italy, at Naples and Rome, where he finished watercolours for Beckford and where he was frequently in the company of Thomas Jones,

Allan Ramsay and Sir George Beaumont, another former pupil of Cozens's father. In the autumn of 1783 Cozens returned to England via the Grande Chartreuse, visiting Beckford at Geneva. Beckford was a capricious and demanding patron, but the 94 watercolours he owned by Cozens, such as the *View from Mirabella, Villa of Count Algarotti in the Euganean Hills* (London, V&A) and *St Peter's from the Villa Borghese, Rome* (U. Manchester, Whitworth A.G.), were the most poetic and original watercolours the artist ever produced.

On his return to England, Cozens seems to have stayed in London, continuing to produce finished watercolours from both Continental tours for various patrons. He also painted large, serene watercolours dominated by low horizons and broad expanses of quiet sky. These included views of London from sites traditionally popular with artists, such as Greenwich Park (U. London, Courtauld Inst. Gals), Windsor Park (Bedford, Cecil Higgins A.G.) and the Thames from Richmond Hill (New Haven, CT, Yale Cent. Brit. A.), while others, of Windermere in the Lake District and the Suffolk and Essex countryside, may have been commissioned by Beaumont. He did not exhibit, however, and the only evidence of new activity was at the end of the 1780s, when he published 14 soft-ground etchings of trees. Several sets of proofs (London, BM) were washed with grey or yellow, and later published sets were in aquatint. The landscapes in which he set his examples of trees were not only appropriate to each species but as dramatically and beautifully composed as his watercolours had come to be. His last painting, *Mountainous Landscape with Beech Trees* (London, V&A), dated 1792, was based in part on one of these etchings.

Cozens suffered from bouts of melancholia all his life, but the malaria he caught in Italy in 1782 may have contributed to the mental illness that in February 1794 led to him being placed under the care of Dr Thomas Monro, the physician to Bethlehem Hospital (Bedlam). Several patrons and pupils, both of Cozens and of his father, as well as of the Royal Academy, organized financial support for him and his family. Within four years he died.

2. WORKING METHODS AND TECHNIQUE. The earliest work by Cozens, the sketches made around Nacton and Matlock, provide a clear indication of the method he used throughout his life. The majority were pencil sketches, but some were washed on the spot to record light and shade or later touched up with pen and ink or coloured washes. Figures were inserted to indicate scale, and dimensions were exaggerated or objects moved to conform with the mood or effect Cozens sought. Figures and animals incorporated into finished watercolours were probably chosen by Cozens from his collection of tracings and freehand copies made after figures in prints and drawings by other artists. This practice was recommended by his father, and a large number of animal studies on oiled paper were

1. John Robert Cozens: *Lake Albano*, watercolour, 441×622 mm, *c.* 1780 (Leeds, City Art Gallery)

2. John Robert Cozens: *Shepherd's Hut between Naples and Portici*, watercolour, 268×371 mm, *c.* 1782 (London, Victoria and Albert Museum)

discovered at the back of the National Library of Wales album.

The Alpine views drawn for Payne Knight were first sketched in pencil, then washed in grey or brown (sometimes with blue or green highlights), and finally details of foliage and shading on rocks and edges of mountains were picked out with black or brown pen and ink. Figures, if added, were indicated summarily in order to emphasize the scale of the mountains. The Payne Knight drawings all measured approximately 230×350 mm (or 350× 230 mm), but larger copies, such as the *Ober Hasli Valley from the South-east* (371×530 mm, 1778; London, V&A), were made for other patrons.

In these later copies and in his first Italian watercolours, such as *Lake Albano* (see fig. 1), the monochromatic, cool colours of the Payne Knight drawings are replaced by warm washes of yellow and orange, soft greys and dark blues. The outline of the basic shapes was first sketched in pencil, then broad washes of colour were laid on to set the overall tone. Finally, working from light to dark, forms and shapes were created by successively narrower washes and a build up of tiny strokes of colour to indicate grass, trees, bushes, buildings and figures. Pen was not used at all in these large works; necessary details were drawn in at the end with the finest of brushes. Cozens continued to refine this method for the remainder of his life, learning to use wash and colour like oil paint. The result was works of watercolour on paper that had the presence and effect of oil paintings—even their size rivalled oils, sometimes as

large as 500×700 mm. They evoked a powerful emotional response from viewers, which Cozens prompted through his choice of compositional viewpoints, colour and weather effects, most successfully in the Italian views painted for William Beckford, such as the dramatic *Shepherd's Hut between Naples and Portici* (see fig. 2), with its approaching storm and melancholy shepherd.

3. CRITICAL RECEPTION AND POSTHUMOUS REPU-TATION. Cozens's work was much praised by fellow artists and other contemporaries during his lifetime and for several decades after his death, but by the middle of the 19th century he was forgotten, remaining so until his rediscovery early in the 20th century by Oppé and others. One contemporary, Thomas Grimston, wrote that Cozens's first (and only) Royal Academy exhibit, the *Hannibal*, which he noted was in Cozens's father's style, astounded everyone (letter to his father John, May 1776; Hull, Humberside Co. Rec. Office, Grimston Papers, DDGR 42/26). Turner stated that he learnt more from this oil painting than from anything he had then seen, and there is no doubt it was a significant precursor to Turner's own successful *Snowstorm: Hannibal and his Army Crossing the Alps* (1812; London, Tate).

While Cozens was under Dr Monro's care, the doctor had access to some of Cozen's Continental sketches, and he employed Turner and Thomas Girtin to copy them. This exposure at Monro's 'Academy' to the compositional approach Cozens took toward Alpine and Italian scenery had a formative influence on the work of both artists, particularly on Turner's approach to Sublime and evocative scenery and Girtin's approach to panoramic landscape. Henry Fuseli described Cozens's watercolours as creations of 'an enchanted eye', drawn with 'an enchanted hand'; strong praise also came from John Constable, who knew Cozens's work through their mutual patron Sir George Beaumont and who owned at least one watercolour, the *Valley of the Eisach in the Tyrol, near Brixen* (Ottawa, N.G.).

BIBLIOGRAPHY

A. P. Oppé: *Alexander and John Robert Cozens* (London, 1952)

M. Hardie: *Watercolour Painting in Britain*, i (London, 1966)

John Robert Cozens (exh. cat. by F. W. Hawcroft, U. Manchester, Whitworth A.G.; London, V&A; 1971)

Catalogue of Seven Sketch-books by John Robert Cozens (sale cat., intro. A. Blunt; London, Sotheby's, 1973)

The Art of Alexander and John Robert Cozens (exh. cat., ed. A. Wilton; New Haven, CT, Yale Cent. Brit. A., 1980)

K. Sloan: *Alexander and John Robert Cozens: The Poetry of Landscape* (London, 1986)

——: 'A Cozens Album in the National Library of Wales, Aberystwyth', *Walpole Soc.*, lvii (1995)

KIM SLOAN

Cozza, Francesco (*b* Stilo di Calabria, 1605; *d* Rome, 13 Jan 1682). Italian painter and etcher. He painted religious works and decorative frescoes, in a classical style of exceptional purity and restraint. He probably moved at the end of the 1620s to Rome, where he studied with Domenichino (Pascoli), whose influence is evident in his first dated work, *St Joseph with Child and Angels* (1632; Rome, S Andrea delle Fratte). Here Cozza's isolation from the most modern trends in Roman painting, and his fidelity to Domenichino and to the Roman works of Annibale Carracci, is already established and was to endure throughout his career. In 1634 and 1635 he worked on frescoes of the *Virtues* in the pendentives of the dome of S Ambrogio alla Massima, Rome (*in situ*). Unlike the pendentive figures by Domenichino at S Andrea della Valle and at S Carlo ai Catinari, Rome, which respond to the illusionism of Giovanni Lanfranco's Baroque art, Cozza's *Virtues* retain a sober classicism and emphasize a clear didactic content. He very probably followed Domenichino to Naples in 1635–6. Here he studied the work of Pacecco, whose art has an affinity with his both in feeling and in a concern for the clear and lucid rendering of devotional subjects. Typical of Cozza's work of this period is the *Holy Family in the Carpenter's Shop* (Naples, Capodimonte). His approach was well received in Naples, where the new Baroque art of Lanfranco was not yet established.

Cozza returned in the late 1630s to Rome, where he remained aloof from the most modern developments. His painting retained a quiet naturalism, which sought to evoke in the spectator a serene meditation on sacred themes rather than a sense of awe. In 1640 the Calabrian Minimite fathers commissioned him to fresco the sacristy of S Francesco di Paola, Rome. However, this commission was transferred to Sassoferrato in July 1641, and Cozza executed only a *Crucifixion with St Francis of Paola* in the

Francesco Cozza: *Hagar and Ishmael*, oil on canvas, 1.27×1.80 m, 1664 (Copenhagen, Statens Museum for Kunst)

chapter house (*in situ*). In the 1650s, after the death of Pope Urban VIII and the advent of Pope Innocent X, the intense creativity of the early years of the century was succeeded by a period of consolidation. Cozza looked back to his early sources of inspiration, and in the frescoes of scenes from the *Life of St Carlo Borromeo* (*c.* 1656; Rome, S Andrea delle Fratte) he returned to a pure form of classicism, indebted to Domenichino, which emphasizes clarity of gesture and expression.

From 1659 Cozza won the patronage of Prince Camillo Pamphili. Between July 1658 and March 1659 he was involved with the fresco decorations of the Stanza del Fuoco in the Pamphili palace at Valmontone. Here mythical themes, such as the *Forge of Vulcan*, serve as pretexts for realistic scenes, in this case of men working with fire. At Valmontone, Cozza worked alongside Mattia Preti and Gaspard Dughet, and his later work shows their influence. A small group of landscapes, such as *Hagar and Ishmael* (1664; Copenhagen, Stat. Mus. Kst; see fig.), show his interest in the classical landscapes of Dughet and Salvator Rosa. Between 1667 and 1673 he frescoed the *Triumph of Divine Wisdom*, a celebration of the Pamphili family, on the library ceiling in the Palazzo Pamphili, Piazza Navona, Rome (*in situ*). Here, although the allegorical figures are still in the tradition of Domenichino, the flickering patterns of light and shade and the sense of a vast open sky reveal Cozza's response to Preti's revolutionary treatment of space. In 1675 he frescoed the Salone Verde of the Palazzo Altieri, Rome, with allegories of *Autumn* and *Winter* (both *in situ*), distinguished by their pale colours and silvery light. His last certain work, *St John the Baptist Preaching* (1675; Rome, Pal. Barberini), remains based on the ideals of Domenichino. Five etchings (B. pp. 362–6), after his own works, are known.

DBI

BIBLIOGRAPHY

L. Pascoli: *Vite* (1730–36), ii, pp. 64–75
L. Montalto: 'Gli affreschi di palazzo Pamphili in Valmontone', *Commentari*, vi (1955), pp. 267–302
——: 'Francesco Cozza nella libreria Pamphili a Piazza Navona', *Commentari*, vii (1956), pp. 267–302
——: 'Aggiunte all' opera di Francesco Cozza', *Paragone*, vii/73 (1956), pp. 18–21
J. T. Spike: *Italian Masters of the Seventeenth Century* (1981), 41 [XIX/i] of *The Illustrated Bartsch*, ed. W. Strauss (New York, 1978–) [B.]
L. Trezzani: *Francesco Cozza, 1605–1682* (Rome, 1981)

TIZIANA MANCINI

Cozzarelli. Italian family of artists.

(1) Guidoccio (di Giovanni) Cozzarelli (*b* Siena, 1450; *d* Siena, 1516–17). Painter and illuminator. He trained in the workshop of Matteo di Giovanni, with whom he was associated from about 1470 to 1483 and with whom he is often confused. Early illuminations for the Antiphonals of Siena Cathedral (*c.* 1480; Siena, Bib. Piccolomini, 6F, 15Q, 26R) and a number of securely attributed paintings demonstrate Guidoccio's development of a fine, distinctive style that reflects Tuscan and northern European as well as Sienese influences. A scene from an Antiphonal depicting a *Religious Ceremony* (Siena, Bib. Piccolomini), a fragment of an altarpiece depicting the *Annunciation* and the *Journey to Bethlehem* (Coral Gables, FL, U. Miami, Lowe A. Mus.) and a cassone panel depicting the *Legend of Cloelia* (New York, Met.) all combine masses of rusticated and Classical architectural structures into perspective vistas. The dense cityscapes are played off against open sky and landscape, while porticos, gateways and vaulted spaces form the stage on which tactile and sprightly figures re-enact religious drama or ancient legends. In the *Baptism of Christ with SS Jerome and Augustine* (1470; Sinalunga, S Bernardino) the deep, panoramic landscape and triad of angels suggest Umbrian influences. A connection with Piero della Francesca through Matteo di Giovanni is possible.

Guidoccio's familiarity with contemporary trends in architecture and painting and his fashionable interest in the exploitation of antique subject-matter suggest points of contact with Francesco di Giorgio Martini and another member of his own family, the sculptor (2) Giacomo Cozzarelli, who accompanied Francesco di Giorgio to Urbino around 1476–8. Guidoccio produced manuscript copies of Francesco di Giorgio's architectural texts (Turin, Bib. Reale, C.14B; Florence, Bib. N. Cent., C. Palat. 767), and it has been suggested that he was responsible for colouring Giacomo Cozzarelli's terracotta *Lamentation* group (Siena, Chiesa dell'Osservanza). In accordance with common practice, Guidoccio also produced numerous traditional images of the Virgin and Child. By the end of the 15th century in Siena his workshop produced the majority of secular cupboards and cassone panels depicting scenes from Classical mythology.

BIBLIOGRAPHY

R. van Marle: *Italian Schools* (1923–38)
B. Berenson: *Central and North Italian Schools* (1968), ii, pp. 97–101
G. Scaglia: 'Autour de Francesco di Giorgio Martini, ingénieur et dessinateur', *Rev. A.*, xlviii (1980), pp. 7–25
M. Ciatti: 'I costumi e i tessuti: Proposte di lettura', *Restauro di una terracotta del quattrocento: Il* Compianto di Giacomo Cozzarelli (exh. cat. ed. A. M. Giusti; Florence, Mus. Opificio Pietre Dure, 1984), pp. 115–39
Painting in Renaissance Siena, 1420–1500 (exh. cat. by K. Christiansen, L. Kanter and C. B. Strehlke, New York, Met., 1988), pp. 282–5

VIRGINIA ANNE BONITO

(2) Giacomo [Jacopo] Cozzarelli (*b* Siena, 20 Nov 1453; *d* Siena, 25 March 1515). Sculptor, painter and architect. His brother, Battista Cozzarelli (*b* 1483), was a goldsmith: his relationship to (1) Guidoccio Cozzarelli is unclear. His own activity began with the painting of cassoni and processional chariots, and extended to sculpture and architecture. His direct contact with Francesco di Giorgio Martini is first documented in October 1471 in connection with the Ospedale di S Maria della Scala in Siena. Giacomo followed Francesco to Urbino around 1476, and in 1477, in his tax return to Siena, declared that he was in Urbino 'to paint'. In 1488 he stated in another tax return: 'I have been in Urbino with Francesco di Giorgio di Martino, and I have been already 10 years' (Bacci). No evidence of Giacomo's work in Urbino has been found and the attributions to him of decorative works in the Palazzo Ducale are not entirely convincing. In 1489 he collaborated with Francesco di Giorgio, with whom he had returned to Siena just after 1488, on the production of two large bronze *Angels* (Siena Cathedral), which, together with another two (*in situ*) by Giovanni di Stefano, were placed at the sides of the main altar. In 1490 Giacomo supervised the casting of Francesco's *Angels* (see Fumi) and from 1491 to 1495 he cast cannon for the Siena commune.

Cozzarelli's work is not easily distinguished from that of Francesco di Giorgio, for whom he may have painted panels and perhaps also illustrated pages of his architectural treatise. Cozzarelli successfully followed Francesco's dynamic interpretation in his sculptural works, accentuating the popular character of the figures also through the technique of polychrome terracotta. The most notable example of this is his group of seven statues comprising the very expressive *Lamentation* in the Petrucci Chapel (1498; Siena, Osservanza; see fig.) connected with Francesco di Giorgio and his *Pietà* di Querciagrona. With Francesco, Giacomo probably worked also on the *Virgin and Child* (Torrita di Siena, church of S Leonard in Montefollonico). Among the numerous other Sienese works latterly attributed to him are the *St Lucia* (S Niccolò e Lucia) and the *St Margherita* (Santi Matteo e Margherita ai Tufi), while the monochrome terracotta of *St Sigismund* (completed 1507; Siena, Carmine), the tomb plaque of *Giovan Battista Tondi* (Siena, Ospedale S Maria della Scala) and the polychrome wooden statue of *St Vincenzo Ferreri* (completed 1512; Siena, Santo Spirito) may be considered to be among his most mature and independent works. In 1505–6 he was working on bronze statues (unexecuted)

of the twelve Apostles, designed for Siena Cathedral by Francesco di Giorgio.

The distinction between the two artists is similarly unclear with regard to some architectural works in Siena, in particular the church of the Osservanza, which Francesco may have planned in 1476. From 1495 Giacomo also directed new fortifications in Montepulciano, where Francesco made a tour of inspection in 1496. Both S Sebastiano in Valle Piatta, begun around 1493, and Villa Chigi (1496–1505) at Le Volte were probably designed by Francesco, but were probably more likely continued by Baldassarre Peruzzi rather than by Cozzarelli. Certain simplifications introduced into the architectural language of Francesco di Giorgio make it seem more plausible that Cozzarelli designed the church of S Spirito, Siena, rebuilt between 1498 and 1504. Cozzarelli was employed by the commune in 1508, when he began the church of S Maria Maddalena (destr. 1526) outside Porta Tufi. In the same year the Palazzo del Magnifico, the massive residence commissioned by Pandolfo Petrucci and situated opposite the baptistery in Siena, was being completed by Giacomo. This house, which again echoes Francesco di Giorgio's architectural solutions, was partly altered after the sack and ruin following Petrucci's death (1512), but Cozzarelli's bronze fittings (*bracciali* and *portatorce*) are preserved on the exterior.

DBI   BIBLIOGRAPHY

P. Bacci: 'Commentarii dell'arte senese: I. Il pittore, scultore e architetto Iacopo Cozzarelli e la sua permanenza in Urbino con Francesco di Giorgio Martini dal 1478 al 1488; II. I due "angioletti" di bronzo (1489–1490) per l'altare del Duomo di Siena', *Bull. Sen. Stor. Patria*, n.s., iii (1932), pp. 97–112

L. Bersano: 'L'arte di Giacomo Cozzarelli', *Bull. Sen. Stor. Patria*, lxiv (1957), pp. 109–42

A. Cecchi: 'Giacomo Cozzarelli (Siena, 1453–1516): Bracciali', *Mostra di opere d'arte restaurate nelle provincie di Siena e Grosseto*, ii (Genoa, 1981), pp. 128–31

F. Fumi: 'Nuovi documenti per gli angeli dell'altar maggiore del Duomo di Siena', *Prospettiva*, xxvi (1981), pp. 9–25

Restauro di una terracotta del quattrocento: Il 'Compianto' di Giacomo Cozzarelli (exh. cat., ed. A. M. Giusti; Florence, Mus. Opificio Pietre Dure, 1984)

A. Ferrari, R. Valentini and M. Vivi: 'Il Palazzo del Magnifico a Siena', *Bull. Sen. Stor. Patria*, xcii (1985), pp. 107–53

C. Sisi: 'Giacomo Cozzarelli', *Domenico Beccafumi e il suo tempo* (Milan, 1990), pp. 540–47

A. Bagnoli: 'Gli angeli dell'altare del Duomo e la scultura a Siena alla fine del secolo', *Francesco di Giorgio e il rinascimento a Siena, 1450–1500*, ed. L. Bellosi (Milan, 1993), pp. 414–19

F. Cantatore: 'Opere bronzee', *Francesco di Giorgio architetto*, ed. F. P. Fiore and M. Tafuri (Milan, 1993), pp. 326–8

FRANCESCO PAOLO FIORE

Cozzi Porcelain Factory. Italian porcelain factory. It was established in the Cannaregio area of Venice by the banker and ceramic technician Geminiano Cozzi (1728–97) in 1764. Cozzi had been trained at the Vezzi Porcelain Factory in Venice and later established a partnership with the Saxon potter Nathaniel Friedrich Hewelke, a porcelain expert. The factory produced mostly hard-paste porcelain but also some maiolica and cream-coloured earthenwares in the English style. Tablewares and vases were decorated with chinoiseries, carnival scenes and floral designs in bright colours and thick gilding. Painters and sculptors such as Domenico Bosello worked at the factory. Cozzi's brother Vincenzo Cozzi also worked with him, and the

Giacomo Cozzarelli: *Lamentation*, polychrome terracotta group, 1498 (Siena, Church of the Osservanza, Petrucci Chapel)

factory is known to have remained in production until 1812.

BIBLIOGRAPHY

G. M. Urbani De Ghelthof: *Studi intorno alla ceramica veneziana* (Venice, 1876)

N. Barbantini: *De porcellane di Venezia e delle Nove* (Venice, 1936)

F. Stazzi: *Le porcellane veneziane di Geminiano e Vincenzo Cozzi* (Venice, 1982)

CARMEN RAVANELLI GUIDOTTI

Crabbe (van Espleghem) [Minnebroer], **Frans** [Master of the Crayfish; Master F.C.] (*b* Mechelen, *c.* 1480; *d* Mechelen, 1553). South Netherlandish printmaker. Friedländer first identified the Master of the Crayfish (Flem. *Crabbe*) as Frans Crabbe in 1921. It seems likely that Crabbe met and was influenced by Albrecht Dürer during the latter's visit to Mechelen in June 1521. In 1539 Crabbe acquired the workshop of Nicholas Hogenberg; he is recorded in Mechelen as a master in the Guild of St Luke and head of the Brotherhood of Our Lady. His work is transitional, combining late northern medieval subjects and compositions with a style and technique showing the influence of the Italian Renaissance. He was especially indebted to Lucas van Leyden in his concern for atmosphere and depth in landscape, and to Jan Gossart for Italianate figure types. He worked as an engraver, woodcutter and etcher but is noted for etching because of his unusual success in a medium considered by his contemporaries to be limited. His achievement lies in his ability to create graphic equivalents for a painterly style in this experimental medium (e.g. *Solomon and the Queen of Sheba*, *c.* 1525, see Popham, no. 26) and in his ambitious compositions, which show his ability to depict striking lighting and atmospheric conditions. Surviving examples of his work are rare.

Thieme–Becker

BIBLIOGRAPHY

M. J. Friedländer: 'Nicholas Hogenberg and Frans Crabbe, die Maler von Mecheln', *Jb. Kön.-Preuss. Kstsamml.*, xlii (1921), pp. 161–8

A. E. Popham: 'Catalogue of Etchings and Engravings of Frans Crabbe', *Pr. Colr Q.*, xxii (1935), pp. 194–211

——: 'The Engravings of Frans Crabbe van Espleghem', *Pr. Colr Newslett.*, xxii (1935), pp. 92–115

The Prints of Lucas van Leyden and his Contemporaries (exh. cat. by E. S. Jacobowitz and S. Loeb Stepaneck, Washington, DC, N.G.A.; Boston, MA, Mus. F.A.; 1983), pp. 277–86

ELLEN S. JACOBOWITZ

Crabeth. Dutch family of artists. With a striking, personal style that sets him apart from his contemporaries, (1) Dirck Crabeth was the most important Dutch stained-glass artist of the 16th century. His younger brother (2) Wouter Crabeth (i) was a less individual designer, whose work has a pleasant spaciousness, but the rendering of detail is not always satisfactory. The impressive windows (1555–71) of the St Janskerk, Gouda, executed largely by the Crabeth brothers, constitute one of the highpoints of Dutch art of that period. Their father was the glass painter Pieter Dircksz., nicknamed Crepel Pier. Van Mander devoted a few lines to Adriaen Pietersz. Crabeth (*d* 1553), apparently the eldest son and a painter who has so far remained obscure and is said to have been apprenticed to Jan Swart. Wouter Crabeth's son, Pieter (Woutersz.) Crabeth, fulfilled many important political functions in Gouda, including that of burgomaster. Pieter's son (3) Wouter Crabeth (ii) was also a painter; he travelled to Italy and worked in the Caravaggesque style practised by the Utrecht Caravaggisti.

(1) Dirck (Pietersz.) Crabeth (*fl* Gouda, 1539; *d* Gouda, 1574). Stained-glass and tapestry designer and cartographer. He is first mentioned in 1539 in connection with a window design commissioned by Count Floris van Egmond (1469–1539) for the Catherijnekerk in Utrecht. A drawing, the *Adoration of the Magi* (Haarlem, Teylers Mus.), which must be dated very early on stylistic grounds, makes it clear that Dirck had studied the work of Jan van Scorel in Utrecht. The same drawing also reveals how strongly the young artist was influenced by Jan Swart. Dirck's first important work is a group of stained-glass windows (1543; Paris, Mus. A. Déc.) for the cross-windows in the house of the Leiden bailiff Adriaen Dircksz. van Crimpen. The small scenes, framed by imaginary architecture, depict scenes from the *Lives of the Prophet Samuel and the Apostle Paul* and are stylistically so close to the work of Jan Swart that personal contact between the two artists can be assumed. The frames, unusual in the decorative arts of that time, demonstrate Crabeth's qualities as a designer of ornament. Judging from a number of preparatory drawings and a few small panes, mostly executed by others after his designs, Dirck must have designed other small stained-glass windows later in his career. A series of interesting allegories, made presumably in the early 1550s and including the *Allegory with Christ as Salvator mundi* (Amsterdam, Rijksmus.), is related to allegories compiled at about the same time by Maarten van Heemskerck and Dirck Volkertsz. Coornhert.

It is possible to get an idea of Dirck's monumental work done before 1555 from a number of preparatory drawings and surviving fragments of the window showing the *Virgin Mary as the Woman of the Apocalypse with Charles V as Donor* (1547; The Hague, St Jacobskerk). This must have been a formative period for the artist: besides being influenced by Jan Swart, he seems also to have admired an anonymous artist, whose *Judgement of Solomon* (London, V&A) served as a design for one of his windows in St Jacobskerk. The influence is especially obvious in the arrangement of figures in small groups. In 1555 the window with the *Death of the Virgin* was installed in the Oude Kerk in Amsterdam. On this occasion Dirck worked alongside Lambert van Noort, as he was to do shortly afterwards in Gouda.

The rebuilding of the St Janskerk, Gouda, which had burnt down in 1552, was approached with great enthusiasm. The Dean of the St Mariakerk in Utrecht, Herman Lethmaat, was probably instrumental in finding donors for the windows and was himself one. Apart from the workshop of the Crabeths, various Antwerp workshops and Lambert van Noort were called upon to help. During the first five years, six designs by Dirck were executed, of which the three windows in the choir make a particularly beautiful group: the *Baptism* (1555; see fig.) with, on either side, *St John Recognizing Christ* (1556) and *St John Preaching* (1557). They combine an almost ascetic austerity with a love of landscape and a clever use of light effects. The hieratic figures recall the work of the Liège artist Lambert Lombard. The royal window in the transept, nearly 20 m high, dates from 1557 and was donated by

Dirck Crabeth: *Baptism* (detail), stained-glass window, 9.90×4.03 m, 1555 (Gouda, St Janskerk)

Philip II, then ruler of Holland. It shows the *Building of King Solomon's Temple* and the *Last Supper*. The majestic *Last Supper*, which features Mary Tudor, Philip II and his patron saint, is flanked by the building of the ideal church and a skilfully designed decorative cartouche. The *Baptism of the Eunuch* (1559) demonstrates Crabeth's distinctive manner of depicting compact rows of figures with individually characterized heads.

Although the Gouda windows survived the iconoclastic outbreak in 1566 and work on them continued afterwards, the glazing gradually came to a standstill. Dirck's design for *Christ Driving the Money-changers from the Temple*, probably commissioned as early as 1562, is dated 1567 but was not installed until 1569. Its donor, William the Silent of Orange Nassau, had by then instigated the resistance in the northern Netherlands to Philip II's rule. The donor's frame for the window was probably never installed, and William presumably never paid for the window. One more window, with *Judith and Holofernes* (1571), shows the full range of Dirck's skills. The artist used a relatively simple composition as an opportunity to provide eye-catching decoration and a brilliant landscape background, containing a view of the siege of the town of Bethulia. After the installation of this window the glazing work was suspended for 20 years. Full-size cartoons for most of the windows are kept at the church in Gouda, a unique but virtually

inaccessible collection. Dirck lavished much care on these cartoons, occasionally changing minor aspects of the composition and, as appears from his study for the background of the *Judith and Holofernes*, devotedly putting in more detail than was required for the actual window. That neither the windows nor the cartoons at Gouda have ever been fully published is surprising.

Apart from designing windows, Dirck drew maps and also made tapestry designs for Willem Andriesz. de Raedt (*fl* 1541–73/4), a Leiden weaver.

(2) Wouter (Pietersz.) Crabeth (i) (*fl* Gouda, 1559; *d* Gouda, 1589). Stained glass designer and draughtsman, brother of (1) Dirck Crabeth. He is presumed to have been taught by Frans Floris and before that probably assisted Dirck. He designed four windows for the St Janskerk in Gouda, in a style that was more spacious and more influenced by Renaissance ideas than was his brother's. *The Adoration of the Shepherds* (1564), an attractive composition combining bright colours with an uncomplicated arrangement of figures, owes much to the work of Lambert van Noort, while *Heliodorus Driven from the Temple* (1566) suggests the inescapable influence of Raphael. Wouter is known to have made a journey on Dirck's behalf to draw portraits of several donors for the windows, and of his surviving cartoons the portraits (e.g. *Margaret of Parma*) are the most distinguished. He must also have designed small independent windows. A few drawings have been ascribed to him, of which *The Art of Measurement* (Paris, Ecole N. Sup. B.-A., inv. no. M 1353) is the most attractive.

BIBLIOGRAPHY

J. Q. van Regteren Altena and others: *De Goudse glazen, 1555–1603: Beschouwingen over Gouda, haar Sint Janskerk en de gebrandschilderde glazen* (The Hague, 1938)

A. van de Boom: *Monumentale glasschilderkunst in Nederland*, i (The Hague, 1940)

A. A. J. Rijksen: *Gespiegeld in kerkeglas* (Lochem, 1947)

Z. van Ruyven-Zeman: 'Some Drawings Attributed to Wouter Crabeth, the Glass Painter from Gouda', *Master Drgs*, xxiii–xxiv (1985–6), pp. 544–51

Kunst voor de beeldenstorm: Noordnederlandse kunst, 1525–1580 (exh. cat., ed. J. P. Filedt Kok, W. Halsema-Kubes and W. Th. Kloek; Amsterdam, Rijksmus., 1986), pp. 282–95, 359–67

WOUTER TH. KLOEK

(3) Wouter (Pietersz.) Crabeth (ii) (*b* Gouda, *c.* 1594; *d* Gouda, 18 June 1644). Painter, grandson of (2) Wouter Crabeth (i). According to the early 18th-century Gouda historian Ignatius Walvis, his teacher was Cornelis Ketel. This may be a reference either to the well-known Amsterdam painter or to his lesser-known relative and namesake from Gouda, who was also an artist.

In 1615, in Paris, Wouter Crabeth (ii) wrote a poem in the *album amicorum* of Wybrand de Geest I, a former pupil of Abraham Bloemaert in Utrecht. The next entry in the album, dated 15 February 1616, was made by the Delft painter Leonard Bramer in Aix-en-Provence. It is likely that de Geest, Bramer and Crabeth travelled to Italy together; in 1619 Crabeth and Bramer were recorded as living in the same house on the Strada della Croce in the Roman parish of S Lorenzo in Lucina. The same two artists were living in a house on the Via dei Pontifici in 1621 and 1622. It is also likely that Crabeth is the 'Signor Gualtiero, pittore' listed as living on the Via Ferratine in the spring of 1625. In 1623 Crabeth was a founder-member of the Schildersbent, the association of Netherlandish artists in Rome, where he was given the Bent-name 'Almanack'. His portrait appears next to that of the Utrecht artist Cornelis van Poelenburch in a drawing of the Bent founders (Rotterdam, Mus. Boymans–van Beuningen). Crabeth was back in Gouda by 27 July 1626, when he became a member of a Civic Guard company.

Although Crabeth's earliest certain work is the signed and dated altarpiece *Assumption of the Virgin* (1628; Gouda, Old Catholic church, on loan to the Stedel. Mus. Catharina Gasthuis), several works have been tentatively assigned to his Italian period, including *Christ among the Doctors* (Vienna, Ksthist. Mus.), which reveals close stylistic affinities with the work of the Utrecht artist Dirck van Baburen, who had also travelled to Rome. The large *Incredulity of Thomas* (Amsterdam, Rijksmus., on dep. Gouda, Stedel. Mus. Catharina Gasthuis; see fig.), which bears traces of a signature and is firmly documented to Crabeth in a reproductive engraving by Cornelis van Dalem I, appears to bridge the stylistic gap between the Vienna picture and the altarpiece of 1628. It also reveals contacts with such Caravaggesque artists as the Liège painter Gerard Douffet and the enigmatic master, probably French, known as the Master of the Judgement of Solomon, both of whom Crabeth could have met in Rome. Besides the 1628 altarpiece, other pictures by Crabeth, possibly including the *Incredulity of Thomas*, have provenances going back to the Old Catholic parish of St Janskerk in Gouda. Among these are the signed *Adoration of the Magi* (1631; untraced) and the unusual, signed historiated portrait *St Bernard of Clairvaux and the Duke of Aquitaine* (1641; Ghent, priv. col.), in which Petrus Purmerent, apparently Crabeth's patron for these religious works, is represented as St Bernard and shown wearing a chasuble, from the Old Catholic church, that still survives (on loan to the Stedel. Mus. Catharina Gasthuis, Gouda).

Crabeth also painted a number of genre pictures, for example the signed *Cheating Card Players* (Warsaw, N. Mus.) and a closely related composition of the same subject (Berlin, Bodemus.), which suggest that he was in contact with the artists known as the UTRECHT CARAVAGGISTI. These works reveal the influence of van Baburen and Hendrick ter Brugghen in subject-matter and in the strong, dramatic lighting. There are also several other portraits executed by Crabeth; the most interesting of these are the historiated portrait of the Gouda glassmaker

Wouter Crabeth (ii): *Incredulity of Thomas* 2.4×3.1 m, 1630–44 (Amsterdam, Rijksmuseum: on deposit at Gouda, Stedelijk Museum Het Catharina Gasthuis)

Jan Dirx Westerhout and his wife, who appear as the bridal couple in the *Marriage at Cana* (1641; Gouda, Stedel. Mus. Catharina Gasthuis), and his group portrait of the Gouda civic guard company, the *St Joris Doelen* (Gouda, Stedel. Mus. Catharina Gasthuis), completed shortly before Crabeth's death.

BIBLIOGRAPHY

I. Walvis: *Beschrijving der stad Gouda* (Gouda, 1714)

A. von Schneider: *Caravaggio und die Niederländer* (Marburg, 1933)

G. J. Hoogewerff: *Nederlandsche kunstenaars te Rome (1600–1725): Uittreksels uit de parochiale archieven* (The Hague, 1942)

J. Schouten: 'Goudse schilderkunst in der tweede helft van de zestiende en de eerste helft van de seventiende eeuw', *Gouda zeven eeuwen stad: Hoofdstukken uit de geschiedenis van Gouda* (Gouda, 1972), pp. 381–428

B. Nicolson: *The International Caravaggesque Movement* (Oxford, 1979); review by L. J. Slatkes in *Simiolus*, xii (1981–2), pp. 167–83

Holländische Malerei in neuem Licht: Hendrick ter Brugghen und seine Zeitgenossen (exh. cat., ed. A. Blankert, L. J. Slatkes and others; Utrecht, Cent. Mus.; Brunswick, Herzog Anton Ulrich-Mus., 1986)

Portretten van echt en trouw [Portraits of matrimony and betrothal] (exh. cat., ed. E. de Jongh; Haarlem, Frans Halsmus., 1986)

Vouwblad Wouter Pietersz. Crabeth II (exh. cat. by X. van Eck, Gouda, Stedel. Mus. Catharina Gasthuis, 1986)

X. van Eck: 'Wouter Pietersz. Crabeth II en de parochie St Johannes de Doper in Gouda', *Oud-Holland*, ci (1987), pp. 35–49

LEONARD J. SLATKES

Crac de Montréal. *See* KRAK DE MONREAL.

Crace. English family of interior decorators. During the 19th century members of the family headed the most important decorating firm in Britain. For 131 years the business was handed down from father to son, and commissions included interiors for a number of royal palaces, aristocratic seats and major public buildings. The family worked with leading architects and designed interiors in the most advanced styles of the day, their work informed by careful study of major European architectural monuments. Sketchbooks and drawings document the individual role each Crace played as a designer.

In 1718 Thomas Crace (*b c.* 1695) set up as a coachmaker in Rochester Row, London. His eldest son, Edward Crace (*b* London, 1725; *d* London, 7 Dec 1799), was apprenticed in 1741 to the artist William Atkinson and in 1752 became a coach decorator in Long Acre, Covent Garden, London. An extant sketchbook (*c.* 1760; priv. col.) illustrates the facility with which Edward Crace designed in the French Rococo style.

Edward Crace made the natural transition to house decoration, establishing a decorating firm in 1768 in his Long Acre premises. In 1770 he provided gilt furniture, rich scagliola columns and arabesques in grisaille for the Pantheon (destr.), London, which was designed by James Wyatt and was the first major Neo-classical public building in Britain. The success of the scheme, Crace's most important commission, led to his appointment before 1778 as Keeper of Paintings to George III. Crace retired in the late 1780s.

Edward Crace was succeeded by his eldest son, (1) John Crace, who traded as John Crace & Co. His three sons, (2) Frederick Crace, Alfred Crace (*b* London, 13 July 1782; *d* Canada, 1849) and Henry Crace (*b* London, 23 Sept 1790), traded as John Crace & Sons from 1812 to 1826. Frederick's eldest son, (3) John Gregory Crace, became a full partner in Frederick Crace & Son in 1830

and continued to head the firm until his retirement *c.* 1880. His son (4) John Dibblee Crace began his professional career in 1854. The Crace firm reached its largest extent in 1873, having 101 regular employees. This number declined towards the end of the 19th century, particularly after the death of John Gregory Crace. In 1899 John Dibblee Crace closed the firm.

UNPUBLISHED SOURCES

Brighton, A.G. & Museums [designs and sketches]

London, V&A [designs and drgs by J. G. Crace; diaries, letters, geneal. mat. and other MSS; sketchbooks; photographs]

New York, Cooper-Hewitt Mus. [drgs and prts]

New York, Met. [drgs, prts and photographs]

Windsor Castle, Royal Lib. [watercolours of inter.]

BIBLIOGRAPHY

J. Morley: *The Making of the Royal Pavilion, Brighton* (London, 1984)

M. Aldrich: *The Crace Firm of Decorators, 1768 to 1899* (diss., U. Toronto, 1987)

——: 'Fit for an Emperor at Windsor', *Country Life*, clxxxii (8 Dec 1988), pp. 56–9

——: 'The Marquess and the Decorator', *Country Life*, clxxxiii (7 Dec 1989), pp. 162–7

M. Aldrich, ed. *The Craces: Royal Decorators, 1768–1899* (London, 1990)

The Craces: Royal Decorators, 1768–1899 (exh. cat. by M. Aldrich, Brighton, A.G. & Mus., 1990)

M. Aldrich: 'The Furniture of J. G. Crace and Son', *Antiques*, cxxxix (1991), pp. 1140–49

(1) John Crace (*b* Greenwich, 1 Nov 1754; *d* London, 8 May 1819). He briefly ran his own house-decorating business in London (1776–8) before taking over the family firm. By 1780 John Crace & Co. had a small number of regular employees, including a cousin also called John Crace. Country-house commissions with the architect Henry Holland included Althorp (*c.* 1790), Northants, and Woburn Abbey (*c.* 1790–95), Beds. At Woburn, Crace decorated Holland's Chinese Dairy (*c.* 1789) with bold chinoiseries that anticipated his work at the Royal Pavilion in Brighton. John Crace was also closely linked to the circle of John Soane, and he executed decorative schemes for Soane at 12 Lincoln's Inn Fields (*c.* 1792), London, and Pitzhanger Manor (*c.* 1802), Ealing, Middx. He also worked for Soane on the Bank of England (*c.* 1794), London, in his capacity as Painter to the Board of Works, and held the appointment of Painter to the Royal Hospital at Greenwich.

John Crace's most important work was for George, Prince of Wales (later Prince Regent and George IV, King of England), at Carlton House (*c.* 1785–95; destr.), London, and the Royal Pavilion (*c.* 1802–4), Brighton, where he created the first series of chinoiserie interiors with his son (2) Frederick Crace. John Crace also supplied furniture and Chinese works of art for the Pavilion. A group of drawings (New York, Cooper-Hewitt Mus.) executed in a bold, linear style can be attributed to him.

(2) Frederick Crace (*b* Greenwich, 3 June 1779; *d* London, 18 Sept 1859). Son of (1) John Crace. After an apprenticeship with Richard Holland, he began work for his father in 1793. He was particularly talented at gilding, marbling, graining and decorative painting, and in 1794 his work at Carlton House drew the attention of the Prince of Wales. From this time he worked almost exclusively for the Prince: he designed some of the interior decoration (*c.* 1802–4) at the Royal Pavilion, where he was recalled in 1815 to begin a new series of interiors in a spectacular

Chinese style including the downstairs Corridor (*c.* 1815) and the Music Room (*c.* 1817–20; both altered). For the latter he designed curtains, a carpet (rewoven) and a large suite of furniture, made by the firm of Bailey & Saunders of London.

In 1826 Frederick Crace became the sole head of the firm and between 1827 and 1834 carried out decorative painting and gilding at Windsor Castle, Berks, under the direction of the architect Jeffry Wyatville, in the Gothic and 'Old French' styles. He later became increasingly occupied with assembling and cataloguing an extensive collection of *c.* 6000 topographical views of London, now known as the Crace Collection (London, BM).

MEGAN ALDRICH

(3) John Gregory Crace (*b* London, 26 May 1809; *d* Dulwich, 13 Aug 1889). Son of (2) Frederick Crace. He joined the family decorating business in London in 1826 and became a full partner in 1830. In 1827 and 1829 Crace travelled to the Continent, where he was impressed by French decorative work of the 18th century, and after a visit to Paris in 1837 he decorated the firm's Wigmore Street showroom in a French Renaissance manner. Crace's first important patron was William Spencer Cavendish, 6th Duke of Devonshire, for whom he worked at Devonshire House (1840–45) in London and Chatsworth (1840–48), Derbys, providing carpets, upholstery, painted walls and ceilings, and some furniture. In 1843 Crace went to Munich to examine the processes involved in encaustic and fresco painting, and was strongly influenced by the way Bavarian decorative artists used colour to emphasize internal architectural forms. From this period he tended to use strong colours in preference to the French-inspired pastels of his early work, as in the State Drawing-room at Knebworth House, Herts, for example, redecorated in a medieval style in 1843–4 for Edward Bulwer Lytton, 1st Baron Lytton (1803–73).

Crace's most important work was for A. W. N. Pugin (*see* PUGIN, (2)), with whom he worked at Alton Towers, Staffs, in 1844. In the same year Frederick Crace & Son began to make furnishings in the Gothic style for Pugin's own house, The Grange, Ramsgate, Kent, and in 1846 they were awarded the contract for painting and gilding the New Palace of Westminster (*see* LONDON, §V, 3(iii)), designed by Sir Charles Barry and Pugin. Crace also collaborated with Pugin at Eastnor Castle, Heref. & Worcs (begun 1849) and Lismore Castle (1849–52), Co. Waterford, again for William Spencer Cavendish. At both houses Crace departed from Pugin's designs to some extent; Crace tended towards a more ornate and luxurious version of Gothic than did Pugin. At the Great Exhibition of 1851 (where he was a juror), Crace supervised the decoration of Pugin's Medieval Court, which included hangings, a prie-dieu and an oak armoire (all London, V&A) designed by Pugin and made by the Crace firm. After Pugin's death in 1852, Crace continued to work in the Gothic manner. At Abney Hall (nr Manchester), redecorated from 1852 to 1857, some Pugin designs were used, but much of the final scheme was by Crace.

Crace designed and executed the colour schemes for the buildings housing the Manchester Art Treasures Exhibition of 1857 and the International Exhibition of 1862

in London, where much stencilled decoration was used. He designed Queen Victoria's throne and canopy for the latter, and the firm exhibited furniture in both Gothic and Italian Renaissance styles. An important commission of the 1870s was the redecoration of the principal rooms of Grosvenor House, London, around the collection of Old Masters of Hugh Lupus, 3rd Marquess of Westminster. Through lectures and published articles, as well as through his own work, Crace was influential in the establishment of interior decoration as a profession. He was also a founder member of the Photographic Society of London and took some of the earliest photographs of the architecture of Moorish Spain during a visit in 1835.

UNPUBLISHED SOURCES

London, RIBA [letters from Pugin to Crace; designs]
London, V&A, Archv A. & Des. [designs]

WRITINGS

DNB
'On the Decoration of the International Exhibition Building', *J. Soc. A.*, x (1862), pp. 339–43
'On Colour', *The Builder* (30 Nov 1867), pp. 874–5; (7 Dec 1867), pp. 888–9

BIBLIOGRAPHY

Obituary, *The Builder* (17 Aug 1889), pp. 122–3
M. Aldrich: 'Gothic Interiors of the 19th Century: John Gregory Crace at Abney Hall', *V&A Mus. Album*, v (1986), pp. 76–84

MEGAN ALDRICH, ROSAMOND ALLWOOD

(4) John Dibblee Crace (*b* London, 1838; *d* London, 18 Nov 1919). Son of (3) John Gregory Crace. He was apprenticed to (2) Frederick Crace. He first came to public notice through his Gothic- and Renaissance-style furniture for the International Exhibition of 1862 in London. Of scholarly inclinations, John Dibblee Crace executed creditable work in the Gothic style at the Palace of Westminster (1869), London, and at Knightshayes (1874–82), Devon, after the dismissal of the architect William Burges. His passion for Italian Renaissance art culminated in the publication of *The Art of Colour Decoration* (London, 1912). John Dibblee Crace's greatest patron was John Alexander Thynne, 4th Marquess of Bath (1831–1915), for whom he transformed the state rooms and east range (1874–82) of Longleat, Wilts, creating some of the most important Renaissance Revival interiors in Britain. Crace's travels to the Middle East in 1868–9 later inspired his interiors in the Islamic style, most notably his work at the Royal Pavilion (1884–98). At the end of his career he worked for William Waldorf Astor, decorating Cliveden (*c.* 1895), Bucks, 18 Carlton House Terrace, London (1895–6), and the Astor Estate Office (*c.* 1892–5), London, in a sumptuous French Renaissance style, and designing for Astor many items of furniture. Like his father, John Dibblee Crace was a Master of the Painter-Stainers' Company in London and belonged to many other professional bodies and published a number of articles on art and design. After the closure of the firm, he acted as a consultant until his death.

MEGAN ALDRICH

Cracow. *See* KRAKÓW.

Cradle (i). Bed for an infant. In noble households during the Middle Ages cradles possessed much the same social significance as state beds. Aristocratic families generally had a splendid daytime cradle, in which the infant could be shown to visitors, and a simpler night cradle, in which the baby slept. Alienor de Poitiers (*d* 1506 or 1508), in *Les honneurs de la cour* (see Eames, 1977), written between 1484 and 1491, described how the textiles and furs used for draping state cradles reflected appropriate degrees of honour: for example, a princess's cradle had a counterpane of ermine that touched the ground, while that of a countess was of miniver and should, on no account, reach the floor. State cradles were high, generally being suspended between wooden, inverted T-shaped standards, whereas ordinary cradles set on base rockers were low, permitting the nursemaids to attend the baby. Very few Gothic cradles of estate have survived; however, the British Royal Collection includes an oak high cradle (Brit. Royal Col., on loan to London, Mus. London, see fig.) traditionally believed to have been used by the infant Henry V, born in 1388, but apparently dating from the late 15th century. The box, constructed of ribbed boards, swings between buttressed uprights surmounted by birds. An important state cradle (of the same design but now lacking its stand) of 1478–9 (Brussels, Musées Royaux A. & Hist.), made for either Philip the Fair or Margaret of Austria, is embellished with tracery, lavishly painted decoration and gold leaf.

Cradles of the 16th and 17th centuries were usually of box form, set on rockers, often with turned corner posts headed by ball finials so that the cradle could be easily rocked by hand. Many have a hood at one end (sometimes hinged or made to slide), and the exterior might have been covered with fringed and panelled velvet with gilt nails. The tomb of Princess Sophia (*d* 1607), daughter of James I, in Westminster Abbey, London, is carved in the form of a richly draped cradle, while a cradle (untraced) belonging to Charles I was 'covered with carnation vellvet'. The commonest form of decoration at this time was bas-relief carving. A fine example at Townend, a manor house in Cumbria (NT), displays characteristic regional carvings, featuring the date 1670 and initials B over G E for George and Elizabeth Browne.

A report of the christening of Princess Augusta (1737–1806), daughter of Frederick, Prince of Wales, in the *Gentleman's Magazine* (Aug 1737) noted: 'The Cradle, valued at £500 was made by Mr Williams, his Majesty's Cabinet-Maker, the Inside and Curtains white satin, lac'd with Silver Lace: the Covering, Crimson Velvet, with Gold Lace, Fringes and Tassels: At the Feet four Lyons, finely carv'd and gilt.' Poor families, however, made cradles of wicker or straw, known as bassinets, sometimes raised on simple stands. Although few survive, they are often depicted in paintings of cottage interiors. Many late 18th-century provincial cabinetmakers' books of prices include specifications for cradles. If these were made of pine the surface was normally grained. Thomas Sheraton published a design for a 'Swinging Crib Bed' in his *Cabinet Dictionary* (1803), which marked a return to the medieval system of suspending a cot between uprights. He recommended fitting a special clock spring, claimed to make the cradle swing for one and a half hours.

Royal cradles were still magnificent in the early 19th century. The cradle (Paris, Louvre) of Napoleon II, King of Rome, by François-Honoré-Georges Jacob-Desmalter

Oak high cradle, 865×1170×710 mm, late 15th century (British Royal Collection: on loan to London, Museum of London)

and Pierre-Philippe Thomire, made of amboyna with gilt-bronze mounts, is of hooded design, fabric-lined, raised on an X-frame and surmounted by a figure of Fame. It is a simplified version of the silver gilt cradle given to him by the City of Paris (Vienna, Schatzkam.). During the late 19th century wicker cribs and cradles with canework sides were popular in wealthy households.

BIBLIOGRAPHY
R. Edwards: *Dictionary of English Furniture* (London, 1954)
P. Eames: *Medieval History* (London, 1977) [incl. Alienor de Poitiers: *Les honneurs de la cour*, pp. 257–68, 268–71]
E. Joy, ed.: *Pictorial Dictionary of British 19th Century Furniture Designs* (Woodbridge, 1977)

CHRISTOPHER GILBERT

Cradle (ii). Additional support applied to the back of a wooden panel painting to prevent or correct warping or splitting. It consists of a latticework of wooden batons, which are designed to allow some movement perpendicular to the grain of the panel in response to changes in humidity. Cradling has been used extensively since the 18th century or earlier, and many panel paintings have been thinned to accept a cradle, often with damaging long-term results. Because of the inevitable constraints on the expansion and contraction of the painting, cradling may cause more damage than it prevents and is thus no longer considered an acceptable method of reinforcement or repair (for further discussion and illustration *see* PANEL PAINTING, §3 and fig. 4).

RUPERT FEATHERSTONE

Cradock, Marmaduke [Luke] (*b* Somerset, *c.* 1660; *d* London, *bur* 24 March 1717). English painter. He was self-taught and worked mostly for dealers, producing paintings of exotic birds and animals in landscape settings, frequently with Classical ruins, much in the manner of Peter Casteels. Works ascribed to Cradock often appear in the sale-rooms, but signed paintings are rare; one such is *Exotic Fowl* (New Haven, CT, Yale Cent. Brit. A.).

BIBLIOGRAPHY

Waterhouse: *18th C.*

E. Croft-Murray and P. Hulton: *Catalogue of British Drawings, I: XVI & XVII Centuries*, 2 vols, London, BM cat. (London, 1960)

MARC JORDAN

Craesbeeck [Craesbeke]**, Joos van** (*b* Neerlinter, ?1605–6; *d* Brussels, 1654–61). Flemish painter. He was the son of an alderman and baker. In 1631 he became a citizen of Antwerp and was entered as a journeyman baker, probably at the age of about 25, though a *Self-portrait in front of a Mirror* (ex-Ksthalle, Bremen; untraced) had an old inscription on the back (not in the artist's hand) stating that Craesbeeck was 39 in 1647. He married Johanna Tielens, the daughter of the deceased Antwerp prison baker, in the chapel of Het Gasteel, the Antwerp prison, in January 1631. In 1633–4 he was enrolled as a baker and painter in the Guild of St Luke at Antwerp, and in 1637 he was listed as the proprietor of a new house with a bakery there. He subsequently moved to Brussels, where he became a master in the painter's guild in 1651. In 1653–4 he registered two pupils with the guild.

According to de Bie and Houbraken, Craesbeeck was probably taught by Adriaen Brouwer; he may have met him in 1633 when Brouwer was in prison for tax debts (Craesbeeck baked bread for the prison). This is also borne out by a certain stylistic similarity in his early pictures to Brouwer's work. Like Brouwer, Craesbeeck found his subject-matter in tavern interiors with simple people, but

Joos van Craesbeeck: *Peasants Smoking*, oil on panel, 329×268 mm (Munich, Alte Pinakothek)

he subsequently turned completely to the middle-class world, which was depicted both carousing at the inn and in domestic genre scenes. He occasionally painted a studio scene (e.g. *Artist's Studio*, Paris, Fond. Custodia, Inst. Néer.), and there are a few New Testament stories, such as the *Massacre of the Innocents* (Linz, Abbey of St Florian) and *Ecce homo* (sold London, Christies, 14 May 1971, lot 43), painted in the style and manner of the Rembrandt school. There is also the occasional unmistakable Christian allegory among the genre pictures, such as *Brawl at an Inn: 'Death is Fierce and Quick'* (Antwerp, Kon. Mus. S. Kst.).

The *Company of Drinkers* (Kassel, Schloss Wilhelmshöhe) is signed with Craesbeeck's full name, and about 30 other paintings have the monogram CB or JVCB (e.g. *Flemish Tavern* and *At the Antwerp Arms*, both Antwerp, Kon. Mus. S. Kst.). However, except for the missing *Self-portrait in front of a Mirror*, none of the pictures is dated, nor it is possible to link them to a fixed date; their chronology is therefore hard to establish with any certainty. Pictures that still show the influence of Brouwer clearly must be earlier. At first, the figures correspond to Brouwer's figure types (e.g. *Peasant in a Felt Hat*, Berlin, Bodemus.). In *Peasants Smoking* (Munich, Alte Pin.; see fig.) Craesbeeck treated the same subject as Brouwer, like him concentrating on depicting the emotions revealed in the expression, but failing to achieve the same trenchancy and sureness of touch. The composition of the picture, with its four figures, is also reminiscent of Brouwer, and the colouring follows Brouwer's later works in the subtly harmonized toning with occasional gleaming highlights. The technique is also influenced by him, especially the thin application of colour that often leaves the ground partly visible. Craesbeeck's *Smoker* (Paris, Louvre), directly influenced by Brouwer's *The Smokers* (New York, Met.), is a facial study of a smoker with eyes rolling and an open mouth with smoke welling up out of it.

Brouwer's influence is less evident in paintings that are obviously later. The colours used tend increasingly towards browns and greys. Probably following on from that phase, carried out under the influence of painting in Brussels, is a group of pictures in vivid colours: dazzling white, yellow, a cool light blue and salmon red dominate the palette. In his mature work, which was independent of Brouwer, Craesbeeck used an individual, unmistakable and firmly established repertory of figures that makes his work easy to recognize: bearded men with flat or fur-decked caps, women with white bonnets or a particularly conspicuous straw hat. In these pictures, too, he tried to emulate Brouwer's mimic narrative, but the rolling eyes and roaring mouths never achieve the deft trenchancy of his model.

BIBLIOGRAPHY

C. die Bie: *Het gulden cabinet* (1661), pp. 109–10

A. Houbraken: *De groote schouburgh* (1718–21), i, pp. 333–5

F. J. Van den Branden: 'Adriaan de Brouwer en Joos van Craesbeeck', *Ned. Kstbode*, iii (1881)

——: *Geschiedenis der Antwerpse schilderschool* (Antwerp, 1883), pp. 857–63)

K. Z. von Manteuffel: 'Joos van Craesbeeck', *Jb. Kön. Preuss. Kstsamml.*, xxxvii (1916), pp. 315–37

Adriaen Brouwer und das niederländischen Bauern-genre, 1600–1660 (exh. cat. by K. Renger, Munich, Alte Pin., 1986), pp. 52–3, 103–5

The Age of Rubens (exh. cat. by P. C. Sutton and others, Boston, MA, Mus. F.A., and Toledo, OH, Mus. A., 1993–4), pp. 430–33, *passim*

KONRAD RENGER

Cragg, Tony (*b* Liverpool, 9 April 1949). English sculptor. His work is notable for its exploration of different materials, including found objects and raw matter of various kinds. Cragg's method of dispassionate ordering and composing seeks to make evident the vast array of objects and images that surround us, but with which he feels modern man has only a superficial relationship, based on function alone. In order to enhance our imaginative and emotional relationship with the world at large, Cragg proposed beginning with physical matter as the fundamental basis of experience. To this end, in the early 1980s, he began to work with objects arranged on the floor or wall in simple configurations, such as *Postcard Union Jack* (1981; Leeds, C.A.G.), made from sherds of plastic, or an axehead composed of various real and fake wooden elements. By 1985 he had extended his range to include carved and machine-cut stone and cast bronze and iron to make sculpture of simple, generic images or standardized prototypes, such as a house or a test-tube.

BIBLIOGRAPHY
Tony Cragg (exh. cat., ed. A. Pohlen; Brussels, Pal. B.-A., 1985)
M. J. Jacob: 'Tony Cragg: First Order Experiences', *A Quiet Revolution: British Sculpture since 1965*, ed. T. A. Neff (London, 1987), pp. 54–71
Tony Cragg (exh. cat. by L. Cooke, London, Hayward Gal., 1987)

LYNNE COOKE

Craig, Edward Gordon (*b* Stevenage, 16 Jan 1872; *d* Vence, France, 29 July 1966). English theatre director, designer, theorist, printmaker and typographer. He was one of the great, if controversial, innovators of the modern theatre movement. The son of the actress Ellen Terry and the architect Edward William Godwin, Craig was born into a strong theatrical tradition. He abandoned a promising career as an actor with Henry Irving's Lyceum Company in 1897 to concentrate on directing and developing ideas about 'the theatre of the future'. Inspired by Hubert von Herkomer's scenic experiments with auditorium lighting and three-dimensional scenery in productions at the Bushey Art School, Herts, Craig exchanged the conventions of realistic scenery for a suggestive, abstract interplay of form, light, movement and music. This new total theatre drew on the imagination to create an architectonic vision of choreographic movement, colour harmony, visual simplicity and atmospheric effect united under the sole control of a single artist. Influenced by his relationship with the dancer Isadora Duncan, he also proposed a concept of the rhythms and movements in nature acting as the vehicle for an emotional and aesthetic experience.

These principles were given practical shape in six early productions in which Craig successfully collaborated with the composer Martin Shaw (founder of the Purcell Operatic Society, London) to direct and design Purcell's *Dido and Æneas* (1900) and *The Masque of Love* (1901), Handel's *Acis and Galatea* (1902), Laurence Housman's *Bethlehem* (1902), *Much Ado about Nothing* and Ibsen's *The Vikings of Helgeland* (both 1903). Craig was unwilling to compromise or relinquish the concept of complete directorial control, and much of his subsequent work was aborted or unrealized, with the exception of Otway's *Venice Preserv'd* for the German director Otto Brahm in 1905, Ibsen's *Rosmersholm* for the actress Eleanora Duse in 1906, *Hamlet* for the Moscow Arts Theatre in 1912 and Ibsen's *The Crown Pretenders* for the Royal Copenhagen State Theatre in 1926, though these too were dismissed by their producer as unsatisfactory. Instead the scope of Craig's theories was most fully realized in the writings that absorbed him during the later part of his life, in particular the influential *On the Art of the Theatre* (1911) and the theatrical journal *The Mask* (1908–29), and in drawn, etched and engraved designs (collections in London, V&A; Paris, Bib. N.). The pre-eminence of the director's role and the complete rejection of spectacular detailed realism remain Craig's most significant contributions to the modern theatre and can be directly related to the work of Bertolt Brecht and Peter Brook.

As a printmaker and typographer Craig was no less forceful in breaking away from the Victorian taste for elaborate artifice. Introduced to the medium of wood-engraving by the Beggarstaff Brothers, William Nicholson and James Pryde, he produced his first marketable print of *Walt Whitman* in 1895, followed by a prodigious period of engraving, which resulted in nearly 250 prints between 1898 and 1901. Most of these simplified, sometimes tinted, black-and-white images of literary and historical subjects, portraits and bookplates were subsequently illustrated in *The Page*, a miscellaneous arts periodical written, illustrated and published by Craig under various pseudonyms between 1898 and 1901. The influence of Nicholson and Joseph Crawhall (1821–96) is seen in *Gordon Craig's Book of Penny Toys* (1899), a children's book with 20 bold hand-coloured illustrations accompanied by elephant type and printed on thick sugar paper; this volume is now recognized as a significant landmark in the development of British book design. The expressive tonal qualities of black are imaginatively explored in the *Black Figure Series* (from 1907), a series of woodcuts printed from thin planks of holly, originally used to work out movements in Craig's model stages. This included the *Hamlet Series* of single dramatic figures and scenes that Harry Graf Kessler (1868–1937) eventually published in book form as *Die tragische Geschichte von Hamlet* at the Cranach Presse, Weimar, in 1928. Less familiar are the etchings reproduced in Craig's book *Scene* (1923) and the related wood-engravings such as *Design for a Stage Scene* (London, V&A), which convey the progression of moving scenes of geometric shapes and projected light. Craig used these prints as a means of visualizing and developing ideas about theatre movement, but they also show his instinctive ability to work creatively with the woodblock. As one of the early figures who contributed to its revival in England at the beginning of the 20th century, he was elected to the exclusive Society of Twelve (1903) and was a founder-member of the Society of Wood-Engravers (1920).

WRITINGS
On the Art of the Theatre (London, 1911/*R* 1958)
Towards a New Theatre (London and Toronto, 1913)
Scene (London, 1923)
Nothing or the Bookplate (London, 1924)
Woodcuts and Some Words (London, 1924)
Index to the Story of my Days (London, 1957)

BIBLIOGRAPHY

H. MacFall: 'Concerning the Woodcuts of Gordon Craig', *Print Colr Q.*, ix (1922), pp. 407–32

D. Bablet: *The Theatre of Edward Gordon Craig* (London, 1966/R 1981)

Edward Gordon Craig (exh. cat., ed. G. Nash; London, V&A, 1967)

E. A. Craig: *Gordon Craig: The Story of his Life* (London, 1968)

A. Rood: *Gordon Craig on Movement and Dance* (London, 1977)

Edward Gordon Craig: An Exhibition of Wood-engravings and Woodcuts (exh. cat., ed. T. Sidey; U. York, Heslington Hall, 1982)

C. Innes: *Edward Gordon Craig* (Cambridge, 1983)

L. M. Newman, ed.: *The Black Figures of Edward Gordon Craig* (Wellingborough, 1989) [with photographs by H. Craig]

TESSA SIDEY

Craig-Martin, Michael (*b* Dublin, 28 Aug 1941). Irish sculptor and painter, active in England. He moved to the USA with his family in 1945 and studied painting at Yale University, CT (1961–3; 1964–6); his tutors included Al Held and Alex Katz.

Craig-Martin moved to England in 1966 to teach at the Bath Academy of Art in Corsham, Wilts, and he eventually taught from 1973 at Goldsmiths' College in London, where he remained a powerful influence on students through the 1980s and 1990s. His early work made deliberate reference to the American artists he most admired, such as Donald Judd, Jasper Johns and Robert Morris (ii). Although he was particularly affected by Minimalism and used ordinary household materials in his sculptures, he played against the logic of his sources; in *Four Identical Boxes with Lids Reversed* (painted blockboard, 1969; London, Tate), for example, he created a curious progression by slicing into four identical boxes at different angles and then exchanging their halves.

Craig-Martin moved closer to conceptual art with such works as *An Oak Tree* (1973; Canberra, N.G.), a glass of water placed on a glass shelf that he claimed in an accompanying text to have transformed in identity without altering the 'accidents' of its appearance. In a series of large-scale 'wall drawings' begun in 1978, such as *Reading (with Globe)* (1980; London, Tate), in which a jumble of ordinary objects is pictured outlined with black tape, he played with the relationship between an image and its physical materialization. By the mid-1980s, in such works as *Man* (1984; Hull, Ferens A.G.), he had these outlined shapes made from steel rods, their contours set against the geometric designs formed by painted aluminium panels. He continued working in various forms, always maintaining an elegant restraint and conceptual clarity.

BIBLIOGRAPHY

Michael Craig-Martin: Selected Works, 1966–1975 (exh. cat. by A. Seymour, Leigh, Turnpike Gal.; Bristol, Arnolfini Gal.; London, ICA; and elsewhere, 1976–7)

Michael Craig-Martin (exh. cat., essay L. Cooke, interview R. Rosenblum; London, Whitechapel A.G., 1989–90) [incl. sel. writings]

MARCO LIVINGSTONE

Cram, Ralph Adams (*b* Hampton Falls, NH, 16 Dec 1863; *d* Boston, 22 Sept 1942). American architect and writer. He was the leading Gothic Revival architect in North America in the first half of the 20th century, at the head of an informal school known as the Boston Gothicists, who transformed American church design.

In 1881 Cram was apprenticed to the firm of Rotch & Tilden in Boston. His letters on artistic subjects to the *Boston Transcript* led to his appointment as the journal's

Ralph Adams Cram: cathedral of St John the Divine, New York, 1912–41, interior looking east

art critic by the mid-1880s. In 1886 he began his first European tour. In 1888 he founded the firm of Cram & Wentworth with Charles Wentworth (1861–97). With the arrival of BERTRAM GOODHUE, the firm became Cram, Wentworth & Goodhue in 1892, and in 1899 Cram, Goodhue & Ferguson, Frank Ferguson (1861–1926) having joined the office as business and engineering partner following the death of Wentworth.

Cram was strongly influenced both by the philosophies of John Ruskin and William Morris and by the architectural images of H. H. Richardson, Henry Vaughan (1846–1917) and, behind Vaughan, the English Gothic Revival architects J. L. Pearson, G. F. Bodley and J. D. Sedding. Cram became an ardent Anglican, following the precepts of the Oxford Movement. He believed that the development of Gothic had been sundered prematurely at the Renaissance and argued that Gothic Revival should continue the Gothic style. His first work, All Saints (1891), Ashmont, Boston, built of irregular brown granite, is a powerful adaptation of the English Perpendicular style.

Cram's most successful designs were for small village churches and chapels that combined overall strength and simplicity while nonetheless including some rich detail. Examples include Our Saviour's (1897), Middleborough, MA, and the Day Chapel (1902), Norwood, MA. Among his large urban churches are the House of Hope (1912), St Paul, MN, Central Church (1920), Honolulu, HI, and

First Presbyterian (1922), Tacoma, WA. His output was prolific and he undertook commissions for many denominations in a wide variety of styles. For the stained glass and fittings of his churches, he secured exceptionally talented collaborators, including the stained glass makers Charles Connick, Wilbur Burnham and Reynolds, Francis & Rohnstock and the architectural sculptor and carver Johannes Kirchinayer.

Two of Cram's most outstanding contributions to Gothic Revival are in New York: St Thomas (1905–14), Fifth Avenue, and work on the cathedral of St John the Divine (1912–41), Amsterdam Avenue. At St Thomas he showed how, even without a tall tower, a Gothic Revival church could still dominate its surroundings, with a majestic and elegant massing of strong forms.

St John the Divine was begun by Heins & La Farge in 1892–1911 in a Romanesque style. Cram took over in 1912 with a new Gothic design. He remodelled the chancel and was responsible for the nave, west front, baptistery and synod house. His intended towers were not built, but the awkward façade is nonetheless imposing. The impressive, spacious nave is tall and narrow (see fig.), with the aisles rising to the height of the nave itself.

Cram was also an important college architect. His educational commissions include the campuses at Wheaton College (1900), Norton, MA, and Sweet Briar College (1902), VA. The magnificent Gothic Revival ranges at the United States Military Academy (1903) at West Point, New York, were the result of the winning competition entry that brought the firm national fame. His Graduate College at Princeton University (1910) is an important work in the tradition of the Anglo-American residential college.

Other significant work by Cram includes Richmond Court (1899), Brookline, MA, possibly the first courtyard apartment house in the eastern United States; Harbourcourt, the John Nicholas Brown House (1904, Newport, RI); and the Japanese garden court and temple room of the Museum of Fine Arts (1910), Boston, MA, which shows his interest in Japanese architecture.

The initial plans for the firm's commissions were prepared by Cram; he outlined the mass, scale and proportions and left the detail to his partners. From 1902 to 1913, when Cram and Goodhue dissolved their partnership, the firm maintained a New York office under Goodhue's charge, Cram remaining in Boston. After 1913 the firm became Cram & Ferguson, Frank Cleveland (1878–1950) and Alexander Hoyle (1881–1969) becoming Cram's designing partners. The firm continued after Cram's death, with John Doran and Maurice Berry, and Hoyle, Doran & Berry remains one of few American architectural firms to have lasted more than a hundred years, continuing work on St John the Divine.

Cram was the author of nearly two dozen books and many articles on various subjects, including art criticism and Japanese architectural history, on which he was an authority. He was Professor of the Philosophy of Architecture and Head of the School of Architecture at the Massachusetts Institute of Technology. His work was eclectic but his passionate medievalism was the sphere of his greatest influence. He persuaded Henry Adams (1838–1918) to publish privately his *Mont Saint–Michel and*

Chartres (1904) and wrote the introduction to it. He also played a leading role in inspiring Kenneth Conant's work on Cluny at Harvard. A founder of the Medieval Academy of America, Cram was also led by his medievalism to an interest in conservative social philosophy, about which he wrote widely. His influence in this field alone has generated considerable scholarship since World War II.

WRITINGS
Church Building (Boston, 1901–2, 2/1914, 3/1924)
Impressions of Japanese Architecture (New York, 1905/R 1966)
Ministry of Art (Boston, 1914/R Freeport, NY, 1967)
Heart of Europe (New York, 1915)
The Substance of Gothic (Boston, 1917)
The Catholic Church and Art (New York, 1930)
The End of Democracy (Boston, 1935)
My Life in Architecture (Boston, 1936/R New York, 1969)

BIBLIOGRAPHY
M. Schuyler: 'The Works of Cram, Goodhue and Ferguson', *Archit. Rec.*, xxix (1911), pp. 1–112
The Work of Cram and Ferguson (New York, 1929)
R. Muccigrosso: *Ralph Adams Cram* (New York, 1931)
D. Shand-Tucci: *Ralph Adams Cram: American Medievalist* (Boston, 1975)
A. M. Daniel: *The Early Architecture of Ralph Adams Cram, 1889–1902* (diss., U. North Carolina, 1978)
R. Muccigrosso: *American Gothic: The Mind and Art of Ralph Adams Cram* (Washington, DC, 1980)
DOUGLASS SHAND-TUCCI

Cramillion, Bartholomew (*fl* Dublin, 1755–72). Stuccoist, active in Ireland. In 1755 he was engaged by Bartholomew Mosse (1712–59), Master Builder of Dublin's Rotunda Hospital, to 'execute the stucco-work which is to be done in the chapel'. He was further employed in 1757 to 'execute the stucco-work of the altar-piece ... according to the plan and draft made by him'. In the Rotunda accounts he is described as a 'statuary and stuccoman'. This is significant since the modelling of the figures in the chapel is by a different hand from that of the framework, foliage and other ornament, and there would appear to have been two plasterers at work on the background, both of them less assured than the modeller of the figures. The chapel's ceiling plasterwork is full of Rococo movement, where allegorical groups of Faith, Hope and Charity are framed by angelic caryatids bearing texts. These caryatids have decisive gestures and keen expressions and yet wear an air of languid elegance, while the putti heads might easily have been modelled from those of babies in the Hospital. The ceiling's centre and four corner panels were left empty in order to receive paintings by Giovanni Battista Cipriani, but these were never executed. The altarpiece itself displays angels adoring a lamb and is placed against a curtain hanging from a lambrequin. No further stucco work by Cramillion has been identified. However, in 1772 he is known to have exhibited a statue at the Society of Artists in Dublin.

BIBLIOGRAPHY
C. P. Curran: *The Rotunda Hospital, Dublin* (Dublin, 1946)
——: *Dublin Decorative Plasterwork* (London, 1967)
WILLIAM GARNER

Cranach. German family of painters, draughtsmen and printmakers. They were active in Saxony during the 16th century. (1) Lucas Cranach I adopted his surname from his birthplace, Kronach, a town of Upper Franconia in the diocese of Bamberg. He was the foremost member of the family of artists by that name. His father and teacher was a painter by the name of Hans Moller or Maler (1448–1491/2). None of his work is known to survive, but his large house in Kronach on the Marktplatz suggests that he was successful. The name Maler ('Painter') has led to some uncertainty as to whether it was simply a reference to Hans's profession, but contemporary references to 'pictor Lucas Moller' or 'maler Moller' confirm that it had become the family surname. The still repeated belief that the name was Sonder or Sunder apparently results from a confusion with another family in Kronach, which was related to Lucas the elder through marriage (Koepplin, 1966).

After a brief period of activity in Vienna (1502–45), which was seminal for the development of the Danube school, Lucas I settled in 1505 in Wittenberg, where he became court artist to the Saxon electors and established a highly productive workshop. There he developed a distinct manner of painting that essentially defined the art of Saxony for the rest of the century. His two sons, (2) Hans Cranach and (3) Lucas Cranach II, closely emulated their father's art, and Lucas the younger took over the workshop in 1550. Augustin Cranach (1554–95), son of Lucas the younger, was the only member of the third generation and the only one of nine children from two marriages to become a painter. His oeuvre has been only surmised insofar as it has survived. Augustin's son, Lucas Cranach IV (1586–1645), also became a painter, but nothing is known of his work.

In 1508 the elector Frederick the Wise conferred a coat of arms on Lucas Cranach the elder, which displayed a crowned serpent carrying a ring in its mouth. The artist had already used an angular, serpent-like device as a signature on his woodcut of the *Crucifixion* (1502). After 1508 the elaborated form of the winged serpent became the standard Cranach signature, occasionally in combination with the initials L.C. The batlike wings of the serpent underwent a change after 1537. The raised and flared wings were folded back in a horizontal position. The suggestion that this change was related to the death of Hans Cranach in 1537 is contradicted by the fact that at least four paintings from 1535 and 1536 already bear the redesigned signature (1974–6 exh. cat., p. 574). The use of the later form of the signet coincides with Lucas the younger's activity in the workshop, but the view (Giesecke) that all the signed work after 1537 is his and none of it is any longer that of Lucas the elder defies both visual and documentary evidence.

BIBLIOGRAPHY
W. Schade: *Die Malerfamilie Cranach* (Dresden, 1974); Eng. trans. by H. Sebba as *Cranach: A Family of Master Painters* (New York, 1980) [with bibliog. and docs]

(1) Lucas Cranach I [the elder] (*b* Kronach, 1472; *d* Weimar, 16 Oct 1553). Painter, engraver and designer of woodcuts.

I. Life and work. II. Workshop.

I. Life and work.

1. Vienna, *c.* 1501–4. 2. Wittenberg, 1505 and after.

1. VIENNA, *c.* 1501–4. No works are known by Lucas Cranach the elder before his arrival in Vienna in 1501 or 1502, when he was already about 30 years old (but *see* MASTERS, ANONYMOUS, AND MONOGRAMMISTS, §III: MASTER L.CZ.). His earliest surviving painting is presumably a small panel of the *Crucifixion* (before 1502; 585×450 mm; Vienna, Ksthist. Mus.) from the Schottenstift in Vienna. This picture reveals the expressive and vigorous handling of the brush that marks his painting technique during this intense two- or three-year period of activity. The rendering of the figures, especially the bloody, crucified bodies, and the composition with its rugged landscape are likewise calculated for an emotional impact. How the artist came by this manner of painting may in part be explained by the colouristically strong and brutal scenes of the *Passion* by Jan Polack, such as the *Crucifixion* (1492; Munich, Alte Pin.), which Cranach could have seen in the Franciscan church in Munich en route to Vienna. Otherwise his early stylistic sources are as hard to specify as those for the emerging DANUBE SCHOOL, of which Cranach was a principal founder.

Under the inspiration of Dürer's woodcuts from *c.* 1498 for the *Large Passion*, Cranach turned to the same medium with distinctly individual results. His two woodcuts of the *Crucifixion* (Hollstein, nos 25–6), one of which is dated 1502, and the contemporary *Christ on the Mount of Olives* (Hollstein, no. 24) transform Dürer's finely controlled graphic style into a surface of fractured linear movements and turbulent patterns of light and dark in keeping with the physical and mental anguish of the protagonists. Two chalk drawings of the *Crucified Thieves* (both *c.* 1502; Berlin, Kupferstichkab.), closely related to the thieves in both the woodcuts and the preceding painting, reaffirm the artist's painterly execution and freely expressive rendering of the bodies.

The rapid development of Cranach's Viennese manner of painting coincided with his mastery of landscape. The small panel of *St Jerome in Penitence* (555×415 mm, 1502; Vienna, Ksthist. Mus.) gives nearly as much prominence to the forested setting as to the half-nude penitent. Similarly, in the *Stigmatization of St Francis* (*c.* 1502; Vienna, Akad. Bild. Kst.) the figures are completely immersed within the landscape. A large tree trunk in the foreground bends in a way that reinforces the saint's own recoiling at the vision of Christ on the cross. In the much larger *Crucifixion* (1503; Munich, Alte Pin.; see fig. 1) landscape combines with an eccentric view of the otherwise familiar subject to generate a fresh response. If Cranach were indebted for the oblique view of Christ on the cross to Dürer's *Crucifixion* (Dresden, Gemäldegal. Alte Meister) from the altarpiece of the *Seven Sorrows*, he raised the idea into a dramatic encounter. Seeing Christ from the side and only glimpsing part of the near thief's swollen body, the beholder observes the scene as if having come on it unexpectedly. Dark clouds hang over the cross, and the land appears heaving still from the earthquake that struck at the moment of death. The use of landscape to set the mood and as a bridge to the beholder is also found in the intimate monogrammed and dated panel of the *Rest on the Flight into Egypt* (707×530 mm, 1504; Berlin, Gemäldegal.), where the Holy Family pauses by a spring in a conifer forest, as angels descend for a musical interlude. Joseph, hat in hand, looks towards the beholder who would seem to be passing through the same terrain.

1. Lucas Cranach I: *Crucifixion*, oil on panel, 1.38×0.99 m, 1503 (Munich, Alte Pinakothek)

Two pairs of portraits, those of *Dr Johannes Cuspinian* and his wife *Anna Cuspinian*, which are joined as a diptych (1502–3; Winterthur, Samml. Oskar Reinhart), and the *Portrait of a Scholar* (1503; Nuremberg, Ger. Nmus.), formerly identified as depicting the professor of law Stephan Reuss, and that of his wife (*c.* 1503; Berlin, Gemäldegal.), show that Cranach had entered the circle of humanists at the University of Vienna. Cuspinian, in particular, known for his fascination with cosmography, must have contributed to the idea of placing the scholars and their wives in a landscape inhabited by numerous astrological, pagan and Christian symbols. By the age of 29 Cuspinian was professor of both medicine and rhetoric, rector of the university and designated poet laureate by the Emperor. His portrait and that of his 16-year-old bride were presumably painted on the occasion of their marriage near the end of 1502. Cranach absorbed the scholar's erudite symbolism into a visually poetic landscape and painted the figures as though their presence in nature were a matter of spirit as much as body. As exemplars of Renaissance portraiture in Germany, the young, somewhat dreamy, yet worldly images of Johannes and Anna Cuspinian never found their equivalent, least of all in the new directions taken by Cranach after his move to Saxony.

2. WITTENBERG, 1505 AND AFTER. In 1504 Cranach was called to the electoral capital of Saxony by Duke Frederick the Wise. His appointment as court artist, successor to the peripatetic Jacopo de' Barbari, indicates

that Cranach had already established a far-reaching reputation. Without delay he enlarged that reputation by his prolific achievements in portraiture, panel painting of religious and mythological subjects, mural designs for the Saxon palaces and hunting lodges (Lochau, Torgau and Veste Coburg, though none of these paintings survives) and prints, especially woodcuts. He was admired for the ability to work quickly, as his tombstone recorded: '*pictor celerimus*'. By 1507 he had begun to develop his workshop with a growing number of assistants and pupils (*see* §II below). In 1508 the Duke conferred on him the coat of arms with the winged serpent that became the basis of his standard signature. Already in 1509 Christoph Scheurl and Andreas Bodenstein von Karlstadt were outdoing each other to praise Cranach in their erudite way of comparing him to the most renowned painters of antiquity, Zeuxis, Parrhasius and Apelles. Karlstadt even claimed that Cranach could hold forth in Latin.

(i) Altarpieces, portraits and religious prints. (ii) Nudes and mythological subjects.

(i) Altarpieces, portraits and religious prints.

(a) Before c. *1520.* The first paintings that Cranach made in Wittenberg, such as the signed and dated triptych of the *Martyrdom of St Catherine* (1506; Dresden, Gemäldegal. Alte Meister), not surprisingly still resemble works of the Vienna period, especially in their vivid colouring and forested landscape. Less expected, however, is the sudden departure from the expression of emotion and the painterly brushwork that had enlivened and unified the forms of those earlier paintings. The central panel of the triptych is visually active in a complex way that reveals a debt to Dürer's woodcut of the same subject (*c.* 1497–9; B. 120), but the figures are painted with sharp contours and the surfaces are much smoother than before. The figures are also crowded and pushed near the picture surface, but the parts, while collectively massed, remain individually distinct. The faces of the men are strongly characterized and have been variously identified with members of the court circle, but they show little or no emotion despite the hail of brimstone and the saint's imminent beheading. The wings of the altarpiece are occupied by three full-length figures of saints on the interior and two against a plain black ground on the exterior. Behind SS Barbara, Ursula and Margaret on the right panel rises the huge, turreted castle of Veste Coburg, from which the saints themselves might well have stepped forth to judge by the finery of their dress. In contrast to the strong and individualized faces of men, these young women are typical of Cranach's new feminine ideal, fair and finely featured, unblemished even by the traces of a passing thought. Their costumes, too, however richly detailed, are stiff and painted with linear precision.

Individual portraits, such as the arresting full-length pair of *Henry the Pious, Duke of Saxony* and *Catherine of Mecklenburg, Duchess of Saxony* (1514; both Dresden, Gemäldegal. Alte Meister), epitomize this courtly art. Henry's face, the work of a master portraitist, makes his human presence strongly felt, but his body could pass for that of a magnificently dressed manikin, posed to draw the sword that never moves. His costumed stance, like an elaborate escutcheon, is, above all, a signifier of rank.

In autumn 1508 Cranach was in the Netherlands, a journey taken on behalf of Duke Frederick. Reportedly he made a portrait then of the future emperor Charles V at the age of eight (untraced). Cranach's encounter with Netherlandish art was reflected on his return in the triptych of the *Holy Kinship*, otherwise known as the Torgau Altarpiece (1509; Frankfurt am Main, Städel. Kstinst. & Städt. Gal.). He proudly signed and dated the work uncustomarily in Latin: LUCAS CHRONUS/FACIEBAT/ANNO 1509. His choice and treatment of the subject suggest that he knew the *St Anne* altarpiece (1509; Brussels, Mus. A. Anc.) by Quinten Metsys while it was still in the master's Antwerp studio. The relatively soft modelling of forms and the layout of the architecturally defined space also point to an influence, albeit short-lived, from the southern Netherlands. However, Cranach gave his scene an explicitly German identity by means of the forested and mountainous landscape in the background and especially by including portraits of Emperor Maximilian, Elector Frederick the Wise and his brother, Duke John the Steadfast, among members of the Holy Family. A year or two later he painted another version of this subject on a single panel (Vienna, Akad. Bild. Kst.) apparently occasioned by his marriage; in this version the visibly affluent and confident artist himself stands in for Alphaeus.

Cranach was engaged in the design and production of prints throughout his career, but during the first five to seven years of his activity in Wittenberg he devoted special care to their execution, beginning with a devotional image of the *Adoration of the Heart of Jesus* (1505; Hollstein, no. 69). Like most of his woodcuts from this period, this one bears the two coats of arms of Electoral Saxony. Two woodcuts from 1509, *St Jerome in Penitence* (Hollstein, no. 84) and the *Holy Family Resting on the Flight into Egypt* (Hollstein, no. 7), reveal Cranach's indebtedness to and rivalry with Dürer. The religious subjects are characteristically embedded within the landscape, which vibrates with linear energy and flickering contrasts of light and shadow. In the same year, Cranach dated his first two engravings, of which only seven are known. One of these, the *Penance of St John Chrysostom* (see fig. 2), is a masterpiece of lively burin work. The highlights sparkle amid the dense foliage and the linear patterns vary according to the shapes and surfaces of the myriad floral motifs.

The prominent stag and other animals in the foreground of this engraving, like those in the woodcut of *Adam and Eve* (1509; Hollstein, no. 1), represent an aspect of Cranach's work for which he received special praise from his contemporaries; (his skilful portrayal of hunts and hunting trophies was the subject of much of the no longer surviving mural decoration that he painted for his Saxon patrons). A reflection of these wall paintings may be seen in one large woodcut of a *Stag Hunt* (*c.* 1506; Hollstein, no. 15). Christoph Scheurl's encomium of 1509, in which Cranach is compared with Zeuxis and Apelles, claims that birds fell to the ground when they tried to land on the antlers of the stags painted on the walls at Coburg and that Duke George of Saxony refused to believe that they were not real until he felt them for himself. When Cranach was commissioned in 1515, along with Dürer, Altdorfer and other German masters, to provide marginal designs for

2. Lucas Cranach I: *Penance of St John Chrysostom*, engraving, 256×200 mm, 1509

the Prayerbook of the Emperor Maximilian (Munich, Bayer. Staatsbib.), he contributed his eight pages, as evidently expected of him, with lively animals in their natural habitat. Paintings of a *Stag Hunt* in several versions (two dated 1544 and 1545; both Madrid, Prado) show that this subject remained a lifelong, standard part of his repertory.

Cranach played a key role in the initial development of printing woodcuts with colour, a development that led to the chiaroscuro woodcut (*see* PRINTS, §III, 6), in which a tone block is cut to leave areas of the white paper exposed for highlights. In 1507 he produced a woodcut of *St George on Horseback* (Hollstein, no. 82), printed from two blocks on blue-prepared paper. One block printed the black lines and the other a tacky substance on which powdered silver or gold was sprinkled to provide highlights. This print gave Hans Burgkmair I in Augsburg the incentive to imitate the technique, then to embark in 1508 on experiments with colour printing by means of a tone block. Two of the five woodcuts by Cranach printed with tone blocks in the chiaroscuro manner are dated 1506, namely *St Christopher* (Hollstein, no. 79) and *Venus and Cupid* (Hollstein, no. 105), but there is reason to think that he designed tone blocks only after seeing Burgkmair's examples. Moreover, the existence of the winged serpent on prints both dated 1506 (i.e. two years before Cranach had been granted this heraldic insignia) cast doubt on the accuracy of those dates and on his possible claim to have pioneered the technique of chiaroscuro printing, despite his early application of it and his path-breaking *St George*.

Cranach's prints between 1509 and *c.* 1512 provide a revealing picture of the religious attitudes and practices at the Wittenberg court on the eve of the Reformation. The 14 woodcuts of the *Passion* (1509) offer dramatic portrayals of the events leading up to Christ's death and resurrection. In this work Cranach adhered to the recent precedents of Dürer and Hans Schäufelein. Similarly, the 14 woodcuts of *Christ, the Apostles and St Paul* (Hollstein, nos 31–44) or the 12 of the *Martyrdom of the Apostles* (Hollstein, nos 53–64), both series from *c.* 1512, responded to widespread popular interest in such images. The *Celestial Ladder of St Bonaventura* (*c.* 1510) shows how printed images combined with short passages of text could turn a difficult religious idea into a simplified visual lesson, not unlike a modern poster showing how to administer artificial respiration.

Three woodcuts of *Jousting Tournaments* (1509; Hollstein, no. 116) initially seem to be simple depictions of a rather chaotic and bone-shattering, courtly sporting event, but these tournaments were organized by Duke Frederick in association with the Feast of All Saints, when his famous collection of relics was put on display in his new church. Moreover, the tournament reflected a 10th-century tradition, in which the event was conceived as preparation for crusaders. Published the same year as the *Tournament* woodcuts was the so-called *Wittenberger Heiligtumsbuch*, a catalogue of Frederick's relic collection, with 117 illustrations of his reliquaries by Cranach. Given the focus that came to be directed against the granting of indulgences for devotion to relics during the Reformation, it is noteworthy that the *Heiligtumsbuch*, which numbered 5005 examples, ranging from a drop of the Virgin's milk to a complete child's body from the Massacre of the Innocents, offered an indulgence of 1443 years' release from purgatory for devoutly beholding these relics. In his boundless passion to increase his collection, Frederick offered to trade paintings by Cranach to Louise of Savoy, the mother of Francis I, in exchange for a gift of relics to his church, which contained some 19,000 of them by the year 1520.

(b) c. 1520 and after. As court painter in Wittenberg, Cranach found himself at the very centre of the Protestant Reformation. His patrons, the Saxon Electors, were also the protectors of Martin Luther and champions of his cause, notwithstanding Duke Frederick's obsession with relics. Cranach and Luther were close personal friends and godfathers to each other's children. Cranach became the *de facto* official portraitist of Luther. Two engravings (both 1520; Hollstein, nos 6–7), dated three years after Luther posted the 95 theses at the castle church, show the Reformer as an emaciated Augustinian. The year Luther was excommunicated and took his stand at the Diet of Worms, Cranach portrayed him in another engraving, this time in profile, wearing the distinctive cap of the learned doctor of theology (1521; Hollstein, no. 8), and he recorded Luther's likeness in disguise as Junker Jörg while sequestered for his own safety at the Wartburg in a woodcut of 1522 (Hollstein, no. 132). Numerous versions of painted portraits by Cranach show Luther as monk, as Junker Jörg, in pendant with Katharina von Bora, whom he married in 1525, and in pendant with Philip Melanchthon. He also painted companion portraits of Luther's parents, *Hans Luther* (1527) and *Margaretha Luther* (*c.* 1527; both Eisenach, Wartburg Stift.); the preliminary

study for *Hans Luther* (Vienna, Albertina) shows how well Cranach could deliver physiognomic detail and character with the same rapid, energetic strokes of the brush.

To an unprecedented extent the Reformation was a conflict waged with the printing press. Woodcut illustrations were an essential component of the propaganda of both sides. In 1519 Cranach designed the first known Reformation broadsheet, the *'Fuhrwagen'* (the *Chariot to Heaven and the Chariot to Hell*; Hollstein, no. 95), to illustrate Andreas Karlstadt's argument that redemption is the gift of God's grace and not the result of human will. Such visual antitheses were typical of Reformation disputation. In the polemic booklet *Passional Christi und Antichristi* (Wittenberg, Johannes Grunenberg, 1521), text and pictures on facing pages contrast the acts of Christ and those of the pope as the antichrist. Speed and economy of production generally took precedence over refinement and careful execution in these woodcuts, as with many others of their type, so that Cranach's contribution is discernible more in the planning than in the hand.

In the painted *Allegory of the Law and the Gospel* (1529; Gotha, Schloss Friedenstein) and a contemporary woodcut of the same composition (Hollstein, no. 14), Cranach gave indelible form to a central tenet of Protestant theology. Two landscapes, divided by a tree whose branches are leafless on one side and flourish on the other, contain contrasting images illustrating Luther's teaching that sinful mankind can be redeemed only by grace through faith. On one side a terrified, naked figure is driven by Death and the Devil into the flames of Hell, despite the presence of Moses, while on the other side the same naked man, his attention now directed by John the Baptist to a figure of Christ on the cross, is showered by the blood of salvation. Among the subjects, previously seldom seen in art, that suddenly began to appear due to their special meaning for the Wittenberg Reformers was the scene of *Christ Blessing the Children*, of which Cranach painted many versions (e.g. 1538; Hamburg, Ksthalle). Its twofold message reaffirmed that faith was a divine gift and upheld the belief in infant baptism in opposition to the Anabaptists.

The most important publishing event in Wittenberg as well as for the Protestant Reformation itself, at least in Germany, was Luther's translation of the Bible, which appeared over a 12-year period between 1522 and 1534. For the first edition of the New Testament, known as the 'September Testament' because it was published in that month in 1522, Cranach provided the illustrations—21 full-page woodcuts, all for the Book of Revelation. His debt to Dürer's *Apocalypse* is unconcealed, and the cutting of the blocks betrays a haste to bring the edition out. Cranach and the goldsmith Christian Döring undertook financial responsibility for the 'September Testament', and the following year they installed a press in Cranach's house, where they printed and published in 1524 the part of Luther's Old Testament known as *Das ander Teyl des alten Testaments*, among other Reformation texts. All the illustrations published in the first editions of Luther's New and Old Testaments were produced in Cranach's workshop, as were many title borders used for other publications. The Cranach–Döring publishing enterprise

3. Lucas Cranach I: triptych with the *Three Electors of Saxony*, oil on panel, 675×670 mm (central panel), 687×323 mm (each wing), *c.* 1535 (Hamburg, Hamburger Kunsthalle)

was dissolved by 1525 or 1526, but the Cranach shop continued to work closely with other publishers.

Cranach himself was simultaneously engaged in many civic and commercial activities. From 1519 to 1545 he served on the Wittenberg city council and on three occasions was elected to the office of burgomaster. He owned several houses and an apothecary that held a monopoly on the sale of medicine, herbs and wine. The tax records of 1528 indicate that he was one of the city's two wealthiest citizens.

Cranach's friendship with Luther and personal involvement with the Reformation created no impediment to his continuing work for Catholic patrons, such as members of the Albertine line of Saxon princes or Cardinal Albrecht of Brandenburg, one of Luther's principal foes. In fact, Cranach executed more versions of the standard Catholic devotional theme, the Virgin and Child, after 1520 (*c.* 43) than before (*c.* 16). Following the dedication in 1523 of the Cardinal's Stiftskirche in Halle an der Salle, Cranach was commissioned to provide numerous altarpieces for the church. He generally turned over the execution of the altar panels to one or more assistants, who worked from his designs, of which a considerable number survive (see Rosenberg, 1960, nos 29–37), with one known exception: a *Man of Sorrows* (1524; Freiburg im Breisgau, Augustinmus.), which he painted himself as the central panel of an altarpiece, for which the wings (both Aschaffenburg, Schloss Johannisburg, Staatsgal.) were carried out by an assistant, known as the Pseudo-Grünewald or the Master of the Mass of St Gregory. Cardinal Albrecht, from whom Dürer and Grünewald also received commissions, chose Cranach to paint him as he wished to be seen, devout and scholarly. Cranach, who may never have laid eyes on the man and seems to have relied on Dürer's portrait engraving of him (1519; B. 102) as a model for the face, depicted him praying before a Crucifix (*c.* 1524; Munich, Alte Pin.); as *St Jerome in the Wilderness* (1527; Berlin, Gemäldegal.;

see PORTRAITURE, fig. 3); and twice as *St Jerome in his Study* (1525; Darmstadt, Hess. Landesmus.; and 1526, Sarasota, FL, Ringling Mus. A.), both modelled directly on Dürer's engraving of 1514 (B. 60).

The increasing tendency towards patternistic design in Cranach's portraits from after 1520 was held in balance by the artist's lifelong appreciation for individual physiognomy, especially in the portraits of men. In the unidentified pendant *Portrait of a Man* and *Portrait of a Woman* (1522; both Washington, DC, N.G.A.), the faces emerge with clear features and fine modelling from the relative flatness of the strong silhouettes of their upper torsos, which are darkly clad and set against a bright, fresh green background. Although the man's dominance is evident from the way his body fills a larger portion of the panel, both figures appear gentle, with fine features. This remains true for Cranach's portraits of women, but the male portraits, especially the rulers and other prominent men of political and religious affairs, are strikingly assertive, their bodies and heads filling up the available space. This can be seen in the sympathetic portrait of *Gregor Brück* (1533; Nuremberg, Ger. Nmus.), the electoral chancellor whose daughter, Barbara, was to marry Lucas Cranach the younger in 1541 and whose son, Christian, married Cranach's daughter, Barbara, in 1543.

From the beginning of his appointment to the court at Wittenberg, Cranach and his shop produced hundreds of portraits of his three electoral patrons in Wittenberg: Frederick the Wise (1463–1525); his brother, co-ruler and successor, John the Steadfast (1468–1532); and the latter's son and successor, John Frederick the Magnanimous (1503–54). On his succession to the electoral office in 1532, John Frederick ordered 60 portrait pairs of his deceased uncle and father, which were delivered and paid for the following year. He also commissioned a portrait of himself together with his two predecessors in a triptych format (*c.* 1535; Hamburg, Ksthalle; see fig. 3), in which the electors appear half-length, sturdy and resolute, with a view of their lands extending to the horizon behind them.

Following John Frederick's defeat and capture by Charles V at Mühlberg in 1547, Cranach no longer enjoyed his salaried position as court artist. In 1550 he joined his captive patron first in Augsburg, then in Innsbruck, where he continued to paint mythologies, hunting scenes and portraits, including one of *Titian* (untraced), who was in Augsburg at the same time. In 1552 John Frederick was freed, and Cranach moved with him to Weimar, where he lived in the house of his son-in-law, Christian Brück, and died the following year, at the age of 81.

(ii) Nudes and mythological subjects. As far as the defining criteria of Cranach's style of painting in Wittenberg are concerned, no subject is quite so telling as the nude, whether taken from Classical mythology or the figures of Adam and Eve. In his depictions of the nude, Cranach, like other German Renaissance artists, was stimulated especially by Dürer's engraving of *Adam and Eve* (1504; B. 1). However, in Cranach's work the nude developed away from Renaissance sources and towards a figural type whose appearance seems at once sophisticated and naive, just as its anti-Classical shape suggests a selfconscious return to the innocent youthfulness and courtly grace of the German Soft style or International Gothic of *c.* 1400.

Cranach's vision of the idealized, female nude first took shape in the life-size *Venus and Cupid* (1509; St Petersburg, Hermitage). Standing on a pebbly strip of earth and silhouetted against a solid black background, the Venus recalls Dürer's painting of *Eve* (1507; Madrid, Prado), but her body is fuller in the manner of an engraved figure by Jacopo de' Barbari, whose path had already crossed Cranach's in Wittenberg. As forthright as this nude appears to be, the painting contains a moralizing admonition in the form of a Latin inscription along the top, which says 'Avoid Cupid's lust with all your might/ That your breast be not possessed by amoral Venus'. This inscription also gives forewarning of the future enticements of the nude as it was conceived in some of Cranach's most popular subjects.

Similar proportions and contours are found in the woodcut of the same subject, dated 1506 (actually ?1509; Hollstein, no. 105), where Venus makes a similar restraining gesture towards Cupid, and also in woodcuts of the *Judgement of Paris* (1508; Hollstein, no. 104) and of *Adam and Eve* (1509; Hollstein, no. 1). Soon thereafter the figures began to change in form, taking on slimmer proportions and rather adolescent contours, the women having more slender hips and smaller breasts. After 1520 the early Venus type was replaced by a younger, more coquettish sister, as in the *Venus* (1532; Frankfurt am Main, Städel. Kstinst. & Städt. Gal.), where she draws attention to her nakedness by leaving her jewellery on and covering herself with a length of transparent drapery. Yet given the nearly childlike shape of her body, she could very well join in with the innocent, playful nude figures in

4. Lucas Cranach I: *Golden Age*, oil on canvas, laid on to panel, 0.73×1.05 m, *c.* 1530 (Munich, Alte Pinakothek)

the painting of the *Golden Age* (*c.* 1530; Munich, Alte Pin.; see fig. 4).

The thin line that Cranach liked to draw between the expression of innocence and seductiveness in these female nudes also leads to the choice of certain themes, such as the *Nymph of the Spring*, to which he turned repeatedly from *c.* 1516 onwards. No fewer than 17 versions survive from his hand (e.g. 1534; Liverpool, Walker A.G.) or those of his assistants. The subject evolved from a pseudo-Classical epigram that appears in abbreviated form as an inscription, saying: 'Here I rest, nymph of the spring, do not disturb my sleep.' Yet the nymph happens to be lying on a stylish dress that she has taken off, and her admonition not to disturb her sleep is contradicted by her partly opened eyes, as if she intended to make sure that the beholder was not able to resist her. The contemporary appetite for Cranach's *Venus with Cupid, the Honey Thief* is attested by 22 known versions. It, too, bears an inscribed warning, taken from the Nineteenth Idyll of Theocritus: 'As Cupid was stealing honey from the hive,/ A bee stung the thief on the finger;/ And so do we seek transitory and dangerous pleasures/ That are mixed with sadness and bring us pain.' In one version (1531; Rome, Gal. Borghese) Venus appears as a tall, elegant courtesan, wearing only a large red hat and gold necklace. If that were not enough to make the message clear, Cupid is shown having stolen the honeycomb from a prominent slit in the tree trunk adjacent to Venus's thigh.

In the equally popular moralizing theme of the *Unequal Lovers*, where an old man's money is exchanged by consent or stealth for the promise of a young woman's love, decorum forbade nudity, so allurement was expressed by fashionable clothing. By the 1530s the faces and figural types of Cranach's women were scarcely differentiated among 'portraits' of aristocratic ladies, goddesses, heroines or courtesans. But he was not unmindful of the transitoriness of their youthful beauty, especially at the age of 74, when he painted the *Fountain of Youth* (1546; Berlin, Gemäldegal.). Feeble, wrinkled old women are carried and carted to the pool of water, where they shed their clothes and enter. Halfway across they begin to frolic like the girls back into which they have been changed, and they emerge on the other side to the attentions of gallant young men and to a new life of courting and gaiety.

II. Workshop.

Documents and surviving works attest to Cranach's large and productive workshop in Wittenberg. His first pupil is mentioned in 1507. During the work at Torgau in preparation for the marriage of John the Steadfast and Margaret of Dessau, he was paid for ten assistants. The size of his staff undoubtedly varied according to the projects at hand, but every indication points to several or more assistants and pupils every year. Not surprisingly, then, the number of 'Cranach school' works defies tally. The fact that after 1520 it becomes increasingly difficult to be sure about attributions to the master among multiple versions of a single composition has led many commentators to conclude that Cranach was delegating more of the execution of paintings to the workshop. Clearly, when he was able to deliver 60 double portraits of Frederick the Wise and

John the Steadfast within a single year, both the staffing and the working system in the shop were intended for rapid production. It may well be that Cranach developed aspects of his later style in order to facilitate standardized execution and easy replication of the work. In any case he stocked the workshop with portrait drawings, studies of animals for hunting scenes and presumably other drawings or prototypes for use as needed.

From the point of view of stylistic uniformity, if not always uniform quality, Cranach's artistic identity subsumed that of virtually all the other artists who worked with him. Even his talented sons Hans and Lucas the younger scarcely established a profile of their own, except for Lucas the younger after his father's death. Names of a few other followers, who probably worked in the shop, such as Hans Döring or Wolfgang Krodel (*fl* 1528–61), are linked to a handful of works but without the promise of emerging as significant personalities in their own right. Much effort has been directed towards distinguishing the hands of the assistants who executed Cranach's designs in Halle for Cardinal Albrecht of Brandenburg; these paintings have also been attributed to the Master of the Pflock Altarpiece and the Master of the Martyrdom of St Erasmus. Tacke (1992) argued that the principal artist who carried out Cranach's designs in Halle was Simon Franck.

BIBLIOGRAPHY

EWA; Thieme–Becker

MONOGRAPHIC STUDIES AND DOCUMENTS

J. Heller: *Lucas Cranachs Leben und Werke* (Bamberg, 1821, 2/Nuremberg, 1854)

C. Schuchardt: *Lucas Cranach des Ältern: Leben und Werke, nach urkundlichen Quellen bearbeitet* Leipzig, pt 1 and 2, 1851, pt 3, 1871)

E. Flechsig: *Cranachstudien*, i (Leipzig, 1900) [nothing more published]

C. Glaser: *Lukas Cranach* (Leipzig, 1921)

M. J. Friedländer and J. Rosenberg: *Die Gemälde von Lucas Cranach* (Berlin, 1932); rev. 2 and Eng. trans. by H. Norden and R. Taylor (Ithaca, 1978)

C. Posse: *Lucas Cranach d. Ä* (Vienna, 1942)

H. Lilienfein: *Lukas Cranach und seine Zeit* (Bielefeld, 1944)

H. Lüdecke: *Lucas Cranach der Ältere im Spiegel seiner Zeit* (Berlin, 1953)

H. Lüdecke, ed.: *Lucas Cranach der Ältere: Der Künstler und seine Zeit* (Berlin, 1953) [docs and bibliog.]

A. Giesecke: 'Wappen, Siegel und Signet Lucas Cranachs und seiner Söhne und ihre Bedeutung für die Cranach-Forschung', *Z. Kstwiss.*, ix (1955), pp. 181–92

J. Rosenberg: 'The Problem of Authenticity in Cranach's Late Period', *A. Q.* [Detroit], xviii (1955), pp. 165–8

E. Ruhmer: *Cranach* (London, 1963)

F. Thöne: *Lucas Cranach der Ältere* (Königstein im Taunus, 1965)

D. Koepplin: 'Lucas Cranachs Heirat und das Geburtsjahr des Sohnes Hans', *Z. Dt. Ver. Kstwiss.*, xx (1966), pp. 79–84

U. Steinmann: 'Lucas Cranachs Eheschliessung und das Geburtsjahr des Sohnes Hans', *Forsch. & Ber.: Staatl. Mus. Berlin*, ii (1968), pp. 124–34

J. Rosenberg: 'Lucas Cranach the Elder: A Critical Appreciation', *Rec. A. Mus., Princeton U.*, xxviii (1969), pp. 27–53

G. Fehr, F. Winzinger and F. Seibt: *Lucas Cranach, 1472/1972* (Munich, 1972)

J. Wirth: 'Cranach reconsidéré', *Rev. A.*, xxxvii (1977), pp. 83–99

E. Ullmann: 'Lucas Cranach der Ältere: Bürger und Hofmaler', *Kunst und Reformation* (Leipzig, 1982), pp. 41–52

PRINTS AND DRAWINGS

Hollstein: *Ger.*

C. Dodgson: *Catalogue of Early German and Flemish Woodcuts*, ii, London, BM cat. (London, 1911), pp. 274–321

M. Geisberg: *Der deutsche Einblatt-Holzschnitt in der 1. Hälfte des 16. Jahrhunderts* (Munich, 1923–30); Eng. trans. and ed. by W. L. Strauss as *The German Single-leaf Woodcut, 1500–1550*, ii (New York, 1974), pp. 503–614

J. Jahn: *Lucas Cranach als Graphiker* (Leipzig, 1955)

J. Rosenberg: *Die Zeichnungen Lucas Cranachs d. Ä.* (Berlin, 1960)

J. Jahn and M. Bernhard: *Lucas Cranach d. Ä.: Das gesamte graphische Werk* (Munich, 1972)

D. Koepplin: 'Zu Cranach als Zeichner: Addenda zu Rosenbergs Katalog', *Kstchronik*, xxvi (1972), pp. 345–8

M. B. Pope: *Woodcuts by Lucas Cranach the Elder and his Workshop* (diss., Philadelphia, U. PA, 1976, Ann Arbor, 1978)

From a Mighty Fortress: Prints, Drawings and Books in the Age of Luther, 1483–1546 (exh. cat. by C. Andersson and C. Talbot, Detroit, MI, Inst. A., 1983)

G. Seebass: *Die Himmelsleiter des hl. Bonaventura von Lukas Cranach d. Ä.* (Heidelberg, 1985)

H. Sieveking: *Das Gebetbuch Kaiser Maximilians: Der Münchner Teil mit den Randzeichnungen von Albrecht Dürer und Lucas Cranach d. Ae.* (Munich, 1987)

Albrecht Altdorfer: Zeichnungen, Deckfarbenmalerei, Druckgraphik (exh. cat. by H. Mielke, Berlin, Kupferstichkab., 1988)

K. Löcher: 'Cranachs Holzschnitt-*Passion* von 1509: Ihre Wirkung auf die Künste', *Anz. Ger. Nmus.* (1990), pp. 9–52

EXHIBITIONS AND SYMPOSIA

Katalog der Lucas-Cranach-Ausstellung (exh. cat. by W. Scheidig, Weimar, Schlossmus.; Wittenberg, Staatl. Lutherhalle; 1953)

Lucas Cranach d. Ä. (exh. cat., Weimar, Schlossmus., 1972)

Lucas Cranach der Ältere und seine Werkstatt (exh. cat. by K. Schütz, Vienna, Ksthist. Mus., 1972)

Lucas Cranach d. Ae., 1472–1553: Graphik aus dem Kupferstichkabinett der Kunstsammlungen der Veste Coburg (exh. cat. by H. Maedebach, Coburg, Veste Coburg, 1972)

Lucas Cranach: Künstler und Gesellschaft: Wittenberg, 1972 (Wittenberg, 1973)

Lukas Cranach, 2 vols (exh. cat. by D. Koepplin and T. Falk, Basle, Kstmus., 1974–6)

Akten des Kolloquiums zu Basler Cranach-Ausstellung: Basle, 1974 (Basle, 1977)

Cranach och den tyska renässansen [Cranach and the German Renaissance] (exh. cat., Stockholm, Nmus., 1988)

Lucas Cranach: Ein Maler–Unternehmer aus Franken (exh. cat., ed. C. Grimm and others; Augsburg, Haus Bayer. Gesch., 1994)

RELIGIOUS THEMES AND THE REFORMATION

A. Schramm: *Luther und die Bibel, I: Die Illustration der Lutherbibel* (Leipzig, 1923)

O. Thulin: *Cranach-Altäre der Reformation* (Berlin, 1955)

H. von Hintzenstern: *Lucas Cranach d. Ä.: Altarbilder aus der Reformationszeit* (Berlin, 1972)

C. C. Christensen: *Art and the Reformation in Germany* (Athens, OH, 1979)

C. D. Andersson: 'Religiöse Bilder Cranachs im Dienste der Reformation', *Humanismus und Reformation in der deutschen Geschichte*, ed. L. W. Spitz, Veröff. Hist. Kommiss. Berlin, 51 (Berlin, 1981), pp. 43–79

D. Bax: *Hieronymus Bosch and Lucas Cranach: Two 'Last Judgement' Triptychs* (Amsterdam, 1983)

P. Martin: *Martin Luther und die Bilder zur Apokalypse: Die Ikonographie der Illustrationen zur Offenbarung des Johannes in der Lutherbibel, 1522 bis 1546* (Hamburg, 1983)

Kunst der Reformationszeit (exh. cat., Berlin, Altes Mus., 1983)

Martin Luther und die Reformation in Deutschland (exh. cat., ed. G. Bott; Nuremberg, Ger. Nmus., 1983)

Luther und die Folgen für die Kunst (exh. cat., ed. W. Hofmann; Hamburg, Ksthalle, 1983–4)

M. Warnke: *Cranachs Luther* (Frankfurt am Main, 1984)

F. Ohly: *Gesetz und Evangelium: Zur Typologie bei Luther und Lucas Cranach: Zum Blutstrahl der Gnade in der Kunst*, Schrreihe Westfäl. Wilhelms-U. Münster (Münster, 1985)

A. Perrig: 'Lucas Cranach und der Kardinal Albrecht von Brandenburg', *Forma et subtilitas*, ed. W. Schlink and M. Sperlich (Berlin, 1986), pp. 50–62

C. C. Christensen: *Princes and Propaganda: Electoral Saxon Art of the Reformation* (Kirksville, MO, 1992)

A. Tacke: *Der katholische Cranach: Zu zwei Grossaufträgen von Lucas Cranach d. Ä., Simon Franck und der Cranach-Werkstatt, 1520–1540* (Mainz, 1992)

PORTRAITS

E. Buchner: *Das deutsche Bildnis der Spätgotik und der frühen Dürerzeit* (Berlin, 1953)

D. Koepplin: *Cranachs Ehebildnis des 'Johannes Cuspinian' von 1502* (diss., U. Basle, 1964, pubd 1974)

J. L. Koerner: *The Moment of Self-portraiture in German Renaissance Art* (Chicago, 1993)

NUDES AND MYTHOLOGICAL SUBJECTS

C. Zervos: *Nus de Lucas Cranach l'Ancien* (Paris, 1950)

C. W. Talbot jr: 'An Interpretation of Two Paintings by Cranach in the Artist's Late Style', *N.G.A., Rep. & Stud.* (1967), pp. 67–88

M. Liebmann: 'On the Iconography of the *Nymph of the Fountain* by Lucas Cranach the Elder', *J. Warb. & Court. Inst.*, xxxi (1968), pp. 434–7

D. Wuttke: 'Zu *Huius nympha loci*', *Arcadia*, iii (1968), pp. 306–7

W. Strauss: *Sixteenth-century German Artists* (1980), 10 [XVII/i] of *The Illustrated Bartsch*, ed. W. Strauss (1978–) [B.]

G. Biedermann: 'Die *Paris Urteile* Lucas Cranachs d. Ä', *Pantheon*, xxxix (1981), pp. 310–13

H. Nickel: 'The *Judgment of Paris* by Lucas Cranach the Elder: Nature, Allegory and Alchemy', *Met. Mus. J.*, xvi (1982), pp. 117–29

F. W. G. Leeman: 'A Textual Source for Cranach's *Venus with Cupid the Honey Thief*', *Burl. Mag.*, cxxvi (1984), pp. 274–5

C. Heck: 'Entre humanisme et réforme: La *Mélancolie* de Lucas Cranach l'ancien', *Rev. Louvre*, xxxvi (1986), pp. 257–64

(2) Hans Cranach (*b* Wittenberg, *c.* 1513; *d* Bologna, 9 Oct 1537). Painter and draughtsman, son of (1) Lucas Cranach I. The earliest documentary references to him, from 1533 and 1534, concern his receipt of payments for his father. In 1536 Hans was working at the castle in Torgau with his father, brother and other assistants from the Cranach workshop. Only two signed paintings are known: the monogrammed *Portrait of a Bearded Man* (1534) and the monogrammed *Hercules at the Court of Omphale* (1537; both Madrid, Mus. Thyssen–Bornemisza). His signature also appears in a sketchbook (Hannover, Kestner-Mus.) with studies in silverpoint of portraits and some landscapes of places seen on route to Italy. This evidence reveals that Hans was trained by his father in Wittenberg and began his brief career in the family workshop, before travelling to Italy. At the time of Hans's early death, Johann Stigel (1515–62), who became a professor in Wittenberg, eulogized him in a long poem and favourably compared his inventiveness to that of his father.

The few established works by Hans, however, show neither stylistic nor thematic independence from Lucas the elder. *Hercules at the Court of Omphale*, a variant on Lucas's earlier treatment of the subject (e.g. 1532; ex-Kaiser-Friedrich Mus., Berlin, destr.), replicates the familiar Cranach facial types with a precision and a fine modulation of broken colours, but the bodies of the half-length figures are spatially and proportionally ambiguous. The *Portrait of a Bearded Man*, a stolid-looking figure, was probably one of a pair, its pendant being the *Portrait of a Woman* (Paris, Petit Pal.). This would rule out the possibility (Schade) that the man is a self-portrait, since Hans died unmarried. Based on these works, a handful of other works, including watercolours and a woodcut for a title-page, have been attributed to Hans, but almost always with a question mark (see 1974–6 exh. cat., nos 144–6, 269, 497, 626).

BIBLIOGRAPHY

E. Flechsig: *Cranachstudien* (Leipzig, 1900), pp. 236–50

D. Koepplin: 'Lucas Cranachs Heirat und das Geburtsjahr des Sohnes Hans', *Z. Dt. Ver. Kstwiss.*, xx (1966), pp. 79–84

W. Schade: 'Die Stellung der Söhne innerhalb der Werkstatt Cranachs (1534–1538)', *Lucas Cranach: Künstler und Gesellschaft: Wittenberg, 1972* (Wittenberg, 1973), pp. 116–18

Lukas Cranach, 2 vols (exh. cat. by D. Koepplin and T. Falk, Basle, Kstmus., 1974–6)I.

I. Lübbeke: *The Thyssen-Bornemisza Collection: Early German Painting*, trans. by M. T. Will (London, 1991), pp. 178–89, 406

(3) Lucas Cranach II [the younger] (*b* Wittenberg, 4 Oct 1515; *d* Weimar, 25 Jan 1586). Painter and designer of woodcuts, son of (1) Lucas Cranach I. His work was so closely modelled on that of his father that distinguishing the late style of Lucas the elder from the early works of his son remains in most cases hypothetical. Having first been his father's pupil and assistant, he remained in the workshop his entire career. His responsibilities increased over the 1530s, especially after the death of his older brother Hans in 1537. Lucas II became the *de facto* head of the workshop in 1550, when his father left Wittenberg to join the deposed Saxon elector John Frederick in Augsburg. On his father's death in 1553, he became sole proprietor and chief artist of this family enterprise. In 1541 he married Barbara Brück, the daughter of the electoral chancellor, Gregor Brück. Widowed in 1550, he then married Magdalene Schurff (*d* 1606), a niece of Melanchthon, the following year. Lucas the younger also followed his father's footsteps into high civic office. From 1549 through 1568 he served on the Wittenberg city council, rising first to chancellor and then to burgomaster. Although he continued to receive many commissions from Saxon princes, unlike his father he did not enjoy the advantages of a court appointment, since John Frederick lost the electoral territory of Wittenberg in 1547, when he and the League of Schmalkalden were defeated by Emperor Charles V at the Battle of Mühlberg. Still, Lucas II remained one of the richest citizens of the city, according to his taxable property in 1573.

Attributions to Lucas the younger from the 1530s and 1540s depend on stylistic connections to his work from and after 1550, when he was in sole charge of the workshop. The *Portrait of a Nobleman* and the *Portrait of a Noblewoman* (1564; both Vienna, Ksthist. Mus.), for example, bear the familiar traits of the Saxon Cranach style but may be distinguished from Lucas the elder's work by the degree of rosy complexions, lighter tonalities, smooth but colouristically softened surfaces, sharp silhouettes and frozen positions, which invite recognition of the same hand in the portraits of *Caspar von Minckwitz* and *Anna von Minckwitz* (1543; both Stuttgart, Staatsgal.). Increasingly these portraits emphasize social standing at the expense of conveying individual character.

Opinions still remain divided, however, on whether the painting of *Lucas Cranach the Elder* (1550; Florence, Uffizi) is a self-portrait by the 77-year-old father or a likeness of the father by the son. A similar disagreement exists over the attribution of the 15 vivid portrait drawings of aristocratic sitters (*c.* 1540; Reims, Mus. St-Denis); these tempera and oil studies on paper provided models for the workshop to use many times over, varying costume and format as required. Those who believe that all fifteen portraits, not just three of them, are by Lucas the younger also attribute to him the similar drawing of a *Bearded Man* (Berlin, Kupferstichkab.). Efforts to shift the attribution of the *Fountain of Youth* (1546; Berlin, Gemäldegal.) from father to son (Hartlaub) are generally rejected on stylistic grounds.

Two signed panels with scenes of *Hercules in Combat against an Army of Dwarfs* (1551; both Dresden, Gemäldegal. Alte Meister) count among Lucas II's earliest authenticated, independent works. Painted for the new elector, Maurice of Saxony, they show the younger artist's predisposition for large paintings (each panel, *c.* 1.9×1.6 m) and his ready access to commissions from the rival, Albertine house of Saxony, which received the electoral title after the defeat of the Cranach family's Protestant patron John Frederick. As a memorial to John Frederick, however, and as a confession of the new faith, he painted a large triptych (central panel, 3.6×3.11 m, 1555; Weimar, SS Peter and Paul), showing the former Elector and his wife on one of the flanking wings and their three sons on the other. In the centre panel Christ on the Cross divides the foreground between Christ vanquishing the devil on the left and John the Baptist standing under the cross in the company of Lucas Cranach the elder and Martin Luther on the right. In the absence of traditional religious painting for Protestant churches, Lucas the younger continued to receive commissions for memorial pictures in which the reformers appeared in biblical scenes, such as the *Last Supper* (1565; Dessau-Mildensee, Parish Church), a memorial to Joachim of Anhalt, in which Prince George of Anhalt appears alongside Luther and Melanchthon, among others, in place of the Apostles.

Lucas the younger also continued to meet the demand for replications of images made popular by his father, such as portraits of the reformers, religious allegories and Classical themes. These were often small panels, such as the *Allegory of the Law and the Gospel* (*c.* 1550; priv. col., see 1974–6 exh. cat., no. 355, fig. 275), based on the prototype of Lucas the elder (*c.* 1530; Gotha, Schloss Friedenstein), or the *Adam and Eve* (1549; priv. col., see Friedländer and Rosenberg, 1978, no. 432), perhaps the earliest dated work by Lucas the younger. The moralizing and pseudo-Classical theme of the *Nymph of the Spring* exists in no fewer than 17 versions, of which at least one (New York, Met.) bears the traits of Lucas the younger's hand.

The hand of the younger Lucas may also be seen in woodcut book illustrations from as early as 1538 (1974–6 exh. cat., no. 277) and certainly no later than the following year when Fabian von Auerswald's *Ringer Kunst* (Wittenberg, 1539) was published with its 85 illustrations of wrestling positions plus the author's portrait on the title-page. Lucas II also contributed illustrations to two editions of Luther's translation of the Bible in 1541, one published by Hans Lufft in Wittenberg and the other by Nikolaus Wolrab in Leipzig. His single-leaf woodcuts, like the title-page of the Wittenberg Bible, include several Protestant allegories. One of these (Geisberg, no. 653) from *c.* 1546 represents Luther in a pulpit pointing on his right to a Protestant celebration of the Eucharist and on his left to the Catholic clergy's descent into Hell's maw. Unlike many polemical prints of the period, these by Lucas are carefully designed and executed. He also published full- and half-length woodcut portraits of reformers and Saxon princes, notable for the precision and clarity of their draughtsmanship.

BIBLIOGRAPHY
Hollstein: *Ger.*
M. Geisberg: *Der deutsche Einblatt-Holzschnitt in der 1. Hälfte des 16. Jahrhunderts* (Munich, 1923–30); Eng. trans. and ed. by W. L. Strauss as *The German Single-leaf Woodcut, 1500–1550* (New York, 1974), ii, pp. 615–51.

M. J. Friedländer and J. Rosenberg: *The Paintings of Lucas Cranach* (Berlin, 1932); rev. 2 and trans. by H. Norden and R. Taylor (Ithaca, 1978)

H. Lüdecke, ed.: *Lucas Cranach der Ältere: Der Künstler und seine Zeit* (Berlin, 1953) [with bibliog. for Lucas Cranach the younger]

H. Zimmermann: 'Beiträge zum Werk Lucas Cranachs d. J.', *Z. Kstwiss.*, vii (1953), pp. 209–15

G. F. Hartlaub: *Lucas Cranach d. J.: Der Jungbrunnen* (Stuttgart, 1958)

H. Zimmermann: 'Über einige Bildniszeichnungen Lucas Cranachs d. J.', *Pantheon*, xx (1962), pp. 8–12

W. Schade: 'Maler am Hofe Moritz 'von Sachsen', *Z. Dt. Ver. Kstwiss.*, xxii (1968), pp. 29–44

H. Zimmermann: 'Zur Ikonographie von Damenbildnissen des älteren und des jüngeren Lucas Cranach', *Pantheon*, xxvii (1969), pp. 283–93

W. Schade: 'Die Stellung der Söhne innerhalb der Werkstatt Cranachs (1534–1538)', *Lucas Cranach: Künstler und Gesellschaft: Wittenberg, 1972* (Wittenberg, 1973), pp. 116–18

Lukas Cranach, 2 vols (exh. cat. by D. Koepplin and T. Falk, Basle, Kstmus., 1974–6)

W. Schade: 'Der jüngere Cranach und die *Ringer-Kunst* des Fabian von Auerswald', *Ringer-Kunst: 85 Stücke...durch Fabian von Auerswald* (Weinheim, 1987), pp. 13–18 [facs. repr.]

F. Baron: 'Ein Einblattdruck Lucas Cranachs d. J. als Quelle der Hexenverfolgung in Luthers Wittenberg', *Poesis et Pictura: Festschrift Dieter Wuttke* (Baden-Baden, 1989), pp. 277–94

CHARLES TALBOT

Cranbrook Colony. Group of English painters working *c.* 1855–1900. The name was attached in the early 1860s to an informal group of genre painters who spent their summers working in the village of Cranbrook in Kent. The brothers George Hardy (1822–1909) and Frederick Daniel Hardy (1826–1911) were disciples of Thomas Webster. F. D. Hardy first settled in Cranbrook about 1854. Webster moved there in 1857 and introduced his friend J. C. Horsley to the Hardys. G. B. O'Neill, who had married Horsley's cousin, joined them in the late 1850s. Augustus E. Mulready and G. H. Boughton (1833–1905) were also frequent visitors.

Cranbrook's attractions were the same as those of other contemporary artistic centres in the home counties: picturesque countryside, a wealth of old houses and cottages and easy access to London by railway. This was an important consideration for such artists as Horsley and O'Neill who also had houses in London.

Although Dutch 17th-century genre painting was a fundamental influence on the whole group, it was united more by family links than by artistic sympathies. In terms of stylistic cohesion, talent and sophistication, its artists had little in common. Horsley was the most successful. F. D. Hardy's earliest cottage interiors reveal an almost Pre-Raphaelite seriousness and objectivity, but he and O'Neill seldom rose above the anecdotal. The Cranbrook Colony was primarily a social group, but important professional contacts could be established through it. For example, Richard Norman Shaw owed the foundation of his country-house practice to the additions he made to Horsley's house in Cranbrook, Willesley, in 1864–9.

BIBLIOGRAPHY
The Cranbrook Colony (exh. cat., ed. A. Greg; Wolverhampton A.G., 1977)

ANDREW GREG

Crane. *See under* CONSTRUCTION MACHINERY.

Crane, Walter (*b* Liverpool, 15 Aug 1845; *d* Horsham, W. Sussex, 14 March 1915). English painter, illustrator, designer, writer and teacher. He showed artistic inclinations as a boy and was encouraged to draw by his father, the portrait painter and miniaturist Thomas Crane (1808–59). A series of illustrations to Tennyson's *The Lady of Shalott* (Cambridge, MA, Harvard U., Houghton Lib.) was shown first to Ruskin, who praised the use of colour, and then to the engraver William James Linton, to whom Crane was apprenticed in 1859. From 1859 to 1862 Crane learnt a technique of exact and economical draughtsmanship on woodblocks. His early illustrative works included vignette wood-engravings for John R. Capel Wise's *The New Forest: Its History and its Scenery* (1862).

During the mid-1860s Crane evolved his own style of children's book illustration. These so-called 'toy books', printed in colour by Edmund Evans, included *The History of Jenny Wren* and *The Fairy Ship*. Crane introduced new levels of artistic sophistication to the art of illustration: after *c.* 1870 his designs show the influence of Japanese prints in the use of flat areas of colour and simple, often asymmetrical compositions, and of classical sculpture in the figures and draperies; they also display the styles and schemes of decoration associated with the emergent Aesthetic Movement (for illustration by Crane *see* AESTHETIC MOVEMENT). Among his best-known works were *The Baby's Opera* (1877) and *The Baby's Bouquet* (1878). In the 1880s Crane compiled various books of drawings for his own children, among them *Legends for Lionel* (Cambridge, MA, Harvard U., Houghton Lib.) and *Lancelot's Levities* (New Haven, CT, Yale U., Beinecke Lib.). By this time Kate Greenaway and Randolph Caldecott were competing with Crane for the juvenile audience. Crane's last outstanding book of illustrations for children was *Flora's Feast* (1889). He later worked with William Morris at the Kelmscott Press on wood-engravings for Morris's *The Story of the Glittering Plain* (1894) and for Spenser's *The Faerie Queene* (1894–7); these Gothic images were among his finest works as an illustrator.

Despite the success of his books, Crane's principal ambition was as a painter. In 1862 his painting *The Lady of Shalott* (untraced) was favourably received at the Royal Academy; however, his only subsequent Royal Academy exhibit was *At Home: A Portrait* (1872; Leeds, C.A.G.), and therefore he depended on the Dudley, Grosvenor and New galleries, and on the two watercolour societies, to show his works. Crane's early landscapes and figurative subjects show the influence of the Pre-Raphaelites and Edward Burne-Jones. George Howard, later 9th Earl of Carlisle, commissioned Crane to complete Burne-Jones's *Cupid and Psyche* decorations for his house in Palace Green, Kensington (1872–81; Birmingham, Mus. & A.G.), and introduced Crane to fellow artists and patrons.

In 1871 Crane married Mary Frances Andrews, and during a protracted Italian honeymoon he evolved a personal style of gouache landscape painting. In common with his new friends Frederic Leighton and Giovanni Costa, he reduced the range of colour and simplified the forms of the landscape to convey the sun-baked but luxuriant character of the Italian countryside. Crane's larger-scale pictures increasingly reveal his belief that art might be used as a metaphor for the human condition. The *Renascence of Venus* (1877; London, Tate; see fig.) shows both his study of Botticelli and his hope that a new

Walter Crane: *Renascence of Venus*, tempera on canvas, 1384×1841 mm, 1877 (London, Tate Gallery)

appreciation of beauty in art and decoration was coming about in England. However, many of his allegorical paintings of the 1880s, such as *The Bridge of Life* (1884) and *Freedom* (1885; both untraced), suffer from sombre mood and banal symbolism and were criticized on these accounts. Crane's draughtsmanship became less precise and his treatment of figures crude.

Crane's great skill was in the designing of decorative patterns and ornament. Among his finest works were the wallpapers printed by Jeffrey & Co., which he worked on from 1875 (*see* WALLPAPER, colour pl. V, fig. 1); the designs for pottery for Maw & Co., Pilkington and Wedgwood; and the decorative schemes that he created. His view of the usefulness and purpose of works of art was derived from the theories of Ruskin: like William Morris, Crane believed that the dignity and pride of a craftsman were reflected in what he made and would thus inspire the user. He was committed to the improvement of art education and the application of design to the processes of industrial manufacture. In 1884 Crane became a member of the Art Workers' Guild, serving as Master of the guild in 1888–9. In 1886 he campaigned with William Holman Hunt for the foundation of a 'national exhibition' where pictures and decorative arts might be shown together: this idea, which stemmed from a dissatisfaction with the Royal Academy, led to the foundation of the Arts and Crafts Exhibition Society, which held exhibitions at

the New Gallery and elsewhere from 1888. Crane served as part-time director of the Manchester School of Art (1893–6) and briefly succeeded Thomas Armstrong as principal of the Royal College of Art in 1898. Crane was the author of various influential theoretical treatises, as well as an indefatigable campaigner in the causes of art and socialism; he was a habitual traveller and exhibition organizer, making lecture tours in the USA and Europe.

WRITINGS
The Claims of Decorative Art (London, 1892)
Of the Decorative Illustration of Books (London, 1896)
Line and Form (London, 1900)
An Artist's Reminiscences (London, 1907)

BIBLIOGRAPHY
P. G. Konody: *The Art of Walter Crane* (London, 1902)
O. von Schleinitz: *Walter Crane* (Bielefeld, 1902)
G. C. E. Massé: *Bibliography of First Editions of Books Illustrated by Walter Crane* (London, 1923)
I. Spencer: *Walter Crane* (London, 1975) [bibliog. supplements that comp. by Massé and incl. writings]

CHRISTOPHER NEWALL

Cranfield Sackville, Lionel. *See* SACKVILLE, (1).

Cranke, James (*b* Urswick, Lancs, 23 June 1707; *d* Urswick, 28 Oct 1780). English painter. A self-taught artist who began work as a plasterer, by the 1730s or 1740s he was in London, where he attended the St Martin's Lane Academy. After marrying an heiress in *c.* 1744, he set up a studio in Bloomsbury Square. His earliest known paintings are portraits of *Foster Cunliffe* and *Mrs Foster Cunliffe* (priv. col., see Dibdin, pp. 203, 206). The seated full-length portrait of the well-known bookseller *Thomas Osborne* (1747; New Haven, CT, Yale Cent. Brit. A.) is among his rare signed works and has the solid accomplishment of contemporary portraits by Thomas Hudson, with something of William Hogarth's realism as well. The quality of the drapery painting, however, suggests that (unlike Hudson) Cranke did this part of the work himself.

Cranke returned to Lancashire in 1751 and worked for the Stanley family at Knowsley Hall. He painted several portraits and also made large copies of works by Raphael, Peter Paul Rubens and Correggio (probably derived from earlier copies or engravings) as well as executing his only known religious work—an altarpiece of the *Last Supper* (Urswick, St Mary's). His last known portrait is of *Isabell Tetlaw* (1757; priv. col., see Dibdin, p. 208). There is some evidence that Cranke gave lessons to George Romney, who was in the area until 1762.

BIBLIOGRAPHY

Waterhouse: *18th C.*

E. R. Dibdin: 'James Cranke the Elder: A Forgotten Lancashire Painter', *Connoisseur*, lxiv (1922), pp. 199–208

HUGH BELSEY

Craquelure [Fr.: 'cracking']. Pattern or network of small cracks on a painting. This may be due entirely to ageing of the structure of the painting, or it may have been provoked by defective or unsuitable materials, poor storage, technical error or the painter's incompetence. As a consequence of ageing alone, craquelure is seldom disfiguring and is simply regarded as a characteristic feature of older paintings (for which reason it has been faked). Movement of the support and shrinkage or embrittlement of the ground, paint and varnish are the main causes. The cracks occur in distinctive formations related to the type of support or to weaknesses and irregularities that act as focal points for stress. A circular pattern of cracks, known as 'rivelling', occurs on Vermeer's *Guitar Player* (c. 1672–5; London, Kenwood House) and Reynolds's *Mrs Siddons as the Tragic Muse* (1784; San Marino, CA, Huntington Lib. & A.G.). Cracks that originate within the paint layer, often due to poor technique, are more likely to detract from the painting's appearance. Reynolds's use of bituminous pigments provides many examples of '*craquelure anglaise*'. Premature overpainting, especially of thick layers of oil paint, and not painting 'fat over lean' are other common causes. Sometimes another colour is revealed through the cracks, for example in the *Bellelli Family* (1858–67; Paris, Mus. d'Orsay) by Degas, in which an underlayer of red is visible through a fractured layer of black. Acrylic paints are affected by low temperatures and can evolve a form of craquelure despite their elasticity.

Craquelure is often produced intentionally as a decorative effect in glazes, particularly on ceramics (*see* GLAZE).

BIBLIOGRAPHY

E. M. Gilberte: *The Restorer's Handbook of Easel Painting* (London, 1976)

JONATHAN STEPHENSON

Crauk, Charles-Alexandre (*b* Douchy, 27 Jan 1819; *d* Paris, 30 May 1905). French painter. He was a pupil of Jacques-François Momal (1754–1832) and of Antoine-Julien Potier (1796–1865) at the Académie in Valenciennes, which gave him a grant, and he then went to the Ecole des Beaux-Arts in Paris in 1840, where he studied under François-Edouard Picot. He exhibited regularly at the Salon from 1845, including such works as *Antoine Watteau, Dying, Gives his last Advice to Jean-Baptiste Pater*. In 1846 he won the Deuxième Prix de Rome for *Alexandre, Ill, with his Doctor, Philip* (sketch Paris, priv. col.), though the Première Prix de Rome was not awarded that year. He is known mainly for his religious paintings, among them the *Ecstasy of St Lambert*, commissioned by the Interior Minister in 1852, and the *Baptism of Christ* (church of Lescas, Basses Pyrenées), commissioned by the Minister of State in 1852. He also painted the *Martyrdom of St Piat* for the cathedral in Angers and four scenes from the life of the eponymous saint for the choir of St Francis Xavier in Paris, as well as numerous cartoons for stained glass in churches at Compiègne, Versailles, Chartres and elsewhere. Crauk executed several civic decorative works for the Galerie des Machines at the Exposition Universelle in Paris in 1889, producing the cartoon for a large stained-glass window on the theme of the *Chariot of the Sun*. He also painted a ceiling for the Musée des Beaux-Arts in Amiens. He was appointed professor of drawing at the Ecole de Saint-Cyr in 1875 and exhibited regularly at the Salon until 1902, with one break in 1893.

BIBLIOGRAPHY

Bénézit; *DBF*; Thieme–Becker

A. DAGUERRE DE HUREAUX

Crauk, Gustave-Adolphe-Désiré (*b* Valenciennes, 16 July 1827; *d* Meudon, 17 Nov 1905). French sculptor. An artist noted more for productivity than originality, he won the Prix de Rome in 1851. He was most successful with commemorative statues in historical, military or ecclesiastical costume, such as the *Intendant d'Etigny* in front of the thermal baths at Bagnères-de-Luchon, Haute-Garonne (1873), *General Chanzy* at Le Mans (1885; Place de la République) and the tomb of *Cardinal Lavigerie* in the basilica of St Louis, Carthage (1899). Crauk was a compatriot and contemporary of Jean-Baptiste Carpeaux, and both received their first artistic training at the Académie de Peinture et de Sculpture, Valenciennes. Crauk's relationship with his birthplace was commemorated in the town's Musée Crauk, which housed the artist's bequest of his studio contents. Following damage sustained by the museum in World War II, the exhibits were removed to the Musée des Beaux-Arts, Valenciennes.

BIBLIOGRAPHY

Lami

De Carpeaux à Matisse: La Sculpture française de 1850 à 1914 dans les musées et les collections publiques du nord de la France (exh. cat., Calais, Mus. B.-A.; Lille, Mus. B.-A.; Arras, Mus. B.-A.; Paris, Mus. Rodin; 1982–3), pp. 172–7

PHILIP WARD-JACKSON

Cravo Neto, Mario (*b* Salvador, Bahia, 1947). Brazilian photographer. In 1964 he trained as a photographer in Berlin, returning to Brazil in 1966. He worked with the photographer Hans Mann in Rio de Janeiro, and as Fulvio Roiter's assistant on the latter's journey to Bahia. In 1969 he visited New York, and in the 1970s worked as a sculptor and photographer in São Paolo. In 1980 Cravo Neto won the prize for the best photographer of 1980 from the society of Brazilian art critics. This was in recognition of his extraordinary work in portrait studies, which he produced in front of a dramatic black background, as in *Tep, the Indian* (1980; see 1988 exh. cat.).

PHOTOGRAPHIC PUBLICATIONS
La Ciudad de Bahia (Brasília, 1980)
Mario Cravo visto da Mario Cravo Neto (Brasília, 1983)

BIBLIOGRAPHY
Brasil, fotografie di Mario Cravo Neto (exh. cat., intro. J. Amado; Venice, Pal. Fortuny, 1988)

ERIKA BILLETER

Crawford, 25th Earl of. *See* LINDSAY, ALEXANDER.

Crawford, Ralston (*b* St Catharines, nr Niagara Falls, 5 Sept 1906; *d* New York, 27 April 1978). American painter, printmaker and photographer of Canadian birth. After attending high school in Buffalo, NY, Crawford worked on tramp steamers in the Caribbean. In 1927 he enrolled at the Otis Art Institute in Los Angeles, CA, and worked briefly at the Walt Disney Studio. Later that year he moved to Philadelphia, PA, where he studied at the Pennsylvania Academy of the Fine Arts and at the Barnes Foundation in Merion Station until 1930. Crawford's paintings of the early 1930s, such as *Still-life on Dough Table* (1932; artist's estate, see 1985 exh. cat., p. 19), were influenced by the work of Cézanne and Juan Gris, which he had studied at the Barnes Foundation. He was also attracted to the simplified Cubism of Stuart Davis, with its restricted primary colour schemes. After a trip to Paris in 1932–3, where he studied at the Académie Colarossi and the Académie Scandinave, Crawford's flat, geometric treatment of architectural and industrial subjects in paintings such as *Vertical Building* (1934; San Francisco, CA, MOMA) led him to be associated with Precisionism. After 1940 he almost eliminated modelling from his work in favour of flat and virtually abstract architectural renderings, for example *Third Avenue Elevated* (1949; Minneapolis, MN, Walker A. Cent.). He taught at several schools in the United States and worked extensively in lithography and photography, in many cases using his highly formal black-and-white photographs as source material for his paintings.

BIBLIOGRAPHY
R. B. Freeman: *Ralston Crawford* (Tuscaloosa, AL, 1953)
——: *The Lithographs of Ralston Crawford* (Lexington, KY, 1962)
H. H. Arnason: *Ralston Crawford* (New York, 1963)
W. C. Agee: *Ralston Crawford* (Pasadena, CA, 1983)
Ralston Crawford: Photographs/Art and Process (exh. cat. by E. A. Tonelli, College Park, U. MD A.G., 1983)
Ralston Crawford (exh. cat. by B. Haskell, New York, Whitney, 1985)

ANDREW KAGAN

Crawford, Thomas (*b* New York, ?1813; *d* London, 10 Oct 1857). American sculptor. One of the major American Neo-classical sculptors, he learnt wood-carving in his youth. In 1832 he became a carver for New York's leading marble shop, operated by John Frazee (1790–1852) and Robert E. Launitz (1806–70). He cut mantelpieces and busts, and spent his evenings drawing from the cast collection at the National Academy of Design. In 1835 Crawford became the first American sculptor to settle permanently in Rome. Launitz provided Crawford with a letter of introduction to Bertel Thorvaldsen, who welcomed Crawford into his studio, gave him a corner in which to work, and provided occasional criticism including the advice to copy Antique models and not Thorvaldsen's own work. It is not known precisely how long Crawford remained under Thorvaldsen's tutelage, but it was probably less than a year. Crawford always esteemed Thorvaldsen's sculpture and continued friendship.

Once in his own studio, Crawford at first eked out a living by producing portraits, such as his bust of *Mrs John James Schermerhorn* (1837; New York, Hist. Soc.). By 1839 he had executed a full-scale plaster of his first major ideal work, *Orpheus* (Boston, MA, Mus. F.A.). Charles Sumner, the future United States senator and abolitionist, persuaded a group of literati to present an over life-size marble version of *Orpheus* to the Boston Athenaeum, where it was unveiled in 1844 with other sculpture by Crawford: the first one-man exhibition by an American sculptor. With its touching subject, careful nudity and echoes of the *Apollo Belvedere* (Rome, Vatican, Cortile Belvedere)—the statue most revered by Neo-classical artists—*Orpheus* won Crawford a reputation in Roman, British and, most importantly, American art circles. His rise to eminence was steady, and he found ready American patronage for ideal sculptures. Crawford attained particular success with figures of children, such as the *Genius of Mirth* (1842; New York, Met.).

Crawford was singular among the first generation of American Neo-classical sculptors in his success with public statuary. In 1850 he won a competition in Richmond, VA, for his bronze equestrian *George Washington*. Crawford's pediment design of the *Progress of Civilization* was commissioned for the Senate of the US Capitol in 1854. This pediment, composed of figures from America's past and present, dressed in contemporary costume, was thought eminently suitable for public statuary, and Crawford received subsequent Capitol commissions including *History and Justice* (a pediment); bronze doors for the House of Representatives and Senate; and the colossal bronze *Armed Freedom* for the dome (all begun 1855). Crawford continued to execute ideal figures such as *Flora* (1847; Newark, NJ, Mus.) and the *Peri* (1854; versions at Washington, DC, Corcoran Gal. A., and Philadelphia, PA Acad. F.A.), in which his earlier severe Neo-classicism was sweetened by sentimentality, but his career was cut short by his death from cancer at the age of 44. Many of his projects were completed by colleagues in Rome under the supervision of his widow. His plaster models were presented to the New York Central Park Commissioners and were exhibited until 1881, when a fire destroyed many of them.

BIBLIOGRAPHY
R. L. Gale: *Thomas Crawford, American Sculptor* (Pittsburgh, 1964)
W. Craven: *Sculpture in America* (New York, 1968, rev. Newark, 2/1984), pp. 123–35
L. Dimmick: *The Portrait Busts and Ideal Works of Thomas Crawford (1813?–1857), American Sculptor in Rome* (diss., U. Pittsburgh, 1986)
——: 'Thomas Crawford's *Orpheus*: The American *Apollo Belvedere*', *Amer. A. J.*, xix/4 (1987), pp. 47–79

——: '"An Altar Erected to Heroic Virtue Itself" Thomas Crawford and his *Virginia Washington Monument*', *Amer. A. J.*, xxiii/2 (1991), pp. 4–73

LAURETTA DIMMICK

Crawhall, Joseph (*b* Morpeth, Northumb., 20 Aug 1861; *d* London, 24 May 1913). English painter, active in Scotland. He was brought up in Newcastle upon Tyne and was encouraged by his father and by Charles Keene, the cartoonist for *Punch*, studying at King's College School in London under P. H. Delamotte. There he met E. A. Walton, with whom, joined by James Guthrie, he painted at Roseneath, near Glasgow, in 1879. Crawhall also collaborated with Walton and Guthrie on illustration. His association with the Glasgow Boys was consolidated during the early 1880s on further painting trips in the Trossachs, Berwicks, and Crowland, Lincs. A keen huntsman and rider, Crawhall specialized in bird, animal and humorous subjects, and his work, with that of Arthur Melville, exemplifies the achievement of the Glasgow Boys in watercolour. After studying in Paris in 1882 under Aimé Morot (1850–1913), Crawhall exhibited for the first and only time at the Royal Academy, probably showing *A Lincolnshire Meadow* (1883; Glasgow, A.G. & Mus.). He then virtually abandoned oil painting and the *plein-air* technique, working instead from memory and using line and watercolour. From 1887 to 1893 he was a member of the Royal Scottish Water Colour Society.

On his regular visits to Morocco and Spain, Crawhall evolved a distinctive gouache technique of fluid paint applied in calligraphic brushstrokes with accents of high colour, as in *The Bullfight* (1890–93) and *The Aviary, Clifton* (1888; both in Glasgow, Burrell Col.). After 1888 he painted on brown holland cloth, developing a more highly finished style with increasingly subtle colour modulation. He was much influenced by Melville, by Chinese art, and by Whistler, becoming a member of Whistler's International Society. From *c.* 1889 he produced a small series of pastels, including *Hen and Chickens* (1889; Glasgow, Burrell Col.), probably under the stimulus of Guthrie and the French art exhibitions of the Glasgow art dealer ALEX REID.

Crawhall's first public success was through Reid's exhibition of his work in 1894; he won great acclaim subsequently in London and in continental exhibitions. Sir William Burrell became his chief patron and owned more work by Crawhall than by any other artist.

BIBLIOGRAPHY
A. Bury: *Joseph Crawhall: The Man and the Artist* (London, 1958)
M. Hardie: *Watercolour Painting in Britain*, iii (London, 1968), pp. 204–7
D. Irwin and F. Irwin: *Scottish Painters at Home and Abroad, 1700–1900* (London, 1975), pp. 383–5
V. Hamilton: *Joseph Crawhall: One of the Glasgow Boys* (London, 1990)
For further bibliography see GLASGOW BOYS.

CLARE A. P. WILLSDON

Craxton, John (*b* London, 3 Oct 1922). English painter. Rejected from military service in 1941, he shared a studio in London with Lucian Freud, provided by their patron and friend Peter Watson, a figure of immense importance to Craxton's early development. Through Watson he met with other artists associated with NEO-ROMANTICISM and like many of his generation he fell heavily under the influence of Graham Sutherland and Samuel Palmer, as seen in *Poet in a Landscape* (1941; London, Christopher Hull Gal.). By 1943, in such works as *Welsh Estuary Foreshore* (Edinburgh, N.G. Mod. A.), a marked departure could be recognized. Its reference to the work of Pablo Picasso and Joan Miró placed him in a more European context. After World War II he travelled around the Mediterranean, finally settling in Crete in 1960, where he continued to develop his Romantic pastoral themes. The influence of William Blake gave way to that of Cubism, and he also became interested in Byzantine art. His paintings of Cretan life, such as *Vokos II* (1984; London, Christopher Hull Gal., see exh. cat., no. 3), still reveal a humanist if not pantheist philosophy.

BIBLIOGRAPHY
A Paradise Lost: The Neo-Romantic Imagination in Britain, 1935–55 (exh. cat., ed. D. Mellor; London, Barbican A.G., 1987)
M. Yorke: *The Spirit of the Place: Nine Neo-Romantic Artists and their Times* (London, 1988), pp. 300–26, *passim*

VIRGINIA BUTTON

Crayer, Gaspar [Caspar] **de** (*b* Antwerp, 18 Nov 1584; *d* Ghent, 27 Jan 1669). Flemish painter and draughtsman. He was active in the southern Netherlands at the time when demand was high for decorative schemes embodying the tenets of the Counter-Reformation: altarpieces and other religious paintings form the largest part of his considerable oeuvre. To a significant extent he owes his reputation to the fact that he was one of the earliest and most consistent followers of Rubens, whose formal idiom he disseminated beyond Antwerp's artistic circles.

1. LIFE AND CAREER. In his youth de Crayer moved from Antwerp to Brussels, probably attracted by the opportunities offered in the capital. According to Cornelis de Bie, he apprenticed himself there to Raphaël Coxcie (*c.* 1540–1616), court painter to Archdukes Albert and Isabella. De Crayer's earliest work included portraits of the Spanish kings and of the governors and Spanish officials who were stationed in the southern Netherlands, for example the Marqués de Leganès (portrait *c.* 1628–30; Vienna, Ksthist. Mus.), as well as members of the Brussels town council. In addition, from the beginning of his career de Crayer received commissions for altarpieces to decorate several churches and monasteries in and around Brussels. Not until 1635 did he establish a closer relationship with the court in Brussels, becoming court painter first to Cardinal-Infante Ferdinand and later to Archduke Leopold William.

De Crayer must have been a man of considerable stature in Brussels, as is apparent from the volume of his production and from his appointment as dean of the painters' guild from 1611 to 1616. He also held important positions on several of the town's governing bodies, for example as a member of the town council (1626–7). De Crayer also retained contact with his home town of Antwerp, then the most important centre of art in Flanders: apart from his family connections, he was a friend and business associate of the art dealer Matthijs Musson (*c.* 1600–78), who was also his patron. De Crayer must also have possessed some measure of business sense; he played a role in the sale of paintings from Rubens's estate to Philip IV of Spain. He must also have known Rubens personally, for his work, especially that of the 1620s, strongly reflects Rubens's influence and includes copies of paintings that could only have been seen in the master's studio.

In 1664 de Crayer moved to Ghent, where, despite his age, he received more important commissions for altarpieces. He had already established a reputation in Ghent: starting before 1620 he had regularly carried out commissions for various religious and secular institutions of the town. De Crayer's fame there is reflected, above all, by the large role that he was given in the execution of the monumental decorations for the Joyous Entry of the Cardinal-Infante in 1635. Nevertheless, altarpieces and other religious works form the largest part of de Crayer's oeuvre. He profited from the establishment of the Counter-Reformation in the southern Netherlands immediately after the consolidation of Spanish power in 1585, after which many of the churches in Brussels and elsewhere had to be redecorated in the spirit of the Council of Trent. Moreover, in Brussels, as in other southern Netherlandish towns, many newly founded religious institutions commissioned cycles of paintings in which Counter-Reformation beliefs were given forceful visual expression. Abbey churches became important patrons of de Crayer, not least towards the end of his career, especially after 1650. In particular the Benedictines (at Afflighem), the Norbertines (at Averbode and Vicoigne) and the Cistercians (at Nazareth, Zwijveke, Villers-la-Ville and Florival) commissioned important works from him.

Commissions also came to de Crayer from outside the southern Netherlands. In 1647 Jacob van Campen enlisted his assistance in decorating the Huis ten Bosch (see THE HAGUE, §IV, 3). De Crayer also carried out commissions for Spanish patrons, the largest of which was for at least 17 representations of saints, possibly intended for the Franciscan monastery at Burgos. Another important foreign patron was the German Catholic ruler Maximilian Willibald, Herzog von Wolfegg (1604–67), for whom, between 1658 and 1666, de Crayer executed several large altarpieces for the churches in the Palatinate, including those at Wolfegg, Unteressendorf, Heinrichsburg and Amberg.

2. STYLISTIC DEVELOPMENT. Some five stylistic periods can be distinguished in de Crayer's oeuvre. During the first period, until c. 1618, his work reflects prevailing 16th-century trends: in particular, compositions by Marten de Vos and Hendrik de Clerck were influential. De Crayers' work, like that of his models, is characterized by compositions in which the depiction of space is inaccurate and the foreground is often crowded with rather wooden figures, as in the *Martyrdom of St John the Baptist* (Brussels, Mus. A. Anc.).

From 1619, however, de Crayer's style took a different turn. His compositions became more harmonious and balanced, his figures were rendered in a more monumental fashion and with a greater sense of volume, and his palette was determined by contrasting areas of local colour. Important works of this period include the *Mocking of Job* (1619; Toulouse, Mus. Augustins), the *Judgement of Solomon* (1620–22; Ghent, Mus. S. Kst.), the *Martyrdom of St Catherine* (1622; see fig. 1) and *Diogenes and Alexander*

1. Gaspar de Crayer: *Martyrdom of St Catherine*, oil on canvas, 2.42×1.88 m, 1622 (Grenoble, Musée des Beaux-Arts)

the Great (Cologne, Wallraf-Richartz-Mus.). The changes in de Crayer's style are attributable to the profound influence on him of the work of Rubens, especially the latter's classicizing compositions of 1612–18. Rubens's oeuvre in Brussels remained of great significance to de Crayer throughout the remainder of his career. A further debt to Rubens is evident in de Crayer's portraits of this period.

After c. 1631 a new stylistic change became apparent in de Crayer's oeuvre, which, in contrast to his previous work, became much more dynamic in conception. The strongly modelled character of his figures, however, was retained. In addition to Rubens, van Dyck, who was in Antwerp for a brief period from 1627 to 1632, became an important model for him, especially the emotionally charged interpretations of religious themes. Paintings made by de Crayer in emulation of van Dyck include the *Raising of the Cross* (Rennes, Mus. B.-A. & Archéol.), the *Crucifixion* (Paris, Louvre) and the *Vision of St Simon Stock* (Ghent, Carmelite Church). In several painted portraits de Crayer also drew on van Dyck's *Iconography* series (c. 1632–44).

Between 1638 and 1648 de Crayer's compositions once again became calm and balanced, while his palette changed dramatically. In particular, the areas of bright local colour were replaced by softer hues and less abrupt areas of transition, which were more in harmony with the generally sentimental character of the images. During this period de Crayer was again inspired by Rubens, specifically by the Antwerp master's late works, which displayed similarities to his own. The many variants of the *Virgin and Child*

Adored by Saints (see fig. 2) were influenced by Rubens's *Mystic Marriage of St Catherine* (1628; Antwerp, Kon. Mus. S. Kst.) as well as his *St Ildefonsus* triptych (1630–32; Vienna, Ksthist. Mus.). During this period de Crayer also showed a strong interest in the great 16th-century Venetian painters Titian and Veronese, whose works he knew through the prints of Agostino Carracci. It is probable that Rubens's late work, which owed much to the Venetian formal idiom, prompted de Crayer to emulate these sources.

After *c.* 1649 de Crayer's works exhibit an even stronger emotional character. The action is carried by a relatively large number of figures deployed at various planes within the picture space, their gestures strongly emphasized. Because certain dramatic formulae are repeated, these late works make an unmistakably stereotypic impression, many of the compositions constituting replicas or variants with only slight alterations, in which it is often difficult to distinguish de Crayer's hand from those of his assistants. The stately monumentality of his early work was completely replaced by a hollow theatricality. The rich, warm palette of his early years gave way to increasingly dull and washed-out tonalities.

3. WORKING METHODS AND TECHNIQUE. De Crayer ran a prominent studio in Brussels, and between 1610 and 1661 he taught a large number of pupils. By 1634–5 he had, in his own words, set 'many boys' to work. In Ghent he collaborated with Jan van Cleef (1646–1716), who continued to work in a similar style after de Crayer's death. In preparation for his many large compositions de Crayer made preliminary pen-and-ink drawings, some of which are squared for transfer, and oil sketches. That the latter are often in colour is undoubtedly due to Rubens's influence. De Crayer also continued to practise the technique of making oil sketches in grisaille, which was more popular in Flanders than anywhere else.

BIBLIOGRAPHY

C. de Bie: *Het gulden cabinet* (1661), pp. 244–5

H. Vlieghe: *Gaspar de Crayer: Sa vie et ses oeuvres*, 2 vols (Brussels, 1972)

——: 'Gaspar de Crayer: Addenda et corrigenda', *Gent. Bijdr. Kstgesch.*, xxiv (1979–80), pp. 159–207

R. De Man: 'Documenten over het mecenaat van R. Braye (ca. 1550–1632) te Kortrijk en de schilderijen van G. de Crayer en A. van Dyck', *Jb.: Kon. Mus. S. Kst.* (1980), pp. 233–59

H. Vlieghe: 'Drawings by Gaspar de Crayer from the Ghent Album', *Master Drgs*, xxvi (1988), pp. 119–32

J. S. Held: 'More on Gaspar de Crayer', *Master Drgs*, xxvii (1989), pp. 53–63

E. Mai: 'Gaspar de Crayer: *Alexander und Diogenes*, ein Bild macht Politik', *Köln. Mus.-Bull.*, ii (1991), pp. 25–40

HANS VLIEGHE

2. Gaspar de Crayer: *Virgin and Child Adored by Saints*, oil sketch on canvas, 740×530 mm, 1646 (Munich, Alte Pinakothek: on deposit in Munich, St Kajetan)

Crayon. Except for consistent reference to a stick of dry colour, the term 'crayon' is ambiguous. Historically it has denoted various fabricated, direct-line drawing instruments, made of ground pigment and binder, that are cut or moulded into cylindrical rods or straight-sided sticks about 60–70 mm in length and 10 mm in thickness. Included in this definition are PASTEL, red and black CHALK and *crayons de couleur* (wood-encased crayons), also oil, CHARCOAL, conté, lithograph and wax crayons. 'Crayon' has become a generic term for colour sticks made with oily, fatty or waxy binding media, such as lithograph, conté or children's wax crayons.

1. TYPES AND PROPERTIES. The type and percentage of the binder in a crayon determines and modifies its physical and optical properties, such as texture, tenacity, light reflection and colour saturation (see fig.). A high percentage of an oleo-resinous medium, such as wax, oil, fat or soap, will produce a greasy or dense stroke, whereas a small amount of a gum or clay binder produces dry, friable crayons, such as pastel, fabricated chalk and charcoal, because the particles lack adhesion.

Coloured oleo-resinous crayons were never in widespread use and are rarely mentioned in treatises on artists' materials. The earliest reference to wax crayon is in Leonardo da Vinci's notebooks (*c.* 1492–1515): 'To make points for colouring dry. Temper with a little wax and it will not come off...; you will thus make good crayons...' (J. P. Richter, ed: *The Literary Works of Leonardo da Vinci*, i (London, 1888, rev. 1970), pp. 301, 359). In the 16th and 17th centuries references exist only to modifying pastel to increase its hardness and tenacity by varying the binder (Gregorius recommends fish glue, fig juice and gum arabic, and Norgate refers to milk, beer, wort and gum). Hard pastel was soaked in olive or linseed oil to improve its

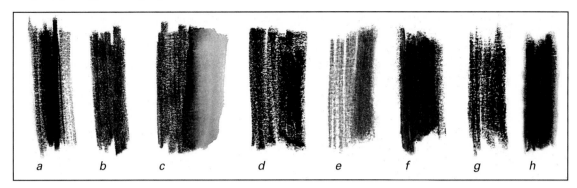

Crayon types: (a) conté crayon; (b) wax crayon; (c) water-soluble wax crayon; (d) oiled pastel; (e) compressed charcoal; (f) oiled compressed charcoal; (g) lithographic crayon; (h) pastel

working and visual properties. Browne described this process in 1675 in *Ars pictoria*: '[When dry] take a feather and some sallet Oyl and oyl them lightly over, let dry till the oyl be soaked well into them which will make them work free and easie'. Salmon in 1685 claimed that this 'will not rub off, nor any part of it stir. [These crayons] are extremely neat, brisk, lively and (like Oyl-painting) very strong'. He also described an early method for producing fatty crayons by preparing a paste of finely ground chalk or pigment tempered with oil. A more typical process was to soak charcoal in a fatty binder (Volpato specified common oil) to increase its smudge resistance, enhance its tone and yield broader, softer lines; Guercino, Tintoretto, Peter Paul Rubens and Hendrick Goltzius used such a crayon. Van Hoogstraten and Goree noted that coal soaked in linseed oil is suitable for life-size nudes: this medium was used by Nicolaes Berchem and Hermann Saftleven.

In 1764 Dossie, in *The Handmaid to the Arts*, referred disparagingly to pastel with a beeswax binder: '[It will] render the cartoon secure from flaking off and [will] bear rubbing with a brush—but such crayons cannot make delicate touches and thus can be employed only for coarse purposes'. In the late 18th century other tenacious crayons were produced. In 1797 Hochheimer gave recipes for crayons made with wax, tallow and spermaceti. Developing concurrently (1796–1800) were Alois Senefelder's experiments with lampblack, tallow, soap and various waxes cast into hard, or soft and greasy sticks. Intended for lithographic stone, their rich colour and lustrous texture encouraged such artists as George Bellows and Käthe Kollwitz to use them for drawing on paper.

The early wood-encased conté, patented by the French engineer Nicolas-Jacques Conté in 1795 as a substitute for embargoed Burrowdale GRAPHITE, was made from compressed and fired graphite and clay. In 1840 the fluidity of its stroke was enhanced by impregnation with spermaceti. Fatty oils are now also used for this purpose. Conté crayons, widely employed in the 19th century, most notably by Georges Seurat, while not powdery like natural chalk blend readily to produce delicate tonal gradations.

The scarcity of graphite and the popularity of conté stimulated further invention. In 1818 a method was published in *Annales de chimie et physique* for controlling hardness by immersing charcoal in mixtures of wax and resins, tallow or butter. In the 1840s the first compressed charcoal, available as a greasy (*trempê*) or dry stick, was marketed, and it was used extensively by academicians. In 1835 J. S. Staedtler developed a wood-encased coloured crayon, now called PENCIL, with a wax-impregnated 'lead'. The hardness of these crayons causes them to have a limited valve range because the pigments are tightly bound with wax and other additives. This compresses the pigments, optically reducing the amount of light the colours reflect, and limiting the amount of powder obtained from the stick as it is drawn across a drawing surface. These crayons were used by late 19th-century artists, including Henri de Toulouse-Lautrec and Jacques Villon. Modern coloured pencils are mixtures of waxes, kaolin and other clays, to which dyes or pigments have been added. In the late 19th century the Realist painter Jean-François Raffaëlli developed a modified pastel: a soft crayon containing cocoa butter, tallow, Japan wax and non-drying oils. They have been referred to as Raffaëlli colours, oil pastels and oil crayons. They were claimed to have the durability and lustre of oil painting, but no work in this medium is extant, presumably because the colours darkened. Oil crayons became popular from the 1940s despite the tendency of the binders to seep into the paper.

In 1903 extruded, paper-wrapped wax crayons were developed, composed of high percentages of paraffin and stearic acid and low percentages of pigment and synthetic lakes. They require bearing down to produce strong colour, the palette is limited and mixing restricted, hence they are more frequently associated with the work of children than of professional artists, though they were used by Henry Moore (*see* DRAWING, colour pl. II, fig. 2), Pablo Picasso, Roberto Matta and Arshile Gorky. Some wax, wood-encased crayons are water-soluble and thus may be used dry or in washes, as in the work of Jackson Pollock and Frank Lloyd Wright.

2. CONSERVATION. There is no standard technique for cleaning crayon drawings. The type of crayon must be tested to determine the solubility and friability of the medium and pigment, and the condition of the support must also be examined. Even familiar materials must be tested, since drawings executed in the same type of crayon will age at different rates depending on environmental factors, such as light and humidity, and on the components

of the support and mount. Surface cleaning is usually inadvisable because of the tendency of these media to smudge. As with any work on paper, the feasibility of either local or general cleaning will depend on finding a suitable method and the correct aqueous solution or organic solvent for the type of discoloration. (*See also* PAPER, §VI.)

The preservation of crayon drawings rests equally on safeguarding the support and the medium. Many wax crayons and coloured pencils are made with dyes and pigments of questionable lightfastness, hence limited exhibition time (two to three months) and light intensity (50 lux maximum) is necessary. Framing should be under ultraviolet-filtering acrylic sheeting separated from the surface of the art work by at least 3.18 mm. Conté crayons and oiled charcoal are light stable, but their slightly powdery nature requires framing with glass. Acid-free mounting materials are essential for storage and framing.

BIBLIOGRAPHY

P. Gregorius: *Syntaxeon artis mirabilis* (Lyon, 1574) [see J. Meder: *Die Handzeichnung* (Vienna, 1919); Eng. trans. as *The Mastery of Drawing*, abridged, by W. Ames (New York, 1978), p. 100]
E. Norgate: *Miniatura, or the Art of Limning* (London, 1648–50), p. 75
A. Browne: *Ars pictoria* (London, 1675), p. 30
S. van Hoogstraten: *Inleyding tot de hooge schoole der schilderkonst, anders de zichtbaere werelt* [Introduction to the academy of painting, or the visible world] (Rotterdam, 1678/*R* Soest, 1969); Ger. trans. by E. von Gosen in *Einführung in die hohe Schule der Malerei* (Ann Arbor, 1980), p. 32
W. Salmon: *Polygraphice* (London, 1685), p. 6
W. Goree: *Inleyding tot de al-ghemeene teyckenkonst* [Introduction to the general art of drawing] (Middelburg, 1697), p. 94
G. B. Volpato: *Modo da tener nel dipinger* (Bassano, *c.* 1700); Eng. trans. by Mrs Merrifield as *Original Treatises on the Arts of Painting*, ii (London, 1849), p. 752
R. Dossie: *The Handmaid to the Arts* (London, 1758, 2/1764), p. 205
C. F. A. Hochheimer: *Chemische Farben-lehre* (Leipzig, 1797), p. 234
An. Chim. & Phys., 2nd ser., ix (1818), pp. 334–5
K. Robert: *Charcoal Drawing* (Cincinnati, 1880)
M. Doerner: *Materials of the Artist* (New York, 1934)
E. Voice: 'The History of the Manufacture of Pencils', *Newcomen Soc. Trans.*, xxvii (1949–51), pp. 131–41
J. Watrous: *The Craft of Old Master Drawings* (Madison, 1957)
C. Hayes: *The Complete Guide to Painting and Drawing Techniques and Materials* (New York, 1976)
P. Schatborn: *Dutch Figure Drawings from the 17th Century* (The Hague, 1981)

MARJORIE SHELLEY

Crayon manner. Type of copperplate-engraving process that reproduces a drawing in chalk or pencil in facsimile. It was invented in the 18th century, but it was superseded by the stipple technique (*see* STIPPLE (i), §1).

1. Materials and techniques. 2. History.

1. MATERIALS AND TECHNIQUES. The crayon manner aims to imitate drawing as the collection of a multitude of dots corresponding to marks left by a pencil on the grain of paper rather than as an assemblage of lines. It can be executed directly on to the bare copper but is more often prepared by etching. The engraver counterproofs the drawing that he is using as a model (or a copy if he has made one) on to the ground; he then follows the marks of the main contour lines using single or multiple-point punches, or an instrument made of various sized needles fastened together. Rather than tracing a line, dots are hammered out close together right along the line,

which gives the contours the grainy appearance of a drawing. The dark masses of shadow and the half-tones are then distributed by using mattoirs (for illustration of engraving tools *see* ENGRAVING, fig. 1); the large number of points of various sizes irregularly distributed on the end of the mattoir makes it possible to engrave dots that are irregular in shape and depth. The work can be speeded up by using roulettes, mattoirs with wheels embellished with the same type of points as the mattoir. The engraver uses these tools to follow all the pencil lines that make up the drawing. Once the plate has been bitten by the acid, work on the bare copper is completed with the help of these same instruments. A hammer may also be used to knock the needles and punches into the plate. Some engravers execute the whole engraving in this way.

Whatever the method, the engraver keeps to the same basic rules: first he must lay down the main lines and hatching of the drawing that serves as the model and then distribute dots across the rest of the engraving as irregularly as possible. In the dark parts the different dots may tumble over each other; in the half-tones they are not so deep, and the untouched areas that are not engraved are usually limited. The engraved plate is then printed by a copperplate press. Use of a dark grey ink makes it possible to imitate a black pencil drawing, while ochre or red give the appearance of a sanguine drawing. The presence of numerous shallow dots makes the plate relatively fragile, and the number of prints pulled has to be limited. In the late 20th century one might pull 50 proofs, but 18th-century engravers seem to have continued using their plates after pulling 200 prints.

Crayon manner was also used for multiple-plate printing. Its most immediate application was the reproduction of drawings in several colours (sanguine, black, and white highlights). Using the techniques described above, the line of each colour was engraved on each plate; having been coated with an ink corresponding to the desired colour, each plate was then pulled in succession. Like mezzotint or aquatint, crayon manner makes colour printing possible with the use of several juxtaposed plates; this is referred to as pastel manner. Printing is done by following guiding marks. The number of plates can vary from three to eight, according to the subject engraved and the quality of gradation desired by the artist. Using principles of prismatic analysis of primary colours based on the theories of Sir Isaac Newton, the engraver invariably uses four plates, successively coated in black, yellow, blue and red ink. However, a more delicate approach allows the engraver to juxtapose rather than blend colours, in the manner of a pastellist; the number of plates is then greater, and, by inking with a dauber, each one can contain several colours. Although using the same mattoirs and roulettes as for the crayon manner, the results are different, especially on the first plates to be printed, being engraved in a looser manner. The sheet has to be passed under the press several times, and the dots appear smudged, which gives the hatchings the blurred effect of pastel drawings. Pastel-manner engraving allows for only a small number of good proofs: as soon as the least deeply engraved plate is worn, the colour of the prints is set at variance.

The crayon-manner technique is clearly faster than traditional copperplate engraving, the roulettes and mattoirs allowing for swifter work. The same effects can, however, be produced more quickly by soft-ground etching and by lithography; the latter has made crayon manner virtually disappear. The investigations it prompted originated an increasing use of stipple engraving and other methods of engraving with tools (e.g. GOUACHE MANNER).

2. HISTORY. Although the technical invention of crayon manner dates from the 18th century, as early as the 16th century certain engravers, in particular Domenico Campagnola and Giulio Campagnola, favoured the use of dots, as opposed to strokes, and their work resembles crayon-manner engraving. In the 17th century some engravers, including Johannes Lutma (ii), used several goldsmiths' tools, such as punches and mattoirs with wheels, in their work, but it is hard to speak of their engravings as facsimiles of pencil drawings, if only because of the excessive regularity of the dots. In the 18th century the interest shown in drawings as works of art worth collecting led certain engravers to seek means of reproducing them with the greatest possible fidelity. Drawings by Watteau were the object of the first attempts. Around 1727 Benoît Audran II (1698–1772) engraved a woman sitting on the ground (*Figures de différents caractères*, ii, no. 154) by working in very fine parallel strokes, completed with short crosshatchings. This mixture of strokes made it possible to imitate a pencil stroke broken down into a multitude of lines rather than dots. In London, Arthur Pond made similar attempts between 1736 and 1742, notably in engraving *Dr Misabin* (1739; Dacier and Vuaflait, i, fig. 81) after Watteau. He perfected Audran's system by using irregularly shaped strokes completed with dots and therefore better suited to imitating pencil strokes.

The invention of this new manner of engraving must, however, be ascribed to Jean-Charles François. His first efforts resulted in his book *Principes de dessein faciles et dans le goût du crayon* (Lyon, 1748). At this time his technique was rudimentary, with his models engraved in fine parallel strokes by a burin; the print was then counterproofed, so that the strokes that merged into each other gave the impression of a relatively thick and fluid line. Despite the various improvements that François made to this technique until the 1750s, it was insufficient. He owed to Gilles Demarteau the idea of using goldsmiths' chasing-tools and marking-wheels. Demarteau, a former goldsmith's apprentice, had used them in 1736 to shade the lines in a series of *Trophies* (e.g. Hérold, no. 12). François, by then a partner of Demarteau, conceived of using such tools to engrave the entire plate. He had the mechanic Alexis Magny (1711–95) make him tools that were better adapted to his needs and that allowed him to engrave in irregular dots; in 1757 he engraved his first three plates in crayon manner, directly on to the copper. To accelerate the work, he etched three other plates using different-size needles bound together. These six plates, published in the book *L'Amour du dessein ou cours du dessein dans le goût du crayon* (Paris, 1757), were submitted to Abel-François Poisson de Vandières, Marquis de Marigny, and to the Académie Royale de Peinture et de Sculpture.

François's invention was swiftly contested. Magny, who had made François's instruments, perfected and then exploited them. He made an articulated machine, in which pressure on the mattoir was obtained with a lever worked by a foot pedal. The engraver had only to move his tools with his hand, but the cutting itself required no effort. Magny became a partner of Jean-Baptiste Delafosse (1721–1806) in order to exploit his machine, and his first engraving, a *Head of an Old Man* after Boucher (Hérold, no. 19), appeared in November 1757. Magny and Delafosse separated after their second engraving had appeared, and it was not until after legal proceedings lasting until 1761 that Magny, by then in partnership with another engraver, Pierre Gonord, began once more to publish engravings in the crayon manner. He then tried unsuccessfully to challenge the anteriority of François's invention. By refining his tools, Magny published the first imitation of stump drawing: a *Women's Academy* after Cochin (1762).

François was also rivalled by Demarteau. The two engravers separated in 1757, and in 1759 Demarteau brought to his studio Louis-Marin Bonnet, who had been a student of François and was acquainted with his processes. In 1759 Bonnet engraved his first plate for Demarteau, and the latter executed the first of c. 300 plates after Boucher (see fig.), which would constitute the major part of his work. Despite not inventing the crayon manner,

Crayon-manner engraving by Gilles Demarteau: *Head of a Woman*, after Boucher, c. 1759 (Paris, Bibliothèque Nationale)

Demarteau was its main exponent in France. A better draughtsman and engraver than François, he was also capable of recognizing public taste.

The success of crayon-manner engraving soon led to attempts to improve it. In 1760 François wanted to execute engravings with two pencils, black and white, on coloured paper, but neither he nor Joseph Varin (1740–1800), who published this type of engraving in 1761, succeeded in finding a white ink that did not turn yellow. Bonnet did succeed and in 1764 published a two-colour engraving. He was, moreover, the first to make a multiple-plate print, pinning the plates in place rather than fitting the second into the plate mark made on the paper by the first plate. In April 1767 Demarteau submitted his first two-colour plates (sanguine and black) to the Académie and received its approval, which encouraged Bonnet to publish a three-colour head the same year. After several attempts at five-plate engravings (black, blue, red, yellow and white), in July 1769 Bonnet published a pastel-manner engraving using eight plates, a *Head of a Woman* after Boucher. In the 1770s his investigations led him to the GOUACHE MANNER. François also continued to search for new techniques. A mediocre engraver, he perfected a method using no metal tools, which he kept secret; it was probably soft-varnish engraving. He failed in his attempts to interest the Académie and the Marquis de Marigny in this invention, but his secret was discovered in the Netherlands by Cornelis Ploos van Amstel (1726–95) and in England by Benjamin Green (c. 1736–1800).

Crayon-manner engraving and its various offshoots were successful mainly in France. It was above all adapted to drawings in wax crayon (sanguine and stone black) used by 18th-century French artists whose work was in great demand. From 1757 the engraver Charles-Nicolas Cochin (ii) had noted in relation to a request from François that most of the early drawings in the Cabinet du Roi could not be used as models. The field for this type of engraving was therefore limited outside France and countries where 18th-century French drawing was appreciated. Moreover, crayon-manner engraving was a fairly quick process: Demarteau engraved nearly 600 plates in less than 20 years, and the work published by Bonnet is more or less comparable. There were therefore enough Parisian artists to satisfy demand in France and Europe, and the development of engraving in the crayon manner in the provinces and overseas remained limited. In England, however, the new technique had important consequences. It was introduced by William Wynne Ryland, who had spent time in Paris in Jacques-Philippe Lebas's studio, where he stayed until 1765, learning the new techniques and engraving several plates. On his return to London he introduced crayon-manner engraving, also practised by Francesco Bartolozzi. However, their association with Angelica Kauffman led to a transformation of the technique into stipple. Although the crayon manner's success was limited to the period between 1757 and the French Revolution (1789–95), it paved the way for most of the technical investigations at the end of the 18th century.

BIBLIOGRAPHY
A. Bosse: *De la manière de graver à l'eau-forte et au burin*, ed. C. N. Cochin (Paris, 1645, 2/1758 [1769])
F. Courboin: *L'Estampe française: Graveurs et marchands* (Brussels and Paris, 1914)
E. Dacier and A. Vuaflart: *Jean de Jullienne et les graveurs de Watteau au XVIIIe siècle*, 4 vols (Paris, 1921–9)
J. Hérold: *Gravure en manière de crayon: Jean-Charles François, catalogue de l'oeuvre gravé* (Paris, 1931)
——: *Louis-Marin Bonnet (1756–1793): Catalogue de l'oeuvre gravé* (Paris, 1935)
R. T. Godfrey: *Printmaking in Britain* (Oxford, 1978)
V. Carlson and others: *Regency to Empire: French Printmaking, 1715–1814* (Baltimore, 1984)

CHRISTIAN MICHEL

Creangă, Horia (*b* Bucharest, 1 Aug 1893; *d* Vienna, 1 Aug 1943). Romanian architect. He studied (1913–16) at the Academy of Architecture, Bucharest, continuing after World War I at the Ecole des Beaux-Arts, Paris, and between 1919 and 1924 in the studio of Gustave Umbdenstock and obtaining a diploma. In 1925 he was hired by Umbdenstock and worked in the architectural bureau of the Northern Railways Company on the Tergnier Aisne Railroad Station project. Creangă was a follower of the Modernist architectural ideas formulated principally by Le Corbusier, which he promoted in his own works after returning to Romania in 1926, for example in the Asigurarea Românească (ARO) block (1929–33; now Patria), Bucharest. Many large commissions came from the functional and aesthetic values of the International Style, which he propagated, and his widely discussed constructive and formal solutions conferred a distinctive profile on Bucharest's architecture before World War II. He also influenced his contemporaries Marcel Iancu and G. M. Cantacuzino, as well as younger architects. In response to housing needs Creangă developed blocks of flats with additional functions: the ARO block, for example, includes a 1200-seat cinema, and the block (1935–7) at Boulevard N. Bălcescu 35, Bucharest, has shops on the ground floor. Exterior structures are of reinforced concrete, glass and metal, with interiors finished with high-quality stone and marble. He adopted almost exclusively a rectilinear aesthetic, giving great importance to the balance of large, simple volumes particularly with regard to the façades. The latter are structured in horizontal bands marked by the alternation of window openings and continuous, smooth, undecorated wall surfaces. He also offered Modernist solutions in other building types, for example in the Hotel ARO (1938–9; now Hotel Carpaţi), Braşov, with Haralamb Georgescu (1908–77), and the Malaxa locomotive works (1933; now FAUR) and the Malaxa pipeworks (1936–8; now Republica), both in Bucharest.

BIBLIOGRAPHY
Către o arhitectură a Bucureştilor: Creangă Horia, Iancu Marcel, Doicescu Octav [Towards an architecture of Bucharest: Horia Creangă, Marcel Iancu, Octav Diocescu] (Bucharest, c. 1934)
R. Patrulius: *Horia Creangă: Omul şi opera* [Horia Creangă: the man and his work] (Bucharest, 1980)
Horia Creangă: 100 ani de la naştere [Horia Creangă: centennial exhibition] (exh. cat., Bucharest, Gal. A. Dalles, 1993)

CODRUŢA CRUCEANU

Crease, Josephine (*b* New Westminster, BC, 7 Aug 1864; *d* Victoria, BC, 24 Dec 1947). Canadian painter and administrator. From 1889 to 1891 she attended art classes at King's College, London. Crease exhibited regularly in

British Columbia and was noted for her watercolour landscapes and domestic interiors. She also taught occasionally and executed commercial commissions. Crease is important for her lifetime promotion of the arts in Victoria. She was a founder-member of the (Vancouver) Island Arts and Crafts Society in 1909 (*see* VICTORIA), the leading art organization in British Columbia, and she served on the Society's executive for 35 years.

BIBLIOGRAPHY

C. Johnson-Dean: 'Josephine Crease and the Arts in Victoria' (MA thesis, U. Victoria, BC, 1981)

——: *The Crease Family Archives* (Victoria, BC, 1982)

KATHRYN BRIDGE

Creatura di Baciccia, il. *See* BIANCHI, PIETRO (i).

Creccolini [Crecolini; Cricolini; Grecolini], **Giovanni Antonio** (*b* Rome, 16 Jan 1675; *d* Rome, 24 May 1725). Italian painter. According to contemporary and later sources, he was a pupil of the Roman painter Giovanni Battista Lenardi (1656–1704), of Lazzaro Baldi and, following Lenardi's death, of Benedetto Luti. As well as reflecting the dominant classicism of the Late Baroque exemplified by Carlo Maratti, his style was particularly strongly influenced by the early teachings of Lenardi, to whom he owed the rhetorical gestural quality of some of his paintings. His subsequent period as a pupil of Luti succeeded only partly in making his work more 'pleasing' by influencing his portrayal of faces and lightening the tones of his paintings. By 1694 he was already taking part in the competitions announced by the Accademia di S Luca (now the Accademia Nazionale di S Luca), the archives of which contain some of his drawings. He was active mainly in Rome: among his most important works are the two canvases on the side walls of the baptismal chapel in S Lorenzo in Lucina and the decoration of the third right-hand chapel in S Francesco di Paola. He obtained his most prestigious commission in 1716, when he participated in the decoration of the nave of the basilica of S Clemente, in which he was responsible for the fresco depicting the *Martyrdom of St Clement*. His *Miracle of St Vincent Ferrer* (Rome, S Rocco) dates from 1720, while documents mention him as working on the Palazzo Reale in Turin from 1721 to 1723. He also painted the ceiling of the chapel of the Sacrament in Assisi Cathedral and drew numerous portraits of artists for Nicola Pio.

BIBLIOGRAPHY

N. Pio: *Vite* (1724); ed. C. Enggass and R. Enggass (1977)

L. Pascoli: *Vite* (1730–36)

A. M. Clark: 'The Portraits of Artists Drawn for Nicola Pio', *Master Drgs*, v/1 (1967), pp. 3–23 [esp. pp. 18–19]

J. Gilmartin: 'The Paintings Commissioned by Pope Clement XI for the Basilica of San Clemente in Roma', *Burl. Mag.*, cxvi (1974), pp. 305–10

V. Casale: 'Diaspore e ricomposizioni: Gherardi, Cerruti, Grecolini, Garzi, Masucci ai Santi Venanzio ed Ansuino in Roma', *Scritti di storia dell'arte in onore di Federico Zeri*, ed. M. Natale, ii (Milan, 1984), pp. 736–55 [esp. pp. 744–7]

F. Arisi: *Gian Paolo Panini e i fasti della Roma del '700* (Rome, 1986)

GERARDO CASALE

Credi, Lorenzo di. *See* LORENZO DI CREDI.

Creeft, José de (*b* Guadalajara, Spain, 27 Nov 1884; *d* New York, 11 Sept 1982). American sculptor, painter and draughtsman of Spanish birth. After being apprenticed to a religious figure-carver and then in a foundry, in 1900 he moved to Madrid, where he became a student of Augustín Querol y Subirats. He also studied with Ignacio Zuloaga before acquiring his own studio in Madrid in 1902. In 1903 he had his first one-man show at the Círculo de Bellas Artes in Madrid and in 1905 moved to Paris. Shortly afterwards he settled in the Bateau-Lavoir in Paris, where Picasso, Braque and Gris lived. On the advice of Auguste Rodin he studied sculpture at the Académie Julian from 1905 to 1906. He learnt the techniques of copying models into stone at the Maison Gréber workshop in Paris from 1911 to 1914 but in 1915 turned to direct carving in stone. This was to be his main technique thereafter, leading to such works as *Fetish* (*c.* 1916; Washington, DC, Hirshhorn), which showed the influence of non-Western sculpture. Some of his early sculptures moulded the female figure into near abstract forms, as in *Orchid* (1919; New York, Lorrie Goulet priv. col., see Campos, pl. 217).

During the 1920s de Creeft made a number of otherwise rare experiments using avant-garde techniques, producing several sculptures using junk metal elements, for example *Picador* (1925; Barcelona, Fund. Miró). Representing a horse and rider, this is 2.4 m high and made largely from stove pipes. He also made several abstract sculptures, such as *Abstract* (1928; Leesburg, VA, Mr and Mrs Edward Marks priv. col., see Campos, pl. 249), but found this aesthetic uncongenial. In 1929 he settled in New York, becoming an American citizen in 1940. After the move he returned to carved works of the female figure. These were invariably squat and often used in a symbolic role, as in *The Cloud* (1939; New York, Whitney) or *Metamorphosis* (1958; Washington, DC, Hirshhorn). He also used beaten metal as in *Himalaya* (beaten lead, 1942; New York, Whitney) and produced portraits, such as *Rachmaninoff* (1943; Philadelphia, PA Acad. F.A.). From 1932 to 1948 de Creeft taught at the New School for Social Research, New York. In 1955 he was commissioned to design the bronze tableau *Alice in Wonderland* (unveiled 1959), for Central Park in New York. He continued working well into later life, producing such works as *Maternity* (silver, 1973; New York, Lorrie Goulet priv. col., see 1983 exh. cat., p. 55).

BIBLIOGRAPHY

J. Campos: *The Sculpture of José de Creeft* (New York, 1973)

L'aventura humana de José de Creeft (exh. cat. by C. Fontsere, Barcelona, Fund. Miró, 1980)

José de Creeft: Sculpture and Drawings (exh. cat. by A. D. Breeskin and V. M. Mecklenburg, Washington, DC, N. Mus. Amer. A., 1983)

KENNETH W. PRESCOTT

Cregan, Martin (*b* Co. Meath, Ireland, 1788; *d* Dublin, 10 Dec 1870). Irish painter. Together with his older contemporary, William Cuming, Martin Cregan was the best Irish portrait painter of the generation following Hugh Douglas Hamilton. After two years of training in London under his fellow countryman, Martin Archer Shee, and some ten years of exhibiting at the Royal Academy and the British Institution, Cregan returned to Dublin in 1822. He soon became active in the newly formed Royal Hibernian Academy, exhibiting about 300 paintings between 1826 and 1859. He was President of the Academy from 1832 to 1857. Two years after his retirement from the presidency, Cregan's involvement with the Royal

Hibernian Academy was ended when he and Michael Angelo Hayes urged for a reform of the institution; the motion was defeated and a bitter schism followed.

Strickland's *Dictionary of Irish Artists* (1913) lists ten pages of portraits and other paintings that indicate the extent of Cregan's practice and the patrons he worked for. As Portrait Painter to the Lord Lieutenant for Ireland, he painted the obligatory formal portraits for Dublin Castle, such as *Hugh Percy, 3rd Duke of Northumberland* (1830; *in situ*). While lacking the bravura of those by Thomas Lawrence or William Cuming, Cregan's small-scale portraits and head and shoulder portraits convey a solidity of presence which, although tinged by a sobriety of expression, are as effective as the portraits of comparable scale produced by such English contemporaries as Thomas Phillips and John Jackson. This aspect of his work is particularly apparent in his portrait of the architect Joseph Williamson (1825; Dublin, N.G.).

BIBLIOGRAPHY

Strickland

A. Crookshank and the Knight of Glin: *The Painters of Ireland, c. 1660–1920* (London, 1979), pp. 173–4
Illustrated Summary Catalogue of Paintings, N.G. cat. (Dublin, 1981), p. 199

FINTAN CULLEN

Cremer. German family of architects. Markus Cremer (*b* Poppelsdorf, 1753; *d* Aachen, 1819) was architect to the city of Cologne until the French annexed the city in 1799. None of his work is now extant. His eldest son, Johann Peter Cremer (*b* Cologne, 1785; *d* 1863), studied in Paris (1804–6), where he attended the lectures of Jean-Nicolas-Louis Durand and joined the studio of François-Joseph Bélanger, in whose house he lived. He was a building inspector in Düsseldorf (1806–17) but was promoted to Landbauinspektor in Aachen following the Prussian annexation of the Rhineland, remaining there until his retirement as municipal architect in 1861. His designs were subject to interference from the Oberbaudeputation in Berlin, so much so that his Elisenbrunnen (1822–7) in Aachen has subsequently been attributed to Karl Friedrich Schinkel. Cremer considered the theatre (1822–4) at Aachen his most important work. Modelled on a Greek temple with an Ionic portico, its clarity of design is typical of the work of a pupil of Durand. Other works included government offices (1827–31) on the Theaterplatz, composed of thirteen bays with a five-bay pediment, built with little interference from Berlin. Indeed, Schinkel praised both it and Cremer's Rathaus (1827–42) at Elberfeld, which was of a similar size but in a Rundbogenstil manner. Cremer's Hauptzollamt (1846–8), however, was so redesigned by Berlin that probably only the severe grid of its plan is his own work. In addition to these five large buildings, Cremer built a considerable number of houses and at least 15 churches. His Protestant and early Romantic Catholic churches show that when he was able to work unhindered, he made use of all he had learnt in Paris. The church (1822–6) at Geilenkirchen, a cruciform building with barrel vaults, and the handsome church of St Remacle (1834–8) at Verviers, Belgium, a richly decorated basilica of great spatial effect, belong to this period. Later he had to submit to pressure from the Cologne clergy to use Gothic forms, but his designs did not conform to the Cologne Gothic Revival style, instead having their own character and betraying their classical origins. His best church of this period is at Rödingen (1856–8). Cremer was also in charge of the restoration (1842–9) of Aachen Cathedral, where in 1843 he replaced the columns in the octagon that had been stolen in 1794 by the French and designed replacements for those that were missing.

Markus Cremer's younger son, Johann Baptist Cremer (*b* Cologne, 1794; *d* 1870), became municipal architect (1819) at Linnich. He was responsible for five rural counties devastated in the Napoleonic Wars (1803–15), so most of his work consisted of the reconstruction and renovation of buildings, particularly of schools. Although his talents as an architect were appreciated by his superiors, he lacked the will to assert himself, and he resigned in 1836 to become the tax collector in Cornelimünster. Few of his churches survive, although those at Dremmen, a flat-roofed basilica with piers and a richly articulated clerestory, and at Kirchhoven have been preserved in their original state.

Johann Peter Cremer's elder son, Friedrich Albert Cremer (*b* Aachen, 1824; *d* 1891), studied at the Bauakademie, Berlin, and worked under his father at Aachen Cathedral. He was appointed building inspector (1851) for the Ministerial-Baukommission, Berlin, later rising to councillor and planning officer (1868). His work, variously Neo-classical and Renaissance in style, includes the Anatomiegebäude (1863–5) and the debtors' prison (1863–4) in Berlin and the Inhalationshalle (*c.* 1871) of the Militärkurhaus in Wiesbaden. Johann Peter Cremer's younger son, Ferdinand Robert Cremer (*b* Aachen, 1826; *d* 1882), followed the prescribed training for an architect in the Prussian civil service. In 1854 he was appointed regional architect with responsibility also for waterworks and railways. While based at Bad Oynhausen (1855–6) he built his first independent work, the Dampfbadehaus. In 1856 he moved to Cologne, where his design for his only church, a basilica at Bliesheim in a severe Romanesque style, shows the influence of his superior, the Cologne Cathedral architect Ernst Friedrich Zwirner. In 1862 he succeeded his father as municipal architect in Aachen and also as cathedral architect, in which capacity he extended the Kreuzkapelle. His most important works at Aachen were the new prison (1864–72), a Gothic structure of unrendered brick, and the Technische Hochschule (1865–8). Shortly afterwards he was transferred to Koblenz, where his main building was the impressive Dikasterial-Gebäude (1876–8; destr. 1944) in the German Renaissance style.

WRITINGS

J. P. Cremer: 'Einige Nachrichten von dem neuen Schauspielhaus zu Aachen', *J. Baukunst*, i (1829), pp. 68–72
——: 'Beschreibung des Verfahrens beim Ziegelbrennen', *J. Baukunst*, i (1829), pp. 305–8
——: 'Das neue Rathaus in Elberfeld', *Z. Bauwsn*, ii (1852), pp. 81–2

BIBLIOGRAPHY

J. Everling: 'Cremer und Leydel: Zwei rheinische Baumeister vor hundert Jahren', *Z. Rhein. Ver. Dkmlpf. & Heimatschutz*, xx/2 (1927), pp. 35ff
W. Weyres: 'Zur Geschichte der kirchlichen Baukunst im Rheinland', *Studien zur Kölner Kirchengeschichte*, ed. Historischen Archiv des Erzbistums Köln, v (Düsseldorf, 1960), pp. 409ff
I. Schild: *Die Brüder Cremer und ihre Kirchenbauten* (Mönchengladbach, 1965)
W. Weyres and A. Mann: *Handbuch zur rheinischen Baukunst des 19. Jahrhunderts* (Cologne, 1968), pp. 38–9

E. Zinn: *Die Baukunst in Elberfeld während der ersten Hälfte des 19. Jahrhunderts* (Düsseldorf, 1968), pp. 20ff

H. P. Schmitz: *Robert Cremer: Erbauer der Technischen Hochschule und Restaurator des Münsters zu Aachen* (Aachen, 1969)

E. Trier and W. Weyres, eds: *Kunst des 19. Jahrhunderts im Rheinland*, Architektur I and II (Düsseldorf, 1980), pp. 92ff, 115ff

WILLY WEYRES

Cremer, Fritz (*b* Arnsberg, Ruhr, 22 Oct 1906; *d* Berlin, 1 Jan 1993). German sculptor and printmaker. From 1929 to 1934 he studied under Wilhelm Gerstl (1879–1963) at the Kunsthochschule in Berlin-Charlottenburg, and from 1945 to 1950 he was head of the sculpture department at the Akademie der Angewandten Kunst in Vienna. He was made a member of the Akademie der Künste der DDR, East Berlin, in 1950. Cremer was one of East Germany's leading realist sculptors and taught many of the country's important artists, including Wieland Förster. His life and work were imbued with his anti-Fascist views. After World War II he worked mainly on monuments for the victims of Fascism. These included *Man Set Free*, *Grieving Woman* and *Accusing Woman* (all 1948; Vienna, Cent. Cemetery); *Man Defeated*, a monument to the French victims at Ebensee concentration camp in Austria (1950); a monument for the victims of Buchenwald concentration camp near Weimar (1958); and *Oh Germany, Pale Mother*, a monument for Mauthausen, near Linz, in Austria (erected 1964–5). A typical feature of his sculptures is that while outwardly they seem peaceful and restrained they are full of tension in their form. He constructed them in large, clear shapes, using simple gestures.

BIBLIOGRAPHY

D. Schmidt: *Fritz Cremer* (Dresden, 1971)

H.-J. Ludwig, ed.: *Fritz Cremer, Lithographien 1955–1974* (Berlin, 1975) [cat. rais.]

BARBARA BARSCH

Cremona. Italian city in Lombardy, capital of the province of Cremona. Situated on the River Po about 80 km southeast of Milan, the city (population *c.* 85,000) is famous for its medieval and Renaissance buildings and also for a school of painting that flourished there in the 16th century. The original Gallic settlement at Cremona became a Roman colony in 218 BC, its commercial and strategic importance assured by its position on the Po. The city's prosperity in antiquity is attested by many fine surviving artefacts (Cremona, Mus. Civ. Ala Ponzone), and the street pattern in the town centre, around the Piazza del Comune, still retains the grid layout of the original Roman nucleus. During the Byzantine period the city expanded to the north, around the present Piazza Garibaldi, to accommodate a military garrison. The city re-emerged in 1098 as one of the Lombard city states, acquiring a circuit of walls that remained unaltered until the 19th century.

Cremona's first artistic flowering followed its establishment as a free *comune*, recognized in 1114 by Henry V, Holy Roman Emperor (*reg* 1106–25). A wave of building took place, including the reconstruction of the Early Christian church of S Lorenzo and the rebuilding of S Michele (7th–8th century), which had been destroyed in an earthquake in 1117. The cathedral was begun in 1107 with a plan typical of the Romanesque architecture of the Po valley and consecrated in 1190. It was radically altered in the later 12th century and the 14th to the Lombard Gothic style, with rectangular nave bays and deep transepts. The façade (see fig.) was rebuilt several times between the 12th and 16th centuries: in 1274 the rose window by Giacomo Porrata was added, in 1491 Alberto Maffiolo da Carrara (*fl* 1486–99) replaced the classical pediment with an attic storey with four niches, and in 1585 further alterations were made by Sebastiano Nani. The cathedral workshop was also a sculpture studio, and the *Four Prophets* carved by WILIGELMO before 1117, which flank the main door, are outstanding for their complexity. The octagonal Baptistery (begun 1167) is in a mature Romanesque style with Gothic accents; the upper part was rebuilt (1554–6) by Francesco Dattaro. The campanile or Torrazzo (13th century), claimed to be one of the highest in Italy (110 m), has several storeys marked by sculpted decorative elements and is crowned with a spire (see fig.). Near the cathedral in the Piazza del Comune is the arcaded Palazzo del Comune, rebuilt between 1206 and 1246 and restored at the end of the 15th century by Bernardino de Lera (*fl c.* 1480), from 1568 to 1578 by Francesco Dattaro and 1837–47 by Luigi Roghera (*b* 1788). The Palazzo del Popolo was built (*c.* 1250) in the Piazza Garibaldi in the northern part of the city.

In 1334 Cremona was taken by the Visconti family of Milan, passing to the Sforza family in 1441 upon the marriage of Bianca Maria Visconti to Francesco I Sforza (later Duke of Milan). Sforza patronage favoured the development of architecture and the arts in the city for the next century. In 1452 work began on the construction of the Ospedale Maggiore, whose plan probably derives from Filarete's Ospedale Maggiore in Milan; its eclectic

Cremona Cathedral, begun 1107, and the Torrazzo, 13th century

architecture was later unified by the construction of a screen carrying paired pilasters, based on a proposal (1785) by Faustino Rodi with modifications by Giuseppe Piermarini. In 1463 Bianca Maria founded a new church at the abbey of S Sigismondo, c. 2.5 km to the east of Cremona, to commemorate her marriage there. The measured articulation of space that characterizes this building has led to suggestions that Filarete may have been involved in its design. A striking feature of 15th-century architecture in Cremona is the use of terracotta, both as polychrome decoration with plaster and stone inserts, and as tiles stamped with classical motifs used to outline arches, cornices and friezes, for example the terracotta work by Rinaldo de Staulis (fl 1450–94) in the Palazzo Fodri (1488–1500) by Guglielmo de Lera. At this time the city was the Po valley's main centre of production for moulded terracotta tiles, while the building trade was dominated by a few families, including the de Lera (fl early 16th century) and DATTARO (c. 1550–80) families. Several important Renaissance buildings often classified as 'Bramantesque' were also erected in Cremona. They include the Palazzo Raimondi (c. 1496), by a local group of architects led by the building's owner, ELISEO RAIMONDI, who were devoted to the study of Vitruvius; the Cappella di Cristo Risorto (1502) in front of S Luca, attributed to Bernardino de Lera, which reveals the influence of Giovanni di Domenico Battaggio, a Lombard follower of Bramante; and the cloisters of S Pietro al Po (begun 1505) by Cristoforo Solari (see SOLARI (i), (5)) and S Abbondio (c. 1511) by Bernardino de Lera, which were based on Roman models.

In painting, the rapid increase in commissions under the Sforza led to the decline of small family workshops, such as that of the BEMBO, in favour of corporate institutions: the Paratico dei Pittori was founded in 1470. In the 16th century painting in Cremona was distinguished for its openness to outside influences, for example from Bologna, Ferrara, the Veneto, central Italy and Umbria, and also from Germany and Flanders. Rich inspiration and the use of brilliant colour characterize the Cremona school of painting, which for more than a century produced first-class artists, including Boccaccio Boccaccino (see BOCCACCINO, (1)), ALTOBELLO MELONE, Sofonisba Anguissola (see ANGUISSOLA, (2)) and members of the Campi family; many works by these and other artists can be seen in the cathedral and other churches in the city.

In 1535 Cremona came under the domination of the Spanish rulers of Milan, followed by a period of Austrian rule in the 18th century. After 1619 it suffered an economic depression from which it never recovered. This was accompanied by a rapid decline in artistic production, although the city became a noted centre of manufacture of musical instruments, Nicolò Amati (1596–1684), Antonio Stradivari (1644–1737) and Giuseppe Guarneri (1683–1745) all working there. Building projects of the 19th century included the Teatro della Concordia (1808) by Luigi Canonica and the façade of the 15th-century church of S Agata (1845–8) by Luigi Voghera, both in Neo-classical styles. Cremona's art collections are displayed in the Museo Civico Ala Ponzone in the Palazzo Affaitati (probably built c. 1560 by Giuseppe DATTARO), which also houses the cathedral treasury. Other works are exhibited in the Palazzo del Comune. The city's consciousness of its artistic heritage was celebrated in writings, from Antonio Campi's *Cremona fedelissima* (1585) to the guides and biographies written by local scholars between the 17th and 19th centuries.

BIBLIOGRAPHY

Boll. Stor. Cremon. (1931–)
An. Bib. Stat. & Lib. Civ. Cremona (1948–)
L. Cochetti Pratesi: *I profeti di Cremona: Problemi dell'occidente romanico* (Rome, 1976)
L. Grassi: 'Gli Sforza e l'architettura del ducato', *Gli Sforza a Milano* (Milan, 1978), pp. 183–262
Documenti per la storia dell'urbanistica e dell'architettura a Cremona nel primo ottocento (exh. cat., ed. M. L. Corsi; Cremona, Archv. Stato, 1981)
A. Piva, ed.: *Palazzo Affaitati a Cremona: Il nuovo Museo Civico* (Milan, 1984)
I Campi e la cultura artistica cremonese del cinquecento (exh. cat., ed. M. Gregori; Cremona, 1985) [detailed bibliog.]
B. Adorni and M. Tafuri: 'Il chiostro del convento di Sant'Abbondio a Cremona: Un'interpretazione eccentrica del modello bramantesco del belvedere', *A. Lombarda*, lxxix (1986), pp. 85–98
S. Bandera Bistoletti: 'Documenti per i Bembo: Una bottega di pittori, una città ducale del quattrocento e gli Sforza', *A. Lombarda*, lxxx/lxxxii (1987), pp. 155–81
G. Voltini: 'San Lorenzo in Cremona: Strutture architettoniche e reperti decorativi tra la fine del X e l'inizio dell'XI secolo', *A. Med.*, n. s. 2, i/1–2 (1987), pp. 215–57

STEFANO DELLA TORRE

Cremona, Girolamo da. *See* GIROLAMO DA CREMONA.

Cremona, Nebridio da. *See* NEBRIDIO DA CREMONA.

Cremona, Tranquillo (*b* Pavia, 10 April 1837; *d* Milan, 1 June 1878). Italian painter.

1. LIFE AND WORK. The son of an Austrian government official, Cremona began his artistic education in 1849 at the art school in Pavia, where he encountered three Lombard artists who were an important influence on his early studies: Giacomo Trécourt (1812–82), head of the school; Giovanni Carnevali, Trécourt's friend and a frequent visitor to Pavia; and Federico Faruffini, also a student at Pavia. All three were interpreters of the curiously soft and subtle form of Romanticism, derived from Andrea Appiani, that was to be found in this specific form only in Italy. In 1852 Cremona moved to Venice, where he enrolled at the Accademia. His teachers, who included Ludovico Lipparini (1800–56), Michelangelo Grigoletti (1801–70) and Antonio Zona (1814–92), were well versed in the more academic form of Romanticism expressed by Francesco Hayez, although in Zona the rather rigid, academic linearity was attenuated by a softer sense of form and colour. The Venetian Old Masters were a greater influence on Cremona's ultimate use of colour than was his academy training. In 1859, to avoid military service with the Austrian Army, Cremona moved to Piedmont. As soon as Lombardy had been freed from Austrian rule he transferred to Milan, where he remained for the rest of his life. In Milan Cremona enrolled at the Accademia di Belle Arti di Brera, where he was taught by Hayez and Giuseppe Bertini, in whose private studio he was also permitted to work. Fellow students included Daniele Ranzoni and Mosè Bianchi.

Cremona exhibited for the first time at the annual Brera exhibition of 1859, showing *The Falconer* (Milan, Gal. A.

Mod.). In 1862, having established his own studio, Cremona exhibited his first large-scale oil painting at the Brera Annual: *A Visit to the Tomb of Romeo and Juliet* (Milan, Gal. A. Mod.), a literary–historical subject depicted in a 'classical–romantic' vein. Very clearly the product of the stimuli assimilated from Cremona's previous artistic experiences, it nevertheless revealed an independent mind at work. At the Brera Annual the following year Cremona showed two canvases that received considerable attention from the critics: the large-scale *Marco Polo Presented by his Father to Kublai, Grand Khan of the Tatars* (1863; Rome, G.N.A. Mod.), which was partly a product of the current vogue for large history paintings, preferably celebrating the glories of Italy, and partly derived from the examples of Hayez, Trécourt and Faruffini; and his second, more complex version of *The Falconer* (1863; Milan, Gal. A. Mod.), in which Cremona can be seen to be moving towards his own, less distinctly derivative style. Cremona had by now rejected the popular form of anecdotal genre painting practised in Milan by the Induno brothers and their followers, and he was looking more closely at the softness of outline achieved by Carnevali. The passionate but at the same time guarded expressions of the lovers and the pervasive sense of nostalgia, conveyed in muted tones, create a charged atmosphere that recurs throughout the artist's oeuvre.

In Milan, Cremona had become friendly with GLI SCAPIGLIATI. He had also begun producing drawings, and especially caricatures, for several Milanese newspapers and periodicals such as *Farfulla* and *Uomo di pietra*, to which a number of the Scapigliati writers contributed. Cremona, along with Ranzoni and the sculptor Giuseppe Grandi, rapidly became identified as one of the official artists of the Scapigliatura movement. Its literary members included Guido Pisa, Cremona's first serious biographer, and Alberto Pisani Dossi, with whom Cremona became especially friendly. Through the Scapigliati, a number of whom were socially well-connected, Cremona received several commissions for portraits from the Milanese bourgeoisie, for example the lawyer *Emilio Marozzi* (1869; Milan, E. Marozzi priv. col.). The muted tones, soft outlines and concentration on the subject rather than on surrounding details showed that Cremona had been looking still more closely at Carnevali. Most Milanese patrons, however, accustomed to the more elaborately 'finished' pieces by Hayez and Giuseppe Molteni, refused to be drawn to Cremona's more subtle, alternative form of portraiture. Cremona's sitters were frequently Scapigliati themselves or members of their families. Most notable among these portraits, for their psychological penetration of character and rendering of colour and space, are those of *Alberto Carlo* and *Guido Pisani Dossi* (both 1867; priv. col., see 1986 exh. cat., figs 67, 68).

In 1870 Cremona again attracted the attention of the critics with *The Kiss*, later retitled the *Two Cousins* (1870; Rome, G.N.A. Mod.; see fig. 1). This success led Cremona in two directions: first, he expanded his activity as a portrait painter, the most important commission being for portraits of *Signor Deschamps* (1875; Milan, Gaspare Gussoni priv. col.) and *Signora Deschamps* (1875; Milan, Gal. A. Mod.), which is one of Cremona's most outstanding mature works. Secondly, he executed a series of

1. Tranquillo Cremona: *Two Cousins*, oil on canvas, 1870 (Rome, Galleria Nazionale d'Arte Moderna)

paintings and watercolours, a medium with which he had recently begun to experiment, in which he investigated not only the effects of light and colour but also the various forms of sentiment expressed between children and young people, frequently turning his attention to the repressed sensuality of their emotions, as in *Attraction* (1874; Milan, Gal. A. Mod., see fig. 2). These works were frequently supplied with frivolous or allegorical titles. Cremona extended this interest in personal relationships by investigating (in secular rather than religious terms) the mother and child theme, for example *Maternal Love* (1873; Milan, Gal. A. Mod.). This may have been prompted by the birth of his first child in 1873. Through these two series Cremona developed a penetrating insight into emotions. At times his work was overpoweringly sentimental, but at his best he produced such impressive pieces as *Ivy* (1878; Turin, Gal. Civ. A. Mod.). This work, commissioned by Benedetto Junck, was his last completed oil painting, and it made an immense impact on Milanese cultural circles. The way in which Cremona portrayed the two lovers, a common theme in his work, was completely alien to the Realist painters. *Ivy* marked the culmination of Cremona's attempts, influenced by Scapigliati ideas, to produce passionate yet ambiguous intensity using evanescent luminosity and simplified forms.

In 1878 Cremona was nominated head of the art school at Pavia, but he died a few months later, reportedly as a result of the poison accumulated from his habit of mixing lead-based paints on his arm. Vittore Grubicy organized a retrospective exhibition of Cremona's paintings in the

Ridotto della Scala in the same year. This exhibition was highly successful, and as a result the prices of Cremona's paintings rose considerably. Grubicy continued to promote Cremona's work in his articles and the exhibitions he organized, and Cremona remained popular for many years.

2. WORKING METHODS AND TECHNIQUE. Cremona introduced to Lombardy a dynamically new way of approaching a painting. In his attempt to capture the feeling of the moment, the innuendo behind each brief glance and gesture, he is said to have virtually thrown his paint on to the canvas (which usually lay on the floor, as he disliked working from an easel); he worked furiously, frequently working on more than one canvas, directed only by the inspiration of the moment. This is undoubtedly an over-romanticized view of Cremona as the authentic bohemian artist, but one based in reality, as he apparently preferred to transfer his ideas directly on to the canvas; indeed, few sketches survive for his completed canvases. Similarly, most of his drawings, if at all related to the completed article, can only be regarded as very preliminary sketches. Intimately connected with this working method was Cremona's highly developed ability to paint in watercolour. He was able to superimpose colours without losing the quality of transparency and translucency so important to the medium. *High Life* (1877; Milan, Gal. A. Mod.) and *Curious Girls* (Codogno, Fond. Lamberti) are superbly delicate, remarkable examples of late 19th-century Italian watercolour painting. Highly prized, these works became more valuable than the artist's oil paintings.

In his oils Cremona also succeeded in maintaining a sense of luminosity by using 'vaporous', superimposed brushstrokes. Expansive, interlayered but still translucent brushwork and a greater fluidity are visible in all of Cremona's mature works. This method, in which Cremona was clearly more interested in defining space through luminous colour effects rather than sharply delineated form, was, inevitably, misunderstood by the majority of his contemporaries. Many patrons and fellow artists clung to the traditional interpretation of what was intended by a 'finished' painting—the work of Hayez, for example—to which Cremona's work definitely did not correspond. The artist was frequently accused of presenting worked-up preparatory studies as finished paintings, although when it came to rendering the appearance and quality of a lady's attire Cremona was by no means inferior to Hayez, merely different in approach. This lack of comprehension was partially due to the inability of language to express what Cremona was visually attempting to do. Many critics fell back on the literary–musical vocabulary formulated by the Scapigliati writers.

Cremona differed from many of his contemporaries also in his choice of subject-matter, which relates to his style and technique. He produced virtually no landscapes (unlike Ranzoni); relatively few works inspired by religious, mythological, historial or literary themes; a very large number of portraits (characteristic of all the Scapigliati artists); and many figure studies, especially among his watercolours. Common to his portraits and figure studies (and perhaps also deriving from his watercolour technique) was Cremona's elimination of all irrelevant detail.

2. Tranquillo Cremona: *Attraction*, oil on canvas, 575×700 mm, 1874 (Milan, Galleria d'Arte Moderna)

His barren backgrounds and surroundings, so completely at variance with those of Mosè Bianchi or the Induno brothers, are rendered by large areas of luminous colour that force the viewer to concentrate on the psychological content of the picture. Cremona probably limited his subject-matter in order to focus more closely on the qualities of the light reflected by his sitters.

The nature of the artistic relationship between Cremona and Ranzoni and the extent to which one influenced the other are unclear. The two artists were intimate friends and at one stage even shared a studio; both were closely connected with the literary–musical set of the Scapigliati; and their work displays many similarities in approach. Cremona is known to have proclaimed Ranzoni as his real master on more than one occasion, but the situation was probably far more complex; at the very least, a continuous exchange of ideas must have existed.

BIBLIOGRAPHY

DBI

G. Pisa: *Tranquillo Cremona* (Milan, 1899)

Mostra della Scapigliatura: Pittura, scultura, letteratura, musica, architettura (exh. cat., ed. A. M. Brizio and D. Isella; Milan, Pal. Permanente, 1966)

L. Luciani and F. Luciani: *Dizionario dei pittori italiani dell'ottocento* (Florence, 1974), pp. 150–52 [with bibliog.]

L. Caramel and C. Pirovano: *Opere dell'ottocento*, Milan, Gal. A. Mod. cat. (Milan, 1975), i, pp. 44–5 [with bibliog.]

1886–1986—La Permanente: Un secolo d'arte a Milano (exh. cat., Milan, Pal. Permanente, 1986)

CLARE HILLS-NOVA

Cremonese, il. *See* CALETTI, GIUSEPPE.

Crenellation [battlementing]. Name given to a treatment of the outer wall of a parapet that produces a series of merlons and the spaces left between them. The merlons, or upright sections, provided an immediate cover for the defender, armed usually with bow or crossbow, while the open section gave him his view for shooting. Crenellation is found universally about the summit of the walls and towers of castles and fortified towns (and fortified churches, e.g. Béziers, Herault) as an essential part of the wall-walk, without which active defence would scarcely have been possible. The technique was inherited from the Classical past and no doubt had its equivalent in the timber stockades of some early medieval fortresses. However, it long outlived its practical use to survive into the modern period as a mere architectural motif, at first signifying nobility and then just a general medieval romanticism. In the medieval period it was so common a feature of fortification and its serrated outline so marked that it evidently acquired a symbolism of its own as the sign of castellation and of lordship and gentility. In England a 'licence to crenellate', which it was necessary or at least desirable to obtain before building a castle or fortifying a house, gave such prominence to the word as to suggest that crenellation was taken to be the line of demarcation between a fortified or unfortified residence. Thus a licence of Edward I to Stephen of Penchester, dated 23 May 1281, empowered him to fortify and crenellate his house at Allington (Kent) with a wall of stone and lime.

The familiar outline of crenellation (i.e. the shape of both the merlons and the spaces between them) is almost always rectangular, though the more fancifully shaped merlons of so-called Moorish crenellation are found in Spain, for example Ávila (town walls) and the castles of Clavizo and S Servando (Toledo); at Guimarães in Portugal; and at Frederick II's castle of Prato in Tuscany (c. 1237). Optional extras include arrow slits set in the merlons themselves and shutters to be raised and lowered diagonally between the merlons, both devices for the further protection of the defenders. Working shutters, albeit restorations, can be seen at Gravensteen (Castle of the Counts of Flanders, Ghent), and the original hinges or sockets can sometimes be seen on the merlons, as on Henry II's keep at Orford, Suffolk (1160s). The crenellated parapets of curtains, towers and gateways could also be combined with timber hoarding or later stone machicolation to form a projecting gallery to cover their bases.
See also CASTLE, §I.

R. ALLEN BROWN

Creole. In the strictest sense the term denotes people of fully European descent born in French, Portuguese and Spanish colonies (or former colonies), mostly in South America, the Caribbean and Africa (for associated art forms see under relevant country surveys). The term is applied far more loosely, however, to people of mixed race born in these regions; its usage for people of African descent born in America is now almost obsolete. The designation 'creole' is also applied to the various languages, originally colonial-based, spoken in such regions.   □

Créquy, Charles de Blanchefort, Maréchal **de.** See LESDIGUIÈRES, DUCS DE, (2)

Crescenzi. Italian family of patrons and artists. They played a prominent part in the life of Rome from the 10th century, if not earlier, and by the 17th century were regarded as one of the oldest and most illustrious of the city's patrician families. Under the leadership of Virgilio Crescenzi (d 1592) and his sons Giacomo Crescenzi (c. 1570–18 April 1638), (1) Pietro Paolo Crescenzi, (2) Giovanni Battista Crescenzi and (3) Francesco Crescenzi, the family, which supported Filippo Neri, the founder of the Oratorians, was distinguished both for its dedication to the work of reform within the Church and for its interests in the arts. Cristoforo Roncalli ran an academy at the Palazzo Crescenzi, at which the Crescenzi brothers, among others, studied (Baglione).

In his will of 1585 Matteo Contarelli appointed Virgilio Crescenzi as his heir and executant for the completion of the Contarelli Chapel in S Luigi dei Francesi, Rome, situated near the Palazzo Crescenzi at 23 Via della Rotonda. In 1591 the Cavaliere d'Arpino began to decorate the chapel but little progress was made until it was put under the control of the Fabbrica of St Peter's in 1597. However, the Crescenzi again became involved and on 7 February 1602 Abbot Giacomo Crescenzi, acting for Francesco Contarelli, signed a contract with Caravaggio for an altarpiece of *St Matthew and the Angel* (destr.). When completed this painting was rejected by the clergy and a second version (*in situ*) was painted. The family continued until the mid-18th century, but became extinct with the death in 1768 of Cardinal Marcello Crescenzi.

(1) Cardinal **Pietro Paolo Crescenzi** (*b* Rome, 1572; *d* Rome, 19 Feb 1645). Patron and collector. He was appointed cardinal by Pope Paul V in 1611. His name is associated in particular with that of Cristoforo Roncalli, for whom he used his influence to win an important commission to decorate the sacristy of the basilica of S Maria at Loreto (for illustration see RONCALLI, CRISTOFORO). Crescenzi was also a keen student of antiquity and a collector of epitaphs, an interest shared with his friend, the antiquarian Giovanni Zaratino Castellini (1570–1642). During the pontificate of Gregory XV (1621–3), Pietro Paolo and his brother Giacomo were appointed members of a special commission to regulate the dispensation of licences for excavating the catacombs.

Pietro Paolo was also an early patron of Claude Lorrain whom, in the late 1620s, he commissioned to paint frescoes in the Palazzo Crescenzi: a frieze of seven small landscape frescoes (*in situ*) has been plausibly attributed to Claude.

BIBLIOGRAPHY
DBI
G. Baglione: *Vite* (1642); ed. V. Mariani (1935), p. 291
I. Toesca: 'Pomarancio a Palazzo Crescenzi', *Paragone*, viii (1957), pp. 41–5
A. Grelle: 'I Crescenzi e l'Accademia di via S Eustachio', *Commentari*, xii (1961), pp. 120–38

JANET SOUTHORN

(2) **Giovanni Battista Crescenzi** (*b* Rome, 17 Jan 1577; *d* Madrid, 17 March 1635). Painter and architect, brother of (1) Pietro Paolo Crescenzi. Like his brothers, he studied painting with Cristoforo Roncalli, and he painted frescoes and canvases (untraced) for the Palazzo Crescenzi (Baglione). He was Superintendent of Works at the Pauline Chapel (1610–13) in S Maria Maggiore, Rome, and also supervised the artistic projects commissioned by Pope Paul V (see BORGHESE, (1)). He founded a school of painting from life in his palazzo.

In 1617 he moved to Spain to work for King Philip III, and in 1618 he became involved in the construction of the Pantheon for the Spanish Habsburgs (see ESCORIAL,

§2). In this connection he returned to Italy briefly in 1618 to recruit bronze- and silverworkers and smelters. In 1626 Philip IV made him Marques de la Torre. In 1630 he was named Superintendent of Royal Works, in which year he can be connected with the decoration of the Buen Retiro palace on the outskirts, at that time, of Madrid (*see* MADRID, §II, 1). He has been associated with the commissioning of 12 landscape paintings from Rome (paid for in 1634) for the decoration of this palace.

As to Giovanni Battista's work as a painter, only one secure attribution exists: *St Anthony Abbot* (1596; Piedivalle, S Giovanni Battista). Some figurative paintings and numerous Caravaggesque still-lifes have been proposed as his, but all of the latter are also attributed to other artists such as the MASTER OF THE PALAZZO S GERVASIO (*see* MASTERS, ANONYMOUS, AND MONOGRAMMISTS, §I) and Pietro Paolini.

BIBLIOGRAPHY

DBI [with full bibliog. to 1984]

G. Baglione: *Vite* (1642); ed. V. Mariani (1935), pp. 364–7

R. Taylor: 'Juan Bautista Crescenzio y la arquitectura cortesana española (1617–1635)', *Academia: Bol. Real Acad. B.A. San Fernando*, xlviii (1979), pp. 503–66

E. Harris: 'G. B. Crescenzi, Velazques and the "Italian" Landscapes for the Buen Retiro', *Burl. Mag.*, cxxii (1980), pp. 562–4

M. Marini: 'Del Signor Giovanni Battista Crescentij, pittore', *Getty Mus. J.*, x (1981), pp. 127–32

L. Spezzaferro: 'Un imprenditore del primo seicento: Giovanni Battista Crescenzi,' *Ric. Stor. A.*, xxvi (1985), pp. 50–73

A. Cottino: *La natura morta in Italia*, ii (Milan, 1989), pp. 710–11

Pittura del seicento: Ricerche in Umbria (exh. cat., ed. L. Barrocro; Spoleto, Rocca Albornoziana, 1989), pp. 262–4

ELENA FUMAGALLI

(3) Francesco Crescenzi (*b* Rome, 8 Sept 1585; *d* Naples, Jan 1648). Amateur artist, brother of (1) Pietro Paolo Crescenzi. A poem by G. F. Maja Malestona published in 1629 described Francesco as a 'most excellent painter', a reference to artistic talents which found expression as part of his wider cultural interests, including his membership, together with his friend Pietro della Valle, of the Accademia degli Umoristi, and his friendship with the poet Giambattista Marino. When Marino died in 1625, he left his collection of drawings to Francesco and most of his paintings collection to Francesco's relative Crescentio Crescenzi, whose brother Melchiorre had been one of the poet's earliest patrons. Among these paintings, inherited by Francesco in 1641, are portraits of *Crescentio Crescenzi* and *Giambattista Marino* (untraced) attributed in the will to Caravaggio. In 1625 the Accademia degli Umoristi had organized a commemoration of Marino to which Francesco contributed a life-size portrait in which he showed the poet seated at work on a composition, with books at hand to indicate his poetic range. In 1640 Francesco's *Innocence* (see Grelle, pl. xlvii, fig. 1) was one of a number of drawings by various artists (including the Cavaliere G. B. Muti, another noble Roman amateur, who contributed *Patience*) engraved by Cornelis Bloemaert II; these were illustrations to a new edition of the 14th-century poem *Documenti d'amore* by Francesco da Barberino, published in Rome by Federico Ubaldini. The composition of a female figure (perhaps representing Envy; Grelle) seated in a landscape with a putto and a dog departs from the usual presentation of Innocence (as described, for example, in the *Iconologia* by Cesare Ripa) and may indicate

Crescenzi's originality as an artist. Francesco shared the family interest in the work of Claude; the *Rest on the Flight into Egypt* (mid-1640s; Cleveland, OH, Mus. A.), which draws on a picture the artist had painted for Philip IV of Spain, was commissioned by Francesco.

BIBLIOGRAPHY

DBI

G. Baglione: *Vite* (1642); ed. V. Mariani (1935), p. 366

I. Toesca: 'Pomarancio a Palazzo Crescenzi', *Paragone*, viii (1957), pp. 41–5

A. Grelle: 'I Crescenzi e l'Accademia di via S Eustachio', *Commentari*, xii (1961), pp. 120–38

E. Schleier: 'Charles Mellin and the Marchesi Muti', *Burl. Mag.*, cxviii (1976), pp. 837–44

G. Fulco: 'Il sogno di una galleria: Nuovi documenti sul Marino collezionista', *Ant. B. A.*, iii (1979), pp. 84–99

JANET SOUTHORN

Crescenzi, Bartolomeo del. *See* CAVAROZZI, BARTOLOMEO.

Crescenzio, Pietro (*b* Bologna, *c.* 1233; *d* Bologna, between 23 June 1320 and 25 Feb 1321). Italian writer. He studied logic, medicine, natural science and law at the University of Bologna. After retiring from public life Crescenzio wrote the *Liber ruralium commodorum* (*c.* 1304–9), better known as the *Trattato della agricoltura*, the first agricultural treatise composed in Europe since the 5th century AD. Parts of an autograph manuscript (Bologna, Bib. U., MS. 1494) survive. The treatise enjoyed enormous success. It was translated into French in 1373 for King Charles V; the manuscript (Paris, Bib. Arsenal, MS. 5064) has 14 miniatures and coloured, decorated initials, embellished with gold. The *Trattato* was subsequently translated into most other European languages. The great number of manuscript copies (132 according to one estimate) that survive in libraries in Austria, England (e.g. Oxford, Bodleian Lib., MS. Canon. Italiani 149), France (e.g. Dijon, Bib. Mun., MS. 453(271)), Germany, Holland, Italy (e.g. Rome, Vatican, Bib. Apostolica, MS. lat. 7303), Poland, Switzerland and Spain indicate its wide appeal both as a practical treatise and as a subject for manuscript illumination. The manuscripts contain several portraits of Crescenzio; in one (Rome, Vatican, Bib. Apostolica, MS. lat. 1529) he is depicted bareheaded, wearing a red overgarment and a green cowl, and presenting his work to the head of the Dominican Order. The *Trattato* was first printed in Augsburg in 1471.

WRITINGS

Trattato della agricoltura (*c.* 1304–9), ed. G. L. Monti (Bologna, 1804) [incl. a life of Crescenzio, pp. 1a–49]

BIBLIOGRAPHY

DBI

L. Frati: 'Pietro de' Crescenzio e l'opera sua', *Atti & Mem. Stor. Patria Prov. Romagna*, ix (1919), pp. 146–64

L. Savastano: *Contributo allo studio critico degli scrittori agrari italici: Pietro dei Crescenzi* (Acrireale, 1922)

T. Alfonsi and others, eds: *Pier de' Crescenzi, 1233–1321: Studi e documenti* (Bologna, 1933) [incl. a list of manuscripts and printed editions, pp. 265–369]

JANET SOUTHORN

Crescione. *See* CRISCUOLO.

Crespi (i). Spanish family of illuminators. They were active in Valencia. Domingo Crespi (*fl* 1383–1438) was the founder of the dynasty, which was continued by his son Lleonard (*fl* 1424–59); another son Pedro was also a miniaturist. Pere Crespi and Miguel Crespi, who may also have been members of the family, are cited in documents in 1428 and 1432 respectively. The Crespi workshop enjoyed royal and ecclesiastical patronage and was the source of work for many local illuminators. Domingo must already have been a prominent miniaturist by 1383 because he was then engaged in the illumination of a lectionary (untraced) for King Peter IV of Aragon, 'el Ceremonioso'. Other prestigious commissions followed: a psalter for the church at Quart (1397), two psalters for Valencia Cathedral (1398) and a Book of Hours for Fray Juan de Casanova, Cardinal of S Sixto and Bishop of Elna (1437; all untraced). The *Libre del Consolat de Mar* (1408–12; Valencia, Archv Reino) is the only surviving authenticated work by Domingo. Lleonard Crespi's achievements were comparable to those of his father, as witness his steady production of manuscripts from 1424 to 1454, including the completion of the BREVIARY OF KING MARTIN (Paris, Bib. N., MS. Rothschild 2529). The influence of Franco-Flemish manuscript illumination on the style of the Crespi workshop is evident in the figure types, the spatial compositions and the decorative elements employed in their works. Yet traces of Valencian Gothic can also be detected in the tendency towards frontally orientated and strictly symmetrical arrangements of figure groups.

BIBLIOGRAPHY

A. Villalba Dávalos: 'Flors Sanctorum. Cod. 84 del Archivo Catedral de Valencia', *Archv A. Valenc.* (1957), pp. 36–44

——: 'Los comienzos de la miniatura valenciana: Domingo Crespí', *Archv Esp. A.*, xxxi (1958), pp. 23–38

P. Bohigas y Balaguer: *La ilustración y la decoración del libro manuscrito en Catalunya* (Barcelona, 1960–67), ii, pp. 12–41

A. Villalba Dávalos: *La miniatura valenciana en los siglos XIV y XV* (Valencia, 1964)

J. Madurell Marimón: 'El misál de Santa Eulália en la Seo de Barcelona', *Cuad. Arqueol. Hist. Ciudad*, xviii (1980), pp. 141–51

LYNETTE BOSCH

Crespi (ii). Italian family of artists and writers. The painter and printmaker (1) Giuseppe Maria Crespi was the most original Bolognese artist of his time, producing religious, mythological and genre works, these last being particularly innovative. Of his four sons, Antonio Crespi (1712–81) and (2) Luigi Crespi assisted their father in his later years and adopted his style. Luigi was also a writer, producing, among other works, a collection of biographies of his father and various contemporary Bolognese artists.

(1) Giuseppe Maria Crespi [lo Spagnuolo] (*b* Bologna, 14 March 1665; *d* Bologna, 16 July 1747). Painter, draughtsman and printmaker. His religious and mythological works are distinguished by a free brushstroke and a painterly manner. He also painted spirited genre scenes, which by their quality, content and quantity distinguish him as one of the first Italian painters of high standing to devote serious attention to the depiction of contemporary life. Such paintings as *Woman Laundering* (1700–05; St Petersburg, Hermitage) or *Woman Washing Dishes* (1720–25; Florence, Uffizi) offer straightforward glimpses of domestic chores in images that are startlingly novel for the period and look forward to the art of Jean-Siméon Chardin, Jean-François Millet and Honoré Daumier.

1. Life and work. 2. Working methods and technique.

1. LIFE AND WORK.

(i) Training and first independent works, 1665–1700. (ii) Bologna, 1700–08: professional success. (iii) Florence and Bologna, 1708–9: the patronage of Grand Prince Ferdinando. (iv) Bologna, 1709–22: genre painting, prints and the *Seven Sacraments*. (v) Later career, 1722–47.

(i) Training and first independent works, 1665–1700. Giuseppe Maria was the youngest of four children born to Girolamo Crespi, a Bolognese miller, and Ippolita Cospi. His childhood was relatively comfortable, and he lived his entire life in the house that his mother's dowry had provided. At around the age of 12 he learnt to draw from the little-known painter Angelo Michele Toni (1640–1708). In the early 1680s he studied with Domenico Maria Canuti and later (*c.* 1684–6) in the drawing academy headed by Carlo Cignani. In the late 1680s he attended the life drawing academy in the Palazzo Ghislieri. Independently, he immersed himself in the late 16th-century works of the founders of the Bolognese school and copied the Carracci frescoes (*c.* 1583/4) in the Palazzo Fava, those of Ludovico Carracci and his pupils in the cloister of S Michele in Bosco (1592), and the early altarpieces of Guercino. In these years his fellow students dubbed him 'lo Spagnuolo' ('the Spaniard') because of his manner of dress. He set up on his own in 1686, renting a studio with Gian Antonio Burrini, nine years his senior, who introduced him to the Bolognese merchant and amateur, Giovanni Ricci. Financial support from the latter enabled Crespi to further his artistic education: in 1688–90 he made trips in Emilia and to Venice, following the itinerary taken earlier by the Carracci, to study the great masters of north Italian tradition: Correggio, Titian and Veronese. Like the young Carracci, too, he went to the Marches and made many copies after Federico Barocci, which were said to have sold later at high prices and in some cases even as originals. The unusually liberal terms of Crespi's contract with Ricci provided him with a ready buyer for any of his uncommissioned works, and the first of these, the *Wedding at Cana* (*c.* 1686–8; Chicago, IL, A. Inst.), reveals the results of his study of Venetian painting and of Barocci. Its composition paraphrases the lower left third of Paolo Veronese's great canvas of the same subject (1562/3; Paris, Louvre) and its luminous, high-keyed palette echoes that of Barocci. Already evident are two elements that remained constants in his oeuvre: the feathery brushwork, especially in the gauzy fabrics, and the attention to genre detail, seen in his treatment of the lively cat and dog.

The early sources attest that Crespi painted genre themes at the beginning of his career, but none of these survive. He chose quotidian subjects that had some precedent in the Carracci's early works but were ignored by contemporary Bolognese artists. In 1688 he exhibited pictures of a butcher's shop and of a wine cellar, with rough men squeezing grapes in a large press (see Zanotti). His first essay in printmaking—five prints from an aborted project to portray the craftsmen of Bologna—dates to these earliest years.

Two important events in 1690 signal the turning-point in Crespi's career from student to independent master: his election to the Compagnia dei Pittori and the commission for his first major altarpiece in Bologna, the *Temptation of*

St Anthony (1690; Bologna, S Nicolò degli Albari). According to Crespi's son Luigi Crespi, this was commissioned by Conte Carlo Cesare Malvasia, who was a director of the Palazzo Ghislieri drawing academy. It openly imitates the forceful style of Ludovico Carracci and thus must have pleased Malvasia, who had accredited Ludovico with the founding of the Bolognese school (see Crespi). The monumental figure of St Anthony, seen from below, looms up to fill the foreground; his and Christ's body are arranged along opposing diagonals. Strong contrasts of lighting and emphatic gesture further dramatize the saint's triumph. Shortly after the altarpiece's completion, Crespi alienated his patron by caricaturing him as a dead chicken. The ensuing scandal resulted in Crespi's break with the Ghislieri academy in 1691. Sometime during the mid-1690s Crespi was invited, along with three older Bolognese painters (Burrini, Benedetto Gennari II and Giovanni Gioseffo dal Sole) to decorate Prince Eugene of Savoy's newly acquired (1694) Winter Palace in Vienna with paintings on a theme from Greek mythology. Recent research has established that Crespi's part in this prestigious commission, pendants depicting *Chiron Teaching Achilles to Draw the Bow* (see fig. 1) and *Aeneas, Sibyl and Charon* (both 1695–1700; Vienna, Ksthist. Mus.), hung as two of three overdoors in an audience chamber. The interpretation of the themes is on a human rather than a heroic scale and includes the novel conceit of showing Chiron about to give his pupil a reproving kick: a feature that was judged by some critics to have offended decorum (see Zanotti; Algarotti) but appears to have pleased Prince Eugene as he proceeded to commission its pendant. Crespi's two pictures are similar in format, composition (reduced number of figures) and dark tonality to those by his Bolognese colleagues, which suggests that they all followed specific directives regarding form as well as subject. Crespi was clearly experimenting with dramatic lighting: his figures barely emerge from shadowy backgrounds, and their arms, legs and torsos are illuminated as if by lightning flashes. Only the tip of Aeneas' nose and his cheek are lit in the second painting. These effects are borrowed from Ludovico Carracci, as is the powerful figure of Charon, who mirrors the latter's St Jerome in the *Madonna degli Scalzi* (Bologna, Pin. N.).

Early in the 1690s Crespi made his first essays in fresco, a medium he only employed early in his career. In collaboration with Marcantonio Chiarini (1652–1730) he painted a ceiling fresco (1691; untraced) for S Francesco di Paola, Pistoia. His only surviving frescoes, two ceilings in the Palazzo Pepoli in Bologna, probably date to the end of the decade. They consist of scenes aggrandizing Marchese Ercole Pepoli and his family: the *Triumph of Hercules*, which shows Ercole's mythological namesake attaining immortality, borne in a chariot beyond the mortal realm of the Four Seasons, and the *Banquet of the Gods*, which implies (by its inclusion of the Pepoli arms in the scene) the family's place among the gods on Olympus and beyond the reach of the Fates. Using the illusionistic devices of Baroque ceiling painting, Crespi opened up the centre of each vault to show airborne figures in an uninterrupted expanse, moving up and away from the steeply foreshortened figures representing the Seasons and Fates, who seem to stand bound to the edge of their respective

1. Giuseppe Maria Crespi: *Chiron Teaching Achilles to Draw the Bow*, oil on canvas, 1.26×1.24 m, 1695–1700 (Vienna, Kunsthistorisches Museum)

ceilings. These female personifications are among Crespi's most memorable creations: Spring and Summer are young peasant girls, their coarse features alive with infectious good humour; similarly laughing girls improbably represent the Fates. This irreverent approach to the gods and demi-gods of Classical mythology sets these ceilings apart from the distinguished tradition of Bolognese decorative painting upheld by his contemporaries. Also unusual was Crespi's refusal on this and subsequent occasions to collaborate with a specialist in *quadratura*.

Crespi's untraditional approach is further demonstrated in his treatment of the pastoral themes that he began to explore in small easel paintings of the 1690s. He took up the mode that had been formulated by Francesco Albani earlier in the century and had gained popularity in Bologna by the 1690s in the works of Cignani, Marcantonio Franceschini, Lorenzo Pasinelli and dal Sole. His *Sleeping Cupids Disarmed by Nymphs* (1695–1700; Bologna, Pin. N.), in which the mythological theme provides a pretext for painting pretty young nymphs and innumerable cupids in idyllic landscapes, exemplifies the genre. He subverted the tradition by producing a humorous inversion: mischievous cupids discover and toy with sleeping nymphs (e.g. *Cupid with Sleeping Nymphs*, 1695–1700; Washington, DC, N.G.A.). At least eight of his variations on this theme survive, five from the 1690s and three from the 1730s.

(ii) Bologna, 1700–08: Professional success. By 1700 Crespi had become successful enough to open his own school (which he closed in the 1720s), immediately attracting as many as 30 students. In 1707 he married Gioanna Cuppini, legitimizing the birth of their first son, who had been born in 1703. In 1701 Grand Prince Ferdinando de' Medici's

Bolognese agent, as part of a project to remove famous altarpieces from churches into the Prince's collection, arranged for Crespi to paint the replacement for Giovanni Lanfranco's *Ecstasy of St Margaret of Cortona* (Florence, Pitti), then in the church of S Maria Nuova in Cortona. Crespi's *Ecstasy of St Margaret of Cortona* (Cortona, Mus. Dioc.) was unveiled to public acclaim shortly before 1 January 1702 (see Chiarini; 1986 exh. cat.), which date provides a reference point for the artist's still uncertain chronology between 1695 and 1706. Crespi's altarpiece is not a copy of Lanfranco's, although its composition, predicated on a diagonal juxtaposition of Christ at upper left and the saint at lower right, implies his familiarity with the original or a copy of it. Significant differences, however, lie in conception and handling. Crespi reinterprets the spiritual experience in quotidian terms: Margaret kneels, not supported by angels, calmly acknowledging the celestial vision. Nocturnal lighting, shadowy recesses that dissolve form and a selective layering of transparent, luminous highlights create a sense of the figures' immateriality and confer mystic overtones. Prince Ferdinando expressed his pleasure at the commission's successful completion. Four years later Crespi hoped to attract the Prince's patronage again with the *Massacre of the Innocents* (see fig. 2), commissioned by Don Carlo Silva, a Florentine priest, as a present for the Prince. This ambitious, multifigured composition with over 100 figures marks the watershed in Crespi's career. A tangled skein of soldiers, mothers and babies fills the picture's lower left quadrant, while a pair of mothers lamenting over a child stand in isolation at the lower right, their quiet, vertical forms providing a counterpoise to and a dramatic commentary on the tumultuous violence. Crespi explored the theme in successive versions throughout his career (e.g. 1735–40; Bologna, Pin. N.), varying the scale of the figures and describing the setting in more detail.

(iii) Florence and Bologna, 1708–9: The patronage of Grand Prince Ferdinando. Once the *Massacre of the Innocents* had been completed, Don Carlo Silva proved reluctant to part with it, so in 1708 Crespi wrested it from him and delivered it to the Prince personally, surprising the Florentine court by his informality. The Grand Prince approved the painting, delighted in the artist's unconventional approach and invited him to return to Florence on an extended visit. For a while Crespi worked for Ferdinando from Bologna, sending him various works, including the unusually informal and light-hearted *Self-portrait with Family* (1708; Florence, Uffizi), in which his laughing wife watches as he pulls his eight-month-old son, Luigi, in a wagon. In 1709 the Crespi family moved to Florence, where they spent eight months living in rooms in the Grand Prince's villa at Pratolino and where their third son was born. He was named Ferdinando after his royal godfather.

In Florence, Crespi, encouraged by Ferdinando (who called him his 'pittore attuale') and inspired by the Prince's collection of paintings by the Bamboccianti, renewed his interest in depicting genre subjects, which he had neglected since 1690. His most intense activity in this field dates to

2. Giuseppe Maria Crespi: *Massacre of the Innocents*, oil on canvas, 1.33×1.89 m, 1706 (Florence, Galleria degli Uffizi)

his stay in Florence and to the period immediately afterwards. He painted both directly observed subjects and scenes with implicit narrative content, usually with satiric or comic implications. Two important works from his stay in Florence are the *Fair at Poggio a Caiano* (1709; Florence, Uffizi) and the *Flea Hunt* (1709; Pisa, Mus. N. S Matteo). The *Fair at Poggio a Caiano* represented the many colourful individuals and episodes at the annual fair and market near the Medici country villa. Rich in incident, the crowded scene includes portraits of courtiers: for example, Ferdinando and his court would have recognized Antonio Morosini, the Prince's 'fool', who at one fair had in fact impersonated a local charlatan, much to everyone's amusement, and who is shown acting out this practical joke. Anonymous anecdotes also unfold: in the left foreground the outcome of an encounter between two peasants is broadly hinted at by bawdy gestures, while in the right foreground the upper classes, represented by a young, well-dressed lady, mingle with the lower classes, represented by a market woman offering wares.

(iv) Bologna, 1709–22: genre painting, prints and the 'Seven Sacraments'. The Accademia Clementina, the first official Bolognese academy of art, was inaugurated in 1710, and Crespi became one of its first directors. However, he disagreed with his fellow administrators over the policy of admitting artisans and amateurs as well as professional artists and ceased to attend after 1711.

Despite the death of Ferdinando in 1713, Crespi continued to explore a variety of genre themes in this decade, picturing the working class at their labour: pressing wine grapes, making silk, doing laundry. Soon after his return from Florence, *c.* 1710, he began to make prints illustrating *Bertoldo e Bertoldino*, a popular book of stories by the Bolognese writer, Giulio Cesare Croce (*c.* 1550–1609). He pictured the exploits of the shrewd but crude peasant Bertoldo and his son in three separate sets of 20 episodes: etched (Bologna, Pin. N.), in oil on copper (Rome, Gal. Doria-Pamphili) and in watercolour on parchment (Bologna, Bib. Cassa di Risparmio). The sequence and date of these sets remain controversial. Possibly Crespi identified with the salty folk hero whose non-conformity found echoes in his own often individualistic behaviour and dress.

Crespi must have lavished his most comic effects on the lost cycle of paintings that reduced his biographer, Zanotti, to side-splitting laughter, in which he illustrated the rise and fall of an opera singer. Two extant paintings have been associated with the series: the *Flea Hunt*, as known in three replicas (Pisa, Mus. Civ.; Paris, Louvre; see fig. 3); Naples, Capodimonte), probably represents the opening scene in the story, and the *Singer at the Spinet with an Admirer*, known in two replicas (Florence, Uffizi; Bologna, priv. col.), may reflect a later episode. In the first, a young woman performs her intimate morning ritual in a humble room in which the unexpected presence of a spinet and printed announcements of concerts allude to her musical talents, while tokens of gallantries signal her route to future success. In the second an elegantly dressed and coiffed woman interrupts her singing to receive the admiring attentions of the aristocratic lover responsible for her sudden prosperity. The dating of the project and

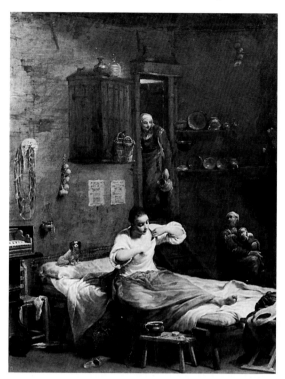

3. Giuseppe Maria Crespi: *Flea Hunt*, oil on canvas, 550×410 mm, *c.* 1720–25 (Paris, Musée du Louvre)

of the surviving versions of the *Flea Hunt*, as well as the chronological sequence of the latter's known variant compositions, has yet to be fully resolved. According to Zanotti, the series was commissioned by an Englishman, to judge from circumstantial evidence not earlier than 1716. It seems likely that the Englishman requested a repetition of existing works, as Crespi's involvement with the theme began earlier with the *Flea Hunt* painted in Florence in 1709. Apart from tracing its genesis and establishing its place in the artist's oeuvre, the dating of the cycle would help to clarify Crespi's contribution to the genre of narrative satire, for thematic parallels exist that link the lost cycle to William Hogarth's series of engravings, the *Harlot's Progress* (1731), in which he claimed to have invented the 'modern moral subject'.

Probably in 1712 Crespi painted his most famous cycle, the *Seven Sacraments* (Dresden, Gemäldegal. Alte Meister), which originated as an exercise in genre. Its remarkable novelty lies in the casting of the liturgical theme in an everyday idiom. According to Zanotti, the inspiration for the composition occurred in S Benedetto when Crespi observed a ray of sunlight from a broken window falling across the head and shoulder of a man in the confessional booth. Struck by the beauty of the lighting, he returned to his studio to reproduce the effect in a drawing, and subsequently in a painting, for which he borrowed the confessional, re-created the same lighting and posed the original priest and a friend. He sent the painting to the noted collector Cardinal Pietro Ottoboni in Rome, who was so impressed that he commissioned paintings of the other sacraments to be done in the same manner. Crespi accordingly produced six further canvases, usually dated to 1712, all, like the *Confession*, genre-like in tone and featuring only a few, almost life-size figures. Comments by Zanotti and Luigi Crespi indicate that contemporaries admired the paintings but were nonplussed by the originality of presenting religious subject-matter in terms of contemporary experience. They found it hard to believe that Crespi, so often ready to depict the comic and satirical, was being serious. Hence they interpreted the works as examples of the genre of narrative satire and discovered comic elements (particularly in the *Matrimony*) where a modern viewer can find none.

(v) Later career, 1722–47. After his wife's death (1722), Crespi rarely left his house except to attend daily mass. He became increasingly reclusive and pious for the last 20 years of his life. Altarpieces, which provide the few fixed points in his later chronology, formed the main part of his work, though he continued to paint genre scenes. The two altarpieces he painted for the church of the Gesù in Ferrara (*in situ*) were done, like several others, for a small sum in return for masses for the souls of deceased friends. The

earlier of the two, the *Ecstasy of St Stanislaus Kostka* (1727), executed one year after the Polish saint's canonization, represents a mystic vision experienced by the young Jesuit novitiate. Its balanced composition and relatively diminutive figures are characteristic of his later religious paintings and in contrast to his earlier preference for oblique, dynamic arrangements and figures that fill the frame. His visualization of ecstasy is more mystical than in the *Ecstasy of St Margaret of Cortona*. Vaporous clouds transport the heavenly realm to earth and blur its separation from tangible reality, while the saint, his eyes closed, leans back in the embrace of angels.

In the 1720s Crespi returned to the pastoral mode that he had practised in the first decade of the century. His earlier irreverent treatment of Classical mythology yielded to a new seriousness, evident in his choice and formulation of traditional subjects. A centralized and symmetrically balanced grouping of figures structures *Jupiter among the Corybantes* (see fig. 4). Carefully choreographed poses and gestures, controlled by selective accents of light, lead the viewer's gaze into the painting from the left, around the semicircle of nymphs, to the seated figure at lower right.

4. Giuseppe Maria Crespi: *Jupiter among the Corybantes*, oil on canvas, 1.86×2.15 m, 1728–9 (Stuttgart, Staatsgalerie)

From the 1730s Crespi's religious themes become more violent, focusing in particular on the sufferings of Christ and the saints at the hands of their brutal tormentors, as for example in the *Mocking of Christ* (1735–40; Bologna, Pin. N.). At the end of the 1730s he acquired a new and influential patron and friend in Cardinal Prospero Lambertini, archbishop of Bologna in 1731, who referred to him as 'suo pittore della mensa arcivescovile'. Crespi prepared the Cardinal's portrait in a lively oil sketch (1739; Bologna, Pal. Com.) that conveys the sitter's intelligence and forceful personality. The finished portrait (1740; Rome, Pin. Vaticana) has Lambertini, who had been elected as Pope Benedict XIV, in appropriately altered vestments and papal tiara. The Pope conferred a knighthood on the painter in 1741.

At the end of his career Crespi reinterpreted his earlier genre-like representation of confession in his *St John of Nepomuk Confessing the Queen of Bohemia* (1743; Turin, Gal. Sabauda), a historic sacred subject commissioned by Charles-Emanuel III, King of Sardinia and 17th Duke of Savoy. In 1745 Crespi suffered a stroke that left him blind for the last two years of his life. He was buried in the church of the Confraternity of St Mary Magdalene, Bologna.

2. WORKING METHODS AND TECHNIQUE. Trained in the traditional workshop manner, Crespi was skilled in the technique of both fresco and oil painting, though he received few fresco commissions, possibly because he was unwilling to collaborate with a *quadratura* specialist. Most of his oeuvre is executed in oil on canvas and ranges in size from monumental altarpieces to miniaturist cabinet pictures. Small oils on copper for private patrons (e.g. *Self-portrait with Family*, 1708; 280×240 mm) account for some 15% of his production and are typically on devotional themes, pastoral or genre subjects.

From early in his career Crespi explored painterly devices derived from Venetian pictorial tradition, such as layering coloured glazes to achieve luminous effects. Contrary to contemporary practice he mixed his media, blending water- and oil-based emulsions. For light landscape passages and for flesh tints he even seems on occasion to have used tempera covered with transparent glazes to achieve a porcelain-like translucence. The poor condition of many of his works is due to injudicious attempts at restoration in the past that have removed the final glaze and thereby disturbed the tonal harmony. Works that have escaped this fate (e.g. the two small oils on copper, *Cupids at Play*, 1695–1700; El Paso, TX, Mus. A.) are in excellent condition.

To achieve the extreme contrasts of light and shadow that he often required in his compositions, Crespi built up impasto in the brightest areas and applied pigment thinly in the shadows and half-tones, sometimes exploiting the reddish ground. He veiled the resulting transitions with a final transparent glaze. According to Luigi Crespi, he made a daily practice of observing natural light and used aids, including the camera obscura, for reproducing desired effects in the studio. After his death Crespi was singled out by the Venetian critic Francesco Algarotti (1764) for his pioneering use of this method, for which he darkened a room in his house, inserted a lens into a hole in the door leading outside and placed a canvas opposite the lens at the focal point, so that he could study the effects of light projected from outdoors on to the canvas. His familiarity with the camera obscura probably dates to 1708–12, when scientific experimentation was encouraged in Bologna by General Ferdinando Marsili, who introduced artists, poets and scientists to the latest optical inventions following his return from Holland in 1708. The direct impact on his painting can be seen in *Courtyard Scene* (1710–15; Bologna, Pin. N.), with its 'almost photographic rendering of the crumbling stones' (Merriman, 1980). His fascination with singular lighting effects also led him to set up an overhead light in his studio to reproduce the fall of sunlight from high church windows.

As a young man Crespi attended drawing classes with Cignani and at the Palazzo Ghislieri. According to Luigi Crespi, he continued to draw from life models, and many 18th-century Bolognese collectors possessed examples of his drawings. Few are known nowadays, however, which has posed problems for scholars. Among the handful of sheets that may be associated with paintings, several pen-and-wash drawings on brown ground and roughed out in red chalk (sold London, Christie's, 29 March 1966, lot 164) are preparatory studies for the two frescoed ceilings in the Palazzo Pepoli. The largest surviving group, more interesting for content than for style, consists of nine red chalk studies for a set of prints (c. 1710) to illustrate Croce's *Bertoldo e Bertoldino* (New York, Met.; Stuttgart, Koenig-Fachsenfeld priv. col.; Orléans, Mus. B.-A.; Hamburg, Ksthalle).

With regard to prints, Crespi's early portrayals of craftsmen of Bologna are crudely handled. He returned to printmaking with more success in 1710–15, and the 20 etchings for the *Bertoldo e Bertoldino* series reveal greater mastery of the medium. His plates were later re-etched in a second set by his friend Ludovico Mattioli for the 1736 republication of Croce's book. Crespi's total responsibility for the original set of etchings, although attested to by the sources, has been questioned by Merriman. More recently, the set has been reattributed to Crespi's hand alone and his use of the etching needle characterized as delicate and feathery, reminiscent of contemporary Venetian artists (see 1982 exh. cat.).

Crespi's workshop must have been small, and his assistants were called on to imitate the master's style as closely as possible. His most talented student was Antonio Gionima, who worked in the studio from 1719 until his early death (1732). By c. 1730 Crespi's chief pupils and assistants were his two sons, Luigi and Antonio. Their faithful adoption of their father's figural types, repertory of gesture and classicizing compositions obscures the certain attribution of Crespi's later altarpieces, although Luigi's assistance betrays itself in mechanical repetition, the dilution of expression and a hardening of forms.

BIBLIOGRAPHY

G. Zanotti: *Storia dell'Accademia Clementina di Bologna*, ii (Bologna, 1739), pp. 31–73

F. Algarotti: *Saggio sopra la pittura* (Livorno, 1764), p. 62

L. Crespi: *Felsina pittrice: Vite de' pittori bolognesi, tomo terzo* (Rome, 1769), pp. 201–32

M. Marangoni: 'Giuseppe Maria Crespi detto lo Spagnolo', *Dedalo*, i (1920–21), pp. 575–91, 647–68

C. Gnudi: 'Sebastiano Mazzoni e le origini del Crespi', *Com. Bologna*, i (1935), pp. 18–36 [Ven. sources]

Three Baroque Masters: Strozzi, Crespi, Piazzetta (exh. cat. by H. Tietze, Baltimore, MD, Mus. A., 1944)

Mostra celebrativa di Giuseppe Maria Crespi (exh. cat. by F. Arcangeli and C. Gnudi, Bologna, Pal. Com., 1948) [first monographic exh.]

F. Arcangeli: 'Nature morte di Giuseppe Maria Crespi', *Paragone*, iii/25 (1952), pp. 20–32

C. Volpe: 'Antefatti bolognesi ed inizi di Giuseppe Maria Crespi', *Paragone*, viii/91 (1957), pp. 25–37

F. Haskell: *Patrons and Painters* (London, 1963, rev. New Haven and London, 1980)

A. M. Matteucci: *Giuseppe Maria Crespi*, Maestri Colore, xcii (Milan, 1965) [good illustrations]

J. Bean: 'Drawings by Giuseppe Maria Crespi', *Master Drgs*, iv (1966), pp. 419–21

M. P. Merriman: 'Two Late Works by Giuseppe Maria Crespi', *Burl. Mag.*, cx (1968), pp. 120–25

Natura ed espressione nell'arte bolognese-emiliana (exh. cat. by F. Arcangeli, Bologna, Pal. Archiginnasio, 1970)

P. Rosenberg: 'La Femme à la puce de G. M. Crespi', *Rev. Louvre*, xxi (1971), pp. 13–20

M. Chiarini: 'La data esatta dell'Estasi di S Margherita da Cortona di G. M. Crespi', *A. Illus.*, vii (1973), pp. 385–6

A. Emiliani, ed.: *Le collezioni d'arte della Cassa di Risparmio in Bologna: I disegni: I. Dal cinquecento al neoclassicismo* (Bologna, 1973)

R. Roli: 'Disegni di Giuseppe Maria Crespi per la serie incisoria delle "Storie di Bertoldo"', *Atti & Mem. Accad. Clementina Bologna*, xi (1974), pp. 1–6

M. Liebmann: *Giuseppe Maria Crespi* (Dresden, 1976)

M. P. Merriman: 'Giuseppe Maria Crespi's *Jupiter among the Corybantes*', *Burl. Mag.*, cxviii (1976), pp. 464–73

R. Roli: *Pittura bolognese, 1650–1800: Dal Cignani al Gandolfi* (Bologna, 1977) [contemp. Bologn. context]

L'arte del settecento emiliano: La pittura: L'Accademia Clementina (exh. cat. by A. Emiliani and others, Bologna, Pal. Podestà, 1979)

M. P. Merriman: *Giuseppe Maria Crespi* (Milan, 1980) [with cat.]; review by D. Miller in *A. Bull.*, lxvii (1985), pp. 339–42

F. Petrucci: 'La ragione trionfante alla corte medicea: Il Gran Principe Ferdinando e Giuseppe Maria Crespi', *Artibus & Hist.*, v (1982), pp. 109–23

Bolognese Drawings in North American Collections, 1500–1800 (exh. cat. by M. Cazort and C. Johnston, Ottawa, N.G., 1982)

M. P. Merriman: 'Additions to Giuseppe Maria Crespi's Oeuvre', *Paragone*, xxxvi/419, 421, 423 (1985), pp. 253–7

D. Dwyer and M. Modestini: 'Rapporto sui Crespi esposti in Texas', *G.A.*, xl (1986), pp. 31–2 [on artist's tech. by two restorers]

The Age of Correggio and the Carracci: Emilian Painting of the Sixteenth and Seventeenth Centuries (exh. cat., Washington, DC, N.G.A.; New York, Met.; Bologna, Pin. N.; 1986)

Giuseppe Maria Crespi and the Emergence of Genre Painting in Italy (exh. cat., ed. J. T. Spike; Fort Worth, Kimbell A. Mus., 1986)

CATHERINE R. PUGLISI

(2) Luigi Crespi (*b* Bologna, 23 Jan 1708; *d* Bologna, 2 July 1779). Writer, art dealer and painter, son of (1) Giuseppe Maria Crespi. Like his father, he painted portraits, although he favoured a style that was more fashionable and 'international' than that of Giuseppe Maria. He is alleged to have imitated his father's genre and religious paintings in order to sell them as works by the latter. He was a member of several art academies (Florence, Parma and Venice) but was never admitted to the Accademia Clementina in Bologna. As an art dealer he was one of the earliest to promote the trade in Emilian 15th-century paintings. His most important client was Augustus III, King of Saxony and Poland, for whose gallery in Dresden he secured Francesco del Cossa's *Annunciation* (1473) and the predella associated with this altarpiece by Ercole de' Roberti, depicting scenes from the life of *St Vincent Ferrer* (1473; Rome, Pin. Vaticana). There are several letters by Crespi on art, collecting, restoration and art literature in Giovanni Gaetano Bottari's *Raccolta di lettere*, for which he also tracked down lost documents and secured contributions from other writers. Under Bottari's protection he published his most notorious book, *Felsina pittrice: Vite de' pittori bolognesi, tomo terzo* (1769), using it as a vehicle to express his resentment of certain contemporary Bolognese artists and to criticize the didactic methods of the Accademia Clementina. The hostile reaction to it provoked his defence, *Dialoghi di un amatore della verità* (1770). His subsequent continual engagement in controversy finally alienated Bottari and provoked an attack from Giovanni Lodovico Bianconi (published in 1802, after the death of its author). His most interesting projects remained unpublished: he supervised a series of guidebooks to minor towns in central Italy, planned to publish reproductions of the most famous altarpieces in Bologna (with a commentary) and prepared an annotated edition of Girolamo Baruffaldi's *Vite dei pittori ferraresi* (MS. 177?; Bologna, Bib. Com. Archiginnasio, B 77) and a general catalogue of Filippo Hercolani's collection of paintings (MS. 1774; Bologna, Bib. Com. Archiginnasio, B 384, pt 2).

WRITINGS

G. Bottari, ed.: *Raccolta di lettere sulla pittura, scultura ed architettura*, ii–iv (Rome, 1757–64) [incl. corr. by Luigi Crespi]

Felsina pittrice: Vite de' pittori bolognesi, tomo terzo (Rome, 1769)

Dialoghi di un amatore della verità in difesa del terzo tomo della Felsina pittrice (Bologna, 1770)

La Certosa di Bologna descritta nelle sue pitture (Bologna, 1772)

BIBLIOGRAPHY

DBI [incl. bibliog. to 1983]

G. L. Bianconi: *Otto lettere riguardanti il così detto terzo tomo della Felsina pittrice del Cav. Luigi Crespi* (Milan, 1802)

R. Roli: *Pittura bolognese, 1650–1800: Dal Cignani ai Gandolfi* (Bologna, 1977), pp. 108, 145–7, 171–3, 179, 216 [incl. good bibliog.]

S. Prosperi Valenti Rodinò: 'Le lettere di Luigi Crespi a Giovanni Gaetano Bottari nella Biblioteca Corsiniana', *Paragone*, xxxv/407 (1984), pp. 22–50

G. Perini: 'Luigi Crespi inedito', *Il Carrobbio*, xi (1985), pp. 236–61

GIOVANNA PERINI

Crespi, Cristoforo Benigno (*b* Busto Arsizio, 18 Oct 1833; *d* Milan, 5 Jan 1920). Italian businessman and collector. His family owned a successful cotton-spinning business, which Crespi and his four younger brothers inherited and ran as a flourishing concern. With the help of such friends as the art historian Giovanni Morelli and the painter Giuseppe Bertini, who was also curator of the Accademia di Belle Arti di Brera and the Museo Poldi Pezzoli, Crespi created one of the finest private collections of turn-of-the-century Milan and displayed it on the first floor of his palazzo at 18 Via Borgonuovo. An illustrated catalogue by Adolfo Venturi, published in 1900, shows that the collection included a wide range of Italian art from the 16th to the 18th century. Lombard painters were particularly well represented, with paintings, for example, by Giovanni Antonio Boltraffio, Daniele Crespi and Luigi Crespi (ii). Examples of Venetian painting included a *Risen Christ* (Florence, Contini-Bonacossi priv. col., see Wethey, p. 177, cat. no. X-31) by Palma il Vecchio, four views of the Grand Canal by Canaletto and his studio, and a *Blessed Ludwina* (untraced, see Morassi, p. 27 and fig. 425) by Giambattista Tiepolo. There were several examples of Dutch 17th-century painting. The family decided to sell the collection in 1910, when the business ran into financial difficulties. Some of the paintings, including Correggio's *Nativity* (1512; Milan, Brera), Domenico Morone's *Expulsion of the Bonacolsi in 1328* (1494; Mantua, Gal. & Mus. Pal. Ducale) and Francesco Granacci's *Entry of Charles VIII into Florence* (Florence, Uffizi), were offered to state collections. The remaining 185 pictures were sold by Georges Petit in Paris on 6 June 1914.

DBI

BIBLIOGRAPHY
A. Venturi: *La Galleria Crespi in Milano* (Milan, 1900)
C. E. Pirovano: *Il Palazzo Crespi in Milano* (Milan and Rome, [1928])
A. Morassi: *A Complete Catalogue of the Paintings of G. B. Tiepolo* (London, 1962)
H. W. Wethey: *The Paintings of Titian, I: The Religious Paintings* (London, 1969)

JANET SOUTHORN

Crespi, Daniele (*b* ?Milan, 1597–1600; *d* Milan, 19 July 1630). Italian painter and draughtsman. He was the most original artist working in Milan in the 1620s, the first to break with the wilfully exaggerated manner of Lombard Mannerism and to develop an early Baroque style, distinguished by clarity of form and content. In this context his *Supper of St Carlo Borromeo* (Milan, S Maria della Passione; see fig. 1 below) is one of the most famous early 17th-century pictures in northern Italy. Crespi's style, both as a painter and as a draughtsman, is a fusion of Lombard and Emilian sources.

In the Milanese census of 1610 Crespi was listed as a ten-year-old living with his family in the parish of S Eufemia. The family is thought to have come from Busto Arsizio, north of Milan, but Daniele may have been born in the Lombard capital; certainly his education should be considered Milanese. His teacher is unknown, but in 1619 Crespi was already described as a promising painter (Borsieri) and is documented (Delfinone) as working with Guglielmo Caccia, called Moncalvo, in S Vittore al Corpo, Milan. Moncalvo frescoed *Sibyls and Angels* (1617) in the cupola of the church; the *Four Evangelists* in the pendentives are traditionally attributed to Daniele. These heavily restored frescoes of rather awkward muscular figures have little in common with Moncalvo's style and, in their present state, are awkwardly Emilian in character. More significant for understanding Crespi's later development are the three canvases of scenes from the *Life of St Anthony* and his fresco decorations (*c.* 1619) in the chapel of S Antonio in the same church. These pictures are typical of a young painter grappling with the style of his elders; the large, rhythmic and rather flat forms reflect a study of the work of Giovanni Battista Crespi, called Cerano, and particularly of Giulio Cesare Procaccini. Other early works, such as the frescoes of the *Four Evangelists* in the pendentives of the chapel of the Annunciation in S Eustorgio, Milan (1621; the altarpiece, the *Annunciation*, was found in S Maria del Paradiso, Milan), and the fresco of the *Adoration of the Magi* (*c.* 1621) in the sacristy of S Alessandro, Milan, display similar features. The *Adoration* reworks an *Adoration of the Magi* by Cerano (ex-Parish Church, Pusiano, destr. 1943); the frescoes in S Eustorgio are indebted to Cerano, Procaccini and the Emilian followers of Correggio.

1. Daniele Crespi: *Supper of St Carlo Borromeo*, oil on canvas, ?early 1620s or *c.* 1628 (Milan, S Maria della Passione)

In 1623 Crespi received the first of two payments (the second was in 1626) for painting part of a frieze in S Maria di Campagna, Piacenza. The chapel of S Giovanni Battista, formerly in S Protasio ad Monachos, Milan, also dates from 1623. The altarpiece, *St John the Baptist Preaching in the Desert*, two lateral canvases, *St John Pointing to Christ* and the *Infant St John in the Wilderness*, and two detached frescoes, *St Bartholomew* and *St James* (all Busto Arsizio, S Giovanni Battista), with their stark, simple narratives and new clarity of form, mark the point at which Crespi abandoned the formal, rhythmic exaggerations of his earlier work. Gregori has suggested that this change of style may have been inspired by a trip to Rome. Certainly, Crespi's contact with Piacenza must have been relevant, for there he would have seen work, now scattered, by Giovanni Lanfranco. It is clear from his paintings of St John the Baptist that Crespi admired Lanfranco's combination of Emilian clarity and Caravaggesque naturalism and chiaroscuro.

Crespi drew on a wide range of Lombard and Emilian sources, and the chronology of his oeuvre is hard to determine. The remarkable works painted for S Maria della Passione, Milan, probably date also from the early 1620s. A set of organ shutters for the south organ depict *Christ Washing the Feet of the Disciples* when closed; when open they show the *Raising of the Cross* and the *Deposition*. The latter, single, compositions crowd the tall and narrow shutters with passionate and intensely dramatic figures; they are intelligent reconsiderations of Lombard sources. By contrast, the *Christ Washing the Feet of the Disciples* is a stark, architecturally ordered presentation. Less secure is an early dating for the *Supper of St Carlo Borromeo*, a large picture painted for the same church (*in situ*; see fig. 1). This, painted in simple blacks, reds and whites, shows a steeply foreshortened room containing a strikingly immediate image of the saint, seated alone at a table. Two figures in the background are amazed to see his frugal meal, and the viewer, coming on the saint from the opposite direction, seems also to be a secret witness to his austerity. Parallels have been drawn between this painting and the work of Francisco de Zurbarán, but no direct contact between the two artists has been demonstrated.

Crespi's other works of the 1620s never achieved this pitch of psychological tension. The *Martyrdom of St Mark* (1626; Novara, S Marco) is again based on Milanese models; it is the logical, reformed continuation of such large pictures as Cerano's *Baptism of St Augustine* and Camillo Procaccini's *SS Ambrose and Augustine Disputing* (both 1618; Milan, S Marco). Throughout the 1620s Crespi's production continued to be prolific. Such works as the *Road to Calvary* (Milan, Brera), the *Entombment* (Budapest, Mus. F.A.) and the *Pietà* (Madrid, Prado) are possibly from the middle of the decade. The last two are remarkably indebted to the melting, emotional tenor of Giulio Cesare Procaccini's work. Other altarpieces, probably from the very end of the 1620s (*DBI*), are grander and more classical. These include the *Last Supper* (Milan, Brera), the *Coronation of the Virgin* (Modena, Gal. & Mus. Estense), the *Baptism* (Milan, Brera; see fig. 2) and the *Virgin and Child with SS Francis and Carlo Borromeo* (Milan, Brera).

2. Daniele Crespi: *Baptism*, oil on canvas, 2.04×1.34 m, late 1620s (Milan, Pinacoteca di Brera)

In 1629 Crespi completed a large fresco cycle for the Carthusian Order in the nave of the Certosa di Garegnano. A year later, in 1630, he painted a second, larger cycle for the same Order in the apse and choir of the Certosa di Pavia, where there is also an altarpiece by the artist, *Christ in Glory with Ten Saints*, dedicated in 1628. According to Gregori, Crespi may have been working for the Order for some time, possibly since 1626. The frescoes, among the first artistic results of the Carthusian reorganization in the 1620s, are painted in light, almost pastel colours. Along the nave and entrance wall of the Certosa di Garegnano are seven scenes from the *Life of St Bruno*, the founder of the Carthusians, and full-length portraits of monks and nuns. The ceiling is elaborately divided into hexagonal fields with representations of the *Resurrected Christ*, the *Magdalene in Glory*, the *Sacrifice of Isaac* and *St John the Baptist*. The figures are further divided from one another by bands of half-length portraits of Carthusians and triangular fields of angels. Crespi placed the events of St Bruno's life in the context of the saints of the Order and of sacred figures representing the Carthusian virtues: sacrifice, obedience and contemplation. His artistic sources are those that always inspired him: Cerano, Giulio Cesare Procaccini and Lanfranco. His art is close to that of Alessandro Tiarini, a painter whose work Crespi would have known and, in the case of the Carthusian cycles, to

Vicente Carducho's paintings (1626–32; e.g. Madrid, Prado) for the charterhouse at El Paular, near Segovia, though direct contact with the latter has not been demonstrated. The frescoes Crespi made for the Certosa di Pavia are increasingly monumental and simplified, close in style to the late altarpieces. The cycle, presumably begun in the spring of 1629, is iconographically more complex than that at Garegnano and includes scenes from the *Life of Christ* (the *Christ Disputing in the Temple* is dated 1630) below those from the *Life of St Bruno*. In June 1630 Crespi left Pavia to return to his family in Milan, where plague had broken out. He perished in the epidemic, along with his mother, wife and two sons.

Crespi was also well known as a portrait painter. Though much work on attribution and identification remains to be done, it is documented that his portraits were sought after and that he was admired by learned patrons. In 1625 Sigismondo Boldoni, professor of philosophy at the University of Pavia, wrote to request Alessandro Monti's help in procuring a reduced version of one of Crespi's portraits (Sparrow). That the artist moved in scholarly circles is also suggested by the inventory of his books made after his death, which shows that he possessed all the standard late 16th-century treatises on art.

Unlike most of the Lombards, Daniele often made preparatory drawings for his paintings. A number of compositional studies survive as do studies of details and single figures. Such a method of working is typical of the academies in Bologna and central Italy and constitutes a significant link between Crespi and the Emilian early Baroque. Some of his drawings have been attributed to Emilian painters, such as Alessandro Tiarini or even Correggio, though others have been identified under the names of Giulio Cesare Procaccini and Morazzone.

UNPUBLISHED SOURCE

Milan, Archv Stato, fondo religione, registri 43, i, MS. 1679 [G. A. Delfinone: *Il copioso et esatto regestro del grade archivio del insigne monastero di S Vittore al Corpo*]

BIBLIOGRAPHY

DBI

G. Borsieri: *Il supplimento alla nobiltà di Milano* (Milan, 1619)

L. Lanzi: *Storia pittorica della Italia* (Bassano, 1795–6); ed. M. Capucci, 2 vols (Florence, 1970)

V. Forcella: *Iscrizioni delle chiese e degli altri edifici di Milano dal secolo VIII ai giorni nostri*, 13 vols (Milan, 1889–90)

G. Nicodemi: *Daniele Crespi* (Busto Arsizio, 1914, rev. 2/1930) [the only monograph, now out of date]

F. R. Pesenti: *La Certosa di Pavia* (Milan, 1968), pp. 83–113

U. Ruggeri: 'Per Daniele Crespi', *Crit. A.*, xv/93 (1968), pp. 45–56; xv (1968), pp. 43–58

J. Sparrow: 'Daniele Crespi: Portraits Lost and Identified?', *A. Lombarda*, xiii/2 (1968), pp. 63–6

N. W. Neilson: 'A Source for Daniele Crespi', *A. Lombarda*, xiv/1 (1969), pp. 71–4

M. Gregori: *Affreschi della Certosa di Garegnano* (Modena, 1973)

N. W. Neilson: 'Some Drawings by Daniele Crespi', *Burl. Mag.*, cxv (1973), pp. 382–5

Il seicento lombardo: Catalogo dei dipinti e delle sculture (exh. cat., ed. M. Valsecchi; Milan, Pal. Reale, 1973)

Il seicento lombardo: Catalogo dei disegni, libri, stampe (exh. cat., ed. G. Bora; Milan, Ambrosiana, 1973)

U. Ruggeri: 'Nuovi disegni di Daniele Crespi', *A. Lombarda*, xl (1974), pp. 101–9

Lombard Paintings, c. 1595–c. 1630: The Age of Federico Borromeo (exh. cat., ed. P. Cannon-Brookes; Birmingham, Mus. & A.G., 1974)

H. Brigstocke: 'G. C. Procaccini et D. Crespi: Nouvelles découvertes', *Rev. A.* [Paris], xlviii (1980), pp. 30–39

L. Turčić: 'Putti by Daniele Crespi for Pavia', *Master Drgs*, xix/1 (1981), pp. 23–5

G. Bora: 'Ruolo e significato del disegno in Daniele Crespi', *Fra rinascimento, manierismo e realtà: Scritti di storia dell'arte in memoria di A. M. Brizio* (Florence, 1984), pp. 157–66

F. M. Ferro: 'I quadroni della chiesa di San Marco a Novara, I: Daniele Crespi e Francesco Carloni a confronto', *Paragone*, xxxvii/441 (1986), pp. 64–71

G. Pacciarotti: *Il pittore Daniele Crespi* (Busto Arsizio, 1988)

G. Bora: 'Daniele Crespi', *Pinacoteca di Brera: Scuole lombarda, ligure e piemontese, 1535–1796* (Milan, 1989), pp. 204–21

Daniele Crespi nelle raccolte private (exh. cat. by G. Testori and F. Frangi, Busto Arsizio, 1989)

N. W. Neilson: 'Daniele Crespi's *Annunciation* for S Eustorgio, Milan', *A. Lombarda*, n.s., 102–3 (1992–4), pp. 42–4

NANCY WARD NEILSON

Crespi, Giovanni Battista. *See* CERANO.

Crespin, Paul (*b* London, 1694; *d* Southampton, 25 Jan 1770). English goldsmith. He was the son of French Huguenot refugees who had settled in England in 1687. Apprenticed in June 1713 to Jean Pons, he entered his first marks between July 1720 and December 1721 and established a workshop in Old Compton Street, Soho, London, close to that of NICHOLAS SPRIMONT. During the 1720s Crespin's reputation grew rapidly, and he attracted a number of commissions from the Portuguese court. An early example of his chasing skill can be seen on a cruet stand (1721; Colonial Williamsburg, VA), the rim of which is decorated with hunting scenes. Although brought up in England, he corresponded with clients in French and was aware of, and responsive to, stylistic developments in France. The silver gilt ice buckets (1732; Blenheim Pal., Oxon), for example, which he made for Charles Spencer, 3rd Duke of Marlborough (1706–58), relate closely to a Parisian engraving published in the 1720s. He maintained a high standard of workmanship and was an innovative designer, one of the few English goldsmiths to adopt the Rococo manner as early as the mid-1730s. His clients included Robert Walpole, 1st Earl of Orford, and many English aristocratic families to whom he supplied table services, ornate centrepieces, two-handled cups, tureens, candlesticks and such smaller items as spice-boxes. Among the most remarkable of these items are the tureen and salver (1741; Toledo, OH, Mus. A.) made for Charles Seymour, 6th Duke of Somerset, executed at the peak of his career. The tureen is majestically supported on the backs of two goats amid a profusion of fruits. Crespin may have collaborated with Sprimont on a silver gilt centrepiece made for Frederick, Prince of Wales (1741; London, Brit. Royal Col., Buckingham Palace). He retired in 1759 and moved to Southampton.

BIBLIOGRAPHY

C. Lever: *Goldsmiths and Silversmiths of England* (London, 1975)

A. Grimwade: *London Goldsmiths, 1697–1837* (London, 1976, rev. 1990)

P. Glanville: *Silver in England* (London, 1987)

☐

Cressant [Cresant; Cressent; Croisant], **Jacob** (*b* ?Abbeville, Somme; *fl* 1714–56). French sculptor, active in the northern Netherlands. His earliest known works are two signed and very elegant Louis XIV garden vases decorated with allegories of the seasons (1714; Amsterdam, Rijksmus.); they were commissioned by David van Mollem

150   Cressant, Jacob

(1670–1746), a silk merchant, who was laying out a fine garden for the country house on his estate of Zijdebalen, near Utrecht. Cressant's name is first mentioned in Utrecht c. 1730–31 in connection with his statue of *Justice* for the Stadhuis; it is now in the Paleis van Justitie in Utrecht. The many commissions for garden sculpture that Cressant received from van Mollem probably account for his settling in Utrecht: other artists who made sculptures and vases for these gardens are Jan-Baptiste Xavery, Jan van der Mast (*fl c.* 1736) and J. Matthijsen. Cressant made for van Mollem, among other things, vases, putti and a wooden *Neptune*: very little of this work survives.

In 1736 Cressant applied to become a citizen of Utrecht, having lived there for eight years. In that same year he was admitted to the Guild of St Luke without having submitted a masterpiece. In 1740 he made powerful and realistic terracotta busts of *David van Mollem* (Utrecht, Cent. Mus.) and his kinsman *Hendrik Grave* (untraced). In 1741 he made for the city of Utrecht two coats-of-arms in stone (both untraced). By 1742 Cressant was living in Amsterdam, having moved there probably in search of new commissions, now that the Zijdebalen gardens were finished. He was registered as a citizen in 1743 and in that year submitted a masterpiece—a wooden figure of a woman—to the Guild of St Luke. Before 1745 van Mollem commissioned him to make four terracotta portrait busts of Utrecht professors; they were remarkably realistic, and van Mollem donated them to Utrecht University (Rijksuniv. Utrecht, Umus.).

In 1746 Cressant completed a large marble statue representing *Neptune* for the Hôtel Champbel-Beau-Séjour in Geneva (terracotta model, Amsterdam, Col. Six; variant version, Amsterdam, Rijksmus.). The following year he made four of a set of twelve gilded lead putti for the gardens of Schloss Wilhelmstal near Kassel; a signed terracotta group representing *Charity* (Kassel, Hess. Landesmus.) dates from roughly the same time. Cressant made many small terracottas, ten of which were in the sale catalogue of the collection of Gerrit Braamcamp (31 July 1771).

While in Amsterdam, Cressant made a number of wood sculptures for the church of St Anne (de Pool), the French church in Amsterdam: *St Peter* and *St Paul*, a head of *God the Father* and the *Lamb of God* (Amsterdam, Mus. Amstelkring). These powerful late Baroque figures were probably intended for an altar. In 1750 he made a marble chimney-piece for Amsterdam's Stadhuis, now the Koninklijk Paleis (Royal Palace). In 1751 he designed the model for the splendid white marble pulpit of the Grote Kerk in Dordrecht: the actual pulpit was executed by Asmus Frauen (*fl c.* 1756), probably because Cressant had left for Paris, where he had been appointed assistant professor at the Académie de St Luc. He entered work for exhibitions at the Académie in 1753 and 1756. Cressant was the most important sculptor in Utrecht in the first 40 years of the 18th century. After his move to Amsterdam he filled the gap created by the death of Jan van Logteren, gaining many commissions from private individuals and Roman Catholic churches. His son, Jacob Matheus Cressant (1732–94), was also a sculptor.

BIBLIOGRAPHY

J. Knoef: 'De beeldhouwer Jacobus Cresant', *Oud-Holland*, lviii (1941), pp. 169–77
Het beeld in de Nederlandse barok [Sculpture at the time of the Dutch Baroque] (exh. cat. by F. Haks, Utrecht, Aartsbisschoppelijk Mus., 1963), nos 16, 17
J. Leeuwenberg and W. Halsema-Kubes: *Beeldhouwkunst in het Rijksmuseum: Catalogus* [Sculpture in the Rijksmuseum: a catalogue] (The Hague and Amsterdam, 1973), no. 393–4
Zijdebalen: Lusthof aan de Vecht [Zijdebalen: pleasure garden by the Vecht] (exh. cat. by E. de Jong, D. P. Snoep and P. J. M. van Gorp, Utrecht, Cent. Mus., 1981), nos 59–65 and pp. 3, 9, 32, 34, 40, 58, 64 and 76
J. van Cauteren: 'De beelden van het hoofdaltaar uit de voormalige Franse kerk te Amsterdam' [The sculptures of the high altar in the former French church in Amsterdam], *Antiek*, xix (1984–5), pp. 524–30

WILHELMINA HALSEMA-KUBES

Cressent, Charles (*b* Amiens, 16 Dec 1685; *d* Paris, 10 Jan 1768). French cabinetmaker and sculptor. He was taught by his father, François Cressent, a sculptor in Amiens, and became a *maître-ébéniste* on 9 January 1708. He subsequently became a pupil of François Girardon and became a *maître sculpteur* in the Académie de Saint-Luc, Paris, on 14 August 1714. He obtained the title of Ebéniste du Régent in 1719, which allowed him to trade as a cabinetmaker free from guild restrictions. The richest French patrons, the Portuguese Court and many German princes bought furniture from him. His work is of exceptional quality and epitomizes the Régence and early Louis XV styles, to which he remained faithful throughout his career. The forms of his pieces were perfectly curved and rendered sumptuous by abundant, virtuoso bronze mounts and emphatically serrated agraffe ornaments and mouldings. His lavish mounts to some extent obscured the restrained veneering or geometric marquetry, for which he almost always used rose-wood, purple-wood or satinwood. Above all, however, he was a sculptor, and he contravened guild restrictions by modelling the bronzes that adorn his furniture himself; these included terminals depicting the *Four Continents* (e.g. book-cabinet; Lisbon, Mus. Gulbenkian), *Child Musicians* (e.g. commode) and *Seated Women Holding Cornucopias* (e.g. commode; both Munich, Residenzmus.), all *c.* 1740. These figures were combined with vegetation consisting of palms, vines and garlands of flowers, which emphasized the furniture's contours. He also mounted furniture with busts of *Mars* (e.g. desk, *c.* 1740; Paris, Louvre) and *espagnolette* heads (female head surrounded by a stiff ruff; e.g. commode, *c.* 1730; London, Wallace). He also made many, predominantly bronze, cartel-clocks, the most remarkable of which depicts the theme of *Love Conquering Time* (*c.* 1747; London, Wallace).

For an illustration of Cressent's work *see* RÉGENCE STYLE.

BIBLIOGRAPHY

M. J. Ballot: 'Charles Cressent, sculpteur, ébéniste et collectionneur', *Archvs A. Fr.*, x (1919) [whole issue]
J. Viaux: *Bibliographie du meuble (Mobilier civil français)*, 2 vols (Paris, 1966–88)
T. Dell: 'The Gilt Bronze Cartel Clocks of Charles Cressent', *Burl. Mag.*, cix/4 (1967), pp. 210–15
J. D. Augarde: 'Charles Cressent et Jacques Confesseur', *L'Estampille*, cxcv (1986), pp. 54–8

JEAN-DOMINIQUE AUGARDE

Cresti, Domenico. *See* PASSIGNANO, DOMENICO.

Creswell, H(arold) B(ulkeley) (*b* 16 May 1869; *d* 7 July 1960). English architect and writer. He was articled in the large London office of Sir Aston Webb, worked as an architect for the Post Office and then in 1900 established his own practice in Rugby. His design for the Queensferry Turbine Factory, Clwyd (1901), a flat-roofed building with horizontal strip windows separated by battered buttresses, was described by Nikolaus Pevsner as a rare English precursor of Functionalism. Creswell worked for the government during World War I and afterwards gained a post in London as an architectural and engineering consultant with the Crown Agents for the Colonies in addition to running a private practice until the end of the 1920s. He also took up architectural journalism, and it is as a humourist that he is best known. In 1929 he published *The Honeywood File*, an imaginary correspondence between the architect James Spinlove, his client Sir Leslie Brash and the builder John Grigblay. Spinlove, a young and inexperienced architect, is struggling to make his mark with a commission for a businessman's private house. The letters are interspersed with a world-weary commentary pointing to Spinlove's bad management and speculating on how various pitfalls might have been avoided. Creswell highlighted the failure of communication between Spinlove and Sir Leslie, revealing fundamental truths about the conflicts of interest and attitudes between architect and client. Creswell wrote a sequel in the same vein and several other books, but it is the *Honeywood File* that endures as a classic of its type.

WRITINGS

The Honeywood File: An Adventure in Building (London, 1929)
The Honeywood Settlement: A Continuation of the Honeywood File (London, 1930)
Jago v Swillerton & Toomer (London, 1931)
Diary from a Dustbin (London, 1935)
Grig (London, 1942)
Grig in Retirement (London, 1943)

BIBLIOGRAPHY

N. Pevsner: 'Nine Swallows—No Summer', *Archit. Rev.* [London], xci (1942), pp. 109–127
Obituary, *Builder*, cxcix/6113 (1960), p. 108
A. Saint: *The Images of the Architect* (New Haven, 1983), pp. 98–104

LOUIS HELLMAN

Creswell, K(eppel) A(rchibald) C(ameron) (*b* London, 13 Sept 1879; *d* Acton, 8 April 1974). English historian of Islamic architecture. Born in modest circumstances, Creswell attended Westminster School, where he was active in science and mathematics, and the City and Guilds Technical College at Finsbury, where he studied electrical engineering. He became fascinated with the Orient and specifically the Islamic world, gathering systematic notes on every known monument. In 1913 and 1914 his first publications dealt with domes in Iran, concentrating on their 'origin' and 'evolution', two terms that became essential concerns of his later work. He applied for a job in the Archaeological Survey of India, but World War I intervened, and he went to Egypt in April 1916 as a member of the Royal Flying Corps. In July 1919 he was appointed Inspector of Monuments in the area (occupied by the British Army) that had formerly been Ottoman territory. With the forceful energy that stayed with him until his early nineties, he traversed Syria and Palestine,

measuring buildings, recording their condition and photographing them. Out of his Syrian experience, Creswell made plans for a history of the Muslim architecture of Egypt, and after his demobilization found a patron in Fu'ad I (*reg* 1917–36) of Egypt. He returned to Cairo on 13 October 1920, where he stayed for 53 years. He was associated with Cairo University and, after the 1956 Suez crisis, with the American University in Cairo, where his extraordinary library is preserved. He was known less as a teacher than as an institution, the one individual who had walked and understood every street and alley of Cairo and for whom all architectural remains in the Muslim world became a sacred cause. He was one of the most vocal members of the Committee for the Conservation of Monuments of Arab Art in Cairo.

An extraordinary personality, Creswell was opinionated and prejudiced and his patriotism childishly chauvinistic, yet his passion for Islamic architecture, the monuments of Cairo and almost all other aspects of Islamic art was so thorough that the Egyptian government did not require his departure from Egypt in 1956 when nearly all other French and British nationals were compelled to leave. He published a huge bibliography of Islamic art and enormous volumes on Islamic architecture. In this meticulous series, monographs on individual monuments are set in a rigid chronology with occasional excurses into such issues as function or the origin of a type of dome. Causality is defined by chronology, and style and quality are measurable. His matter-of-fact positivism stopped short of the imaginative visions of architecture that were developed by others, and he took refuge in an archaeology of building from which architecture was absent and which saw virtue in the thorough and prosaic recording in two dimensions of everything that remained. Although he failed to inspire, his work will probably outlast that of his more gifted contemporaries.

WRITINGS

'A Brief Chronology of the Muhammadan Monuments of Egypt to AD 1517', *Bull. Inst. Fr. Archéol. Orient.*, xvi (1919), pp. 39–164
Map of Cairo Showing Mohammedan Monuments to AD 1517 (Cairo, 1924)
Early Muslim Architecture: Umayyads, Early 'Abbasids and Tulunids. Pt. I: Umayyads, A.D. 622–750 (Oxford, 1932; rev. 1969 in 2 vols/R New York, 1979)
Early Muslim Architecture: Umayyads, Early 'Abbasids and Tulunids, Pt. 2: Early 'Abbasids, Umayyads of Cordova, Aghlabids, Tulunids, and Samanids, A.D. 751–905 (Oxford, 1940/R New York, 1979)
'The Lawfulness of Painting in Early Islam', *A. Islam.*, xi–xii (1946), pp. 159–66
The Muslim Architecture of Egypt. I. Ikhshids and Fatimids, A.D. 939–1171 (Oxford, 1952/R New York, 1978)
'Fortification in Islam before A.D. 1250', *Proc. Brit. Acad.*, xxxviii (1952), pp. 89–125
A Short Account of Early Muslim Architecture (Harmondsworth, 1958/R Beirut, 1968, rev. Aldershot, 1989)
The Muslim Architecture of Egypt. II. Ayyubids and Early Bahrite Mamluks, A.D. 1171–1326 (Oxford, 1959/R New York 1978)
Bibliography of the Architecture, Arts and Crafts of Islam to 1st Jan 1960 (Cairo, 1961/R Vaduz, 1978); *Supplement Jan 1968 to Jan 1972* (Cairo, 1973); *Second Supplement Jan 1972 to Dec 1980 (with omissions from previous years)* by J. D. Pearson (Cairo, 1984)

BIBLIOGRAPHY

Studies in Islamic Art and Architecture in Honour of Professor K. A. C. Creswell (Cairo, 1965), pp. xiv–xix [bibliog. to 1965]
K. Brisch: Obituary, *Kst Orients*, ix (1973–4), pp. 176–82
R. W. Hamilton: Obituary, *Proc. Brit. Acad.*, xl (1974), pp. 3–20; also in *Muqarnas*, viii (1991), 128–36
Muqarnas, viii (1991) [whole issue entitled *K. A. C. Creswell and his Legacy*]

D. M. Reid: 'Cultural Imperialism and Nationalism: The Struggle to Define and Control the Heritage of Arab Art in Egypt', *Int. J. Mid. E. Stud.*, xxiv (1992), pp. 57–76

OLEG GRABAR

Creswick, Thomas (*b* Sheffield, 5 Feb 1811; *d* London, 28 Dec 1869). English painter and etcher. His contributions to the Birmingham Exhibition (*c.* 1826) attracted considerable attention. Arriving in London in 1828, he showed two paintings at the Royal Academy the same year, *Llyn Gwnart, North Wales* and *Storm Coming On—Boats off Caernarvon Castle* (both untraced). He exhibited at the Academy until his death, being elected ARA in 1842 and RA in 1851. He also exhibited at the British Institution (1828–69) and the Birmingham Society of Artists (1829–38).

The paintings of Creswick's formative years (*c.* 1828–40) owe much in style and subject-matter to the work of the 18th- and early 19th-century English landscape painters. He mainly painted scenes in Wales or northern England, invariably including water. After a visit to Ireland in 1836–7, 34 of his Irish landscapes were engraved in Leitch Ritchie's 'Ireland: Romantic and Picturesque', published in Charles Heath's *Picturesque Annual* (London, 1837–8). Creswick became known as a book illustrator and from *c.* 1838 was a member of the Etching Club, for whom he etched many plates, including fifteen for Oliver Goldsmith's the *Deserted Village* (London, 1841) and five for Milton's *L'Allegro* (1859). He also produced etchings for the Art Union of London.

During the 1840s Creswick may have been associated with the artists of THE CLIQUE and abandoned his early, somewhat mannered, style in favour of a more direct response to nature, developing a *plein-air* technique: the *Course of the Greta through Brignal Woods* (1842; untraced) was much praised for its lyricism and truth to nature. *England* and *London Road a Hundred Years Ago* (exh. RA 1847; both untraced) mark the acme of his career. After a brief flirtation with coastal subjects (*Squally Day at the Seaside*, 1848; Rochdale, A.G.), he returned to landscape painting, although his work lost much of its freshness and vitality. Creswick's later paintings often display a mechanical, sentimental response to their subject, owing more in spirit to pastoral mythology (*Mouth of an English River*, 1855; Manchester, C.A.G.) and historical nostalgia (*Relic of Old Times—Barnard Castle*, *c.* 1860; Barnard Castle, Bowes Mus.) than to the realities of contemporary rural life and landscape.

BIBLIOGRAPHY

'British Artists, their Style and Character: Thomas Creswick R.A.', *A. J.* [London], n.s., ii (1856), pp. 141–4

G. Reynolds: *Victorian Painting* (London, 1966), pp. 152, 159 (incl. pl.), 175

J. Maas: *Victorian Painters* (London, 1969), p. 49

NEIL MARCHANT

Cret, Paul (Philippe) (*b* Lyon, 23 Oct 1876; *d* Philadelphia, PA, 8 Sept 1945). French architect, active in America. He first studied architecture at the Ecole des Beaux-Arts in Lyon and then at the Ecole des Beaux-Arts in Paris (1897–1903), where he was in the atelier of Jean-Louis Pascal. After receiving his diploma in 1903 he emigrated to the USA to teach architectural design in Philadelphia at the University of Pennsylvania. He taught there until 1937, when he retired due to ill health, and gained a national reputation as a teacher; Louis I. Kahn was his best-known student. A number of influential French critics taught in the USA in the late 19th century and early 20th, but Cret also achieved prominence as a practising architect and received the Gold Medal of the American Institute of Architects in 1938. His designs, even for those competitions that he entered but did not win, such as for the Nebraska State Capitol (1920), Lincoln, NE, the Kansas City Liberty Memorial (1921) and the Smithsonian Gallery of Art (1939), Washington, DC, furthered his distinctive ideas about typology and style. His writings about the Beaux-Arts method of design and about the possibilities of achieving a modern classicism complement and explicate his buildings and teaching.

Cret's civic buildings, for example the Indianapolis Public Library (1913–17), the Detroit Institute of Arts (1919–27; for illustration *see* DETROIT) and the Pan American Union Building (1907–10) in Washington, DC, are all notable for the hierarchical lucidity of their designs. Following Beaux-Arts conventions, he composed his buildings as a succession of volumes organized on an armature of major and minor axes. He created legible sequences of rooms with subtly varying light, ornament and proportions that prepared visitors for the most important space in the building, the one that characterized each institution.

In keeping with Beaux-Arts theory, Cret saw architectural design as a process in a dialectical evolution of building types. He felt that it was the architect's responsibility to penetrate the complex and contradictory programmes of modern civic clients in order to understand and to make architecturally legible the present state of an institution's development. For example, although American public libraries had formerly been characterized by the prominence of their reading rooms, at the Indianapolis Public Library Cret displaced the reading rooms to the sides of the building and placed, in the central location, a double-storey book delivery room. The giant Doric order of the main façade not only deferred to contemporary American stylistic preferences but, more importantly for Cret, emphasized further the importance of this space, giving it a new prominence that articulated the shift in function of public libraries from reading to lending institutions.

The problem of the appropriate architectural representation for modern public institutions occupied Cret throughout his career, but in the mid-1920s he began to focus equal attention on the issue of the appropriate stylistic language for his time. In response to the argument that new materials and methods of construction had made the historical styles obsolete, Cret proposed the viability of a modern classical style. In bridges, such as the Delaware River Bridge (1920–26), Philadelphia, which he designed with the engineer Ralph Modjeski (1861–1940), he rationalized the form of the stone piers in terms of the forces of tension and compression. In the County Building, Hartford, CT, he developed a modern Greek classicism of unfluted piers to signify the steel frame, thus emphasizing the congruence between modern structure and classical form. His much-publicized Folger Shakespeare Library,

Washington, DC, however, addressed the conventionality of the classical language; the fluted pilaster strips set into the plane of the walls read, like the sculptural plaques beneath them, as independent symbolic elements. In this building the issue is classicism as symbol rather than as structure. Cret's modern classicism may thus be understood as participating in the continuing debate about the origin and cultural function of classicism.

BIBLIOGRAPHY

Macmillan Enc. Architects

J. Harbeson: 'Paul Cret and Architectural Competitions', *J. Soc. Archit. Hist.*, xxv (1966), pp. 305–6

T. B. White: *Paul Philippe Cret: Architect and Teacher* (Philadelphia, 1973)

J. Esherick: 'Architectural Education in the Thirties and Seventies: A Personal View', *The Architect*, ed. S. Kostof (New York, 1977)

D. Van Zanten: 'Le Système des beaux-arts', *Archit. Des.*, xviii (1978), pp. 11–12, 66–79

E. Grossman: 'Paul P. Cret and the Pan American Union Competition', *Modulus* (1982), pp. 30–39

C. McMichael: *Paul Cret at Texas* (Austin, 1983)

E. Grossman: 'Architecture for a Public Client: The Monuments and Chapels of the American Battle Monuments Commission', *J. Soc. Archit. Hist.*, xliii (1984), pp. 119–43

——: 'Two Postwar Competitions: The Nebraska State Capitol and Kansas City Liberty Memorial', *J. Soc. Archit. Hist.*, xlv (1986), pp. 244–69

ELIZABETH GROSSMAN

Crete. Largest island in the Greek archipelago; home of the Minoan civilization (for map of Minoan sites *see* MINOAN, fig. 1) and subsequently associated with an important school of Byzantine iconographers (*see* §4 below). The island, which is the fourth largest in the Mediterranean, owes its historical importance primarily to its focal position between Europe, Asia and Africa. Lying at 35° latitude, some 100 km south-east of the Peloponnesian mainland of Greece, Crete forms the southern boundary of the Aegean Sea and links the Peloponnese to the mainland of Asia Minor through a chain of smaller islands; the Libyan coast is *c.* 300 km to the south over open sea .

Crete extends *c.* 250 km east–west and a maximum of 57 km north–south, with sheltered anchorages chiefly along the north coast. Four mountain ranges constitute the island's spine: westernmost are the White Mountains, with ten peaks above 2000 m; then Mt Ida (2456 m); the Lasithi Range, with Mt Dikte (2148 m); and finally, east of the narrow (12 km) isthmus of Ierapetra, Mt Ornon (1476 m). Isolated upland plains drained by swallow-holes include the Omalos in the White Mountains, 1100 m high and snowbound in winter, and the Lasithi Plateau (*c.* 850 m). The fertile Mesara Plain lies north of the Asterousia Range, which runs parallel to the central southern coast. Crete was renowned in antiquity for its climate and fertility, especially for wine, oil, cypress forests and cereals. The island lies in a geological fault zone, and severe earthquakes feature in its history.

1. Neolithic and Minoan, *c.* 7000–*c.* 1050 BC. 2. Sub-Minoan to Hellenistic, *c.* 1050–67 BC. 3. Roman, 67 BC–*c.* AD 300. 4. Byzantine, *c.* AD 300–1204. 5. Venetian, 1204–1669. 6. Turkish rule, independence and union with Greece, from 1669.

1. NEOLITHIC AND MINOAN, *c.* 7000–*c.* 1050 BC. Crete had been visited during the Mesolithic period, but Neolithic (*c.* 7000–*c.* 3500/3000 BC) settlers, probably from western Anatolia or Syria, introduced the essentials of a mixed farming economy. They built villages of mud-brick houses (later on stone foundations) favouring knolls as at Phaistos and Knossos, where Neolithic levels 7 m deep indicate conservatism and isolation from outside influence. Burials were in caves.

After an initial aceramic phase huge quantities of a dark-surfaced, burnished ware were produced in an apparently well-developed tradition of potting; later decoration consisted of incisions filled with white paste or applied knobs and ribs. Stone tools were almost entirely of local materials, except for obsidian from the Cycladic island of MELOS. Fine bone tools (e.g. Rethymnon, Archaeol. Mus.) are preserved, as well as spinning and weaving equipment of clay. Cult objects include a stone phallic idol (Ayios Nikolaos, Archaeol. Mus.) found at Pelekita (nr Zakros) and violin-shaped and steatopygous idols (Herakleion, Archaeol. Mus.) from Knossos, Phaistos and the cave sanctuary of Eileithyia at Amnisos.

Around 3500 BC, with increasing metal technology, a transformation began towards the more highly organized society of the Cretan Bronze Age. In the Early Minoan period (*c.* 3500–*c.* 2050 BC; *see* MINOAN, §I, 4(i)) there were developments in architecture, both domestic (e.g. at VASILIKI, Phournou Koriphi) and funerary (e.g. the MESARA), and in craft specialization such as the earliest painted decoration on pottery and the production of cult vessels, stone vases, bronze weapons and tools, jewellery and engraved seals (for detailed discussions *see* MINOAN, §§III, 3; VIII; IX, 1(i) and 2; and X).

The founding of the first Minoan palaces (*c.* 1900 BC; *see* MINOAN, §II) marked a new level of civilization and heralded half a millennium of extraordinary artistic achievement. Sophisticated architecture, sometimes with wall paintings, has been uncovered at the four great palaces of Knossos, Phaistos, Mallia (for illustration *see* MALLIA) and Zakros, at sites such as GOURNIA and Palaikastro, and at town and country mansions across the island (e.g. TYLISSOS, AMNISOS, Nirou Khani, MYRTOS and AYIA TRIADA), as well as deposits in cemeteries (e.g. Arkhanes and Mochlos), peak sanctuaries (e.g. Juktas, Petsophas, Vrysinas and Kophinas) and sacred caves (e.g. KAMARES, Skoteino and Psykhro). Works of art in pottery, gold, bronze, stone, faience and ivory (*see* MINOAN, figs 20, 21, 26 and 27) are further evidence of the wealth, power and trading contacts of the Minoans in the Mediterranean world.

Around 1425 BC most of the major Minoan sites on the island were destroyed except Knossos, which continued in diminished splendour until *c.* 1360 BC or even to *c.* 1200 BC (*see* MINOAN, §I, 4(iii)). Apparently the rival power of MYCENAE overran the island (*see* HELLADIC, §I, 4(iii)), which it ruled from Knossos and later from Kydonia (now Chania). Crete never regained its former brilliance, and the last centuries of the Late Bronze Age (*c.* 1580–1100 BC) were a period of disturbance and decline.

2. SUB-MINOAN TO HELLENISTIC, *c.* 1050–67 BC. During the Early Iron Age Crete advanced from relative poverty, isolation and illiteracy to the dawn of recorded history associated with the adoption of a Semitic script for Greek alphabetic writing, the political organization of the city-state and the codification of laws.

In the Sub-Minoan period (*c.* 1050–*c.* 1000 BC) the Minoan–Mycenaean bronzeworking culture began to give way to an iron-based economy. Improved metalworking technology led to the adoption of iron for weapons and tools, though bronze persisted for ornamental pieces (e.g. figurines and cauldrons); fibulae were produced in both materials.

Pottery of the Protogeometric and Geometric periods (*c.* 1050–*c.* 700 BC; *see* GREECE, ANCIENT, §V, 2(iii) and 3(iv)), while not attaining the sophistication of the Attic school, is seen at its best in the corpus of cremation urns and other vases from tombs (Sub-Minoan–Late Orientalizing; *c.* 1050–*c.* 630 BC) in the North Cemetery of Knossos (Herakleion, Archaeol. Mus.). The typical patterns of the Protogeometric vase painters, dark parallel bands and precise concentric circles or semicircles, were succeeded by elaborate compositions of rectilinear motifs (meander, triangles etc) combined in zones and panels. Mycenaean pictorial decoration virtually disappeared, though the female divinity is occasionally represented on Cretan Protogeometric vases (e.g. Knossos, Archaeol. Mus.), and by the 8th century BC bird motifs are not uncommon.

Orientalizing influences, associated with the renewal of eastward commerce in the 7th century BC, resulted in the introduction of animals, real and imaginary (occasionally as *protomes*), and curvilinear designs, such as the cable, lotus, volute and the Tree of Life (*see* GREECE, ANCIENT, §V, 4(iv)). Polychrome decoration was popular, employing red, bluish-grey and occasionally yellow over a thick white slip. Vases from the Arkades cemetery (Herakleion, Archaeol. Mus.) have complex figural scenes on a funerary theme. Imported pottery, including Proto-Corinthian and 'Wild Goat' wares, suggests renewed contact with the wider Aegean world. After 630 BC Cretan vase painting declined, but coarse ware giant pithoi (8th–6th century BC; examples in Herakleion, Archaeol. Mus.) were decorated in relief with Oriental motifs.

During this Orientalizing period (700–630 BC) figural art also embellished bronze and ivory objects, seals and jewellery, such as the bronze shields hammered in relief from the Idaian Cave and jewellery from a tomb at Teke, which was possibly the family vault of a guild of metalworkers of Near Eastern origin (both at Herakleion, Archaeol. Mus.).

Given the island's Minoan tradition of building in stone rather than mud-brick, traces of architecture from the 8th and 7th centuries BC are often more substantial on Crete than elsewhere in Greece. Excavated sites include Early Iron Age villages (e.g. Phaistos, Vrokastro, Kavousi), an 8th-century temple at Dreros and a 7th-century example of civic planning with stoa, temple and prytaneion around an agora at Lato.

In sculptural techniques the island was ahead of the contemporary Aegean world. Three early 7th-century bronze statuettes (Herakleion, Archaeol. Mus.) from Dreros, executed in the sphyrelaton technique (*see* GREECE, ANCIENT, §IV, 1(iv)), are the first Cretan sculptures in the round. Terracottas in the Daedalic style, which had a significant influence on the evolution of Archaic Greek sculpture (*see* GREECE, ANCIENT, §IV, 2(i)(c)), appeared on the island *c.* 700 BC (important examples from Gortyn, Eleutherna, Astretsi at Herakleion, Archaeol. Mus.). The

two seated deities with panther frieze and mounted procession (Herakleion, Archaeol. Mus.) from the late 7th-century Temple A at Prinias are early examples of Daedalic sculptural decoration on a sacred building.

During the 6th century BC there was an artistic decline on Crete. Isolated examples of quality in Archaic workmanship include the Gortyn *Athena*, terracotta figurines from Praisos, ivories among votive material from the Idaian Cave, a chariot scene on a clay sima from the Temple of Diktaian Zeus at Palaikastro and a bronze helmet from Axos with winged horses embossed on its cheek pieces (all Herakleion, Archaeol. Mus.).

In the 8th century BC, the city-state became the basis of Cretan society, and it was to remain so for the next 1000 years. Each self-governing community developed its own traditions, laws, cults, calendar and often, by the 5th century BC, coinage. Their oligarchic Dorian rulers gave little importance to art patronage, and the island, politically a backwater during the Archaic, Classical and Hellenistic periods (*c.* 750–67 BC), was absorbed culturally into the wider Aegean civilization. Fragments of inscribed blocks (7th–4th century BC), indicating the early codification of laws, have survived from nine cities, but the 5th-century Code of Gortyn has a scope that is unparalleled in contemporary Greece.

The simple cella plans of Archaic temples often survived with few alterations until the establishment of Christianity in the 4th century AD: for example, Gortyn's 7th-century Temple of Apollo Pythios remained the city's religious centre for 1000 years. Among known temples originating in the Hellenistic period (323–67 BC), only Axos follows the conventional Classical Greek plan of pronaos, cella and opisthodomos. Cult statues from temple sites include the Gortyn *Apollo* (Herakleion, Archaeol. Mus.) and the Hyrtakina *Pan* (Chania, Archaeol. Mus.).

Other sites of Classical or Hellenistic interest are: Praisos (3rd-century BC architecture), Apollonia (city, destr. 171 BC), Aptera (2nd-century double-cella temple, and 3.80 km circuit of bastioned walls), Prinias (Hellenistic fort) and Phalasarna (4th–3rd-century artificial harbour). In the treasury of the Temple of Asklepios at Lebena (now Lendas) is a 4th–3rd-century pebble pavement depicting a seahorse. A striking bronze statue of a young boy (1st century BC; Herakleion, Archaeol. Mus.) was found at the site of the ancient city of Ierapytna (now Ierapetra), but in general Cretan Hellenistic sculpture is of a provincial quality.

3. ROMAN, 67 BC–*c.* AD 300. In 67 BC Crete was annexed by Rome after a two-year campaign by Quintus Caecilius Metellus Creticus (*d* late 50s BC), in the course of which Knossos was destroyed. Gortyn became capital of the praetorian province of Crete and Cyrene, and Roman colonists resettled Knossos *c.* 27 BC. Under Roman administration the island, which lay on the main sea route between Rome and her eastern empire, enjoyed prosperity and peace.

The main building activity at Gortyn (for illustration *see* GORTYN) dates from the first and second centuries AD. As at Knossos, the city was embellished with the usual public buildings: praetorium, civil basilica, temples, theatres, baths, fountains and aqueducts. Existing Hellenistic buildings were often reconstructed in the Roman period, as for example Gortyn's Odeum and Temple of Isis and Serapis, Lebena's Temple of Asklepios, and probably the pseudoperipteral temple at the Dictynnaeum (on Cape Spada).

Much information about destroyed Roman buildings comes from the writings (*c.* 1417) of the Florentine monk CHRISTOPHER BUONDELMONTE and drawings by a 16th-century Venetian physician and antiquary, Onorio Belli (see Falkener). The majority of the planned theatres were of a similar type, with deep postscenia, elaborate porticos, and façades that suggest parallels with Asia Minor (e.g. Ephesos) and Athens (Odeion of Herodes Atticus; *see* ATHENS, §I, 3); some of the marbles were probably shipped from Asia Minor in roughed-out form. Western influence, however, appears in the preference from *c.* AD 100 for brick-faced concrete, despite the availability of stone.

Mosaics in the Villa Dionysus at Knossos (2nd–3rd century AD) are of a technical and artistic quality unequalled elsewhere on the island, but noteworthy examples come from the villas at Kydonia (Chania, Archaeol. Mus.) and also decorate a pyramidal fountain at Chersonisos. A few Roman sculptures survive and many dedications from lost works: busts and statues of the emperors and their families reflect the link with Rome. Nine extant heads or cuirassed statues of Hadrian were all probably from an Attica workshop; the finest (Herakleion, Archaeol. Mus.) comes from the Villa Dionysus at Knossos and has Rome, not the usual Athena, on the breastplate. Other categories include funeral reliefs of local citizens; cult figures (e.g. Isis and Serapis, Asklepios); decorative, often mythological, pieces such as *Europa and the Bull* and the Inatos *Niobe* group (Herakleion, Archaeol. Mus.). Although the existence of local workshops is not ruled out, some sculpture was imported from Greece or Asia Minor. Imported stone sarcophagi of the 2nd and 3rd centuries AD, comprising twelve Attic and two Asiatic examples against one Italian (Cambridge, Fitzwilliam), provide further indication of Crete's artistic and architectural position within the eastern empire.

4. BYZANTINE, *c.* AD 300–1204. Crete's First Byzantine period (AD 300–827) began with major reconstruction after 4th-century earthquakes. In many towns the resettlement extended below the acropolis, disregarding defence (e.g. Gortyn and Phaistos), and elsewhere revived coastal sites (e.g. Mochlos) that had in some cases remained uninhabited since Minoan times. The first villas appeared in remote rural areas such as the Amari Valley.

The Bible records St Paul's shipwreck on Crete (Acts 27) and his appointment of Titus as its first bishop (Titus 1:5). After 313 Christianity was the religion of the Empire, but though the Temple of Apollo Pythios became the 4th-century metropolitan church of Gortyn most of the *c.* 70 basilica churches known from Byzantine Crete date to 450–550. The most important, Hagios Titos at Gortyn, is, however, from the late 6th century or early 7th. The basilican plan on Crete occasionally includes the tripartite transept, with or without pastophoria or atrium (e.g. Panormos and Chersonisos); Vizari has apsed side aisles. Churches with triconch plans (e.g. Gortyn, Mitropolis) are

interpreted as martyria. Cretan baptisteries were usually annexed to the narthex but were occasionally free-standing and later sometimes housed in the pastophorion to the south of the sanctuary. Construction was usually of mortared rubble, often (until the mid-6th century) with marble inlay floors (e.g. Olous and Souyia). These mosaic pavements, as well as architectural fragments, point to possible stylistic influences from the eastern empire (north Syria) and the Aegean.

After the 7th-century Arab conquest of north Africa the eastern Mediterranean was increasingly exposed to marauders, and refortification was attempted at some Cretan cities (e.g. Lyttos, Mochlos and Pseira); but in 827 the island fell to Arab invaders and became a centre of piracy. In 961 Crete was recaptured for Christendom by the Byzantine general and later emperor Nikephoros Phokas (*reg* 963–4). Jurisdiction of the Cretan Church had been transferred in 732–3 from Rome to Constantinople, and after the Arab devastation Crete's Second Byzantine period (961–1204) was one of intensive reconstruction by Christian nobility from Constantinople, local evangelists (e.g. St John the Hermit) and, after 1088, the monastery of Hagios Ioannis on Patmos.

Although three-aisled basilicas were still built, often using the sites and/or materials of earlier basilicas (e.g. Viran Episkopi, Piyi (formerly Bizariano) and the episcopal Church of the Virgin near the village of Ayia), churches increasingly adopted the typical Byzantine dome raised on a cylindrical or octagonal drum, often arcaded; at Stylos (Church of the Virgin, Panayia Serviotissa) and Rukani a dome completes the basilican ground-plan. More simply a single nave may be divided into bays, the central bay supporting the drum—five bays at Chromonastiri, three at Kyriakoselia and at Ayios Nikolaos. The central domed space is elsewhere achieved by a cruciform ground-plan (e.g. Ayios Ioannis (Sphakia), Hagios Paolos; Myriokephala; Kalamas; and Alikianos, Hagios Ioannis Erimitis). At Episkopi, Kisamos, a rotonda with a stepped dome of five concentric rings is unique on Crete.

Only traces remain of wall painting in the Iconoclastic style (e.g. Ayios Nikolaos, Hagios Nikolaos), but fine examples of fully developed Middle Byzantine fresco decoration, in the conservative linear style diffused from Constantinople under the MACEDONIAN DYNASTY and Komnenian dynasty (*see* KOMNENOS), are preserved in the churches at Myriokephala, Chromonastiri, Kalamas and Kurnas.

5. VENETIAN, 1204–1669. In the division of Byzantine lands after the capture of Constantinople (1204) by the armies of the Fourth Crusade, Crete was sold to the Venetians by Boniface, Marquis of Montferrat (*d* 1207). The Genoese briefly established strongholds on the island, but by 1210 Venice had gained control, and Crete remained a part of the VENETIAN EMPIRE until the Turkish conquest in 1669. The island occupied a vital position along the shipping lanes from the Adriatic to Asia Minor and the oriental trade route on which Venice's extraordinary wealth depended. Venice gave the name Candia to both the island and its capital, present-day Herakleion, and appointed a Duke of Candia to govern with the aid of an administration modelled on that of the Serene Republic, while colonists

from Venetian noble families appropriated Cretan estates to counterbalance the continuing influence of Byzantine feudalism.

Venetian rule was at first ferociously challenged. Venice established the Western Church on Crete, building new episcopal churches and banishing the Orthodox bishops, but Cretan loyalties remained firmly with the Orthodox emperors and their patriarchs up to the Fall of Constantinople in 1453. At that time many scholars and clerics fled to Crete, and, by strengthening its Byzantine element, played a crucial role in preserving and transmitting the elements of Greek thought and art that were seminal to the development of the Italian Renaissance.

(i) Architecture. Urban architecture was the Venetians' most lasting contribution to Crete. They built walled cities for the north-coast harbours of Candia, La Canea (now Chania) and Retimo (now Rethymnon). Candia's ducal palace no longer exists, but restored Venetian buildings include the basilica of St Mark (1239; most recently rest. 1956; now used as a concert and exhibition hall) and the Armoury (17th century; reconstructed as town hall, 1934) and Loggia (1629; rest. 1980s). Outside St Mark's stands a fountain built in 1628 for the Venetian governor Francesco Morosini, with 14th-century sculptured spouts in the shape of lions set above an eight-lobed basin carved with mythological marine scenes and originally completed by a marble statue of Neptune (destr.).

The harbour fortress Rocca al Mare was built in the early 13th century by the Venetians to defend the dockyard arsenals. Destroyed in 1303 by an earthquake but frequently rebuilt (notably 1523), it is embellished by three high-relief carvings of the lion of St Mark. Candia's defences—a 3 km star-shaped circuit—were constructed between the 14th century and the 17th, with an important phase (1538) designed by the Venetian MICHELE SANMICHELI. In 1647 Candia was besieged by the Turks, but it held out for 22 years. Fortresses across the island protected its rulers first against revolt and later against the Turkish threat; the largest example, a six-bastioned fort with loopholed battlements (1573–80), dominated Retimo. Among the military engineers responsible were Venetians of the ORSINI and Sforza Pallavicini families. At Retimo, Venetian remains include the Rimondi Fountain (1629) and a 17th-century portal following the *Extraordinario libro di architettura* (Venice, 1537) of Sebastiano Serlio.

Monastic communities are documented from the 11th century. The Venetians established Latin monasteries (376 are recorded by the 16th century), but usually only the church survives, as for example the churches of the Franciscans (begun 1595) and the Dominicans (Hagios Nikolaos) at La Canea; the former's severely plain vaulted nave with narrow side aisles (the largest Venetian nave on the island) houses the Chania Archaeological Museum. Monasteries of the Eastern Rite flourished, especially during the decreasing religious tension that followed the Decree of Union signed at Florence in 1439; the early 17th-century monastery of Hagia Triada (also known as Zangaroli) near Chania was founded by Venetian converts to Orthodoxy.

Larger churches frequently grew by additions to single-naved chapels, as at the church of the Virgin (Panagia) of Kera at Kritsa, or the monastic churches at Vrondisi and Valsamonero at Kera (Pediada) and at the Akimbo Monastery of Toplou. Others were built to a clear Byzantine design (e.g. the domed cruciform church at Potamies). Although the old-fashioned three-aisled plan persisted into the Venetian period (e.g. the 13th-century church of Paliani Monastery and the 13th–14th-century church at Ayii Deka), the domed cruciform plan was developing towards the cross-in-square, as in the 14th-century church of the Virgin (Panagia) at Lambini. External brick or tile decoration was employed. Wood-carving was highly developed. Western influence in Venetian architectural detail is exemplified by the quatrefoil windows and pointed arches at Valsamonero, Potamies and Meronas, and in such features as the monumental gateway at Ayia Triada or the paired columns and twin pediments on the façade of the monastery church at Arkadi, where the Corinthian order is adapted to a two-aisled Cretan church.

(ii) Wall paintings and icons. Despite the arrival of a Latin hierarchy, fresco decoration of churches continued strictly in the traditions of Byzantine style and iconography. The aristocratic Komnenian style evident in the late 12th-century frescoes in the church of the Virgin (Panagia) at Myriokephala persisted at Hagios Nikolaos (1230–36), Kyriakokselia, while the conservative linear style survives at Hagia Anna (1225), Amari, and Hagios Georgios (1284), Vathi.

Crete has some 900 churches with wall paintings, the majority painted during the 14th and 15th centuries. After 1300, some artists were influenced by the realism and liveliness associated with the art of the PALAIOLOGAN dynasty. This development is illustrated by comparison of the two phases of decoration (1303 and *c.* 1471) in the church of Our Saviour Christ (Sotiros Christos) at Meskla and of the four (mid-13th–mid-14th century) at the Virgin (Panagia) of Kera at KRITSA. Only rarely (e.g. in representations of St Francis) does iconography or compositional detail (e.g. the glassware in the *Last Supper* at Kritsa) suggest Venetian cultural influence.

Most Cretan painters are anonymous, but Ioannis Pagomenos is known from inscriptions (1315–47) in seven churches in west Crete, and his work is recognized at others, especially in Sphakia and Selinos; his frescoes demonstrate Palaiologan influence on a strongly conservative tradition. A century later Manuel Phokas decorated the churches of Hagios Georgios at Embaros (1436) and Apano Symi (1453), and with his brother Ioannis the church of Hagios Konstantinos (1445) at Avdou. Their erudite iconography and aristocratic refinement reflect close contact with Constantinople.

By the mid-14th century variations in technique, such as the modelling of flesh with dense highlights on dark brown underpaint and the use of emphasized outlines, marked the evolution of a recognizably Cretan style of painting which was to dominate post-Byzantine art (*see* POST-BYZANTINE ART, §II). This development may be seen in the church at Vrondisi Monastery; the church of the Dormition at Spilia; the narthex of Hagios Phanourios at Valsamonero, which was painted by Konstantinos Rikos in 1428–31; and the church of Hagios Georgios at Sklaverokhori. The elongated figures of the emerging style convey inner emotion through disciplined restraint. Among Cretan painters in demand abroad were THEOPHANES THE CRETAN (*fl* 1527; *d* 1559), who worked at the Meteora and on Mt Athos (*see* MT ATHOS, §3 and POST-BYZANTINE ART, fig. 4). On the island the last dated mural (1565) is in the church of Hagia Paraskevi at Ziros.

Portable icons are documented on Crete from 1025, but after 1453 Candia became a major centre of icon painting (*see* POST-BYZANTINE ART, §II, 1). Production was efficiently organized in workshops, which completed not only large consignments for the Orthodox world—Mt Athos, Meteora, Mt Sinai and Patmos—but also others 'in the Latin style' for patrons from the Western Church. Their products generally remain dispersed outside Crete.

Outstanding among icons still on the island is the work of the 15th-century painters Angelos Akotantos (*see* POST-BYZANTINE ART, fig. 2) and Andreas Ritzos. Six icons in the collection of the former Sinaiite church of St Catherine in Herakleion are late works signed by Michael Damaskinos (*fl* 1555–91; see fig.); others (unsigned but confidently attributed to him) hang in the nearby church of Hagios Matthaios. After a period in Venice (1577–82), where he encountered Renaissance art, Damaskinos returned to Crete and in his mature work brought a fresh approach to the treatment of traditional subjects. His younger contemporary Dominikos Theotokopoulos left Crete never to return, achieving fame as EL GRECO.

6. TURKISH RULE, INDEPENDENCE AND UNION WITH GREECE, FROM 1669. In 1669 the Venetians surrendered Candia to the Ottoman Empire. The Turks concentrated in the cities, but few traces remain of this period of hated foreign domination, which led to several attempted revolts. Apostasy divided the Cretan population. Churches were converted to mosques (e.g. Chania, Hagios Nikolaos, which retains both bell-tower and minaret), while the monasteries strove to preserve Greek art and learning, and the clergy actively supported the struggle for liberation. In 1898 the island finally gained independence, under the protection of Britain, France and Russia, and in 1913 it achieved union with Greece. European awareness of the island's antiquities had been revived by the writings of 19th-century travellers (see bibliography), and with independence the way was clear for archaeology, art-historical research and restoration, and the establishment of museum collections for the understanding and protection of Crete's cultural heritage (e.g. Ayios Nikolaos, Archaeol. Mus.; Herakleion, Archaeol. Mus., Hist. Mus. Crete; Ierapetra, Archaeol. Col.; Chania, Archaeol. Mus., Naval Mus., Hist. Mus. & Archv.; Rethymnon, Archaeol. Mus.; Síteia, Síteia Mus., Flklore Mus.; Vori, Mus. Cret. Ethnol.). Respected 20th-century Cretan painters include Thomas Fanourakis (1915–93), Georgios Manousakis and Ioannis Migadis (*b* 1921).

BIBLIOGRAPHY
F. Cornelius: *Creta sacra* (Venice, 1755)
R. Pashley: *Travels in Crete*, 2 vols (London, 1837/*R* Amsterdam, 1970)
E. Falkener: *A Description of Some Important Theatres and other Remains in Crete* (London, 1854) [incl. repr. of 16th-century drgs by Onorio Belli]
T. A. B. Spratt: *Travels and Researches in Crete*, 2 vols (London, 1865/*R* 1965)
G. Gerola: *Monumenti veneti nell'isola di Creta*, 5 vols (London, 1905–32)
W. Miller: *Essays on the Latin Orient* (Cambridge, 1921)

Cretan icon by Michael Damaskinos: *Virgin and Child*, late 16th century (Herakleion, St Catherine, Icon Collection)

J. D. S. Pendlebury: *The Archaeology of Crete: An Introduction* (London, 1939/*R* 4/1971)
J. K. Brock: *Fortetsa: Early Greek Tombs near Knossos* (Cambridge, 1957)
K. Kalokyris: *Ai Byzantinai toichographiai tes Kritis* [The Byzantine wall paintings of Crete] (Athens, 1957; Eng. trans., New York, 1973)
S. Marinatos and M. Hirmer: *Crete and Mycenae* (London, 1960)
J. Boardman: *The Cretan Collection in Oxford: The Dictaean Cave and Iron Age Crete* (Oxford, 1961)
R. W. Hutchinson: *Prehistoric Crete* (Harmondsworth, 1962, rev. 3/1968)
R. Higgins: *Minoan and Mycenaean Art* (London, 1967)
C. M. Woodhouse: *The Story of Modern Greece* (London, 1968); rev. as *Modern Greece: A Short History* (London, 1977, rev. 3/1984)
K. Branigan: *The Tombs of Mesara: A Study of Funerary Architecture and Ritual in Southern Crete, 2800–1700 BC* (London, 1970)
S. Hood: *The Minoans: Crete in the Bronze Age* (London, 1971)
C. Davaras: *Guide to Cretan Antiquities* (New Jersey, 1976)
R. F. Willetts: *The Civilisation of Ancient Crete* (London, 1977)
I. F. Sanders: *Roman Crete: An Archaeological Survey and Gazetteer of Late Hellenistic, Roman and Early Byzantine Crete* (Warminster, 1982)
A. Brown: *Arthur Evans and the Palace of Minos* (Oxford, 1983)
K. Gallas, K. Wessel and M. Borboudakis: *Byzantinisches Kreta* (Munich, 1983)
Creta antica: Cento anni di archeologia italiana a Creta (1884–1984) (exh. cat., ed. A. Di Vita, V. La Rosa and M. A. Rizzo; Athens, It. Sch. Archaeol., Eng. trans., 1985)
From Byzantium to El Greco: Greek Frescoes and Icons (exh. cat., ed. M. Acheimastou-Potamianou; trans. D. A. Hardy; London, RA, 1987)
T. E. Detorakis: *History of Crete* (Iraklion, 1994)

PATRICIA CAMERON

Cretey, Pierre-Louis (*b* ?Lyon, ?1645; *d* Paris, 1721). French painter. He is recorded in Rome between 1672 and 1679, in Modena in 1677, and he probably also worked in Florence. On his return to France most of his career was spent in Lyon, where he was renowned as a history painter in the 1680s. He produced altarpieces such as the *Road to Emmaus* (Lyon, Ste Blandine) and became the principal collaborator of Thomas Blanchet on a number of decorative schemes, including work at the Palais de Roanne (now Palais de Justice). The most important of these, however, was a series of paintings (now Lyon, Mus. B.-A.) for the refectory of the Benedictine abbey of St Pierre. Here he executed a *Last Supper*, a *Multiplication of the Loaves*, an *Assumption of the Virgin*, an *Ascension of Christ* and an *Elias* between 1684 and 1686. The style of these powerful canvases, with figure groups brilliantly but irregularly lit against dark and brooding backgrounds, is suggestive both of 16th-century Venetian prototypes and of the sharp chiaroscuro of Simon Vouet's early Italian works.

BIBLIOGRAPHY

P. Rivière de Brinais [Clapasson]: *Description de la ville de Lyon* (Lyon, 1741), p. 71
M. Audin and E. Vial: *Dictionnaire des artistes et ouvriers d'art*, i (Paris, 1918), p. 23
J. Bousquet: 'Les Artistes français à Rome au XVIIe siècle à travers quelques exemples lyonnais', *L'Art baroque à Lyon. Actes du colloque: Lyon, 1973*, pp. 177–99
D. Tennois: 'Les Tableaux des églises et des couvents de Lyon', *L'Art baroque à Lyon. Actes du colloque: Lyon, 1973*, pp. 201–88
L. Galacteros de Boissier: 'Les Peintures du Palais de Roanne à Lyon au XVIIe siècle: Problème d'iconographie et d'attribution (Th. Blanchet et P.-L. Cretey)', *La Peinture à Lyon aux XVIIe et XVIIIe siècles*, iii of *Le Rôle de Lyon dans les échanges artistiques* (Lyon, 1977), pp. 1–26

THOMAS NICHOLS

Creti, Donato (*b* Cremona, 24 Feb 1671; *d* Bologna, 29 Jan 1749). Italian painter and draughtsman. His individual and poetic art represents, with that of Marcantonio Franceschini, the last significant expression of the classical–idealist strain in Bolognese painting. His activity was almost wholly confined to Bologna, where he painted decorative frescoes, altarpieces and easel pictures for private collectors. Two qualities are paramount: a perfected finesse of handling and poetic suggestiveness of situation and mood. He sought the ideal beauty of the individual figure and was thus at his best in meditative pictures with few figures; his subjects combine grace of form and precision of contour with flesh that attains the surface delicacy of porcelain and colours that have a mineral-like refulgence. He was a prolific draughtsman with a distinct personal manner, who drew for pleasure as well as to prepare his compositions, usually using a quill-pen and producing shadowing by hatching.

1. TRAINING AND EARLY WORKS, 1685–1710. Creti's father, Gioseffo (1634–1714), was a painter 'di mediocre fama' (Zanotti) who specialized in architectural painting. The family moved to Bologna when Donato was two. He trained with the minor painter Giorgio Rasparini and then entered the studio of Lorenzo Pasinelli; Pasinelli had studied with Simone Cantarini, Guido Reni's most gifted pupil. Creti was a precocious artist, affectionately nicknamed 'ragazzino' as the youngest and most gifted of Pasinelli's students. His talent was soon noticed by Conte Alessandro Fava, whose son, Pietro, studied with Creti in Pasinelli's life drawing classes. A study of the Carracci's

frescoed friezes in the Palazzo Fava, Bologna, showing stories of *Europa* and *Jason*, was an established part of a Bolognese artist's training. Creti was invited to live in the palazzo and given a small stipend, and before 1700, according to Zanotti, he benefited from a study visit to Venice with Pietro Fava.

In return for this generous support, Creti gave Conte Alessandro paintings and drawings. Fava inscribed and dated some of these works, providing important evidence for Creti's early chronology. The picture of a *Youth Holding Two Candles* (1688; Bologna, priv. col.; see Roli, *Donato Creti*, 1967, fig. 1), inscribed and dated by Fava, is Creti's earliest documented painting. A *Self-portrait* of the artist as a young man (Bologna, Pin. N.) seems to date from the same period. Among the drawings inscribed by Fava are *Two Seated Boys*, a *Study of Heads* (1685; both Florence, Uffizi) and a *Martyrdom of a Saint* (1691; Bologna, ex-col. Zanassi; see Roli, *Donato Creti*, 1967, pl. 110), with, on the *verso*, a series of heads executed with the brilliant calligraphic flourish that characterizes one aspect of Creti's draughtsmanship. The most masterly work painted for Fava, which established Creti's fame with his contemporaries, was *Alexander Menaced by his Father, Philip of Macedonia* (before 1705; Washington, DC, N.G.A.; see fig. 1), a picture distinguished by the theatrical grandeur of the architectural setting, which is indebted to Veronese, and by the richness and variety of expression and gesture.

During these early years Creti also painted decorative frescoes. When he was 17 he decorated a room in the

1. Donato Creti: *Alexander Menaced by his Father, Philip of Macedonia*, oil on canvas, 1.29×0.95 m, before 1705 (Washington, DC, National Gallery of Art)

Palazzo Fava with a frieze of landscapes with figures (untraced). A little later (*c.* 1690) he worked with the *quadratura* painters Tomasso Aldrovandini (1653–1736) and Ercole Graziani the elder (1651–1726) on decorations in the Palazzo Zaniboni-Pichi (now Bianconi), Bologna. In the palazzo of the Conte di Novellara he painted 'varie imprese d'Alessandro' (Zanotti); one of these scenes is recorded in a *bozzetto*, the *Family of Darius before Alexander* (*c.* 1700; priv. col.; see Roli, *Donato Creti*, 1967, fig. 6). In 1708 he frescoed the ceilings of three rooms in the Palazzo Pepoli-Campogrande, Bologna, for Conte Ercole Pepoli. Two of these, *Nobiltà* and *Gloria*, are no longer visible. The third, *Alexander Cutting the Gordian Knot*, is Creti's only surviving large-scale decorative fresco. It is seen in steep *di sotto in sù* perspective and is impressive evidence of his ability as a fresco decorator. The scene is set in a fantastic, almost surreal, domed chamber, which was painted by the *quadratura* painter Marcantonio Chiarini (1652–1730).

In these years Creti also painted astonishingly accomplished, glacially elegant pictures of subjects from ancient and biblical history and from mythology. He painted some genre scenes, mainly of musical gatherings. His *Old Woman Recounting the Story of Psyche to a Young Woman* (1705; Bologna, priv. col.; see Roli, *Donato Creti*, 1967, fig. 16), painted for the Bolognese Senator Paolo Magnani, is an unusual blending of the real and the ideal. He set the naturalism of the old woman against the ideal beauty of the younger and enriched a severely classical composition with anecdotal detail (Roli, *Donato Creti*, 1967). In a preparatory drawing (Bologna, Pin. N.) the shading is carried out by careful hatching. Zanotti, who knew Creti, noted his anxiety over this picture and his fear that it would be unworthy of other works in the collection. Throughout his account Zanotti stressed Creti's melancholy disposition.

2. MIDDLE YEARS, 1711–20. In 1711 a distinguished fellow citizen, General Luigi Marsili, commander of the papal forces during the pontificate of Clement XI, commissioned Creti to paint eight small pictures illustrating astronomical observations made of the moon and other planets (all Rome, Pin. Vaticana). The pictures showed the instruments used for these observations, which Marsili, himself a scientist, had given to Bologna's Istituto delle Scienze. These extraordinary little nocturnes, magically atmospheric, were a gift to the Pope, to encourage him to establish an astronomical observatory for the institute.

In 1713 Creti painted a mural in a corridor of the University of Bologna, now the Biblioteca Comunale dell'Archiginnasio, commemorating a distinguished member of the Sbaraglia family, Giovanni Gerolamo Sbaraglia (1641–1710), a celebrated anatomist. There followed a series of pictures painted for Marco Sbaraglia, who was to become Creti's most enthusiastic patron. The four large and imposing narrative pictures (Bologna, Pal. Com.) form an unrivalled display of the artist's distinction. They illustrate episodes from the *Story of Achilles*, in which Creti employed to the full all the learning, artifice and poetic sentiment at his command. The female figures are strikingly beautiful and, according to Zanotti, were modelled on Francesca Zani, whom Creti had married in 1713. Her

death in 1719 caused the artist the greatest distress. His pictures for Marco Sbaraglia also include four lovely tondi, *Charity*, *Temperance*, *Humility* and *Prudence*, and the large companion paintings of *Mercury Bringing the Head of Argus to Juno* and *Mercury Bringing the Golden Apple to Paris*. In the latter the figure of Paris superbly paraphrases Reni's celebrated Samson in *Samson Victorious* (*c.* 1618–19; Bologna, Pin. N.).

3. LATE YEARS: SUCCESS BEYOND BOLOGNA, 1721–49. Creti enjoyed considerable success in his later years. He had been among the founder-members of the Accademia Clementina in Bologna and was active in its functions. Between 1713 and 1727 he was seven times director of studies and often judge of student competitions. In 1728 he was appointed the eleventh principe of the Accademia. In these years his reputation grew outside Bologna. Cardinal Tomasso Ruffo, papal legate to Bologna from 1721–7, commissioned from Creti the *Dance of Nymphs* (*c.* 1724; Rome, Pal. Venezia) and two large and impressive companion pictures, *Solomon and the Queen of Sheba* and *Solomon's Idolatry* (before 1727; both Clermont-Ferrand, Mus. Bargoin). About 1725 Ruffo honoured Creti with the title of Cavaliere. The *Dance of Nymphs* and such other pastoral idylls as the *Country Idyll* (*c.* 1730; Bologna, Pin. N.) are perhaps Creti's most appealing works. The idealized figures are displayed in hauntingly evocative arcadian settings, at twilight, suffused by a mood of sadness (see fig. 2). It was such works that inspired Longhi (1935, p. 133) to describe Creti as the 'Italian Watteau'. His landscape drawings of the period are similar in mood; in his *Sleeping Endymion* (Bologna, Pin. N.) the rendering is quite painstakingly detailed and brings to mind the technique of engraving.

In the 1720s the Irish theatre impresario Owen McSwiny promoted a plan for a series of large pictures, each dedicated to the memory of a British 'worthy' deceased in recent times and presenting his tomb with appropriate allegorical allusions to greatness. McSwiny hired teams of Italian artists, and figure painters collaborated with landscape and architectural specialists. Venetian masters were prominent, among them Sebastiano and Marco Ricci, Giambattista Pittoni, Giovanni Battista Piazzetta and Canaletto. Creti contributed five pictures, the *Tombs of Locke, Boyle and Sydenham* and the *Tomb of the Duke of Marlborough* (both 1729; Bologna, Pin. N.), the *Tomb of Joseph Addison* and the *Tomb of the Marquis of Wharton* (both *c.* 1730; Rome, Villa Wolkonsky; see Roli, *Donato Creti*, 1967, figs 73–4) and the *Tomb of Charles Montagu, Count of Halifax* (*c.* 1730; Rome, priv. col.; see Roli, *Donato Creti*, 1967, fig. 75), in which he collaborated principally with the Bolognese landscape and architectural painters Carlo Besoli (1709–54) and Nunzio Ferraiolo. A volume of plates reproducing the pictures was planned, and in 1741 *Tombeaux des princes, grands capitaines et autres hommes illustres qui ont fleuri dans la Grande Bretagne vers la fin du XVII et le commencement du XVIII siècle* was published. Twenty-four plates were planned, but only nine, including engravings after Creti's two pictures in Bologna, were completed.

Creti was perhaps less successful in his large altarpieces, most of which were painted in his later years. Pictures

2. Donato Creti: *Sigismonda*, oil on canvas, *c.* 1740 (Bologna, Palazzo Comunale, Collezioni Comunali d'Arte)

such as the *Virgin with St Ignazio* (1737), the *Charity of St Carlo Borromeo* (1740; both Bologna, S Pietro) and the *Coronation of the Virgin* (1740–45; Bologna, Santuario della Madonna di S Luca) lack the authority necessary to activate and unify such large, multifigured compositions. Creti's attempt to adapt an essentially classical idiom to the purpose of the religious art of the Counter-Reformation was not successful, for the beauty of the individual figure, so essential to his art, was not allowed sufficient autonomy. In his later years Creti, whose nature was painfully sensitive, was afflicted with sleeplessness and depression. His most successful pupils were Ercole Graziani (the younger) and Domenico Fratta (1696–1763).

UNPUBLISHED SOURCE

Bologna, Bib. Com. Archiginnasio, MS. B 130 [M. Oretti: *Notizie de' professori del disegno*; contains a copy of Zanotti with marginal annotations]

BIBLIOGRAPHY

DBI; Thieme–Becker
G. P. Zanotti: *Storia dell'Accademia Clementina di Bologna* (Bologna, 1739), i, pp. 17, 100; ii, pp. 98–122 [see also Zanotti's personal MS. (Bologna, Bib. Com. Archiginnasio, MS. B 6) and his marginal annotations to the printed edn (Bologna, Bib. Com. Archiginnasio, MS. B 11–12)]
L. Crespi: *Vite de' pittori bolognesi non descritte nella 'Felsina pittrice'* (Rome, 1769), pp. 257–9
L. Lanzi: *Storia pittorica della Italia* (Pisa, 1816), v, pp. 177–9
K. Alcsuti: 'Donato Creti bolognai festo', *Com. Bologna* (Sept 1932) [It. trans.]
G. Zucchini: 'Quadri inediti di Donato Creti', *Com. Bologna* (Oct 1933)
R. Longhi: 'Momenti della pittura bolognese', *Archiginnasio*, xxx (1935), pp. 111–35
Mostra del settecento bolognese (exh. cat., ed. R. Longhi; Bologna, Pal. Com., 1935–8)
O. Kurz: *Bolognese Drawings at Windsor Castle* (London, 1955), nos 190–203
G. Rivani: 'Opere di Donato Creti nella raccolta della Cassa di Risparmio di Bologna', *Strenna Stor. Bologn.*, ix (1959)
R. Roli: 'I disegni di Donato Creti agli Uffizi', *Boll. A.*, xlvii (1962), pp. 241–50
F. Haskell: *Patrons and Painters* (London, 1963)
R. Roli: 'Dipinti inediti di Donato Creti', *A. Ant. & Mod.*, xxiii (1963), pp. 247–53
——: 'Donato Creti: Un *Bacco* in terracotta', *A. Ant. & Mod.*, xxv (1964), pp. 101–2
——: *Donato Creti* (Milan, 1967); review by D. Miller in *Burl. Mag.*, cxi (1969), pp. 306–8
——: 'Peintures de Donato Creti dans les musées de France', *Rev. Louvre* (1967), pp. 249–56
——: *Donato Creti: 46 disegni inediti* (Bologna, 1973)
L'arte del settecento emiliano: La pittura: L'Accademia Clementina (exh. cat., ed. A. Emiliani; Bologna, Pal. Podestà, 1979), pp. 55–68, nos 84–129 [entries by R. Roli]

DWIGHT C. MILLER

Creussen [Kreussen]. German centre of ceramics production. Stoneware was produced at Creussen, near Bayreuth, as early as the end of the 15th century. Brown-glazed stoneware, however, was not manufactured until the end of the 16th century. The oldest-known dated piece was made in 1614. During the first quarter of the 17th century output was at its finest, and the most famous potteries belonged to the Vest and Speckner families. A number of special forms were developed, including the *Krause* (a low, wide tankard) and *Schraubflasche* (a globular-shaped flask with four or six flattened sides). Another speciality was vessels for chemists' shops, as Creussen wares were resistant to acids. The majority of the potteries' output consisted of wine jugs and tankards. Typical wares were decorated in relief and brightly coloured enamels. Favoured motifs included the Apostles (*Apostelkrüge*), biblical scenes, representations of the seven planets (*Planetenkrüge*), the Emperor with the seven Electors (*Kurfürstenkrüge*; e.g. of 1690; Hannover, Kestner-Mus.), hunting scenes and coats of arms. The manufacture of stoneware ceased in the 1730s. From 1618 to *c.* 1669 high-quality blue-and-white faience was also produced in Creussen at the workshop of Lorenz Speckner (1598–1669).

BIBLIOGRAPHY
J. Kröll: *Creussener Steinzeug* (Brunswick, 1980)

WALTER SPIEGL

Creutz [Crutz], Comte **Gustav Filip** [Philip] (*b* Anjala, Finland, May 1731; *d* Stockholm, 30 Oct 1785). Swedish diplomat, poet, patron and collector. He studied arts and sciences in Åbo (now Turku), and in 1751 arrived in Stockholm, where he was employed in the Chancellery. Between 1757 and 1762 he was a knight at the Swedish court. In Stockholm, Creutz wrote poems, the elegance of which won him the reputation of national poet. In 1762 he was appointed Swedish Minister at the Spanish court and in 1766 he took up the post of Minister and later Ambassador of Sweden at the French court. In Paris he was well known and highly esteemed and acted as a patron of arts and letters. His house, a meeting-place for the most famous artists and writers, was adorned with paintings and busts by such artist friends as François Boucher, Louis Lagrenée, Jean-Baptiste Oudry, Nicolas Pineau, Guillaume-Thomas Taraval, Joseph Vernet, Philippe Jacques de Loutherbourg, Elias Martin (iii), Alexander Roslin and Johan Tobias Sergel. Some of his canvases and drawings are now in the Nationalmuseum, Stockholm. Gustav III (*reg* 1771–92) bought from Creutz, among other items, a silver service (1775–6; Stockholm, Kun. Slottet) by Robert-Joseph Auguste. The King, whose interest in French culture is well known, esteemed Creutz greatly, especially for his taste, and entrusted him with numerous commissions. Creutz commissioned and sent to Sweden paintings, furniture, busts of writers and jewellery made by Jolivet, his favourite jeweller. A wealth of correspondence has survived from Creutz's ambassadorship in France. In 1783 he was recalled to Stockholm and appointed President of the Chancellery.

WRITINGS
M. Molander, ed.: 'Le Comte de Creutz: Lettres inédites de Paris, 1766–1770', *Romanica Gothoburg.*, xxxiii (1987)
G. Mary, ed.: 'Un Ambassadeur à la cour de France, le Comte de Crutz: Lettres inédites à Gustave III, 1779–1780', *Romanica Gothoburg.*, xxxiv (1987)

BIBLIOGRAPHY
G. Castrén: *Gustav Philip Creutz* (Helsinki, 1917)
O. Granberg: *Svenska konstsamlingarnas historia* [History of the Swedish art collections], 3 vols (Stockholm, 1929–31)
G. Lundberg: *Roslin liv och verk* [Roslin, life and work], 2 vols (Malmö, 1957)

MARIANNE MOLANDER

Crevalcore, Antonio da. *See* ANTONIO DA CREVALCORE.

Criard, Mathieu (*b* ?Brussels, 1689; *d* Paris, 30 Jan 1776). French cabinetmaker of Flemish origin. He worked independently before becoming a *maître-ébéniste* on 29 July 1738. He mainly worked for the Garde Meuble de la Couronne, through his colleagues Antoine-Robert Gaudreaus, Gilles Joubert and Jean-François Oeben and through such dealers as Hébert. His extant works, stamped

with his mark M CRIAERD, include luxurious furniture, in general characterized by very turbulent forms and exuberant, fantastic decoration. Chequered marquetry or, more rarely, floral marquetry was used, as well as some varnished panels, either imitating Chinese lacquer or in *vernis Martin* with European decoration. In particular, he made beautiful commodes, including one (Versailles, Château) for the Dauphin's Cabinet de Retraite, which is typical of his work, as is the commode (Paris, Louvre) decorated with blue and silvered-bronze birds made for Madame de Mailly.

BIBLIOGRAPHY
F. de Salverte: *Les Ebénistes du XVIIIème siècle, leurs oeuvres et leurs marques* (Paris, 1923, rev. 5/1962)
J. Viaux: *Bibliographie du meuble (Mobilier civil français)*, 2 vols (Paris, 1966–88)

JEAN-DOMINIQUE AUGARDE, JEAN NÉRÉE RONFORT

Crichton-Stuart, John Patrick. *See* STUART, (2).

Cricolini, Giovanni Antonio. *See* CRECCOLINI, GIOVANNI ANTONIO.

Crimca [Crimcovici], **Anastasie** (*b* Suceava, ?mid-16th century; *d* Dragomirna Monastery, Moldavia, 1629). Romanian calligrapher, illuminator and writer. He was Metropolitan of Moldavia (1608–17; 1619–29) and the founder of Dragomirna Monastery (1609), where he initiated a scriptorium remarkable for the stylistic unity of the work produced over two decades. The great similarity of the works has caused them to be attributed to Crimca, although some scholars have disputed this. The accepted opinion is that nine codices can be attributed to him: five of these are at Dragomirna Monastery, three are in Bucharest, and the Acts of the Apostles (1610) is in Vienna (Österreich. Nbib.).

Crimca assimilated elements from the copyists' tradition, from Moldavian mural painting of the time and from apocryphal and popular texts, and in so doing he widened the thematic repertory and adopted the formula of full-page narrative illustration interspersed with the text. He replaced plastic modelling with a graphic device based on groups of parallel lines arranged in various ways, with the extensive use of gold to enhance the whole page. The finesse of the drawing and general decorativeness of the images make Crimca's work, and that of the Dragomirna school, outstanding in Romanian art. His best-known achievements are a Gospels (1609; Dragomirna Monastery, inv. 1/1934, din 7118), a liturgical book (1610, Dragomirna Monastery, inv. 5/1934, din 7118; 1616, Dragomirna Monastery, inv. 3/1934, din 7124) and the Acts of the Apostles (1609, Bucharest, Lib. Acad. Social. Repub. Romania, MS. Slav., inv. 22; 1610).

BIBLIOGRAPHY
G. Popescu-Vilcea: *Anastasie Crimca* (Bucharest, 1972)
——: *Miniatura românească* [Romanian miniatures] (Bucharest, 1982), pp. 37–46

TEREZA-IRENE SINIGALIA

Crippa, Roberto (*b* Monza, 17 May 1921; *d* Milan, 19 March 1972). Italian painter and sculptor. He studied at the Accademia di Belle Arti di Brera in Milan under Aldo Carpi, Carlo Carrà and Achille Funi. Initially attracted by the work of Picasso, he created a number of works influenced by Cubism; however, in 1946 he discovered a personal form of expression in his 'spirals' (e.g. *Dream of Anne Boleyn*, 1948–9; priv. col., see 1971 exh. cat., p. 25). These comprised tangles of lines influenced by Surrealist automatism, and are among the first Italian examples of action painting. Crippa's first exhibition was at the Bergamini Gallery in Milan in 1947, when his works excited the enthusiasm of Lucio Fontana, who bought a 'spiral' and invited him to join the movement SPAZIALISMO. In the following year Crippa took part, for the first time, in the Venice Biennale, where he was to exhibit without interruption until 1954, and then in a room of his own in 1964 and finally in 1968. In 1950 he travelled to the USA, where he exhibited at the Alexander Iolas Gallery in New York and met Max Ernst and Marcel Duchamp; he later met Wifredo Lam and Victor Brauner in Paris. As a result of these experiences, in 1953 his lines began to take on an anthropomorphic quality, which led to his *Totems* (1955–6), *c.* 60 works created by pouring bronze and copper over iron structures. In 1957, however, he began producing collages and assemblages, in which he used different materials including cork, metal and wood (e.g. *Mimicry of Knowledge*, wood and paint, 2×2 m, 1959; New York, MOMA). The preoccupation with texture and limited colours shows the influence of Alberto Burri. In the late 1960s he began to use intense colours in flat abstract compositions, with lunar and marine references. An acrobatic pilot at international level, Crippa died in an air accident.

DBI
M. Tapié: *Crippa* (Milan, 1969)
Roberto Crippa (exh. cat. by G. Ballo, Milan, Pal. Reale, 1971)

DANIELA DE DOMINICIS

Criscuolo [Crescione]. Italian family of painters. They were active in Naples and southern Italy in the 16th century. (1) Giovan Angelo Criscuolo is recorded as a notary who later turned to painting as a minor exponent of Mannerism. His brother (2) Giovan Filippo Criscuolo painted in a style derived from the followers of Raphael and Perino del Vaga. A number of paintings in the style associated with Giovan Filippo's workshop have been attributed to Mariangela Criscuolo (*fl c.* 1550–*c.* 1580), who was probably his daughter.

(1) Giovan Angelo Criscuolo (*b* Naples, ?1500–10; *d* Naples, after 1577). He is documented as a notary between 1536 and 1560, but, according to de Dominici, Criscuolo abandoned that profession and spent five years in the workshop of Marco Pino, who later helped him obtain his first public commission, the signed and dated *Adoration of the Magi* (1562; untraced, but described by early Neapolitan sources) for S Luigi di Palazzo, Naples (destr.).

Criscuolo's earliest work, the *Stoning of St Stephen* (Naples, Capodimonte), commissioned in 1558, is executed in the Mannerist style of Pino, but later works such as the *Annunciation* (1567; Aversa, Seminario), *St Jerome* (1572; Naples, church of Montecalvario) and the *Assumption of the Virgin* (*c.* 1577; Naples, S Giacomo degli Spagnoli) reveal the delicate manner of the Neapolitan

painters Silvestro Buono (*fl* 1575–82) and Giovan Bernardo Lama (1508–79). In the *Annunciation* Criscuolo appears to have been influenced by the Flemish devotional tradition in his handling of facial expressions and in the delicacy of the features. The *St Jerome*, on the other hand, is closer to Lama's style, especially in the working of the landscape, an aspect that is also important in such works as the S Giacomo *Assumption* and the *Nativity* (Naples, S Paolo Maggiore). In the context of mid-16th-century Neapolitan painting, Criscuolo was a painter of secondary importance, whose work falls within the Mannerist tradition, a style that later adapted itself in Naples to suit the requirements of the Counter-Reformation.

BIBLIOGRAPHY
DBI; Thieme–Becker
C. D'Engenio: *Napoli sacra* (Naples, 1624)
G. C. Capaccio: *Il forestiero* (Naples, 1634)
F. de Petri: *Historia napoletana* (Naples, 1634)
B. de Dominici: *Vite* (1742–5), ii, pp. 154–62
G. Previtali: *La pittura del cinquecento a Napoli e nel Vicereame* (Turin, 1978), pp. 73, 90

(2) Giovan Filippo Criscuolo (*fl c.* 1529–61). Brother of (1) Giovan Angelo Criscuolo. The main influence during his formative years in Naples was Lombard art, especially Bramantino, and he was associated with the workshop of Andrea Sabatini. Works of this early period include a *St Andrew* (1529; Naples, Capodimonte) and *St Dominic* (Naples, S Domenico Maggiore). From the 1530s he was active in the region of Gaeta. His first important cycle comprises 19 panels with scenes from the *Life of the Virgin* and the *Life of Christ* (signed and dated 1531) in the Grotta d'Oro at SS Annunziata, Gaeta. These reflect Lombard influence and the styles of Sabatini and Polidoro da Caravaggio, who was in Naples in 1527. References to Tuscan painting also support the account that he went to Rome and saw works by Raphael and followers of Perino del Vaga (de Dominici). A contemporary altarpiece (Ausonia, S Maria del Piano; dispersed) was crowned with a lunette of the *Death of the Virgin* and the *Assumption of the Virgin* (*in situ*), a theme to which he returned (e.g. Budapest, Mus. F.A.; 1534, Fondi, S Maria Assunta; Lipari Cathedral). A large altarpiece (1540; Vallo della Lucania, Mus. Dioc.; disassembled) reflects Spanish taste in its division into many compartments; the central panel is a copy of Raphael's *Madonna of the Fish* (1513–14; Madrid, Prado), which was then in S Domenico Maggiore, Naples. The style developed in these altarpieces remained substantially unchanged in the altarpiece of *SS Sebastian and Mary Magdalene* (Ravello Cathedral) and the triptych with the *Nativity* (1545; Naples, Capodimonte). His late works, such as the scenes from the *Life of Christ* (Naples, S Paolo Maggiore), are pervaded with the eccentric manner of Polidoro and Perino.

BIBLIOGRAPHY
B. de Dominici: *Vite* (1742–5), ii, pp. 174ff
P. Leone de Castris: 'Giovan Filippo Criscuolo', *Andrea da Salerno nel rinascimento meridionale* (exh. cat., ed. G. Previtali; Padula, Certosa di S Lorenzo, 1986), pp. 229–33
—: 'La pittura del cinquecento nell'Italia meridionale', *La pittura in Italia: Il cinquecento*, ed. G. Briganti (Milan, 1987), pp. 480–81, 689–90

GENNARO TOSCANO

Crissé, Lancelot-Théodore Turpin de. *See* TURPIN DE CRISSÉ, LANCELOT-THÉODORE.

Cristall, Joshua (*b* Camborne, Cornwall, ?1768; *d* London, 18 Oct 1847). English painter. He was brought up in Rotherhithe (London), where his father was a sailmaker. He worked initially painting china, first in Aldgate (London) and later in Shropshire, and was expected to become manager of a china works. Instead he chose an artistic career and in 1792 attended the Royal Academy Schools, London. By 1795 he was working as a professional artist. In the 1790s he also attended Dr Monro's Drawing Academy where he met John and Cornelius Varley. In 1802 and 1803 he sketched in Wales with the Varleys and in 1805 co-founded with them the Society of Painters in Water-colours, where he exhibited regularly for the rest of his life. He was president of the Society in 1816 and 1819 and again between 1821 and 1831. He exhibited a portrait at the Royal Academy in 1803, but thereafter his work consisted mainly of landscapes and figure studies in watercolours as well as numerous pencil and ink sketches. He was also fond of classical subjects, particularly with a pastoral flavour (e.g. *Arcadian Shepherds*, exh. Society of Painters in Water-colours 1811; Dyer priv. col.). His early work shows affinities with Samuel Prout and David Cox, although he soon developed his own distinct style which combined neat draughtsmanship with a stylized, classical treatment of form. *Girl Peeling Vegetables* (*c.* 1810–15; New Haven, CT, Yale U. A.G.) is typical of his exhibited watercolours.

Cristall made a precarious living as a painter over the next 20 years, subsisting for a while on a diet of water and potatoes. During this time he made sketching tours of the Isle of Wight, Scotland and Wales (he may also have visited Paris in 1814). In 1823 he moved to Goodrich in the Wye Valley (Hereford & Worcs). After his wife's death in 1841, Cristall moved back to London and painted portraits for a living, but by this time his style had become outdated. The contents of his studio were auctioned at Christie's in November 1848.

BIBLIOGRAPHY
W. G. S. Dyer: *Joshua Cristall* (London, 1959)
Joshua Cristall: Drawings and Watercolours (exh. cat. by B. Taylor, London, V&A, 1975)

MARTIN POSTLE

Cristina of France. *See* SAVOY, §II(7).

Cristino da Silva. Portuguese family of artists. The painter (1) João Cristino da Silva was one of the first generation of Romantic artists in Portugal. His son, João Ribeiro Cristino da Silva (*b* 1858), was also a painter, while his grandson, (2) Luís Cristino da Silva, practised as an

(1) João Cristino da Silva (*b* Lisbon, 24 July 1829; *d* 12 May 1877). Painter. He studied in Lisbon from 1841 to 1847 at the Academia de Belas-Artes, where he was a pupil of António Manuel de Fonseca and André Monteiro da Cruz (1770–1843). He belonged to the first generation of Romantic artists in Portugal, and as a form of Romantic protest he left the Academia in 1847. He worked for two years as an engraver in the Arsenal do Exército (Arsenal of the Army) and then returned to painting in 1849, but the quality of his work was uneven. In the painting that became famous as the manifesto of Romanticism, *Five Artists at Sintra* (1855; Lisbon, Mus. N. A. Contemp.), he

portrayed his contemporaries—the painters Tomás José Anunciação, Francisco Metrass and José Rodrigues and the sculptor Vítor Bastos—as well as himself. In the centre foreground Anunciação, to whom this work is a homage, is painting in the open air, surrounded by a group of curious country people against the background of the Gothic-style Pena Palace, Sintra, built by Ferdinand II in 1839 and the archetypal Romantic building in Portugal. In 1855 King Ferdinand bought the painting, which was shown at the Exposition Universelle in Paris in the same year.

Cristino had adopted the new aesthetic of sanctifying nature, but this painting, which is a study of nature as well as a group portrait, combining landscape and a scene of everyday life, reflects his inability to accept the autonomous value of landscape. His landscapes are dominated by their structures, which are rather theatrical, with contrived, artificial lighting, as is evident in *View of Lisbon from Entremuros* (1859; Lisbon, Mus. N. A. Contemp.), which he submitted in competition for the Chair of Landscape at the Academy in 1859. His feeling for nature gradually deepened as he considered its grander manifestations, and he chose to paint the kind of scenes in the hills around Sintra that were described by Byron in *Childe Harold* (1812). Cristino was one of the few painters of his generation who responded to the dramatic mountain scenery of the area, as in *Cattle Crossing* (1867; Lisbon, Mus. N. A. Contemp.). Here he depicted the mountain range at Sintra in all its grandeur and the earthy colouring of the ravine rock-face. The painting conveys a feeling of romantic solitude, which contrasts with the diffused natural light over the mountains heralding the approach of nightfall. This idealized depiction of nature in a golden haze of light identifies Cristino as a landscape artist of the new generation.

The election of Anunciação (1852) and Cristino (1859) to the Academia marked the acceptance of Romanticism by the establishment, but Cristino did not adapt to this situation. Accustomed to a more wayward Romanticism, he soon abandoned his professorship, although he continued to exhibit at the Salons of the Sociedade Promotora de Belas-Artes from 1863 to 1876.

BIBLIOGRAPHY
R. de Lima: *A arte* (Lisbon, 1879)
Z. d'Aça: *Lisboa moderna* (Lisbon, 1906)
D. de Macedo: *João Cristino da Silva e Manuel Bordalo Pinheiro* (Lisbon, 1952)
J.-A. França: *A arte em Portugal no século XIX*, i (Lisbon, 1966), pp. 265–7

LUCÍLIA VERDELHO DA COSTA

(2) Luís (Ribeiro Carvalhosa) Cristino da Silva (*b* Lisbon, 25 May 1896; *d* Lisbon, 1976). Architect, grandson of (1) João Cristino da Silva. He was the son of João Ribeiro Cristino da Silva and trained at the Escola de Belas Artes, Lisbon. He was then awarded a Valmôr scholarship to Paris (1920–23), where he studied with Victor Laloux, and Rome (1924), where he studied and drew Roman ruins in great detail. In 1925 he returned to Lisbon and began work on the Capitólio (1926–31; later altered), Lisbon, a concert hall with an open-air cinema on a terrace above that was designed with a solid cubist treatment of mass, with mobile window panels of Art Deco glass and innovative access escalators. In 1933 he became a professor of architecture at the Escola de Belas Artes, winning the appointment in competition with Carlos Ramos. During the 1930s he continued to design Modernist buildings, including the Functionalist Liceu de Fialho de Almeida (1930) at Beja; a house (1932–3) for Amadeu Gaudêncio in the Rua Alexandre Braga, Lisbon; and the Café Portugal (1938; partly destr.) and the Diário de Noticias office (1938), both in Rossio, Lisbon. With the Praça do Areeiro (1938–48) in Lisbon (residential blocks around a large square) he moved towards a revival of 18th-century style that he repeated in the provinces, for example in branches of the Caixa Geral de Depósitos at Guarda (1943) and Leiria (1944; destr.). In 1941 he was inspired by a travelling exhibition of Nazi architecture, *Moderna Arquitectura Alemã*, brought to the Sociedade Nacional de Belas Artes, Lisbon, by Albert Speer. Official Portuguese architecture of the 1940s was influenced by this exhibition, and Cristino da Silva became its principal exponent. Such buildings as the CML building, Rua 1 de Dezembro, Lisbon, and the Cidade Universitária (1943–8; with Cottinelli Telmo), Coimbra, exemplify his experiments with monumentalist designs. Later works include the Ministerios das Obras Públicas e das Comunicaçoes (1951), Lisbon, and urban development projects (1953–61) at Belém.

BIBLIOGRAPHY

'Cristino da Silva: Entrevista', *Arquitectura* [Lisbon], cxix (1971), pp. 2–8
J.-A. França: *A arte em Portugal no século XX* (Lisbon, 1974), pp. 221–9

JOSÉ MANUEL FERNANDES

Cristofano dal Borgo. *See* GHERARDI, CRISTOFANO.

Cristofano dell'Altissimo. *See* ALTISSIMO, CRISTOFANO DELL'.

Cristofano di Michele Martini. *See* ROBETTA.

Cristoforo di Geremia (*fl* 1456–76). Italian medallist, goldsmith and metalworker. Originally from Mantua, he worked most of his life in Rome. In the capacity of metalworker, he repaired the antique Roman statue of *Marcus Aurelius* (Rome, Piazza del Campidoglio; *see* ROME, ANCIENT, fig. 61) in 1468. He is known to have visited Florence in 1462 and was making jewellery for Borso d'Este, Duke of Ferrara, in 1466.

Cristoforo went to Rome in 1456 and seems first to have been employed by Lodovico Scarampi Mezzarota, Cardinal of S Lorenzo and Patriarch of Aquileia (*d* 1465). An unsigned medal with a forceful portrait of this cleric is usually attributed to the artist (Hill, *Corpus*, no. 756). He then entered the papal service and in 1469 received payment for medals of *Paul II* to be buried in the foundations of the Palazzo Venezia, Rome. None of the many surviving medals of this pope, who was an enthusiastic collector of ancient coins, bears Cristoforo's signature. Nonetheless, a large number of medals of Paul II have been attributed to him (Hill, *Corpus*, nos 759–74). Although they follow the normal serial production of papal medals, the portraiture has the strength and individuality of Scarampi's medal.

Cristoforo signed two of his medals. The first, which was probably cast around 1458, shows a splendid bust of *Alfonso V of Aragon, King of Naples* (Hill, *Corpus*, no. 754) and is related to Pisanello's medals of the same subject (Hill, *Corpus*, nos 41–3). The reverse shows Alfonso enthroned and crowned by Bellona and Mars. Although the composition is crowded within the confines of the medal, the suggestion of three-dimensionality achieved through the placement of the figures on a three-quarter axis in depth, and the rich modelling of the bodies of Mars and Alfonso, combine with the draperies of Bellona to create an impressive relief.

The second signed medal, *c.* 1468, is of *Constantine the Great* and, as an imaginary portrait, is rather less impressive (Hill, *Corpus*, no. 755). The reverse shows the dignified figures of the Emperor and the Church clasping hands and demonstrates Cristoforo's ability to give monumentality to his figures. Two further medals are attributed to the artist: *Cardinal Guillaume d'Estouteville, Bishop of Ostia* (London, V&A; Hill, *Corpus*, no. 757) and *Paolo Dotti of Padua* (Hill, *Corpus*, no. 758). The simple and effective reverse of the latter, showing the figure of Constantia, was copied by Andrea Guacialoti for his medals of *Sixtus IV* (Hill, *Corpus*, no. 751) and *Alfonso of Calabria* (Hill, *Corpus*, no. 752).

Cristoforo di Geremia's influence was considerable; Hill called him the founder of the Roman school of medallists. The medallist Lysippus the younger was his nephew, who, together with Guacialoti and possibly Niccolò di Forzore Spinelli, borrowed figures and compositions from Cristoforo.

BIBLIOGRAPHY

Forrer
G. F. Hill: *Medals of the Renaissance* (London, 1920); rev. and enlarged by G. Pollard (London, 1978), pp. 68–70
——: *Corpus*, i (1930), pp. 195–201
G. Pollard: *Italian Renaissance Medals in the Museo Nazionale del Bargello*, i (Florence, 1984), pp. 314–26
J. Woods-Marsden: 'Art and Political Identity in Fifteenth-century Naples: Pisanello, Cristoforo di Geremia, and King Alfonso's Imperial Fantasies', *Art and Politics in Late Medieval and Early Renaissance Italy, 1250–1500*, ed. C. M. Rosenberg (London, 1990), pp. 11–37
The Currency of Fame: Portrait Medals of the Renaissance (exh. cat., ed. S. K. Scher; Washington, DC, N.G.A.; New York, Frick; 1994), pp. 119–120, 381

STEPHEN K. SCHER

Cristoforo di Jacopo Biondi [Benintendi] **da Bologna** (*fl* 1360–1415). Italian painter. He was recorded with his father, the Bolognese painter Jacopo Biondi, in the militia records of 1360, and independently as a painter in 1363. At this date he probably painted most of the frescoes of the *Life of Joseph* from S Apollonia, Mezzaratta (Bologna, Pin. N.), signed *Jacobus*, presumably by his father. He is subsequently documented regularly in Bologna until 1415, both as a painter and as the holder of various civic offices. He was Master of the Town Clock in 1381 and 1393. A *Virgin* from the Palazzo Comunale (Bologna, S Antonio) probably resulted from Cristoforo's employment as a civic artist.

His oeuvre may be reconstructed around a small signed *Crucifixion and Deposition* (Ferrara, Pin. N.), the *Madonna of Mercy* from S Maria Vergine, Mezzaratta, signed and dated 1380 (Bologna, Pin. N.), and the *St Christopher*, signed and dated 1395 (S Cristoforo, Montemaggiore), ycertainly by the same artist. His style is derived predominantly from Vitale da Bologna's, with neat, clean contours, precise drawing and fresh colours almost invariably dominated by mid-yellow, scarlet and light green.

BIBLIOGRAPHY

E. Riccomini: *La pittura bolognese del trecento*, Maestri Colore, 245 (Milan, 1966)

F. Arcangeli: *Pittura bolognese del '300* (Bologna, 1978), pp. 210–23 [with notes by M. Ferretti]

R. Gibbs: 'Cristoforo da Bologna or Dalmasio?', *Burl. Mag.*, cxxiv (1982), pp. 584–90

ROBERT GIBBS

Crişul Alb, Mihu de la. *See* MIHU DE LA CRIŞUL ALB.

Critz, de. English family of painters of Flemish origin. John de Critz (i) (*b* Antwerp, 1551–2; *d* London, *bur* 14 March 1642) was brought to England as an infant in 1552. In or about 1567 he was apprenticed to the Flemish Mannerist painter Lucas de Heere, then resident in England. De Critz stayed with him for at least four years; it was probably de Heere who introduced him to the statesman Sir Francis Walsingham (?1530–90), for whom he worked in Paris (and perhaps in Italy) on at least six occasions (1582–8). He supplied his patron with several works by his own hand and perhaps by others: 'I might go to Fontainebleau, from whence I might send you some rare piece of work.' The works he sent back to England, documented in letters of 1582 from Paris, included a *St John* and a *Neptune and Coenis*. It may be inferred from his training and from his trips to France that de Critz was fully aware of European Mannerism and the school of Fontainebleau. Thus it may well be that his was the driving force behind the development in England of the exotic, courtly and highly mannered Elizabethan portrait style.

In 1603 de Critz was appointed Serjeant-Painter, a post that from 1607 he shared with Robert Peake. Evidence from parish registers suggests that de Critz shared Peake's studio in Holborn Conduit, London. From 1603 onwards de Critz's name occurs regularly in royal accounts. Most of the evidence suggests that he progressively took on the role of an organizer rather than a producer of art; the vast majority of payments to him are for decorative work at the various royal palaces. It is unlikely that he undertook much of the manual labour himself: he is known to have employed numerous assistants and apprentices, and from about 1612 (when he was in his 60s) there are no references to his painting portraits. Nevertheless, he continued, almost to the end of his life, to receive large sums regularly from the Lord Chamberlain's office for preparing decorations and restoring works of art.

No signed or fully documented work by de Critz is known, but the first works that may reasonably be attributed to him date from the 1580s. These are the numerous portraits of Walsingham, variants of a standard portrait pattern; the latest example (ex-Lord Wharton priv. col., sold Christie's, 17 Nov 1948, lot 72) is dated 1589. The composition and technique of most of these (many of them probably studio copies) do little to justify the naming of him by Francis Meres in *Palladis Tamia* (1598) as 'very famous. . .for painting'. There are, however, many English courtly portraits of very high quality from the last two decades of the 16th century and later, which defy attribution for lack of evidence. Considering his exalted patronage (he worked extensively for the Cecils at Hatfield House,

Herts), de Critz was probably responsible for some of these (see fig.). Recent attempts (e.g. Strong) to group together a suggested oeuvre for him seem highly speculative. Nevertheless, records survive among the Cecil papers of payments to de Critz in 1606 for full-length portraits of *King James I, Queen Anne of Denmark* and *Henry, Prince of Wales*, and of *Robert Cecil, 1st Earl of Salisbury*, and his father, *William Cecil, 1st Baron Burleigh*. Portraits fitting these descriptions are to be seen at Hatfield House; although they have not been identified as by de Critz, and it is not known whether they are original paintings or studio copies, they make possible reasonable assumptions of what de Critz's compositions were like. For want of authenticated autograph works, de Critz's personal contribution to the art of painting in England is impossible to gauge. However, since he was at the head of the most substantial artistic studio in London at the turn of the 17th century, his influence must have been seminal.

Of the 16 children (by three wives) of John de Critz (i), three sons are known as painters. His eldest son, John de Critz (ii) (*c.* 1591–*c.* 1642), was briefly Serjeant-Painter

John de Critz (i) (attrib.): *James I*, oil on canvas, 2.03×1.16 m, *c.* 1605–10 (London, private collection)

after his father's death: all available documentation suggests he was a decorator rather than a portrait painter. Thomas de Critz (1607–53) was also a decorative painter and was entrusted with the restoration and cleaning of King Charles I's paintings, including works by Titian. Mary Edmond has convincingly argued that he was the author of the surprising and beautiful series of portraits (*c.* 1645) of the Tradescant family in the Ashmolean Museum, Oxford (e.g. *Hester Tradescant and her Stepson John Tradescant*), which are among the highest achievements of native English painting of the period. Emanuel de Critz (1608–65) was a portrait painter (e.g. the signed and dated full-length portrait of *Sir John Maynard*, 1657; Helmingham Hall, Suffolk, see Waterhouse); he has been suggested (Lane-Poole), probably erroneously, as the author of the Tradescant pictures. He bought paintings and sculpture at the sale of the collection of Charles I and was probably a dealer.

BIBLIOGRAPHY

R. Lane-Poole: 'An Outline of the History of the de Critz Family of Painters', *Walpole Soc.*, ii (1912–13), pp. 45–68

E. Waterhouse: *The Collection of Pictures at Helmingham Hall* (Helmingham Hall, 1958)

R. Strong: *The English Icon* (London, 1969), pp. 259–68

M. Edmond: 'Limners and Picturemakers', *Walpole Soc.*, xlvii (1978–80), pp. 63–225

CHRISTOPHER FOLEY

Crivelli. Italian family of painters. The most eminent member of the family was (1) Carlo Crivelli. His brother (2) Vittore Crivelli also attained distinction as a painter. Their father Jacopo (*fl* Venice, 1444–9) and Vittore's son Giacomo (*fl* Fermo, 1496–1502) were also painters; no works by them are known to survive. Documentation concerning a third brother, Ridolfo (*fl c.* 1487), who may have been a painter, was apparently known to 19th-century authorities; nothing substantiating this figure has come to light.

I. Family members. II. Workshop organization. III. Critical reception and posthumous reputation.

I. Family members.

(1) Carlo (Giovanni) Crivelli (*b* ?Venice, ?1430–35; *d* Ascoli Piceno, before 3 Sept 1495). He produced many large, multi-partite altarpieces in which his highly charged, emotional use of line, delight in detail, decoration and citric colours, often set against a gold ground, convey an intensity of expression unequalled elsewhere in Italy. His mastery of perspective was also used for dramatic impact. As he worked in isolation in the Marches, his style only had local influence. In the 19th century, however, he was one of the most collected of 15th-century Italian painters.

1. Life and work. 2. Technique and style.

1. LIFE AND WORK.

(i) Training and early work, before 1465. On 7 March 1457 a legal suit was brought against Crivelli in Venice for having committed adultery with the wife of a sailor; he was fined and sentenced to six months' imprisonment. Since the proceedings of the trial refer to him as an independent painter, and he is known to have died in 1495, it has been estimated that he was born in the early 1430s, presumably in Venice. Although he always signed himself as a Venetian, no later document mentions him in Venice.

Crivelli presumably learnt the rudiments of painting from his father, Jacopo, who was active in the S Moisè district of Venice in the 1440s. It is assumed that Carlo was then apprenticed to some figure of greater distinction early in life. Ridolfi (1648) claimed that he was a pupil of Jacobello del Fiore; but Jacobello died in 1439, so this must be discounted. Crowe and Cavalcaselle (1871) suggested that Giambono was his master, emphasizing the taste both artists share for lavish costumes and intricate textile patterns. Davies (1972) and others proposed that Crivelli was connected with the Vivarini workshop, since works by him from the 1470s share many characteristics with earlier Vivarini workshop paintings in their treatment of figure types. Crivelli soon came under the influence of the school of Squarcione at Padua. This is evident not so much from stylistic affinities with Squarcione himself, but with his pupils, including Mantegna, Marco Zoppo and Giorgio Schiavone. Schiavone's work *c.* 1460 shows many connections with Crivelli's early style, especially in figure types and characterization, and Zampetti (1961) conjectured that the two may have emigrated to Dalmatia together. This would help to explain how Crivelli was often able to draw on sources from regions in which he is not known to have worked. Squarcione possessed a considerable and diverse collection of drawings for the purpose of teaching, and when Schiavone left Squarcione's workshop he took with him 19 of these drawings, which may have become available to Crivelli during his Dalmatian period. One of these drawings showed 'certain nudes by Pollaiuolo', and this possibly provided the model for the nude figures in the *Martyrdom of St Sebastian* from the predella of Crivelli's Odoni Altarpiece (*c.* 1491; London, N.G.).

Most of these early influences on Crivelli's style may be seen in one of only two signed works datable before his time in the Marches, the *Virgin and Child* (*c.* 1460; Verona, Castelvecchio; see fig. 1), originally from S Lorenzo in Venice. Like many of his paintings, this is iconographically a complicated work, combining two disconnected themes, the infancy and the Passion of Christ. The Virgin stands behind a parapet on which seven minute children, perhaps representing Holy Innocents, present instruments of the Passion to the Child. Behind the Virgin, a cloth of honour and a swag of fruit hang from a curious classicizing structure. Here, as elsewhere in Crivelli's work, fruits and similar objects are not used merely in a decorative manner, but also serve a symbolic function, enhancing the devotional significance of the image. To the right, an arch frames a view of the outskirts of a city, in the middle ground the episode of Peter cutting off the ear of Malchus is enacted, and in the distance the Crucifixion takes place. Van Marle (1923–38, xviii) related the painting to works by Giambono, but Paduan elements are much more prominent: swags and parapets are frequently found in works by Squarcione's pupils, where they are used to construct the spatial context. Mantegna's influence is particularly evident in details such as the raven perched in a defoliated tree, the angel foreshortened from below and the dilapidated wall, here used to mark off the middle

1. Carlo Crivelli: *Virgin and Child, c.* 1460 (Verona, Museo Civico di Castelvecchio)

ground. All of these features have possible parallels in Mantegna's *Agony in the Garden* (London, N.G.)

Possibly of greater significance for his later work than any one of these influences is Crivelli's dependence on aspects of the work of Jacopo Bellini, in whose workshop he may well have received some training. In the picture at Verona the Virgin's facial type and expression correspond with works by Jacopo such as the *Virgin and Child* (Florence, Uffizi), while the treatment of the landscape and the extraordinary perspectival arrangement echo types found in Jacopo's sketchbooks. Several of Crivelli's narrative scenes depend on compositions known from Jacopo's drawings.

(ii) Mature work, 1465 and after. By 1465 Crivelli was living in Zara in Dalmatia (now Zadar, Croatia), then a province of the Venetian Republic. A document dated 11 September 1465 refers to him as a master painter from Venice and a citizen of Zara, indicating that he had been resident there for some time. By 1468 he was working at Fermo in the Marches on his earliest dated work, the Massa Fermana Altarpiece (on dep. Urbino, Pal. Ducale), a small polyptych commissioned by a local patron. Interesting comparisons may be made between this altarpiece and the four triptychs painted in the 1460s for S Maria della Carità, Venice, which have been attributed to the studio of Jacopo Bellini. Crivelli was also familiar with the early work of Giovanni Bellini, who probably contributed to the Carità triptychs. Giovanni's early representations of the Pietà furnished Crivelli with ideas on which his own highly emotional Pietà compositions are based. It is likely that Crivelli maintained some contact with Giovanni in later life.

In 1469 Crivelli executed two more altarpieces at Fermo, one for the parish church at Porto San Giorgio (dispersed) and the other for the Franciscan church at Macerata, of which only a fragment survives (Macerata, Pin. & Mus. Com.). These works established him as a major artist in the Marches. By the end of his career most of the larger towns in the region could boast examples of his work in their principal churches. He achieved his success by satisfying a demand from local ecclesiastics and members of the minor nobility for religious panel paintings, chiefly altarpieces, which could attract attention through devotional appeal and a dazzling display of decorative effects.

Between 1468 and 1473 Crivelli completed no fewer than eight altarpieces, each one showing greater confidence in technique and stylistic refinement. In these works he developed the distinctive characteristics for which his work is most admired, seen to advantage in the polyptych of 1473 in the cathedral of S Emidio, Ascoli Piceno, one of his few altarpieces to remain intact, retaining its original Gothic frame. Like several of Crivelli's early altarpieces, this is an ancona in three tiers, the principal tier showing in separate compartments the Virgin and Child surrounded by four saints. Although this was an old-fashioned format, he gave it new relevance by imbuing the figures with a compelling vitality, as in the *Pietà* depicted in the central panel at the top of the polyptych (see fig. 2).

Crivelli perhaps continued to be based in Fermo for the next few years. Works dating from the early 1470s, such as the polyptych from S Francesco at Montefiore dell'Aso

2. Carlo Crivelli: *Pietà*, central panel from the top of a polyptych, tempera on panel, 610×640 mm, 1473 (Ascoli Piceno, Cathedral of S Emidio)

(dispersed), were destined for churches in the vicinity. By 1483 he had settled in Ascoli Piceno, the largest city in the southern Marches, where local prosperity probably guaranteed superior commissions. The earliest work (untraced) that he seems to have executed in the city was in 1471 for the church of S Gregorio. From 1473 until 1488 his presence in the city is frequently recorded. In June 1478 he bought a house near the cathedral. Documents dating from this year and from 1487 explicitly refer to Carlo Crivelli as a citizen of Ascoli; however, he also received commissions from outlying towns, suggesting a fairly peripatetic life.

Ascoli lay just north of the kingdom of Naples, but was under the Pope's sovereignty. In 1482 Sixtus IV granted the city the right of self-government in return for acknowledgement of his suzerainty. The city celebrated the event by instituting an annual procession held on the feast of the Annunciation, when news of the agreement reached the city. A phrase was coined, *Libertas ecclesiastica* ('Freedom under the Church'), to describe the arrangement. This is inscribed on two commemorative paintings, both depicting the *Annunciation*: one is by Crivelli's follower Pietro Alemanno (1484; Ascoli Piceno, Pin. Civ.); the other is one of Crivelli's most sumptuous and powerful compositions and his largest work devoted to a biblical narrative (1486; London, N.G.; see fig. 3). Painted for SS Annunziata, the church where the procession ended, it is notable for its spectacular perspective scheme, based on a composition in Jacopo Bellini's sketchbook, and is Crivelli's most ambitious attempt at integrating figures and architectural setting. Its use of extra-narrative elements, such as citizens dressed in contemporary costumes and St Emygdius, patron saint of Ascoli, indicates that the work was intended to have special significance for the people of Ascoli. Rushforth (1900) conjectured that Crivelli may

3. Carlo Crivelli: *Annunciation*, egg and oil on canvas, transferred from panel, 2.07×1.47 m, 1486 (London, National Gallery)

4. Carlo Crivelli: altarpiece from S Francesco, Fabriano, with *Pietà* lunette (1.28×2.41 m) above the *Coronation of the Virgin with Saints* (2.25×2.55 m), tempera on panel, 1493 (Milan, Pinacoteca di Brera)

have been involved in political events. In 1490 the anti-papal party gained control in Ascoli, and Neapolitan forces took command. In April 1490 Prince Ferrante of Capua, the future King of Naples, knighted Crivelli at Francavilla. He is also referred to as the Prince's *familiaris* (companion), an honour unlikely to be connected with recognition of artistic distinction—there being no evidence that Ferrante commissioned anything from him—but rather with some service to do with the surrender of the city. Furthermore, it seems significant that Crivelli appears not to have returned to Ascoli until 1495, the year of his death.

During the last five years of Crivelli's life he accepted commissions from towns in the northern Marches, such as Fabriano and Camerino. In most of these works he added the title *miles* (knight) to his signature. On one panel, the *Madonna della candeletta* (Milan, Brera), part of a large altarpiece from Camerino Cathedral and possibly his last completed work, his signature is followed by another title, *Eques aureatus*, perhaps indicating that he had been granted a still greater honour. The enormous cost of his late works is confirmed by an inscription on

the Becchetti Altarpiece (1491; London, N.G.), referring to the considerable expense that the patron incurred in ordering it. His last dated work, the *Coronation of the Virgin with Saints* surmounted by a *Pietà* (1493; Milan, Brera; see fig. 4), originally from S Francesco at Fabriano, is one of only three altarpieces by Crivelli for which records of contracts have survived. On 9 February 1493 he committed himself to completing this commission within two years at a cost of 250 ducats; the altarpiece was delivered in August 1494. The speed of the work suggests that Crivelli ran an exceptionally efficient workshop. Its form was certainly influenced by Giovanni Bellini's altarpiece painted for Pesaro in the 1470s; this originally consisted of a large *Coronation of the Virgin* (Pesaro, Mus. Civ.) surmounted by a panel of the *Pietà* (Rome, Pin. Vaticana). The expressive interlacing of hands in Bellini's *Pietà* was exploited in Crivelli's late works, particularly in the *Pietà* of 1493.

2. TECHNIQUE AND STYLE. Crivelli is often treated as an isolated figure, worthy of attention on account of his unmistakable style and fanciful sense of decoration, but standing apart from the main developments in Italian art because his oeuvre, which is exclusively religious, shows little evidence of concern with the prevailing interests of Renaissance artists. The choice of Ascoli as a base for his operations cut him off from major centres of artistic activity, and consequently several aspects of his work seem old-fashioned by comparison with contemporary painting in Venice or Florence. Unlike many Venetian artists, he never took up oil by itself as a medium, always employing tempera on panel. He also favoured devices such as raised gesso-work to heighten the three-dimensional effects of such details as saints' attributes, gold backgrounds and pieces of coloured glass to simulate jewels, all of which had fallen out of use in Venice soon after he settled in the Marches. Nonetheless, from a technical standpoint he was a highly accomplished artist, bringing traditional techniques to a new peak of refinement. His palette is especially notable, expertise in the handling of pigments being evident from the wide range of rich and brilliant colours he brought to his work.

Crivelli's very individual style is characterized by vigorous draughtsmanship, bold modelling and great attention to such naturalistic details as veins and wrinkles. Each figure is carefully worked out so that no pose or gesture is repeated, a variety emphasized by the use of a wide range of vivid, almost garish colours. But it is the inclination to exaggerate form, sometimes to the point of contortion, yet always with expressive results, that makes these figures memorable. This tendency towards exaggeration may have been deliberately developed to satisfy the devotional needs of the Dominicans and Franciscans, Carlo's major patrons, who advocated the use of striking images as an aid to devotion. However, the immediate source for this kind of treatment of the figure was probably Donatello's altarpiece in Il Santo at Padua (*in situ*), which had a profound effect on many artists of Crivelli's generation, including some who shared these qualities of exaggeration, for instance Cosimo Tura.

Although in his later career Crivelli adopted the Renaissance type of altarpiece, integrating the principal figures into a single space as in the Odoni Altarpiece (London, N.G.), his figure style remained remarkably consistent. The tendency to exaggerate, however, gradually became more prominent, some figures appearing neurotic, even hysterical. Ornamental qualities were also developed further, perhaps inspired by contemporary schemes of architectural decoration in the Palazzo Ducale at Urbino. While it is clear that the major developments in Italian art had little effect on Crivelli's later work, it is sometimes possible to detect isolated new influences. Still-life details in the *Annunciation*, for example, suggest familiarity with Flemish paintings, available to him at Urbino, and the musician angels in the *Coronation of the Virgin* may owe something to Melozzo da Forlì, whose work of the 1480s at Loreto was accessible to him.

(2) Vittore [Vittorio] **Crivelli** (*b* Venice, 1444–9; *d* Fermo, after 10 Nov 1501). Brother of (1) Carlo Crivelli. Like Carlo, Vittore always signed himself as a Venetian. He followed his brother to Zara, where he is documented from 1465. He probably spent some time in Carlo's workshop, although there is only one surviving collaborative work, a polyptych for the church of S Martino at Montesanmartino (*in situ*). In 1469 Vittore took on a pupil in Zara whom he agreed to train for eight years. In 1476 he bought a house there. By 1481 he had moved to the Marches. In that year he signed a contract to paint a polyptych with the *Virgin Enthroned with Saints* (Rome, Pin. Vaticana) for the church of the Madonna di Loreto in Montelparo, and from the same year also dates a polyptych painted for S Francesco in Fermo (Philadelphia, PA, Mus. A.). Vittore settled in Fermo, where he spent most of the rest of his life, apparently in comfortable circumstances. He was first mentioned as an inhabitant of the city in 1489. From this period there survives a series of signed works, mostly depicting the Virgin and Child, a small number of which are dated, including two further polyptychs for churches in Montesanmartino, one of 1489 (S Maria del Pozzo) and the other of 1490 (S Martino). In August 1501 he received a commission for an altarpiece (destr.) destined for S Francesco at Osimo for which he was to be paid 200 ducats, slightly less than Carlo received for his altarpiece of 1493, but an indication that Vittore was similarly held in high esteem. In November 1501 Vittore was paid an advance of 55 ducats for this work, but he must have died not long afterwards, because the following year his son Giacomo Crivelli asked Antonio Solario to finish the altarpiece, which was completed in 1506.

Vittore's last dated work, a *Virgin and Child* (1501; Paris, Louvre), indicates how little his style changed from works dated 20 years earlier. His oeuvre, which is variable in quality, may be seen at its best in the early polyptych painted for S Francesco in Fermo, now dismembered (Philadelphia, PA, Mus. A.). The high quality of this work was recognized during his lifetime, since a contract of 1491 cites it as an exemplar. In the central panel, a *Virgin and Child Enthroned with Angels*, many features, such as the symbolic use of fruit and flowers and the lavish decorative effects, are clearly borrowed from Carlo. A certain angularity in the figure style is also derived from his brother, but without such expressive results. The

draughtsmanship, though at times good, is never as powerful as in Carlo's work, and his figures tend to lack vitality. Colours are also more subdued, and in Vittore's work linear qualities tend to be more pronounced than in Carlo's, since his technique of modelling in tempera is less refined. However, while many of Vittore's figures are simply lightweight adaptations of his brother's types, his own compositions have a sweetness and charm that gives them a character of their own. Such features as flushed pink cheeks, languid expressions and small, delicate hands also help to make his best work immensely appealing.

II. Workshop organization.

The scale of Carlo Crivelli's later works and the degree to which they make use of routine but time-consuming techniques, such as details in relief, punched gold backgrounds and stencilling, suggest that he ran a large workshop, members of which continued employing his stylistic traits long after his death. One follower, the Austrian Pietro Alemanno, actually signed himself on one occasion as a disciple of Carlo, though he was probably never formally a pupil. Carlo's closest and most successful adherent was his brother (2) Vittore Crivelli. Although the two collaborated on only one occasion, on the large polyptych for the church of S Martino at Montesanmartino (*in situ*), Vittore's style is heavily indebted to his brother's, so it is likely that he spent a period in Carlo's shop, perhaps in the early 1460s. The efficiency of the workshop is suggested by the speed with which the commission for the *Coronation of the Virgin* (1493; Milan, Brera) was completed (*see* §I(2)1 above).

III. Critical reception and posthumous reputation.

The large number of commissions that the Crivelli brothers undertook and the enormous prices they could command suggest that both artists enjoyed considerable reputations, although they remained unknown beyond the region of their activity. Their works particularly suited the devotional aims of local religious orders, probably the most significant patrons in the Marches, and, perhaps because of their attractive decorative effects, they were also favoured by the minor nobility. However, there is little evidence that their work was acceptable to patrons in larger cultural centres used to more cosmopolitan tastes. This is perhaps one reason why Giovanni Santi did not mention either Carlo or Vittore in the list of notable artists of his time included in his rhymed chronicle, even though he undoubtedly knew Carlo's work. Neither did Vasari mention them, possibly because he was unfamiliar with their region, but more likely because he considered their achievement insignificant to his notion of the progress of art. It would be wrong to assume from this silence, however, that they were totally forgotten. Some brief 16th-century references have come to light, and several 17th-century sources cite Carlo, notably the historians of Venetian painting Ridolfi (1648) and Boschini (1664), both of whom mentioned lost works by him in Venice; in the Marches, the historian Andreantonelli (1676) made a record of his knighthood. In a history of Montefeltro, Guerrini (1667) described a panel by Carlo at Carpegna.

In the 18th century historians of Ascoli mention Carlo enthusiastically, and he is included in Lanzi's history of Italian painting (1795–6). In the 19th century, however, Carlo's works were neglected and many dispersed. This was due in part to the suppression of convents for which they had been painted, and more particularly to Napoleon's Italian campaigns, resulting in numerous Marchigian paintings being removed to the Brera, Milan, which still possesses one of the largest collections of Carlo's works. Many other works by him were taken to Rome; some are now in the Vatican. By 1801 Cardinal Zelata possessed 13 panels by Carlo. These later (1852–c. 1866) belonged to Prince Anatoly Demidov who formed them into a composite Altarpiece, the Demidoff Altarpiece (London, N.G.) for his villa near Florence. In 1823 the *Virgin and Child* from this ensemble was reproduced in Seroux d'Agincourt's *Histoire de l'art*, and this seems to have provoked interest in Carlo's works among collectors, particularly in England. As a result of the popularity of his work with wealthy Englishmen in the 19th century, the National Gallery, London, has one of the finest collections of his paintings, including the *Annunciation* of 1486 and the Demidoff Altarpiece, both acquired in the 1860s. By the end of the 19th century demand for Carlo's paintings was such that works were reaching very high prices. One altarpiece (Berlin, Gemäldegal.), which sold for 920 guineas in 1849, reached 7000 guineas at a sale in 1892. To satisfy the market for Carlo's works, many polyptychs were dismantled for sale as individual panels; by using antiquarian descriptions and old inventories, later scholars succeeded in reconstructing the original arrangements of these polyptychs.

BIBLIOGRAPHY

EARLY SOURCES AND DOCUMENTS

C. Ridolfi: *Le meraviglie dell'arte* (Venice, 1648); ed. D. von Hadeln, i (Berlin, 1914)

M. Boschini: *Le miniere della pittura veneziana* (Venice, 1664), p. 186

P. A. Guerrini: *La Carpegna abbellita e il Montefeltro illustrato*, i (Urbino, 1667)

S. Andreantonelli: *Breve ristretto della storia di Ascoli* (Ascoli Piceno, 1676)

T. Lazzari: *Ascoli in prospettiva, colle sue più singolari pitture, sculture e architetture* (Ascoli Piceno, [1724])

B. Orsini: *Descrizione delle pitture, sculture, architetture . . . della insigne città di Ascoli* (Perugia, 1790)

A. L. Lanzi: *Storia pittorica dell'Italia* (Bassano, 1795–6, 3/1809)

A. Ricci: *Memorie storiche delle arti e degli artisti della Marca di Ancona*, i (Macerata, 1834)

G. Cantalamessa: 'Artisti veneti nelle Marche', *Nuova Antol.*, xli (1892), pp. 401–31

R. Sassi: 'Arte e storia fra le rovine di un antico tempio francescano', *Rass. March.*, v (1927), p. 348

G. Fabiani: *Ascoli nel quattrocento*, 2 vols (Ascoli Piceno, 1950–51)

P. Zampetti: 'Carlo Crivelli a Zara', *A. Ven.*, xiii-xiv (1960), pp. 227–8

L. Dania: 'Nuovi documenti sui Crivelli', *Appennino Camerte* (31 Jan 1970), p. 3

GENERAL WORKS

DBI; Thieme–Becker

J. A. Crowe and G. B. Cavalcaselle: *History of Painting in North Italy* (London, 1871); ed. T. Borenius, i (London, 1912)

R. van Marle: *Italian Schools*, xviii (1923–38), pp. 3, 32, 42, 44, 48, 50, 65, 81, 88, 97

F. M. Godfrey: *Early Venetian Painters, 1415–1495* (London, 1954)

L. Dania: *La pittura a Fermo e nel suo circondario* (Fermo, 1968)

MONOGRAPHS AND CATALOGUES

G. Rushforth: *Carlo Crivelli* (London, 1900, rev. 2/1910)

F. Drey: *Carlo Crivelli und seine Schule* (Munich, 1927)

A. Bovero: *Tutta la pittura del Crivelli* (Milan, 1961)

P. Zampetti: *Carlo Crivelli* (Milan, 1961) [the principal monograph]

Crivelli e i crivelleschi (exh. cat., ed. P. Zampetti; Venice, Doge's Pal., 1961)

L. Murray: *Carlo Crivelli* (London, 1966)

M. Davies: *Carlo Crivelli* (London, 1972)

S. Di Provvido: *La pittura di Vittore Crivelli* (L'Aquila, 1972)

A. Bovero: *L'opera completa del Crivelli*, Class. A. (Milan, 1975)

P. Zampetti: *Carlo Crivelli* (Fermo, 1986)

SPECIALIST STUDIES

C. Grigioni: 'Notizie biografiche ed artistiche intorno a Vittorio e Giacomo Crivelli', *Rass. Bibliog. A. It.*, ix (1906), pp. 109–19

H. Friedmann: 'The Symbolism of Crivelli's *Madonna and Child Enthroned with Donor*', *Gaz. B.-A.*, 6th ser., xxxii (1947), pp. 65–72

P. Zampetti: 'Un polittico poco noto di Carlo e Vittore Crivelli', *Boll. A.*, xxxvi (1951), pp. 130–38

F. Zeri: 'Cinque schede per Carlo Crivelli', *A. Ant. & Mod.*, iii (1961), pp. 158–76

J. F. Omelia: 'Addenda to a Recent Reconstruction of the Demidoff Altar-piece', *Marsyas*, xi (1962–4), pp. 10–24

S. Legouix: 'Vittore Crivelli's Altar-piece from the Vinci Collection', *Burl. Mag.*, cxvii (1975), pp. 98–102

G. Crocetti: 'Vittore Crivelli e l'intagliatore Maestro Giovanni di Stefano da Montelparo', *Not. Pal. Albani*, v/2 (1976), pp. 17–28

F. V. Lombardi: 'Un capolavoro di Carlo Crivelli e la sua origine', *Antol. B. A.*, iii/9–12 (1979), pp. 43–7

THOMAS TOLLEY

Crivelli, Taddeo [Taddeo da Ferrara] (*fl* 1451; *d* Bologna, by 1479). Italian illuminator and painter. Bertoni hypothesized a Lombard origin for the artist on orthographic grounds, and Crivelli's style seems to support this, although at least 20 years of his working life were spent in Ferrara. The earliest surviving document concerning Crivelli is his personal account book for 1451–7 (Modena, Archv Stor.). Ljuba Eleen (*DBI*) calculated that during this period Crivelli was engaged in more than 100 projects. In carrying out these commissions, he employed a sizeable shop of apprentices and assistants, including Cristoforo Mainardi (*fl* 1454) and Jacopo Filippo d'Argenta. In 1452 Crivelli contracted to illuminate 'uno trato sopra lo evangelio di san zoane che fe santo agostino' for Novello Malatesta. This has been identified with a copy of St Augustine's *Sermons on the Gospel of St John* (Cesena, Bib. Malatestiana, MS. D.III.3).

In 1455 Crivelli received his most important commission, and until 1461, with Franco dei Russi, he was responsible for the illumination of the BIBLE OF BORSO D'ESTE (Modena, Bib. Estense, MS. V.G. 12–3, lat. 422–3). A final summary payment indicates that he was responsible for the execution of $42\frac{1}{2}$ gatherings (quinternions) out of a total of 60. His style can best be seen in the double-folio incipit for Genesis (I, fols 5*v*–6*r*) and the single-page incipits for Psalms (I, fol. 214*r*) and Ecclesiastes (I, fol. 280*v*). Figures are small, with spindly legs and rather large heads with fine features. Costumes tend to be aristocratic, possibly reflecting the patron's taste for luxury. The interest in line visible in details of drapery, golden goffered clouds and wavelike rocks suggests a Lombard background. Architectural spaces, though fragile in appearance, display a grasp of artificial perspective. Colours tend to be opaque and saturated.

In 1467 Crivelli was commissioned to illuminate a copy of Boccaccio's *Decameron* for Teofilo Calcagnini (1441–88), a member of Borso's court. This is generally acknowledged to be a manuscript in Oxford (Bodleian Lib., MS. Holkham misc. 49; see fig.), with miniatures demonstrating the same courtly style as Crivelli's illuminations in the

Taddeo Crivelli: *Ten Protagonists Meet in S Maria Novella*, 80×169 mm, miniature from Boccaccio: *Decameron*, begun 1467 (Oxford, Bodleian Library, MS. Holkham misc. 49, fol. 5*r*)

Bible of Borso d'Este. The last reference to Crivelli in the Este accounts of 1472 records the redemption of eight quinternions of a Breviary that he had pawned in Ferrara. This suggests a hasty and perhaps ignominious exit from the city where his commissions may well have diminished with the death of Borso in 1471. Nonetheless, Crivelli is generally acknowledged as one of the founders of the Ferrarese school of illumination. Bertoni published a letter that indicated that Crivelli also executed larger-scale paintings for Borso, but none has been identified.

Crivelli was recorded in Bologna in 1473 when he and Domenico Pagliarolo (*fl* 1471–97) were commissioned to illuminate a Gradual for the monks of S Procolo. In the same year Crivelli contracted to decorate maps and nautical charts. He may also have been engaged in the production of the first printed maps in Bologna, though the evidence for this is slight. In 1476 he contracted with the clerics of S Petronio for work on a new set of choir-books for the church and, with Bornio de' Bianchi, to illuminate an *Hours of the Virgin*. Some historians have discerned Crivelli's hand in a portion of a Gradual (Bologna, Mus. S Petronio, MS. Cor. III), a manuscript completed by Martino da Modena (*fl* 1477–89). A document of 1479 refers to Crivelli as deceased.

DBI   BIBLIOGRAPHY
H. J. Hermann: 'Zur Geschichte der Miniaturmalerei am Hofe der Este in Ferrara', *Jb. Ksthist. Samml. Allhöch. Ksrhaus.*, xxi (1900), pp. 121–271
G. Bertoni: *Il maggiore miniatore della Bibbia di Borso d'Este 'Taddeo Crivelli'* (Modena, 1925)
M. Salmi: *Pittura e miniatura a Ferrara nel primo rinascimento* (Milan, 1961)
                    CHARLES M. ROSENBERG

Crizzling. Fine network of cracks on the surface of old glass caused by progressive degeneration of the material (*see* GLASS, §V, 1).

Crnčić, Menci Clement [Clements; Klement] (*b* Bruck na Muri [now Bruck an der Mur, Austria], 3 April 1865; *d* Zagreb, 9 Nov 1930). Croatian painter, printmaker, teacher and museum director, of Austrian birth. After graduating from the military academy in Vienna he studied painting at the academies of fine art in Vienna and Munich. In 1886–7 he painted sets for the Landestheater in Coburg. For a short time he taught painting in the School of Arts and Crafts in Zagreb, but he left in 1894 to take up a scholarship at the academy in Vienna, studying etching and engraving. He was the first artist in the Croatian graphic tradition to abandon a strictly linear style and use tonal variation to create contrasting areas of light and shade. He first established himself as a marine artist with a series of paintings of the Istrian peninsula and the Adriatic coast. In 1903, with the painter Bela Čikoš-Sesija (1864–1931), he opened the first private painting school in Zagreb, which eventually developed into the Academy of Fine Arts. He taught there until the end of his life. He became a member of the Yugoslav Academy of Arts and Sciences in 1919 and was the Director of the Strossmayer Gallery of Old Masters from 1920 to 1928. His early work shows the influence of the Realism characteristic of the Munich circle of painters and uses a subdued palette, as in *The Girl* (1890) and *Old Men Shelling Corn Cobs* (1891; both Zagreb, Gal. Mod. A.). While painting his coastal landscapes *en plein air*, he gradually used bolder and brighter colours, and the influence of the Zagreb Colourist school of painting led by Vlaho Bukovac is also evident. Crnčić is unsurpassed as a marine painter in Croatian art (e.g. *Island of St Mark* and *The View from Plasa*).

BIBLIOGRAPHY
A. G. Matoš: *Menci Clement Crnčić* (Savremenik, 1910)
Lj. Babić: *Umjetnost kod Hrvata u XIX. stoljeću* [Art in 19th-century Croatia] (Zagreb, 1934), pp. 119–23
M. Peić: *Slikar našeg pejzaža* [Painter of our landscape] (Vjesnik, 1965)
                    BORIS VIŽINTIN

Crngrob, Bolfgangus of. *See* BOLFGANGUS OF CRNGROB.

Croatia [Hrvatska]. Republic of the former Yugoslavia in south-eastern Europe. It covers 56,538 sq. km (mainland and islands), including the regions of Dalmatia, Slavonia and most of Istria, and it has a population of *c.* 4.8 million, of whom over 75% are Roman Catholics. Much of northern Croatia is a plain, while the Dinaric Alps in the south adjoin the country's Adriatic coast. Croatia is bordered by Slovenia to the north-west, Hungary to the north-east, Serbia to the east and Bosnia–Herzegovina to the south (see fig. 1). The capital is ZAGREB.

I. Introduction. II. Architecture. III. Painting, graphic arts and sculpture. IV. Decorative arts. V. Collections and institutions.

I. Introduction.

Greek culture began to spread along the eastern Adriatic as early as the 8th century BC, with important Greek settlements at such sites as Zadar, Hvar, Vis and Korčula.

The Roman occupation of the Dalmatian coast began in the 2nd century BC, and Roman civilization survived there into the 5th century AD (*see* ROME, ANCIENT, §II, 2(ii)(a)). After the collapse of the Roman empire, various cultural influences held sway. According to the Byzantine emperor Constantine VII, the Croats, whose origins are as yet unknown, settled the region of Croatia and Bosnia in the early 7th century AD. An independent kingdom was established there in 925 and survived until 1102, when Croatia entered into a union with Hungary under the Hungarian king Koloman (*reg* 1095–1116). Hungary and Venice fought over Dalmatia from the 12th century until the 15th; with the exception of northern Dalmatia and DUBROVNIK, the area fell to Venice in 1420.

After the invasion of Bosnia by the Ottomans in 1463, the Croatian population of Bosnia (*c.* 750,000) was halved by emigration to Dalmatia, Slavonia, Italy and Austria. Croatia became part of the Habsburg empire in 1526. Warfare continued along the Ottoman frontier and led to further depopulation, but by the end of the 17th century the frontier between the Turkish and Habsburg empires

1. Map of Croatia; those sites with separate entries in this dictionary are distinguished by CROSS-REFERENCE TYPE

had stabilized. After the demise of the Habsburg empire at the end of World War I, Croatia was incorporated into the newly formed Kingdom of Serbs, Croats and Slovenes (known from 1929 as the Kingdom of Yugoslavia). In 1941 the Independent State of Croatia was established, but in 1945 the country became part of the People's Republic of Yugoslavia. In 1991 Croatia's declaration of independence was followed by Serbian invasion and a war during which many architectural monuments and works of art were damaged or destroyed.

II. Architecture.

One of the earliest surviving examples of Byzantine architecture in Croatia is the 6th-century basilica of Bishop Euphrasius at Poreč (for illustration see POREČ). The first significant period of building, however, began in 880 AD, when Croatia became independent of Byzantine domination and came under the jurisdiction of the Roman Catholic Church. Building activity intensified in the 10th century, when King Tomislav (reg 925–30) united northern Croatia with Dalmatia. Most surviving constructions from this period are rustic, vaulted, single-domed churches, many of them adaptations of earlier ruins, such as St Barbara at Trogir, St Donat at Zadar (a monumental circular structure) and the small but refined cruciform church of the Holy Cross at Nin. Larger buildings were the basilicas at Knin, Biograd na Moru and Bribir. Croatia joined the Hungarian Union in 1102, although Dubrovnik remained an independent city state until 1808. Owing to the variety of cultural influences, architecture in the regions—Slavonia on the Panonnian Plain, Dalmatia with its fortified cities, and Istria—developed at different rates. Feudalism activated expansion and the building of such new cities as Grič-Zagreb (1266) and Kaptol-Zagreb (1387), with fortifications built on the pattern of Central European towns. In Istria and Dalmatia, where cities had been founded as early as 400 BC, building activity consisted mainly of infills (Poreč, PULA, Rijeka, Senj, Cres, Osor, Krk, Rab). Split, which was formed by multi-storey infills in Gothic and Romanesque styles within the walls of Diocletian's Palace, is the first proto-modern conurbation (11th century; see SPLIT, §2). It was DUBROVNIK, however, with its Mediterranean and south Balkan links, that developed most rapidly. Here, between the 10th and 12th centuries, a unique urban whole, with a magnificent marble paved axis, was formed, and from 1272 the city was regulated by building statute.

In ecclesiastical architecture, churches in Istria and Kvarner show proto-Romanesque and early Romanesque characteristics (with simple rectangular plans and internal or external apses), such as at the Benedictine church (1060) on Rab. A monumental Romanesque church from about the same date is the basilica of St John on Rab. Romanesque basilicas of Apulian, Anconian and Lombardian type are St Mary's (1105), St Krševan (1175; rebuilt) and St Stošija (1285), all in Zadar. Diocletian's mausoleum in Split (c. AD 300) was converted into a cathedral in the 8th century, although the campanile, in Romanesque/Gothic transitional style, dates from the 13th century.

Other outstanding Romanesque buildings include Dekumanska Street 32 and the Canonika (1252), both in Poreč; the town hall built around the Roman temple of Diana in Pula and the nucleus of the Rector's Palace in Dubrovnik.

In the late 13th century there was a boom in church building in Gothic style, as in the Franciscan churches at Pula and Poreč and in the chapel of St Stephen (13th century), the cathedral (begun 1263) and St Mark's Church (14th–15th century), all in ZAGREB. The transition from Romanesque to Gothic is also evident in many public buildings in Dalmatia, such as the loggia (begun 14th century) in Trogir. During the 15th and 16th centuries the Gothic style continued to dominate the architecture of northern Croatia, and between the 11th and 16th centuries the older urban nuclei were fortified. In the coastal region, however, from the mid-15th century, the influence of the Renaissance gradually fused with the Gothic to create a unique, idiosyncratic style. After a period of stagnation under Venetian domination, this period was one of great activity. In Šibenik the magnificent cathedral was built in Venetian Gothic style (begun 1443; damaged 1991; for discussion and illustration see GIORGIO DA SEBENICO). The arsenal (1559; rebuilt 1611), city tower (1466) and loggia (1517) were erected in Hvar, and the fountain (1436–8) in Dubrovnik was built by Onofrio di Giordano della Cava (fl 1430s). Renaissance elements began to appear on residential buildings as additions to existing Gothic structures. Patrician palaces and public buildings were imbued with the humanist spirit: in Dubrovnik both the Rector's Palace (before 1435; by della Cava; for illustration see DUBROVNIK) and the Sponza Palace (begun 1516) fuse Gothic and Renaissance styles. Architects whose works show the new Renaissance influences include ANDREA ALESSI (e.g. baptistery in Trogir Cathedral, 1466–7), and Michelozzo di Bartolomeo (e.g. Fort Bokar, Dubrovnik, begun 1461). The chapel of Blessed Giovanni Orsini in Trogir Cathedral (1468; completed c. 1497) by the sculptor and architect NICCOLÒ DI GIOVANNI FIORENTINO is a highly developed Renaissance work (see TROGIR, §1). In 1475 Niccolò succeeded Giorgio da Sebenico as architect in charge of the cathedral in Šibenik, a post he held until his death.

In the 16th century and for much of the 17th, both northern Croatia, orientated towards Central Europe, and Dalmatia, dominated by Venice, were under constant threat from the Ottomans, but in the late 17th century there was rapid urban expansion. Dubrovnik, which suffered an earthquake in 1667, was restored and energetically rebuilt. This was the era of Viennese Baroque in the north, Venetian Baroque in Istria and Dalmatia and Roman Baroque in Dubrovnik. Zagreb assumed the contours of a Baroque town, as did provincial cities such as Vukovar (destr. 1991), while fortifications were reinstated in Renaissance style around old cities such as Novi Grad and Kraljevica. Fortified manor houses became a feature of Trogir and Starigrad. The new city hall in Kaptol, Zagreb, the city hall in Rovinj, the loggia and clock tower in Zadar, the arsenal and the theatre in Hvar (all 17th century) and the Baroque military barracks in Osijek (1726) were all public buildings developed by the military and bureaucratic authorities. During the Baroque period a number of manor houses and palaces were also built, usually with an articulated *piano nobile*; outstanding examples are the Archbishop's Palace (1730), the Oršić-Rauch Palace (1740–80) and the Kulmer Palace (17th–18th centuries), all in Zagreb; the Sinčić Palace in Poreč; the Zmajević Palace in Zadar; and the Cindro Palace in Split. All have central entrance halls and imposing staircases. Outstanding Baroque ecclesiastical buildings include the Jesuit churches of St Catherine in Zagreb (1620–32; for illustration *see* ZAGREB) and St Ignatius in Dubrovnik (1699–1725; by Andrea Pozzo; damaged by mortar shells 1991). Also of note is the Baroque Franciscan monastery at Vukovar (18th century; destr. 1991).

In the 19th century, capitalist investment in Croatia resulted in the building of a rail link between Vienna and Zagreb and Rijeka, which encouraged shipping in the main Adriatic ports. City fortifications had by this time lost their function, and urban development was governed by new economic principles, with Zagreb being expanded on a grid plan. Often, though, it should be said, foreign developers were unsympathetic to the architectural context provided by small Dalmatian towns and erected some incongruous buildings. Notable public architecture of this period in Zagreb included the Old Theatre (1834), as well as two Neo-classical buildings by BARTOL FELBINGER: the Draškovic-Jelačić Palace (1830) and the Domotörffy Palace (1820–30). These marked Zagreb as the centre of a stylistic transformation, but Neo-classical buildings were

also built elsewhere in Croatia, such as the Januševac Manor House (1828) in Novi Marof, also by Felbinger, the Pejačević Palace (1812) in Našice and the Esterhazy Palace (18th century) in Darda (architects of the last two buildings unknown). In the mid-19th century, however, Neo-classicism gradually gave way to eclectic and revivalist styles, such as Gothic Revival, Renaissance Revival and neo-Baroque, as in the Vraniczany Mansion (1881–2; by Otto von Hofer; now the Gallery of Modern Art, Zagreb). In the second half of the century a number of massive public buildings were erected in a variety of revival styles in Zagreb, including the Renaissance Revival Croatian Academy of Arts and Sciences (1880; by Friedrich von Schmidt) and the neo-Baroque Croatian Opera House (1895; by Hermann Helmer and Ferdinand Fellner). In 1880 the cathedral in Zagreb was destroyed by an earthquake; it was subsequently rebuilt in a Gothic Revival style by Hermann Bollé.

Towards the end of the 19th century, many Croatian architects returned from studying abroad; they included Martin Pilar (1861–1942), Ćiril Iveković (1864–1933), Josip Vancaš (1859–1932), Janko Josip Grahor (1855–1918) and Janko Holjac (1865–1939). A notable new influence was that of the Vienna Secession, which found expression in residential buildings (e.g. the Kalina and Popović blocks in Zagreb). A key figure in this change in architectural thinking was VIKTOR KOVAČIĆ, who returned to Zagreb from Vienna in 1899 and built St Blaise

2. Viktor Kovačić: design drawing of St Blaise, Zagreb, 1912

(1912; see fig. 2) in Zagreb. However, in 1918, when Croatia was absorbed into the new Kingdom of Serbs, Croats and Slovenes, it was cut off from its Western European architectural links, giving rise to the mediocre development of cheap populist housing at the expense of cultural buildings. The only progressive institution was the Faculty of Architecture (1919) at the University of Zagreb, the professors of which had international status: ALFRED ALBINI, JURAJ DENZLER and others. Logical, functional analysis, clean structure and well-designed space were its main characteristics. Many 20th-century Croatian architects were educated abroad, among them JURAJ NEIDHARDT, ZDENKO STRIŽIĆ and DRAGO IBLER. World War II caused widespread destruction, and the subsequent Socialist policies gave priority to industrial buildings and public housing that were often architecturally superior to equivalent buildings in Western Europe in the 1950s and 1960s. A talented new generation of architects also produced impressive work, for example I. Emili (office building, Rijeka, 1970), I. Crnković (kindergarten, Samobor, 1975), N. Segvić (museum, Rijeka, 1976), B. Magaš (stadium, Split, 1979), M. Pecotić (department store, Korčula, 1979), E. Smit (private house, Brezje, 1981) and D. Mance (crematorium, Zagreb, 1985). Numerous other Croatian architects settled abroad and achieved considerable success in Western European centres, e.g. Paul Tvrtković's New London Theatre (1972; with Sean Kenny and Chew & Percival). Many buildings in Croatia were damaged during the war with Serbia in 1991.

BIBLIOGRAPHY

E. Laszowski: *Hrvatske povijesne gradjevine* [The historical buildings of Croatia], i (Zagreb, 1902)

C. Fisković: *Romaničke kuće u Splitu i Trogiru* [Romanesque houses in Split and Trogir], ii (Zagreb, 1952)

L. Karaman: 'Juraj Dalmatinac', *Hrvatsko kolo*, 3rd ser., v/2 (1952), pp. 99ff

A. Mohorovičić: *Analiza historijsko-urbanističkog razvoja grada Zagreba* [An analysis of the historical and urban development of the city of Zagreb] (Zagreb, 1952)

A. Albini: *Uslovi razvitka nove arhitekture u NRH* [The preconditions for the development of modern architecture in the People's Republic of Croatia] (Zagreb, 1953)

L. Beritić: *Utvrdjenja grada Dubrovnika* [The fortifications of the town of Dubrovnik] (Zagreb, 1955)

C. Fisković: *Prvi dubrovački graditelji* [The first known Dubrovnik builders] (Dubrovnik, 1955)

A. Mohorovičić: *Problemi tipološke klasifikacije objekata srednjovjekovne arhitekture na području Istre i Kvarnera* [Problems of typological classification of the buildings of the medieval period in the region of Istria and Kvarner] (Zagreb, 1957)

K. Prijatelj: 'Dokumenti za historiju dubrovačke barokne arhitekture' [Documents for the history of Dubrovnik Baroque architecture], *Tkalčićev Zborn.*, ii (1958)

Enciklopedija likovnih umjetnosti [Encyclopedia of fine arts], ii (Zagreb, 1962), pp. 587–600

Arhitektura v Hrvatskoj, 1945–1985 [Architecture in Croatia, 1945–1985] (Zagreb, 1986)

Croatia, Bosnia-Herzegovina—Sacral Institutions on Target: Deliberate Military Destruction of Sacral Institutions in Croatia and Bosnia-Herzegovina (Zagreb, 1993)

PAUL TVRTKOVIĆ

III. Painting, graphic arts and sculpture.

1. BEFORE 1800. Croatian art developed from the 7th century AD on the rich layers of Greek and Roman cultural traditions and combined Byzantine and Western influences. After the Croats converted to Christianity (second half of 9th century AD), pre-Romanesque sculpture began to appear along the Adriatic coast of the territory they inhabited as an integral part of ecclesiastical architecture and liturgy. Examples are screens, ciboria and fonts, often decorated by polychrome ornamental plaitwork in low relief. During the 11th century, flat geometric forms gave way to the figurative and richer modelling of early Romanesque art, as in the screen (c. mid-11th century; now Zadar, Permanent Exh. Eccles. A.) from St Nediljica, Zadar, and in the screen in the baptistery of Split Cathedral (see fig. 3). A similar process can be seen in the liturgical manuscripts (8th–11th century) written in either Beneventan or Carolingian script. At the beginning of the 11th century, manuscripts were illuminated with rich animal and plant motifs, as in the Šibenik sacramentary (Šibenik, Franciscan Monastery; monastery damaged 1991). There are few examples of Romanesque art in northern, continental Croatia, while the Dalmatian coast provides the main focus for the development of the style. Andrija Buvina (first half of 13th century) and RADOVAN produced the most important sculptural works of the Romanesque period in Croatia: Buvina carved 28 scenes from the *Life of Christ* (1214) in walnut for the doors of Split Cathedral (see SPLIT, §2), while Radovan executed the west portal (1240) of Trogir Cathedral (see TROGIR, §1). Wall paintings, icons and manuscript illumination, however,

3. Screen panel with relief of a Croatian king, stone, Split Cathedral, baptistery of St John, second half of the 11th century

continued to be influenced by the Byzantine tradition, gradually absorbing the influence of the early Italian Renaissance in the 15th century.

Inland Croatia, with Zagreb as its centre, came under the influence of the mid-European Gothic style in the 14th century. While the oldest paintings in Zagreb Cathedral (in the Sacristy) are of the 13th century, the wall paintings in the chapel of St Stephen date from the 14th century and are Gothic in style. In Istria, Gothic wall painting developed separately, combining a traditional, refined Gothic style with a strong folk element, as in the wall paintings (1474) by Vincent of Kastav in St Mary on Škrlinah, Beram. In Dalmatia, the Gothic style began to establish itself in the 14th and 15th centuries under the influence of Venice, southern Italy and Lombardy. The sculptor and architect Giorgio da Sebenico is a central figure in the art of that period; his tomb of *St Anastasius* (1448) in Split Cathedral and the apsidal frieze of heads (1443–4) on the exterior of Šibenik Cathedral (cathedral partly destr. 1991) combine Late Gothic and Renaissance styles (for discussion and illustration *see* GIORGIO DA SEBENICO). The influence of Venice is clearly evident in the work of many Croatian painters who were educated there, probably including Blaž Jurjev Trogiranin (*c.* 1390–1450), whose paintings can be found in Trogir, Korčula, Zadar and Dubrovnik. In the 15th century and early 16th there were several painters in Dubrovnik who successfully combined Late Gothic and Renaissance styles, notably Lovro Dobričević (*d* 1478), Nikola Božidarević (*c.* 1460–1517/18) and Mihajlo Hamzić (*d* 1518). In their work the local Renaissance style achieved its pinnacle; thereafter the quality of painting declined, and art in Dalmatia became provincial in comparison with the maturing of Renaissance art in Italy.

In Croatia, Renaissance ideas were more clearly expressed in sculpture, for example in the work of ANDREA ALESSI, who executed the monumental baptistery (1467) in Trogir Cathedral. The most important sculptural and architectural work by NICCOLÒ DI GIOVANNI FIORENTINO is the chapel of the Blessed Giovanni Orsini (completed *c.* 1497) in Trogir Cathedral. The chapel also includes sculptures by GIOVANNI DALMATA and by Alessi. The most important Croatian painters of the High Renaissance were ANDREA SCHIAVONE and GIULIO CLOVIO (Juraj Klovic). Schiavone worked in Venice, where he completely absorbed the Venetian style; Clovio, an illuminator, worked mainly in Rome, where he executed the Farnese Hours (1546; New York, Pierpont Morgan Lib., MS. M.69).

During the 17th century the focus of artistic activity shifted from the Adriatic coast to inland Croatia (Zagreb, Varaždin), where the Jesuits and Paulists made their impact on religious art. The area had not been exposed to the influence of the Renaissance, instead retaining Late Gothic elements that slowly evolved into the Baroque. FEDERICO BENCOVICH was one leading figure, while the large wall paintings of IVAN RANGER are in a distinctive illusionistic style, as in the choir of the Paulist monastery, Lepoglava (1735–7), and in St Mary of the Snows, Belec (1740–43). Secular themes began to appear around this time, mainly comprising portraits of the nobility. The Baroque style is particularly evident, though, in sculpture, for example at

St Catherine's, Zagreb (17th century), the Paulist church, Lepoglava, and St Mary of the Snows, Belec (both early 18th century).

2. 1800 AND AFTER. Painting in the first half of the 19th century in Croatia followed the Viennese Biedermeier style. Many foreign painters who visited Croatia settled there, such as Carmel Reggio (*d* 1813) in Dubrovnik, Franjo Conrad von Hetzendorf (1770–1841) in Osijek and Mihael Stroj in Zagreb. The most important painter of the time was VJEKOSLAV KARAS, who studied in Rome and whose paintings were close in spirit to those of the Nazarenes and to Italian academic painting. Private drawing schools were founded in large towns, and as a result of the patronage of Bishop Josip Juraj Strossmayer, art life in Croatia experienced a revival. Young painters were enabled to study in Italy, and the Bishop founded a gallery of Old Master paintings in Zagreb (1884; now the Strossmayer Gallery of Old Masters). In the second half of the 19th century, painting was dominated by historical and romantic subject-matter, while towards the end of the century a tendency towards realism appeared, notably in the work of FERDO QUIQUEREZ and NIKOLA MAŠIĆ. In 1879 the Art Society was founded in Zagreb, while the foremost painter of the period, VLAHO BUKOVAC, campaigned for the building of studios for artists and of the Art Pavilion (1898) in Zagreb. His works are exceptional for their refined colours, as in *Gundulić's Dream* (1894; Zagreb, Gal. Mod. A.; see fig. 4). Important graphic work in Croatia followed the founding of lithographic workshops in Zagreb (1850). Townscapes and themes from Croatian history were the main subjects.

Until the arrival in Croatia of the Viennese sculptor Anton Dominik Fernkorn in the mid-19th century, sculptural activity in Croatia had been largely undistinguished. The most prolific sculptor during the second half of the 19th century was Ivan Rendić, who lived from 1881 to 1921 in Trieste, where he made monuments for towns in Croatia, such as the memorial to *Ivan Gundulić* (1893) in Dubrovnik, as well as many busts and tombstones. With the emergence of the Secession and modernism in Vienna and Munich and the founding of the School for Applied Arts (1882) and the Art School (1907; later the Academy of Arts) in Zagreb, sculptors who had been educated in Vienna, Munich and Paris began to arrive in Zagreb. They included Robert Frangeš Mihanović (1872–1940), Rudolf Valdec (1872–1929) and Branislav Dešković (1883–1939). At the end of the 19th century, Post-impressionism and the work of Paul Cézanne influenced Croatian painting via Munich, where many Croatian artists studied. The 'Munich circle' of Croatian painters was made up of Josip Račić (1885–1908), MIROSLAV KRALJEVIĆ and Oskar Herman (1886–1974). Expressionist ideas first appeared at the Croatian Spring Salon in Zagreb in 1916, and Expressionist painters produced lithographs and etchings equally as powerful as their paintings.

In the inter-war period, art in Croatia retained its individuality in relation to other artistic centres in the Kingdom of Yugoslavia (1918–41). The avant-garde magazine *Zenit* was published in Zagreb from 1921–3, then in Belgrade until 1926. Art life was dominated by a tendency towards realism and social concerns, following the example

4. Vlaho Bukovac: *Gundulić's Dream*, oil on canvas, 1.85×3.10 m, 1894 (Zagreb, Gallery of Modern Art)

of George Grosz. In 1929 the EARTH GROUP was founded in Zagreb. It brought together progressive architects, left-wing artists and some naive artists. One of its co-founders, KRSTO HEGEDUŠIĆ, was the leading artistic force in Zemlja and acted also as its secretary until the group was banned in 1935. Perhaps the most important Croatian artist of the time, however, was the sculptor IVAN MEŠTROVIĆ, whose work ranged from Symbolism to Art Deco and whose artistic and teaching career spanned the first half of the 20th century, until he moved to the USA after World War II. Among the artists he influenced, two sculptors particularly stand out: FRANO KRŠINIĆ and Antun Augustinčić (1900–79).

From 1945 until 1956–7, art in Croatia was dominated by Socialist Realism, but in 1951 the group EXAT-51 appeared in Zagreb, seeking geometric abstraction and greater freedom of artistic creativity. Four members of this group, IVAN PICELJ, Vlado Kristl (*b* 1923), Božidar Rašica (*b* 1912) and Aleksandar Srnec (*b* 1924), exhibited in 1953 at the first exhibition of geometric abstraction in Croatia. Another new influence was Abstract Expressionism, which earned EDO MURTIĆ an international reputation. Dark, dreamlike Surrealism can be found in the work of Miljenko Stančić (1926–77). Meanwhile the screenprint revived graphic production. The Gorgona group was formed in Zagreb in 1961; their activity was similar to that of the Fluxus group. The same year an informal group of artists gathered to develop styles based on geometric abstraction, neo-Constructivism and kinetic art. Artistic activities were no longer concentrated in the capital. Osijek, Rijeka and Dubrovnik became equally important, and alternative galleries staged radical and experimental shows, including happenings. The renewal of naive art and the

expansion of the circle of primitive artists, for example by the HLEBINE SCHOOL, was prompted by the opening of the Gallery of Primitive Art in Zagreb in 1952.

Sculpture after 1945 was largely controlled by the Academy of Arts in Zagreb, and, until the 1950s, had to be ideologically correct. Radical innovations were nevertheless introduced by DUŠAN DŽAMONJA, VOJIN BAKIĆ and Ivan Kožarić (*b* 1921), who made a significant and genuine contribution to sculpture of the period. Šime Vulas (*b* 1932) was more traditional in his approach. Multimedia experiments and procedural techniques began to appear in Croatian art *c*. 1970. The younger generation of artists, such as BRACO DIMITRIJEVIĆ and Goran Trbuljak (*b* 1948), took conceptual art as their starting-point. In 1973–4 Dalibor Martinis (*b* 1947) and Sanja Iveković (*b* 1949) began working with video art. Around 1980, art in Croatia was enriched by the diversity of approaches that characterized Post-modernism.

BIBLIOGRAPHY

L. Karaman: *Iz kolijevke hrvatske prošlosti* [From the cradle of the Croatian past] (Zagreb, 1930)
E. Dyggve: *History of Salonitan Christianity* (Oslo, 1951)
L. Karaman: *Pregled umjetnosti u Dalmaciji: Od doseljenja Hrvata do pada Mletaka* [Overview of art in Dalmatia: from the arrival of the Croats to the fall of Venice] (Zagreb, 1952)
M. Prelog: 'Izmedju antike i romanike' [Between antiquity and the Romanesque], *Peristil*, i (1954), pp. 5–14
I. Petricioli: *Pojava romaničke skulpture u Dalmaciji* [The appearance of Romanesque sculpture in Dalmatia] (Zagreb, 1960)
Slikarstvo XIX. stoljeća u Hrvatskoj [19th-century painting in Croatia] (exh. cat., Zagreb, Gal. Horvat, 1961) [with Fr. summary]
B. Fučić: *Istarske freske* [Istrian frescoes] (Zagreb, 1963)
A. Horvat: *Izmedu gotike i baroka: Umjetnost kontinentalnog dijela Hrvatske od oko 1500 do oko 1700* [Between Gothic and Baroque: the art of continental Croatia between *c*. 1500 and *c*. 1700] (Zagreb, 1975) [with Ger. summary]

The New Art Practice in Yugoslavia, 1966–1978 (exh. cat., Zagreb, Gal. Contemp. A., 1978)

Enciklopedija Hrvatske povjesti i kulture [Encyclopedia of Croatian history and culture] (Zagreb, 1980)

A. Horvat, R. Matejčić and K. Prijatelj: *Barok u Hrvatskoj* [The Baroque in Croatia] (Zagreb, 1982)

Inovacije u hrvatskoj umjetnosti sedamdesetih godina [Innovations in Croatian art during the seventies] (exh. cat., Zagreb, Gal. Mod. A., 1982)

K. Prijatelj: *Dalmatinsko slikarstvo 15. i 16. stoljeća* [Dalmatian painting of the 15th and 16th centuries] (Zagreb, 1983)

Z. Rus and J. Denegri: *Apstraktna umjetnost u Hrvatskoj* [Abstract art in Croatia], 2 vols (Split, 1985)

R. Ivančević: *Art Treasures of Croatia* (Motovun, 1986)

G. Gamulin: *Hrvatsko slikarstvo XX stoljeća* [Croatian painting of the 20th century], 2 vols (Zagreb, 1987)

I. Fisković: *Romaničko slikarstvo u Hrvatskoj* [Romanesque painting in Croatia] (Zagreb, 1989)

J. Dec. & Propaganda A., xvii (1990) [issue devoted to Yugoslavia]

M. Prelog: *Djela: Prostor Vrijeme* [Works: space-time] (Zagreb, 1991)

ZELIMIR KOŠČEVIĆ

IV. Decorative arts.

Both the northern and southern parts of Croatia, including the Adriatic coast, reflect the historic influences of Asia Minor and the Aegean region. Ceramics are the most important survivals from the Neolithic age in Croatia. The oldest examples are from the Starcevacka culture from the northern region, which produced highly polished painted vessels. In the coastal areas, the Danilo culture produced pottery with a characteristic incised decoration. The transitional Aeneolithic period (3500–2300 BC) is identified by strong, naturalistic forms with incised, polychromatic ornament, seen for example in a vessel (Zagreb, Archaeol. Mus.) in the form of a dove, from Vucedol.

In the 9th century AD and for the following 200 years Croatian goldsmiths produced very distinctive jewellery. The type of earrings worn then became a standard form of folk jewellery for centuries thereafter. The first Croatian goldsmiths' guild was established in Zadar in the 12th century. The Zadar, Nin and Dubrovnik treasuries contain the most important collections of early Croatian goldsmiths' work, the Dubrovnik Cathedral Treasury, for example, housing three reliquaries of St Blaise dating from the 9th to the 12th century. The first time artists can be positively identified occurs in the Middle Ages. The wooden doors of Split Cathedral, completed in 1214, were executed by the highly respected painter and sculptor Andrija Buvina. The 28 relief panels, each within its own Romanesque frame, represent the *Life of Christ* and are derived from Byzantine and Western European sources.

In the 14th century the Adriatic coast became an important centre in the production of decorative arts, influenced by Italian culture. The reliquary of St Simeon in Zadar, made of embossed silver-gilt panels and completed in 1380 by Francesco di Antonio of Milan with the assistance of such local craftsmen as Andrija Markov of Zagreb and Stipan Pribčev, is a particularly noteworthy example. The international exchange of craftsmen is further illustrated by the work of Pavao of Dubrovnik (*b c.* 1420), who assisted Donatello in his Padua workshop and collaborated with Pisanello in Naples in the production of medals. From 1463 to 1479 he was the principal diecutter for the Dubrovnik Mint. In the second half of the 16th century one of the most outstanding European goldsmiths was Horatio Fortezza (*c.* 1530–96). His most

accomplished work incorporates highly detailed figurative scenes, framed within elaborate strapwork borders, and was at the forefront of Mannerist decoration.

Throughout the Renaissance period, Dubrovnik, Pag and Lepoglava were important lacemaking centres. During the 17th and 18th centuries Zagreb established itself as a major centre for embroidery. Magnificent examples can be seen in the Cathedral Treasury and the Museum of Arts and Crafts in Zagreb. Glass production is also recorded in Dubrovnik during the Renaissance period, but the most important period dates from the early 18th century, when a factory was established in Gorski Kotar (1728). It flourished particularly in the 19th century, when several major manufactories were founded, producing extensive ranges in all the current styles through to Art Nouveau. Ceramic production closely paralleled the development of glass. The Zagreb School of Arts and Crafts, founded in 1882, sought to improve artistic standards in manufacturing and marked the beginning of a new craft tradition that continued to flourish in the late 20th century.

BIBLIOGRAPHY

Enciklopedija likovnih umjetnosti [Encyclopedia of fine arts], 4 vols (Zagreb, 1959–66)

L'Art en Yugoslavie de la préhistoire à nos jours (exh. cat., Paris, 1971)

R. Ivančević: *Art Treasures of Croatia* (Motovun, 1986)

FLORA TURNER

V. Collections and institutions.

The philosopher Pavao Ritter Vitezović arranged the first private museum in Croatia in his house in Zagreb (1693). Ivo Aletić in Dubrovnik owned a similar museum, but more significant were the treasuries of the Roman Catholic Church, many of which developed into national museums and galleries. Important Church collections are still held, however, in the cathedrals in Dubrovnik, Split and Zagreb, in the Franciscan and Dominican monasteries on Hvar, at St Mark's in Korčula and at the convent of St Mary and the monastery of St Francis in Zadar. The earliest 'modern' museum was the Archaeological Museum in Split (1818), which was succeeded by archaeological museums in Zadar (1830), Zagreb (1846), Dubrovnik (1872), Osijek (1877), Poreč (1884), Rijeka (1892) and Pula (1902). From 1819 to 1919, 24 new collections were formed in Croatia, among them the Museum of Arts and Crafts in Zagreb (1879). The total number is now over 200, including the National University Library Graphic Arts Collection and the Gallery of Primitive Art, both in Zagreb. Other important collections in Zagreb include the Theatre Museum collection and the collection of the patron Bishop J. J. Strossmayer (1815–1905), which is housed in the Strossmayer Gallery of Old Masters (est. 1884). Strossmayer, a great patron of the arts in Croatia, had presented his extensive collections of paintings and other works of art to the newly established Academy of Art in Zagreb in 1866, and he also financed the building of the neo-Gothic cathedral (1866–70) in Djakovo. Also in Zagreb, the Gallery of Modern Art (est. 1905) contains over 2000 works from the 19th and 20th centuries, and the Mimara Museum (est. 1986) holds the gift of the Croatian émigré Ante Mimara. The collection also contains 3750 works, including Old Master paintings, drawings, sculpture and applied arts, porcelain and textiles.

Other important galleries are the Split Gallery of Fine Art (1928), where icons and Renaissance and modern Croatian paintings are shown, and the Osijek Gallery of Fine Art, with some 950 works from the 18th and 19th centuries. The Art Gallery in Dubrovnik contains the works of local and Venetian painters of the 16th and 17th centuries, and the Municipal Art Gallery in Zagreb (1947) contains Renaissance and Baroque art of the 15th–17th centuries. There are also galleries dedicated to the work of Vlaho Bukovac, in Cavtat and to Ivan Meštrović, in both Zagreb and Split. A number of private collections in Zagreb allow public access, such as those of Dagmar Chavrak, Rafael Dolinsek and Tilla Durieux. However, the Bauer Collection and Fine Art Gallery in Vukovar, which contained 150 paintings, was destroyed in 1991, as were 27 other galleries, 13 library buildings and 7 archives. Many Croatian art works were also removed to Belgrade.

Historically, arts and crafts education in Croatia was based on the guild and master workshop principle, as elsewhere in Europe, and was centred on Zagreb and Dubrovnik and in the region of Istria. The first Academy of Arts in the former Yugoslavia was founded in Zagreb in 1921. It developed from the School for Arts and Crafts established there in 1882 by IZIDOR KRŠNJAVI. The new Academy, which has university status, has departments devoted to a foundation course, painting, sculpture, architecture and applied arts. The greatest influence on the teaching there was that of the painters Josip Račić (1885–1908), MIROSLAV KRALJEVIĆ and Vladimir Becić (1886–1954), who had studied in Paris. In 1923 Ivan Meštrović became the rector and gathered around him artists from all over south-eastern Europe.

BIBLIOGRAPHY

A. Bauer and D. Kečkemet: *Muzeji i arhivi* [Museums and archives] (Zagreb, 1957)
Enciklopedija likovnih umjetnosti [Encyclopedia of fine arts], ii (Zagreb, 1962), p. 346; iii (1964), pp. 516, 587
Historical Sites and Cities Damaged and Destroyed during the War in Croatia (Zagreb, 1991) [documentation by the Croatian Institute for the Protection of Cultural Monuments]

PAUL TVRTKOVIĆ

Croce, Aflalo and Gasperini. Brazilian architectural partnership formed in 1962 in São Paulo by Plínio Croce (*b* Tietê, 26 Feb 1921; *d* São Paulo, May 1984), Roberto Aflalo (*b* São Paulo, 18 Sept 1926; *d* São Paulo, 14 Nov 1992) and Gian Carlo Gasperini (*b* Castellamare, Italy, 1926). Croce, the founder of the practice, graduated in architecture in 1946 from the Mackenzie School of Engineering (now Mackenzie University), São Paulo, where the course was extremely conservative; he nevertheless followed the teachings of the modern masters and the influence of Mies van der Rohe is evident in his early work. He then gained experience in professional practice with Rino Levi in São Paulo. Aflalo graduated in 1950 from the School of Architecture at Mackenzie University, São Paulo, and began to work with Croce on many projects for blocks of flats. One of these, the João Ramalho Building (1953), São Paulo, on which Salvador Cândia (1924–91) also collaborated, won the International Prize for Collective Housing at the 6th São Paulo Biennale in 1961. It was a work of great formal purity in the style of the European Rationalist masters.

In 1962 Croce and Aflalo were joined by Gasperini, who had trained at the University of Rome and the Federal University of Rio de Janeiro, graduating in 1950; he had already worked in São Paulo, on his own and with the French architect Jacques Pilon (1905–62). The partnership of Croce, Aflalo and Gasperini was very productive, with a wide variety of clients; in the next 25 years more than 500 architectural projects were completed, as well as others in the field of regional and urban planning and work outside Brazil. Under the influence of Gasperini and his international experience, including commissions from the Union Internationale des Architectes, they abandoned the severity of extreme Rationalism and began to adopt unconventional formal solutions, often using bold exposed concrete frames articulated with beams and fins. They tended to ignore local trends, particularly the sculptural forms of Oscar Niemeyer, and they were notable for being the first in Brazil to follow an independent internationalist line, open to aesthetic developments in architecture in other countries. While all their projects were thoroughly practical and executed to a high standard, there is no consistent style that gives uniformity to their work, which is characterized by a readiness to vary formal solutions according to the requirements of each individual problem.

Croce, Aflalo and Gasperini won many competitions, including those for the Peugeot Building (1961–2), Buenos Aires, a Miesian glass box; and the headquarters of IBM (1970), on the corner of Avenida 23 de Maio and Rua Tutóia, the constructional solution of which suggested the Parque Iguatemi office building (1971), São Paulo; the latter has a splayed base to accommodate shops and parking on a site that did not permit excavation. In the Tribunal de Contas do Municipio Building (1971), São Paulo, they began to move away from conventional solutions and towards a Post-modernist stance. The Citibank Building (1983–6) in São Paulo, for example, illustrates the international trend in the 1980s towards a sophisticated surface treatment for commercial buildings; its smooth granite cladding, incorporating square windows, is contrasted with a staggered corner section of dark glass and a glazed quadrant vault at roof level.

BIBLIOGRAPHY

F. Bullrich: *New Directions in Latin American Architecture* (London and New York, 1969)
'Modern Brazilian Architecture', *Process: Archit.*, 17 (1980), pp. 116–25 [special issue]
A. Xavier, C. Lemos and E. Corona: *Arquitetura moderna paulistana* (São Paulo, 1983)
'Brésil: Etat des lieux', *Archit. Aujourd'hui*, 251 (1987), pp. 42–4
N. C. Oliveira: 'Citicorp Centre', *Projeto*, 97 (1987), pp. 64–86
Croce, Aflalo e Gasperini: Arquitetos, 25 anos depois, CVS Artistas Asociados (São Paolo, 1989)

CARLOS A. C. LEMOS

Croce, Baldassarre (*b* Bologna, 1553–8; *d* Rome, 8 Nov 1628). Italian painter. He is first recorded in 1575 in Bologna, where he trained in the local Mannerist style of such painters as Lorenzo Sabatini, Orazio Sammachini, Pellegrino Tibaldi and Denys Calvaert. During the papacy of Gregory XIII he went to Rome and worked at the Vatican on the decoration of the Cortile di S Damaso, under the supervision of Sabatini (1576–7), and on that of the Galleria delle Carte Geografiche, under Girolamo Muziano and Cesare Nebbia (1580–83). In Rome, he became a member of the Accademia di S Luca (1581) and of the Virtuosi al Pantheon (1584). His fresco for the oratory of the Crocifisso there, the *Approval of the Statutes* (*c.* 1583), reflects the Roman Mannerist style of Federico Zuccaro. He executed frescoes in S Giacomo degli Spagnoli, Rome (1583–4), and took part in projects of Sixtus V, including the decoration of the Scala Santa, Rome (1586–9), where his style is close to Bolognese Mannerism, but with echoes of Muziano, via Nebbia (Scavizzi). In 1592 he completed the decoration of the Sala Regia in the Palazzo Comunale, Viterbo: he painted the six scenes as fictive tapestries within an elaborate architectonic border, including festoons, portrait medallions, putti and niches with historical figures. Two of his frescoes, the *Cruxifixion* and the *Pietà* (both 1593), in the central nave of S Maria Maggiore, Rome, show the influence of Zuccaro and Muziano, especially in the draperies.

Generally considered his most important works are his frescoes in S Susanna, Rome, commissioned by Cardinal Girolamo Rusticucci: the *Martyrdom of St Gabino* in the apse (1595) and the scenes from the *Life of St Susanna* in the nave (1588–1600; see fig.) show close links with the theatrical scenery of the oratory of the Gonfalone, Rome. The *Christ Crowned with Thorns* (1594; Rome, S Prassede, main nave), the frescoes (1599) in the chapel of S Francesco di Assisi, Il Gesù, Rome, as well as the later frescoes in S Maria degli Angeli at Assisi and his probable participation in the decoration of S Cesareo, Rome, indicate that Croce reached the peak of his success at the end of the 16th century and the beginning of the 17th. The *Miracle of St Martin* (Foligno Cathedral) recalls the

work of the Cavaliere d'Arpino; the *St Gregory* (1608; Rome, Santa Trinità dei Pellegrini) and the *Miracle of the Foundation of the Church*, the *Procession* and the *Vision of the Angel* (all Rome, S Maria Maggiore, New Sacristy) can be dated to 1608–10. Under the supervision of Arpino, Croce also took part in the decoration of the Pauline Chapel of S Maria Maggiore (*Death of the Virgin*). The frescoes (1611–12) in the small chapel on the ground-floor of the Palazzo Quirinale, Rome, reveal strong influences from Guido Reni to Domenico Passignano. The frescoes (damaged) in the chapel of S Niccolò, S Luigi dei Francesi, Rome, date from about 1615. In the service of Cardinal Alessandro Peretti–Montalto, Croce frescoed a room in his villa (destr.) on the Esquiline Hill. The *Coronation of the Virgin* (*c.* 1625) in the vault of the Colonna Chapel, S Giovanni in Laterano, Rome, was probably his last work. From 1 January 1628 to August 1628 Croce was Principe of the Accademia di S Luca, Rome.

BIBLIOGRAPHY

DBI; Thieme–Becker
G. Scavizzi: 'Gli affreschi della Scala Santa ed alcune aggiunte per il tardo manierismo romano', *Boll. A.*, xlv (1960), pp. 111–22, 325–35, fig. 9
A. M. Corbo: 'I pittori della Cappella Paolina in S Maria Maggiore', *Palatino*, xi (1967), pp. 301–13
J. von Henneberg: *L'oratorio dell'Arciconfraternità del SS Crocifisso di Roma* (Rome, 1974), pp. 79–83, fig. 28
A. M. Martinelli: *S Maria Maggiore* (Rome, 1975), figs 103–7
C. Strinati: *Quadri romani tra '500 e '600: Opere restaurate e da restaurare* (Rome, 1979), pp. 10, 12, 14–17
——: 'Roma nell'anno 1600: Studio di pittura', *Ric. Stor. A.*, x (1980), pp. 26, 45, n. 29
M. C. Abromson: *Painting in Rome during the Papacy of Clemente VIII* (New York, 1981)

ANTONIO VANNUGLI

Croce, Benedetto (*b* Pescasséroli, Abruzzi, 25 Feb 1866; *d* Naples, 20 Nov 1952). Italian historian, critic, philosopher and statesman. He began his intellectual career as a historian, and his concern for whether history is an art or a science led him to inquire into the nature of art and to produce, in 1902, his first major work in aesthetics, *Estetica come scienza dell'espressione e linguistica generale*. Here he distinguished between the 'intuitive' knowledge of things in their concrete particularity and the 'logical' knowledge of general concepts. Croce proposed that human beings passively receive bombardments of sensory stimuli and, using the faculty of intuition, produce from them objects he called 'intuitions' or 'representations', which give a particular form to otherwise unintelligible stimuli. A painter, using this faculty of intuition or representation, gives the otherwise inchoate welter of stimuli produced by, for example, a moonlit countryside, the particular form of a painting, which is an intuition or representation of that countryside. Intuiting the scene involves giving articulate expression to the otherwise incoherent mass of stimuli received on such occasions, and so intuition and expression are identical. All uses of language to express thoughts and feelings, as well as the visual arts or music, are acts of intuition, which master the flood of sensations to which we are continually subjected.

Croce maintained that all works of art are intuitions and that all intuitions are works of art. This account prefigures later claims that an aesthetic interest in a representation is

Baldassarre Croce: *Susanna and the Elders* (1598–1600), fresco, S Susanna, Rome

not an interest in whether it corresponds to some pre-existing thing, for in Croce's view there are no formed objects prior to the act of representation. His account also involves the notion of 'organic unity', which became influential in criticism partly through the American critic J.E. Spingairn (1875–1939). This notion proposes that a work of art can be apprehended, not by dividing it into the elements from which it is composed, but only by taking account of the overall effect emerging from the fusion of these elements into an organic whole, and so by grasping what Croce called its 'individual physiognomy'. Once that is done, a taxonomist may discuss the resemblances between works, but this is relevant to the study of art only if a prior decision has been made that the works are art. Thus Croce asserted, controversially, that discussions of genre are irrelevant to questions about the artistic status of a work. The question of whether an object is a tragedy, comedy, epic, landscape, portrait and so on always follows in the wake of the question of whether the object is a work of art, namely, an achieved intuition with its own individual physiognomy. Since the sole criterion of artistic success is whether expression is achieved, then this is independent of how the materials with which the artist works, or the effects produced by their fusion, are morally assessed. A representation of the immoral can be a fine work of art just as the representation of an ugly face can be a fine painting.

Croce apparently believed intuition could be achieved purely in the mind, externalization being merely optional. This may be hard to reconcile with the way in which artists solve their artistic problems as they work on or with physical material. Since there are no degrees of success in intuition, it raises the question of what criticism is to do. In *Estetica* Croce maintained that the critic can only 'retrieve' the work by putting her- or himself in the artist's original situation and by re-enacting the artist's original act of intuition. Shortly afterwards, however, Croce tried to distinguish more carefully the nature of artistic intuition, calling it firstly 'lyrical' intuition and later also 'cosmic' intuition. Croce worked on the ideas of *Estetica* for the following 50 years in his contributions to practical criticism in the journals he founded, *La critica* and *Quaderni della critica*, and in a series of works in aesthetics, culminating in *La poesia*. His work in aesthetics reached the English-speaking world largely through his influence on R. G. Collingwood (*see* COLLINGWOOD, (2)).

WRITINGS
Estetica come scienza dell'espressione e linguistica generale (Palermo, 1902, rev. Bari, 3/1909); Eng. trans. by D. Ainslie as *Aesthetic as Science of Expression and General Linguistic* (Boston, MA, 1978)
Problemi di estetica e contributi alla storia dell'estetica italiana (Bari, 1910)
Breviario di estetica: Quattro lezioni (Bari, 1913); Eng. trans. as *Guide to Aesthetics* (1965)
Nuovi saggi di estetica (Bari, 1920)
'Aesthetics', *Encyclopaedia Britannica* (London, 14/1929)
La poesia (Bari, 1936); Eng. trans. as *Poetry and Literature* (Carbondale, 1981)
Filosofia, poesia, storia (Milan, 1951; Eng. trans., London, 1966)
F. Nicolini, ed.: *'L'edizione varietur' delle opere di B. Croce* (Naples, 1960) [complete list]

BIBLIOGRAPHY
E. Carritt: *The Theory of Beauty* (London, 1914)
B. Bosanquet: *Three Lectures on Aesthetic* (London, 1915)
G. Orsini: *Benedetto Croce: Philosopher of Art and Literary Critic* (Carbondale, 1961)
M. E. Brown: *Neo-Idealist Aesthetics: Croce, Gentile, Collingwood* (Detroit, 1966)
R. Zimmer: *Einheit und Entwicklung in Benedetto Croces Ästhetik: Der Intuitionsbegriff und seine Modifikationen* (Frankfurt am Main, [1985])
M. Moss: *Benedetto Croce Reconsidered* (London, 1987)

COLIN LYAS

Crocefissi, Simone dei. *See* SIMONE DEI CROCEFISSI.

Crocket [Fr. *croc, crochet*: 'hook']. Decorative device used in Gothic art and architecture, attached to a capital or a gable, an arch, piece of tracery or coping. The term was used in medieval England in the forms *crockytt* and *crockett*. English writers of the Gothic Revival period, however, suggested a connection with the crook, noting that some of the earliest English examples take the form of the pastoral crosier, but this is probably a misinterpretation.

Crocket capitals developed during the period of transition from Romanesque to Gothic architecture from the mid-12th century, with small curled, twisted fronds of vegetation projecting from the body of the capital, in a form suggesting the much older use of curved floral decoration in the Corinthian order (*see* ORDERS, ARCHITECTURAL, §I, 1(iii)). After *c.* 1250 the crocket emerged as a curve of foliage that twisted or hooked back, turning the opposite way to the arch or gable out of which it rose (see fig.), reminding Gwilt of 'the buds and boughs of trees in the spring season'. In the course of its development, the crocket lost its hook-shape and began to curve upwards rather than downwards, becoming richer and more florid. Thus after *c.* 1250 crockets were used to decorate members that themselves might be more decorative than structural. In the chapter house of Southwell Minster (*c.* 1290) the gables of the stall canopies are crowned with very large, flowing crockets; and in the ornate, decorative tomb-structures of this period the crocket became just one of a host of features and devices that produced exceedingly rich compositions, for example on the Percy tomb (*c.* 1340) in Beverley Minster (*c.* 1340). In some Late Gothic versions, such as the forms set on the large ogee arches in the Condestable Chapel, Burgos Cathedral (begun 1482), the crocket became rectangular in composition. In most cases the form was vegetable (ferns, leaves, buds, lilies, even pomegranates), but animal

Crockets over the north arcade of the choir, Sées Cathedral, France, 1278–94

forms, or equivalents, do exist. Although crockets were normally set on raking, arching members, they also decorated vertical forms, such as the piers of St Hugh's Choir and the central tower of Lincoln Cathedral. In manuscripts they are also used on architectural forms: the Psalter of Yolande of Soissons (1280–90; New York, Pierpont Morgan Lib., MS. M.729) depicts gables with crockets in the form of trefoils, ivy, oval leaves etc (*Harrowing of Hell*, f. 7r; *Entombment*, f. 341v)).

In Gothic Revival architecture, crockets were included with the many other motifs and features of the style; many 19th-century examples imitated earlier crockets, but later examples are more varied. The gables of the central portal of the cathedral of St John the Divine (from 1912, by Ralph Adams Cram) in New York are decorated with numerous attenuated stalklike floral crockets. At Liverpool Cathedral (1904–80), Giles Gilbert Scott devised many varieties of crocket that are highly stylized, sculptural and chunky in form—and wholly original.

BIBLIOGRAPHY

M. H. Bloxham: *The Principles of Gothic Architecture Elucidated by Question and Answer* (London, 1829); rev. as *Companion to the Principles of Gothic Architecture*, 3 vols (London, 11/1882)

[J. H. Parker]: *A Glossary of Terms Used in Grecian, Roman, Italian, and Gothic Architecture* (Oxford, 1836, rev. 5/1850)

J. Gwilt: *An Encyclopaedia of Architecture: Historical, Theoretical, and Practical* (London, 1842); ed. W. Papworth (London, 4/1867, rev. 6/1888)

JOHN THOMAS

Croisant, Jacob. *See* CRESSANT, JACOB.

Croker, John [Crocker, Johann] (*b* Dresden, 21 Oct 1670; *d* London, 21 March 1741). British medallist of German birth. Trained as a jeweller, he arrived in England in 1691 and learnt the art of die-engraving. He became assistant engraver at the Royal Mint, London, in 1697, the year in which he executed a silver and bronze medal for William III symbolizing the *State of Britain after the Peace of Ryswick* (see Hawkins, Franks and Grueber, ii, pp. 192, 499). Such medals as those commemorating the accession and the coronation (both gold, silver and bronze, 1702; see HFG, ii, pp. 227–8) of Queen Anne, together with the medal celebrating the *Battle of Blenheim* (silver and bronze, 1704; see HFG, p. 256), ensured that he was given the post of Chief Engraver at the Royal Mint when it became vacant in 1705. For the next 30 years he produced single-handedly most of the British official medals, as well as engraving the dies for the coinage of Queen Anne, George I and the first issue of George II. He also modelled a large cast medallic portrait of *Queen Anne* (*c.* 1704). The influence of the medallic histories of Louis XIV is evident in his work, with its classical style and ordered presentation of the military victories of the monarchs, but Croker succeeded in injecting new life into this formula through his skill as a designer and engraver. The drawings for many of his medals survive (London, BL).

BIBLIOGRAPHY

DNB; Thieme–Becker

E. Hawkins, A. W. Franks and H. A. Grueber: *Medallic Illustrations of the History of Great Britain and Ireland* (London, 1885) [HFG]

L. Forrer: *Biographical Dictionary of Medallists* (London, 1902–30), i, pp. 472–9; vii, p. 197

P. Barber: 'Commemoration and Control', *Medal*, vi (1985), pp. 2–5

C. E. Challis, ed.: *A New History of the Royal Mint* (Cambridge, 1992)

D. Pickup: 'John Croker and the Alchorne Manuscript', *Medal*, xx (1992), pp. 19–31

PHILIP ATTWOOD

Crolius and Remmey. American pottery established by William Crolius [Johan Willem Crollius] (*b* Neuwied, near Koblenz, *c.* 1700; *d* New York, *c.* 1776) and John Remmey [Remmi] (*d* New York, Nov 1762). Crolius arrived in New York *c.* 1718 and established a stoneware pottery on Pot-Bakers Hill. Bound by intermarriage to the Corselius and Remmey families, who were also in the pottery business, the Crolius family figured prominently in Manhattan pottery history until about 1850. From *c.* 1735 William Crolius and John Remmey were in business together. Although salt-glazed stoneware was the principal product, lead-glazed earthenware was also made in the early years of the Crolius and Remmey potteries. Before the American Revolution their stoneware closely resembled Rhenish stoneware with incised decoration filled in with a blue cobalt oxide glaze, but subsequent generations usually painted simple blue embellishments (e.g. pitcher, 1798; New York, Hist. Soc.). Remmey's grandson Henry Remmey sr (*b c.* 1770; *d c.* 1865) and great-grandson Henry Remmey jr left New York before 1817, when they were working in Baltimore. In 1827 the latter purchased a pottery in Philadelphia and established the Remmey name there.

BIBLIOGRAPHY

W. C. Ketchum jr: *Early Potters and Potteries of New York State* (New York, 1970); rev. as *Potters and Potteries of New York State, 1650–1900* (Syracuse, 1987)

ELLEN PAUL DENKER

Crome, John (*b* Norwich, 22 Dec 1768; *d* Norwich, 22 April 1821). English painter, printmaker, collector and teacher. The son of a journeyman weaver, he was apprenticed to a coach and sign painter, Francis Whisler, from 1783 to 1790. He presumably continued in this trade and during the 1790s consolidated his artistic training. Early local influences upon Crome included William Beechey and John Opie, but the friendship of Thomas Harvey, a patron, collector and amateur artist, was the most significant. Harvey's collection included works by Dutch 17th-century masters such as Aelbert Cuyp, Jacob van Ruisdael and Meindert Hobbema, and also works by Gainsborough and Richard Wilson. The earliest record of Wilson's influence is provided by two oils entitled *Composition in the Style of Wilson* (untraced), dated 1796 and 1798 in Crome's Memorial Exhibition of 1821. The Dutch influence was also strong throughout Crome's career. Crome's early acquaintance with Harvey and his collection almost certainly encouraged him to become a collector, and the Yarmouth banker Dawson Turner recorded buying pictures from Crome, including Old Masters as well as the artist's own work.

Like many of his contemporaries, Crome established a practice as a drawing-master. According to Dawson Turner, he became a teacher on marrying Phoebe Berney in 1792. Members of the Gurney family of Earlham Hall, Norwich, were among his earliest pupils, and in 1802 he accompanied them on a visit to the Lake District. In 1804 he visited Wales with Robert Ladbrooke, his brother-in-law and co-founder of the Norwich Society of Artists. His

John Crome: *Back of the New Mills, Norwich*, oil on canvas, 413×540 mm, *c*. 1814–17 (Norfolk Museums Service, Norwich Castle Museum)

one trip abroad took place in 1814, when he visited the art collections brought to Paris by Napoleon.

The local press credited Crome early for his role as a founder of the Norwich Society of Artists in 1803 and the Norwich school of painters. Crome's monochromatic paintings, such as his magnificent *View of Carrow Abbey, near Norwich* (1805; Norwich, Castle Mus.), did not find universal acceptance. Although he later lightened his palette his work was criticized for its 'unfinished' appearance even towards the end of his career. Within weeks of his death, however, people were reported to be 'crazy for his pictures' (Rev. W. Gunn to J. Flaxman, 4 May 1821; Cambridge, Trinity Coll. Lib.). Crome's work was entirely original, exhibiting a fresh vision, clear colour and strong design, derived as much from the direct observation of nature as from the study of Old Masters. His subject-matter was invariably the local landscape, including buildings and intimate scenes on the rivers Yare and Wensum, such as *Back of the New Mills, Norwich* (*c.* 1814–17; see fig.) and *New Mills: Men Wading* (*c.* 1812; *see* NORWICH, fig. 3; both Norwich, Castle Mus.).

Crome did not sign his paintings and the chronology of his oeuvre is not easy to determine. His 34 etchings, published posthumously on behalf of his wife in 1834, are important in this respect. His earliest dated print, *Colney* (1809), is in soft-ground, and a few of his etchings bear the dates 1812 or 1813. These works place Crome at the forefront of the 19th-century revival in etching in Britain. A number of fakes derive from Crome's etched compositions, and his watercolours have sometimes been confused with those of John Sell Cotman of *c.* 1802.

John Crome has sometimes been called 'Old Crome', to distinguish him from his eldest son John Berney Crome (1794–1842). John Berney was hailed as Crome's true successor within 18 months of his father's death. Popularly known for his moonlight views, his painting did not, however, achieve the promise of the early 1820s. The Crome family tradition was also taken up by John Berney's younger brothers, Frederick James Crome (1796–1832) and William Henry Crome (1806–67). Frederick helped John Berney continue their father's teaching practice but died young. He possibly worked as an etching apprentice to John Sell Cotman and is mainly remembered for his etchings. William Henry's landscapes are solidly within the Victorian tradition. John Crome's oldest daughter to survive infancy also became a painter: Emily Crome (1801–41) specialized in still-lifes, exhibiting annually with the Norwich Society from 1816. Crome's most talented pupils were George Vincent and James Stark.

BIBLIOGRAPHY
H. S. Theobald: *Crome's Etchings: A Catalogue and an Appreciation with Some Account of his Paintings* (London, 1906)

C. H. Collins Baker: *Crome* (London, 1921)

S. C. Kaines Smith: *John Crome* (London, 1923)

R. H. Mottram: *John Crome of Norwich* (London, 1931)

F. Hawcroft: 'Crome and his Patron: Thomas Harvey of Catton', *Connoisseur*, cxliv (1959), pp. 232–7

H. A. E. Day: *East Anglian Painters*, 2 vols (Eastbourne, 1967–9)

D. Clifford and T. Clifford: *John Crome* (London, 1968)

John Crome, 1768–1821 (exh. cat. by F. Hawcroft, ACGB, 1968)

N. L. Goldberg: *John Crome the Elder*, 2 vols (New York, 1978)

A. Hemingway: *The Norwich School of Painters, 1803–1833* (Oxford, 1979)

A. W. Moore: *The Norwich School of Artists* (Norwich, 1985)

——: *Dutch and Flemish Painting in Norfolk: A History of Taste and Influence, Fashion and Collecting* (London, 1988)

For further bibliography *see* NORWICH, §2.

ANDREW W. MOORE

Cromek, Robert Hartley (*b* Kingston upon Hull, 1770; *d* London, 12 or 14 March 1812). English publisher and engraver. He studied in London under Francesco Bartolozzi and engraved a number of book illustrations but was best known as a publisher, issuing the designs by William Blake for Robert Blair's poem *The Grave* (London, 1743). In 1805 Cromek commissioned Blake to draw and engrave the designs, but Blake felt betrayed when Cromek engaged Luigi Schiavonetti instead because he saw that Blake's style of engraving would not please the public (for further discussion *see* BLAKE, WILLIAM). Blake was further annoyed when Cromek commissioned Thomas Stothard to paint the *Canterbury Pilgrims* (1806; London, Tate; for illustration *see* STOTHARD, (1)), an idea that Blake thought had been stolen from him; in 1809 Blake published a very successful singly issued print of it. Bentley has shown that although Cromek had considerable understanding and sympathy for Blake his treatment of him helped to increase the artist's isolation.

UNPUBLISHED SOURCES

London, BM [MS. cat. of engrs by Robert Hartley Cromek, comp. Thomas Hartley Cromek, his son, 1862]

BIBLIOGRAPHY

DNB; Thieme–Becker

G. E. Bentley: 'Blake and Cromek: The Wheat and the Tares', *Mod. Philol.*, lxxi (1974), pp. 366–79

DAVID ALEXANDER

Cromlech. Term for a monument of huge stones of uncertain or prehistoric date.

Cromwell, Oliver (*b* Huntingdon, 25 April 1599; *d* London, 3 Sept 1658). English politician and patron. He first entered Parliament in 1628 as the member for Huntingdon. From 1640 he represented Cambridge in the Short and Long Parliaments. After the Civil War he was a signatory of Charles I's death warrant in 1649, and following the dissolution of the Long Parliament in 1653 he was appointed head of state, with the title of Lord Protector.

Cromwell showed a keen interest in music, but there is less evidence for a personal interest in the visual arts. However, in 1643 he sat for a portrait by Robert Walker (Burghley House, Cambs) and from 1650 Samuel Cooper worked for the Cromwell family (e.g. unfinished miniature, Duke of Buccleuch priv. col.). Cromwell did not engage in architectural works, and those of his homes that survive are unremarkable. His main importance as a patron of the arts dates from his appointment as Protector; the Commonwealth policy of disposing of the assets of the Stuart monarchy ceased and, in some cases, was even reversed. Windsor Castle, Greenwich House, Somerset House, the Manor at York, St James's House and, more significantly, Whitehall Palace and Mews and Hampton Court were all placed at Cromwell's disposal. The maintenance of the Protectoral Court and, from November 1655, of Cromwell's residences at Hampton Court and Whitehall was paid for by a Parliamentary grant, which rose from an initial £64,000 to £100,000 in 1657. Repairs and furnishing were in the hands of a surveyor's department and a wardrobe, both of which were smaller versions of their Stuart counterparts. Colvin concludes that Parliament got very little actual work in return for the money; a contemporary picture (Colvin, IV/ii, pl. IIB) shows rainwater heads dated 1656 on the Queen's Long Gallery, but these and any related works were destroyed by Christopher Wren's later alterations. Some minor works were carried out at Whitehall, and Westminster Hall was repaired and fitted out for a new High Court and the High Court of Justice.

The Protectoral court adopted many of the trappings of the Stuart regime. Cromwell chose works from the royal collection to decorate his residences, including the *Triumph of Julius Caesar* by Andrea Mantegna (London, Hampton Court, Royal Col.) and Raphael's cartoons of the *Acts of the Apostles* (London, V&A). Works were brought from elsewhere to Hampton Court: in 1656 a fountain, now in Bushey Park, was moved from Somerset House, and the organ in the Banqueting Hall was brought from Magdalen College, Oxford. Cromwell chose tapestries, including a set depicting *Mars, Vulcan and Venus*, for his lodgings in Whitehall. New works were commissioned to embellish the court. The Mortlake Tapestry Manufactory, with Cromwell's Lord Chamberlain of the Household, Sir Gilbert Pickering (*c.* 1611–68), as its Director, produced works at the instigation of the Council of State and of the Protector himself. However, the amount spent on tapestries did not compare with the Stuarts' expenditure, being measured in hundreds rather than thousands of pounds. In 1654 some £6000 was spent on plate for the court. The Council of State commissioned from the official engraver and medallist Thomas Simon images of the Protector in the form of medals, coins and seals, such as the Protectoral Medal (1653; London, BM) and the Scottish Protectoral Seal (1656; Edinburgh, Register House, see Fraser). Simon also made Cromwell's wax funeral effigy. The court had no official painter, but Samuel Cooper, Robert Walker and Peter Lely were all commissioned to paint portraits of Cromwell; the Lely portrait, presented to Ferdinando II de' Medici, Grand Duke of Tuscany, is now in the Palazzo Pitti, Florence.

BIBLIOGRAPHY

A. Fraser: *Cromwell: Our Chief of Men* (London, 1973/*R* 1989)

A. Haynes: 'The Mortlake Tapestry, 1619–1705', *Hist. Today*, xxxiv (1974), pp. 32–40

R. Sherwood: *The Court of Oliver Cromwell* (London, 1977)

H. M. Colvin: *The History of the King's Works*, III (London, 1975), IV/ii (1982)

GILES CLIFFORD

Cromwell, Thomas, Earl of Essex (*b c.* 1485; *d* London, 28 July 1540). English politician and patron. Little is known of his early life except that he travelled abroad *c.* 1503–14 and served as a soldier in Italy. Following his return to England he rose to prominence through the household of Cardinal Thomas Wolsey. In the 1530s he was the chief royal minister during the Reformation Parliament and he presided over the Dissolution of the monasteries. His fall, brought about by the conservative faction at court but compounded by Henry VIII's own dissatisfaction with Cromwell's part in the political alliance with Anne of Cleves, came less than two months after he was created Earl of Essex in June 1540; his execution followed convictions for treason and heresy.

Cromwell was less ostentatious in his patronage than some of Henry VIII's other ministers, but he was building extensively in the mid-1530s. His main London residence (destr.), in Throgmorton Street, is quite well recorded, since it was later the Hall of the Drapers Company and is mentioned in John Stow's *Survey of London* (1598); it was built mainly of brick with stone window dressings. Houses were also being constructed or refurbished for Cromwell at Stepney in London, and at Mortlake, Surrey, and Ewhurst, Hants, though no visual records survive. A mutilated record of his household goods mentions a handful of religious images, a few pieces such as 'a great table of misery of Italy', and the fashionable 'antick' decoration that was applied to 'a goodly table of the King's arms', namely 'two naked children standing upon whelks, painted and gilded'. Cromwell sat for his portrait to Hans Holbein (ii) in 1533–4 (original untraced; important copies: New York, Frick; London, N.P.G.).

DNB
BIBLIOGRAPHY
J. Gairdner and R. H. Brodie, eds: *Letters and Papers, Foreign and Domestic, of the Reign of Henry VIII, 1509–47*, xv (London, 1896) [on Cromwell's houses and household goods]
B. W. Beckinsale: *Thomas Cromwell, Tudor Minister* (London, 1978)
S. Bindoff, ed.: *The History of Parliament: The Commons, 1509–1558*, i (London, 1982)
MAURICE HOWARD

Cronaca [Simone di Tomaso del Pollaiuolo] (*b* Florence, 30 Oct 1457; *d* Florence, 27 Sept 1508). Italian architect and mason. He trained as a stone-carver and seems to have spent his early years (*c.* 1475–85) in Rome after a sodomy charge. According to Vasari, his nickname (literally 'the Chronicle') was derived from his study of antiquity and his skill in recounting 'the marvels of Rome' on his return to Florence. In 1486 Cronaca matriculated as a stonecutter in the Florentine Guild of Stonecutters and Woodworkers (Arte dei Maestri di Pietra e Legname), by which time he was already married to the daughter of the builder Jacopo Rosselli, who worked on the early stages of the Palazzo Strozzi and who may have introduced him to Filippo Strozzi I.

Cronaca's first documented activity was in the workshop of Florence Cathedral, but in February 1490, six months after work began on the Palazzo Strozzi, Cronaca was engaged by Strozzi as chief stonecutter, assuming the role of Capomaestro (chief architect) from 1497 until work on the first phase stopped in 1504. He was paid 36 florins per annum to supervise quarrying, stone-carving and construction, supplying models and designs when required. Giuliano da Sangallo's wooden model (1489; Florence, Pal. Strozzi) established the basic plan (bilaterally symmetrical to provide houses for Strozzi's sons from his two marriages) and the three-storey rusticated façade. In execution, vaulting on the first floor greatly increased the height of the building and necessitated the steep stairs disparaged by Vasari. Certainly designed by Cronaca are the upper levels of the courtyard and the exterior cornice. The latter is the most impressive constructed in the 15th century, both for its assimilation of an accurately observed ancient prototype (from the Forum of Nerva, Rome) and for the intricate constructional geometry that keys in its enormous weight. The superb courtyard is three bays wide and five deep, and on the ground floor it is relatively conventional, with arches carried on Composite columns in the manner of the Palazzo Medici. On the first floor the system changes to one of arches and plain piers, originally open loggias at front and back, and closed at the sides by rectangular cross-mullioned windows with oculi above. The top storey remains open, with slender Composite columns on high pedestals linked by a balustrade. Although the sequence lacks real coherence, it gives a convincing impression of tight organization through the use of robustly articulated elements and strong projections.

From 1495 to 1497 Cronaca was joint chief architect of the Hall of the Great Council in the Palazzo della Signoria (now Palazzo Vecchio) for the new republican assembly. This was the most important civic architectural project in Florence after the expulsion of the Medici in 1494. Here Cronaca helped to supervise construction of the enormous wooden roof, the carpentry of which Vasari admired and reused when the Hall was raised and transformed (1563–5) into the Salone del Cinquecento. Traces of Cronaca's windows are visible on the exterior of the Hall. From 1495 until his death Cronaca was Capomaestro at Florence Cathedral. The cathedral works in these years were minor, largely confined to the construction of marble altars, the paving of the choir and general repairs: Cronaca's conscience therefore impelled him to negotiate a reduction in his salary in 1502. As cathedral architect he also designed a house (1503–4) for Michelangelo and collaborated with Giuliano da Sangallo and Baccio d'Agnolo on the model (1507) for the arcaded gallery of the cupola. In 1504 he and Antonio da Sangallo (i) were entrusted with the design and construction of the plinth for Michelangelo's *David* (1504).

Vasari also attributes to Cronaca the design of S Salvatore al Monte (*c.* 1490–1504; see fig.), the observant Franciscan church next to S Miniato: its powerfully simple handling accords well with his style, and in 1504 Cronaca was officially elected architect of the Calimala (Cloth Merchants' Guild), which undertook the construction of the church. He is also described as having consistently advised the guild about architectural matters before that date. The plan of S Salvatore, with its single, flat-roofed nave, interconnecting side-chapels and friars' choir behind the altar, is of a type favoured by the observant orders and influential in the next century (cf. Sansovino's S Francesco alla Vigna, Venice). Of particular interest is the square Nerli Chapel to the right of the choir, which, with its groin

Cronaca: interior of S Salvatore al Monte, Florence, c. 1490–1504

vault supported by four columns in the corners, makes direct reference to the early Christian church of S Salvatore at Spoleto, much studied as an antiquity by Renaissance architects. On the exterior, S Salvatore has a Tuscan simplicity expressive of the reforming nature of the observant Franciscans, adorned only by the tabernacle windows at clerestory level with alternating triangular and segmental pediments, refined from the Florentine Baptistery. These appear again on the interior, which is fully articulated with a two-storey superimposed Tuscan Doric order of pilasters, with fluted capitals. The nave is dominated by the chancel arch, its tough, wide mouldings enlivened by the Calimala eagle at the apex. The energetic simplicity of the brown stone detailing belies its actual sophistication: characteristic are the keystone brackets of the nave chapels, which incorporate the knotted cord of the Franciscan order.

Undocumented works attributed to Cronaca since the 19th century include the Palazzo Corsi (now Museo Horne) and the Palazzo Guadagni (1503–6) built for the Dei family, the splendidly severe façade of which became characteristic of 16th-century Florentine town houses (e.g. the early palaces of Baccio d'Agnolo). Cronaca's known allegiance to Savonarola, and his association with the Hall of the Great Council, make it tempting to see his soberly robust forms as an expression of Savonarolan piety. Vasari's characterization of Cronaca as 'a good imitator of

antiquity, an observer of the rules of Vitruvius and the works of Brunelleschi' is borne out by his few surviving drawings, which show him studying a strikingly Brunelleschian range of buildings, including the Baptistery and SS Apostoli in Florence and such celebrated Roman structures as the Pantheon, Septizodium and the Castel Sant' Angelo (which was miniaturized to compose a chimney-piece in the Palazzo Strozzi). Along with Giuliano da Sangallo, Cronaca was a key influence on the early architecture of Michelangelo.

UNPUBLISHED SOURCES

Berlin, Kupferstichkab. [drgs]
Florence, Uffizi [drgs]
Montreal, Cent. Can. Archit. [drgs]

Thieme–Becker
BIBLIOGRAPHY
G. Vasari: *Vite* (1550, rev. 2/1568); ed. G. Milanesi (1878–85)
H. von Geymüller and C. von Stegmann: *Die Architektur der Renaissance in Toskana*, iv (Munich, 1885)
C. von Fabriczy: 'Simone del Pollaiuolo, il Cronaca', *Jb. Kön.-Preuss. Kstsamml.*, xxvii (1906) [suppl.], pp. 45–69
G. Marchini: 'Il Cronaca', *Riv. A.*, xxiii (1941), pp. 99–136
L. Grassi: 'Disegni inediti di Simone del Pollaiuolo', *Palladio*, vii (1943), pp. 14–22
R. Goldthwaite: 'The Building of the Strozzi Palace: The Construction Industry in Renaissance Florence', *Studies in Medieval and Renaissance History*, x (1973), pp. 99–194
A.-I. M. Radice: *Il Cronaca: A Fifteenth-century Florentine Architect* (PhD diss., U. NC, Chapel Hill, 1976) [useful annotated bibliog.]
L. P. Najemy: 'The First Observant Church of S Salvatore al Monte in Florence', *Mitt. Ksthist. Inst. Florenz*, xxiii (1979), pp. 273–96

A. Nesselrath: 'I libri di disegni di antichità: Tentativo di una tipologia', *Memorie dell'antico nell'arte italiana*, iii, ed. S. Settis (Turin, 1986), pp. 89–147

CAROLINE ELAM

Crone, Peter (*b* Melbourne, 18 May 1944). Australian architect. After training with Bernard Joyce (*b* 1930) from 1967–71, he travelled overseas in 1971 to study Le Corbusier's buildings. After his return in 1973 and a brief partnership with Max May (*b* 1941), Crone commenced private practice in 1977. His early works, the Huebner house (1974), Olinda, and Coakley house (1975), Hampton, were highly acclaimed examples of progressive domestic design in Melbourne. These concrete-block houses blended bold chamfered roof forms and angled glazing with a meticulous sense of detail and spatial manipulation. The later Porrit house (1978), Mt Martha, Briggs house (1979), Lancefield, and Robson house (1987), Point Lonsdale, employ abstracted vernacular forms similar to the transformed Corbusian vocabulary of American architect Charles Gwathmey. Major commissions that developed this regionalized Modernism include the Administration Building (1977) and Mater Christi College, Belgrave, Victoria; Visitor Information Centre (1983) and National Botanical Gardens, Canberra; and a primary school (1986), Isabella Plains, Canberra.

BIBLIOGRAPHY

C. Hamann and J. Duncan: 'Seven in the Seventies', *Archit. Australia*, lxxi/1 (1982), pp. 51–9
J. Taylor: *Australian Architecture since 1960* (Sydney, 1986), pp. 184–6, 192–4

PHILIP GOAD

Cronqvist, Lena (*b* Karlstad, 31 Dec 1938). Swedish painter, sculptor, printmaker and weaver. She began her studies in 1958 at the Konstfackskolan, Stockholm, continuing from 1959 to 1960 at the Kungliga Akademien för de Fria Konsterna, Stockholm. Cronqvist's main subject-matter was the human figure. She first attracted attention for her sensuous use of bright, fleshy colours, evoking an air of humorous absurdity by distorting form and perspective. Although adhering to traditional forms and themes, such as landscape, still-life and self-portrait, her continuous dialogue with tradition led her to question the latter's implicitly patriarchal function and to dispute its representation of women as objects. In 1969–70 she became absorbed with the crucially conflicting themes of being an artist and a mother. She went on to depict her own childhood in a manner reminiscent of Edvard Munch, capturing not only its atmosphere of discolouring depression but also the distortion of memory. For this new imagery she used a darker range of colours and a larger scale to give a sense of constraint, dominated by a rigidly accomplished central perspective. In the self-portrait *The Mother* (tempera and oil on canvas, 1975; Norrköping, Kstmus.) she echoed a *Virgin* by Piero della Francesca. By replacing Christ with the image of her own aged mother she inverted the traditional signification of the Virgin, thereby representing woman's desperate confinement within a symbolic space dominated by the male perspective. In the 1980s Cronqvist pushed this psychological–existential imagery further by following the death process of her parents in two separate series of tempera and oil paintings that combine realistic detail with luminous,

almost magic expressionism: the *Day of Judgement* (1980; Stockholm, Karolinska Sjukhuset) and *1 August 1986* (1986; Stockholm, Mod. Mus.). She also investigated the changes of pictorial meaning achieved by turning the traditional theme of the artist and his model into its rebellious counterpart in a vast series of self-portraits titled the *Painter and her Model* (1982–6). The 'Tanztheater' of the 1980s, created by the German choreographer Pina Bausch, vitally inspired her painting. In 1988–9 she illustrated August Strindberg's classic play *Ett Drömspel* with a series of 30 lithographs, combining her sense of absurd pictorial humour with an atmosphere of painful loss and sorrow. Picasso's play *Les Quatre Petites Filles* (*c*. 1948) inspired her in 1990 to create a series of paintings of small girls, bathing and playing with cats and toys. These naked, lonely children are enclosed in a strange, luminous atmosphere, recalling both Italian 15th-century fresco painting and the art of Balthus. Adding parental figures and apes, she elaborated the theme of the young bathing girls in 40 small bronzes (1993–4), reinforcing the ambiguous expression of sensuous approach and abandonment.

Cronqvist also produced several weavings, mainly in the 1970s. Her technique was inspired by the art of the Norwegian weaver Hanna Ryggen, and she dyed the yarns herself. The main themes of her weavings are the biblical subjects of Adam and Eve and the Fall of Man, although she transferred a number of compositions from her paintings of the late 1970s into versions in wool.

BIBLIOGRAPHY

C.-J. Bolander, ed.: *Lena Cronqvist: En presentation* (Västerås, 1979) [incl. poems and ess. by T. Berggren, G. Sonnevi, G. Tunström and L. Cronqvist].
M.-B. Wadell: 'Om att söka sitt jag: Ett tema i Lena Cronqvists konst' [To seek one's self: a theme in Lena Cronqvist's art], *Ksthist. Tidskr.* (1986), pp. 27–37 [first extended essay on the artist, incl. Eng. summary]
Lena Cronqvist: Ett drömspel [Lena Cronqvist: a dream play] (exh. cat., Stockholm, Prins Waldemarsudde, 1989) [incl. list of exhibitions and a bibliog.]
S. Nordgren: *Lena Cronqvist* (Århus, 1990) [monograph devoted to the art of the 1980s]
N. Weibull: 'Barnet, kvinnan, masken' [The child, the woman, the mask], *Divan*, 1 (1990), pp. 4–23 [study of the theme of loss in Cronqvist's art]
Lena Cronqvist: Målningar, 1964–1994 (exh. cat. by I. Lind, Stockholm, Galleri Lars Bohman)
Lena Cronqvist: Skulpturer, 1993–94 (exh. cat. by L. Nylén, Stockholm, Galleri Lars Bohman)
Lena Cronqvist: Teckningar, 1969, 1979 (exh. cat. by B. Trotzig and G. Tunström, Stockholm, Galleri Lars Bohman)

NINA WEIBULL

Cronstedt, Carl Johan (*b* Stockholm, 25 April 1709; *d* Stockholm, 9 Nov 1777). Swedish architect, administrator, designer and collector. Considered the most technically orientated of 18th-century Swedish architects, he studied mechanics under the engineer Christoffer Polhem (1661–1751) and architecture and drawing with Carl Hårleman and continued his studies in Paris and Rome, while recruiting artisans for work on the Royal Palace, Stockholm. He became Hårleman's assistant during the construction of the palace and succeeded him as Superintendent of Works (1753–68). He used the Baroque style in his refurbishment of the interior of the church of St Mary, Stockholm (1760). He was also responsible for the Rococo interiors of the royal palaces of Drottningholm and Stockholm and designed several country houses, such as Svenneby in Östergötland and Myrö in Närke (both 1770). As an urban planner he is best known for his designs for bridges. He also invented (1767) a type of tiled stove that remained a typical feature of Swedish interiors (*see* SWEDEN, §V) for 200 years. A collection of maps and drawings of Cronstedt's official commissions is extant (Stockholm, Riksarkv); he also formed a personal collection of architectural drawings (Stockholm, Nmus. and Tek. Mus.) during his travels. His country house, Fullerö, in Västmanland, remains in the ownership of his descendants.

UNPUBLISHED SOURCES
Stockholm, Riksarkv [personal letters, 1730s; *Otto Waldes Katalog*: catalogue of priv. archives]

SBL; *SVKL*
BIBLIOGRAPHY
H. Andersson and F. Bedoire: *Svensk arkitektur ritningar, 1640–1970/Swedish Architectural Drawings, 1640–1970* (Stockholm, 1986), pp. 62–5, 68–9 [bilingual text]

MARTA GALICKI

Cronström, Daniel (*b* Avesta, 29 Sept 1655; *d* Paris, 30 Aug 1719). Swedish diplomat and agent. From March 1679 he worked in Paris at the Swedish Embassy and acquired a profound knowledge of French cultural policy. Being a close friend of Nicodemus Tessin (ii), he continually tried to further the artistic connections between France and Sweden. He visited the studios of such prominent artists as François Girardon and Jean Bérain I and also introduced French artists to Sweden, including the painter René Chauveau and the sculptor Bernard Fouquet (*b c.* 1640). He brought sculptures, architectural designs and engravings to his country, most of his copies of Classical statues being located in the Kungliga Akademi för de Fria Konsterna, Stockholm. Tessin's first design for rebuilding the Louvre was introduced by Cronström, who received it in 1694, to Louis XIV, as was a second design, together with a project for a museum at Versailles. He also assisted young Swedish artists in Paris. His patriotic ambitions have been linked to his disapproval of a relief (Paris, Louvre) that formed part of Martin Desjardins's monument to *Louis XIV* in the Place des Victoires, Paris, which showed Karl XI, King of Sweden, in a humiliating attitude before Louis XIV. It has been suggested that the relief was removed as a result of Cronström's remarks to the commissioner, François d'Aubusson, Duc de la Feuillade; however, sources in the Riksarkiv in Stockholm show that this was in fact due to the efforts of Nils Lillieroot, the Swedish ambassador.

WRITINGS
Les Relations artistiques entre la France et la Suède, 1693–1718: Nicodème Tessin le jeune et Daniel Cronström, correspondance (extraits), ed. C. Hernmarck (Stockholm, 1964)

BIBLIOGRAPHY
M. J. Crusenstolpe: 'Påpasslighet fordomdags av en svensk agent' [The alertness of a Swedish agent in times past], *Portefeuille*, iii (Stockholm, 1842)
A. Ellenius: *Karolinska bildidéer* [Caroline concepts of painting] (Uppsala, 1966)

ALLAN ELLENIUS

Cropsey, Jasper F(rancis) (*b* Rossville, Staten Island, NY, 18 Feb 1823; *d* Hastings-on-Hudson, NY, 22 June 1900). American painter and architect. He was a practising architect by 1843 but in that year he also exhibited a landscape painting, to favourable reviews, at the National Academy of Design, in New York. He greatly admired Thomas Cole for his dramatic use of the American landscape, but Cropsey brought to his panoramic vistas a more precise recording of nature, as in *View of Greenwood Lake, New Jersey* (1845; San Francisco, CA, de Young Mem. Mus.). Such vastness and detail impressed the viewer with both the grandeur and infinite complexity of nature and indicated a universal order. In 1847 Cropsey made his first trip to Europe, settling in Rome among a circle of American and European painters. His eye for detail in recording nature was encouraged by the Nazarenes, and his American sympathy for historical and literary subjects was sharpened by the antiquities of Italy. In 1848 Cropsey was in Naples, where the work of contemporary painters may have inspired the bold massing, deep space and brilliant lighting in *View of the Isle of Capri* (1848; New York, NY, Alexander Gal.)

After his return to America in 1848 Cropsey painted landscape subjects, including a keenly observed view of a serene and sun-drenched harvest scene, *Bareford Mountains, West Milford, New Jersey* (1850; New York, Brooklyn Mus.), and a dramatic thunderstorm and waterfall in *Storm in the Wilderness* (1851; Cleveland, OH, Mus. A.). He also painted canvases after sketches made in Europe, one of the largest being *The Coast of Genoa* (1854; Washington, DC, N. Mus. Amer. A.). The strain of idealism characteristic of America found expression in such allegories as *Spirit of War* (1851; Washington, DC, N.G.A.).

Cropsey spent 1856 to 1863 in England, painting American and Italian subjects as well as the English landscape. He provided 16 scenes of America for lithography by Gambart & Co., drew the rugged coast at Lulworth, Dorset, and captured the charm of the Isle of Wight in *Beach at Bonchurch* (1859; Hastings-on-Hudson, NY, Newington Cropsey Found.). The detailed clarity and intense colour of the Pre-Raphaelites impressed Cropsey, and his inclination towards truth to nature was encouraged by his personal acquaintance with John Ruskin. Cropsey portrayed, for an enthusiastic English public, the blazing colours of New England autumn in the vast painting called *Autumn—On the Hudson River* (1860; Washington, DC, N.G.A.; see fig.). Returning to America in 1863, Cropsey repeated his success with such large, crisply drawn and vigorously painted scenes of America as *Indian Summer* (1866; Detroit, MI, Inst. A.). Many of his paintings were modest in size, peopled with boaters or fishermen, sharp in detail but with a serene, burnished, atmosphere as in *Autumn Greenwood Lake* (1866; Hastings-on-Hudson, NY, Newington Cropsey Found.). During the 1860s and 1870s Cropsey became increasingly concerned with depicting the appearance of landscape strongly modified by sun and atmosphere. Air and light became chief elements in his Luminist pictures, such as *Lake Wawayanda* (1874; Amherst Coll., MA, Mead A. Mus.).

Cropsey revived his architectural practice soon after 1863 and built his own house, Aladdin, Warwick, NY (completed by 1869), in Gothic Revival style. His scheme (1867) for a five-storey apartment house was one of the first in America without shops on the ground floor. He also designed the 14 stations of New York's Sixth Avenue

Jasper F. Cropsey: *Autumn—On the Hudson River*, oil on canvas, 1.53×2.75 m, 1860 (Washington, DC, National Gallery of Art)

Elevated Railway (1876, destr. 1939), with much curving ironwork.

In later years Cropsey turned increasingly to watercolour, often with highlights in white gouache and solidly painted darks. An inclination toward the dramatic and imaginative rather than the calm and lyrical is evident in such watercolours as *Under the Palisades* (*c.* 1891; San Francisco, CA, de Young Mem. Mus.). Despite the growing Tonalist concern for projection of individual temperament and the Impressionist preoccupation with perception of light in the second half of the 19th century, Cropsey's descriptive clarity, spirited handling of paint and expansive vistas brought great vigour to American painting.

BIBLIOGRAPHY
Jasper F. Cropsey, 1823–1900 (exh. cat. by W. S. Talbot, Cleveland, OH, Mus. A.; Utica, NY, Munson–Williams–Proctor Inst.; Washington, DC, N. Col. F.A.; 1970–71)
W. S. Talbot: *Jasper F. Cropsey, 1823–1900* (New York, 1977) [catalogues 245 works]
                                    WILLIAM S. TALBOT

Croquison, Pierre Nicolas (*b* Courtrai [Flem. Kortrijk], 6 Dec 1806; *d* Courtrai, 24 March 1887). Belgian architect. He probably attended the Academie voor Schone Kunsten at Courtrai and then worked in Ghent under the direction of Louis Joseph Adrien Roelandt, whom he assisted as a superintendent of the municipal works in the building of the Ghent Opera (begun 1836), Schouwburgstraat, and the Law Courts (begun late 1830s), Koophandelsplein. Appointed Town Architect of Courtrai in 1842 and Provincial Architect for the districts of Courtrai and Ypres in 1858, Croquison was also a member of the Royal Commission on Monuments and so exercised wide control over building activity in southern Flanders. Apart from churches, he built numerous court houses, school buildings, hospitals, town halls, private houses and a château at

Proven (1859), and he was responsible for the restoration of monuments such as the town halls and churches at Courtrai, Furnes and Dixmude. As early as 1847 he published a drawing of the rich Gothic tabernacle (1585), by Hendrik Mauris, in St Martin's at Courtrai, before making a journey *c.* 1851 to study English Gothic Revival architecture. Of the many Gothic Revival churches that he erected (Luingne, 1848–50; Ingooigem, 1854–6; Kruishoutem, 1855; Dentergem, 1855–6; Bossuit, 1857–8; Egem, 1867–9; Deerlijk St Louis, 1868–9), the best is probably St Hilonius at Izegem (1852–5), with its interesting iron steeple. Later he also designed the churches at Herseaux (1870–72) and Wevelgem (1883) in a Romanesque Revival mode. Croquison collaborated with JEAN-BAPTISTE-CHARLES-FRANÇOIS BETHUNE on the church at Sint Kruis-Brugge (1853–6) but later failed to conform to the new archaeological standards of the mature Gothic Revival. His collaboration with E. W. Pugin on the church of Our Lady, Dadizele (1857), was not a success, and in 1862 his restoration of the town hall at Courtrai was heavily criticized by W. H. J. WEALE. Croquison's son, Arthur Croquison (1845–77), was also an architect.

BIBLIOGRAPHY
D. Sabbe: 'J. B. Bethune, promotor van de neogotische beweging', *Hand. Kon. Gesch. & Oudhdknd. Kring Kortrijk*, lxviii (1979), p. 292
J. van Cleven: 'Vlaamse neogotiek, in Europees perspectief', *Vlaanderen*, xxix/174 (1980), pp. 8–9
——: 'Nineteenth-century Architecture', *Flemish Art*, ed. H. Liebaers (Antwerp, 1985), p. 504
                                    JEAN VAN CLEVEN

Cros, (César-Isidore-)Henri [Henry] (*b* Narbonne, 16 Nov 1840; *d* Sèvres, 20 Jan 1907). French sculptor and writer. He was the elder brother of the eccentric poet and inventor, Charles Cros (1842–88), and he received a traditional training under the painter Jules-Emmanuel

Valadon (1826–1900) and under the sculptors François Jouffroy and Antoine Etex. He first exhibited at the Salon of 1861 in Paris, showing a plaster bust of his brother (untraced), and in 1863 he participated in the Salon des Refusés. Between 1869 and 1880 he researched techniques of making sculpture in polychromed wax. At the Salon of 1873 he exhibited the *Prize of the Tournament* (Paris, Mus. d'Orsay), a polychromed wax relief studded with pearls, which was purchased for the State. It depicts a stylized group of medieval women in court costumes occupying a box at a tournament. He produced 12 works in this medium, and although few have survived, they served as technical prototypes for the work of other sculptors, notably Degas and Désiré Ringel d'Illzach. His investigations into the way wax had been used in earlier art culminated in a study, undertaken in collaboration with the scientist Charles Henry, of the use of encaustic in the ancient world. From the mid-1880s Cros became interested in another ancient technique, that of making polychrome sculpture from fired glasspaste imbued with metal oxides. He sought State sponsorship for his research and was rewarded in 1891 by being provided with a studio at the Sèvres Porcelain Factory, for the production of *pâte de verre* sculpture and decorative work. His most substantial surviving pieces in this medium are the *History of Water* (1892–4; Paris, Mus. d'Orsay), a relief for a fountain, and the *History of Fire* (1894–1900; Paris, Mus. A. Déc.), a lunette relief. Unlike the medievalism of his wax pieces, these display a painterly classicism and a free, Symbolist approach to mythological themes. His use of decorative media to break down the boundaries between painting and sculpture is symptomatic of a wider endeavour throughout Europe at the end of the 19th century to unite the fine and the applied arts.

WRITINGS

with C. Henry: *L'Encaustique et les autres procédés de peinture chez les Anciens, histoire et technique* (Paris, 1884)

BIBLIOGRAPHY

A. Bourdelle: 'Un Grand Artiste méconnu: Henri Cros', *La Vie*, 8 (1917)
J.-L. Olivié: 'Un Atelier et des recherches subventionnés par l'état: Henry Cros à Sèvres', *La Sculpture du XIXe siècle, une mémoire retrouvée: Les Fonds de sculpture. Rencontres de l'école du Louvre: Paris, 1986*, pp. 193–9

PHILIP WARD-JACKSON

Crosato, Giovanni [Gian] **Battista** [Giambattista] (*b c.* 1685–6; *d* Venice, 15 July 1758). Italian painter and stage designer. His earliest known work, the *Flagellation of Christ* (*c.* 1706; Venice, Mus. Diocesano S Apollinia), for the Scuola del Cristo of S Marcuola, is a dark, shadowy painting that reveals the strong influence of tenebrist trends of the 17th century. Crosato, however, belonged to the generation of Venetian painters such as Jacopo Amigoni, Sebastiano Ricci and Giovanni Antonio Pellegrini, who were developing a lighter, more colourful style. His tonality changed from the darkened shadows of the

Giovanni Battista Crosato: *Chariot of Apollo* (1750s), ceiling fresco, Ca' Rezzonico, Venice

Flagellation to the light-filled frescoes for Stupinigi, the hunting palace of the Duke of Savoy, near Turin, which constitute his next known work. The most successful of these, the *Sacrifice of Iphigenia* (begun 1733), on the vault of the antechamber of the queen's apartment, is a highly dramatic work full of bright bold colours accentuated against the blue sky and white clouds. The gold, blue and red tones are effectively placed so as to lead the eye around the room and guide it through the narrative, which is related through the specific gestures or glances of a few figures, at the same time suggesting the idea of greater numbers. Equally direct is Crosato's use of sharply defined, highly saturated colours, which remain constant in their intensity and effective in providing visual unity; his linear style defines solidly modelled forms. Other rooms at Stupinigi decorated by him included the antechapel of S Umberto, with figures of hunters and lady companions, and the Sala degli Scudiere, with the story of *Apollo and the Python* on the ceiling. These works established Crosato's career in Savoy. He received further commissions for fresco cycles in the vestibule of the Villa Regina and in the Palazzo Reale in Turin.

Crosato returned to Venice in 1736, where he was admitted to the Venetian painters' guild (the Fraglia). Soon after, he received commissions for decorations in the churches of S Maria dei Servi and S Moise and in Ca' Pesaro. Returning to Turin in 1740, he began working on commissions he received for the churches and homes located in and around the city. Between 1740 and 1742 he decorated several churches—La Consolata, SS Marco e Leonardo, the Immacolata Concezione, S Andrea in Chieri, the Visitazione in Pinerolo and the Palazzo Birago di Borgaro (now Palazzo della Valle).

With the one possible exception of a third trip to Turin in 1749–50, Crosato remained in Venice from 1746 until his death. He was busy with commissions for churches in the city and many of the villas that surround it. Documents record that in 1748 he decorated the parish church in Ponte di Brenta. He also painted frescoes in the Villa Algarotti in Mestre about this time, and in the Villa Marcello in Levada he painted a ceiling decoration depicting the gods and goddesses of Olympus and four wall frescoes of scenes from the *Life of Alexander the Great*.

During the 1750s he completed the fresco of the *Triumph of Juno* in the Palazzo da Mosto and the spectacular ballroom of Ca' Rezzonico, both in Venice. The ballroom ceiling fresco portrays the *Chariot of Apollo* (see fig.) with a brilliant display of light-orange rays emanating from the head of the sun god as he guides the chariot pulled by four grey-white horses through the four corners of the world. Crosato was a master of illusionism, and here he created vast expanses of blue sky with putti and clouds spilling over the edges of the framework. These late works show that neither his abilities nor his use of vibrant colours diminished with age. In 1755 he was invited to become a member of the Venetian Academy, of which Giambattista Tiepolo was president. Crosato continued to attend meetings until the beginning of 1758, when he became fatally ill.

In addition to being a fresco painter, Crosato was involved in making sets (all destr.) for the Royal Theatre in Turin and S Giovanni Crisostome in Venice and designed engravings for Pietro Monaco and others. He rarely changed his pleasing combination of bright bold colours, clear even lighting and hard linear forms. By his travels, he helped to spread the light and airy Venetian Rococo style. Bernardino Galliari in particular imitated Crosato's brilliant manner in his own set designs for the Royal Theatre in Turin and his decorations for villas in Lombardy.

BIBLIOGRAPHY

A. M. Zanetti: *Delle pitture veneziane* (Venice, 1771), p. 454
F. S. Bartoli: *Notizie delle pitture, sculture, ed architetture d'Italia* (Turin, 1776)
O. De Rossi: *Nuova guida per la città di Torino* (Turin, 1781)
G. A. Moschini: *Guida della città di Venezia* (Venice, 1815)
E. A. Cicogna: *Delle inscrizioni veneziane*, 6 vols (Venice, 1824–53), v, pp. 598, 606
F. De Boni: *Biografia degli artisti* (Venice, 1840), p. 262
G. Avogadro: *Cenni sulla vita e sulle opere di Bernardino Galliari* (Turin, 1847)
G. Fiocco: *Giambattista Crosato* (Venice, 1941, 2/1944)
N. Ivanoff: 'Un ignoto ciclo pittorico di Giovanni Battista Crosato', *A. Veneta*, v (1951), pp. 170–71
R. Pallucchini: *La pittura veneziana del settecento* (Bologna, 1951), ii, pp. 21–4
C. Donzelli: *I pittori veneti del settecento* (Florence, 1957), pp. 71, 73–4, 252
M. Bernardi: *La palazzina di caccia di Stupinigi* (Turin, 1958)
A. Griseri: 'Il rococò a Torino e Giovan Battista Crosato', *Paragone*, xi (1961), pp. 42–65
L. Mallé: *I dipinti del Museo d'arte antica* (Turin, 1963)
B. di Vesme: *Schede Vesme—l'arte in Piemonte dal XVI al XVIII secolo* (Turin, 1963–8), i, pp. 377–8
E. Martini: *La pittura veneziana del settecento* (Venice, 1964), pp. 34, 73, 149, 174, 237
L. Mallé: *Stupinigi* (Turin, 1968)
Dal Ricci al Tiepolo (exh. cat. by P. Zampetti, Venice, Doge's Pal., 1969), pp. xlvi, 191–200
L. Mallé: *Palazzo Madama in Torino* (Turin, 1970)
M. Precerutti-Garberi: *Frescoes from Venetian Villas* (London, 1971)
P. Mattarolo: 'La formazione emiliana di Giambattista Crosato', *A. Veneta*, xxv (1971–2), pp. 194–202
I. Chiappini di Sorio: 'Affreschi settecenteschi veneziani: Gian Battista Crosato in Palazzo da Mosto', *Not. Pal. Albani*, iv (1975), pp. 38–43
G. M. Pilo: *Sebastiano Ricci e la pittura veneziana del settecento* (Pordenone, 1976)
F. D'Arcais, F. Zava Boccazzi and G. Pavanello: *Gli affreschi nelle ville venete dal seicento all'ottocento* (Venice, 1978)
M. Viale Ferrero: *La scenografia dalle origini al 1936* (Turin, 1980)
N. S. Harrison: *The Paintings of Giovanni Battista Crosato* (diss., U. Georgia, 1983)

SUSAN HARRISON KAUFMAN

Crosier. Crook or pastoral staff of a bishop, abbot or abbess. It was originally a wooden staff used by itinerant monks, priests and bishops (and also teachers), possibly as an aid to walking and also as a badge of office. The use of such staves is first recorded during the 4th century AD by Gregory of Nazianzus (*Oratio* xlii). Descriptions are ambiguous: crosiers may have been straight, crook-headed or cross-headed, and it is possible that all forms were used. There are indications that by the 9th century a crook-headed form was common, as the term *cambutta* ('little curve') had come into popular use (Strabo's *Vita Sancti Galli*).

In the second half of the 11th century a new term, *crocia* ('crook' or 'cross'), had become popular, and tau-headed (T-shaped) crosiers began to appear alongside the crook-headed form. Some doubt has been expressed as to whether these tau-headed staves were indeed for pastoral use, but they are decorated with precisely the same imagery as contemporary crook-headed staves, and there are contemporary illustrations of tau-headed staves being carried by clerics. By the end of the 12th century this tau-headed form (also known as the tau-crosier or tau-cross) had ceased to be made.

There is evidence that crosiers were occasionally carried by popes until the end of the 12th century, when the practice was abolished by Innocent III (*De Sacro Alteris, De Mysteriis Missae, Decretales* I, i, 15). From then onwards, they were carried only by bishops, abbots and abbesses. In the Roman Catholic Church crosiers remained in use until well into the 20th century, but the practice now seems to be declining. Crosiers were abolished in the Anglican Church, along with many other appurtenances of the Roman Catholic Church, by King Henry VIII, and it was not until the revival of outward form stimulated by the Oxford and Liturgical movements that they again came into use.

From an early period, the plain wooden crosiers of the saints were treated as relics and were encased in precious metal and encrusted with gems. The precious covering of the crosier of St Austreberthe of Montreuil-sur-Mer (Montreuil-sur-Mer, St Sauve) is supposed to date from the 7th century, and a Merovingian *Life of St Sylvanus* (Knögel, no. 737) records the posthumous encasing of the saint's crosier in silver. This practice seems to have become common, and it may have had an influence on later crosiers, which, from about the 9th century, began to be made of semi-precious materials.

The earliest surviving crosiers that do not appear to have been thought relics are Frankish. They are made of various materials, such as jet (New York, Met.) and gilt bronze (Hildesheim Cathedral Treasury). Their heads are small and tightly curled into spiral form, unlike the encased relics, which have heads that are relatively large and just slightly bent. Crosiers survive in large quantities from the 11th century onwards. Throughout the medieval period ivory and enamel were the most common media, and the most common imagery was of serpents, fruit and foliage (a clear example is a 12th-century English crosier head in Florence, Bargello; see fig.). This raises the question of interpretation.

All authorities on the significance of crosiers, from Gregory of Nazianzus in the 4th century onwards, have argued that the crosier is shaped like a shepherd's crook and have developed a symbolism for it based on this analogy: the bishop is the shepherd, and the ordinary people are his flock; he uses his crook to catch them by the neck or the heel when they go astray, to beat them when they need punishment and to support them when they are weary. This being the case, it is surprising to find that crosiers only looked like shepherds' crooks in the 20th century and that shepherd imagery was absent from them until the 19th, when the Good Shepherd appears on some of the more ornate examples. The serpents and foliage that appeared on most crosiers during their formative period between the 9th and 12th centuries probably refer to Aaron's rod, which became a serpent on several occasions (Exodus 4: 2–4, 30–31; 7: 9–13). On the last occasion, Pharaoh's magicians also turned their rods into serpents, but Aaron's serpent devoured them before becoming a rod again. Later, when the Hebrews were

Crosier head, walrus ivory, h. 175 mm, English, mid-12th century (Florence, Museo Nazionale del Bargello)

electing their priesthood, the choice fell on Aaron and his descendants because his rod budded, bloomed and produced ripe almonds overnight (Numbers xvii. 8). So it would seem that there was some conflict between popular perception of the significance of the crosier and the official interpretation. Only Honorius Augustodunensis in the 12th century made any connection between the pastoral staff and Moses and Aaron (*Gemma Animae* i, chaps 217–20).

In later periods, the serpent ceased to appear on crosiers, although foliage remained widespread. Crosiers became increasingly precious and ornate until the later 20th century, when it became fashionable to bear an 'authentic' wooden shepherd's crook, except in the case of the Anglican Bishop of Lynn, who carried a boat-hook on the grounds that there were more boats than sheep at Lynn.

BIBLIOGRAPHY
Walafridus Strabo: *Vita Sancti Galli* [Life of Saint Gall] (9th century); ed. in *PL*, cxiv (1879), cols 975–1030
Honorius Augustodunensis: *Gemma animae* (12th century); ed. in *PL*, clxxii (1895), col. 609
Abbé Barraud and A. Martin: 'Le Bâton pastoral: Etude archéologique', *Mélanges d'archéologie, d'histoire et de littérature*, ed. A. Martin and H. Cahier, iv (Paris, 1856), pp. 145–257
W. Smith and S. Cheetham, eds: *A Dictionary of Christian Antiquities* (London, 1880), col. 1565
E. Knögel: 'Schriftquellen zur Kunstgeschichte der Merovingerzeit', *Bonn. Jb. Rhein. Landesmus. Bonn & Ver. Alterfreunden Rheinlande*, cxl–cxli (1936), pp. 1–258
C. du F. Du Cange: 'Crocia', *Glossarium mediae et infimae latinitatis*, 8 vols (Paris, 1940–50)
F. Cabrol and H. Leclercq, eds: *Dictionnaire d'archéologie chrétienne et de liturgie*, iii (Paris, 1948), cols 3144–60
D. Gaborit Chopin: 'Bâtons pastoraux', *Trésors des abbayes normandes* (Rouen, 1979), pp. 233–4, 243
P. E. Michelli: *The Pre-Norman Crosiers and Metalwork of Ireland* (Norwich, 1987)

PIPPIN MICHELLI

Cross. Symbol of Christianity, widely represented in art in a great variety of types, contexts and materials. This article is concerned with the cross as a three-dimensional object, both of the monumental and portable type. Although in its narrow sense the term denotes a cross without the *corpus* (figure of the crucified Christ), it is also commonly used to refer to a crucifix (a cross with a representation of the *corpus*), a subject that is covered elsewhere (*see* CRUCIFIX). The cross was also adopted as the typical form for reliquaries of the True Cross (for a discussion of reliquary crosses *see also* RELIQUARY, §I, 1).

I. Introduction. II. Monumental. III. Portable.

I. Introduction.

Christ's execution by crucifixion is described in all four Gospel accounts, although none is specific about the shape of the cross. The New Testament Greek word for cross or crucifix, *stauros*, can also simply denote a post, and does not necessarily imply the cruciform shape of the vulgate Latin *crux*. The prevalence of the latter in Christian thought and art may be connected with the symbolic potential of a quadripartite symmetrical form comprising both a vertical and a horizontal member. The image of Christ with arms stretched out on a cross also presents a stylized representation of the Early Christian *orans* position of prayer.

The many different types of cross can be divided into two main groups: Greek crosses with arms of equal length and Latin crosses with a longer vertical arm. The former group includes the *crux ansata* with a small ring at the top, and the *crux gammata*, better known by its Hindu name of swastika; the origins of both predate the Christian period. The Maltese cross has flared ends, while the cross of St Andrew (or the Burgundian cross) is in the shape of an X and is associated with the martyrdom of St Andrew. Of the Latin crosses, the most important are the *crux commissa*, or St Anthony's cross, which takes the shape of the Greek letter *tau* (T); according to a tradition dating from the 10th century the thieves crucified beside Christ were crucified on *tau* crosses. The *tau* is also significant in crucifixion typology as the Old Testament symbol of salvation. Christ was frequently depicted on a *tau* cross

from the 13th century. Other variants include the Patriarchal cross, also known as the cross of Anjou or of Lorraine, with two horizontal arms (e.g. *see* JERUSALEM, LATIN KINGDOM OF, fig. 1), and the Papal cross, which has three. This multiplication can be explained by the addition of the *titulus* (inscription) and the *suppedaneum* (footrest) to the cross. The Russian Orthodox cross also has three hortizontal arms, but the lowest is set at an angle.

According to early legends Christ's cross was made from the wood of the Tree of Life in the Garden of Eden and from the 6th century AD the cross is often depicted as the *arbor vitae*, with stylized stumps of branches on the surface of the wood. The Y-shaped cross which occurs from the 12th century, mostly in Germany, is also usually represented in this way. From the 12th century, but more commonly from the 14th, some *arbor vitae* crosses were shown to grow branches with fruit and flowers and they often incorporated vine motifs or, less commonly, a rose. The Living cross, a type that appeared early in the 15th century, has four human hands projecting out of the ends of the cross arms.

In the Early Christian period the cross was exclusively a symbol of victory. It appears in 4th-century sarcophagus sculpture in combination with a laurel crown and the chi-rho symbol, which derives from the story of Constantine the Great, who, before the battle at the Milvian Bridge, ordered the Christian monogram to be placed within a triumphal garland and fixed to his cruciform imperial standard. Christ was also shown holding the cross like a standard of victory, a tradition that continued in images of Christ Treading the Beasts in Anglo-Saxon and Carolingian art with Christ carrying the cross over his shoulder. The importance of the cross as a central image in Christian iconography was increased by the spread of the legend of the Invention of the True Cross by Constantine's mother, Helena, in the 4th century and the subsequent circulation of relics. A great commemorative cross set up on Calvary and replaced with a jewelled cross in the mid-5th century was, like the relic, an object of veneration. It inspired an image known as the Adoration of the Cross, in which the cross was initially adored by the Apostles, but later usually by angels.

BIBLIOGRAPHY
LCI; *LM*; *RBK*; *RDK*
F. Cabrol and H. Leclerq, ed.: *Dictionnaire d'archéologie chrétienne et de liturgie*, iii (Paris, 1913)
L. Réau: *Iconographie de l'art chrétien*, ii (Paris, 1957)
C. E. Pocknee: *Cross and Crucifix* (London, 1962)
G. Schiller: *Ikonographie der christlichen Kunst*, 4 vols (Gütersloh, 1966–80; Eng. trans., London, 1972)
E. Dinkler: *Signum crucis* (Tübingen, 1967)
R. Schneider Berrenberg: *Kreuz, Kruzifix: Eine Bibliographie* (Munich, 1973)
B. Montevecchi and S. Vasio Rocca, eds: *Suppellettile ecclesiastica*, Dizionari terminologici, i (Florence, 1987)

CATHERINE OAKES

II. Monumental.

Large cross, usually of wood or stone, often free-standing.

1. High cross. 2. *Montjoie*. 3. Eleanor cross. 4. *Khatchk'ar*.

1. HIGH CROSS.

(i) Anglian. Carved stone cross found in Northumbria, Mercia, and East Anglia *c.* 650–775. The term is sometimes

also applied to monumental stone slabs with a prominent cross carved in high relief. Hundreds of fragments of both types have been discovered and classified (Cramp). The crosses do not have any clear distinguishing characteristics, but they are not usually carved on all sides and the vertical shafts are almost invariably square or nearly square in section. According to some authorities the four arms of these crosses were not linked by a ring (as was common in the Celtic examples, *see* §(ii) below), although the Lindisfarne crosses (Cramp, i, nos 45–6) do have ringed heads. Ornamental motifs were frequently based on those in the LINDISFARNE GOSPELS (*c.* 698; London, BL, Cotton MS. Nero D. IV) as well as on earlier Northumbrian models, with filigree ornamental patterns being copied from metalwork. The RUTHWELL CROSS (early 8th century; Ruthwell Church, Dumfries and Galloway) is one of the most representative examples; it combines vine and scroll motifs with birds and animals as well as biblical scenes and a runic poem. Other important crosses include the contemporary Bewcastle Cross (Cumbria; *see* ANGLO-SAXON ART, fig. 4), believed to be a monument to King Aldfrith (*d* 704). Its ornamental decoration is related to the Lindisfarne Gospels, while the figures recall those of the Book of Durrow (second half 7th century; Dublin, Trinity Coll. Lib., MS. 57), although they are more naturalistic. Another example, the Rothbury Cross (Newcastle upon Tyne, Black Gate Mus.), has reliefs with such representations as *Christ Healing the Blind Man* and *Christ the Judge*; a relief with the *Ascension* has been incorporated into a font at the church at Rothbury, Northumberland.

BIBLIOGRAPHY

G. Stephens: *The Old Northern Runic Monuments* (1866–1901)
W. Vietor: *Die northumbrischen Runensteine* (Marburg, 1895)
G. B. Brown: *Arts of Early England*, 6 vols (London, 1903–37)
E. T. Leeds: *Early Anglo-Saxon Art and Architecture* (Oxford, 1937)
T. D. Kendrick: *Anglo-Saxon Art to AD 900* (London, 1938)
R. J. Cramp, ed.: *Corpus of Anglo-Saxon Stone Sculpture*, 3 vols (Oxford, 1984)

JOHN N. LUPIA

(ii) Irish. Stone cross, usually with carved decoration, produced in Ireland from the 8th to the 12th century. At least 70 free-standing crosses survive, as do hundreds of fragments. Most belong to the category of so-called Celtic ringed crosses, a form particularly associated with Ireland. While a few crosses are plain, most are decorated with panels of abstract ornament and Christian iconography. A typical example comprises three pieces of stone: a cubical or square base with sloping sides (*see* INSULAR ART, fig. 4), a cross with hollowed angles and with an open ring linking the four arms, and a capstone surmounting the main shaft. When the elements are well proportioned the result is an extremely satisfying work of art. The tallest crosses, for example those at Arboe, Co. Tyrone, and MONASTER-BOICE (*see* INSULAR ART, fig. 5), rise to almost seven metres, but a height of two to three metres is more common. Some examples are distinguished by large decorated bosses applied to the faces of the cross and ring, a feature that appears to be derived from contemporary metalwork (see fig. 1). Others have rolls or discs placed either within the hollowed angles or on the inside face of the ring, vestigial references to the gems that protruded from the sides of Early Christian jewelled crosses. On the basis of geography, structure, style and iconography, the

1. Irish high cross showing ?*Adam Naming the Animals*, sandstone, h. 3.7 m, 8th or 9th century, Ahenny, Co. Tipperary; south face of the north cross

crosses have been divided into a series of groups (such as the Barrow Valley Crosses, the Midland Scripture Crosses, and the Ahenny Crosses), but the relationship between them is open to argument. The 12th-century crosses are more easily distinguished, as at that time there was a tendency to reduce the diameter of the ring or even abandon it altogether.

The origin and chronology of the crosses remains a controversial subject. Some authorities believe the ringed cross was an indigenous development, evolving in the 8th century from earlier standing stones, while others hold that it emerged first on Pictish slabs (for illustration *see* PICTISH ART) and subsequently spread to Ireland in the 9th century via IONA. Such hypotheses ignore the role of wooden prototypes, the existence of which is suggested both by documentary references and the survival on stone crosses of mortice and tenon jointing. It has been argued that the ring evolved from diagonally placed struts used to brace the arms of wooden crosses, but most modern scholars tend to the view that it was inspired by Early Christian designs in which crosses and chi-rho symbols were set within circular wreaths. There is no doubt that the ringed cross was familiar to Irish metalworkers by *c.* 700, and that processional crosses of this type were to be found in Irish monasteries.

The functions of the high cross were varied. It was common for monasteries to have several crosses, as a way of defining their sacred precinct. Some, like the altars in a medieval cathedral, were dedicated to specific saints. There is little doubt that they played an important didactic and liturgical role, but the exact nature of this remains unclear. They do not usually mark burials, although sometimes inscriptions commemorate the patrons who erected them.

See also CASHEL OF THE KINGS, §2; CLONMACNOIS MONASTERY, §2; and KELLS.

BIBLIOGRAPHY
A. Kingsley Porter: *The Crosses and Culture of Ireland* (New Haven, 1931)
E. H. L. Sexton: *Irish Figure Sculpture of the Early Christian Period* (Portland, MA, 1946)
R. Flower: 'Irish High Crosses', *J. Warb. & Court. Inst.*, xvii (1954), pp. 87–97
R. B. K. Stevenson: 'The Chronology and Relationship of some Irish and Scottish Crosses', *J. Royal Soc. Antiqua. Ireland*, lxxxvi (1956), pp. 84–96
F. Henry: *Irish High Crosses* (Dublin, 1964)
——: *Irish Art in the Early Christian Period, to 800 AD* (London, 1965)
——: *Irish Art during the Viking Invasions, 800–1020 AD* (London, 1967)
——: *Irish Art in the Romanesque Period, 1020–1170 AD* (London, 1970)
K. Hughes and A. Hamlin: *The Modern Traveller to the Early Irish Church* (London, 1977), pp. 80–101
A. Hamlin: 'Crosses in Early Ireland: The Evidence from Written Sources', *Ireland and Insular Art, AD 500–1200*, ed. M. Ryan (Dublin, 1987), pp. 138–40
H. Richardson and J. Scarry: *Irish High Crosses* (Cork, 1990)
R. A. Stalley: *Irish High Crosses* (Dublin, 1991)
P. Harbison: *The High Crosses of Ireland* (Bonn, 1992)

ROGER STALLEY

2. 'MONTJOIE'. Small, free-standing stone monument forming part of a series of seven (or possibly nine), erected by Philip III (*reg* 1270–85) between 1271 and 1285 along the route of Louis IX's funeral procession to Saint-Denis Abbey. These Rayonnant structures were hexagonal in section. They incorporated statues of kings and were surmounted by elevated crosses. Although the crosses were dismantled during the Wars of Religion (second half of the 16th century) and all traces of the royal signposts were destroyed in 1793, it is possible to reconstruct their original appearance from 17th-century engravings and from the extant Eleanor crosses that were erected in England in the 1290s in direct emulation (*see* §3 below). There is no consensus regarding the function of the *montjoies*. Branner traced them to the crosses erected on the trail of miracles wrought by St Remi's relics, while Lombard-Jourdan linked them to the stops made by the decapitated body of St Denis. Both interpretations connect the *montjoies* to the sacred origins of France and the

saintliness of the Capet kings. Members of that dynasty were represented by statues placed in niches above the bases of the *montjoies*. Although the statues were not individualized, later sources identified the kings as Louis VIII (*reg* 1223–6), Louis IX and Philip III. Branner suggested, however, that all the figures represented Louis IX, whereas Lombard-Jourdan assigned the royal statues a more generic identity, that of the royal forebears represented in the galleries of kings in French Gothic cathedrals. The *montjoies* were symbols of royalty and signalled the miracles performed by Louis IX's relics; in exchange for homage to the cult of ancestors, the *montjoies* offered protection to pilgrims travelling to Saint-Denis Abbey.

BIBLIOGRAPHY
P. Irigoin: 'Montjoies et oratoires', *Bull. Mnmtl*, xciv (1935), pp. 145–70
R. Branner: 'The Montjoies of Saint Louis', *Essays in the History of Architecture Presented to Rudolf Wittkower* (New York, 1969), pp. 13–16
A. Lombard-Jourdan: '"Montjoies" et "Montjoie" dans la Plaine Saint-Denis', *Paris & Ile-de-France: Mém.*, xxv (1974), pp. 141–81
J. Zukowsky: 'Montjoie and Eleanor Crosses Reconsidered', *Gesta*, xiii (1974), pp. 39–44
J. Bony: *The English Decorated Style: Gothic Architecture Transformed, 1250–1350* (Ithaca, 1979), pp. 1–29

DONNA L. SADLER

3. ELEANOR CROSS. Stone cross made on the orders of Edward I of England to mark the stages in the funeral journey of his wife, Eleanor of Castile (*d* 1290). Of the twelve crosses set up between Lincoln and London, nine are documented and the bases of three survive: Geddington (Northants), Northampton (also known as the Hardingstone Cross) and Waltham (Essex). Fragments of the Cheapside Cross survive in the Museum of London.

The cross bases are raised on steps, and originally supported tall shafts. The survivors share enough details to suggest that they were made to a common plan, but several masons were involved, sometimes more than one craftsman on one cross. They are composed of receding tiers, on a polygonal ground-plan, the lower tier solid and the upper with open tabernacles housing large-scale statues of the Queen. The bases are decorated with blind tracery motifs, the arms of Ponthieu, Castile, England and León, gables, miniature battlements, diaper ornament, foliage and cresting. The Northampton Cross has sculptured open books (presumably once inscribed), and displays the earliest use in English monumental art of the ogee, or reversed, curve (see fig. 2). The surviving statues of Eleanor have a swaying pose and drapery arranged in broad, flat folds. The two London crosses, at Charing and Cheapside, were the most lavish, using quantities of Purbeck marble. The decorative motifs on the bases were in part derived from contemporary north French architectural decoration, and although single memorial crosses had occasionally been set up in England before, the Eleanor crosses seem to have been part of Edward I's response to the use of art by the French monarchy for elaborate visual display. The funeral route of Louis IX in 1270 had been marked by similar crosses (*montjoies*; *see* §2 above).

The documented Eleanor crosses were made between 1291 and 1294 by masons who were with one exception closely associated with Royal building works: JOHN OF BATTLE, for instance, who made five crosses including

Age of Chivalry: Art in Plantagenet England, 1200–1400 (exh. cat., ed. J. Alexander and P. Binski; London, RA, 1987–8)

D. Parsons, ed.: *Eleanor of Castile, 1290–1990: Essays to Commemorate the 700th Anniversary of her Death* (Stamford, 1991)

N. Coldstream: *The Decorated Style: Architecture and Ornament* (London, 1994)

NICOLA COLDSTREAM

2. Eleanor cross, Hardingstone, Northampton, 1291–4

Northampton, had been undermaster at Edward I's Vale Royal Abbey. MICHAEL OF CANTERBURY, maker of the Cheapside Cross, was master mason of St Stephen's Chapel in the Palace of Westminster. ALEXANDER OF ABINGDON, maker of the Charing and the surviving Waltham statues, did other sculptural work on Eleanor's funerary monuments. The crosses were cut down or destroyed in 1643; the Charing and Cheapside crosses had already been reworked since the 14th century.

BIBLIOGRAPHY

B. Botfield: *Manners and Household Expenses of England*, ed. T. Hudson Turner (London, 1841)

H. M. Colvin, ed.: *History of the King's Works*, i (London, 1963)

J. Bony: *The English Decorated Style* (London, 1979)

4. 'KHATCHK'AR' [Armen.: 'cross-stone']. Typical Armenian stone monument, comprising an upright slab (h. *c.* 1–3 m) carved with a cross design, usually set on a plinth or rectangular base (*see* ARMENIA, §IV, 1(ii) and fig. 8). *Khatchk'ars* were made from the 9th century AD onwards and occur in large numbers throughout Armenia and areas with Armenian settlement, such as Isfahan (Iran) and Jerusalem. These monuments are of basalt or tufa in shades of grey, pink and yellow, the softness of the tufa making it possible to drill patterns of exquisite fineness. They always face west and are decorated on the front surface only. Their marked similarity in appearance, however, is superficial and hides endless variations in treatment. The main motif is a central cross, usually quite large, set against a background of elaborately ornamented stone. The cross may be accompanied by other crosses and surrounded by designs in ribbon interlace, geometric and floral patterns, or figurative scenes. Inscriptions record the date or occasion for which the slab was erected, the name of the patron who commissioned the work and the name of the stonecutter, such as Momik at Noravank' Monastery (1308) and Poghos at Goshavank' (1291).

The *khatchk'ar* follows a long lineage of sculptured monuments in Armenia, leading to the erection between the 5th and 7th centuries AD of many carved votive stelae, surmounted by a cross. The *khatchk'ar* proper emerged as a definite type in the 9th century; it continued the tradition of carved stelae but developed as an art form in its own right. It flourished most prolifically between the 11th and 14th centuries, when the carving of ornamental motifs achieved a supreme virtuosity, with some patterns so fine they resemble lace. *Khatchk'ars* produced after Armenia lost its independence and up to the 18th century are less innovative, showing influences from Iranian art.

Khatchk'ars are important sources of historical information since they were erected to commemorate victories in battle, the building of bridges, donations to monasteries, and as landmarks or thank-offerings. Although popular belief sometimes gave them protective powers, their most common function was as gravestones, particularly later, when foreign domination allowed fewer opportunities to set up commemorative stones. Cemeteries such as those at Noraduz near Lake Sevan or New Julfa (16th–18th centuries) contain thousands of *khatchk'ars*. Sometimes these form part of an architectural complex, or may be incorporated into the walls of a church, for example at Geghard (1215), where they even cover the natural rock outcrops above the monastery.

The carving of *khatchk'ars* began as an assertion of the Christian faith. An elaborate symbolism lies behind the designs, which, although essentially ornamental, are interwoven with abstract motifs expressive of eternal life. The Tree of Life or winged cross is a favourite device, with leaves sprouting from the base of the cross. Golgotha is usually represented by a series of stylized steps below the cross. The intricately carved motifs include rosettes, hands and myriads of cross patterns. In the 13th century the Saviour of All (Amenap'rkitch) type appeared, in which a Crucifixion scene takes the place of the central cross, for example at Haghpat (1273) and Ēdjmiadzin (1279).

BIBLIOGRAPHY

L. Azarian and A. Manoukian: *L'arte dei khatchar, croci di pietra*, Documenti di architettura armena, 2 (Milan, 1969) [Eng. and It. texts]
L. Azaryan: *Armenian Khatchkars* (Ēdjmiadzin, 1973)
Khatchk'ar (exh. cat. by G. Ieni, Venice, 1981)

HILARY RICHARDSON

III. Portable.

Cross that is not permanently fixed. The main types of portable cross are the altar, processional and pectoral cross. All these may incorporate a figure of Christ (for further discussion *see* CRUCIFIX). The function of the so-called hand cross, which is without fittings and mounts, is unclear, but it may have been used for blessing.

1. Altar and processional. 2. Pectoral.

1. ALTAR AND PROCESSIONAL. The altar cross stands on the altar at all times or sometimes only during the celebration of mass. It marks the altar as the place where Christ's death on the cross is re-enacted through the celebration of the Eucharist; thus in a great many cases it includes the figure of Christ crucified on it. The processional cross is fixed on to a tall pole by means of a pin and carried at the front of processions. It is often difficult to distinguish between these two types of cross, particularly since the function and appearance of individual crosses mentioned in treasury inventories and other sources are not generally specified. In addition, most surviving crosses have or once had a pin, so that they could have been fixed either on to a pole or into a pedestal or a slot in the altar, a practice also corroborated by miniatures (Springer).

(i) Byzantine and medieval. (ii) Renaissance and later.

(i) Byzantine and medieval.

(a) *Eastern Church*. Crosses were carried during church processions following Emperor Galerius' Edict of Tolerance (AD 311) and Emperor Constantine the Great's agreement with Licinius to follow this edict in Milan (AD 313), after which such processions were permitted; previously crosses could be carried only at funeral processions. Emperor Justinian I elevated the custom to ecclesiastical law (*Novellae* 123. xxxii), and as the Christian faith spread, processional crosses came to be used in the liturgy. There is evidence that as early as the 5th century it was customary to direct prayer towards a cross, although it might be painted or built into a wall. The custom of placing crosses on altars (although not necessarily on the altar where the Eucharist was celebrated) is already mentioned in 5th- and 6th-century texts from Syria. A number of silver crosses dating from the 6th and 7th centuries have been preserved (e.g. Washington, DC, Dumbarton Oaks); as well as serving as altar or processional crosses, they may also have been placed above the iconostasis or in the narthex, where people also prayed. The Moses Cross (1.04×0.79 m, 6th century; Mt Sinai, Monastery of St Catherine) is a superb example. It is a bronze cross with

flaring arms, decorated on the front with a Greek inscription from Exodus and a dedication. At the ends of the cross arms are three engravings: one on the left depicts Moses ascending Mt Sinai, and one on the right shows him loosening his sandal. The reverse is blank.

From around the 6th or 7th century the preferred material for altar and processional crosses was silver with niello decoration or gilding, although bronze was more widely used from the 10th century. Most of these crosses have widened ends, although there are also examples with straight ends. They are often decorated with engraved or niello representations of the *Trisagion* [Gr.: 'thrice holy'], donors' monograms and dedicatory inscriptions (e.g. Washington, DC, Dumbarton Oaks), or occasionally with an engraved image of Christ crucified. Examples with a three-dimensional figure of the crucified Christ do not occur before the 10th century; such crucifixes often also include busts of the apostles or the evangelists as well as figures of the Virgin and St John the Baptist. The latter usually flank the central figure of Christ thus forming a Deësis arrangement. The Virgin or saints may be shown on the back of the cross, and other frequent depictions include the Virgin and Child, Christ Pantokrator and angels. Jewelled crosses were much less common. The

3. Cross of Justin II, silver and hardstones, AD 565–78 (Rome, Vatican, Museo Storico Artistico—Tesoro di San Pietro)

earliest surviving *crux gemmata* is that of Emperor Justin II (see fig. 3); it has a relic container with a fragment of the True Cross as well as hardstones and inscriptions on the front, while on the reverse are medallion busts of *Justin* with his wife *Sophia, Christ*, and in the middle the *Agnus Dei*.

(b) Western Church. From the 7th century it was customary to place a fairly large cross behind or near the altar of the cross; documentary sources do not, however, indicate when it became usual to place a cross on the altar. While it is known that at the beginning of the 9th century the Bishop of Liège decreed that every priest should try to obtain a cross as part of his church furnishings, there are no indications as to typical usage and appearance. Such a cross certainly did not form part of the permanent furnishings of the altar, for in the *Admonitio synodalis*, probably written by Pope Leo IV (*reg* 847–55), only reliquaries, the Gospel book and the pyx holding the consecrated host were named as objects that could stand on the altar; that such an admonition was deemed necessary suggests that there was a tendency for other objects to be placed on the altar. Even so, it may be assumed that crosses were associated with the altar during mass, as is shown in some Carolingian manuscript illustrations (e.g. Stuttgarter Psalter, Stuttgart, Württemberg. Landesbib., MS. bibl. fols 23, 31*v* and 130*v*).

There are many references to crosses standing on altars in the 11th century, but still there is no information as to their appearance, and in particular as to whether or not they had a crucified figure of Christ. Around 1164 the liturgist Johannes Beleth mentioned several crosses as altar decorations (*Summa de ecclesiasticis officiis* cxv), while Pope Innocent III described a cross being displayed on the altar between two candlesticks (*De sacro altaris mysterio* II.xxi), and the canonist William Durandus (1230–96) provided a description of a cross being carried into church during the introit and displayed on the altar (*Rationale divinorum officiorum* I.iii.31). According to the monk and writer Honorius Augustodunensis (*c.* 1080–*c.* 1156) the cross was displayed on the altar for three reasons (*Gemma animae* cxxxv): as a symbol of Christ it was the focus of prayer, it was a visual reminder of the Passion and it encouraged people to follow Christ.

Notable changes in devotion and theology may have contributed to the increasingly widespread custom of displaying a cross on the altar in the 11th century. The first important change occurred in connection with the Carolingian controversy over transubstantiation, which continued until 1215 when transubstantiation was accepted as dogma at the Fourth Lateran Council. A cross (especially with the crucified figure of Christ) could thus serve to illustrate the actual presence of Christ during the celebration of the Eucharist, when his sacrifice was re-enacted. There were also changes in devotional practice in the 11th century. Faith became increasingly a personal experience, with the individual turning to God in prayer. Christ, having suffered for the sins of mankind, was the object of much of this devotion and prayer. For this reason, too, there was a need for the cross, preferably with the figure of Christ crucified, to be displayed on the altar. These observations are supported by the fact that there is

a great increase in the number of crosses that survive from the 11th century; the silver Bernward Cross (see fig. 4) may be considered the earliest surviving example of an altar cross.

Altar crosses were particularly widespread in the territory of the Holy Roman Empire, in Tuscany and Lombardy as well as in Denmark and Scania (Skåne, now Sweden). Surprisingly few Romanesque examples have been preserved in England, France and Spain. There were no regulations in the medieval period regarding the material to be used for altar and processional crosses. Most of those that survive are made of bronze, copper or brass, usually gilt. Records frequently mention crosses made of silver gilt or gold, although the latter may also have only been gilt as hardly any solid gold crosses survive. In poorer communities wooden crosses must also have been used. A few isolated examples survive of crosses or crucifixes

4. Altar cross known as the Bernward Cross, silver, 310×140 mm, *c.* 1007–8 (base, 14th century) (Hildesheim, Diözesanmuseum mit Domschatzkammer)

century; the earliest examples are the cross of Abbess Mathilde and Duke Otto (see fig. 5) and the silver Bernward Cross at Hildesheim (see fig. 4). The figure of the crucified Christ may be accompanied by renderings of the Virgin and St John the Baptist, the Hand of God, Adam resurrected or angels. Usually the back is either completely undecorated or shows such images as the *Agnus Dei* or the symbols of the Evangelists, often with inscriptions and vine tendrils or similar decorative motifs.

BIBLIOGRAPHY

LM: 'Kreuz', 'Kruzifix'

J. Braun: *Das christliche Altargerät in seinem Sein und in seiner Entwicklung* (Munich, 1932)

K. Weitzmann and I. Sevcenko: 'The Moses Cross at Sinai', *Dumbarton Oaks Pap.*, xvii (1963), pp. 385–9

D. I. Pallas: *Die Passion und die Bestattung Christi in Byzanz: Der Ritus— Das Bild*, Miscellanea Byzantina Monacensa, ii (Munich, 1965)

H. Buschhausen: 'Ein byzantinisches Bronzekreuz in Kassandra', *Jb. Österreich. Byz. Ges.*, xvi (1967), pp. 281–96

P. Springer: *Kreuzfüsse: Ikonographie und Typologie eines hochmittelalterlichen Geräts*, Bronzegeräte des Mittelalters, iii (Berlin, 1981)

Splendeur de Byzance (exh. cat., ed. J. Lafontaine-Dosogne; Brussels, Musées Royaux A. & Hist., 1982)

T. Jülich: 'Gemmenkreuze: Die Farbigkeit ihres Edelsteinbesatzes bis zum 12. Jh.', *Aachen. Kstbl.*, liv–lv (1986–7), pp. 99–258

E. Cruikshank Dodd: 'Three Early Byzantine Silver Crosses', *Dumbarton Oaks Pap.*, xli (1987), pp. 165–79

R. Marth: *Untersuchungen zu romanischen Bronzekreuzen: Ikonographie— Funktion—Stil* (Frankfurt, 1988)

P. Bloch: *Romanische Bronzekruzifixe*, Bronzegeräte des Mittelalters, v (Berlin, 1992)

REGINE MARTH

5. Altar cross of Abbess Mathilde and Duke Otto, silver gilt, hardstones and enamels, 973–82 (Essen, Münsterschatzkammer)

made of walrus ivory; a splendid example is the Cloisters Cross (mid-12th century; New York, Cloisters; *see* RO-MANESQUE, §VIII, 3 and fig. 80), of English workmanship; other examples have originated in the Scandinavian countries (e.g. Gunhild Cross, before 1076; Copenhagen, Nmus.). Limoges enamel crosses became more widespread from the second half of the 12th century, and were exported all over Europe. Processional crosses were often decorated with gems and pearls; the intersection frequently containing relics, as in the Great Bernward Cross (*c.* 1130–40; Hildesheim, Diözmus. & Domschatzkam.), or emphasized by gems, as exemplified by the Lothair Cross (*c.* 1000; Aachen, Domschatzkam.).

The basic form for both altar and processional crosses is the Latin cross with straight ends, although variations are also found; the ends can, for example, be widened, trapeziform, crutch-headed or rounded. Widened ends are particularly frequent on early examples, for instance the jewelled crosses (9th–11th centuries) at the Camara Santa in Oviedo Cathedral and in the Münsterschatzkammer, Essen. The Imperial Cross (*c.* 1024; Vienna, Schatzkam.) is the earliest surviving cross with crutch-head ends. Lily or trefoil-shaped ends became more common from the 13th century and a few isolated crosses with branches appearing to grow from the sides have also been preserved (e.g. the Soltikoff Cross, 1150–60; London, V&A). The figure of the crucified Christ was not represented on altar and processional crosses before the end of the 10th

(ii) Renaissance and after. Altar and processional crosses continued to be predominantly made of gold, silver and silver gilt, and were occasionally decorated with hardstones, precious gemstones and enamels. As in the earlier period, the adjustable fittings that survive on a number of crosses show that in many cases the same object was used on the altar and in processions, although some crosses were apparently designed specifically for one purpose rather than both. Reliquary crosses were sometimes converted into altar crosses: for example the silver cross (Florence, Mus. Opera Duomo) from Florence Baptistery is thought to have been made in 1457 by Antonio Pollaiuolo as a reliquary cross and adapted by the same artist *c.* 1470 to serve as an altar cross (Passavant).

The great demand for processional and altar crosses in the 15th century led a number of major sculptors and goldsmiths, including NICOLA GALLUCCI, to specialize in their production. These artists developed new types that were then repeated by others, often for decades, with the result that numerous crosses from the period have the appearance of mass-produced objects. There are also, however, a great number of high-quality examples that are unique or unusual in design, for example the processional cross (see fig. 6) from Lislaughtin Abbey, Co. Kerry, with a long inscription on the arms stating that it was made by William, son of Cornelius. The cross has a finely modelled figure of the crucified Christ and is incised with a delicate vine motif with pierced leaves; the symbols of the Evangelists are represented in quatrefoils at the ends of the arms. The cross foot is shaped like a crown around which is repeated the figure of a priest blessing and holding a cross in his left hand. The crown rests on a twisted knop that has rhomboid silver panels decorated with floral motifs and a socket for fixing a wooden staff.

A great number of very ornate crosses survive from the 16th century, for example the processional cross (*c.* 1547; London, V&A; *see* SPAIN, fig. 51) by Juan Francisco. Important Italian examples include the gold cross (*in situ*) made by Manno di Bastiano Sbarri (*fl* 1548–61) and Antonio Gentili for the high altar of St Peter's, Rome. (This cross was turned into a crucifix in the 17th century when a 16th-century *corpus* by Giacomo della Porta was affixed to it.) Around 1657 Pope Alexander VII ordered two new altar crosses (*in situ*) for St Peter's, and they were produced to designs by Gianlorenzo Bernini and cast in bronze by Paolo Carnieri (*fl* 1658–61) from moulds by Ercole Ferrata. One cross shows the living Christ while the other depicts Christ dead, showing signs of suffering.

In the 18th century such materials as porcelain were also used for making crosses. King Augustus III of Poland made at least two lavish gifts of porcelain altar sets designed by Johann Joachim Kändler. The smaller of the sets (1736; Urbino, Mus. Duomo) includes an altar cross, candlesticks and two statues of apostles and was given to Cardinal Annibale Albani. In the 19th century a tendency towards more simplified forms co-existed with a renewed interest in medieval designs, which was particularly strong in northern Europe where the GOTHIC REVIVAL flourished. In England the best examples of 'medieval' church furnishings, including crosses, were produced by A. W. N. Pugin. Many of his designs, including the silver plate processional cross (1850; London, V&A, M.107-1978), were produced by John Hardman (1811–67), director of a Birmingham metal workshop specializing in

7. Altar cross by Gerald Benney, parcel gilt, h. 820 mm, 1982 (Godalming, Charterhouse School)

Gothic Revival plate. Designs in the 20th century were characterized by more simplified forms, well-exemplified by the parcel gilt altar cross (see fig. 7) by Gerald Benney (*b* 1930).

BIBLIOGRAPHY

T. H. Clarke: ' "Die Römische Bestellung": Die Meissenser Altar-Garnitur die August III. dem Kardinal Annibale Albani im Jahre 1736 schenkte', *Keramos*, lxxxvi (1979), pp. 3–52

A. Parronchi: 'La croce d'argento dell'altare di San Giovanni', *Atti del convegno internazionale. Lorenzo Ghiberti nel suo tempo: Firenze, 1980*, pp. 195–217

W. Gramberg: 'Notizen zu den Kruzifixen des Guglielmo della Porta und zur Entstehungsgeschichte des Hochaltarkreuzes in S Pietro in Vaticano', *Münchn. Jb. Bild. Kst*, xxxii (1981), pp. 95–114

U. Schlegel: 'I crocifissi degli altari in San Pietro in Vaticano', *Ant. Viva*, xx/6 (1981), pp. 37–42

G. Passavant: 'Beobachtungen am Silberkreuz des Florentiner Baptisteriums', *Studien zum europäischen Kunsthandwerk: Festschrift Yvonne Hackenbroch*, ed. J. Rasmussen (Munich, 1983), pp. 77–105

JOHN N. LUPIA

2. PECTORAL. Small cross worn on a chain or ribbon around the neck. It often comprises two hinged halves holding a relic, but it can also be solid.

(*i*) *Byzantine and medieval.* Pectoral crosses that were not part of liturgical dress are known to have existed both in the East and the West in the Early Christian period. They evolved from the practice of wearing amulets to ward off evil, a custom persisting since antiquity. By the time of the early Christian martyrs such pendants may already have held relics; increasingly they came to be decorated with

6. Processional cross, silver gilt, h. 680 mm, from Lislaughtin Abbey, Co. Kerry, 1479 (Dublin, National Museum of Ireland)

Christian symbols. The earliest surviving examples, dating from the 5th and 6th centuries AD, are small and simple. They include a gold pectoral cross with a niello pattern (Rome, Vatican, Mus. Sacro) from a grave in S Lorenzo fuori le Mura, Rome, and a gold pectoral cross showing *Christ the Judge* (*see* EARLY CHRISTIAN AND BYZANTINE ART, fig. 88).

Pectoral crosses are mentioned in various written accounts. It is known, for example, that *c.* 600 Pope Gregory I presented Queen Theodolinde of Lombardy with a pectoral cross, which may be identifiable with the one preserved in the cathedral treasury at Monza. There is evidence that Byzantine emperors also presented such crosses to imperial dignitaries. Such reports indicate that pectoral crosses were not originally a liturgical badge of office, although they were very popular with bishops, who valued them primarily for the relics they contained. Bishop Gregory of Tours (*d* 594–5), for example, is known to have worn a reliquary cross beneath his clothes.

The pectoral cross was first mentioned as part of the liturgical insignia in the Life of Bishop Arnold of Mainz (written 1170), and one of the earliest representations of it as such is on the mosaic tombstone of *Abbot Gilbert of Maria Laach* (*d* 1152; Bonn, Rhein. Landesmus.). In later centuries the pectoral cross was mentioned repeatedly among the episcopal insignia, for instance by Pope Innocent III and the canonist William Durandus (1230–96), but it became an established, obligatory component of episcopal dress only as a result of Pope Pius V's *Missale Romanum* (1570; *see* §(ii) below). In the East, however, the pectoral cross never became part of a bishop's insignia; when bishops were consecrated they were given an oval *encolpion* (small case containing an amulet, worn on the breast; such amulets were already known in pre-Christian times) with an image of the cross. The numerous surviving eastern pectoral crosses may be regarded as an expression of private piety.

Most surviving pectoral crosses are made of metal, especially bronze, silver and gold, but it can be assumed that less expensive examples were made of wood or bone. Most have curved, straight or medallion-shaped ends, and in later examples these might also take the form of a crook or a lily. The crosses often have engraved or low-relief images, and less frequently are decorated with enamel (such as the 8th/9th-century Beresford Hope Cross; London, V&A; see fig. 8) or niello (for example the 6th/7th-century bronze cross; Providence, RI Sch. Des., Mus. A.). Examples set with precious stones or pearls are less common. Although some simple pectoral crosses have only geometric patterning, most are decorated with figures, and frequently show Christ on the cross accompanied by the Virgin and St John the Evangelist or the Four Evangelists; the standing figure of the Virgin at prayer with apostles or saints is often shown on the reverse. Some 6th- or 7th-century examples survive with Christ the Judge flanked by the Virgin and St John the Baptist. Saints who were particularly venerated in a certain area may also be depicted; for example SS Boris and Gleb were often represented on Russian pectoral crosses from the 11th century and later.

8. Pectoral cross known as the Beresford Hope Cross, cloisonné enamel mounted in gold, with silver gilt frame, Byzantine or Roman, 85×55 mm, 8th century or early 9th (London, Victoria and Albert Museum)

BIBLIOGRAPHY

LM: 'Brustkreuz'; *RBK*: 'Enkolpion'; *RDK*: 'Brustkreuz'
M. von Bárány-Oberschall: 'Byzantinische Pektoralkreuze aus ungarischen Funden', *Wandlungen christlicher Kunst im Mittelalter* (Baden-Baden, 1953), pp. 207–51
K. Wessel: 'Die Entstehung des Kruzifixus', *Byz. Z.*, liii (1960), pp. 95–111
O. Nussbaum: *Das Brustkreuz des Bischofs: Zur Geschichte seiner Entstehung und Gestaltung* (Mainz, 1964)
K. Wessel: *Die byzantinische Emailkunst* (Recklinghausen, 1967)
Byzantinische Kostbarkeiten (exh. cat., ed. A. Effenberger; Berlin, Bodemus., 1977)
Z. Lovag: *Mittelalterliche Bronzekunst* (Budapest, 1979)
——: 'Bronzene Pektoralkreuze aus der Arpadenzeit', *Acta Archaeol. Acad. Sci. Hung.*, xxxii (1980), pp. 363–72
——: 'Die Einflüsse byzantinischer Pektoralkreuze auf die Bronzekunst Ungarns im 11./12. Jh.', *Metallkunst von der Spätantike bis zum ausgehenden Mittelalter*, ed. A. Effenberger (Berlin, 1982), pp. 159–65
1000 Jahre russische Kunst (exh. cat., ed T. Meyer; Frankfurt am Main, Hist. Mus., 1988)

REGINE MARTH

(ii) Renaissance and after. The Western custom of wearing the pectoral cross as a sign of office followed the publication of Pius V's *Missale Romanum* (1570), which prescribed that bishops should wear a pectoral cross over the alb; this was reaffirmed by Pope Clement VIII in the *Ceremonial of Bishops* (1600). Such crosses also came to be used as ornamental insignia by other high-ranking clergy, including the pope, cardinals, abbots and prelates

and consequently are sometimes referred to as archiepis-copal crosses. In the Eastern Church in this period they were worn by archimandrites and archpriests, and in Russia by all priests. Renaissance and Baroque pectoral crosses were usually made of gold or silver and frequently deco-rated with hardstones and enamels. A fine gold example (Berlin, Schloss Köpenick) was made in the 16th century by the Netherlandish goldsmith Hieronymus Jacobs of Antwerp; it was purchased in 1562 by Abbot Mattheus Volders for the Premonstratensian Abbey of Averbode. A good example of a 17th-century archiepiscopal cross (Florence, Archv Opera Duomo) is the silver and gold cross made by Cosimo Merini (1580–1641). There were no great changes in the design and usage of pectoral crosses in the 18th, 19th and 20th centuries. They contin-ued to be predominantly made of gold with hardstones, although such other materials as enamel and ivory were also used. Twentieth-century designers include Meinard Burch, who produced a gold pectoral cross with enamel figures and a quartz crystal in the centre, while Hildegard Domizlaff made a pectoral cross of gold and ivory with a green feldspar stone mounted in the centre (McDonald).

BIBLIOGRAPHY

W. J. McDonald, ed.: *New Catholic Encyclopedia* (Washington, DC, 1967), v, p. 486; viii, p. 882

F. von Molle: 'De Pax van Averbode in de Hofkirche te Innsbruck en het borstkruis van abt Mattheus Volders', *Rev. Belge Archéol. & Hist. A.*, xli (1972), pp. 3–20

R. Tarchi and C. Turrini: 'Nuovi contributi sull'attività dell'orafo Cosimo Merlini tra committenza granducale ed ecclesiastica', *An. Scu. Norm. Sup. Pisa*, n. s. 2, xvii/3 (1987), pp. 735–70

JOHN N. LUPIA

Cross, Henri Edmond [Delacroix, Henri-Edmond-Jo-seph] (*b* Douai, 20 May 1856; *d* Saint-Clair, 16 May 1910). French painter and printmaker. The only surviving child of Alcide Delacroix, a French adventurer and failed businessman, and the British-born Fanny Woollett, he was encouraged as a youth to develop his artistic talent by his father's cousin, Dr Auguste Soins. He enrolled in 1878 at the Ecoles Académiques de Dessin et d'Architecture in Lille, where he remained for three years under the guidance of Alphonse Colas (1818–87). He then moved to Paris and studied with Emile Dupont-Zipcy (1822–65), also from Douai, whom he listed as his teacher when exhibiting at Salons of the early 1880s. His few extant works from this period are Realist portraits and still-lifes, painted with a heavy touch and sombre palette (example in Douai, Mus. Mun.).

To avoid working under the shadow of his celebrated namesake, Eugène Delacroix, in 1881 he adopted an abbreviated English version of his surname, signing his works 'Henri Cross' until around 1886, when he adopted 'Henri Edmond Cross' to avoid being confused with the painter Henri Cros.

In 1884 Cross helped to found the Société des Artistes Indépendants and through it became friends with many of the Neo-Impressionists. However, he only gradually assimilated avant-garde stylistic innovations. He lightened his palette and began painting figures *en plein air* in the mid-1880s. *Monaco* (1884; Douai, Mus. Mun.) reveals his study of both Jules Bastien-Lepage and Manet. Towards

the end of the decade, when he was increasingly influenced by Monet and Pissarro, he began to paint pure landscapes.

Cross's career took a decisive turn in 1891, when he adopted the Neo-Impressionist technique and showed at the Indépendants exhibition his first large work in this style, the portrait of *Mme H. F.* (now titled portrait of *Mme Cross*; Paris, Mus. d'Orsay). Also in this year, he moved to the south of France, staying first at Cabasson and then settling in Saint-Clair, a small hamlet near St Tropez where Signac also took up residence in 1892. Cross lived in Saint-Clair for the rest of his life, travelling twice to Italy (1903 and 1908) and annually to Paris for the Indépendants shows.

In the early and mid-1890s, as he developed the Neo-Impressionist method, Cross concentrated on seascapes and scenes of peasants at work. The *Beach of Baigne-Cul* (1891–2; Chicago, IL, A. Inst.) is characteristic of his highly regular technique: over a densely painted ground he placed small and relatively round touches in rows, more or less equally spaced, and mixed colours with white to express the bleaching action of sunlight. *The Farm (Eve-ning)* (1893; priv. col., see Compin, p. 129) exhibits his decorative use of sensuous silhouettes and recalls the Japanese prints and Art Nouveau designs that inspired other Neo-Impressionists at this time.

After the mid-1890s Cross ceased to depict peasants but continued to paint seascapes while exploring such new subjects as the everyday dances shown in *Village Dance* (1896; Toledo, OH, Mus. A.). Working with his neighbour Signac, he gradually abandoned the dot of earlier Neo-Impressionism and employed instead large and blocky strokes; this technique allowed for intense colour contrasts and created decisively decorative, mosaic-like surfaces. Now associated with the so-called 'second' Neo-Impres-sionist style, these developments inspired Matisse and the other Fauves who visited the south of France in the early 1900s. Also influential on these painters were the nude bathers and mythological figures, particularly the nymphs and fauns, which Cross introduced into his late seascapes.

Cross shared the utopian and anarchist beliefs of many of the Neo-Impressionists. In 1896 he contributed an anonymous lithograph entitled *The Wanderer* (see Compin, p. 337) to Jean Grave's anarchist publication, *Temps nou-veaux*. Later he created cover illustrations for several brochures issued by the same journal. Interpretations of Cross's large painting, the *Air of Evening* (1893–4; Paris, Mus. d'Orsay), have stressed the presence of anarchist-inspired sentiments. Like Signac's *In the Time of Harmony* (Montreuil, Mairie) from the same period, Cross's depic-tion of languorous seaside leisure seems designed to suggest the joy that would be unleashed by anarchy.

The comparatively small size of Cross's oeuvre can be partly attributed to his ill health. Eye problems, which emerged in the early 1880s, worsened in the early 1900s, and bouts of arthritis also kept him from working. Nonetheless, during the last decade of his life he mounted important one-man shows in Paris (Galerie Druet, 1905; Bernheim-Jeune, 1907) and as a result began finally to find a market and enthusiastic critical response.

BIBLIOGRAPHY

Exposition H.-E. Cross (exh. cat., preface E. Verhaeren; Paris, Gal. Druet, [1905])

Exposition Henri-Edmond Cross (exh. cat., preface M. Denis; Paris, Bernheim-Jeune, 1907); preface repr. in M. Denis: *Théories* (Paris, 1913, rev. 4/1920), pp. 157–60

C. Angrand: 'Henri-Edmond Cross', *Temps Nouv.*, xvi (23 July 1910), p. 7

E. Verhaeren: 'Henri Edmond Cross', *Nouv. Rev. Fr.* (July 1910), pp. 44–50; repr. in E. Verhaeren: *Sensations* (Paris, 1927), pp. 204–8

Exposition Henri-Edmond Cross (exh. cat., preface M. Denis; Paris, Bernheim-Jeune, 1910); preface repr. in M. Denis: *Théories* (Paris, 1913, rev. 4/1920), pp. 161–5

L. Cousturier: 'H.-E. Cross', *A. Déc.*, xxix (1913), pp. 117–32; as book (Paris, 1932)

F. Fénéon, ed.: 'Le Dernier Carnet d'Henri-Edmond Cross' and 'Inédits d'Henri-Edmond Cross', *Bull. Vie A.*, iii, 10–22 (1922)

M. Saint-Clair [M. van Rysselberghe]: 'Portrait du peintre Henri-Edmond Cross', *Nouv. Rev. Fr.*, liii (1939), pp. 123–7; repr. in M. Saint-Clair: *Galerie privée* (Paris, 1947), pp. 25–38

J. Rewald, ed.: *H.-E. Cross: Carnet de dessins*, 2 vols (Paris, 1959) [sketchbook facs.]

R. Herbert and E. Herbert: 'Artists and Anarchism', *Burl. Mag.*, cii (1960), pp. 473–82

I. Compin: *H.-E. Cross* (Paris, 1964) [cat. rais. and detailed bibliog.]

MARTHA WARD

Cross(e), Peter [Peeter; Luke, Laurence] (*b* ?*c*. 1645; *d* London, *bur* 3 Dec 1724). English painter. It used to be believed that there were two artists, Peter Cross and Laurence Cross(e); the miniatures once divided between them are now all assigned to Peter Cross. The confusion was started by Vertue, who read the entwined initials *PC* of his signature as *LC*. The full signature *Peeter Cross* on a miniature of *Sir James Ogilby* (1698; Daphne Foskett priv. col.) resolved this long-standing mistake. An early example of Cross's mature style is found in his portrait of *William Gore* (1670; London, V&A). Painted when Samuel Cooper was the dominant artist in the field, this miniature shows his individual preference for stippling, in contrast to Cooper's broad hatching. As Cross's career developed he elaborated this method, juxtaposing dots of red, blue and green and allowing the white ground of the vellum support to shine through the pigment. He continued to work in the same manner well into the second decade of the 18th century and was the last notable exponent of the 17th-century tradition of miniature painting on vellum.

BIBLIOGRAPHY

M. Edmond: 'Peter Cross, Limner: Died 1724', *Burl. Mag.*, cxxi (1979), pp. 585–6

J. Murdoch: 'Hoskins and Crosses', *Burl. Mag.*, cxl (1981), pp. 288–90

J. Murdoch and others: *The English Miniature* (New Haven and London, 1981), pp. 157–62

GRAHAM REYNOLDS

Cross foot. Device for supporting a cross on the altar; by extension, any device for supporting or fixing a cross at or near the altar. The eastward-facing position of the priest at the altar is a prerequisite but not the actual cause of the placing of the cross on the altar table; it is rather that the characteristic affinity of the cross foot with the iconography of the altar (of the cross or the lay altar) generally makes it seem like a continuation of it. As far back as the 5th and 6th centuries there is evidence in Byzantine art of partly combined crosses and candlesticks, which are the precursors of the cross foot as it developed in the later Middle Ages. Images showing altar crosses suggest that by the Carolingian period (if not earlier), cross stands close to those in use in the high Middle Ages were in existence, alongside combinations of the cross foot and

the reliquary. The most famous example of this is associated with EINHARD. This form and design is at least partly derived or adapted from candlesticks following Late Antique models. Both cross foot and candlestick were linked to one another in their arrangement and in their symbolic interpretation, although either could equally well occupy a place on the altar table without the other. The great disparity between the small number (barely 60) of cross feet that survive from the period and the abundance of altar crosses and crucifixes suggests that crosses were also supported on, near or behind the altar by other means (e.g. with pins, or they could be placed on columns flanking the altar or standing behind it, or hung from the ciborium enclosing the altar). The cross feet that were placed on the altar fall into four main groups: in plan they could be four-sided, three-sided or circular, or they could be architectural, i.e. in the form of a building, usually alluding to the Holy Sepulchre. Two bronze gilt examples, thought to be from Hildesheim (second half of the 12th century, Budapest, N. Mus., 1870 inv., no. 25.2; second quarter of the 12th century, Berlin, Schloss Köpenick, SMPK inv. no. 4165), exemplify the three-sided and the architectural type respectively. Common to all of these types is their relationship, formally and in content, to the cross they supported, as the combination of cross and cross foot symbolized salvation through Christ's sacrifice on Golgotha. In this sense the two elements always formed a single entity. The development of the cross foot after the 13th century was characterized by a diminishing relationship between its form and its Christian significance. Consequently, in almost all cases functional and decorative elements became the principal factors influencing the appearance of the cross foot, so that it was no longer meaningfully integrated with the cross but came to be perceived as a subsidiary element.

BIBLIOGRAPHY

P. Springer: *Kreuzfüsse: Ikonographie und Typologie eines hochmittelalterlichen Gerätes*, Bronzegeräte des Mittelalters, iii (Berlin, 1981) [with bibliog.]

Ornamenta Ecclesiae: Kunst und Künstler der Romanik (exh. cat., ed. A. Legner; Cologne, Schnütgen-Mus., 1985), nos B57, C46, F19, H29, H34

O. ter Kuile: *Koper & brons*, Amsterdam, Rijksmus. cat. (The Hague, 1986), pp. 22–5, nos 15–16

S. Marth: *Untersuchungen zu romanischen Bronzekreuzen: Ikonographie–Funktion–Stil* (diss., Berlin, Freie U., 1988)

PETER SPRINGER

Crosshatching. *See* HATCHING.

Crotti, Jean (*b* Bulle, Switzerland, 24 April 1878; *d* Paris, 30 Jan 1958). French painter of Swiss birth. From 1901 he spent almost all his life in Paris, studying there at the Académie Julian. His early work was influenced first by Impressionism, then by Fauvism and Art Nouveau, and included a number of rhythmically stylized female heads in pastel colours, followed from *c.* 1910 by a more strongly constructed Cubist phase. He spent two years in New York (1914–16), where he met MARCEL DUCHAMP—whose sister Suzanne (1889–1963) he married in 1919—and Francis Picabia, and became involved in the DADA movement until 1921; his Dada paintings and reliefs are delicate and poetic and often combine the forms of objects, such as mechanical instruments, with words and typography, as in his portrait of *Thomas Edison* (1920; London, Tate).

In the 1920s, seeking to create a visionary art that would transport the artist and viewer into unknown worlds expressive of the aspirations of the soul, Crotti began to produce pictures in a variety of styles, sometimes completely abstract, like *Composition* (1925; New Haven, CT, Yale U., A.G.), and sometimes with very stylized or ectoplasmic figures. After various experiments in the 1930s with kaleidoscopes and colour light projections he invented a technique for making pictures out of coloured glass, which he called *Gemmaux* and patented in 1939. The pictures made at the end of his life include cosmic visions of creation, death and the galaxies.

BIBLIOGRAPHY

W. George: *Jean Crotti et la primauté du spirituel* (Geneva, 1959)
Rétrospective Jean Crotti (exh. cat., Paris, Pal. Galliéra, 1959–60)

RONALD ALLEY

Crouwel, Joseph, jr (*b* Utrecht, 15 March 1885; *d* The Hague, 16 Feb 1962). Dutch architect. He studied at the Quellinusschool in Amsterdam, where he took the 'Higher Education' course for architecture. Between 1899 and 1902 he worked for T. Hanrath, then K. P. C. de Bazel and finally H. P. Berlage. In 1917 he joined the Landsgebouwen (Department of State Building). In 1920 he was appointed Deputy Government Architect and, in 1923, Government Architect with responsibilities including the building of post offices. He built the post office (1917–24) on the Neude, Utrecht, as well as a number of buildings (1918) on Alexander Numankade and Bekkerstraat, Utrecht, for the Veterinary College. These were in the style of the Amsterdam school, which became somewhat cold and contrived in the hands of Crouwel. Under the influence of the Modernist W. M. Dudok, his work became more rigid, for example the secondary school (1926) in Harlingen, and he gradually adopted the style of Functionalism, for example in his post office (1938; destr. 1987) on the Stationsplein, Utrecht. After 1935 there was a noticeable decline, however, in the quality of Crouwel's work, possibly associated with the death of Berlage and the growing influence of Marinus Jan Grandpré Molière. Crouwel had difficulty in adopting the Rationalist ideas and the Functionalism of the De Stijl movement, particularly its striving for simplification, without lapsing into triviality.

BIBLIOGRAPHY

'C. J. Blaauw, J. Grouwel, J. M. Luthmann: Oudheidsbouwkunst', *Wendingen*, v/11–12 (1923), pp. 1–28
H. P. Berlage and W. M. Dudok, eds: *Moderne bouwkunst in Nederland*, xii (Rotterdam, 1932–5), p. 24
G. Fanelli: *Architettura moderna* (1968)
Postkantoor aan het Neude (Utrecht, 1981)

DIANNE TIMMERMAN, FRANK VAN DEN HOEK

Crowe. English family.

(1) Eyre Crowe (*b* London, 3 Oct 1824; *d* London, 12 Dec 1910). Painter. His childhood was spent in Paris, where his father, the historian Eyre Evans Crowe, was foreign correspondent for the *Morning Chronicle*. In 1839 he became a pupil of Paul Delaroche, with whom he visited Rome in 1843. A fellow pupil on this trip was Jean-Léon Gérôme, who remained a lifelong friend. On his return to London in 1845 Crowe entered the Royal Academy Schools, exhibiting his first picture at the Royal Academy the following year.

In November 1852 Crowe accompanied his cousin, William Makepeace Thackeray, as his secretary and factotum on a six-month lecture tour of the USA. He described this tour in his book *With Thackeray in America*, published in 1893 with his own illustrations. Thackeray's interest in the 18th century clearly communicated itself to Crowe. For the next 30 years he painted a series of pictures based on the lives of such figures as Daniel Defoe, Samuel Johnson, Oliver Goldsmith and Sir Joshua Reynolds (e.g. *William Hogarth*, n.d.; London, V&A). In the USA, Crowe had looked sympathetically at the plight of black slaves and in 1861 exhibited at the Royal Academy the *Sale of Slaves at Richmond, Virginia* (Washington, DC, Heinz priv. col.), a picture based on sketches he had made in 1853. He pursued this social commentary with such works as the *Dinner Hour, Wigan* (1874; Manchester, C.A.G.), which presents an unusual and unsentimental view of factory workers. Later in life Crowe acted as an inspector and examiner at the South Kensington schools. He was elected ARA in 1876.

WRITINGS

With Thackeray in America (London, 1893)

BIBLIOGRAPHY

J. Dafforne: 'British Artists: Their Style and Character, no. lxxii: Eyre Crowe', *A. J.* [London] (1864), pp. 205–7
Hard Times (exh. cat. by J. Treuherz, Manchester, C.A.G., 1987–8), pp. 104–6

MARTIN POSTLE

(2) Sir J(oseph) A(rthur) Crowe (*b* London, 20 Oct 1825; *d* Gamburg an der Tauber, Baden, 6 Sept 1896). Journalist, diplomat and art historian, brother of (1) Eyre Crowe. He is primarily remembered for the volumes on Flemish and Italian art he wrote with GIOVANNI BATTISTA CAVALCASELLE. Soon after he was born his family moved to France, where Crowe grew up, returning to England in 1843 to follow his father's career as a press correspondent. He later pursued a successful career as a diplomat and was made a KCMG in 1890. Yet all his life Crowe had taken a keen interest in art, being encouraged by his father as early as 1846 to gather materials for a history of early Flemish art. In 1847 he met Cavalcaselle on the way to Berlin, where the latter was a student of art. Their friendship developed later in London, when Cavalcaselle sought refuge as a penniless fugitive from the troubles in Italy. Crowe gave him a home, and in the years that followed they travelled together all over Europe to libraries and collections, searching out paintings and manuscripts. Cavalcaselle occasionally went by himself, recording by drawings in his notebooks the paintings to be mentioned and recorded. Their first publication was *The Early Flemish Painters*; this was followed by the *A New History of Painting in Italy* and the *History of Painting in North Italy*. Both agreed on the details and conclusions, Crowe always being a little more personal in his commentaries than Cavalcaselle, but the texts were actually written by Crowe. Their works, many of which were translated, exerted considerable influence, not only because they examined unknown paintings but also because they recalled many artists, especially from north and central Italy, who had long been overshadowed by more famous contemporaries. To present-day readers these histories, with their careful conclusions and simple line-engravings, may seem dry, but they provided inspiration and invaluable assistance to later scholars, such as Giovanni Morelli, Roger Fry, Robert Langton Douglas and Bernard Berenson. Crowe also edited Jacob Burckhardt's *Cicerone* and Franz Kugler's *Handbook on German, Flemish and Dutch Painting*. His memoirs, which are of considerable interest and contain an account of his collaboration with Cavalcaselle, were published in the year before his death.

WRITINGS

with G. B. Cavalcaselle: *The Early Flemish Painters: Notices of their Lives and Works* (London, 1857, 2/1872, 3/1879; Fr. trans., Brussels, 1862; Ger. trans., Leipzig, 1875; Ital. trans., Florence, 1899)
——: *A New History of Painting in Italy, from the Second to the Sixteenth Century*, 3 vols (London, 1864–6); ed. R. L. Douglas and others (2/1903–14); ed. E. Hutton (3/1908–9)
——: *A History of Painting in North Italy, from the Fourteenth to the Sixteenth Century*, 2 vols (London, 1871, 2/1912, ed. T. Borenius)
——: *Titian, his Life and Times* (London, 1877, 2/1881; Ger. trans., Leipzig, 1883; Ital. trans., Florence, 1884–91)
ed. F. T. Kugler: *Handbook of Painting* (London, 1874, 2/1879)
ed. J. Burckhardt: *The Cicerone* (London, 1879)
Reminiscences of Thirty-five Years of my Life (London, 1895)

BIBLIOGRAPHY

DNB
U. Kulturman: *Geschichte und Kunstgeschichte* (Vienna and Düsseldorf, 1966), pp. 199–206
D. Robertson: *Sir Charles Eastlake and the Victorian Art World* (Princeton, 1978), pp. 185–6
C. J. Gibson-Wood: *Studies in the Theory of Connoisseurship from Vasari to Morelli* (London, 1988)
D. Levi: 'Mercanti, conoscitori, "amateurs" nella Firenze di metà ottocento: Spence, Cavalcaselle e Ruskin', *Idea di Firenze: Temi e interpretazioni nell'arte straniera dell'ottocento*, ed. M. Bossi and others (Florence, 1989), pp. 105–16

DAVID CAST

Crowe, Sylvia (*b* Banbury, Oxon, 15 Sept 1901). English landscape architect and writer. She attended Swanley Horticultural College in 1920–22 to study fruit farming, but after travelling through Italy she was inspired to design gardens. After returning to England in 1926, she became a pupil of the landscape gardener Edward White (1876–1952) and also worked for Cutbush Nurseries, Barnet, in 1939. From 1945 she practised landscape architecture in London with the assistance of Brenda Colvin. Small projects eventually led to her appointment as landscape consultant to the new towns of Harlow and Basildon (1948–58) and the Central Electricity Generating Board (1948–68). In 1964 she became the Forestry Commission's first landscape consultant, a post she held until 1976 and where her work broke new ground. Crowe regarded aesthetic and ecological principles as inseparable and she believed that forestry planting should relate to land form. As a result of her influence at the Forestry Commission, landscape considerations were taken into account whenever land was acquired, so that natural rather than artificial boundaries would be used. In 1969 Crowe became consultant to Southern and South West Water Authorities. Other notable works included the master plan (1966) for the Commonwealth Gardens, Canberra, and landscape for the Scottish Widows Fund building, Edinburgh, in 1976. Crowe won a number of awards and was President of the Institute of Landscape Architects (now Landscape Institute) from 1957 to 1959 and Vice-President of the International Federation of Landscape Architects (1958–70). Regarding her writings, Crowe said that she tried to enter into the spirit of each landscape and to express its individual character in her books. These became standard works in their field. *The Pattern of Landscape* provides an overview of her philosophy of landscape based on a lifetime's work.

WRITINGS

Garden Design (London, 1958, rev. Chichester, 3/1994)
The Landscape of Power (London, 1958)
The Landscape of Roads (London, 1960)
with M. Mitchell: *The Pattern of Landscape* (Chichester, 1988)

BIBLIOGRAPHY

Contemp. Architects
S. Harvey, ed.: *Reflections on Landscape: The Lives and Work of Six British Landscape Architects* (Aldershot, 1987)
M. E. Rutz, comp.: *Landscapes and Gardens: Women who Made a Difference* (Michigan, 1987)

SHEILA HARVEY

Crowley, Nicholas Joseph (*b* Dublin, 6 Dec 1819; *d* London, 4 Nov 1857). Irish painter and designer of stained glass. He began his training at the Dublin Society's Art Schools in 1827 (aged eight) and in 1837, when only eighteen, was made a Royal Hibernian Academician. He was a highly successful portrait painter and received much of his patronage from the Roman Catholic hierarchy, which had been liberated as a result of the Catholic Emancipation Act (1829). From the age of ten or eleven he exhibited portraits of these senior churchmen at the newly formed Royal Hibernian Academy, and he showed regularly there until his early death. His portraits of distinguished leaders of Irish Catholic society include that of *Daniel Murray, Archbishop of Dublin* (1846; Dublin, N.G.). Crowley also designed stained-glass windows for a number of the new post-Emancipation Roman Catholic churches in Dublin, for example the Baptisterium in St Nicholas of Myra (1840). In 1836 Crowley moved to London, where he exhibited at the British Institution (1839–57). Most of these paintings were based on episodes from the sentimental literature of the time, a good example being a portrait of the actor *Tyrone Power as Connor O'Gorman* (1838; exh. British Institution, 1840; ex-Tyrone Guthrie priv. col.) in Anna Maria Hall's *The Groves of Blarney*. These genre pieces have a distinctive charm that is probably derived from a thorough knowledge of Wilkie and Mulready. Crowley's *Invitation, Hesitation and Persuasion* (*c.* 1846; Dublin, N.G.) shows a successful merging of group portraiture and theatrical sentiment. Broadly painted, animated and colourful, his figures are charming but rarely go further than a glossy surface observation.

BIBLIOGRAPHY

Strickland
A. Crookshank and the Knight of Glin: *The Painters of Ireland, c. 1660–1920* (London, 1978), pp. 227, 231–3
A. Stewart: *Royal Hibernian Academy of Arts: Index of Exhibitors, 1826–1979*, i (Dublin, 1985), pp. 183–4

FINTAN CULLEN

Crowns. *See* REGALIA, §2.

Cröy. South Netherlandish family of patrons and collectors. Throughout the 15th and 16th centuries members of this aristocratic family played an important role in politics and were closely involved with the Burgundian court. Their collection of manuscripts was one of the most important of the time. It is difficult, however, to establish which manuscripts were acquired by whom. Jean, Count of Chimay (1395–1473), began the collection and ordered many manuscripts on behalf of Charles the Bold, Duke of Burgundy. Jean's son, Philippe, Count of Chimay (d 1482), commissioned eminent translators, scribes and illuminators, including Jean Wauquelin, Jean Miélot (fl 1448–63), David Aubert (c. 1435–79), Jacquemart Pilavaine (fl 1450–85) and Simon Marmion, to enrich the Cröy library. In addition, some of the manuscripts from the ducal library found their way into the Cröy collection. The library was inherited by Philippe's son, Charles, Prince of Chimay (1455–1527), who also inherited a number of manuscripts that had belonged to Jean, bastard son of Wavrin. Charles put his *ex libris*, a bell, on all the manuscripts in the Cröy collection. In 1511 he sold part of his collection, 78 bound volumes and an unknown number of unbound manuscripts, to Margaret of Austria, ruler of the Netherlands. After her death, the collection passed to her niece, Margaret of Hungary, and in 1559, on the instructions of Philip II of Spain, the manuscripts were placed in the collection of the Dukes of Burgundy at Brussels, where they remain (Brussels, Bib. Royale Albert 1er).

The manuscripts that Charles had kept in Chimay were inherited by his daughter Anna. She married Philippe II de Cröy, 1st Duke of Aarschot and Prince of Chimay (1495–1549), and as a result the most important family estates fell to the Cröy van Aarschots. The influential patronage of this branch of the family reached its peak under Philippe II's grandson, Charles III de Cröy, Duke of Cröy and Aarschot and Prince of Chimay (b château of Beaumont, 1 July 1560; d château of Beaumont, 13 Jan 1612). In his châteaux at Heverlee and Beaumont, Charles assembled an enormous collection of jewels, precious objects, medals, coins, furnishings and manuscripts. An inventory after his death listed 234 paintings, including 11 works by Veronese. From 1590 onwards Charles had all his estates and other areas where he held important positions or kept valuable possessions mapped. Adriaan de Montigny, a painter from Valenciennes, was asked to make watercolour versions of these sketches on parchment, and between 1590 and 1609 the 23 Albums de Cröy were made. These contained some 2500 views of estates, settlements and cities in the southern Netherlands and northern France.

After Charles's death, the family library was almost completely dispersed. Most of the manuscripts and books were offered for sale in Brussels in 1614. Charles's albums were also auctioned and dispersed among various libraries and collections (e.g. Paris, Bib. N.; Vienna, Österreich. Nbib.). Only a few manuscripts and albums subsequently remained in the hands of the Cröy family. Eighty-five manuscripts can be identified as having come from the Cröy library, and they show how important and varied the collection was. In addition to those identified by Bayot, they include the *Statutes of the Golden Fleece* (Brussels, Bib. Royale Albert I, MS. IV 125), a *Miroir d'humaine salvation* (Le Roeulx, Prince Etienne de Cröy priv. col.), Jacques de Guise's *Chronicles of Hainault* (London, BL, Landsdowne

MS. 214), Christine de Pizan's *Epistre d'Othéa* (sold London, Quaritch 1871, lot 140), a Book of Hours (Oxford, Bodleian Lib., MS. Rawl. liturg. vol. 2), Raoul Lefèvre's *Histoire de Jason* (Paris, Bib. N., MS. fr. 12570) and an *Anthology of Historical and Moral Texts* (Vienna, Österreich. Nbib., Cod. 2579).

BIBLIOGRAPHY
E. Van Even: 'Notice sur la bibliothèque de Charles de Cröy, duc d'Aarschot (1614)', *Bull. Bibliph. Belg.*, ix (1852), pp. 380–93, 436–51
A. Bayot: *Martin le Franc l'estrif de fortune et de vertu: Etude du manuscrit 9510 de la Bibliothèque royale de Belgique, provenant de l'ancienne 'librairie' des Cröy de Chimay* (Brussels, 1928)
R. Born: *Les Cröy* (Brussels, 1981)
J.-M. Duvosquel, ed.: *Bezittingen der Cröy's in Brabant, Vlaanderen, Artesië an het Naamse* (Brussels, 1985)
De librije van Margareta van Oostenrijk (exh. cat., ed. M. Debae; Brussels, Bib. Royale Albert 1er, 1987)
Een stad en een geslacht: Leuven & Cröy [A city and a family: Leuven and Cröy] (exh. cat., Leuven, Stedel. Mus. Vander Kelen-Mertens, 1987) [essay by P. Valvekens, pp. 27–31]

PATRICK VALVEKENS

Crozat. French family of bankers, patrons and collectors. The brothers Antoine Crozat (1655–1738) and (1) Pierre Crozat were the second generation of a wealthy banking family in Toulouse. They were the sons of Antoine Crozat, the magistrate of Toulouse, and themselves became treasurers of the Languedoc states. Around 1700 the two brothers moved to Paris, where they were among the most successful financiers of the early 18th century. Both built notable hôtels in Paris, Antoine in the Place Vendôme and Pierre in the Rue de Richelieu. Pierre, who became treasurer of France in 1704, formed a collection of paintings, prints, sculpture, engraved gems, ceramics and, above all, drawings that made him the most famous private collector of his century. Although the drawings were sold on Pierre's death (many of the best now Paris, Louvre), his paintings were inherited by other members of the family, in particular his nephew (2) Louis-Antoine Crozat, Baron de Thiers. On the latter's death, they were bought by Catherine the Great of Russia (most now in St Petersburg, Hermitage).

(1) Pierre Crozat (b Toulouse, ?March 1665; d Paris, 24 May 1740). His hôtel in the Rue de Richelieu (1704–14; destr. after 1772) was built by JEAN-SYLVAIN CARTAUD and included a gallery overlooking the garden to house Crozat's magnificent art collection. The vault of the gallery was decorated (1704–7) by Charles de La Fosse, who later worked at Crozat's country house at nearby Montmorency (rebuilt from 1709 by Cartaud and Gilles-Marie Oppenord). Antoine Watteau painted a series of the *Four Seasons* (c. 1715–16; e.g. *Summer*, Washington, DC, N.G.A.) for the dining-room of Crozat's Paris house. Both artists lived in Crozat's house at different times and studied his collection of Old Master drawings. At the Paris hôtel and at the country house at Montmorency, Crozat played host to countless artists and connoisseurs, including the Comte de Caylus, Jean de Jullienne and Pierre-Jean Mariette. The Italian artists Antonio Pellegrini and Rosalba Carriera stayed with Crozat when they visited Paris in 1720–21. Crozat's musical parties were also famous.

In 1714 Crozat travelled to Rome on behalf of the Regent, Philippe II, Duc d'Orléans, to buy from the heirs of Prince Livio Odescalchi, to whom she had bequeathed it, the collection formed by Queen Christina of Sweden. Although the delicate negotiations did not finally bear fruit until 1721, Crozat's visit to Italy influenced decisively the direction of his own collection, which he enriched with many Italian works. In Rome he met the painter Benedetto Lutti and the sculptor Pierre Legros (ii), both of whom subsequently worked for him. He acquired engraved gems and antique and modern sculpture, including terracotta models by François Du Quesnoy. Most of all, however, he bought drawings: in Bologna he purchased the collection of Conte Carlo Cesare Malvasia, which included numerous studies by Annibale Carracci for the Farnese Gallery, Rome, and in Urbino he was able to buy some of Raphael's finest drawings from the family of one of his pupils. In Venice, another decisive influence on the direction of his taste, he was able to buy drawings by Federico Barocci, and through Anton Maria Zanetti the elder he met Rosalba Carriera and the painter Sebastiano Ricci. Zanetti later acted as Crozat's agent in the purchase of the contents of the studio of Gregorio Lazzarini, which included drawings attributed to Giorgione and Titian.

Crozat added to his cabinet of drawings (which by the time of his death numbered nearly 19,000 items, two thirds of them Italian) by buying in France under market conditions that were never to be repeated. Seeking quality and historical interest, he acquired part of Everard Jabach's second collection, which included 100 drawings by Dürer and a similar number by Poussin, and bought from the collections of the Abbé Desneaux de La Noue and from the Abbé Quesnel, whose cabinet yielded drawings by Michelangelo once owned by Vasari. Crozat also sent agents to foreign sales, buying at the sale of John, Lord Somers (1651–1716), in London in 1717, at that of S. van der Schelling in Amsterdam in 1719, and also in Antwerp, Ghent and Venice. Crozat's collection of prints, of all schools, was equally important and included Roger de Piles's unique group of Rembrandt etchings.

Crozat's collection of paintings was comparable neither in size nor in quality. Of his 500 pictures, about 30 were masterpieces. Works by Bolognese and Roman artists (which comprised about two thirds of the total) included Annibale Carracci's *Rest on the Flight into Egypt*, Guido Reni's *Virgin Sewing* and Raphael's *Holy Family* (all St Petersburg, Hermitage). He also owned Raphael's small *St George and the Dragon* (Washington, DC, N.G.A.). Among the pictures from the Venetian school, which was well represented in Crozat's collection, were Giorgione's *Judith* and Tintoretto's *Birth of the Virgin* (both St Petersburg, Hermitage) and Veronese's *Finding of Moses* (Washington, DC, N.G.A.). Works by Flemish and Dutch masters were less numerous: there were about 100 pictures, including 9 by Rembrandt, 10 by van Dyck and 15 by Rubens, including his portrait of *Isabella Brandt* (Washington, DC, N.G.A.). There were approximately 20 German paintings, among them Dürer's *Road to Calvary* and Elsheimer's *Tobias and the Angel* (both Moscow, Pushkin Mus. F.A.).

In the period between 1720 and 1725 Crozat was the instigator of one of the most famous art publishing projects, the 'Recueil Crozat' (*Recueil d'estampes d'après les plus beaux tableaux et les plus beaux dessins qui sont en France dans le cabinet du Roy, dans celui de Monseigneur le Duc d'Orléans et en autres cabinets*, 2 vols, Paris, 1729

and 1742). The impetus for this project to publish the most famous Italian paintings and drawings in France came from the Regent with the encouragement of Mariette and the Comte de Caylus. It was originally intended that Watteau should be one of the principal engravers, but this scheme was changed after his death, with various artists contributing reproductive engravings of the paintings and Caylus making etchings after the drawings. The first volume, devoted to the Roman school, was issued in 1729. The second was abandoned in 1733 after the death of the main engraver, Paul-Ponce Robert. The 42 plates already completed were issued to subscribers, but the volume was not published in its entirety until 1742, with a text by Mariette.

Crozat, wanting his collection of drawings to remain in France to continue to be a resource for artists and connoisseurs, offered it to Louis XV for 100,000 livres, the money to be given to the poor. The offer was, however, refused, and much of the collection, recorded in an inventory compiled after his death in 1740 by Louis-Petit de Bachaumont, was dispersed in the three decades following. He bequeathed the proceeds of the sale of the engraved gems and the drawings to the poor. The former, catalogued by Mariette in 1741, were bought *en bloc* by Louis, Duc d'Orléans (1703–52), and are recorded in the *Description des pierres gravées du Duc d'Orléans* (Paris, 1780). In 1787 the Duke's grandson Philippe Egalité sold them to Catherine the Great (now St Petersburg, Hermitage). Mariette also produced a remarkably detailed catalogue of the drawings for their sale in 1741, with full descriptions and, in many cases, provenances. The main buyers at the sale were Count Tessin, Gabriel Huquier, Jullienne and Mariette. Many of the finest Italian drawings were bought by the Crown at Mariette's sale (now Paris, Louvre). Crozat does not seem to have put a collector's mark on his drawings. The initials followed by a number thought by Lugt to be Crozat's (L. 2951) are now associated with Antoine-Jean Dezallier d'Argenville; however, ex-Crozat drawings do carry a characteristic number in pen and ink at the lower right, which is now generally recognized by drawings connoisseurs. Pierre Crozat never married, and his principal heir was his brother Antoine's son Louis-François Crozat, Marquis du Châtel (1691–1740), who also inherited the hôtel in the Rue de Richelieu. On the latter's death, the hôtel and some pictures, notably Watteau's *Summer* and Tintoretto's *Judith and Holfernes* (Madrid, Prado), passed to his daughter Louise-Honorine, Duchesse de Choiseul, passing out of the Choiseul collection at the sale of 1772. The largest part of Pierre Crozat's paintings, however, was inherited by the Marquis du Châtel's brother (2) Louis-Antoine Crozat, Baron de Thiers.

(2) Louis-Antoine Crozat, Baron de Thiers (*b* Toulouse, 1699; *d* Paris, 15 Dec 1770). Nephew of (1) Pierre Crozat. A respected connoisseur, he inherited from his eldest brother the bulk of the collection of paintings formed by his uncle. In addition, the collection of another brother, Joseph-Antoine Crozat, Marquis de Tugny (*b* Toulouse, 1696; *d* Paris, 1751), passed to him. This consisted of northern, mainly Dutch pictures, including such masterpieces as Rembrandt's *Danaë* (St Petersburg,

Hermitage; *see* REMBRANDT VAN RIJN, fig. 3) and Poussin's *Triumph of Amphitrite* (Philadelphia, PA, Mus. A.). On the death of the Marquis de Tugny, Louis-Antoine organized a sale, keeping for himself only the best of his two brothers' paintings. He had Jean-Sylvain Cartaud redecorate the old Paris hôtel of his father in the Place Vendôme and continued to add important works to the family collection. His hôtel could be visited on request, and a guide was prepared in 1753. A copy of this with marginal illustrations in pen and ink by Gabriel de Saint-Aubin is preserved (Paris, Petit Pal.). On the death of the Baron, his heirs sold the collection to Catherine the Great of Russia in 1772, through the mediation of Denis Diderot and the collector François Tronchin, for 460,000 livres; the nucleus of the Hermitage collection in St Petersburg was thus formed by ex-Crozat pictures. They included a notable selection of works by 18th-century French painters, including Watteau, Largillierre, Boucher and Chardin. During the 1920s and 1930s the Soviet authorities sold abroad a number of works to earn hard currency, including a dozen important paintings bought by the American collector Andrew Mellon (now Washington, DC, N.G.A.).

BIBLIOGRAPHY

P.-J. Mariette: *Description sommaire des desseins…du cabinet de feu M. Crozat* (sale cat., Paris, 10 April–13 May 1741) [also incl. description of the engraved gems]

——: *Description sommaire des statues…du cabinet de feu M. Crozat* (sale cat., Paris, 14 Dec 1750)

——: *Catalogue des tableaux et sculptures…du cabinet de feu M. le Président de Thugny et de M. Crozat* (sale cat., Paris, June 1751)

F. Lugt: *Marques* (1921), pp. 86, 544–9

Le Dessin français dans les collections du XVIIIème siècle (exh. cat., Paris, Louvre, 1935)

M. Stuffmann: 'Les Tableaux de la collection de Pierre Crozat', *Gaz. B.-A.*, n. s. 5, lxxii (1968), pp. 11–143

B. Scott: 'Pierre Crozat: A Maecenas of the Régence', *Apollo*, xcvii (1973), pp. 11–19

J. Labbé and L. Bicart-Sée: *La Collection Saint-Morys au cabinet des dessins du Musée du Louvre*, i (Paris, 1987), pp. 133–5

H. Meyer: 'La Collection de Louis Antoine Crozat, baron de Thiers', *L'Age d'or flamand et hollandais: Collections de Catherine II, Musée de l'Ermitage, Saint-Petersbourg* (exh. cat., Dijon, Mus. B.-A., 1993), pp. 49–56

ANNE LECLAIR

Crozet, René (*b* Romorantin, Sologne, 26 April 1896; *d* Poitiers, 26 March 1972). French art historian. He was a DLitt (1932) and professor of the history of medieval art (1946–66) at Poitiers University; he was also director (1954–66) of the Centre d'Etudes Supérieures de Civilisation Médiévale (CESCM), Poitiers. Crozet published some 400 works, but he was a specialist above all in Romanesque art and wrote three fundamental volumes on the Romanesque in central and western France: Berry (1932), Poitou (1948) and Saintonge (1971). He was also interested in geography, urban development, history, liturgy, methodology and even aviation and the railways. His research was founded on an exemplary working method: observation, analysis and classification of facts. He sanctioned the study of texts in order to identify chronological data with the greatest possible accuracy. Systematically sceptical, he accepted stylistic similarities and symbolic interpretations only in cases supported by substantial evidence. With Edmond-René Labande, Crozet contributed to the reputation and appreciation of the CESCM at Poitiers.

WRITINGS

L'Art roman en Berry (Paris, 1932)

L'Art roman en Poitou (Paris, 1948)

L'Art roman en Saintonge (Paris, 1971)

BIBLIOGRAPHY

Mélanges René Crozet, 2 vols (Poitiers, 1966) [contains cat. of Crozet's pubns, pp. xix–xxxi]

E. R. Labande, C. Heitz and F. Salet: 'Nécrologie', *Cah. Civilis. Méd.*, xv (1972), pp. 174–8 [incl. cat. of Crozet's writings from 1966]

M. T. CAMUS

Crucifix. Cross with a figure of the crucified Christ. Throughout its history, the form of the Crucifix varied widely in size, material and function, ranging from a small, portable object of private devotion to a monumental work, usually for liturgical use. This article focuses on the larger Crucifixes, both painted and sculpted, predominantly for ecclesiastical use.

1. Introduction. 2. Painted. 3. Sculpted.

1. INTRODUCTION. Christ's Crucifixion was not depicted in the first centuries of Christianity; the earliest surviving examples are Italian and date from the 5th century AD. The Crucifix as an independent art form developed somewhat later. Although chiefly a Western phenomenon, its iconography was closely related to that of the Crucifixion in Byzantine art. Christ was initially shown as if he were alive, with his head and body erect and eyes wide open. There is evidence that in some early Crucifixions he was shown naked; however, while this may be more accurate historically, from the 5th century he was almost invariably shown wearing either an ankle-length tunic (*colobium*) or, later, a loincloth (*perizoma*). In the East this had a central knot, but in the Western version the knot was shown to one side. The shift from depicting a living to a dead Christ in Byzantine Crucifixions dates from the second half of the 8th century. This development was connected with the Monophysite heresy of the 7th century, when Christ's human nature was denied. To counter this, Christ's mortal nature was emphasized by focusing on his physical death. Opponents of Iconoclasm in 8th-century Byzantium defended images of Christ on the Cross as representing Christ Incarnate. In the Carolingian period, debates over the Real Presence in the sacrament further drew attention to the redemptive virtue of Christ's death on the Cross. At this time the fully developed Christ, dead but not showing signs of suffering, appeared in Western art alongside the living Christ.

Early scenes of the Crucifixion were often flanked by other scenes and figures, for example the Virgin and St John the Evangelist were often shown (from the end of the 6th century) and the thieves, the sponge-bearer, the lance-bearer and the soldiers casting lots were also represented from early on. Such symbolically significant images were often included in crucifixes. The beginning of the compositional division into left and right sides and the pairing of figures so that the positive are always to Christ's right dates from this period. In the 9th century other symbolic images such as Ecclesia and Synagoga, a dead serpent or Adam's skull at the foot of the Cross were also included. At around the same time 'types' of the Crucifixion were introduced (*see* TYPOLOGICAL CYCLES) and these were developed and expanded during the 12th century (e.g. the Meeting of Abraham and Melchizedeck, the Sacrifice of Isaac, the Killing of Abel and, later, Moses Raising the Brazen Serpent and Jacob Blessing Ephraim and Manasseh). From the 13th century artists usually emphasized Christ's suffering on the Cross; furthermore, from the mid-13th century the number of nails was often reduced from four to three by placing one foot over the other, and this powerfully affected the hanging, buckled posture of Christ's body. At about the same time the Virgin began to be depicted fainting at the foot of the Cross, sometimes with a sword piercing her breast, as prophesied by Simeon. These changes were connected with a more intimate and emotional piety inspired by the writings of St Bernard and St Francis and later also by the 14th-century mystics.

See also CROSS, §§I and III.

BIBLIOGRAPHY

RDK

F. Cabrol and H. Leclerq: *Dictionnaire d'archéologie chrétienne et de liturgie*, iii (Paris, 1913)
L. Réau: *Iconographie de l'art chrétien*, ii (Paris, 1957)
C. E. Pocknee: *Cross and Crucifix* (London, 1962)
G. Schiller: *Ikonographie der christlichen Kunst*, 4 vols (Gütersloh, 1966–80; Eng. trans., London, 1972)
E. Dinkler: *Signum crucis* (Tübingen, 1967)
R. Schneider Berrenberg: *Kreuz, Kruzifix: Eine Bibliographie* (Munich, 1973)

CATHERINE OAKES

2. PAINTED. In its simplest form, a painted Crucifix is a painted wooden panel in the form of a cross, with a central figure of the crucified Christ. Other figures or scenes are sometimes also shown, usually on the apron (a broadening of the upright, either side of Christ's lower body) and on the terminals (rectangular extensions of the cross arms); there may also be a roundel with a representation of God the Father or Christ Logos above the upper terminal. This form of Crucifix developed following the opposition to three-dimensional images in the Eastern Orthodox Church, but it was a type almost exclusively confined to Italy, where it was widespread from the early 12th century to the late 14th. Painted Crucifixes were commonly either placed behind the altar or suspended from the chancel arch, as in Santa Croce, Florence (*see* FLORENCE, fig. 18). The double-sided construction of some painted Crucifixes suggests that they may also have been carried in liturgical processions. The iconography of the Crucifix was dominated by theological expressions of the incarnation and resurrection. In the 13th century the development of Franciscan theology, stressing Christ's humanity, and the renewal of Byzantine artistic influences prompted not only the transition from a triumphant to a suffering Christ but also the changes in number and arrangement of secondary figures and scenes.

The earliest painted Crucifixes follow the *Christus triumphans* (Christ triumphant) iconography, with Christ portrayed as if alive, and reminiscent of a priest: his eyes are open, his head and body are erect, and his hands are spread horizontally, with the palms facing the viewer. Characteristic examples of this type include Guglielmo's *Crucifix* (1138; Sarzana Cathedral) and the Accademia *Crucifix* (1180–90; see fig. 1), in which the position of the body follows that in the earliest extant wall painting of the *Crucifixion* (mid-8th century; Rome, S Maria Antiqua).

1. Accademia *Crucifix* showing *Christus triumphans*, tempera on panel, 1180–90 (Florence, Galleria dell'Accademia)

Yet the slight bending of the elbows, the tilted head and averted gaze that characterize these 12th-century Crucifixes reduce the hieratic effect of the earliest wall paintings. Another notable change in relation to earlier Crucifixion scenes is that Christ is no longer shown wearing the *colobium* or tunic as was customary in the Eastern Orthodox Church; instead he is usually portrayed naked except for a loincloth, in keeping with a Western tradition shown in the earliest preserved *Crucifixion*, which is carved on the 5th-century wooden doors of S Sabina, Rome. Here, Christ represents Adam, who was naked in innocence but wore a loincloth after the Fall. Christ's identification with all sinners is symbolized by the loincloth and the Cross (the latter also a reminder of the Tree of Knowledge in the Garden of Eden).

Schiller suggested that the iconographic programme of crucifixes followed that of chancel wall paintings: the Christ usually represented in the apse appeared in the centre of the Crucifix while the scenes from the side walls were reduced in size and shown on the apron and terminals. In the simplest type, represented (for example) by Alberto di Sozio's *Crucifix* (1187; Spoleto Cathedral), only the standing figures of the Virgin and St John the Evangelist are shown on the apron on either side of Christ; Adam's skull appears in a cave beneath Christ's feet, and the *Ascension* is shown in the upper terminal. A more complex type is represented by Guglielmo's *Crucifix* of

1138 and the Accademia *Crucifix* of 1180–90 mentioned above, both of which show a series of *Passion* scenes that include the *Betrayal,* the *Flagellation, Christ Carrying the Cross,* the *Deposition* and the *Entombment.* Whereas the Virgin and St John the Evangelist are positioned on opposite sides of the apron in the earlier work, in the later example they are both shown in one terminal, facing each other and demonstrating their grief by wringing their hands.

The shift towards displaying more emotion and humanity in the subsidiary scenes prefigured a major change in the iconography that took place in the late 12th century and early 13th, when painters began to show Christ as suffering (*Christus patiens*). Portrayed as dead, he is shown with his head resting on his right shoulder, his body curved and the pelvis turned slightly (or, later, dramatically) to his right. Innumerable variations of this type survive, including Enrico di Tedice's *Crucifix* (first quarter 13th century; Pisa, S Martino), Giunta Pisano's *Crucifix* (1230–35; Assisi, S Maria degli Angeli) and the Master of St Francis's *Crucifix* (late 1260s; London, N.G.; for illustration *see* MASTERS, ANONYMOUS, AND MONOGRAMMISTS, §I: MASTER OF ST FRANCIS). By the end of the 13th century Italian artists were creating masterful representations of the suffering Christ, typically with a very accentuated curving of the body, as in Deodato Orlando's *Crucifix* (1288; Lucca, Villa Guinigi; for illustration *see* DEODATO ORLANDI) and in Cimabue's *Crucifix* (*c.* 1285; Florence, Mus. Opera Santa Croce; *see* CIMABUE, fig. 3 and CONSERVATION AND RESTORATION, colour pl. IX), which owes much to Giunta Pisano's work. The emphasis on Christ's humanity in the newly developing Franciscan theology influenced the predominance of the suffering Christ image in the 13th century. This development paralleled an earlier one in the Eastern Orthodox Church, following the iconoclastic controversies (726–843). Thus iconographic precedents for the suffering Christ existed in such Byzantine works as the narthex mosaic *Crucifixion* (*c.* 1025) at Hosios Loukas, Phokis, and among the icons at St Catherine's Monastery, Sinai.

The development of the curved body of Christ in the 13th century was often accompanied by a change in the positioning of secondary figures. In Cimabue's Santa Croce *Crucifix* of *c.* 1285 mentioned above, for example, the figures of the Virgin and St John the Evangelist were reduced in size and placed in the terminals, so that the emphasis remains firmly on the figure of Christ. Such changes were not necessarily dictated by the curving body of Christ, however, as is shown by the Accademia *Crucifix* (see fig. 1) and by the Master of Oblate's *Crucifix* (*c.* 1250; Florence, Convent of the Suore Oblate), where the Virgin and St John the Evangelist are still shown in the apron, flanking the very prominently curved body of Christ. Scenes paralleling the Passion were sometimes included in later crucifixes; for example St Francis was often shown embracing Christ's feet, as in the Master of St Francis's *Crucifix* (1272; Perugia, G.N. Umbria; *see* GILDING, colour pl. III, fig. 1), and the pelican plucking its breast as a symbol of the Eucharist is shown at the top of a *Crucifix* of *c.* 1400 (St Louis, MO, A. Mus.).

Some aspects of the living Christ iconography persisted in most renderings of the dead Christ until the early 14th

2. *Crucifix* by Coppo di Marcovaldo, showing *Christus patiens,* tempera on panel, h. 2.8 m, 1274 (Pistoia Cathedral)

century, when Giotto depicted Christ's body hanging heavily from outstretched arms in his *Crucifix* of *c.* 1300 (Florence, S Maria Novella; *see* GIOTTO, fig. 10) and in his early 14th-century *Crucifix* (Rimini, S Francesco). Elements of such naturalism had been attempted before; for example, Coppo di Marcovaldo had shown limply hanging hands in his Pistoia *Crucifix* (1274; see fig. 2), and Cimabue, in his Arezzo *Crucifix* (*c.* 1273; Arezzo, S Domenico), had accentuated the emotive curve of the body. However, in both cases the shoulders rise above the arms and lift up the torso, instead of allowing it to sag as Giotto did. Notwithstanding these innovative developments of the early 1300s and the works of such continuators of Giotto's achievement in this genre as GUARIENTO, the painted *Crucifix* was in decline by the end of that century. SIMONE DEI CROCEFISSI produced four great Crucifixes from *c.* 1360 to *c.* 1380, but only isolated examples after *c.* 1400 are known.

BIBLIOGRAPHY
A. Jameson: *The History of Our Lord as Exemplified in Works of Art,* ii (London, 1872)
E. Sandberg-Vavalà: *La croce dipinta italiana e l'iconografia della Passione,* 2 vols (Verona, 1929)
E. B. Garrison: *Italian Romanesque Panel Painting: An Illustrated Index* (Florence, 1949)
G. Schiller: *Ikonographie der christlichen Kunst* (Gütersloh, 1966–80; Eng. trans., London, 1972), ii
T. J. Herbst: *The Humanization of Christ in the Central Italian Panel Crucifixes of the Twelfth and Thirteenth Centuries Reflected in the Development of Franciscan Christology* (Berkeley, 1989)

DOUG ADAMS

3. SCULPTED.

(i) Medieval. (ii) Renaissance. (iii) Baroque and after.

(i) Medieval. Crucifixes sculpted in the round were a Western phenomenon, as the Byzantine world had condemned three-dimensional imagery at the Second Council of Nicaea (AD 787). They were also rare in Italy, where the influence of Eastern Christendom was very strong and where painted Crucifixes prevailed (*see* §2 above). Although there are literary references to Carolingian Crucifixes with the body of Christ carved in the round, the earliest surviving example is the wooden Crucifix known as the Gero Cross (*c.* 969–76; Cologne Cathedral; see fig. 3). About a third of surviving early Crucifixes, including that of Gero, contain a compartment for a relic, usually a consecrated Host. This was considered to be a relic of Christ himself, and thus would have given the observer a greater sense of Christ's presence. The Gero Cross follows Carolingian tradition in showing Christ dead, but the emphasis on suffering conveyed by the hanging head with closed eyes and the disjointed, sagging body is much greater than previously expressed. This shows it to be entirely independent of Byzantine iconographic models, where Christ's body is never depicted disfigured. The Gero Cross was very influential on later Crucifixes, especially during the 11th century in Germany, and they were used with increasing frequency as both processional crosses and altar crosses (*see* CROSS, §III, 1 and ROMANESQUE, fig. 48). The natural, rounded style of the Gero

3. Crucifix, known as the Gero Cross, polychrome oak, h. 1.88 m, *c.* 969–76 (Cologne Cathedral)

Cross gave way to a harder, more mannered rendering of the subject at the end of the 11th century, as represented by a large, late Ottonian bronze Crucifix (Essen-Werden, St Liudger).

Many monumental Crucifixes have survived from the 11th and 12th centuries, especially in Spain. A common type shows the living Christ in Majesty, often crowned, with eyes open and body almost erect. The footrest (*suppedaneum*) is frequently omitted. The large ivory cross of King Ferdinand I and Queen Sancha (1063; Madrid, Mus. Arqueol. N.; *see* SPAIN, fig. 20) is a splendid variation on this type. Where Christ is shown dead, with his eyes closed, the strong, rhythmic lines of the Romanesque style impart a sense of nobility to his suffering, as can be seen in the head (12th century; South Cerney, Glos, All Hallows) from a small wooden Crucifix of Spanish or English workmanship. Typological images and inscriptions are found on the reverse and on the terminals of many Crucifixes, especially those that were also used on altars and in processions; this reflected the didactic nature of religious art during the period. An elaborate example is the walrus ivory cross (mid-12th century; New York, Cloisters) that is usually thought to be from Bury St Edmunds; it combines figures of Old Testament *Prophets* bearing scrolls and such images as *Moses Raising the Brazen Serpent* (*see* ROMANESQUE, fig. 80) with New Testament scenes and figures. Areas of damage on the cross show that it was originally a Crucifix, and a contemporary corpus (Oslo, Kstindustmus.) has been associated with it (Lasko). There is a large group of 12th- and 13th-century Crucifixes in which Christ is shown clothed. These works, mainly from Catalonia, Roussillon and Germany, were influenced by the venerated wooden *Volto Santo* (Lucca Cathedral), a famous Crucifix believed to have been carved from an impression of Christ's body on the shroud. The original Crucifix probably dated from the late 11th century but now only exists in a 13th-century copy. It shows Christ dressed in a garment similar to the Early Christian full-length tunic or *colobium*, but with a knotted belt. His eyes are open and there is no indication of suffering; he seems to be standing in front of the Cross, since there are no nails in the feet and no footrest. The garment and the triumphant posture might well refer to a New Testament description of the risen Christ (Revelations 1:13).

From the end of the 12th century it became customary to place a monumental Crucifix on a beam below the chancel arch or, after its introduction, on top of the rood screen. The figures of the Virgin and St John the Evangelist were frequently placed either side. By the middle of the 13th century the suffering Christ, with closed or sightless eyes, had completely replaced the majestic Christ of the earlier period, reflecting the growing importance of Christ's human death in popular piety. The earliest examples of the crown of thorns probably date from the late 12th century (although in some cases they were added later) and around this time variations in the shape of the cross were introduced, usually with the effect of adding to the impression of suffering. The T-shaped cross appeared in the 13th century, and the Y-shaped cross became especially popular in Germany in the 14th century. The latter was frequently associated with attacks of plague, when it was set up as a focal point of prayer for an

4. Crucifix with the Virgin and St John the Evangelist, attributed to the Naumburg Master, stone, life-size, c. 1250–60, rood screen, Naumburg Cathedral

abatement of God's wrath. In this period Christ was generally shown to be crucified with three nails (rather than four), the nails becoming among the most important of the venerated *Arma Christi*. The life-size stone Crucifix (*c.* 1250–60; see fig. 4) in Naumburg Cathedral, attributed to the Naumburg Master, is an early and highly accomplished example of the new trend. Christ, flanked by the Virgin and St John the Evangelist, stands at eye-level within the rood screen, so that those walking through the screen encounter the stone figures directly; the effect is heightened as all three figures convincingly express suffering and grief. This contrasts with the much more exaggerated approach that became popular *c.* 1300, when Christ's wounds were shown in an increasingly harrowing way, for example the wooden Crucifix (*c.* 1304) in St Maria im Kapitol, Cologne. The venerated Crucifix at Burgos Cathedral, particularly realistic since the figure of Christ is made from oxhide and hair, is typical of this type.

A small group of 14th-century Crucifixes show Christ holding his arms open in a gesture of embrace. This iconography may be associated with St Bernard, St Francis and St Thomas Aquinas, who all reported visionary experiences of being embraced by the crucified Christ. In some examples, however, the eyes are closed and the arms are too close to the chest for this to be the direct source of inspiration. The tradition of showing intense suffering continued until the end of the medieval period and is still evident in the late 15th century in the work of such sculptors as Veit Stoss (*see* §(ii) below). The size of monumental Crucifixes continued to increase; for example, all the figures in Bernt Notke's Crucifix (1477; Lübeck Cathedral) are twice life-size.

BIBLIOGRAPHY

M. Durliat: *Christs romans du Roussillon et de Cerdagne* (Perpignan, 1956)
J. Eric Hunt: *English and Welsh Crucifixes, 670–1550* (London, 1956)
E. Carli: *La scultura lignea italiana dal XII al XVI secolo* (Milan, 1960)
R. Hausherr: *Der tote Christus am Kreuz: Zur Iconographie des Gerokreuzes* (Bonn, 1963)
G. Schiller: *Ikonographie der christlichen Kunst* (Gütersloh, 1966–80; Eng. trans., London, 1972), ii
P. Lasko: *Ars sacra, 800–1200*, Pelican Hist. A. (Harmondsworth, 1972)
D. Gaborit-Chopin: *Ivoires du moyen âge* (Fribourg, 1978)
English Romanesque Art, 1066–1200 (exh. cat., ed. G. Zarnecki, J. Holt and T. Holland; London, Hayward Gal., 1984), nos 206–8 [entries by P. Lasko]

CATHERINE OAKES

(ii) Renaissance. Florentine sculptors of the Renaissance created southern Europe's first major sculpture in the round on the theme of the Crucifix. Although the condemnation of three-dimensional sculpture by the Council of Nicea (AD 787) governed only branches of the Eastern Orthodox Church, until the Renaissance it had the effect of also discouraging the development of such religious sculpture in Italy. In northern Europe the sculpted Crucifix followed in the tradition of Carolingian and Ottonian art, which treated the dead figure of Christ differently from the Eastern tradition. In Germany during the Renaissance the established tradition of Late Gothic limewood sculpture developed in the crucifix a heightened expression of human emotion.

In Byzantine art the idealized beauty of the dead Christ's body showed no injury, but Crucifixes of northern Europe, such as the 10th-century Gero Cross, portrayed a body that had suffered (see fig. 3 above). A large number of such sculptures continued to be produced in Germany and France, often serving as reliquaries. The carrying of the Crucifix in religious rituals and dramatic re-enactments of the Passion further elevated its significance. During the Renaissance one of the most prolific German producers of the sculpted limewood Crucifix was Tilman Riemenschneider. His Crucifix (*c.* 1500) in Mariae Himmelfahrt, Aub, disrupts idealization in several subtle ways, as also found in the earlier Gero Cross: Christ's left hand is higher than the right, so that the line of the body is not vertical; and the head hangs to the right. Christ's long swirling hair and billowing carved loincloth add emotional and sensual effects, while the crown of thorns adds to the sense of pain. As Riemenschneider continued to work on this theme, he intensified the impression of grief and made Christ's head hang still lower; examples are the Crucifix (*c.* 1500) in the parish church, Eisingen, and the Crucifix (1516) in the parish church, Steinach. The sculptures of Veit Stoss are even more emotionally realistic than those of Riemenschneider. Stoss's wooden Crucifix (1520; Nuremberg, St Sebaldus) portrays a most tortured face of Christ, with greatly agitated lines in the partly open mouth, the brow and the hair, and even in the crown of thorns.

In Italy in the early 15th century Donatello and Brunelleschi carved strikingly different life-size polychrome wooden Crucifixes (the attribution to Donatello, however, has been questioned). The difference between the 'Donatello' Crucifix (1.78×1.73 m, *c.* 1410–15; Florence, Santa Croce) and the Brunelleschi Crucifix (*c.* 1410–15; Florence, S Maria Novella; see fig. 5) is partly captured in the criticism attributed to Brunelleschi by Vasari, that Donatello's Christ resembled a peasant; the dark skin and the

5. Crucifix by Brunelleschi, polychrome wood, figure 1.7×1.7 m, *c.* 1410–15 (Florence, S Maria Novella)

muscular chest and limbs of Donatello's Christ contrast with the white skin and thin limbs and torso of Brunelleschi's version. While in both the head hangs towards the right, it is bowed more deeply in Brunelleschi's rendering, which presents the legs also turned towards the right. Donatello's Christ confronts the viewer, while Brunelleschi's Christ turns slightly away and invites attention without engaging the viewer in a dialogue. There is power in each Christ; but it is a power of life in Donatello's and of death in Brunelleschi's. A much later sculpture by Donatello, a bronze Crucifix (1441–9; Padua, S Antonio), contains the substantial legs of his earlier work, but they turn towards the right, and the head bows more deeply in that direction, as in Brunelleschi's sculpture. The earliest Donatello work is in keeping with the frontality of the Eastern Church's images, reminding the viewer of other face-to-face encounters, such as receiving the Host from a priest. Brunelleschi's Crucifix and Donatello's later Crucifix reject this frontal view in favour of a detached perspective. The influence of Brunelleschi's form of the crucifix is evident in many later sculptures.

The sculpted figure of the crucified Christ usually included a loincloth, which might be part of the sculpture itself or a separate piece of fabric. Brunelleschi intended his Crucifix to have such a fabric loincloth, and so did not sculpt details in the genital area. However, the leading theologians of the early Christian Church, including St Augustine, were certain that Christ had died totally naked, for that was a feature of the customary Roman mode of crucifixion, as well as being theologically appropriate to express Christ's innocence. While the influence of the Eastern Church had tended towards a clothed Christ on the Cross, the followers of St Francis of Assisi had once again affirmed Christ's nakedness, in order to assert not only the humanity of Christ but also an affinity between Christ and the poor. All of these interpretations may be seen in the nakedness of a Crucifix attributed to Michelangelo (polychrome wood, 1.35×1.35 m, *c.* 1492–4; Florence, Casa Buonarroti). In this sculpture Christ is depicted with an adolescent body, conveying a minimal sense of suffering; the small wound in the side appears nearly healed. The lithe body has often been compared to the idealization in Donatello's bronze *David* (1450s; Florence, Bargello; *see* STATUE, fig. 1). In the wooden Crucifix the head hangs to the right, as is customary; but the legs turn towards the left, giving Christ a dancing movement.

BIBLIOGRAPHY

H. W. Janson: *The Sculpture of Donatello* (Princeton, 1957/*R* 1963)
M. Baxandall: *The Limewood Sculptors of Renaissance Germany* (New Haven and London, 1980/*R* 1985)
G. Andres, T. Hunisak and A. Turner: *The Art of Florence*, 2 vols (New York, 1988)

DOUG ADAMS

(iii) Baroque and after. From the end of the 16th century a Crucifix was required to be placed on the altar of a Catholic church, and this greatly stimulated its artistic development. There was an increased production of small and medium-sized Crucifixes, while the large-scale celebratory Crucifixes gradually disappeared from church interiors. Expensive materials were predominantly used; increasingly, stone and wood gave way to gold, silver and ivory, although poorer churches still used wood, while

ivory and wood, sometimes encased in tortoise-shell, were also used for the Crucifixes that began to appear in bourgeois interiors.

The Council of Trent (1545–63) prohibited the showing of Christ's body naked and stipulated that it should always be shown with a loincloth. Giambologna was the first to exploit the sculptural possibilities of this requirement by focusing on the drapery. In the bronze Crucifix (1.8 m, c. 1598) that he made for his own tomb (Florence, SS Annunziata) the loincloth is reduced to a modest piece of drapery around the loins, pleated horizontally, with a long section hanging at the side. The loincloth gradually lost its chastening significance, however, and became a compositional element that provided a contrast with Christ's anatomy. In the Baroque period and later, emphasis was placed on showing Christ as both human and divine. Giambologna developed a type of Crucifix (e.g. 1588; Florence, S Marco) that expressed this duality and became very influential. Typically, he showed an idealized Christ with a serene expression and an athletic build, his head either lifted in a hopeful gesture towards heaven or hanging on the chest. In general terms, there was a move away from the portrayal of Christ as a suffering figure.

Giambologna's type was extremely popular with Baroque sculptors both in Italy and in northern Europe, partly because it allowed them to display their knowledge of anatomy. The type persisted well into the 17th century, with many variations, especially in the treatment of the loincloth. This was at first more pleated, with long sections of cloth hanging unnaturally at the side. Later the knot at the side was replaced by a rope that held the drapery together. Gradually, the rope was less tightly tied, so that the cloth no longer covered the side of the thigh, but slid down gently. The bronze altar Crucifixes by Gianlorenzo Bernini (1658–9; Rome, St Peter's) show that he was among the numerous sculptors who continued the type (with its idealized Christ) created by Giambologna. François Du Quesnoy was also inspired by Giambologna's designs, but his chosen material, ivory, led him to change the iconography. His ivory Crucifix in the treasury of S Giovanni in Laterano, Rome, shows the limitations of the material and is representative of Du Quesnoy's numerous ivory crucifixes: the sculptor was obliged to work with the grain of the ivory, so that figure is invariably shown with arms stretched above the head, legs slightly bent, the head usually lifted and the feet parallel or overlapping.

In contrast to the crucifixes in Italy and northern Europe, Spanish Crucifixes retained a degree of theatrical realism, with a strong emphasis on the suffering of the emaciated Christ. A good example is the life-size wooden Crucifix (1688–9; Seville Cathedral) by Francisco Ruiz Gijón (fl 1671–92). Elsewhere in Europe large stone and wooden crucifixes did not become popular again until the late 17th century and the early 18th, when calvaries (large-scale Stations of the Cross built on hillsides and culminating in a Crucifixion) became increasingly widespread. In the 18th century the musculature of the Christ figure became smoother and the body more delicate and decorative in line, while the strength of emotional expression was reduced. The Crucifix by a follower of Gabriel Grupello (Kleve, St Maria Himmelfahrt) is a good example of this type, which dominated the 18th century. Some

Crucifixes produced towards the middle of the century in Germany demonstrate the return of a more realistic approach. Egid Quirin Asam, for example, in his contribution to the *Gesamtkunstwerk* created in 1729–46 at St Johann Nepomuk, Munich, showed the crucified Christ as a dead, emaciated figure crowned with thorns, with blood streaming from the wounded side. The loincloth, a mere symbol, hangs loosely around the body (*see* ASAM, (2), fig. 2).

Two types of Crucifix continued to be produced throughout the 18th century: with an athletically proportioned, idealized Christ or, particularly in Germany and Spain, with a more realistic, emaciated figure of the dead Christ, usually with a crown of thorns. There was considerable diversity during the 19th century owing to the co-existence of various artistic styles, and an increasingly wide range of materials was considered acceptable for a Crucifix, including glass, wax, tin and papier mâché. An interest in medieval art stimulated the renewal of earlier forms, but the great demand for Crucifixes led to mass production, with the result that few high-quality examples were made. In the 20th century, Art Deco made use of the stylized forms that derived from the Gothic and Romanesque styles, and Expressionism later lent itself to images of a convulsed and suffering Christ.

BIBLIOGRAPHY

G. Schönermark: *Der Kruzifixus in der bildenden Kunst* (Strasbourg, 1908)
L. Zumkeller: *Il crocifisso nell'arte* (Florence, 1911)
A. G. Braun: *Das christliche Altargerät in seinem Sein und in seiner Entwicklung* (Munich, 1932), pp. 466–92
P. Thoby: *Le Crucifix des origines au Concile de Trente: Etude iconographique* (Nantes, 1959)
S. Bessenburg: *Rüdiger, Kreuz, Kruzifix: Eine Bibliographie* (Munich, 1973)
Christus im Leiden, Kruzifixe, Passionsdarstellungen aus 800 Jahren (exh. cat., Stuttgart, Württemberg. Landesmuseums, 1988)

IRIS KOCKELBERGH

Crucy, Mathurin (*b* Nantes, 22 Feb 1749; *d* Paris, 7 Nov 1826). French architect. He was the son of a carpenter from Nantes, and he trained initially in Nantes under Jean-Baptiste Ceineray (1722–1811); he later studied at the Ecole des Beaux-Arts, Paris, under Etienne-Louis Boullée. In 1774 he won the Prix de Rome with a design for some public baths. In 1775 he left for Rome, where he spent three years studying the great monuments of antiquity and the Renaissance. The contact with Italian architecture, particularly the work of Andrea Palladio, was to have a decisive impact on his work. In 1778 Crucy returned to Nantes, where he remained for the greater part of his life. Innovative architecture was beginning to spread outside Paris to the major towns throughout France. In 1780 he replaced Ceineray as architect-surveyor of Nantes. Ceineray had overseen the considerable expansion of the city, which was continued by Crucy, who introduced a Neoclassicism that showed evidence of the Palladian revival.

Crucy's work in Nantes included restoration, small individual buildings and great urban schemes. In 1784 he was involved in the restoration of the cathedral. By 1785, however, he had drawn up plans for his major work, the new Graslin district, centred around the Place Graslin (1785) and the Grand Théâtre (1788), an imposing Neoclassical building, the façade of which featured a portico of eight Corinthian columns and a heavy cornice. The theatre was destroyed by fire in 1796 but was restored by Crucy in 1811. In 1786 he built the Halle au Blé and, after a brief period working on the restoration of Rennes Cathedral, he submitted a scheme (1787; later modified) for the Place Royale, Nantes, in the semicircular part of which he planned a cylindrical guard-house, from which a further cylinder projected upwards in a style that derived from Boullée's manipulation of geometrical forms.

From 1788 to 1790 Crucy worked on the restoration of prisons and the college at Nantes. In 1792 he started to design the Bourse, a project that was not completed until 1810. During this period he also built the façade (1808) of the Hôtel de Ville, the former Hôtel Bezard. In 1809 he was appointed architect for the département of Loire-Inférieure. His best-known work, however, continued to be carried out in Nantes. Apart from the Bourse, his most important works include the Pont de la Révolution (now the Pont de l'Ecluse), the church of St Louis, the market hall, the Musée des Beaux-Arts de Nantes (1821), the Hôtel de Comméquiers in the Rue Royale, plans for the Place Louis XVI and the church of Lovoux; together these make Nantes one of the most complete examples of French Neo-classical urban planning carried out on such a grand scale.

Crucy's brothers Jean Crucy and Louis Crucy were also architects and worked in Nantes, although they were less well known than Mathurin; Mathurin Crucy's son Felix Crucy (1798–1867) also became an architect.

BIBLIOGRAPHY
Bauchal; *Macmillan Enc. Architects*; Thieme–Becker
L. Hautecoeur: *Architecture classique*, iv (1952)
E. Kaufmann: *Architecture in the Age of Reason* (Cambridge, MA, 1955/*R* New York, 1968), pp. 196–7
D. Rabreau: 'Le Théâtre et la place Graslin de Mathurin Crucy à Nantes', *Congr. Archéol. France*, cxxvi (1968), pp. 89–135
Mathurin Crucy, 1749–1826: Architecte nantais néo-classique (exh. cat., Nantes, Mus. Dobrée, 1986)
A. Picon: *Architectes et ingénieurs au siècle des lumières* (Marseille, 1988)

Cruet. Small bottle with a stopper, used for oil, vinegar and other condiments. Its earliest use was ecclesiastical, for wine, oil and water; some medieval examples survive (*see* RELIQUARY, §II, 1). Cruets were used domestically from the late 17th century, from which time they were made of glass imported from Italy, often with silver or silver-plated mounts. Cruets were grouped together on a stand in a frame or rack, sometimes with a central vertical handle and supporting feet. The number of bottles could vary from two to six or more, and they were often combined with casters. Their popularity was so great that by the late 18th century hundreds of different patterns were made by a single manufacturer. The term also refers to a condiment set for salt, pepper and mustard.

□

Crüger, Dietrich. *See* KRÜGER, DIETRICH.

Cruikshank. English family of artists.

(1) Isaac Cruikshank (*bapt* Edinburgh, 14 Oct 1764; *bur* London, 16 April 1811). Printmaker and draughtsman. He moved to London, probably *c.* 1785, to work as a caricaturist, illustrator and engraver. He was successful as a cartoonist, working first for S. W. Fores in Piccadilly and then for Laurie & Whittle in Fleet Street. He exhibited at the Royal Academy, London, in 1790 and 1792. The initials of his daughter, Eliza Cruikshank (*b* 1807; *d* Aug 1825), appear on the *Four Mr Prices* (1825; London, BM), a caricature etched by his son (3) George Cruikshank.

(2) (Isaac) Robert Cruikshank (*b* London, 27 Sept 1789; *d* 13 March 1856). Printmaker and painter, son of (1) Isaac Cruikshank. He served as midshipman in the East India Company, then settled in London where he worked as a painter and illustrator. With his brother (3) George Cruikshank he illustrated Pierce Egan's *Life in London* (London, 1820–21) with hand-coloured etchings and aquatints and then provided 68 aquatint plates for Charles Molloy Westmacott's *The English Spy* (London, 1825–6). He illustrated 17 books but never matched his brother George's skills and died in poverty.

(3) George Cruikshank (*b* London, 27 Sept 1792; *d* London, 1 Feb 1878). Printmaker and draughtsman, son of (1) Isaac Cruikshank. From an early age he helped his father, learning to use an etching needle before the turn of the 18th century. He was employed by Hannah Humphrey, James Gillray's publisher and landlady, to finish plates Gillray was too ill to complete: their style is so close as sometimes to be indistinguishable. His early work also owes a considerable debt to Hogarth. Cruikshank was a successful juvenile actor and at one time intended to make his career on the stage. His lifelong gift for play-acting, mimicry and story-telling informed all his illustration.

The Napoleonic Wars provided Cruikshank with the inspiration for many of his most memorable cartoons, for example *Boney Hatching a Bulletin* (1812; London, BM), inspired by the ghastly retreat from Moscow, and *Little Boney Gone to Pot* (1814; London, BM), showing Napoleon sitting on a huge chamberpot, labelled 'Imperial Throne', on Elba. In domestic politics George IV was a natural target. In 1820 Cruikshank signed a receipt for £100 of the royal money 'in consideration of a pledge not to caricature His Majesty in any immoral situation' (Wardroper, p. 16), which did not inhibit him from continuing to ridicule the King. The *Royal Extinguisher, or the King of Brobdingnag and the Lilliputians* (1812, London, BM), however, shows the King as almost handsome, together with powerful portraits of Arthur Wellesley, 1st Duke of Wellington, Robert Stewart, Viscount Castlereagh, and Robert Banks Jenkinson, 2nd Earl of Liverpool. Cruikshank had a long and close collaboration with the anti-government publisher William Hone (1780–1842), who inspired some of his most influential cartoons, for example the *Bank Restriction Note* (1819; London, V&A), which denounced the execution of women for passing forged banknotes.

In 1820 Cruikshank began working with his brother, (2) Robert Cruikshank, and Pierce Egan, the sporting journalist, on *Life in London* (London, 1820–21), which was published from October 1820 in monthly parts and has 36 hand-coloured aquatints. This widely popular publication marked the beginning of Cruikshank's move from political caricature to social observation and book illustration. The heroes of *Life in London*, Tom and Jerry, gave their names to the age. The plates document the times in gripping detail, as indeed do many of Cruikshank's other etched plates, such as *Inconveniences of a Crowded Drawing-room* (1818; London, BM), showing a reception in Buckingham House, London, and *Sailors Carousing*, one of 12 plates in Matthew Henry Barker's book of naval reminiscences, *Greenwich Hospital* (London and Dublin, 1826).

Cruikshank's book illustrations brought him recognition as the leading exponent of the art in Europe. His output was prodigious, his inventiveness never-failing, and he regularly produced images of unforgettable power. Besides a multitude of other work, he illustrated *German Popular Stories* (London, 1823), the first edition in English of *Kinder- und Hausmärchen* (Berlin, 1812–15) by Jacob Ludwig Carl Grimm and Wilhelm Carl Grimm, the plates for which Ruskin thought the best etchings since those of Rembrandt. He also illustrated Walter Scott's *Waverley* novels (Paris and London, 1836–8), Robert Southey's *Life of Nelson* (London, 1830), Daniel Defoe's *Robinson Crusoe* (London, 1831) and, for Thomas Roscoe's *Novelists' Library*, he produced plates for works by Tobias George Smollett (1831), Henry Fielding (1832), Oliver Goldsmith (1832), Laurence Sterne (1832) and Miguel de Cervantes (1833), all published in London. Many of his book illustrations were small but telling and usually packed with detail. He could also produce large folding plates, as in *1851, or the Adventures of Mr and Mrs Sandboys and Family* (London, 1851) by Henry Mayhew and George Cruikshank, which is packed with crowd scenes containing an astonishing profusion of detail. Most of his work was on copper, etched by himself, but the illustrations on wood were engraved by others.

Cruikshank illustrated Charles Dickens's first book, *Sketches by Boz* (London, 1836), and his third, *Oliver Twist*. The 24 etchings for *Oliver Twist* (London, 1838), including the famous *Fagin in the Condemned Cell*, are considered the finest illustrations ever made for Dickens. It was also the last of the author's novels that Cruikshank illustrated, as Dickens disliked the increasingly grim visualization of his characters in the final plates. Furthermore, Cruikshank desired a greater control over the text than Dickens was prepared to allow. In later life Cruikshank dubiously claimed to have been the originator of various aspects of *Oliver Twist*.

At the age of 55 Cruikshank suddenly and passionately espoused the temperance movement and gave up tobacco. This did not lead to any diminution of his skills or changes in his style: *George Cruikshank's Fairy Library* (London, 1853–4), with beautiful etchings for *Hop o'my Thumb*, *Jack and the Beanstalk*, *Cinderella* and *Puss in Boots* is among the finest things he ever did and more than compensates for his rewriting of the stories themselves on temperance lines. For *The Drunkard's Children* (London, 1848), which contained a poem by Charles Mackay, Cruikshank produced eight glyphographs (*see* PRINTS, §III, 1), of which the terrible final drawing of the poor homeless girl throwing herself off Waterloo Bridge is particularly powerful. Horror and fright were Cruikshank's speciality, but he was also a supremely good comic artist, as shown by the *Cat Did It* and other plates in Horace Mayhew and Henry Mayhew's *The Greatest Plague of Life* (London, 1847).

Cruikshank never attempted to follow changing tastes. Like all competent illustrators he modified his style according to the job in hand and the medium of reproduction, but he never pandered to fashion. There are over 6000 published graphic works and thousands of pencil sketches, scribbles and watercolours, now dispersed all over the world. The most important collection of his work is in the British Museum, London.

BIBLIOGRAPHY

G. W. Reid: *Descriptive Catalogue of the Works of George Cruikshank*, 3 vols (London, 1871) [incl. works produced collab. (1) Isaac and (2) (Isaac) Robert]

B. Jerrold: *The Life of George Cruikshank* (London, 1882)

A. M. Cohn: *George Cruikshank: A Catalogue Raisonné* (London, 1924)

R. McLean: *George Cruikshank: His Life and Work as a Book Illustrator* (London, 1948)

K. T. Parker: *The Drawings of Cruikshank at Windsor Castle* (London, 1948)

E. B. Krumhaar: *Isaac Cruikshank: A Catalogue Raisonné* (Philadelphia, 1966)

The Inimitable George Cruikshank: An Exhibition of Illustrated Books, Prints, Drawings and Manuscripts from the Collection of David Borowitz (exh. cat. by R. A. Vogler, Louisville, KY, Speed A. Mus., 1968)

J. R. Harvey: *Victorian Novelists and their Illustrators* (London, 1970), pp. 30–49, 199–210

R. L. Patten, ed.: 'George Cruikshank: A Re-evaluation', *Princeton U. Lib. Chron.*, xxxv/1–2 (1973–4) [issues ded. (3) George Cruikshank]

George Cruikshank (exh. cat. by W. Feaver, ACGB, 1974)

J. Wardroper: *The Caricatures of George Cruikshank* (London, 1977)

H. Evans and M. Evans: *The Man who Drew the Drunkard's Daughter* (London, 1978)

R. A. Vogler: *Graphic Works of George Cruikshank* (New York, 1979)

J. Buchanan Brown: *The Book Illustration of George Cruikshank* (Newton Abbot, 1980)

J. R. Cohen: *Charles Dickens and his Original Illustrators* (Columbus, OH, 1980), pp. 15–38

M. Bryant, ed.: *The Comic Cruikshank* (London, 1992)

R. L. Patten: *George Cruikshank's Life, Times and Art*, i: *1792–1835* (Cambridge, 1992)

Cruikshank 200: An Exhibition to Celebrate the Bicentenary of the Artist George Cruikshank (exh. cat. by J. Wardroper, London, Mus. Order St John; Burnley, Towneley Hall A.G. & Mus.; Maidstone, Mus. & A.G.; Sheffield, Graves A.G.; 1992–3)

Isaac Cruikshank and the Politics of Parody: Watercolours in the Huntington Collection (exh. cat., ed. E. J. Nygren; Los Angeles, USC, Fisher Gal., 1994)

RUARI McLEAN

Crusader States. *See* JERUSALEM, LATIN KINGDOM OF.

Crusades. Wars conducted against the enemies (mainly Muslims) of the Western Christian Church from the late 11th century to the 16th. The papacy authorized these holy wars, and participants were given a series of privileges by the Church, notably indulgences. The Church had long developed arguments justifying wars fought in its defence against heretics and infidels. What distinguished the Crusades from other 'just' wars was the association of war and pilgrimage, a popular form of penance in the 11th century; Jerusalem was particularly attractive to pilgrims. In 1095 Pope Urban II (*reg* 1088–99) sought to raise an army among the knights of western Europe to assist the Greek Byzantine empire against the Saljuq Turks and made Jerusalem, which had been in Muslim hands since the 7th century, the ultimate military goal of the expedition. He offered recruits the same spiritual advantages and ecclesiastical protection enjoyed by pilgrims to the Holy Land, making the campaign an armed pilgrimage. The soldiers signalled their commitment by sewing a cross on to their clothes, thus becoming *crucesignati*, or crusaders.

Urban's call touched the knights' imagination. The first crusaders fought to avenge the insult done to Christ by the occupation of his Holy Land and to earn themselves salvation. Throughout the subsequent centuries crusaders' motives remained mixed: the crusade offered spiritual and earthly advancement, a combination of pilgrimage, war, adventure, tourism and, for some, territorial and material gain. Crusades became the highest expression of the martial values they had been invented to contain. The First Crusade (1096–9) was spectacularly successful. The so-called Peasants' Crusade (1096) failed dismally, but the main army captured Antioch (now Antakaya) in Syria (1097–8) and took Jerusalem on 15 July 1099. The First Crusade established both the LATIN KINGDOM OF JERU-SALEM and other Crusader States, and the crusading tradition. With its attendant visions, miracles, deeds of heroism and signs of God's favour, the expedition quickly entered legend and romance.

The capture of Edessa (now Urfa) in 1144 by Zangi of Mosul (*d* 1146) provoked the Second Crusade (1145–9). It was carefully prepared, yet the only gain from the Muslims was the recapture of Lisbon (1147) by Alfonso I, King of Portugal (*reg* 1139–85), aided by a crusader fleet. The failure of the Second Crusade caused disappointment and disillusion and left Outremer, the Crusader States in the East, insecure. After the Ayyubid sultan Salah-al-Din (*reg* 1169–93) united Muslim Syria and Egypt, the Military Orders of the KNIGHTS TEMPLAR and KNIGHTS HOSPI-TALLER adopted increasing responsibility for the defence of the Crusader States. Nevertheless, Salah-al-Din won the Battle of Hattin in July 1187 and captured Jerusalem three months later.

The Third Crusade (1189–92) was dominated by Richard I of England (*reg* 1189–99); it did not recapture Jerusalem, but it brought Cyprus under western control, which lasted until 1571, and, by retaking Acre (now 'Akka) in 1191, reconstituted the Kingdom of Jerusalem. The Fourth Crusade (1202–4), originally intended as an attack on Egypt, was diverted to Constantinople (now Istanbul) and ended in the shameful sack and looting of the city. The Fifth Crusade (1217–21) and the first crusade of Louix IX of France (1248–54), or the Seventh Crusade, both succeeded in briefly capturing the Egyptian port of Damietta (now Dumyât), but ended in ignominious defeat. Only the crusade (1228–9) of Emperor Frederick II and those of Theobald IV, Count of Champagne (*reg* 1201–53), in 1239–40, Richard, Earl of Cornwall (1209–72), in 1240–41 and the future Edward I of England (1270–72) were aimed directly at the Holy Land; all ended with little more than negotiated treaties with local Muslim rulers. The loss of mainland Outremer (1268–91) was not regarded as final: Peter I, King of Cyprus (*reg* 1359–69), for example, recruited Western crusaders for an assault on Alexandria in 1365, but there was no concerted action. After the last serious attempt to recover the Holy Land ended in the slaughter of the Christian army by Ottoman forces at Nicopolis on the Danube (1396), the ideal persisted but was no longer a political priority. The papacy employed crusading privileges associated with the recovery of the Holy Land in various other contexts between the

12th and 15th centuries. Men still took the cross in the 16th century, and the Knights Hospitaller remained at Rhodes until 1522 and at Malta from 1530, until expelled by Napoleon I in 1798.

Crusades also took place within Europe: under the guise of crusading, Prussia and Livonia were opened to German colonization (*see* TEUTONIC ORDER); the rulers of northern France subjugated the Languedoc after the crusades against the Albigensian heretics (1209–29); and the Christian kings of the Iberian peninsula gained money, men and religious justification for the Reconquest of Muslim Spain (*c.* 722–1492) and Portugal (completed 1249). The Crusades to the East were generally unsuccessful at colonization, however, based as they were on the principles of the pilgrimage, from which most intended to return home. Anti-Semitic pogroms, first seen when the Peasants' Crusade massacred Jewish communities in the Rhineland, were one result of the First Crusade; the Crusades were born of a rough, uncompromising faith and reflected intolerant and violent social attitudes.

The effect of the Crusades upon art was indirect and coincidental. In Syria and Palestine under the crusaders there existed a narrow dominance rather than cultural exchange. Even in Spain and Sicily, on the traditional frontiers of Christendom and Islam, separate development predominated. In the East the eclectic crusader style fed on Western and Byzantine traditions and ignored local ones; the artists and craftsmen were either foreign or influenced by foreign models. In the scriptoria of Jerusalem (12th century) and Acre (*c.* 1250–91), Byzantine, Italian, French and English styles were mingled with varying degrees of harmony to create less a synthesis than a hybrid (for example *see* MELISENDE PSALTER; *see also* JERUSALEM, LATIN KINGDOM OF, fig. 2). Churches, palaces and castles were influenced by local conditions and relative isolation from contemporary artistic changes in the west. Western domination is shown by, for example, the Romanesque remodelling of the church of the Holy Sepulchre in Jerusalem (*see* ROMANESQUE, §III, 1(vii)), which was then copied in Europe (*see* JERUSALEM, §II, 2). Castle design was influenced by existing Arab and Greek structures and was dependent on local circumstances and site; they were the result of pragmatism, not of fashion (*see* CASTLE, §I, 3(iii)). Although the labour and materials were local, plans and techniques show little cross-fertilization; Arab, Greek and Frankish work co-existed rather than combined to form an integrated artistic whole. Given this cultural apartheid, the idea that the Crusades allowed eastern influences to civilize the West appears unconvincing. The genesis of Gothic cannot be demonstrably traced to the Crusades. Greek styles and models were more easily available in Sicily and Calabria than in Outremer, as was Moorish architecture in Spain. Western castle builders discovered their own solutions to problems of fortification. The Crusades did not exert a profound or direct influence on art outside their own hybrid, often beautiful and impressive creations (for an alternative view *see* JERUSA-LEM, LATIN KINGDOM OF, §II).

BIBLIOGRAPHY

R. C. Smail: *Crusading Warfare, 1097–1193* (Cambridge, 1956/*R* 1972)
H. Buchthal: *Miniature Painting in the Latin Kingdom of Jerusalem* (Oxford, 1957/*R* London, 1986)

K. M. Setton, ed.: *A History of the Crusades*, 6 vols (Madison and London, 1962–89)
J. Prawer: *The Latin Kingdom of Jerusalem: European Colonialism in the Middle Ages* (London, 1972)
J. Folda, ed.: *Crusader Art in the Twelfth Century*, Brit. Archaeol. Rep., Int. Ser., 152 (Oxford, 1982)

For further bibliography *see* JERUSALEM, LATIN KINGDOM OF.

CHRISTOPHER TYERMAN

Crutcher, Richard (*b c.* 1660; *d* 1725). English sculptor. He was apprenticed to William King, a mason in London, from 1674 to 1680, when he transferred to serve under the sculptor Edward Pierce (ii), becoming free of the Masons' Company in 1681. He held a variety of offices in the Masons' Company, becoming steward in 1691 and master in 1713. Between 1716 and 1719 he was the mason responsible for the rebuilding of Bakers' Hall, London. His only surviving signed work is the marble tomb (1705) of *Sir Robert Clayton, Lord Mayor of London, and Lady Clayton* at the church of St Mary the Virgin, Bletchingley, Surrey. This fine Baroque monument portrays the two standing figures in contemporary dress; behind them is a Corinthian aedicula with a broken segmental pediment decorated with flaming urns, cherubs and angels. The influence of Pierce is evident in the lively style of cutting and the expressive quality of the portraiture. Crutcher's son Michael Crutcher (*d* before 1725) became free of the Masons' Company in 1712; he worked as his father's assistant.

Gunnis
BIBLIOGRAPHY
K. A. Esdaile: *English Church Monuments, 1510 to 1840* (London, 1946), pp. 28–30
M. Whinney: *Sculpture in Britain, 1530 to 1830*, Pelican Hist. A. (Harmondsworth, 1964, rev. J. Physick, 1988), pp. 106–8, 142, 245, 441

□

Cruyl, Lieven [Liévin] (*b* Ghent, ?1640; *d* Ghent, ?1720). Flemish priest, draughtsman and etcher, active also in Italy and France. While living in Wetteren (nr Ghent), he was involved in the completion of the Gothic St Michielskerk in Ghent. The construction of the western tower had been interrupted in 1566 because of religious unrest, and in 1652 steps were taken to complete it. After a Renaissance design was proposed in 1653, Cruyl submitted a drawing in Brabantine Late Gothic style (Ghent, Bib. Rijksuniv.) in 1662. His tower was to have been 134 m high, higher than the north tower of Antwerp Cathedral (1521). However, the project was never realized because of lack of funds. Although unoriginal and of an outdated style, the design had elegance and grandeur.

In 1664 Cruyl left for Rome, where he lived until *c.* 1670. During this time he drew many views of the city (e.g. 18 sheets, Cleveland, OH, Mus. A.) and etched ten plates representing the *Triumph of Caesar* after Andrea Mantegna's series (Hollstein, nos 1–10). His etched views of Rome and its surroundings appeared in several contemporary publications. For instance, two series of 25 prints (Hollstein, nos 27–76) were first published in 1667 and were later included in Graevius's *Thesaurus antiquitatum Romanarum* and in F. Desseine's *Het oude en heden daagsche Rome*. In 1672–3 Cruyl was probably in Florence, then in Naples in 1673 and Venice in 1676. Two years later he returned to Ghent, but in 1680 he left for France, which

he visited on several occasions, making drawings and etchings, until he returned to Ghent for good in 1688. Under the influence of his stay in Rome, he designed an altarpiece (unexecuted) for St Bavo's, Ghent, and in 1684 the city magistrates of Ghent commissioned him to design a belfry for the bell-tower, but again the design, this time in a Baroque style, was never executed.

PRINTS
L. Cruyl and G. Testone: *Pianta di Roma come si trova al presente colle alzate delle fabbriche più notabili così antiche come moderne* (Rome, 1665)
G. B. Falda: *Il nuovo teatro delle fabbriche*, 3 vols (Rome, 1665–9)
M. G. de Rossi and L. Cruyl: *Prospectus locorum urbis Romae insign[ium]*, i (Rome, 1666, 2/1692–8, 3/1773)
G. B. Falda: *Recentis Rome ichnographia et hypsographia* (Rome, [1667])
M. G. de Rossi [and L. Cruyl]: *Nuova pianta di Roma presente* (Rome, 1668)
P. Ferrerio and G. B. Falda: *Nuovi disegni dell'architetture, e piante de' palazzi di Roma de più celebri architetti* (Rome, [1670–77])
G. B. Falda: *Nuova pianta ed alzato della città di Roma* (Rome, 1676)
A. Kircher: *Turris Babel* (Amsterdam, 1679)
J. G. Graevius: *Thesaurus antiquitatum Romanarum*, iv (Amsterdam and Utrecht, 1697)
F. Desseine: *Het oude en heden daagsche Rome* (Amsterdam, 1704, 2/1713)

BIBLIOGRAPHY
Bénézit; *BNB*; Hollstein: *Dut. & Flem.*; *NKL*; Thieme–Becker
F. de Potter: *Gent van de ousten tijd tot heden* [Ghent from ancient times to the present day], 5 vols (Ghent, 1882–9/*R* 1969)
E. Mareuse: 'Trois vues de Paris de Liévin Cruyl en 1686', *Bull. Soc. Hist. Paris & Ile-de-France* (1919), pp. 64–71
T. Ashby: 'Lieven Cruyl e le sue vedute di Roma, 1664–1670', *Mem. Pont. Accad. Romana Archeol.*, 3rd ser., i/1 (1923), pp. 221–9
H. Egger: 'Lieven Cruyls römische Veduten', *Meded. Ned. Hist. Inst. Rome*, vii (1927), pp. 183–96
H. S. Francis: 'Drawings by Lievin Cruyl of Rome', *Bull. Cleveland Mus. A.*, xxx (1943), pp. 152–9
K. Langedijk: 'Eine unbekannte Zeichnungsfolge von Lieven Cruyl in Florenz', *Mitt. Ksthist. Inst. Florenz*, x (1961), pp. 67–94
C. Pietrangeli: 'Vedute romane di Lievin Cruyl al Museo di Roma', *Boll. Mus. Com. Roma* (1972), pp. 7–21
G. Walton: 'Liévin Cruyl: The Works for Versailles', *Art, the Ape of Nature: Studies in Honor of H. W. Janson*, ed. M. Barasch (New York, 1981), pp. 425–37
Vedute romane di Lieven Cruyl: Paesaggio urbano sotto Alessandro VII (exh. cat. by M. Miller, B. Jatta and J. Connors, Rome, Amer. Accad., 1989)

J.-P. ESTHER

Cruz, Diego de la. *See* DIEGO DE LA CRUZ.

Cruz, Juan Pantoja de la. *See* PANTOJA DE LA CRUZ, JUAN.

Cruz, Luis Hernández. *See* HERNÁNDEZ CRUZ, LUIS.

Cruz, Marcos da (*b* Lisbon, *fl* 1649; *d* Lisbon, 1683). Portuguese painter. In 1649 he held the post of judge at the Irmandade de S Lucas, the guild of painters of Lisbon. He was a prolific artist, much praised by his clients, but he was never appointed to the court. Nevertheless, he led an active and lucrative professional life working for religious patrons in Lisbon. In his youth he painted 10 small panels representing scenes from the *Life of the Virgin*, of which he signed the *Visitation*, for the Oratório de Dona Catarina at the ducal palace of Vila Viçosa (*in situ*). Around 1663 he probably painted the 12 scenes from the *Life of St Francis* in the transept of the church of Mercês, Lisbon, for the Irmandade de S António. These won the praise of Atanazy Raczynski and reveal their author as a dexterous painter whose tenebrist manner and skilful modelling are reminiscent of Bartolomé Murillo.

Their attribution to da Cruz remains uncertain, however, as they are far superior in quality to the tighter Baroque style of the documented panels at the ducal palace, which are the only firm basis for an assessment of his work. In 1677 da Cruz painted an altarpiece (destr.) for the Irmandade de Nossa Senhora de Guadalupe e Benedito in the monastery of S Francisco, Lisbon. Félix da Costa Meesen cited the panel from the altarpiece at the church of S Nicolau and the paintings at the church of S Paulo and the Royal Chapel in Lisbon as da Cruz's best works, but these were destroyed in the earthquake of 1755. In 1721 Fray Manuel de Sá praised da Cruz's painting *St Madalena of Pazzi* (untraced) at the convent of Carmo in Lisbon, and Francisco Vieira de Matos mentioned a signed *Assumption of the Virgin* (untraced) that in 1758 was in the collection of the Marquis of Penalva. Bento Coelho da Silveira was probably among da Cruz's followers.

BIBLIOGRAPHY

F. da Costa Meesen: *Antiguidade da arte da pintura* (Lisbon, 1696); ed. G. Kubler (New Haven and London, 1967), pp. 271–2

M. de Sá: *Memória histórica da Ordem do Carmo*, ii (Lisbon, 1721), chap. x, no. 251

R. dos Santos: *Oito séculos de arte portuguesa*, i (Lisbon, 1967), p. 160

J. Teixeira: *O paço ducal de Vila Viçosa* (Lisbon, 1983), p. 183

VITOR SERRÃO

Cruz Azaceta, Luis (*b* Havana, 5 April 1942). Cuban painter, active in the USA. He left Cuba in 1960 and settled in New York where from 1966 to 1969 he studied at the School of Visual Arts. He was a protagonist of the neo-expressionist movement that emerged in New York in the 1970s. His work of this date is characterized by a humour lacking in some of the work by European exponents, for example the *Dance of Latin America* (acrylic on canvas, 1.96×2.34 m, 1983; New York, Met.). In 1985 he won a Guggenheim Fellowship in painting. Works by Cruz Azaceta are in a number of collections (e.g. *A Question of Colour*, acrylic on canvas, 3.05×3.66 m, 1989; Houston, TX, Mus. F.A.) including those of the Metropolitan Museum of Art, New York; Rhode Island School of Design, Providence; Boston Museum of Fine Arts, MA; and the Houston Museum of Fine Arts, TX.

BIBLIOGRAPHY

Azaceta's Tough Ride around the City (exh. cat., New York, Mus. Contemp. Hisp. A., 1986)

The Art of the Fantastic: Latin America, 1920–1987 (exh. cat. by H. T. Day and H. Sturges, Indianapolis, Mus. A., 1987)

RICARDO PAU-LLOSA

Cruz-Diez, Carlos (*b* Caracas, 17 Aug 1923). Venezuelan painter and kinetic artist. He studied in 1940 and 1941 at the Escuela de Artes Plásticas y Aplicadas in Caracas, producing Socialist Realist paintings while working as art director to the McCann Erickson advertising agency in Venezuela, where he became interested in the effect of colour in advertising. In 1955–6 he visited Paris and Barcelona, where his interest was aroused by theories of geometric abstraction, scientific colour theory and Bauhaus ideas on the integration of the arts and crafts. On returning to Caracas he opened the Estudio de Artes Visuales, where he began to investigate the role of colour in kinetic art. Cruz-Diez's wide experience in advertising, industrial applications of colour, cinema and photographic

and photo-mechanical processes, together with his study of work by Georges Seurat and Josef Albers and of Edwin Land's (*b* 1909) scientific ideas on colour perception, led him to produce such constructions as the *Physichromy* series, which was initiated in 1959, immediately after a group of geometric works based on the repetition and serialization of flatly painted trapezoids. The *Physichromies* explored additive, subtractive and reflective colour relationships that could be altered by the relative positions of the light source and viewer.

In 1964 Cruz-Diez began to create *Chromointerferences*, characterized by mechanically produced movement and by programmed additive colour changes, constructing such works as the *Chromointerference Column* (1971; Paris, U. Paris XIII). In 1965 he introduced *Sensory Deconditioning Rooms*, environments inducing acoustic, visual and tactile perception. The *Chromosaturation* series isolates the viewer in an atmosphere of intense colour, as in the *Chromatic Ambience* (1973), constructed for the hydroelectric plant at Santo Domingo in the Barinas State, Venezuela. His *Transchromies* consist of wide sheets of perspex superimposed on a rotating axis to produce different optical mixtures of colour. Cruz-Diez also produced works integrated with architecture, as in the headquarters of the Union de Bancos Suizos (1975–9) and the international airport at Caracas.

BIBLIOGRAPHY

R. Bordier: *Cruz-Diez ou la couleur comme événement* (Paris, 1972)

Carlos Cruz-Diez: Génesis, eclosión y absoluto del color (exh. cat. by R. Guevara, Caracas, Mus. A. Contemp., 1974)

A. Boulton: *Cruz-Diez* (Caracas, 1975)

For further bibliography see KINETIC ART.

BÉLGICA RODRÍGUEZ

Cruzeiro Seixas(, Artur Manuel Rodrigues do) (*b* Lisbon, 3 Dec 1920). Portuguese painter, draughtsman, illustrator and poet. After a Neo-Realist phase, he joined the dissident group The Surrealists, founded in Lisbon in 1948 by MÁRIO CESARINY. Cruzeiro Seixas participated in the two exhibitions held by this group in 1949 and 1950, with works inspired by the poetry of Lautréamont.

In his paintings and, more especially, drawings, for example *La Variété en dehors d'elle-même* (1947; Lisbon, Mus. Gulbenkian), he aimed to create a personal and often erotic imagery in the metamorphosis of human, plant and animal forms. These works seldom transcend the commonplace or contrived. His collages, such as *The Basis of Language* (1960; artist's col., see Wohl, 1978 exh. cat., p. 83), resemble those of Max Ernst.

Between 1952 and 1964 he lived in Luanda, where he was a curator in the Museum of Angola. In 1965 he lived in Paris and returned to Portugal in 1966, where he illustrated several books that year: *Alguns mitos maiores, alguns mitos menores* (Some major myths, some minor myths) by Cesariny, and Natália Correia's *Antologia erótica e satirica* (Erotic and satirical anthology). He wrote *Rencontres angoissantes dans une ville — rencontres manquées, scenario* (1973). In 1986 he designed the costumes and painted the stage sets for a production of Tchaikovsky's *Swan Lake* for the Teatro Nacional de São Carlos, Lisbon.

BIBLIOGRAPHY
Cruzeiro Seixas (exh. cat., Castelo Branco, Mus. Tavares Proença, 1978)
Portuguese Art since 1910 (exh. cat., ed. H. Wohl; London, RA, 1978)

RUTH ROSENGARTEN

Cruz González, Manuel de la. *See* GONZÁLEZ, MANUEL DE LA CRUZ.

Crypt. Subsidiary vaulted room normally below the main floor level but not necessarily wholly subterranean. The term is normally used of church architecture. Crypts are found throughout western Europe, until the 11th century associated with funerary rites and in particular with the cult of relics, simulating the form of a tomb if not an actual one. In some instances, churches were built around the existing tomb of a saint or a holy place. The most important example of this is the Anastasis Rotunda on Golgotha built by Constantine the Great around the tomb of Christ, now the Church of the Holy Sepulchre (*see* JERUSALEM, §II, 2). The function of early crypts was to keep relics secure and to allow the circulation of pilgrims. As the cult of relics and its liturgical implications grew, the crypt tended to lose its specific function as reliquary. Nevertheless crypts continued to be built, simply providing extra space for altars and chapels. Their size increased, and in some cases they lay beneath the entire eastern arm of a major church, for example Archbishop Anselm's vast extension to Canterbury Cathedral (1096–1130).

1. Before *c.* AD 1000. 2. Later developments.

1. BEFORE *c.* AD 1000. As early as in the 4th century AD relics were being deposited in churches, sometimes in tiny, inaccessible vaults beneath the altar. From the 4th century AD to the 6th crypts were particularly popular in North Africa, while during the heyday of their development (7th–12th centuries) they were confined to western Europe. At the cathedral of Orléansville (now El-Asnam, Algeria; founded 324) a small crypt existed beneath the apse, while the church at Bénian (now Ala Miliara, Algeria; 434–9) had a room beneath the apse connected to the tomb of St Robba by a small window (fenestella) through which the saint's tomb was viewed by the faithful.

The earliest evidence of crypts in western Europe is in the writings of GREGORY during the late 6th century. Although his descriptions of churches in Gaul are difficult to interpret, they confirm the existence of purpose-built crypts there during the 6th century. Gregory mentioned the church of St Etienne at Déols (Indre), the surviving crypts of which are two simple chambers: the northern one with a single access stair, that to the south with two. Related to this type are the crypts at Ripon (N. Yorks) and Hexham (Northumb.), both built by the energetic Bishop Wilfrid (634–709). There are two access stairs at Ripon, one of which leads to a small room from where the barrel-vaulted relic chamber (confessio) can be viewed. The other stair, which may have been reserved for priests, leads directly into the confessio. At Hexham the arrangement is more sophisticated with two stairs leading to and from the viewing chamber, allowing the efficient circulation of pilgrims, and another leading directly into the confessio for the officiating priests (for illustration *see* HEXHAM ABBEY).

This deliberate allowance for the circulation of pilgrims is perhaps more logically achieved by the annular or ring crypt. This type was first installed in Old St Peter's, Rome (see fig. 1), by the future Pope Gregory the Great in the late 6th century. It consisted of a partly subterranean vaulted passageway following the internal face of the apse; on the main axis a passageway led back to the confessio, which was positioned on the chord of the apse. Pilgrims would have viewed the tomb of St Peter along this passageway and afterwards continued along the corridor that bordered the apse. This type of crypt was widely copied, for example in S Crisogono (731–41), Rome; in S Apollinare in Classe (9th century) near Ravenna; and in the Carolingian empire at Seligenstadt (831–40) and Werden (after 809), near Essen.

During the Carolingian period a new form of crypt, known as the outer crypt, was introduced. It consisted at first of the normal elements of a crypt with vaulted corridors and confessios, the significant difference being that they were constructed outside the main body of the church and connected to it by corridors or simple doorways in the wall of the church. The earliest documented example appears to have been Abbot Hilduin's addition to Saint-Denis Abbey in 832, to which access was gained by doorways on each side of the apse. A partially surviving example of a simple outer crypt possibly belonging to the 8th century can be seen at ALL SAINTS' CHURCH, BRIXWORTH, where a vaulted corridor similar in function to the ring crypt is attached to the outside face of the apse. Access was gained by doorways on each side of the apse.

The outer crypt rapidly became more complicated and extensive, providing multiple oratories and tortuous passages answering the needs of an increasingly complex liturgy, as illustrated by the abbey church at Saint-Philbert-de-Grand-Lieu (Loire-Atlantique). The first church on this site was built between 814 and 819. About 836 the original east end was rebuilt with a crypt beneath the apse to contain the body of St Philibert. Shortly afterwards the whole eastern arm was surrounded by a corridor with several apses protruding from it, the whole construction on the same level as the crypt and connected to it by a cruciform vestibule beneath the apse of the upper church. The outer crypts of the abbeys of St Germain at Auxerre (841–59; *see* AUXERRE, §2) and St Pierre at Flavigny-sur-Ozerain (864–78; Côte d'Or) are similar to Saint-Philbert-de-Grand-Lieu insofar as they surround earlier crypts that house important relics. They are, however, much more elaborate, being two-storey constructions, and their eastern extremities consist of single rotundas. The notion of upper and lower crypts appears strange, but contemporary texts refer to them as *cryptae inferiores* and *cryptae superiores*, and although an upper crypt might be above ground level it retains the appearance of a crypt, being small-scale, vaulted and, above all, separated from the main body of the church.

Towards the mid-10th century a specific type of purpose-built, two-storey outer crypt was created in Lotharingia associated with the ORDER OF GORZE reform movement, which disseminated new, more rigorous monastic customs to abbeys and convents in the region and further afield. The liturgy promoted by the Gorze reform

1. Ring crypt, Old St Peter's, Rome, late 6th century AD; isometric reconstruction

appears to have required abbey churches to have two-storey outer crypts in order to perform complex rituals pertaining particularly to the celebration of the Crucifixion, Deposition and Resurrection. The Ottonian abbey church at Gorze has not survived, and the earliest example of an outer crypt inspired by Gorze appears at St Maximin in Trier (consecrated 952; destr. 1674), which is known only from excavations and a 17th-century engraving (for drawings, see Heitz). It consisted of a three-aisled, groin-vaulted upper crypt divided by arcades of three bays. The wider lower crypt consisted of five barrel-vaulted aisles. In comparison with the Carolingian crypts it was ordered and coherent and may be seen as an architectural entity in its own right. Although the construction of outer crypts was linked to the monastic reform, the individual designs differed considerably. For example, a surviving, almost centrally planned, single-storey crypt was erected at St Emmeram in Regensburg (c. 980) and a five-aisled, single-storey version was built at Essen Abbey (now Minster; c. 965). One common characteristic is their structural independence from the main body of the church, like miniature chapels barely linked to the eastern end of the abbey church. The outer crypt continued to be popular until the second half of the 11th century. A particularly good example from the middle years of the century is the replacement crypt at Essen Abbey. Of the original two storeys only the lower crypt survives, consisting of five groin-vaulted aisles supported on columns, with the middle

bays of the outermost aisles left open as octagonal wells connecting with the upper crypt.

The architectural innovations that introduced the Romanesque style in the 11th century affected the design of crypts (see ROMANESQUE, §II, 2(ii)). In Lotharingia a small group heralded one aspect of the style with highly original pier forms: St Martin (c. 1050), Emmerich, the Pieterskerk (consecrated 1048), Utrecht, and St Lebuïnus (1040), Deventer, have small three-aisled, four-bay crypts unremarkable in plan yet with interesting piers. At St Martin there are three pairs of piers: the westernmost has four attached shafts to each pier, the middle has eight and the easternmost sixteen. At the Pieterskerk and St Libuinus the piers are columnar yet decorated with complex geometric grooved patterns, mainly zigzag and helical. It is significant that these otherwise plain churches should display such sophistication in the designs of their crypts, using forms and patterns that, towards the end of the 11th century, were being used on the main arcades of the greater churches of France and Anglo-Norman Britain.

Another development in crypt design related to the emergence of Romanesque occurred first in France. With ancestry going back to the Carolingian annular crypt and such outer crypts as that of Saint-Philbert-de-Grand-Lieu, the Romanesque ambulatory with radiating chapels was first used in the design of crypts. This consists of a groin-vaulted hall with an apsidal end bordered by aisles carried round the apse to form the ambulatory. Protruding from the ambulatory are symmetrically arranged chapels. The principal early examples occur at St Pierre-le-Vif (920–40; destr.), Sens (Yonne); Thérouanne Cathedral (mid-10th century; destr.; Pas-de-Calais); Clermont-Ferrand Cathedral (consecrated 964; destr.; Puy-de-Dôme); St Philibert (960–79), Tournus (Saône-et-Loire); and St Aignan (989–1029), Orléans (Loiret). The last three examples are, or were, of two storeys, the upper storey forming the main sanctuary of the church. The form became common in major churches during the 11th and 12th centuries.

2. LATER DEVELOPMENTS. By the late 11th century the cult of relics was no longer associated solely with crypts; the growing popularity of pilgrimages and their economic importance tended to bring the veneration of relics into the main body of the church. Nevertheless, the crypt remained an important element in major churches, serving to increase the number of altars and continuing to play a part in liturgical customs. Crypts tended to become much larger and less subdivided. These hall-crypts were divided into square, groin-vaulted bays supported on free-standing columns, in some cases covering very large areas. The earliest hall-crypt, and one of the largest, is at Speyer Cathedral (*c.* 1030–61; see fig. 2), covering the area of the east end and transepts; its spaciousness articulated by dozens of columns with cushion capitals supporting ashlar transverse arches, it is one of the most impressive monuments of Romanesque architecture. Archbishop Anselm's crypt at Canterbury Cathedral (1096–1130) also covers a vast area: the plan, reflecting the choir above, is of the ambulatory with radiating chapels type, and it also covers the area of the eastern transepts. About 30 columns and 26 piers support the vaulting. Large Romanesque crypts survive in France at Auxerre Cathedral (begun 1023), with

2. Hall-crypt, Speyer Cathedral, *c.* 1030–61

early Romanesque quadrilobe piers and soffit rolls, and at St Eutrope (late 11th century), Saintes, in a more developed form of the same technique.

In southern Europe and especially Italy many churches were provided with 'raised crypts' during the 11th and 12th centuries. This type is accommodated in the chancel of the church only slightly below the level of the nave floor. The high altar is situated above it and reached by steps. The crypt is often open to the nave. Among the most remarkable of the numerous surviving examples are S Miniato al Monte (second half of the 12th century), Florence; Modena Cathedral (1099–1106); S Zeno (*c.* 1122), Verona; and a particularly expansive version at Parma Cathedral (mid-12th century).

By the late 12th century crypts were no longer in fashion and were rarely built. In the Gothic period such functions as the cult of relics were transferred from the crypt to the choir. It is partly for this reason that early choirs were often extended and newly built choirs were larger than their Romanesque counterparts.

Crypts did not recover an important liturgical role in the post-medieval period. An exception to this rule is Bramante's Tempietto in the cloister of S Pietro in Montorio (1502), Rome, which incorporates a small crypt (remodelled 1628) marking the site of St Peter's martyrdom in the centre of the circular building. A fenestella in the floor of the church communicates with the crypt, probably a deliberate reference to Early Christian practice. Similarly, the association of crypts with Early Christian and medieval churches brought about an attempted revival during the second half of the 16th century as an expression of the Counter-Reformation. Notable examples are Pellegrino Tibaldi's confessio at Milan Cathedral (1570); Domenico Fontana's crib crypt (from 1581) in the Sistine chapel at S Maria Maggiore, Rome; and Carlo Maderno's crypt (*c.* 1604) at S Susanna, Rome.

The purely funerary purposes of crypts survived into the modern period in major European churches. At St Paul's Cathedral (1675–1711), London, by Christopher Wren, the crypt extends under the whole church. Massive piers support groin and barrel vaults, and the vault at the crossing is supported on a circle of eight Tuscan columns. The crypt is filled with fine monuments and tombs commemorating famous national personages.

The 20th century has very few examples of crypts. Edwin Lutyens's crypt to the Roman Catholic cathedral of Liverpool, as projected between 1933 and 1940, consists of three large aisled chapels, vaulted with red engineering brick. The perfectly turned vaults and the Penrith granite walls and dressings are an impressive, if fragmentary, testimony to an inspired and important architectural design. Among the many memorials to World War II, the Deportation Memorial (completed 1962) in the Ile de la Cité, Paris, was designed by Georges-Henri Pingusson in the form of a crypt. It consists of a long subterranean corridor lined with 200,000 glass rods representing the French victims who died in Nazi concentration camps. At its entrance is the tomb of the Unknown Prisoner. The small doorway is closed by a grille and preceded by a hexagonal vestibule. It is essentially designed for pilgrims, and the architect has chosen, perhaps unconsciously, an early medieval layout with confessio, fenestella and vestibule with three access corridors ensuring the smooth circulation of pilgrims and ceremonial processions.

See also CHURCH, §II, 3(i).

BIBLIOGRAPHY

B. Fletcher: *A History of Architecture . . . being a Comparative View of the Historicist Styles from the Earliest Period* (London, 1896); rev. as *A History of Architecture on the Comparative Method* (London, 5/1905); rev. by J. Musgrove (London, 19/1987)

F. Deshoulières: 'Le Mystère de l'Eglise de Déols (Indre)', *Bull. Mnmtl*, xcvi (1937), pp. 45–53

A. Grabar: *Martyrium: Recherches sur le culte des reliques et l'art chrétien antique*, 2 vols (Paris, 1943–6)

J. Hubert: '*Cryptae Inferiores* et *Cryptae Superiores* dans l'architecture religieuse de l'époque carolingienne', *Mélanges d'histoire du Moyen Age dédiés à la mémoire de Louis Halphen* (Paris, 1951), pp. 351–7

K. J. Conant: *Carolingian and Romanesque Architecture, 800–1200*, Pelican Hist. A. (Harmondsworth, 1959, rev. 2/1974)

'War Memorial, Paris: A Monument to the French Victims of Nazi Concentration Camps', *Archit. Rev.* [London], cxxxiii/791 (Jan 1963), pp. 186–9

R. Krautheimer: *Early Christian and Byzantine Architecture*, Pelican Hist. A. (Harmondsworth, 1965, rev. 2/1975)

H. M. Taylor and J. Taylor: *Anglo-Saxon Architecture*, 3 vols (Cambridge, 1965–78)

F. Oswald and others: *Vorromanische Kirchenbauten* (Munich, 1966)

W. Sanderson: 'Monastic Reform in Lorraine and the Architecture of the Outer Crypt, 950–1100', *Trans. Amer. Philos. Soc.*, n. s., lxi/6 (1971), pp. 3–36

M. Magni: 'Cryptes du Haut Moyen Age en Italie: Problèmes de typologie du IXe jusqu'au début du XIe siècle', *Cah. Archéol.*, xxviii (1979), pp. 41–85

J. S. Curl: *A Celebration of Death: An Introduction to Some of the Buildings, Monuments and Settings of Funerary Architecture in the West European Tradition* (London, 1980)

C. Heitz: *L'Architecture religieuse carolingienne: Les Formes et leurs fonctions* (Paris, 1980)

J. Summerson: 'Arches of Triumph: The Design for Liverpool Cathedral', *Lutyens: The Work of the English Architect Sir Edwin Lutyens (1869–1944)* (exh. cat., London, Hayward Gal., 1981), pp. 45–52

E. C. Fernie: *The Architecture of the Anglo-Saxons* (London, 1983)

STEPHEN HEYWOOD

Cryptoporticus. Enclosed portico, underground passage or a gallery enclosed by walls with windows.

☐

Csaba, Vilmos Perlrott. *See* PERLROTT CSABA, VILMOS.

Csáky, Joseph [József] (*b* Szeged, 18 March 1888; *d* Paris, 1 May 1971). French sculptor of Hungarian birth. He studied at the school of Decorative Arts in Budapest from 1904 to 1905. In 1908 he went to Paris and settled in the block of studios La Ruche, where he was a neighbour of Fernand Léger, Alexander Archipenko, Henri Laurens, Marc Chagall and Chaim Soutine. He joined the Cubist movement in 1911, and he was included by Marcel Duchamp in the Salon de la Section d'Or in 1912. Only three of his pre-1914 sculptures survive, two *Heads* (e.g. 1914; Saint-Etienne, Mus. A. & Indust.) and a *Clothed Figure* (1913; Paris, Pompidou), which show a progression from a style still influenced by Rodin to a blocklike simplification and Cubist faceting. Volunteering for the French Army in 1914, he was unable to make any more sculptures until his return to Paris in 1919, when he acquired French citizenship; his immediate post-war work was much more abstract. After making in 1919 several columnar sculptures with a Léger-like dynamic, tumbling accumulation of pure cylinders, cones, spheres and discs,

he began to make a series of bas-reliefs, heads and figures of an almost crystalline structure, sometimes completely symmetrical; smooth, flat planes and straight edges are contrasted with meandering curves. This phase, related to Art Deco and to ancient Egyptian and Assyrian art, lasted until the late 1920s; his later sculptures, partly under the influence of Laurens, were of figures and animals in a more figurative, curvilinear and rhythmical style.

BIBLIOGRAPHY

D. Karshan: *Csáky* (Paris, 1973)

RONALD ALLEY

Csók, István (*b* Sáregres, 13 Feb 1865; *d* Budapest, 1 Feb 1961). Hungarian painter. He studied (1882–5) at the Academy of Fine Arts in Budapest, then (1886–7) at the Akademie in Munich, and finally (1888) attended the Académie Julian in Paris. In 1890 he returned to Munich, where he painted *Holy Communion* (1890; Budapest, N.G.) in a style reminiscent of the refined Naturalism of the French painter Jules Bastien-Lepage. The somewhat more sentimental *Orphans* (1891; Budapest, N.G.) is another work in this spirit. Csók's large, colourful history painting, *Erzsébet Báthory* (1895; destr., see Farkas, pl. 9), was produced for an exhibition in Budapest in 1896 to commemorate a thousand years of Hungarian statehood. Besides its Romantic qualities, this picture also reveals the influence of German *Jugendstil*.

From 1897 Csók spent three summers working at NAGYBÁNYA COLONY, primarily concerned with the problems of *plein-air* painting, and taking peasant life as one of his main themes. From 1903 to 1910 Csók was in Paris: here he painted one of his most accomplished works, *Studio Corner* (1905; Budapest, N.G.), which combines a self-portrait of the artist at work, a nude study of the reclining model, and a still-life of flowers, drapery and other foreground objects. Each summer he returned to Hungary where some of his most constant subjects were the country girls of the Sokác, in their brilliantly coloured folk costumes (e.g. *Young Sokác Bride*; *c.* 1910, untraced, see Farkas, pl. 23). Returning to Hungary permanently in 1910, Csók painted some striking interiors and figure scenes: especially charming are the pictures of his daughter *Züzü with a Rooster* (1912) and *Züzü's Christmas* (1914; both Budapest, N.G.). From this time Csók's style was characterized by a vigorous brushstroke and brilliant colours. His later work also includes some notable landscapes, especially powerful impressions of sky and water observed from the shores of Lake Balaton (e.g. *Rainbow over Lake Balaton*; 1930, Budapest, N.G.). From 1923 to 1932 he was a professor at the Academy of Fine Arts, Budapest. In the late triptych *War and Peace* (1951; Budapest, N.G.), symbolic scenes of death and destruction enclose a boldly painted rural idyll based on Csók's composition of 1890, *Haymakers* (Budapest, N.G.).

WRITINGS

Emlékezéseim [My reminiscences] (Budapest, 1945)

BIBLIOGRAPHY

I. Farkas: *Csók István* (Budapest, 1957)

A. Székely: *Csók István* (Budapest, 1977)

MÁRIA SZOBOR-BERNÁTH

Csontváry (Kosztka), Tivadar (*b* Kisszeben [now Sabinov, Slovak Republic], 5 July 1853; *d* Budapest, 20 June 1919). Hungarian painter and draughtsman. He was born Tivadar Kosztka and adopted the name Csontváry in 1900. A practising chemist, he had a mystical experience at the age of 41, which gave him a sense of mission. He took up regular studies in art, determined to become the world's greatest *plein-air* painter with a reputation surpassing that of Raphael. Csontváry's mission was to legitimize the historical existence of the Hungarian nation through his art. His idiosyncratic world view and his sense of vocation, which concentrated all his efforts into a single aim, underline the grandeur of his oeuvre; he asserted artistic sovereignty by disregarding all rules, and he defied attempts to categorize him as a naive painter.

For a short period Csontváry studied art intensively, first in Budapest (at Simon Hollósy's School, 1894–5), then in Munich, in Paris (at the Académie Julian) and in Düsseldorf. His training is evident in some virtuoso drawings made during his time at the academies (Pécs, Csontváry Mus.). Yet, as he later stated in his autobiography, he still considered nature to have been his real master. From 1895 he perfected his basic techniques by painting popular tourist motifs in Pompeii, in Taormina, on the

Dalmatian coast and in Serbia. During what is considered his preparatory period he painted such important pictures as his *Self-portrait* (Budapest, N.G.), *Moonlight Night in Taormina* (Budapest, priv. col., see Lehel) and *Almond Blossoms in Taormina* (Pécs, Csontváry Mus.). These early naturalistic paintings already reveal his feel for colour.

Csontváry's prime concern was *plein-air* painting, and two tendencies can be discerned in his work: the pantheistic appraisal of the beauty of nature, as in the *View of Selmecbánya* (1902; Budapest, N.G.), and the projection of his psychic responses on to natural scenes, as in *Castellamare di Stabia* (1902; Pécs, Csontváry Mus.). The two tendencies are united in his *Storm on the Great Hortobágy* (1903; Pécs, Csontváry Mus.), a painting suffused with a romantic atmosphere. This is also the last picture from his preparatory period. In a number of pictures he was concerned with unusual effects of light, as in *Electricity Works in Jajce at Night* (1903) and *Trees in Jajce Illuminated by Electric Lights* (1903; both Pécs, Csontváry Mus.).

Csontváry spent 1903 studying in the great museums of western Europe, then he decided to travel to Bethlehem and paint, from local observation, a large-scale composition of the birth of Jesus, with the avowed aim of surpassing the great masters of the Renaissance. At one

Tivadar Csontváry: *Solitary Cedar*, oil on canvas, 1.94×2.48 m, 1907 (Pécs, Csontváry Museum)

point during the sea passage his life was endangered; the derangement induced by this experience is reflected in the expressive, visionary *Supplicating Saviour* (1904; Pécs, Csontváry Mus.), which is a concealed self-portrait. He followed this with *At the Entrance to the Wailing Wall in Jerusalem* (1904; Pécs, Csontváry Mus.), a monumental composition with many figures, in which he articulated his strident social criticism. In an expressive, large-scale picture painted in the Tatra Mountains, *The Great Tar-Beck in the Tatras* (1905; Pécs, Csontváry Mus.), he came closest to the Secessionist style, which at the time dominated central Europe.

In 1905 Csontváry travelled to Athens, where he produced *Promenade in a Carriage at the New Moon in Athens* (Pécs, Csontváry Mus.), one of his most harmonious and aesthetically pleasing works. Following his mystical calling, he set out to seek great motifs in nature and to paint only monumental compositions. The first canvas in this series was *The Ruins of the Greek Theatre at Taormina* (1905; Budapest, N.G.), which was followed by the 32 sq. m *Baalbek* (1906; Pécs, Csontváry Mus.), a successful synthesis of realistic detail, Divisionist composition and decorative outlining: a grandiose summary of his idiosyncratic mythology. Csontváry believed this work to have surpassed that of the greatest artists, thereby legitimizing the European presence of the Hungarian nation and fulfilling his mission.

In 1907 an exhibition of Csontváry's work was held in Paris, and, enthused by its apparent success, he travelled to Lebanon. There he painted the 'icons' of his syncretic world view, *The Pilgrimage to the Cedars in Lebanon* (Budapest, N.G.) and the *Solitary Cedar* (Pécs, Csontváry Mus., see fig.), both suggestive of the tragic isolation of the artist. These cedar pictures are generally considered to be forerunners of Surrealism. His last paintings are grandiose attempts to create a monumental style (*The Well of Mary in Nazareth*, 1908) and symbolic messages from his dream world (*Joy-ride at the Seaside*, 1909; both Pécs, Csontváry Mus.). After 1910 Csontváry's psychosis became worse, and, although his symbolic drawings are still aesthetically pleasing in their detail, their content is increasingly schizoid. In one charcoal drawing, for example, he represented his own apotheosis: *The Arrival of the Magyars* (untraced, see Lehel) shows the artist leading the incoming Hungarian tribes on the back of a camel. He also published pamphlets in which he voiced his opposition to modernity and asserted his genius (*Energia és művészet*, 'Energy and art', 1912, and *A lángész*, 'Men of genius', 1913).

Although Csontváry exhibited works in Budapest in 1905, 1908 and 1910, and in Paris in 1907, he was not appreciated by his contemporaries and was only truly discovered at a posthumous exhibition devoted to him in 1930 at the Ernst Museum in Budapest. His paintings met with great approval at an exhibition in Paris in 1949 and at the Exposition Universelle in Brussels in 1958, but in Hungary his significance was not fully understood until exhibitions held in Székesfehérvár (1963) and at the Hungarian National Gallery, Budapest (1964). Csontváry's expressive Symbolist art, which was influenced to some extent by the stylistic aims of the Secession and blends elements of Post-Impressionism and Divisionism in an idiosyncratic manner, came to be seen as a great achievement in Hungarian art.

UNPUBLISHED SOURCES
Pécs, Csontváry Mus. [autobiographical fragments]

WRITINGS
Energia és művészet: A kultur ember tévedése [Energy and art: the mistake of men of culture] (Budapest, 1912)
A lángész: Ki lehet és ki nem lehet zseni [Men of genius: he who can and he who cannot become a genius] (Budapest, 1913)

BIBLIOGRAPHY
F. Lehel: *Csontváry Tivadar, a poszt-impresszionizmus magyar előfutára* [Tivadar Csontváry, Hungarian forerunner of Post-Impressionism] (Paris, 1931)
F. Gachot: *Csontváry* (Budapest, 1944)
J. Marcel and A. Mezei: 'Csontváry, 1853–1919', *Cah. A.*, 1 (1949), pp. 89–98
E. Ybl: *Csontváry Tivadar* (Budapest, 1958) [in Hung. and Eng.]
M. Brion: 'Czontváry, le rêveur éveillé', *Jard. A.*, 113 (April 1964), pp. 18–25
L. Németh: *Csontváry Kosztka Tivadar* (Budapest, 1964, rev. 1971) [in Hung., Eng., Ger. and Fr.; with cat. of works]
G. Jászai: *Csontváry kritikai jegyzetek* [Critical notes on Csontváry] (Munich, 1965)
R. Pertorini: *Csontváry patográfiája* [The pathography of Csontváry] (Budapest, 1966)
O. Mezei and others: 'Csontváry', *Müvészet*, 20 (Jan 1979), pp. 2–30
L. Németh: *Baalbek* (Budapest, 1980)
J. Szabó: 'Cedrus aeternitatis hieroglyphicum' [Iconology of a natural motif], *Acta Hist. A. Acad. Sci. Hung.*, xxvi/1–2 (1981), pp. 3–127

LAJOS NÉMETH

Ctesiphon. *See* KTESIPHON.

Cualladó, Gabriel (*b* Massanassa, nr Valencia, 20 May 1925). Spanish photographer. He began photographing as an amateur *c.* 1956 and in 1959 joined the Palangana group of photographers in Madrid. Working predominantly in black and white, he based most of his work on portraits of people in their daily lives, portrayed with a poetic intimacy, for example *Little Girl on Path* (1957, see 1985 Bilbao exh. cat., p. 15). Cualladó's work has been widely published in such magazines as *Stern*, *Photographies* and *Photo-Vision*, and he has been awarded a number of prizes.

BIBLIOGRAPHY
Gabriel Cualladó (exh. cat. by L. Revenga, Bilbao, Mus. B.A., 1985)
Gabriel Cualladó: Fotografías (exh. cat. by L. Revenga, Madrid, Mus. A. Contemp., 1985)

JOAN FONTCUBERTA

Cuba. *See* QUBA (i).

Cuba, Republic of. Country situated in the Caribbean Sea between North and South America, near the Tropic of Cancer. It comprises over 1600 cays (low coral banks) and islands, with a total land area of 110,922 sq. km. The main island, the largest of the Caribbean islands, is known as Isla de la Juventud (see fig. 1). The capital is HAVANA.

See also CARIBBEAN ISLANDS.

I. Introduction. II. Cultures. III. Architecture. IV. Painting, graphic arts and sculpture. V. Furniture. VI. Ceramics. VII. Metalwork. VIII. Patronage. IX. Art institutions.

I. Introduction.

Cuba is characterized by fertile territory that until the 19th century was covered with forests of valuable timber; these have been replaced by orchards and extensive plantations of sugar cane, tobacco and coffee. The mountains, of

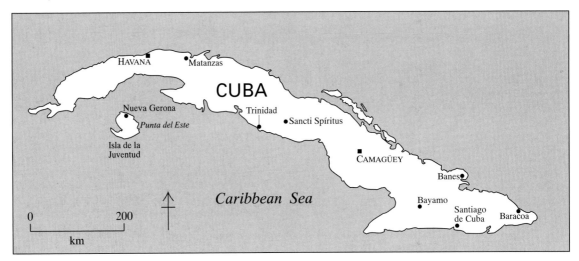

1. Map of Cuba; those sites with separate entries in this dictionary are distinguished by CROSS-REFERENCE type

moderate height, include the Guaniguanico range, the Sierra de los Organos and the Sierra del Rosario in the west; the Sierra del Escambray in the centre; and the Sierra Maestra in the east. The most important rivers are the Cayagualeje, Almendares, Mayabeque, Hatiguanico, Canimar, Sagua la Grande, Toa and Cauto. The climate is moist and subtropical, and there are two main seasons: dry, from November to April, and rainy, from May to October. The islands are also sporadically swept by hurricanes and cyclones.

When Christopher Columbus landed in 1492 in Cuba, the native population consisted of Ciboney and Taino peoples (*see* §II, 1 below). In 1510 Governor Diego Velázquez took possession of the islands and went on to found the first seven towns: Baracoa, Santiago de Cuba, Bayamo, Puerto Príncipe, Sancti Spíritus, Trinidad and Havana. The *encomienda* system of forced labour exploited the indigenous population, ultimately leading to its extinction.

During the 16th and 17th centuries Cuba's economy had been determined by the direct extraction of natural resources to supply the Spanish fleet, but the rapidly increasing importation of African slaves in the 18th century inaugurated the plantation phase, with the growing of coffee, tobacco and sugar cane. The capture of Havana by the English in 1762, the reforms introduced by the Spanish ruler Charles III (*reg* 1759–88) and the Haitian Revolution (1804) all made Cuba a prosperous island with a class of educated and refined Creole (native-born white) landowners who fostered the arts and letters. The need to promote exports to neighbouring countries, particularly the USA, and the liberation of Latin America from colonial rule encouraged independence and reform movements led by Félix Varela, José Antonio Saco and Domingo Delmonte. In 1868 Carlos Manuel de Céspedes freed slaves, leading to a ten-year war.

After a truce (the Pact of El Zanjón) in 1878, José Martí created the ideological basis of the movement that culminated in the War of Independence of 1895. However, in 1898 the USA intervened and occupied Cuba until 1902, marking the beginning of the Republican phase.

This was characterized by a new economic and political dependence of the country, maintained by the dictatorships of Gerardo Machado y Morales (1925–33) and of Fulgencio Batista (1952–9). In 1953 Fidel Castro led a revolutionary guerrilla movement that succeeded in ousting the Batista regime in 1959. In 1961 the Socialist character of the Cuban state was established. The country was divided into 14 provinces in 1976, and by 1990 the population had exceeded 10 million. In the 1990s the demise of the USSR led to economic difficulties and an increase in the number of artists leaving the country.

BIBLIOGRAPHY
I. Wright: *The Early History of Cuba, 1492–1586* (New York, 1916)
F. Portuondo: *Historia de Cuba, 1492–1898* (Havana, 1957)
H. Thomas: *Storia di Cuba, 1762–1970* (Turin, 1970)
M. Moreno Fraginals: *El ingenio* (Havana, 1978)
J. M. Macías: *Diccionario cubano* (Havana, 1986)
F. López Segrera: *Sociología de la colonia y la neocolonia cubana, 1510–1959* (Havana, 1989)

ROBERTO SEGRE

II. Cultures.

1. Indigenous. 2. Afro-Caribbean.

1. INDIGENOUS. The small indigenous population of Cuba was exterminated by the colonizing Spaniards as early as the 17th century. Their contribution to Cuban culture had been limited to rural dwellings, some utensils, crops, eating customs and the use of tobacco, although many place names and other terms are derived from indigenous language. Two groups of people co-existed in Cuba at the time of the arrival of the Europeans. The first group, sometimes known as Ciboney, probably arrived *c*. 4000 BC. Their origin is unknown, although the most commonly accepted hypothesis links them to Central America. They were fishers, hunters and gatherers who lived naked in caves, usually in coastal mangrove swamps; their older sites are characterized by a stone-tool industry, though at later sites shell implements were more commonly used. This group also created a geometric style

expressed in carved stone clubs, stone-carvings and extraordinary rock paintings. The most important rock art site is Cave 1 at Punta del Este, Isla de la Juventud, which is painted with hundreds of designs in red and black with a predominance of concentric circles (see fig. 2).

The other group were the Arawak Taínos, who came from the Orinoco Delta *c.* AD 500. These people were farmers who lived in circular or rectangular huts of wood and straw and shared the figurative art style common to the Greater Antilles (*see* individual island surveys). Their ceramics included unpainted bowls modelled with figures on the handles as well as figurines with strongly marked feminine features. Among their wood products were the famous *dujos* (carved anthropomorphic or zoomorphic ceremonial seats), ritual tables and trays, decorated oars and *zemis*, images of gods carved in stone, shell and bone. Some *zemis* have been identified with the myths sung during *areytos*, ceremonies accompanied by dancing and music. Other aesthetic–religious objects include small pendant figures and beads, as well as sticks (made of manatee ribs and carved with faces) used to induce 'purifying' vomiting in *cohoba* ceremonies, at which a hallucinogenic powder was inhaled. Wooden anthropomorphic figures were made to hold the drug before inhalation. The Taínos also made polished stone axes (celts), occasionally carved with anthropomorphic figures. However, no examples of *trigonolitos*, the triangular carved stones typically made by the Arawaks of the Antilles, have been found in Cuba, although petroglyphs and rock paintings are known. The principal collections of indigenous Cuban art are held by the Museo Antropológico Montané, Havana, the Museo de los Indios Cubanos, Banes, the Universidad de Oriente, Santiago de Cuba and the Smithsonian Institution, Washington, DC.

BIBLIOGRAPHY
J. Juan Arrom: *Mitología y artes prehispánicas de las Antillas* (Mexico City, 1975)
A. Núñez Jiménez: *Cuba: Dibujos rupestres* (Lima, 1975)
G. Mosquera: *Exploraciones en la plástica cubana* (Havana, 1983)
R. Dacal Moure and L. Domínguez Gonzáles: 'El arte agroalfarero de Cuba', *Revolución & Cult.*, ii (1988), pp. 32–7

2. AFRO-CARIBBEAN. Cuba's national culture preserves some of the purest and most varied traditions of the entire African diaspora. Africans were first brought to Cuba as slaves in the 16th century and were imported in increasing numbers with the growth of the sugar and coffee plantations in the 19th century. It is calculated that *c.* 800,000 Africans from very diverse backgrounds were brought as slaves, although from early times there were also free blacks and mulattos (people of mixed race) who worked as craftspeople in the cities. Despite a process of creolization that helped the slaves adapt to the new milieu, at the peak of sugar production they were exploited at a pace that quickly shortened their lives. Rebellions and flights on the part of the slaves were initially unsuccessful because of the islands' geography and a lack of organization. However, at the end of the 18th century a Cuban national consciousness shared by blacks, mulattos and white creoles began to take shape. Despite the fear of a 'Cuban Haiti' coming into existence—a decisive factor in retarding the Wars of Independence—when these struggles were eventually initiated by the landowners they united all

2. Central motif of Ciboney rock painting, Cave 1, Punta del Este, Isla de la Juventud, Cuba, ?*c.* AD 800

classes and ethnic groups; freed slaves made up 70% of the rebel troops. Such anti-colonial exploits acquired an increasingly popular character and became a crucible in which the national identity was fused. The final abolition of slavery in 1886 contributed further to this identity and helped to forge a culture in which the dominant Western component was conditioned from within by Black African components.

In the fine arts, the African component was expressed in some characteristics of painting at the end of the 1920s when modernism appeared on the Cuban scene. It was not, however, until the 1940s that WIFREDO LAM created a truly Afro-Cuban vision. Lam was followed by Roberto Diago (1920–57), another painter, and in the mid-1950s AGUSTÍN CÁRDENAS put the stamp of African sensibility on abstract sculpture. Around the mid-1960s Manuel Mendive (*b* 1944) began a series of paintings, sculptures, performances and mixed-media works based particularly on myths. From the early 1980s José Bedia (*b* 1959), Juan Francisco Elso (1956–88), Marta María Pérez (*b* 1959), Ricardo Rodríguez Brey (*b* 1955) and Santiago Rodríguez Olazábal (*b* 1955) based their work on an Afro-Cuban world view. Explicit African elements can be discerned in the works of other artists, but from the 1960s a parallel 'Africanism' of a superficial and often touristic nature also flourished.

The four main Afro-Cuban religious traditions, known as 'Rules', perpetuate African traditions with a certain purity. These groupings arose from the *cabildos de nación*, which had come into being under Spanish colonialism, grouping together Africans of the same ethnic background, but gradually disappeared in the 20th century. Afro-Cuban religions and societies are notable for their popular character, even though all social groups and races take part in them, and they lack a centralized ecclesiastical organization or hierarchy, so that their 'churches' are usually the believers' own houses. Although these cults mingle diverse elements of popular Roman Catholicism and European spiritualism, their essence, structure and ritual remain very close to specific African sources. Thus, the best-known of these religions, the *Santería* (Rule of Ocha), is an adaptation of the religion of the YORUBA people, which is based on the cult of a pantheon of deities known as *orishas*. It is related to the *Candomblé*, *Xango* and *Batuque* religions of Brazil (*see* BRAZIL, §III) and the *Shango* cult of Trinidad (*see* TRINIDAD AND TOBAGO, §II, 2). Although the deities have been syncretized with Catholic saints and types of the Virgin, they retain their personal mythological features; their cults are performed as in Yoruba culture through the settling of their powers in receptacles, personal initiation, spirit-possession during dances, propitiatory sacrifices and the belief in the intervention of the gods in daily life and their communication with, and advice to, humans. In Cuba, however, the clan, tribal and regional character of the African religion has been lost in the synthesis of the different cults that has taken place. Nonetheless, Cuba is the only country of the African diaspora to have preserved the *babalaos*, high priests of prophecy who operate through the system of *Ifá*, based on a body of myths. The oral literature, dances, songs and music accumulated and recreated in the ritual of the *Santería* are extremely rich; in addition, archaic Yoruba has been retained as the ritual language.

The outstanding cult-related artefacts are the altars, complex installations comprising arrangements of the most diverse objects, freely invested with new meanings to create a complex symbolic and aesthetic vocabulary in which religious canons do not obstruct the formation of a new vernacular uniting the traditional and the contemporary. Thus, while various ritual implements and divine attributes retain Yoruba elements, these are often reinterpreted. For the Yoruba, *batá* drums are the drums of Sango, but in Cuba they are used in the rites for all the deities. These hour-glass-shaped, two-membrane instruments are of different sizes, called *ayá*, *atótele* and *okónkolo*, and are struck with the bare hand. Of exclusively religious use, they are inhabited by a power or spirit called *Aña*. Also of great interest are the bead-embroidered cloths that decorate the drums, images of the gods Elegguá (see fig. 3)

and Changó, necklaces, metal objects related to Oggún, Inle, Ochosi and other deities, ritual fly-whisks, garments and initiation thrones. This type of worship is characteristic of the western half of Cuba, from where it spread to the remainder of the island. The widespread nature of this practice has led to the dissemination of 'pure' forms that have spread with Cuban emigration into the USA, Latin America and Spain, as well as to hybridization with popular spiritualism within Cuba.

The Arará Rule is the religion of the Ewe-fon of Benin, Togo and Ghana, practised in Cuba without being structured in 'houses', as it is in Brazil and Trinidad. Proximity and prolonged contact have made the Yoruba and Ewe-fon cultures very similar, and this convergence continued in Cuba, where the Arará Rule and the Rule of Ocha have tended to blend. Fongbé is used as the ritual language, special songs, dances, music and instruments are employed, and a pantheon like that of the Rule of Ocha is worshipped with a similar liturgy. The drums, engraved and painted in the Fon style, are particularly notable. The Rule of Palo Monte originates in the Kongo *minkisi* (spirit) cult of Zaïre, Congo, Angola and other regions, but outside Africa it exists in a fully structured form only in Cuba. The spirit is held by its owner in a receptacle, together with materials that contain and direct it; during songs it enters the owner to counsel him. There is no mythology, but there is a complicated use of magic and herbalism. Kikongo mixed with Spanish is used as the ritual language, and unique songs, music and instruments are employed. The Rule of Palo Monte is divided into three sects known as *Mayombe*, *Briyumba* and *Kimbisa*: the last, created in the 19th century, combines the spirit worship and Catholicism in the Kongo cult, giving rise to 'Crossed Palo Monte', which spread to other sects. In Crossed Palo Monte Yoruba-type deities are set into *minkisi* receptacles, with additional borrowings from Catholicism; the liturgy, however, remains Kongo. Some wall paintings in the areas of worship represent curious popular painted versions of the Kongo concept of the universe. Wooden figures are

3. Afro-Caribbean Cuban images of Elegguá, cement, stone, cowrie shells, metal, feathers, ceramic bowls, h. *c.* 200–450 mm, early 20th century (Havana, Casa Africa)

also found, along with 'signatures', abstract ceremonial emblems drawn on the ground and the objects of worship. These symbols derive from writing systems of Kongo origin, developed in Mestizo Baroque style in Latin America, with the incorporation of Western elements. They also form the basis of the Haitian *vèvès* (*see* HAITI, §II, 2), the ground drawings of the Trinidadian Shouters, the 'Pontos riscados' of Brazil and the 'Ereniyó' system of the Abakuás, representing a complete and uniquely Afro-American graphic tradition.

The Abakuá Secret Society is a reconstitution of an African male secret society in the African diaspora. Based on the leopard society of the EJAGHAM, Efik, Efut and other peoples of the Cross River area of Nigeria and Cameroon, it provides the only true survival of masked dances as the incarnation of spirits; celebrated during funeral and initiation ceremonies, these dances involve predramatic performances. The Abakuá mystery is based on an esoteric power, *Ekue*, and the mythology surrounding the origin and possession of its secret by the society. Terms from Calabar languages form a ritual language, and there are also specific dances, songs and music. From a visual point of view, the clothing of the masked dancers, their sceptres and drums and the numerous stylized designs drawn on the ground, on cloths and on their bodies are the most interesting. These designs probably derive from the Nsibidi ideographic writing of Calabar, with Congolese and Western assimilations and creole inventions. The principal collections of Afro-Cuban artefacts are held at the Casa de Africa, Museo Histórico de Guanabacoa and Museo Municipal de Regla, all in Havana.

BIBLIOGRAPHY
R. Lachatañeré: *El sistema religioso de los lucumís y otras influencias africanas en Cuba* (Havana, 1940)
F. Ortiz: *Los bailes y el teatro de los negros en el folklore de Cuba* (Havana, 1951)
L. Cabrera: *El Monte* (Havana, 1954)
——: *La sociedad secreta Abakuá narrada por viejos adeptos* (Havana, 1958)
R. Bastide: *Les Amériques noires* (Paris, 1967)
L. Cabrera: *Anaforuana* (Madrid, 1975) [reproduces 512 signs of the 'Ereniyó' system and describes the Abakuá initiation ritual]
M. Dornbach: 'Gods in Earthenware Vessels', *Ethnog. Acad. Sci. Hung.*, xxvi (1977), pp. 285–308
L. Cabrera: *Reglas de Congo, Palo Monte, Mayombe* (Miami, 1979)
R. Martínez Furé: *Dialogos imaginarios* (Havana, 1979), pp. 79–238
P. Fatumbi Verger: *Orisha* (Paris, 1982) [text and pict. on the myths and ceremonies of main Yoruba gods in Africa and America]
R. Farris Thompson: *Flash of the Spirit* (New York 1983) [general study of traditional Afro-American art and its underlying religious philosophy]
R. L. López Valdés: *Componentes africanos en el etnos cubano* (Havana, 1985)
G. Mosquera: 'Africa dentro de la plástica caribeña', *Plástica del Caribe: Havana, 1989*
——: 'Africa in the Art of Latin America', *A. J.* [New York], li (1992), pp. 30–38

GERARDO MOSQUERA

III. Architecture.

1. COLONIAL PERIOD, 1514–1902. HAVANA was founded on its present site in 1519 and became the capital in 1552. By the end of the 16th century it had eclipsed Santo Domingo, on the island of Hispaniola, as the pivot of Spain's Caribbean fortifications. Such early structures as the Fortaleza Vieja (1537; destr.) were replaced by the Real Fuerza (1558–60) designed by Ochoa de Luyando on the model of the ideal Renaissance fort and built by the engineer Bartolomé Sánchez. As foreign incursions grew more serious, King Philip II of Spain employed Bautista ANTONELLI. He worked out a protective system for the entrance to Havana Bay with the large fortified towers of Los Tres Reyes del Morro and San Salvador de la Punta (both *c.* 1590), constructed by local master Juan de la Torre; the same model was subsequently applied to El Morro (1633) in Santiago de Cuba. Sixteenth-century buildings, especially military and naval barracks and service buildings, had heavy masonry walls and roofs of palm thatch. The same is true of the buildings of the religious orders, including the Franciscan Hospital (1544–58), Havana. The town hall and the prison (begun 1580) and the customs house (1582) were among the earliest public buildings in the city. Havana's oldest extant church, Espíritu Santo (dedicated 1638; façade 1674), the S Domingo (1643–4), the Franciscan monastery (1638–44) and the convent of S Clara de Asís (begun 1638) are all noted for their fine MUDÉJAR carpentry, profusely decorated in geometric patterns. Urban houses with enclosed, arcaded courtyards include the house of Don Martín Calvo de la Puerta (1679) on Calle Obrapía, which has an almost Rococo frame to its great portal; a mansion in Calle San Ignacio, also Havana; and the house of Diego Velázquez, Santiago de Cuba (both late 17th century). Bracketed *Mudéjar* timber roofs continued to be built during the 18th century, although there are examples of churches with transverse masonry arches to reinforce the nave arcades, as in the parish church of Guanabacoa (1714–21). The two-storey façade of S Francisco de Asís (1719–38) retains some of the severity of earlier Renaissance models, and the lower storeys of the high central tower, on which the Cuban architect José Arcés worked, is heavy and sober: the church (1730–45) of the hospital of S Francisco de Paula has a more typical Baroque two-storey façade from which cornices sweep up to a three-bell bellcote (*espadaña*). Although often unadorned, Cuban Baroque church towers are frequently characterized by pyramidal cupolas with an arched aedicula on each face and a pinnacle at each corner.

There were a number of cathedral projects in the 17th century, three of which were by Juan de la Torre. In 1789 the Jesuit church of La Compañía (begun 1748) was accorded cathedral status. Two figures associated with its development are the Spanish architect Pedro de Medina (1738–96) and a local engineer Antonio Fernández Trevejos (1764–1800). Kubler suggests that the outward-sweeping walls applied to the original centre section of the façade (destr.) may have been the work of Medina; its character is reminiscent of the work of Borromini and may have been executed in the 1760s. Trevejos and de Medina are also thought to have been responsible for two of Havana's finest colonial civic buildings: the Palacio de los Capitanes Generales (1776–92) and the Palacio del Segundo Cabo (1770–92), both on the Plaza de Armas. They are Neo-classical, with mezzanines between the ground and principal upper floors, reflecting Andalusian models. Similar houses include the Havana town houses of Don Mateo Pedroso (1780) and the Condesa de Reunión (1785), both of which have tile-roofed timber balconies above their mezzanine floors. The cathedral at Santiago de Cuba (destr. 1770) was rebuilt with a Baroque façade under the direction of Pedro Fernández from 1806; the present Neo-classical façade was remodelled in 1922.

In the 19th century colonial dependence on Spain persisted. However, Neo-classicism came to Cuba via a growth in trade with North America. The French influence is obvious in such buildings as the mid-century Teatro Tacon, Havana, which is built on an elliptical plan. In 1906 a hurricane destroyed many buildings. Notable surviving houses in Havana include the Aldama mansion (1840) by Manuel José Carrerá, Casa-Moré (1872) by Eugenio Rayneri y Piedra (1883–1960) and the Balaguer mansion (1873) by Pedro de Balboa.

2. REPUBLICAN PERIOD, 1902–59. Peninsular eclecticism persisted with neo-colonial references in such culturally symbolic buildings as the Centro Gallego (1907) by Paul Beleau. There was also a flourishing of Art Nouveau in Havana in the 1910s: typical examples include the house on the Loma del Mazo by Mario Rottland and the Cetro de Oro flats by Eugenio Dediot (1871–1931). More redolent of North American academicism are the Palacio Presidencial (1920) by Beleau and the monumental National Capitol (1929) by Eugenio Rayneri y Sorrentino, Raúl Otero and José María Bens (b 1893), both in Havana. The neo-colonial influence arising from close bonds with the USA is evident in Havana in the plateresque style tower of the Cuban Telephone Company (1928) by Leonardo Morales (1887–1965) and the Hotel Nacional (1930) by McKim, Mead and White. The Modern Movement made itself felt in Cuba in the 1920s and 1930s, initially through Art Deco, as in the Bacardi offices (1929) by Esteban Rodríguez Castell (b 1887) and the López

Serrano flats (1932) by Ricardo Mira (1898–1945) and Miguel Rosich. In the 1940s it was part of the assimilation of the repertory of forms of Rationalism, seen, for example, in Manuel Copado's flats in San Lázaro and houses by Rafael de Cárdenas (1902–57) in Miramar and by Emilio de Soto (1889–1961) on the Avenida de los Presidentes. Eugenio Batista (1900–92) was an influential teacher of architecture in the 1950s. In his Falla Bonet (1938) and Alvarez Tabio (1941) residences he introduced a 'regionalist' aspect to Rationalism, in accordance with the tropical climate and natural materials. Notable experiments in housing include the Noval house (1949) and the Vidaña house (1955) by Mario Romañach (1917–84). Such architects as Max Borges (b 1918) catered to the booming tourist trade. In Havana interesting public buildings include the Tribunal de Cuentas (1954) by Aquiles Capablanca (1907–62) and the Retiro Odontológico (1953) and Seguro del Médico (1955) by ANTONIO QUINTANA.

3. POST-REVOLUTIONARY PERIOD, 1959 AND AFTER. The social and economic transformations that followed the Revolution radically changed the direction of architecture. The need for mass housing, schools and hospitals fostered the use of industrialized building techniques. The best-known examples include the large, prefabricated structures built by groups led by FERNANDO SALINAS, such as his four-storey housing at Manicaragua, Las Villas (1963), and the Multiflex housing system. However, despite severely limited resources, Cuban architects of the 1960s produced memorable works in their search for a cultural identity, especially in a series of buildings for the Escuelas Nacionales de Arte (1961–5).

4. Ricardo Porro: Escuela Nacional de Bellas Artes, Cubanacán, Havana, 1961–3

Those by RICARDO PORRO are outstanding for their exploitation of short-span domes linked into amorphous clusters by barrel-vaulted corridors, all constructed in economical local materials (see fig. 4). Vittorio Garatti's ballet and music schools and that by ROBERTO GOTTARDI for drama subscribe to the same aesthetic, as does the Casa Cultura de Velasco (1965) by Walter Betancourt (1932–78), all of which are in or near Havana. Serialized components were also used by Salinas in the Oficinas de Mecánica Agrícola (1962) and, to a lesser extent, on José Antonio Echevarria University campus (begun 1960), the Palacio de las Convenciones (1977) by Antonio Quintana (*b* 1919) and in the Faculty of Farming and Animal Husbandry Sciences (1968) by Juan Tosca (*b* 1928), as well as the Coppelia ice-cream parlour (1966) by Mario Girona (*b* 1924). From the 1980s a generation of young professionals followed the path of contextualism in response to the abundant classical vocabulary provided by Havana's historical architecture. In Santiago de Cuba, José Antonio Choy (*b* 1949) built the Santiago Hotel (1990); in Havana new buildings were designed and constructed in the historical town centre by Eduardo Luis Rodríguez (*b* 1959), Emma Alvarez Tabio (*b* 1962), Juan Luis Morales (*b* 1960), Abel Rodríguez (*b* 1963) and Francisco Bedoya (*b* 1959).

BIBLIOGRAPHY

L. de Soto: *The Main Currents in Cuban Architecture* (New York, 1929)
D. Angulo Iñiguez, E. Marco Dorta and M. J. Buschiazzo: *Historia del arte hispano-americano*, 3 vols (Barcelona, 1945–56)
F. Prat Puig: *El prebarroco en Cuba* (Havana, 1947)
J. E. Weiss: *Arquitectura cubana contemporánea* (Havana, 1947)
——: *Medio siglo de arquitectura cubana* (Havana, 1950)
H.-R. Hitchcock: *Latin American Architecture since 1945* (New York, 1955)
G. Kubler and M. Soria: *Art and Architecture in Spain and Portugal and their American Dominions, 1500–1800*, Pelican Hist. A. (Harmondsworth, 1959), pp. 62–8, 165
J. E. Weiss: *La arquitectura cubana del siglo XIX* (Havana, 1960)
N. Quintana: 'Evolución histórica de la arquitectura en Cuba', *La enciclopedia de Cuba*, v (Madrid, 1974), pp. 1–115
J. E. Weiss: *La arquitectura colonial cubana*, i–ii (Havana, 1979)
R. Segre: *Arquitectura, historia y revolución* (Guadalajara, 1981)
E. Tejeira-Davis: *Roots of Modern Latin American Architecture: The Hispano-Caribbean Region from the Late 19th Century to the Recent Past* (Heidelberg, 1987)
L. Castedo: *Historia del arte ibero-americano*, 2 vols (Madrid, 1988)
E. Alvarez Tabio: *Vida, mansión y muerte de la burguesía cubana* (Havana, 1989)
R. Segre: *Aquitectura y urbanismo de la revolución cubana* (Havana, 1989)

ROBERTO SEGRE

IV. Painting, graphic arts and sculpture.

Apart from the rock paintings and carvings of the Native American population (*see* §II, 1 above), the earliest Cuban art works were 16th-century altarpieces and gravestones. Local bronze-casting and graphic art began in the 17th and 18th centuries respectively. Until the early 19th century Cuban art remained basically religious, consisting of altarpieces, paintings of Virgins and saints, all executed in the Baroque style, although there were also popular propaganda murals and decorative architectural paintings; all these forms continued into the 19th century. In the same century a special category of lithographs portraying local customs and other motifs was developed by the tobacco industry for use in packaging, while portrait painting, landscapes and other genres emerged. Academic painting gradually superseded the naive Baroque style, but colonial art remained derivative and imitative of European schools. It rarely achieved a distinctive character, although glimpses of originality are visible in the paintings of GUILLERMO COLLAZO. Only a few artists (the Spaniard VÍCTOR PATRICIO DE LANDALUZE being the best example) took a direct interest in the human and natural environment.

In the 20th century graphic arts declined, and painting and what little sculpture there was were fettered by the academic style. However, at the end of the 1920s modernism burst on to the Cuban scene as part of the critical movement of national regeneration that arose in opposition to the dictatorship of Gerardo Machado, American neo-colonial control and the consequent economic crisis. Leading figures included EDUARDO ABELA, Rafael Blanco (1885–1955), VÍCTOR MANUEL and Marcelo Pogolotti (1902–88). Their avant-garde activity, although also formally derived from diverse European movements, was driven by an enthusiasm for discovering and expressing qualities uniquely their own: a preoccupation with social issues, an interest in the workings of culture and a will to incorporate the popular into learned discourse. This new consciousness shattered the colonial vision and gave rise to a truly Cuban mode of expression. Among the prominent features of this movement are the expressive use of colour, the importance of the role of light, a quality of sensuality, a baroque style, a deeper exploration of the environment and an imaginative vision of popular origin. The writer Alejo Carpentier was one of the chief promoters of this nationalist modernism, although it was mainly pictorial, with AMELIA PELÁEZ and CARLOS ENRÍQUEZ as its most notable exponents.

A second group of artists with a more internalized aesthetic sense appeared at the end of the 1930s, in keeping with the new intellectual movement formed around the writer José Lezama Lima and the review *Orígenes*; the most outstanding painters included WIFREDO LAM and RENÉ PORTOCARRERO. In the 1950s this movement became schematized into a sort of manneristic 'School of Havana', which was opposed in turn by the Grupo de los Once, motivated by American Abstract Expressionism. Throughout the decade and until the early 1960s lyrical abstraction was the main movement in Cuban art, although in practice the process of abstraction was often taken as far as a radical form of Concrete art; abstraction brought sculpture, which previously had been unable to free itself of academic mannerisms, into the foreground, notably in the work of AGUSTÍN CÁRDENAS. Graphic arts also gained new impetus in this period with the establishment of the workshop of the Associación de Grabadores de Cuba in 1949.

The Revolution (1959) did not disrupt the artistic process, which continued to develop along its own lines, strengthened by generous government support. Freedom of creativity was guaranteed by cultural policy, and the idea of establishing such an official art style as SOCIALIST REALISM was rejected as contradictory to the liberal tradition of Cuban culture, in which modernism united radical social and political positions. The only notable exception in this context was the public art of the 1960s, posters and public bulletin boards combining the political, the aesthetic and the communicative. Some experiments

5. Raúl Martínez: *Fénix*, oil on canvas, 2.0×1.6 m, 1968 (Havana, Museo Nacional de Bellas Artes)

in the integration of the arts were made at the end of the decade. Abstract art gave way to an expressionist, neo-figurative style typified by the work of Antonia Eiriz (*b* 1929; e.g. *The Annunciation*, *c.* 1963–4; Havana, Mus. N. B.A.) and the Pop art of Raúl Martínez (*b* 1927; see fig. 5) and Umberto Peña (*b* 1937). Other styles included an epic, figurative art inspired by the revolution and exemplified by the work of Servando Cabrera Moreno (1923–81) and the imaginative, mythologizing paintings of Angel Acosta León (1930–64; e.g. *La Nave*, 1961; Havana, Mus. N. B.A.) and Manuel Mendive (*b* 1944). Graphic arts, especially lithography, flourished in new workshops, while photography gave fresh expression to the revolutionary epic with a mixture of journalistic reportage and aesthetic preoccupations. Drawing, too, assumed great importance, which increased in the following decade.

This art boom can be interpreted as a response to the optimistic atmosphere of the 1960s; however, a combination of economic chaos and the collapse of Latin American guerrilla-warfare campaigns over the next decade acted as a restraint. As Cuba entered the orbit of Soviet influence the country's social administration was reorientated in a process of institutionalization. This resulted in a shift in cultural policy in favour of a propagandist art and the superficial proclamation of national identity, leading to a 'dark decade' that stifled existing artistic energy. The only development of note during this period was the burgeoning of the ceramic arts, which had very little local tradition (*see* §VI below). The appearance of Photorealism soon afterwards also testified to an anxious desire for change. This was shortly answered by a new movement that broke through existing forms with an art of conceptual poetics concerned with the Afro-American and Native American vision of the universe as explored in the work of José Bedia (*b* 1959) and Juan Francisco Els (1956–88; e.g. *The Traveller*, installation, 1986; Mexico City, Cent. Cult. A. Contemp.), the popular kitsch of Flavio Garciandía (*b* 1954; e.g. *Tropicalia*, installation, 1990; Mexico City, Cent. Cult. A. Contemp.) and the philosophical reflection of Arturo Cuenca (*b* 1955); performance art and installations were also popularized. The establishment of the Ministry of Culture in 1976 coincided with a cultural revival: the *Volumen I* exhibition of 1981 was a landmark in the boom of Cuban fine arts. In the 1980s and 1990s trends were numerous and varied, ranging from the appropriation of images seen in the work of Consuelo Castañeda (*b* 1958; e.g. *Lichenstein and the Greeks*, wood, plaster and acrylic on canvas, 1985; Havana, Mus. N. B.A.) to the Neo-expressionism of Tomás Esson (*b* 1963). From the mid-1980s the tone was set by an art of social, cultural and political criticism with a Post-modernist aesthetic derived from the popular and recontextualized, as exemplified by the work of Carlos R. Cárdenas (*b* 1962), Glexis Novoa (*b* 1964; e.g. *Untitled*, installation, 1990; Aachen, Ludwig Forum Int. Kst) and Ciro Quintana (*b* 1964). Utopian attempts to transform art into a direct social activity include the work of Abdel Hernández (*b* 1968). In the 1990s the crisis in Cuba led to an exodus of artists.

See also LATIN AMERICAN ARTISTS OF THE USA, §4.

BIBLIOGRAPHY
A. Barr: 'Modern Cuban Painters', *MOMA Bull.*, xi (1944), pp. 1–14
J. Gómez Sicre: *Pintura cubana de hoy* (Havana, 1944)
G. Pérez Cisneros: *Características de la evolución de la pintura en Cuba* (Havana, 1959)
E. Desnoes and O. Hurtado: *Pintores cubanos* (Havana, 1962)
A. de Juan: *Introducción a Cuba: Las artes plásticás* (Havana, 1968)
J. Rigol: 'Pintura cubana', *Museo Nacional de Cuba: Pintura* (Leningrad, 1978)
——: *Apuntes sobre la pintura y el grabado en Cuba* (Havana, 1982)
L. de la Torriente: *Imagen de dos tiempos* (Havana, 1982)
G. Mosquera: *Contemporary Art from Havana* (London, 1989)
——: 'Problemas del nueve arte cubano', *Temas*, xx (1990), pp. 57–63
Cuba O.K. (exh. cat. by G. Mosquera and others, Düsseldorf, Städt. Ksthalle, 1990)
Third Text, 20 (Autumn 1992) [special issue on Cuba]

GERARDO MOSQUERA

V. Furniture.

Cuban furniture of the 16th, 17th and 18th centuries is strongly indebted to popular Spanish traditions, especially those found in the south of Spain. Spacious interiors contained relatively few pieces of furniture, limited to a small range of chairs, beds and chests. The woods used for furniture were principally cedar and mahogany; jacaranda and Jamaican ebony were also used, particularly for beds. Most surviving 17th-century furniture was commissioned for churches and convents and is therefore conservative in character. While devotional pieces were often very richly styled, objects made for domestic monastic use were simple in form and decoration. Certain pieces of furniture, regarded in the 20th century as primitive—such as Havana chests with step-profiled dovetails, which rely for their effect on plain joinery combined with handsome iron fittings—were highly esteemed at the time and were often exported to South America. Superior examples of these chests (17th-century example, Havana, Mus. N. B.A.) have domed lids and are decorated with flat, geometrical chip-carving, known as *montañesa* or high-lander carving, similar to that on furniture from northern Spain. Similar ornament was also used frequently on the backs and rails of chairs (examples in the sacristy of the church at Escolapios, Guanabacoa, Havana), which followed Spanish models closely, except that lavish textiles were normally replaced by leather upholstery. Beds were mostly simple wooden frames with decorative drapes; some featured elaborately turned reel-and-bobbin posts. Limited numbers of tables and wardrobes were made. Surviving examples of the former often have lyre-shaped supports, reflecting the influence of contemporary Spanish prototypes. The design and decoration of the few extant wardrobes is similar to the workmanship found on doors and windows. These pieces, together with documented payments to carpenters, indicate that the Cuban craftsmen who made furniture during this period were the same tradesmen responsible for doors, windows and general home carpentry.

The austerity of traditional 17th-century furniture underwent a dramatic change when mouldings, reliefs and curvilinear impulses began to appear in the mid-18th century, inspired by current European styles. Different styles coexisted and were occasionally combined in single pieces of Cuban furniture. Other pieces were influenced by the English Queen Anne and Chippendale styles or reflected French designs or the Provençal style. Dutch influence is also discernible, but the persistence of Spanish decorative traditions is most obvious. These stylistic trends were partly the result of trade with Europe but may also have been due to immigrant tradesmen. During the 18th century master craftsmen, varnishers and gilders flourished, many of Creole or Spanish origin. Foreign craftsmen introduced many new decorative techniques, and furniture inventories of the period describe numerous pieces embellished with inlays, marquetry and gilding. Wickerwork was sometimes used for seat furniture.

Technical developments during the 18th century led to a marked increase in the repertory of available furniture, and this diversity created richer ensembles to equip fashionable interiors. New items recorded in contemporary documents include large mirrors, musical instruments and elaborate lamps. Traditional pieces of furniture were superseded: chests were replaced by chests-of-drawers; desks and writing tables by bureaux; and multi-chairback settees evolved. Cupboards used for both clothes and household goods proliferated. A wide range of tables was produced, such as the folding or console varieties. Chairs multiplied in number and type, while beds increasingly became objects held in high esteem, with delicate carvings and lavish hangings. Elements derived from Cuban architecture are often present in furniture dating from this period; the Baroque Havana jamb was frequently copied on cupboard crestings, cabinets and beds, while the relief

6. Drawing-room decorated in the Cuban Medallion style, *c.* 1870 (Santiago de Cuba, Museo de Ambiente Histórico Cubano)

work and fine mouldings found on doors and window-frames were used as surface decoration. During the 18th century Cuban furniture, notably chests-of-drawers, gained wide acceptance throughout Hispanic America.

In the first half of the 19th century an increase in trade with North America was directly responsible for the transmission of Neo-classical taste to Cuba. Initially, furniture reflecting the French Empire style co-existed with English Regency-style pieces, as well as items in the American Federal style. These fashions were followed by variations of Biedermeier and French Restoration-style furniture. Many advertisements appeared in Cuban newspapers announcing the arrival of ships from the north with cargoes of furniture. The low price of imported furniture inevitably accelerated demand, and this factor had a powerful influence on Cuban craftsmanship; spectacular items of carved and inlaid furniture were produced as the industry expanded and diversified. Wardrobes, chairs and beds in particular proliferated, and the use of wickerwork instead of textiles became widespread. Comfort, luxurious decoration and ambitious styling came to be highly regarded. An impressive and freely interpreted version of the Louis XVI style, known as the Medallion style, emerged (see fig. 6). Early examples combined a large scale with lavish carving, gilding and often rich textiles. Later decorative schemes were on a more domestic scale and made exclusive use of wickerwork. A simpler, widely popular version of this style, known as *perilla*, was used well into the 20th century.

During the late 19th century the Gothic Revival, the Neo-Romantic and the Spanish style (combining Cuban Renaissance and Baroque elements) became significant. The colonial tradition was effectively terminated by this exploration of European revival styles, and by the end of the 19th century many wealthy families were importing furniture from Europe. During the Republican period (1902–59) Art Nouveau furniture was fashionable; this style was widely copied in middle-class homes and marked the modernization of Cuban furnishing schemes. By the

1930s a style known as the 'Modern Line' became widespread and ushered in a period when furniture was dominated by North American design attitudes. The political, economic and social changes that occurred in Cuba as a result of the Revolution of 1959 led to an attempt to create a distinctive national style exemplified by the work of EMPROVA (Empresa de Producciones Varias), which produced furniture using such indigenous materials as fine woods, leather, marble and various fibres, and by the functional furniture developed by the Ministry of Light Industry.

BIBLIOGRAPHY

J. M. F. de Arrate: *Llave del Nuevo Mundo y antemural de las Indias Occidentales* (1761/*R* Mexico, 1949)
E. Pichardo: *Diccionario provincial de voces cubanas* (Havana, 1836)
Directorio de artes, comercio e industrias de La Habana (Havana, 1860)
Directorio criticón de La Habana (Havana, 1883)
Directorio mercantil de la isla de Cuba (Havana, 1888–96)
A. Stapley and M. Byne: *Repertorio de muebles e interiores españoles (siglo XVI–XVIII)* (Mexico City, 1958)
W. C. Briant: 'Cartas de un viajero', *Rev. Bib. N.*, lvi (1965), pp. 35–68
M. Arola: *Historia del mueble* (Barcelona, 1966)
C. F. Duarte: *Muebles venezolanos de los siglos XVI, XVII y XVIII* (Caracas, 1978)
J. Pérez de la Riva: *La isla de Cuba en el siglo XIX vista por los extranjeros* (Havana, 1981)

ERNESTO CARDET

VI. Ceramics.

After the colonization of Cuba in the early 16th century, new influences were introduced by the Spanish and by African slaves; new styles became intertwined and mixed with the vestiges of indigenous ceramics. This gave rise to a new type of pottery that was initially limited to domestic utensils and construction materials. During the 17th century the potter's wheel was introduced into Cuba. No noticeable artistic developments occurred during the Colonial period, as the Creoles and Spaniards imported their ceramics from Europe, in particular from Spain and France. National production was limited to the manufacture of cheap earthenware. The only type of ware from this period that can be defined as typically Cuban is the *tinajón* (a large earthenware jar with a narrow base that broadens out and is closed by a narrow neck), which was placed in the inner courtyards of houses to collect rainwater. Ceramic production spread to all the towns; important kilns were established at Santa María del Puerto Príncipe, and in the 18th century a factory was founded by Mateo Santander Pérez, in the town of Trinidad.

There were no great artistic advances during the 19th century, nor did the establishment of the Republic contribute any great ceramic developments. Small factories were set up during this period by such Catalans as Pablo Bergolat in Calabazar (now in Havana) and Mateo Fugarolas in Camagüey. Both factories manufactured earthenwares that lacked any distinctive traits. Similarly, many other kilns proliferated on the island without making any great contributions.

In the early 20th century ceramic production was affected by the move in Cuban art, to create designs with national character. The origins of this movement lay in a workshop founded in 1930 by the Catalans Jaime Xart and Castor González Darna in the colony of Santiago de las Vegas (now in Havana). In 1941 they were joined by the Russian Michel Kratchenko. This workshop was converted into a manufacturing centre for industrial earthenware, and José Miguel Rodríguez de la Cruz (1902–90) and Filiberto Ramírez Corría (1902–76) became the central figures in the factory. Rodríguez de la Cruz contributed to the development of ceramic wares through his studies of clay, tin deposits, pastes and pigments and of industrial processes and the construction of kilns.

It was during the 1950s that Cuban ceramics began to develop. The Santiago de las Vegas Workshop became the main centre, where artists who had graduated from the Academia de S Alejandro in Havana and young enthusiasts met to produce and decorate ceramic wares. The work of the painter AMELIA PELÁEZ, for example, includes a *porrón* (1951; Havana, Mus. A. Dec.; see fig. 7)), which is a drinking vessel traditionally made of glass. Other such painters as Wifredo Lam, RENÉ PORTOCARRERO, Mariano Rodríguez and Luis Martínez Pedro made frequent use of this workshop, together with such young artists as Marta Arjona (*b* 1923), María Elena Jubrías (*b* 1930), Mirta García Buch (*b* 1919) and Rebeca Robés (*b* 1923), who developed new techniques and forms. However, the country's political situation prevented any further development, and the production of ceramics was confined to small, household kilns.

In the 1960s workshops, schools and factories for the industrial manufacture of ceramics were established all over the island. In 1965 the Cubanacán Ceramic Workshop was founded in Havana and attracted such principal potters from the Revolutionary period as Alfredo Sosabravo (*b* 1930), Reinaldo Calvo (*b* 1942), José Rodríguez Fuster (*b* 1943) and Julia González (*b* 1934). The potter Nazario Salazar (*b* 1942) produced thrown wares in the province of Camagüey. In the 1970s several factories producing industrial ceramics were established, and specialist ceramic

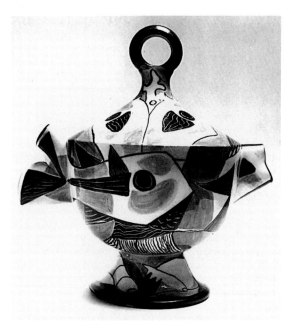

7. Amelia Peláez: glazed ceramic *porrón*, h. 340 mm, 1951 (Havana, Museo de Artes Decorativas)

technology was created and subsequently taught in elementary art schools. These developments led to the creation of a movement that culminated in the annual Feria de la Cerámica held at Nueva Gerona, Isla de Pinos. In the 1980s Angel Norniella (*b* 1947), José Ramón González (*b* 1953), Amelia Carballo (*b* 1951) and Agustín Villafaña (*b* 1952) settled on the island and became the leading figures in avant-garde ceramics.

BIBLIOGRAPHY
M. R. Harrington: *Cuba antes de Colón* (Havana, 1935)
B. Tomás: 'Antecedentes e inicios de la cerámica artística en Cuba', *Encuentro de Investigadores de Museos: La Habana, 1976*
Retrospectiva de la cerámica cubana (exh. cat., Havana, Mus. A. Dec., 1976)
L. Romero Estébanez: 'Sobre las evidencias arqueológicas de contacto y transculturación en el ámbito cubano', *Rev. Santiago*, 44 (Dec 1981), p. 71
G. Valdés: *Panorama de la cultura cubana* (Havana, 1983)

REBECA GUTIÉRREZ

VII. Metalwork.

Post-conquest metalwork in Cuba derived little from native traditions, owing to the near extermination of the indigenous peoples. According to records of passengers going to the West Indies, master silversmiths began to settle in the American continent from the earliest years of colonization, and, despite a lack of rich deposits of precious metals, Cuba was one of the first places in which this happened. Under a Spanish royal decree dated 1 June 1513, Cristóbal de Rojas, a silversmith by trade, was allowed to go to Cuba to practise as a founder and hallmarker, and, in order to establish himself on the island, he was given a residence with land, as well as being assigned servants.

In the 16th century Havana supported the activity of about 20 metalworkers. Although there are references before 1550 to the production of such silver objects as vases, pots, small holy-water vessels and jewellery, it was only in that year that the first Havana-based silversmith is recorded: Juan de Oliver, who was responsible for hallmarking silver. The oldest extant pieces of Cuban metalwork are chapter house maces (1631; Havana City Hall; see fig. 8), made by the master silversmith Juan Díaz Maldonado (*fl* 1631–50). They clearly illustrate the artistic and technical skill that had been achieved by that time. Other surviving examples, although later in date, are the silver filigree cross (*c.* 1662–5; Icod de los Vinos, Canaries, S Marco), crafted by Gerónimo de Espellosa (1613–80) and sent to Icod by the Dean of Santiago de Cuba, Nicolas Estévez Borges, and the silver filigree objects (1756) in the cathedrals of Havana and Santiago de Cuba, produced by Antonio Pérez.

In 1665 the Hermandad de S Eloy was constituted in Cuba, and *c.* 1759 the Gremio de Plateros de la Ciudad was founded in Havana, testifying to the number of silversmiths working in that city in the 18th century and to their artistic drive. The Gremio was subsequently accused by the Governor of not working metals in accordance with the law. It was alleged that, because of Cuba's shortage of rich mineral deposits, the proportion of precious metal included in quality objects was not sufficient. Thus it was decided to import annually a certain quantity of gold and silver from Mexico.

8. Macehead by Juan Díaz Maldonado, silver, 380×240 mm, 1631 (Havana City Hall)

In the 1830s the Gremio was dissolved, which left metalworking open to anyone who had the financial means to establish a shop and withstand local and foreign competition. In spite of the importation of gold and silver objects, principally from France, England, the USA and Spain (especially Barcelona), there were around 350 metalworkers in Havana in the later part of the 19th century.

The largest quantities of surviving pieces of Cuban metalwork date from the 19th, 18th and 17th centuries respectively. They are mainly ecclesiastical examples—less given to changes in fashion, as well as being less subject to economic fluctuations—fashioned out of a heavy metal and nearly always worked with a hammer. As demand increased, a marked contrast developed between the pieces that were finely cut and engraved, and others that were extremely simple or on which such industrial techniques as the engraving of borders and other ornamental motifs were used. With the exception of jewellery production, no major contributions to metalwork were made in the 20th century in Cuba.

BIBLIOGRAPHY

H. Hutchinson: 'Spanish and Spanish American Colonial Silver', *Int. Studio*, xcvi (1930), pp. 48–51
J. Torre Revello: *El gremio de plateros en las Indias Occidentales*, U. Buenos Aires, Inst. Invest. Hist., no. 61 (Buenos Aires, 1932)
——: *La orfebrería colonial en hispanoamérica y particularmente en Buenos Aires* (Buenos Aires, 1945)
D. C. Bayón: *América Latina en sus artes*, UNESCO (Paris, 1974)
Raíces antiguas, visiones nuevas/Ancient Roots, New Visions (exh. cat., Tucson, AZ, Mus. A., 1977) [bilingual text]
L. Romero: 'Orfebrería habanera en las Islas Canarias', *Rev., U. La Habana*, 222 (1984), pp. 390–407

MARTA AGUILERA

VIII. Patronage.

From the 16th century local councils and churches commissioned altarpieces and commemorative works; additionally, during the 18th and 19th centuries painters were employed to decorate mansions with wall paintings and to paint advertisements for commercial establishments. Even after the end of the 18th century, when an economic boom led to an increase in the commissioning by businessmen, landowners and other professionals of portraits and other works, the Church and the colonial administration remained the principal patrons of the arts. After independence, however, artists relied chiefly on commissions from the upper class and a few more enlightened patrons, although scarcity of work often obliged them to seek parallel occupations. There was support by some private institutions, but government sponsorship was almost non-existent until the 1940s and only became meaningful at the beginning of the 1950s with the creation of the Museo Nacional de Bellas Artes, Havana.

Although the first private collections were formed at the end of the 19th century, it was during the 20th century that the most important collections were assembled. These included collections of 17th–19th century European paintings, Classical antiquities, French decorative art and Cuban academic art. Modern fine arts were also collected, particularly by the middle class. The first permanent commercial outlets for paintings emerged in the 20th century as part of luxury stores or art supply shops, but it was not until the beginning of the 1940s that organized galleries appeared. At the same time, the acquisition of Cuban avant-garde painting by MOMA in New York stimulated the market for Cuban art in the USA. Internationally successful artists could survive on the proceeds of their work by working for foreign patrons or by living abroad. In 1954 the 2nd Bienal Hispanoamericano, organized by the Spanish government, was held in the Palacio de Bellas Artes, Havana.

After the Revolution a number of new galleries were set up, among them the Galería Habana and the Centro de Arte Internacional, both in Havana, the Galería Oriente in Santiago de Cuba, and galleries in casas de cultura throughout the country; these were for exhibition, rather than commercial, purposes, although the artists could sell the pictures on display. Government institutions such as the Ministries of Foreign Relations and the Sugar Industry,

the Cuban Communist Party and the Federación de Mujeres Cubanas also made collections of contemporary paintings, and the State became the principal promoter of art through museums, institutions and public commissions. The Ministry of Culture was established in 1976. However, although support of cultural activities increased considerably, and artists were guaranteed appropriate employment, it was still the case that few were able to make a living from their work. In 1978 the Fondo Cubano de Bienes Culturales, a state organization for commercial art transactions, was created to foster the sale of Cuban art, both in Cuba and abroad, through negotiations with galleries and dealers and its own exhibitions. The numerous new professionals replaced the middle class as patrons, and from the mid-1970s the number of full-time artists increased, thanks to government orders and an increasing international demand for Cuban fine arts.

IX. Art institutions.

The first school of fine arts, the Academia de S Alejandro, Havana, was officially established in 1818; before that, artists either trained in the studios of master painters or were self-taught. The Academia was public and free; its first Director was Jean-Baptiste Vermay (*fl* 1808; *d* 1833), a French pupil of Jacques-Louis David. There were also private art schools in Matanzas and Santiago de Cuba from the 19th century, and in the latter city an official academy was established at the end of the century. Despite changes and interruptions both the Academia (renamed the Escuela Nacional de Bellas Artes S Alejandro) and the Santiago school survive. From 1937–8 avant-garde artists sponsored the Free Studio for Painters and Sculptors in Havana; inspired by the Escuelas de Arte Libre in Mexico, it represented the first anti-academic teaching experiment aimed at establishing a Cuban national form of artistic expression. In 1962 the Escuelas Nacionales de Arte were established in Havana, and subsequently a free, modern, country-wide system of art teaching came into operation; in 1976 the Instituto Superior de Arte opened in the capital. Art training is offered on four levels: three years' study at secondary level in the Escuelas Elementales de Arte is followed by four years at the Escuelas Nacionales de Arte, then five years at the Instituto Superior de Arte to obtain a degree; postgraduate work may then be undertaken at the same institute.

The first public art collection in Cuba was of European paintings. It was originally assembled for teaching purposes in 1842 by the Academia S Alejandro, Havana, and continued to grow throughout the century; however, despite its importance, it did not function as a museum. The first true museums, established in Cárdenas and Santiago de Cuba at the end of the 19th century, included works of art among their wide-ranging collections, and in 1913 the Museo Nacional in Havana was founded on the same basis. In addition to a permanent exhibition of part of the San Alejandro collection, the Museo Nacional increased its reserves by acquiring modern Cuban artworks. In 1954 the fine arts collections were transferred to the new Palacio de Bellas Artes, inaugurated that year in Havana and renamed the Museo Nacional de Bellas

Artes. Some of the best private collections were also exhibited there.

After the Revolution the Museo Nacional was reorganized and enlarged to accommodate collections confiscated from the exiled upper class. Some of these collections formed the nucleus of new museums, such as the Museo de Artes Decorativas, which later enlarged their collections. The Museo Nacional holds the largest and most valuable collection of Cuban art in the world, together with collections of Egyptian antiquities, Greek and Roman artefacts and European paintings from the 17th–19th centuries. It has outstanding holdings of English 18th-century portraits and one of the most noteworthy collections of ancient Greek ceramics in Latin America. There are more than 250 museums in Cuba; some—such as that of Camagüey—specialize in art, others in colonial art and architecture or photography (e.g. the Fototeca de Cuba, Havana). Some multi-purpose galleries also have displays of art.

BIBLIOGRAPHY
Los museos en Cuba, Consejo Nacional de Cultura (Havana, 1972)
J. Rigol: *Museo Nacional de Cuba: Pintura* (Leningrad, 1978)
J. Saruski and G. Mosquera: *La política cultural de Cuba* (Paris, 1979)
J. Rigol: *Apuntes sobre la pintura y el grabado en Cuba* (Havana, 1982)
O. López Núñez: *Escuela San Alejandro: Cronología* (Havana, 1983)
GERARDO MOSQUERA

Cubas y González-Montes, Francisco, Marqués de Fontalba (*b* Madrid, 13 April 1826; *d* Madrid, 2 Jan 1899). Spanish architect and politician. He graduated in 1855 from the new Escuela de Arquitectura, Madrid, which though separate from the Academia de Bellas Artes continued the latter's pursuit of Italianate classical ideals. His principal teacher was Narciso Pascual y Colomer, whose style is reflected in Cubas's early works. Cubas travelled in Italy and Greece on a Spanish government scholarship and on a second tour visited various European countries, including a longer stay in Munich.

His first architectural period coincides with the latter years of the reign of Isabella II (*reg* 1833–68), during which he built a number of palatial Renaissance Revival houses in the Salamanca district of Madrid. Examples include those of the Duque de Sesto and the Duque de López-Dóriga. Typically they are terraced houses of three storeys and a semi-basement. A gallery of arches with Renaissance Revival decoration, usually on the first storey, forms the high point of the façade.

With the Isern House (1865) in the Carrera de San Jerónimo, Madrid, Cubas began to move towards a Gothic Revival style influenced by Viollet-le-Duc. Thereafter Gothic was employed on his major religious projects, through which he became the favourite architect of the Church, while Neo-classicism was largely reserved for his secular works. This duality of styles was to characterize the development of his mature work during the remainder of the 19th century. Cubas's outstanding essays in Gothic Revival architecture are the asylum of the Sagrado Corazón de Jesús (1880), the unfinished Almudena Cathedral (begun 1883) and the church of Santa Cruz (begun 1902), also unfinished. The cathedral was an over-ambitious attempt to reproduce aspects of 13th-century French and Spanish models, with three naves, ambulatory and an extremely high dome. Cubas's secular buildings include

the restoration in a grandiose medieval style of the Castillo de Butrón, Gatica, Vizcaya, and the Palacete Arenzana (1876; now the French Embassy), Madrid, which belongs to the last stage of his use of Renaissance Revival. In other works, however, he tended to eliminate superfluous ornamentation to allow the structural elements characterizing the actual construction of his edifices to become more plainly visible. The best example is the sober, Greek Revival Museo Antropológico González Vázquez (1875; now Museo Etnológico), Madrid.

Cubas was politically active in the Conservative Union Party and was successively elected Senator for the province of Avila, Deputy Senator for the province of Madrid and, in 1892, Mayor of Madrid. In the latter post he distinguished himself by a campaign to improve hygiene. He was also a director of the Comisión Central de Monumentos and president of the Sociedad Central de Arquitectos. He was created Marqués de Fontalba in 1893.

BIBLIOGRAPHY
J. A. Gaya: *Arte del siglo XIX* (Madrid, 1966)
P. Navascués: *Arquitectura y arquitectos madrileños del siglo XIX* (Madrid, 1973)
P. Navascués and others: *Del Neoclasicismo al Modernismo* (Madrid, 1979)
M. Gómez-Morán: 'Arquitectura del siglo XIX', *Historia de la arquitectura española* (Barcelona, 1987)
ALBERTO VILLAR MOVELLÁN

Cubero, José Alvarez. *See* ALVAREZ, (1).

Cubiculum (i). Bedroom in an ancient Roman house.

Cubiculum (ii). Burial chamber in a catacomb or a chapel.   □

Cubism. Term derived from a reference made to 'geometric schemas and cubes' by the critic Louis Vauxcelles in describing paintings exhibited in Paris by Georges Braque in November 1908; it is more generally applied not only to work of this period by Braque and Pablo Picasso but also to a range of art produced in France during the later 1900s, the 1910s and the early 1920s and to variants developed in other countries. Although the term is not specifically applied to a style of architecture except in former Czechoslovakia (*see* CZECH CUBISM), architects did share painters' formal concerns regarding the conventions of representation and the dissolution of three-dimensional form (*see* §II below). Cubism cannot definitively be called either a style, the art of a specific group or even a movement. It embraces widely disparate work; it applies to artists in different milieux; and it produced no agreed manifesto. Yet, despite the difficulties of definition, it has been called the first and the most influential of all movements in 20th-century art.

I. Painting, sculpture and collage. II. Architecture.

I. Painting, sculpture and collage.

1. Origins and application of the term. 2. Cubist milieux: Kahnweiler's Cubists and the Salon Cubists. 3. Technical and stylistic innovations. 4. Meanings and interpretations. 5. Late Cubism.

1. ORIGINS AND APPLICATION OF THE TERM. The question of when Cubism began and who led the way in its development is inextricably tied up with the question

of what distinguishes Cubist art, how it can be defined and who can be called Cubist. The beginnings of Cubism have variously been dated 1907, 1908, 1909 and 1911. In 1907 Picasso painted *Les Demoiselles d'Avignon* (New York, MOMA), which has often been considered a proto-Cubist work. In 1908 Braque produced *Houses at L'Estaque* (Berne, Kstmus.) and related landscapes, which prompted the reference by Vauxcelles to 'cubes'. The landscapes made by Picasso at Horta de Ebro in 1909, such as *Reservoir at Horta de Ebro* (New York, priv. col., see 1983 exh. cat., p. 245), were regarded by Gertrude Stein as the first Cubist pictures. The first organized group showing by Cubists took place in a separate room, 'Salle 41', at the Salon des Indépendants in Paris in 1911; it included work by Fernand Léger, Robert Delaunay, Henri Le Fauconnier, Jean Metzinger and Albert Gleizes, but nothing by Picasso or Braque.

By 1911 Picasso was accepted as the inventor of Cubism, a view that began to be challenged only with the publication of John Golding's influential history of Cubism in 1959; here Braque's importance and possible precedence was recognized for the first time. A later interpretation of Cubism associated especially with William Aubin, the impact of which has been considerable, identifies Braque categorically as the first. According to this view, the major breakthrough represented by Cubism centres on the depiction of space, volume and mass, especially as it occurred in Braque's L'Estaque landscapes. This view of Cubism is associated with a distinctly restrictive definition of which artists are properly to be called Cubists. Marginalizing the contribution of the artists who exhibited at the Salon des Indépendants in 1911, it focuses attention strictly on those who took a leading part in the development of this new mode of depiction, usually identified as Braque, Picasso, Juan Gris (from 1911) and, to a lesser extent, Fernand Léger (especially in 1911–12). DOUGLAS COOPER coined the terms 'true' Cubism and 'essential' Cubism to distinguish the work of these Cubists; the implied value judgement was intentional.

This restricted view of Cubism is linked to a formalist interpretation of its significance in 20th-century art. The assertion that the Cubist depiction of space, mass and volume supports rather than contradicts the actual flatness of the picture surface or the material qualities of the medium was made as early as 1920 by Daniel-Henry Kahnweiler, but it is also closely attuned to the art criticism of the 1950s and 1960s, especially that of Clement Greenberg. Contemporary views of Cubism were, in fact, complex and heteroclite; they were formed to some degree in response to the more publicized 'Salle 41' Cubists, whose methods were too distinct from those of the 'true' Cubists to be considered merely secondary to them. Alternative interpretations of Cubism have therefore developed. Such wider views of Cubism take in others who were later associated with the 'Salle 41' artists, most conspicuously Francis Picabia; the brothers Jacques Villon, Raymond Duchamp-Villon and Marcel Duchamp, who from late 1911 formed the core of the PUTEAUX GROUP; the sculptors Alexander Archipenko, Ossip Zadkine and Joseph Csaky as well as the two regarded as 'essential' Cubist sculptors, Jacques Lipchitz and Henri Laurens; and painters such as Louis Marcoussis, Roger de

La Fresnaye, František Kupka, Marc Chagall, Diego Rivera, Léopold Survage, Auguste Herbin, André Lhote, Gino Severini (after 1916), María Blanchard (after 1916) and Georges Valmier (after 1918). More fundamentally, the notion of 'essential' Cubism was later undermined by interpretations of the work of Picasso, Braque, Gris and Léger that stress iconographic and ideological questions rather than methods of representation.

Before 1914 the image of Cubism both in France and internationally was based on an extremely broad definition. A more heterogeneous view of Cubism is certainly encouraged by the earliest promotional writings by its practitioners and associates. Picasso, Braque and Gris made almost no published statements on the subject before 1914. The first major text, *Du cubisme*, was produced by two 'Salle 41' Cubists, Gleizes and Metzinger, in 1912; this was followed in 1913 by a far from systematic collection of reflections and commentaries by the poet and critic Guillaume Apollinaire, who had been closely involved with Picasso (from 1905) and Braque (from 1907), but who gave as much attention to artists such as Delaunay, Picabia and Duchamp. Along with Léger he identified these three with a new tendency, which he labelled Orphic Cubism or ORPHISM and which he considered of special significance for the future. Painters such as Gleizes, Metzinger, Delaunay and Duchamp were powerful influences alongside Picasso, Braque, Gris and Léger in the development of art related to Cubism in Russia, Czechoslovakia, Italy, the Netherlands, Britain, Spain and the USA.

2. CUBIST MILIEUX: KAHNWEILER'S CUBISTS AND THE SALON CUBISTS. Picasso, Braque and Gris (and to a lesser extent Léger) were nevertheless distinct in important ways from the other Cubists. Braque and Gris were based in Montmartre until after World War I, while Picasso remained there until 1912. Most of the others, including Léger, were based on the Left Bank, in Montparnasse and in the Parisian suburbs of Puteaux and Courbevoie, and they moved in different, if overlapping, milieux. Before 1914 Picasso, Braque, Gris and Léger further distinguished themselves from the other Cubists by gaining the backing of a single committed dealer in Paris, the German Daniel-Henry Kahnweiler, who paid each of them a guaranteed annual income for the exclusive right to buy their work and who sold only to a small circle of well-informed clients. Kahnweiler's support gave his artists the freedom to experiment in relative privacy.

The other Cubists, by contrast, concentrated before World War I on building their reputations by showing regularly at the major non-academic Salons in Paris, the Salon des Indépendants and the Salon d'Automne, and for this reason they are sometimes referred to as 'Salon' Cubists. Inevitably they were more aware of public response and the need to communicate. The first public controversies generated by Cubism resulted from Salon showings, not only at the Indépendants of 1911 but also at the Salon d'Automne of 1912; the latter occasion led to Cubism being debated in the Chambre des Députés, since the Salon d'Automne was held in the State's Grand Palais and the State could, therefore, be said to have subsidized the scandal. It was against this background of public anger that Gleizes and Metzinger wrote *Du cubisme* (1912), not necessarily to explain Cubism but to persuade a general audience that their intentions were serious.

3. TECHNICAL AND STYLISTIC INNOVATIONS. Technical and stylistic innovations in Cubist painting and sculpture are easier to grasp than Cubism as a concept or art-historical category, particularly as a clear sequence can be outlined. The fact that almost all of these were introduced by Braque or Picasso reinforces the notion of an 'essential' Cubism, but the methods they devised were widely influential precisely because they were so open to different and often contradictory adaptations. The geometric simplifications of form that led to Vauxcelles's references to 'cubes' in 1908 were not in themselves innovative. The two basic methods favoured in early Cubism—the rendering of three dimensions by shifting viewpoints and of volume or mass in terms of flat planes—led to the complication, not the simplification, of the problem of depiction. Early Cubism, with its stress on multiple viewpoints and planar faceting, and its retention of model, landscape or objects as starting-points, has misleadingly been referred to as Analytical Cubism (see below), although the artists themselves did not use this term.

The role assigned to Picasso's *Les Demoiselles d'Avignon* (1907) as the painting that opened the way to Cubism is based above all on the exaggerated changes of viewpoint applied to the figures, especially the crouching nude on the right, whose head appears almost to have swivelled free from the shoulders so that it can be confronted in three-quarter view. The use of contrasting vantage-points for different features became a central factor in the practice of all Cubists, leading to the assertion that Cubist art was essentially conceptual rather than perceptual. The critic Maurice Raynal, a supporter of Cubism, was most responsible for the emphasis given to this claim from 1912. Raynal argued that the rejection of consistent perspective represented a break with the insistence on instantaneity that characterized Impressionism. The mind now directed the optical exploration of the world as never before. Art was no longer merely a record of the sensations bombarding the retina; it was the result of intelligent, mobile investigation.

Arguments for Braque's L'Estaque landscapes of 1908 as the first Cubist paintings rest, by contrast, on their depiction of space, mass and volume. In works such as *Houses at L'Estaque*, a restrained use of shifting viewpoints is combined with a rendering of forms in space in terms of a continuous pattern of flat surfaces, subdued in colour, that tilt in and out across the picture plane. Such methods, which were taken further in pictures such as *The Port* (spring 1909; Chicago, IL, A. Inst.), clearly provided a stimulus for Picasso's faceting of buildings and sky in his Horta de Ebro landscapes of summer 1909, for example *Factory at Horta de Ebro* (St Petersburg, Hermitage). A crucial technique here, later referred to as 'passage', involves the breaking of the contours defining both the things depicted and the overall faceting so that surfaces appear to flow together, blurring above all the distinctions between solid form and space, foreground and background. The emphasis later placed on the planar depiction

of space, mass and volume arose from its usefulness in asserting the flatness of the support. The painting is seen both to capture the palpable three-dimensionality of the world revealed to the eyes and to draw attention to itself as a two-dimensional thing, so that it is both a depiction and an object in itself. From 1911 this emphasis on the status of the picture as an object was sometimes reinforced by Picasso and Braque by means of the admixture of sand and gesso in their paint to accentuate unevenness and tactility of surface. Picasso was the quickest, if not the first, to realize the implications of the planar depiction of space, volume and mass at their most extreme. In summer 1910, at Cadaqués in Catalonia, he produced pictures that so comprehensively broke down the distinctions between figures and spatial settings that the very identity of the subject was obscured; a major instance is *Female Nude* (Washington, DC, N.G.A.). From 1910 to 1912 the work produced by both Picasso and Braque was characterized by difficulties in the legibility of images that arose partly from the decision to open form fully out into space. Kahnweiler later referred to this kind of Cubist painting as Hermetic Cubism.

Early Cubism has been related to very different kinds of model or source. Picasso's work, for instance, has been linked above all to primitivism, that is to say to non-Western sources (see PRIMITIVISM, §2); the stylizations and distortions of *Les Demoiselles d'Avignon* seem to have come about in response to African sculpture, examples of which he knew in the collections of friends such as André Derain and in the Musée d'Ethnographie du Trocadéro in Paris, and to 'primitive' Iberian stone-carvings. The relation to African art has also been associated with the conceptual view of Cubism, since such sculptures were held to represent the figure emblematically rather than naturalistically, in terms of simple signs for facial features, limbs and other parts of the body. By contrast, Picasso's use of distortion from 1910 has also been related to the liberties taken by Ingres in idealizing human form. Yet, by general consent the major source for both the distortions created by the use of multiple perspective and for the depiction of forms in terms of planes is the late work of Paul Cézanne, who was the subject of a major retrospective at the Salon d'Automne in 1907. There is little doubt that the concentration by Braque and Picasso between 1909 and 1912 on Cézanne's range of subjects—the posed model, still-life and landscape—was intended as a deliberate homage. Yet the extreme to which they exaggerated these formal strategies led to a fundamental change in the relationship between artist and subject not anticipated by Cézanne. They used these techniques not merely in response to things seen but positively to manipulate and even reconstruct their subjects, hence their temporary willingness to dispense with representational clarity in their Hermetic Cubist phase.

Later inventions in Cubism arose from a desire to emphasize further the material identity of the art object and to convey the subject-matter more lucidly. Probably in spring 1912 Picasso glued a factory-made piece of oilcloth printed with a realistic chair-caning pattern on to a small still-life, *Still-life with Chair-caning* (Paris, Mus. Picasso; see fig. 1). This is generally regarded as the first Cubist COLLAGE. Later in 1912 Braque stuck a piece of

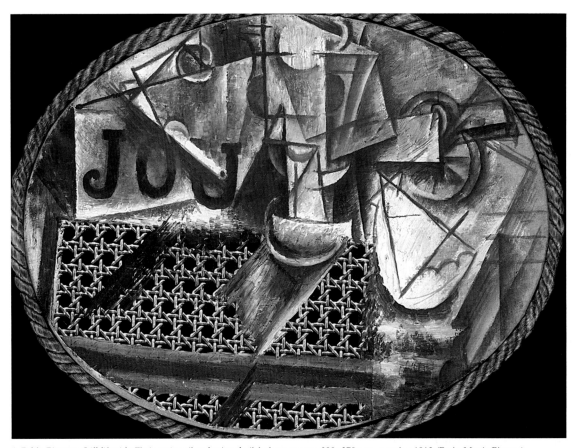

1. Pablo Picasso: *Still-life with Chair-caning*, oil and printed oilcloth on canvas, 290×370 mm, *c.* spring 1912 (Paris, Musée Picasso)

cut-out wallpaper printed with wood-grain patterns on to a still-life drawing, *Fruit-dish with Glass* (Sept 1912; priv. col., see 1983 exh. cat., p. 85). This was the first Cubist papier collé. Papier collé differed from collage in that there was a more arbitrary relationship between the cut-out and stuck-on shapes and the things depicted: newspaper could stand for itself, but it could also depict anything from a glass to a soda-syphon; wood-grained wallpaper could depict the surface of a guitar or violin without being cut to the shape of either. Moreover, the broad areas of cut-out paper used in papier collé led to simpler compositions in which the flatness of the constituent planes was taken for granted, leading to more schematic signs for the representation of things. Linear configurations could denote figures and still-life objects in easily legible ways, as in Picasso's *Man with a Hat* (autumn–winter 1912; New York, MOMA), while remaining both obviously two-dimensional and capable of combining different viewpoints. At the same time, the use of cut-out shapes led to a novel development in the Cubist depiction of space: effects of depth could be achieved by contrived overlappings of one flat shape by another, and indeed it became possible to suggest the illusion of space in front of the picture surface by, as it were, piling planes up one over another, apparently outwards, as in Braque's *The Clarinet* (1913; New York, MOMA; for illustration *see* BRAQUE, GEORGES, fig. 1). Complications of another kind were

created by the insertion of words, a development that preceded collage and papier collé but that was fully elaborated only with their invention.

Between 1912 and 1914 Picasso, Braque and Gris were stimulated by the possibilities opened up by these new techniques to produce a kind of Cubism different in many ways from that of the preceding four years. The subject-matter and the question of representation are not obscured, but the range of spatial effects made possible and the range of reference allowed by the insertion of words and of fragments from the 'real world' led to paradoxical, highly subtle and complex results. Later these developments stimulated other artists to investigate very different, even contradictory, directions. The simple compositions and overlapping planes of Cubist papiers collés were important for the geometric abstraction of both De Stijl and the Suprematism of Kazimir Malevich in Russia. The Cubist use of schematic signs and word play was equally significant for the Dada and early Surrealist work of artists such as Picabia, Max Ernst and Joan Miró.

The changes effected in 1912 in the Cubism of Picasso, Braque and Gris have tempted historians to make a clear distinction between Cubism executed before and after that date. Because of the technical basis of the change in collage and papier collé, the tendency has been to make the distinction in terms of procedural differences. It has been suggested that up to 1912 Cubist method was 'analytical', entailing the part-by-part, viewpoint-by-viewpoint dissection of the subject, while after 1912 it was 'synthetic', based on the construction or invention of representational signs using elementary and sometimes geometric shapes. Explained in these terms, the earlier work was based empirically on the study of things, while the later work was more purely inventive and free of such primary study. This distinction, from which the terms Analytic Cubism and Synthetic Cubism originated, was first developed by Gris and Kahnweiler from 1915 to 1921, and broadly speaking Picasso, Braque and Gris did tend more to 'synthetic' procedures after 1912. Their work prior to 1912, however, was not exclusively 'analytical', and synthesis or invention was a key factor in their Cubism from the beginning.

Invention and a conceptual rather than perceptual view of art are related preoccupations in Cubism. Moreover, since Cubist art consistently stressed the directing role of the artist's will, the assertion of the independent status of the work was accompanied by a corresponding emphasis on the degree of control exerted by the person making it. The practice of metamorphosis, introduced and developed above all by Picasso between 1912 and 1914, further underlined the importance of this subjectivity. The simpler the signs used in the process of depiction, the more similar and therefore the more interchangeable they became. As early as 1909 Picasso developed a major still-life from sketches for a figure composition. *Table with Loaves and Bowl of Fruit* (early 1901; Basle, Kstmus.) has its origins in a series of studies for a painting, *Carnival at the Bistro*, which Picasso never executed. The inanimate items laid here upon the table are transformations of the *commedia dell'arte* figures ranged behind the table. After 1912 Picasso consistently exploited and made clear the interchangeability of figures and objects in his work. The determining role of the artist's imagination was made still more explicit. The use of metamorphosis by Picasso and to some extent by Gris was to influence the Surrealists in the 1920s, especially Joan Miró and André Masson.

In sculpture, two Cubist pictorial innovations were of particular significance: first, the fusion of solid and space, and second, collage and papier collé. From the first followed the positive treatment of space in sculpture and the development of positive/negative reversals (positive features depicted by negative spaces and vice versa). Picasso anticipated this with a *Head of a Woman (Fernande)* (bronze, autumn 1909; Paris, Mus. Picasso), but the earliest to exploit it ambitiously in sculpture was Alexander Archipenko in 1910–11 and especially in 1912–13, for example in *Medrano II* (1913; New York, Guggenheim; for illustration *see* ARCHIPENKO, ALEXANDER). From collage and papier collé came Cubist construction and ASSEMBLAGE. Archipenko was again important in this respect, but Picasso's role was more central and influential. His first substantial construction was a metal *Guitar* (1912; New York, MOMA; *see* IRON AND STEEL, fig. 6), but for the most part his early Cubist constructions, starting late in 1912, were made from varied materials and came directly out of collage and papier collé. The additive nature of collage, coupled with the suggestion of space in front of the picture surface achieved by overlapping planes in papier collé, led to the actual building of elements out

from the support to form reliefs such as *Mandolin and Clarinet* (painted wood and pencil, 1913; Paris, Mus. Picasso).

The additive and improvisational insouciance of these three-dimensional compositions, which were often left deliberately untidy in appearance, contrasts strikingly with sculpture produced by traditional modelling and carving techniques that entailed either moulding or cutting away from a homogeneous, usually dense material such as clay, plaster, stone or wood. By contrast with such traditional methods, which required an elaborate craft training and often the collaboration of others for carving or casting, these Cubist constructions could be easily assembled using basic non-specialized skills. They were, moreover, characteristically flimsy and open, as in the case of two *Guitars* made of paper and string in late 1912 (Paris, Mus. Picasso), not heavy, durable and monolithic. Of the Cubist sculptors working in France it was Laurens who responded most inventively to Picasso's constructions, especially between 1915 and 1919 with works such as *Bottle and Glass* (1918; Paris, Pompidou) and *Guitar* (1917–18; Cologne, Mus. Ludwig; for illustration *see* LAURENS, HENRI); but as they could be seen by visitors in the studio or as illustrations in the periodical *Soirées de Paris* in 1914, their impact was also felt outside France. Indeed, Cubist construction was as influential as any pictorial Cubist innovation. It was the stimulus behind the proto-Constructivist work of both Naum Gabo and Vladimir Tatlin and thus the starting-point for the entire constructive tendency in 20th-century modernist sculpture.

4. MEANINGS AND INTERPRETATIONS. The Cubism of Picasso, Braque and Gris had more than a purely technical or formal significance, and the often distinct attitudes and intentions of the other Cubists produced not so much a derivative of their work as different kinds of Cubism. It is by no means clear, in any case, to what extent these other Cubists depended on Picasso and Braque for their development of such techniques as faceting, 'passage' and multiple perspective; they could well have arrived at such practices with little knowledge of 'true' Cubism in its early stages, guided above all by their own understanding of Cézanne. The works shown at the Salons of 1911 and 1912 by these other Cubists extended beyond the conventional Cézanne-like range of subjects favoured by Picasso and Braque to include large-scale modern-life subjects and even allegory. Aimed at a large Salon public, these works made clear use of Cubist techniques of faceting and multiple perspective for expressive effect in order to preserve the eloquence of subjects that were richly endowed with literary and philosophical connotations.

At the Indépendants of 1911, Le Fauconnier's *Abundance* (1910–11; The Hague, Gemeentemus.) gave allegorical expression to a theme that concerned not only the 'Salle 41' Cubists but also the ABBAYE DE CRÉTEIL, a group of writers and artists that included Alexandre Mercereau, Jules Romains, Henri-Martin Barzun, René Arcos, Charles Vildrac and Georges Duhamel (1884–1966). Le Fauconnier here used the allegory of fruitfulness to represent life as a process of incessant birth and rebirth, giving symbolic expression to the key notion of 'duration' proposed by the philosopher Henri Bergson according to which life is subjectively experienced as a continuous forward movement in time, with the past flowing into the present and the present merging into the future. The other Salon Cubists were also attuned to this concept—in *Du cubisme* Gleizes and Metzinger explicitly related this sense of time to multiple perspective—and to Bergson's insistence on the elasticity of our consciousness of both time and space. They gave physical expression to this blurring of distinctions by means of 'passage', using the faceted treatment of solid and space, and effects of planar interpretation to convey a physical and psychological sense of the fluidity of consciousness in Bergson's terms. These concerns are related to Jules Romains's theory of Unanimism, which stressed the power of collective feelings to break down the barriers between people. The one major innovation that one can be sure was made independently by the Salon Cubists, that of 'simultaneity', came of a conviction also rooted in their understanding of Bergson that the divisions of space and time should be comprehensively challenged.

Delaunay's *City of Paris* (1910–12; Paris, Pompidou) and Léger's *The Wedding* (c. 1911; Paris, Pompidou, see fig. 2), both shown at the Salon des Indépendants in 1912, give form to this concept of simultaneity by presenting different motifs as occurring within a single time frame: Delaunay brings together the quais on the Seine, the three Graces, a view across the roofs and the Eiffel Tower, while Léger unites a wedding group with fragmentary views of a village setting. The subjects themselves again carry strong overtones of ideas derived from Bergson and Unanimism: for Romains the city was a Unanimist entity, a psychological as well as a physical fact, where responses

2. Fernand Léger: *The Wedding*, oil on canvas, 2.57×2.06 m, c. 1911 (Paris, Pompidou, Musée National d'Art Moderne)

to the past and the present interpenetrate; an event like a wedding was seen as a powerful emotional occasion through which the past is precipitated into the future with collective force. The conjunction of such subject-matter with simultaneity aligns Salon Cubism with early Futurist paintings by Umberto Boccioni, Gino Severini and Carlo Carrà; these Italian works, though themselves made in response to early Cubism, led the way in the application of techniques of simultaneity in 1911–12.

The Cubist work produced before 1912 by Picasso, Braque and Gris had little to do with Bergson, but wide cultural, literary, philosophical and even scientific and mathematical connotations have also been attributed to it. The scientific and mathematical connection was something made very generally in relation to Cubism. In the case of Picasso, Braque and Gris it followed from their known involvement with an amateur mathematician, Maurice Princet, around 1910–11. Princet introduced them to new mathematical developments popularized by Jules Henri Poincaré (1854–1912) and to currently fashionable theories of the FOURTH DIMENSION and the 'hypercube', although they were unaware of the theories of Albert Einstein. Ancient and Renaissance theories of proportion were also considered relevant, especially to the Duchamp brothers and others involved in the *Salon de la Section d'Or* in late 1912 (*see* SECTION D'OR (ii)), though of the Montmartre Cubists only Gris was drawn to them.

These quasi-scientific and mathematical interests were linked with the 'hermetic sciences', the occult and alchemy. Of the writers sympathetic to Cubism, Mercereau and Gleizes's brother-in-law Jacques Nayral were actively engaged in Occultism, while Apollinaire and Jacob are known to have dabbled in the cabbala, alchemy and the writings of hermeticists such as Eliphas Lévi. Apollinaire's concept of Orphism had a clear mystical aspect, which followed from its roots in Greek myth, and alchemical themes seem to have been touched on in Duchamp's subject-matter from 1912 and in works by Marc Chagall such as *Homage to Apollinaire* (1913; Eindhoven, Stedel. Van Abbemus.). Picasso is also thought to have shared the enthusiasm of Apollinaire and Jacob for magic and the occult; indeed, it is possible that, like them, he thought of his Cubist works as magical mediators between himself and a hostile world.

Just as the Salon Cubists were linked with the Abbaye de Créteil group, so the early Cubist work of Picasso, Braque and Gris was associated with the post-Symbolist and sometimes proto-Surrealist poetry of Apollinaire and Jacob, and also with 19th-century Symbolist poetry, especially that of Stéphane Mallarmé. Their interest in Mallarmé has often been corroborated, and the obscurity of their 'hermetic' Cubism of 1910–12 has been related to Mallarmé's late poetic practice, by which things are not named but evoked through the images or sensations stimulated by their presence. Apollinaire's lyrical variant on these methods, arising from his ability to take ordinary things as a starting-point for series of images possessing 'supernatural' qualities, clearly relates to the use of banal subjects by Picasso and Braque as the springboard for arcane yet suggestive clusters of lines and planes. Indeed the poet Pierre Reverdy, who was also close to Picasso, Braque and Gris, could claim that the importance of Cubism lay essentially in the fact that it had consolidated changes wrought first in poetry by Mallarmé and Arthur Rimbaud. It is also clear that the emphasis placed by these painters on the autonomy of the elements of their art (colours, lines, forms) and their belief in the directing role of the subjective imagination were extensions of Symbolist attitudes. This association between Cubism and Symbolism relates closely to the association often made between Cubism and the aesthetic theories of Immanuel Kant, particularly his theory of form as the key to beauty as elaborated in *Kritik der Urteilskraft* (Berlin, 1790).

The most extreme directions suggested by Cubism were not those followed by Picasso and Braque, who resisted the invitation to abstraction inherent in their most obscure Hermetic work. For them, the assertion of the autonomy of the work as an object was no more important than the task of representing things as informatively, suggestively and from as many different aspects as possible. Collage and papier collé resulted in part from a desire to shift the balance back towards 'real' things. The other Cubists, by contrast, especially Jacques Villon's Czech neighbour, František Kupka, and those grouped together as Orphists by Apollinaire (Delaunay, Léger, Picabia and Duchamp), accepted the invitation to abstraction with some enthusiasm.

Kupka's painting from 1912, rooted in his formative years in Prague and Vienna, was metaphysical in orientation. Duchamp in 1912 and Picabia from 1912 to 1914 developed an expressive and allusive abstraction dedicated to complex emotional and sexual themes, and in Duchamp's case to theories of the fourth dimension. From 1912 Delaunay painted a series of paintings entitled *Simultaneous Windows* (e.g. 1912; Hamburg, Ksthalle; for illustration *see* ABSTRACT ART, fig. 1), in which he combined planar structures derived from Hermetic Cubism with bright prismatic hues based on Michel-Eugène Chevreul's theories of simultaneous colour contrasts; the colour in early Cubist paintings had been distinctly subdued. In 1913–14 Léger produced a series entitled *Contrasts of Forms* (e.g. 1913; Philadelphia, PA, Mus. A.), which were also based on a theory of contrasts but which gave equal stress to colour, line and form. His Cubism, even in this abstract guise, was explicitly associated with themes of mechanization and the celebration of modern life. Apollinaire supported all these developments in *Les Peintres cubistes* (1913), writing of a new 'pure' painting in which the subject no longer counted, but in spite of his use of the term Orphism these kinds of abstract Cubism were so varied that they defy attempts to treat them as a single category.

Although the importance of the subject was played down in the 'pure' painting practised in 1912–14, such art in its several forms was considered to carry meanings beyond the simply aesthetic. Picabia and Duchamp were dedicated to an expressive project with psychological and arcane overtones. Léger declared that he wanted to convey the dissonant energy of the modern by means of pictorial contrasts, and in his essay 'La Lumière' (first published in German translation in *Der Sturm* in 1913) Delaunay wrote in terms reminiscent of Bergson of his simultaneous contrasts as conveying 'the movement of the world'. It is

understandable, therefore, that Delaunay's Orphism accompanied the ambitious further development of simultaneity in its broader Cubist and Futurist sense, and that it did so as the pictorial complement to developments in the poetry of Apollinaire and the Swiss adventurer-poet, Blaise Cendrars. In 1912–14 Delaunay produced a series of pictures that combined simultaneous contrasts of colour with fragmentary clusters of images of modern life such as aeroplanes, posters, rugby players and the Eiffel Tower, for example in the *Cardiff Team* (1912–13; Eindhoven, Stedel. Van Abbemus) and *Homage to Blériot* (*c*. 1914; Basle, Kstmus.; for illustration *see* DELAUNAY (ii), (1)). Bergson's attack on the divisions of space and time was all-important here still; the Eiffel Tower owed its central role to its function as the radio-mast of Paris, the point at which global distances were nullified. It was the prime symbol of simultaneity.

Duchamp, also labelled an Orphist by Apollinaire, was responsible for a further extreme development based on Cubism: the READY-MADE. The ready-made arose from a consideration of the linked notions of the painting as object and of 'pure' painting alongside the implications of collage and Cubist construction. On the one hand, the work is considered an object in its own right, pure and self-contained; on the other, it takes into itself the material detritus of the world. It was a short step to the decision that an ordinary object could be presented, with irony, as a self-sufficient work of art representing nothing but itself, as Duchamp did in 1913 by attaching a bicycle wheel to a kitchen stool and in 1914 by selecting a bottle-drying rack as a sculpture in its own right.

While stopping short of such extreme conclusions, the works made after 1912 by Picasso, Braque and Gris were wide-ranging in their form and meaning. Braque pursued musical analogies by his use of words, for example in collages such as *Glass, Newspaper, Packet of Tobacco and Sheet Music* (spring 1914; Chicago, IL, A. Inst.) and in his concentration on subjects such as *The Musician* (1917–18; Basle, Kstmus.). Gris produced subtle word plays and introduced references to such disparate interests as Apollinaire's poetry and the popular *Fantomas* novels. Picasso, however, most effectively widened the range of meaning in Cubism, playing on the ambiguous metamorphic relationships between inanimate objects and figures, using bulbous organic shapes and extreme distortion to create comic and even grotesque sexual suggestions, and also using words in a witty manner, sometimes injecting a sexual or scatological humour reminiscent of the *Ubu* plays by Alfred Jarry, as in the highly suggestive placing of the words 'trou ici' (hole here) in relation to department-store lingerie advertisements in the collage *Au Bon Marché* (winter 1912–13; Aachen, Neue Gal.). Early in 1913 Picasso used press-cuttings concerning the Balkan War as a way of alluding to the climate of rising nationalism and international tension that would culminate in World War I. The very heterogeneity of Cubist art by Picasso, Braque and Gris after the invention of collage and papier collé can be thought of as a representation of the disparateness and intensity of early 20th-century urban experience.

5. LATE CUBISM. The most eventful and innovative period of Cubism was before 1914, but after 1918 Cubism

returned as a central issue for artists in France. It continued as such until the mid-1920s, when its avant-garde status was rendered questionable by the advent of geometric abstraction and by the rebarbative presence of the Surrealists in Paris. Many Cubists, including Picasso, Braque, Gris, Léger, Gleizes and Metzinger, while developing other styles, continued on occasion to produce work that was clearly Cubist and that was attacked and defended as such. It is impossible, indeed, to date the end of Cubism, since such artists as Braque, Picasso and Gleizes returned to Cubist modes long after 1925, and since forms of avant-garde art directly responsive to Cubism emerged as late as the end of the 1920s and the 1930s in, for instance, the work of the American Stuart Davis and the Englishman Ben Nicholson. In France, however, a sharp decline in its significance is clear from about 1925.

Cubism was changed, moreover, by World War I. In 1914–15 the Cubists were dispersed either to the Front or abroad; those that continued with their art, including Picasso, Gris, Lipchitz, Laurens and a recent convert to Cubism, the Mexican Diego Rivera, were left relatively isolated. Cubism re-emerged as a significant force in 1917 with the première in Paris of the ballet *Parade*, produced by the Ballets Russes with a scenario by Jean Cocteau, music by Erik Satie and sets and costumes by Picasso (*see* PICASSO, PABLO, fig. 4), and especially with the support given by the dealer Léonce Rosenberg, who took up not only the artists stranded by Kahnweiler's exile in Switzerland but also many others, including Laurens, Lipchitz, Metzinger, Herbin and Severini. Soon after the Armistice on 11 November 1918 Rosenberg mounted a series of Cubist exhibitions at his Galerie de l'Effort Moderne in Paris, culminating in an exhibition by Picasso, all showing wartime work. Cubism was featured in exhibitions devised by organizations such as Lyre et Palette and in new periodicals such as *S.I.C.* (from 1915), *L'Elan* (1915–16) and *Nord-Sud* (from 1917). There were attempts, led by Louis Vauxcelles, to claim that Cubism was finished, but these exhibitions, along with a well-organized Cubist showing at the Salon des Indépendants in 1920 and a revival of the Salon de la Section d'Or in the same year, demonstrated its survival.

By 1920 Cubism had become almost exclusively associated with the question of the autonomy of art. The changes that had occurred in Cubism were remarked by a number of commentators, including the artist and critic André Lhote, who himself was often called a Cubist. By this time Picasso was working in a variety of styles, but he continued occasionally to produce expressive Cubist work, while Léger, after his recovery from war wounds in 1917–18, produced Cubist pictures with references to modern life that were even more explicit than before, as in *The Typographer* (1919; Philadelphia, PA, Mus. A.). Most of those associated with Rosenberg's gallery, however—including Gris, Metzinger, Lipchitz, Laurens, Herbin and Severini—made direct reference to observed reality but were at pains to stress the self-sufficiency of their pictures and sculptures as objects in their own right. Lipchitz, for example, came close to complete abstraction in carvings such as *Standing Personage* (1916; New York, Guggenheim; for illustration *see* LIPCHITZ, JACQUES). There was also a tendency to give priority to the orderly qualities of Cubist composition, so that Cubism became part of a widely noted phenomenon in French culture at the end of the war, a return to classical traditions referred to by Jean Cocteau as a 'rappel à l'ordre'. Gris played a leading role in these developments; the clarity and sense of order of the work he produced between 1917 and 1920 led to its being referred to by the critic Maurice Raynal as 'crystal' Cubism. This narrowing of the frame of reference to a more purely formal one that excluded reference to the types of concerns manifested in Cubism before 1914—for example to Bergson's concept of duration, psychological interpenetration, the occult, the fourth dimension and the dynamism of modern life—coincided with the appearance from 1917 to 1924 of a coherent body of theoretical writing about Cubism; influential texts were published by Pierre Reverdy, Maurice Raynal and Daniel-Henry Kahnweiler and, among the artists, by Gris and Léger. Their theories, supported in the writings of Reverdy and Raynal by reference to Kant and Plato, strengthened the insistence on the autonomous purity of art. The distillation of Cubism and its part in the 'rappel à l'ordre' have been linked to the tendency, shown by many of those left on the home front, to evade the realities of the war and also to the cultural dominance of a classical or Latin image of France during and immediately after the war. Cubism after 1914 can be seen as part of a far wider ideological shift towards a more conservative stance in French society and culture alike.

In the early 1920s confusion was caused by the decision of several Cubists to produce overtly classical figurative work either exclusively or alongside Cubist work; Picasso was the model, having developed parallel classicizing styles from 1914. There was, however, a consistency in the common Cubist and figurative themes of Classicism and order, and in the common accent on formal priorities. The Cubists considered classical styles above all to be structured formal idioms under the control of the artist. Cubist art itself remained extremely varied and changeable both within the oeuvre of a single artist such as Gris and across the work of artists as different from each other as Braque and Léger. Yet, Cubism as a publicly debated concept or movement became relatively unified and open to definition. Its apparent theoretical purity made it a gauge against which not only traditional academic art but such contrasting tendencies as Naturalism, Dada, Surrealism and various forms of abstraction could be measured, even though many of the more radical artists who attacked Cubism were specifically indebted to it. While late Cubism produced no major innovations, its self-imposed limitations and its greater coherence, both as a public phenomenon and in terms of theory and practice, prepared the way for a more general acceptance of Cubism as a whole and particularly of the 'essential' Cubism of the years prior to 1914.

See also ABSTRACT ART.

BIBLIOGRAPHY

EARLY SOURCES

Cubistas (exh. cat., preface J. Nayral; Barcelona, Gal. Dalmau, 1912)
G. Apollinaire: *Les Peintres cubistes: Méditations esthétiques* (Paris, 1913)
P. Reverdy: 'Sur le cubisme', *Nord-Sud*, i (1917); repr. in *Oeuvres complètes, 'Nord-Sud', 'Self-défence' et autres écrits sur l'art et la poésie, 1917–1926*, ed. E.-A. Hubert (Paris, 1975)

M. Raynal: *Quelques intentions du cubisme* (Paris, 1919)

D.-H. Kahnweiler: *Der Weg zum Kubismus* (Munich, 1920; Eng. trans., New York, 1949)

ARTISTS' WRITINGS AND STATEMENTS

A. Gleizes and J. Metzinger: *Du cubisme* (Paris, 1912; Eng. trans., London, 1913)

F. Léger: 'Les Origines de la peinture et sa valeur représentative', *Montjoie!* (29 May 1913), p. 7; (14–29 June 1913), pp. 9–10; repr. in *Fonctions de la peinture* (Paris, 1965; Eng. trans., New York and London, 1973)

——: 'Les Réalisations picturales actuelles', *Soirées Paris*, 25 (1914), pp. 349–56; repr. in *Fonctions de la peinture* (Paris, 1965; Eng. trans., New York and London, 1973)

J. Gris: 'Des possibilités de la peinture', *Transatlantic Rev.* (1924), i/6, pp. 482–8; ii/1, pp. 75–9; repr. in D.-H. Kahnweiler: *Juan Gris: Sa Vie, son oeuvre, ses écrits* (Paris, 1946); Eng. trans. and rev. D. Cooper as *Juan Gris: His Life and Work* (London, 1968–9), pp. 195–200

R. Delaunay: *Du cubisme à l'art abstrait*, ed. P. Francastel (Paris, 1957)

A. Gleizes: *Souvenirs: Le Cubisme, 1908–1911* (Audin, 1957)

J. Lipchitz and H. H. Arnason: *My Life in Sculpture* (London, 1972)

EXHIBITION CATALOGUES

Le Cubisme (1907–1914) (exh. cat., Paris, Mus. N. A. Mod., 1953)

Les Cubistes (exh. cat., Bordeaux, Gal. B.-A.; Paris, Mus. N. A. Mod.; 1973)

W. Rubin: 'Cézannism and the Beginnings of Cubism', *Cézanne: The Late Work* (exh. cat., ed. W. Rubin; New York, MOMA, 1977)

The Planar Dimension (exh. cat. by M. Rowell, New York, Guggenheim, 1979)

Zeichnungen und Collagen des Kubismus: Picasso, Braque, Gris (exh. cat., Bielefeld, Städt. Ksthalle, 1979)

Kubismus: Künstler–Themen–Werke, 1907–1920 (exh. cat., Cologne, Josef-Haubrich-Ksthalle, 1982)

The Essential Cubism, 1907–1920: Braque, Picasso and their Friends (exh. cat. by D. Cooper and G. Tinterow, London, Tate, 1983)

Picasso and Braque: Pioneering Cubism (exh. cat., intro. W. Rubin, ed. J. Leggio; New York, MOMA, 1989) [with doc. chronology by J. Cousins]

GENERAL

A. H. Barr: *Cubism and Abstract Art* (New York, 1936)

C. Greenberg: 'The Pasted-paper Revolution', *ARTnews*, 57 (1958), pp. 46–9, 60–61; repr. as 'Collage' in *Art and Culture* (Boston, 1961), pp. 70–83

J. Golding: *Cubism: A History and an Analysis, 1907–1914* (London, 1959, rev. 1968, 3/1988)

R. Rosenblum: *Cubism and Twentieth-century Art* (New York and London, 1960, rev. 1977)

E. F. Fry: *Cubism* (London and New York, 1966)

D. Cooper: *The Cubist Epoch* (London and New York, 1970)

L. D. Henderson: 'A New Facet of Cubism: "The Fourth Dimension" and "Non-Euclidean Geometry" Re-interpreted', *A. Q.* [Detroit], xxxiv/4 (1971)

R. Rosenblum: 'Picasso and the Typography of Cubism', *Picasso in Retrospect*, ed. J. Golding and R. Penrose (New York, 1973), pp. 49–76

Le Cubisme, Université de Saint-Étienne, Centre Interdisciplinaire d'Etudes et de Recherche sur l'Expression Contemporaine, Travaux iv (Paris, 1973)

L. Steinberg: 'Resisting Cézanne: Picasso's *Three Women*', *A. America*, lxvi/6 (1978), pp. 114–33

V. Spate: *Orphism: The Evolution of Non-figurative Painting in Paris, 1910–1914* (Oxford, 1979)

L. Steinberg: 'The Polemical Part', *A. America*, lxvii/2 (1979), pp. 114–27

L. W. Gamwell: *Cubist Criticism, 1907–1925* (Ann Arbor, 1980)

J. M. Nash: 'The Nature of Cubism: A Study of Conflicting Explanations', *A. Hist.*, iii/4 (1980), pp. 435–47

D. Cottington: *Cubism and the Politics of Culture* (diss., U. London, Courtauld Inst., 1985)

C. Green: *Cubism and its Enemies: Modern Movements and Reaction in French Art, 1916–1928* (London and New Haven, 1987)

M. Roskill: *The Interpretation of Cubism* (Philadelphia, Toronto and London, 1987)

P. Assouline: *L'Homme de l'art: D.-H. Kahnweiler, 1884–1979* (Paris, 1988)

C. Poggi: *In Defiance of Painting: Cubism, Futurism and the Invention of Collage* (New Haven, 1992)

CHRISTOPHER GREEN

II. Architecture.

Architectural interest in Cubism centred on the dissolution and reconstitution of the individual characteristics of three-dimensional form, using simplified geometrical shapes, juxtaposed without resort to the illusions of perspective. To the architect, Cubist paintings suggested that elements of form could be superimposed, made transparent or penetrate each other, while retaining the essence of their unique spatial relationships and context. By 1912 Cubism had become a predisposing factor in the development of the Modern Movement in architecture. While the nature of this influence may be in dispute, Cubism developed in parallel with the work of architects of the early Modern Movement such as Peter Behrens (AEG Turbine Factory, Berlin, 1908–9) and Walter Gropius (Fagus factory at Alfeld, Germany, 1911–13), and thus with the simplification of building forms, the use of components appropriate to industrial production, and the increased use of glass (*see* MODERN MOVEMENT, §2).

Cubist conventions were found relevant to an architecture seeking a non-rhetorical manner appropriate to an increasingly industrialized society, and promised an architectural style that need not refer to the past. Attempts at the direct application of Cubism to architecture and interior design by members of the Puteaux group were superficial, however, and Banham (1960, p. 203) suggested that '. . . it is only in conjunction with Futurist ideas that Cubism was able to make any significant contribution to the mainstream. . .'. Although the ideology and subject-matter of the Italian Futurist painters and sculptors predated their visit in 1911 to Paris, their representational techniques were effectively transformed by it and are reflected in the dynamic brilliance of Antonio Sant'Elia (*see* FUTURISM, §2). Thus, what had become a revolution in painting was applied, as Banham puts it, as part of 'a profound reorientation towards a changed world'. The Cubo-Futurist ideas, widely propagated by Filippo Tommaso Marinetti, coloured aesthetic attitudes in the architectural avant-garde. For example, the influential DE STIJL movement (formed 1917) espoused the formal rigours of Neo-plasticism developed by Piet Mondrian under Cubist influence in Paris, and De Stijl was also linked by the classicizing tendencies of Gino Severini to Cubist theory through the writings of, for example, Albert Gleizes. The linking of elementary geometrical forms with inherent beauty as well as with ease of industrial production, however, which had been foreshadowed from 1914 by the art-objects of Marcel Duchamp and pragmatically codified by Hermann Muthesius, was left to the founders of PURISM (1918), Amédée Ozenfant and Charles Edouard Jeanneret (*see* LE CORBUSIER, §I, 1) who in the same year exhibited paintings together in Paris and published *Après le cubisme* (1918).

BIBLIOGRAPHY

G. Severini: *Du Cubisme au classicisme* (Paris, 1921)

P. R. Banham: *Theory and Design in the First Machine Age* (London, 1960), pp. 202–13

H. Sting: *Der Kubismus und seine Einwirkung auf die Wegbereiter der modernen Architektur* (Aachen, 1965)

JOHN MUSGROVE

Cubist Centre. *See* REBEL ART CENTRE.

Cubist-Realism. *See* PRECISIONISM.

Cubitt, James (William Archibald) (*b* Melbourne, Australia, 1 May 1914; *d* London, 16 Dec 1983). English architect and sculptor. He studied at the University of Oxford (1932–5) and the Architectural Association, London (1935–40), and then served with the Royal Engineers in West Africa and Asia. In 1948 he set up in practice in London with Fello Atkinson (1919–82), Dick Maitland (1918–69) and Stefan Buzas (*b* 1913). From the outset Cubitt drew on his acquired knowledge of tropical countries, designing several schools and colleges in Ghana between 1951 and 1954. The practice rapidly gained a pioneering reputation in this field and, after designing some schools in Sowerby Bridge and Pontefract, Yorkshire (1954–7), it was appointed to plan the University of Nigeria at Nsukka, a project that was not completed until 1971. Other work in the 1950s and 1960s included a factory in Rangoon, office buildings in Sierra Leone and Nigeria and the Faculty of Medicine and Teaching Hospital (1961–7) at the University of Malaysia, Kuala Lumpur. Cubitt's major university buildings in developing countries are landmark schemes demonstrating a detailed understanding and selective use of traditional local materials. He is best known for the University of Garyounis (1966–77) at Benghazi, Libya, which at its inception was one of the largest single contracts for a building of its type, catering for 22,000 students on a 400-ha site. The design combined a bold formalism, using marble, ceramic tiles and mosaics in strong colours, and a sensitivity towards clients and users that was consistent in all his buildings. Modern in style, it incorporated traditional arid-climate design features such as protective, inward-looking courtyards and was the first project of its kind to fit physically and psychologically into the desert landscape. Cubitt was also a practising sculptor, holding exhibitions of his work in London and New York. He was President of the Architectural Association from 1965 to 1966.

WRITINGS

'The Need for Self-Awareness', *Arena*, lxxxi/898 (1966), pp. 162–6
with F. Atkinson and D. Sharp: 'University of Benghazi, Libya', *Archit. Assoc. Q.*, vi/3–4 (1974), pp. 81–96

BIBLIOGRAPHY

'University of Nigeria', *Archit. Rev.* [London], cxxv/745 (1959), pp. 132–6
'Medical Centre, Kuala Lumpur', *Archit. Rev.* [London], cxliv/857 (1968), pp. 57–60

□

Cubitt, Thomas (*b* Buxton, Norfolk, 25 Feb 1788; *d* Dorking, Surrey, 20 Dec 1855). English builder. He was the son of a Norfolk smallholder and became the best-known master builder of the 19th century. His family moved to London *c.* 1793 and Thomas was trained as a journeyman carpenter. He made one voyage to India as a ship's carpenter *c.* 1806 and used the proceeds from this trip to set up independently in Eagle Street, Holborn, London, in 1809. In 1814 he became a member of the Carpenters' Company and the same year was joined in business by his brother William Cubitt (1791–1863). The repairing of the roof of the Russell Institution in Great Coram Street, Bloomsbury, in 1812, brought Cubitt much credit for his sound workmanship, and in 1815 he won a

£20,000 contract for building the new London Institution in Moorfields. A stiff penalty clause for non-completion led Cubitt to break with traditional methods of labour organization and take the step for which he is most famous in building history. He leased a large piece of ground in the Gray's Inn Road to use as a builder's yard and engaged a permanent staff of building tradesmen in every trade from bricklayers to paper-hangers, each gang working under its own specialist foreman. Hitherto general contractors had always subcontracted many of the jobs on a large project to independent firms. As his business prospered Cubitt also built up a large civil engineering department and developed his own brickfields.

This large workforce necessitated a constant flow of commissions and Cubitt at once embarked on a long succession of speculative house-building enterprises in various parts of London. Among the earlier jobs were Frederick Street and Ampton Street on the Calthorpe Estate in Bloomsbury (1815); a group of 'genteel and commodious villas' at Highbury Park (1820–23); a mixed development of terraced and semi-detached houses in Albion Road, Stoke Newington (1821–40); and the south side of Tavistock Square for the financier Benjamin Oakley (1820s).

During the 1820s Cubitt's high standard of workmanship earned him substantial contracts for work on the Bedford Estate in the northern parts of Bloomsbury, south of the Euston Road; this included the west side of Tavistock Square, much of Gordon Square, parts of Euston Square and several other streets. The new houses, like all Cubitt's other buildings of this period, were in a classical style and stucco-fronted. The designs for the Bedford Estate work were made in Cubitt's own office by his younger brother Lewis Cubitt (1799–1883), who had been a pupil of Henry Kendall (1776–1875) and who enjoyed a successful career in the 1840s as a railway architect. Lewis's works for various railway companies included the major stations at King's Cross and Bricklayers' Arms. He left the family business in 1832 to join his brother William, who had set up independently as a contractor earlier that year. There were thus two building firms run by the Cubitt brothers (neither had any family connection with Sir William Cubitt, the prominent civil engineering contractor, or with James Cubitt, the Nonconformist church architect).

After the departure of his younger brother, Thomas Cubitt continued to offer a 'design and build' service, but he remained resolutely sceptical of the abilities of independent architects. In 1824 he took his first lease on the Grosvenor Estate, and this connection led directly to his successful speculations, first in Belgravia, then in Pimlico. In Belgravia, Cubitt seems to have been the prime mover and carried much of the responsibility for laying out streets and providing services. Belgrave Square itself was laid out in 1826, and the stately stuccoed terraces and detached mansions designed by George Basevi were largely completed and occupied by 1840. In the streets south of the square—including Eccleston Street, Belgrave Street and Eaton Place—the terraced house fronts mostly conformed to overall designs provided by Lewis Cubitt. The Cubitt firm also built the two tall detached houses at Albert Gate (nicknamed 'Malta' and 'Gibraltar', 'because they will never be taken'). In the 1830s Cubitt continued the expansion of Belgravia westwards by his building activities on the Lowndes Estate, with Lowndes Square as its centrepiece. Pimlico, or 'South Belgravia', was laid out in the later 1830s, but building did not begin in earnest until the 1840s. At this time he was also building the Clapham Park development in south London, in which he turned over 200 acres of bare land into a fashionable suburb of detached villas, where he himself took up residence.

Outside London, Cubitt built houses in Kemp Town at Brighton from 1828 and also a handful of large private mansions which were almost all in the same Italianate or classical Italianate style as his urban terraces and villas. In 1845–8 he designed and built Osborne House in the Isle of Wight for Queen Victoria and Prince Albert, and his good relations with Prince Albert probably secured him the commission to build the substantial additions to Buckingham Palace designed by Edward Blore and James Pennethorne. In the 1850s he was also building himself a large house, Denbies, near Dorking.

Although many of his speculations were extremely risky, Cubitt was consistently lucky and successful. He was also a distinguished public figure and made conspicuous efforts to improve both the condition of the Metropolis and also the reputation of the building trade. He negotiated the purchase of the Brompton site for the Great Exhibition of 1851 and took a leading part in the preparation of the London Building Act of 1855.

Colvin

BIBLIOGRAPHY
H. Hobhouse: *Thomas Cubitt: Master Builder* (London, 1971)

NEIL BURTON

Cubo-Expressionism. Term used to describe a style of Czech avant-garde art, literature, film, dance and cabaret of the period 1909–21. It was introduced by art historians and critics, notably Jiří Padrta and Morislav Lamač, in the early 1970s. The term has two meanings: a general one applicable to the tendency of the age and a specialized one referring to the synthesis of two styles that influenced the development of modern Czech art: French Cubism and German Expressionism.

Expressionism had been in vogue in Bohemia from the 1890s. In 1907 the group known as the Eight, influenced by the Edvard Munch exhibition of 1905, laid down the basic principles for the development of Czech modern art. They were dissatisfied with the prevailing naturalism and sought the reintroduction of colour as the dominant element in art, together with freer brushwork (*see* EIGHT, THE (i)). Most members of the Eight subsequently became joint founders of the Group of Plastic Artists, which was concerned primarily with Cubo-Expressionism. By 1911 the Expressionistic tendencies of Czech art at the beginning of the century had acquired formal direction under the influence of Cubism. The clean morphology of Cubism had impacted on contemporary central European themes: primarily an existential anxiety accompanied by feelings of absurdity and isolation. Cubo-Expressionism is thus an authentic cross-fertilization between foreign influences and the central European intellectual climate, with its conflicting currents of thought.

The influence of Cubism penetrated architecture, sculpture, painting and design. Some artists, such as Emil Filla and Vincenc Beneš, followed the one-sided response to stimuli shown in the work of Picasso and Braque. Others, such as the painters Bohumil Kubišta, Josef Čapek, Jan Zrzavý and the architects Vlastislav Hofman (1884–1964) and Josef Gočár, developed their own variant of Cubism.

A typical example of early Cubo-Expressionism is the sculpture *Anguish* (1911) by OTTO GUTFREUND (see fig.). The anguish in the face of the figure cowering in a Cubistic cloak, as though it had sprung forth from unexplained

Cubo-Expressionist sculpture by Otto Gutfreund: *Anguish*, bronze, h. 1.5 m, 1911 (Prague, National Gallery, Zbraslav Castle)

existentialist horrors, was a frequent theme at the turn of the century. The sculpture drew on some of the emotional sources of the Eight, but its manner of execution was new. In his subsequent work Gutfreund moved from existential subjects to purely Cubistic, athematic sculpture, while Cubo-Expressionism was further developed in the work of Kubišta and Čapek. As early as 1912 Kubišta had shown his opposition to the Cubist aesthetic. His painting *Hanged Man* (1915; Brno, Morav. Mus.; for illustration *see* KUBIŠTA, BOHUMIL) is often cited as demonstrating the way in which Czech Cubo-Expressionism differs from French Cubism and German Expressionism. Kubišta's themes are suffused in the atmosphere of the time, pointing to the dark side of the human psyche, as in *Nervous Lady* (1912; Ostrava, A.G.) and *St Sebastian* (1912; Prague, N.G., Mun. Lib.), which was ignored by those artists who, like the pro-French Emil Filla, were purely Cubistic in their orientation. The *doppelgänger* was a frequent theme in Cubo-Expressionist art and literature, which concerned itself with the minutiae of the split personality. Inspiration, according to Kubišta and Zrzavý, is to be found in the hidden, split-off depths of the human psyche. Zrzavý, who was Kubišta's friend and private pupil, began as a Symbolist but turned to Cubo-Expressionism in *Obsession* (1915), *Suffering* (1916) and *Madman* (1918; all Prague, N.G., Mun. Lib.).

The diagonal was a typical motif in Cubo-Expressionism and acquired an important role, especially in architecture and design. Its possibilities were deduced from the theoretical literature of the time. The German theory of art and aesthetics and Viennese ideas on the history of art, especially the lectures of Alois Riegl, had a hold on many Czech architects; some of the principles of Cubo-Expressionist architecture were analogous to those of the German architects in the Gläserne Kette ('glass chain') group. Cubo-Expressionism had a greater following in Germany than in France. Many of its adherents exhibited at the Sturm-Galerie in Berlin and published articles in such leading German Expressionist journals as *Die Aktion* and *Der Sturm*. German critics especially valued Kubišta and Čapek (the latter both as artist and as writer) and Vlastislav Hofman. Cubo-Expressionism also had a powerful effect on literature, and many important writers were associated with the Group of Plastic Artists, including Karel Čapek, brother of Čapek, František Langer and Richard Weiner. Their collections of stories vividly caught the predicament of the individual tossed about by personal uncertainty regarding his true identity.

BIBLIOGRAPHY

B. Kubišta: *Korespondence a úvahy* [Correspondence and considerations] (Prague, 1960)
J. Opelík: *Josef Čapek* (Prague, 1980)
F. Burkhardt and M. B. Lamerová: *Cubismo cecoslovacco: Architekture e interni* (Milan, 1982)
P. Wittlich: *Česká secese* [The Czech Secession] (Prague, 1982)
M. Nešlhová: *Bohumil Kubišta* (Prague, 1984)
M. Lamač: *Osma a Skupina výtvarných umělců* [The Eight and the Group of Plastic Artists] (Prague, 1988)
1909–1925, Kubismus in Prag (exh. cat., ed. J. Švestka and T. Vlček; Düsseldorf, Kstver., 1991)

KAREL SRP

Cubo-Futurism. Term first used in 1913 in a lecture, later published, by the Russian art critic Korney Chukovsky (1882–1969) in reference to a group of Russian avant-garde poets whose work was seen to relate to French Cubism and Italian Futurism; it was subsequently adopted by painters and is now used by art historians to refer to Russian art works of the period 1912–15 that combine aspects of both styles. Initially the term was applied to the work of the poets Vladimir Mayakovsky, Aleksey Kruchonykh, Velimir Khlebnikov, Benedikt Livshits (1886–1939) and Vasily Kamensky (1864–1961), who were grouped around the painter David Burlyuk. Their raucous poetry recitals, public clowning, painted faces and ridiculous clothes emulated the activities of the Italians and earned them the name of Russian Futurists. In poetic output, however, only Mayakovsky could be compared with the Italians; his poem 'Along the Echoes of the City', for example, which describes various street noises, is reminiscent of Luigi Russolo's manifesto *L'arte dei rumori* (Milan, 1913).

Burlyuk was particularly interested in the stylistic devices of Cubist painting and frequently wrote and lectured on the subject. As a result, several of the poets tried to discover analogies between Cubism and their own poetry. Particularly important in this respect was the work of Khlebnikov and Kruchonykh. Their poems of 1913–14 ignored the rules of grammar and syntax, metre and rhyme; they omitted prepositions and punctuation, used half-words, neologisms, irregular word formations and unexpected images. For some, such as Livshits, who attempted merely 'a cubist shaping of the verbal mass', this approach was too radical. Others preferred to introduce more visual qualities. Kamensky, for instance, divided his sheet of paper with diagonal lines and filled the triangular sections with single words, part words, individual letters, numbers and signs, in a variety of typefaces, imitating the geometrical planes and letters of Analytical Cubism.

The term Cubo-Futurism was subsequently used by artists such as Lyubov' Popova, whose stylistic development was indebted to both Cubism and Futurism. Her *Portrait* (1914–15; Athens, George Costakis priv. col.) includes the words 'Cubo Futurismo' as a conscious homage. Later art historians have used the term to categorize paintings and constructions by the Russian avant-garde in general, in which the influences of both Cubism and Futurism are synthesized. Popova's most important work in this respect is *Seated Figure* (1914–15; Cologne, Wallraf-Richartz-Mus.), in which the treatment of the body recalls the work of Léger and Metzinger. However, her use of cones and spirals and the dynamism of line and plane betray the influence of Futurism.

Notable Cubo-Futurist paintings by other artists include Malevich's the *Knife Grinder* (1913; New Haven, CT, Yale U. A.G.) and Burlyuk's the *Siberian Fleet Sailor* (1912; London, Grosvenor Gal.). The mosaic of planes in the former recalls Analytical Cubism, and the cylindrical treatment of the body suggests the work of Léger, but clear trajectories of movement and the subject of man and machine indicate the influence of Futurism. In the latter the head is depicted from different points of view and is integrated with the background by means of echoed arcs, a technique borrowed from Braque, while the dynamism of the diagonals that fracture the image is clearly Futurist.

Cubo-Futurism was a passing but important phase in Russian avant-garde painting and poetry. Mikhail Larionov, Natal'ya Goncharova, Alexandra Exter, Ol'ga Rozanova and Ivan Klyun also painted in this manner. It acted as a springboard for non-objectivity, with Popova and Malevich progressing to SUPREMATISM and the poets Khlebnikov and Kruchonykh to an 'abstract' poetical language in which meaning was negated and only sounds were important.

BIBLIOGRAPHY

K. Chukovsky: 'Ego-futuristy i Cubo-futuristy' [Ego-Futurists and Cubo-Futurists], *Shipovnik*, xxii (1914), pp. 95–154
Il Futurismo russo (Milan, 1967), v/44 of *L'arte moderna* [good pls]
V. Markov: *Russian Futurism: A History* (London, 1969)
S. Compton: *The World Backwards: Russian Futurist Books, 1912–1916* (London, 1978)
A. Z. Rudenstine: 'Cubo-Futurism', *Art of the Avant-garde in Russia: Selections from the George Costakis Collection* (exh. cat., ed. A. Z. Rudenstine and M. Rowell; New York, Guggenheim, 1981), pp. 46–74
C. Gray: *The Russian Experiment in Art, 1863–1922* (rev. and enlarged edn. London, 1990)
M. Yablonska: *Women Artists of Russia's New Age* (London, 1990)

ANTHONY PARTON

Cubr, František (*b* Prague, 8 Jan 1911; *d* Prague, June 1976). Czech architect and teacher. He studied architecture at the Czech Technical University, Prague (1928–34), and subsequently became a member of the Architects' Club, the Block of Progressive Architectural Groups (BAPS) and the Union of Czech Architects. From 1949 he led the Stavoprojekt socialist design studio in Prague. Most of his work was devoted to exhibition and interior design, in which he developed trends from abroad and attempted to achieve a synthesis of different artistic disciplines. At the same time he experimented with new building materials, evaluating their artistic potential. In 1947 he won a gold medal for the Czechoslovak exhibition at the Milan Triennale. He achieved his most noteworthy success at Expo 58 in Brussels, where his Czechoslovak Pavilion, designed in collaboration with Josef Hrubý and Zdeněk Pokorný, won several major awards. The restrained and elegant layout of the pavilion, with its three steel, glass and laminated plastic cubes connected by glass wings into an L-shape, significantly influenced the development of Czechoslovak architecture as a whole. The pavilion was rebuilt in Prague in 1959 and damaged, in 1991, by a fire. Together with the same team he designed many other exhibition buildings and interiors as well as the Strahov student campus (1960–65) and the International Telephone and Telegraph Exchange (1966–78), both in Prague. In 1960 he became a lecturer at the Czech Technical University and in 1967 Head of the School of Architecture at the Academy of Fine Arts, Prague.

BIBLIOGRAPHY

O. Nový and J. Šetlík: *Cubr-Hrubý-Pokorný* (Prague, 1962)
Architektonické práce z let 1959–1965 architektů Cubra, Hrubého a Pokorného [Architectural works 1959–1965 by Cubr, Hrubý and Pokorný] (Prague, 1965)

RADOMÍRA SEDLÁKOVÁ

Cucchi, Enzo (*b* Morro d'Alba, nr Ancona, 14 Nov 1950). Italian painter, draughtsman and sculptor. He began exhibiting in 1977 after sporadic studies and established his reputation as a figurative painter belonging to the *Transavanguardia* with large oil paintings such as *Ferocious Tongues* (2.10×2.53 m) and *A Painter's Earth Paintings* (2.01×2.19 m, both 1980; Amsterdam, Stedel. Mus.). These were characterized by an economical and simply rendered image, brilliant primary and secondary colours, bold draughtsmanship and abrupt shifts of scale. Motifs were often established in charcoal or pencil drawings as if by stream-of-consciousness, with waves, flames, skulls and roosters figuring prominently in his symbolic imagery. He consistently favoured a titanic scale, heavily textured surfaces and a fundamentally intuitive and anti-intellectual approach, portraying the universe in apocalyptic terms as a battlefield of elemental forces: light against dark, life and death, creation and destruction. The compressed and flattened space of his early paintings gave way to illusions of deep, cavernous space, for example in imaginary landscapes such as the *Flourishing of the Black Rooster* (1983; Amsterdam, Stedel. Mus.); such works also introduced earthy browns, deep greys, velvety blacks and brilliant whites as well as an almost Caravaggesque sense of dramatic light effects. On occasion he incorporated elements made of iron, neon tubing or burnt wood, as in *Prehistoric Dawn* (oil on canvas with wood element, 1983; Amsterdam, Stedel. Mus.); he also created a few sculptures, such as *Untitled* (bronze, 1.2×2.0×10.0 m, 1985; Humlebæk, Louisiana Mus.), a huge, essentially flat shape that gives the impression of having been poured on to its outdoor site.

BIBLIOGRAPHY

Enzo Cucchi (exh. cat., texts by D. Bozo, E. Darragon, B. Corà; Paris, Pompidou, 1986)
Enzo Cucchi (exh. cat. by D. Waldman; New York, Guggenheim, 1986)
Enzo Cucchi (exh. cat., texts by H. Hohl and E. Cucchi; Hamburg, Ksthalle, 1992)

MONICA BOHM-DUCHEN

Cucci, Domenico (*b* Todi, Italy, *c.* 1635; *d* ?Paris, 1704–5). French cabinetmaker, bronzeworker and carver of Italian birth. He may have trained in Rome and was summoned to France *c.* 1660, probably by Cardinal Mazarin, to work at the Gobelins. In 1664 he became a naturalized French citizen. He was granted lodgings at the Gobelins, where he was the head of the workshop that produced opulent, Italianate display cabinets of superb workmanship (*see* GOBELINS, §§3 and 4). Cucci can be seen presenting such a cabinet in the tapestry of *Louis XIV Visiting the Gobelins* (*c.* 1667; Versailles, Château; *see* GOBELINS, fig. 1). This cabinet is probably one of a pair of 'large ebony cabinets inlaid with pewter' with 'four large twisted columns in imitation of lapis and vine scrolls of copper gilt supported by lions' paws', made between 1667 and 1673, described in the royal records. The records provide detailed information on the cabinets produced by Cucci and his workshop, among them the War and Peace cabinets, and the Apollo and Diana cabinets with columns of aventurine marble and jasper. These four cabinets were considered old-fashioned by 1748 and were placed in the Cabinet of Natural History, where they were probably dismantled and the mosaic panels and hardstones turned into mineralogical specimens. The two identifiable works by Cucci that survive are cabinets made between 1681 and 1683 (both Alnwick Castle, Northumb.; *see* GOBELINS, fig. 2). These cabinets were at Versailles, possibly in the

Galerie de Mignard, which Cucci had decorated with lapis lazuli, gilded tortoiseshell and bronze in the early 1680s, until 1751, when they were among items of royal furniture sold by auction.

Cucci also produced decoration in bronze and gilt copper. In 1693 Daniel Cronström wrote a letter to Nicodemus Tessin the younger in which he described Cucci as the ablest worker in gilt copper at the Gobelins and mentioned that Cucci had produced ironwork for the windows and door furniture at Versailles. Cucci was employed on the elaborate marquetry floor designed by Le Brun for the château of Saint-Germain and is known to have carved cases for an organ, a harpsichord and a spinet for the King at Versailles.

BIBLIOGRAPHY

J. Guiffrey, ed.: *Comptes des Bâtiments du roi sous le règne de Louis XIV* (Paris, 1881–1901), ii, col. 65, 217, 269, 373

——: *Inventaire général du mobilier de la couronne sous Louis XIV* (Paris, 1885–6), ii, pp. 160–2, nn. 372–3

M. Jourdain: *Country Life*, 23 August 1930, p. xxxiv

P. Verlet: *French Royal Furniture* (London, 1963), pp. 3–7

R.-A. Weigart and C. Hernmarck: *L'Art en France et en Suède, 1693–1718: Extraits d'une correspondance entre l'architecte Nicodème Tessin le jeune et Daniel Cronström* (Stockholm, 1964), pp. 15, 16, 39, 41

A. Gonzalez-Palacios: 'La manifattura di Luigi XIV ai Gobelins', *Splendori di pietre dure* (exh. cat., ed. A. Giusti; Florence, Pitti, 1988), pp. 242–5

BET MCLEOD

Cucuteni. Site of a prehistoric settlement that flourished in the 5th millennium BC in north-east Romania. It is of interest for the sequence of painted pottery found there. Cucuteni is near Tîrgu-Fromoş in the district of Iaşi, between the Prut and Siret rivers. It was first excavated by Hubert Schmidt in 1909–10 and then by Mircea Petrescu-Dîmboviţa in 1961–8. Material recovered from the site is held in museums in Iaşi, Bîrlad and Bucharest in Romania as well as in Berlin. The settlement is stratified, revealing several phases of agriculture-based occupation, although this did not result in the build-up of a mound. The site has given its name to the Cucuteni culture, which is usually linked with the Tripolye culture of Moldova and the western Ukraine and had several phases; Cucuteni itself was occupied in the main phases. Cucuteni pottery took various shapes, from bowls and pedestalled bowls to tripartite pots and large bellied jars. Early 'Pre-Cucuteni' forms had incised decoration on fine dark wares, a feature that continued into later phases. Most striking, however, are the polychrome vessels of the main phases of the Cucuteni culture (*see* PREHISTORIC EUROPE, fig. 23). In the Cucuteni A phase, painting was both bichrome and trichrome, using red, black and white; in Cucuteni A-B and B it was mainly bichrome, using black and orange. Some Cucuteni A pots were painted in white slip over an unslipped orange surface, with black lines for borders; the paint was applied before firing. The decoration is dominated by abstract, interlocking spiral and curvilinear motifs, which usually cover most of the outside of the vessel. The amount of variation and the rate of innovation are as interesting as the technical details. It is not known if pottery production in the region was in the hands of specialists. In addition to the pottery, small fired-clay anthropomorphic figurines, skilfully made flintwork and copper tools and ornaments were produced.

For further discussion of the arts and architecture of Neolithic Europe *see* PREHISTORIC EUROPE, §IV.

BIBLIOGRAPHY

H. Schmidt: *Cucuteni* (Berlin, 1932)

M. Petrescu-Dîmboviţa: *Cucuteni* (Bucharest, 1966)

ALASDAIR WHITTLE

Cuenca [Lat. Conca]. City in east central Spain, capital of Cuenca Province.

1. HISTORY AND URBAN DEVELOPMENT. Cuenca was founded by the Romans on a rocky massif above the confluence of the Júcar and Huécar rivers. The settlement was given by Muhammad II al-Mu'tamid of Seville (*reg* 1069–91) to Alfonso VI of León and Castile (*reg* 1065–1109). In 1177 the city was finally reconquered from the Moors by Alfonso VIII of Castile (*reg* 1158–1214), and Pope Lucius III (*reg* 1181–5) made it an episcopal see in 1183. In the Middle Ages, Cuenca was a flourishing centre of the wool trade and expanded considerably. From the 13th century to the 18th the city was one of the most important centres of the production of handwoven carpets. The cathedral (see §2 below) was built in the first half of the 13th century. The characteristic *casas colgadas* or 'hanging houses' with wooden balconies date from the 14th century. The city declined after the 18th century: between 1808 and 1811 Cuenca was sacked three times by Napoleonic troops, and in 1873–4 it was sacked again by the Carlists. In the 19th century the city began to expand on the Júcar Valley, where the medieval market gardens had been laid out.

2. CATHEDRAL. The starting date for the construction of the cathedral is not recorded. The series of donations from Alfonso VIII between 14 November 1183 and 21 November 1214 does not mention any building activity. There was no hurry to build a cathedral as, according to the mid-13th-century antiquary Ascensio de Morales, immediately after Alfonso VIII's capture of the city (1177) he had provided it with a church by placing an image of the Virgin in its Great Mosque and dedicating the building to S Maria de Gracia; its site is thought to be that of the Capilla Honda in the cathedral. Tradition states that the high altar was consecrated in 1207 or 1208, but the sources are late and contradictory and cannot be trusted. The earliest documentary evidence of construction was the grant the town council made of part of the tithe for the maintenance of churches for ten years to Bishop Cronzalo Palomeque on 25 April 1231. In 1271 Alfonso X of León and Castile (*reg* 1252–84) provided for ashlar to be transported to the cathedral, and on 4 May 1284 Sancho IV (*reg* 1284–95) exempted five of its builders from tolls.

The fabric bears out this chonology. The east end falls into two parts. The choir, choir aisles and walls of the transepts—excluding the entrances to the nave aisles—have different abaci to the transept vaults. Similarities between these sections and parts of S Maria de Huerta (Soria), dated to the 1220s, in which masons from Cuenca appear to have participated, and in addition the earliest work at Toledo Cathedral (*c.* 1215/20–38), suggest a probable date of the 1220s for this first phase. The nave is distinct from the east end in that it possesses flying buttresses rather than wall buttresses. This building campaign must have included the construction of La Torre de Angel as the rib profile of its octopartite vault is the same as that of the nave. A date of *c.* 1280 is likely as connections abound between it and the latest work at Burgos Cathedral (consecrated 20 July 1260).

The cathedral, 109 m long, 20 m high and built of limestone, is situated on a spur formed by the confluence of the rivers Júcar and Huécar. Its present plan consists of an aisled nave, projecting transept, deep, twin-aisled choir and double ambulatory, the latter a Late Gothic addition; originally, as Lambert has argued, the choir was probably flanked by an echelon of chapels. The elevation of the east end consists of an arcade and short clerestory; the nave is the same except that the clerestory has an interior passageway. The first 13th-century architect seems to have set out to build as modern, expensive and grand a building as the restricted site allowed. Thus, a compact Romanesque plan was updated by the adoption of double aisles, a feature of French High Gothic buildings.

As originally conceived, the cathedral belongs to that current of artistic exchange, identified by Bony, which extended around the Ile-de-France and eschewed Chartres Cathedral. This is clear from the two-storey elevations of both the choir and nave, the wall buttresses, colonnettes *en délit* and, in the transept, compressed sexpartite vaults. More specifically, the first master knew of the architecture around Soissons and Laon in nothern France: the sexpartite vaults of the choir have supports similar to those of Laon Cathedral. Cuenta Cathedral later came to belong to the Castilian Gothic style of the reign of Alfonso X, which drew on the latest French buildings but delighted in sculptural embellishments, as is apparent from the smiling angels and crockets in the interior clerestory passageway and the original design of the west façade. The present one is an early-20th-century reconstruction by V. Lamperez y Romea, but there is evidence that it used to have glazed tympana like the west façade of Reims Cathedral. Cuenca was one of the first Spanish cathedrals to be initiated in the French Gothic style. The east end influenced a number of buildings in New Castile and further north in the first half of the 13th century; for example, the pattern of its south transept rose was repeated at S Salvador Cifuentes (Guadalajara.)

Three main alterations to the cathedral were subsequently made. First, the double ambulatory, with the arches on to the last straight bay of the choir, was constructed, the escutcheons on the bosses indicating a date in the episcopacy of Lope de Barrientos (*reg* 1444–69). The architect was probably Hanequin de Bruselas, Master of the Works of Toledo Cathedral: the double ambulatory with its stepped cross-section and alternation of rectangular and triangular bays was obviously modelled on the 13th-century chevet of Toledo. On 6 March 1454 Hanequin de Bruselas and Egas Cueman contracted to provide the *coro* with new stalls (sold to the Prior of Belmonte in 1754). This enlargement was part of a bigger programme to turn Cuenca into a Late Gothic cathedral.

Second, the north side of the choir and transept were lined with three Plateresque chapels: the Capilla de los Caballeros, restored in 1520–22 by Canon Carrillo de Albornoz; the Capilla del Doctor Muñoz, begun in 1537

by the sculptor Diego de Tiedra (*fl* 1537–70); and the Arco de Jamete (1546–50; see fig.) built by Bishop Sebastián Ramírez de Fuenleal (*reg* 1542–7). Antonio Flores, responsible for the other notable Plateresque chapel, the Capilla de los Aposteles (1527–38), off the south aisle, probably executed the portal and altars of the Capilla de los Caballeros.

The most important of these works is the Arco de Jamete. A combination of a triumphal arch, chapel and portal for the cloister, it is traditionally attributed to Esteban Jamete (*b* Orléans, 1515) but Azcárate has suggested that it was designed by Alonso de Covarrubias. The Renaissance architecture is fused with medieval iconography in a typically Plateresque manner. For example, the arch flanked by Corinthian columns with cabled fluting on consoles has busts of *Christ* and the 12 *Apostles*; but it is unusual in balancing the dense, crisp ornamentation characteristic of Plateresque with a monumental structure.

Last, the Capilla Mayor was refurbished. The *coro* was moved from the presbytery in 1576–8 but it was not until 1753–60 that the Capilla Mayor took its present form. Then, Gabriel González and Pedro Incharraundiaga, executing the plans of Ventura Rodríguez, created the retable

Cuenca Cathedral, Arco de Jamete, 1546–50

and behind it the Capilla del Transparente with a connecting aperture that allowed the urn of St Julian of Cuenca to be viewed from the Capilla Mayor.

BIBLIOGRAPHY

E. Lambert: *L'Art gothique en Espagne aux XIIe et XIIIe siècles* (Paris, 1931)
J. M. de Azcárate: 'Sobre el Arco de Jamete, en la Catedral de Cuenca', *Archv Esp. A. & Arqueol.*, xvii (1945), pp. 178–80
J. Bony: 'The Resistance to Chartres in Early Thirteenth-century Architecture', *J. Brit. Archaeol. Assoc.*, n. s. 3, xx–xxi (1957–8), pp. 35–52
J. Bermejo Díaz: *La Catedral de Cuenca* (Cuenca, 1977)

CHRISTOPHER WELANDER

Cuer. *See* CURE.

Cueto, Germán (*b* Mexico City, 9 Feb 1893; *d* Mexico City, 14 Feb 1975). Mexican sculptor, painter and decorative artist. He studied briefly at the Academia de Bellas Artes de S Carlos in Mexico City but was fundamentally self-taught. In 1925 he was associated with ESTRIDENTISMO, an avant-garde literary and artistic movement with which he exhibited caricature masks painted in strong expressive colours on glossy card, for example *Germán List Arzubide* (1926; Mexico City, priv. col., see List Arzubide, p. 6). Between 1927 and 1932 he lived in France and Spain; he visited the studios of Brancusi, Gargallo and Lipchitz in Paris, but he was especially influenced by his contact there with Joaquín Torres García. It was during this time that he became committed to abstraction, for example in his stone carving *Napoleon* (1931; Mexico City, priv. col., see 1981 exh. cat., no. 1).

Cueto produced not only sculptures in a variety of materials, but also mosaics and puppets. The avant-garde aesthetics of his exclusively abstract art failed to find acceptance, however, on his return to Mexico, and he was likewise unwilling to yield to the ideologically committed art that was then dominant. Instead he continued his experimental work in a variety of techniques and materials, as in the undated *Tehuana* (Mexico City, Mus. A. Mod.), constructed from bronze, aluminium and copper sheets, and in *Figure* (1967; Mexico City, Acad. A.). From *c.* 1950 he came to be regarded as a precursor of younger Mexican artists dedicated to the avant-garde.

BIBLIOGRAPHY

G. List Arzubide: *El movimiento estridentista* (Jalapa, 1927)
Exposición Germán Cueto (exh. cat. by X. Moyssén, Mexico City, Mus. A. Mod., 1981)

Cuevas, José Luis (*b* Mexico City, 26 Feb 1934). Mexican draughtsman, printmaker and painter. He showed early artistic talent and briefly attended the Escuela Nacional de Pintura y Escultura 'La Esmeralda' in Mexico City, which he left because he did not agree with its teaching methods; he was thus essentially self-taught. He studied graphic arts at the Institución de Enseñanza Universitaria in Mexico City *c.* 1948. At the Galería Prisse in Mexico City he joined a group of young artists, including Alberto Gironella, Enrique Echeverría, Pedro Coronel, Manuel Felguérez and Francisco Icaza (*b* 1930), who were opposed to the socialist artists favoured by the Government and whose rebellion against the offical mural art was instrumental in modifying the contemporary artistic panorama. Cuevas conducted an aggressive polemic against David Alfaro Siqueiros and his more dogmatic followers, publishing the manifesto 'La cortina de nopal' (*Novedades*, 1957). In 1953 he had his first exhibition at the Galería Prisse; its success led to its being shown the following year at the Pan American Union, Washington, DC, and later to Cuevas's receiving worldwide exposure and recognition as a draughtsman and graphic artist. He was subsequently invited to work in various workshops worldwide, including the Tamarind Workshop in Los Angeles, CA, and Poligrafa in Barcelona in 1981, while in Mexico he worked at the Taller Kyron, among others.

Cuevas produced numerous self-portraits, but he also depicted a variety of characters and scenes in his drawings and prints, some drawn from reality and others from his imagination. His work is satirical, incisive and grotesque in style, and he sometimes visited mental asylums, old people's homes and brothels to seek inspiration in deformity and sordidness. His literary sources included Franz Kafka, the Marquis de Sade and Francisco de Quevedo, while his chief artistic influences were Goya, Rembrandt, Picasso and Orozco. He was a skilled draughtsman with both pencil and ink pen, and in his printmaking he experimented constantly with new materials and techniques.

WRITINGS

The World of Kafka and Cuevas (Philadelphia, 1959)
Cuevas por Cuevas (Mexico City, 1965)
Crime by Cuevas (New York, 1968)
Homage to Quevedo (San Francisco, 1969)
Cuevario (Mexico City, 1973)

BIBLIOGRAPHY

M. Traba: *Los cuatro monstruos cardinales: Bacón, Cuevas, Dubuffet y De Kooning* (Mexico City, 1965)
C. Fuentes: *El mundo de José Luis Cuevas* (Mexico City, 1969)
J. Gómez Sicre: *José Luis Cuevas* (Barcelona, 1982)

XAVIER MOYSSÉN

Cuevas, Pedro de las (*b* Madrid; *d* Madrid, 28 July 1644). Spanish painter. Although no work by him has been identified, he was, according to Palomino, one of the most notable masters 'in the art of teaching', and many of the leading artists in Madrid in the second third of the 17th century were his pupils. He married the widowed mother of the painter Francisco Camilo, and they had a son, Eugenio de las Cuevas, who was also a painter. Among those who trained in de las Cuevas's workshop, besides his stepson Francisco and his son Eugenio, were Jusepe Leonardo, Antonio de Pereda, Antonio Arias Fernández, Juan Carreño de Miranda and Francisco de Burgos Mantilla. He worked as a painter in the service of the Real Cárcel de la Corte de Madrid, producing seven large canvases including the *Crucifixion of St Peter*, *Christ at the Column* and the *Crowning with Thorns* (1643; destr.). It can be assumed that his art was not far removed from that of his contemporaries Vicente Carducho and Eugenio Cajés, with whom he maintained relations that are documented.

BIBLIOGRAPHY

M. Agulló y Cobo: *Noticias sobre pintores madrileños de los siglos XVI al XVIII* (Madrid, 1978), pp. 38, 54–5
——: *Más noticias sobre pintores madrileños de los siglos XVI al XVIII* (Madrid, 1981), p. 67

JESUS URREA

Cuffle, Pierre de la. *See under* MILAN, PIERRE.

Cui Bo [Ts'ui Po; *zi* Zixi] (*b* Haoliang, now Fengyang, Anhui Province; *fl* mid-11th century). Chinese painter. After establishing a considerable artistic reputation, Cui was appointed to the post of assistant teacher (*yixue*) at the court of Emperor Shenzong (*reg* 1067–85) at Bianliang (now Kaifeng, Henan Province). Dissatisfied with his post in the imperial Hanlin Painting Academy, Cui was given permission by the Emperor to resign but continued to paint imperial commissions.

Cui established a new standard for painting within the Northern Song (960–1127) Academy. In contrast to the Tang (AD 618–907) style of animal, bird and plant painting (*see* CHINA, §V, 3(v)(b)), which stressed central, static compositions and employed strong ink outlines filled with luxuriant colour, Cui introduced a new sense of action in his natural scenes, which were painted directly on to silk without underdrawing. In 1061 he produced one of the extant masterpieces of Northern Song painting, *Shuangxi tu* ('Magpies and hare'; Taipei, N. Pal. Mus.; *see* CHINA, fig. 122). This painting presents a confrontation between a hare and two magpies on a windy autumn day. The preciseness of a moment in time is emphasized by the backward and upward glance of the hare and the precarious thrusting forward of the bird above it. The effect of transience is heightened by the wind-bent bamboos and grasses, the decaying leaves and the linear movement of the elements of this seemingly unarranged scene. The dramatic interaction between animals is unprecedented in earlier paintings. The colouring is subdued, and the hare and magpies are textured with hair-thin lines, appearing more lifelike than in any other previous example. Stories record Cui's broad competence and versatility in subject-matter. He painted narrative and religious themes, landscapes and animals, birds and plants, setting new standards of realism for subsequent generations of Chinese painters.

BIBLIOGRAPHY
A. Soper: *Kuo Jo-hsü's Experience in Painting* (Washington, DC, 1951)
J. Cahill: *Chinese Painting* (Geneva and New York, 1960)
——: *An Index of Early Chinese Painters and Paintings: T'ang, Sung, and Yüan* (Berkeley, 1980)
S. Bush and H. Y. Shih: *Early Chinese Texts on Painting* (Cambridge, MA, 1985)

JAMES ROBINSON

Cuicuilco. Pre-Columbian site in Mexico, on the southern periphery of modern Mexico City. It flourished in the Late Pre-Classic period (*c.* 300 BC–*c.* AD 250), until overshadowed by the city of TEOTIHUACÁN in the north-east Basin of Mexico. Few of Cuicuilco's structures have been excavated. Excavations were carried out by Manuel Gamio and Byron Cummings in 1922 and 1925, and by Eduardo Noguera, Hugo Moedano and Robert Heizer in the 1950s. Further study and new interpretations of the results of these excavations were completed in the 1970s.

Cuicuilco's occupation began *c.* 900 BC as early agriculturists settled at the site. By the time of its apogee it covered a wide region close to an already drained ancient lake in the southern Basin of Mexico and controlled up to 40,000 people. In the final centuries BC and the 1st century AD Cuicuilco was a serious rival to Teotihuacán for control of the Basin of Mexico. The eruption of nearby Xitle volcano caused the first destruction of the city, and another eruption at the beginning of the 4th century AD partially covered the site.

The principal ceremonial construction was a round 'pyramid', ultimately 135 m in diameter at the base, comprising four stacked, sloping, circular tiers built in stages up to *c.* 20 m high. Two ramps, one possibly a staircase, ascended the east and west sides. Several oval altars were built in succession at the summit, and a double line of large vertical stone slabs encompassed the base. The core of the mounds consists of light volcanic rubble, covered in a thick layer of mud, then a facing of large river boulders. Traces of reed and grass huts, and numerous radial burials were found around the base of the pyramid, together with stone tools. At the base of the western ramp a circular structure of unknown use was built. It comprises several huge, irregular stones buried deep in the ground and sloping towards the centre. Other large stones were presumably used to form a roof. Inside, spiral-like designs in red paint were applied directly to the stones.

Cuicuilco's primary craft product was pottery. As well as utilitarian vessels, a wide variety of figurines was made, especially of females in a style similar to those found at TLATILCO. Some are in dancing poses, and others wear rich garments and have elaborate hairstyles. Some appear to be ball-players, early evidence of the spread of the Mesoamerican game played with a solid rubber ball (*see* BALLCOURT, §1). Many others are naked, and some may represent deities including the pan-Mesoamerican Old Fire God, Huehueteotl or Xiuhtecuhtli. Their purpose is unknown.

For discussion of the arts of Pre-Columbian Mexico *see also* MESOAMERICA, PRE-COLUMBIAN.

BIBLIOGRAPHY
B. Cummings: 'Cuicuilco and Archaic Cultures in Mexico', *Soc. Sci. Bull.*, iv (1933), pp. 1–56
I. Marquina: *Arquitectura prehispánica* (Mexico City, 1950, 2/1964/*R* 1981), pp. 47–55
G. Kubler: *The Art and Architecture of Ancient America*, Pelican Hist. A. (Harmondsworth, 1962, rev. 3/1984), pp. 46–8, 51, 56, 63
W. Sanders, J. Parsons and R. Santley: *The Basin of Mexico: Ecological Processes in the Evolution of a Civilization* (New York, 1979)
J. Kelly: *The Complete Visitor's Guide to Mesoamerican Ruins* (Norman, 1982), pp. 79–81
D. Schávelzon: *La pirámide de Cuicuilco: Album fotográfico* (Mexico City, 1983)

DANIEL SCHÁVELZON

Cuicul. *See* DJEMILA.

Cuijp. *See* CUYP.

Cuipers. *See* CUYPERS.

Cuixart, Modest (*b* Barcelona, 2 Nov 1925). Spanish Catalan painter. He studied medicine from 1944 to 1946 at the University of Barcelona but abandoned these studies in order to devote himself to painting, which he had taken up in 1941. His early works tended towards a decorative calligraphic abstraction, but on becoming a founder-member of the DAU AL SET group in 1948 he underwent the influence of Surrealism in such works as *Fishermoons* (1949; *see* Caballero Bonald, pl. 15). He settled in France in 1951, and from 1955 to *c.* 1965 he produced paintings in different techniques related to *Art informel* and matter painting. A favourite technique was that of drip painting;

often the drips were in light colours or in metal-based paints against dark backgrounds, as in *Gran Barroco* (1.62×1.30 m, 1959; Madrid, Fund. Juan March). In the mid-1960s he returned to a more overt figuration while on occasion still using techniques adapted from his informal abstractions of the late 1950s.

BIBLIOGRAPHY

J. E. Cirlot: *La pintura de Modest Cuixart* (Barcelona, 1958)
J. J. Lerrant: *Modest Cuixart* (Barcelona, 1960)
J. E. Cirlot: *Visión de Cuixart* (Barcelona, 1963)
P. Chamorro: *Conversación con Cuixart* (Madrid, 1975)
J. M. Caballero Bonald: *Cuixart*, intro. B. Porcel (Madrid, 1977)

LOURDES CIRLOT

Cularo. *See* GRENOBLE.

Ćulinović, Juraj. *See* SCHIAVONE, GIORGIO.

Cullen, (Thomas) Gordon (*b* Yorks, 9 Aug 1914; *d* 11 Aug 1994). English writer and urban planning consultant. He studied architecture at the Polytechnic of Central London and subsequently worked as a draughtsman in various architects' offices including that of Berthold Lubetkin and Tecton, but he never qualified or practised as an architect. From 1944 to 1946 he worked in the planning office of the Development and Welfare Department in Barbados, then returned to London and joined the *Architectural Review*, first as a draughtsman and then as a writer on planning policies and principles. He produced a large number of influential editorial features and case studies on the theory of planning and the design of towns, including criticism of the disregard by local planning authorities of aesthetic and other considerations. Many improvements in the urban and rural environment in Britain during the 1950s and 1960s were due to his influence. The features consisted largely of drawings that conveyed a particularly clear understanding of his ideas, and these had a considerable influence on subsequent architectural illustration styles. He also illustrated several books by other authors. Cullen became a freelance writer and consultant in 1956 and, in the years immediately following, he advised the cities of Liverpool and Peterborough on their reconstruction and redevelopment plans. In 1960 he was invited to India to advise on the planning aspects of the Ford Foundation's work in New Delhi and Calcutta (1962). His later work included planning advice to the city of Glasgow and the London Docklands Development Corporation during the 1980s. He was elected Honorary Fellow of the RIBA (1972), appointed Royal Designer for Industry and awarded the Gold Medal of the American Institute of Architects (both 1976) and appointed CBE in 1978.

WRITINGS

Townscape (London, 1961); rev. as *The Concise Townscape* (London, 1971)

J. M. RICHARDS

Cullen, Maurice (*b* St John's, Nfld, 6 June 1866; *d* Chambly, Qué., 28 March 1934). Canadian painter. In 1870 he moved with his family to Montreal, which became his principal home. After taking drawing lessons in local art schools and studying sculpture with Louis-Philippe Hébert from 1884 to 1887, he went in 1888 to study in Paris. He was elected an associate of the Société Nationale des Beaux-Arts in 1895. On his return to Montreal, he found his preferred subject-matter: the tempered winter landscape (e.g. *Logging in Winter, Beaupré*, 1896; Hamilton, Ont., A.G.). Later trips to Europe in 1896 and from 1900 to 1902 reinforced his admiration for late Impressionism. In his views of Québec (*c.* 1900–1910), typified by *The Old Ferry, Louise Basin* (1907; Ottawa, N.G.), Cullen infused the atmospheric, inhabited landscape with the grandeur of panorama painting. Unlike his friend J. W. Morrice, he sought to convey good design in nature rather than impose it on his landscape compositions. In his cityscapes of Montreal (1909–16), Cullen successfully reconciled man and nature, Impressionism and the academic tradition; but he also retained a sense of the romantic and the picturesque. Cullen exhibited with the CANADIAN ART CLUB. In the early 1920s, after serving in Europe as a war artist, his painting became more conservative with increasing emphasis on the factual. When Cullen died, his 'tempered Impressionism' had long been rejected, but his evocation of the familiar later influenced Canadian modernism.

BIBLIOGRAPHY

Maurice Cullen, 1866–1934 (exh. cat., ed. S. Antoniou; Kingston, Ont., Queen's U., Agnes Etherington A. Cent., 1982)
S. Paikowsky: 'Maurice Cullen', *Artmagazine*, xiv (1983), pp. 54–7

SANDRA PAIKOWSKY

Cullinan, Edward (*b* London, 17 June 1931). English architect and teacher. He studied at Cambridge University (1951–4), then briefly at the Architectural Association School, London; this was followed by a fellowship at the University of California, Berkeley (1954–6). Cullinan was an admirer of William Morris, and his practice evolved on a co-operative basis. His first major commission (1971) was from the Olivetti Company and led to designs for workshops in Dundee, Belfast, Derby and Carlisle, as well as five further projects, including the two-stage Training Centre Residential Wing at Haslemere, Surrey. Cullinan was also involved in residential architecture, while a number of projects for older people—such as the older people's flats (1971; with Phil Tabor), Northwood, Middlesex, the Community Care Centre (1983; with Robin Nicolson), Lambeth, London, and the Elderly Persons' Day Care Centre (1984), Lambeth, London—as well as buildings for the mentally handicapped, brought his practice to prominence in the field of design for social welfare. He also designed various heritage projects: the Minster Lovell Conference Centre (1969) for the Cotswold National Park, which incorporated domestic scale into a public sphere, the successful rebuilding (1982) of St Mary's Parish Church, Barnes, London, and a Visitors' Centre (1992), Fountains Abbey, N Yorks. In the latter the cantilevered, curved roof obviates the need for load-bearing walls, providing clear views and creating a distinct visual identity that nevertheless harmonizes with its surroundings at a formal and material level.

BIBLIOGRAPHY

Contemp. Architects
S. Cantacuzino, ed.: *British Architecture: Arts and Leisure* (London, 1977)

MICHAEL SPENS

Culot, Maurice (*b* Seville, 7 Dec 1938). Belgian architect, urban planner, historian and teacher. He graduated in architecture in 1964 and until 1967 lived in the USA, where he worked at the Frank Lloyd Wright Foundation and with Paolo Soleri in Scottsdale, AZ. On his return to Brussels, he began to teach urban planning at the Institut Supérieur des Arts Decoratifs de la Cambre (now the Ecole N. Sup. A. Visuels), Brussels; an ardent promoter of urban reconstruction in Europe, he favoured alternative approaches in support of the preservation of traditional urban structures. In 1969 he founded the Archives d'Architecture Moderne in Brussels, a research and conservation centre and a publishing house specializing in the architecture of the 19th and 20th centuries; in 1975 he became editor of the journal *Archives d'architecture moderne*, which discusses mostly classical and vernacular architectural projects. A friend of Léon Krier, Culot published a number of works with him, such as *Architecture rationnelle* (1978) and *Albert Speer* (1985), and they worked together on the Südliche-Friedrichstadt project for the Internationale Bauausstellung (IBA 1981) in Berlin. In 1980 Culot was invited to Paris to become Director of the Archives and History Department of the Institut Français d'Architecture, where he set up a centre for the conservation of architects' archives. He created and directed collections devoted to French towns, including Toulouse and Amiens, and to architects, including Henri Sauvage and Louis Bonnier. At the same time he opened the Musée des Archives d'Architecture Moderne in Brussels (1984), which gathered together the archives of the most important Belgian architects since the end of the 19th century. In 1986 he became President of the Fondation pour l'Architecture, created by Philippe Rotthier to give the capital of Europe a site for architectural exhibitions and debate.

BIBLIOGRAPHY
R. Maxwell: 'Tafuri/Culot/Krier: The Role of Ideology', *Archit. Des.*, xlvii/3 (1977), pp. 187–99

ANNE VAN LOO

Cult of carts. Acts of piety that assisted church-building in western Europe during the 11th and 12th centuries. The expression was first used by Arthur Kingsley Porter in 1909 to characterize the phenomenon of people, under close supervision, serving as beasts of burden to haul materials to church building sites.

In a true cult of carts event the faithful pulled cartloads of materials rather than just the materials themselves. Of the fourteen superficially similar instances recorded between 1066 and 1308 (twelve religious and two secular), seven took place at Benedictine churches or were reported by Benedictine chroniclers, and the link may be significant. The cult of carts was short-lived; the concept is justified by five historically related examples that occurred in France between *c.* 1140 and 1171, at Saint-Denis, Chartres, Rouen, Saint-Pierre-sur-Dives (Normandy) and Châlons-sur-Marne (Champagne). The account of people dragging stones to help rebuild the church of St Cuthbert at Lindisfarne (England) after 1093 does not fall within this definition, nor do manifestations reported after 1200 in France, at Calais, Beaucaire and the cathedrals of Auxerre and Le Mans.

The 12th-century events were inspired by two 11th-century occurrences, at Montecassino Abbey (Italy) and Saint-Trond Abbey (Lorraine). The event at Montecassino was reported by Peter the Deacon in *Chronica monasterii Casiensis*. In 1066, after the arrival of marbles purchased in Rome by Abbot Desiderius for the new monastery church, 'a group composed solely of the faithful carried up the first column on the strength of their necks and arms'. This was a single, symbolic act of support. Peter may have known the account of a similar event at the Cathedral of St Irene at Gaza, Judaea, between 402 and 407, when the faithful dragged columns from the beach to an inland construction site. At least one Greek version of Mark the Deacon's life of Bishop St Porphyry of Gaza (Vienna, Österreich. Nbib., Vind.hist.gr.3) existed in Italy by *c.* 1100. Peter may also have been inspired by the account in Suetonius (*Vespasian* 5) of Emperor Vespasian's carrying away the first basketful of rubble from the Temple of Jupiter Capitolinus, Rome, which was burnt AD 68–70. Although the Montecassino event was not a strict cult of carts, many aspects of Peter's account are echoed in accounts of the 12th-century occurrences.

A possibly earlier cult of carts event took place between 1055 and 1082 at the Benedictine abbey of Saint-Trond under Abbot Adelhard II. The account was written between 1108 and 1138 by Abbot Rudolf, who may have been an eye-witness. Building materials, purchased by the faithful at their own expense, were carried on their shoulders and in carts. He described how 'the people in their villages, their voices raised in hymns, took [the columns] up with a most eager enthusiasm, their ropes attached to wagons, without the least use of oxen or pack animals'.

The Saint-Trond event constituted longer-lasting support of the building project. It is historically related to the main group of 12th-century events in France, but Abbot Suger's account of the earliest of these, at Saint-Denis between 1140 and 1144, looks back to Montecassino: after the miraculous discovery of columns in a Roman quarry at Pontoise, Suger's workmen and the pious faithful of all ranks tied ropes to them and dragged them to the centre of Pontoise to load them onto carts. There are other similar details and Suger certainly knew the *Chronica monasterii Casiensis* from a visit to Montecassino in 1123.

The cult of carts activity at Chartres Cathedral in 1145 is best documented in a letter of Haymo, Abbot of Saint-Pierre-sur-Dives. Haymo was an eye-witness, although his account borrowed from that of Rudolf of Saint-Trond. He described the thousands of participants from different social ranks at Chartres who sang as they laboured under the strict control of the clergy; one priest was assigned to each cart, to which people were harnessed, perhaps in a similar manner to that shown in the Bayeux Tapestry (see fig.). The whole event was a carefully supervised act of penance, and adults and children welcomed scourging. Haymo understood clearly that the hysteria for salvation had practical value, saying that the monks of Saint-Pierre-sur-Dives constructed a cart of the new type built at Chartres so that their neighbours could help them to complete their church.

The spread of the cult of carts phenomenon from Chartres to Normandy was discussed in a letter written in

...ORIANT:ARMAS: ADNAVES: ET HIC
TRAhVNT: CARRVM
CVM VINO: ET ARM IS:

Cult of carts: humans serving as draught-animals, detail from the Bayeux Tapestry (scene 37), linen with wool embroidery, h. 510 mm, probably before 1082 (Bayeux, Musée de la Tapisserie de la Reine Mathilde)

1145 by the Archbishop of Rouen, Hugo of Amiens, a former Benedictine monk, who reported that some of his people went to help at Chartres and that he later put their faith to use at home. The last recorded 12th-century cult of carts manifestation in France was at Châlons-sur-Marne, associated with the building of the Benedictine abbey church and reported in a letter by Guy of Bazoches, canon of Châlons Cathedral from 1162 to 1171. Guy's account shows familiarity with Haymo's. In the 1180s the chronicler Robert of Torigny, whose sources were the letters of Archbishop Hugo and Abbot Haymo, made it clear that the cult was over.

In 1223 a distant reflection of Montecassino may have been seen at the Franciscan church in Reggio nell'Emilia in Italy, where the townspeople carried building materials on their backs and helped to build the foundations. The last reported true cult of carts event in the Middle Ages, however, was in Rome in 1308 when, according to contemporary accounts, after the fire in the basilica of S Giovanni in Laterano, 'women hauled four-wheeled carts loaded with stone into the church, not permitting animals to defile it'.

BIBLIOGRAPHY

EARLY SOURCES

Gaza

Mark the Deacon: *Bios tou agiou Porphuriou* [Life of St Porphyry]; in H. Grégoire and M. Kugener, eds: *Vie de Porphyre* (Paris, 1930), chaps 75–9, 84 [with Fr. trans.]; Eng. trans. in C. Mango: *The Art of the Byzantine Empire*, Sources & Doc. Hist. A. (Englewood Cliffs, 1972), pp. 30–32

Montecassino

Leo of Ostia: *Chronica monasterii Casiensis*; in J. von Schlosser, ed.: *Quellenbuch zur Kunstgeschichte des abendländischen Mittelalters*, Quellenschr. Kstgesch., vii (Vienna, 1896), pp. 202–3; Eng. trans. in C. Davis-Weyer: *Early Medieval Art, 300–1150*, Sources & Doc. Hist. A. (Englewood Cliffs, 1971), p. 136 [the account of the events of 1066 is by Peter the Deacon]

Saint-Trond

Rudolf of Saint-Trond: *Gesta abbatum Trudonensium*; ed. D. R. Koepke in Mnmt. Ger. Hist., Scriptores, x (Hannover, 1852), pp. 234–5; excerpt in V. Mortet and P. Deschamps, eds: *Recueil des textes relatifs à l'histoire de l'architecture et à la condition des architectes en France au moyen âge*, ii (Paris, 1929), pp. 157–8

Lindisfarne

Reginald of Durham: *Reginaldi monachi Dunelmensis libellus de admirandis beati Cuthberti virtutibus*; ed. J. Raine (London, 1835), p. 45; Eng. trans. in L. Salzman: *Building in England down to 1540* (London, 1952)

Saint-Denis

Suger of Saint-Denis: *Libellus alter de consecratione ecclesiae sancti Dionysii*; ed. in E. Panofsky: *Abbot Suger on the Abbey Church of Saint-Denis and its Art Treasures* (Princeton, 1946, rev. 2/1979/R 1986), pp. 90–95, 215 [with Eng. trans.]

Chartres, Rouen and Saint-Pierre-sur-Dives

Haymo of Saint-Pierre-sur-Dives: *Relatio de miraculis beatae Mariae*, ed. L. Delisle in *Bibliothèque de l'Ecole des Chartes*, v/i (Paris, 1860), pp. 120–39; Lat. excerpt and Eng. trans. in A. K. Porter (1909), pp. 151–6; Eng. trans. in G. Coulton: *Art and the Reformation* (Oxford, 1928), pp. 339–41

Hugo of Amiens: *Epistola Hugonis Rotomagensis archiepiscopi ad Theodoricum Ambianensem episcopum*; ed. in M. Bouquet: *Recueil des historiens des Gaules et de la France*, xiv (Paris, 1877), pp. 318–19; Lat. with Eng. trans. in A. K. Porter (1909), pp. 156–7; Eng. trans. in T. Frisch (1971), p. 25, and in R. Branner, ed.: *Chartres Cathedral*, Norton Crit. Stud. A. Hist. (New York, 1969), p. 94

Robert of Torigny: *Ex chronico sanctis Michaelis in periculo maris*; ed. D. L. C. Bethmann in Mnmt. Ger. Hist., Scriptores, vi (Hannover, 1844), p. 496; and in L. Delisle, ed.: *Société de l'histoire de France*, i (Paris, 1872), p. 238; Lat. with Eng. trans. in A. K. Porter (1909), p. 159; Eng. trans. in R. Branner, op. cit., p. 93 [Robert of Torigny's account is in a continuation of the *Chronicle* of Sigebert of Gembloux]

Additional, less specific 12th-century texts referring to cult of carts activities at Chartres and in Normandy are given in V. Mortet and P. Deschamps, op. cit., p. 65, no. 1.

Châlons-sur-Marne

Guy of Bazoches: *Epistola*; ed. in L. Demaison: 'Les Chevets des églises Notre-Dame de Châlons et Saint-Remi de Reims', *Bull. Archéol. Com. Trav. Hist. & Sci.* (1899), pp. 106–7

Calais

Lambert of Ardres: *Historia comitum Ghisnensium et Ardensium dominorum*, ed. J. Heller in Mnmt. Ger. Hist., Scriptores, xxiv (Hannover, 1883), p. 640; Eng. trans. in G. Coulton: *Life in the Middle Ages*, ii (Cambridge, 1910), pp. 18–20

Beaucaire

Guillaume of Tudèle: *La Chanson de la croisade contre les Albigeois*, ed. P. Mayer in *Société de l'histoire de France*, I, v (Paris, 1875), p. 406; excerpt with Fr. trans. in V. Mortet and P. Deschamps, op. cit., pp. 225–6

Auxerre

Gesta pontificum Autissiodorensium; ed. in L. Duru: *Bibliothèque historique de l'Yonne*, i (Auxerre, 1850), pp. 475–6; Lat. excerpt in V. Mortet and P. Deschamps, op. cit., pp. 204–9; Eng. trans. in T. Frisch (1971), pp. 27–8

Reggio nell'Emilia

A. Bertani, ed.: *Cronica regii* (Parma, 1857), pp. 34–5 [see V. Mortet and P. Deschamps, op. cit., p. 63, no. 2]

Le Mans

G. Busson and A. Ledru, eds: *Actus pontificum Cenomannis in urbe degentium* (Mamers, 1901), pp. 489–92; Lat. excerpt in V. Mortet and P. Deschamps, op. cit., pp. 257–8; Eng. trans. in T. Frisch (1971), pp. 28–30

Rome

Ptolemy of Lucca: *Historica ecclesiastica*; ed. in G. Mollat: *Vitae paparum Avenionensium*, i (Paris, 1914), pp. 31–2

GENERAL

A. K. Porter: *Medieval Architecture*, ii (New York, 1909), pp. 150–60 [first pubd ref. to the cult of carts]

H. Adams: *Mont-Saint-Michel and Chartres* (New York, 1913) [popularized the cult of carts concept although Adams did not use the term]

T. Frisch: 'On the Question of the Participation of the Common People in the Building of Gothic Churches', *Gothic Art, 1140–c. 1450*, Sources & Doc. Hist. A. (Englewood Cliffs, 1971), pp. 23–30 [gen. review with trans. of some of the doc.]

CARL F. BARNES JR

Cult of relics. Christian belief in the power of the physical remains of saints or objects that come into contact with them. Fuelled by belief in the afterlife, resurrection, the power of the soul and the role of saints as advocates in heaven for mankind, the veneration of relics came to rival the sacraments in their importance in the daily life of the Church in the Middle Ages.

1. HISTORY AND DEVELOPMENT. The New Testament refers to the healing power of objects that had come into contact with Christ or his Apostles: touching the hem of Christ's robe healed a woman suffering from an issue of blood (Matthew 9:20–22); cloth that touched St Paul was endowed with curative power (Acts 19:11–12). It was the new Christian attitude towards the meaning of death, however, that led to the belief in the abiding power of saints and their physical remains, even after death. The account by Eusebios of Caesarea of the martyrdom of St Polycarp (*d c.* 155) is often used to reveal Early Christian attitudes towards the holy dead. Like the Apostles after the Crucifixion, the followers of Polycarp reverently sought the martyr's body: '. . . we gathered up his bones that were more valuable than precious stones and more to be esteemed than gold, and we placed them where it was suitable'.

The presumption that the bodies of saints (primary relics) and objects associated with the saints (secondary relics) are to be honoured, and that they are endowed with spiritual power, runs throughout patristic thought in both the Eastern and Western Churches. According to St Augustine of Hippo (354–430), the remains of a saint's body were to be treasured because the Holy Spirit affected both the soul and body. The growing importance attached to relics is reflected in Augustine's writings. In 390 he asserted that the types of miracles witnessed in apostolic days were no longer allowed (*De vera religione*). As Bishop of Hippo (*reg* 396–430), however, he began systematically to document miraculous cures in Africa. In the *City of God* he refers to miracles wrought by flowers that had touched a reliquary or been set on altars, and by oil from the lamps of a martyr's church. One of the earliest and most celebrated justifications of relics is the *Contra vigilantium*, written by St Jerome (*c.* 342–420), in which relics were proclaimed to be an aid to the veneration of martyrs.

Relics became an integral part of Christian ceremony (*see* CHURCH, §II, 3(i)). The sixth Synod of Carthage (393) declared that every altar must have a relic, a practice adopted by St Ambrose (*c.* 339–97) and St Paulinus of Nola and reiterated in 787 at the second Council of Nicaea. The connection that this created between the veneration of relics and the principal sacrament of the Eucharist is manifest in such works of art as the Carolingian Golden Altar (*c.* 835) of S Ambrogio, Milan, which, according to its inscription, is both an altar and a reliquary (*see* CAROLINGIAN ART, fig. 11), or in the numerous portable altars that enshrine relics. Pope Gregory I sent to England 'all things that were necessary for the furniture and ministry of the church, as holy vessels and altarcloths, . . . relics too of the holy apostles and martyrs as well as many books'. Gregory recommended that processions with saints' relics be staged by the Church instead of pagan sacrificial feasts.

The Venerable Bede (*c.* 673–735) similarly refers to replacing idols with holy relics. In the Middle Ages relics were principally used in the consecration of the altar and as part of liturgical equipment and ceremony; these functions—one commemorative, one active—informed the development of works of art associated with the devotion to relics.

Veneration of the holy dead notwithstanding, the Western Church inherited from Roman imperial law certain restrictions on the movement of mortal remains. Veneration of the saints in the Western Church was initially localized at the burial place. When barbarian tribes threatened Rome, this policy began to change, as the accounts of the *Liber Pontificalis* attest. Under Boniface IV (*reg* 608–15), 28 wagons filled with the bones of martyrs were taken to the Pantheon, which was then converted into the church of S Maria ad Martyres. Pope Paul I (*reg* 757–67) had more than 100 relics moved inside the city walls. Additionally, there had been a reluctance in the West to divide saints' relics. Pope Hormisdas (*reg* 514–23) refused a request from Emperor Justinus I (*reg* 518–27) for bones of SS Peter, Paul and Lawrence (*d* 258) because it was contrary to Roman custom. This, too, began to change, perhaps under the influence of eastern popes: the heads of SS George and Anastasius the Persian (*d* 628) had already been brought to Rome by 682. Thus by the 7th century the veneration of the body at the tomb and the dispersal and distribution of individual relics were established tendencies.

A major component of Charlemagne's effort to strengthen the Empire was the acquisition of relics of Roman saints for his churches and monasteries in the north. These efforts were facilitated by merchants of relics, of whom the deacon Deusdona (*fl* 827) was the most celebrated. Bodies of biblical saints also were established in sanctuaries outside Italy through what were believed to be miraculous circumstances; thus, for example, the cults of SS Mary Magdalene and Lazarus were established in France. In northern Spain the cult of St James the Greater developed; his body was miraculously washed ashore near Santiago de Compostela, which rivalled Rome in importance as a goal of pilgrimage after 813. Early bishops and abbots emerged as principal saints in their own regions. Where their veneration was fostered by local nobility or by a strong church community, their cults flourished. Councils convened at Limoges from the 11th century declared that St Martial (*fl*?3rd century), the city's first bishop and the apostle of Aquitaine, was equal in rank to the disciples: it was even maintained that Martial had been present at the Last Supper. It was often politically expedient to foster devotions that strengthened the authority of a cause. Thus the devotion to St Denis was ardently supported by the French monarchy, while the cult of Charlemagne as a saint was encouraged by the Holy Roman Emperors.

Although *De pignoribus sanctorum* by Guibert de Nogent (1053–1124) is often cited as evidence of the opposition of church officials to relics, his critique was highly selective: he condemned a relic of the milk tooth of Christ at St Médard, Soissons, but not the relics under his own authority, which included fragments of the Virgin's tunic. His treatise clearly had little impact—it is known from only one copy, from his own monastery of Nogent-sous-Covey. A codification of the medieval attitude towards relics can be found in the writings of St Thomas Aquinas in the mid-13th century: relics are primarily to be revered as mementos of the holy departed and as links to them. They are also sacred in themselves because the Holy Spirit worked through both the soul and body of the saint. For Aquinas, the miracles wrought at the tombs of saints were additional proof of the will of God that his saints be venerated.

Saints and their relics at different pilgrimage sites came to be renowned for particular cures. At his shrine at Saint-Léonard-de-Noblac, St Leonard of Noblac (*d c.* 559) was invoked by prisoners, as was St Faith at Ste Foy, Conques. Secondary relics of the Virgin, such as her belt at Le Puy Cathedral and breast milk at Evron Abbey, were venerated by women hoping to conceive and those having difficulty nursing. Similarly, devotion to St Margaret in the late Middle Ages depended on her reputation for helping women through childbirth.

2. RELATION TO ART AND ARCHITECTURE. As the devotion to relics grew, the ecclesiastical art form of reliquaries developed with extraordinary richness and variety as a natural consequence of the Christian belief that holy remains—the tangible reminders of death, decay and disease in the unsaintly—themselves became precious materials. Eusebios likened the burning flesh of St Polycarp to 'gold and silver being refined in a furnace' with 'such a fragrant odour as the fumes of frankincense or of some other of the precious spices'. SUGER, Abbot of Saint-Denis, considered it part of his mission to encase 'the most sacred ashes of those whose venerable spirits, radiant as the sun, attend upon the Almighty God with the most precious material we possibly can: with refined gold and a profusion of hyacinths, emeralds and other precious stones'. (For a discussion of the form and development of reliquaries see RELIQUARY, §I,1.)

The fabrication of reliquary containers was a function solely of the devotion to saints; in the creation of medieval ecclesiastical architecture, the cult of relics was but one of a number of possible factors affecting a building's form. Indeed, the existence of a saint's relics could be the motivating factor in the creation of a church, as at St Peter's in Rome (see ROME, §V, 14(i)(a)), Santiago de Compostela Cathedral, or S Nicola at Bari (see BARI (ii), §2). The sites of many Early Christian buildings in the West were determined by the localization of saints' cults at the burial place. Churches were built where cemeteries lay, outside the walls. The Constantinian church of St Peter in Rome was built so that its apse lay directly over St Peter's tomb; by the time of Gregory I a grilled window allowed Christians to look down upon it (see also CRYPT, fig. 1). In S Ambrogio, Milan, the altar is directly over the relics of martyred saints, next to whom St Ambrose wished to be interred. The setting of the high altar over a tomb was widespread, and plans for the expansion of churches over the centuries, as at Saint-Denis Abbey, had to take into account the location of the original crypt.

Expansion of such early, important Christian monuments as S Lorenzo fuori le Mura (*c.* 330; altered 13th century; rebuilt 1864–70 and 1945–61), Rome, was repeatedly required to allow for greater numbers of pilgrims. The basilica was set into the hill where the tomb of St Lawrence was located, so that the galleries were level with the top of the hill, allowing the faithful to move into the gallery above the tomb at ground-floor level. The accommodation of pilgrims inspired medieval building campaigns and affected the form of church buildings. The church architecture of the pilgrimage road to Santiago de Compostela consistently features wide transepts to accommodate visitors, and ambulatories to allow for circulation of the faithful past saints' relics, lists of which were to be found in the pilgrims' guide contained in the *Liber Sancti Jacobi* (*c.* 1130; *see also* CRYPT, §1; for discussion and illustration *see* AMBULATORY). The guide also specifies that the gallery level at Santiago de Compostela Cathedral, the only pilgrimage church where it was fully developed, was used by visiting pilgrims moving through the building. At the beginning of the Gothic era, Abbot Suger wrote of the danger of overcrowding at Saint-Denis Abbey as he undertook the expansion of the church with its double ambulatory. The Late Gothic choir added to the palatine chapel at Aachen was also necessitated by the numbers of pilgrims, in this case coming to the shrine of Charlemagne.

In the Early Christian churches of northern Italy, a martyr's chapel was sometimes appended to the basilica near the end of an aisle, as at S Ambrogio, which has a domed room dedicated to St Victor. Special chapels to individual saints were a standard feature encircling the apses of many Romanesque churches, and they proliferated in Gothic church buildings (*see* CHURCH, §II, 3(i)(c)). In some instances, the growing devotion to particular saints occasioned the addition of chapels. At Canterbury Cathedral devotions to a head reliquary of St Thomas Becket were accomplished in the Corona Chapel, while the tomb and shrine were in the Trinity Chapel. At Lincoln Cathedral, those to the head of St Hugh (*d* 1200; *can* 1220) took place in the Angel choir after 1280.

It has long been recognized that the form of pilgrimage churches was adapted to their function. The architecture is but one element in an ensemble dedicated to the cult of a particular saint. Such an ensemble could include programmes of monumental painting and of sculpture, but it necessarily included the shrines of saints (*see* SHRINE (i), §I). Too often, many of these components have been destroyed, and what remains represents an incomplete picture of the full range of medieval devotions to saints.

See also MARTYRIUM.

BIBLIOGRAPHY

EARLY SOURCES
Eusebios of Caesarea: *Ecclesiastical History* (early 3rd century AD); Eng. trans., ed. K. Lake, J. E. L. Oulton and H. J. Lawlor, 2 vols (London, 1926–32)
Augustine of Hippo: *De vera religione* (AD 390); ed. in *PL*, xxxiv (1845), cols 121–72
Jerome: *Contra vigilantium* (*c.* AD 400); ed. in *PL*, xxiii (1845), cols 337–52
Augustine of Hippo: *De cura pro mortuis gerenda* (AD 421); ed. in *PL*, xl (1845); Eng. trans., *Saint Augustine: Treatises on Marriage and Other Subjects*, The Fathers of the Church, xxvii (New York, 1955)
Guibert of Nogent: *De pignoribus sanctorum* (*c.* 1100); ed. in *PL*, clvi (1853), cols 607–80
Liber Sancti Jacobi, v (*c.* 1130; Santiago de Compostela, Cathedral Lib.); ed. and Fr. trans. by J. Viellard as *Le Guide du pèlerin de Saint-Jacques de Compostelle* (Mâcon, 1963)
Thomas Aquinas: *Summa Theologiae* (*c.* 1265–74); ed. and trans. by T. Gilbey and others (London and New York, 1964–80)

STUDIES
S. Beissel: *Die Verehrung der Heiligen und ihre Reliquien in Deutschland*, 2 vols (Freiburg im Breisgau, 1890–92)

J. Guiraud: 'Le Commerce des reliques au commencement du IXe siècle', *Mélanges G. B. de Rossi: Recueil de travaux publiés par l'école française de Rome en l'honneur de M. le Commandeur Giovanni Battista de Rossi* (Paris and Rome, 1892), pp. 73–95
P. Lefeuvre: *Courte histoire des reliques* (Paris, 1932)
E.Panofsky, ed.: *Abbot Suger on the Abbey Church of Saint-Denis and its Art Treasures* (Princeton, 1946); 2nd rev. edn ed. G. Panofsky-Soergel (Princeton, 1979)
A. Frolow: *La Relique de la vraie croix* (Paris, 1961)
P. Héliot and M.-L. Chastang: 'Quêtes et voyages de reliques au profit des églises françaises du moyen âge', *Rev. Hist. Ecclés.*, lix (1964), pp. 789–822; lx (1965), pp. 5–32
N. Hermann-Mascard: *Les Reliques des saints: Formation coutumière d'un droit* (Paris, 1975)
P. Geary: *Furta Sacra: Thefts of Relics in the High Middle Ages* (Princeton, 1978)
P. Brown: *The Cult of Saints: Its Rise and Function in Latin Christianity* (Chicago, 1981)
M.-M. Gauthier: *Les Routes de la foi: Reliques et reliquaires de Jérusalem à Compostelle* (Fribourg, 1983)
J. C. Cruz: *Relics* (Huntington, IN, 1984)
J. Bentley: *Restless Bones: The Story of Relics* (London, 1985)
Reliquien: Verehrung und Verklärung, Skizzen und Noten zur Thematik (exh. cat. by A. Legner, Cologne, Schnütgen-Mus., 1989)
B. D. Boehm: *Medieval Head Reliquaries of the Massif Central* (diss., U. New York, 1990; microfilm, Ann Arbor, 1990)
B. Abou-el-Haj: 'The Audiences for the Medieval Cult of Saints', *Gesta*, xxx/1 (1991), pp. 3–15

BARBARA DRAKE BOEHM

Cult statue. Image of a divinity that served in antiquity as a focal-point for worship and cult rituals. Most cult statues were housed in temples or shrines, although outdoor worship of images is also attested. Although aniconic worship (i.e. of a non-anthropomorphic symbol of a deity such as a rock or pillar) is known in Near Eastern, Greek and Roman cults, most deities by the late 2nd millennium BC were worshipped in an anthropomorphic form and were, as such, earthly substitutes or humanized manifestations of the presence of a deity.

Anthropomorphic cult statues are well attested in the Ancient Near East, Anatolia, the Levant and Egypt. Near Eastern cuneiform records going back at least to the 2nd millennium BC indicate that Mesopotamian cult images were made of wood and opulently clad in tiaras, robes and jewellery. The garments of the statue were ceremonially changed, and ritual meals were served up to the cult image. Specific attributes and attire aided identity. From Hittite texts of the 14th or 13th century BC we know of cult images that were carried in processions, bathed and clothed. Large stone cult statue bases survive in the temples of the Hittite capital at Boğazköy, although no cult statues have been preserved. The sizes of these bases indicate that life-size or larger images would have served the cult, at least at this major site, while provincial shrines might have been equipped with statuettes. Gold and silver seem to have been the primary materials used. In Late Bronze Age Canaanite cult (2nd millennium BC), statues of deities are known from temples, such as the male statue (h. 400 mm) from the Stelae Temple at HAZOR, but more often aniconic symbols of the presence of the gods were placed alone on daises or in niches in temple cellas. In ancient Egypt the gods were being worshipped increasingly in the form of statues by the New Kingdom (*c.* 1540–*c.* 1075 BC). There is evidence for the feeding, washing, dressing and processioning of Egyptian cult statues, which were made primarily of precious metals, especially gold, and precious stones and hardstones.

Anthropomorphic statues certainly existed in the Aegean Bronze Age in terracotta, bronze and limestone, but it is unclear whether these served as cult images for a specific cult or whether, rather, these multiple statues were devotees of the divinity or votive gifts. It is likely that the stimulus for the use in early Greek Iron Age practice of a single sacred anthropomorphic cult image as the substitute for the deity came from the Near East by the 8th century BC, as is evidenced by the similarities in cult practices (processioning, dressing, feeding, bathing). Although aniconic symbols of deities existed in Iron Age Greece, most Greek deities were worshipped in anthropomorphic form and mainly in temples.

It seems from Greek literary sources that many of the *xoana* (Gr.: cult statues) before the end of the 6th century BC were wooden. Only a few Greek wooden statues survive, and none of these is likely to be a cult image. *Xoana* could be gilded, and they may have been painted. The earliest examples were in general less than life-size, but by the late 7th century BC or the 6th larger than life-size and colossal idols are known and remained the preferred sizes for cult images through the Classical, Hellenistic and into the Roman periods. Greek cult images could be either in standing or in seated positions, although specific deities are associated with seated types, for example the enthroned Zeus or Hera. Greek cult images in general carried attributes to aid identification and were often, especially in early cases, provided with real costume and jewellery.

By the end of the 6th century BC the popularity of wood was being eclipsed by that of other materials such as bronze and stone (especially marble), or of combined materials such as gold and ivory (chryselephantine) or stone with other materials (acrolithic). Two bronze statues of Apollo that can probably be identified as cult images survive, illustrating two different manufacturing techniques: in sphyrelaton (hammered sheet metal), a statuette from Dreros, Crete (see fig.); in hollow-cast bronze, a just over life-size late 6th-century BC image from the Peiraeus (Peiraeus, Archaeol. Mus.; for illustration *see* PEIRAEUS). Chryselephantine cult statues are often associated only with the Classical period and the famous statues of *Zeus* in Olympia and *Athena Parthenos* in Athens by PHEIDIAS, but these colossal 5th-century BC and other 4th-century BC works were foreshadowed in the 6th century BC by chryselephantine idols. Stone cult statues are well known in Greece from the end of the 6th century BC to the Hellenistic period and survive in greater numbers than do the more valuable and fragile bronze, chryselephantine and wooden statues, for example large portions of a colossal Hellenistic marble cult group of *Apollo, Artemis and Leto* from Klaros in Asia Minor (*in situ*) and the fragmentary, 5th-century BC *Nemesis* by Agorakritos at Rhamnous (Athens, N. Archaeol. Mus.). By the time of the Pheidian *Athena Parthenos*, attitudes towards cult statues in Greece had changed. Through the Hellenistic age and into the Roman period new extravagant and theatrical images were manufactured, designed as much to

Cult statue of *Apollo*, bronze, h. 800 mm, from Dreros, 8th century BC (Herakleion, Archaeological Museum)

provide worshippers with a sacred image as to attract worshippers to the sanctuary or to bring prestige to the city state or shrine.

While the Roman practice of making cult images of divinities remained essentially the same as that of the Greeks, sacred images of the deified emperors, either in the form of a divinity, or of a divinity combined with a portrait head of the emperor or in the form of the emperor himself, were made to serve the imperial cult in temples throughout the Empire. According to M. Terentius Varro

(Pliny: *Natural History* XXXV.xlv.157) the first cult image in Rome was a red-painted terracotta statue by Vulca of Veii, brought by the Etruscan king Tarquinius Priscus in the 6th century BC for the Temple of Jupiter on the Capitoline Hill. The traditional wisdom was that the Romans worshipped gods without images before this time, thus crediting the Etruscans with the innovation and transmission to the Romans of cult images. The first documented Etruscan cult images date to the second half of the 6th century BC, such as the limestone, half life-size nude goddess from Orvieto (*see* ETRUSCAN, fig. 2). Many Greek cult statues and other art works were taken to Rome, especially in the 2nd and 1st centuries BC (*see* ROME, ANCIENT, §IV, 2(i)), thus defining cult image types for many deities and sanctuaries. Most Roman cult images, especially of the early Empire, were based on Greek prototypes, or even taken from Greek temples and reused in Roman temples. Other statues were brought to Rome as works of art and later attained the status of cult image.

In general Roman cult images were conservative but stylistically eclectic figures reflecting the conflated Greek styles of the Archaic, Classical and Hellenistic periods. Preferences for specific Greek styles can be traced, for example the archaistic style, conflated with 5th- and 4th-century BC types, in the 1st century BC to 1st century AD, and the High Classical style in the Hadrianic period (AD 117–38). Standing males and females were normally the rule, although specific deities were shown in seated poses, such as Jupiter (patterned after the Olympian *Zeus* of Pheidias) and Serapis (adapted from the Ptolemaic version by Bryaxis). Female cult images were usually engulfed in drapery. Life-size to colossal was the preferred size in Roman temples, while smaller shrines would have been equipped with appropriately scaled images.

Roman cult images were made of a variety of materials. According to Pliny, gold and silver images were popular in his day (1st century AD; *Natural History* XXXV.157), and a cult image of the god Veiovis on the Capitoline Hill was made of cypress wood (*c.* 193 BC; *Natural History* XVI.26). Chryselephantine cult images, imitating those of the Classical and Hellenistic periods, are also known from literary sources (e.g. Pausanias: *Guide to Greece* I.xviii.6: a colossal Hadrianic statue of *Zeus* in the Temple of Olympian Zeus at Athens). Examples of Roman cult statues survive in bronze, such as the *Hercules Victor* from the Forum Boarium (2nd century BC; Rome, Mus. Conserv.); and in a combination of alabaster, 'basalt' and Luna marble, such as the colossal seated goddess of the post-Trojanic period from the Piazza dell' Emporio (Rome, Mus. N. Romano); and in an acrolithic technique, such as the probably Greek-manufactured statue from the 2nd-century BC Temple of Fortuna (Temple B) in the Largo Argentina, Rome (Rome, Mus. Capitolino).

BIBLIOGRAPHY

Pauly–Wissowa: 'Kultbild'
F. Willemsen: *Frühe griechische Kultbilder* (Munich, 1939)
W. F. Leemans: *Ishtar of Lagaba and her Dress* (Leiden, 1952)
A. Spycket: *Les Statues de culte dans les textes mésopotamiens des origines à la 1ère dynastie de Babylone* (Paris, 1968)
N. Leipen: *Athena Parthenos: A Reconstruction* (Toronto, 1971)
E. T. Vermeule: 'Götterkult', *Archeol. Homer.*, III/v (Göttingen, 1974)
W. Helck and E. Otto, eds: *Lexikon der Ägyptologie* (Wiesbaden, 1975–)
I. B. Romano: *Early Greek Cult Images* (diss., University Park, PA State U., 1980)
N. Marinatos and R. Hägg: 'Anthropomorphic Cult Images in Minoan Crete?', *Minoan Society: Proceedings of the Cambridge Colloquium: Cambridge, 1981*, pp. 185–201
B. Rutkowski: *Frühegriechische Kultdarstellungen* (Berlin, 1981)
W. W. Hallo: 'Cult Statue and Divine Image: A Preliminary Study', *Scripture in Context*, ii, ed. W. W. Hallo, J. C. Moyer and L. G. Perdue (Pittsburgh, 1983), pp. 137–215
S. Hiller: 'Mycenaean Traditions in Early Greek Cult Images', *The Greek Renaissance of the Eighth Century BC: Tradition and Innovation*, ed. R. Hägg (Stockholm, 1983), pp. 91–9
B. Gladigow: 'Präsenz der Bilder, Präsenz der Götter: Kultbilder und Bilder der Götter in der griechischen Religion', *Visible Relig.*, iv–v (1985–6), pp. 114–33
H. G. Martin: 'Römische Tempelkultbilder: Eine archäologische Untersuchung zur späten Republik', *Stud. & Mat. Mus. Civil. Romana*, xii (1987)
C. C. Vermeule: *The Cult Images of Imperial Rome* (Rome, 1987)
A. A. Donohue: *Xoana and the Origins of Greek Sculpture* (Atlanta, 1988)
I. B. Romano: 'Early Greek Cult Images and Cult Practices', *Proceedings of the 5th International Symposium 'Early Greek Cult Practice' at the Swedish Institute, Athens: 1988*, pp. 127–33
B. S. Ridgeway: 'Images of Athens on the Acropolis', *Goddess and Polis*, ed. I. Neils (Hanover, NH, and Princeton, 1992), pp. 119–42

IRENE BALD ROMANO

Cumae. Greek colony on the Bay of Naples in southern Italy, which flourished from the late 8th century BC until around 300 BC. It was the oldest and most northerly Greek settlement on the Italian mainland, though Eusebius' date for its foundation (*c.* 1050 BC; see Schoene) cannot be accepted. The oldest extant remains date no earlier than around 725 BC, while Livy's hint (*History of Rome*, VIII.xxii.5–6) that its Chalkidian founders came from PITHEKOUSSAI is strongly supported by the archaeological discoveries made there. The site had a naturally defensible acropolis, already used by an indigenous Iron Age community, and convenient access to a good harbour, now silted up. Cumae took over and developed Pithekoussai's role as a trading centre, and until around 500 BC played a major part in the spread of Greek religious cults, art and culture to the region. Indeed, it was from Cumae that the Etruscans adopted the Euboean alphabet around 700 BC, taking it eventually to Rome and north Italy, and bringing it back to Campania during their period of hegemony (*c.* 650 BC onwards). During this era the Cumaeans established the nearby city of Neapolis (*see* NAPLES, §I, 1) and fought a series of actions against the Etruscans, scoring notable victories in 524 BC and, with Syracusan assistance, in a sea battle of 474 BC, when a captured Etruscan helmet was dedicated in the sanctuary of Zeus at Olympia (London, BM). In 421 BC Cumae itself was captured by native Samnite highlanders from the interior, but Greek traditions persisted, and with the decline of Athenian pottery exports to the West a major pottery workshop was established at Cumae itself. It flourished from about 350 to 300 BC, and around 1500 extant Red-figure vases have been attributed to it (*see also* GREECE, ANCIENT, §V, 6(ii)(d)).

In Roman times Cumae's importance dwindled, while that of Puteoli increased. However, in 38–36 BC Agrippa restructured its harbour in a remarkable engineering project, which included the construction of two long tunnels linking Lake Avernus and Lake Lucrinus to the sea. The extraordinary volcanic landscape of the Phlegraean Fields around Cumae was regarded as the site of the entrance to the underworld, and formed the setting for the 'cave' of the Cumaean Sibyl, the prophetess of Apollo made famous by Virgil (*Aeneid* VI.9–155). This 'cave' may have been the long trapezoidal gallery below the acropolis: its stone-cutting resembles the best Archaic Greek work, thus implying a date before *c.* 500 BC.

BIBLIOGRAPHY

A. Schoene, ed.: *Eusebi Chronicorum libri duo*, ii (Berlin, 1866), p. 61
R. F. Paget: 'The Ancient Ports of Cumae', *J. Roman Stud.*, lviii (1968), pp. 152–69
M. W. Frederiksen: *Campania* (London, 1984)
C. Albore Livadie: 'Cuma preellenica', *Napoli antica* (exh. cat., Naples, 1985), pp. 62–75
G. Tocco Sciarelli: 'La fondazione di Cuma', *Napoli antica* (exh. cat., Naples, 1985), pp. 87–99

DAVID RIDGWAY

Cumberland, Duke of. *See* HANOVER, (2).

Cumberland, Frederic W(illiam) (*b* London, 10 April 1820; *d* Toronto, 5 Aug 1881). Canadian architect of English birth. He was articled for five years to a civil engineer, William Tress, and then worked as a railway engineer before joining the Engineering Department of the Admiralty (1844). He moved to Canada in 1847, and in 1848 he was appointed engineer to the County of York in Ontario. By 1850 he had established an architectural practice with offices in Toronto and Hamilton. His partner from 1850 to 1852 was Thomas G. Ridout jr, and from 1852 to 1863 he worked with William George Storm (1826–92). Cumberland's three churches, St James's Anglican Cathedral (1849–53), Toronto, the Church of the Ascension (1850–51), Hamilton, Ontario, and the Chapel of St James the Less (1857–60), St James's Cemetery, Toronto, are all Gothic Revival and show an awareness of current developments in England. His auditorium of the Normal and Model Schools (1851; destr. except for main façade), Toronto, was also Gothic Revival, with delicate cast-iron columns. The façade of the building, however, is classical, with colossal Doric pilasters, a favourite motif, which he employed in his court-houses in Toronto (1852), Cayuga (1850–51) and Whitby (1852). He used Ionic columns in the Seventh Post Office (1851–3), Toronto. In his house for J. Lukin Robinson (1855), Toronto, and in the Mechanics' Institute (1853–5; after 1883 Toronto Pub. Lib.), he used an adaptation of Italian Renaissance architecture, whereas the façade of the lavish central block of Osgoode Hall (1857–60), Toronto, is based on the garden front of the palace of Versailles (remod. from 1678 by Jules Hardouin Mansart). Cumberland's major work, University College (1856–9), University of Toronto, was inspired by the University Museum by Deane & Woodward, Oxford, but also incorporates details from Romanesque sources including the gate-house of Bury St Edmunds Abbey. After the early 1860s Cumberland became increasingly involved in the development of the Canadian railways, an interest that ultimately took over from architecture completely. Drawings from the Cumberland and Storm partnership can be seen in the Horwood Collection (Toronto, Archvs Ont.).

DCB
S. G. Morriss: 'The Nine-year Odyssey of a High Victorian Goth: Three Churches by Fred Cumberland', *J. Can. A. Hist.*, ii/1 (1975), pp. 42–52
M. MacRae and A. Adamson: *Cornerstones of Order* (Toronto, 1983)

MALCOLM THURLBY

Cumberland, George (*b* London, 1754; *d* Bristol, 1848). English writer, collector and amateur artist. He became a clerk on the death of his father in 1771, until freed from financial necessity by a legacy in 1785. In 1788 he left for Rome, where he studied the work of Raphael, Marcantonio Raimondi and Giulio Bonasone, and collected prints and curios. Cumberland returned to England in 1790 and lived near Southampton, adding to his collections and corresponding with Thomas Johnes (1748–1816) of Hafod in Cardiganshire (now Dyfed), who praised his *Poem on the Landscapes of Great Britain*, written in 1780 but not published until 1793. By this time he was living near Windsor and proximity to London allowed him greater intimacy with William Blake, whom he had met through Thomas Stothard before 1788. In 1793 he published *Some Anecdotes of the Life of Julio Bonasoni*, prefaced by *A Plan for the Improvement of the Arts in England*, which urged the establishment of a national gallery. *An Attempt to Describe Hafod* (1796), Johnes's estate, contains a folding map engraved by Blake, who also provided eight of the 24 plates illustrating *Thoughts on Outline* (1796), a subject to which he returned in *Outlines of the Ancients* (1829), which contains three further Blake engravings. In 1808 Cumberland settled in Bristol, where he became an influential figure in artistic circles. His landscape sketches and watercolours produced at this time have a simple directness of vision, reminiscent of those of his friend John Linnell (e.g. Bristol, Mus. & A.G.). He catalogued his collection of prints, which he presented to the Royal Academy and the British Museum, in the *Utility of Collecting the Best Works of the Ancient Engravers of the Italian School* (1827).

WRITINGS

A Poem on the Landscapes of Great Britain (London, 1793)
Some Anecdotes of the Life of Julio Bonasoni, a Bolognese Artist (London, 1793)
An Attempt to Describe Hafod (London, 1796)
Thoughts on Outline (London, 1796)
An Essay on the Utility of Collecting the Best Works of the Ancient Engravers of the Italian School (London, 1827)
Outlines of the Ancients (London, 1829)

BIBLIOGRAPHY

C. Black, ed.: *The Cumberland Papers* (London, 1902)
G. Keynes: 'George Cumberland', *Bk Colr*, xix/1 (1970)
The Bristol School of Artists: Francis Danby and Painting in Bristol, 1810–1840 (exh. cat., ed. F. Greenacre; Bristol, Mus. & A.G., 1973), pp. 250–54
Edward Bird (exh. cat. by S. Richardson, Wolverhampton, A.G., 1982)

DAVID RODGERS

Cumberland Market Group. British group of painters. They took their subject-matter from everyday life, particularly that of north-west London, where Robert Bevan had his studio and held 'At Homes' for artist-friends. These formalized in late 1914 when Bevan, Charles Ginner and Harold Gilman established the group, joined in 1915 by John Nash. Christopher Nevinson and E. McKnight Kauffer attended meetings and compared works, although they did not exhibit with the group. Members consciously embraced the style called 'Neo-Realism', exploring the spirit of their age through the shapes and colours of daily life. Their intentions were proclaimed in Ginner's manifesto in *New Age* (1 Jan 1914), which was also used as the preface to Gilman and Ginner's two-man exhibition that year: it attacked the academic and warned against the 'decorative' aspect of imitators of Post-Impressionism.

Although the Cumberland Market Group developed from Walter Sickert's CAMDEN TOWN GROUP, its members sought more rigorous attention to natural facts, though not neglecting compositional selection and design and insisting on a love of the medium as essential to expressive painting. Characteristic paintings are Ginner's *Leeds Canal* (1914; Leeds, C.A.G.) and Gilman's *The Eating House* (*c*. 1914; Sheffield, Graves A.G.), which achieve equal weighting of form and content through strict control of colour and composition and through sensitivity to atmosphere and location. Their practices were briefly the basis of their School of Painting in Soho, London (1916–17). The group's only public exhibition took place in April 1915 at the Goupil Galleries in London, the location of their later meetings. Commitment to the group was not exclusive: Gilman was a founder-member of the LONDON GROUP; Ginner joined the avant-garde GROUP X. In 1921 Bevan and Ginner organized an exhibition of *Peintres modernes anglais* at the Galerie Druet, Paris, which included work by members of the group, as well as by William Roberts and Edward Wadsworth. However, after Gilman's death in 1919 the group lapsed, although it never officially disbanded.

BIBLIOGRAPHY
An Exhibition of Paintings by Harold Gilman and Charles Ginner (exh. cat., London, Goupil Gals, 1914)
Paintings by the Cumberland Market Group (exh. cat., London, Goupil Gals, 1915)

JUSTINE HOPKINS

Cuming, William (*b* 1769; *d* Dublin, 5 April 1852). Irish painter. He received his artistic training at the Dublin Society Drawing Schools, winning a silver medal for figure drawing in 1790. He soon set himself up as a portrait painter, his early works being similar in manner to those of his main Dublin rival, Hugh Douglas Hamilton. It was probably in these early years that he completed Tilly Kettle's portrait of the architect *James Gandon* (Dublin, N.G.). Cuming was among the artists of Dublin who in 1800, after an absence of 20 years, re-established annual exhibitions in the city. He exhibited a large number of portraits, one of the most notable being that of *Vincent Waldrè* (1800; Dublin, N.G.). The forceful, rich brushwork of this portrait (somewhat similar to Raeburn in the loose handling of the paint) with the brilliant red chaircover and the prominent palette and brushes, is in marked contrast to Hamilton's style of controlled conviction and smooth finish which was then dominant. Throughout his career Cuming could be relied upon to paint an excellent face, but beneath the dash of his colourful palette there lay little power of observation.

A sociable, active man, Cuming enjoyed literary company and frequently travelled abroad. He was a founder-member of the Royal Hibernian Academy, exhibiting at the first exhibition in 1826; he was President from 1829 to 1832. His output for the Academy was by no means prolific; in his six years of exhibiting there he showed only 15 paintings. Although a portrait such as that of Waldrè has a bravura that gives it a special place in the history of Irish portraiture, the bulk of Cuming's work was official portraiture which was often quite dreary. His sitters included lord lieutenants of Ireland, lord mayors of Dublin and provosts of Trinity College, Dublin.

BIBLIOGRAPHY
Strickland
M. Wynne: 'Tilly Kettle's Last Painting?', *Burl. Mag.*, cix (1967), pp. 532f
Irish Portraits, 1650–1850 (exh. cat., ed. A. Crookshank and the Knight of Glin; London, N.P.G.; Belfast, Ulster Mus.; Dublin, N.G.; 1969)

FINTAN CULLEN

Cumming, Robert (*b* Worcester, MA, 7 Oct 1943). American photographer and conceptual artist. He studied painting at the Massachusetts College of Art, Boston (1961–5), and the University of Illinois, Urbana (1965–7). He first won recognition for his 8 × 10 view camera photographs, for example *Chair Trick* (1973; see Alinder, pl. 12). In such works as these, where he constructed the objects and their settings and then photographed them, Cumming explored perception, illusion, logic, time and motion. In the 1980s he began using drawing, printmaking and colour photography, for example *X-ray Crystallography Mounts (DNA Molecule Research) MIT* (photograph, 1986; Cambridge, MA, MIT; see 1988 exh. cat., pl. 24), with the same attention to pragmatic detail and often magical humour. His interest in narrative fantasies first provided storylines for photo-sequences and later led him to write, illustrate, and publish five books including *Discourse on Domestic Disorder* (Orange, CA, 1975).

BIBLIOGRAPHY
J. Alinder: *Cumming Photographs: Untitled 18* (Carmel, 1979)
Three on Technology: New Photographs by Robert Cumming, Lee Friedlander, Jan Groover (exh. cat., essay by A. Trachtenberg; Cambridge, MA, MIT, List Visual A. Cent., 1988)
Robert Cumming: Cone of Vision (exh. cat., essay by H. M. Davies and L. Forsha; San Diego, CA, Mus. Contemp. A.; Houston, TX, Contemp. A. Mus.; 1993)

CONSTANCE W. GLENN

Cummings & Sears. American architectural partnership formed in 1857 by Charles A. Cummings (*b* Boston, MA, 26 June 1833; *d* Northeast Harbor, ME, 11 Aug 1905) and Willard T. Sears (*b* New Bedford, MA, 15 Nov 1837; *d* Boston, MA, 21 May 1920). Charles A. Cummings graduated from the Rensselaer Polytechnic Institute, Troy, NY, in 1853. Following a two-year tour of Europe and Egypt he returned to Boston and began work in the office of Gridley J. F. Bryant. There he met Willard T. Sears, and the two set up in practice together. The partnership lasted until Cummings retired in 1889. Like most Boston architects of the time, Cummings & Sears profited from the destruction caused by the Great Fire of 1872 and from the new land being created by the filling of Boston's Back Bay. They built commercial blocks, apartment hotels and houses throughout the 1870s and 1880s. They also undertook many suburban house commissions. Cummings, who did most of the firm's design work, was strongly influenced by his travels in Italy. His style can best be seen in the New Old South Church (1876), Boston, with its pointed arches, polychromatic stonework, fine floral and foliate decoration and tall Italian campanile. This free Italianate Gothic is typical of most of the firm's work.

Cummings was a prominent member of the Boston Society of Architects. He retired from architectural practice in 1889 in order to devote himself full-time to writing, particularly on Greek and Italianate architecture. Sears continued to practise alone after 1889, with the Italian Gothic bent of his practice culminating in Fenway Court (now the Gardner Museum), Boston, a mansion built in 1901–3 for Mrs Isabella Stewart Gardner, which housed her important collection consisting largely of Renaissance paintings, sculpture and decorative art. The house, a four-storey stuccoed building with a covered interior courtyard, utilized European architectural fragments throughout its vast interiors.

WRITINGS

C. A. Cummings and W. P. P. Longfellow: *Cyclopaedia of Works of Architecture in Italy, Greece and the Levant* (New York, 1895)
C. A. Cummings: *A History of Architecture in Italy*, 2 vols (Boston, 1901)
——: contributions to Winsor and Sturgis

BIBLIOGRAPHY

J. Winsor: *The Memorial History of Boston*, 4 vols (Boston, 1881)
R. Sturgis, ed.: *A Dictionary of Architecture and Building* (Boston, 1901)
W. P. P. Longfellow: 'Charles A. Cummings', *Q. Bull. Amer. Inst. Archit.*, vi/10 (1905), pp. 169–73

JEAN A. FOLLETT

Cumont, Franz (Valéry Marie) (*b* Aalst, 3 Jan 1868; *d* Woluwe, Brussels, 20 Aug 1947). Belgian archaeologist and religious historian. Educated in Ghent, Bonn, Berlin and Paris, he taught at the University of Ghent from 1896 to 1910. He made a fundamental contribution to the understanding of the complexity of ancient paganism and its symbols, and he travelled widely in Syria and Turkey in search of ancient astrological drawings and symbols. Other important early works of this prolific scholar focused on the influence of ancient oriental cults, particularly Mithraism, on the Roman world and on Christianity. He developed an interest in pagan representations of the afterlife and collected widely dispersed information for his great work *Recherches sur le symbolisme funéraire des Romains*. This broke decisively with the tradition of romantic scholarship, which had concentrated on style, aesthetic quality and dating: Cumont marshalled his impressive archaeological knowledge to present a scientific categorization of the material remains of ancient funerary art, including sculpture, painting and sarcophagus reliefs, together with a penetrating and influential analysis of the selection and meaning of the artistic themes used.

WRITINGS

L'Art dans les monuments mithraïques (Paris, 1899)
L'Adoration des Mages et l'art triomphal de Rome (Rome, 1932)
Mélanges Franz Cumont (Brussels, 1936) [with extensive Cumont bibliog.]
L'Egypte des astrologues (Brussels, 1937)
Recherches sur le symbolisme funéraire des Romains (Paris, 1942)

BIBLIOGRAPHY

A. J. Festugière: 'Franz Cumont', *Gnomon*, xi (1949), pp. 272–4
F. Mayence: 'Hommage à la mémoire de Franz Cumont, à l'occasion de la remise de son buste à la classe', *Cl. Lett. & Sci. Mor. & Polit.: Bull. Cl. Lett. & Sci. Mor. & Polit. & Cl. B.-A.*, xiii (1956), pp. 363–77

JOHN CURRAN

Cun. See KUN.

Cundy. English family of artists.

(1) Thomas Cundy (i) (*b* St Dennis, Cornwall, 1765; *d* London, 28 Dec 1825). Architect and builder. He trained as a builder in Plymouth and went to London in the 1790s. He was employed for a time by Samuel Pepys Cockerell as Clerk of Works at Normanton, Leics, but *c.* 1800 set up on his own in London as an architect and builder in Ranelagh Street, Pimlico. During the next two decades he built up a substantial country house practice in association with his three sons, of whom (2) Thomas Cundy (ii) became an architect, while James Cundy (1792–1826) and Joseph Cundy (1795–1875) were trained respectively as mason and carpenter. Much of the work consisted of altering and remodelling existing houses, for which Cundy used either a picturesque Gothic style—as at Hawarden Castle, Clwyd (1804–9), Wytham Abbey, Berks (1809–10), and Syon House, London (1819–26)—or a rather conventional classical style—as in his alterations to Middleton Park, Oxon (1806–10; destr. 1938).

In 1821 Cundy sr was appointed Surveyor to the Grosvenor Estate in succession to William Porden. This was at a time when the major redevelopment, which ultimately produced the districts of Belgravia and Pimlico, was just beginning. He exerted a controlling influence on the early stages of the development, even if no specific works are attributable to him.

(2) Thomas Cundy (ii) (*b* Pimlico, London, 1790; *d* Bromley, Kent, 15 July 1867). Architect, son of (1) Thomas Cundy (i). He succeeded his father as Surveyor to the Grosvenor Estate in 1825. He kept up the country house side of the business but also designed much on the estate, including several private speculations. One early estate job, for Richard Grosvenor, Viscount Belgrave (eldest son of Robert Grosvenor, 1st Marquis of Westminster), was the formation of Belgrave House (1823–4) out of two terraced houses in Grosvenor Square. In the later 1820s Cundy prepared plans for rebuilding Grosvenor House, of which only the picture gallery and the handsome Doric columned screen were eventually executed, and developed the south side of Chester Square in partnership with his brother Joseph.

Cundy designed seven churches in Gothic style, five on the Grosvenor Estate. The earlier ones, such as St Paul's, Knightsbridge (1840–43), showed little awareness of current liturgical developments, but in St Barnabas, Pimlico (1847–50), Cundy produced what the *Ecclesiologist* described as 'the most sumptuously and correctly fitted church erected in England since the Reformation'. There is no evidence for the rumour that William Butterfield was Cundy's assistant, a position more likely to have been filled by Cundy's third son, (3) Thomas Cundy (iii). During the 1850s many of the old Grosvenor leases expired, and Cundy provided designs for re-fronting over 40 of the larger houses in a harsh yellow-brick Italianate style epitomized by 26 Grosvenor Square. In his last years he retired to live at Bromley, Kent, but retained the estate surveyorship until his death.

(3) Thomas Cundy (iii) (*b* London, 17 Oct 1820; *d* Brighton, 4 Oct 1895). Architect, son of (2) Thomas Cundy (ii). He carried out what was probably his most notable contribution to architecture during the early 1860s, with the rebuilding of the Grosvenor Gardens area immediately west of the new Victoria Station. After a limited competition in 1864, he was given the job of planning the layout and designing the façades of several large stone ranges of terraced houses. In part taking his cue from J. T. Knowles's new Grosvenor Hotel, Cundy adopted the French style of Louis Tullius Joachim Visconti's and Hector-Martin Lefuel's New Louvre (1852–71), and his terraces had Parisian ornament and high mansard roofs with iron roof crestings. They also sported coloured slate roof coverings and terracotta cornices as a nod in the direction of High Victorian polychromy. After succeeding his father as Surveyor in 1867, his designing activity diminished, but he fulfilled his supervising functions on the Grosvenor Estate with stringent efficiency.

UNPUBLISHED SOURCES

London, RIBA Lib. [sketchbook of (2) Thomas Cundy (ii)]
ex-T. J. Cundy priv. col., Brant Broughton, Lincs [O. F. Cundy: *Account of the Cundy Family* (MS., 1874)]

BIBLIOGRAPHY
Colvin; Papworth
Obituary, *Builder*, xxv (1867), p. 607
A. Saint: 'The Grosvenor Estate II: The Cundy Era', *Country Life*, clxii (17 Nov 1977), pp. 1474–7

NEIL BURTON

Cunego, Domenico (*b* Verona, 1724–5; *d* Rome, 8 Jan 1803). Italian printmaker. He was the pupil of an otherwise unknown painter by the name of Francesco Ferrari. When he was 18, and after executing several paintings (untraced), he turned to engraving, an art in which he may have been self-taught (Gori Gandellini). Between 1752 and 1760 he collaborated with Dionigi Valesi on the illustrations for a three-volume catalogue of the coin collection of Giacomo Muselli, published in Verona (1752, 1756, 1760; e.g. Verona, Mus. Muselli). Also from the 1750s are several *Views of Verona* after drawings by T. Majeroni and the *St Thomas of Villanova* (1757) after Antonio Balestra. This Veronese painter was frequently a source of inspiration for Cunego, who often reproduced works by his contemporaries, for example Francesco Solimena and Felice Boscaratti (1721–1807).

In October 1760 Cunego came into contact with James Adam, younger brother of Robert Adam, who was visiting Verona. Together with Adam and his travelling companions, Charles-Louis Clérisseau, Antonio Zucchi and the Veronese draughtsman Giuseppe Sacco (1735–98), Cunego visited Florence and Siena, and in February 1761 he arrived in Rome. He remained in the service of Adam for about two years, during which time he engraved two plates for Robert Adam's *Ruins of the Palace of the Emperor Diocletian at Spalatro in Dalmatia* (London, 1764), as well as 14 views of towns in the region of Campania after drawings by Clérisseau, printed about 1763. Adam returned to London in 1763, but Cunego preferred to remain working independently in Rome. He remained on good terms with his former patron, however, and with the world of English publishing in general. Between 1764 and 1778 he executed many engravings after Gavin Hamilton's paintings; most important are several pictures based on Homeric incidents (see Irwin, figs 2, 4–6; for illustration *see* HAMILTON, GAVIN). Cunego was commissioned in 1769 to produce several plates for the *Collection of Prints Engraved after the Most Capital Paintings in England*, published in London by John Boydell, and 22 plates for the *Schola Italica picturae* by Gavin Hamilton, a collection

of engravings of 16th- and 17th-century Italian paintings (Rome, 1773). During the same period Cunego also made a large number of engravings after the work of famous artists of the past such as Giorgione, Titian, Reni, Domenichino, Guercino and (in 1780) after Michelangelo's *Last Judgement* (Rome, Vatican, Sistine Chapel). He produced plates of portraits, particularly those of popes: *Clement XIII* (after Piranesi), *Clement XIV* and *Pius VI* (after Giovanni Domenico Porta).

By this time Cunego was famous in Rome and well established in Neo-classical circles. He was the favourite engraver of Anton Raphael Mengs, many of whose works he reproduced in engravings and etchings. Mengs's tracings were the basis for Cunego's 40 engravings of the heads of figures from Raphael's *School of Athens* (Rome, Vatican, Stanza della Segnatura). In 1785 Cunego travelled to Berlin, where he was invited to manage the copperplate printing works of someone named Pascal; he returned to Rome, however, four years later. In Germany he experimented with engraving in the *manière noire* (mezzotint), which became the predominant mode of expression in his later Roman works. A number of plates date from the 1790s, notably 27 *Views of Rome* as well as some devotional engravings. His last engraved work may have been the *Tomb of Bishop de Fatatis* (1800), after a drawing by Ciaffaroni. He continued to run his own school until his death and numbered among his pupils Gian Carlo Colombo, Camillo Tinti (1738–96) and his sons by his first marriage Luigi Cunego (1750/57–after 1819) and Giuseppe Cunego (*b* 1760).

BIBLIOGRAPHY

DBI [with list of dated works and bibliog.]
G. Gori Gandellini: *Notizie istoriche degli intagliatori*, i (Siena, 1771)
M. Pittaluga: *Acquafortisti veneziani del settecento* (Florence, 1952), p. 41
Il settecento a Roma (exh. cat., ed. E. Lavagnino; Rome, Pal. Espos., 1959), pp. 101–4
D. Irwin: 'Gavin Hamilton: Archaeologist, Painter and Dealer', *A. Bull.*, xliv (1962), pp. 87–102
Aspetti dell'incisione veneziana del settecento (exh. cat. by G. Dillon, Venice, Scu. Grande S Teodoro, 1976), p. 35

FILIPPO PEDROCCO

Cunelachi, Nicolas. *See* KOUNELAKIS, NICOLAS.

Cúneo (Perinetti), José (*b* Montevideo, 11 Sept 1887; *d* Bonn, 19 July 1977). Uruguayan painter. He first studied art at the Círculo de Bellas Artes in Montevideo under the Uruguayan painter Carlos María Herrera (1875–1914) and the Uruguayan sculptor Felipe Menini (1873–1940). In 1907 he travelled to Europe, and after studying in Turin at the workshops of Leonardo Bistolfi and the Italian painter Anton Maria Mucchi (*b* 1871), and meeting Auguste Rodin in Paris, he returned to Montevideo and had his first show at the Galería Moretti in 1910. He returned to Paris in 1911, studying with Hermen(egild) Anglada Camarasa and Kees van Dongen at the Academia Vity.

Around 1914 Cúneo began painting the Uruguayan countryside, an unspectacular landscape of ranches and fields, in an expressionist style, often enlarging the size of the moon and distorting the land and the sky to create a sensation of instability. Typical examples of this highly personal form of perspective include *Moon and Ranch* (1942), *Ranches in the Gully* (1940) and *Outskirts of Florida*

(1931; all Montevideo, Mus. N. A. Plást. & Visuales). He returned in 1938 to Europe, where he painted Venetian canals and exhibited in Paris and Milan, but during World War II went back to Uruguay, where he taught at the Círculo de Bellas Artes and the Escuela Nacional de Bellas Artes. In 1957, after seeing an exhibition of Pablo Picasso's *Guernica* (1937) and related studies, he began to produce abstract paintings, which he signed *Perinetti* (his maternal surname) and exhibited in Yugoslavia in 1962. His rejection of figuration was decisively demonstrated in the thickly painted and elaborately textured paintings, such as *Serpentine* (1964; Montevideo, Mus. N.A. Plást. & Visuales), that he began to produce in the mid-1960s, using *José Cúneo Perinetti* as his signature. In 1969 he won the Latin American Grand Prize at the São Paulo Biennale.

BIBLIOGRAPHY

J. P. Argul: *Las artes plásticas del Uruguay* (Montevideo, 1966); rev. as *Proceso de las artes plásticas del Uruguay* (Montevideo, 1975), pp. 148–54, 162–6

Seis maestros de la pintura uruguaya (exh. cat., ed. A. Kalenberg; Buenos Aires, Mus. N. B.A., 1985), pp. 139–56

R. Pereda de Nin: *José Cúneo* (Montevideo, 1988)

ANGEL KALENBERG

Cungi, Leonardo (*b* Borgo San Sepolcro; *fl* 1540s; *d* Rome, June 1569). Italian painter and draughtsman. Vasari mentioned him among the painters who decorated the Vatican Belvedere in the 1560s. This was an important collaborative project involving Pirro Ligorio, Taddeo and Federico Zuccaro, Federico Barocci and Santi di Tito and may be the work for which Cungi received a payment from the papal datary in 1566. In 1569 Cungi was asked to complete the ceiling gilding in the nave of S Giovanni in Laterano for Pope Pius IV, a project first assigned to Daniele da Volterra. Cungi died before the commission was completed, and it was undertaken by Cesare Trapasso (*fl* 1570s). Vasari recognized a drawing by Cungi of Michelangelo's fresco of the *Last Judgement* in the Sistine Chapel in the collection of Perino del Vaga at Perino's death in 1547. According to Giovanni Battista Armenini, the drawing would have formed part of Perino's collection of drawings sold by his daughter to the Mantuan antiquary and collector Jacopo Strada in 1566. Vasari assembled other designs by Cungi in his *Libro dei disegni*. A number of Cungi's drawings of the *Last Judgement* and of Michelangelo's Pauline Chapel frescoes survive (Florence, Uffizi; Cleveland, OH, Mus. A.; Paris, Louvre) as do several other sheets (Cleveland, OH, Mus. A.; Paris, Louvre). The draughtsmanship is characterized by figures with blank eyes and scalloped outlines for hands and feet. The use of a loose, ornamental line for interior modelling often results in lyre-shaped abdomens, and short, widely spaced parallel strokes are used for shading. Cungi's brother, Giovanni Battista Congi (*fl* 1539–46), was also a painter.

BIBLIOGRAPHY

Thieme–Becker

G. Vasari: *Vite* (1550, rev. 2/1568); ed. G. Milanesi (1878–85)

G. B. Armenini: *De' veri precetti della pittura* (Ravenna, 1587/*R* New York, 1971); Eng. trans. and ed. E. Olszewski (New York, 1977), pp. 134–7

B. Berenson: *Drawings of the Florentine Painters*, 3 vols (Chicago, 1938)

The Draughtsman's Eye: Late Italian Renaissance Schools and Styles (exh. cat. by E. J. Olszewski, Cleveland, OH, Mus. A., 1979), pp. 68–70

EDWARD J. OLSZEWSKI

Cunha, Domingos da (*b* Lisbon, 1598; *d* Cotovia, 11 May 1644). Portuguese painter and Jesuit priest. He was apprenticed in Madrid to Eugenio Cajés, in whose studio he became familiar with the tenebrist style characterized by sharply contrasting figures, strong gradations of chiaroscuro and naturalistically rendered background and drapery. He returned to Lisbon around 1625. In 1632 he became a Jesuit, and in 1644 he died in the Noviciado da Cotovia, renowned for his saintliness. The naturalism of his works quickly gained him fame, and he was nicknamed *cabrinha* (little goat) by his contemporaries because of his 'oriental features'. An early work is the beautiful *Visitation* (*c.* 1630; Lisbon, S Mamede, Sacristy). Among his patrons and collectors were the Inquisitor General, Dom Francisco de Castro, and the Capelão-mor (royal chaplain) and future Bishop of Elvas, Dom Manuel da Cunha.

Like the work of André Reinoso, that of Domingos da Cunha clearly reflects the innovative spirit of the Portuguese painters trained at the school of Madrid. Félix da Costa Meesen noted that 'he is a good colourist' and a 'great imitator of the natural', although 'narrative was not his strong point'. These qualities are seen in the series of scenes from the *Life of St Ignatius Loyola* (*c.* 1640–44) that he painted for the church of S Roque, Lisbon. These naturalistic paintings, with detailed backgrounds, luminous colours and firm drawing, recall the style of Cajés and of Bartolomé Carducho. Da Cunha painted another series on the *Life of St Ignatius* for the church at the Noviciado da Cotovia, now in the sacristy of the church of S Roque, Lisbon, as well as the high altar for the same church at Cotovia, depicting the *Assumption of the Virgin* (*c.* 1640–44), which survived the fire at the Noviciado. In 1641, immediately after the restoration of the crown, he was commissioned to paint the portrait of *John IV* (untraced).

BIBLIOGRAPHY

F. da Costa Meesen: *Antiguidade da arte da pintura* (MS. 1696), ed. G. Kubler (New Haven and London, 1967), pp. 268–9

Fray António Franco: *Imagem da virtude em o Noviciado de Lisboa*, iii (Coimbra, 1717), chap. 15

J. Da Costa Lima: 'Para a identificação da obra do Mestre Cabrinha', *Brotéria*, xxiii (1936), pp. 18–36

R. dos Santos: 'A pintura da segunda metade do século XVI ao final do século XVII', *Arte Port.*, ed. J. Barreira (Lisbon, 1951), pp. 293–4

VITOR SERRÃO

Cunha, Félix Adaústo (*b* Lisbon, *c.* 1680; *fl c.* 1725–50). Portuguese sculptor and wood-carver. He was best known for his Italianate interpretation of the Joanine style. His most important works include the carving of the pulpit and chancel of the church of the convent of Nossa Senhora de Jesus, Lisbon (1725), and in the 1740s the sacristy of the church of the Madre de Deus, Lisbon. The nave and the elegant, gilded pulpit of the latter are also attributed to Cunha. The design was based on an engraving by Filippo Passarini (*d* 1698) that was published in Rome (1698). The carved volutes and the mass of foliage offer a foretaste of the rich Rococo style. Also attributed to Cunha are the organ cases and two pulpits in the church of the convent of Nossa Senhora de Jesus, Lisbon, which were produced in partnership with his son João Cipriano Cunha and gilded by the painter José Gonçalves Soares in 1731.

BIBLIOGRAPHY

A. de Carvalho: 'Novas revelações para a história do Barroco em Portugal', *Belas A.*, n. s. 2, xx (1964), pp. 13–81

NATÁLIA MARINHO FERREIRA ALVES

Cunha Correia Vale, da. *See* VALE.

Cunill, Josep Gudiol i. *See* GUDIOL I CUNILL, JOSEP.

Cunningham, Sir Alexander (*b* London, 23 Jan 1814; *d* London, 28 Nov 1893). British archaeologist, numismatist and engineer. He obtained an Indian cadetship in 1828 through the patronage of Sir Walter Scott and received his commission as Second Lieutenant, Bengal Engineers, in 1831. After training at Addiscombe and Chatham, he was sent to India in 1833. Friendship with James Prinsep encouraged an immediate interest in Indian antiquities and led to his excavation of the Sarnath stupa (1835–6). After three years with the Sappers at Calcutta, Delhi and Benares (Varanasi), he was appointed an aide-de-camp (1836–40) to Lord Auckland. A geographical mission (July–September 1839) to trace the sources of the Punjab rivers in Kashmir provided access to the antiquities of the region. While Executive Engineer to Muhammad 'Ali Shah, the ruler of Avadh (1840–42), he discovered the Buddhist site of Sankasya (Sankisa).

As a field engineer, he saw action during the Bundelkund rebellion (1842), at Punniar (1843), Sobraon (First Sikh War 1846), Chilianwala and Gujarat (Second Sikh War 1848–9). He served as Political Officer at Kangra (1846) and on a boundary commission (1846–8), which was combined with a survey of Ladakh and adjacent regions. He was Executive Engineer at Gwalior (1844–5; 1849–53) and Multan (1853–6), during which time he excavated at Sanchi, Mathura and Harappa. In 1856 he was sent as Chief Engineer to Burma, and then to the North-Western Provinces (1858–61). He retired from the army in 1861 as a Major-General.

At his own behest, Cunningham then became the first Archaeological Surveyor to the Government of India (1861–5). In 1870 he was appointed Director General of a permanent Archaeological Survey department. He concentrated throughout on the Buddhist sites in the north of the subcontinent, a major preoccupation being the identification of places visited by the Chinese monk Xuan zang (7th century AD). He usually spent three to six days at each site, exploring up to thirty locations in one touring season, and recommending promising sites for excavation by the public works departments. Though many of his interpretations have been challenged, Cunningham's detailed published record of sites and finds remains valuable. His systematic study produced the first understanding of the nature of many ruins and enabled him to identify correctly such ancient sites as Taxila and Pataliputra (Patna). He discovered several Gupta-period temples and the use of the arch in early Hindu architecture, contributed to the decipherment of Kharoshthi and identified the iconography of many Gandharan and early Indian Buddhist bas-reliefs. After his retirement in 1885, Cunningham concentrated on coins, his work providing the first chronological framework for Indian numismatics. In 1887 he was created a Knight Commander of the Indian Empire.

Much of his personal collection of Indian antiquities is now in the British Museum.

WRITINGS

The Bhilsa Topes (London, 1854)

Ladak, Physical, Statistical and Historical: With Notices of the Surrounding Countries (London, 1854)

Archaeol. Surv. India Rep., i–ii (1862–5); iii–v (1871–3); ix–xi (1873–8); xiv–xvii (1878–82); xx–xxi (1882–5)

The Ancient Geography of India (London, 1871), ed. Surendranath Majumdar Sastri (Calcutta, 1924)

Inscriptions of Aśoka, Corp. Inscript. Indic., i (Calcutta, 1877)

The Stūpa of Bharhut (London, 1879)

Book of Indian Eras (Calcutta, 1883)

Coins of Alexander's Successors in the East (London, 1884)

Coins of Ancient India from the Earliest Times Down to the Seventh Century AD (London, 1891)

Coins of the Indo-Scythians (London, 1892)

Mahabodhi or the Great Buddhist Temple under the Bodhi Tree at Buddhagaya (London, 1892)

'Later Indo-Scythians', *Numi. Chron.*, 3rd ser., xiii (1893), pp. 93–128, 166–202, pls VIII–X, XIII–XV; xiv (1894), pp. 243–93, pls IX–XII; ed. A. K. Narain (Varanasi, 1962)

Coins of Mediaeval India from the Seventh Century Down to the Muhammadan Conquests (London, 1894)

BIBLIOGRAPHY

DNB suppl. ii

Abu Imam: *Sir Alexander Cunningham and the Beginnings of Indian Archaeology* (Dhaka, 1966)

P. Chandra: *On the Study of Indian Art* (New York, 1983)

E. ERRINGTON

Cunningham, Allan (*b* Keir, Dumfries & Galloway, 7 Dec 1784; *d* London, 30 Oct 1842). Scottish writer. His literary ambitions may have been initially stimulated by the poet Robert Burns, who was a friend and neighbour at Dalswinton. He was interested in Scottish ballads and the poetry of Sir Walter Scott and turned to writing after completing an apprenticeship as a mason. He published several collections of Scottish songs and ballads, both traditional and modern (including many of his own), as well as folk tales, romances (of the kind made popular by Scott) and an edition of Burns's poetry in eight volumes.

In 1810 Cunningham moved to London, where he was introduced to the sculptor Francis Chantrey, who employed him from 1814 to 1841 as his secretary and superintendent of his workmen. Through Chantrey he met many leading artists of the period and incorporated his personal knowledge of them, together with contemporary critical opinions, into the six volumes of artists' biographies he published between 1829 and 1833. These and his account of the painter Sir David Wilkie (published posthumously in 1843) provide useful evidence of the artistic and critical attitudes prevalent in his time.

WRITINGS

Lives of the Most Eminent British Painters, Sculptors and Architects, 6 vols (London, 1829–33)

M. Pilkington, ed.: *A General Dictionary of Painters: A New Edition, Corrected and Revised, with an Introduction, Historical and Critical, and Twenty-six New Lives of Artists of the British School, by A. Cunningham* (London, 1841)

The Life of David Wilkie: With his Journals, Tours, and Critical Remarks on Works of Art, 3 vols (London, 1843)

BIBLIOGRAPHY

D. Hogg: *The Life of Allan Cunningham* (London, 1875)

M. J. H. LIVERSIDGE

Cunningham, Imogen (*b* Portland, OR, 12 April 1883; *d* San Francisco, CA, 23 June 1976). American photographer. She studied at the University of Washington, Seattle, where she became interested in photography. She had been inspired by the work of Gertrude Käsebier, whose Pictorial images were reproduced in Alfred Stieglitz's *Camera Work* and in *The Craftsman*. Cunningham took her first photographs about 1906 and became a professional photo-technician at the Edward Curtis Studio in Seattle from 1907 to 1909, where she printed Curtis's negatives of North American Indians. She was awarded a scholarship to study with Robert Luther (1868–after 1932) at the Technische Hochschule, Dresden (1909–10), where she studied platinum printing, art history and life drawing. In late 1910 Cunningham returned to Seattle and opened a portrait studio. From 1910 to 1915, in addition to her commercial portraiture, she produced a body of Pictorial, Symbolist works inspired by the poetry and prose of William Morris. These depict her friends dressed as mythical characters in bucolic settings. She married the etcher Roi Partridge (1888–1984) in 1915. (They were divorced in 1934.) Her nude photographs of her husband on Mt Rainier, WA, caused a local scandal when they were published in a Seattle periodical that same year. Cunningham moved to San Francisco in 1917, and in 1918 she worked with Francis Bruguière in his local studio.

Cunningham became an innovator in West Coast photography. By 1921 she discovered her interest in detailing natural forms, such as trees at Point Lobos, as well as poised snakes, zebra stripes and close-up botanical studies. She also experimented with pure light abstractions and double exposures. During the 1920s she produced her famous images of magnolia blossoms and calla lilies. Her work was prominent in the exhibition *Film und Foto* held at the Deutscher Werkbund, Stuttgart, in 1929. She was one of the seven original members of GROUP f.64 who created a corpus of sharply focused, unmanipulated imagery. She photographed for *Vanity Fair* in the early 1930s and after that time became increasingly interested in portraiture integrating subject and setting. She became a popular San Francisco figure over the decades, especially among student photographers.

BIBLIOGRAPHY

E. T. Daniel: *Imogen Cunningham: Portraits, Ideas and Design* (Berkeley, 1961)
G. M. Craven: 'Imogen Cunningham', *Aperture*, xi/4 (1964), pp. 134–74
Imogen Cunningham: Photographs, 1921–1967 (exh. cat., intro. B. Newhall; Stanford, CA, U. A.G. & Mus., 1967)
Imogen Cunningham: Photographs, intro. M. Mann (Seattle, 1970)
Imogen!...Imogen Cunningham Photographs, 1910–1973 (exh. cat., intro. M. Mann; Seattle, U. WA, Henry A.G., 1974)
J. Dater: *Imogen Cunningham: A Portrait* (Boston, 1979)
R. Lorenz: *Imogen Cunningham: Frontiers, Photographs, 1906–1976* (Washington, DC, 1987)

RICHARD LORENZ

Cunningham, Merce [Mercier] (*b* Centrala, WA, 16 April 1919). American dancer and choreographer. A master of modern dance, he set the precedent for artistic invention involving the interaction of dance, music, and the visual arts. He trained at Cornish School, Seattle, WA, where he met the musician and composer John Cage. In 1939 he joined the Martha Graham Company in New York. His début as a choreographer and solo dancer came in 1944 when he and Cage presented a programme of music and dances in a small theatre on 16th Street, New York. In 1948 he was commissioned by the New York Ballet Society to choreograph *The Seasons*, for which Cage wrote the score and Isamu Noguchi designed the sets. When the Cunningham Dance Company was formed at BLACK MOUNTAIN COLLEGE, NC, in 1953, Cage became its composer, conductor and musical director. An untitled 'event' in the previous year had been organized by, among others, Cage, Cunningham, Robert Rauschenberg and poet Charles Olson (1910–70) and had included music, film, dance and poetry.

Cunningham exerted a powerful physical presence based on a muscular grace and almost sculptural attitude. Although he was never a collaborator in the strictest sense, he consistently created performances and theatrical 'events' which exploited individuality and autonomy of musicians, dancers and artists. He was among the first to employ programmed chance, or structured disorder, as a creative methodology. His most noted partnership in the visual arts was with Rauschenberg, who travelled with the company, designing sets, costumes and lighting (1961–4). Jasper Johns succeeded Rauschenberg as Cunningham's artistic director and provided design opportunities for artists such as Frank Stella (*Scramble*, 1967), Andy Warhol (*Rainforest*, 1968) and Bruce Nauman (*Tread*, 1970). In 1986 a Cunningham/Cage collaboration, *Roaratorio: An Irish Circus on 'Finnegans Wake'*, opened the Next Wave Festival at the Brooklyn Academy of Music, New York.

BIBLIOGRAPHY

'Essays, Stories and Remarks about Merce Cunningham', *Dance Persp.*, xxxiv (1968) [issue devoted to Cunningham]
J. Klotsky, ed.: *Merce Cunningham* (New York, 1975)
Dancers on a Plane: Cage-Cunningham-Johns (exh. cat., foreword by S. Sontag, London, Anthony d'Offay Gallery, 1989)

CONSTANCE W. GLENN

Cupboard. A piece of case furniture enclosed by doors, generally used for storage. The word 'cupboard' derives from the term applied during Tudor and Jacobean periods to an open structure of shelves used to display plate, a type of furniture now known as a court cupboard (e.g. oak, *c*. 1620; London, V&A). Cupboards, in the modern sense, were widely used by the Romans. During the Byzantine period most cupboards were used for such specialized functions as the storing of books or vestments, as depicted in a mosaic of St Lawrence (early 5th century; Ravenna, S Vitale, mausoleum of Galla Placidia). Typically of plank construction, although sometimes panelled, they were often of architectural form and might be decorated with paintings. When used for storing books the interiors were fitted with shelves. Large cupboards continued to be used for ecclesiastical purposes in the Romanesque and Early Gothic period (e.g. sacristy cupboard, *c*. 1200; Halberstadt, Dom & Domschatz). The doors were generally symmetrical around a central axis and of plank construction bound by iron hinges. The sides could be panelled and carved with arcading. In northern Europe during the Middle Ages the ironwork covering the doors became increasingly elaborate and could be wrought into scrolls, and cast with such naturalistic details as fruit and foliage (e.g. cupboard doors, originally from the church of St

Quentin, Somme, *c.* 1290–1320; Paris, Mus. A. Déc.). In Germany and Austria cupboards often assumed an architectural character, with two sets of doors one above the other, topped by a crenellated cornice and carved with Gothic motifs (*see* GERMANY, §VI, 1 and AUSTRIA, §VI, 1). In the Low Countries, France and England linenfold panelling was a common way of facing cupboards during the late 15th century and early 16th.

During the Renaissance shelves that had been open in court cupboards were frequently enclosed, creating cupboards in the modern sense. Livery cupboards, an adaptation of this form, were installed in bedrooms to hold 'livery'—food and drink left overnight for members of the household and guests (e.g. livery cupboard, late medieval; London, V&A). In France furniture of this type was known as a buffet or dressoir. In Italy large cupboards generally had a pair of panelled doors flanked by pilasters and topped by a cornice (*see* ITALY, §VI, 2). The doors and sides could be decorated with applied panels of intarsia (e.g. cupboard with intarsia decoration, 1502; Monte Oliveto Maggiore, Abbey). In France various types of buffet and dressoir or *armoires à deux corps* were decorated with elaborate Mannerist carving of caryatids and grotesques, under the influence of Jacques Androuet Du Cerceau, but cupboards proper, or armoires, remained relatively plain (*see* FRANCE, §VI, 1). They usually had a single door flanked by thin columns. In southern Germany the Gothic two-tiered cupboard was quickly adapted to Renaissance motifs under the influence of the designer Peter Flötner of Nuremberg (e.g. 1541; Nuremberg, Ger. Nmus.; see fig.). Other impressive Gothic and early Renaissance cupboards have survived in Austria (*see* AUSTRIA, fig. 29). In northern Germany cupboards became more complex in form (*see* GERMANY, §VI, 2). They were increasingly faced by a multitude of smaller doors, often arranged on different axes, while ornament became more sculptural, with small, densely packed scenes carved in relief.

In the Low Countries a distinctive type of oak cupboard emerged in the early 17th century, featuring a deep cornice and heavily panelled doors divided by half columns often of a darker wood such as ebony (e.g. Dutch cupboard, *c.* 1620–50; London, V&A). The form of German cupboards was simplified during the same period, and by 1660 they were usually faced by two long, panelled doors divided by three pilasters above a base containing a pair of drawers. Although oak was used earlier in the century it began to be replaced by walnut *c.* 1670. The shape of the cornice varied according to region. Cabinets made in Frankfurt had particularly distinctive door panels faced with heavily moulded concentric rectangles (e.g. *c.* 1700; Frankfurt am Main, Hist. Mus.). This type of cupboard was developed well into the 18th century, by which time it was decorated with fine walnut veneers inlaid with strapwork and marquetry panels. The grandest cupboards of this period were those associated with the workshops of André Charles Boulle (e.g. *c.* 1700; Paris, Louvre; *see also* MARQUETRY, colour pl. VII). Initially their form was relatively simple, with a pair of doors faced by panels. The decoration of the panels, however, was particularly lavish, often combining brilliantly stained floral marquetry with panels of

Two-tiered cupboard by Peter Flötner, pine and oak with ash veneer, 2.35×1.75×0.58 m, 1541 (Nuremberg, Germanisches Nationalmuseum)

boullework. Later these armoires acquired elaborate crestings, and although floral marquetry fell from favour the boullework panels became more elaborate and were framed by gilt-bronze mounts.

During the 18th century grand cupboards were replaced as decorative pieces by such other types of case furniture as commodes and cabinets. In the Netherlands, however, cupboards remained relatively important; they were usually veneered with walnut and had a domed upper part and a *bombe* lower section fitted with drawers (*see* NETHERLANDS, THE, §VI, 2). In France armoires were usually of oak, walnut or fruit-wood and not veneered. They were given a domed cresting and carved with scroll ornament and set with shaped panels. In England the 'gentleman's press', or wardrobe, with its pair of doors above an arrangement of drawers, was the main form of storage cupboard.

BIBLIOGRAPHY
W. M. Odom: *A History of Italian Furniture from the Fourteenth to the Early Nineteenth Century*, 2 vols (New York, 1918–19, 2/1966–7)
P. Macquoid and R. Edwards: *The Dictionary of English Furniture*, 3 vols (London, 1924–7, rev. 1954/*R* 1983)
H. Kreisel: *Die Kunst des deutschen Möbels*, 3 vols (Munich, 1968–73)
P. Eames: 'Furniture in England, France and the Netherlands from the Twelfth to Fifteenth Century', *Furn. Hist.*, xiii (1977) [whole issue]
P. Thornton: *Seventeenth Century Interior Decoration in England, France and Holland* (New Haven and London, 1978)
N. de Reyniès: *Le Mobilier domestique*, 2 vols (Paris, 1987)

J. W. TAYLOR

Cupisnique. Pre-Columbian culture and art style of South America. It was centred on a small, dry valley *c.* 50 km

Cupisnique clay pottery vessel with stirrup-spout, h. 200 mm, *c.* 800–300 BC (Cambridge, MA, Peabody Museum of Archaeology and Ethnology)

north of the Chicama Valley, Peru. Various sites were located and excavated in the 1930s by Rafael Larco Hoyle. Ceramics from Cupisnique burials and stone-walled structures in the Chicama Valley were attributed to the north-coast version of the CHAVÍN style in the Central Andean area. Lumbreras suggested that Cupisnique ceramics were contemporaneous with the 'Ofrendas' style of Chavín and therefore dated between *c.* 800 and *c.* 300 BC. Cupisnique pottery has also been found in the Moche and Nepeña valleys south of Chicama. The earliest date for the Cupisnique culture has been pushed back to *c.* 1000 BC using radiocarbon measurements from such temples as the Huaca de Los Reyes in Moche with its enormous unbaked clay feline heads. Both Larco and A. R. Sawyer proposed chronologies for Cupisnique ceramics. Sawyer defined Early Cupisnique pottery (*c.* 800–*c.* 600 BC) as similar to highland Chavín, being well-made and polished but usually thick-walled. Colours caused by varying degrees of reduction in firing range from brownish grey to carbon black, and decoration is bold and curvilinear, depicting human, feline and raptorial bird heads like those on large Chavín stone carvings (*see* CHAVÍN DE HUÁNTAR). Lines are broad and incised on a textured background. The few vessel shapes in this early style consist of simple bowls, stirrup-spout bottles (see fig.) and flask-like bottles similar to bottle gourds. Middle Cupisnique pottery (*c.* 600–*c.* 500 BC) is decorated with fine, incised lines, and there is

relief and modelled pottery with three-dimensional forms. Late Cupisnique pottery (*c.* 500–*c.* 300 BC) includes some pieces combining red and black slips as painted bands separated by incised lines. There is greater variety in modelled forms—including human, vegetable, marine and architectural subjects—and redware occurs; this was painted with graphite or other red pigment, then polished and incised with wide lines. Two-piece moulds were used to make bottle chambers, while stirrup spouts were added separately before firing. (For further discussion of Pre-Columbian Central Andean pottery *see* SOUTH AMERICA, PRE-COLUMBIAN, §III, 5.)

The finest early metalwork from Peru has come from the late Cupisnique culture, in which gold was made into ornaments and tools, such as earrings, pectorals and tweezers, by hammering, repoussé, annealing and soldering. The best examples (e.g. ex-Mus. Amer. Ind., New York, now Washington, DC, Smithsonian Inst.) are from Chongoyape, *c.* 170 km north of Chicama, presumably from looted burials.

BIBLIOGRAPHY
R. L. Burger: *Chavín and the Origins of Andean Civilization* (London, 1922), pp. 248ff
R. Larco Hoyle: *Los Cupisniques* (Lima, 1941)
Ancient Peruvian Ceramics: The Nathan Cummings Collection (exh. cat. by A. R. Sawyer, New York, Met., 1966), pp. 17–18
J. H. Rowe: 'Form and Meaning in Chavín Art', *Peruvian Archaeology: Selected Readings*, ed. J. H. Rowe and D. Menzel (Palo Alto, 1967), pp. 72–103
L. G. Lumbreras: *De los pueblos, las culturas y las artes del antiguo Perú* (Lima, 1969; Eng. trans. by B. J. Meggers, Washington, DC, 1974), pp. 67–77
C. B. Donnan and C. J. Mackey: *Ancient Burial Patterns in the Moche Valley, Peru* (Austin, 1978), pp. 21–3
T. Pozorski and S. Pozorski: 'Chavín: The Early Horizon and Initial Period', *The Origins and Development of the Andean State*, ed. J. Haas, S. Pozorski and T. Pozorski (Cambridge, 1987), pp. 36–46
GEORGE BANKES

Cupola. *See* DOME.

Curaçao. *See under* ANTILLES, LESSER.

Curatella Manes, Pablo (*b* La Plata, 14 Dec 1891; *d* Buenos Aires, 14 Nov 1962). Argentine sculptor. He entered the Escuela Nacional de Bellas Artes in Buenos Aires in 1907 and won a scholarship to study in Italy, where he was in the habit of creating and destroying monumental sculptures in a single day. In spite of the prohibition against holders of scholarships absenting themselves from the country to which they were sent, he travelled widely, visiting major museums and galleries and from 1914 to 1926 coming into contact with Aristide Maillol, Emile-Antoine Bourdelle, Maurice Denis, Paul Sérusier, Henri Laurens, Gris, Brancusi and Le Corbusier. Only his seriousness as an artist saved him from being penalized for breaking the terms of his scholarship.

In 1920 Curatella Manes settled in Paris, where he remained until after World War II. Between 1921 and 1923 he produced accomplished sculptures in a Cubist style, concentrating on representations of figures such as *The Guitarist* (1921) and *The Acrobats* (1923). After 1923, in works such as *Dance* (1925) and *Rugby* (1926), he treated mass in a lighter, more rhythmic way, although in works such as *Feminine Torso* (1932) and *The Prophet*

(1933) he returned to a heavier expression of mass. His final works, apparently geometrical but with an organic sense of structure, were virtually abstract. In 1949 he gave 31 sculptures to the Museo Nacional de Bellas Artes in Buenos Aires, including all of the works cited above.

BIBLIOGRAPHY
O. Svanascini: *Curatella Manes* (Buenos Aires, 1963)
J. Romero Brest: *Curatella Manes* (Buenos Aires, 1967)
J. López Anaya: *Curatella Manes* (Buenos Aires, 1981)

HORACIO SAFONS

Cure [Cuer]. English family of masons and sculptors of Dutch origin.

(1) William Cure (i) (*b* Holland, 1514–15; *d* London, 1579). He was summoned to England in 1541 to work on Nonsuch Palace for Henry VIII, and in 1552 he became an English citizen. By 1559 he was living across the Thames from the City of London in Southwark, where an émigré artistic community grew up in the late 16th century, and he remained in the area. He did unspecified work for Edward Seymour, Duke of Somerset, at old Somerset House (built 1547–52; destr. *c.* 1777) in the Strand, London, and may have been the person of his surname who made a fountain (1568) for Sir Nicholas Bacon's garden at Redgrave, Suffolk.

(2) Cornelius Cure (*b* London; *fl* from *c.* 1574; *d* London, *c.* 1609). Son of (1) William Cure (i). He is probably the 'Cure' who in 1574 was paid for drawing plans and elevations for an unexecuted funerary monument to *Henry VIII*, and a design for an unexecuted monument to *Edward VI* (Oxford, Bodleian Lib., Gough Maps 45 no. 63). This drawing is stylistically related to three church monuments of exceptional quality, with kneeling effigies set up against a wall, that are certainly from the same workshop and may be Cornelius's work: *Richard Alington and his Wife* (*c.* 1561; London, PRO), *Sir Richard and Lady Blount* (*c.* 1574; London, Tower, St Peter ad Vincula) and *Sir Anthony Coke and his Family* (*c.* 1576; Romford, St Edward Confessor). Cure was among the freemen of the Marblers' Company of London when it was amalgamated with the Masons' Company in 1585. William, Lord Burghley, chief minister to Elizabeth I, employed him, and his workshop was probably responsible for the monuments to Burghley himself, to his parents (both *c.* 1587; Stamford, Lincs, St Martin) and to his wife Mildred and daughter Anne (*c.* 1589; London, Westminster Abbey). The last of these was intended to overwhelm with bright colour, architectural display and an abundance of carved ornament in a north European Mannerist style. Burghley recommended Cure for the post of Master Mason to the Crown, to which he was appointed in 1596, but his only major royal commission appears to have been for the monument to *Mary, Queen of Scots* (1605) in Westminster Abbey. This was clearly intended to complement Maximilian Colt's tomb of *Elizabeth I*, which is of similar design.

(3) William Cure (ii) (*b* London; *fl c.* 1605; *d* London, *bur* 6 Aug 1632). Son of (2) Cornelius Cure. He joined his father as Master Mason in 1605 and became the sole holder of the office after the latter's death, completing the monument to *Mary, Queen of Scots* (*c.* 1613). He repaired and re-erected two fountains in coloured marble for Hampton Court Palace in 1607–9 (destr.) and made two more, each embellished with eight leopard's heads, for the same palace in 1615–16 (destr.). From June 1619 until the end of February 1621 Cure's wages were suspended because he had failed to undertake the mason's work on the King's new Banqueting House in Whitehall, London, and in 1622 it was said that he had continued to be 'careless and negligent' about the royal works elsewhere. He probably neglected Whitehall because he was late in completing three tombs for Francis Russell, the future 4th Earl of Bedford, for which he had contracted in 1618; the tombs were almost certainly those of the 4th Earl himself, the 2nd Earl and *Anne, Countess of Warwick* (Chenies, St Michael, Bedford Chapel). He was also responsible for the memorial to *Sir Roger Aston and his Two Wives* (1612–13, Cranford, Middx, St Dunstan), which has kneeling effigies in a setting derived from the canopy of the *Mary, Queen of Scots* memorial. With Nicolas Johnson he executed the monument to *Bishop Montagu* (1618–19, Bath Abbey), with its unusual columns bearing heraldic devices at the four corners. His least creditable works are the statues (1614–15) of *Henry VIII*, *Anne of Denmark* (wife of James I) and *Charles, Prince of Wales* (later Charles I) on the Great Gate of Trinity College, Cambridge.

BIBLIOGRAPHY
K. A. Esdaile: 'William Cure II and his Work at Trinity College, Cambridge', *Burl. Mag.*, lxxxi (1942), pp. 21ff
M. Whinney: *Sculpture in Britain, 1530–1830*, Pelican Hist. A. (Harmondsworth, 1964), pp. 16–17
H. M. Colvin, ed.: *The History of the King's Works*, iii (London, 1975), iv (London, 1982)
A. White: 'Classical Learning and the Early Stuart Renaissance', *Ch. Mnmt*, i (1985), pp. 20–33 (20–23)

ADAM WHITE

Curfew. *See under* FIREPLACE FURNISHINGS.

Curjel, Robert. *See under* MOSER (ii), (2).

Curnoe, Greg (*b* London, Ont., 19 Nov 1936; *d* Nov 1992). Canadian painter and printmaker. He attended the Doon School of Art, Kitchener, Ontario, from June to October 1956, and the Ontario College of Art in Toronto (1957–60). He then returned to London, establishing a studio and joining with a number of other young artists living in the city to form a small but vital community: he founded a magazine, *Region* (nine issues, 1961–9), and with six other artists ran an artists' gallery, also called Region, from November 1962 to the end of 1963. His works of this period, sometimes linked to Pop art in their style and contemporary references, were often intimate in their subject-matter and unconventional in technique, as is the case with *On the Bed* (oil and stamp pad on hardboard, 1963; Vancouver, U. BC, Students' Un.).

Motivated by his interest in the Dada movement and encouraged by the writer Michel Sanouillet, Curnoe directed his paintings, drawings and prints towards a closely observed response to the events, relationships and surroundings of his life in London. He advocated a particular definition of the term 'regionalism' not as the isolationism of the provincial but as the reality of individual and collective existence. His interest in popular culture, reflected in his work on many levels, led him to regard art as a response to the broad cultural reality of everyday life rather than as a separate entity. In *The Camouflaged Piano or French Roundels* (1966; Ottawa, N.G.), for example, he portrayed two friends playing jazz on piano and saxophone surrounded by a variety of images, including an early 20th-century Brazilian airship and a hotel sign salvaged from the streets of London. He became closely associated with the activities of the Canadian Artists Representation, founded in 1967 by his friend and fellow London artist Jack Chambers, which advocated the professional status of artists and asserted their rights to fees for the use of their works both in reproduction and exhibition.

BIBLIOGRAPHY
Greg Curnoe (exh. cat. by P. Theberge, Ottawa, N.G., 1982) [incl. comprehensive bibliog.]

DAVID BURNETT

Curradi. Italian family of artists.

(1) Taddeo Curradi [Taddeo di Francesco di Piero di Taddeo Curradi] (*b* Florence, 25 Oct 1529; *d* Florence, 12 Sept 1596). Sculptor. His initial training was as a goldbeater, but he later learnt the art of sculpture. His main work consisted of wooden crucifixes, usually of limewood. According to Filippo Baldinucci, Giovan Battista Naldini, on seeing Curradi's rather stiff crucifixes, showed him a drawing by Pontormo, and with his help Curradi's work improved, softened and gained in grace and piety. Baldinucci also relates that Curradi's work was complimented by Giambologna. Baldinucci was acquainted with crucifixes by Curradi in various Florentine churches and private chapels, including the oratory of the Concezione in S Maria dei Servi (where one crucifix was located above the altar of the Curradi family, with another small one in the sacristy); the Donne di S Bonifacio hospital; the Gaddi Chapel in Santa Croce; and the oratory of the Confraternità di S Bonaventura. Baldinucci also referred to another crucifix in the possession of Grand Duke Francesco I. There was also a large gilded crucifix, in S Maria Novella, which was accompanied by frescoes by Alessandro Allori and an altarpiece by Bronzino. None of Curradi's works is known to have survived.

BIBLIOGRAPHY
Thieme–Becker
F. Baldinucci: *Notizie* (1681–1728); ed. F. Ranalli (1845–7), ii
W. E. Paatz: *Die Kirchen von Florenz* (Frankfurt am Main, 1940–57), i, pp. 401, 409, 610; iii, p. 743
D. Carl: 'Die Kruzifixe des Taddeo Curradi in der Kirche der SS Concezione zu Florenz', *Mitt. Ksthist. Inst. Florenz* (1984), pp. 394–401

JULIA WATSON

(2) Francesco Curradi (*b* Florence, 15 Nov 1570; *d* Florence, 1661). Painter, son of (1) Taddeo Curradi. He produced many devotional works and had a large clientele. At their best, the works are distinguished by lucid draughtsmanship, simple compositions and elegant, melancholy figures. Curradi was trained in the studio of Giovan Battista Naldini and in 1590 matriculated from the Accademia del Disegno, Florence. His first independent works include a *Virgin and Child with Saints* (1597; Volterra, S Lino) and a *Birth of the Virgin* (1598; Volterra Cathedral), both signed and dated. These paintings reflect the new clarity and directness introduced into Florentine painting by such artists as Santi di Tito and Jacopo Ligozzi. Subsequent works include a *Crucifixion* (1600) and a *Virgin and Saints* (1602; both Legnaia, S Angelo). In these the influence of Naldini yielded to that of Lodovico Cigoli and his circle, while the mildness of expression in the figures was inspired by Domenico Passignano. An album of 87 red chalk drawings, with scenes from the *Life of St Mary Magdalene dei Pazzi* (1606; Florence, convent of the Carmelites at Careggi) distinguished by their precision and clear, characteristically Florentine compositions, contributed to the iconography of this popular Counter-Reformation saint. In 1607 Curradi was commissioned to portray her mortal remains, and this painting, together with the drawings, established an authoritative pattern for later treatments of her life. Curradi's *St Lawrence* and *St Albert* (1608; Florence, S Maria Maddalena dei Pazzi) are devotional images, distinguished by the simplicity of the forms and sweetness of expression. *Adam and Eve* (1609; priv. col., see exh. cat., p. 175) depicts Adam and Eve and their sons after the Fall; the union of religious art and genre painting in this work was much admired and widely influential. Many dated paintings record the artist's development from 1610 to 1620; they include the *Annunciation and Saints* (1610; San Miniato al Tedesco, SS Miniato e Francesco), the *Crucifixion* (1611; Volterra Cathedral), the intense, commemorative *Portrait of a Young Man* (1611; Stuttgart, Staatsgal.; see fig.) and the *Assumption of the Virgin* (1613; Dicomano in Val di Sieve, S Maria).

Francesco Curradi: *Portrait of a Young Man*, oil on canvas, 1.04×0.80 m, 1611 (Stuttgart, Staatsgalerie)

From June 1616 to October 1617 Curradi participated in the decoration of the Casa Buonarroti, Florence, to which he contributed a canvas showing *Fame Raising Michelangelo above other Painters*. In 1622 he executed a major work, distinguished by new vigour and enriched by lively figures: the *St Francis Xavier Preaching to the Indians* (Florence, S Giovannino degli Scolopi). In the same year, he fulfilled a commission from Cardinal Carlo de' Medici for a *Narcissus at the Spring* (Florence, Pitti), a lyrical and melancholy work that was probably intended, along with *Erminia among the Shepherds* (Petraia, nr Florence, Castello), for the Casino di S Marco. His newly dramatic art, with bolder chiaroscuro and a diagonally based composition, culminated in the *Beheading of St Paul* (*c.* 1627; Volterra Cathedral). In 1632 Curradi painted a series of lunettes on canvas depicting scenes from the *Life of St Mary Magdalene* for the Medici Villa di Poggio Imperiale (Florence, Depositi Gal.), and possibly soon after executed another cycle of scenes from the *Life of the Virgin* (Florence, S Maria degli Angiolini). For his *St Mary Magdalene dei Pazzi Receiving a Veil from the Virgin* (1633; Rome, S Giovanni dei Fiorentini) he received the title of Cavaliere dell' Ordine di Cristo.

Curradi's late works, despite the warm Florentine reception accorded to the new art of Pietro da Cortona at this date, show little stylistic development, although his colour is perhaps more severe and his draughtsmanship more simplified. In 1649 he executed for the chapel of the Ronconi in Santa Trinita, Florence, the altarpiece *St John the Baptist Preaching*. An inscription, probably not in his own hand, asserts his authorship of a *Landscape with Figures* (Louisville, KY, W. Hughes priv. col., see Gilbert) and the date 1658, which is the latest found on any painting attributed to him.

BIBLIOGRAPHY
F. Baldinucci: *Notizie* (1681–1728); ed. F. Ranalli (1845–7), iv, pp. 173–4
F. M. N. Gabburri: *Vite di pittori* (MS.; 1719–41); ed. *Serie degli uomini i più illustri nella pittura, scultura e architettura* (Florence, 1784), viii, p. 134
C. Gilbert: 'Francesco Curradi e la tipologia del paesaggio nel '600', *Commentari*, ii (1952), p. 135
P. Pacini: 'Contributi per l'iconografia di Santa Maria Maddalena de' Pazzi: Una "vita" inedita di Francesco Curradi', *Mitt. Ksthist. Inst. Florenz*, xxviii/3 (1984), pp. 279–350
S. Cuzzocrea: 'Francesco Curradi ovvero la pittura di devozione', *Paradigma*, vi (1985), pp. 107–29
Il seicento fiorentino: Arte a Firenze da Ferdinando I a Cosimo III, 3 vols (exh. cat., Florence, Pal. Strozzi, 1986), i, 65–7; ii, 166–79; iii, 168–9 [with bibliog.]
M. Gregori: 'Qualche avanzamento sul periodo giovanile di Francesco Curradi', *Ant. Viva*, xxvi/5–6 (1987), pp. 40–43
BRUNO SANTI

Curri, Antonio (*b* Alberobello, nr Bari, 9 Oct 1848; *d* Naples, 16 Nov 1916). Italian architect and decorator. He attended the school of painting at the Istituto di Belle Arti, Naples (1865–9), and after a period spent in his native town, where he apparently began his architectural activity, he moved permanently to Naples. His earliest works included the façade decoration (1874) for Naples Cathedral and a plan for the building's restoration, which was a prize-winning exhibit at the Esposizione Nazionale di Belle Arti (1877) in Naples. He later carried out many restoration works in religious buildings in Naples. In collaboration with Ernesto di Mauro he also decorated

the Galleria Umberto I, which was built (1887–92) from designs by the architect Emanuele Rocco and the engineer Francesco Paolo Boubée. He became a decorative painter with a design (*c.* 1869) for the cradle of Prince Victor-Emanuel (later Victor-Emanuel III (*reg* 1900–46)), which was realized in collaboration with the sculptor Vincenzo Gemito. Curri's most famous work of this kind is the decoration, in tempera and pastel, of the interior of the Caffè Gambrinus (1890), Naples; at the time the rooms were said to be better suited for an art gallery than for a café or beer hall. Curri's prolific activity extended outside Naples, to the province of Campania and to Alberobello, and he was also a lecturer in architecture and decoration at the University of Naples. Among his last works was the pavilion of Campania, Basilicata and Calabria for the Esposizione Nazionale in Rome (1911; with Alfonso Guerra and a team of painters and sculptors).

BIBLIOGRAPHY
C. Villani: *Scrittori ed artisti pugliesi antichi, moderni e contemporanei* (Trani 1904), pp. 302ff
G. Tesorone: *Il padiglione della Campania, Basilicata e Calabria all'Esposizione di Roma del 1911* (Milan, 1913)
E. Giannelli: *Artisti napoletani viventi* (Naples, 1916), pp. 712ff
F. De Filippis: *Ottocento napoletano: Il Gambrinus* (Naples, 1939), pp. 8, 11, 15, 36, 39
C. Lorenzetti: *L'Accademia di Belle Arti di Napoli (1752–1952)* (Florence, 1952), p. 326
R. De Fusco: *L'architettura dell'ottocento* (Turin, 1980), pp. 165, 244
ANTONELLA D'AUTILIA

Currier, J(oseph) Frank (*b* Boston, MA, 21 Nov 1843; *d* Waverley, MA, 15 Jan 1909). American painter. He first studied art in the late 1860s after working briefly as a stone-cutter (his father's profession) and as a banking apprentice. In 1869, after a short stay in England, he arrived in Antwerp, where he studied at the Koninklijke Academie and benefited especially from the example of Antoine Wiertz. Currier visited Paris in the spring of 1870, perhaps intending to undertake a lengthy period of study. With the outbreak of the Franco-Prussian War in August 1870, however, he moved to Munich, where he studied at the Akademie der Bildenden Künste until 1872. He became part of the American contingency of Munich painters, which included Frank Duveneck, Walter Shirlaw and William Merritt Chase. Like them, he became a notable practitioner of Munich realism as taught by Wilhelm Leibl and others. To this style, based on the chiaroscuro and dramatic brushwork of Frans Hals, Currier brought an expressionistic, individual manner, bolder in technique and more emotional and visionary in character. The *Head of a Boy* (1873; New York, Brooklyn Mus.) and *Peasant Girl* (*c.* 1878; Waterford, CT, Mr & Mrs Henry C. White priv. col., see Neuhaus, p. 126, fig. 93) are representative of his Munich style at its best. In 1877 Currier moved to the Bavarian town of Polling. There, as in Dachau and Schleissheim (located a few kilometres west of Dachau) in the early 1880s, he assumed leadership of the American art colony after the departures of Duveneck and Chase. Currier returned to Boston in 1898, and subsequently gave up painting entirely. In 1909 he took his own life.

BIBLIOGRAPHY
N. C. White: *The Life and Art of J. Frank Currier* (Cambridge, MA, 1936)
M. Quick: 'Munich and American Realism', *Munich and American Realism in the 19th Century* (Sacramento, CA, 1978), pp. 21–36

R. Neuhaus: *Unexpected Genius: The Art and Life of Frank Duveneck* (San Francisco, CA, 1987)

JAMES C. COOKE

Currier & Ives. American firm of printmakers. It was founded in New York in 1835 by Nathaniel T. Currier (1813–88), who had been apprenticed as a youth to the Boston lithographic firm of William S. & John Pendleton. Currier & Ives lithographs initially appeared under Currier's imprint (his earlier lithographs had been issued in 1834 under the name of Stodart & Currier), and the name Currier & Ives first appeared in 1857, when James Merritt Ives (1824–95), the company's bookkeeper and Currier's brother-in-law, was made a partner. Currier supervised production while Ives handled the business and financial side. In 1840 the firm began to shift its focus from job printing to independent print publishing, to which it was exclusively devoted from 1852 to 1880.

Currier & Ives prints were decorative and inexpensive, ranging in price from twenty cents to three dollars. Their subject-matter ranged from rural life, ships, trains, animal and sporting scenes to religious images and spectacular news events. The firm produced more than 7000 titles, many in runs of hundreds of thousands, and became the largest and most successful American lithographic publishing company of the 19th century. Vigorous marketing through published catalogues, a sales staff and agents throughout the USA, as well as in London, enabled Currier & Ives to capture approximately three-quarters of the American print market in the peak years of the firm's popularity. Both black-and-white and coloured prints were sold; colour was usually applied by a staff of women working in a production line from a model, although some prints were sent out for hand colouring. Chromolithographs were also published by the firm, but colour-printing was not done on the premises.

Although many of the large number of artists employed by Currier & Ives simply copied the designs of others on to the stone, original works were also commissioned. These occasionally included pictures by well-known artists, such as Arthur Fitzwilliam Tait's *The Life of a Hunter: A Tight Fix* (pubd 1861) and George Henry Durrie's *New England Winter Scene* (pubd 1861), but more often commissions went to artists closely associated with the firm. Significant among these were FRANCES PALMER; Thomas Worth (1834–1917), whose speciality was comic scenes; Charles Parsons (1821–1910), noted for his sailing ships and steam vessels, for example *A 'Crack' Sloop in a Race to Windward* (pubd 1882); and Louis Maurer (1832–1932), creator of the series *Life of a Fireman* (see fig.) and of a popular group of prints featuring trotting horses.

By the time Currier retired in 1880 in favour of his son Edward West Currier, chromolithography and photography had already begun to challenge the Currier & Ives market. Broader cultural changes also hastened the decline in appeal of the company's products: exuberant self-confidence and belief in the simple values and homely virtues that the Currier & Ives image had come to symbolize had largely passed from the scene. Ives stayed with the firm until his death, succeeded by his son Chauncey Ives, who purchased the firm in 1902 and sold it in 1907.

Currier and Ives: print of *Life of a Fireman: The Metropolitan System* by Louis Maurer, hand-coloured lithograph, 482×670 mm, 1866 (Washington, DC, Library of Congress)

BIBLIOGRAPHY

H. T. Peters: *Currier & Ives: Printmakers to the American People*, 2 vols (New York, 1929–31)
W. Rawls: *The Great Book of Currier & Ives' America* (New York, 1979)
C. Carter Smith and C. Coshion, eds.: *Currier & Ives: A Catalogue Raisonné* (Detroit, 1984)

ANNE CANNON PALUMBO

Curry, John Steuart (*b* nr Dunavant, KS, 14 Nov 1897; *d* Madison, WI, 29 Aug 1946). American painter and illustrator. As one of the 'Regionalist triumvirate', with Thomas Hart Benton and Grant Wood, he has been most often characterized as a faithful chronicler of rural life in Kansas. From 1916 to 1918 he was at the School of the Art Institute of Chicago. In 1919 he began study in the studio of Harvey Dunn (1884–1952) in Tenafly, NJ. After seven years as an illustrator in and around New York, he went to Paris in 1926 to study with the Russian Academician Vasily Shukhayev. Ironically, it was on Curry's return to the East Coast the following year that he began to earn his reputation as a Regionalist by painting memories of Kansas from his studio in the fashionable art colony of Westport, CT. *Baptism in Kansas* (1928; New York, Whitney, for illustration *see* AMERICAN SCENE PAINTING) shows a country child being baptized in a cattle trough. Such paintings of early American life appealed to certain East Coast urban viewers seeking to recover a lost past.

From 1936 to 1946 Curry was artist-in-residence at the University of Wisconsin, Madison. From 1936 to 1938 he executed mural cycles for the Departments of Justice and of the Interior (Washington, DC) under New Deal patronage. In 1937 he was commissioned to paint murals for the Kansas State Capitol building, but Kansas gave its truant Regionalist such a hostile reception that the ambitious cycle (featuring John Brown and the history of settlement on the plains) was never fully completed.

BIBLIOGRAPHY

L. E. Schmeckebier: *John Steuart Curry's Pageant of America* (New York, 1943)
John Steuart Curry (exh. cat., ed. B. Waller; Lawrence, U. KS, Spencer Mus. A., 1970)
M. S. Kendall: *Rethinking Regionalism: John Steuart Curry and the Kansas Mural Controversy* (Washington, DC, 1986)

M. SUE KENDALL

Curstgen. *See* KNÜTGEN.

Curtain wall (i). Stretch of wall in a castle, usually the whole perimeter wall or enceinte. To defend a great residence (or town or city) by raising a strong wall about it was a basic principle of fortification, especially before the 14th and 15th centuries, when the components of a seigneurial house (hall, chambers, kitchen, chapel, stables etc) were almost always separate, non-integrated buildings. In concentric fortification there are two curtain walls, one within the other, the inner stronger and loftier to command the outer screen. In many of the earliest castles of the late 10th century and the 11th the precursor of the stone curtain wall was the timber palisade, defended by wall-walk and towers in a similar way.

The active defence of the curtain wall and its exposed outer face required at least a wall-walk with a crenellated parapet towards the field to give the defenders both cover

and sighting. A projecting gallery of timber (hoarding) might also be fitted along the wall-head (see fig.), as also on the summit of the towers and gatehouses, to allow the outer base of the wall to be defended against picks, bores and battering rams. That base might also be battered or splayed out farther to strengthen and defend it and so that projectiles dropped from the apertures or murder-holes could ricochet or splinter to do more widespread damage to the assailants. Sometimes the whole face of the bank on which the curtain wall commonly stood was revetted with stone to make a glacis or talus (e.g. Krak des Chevaliers, Syria); in any case, such a bank was formed by the spoil of a deep, wide ditch, fosse or moat dug in front of the wall to keep an enemy at his distance. Original and perishable timber hoarding seldom survives (a possible example, now integrated with the building, occurs about the north tower at Stokesay, Salop), although it can be

Timber hoarding in position on the inner and outer curtains of the city of Carcassonne and rectangular flanking tower (Tour l'Evêque); from E.-E. Viollet-le-Duc: *Dictionnaire raisonné de l'architecture française du XIe au XVIe siècle*, ix (Paris, 1868), p. 99

restored or replaced, and putlog holes for the original timbers are often visible, as about the keeps at Rochester and Issoudun. MACHICOLATION is the more sophisticated corbelling out of a projecting gallery in stone instead of timber. It is evidently later, scarcely appearing before the late 12th century (e.g. Richard I's donjon at Château-Gaillard), but did not entirely replace hoarding, especially in England and Wales, where it appears less frequently than in France. There are, nevertheless, plenty of English examples, including the 15th-century Raglan. In addition, arrow slits (apertures for the crossbow or, from the 14th century, loops for guns) could be pierced through the wall, although their field of 'fire' was limited to a few degrees on either side, and they could only be at ground-level unless a gallery were constructed within the thickness of the wall, as at Caernarfon in the late 13th century.

By far the most important adjunct of the curtain wall, without which the effective defence of a long stretch would scarcely have been possible, was the mural or flanking tower. Projecting forward to the field and equipped not only with a crenellated fighting platform on the summit but also with arrow slits (and/or apertures or loops) at heights corresponding to the levels and floors within, flanking towers systematically placed could cover the outer face of the entire length of wall. They also covered the wall-walk from a superior height, should an intrepid foe gain it by escalade or belfry. Strong-points on the perimeter themselves, they could also help to seal a breach made in the wall between them. The technique of the flanking tower was inherited from the Romans and is found in medieval military architecture from the beginning, although its application became increasingly sophisticated and formidable, for example at mid-13th-century Angers, where no approach seems possible; or at Caerffili late in the same century, where the four angle towers of the quadrangular castle are self-sufficient strong-points almost on the scale of *donjons circulaires*; or in the great Marten's Tower at Chepstow (*c.* 1300).

The towers of the curtain wall were constructed with doorways and passages so as not to block the rapid movement of men-at-arms about the wall-walk, and most contained residential accommodation of high quality. Their varying design follows the same pattern as that of the great tower or keep; early towers were rectangular, and the cylindrical tower was very fashionable in the 13th century, although rectangular towers continued to be built, and variants from the late 12th century onwards included polygonal and *à bec* types (the latter at Loches (*see* LOCHES, §1) and DOVER CASTLE, for example). At CHÂTEAU-GAILLARD (1196–8) the curtain of the inner bailey exploits the principle of flanking and enfilading fire in a manner that appears to be unique: there are no mural towers because the extraordinary elliptical construction of the wall itself renders them unnecessary.

See also CASTLE, §I; CRENELLATION; and DONJON.

R. ALLEN BROWN

Curtain wall (ii). Non-load-bearing exterior wall supported by the primary structural system and providing enclosure. It came into widespread use after World War II and was adopted throughout the world. Although a curtain wall does not afford any structural support to the building, it must act in a semi-structural and load-bearing way. It must carry its own weight without cracking, and it must resist wind loads acting on the enclosure and transfer these loads safely to the supporting structure of the building. These loads are usually transferred to structural columns via horizontal members, either the outer beams of the structure itself or intermediate members known as 'girts'. The predecessor of the 20th-century curtain wall can be found in prefabricated metal building fronts of the 19th century such as those erected in the SoHo district of Manhattan by James Bogardus. These, however, still provided structure as well as enclosure. True curtain walls began to evolve at the end of the century; a notable early example is the Reliance building (1894–5; *see* SKYSCRAPER, fig. 1) at State and Madison Streets, Chicago, by John Wellborn Root and Charles B. Atwood. The technique remained dormant until it came into common use in the late 1940s and 1950s.

Curtain walls are usually assembled from prefinished panels; these can be made from a variety of materials including precast concrete, preformed metal (steel or aluminium), preformed glass-fibre reinforced polyester (GRP) or from combinations of metal and glass. A well-known example of the precast concrete form is the US Embassy (1955–60), Grosvenor Square, London, by Eero Saarinen. Preformed metal panels were pioneered by Jean Prouvé, and their first use in a large building was in the Alcoa building (1953), Mellon Square, Pittsburgh, PA, by Harrison & Abramovitz. In precast concrete curtain walls the panels are supported directly from the beams of the primary structure at top and bottom, usually by some combination of metal parts that are cast into the concrete. With preformed metal panels, they are usually connected to separate horizontal girts. Typically the panel has a core that may or may not be structural but has high thermal-insulation qualities. The facing skins are of steel or aluminium bonded to this core. The skins or liners may also be corrugated or ribbed for additional strength. Deep corrugations or ribs can form very strong panels that can span directly between structural members. GRP or plastic panels are very light, and they can be moulded complete with insulation and flanges for connection and are easily erected. However, their properties in a fire, which include the emission of toxic smoke, are questionable; they often undergo severe changes in colour and appearance through weathering and exposure to ultra-violet radiation.

By far the most commonly used curtain wall system is the composite assembly of glass and a metal, usually aluminium. The low cost and availability of the latter after World War II sparked an upsurge in the use of curtain walls, as did the wide publication of the metal-and-glass façades of the UN Secretariat building (1947–53; *see* GOVERNMENT BUILDINGS, fig. 2), New York. In single-storey buildings this system is also sometimes referred to as 'storefront' construction. The wall and window sashes are built up from formed metal pieces that serve to hold the glazing and transfer wind forces to the beams of the primary structures. There are few limitations on the design of such systems, and their light weight and availability make them economical. Framing elements can be hidden so that the wall appears to be completely of glass; reflective

Glass curtain wall at Willis Faber & Dumas Building by Norman Foster, Ipswich, 1974

glass is often used in this form. Glass cannot be set directly into metal frames because the materials have different expansion rates. Composite curtain walls use a variety of glazing methods; these range from systems in which soft sealants act more or less like putty in traditional windows, to systems, more closely resembling car windows, in which the glass is set with preformed pads or gaskets of neoprene or other flexible materials. Although most composite curtain walls use fixed windows, they can also accommodate operable sash assemblies. In either case the most critical detail of the entire wall system is the point of connection between glass and framing position; wind pressures against a large building, both inward and outward by suction, can be strong and erratic, and failures occur when glass breaks or is pulled completely out of the wall.

Because curtain-wall assemblies are by their nature repetitive, they tend to impose this quality on the appearance of buildings using them. From World War II until the late 1960s this repetition of elements was considered a positive aesthetic motif by many architects; curtain walls were especially used to give horizontal emphasis to façades, although in fact most systems can be detailed to emphasize either horizontality or verticality, and in the Willis Faber & Dumas Building (1974; see fig.), Ipswich, a glazed wall was designed to follow the curve of the street. In the 1970s and 1980s Post-modernist architecture, with its concern for ornament and irregularity, did not easily incorporate curtain walls; on the other hand the High Tech style exaggerated the connections between components for expressive purposes. In general, one of the fundamental points of 20th-century architecture was the separation of structural and enclosing elements; the curtain wall was both the result of this tendency and the technical means that made its wide application possible.

BIBLIOGRAPHY
Curtain Walls of Stainless Steel, Princeton University School of Architecture (Princeton, 1955)
A. E. J. Morris: *Precast Concrete Cladding* (London, 1966)
K. Gatz: *Curtain Wall Construction* (New York, 1967)
B. S. Benjamin: *Building Construction for Architects and Engineers*, 2 vols (Lawrence, KS, 1978–9)
H. Sands: *Wall Systems: Analysis by Detail* (New York, 1986)

B. S. BENJAMIN

Curtea de Argeş. Romanian town, capital of the Argeş district. Between the late 13th century AD and the mid-15th it served as the capital of the Wallachia Principality. The most important remains belong to the Princely Court (Curtea Domnească), which comprised houses (14th–16th century; in ruins) and the princely church of St Nicholas (*see* ROMANIA, fig. 2). The date of its construction and decoration and the identity of its founders remain controversial. The present cross-in-square church replaced an earlier building (1290–1300; destr. 1330) and is generally attributed to Voivode Vladislav I (*reg* 1364–*c*. 1377). It is marked by the harmony of its external aspect and well-proportioned nave tower, in contrast to similar churches in the Balkans. The walls are of alternating courses of stone and brick and, like the interior wall paintings, are probably by a workshop from Constantinople. Iconographically these paintings are similar to the mosaics (*c*. 1321) in the monastery of Christ the Saviour in Chora (*see* ISTANBUL, §III, 3(ii)) and reflect the influence of the Palaiologan style.

In 1512–17, Voivode Neagoe Basarab (*reg* 1512–21) built the Argeş Monastery on the outskirts of the town; it became the episcopal seat in 1794. Only the monastic church of the Assumption of the Virgin and the holy water font in front of it survive. The church is one of the most elaborate monuments in Romania and is attributed to the legendary Master Manole. It is constructed of worked stone blocks and decorated with sumptuous sculptural motifs of Caucasian and Islamic origin, transmitted through an Ottoman channel. The nave has a trefoil plan surmounted by a central tower on squinches; it is preceded by an enlarged narthex, with a secondary domed tower over the central bay and two smaller domes over the western corners. Twelve stone columns with motifs of Islamic inspiration surround the central bay. The lateral spaces of the narthex were used as the voivodal burial ground, and they contain the tombstones of Neagoe Basarab, his family and his son-in-law Radu V (*reg* 1522–3; 1524–9); that of Vladimir I was removed (Bucharest, N. Mus. A.). King Carol I of Hohenzollern and Sigmaringen (*reg* 1866–1914) and King Ferdinand (*reg* 1914–27) and their wives, respectively Elizabeth and Maria, were also buried here. Only fragments of the original wall paintings (1526; Bucharest, N. Mus. A.) by Dobromir of Tîrgovişte survive; they show votive portraits of the founders and saints. These paintings were replaced during the church's restoration (1875–86) by the French architect Lecomte du Nouÿ with works of inferior quality.

Other buildings preserved in the town include the ruined church of St Nicoară (14th century), with its rectangular plan and bell-tower above the narthex; the parish churches of Olari (before 1687), Drujesti (*c.* 1720) and St Angels (1717), all with external wall paintings (late 18th century–early 19th), and the monastery church of Flămânzeşti (1752).

BIBLIOGRAPHY

L. Reissenberger: *L'Eglise du monastère épiscopal de Kurtea d'Argis en Valachie* (Vienna, 1867)
O. Tafrali: *Monuments byzantins de Curtéa de Arges* (Paris, 1931)
V. Drăgut: *Romanian Art* (Bucharest, 1984), pp. 239–41

TEREZA-IRENE SINIGALIA

Curti, Girolamo [Dentone] (*b* Bologna, 4 April 1575; *d* Bologna, 18 Dec 1632). Italian painter and stage designer. A specialist in illusionistic architectural settings, or *quadratura*, he trained with Cesare Baglione (*c.* 1550–1615). His dramatically lit settings, which display realistic and well-proportioned architecture, departed from Baglione's Mannerist fantasy and established classical ceiling decoration in Bologna. His *quadratura* combined a recessed frame as the immediate surround of the ceiling crown, with a substantial, deeply foreshortened frame, which simulates height.

Curti's first surviving ceilings, at the Casino Malvasia at Trebbo di Reno (*c.* 1610–22) and the Villa Paleotti at San Marino (*c.* 1616–22), were influenced by his earliest model, Tommaso Laureti's frescoed ceiling in the Palazzo Vizzani, Bologna (*c.* 1562; destr.), which first combined a wall frieze, based on Palladian windows, with a foreshortened ceiling frame. In 1618 Curti travelled to Parma, where he was involved in the decoration of the Teatro Farnese, and in 1623, at the invitation of Cardinal Ludovico Ludovisi, he went to Rome, where a ceiling in the Palazzo Odescalchi has been attributed to him. In the 1620s and early 1630s he worked as a decorator and stage designer in Bologna, Ferrara (1627), Parma (1628–9) and Modena, where in 1631–2 he worked on the decoration of S Biagio and on the decoration (destr. 1634) of the old castle of S Pietro.

Only the staircase of S Francesco remains from his Bolognese activity of 1623–9; his most splendid surviving work is the ceiling of the Sala Urbana, Palazzo Comunale, Bologna (1630). His most influential heirs were ANGELO MICHELE COLONNA and Agostino Stanzani Mitelli, who elaborated his restrained style; Marcantonio Chiarini (1625–1730) and Mauro Antonio Tesi were prominent classicist followers.

BIBLIOGRAPHY

DBI [good bibliog.]; *Enc. Spettacolo*
C. C. Malvasia: *Felsina pittrice*, 2 vols (1678); ed. G. Zanotti (1841), pp. 105–16
G. Soli: *Chiese di Modena* (Modena, 1974), i, pp. 182, 224; iii, p. 362
E. Feinblatt: 'Contributions to Girolamo Curti', *Burl. Mag.*, cxvii (1975), pp. 342–53
R. Roli: *Pittura bolognese, 1650–1800* (Bologna, 1977), pp. 39, 49, 72–4, 76, 88, 205

E. FEINBLATT

Curtis, Edward S(heriff) (*b* White Water, WI, 1868; *d* Los Angeles, CA, 21 Oct 1954). American photographer. A self-taught photographer, he became a partner in a portrait studio in Seattle in 1887, where he experimented with new subject-matter. He decided to make the photography of native peoples his speciality and accompanied anthropologists on the Harriman Expedition to Alaska in 1899 and to Montana in 1900. In 1901 he conceived a vast project to document photographically the lives, customs and folklore of the native American tribes and to record their customs. President Theodore Roosevelt introduced him to J. Pierpont Morgan, who sponsored Curtis's work and his publication of the luxurious 20-volume compendium *The North American Indian* (1907–30).

Curtis's photographs in *The North American Indian* reflected the contemporary view of Native Americans as 'noble savages'. He judged his methods to be far superior to those of his predecessor, George Catlin. In wishing to document the vanishing culture of the rapidly Europeanized Native American, he romanticized the settings of his photographs, sometimes adding props consisting of 'scalps', head-dresses and ceremonial costume, suggesting, for example, the inherent warrior nature of the men and the promiscuity of the young women. To reduce the intervention of contemporary settings, he freely altered negatives and reduced the depth of field using a large aperture to soften the surroundings of his subject. His portraits adopted the tight cropping and full-face or profile formats characteristic of ethnographic photography. His formal mastery and his concern with creating works of art as well as documents of a culture distinguished him from other contemporary photographers of the 'vanishing race'. He also made a film of the Kwakiutl people called *In the Land of the Headhunters*, first presented in 1914.

For an illustration of his work *see* DAT SO LA LEE.

PHOTOGRAPHIC PUBLICATIONS

The North American Indian, intro. T. Roosevelt, 20 vols (Norwood, 1907–30)

FILMS

In the Land of the Headhunters (1914)

BIBLIOGRAPHY

F. C. Graybill and V. Boesen: *Edward Sheriff Curtis: Visions of a Vanishing Race* (New York, 1976)
C. M. Lyman: *The Vanishing Race and Other Illusions* (New York, 1982)
B. Davis: *Edward S. Curtis* (San Francisco, 1985)

MARY CHRISTIAN

Curvilinear perspective. *See* PERSPECTIVE, §II, 3.

Curzon, (Paul-)Alfred de (*b* Le Moulinet, Vienne, 7 Sept 1820; *d* Paris, 4 July 1895). French painter. He belonged to the provincial aristocracy of south-east France. As a schoolboy in Paris, he was impressed by Delacroix's *Medea* (Lille, Mus. B.-A.) in the Salon of 1838. In September of that year he began to experiment with pastel and decided to become a painter. As Ingres no longer ran a teaching studio, he was sent to Michel-Martin Drolling, who presented him at the Ecole des Beaux-Arts on 1 April 1840; but Drolling was never a very successful teacher, and Curzon's fellow student Louis-Georges Brillouin (1817–93) persuaded him to leave in 1845 for the atelier of the landscape painter Louis Cabat. Curzon made his début at the Salon in 1845 with a landscape.

In 1846 Curzon made his first visit to Italy, travelling from Rome, where he met the Bénouville brothers, Alexandre Cabanel and Louis Français, to Venice and Florence. Back in France, he entered the competition in 1848 for a figure of the Republic, without success; he also put his name down for the Prix de Rome competition in historical landscape in 1849. Charles-Joseph Lecointe (1823–86) won the prize, but the critics preferred Curzon's entry (*The Death of Milo of Crotona*; Paris, Ecole N. Sup. B.-A.) and, after a complaint by Paul Delaroche, Curzon was given a vacancy. During his four years at the Académie de Rome (1850–53), Curzon travelled in search of views. In 1852 he visited Athens with Charles Garnier. Works inspired by this period in Italy and Greece, picturesque genre scenes and landscapes, appeared in the Paris exhibitions of the 1850s.

Landscape was Curzon's first love, but he successfully explored other genres. On his return to France in 1853, he collaborated with Eugène Froment in decorating the chapel of the seminary at Autun; his only other religious work of this kind and his only commission for a religious picture, *Christ Showing his Wounds to St Thomas*, was painted in 1860 for the Paris church of St Nicolas-du-Chardonnet. This large, understated picture, dominated by the delicately modelled group of Christ and his apostles, shows Curzon's excellence in figure painting. It is curious that he did no more work like this. His four allegorical panels, executed in mosaic in the *avant-foyer* of the Opéra for his friend Charles Garnier, was also his only effort in secular decorative art.

In the Salon of 1859, *Psyche* (Sermaize-les-Bains, Hôtel de Ville), a pale, luminous sylph drifting towards the spectator, proved Curzon's talent as a painter of classical mythology in rivalry with Paul Baudry and William-Adolphe Bouguereau. The picture was a huge popular success, but this did not divert him from his memories of Greece and Italy, which he continued to illustrate throughout the 1860s and 1870s. *Dream in the Ruins of Pompeii* (1866; Bagnères-de-Bigorre, Mus. A.), inspired by a visit to Pompeii in 1851 with Bouguereau, depicts a company of ghosts wandering in the ruins of the town with the quiet, elegiac poetry which is characteristic of his work. The State recognized his talent: in 1865 he was made an officer of the Légion d'honneur, and his *Dominican Monks Decorating their Chapel* (Poitiers, Pal. Justice) was bought by the State, as was his *View at Ostia* (exh. Salon, 1868;

untraced) in 1869. He was a landscape painter with an unusual talent in figure painting and a striking draughtsman with a liking for highly worked effects in watercolour and charcoal. The Musée Sainte-Croix, Poitiers, owns a large number of his drawings.

BIBLIOGRAPHY
H. de Curzon: *Alfred de Curzon, peintre (1820–1895): Sa vie et son oeuvre d'après ses souvenirs, ses lettres, ses contemporains*, 2 vols (Paris, [1916])
L'Art en France sous le Second Empire (exh. cat., Paris, Grand Pal., 1979), pp. 337–8, 432–3
JON WHITELEY

Curzon, Nathaniel, 1st Baron Scarsdale (*b* Kedleston Hall, Derbys, 23 Dec 1726; *d* 6 Dec 1804). English patron and collector. He became 5th Baronet in November 1758 and took over the family's early 18th-century house in Derbys. He immediately hired Matthew Brettingham (i) to make plans for redesigning it; these were based on Andrea Palladio's Villa Mocenigo. Scarsdale became disillusioned with Brettingham and instead in 1758–9 employed James Paine. Brettingham and Paine in turn oversaw the demolition of part of the old house and began supervision of the construction of a new central block. Only a small part of their designs had been executed, however, when in 1760 Scarsdale turned the commission over to Robert Adam. Scarsdale's generous patronage during the next 10 years allowed Adam to experiment with architecture, landscape gardening and interior decoration; it resulted in Kedleston Hall, an elegant Neo-classical house. In 1761 Scarsdale was made Baron, and, conscious of both style and status, he spent large sums on making his house as fashionable as possible. Adam was responsible for the south (garden) façade (1760–61; *see* ADAM (i), (3), fig. 1), which combined Baroque rhythmic grace with classical restraint. Working with the landscape gardener William Emes, Adam also removed Charles Bridgeman's formal gardens and replaced them with a more natural landscape vista. He designed a fishing house, a Gothic temple, a bridge and a cascade as points of interest in the garden. Adam's most striking work at Kedleston, however, is the interior decoration, in which he used Pompeiian Revival motifs. Scarsdale employed a large staff to work under Adam on the interiors, including numerous stone- and wood-carvers and such distinguished history painters as William Hamilton (ii) and Antonio Zucchi.

Scarsdale was also a collector, and he arranged for the interior decoration to be realized with his collection of paintings in mind. In addition to over 100 pictures inherited from his father, he purchased paintings in London sales between 1753 and 1759 and commissioned over 30 works from popular contemporary artists, such as Gavin Hamilton, Joshua Reynolds and Francesco Zuccarelli. He acquired paintings from Italy through a picture dealer and also collected casts made after the Antique. His taste in art was eclectic but fashionable, embracing 17th-century Dutch (e.g. a *Landscape* by Aelbert Cuyp) and Italian (e.g. the *Triumph of Bacchus* by Luca Giordano) paintings.

Colvin

BIBLIOGRAPHY
E. Croft-Murray: *The 18th and Early 19th Centuries*, ii of *Decorative Painting in England* (London, 1970)
Robert Adam and Kedleston (exh. cat., ed. L. Harris; Kedleston Hall, Derbys, 1987)
SHEARER WEST

Cusae. *See* MEIR.

Cushing, Frank Hamilton (*b* north-east Erie County, PA, 22 July 1857; *d* 10 April 1900). American ethnologist and writer. Cushing was of frail health, and his schooling was irregular; he was briefly enrolled at Cornell University, NY, in 1875, but was enlisted as an assistant to Charles Rau to help with the Philadelphia Centennial in 1876 and served as curator until it closed. In 1879 he went to the Zuni Pueblo of the US Southwest, where he remained for four and a half years, moving into the governor's house and becoming an accepted member of the Zuni tribe. He learnt their language and customs to the extent that he was able to call himself 'War Chief' and act as an aide to the governor and the tribe in its many quarrels with the US Army and with the Bureau of Indian Affairs. He won the Zuni name Tenatsali or 'Medicine Flower', a reference to the curative powers of the jimson weed. He fell foul of Senator John A. Logan, who forced him to leave the Zunis in 1884 and return to Washington, DC. From 1887 to 1889 he was co-director of the Hemenway Southwestern Archaeological Expedition with Adolph Bandelier, Hermann F. C. Ten Kate and Frederick Webb Hodge in southern Arizona and New Mexico, but his health continued to afflict him and he returned east. In 1895–6 he began to conduct explorations at KEY MARCO, FL, but died at the age of 42. His major ethnological writings include an account of his life in the Zuni village (1882); one of the first books of Indian mythology (1901); and a rare inside account of life in the Southwest Pueblos at the turn of the century (1920).

For general discussion of the study and collection of Native American art *see* NATIVE NORTH AMERICAN ART, §XVI.

WRITINGS

My Adventures in Zuni (Santa Fe, NM, 1882, 2/1951)
Zuni Folk Tales (New York, 1901, 2/1931)
Zuni Breadstuff, Contributions from the Museum of the American Indian, Heye Foundation, viii (New York, 1920)

FREDERICK J. DOCKSTADER

Cusp. Point formed by the intersection of the curves in Gothic TRACERY (*see* LAON, fig. 2).

Custodis, Hieronimos (*b* Antwerp; *d* ?London, ?1593). Flemish painter, active in England. He probably went to England because of religious persecution, perhaps soon after the surrender of Antwerp to the Duque de Alba in 1585. Three signed and dated portraits survive, all painted in 1589: *Sir John Parker* (London, Hampton Court, Royal Col.), dated 10 August, almost certainly the Sir John Parker of Ratton in Sussex, who was a Gentleman Pensioner at Court and captain of St Denis Castle in Cornwall; and *Sir Giles Brydges, 3rd Lord Chandos,* of Sudeley, Glos, and his 14-year-old daughter *Elizabeth Brydges,* later Lady Kennedy (both Woburn Abbey, Beds), both dated 8 July. A fourth, unsigned, portrait at Woburn, *Frances, Lady Chandos,* also dated 1589, is almost certainly by the same hand. The elaboration of the dress of mother and daughter, the cool colours and the meticulous delineation of jewellery are reminiscent of the work of Nicholas Hilliard, and Custodis also seems to owe something to the English

portrait painter George Gower. Elizabeth, whose charming portrait is embellished with a little dog and a finch on a spray of eglantine, was the 'fair Mrs Brydges' to whom the Earl of Essex showed so much attention as to offend Queen Elizabeth. Her younger sister Catherine became the wife of Francis Russell, 4th Earl of Bedford, through whom the three portraits presumably passed to Woburn; they were first noted there by Vertue in 1727.

Strong has attributed to Custodis the painting of *Lady Chandos* and nine other portraits dated between 1587 and 1593, including *Edward Sheldon* (1590; Major C. Fellows priv. col., see Strong, p. 199) and companion portraits of *Sir Francis Hynde* and *Lady Hynde* (1591; priv. col., see Strong, pp. 201, 202), on the basis of the distinctive inscriptions giving the age of the sitter. Waterhouse suspected that the inscriptions were the responsibility of an assistant who was perhaps employed by more than one studio, since similar inscriptions are to be found on portraits dating from after Custodis's death.

Jacobus Custodis, son of 'Jeremye A Paynter' (presumably Hieronimos), was baptized at St Botolph-without-Aldgate in the City of London on 2 March 1591. Hieronimos was recorded as a member of the Dutch church of Austin Friars in 1592; his widow, a native of Brussels, was married there to Jan Jems of Antwerp on 27 December 1593. The artist may have been a victim of the outbreak of plague in that year. Francis Meres, in *Palladis Tamia* in 1598, listed a painter 'Hieronimo', who has sometimes been assumed to be Custodis. (Meres's later addition of the name 'Bye', which has caused confusion with Hieronimos de Bye, appears to be founded on his lack of acquaintance with artists.) Strong has attributed a number of inscribed works, dated from 1593 to 1612, to an unknown follower of Custodis who may have inherited his pattern book.

BIBLIOGRAPHY

E. Waterhouse: *Painting in Britain, 1530 to 1790,* Pelican Hist. A. (Harmondsworth, 1953, 4/1978/*R* 1986), pp. 34–5
O. Millar: *The Tudor, Stuart and Early Georgian Pictures in the Collection of HM the Queen,* i (London, 1963), p. 70
R. Strong: *The English Icon: Elizabethan and Jacobean Portraiture* (London, 1969), pp. 195–206, 349

MARY EDMOND

Custodis, Pieter. *See* BALTENS, PEETER.

Cutileiro, João (*b* Lisbon, 26 June 1937). Portuguese sculptor. Between 1955 and 1970 he lived in London, where he attended the Slade School of Fine Arts for a year (1959) and worked with Reg Butler. In the early 1960s he made sculptures in soldered iron representing eroded and fragmented human parts. These were followed by articulated figures in marble, such as *Torso of a Woman to Assemble at Home* (1964). Thereafter he continued to favour marble anatomical fragments with erotic overtones. In 1970 he returned to Portugal, settling first in Lagos and in 1985 in Evora. His monumental sculpture of *King Sebastian* (*see* PORTUGAL, fig. 11) in Lagos won wide acclaim. His growing national popularity may have caused the lyricism, humour and investigative power of his work to give way to a blander and more crudely executed form of expression. The predominating subject of his free-standing sculptures, wall pieces and mosaics is the titillating female figure, partially dressed or nude. Marble of various colours is used only to literal and descriptive ends. The Museu de Evora houses some of his best works of the late 1960s and 1970s.

BIBLIOGRAPHY

S. Chico: *João Cutileiro* (Lisbon, 1982)
João Cutileiro—45 recortes em mármore (exh. cat., Almansil, Cent. Cult. S Lourenço, 1983) [includes an interview with the artist]
João Cutileiro (exh. cat., Lisbon, Fund. Gulbenkian, 1990)

RUTH ROSENGARTEN

Cutlery. Domestic implements, predominantly of metal, used for a variety of purposes, particularly for eating. The term generally describes knives, forks and spoons for dining but also refers to scissors, edged tools and, formerly, edged weapons. This article for the most part describes cutlery in the Western European tradition.

1. Knives, forks and spoons. 2. Scissors.

1. KNIVES, FORKS AND SPOONS. Cutlery, in particular knives, probably has the longest history of any artefact (see figs. 1 and 2). Edged implements made of stone (eoliths) for cutting or scraping animal carcasses were probably in existence about 2.5 million years ago or even earlier. The making of stone blades, predominantly of flint, developed slowly throughout the Palaeolithic and Mesolithic periods. Neolithic blades show more sophistication in the preparation of the cutting edge and were usually polished. To prevent self-damage, users devised means of hafting stone blades with animal skin, moss, wood, bone and horn. Neolithic spoons and ladles fashioned from mollusc shells, hollowed-out ends of bone and antlers or carved from wood have also been discovered (London, BM). In the following centuries a general European style of cutlery developed, but stone implements continued to be used by less sophisticated cultures long after they had been superseded elsewhere by those in metal.

The first metal blades were made during the Copper Age and evolved during the Bronze Age. These were generally bilaterally symmetrical, but some extant wave-shaped blades (Solingen, Dt. Klingenmus.), sometimes engraved with linear designs (using flint-tipped burins), illustrate technical and stylistic advances; these blades were also the first to have integral bolsters. Wood, horn or bone hafts were attached to blades by insertion into a socket, riveting on to a scale tang or hollowing out and pushing on to a whittle tang. Early metal spoons were made with deep, circular bowls abutting on to a flattened flange of metal; some were decorated with designs derived from Celtic art. Spoons from this period carved from wood or bone or made from fired clay also survive.

Iron Age knives still tended to be spear-pointed, with either socketed hafts or whittle tangs; many later Iron Age blades were triangular in outline. The rapid spread of the Roman Empire led to the widespread introduction of many innovative designs for knives and spoons (*see* ROME, ANCIENT, §IX), including the first folding types. For the

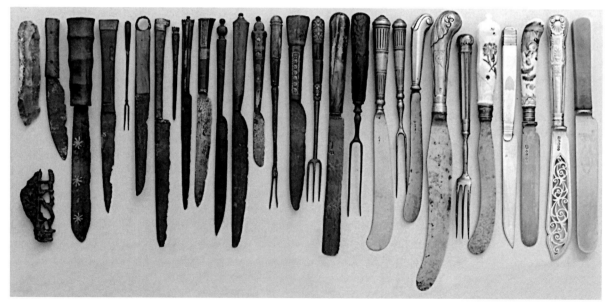

1. Knives and forks, from left to right: Mesolithic knife blade (10,000 BP–6500 BC); Roman knife and (below) Roman folding knife with bronze haft cast as a hound catching a rabbit; Anglo-Saxon knife; knife, 14th century; sweetmeat fork, 14th century; knife with ring terminal, 13th century; knife with dog's-head terminal, late 15th century; knife sharpener (knife steel) with clenched-fist terminal, late 15th century; Flemish-style knife, early 16th century; knife with Flemish/Dutch terminal, mid-16th century; iron knife, mid- to late 16th century; knife with engraved bone haft and latten (brass) pommel, late 16th century; knife with ivory haft, coral roundels and latten pommel, early 17th century; sweetmeat fork with ivory phallic haft, late 16th century; knife with ivory haft and long bolster inlaid with pewter, early 17th century; sweetmeat fork with silver inlaid bolster and ivory and ebony haft, early 17th century; knife with square tip and ivory club haft, mid- to late 17th century; fork with horn haft, late 17th century; knife and fork with silver hafts, late 17th century; dessert/cheese knife with silver haft, early to mid-18th century; silver-hafted table-knife, early to mid-18th century; table-fork with green-stained ivory and silver-banded haft, *c.* 1770; table-knife with Meissen porcelain haft, *c.* 1780; fruit-knife with silver gilt blade and mother-of-pearl haft, French, *c.* 1830; gilt-brass dessert knife with porcelain haft, mid-19th century; silver fish-knife with openwork patterned blade, 1863; table-knife with bone haft, late 19th century (private collections)

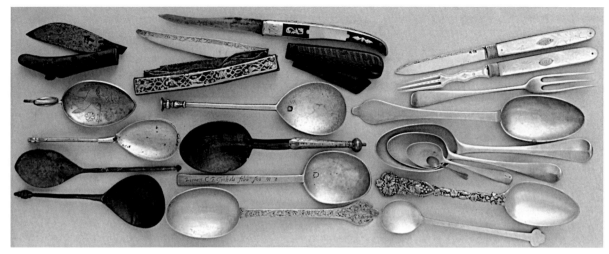

2. Knives, forks and spoons, from top to bottom: (left) medieval folding knife with bone haft; curl-handled Roman silver spoon; Roman silver folding spoon; pewter spoon with diamond knop, 13th century; pewter spoon with acorn knop, 14th or 15th century; (centre) pocket-knife with mother-of-pearl and tortoiseshell haft, mid-18th century; spring-backed multi-bladed folding knife with silver tracery on tortoiseshell haft, French, c. 1690; pocket-knife with bone haft, c. 1820; silver seal-top spoon, London, 1592; northern European spoon with silver haft and horn bowl, early 17th century; silver 'Puritan' spoon, London, 1652; trefid spoon with engraved handle, London, 1682; (right) folding fruit-knife and fork with mother-of-pearl hafts and silver blades, c. 1790; dessert fork, Dublin, 1749; 'Dognose'/shield-top tablespoon, London, 1704; four Hanoverian spoons: table, dessert, tea and snuff, c. 1720–70; vine-leaf pattern spoon (based on a 'fiddle' pattern), 1837; Art Nouveau spoon based on a design by Charles Rennie Mackintosh, c. 1900 (private collections)

first time knives were made for specific purposes—trimming horses' hooves, fletching, tanning, candlemaking, surgery, kitchen use, eating, scribing and personal hygiene, including shaving. In ancient Rome spoons were also specially made for eating, measuring, pharmacy, pouring libations and personal hygiene. Later spoons were often beautifully engraved or embossed and were capped with a metal finial or knop to prevent them slipping into a large dish.

As the Roman Empire declined, invaders from Scandinavia introduced new designs of knives and spoons. In the early medieval period knives largely followed weapon styles, many with slope-pointed blades inlaid with bands of coloured metals and wood or bone hafts carved with scroll decoration, although zoomorphic subjects were also frequently used. An essential everyday tool, a knife was carried by everyone, either slung on its own or, more usually, in a leather sheath worn from the belt. Folding knives appear to have been out of favour at this time. Spoons retained their Roman style until about the 9th or 10th century AD.

Surviving late medieval knives and spoons show that experiments in cutlery-making occurred at this time: new blade styles, although many evolved from Anglo-Saxon, Roman and even Bronze Age designs, were introduced. Knife blades were normally strip-tanged, the haft, comprising two 'scales' of material, riveted on to the tang. Furthermore, cutlers in London, for example, were obliged, from c. 1350, to strike a trademark on to knife blades. In the late 15th century brass knops were added to the ends of many knife hafts, a style that originated in the Netherlands or Flanders. Elaborate carving sets (examples in London, BM; Paris, Louvre) became popular at this time; noble households often included a pantler, who

prepared diners' bread, and a carver, who set diners' places and carved their meat. Guests brought their own knives and spoons, the knife for cutting off pieces of meat, the spoon for eating broth or other liquid foods. Spoons were made from bone, wood and horn, although the majority were of base metal, frequently pewter and tinned brass. Those made from silver (and often also those in base metal) were often knopped in the Roman style. Medieval spoon shapes appear to have evolved from some late Roman designs with a slender handle (stele) joining on to a nearly circular to fig-shaped (ficulate) bowl. Ficulate spoon bowls (re-)appeared during the early 14th century. Earlier spoon bowls were either round (French influence) or leaf-shaped (11th–12th centuries). During the medieval period Middle Eastern knives were characterized by long blades set into disproportionately short but heavy hafts. In East Asia knives only were used as preparatory tools for a meal; at table they were supplanted by chopsticks.

By the 16th century the uniformity of knife and spoon styles throughout Europe was declining; consequently, cutlery dating from this period onwards can be assigned to individual countries within (as well as outside) Europe. Netherlandish genre painters, particularly Pieter Bruegel the elder, depicted many items of cutlery in their work. In England, as dining halls were replaced by dining-rooms, knives and spoons became more refined and were fitted with such materials imported from newly explored lands as ivory, which became important for hafts. Knives with bolsters and whittle tangs largely replaced those with strip tangs. Slender knives tended to be made entirely from ferrous materials, with a steel blade forged on to a wrought-iron haft.

Towards the end of the 16th century the fashion for pairs of knives, given from groom to bride at weddings, stimulated the production of knives of great artistry—blades and bolsters inlaid with precious metals and with ivory or amber hafts often carved into figures. The tradition of owning fine sets of knives started at about this time; a host of social standing was required to provide table cutlery, rather than the guests supplying their own. In England larger forks assisted in carving, while smaller ones were used to eat sticky sweetmeats. Spoons remained largely unchanged in style from their medieval forbears, although knops were more adventurous in form—seated lions, saints and other figures were popular.

In the early 17th century knives and spoons gradually became more austere in style; knife hafts made of ivory or bone were carved into simple club and cylinder shapes. After 500 years spoons with slender handles and fig-shaped bowls were phased out in favour of a type of spoon with an elliptical bowl and flattened plain handle, known as the 'Puritan' spoon. Its ancestry can also be traced back to the late Roman spoon period (5th–7th centuries AD); it was the prototype for modern table spoons.

With the Restoration in 1660 the English court, returning from exile on the continent, introduced the European trefid spoon, with Roman-style rat-tail bowl support down the centre of the bowl underside, which readily became popular. Soon after (1680–1700), the table-fork, another European refinement, began to find favour at English dining tables after many years of unpopularity. Matching sets of six or twelve spoons and a few sets of forks were made at this time. (The term 'flatware' is often applied to sets of matching spoons and forks made from metals other than steel.) At this time blades of eating knives became more varied, with triangular points or square or rounded ends; hafts tended to be cylindrical and, if made of metal, often engraved.

In the mid-17th century folding knives incorporated a backspring to hold the blade open or closed. The practicality of this invention encouraged a renaissance in the manufacture and use of the folding knife, which, for general purposes, gradually replaced the personal eating knife carried in a sheath. Folding knives generally resembled their table counterparts; many included more than one blade and were made in different sizes, mainly at Sheffield in England.

At the end of the 17th century a new style of knife blade, curving up at the end like a scimitar, was made. Although originally with a traditional cylindrical or cannon-shaped haft, the new type of blade was better balanced with a haft that turned down at the end like a pistol butt. 'Pistol-grip' hafts, as they became known, were made from bone, ivory (sometimes stained green or black), silver or ceramic; this style remained unchanged until about the 1770s. Spoon bowls, however, became more elongated, while the ends of handles of both spoons and forks were shaped like the top of a shield or a dog's nose. The latter type was soon phased out in favour of a spoon with the standard, round-ended handle that turns up at the end and is known as Hanoverian, since its introduction coincided with the accession in 1714 of George I; this type of spoon continues to be produced. During the 1740s spoons were also made with downturned handles; this form became known as the 'Old English' pattern. Forks to match

'Dognose' and 'Hanoverian' spoons were generally made with three tines, and although 'Old English' forks were made with four tines, the handles were still turned up at the end, ensuring that they were comfortable to hold. In the 18th century knives, forks and spoons were made in sizes according to their function at table: spoons, especially, varied in size from the huge 'baster', 600 mm in length, stuffer and table (soup) spoons to the much smaller dessert, tea, snuff and toy spoons (the last two about 25 mm long).

The form of folding knives continued to evolve in the 18th century; some were effectively pocket tool kits, as cutlers skilfully crammed in more blades. Fine folding knives with silver or gold blades, as well as folding forks for eating fruit were also developed at this time. In France, particularly elegant examples with two blades (one steel, one silver or gold) and superbly enamelled and jewelled hafts were made as an offshoot of the manufacture of snuff-boxes. A few Swiss examples even contain a tiny musical box movement.

With the advent of machine production towards the end of the 18th century knife styles became more simple—straight-bladed and the hafts with slightly curved sides. Silver handles were cheaper and easier to make as silver sheets stamped out of moulds then filled with resin. In the 1780s the 'Fiddle' pattern spoon, similar to the 'Old English' but with a broader-ended handle and a pair of 'shoulders' on the handle just above the bowl, was introduced. At the same time a method for die-stamping spoons from sheet silver was devised by William Darby in Sheffield.

In the 19th century new methods of refining large quantities of steel were introduced by Henry Bessemer (1813–98) in Sheffield, reducing the amount of extra work in hand-processing blades, although such smaller items as knife and tool blades continued to be made from crucible steel well into the 20th century. Knives of a simpler form, with round-ended and parallel-sided blades, were made. Bolsters and tangs continued to be die-stamped as one unit and then forged on to the steel blade. Hafts were made from ivory, bone, horn and wood, although, with the invention of Bakelite and other plastics, ivory was soon substituted by cheaper ivorine or celluloid xylo. In 1914 the first knife blades of stainless steel were made, and during the following years cutlery firms marked their blades in deference to the inventor, Harry Brearley (1871–1948), and the firm of Thomas Firth & Sons for whom he worked. Stainless steel was quickly adopted for the manufacture of cutlery throughout the world.

See also TABLE SERVICES AND ORNAMENT.

SIMON MOORE

2. SCISSORS. There are two types of scissors: those that work with a spring action (known as shears), which, although originally intended for general use, are employed for a limited number of purposes (e.g. carpet-making and weaving), and those with pivoted blades (see fig. 3). The latter type dates from Roman times while the former may have evolved much earlier. Both types were used by the Romans and are usually described in ancient written

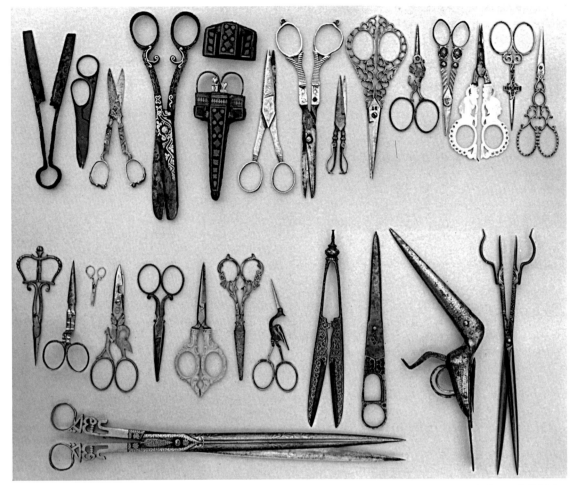

3. Scissors, from left to right (top row): iron shears edged with steel, 14th century; late medieval scissors; scissors with silver and gilt blades, German or Flemish, *c.* 1520; iron scissors edged with steel and ornamented with gold, English, *c.* 1540; 'drizzling' kit in leather case, possibly Italian, 17th century; scissors close-plated with silver and engraved, English, late 18th century; scissors with silver handles, Dutch, late 18th century; étui scissors with folding handles, 18th century; scissors with cut-steel handles, maker's mark of BT, Italian, 18th century; steel scissors with lion rampant shanks, French, 18th century; steel scissors with cut-steel decoration, French, late 18th century; steel scissors with mother-of-pearl mounts carved with Roman emperors' heads, Paris, *c.* 1800; cut-steel scissors, French, *c.* 1830; steel scissors decorated with gold studs, English, *c.* 1830–40; (middle row) steel scissors with bows forming a crown, English, *c.* 1840; cranked-steel scissors for lace, English, *c.* 1830; miniature steel scissors, Sheffield, *c.* 1850; steel buttonhole scissors with gilt figural shanks, Sheffield, late 19th century; 'Carrickmacross' scissors, Sheffield, 19th century; scissors with ivorine handles, German, late 19th century; gilt-steel scissors with blade guard, French, 19th century; blued-steel and gilt stork scissors by Henckels of Solingen, *c.* 1900; shears inlaid with gold, Iran, 18th century; dagger scissors with pierced decoration, Iran, late 18th-century/early 19th; steel 'bird' scissors inlaid with silver, Iran, 19th century; blued-steel scissors with folding handles, Iran, late 19th century; (bottom) long scissors with damascened hollow-ground blades and brass mounts, Iran, 19th century (private collections)

sources as being made of iron, although scissor blades may have been made from or edged with steel.

Early scissors were relatively simple in design and construction: the bows or finger loops consisted of rings attached to the shanks of the blades; a rivet or screw held the two blades together. From the medieval period scissors were produced in a number of European centres, for example Solingen in Germany, and in 16th-century France cutlers in Moulins produced high-quality steel for scissors. According to an order dated 1560, the king's nails were trimmed with scissors made in the town. Large decorated scissors, often engraved with the owner's name and the date, were made in Spain in the 17th century. Some were damascened at Toledo, while others had pierced decoration. The records of the Cutlers' Company of London (1624) refer to scissor-making in the city, although the quality of English-made scissors did not match that of continental scissors for another 100 years. A few English firms of scissor-makers, notably those of Beach, Macklin and Neesham, established a small but notable industry at Salisbury, Wilts, from the mid-17th century until the early 20th.

The 18th and 19th centuries represented the period of the greatest variety in construction and decoration of scissors throughout the world. Steel scissors inlaid with silver and resembling birds, the blades forming the beak while the bows formed part of the underbelly and the back, were produced in Iran. 'Dagger' scissors, the bows set one over the other, were also first produced in this region. Persian blades were ground hollow, it is said, for secreting notes. In Europe, scissors were often kept in attractive metal cases, so that they could be worn as part of the daily costume. Some of these cases also contained a small knife and spike, which were used to unpick gold and silver thread from fine material—a practice that, although popular in the 17th century, developed into near mania during the early 18th century and was known as 'drizzling' or *parfilage*. New methods of production were also developed: towards the end of the 18th century the bows and shanks of scissors began to be made in one piece, either in silver or steel.

The best quality English scissors were made in Sheffield from the end of the 18th century to the end of the 19th by such companies as Joseph Rodgers & Sons and Thomas Wilkinson & Sons. In 1837, to commemorate her coronation, Queen Victoria was presented with elaborately decorated scissors (which apparently took four months to make) by James Atherton, who was the chief scissor-maker for Wilkinson. The firm also had a fine display at the Great Exhibition of 1851 in London, including six pairs of scissors less than 50 mm long; the smallest were only *c.* 1.5 mm long and weighed 0.04 g, in contrast to a pair 600 mm long, weighing almost 4 kg.

The Victorians invented many gadget scissors, including lace scissors with a protruding tip to one blade for use in 'Carrickmacross' appliqué work, where the top layer of fabric has to be removed without damaging the net base, and 'stork' scissors in all sizes, which continue to be popular. Cases containing three scissors—nail, embroidery and paper—were a popular gift.

In the 18th and 19th centuries the most important French centres of steel production were Paris, Langres, Moulins and Thiers. In Paris, mother-of-pearl was also worked in the area around the Palais Royal, where ornate, fretted scissor shanks and bows in this material, depicting swans, dolphins, urns and other classical motifs, were made and fitted with steel blades. By the end of the 19th century in Germany, 3200 cutlers in Solingen specialized in the production of scissors; manufacture in Germany outstripped that of Britain, with cheaper products that were exported to the Americas, Italy and even to England. The multi-bladed 'Universal', incorporating many sewing and personal tools, was also invented in Germany. Some included a 'Stanhope' or peep featuring a local view. In the early 20th century pinking 'shears', which do not have a spring action, were invented to cut a zigzag or scalloped edge to prevent fraying.

MIN MAUDE

BIBLIOGRAPHY

GENERAL

C. Pagé: *La Coutellerie depuis l'origine jusqu'à nos jours*, 6 vols (Châtellerault, 1896–1905)
H. R. Schubert: 'Anglo-Saxon Cutlery', *J. Iron & Steel Inst.*, clvii (1947), pp. 22–6
J. B. Himsworth: *The Story of Cutlery, from Flint to Stainless Steel* (London, 1953)
J. F. Hayward: *English Cutlery, 16th to 18th Century* (London, 1957)

E. Lassen: *Knives, Forks and Spoons* (Copenhagen, 1960)
H. R. Singleton: *A Chronology of Cutlery* (Sheffield, 1973)
G. Benker: *Alte Bestecke* (Munich, 1978)
M. Pearce: 'Neglected Cutlery', *Ant. Collct.*, xiv (1979), pp. 20–22
Masterpieces of Cutlery and the Art of Eating (exh. cat., London, V&A, 1979)
S. J. Moore: 'English Table Cutlery', *Ant. Dealer & Colr's Guide* (May 1980), pp. 64–8; (June 1980), pp. 67–9
I. Pickford: *Silver Flatware* (Woodbridge, 1983)
S. J. Moore: 'Carriers and Containers for Eating Cutlery', *N. Knife Mag.* (Nov 1988), pp. 13–15; (Dec 1988), pp. 13–17
——: *Table Knives and Forks* (Aylesbury, 1995)

INDUSTRY AND TRADE

J. Smith: *Explanation or Key, to the Various Manufactories of Sheffield, with Engravings of each Article* (Sheffield, 1816/R South Burlington, VT, 1975)
G. Saint-Joanny: *La Coutellerie thiernoise de 1500 à 1800*, i (Clermont-Ferrand, 1863)
R. E. Leader: *History of the Company of Cutlers in Hallamshire in the County of York*, 2 vols (Sheffield, 1905)
C. Welch: *History of the Cutlers' Company of London and of the Minor Cutlery Crafts with Biographical Notices of Early London Cutlers* (London, 1916, 2/1923)
M. V. H. Taber: *A History of the Cutlery Industry in the Connecticut Valley* (Northampton, MA, 1955)
P. Smithurst: *The Cutlery Industry* (Aylesbury, 1985)
G. Tweedale: *Giants of Sheffield Steel* (Sheffield, 1986)
D. Hey: 'The Origins and Early Growth of the Hallamshire Cutlery and Allied Trades', *English Rural Society, 1500–1800: Essays in Honour of Joan Thirsk*, ed. J. Chartres and D. Hey (Cambridge, 1990), pp. 343–67

KNIVES AND FORKS

C. T. P. Bailey: *Knives and Forks* (London, 1927)
C. R. Beard: 'Wedding Knives', *Connoisseur*, lxxxv (1930), pp. 91–7
G. B. Hughes: 'Old English Table Knives and Forks', *Country Life*, cvii (17 Feb 1950), pp. 450–52
Knives and Forks in the Netherlands, 1500–1800, The Hague, Gemeentemus., (The Hague, 1972)
Y. de Riaz: *Le Livre des couteaux* (Lausanne, 1978; Eng. trans., New York, 1981)
S. J. Moore: 'The History of the Folding Knife', *N. Knife Mag.* (Dec 1983), pp. 5–7; (Feb 1984), pp. 8–13; (April 1984), pp. 8–10
——: 'The Evolution of Mediaeval English Knives', *N. Knife Mag.* (July 1985), pp. 15–17, 29–31
G. Boggiali: *La Posata* (Milan, 1987)
J. Cowgill, M. de Neergard and N. Griffiths: *Knives and Scabbards* (London, 1987)
S. J. Moore: *Penknives and Other Folding Knives* (Aylesbury, 1988)
——: 'French Folding Fruit Knives', *Ant. Colr*, lx (1989), pp. 58–63
——: 'Folding Knives', *Times Past*, vii (1990), pp. 2146–53
A. Stevenson: 'A Review of Chelsea, Chelsea–Derby and Derby Knife and Fork Hafts', *Trans. Eng. Cer. Circ.*, xiv (1990), pp. 50–58
S. J. Moore: 'A Taste for Music (Musical Fruit Knives)', *Ant. Dealer & Colr's Guide* (Aug 1994), pp. 22–3

SPOONS

C. J. Jackson: *The Spoon and its History* (London, 1892)
N. Gask: *Old Silver Spoons of England* (London, 1926/R Feltham, 1973)
M. Snodin: *English Silver Spoons* (London, 1974)
R. F. Homer: *Five Centuries of Base Metal Spoons* (London, 1975)
G. Belden and M. Snodin: *Spoons* (London, 1976)
J. Emery: *European Spoons before 1700* (Edinburgh, 1976)
D. T. Rainwater and D. H. Felger: *A Collector's Guide to Spoons around the World* (Pennsylvania, 1976)
V. Houart: *Antique Spoons: A Collector's Guide* (London, 1982)
E. Riha and W. B. Stern: 'Die römische Löffel aus Augst und Kaiseraugst', *Forsch. Augst*, 5 (1982)
S. J. Moore: *Spoons, 1650–1930* (Aylesbury, 1987)
——: 'Folding Spoons', *Ant. Dealer & Colr's Guide*, xliii (1990), pp. 46–9

SIMON MOORE

SCISSORS

H. R. D'Allemagne: *Les Accessoires du costume et du mobilier* (Paris, 1928/R 1970)
M. Andrere: *Old Needlework Boxes and Tools* (Newton Abbot, 1971)
S. Groves: *History of Needlework Tools and Accessories* (Newton Abbot, 1973)

M. Pearce: 'Needlework Tools Made by Joseph Rodgers & Sons', *Ant. Collct.*, xiv (1979), pp. 25–7

G. A. Rogers: *An Illustrated History of Needlework Tools* (London, 1983)

E. Zalkin: *Thimbles and Sewing Implements*, Warman (1989)

MIN MAUDE

Cuvelier, Hugues [Huguet] (*fl* 1489/90–1502). French architect. He was the lieutenant of Martin Chambiges (*see* CHAMBIGES, (1)) in the construction work on the transept arms of Sens Cathedral, and he was presumably the *compagnon* mentioned in the fabric account for 1489–90, when Chambiges came from Paris to Sens to draw up the plan. He worked with Chambiges on the new south transept arm until 1494 when Chambiges left Sens; Cuvelier continued the work, installing the vaults in 1497 and the window tracery in 1499–1500. By September 1500 the masons had transferred their attention to the north transept, which was constructed in the first two decades of the 16th century. Whereas Chambiges devised the plans and supervised the work as Maistre de l'Entreprise et Conducteur de la Croisée, maintaining control through periodic visits (1497, 1498, 1502 and 1506), Cuvelier worked on the site as the Maître de l'Oeuvre de la Croisée, completing complex tasks of stonecutting, including the elaborate tabernacles for the north transept portal. The relationship between the two masters is documented in the accounts of the visit that Cuvelier made with Chambiges to Troyes in 1502, where the latter was beginning work on the west front. Cuvelier is here designated as the assistant of Martin Chambiges. Thus it is impossible to separate Cuvelier's artistic identity from that of his master.

UNPUBLISHED SOURCES

Archives départementales de l'Yonne, MSS G 1137–43

BIBLIOGRAPHY

Bauchal

A. Lance: *Dictionnaire des architectes français* (Paris, 1872)

C. Porée: 'Les Architectes et la construction de la cathédrale de Sens', *Congr. Archéol. Dauphiné*, lxxiv (1907), pp. 559–98

L. Bégule: *La Cathédrale de Sens: Son architecture, son décor* (Lyon, 1929)

STEPHEN MURRAY

Cuvilliés, (Jean) François (Vincent Joseph) de, I (*b* Soignies [Hainault], nr Brussels, 23 Oct 1695; *d* Munich, 14 April 1768). French architect of Flemish origin, active in Bavaria. A discriminating and imaginative artist, he successfully imported the Parisian Rococo, at the height of its popularity, into the Munich area: his glittering adaptations of French ideas far surpass the original models. In the 18th and 19th centuries de Cuvilliés's work was known chiefly from collections of his ornamental designs, which were made between 1738 and 1768.

1. EARLY CAREER, BEFORE 1739. At the age of 11, de Cuvilliés entered the service of Maximilian II Emanuel (*reg* 1679–1726), exiled Elector of Bavaria, as a court dwarf and was educated by him. In 1714 he returned with Maximilian to Munich, where he was taught mathematics and fortification design. In 1715 he was appointed draughtsman to the Bavarian Director General of Building, Graf Ferdinand von der Wahl. Two years later he served as an ensign in the Bavarian army, apparently in the position of a fortifications engineer. During 1720–24 he studied architecture in Paris at Maximilian Emanuel's expense, and he was a fellow-student of Jacques-François

Blondel, with whose engravings his own work exhibits parallels and borrowings.

In 1724 de Cuvilliés designed stucco ceilings at Schloss Schleissheim near Munich. The following year he was appointed to the post of architect under the chief court architect in Munich, Joseph Effner, who had also trained in Paris. In 1726 the Elector died and was succeeded by Charles Albert (*reg* 1726–45; as Charles VII from 1740), who continued his patronage. In the same year de Cuvilliés received his first important court commission, the Palais Piosasque de Non (1726–32; destr. World War II). Between 1727 and 1729 he built the pavilion in the gardens of Schloss Ismaning near Munich for Prince Bishop Johann Theodor von Freising, one of the Elector's brothers. Charles Albert's other brother, Clemens August, Elector of Cologne, called in de Cuvilliés to impart the latest French style to his palace at Brühl (1728), which had been converted by Johann Conrad Schlaun from an old moated castle (*see* BRÜHL, SCHLOSS). De Cuvilliés changed the layout and gave the Gelbes Appartement in the north wing a new, modern look. In March 1728 Charles Albert placed de Cuvilliés on an equal footing with Joseph Effner; in October, while he was in Brühl, de Cuvilliés was appointed court architect and Lord High Steward (Truchsess) to the court of Cologne and was ennobled. Between 1728 and 1733 he collaborated on the design of the Falkenlust, a hunting-lodge near Brühl.

De Cuvilliés introduced the French 'goût nouveau' (or ROCOCO) style of decoration into Bavaria via his work in Munich. As architect to the court he worked under contract for Elector Charles Albert on the Munich Residenz (*see* MUNICH, §IV, 2), where he built the Gelbes Appartement (1726; destr.) and parts of the Trierzimmer (1725–35; destr.) and designed the ceiling of the Ahnengalerie (1729). He also created a new façade for the Grottenhof (*c.* 1730), one of the eight courtyards of the Residenz. His first major task there was the modification of the state apartments known as the Reiche Zimmer (1730–37), following a fire in December 1729. In 1730 the Schatz-Gewölb had been built at the end of the Ahnengalerie: de Cuvilliés's playful décor in this room, from the free development of the cove into the ceiling, to the individual motifs—of springs, swinging putti and dragons—influenced his choice of décor in the Reiche Zimmer, for which he also created new types of rooms, not based on Parisian models. For example, he built the Grüne Galerie with an H-shaped ground-plan (1733), a vestibule on the ground-floor, which opened out on to an Italianate grand staircase with three flights of stairs (destr. 1764), and the Spiegelkabinett (1731–2). In the latter, the framed panels usually employed to articulate walls are replaced (except for the dados) by mirrors. The miniature cabinet known as the Rotes Kabinett is equally unusual (stucco completed 1733), for here the rectangular pictures are framed with a network of ROCAILLE, which completely covers the red lacquered walls.

The décor in the Reiche Zimmer was very much in keeping with the *genre pittoresque*: the ornamentation consists of such a wealth of figures that, in addition to the masks, vases and trophies, allegories were realized in the stucco décor rather than in painted pictures. This effect was made possible only by de Cuvilliés's collaboration with gifted artists such as the stuccoist Johann Baptist

1. François de Cuvilliés I: Amalienburg Pavilion, in the gardens of Schloss Nymphenburg, Munich, 1734–9

Zimmermann and the wood-carvers Johann Adam Pichler (*fl* 1717–61), Wenzeslaus Miroffsky and Joachim Dietrich. Such a collaboration was of equal importance when de Cuvilliés was creating his most significant work, the Amalienburg Pavilion (1734–9) in the gardens of Schloss Nymphenburg. The Amalienburg combines French ideas, taken from the Pavillon d'Aurore in Sceaux and the Trianon de Porcelaine in Versailles, with the new shape of the mirrored hall, which was round in the centre and flanked by connecting rooms which form two *appartements en enfilade*. The subdued exterior (see fig. 1) is marked by contrasts, particularly between convex and concave shapes. In the interior the corners of the rooms are rounded for the first time, and the rocaille is employed with an especial emphasis on its asymmetry. In the Spiegelsaal both the articulation of the wall bays and their border with the vaulting disappear.

De Cuvilliés was also responsible for introducing the French hôtel to Munich, where it eventually became an indigenous feature. As available sites tended to be small and narrow, he based his ground-plans on Effner's Palais Preysing (1723–9), Munich, and on Viennese town palaces such as the one belonging to Prinz Eugen (by Johann Bernhard Fischer von Erlach; 1695–8), rather than on the typical Parisian hôtel. He followed the pattern of four wings with a gateway to a small inner court in the Palais Piosasque de Non and the Palais Holnstein (1733–7; now the Erzbischöfliches Palais). Architecturally, his façades are reminiscent of Italian buildings, not only when he altered older palaces (Palais Portia, 1731–3; destr.) but also in his new work (Holnstein); only the façade of the Palais Piosasque de Non was French. The plans for the Palais Törring in Munich (1736; not executed) survive.

The design for the décor of some rooms at Schloss Alteglofsheim near Regensburg (*c*. 1730–35) may also be attributed to de Cuvilliés.

2. LATER WORKS, 1739 AND AFTER. The project at Amalienburg ended for de Cuvilliés the first phase of large commissions from Elector Charles Albert. From then until 1751, a period that encompassed the Austrian War of Succession (1742–5), de Cuvilliés continued to honour his contracts with the court in Munich—overseeing official building work (eastern part of the monastery church of Schäftlarn, 1733–40)—and with Clemens August (inspection and approval of Johann Michael Fischer's project for the collegiate church of Berg am Laim, 1738–44; consultant to the scheme for the church and Residenz for the Deutscher Orden in Mergentheim, 1734–5). He also delivered plans for the layout of Schloss Wilhelmstal near Kassel (grotto, 1743; Chinese houses, 1747; picture gallery, 1749) and completed drawings (from 1747) for rebuilding Schloss Haimhausen outside Munich.

From 1738 de Cuvilliés assembled three series of bound collections of engraved designs of Rococo decorative devices. *Series I* appeared from 1738 to 1742, *Series II* from 1742 to 1754 and *Series III* from 1755. A proportion of the engravings were assembled and after his death reproduced in the anthology *Architecture bavaroise* (unpublished) by de Cuvilliés's son François de Cuvilliés II (1731–77). The engravings were widely viewed and hugely influential. Essentially they deal with suggestions for the design of architectural features (e.g. frames, panelling, iron lattice-work), as well as furniture and caprices, which were fantasy landscapes in rocaille frames. The anthology, like the series, became dispersed (Munich, Staatsbib., Berlin, Kstbib.; Nuremburg, Ger. Nmus.; priv. cols; see Schnell, 1961).

After the destruction by fire of the theatre in the Georgssaal at the Munich Residenz (5 March 1750), de Cuvilliés was commissioned to build a new theatre by Elector Maximilian III Joseph. His Residenztheater (1750–53; see fig. 2; destr. World War II; rebuilt on a new site) was designed with boxes, like the opera house (rebuilt 1685; destr.) in the Salvatorplatz, Munich; the main tier, set off by drapes in carved work, is supported by herms. In 1749 de Cuvilliés had proposed plans (Marburg, Hess. Staatsarchv) for a new opera house (not executed) in Kassel, and he borrowed elements from these drawings (e.g. royal box, balustrade drapery) for the Residenztheater. Between the sculptural accents of the royal box and the proscenium box stretched a line of boxes with accentuated balustrades, stepped according to status and resting on delicate supports. In conjunction with the white, gold and red colour scheme, they created the effect of a framed picture, imparting a feeling of splendour while remaining light and elegant. Once again Johann Baptist Zimmermann formed part of de Cuvilliés's team, as did Johann Adam Pichler and Joachim Dietrich, accompanied in this instance by the court sculptor Johann Baptist Straub. At one time the auditorium of the theatre could be lifted from a sloping position to a horizontal one, to create a dance floor. De Cuvilliés's early training as an engineer was evident in his skilful construction of the lifting device. Apart from several small projects, including the aviary at Schloss Nymphenburg (1751–7) and amendments to the stuccowork at both Nymphenburg and Schloss Schleissheim (1756–7), the court in Munich had no further commissions for de Cuvilliés in the following decade.

From 1753 de Cuvilliés built the *corps de logis* at Schloss Wilhelmsthal (nr Kassel) and planned the summer palace of Seraing (nr Liège) for Johann Theodor, Bishop of Freising and Liège. In addition, he delivered a plan and a model (1755) for the Residenz in Würzburg. In 1759 his façade (1741; destr. 1944) was constructed for the Palais Fugger-Zinneberg. Here, de Cuvilliés broke away from the Rococo style (which was then waning in popularity): his design had windows all of the same size without any central points of emphasis and also had a new, rigid look. In 1760 he received another government commission, to rebuild the royal suite in the Munich Residenz using the old panelling. At the same time he produced an engraving of a new urban plan for Dresden, the home of the wife of Elector Maximilian III Joseph. From 1761 to 1765 the von Seinsheim family had their castle at Sünching, near Regensburg, redecorated from designs by de Cuvilliés (chapel and great hall). Having been passed over in favour of Johann Baptist Gunetzrhainer (1692–1763) for the post of chief court architect on the death of Joseph Effner in 1745, de Cuvilliés ultimately achieved that position on Gunetzrhainer's death some 18 years later. Almost immediately he received a new commission of great importance for the extension and rebuilding of the Munich Residenz (plans 1764–5; wooden model paid for in 1767). The building work, however, was never executed. De Cuvilliés had envisaged finishing the residential complex with a façade looking on to the royal gardens and a large castle building with a façade looking on to a *cour d'honneur* to the east, but the project was only taken up again during 1825–48 by Leo von Klenze, who continued the work in a contemporary classical revival form. The last completed work by de Cuvilliés was the façade (1765–7) of the Theatinerkirche in Munich, which had remained unfinished until then. While keeping to the original sketch by Enrico Zuccalli (*c.* 1690) for the general outlines, de Cuvilliés made decisive modifications that are characteristic of his skill as a discriminating and imaginative architect.

UNPUBLISHED SOURCES

Munich, Staatsbib.; Berlin, Kstbib.; Nuremberg, Ger. Nmus.; priv cols [parts of *Series I, II, III*]

BIBLIOGRAPHY

Macmillan Enc. Architects
Bérard: 'Catalogue de l'oeuvre de Cuvilliés père et fils', *Rev. Univl A.*, viii (1859), pp. 429–49
O. Aufleger and K. Trautmann: *Die reichen Zimmer der königlichen Residenz in München* (Munich, 1893)
K. Trautmann: 'Der kurfürstliche Hofbaumeister Franz Cuvilliés der Ältere und sein Schaffen in Altbayern', *Mschr. Hist. Ver. Oberbayern*, iv (1895), pp. 86–136
J. Laran: *François de Cuvilliés: Dessinateur et architecte*, Les Grands Ornemanistes (Paris, [1930]) [100 pls]
F. Kimball: *The Creation of the Rococo* (Philadelphia, 1943)
H. Bauer: *Rocaille* (Munich, 1955)
L. Hager: *Nymphenburg: Schloss, Park und Burgen* (Munich, 1955)
H. Brunner: *Altes Residenztheater in München* (Munich, 1958)
K. Kosel: 'Ein Spätwerk François de Cuvilliés', *Verh. Hist. Ver. Oberpfalz & Regensburg*, cvii (1961), pp. 103–20
J. Schnell: *François de Cuvilliés' Schule Bayerischer Architektur: Ein Beitrag zum Stickwerk und zur Architekturtheorie beider Cuvilliés* (Munich, 1961)

2. François de Cuvilliés I: interior of the Residenztheater, Munich, 1750–53 (destr. World War II; rebuilt on a new site)

J. Gamer: 'Entwürfe von François Cuvilliés d. Ä. für den Kurfürsten Clemens August von Köln und den Kardinal Fürstbischof Johann Theodor von Lüttich', *Aachen. Kstbl.*, xxxii (1966), pp. 126–62

F. Wolf: 'François de Cuvilliés: Der Architekt und Dekorschöpfer', *Oberbayer. Archv*, lxxxix (1967)

W. Hansmann: *Schloss Falkenlust* (Cologne, 1972)

C. Thon: *Johann Baptist Zimmermann als Stukkator* (Munich and Zurich, 1977)

E. D. Schmid: *Nymphenburg* (Munich, 1979)

G. Dischinger and L. Koch: *Zwei Münchner Adelspalais: Palais Portia, Palais Preysing* (Munich, 1984)

W. Braunfels: *François de Cuvilliés* (Munich, 1986)

G. Hojer: *Die Amalienburg* (Munich, 1986)

U. Kretzschmar: *Das alte und das neue Schloss Heimhausen* (Munich, 1986), pp. 36–53

H. Mellenthin: *François Cuvilliés–Amalienburg: Bezug zur französische Architekturtheorie* (diss., U. Munich, 1989)

A. Schick: *Cuvilliés–Möbel* (Munich, 1993)

GERHARD HOJER

Cuvillon, Louis. *See* QUÉVILLON, LOUIS.

Cuxa, St Michel. *See* SAINT-MICHEL-DE-CUXA.

Cuyp [Cuijp; Kuyp]. Dutch family of artists. Gerrit Gerritsz. (*c.* 1565–1644), whose father (*d* 1605) was probably an artist, was a glass painter from Venlo who moved to Dordrecht around 1585. He married and joined the Guild of St Luke there that same year, serving as the Guild's deacon in 1607 and 1608. He designed and executed numerous stained-glass windows in Dordrecht and other towns until 1639, but only his cartoon for a window in St Janskerk, Gouda, survives (1596; Gouda, Archf Ned. Hervormde Gemeente). His eldest son, Abraham Gerritsz. (1588–*c.* 1647), was also a glass painter; his second son, (1) Jacob Gerritsz., was a painter. Gerrit Gerritsz. married a second time in 1602; children from this marriage included the artists Gerrit Gerritsz. the younger (1603–51), also a glass painter, and the painter (2) Benjamin Gerritsz. By 1617 Jacob Gerritsz. had adopted the surname Cuyp, and the rest of the family seems eventually to have followed this practice. (3) Aelbert Cuyp, the most important artist in the family, was the only child of Jacob Gerritsz. Cuyp.

BIBLIOGRAPHY

A. Houbraken: *De groote schouburgh* (1718–21), i, pp. 237–8, 248

G. H. Veth: 'Aelbert Cuyp, Jacob Gerritsz. Cuyp en Benjamin Cuyp', *Oud-Holland*, ii (1884), pp. 233–90; vi (1888), pp. 131–48 [documentary evidence]

Aelbert Cuyp en zijn familie (exh. cat., intro. J. M. de Groot; Dordrecht, Dordrechts Mus., 1977) [source mat. and a surv. of the fam.]

De zichtbaere werelt [The visual world] (exh. cat., Dordrecht, Dordrechts Mus., 1992)

(1) Jacob (Gerritsz.) Cuyp (*b* Dordrecht, Dec 1594; *d* Dordrecht, ?1652). Painter and draughtsman. Probably taught by his father, he entered the Guild of St Luke in Dordrecht in 1617, the same year that he executed an important commission to portray the masters of the Holland Mint (Dordrecht, Mus. van Gijn). He was the Guild's bookkeeper in 1629, 1633, 1637 and 1641 and, according to Houbraken, led Dordrecht's fine painters in their separation from the Guild in 1642. Jacob married Aertken van Cooten from Utrecht in 1618; his only child, (3) Aelbert Cuyp, was born two years later.

Much of Jacob's work consists of single bust-length portraits, executed in a direct, rather sober style. These date from throughout his career and include at least two sets of portraits of the powerful Dordrecht merchant Jacob Trip and his wife, Margaretha de Geer (e.g. Amsterdam, Rijksmus., and Denver, A. Mus., on loan); they were also portrayed by Nicolaes Maes and by Rembrandt. Jacob Cuyp also painted a few portraits of children in landscapes, occasionally accompanied by animals (e.g. the *Portrait of Two Children*, 1638; Cologne, Wallraf-Richartz-Mus.), but many such portraits are assigned to him incorrectly.

Around 1627 Jacob's work began to be strongly influenced by Utrecht painters, especially Abraham Bloemaert and Hendrick ter Brugghen. Houbraken stated that Jacob actually studied with Bloemaert. A number of pastoral landscapes with shepherds (e.g. Amsterdam, Rijksmus.) and history paintings betray the effects of Utrecht Mannerism. A series of Jacob's animal drawings, etched by Reinier van Persijn (*c.* 1615–88) in 1641, closely resemble similar print series after Bloemaert. Also from *c.* 1627 are several paintings, for example the *Man with a Jug* (Stockholm, Nmus.), done in the Caravaggesque style practised by Hendrick ter Brugghen and other Utrecht Caravaggisti. The man's face in the picture is strongly lit from the side by candlelight, a convention favoured by the Utrecht artists. Their influence is also apparent in Cuyp's simple, yet dramatic half-length depictions of the apostles *Peter* and *Paul* (both Dordrecht, Dordrechts Mus.) and the evangelist *Luke* (Karlsruhe, Staatl. Ksthalle). Perhaps his most remarkably Caravaggesque conception is his genre scene of *Two Cavaliers Seated at a Table* (St Petersburg, Hermitage), in which careful attention is paid to the still-life details of the setting.

By 1630 Jacob Cuyp's style of figural painting had altered under the influence of Claes Moyaert and Pieter Lastman, resulting in compositions that arranged weighty, bulky figures in landscapes. An allegory of the capture of the city of 's Hertogenbosch (1630; 's Hertogenbosch, Stadhuis) depicts the stadholder Frederick Henry as David holding the head of the slain Goliath (symbolizing Spain), surrounded by Muses representing the seven provinces of the united Netherlands. This work may have been commissioned by the government or court since it appears in an inventory (1751) of a royal Dutch collection.

Jacob Cuyp's extremely varied output also included numerous still-lifes and genre scenes, two forms of subject-matter that are combined in the *Fish Market* (1627; Dordrecht, Dordrechts Mus.). The artist also painted kitchen, flower and poultry still-lifes. Curious examples of the latter are the pairs of paintings of a *Boy Holding a Goose* and a *Girl Holding a Chicken* (e.g. Paris, Louvre), with an inscription *Mon oye faict tout* (a French pun on money and goose).

Jacob provided instruction not only for his half-brother (2) Benjamin Cuyp and his son Aelbert, but also for Ferdinand Bol, Paulus Lesire (1611–after 1656) and others. He collaborated with Aelbert on several paintings: three group portraits, two dated 1641 and another of 1645, and several landscapes with shepherds. In such works, Jacob painted the figures and Aelbert the landscapes.

Jacob's last signed and dated work, *Boy with a Wineglass and Flute* (priv. col., see bibliog. above, 1992 exh. cat., no. 28), is from 1652; later the same year his wife is referred to as a widow.

BIBLIOGRAPHY

M. Balen: *Beschryvinge der stad Dordrecht* [Description of the town of Dordrecht] (Dordrecht, 1677), pp. 666, 682

J. Heyligers: *Jacob Gerritsz. Cuyp: Porträt, Genre- und Historienmaler zu Dordrecht* (diss., U. Rostock, 1924)

Portret van een meester (exh. cat., Dordrecht, Dordrechts Mus., 1975)

A. Chong: 'De *Apostel Paulus* uit 1627 door Jacob Cuyp', *Dordrechts Mus. Bull.*, xiii/4–5 (1988); Eng. trans. in *Hoogsteder-Naumann Mercury*, 7 (1989), pp. 10–18

(2) Benjamin (Gerritsz.) Cuyp (*bapt* Dordrecht, Dec 1612; *d* Dordrecht, *bur* 28 Aug 1652). Painter, half-brother of (1) Jacob Cuyp. Houbraken stated that he studied with his half-brother Jacob. Benjamin entered the Guild of St Luke on 27 January 1631, at the same time as his brother Gerrit Gerritsz. the younger. In 1641 Benjamin gave evidence in a medical affair, which has prompted speculation that he may have trained as a doctor, but in 1643 he is twice recorded in The Hague as a painter, living with other artists. Seventeen of his paintings appeared at auction at Wijk-bij-Duurstede in 1649. At the time of his death, he was living in Dordrecht with another half-brother, who was a glassmaker.

As no dated works by Benjamin are known, it is difficult to chart the artist's development accurately, although several different styles of painting can be isolated. In his handling of religious subjects, Benjamin may be considered an important follower of Rembrandt, with whom, however, he seems to have had no direct contact. His fellow townsmen Paulus Lesire (1611–after 1656) and Hendrik Dethier, who also entered the Guild in 1631, were also strongly influenced by Rembrandt's early work, as indeed were such later Dordrecht artists as Ferdinand Bol, Nicolaes Maes, Samuel van Hoogstraten and Aert de Gelder. Benjamin constructed several variations of Rembrandt's compositions from the late 1620s and early 1630s, in particular *Judas and the Thirty Pieces of Silver* (1629; GB, priv. col., see J. Bruyn and others, *A Corpus of Rembrandt Paintings*, i (The Hague, 1982), no. A15), an especially common source for Rembrandt's early followers. Benjamin borrowed not only Rembrandt's deeply shadowed lighting but also his characteristic huddled figures and piled-up compositions (see Ember, figs 5–7). Benjamin's paintings of the *Flight into Egypt* (ex-art market, Paris, 1951, see Ember, fig. 1) are similarly derived from the nocturnal setting of a Rembrandt school painting (Tours, Mus. B.-A., see Bruyn and others, no. C5).

In other paintings tentatively assigned to Benjamin's early career, the influence of Leonaert Bramer can be felt in dark monochromatic works consisting of a few figures (Ember, figs 2–3). These various stylistic elements are combined in the large, ambitious *Adoration of the Magi* (Dordrecht, Dordrechts Mus.), which displays free, quick

Benjamin Cuyp: *Conversion of Saul*, oil on canvas, 1.17×1.53 m (Vienna, Gemäldegalerie der Akademie der Bildenden Künste)

brushwork and deeply saturated colours. The influence of Adrian Brouwer and Adrian van Ostade is added to that of Rembrandt and Bramer. Benjamin's achievement was the marriage of a sketchy brush technique with an intensity of light and colour. He came to favour biblical and historical scenes featuring dramatic bursts of light, such as the Annunciation to the Shepherds, the Raising of Lazarus, the Resurrection, the Liberation of St Peter and the Conversion of Saul. A tumble of figures, one boldly silhouetted, and dramatic flashes of light characterize, for example, the *Conversion of Saul* (Vienna, Gemäldegal. Akad. Bild. Kst.; see fig.). Another group of Benjamin's paintings, also conceived in a painterly style but employing delicate pastel shades of blue, pink and orange, seems to have been strongly influenced by Adrian van Ostade, for example the *Liberation of Peter* (Kassel, Schloss Wilhelmshöhe), which is more brightly and evenly lit than the majority of Benjamin's paintings.

Benjamin Cuyp also painted religious and history scenes in a monochrome palette with heavy impasto highlights, for example the *Annunciation to the Shepherds* (Hannover, Niedersächs. Landesmus., see Ember, fig. 37), which is constructed in various shades of brown. These works resemble grisailles, with a complex overlay of sketchy white strokes, as in the *Adoration of the Shepherds* (Berlin, Gemäldegal.). In smaller-scale interior scenes the influence of Adrian Brouwer and Daniel Teniers can be felt. These include biblical subjects (e.g. *Tobias*; Dordrecht, Dordrechts Mus.) but more often are genre paintings, usually of peasants, inn scenes (e.g. Budapest, Mus. F.A.) or depictions of soldiers (e.g. Cologne, Wallraf-Richartz-Mus.). Benjamin also painted a number of battle or encampment scenes in a loose style influenced by painters such as Gerrit Claesz. Bleker and more generally Esaias van de Velde. Closely connected with these are Benjamin's beach scenes, which usually feature the unloading of fish from boats overseen by gentlemen on horseback. The landscapes that form the settings for these themes show some influence from (1) Jacob Cuyp and, in turn, may have influenced (3) Aelbert Cuyp's early work.

BIBLIOGRAPHY
K. Boström: 'Benjamin Cuyp', *Ksthist. Tidskr.*, xiii (1944), pp. 59–74
I. Ember: 'Benjamin Gerritsz. Cuyp', *Acta Hist. A. Acad. Sci. Hung.*, xxv (1979), pp. 89–141; xxvi (1980), pp. 37–73
Gods, Saints and Heroes: Dutch Painting in the Age of Rembrandt (exh. cat., ed. A. Blankert; Washington, DC, N.G.A., 1980), pp. 253–4, 270–71
W. Sumowski: *Gemälde der Rembrandt-Schüler*, i (Landau, 1983)

(3) Aelbert [Albert] **Cuyp** (*b* Dordrecht, *bapt* late Oct 1620; *d* Dordrecht, *bur* 15 Nov 1691). Painter and draughtsman, son of (1) Jacob Cuyp. One of the most important landscape painters of 17th-century Netherlands, he combined a wide range of sources and influences, most notably in the application of lighting effects derived from Italianate painting to typical Dutch subjects. Such traditional themes as townscapes, winter scenes, cattle pieces and equestrian portraits were stylistically transformed and given new grandeur. Aelbert was virtually unknown outside his native town, and his influence in the 17th century was negligible. He became popular in the late 18th century, especially in England.

1. Life and work. 2. Working methods and technique. 3. Critical reception and posthumous reputation.

1. LIFE AND WORK. No record exists of his training or entry into the painters' guild, but it is clear that he was taught by his father, for whom he painted the landscape backgrounds in two family group portraits from 1641 (Jerusalem, Israel Mus.; and priv. col., see Reiss, nos 16–17). By this time Aelbert had begun to travel in Holland and along the Rhine, making sketches of Rhenen, Arnhem, Amersfoort, Utrecht, Leiden and The Hague. In late 1651 or in 1652 he again journeyed up the Rhine and the Waal past Rhenen to Nijmegen, as far as Cleve, Elten and Emmerich. The numerous drawings made on this trip provided motifs for many of the painter's later landscapes. In 1658 Cuyp married Cornelia Boschman (1617–89), the widow of Johan van den Corput (1609–50), a wealthy regent by whom she already had three children. In 1663 the family bought a larger house in the Wijnstraat. Cuyp's marriage left him financially well-off and socially prominent, and he and his wife owned large tracts of land around Dordrecht. He became a deacon (1660) and an elder (1672) of the Reformed Church, a regent of the sickhouse (1673) and a member of the High Court of South Holland (1679). With the fall of the de Witt brothers and their faction in 1673, Cuyp's name was put on a list of 100 candidates approved by supporters of the stadholder William III, although he did not actually assume municipal office. At the death of his wife, Cuyp's estate was worth 42,000 guilders. Their only child, a daughter, Arendina (*b* 1659), married Pieter Onderwater (1651–1728) in 1690; she died in 1702, her only son having died at the age of four.

(i) Early work, 1639–c. 1645. (ii) Mature work, c. 1645–mid-1650s. (iii) Last works, late 1650s and after.

(i) Early work, 1639–c. 1645. Cuyp's earliest works are three landscape paintings signed and dated 1639: a *Farm Scene* (Besançon, Mus. B.-A.), a *Harbour Scene* (London, Johnny van Haeften Ltd) and a *River Valley with a Panorama* (the Netherlands, priv. col., see 1992 exh. cat., no. 15), the last of which shows his interest in the work of Josse de Momper II, Hercules Segers and Esaias van de Velde. The only works that can be convincingly dated before these paintings are a *Rocky Landscape with Cows* (ex-art market, Brussels, 1928; see Chong, 1991, fig. 42) and a similar drawing (Bremen, Ksthalle), which are especially close to de Momper's work. A painting dated 1640 with shepherds, tall cliffs and a distant panorama (USA, priv. col., see Chong, 1991, fig. 45) shows the clear influence of Cornelis van Poelenburch. Directly related in style and composition are two paintings of *Orpheus in a Landscape* (Dessau, Staatl. Gal.; the other sold at London, Sotheby's, 6 July 1994), the first of Cuyp's historical subjects. At about the same time he also painted the distant background in his father's *Landscape with Two Shepherds* (Montauban, Mus. Ingres).

The bulk of Cuyp's output from the early 1640s until *c.* 1645 is based on the tonal landscapes of Jan van Goyen, Salomon van Ruysdael and Herman Saftleven II, although Cuyp constantly sought brighter and stronger contrasts of light. Van Goyen seems to have visited Dordrecht on numerous occasions, and his son-in-law Jacques de Claauw (*fl* 1642–76) was a Dordrecht artist associated with Jacob Cuyp. Aelbert may therefore have had direct contact with

1. Aelbert Cuyp: *River Scene with Distant Windmills*, oil on panel, 356×524 mm, *c*. 1642 (London, National Gallery)

van Goyen. Cuyp commonly depicted quiet waterways and inlets (e.g. *River Scene with Distant Windmills*; London, N.G.; see fig. 1). Several paintings, for instance the *View of the Mariakerk, Utrecht* (Salzburg, Residenz Gal.), are based on sketches made in Utrecht. Cuyp must have visited the city on several occasions; his mother was from Utrecht, his father had studied there, and he himself seems to have been influenced by a series of Utrecht painters, including Poelenburch, Saftleven and, later, Jan Both. Cuyp also began to depict his home town of Dordrecht in paintings delicately tinged with pastel colours (e.g. Malibu, CA, Getty Mus., and Leipzig, Mus. Bild. Kst.). Much larger in scale is a *Farm Scene* (Melbury House, Dorset, see 1987–8 exh. cat., no. 20), rendered in rich green tones and showing greater compositional complexity. Closely connected with this is the *Baptism of the Eunuch* (Houston, TX, Menil Col.).

(ii) Mature work, c. 1645–mid-1650s. Around 1645 Cuyp became influenced by the light and compositions of Dutch Italianate landscape painters, especially Jan Both and, to a lesser degree, Saftleven and Herman van Swanevelt. Cuyp's first Italianate landscapes are cast with a smoky orange sunlight, with shepherds and their flocks occupying a prominent place in the composition. The treeless rocky plains he painted resemble the work of Jan Asselijn and Nicolaes Berchem, although, in fact, he predated these two Italianate artists. *Two Herdsmen and Cattle in a Wide Landscape* (London, Dulwich Pict. Gal.) shows a brilliant sun *contre-jour* over a misty landscape; the *Ruins on a Hill*

with Sheep and Two Horsemen (Amsterdam, Rijksmus.) introduces the theme of horsemen that Cuyp so often used later in his career. Also among Cuyp's first Italianate paintings is another painting of *Orpheus* (priv. col., see Reiss, no. 48).

Two paintings are dated 1645: a *Portrait of Four Children in a Landscape* (Devon, priv. col., see Chong, 1991, fig. 54), signed and dated by both Jacob and Aelbert Cuyp, Jacob again being responsible for the figures; and a *View of Rijnsburg Abbey* (priv. col., see Chong, 1991, fig. 51). These introduce a series of landscapes lit by a strong, almost monochromatic sun, but with clear blue skies. Milking became a dominant theme in Cuyp's work in the years just after 1645 (e.g. *Milking Scene near a River*; Karlsruhe, Staatl. Ksthalle). The *Distant View of Dordrecht* (the '*Large Dort*', London, N.G.) combines a milking scene with a profile of the artist's native city. These scenes were succeeded *c*. 1650 by very simple landscapes consisting almost wholly of herds of cattle, placed on river banks (e.g. Washington, DC, N.G.A.) or actually in a river (e.g. Budapest, N.G.). Cuyp also paired paintings of cows in a river with representations of bulls on a river bank (e.g. GB, priv. col., see 1987–8 exh. cat., p. 294). The dairy industry near Dordrecht was expanding in the mid-1600s through ambitious land reclamation programmes, and these paintings must have reminded viewers of this.

Around 1650 Cuyp also painted a number of figural scenes and portraits (e.g. 1649; London, N.G.). A *Portrait of a Man with a Rifle* (Amsterdam, Rijksmus.) has a pendant showing a *Woman Dressed as a Huntress* (1651;

priv. col., on loan to Boston, MA, Mus. F.A.). Cuyp also portrayed *Jacob Trip* (the Netherlands, priv. col., see 1977 exh. cat., no. 20), whom Jacob Cuyp, Nicolaes Maes and Rembrandt also painted. Cuyp's last dated work is a *Portrait of a Child with a Sheep* (1655; London, John Mitchell & Sons). There are also a few paintings of poultry (e.g. London, Leger Gals) and several stable interiors with cattle in their stalls, the latest of which shows a *Woman Scouring a Pot* (Dordrecht, Dordrechts Mus.), with brilliant light entering from an open door. Around this time Cuyp also painted two copperplates showing *Apollo* and *Mercury* (both priv. col., see de Mirimonde, figs 1 and 2), which were originally fitted as doors to a cabinet. He also painted two versions of the *Conversion of Saul*, based generally on the many representations by his uncle (2) Benjamin Cuyp. The example in Amiens (Mus. Picardie), full of brilliant light and gesticulating figures, is Aelbert's only true figural composition (the other version is in the Netherlands, priv. col., see 1977 exh. cat., no. 27).

Cuyp's first equestrian portrait is of *Pieter de Roovere* (The Hague, Mauritshuis); the sitter died in 1652, and the style of the portrait resembles the cattle pictures of *c.* 1650. De Roovere is depicted inspecting a large fish held by a boy, a motif often used by Benjamin Cuyp in his beach scenes. Here it takes on added significance, since fishing and the smoking of fish were major industries in the area

around Dordrecht, including de Roovere's estate at Hardinxveld. Aelbert's chronology after *c.* 1652 is impossible to determine with any certainty. Nevertheless, the portrait of de Roovere must soon have been followed by the equestrian portrait of *Michiel and Cornelis Pompe van Meerdervoort with their Tutor and Coachman* (*c.* 1652–3; New York, Met.; see fig. 2), the background of which is derived from a sketch of Elten (Paris, Fond. Custodia, Inst. Néer.), which also served as the basis for the *Draughtsman near Elten* (Woburn Abbey, Beds). Inventories in 1680 and 1749 provide a precise identification of the Pompe van Meerdervoort boys, the elder of whom died in 1653. Hunting forms the primary theme in most of Cuyp's equestrian portraits, to which figures in Turkish garb lend an exotic as well as elegant atmosphere. No less prestigious African pages appear in other portraits of riders (e.g. London, Buckingham Pal., Royal Col., and Birmingham, Barber Inst.). Another double portrait, of a *Lady and Gentleman on Horseback* (Washington, DC, N.G.A.), is problematic since the figures were repainted by Cuyp at a later stage, and hunting figures in the distance were altered. Related to these works is a painting, perhaps a portrait, of an *Officer Tying Ribbons on his Horse* (London, Buckingham Pal., Royal Col.). Cuyp's second version of the *Baptism of the Eunuch* (Anglesey Abbey, Cambs, NT) is based on treatments of the subject by Rembrandt and

2. Aelbert Cuyp: *Michiel and Cornelis Pompe van Meerdervoort with their Tutor and Coachman*, oil on canvas, 1.10×1.56 m, *c.* 1652–3 (New York, Metropolitan Museum of Art)

Benjamin Cuyp, but its Italianate landscape with numerous riders is indebted to Jan Both's painting of the same subject (London, Buckingham Pal., Royal Col.). Aelbert also painted a *Riding School* (Toledo, OH, Mus. A.) near a Romanesque church and surrounded by Classical statuary. In all these equestrian paintings, well-dressed riders are represented with accessories that enhance their status and lend an elegant, almost classicizing atmosphere to the scene.

One of Aelbert Cuyp's favourite motifs in his later career was the town of Nijmegen in Gelderland. The town, especially the medieval citadel Valkhof, was familiar from maps and prints and the many paintings of van Goyen and Salomon van Ruysdael: the popularity of the site was due to its importance in the history of the Netherlands, especially as the supposed seat of Claudius Civilis, leader of the Batavian revolt against the Romans. The subject thus had strongly patriotic associations for citizens of the newly independent Dutch State. On the journey of 1651 or 1652 Cuyp made numerous sketches of Nijmegen from different vantage-points. He painted two versions of the *View of the Valkhof from the North-east* (Woburn Abbey, Beds, and Indianapolis, IN, Mus. A.), based on a drawing (sold Amsterdam, Sotheby's, 25 April 1983, lot 73); these are similar to van Goyen's pictures but arranged with greater classical repose and rendered in Cuyp's rich Italianate light. The earlier of Cuyp's versions with pastoral herders (Indianapolis) has as its pendant a *View of Nijmegen from the East* (USA, priv. col., see Reiss, no. 129). The second and larger view from the north-east (Woburn

Abbey) shows elegant gentlemen on horseback; its pendant is a deeply shadowed *View of the Valkhof from the South-east* (Edinburgh, N.G.). A scene of *Ships before the Valkhof* (Scotland, priv. col.), similar to depictions of the fleet at Dordrecht, completes the group of depictions of Nijmegen and probably refers to the visit in 1647 of the Stadholder Frederick Henry in the company of Elector Friedrich Wilhelm of Brandenburg.

Cuyp meanwhile continued to paint ships and views of Dordrecht. Occasionally shown in stormy weather (e.g. London, Wallace), the town is more typically seen with glassily still water. Two views of *Dordrecht at Sunset* (London, Kenwood House, and Ascott, Bucks, NT) are early contributions to the development of the pure townscape, preceding, for example, Vermeer's *View of Delft* (*c.* 1661; The Hague, Mauritshuis; *see* DELFT, fig. 2). The careful attention Cuyp paid to the fall and reflection of light and to the calm shapes of the ships and floating log rafts is especially striking. In the *Gathering of the Fleet at Dordrecht* (mid-1650s; Washington, DC, N.G.A.; see fig. 3) Cuyp depicted the arrival of a dignitary, perhaps an evocation of a rendezvous of 1646 (a type of picture favoured by Simon de Vlieger and Jan van de Cappelle), which Frederick Henry did not himself attend but which was marked by great festivities and celebrations. The work may, however, also recall other visits of the Stadholder and his family to the town. Cuyp twice painted winter scenes near Dordrecht. Although other Dutch Italianate artists occasionally painted winter landscapes (e.g. Asselijn and Berchem), Cuyp uniquely was able to impart a golden

3. Aelbert Cuyp: *Gathering of the Fleet at Dordrecht*, oil on canvas, 1.15×1.70 m, mid-1650s (Washington, DC, National Gallery of Art)

4. Aelbert Cuyp: *River Landscape with Horseman and Peasants*, oil on canvas, 1.23×2.41 m, 1655–60 (London, National Gallery)

glow to ice landscapes. The *Ice Scene near the Huis te Merwede* (Brocklesby Park, Lincs) is based on a sketch of the ruins (London, BM) and shows skaters on the ice; the other winter landscape shows *Fishing under the Ice* (Woburn Abbey, Beds).

(iii) Last works, late 1650s and after. Costumes or other forms of external evidence provide little clue as to when Cuyp stopped painting, although his marriage in 1658, with its increasing social responsibilities, seems to have marked a slowing of production. His last works, probably from the late 1650s, consist of broad, open landscapes populated by elegant riders and shepherds: the *River Landscape with Two Horsemen* (Amsterdam, Rijksmus.) is directly transcribed from a sketch made near Cleve, but other works are imaginary, although still based on Rhineland scenery. *Peasants on a Road* (London, Dulwich Pict. Gal.) shows a screen of trees with mountains in the distance; the composition and the crystalline Italianate light are derived directly from the work of Jan Both. Unlike Both, however, Cuyp almost always employed a flat foreground on which to arrange his staffage. In what are probably Cuyp's last landscapes, a strong silvery light casts a monochromatic glow over the entire scene. This is clearly seen in the *Hilly Landscape with Shepherds and Travellers* (London, Buckingham Pal., Royal Col.), in which the ridges and horsemen are influenced by an etching by Jan Both. The same light gilds the *River Landscape with Horseman and Peasants* (London, N.G.; see fig. 4), Cuyp's largest landscape, in which the distant mountains and the town on the far side of the lake are not topographically accurate transcriptions but evocations of an idyllic pastoral land, populated by a hunter, an elegant rider and shepherds.

2. WORKING METHODS AND TECHNIQUE. Most of Cuyp's early paintings are based on drawings of rivers, forests and towns, rendered in black chalk and usually worked up in green, brown and a characteristic mustard-yellow wash. More than most Dutch landscape artists, Cuyp made drawings as an integral part of his creative process, beginning with sketches made on the spot, later worked up in the studio and then transformed into paintings. He also produced a number of figure studies (e.g. Paris, Fond. Custodia, Inst. Néer.) that were used in the same fashion. During his 1652 journey up the Rhine and the Waal, he filled sketchbooks with dozens of drawings done on the spot, often continuing a sketch across to the back of the adjacent page, allowing the sequence of drawings to be partially reconstructed. Most of Cuyp's later paintings can be connected with these sketches or similar ones made in or near Dordrecht. The first painting that appears to show high cliffs above the Rhine (Rotterdam, Mus. Boymans–van Beuningen) has no preliminary drawing, but, instead, a sketchier version in oil (Paris, Fond. Custodia, Inst. Néer.); dendrochronology indicates that the work dates from just after 1649. Cuyp's drawing of *Ubbergen Castle near Nijmegen* (Vienna, Albertina), used for the painted version (London, N.G.) of the site where an important battle against the Spanish took place in 1591, shows how the artist elaborated the original sketch (1652) from nature, later adding the background hills and framing trees.

The broken, blond brushwork in Cuyp's early painted work shows his indebtedness to Jan van Goyen, as does the monochromatic colouring; this is clearly evident by 1641 in the two group portraits with figures by Jacob Cuyp. Aelbert gradually replaced the brushwork of this van Goyen phase with deeper colours and greater contrasts of light, allied to a greater solidity of structure. Many paintings are devoted to nature's specialized light effects: his evening and night scenes, typically set in harbours, are highlighted with rich pastel tones (Toledo, OH, Mus. A., and Cologne, Wallraf-Richartz-Mus.), and he painted two storm scenes streaked with lightning (*c.* 1644; Zurich, Stift. Samml. Bührle; and early 1650s; London, N.G.). Cuyp's later technique seems to have moved from a brushy calligraphic touch towards a harder style.

3. Critical reception and posthumous reputation. In his own lifetime Cuyp seems to have been almost unknown outside Dordrecht. His principal pupil was probably Abraham van Calraet (a number of whose works were previously attributed to Cuyp), although Houbraken recorded Abraham's brother Barent van Calraet (1650–1737) as a student. Houbraken provided the first account of the career of his fellow-townsman in 1718, and for nearly a century this brief discussion remained the only biography of the artist. Although a few paintings attributed to Cuyp began to appear at auctions in the Netherlands and London in the 1750s, Cuyp escaped the attention of nearly all 18th-century writers of lexica and landscape surveys. Richard Wilson noted that Cuyp was still little known and appreciated. Towards the end of the 18th century the situation altered dramatically: in 1774 a sale catalogue termed Cuyp the equal of Claude; and in Dordrecht, Johan van der Linden van Slingeland's sale (22 Aug 1785) of 41 works catalogued as being by Cuyp (of which at least 17 are genuine) fetched high prices, as did paintings occasionally sold in England. By the late 18th century writers had already begun to complain of numerous imitations and copies being passed off as genuine works by Cuyp; in Dordrecht, artists such as Dionys van Dongen (1748–1819), Arie Lamme (1748–1801), Aert Schoumann and Jacob van Strij were responsible for copies and pastiches of Cuyp's work.

John Smith's remarkable catalogue of 1834 was the first attempt to define Cuyp's oeuvre systematically; Waagen's survey of British collections added significantly to this. Set against these works, which catered primarily for art dealers and aristocratic collectors, were critics who felt that living artists were being ignored in the scramble to buy Old Masters. Pamphleteers attacked collectors and criticized Cuyp's work, although painters themselves, most notably J. M. W. Turner and John Constable, praised Cuyp and borrowed from his pictures. John Ruskin, while conceding Cuyp's value as a pastoral landscape painter, found him lacking in realism when compared with British painters, especially Turner.

BIBLIOGRAPHY

J. Smith: *A Catalogue Raisonné of the Works of the Most Eminent Dutch Flemish and French Painters*, v (1834), pp. 279–368, 443–52; suppl. ix (1942), pp. 649–67, 868–70
G. F. Waagen: *Treasures of Art in Great Britain*, 3 vols (London, 1854)
C. Hofstede de Groot: *Holländische Maler*, ii (1908), pp. 5–246
A. P. de Mirimonde: 'Un Phébus énigmatique de Cuyp', *Oud-Holland*, lxxx (1965), pp. 181–8
J. Nieuwstraten: 'Een ontlening van Cuyp aan Claude Lorrain' [Cuyp's borrowing from Claude Lorrain], *Oud-Holland*, lxxx (1965), pp. 192–5
W. Stechow: *Dutch Landscape Painting of the 17th Century* (London, 1966), pp. 40, 61–4, 161, 181
D. G. Burnett: 'The Landscapes of Aelbert Cuyp', *Apollo*, lxxxix (1969), pp. 372–80 [gen. survey, with some inaccuracies]
J. G. van Gelder and I. Jost: 'Vroeg contact van Aelbert Cuyp met Utrecht' [Aelbert Cuyp's early contact with Utrecht], *Miscellanea I. Q. van Regteren Altena* (Amsterdam, 1969), pp. 100–03
——: 'Doorzagen op Aelbert Cuyp' [Comments about Aelbert Cuyp], *Ned. Ksthist. Jb.*, xxiii (1972), pp. 223–39
S. Reiss: *Aelbert Cuyp* (London, 1975); review by C. Brown in *TLS* (28 Nov 1975) [best source for illus., but controversial]
Aelbert Cuyp en zijn familie (exh. cat., intro by J. M. de Groot, Dordrecht, Dordrechts Mus., 1977)
Masters of 17th-century Dutch Landscape Painting (exh. cat., ed. P. Sutton; Amsterdam, Rijksmus.; Boston, MA, Mus. F.A.; Philadelphia, PA, Mus. A.; 1987–8) [entries on Cuyp by A. Chong]
A. Chong: '"In 't verbeelden van slachtdieren"' [Depicting farm animals], *Meesterlijk vee* [Masterly cattle] (exh. cat., Dordrecht, Dordrechts Mus.; Leeuwarden, Fries Mus.; 1988–9)
——: 'New Dated Works from Aelbert Cuyp's Early Career', *Burl. Mag.*, cxxxiii (1991), pp. 606–12
——: *Social Meanings in the Paintings of Aelbert Cuyp* (diss., New York U., 1992)
De zichtbare werelt [The visual world] (exh. cat., Dordrecht, Dordrechts Mus., 1992)

ALAN CHONG

Cuypers [Cuipers]. Dutch family of architects and designers. (1) P(etrus) J(osephus) H(ubertus) Cuypers, his nephew (2) Eduard (Gerard Hendrik Hubert) Cuypers, his son (3) Joseph (Theodorus Johannes) Cuypers, and his grandson Pierre Cuypers jr trained a generation of Dutch architects and decorative artists, including K. P. C. de Bazel and J. L. M. Lauweriks.

(1) P(etrus) J(osephus) H(ubertus) Cuypers (*b* Roermond, 16 May 1827; *d* Roermond, 3 March 1921). Known as 'the Dutch Viollet-le-Duc' because he restored numerous medieval buildings and followed the French theorist's principles of structural rationalism and geometric proportion, he could also be dubbed the Dutch William Morris because of his decisive role in revitalizing the arts and crafts in the Netherlands. Cuypers was a devout Roman Catholic, and he was aided in his architectural practice by the increased building of churches after the restoration of the Episcopal hierarchy (1853); he designed some two dozen throughout the Netherlands, all in the Gothic Revival style, which in his interpretation became a supple instrument of artistic and religious expression. In his secular commissions he revived Northern Renaissance motifs to create a lively, polychromatic Dutch national style for the second half of the 19th century. Cuypers's success as an architect was greatly helped by his brother-in-law, Joseph Alberdingk Thijm (1820–89), a leading Catholic intellectual and writer who supported Cuypers's revival of Gothic forms as the only ones appropriate for religious purposes; and by Victor E. L. de Stuers, a nobleman who used his powerful position in the Ministry of the Interior to secure for Cuypers important government commissions.

Cuypers attended the Koninklijke Academie voor Schone Kunsten in Antwerp and in 1848 won the prize for excellence. Returning to Roermond in 1850, he was asked to restore the local minster (Onze Lieve Vrouwe Munsterkerk). As preparation he visited Gothic churches in the Rhineland, and in Cologne he discovered the work of the Dombauhütte (cathedral building lodge). This inspired him to found in Roermond in 1853 Cuypers & Stolzenberg, the modern equivalent of a guild for liturgical design that would reunite architecture with the decorative arts; it survived until 1892, when it was replaced by Cuypers & Co., in which his son Joseph became a partner. P. J. H. Cuypers's restoration of the minster brought him into contact with Eugène-Emmanuel Viollet-le-Duc, who advised him on various technical and architectural details.

In the rectory (1854) of St Lambertus, Veghel, he became the first Dutch architect since the 16th century to employ brick vaults. Cuypers played an essential role in reviving brickmaking and bricklaying in Holland by encouraging the manufacture of vividly coloured profile bricks and by training the workmen to use them. His ability to make the most of his masons' skills is seen in the interior of the Heilige Hart or Vondelkerk (1870–73), Vondelstraat, Amsterdam; the brilliant greens, yellows and reds and the virtuoso play of ribbed vaults create an effect that rivals the most sophisticated work of William Butterfield or G. E. Street, whose work Cuypers knew through his membership of the Ecclesiological Society.

Cuypers initially based his church plans either on medieval French basilicas or on Viollet-le-Duc's ideal Gothic cathedral. St Lambertus (1855–62), Veghel, St Catherine (1859), Eindhoven, and St Barbara (1865), Breda, are examples of the former; St Willibrordus-outside-the-Walls (1864–73; destr.), Amsterdam, of the latter. Cuypers eventually produced astonishingly original creations. Two churches in Amsterdam displayed his sophisticated handling of space. The swelling volumes of the Vondelkerk yield a Baroque dynamism. The cramped triangular site of the Maria Magdalenakerk (1889–91; destr.; see fig.) inspired Cuypers to produce a building more conventionally Gothic in its soaring height but singular in its complex plan; a polygonal entrance with ribbed vaults leads to a three-aisled church with narrow

P. J. H. Cuypers: Maria Magdalenakerk, Amsterdam, 1889–91 (destr.; from a photograph of 1964)

transepts and radiating chapels around the choir. A tempered polychromy prevails on the exterior of Cuypers's churches produced mainly by red brick trimmed with stone or brown brick dressed with bright yellow. Within, the colour is more insistent because of the rich hues of the structural materials, the glowing stained-glass windows and the brightly painted sculpture and liturgical accessories provided by Cuypers's firm in Roermond. The complex spaces can be read clearly in the rationally composed exterior masses. The vertical emphasis makes these churches important urban focal points.

For two secular buildings in Amsterdam commissioned by government authorities—the Rijksmuseum (1876–85; see NETHERLANDS, THE, fig. 10) and the Central Station (1882–9; with Adolph Leonard van Gendt)—Cuypers created an influential national style by combining such medieval, Renaissance and Baroque motifs as pointed ribbed vaults, round-headed windows and mansard roofs, with modern materials such as iron and glass. The complex decorative programmes for these two works required the talents of a host of artists and artisans working in a variety of media; within and without, the two buildings are consummate examples of the 19th-century ideal of the *Gesamtkunstwerk*. Cuypers also designed private houses; a group from the period of 1876 to 1880 survives in the wealthy neighbourhood by Amsterdam's Vondelpark, to the south-west of the inner city. He restored the Château de Haar (1891–6) at Haarzuylens, near Amsterdam, and, like Viollet-le-Duc at Pierrefonds, provided a new Gothic Revival construction that makes the castle a resolutely 19th-century recapitulation of the romantic image of the Middle Ages. In 1894, after 30 years in Amsterdam, he returned to Roermond, completing his last building there, the Juvenaat, in 1919.

(2) Eduard (Gerard Hendrik Hubert) Cuypers (*b* Roermond, 18 April 1859; *d* The Hague, 1 June 1927). Nephew of (1) P. J. H. Cuypers. He trained in his uncle's office before establishing an independent practice in Amsterdam in 1878. He had proportionally more secular and private commissions than his uncle and his cousin Joseph. Eduard Cuypers was particularly interested in domestic architecture; in 1903 he established *Het Huis*, his own periodical devoted to the subject, which illustrated exclusively the residences and interior decoration emanating from the studio of the same name that he opened in 1900. From 1905 to 1927 the magazine, renamed *Het Huis oud en nieuw*, included articles on historical buildings and furnishings and the architecture of the Dutch Indies. The contents kept pace with his increasingly eclectic preferences. At the turn of the century Eduard Cuypers worked in Nieuwe Kunst, Dutch Art Nouveau, and was influenced by the work of Joseph Maria Olbrich in his studio and house at Jan Luykenstraat 2 (1899), in the house at van Eeghenstraat 22 and in the headquarters (1902) for the *Algemene Handelsblad* newspaper, all in Amsterdam. Next he began to emulate 16th- and 17th-century styles, as in his competition project for the Vredespaleis (1906) in The Hague and the country house Die Hooge Vuursche (1910) at Baarn. Nevertheless, the office of this increasingly historicist architect was a training ground for half a dozen future members of the

Amsterdam school, and in his role as mentor, as in his interest in the *Gesamtkunstwerk*, Cuypers carried on his uncle's legacy.

(3) Joseph (Theodorus Johannes) Cuypers (*b* Roermond, 10 June 1861; *d* Roermond, 1949). Son of (1) P. J. H. Cuypers. He was trained at the Technische Hogeschool in Delft and began his practice in his father's office. He updated his father's vocabulary, in religious architecture moving from the Gothic Revival to the Romanesque Revival and in secular commissions from Dutch Renaissance to Dutch classicism. His major church was the new St Bavo Cathedral (begun 1895), Leidsevaart, Haarlem; in medieval fashion this vast, five-aisled basilica with radiating chapels and domed lantern was not completed until 1930. Designed with Jan Stuyt, his partner from 1900 to 1909, the cathedral demonstrates the influence in the Netherlands of the Romanesque Revival style adopted by H. H. Richardson, an influence that can be seen in contemporary work by A. W. Weissman and H. P. BERLAGE, as well as in other churches by Cuypers at Dongen (1919), Bussum (1921) and Beverwijk (1922). St Bavo shows the impact of Berlage's call for repose after the restlessness characteristic of the picturesque Gothic Revival: here, round arches and low stair-towers, subordinated to the dome, which resembles those of 12th-century Aquitaine, contribute to a monumental harmony contrasting with the tense drama of P. J. H. Cuypers's pointed-arch creations.

Joseph Cuypers scored a major professional success when invited in 1909 to design a new stock exchange. Completed in 1912, his building is located next to Berlage's Beursgebouw (1896–1903); with its historicizing forms based on 17th- and 18th-century Dutch Palladianism, it seems a reproach to Berlage's *Zakerlijkheid* ('objectivity') and modernity. In town houses in Amsterdam, for example Museumplein 9 (1907) and Hobbemastraat 20 (1913), and in country villas, such as 'De Pauwhof' in Wassenaar, Cuypers responded to a taste for historicism on the part of his wealthy clients by producing designs based on 18th-century Dutch sources, which in turn had derived from French and English Palladianism.

BIBLIOGRAPHY

Thieme–Becker
J. W. V. de Stuers: *Dr P. J. H. Cuypers* (Haarlem, 1897)
J. Kalf: *De katholieke kerken in Nederland* (Amsterdam, 1906)
J. T. J. Cuypers: *Het werk van Dr P. J. H. Cuypers* (Amsterdam, 1917)
J. H. W. Leliman: *Het stadswoonhuis in Nederland gedurende de laatste 25 jaren* (The Hague, 1920, rev. 2/1924)
Nederland bouwt in baksteen, 1800–1940 (exh. cat., Rotterdam, Mus. Boymans, 1941)
H.-R. Hitchcock: *Architecture: 19th and 20th Centuries* (London, 1958/R Harmondsworth, 1977)
H. P. R. Rosenberg: *De 19de-eeuwse kerkelijke bouwkunst in Nederland* (The Hague, 1972)
H. Searing: 'Berlage or Cuypers? The Father of them All', *In Search of Modern Architecture: A Tribute to Henry-Russell Hitchcock*, ed. H. Searing (Cambridge, MA, 1982), pp. 226–44
G. Hoogewoud, J. Jaapkuyt and A. Oxenaar: *P. J. H. Cuypers en Amsterdam: Gebouwen en ontwerpen, 1860–98*, Cahiers van het Nederlands Documentiecentrum voor de Bouwkunst (Assen, 1985)

HELEN SEARING

Cuzco. Site in Peru, in the heart of the southern Andes, 3560 m above sea-level. It was the capital of the INCA empire. Cuzco occupies the head of the fertile valley of the Huatanay River, where it is connected by a low pass with the Anta Basin and Valley. The climate is temperate, with a rainy season from December to March. Now a city of over 275,000, a majority of whom are Indians, it is the present-day capital of the department of Cuzco.

1. PRE-COLUMBIAN.

(i) Introduction. In pre-Inca oral traditions Cuzco was known as Acamana and considered to have been inhabited by three ethnic groups: Sahuasiray, Antasayas and Huaylla. Archaeological evidence shows that the area was inhabited by *c.* 1200 BC; this early phase is represented by pottery in the Marcavalle style and subsequently the Chanapata style. There is also evidence for settlements of later pre-Inca cultures in the valley, such as Huari, and the Quotacalle style and Killke ceramic styles have been defined as precursors of the Inca style. Most archaeological investigations have been concentrated in and around the Coricancha (Sun Temple) and Sacsahuaman fortress. Initially work was carried out under the auspices of the Patronato de Arqueología de Cuzco and subsequently by the Instituto Nacional de Cultura.

Around AD 1200 the Inca tribe, led by Manco Capac, settled on the site of the later Coricancha (see fig. (a)), naming the new settlement Cuzco. From 1438 Pachacutec, the ninth Inca, reorganized and rebuilt Cuzco into a suitable capital for the expanding Inca empire, extending the settlement northwards by draining a swamp and using a worked masonry style developed during the reign of his father Viracocha Inca. The only permanent residents of Cuzco were the rulers and Inca nobility, including priests and important government officials. Temporary residents included some servants and attendants to the shrines, but the majority lived in the outlying districts. Outside the central nucleus, settlements or suburbs were considered parts of the capital. The suburbs were the homes of the native lords of subject provinces, considered 'Incas by privilege'. The lords were required to live for four months of the year in the suburbs and maintain a permanent embassy and servants. These embassies were distributed around the capital in an order based on the administrative and geographical divisions of the empire.

(ii) Planning and architecture. The city devised by Pachacutec to be the microcosm of the empire was situated between the canalized sections of the Huatanay and Tullumayo rivers and divided into four quarters representing the empire's four great districts or *suyu*. There was also a division of Cuzco into two sectors: Hanan (upper), occupied by the new Inca leaders; and Hurin (lower), representing the older inhabitants. The inner city covered an area of 2000×400–600 m and contained approximately 4000 structures. The layout of the inner city took the shape of a puma, with the fortress of Sacsahuaman (the puma's head; (b)) to the north, overlooking the main body of the town and the southernmost ward, Pumachupan (puma's tail; (c)) at the confluence of the two rivers. The heart of the new city in the main body of the puma was Huacaypata ('holy place'; (f)), a central plaza of approximately 2500 sq. m, surrounded by the royal palaces of the Inca, where all important occasions and state events were celebrated. Adjacent to Huacaypata and extending from it was a secondary square, the Cusipata ('joy place'; (g))

reached by a flight of steps. The Cusipata occupied approximately 4000 sq. m between the puma's back and front legs, was paved with pebbles and was used for social gatherings and markets.

The greatness of Pachacutec Inca's Cuzco was reflected in the impressive palaces, the primary function of which was royal, although they were also used as administrative, religious and academic centres. The important buildings of the inner city were constructed of finely fitted, dressed masonry (*see also* SOUTH AMERICA, PRE-COLUMBIAN, §III, 2(iii)). Building stone included diorite porphyry, Huaccoto basalt, Yucay limestone, andesite from the south-east, and rubble. Upper storeys may sometimes have been of adobe; the roofs were always thatched, occasionally decoratively, and interiors could be generously ornamented with gold and silver.

The two most important buildings were the Coricancha (a), built by Pachacutec on the most prominent site in Hurin Cuzco, and the monumental fort of Sacsahuaman (b) in Hanan Cuzco, built on the hill by Tupac Inca Yupanqui after 1471 and representing the head of the puma and Inca power. Other temples included the Quishuarcancha ((h); the Temple of Viracocha, the Creator, and present site of Cuzco Cathedral) beside the *Usnu* (platform) on the main square, and Illapa (the Temple of the Thunderbolt in the Pucamarca palace; (d)). The Coricancha (later a colonial church and monastery of S Domingo) has been restored since the 1956 earthquake that destroyed parts of the convent. Its main gateway supposedly faced approximately north, connecting a small entrance court with the Huacaypata. An enclosure wall contained the main Sun Temple of the empire, four shrines (for the Moon; Venus and the Pleiades; the Thunderbolt; and the Rainbow) and the building used by the priests attending the shrines. The Sun Temple, a rectangular structure with a curved western end, or enclosure wall, which also acted as a retaining wall where the ground falls steeply, contained the image of the Sun on a gold plate covering much of the western wall, facing the rising Sun. This structure was surrounded by the mummies or idols of dead rulers; it was still standing in 1560. It may originally have contained a painted cosmic map and a painted history of the Incas on wooden boards. On opposite sides of the Coricancha's inner courtyard were pairs of buildings with an alcove between them. The shrine of the Moon contained a large silver plate decorated with the Moon's image and was surrounded by the mummies or idols of the Inca *Coyas* (queens). All the shrines were lined with niches and were richly ornamented with gold or silver plaques and with decorative features and statues set with precious stones. The thatch was thick and the *ichu* grass was woven in designs intermingled with gold. In the courtyard, nailed around the outside of the temple walls, was a wide band (two palms in width according to Pedro Pizarro's report) of gold. On the south side of the courtyard was the priest's building. The proportions of the buildings and their internal features are perfectly regular and symmetrically distributed according to the most exacting canons of Inca architecture. The enclosure wall on the north-east side is preserved almost to its original height, *c.* 4.5 m above the street and 3 m above the temple floor; it is 810–910 mm thick, the width decreasing with height, and has 12 courses

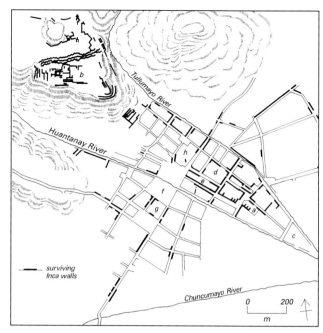

Cuzco, plan, *c.* AD 1438–*c.* 1550: (a) Coricancha; (b) Sacsahuaman; (c) Pumachupan; (d) Pucamarca; (e) Acllahuasi; (f) Huacaypata; (g) Cusipata; (h) Quishuarcancha; (i) Amarucancha

of cut and unusually large rectangular blocks of dark andesite. The finely fitted masonry of the surviving parts of the enclosure walls exhibits an unusually smooth finish. Small buildings around the temple were occupied by those assigned to its service. According to Cobo, there was adjacent a ceremonial garden, in which sacrifices were made, ornamented with gold flowers, crops, birds, animals and a shepherd. The garden had a fountain supplied with water brought underground from the Huatanay. The Acllahuasi ((e); convent of the Sun Virgins) lay to the north of the Coricancha, adjacent to Pucamarca palace (d). Numerous shrines or *huacas* were grouped along arbitrary lines (*ceques*) radiating from the Sun Temple.

Outlying buildings, for example the provincial embassies, were constructed mainly of rubble and mortar covered with a mud stucco finish. Shortly after the Conquest a census conducted by the King of Spain's inspector recorded 100,000 such houses, although this may have included houses in settlements in the entire valley. Storehouses (*collcas*) built to store tribute from all over the empire were built in rows on a hill to the south-west, overlooking the city.

BIBLIOGRAPHY

P. Sancho: *Relación para S.M. de lo sucedido en la conquista y pacificación de estas provincias de Nueva Castilla y de la calidad de la tierra* (1543); ed. C. Romero and H. Urteaga (Lima, 1917); Eng. trans by P. A. Means (New York, 1917)

J. de Betanzos: *Suma y narración de los Incas* (1551); ed. M. del Carmen Rubio (Madrid, 1987)

P. Pizarro: *Relación del descubrimiento y conquista de los reinos del Perú y del gobierno y órden que los naturales tenían* (1571); ed. M. Menéndez Pelayo (Madrid, 1905–65); Eng. trans. by P.A. Means (New York, 1921)

Garcilaso de la Vega [El Inca]: *Commentarios reales de los Incas* (i, Lisbon, 1609; ii, Córdoba, 1617); Eng. trans., intro. by H. V. Livermore, Texas Pan American Series (Austin, 1966)

B. Cobo: *Historia del nuevo mundo* (1653); ed. L. Pardo, 4 vols (Cuzco, 1956); Eng. trans. by R. Hamilton (Austin, 1979)

J. H. Rowe: *An Introduction to the Archaeology of Cuzco*, Pap. Peabody Mus. Amer. Archaeol. & Ethnol., xxvii/2 (Cambridge, MA, 1944)

R. T. Zuidema: *The Ceque System of Cuzco: The Social Organization of the Incas*, Int. Archv Ethnog., l (1964), suppl.

O. Ladrón de Guevara Avilés: 'La restauración de Coricancha y templo de Santo Domingo', *Rev. Inst. Arqueol. Cuzco* (1967)

J. H. Rowe: 'What Kind of Settlement Was Inca Cuzco?', *Ñawpa Pacha* (1967), pp. 59–76

M. Chávez Ballón: 'Ciúdades incas: Cuzco capital del imperio', *Wayka*, iii (1970), pp. 1–14

A. Kendall: *Everyday Life of the Incas* (London, 1973)

G. Graziano and L. Margolies: *Arquitectura inka* (Caracas, 1977; Eng. trans by P. J. Lyon, Bloomington and London, 1980)

S. Agurto Calvo: *Cuzco: La traza urbana de la ciudad inca* (Cuzco, 1980)

J. Hemming and E. Ranney: *Monuments of the Incas* (Boston, MA, 1982)

A. Kendall: 'An Archaeological Perspective for the Late Intermediate Period Inca Development in the Cuzco Region', *Structure, Knowledge and Representation in the Andes*, ed. G. Urton and D. Poole, i (Hamilton, NY, 1993)

ANN KENDALL

2. COLONIAL AND AFTER. In late 1533 the Spaniards sacked Cuzco. Several periods of destruction were followed by burning and earthquakes. In the mid-16th century the city was rebuilt as a colonial town, preserving the original lines of the streets and reusing the solid masonry foundations. In 1650 Spanish Cuzco was destroyed by an earthquake, and the whole town had to be rebuilt; nevertheless, the remains of Inca walls, arches and doorways are still evident throughout the city.

Colonial architecture and painting flourished in Cuzco during the latter half of the 17th century and is partially preserved today. The city contains many colonial churches, monasteries and convents (*see also* PERU, §III, 1). At its heart is the Plaza de Armas, with colonial arcades and four churches situated around it. The cathedral, built on the site of the Temple of Viracocha (see fig. (h)) and completed in the 17th century, exhibits both Renaissance and Baroque elements. It has a solid silver altar and a beautifully carved original wooden altar retable. In the sacristy are paintings of all the bishops of Cuzco. On the east side of the plaza is the twin-towered La Compañia de Jesus, a Jesuit church built on the Inca site of the Amarucancha ((i); Palace of the Serpents) in the late 17th century. Considered by many to be the finest church in Peru, it is filled with exceptional murals, paintings and carved altars. On the south side of the cathedral lies the church of El Triunfo, which contains a Churrigueresque high altar made of granite and gold.

Among Cuzco's many other fine churches, La Merced, founded in 1536 and rebuilt in the late 17th century after an earthquake, contains one of the few existing Platersque choir stalls and many paintings of the CUZCO SCHOOL. In the 17th century S Domingo was built on the walls of the Temple of Coricancha (a), using its stones. In the convent the ancient temple walls can be seen, and the Baroque cloister has been opened up to disclose four of the original temple chambers. Belen de los Reyes, also dating from the 17th century, has a particularly beautiful main altar with silver embellishments at the centre and goldwashed retables at the sides.

City museums include the Museo de Arte Religioso, a collection of colonial paintings and furniture housed in the Palacio Archiespiscopal, and the Museo Arqueologica, located in the impressive Palacio del Almirante and exhibiting an excellent collection of Pre-Columbian artefacts.

EWA

BIBLIOGRAPHY

G. Kubler: *Cuzco: Reconstruction of the Town and Restoration of its Monuments* (Paris, 1952)

M. Kropp: *Cuzco: Window on Peru* (New York, 1956)

J. de Mesa and T. Gisbert: *Historia de la pintura cuzqueña* (Buenos Aires, 1962)

E. Miranda Iturrino, ed.: *La arquitectura peruana a través de los siglos* (Lima, 1964)

B. Box, ed.: *South American Handbook* (Bath and New York, 1992)

Cuzco school. Term used to refer to the Peruvian painters of various ethnic origins active in CUZCO from the 16th to the 19th century. When Viceroy Toledo reached Cuzco in 1570, he commissioned a series of paintings (destr.) to be sent to Spain, which included depictions of the conquest and capture of Atahuallpa (*d* 1533) and portraits of the Inca rulers. These works were painted by Indians who had been taught by such Spanish masters as Loyola. From the beginning of Spanish colonization until the end of the 16th century two currents existed in painting in Cuzco: that of the Spanish masters, influenced by Netherlandish and Late Gothic art; and the indigenous tradition. Both influences persisted simultaneously until Roman Mannerism reached Peru through the work of three Italian painters based in Lima: Mateo Pérez de Alesio, Bernardo Bitti and Angelino Medoro. Bitti, a Jesuit, worked in Cuzco with, among others, two disciples of Medoro: the Indian Loayza and the Lima painter Luis de Riaño (*b* 1596). The influence of Bitti and the popularity of Flemish engravings as inspiration for compositions overwhelmed indigenous art, which was evident only in the drawings in the *Primer nueva crónica y buen gabierno* (*c*. 1580–1613) by Guaman Poma de Ayala. Medieval styles were also perpetuated through the work of such monks as Diego de Ocaña, who popularized the image of the *Virgin of Guadalupe*.

Despite these influential models, the Indian painter DIEGO QUISPE TITO, who took pride in his Inca ancestry, created a personal style in his landscapes embellished with gold leaf and abounding with birds. He lived outside the city itself and maintained a distance from foreign tendencies. His followers included such Indian masters as Chihuantito, Chilli Tupac and the Master of the *Procession of Corpus Christi* (before 1700; Cuzco, Mus. A. Relig.), one of the most important social, historical and artistic documents of Cuzquenian art. Another Indian painter, Basilío de Santa Cruz Pumacallao, produced paintings for Bishop Manuel de Mollinedo y Aungulo (*d* 1699). The latter had seen works by Velázquez and Rubens, and the works of Pumacallao were similar to paintings being produced in Europe at that time. They were also often superior to those of the Spanish and Creole artists active in Cuzco, among whom Marcos Ribera is notable for his use of dramatic chiaroscuro.

Wall painting was practised from the 16th century, following the Indian tradition and using Italian influences. It had developed in the poorer towns, where canvases would have been too expensive for church decoration. The most important groups include those by Riaño at the church in Andahuaylillas (1618–26), inspired by the priest

Juan Pérez de Bocanegra, and those by Tadeo Escalante at S Juan, Huaro (1802). Escalante also painted portraits of 12 Incas and of noble Indian women at a mill in Acomayo. Pumacahua, the chief of Tinta, commissioned a wall painting on the façade of his village church, which depicted the battle in which he conquered Tupac Amaru, and portraits of him and his family.

Spanish and Creole painters were in the same guild as Indian painters until 1684, when the latter group objected to a compulsory examination that required knowledge of the architectural orders and the drawing of a male and a female nude. The Indians began to work independently under the patronage of local leaders, who dedicated themselves to selling their works in other towns, including the mining centres of the Audiencia de Charcas (now Bolivia). Works from this school also reached the north of Argentina, Chile and Lima. The Indian painters abandoned European perspective and returned to characteristically flat compositions filled with figures, birds and trees, which they also gilded.

In the 18th century such Indians as Mauricio García y Delgado (*fl c.* 1760) set up large workshops, which produced up to 100 paintings per month. The quality and colouring of the paintings declined, but their prices also fell, allowing their work to become popular among even the poorest. Marcos Zapata painted *c.* 200 works on the *Litanies of the Virgin* for Cuzco Cathedral (1755) and a series on the *Life of St Ignatius* (*c.* 1762) with Cipriano Toldeo y Gutiérrez (*fl* 1762–73) for the church of La Compañia in Cuzco (both *in situ*). Antonio Vilca, another notable painter, was apprenticed to Zapata. The popular secular theme of portraits of the Inca kings continued until well into the 19th century. They were initially painted alongside those of the Spanish kings until the latter were discontinued, and the Inca dynasty continued from Manco Capar to Atahuallpa. Cueva and Juan y Ulloa made engravings on the theme; Ulloa's was published in *Viaje a la América meridional.*

BIBLIOGRAPHY
C. del Pomar: *Pintura colonial* (Lima, 1928)
R. Vargas Ugarte: *Ensayo de un diccionario de artífices de la América meridional* (Lima, 1947)
Mariategui: *Pintura cuzqueña del siglo XVII* (Lima, 1951)
E. Marco Dorta: *Arte en América y Filipinas* (Madrid, 1973)
P. Macera: 'El arte mural cuzqueño, de los siglos XVI al XX', *Trabajos Hist.*, ii (1977), pp. 343–460
J. Mesa and T. Gisbert: *Historia de la pintura cuzqueña*, 2 vols (Lima, 1982)
J. Bernales Ballesteros: *Historia del arte hispanoamericano: Siglos XVI a XVIII*, ii (Madrid, 1987)

TERESA GISBERT

Cwenarski, Waldemar (*b* Lwów [now L'viv, Ukraine], 6 Oct 1926; *d* Wrocław, 4 April 1953). Polish painter and printmaker. He trained at the Art Lyceum in Wrocław (1947–9) and from 1949 to 1953 under Stanisław Dawski (*b* 1905) and Eugeniusz Geppert (1890–1979) at the State Higher School of Fine Arts in Wrocław. He was a member of the Wrocław Group. His very short but prolific career embraced portraits (e.g. *Portrait of the Artist's Mother,* before 1947; Wrocław, N. Mus.), landscapes, still-lifes and figurative and devotional paintings, all created at variance with the official, epic Socialist Realist style. His own style, reminiscent of that of Georges Rouault, evolved towards greater expressiveness of forms and colours. He painted with broad, quick brushstrokes, applying paint thickly and leaving it to run randomly, and he built up forms with simple, geometric planes and strong black outlines (e.g. *Self-portrait*, 1952; Wrocław, N. Mus.). His red ochre and blue *Pietà* (1951; Wrocław, N. Mus.) shows two faceless figures so arranged and simplified that they appear like a cross (the outstretched arms of the Madonna) and an altar table (the body of Christ). Two series of black-and-white paintings, entitled *Studies* and *Heads* (both 1952; Wrocław, N. Mus.), inspired by tragic experiences of war and concentration camps, depict the pain of human existence, a recurring theme in Cwenarski's work.

BIBLIOGRAPHY
Waldemar Cwenarski, 1926–1953 (exh. cat., text by B. Kowalska, Wrocław, N. Mus.; Warsaw, N. Mus.; 1967)
H. Hermansdorfer: *Waldemar Cwenarski* (Wrocław, 1976)

ANNA BENTKOWSKA

Cyanotype. *See under* PHOTOGRAPHY, §I.

Cybei [Cibei], **Giovanni Antonio** (*b* Carrara, 3 Feb 1706; *d* Carrara, 7 Sept 1784). Italian sculptor. His father died when Cybei was young and it was his uncle, the sculptor Giovanni di Isidoro Baratta (*see* BARATTA, (3)), who suggested that the talented boy pursue a career in art. In about 1721 Cybei travelled to Rome to study with Agostino Cornacchini, whom he assisted in the carving of the marble equestrian statue of *Charlemagne* (*c.* 1720–25; Rome, St Peter's, portico). Cybei also studied painting. After a stay in Rome of about seven years, he returned to Carrara and worked with Baratta for nearly a decade. He assisted his uncle on several projects, including the *Four Doctors of the Church* (1728) for the chapel of S Uberto at Venaria Reale, a royal hunting-lodge near Turin, but he also created works of his own design when not working for Baratta. Among these is the marble figure of *St Augustine* for the altar niche of the Caraffa Chapel in Sarzana Cathedral. In 1739 Cybei took holy orders, determining at that point to give up sculpture; but a second trip to Rome renewed his interest, and he remained active in the art for the rest of his life. A few years after his uncle's death in 1747, Cybei became an independent artist with his own workshop. His numerous statues and ornamental sculptures of urns and trophies decorated gardens across Europe and even in Moscow, although many are of indifferent quality. One of Cybei's first major independent works is the funerary monument to *Cardinal Giulio Alberoni* (1753; Piacenza, S Lazzaro), which features a marble likeness of the deceased. Cybei also realized his abilities in portraiture with busts of many contemporary figures such as *Lodovico Antonio Muratori* (1774; Modena, Bib. Estense). In the same year he produced another equestrian statue, the colossal *Francesco III d'Este, Duke of Modena*, erected in the Piazza S Agostino in Modena. Destroyed during the French occupation in 1796, the composition is known through a gesso modello (Carrara, Accad. B.A. & Liceo A.). Cybei became the first director of the Accademia at Carrara in 1769. His works generally follow the late Baroque style of Camillo Rusconi and Baratta. However, he was aware of the increasing classical tendencies in mid-18th-century Italian art, and his portraits in particular demonstrate a more classical style.

BIBLIOGRAPHY

G. Tiraboschi: *Biblioteca modense: O, notizie della vita e delle opere degli scrittori nati negli stati del serenissimo signor Duca di Modena*, VI/ii (Modena, 1786/*R* Bologna, 1970)

E. Gerini: *Memorie storiche d'illustri scrittori e di uomini insigni dell'antica e moderna Lunigiana*, i (Massa, 1824)

G. Campori: *Memorie biografiche degli scultori, architetti, pittori . . . nativi di Carrara* (Modena, 1873)

Cycladic. Culture that flourished during the Greek Bronze Age in the Cyclades, a large archipelago in the Aegean Sea between southern Greece and Turkey (see fig. 1). The

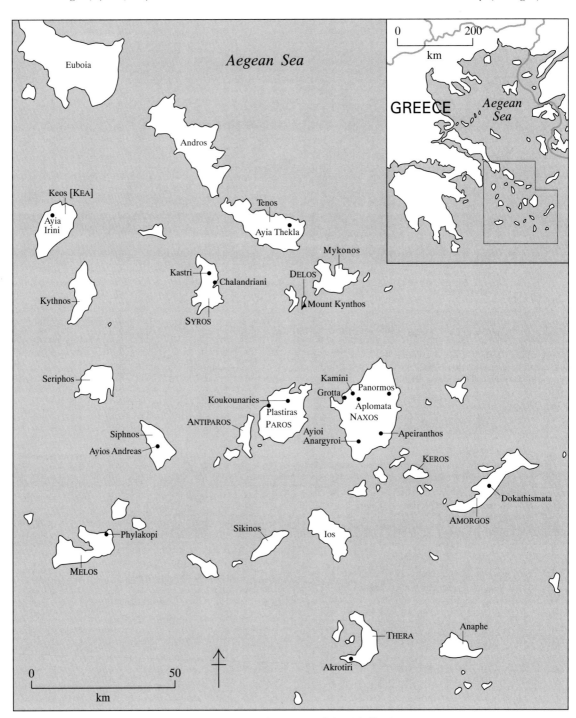

1. Map of the Cyclades; those areas with separate entries in this dictionary are distinguished by CROSS-REFERENCE TYPE

islands, whose name derives from *kuklos* ('circle') because they encircled the holy island of Delos, are bounded to the south by the much larger island of Crete. They were both probably first settled in the Early Neolithic period by peoples from western Anatolia (now Turkey), but in the Bronze Age the Cyclades and Crete (*see* MINOAN) developed their own distinctive art and architecture, in each case strongly influenced by the islands' natural environment.

For the later history of the islands, *see* GREECE, ANCIENT and the modern Hellenic Republic of GREECE.

GENERAL BIBLIOGRAPHY

J. Bent: *The Cyclades* (London, 1885)
U. Kahrstedt: 'Zur Kykladenkultur', *Mitt. Dt. Archäol. Insts: Athen. Abt.*, xxxviii (1913), pp. 148–86
H. R. Hall: *The Civilization of Greece in the Bronze Age* (London, 1928)
E. Vermeule: *Greece in the Bronze Age* (Chicago, 1964, 5/1972)
P. M. Warren: *The Aegean Civilizations: From Ancient Crete to Mycenae* (Oxford, 1975, 2/1989)
C. Zervos: *L'Art des Cyclades du début à la fin de l'âge du bronze: 2500–1100 avant notre ère* (Paris, 1975)
Kunst und Kultur der Kykladeninseln im 3. Jahrtausend v. Chr. (exh. cat., ed. J. Thimme; Karlsruhe, Bad. Landesmus., 1976); Eng. trans. as *Art and Culture of the Cyclades*, ed. P. Getz-Preziosi (Karlsruhe, 1977)
S. Hood: *The Arts in Prehistoric Greece*, Pelican Hist. A. (Harmondsworth, 1978)
J. F. Cherry: 'Four Problems in Cycladic Prehistory', *Papers in Cycladic Prehistory*, ed. J. L. Davis and J. F. Cherry (Los Angeles, 1979), pp. 22–47
C. Renfrew: 'The Cycladic World and its Art', *Cycladic Art: The Ancient Sculpture and Ceramics of the N. P. Goulandris Collection* (exh. cat., ed. C. Doumas; London, BM, 1983), pp. 9–13
J. A. MacGillivray and R. L. N. Barber, eds: *The Prehistoric Cyclades* (Edinburgh, 1984)
H. van Effenterre: *Les Egéens: Aux origines de la Grèce, Chypre, Cyclades, Crète et Mycènes* (Paris, 1986)
R. L. N. Barber: *The Cyclades in the Bronze Age* (London, 1987)

I. Introduction. II. Architecture. III. Pottery. IV. Stone figurines. V. Stone vases. VI. Wall paintings. VII. Metalwork. VIII. Ivory and bone. IX. Museums, collections and exhibitions.

I. Introduction.

1. Environment. 2. Trade. 3. Religion and iconography. 4. Chronological overview.

1. ENVIRONMENT. The islands of the Cyclades are widely scattered, and the early settlements were small and closely knit, giving each island a certain sense of isolation and individualism. The sea served both to divide and unite, a barrier as well as a channel of communication; it was an important source of food but also provided access for the pirates who plundered the islands or used them as a haven. The islands have an arid climate and poor soil that has never been well watered or easily worked. Cycladic landscapes are strikingly rugged (the southern island of THERA is volcanic), with steep limestone hills and often high and impressive cliffs, creating stark contrasts in shape, colour and texture. Colours are bright and vivid, ranging from the deep blue of the ever-visible sea to the white of the natural marble, the verdure of olive trees and vines and the golden glow of the sandy beaches. In the Bronze Age the Cyclades had few natural resources: there were small deposits of copper, but the islands' principal wealth was in silver and lead, in marble and in the black volcanic glass called obsidian.

These environmental factors clearly influenced Cycladic art and architecture from earliest times. From the beginning of the Bronze Age, many Cycladic settlements were sited in naturally defensible locations, presumably to counter the risk of seaborne raids, and some were strengthened by stout walls and projecting towers or bastions; Chalandriani on SYROS is a typical example. Settlements were small, with populations of at most a few hundred people crowded together in irregular houses that hugged the hill slopes. Even in the later Bronze Age, when settlements grew larger and trading ships regularly plied the seas between the islands, the Greek mainland and Crete, the two principal towns—Ayia Irini on the island of KEA and Phylakopi on MELOS—were defended by very substantial walls and towers, within which the tightly packed houses were separated by meandering alleys and passages rather than streets. In the wealthier houses, interior walls were decorated with lively frescoes with brightly coloured scenes of fishermen, boats, dolphins, rugged landscapes and harbour towns, which echoed the world outside.

The influence of the natural environment in which their makers lived is most clearly identified in Early Cycladic artefacts. Most pottery vessels and stone vases are simply shaped and are decorated with restrained and uncomplicated motifs. The exception is the use, on both stone and clay vessels, of free-running spirals; these in some instances at least, were doubtless inspired by the sea, since long-oared ships are depicted cutting through such rolling spirals on the bases of the flat-bottomed dishes known as 'frying-pans' (*see* §III, 1 and fig. 5b below). Though some of these ships display fish emblems on their prows, they are more likely to have been used by traders or pirates than by fishermen. Other sea creatures are surprisingly rare in Early Cycladic art, although a few sea birds apparently occur on the top of pin shafts or occasionally as amulets. Animal life on the islands was restricted, and representations of mammals are rare and confined to some amulets and a handful of stone vases. Apart from two charming hedgehogs holding miniature vases (Early Cycladic II; Athens, N. Archaeol. Mus.) and a single stone vase in the form of a pig (Early Cycladic II–III; Athens, Mus. Cyclad. & Anc. Gr. A.), the only mammals to appear in Early Cycladic art are sheep and goats, which have always been the principal domestic livestock on the islands. The use of hard white marble for the manufacture of vases, amulets and, primarily, figurines no doubt played its part in the development of a repertory of shapes and styles marked above all by its simplicity of line. Even the most elaborate figurines, portraying seated lyre-players (see fig. 2), are remarkably plain and apparently uncomplicated, though they are not the simple products they initially appear to be (*see* §IV below).

BIBLIOGRAPHY

A. Philippson and E. Kirsten: *Die griechischen Landschaften*, 4 vols (Frankfurt, 1950–59)

2. TRADE. Situated between the west coast of Turkey, mainland Greece and the island of Crete, the Cyclades inevitably played an important part in trans-Aegean trade from early times. One of their few useful resources was the obsidian found on MELOS (the best source in the

2. Early Cycladic lyre-player, marble, h. 225 mm, from Keros, Early Cycladic II (Athens, National Archaeological Museum)

Aegean), which was being used both in Crete and on the Greek mainland well before 5000 BC (i.e. before metals were commonplace and before the Cyclades were settled) to make knives, scrapers, razors and arrowheads. Actual commerce between the Cyclades and Crete, and to a lesser extent with the mainland, began sporadically at the end of the Neolithic period. With the development of metalworking in the Aegean in the 3rd millennium BC, however, trading contacts apparently increased significantly, perhaps mainly in consequence of the search for sources of metal. Though both Crete and the Cyclades had a little copper, they had to obtain gold from Macedonia or possibly Anatolia and tin from Iran or even further east. In return, the Cyclades offered obsidian, marble, emery, silver, lead and the products of Cycladic craftsmen. Most frequent among the latter were folded-arm figurines of white marble, whose distribution not only throughout the Cyclades but also in Crete, central Greece and the Dodecanese demonstrates their widespread appeal. Marble vases and boxes and a few clay vases were also exported, together with daggers and spearheads of arsenical bronze, which have been found at sites throughout the Aegean, especially along the northern coast of Crete. On the basis of the archaeological evidence, the tide of trade at this time flowed from the Cyclades to Crete. Most of this trade was apparently conducted in long, high-prowed, low-sterned ships driven by 40 or 50 rowers, judging from several drawings of such ships preserved on 'frying pans' (see fig. 5b below), and three lead models of ships from the island of Naxos (Early Cycladic II–III; Oxford, Ashmolean). At the end of the Early Cycladic period, however, sailing ships appeared in the Aegean apparently for the first time; they were depicted on Minoan sealstones from Crete, and the Minoans may well have been the first to use them in this part of the Mediterranean. Certainly from this time onwards there is evidence of a marked increase in Cretan exports to the Cyclades and a consequent shift in the balance of trade in favour of the Minoans. Kamares-style painted pottery from Crete (see MINOAN, §III, 4) began to be used widely in settlements throughout the Cyclades, along with smaller quantities of attractive Minoan stone vases; other Cretan exports found in Cycladic towns and villages include bronze weapons and trinkets. Cycladic lead and silver were still exported to Crete, but what other Cycladic items found a market there at this time is unknown. Minoan trade with the Cyclades was at its height in the Late Cycladic I–II period, when greater quantities of Cretan pottery and stone vases than ever before reached such islands as Thera, Melos and Keos. Some Minoan traders almost certainly settled in several of the Cycladic harbour towns. In contrast, the handful of contemporary Cycladic bird vases discovered on Crete are the sole evidence of Cycladic exports at this date.

BIBLIOGRAPHY

A. Köster: *Studien zur Geschichte des antiken Seewesens* (Munich, 1934)
R. Barnett: 'Early Shipping in the Near East', *Antiquity*, xxxii (1958), pp. 220–30
K. Branigan: 'Minoan Colonialism', *Annu. Brit. Sch. Athens*, lxxvi (1981), pp. 23–33
N. Gale and Z. Stos-Gale: 'Lead and Silver in the Ancient Aegean', *Sci. Amer.*, ccxliv (1981), pp. 142–52
P. F. Johnston: 'Bronze Age Cycladic Ships', *Temple University Aegean Symposium 7: Philadelphia, 1982*, pp. 1–8
J. C. Overbeck: 'The Hub of Commerce: Keos and Middle Helladic Greece', *Temple University Aegean Symposium 7: Philadelphia, 1982*, pp. 38–49
S. Stucynski: 'Cycladic Imports in Crete: A Brief Survey', *Temple University Aegean Symposium 7: Philadelphia, 1982*, pp. 50–59

KEITH BRANIGAN

3. RELIGION AND ICONOGRAPHY. The cult practices of the Cycladic islanders before the Late Bronze Age are little known, though they clearly had a religious life that developed independently of that on Crete, the major cultural power of the Middle and Late Bronze Age in the Aegean. Early Cycladic I violin-shaped figurines representing rotund women, apparently based on Neolithic prototypes, may have been fertility symbols (see §IV, 1 and fig. 8 below), and the famous marble folded-arm figurines (see fig. 10 below) may also have had a religious function. Many of the marble statues come from tombs, where they would have served as funerary goods, but others, too large for burial in typical Cycladic graves, may have been cult statues; some may also have been in daily use, as indicated by ancient repairs. Apart from figurines, the Early Cycladic 'frying-pans', with markings that have been interpreted as female genitalia, may also have been related to some type of fertility cult.

By the Late Bronze Age, Cycladic art and, evidently, religion were dominated by Minoan culture and iconography (see MINOAN, §I, 3), though some individuality on the part of the islanders can be discerned. Minoan-type pier-and-door partitions and so-called 'lustral basins' (*adyta*; see MINOAN, §II, 3) were constructed at Akrotiri on

Thera, and wall paintings there and at Phylakopi on Melos and Ayia Irini on Kea depicted Minoan themes of nature, the concept of cyclical rebirth, rites of passage and initiation, and cult scenes involving priests or priestesses and deities identical to those found in Minoan art. Lilies, dolphins, blue monkeys and other animals and plants associated with Minoan cult occur frequently. It is interesting to note that while on Crete the blue monkey occurs in what could reasonably be interpreted as a domestic garden scene in the *Saffron Gatherer* fresco from Knossos (Herakleion, Archaeol. Mus.), on Thera the creature is explicitly associated with cult.

Cult equipment used on the islands appears to be the same as that used by the Minoans, including offering tables painted with lilies and other sacred motifs, horns of consecration, even snakes, as depicted on the head of the girl in the *Priestess* fresco in the West House at Akrotiri. Minoan cult statuary is echoed in the terracotta female figures (mostly Late Cycladic II) found in a shrine building (House A) at Ayia Irini on Kea (*see* §4(iii) below).

For more detailed discussion of Cycladic iconography, including 'civic' or secular themes as well as its religious aspects, *see* §VI below; *see also* §4 below. For Minoan religion and iconography *see* MINOAN, §I, 3.

BIBLIOGRAPHY
C. Doumas: *Early Bronze Age Burial Habits in the Cyclades*, Stud. Medit. Archaeol., lxviii (Göteborg, 1977)
Sanctuaries and Cults in the Aegean Bronze Age. Proceedings of the First International Symposium at the Swedish Institute at Athens: Athens, 1980
N. Marinatos: *Art and Religion on Thera* (Athens, 1984)
C. Renfrew: *The Archaeology of Cult: The Sanctuary at Philakopi* (London, 1985)
B. Rutkowski: *The Cult Places in the Aegean* (New Haven and London, 1986)
Early Greek Cult Practice. Proceedings of the Fifth International Symposium at the Swedish Institute at Athens: Athens, 1986
L. Morgan: *The Miniature Wall Paintings from Thera: A Study in Aegean Culture and Iconography* (Cambridge, 1988)

4. CHRONOLOGICAL OVERVIEW. Archaeologists divide the Cycladic Bronze Age into three periods: Early, Middle and Late Cycladic (EC, MC, LC). These are themselves subdivided on the basis of changing pottery styles and are broadly parallel to those adopted for the contemporary cultures of Crete and the Greek mainland (*see* MINOAN, §I, 4 and HELLADIC, §I, 4). Although chronological periods (see fig. 3a) are separated into discrete units, there was some overlap from one phase to the next: the inhabitants of one site might retain older pottery types for many years while another site changed to new styles. This 'regionalism' was particularly common during the Neolithic and EC periods and at the end of LC.

Approximate absolute dates for these chronological periods are derived from radiocarbon analysis and from links first with Crete and indirectly with Egypt and the Near East, where relatively secure dates are based on historical dynastic sequences (*see* EGYPT, ANCIENT, fig. 2, and ANCIENT NEAR EAST, fig. 2). Nevertheless, the field of Aegean Bronze Age chronology has been the subject of considerable scholarly controversy since the 1980s, and many archaeologists believe that dates should be higher by a century. This last argument is based largely on new radiocarbon dates suggesting that the eruption of the volcanic island of THERA took place *c.* 1625 BC instead of

Final Neolithic	*c.* 4000-*c.* 3500/3000 BC
Early Cycladic (EC)	*c.* 3500/3000-*c.* 2000 BC
EC I	*c.* 3500/3000-*c.* 2800/2600 BC
EC II	*c.* 2800/2600-*c.* 2300 BC
EC IIIA	*c.* 2300-*c.* 2150 BC
EC IIIB	*c.* 2150-*c.* 2000 BC
Middle Cycladic (MC)	*c.* 2000-*c.* 1600 BC
Late Cycladic (LC)	*c.* 1600-*c.* 1050 BC
(a) LC I	*c.* 1600-*c.* 1500 BC
LC II	*c.* 1500-*c.* 1390 BC
LC IIIA	*c.* 1390-*c.* 1335 BC
LC IIIB	*c.* 1335-*c.* 1190 BC
LC IIIC	*c.* 1190-*c.* 1050 BC
(b) LC I	*c.* 1700-*c.* 1610 BC
LC II	*c.* 1610-*c.* 1440 BC
LC IIIA-B	*c.* 1440-*c.* 1180 BC

3. Chronological chart showing major Cycladic periods with subdivisions: (a) traditional chronology; (b) alternative chronology of the Late Cycladic period

c. 1525 BC, making the beginning of the Late Bronze Age approximately 100 years earlier (see fig. 3b). However, not all archaeologists are convinced of the efficacy of the new scientific dating methods for the periods in question, not least because the higher chronology tends to weaken proven links between Crete and the mainland and ancient Egypt. The dating system in figure 3a is the traditional chronology accepted by most archaeologists, although individual scholars may vary the details.

C. D. FORTENBERRY

(i) Early Cycladic. (ii) Middle Cycladic. (iii) Late Cycladic.

(i) Early Cycladic. The Final Neolithic period in the Aegean was marked by intense activity in the islands. The centrally located Cyclades acted as a melting pot of diverse cultural elements that the islanders readily absorbed and adapted to their own taste and needs. The distinctive culture that developed there at the beginning of the Early Cycladic (EC) period maintained, at least initially, its integrity and identity, particularly in its art.

The Early Cycladic period is also known as the Early Bronze Age (EBA), that is, the period when metals were first used on the islands. These included a little gold but principally lead, silver, copper and arsenical bronze, all of which were obtained either locally or from the mainland of Greece or Anatolia. Once Cycladic craftsmen had developed the appropriate moulds and techniques, they were able to cast objects into almost any shape. Even so, casting was used mainly for producing functional items, such as tools and weapons, whereas most products made by early Cycladic metalsmiths, particularly objects intended to ornament or embellish, were made partly or entirely by hammering sheet metal (*see* §VII below). Among the latter are many items of EC jewellery, including some charming bronze and silver pins with heads fashioned in the form of rams (see fig. 15 below) or resting sea birds (e.g. Athens, N. Archaeol. Mus.), as well as others crowned with pairs of spirals. Bangles and armlets are for the most part of simple form and decoration, but the repoussé frieze on a silver diadem from the island of Syros (see fig. 14 below) attests to the advanced metalworking skills of the EC craftsman; the frieze mixes abstract or perhaps symbolic motifs with naturalistic representations of animals, including two birdlike figures and two quadrupeds that appear to be dogs (they even have collars!). The piece is unique among extant Cycladic work but resembles some gold diadems from northern Crete (e.g. from Mochlos, EC II; Ayios Nikolaos, Archaeol. Mus.), where animals were far more frequently depicted at this time. Cycladic craftsmen of the EC period also manufactured attractive shallow bowls in silver (e.g. Oxford, Ashmolean); they may have made other vessels in silver, though none survive.

The recurrence of some vase shapes in metal, clay and stone emphasizes the extent to which works in one medium influenced those in another. Until the appearance of bronze and copper, stone had been used largely, though not exclusively, for tools and implements. The introduction of bronze provided a new material that could produce finer cutting edges and be cast into a much wider range of shapes. Yet as the demand for stone tools and weapons declined, so the volume and variety of other products in stone, especially vases and figurines, seems to have grown. Pottery did not face the same challenge from the new materials, but the prestige value of silver vessels is probably reflected by the appearance of clay vessels clearly imitating metallic shapes.

Pottery of the EC period (see §III, 1 below) seems unspectacular when compared to Minoan pottery or to the contemporary products of Cycladic stoneworkers. The repertory of shapes is rather limited. Vessel types from EC I include a globular flask with narrow neck and suspension lugs, normally decorated with incised all-over herringbone pattern (e.g. from Antiparos, London, BM), and a circular, lidded box or pyxis decorated in similar style (see fig. 5a below). In EC II (sometimes called the Keros–Syros culture) two unusual shapes become popular: the enigmatic 'frying-pan' (see fig. 5b below) and the pedestal jar, a simply decorated storage vessel with a rather heavy body and a broad, deep neck, perched on a narrow conical pedestal (e.g. from Chalandriani on Syros; Athens, N. Archaeol. Mus.). The shape is difficult to make in clay and may well have been inspired by contemporary products in stone.

Cycladic stone vase production (see §V below) began in the last centuries of the Neolithic period but reached its height in the late EC I to early EC II, when the repertory of shapes at least equalled that of ceramic shapes. Most stone vases were made from island marble, but a small and interesting group was made of greenish chlorite-schist or bluish steatite, both softer materials that allowed more elaborate shapes and more intricately carved decoration. Chlorite-schist or steatite was used for cylindrical boxes as well as some intriguing boxes apparently representing granaries, cylindrical storage vats built on a raised floor supported on piles and reached by flights of steps (e.g.

from Melos, EC II; Munich, Staatl. Antikensamml.). There are a few simplified marble versions of the 'granary' boxes and one charming marble vase in the shape of a pig. However, the majority of works in marble are less ambitious and consist merely of low bowls, cups and dishes, along with pedestal jars (see fig. 11 below), goblets and cylindrical lidded boxes with slightly more elaborate forms. Few marble vases are decorated; most are elegantly simple.

Elegance and simplicity are also the hallmark of the most outstanding EC works of arts, the marble figurines, which, like stone vases, were produced in EC I and EC II (see §IV, 1 below). The earliest were either flat, 'violin-shaped' figures (see fig. 8 below) or rotund steatopygous seated ladies, both of which were based on prototypes made in the Late Neolithic period. Flat abstractions and full-rounded human figures continued to be modelled in stone throughout the EC period, but a new type, the folded-arm figurine (see fig. 10 below), was far more widely produced. The folded-arm figurines appear in five or six principal varieties, with different chronological or geographical origins. The bodies of these marble figures, which range in size from 100 mm to 1500 mm, are reduced to essential forms and portrayed with a superb blend of harmony and balance. Detailed study suggests that it is possible to identify the work of individual masters from among the Cycladic artists of 4500 years ago.

At the transition from EC II to EC III, Cycladic life and material culture seem to have changed radically, almost certainly owing to the arrival of a new population element. The development of large harbour towns following these disturbances was apparently accompanied by changes in the means of artistic expression. The production of both stone figurines and stone vases decreased considerably and finally ceased, and Cycladic pottery and architecture began to show signs of the influence of Anatolian craftsmen and artists, suggesting that the immigrants had come from Asia Minor. Fortifications also appeared on the islands for the first time at the end of the EC period (probably EC IIIA), though these show similarities with fortified settlements on the Greek mainland.

BIBLIOGRAPHY

C. Renfrew: 'Cycladic Metallurgy and the Aegean Early Bronze Age', *Amer. J. Archaeol.*, lxxi (1967), pp. 1–20
——: 'The Development and Chronology of the Early Cycladic Figurines', *Amer. J. Archaeol.*, lxxiii (1969), pp. 1–32
——: *The Emergence of Civilisation: The Cyclades and the Aegean in the Third Millennium BC* (London, 1972)
Kunst und Kultur der Kykladeninseln im 3. Jahrtausend v. Chr. (exh. cat., ed. J. Thimme; Karlsruhe, Bad. Landesmus., 1976); Eng. trans. as *Art and Culture of the Cyclades*, ed. P. Getz-Preziosi (Karlsruhe, 1977)
Cycladic Art: Ancient Pottery and Sculpture from the N. P. Goulandris Collection (exh. cat., ed. C. Doumas; London, BM, 1983)
J. L. Fitton, ed.: *Cycladica: Studies in Memory of N. P. Goulandris* (London, 1984)
P. M. Warren and V. Hankey: *Aegean Bronze Age Chronology* (Bristol, 1989)
D. A. Hardy and A. C. Renfrew, eds: *Chronology*, iii of *Thera and the Aegean World III* (London, 1990)
P. M. Warren: 'The Minoan Civilisation of Crete and the Volcano of Thera', *J. Anc. Chron. Forum*, iv (1990–91), pp. 29–39 [no. 22 with previous bibliog.]
P. James: *Centuries of Darkness* (London, 1991)

(ii) Middle Cycladic. After the inventive and innovative EC period, Cycladic culture developed steadily but unspectacularly during the Middle Cycladic (MC) period. Little is known of the art and architecture of this period, partly because so little survives. The houses within fortified settlements, such as Ayia Irini on Kea and Phylakopi on Melos, are perhaps better built than their EC predecessors, but they are still small, ill-planned, single-storey buildings with one to four undecorated rooms. The art of the MC period is represented almost entirely by pottery, which is generally uninspired and unattractive. The two most distinctive varieties are Dark Burnished wares and Cycladic White. The burnished pottery, though highly polished, is unimaginative and used on a limited repertory of goblets, bowls and jars. Cycladic White, with a moderately fine pale fabric and matt brown-to-black painted decoration, offered more scope for imaginative surface treatment, but the opportunity was rarely seized. The exceptions to the general mediocrity of MC pottery are the Black-and-red style beaked jugs. They are not elegantly shaped (see fig. 6a below), but their bent-back spouts have a certain haughty vitality, and their decoration is more interesting and more colourful than that of other vessels. The most characteristic Black-and-red jugs are decorated with birds (see §III, 2 below). These bird vases are particularly associated with the island of Melos, but they found their way to other islands and in time to both Crete (e.g. from Knossos, Middle Minoan II–III B; Oxford, Ashmolean) and mainland Greece. Already, however, they were greatly outnumbered by the flow of painted Cretan vases to the Cyclades, a trade reflecting the richness of the Minoan ceramic repertory at this time and the poverty of the Cycladic one.

BIBLIOGRAPHY

R. L. N. Barber: 'The Cyclades in the Middle Bronze Age', *Thera and the Aegean World I*, ed. C. Doumas (London, 1978), pp. 367–79

KEITH BRANIGAN

(iii) Late Cycladic. By Late Cycladic (LC) I, Akrotiri on Thera, Phylakopi on Melos and Ayia Irini on Kea were thriving settlements whose artists drew inspiration from Minoan Crete while expressing native individuality. Major rebuilding was undertaken as Minoan cultural domination grew. The period is traditionally thought to have ended with the volcanic eruption of Thera, the ash from which preserved the town of Akrotiri and its art for posterity. In LC II, Minoan influence at Phylakopi and Ayia Irini was still strong, but at Ayia Irini connections with the mainland Helladic culture (apparent to a lesser degree in the islands in LC I) increased.

Cycladic towns in LC I and II were composed of blocks of houses separated by pathways. The walls were generally of rubble with brick for the upper storeys; internal walls were plastered. At Akrotiri, however, some of the houses are free-standing, and the pathways open on to public squares. This and such features as ashlar masonry, wooden frameworks, central columns, pier-and-door partitions (multiple internal entrances controlling light and space) and 'lustral basins' (sunken areas used for ritual purposes) are Minoan (see MINOAN, §II, 3). As on Crete, the lower floors were used for workshops and storage, the upper rooms for living. Both Phylakopi and Ayia Irini were fortified. At Phylakopi a mansion served as the administrative centre, as did a large building known as House A at Ayia Irini. A free-standing temple stood near the gateway entrance to the town of Ayia Irini, a long narrow building with three rooms, a passage, hearth and benches; it continued in use during LC III.

The wall paintings of Thera (see §VI, 1 below) were stunningly well preserved by volcanic ash. Every building had one or more painted rooms, with scenes from nature, cult and popular festivals. The building Xeste 3 held a complex of paintings relating to initiatory rites of young girls, while the West House had miniature friezes relating to a nautical festival. Festivals and nature were also the subjects of miniature friezes on Kea; other paintings there display a preference for abstract designs. Since many of the walls at Phylakopi were cleared during the Mycenaean occupation, the only building with substantial remains is the Pillar Crypt complex, with nature scenes and a cult scene.

During LC I and II local Cycladic pottery existed alongside imported Minoan wares and their imitations (see §III, 3 below). Typical shapes included the beaked jug and hole-mouthed jar. Motifs were mainly taken from nature but included abstract designs and griffins. There were also Helladic imports, especially on Kea. On Melos, local Black-and-red designs of birds, fish/dolphin and plant motifs were popular. On Thera, spirals and floral motifs predominated, while swallows, dolphins and goats were the subjects of local polychrome pottery. Polychrome tables of offerings—three-legged, flat-toppped vessels—were found on Kea (wave designs), Melos (plant fragment) and Thera (dolphins and marine vegetation). Polychrome kymbe (bath-shaped containers) were found only on Thera, painted with scenes from nature.

Over 50 unique terracotta sculptures of female figures, ranging in height from 600 mm to life-size, were found in the temple on Kea. They stand or dance with their hands on their hips and are dressed in full skirts, heavy girdles and breast-exposing jackets; some have garlands. The statues were built around wooden poles; the skirts are hollow, made up in coils, and the breasts were formed over pieces of wood or, in some cases, conical cups. The finished surface was then painted, though little paint remains. Most were made in LC II.

In LC III settlers arrived from the mainland. The destruction of Ayia Irini *c.* 1450 had been caused by an earthquake, but that of Phylakopi was due to Mycenaean incursion. Both towns were rebuilt, and at Phylakopi a Mycenaean-style megaron was constructed over the earlier mansion (*c.* 1380 BC) (see §II, 3 below). A sanctuary was built near the city wall, composed of a West Shrine (*c.* 1360 BC)—a large room with altars and a smaller room for cult equipment—and a smaller East Shrine (*c.* 1260 BC) reached through a court with a stone bench and a baetyl (holy stone). There was also a megaron at the important settlement at Grotta on Naxos. In the Cyclades, as on the mainland, these were unsettled times: new fortifications were built at Phylakopi, and other defensive sites were occupied at Ayios Andreas on Siphnos and Koukounaries on Paros.

A large, wheelmade, female statuette found in the sanctuary at Phylakopi is painted with motifs from contemporary Mycenaean pottery. Also of Mycenaean type are the wheelmade bovine figures, smaller animal figurines, groups of chariot and oxen, furniture and seated figurines. Two bronze Reshef ('smiting god') figures of Near Eastern origin and a local miniature gold-leaf head were also found (Melos Mus.), as were several sealstones with animal themes. A number of unusual male figures retain local styles. A series of ivory plaques with scenes of warriors and animals in Mycenaean or Cypro-Mycenaean style was found in a votive deposit below the Sanctuary of Artemis on Delos. Gold jewellery, terracotta figurines and a bronze Reshef figure were found in the same deposit. Mycenaean pottery replaced local wares and remained popular throughout the late phase of LC III, although there is increasing evidence of influence from the Dodecanese, Crete and Cyprus as well.

BIBLIOGRAPHY

K. Scholes: 'The Cyclades in the Later Bronze Age: A Synopsis', *Annu. Brit. Sch. Athens*, li (1956), pp. 9–40
R. L. N. Barber: 'Phylakopi 1911 and the History of the Later Cycladic Bronze Age', *Annu. Brit. Sch. Athens*, lxix (1974), pp. 1–53
C. Renfrew: 'Phylakopi and the Late Bronze I Period in the Cyclades', *Thera and the Aegean World I*, ed. C. Doumas (London, 1978), pp. 403–21
J. L. Davis and J. F. Cherry, eds: *Papers in Cycladic Prehistory* (Los Angeles, 1979)
R. L. N. Barber: 'The Late Cycladic Period: A Review', *Annu. Brit. Sch. Athens*, lxxvi (1981), pp. 1–21
The Minoan Thalassocracy: Myth and Reality. Proceedings of the Third International Symposium at the Swedish Institute in Athens: Athens, 1982
E. Schofield: 'The Western Cyclades and Crete: A "Special Relationship"', *Oxford J. Archaeol.*, i (1982), pp. 9–25
J. A. Macgillivray and R. L. N. Barber, eds: *The Prehistoric Cyclades* (Edinburgh, 1984)

LYVIA MORGAN

II. Architecture.

The Cyclades have abundant and accessible sources of stone, which was used for building from the Late Neolithic period. Mud brick was sometimes also used, and structures of perishable material may have existed, though there is little surviving evidence. Floors were mostly earthen, and roofs were made of branches and concrete.

1. EARLY CYCLADIC. The first Early Cycladic (EC) settlements are not well known but were certainly small

4. Triangle Square, Akrotiri, Thera, LC; view looking south with Building Complex Delta on the left and the West House on the right

and unplanned; the houses were modest. By EC II, however, the village at Ayia Irini on KEA was tidily organized, with rather larger houses neatly made from flat slabs of local schist. A curious apsidal house-plan that occurs in EC IIIA was almost certainly one of the innovations introduced by immigrants from Anatolia.

Graves in EC cemeteries were solidly built, simple 'cists', with sides of large slabs or smaller stones or both, and were just large enough for a contracted body. Some had more than one storey, the original level being used as an ossuary once it was full and a new burial level had been added on top. Many had platforms for funerary rites constructed above them. One cemetery, Ayioi Anargyroi on Naxos (*see* NAXOS, §1), had a large public platform serving the entire burial area.

Fortifications began to appear in the later part of the Early Cycladic period (probably in EC IIIA). The remote mountain-top site at Kastri on SYROS was defended by a wall with projecting horseshoe-shaped towers and by an additional outwork. It is unique in the Cyclades but is somewhat similar to the defences at Lerna on the Greek mainland dating from the Early Helladic II period. The tiny fort at Panormos in south-west Naxos and the circuit wall at Mt Kynthos on Delos (*see* DELOS, §1) are probably of the same period.

2. MIDDLE CYCLADIC. In the Middle Cycladic (MC) evidence for house types is sparse. A new settlement at Phylakopi on MELOS (on the site of the EC IIIB 'First City', which had been less elaborately constructed) was laid out on a rough grid-plan and had somewhat larger houses. Cist graves and platforms continue to be found, some, such as those at Ayia Irini, being quite elaborate.

The most spectacular MC architecture is found in the fortifications. Those at Ayia Irini, from the later part of the period, enclosed much of the site, were at least 5 m high and consisted in part of roughly squared ashlar masonry with massive towers at intervals. An earlier MC system at the site enclosed a smaller area and had horseshoe-shaped bastions. Phylakopi may also have had a fortified wall at this time.

3. LATE CYCLADIC. The most substantial Cycladic architectural remains are naturally those of the latest phases of occupation, when recognizable public buildings first appeared. All the major Late Cycladic (LC) settlements—Ayia Irini, Phylakopi and Akrotiri (*see* THERA)—were to some extent divided up into blocks, though in different ways. Phylakopi was rebuilt for the second time at the beginning of the LC period, with a grid-plan as before, but at Ayia Irini the blocks (called 'houses' by the excavators, though they were almost certainly not individual houses in the modern sense) were irregular in size and shape and separated by narrow paved lanes. The roads had extensive drains laid beneath. At Akrotiri the town layout included both irregular blocks and independent structures (see fig. 4) not unlike Cretan 'villas' (*see* MINOAN, §II, 4). Some of these (e.g. the various buildings called 'Xestai') had façades entirely composed of fine ashlar masonry, which was employed sparingly on other Cycladic sites. This and certain other architectural features (pier-and-door partitions between rooms, a 'lustral basin') betray Cretan

inspiration, as indeed do the remarkable frescoed scenes found in some buildings (*see* §VI below). Some of the larger buildings at Akrotiri may have had a public (possibly ritual) function.

The temple at Ayia Irini dates from the beginning of the Late Bronze Age (though it had a precursor of unknown form on the same site). It is an independent structure (*c.* 20×5 m) divided into several rooms, some with stone benches, on which apparently stood a unique series of 50 large terracotta figures, dressed in Minoan style. Sacrificial hearths and some votive offerings were also found in the temple.

At Phylakopi in LC I there was a large 'mansion', on the site of which a palace or 'megaron' of distinctive Mycenaean type was later built. So close is its design to examples from the Greek mainland (e.g. at PYLOS) that it must imply the imposition of Mycenaean authority at the site. From this same period of Mycenaean domination at Phylakopi is a 'shrine' or, more correctly, a sanctuary (since it consists of two separate units linked by a paved courtyard with a standing stone). The structures are not particularly impressive, though the 'West Shrine' is large (*c.* 12×8 m), with a main room separated from a smaller side room by a wall with deep hatches, perhaps for the display of ritual objects, and platform-altars in the corners.

Fortifications continued to be a feature of LC-period architecture. Those at Phylakopi were greatly extended in the 13th century BC and were equipped with bastions, casemates and at least one internal staircase. The fortified settlement on the acropolis of Koukounaries on the island of PAROS also had a defensive wall on the lower slopes of the hill on which it was built, and Ayios Andreas on Siphnos had a wall with square towers. In funerary architecture cist tombs were replaced by rock-cut chamber tombs (e.g. at Aplomata on Naxos) and one or two crude versions of the Mycenaean tholos tomb (e.g. at Ayia Thekla on Tenos).

BIBLIOGRAPHY

T. D. Atkinson and others: *Excavations at Phylakopi in Melos* (London, 1904)

E. Bell: *Prehellenic Architecture in the Aegean* (London, 1926)

J. L. Caskey: 'Investigations in Keos, Part 1: Excavations and Explorations 1966–70', *Hesperia*, xl (1971), pp. 359–96

C. Doumas: 'Notes on Early Cycladic Architecture', *Archäol. Anz.*, lxxxvii (1972), pp. 151–70

——: 'Early Cycladic Architecture' and 'Early Cycladic Burials', *Art and Culture of the Cyclades*, ed. P. Getz-Preziosi (Karlsruhe, 1977), pp. 31–6 [Eng. trans. of *Kunst und Kultur der Kykladeninseln im 3. Jahrtausend v. Chr.* (exh. cat., ed. J. Thimme; Karlsruhe, Bad. Landesmus., 1976)]

C. P. Kardara: *Aplomata Naxou: Kineta euremata taphon A kai B* [Aplomata on Naxos: Portable finds from Tombs A and B] (Athens, 1977)

C. Renfrew: 'The Mycenaean Sanctuary at Phylakopi', *Antiquity*, lii (1978), pp. 7–15

——: 'Phylakopi and the Late Bronze I Period in the Cyclades', *Thera and the Aegean World I*, ed. C. Doumas (London, 1978), pp. 403–21

G. Despinis: 'Anaskaphe Tenou', *Praktika* (1979), pp. 228–35

C. Doumas: *Thera: Pompeii of the Ancient Aegean* (London, 1983)

W. W. Cummer and E. V. Schofield: *Ayia Irini: House A* (1984), iii of *Keos* (Mainz, 1977–)

G. F. Overbeck: 'The Development of Grave Types at Ayia Irini, Kea', *The Prehistoric Cyclades*, ed. J. A. MacGillivray and R. L. N. Barber (Edinburgh, 1984), pp. 114–18

C. Renfrew and others: *The Archaeology of Cult: The Sanctuary at Phylakopi* (London, 1985)

J. L. Davis: *Ayia Irini: Period V* (1986), v of *Keos* (Mainz, 1977–) [fortifications]

III. Pottery.

The Early and Middle Cycladic periods were times of innovation and individuality in island pottery. Subsequently, although local features can be discerned, they are insignificant compared with the stylistic influences of Minoan Crete and, later, Mycenean Greece. Although wheelmade pots from the end of the Early Bronze Age have been found, they were not common until the Late Cycladic period.

1. EARLY CYCLADIC. The earliest Cycladic pottery is relatively crude. The fabric is thick and coarse, though the surfaces are often burnished to a high and attractive lustre, most commonly in black, brown or reddish-brown. All the vessels are handmade, and decoration, when it occurs, always consists of incised rectilinear patterns. There are no curvilinear or figurative motifs. The incisions are filled with a white substance, making the patterns stand out sharply from the dark background, though the original effect is now usually diminished by the loss of the white filling or the deterioration of the burnish over time. The uses of the various vases are not always easy to determine, though pottery containers certainly fulfilled a wide range of functions. Two forms, the purposes of which are unknown, may be taken as examples: a globular flask (of which copies or exported specimens occur in northern Crete) and a circular pyxis (see fig. 5a). Some shapes found more commonly in cemeteries than in settlements may have had some specifically funerary purpose. One example is the 'hat-vase', which resembles an upturned hat and apparently contained offerings.

Towards the end of EC I the range of shapes increased, and some curvilinear motifs, such as running spirals, were introduced. A notable new form was the 'frying-pan', a shallow bowl with flat bottom, straight sides and a projecting handle that varies in form. The circular, flat area of the base was extensively and sometimes elaborately decorated with incised patterns. This vessel type is thought by some to have been filled with water and used as a mirror, though the fact that the handles are sometimes decorated to resemble the female vulva may suggest a more complex function. Later 'frying-pans' sometimes bear representations of boats (fig. 5b), providing some of the earliest evidence for shipping in the Aegean. Others are decorated with a frieze of running spirals encompassing a large star pattern.

During EC II the variety of shapes and motifs again increased, and two new decorative techniques were used: painting and stamping. The painted designs, which are neat and rectilinear, occur on a new fine fabric with a pale surface. Stamps were carved, probably from wood, and their designs were then pressed into the damp clay. In this sense stamping was simply a variation on the traditional practice of incision. A common stamped pattern, the *kerbschnitt*, is composed of a series of solid triangles set alternately in opposite directions. On some EC II 'frying-pans' the exuberance of the earlier incised spiral patterns was replaced by a dull, mechanical repetition of isolated spirals made by stamping. Important new shapes in EC II were the jug (fig. 5c) and 'sauceboat'. The latter is an odd and distinctive shape, again of uncertain function, which

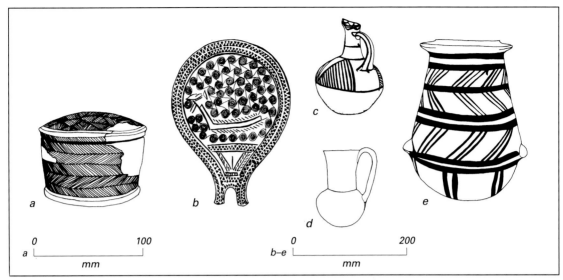

5. Early Cycladic pottery: (a) circular pyxis with incised decoration, h. 83 mm, EC I; (b) 'frying-pan' with incised and stamped decoration, h. 280 mm, EC II; (c) jug with painted decoration, h. 160 mm, EC II; (d) tankard with burnished surface, h. 132 mm, EC IIIA; (e) barrel jar with painted Geometric designs, h. 274 mm, EC IIIB

is often regarded as a typically mainland form (EH II; *see* HELLADIC, fig. 7) but is possibly of Cycladic origin. Another typical shape in EC II was the pedestalled jar with a trumpet-shaped or conical foot. Its decoration was relatively simple, comprising one or two friezes of incised herringbone patterns or running spirals around the neck and shoulder. This shape is also found in stone. Indeed, as in the preceding period, stone and clay vessels shared many forms.

Pottery fabrics, forms and motifs established in EC I and II did not entirely disappear with the radical changes that occurred in EC IIIA (though their range was certainly reduced). But the innovations of this late phase of EC are striking and appear to be due to Anatolian influence. The potter's wheel began to be used, especially for plates, though handmade vases remained predominant. The most interesting new fabric had a highly burnished finish, usually black or red, and some distinctive shapes, including the tankard (fig. 5d), the two-handled tankard (*depas amphikypellon*) and the high-beaked jug, immediately betray their Anatolian origin. There was little decorated pottery, but incised and painted designs persisted, the latter usually in the form of cross-hatching on stemmed cups. Some innovations in this period were purely local, such as the duck vase, a squat, humped vessel with a projecting spout, which became more common later. Spout-ends have an attractive leaf shape, which also continued in fashion.

The last phase of the Early Cycladic period (EC IIIB), which overlaps with the early Middle Bronze Age in neighbouring Aegean areas, is notable for local developments and for the influence it exerted on the Matt-painted pottery of the Greek mainland (*see* HELLADIC, §III, 2(ii)). The tradition of incised decoration continued on roughly burnished 'Dark-faced' vases (e.g. the duck vases, which sometimes bear modest figural scenes), but there was a great expansion of painted designs in the so-called Geometric style, which apparently originated on MELOS. Most

of the designs are in dark matt paint on a light surface, provided by covering the vase with a thin pale wash. (This decorative technique was then widely used in Syria and Cilicia in southern Anatolia.) Initially the painted motifs were probably almost entirely rectilinear, but they increasingly incorporated curvilinear elements. They were applied to some distinctive shapes: the barrel jar (fig. 5e), also found on the mainland, and the beaked jug, a developed version of the earlier type. At the end of the EC period, however, after the use of white-filled incision had ceased, patterns were sometimes painted in white on a dark ground, perhaps in an attempt to reproduce the effect of incising.

2. MIDDLE CYCLADIC. Although some aspects of the pottery of the Middle Cycladic (MC) period are directly derived from that of the preceding phase (e.g. the barrel jar and the beaked jug), some of the similarities are only general (e.g. the widespread use of a dark burnished fabric); and some elements are completely new, such as the Cycladic White fabric and the motifs that decorate it. There is a good deal of variation between the pottery of different islands, mostly in details of fabric and finish.

The two major classes of MC pottery are Cycladic White and Dark Burnished (see fig. 6). Of these, the most conservative is the Dark Burnished. Its fabric is fairly crude, but the surfaces, which were sometimes slipped first, are finely finished and can have a very high lustre. This pottery was most common in the earlier part of the period, when it was occasionally exported to sites in mainland Greece, including Lerna, Athens and Magnesia. Shapes were limited, consisting primarily of bowls, jars, stemmed goblets (fig. 6b) and angular vases imitating those found in Helladic Grey Minyan pottery, which, although imported into the Cyclades, is primarily associated with the mainland (*see* HELLADIC, §III, 2(ii)). Designs, occasionally quite elaborate, were sometimes painted in white and, less frequently, in black on the dark burnished surfaces. This kind of pottery occurs on all Middle Cycladic sites, but at the end of MC and in the Late Cycladic period it was replaced by a less prominent Red-washed variety with a thick, matt, cherry-coloured surface coat.

The finest examples of the second main type, Cycladic White, have a thin, smooth and well-levigated fabric and a consistent creamy colour, though there are many coarser pieces. Cycladic White pots are normally decorated with designs in a rather dusty matt black paint; however, there is an attractive subgroup particularly associated with Melos, the Black-and-red style, which combines burnished red elements, mainly large circles, with other motifs in the standard matt black against a white ground. The shapes of Cycladic White consist partly of adaptations of traditional forms such as the beaked jug (fig. 6a), with a taller neck and a longer spout, flanged at the tip; partly of local innovations (e.g. the 'panelled' cup, so called because the decoration is set in a panel on the visible side); and partly of forms borrowed from other areas, such as the bridge-spouted jar from Crete (*see* MINOAN, fig. 10).

The decorative motifs of Cycladic White are sometimes divided into a 'curvilinear' and a 'naturalistic' style. The earlier, curvilinear style consists mainly of non-figural designs, usually large spirals or irregular running loops arranged in zones, some clearly of Cretan derivation. One striking motif is the 'imp', a figure composed of essentially abstract elements, which appears on some Cycladic White beaked jugs. The later, naturalistic style comprises vegetable, floral and bird motifs, some again with parallels in Crete. Particularly common are the round-bodied birds, with wings, head and legs added in outline, that appear on Black-and-red jugs. Before the end of the MC period, the attractive Cycladic White fabric began to have a more sandy tinge, and some of its painted decoration was almost lustrous, changes that anticipated the most common local decorated pottery of the Late Cycladic period.

3. LATE CYCLADIC. During the two early phases of the Late Cycladic (LC) period Minoan vases were imported from Crete and imitated to a remarkable extent. Minoan teacups, Vapheio cups and bridge-spouted jars (see fig. 7a) were typical shapes, and, as in Crete, many of the decorative motifs were floral or vegetable. Spirals were also common.

Two decorative schemes characterize the copious finds of the early LC period from Akrotiri on THERA. One is arranged in zones and is close to Minoan designs; the other disposes motifs in a free field and seems characteristically Cycladic. The motifs are both abstract and figural, including dolphins, fish, quadrupeds and birds (7b). Colours used are either the traditional matt black or a mixture of red and black, sometimes with added white detail. Pottery of the LC I and II periods is also well represented at Phylakopi on Melos and Ayia Irini on Keos, and local variations of the Minoanizing trends are identifiable.

About the beginning of LC III, the Minoan stylistic influence on Cycladic pottery was replaced by Mycenaean. Typical Mycenaean forms—the kylix and, later, the deep bowl—became common. Though a period of change, it was not one of renewed local artistic initiative, and there were no longer any truly local shapes. It remains unclear how much of the pottery of the earlier part of LC III was

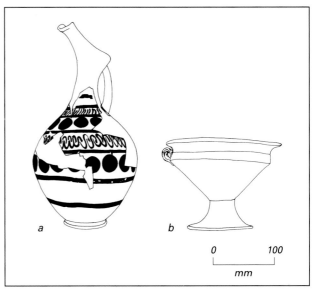

6. Middle Cycladic pottery: (a) Cycladic White beaked jug, h. 330 mm; (b) Dark Burnished stemmed goblet, h. 70 mm

locally produced and how much was imported. The fabric of most of the decorated vases suggests that they were produced abroad, but it seems improbable that all the fine wares were imported. Mycenaean imports certainly declined drastically during the later 13th century BC (LC IIIB), and subsequent production was locally based, even though remaining strongly Mycenaean in character. Cycladic pottery of the final stage of the Bronze Age (LC IIIC) essentially mirrors that of contemporary Mycenaean pottery on the mainland, though there are some local trends, the stirrup jars with stylized octopus decoration (fig. 7c), particularly well known on Naxos, being attractive examples.

BIBLIOGRAPHY

GENERAL

C. C. Edgar: 'The Pottery', *Excavations at Phylakopi in Melos*, ed. T. D. Atkinson and others (London, 1904)

C. Zervos: *L'Art des Cyclades du début à la fin de l'âge du bronze: 2500–1100 avant notre ère* (Paris, 1957) [excellent pls]

R. H. Higgins: *Minoan and Mycenaean Art* (London, 1967, 2/1981)

J. L. Caskey: 'Investigations in Keos, Part 2: A Conspectus of the Pottery', *Hesperia*, xli (1972), pp. 357–401

S. Hood: *The Arts in Prehistoric Greece*, Pelican Hist. A. (Harmondsworth, 1978), pp. 28, 32, 38–40

R. L. N. Barber: *The Cyclades in the Bronze Age* (London, 1987)

EARLY CYCLADIC

J. E. Coleman: 'Early Cycladic Clay Vessels', *Art and Culture of the Cyclades*, ed. P. Getz-Preziosi (Karlsruhe, 1977), pp. 109–17 [Eng. trans. of *Kunst und Kultur der Kykladeninseln im 3. Jahrtausend v. Chr.* (exh. cat., ed. J. Thimme; Karlsruhe, Bad. Landesmus., 1976]

R. L. N. Barber and J. A. MacGillivray: 'The Early Cycladic Period: Matters of Definition and Terminology', *Amer. J. Archaeol.*, lxxxiv (1980), pp. 141–57 [incl. summaries of the pottery of each phase and further refs]

MIDDLE CYCLADIC

R. L. N. Barber: 'The Cyclades in the Middle Bronze Age', *Thera and the Aegean World I*, ed. C. Doumas (London, 1978), pp. 367–79

J. C. Overbeck: 'Stratigraphy and Ceramic Sequence in Middle Cycladic Ayia Irini', *The Prehistoric Cyclades*, ed. J. A. MacGillivray and R. L. N. Barber (Edinburgh, 1984), pp. 108–13

J. L. Davis: *Ayia Irini: Period V* (1985), v of *Keos* (Mainz, 1977–) [incl. pottery of the later MC period only]

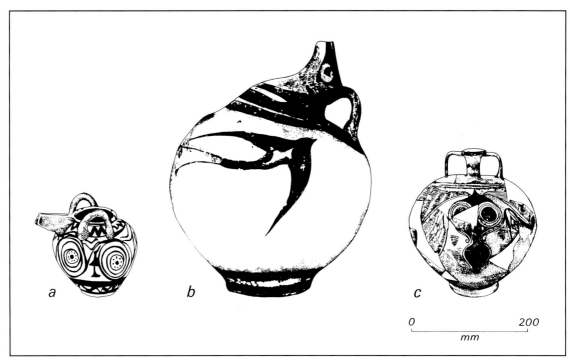

7. Late Cycladic pottery: (a) Minoanizing bridge-spouted jar with Black-and-red style decoration, h. 130 mm, LC I; (b) breasted ewer with painted bird motif, h. 435 mm, from Akrotiri, Thera, LC I; (c) Stirrup jar with stylized octopus decoration, h. 250 mm, LC IIIC

LATE CYCLADIC
C. Kardara: *Aplomata Naxou: Kineta euremata taphon A kai B* [Aplomata on Naxos: Portable finds from Tombs A and B] (Athens, 1977) [numerous illus. of octopus vases]
C. Doumas: *Thera: Pompeii of the Ancient Aegean* (London, 1983), pp. 108–13
P. A. Mountjoy: 'The Pottery', *The Archaeology of Cult: The Sanctuary at Phylakopi*, ed. C. Renfrew (London, 1985), pp. 151–208
J. C. Overbeck: *Ayia Irini: Period IV: 1. The Stratigraphy and the Find Deposits* (1989), vii of *Keos* (Mainz, 1977–)

R. L. N. BARBER

IV. Stone figurines.

The abundance of white marble on most of the Cycladic islands, especially Naxos (*see* NAXOS, §2(ii)) and Paros (*see* PAROS, §2), resulted in a strong tradition of stone-carving in the Early Cycladic (EC) period (*see also* §V below). Stone figurines of the EC period—sometimes referred to as idols—are arguably the best-known and most highly appreciated productions of Cycladic art. Their appeal to modern taste has led to an increased demand for them on the international antiquities market, and extraordinary prices have been paid for individual items at auction (for example, £2.09 million for the Merrin Head, sold New York, Sotheby's, 1 Dec 1988, lot 83). One consequence has been the intensification since the 1960s of illicit digging of EC tombs. But even this proved unable to satisfy the demand, and the manufacture of forgeries has reached the status of a 'growth industry'. Disputes have also arisen over the ownership of authentic pieces: in July 1990, in a precedent-setting case, Greece failed to obtain a court order halting the sale of a private collection of Cycladic sculptures at auction, despite the Greek government's insistence that the works had been removed from Greek soil illegally.

The fact that most Cycladic stone figurines come from illicit excavations has added to the confusion surrounding their function and significance. Several interpretations of their purpose have been proposed, none of which is universally accepted. They may have been magical representations of venerated ancestors, companions for the dead, images of divinities, status symbols or even toys. Those of known provenance are mainly from burials, but not all graves contained them. Moreover, some were evidently repaired in antiquity, suggesting that they were items of personal property for everyday use. Finally, some are too large to have been buried in the small and narrow graves: these may perhaps be cult images of an unknown deity.

1. EARLY CYCLADIC. Figurines of the EC I phase, whose origins can be traced to the Neolithic period, rarely exceed 200 mm in height. Initially they seem to have been fashioned from white flattened beach pebbles, the earliest types being natural pebbles worn by the waves into schematic human forms. Other early types were more substantially worked with tools, probably of obsidian, stone, emery or wood; abrasives such as emery powder and pumice stone were also used. The flat, violin-shaped figurines (see fig. 8), which occasionally have anatomical details such as breasts, genitalia and arms, are more sophisticated than the pebble figurines. Their predecessors were the Neolithic squatting female figures such as the Fat Lady of Saliagos (Paros, Archaeol. Mus.). Later in date, though still in EC I, and far more naturalistic is the

Plastiras type of figurine, named after its place of discovery on Paros. This figurine seems to have evolved from the standing variety of the Neolithic Aegean figurines. Both male and female figures of the Plastiras type have an almond-shaped head with facial details in low relief (nose, eyes, mouth, ears), arms bent at the elbows with hands meeting on the stomach, legs set apart and feet with flat horizontal soles suggesting a simple upright pose (see fig. 9). The introduction of metal tools in EC II enabled sculptors to attempt larger, more three-dimensional figures. But schematic forms, such as the Louros type, which is an abstract version of the earlier Plastiras type, continued.

The most characteristic EC II type is the folded-arm figurine, ranging in size from *c.* 100 mm to almost life-size (*c.* 1500 mm). Its body is three-dimensional but never fully rounded. The main features are a triangular, spade- or almond-shaped head turned upwards, an elongated and stylized nose (no eyes or mouth), arms folded left-over-right across the stomach and legs usually slightly bent at the knees and separated by means of a groove both at the front and back. The feet have slanting soles, suggesting a tip-toe position for the figurine. Few other anatomical details were carved, but some, mainly the facial features and hair, were painted. Variants of this popular type, named after the sites where they were first discovered, are ascribed to different phases of EC II. The Kapsala variety, characterized by narrow shoulders, heavy, convex head and clearly indicated breasts, as well as by generally rounded forms, was common in the central Cyclades, while the Dokathismata group (*see* AMORGOS), consisting of thin, long, angular and very elegant figurines, was more widely distributed among the islands. Spedos-type figurines, which are the most numerous and were produced over the longest period, are well built and have spade-shaped heads (see fig. 10). The Koumasa variety comprises short, broad and rather flat figurines found exclusively on Crete, and the Chalandriani variety consists of figures with rather square, flat torsos and the right arm folded over the left (which gives rise to the group's alternative title of 'post-canonical', to distinguish them from the standard folded-arm type). A small group of typical folded-arm figurines depict pregnant women; another special category, the 'occupational' figurines, depict mainly male figures engaged in a specific activity: common figures include the 'hunter' or 'warrior', the lyre-player (see fig. 2 above), the flautist and the seated figure proposing a toast.

Systematic study of the EC figurines has led to the recognition of individual artists to whom certain pieces can be attributed on stylistic grounds. Among these artists are the Goulandris Master, the Naxos Museum Master, the Ashmolean Master, the Steiner Master and the Copenhagen Master. They all produced figurines of the Spedos variety. It has become clear through study and experimentation that the Cycladic figurines were not sculpted at random but that specific canons were applied in the planning of the various types, in order that standard proportions should be met in their execution.

BIBLIOGRAPHY

D. G. Hogarth: 'Aegean Sepulchral Figurines', *Essays in Aegean Archaeology Presented to Sir Arthur Evans* (Oxford, 1927), pp. 55–62

8. Early Cycladic female figurines of violin shape, marble, h. 94 mm, 98 mm and 42 mm, EC I (Athens, Museum of Cycladic and Ancient Greek Arts)

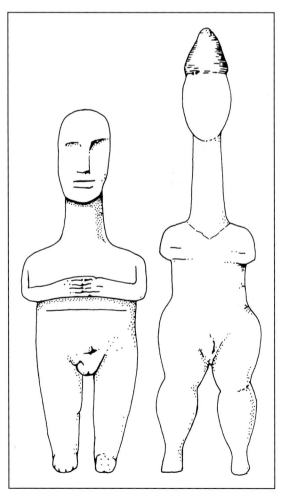

9. Early Cycladic male figurines of Plastiras type, marble, EC I

10. Early Cycladic folded-arm figurine, marble, h. 584 mm, from Spedos cemetery, Naxos, EC II (Athens, National Archaeological Museum)

M. L. Erlenmeyer and H. Erlenmeyer: 'Von der frühen Bildkunst der Kykladen', *Ant. Kst*, viii (1965), pp. 59–71
J. Thimme: 'Die religiöse Bedeutung der Kykladenidole', *Ant. Kst*, viii (1965), pp. 72–86
C. Doumas: *The N. P. Goulandris Collection of Early Cycladic Art* (Athens, 1968)
O. Höckmann: 'Zu Formenschatz und Ursprung der schematischen Kykladenidole', *Berlin. Jb. Vor- & Frühgesch.*, viii (1968), pp. 45–75
C. Renfrew: 'The Development and Chronology of the Early Cycladic Figurines', *Amer. J. Archaeol.*, lxxiii (1969), pp. 1–32
P. G. Preziosi and S. S. Weinberg: 'Evidence for Painted Details in Early Cycladic Sculpture', *Ant. Kst*, xiii (1970), pp. 4–12
F. Zafiropoulou: 'Early Cycladic Finds from Ano Koufonisi', *Athens An. Archaeol.*, iii (1970), pp. 48–51
K. Branigan: 'Cycladic Figurines and their Derivatives in Crete', *Annu. Brit. Sch. Athens*, lxvi (1971), pp. 57–78
J. L. Caskey: 'Marble Figurines from Ayia Irini in Keos', *Hesperia*, xl (1971), pp. 113–26
J. L. Fitton, ed.: *Cycladica: Studies in Memory of N. P. Goulandris* (London, 1984)
P. Getz-Preziosi: *Early Cycladic Sculpture: An Introduction* (Malibu, 1985)
——: *Early Cycladic Art in North American Collections* (Richmond, VA, 1987)
——: *Sculptors of the Cyclades: Individual and Tradition in the Third Millennium BC* (Ann Arbor, 1987)
C. Renfrew: *The Cycladic Spirit* (New York, 1991)

2. MODERN FORGERIES. Just as Greek sculptures were copied in antiquity to meet the demands of the imperial Romans, Early Cycladic figurines were copied for contemporary Cretans. This does not imply, however, that the reproduction or imitation of Cycladic figures in Early Minoan Crete (the Koumasa variety) was an intentional act of deceit. In modern times, by contrast, Cycladic stone figurines are deliberately forged to satisfy the thirst of ignorant collectors, who often purchase the objects for investment. Most EC sculptures have been forged by professional artists inside Greece, where imitations are still made for tourists, but when demand has been high, forgeries have also been produced abroad. In the late 1960s a high proportion of fakes supplied to the market came through Paris, where many young Greek artists had sought refuge from the oppressive regime of the Colonels in Greece. During that decade many private collections, especially in Switzerland, were enriched with fakes.

The most systematically forged figurine is the folded-arm type, but the diversity of genuine stone figurines makes the detection of forgeries on stylistic grounds alone difficult. Much depends on the technical skills of the fakers, though in certain cases they are betrayed by the character of their marble. For example, the large figures that appeared on the Paris market in the 1960s eventually aroused suspicion because they were made of white marble with dark veins, which is unusual for genuine Cycladic sculptures. The difficulties involved in successfully imitating the patina of age on the surface of the marble also facilitate detection, especially under ultraviolet light: freshly cut marble appears as uniform purple, ancient surfaces show as mottled white.

The forging of EC art has often been disclosed in court by antique dealers accused of illicitly exporting Cycladic works of art and hoping for lighter sentences. A famous illegal dealer from Ios—Angelos Batsalis (1885–1953), nicknamed Niotis—whose career started before World War II and ended in the 1950s, was himself an artist, and fakes were rumoured to have been included often among his merchandise. He apparently buried the forged figurines in his garden to give them a convincing patina.

BIBLIOGRAPHY
G. Savage: *Forgeries, Fakes and Reproductions: A Handbook for the Collector* (London, 1963)
C. Doumas: 'Prehistoric Cycladic People in Crete', *Athens An. Archaeol.*, ix/1 (1977), pp. 69–80

CHRISTOS G. DOUMAS

V. Stone vases.

The same high quality of Cycladic white marble that inspired the sculptors of stone figurines (*see* §IV above) also led to the creation of an impressive series of stone vessels with similarly clean lines and simple, elegant forms. Like the figurines, these vases were produced chiefly in EC I and II, although there were a few Late Neolithic prototypes, such as a pointed marble beaker from an early 4th-millennium grave on Kea (Kea, Archaeol. Col.). The most common EC I forms are the rounded jar with a tall collar and pedestal foot (the *kandili*; see fig. 11), plain open bowls, flat-based beakers and rectangular trough palettes. One or two beakers have seemingly anthropomorphic relief decoration, recalling marble figurines of the EC I Plastiras type (see fig. 9 above) as well as Early Minoan (EM) cult statuettes from Crete. The earliest Cycladic stone vessels seem to have functioned mainly as grave offerings. Some are decorated with red ochre, and some contain traces of red or blue pigment used in burial rites. Occasionally the interior of a bowl is coloured red all over; this looks like decoration rather than the result of mixing colouring matter.

During EC II a wider range of forms developed, chiefly elegant open bowls, flaring in profile and sometimes with an open spout or a pedestal foot. Rectangular palettes up to 300 mm long also occur, as do rounded bowls or jars with lug handles (pyxides). The bowls and pyxides are closely paralleled in contemporary pottery shapes. A rarer form is a cylindrical pyxis with horizontal grooves and a close-fitting lid. A special class of lidded box was made of green chlorite or chlorite-schist rather than marble. Such

boxes are decorated with incised herringbone patterns, alternating hatched triangles or finely carved low-relief spirals. One example from Melos (Munich, Staatl. Antikensamml.) appears to be a model of a granary, raised on pillars: it portrays a building with an elaborate entrance porch, seven tall cylindrical storage bins and a central courtyard. Others could be models of huts. Vases of the same stone and similar decoration, but of different shapes, occur at the same time in Crete, where they constitute the earliest stone vessels. This suggests direct links between Cycladic and Minoan workshops (*see* MINOAN, §X). As in Crete, the EC II stone vessels were apparently burial gifts, though this cannot be confirmed, as few EC I and II settlements have been excavated.

There were sudden changes at the beginning of EC III, which resulted in the almost complete abandonment of stone vase production, though there were occasionally stone imitations made of the collared and pedestalled pottery jars. This lapse in production lasted several centuries, making the discovery at Akrotiri on Thera of a complete pithos of local grey-black lava (h. 1.18 m; Akrotiri, Thera Excav. Storerooms) all the more astonishing. The vase came from a settlement immediately below the LC I town. Though a unique survival, the jar presupposes the complete mastery of the craft of carving in a Theran volcanic stone. It heralds the resumption of the vase industries during the LC I period, when two distinct classes of vases were produced. One comprises vessels fashioned from local stones: banded marble on Kea and volcanic rocks (dacite, lava and tuff) on Thera. The best Theran works are three-footed mortars, some exported to Crete. The other class comprises a wide range of vessels in foreign materials, chiefly Cretan serpentine but sometimes more exotic stones, such as *rosso antico*. Either the vessels themselves or the stone to make the vessels were imported to the islands from Minoan Crete. A magnificent unfinished jar in *rosso antico* marble found at Thera (Akrotiri, Thera Excav. Storerooms) was in the course of manufacture by either a Theran or Minoan stone-carver when Akrotiri was destroyed in the volcanic eruption late in LC I.

The excavated towns on Kea and Thera have provided the most evidence of imported Minoan pieces, but a few are known from other islands. A small group of gypsum vessels from Thera appears to have come from the Syro-Palestinian region. After the destruction of Thera and the subsequent Minoan destructions, stone vases ceased to be made on the islands, and the few imported items found in later contexts were simply heirlooms.

11. Stone pedestal jar (*kandili*), marble, h. 280 mm, from Paros, EC I (Athens, National Archaeological Museum)

BIBLIOGRAPHY

C. Zervos: *L'Art des Cyclades du début à la fin de l'âge du bronze: 2500–1100 avant notre ère* (Paris, 1957) [excellent pls]
P. Getz-Preziosi: 'Early Cycladic Stone Vases', *Kunst und Kultur der Kykladeninseln im 3. Jahrtausend v. Chr.* (exh. cat., ed. J. Thimme; Karlsruhe, Bad. Landesmus., 1976); Eng. trans. as *Art and Culture of the Cyclades*, ed. P. Getz-Preziosi (Karlsruhe, 1977)
P. M. Warren: 'The Stone Vessels from the Bronze Age Settlement at Akrotiri, Thera', *Archaiol. Ephemeris* (1979), pp. 82–113
Cycladic Art: Ancient Pottery and Sculpture from the N. P. Goulandris Collection (exh. cat., ed. C. Doumas; London, BM, 1983)
T. Devetzi: 'Stone Carving–sculpture: Vessels', *Cycladic Culture: Naxos in the 3rd Millennium BC* (exh. cat., ed. L. Marangou; Athens, Mus. Cyclad. & Anc. Gr. A., 1990), pp. 117–35, nos 113–41

P. M. WARREN

12. Wall paintings depicting *Boxing Boys* and *Antelopes*, from Room Beta 1 of a shrine complex, Akrotiri, Thera, LC I (Thera, Archaeological Museum: on deposit at Athens, National Archaeological Museum)

VI. Wall paintings.

Cycladic painting had a brief but rich life covering a few decades at the beginning of the Late Bronze Age. Major excavations on the three Cycladic islands of THERA, MELOS and KEA have revealed towns with wall paintings that clearly owe much to Minoan painting on Crete (*see* MINOAN, §IV) yet have distinctively local characteristics. Features that set Cycladic painting somewhat apart from that of Minoan Crete include complexes of rooms with related sequences of paintings, miniature paintings and the juxtaposition between cult activity and the natural world, especially in themes related to the sea and to presentation and robing ceremonies. Although Cycladic paintings share these features, they were clearly painted by different artists. The painters were apparently local rather than specialized travelling artists. Yet a common tradition (perhaps in some cases a shared apprenticeship) and a free exchange of ideas led to the development of characteristically Cycladic formats and themes.

1. Thera. 2. Melos. 3. Kea.

1. THERA. The paintings from Akrotiri on Thera (Thera, Archaeol. Mus.; on long-term dep. Athens, N. Archaeol. Mus.) are extraordinarily well preserved, having been covered in volcanic ash following the eruption that destroyed the settlement. Like Minoan murals, they decorated the upper storeys of houses and were found fallen in small fragments, but their excellent state of preservation has enabled them to be extensively reconstructed. Akrotiri was a town rich in wall paintings. Every house or house-complex had a painted room, and those known as the West House and Xeste 3 had programmes of paintings covering two or three adjoining rooms. All the paintings date from the latter part of LC I.

(i) *Large-scale works.* The theme of nature is expressed in the *Spring* fresco, a painting that ran continuously around three walls in a small house shrine (Delta 2). Red lilies in bud, opening and in bloom perch on top of multicoloured rock formations reminiscent of the bright volcanic rocks of the island. Swallows fly singly or in pairs between the flowers, some in the process of courtship feeding.

Other paintings, such as the *Boxing Boys* and *Antelopes* (see fig. 12) found in a small room of a shrine complex (Beta 1), seem to draw a comparison between human and animal nature in scenes of confrontation or contest. There pairs of male antelopes were painted on three walls; their posture, with their heads turned, eyes meeting and tails raised, expresses the competitive aggression typical of the species. On the south wall a pair of young boys engage in ritualized play: each has a boxing glove and is naked except for knotted belts and jewellery. From their blue (shaved) heads stream long black locks, a distinctive style indicating status and youth. A frieze of ivy leaves ran continuously above the figures, linking the images of each wall.

In the House of the Ladies, two life-size female figures were represented alongside large papyrus plants, which, like lilies, were associated with cult in Aegean iconography. A mature woman bends forward with her arms outstretched, a garment in one hand, the other touching the sleeve of the second woman. The rest of this figure has not survived, but she has been reconstructed as seated. The scene has been interpreted as depicting a robing ceremony, in which a garment is presented to a priestess or goddess. The same ceremony was apparently represented elsewhere, for instance in Xeste 3 at Akrotiri, where a man in a procession holds an offering of a cloth, and at Phylakopi on Melos (*see* §2 below).

Another common motif in Aegean painting was the blue monkey. A painting at Thera of *Blue Monkeys*, in which they are shown climbing among stylized rocks above a river, appears to be a scene from nature (Beta 6). Its prototype is the *Birds and Monkeys* frieze from Knossos (*see* MINOAN, fig. 15), but while some Minoan paintings give the impression that the monkey was an imported pet roaming in parks, at Thera it seems to have had a different iconographic role. In another, fragmentary painting from Akrotiri blue monkeys are shown worshipping before an outdoor shrine with a sacred papyrus column and horns of consecration. Fragments with human scenes—a woman, a man before a palm—came from the same area (Alpha 1).

Blue monkeys were also clearly associated with cult scenes in the cycle of paintings from Xeste 3. This building is divided into areas for domestic and ritual activity. The entrance leads directly to the cult area, suggesting that it was a public rather than a private shrine. A life-size mural of a man was painted in the anteroom, facing towards the stairway that led upstairs to the cult area. Plants among a rocky landscape flanked the stairs. The cult area was itself split into two levels, linked by a small staircase. Entry was from the south on the lower level. The walls on both levels were covered with near life-size figures. On the lower-level west wall was a procession of young men carrying offerings (a similar scene was discovered in the partly excavated building Xeste 4 nearby), and on the upper-level west wall was a fowling scene of birds among reeds. On the south wall was a procession of women.

The main action, with young women in a rocky landscape with crocuses, took place on the north and east walls. Their hairstyles—blue shaven head with locks, short curly hair or long hair tied at the neck—differentiate them according to age. On the lower-level east wall were three female figures (*Adorants*), one woman holding a necklace, one bending down to her bleeding foot and a young girl draped in a transparent cloth turning to look behind her towards an altar with horns of consecration dripping with blood. On the upper level were the *Saffron Gatherers*: young girls collecting crocuses into baskets (*see* THERA, fig. 2). The crocuses were then offered by a blue monkey to a nature goddess seated on a raised platform, with necklaces of ducks and dragonflies and crocuses on her dress and cheek; behind her is a protective griffin. Saffron

was probably exported from the island, and economics and religion are linked in these scenes. The theme of blue monkeys is elaborated in a frieze from near the sanctuary entrance: one monkey holds a lyre, another wields a sword at a snake. Monkeys and crocuses were shown together in wall paintings from Crete (for example the *Saffron Gatherers* from Knossos), but here on Thera the mythic association is explicit. The paintings have been interpreted as initiation scenes for girls approaching womanhood, and it has been suggested that such rituals took place within the sanctuary itself (N. Marinatos, 1984).

Although it is not always possible to relate the activities depicted in the paintings at Akrotiri with rituals that could have taken place indoors, there is evidence to suggest that the paintings reflect Cycladic religious beliefs, which must have revolved around the relationship between humans and the natural world. Even apparently pure nature scenes, such as the *Spring* fresco, relate to a specific time of year of crucial importance in the cyclical life of those dependent on their environment.

(ii) Miniatures. A wealth of information on the culture, environment and cosmopolitan outlook of the Theran people is contained in the miniature friezes that ran above the windows and doorways of one of two painted rooms in the West House. Thera was a central port of call in an international trading network, a maritime role that is reflected in the miniature paintings.

In the *Meeting on the Hill* from the north wall, men in Theran priestly robes and Minoan loincloths are gathered on a rocky summit—the first known representation of rituals at Aegean 'peak sanctuaries'. A pastoral scene on the right shows flocks of sheep led by shepherds and women at a well. Akrotiri had a local wool-producing industry, and sheep were an important commodity. The inhabitants were also sailors, traders and fishermen, and their concern with the sea is expressed in the scene below. Warriors (potential raiders) march up the coast, and in the sea is a shipwreck. This scene has been variously interpreted as an invasion and sea battle (though no fighting is shown) or as a reflection of the typical dangers faced by a coastal people. Depicted on the east wall was a *Landscape* frieze, in which a cat chases birds and a griffin pursues a deer in a river landscape, where the wildness of nature is somewhat domesticated by the inclusion of cultivated palms.

On the south wall was the *Ship Procession* frieze (see fig. 13). There is a town at each end of the frieze, that on the left set in a hilly landscape with trees and a river, the grander, fortified city on the right around a harbour with fishermen and boats. Horns of consecration mark the sanctity of the city wall and the building closest to the sea. Young men walk beneath the wall, one leading a calf for sacrifice. Men run to look-out buildings on top to see the incoming procession of seven large ships, one rowing boat and one sailing ship, as the townsfolk watch from windows and rooftops. In the harbour multicoloured rocks rise from the sea, and dolphins play around the ships, which have been decorated with dress-ship lines, emblems on mast-tops and prows, painted hulls and stern figureheads of lions and griffins. The large ships are paddled, a traditional method used for ceremonial occasions. Elite

13. *Ship Procession* frieze (detail), from the south wall of the West House, Akrotiri, Thera, LC I (Thera, Archaeological Museum: on deposit at Athens, National Archaeological Museum)

passengers sit beneath awnings, some dressed in the ceremonial robes worn by the men in the *Meeting on the Hill*. At the stern of each ship is a cabin, a feature derived from Egyptian ceremonial vessels. This cabin is repeated in large-scale paintings that decorate the walls of the adjoining room. Near them was the painting of a *Priestess*, wearing an oriental-style ceremonial robe; her lips and ear are red, and on her blue head is perhaps a snake, cult symbol of the Minoans. She holds a plant (possibly saffron) over an incense burner, presumably an offering in blessing of the ships.

The occasion represented in this miniature cycle has been variously interpreted. The excavator (Spiridon Marinatos, who began work in 1967) postulated an expedition to Libya, and though that destination was largely rejected, others followed his martial emphasis. Since then, study of the ships' features has led scholars to interpret the scene as a nautical festival, more specifically the resumption of the navigation season in May (Doumas, ed., 1978, pp. 629–44; Morgan, 1983, 1988). This suggestion is based on the seasonal element that runs through the paintings. Lilies in pots were painted on the window-jambs of Room 4. Beneath the miniatures on two walls of Room 5 was a panel of a life-size naked fisherman holding mackerel, which is caught in bulk in early summer. Both the new sailing season and the time for moving flocks to the uplands coincide with the beginning of summer, and both sailors and shepherds participate in the north-wall ritual of the *Meeting on the Hill*. Other scholars have proposed different theories for the festival of ships: a victory celebration (N. Marinatos, 1984), sacred marriage (Säflund), jubilee (Polinger Foster); while still others have sought to link the images with the origins of epic Greek poetry (Morris; Hardy and Renfrew, eds, pp. 229–36).

2. MELOS. At Phylakopi on Melos, the walls of the Pillar Crypt shrine complex were decorated with paintings at the beginning of LC II, but little was found elsewhere in the town (all Athens, N. Archaeol. Mus.). Some pieces of plaster were found outside the city walls, where they must have been dumped at the time of the Mycenaean occupation in LC III. Among them was a fragment of a miniature frieze, showing a man's booted leg and the head of a second figure below. The rest of the frieze is lost, but the fragment suggests that each Cycladic settlement at this time had a cycle of miniatures.

From the original excavations (British School at Athens, 1896–9), fragments of narrow friezes of *Flying Fish in a Seascape* were found in the Pillar Crypt. Dabs of blue paint indicate the sea that surrounds the swooping fish, with marine rocks above and below. Found in the same room was a painting of two half life-size women, one seated facing right and holding a blue cloth. She wears a skirt with designs (now faded) of birds among rocks; the head has not survived. Only the upper torso of the other figure survives. She faces left and extends her arms. The presentation of a garment suggests the figures are part of a robing ceremony (Morgan, in preparation), like that depicted in the House of the Ladies at Thera. The seated figure who has received the cloth offering should thus be understood as the goddess or priestess. The birds and rocks on her skirt, together with the associated *Flying Fish* frieze, suggest the cult of nature, embracing the domains of air, land and sea. Fragments of white lilies, which often occur as offerings in Aegean iconography, were painted on a red background in the adjacent room. They have no stems or leaves, characteristic of ceramics rather than paintings. In the 1970s a stratigraphical sounding in the room immediately to the east was undertaken in order to date the Pillar Crypt paintings. The sounding revealed that a frieze of *Blue Monkeys* had decorated the room with a festoon spiral frieze above or near by.

3. KEA. Compositions of large-scale human figures were apparently not favoured at Ayia Irini on Kea; only a few stray pieces were found (House B). The characteristic format of Kean painting (all Kea, Archaeol. Mus.) was the frieze. *Bluebirds* (doves) and *Dolphins*, shown in various poses against a monochromed background and devoid of context, form the subjects of two friezes (Houses A and J). This abstraction of nature contrasts with the vivid landscapes and seascapes of Minoan paintings of the same subjects (*see* MINOAN, §IV), though it was characteristic of Mycenaean painting some 200 years later (*see* HELLADIC, §IV). The *Bluebirds* frieze ran around three walls of a room, on the fourth of which, on a larger scale, was a painting of a griffin seated within a shrine. A nearby room was decorated with a 'splash pattern': paint flicked on to the wall to imitate marble.

A miniature frieze ran around three walls of a large room within the fortification wall (North-east Bastion), which was perhaps intended for public religious gatherings or banquets. Less well preserved than the Theran miniatures, this frieze is harder to interpret. The theme is again a festival set by the sea, with two building complexes and many figures, mainly male. Some, dressed in long robes, take part in a procession, and others dance. A hunter carries a flank of deer, and there are fragments of a chariot and horses. By the seashore men bend over large cauldrons. Fragments of large ships and a small paddled boat show that activity continued at sea. A scene of deer hunted by dogs was painted on one of the walls. The landscape in which the human activity is set is richly diverse, with a river, a marsh, a variety of plants and multicoloured rocks. In the adjoining room were large painted panels of plant compositions. Some of these features—chariot, hunter and dogs—appear for the first time in Aegean painting at Kea, recurring as popular components of Mycenaean painting.

BIBLIOGRAPHY

GENERAL WORKS

S. Hood: *The Arts in Prehistoric Greece*, Pelican Hist. A. (Harmondsworth, 1978)

S. A. Immerwahr: *Aegean Painting in the Bronze Age* (Pennsylvania and London, 1990)

THERA

S. Marinatos: *Excavations at Thera*, i–vii (Athens, 1968–76)

——: 'Das Schiffsfresko von Akrotiri', *Seewesen*, ed. D. Gray, Archaeologia Homerica (Göttingen, 1974), pp. 140–51

H. G. Buchholz: 'Bemerkung zum Schiffsfresso von Thera', *Hellas ewig unsere Liebe: Freundesgabe für Willy Zschietzschmann zu seinem 75. Geburtstag, 15 Februar 1975*, ed. S. Oppermann (Giessen, 1975)

L. Casson: 'Bronze Age Ships: The Evidence of the Thera Wall Paintings', *Int. J. Naut. Archaeol. & Underwtr Explor.*, iv (1975), pp. 1–10

G. C. Gesell: 'The "Town Fresco" of Thera: A Reflection of Cretan Topography', *Pepragmena tou 4 Diethnous Kretologikou Synedrion: Athina, 1976* [Proceedings of the 4th Annual Cretological Conference: Athens, 1976], pp. 297–304

D. L. Page: 'The Miniature Frescoes from Akrotiri, Thera', *Praktika*, li (1976), pp. 135–52

E. Sapouna-Sakellarakis: 'Oi toíchographiés tés Théras se schesé me tén Minóïké Krété [The wall paintings of Thera in relation to Minoan Crete], *Pepragmena tou 4 Diethnous Kretologikou Synedrion: Athina, 1976* [Proceedings of the 4th Annual Cretological Conference: Athens, 1976], ii, pp. 532–8

M. Benzi: 'Gli affreschi dell'ammiraglio a Thera', *Prospettiva*, x (1977), pp. 3–15

S. A. Immerwahr: 'Mycenaeans at Thera: Some Reflections on the Paintings from the West House', *Greece and the Eastern Mediterranean in Ancient History and Prehistory: Studies Presented to Fritz Schachermeyr on the Occasion of his Eightieth Birthday*, ed. K. H. Kinzl (Berlin and New York, 1977), pp. 173–91

C. Doumas, ed.: *Thera and the Aegean World I* (London, 1978), pp. 571–92, 599–604, 617–56

P. Haider: 'Grundsätzliches und Sächliches zur historischen Auswertung des bronzezeitlichen Miniaturfrieses auf Thera', *Klio*, lxi (1979), pp. 285–307

P. M. Warren: 'The Miniature Fresco from the West House at Akrotiri, Thera, and its Aegean Setting', *J. Hell. Stud.*, xcix (1979), pp. 115–29

G. Säflund: 'Cretan and Theran Questions', *Sanctuaries and Cults in the Aegean Bronze Age. Proceedings of the First International Symposium of the Swedish Institute at Athens: Athens, 1980*, pp. 189–208

A. Sakellariou: 'The West House Miniature Frescoes', *Thera and the Aegean World II*, ed. C. Doumas (London, 1980), pp. 147–53

A. B. Knapp: 'The Thera Frescoes and the Question of Aegean Contact with Libya during the Late Bronze Age', *J. Medit. Anthrop. & Archaeol.*, i (1981), pp. 249–79

N. Marinatos: 'Minoan Threskeiocracy on Thera', *The Minoan Thalassocracy: Myth and Reality. Proceedings of the Third International Symposium at the Swedish School at Athens: Athens, 1982*, pp. 167–76

E. Davis: 'The Iconography of the Ship Fresco from Thera', *Ancient Greek Art and Iconography*, ed. W. G. Moon (Wisconsin, 1983), pp. 1–14

C. Doumas: *Thera: Pompeii of the Ancient Aegean* (London, 1983)

N. Marinatos: 'The West House at Akrotiri as a Cult Centre', *Archäol. Anz.*, xcviii (1983), pp. 1–19

L. Morgan: 'Theme in the West House Paintings at Thera', *Archaiol. Ephemeris* (1983), pp. 85–105

N. Marinatos: *Art and Religion in Thera: Reconstructing a Bronze Age Society* (Athens, 1984)

——: 'An Offering of Saffron to the Minoan Goddess of Nature: The Role of the Monkey and the Importance of Saffron', *Gifts to the Gods: Proceedings of the Uppsala Symposium: Uppsala, 1985*, pp. 123–32

——: 'The Function of the Theran Frescoes', *L'Iconographie minoenne: Actes de la table ronde d'Athènes*, ed. P. Darcque and J.-C. Poursat, *Bull. Corr. Hell.*, suppl. 11 (Paris, 1985), pp. 221–32

E. Davis: 'Youth and Age in the Thera Frescoes', *Amer. J. Archaeol.*, xc (1986), pp. 399–406

L. Morgan: *The Miniature Wall Paintings of Thera: A Study in Aegean Culture and Iconography* (Cambridge, 1988)

K. Polinger Foster: 'Snakes and Lions: A New Reading of the West House Frescoes from Thera', *Expedition*, xxx/2 (1988), pp. 10–20

M. B. Hollinshead: 'The Swallows and Artists of Room Delta 2 at Akrotiri, Thera', *Amer. J. Archaeol.*, xciii (1989), pp. 339–54

S. P. Morris: 'A Tale of Two Cities: The Miniature Frescoes from Thera and the Origins of Greek Poetry', *Amer. J. Archaeol.*, xciii (1989), pp. 511–35

D. A. Hardy and C. Renfrew, eds: *Thera and the Aegean World III* (London, 1990), i, pp. 214–36, 252–82, 309–26; iii, pp. 229–36

MELOS

T. D. Atkinson and others: *Excavations at Phylakopi in Melos* (London, 1904)

L. Morgan: 'The Painted Plasters and their Relation to the Wall Paintings of the Pillar Crypt', *Excavations at Phylakopi, 1974–1976*, ed. C. Renfrew (in preparation)

KEA

K. Coleman: 'Frescoes from Ayia Irini, Keos: Part I', *Hesperia*, xlii (1973), pp. 284–300

K. Abramovitz: 'Frescoes from Ayia Irini, Keos: Parts II–IV', *Hesperia*, xlix (1980), pp. 57–85

E. Davis and L. Morgan: *Keos: The Wall Paintings of Ayia Irini* (in preparation)

LYVIA MORGAN

VII. *Metalwork.*

Precious metals are not common in the Cycladic Bronze Age but are most frequent in the Early Cycladic (EC) period, when Cycladic craftsmen were active in metallurgical innovation. By contrast, the islands have produced quite large numbers of bronze objects, especially of EC date, and some varieties were probably developed locally.

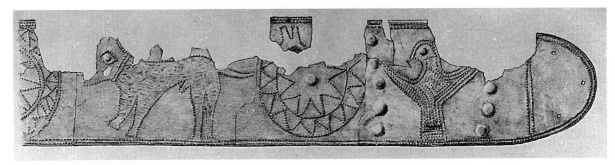

14. Silver diadem with repoussé frieze, h. 24 mm, from Syros, EC IIIB (Athens, National Archaeological Museum)

The production of lead is closely related to that of silver, though only a few objects in lead survive: one or two figurines and some model boats from Naxos (EC II; Oxford, Ashmolean).

1. GOLD AND SILVER. Ancient mines have been located at Ayios Sostis on Siphnos, which is known to have been a source of silver and was reputed in later antiquity to possess gold. The only extant gold objects are an EC bead from Naxos (Athens, N. Archaeol. Mus.) and others from a Middle Cycladic (MC) grave on Kea (Kea, Archaeol. Col.). Silver jewellery is slightly more common, especially in EC graves. Its style is influenced by the gold jewellery produced by the people of the Troad and the Minoans. Other silver artefacts include EC shallow bowls from Amorgos (Oxford, Ashmolean) and others of unknown provenance, some with simple linear decoration (EC–MC; e.g. Athens, N. Archaeol. Mus.). Silver diadems have been found on Amorgos and Syros. One has a neat openwork rim; another, from Chalandriani on Syros (see fig. 14), has an unusual repoussé frieze representing two collared animals (thought to be dogs), ornamental discs with elaborate sun or star patterns and a birdlike figure (possibly of a deity) with raised arms or wings. The piece is unique among extant Cycladic work and seems to imitate a series of gold diadems from Mochlos in eastern Crete. Silver bracelets and beads also occur: these are plain or decorated with simple linear designs (e.g. Oxford, Ashmolean). Pins with ornamental heads, used to secure garments at the shoulder, are much rarer in silver than in bronze. Most pinheads take the form of simple knobs, cages or spirals of wire. Some represent animals or sea birds: a silver pin from a grave on Amorgos is topped by the lively figure of a ram (see fig. 15).

There are few surviving precious metal objects from the MC period, but the Late Cycladic (LC) tombs at Aplomata on Naxos have yielded over 80 rosettes of gold leaf (Naxos Mus.), pierced for attachment to clothing, as well as some gold-leaf lions, probably made to cover figures of wood or other material. Perhaps also a covering for a figure is a tiny gold mask (diam. 40 mm) from the sanctuary at Phylakopi (Melos Mus.).

R. L. N. BARBER, REYNOLD HIGGINS

2. BRONZE. Several Cycladic islands had sources of copper, and there is evidence for mining and smelting at

15. Silver pin with head in the shape of a ram, h. 90 mm, from Amorgos, EC (Athens, National Archaeological Museum)

Siphnos, smelting on Kythnos and casting (moulds, crucibles and hearth) at Kastri on Syros and elsewhere. Tools (chisels, axe heads and a saw) and weapons (dagger or sword blades and spear heads) are the most common artefacts. Tools are prominent in the contents of two EC 'hoards': one (London, BM), long supposed to be from Kythnos, was shown by recent research to be more probably from Naxos; the other was from Kastri (Athens, N. Archaeol. Mus.; Syros Mus.). Notable examples of weapon blades and spear heads were found on Amorgos (London, BM). A number of toilet articles (tweezers) and some items of jewellery (rings, pins) are made of bronze, suggesting that it was considered precious for a long while after its introduction. Like silver pins, those in bronze have ornamental heads, with small animals, spirals etc.

As in other arts the MC period did not produce many bronze objects, but from LC I there is a fine group of bronze vessels from Akrotiri on Thera (Athens, N. Archaeol. Mus.). The shapes, and in one case the decoration, are similar to examples from Knossos and they may have been Cretan imports. Apart from numerous LC tools and weapons, Theran finds include an inlaid dagger blade (Copenhagen, Nmus.) directly comparable to those from mainland Mycenaean shaft graves (*see* HELLADIC, §VII, 2). Also from the LC period are a few 'Minoanizing' statuettes from Kea (Kea, Archaeol. Col.) and some of the Near Eastern Reshef type from Phylakopi (Melos Mus.).

BIBLIOGRAPHY
R. H. Higgins: *Greek and Roman Jewellery* (London, 1961, 2/1980), pp. 47–51
R. H. Higgins: *Minoan and Mycenaean Art* (London, 1967, 2/1981)
K. Branigan: *Aegean Metalwork of the Early and Middle Bronze Age* (Oxford, 1974)
——: 'Metal Objects and Metal Technology of the Cycladic Culture', *Art and Culture of the Cyclades*, ed. P. Getz-Preziosi (Karlsruhe, 1977), pp. 117–22 [Eng. trans. of *Kunst und Kultur der Kykladeninseln im 3. Jahrtausend v. Chr.* (exh. cat., ed. J. Thimme; Karlsruhe, Bad. Landesmus., 1976)]
E. Sapouna-Sakellarakis: 'Cycladic Jewellery', *Art and Culture of the Cyclades*, ed. P. Getz-Preziosi (Karlsruhe, 1977), pp. 123–9 [Eng. trans. of *Kunst und Kultur der Kykladeninseln im 3. Jahrtausend v. Chr.* (exh. cat., ed. J. Thimme; Karlsruhe, Bad. Landesmus., 1976)]
S. Hood: *The Arts in Prehistoric Greece*, Pelican Hist. A. (Harmondsworth, 1978), pp. 190–92
N. H. Gale and Z. A. Stos-Gale: 'Cycladic Metallurgy', *The Prehistoric Cyclades*, ed. J. A. MacGillivray and R. L. N. Barber (Edinburgh, 1984), pp. 255–76
J. L. Fitton: 'Esse quam videre: A Reconsideration of the Kythnos Hoard of Early Cycladic Tools', *Amer. J. Archaeol.*, xciii (1989), pp. 31–9

R. L. N. BARBER

VIII. Ivory and bone.

During the Early Cycladic period ivory is not found in the Cyclades, though bone tubes with incised decoration were used to contain pigments, and bone was fashioned into such minor objects as spindle-whorls, beads and decorative pins. A few examples show that even Cycladic figurines were sometimes made from bone. The Middle and Late Cycladic periods saw continuing use of bone, as well as the appearance of carved ivories in the islands. The influence first of Minoan Crete and later of Mycenaean Greece dominated many aspects of Cycladic art, and it seems probable that all the known ivories, which are mainly of Late Bronze Age date, are imports: no evidence

has yet been found for Cycladic ivory workshops. An important ivory ring (Athens, N. Archaeol. Mus.) was found at Phylakopi on Melos, the bezel engraved with a cult scene showing a woman standing before a platform with Minoan horns of consecration; it is perhaps Cretan work of the Late Minoan IA period. A group of carved ivories found in the Sanctuary of Artemis on Delos is particularly significant for the history of Mycenaean ivory-carving. It includes decorative attachments such as columns, rosettes and inlays of types known from Mycenae itself, as well as plaques engraved with animal combat scenes and the famous relief plaque showing a warrior in a boar's-tusk helmet with a figure-of-eight shield (Delos, Archaeol. Mus.). These plaques show eastern influences and may have been made in Cyprus *c*. 1250–*c*. 1200 BC (*see* CYPRUS, §II, 5(iii)).

See also MINOAN, §XIV, and HELLADIC, §VI.

BIBLIOGRAPHY
J.-C. Poursat: *Les Ivoires mycéniens: Essai sur la formation d'un art mycénien* (Paris, 1977), pp. 152–8
G. Papathanassopoulos: *Neolithic and Cycladic Civilization* (Athens, 1981), pp. 134, 142
Cycladic Art: The N. P. Goulandris Collection (exh. cat., ed. C. Doumas; London, BM, 1983), p. 123
J. G. Younger: 'The Sealstones', *The Archaeology of Cult: The Sanctuary at Phylakopi*, ed. C. Renfrew (London, 1985), pp. 295–6

J. LESLEY FITTON

IX. Museums, collections and exhibitions.

The most important public collections of Cycladic objects are found in Greece. The National Archaeological Museum in Athens has a whole gallery devoted to Cycladic finds, many of them from the excavations of Christos Tsountas in the late 19th century but also including material from the first series of excavations at Phylakopi on Melos (1896–9). The bulk of the Tsountas finds are Early Cycladic (EC), but the Phylakopi material also covers the Middle (MC) and Late Cycladic (LC) phases. Among the exhibits are stone figurines and vases, as well as pottery of all periods and objects of obsidian and metal. The museum also has a separate gallery devoted to the recent spectacular discoveries from Akrotiri on Thera: in addition to much LC I pottery and some small finds, this features the fine and well-preserved frescoes from the site. Also in Athens is the Goulandris Museum of Cycladic Art, which opened in 1986 to display what was originally the private collection of Nicholas P. Goulandris. This contains many fine marble figurines, including one of the largest known (h. 1.4 m), marble vases and pottery of all phases. There are also objects of later periods.

The Naxos Museum has many finds (especially pottery and marble) from EC cemeteries and numerous fine vases and minor objects from the late tombs at Aplomata and Kamini. The small museum at Apeiranthos, also on Naxos, has good EC material. Melos has finds from later excavations at Phylakopi (1911; 1974–7), now housed in a restored Neo-classical building (the island's original secondary school), and Syros has important EC II and IIIA material from the Chalandriani cemetery and the fort at Kastri. The Kea Archaeological Collection contains some finds from Ayia Irini. Some other Cycladic islands have small collections that are less accessible.

Museums with substantial collections of Cycladic objects outside Greece include the British Museum, London, which has a good range of Cycladic sculpture and pottery derived from the excavations of Julia T. Bent in cemeteries on Antiparos and from other sources, including Melos. The Ashmolean Museum in Oxford has important bronzes and silver jewellery and vessels from Amorgos and the Fitzwilliam Museum in Cambridge also has some Cycladic objects. A number of European and American museums, notably the Badisches Landesmuseum in Karlsruhe and the Metropolitan Museum in New York, have groups of Cycladic objects, which vary greatly in size. Small groups of potsherds from Phylakopi are widely distributed throughout the Western world. An idea of the extent and content of private collections containing Cycladic objects can be gained from the list of private lenders to public exhibitions (see bibliog.). Among the larger collections is that of Leonard Stern (Harmon F.A., New York).

BIBLIOGRAPHY

E. Sapouna-Sakellarakis: *Cycladic Civilisation and the Cycladic Collection of the National Archaeological Museum of Athens* (Athens, n.d.)
J. Dorig: *Art antique: Collections privées de Suisse Romande* (Geneva, 1975)
Kunst und Kultur der Kykladeninseln im 3. Jahrtausend v. Chr. (exh. cat., ed. J. Thimme; Karlsruhe, Bad. Landesmus., 1976); Eng. trans. as *Art and Culture of the Cyclades*, ed. P. Getz-Preziosi (Karlsruhe, 1977) [pp. 195–7 list other museums and collections that contributed to the exh.]
Cycladic Art: Ancient Pottery and Sculpture from the N. P. Goulandris Collection (exh. cat. by C. Doumas, Athens, Benaki Mus.; London, BM; Washington, DC, N.G.A.; Tokyo, N. Mus. W.A.; and elsewhere; 1978–84)
Greek Art of the Aegean Islands (exh. cat., Paris, Louvre; New York, Met.; 1979–80)
A. C. Renfrew: 'The Goulandris Museum of Cycladic and Ancient Greek Art', *Archaeol. Rep.: Council Soc. Promotion Hell. Stud. & Managing Cttee Brit. Sch. Archaeol. Athens*, xxxii (1985–6), pp. 134–41
D. von Bothmer and others: *Antiquities from the Collection of Christos G. Bastis* (New York, 1987)
Early Cycladic Art in North American Collections (exh. cat., ed. P. Getz-Preziosi; Richmond, VA Mus. F.A., 1987)
D. von Bothmer: *Glories of the Past: Ancient Art from the Shelley White and Leon Levy Collection* (New York, 1990)
Cycladic Culture: Naxos in the 3rd Millennium BC (exh. cat., ed. L. Marangou; Athens, Mus. Cyclad. & Anc. Gr. A., 1990) [pp. 337–41 list private lenders]

R. L. N. BARBER

Cyclorama. Large-scale panoramic landscape painting, usually on canvas, which is suspended in a circle to form a continuous scene. Some cycloramas were designed to be portable. They were especially popular in the 19th century (for illustration *see* DIORAMA).

RUPERT FEATHERSTONE

Cyfrewas, John de. *See* JOHN DE SIFERWAS.

Cylix. *See* KYLIX.

Cyma. Architectural moulding consisting of a double curve. In the cyma recta profile, the lower part of the curve is convex and the upper part concave; in the cyma reversa (Lesbian cymatium), the lower part is concave and the upper convex. The moulding was commonly used in Classical architecture and its later derivatives (*see* ORDERS, ARCHITECTURAL, §I and fig. 1); the cyma recta profile, for example, was often used to terminate the cornice (*see* GREECE, ANCIENT, fig. 18), and the abacus of the Corinthian capital usually had a cyma recta profile. Cyma reversa profiles were commonly used in the Ionic and Corinthian orders. An example from the early period can be found on the column capitals of the Temple of Artemis at Ephesos (6th century BC), while a later example appears on the entablature and column capitals of the Temple of Athena Polias at Priene (4th century BC). A single convex curve was common in 5th-century BC Athens, as for example on the Erechtheion. Sometimes the moulding was left unworked and undecorated, as in the façade of the Khaznat at Petra (?AD 40). The characteristic carved decoration, however, was leaf-and-dart, which was probably in origin a vegetal pattern. In the Roman period this moulding was characteristically used in the entablature crowning the architrave and frieze of temples of the Corinthian order, such as the Temple of Concord in Rome (ded. AD 10). The form of the cyma reversa moulding is an important criterion for dating, which has been extensively explored for the Roman period. In Gothic architecture, the double-curve profile is known as an ogee moulding.

BIBLIOGRAPHY

D. S. Robertson: *A Handbook of Greek and Roman Architecture* (Cambridge, 1929, rev. 2/1943); *R* as *Greek and Roman Architecture* (London, 1969)
L. Shoe: *Profiles of Greek Mouldings* (Cambridge, MA, 1936)
D. E. Strong: 'Late Hadrianic Architectural Ornament in Rome', *Pap. Brit. Sch. Rome*, xxi (1953), pp. 118–51

Cymru. *See* WALES.

Cyprus [Gr. Kypros; Turk. Kıbrıs]. Third largest island in the Mediterranean (9251 sq. km), 70 km south of Turkey and 103 km west of Syria (see fig. 1). The island's geographical location and its natural resources of copper and shipbuilding timber have had a considerable impact on the destiny of its inhabitants. Cyprus has throughout its history been vulnerable to the geopolitical ambitions of the powers controlling the neighbouring countries, which have not hesitated to exploit its resources and to use it as a stepping stone or place of retreat. Although it possessed a vigorous and distinctive local culture in Neolithic times (*c.* 7000–*c.* 3800 BC), it lacked the population, resources and strength to withstand the external pressures to which it was subjected from the start of the Bronze Age (*c.* 2300 BC). Since then and over the subsequent millennia Cyprus has been invaded and colonized for varying periods by Achaeans, Phoenicians, Assyrians, Egyptians, Persians, Romans, Arabs, Byzantines, Crusaders, Venetians, Turks and the British. While its strategic position has always given it certain commercial and cultural advantages, it has also been the source of most of the island's troubles since the beginning of recorded history, because too often the interests and concerns of the native inhabitants were subordinated to the ambitions and dictates of the powers around it. Yet, despite the ultimate demise of the native Cypriot style in the Late Bronze Age, the Cypriot craftsman's ability to adapt and amalgamate the forms, designs and subject-matter of successive incoming groups produced a range of artefacts that ingeniously blended traditional with foreign concepts. While the forms of Cypriot expression after the introduction of outside influences could be mistaken for provincial imitation, the island's art

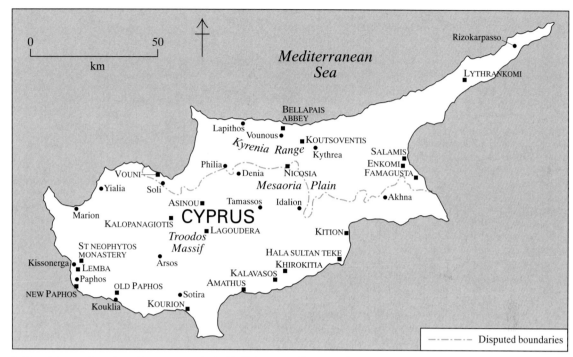

1. Map of Cyprus; those sites with separate entries in this dictionary are distinguished by CROSS-REFERENCE TYPE

never lost its essential native characteristics: a strong underlying sense of inventiveness, superstition and wit. This has left a large body of captivating and whimsical material which, in turn, has inspired not only students and collectors of the island's past art but modern Cypriot craftsmen as well.

GENERAL BIBLIOGRAPHY

T. Spiteris: *The Art of Cyprus* (Amsterdam, 1970)
V. Karageorghis: *Ancient Cyprus: 7000 Years of Art and Archaeoloogy* (Nicosia, 1981)
D. Hunt, ed.: *Footprints in Cyprus* (London, 1990)

I. Introduction. II. Ancient. III. Early Christian and Byzantine. IV. Lusignan and Venetian. V. Ottoman and modern. VI. Museums, collections and exhibitions.

I. Introduction.

1. GEOGRAPHY AND CLIMATE. Cyprus is dominated by two mountain formations—the Kyrenia Range, which runs east–west along the north coast, and the Troodos Massif, which overlooks the south-western part of the island. To the north and east of the Troodos lies a sedimentary plain called the Mesaoria (Gr.: 'between mountains'), which is open to the sea at its western and eastern ends. In antiquity, when the natural vegetation was presumably much denser than now, the Troodos Massif must have been all but impenetrable, and the Kyrenia Range would have been a significant barrier to communication between the north coast and the Mesaoria. Until the Late Bronze Age at least, the only means of transportation was by donkey or on foot, and roads did not become a feature of the Cypriot landscape until Roman times. Moreover, Cyprus has few natural harbours, so that traffic around the coast could have been conducted only by small sailing vessels capable of landing on the shore.

Cyprus today gives little hint of the riches that once existed above and below its surface. Copper has been extracted for more than 5000 years and derives its name from the Roman designation for the island: Latin *cyprium aes* ('cyprian metal'). Although it is no longer a significant element of Cyprus's economy, the contribution it made in the Late Bronze Age and Roman times to the prosperity of the island and the Mediterranean basin at large makes it a resource of great historical importance. Information about Cyprus's other ancient natural resource comes from literary evidence of the Classical period, notably Strabo (*Geography* XIV.vi.5), who indicated that the island was once heavily forested but that the inroads made by timber-cutters for copper smelting and boatbuilding progressively reduced the natural tree cover. The Cypriot cedar is now confined to one small area of the Troodos Massif, but systematic reafforestation since the 19th century has considerably altered and restored the landscape. Nevertheless, the Cypriot climate is now hotter and drier than in antiquity, with an annual seven-month drought that dries up the island's rivers and causes springs to fail. There are no perennial rivers in Cyprus, and lack of water has always been a determining factor in the pattern of human habitation and land development.

Cyprus's natural setting seems to have had significant effects on its ancient inhabitants. It bred deeply into the islanders a rural, even rustic outlook that manifested itself in a less than sophisticated, though not provincial, perception of the environment. There is also a sense of isolation about Cypriot communities before the 1st millennium BC, no doubt fostered by the basic self-sufficiency of rural settlements and the obstacles to movement around the island. Before the mid-20th century it was common to find people who had hardly ever left their villages, and the archaeological record reveals a strong tendency towards insularity and regionalism that only the Hellenization of Cyprus in Ptolemaic times finally broke down.

R. S. MERRILLEES

2. TRADE. Copper was an important source of Cypriot mercantile wealth from prehistoric times until the closure of the mines in the 20th century. The discovery of copper in the Troodos foothills, together with an advantageous position as a staging post for seaborne traffic, brought the island out of its early isolation during the Middle Bronze Age (*c.* 1900–*c.* 1600 BC), when copper mining there is first attested. In this same period 'copper from the mountain of Alashiya', generally assumed to be on Cyprus, is mentioned in the palace archives of Mari in the Syrian hinterland. In the Late Bronze Age (*c.* 1600–*c.* 1050 BC) the metal was exported in the form of ingots shaped like oxhides, a form reproduced in miniature as the attribute of the bronze 'Ingot God' figurine from Enkomi (for illustration *see* ENKOMI).

Cypriot pottery, inventively and imaginatively designed, was copiously exported in the Late Bronze and Geometric (*c.* 1050–*c.* 750 BC) periods. Late Bronze handmade wares attracted many customers in the Levant and Egypt; Base Ring juglets (*see* §II, 4(iii) below), modelled after the head of the opium poppy, advertised their contents. Their wheel-made successors in the Geometric period, the Black-on-red juglets (*see* §II, 4(iv) below), contained perfume marketed in the Levant and the Aegean. When the Greek emporium at Naukratis in the Nile Delta was founded in the 7th century BC, Cyprus profited greatly from her intermediate staging posts, where sculpture dating from the 6th century BC shows influences from both Egypt and Greece (*see* §II, 3(iii) below). Even while it was part of the Persian empire in the 5th century BC, fine Attic pottery was imported in abundance to the island. Cypriot products are less distinctive in the common East Mediterranean idiom of the Hellenistic and Roman periods (323 BC–*c.* AD 330), but a local industry of glass vessels has been identified.

Under the Lusignan dynasty (1192–1489; *see* §IV below), commerce with Cyprus contributed to the mercantile prosperity of Venice, Genoa and Catalonia. Production of sugar, also exploited under Venetian rule, was a notable asset in the island's economy. In modern times, Cypriot craftsmanship in lace frequently attracts foreign custom.

NICOLAS COLDSTREAM

3. RELIGION AND ICONOGRAPHY.

(i) *Bronze Age.* From the earliest Neolithic times (*c.* 7000 BC) Cyprus's inhabitants developed fertility cults intended to enhance human and animal reproduction. From the Early Bronze Age (*c.* 2300–*c.* 1900 BC) the bull, mouflon and snake featured in a wide variety of art forms, no doubt linked with the islanders' preoccupation with fertility. A unique insight into prehistoric Cypriot religion is provided by the Early Bronze Age clay model (known as the Vounous Bowl; *see* §II, 3(ii) below) of an open-air sanctuary from Site B at Vounous (Nicosia, Cyprus Mus.;

see fig. 2). On the wall opposite the entrance (the lack of gates may itself be of cultic significance) are carved reliefs of three cult figures wearing bull masks (a symbol of fertility); snakes (representing death) coil down from their outstretched arms. Presiding figures (perhaps priests or chieftains) sit along the wall to either side of the images, while worshippers, some bearing infants, stand or kneel in the middle of the enclosure. Bulls stand near the entrance awaiting sacrifice, and from the outside a figure peers over the wall, suggesting that the rituals taking place within are reserved for a religious or social élite. As the prehistoric period progressed, the bird became increasingly associated with the most potent symbol of procreation, the naked female figure. What presumably started off in prehistoric tribes as a fertility charm was eventually transformed, after a long evolutionary process of syncretism, into the goddess for which the island was famed in the Classical period, Aphrodite.

While little can be said with great authority about the designs of temples or shrines, since too few have been excavated or preserved, tombs—whether cut into the rock or built—show architectural and sculptural features that imply (in death at least, if not so clearly in life) a certain non-functional indulgence. It is probably no coincidence that pottery and figurines with shapes and decorative designs that depart most radically from the norms of everyday domestic containers were found in graves and evidently made for funerary use. The ancient Cypriots made ample provision in their burial customs for the passage from this life into the next, and this journey may well have been less terminal than transcendental for them; the anticipation of death seems to have freed the artists' imagination from mundane requirements and allowed them to indulge in the humour and exuberance characteristic of Cypriot funerary art.

R. S. MERRILLEES

(ii) *Geometric to Classical.* Massive Aegean migrations at the end of the Bronze Age, followed by the coming of the Phoenicians to Kition *c.* 850 BC, resulted in a widespread religious syncretism compounded of Greek, Levantine and native Eteocypriot elements. The indigenous fertility goddess became equated with the Phoenician Astarte and the Greek Aphrodite, whose sanctuary at Old Paphos remained a major centre of pilgrimage in the Mediterranean world until the advent of Christianity. The Greek Herakles corresponded to the Phoenicians' Melqart, protector of their outpost at Kition; further examples of religious intermingling are the cults of the Egyptian deities Hathor and Bes at Eteocypriot Amathus, and of Zeus the Thunderer at Phoenician Kition.

Worship took place around altars in open courts, whether these sanctuaries adjoined major cities or were sited in rustic isolation. Temples were small and architecturally unpretentious, and cult statues occurred only under Classical Greek influence; otherwise, sculpted figures represented the votary rather than the deity. Even in the remote country sanctuary of Ayia Irini, a forest of terracotta statues acting as substitutes for the worshippers accumulated round the open-air altar. After the island's loss of independence in the early 3rd century BC, the cults

2. Clay model of an open-air sanctuary, Red Polished ware, h. 80 mm, diam. 370 mm, from Bellapais *Vounous* Site B, Tomb 22:26, *c.* 2000– *c.* 1900 BC (Nicosia, Cyprus Museum)

instituted were those of its new rulers, the Ptolemies followed by the Roman emperors.

NICOLAS COLDSTREAM

(iii) Early Christian to modern. By AD 325 the Christian community in Cyprus was already large enough to send at least three bishops to the Ecumenical Council of Nicaea. The spread of Christianity in the island was influenced by St Spyridon (*d c.* AD 348), St Hilarion (*c.* AD 291–371) and St Epiphanios (*c.* AD 315–403). Under the Lusignan dynasty from 1192 the Latin church took over the administration of the dioceses from the Greek Orthodox bishops, Nicosia became the seat of a Latin archbishop (1196), and many Latin monastic foundations followed, although some Greek Orthodox monasteries continued. The early 14th-century Gothic cathedral of Famagusta was an influential architectural model in the island. The 300 years of Turkish rule (1571–1878) relegated Cyprus to a backwater in the Muslim Ottoman empire but left the architectural heritage much as it was; religious tolerance allowed the Orthodox establishment to rise in power, so that the Archbishop came to be regarded as the leader of the Greek population. This tolerance continued in the period of British administration (1878–1960). The island has from 1974 been divided into a Muslim Turkish Cypriot north and an Orthodox Greek Cypriot south.

☐

II. Ancient.

Cypriot antiquity covers the period from the earliest habitation of the island to *c.* AD 330. When referring to ancient sites, the system used in excavation reports has been followed: 'Philia–Drakos A1', for example, signifies site A1 of the excavations at Drakos near the modern village of Philia.

1. Chronology. 2. Architecture. 3. Sculpture and figurines. 4. Pottery and vase painting. 5. Other arts.

1. CHRONOLOGY. Dates for the island's prehistoric sequence (see fig. 3) are now largely derived from radiocarbon (C-14) analysis. This scientific technique was not available when Cyprus's chronological framework was first established, and early accounts assume much later dates than those proposed since the mid-1960s, when scientific dating became widely accepted. More significantly, understanding of the Cypriot cultural sequences has been modified: radiocarbon dates indicate that the evolutionary

Neolithic	c. 7000–c. 3800 BC
Early (Aceramic)	c. 7000–c. 6000 BC
Middle	c. 6000–c. 4500 BC
Late	c. 4500–c. 3800 BC

Chalcolithic	c. 3800–c. 2300 BC
Early	c. 3800–c. 3500 BC
Middle	c. 3500–c. 2800 BC
Late	c. 2800–c. 2300 BC

Bronze Age		c. 2300–c. 1050 BC
Early Cypriot (ECYP)		c. 2300–c. 1900 BC
	ECYP I	c. 2300–c. 2100 BC
	ECYP II	c. 2100–c. 2000 BC
	ECYP III	c. 2000–c. 1900 BC
Middle Cypriot (MCYP)		c. 1900–c. 1600 BC
	MCYP I	c. 1900–c. 1800 BC
	MCYP II	c. 1800–c. 1725 BC
	MCYP III	c. 1725–c. 1600 BC
Late Cypriot (LCYP)		c. 1600–c. 1050 BC
	LCYP I	c. 1600–c. 1450 BC
	LCYP II	c. 1450–c. 1200 BC
	LCYP III	c. 1200–c. 1050 BC

Geometric		c. 1050–c. 750 BC
	I	c. 1050–c. 950 BC
	II	c. 950–c. 850 BC
	III	c. 850–c. 750 BC

Archaic		c. 750–c. 475 BC
	I	c. 750–c. 600 BC
	II	c. 600–c. 475 BC

Classical		c. 475–323 BC
	I	c. 475–c. 400 BC
	II	c. 400–323 BC

Hellenistic	323–c. 30 BC

Roman	c. 30 BC–c. AD 330

3. Chronological chart of ancient Cyprus

approach used to order sites was an oversimplification and that regional variation and collateral traditions in the arts operated from early times.

(i) Neolithic and Chalcolithic (c. 7000–c. 2300 BC). (ii) Bronze Age (c. 2300–c. 1050 BC). (iii) Geometric (c. 1050–c. 750 BC). (iv) Archaic (c. 750–c. 475 BC). (v) Classical (c. 475–323 BC). (vi) Hellenistic (323–c. 31 BC). (vii) Roman (c. 31 BC–c. AD 330).

(i) Neolithic and Chalcolithic (c. 7000–c. 2300 BC). Human occupation on Cyprus is first attested at pre-Neolithic Akrotiri–Aetokremnos c. 8000 BC. There is then a gap in the evidence until the emergence of Aceramic Neolithic villages (Neolithic I, c. 7000–c. 6000 BC; see KHIROKITIA and KALAVASOS), so named because of their lack of pottery, which was then current on the adjacent mainland. Another gap seems to exist between the Aceramic and Late Neolithic (Neolithic II) periods, perhaps denoting a colonizing failure; with the Late Neolithic period (c. 4500–c. 3800 BC) begins an unbroken settlement record on the island of Cyprus.

Throughout these early periods Cypriot art and architecture were resolutely individualistic, and foreign influence, so common in later periods, is conspicuous by its absence. Circular buildings, at times massively proportioned, characterize the walled settlements of the Aceramic Neolithic period (see fig. 5 below), but few artefacts of outstanding artistic merit have survived. Slightly modified pebbles sufficed to render the human, asexual form; energy was expended instead on the creation of pleasing shapes for utilitarian objects. This sense of practicality and functionalism is characteristic of Cypriot art throughout the prehistoric period.

As in other aspects of material culture of the time, the unpretentious architecture of the Late Neolithic period has no affinities with preceding traditions: rectangular buildings with rounded corners became popular, and floors were often sunk below ground-level. Indigenous pottery appeared for the first time in two distinctive regional styles (see §4(i) below): Red-on-white ware (also called Northern Painted) and Combed ware (also known as Southern Monochrome).

The end of the Neolithic period is marked at some sites by evidence of earthquake and at others by abandonment and subsequent reoccupation by squatters. Nevertheless, the transition to the Chalcolithic period (c. 3800–c. 2300 BC) seems to have occurred without major cultural discontinuity. The period takes its name from the appearance of copper tools, weapons and jewellery, alongside the continued use of stone implements; some of the new metal artefacts were probably imported from Anatolia, though local extraction or at least local working of the metal is also indicated.

Chalcolithic buildings were, like those of the Aceramic Neolithic period, almost invariably circular (see §2(i) below). Representative artwork emerged from the poorly articulated Neolithic forms: pendants representing cruciform-shaped humans (see fig. 9 below) and schematized designs such as a 28-rayed disc were carved from picrolite, a native blue–green stone; other stones were sculpted into free-standing statuettes (see §3(i) below). The full vigour of this creative potential appears in Red-on-white pottery, which was fashioned into some of the earliest known figures of women giving birth (see fig. 4), fantastic centaur-like creatures and anthropomorphic vessels. These lively, heterogeneous styles date to the Middle Chalcolithic period (c. 3500–c. 2800 BC), when innovative pottery painters introduced tension into decorative schemes and builders roofed enormous areas. The reasons for this outburst of prehistoric creativity are as yet little understood.

In the Late Chalcolithic period (c. 2800–c. 2300 BC) pottery decoration reverted to monochrome with a subtle interplay of red and black caused by differential firing. The

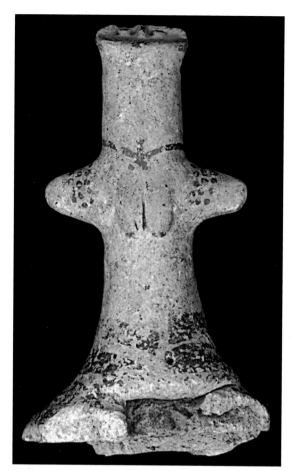

4. Chalcolithic figurine of a woman giving birth, Red-on-white ware, h. 200 mm, from Kissonerga–Mosphilia, *c.* 3000 BC (Nicosia, Cyprus Museum)

earliest phase of glyptic art may be traced to this period. Conical seals incised with linear designs emulate stamp seals from Cilicia, an area with which Cyprus had increasing contact.

(ii) Bronze Age (c. 2300–c. 1050 BC).

Momentous changes at the end of the Chalcolithic period, possibly owing to the arrival of Anatolian settlers on the island's north-west coast, led to the institution of burial in cemeteries. Archaeologists have concentrated on the investigation of these artefact-rich repositories with the result that the nature of the evidence now reflects mortuary concerns. Added to the difficulties of this one-sided picture is the fact that most cemeteries were excavated before the invention of radiocarbon dating. Chronological uncertainty is also fuelled by a dearth of well-dated imports and the likelihood of an increased divergence between regional styles. This situation means that great store has been placed on typological analysis for the chronological ordering of the numerous cemeteries. Following the practice of Aegean archaeology, the Bronze Age material has been divided into the Early Cypriot (ECYP), Middle Cypriot (MCYP) and Late Cypriot (LCYP) periods, each with its

subphases, although this system fails to give appropriate prominence to the radical artistic changes of the LCYP period.

(a) Philia Culture. Conventionally ascribed to the Bronze Age, tombs at Philia, east of the Morphou Plain, yielded only copper items (knives, adzes and jewellery). Some of the associated pottery follows Late Chalcolithic styles, including a transitional version of Red-on-white ware, but most of the vessels are in the new Red Polished ware, which was to become very popular in ECYP and MCYP times. The shapes and designs of the Philia pottery are paralleled in south-western Anatolia and Cilicia, suggesting either the arrival on the island of a group of mainland settlers or the activity of a group of native potters who were eager and adept imitators of Anatolian imports. The finds have been dated to *c.* 2500–*c.* 2300 BC, and the rise of the so-called Philia Culture may be related to the disturbed times around the end of the Early Bronze II period (*c.* 2500 BC) in Anatolia and Cilicia. Philia-style Red Polished ware has also been found at other sites on and around the Morphou Plain, and at Anoyira and Sotira–Kaminoudia to the south of the Troodos Massif. Excavations at Sotira–Kaminoudia have revealed a complex settlement of closely packed suites of rooms, but the associated Red Polished ware is not of the Philia style, although this style was found in nearby tombs. The rectilinear architecture here and, more clearly, at Margi facilitated the emergence of urbanism on Cyprus.

(b) Early Cypriot (c. 2300–c. 1900 BC). ECYP grave goods indicate a thriving economy, perhaps derived from a nascent Cypriot copper industry. A large variety of metal objects occur—weapons, tools and domestic implements—though it is not clear whether some prestige items were imported or locally made. Red Polished pottery gradually became the dominant ware on all sites. Flat terracotta figurines made in this ware were painted or incised to indicate the human form (*see* §3(ii) and fig. 10 below). Similar figurines on the Anatolian mainland have led to suggestions of foreign settlement, and the argument is sustained by other evidence: there are no plank figurines in picrolite, the material *par excellence* for Chalcolithic figurines.

By the end of the ECYP period, sites had spread from the Kyrenia Range and the edges of the Mesaoria Plain throughout the island, and the remains indicate a flourishing agricultural economy. From the Vounous B cemetery comes a clay model in Red Polished ware showing teams of yoked oxen (Nicosia, Cyprus Mus.), one of many images of daily life from the cemetery. The Vounous repertory ranges from single plank or brush-shaped figurines (a notable departure from the traditional Chalcolithic cruciforms) to vases with complete scenes of daily life modelled around their outer rims, while another clay model (*see* §I, 3 and fig. 2 above), which shows a cultic scene taking place in a circular walled courtyard, provides important evidence for the continued survival of the Chalcolithic circular building type, at any rate for ritual purposes.

A new pottery style, White Painted I ware, appeared in northern Cyprus at the end of the ECYP period. Although technically a derivative of Red Polished ware, it was the precursor of an important new sequence of MCYP styles. The increased economic importance of copperworking by the end of the ECYP period is indicated by a cluster of settlements around Ambelikou on the northern edge of the Troodos Massif, where a MCYP metalworking complex has been found. Local transport must have been revolutionized by the introduction of the donkey, as indicated by figurines of such animals supporting panniers (Sarasota, FL, Ringling Mus. A.). External contacts with Crete are indicated by a jar and some dagger blades of Early Minoan III–Middle Minoan I (c. 2200–c. 1800 BC) style (Nicosia, Cyprus Mus.), and faience beads were imported from Egypt.

(c) Middle Cypriot (c. 1900–c. 1600 BC). The transition to the Middle Bronze Age seems to have been peaceful, with continued industrial and agricultural prosperity. But the appearance in MCYP III of forts in the Karpas Peninsula, along the south side of the Kyrenia Range and even as far south as Ayios Sozomenos (c. 15 km south-east of Nicosia in the Mesaoria Plain), points to unrest at the end of the period, the causes of which have yet to be satisfactorily explained. Almost all the earliest excavated Bronze Age settlements—Kalopsida, Episkopi–Phaneromeni and Alambra—date from MCYP times. Their contiguous, rectangular-roomed houses were substantially built and set along straight streets in a way that recalls Cilician styles and anticipates the sophisticated cities of the LCYP period. Red Polished ware continued to be used in the south of the island, while in the north White Painted I gave way to White Painted II (see §4(ii) below). Plank figurines were produced in both Red Polished and White Painted styles and show an increasing sophistication towards the end of the MCYP period, with modelled arms and legs and grotesque facial features (see fig. 10 below).

(d) Late Cypriot (c. 1600–c. 1050 BC). During the disturbed times indicated by the destruction and rebuilding of fortresses at the end of MCYP III and the beginning of LCYP I, there is evidence of a dramatic change in Cypriot circumstances. This coincided with the establishment of the Asiatic Hyksos kings in Egypt (c. 1630 BC). They opened Egypt to foreign trade, a policy adopted by the 18th Dynasty Egyptian kings (c. 1540–c. 1292 BC) and one that enabled Cyprus to increase radically its trading links with the Near East, Egypt and the Aegean and to embark on one of the most prosperous periods in its history. New trading settlements, which had been founded near the east and south coasts at the end of the MCYP period, developed into cosmopolitan industrial centres, creating wealth and patronage that in turn fostered a greatly diversified artistic output. The result of these transmaritime exchanges, no doubt based on the island's rich copper resources, was the growth of eclectic art styles. More importantly for the establishment of a firm chronology, cross-dating of artefacts becomes possible through the occurrence of well-dated imports in Cyprus and of Cypriot exports in well-dated contexts abroad. Quite secure synchronisms are provided by the discovery of Cypriot White Painted V juglets at Tell el-Dab'a, the probable Hyksos capital of Egypt and of Cypriot Base Ring II pottery (?opium vessels;

London, BM; London, U.Coll., Petrie Mus.) at el-Amarna, the capital of the Egyptian king Akhenaten (reg c. 1353–c. 1336 BC).

Symptomatic of the new prosperity and openness of the LCYP period are distinctive Cypriot pottery styles—Bichrome, Base Ring, White Painted and its successor, White Slip (see §4(iii) and fig. 15 below)—that flooded eastern markets. Such was the demand that potters could scarcely provide enough and, perhaps inevitably, quality deteriorated. Exotic pottery such as incised juglets with Nilotic scenes of ducks among lotus blossoms came to the island in return.

The apogee of Cypriot Late Bronze Age civilization came c. 1300 BC, in LCYP II. New cities were founded, including Kalavasos–Ayios Dimitrios, which exhibits a grid-plan and had at least one administrative building with fine ashlar masonry, perhaps the earliest occurrence of this masonry style on the island. Although no LCYP palaces have been discovered, most scholars believe that Cypriot kings are attested in contemporary Egyptian, Hittite and Ugaritic texts, where they are clearly part of the Near Eastern political and economic system. Master craftsmen were likely to have been attached to these royal establishments, but the organization of the production of lesser artistic works is poorly understood. Imported luxury goods such as Hittite rings, Mycenaean and Minoan pottery and Egyptian jewellery, alabaster and glass exemplify the vigorous trade of the period, while native craftsmen simultaneously produced a wide and sophisticated range of gold jewellery combining local styles with foreign elements.

Newly emerged urban society in Cyprus sought inspiration from neighbouring lands—Egypt, the Near East and the Aegean—where states had existed for centuries. Egypt, with which Cyprus by then had diplomatic relations, supplied a rich fund of iconographical detail. Deities such as Bes and Hathor appear on ivories, and the *ankh*-sign is found on seals. Connections with Asia were more intimate, as is evident from buildings and tombs at Enkomi; Cypriot temples also possess plans derived from the Near East (see §2(ii) below). Seal-engravers were influenced by a wide variety of Asiatic styles. Local production was not wholly bound by foreign conventions, however: the oxhide-shaped ingot, for example, is a typically Cypriot symbol, occurring at the base of a bronze statuette from ENKOMI (Nicosia, Cyprus Mus.). Aegean imports evoked so much imitation that there are acute problems in determining whether a particular artefact was made by local or migrant craftsmen: a silver bowl from Enkomi with inlaid gold and niello bucrania (Nicosia, Cyprus Mus.) has a Cypriot shape and yet is technically so close to bowls from Greece that it may be an import. Adaptations of Mycenaean pottery styles led to the formation of the naive Pastoral (or Rude) style in Cypriot vase painting at the end of the 13th century BC (see §4(iii) below). Spirited designs, animals depicted in a 'flying gallop' with front and back legs extended, suggesting great speed, and floral patterns such as the ivy are typical western introductions. Features from several sources are often synthesized on the same work, with the product ascribed to a so-called International style. Thus a faience rhyton from Kition (c. 1250 BC; Nicosia, Cyprus Mus.; for illustration *see*

KITION) has an Aegean shape, Syrian flora and Egyptian glaze colours and polychrome glazing technology.

In the late 13th century BC the raids of the 'Sea Peoples' caused violent disturbances throughout the Mediterranean world. Most of the Mycenaean palace centres and Anatolian coastal cities were destroyed and abandoned. Some Cypriot sites (Kalavassos-Ayios Dimitrios) were destroyed, but most were immediately rebuilt (perhaps by incoming refugees), and whereas the LCYP III period was one of decline elsewhere in the ancient world, it was one of the most brilliant episodes in Cypriot art, one that reflected the island's continued economic prosperity. Undoubted Cypriot masterpieces were executed in ivory and metalwork. Ivory mirror handles with vigorous combat scenes (see §5(iii) and fig. 19 below) and bronze stands with openwork compositions that include the 'woman at the window' motif have been found in post-1200 BC deposits, although many were either heirlooms or were created under the impact of newcomers (see §(iii) below). As in previous periods, there was a lack of monumental art, but Cyprus continued to excel in the applied and decorative fields.

BIBLIOGRAPHY

P. Dikaios and J. R. Stewart: *The Stone and Early Bronze Age in Cyprus* (1962), iv/1a of *The Swedish Cyprus Expedition* (Stockholm, 1934–)
H. -G. Buchholz and V. Karageorghis: *Altägäis und Altkypros* (Tübingen, 1971)
D. Hunt, ed.: *Footprints in Cyprus* (London, 1982), pp. 18–57
V. Karageorghis: *Cyprus from the Stone Age to the Romans* (London, 1982), pp. 16–113
——: *Archaia kypriake techne sto Museio to Idrymatos Pieride* [Ancient Cypriot art in the Pierides Foundation Museum] (Larnaka, 1985)
D. Morris: *The Art of Ancient Cyprus* (Oxford, 1985)
E. J. Peltenburg: *Early Society in Cyprus* (Edinburgh, 1989)
V. Karageorghis, E. J. Peltenburg and P. Flourentzos: *Cyprus before the Bronze Age* (Malibu, 1990)

E. J. PELTENBURG

(iii) Geometric (c. 1050–c. 750 BC). The beginning of the Cypriot Geometric period coincides approximately with a movement of immigrants from the Aegean, which was to transform Cyprus into a predominantly Greek-speaking land. Since the early 12th century BC the island had received a steady infiltration of Aegean newcomers, fleeing the demise of Mycenaean palatial civilization and settling among the indigenous inhabitants at Enkomi and other cities. Then, during the 11th century BC, whole Aegean communities arrived to found new settlements that were destined to become the seats of the historical Greek kingdoms of Cyprus: Kourion, Old Paphos, Marion, Soli, Lapithos, Tamassos, Idalion and Salamis, the last of which superseded Enkomi as the chief settlement in eastern Cyprus.

Greek legends place these new foundations at the close of the Heroic Age. A typical example is that of the city of Salamis, reputedly founded by Teuker, a hero from the Aegean island of Salamis and half-brother of Ajax, who was blown off course during his return from the Trojan War. Such legends usually contain at least a kernel of historical truth. Although the new settlements have hardly been explored, their associated burials, in collective rock-cut chamber tombs of Mycenaean type, have been found to be plentifully furnished with fine painted pottery chiefly of Aegean character, in the style known as Cypro-Geometric I (c. 1050–c. 950 BC; see §4(iv) below). A bronze

spit from a Paphian tomb of this period (Nicosia, Cyprus Mus.) is inscribed in syllabic script with an Arcadian Greek personal name ('of Opheltas'), attesting not only the continuity of literacy in Cyprus from the Bronze Age but also the use of the Greek language there as early as c. 1000 BC. The offerings in these early Greek-Cypriot tombs, especially rich in bronze vessels, jewellery and Levantine imports, show that the new settlers enjoyed a prosperity denied to their impoverished kinsmen in the Aegean at the outset of the Greek Dark Age.

A new settlement was established in the 11th century BC at Amathus, which was to emerge in historical times as the chief stronghold of the indigenous islanders, called Eteocypriots. There they preserved their language (as yet undeciphered) and soon profited from their advantageous position on the main sea route between the Aegean and the mercantile cities of the Levant. After an uneventful period of consolidation and gradual symbiosis between the Greek and indigenous inhabitants, it was the Phoenicians who provided the next external impetus to Cypriot civilization. At some time during the 9th century BC citizens from their leading city, Tyre, established a colony at Kition. A Phoenician inscription on an 8th-century BC bronze bowl (Paris, Bib. N.) gives the name of the colony as Qart Hadasht (Phoenician: 'new town'), the name also given to two later Phoenician outposts in the western Mediterranean, Carthage in Tunisia and Cartagena in Spain. The inscription also reveals that Kition was a colony in the imperial sense, ruled by a governor who was accountable to the king of Tyre. The earliest archaeological evidence for the colony is a large temple to the fertility goddess Astarte (c. 850 BC; see §2(iii) below) built over and incorporating much of the remains of a Late Bronze Age sanctuary deserted since c. 1000 BC; the ground-plan and monumental masonry of the later temple bear some relation to another great Phoenician architectural masterpiece, King Solomon's Temple at Jerusalem (1 Kings 6–8).

The Phoenicians made no immediate attempt to extend their political control beyond Kition, but their impact on Cypriot art was soon felt throughout the island. Ivories of the Phoenician school and Cypro-Phoenician metal bowls with embossed scenes inside became important iconographical sources for Cypriot figured art, ceramic and otherwise. For writing, however, both the Greek Cypriots and the Eteocypriots preferred their syllabic scripts to the more practical alphabet introduced by the Phoenicians.

(iv) Archaic (c. 750–c. 475 BC). For Cyprus, as for Greece and Phoenicia, the 8th century BC was an age of improved communications, expanding horizons and burgeoning prosperity. Cypriot coastal towns profited greatly from eastern and western trade, and the interplay of oriental and Greek influences contributed much to the vitality of Cypriot Archaic art. In their politics, however, the Cypriots were immovably conservative. While Aegean Greeks began to develop the polis, the autonomous city state with its clearly defined republican constitution, Cyprus knew only an absolute monarchy, which owed something to both Mycenaean tradition and eastern despotism. The island was divided into ten petty kingdoms, wholly independent at first and still preserving local autonomy even

during their temporary submission to the Assyrian empire from 709 to *c.* 663 BC.

The 'royal tombs' of SALAMIS (*c.* 750–*c.* 600 BC) illustrate an outstandingly brilliant phase of Cypriot history. The richest burials, accompanied by chariots with sacrificed horse teams and crowned by earth tumuli, echo Greek heroic tradition (as preserved in *Iliad* XXIII). The luxurious offerings, however, are almost wholly of oriental character: thrones and a bed are adorned with Phoenician ivory plaques; bronze vessels (see fig. 21 below) and profusely figured items of bronze harness combine Urartian, Levantine and Egyptian elements (all finds at Nicosia, Cyprus Mus.). Fine ashlar masonry, also of eastern inspiration, lines the tomb-chamber façades and broad entrance passages.

The end of Assyrian rule was followed by a century of complete independence, a flourishing period for all the arts of Archaic Cyprus. In architecture, the rock-cut royal tombs of Tamassos (*c.* 600–*c.* 550 BC) skilfully imitated wooden dwellings, decorated in relief with Phoenician ('Protoaeolic') volute capitals. Large-scale statuary, both in limestone and in terracotta, made its first appearance in sanctuaries, representing worshippers rather than deities (see §3(iii) below). Cypriot pottery painted in the Free Field style (see §4(v) below), which was rich in exotic floral, bird and animal motifs, reached its most creative and decorative stage.

After a brief interlude of Egyptian rule (*c.* 560–*c.* 540 BC) under the Saite dynasty, the island voluntarily submitted to the rising Persian empire. The Cypriot kingdoms at first retained some local autonomy. King Euelthon of Salamis (*reg* 560–525 BC), for example, was not only allowed to mint his own coinage (the earliest in Cyprus) but also to receive foreign embassies. In the arts, especially sculpture, the later 6th century BC was characterized by profound influence from the Ionian Greeks. Relations with Persia deteriorated when Cyprus became embroiled in the abortive Ionian Revolt, when the Ionian Greeks of the east Aegean rebelled from Persian domination (499/8 BC). Outside the walls of Old Paphos the Persian ramp and siege-mound form a vivid memorial to the failure of this uprising.

*(v) Classical (*c. 475–323 BC*).* In spite of two successive attempts by the Athenians to detach Cyprus from the Persian empire, the island remained firmly under Persian control throughout the 5th century BC. Most of its kingdoms, however, were still permitted to mint coins, some of which supply names of local dynasts unknown from historical sources. Semitic royal names on coins of Marion and Lapithos are consistent with a general expansion of Phoenician influence, as seen in Kition's acquisition, with Persian help, of Idalion (*c.* 470 BC) and, in the 4th century BC, of Tamassos. There is no evidence, however, of any rooted hostility between the Greek and Phoenician communities; a cult of Zeus at Kition, for example, indicates some measure of coexistence and mixture of populations. The 5th-century BC palace at Vouni, the plan of which is based on Near Eastern models (see §2(iii) and fig. 7 below), is a fine example of a Cypriot royal despot's residence under the Persian empire.

In 411 BC a Phoenician usurper at Salamis was ousted by a young Teukrid nobleman, Euagoras I (*reg* 411–374/3 BC); during his long reign Euagoras temporarily succeeded, with Athenian and Egyptian help, in expelling the Persians altogether and in uniting the island under his sway, though by force rather than consent. He attracted to his court Athenian writers, public men and artists; marble heads of his time from Salamis, in an elegant Praxitelean style (see SALAMIS, fig. 2), form a welcome contrast to the sub-Archaic mediocrity of most Cypriot sculpture in Classical times.

BIBLIOGRAPHY

E. Gjerstad: *The Cypro-Geometric, Cypro-Archaic and Cypro-Classical Periods* (1948), iv/2 of *The Swedish Cyprus Expedition* (Stockholm, 1934–)
F. G. Maier: *Cypern: Insel am Kreuzweg der Geschichte* (Stuttgart, 1964); Eng. trans. by P. George as *Cyprus from Earliest Time to the Present Day* (London, 1968)
V. Karageorghis: *Excavations in the Necropolis of Salamis*, 4 vols (Nicosia, 1967–78)
J. L. Benson: *The Necropolis of Kaloriziki* (Göteborg, 1973)
E. Gjerstad: 'The Phoenician Colonization and Expansion in Cyprus', *Rep. Dept Ant., Cyprus* (1979), pp. 230–54
V. Karageorghis: *Cyprus from the Stone Age to the Romans* (London, 1982)
——: 'Cyprus', *Camb. Anc. Hist.*, iii/1, ed. J. Boardman and others (Cambridge, 1982), pp. 511–33

NICOLAS COLDSTREAM

*(vi) Hellenistic (323–*c. 31 BC*).* Cyprus was freed from Persian rule in 332 BC by Alexander the Great, but its period of relative independence was brief: by 294 BC it had become a province of the Egyptian kingdom of Ptolemy I Soter (*reg* 304–283/2 BC). The early 3rd century BC was a turning-point in the history of Cyprus, as the influence of Hellenistic Greek culture became paramount on the island; the uncompromising standards of Greek art gradually eradicated the indigenous Cypriot tradition. Seen in perspective, Cypriot art and architecture during the following centuries pose the problem of regional tradition versus cultural conformity.

Although the cities of the island had lost their autonomy, considerable building activity during the Hellenistic period reflects their growing prosperity. Because of earthquakes and large-scale Roman reconstruction, however, only scarce traces survive. At Salamis a Hellenistic gymnasium has come to light below the Roman baths, and at Kourion the remains of a late 2nd-century BC theatre were discovered below a 2nd-century AD Roman building. In a similar way most Hellenistic sanctuaries were completely destroyed by subsequent Roman building, though the remains of the famous Temple of Zeus Olympios at SALAMIS date from the end of the 2nd century BC.

The most conspicuous products of Hellenistic art were statues of rulers, officials, priests and eminent citizens, which filled sanctuary precincts and other public places. Most of these were executed by Cypriot workshops in soft local limestone, though some of the marble sculpture was imported. Strong Athenian influence persisted, but the impact of thriving Hellenistic workshops at Alexandria and later at Pergamon can also be observed. The minor arts reflect the comfortable living standards and cosmopolitan influences of the time. Hellenistic terracotta figurines replaced those from local traditions, Alexandria being a main source of inspiration. Pottery shows a similar if slower development, with local imitations of Hellenistic

East Greek wares gradually becoming dominant in Cyprus. New types of mould-pressed glass bowls occurred in the Late Hellenistic period, but it is still uncertain whether they were imported or manufactured on the island. The magnificent gold and silver jewellery of the period shows clear traces of Eastern influence.

Rock-cut or built Hellenistic chamber-tombs as a rule represent more sophisticated versions of traditional tomb types, but there is one notable exception: the so-called 'Tombs of the Kings' at New Paphos (see §2(iv) and fig. 8 below). These sunken peristyle tombs, cut from the living rock, have no antecedents in Cyprus and doubtless drew inspiration from Alexandria. They show how precarious the hold of indigenous traditions had become: when Hellenistic Cypriot craftsmen aimed at magnificence, they adopted foreign models.

(vii) Roman (c. 31 BC–c. AD 330). Although Cyprus was annexed by Rome in 58 BC, Roman control of the island was not fully established until after the Battle of Actium in 31 BC. Roman rule did not drastically alter conditions on the island. The prosperity of Late Hellenistic times increased with the *pax romana*, reaching its zenith under the Antonine and Severan emperors (AD 138–235). A remarkable burst of activity in arts and architecture took place during these centuries, and elements of Roman-style urban development can be seen across the island: fora, colonnaded squares, theatres, temples, baths and aqueducts (see §2(iv) below). In these public buildings and the sumptuous private residences that have been uncovered at NEW PAPHOS and Kourion can be seen the changing fashions of Roman Imperial architecture. The well-known mosaics adorning these houses are the most impressive examples of Roman art in Cyprus (see §5(vi) below). Statues were also produced in large quantities, often recalling closely the work of Anatolian schools of sculpture. One striking example is the over life-size bronze portrait statue of *Septimius Severus* (reg AD 193–211; Nicosia, Cyprus Mus.) found at Kythrea; its heroic nudity testifies to the survival of Hellenistic traditions as late as the 3rd century AD. Both mosaics and sculpture indicate that the arts of Cyprus conformed ever more closely to the civilization of the Roman Empire. Some works, such as the statues from a rustic sanctuary at Phasoula (4th–5th century AD; Nicosia, Cyprus Mus.), show unconventional elements, but these can hardly be described as specifically Cypriot.

Conformity and loss of local individuality are apparent also in the minor arts. Cypriot pottery workshops reproduced Syrian and Cilician types, and vases sometimes show the influence of Italian *Terra sigillata* ware (see ROME, ANCIENT, §X, 8). From the 2nd century AD onwards fine pottery to a certain extent gave way to glass. The more sophisticated vessels were still imported from Syria, but a local Cypriot glass industry produced large quantities for everyday use. Nevertheless, Cypriot glass was but a regional variety of the standardized domestic glass produced throughout the Empire. Cypriot goldsmiths turned to new fashions in jewellery and adopted such new techniques as pierced work, the use of polychrome stones or niello ornamentation. From the Late Bronze Age to the Classical

period Cypriot art and architecture were clearly distinguished from the models that inspired them by definite and typical local elements. By the 4th century AD, however, most of the island's individual character had disappeared, overwhelmed by the Mediterranean world civilization of the Roman Empire; yet it was of crucial importance for the future history of Cyprus that the Roman East remained Greek in language and cultural traditions.

BIBLIOGRAPHY
O. Vessberg and A. Westholm: *The Hellenistic and Roman Periods in Cyprus* (1956), iv/3 of *The Swedish Cyprus Expedition* (Stockholm, 1934–)
V. Karageorghis: *Cyprus from the Stone Age to the Romans* (London, 1982)
V. A. Tatton-Brown: 'The Hellenistic Period', *Footprints in Cyprus*, ed. D. Hunt (London, 1982), pp. 106–19
——: 'The Roman Period', *Footprints in Cyprus*, ed. D. Hunt (London, 1982), pp. 120–33

FRANZ GEORG MAIER

2. ARCHITECTURE.

(i) Neolithic and Chalcolithic (*c.* 7000–*c.* 2300 BC). (ii) Bronze Age (*c.* 2300–*c.* 1050 BC). (iii) Geometric to Classical (*c.* 1050–323 BC). (iv) Hellenistic and Roman (323 BC–*c.* AD 330).

(i) Neolithic and Chalcolithic (c. 7000–c. 2300 BC). The earliest recovered buildings in Cyprus belong to the Aceramic Neolithic period (*c.* 7000–*c.* 6000 BC); they are circular in plan and were built in villages. When first excavated on a large scale, at KHIROKITIA, they were believed to have domed roofs and were described as tholoi, but work since 1977 at this major site indicates flat roofs. Walls were of rammed mud (pisé) or mud-brick, with stone foundations frequently of massive proportions owing to rebuilding; additional support, perhaps for an upper floor or loft, was provided by free-standing or engaged pillars (see fig. 5). Internal wall faces were often plastered and sometimes painted. At KALAVASOS–Tenta the largest building (diam. 10 m) has an external gallery; it crowns a hillock, on the slopes of which are clustered much simpler huts (diam. only 4 m). The origins of this distinctive building style may lie in widespread prehistoric traditions, in which the first structures of a new settlement were circular. Insular conservatism meant that little architectural evolution occurred in prehistoric Cyprus.

Late Neolithic (*c.* 4500–*c.* 3800 BC) architecture on the island is unpretentious, consisting primarily of small, single-roomed dwellings in villages often bounded by

5. Aceramic Neolithic house at Khirokitia, Cyprus, *c.* 7000–*c.* 6000 BC

stone-built walls and ditches or by natural defences. Where there were few topographical constraints, as at Sotira, buildings tend to be free-standing and are square in plan with rounded corners. At Ayios Epiktitos–Vrysi, however, structures were semi-subterranean; restricted by lack of space, the builders there produced curvilinear and contiguous dwellings, with stone foundations up to 1.5 m in height that supported thin walls of mud. Most Late Neolithic buildings enclose an area of *c.* 15 sq. m, and this uniformity is emphasized by the complete absence of any outstanding, let alone monumental architecture such as occurred on the adjacent Near Eastern mainland.

Circular buildings reappeared in the Chalcolithic period (*c.* 3800–*c.* 2300 BC), but chronological, cultural and architectural evidence demonstrates that this was a new building tradition quite independent from that which had prevailed on the island in the Aceramic Neolithic period. At Kissonerga–Mosphilia, flimsy, pisé-walled structures with flat or conical roofs developed into spacious multi-roomed circular buildings enclosing some 75 sq. m. Even in these structures, however, the largest in prehistoric Cyprus, walls were low and were composed of drystone masonry and pisé. Puddled lime was used to pave floors, and, as shown in a building model (Nicosia, Cyprus Mus.), the earliest from Cyprus, walls might be painted from floor to ceiling with checks, poles with streamers and squares set on diverging base-lines. Increasing social complexity led to the creation of different-sized structures with specialist functions, as well as to entrance passages in tombs, all of which presage developments in the Bronze Age.

BIBLIOGRAPHY

P. Dikaios: 'A Conspectus of Architecture in Ancient Cyprus', *Kyp. Spoudai*, xxiv (1960), pp. 1–30

E. J. Peltenburg: *Recent Developments in the Later Prehistory of Cyprus* (Göteborg, 1982)

——: *Lemba Archaeological Project II.2: A Ceremonial Area of Kissonerga* (Göteborg, 1991)

E. J. PELTENBURG

(ii) Bronze Age (c. 2300–c. 1050 BC). The so-called Philia Culture (*see* §1(ii)(a) above), as characterized by its burial goods, is held to span the Late Chalcolithic and the Early Bronze Age or Early Cypriot (ECYP) periods in Cyprus and to manifest connections with Anatolia. At Sotira–Kaminoudia near the south coast of Cyprus a densely accreted settlement apparently of one or more hectares has been excavated, with individual compartments of all shapes and sizes, their walls curved to subrectilinear. Suites of chambers can be identified only because of the interesting use of long corridors for access and circulation. This radical change from the Chalcolithic type of settlement indicates not so much that Cyprus had entered into contact with the adjacent mainland—it would have been virtually impossible for an island in plain view to remain unvisited—but that the amazingly resilient round-house society had at last lost its vital force and accepted the building form of its neighbours, for example Anatolia and northern Syria–Mesopotamia, where similar dense, hive-like planning occurs. However, the social norms associated with this type of planning on the mainland were not adopted on Cyprus. As far as is known, the island maintained a rural village lifestyle resembling the mainland social conditions of 1000 years earlier and continued to do so for many centuries to come.

No ECYP or Middle Cypriot (MCYP) temple or shrine has yet been excavated, although the recovery of ECYP I terracotta models from tombs demonstrates the existence of simple open-air enclosures with a symbolic gate and such internal installations as benches, offering tables etc. The best-known of these models, that from Vounous (*c.* 2300–*c.* 2100 BC; Nicosia, Cyprus Mus.; *see* §I, 3 and fig. 2 above) shows that by operation of religious conservatism such simple rural sanctuaries remained circular in form. This model is the oldest known representation of the type of rural sanctuary that has also been discovered at Ayios Iakovos and Ayia Irini (in the north-west and north-east of the island respectively); both date from the Late Cypriot (LCYP) period. These sanctuaries endure throughout antiquity to constitute possibly the most distinctive class of buildings in ancient Cyprus. The simplest consist of an enclosure with a sacred object (altar, tree etc) in the court, accompanied perhaps by some shed or shelter (e.g. Ayios Iakovos), or they may have an enclosure containing a built shrine in addition to the sacred object in the court (e.g. Ayia Irini).

Some diversity of domestic building forms evolved during ECYP and MCYP times. At the ECYP III–MCYP site of Alambra, *c.* 20 km south of Nicosia, two complementary house forms have been revealed: a rural two-room cabin in an enclosure (cf. the Chalcolithic house type of Palestine and Syria) and a row of terrace houses—long buildings divided across the middle into a front and rear compartment, not at all unlike poorer, high-density urban housing common in Palestine at the same time. Another house, at Kalopsida in the eastern Mesaoria Plain (*c.* 1600 BC), appears to be something like a fairly large (*c.* 11×14 m) internal-courtyard house, its four-square frontages connoting a regularly laid-out street system, although the nature of the settlement remains uninvestigated.

The process of development from village to urban building is well illustrated at ENKOMI, where excavation has revealed in some areas a succession of buildings from *c.* 1600 BC onwards. Originally there appear to have been several clusters of rural-type dwellings with open-fronted, π-form plans. At the northern edge of the settlement there was a type of blockhouse or fort designed to protect or dominate the settled area; it included premises for metal-working. Other strongholds or fortified centres (e.g. at Nikolides in central Cyprus and at Nitovikla to the north of Enkomi) are known from MCYP III and LCYP I. It is possible that some of these fortresses may have served to dominate rural settlements and control copper production. In the latter part of the 13th century BC (LCYP II) a Cyclopean stone wall was built at Enkomi to enclose an area of *c.* 16 ha, and the interior of the settlement was laid out in a regular series of parallel east–west streets and a main north–south central avenue to produce a series of elongated *insulae* crammed with high-density, urban-style buildings. The plots close to the avenue have revealed large (*c.* 30×30 m), even-fronted residential block buildings containing some 40 rooms and covering over 1000 sq. m (see fig. 6). Much of the construction includes finely dressed (ashlar) masonry orthostates, a very recent development in the Eastern Mediterranean. It is not easy to characterize the social function of such buildings, though something like a Renaissance Italian palazzo or a French

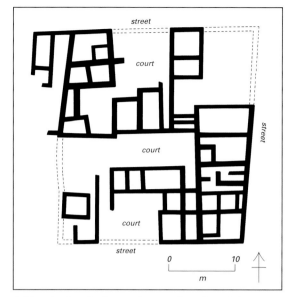

6. Plan showing the Bronze Age transformation of three open-fronted court complexes into a unified residential block at Enkomi, Late Cypriot II, *c.* 1225 BC

hôtel may give the best idea. In one such building (the Ashlar Building, Area I) a sanctuary complex was installed *c.* 1200 BC after an earlier destruction; it comprised two associated chapels to a god and a goddess, perhaps patrons of metalworking. The plan consists essentially of a main public hall for the cult activities of the congregation and a small inner chamber (sacristy or thalamus) for the cult image and sacred objects.

The picture of LCYP urban Cyprus at Enkomi is complemented by discoveries at Kition, the other great east-coast maritime centre. In the northern part of the site a striking urban sanctuary area of the 13th or 12th century BC has been meticulously excavated to reveal five temple buildings, of which four conform to a plan familiar both in Palestine (e.g. at Tel Qasile and Lachish) and in continental Greece (e.g. at Mycenae). Essentially it comprises a hall with an indirect entry (i.e. non-axial or bent) and a small room at the rear that housed the divine image and served as a storeroom for cultic equipment. However, one temple (No. 1) is of a more monumental long-room type (*c.* 31×22 m), which was later restored and redeveloped by the Phoenicians as the metropolitan Temple of Astarte (*see* §(iii) below).

Thus by *c.* 1200 BC the large towns of Enkomi and Kition were in all respects similar to contemporary towns of the neighbouring mainland. This constitutes a momentous transformation from the insular Cypriot tradition of the preceding 5000 years. Within one or two generations during the 13th century BC the rubble and mud-brick construction that had served the island virtually from its colonization was supplemented by finely dressed monumental masonry, and rude wooden props and posts gave place to something like an architectural order consisting of stone capitals and bases with simple stepped mouldings and pillars of monolithic stone or from composite timber scantlings.

BIBLIOGRAPHY

P. Åström: *The Late Cypriote Bronze Age* (1971), iv/1c of *The Swedish Cyprus Expedition* (Stockholm, 1934–)
M. Fortin: *Military Architecture in Cyprus during the 2nd Millennium* (diss., U. London, 1981)
G. Hult: *Bronze Age Ashlar Masonry*, Stud. Medit. Archaeol., lxv (Göteborg, 1983)
I. Ionas: *L'Architecture religieuse au 11e millénaire à Chypre* (diss., U. Lyon, 1983)
S. S. Weinberg: *Bamboula at Kourion: The Architecture* (Philadelphia, 1983)
V. Karageorghis, ed.: *Archaeology in Cyprus, 1960–85* (Nicosia, 1985)
G. R. H. Wright: *Ancient Building in South Syria and Palestine*, 2 vols (Leiden, 1985)
O. Negbi: 'The Climax of Urban Development in Bronze Age Cyprus', *Rep. Dept Ant., Cyprus* (1986), pp. 97–121
G. R. H. Wright: *Ancient Building in Cyprus*, 2 vols (Leiden, 1992)

(iii) Geometric to Classical (c. 1050–323 BC*).* Although some sites may have been abandoned and settlement patterns changed at the end of the Late Cypriot (LCYP) period, there is little evidence of a Dark Age, and tomb finds of the Archaic period again indicate a time of extravagant prosperity. Nonetheless, the archaeological record of the Geometric to Classical periods is conspicuously lacking in free-standing building remains, and it is far from easy to characterize Cypriot building of this time or to specify its relationship with the preceding building tradition. The most significant illustration of the origins and development of Cypriot building in the Geometric period (*c.* 1050–*c.* 750 BC) is found in the sanctuary area at Kition, where the Phoenician-built Temple of Astarte (*c.* 850 BC) must have constituted the metropolitan shrine for that part of the island. Constructed on the ruins and incorporating much of a Bronze Age temple, it repeated the role of Solomon's Temple in Jerusalem in carrying over Bronze Age building forms into the Geometric period. Even more significantly, the Temple of Astarte reveals the continued use of monumental ashlar-faced walls for at least the socle of major public buildings. Thus, although the sanctuary area was neglected or abandoned from *c.* 1000 BC to its redevelopment in *c.* 850 BC, this did not constitute a break in the established building tradition that Cyprus shared with its neighbouring lands.

The only surviving examples of architectural continuity from the Geometric to the Classical periods are provided by masonry tombs and rural sanctuaries. The monumental tombs of the Archaic period (e.g. those at Tamassos and SALAMIS) reveal excellent ashlar masonry revetment (a natural medium for underground construction) and have much in common with tombs in the neighbouring coastal areas of Anatolia. The excavation of the rural sanctuary at Meniko (*c.* 600–*c.* 550 BC), however, shows a typical village-type building with an emphasis on the square cella; this type of architecture seems to be a post-Bronze Age phenomenon and attributable ultimately to Phoenicia. On the other hand, a long hall was uncovered in the sanctuary (*c.* 500 BC) at Golgi in the 19th century; it had a double-square design (*c.* 18×9 m) with three rows of pillars, suggesting a provincial version of the Phoenician Temple of Astarte at Kition.

Although no remains have yet been found of the luxurious palaces built by the Cypriot kings of the Archaic period, the superlative palace building of VOUNI from the Late Archaic and Classical periods (see fig. 7) gives some idea of their grandeur. The original palace was built in the

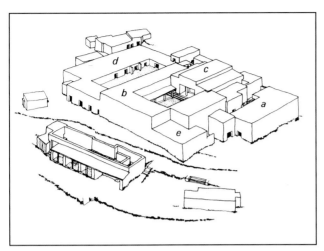

7. Palace at Vouni, final stage (Vouni II), late 5th century BC; isometric reconstruction: (a) original service wings; (b) residential and reception rooms; (c) original entrance block transformed into an inward-facing megaron; (d) service wings; (e) new main entrance leading into north-west corner of the court

first half of the 5th century BC and incorporates striking features of design and construction. The essential continuity these show with LCYP public buildings is telling evidence against any intervening Dark Age. Over its various building phases the palace was provided with extensive service wings (7a and 7d), and a variety of chapels or shrines were set around it. The monumental core of the building was the suite of residential and reception rooms (7b) set out around a central court to form the basic Cypriot open-fronted (π) plan. In its developed form the open front of the court was closed by an entrance block containing state apartments (7c). This design can be seen at LCYP Enkomi (see also fig. 6 above) and Ayios Dimitrios, but at Vouni it was carried out on a truly monumental scale. The total complex was c. 80×60 m, and the core unit was c. 35×30 m, with the entrance block functioning as a magnificent gate-house. A similar development of an existing tradition can be seen in Vouni's construction technique. Some of the service area is built in the 'village' style, with mud-brick walls on rubble foundations or socles. Much of the walling, however, is in the LCYP 'urban' style, with ashlar masonry facing, although in a distinct development at Vouni the facing blocks were set in various patterns involving alternation in the format of blocks in successive courses and/or in successive blocks within one course, which promoted the bonding of the facing and filling in what became (depending on the cementitious properties of the ground mass) a type of concrete construction.

Contemporary with the first phase of the palace at Vouni was a palatial residence built against the city wall in the Hadji Abdullah locality of Old Paphos. The design was modelled on Asiatic prototypes, though the building was in fact an interesting hybrid: its long, narrow halls recall the vaulted mud-brick architecture of Mesopotamia, but it was constructed in the local ashlar-faced masonry tradition common to the eastern Mediterranean.

It was only during the 5th and 4th centuries BC that some isolated echoes of Classical Greek architecture appeared in Cyprus. The rearrangement and enlargement of the palace at Vouni in the second half of the 5th century BC may have been intended to convert the Asiatic entrance block into a Greek megaron (though this interpretation is disputed; see VOUNI), while some of the sanctuary buildings of the period might have been simple, one-room Greek-style temples (e.g. at the Sanctuary of Apollo Hylates near Kourion). Odd pieces of Classical (Ionic) architectural ornament have survived at Tamassos, but nothing like a Classical peristyle temple has been discovered, and it is not easy to say what type of buildings were ornamented with these Classical members. More significantly, there are no examples of those varied public buildings that were the hallmark of the Classical Greek spirit: the theatre and gymnasium, the stoa and bouleuterion etc. All these marks of thorough Hellenization appeared in Cyprus only with the end of Cypriot autonomy and the establishment of Ptolemaic rule in 294 BC.

BIBLIOGRAPHY

M. Ohnefalsch Richter: *Kypros, the Bible and Homer* (London, 1893)
A. Westholm: 'Built Tombs in Cyprus', *Opuscula Archaeol.*, ii (1941), pp. 29–58
E. Gjerstad: *The Cypro-Geometric, Cypro-Archaic and Cypro-Classical Periods* (1948), vi/2 of *The Swedish Cyprus Expedition* (Stockholm, 1934–)
R. Scranton: 'The Architecture of the Sanctuary of Apollo Hylates at Kourion', *Trans. Amer. Philos. Soc.*, n. s., lvii (1967)
V. Karageorghis: 'The Relations between the Tomb Architecture of Anatolia and Cyprus in the Archaic Period', *Proceedings of the 10th International Congress of Classical Archaeology: Ankara–Izmir, 1973*, i, pp. 361–8
——: *Two Cypriote Sanctuaries of the End of the Cypro-Archaic Period* (Rome, 1977)
S. M. S. al Radi: *Phlamoudhi Vounari: A Sanctuary Site in Cyprus* (Göteborg, 1983)
V. Karageorghis, ed.: *Archaeology in Cyprus, 1960–85* (Nicosia, 1985)
G. R. H. Wright: *Ancient Building in Cyprus* (Leiden, 1992)

G. R. H. WRIGHT

(iv) Hellenistic and Roman (323 BC–c. AD 330). The Hellenistic architecture of Cyprus was, like the rest of its culture, characterized by a strong Greek bias, but it also exhibited a diversity of traditions that derived from its own earlier mixed culture and the cosmopolitan nature of the Ptolemaic world. Early evidence of urban planning comes from NEW PAPHOS (founded c. 320 BC), where a street grid-plan created rectangular building plots c. 35×80 m in size. The city was heavily fortified with stone walls and towers partly built and partly hewn out of bedrock. Although Cyprus was by this time heavily influenced by Greek tastes, it appears to have had no traditional Greek temples. Several of the old temples, such as that of Aphrodite at OLD PAPHOS, were in effect sacred precincts, and although they were often remodelled during the Hellenistic period they never lost their traditional character: a roofed cella opening on to one or more courtyards, which were occasionally equipped with porticos. The temples at Soli (early 3rd and mid-1st century BC) were of this type, with a plan developed from the Classical Temple of Athena at Vouni (c. 450 BC). The underground Sanctuary of Apollo Hylates at New Paphos, although different, is equally conservative.

Architecture of a more standard Greek type is also found on the island, most notably at SALAMIS, where a curious mixture of the Corinthian, Doric and Ionic orders occurs in the Temple of Zeus (2nd century BC). Theatres are known at New Paphos and Kourion, the latter similar to that of Priene on the coast of Asia Minor. Hellenistic dwellings were generally small, as at Idalion, but could sometimes be equipped with baths and workshops, as at Ayia Irini. In rich centres such as New Paphos, however, splendid examples of domestic architecture have been found, where the rooms (decorated with frescoes and pebble mosaics) were arranged around a colonnaded portico, as in Greece and Asia Minor. In the 'Tombs of the Kings' at New Paphos (3rd century BC; see fig. 8) funerary architecture imitates these domestic designs, with peristyle atria surrounded by burial chambers cut in the rock. The architecture and painted decoration of the tombs find their closest parallels in Alexandria.

The same diversity characterizes the architecture of the Roman period, in which a strong influence from the eastern Roman Empire, especially Syria and Asia Minor, is evident. Among temples, the traditional sacred enclosures still predominated, but more standard types also appeared, such as the Temple of Apollo Hylates at Kourion (1st and 2nd centuries AD), which had a podium and a tetrastyle façade with Nabataean capitals. The Temple of Aphrodite at AMATHOUS (1st century AD) had a similar colonnaded front and architectural decoration combining Greek, Egyptian Greek and Nabataean elements. The colonnaded gymnasium at Salamis (1st century AD) is one of the most splendid examples of its type. Some new theatres were built during the Roman period, while old ones were occasionally modified to suit the changing tastes of the time: that at Kourion (c. AD 200) was converted to stage gladiatorial and wild-beast contests, while the *orchestra* of the theatre at Salamis was rearranged to accommodate aquatic games. Characteristic Roman buildings of the 1st and 2nd centuries AD were also constructed, such as amphitheatres (Salamis, New Paphos), odeia (New Paphos) and nymphaea (Soli, Kourion). Houses, especially those at New Paphos (e.g. the houses of Orpheus and Dionysos), follow the traditional atrium plan (*see* ROME, ANCIENT, §II, 1(i)(c)) but are of an unprecedented size, with a large number of rooms decorated with superb mosaics, frescoes, statues etc. At New Paphos there is also the gigantic Villa of Theseus, which was built on a plan characteristic of late Roman palaces.

The basic building material in both the Hellenistic and the Roman periods was local stone. Fine ashlar masonry was employed in public and other large buildings, while dressed or rough stone or even mud-brick was used for the rest. Marble was not quarried locally, and its use in Hellenistic times was very limited. Even in the Roman period, imported marble and granite decorated only the wealthiest of buildings.

BIBLIOGRAPHY

A. Westholm: *The Temples of Soli: Studies on Cypriote Art during the Hellenistic and Roman Periods* (Stockholm, 1936)

O. Vessberg and A. Westholm: *The Hellenistic and Roman Periods in Cyprus* (1956), iv/3 of *The Swedish Cyprus Expedition* (Stockholm, 1934–)

A. Hermary: 'L'Architecture religieuse à Chypre à l'époque impériale: Traditions et innovations', *Chypre: La Vie quotidienne de l'antiquité à nos jours. Actes du colloque, Musée de l'Homme: Paris, 1985*, pp. 127–34

8. Hellenistic peristyle atrium of one of the 'Tombs of the Kings', New Paphos, 3rd century BC

V. A. Tatton-Brown: 'Archaeology in Cyprus, 1960–1985: Classical to Roman Periods', *Archaeology in Cyprus, 1960–1985*, ed. V. Karageorghis (Nicosia, 1985), pp. 60–72

G. R. H. Wright: *Ancient Building in Cyprus* (Leiden, 1992)

DEMETRIOS MICHAELIDES

3. SCULPTURE AND FIGURINES.

(i) Neolithic and Chalcolithic (c. 7000–c. 2300 BC). (ii) Bronze Age (c. 2300–c. 1050 BC). (iii) Geometric and Archaic (c. 1050–c. 475 BC). (iv) Classical (c. 475–323 BC). (v) Hellenistic and Roman (323 BC–c. AD 330).

(i) Neolithic and Chalcolithic (c. 7000–c. 2300 BC). The main source of evidence for Neolithic sculpture on Cyprus is the site of Khirokitia; several stone figurines have been found there, belonging mostly to a late phase of the Aceramic Neolithic period (c. 7000–c. 6000 BC). The general aspect of these sculptures is rather abstract: the outline of the body is simplified, facial features are not indicated in great detail and are sometimes completely omitted, and sexual characteristics are normally absent but, when displayed, are female. An exception to this rule is a strikingly naturalistic head of unbaked clay from Khirokitia (Nicosia, Cyprus Mus.) with incised and moulded facial features and hair; it is the only evidence for the existence of accurate figured representations at this time, perhaps made of perishable materials completed with clay. The few surviving anthropomorphic and animal figurines from other Aceramic Neolithic sites are consistent with the style of Khirokitia. However, the limited number of examples from controlled excavations makes it difficult to attribute the many surface finds to this or the succeeding Late Neolithic phase (c. 4500–c. 3800 BC), the latter being characterized by an increasing tendency towards abstraction.

The Early and Middle Chalcolithic periods (c. 3800–c. 2800 BC) are characterized by the production of remarkable anthropomorphic figurines of various types, frequently represented with a long neck and outstretched arms that give the figure its characteristic cruciform shape. Most of these figurines are made of picrolite, a blue-green soft stone. Finds are concentrated in the south-western part of the island where the stone occurs; the main sites of production are Erimi, Souskiou, Lemba and Kissonerga.

Their attractive colour, high level of craftmanship and highly synthetic, almost abstract way of representing the human figure have made them a popular modern symbol of Chalcolithic Cyprus. Most of the figurines are small (h. 40–70 mm), and as a figurine from Yialia (see fig. 9) clearly shows, tiny pendants of the same shape were worn around the neck; these were also combined with other shapes and shells to form necklaces. Clay and limestone figurines are also known, some of the clay ones painted with red patterns, recalling the style of contemporary pottery.

Two exceptional figures show that in Cyprus, as elsewhere, prehistoric anthropomorphic representations often, if not always, have symbolic and religious meanings. An outstanding female statuette of limestone from Lemba–Lakkous (h. 360 mm; Nicosia, Cyprus Mus.) with clear sexual characteristics is an unprecedented example of larger-scale sculpture and could have been the cult image of a fertility goddess. More realistic are the clay models of seated female figures, perhaps divinities, with marks on the breasts that have been interpreted as tattooing. Clay figurines are often painted in the Red-on-white style (*see* §4(i) below) and include some of the earliest representations of women giving birth (see fig. 4 above). While most of the figurines are female, males also appear, including a hollow terracotta figurine of unknown provenance (possibly Souskiou) representing a sitting male figure, known as the 'Great Ejaculator' (Larnaca, Pierides Found. Mus.); liquid poured through its open mouth would flow out of the perforated genitalia, perhaps to simulate ejaculation in a fertility ritual.

BIBLIOGRAPHY

L. Vagnetti: 'Preliminary Remarks on Cypriot Chalcolithic Figurines', *Rep. Dept Ant., Cyprus* (1974), pp. 24–34

J. Karageorghis: *La Grande Déesse de Chypre et son culte* (Lyon, 1977)

E. J. Peltenburg: 'Chalcolithic Figurine from Lemba, Cyprus', *Antiquity*, li (1977), pp. 140–43

L. Vagnetti: 'Figurines and Minor Objects from a Chalcolithic Cemetery at Souskiou-Vathyrkakas (Cyprus)', *Stud. Micenei & Egeo-Anatol.*, xxi (Rome, 1980), pp. 17–72

E. J. Peltenburg: 'The Evolution of the Cypriot Cruciform Figurine', *Rep. Dept Ant., Cyprus* (1982), pp. 12–14

H. Wylde Swiny and S. Swiny: 'An Anthropomorphic Figurine from the Sotira Area', *Rep. Dept Ant., Cyprus* (1983), pp. 56–9

E. J. Peltenburg and others: 'Kissonerga-Mosphilia 1987: Ritual Deposit, Unit 1015', *Rep. Dept Ant., Cyprus* (1988), pp. 43–52

E. Goring: 'Pottery Figurines: The Development of a Coroplastic Art in Chalcolithic Cyprus', *Bull. Amer. Sch. Orient. Res.*, 282–3 (1991), pp. 153–61

L. Vagnetti: 'Stone Sculpture in Chalcolithic Cyprus', *Bull. Amer. Sch. Orient. Res.*, 282–3 (1991), pp. 139–51

LUCIA VAGNETTI

(ii) Bronze Age (c. 2300–c. 1050 BC*).* Cyprus had no true sculpture during the Bronze Age. Both humans and animals were represented in the round but on a small scale, most being between 100 and 300 mm in height. Most were made of terracotta in fabrics akin to those of contemporary vases, though bronze was sometimes used towards the end of the era. Their significance is for the most part elusive. The human figurines are often described as representations of the Mother Goddess, but most of the Early Cypriot (ECYP) and Middle Cypriot (MCYP) examples are sexless, and over the whole era the majority with known find-spots come from tombs. 'Fertility charm' is probably a better description for the female figurines, and their function was doubtless to promote fertility, whether they were in fact charms or images of a goddess; having been treasured possessions during life, they were then deemed suitable for burial with the dead.

The plank figurine was the predominant human type of the ECYP and MCYP periods; like contemporary pottery, it was made of Red Polished or White Painted ware (*see* §4(ii) below). The most typical have a rectangular body on which is set a smaller rectangle for the head; some have two heads (see fig. 10). Red Polished examples have headbands, necklaces, belts and facial features indicated by incised patterns, sometimes enhanced by a chalky white filling. Figurines in either ware may have modelled noses, small ears and crudely formed breasts, and some cradle a child; separately formed arms and, more rarely, legs became common only towards the end of the MCYP period. Another type has a head and body of roughly the same width so that there are no obvious shoulders; others look like combs or brushes with long thin necks and square bodies, the lower halves of which are decorated with vertical lines. Most are sexless, although the examples with breasts and/or children are certainly female.

The introduction of plank figurines in Cyprus has been ascribed to refugees from southern Anatolia, who seem to

9. Chalcolithic cruciform idol, picrolite, h. 153 mm, from Yiala, *c.* 3800–*c.* 2300 BC (Nicosia, Cyprus Museum)

pouring liquids or making bread, and men tending animals or ploughing the land. One vessel, known as the Vounous Bowl, contains an intricate scene of moulded, free-standing figures, which is usually described as a religious ceremony taking place within a circular shrine (*see* §I, 3 and fig. 2 above); this has led to the identification of other 'shrine models'. All of these were found in tombs, and until further evidence from settlement sites is forthcoming it is impossible to say for certain whether or not they had any religious significance. Also of Red Polished ware is a fine model of a ploughing scene (*c.* 2000 BC; Nicosia, Cyprus Mus.). Unique for Cyprus is a relief of a human figure (h. *c.* 1 m) carved in the wall of the entrance passage to a 17th-century BC tomb at Karmi–Palaeolona.

Terracotta human figurines of the Late Cypriot (LCYP) period are radically different from their predecessors. They are obviously female, with a curving outline, wide hips and incised pubic triangle. Many stand with their hands just below their breasts, others cradle a baby and the occasional example is seated. This new type originated in the Near East and reached Cyprus by way of Syria. There are two versions: those with birdlike faces and large ears—often adorned by earrings—are closest to their Syrian prototypes, while those of the other variety have flattened heads with the ears squashed down by a cap, perhaps a sign of Mycenaean Greek influence (examples of each in London, BM).

Towards the end of the LCYP period, probably some time before 1200 BC, the Cypriot bronze industry was revolutionized under foreign influence. The lost-wax process was introduced for the casting of statuettes, and the bronze sculptures show close connections with the Near East (*see* §5(v)(a) below). The terracottas of 11th-century BC Cyprus show marked Minoan influence, suggesting that Cretans were among the immigrants from the Bronze Age Greek world who seem to have arrived in the island in fairly large numbers around 1100 BC (*see* §1(iii) above). Among the figurines are females wearing low crowns (e.g. Limassol, Distr. Mus.), sometimes described as representations of a 'goddess with uplifted arms'. Animal statuettes have wheelmade bodies like those from Minoan sanctuaries of the 12th century BC (and Mycenaean Greek sanctuaries of a century earlier); two examples from Enkomi each have two human heads (Nicosia, Cyprus Mus.).

BIBLIOGRAPHY

H. W. Catling: *Cypriot Bronzework in the Mycenaean World* (Oxford, 1964)
L. Åström: *The Middle Cypriote Bronze Age: Other Arts and Crafts* (Lund, 1972), iv/1d of *The Swedish Cyprus Expedition* (Stockholm, 1934–)
J. des Gagniers and V. Karageorghis: *Vases et figurines de l'âge du bronze à Chypre* (Quebec, 1976)
J. Karageorghis: *La Grande Déesse de Chypre et son culte* (Lyon, 1977)
R. S. Merrillees: 'Representation of the Human Form in Prehistoric Cyprus', *Opuscula Athen.*, xiii (1980), pp. 171–84
A. G. Orphanides: *Bronze Age Anthropomorphic Figurines in the Cesnola Collection at the Metropolitan Museum of Art* (Göteborg, 1983)
H. W. Catling: 'Cypriot Bronzework: East or West', *Acts of the International Archaeological Symposium 'Cyprus between the Orient and the Occident': Nicosia, 1986*, pp. 91–103
R. S. Merrillees: 'Mother and Child: A Late Cypriote Variation on an Eternal Theme', *Medit. Archaeol.*, i (1988), pp. 42–56
V. Karageorghis: *Chalcolithic to Late Cypriot I* (1991), i of *The Coroplastic Art of Ancient Cyprus* (Nicosia, 1991–)

10. Bronze Age plank figurine with two heads, Red Polished ware with incised decoration, h. 300 mm, from Dhenia, Tomb 1, no. 6, 19th–18th centuries BC (Nicosia, Cyprus Museum)

have arrived on the island in the mid-3rd millennium BC and to have been responsible for ushering in ECYP culture, although it is possible that the type evolved independently in the two different areas (*see* §1(ii)(b) above). Some of these figurines were attached to vessels. Of particular interest is a group of Red Polished ware vases made around 1900 BC (e.g. Nicosia, Cyprus Mus.; Sèvres, Mus. N. Cér.; Oxford, D. Morris priv. col.) with scenes modelled around the outside of the rim including women grinding corn,

(iii) Geometric and Archaic (c. 1050–c. 475 BC). The first Geometric and Archaic period figurines in Cyprus were

made at the onset of the era around 1050 BC. Among these were female figures with bell- or bottle-shaped bodies, sometimes wheelmade; those with uplifted arms may represent goddesses or worshippers. Other types included anthropomorphic masks and a few animals (Larnaka, Archaeol. Mus.; Limassol, Distr. Mus.; Nicosia, Cyprus Mus.). To the 10th century BC belong warriors, often helmeted, with bell-shaped bodies and movable legs, a distinctive variety possibly of Greek origin (Nicosia, Cyprus Mus.; Cambridge, Fitzwilliam). Among other types of terracottas (which persisted into the 5th century BC) were females with arms upraised or holding their breasts and males such as warriors, the bearers of offerings, musicians and horsemen. At first all the heads were handmade with prominent noses and often hats, low crowns for the women and pointed bonnets for the men. The bodies were frequently trumpet-shaped or conical, either solid and handmade or hollow and thrown on a fast wheel (Nicosia, Cyprus Mus.; Stockholm, Medelhavsmus.; Paris, Louvre; London, BM). Many attractive animal figurines were also made by hand, especially in the 7th and 6th centuries BC; horses (often with riders), goats, stags, pigs, birds and dogs were all portrayed (Nicosia, Cyprus Mus.; Stockholm, Medelhavsmus.; London, BM).

Moulds for terracottas were introduced from the Near East in the late 8th century BC or the 7th, but it was from the 6th century BC that they were in widespread use. The head or the whole figure might be cast in a mould, resulting in a change of style: female figures were given wiglike hair and, if the body was moulded as well, either a transparent tunic or a robe with a sash, usually under a cloak pulled up over the head. Moulded male figures wore a variety of caps and helmets and were dressed either appropriately to their tasks or in long robes and mantles (London, BM; Nicosia, Cyprus Mus.; Paris, Louvre).

Cypriot sculpture was revolutionized around the middle of the 7th century BC when the production of large-scale (life-size or larger) statues began. The principal materials were locally available limestone and terracotta. Bronze was less common, and marble had to be imported from Greece and Asia Minor, which from the later 6th century BC supplied some finished statues. Cypriot limestone was relatively soft, and details were usually engraved or painted rather than sharply carved. As late as the Hellenistic period the backs of these statues were generally ignored and left virtually flat with little or no carving. Large terracotta statues were handmade in separate pieces and then joined together. Cypriot sculpture from *c.* 650 to *c.* 590 BC was essentially a local creation, although some influence from the Near East is apparent. Faces are triangular or oval with large protruding eyes and severe expressions. Women wear jewellery and a turban or low crown; men are bearded and wear helmets. Both men and women are normally dressed in ankle-length robes, partly covered by a cloak for the men. They stand with their feet together; one arm is at the side and the other is held across the body either holding an offering (women) or tucked into a fold of the cloak, perhaps with a gift (men).

By the early 6th century BC Cyprus's involvement with other Mediterranean powers (*see* §1(iii) above) led to a new style reflecting influence from Egypt, the Near East and East Greece (the Greek cities on the west coast of

Asia Minor and the neighbouring islands). From Egypt came the *klaft* (wig) hairstyle, common for both men and women, and from the Near East many different helmets. East Greek influence accounts for the softer features and slight smile. The costume continued unchanged, but some men now wore a loincloth, of probable Greek origin, and a headband. Statues of lions and sphinxes reflected their Near Eastern forerunners: most were influenced by Phoenician versions, which themselves owed a debt to Egypt. Direct Egyptian influence during the period of her domination of Cyprus in the mid-6th century BC may account for the production of strongly Egyptianizing bronze statuettes (Nicosia, Cyprus Mus.; Paris, Louvre; London, BM).

Cyprus was absorbed into the Persian empire *c.* 525 BC, and freedom of movement within the empire led to increasing contacts with the East Greek cities of Asia Minor and with Syria and Phoenicia, which had also been annexed by the Persians. Cypriot sculptors became more dependent on East Greek models, and many statues were given Greek hairstyles and dress (a linen *chiton* (tunic)

11. Archaic head of a man wearing the Egyptian crown combined with an Assyrian helmet, limestone, h. 300 mm, from the siege mound at Old Paphos, *c.* 525–*c.* 500 BC (Liverpool, Liverpool Museum)

with a wool *himation* (cloak)) and the Greek posture of standing with one leg advanced. There are also some faithful copies of Greek korai, though the Cypriot versions keep their rich jewellery (Nicosia, Cyprus Mus.; London, BM). Other statues have Egyptian crowns and kilts (New York, Met.; Paphos, Distr. Archaeol. Mus.; Liverpool, Liverpool Mus.), which may reflect the fashion of the resident Phoenician population for Egyptianizing statues. The size and particularly elaborate headdress of a head found at Old Paphos (see fig. 11) denote an important personage. The head has been identified as representing the 'Priest King', since it comes from the only city in Cyprus of which the monarch also served as High Priest and which was the site of a renowned sanctuary of Aphrodite, the Cypriot goddess *par excellence*.

Tombstones decorated in relief and pilasters, usually free-standing objects of veneration crowned by the head of the Egyptian goddess Hathor (identified on Cyprus with Aphrodite), were first made on Cyprus in the Late Archaic period (*c.* 600–*c.* 475 BC; Nicosia, Cyprus Mus.). The tombstones were inspired by Greek practice, though the earliest example (Nicosia, Cyprus Mus.) stands apart from its Greek predecessors in both shape and decoration. It shows a frontal figure (itself in the East Greek style) in high relief within a deep niche; the type remained popular in the island for some time. Greek influence is apparent as well in the rendering of the facial features of the Hathor capitals. Sculpted lions and sphinxes also acted as grave guardians.

Much Archaic statuary was dedicated in sanctuaries, and the Cypriots evidently believed that the statues acted as substitutes for themselves as continuous worshippers. Sculptural groups reproduce activities held in the sanctuaries, such as sacred banquets accompanied by music and dancing. Some animal figures may represent offerings, while others are those associated with deities, who are themselves occasionally portrayed. Since Cypriot sanctuaries typically consisted merely of a walled precinct (*temenos*) with small cult buildings and altars, there was little opportunity for architectural sculpture.

(iv) Classical (c. 475–323 BC). In the Classical period Cyprus was poised between Persia and Athens. The best Cypriot sculpture, whether in the round or in relief, reflected the Classical style that had developed in mainland Greece from the early 5th century BC. Imported works of marble or bronze, such as the famous Chatsworth Head from Tamassos (*c.* 470 BC; London, BM), were no doubt sources of inspiration. Some marble pieces may have been carved locally, although the material was always imported. In the second quarter of the 5th century BC a school of sculptors at Golgoi produced a series of limestone reliefs with strong Greek influence. Graves by this time were often given tombstones, and those from Marion rely particularly heavily on Greek prototypes; two marble examples of *c.* 420 BC (Nicosia, Cyprus Mus.) may have been commissioned in Rhodes. Sculptors were probably among the Greek immigrants welcomed by Euagoras, King of Salamis (*reg* 411–374/3 BC); a marble head of *Aphrodite/Hygieia* found at the gymnasium, Salamis, illustrates this Greek influence (*see* SALAMIS, fig. 2). Some distinctly Cypriot limestone statues continued to be made,

however, continuing the traditions established at the end of the 6th century BC. Male figures wear Greek costume and may have beards, sometimes artificially curled; their hair is short and secured by a wreath. This style eventually stagnated, and later examples are poorly carved.

Cypriot ties with Phoenicia were maintained during the Classical period. Mummy-shaped sarcophagi were imported in the 5th and early 4th centuries BC (New York, Met.; Limassol, Distr. Mus.), and Phoenicians at Kition also made their own versions locally (Limassol, Distr. Mus.). Rather different and with specifically Cypriot features, such as the feet supporting the box, is a limestone example from Amathus of the mid-5th century BC (New York, Met.). By the 5th century BC small terracottas were made in moulds, some of which were imported from Greece: the features are Classical, and Greek dress is worn. More obviously Cypriot is a series of horsemen with mould-made faces of the 4th to the 1st century BC: the riders still have prominent noses and wear a variety of headdresses (Episkopi, Kourion Mus.).

BIBLIOGRAPHY

J. L. Myres: *Handbook of the Cesnola Collection of Antiquities from Cyprus* (New York, 1914/*R* 1974)

F. N. Pryce: *Cypriote and Etruscan* (1931), i/2 of *Catalogue of Sculpture in the Department of Greek and Roman Antiquities in the British Museum* (London, 1928–)

E. Gjerstad: *The Cypro-Geometric, Cypro-Archaic and Cypro-Classical Periods* (1948), iv/2 of *The Swedish Cyprus Expedition* (Stockholm, 1934–)

R. H. Young and S. H. Young: *Terracotta Figurines from Kourion in Cyprus* (Philadelphia, 1955)

G. Schmidt: *Kyprische Bildwerke aus dem Heraion von Samos* (1968), vii of *Samos* (Bonn, 1961–)

H. Ergulec: *Large-sized Cypriote Sculpture in the Archaeological Museums of Istanbul* (Göteborg, 1972), iv of *Corpus of Cypriote Antiquities*, Studies in Mediterranean Archaeology, 20 (Lund, 1969–)

M. Yon: *Un Dépôt de sculptures archaïques* (1974), v of *Salamine de Chypre* (Paris, 1969–)

B. Lewe: *Studien zur archäischen kyprischen Plastik* (Dortmund, 1975)

V. Wilson: 'The Kouklia Sanctuary', *Archäol. Anz.* (1975), pp. 446–55

J. Karageorghis: *La Grande Déesse de Chypre et son culte* (Lyon, 1977)

A. Hermary and V. A. Tatton-Brown: *Les Sculptures découvertes avant 1975* (1981), ii/2 of *Amathonte* (Paris, 1981–)

A. Hermary: 'Deux têtes en marbre trouvées à Amathonte', *Bull. Corr. Hell.*, cvii (1983), pp. 289–99

T. Monloup: *Les Figurines de terre cuite de tradition archaïque* (1984), xii of *Salamine de Chypre* (Paris, 1969–)

V. A. Tatton-Brown: 'Sculptors at Golgoi', *Rep. Dept Ant., Cyprus* (1984), pp. 169–73

A. Hermary: 'Un Nouveau Chapiteau hathorique trouvé à Amathonte', *Bull. Corr. Hell.*, cix (1985), pp. 657–99

R. Senff: *Das Apollonheiligtum von Idalion* (diss., U. Munich, 1986)

V. A. Tatton-Brown: 'Gravestones of the Archaic and Classical Periods: Local Production and Foreign Influences', *Acts of the International Archaeological Symposium 'Cyprus between Orient and Occident': Nicosia, 1986*, pp. 439–53

F. Vandenabeele: 'Phoenician Influence on the Cypro-Archaic Terracotta Production and Cypriot Influence Abroad', *Acts of the International Archaeological Symposium 'Cyprus between Orient and Occident': Nicosia, 1986*, pp. 351–60

V. Karageorghis and A. Hermary: *The Terracottas* (1987) and *Statuettes, sarcophages et stèles décorées* (1987), iii/1–2 of *La Nécropole d'Amathonte: Tombes 113–367* (Nicosia, 1987–)

A. Caubet and M. Yon: 'Ateliers de figurines à Kition', *Cyprus and the East Mediterranean in the Iron Age*, ed. V. A. Tatton-Brown (London, 1989)

H. Kyrieleis: 'New Cypriot Finds from the Heraion at Samos', *Cyprus and the East Mediterranean in the Iron Age*, ed. V. A. Tatton-Brown (London, 1989)

R. Laffineur and F. Vandenabeele, eds: 'Cypriote Terracottas', *Proceedings of the First International Conference of Cypriot Studies: Brussels, Liège, Amsterdam, 1989*

A. T. Reyes: 'The Anthropomorphic Statuettes of Archaic Idalion', *Annu. Brit. Sch. Athens*, lxxxvii (1992), pp. 242–57

V. Karageorghis: *The Coroplastic Art of Ancient Cyprus*, 2 vols (Nicosia, 1993)

R. Laffineur, ed., with F. Vandenabeele: 'Cypriote Stone Sculpture', *Papers of the Second International Conference of the Groupe de Contact Interuniversitaire d'Etudes Chypriotes: Liège, Brussels, 1993*

VERONICA TATTON-BROWN

(v) Hellenistic and Roman (323 BC–c. AD 330). Two distinct artistic traditions coexisted in Hellenistic and Roman Cyprus: the old native tradition of votive sculpture and the new international style. Inland sites continued to produce traditional limestone statuary with detailed treatment of the face and formulaic treatment of the body. Uncarved marble and marble statuary in the international style of the time were imported to the coastal centres and used in honorific, decorative and votive contexts.

In the Hellenistic period (323–c. 31 BC) sculptures of soft, chalky stone were dedicated at sanctuaries near the limestone deposits of the Mesaoria Plain. Voni, Lefkoniko, Arsos, Golgi and Idalion yield the majority of votives, but Vitsada, Akhna, Pyla, Potamia and Tamassos also provide examples (collections at Nicosia, Cyprus Mus., and New York, Met.). Sculptures of hard, shelly limestone are concentrated at sanctuaries along the north coast, especially Soli and Mersinaki.

Votive statues depict deities, most frequently Apollo and Aphrodite but also Artemis, Kybele and Pan. Male and female votaries of various ages also occur and may reflect stages of dedication: presentation of the child to the deity at infancy, rites of passage at puberty and entry into adulthood. High-quality adult votaries show sensitively modelled, individualized faces reflecting the influence of Hellenistic portraiture. The extraordinary head from Arsos (3rd century BC; Nicosia, Cyprus Mus.; see fig. 12) illustrates the unique phenomenon caused by the intersection of local tradition with the international Hellenistic style: the generic votary with individualized face. Contemporary relief carving occurs on an altar from Vitsada showing the *Rape of Persephone* (c. 150–c. 50 BC) and on a double-sided stele with Dionysos mask and erotic scene (both Nicosia, Cyprus Mus.). A stele shaped like a small temple from Tremithousa (London, BM) is a rare example of late Hellenistic funerary relief.

The production of large-scale terracottas died out as small figurines of worshippers, divinities and genre types became popular. Horse riders with moulded faces were dedicated at the Sanctuary of Apollo at Kourion, continuing a tradition known from Archaic times. At the Sanctuary of Aphrodite at Amathus, nearly a thousand Greek-style terracottas have been found, representing Aphrodite, Isis and the Dioskouroi, female tambourine- and harp-players, water-bearers and 'Tanagra'-type standing figures (*see* GREECE, ANCIENT, §IX, 2).

The production of limestone votive statues ended in the Roman period, by the first half of the 1st century AD. Local stone was used instead for funerary sculpture, including busts, probably of Julio-Claudian date (AD 14–68), and relief stelae dating from the 2nd century AD. Rare stone portraits include a head of *Augustus* (Boston, MA, Mus. F.A.) and the so-called *Caligula* (Nicosia, Cyprus Mus.).

12. Hellenistic head of a female figure, limestone, h. 270 mm, from Arsos, early 3rd century BC (Nicosia, Cyprus Museum)

Marble was the most popular material for sculpture, especially during late Flavian to Antonine times (late 1st century AD to late 2nd). Quantities of partially worked blocks and statuary were imported to Salamis, New Paphos, Kourion and Soli, where they eventually decorated gymnasia, fountains, colonnades and theatres. During the 2nd century AD the gymnasium at Salamis was adorned with copies of Greek statues, including a 'Farnese' *Herakles*, *Hermes*, *Nemesis* and *Zeus*, while statues of *Apollo Kitharoidus* (Apollo playing his lyre), the *Muses*, *Aphrodite* and *Eros* decorated the theatre (all Nicosia, Cyprus Mus.). A taste for Greek divinities and mythological characters, for Hellenized style and colourful effects in mixed marbles dominated the decoration of large private villas, as attested by marble statuettes of *Artemis, Asklepios, Herakles* and *Aphrodite* from the Villa of Theseus at New Paphos (3rd century AD; Paphos, Distr. Archaeol. Mus.).

The importance of bronze statuary in Roman Cyprus is illustrated by the foundry excavated near the House of Dionysos at New Paphos, the young male head found below the theatre at Soli, the Julio-Claudian head from Salamis and the magnificent statue of *Septimius Severus* (*reg* AD 193–211) found at Kythrea (all Nicosia, Cyprus Mus.).

BIBLIOGRAPHY
O. Vessberg and A. Westholm: *The Hellenistic and Roman Periods in Cyprus* (1956), iv/3 of *The Swedish Cyprus Expedition* (Stockholm, 1934–)

V. Karageorghis and C. C. Vermeule: *Sculptures from Salamis*, 2 vols (Nicosia, 1964, rev. 1966)

C. C. Vermeule: *Greek and Roman Cyprus* (Boston, 1976)

J. B. Connelly: *Votive Sculpture of Hellenistic Cyprus* (Nicosia, 1988)

A. Queyrel: *Les Figurines hellénistiques de terre cuite* (1988), iv of *Amathonte* (Paris, 1981–)

JOAN BRETON CONNELLY

4. POTTERY AND VASE PAINTING.

(i) Neolithic and Chalcolithic (*c.* 7000–*c.* 2300 BC). (ii) Early and Middle Bronze Age (*c.* 2300–*c.* 1600 BC). (iii) Late Bronze Age (*c.* 1600–*c.* 1050 BC). (iv) Geometric (*c.* 1050–*c.* 750 BC). (v) Archaic and Classical (*c.* 750–323 BC). (vi) Hellenistic and Roman (323 BC–*c.* AD 330).

(i) Neolithic and Chalcolithic (c. 7000–c. 2300 BC). A roughly modelled head (Nicosia, Cyprus Mus.) and other unbaked fragments are proof that the Aceramic Neolithic (*c.* 7000–*c.* 6000 BC) inhabitants of Khirokitia were aware of some of the properties of clay. They preferred stone and presumably perishable materials for containers, however, and it is not until the Late Neolithic period (*c.* 4500–*c.* 3800 BC) that the history of Cypriot pottery-making begins. It is not clear from the archaeological evidence when precisely this took place. In early levels at Philia–Drakos A, a Late Neolithic site, Dark-faced Burnished vessels of types recalling those in northern Syria were found. Thereafter, the first completely indigenous regional styles emerge: Red-on-white pottery (also called Northern Painted) in the north and Combed ware (also known as Southern Monochrome) in the south. In both wares simple thick-walled bowls and handleless flasks prevail; all vessels were handmade, many by coil or slab-and-anvil technique (*see* GREECE, ANCIENT, §V, 1(iii)), and most were finished in red paint—the patterned vessels were in red on a white ground. In these as in all early prehistoric Cypriot ceramics, little external influence can be traced.

Red-on-white pottery went through several stages of development, which are most clearly traced at the settlement of Ayios Epiktetos–Vrysi. At first, irregular red dots and lines adorned the surfaces of the vessels; then curvilinear, banded motifs, frequently set in metopal arrangements, predominated; rather later, strictly linear designs prevailed, often incorporating sets of chevrons and displaying the use of the multiple brush. This tool was employed to great effect to produce dazzling ripples as fillers or as lines descending from rim festoons like rain from clouds. On the much less vivacious southern Combed wares the wet red paint was lightly scraped away by a comblike object to reveal a thick white slip beneath the fine, parallel, undulating lines.

New shapes and decorative fashions appeared in the Chalcolithic period (*c.* 3800–*c.* 2300 BC). Bracketed by monochrome styles at the beginning and end of the period is a Fine-line Red-on-white style that is one of the high points of prehistoric Cypriot vase painting. At its best, it transcended the merely decorative, and by judicious location of line it introduced tension and movement, as in a flask from Kissonerga–Mosphilia (see fig. 13). Occasionally flamboyant, sometimes with unexpected appendages attached to bold lattice-filled cruciform motifs, these vases stood on the threshold of a new and more complex style but still eschewed naturalistic designs. Complementing the painters' liveliness, potters fashioned vessels in bizarre forms, perhaps at Old Paphos intended solely for funerary purposes; examples include hollow centaurs with exaggerated facial features and fanciful composite vases consisting of several interconnected vessels of different sizes (e.g. Famagusta, D. Hadjiprodromou priv. col.).

In late Chalcolithic times (*c.* 2800–*c.* 2300 BC) the Fine-line style declined in quality and was largely replaced by unpainted vases, in which a subtle interplay of red and

13. Middle Chalcolithic painted flask in Fine-line Red-on-white ware, h. 265 mm, from Kissonerga–Mosphilia, *c.* 3000 BC (Paphos, District Archaeological Museum)

black was achieved by differential firing (*see* GREECE, ANCIENT, §IV, 1(iii)(d)) in a way that foreshadowed the Red Polished wares of the Early Cypriot I and II periods. At the same time a new style known as Black-slip-and-combed ware developed, a type that was also known in contemporary Tarsus in Anatolia.

BIBLIOGRAPHY
P. Dikaios: 'The Excavations at Erimi, 1933–35', *Rep. Dept Ant., Cyprus* (1938), pp. 1–81
——: *Sotira* (Philadelphia, 1961) [Combed ware]
E. J. Peltenburg: *Vrysi: A Subterranean Settlement in Cyprus* (Warminster, 1982) [Red-on-white ware]

E. J. PELTENBURG

(ii) Early and Middle Bronze Age (c. 2300–c. 1600 BC). Pottery from this period is known largely from tomb deposits. Few contemporary settlement sites have been excavated, and there is insufficient evidence to reconstruct the full range of wares and shapes in domestic use. Nevertheless, what is extant indicates that there was a significant difference between vases manufactured for

everyday purposes and those produced for funerary or ritual functions. This distinction implies that pottery-making was a specialist craft that responded on demand to specific requirements. The functions of the simple utilitarian shapes of the period are relatively easy to determine, although disproportionately large or small versions of these standard containers cannot have been used for household purposes: the handles of the huge jugs would not have supported their filled weight, while the capacity of the miniature specimens is minuscule. (Some scholars have argued, however, that these tiny vessels were designed to hold highly expensive substances, such as perfume or opium.) These types of vessels, together with those of odd shapes or with multiple and scarcely practical components (e.g. several bodies and/or necks; see fig. 14)

14. Early or Middle Bronze Age composite jug, of Red Polished III ware, h. 830 mm, from Vounous, Bellapais, Tomb 19, no. 67, 20th–19th centuries BC (Nicosia, Cyprus Museum)

must have been made for ritual activities, such as burial with the dead. Also found in both tombs and settlement sites are hemispherical bowls and juglets with piriform bodies and tall, narrow necks. Both were evidently modelled on the gourd, the dried shell of which was used until the 20th century in Cyprus to hold liquids; the juglets were no doubt used for the same purpose and show how Cypriot potters drew on nature for their inspiration.

The mechanics of ceramic production cannot yet be established, but it is clear that all indigenous vases were handmade, without the fast wheel. It is usually assumed that these vases were built up in moulds or in coils. That numerous centres of ceramic production were active may be inferred from the pronounced regional differences of the period. While there is a recognizable common theme, there are sufficient variations in fabric, shape and decoration to make it possible to identify individual Early Cypriot (ECYP) and Middle Cypriot (MCYP) schools or styles. For example, a particular ECYP II decorative design called the Panel style is concentrated at Vounous on the north coast: the exterior field of the vase is divided into a number of well-defined zones and filled with carefully and symmetrically incised linear and geometrical patterns, the constituent elements of which characteristically do not join. Elsewhere, a style typified by bold, deeply incised concentric circles and hatched ladder patterns was favoured by potters working at Denia in MCYP I, and a special kind of gourd-shaped bottle with finely incised lozenge designs was produced in the north-eastern corner of Cyprus in MCYP I and II. The development of decoration and shapes was both spontaneous and indigenous, as Cyprus had limited foreign contacts at this time and was little exposed to other cultural influences. The ceramic industry consequently developed very strong regional characteristics towards the end of the MCYP period, to the point at which it is possible to delineate cultural provinces, such as the Red-on-black zone in the Karpas Peninsula.

Despite these regional styles, Cypriot pottery production was united by a common inheritance, which can be broadly divided into a monochrome and a painted tradition (*see* §(i) above). The former, comprising by far the majority of the vases manufactured in ECYP and MCYP times, was represented in nearly all parts of the island by Red Polished ware, distinguished by its burnished red slip, skilfully fired to give a final coloration of red and black and decorated with incised or relief motifs. The style was anticipated in Late Chalcolithic times and was a preponderant feature of the Philia Culture (*see* §1(ii)(a) above); the ware continued to predominate until the end of the MCYP period, when its latest manifestation was a debased fabric called Red Polished IV. During its long history it underwent many changes in quality and appearance, of which the three decorative styles mentioned in the previous paragraph are symptomatic, and it embraced almost every shape and ornamental design known to the potters of the time. Besides a wide range of open and closed shapes, typified respectively by the bowl with suspension lug and the jug with tall, usually narrow neck, a considerable number of clay models were also produced in Red Polished ware, consisting of human figurines, animals and everyday scenes (*see* §3(ii) above).

Unlike Red Polished ware, Chalcolithic Red-on-white styles (*see* §(i) above) do not seem to have continued into ECYP times. Given the gaps in the archaeological record, great significance should not be attached to this, but it is noteworthy that whereas the buff surface and red painted decoration on the Philia Culture Red-on-white ware had a matt finish, its ECYP successor, White Painted I ware, had a burnished, buff-coloured slip with a matt red painted decoration; the technique used in firing the vessel was the same as that for producing Red Polished ware. White Painted II was a brilliantly finished fabric distinguished by its thick lustrous slip and painted ornamentation. The White Painted wares continued throughout the MCYP period in a considerable variety of identifiable regional styles but were characteristically limited to geometrical and linear designs. In contrast to the figured shapes current throughout the Bronze Age, naturalistic motifs were rarely incised or painted on Red Polished or White Painted vases, and it was only in relief or plastic ornamentation that free rein was given to the representation of living things.

The White Painted wares appear to have developed in the north-west and central northern parts of Cyprus and to have spread only gradually, and then not widely, southwards. They are rare on the south coast, where another fabric, Drab Polished Blue Core ware, is found, together with local variants of Red Polished ware. There also developed a black version of Red Polished ware, with a similar but smaller repertory of shapes including miniature vessels; the style was uncommon and confined to the north-west quarter of Cyprus in MCYP I. From this Black Polished ware evolved another fabric characteristic of the MCYP period, Black Slip ware, on which the black slipped exterior surface ceased being burnished and gradually became matt.

BIBLIOGRAPHY

J. R. Stewart: 'The Early Cypriote Bronze Age', *The Stone Age and the Early Bronze Age in Cyprus*, ed. P. Dikaios and J. R. Stewart (1962), iv/1a of *The Swedish Cyprus Expedition* (Stockholm, 1934–), pp. 205–394

P. Åström: *The Middle Cypriote Bronze Age* (1972), iv/1b of *The Swedish Cyprus Expedition* (Stockholm, 1934–)

J. B. Hennessy: 'Cypriot Artists of the Early and Middle Bronze Age', *The Cypriot Bronze Age: Some Recent Australian Contributions to the Prehistory of Cyprus*, ed. J. Birmingham (Sydney, 1973), pp. 10–22

D. Frankel: *Middle Cypriot White Painted Pottery: An Analytical Study of the Decoration* (Göteborg, 1974)

J. des Gagniers and V. Karageorghis: *Vases et figurines de l'âge du bronze à Chypre* (Quebec, 1976)

R. S. MERRILLEES

(iii) Late Bronze Age (c. 1600–c. 1050 BC). At the beginning of the Late Cypriot period the more conservative pottery shows a gradual evolution of such established handmade Middle Cypriot (MCYP) III wares as Red Polished and White Painted IV (see fig. 15a), together with Red-on-black in the Karpas Peninsula. A new departure came *c.* 1600 BC with the introduction of the fast wheel in east Cyprus and the production of Bichrome Wheelmade ware (see fig. 15b); this pottery seems to be an imitation of a Palestinian type, but the clay shows it to be of Cypriot manufacture. Bichrome Wheelmade shapes—heavy tankards and kraters—and the geometric elements in their red and black decoration are paralleled in contemporary White Painted vases; but the representations of trees, animals and men (including scenes of armed combat) in the former

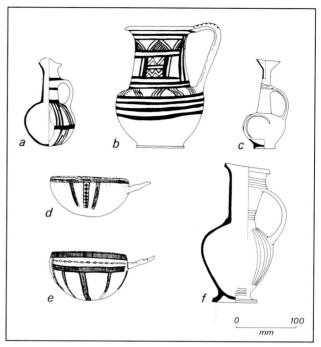

15. Late Bronze Age pottery from Cyprus, *c.* 1600–*c.* 1050 BC: (a) White Painted IV ware, h. 37 mm; (b) Bichrome Wheelmade ware, h. 51 mm; (c) Base Ring I ware, h. 36 mm; (d) White Slip I ware, h. 22 mm (all Stockholm, Medelhavsmuseum); (e) White Slip II ware, h. 28 mm (Larnaca, Archaeological Museum); (f) Base Ring II ware, h. 59 mm (Stockholm, Medelhavsmuseum)

are a significant innovation. Production of the ware, which may have been undertaken by immigrants, seems to have lasted no more than 50 years and to have had no influence on other Cypriot ceramics, which remained handmade and aniconic for nearly four centuries. Imported wheelmade pottery is, however, found: White Painted Wheelmade vessels show Syrian or Palestinian influences, and Black Lustrous Wheelmade ware has connections with Palestine and Egypt.

Around 1600 BC several new wares emerged that probably had their roots in western or central Cyprus: Proto-Monochrome, Proto-Base Ring and Proto-White Slip. These developed over the next century into Monochrome, Base Ring I and White Slip I wares (all handmade), which dominated the next three centuries. Monochrome ware seems to have been derived from Red Polished V. It is characterized by thin walls usually covered in a brown slip (though shades from reddish-brown to plum have been found) and is sometimes mottled; the slip is normally matt, but burnished examples are also known. Bowls are the most common shape, with wishbone handles and angular shoulders that often show knife ripples under the slip. Bowls with similar handles, jugs and juglets were manufactured in Base Ring I fabric (see fig. 15c). This ware gets its name from its applied ring-shaped bases; its thin walls are finished in a highly polished brown slip and were perhaps intended to imitate metal. The decoration was incised or in relief, often with antithetic spirals, and the ware was exported to the Aegean, Anatolia, Syria–Palestine and Egypt: analyses have shown that the elegant, well-made juglets contained opium. White Slip I ware can be seen as a development of the White Painted style: the slip is thicker and creamier, and the thin, neat lines of the decoration in orange, brown and/or black paint achieve a high degree of refinement. The most frequent shape in this ware (which has the same foreign distribution as Base Ring I) is the bowl, perhaps used for milk or yoghurt (see fig. 15d). Typical motifs are framed wavy lines, ladder patterns, framed lozenges and rows of dots.

A common native ware of LCYP I and II is White Shaved ware—so called because of the vessels' knife-trimmed bodies—represented by small jugs and a few spindle-shaped bottles; it has a soft, sandy fabric. The jugs were probably used as dippers to extract liquid from larger vessels. Coarse Monochrome ware for household use was manufactured from LCYP I to the beginning of LCYP III; jugs decorated with antithetic spirals in relief on the shoulders are the most common vessels.

The most characteristic locally made LCYP II pottery is Plain White Wheelmade ware. This was a domestic ware, used most frequently for bowls, jugs and kraters. Among the handmade wares, White Slip II (see fig. 15e) had a richer repertory of shapes than White Slip I: bowls, bridge-spouted bowls, jars, kraters, jugs, tankards and spindle-shaped bottles were made, and the ladder pattern was universally adopted for decoration. Towards the end of LCYP II the decoration and technique of the ware degenerated, and the main motifs were irregular, roughly parallel lines. Similarly, Base Ring II (see fig. 15f) may be regarded as a degenerate form of Base Ring I: the vessels were coarser and clumsier, and decoration was in white paint. Red Lustrous Wheelmade ware was also current in Cyprus during LCYP II. It may have been manufactured on the island, but it was also common in Anatolia and was also imitated there. Bowls, jars, jugs, spindle-shaped bottles and pilgrim flasks have been found, together with arm-shaped vessels intended for ritual use.

During LCYP II a continuous flow of imported wheelmade Mycenaean pottery reached Cyprus, including magnificent Pictorial style kraters (see HELLADIC, §III, 2(iii)) depicting chariot scenes, bulls leaping over rocky ground, and decked ships carrying warriors. Almost the entire repertory of other contemporary Mycenaean shapes has been found on the island, together with locally produced imitations in Base Ring and White Slip wares. Minoan imports are also present, particularly coarse stirrup jars.

Handmade jugs and amphorae in the so-called LCYP Bucchero ware (not related to the Etruscan ware of the same name, though both probably imitated metal proto-types) developed in LCYP II and were common in LCYP III. The vases are decorated with vertical ribs or grooves and were originally manufactured in the grey clay of Base Ring II; by the opening of the Iron Age (c. 1050 BC) they were wheelmade in the buff clay characteristic of Black Slip and Red Slip ware. Pithoi with relief bands on the shoulder were also typical of later LCYP II and LCYP III. So-called Canaanite wine jars were imported from Egypt and Syria–Palestine and were also manufactured on Cyprus. Wheelmade bell kraters in the Pastoral (or Rude) style began to be manufactured on the island, depicting animals, birds and flowers. Their production lasted from the end of LCYP II to shortly after c. 1200 BC. The disturbed international situation at the end of LCYP II and the opening of LCYP III led to a radical decline in Mycenaean imports. The production of Mycenaean-style bowls decorated with antithetic spirals, probably by Mycenaean immigrants, continued until the end of the Bronze Age. In late LCYP III a new wheelmade Cypriot ware appeared, called Proto-White Painted, decorated with black paint on a white slip. The sheen of the paint and the decorative motifs employed point to Mycenaean influence, as they do on the rarer Bichrome ware, on which reddish-brown paint was used. The Bichrome technique, however, and some of the shapes are of Levantine origin. These two wares are the precursors of the Geometric period White Painted and Bichrome wares (see §(iv) below).

BIBLIOGRAPHY

E. Sjöqvist: *Problems of the Late Cypriote Bronze Age* (Stockholm, 1940)
P. Åström: *The Late Cypriote Bronze Age: Architecture and Pottery* (1972), iv/1c of *The Swedish Cyprus Expedition* (Stockholm, 1934–)

PAUL ÅSTRÖM

(iv) Geometric (c. 1050–c. 750 BC). Cypriot painted pottery dating to the period from the end of the Bronze Age to the beginning of Archaic times is referred to as Cypro-Geometric. Throughout this period the two most usual wares were White Painted (dark decoration on a pale clay ground) and Bichrome (similar, but with the addition of a second, purplish-red colour in the decoration). In Cypro-Geometric III (*c.* 850–*c.* 750 BC) these were joined by Black-on-red ware, with dark matt ornament applied above an orange-red slip.

Copious offerings in rock-cut family tombs have enabled many thousands of Cypro-Geometric vessels to survive intact. The chief sources of Cypro-Geometric I pottery (*c.* 1050–*c.* 950 BC) are the tombs of early Greek settlers at Old Paphos, Kourion, Lapithos and Salamis. The repertory of shapes, inherited from the main period of Aegean immigration at the close of the Bronze Age, resembles Greek Protogeometric (see GREECE, ANCIENT, §V, 2), though with some additions from the Levant and some influence from native Cypriot tradition. The leading closed forms, both of Mycenaean derivation, are the belly-handled globular amphora with concave neck and the broad-necked amphoroid krater; both also occur in miniature form. The tall pyxis was borrowed from the Cretan repertory. Pouring vessels include the trefoil-lipped jug for wine and various narrow-necked unguent flasks of Levantine type, with a ridge on the neck; their bodies, usually rounded underneath, may be globular, lentoid or barrel-shaped. Zoomorphic askoi represent native Cypriot fantasy. The usual open shapes are flat-based plates, shallow dishes, bowls (or skyphoi) with two horizontal handles and cups with a single vertical handle; the bowls and cups rest on high conical feet.

The more adventurous painters of Cypro-Geometric I occasionally attempted representational motifs including birds—as on a White Painted bowl from Lapithos–Ayia Anastasia (see fig. 16)—trees, snakes, goats, bulls and human figures; a plate from Old Paphos (Nicosia, Cyprus Mus., Skales T. 58.104) even portrays a mythical scene recalling Herakles' encounter with the Lernaean Hydra. Otherwise, geometric ornament is the rule, confined mainly to latticed triangles and lozenges, and wavy lines; the oriental flasks carry sets of large circles on their flanks. The increasing popularity of Bichrome ware followed Levantine precedent. Other features look back to the Cypriot Bronze Age: for instance, the placing of geometric ornament in vertical columns and the ribbed vessels in Black Slip ware, which simulated the appearance, though not the fabric, of Bucchero pottery of Late Cypriot III (*see* §(iii) above).

No fresh impulse enlivened the pottery of Cypro-Geometric II (*c.* 950–*c.* 850 BC); rather, the wares and style of the preceding period continued at a lower standard of craftsmanship. Large closed vessels lost their taut contours, decorated zones became narrow and perfunctory, and figured motifs were very rare.

During Cypro-Geometric III two dark-faced wares, Black-on-red and its undecorated counterpart Red Slip, entered the Cypriot repertory. The island had already received Levantine imports of both wares, but the beginning of local Cypriot production was stimulated by the arrival of the Phoenicians at Kition early in Cypro-Geometric III. The most frequent Black-on-red shape, a globular unguent flask with flat base, ridged neck and neat sets of concentric circles on the shoulder with fine lines below, was widely exported to the Levant and the Aegean through Cypro-Phoenician maritime enterprise. Other important Black-on-red novelties include a tall trefoil-lipped jug with ovoid body and straight neck, decorated with an intricate combination of large and small sets of concentric circles, and a bowl with offset lip, concentric circles outside and fine lines inside. These shapes were soon reproduced in the older White Painted and Bichrome fabrics; conversely, the open shapes of those wares were imitated in Black-on-red.

By Cypro-Geometric III, Bichrome ware was becoming as popular as White Painted, and regional variation had developed between eastern and western Cyprus. A relatively conservative western style of decoration, favouring old rectilinear motifs such as lozenges placed in long panels, is well represented in the cemetery of Ktima near Paphos. Potters of eastern Cyprus preferred subdivision into smaller square panels resembling architectural metopes, in which were painted light and airy motifs such as small swastikas and rosettes, or diagonal crosses vertically bisected. Amphorae and other closed vessels developed graceful ovoid bodies, with taller and straighter necks; bowls assumed a more vertical profile, turning in sharply towards a high stemmed foot.

After a lull during the preceding period, representational motifs became more frequent in Cypro-Geometric III. Most pictorial work occurs on Bichrome ware in eastern Cyprus. Especially popular were elegant birds with raised wings, decoratively rather than anatomically rendered in the two colours; individual workshops have been recognized. Bulls, stags, horses and lions were more rarely attempted, and the drawing of human figures, sometimes in silhouette but more often in outline, usually displays a helpless naivety. Singly, they may appear as warriors, archers, huntsmen, fishermen or lyre-players, while the more extended compositions occasionally defy sure identification, such is the crudity of the style; thus the scene on a krater (Nicosia, Cyprus Mus., CM 1988) has been variously interpreted as a tripartite temple, as sacred courtesans with combs, and as fowlers entrapping birds in

16. Cypro-Geometric I footed bowl, White Painted ware, h. 140 mm, from Lapithos–Ayia Anastasia, Tomb 2, no. 29, *c.* 1050–*c.* 1000 BC (Nicosia, Cyprus Museum)

cages. More accomplished is the drawing on the Hubbard Amphora (Nicosia, Cyprus Mus., CM 1938/XI–2/3) showing a ritual performance of Near Eastern character, strongly influenced by the iconography found on Cypro-Phoenician embossed bowls: an enthroned goddess, attended by a winged sphinx, receives a libation through a siphon, and the composition continues on the reverse side with four dancing girls accompanied by a lyre-player.

(*v*) *Archaic and Classical (c. 750–323 BC).* The wares produced in Cypro-Geometric times continued into the Archaic period; the only innovation was Bichrome Red ware, an elaboration of Black-on-red, on which white paint was added over the red ground for subsidiary decoration. The Cypro-Archaic I style (*c.* 750–*c.* 600 BC) represents the climax of the Iron Age potter's art in Cyprus. Like the largely contemporary Orientalizing pottery of Greece (*see* GREECE, ANCIENT, §V, 4), it drew fresh inspiration from the floral ornament of Levantine artefacts in more precious materials. The chief new motifs were the lotus bloom, the cable and the rosette, as on a 7th-century BC Bichrome ware stemmed bowl (see fig. 17); their immediate sources were probably Phoenician ivories such as those made for the furniture in the 'royal tombs' of Salamis (*see* §5(iii) below), and Cypro-Phoenician bowls in silver and bronze. These plant motifs were combined with the old rectilinear Cypro-Geometric stock to form a harmonious Orientalizing style that flourished in the east and south of the island, especially on Bichrome amphorae and stemmed bowls. Circle decoration, however, still persisted on Black-on-red shapes and on their imitations in other wares. Orientalizing ornament rarely occurred in conservative western Cyprus, where more use was made of Black-on-red; its characteristic circles were applied indiscriminately to the shapes of all other painted wares.

As in Cypro-Geometric III, figured decoration was practised mainly in outline on Bichrome ware in eastern Cyprus. These outlines were more rounded and naturalistic than before, but within them the vase painters exploited the black and red colours for decorative effect rather than out of any desire for anatomical accuracy. Birds and

17. Cypro-Archaic I stemmed bowl, Bichrome ware, h. 165 mm, 7th century BC (Larnaca, Pierides Foundation Museum)

animals are always more plausibly rendered than human figures; indeed, the human body caused insuperable difficulties for most Cypriot vase painters, as did the spatial relationship between one figure and another. There was no breakthrough on Cyprus into narrative vase painting, whether mythical or otherwise, as there was in Greece during this period. On the contrary, the iconography of Cypro-Archaic I figured work has much more of the East than of Greece. In the most extended human scenes, oriental grandees hunt assorted prey from chariots, as on Assyrian sculpted reliefs, and seated goddesses or priestesses preside over libation ceremonies, as on Cypro-Phoenician metal bowls. Other purely decorative subjects typical of the time include women and bulls smelling flowers.

Especially noteworthy is the Cypro-Archaic I Free Field style, not only because of the frequency of its figured decoration but also for the effective way in which the figures are arranged, floating freely in the field with no ground-line and a minimum of subsidiary ornament. The usual shape is a baggy jug, often with a circular 'eye' painted near the trefoil lip. Charioteers, huntsmen and warriors were sometimes attempted, but the most successful subjects are the bird and the bull. Huge birds, well suited to the curve of the vase, often have an ominous and predatory look; they are exuberantly and elaborately rendered, with a wealth of rather schematic interior detail. One fine Free Field jug (see fig. 18) shows a bull sniffing a lotus flower. The animal has an expressive eye and an air of enjoying life; a typical feature of the style is the accumulation of reserved arcs marking its dewlap and rump. The Free Field style is a fine expression of indigenous Cypriot invention at a time of high prosperity and of strong influence from the island's eastern neighbours.

Orientalizing ornament and the later manifestations of the Free Field style both reached an over-ripe stage in the

Cypro-Archaic II period (c. 600–c. 475 BC). The sprawling Phoenician palmette was much in evidence; lotuses and other floral motifs often spread over a vessel's surface in a carpet-like design. Human figures became rarer and somewhat repetitious in their compositions. The most elaborate decoration occurred mainly in eastern Cyprus on Bichrome and Bichrome Red wares. In the west, concentric circles still predominated.

Some distinctive types of Cypro-Archaic vessel are peculiar to Amathus, city of the indigenous Eteocypriots. Small plump jugs, simply decorated with long-legged birds in a Subgeometric manner, represent a local version of the Cypro-Archaic I Free Field style. In Cypro-Archaic II Amathus produced its own class of small globular amphorae decorated in various ways: with either a close network of lotuses and sacred trees, a central panel containing a frontal bust of the Egyptian goddess Hathor or incised silhouette scenes in imitation of the Greek Black-figure technique (see GREECE, ANCIENT, §V, 5).

From the late 6th century BC onwards Greece became the chief source of external influence on Cypriot pottery and vase painting. A series of Bichrome Red jugs from Marion (e.g. Stockholm, Medelhavsmus.) carry on the shoulder a moulded figure of a Greek kore pouring liquid from a miniature jug; these figures follow contemporary Greek sculptural styles, from Late Archaic through to Early and High Classical. The idea of three-dimensional figured decoration, however, has firm roots in the island's prehistoric past (see §3(i) and (ii) above).

18. Cypro-Archaic I jug, Free Field style, Bichrome ware, h. 235 mm, c. 700–c. 650 BC (Nicosia, Cyprus Museum)

Cypro-Classical pottery, also divided into two phases (I, c. 475–c. 400 BC; II, c. 400–323 BC), displays a decline of ceramic invention and a gradual loss of characteristically Cypriot features. Gone are the figural style, the traditional stemmed bowls and the Near Eastern unguent shapes; amphorae and jugs assume slimmer proportions. White Painted ware enjoyed a revival at the expense of Bichrome, but its decoration rarely progressed beyond bands and lines, short strokes and wavy lines; circular motifs disappeared. Only Bichrome Red received any elaborate decoration. Here the subsidiary floral motifs of Attic Red-figure played an important part, especially in Cypro-Classical II (see GREECE, ANCIENT, §V, 6): the most frequent are myrtles, palmettes, olive leaves and ivy sprays.

BIBLIOGRAPHY

J. R. Stewart: 'Cyprus', *Handbook to the Nicholson Museum*, ed. A. D. Trendall (Sydney, 1945, rev. 1948), pp. 174–99

E. Gjerstad: *The Cypro-Geometric, Cypro-Archaic and Cypro-Classical Periods* (1948), iv/2 of *The Swedish Cyprus Expedition* (Stockholm, 1934–)

——: 'Pottery Types, Cypro-Geometric to Cypro-Classical', *Opuscula Athen.*, iii (1960), pp. 105–22

J. Birmingham: 'The Chronology of Some Early and Middle Iron Age Cypriot Sites', *Amer. J. Archaeol.*, lxvii (1963), pp. 15–42

J. Deshayes: *La Nécropole de Ktima* (Paris, 1963)

F. Vandenabeele: 'Quelques particularités de la civilisation d'Amathonte à l'époque du Chypro-Géométrique', *Bull. Corr. Hell.*, xcii (1968), pp. 103–14

——: 'Premiers indices d'une division de Chypre en deux provinces culturelles au Cypro-Géométrique', *Ant. Class.*, xxxviii (1969), pp. 5–15

J. L. Benson: *The Necropolis of Kaloriziki* (Göteborg, 1973)

V. Karageorghis and J. des Gagniers: *La Céramique chypriote de style figuré: Age du fer, 1050–500 av. J.-C.*, 3 vols (Rome, 1974–9)

J. L. Benson: 'Birds on Cypro-Geometric Pottery', *The Archaeology of Cyprus: Recent Developments*, ed. N. Robertson (Park Ridge, NJ, 1975), pp. 129–50

A. Dimitriou: 'A Cypriote 8th–7th Century Bird-workshop', *Deltion Archaiol.*, xxx/1 (1975), pp. 21–34

C. M. Adelman: *Cypro-Geometric Pottery: Refinements in Classification* (Göteborg, 1976)

J. L. Benson: 'A Cypro-Geometric Workshop Reconsidered', *Studies Presented in Memory of Porphyrios Dikaios*, ed. V. Karageorghis (Nicosia, 1979), pp. 129–38

V. Karageorghis: *Palaeopaphos-Skales: An Iron Age Cemetery in Cyprus* (1983), iii of *Ausgrabungen in Alt-Paphos auf Cypern* (Konstanz, 1977–)

P. M. Bikai: *The Phoenician Pottery of Cyprus* (Nicosia, 1987)

M. Iacovou: *The Pictorial Pottery of 11th Century BC Cyprus* (Göteborg, 1988)

(vi) Hellenistic and Roman (323 BC–c. AD 330). During the Hellenistic period (323–c. 31 BC) Cypriot pottery conformed largely to the common idiom of the eastern Mediterranean world. The most ornate and sophisticated ware imitated the West Slope pottery of Athens, in which ivy and vine motifs were painted in white over a dark lustrous coating (see GREECE, ANCIENT, §V, 9). Likewise, the fine red wares of Roman times, (c. 31 BC–c. AD 330; see ROME, ANCIENT, §X, 8) decorated with rouletting, stamped motifs (sigillata) or, more rarely, moulded relief designs, display virtually no regional individuality.

BIBLIOGRAPHY

O. Vessberg and A. Westholm: *The Hellenistic and Roman Periods in Cyprus* (1956), iv/3 of *The Swedish Cyprus Expedition* (Stockholm, 1934–), pp. 53–81

5. OTHER ARTS.

(i) Coins. (ii) Faience. (iii) Ivories. (iv) Jewellery. (v) Metalwork. (vi) Mosaics. (vii) Seals. (viii) Wall paintings.

(i) Coins. The first Cypriot coins were minted in silver by king Euelthon of Salamis (reg 560–525 BC) and bore his name in the local syllabic script. The island's other city-kingdoms followed his example in the 5th century BC, even though they were then under Persian rule. Except for Soloi, a ringleader in the Ionian revolt against Persia (499/8 BC), each city-kingdom was permitted to mint its own silver coins, inscribed with the local ruler's name. Gold is exceptional, known only in some mints of Salamis and Kition in the 4th century BC. The Greek Cypriot kingdoms, as well as Phoenician Kition and Eteocypriot Amathus, regularly followed current Greek artistic style in the obverse and reverse devices of their Classical coins (see GREECE, ANCIENT, §X, 2(ii)(b)). They are thus easily datable and often supply names of local kings not mentioned in historical sources.

Under the Ptolemies (3rd to mid-1st century BC), Cypriot coins were struck in silver and in bronze, bearing the ruler's head on the obverse and an eagle on the reverse. A hoard of 2484 silver tetradrachms (Nicosia, Cyprus Mus.), mainly of the 2nd century BC, was found under a Roman mosaic floor at New Paphos. Under the Roman Empire, silver and bronze coins were minted in Cyprus between the reigns of Augustus (27 BC–AD 14) and Elagabalus (AD 218–22). The reigning emperor's bust occupies the obverse, while the reverse shows either a Winged Victory, a statue of Zeus Salaminios or the tripartite façade of the temple of Aphrodite at Old Paphos.

BIBLIOGRAPHY

G. F. Hill: *Catalogue of the Greek Coins of Cyprus in the British Museum* (London, 1904)

I. Nicolaou and O. Mørkholm: *A Ptolemaic Coin Hoard* (1976), i of *Paphos* (Nicosia, 1976–)

M. Iacovou: *Cypriote Coinage from Evelthon to Marc Antonio Bragadino* (Nicosia, 1991)

NICOLAS COLDSTREAM

(ii) Faience. This blue-glazed synthetic material first appeared on Cyprus c. 2500 BC as small ring beads in Late Chalcolithic deposits at Kissonerga. Tiny beads and pendants continued to be imported sporadically from the Levant or Egypt until c. 1400 BC, when the repertory, styles and techniques were considerably developed. This florescence lasted for some 200 years and was associated with the prosperity achieved by Cypriots during the Late Bronze Age. Luxury vases with monochrome and polychrome alkaline glazes constitute the most outstanding works of this period. They are divided into three major styles, each betraying the distinct foreign influences to which Cyprus was so prone (see §II, 1(ii)(d) above).

The international western Asiatic style was prevalent all over western Asia, and examples even reached Greece, probably through Cyprus. They are distinguished principally, though not exclusively, by relief decoration and blue, black–brown and golden-yellow glazes laid directly on the silicate bodies. Egyptian faience traditions are completely absent. Common shapes include blossom bowls and goblets with raised pentagonal petals, lidded pyxides and duck-shaped vessels. The style drew its inspiration from varied sources. Cyprus, in particular, may have played a leading role in the development of one of its most exuberant exemplars, female-headed goblets. The bodies of these gaudy drinking vessels, mostly from tombs at Enkomi, were modelled with bejewelled heads sporting cheek curls and tall *poloi* (headdresses). The polychrome vessels of the north Levantine style are technically similar, but they are found only in Cyprus and coastal Levantine regions, and the shapes, which include stirrup jars and juglets, are clearly derived from the Aegean.

Monochrome vessels in the Egyptian and Egyptianizing style have brown line-drawn designs on blue backgrounds; polychrome vessels have inlaid glazes with brown outlines. They are characterized by cursorily executed popular themes: Nilotic waterscapes, standard floral motifs and figural genre scenes including lutists, the Egyptian god Bes, ducks alighting and bulls charging through marshlands. Because of the large number of plates, bowls, cups, kohl pots and pilgrim flasks in Cyprus, it is not easy to establish which are local and which are imports. One outstanding polychrome group from 13th-century BC KITION epitomizes the problem of the source of Late Bronze Age Cypriot faiences. Its colourful amphorae, jars and rhyta (conical vessels) are distinguished by novel shapes, Asiatic decorative motifs and Egyptian faience-working techniques. The usual pleasing, but staid, patterns give way here to lively hunting scenes in which bearded Asiatics lasso bulls and confront lions. Such scenes are the prerogative of the king in Egyptian iconographical conventions, and it is unlikely therefore that, despite the use of Egyptian colours—blue, lemon yellow, green and red—and esoteric techniques, these faiences were produced in Egypt. Mixed production traditions such as this may best be explained by the exchange of craftsmen between the palace courts of Late Bronze Age society.

During the same period, glazed pottery and glass vessels made their appearance. Subsequently, in the Geometric and Archaic periods, faiences became much rarer in Cyprus. They display little individuality and they were all probably imported from Egyptian or Phoenician production centres.

BIBLIOGRAPHY

E. Peltenburg: 'On the Classification of Faience Vases from Late Bronze Age Cyprus', *Praktika tou A diethnous kyprologikou synedriou* [Proceedings of the first international Cypriot conference]: *Nicosia, 1969*, pp. 129–37

H. G. Buchholz and V. Karageorghis: *Altägäis und Altkypros* (Tübingen, 1971)

J. C. Courtois, J. Lagarce and E. Lagarce: *Enkomi et le bronze récent à Chypre* (Nicosia, 1986)

E. J. PELTENBURG

(iii) Ivories. Ivory appears scarcely to have been used in Cyprus before *c.* 1375 BC (Late Cypriot (LCYP) II). Probably imported from Syria at that time, it was then employed, like bone, for gaming boxes, cosmetics boxes of many forms, combs, mirrors, pins, buttons, spindles and spindle whorls. Until at least the end of the 13th century BC decorative ivories were engraved. The best example is a series of small discs, with or without a central hole, frequently decorated with a C-spiral design that was sometimes accompanied by palmettes or stylized lotus or pomegranate flowers; the decorated parts could also be painted. These discs—box lids or ornamental pieces—have been found at many sites (e.g. Enkomi, Kition, Lapithos,

19. Carved ivory mirror handle, h. 200 mm, from Enkomi, *c.* 1200 BC (London, British Museum)

Morphou; examples at Nicosia, Cyprus Mus.); the C-spiral decoration, of Aegean inspiration, distinguishes them from similar examples known in the Near East.

Towards the second half of the 13th century BC, pictorial designs appeared on a group of engraved ivories that closely combined Aegean and Near Eastern traditions. These designs, principally animal combats (e.g. lion–bull, griffin–bull, dog–deer), decorate the pyxis lids from Kition and Old Paphos (Nicosia, Cyprus Mus.), as well as furniture appliqués in the form of fretwork plaques discovered at Kition (Nicosia, Cyprus Mus.) and on Delos (Delos, Archaeol. Mus.). The animals in this series are represented in a stylized manner (with a 'flame' design on their thighs, for example), which are paralleled on some contemporary engraved ivories from Megiddo and on some Mycenaean carved ivories. The Cypriot origin of these engraved ivories, which influenced vase painting of the so-called Pastoral (or Rude) style (*see* §4(iii) above), appears certain since the discovery of the remains of workshops at Old Paphos; furthermore, a fretwork plaque from Kition representing the Egyptian god Bes (*c.* 1200 BC; Nicosia, Cyprus Mus.), which closely resembles plaques from Megiddo, carries an inscription in Cypro-Minoan; another inscription occurs on a cylindrical pipe with engraved geometrical designs (*c.* 1200 BC; Nicosia, Cyprus Mus.).

The appearance in the late 13th century BC of carved Cypriot ivories probably reflects the increased influence in LCYP III of Mycenaean art, in which ivory relief sculpture was common. The style of decoration nevertheless remained essentially Cypriot and developed directly from that of the earlier engraved works. Several fine mirror handles of Near Eastern type from Enkomi (London, BM; see fig. 19) and from Old Paphos (*c.* 1200 BC; Nicosia, Cyprus Mus.) are carved with scenes of animals or battles between a warrior and a lion or griffin; this theme is also found on the exterior surfaces of pyxides. A few pieces reproduce subjects from the Mycenaean repertory: a pyxis with a sphinx held on a lead from Enkomi (London, BM) and a plaque with a striding warrior in profile from Delos (Delos, Archaeol. Mus.). A large gaming box from Enkomi (London, BM), depicting a hunt by chariot directly inspired by Near Eastern iconography, with animals leaping in the Aegean 'flying gallop' pose (*see* §1(ii)(d) above), shows clearly the mixture of Syrian, Egyptian and Aegean elements in the decoration of Cypriot ivories.

The art of decorated ivories seems to have disappeared from Cyprus after the 12th century BC, though Aegean and Cypriot artistic traditions continued in the Near East. It was only after the extension of Assyrian power over the island under Sargon II (*reg* 722–705 BC), towards the end of the 8th century BC, that decorated ivories appeared again on Cyprus; these are similar in style to the Egyptianizing ivories of Nimrud and were probably executed by Phoenician artists. Several remarkable pieces of carved ivory have been discovered in the 'royal tombs' at Salamis; most of them were originally attached to wooden furniture (thrones and a bed) deposited in the entrance passage of Tomb 79 (*c.* 700 BC; Nicosia, Cyprus Mus.). Some openwork specimens probably adorned the arms of a throne; they represent passant sphinxes (*see* SALAMIS, fig. 1) and 'Tree of Life' designs executed in cloisonné technique, with inlays of coloured paste and areas of gilding. Few ivories are known from the end of the Archaic period, though a carved knife handle was found in a tomb in the necropolis at Idalion (*c.* 500 BC; Nicosia, Cyprus Mus.), which shows a hero fighting a lion in a style close to that of Near Eastern ivories. In the following periods, decorated ivory objects simply reflect the stylistic currents of the Greco-Roman world.

BIBLIOGRAPHY

A. Pierides: 'Observations on Some Mycenaean Ivories from Cyprus', *The Mycenaeans in the Eastern Mediterranean. Acts of the International Archaeological Symposium: Nicosia, 1972*, pp. 274–7

V. Karageorghis: *Excavations in the Necropolis of Salamis*, iii (Nicosia, 1974)

J.-C. Poursat: *Les Ivoires mycéniens* (Paris, 1977)

M.-J. Chavane: 'L'Os et l'ivoire à Chypre de l'époque néolithique à l'époque classique: Inventaire', *Objets en os historiques et actuels*, ed. D. Stordeur (Lyon, 1980), pp. 19–40

JEAN-CLAUDE POURSAT

(iv) Jewellery. Cypriot jewellery of the Neolithic and Chalcolithic periods is comparatively rare, but much survives from the Bronze Age and later (after *c.* 2300 BC), probably reflecting excavation patterns as well as the accident of survival. Most examples have been recovered from tombs or occasionally sanctuaries; finds from settlements are rare and are chiefly the result of chance losses. This imposes a bias on interpretation, since types and materials used for burial or dedication may not be representative of those used in daily life. Because of natural or human disturbance or inadequate past excavation techniques, little tomb jewellery has been found *in situ* on the body, and the distribution of types between the sexes and age and status groups remains unclear. Dating of jewellery is difficult because many items were probably heirlooms, and the effects of conservatism or fashion can be obscured when dealing with ritual contexts. Fortunately, the evidence is greatly amplified by the existence of numerous figurines and sculptures, often lavishly adorned. These confirm that both men and women wore jewellery, including earrings, and that necklaces and earrings were often worn *en masse*. The importance of jewellery as a symbol of status or wealth can only be surmised.

(a) Materials and techniques. In Chalcolithic times figures made of picrolite (*see* §3(i) and fig. 9 above) were worn as single neck pendants or grouped with clusters of dentalium shells to form necklaces. Throughout the Bronze Age and later, jewellery was made from a wide variety of materials, including glass and faience, stones such as carnelian, picrolite and agate, and metals such as bronze, silver and gold. Glass and stone were used chiefly for beads and pendants, but metals were employed for a great variety of forms, including diadems, necklaces, pins, bracelets, armlets, anklets, earrings and finger-rings. In the Early Cypriot (ECYP) and Middle Cypriot (MCYP) periods, when gold was apparently uncommon, bronze (introduced in ECYP II) was used as an attractive metal in its own right. From the Late Cypriot (LCYP) period it was often gold-plated.

From the beginning of the LCYP period there was an enormous increase in the amount of gold jewellery buried in tombs. Whether this reflects a change in burial customs or easier access to sources of the metal is unknown. A more cautious use of gold in burial contexts is apparent in the Geometric period, when there was a noticeable reduction in the thickness of the metal sheet and more frequent gilding. Gold was again used on a lavish scale from the Archaic period, a fact reflected by the richly adorned figurines and sculptures of the time. Most gold jewellery was created from sheet-metal and embellished with freehand decorative techniques such as repoussé or mechanical techniques such as stamping. Granulation and filigree were used from early LCYP times, the former technique reaching its height in the Archaic period. Casting was also employed, although even in the LCYP period some heavier items were gold-plated over a bronze core.

20. Enamelled gold finger-ring, diam. 22 mm, from Kouklia–Evreti, Tomb 8, 12th century BC (Nicosia, Cyprus Museum)

The appearance of cloisonné enamelling in the 12th century BC in Cyprus marks a notable technical development. Although a simple form of the technique was known earlier in the Aegean, the set of six rings from Kouklia–Evreti (see fig. 20) provides the first known examples of a more complex variety. A network of open-backed gold cloisons was placed in a crucible, filled with tiny fragments of glass and fired. The glass fused to the cloisons, and the whole was inverted and set into the rings. This technique is fundamentally different from the more standard cloisonné technique so skilfully employed in the round on the Kourion sceptre (believed to be of the early 11th century BC; Nicosia, Cyprus Mus.), on which cloisons formed by thin, flat wire were soldered directly to a backplate. Powdered glass was placed within these and heated until it melted and eventually fused to the metal.

(b) Stylistic development and forms. ECYP and MCYP jewellery was simple and limited in range, giving little hint of the spectacular development that occurred in the LCYP period, with its enormous expansion in the range of types and the sophistication of techniques and decoration. Levantine, Aegean and Egyptian ideas were borrowed and combined with specifically local styles. Forms of the Geometric period were derived from LCYP types but were simpler and more fragile. From about the Geometric III period, Cypriot jewellery was strongly influenced by Phoenician work, and by the Archaic period elaborate and technically sophisticated jewellery was again being produced. From the Bronze Age to the Archaic period a vibrant Cypriot individuality was always evident; even when techniques or types were borrowed from elsewhere, they were often adapted in a typically Cypriot manner. By the Classical period, however, Cypriot jewellery had lost much of its individuality. By the Hellenistic and Roman periods, although jewellery was lavish and abundant, it was part of a universal style, following widespread cosmopolitan fashions. It is often difficult to distinguish locally made items from those that were imported.

Gold funerary diadems and mouthpieces are common finds in rich LCYP tombs; they consist of rectangular or oval strips decorated with repoussé or stamping. Motifs range from simple circles or dots to elaborate figural motifs such as sphinxes; the mouthpieces were occasionally adorned with lips, moustaches or beards. The strips may have been intended to preserve some spiritual aspect of the deceased by association, since it must have been observed that gold does not visibly decay after burial. Decorated diadems were also used in Geometric and Archaic times, often more elaborate in shape than the LCYP examples. A new type, consisting of linked decorated plaques, appeared in the Geometric period.

There was a limited range of earrings. The earliest were simple hoops or crescents, which continued in bronze, silver or gold throughout antiquity. Another early type has a pendant of metal granules; this form also continued after the Bronze Age, though later granules were often hollow. Specific to the LCYP period are earrings with bull's-head pendants, 'leech' earrings and a type with a richly granulated conical pendant. Post-Bronze Age earrings were influenced by Near Eastern forms.

Hair spirals were worn from the ECYP period. The earliest were made of broad, flat strips with repoussé decoration. Plain wire spirals were common later. Cypriot beads are generally simple and of forms common in both the Aegean and the Levant. Those from an Archaic necklace (7th century BC; Nicosia, Cyprus Mus.) found in the sanctuary of Aphrodite at Arsos are among the finest in terms of technique and decoration. Pendants were more varied, and some specifically ritual types, such as rayed discs, crescents and Astarte plaques, were imported from the Near East.

Dress pins were common in the Bronze Age. Eyelet pins are indistinguishable from their Levantine counterparts, but pins with a central loop and heavy terminals are unique to Cyprus. Fibulae were introduced at the end of the LCYP period; fine examples in precious metals and bronze are known from Geometric times. Bracelets, armlets and anklets were also worn from the Late Bronze Age. The earliest finger-rings were simple bronze bands or spirals. Later types include rings with incised or inlaid bezels, signet rings (often in gold or silver) and a type with a swivelling bezel, derived ultimately from Egypt. Gold and silver toe-rings are known from LCYP deposits.

BIBLIOGRAPHY

F. H. Marshall: *Catalogue of the Jewellery, Greek, Etruscan and Roman, in the Department of Antiquities, British Museum* (London, 1911)
R. A. Higgins: *Greek and Roman Jewellery* (London, 1961, rev. 2/1980)
H. W. Catling: 'Kouklia Evreti Tomb 8', *Bull. Corr. Hell.*, xcii (1968), pp. 162–9
J. Boardman: 'Cypriot Finger Rings', *Annu. Brit. Sch. Athens*, lxv (1970), pp. 5–15
K. R. Maxwell-Hyslop: *Western Asiatic Jewellery, c. 3000–612 BC* (London, 1971)
A. Pierides: *Jewellery in the Cyprus Museum* (Nicosia, 1971)
L. Åström: *The Late Cypriote Bronze Age: Other Arts and Crafts* (1972), iv/1a of *The Swedish Cyprus Expedition* (Stockholm, 1934–)
E. S. Goring: *Late Cypriot Goldwork* (diss., U. London, 1983)

ELIZABETH GORING

(v) Metalwork. Ancient Cyprus was famous for its plentiful deposits of copper, and from the Bronze Age it developed a flourishing metalworking industry. Indeed, the name for copper itself is derived from that of the island (Lat. *cyprium aes*: 'metal of Cyprus').

(a) Bronze Age (c. 2300–c. 1050 BC). The earliest copper objects found in Cyprus are of pure unalloyed metal and date from the Chalcolithic period, some from the earliest phase. They include a copper hook, spiral bead, a blade and chisels. Although the origins of copper metallurgy on the island remain obscure, it was probably an

indigenous development, occurring somewhat later than in surrounding lands but probably independent of external influence.

Around 2700–2600 BC an influx of Anatolian refugees may have brought about a change in copperworking on Cyprus (*see* §1(ii)(a) above): from about 2500 BC tools and weapons were made of arsenical copper (i.e. copper mixed with arsenic sulphides). Early Cypriot (ECYP) cemetery sites such as Vounous have produced daggers, knives, axes, chisels, tweezers and razors. All the Vounous material is of arsenical copper except for one tin and bronze object (Nicosia, Cyprus Mus.), which dates from *c.* 2000 BC (ECYP III) and shows that tin was beginning to be imported. To the Middle Cypriot (MCYP) period belongs the earliest evidence for the smelting of copper on Cyprus, at the site of Ambelikou–Aletri. Tin replaced arsenic as the mixing agent, thus making a true bronze. Even after this change, however, the Cypriots preferred using arsenical copper to bronze, and it was not until *c.* 1600 BC, the beginning of the Late Cypriot (LCYP) period, that bronze replaced copper for weapons in Cyprus. The range of MCYP weapons produced in Cyprus included swords, dirks, daggers and spearheads. Hooked tang weapons had their blades cast in moulds and then hammered. Tools were also made, including axes, awls, drills and punches, as well as domestic items such as dress pins, tweezers and razors.

In the LCYP period there is evidence for intense metallurgical activity on Cyprus; the island was probably exporting quantities of copper to other countries in the eastern Mediterranean in the form of oxhide ingots. Settlement sites such as Enkomi, Hala Sultan Teke, Maroni, Kition and Old Paphos all have areas where copper-smelting took place. Despite the smelting evidence in the settlements, however, little securely dated bronze has been found from *c.* 1450 to the late 13th century BC, when the Cypriot bronze industry was transformed by new techniques from Greece, Egypt and the Near East. This combination of influences from east and west allowed the Cypriot bronze industry to produce a variety of high-quality metal goods. The few surviving examples of fine vessels of sheet-metal include a jug with a beaked mouth from Enkomi (h. 308 mm; LCYP III; London, BM) and jugs with vertically ribbed bodies from Hala Sultan Teke and Kition. Casting in two-piece moulds allowed tools and weapons to be made with a central socket for inserting the handle. In the late 13th century BC and the 12th the European 'cut and thrust' sword was introduced to Cyprus. Spearheads were made with socketed bases, as was a large bronze trident with tubular socket and barbed points from a LCYP III tomb at Hala Sultan Teke. The introduction of the lost-wax casting technique permitted the manufacture of lead-filled weights in the form of animals and human heads, as well as statuettes. The latter included such forms as bulls, goats and a seated lion, and divinities. Two statues of horned gods from Enkomi, the 'Horned God' and the 'Ingot God' (13th and 12th century BC, respectively; Nicosia, Cyprus Mus.; for illustration of the 'Ingot God' *see* ENKOMI), are probably the finest of the statuettes and must represent divine protectors of the copper industry. When the new hard-soldering technique was introduced to Cyprus, metalworkers were able to produce a series of fine rod-and-cast tripods and four-sided stands with a ring on top. The stands, sometimes on wheels, are some of the greatest achievements of the Cypriot bronze industry. Their openwork decoration includes a pictorial scene on each side, such as a man carrying an oxhide ingot, a lyre player, sphinxes, bulls and fighting lions and griffins.

(b) Geometric to Roman (c. 1050 BC–c. AD *330).* Iron was already beginning to be used in Cyprus for certain classes of object by the end of the LCYP period in, for example, knife blades that were fixed to handles with bronze rivets; by the 11th century BC ironworking was clearly becoming more common in the island. Excavations of tombs from the Early Geometric period at the cemetery of Skales at Old Paphos reveal flourishing metallurgical activity with a combination of bronze and iron objects, including bronze bowls, spearheads and a tripod cauldron, and iron daggers and flange-hilted swords. There were copper workshops at Kition between *c.* 650 and *c.* 450 BC and associated with the Sanctuary of Aphrodite–Astarte at Tamassos from the 7th century BC until the Hellenistic period. High-quality products in bronze include bowls with lotus-flower handles, lampstands decorated with lotus flowers and bronze horse trappings, and widely exported triangular fibulae with added beads. Despite the continuing use of bronze for certain classes of object, Cypriot metalworkers were also making increasing use of iron in this period and probably introduced ironworking to Greece in the 11th century BC. The metal seems to have been popular initially for the making of weapons, following its use in the mid-12th century BC for knife blades, and it became the principal metal for swords and spearheads in the 11th century BC. These first iron swords were versions of the earlier bronze 'cut and thrust' type, although long-swords continued to be used until the 6th century BC.

The Archaic period in Cyprus has yielded many works in bronze, iron and precious metals. Bronze and silver bowls decorated in repoussé and engraved technique with figural compositions showing cult scenes were made from the mid-8th century BC to the mid-6th (*see* PHOENICIAN, fig. 2). The 'royal tombs' of Salamis (8th–7th century BC) were a rich source for fine bronze vessels, which show local Cypriot artists working in an international milieu of Egyptian, Assyrian and Urartian styles. The finest of the Salamis vessels is a cauldron of double sheet bronze standing on an iron tripod (see fig. 21); it has twelve protomes on its rim, eight cast griffins and four hammered double-faced sirens or bird-men. Bronze was also used to decorate the chariots, hearses and horse trappings buried in the tombs. Iron objects were found in the tombs as well, including an iron sword (l. 920 mm) fixed to a perishable pommel by silver-plated bronze nails, a pair of iron fire-dogs and 12 spits (all Nicosia, Cyprus Mus.).

Statuettes of bronze, iron, gold, silver or a combination of these have been found dedicated at sanctuaries. Two particularly fine examples are a pair of bull figurines (7th century BC), one silver and one gold, from the Archaic Sanctuary of Apollo Hylates at Kourion. Sanctuaries have also yielded many fine bronze statuettes from the Classical period, including a bearded satyr of the 5th century BC from Kourion and, from the palace at Vouni, a relief of two lions attacking a bull and an extremely realistic figure

21. Archaic bronze cauldron on an iron tripod, combined h. 1.25 m, from Salamis, 'Royal tomb' 79, late 8th century BC (Nicosia, Cyprus Museum)

of a cow (5th century BC; Nicosia, Cyprus Mus.). In the Hellenistic period an interesting combination of metals was used to great effect in the head of *Zeus Ammon* from Soli (3rd century BC): made mainly of bronze, it has silver inlaid eyes and red copper lips.

Under the Ptolemies, large-scale bronze statues were made on Cyprus from the 1st century BC, hollow cast by the lost-wax process. Copper was one of the resources that brought the Romans to the island. A bronze foundry of late Hellenistic to early Roman date was found in the House of Dionysos at New Paphos. Cypriot bronzes of the Roman period lost much of their individuality and became part of the rather uniform style of the Roman Empire. Surgical instruments, toilet articles and statuettes have been found, as well as life-size and over life-size statues, including the head of a youth from Soli and the statue of *Septimius Severus* (*reg* AD 193–211) from Kythrea (Nicosia, Cyprus Mus.).

BIBLIOGRAPHY
H. Catling: *Cypriot Bronzework in the Mycenaean World* (Oxford, 1964)
J. C. Waldbaum: *From Bronze to Iron: The Transition from the Bronze Age to the Iron Age in the Eastern Mediterranean* (Göteborg, 1978)
T. Wertime and J. Muhly, eds: *The Coming of the Age of Iron* (New Haven, 1980)
A. M. Snodgrass: 'Early Iron Swords in Cyprus', *Rep. Dept Ant., Cyprus* (1981), pp. 129–34
J. Muhly, R. Maddin and V. Karageorghis, eds: *Early Metallurgy in Cyprus, 4000–500 BC* (Nicosia, 1982)

LOUISE SCHOFIELD

(vi) Mosaics. The earliest example of mosaic decoration on Cyprus is a floor mosaic from New Paphos, dating from the late 4th century BC or the early 3rd. Made of black and white pebbles, it depicts the sea monster Scylla and two pairs of dolphins within a rectangular frame of meander pattern. The lack of evidence for any local mosaic tradition implies that the Paphos example was executed by a migrant Greek artist: both the style and the subject of its decoration fall within the repertory of Hellenistic Greek art. A second Hellenistic pebble mosaic in black and white was discovered at Kourion, with a representation of a dolphin, fish and vase within a geometric frame; it has been dated to between 215 and 185 BC. In 1990 yet another Hellenistic mosaic, with a black rectangular frame on a white background, was found at New Paphos; it is made of irregular fragments of stone and is probably of the 2nd century BC. The only other mosaic of the period on Cyprus is a circular one from Kition (?1st century BC) made of tesserae (cubes of cut stones) with black and white geometric and floral ornaments.

The rest of Cyprus's mosaics belong to the Roman period and come from all over the island: New Paphos, Salamis, KOURION, Soli, Old Paphos, Mansoura, Lambousa and Alassa. All the Roman mosaics were executed exclusively of tesserae, in this case made of local stones in a variety of colours, the size of the cubes ranging from 20 to 25 mm; rare colours were provided by tinted glass tesserae (*see* ROME, ANCIENT, §VI, 1(i)). Mosaic decoration was particularly favoured for floors but was also used on walls; examples of the latter were discovered in a 3rd-century AD bath at Salamis. Most of the mosaics had geometric designs, but figural representations were also common, the latter always possessing the character of picture panels set within large geometric frames. While themes such as hunting, gladiatorial combats and personified abstractions appeared only sporadically, subjects derived from Greek mythology were frequent and included scenes with gods, especially Dionysos, and the best-known mythological heroes, Achilles, Theseus, Herakles etc. The influence of the eastern Mediterranean, especially Syria, as well as of the west (Italy and to a lesser extent North Africa) is discernible in the geometric repertory and in some of the figural compositions. In spite of influence from East and West, however, Cyprus managed to preserve its own identity in this field.

Most of the Roman mosaics on Cyprus were uncovered at NEW PAPHOS. The largest series was found in the House of Dionysos and was probably executed by the end of the 2nd century AD (although some scholars have assigned it to the later 3rd century AD or even early 4th); themes include dionysiac subjects, famous mythological and literary love stories and hunting scenes. Also of the late 2nd century AD or the early 3rd and probably executed partly by the same artists are the mosaics that gave the House of Orpheus its name. A mosaic of *Leda and the Swan* (Nicosia, Cyprus Mus.) from Old Paphos is of similar date. Important mosaics were uncovered in the Roman palace at New Paphos known as the Villa of Theseus: three mythological panels date from the later 3rd century AD, the late 4th and

22. Roman mosaic showing *Hermes passing the Infant Dionysos to Tropheus and the Nymphs*, in the House of Aion, New Paphos, mid-4th century AD

the 5th centuries and include scenes of *Theseus and the Minotaur* and the *Birth of Achilles*. A set of five mythological mosaics of exceptional quality was found in the House of Aion, also at New Paphos, showing scenes of *Cassiopeia and the Nereids*, the *Infant Dionysos* (see fig. 22), *Apollo and Marsyas* and *Leda and the Swan*; these can be dated to the mid-4th century AD. At Kourion, mosaics with gladiatorial and mythological scenes are assigned to the late 3rd century AD and the 4th.

BIBLIOGRAPHY

V. Karageorghis: *Salamis in Cyprus: Homeric, Hellenistic and Roman* (London, 1969)

W. A. Daszewski: 'Polish Excavations at Kato (Nea) Paphos in 1970 and 1971', *Rep. Dept Ant., Cyprus* (1972), pp. 204–36

——: 'Les Fouilles polonaises à Nea Paphos, 1972–1975: Rapport préliminaire', *Rep. Dept Ant., Cyprus* (1976), pp. 185–225

——: *Nea Paphos II: La Mosaïque de Thésée* (Warsaw, 1977)

G. S. Eliades: *The Villa of the Mosaics in New Paphos: The House of Dionysos* (Paphos, 1980)

K. Nicolaou: 'Three New Mosaics at Paphos, Cyprus', *III Colloquio internazionale sul mosaico antico: Ravenna, 1980*, pp. 219–25

C. Kondoleon: 'The Mosaics: Areas I and II', *Ancient Kourion Area: An Archaeological Guide*, ed. H. Wylde Swiny (Nicosia, 1982), pp. 98–105

D. W. Rupp: 'Eustolius Complex: Area IV', *Ancient Kourion Area: An Archaeological Guide*, ed. H. Wylde Swiny (Nicosia, 1982), pp. 132–9

W. A. Daszewski: *Dionysos der Erlöser* (Mainz, 1985)

D. Michaelides: *Cypriot Mosaics* (Nicosia, 1987)

W. A. Daszewski and D. Michaelides: *Guide to the Paphos Mosaics* (Nicosia, 1988)

——: *Mosaic Floors in Cyprus* (Ravenna, 1988)

WIKTOR A. DASZEWSKI

(vii) Seals. Cylinder seals, introduced from the Near East (*see* ANCIENT NEAR EAST, §II, 1(ii)) *c.* 1600 BC, constitute the most abundant source for the religious and mythical iconography of Cyprus during the Late Bronze Age. Two groups, termed Elaborate and Common, are distinct in technique and style. The modelling is finer and more delicate on the Elaborate cylinders, which use haematite and other hardstones. Deities of Western Asiatic appearance are frequently portrayed, whether receiving worshippers or subduing animals, as are heroes fighting animals, demons or monsters. External influences, often mixed on the same seal, are apparent from Syrian, Mitannian, Egyptian and Aegean sources, but the frequent insertion of Cypro-Minoan syllabic signs is a guarantee of Cypriot manufacture. On cylinders of the Common group, simpler Asiatic themes are represented in a rougher and more angular style on softer stones such as chlorite. By the late 13th century BC cylinders had been superseded by conoid stamp seals of Anatolian character, which became common in the 12th century BC. Metal signet rings, with long, oval bezels in line with the hoops and portraying Egyptian themes, were also manufactured in Cyprus at this time.

After a long interval during which seals fell out of use, seal-engraving on metal signets was revived in the 7th century BC under strong influence from the Egyptianizing art of the Phoenicians; the bezels, now separately made, took the form of cartouche scarabs. By the late 6th century

BC signets were produced in an accomplished Archaic Greek style with leaf-shaped bezels, possibly made by expatriate craftsmen from the Greek cities of Asia Minor. Thereafter, Greek inspiration remained paramount.

BIBLIOGRAPHY

E. Porada: 'The Cylinder Seals of the Late Cypriot Bronze Age', *Amer. J. Archaeol.*, lii (1948), pp. 178–98

J. Boardman: 'Cypriot Finger Rings', *Annu. Brit. Sch. Athens*, lv (1970), pp. 5–15

NICOLAS COLDSTREAM

(viii) Wall paintings. Evidence for wall paintings on Cyprus goes back to the Neolithic period: traces of a human figure in red pigment on cream-coloured plaster were found on a pier within a building excavated at Kalavasos–Tenta (*c.* 5500 BC; Nicosia, Cyprus Mus.). The figure has upraised arms and a square head with no facial details. More recent remains of wall paintings were found at Salamis, Tomb 80 (later 6th century BC); the walls were decorated with stylized blue and purple lotus flowers, while the ceiling was painted with crosses and rosettes that recall Egyptian prototypes. Plaster fragments with painted geometric motifs from the 5th century BC were found near the Sanctuary of Aphrodite–Astarte at Tamassos.

Numerous examples of painted decoration survive in Hellenistic tombs at NEW PAPHOS, with either geometric motifs—meanders, wave-crests, guilloches—in red, green, yellow, blue and black, or architectural elements such as pilasters imitated in paint. Tomb B at Ammoi in New Paphos was exceptionally fine: the lower parts of the walls had painted imitations of alabaster slabs, above which ran floral garlands, while on the ceiling a cloth spangled with stars in a geometric frame was painted. This type of decoration finds parallels on Delos and in Alexandria.

The painted decoration of Roman tombs was usually concentrated within the arched niches that held sarcophagi. One tomb in the Glyky Nero area of New Paphos had representations of a dog, an open casket, a pomegranate, a throne and a bird, recalling the Columbarium style of the 2nd–3rd century AD (named after the painted decoration of the Columbarium (tomb) of Pomponius Hylas at Rome). Scattered fragments of wall paintings have been found in ruins of late Hellenistic and Roman houses in New Paphos and Amathus. The decoration was mainly geometric and floral, but small fragments of figured panels were also uncovered. Remains of a mythological scene showing *Hylas and the Nymphs* were painted on the walls of a late 3rd-century AD bath at Salamis. Representations of Muses were uncovered in the House of Aion in New Paphos (mid-4th century AD).

BIBLIOGRAPHY

V. Karageorghis: *Salamis in Cyprus: Homeric, Hellenistic and Roman* (London, 1969)

——: 'Fouilles de Nea Paphos: "Tombeaux des Rois"', *Bull. Corr. Hell.*, ciii (1980), p. 794

I. A. Todd: 'A Cypriote Neolithic Wall-painting', *Antiquity*, lv (1981), pp. 47–51

S. Hadjisavvas: 'A Unique Roman Built Tomb in Paphos', *Rep. Dept Ant., Cyprus* (1982), pp. 202–6

V. Karageorghis: 'Chronique de fouilles et découvertes archéologiques à Chypre en 1981', *Bull. Corr. Hell.*, cvi (1982), p. 7

WIKTOR A. DASZEWSKI

III. Early Christian and Byzantine.

This subsection covers the period from *c.* AD 330 to 1191: Byzantine art and architecture after that date are discussed in §IV below.

1. Introduction. 2. Architecture. 3. Painting and mosaics. 4. Gold and silver.

1. INTRODUCTION. By AD 325 the Christian church in Cyprus was already well enough established to be able to send at least three bishops to the Ecumenical Council of Nicaea (now Iznik). One of these was St Spyridon, bishop of Trimithos (*d c.* AD 348) who, together with St Hilarion (*c.* AD 291–371) and St Epiphanios (*c.* AD 315–403), influenced the spread of Christianity on the island. The first half of the 4th century AD, however, was a difficult period for Cyprus. It suffered a long period of drought, and in 332 and 342 earthquakes destroyed Salamis and other important cities. Salamis was rebuilt, renamed Constantia, and the capital was transferred there from Paphos. Cyprus came under the command of the praetorian prefect of the East residing in Antioch until AD 535, when Justinian I joined Cyprus, Moesia, Caria and the Cycladic islands to Scythia. It is not known how long this arrangement stayed in force. After the death of St Epiphanios, the church of Antioch tried to subjugate the church of Cyprus, but the Ecumenical Council of Ephesos (431) decided that the church of Cyprus should remain autocephalous. The matter was not finally settled, however, until Emperor Zeno (*reg* AD 474–91) gave his support to the building of a church and a monastery near the tomb of St Barnabas, west of Salamis–Constantia.

In the 6th century AD the island became a centre of silk production after silkworms had been smuggled into the Byzantine empire from East Asia during Justinian's reign. In AD 610 Heraklios (*reg* 610–41) stayed on his way from Egypt to Constantinople in Salamis–Constantia and contributed towards the construction of an aqueduct between Kythrea and Salamis–Constantia (40 km). The prosperity of Cyprus came to an end in the middle of the 7th century AD. In 649 the Arabs attacked the island, destroying Salamis–Constantia and plundering other areas. In 653 they returned, occupied the whole island, destroyed the towns and massacred the population. They established a garrison that remained until 680–81. In 688–9 the caliph Abd al-Maliq (*reg* 685–705) signed an agreement with Justinian II (*reg* 685–95; 705–11) in which Cyprus was neutralized and Cypriots were obliged to pay an equal amount of tribute to Arabs and Byzantines. The neutrality of Cyprus was not always respected, however, and several Arab attacks were reported between the 8th century and the early 10th.

Owing to its neutral status, Cyprus was largely unaffected by the iconoclast controversy (730–843). The island became a refuge for the iconophiles of Asia Minor and a place of exile for iconophile monks sent there by the imperial administration. Christians from Syria and Palestine, persecuted by the Arabs, also took refuge in Cyprus. In 965 the island once again became a province of the Byzantine empire, and in the 11th century Nicosia became its capital. With the loss of Asia Minor to the Saljuqs (1071–80) and the beginning of the Crusades in 1095,

Cyprus became an important strategic centre for the empire, and the castles of St Hilarion, Buffavento and Kantara were built on the island's northern range of mountains. During the mid-12th century Cyprus was raided by Raynald of Châtillon (*reg* 1153–60) in 1155–6, by the Egyptian fleet in 1158 and by Raymond III, Count of Tripoli (*reg* 1152–87), in 1161. According to the sources, a three-year drought followed in the 1170s.

In 1184 Isaak Komnenos proclaimed himself King of Cyprus, and for seven years the Cypriots suffered at his hands. In 1191 Richard II, King of England, defeated him and occupied the island, taking with him a large booty to the Holy Land. There he sold Cyprus, which was held briefly by the Knights Templar and then, in 1192, ceded to Guy de Lusignan (*reg* 1192–4), who established a Frankish kingdom there.

2. ARCHITECTURE. According to the literary sources, small churches existed on Cyprus in the first half of the 4th century AD, but the earliest surviving remains belong to what was probably part of the mid-4th-century AD martyrium of St Herakleidios in the monastery of Hagios Herakleidios (largely 18th century) at Politiko. Excavations have revealed the remains of numerous churches from the late 4th century to the 6th. They are all of the wooden-roofed basilican type; no vaulted basilicas or centralized buildings were built. Most of these Early Christian basilicas have only three aisles, such as Hagios Spyridon (late 4th century) at Tremetousia (anc. Trimithos), Hagios Herakleidios at Politiko, Hagios Philon at Rizokarpasso and the basilicas at Hagia Trias, Amathus, Soli, Pegia, Paphos, Polis, Kourion, Marathovouno, Lysi and on the Akamas Peninsula. The aisles were originally separated from the nave by colonnades, except in the basilica at Marathovouno, where masonry piers replaced the columns.

The largest three-aisled basilica is at Soli, in which the colonnades flanking the nave each had 12 huge stone columns (see fig. 23). To the west lies a partially excavated atrium surrounded by porticos; in the middle was a hexagonal phiale (fountain) on a platform. Another important three-aisled basilica is the cathedral of Kourion. Its polygonal apse was flanked by *pastophoria* (service rooms), common in Syria but unknown elsewhere in Cyprus. The narthex communicated to the west with an open space containing a hexagonal phiale and to the north with the atrium of the baptistery. Corridors with benches along the south and north walls of the basilica were probably used as catechumena. The most sumptuous of the three-aisled basilicas is that of Kampanopetra at Salamis, with its columns, bases and capitals of Proconnesian marble. Its narthex has apsidal ends and is preceded to the west by an atrium and a vast yard. Along the north and south walls of the basilica two corridors link the narthex with another atrium at the east end. The east portico of this second atrium contains a ciborium. Baths and a monumental staircase leading down to the sea lie beyond the east atrium.

Among the few five-aisled basilicas, one example, at Soli, was replaced in the 5th century by the three-aisled basilica. The excavations of the five-aisled basilica of Acheiropoiitos at Lambousa (anc. Lapithos) have revealed that the three eastern semicircular apses are enclosed

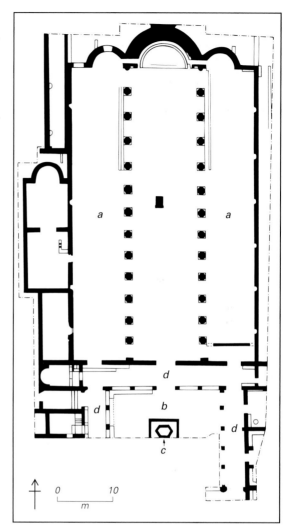

23. Plan of the three-aisled basilica at Soli, 5th century AD: (a) basilica; (b) atrium; (c) phiale (fountain); (d) porticos

within rectilinear walls, as in the churches of Syria–Palestine, and that the outermost aisles are shorter than the nave and the two inner aisles. The basilica of Hagia Kyriaki (or Chrysopolitissa) at Paphos originally had seven aisles, which were reduced to five in the 6th century. An unusual feature is that it had two apses at the east end of the central nave: an outer apse and an inner one 12 m to the west. In the space between the two apses four granite columns (h. 7.10 m) supported a higher roof and separated the nave from the inner aisles. Marble columns (h. 5.80 m) flanked the rest of the nave. The narthex to the west linked the basilica to the bishop's house to the south. To the west was an atrium with four porticos and a circular phiale. Another seven-aisled basilica is that of Hagios Epiphanios at Salamis. A semicircular synthronon was inserted in the main apse in the 6th century, and the baptistery to the east of the south aisles contains a cruciform font with a hypocaust underneath.

These basilicas were all destroyed by the Arab raids of the 7th and 8th centuries. Although some were later restored, the colonnades between the nave and aisles were replaced by masonry piers, as in the basilicas of Panagia Kanikaria, Lythrankomi, Hagios Spyridon and Hagios Herakleidios. Others were rebuilt as vaulted basilicas, as in the Panagia and Asomatos churches at Aphendrika, Panagia Syka at Rizokarpasso and Hagia Varvara near Korovia. During the period of the Arab raids, new church plans were introduced into the island, such as the vaulted church with five domes. Hagia Paraskevi (9th century) at Yeroskipos, for example, is a three-aisled vaulted basilica with five domes; three larger domes replaced the vault of the nave and two smaller domes rest on the vaults of the aisles on either side of the central dome of the nave. Another church type introduced into Cyprus in this period was the domed cross-in-square, as in Hagios Antonios (9th century) at Kellia, near Larnaca (anc. Kition). The church was destroyed in 1425 and was rebuilt in the 16th century with a transverse vault in place of the dome.

Slightly later in date are the churches that combine the cross-in-square plan with three domes, as in Hagios Lazaros at Larnaca (9th century; rebuilt 17th century) and Hagios Varnavas (with only two surviving domes) near Salamis. Excavations have revealed that, following its destruction by the Arabs, Hagios Epiphanios at Salamis was rebuilt as a vaulted basilica with three domes over the nave. In addition to the basilican churches, small vaulted chapels were built, such as the chapel (8th century) in an annexe of the basilica at Hagia Trias. Still standing is the chapel of Hagia Solomoni (9th century) at Koma tou Yialou. By the early 10th century, domed, single-aisled churches known as 'inscribed-cross in embryo' were also being built, such as Hagios Giorgios at Aphendrika near Rizokarpasso.

The re-establishment of Byzantine rule in Cyprus in 965 strengthened the ties between Cyprus and Constantinople. New church types were introduced and existing types, such as the domed cross-in-square, became widespread. Examples of this type include Hagios Philon (10th century) near Rizokarpasso; Hagios Giorgios in Kyrenia Castle, the only example in Cyprus in which the dome is supported by four marble columns instead of masonry piers; Hagios Nikolaos tis Stegis ('of the roof'; 11th century) near Kakopetria; Hagios Herakleidios (11th century) in the monastery of St John Lampadistis at KALOPANAGIOTIS; and the churches of Acheiropoiitos at Lambousa, Angeloktistos at Kiti, Hagios Giorgios (11th–12th century) at Chortakia near Sotira and Hagios Synesios (12th century) at Rizokarpasso. Domed, single-aisled churches also became more common, as evidenced by the parekklesion of Hagia Trias (c. 1090) in the monastery of ST JOHN CHRYSOSTOMOS, KOUTSOVENTIS, the ruined church of Hagios Theodoros at Chortakia, Panagia (partly early 12th century) at Trikomo, the Holy Apostles (late 12th century) at Pera Chorio, PANAGIA TOU ARAKOU, LAGOUDERA, the church of the Archangel Michael at Kato Lefkar and others. The cruciform church type is represented by the church of Panagia tis Kyras or Kyriotissa near Livadia, the ruined church of Hagios Giorgios near Koili and the predecessor of the present Hagia Kyriaki (11th–12th century) at Paphos.

In the late 11th century octagonal churches were introduced to Cyprus from Constantinople. Only the octagonal plan of the katholikon (c. 1090; destr.) of the monastery of St John Chrysostomos, Koutsoventis, survives. Other examples include the roofless church in the castle of St Hilarion and the church of Christ Antiphonitis (12th century) near Hagios Ambrosios in the district of Kyrenia. A local modification of the octagonal church is the hexagonal church of Panagia Apsinthiotissa (12th century) near Sukari. Numerous single-aisled, vaulted chapels were also built in the 11th and 12th centuries, for example at Asinou, Hagios Giorgios at Sakkas near Yialoussa, Hagios Philon at Agridia, Hagia Marina near Yialoussa and Panagia Amasgou (early 12th century; rest. early 16th century) near Monagri. A characteristic of the Cypriot churches of the Middle Byzantine period is that they were built without narthexes, which were sometimes added later, as in the Panagia Phorbiotissa (c. 1105) at Asinou; here the domed narthex is dated c. 1200.

BIBLIOGRAPHY

G. Soteriou: *Ta byzantina mnimeia tis Kyprou* [The Byzantine monuments of Cyprus] (Athens, 1935)
——: 'Les Eglises byzantines de Chypre à trois et à cinq coupoles et leur place dans l'histoire de l'architecture byzantine', *Atti del v congresso internazionale di studi bizantini: Roma, 1936*, ii, pp. 401–9
——: 'O naos kai o taphos tou Apostolou Varnava para tin Salmina tis Kyprou' [The church and grave of Apostle Barnabas near Salamis in Cyprus], *Kyp. Spoudai*, i (1937), pp. 175–87
A. Stylianou and J. Stylianou: 'O naos tou Agiou Nikolaou tis Stegis para tin Kakopetrian' [The church of Hagios Nikolaos of the Roof near Kakopetria], *Kyp. Spoudai*, i (1946), pp. 95–196
A. H. S. Megaw: 'Three Vaulted Basilicas in Cyprus', *J. Hell. Stud.*, lxvi (1948), pp. 48–56
A. Papageorghiou: 'Ereuna eis ton naon tou Agiou Spyridonos en Tremetousia' [Findings from the church of Hagios Spyridonos at Tremetousia], *Kyp. Spoudai*, xxx (1966), pp. 17–33
C. Delvoye: 'La Place de Chypre dans l'architecture paléochrétienne de la Méditerranée', *Praktika tou A diethnous kyprologikou synedriou* [Proceedings of the first international Cypriot conference]: *Nikosia, 1969*, ii, pp. 17–21
A. H. S. Megaw: 'Byzantine Architecture and Decoration in Cyprus: Metropolitan or Provincial?', *Dumbarton Oaks Pap.*, xxviii (1974), pp. 57–85
A. Papageorghiou: 'Constantinopolitan Influence on the Middle Byzantine Architecture of Cyprus', *Akten, XVI. internationaler Byzantinistenkongress: Wien, 1981*, ii/4, pp. 469–78
——: 'The Narthex of the Middle Byzantine Churches of Cyprus', *Rayonnement grec: Hommage à Charles Delvoye* (Brussels, 1982), pp. 437–48
——: 'L'Architecture paléochrétienne de Chypre', *Corsi Cult. A. Ravenn. & Biz.*, xxxii (1985), pp. 299–324
——: 'L'Architecture de la période byzantine à Chypre', *Corsi Cult. A. Ravenn. & Biz.*, xxxii (1985), pp. 325–35
C. Delvoye: *La Place de Chypre dans les grandes basiliques de Salamine de Chypre dans l'architecture paléochrétienne* (1986), xii of *Salamine de Chypre: Histoire et archéologie* (Paris, 1969–)
A. Papageorghiou: 'Foreign Influences on the Early Christian Architecture of Cyprus', *Acts of the International Archaeological Symposium: Cyprus between the Orient and the Occident: Nikosia, 1986*, pp. 490–503
——: 'I ekklisia tou Archangelou, Kato Leukara' [The church of Archangelos, Kato Leukara], *Rep. Dept Ant., Cyprus* (1990), pp. 189–230

3. PAINTING AND MOSAICS. Despite the establishment of Christianity in Cyprus in the early 4th century AD, excavations in the Villa of Theseus and House of Aion at New Paphos have revealed mosaic floor panels of the mid-4th century AD to the early 5th that depict mythological scenes (*see* PAPHOS, NEW and §II, 5(vi) above). The floor mosaic (mid-5th century) in the complex of Eustolios at Kourion is decorated with geometric ornament, fish, birds, a personification of Creation (Ktisis) and inscriptions, including one referring to Christ. Fragments of

mosaic pavement with geometric designs, sometimes combined with representations of birds and animals, have also been found in the remains of Early Christian basilicas at Paphos, Soli, Kourion and of Hagios Giorgios at Pegia.

Most wall paintings and mosaics were destroyed, together with the churches, during the Arab raids of the 7th and 8th centuries. Of the surviving fragments, not all are now *in situ*. The underground shrine of Nikodemos (6th century) at Salamis contained a painted panel of an aquatic scene below a roundel with a bust of a bearded Christ. The earliest known mosaic decoration is in the apse of a basilica incorporated into the PANAGIA KANIKARIA, LYTH-RANKOMI. Here in a paradisaical landscape indicated by palm trees the *Virgin and Child Enthroned* appear in a frontal pose, set off from the attending angels in a panel of light. The border contains roundels with the heads of the Apostles. The bold stylization and the use of large tesserae suggest a date for this mosaic of *c.* 525–30.

The best-preserved mosaic (late 6th century) is that in the apse of the Panagia Angeloktistos at Kiti. The Virgin stands on a footstool holding the Child on her left arm, flanked by the archangels Michael and Gabriel (see fig. 24). A decorative border including fountains of life and pairs of ducks, parrots and stags surrounds the composition. Another mosaic (early 7th century; partly destr.) in the apse of the Panagia tis Kyras near Livadia depicted a full-length *Virgin* with her hands raised in prayer against a golden background. Part of a mosaic perhaps representing three Apostles was found in a niche of an annexe of the episcopal basilica at Kourion.

Few wall paintings from the period of the Arab raids have survived. To the 8th century belong a fragment in the church of the monastery of Hagios Herakleidios, showing the lower half of a full-length Apostle, and the first layer of wall paintings in the chapel of Hagia Solomoni at Koma tou Yialou. The paintings on the second layer show Cappadocian influences and probably date from the 9th century. Of a similar date are the *Crucifixion*, two standing saints and a female saint in the church of Hagios Antonios at Kellia and the aniconic paintings in the eastern dome of the church of Hagia Paraskevi at Yeroskipos. The fragmentary wall paintings in the rock-cut chapel of Hagia Mavra in Kyrenia are more typical of 10th-century Byzantine painting. They show part of an *Ascension* and a poorly preserved *Pantokrator* surrounded by four angels, of which only one is preserved. Paintings of two saints in Hagia Paraskevi and of one saint in Hagios Antonios at Kellia also date from the 10th century.

Only wall paintings and some icons survive from the period following the Byzantine reconquest of Cyprus (AD 965). The earliest wall paintings (11th century) are in Hagios Nikolaos tis Stegis and depict the *Transfiguration*, the *Raising of Lazarus*, the *Entry into Jerusalem*, the *Ascension*, the *Deposition*, the *Entombment*, the *Dormition*, *Pentecost* and some portraits of saints. There are also several 11th-century wall paintings in Hagios Antonios at Kellia. Of greater importance are the wall paintings of the late 11th century to the 12th, when the Byzantine governors of Cyprus and other officials erected numerous chapels and churches and brought painters from Constantinople to decorate them. The paintings in the parekklesion

24. Mosaic showing the *Virgin and Child* flanked by the archangels Michael and Gabriel, from the apse of the Panagia Angeloktistos, Kiti, late 6th century AD

of Hagia Trias in the monastery of ST JOHN CHRYSOSTO-MOS, KOUTSOVENTIS, are of an unsurpassed quality (see fig. 25) and were probably by the artist who painted the Panagia Apsinthiotissa and the ruined chapel of Panagia Aphendrika near the monastery.

Another artist who painted in an elegant and expressive style, using harmonious colours, was responsible for both the earliest layer of wall paintings (1105–6) in the Panagia Phorbiotissa at Asinou and those in the Panagia at Trikomo. Other paintings of the first half of the 12th century are preserved in the churches of Hagios Nikolaos tis Stegis, Hagioi Joachim and Anna at Kalliana and Hagia Mavra at Rizokarpasso. Slightly later in date (third quarter of the 12th century) are wall paintings in the church of the Holy Apostles at Pera Chorio. The underdrawings are done so skilfully that they could be mistaken for the final paintings. Among examples of paintings in the late Komnenian style are those in the Enkleistra (1183) of ST NEOPHYTOS MONASTERY and in the PANAGIA TOU ARAKOU, LAGOUDERA. The Enkleistra paintings are by Theodoros Apsevdis, whose work retains a monumental character despite its unusually small scale and whose treatment of drapery is in an exaggerated 'rococo' style. He may also have painted the walls of the Panagia tou Arakou (1192), in which the elongated figures are both elegant and animated.

The earliest surviving icons, the *Virgin Vlachesnitissa* (9th century AD; Nicosia, Mus. Byz. Icons) and *St Maria* (9th century; Paphos, Byz. Mus.), reflect Eastern influences, while later icons were all influenced by contemporary Constantinopolitan painting: these include the *Virgin Hagiosoritissa* (10th century; Machairas Monastery), *Hagioi Anargyroi* (10th century; Nicosia, Mus. Byz. Icons), the *Apostles* (11th century; Nicosia, Mus. Byz. Icons), the 12th-century icons *St John the Baptist*, *Christ* and the *Virgin Arakiotissa* (Nicosia, Mus. Byz. Icons), *Christ* and the *Virgin* in the Enkleistra of St Neophytos Monastery, and the *Annunciation* in the church of the Holy Cross at Lefkara.

See also EARLY CHRISTIAN AND BYZANTINE ART, §III, (3)(i).

BIBLIOGRAPHY

M. Bardswell: 'The Byzantine Paintings in a Water Cistern, Salamis, Cyprus', *Antiqua. J.*, xix (1939), pp. 443–5

M. R. Sakopoulos: 'La Fresque chrétienne la plus ancienne de Chypre', *Cah. Archéol.*, xiii (1952), pp. 61–83

A. H. S. Megaw: 'Twelfth Century Frescoes in Cyprus', *Actes du XIIe Congrès international d'études byzantines: Ochride, 1961*, iii, pp. 257–66

A. H. S. Megaw and E. J. W. Hawkins: 'The Church of the Holy Apostles at Perachorio, Cyprus, and its Frescoes', *Dumbarton Oaks Pap.*, xvi (1962), pp. 279–348

A. Stylianou and J. Stylianou: *The Painted Churches of Cyprus: Treasures of Byzantine Art* (Nicosia, 1964, rev. London, 1985)

A. Papageorghiou: *Masterpieces of the Byzantine Art of Cyprus* (Nicosia, 1965)

D. C. Winfield: 'Middle and Later Byzantine Wall Painting Methods: A Comparative Study', *Dumbarton Oaks Pap.*, xxii (1968), pp. 61–139

H. Grigoriadou: 'Affinités iconographiques des décors peints en Chypre et en Grèce au XIIe siècle', *Praktika tou A diethnous kyprologikou synedriou* [Proceedings of the first international Cypriot conference]: *Nicosia, 1969*, ii, pp. 37–41

A. Papageorghiou: *Icons of Cyprus* (Paris, Geneva and Munich, 1969/R Nicosia, 1992)

A. H. S. Megaw and E. J. W. Hawkins: 'A Fragmentary Mosaic of the Orant Virgin in Cyprus', *Actes du XIVe Congrès international des études byzantines: Bucarest, 1971*, iii, pp. 363–6

A. Papageorghiou: 'Recently Discovered Wall-paintings in 10th–11th Century Churches of Cyprus', *Actes du XIVe Congrès international des études byzantines: Bucarest, 1971*, iii, pp. 411–14

S. Boyd: 'The Church of the Panagia Amasgou, Monagri, Cyprus, and its Wall Paintings', *Dumbarton Oaks Pap.*, xxviii (1974), pp. 277–349

M. Sakopoulos: *La Theotokos à la Mandorle de Lythrangomi* (Paris, 1975)

C. Delvoye: 'L'Art paléochrétien de Chypre', *XVe Congrès international des études byzantines: Rapports et co-rapports: Athènes, 1976*, pp. 52–101

A. H. S. Megaw: 'Interior Decoration in Early Christian Cyprus', *XVe Congrès international d'études byzantines: Rapports et co-rapports: Athènes, 1976*, pp. 129–54

T. Velmans: 'Quelques programmes iconographiques de coupoles chypriotes du XIIe au XVe siècle', *Cah. Archéol.*, xxxii (1984), pp. 137–62

L. Hadermann-Misquish: 'La Peinture monumentale du XIIe siècle à Chypre', *Corsi Cult. A. Ravenn. & Biz.*, xxxii (1985), pp. 233–58

V. Pace: 'Presenze e influenze cipriote nella pittura duecentesca italiana', *Corsi Cult. A. Ravenn. & Biz.*, xxxii (1985), pp. 259–98

4. GOLD AND SILVER. The wealth of Cyprus in the late 6th century AD and the early 7th is reflected in the two treasure hoards, mostly ecclesiastical plates, found at Lapithos (now Lambousa), which was noted for its gold and silver works. The first discovery, made in the late 19th century, included gold and silver objects bearing the imperial control stamps of Tiberios II (*reg* AD 578–82), Phokas (*reg* AD 602–10) and Constans II (*reg* AD 641–68). Notable pieces are a hexagonal silver censer (diam. 106 mm; AD 602–10; London, BM) chased on each side with a medallion containing a bust of one of the following: *Christ*, the *Virgin*, *St Peter*, *St Paul*, *St John the Evangelist* and *St James*, and a silver bowl (diam. 247 mm; AD 641–51; London, BM) with a central medallion in low relief showing the frontal bust of a saint. The second discovery (1902) comprised several gold objects and a set of nine silver plates (AD 610–29; Nicosia, Cyprus Mus. and New York, Met.). They depict scenes in relief from the life of David, such as *David Slaying the Lion*, *David as a Shepherd*, the *Marriage of David and Michal*, the *Anointment of David* and *David and Goliath* (*see* EARLY CHRISTIAN AND BYZANTINE ART, fig. 85). Despite the religious subject-matter, both human and animal forms are executed in a classicizing style. It has been suggested that these plates were produced in Constantinople, but since their hallmarks date them to the reign of Heraklios (*reg* AD 610–41), who is known to have spent some time on Cyprus

25. Wall painting from the parekklesion of Hagia Trias in the monastery John Chrysostomos, Koutsoventis, early 12th century

during his war against the Iranians, they may well have been made for him at Lapithos.

BIBLIOGRAPHY

A. Stylianou and J. Stylianou: *The Treasure of Lambousa* (Nicosia, 1969)

S. H. Wander: 'The Cyprus Plates: The Story of David and Goliath', *Met. Mus. J.*, viii (1973), pp. 89–123

A. PAPAGEORGHIOU

IV. Lusignan and Venetian.

When Richard I (the Lionheart), King of England (*reg* 1189–99), occupied Cyprus in 1191, the island was already an entrepôt of Levantine trade and a staging point for Western pilgrims and crusaders. After a brief period under the Knights Templar and the ceding of the island to Guy de Lusignan (*reg* 1192–4), French-speaking Lusignan kings ruled for almost three centuries, successfully managing the competing demands of their Greek Orthodox subjects, the papacy, the Knights Hospitaller and other military orders, the Italian trading republics and the Egyptian sultanate. The Lusignan kingdom declined in the second half of the 14th century and owed tribute to the Mamluks after the invasion of 1426. Caterina Cornaro, widow of James II (*reg* 1460–73), abdicated in 1489 and retired to her native Venice (*see* CORNARO, (2)). The Venetian occupation was short-lived; Cyprus was annexed to the Ottoman empire in 1571.

1. Architecture. 2. Other arts.

1. ARCHITECTURE.

(i) Secular. Once the Lusignan rulers secured power they prudently began to extend and modify the Byzantine castles on the island. Little of this work is preserved. The most complete specimen is the north-west tower of Kyrenia Castle, which has a sloping scarp and high walls pierced by arrow slits; the chambers within carry pointed barrel vaults with square ribs. Other chambers (those on the east side are fairly complete) have barrel and groin vaults in two storeys. A gate-house, inserted into a section of Byzantine wall, is also reasonably well preserved. The window openings are simply moulded and lack carved decoration, a common feature of Lusignan military architecture.

Similar developments can be seen at other sites. At Nicosia, the capital city, a Byzantine fort was under reconstruction as early as 1211; Peter II (*reg* 1369–82) replaced this early building *c*. 1380. By 1372 the city was walled, but all these fortifications were razed by the Venetians in 1564, when the city was made smaller and enclosed by a circular wall with heart-shaped bastions (*see* NICOSIA, §1). At Famagusta, the chief seaport in the 14th century, the Lusignan walls were completely removed when the Venetians refortified the city between 1492 and 1544 (*see* FAMAGUSTA, §1). Low angle bastions of great thickness were built to withstand artillery fire and to house cannon. The Martinengo bastion at the north-west, with its splayed embrasures and arrow-headed plan, is the most impressive and original to have survived: the Ottoman barrage in 1571 focused on the barbican at the south-west corner of the city. The citadel, next to the harbour, also has Venetian towers. A vaulted chamber inside, which may be dated to the late 13th century or the early 14th, has unusual groin vaults with non-structural ribs appended to them; the latter have mostly fallen away.

The mountain castles of St Hilarion, Buffavento and Kantara were also of Byzantine origin and were modified in varying degrees by the Lusignan kings. The royal retreat of St Hilarion, dramatically located overlooking Kyrenia, is similar to coeval structures in that carved decoration, moulded arches and rib vaults were avoided. The most notable portion is a barrel-vaulted chamber (ruined), apparently a royal hall; one window (probably 13th century) retains its tracery. There were also significant early castles at Limassol (rebuilt early 14th century) and Paphos, notably the fortress known as Saranda Kolonnes (destr. 1222), but repeated earthquakes reduced their importance. The most complete later building is in the complex at Kolossi, the principal seat of the Knights Hospitaller in Cyprus. The donjon (mid-15th century) is a crenellated three-storey tower. The chambers inside have pointed barrel vaults and are unornamented except for large fireplaces. A barrel-vaulted sugar mill (rest. 1591) stands near the donjon.

Civil architecture is poorly represented in Cyprus, as the official residences of the trading communities and individual merchants have mostly been destroyed, together with the royal palaces of the Lusignans and their nobles. An exception is the hall (destr. 1426; rest.) of the Royal Manor at Kouklia (Old Paphos) and its accompanying sugar mill at nearby Stavros. A number of portals, some showing influence from Mamluk Egypt, may mark noble houses in Nicosia, although little survives other than the entrances and lower façades. The royal palace at Famagusta stood opposite the main cathedral; the façade was rebuilt in the Venetian period and incorporated into the Palazzo del Provveditore; its entablature was restored by the British. Some Renaissance portals are also preserved in Famagusta.

(ii) Religious. Chroniclers disagree as to the exact foundation date of St Sophia (now the Selimiye Mosque) in Nicosia, but its establishment and proper endowment was a concern of both Rome and the early Lusignans (*see* NICOSIA, §1). St Sophia became the seat of the Latin archbishop, and coronation ceremonies were performed before the west doors. Work had progressed sufficiently for Amalric (*reg* 1194–1205) to be buried there, and by the mid-13th century the apse, ambulatory and three bays of the nave were complete (for illustration *see* NICOSIA). Instead of a transept, low apsed chapels are appended to the north and south aisles; an additional chapel on the north side may have been used as a burial-place for the earliest Lusignan rulers. The simple, two-storey elevation does not look to the great French cathedrals of the day, such as Chartres and Bourges, but to humbler and older churches in west central France (see Gardner). To this were added details from mid-12th-century cathedral architecture: the early flying buttresses, for example, were derived directly from those of Laon Cathedral.

Work on St Sophia appears to have been interrupted in the mid-13th century when Henry I (*reg* 1218–53) and Hugh II (*reg* 1253–67) built an extensive Dominican monastery in Nicosia. The church became the favoured burial-place for the Lusignan rulers and many of their nobles. The whole complex, east of the present Paphos Gate, was pulled down by the Venetians in 1567. A modest example of 13th-century monastic architecture is preserved at BELLAPAIS ABBEY, which enjoyed royal patronage. The church was built on a Byzantine site, as shown by a reused carved lintel over the north door, and is notable for its square sanctuary pierced by three identical windows, a design of Cistercian derivation. As at St Sophia, cylindrical piers were used, but instead of colonnettes the arches spring from corbels, a device used frequently in later architecture. The non-projecting transept bays have barrel vaults, as if to emphasize the unimportance of this feature in Cyprus. The builders may have intended to extend the nave as far as the monastery's west gate, but only three bays were constructed.

Cyprus became increasingly important after the fall of Acre (now 'Akko in Israel) in 1291, with Famagusta emerging as one of the leading ports in the eastern Mediterranean. Many churches were built as the city developed in the 14th century. The first and most important undertaking was the cathedral, dedicated to St Nicholas. An inscription to the side of the south door indicates that three aisle vaults on each side of the nave were complete in 1311; the location of the inscription suggests that the church was built from west to east (for further discussion and illustration *see* FAMAGUSTA). While the west front distantly echoes Reims in its general configuration, the immediate stylistic sources are from the Rhineland: the window tracery, the flying buttresses topped with quatrefoils and the clerestory gables are closely related to Cologne. Other features, such as the ground-plan without a transept and the two-storey elevation, are more characteristic of Cyprus.

The cathedral of St Nicholas, probably finished by *c*. 1320, had a significant impact. In Famagusta, St George of the Latins and some smaller churches (all ruined) were probably built by members of the cathedral workshop. In Nicosia, St Sophia was finished using variations on the designs introduced at Famagusta; the consecration in 1326 indicates that most of the work was finished. The west portals, however, tentatively assigned to *c*. 1347, when Pope Clement VI issued a bull referring to the restoration and completion of the church, introduce a more detailed and decorated style. The dogtooth ornament on the portals became a frequent feature in the second half of the 14th century. Equally influential were the framed panels for painted images (destr.) in the tympana. The conventual buildings at Bellapais Abbey, which were commissioned by Hugh IV (*reg* 1324–59) and probably completed in the 1350s (for illustration *see* BELLAPAIS ABBEY), more fully exemplify the developments seen in the St Sophia portals. Architectural spaces carry forward the lightness and delicacy of Famagusta Cathedral, but the sculpture is handled in a cramped and somewhat rustic manner. The refectory door has dogtooth ornament and a particularly striking chevron moulding, the first of many examples in Cyprus.

The readoption of earlier motifs is symptomatic of the dramatic reformulation of architecture that emerged in the time of Peter I (*reg* 1358–69). No royal buildings from his reign have survived in Nicosia or elsewhere, and the development is best illustrated by St George of the Greeks (ruined; see fig. 26), Famagusta. This was apparently the largest Orthodox church built during the 14th century and ranks as the most remarkable product of the Lusignan period in its adaptation of the Gothic style to Orthodox requirements in a dynamic and highly original manner. The church was built next to an earlier Orthodox shrine and laid out as a grand basilica without an ambulatory or transept. Recalling earlier traditions, the piers were reduced in diameter so as to resemble monolithic columns, and a large dome was placed over the central bay and half domes over the apses. The windows (especially in the apses) were made smaller to provide space for extensive narrative frescoes in the Byzantine manner. The interior and exterior were purged of carved ornament and the west front reduced to a plain wall pierced by three doors and a small oculus. Rib vaults and simple flying buttresses were effortlessly integrated into this scheme; the quality of masonry and command of vaulted space show that the lessons of Famagusta Cathedral had been fully assimilated. The building served as a model for later churches, notably

26. St George of the Greeks, Famagusta, 1360s; view from the north-west

St Mammas (15th century; rebuilt from 1725) at Morphou and the Katholikon (early 16th century) at St Neophytos Monastery. St George of the Greeks can be assigned to the 1360s owing to its similarity to the Nestorian church in Famagusta, known to have been constructed before the Genoese occupation of the city in 1371. St George is also closely related to SS Peter and Paul in Famagusta, which was built in the time of Peter I and shows that the new style was used for churches of the Roman rite. Its appearance can be explained by Peter I's anachronistic attempt to resuscitate the crusading enterprise, an effort which appears to have fostered the use of older forms. Certainly Peter's ill-conceived economic policies contributed to the kingdom's decline and were instrumental in encouraging a chaste architectural style. Plague ravaged the island during his reign, and while its effects on architecture cannot be directly measured, the disease seems to have reinforced the conservative outlook that dominated much of the eastern Mediterranean from the 14th century (see Meyendorff).

The kingdom of Cyprus declined dramatically with the death of Peter I and the Genoese occupation of Famagusta. During the 15th century the most notable building took place after the marriage of John II (*reg* 1432–58) to Helena Palaiologina (*d* 1458), daughter of Theodore II, Despot of Morea and Duke of Sparta (*reg* 1407–43). Helena, who arrived in Cyprus in 1442, sought to promote Orthodoxy and was encouraged by the reconciliation that had been effected between the Greek and Latin churches at the Council of Florence (1439). An architectural residue of this rapprochement can be seen in the church of Panagia Hodegetria (now known as the Bedesten) next to St

Sophia in Nicosia. The church was founded in the Byzantine period, and there had been several campaigns of reconstruction under the Lusignans (see Willis). The north façade was completely replaced in the mid-15th century and fitted with three elaborate portals. This effectively turned the conceptual orientation of the church towards the square in front of the cathedral and thereby presented the Orthodox claim to equal participation in the affairs of the kingdom. The main portal is a close copy of the southwest portal of St Sophia, while the windows and other entrances were inspired by the cathedral and other important buildings in Nicosia. It is the clearest demonstration of how 15th-century Cypriot architecture drew exclusively on its own traditions and resources. The royal chapel of Hagia Ekaterina at Pyrga, constructed in the time of Janus (*reg* 1398–1432), is a simple, barrel-vaulted cell that exemplifies the humble nature of later building outside the capital. Under Venetian rule (1489–1571) the fortifications were extensively rebuilt, but there were no significant additions to church architecture.

BIBLIOGRAPHY

C. Enlart: *L'Art gothique et la renaissance en Chypre* (Paris, 1899; Eng. trans. by D. Hunt, intro. by N. Coldstream, London, 1987)

G. Jeffery: *A Description of the Historic Monuments of Cyprus* (Nicosia, 1918/*R* London, 1978)

G. Hill: *A History of Cyprus*, 4 vols (Cambridge, 1940–52) [short but useful section on archit.]

J. Meyendorff: 'Spiritual Trends in Byzantium in the Late Thirteenth and Early Fourteenth Centuries', *The Kariye Djami*, ed. P. A. Underwood (New York and Princeton, 1966–75), pp. 95–106

A. C. N. Borg: 'The Development of Chevron Ornament', *J. Brit. Archaeol. Assoc.*, xxx (1967), pp. 122–40

A. H. S. Megaw: 'Military Architecture in Cyprus', *The Art and Architecture of the Crusader States*, ed. H. W. Hazard (1977), iv of *A History of the Crusades*, ed. K. M. Setton (Madison and London, 1962–89), pp. 196–207

M. D. Willis: 'Byzantine Beginnings of the Bedesten', *Kyp. Spoudai*, 57 (1981), pp. 186–9

A. H. S. Megaw: 'Excavations at Saranda Kolonnes', *Report of the Department of Antiquities, Cyprus* (Nicosia, 1982), pp. 210–16

S. Gardner: 'The Church of St Etienne in Dreux and its Role in the Formation of Early Gothic Architecture', *J. Brit. Archaeol. Assoc.*, cxxxviii (1984), pp. 86–113

P. W. Edbury: *The Kingdom of Cyprus and the Crusades* (Cambridge, 1991)

A. Luttrell: *The Hospitallers of Rhodes and their Mediterranean World* (Aldershot, 1992)

N. Coldstream: *Nicosia: Gothic City to Venetian Fortress* (Nicosia, 1993)

2. OTHER ARTS. The turmoil surrounding the Ottoman conquest in 1571 led to the destruction and dispersal of many works of art. Historical accounts indicate that tombs in the Latin churches were pulled down by the Turks when the buildings were turned into mosques; the only funerary objects to survive (aside from a few carved fragments) were incised tomb slabs, most dating to the 14th century (see Chamberlayne). Figurative sculpture was also destroyed: other than several large lions of St Mark, which were apparently preserved as trophies, there are only two specimens of note. A tympanum from Larnaka (1210–20; London, V&A) shows stylistic links with northern Italy, and a damaged standing figure (mid-13th century), possibly from the destroyed church of St Dominic, is purely French in style (see Boase).

There are literary accounts of numerous objects from Lusignan and Venetian times, but in most cases connections cannot be made to surviving pieces. For example, a mid-13th century inventory (Rome, Vatican, Bib. Apostolica, Cod. P. Gr. 367) enumerates the vessels, books, images, candelabra etc from a church in Nicosia, but none of these objects has been located. Similar problems surround the silk, brocade, taffeta, linen and *camlet* for which Lusignan Cyprus had a wide reputation. Few samples seem to have been preserved, but it has been suggested that the Berne altar frontal (excepting the later end panels) was produced in Cyprus (see Folda). Recognizably Cypriot characteristics of this work have yet to be determined, and it is difficult to establish a corpus given the paucity of documentation.

Many luxury objects were imported. Glazed ceramics from Italy were brought to Cyprus well into the Ottoman period, and accounts of 15th-century travellers mention a vessel in Nicosia similar to the celebrated Alhambra vases (*see* ISLAMIC ART, §V, 4(iv) and fig. 176). Manuscripts also seem to have been imported for the Lusignans. When the barons of the Holy Land wanted a coronation gift for Henry II (*reg* 1285–1324) they turned to the workshops in Acre (now 'Akko in Israel) for a sumptuous *Histoire Universelle*.

Irrefutable evidence for local manuscript production survives in the earliest musical manuscripts of the Cypriot Orthodox church (16th century). Luxury metal objects were both imported and locally made. In 1397 the goldsmiths of Nicosia produced a model ship in gold, which was presented to the Ottoman sultan Bayazid I (*reg* 1389–1403) by James I (*reg* 1382–98). A reliquary from Famagusta, carried to Diyabakir by Armenians in the 16th century, was also likely the work of Cypriot craftsmen (see Willis). The most impressive piece of metalwork from the Crusader period is the brass basin with gold and silver inlay (Paris, Louvre) made for Hugh IV (*reg* 1324–59). Incised with Arabic and French inscriptions and evidently intended as a gift for Hugh, the basin is closely related to those produced in Mamluk Egypt or Syria (*see* ISLAMIC ART, §IV, 3(iii)(a)). A second basin made for Hugh is in the L. A. Mayer Memorial Institute, Jerusalem.

BIBLIOGRAPHY

T. J. Chamberlayne: *Lacrimae Nicossienses* (Paris, 1894)

C. B. Cobham: *Excerpta Cypria* (London, 1908)

C. Enlart: 'Deux souvenirs du royaume de Chypre', *Mém. Soc. N. Antiqua. France*, lxix (1910), pp. 1–16

——: 'Boucle d'argent à la devise de l'ordre de l'épée au Musée du cinquantenaire', *An. Soc. Royale Archéol. Bruxelles*, xxiv (1910), pp. 209–12

G. Hill: *A History of Cyprus*, 4 vols (Cambridge, 1940–52)

D. S. Rice: 'Arabic Inscriptions on a Brass Basin made for Hugh IV de Lusignan', *Studi orientalistici in onore di Giorgio Levi della Vida*, 2 vols (Rome, 1956), ii, pp. 390–402

R. H. Hoppin: *The Cypriot-French Repertory of the Manuscript Turino, Biblioteca Nazionale, J. II. 9* (Rome, 1960–63) [MS. made for King Janus in northern Italy]

J. Folda: *Crusader Manuscript Illumination at Saint-Jean d'Acre, 1275–1291* (Princeton, 1976)

T. S. R. Boase: 'The Arts in Cyprus: Ecclesiastical Art', v of *A History of the Crusades*, ed. K. M. Setton (Madison, WI, 1977)

M. Willis: 'A New Document of Cypriote History: The Journal of Ambrosio Bembo', *Kyp. Spoudai* (1978), pp. 35–46

P. Williamson: *Catalogue of Romanesque Sculpture* (London, 1983) [Romanesque sculpture in London, V&A]

A. Jakovljevic: *Catalogue of Byzantine Chant Manuscripts in the Monastic and Episcopal Libraries of Cyprus* (Nicosia, 1990)

MICHAEL D. WILLIS

V. Ottoman and modern.

1. Introduction. 2. Architecture, painting and sculpture. 3. Interior decoration and furniture. 4. Metalwork. 5. Textiles.

1. INTRODUCTION. In 1571 Cyprus was seized by the Ottoman empire, and the island entered a period of decline. Such churches as the cathedrals of Nicosia and Famagusta were converted into mosques, and the Orthodox Church replaced the Latin Church; at the same time the Archbishop was gradually given increasing power by the Ottoman rulers. In the first half of the 19th century the British intervened to bolster the Ottoman empire against the threats of Egypt and Russia; the price of this support was greater official tolerance of the Greek Cypriots. In 1878 Britain assumed control of the island under the Cyprus Convention, and its formal annexation in 1914, when the Ottoman empire sided with Germany in World War I, was confirmed in 1923 by the Treaty of Lausanne. The island's economy gradually improved.

The Treaty of Zurich established the Republic of Cyprus in 1960, but Greek and Turkish intercommunal violence resulted in the installation of a United Nations peacekeeping force in 1964. Despite the island's growing prosperity, tension between the Greek and Turkish communities increased until, in response to an attempt by the Greek government to overthrow the President, Archbishop Makarios III Mouskos (1913–77), Turkey invaded northern Cyprus in 1974 and established the Attila Line, which partitioned the island; the capital, Nicosia, was divided by the so-called Green Line. The Republic of Cyprus retained the districts of Limassol and Paphos, together with most of Larnaka and Nicosia, while the majority of Famagusta and Kyrenia were in Turkish hands. In 1983 Turkey unilaterally declared the latter areas the Turkish Republic of Northern Cyprus, a move repeatedly condemned in the United Nations.

BIBLIOGRAPHY
C. W. J. Orr: *Cyprus under British Rule* (London, 1918/*R* London, 1972)
H. Luke: *Cyprus under the Turks, 1571–1878* (1921/*R* 1969)
C. Hitchens: *Cyprus* (London and New York, 1984)
C. P. Kyrris: *History of Cyprus* (Nicosia, 1985)

2. ARCHITECTURE, PAINTING AND SCULPTURE. Under Ottoman rule (1571–1878) architecture, painting and sculpture were constrained by the island's impoverished conditions and were limited to local religious and vernacular traditions. Orthodox churches were still built in the Byzantine style, retaining some Gothic decorative motifs (*see* §IV, 1(ii) above), and became more elaborate during the 19th century. Some, such as Hagios Ioannis (1718–59) in Nicosia, were painted with frescoes, but usually the icons and iconostases of carved, painted and gilded wood were more noteworthy. Mosques, other than converted Latin churches, have rectangular, transverse plans and pitched roofs, although the Arabamet Mosque (17th century) in Nicosia is an example of the classical Ottoman style. Grandiose town houses of dressed stone masonry with elaborate courtyards, such as the house (1793) in Nicosia of Hadjigeorgakis Kornessios, Great Dragoman from 1779 to 1809, were richly decorated and furnished. The vernacular housing was of mud-brick, with decoration restricted to carved and painted furniture (*see* §3 below).

During the British colonial period (1878–1960), Cypriot painters and architects studied abroad and returned to teach and practise their skills. Early descriptive painters, such as Ioannis Kissonergis (1889–1963), were followed by a generation of painters who combined the formal influences of the European avant-garde with Byzantine art and folk traditions to portray the life and landscape of rural Cyprus. The folk tradition was sustained through strong works by naive painters, notably Michael Kashalos (1885–1974). ADAMANTIOS DIAMANTIS produced a series of works expressing the customs and manners of the Cypriot people, culminating in the epic *World of Cyprus* (1967–72). Yeoryios Pol. Yeoryiou (1901–72) combined religious and historical traditions of Cyprus with mannerist and Expressionist sources, while TELEMACHOS KANTHOS divided his work between impressionistic depictions of Cypriot life and landscape and atmospheric, often dramatic, engravings. Architects introduced formal concepts from European design and planning practices: the façades of the private villas and public schools built by THEODOROS FOTIADES after 1919, for example, have precise Neoclassical detailing. Odysseus Tsangarides (1907–74), municipal architect of Nicosia from 1930 to 1935, introduced ideas that later formed the basis of the island's urban planning ordinances. These painters and architects helped to introduce contemporary approaches to artistic and architectural design and inspired others to express their creative talents.

The next generation of artists and architects studied in Europe in the years immediately before and after World War II and experimented enthusiastically with new concepts and approaches after their return. Of particular note was CHRISTOFOROS SAVVA, who experimented with Fauvism and Cubism, combining geometric and organic forms to create an individual style. The powerful style of Stass Paraskos (*b* 1933) draws on similar influences and shows an interest in Cyprus's artistic and archaeological heritage. Modern theories and conceptions of art all had their adherents and experimenters on Cyprus; particularly influential on other Cypriot painters were the Constructivism of Stelios Votsis (*b* 1929) and Nikos Kouroushis (*b* 1937), the abstract Expressionism of Vera Hadjida (*b* 1936) and the Surrealism of George Skoteinos (*b* 1937). The first notable Cypriot sculptors belonged to this generation, including Andreas Savvides (*b* 1930), whose work encompasses monumental sculpture and abstract compositions combining different materials, and Andy Adamos (or Hadjiadamos; 1936–90), who studied and lived in South Africa and was much influenced by African art.

Architects wholeheartedly implemented the various interpretations of International Style to which they had been exposed during their studies abroad. The buildings of PANAYIOTIS STAVRINIDES reflect a familiarity with the Amsterdam school. CHARILAOS DIKAIOS studied at the Ecole des Beaux-Arts, Paris; his work shows the influence of Tony Garnier and Perret. The structures of N. A. MICHAELIDES have a sense of formal rationalism that was acquired in Milan, while those of AHMET BEHAEDDIN represent an awareness of principles expressed by Gropius and Le Corbusier. This pursuit of modern Western styles epitomized Cyprus's desire to appear a fully fledged modern state, especially after independence in

1960, although it often distanced artists and architects from their traditional heritage and the Cypriot public.

Most of the artists who studied abroad during the 1960s and early 1970s returned and experienced the social upheaval resulting from the schism of 1974. They countered this upheaval with a search for a new identity and its expression in art and design, combining influences from abroad with specifically Cypriot themes. The earlier abstract and Constructivist painting of Andreas Ladommatos (*b* 1940) developed into a series of dreamlike, surrealistic details from Cypriot architecture and landscape, for example in his *Windows and Doors* cycle. Emin Çizenel (*b* 1949) used both figured and abstract forms and had an interest in symbolism, while Andreas Charalambous (*b* 1947) produced philosophical compositions reflecting on the artist's role in the world. Furthermore, the most monumental sculpture in Cyprus was created at this time, the bronze statue of *Archbishop Makarios* (h. 10 m) by Nikos Kodjiamani (*b* 1946) outside the Archbishop's Palace in Nicosia. While modern architectural techniques remain dominant, some architects, such as Pefkios Georgiades (*b* 1935), have endeavoured to reconcile contemporary design with attitudes and practices from within the native building tradition.

Cypriot art, sculpture and architecture are inspired by enthusiastic cosmopolitan interests, which encourage energetic experiments with alternative media and compositions. This eclecticism, however, is periodically tempered by an awareness of native traditions and themes, which ultimately may stimulate the forging of a coherent and distinctly Cypriot artistic style.

BIBLIOGRAPHY

'Türkische Mädchenoberschule mit Internat in Nicosia auf Cypern', *Baumeister* (1964), pp. 350–55

P. Georgiades: 'Modern Architecture', *Architektoniki*, lv (1966), pp. 54–88

C. Christou: *Mia sindomi istoria tis neoteris kai synchronis kypriakis technias* [A brief history of modern and contemporary Cypriot art] (Nicosia, 1983)

I. Ionas: *La Maison rurale de Chypre (XVIIIe–XXe siècle): Aspects et techniques de construction* (Nicosia, 1988)

Kıbrıs Türk resim sanatından bir resit [A review of Turkish Cypriot painting] (Nicosia, 1988)

MICHAEL GIVEN, ELISE MARIE MOENTMANN,
KENNETH W. SCHAAR

3. INTERIOR DECORATION AND FURNITURE. Until the early 20th century Cyprus had an agrarian economy, so storerooms and stables occupied most of the space in the houses, and the living area was kept to a minimum. Traditional Cypriot furniture, as demonstrated by surviving examples from the 18th century to the early 20th, was restricted to a few utilitarian types made of pine, cypress or walnut wood. Apart from the simple bedsteads used by the poor, the earliest surviving beds are wooden with projecting carved posts. These were later replaced by wrought-iron beds with painted decoration. Chests were used for storing household linen, wall cupboards and shelves of wood or plaster for other household goods. By the early 20th century, wardrobes, chests-of-drawers and mirrors were in general use, and chairs with plaited rush seats were made. Tables were plain or had carved drawers. Sometimes a straw tray was set on a stool as a table.

Wood-carving developed principally for items of ecclesiastical use, so similar techniques and iconography were applied to domestic work. There were several local styles, the outstanding being the high-relief work of Lapithos and the relief and painted decoration of Akanthou. (Both these centres are in the Kyrenia District.) In poor areas the decoration of the chests was confined to shallow incised geometric patterns. Other motifs, such as arches, vases of flowers, rosettes, cypresses, vines, angels, double-headed eagles, crosses and lions were used on chests, shelves and wall cupboards. In the grander houses, which tended to be in Nicosia, Ottoman influences could be seen in the divan rooms and in the carved and painted ceilings. This was true of both Greek and Turkish houses. From 1878, when the island came under British rule, European influences became apparent, and imitation Victorian styles were produced. Increasing urbanization and industrialization eventually caused the decline of traditional furniture in the early 20th century.

BIBLIOGRAPHY

G. Charalambous: *I kypriaki ikia* [The Cypriot house] (Nicosia, 1968)

H. Papademetriou: 'I laiki techni tou Karava' [Folk art of Karavas], *Karavas*, eds A. Stylianou and K. Harmanda (Nicosia, 1969), pp. 115–37

A. Pieridou: *Kypriaki laiki techni* [Cyprus folk art] (Nicosia, 1980), pp. 161–7

T. Kanthos: *Laikoi technites tis Kyprou* [Craftsmen of Cyprus] (Nicosia, 1981), pp. 67–87

4. METALWORK. Native sources of copper were known in Cyprus from the 4th millennium BC and in the form of bronze were used abundantly in antiquity and the Middle Ages. Copper utensils constituted an indispensable part of any household; more elaborate objects were used by wealthy families and the Church. Typical products of the Ottoman period (1571–1878) included trays, goblets, plates, bowls, cauldrons and various types of cooking vessels. They were usually hammered into shape (less often cast) with a variety of mallets, hammers and anvils. Decoration consists of geometric designs and more composite motifs of Islamic origin. The main centre for metalwork was Nicosia, where, according to Louis Salvator (1873), 'the coppersmiths make small and large flat plates and dishes for the Turks, partly of tin, of very handsome workmanship and nicely ornamented'. Gold- and silversmithing flourished in Cyprus, reaching especially high standards from the 17th century to the 19th. Fine jewellery and articles of both ecclesiastical and domestic use were made from silver, pure or mixed with copper, gold or gold-plated silver and were adorned with incised, applied or repoussé designs. The predominant technique was filigree, often combined with cloisonné enamel and inset stones, on such objects as cup-holders, belt-buckles, crosses and earrings. Rosewater bowls in silver and incense burners used by women to welcome guests were considered precious household items. Silver and jewellery—used to complement official dress—were made in several parts of Cyprus, but the most important centre was Nicosia.

BIBLIOGRAPHY

Louis Salvator, Archduke of Austria: *Levkosia, die Hauptstadt von Cypern* (Prague, 1873); Eng. trans. as *Levkosia, the Capital of Cyprus* (London, 1983), p. 69

A. Pieridou: 'I laiki techni sti Levkosia kata ton 18o ke 19o aiona' [Folk art in Nicosia during the 18th and 19th centuries], *Kypriaki laiki techni* [Cypriot folk art] (Nicosia, 1980), pp. 112–14

T. Kanthos: *Laikoi technites tis Kyprou* [Craftsmen of Cyprus] (Nicosia, 1981), pp. 45–51

S. Papadopoulos: 'Syllogi neoteron chalkinon skevon archaeologikou Mousiou Kyprou' [Collection of copper utensils in the Cyprus Museum], *Rep. Dept Ant., Cyprus* (1986), pp. 222–9

E. Papademetriou: 'Art populaire chypriote', *Chypre: 9000 ans de civilisation: Tours, 1990*, pp. 17ff

5. TEXTILES. On account of its fertility and geographical position, Cyprus was an important centre of textile manufacture from antiquity. It produced good quality wool, flax, cotton and, from the Byzantine period, silk. These materials were woven into both single-fibre fabrics and such mixed cloths as *camlet* (a combination of wool, silk and, sometimes, goat or camel hair). Fine cloth was manufactured in Nicosia and Famagusta to be traded throughout the eastern Mediterranean and into the Near East; Cyprus may also have been the source of some of the *camlet* imported to Europe in the medieval period. The production of fine wool and silk fabrics declined from the late medieval period, but coarse linen continued to be woven, and a printed cotton industry was developed at Nicosia by the 19th century. Early travellers to Cyprus admired the embroidery, which reflected the influences of the various conquerors of the island. It had been important from at least the Byzantine period, but it declined in the 18th and 19th centuries. Giovanni Mariti, who visited in the 1760s, commented on the Turkish dress worn by the ladies (*see* ISLAMIC ART §VI, 3(v)(b)). The light polychrome silk embroidered veils and scarves of their elaborate headwear were probably worked on the island. Surviving pieces are somewhat coarser than the Turkish originals. Most notable was the fine whitework. In this, the linen ground was decorated with cutwork and drawn-thread-work to make open, almost lacelike fabrics known as *lefkaritika*, from Lefkara village in the Larnaca District. In the 20th century this was revived as a cottage industry. Another type was the counted-thread embroidery with zigzag floral stem designs worked with red silk in cross-stitch. It is called *phythkiotika* from the village of Phyti in the Paphos District. Both these types of embroidery are clearly derived from 16th-century Italian originals. Renaissance patterns also underlie the geometric designs decorated with coloured glass beads that were worked on the Karpas peninsula. The patterns on these textiles, which are repeated generation after generation, are mainly geometric; stylized floral designs or human figures are rare. The names of the patterns, for example 'river' or 'palmette', suggest the source of their inspiration. These locally produced fabrics met all the needs of the household and formed the main part of the dowry. However, a decline in handmade textiles began in the early 20th century with increasing industrialization and the importation of manufactured fabrics.

BIBLIOGRAPHY

G. Mariti: *Viaggi per l'isola di Cipro e per la Siria e Palestina, fatti . . . dall'anno 1760 al 1768*, 9 vols (Lucca and Florence, 1769–76)

A. Pieridou: 'Kypriaki laiki ifantiki' [Traditional Cypriot weaving], *Kyp. Spoudai*, xxiii (1959), pp. 187–214

——: *Cyprus Embroidery* (Nicosia, 1976)

H. Papademetriou: 'Kypriaki ifantiki' [Cypriot weaving], *Kyp. Spoudai*, xlvi (1982), pp. 153–61

A. Aristidou: 'Production and Trade in Cyprus during the 18th and 19th Centuries', *I zoi stin Kypro ton IH' kai TH' aiona* [Life in Cyprus in the 18th and 19th centuries] (Nicosia, 1984), pp. 33–62

A. Hadjiyiasemi: *Lefkara Lace Embroidery: Historical Development, Designs, Technique* (Nicosia, 1987)

EUPHROSYNE RIZOPOULOU-EGOUMENIDOU

VI. Museums, collections and exhibitions.

The wealth and diversity of archaeological finds on Cyprus attracted the attention of diplomats, collectors, excavators and treasure-hunters in the late 19th century. The most celebrated of these, Luigi Palma di Cesnola (1832–1904), had the island's earliest museum in his Larnaka residence. He sold some of his collection to the Louvre and the British Museum; much of the rest formed the nucleus of the Metropolitan Museum of Art in New York.

The first Cypriot antiquities law (1874), introduced by the Ottoman authorities, required that one-third of excavation finds go to the government, resulting in the establishment of the first Cyprus Museum in Nicosia. Today it exhibits the national antiquities collection, with artefacts dating from the earliest settlement of the island to the late Roman period (*c.* 8500 BC–*c.* AD 400). One of its founders, Demetrios Pierides (1811–95), began assembling in 1839 what has become the island's finest private archaeological collection, spanning the Chalcolithic period to the Middle Ages, housed in the Pierides Foundation Museum, Larnaka; his decendants enlarged the holdings, which now include folk art.

Further legislation in 1905 and 1935 made all antiquities the property of the government, established the Department of Antiquities and provided for the creation of museums. Sites and buildings of historic and artistic merit, declared Ancient Monuments, subsequently became ideal venues for the growing collections. The major museums in the Republic are government-owned; others are municipal or private, belonging to individuals, societies, foundations and cultural centres or the Greek Orthodox Church.

From 1936 onwards the largest and most comprehensive assemblage of Cypriot folk art, supplemented by 4000 photographs and archival material dating from the 1800s, was gathered by the Society of Cypriot Studies and is now housed in the Old Archbishopric of Nicosia. The national collection, however, is in the Museum of Folk Art, established in a traditional 19th-century house in the village of Yeroskipou, Paphos District.

The 1960s, early 1970s and 1980s were marked by the development, growth and increasing variety of museums. Medieval artefacts were accorded a place of their own under the purview of the Cyprus museums after independence in 1960. The Cyprus Medieval Museum in Limassol Castle (13th century) displays the national collection of art and artefacts dating from *c.* AD 400 to *c.* 1850. District archaeological museums were built in Paphos, Famagusta, Larnaka and Limassol. Government site museums were created for Old Paphos at the Kouklia Royal House, the necropolis at Salamis, and the greater Kourion area in Episkopi village culminating with the reconstructed Chalcolithic houses (*c.* 2500 BC) at Lemba Experimental Village and the innovative museum at Maa–Palaeokastro, both in the Paphos District. The Greek Orthodox Church established the Byzantine Museum in 1982 as a part of the Archbishop Makarios III Foundation and Cultural Centre in Nicosia, with the most representative collection of Cypriot icons dating from the 8th to the 18th century. Religious accoutrements are held by numerous monasteries and are displayed at Kykko (founded *c*. 1100) and at Hagios Neophytos near Tala, where the creative exhibits also include antiquities. The village of Koilani near Limassol and the Holy Bishopric of Paphos also display their ecclesiastical collections. Specialized ethnographic museums have been established, inlcuding the Rural Museum of Phikardou, where a typical late 19th-century mountain village is preserved; the Ethnological Museum in the House of the Dragoman Hadjigeorgakis Kornessios (1779–1809); the Cyprus Jewellers Museum in the old city of Nicosia with an exhibition of traditional 19th- and 20th-century silverwork; and the Lefkara Museum, featuring traditional Cypriot embroidery. In addition, there are numerous other local museums devoted to Cypriot folk art, industries and crafts.

New trends in museum development, including educational programmes, are exemplified by the Leventis Municipal Museum (1989), the island's first historical museum, devoted to the social development of the capital, Nicosia. The concept of a fine arts museum came late to the island, when the Cyprus State Art Gallery opened in 1990 within the old Majestic Hotel (1925), Nicosia. It contains an expanding collection of works by 20th-century Cypriot painters, sculptors and graphic designers; such contemporary work can also seen in the Limassol Municipal Art Gallery. The east gate of Venetian Nicosia, the Porta Giuliana, has been converted into the Famagusta Gate Municipal Cultural Centre, which hosts numerous art exhibitions, as does the capital's former electrical power station, now the Municipal Art Centre. Major Cypriot banks are also involved in the island's cultural heritage. The Bank of Cyprus Cultural Foundation owns maps, charts and rare books dating from the 15th to the 19th century and displays its specimen collection of coins, dating from the 6th century BC to the present day, in the bank's Museum of the History of Cypriot Coinage, Nicosia. The Popular Bank Cultural Centre has a collection of works by contemporary Cypriot artists supplemented by the most comprehensive collection of old photographs of the island. Finally, there are numerous registered private collections on Cyprus; these are not open regularly to the public, but they may be viewed by appointment.

Geopolitical changes in 1963 and 1974 resulted in the division of the island. In the Turkish Cypriot sector of Nicosia, the Lapidary Museum, a restored 15th-century Venetian house, contains a collection of medieval and Gothic architectural fragments from vanished palaces and churches gathered by Geroge Jeffrey (1855–1935), Curator of Ancient Monuments under the British. An ethnographic museum was opened in 1963 within the Mevlevi Tekke, an early 17th-century centre of the Sufi Muslim mystic 'whirling' Dervish sect; the tekke is arguably the most attractive example of Turkish architecture on Cyprus. A picture of Ottoman domestic life is provided by the Mansion of Dervish Pasha, built in 1802 in the Arabamet quarter of old Nicosia and restored as a museum of folk art in 1988.

Kyrenia Castle contains the remains of a unique 4th-century BC ship, excavated and reassembled before 1974. A new Museum of Archaeology and Natural History was established in 1979 within the Bishop's Palace at Morphou and exhibits of ecclesiastical furnishings, especially icons, and antiquities opened in the church and the cloisters of the monastery of Apostolos Barnabas at Salamis in 1992.

BIBLIOGRAPHY

J. D. Stewart: 'Museums and Archaeology in Cyprus', *Mus. J.*, lxxxi/1 (1981), pp. 39–41
V. Karageorghis and others: *Ancient Cypriot Art in the Pierides Foundation Museum* (Larnaca, 1985)
V. Karageorghis, ed.: 'The Cyprus Department of Antiquities, 1935–1985', *Archaeology in Cyprus, 1960–1985* (Nicosia, 1985), pp. 1–10
P. Gaber: 'The Museums of Cyprus', *Bibl. Archaeol.*, i/4 (1989), pp. 170–78
V. Karageorghis: *The A. G. Leventis Foundation and the Cultural Heritage of Cyprus* (Athens, 1990)
M. C. Loulloupis: 'Les Musées archéologiques publics de Chypre', *La France aux portes de l'orient: Chypre XIIème–XVème siècle* (Paris, 1991), pp. 145–55
R. Hanworth: *The Heritage of North Cyprus* (Nicosia, 1993)

HELENA WYLDE SWINY

Cyrene [Arab. Shaḥḥāt]. City in Libya, 8 km from the coast and 620 m above sea-level on a plateau of the al-Jabal al-Akhdar (Green Mountain). The Greek city flourished from its founding as a Dorian colony *c*. 630 BC to Hellenistic times, and its Greek culture was maintained

1. Cyrene, Temple of Zeus, late 6th century BC

during the long period of Roman rule, when its fortunes declined somewhat.

1. ARCHITECTURE. Cyrene's principal monuments, restored by their Italian excavators, reveal the splendours of the Greek city. It changed only superficially in Roman times, when alterations to existing buildings were more common than new projects.

(i) Greek. Herodotus (IV. cl–clviii) related how a party of Therans, forced by drought to leave their native island, settled at Cyrene because of its high rainfall. Their leader, Battos, became king and established a dynasty that lasted until 440 BC. The site is protected on three sides by gorges with gently sloping ground to the east. A low hill, the acropolis, rises to the west and immediately below its north slopes is the Sanctuary of Apollo. Springs emerge from the rock at this point, ensuring a constant water supply. The plateau is divided by the valley street, which runs from the east gate down to the Sanctuary of Apollo and then past the north necropolis to the port of Apollonia, 19 km away. Parallel to the valley street is the Street of Battos, which runs from the south-east gate through the agora to the acropolis. A main transverse street intersected both streets just east of the Hellenistic gymnasium. The earliest settlers presumably occupied the acropolis, and the eastern fringe of the later agora seems to have been used as a burial ground, which suggests that the early town could not have extended far to the east. Other evidence for the early city is pottery from *c.* 600 BC found in the extramural sanctuary of Demeter in the wadi Bel Gadir south of the agora. Cyrene's eventual size can be judged by the four massive cemeteries surrounding the city, which contain over 1200 tombs and several thousand individual sarcophagi. Some rock-cut tombs of the 6th century BC have fine façades with Doric and Ionic columns. There are also free-standing rectangular and circular tombs. The city owed much of its prosperity to the production of corn, wool, dates and silphium, a much sought-after medicinal plant that appears as the symbol of Cyrene on her coinage. A famous Lakonian cup (*c.* 560 BC; Paris, Bib.

2. Cyrene, Caesareum, aerial view, 1st–2nd centuries AD

N., Cab. Médailles; *see* GREECE, ANCIENT, fig. 103) shows King Arkesilaos of Cyrene supervising the weighing of silphium.

Cyrene's wealth is reflected in such buildings as the Temple of Apollo (late 6th century BC), the theatre (early 5th century BC) west of the Sanctuary of Apollo, and the hippodrome (5th–4th century BC). A large octastyle Doric Temple of Zeus (see fig. 1) was built on high ground to the north-east of the valley street, perhaps after the Persian destruction of an earlier shrine in 515–514 BC. Measuring 69.68×31.77 m, it is slightly larger than the Temple of Zeus at Olympia. Buildings constructed after the fall of the monarchy (440–323 BC) include the marble-clad altar of Apollo, the small Strategeion, so called because it was dedicated by three generals (*strategoi*), and the gateway of the Sanctuary of Apollo. To this period or to a slightly later date belongs the rock-cut bathing establishment with its rows of small hip-baths south-east of the Sanctuary of Apollo. When the surrounding kingdom of Cyrenaica was annexed by Ptolemy I after the death of Alexander the Great (323 BC), many additions were made to the city, especially the area around the agora, including the north stoa, the naval monument and the two *tholoi* (circular structures), one with statues connected with the cult of Demeter (*in situ*). One of the most splendid Hellenistic monuments is the 2nd-century BC gymnasium with its outer walls of fine isodomic masonry and porticos of slender Doric columns. A running track with a façade formed by statues of Hermes and Herakles dates from the same period.

(ii) Roman. In 96 BC Cyrenaica was bequeathed to Rome by its ruler, Ptolemy Apion. Under Augustus (*reg* 27 BC– AD 14) it became a senatorial province governed from Gortyn on Crete. At the end of Augustus' reign a wealthy citizen, M. Sufenas Proculus, and the proconsul, Rubellius Blandus, rebuilt the Hellenistic gymnasium, which became known as the Caesareum (see fig. 2). At the end of the 1st century AD the rooms on the north-east side were replaced by a large apsed basilica, and in the 2nd century AD a small temple dedicated to the imperial cult was added in the middle of the courtyard. At the time of Trajan (*reg* AD 98– 117) a large bath complex was built in the north-east corner of the Sanctuary of Apollo, where the *Venus of Cyrene* was found. The hot rooms are grouped together in a single circulation system to the south-west, while the cold room runs the whole length of the north-east side of the complex, and leading off it is a long, colonnaded palaestra which also acts as the entrance corridor into the complex. Because the baths had reduced the size of the sanctuary itself, a new propylaeum was built near by.

In AD 115 the large Jewish community of Cyrenaica revolted and the public buildings of Cyrene were systematically destroyed. Thousands of lives were lost and Hadrian (*reg* AD 117–38) brought in new settlers, including 3000 army veterans, to rebuild the shattered city, a project in which he seems to have taken a personal interest. The Temple of Apollo was rebuilt with unfluted columns, but a similar project to rebuild the Temple of Zeus seems to have been abandoned. The Greek theatre was enlarged and later transformed into an amphitheatre by turning the *orchestra* into an arena and adding seats opposite the existing ones. In AD 134 Cyrene was given the title of Metropolis, and by the end of the 2nd century AD it seems largely to have recovered from its earlier misfortunes, although it never attained the prosperity of other great North African cities such as Leptis Magna and Sabratha. In the Severan period (AD 193–235) a grand peristyle house, the House of Jason Magnus, was created by amalgamating two earlier houses. It was richly decorated with fine mosaic and pavements in *opus sectile* (cut marble inlay). To the same period belongs an elaborate propylaeum on the valley street with spirally fluted columns and windswept acanthus capitals. Its frieze shows battles between the Romans and the Parthians in celebration of Septimius Severus' eastern victories (AD 197–9). Cyrene was damaged by an earthquake in AD 262, and in AD 297 Diocletian reorganized the coastal regions of Cyrenaica into the province of Libya Pentapolis with Ptolemais as its capital. Declining population, incursions of desert tribesmen and a severe earthquake in AD 365 all took their toll of the city. A large basilica with fine mosaics of rural and animal scenes (some *in situ*; some in Cyrene, Mus. Ant.) was built on the eastern edge of the city during the 5th century AD, but after Justinian's reconquest of North Africa in the 560s AD the wall circuit was reduced so that the basilica was excluded and had to be fortified. Cyrene fell to the army of the Arab general Amr ibn el-Aasi in AD 643.

BIBLIOGRAPHY

R. M. Smith and E. A. Porcher: *History of the Recent Discoveries at Cyrene* (London, 1864)
R. Norton: 'The Excavations at Cyrene, First Campaign, 1910: Preliminary Reports', *Bull. Archaeol. Inst. America*, ii/4 (1911), pp. 141–63
P. Romanelli: *La Cirenaica romana* (Verbania, 1943)
F. Chamoux: *Cyrène sous la monarchie des Battiades* (Paris, 1953)
J. Cassels: 'The Cemeteries of Cyrene', *Pap. Brit. Sch. Rome*, xxiii (1955), pp. 1–43
A. Rowe, D. Buttle and J. Gray: *Cyrenaican Expedition of the University of Manchester, 1952* (Manchester, 1956)
G. R. H. Wright: 'Cyrene: A Survey of Certain Rock-cut Features to the South of the Sanctuary of Apollo', *J. Hell. Stud.*, lxxvii (1957), pp. 300–10
A. Rowe, D. Buttle and J. Gray: *Cyrenaican Expeditions of the University of Manchester, 1955, 1956, 1957* (Manchester, 1959)
S. Stucchi: *L'agora di Cirene*, i: *I lati nord ed est della platea inferiore* (Rome, 1965)
P. Mingazzini: *L'insula di Giasone Magno a Cirene* (Rome, 1966)
S. Stucchi: *Cirene 1957–1966: Un decennio di attività della Missione Archeologica Italiana a Cirene* (Tripoli, 1967)
——: 'I lavori nel temenos di Zeus a Cirene', *Libya Ant.*, v (1968), pp. 105–7
J. H. Humphrey, ed.: *Apollonia, the Port of Cyrene: Excavations by the University of Michigan, 1965–67, Libya Ant.*, suppl. iv (Tripoli, n.d.)
R. G. Goodchild: *Cyrene and Apollonia: An Historical Guide* (Tripoli, 3/1970)
D. White: 'Excavations of the Demeter Sanctuary at Cyrene: A Preliminary Report', *Libya Ant.*, viii (1971), pp. 85–104; '2nd and 3rd Preliminary Reports', *Libya Ant.*, ix–x (1972–3), pp. 171–219; '4th and 5th Preliminary Reports', *Libya Ant.*, xiii–xiv (1976–7), pp. 265–330
M. Vickers and J. M. Reynolds: 'Cyrenaica 1962–72', *Archaeol. Rep.: Council Soc. Promotion Hell. Stud. & Managing Cttee Brit. Sch. Archaeol. Athens*, xviii (1971–2), pp. 27–47
S. Stucchi: *Architettura cirenaica* (Rome, 1975)
J. M. Reynolds, ed.: *Libyan Studies: Select Papers of the Late R. G. Goodchild* (London, 1976)
J. B. Ward-Perkins and S. Gibson: 'The Market-theatre at Cyrene', *Libya Ant.*, xiii–xiv (1976–7), pp. 331–75

F. B. SEAR

2. SCULPTURE. Cyrene's strong cultural and commercial ties within the eastern Mediterranean are attested by the extensive amounts of sculpture, pottery, coins, glass and other small finds uncovered there, which date from the 6th century BC to the early 4th century AD. Several korai and kouroi, some imported and others carved locally, date from the Archaic period. Two fine male portraits in bronze are indicative of the high quality of works on display in the city in the Late Classical period. A wide range of reliefs, statuettes and large-scale portrait statues shows the variety of style and quality available for purchase at Cyrene in the Hellenistic and, most particularly, the Roman period. Marble is the most frequently used material, then bronze and local limestone. This distribution is striking since marble is not found in the Cyrenaican region and therefore had to be imported, mainly from Athens and the islands of Paros and Thasos but also from Italy and Asia Minor. Works were produced both by native sculptors and by visiting foreign artists. Some pieces, such as Attic sarcophagi, were imported in a nearly finished state. Although Cyrenean sculpture was heavily influenced by styles from Athens and Alexandria, the recurrence of certain stylistic and technical features, the popularity of certain types, the existence of unfinished, near duplicate, or reused works, and the discovery of artists with Cyrenean names support the argument for local, inherently conservative, styles and workshops. Important indigenous types include a series of veiled or aniconic female busts (mainly Cyrene, Mus. Ant.) of Late Classical to early Roman date and an uneven collection of Roman funerary portraits, both of which decorated the tomb façades in the city's extensive necropoleis.

BIBLIOGRAPHY

E. Paribeni: *Catalogo delle sculture di Cirene: Statue e rilievi di carattere religioso* (Rome, 1959)
E. Rosenbaum: *A Catalogue of Cyrenaican Portrait Sculpture* (London, 1960)
G. Traversari: *Statue iconiche femminili cirenaiche* (Rome, 1960)
L. Beschi: 'Divinità funerarie cirenaiche', *Annu. Scu. Archeol. Atene & Miss. It. Oriente*, xlvii–xlviii (1969–70), pp. 133–341
J. Huskinson: *Corpus Signorum Imperii Romani: Great Britain*, II/i of *Roman Sculpture from Cyrenaica in the British Museum* (London, 1975)

SUSAN KANE

Cyriac of Ancona [Ciriaco d'Ancona; Ciriaco di Filippo de' Pizzicolli] (*b* Ancona, 1391; *d* Cremona, ?1455). Italian traveller and antiquarian. A self-educated merchant and occasional papal diplomatic agent, he played a central role in the rediscovery of the ancient world during the 15th century, travelling extensively in Italy, Greece and the Near East between 1412 and 1449. He learnt Latin and Greek and became the first great amateur classicist, as well as the undisputed father of modern archaeology and epigraphy. His explorations in Greece and the Levant resulted in the recovery of a number of manuscripts by ancient authors, though his most important contributions to the study of ancient art were his detailed notes on the antiquities he observed during his travels. Among the monuments of greatest interest to him were the antiquities of Athens, where he drew the Parthenon, the Philopappos Monument and the Temple of Olympian Zeus when it had 21 columns. He also recorded the Temple of Artemis at Didyma in Turkey before it was toppled by an earthquake, the ruins of Kyzikos on the Sea of Marmara, Hagia Sophia in Istanbul and the monuments of ancient Egypt.

He devoted himself as well to searching for and recording the antiquities of Italy, assembling a substantial corpus of drawings of ancient monuments and inscriptions. His relatively analytical and precise approach to antiquity sets him apart from late medieval tradition, especially in regard to the exactness with which he copied inscriptions. While he made use of historical texts, Cyriac preferred to study monuments and inscriptions directly, thus laying the foundations of the antiquarian approach to antiquity that became standard in the following centuries.

Cyriac's notebooks are invaluable for their descriptions and drawings of monuments that have since been lost or damaged. Among the few extant autograph texts are his descriptions and drawings of Athenian antiquities, especially the Parthenon (see fig.), of which his is the earliest surviving drawing. Nonetheless, much of his material has survived in the form of copies, for his work was already admired and imitated by the second half of the 15th century, shortly after his death. Among those who read and copied his manuscripts and imitated his cultural attitudes were FELICE FELICIANO and Giovanni Marcanova. These men journeyed with Samuele da Tradate and Andrea Mantegna to search for antiquities on Lake Garda—a famous episode clearly reflecting Cyriac's interests that inspired Feliciano's compilation of inscriptions for Mantegna. This line of antiquarian and epigraphic research led, in northern Italy and especially in the Veneto, to that climate of admiration for and recording of ancient monuments that later found expression in the *Hypnerotomachia Poliphili* (1499) by the Dominican monk Francesco Colonna of Venice.

In addition to his records of ancient monuments, Cyriac is known for his description of smaller objects and for his own collections. He probably bought and sold ancient coins, and he was often in Venice, where collectable antiques circulated before this interest developed elsewhere. He certainly owned various small artefacts, such as a head of Medusa and an engraved gem depicting the monster Scilla. He also had casts made from these objects, which he presented to friends such as Teodoro Gaza.

Cyriac knew many of the most important political and cultural figures of the age, such as the Giustiniani family, who ruled the island of Chios, and Pope Eugenius IV, whom he lobbied for a crusade against the Turks in order to prevent further defilement of the antiquities under their control. He was also for a time companion to Sultan Mehmet II and may have entered Constantinople (now Istanbul) with him when it fell to the Turks in 1453. Other acquaintances included Ambrogio Traversari and the humanist NICCOLÒ NICCOLI. To Cyriac we also owe some important information on the 15th-century figurative cycle begun for the Marchese of Ferrara, Lionello d'Este, in 1447; Cyriac saw two of the paintings before the cycle was complete.

BIBLIOGRAPHY

A. Momigliano: 'Ancient History and the Antiquarian', *J. Warb. & Court. Inst.*, xiii (1950), pp. 285–315
B. Ashmole: 'Cyriacus of Ancona and the Temple of Hadrian at Cyzicus', *J. Warb. & Court. Inst.*, xix (1956), pp. 179–91
A. Campana: 'Giannozzo Manetti, Ciriaco, e l'Arco di Traiano ad Ancona', *Italia Med. & Uman.*, iii (1959), pp. 484–504
E. W. Bodnar: *Cyriacus of Ancona and Athens* (Brussels, 1960)
C. Mitchell: 'Ex libris Kiriaci Anconitani', *Italia Med. & Uman.*, v (1962), pp. 283–99
R. Weiss: *The Renaissance Discovery of Classical Antiquity* (Oxford, 1969)
A. Campana: 'Ciriaco d'Ancona e Lorenzo Valla sull'iscrizione greca del Tempio dei Dioscuri a Napoli', *Archeol. Class.*, xxv–xxvi (1973–4), pp. 85–102
E. W. Bodnar and C. Mitchell: 'Cyriacus of Ancona's Journeys in the Propontis and Aegean, 1444–1445', *Mem. Amer. Philos. Soc.*, cxii (1976) [whole issue]
J. Colin: *Ciriaque d'Ancône* (Paris, 1982)
M. Manfredini: 'Ciriaco d'Ancona e l'epitaffio per i Corinzi a Salamina', *An. Scu. Norm. Sup. Pisa*, 3rd ser., xiii (1983), pp. 1003–5
C. R. Chiarlo: '"Gli frammenti della sancta antiquitate": Studi antiquari e produzione delle immagini da Ciriaco d'Ancona a Francesco Colonna', *Memoria dell'antico nell'arte italiana*, i (Turin, 1984), pp. 271–303
K. A. Neuhausen: 'Cyriacus und die Nereiden: Ein Auftritt des Chors der antiken Meernymphen in der Renaissance', *Rhein. Philol.*, cxxxvii (1984), pp. 174–92
C. A. Smith: 'Cyriacus of Ancona's Seven Drawings of Haghia Sophia', *A. Bull.*, 69 (1987), pp. 16–32

CARLO ROBERTO CHIARLO

Cyriac of Ancona (attrib.): earliest surviving drawing of the west front of the Parthenon, silverpoint, 1436–7 (Berlin, Deutsche Staatsbibliothek, Cod. Berolinensis Hamiltonianus 254, fol. 85*r*)

Cythera. *See* KYTHERA.

Czajkowski, Józef (*b* Warsaw, 27 Jan 1872; *d* Warsaw, 27 July 1947). Polish architect, interior designer, teacher and painter. In 1891 he left Poland to study painting at the Akademie der Bildenden Künste, Munich, and later in Paris, under Jean-Paul Laurens, Benjamin Constant and James McNeill Whistler. He then studied (1894–5) at the School of Fine Arts, Kraków, and at the School of Industrial Art, also in Kraków. He was co-founder of the

Polish Applied Arts Society (1901–14), a pioneering institution set up to develop the crafts in Poland. With other members of the society, including Tadeusz Stryjeński, he designed the interiors (1903–6) of the Old Theatre, Kraków, in a style influenced by Art Nouveau. He was also a co-founder of the Kraków Workshops (1913–26), which were housed in the town's Museum of Technology and Industry, and he designed stucco reliefs for the façade of this building. Czajkowski was a leading supporter of the Arts and Crafts Movement in Poland, but he increasingly inclined towards the Polish 'mansion house' style, for example his design (1908; unexecuted) for a house at Opinogóra, Ciechanów. This trend continued in the buildings he designed for an exhibition in Kraków on architecture and interiors in a garden setting (1912), which he helped organize, and in his award-winning Polish Pavilion (destr.) for the Exposition Internationale des Arts Décoratifs et Industriels Modernes (1925), Paris. In this building he combined the principles of classical composition with stylized folk ornament and simplified, crystalline forms; he also designed a room at the exhibition (see POLAND, §V and fig. 16). Czajkowski established and was professor (1913–19) at the Department of Architecture, Academy of Fine Arts, Kraków; he subsequently taught (1919–23) at the University of Stephan Batory, Wilno (now Vilnius, Lithuania), and was a professor at the School of Fine Arts, Warsaw (1922–38), where he introduced elements of vernacular art to the curriculum. He also co-founded (1926) the Ład Cooperative, designed furniture, tapestry and stained-glass windows and painted—mainly oil portraits, landscapes and rural scenes.

WRITINGS

Szkoła Sztuk Pięknych w Warszawie: Cele i zadania [School of Fine Arts in Warsaw: aims and tasks] (Warsaw, 1928)

SAP
BIBLIOGRAPHY
S. Łoza: Architekci i budowniczowie w Polsce [Architects and builders in Poland] (Warsaw, 1954), p. 54
L. Lameński: 'Tadeusz Stryjeński i Josef Czajkowski', Roc. Human., xxxv/4 (1987), pp. 323–36
A. K. Olszewski: Polish Art and Architecture, 1890–1980 (Warsaw, 1989)

WOJCIECH WŁODARCZYK

Czapski, Józef (b Prague, 3 April 1896; d Paris, 12 Jan 1993). Polish painter and writer. He intended to be a pianist and then a lawyer, and finally chose an artistic career. A course at the Warsaw Academy of Fine Arts was interrupted when he was sent with a military mission to Russia in search of missing Polish officers (1918). On his return he studied at the Academy of Fine Arts in Kraków (1920–24) as a student of Józef Pankiewicz and then joined the KAPISTS, with whom he went to Paris (1924–31). He wrote about the painting of Pankiewicz (1936) and Cézanne (1937), whose art he particularly admired, and stressed the importance of conscious creation, its intellectual background and the need for direct observation of nature to eliminate random effects. He valued, in opposition to other Kapists, modelling with light and shade. His brushwork was always expressive and impulsive; he used vivid, contrasting colours and depicted scenes from unusual angles, as in Woodland Opera in Sopot (1937; Warsaw, N. Mus.). During World War II he served in the Polish Army and was imprisoned in Starobielsk; he described these experiences in two volumes of memoirs (1944 and 1949). In 1945 he settled in Paris, dedicating himself to writing and painting. His style of painting became increasingly Expressionistic as he was drawn towards representing movement and transitory situations, although his subjects remained simple and unembellished: a man at an underground station (e.g. Métro Pasteur, 1953; Warsaw, N. Mus.), a sleeping warden in a museum room, the concierge on a doorstep of a Paris house. He found felt-tip pens and watercolours particularly suitable for his later sketches, for example drawings in his diary, in which he recorded the faces of people he met as well as colours and shapes that struck him the most in everyday observation.

WRITINGS

Pankiewicz (Warsaw, 1936)
O Cézanne'ie i świadomości malarskiej [On Cézanne and pictorial awareness] (Warsaw, 1937) [repr. in Oko, 1960]
Wspomnienia Starobielskie [Memoirs from Starobielsk] (1944; Fr. trans., Paris, 1945)
Na nieludzkiej ziemi [The inhuman land] (Paris, 1949; Fr. trans., Paris, 1949; Eng. trans., London, 1951)
Oko [The eye] (Paris, 1960; Fr. trans., Lausanne, 1982)

BIBLIOGRAPHY
M. Werner-Gagnebin: Czapski, la main et l'éspace (Lausanne, 1974)
Joseph Czapski: Retrospective (exh. cat., ed. J.-L. Kuffer; Vevey, Mus. Jenisch, 1990)
J. Pollakówna: Czapski (Warsaw, 1993)

ANNA BENTKOWSKA

Czartoryski. Polish family of patrons and collectors. They were active in the 18th and 19th centuries and formed an extensive and varied collection of fine and decorative arts and curiosities, much of which was housed at Puławy, their country estate. Many pieces were removed to France in the mid-19th century and were not brought back to Poland until the 1870s, at which time they formed the basis of the Czartoryski Collection in Kraków and at Gołuchów. The Czartoryski Foundation, established in 1991, includes the Cartoryski Library and, in the National Museum and other buildings, the Cartoryski collection of art. It constitutes Poland's oldest collection of art and artefacts.

(1) Prince **Adam Casimir** [Kazimierz] **Czartoryski** (b Gdańsk, 1 Dec 1734; d Sieniawa, nr Jarosław, 19 March 1823). He was born into a wealthy and influential family, and was brought up as a potential ruler of Poland; however, he declined to compete for the throne against his cousin Stanisław II Augustus Poniatowski (elected King in 1764) and, although he was active in public life, he never sought high office. He was fascinated by all areas of knowledge and indulged this taste by travelling widely and often. He surrounded himself with writers and learned men and was in frequent contact with Jean-Jacques Rousseau, Johann Kaspar Lavater and Benjamin Franklin, introducing many of their ideas to Poland. He was particularly concerned with promoting public education: he was an active member of the Committee of National Education from its foundation in 1773 and was later associated with the University of Wilno (now Vilnius University, Lithuania).

(2) Princess **Izabela** [Elżbieta; Isabella] **Czartoryska** [née Fleming] (b Warsaw, 3 March 1746; d Wysock, nr Jarosław, 17 June 1835). Wife of (1) Adam Casimir Czartoryski. In her youth she received no formal education and married at 15. She initially took little interest in her husband's activities or their journeys abroad; however, during the 1770s, under her husband's influence, her artistic tastes began to evolve. In 1774 JAN PIOTR NORBLIN DE LA GOURDAINE returned with the couple from a trip to Paris to become court artist and teacher to their children. Over the next decades, the Czartoryskis extended their patronage to artists of different nationalities, including Louis Marteau (c. 1715–1805), Józef Grassi, Josef Abel, Greuze, Elisabeth-Louise Vigée Le Brun, Maurice-Quentin de La Tour, Richard Cosway, Jean-Baptiste Le Prince, Aleksander Kucharski and Kazimierz Wojniakowski. Izabela also discovered the precocious talent of Aleksandr Orlovsky and became his patron. She attracted a group of artists that complemented her husband's intellectual and literary entourage, entertaining them at the Pałac Błękitny (Blue Palace) in Warsaw and particularly at Puławy (now the Institute of Cultivation, Fertilization and Soil Science), their country estate west of Lublin. During the 1780s the Czartoryskis became increasingly active in public life, and Puławy eventually rivalled the court of Stanisław II Augustus Poniatowski artistically and intellectually. At the same time, Izabela began to take an interest in the condition of the peasants, rebuilding houses and establishing schools.

As a result of the Czartoryskis' political activities and support for the Constitution of 3 May 1791, some of their estates were confiscated, and Puławy was devastated by Russian troops during the invasion of 1794. Izabela was horrified by the partition of Poland by Russia, Austria and Prussia, and she determined to re-create a 'scrap of Poland' at Puławy, focusing on relics of the country's past greatness. She had begun collecting works of art in the 1780s, often for their historical or sentimental value. During a visit to Britain in 1790, she had acquired a number of fine paintings, as well as such items as a fragment of Stonehenge and a chair owned by Shakespeare. She began to collect objects and memorabilia of every kind from Poland and from many European countries. For the park at Puławy, she commissioned from CHRYSTIAN PIOTR AIGNER a Temple of Memory (known as the Temple of the Sibyl) modelled on the Temple of Vesta (early 1st century BC) at Tivoli, and in 1801 she opened it to the public. The temple was a pantheon in which great kings, warriors, statesmen, writers and other figures of the past were represented by fragments of tombs, arms, portraits, allegorical trophies and sarcophagi containing relics (see also POLAND, §XIII). Near by she built 'The Gothick House', which was opened in 1809 as a museum of European history. It housed an assortment of objects of historical, scientific and sentimental interest, as well as sculpture, enamels, armour, objets d'art and early manuscripts, and a fine collection of European paintings, the principal pieces of which were Leonardo's Portrait of a Lady (c. 1485; Kraków, Czartoryski Col.; see LEONARDO DA VINCI, fig. 3) and Raphael's Portrait of a Young Man (c. 1511; ex-Czartoryski Col., Kraków, 1945; untraced; see RAPHAEL), both purchased in Venice in 1799 by her son Adam Jerzy Czartoryski (b Warsaw, 14 Jan 1770; d Montfermeil, nr Paris, 15 July 1861), as well as Rembrandt's Landscape with the Good Samaritan (1638; Kraków, Czartoryski Col.; see REMBRANDT, fig. 4). Despite its diversity of scope, the collection did have a unified theme, epitomizing the Romantic

perception of a European community of culture and of the human element in history. Izabela's concept, although naive, was in tune with emerging ideas, and the museum was one of the first to mark the transition from the Wunderkammer to a more modern version of the museum. After the Polish Insurrection of 1830, Puławy was again sacked by the Russians, who confiscated it; however, much of the collection was saved by Izabela and her servants. It was taken to France when Adam Jerzy Czartoryski went into exile and was housed until the 1870s in the Hôtel Lambert in Paris.

(3) Prince **Władysław Czartoryski** (b Warsaw, 3 July 1828; d Boulogne-Billancourt, nr Paris, 23 June 1894). Grandson of (2) Izabela Czartoryska. In 1861 he inherited from his father, Adam Jerzy Czartoryski, the remnants of his grandmother's collections that were originally at Puławy but were dispersed after the Insurrection of 1830 (see (2) above). He decided to repatriate these and other works of art that he had accumulated by creating a new museum in Poland to house them. He chose the city of Kraków, then under Austrian rule, and between 1874 and 1886 acquired the medieval arsenal and four neighbouring buildings. Though Viollet-le-Duc submitted projects, the conversion of the buildings was entrusted to François Maurice Ouradou (1822–84) and the Polish architect Albert Bitner (1845–1902), both of whom created a Gothic Revival ensemble incorporating elements drawn from the Renaissance architecture of the old city. The museum was finally opened to the public in 1876. The greater part of the collection was acquired in the second half of the 19th century by Władysław, whose motivations were similar to his grandmother's at Puławy, although he was more concerned with quality and authenticity. As a result, he created a museum that held an eclectic grouping of objects of interest and of artistic value, as well as functioning as a reliquary of national mementos. He also built up one of the finest collections of prints and drawings in Poland and added a large number of early manuscripts and books to the family archive and library, which established them as important institutions in their own right.

PSB

BIBLIOGRAPHY

M. Sokołowski: Muzeum Czartoryskich w Krakowie (Lwów, 1892)
Z. Żygulski: Dzieje zbiorów Puławskich [History of the Puławy collections] (Kraków, 1962)
——: 'Shakespeare's Chair and the Romantic Journey of Isabel Czartoryska', Apollo, lxxxii (1965), pp. 392–7
——: 'Princess Isabel and the Czartoryski Museum', Connoisseur, clxxxii (1973), pp. 15–24
M. Rostworowski, ed.: Muzeum Narodowe w Krakowie: Zbiory Czartoryskich: Historia wybór zabytków [The National Museum in Kraków: the Czartoryski collection: history and selections from the collection] (Warsaw, 1978) [extensive bibliog.]

ADAM ZAMOYSKI

Czech, Hermann (b Vienna, 10 Nov 1936). Austrian architect and writer. After studying architecture at the Technical University and the Akademie der Bildenden Künste in Vienna, he went on to study film at the Hochschule für Musik und Darstellende Kunst, Vienna, between 1954 and 1956. He then read philosophy at the University of Vienna until 1960. He returned to architecture, and much of his work of the 1960s and 1970s was for interior designs (e.g. Restaurant Ballhaus, 1961–2;

Kleines Café, 1973–4; Dicopa offices, 1974–5; Café Wunder-Bar, 1975–6; all Vienna). The café interiors have traditional 19th-century features and detailing in a plain and modern but almost playful manner. They have been praised for their 'ironic quotations' (Sanderson). From 1963 to 1967 Czech worked as architectural critic for *Die Furche* (Vienna) and as a correspondent for *A and U* (Tokyo). In 1974 he became assistant professor at the Kunstgewerbeschule, Vienna. His writings concentrated to a large extent on Austrian architecture of the late 19th century and the early 20th, in particular on the work of Adolf Loos and Otto Wagner. In modern architecture he favoured mannerism, which he saw as 'a sense of the irregular and the absurd' (see 1980 exh. cat., p. 60). For Czech, existing historical architecture and its re-use and renovation offered the opportunity of reinterpretation and the 'opening of our eyes to ambiguity and complexity' (see 1980 exh. cat., p. 60). This is best illustrated in his addition (1977–9) to the Villa Plaum, Altendorf, a flamboyant Venetian Gothic villa of 1848. Czech's extension expresses his restrained Post-modernist tendencies. His design is carefully detailed and clearly indebted to the early Austrian Modernists in its use of the plain surfaces and cubic forms of such architects as Josef Hoffmann and Loos.

WRITINGS
with W. Mistelbauer: *Das Looshaus* (Vienna, 1976)
'Otto Wagner's Metropolitan Railway', *A + U*, vii (1976)

BIBLIOGRAPHY
A New Wave of Austrian Architecture (exh. cat., New York, Inst. Archit. & Urb. Stud., 1980)
W. Sanderson: *International Handbook of Contemporary Developments in Architecture* (London, 1981)

CLAUDIA BÖLLING

Czech Cubism. Term used to describe a style in architecture and the applied arts, directly inspired by Cubist painting and sculpture, which was developed by architects and designers active in Prague shortly before World War I; the term itself was not used until the 1960s. The leaders of the style were the members of the Group of Plastic Artists (1911–14), which broke away from the Mánes Union of Artists in 1911 and for two years published its own journal, *Umělecký měsíčník* ('Art monthly'). The architects in the group were Josef Gočár, Josef Chochol, Vlastislav Hofman (1884–1964) and Pavel Janák; other members included Emil Filla, Václav Špála, Antonín Procházka and Otto Gutfreund. The group was reacting against the austere rationalism of such architects as Jan Kotěra, seeking instead to sustain architecture and the applied arts as branches of art rich in content. Their approach was expounded in various articles, particularly by Janák, who developed the principles of architectural Cubism; based on the thesis of Cubism in painting and sculpture, that art should create a distinctive, parallel picture of reality, it attempted to dematerialize a building's mass by the three-dimensional surface sculpturing of the façade with abstract, prismatic forms.

The principal buildings to embody these ideas include Gočár's sanatorium (1911–12) at Bohdaneč, and Black Madonna House (1911–12), Prague; three houses by Chochol (1911–13) beneath Vyšehrad in Prague (for illustration *see* PRAGUE, fig. 6); and Janák's rebuilding (1913) of an existing Baroque house in Pelhřimov with Cubist details. Later works include three teachers' houses (1917–19), Prague, by Otakar Novotný. Jiří Kroha also acknowledged Cubism in some of his studies but soon moved away to develop an expression of his own. Architectural Cubism, unmatched in any other country, was a significant step in the evolution of Czech architecture, contributing to the demise of 19th-century academicism and historicism. At the same time it amounted to a break with other developments of the early 20th century, including the Viennese Secession as well as rationalism. However, while it brought architectural form to artistic abstraction, dynamizing mass and elaborating the spatial plasticity of façades and their detail, it had no profound effect on the interior planning of buildings or on their structure.

The principles of Czech Cubism found more prolific expression in the applied arts and in furniture design. In 1912 Gočár and Janák set up the Prague Art Workshops (PUD) for the design of arts, crafts and furniture; it was intended to concentrate on the furnishing of the complete house, with the contention that furniture should not only meet the demands of utility and good taste but also be serious art of substantial content. Distinctive Cubist furniture designs were produced by several architects including Janák (*see* CZECH REPUBLIC, fig. 23). They also designed lighting, tableware, vases and other products. The style gained international recognition with the dining-room interior presented by Gočár and František Kysela (1881–1941) at the Deutsche Werkbundausstellung (1914) in Cologne.

After World War I and the formation of the Czechoslovak Republic (1918), the Cubist style underwent a major change. The pyramid was replaced by the cylinder and sphere in the rich plastic decorativeness of Rondocubism, which laid claim to become a national style in architecture. It is associated with the same group of names: Gočár, for example, used the circle as a generating motif for the Legiobanka (1921), Prague, with façade sculpture by Otto Gutfreund; Janák employed the style for the crematorium (1921) in Pardubice and the building of the Riunione Adriatica di Sicurtà (1922–4), Prague; and Novotný built a block of flats (1921) in Prague. This attempt to create a national style, together with the concept of architecture as primarily an art form, culminated in 1925 with the interiors of the Czechoslovak Pavilion at the Exposition Internationale des Arts Décoratifs et Industriels Modernes (1925), Paris, designed by Janák and Kysela; the Pavilion was designed by Gočár. It then yielded to the more vigorously evolving Functionalism of avant-garde Czechoslovak architecture in the 1920s and 1930s, supported by Devětsil, the group centred on the figure of Karel Teige that was formed in 1920.

BIBLIOGRAPHY
P. Janák: 'Hranol a pyramida' [The prism and the pyramid], *Umělecký Měsíčník*, 1 (1911)
I. Margolius: *Cubism in Architecture and the Applied Arts: Bohemia and France, 1910–1914* (London, 1979)
Filla, Gutfreund, Kupka och tjeckisk kubism, 1907–1927 (exh. cat., Malmö, Ksthall, 1982)
V. Šlapeta: 'Cubismo Bohemio', *Quad. Arquit. & Urb.*, 169–70 (1986), pp. 48–55
Český kubismus, 1909–1925 (exh. cat., eds J. Švestka and T. Vlček; Brno, Morav. Gal.; Düsseldorf, Kstver.; Prague, N.G.; 1991–2)
A. von Vegesack, ed.: *Czech Cubism: Architecture, Furniture and Decorative Arts, 1910–1925* (London, 1992)

Prague, 1891–1941: Architecture and Design (exh. cat., Edinburgh, City
   A. Cent., 1994)

RADOMÍRA SEDLÁKOVÁ

Czechowicz, Szymon (*b* Kraków, *bapt* 22 July 1689; *d*
Warsaw, 21 July 1775). Polish painter. He worked in Rome
c. 1711–30, primarily on commissions from Poland and
for the Polish Church in Rome. In 1716 he won an award
in a competition organized by the Accademia di S Luca,
and from 1725 he was a member of the Congregazione
dei Virtuosi. He apparently painted only altarpieces and
scenes from the Old Testament, working from prints of
famous works and making copies from the Old Masters.
His paintings, such as the *Entombment* (before 1731;
Kraków, N. Mus.), exhibit a great eclecticism.

   Czechowicz was back in Poland by 1731. During a long
working life he was overwhelmed with commissions for
altarpieces throughout Polish territory, such as the *Mystical
Marriage of St Catherine* (1759; Vilnius, St Catherine). He
lived mainly in Warsaw but frequently visited the provinces. In his portraits, for example of the chancellor *Jean-
Frédéric Sapieha* (engraved 1741) and of *Bishop Antoine
Dembowski* (engraved 1743), he adhered to the traditional
formulae for Polish portraiture. He had numerous pupils
(including Franciszek Smuglewicz) and imitators.

BIBLIOGRAPHY

J. Orańska: *Szymon Czechowicz, 1689–1775* (Poznań, 1948)

ANDRZEJ RYSZKIEWICZ

Czech Republic [Česká Republika; formerly part of
Czechoslovakia]. Central European country comprising
Bohemia and Moravia. It is landlocked and bounded by
Austria, Germany, Poland and Slovakia and has a population of approximately 10 million. The independent
republic of Czechoslovakia was founded in 1918; on 1
January 1993 it was divided into the Czech Republic and
SLOVAKIA. The capital is PRAGUE, in Bohemia, while the
main city in Moravia is BRNO. The country's border areas
are wooded and mountainous, the central areas gently
rolling. Its historical and cultural development has been
determined by its geographical position between Western
and Eastern Europe (see fig. 1).

I. Introduction. II. Architecture. III. Sculpture. IV. Painting and
graphic arts. V. Interior decoration and furniture. VI. Ceramics. VII.
Glass. VIII. Metalwork. IX. Objects of vertu. X. Textiles. XI.
Patronage. XII. Collecting and dealing. XIII. Museums. XIV. Art
libraries and photo collections. XV. Art education. XVI.
Historiography.

I. Introduction.

The first evidence of settlement in the area of the Czech
Republic dates to 750,000 BC. The earliest artefacts—
female idols, sculptures of animals, petroglyphs—date to
the Palaeolithic period, while the earliest ceramic artefacts
date to the Neolithic period and the earliest metal objects
to the Late Neolithic period. The Celts settled in the
country *c.* 400 BC but were conquered by the Marcomanni
tribe in the 1st century BC. The Slavs arrived in Bohemia
in the 5th and 6th centuries AD. The Great Moravian
empire (Great Moravia) was formed on the territory of

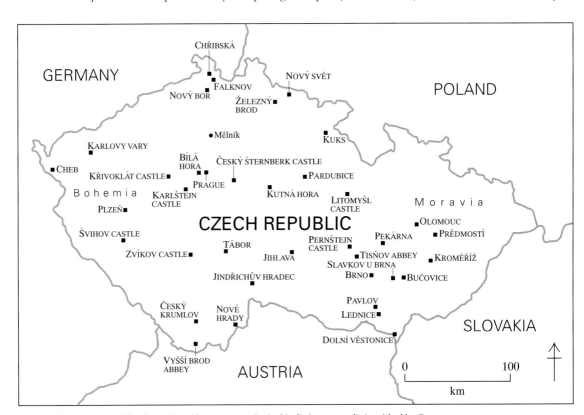

1. Map of the Czech Republic; those sites with separate entries in this dictionary are distinguished by CROSS-REFERENCE TYPE

present-day Moravia, Bohemia and part of Slovakia *c.* AD 830, and the Byzantine missionaries SS Cyril and Methodius brought Christianity to Moravia in AD 863. In centres throughout Great Moravia, such as Velehrad, ecclesiastical buildings (rotundas and basilicas) were built, secular architecture developed and crafts blossomed.

The empire disintegrated under the Magyars' attack *c.* 906. Bohemia, which had broken away, was united under the Přemyslid family in the 9th century, while Slovakia came under Hungarian rule (until 1918). The Přemyslids moved their seat from Levý Hradec to Prague in the late 9th century. In 973 Prague became the seat of the metropolitan bishop, and Benedictine monasteries were founded there in the last third of the 10th century. Between the late 9th century and the 1240s art in Bohemia and Moravia was predominantly Romanesque, under the influence of Germany, France and Italy. Bohemia was proclaimed a kingdom in 1198.

The Early Gothic style was introduced into Bohemia in the mid-13th century from France, Germany and Italy and spread under the auspices of rulers and monastic orders such as the Cistercians. Přemysl Ottakar II (*reg* 1253–78) founded towns and built castles (e.g. ZVÍKOV CASTLE). The country's significance grew under Wenceslas (Václav) II (*reg* 1278–1305), who was king of Bohemia, Poland and Hungary and made full use of the resources provided by ore mining in Bohemia, but with the murder of Wenceslas III in 1306 the Přemyslid dynasty ended. After the short reign of Henry of Carinthia (*reg* 1307–10), John of Luxembourg was chosen as king. During his reign (1310–46) the construction of Prague's cathedral began, and Prague became an archbishopric. Charles IV (*reg* 1346–78), Holy Roman Emperor, transformed Prague into a leading European metropolis in which there occurred a creative synthesis of local artistic traditions and influences from France and Germany (architecture and sculpture) and Italy (panel and wall painting). Under Wenceslas IV (*reg* 1378–1419) Bohemia became one of the centres of the International Gothic style.

The death at the stake of the Church reformer Jan Hus in 1415 gave impulse to the Hussite Wars (1420–36), during which several castles and churches were destroyed. A period of confusion led to the election of George of Poděbrady as king (*reg* 1457–71). At that time the Catholics were in a minority. In the first half of the 15th century the International Gothic style began to decline, while Late Gothic penetrated from Germany and the Danube region under Vladislav Jagiellon (*reg* 1471–1516) and Louis Jagiellon (*reg* 1516–26).

The Renaissance style was introduced from Italy and Saxony in the last decade of the 15th century and dominated art in Bohemia and Moravia in the 16th century. The Habsburgs were elected to the Czech throne in 1526 and ruled until 1918. Towns blossomed, and the nobility built luxurious Renaissance châteaux. The court of Rudolf II (*reg* 1575–1612) was one of the major artistic centres of Europe. The failed uprising of the Protestant nobility (1618–20) ushered in the Thirty Years War (1618–48), which put an end to Bohemian independence; about 30,000 Protestant families left the country.

A strong Counter-Reformation developed in the early 17th century, followed by the introduction of the Baroque style (Early Baroque, 1620–70; High Baroque, 1670–1720). After the destruction caused by the Thirty Years War, the country gradually acquired Baroque monasteries, places of pilgrimage, castles and country houses, the interiors of which were embellished by Czech and foreign artists. The Austrian Late Baroque style strongly influenced art in Moravia in the 18th century. Under Maria-Theresa (*reg* 1743–80) Late Baroque art spread throughout the country. During his reforms (1782–90) Joseph II (*reg* 1765–90) abolished serfdom, issued a decree for religious tolerance, closed the monasteries, increased centralization and insisted that teaching be conducted in German. Artistic activity declined, and Neo-classicism made little impact in Bohemia at the turn of the 18th and 19th centuries.

The nation's gradual cultural renewal began in the early 19th century, marked by the founding of the National Museum in 1818. Artists such as Josef Mánes and the National Theatre Generation sought national forms, and historical eclecticism developed after the mid-19th century. In the 1870s and 1880s French Realism, Impressionism and Symbolism were influential. At the turn of the 19th and 20th centuries Czech industry gained a leading position in the Austro-Hungarian empire, and Art Nouveau blossomed; in 1900–18 European Expressionism and Cubism were introduced.

In 1918 the independent Czechoslovak Republic was founded, with Tomáš Masaryk (1850–1937) as its first president. The period before World War II was one of economic, democratic and cultural prosperity. In 1938–45 Bohemia and Moravia were occupied by Nazi Germany. After 1945 political developments led to the Communist putsch of February 1948. The 1948–53 period was one of Socialist construction and Stalinist deformation, and Socialist Realism dominated artistic output. In the late 1950s and 1960s links with Western Europe were resumed, and several artists began to work within the context of modern European art.

BIBLIOGRAPHY
J. Pavel: *Dějiny umění v Československu* [History of art in Czechoslovakia] (Prague, 1971)
Dějiny českého výtvarného umění [History of Czech fine arts] (Prague, 1984–)

JAN ROYT

II. Architecture.

Late Gothic architecture in Bohemia and Moravia began to succumb to Renaissance influences in the late 15th century, and after 1620 Baroque elements were introduced. The Neo-classicism of the 1780s and 1790s gave way to Gothic Revival and eclectic styles in the 19th century, and Cubism was influential in the early 20th.

1. Before the 1620s. 2. 1620s–1780s. 3. 1780s and after.

1. BEFORE THE 1620s. Evidence of massive walled architecture in the Czech lands dates to the last quarter of the 9th century AD, during the period of the Great Moravian empire. At Mikulčice, for example, apart from a fortification system, a bridge and a palace, the foundations of 20 churches have been discovered. Christianity and stone ecclesiastical architecture spread from Great Moravia into Bohemia in the late 9th century (e.g. the

2. Karlštejn Castle, 1348–57, restored 1887–96; view from the south-east

rotundas at Levý Hradec, Budeč and Znojmo). The most important structures of this period were the group of buildings in Prague Castle (Hradčany), the centre of the PŘEMYSLID dynasty (*see* PRAGUE, §IV, 1).

Examples of late Romanesque architecture are the basilica at Tismice, the Premonstratensian monastery at Strahov (founded 1140; *see* PRAGUE, §IV, 5) and the convent of Doksany (founded 1144). This phase of building culminated in the late 12th century in Prague when the Judith Bridge (now Charles Bridge) and several Romanesque stone houses below Hradčany were built. Romanesque rotundas were constructed at Říp, Holubice and Přední Kopanina, while basilican churches with galleries were built at Kyje, Mohelnice and Vinec. This Late Romanesque style developed further alongside the newly introduced Gothic style in the 13th century, as at the monasteries of Osek and Teplá. The main building material was slate ashlar masonry. An example of the transitional Romanesque style is the monastic church (mid-13th century; rest.) at Třebíč, which has similarities with Rhenish Romanesque architecture.

The introduction of Gothic architecture in Bohemia was associated with the development of feudalism in the first half of the 13th century. The Cistercian monasteries of Osek (founded 1199) and Velehrad (founded 1202), with their generous use of space, their plain, solid forms and closely integrated design, were influential. The monumental scale of the porch at Předklášteří u Tišnova and its rare plasticity indicate the foreign provenance of its builders, who went on to build another royal foundation, the convent of the Minorites and Poor Clares (founded 1233) in Prague's Old Town. The design of the presbytery of the neighbouring St Saviour, completed *c.* 1285 as a mausoleum for the Přemyslids, shows the influence of northern French Gothic. Přemysl Ottakar II (*reg* 1253–78) founded several royal towns with spacious and well-proportioned urban plans, such as Vysoké Mýto, České Budějovice and Písek. Gothic architecture spread and developed: churches were built at Kolín, Kouřim and JIHLAVA, the Staronová (Czech: 'old-new') Synagogue was

erected before the mid-13th century (*see* PRAGUE, §IV, 4), while burghers' houses and city walls were constructed at Nymburk and Žatec. The impressive, well-preserved 13th-century castles at Zvíkov (*see* ZVÍKOV CASTLE), Horšovský Týn (1260–70; rest.), Bezděz (1264–78) and Buchlov were built by the Přemyslids. In the early 14th century the cathedrals at Zbraslav and Sedlec were begun, and the older monasteries of Zlatá Koruna and VYŠŠÍ BROD ABBEY were expanded.

In 1348 Charles IV, Holy Roman Emperor (*see* LUXEMBOURG, (3)), founded the Prague New Town as a way of enhancing the importance and prestige of the royal seat (*see* PRAGUE, §I, 1). The Charles Bridge (1367), a work of exceptional quality in both engineering and design, became the symbol of the city (*see* PRAGUE, fig. 2). St Vitus' Cathedral in Prague, inspired partly by French models such as Narbonne Cathedral, expresses the artistic trends of the second half of the 14th century (*see* PRAGUE, §IV, 2(i)). Its first architect, MATHIAS OF ARRAS, who was grounded in the French Rayonnant style, apparently began work in 1342. Peter Parler, who took charge in 1356, incorporated advanced elements such as more elaborate window tracery and complicated reticulated vaulting (*see* PARLER, (3)). The influence of the Prague Cathedral lodge is to be seen in buildings elsewhere in Bohemia, for example the choir in the cathedrals of Kolín, Kutná Hora (*see* KUTNÁ HORA, §2) and Hradec Králové, or in Moravia at Olomouc and Dolní Kounice.

Charles IV's striving for territorial stabilization is evident in a series of massive castles (Kost, Lipnice, Veveří) and, most notably, in the impregnable Karlštejn Castle (see fig. 2). Late Gothic influence is evident in the architecture of the court circle of Charles's son, Wenceslas IV (*reg* 1378–1419), especially in the use of centralized ground-plans and subtly moulded pier forms. The trend became established in the 1380s in such churches as those at Třeboň, Soběslav and Vetla. The airy ornamentation of patterned vaulting reached its peak in the 15th-century churches of St Giles at Milevsko and St Vitus at Český Krumlov.

The most common building materials in Bohemian Gothic architecture were local granite and sandstone. Timber and plaster buildings were also erected, while houses gradually began to be built in stone, even in the countryside. In the north of the country, architecture was usually of brick, as at Hradec Králové and Opava. Builders' guilds formed a monopoly that went unchallenged except by the workshops set up by the nobility or large monasteries. Few individual figures stand out from the general mass, but the broad range of 15th-century local architecture indicates that able builders and masons were active in regions that gradually grew in significance with the decline of court influence.

During the rule of the Luxembourg dynasty (1310–1437), the Czech lands became a centre of cultural importance for the surrounding Hungarian lands, Silesia and Poland, as well as for Austria and southern Germany. The Hussite Wars (1420–36), however, violently interrupted artistic activity. Many buildings were destroyed or severely damaged, and a number of grandiose designs remained incomplete. When building work started again it was predominantly undistinguished and schematic, as in

3. Relief decoration on a house in Pernštejn Square, Pardubice, 16th century

the church of the Transfiguration (begun 1440) at Tábor. At the end of the 1470s, however, after the accession of Vladislav II Jagiellon to the Bohemian throne, fresh artistic forces arrived from abroad, for instance Hans Spiess from Frankfurt, who built the oratory at Prague Cathedral, the chapel at Křivoklát Castle and the church at Mělnice. The most important of the Bohemian masters was the skilful decorator MATĚJ REJSEK, architect of the Powder Tower (begun c. 1475) in Prague. His main competitor was Benedikt Ried, the leading figure in Czech Late Gothic architecture. Ried's finest work was the magnificent Vladislav Hall in Hradčany, with its bold, dynamic vaulting (for illustration see RIED, BENEDIKT). After the closure of the Prague lodge in 1511, Ried was commissioned by the prominent feudal lords of Blatná, Švihov and Rábí castles and by wealthy royal towns such as Kutná Hora and Louny to create dynamic groin vaulting in their properties and churches (for illustration see KUTNÁ HORA). Ried's work was continued by his pupils and imitators, in the north particularly by Jacob Haylmann, architect of the church of the Assumption at Most (1517–94), whose work was linked with the tradition of Saxon Late Gothic architecture. Under the influence of neighbouring Míšně, a specific type of cellular or diamond vaulting appeared, as at Kadaň and Bechyně.

Late Gothic architecture reached its peak under the hegemony of the powerful ROŽMBERK family in southern Bohemia. In ČESKÝ KRUMLOV this came about under the direct influence of the members of the Pasov lodge, who provided the Rožmberks with a series of churches vaulted with net patterns over shallow barrels, as at Kájov,

Dvořiště and Rožmberk. The influence of this lodge spread into neighbouring Moravia (Český Rudolec, Lidéřovice) and as far as Znojmo. Olomouc and Brno (St James's Church, early 16th century; Town Hall, 1511; for illustration see BRNO, fig. 2) were also important centres of Late Gothic architecture. The early 16th-century reconstruction of PERNŠTEJN CASTLE and of the nearby hall church at Doubravník is also Late Gothic.

By the end of the 15th century Renaissance influences had begun to spread from various centres into the Czech lands. The influence of the architect Luciano Laurana spread from the court at Budapest to Prague, where it is evident in the work of the lodge headed by Benedikt Ried. The so-called Ludwig wing (1501–9) of Prague Castle is in Early Renaissance style, as is the restoration work on the town halls in the New Town and Old Town. Northwestern Bohemia, especially around the wealthy town of Krušná Hora, was directly influenced by Saxony, as is evident from the building activity of the Barons Schlick in Jáchymov and Slavkov u Brna (Ger. Austerlitz). Elements of northern and Italian Renaissance styles appeared in unique synthesis in the reconstruction of the east Bohemian towns of PARDUBICE and Nové Město nad Metují, where they found expression in the typical ornamental window surrounds, portals and cornices (see fig. 3).

The accession of the Habsburgs to the crown of Bohemia in 1526 was a further stimulus to the spread of Renaissance ideals. Ferdinand I (reg 1526–64) called in Giovanni Spazio and, shortly afterwards, PAOLO STELLA and a group of Italian masons, who built in Hradčany the airy arcaded loggia of the 'Belvedere' Summer Palace (1538–63; see PRAGUE, §IV, 1), the first fully Italian Renaissance building north of the Alps. FLORIÁN GRIESBECK VON GRIESBACH, who directed the court workshop, brought Italian masons to work on the castles at Kaceřov

4. Houses in the market square, Telč, 16th century, with later additions

(1540) and Nelahozeves (1553) and on the church at Kralovice (1575–81). In the mid-16th century BONIFAZ WOLMUT became court architect. He had already proved his knowledge of Gothic as well as his ability in pure Palladianism in the Ballcourt (Míčovna) in Hradčany. New buildings were constructed in the Little Quarter in Prague and in Hradčany after the fire of 1541, including new Rožmberk and Schwarzenberg-Lobkovice palaces (*see* PRAGUE, §I, 2). The façades of numerous Czech and Moravian castles (JINDŘICHŮV HRADEC, Opočno, Litomyšl, Moravský Krumlov, Buchlovice) are decorated with *sgraffito*, while the courtyards have arcaded galleries. The Renaissance transformation of country towns created ensembles of memorable urban design, notably at Slavonice and Telč (see fig. 4). The Italian architects brought new technology with them, with the result that bricklayers gradually superseded masons.

Under Rudolf II (*reg* 1576–1612), Prague again became a European cultural metropolis (*see* HABSBURG, §I(10)). There was intense building activity and, in the mid-1580s, a move away from the traditional northern Italian orientation in favour of the Mannerism of Tuscany and Rome. GIOVANNI GARGIOLLI, who devised the imperial mill (*c.* 1586), looked to Florence for his models, notably Bartolomeo Ammanati and Bernardo Buontalenti. Many Italian craftsmen set up their workshops in Prague. In the late 16th century, the influence of northern Mannerism appeared in secular buildings such as Frýdlant Castle and, later, in the Town Hall (1617–19) in the Little Quarter.

Protestant churches retained many Gothic elements and include SS Simon and Jude (1615–20) and St Saviour (1611–14) in Prague. The leading architect in the planning office of Rudolf II and Matthias (*reg* 1612–19) was Giovanni Maria Filippi. The design for Holy Trinity Church (1609–13) in the Little Quarter follows Il Gesù, Rome, in its spatial arrangement (*see* ROME, §V, 16) and may be by Filippi. A similar design is to be found in the Catholic church at Stará Boleslav, which became a forerunner for the early Baroque.

2. 1620s–1780s. After the Catholic victory at the Battle of the White Mountain (1620), a new cultural orientation was imposed under the slogan of Counter-Reformation and absolutism. The most important buildings of the time, such as the Michnov and Valdštejn (Wallenstein) palaces (*see* PRAGUE, §IV, 7), demonstrate the development in style before and after the battle. Their conception is still Mannerist, but the scale and emphasis on spatial relationships point to the Baroque. The Counter-Reformation brought in new types of architecture, as in the Loreto church (begun 1626) in Prague, but in this period of uncertainty, architectural activity concentrated on fortifications, as at Prague and Uherské Hradiště.

The Peace of Westphalia (1648) led to the arrival in Bohemia of members of wealthy northern Italian families who formed well-organized architectural associations. Carlo Lurago, for example (*see* LURAGO (ii), (1)), was an able and resourceful architect known especially for his work for the Jesuits, as at Březnice, Hradec Králové and the Clementinum (now the State Library) in Prague. His younger competitor, GIOVANNI DOMENICO ORSI, was the architect of unique groupings of buildings, as at the Nová

Bystřice Monastery (from 1667). The work of Antonio Porta and FRANCESCO CARATTI, such as the Černín Palace (1668–77; now the Foreign Ministry), Prague, harks back to Palladianism.

In the last quarter of the 17th century the building boom brought to Prague architects from abroad who broke the Italians' monopoly and introduced a greater variety of building. JEAN-BAPTISTE MATHEY, for example, designed the innovative church of St Francis (1679–88) in Prague, which was to dominate architecture at the turn of the century. Prominent architects commissioned by the aristocracy in Bohemia and Moravia included Carlo Fontana (*see* FONTANA (v), (1)), DOMENICO MARTINELLI, Jakob Prandtauer and Johann Bernhard Fischer von Erlach, whose work was carried on by Giovanni Battista Alliprandi. In 1699 Johann Lukas von Hildebrandt drew up plans for St Lawrence at Jablonný v Podještědí. This was the first of the so-called Czech radical group of churches, which also includes those at Obořiště (1699–1712), St Nicholas (1703–11; 1737–52; see fig. 5) in the Little Quarter of Prague and St Clare (1707) at Cheb, all characterized by their dynamic use of materials and their convex–concave curves. Research has identified the architect of the last three buildings as Christoph Dientzenhofer (*see* DIENTZENHOFER, (1)), who was influenced by the Italian radical Baroque of Guarino Guarini.

One of the most innovative architects of 18th-century Bohemia was GIOVANNI SANTINI, whose work, for example the monastery (begun 1711) at Plasy and the castle at Chlumec nad Cidlinou, is remarkable for its adventurous conception. He combined the plasticity of the Baroque

5. St Nicholas in the Little Quarter, Prague, west front by Christoph Dientzenhofer, 1703–11

with the resources of Gothic form to create the unique phenomenon of 'Baroque-Gothic', as in the abbey church (1703) at Sedlec, the monastery (1712–26) at Kladruby and the abbey at Želiv (1712–20; for illustration *see* SANTINI, GIOVANNI). His work influenced such contemporaries as Ottaviano Broggia (1668–1742) in northern Bohemia (Osek), Jakub Auguston in Plzeň (Trpisty, Nebílovy) and FRANTIŠEK MAXIMILIÁN KAŇKA. The chief representative of the later phase of this style in Bohemia was Kilian Ignaz Dientzenhofer (*see* DIENTZENHOFER, (3)), creator of an original synthesis of Bohemian and Austrian traits.

In the mid-18th century, Rococo miniaturization and delicacy of decoration were introduced. In Bohemia, however, Rococo never achieved the importance it had in France or Bavaria, because it was combined with Baroque ground-plans and expressed itself merely in ornament, for example in buildings by Anselmo Martino Lurago (*see* LURAGO (ii), (2)) such as Hořín Castle. Simultaneously, French Neo-classicism spread into Bohemia from Vienna, as at Dobříš Castle and in the remodelling of Prague Castle (1755–6) by NIKOLAUS PACASSI. The two styles, the Rococo and the Neo-classical, influenced each other and finally merged, as in the façade (1764–5) of the Archbishop's Palace in Prague by Johann Josef Wirch.

The architectural monuments of the 17th and 18th centuries in Bohemia are the most numerous, most homogeneous and best-preserved examples of the country's artistic heritage: the Baroque can be said to have completed the artistic image of the country. The characteristic materials of Bohemian Baroque architecture were brick with lime plasterwork, which probably helped to produce its softness and sculptural quality. As a result of the limited supply of suitable material, stone façades became the exception, as in the church of St Francis in Prague and buildings at KUKS. In spite of the large number of foreign architects working in Bohemia, the majority of buildings were constructed by local builders, whose names are often not known. Vernacular architecture was still largely of wood.

3. 1780s AND AFTER. In the 1780s and 1790s Neoclassical influences predominated, as in the Strahov Library, Prague, while elements of late Baroque and Rococo ornament were often added, as at the Mitrovský summer palace at Brno. Pre-Romantic tendencies were manifested in parks with diminutive exotic architecture, as at Krásný Dvůr, Veltrusy and Valtice-Lednice. The peak period of Neo-classicism in the early 19th century began with Kačin Castle, by the Saxon architect Christian Friedrich Schuricht. Whole towns were modernized, such as České Budějovice and Jihlava, and official buildings and apartment houses were erected by a generation of trained engineers. Building regulations and the influence of model patterns led to stylistic unity in late Neo-classicism, as at the castles at Kynžvart, Kostelec nad Orlicí and Boskovice. Meanwhile, in the 1830s, Romantic medievalism is evident in, for example, the parks at Cibulka and Kroměříž Castle. Wrought iron and cast iron were introduced at the end of the 1820s with the construction of the first suspension bridges at Žatec, Loket and Ostrava.

In the 1840s Gothic Revival elements became more marked in new buildings, and castles were restored in Tudor-Gothic style, as at Žleby, Sychrov, Bítov and Velké Uherce. Interest in the Middle Ages is also reflected in the stylistic purity with which JOSEF MOCKER and August Prokop restored important medieval monuments in Gothic style, such as Karlštejn Castle (1887–94) and the cathedrals at Brno, Olomouc and Prague. Romantic historicism was replaced by a strict historicism that was based on an exact study of form, and the stylistic spectrum incorporated Antique, Early Christian, Renaissance and Baroque models. In the Klein Palace (1848; by Ludwig von Forster) at Brno this striving after a new style produced a symbiosis of historicism and engineering, while the Renaissance Revival style symbolized the enterprise of the rising bourgeoisie against the feudal Gothic. In Prague it is represented by the work of Ignaz Ullmann (1822–97) and Antonín Barvitius (*see* BARVITIUS, (1)).

The outstanding architect of this period was JOSEF ZÍTEK, who combined a modern, functional approach with a sense of proportion derived from the Italian Renaissance. His main buildings, in particular the National Theatre (1868–83; *see* PRAGUE, fig. 5) and the Rudolfinum (1875–84), became symbols of Czech nationalism. The Renaissance Revival style is also expressed in the National Museum (1886–90) in Prague, built by Zítek's collaborator JOSEF SCHULZ. In the 1870s the style spread, as in the Town Hall at Kolín and a school in Kroměříž. Meanwhile, the so-called Czech Renaissance Revival, the main proponent of which was ANTONÍN WIEHL, was characterized by *sgraffito* decoration. In the 1880s strict stylistic canons declined in favour of eclecticism, together with an emphasis on ornament. The new phenomenon of imperial Baroque is evident in the work of FRIEDRICH OHMANN, Antonín Balšánek (1865–1921), Osvald Polívka and JOSEF FANTA; the last transformed late historicism into Secessionist or Art Nouveau style.

In the 1890s a break with the past occurred, signalling the arrival of the modern. The development of the work of engineers, the Arts and Crafts Movement and the national folklore movement all had a role to play. The architect JAN KOTĚRA succeeded in transmitting modern trends to conservative Bohemia: by 1910 he had made his own adaptation of the ideas of modern architectural pioneers, including Frank Lloyd Wright. In Bohemia the geometrical modern style is considered the second phase of the Secession, although in many respects it points to Cubism and Purism. The style is evident in Bohemia in the work of Bohumil Hypšman and Josef Zasche and in Moravia in work by Joseph Maria Olbrich, JOSEF HOFFMANN and the Gessner brothers.

In the first decade of the 20th century, historicism, the late Secession (e.g. Municipal House (Obecní dům), Prague) and the modern co-existed. In the increasingly international environment of Prague the principles of the Dutch modernist school (e.g. Štenc House, Prague, by OTAKAR NOVOTNÝ) clashed with the Constructivist principles of Walter Gropius (e.g. Gočár department store at Jaroměř), the work of the German Expressionists and the influence of French Cubism. In 1911–12, Cubism dominated Czech architecture. The theoretical and practical

6. Garden façade of the Tugendhat House, Brno, by Ludwig Mies van der Rohe, 1928–30

activity of the protagonists of CZECH CUBISM, PAVEL JANÁK, JOSEF GOČÁR, Vlastislav Hofman (1884–1964) and JOSEF CHOCHOL, resulted in innovative buildings such as Gočár's sanatorium at Bohdaneč (1911–12), the Black Madonna House (1911–12) in Prague and houses below Vyšehrad in Prague (1911–13; by Chochol; *see* PRAGUE, fig. 6). In the 1920s Gočár and Janák created a specifically Czech style with folk elements, Rondo-Cubism, as in the Legiobank (1921–3; by Gočár) in Prague. Purism had originated in France in 1917 as a counterweight to Cubism. Following the sketches from the circle of the Four Purists, Karel Honzík, EVŽEN LINHART, JAROSLAV FRAGNER and Vít Obrtel (1901–88), it penetrated into architectural practice from the beginning of the 1920s, owing mainly to the work of BEDŘICH FEUERSTEIN (e.g. the crematorium at Nymburk).

The Czechoslovak Republic, established in 1918, was immediately faced with the need to construct new official buildings, especially in Prague, where there had been a marked preference for garden suburbs (e.g. Ořechovka and Dejvice) and for monumental Neo-classical government buildings. Interesting results were achieved through the care devoted to restoring historical buildings, especially when the work was linked to an appropriate modern style, as for instance in Janák's reconstruction (1920s) of the Černín Palace in Prague and the restoration (1922–34) by JOŽE PLEČNIK of Prague Castle.

Mainly for economic reasons, public competitions were introduced that resulted in Functionalist solutions such as the Prague Trade Fair building (1926–8; now housing the

modern Czech collections of the National Gallery) by Oldřich Tyl and Josef Fuchs (*b* 1894). The left-wing intelligentsia, among them JIŘÍ KROHA, developed contacts with the Soviet Union, and there was mutually beneficial cooperation with the Bauhaus, where many Czech architects and theoreticians, such as Karel Teige, were active. Czech architects of this period developed a technically orientated Functionalism exemplified in the General Pensions Institute building (1929–34) in Prague, designed by JOSEF HAVLÍČEK and Karel Honzík. Functionalist architecture outside Prague includes work at Ústí nad Orlicí by KAMIL ROŠKOT and the Kolín power station (1930–41) by Jaroslav Fragner. Regional differences gradually disappeared with the spread of communications, and from the end of the 1920s there are examples of highly progressive Functionalist architecture at Brno, Ostrava and Zlín in Moravia. The Brno avant-garde was represented by ARNOŠT WIESNER (e.g. the Bank of Moravia; 1929–31) and BOHUSLAV FUCHS (e.g. the Avion Hotel; 1927–8). The Tugendhat House (1928–30) at Brno by Ludwig Mies van der Rohe (see fig. 6) established the architect's international status, while the town of Zlín, brought into being with the aid of Le Corbusier, became a symbol of efficient modern architecture, with work by František L. Gahura (1891–1958) and VLADIMÍR KARFÍK.

The outbreak of World War II prevented Functionalist architecture from fully achieving its aim, while post-war development followed largely in the spirit of the inter-war period, as in the Children's Teaching Hospital (1947–53; by BEDŘICH ROZEHNAL) at Brno. After the Communist putsch of February 1948 a monopolistic state sector for planning and building was established; it introduced standardized and prefabricated buildings, with emphasis on gigantic collective constructions after the Soviet example. The first buildings, which still used conventional technology, were largely traditional, but with elements of Stalinist Neo-classicism and folklorism, as in the International Hotel (1967–73) in Prague. By the end of the 1950s the use of prefabricated structures had reduced architects to the level of draughtsmen, although the restoration of listed buildings, such as the Carolinum (by Jaroslav Fragner), remained a professionally satisfying activity.

A significant architectural event was the construction of the television mast on Mt Ještěd, which was awarded the Auguste Perret prize in 1969. Its architect, Karel Hubáček, also played an important part in the establishment of the Liberec school of architecture. In the short period of greater freedom at the end of the 1960s architects attempted to come into line with practice in Western Europe with such buildings as the Kotva department store (1966–74; by V. Machonin and O. Machonin), but in the 1970s and 1980s Czech architecture reverted to the construction of gigantic housing projects or expensive, grandiose official buildings. Some buildings stood out from the monotonous stream of humdrum production and had a positive influence, for example the building (1974–83) at Na můstku (On the footbridge) in Prague by JAN ŠRÁMEK and Alena Šrámková or the House of Culture (Kulturní dům) at Teplice by Karel Hubáček. Some younger architects were inclined towards Post-modernism (Martin Rajniš); some rejected the restraints of Functionalism (Emil Přikryl, Jiří Suchomel) or launched into the struggle against prefabrication in an effort to give new meaning to architecture. Sometimes this was achieved by a search for self-expression (Václav Králíček, Michal Brix), sometimes by unrelenting tenacity (Jan Línek, Vlado Milunič), by sheer complexity (Ivo Oberstein) or by expressive technical elements (Jan Louda, Zbyšek Stýblo and Tomáš Kulík).

Moravian architecture remained in Prague's shadow, although in the 1960s attempts were made to revive the roles of Brno and Zlín as progressive architectural centres.

BIBLIOGRAPHY

Z. Wirth and A. Matějček: *Česká architektura XIX století* [Czech architecture of the 19th century] (Prague, 1922)

J. E. Koula: *Nová česká architektura a její vývoj ve 20. století* [The new Czech architecture and its development in the 20th century] (Prague, 1940)

D. Líbal: *Gotická architektura v Čechách a na Moravě* [Gothic architecture in Bohemia and Moravia] (Prague, 1948)

V. Mencl: *Onze cent années d'architecture en Tchécoslovaquie* (Prague, 1957)

E. Šamánková: *Architektura české renesance* [The architecture of the Czech Renaissance] (Prague, 1961)

Z. Wirth and A. Müllerová: *Architektura v českém národním dědictví* [Architecture in the Czech national heritage] (Prague, 1961)

H. G. Franz: *Bauten und Baumeister der Barockzeit in Böhmen* (Leipzig, 1962)

O. Dostál: *Moderní architektura v Československu* [Modern architecture in Czechoslovakia] (Prague, 1967)

D. Líbal: *Starobylá města v Československu* [The old towns of Czechoslovakia] (Prague, 1970)

A. Merhautová: *Raněstředověká architektura v Čechách* [Early medieval architecture in Bohemia] (Prague, 1971)

V. Richter and Z. Kudělka: 'Die Architektur des 17. und 18. Jahrhunderts in Mähren', *Sborn. Prac. Filoz. Fak. Brn. U.*, xxi (1972), pp. 91–130

B. Syrový: *Architektura: Svědectví dob* [Architecture: Testimony of the ages] (Prague, 1974)

J. Krčálová: *Centrální stavby české renesance* [Key buildings of the Czech Renaissance] (Prague, 1976)

V. Mencl: 'Architektura', *Pozdně gotické umění v Čechách* [Late Gothic art in Bohemia] (Prague, 1978)

J. Pechar: *Československá architektura* [Czechoslovak architecture] (Prague, 1979)

V. Mencl: *Lidová architektura v Československu* [Folk architecture in Czechoslovakia] (Prague, 1980)

J. Dekan: *Velká Morava* [Great Moravia] (Prague, 1981)

J. Krčálová: 'Die rudolfinische Architektur', *Leids Ksthist. Jb.*, i (1982), pp. 271–302

M. Benešová: *Česká architektura v proměnách dvou století* [Czech architecture over two centuries] (Prague, 1984)

R. Švácha: *Od moderny k funkcionalismu* [From the modern to Functionalism] (Prague, 1985)

ABC kulturních památek [An ABC of cultural monuments] (Prague, 1985)

JIŘÍ T. KOTALÍK

III. Sculpture.

The earliest figurines found in the area of the Czech Republic date to the Upper Palaeolithic period and were discovered in southern Moravia. The finds include the so-called Věstonice Venus, a head made from mammoth tusk and a mammoth-tusk sculpture of a woman in geometric style. Neolithic sculptures of female worshippers and a Late Bronze Age sculpture of a bull were found in the same region. The Celtic settlement in Bohemia is represented by an argillite head of a man (2nd century BC). Later sculpture in Bohemia achieved three distinctive peaks of development: in the second half of the 14th century, when the *Schöne Stil* evolved, which influenced the whole of central Europe; in the first third of the 18th century, when Bohemian Baroque was at its height; and in the late 19th century, when the work of Josef Václav Myslbek embodied the ideals of the national revival.

1. *c*. 1100–*c*. 1450. 2. *c*. 1450–early 1620s. 3. 1620s–1780s. 4. 1780s and after.

1. *c*. 1100–*c*. 1450. The first record of a sculptor in Bohemia dates to the late 11th century AD and refers to Božetěch, abbot of the Benedictine monastery on the Sázava River. He may be linked with the relief *Christ Enthroned with SS Peter and Paul* from the tympanum of St John the Baptist at Oldříš Castle (*c*. 1150; Prague, Lapidarium Hist. Mus.), which shows Byzantine influence. Reliefs and sculptures of the late 12th century and early 13th reveal both western and southern influences and include the reliefs (*c*. 1165) of *Christ with Bohemian Saints* on the southern façade of St James, Kutná Hora, the embellishment (*c*. 1200) on the portal of the church of St Procopius at Záboří and the *Virgin Enthroned with Abbesses and King Ottakar Přemysl I* (after 1220) in the tympanum of the church of St George in Hradčany, Prague. The relief (*c*. 1170–after 1250) of a ruler with a kneeling donor from the Little Quarter tower of the Charles Bridge is the most important Romanesque sculpture in Bohemia (Prague, Mus. City; see fig. 7; *see also* ROMANESQUE, §III, 1(x)(c)).

The first monumental sculptures in the Gothic style were linked to the building of the monasteries, as in the west tympanum of the church at TIŠNOV ABBEY (after 1240), with *Christ Enthroned* in a nimbus borne by symbols

7. Stone relief of a ruler with a kneeling donor, from the Little Quarter tower of the Charles Bridge, Prague, *c.* 1170–after 1250 (Prague, Museum of the City of Prague)

of the Evangelists, and the crowned male and female heads on the capitals (*c.* third quarter of the 13th century) of the triumphal arch of the convent of St Agnes in Prague. An example of a work from a slightly later period is the standing, over life-size statue of the *Virgin* from the church of the Knights of St John in Strakonice (Prague, N.G., Convent of St George), which shows the influence of French cathedral sculpture. Wooden carved Crucifixes appeared in the late 13th century and early 14th, including the expressive Přemysl Crucifix (*c.* 1300) at St Ignatius, Jihlava, and the harmoniously carved Crucifix in St James, Brno. Dramatic wooden *Pietà*s, in which Christ's body is convoluted, are from the Dominican monastery in Cheb, St James in Jihlava and the church of the Knights of St John in Strakonice and date to a slightly later period.

Monumental stone sculptures from before the mid-14th century include fragments from the house At the Bell (U Zvonu), Prague, which may be the images of John of Luxembourg and his wife Elizabeth. The high quality of Bohemian sculpture of that period is evident also in the reliefs from the tympanum of the north portal of the church of Our Lady of the Snows, Prague (Prague, N.G., Convent of St George); the rich articulation with minute parallel folds in these reliefs influenced a group of wooden standing Virgins (from Buchlovice, Michle, Velké Meziříčí). Until the mid-14th century western influences are evident in Bohemian art, but from the accession of Charles IV in 1346 an autonomous style emerged (*see* LUXEMBOURG, (3)). Sculptural mass increased, while movement

became softer and continuous, with the emphasis on the three-dimensional character of a work. The austere monumentality inspired by French cathedral sculpture alternated with the graceful intimacy demanded by the new religious spirit, as in the *Virgin and Child* from the church of St James, Jihlava, but gradually movement prevailed, probably under the influence of the Silesian sculptures of the *Virgin and Child Standing on a Lion.* This development is obvious in, for example, the standing Broumov *Madonna and Child* (after 1350) and the nursing Konopiště *Madonna and Child* (after 1380; Prague, N.G., Convent of St George).

The extraordinary talent of Peter Parler and his embellishment, with his workshop, of St Vitus' Cathedral in Prague introduced a new spirit of monumentalism in sculpture (*see* PRAGUE, §IV, 2(ii)). The sculptural programme was ambitious: the triforium inside the cathedral contains portrait busts of members of the imperial family as well as of the higher clergy and the architects of the cathedral, Mathias of Arras and Parler himself (*see* PARLER, (3), fig. 2). Six tombs in the chapels of the ambulatory with reclining figures of the Přemyslids (before 1373; *see* GOTHIC, §III, 1(iii)(c)) are also by the Parler workshop. The standing statue of *St Wenceslas* (probably after 1373) in the Wenceslas Chapel is thought to be by Heinrich Parler of Gmünd, Peter's nephew. It is both monumental and delicate and represents the ideal of Bohemian High Gothic sculpture. Numerous gargoyles, consoles and capitals in the cathedral illustrate the relaxation of Gothic forms.

The work of the Parlers inspired the development of Bohemian High Gothic in the 1370s and 1380s, for example the *Pietà* (after 1370) at St Thomas, Brno, the bronze *St George and the Dragon* in the third courtyard of Prague Castle and the monumental *Virgin* (before 1381) on the corner of the Old Town Hall in Prague. A specific Bohemian type of *Virgin and Child* and *Pietà* emerged in that period. Among the first of these Virgins are the Plzeň *Madonna and Child* (*c.* 1395) on the high altar of St Bartholomew, Plzeň, and the Všeměřice *Madonna and Child* (perhaps originally from Vyšší Brod Abbey). Over the ensuing 20 years the two types became more dynamic, and their three-dimensional character was emphasized while their robes became less decorative. The paintings of the Master of Třeboň, with their elegant figures and elaborate draperies, inspired sculptors and influenced the developing *Schöne Stil*, in which two trends are discernible. The first emphasized fragile playfulness and ornamentally embellished surfaces and is represented by the Český Krumlov *Madonna and Child* (after 1390; Vienna, Ksthist. Mus.). Among the works attributed to the Master of the Český Krumlov Madonna is *St Catherine* (before 1400) from St James, Jihlava. The second trend is usually linked to the work of the Master of Beautiful Madonnas, whose *Sancta Maria Gravida* (*c.* 1400) has been missing from the Toruń Museum, Poland, since 1945. Such sculptures are animated by an inner movement, while the Virgin's robes form a flowing system of dished folds.

The type of *Pietà* in which Christ's body is almost horizontal on his mother's lap gradually superseded the type in which his body was vertical. The stone *Pietà* from Dlouhá Ves, probably influenced by Parler, shows the transition; in it Christ's body is in a diagonal position. A group of large and small *Pietà*s of the horizontal type were developed from the 1380s; the *Pietà* (c. 1400; see fig. 8) from St Ignatius, Jihlava, is the most refined. The Bohemian scheme of the *Pietà* was in demand throughout central Europe. Statues of the *Ecce homo* type were made for Bohemian town halls. After 1400 Crucifixes were smaller and more appropriate for private devotion. The monumental sculptural group *Calvary* (c. 1410–20; Prague, N.G., Convent of St George) was made for the Týn church in Prague shortly before the outbreak of the Hussite Wars (1420–36). The artist expressed the drama of the time by abandoning the decorative character of the *Schöne Stil* in favour of the realistic depiction of faces.

2. *c.* 1450–EARLY 1620s. Sculpture in Bohemia was slow to recover from the period of Hussite iconoclasm. In the Catholic parts of the country, forms of *Schöne Stil* survived until the mid-15th century (e.g. the Borovany *Pietà*), but the style had become debased, and Bohemia emerged as a cultural province of the German Late Gothic. Though Prague attempted to pay homage to the new king, George of Poděbrady, by building two monuments (his statue on the façade of the Týn church and his equestrian statue on the Charles Bridge), these were not successful. Some important works appeared in the Catholic towns around the mid-15th century, such as the *Calvary* in St Bartholomew, Plzeň, and the sandstone group of the *Agony in the Garden* in St Maurice, Olomouc. The arts revived after 1471, when Vladislav II Jagiellon succeeded to the throne of Bohemia. Matěj Rejsek designed and decorated the Powder Tower (1475) in Prague in Vladislav's honour. From the 1480s Vladislav II employed Hans Spiess from Frankfurt, who probably cooperated with the architect Benedikt Ried on the decoration of the Royal Oratory (1490–93) in St Vitus' Cathedral. Wood-carvings from the Catholic Rožmberks' estates in southern Bohemia were influenced by the work of the Austrian Master of the Kefermarkt Altar (*fl c.* 1470–1510). Sculptures from Český Krumlov and other centres were influenced by the Vienna workshop of Nicolaus Gerhaert. Contacts with the Danube school increased around 1500. Western Bohemia (Plzeň and near by) was influenced by Nuremberg wood-carving, while north-western Bohemia came under the influence of neighbouring Saxony.

Wood-carving in Bohemia culminated after 1500 in the oeuvre of the Master of the Žebrák Lamentation, who was one of the leading artists of the Danube school. His fragile yet dynamic *Lamentation* (Prague, N.G., Convent of St George; see fig. 9) influenced numerous wood-carvings (mostly Hluboká nad Vltavou, Aleš Gal.). The Master of the Zvíkov Lamentation was another significant artist of that period who worked mainly in south-western Bohemia. Master I.P. also belonged to the Danube school and was active in the period of transition from Late Gothic to Renaissance, producing intricately carved reliefs (Prague, N.G., Convent of St George). Anton Pilgram worked in Brno (e.g. the wood-carvings of the *Death of St Peter the Martyr* and of a Dominican saint, c. 1511). The stone reliefs of the *Crucifixion* (1519) and *Lamentation* (1518) in St James, Brno, represent the end of Late Gothic sculpture.

8. *Pietà*, wood with polychromy and gilt, h. 1.2 m, c. 1400 (Jihlava, St Ignatius)

9. Žebrák *Lamentation*, wooden relief, after 1500 (Prague, National Gallery, Convent of St George)

In 16th-century Bohemia the ideal was the expression of spiritual grandeur rather than physical beauty, and Renaissance values made little impact. In Moravia, examples of work in the style of the Florentine Renaissance, as in the portrait medallions (c. 1490) on the portals at Tovačov and those at Moravská Třebová (1495), had no greater impact. The local Utraquism continued to look to

Late Gothic examples until the influence of the Lutheran Reformation drew attention to new Saxon forms. Early Lutheranism in Prague (*c.* 1520) provoked a new wave of iconoclasm, to which Ferdinand I, Holy Roman Emperor, reacted after his succession to the throne of Bohemia in 1526 by attempting to strengthen Catholicism. He had to look for his artists abroad, however. The carved altarpiece of the restored monastery church in Zbraslav was made in the Hans Daucher workshop in Augsburg *c.* 1530 and was probably financed by Ferdinand. From the 1520s works in brass for Prague's St Vitus' Cathedral were commissioned from the Vischer foundry in Nuremberg, such as the brass candlestick (1534) with a statue of *St Wenceslas* (*see* VISCHER, (5)) and in 1558 the *Ludmila Berková* tomb, which is among the most important 16th-century transalpine sculptures.

Ferdinand I employed Paolo Stella to work on the Royal Summer Palace ('Belvedere'), Prague, for which Stella and his group of Italian masons made over a hundred sandstone reliefs (1538–52) depicting mythological and contemporary scenes. The example of the Dresden court circle was followed by the powerful lords of Pernštejn in the embellishment (1529–43) of their castle and the church of St Bartholomew in Pardubice. They were exceptional in employing an Italian sculptor, whose tomb of *Žofia of Těšín* (1541) is one of the purest works of the Italian Late Renaissance in Bohemia. The reliefs on the castle bridge, which were influenced by Saxon art, are rough in comparison. By the late 15th century north-western Bohemia had established a cultural link with Saxony; later this connection was strengthened, and its impact is evident as far away as Prague, in the cathedral tombs (*c.* 1550). Silesian and Austrian influences are revealed on gravestones in Moravia.

The imperial court at Prague defended itself against the influence of Lutheran Saxony by turning its attention to Italy. The most important work in this context is the stucco embellishment (from 1556) of the Hvězda summer house in Prague. Numerous works were commissioned by the newly arrived Jesuit Order, ranging from triumphal arches to theatre sets and new altarpieces. During the tolerant reign of Maximilian II a temporary mixing of forms occurred, as in the *Singing Fountain* in the garden of the Royal Summer Palace, Prague. It was designed in 1562 by Francesco Terzio, modelled by HANS PEISSER from Nuremberg and cast in bronze by Tomáš Jaroš (*d* 1570) in 1568. The court's interest gradually switched to Netherlandish artists. In 1566 Maximilian II commissioned the Fleming Alexander Colin to sculpt a marble memorial to his parents *Ferdinand I and Anna Jagiellon* for St Vitus' Cathedral. The work, in Mannerist style, was completed in 1573, but after Maximilian's death his effigy was added (1585–7), as were medallions of kings and queens of Bohemia (1587–9).

In Utraquist Bohemia the type of tomb established in Saxony was widespread. Around the mid-16th century it most often represented a knight in armour kneeling in front of a crucifix. From the 1560s thousands of oblong stone plaques with images of standing men, women and children were produced. No attempt was made to portray the deceased, but Czech inscriptions gave their social status and age. These simple works embodied the democratic ideals of Hussite Bohemia and were understood by the Catholics as an expression of Reformation ideas. Efforts were made to destroy them during the Counter-Reformation after the Battle of the White Mountain (1620).

The decoration of Protestant churches was also influenced by Saxony. High altars were ornamented with reliefs of the *Last Supper* on their predellas, the *Crucifixion* in the centre and the *Resurrection* on their extension pieces. Epitaphs appeared on side altars, frequently representing the *Last Judgement* and sometimes the *Vision of Ezekiel*. Pulpits with reliefs of the Evangelists were often sustained by a statue of *Moses*. These well-crafted but conformist works were usually supplied by workshops in Dresden, Meissen, Freiburg and Pirna, mainly to western Bohemia but also to Prague. Works produced in Wrocław in Silesia (now Poland) also had an influence on Bohemian sculpture, largely because of their affinity with the middle class. The large epitaph for *Václav Morkovský* in Boskovice, Moravia, was made *c.* 1600 from a range of coloured marble, probably by a stonemason from Wrocław. The Late Mannerist *Redern* monument (1605–10; damaged in the Thirty Years War) in the church of the Holy Cross at Frýdlant Castle was by Gerard Hendrik from Amsterdam, who settled in Wrocław. Adriaen de Vries, however, was the principal sculptor of the Mannerist period at the Prague court. He worked at first for Rudolf II and then, after his death, for Count Albrecht von Wallenstein (1583–1634), for whom he designed several fountains and bronze sculptural groups (1623–6) for the garden of the Wallenstein (Valdštejn) Palace in Prague (*see* PRAGUE, §IV, 7).

3. 1620s–1780s. The development of sculpture was disrupted by the Battle of the White Mountain, which was followed by the harsh Counter-Reformation and the introduction of Baroque art. In the 1620s the decoration of St Vitus' Cathedral in Prague was resumed by Daniel Altman from Eydenberg and by Kašpar Bechteller, who made the reliefs of the *Looting of the Cathedral by the Calvinists in 1619* and the *Flight of Frederick the Palatine from Prague*. ERNST JOHANN HEIDELBERGER carved a wooden altarpiece (1630–32) for the chapel of the Wallenstein Palace and possibly the large altarpiece (*c.* 1650) for St Mary of the Snows, Prague. Immediately after the end of the Thirty Years War in 1648 the production of sculpture increased, first in Prague. The Marian column for the Old Town Square in Prague by Jan Jiří Bendl, Abraham Melber and Stanislav Goldschneck was one of the first examples of pure Baroque (1650; Prague, Lapidarium Hist. Mus.; *see* BENDL, (1)). The growing emphasis on mass and dynamism in sculpture is reflected in the works of Bendl, who was the leading sculptor in Bohemia until his death in 1680. In the countryside the flat-modelled figures of the Saxonian Renaissance were still produced.

The art of Catholic Bavaria began to influence southern Bohemia in the mid-17th century. The style spread and is expressed in an equestrian statue of *St Wenceslas* by Bendl (stone, before 1680; original Prague, Mun. Gal.). The style was considerably refined by Heidelberger's apprentice Hieronymus Kohl, who subsequently became court sculptor. His statue of *St Ursula* (1677) above the portal of the

Ursuline convent in Prague shows his ability to combine a Mannerist figure with the sharp modelling of a Baroque robe. His atlantids in the fountain (1686) in the second courtyard of Prague Castle indicate that he also came to terms with Bendl's legacy. Stucco decoration was the domain of the Italians gathered around the architect Carlo Lurago. Bartholomäus Cometa (*fl* 1665–84), for example, made reliefs for the Loreto church in Prague and stucco altarpieces for the church of St Mary at Stará Boleslav.

Architectural activity increased in Bohemia during the last quarter of the 17th century, and this attracted sculptors from neighbouring countries. The first was probably Jan Brokof, an ardent Lutheran, who arrived from Slovakia in 1675 and converted to Catholicism while working on the statue of *St John of Nepomuk* for the Charles Bridge. Its model was supplied in 1681 by MATHIAS RAUCHMILLER, and Brokof's carving was subsequently cast in bronze. Brokof went on to work on other statues for the Charles Bridge but remained faithful to the austerity of 17th-century Lutheran sculpture. The dramatic Baroque style of Bernini was introduced to Prague by the Heermanns and Süssners from Saxony and the Italian Ottavio Mosto. Johann Georg Heermann (*fl* 1683–1700) and his nephews Paul (*d* 1732) and Zacharias, all from Dresden, embellished the staircase of the Trója château in Prague. The brothers Jeremias Süssner (*d* 1690) and Konrad Max Süssner supplied statues for the interior of the Prague church of St Francis, and Ottavio Mosto made a sculptural group of *St Wenceslas* for the Charles Bridge. MATĚJ VÁCLAV JÄCKEL, who had probably studied Roman Baroque sculpture in southern Germany, influenced the development of Bohemian sculpture with his numerous wooden and stone statues in Prague and elsewhere in Bohemia. František Preiss (*d* 1712) successfully combined Bohemian traditions with foreign influences in his expressive figures with their richly articulated drapery.

Matyáš Bernard Braun and Ferdinand Maximilián Brokof were the foremost Baroque sculptors in Bohemia, representing the culmination of two opposing traditions in transalpine Europe. Using soft Bohemian sandstone, Braun brought Bernini's drama to its maximum effect (for illustration *see* BRAUN, MATYÁŠ BERNARD), while Brokov perfected the statuesque seriousness of sculpture from Lutheran Saxony, thus becoming a predecessor of Georg Raphael Donner as well as of the official art of the 19th century. Both sculptors received the most important commissions of the period, making sculptures for the Charles Bridge representing Bohemian saints as well as Counter-Reformation saints (for illustration *see* BROKOF, (2)), and working for the Jesuits and the nobility. Braun's principal patron was the Jansenist Count Franz Anton von Sporck at KUKS. Over the years Braun and Brokof influenced each other: the dynamism of Brokof's works increased (e.g. tomb of *Vratislav z Mitrovic* in St James, Prague, and the Moorish atlantids (1714) on the Morzin Palace, Prague; see fig. 10), while Braun's statues became more robust.

By the mid-1720s both Braun and Brokof were ill and passed their commissions to their workshops and to their contemporaries Jan Oldřich Mayer, Ondřej Filip Quitainer and Johann Friedrich Kohl-Severa, who copied their style but failed to develop it. The spirit of Bohemian Baroque

10. Ferdinand Maximilián Brokof: Moorish atlantid on the Morzin Palace, Prague, 1714

sculpture changed. The monumental style was replaced by a softer, more playful approach that turned the interiors of churches into theatres welcoming their visitors. Michal Jan Brüderle (*d* 1740), for instance, made fountains for the courtyard of the Loreto church in Prague that are almost jocular in their robust exaggeration.

From the end of the 17th century sculptural production in the countryside became immensely rich. Every town put up its own Marian or Trinity column; every village acquired its own statue of St John of Nepomuk; many churches commissioned additional altarpieces. Artists in the countryside initially drew on the work of Prague artists, as did the Jesuit František Baugut (1668–1726) at Kutná Hora, Osvald Josef Venda (*d* 1721) in western Bohemia, and Kristián Widman (*d* 1725), but artists of importance later emerged from the countryside itself. Franz Anton Kuen, for example, worked first at Osek Monastery (1713–16) and later throughout north-western Bohemia, and

G. B. Bulla established a great sculptural tradition in eastern Bohemia after 1711, as did Jan Pavel Cechpauer in Chrudim. From the first quarter of the 18th century eastern Bohemia became the domain of Braun's apprentices or followers, including the Jelínek family; Ignác Rohrbach (1691–1747), who produced hundreds of dynamic wood-carvings reflecting Braun's style, as did Řehoř Thény (1680–1756); Jiří František Pacák (1670–1742); and Severin Tischler (1705–before 1752). In western Bohemia the most pronounced follower of Braun was Jakub Artschlag; Josef Herscher (1688–1756) created works for Manětín after 1720, while Plzeň-based LAZAR WIDMAN looked for guidance both to Braun's works and to historicizing styles. This development of sculpture in the countryside ceased around the mid-18th century, when signs of social reform emerged.

The transitional style between late Baroque and early Rococo appeared first in Prague in the second quarter of the 18th century and was expressed in the work of KARL JOSEF HIERNLE as well as in the sculptures of Jan Antonín Quitainer, who around 1750 was considered the best Prague-based sculptor (see QUITAINER, (2)). František Ignác Weis (c. 1695–1756) produced Rococo sculptures that are both monumental and quietly delicate. The court sculptor Josef Klein (c. 1700–70) made similarly gracious statues, while figures by the Tyrolean Matyáš Schönherr (1701–43) are excessively distorted. The Bavarian Richard Prachner (1705–82) made statues that combine a playful dynamism with a statuesque austerity. František Platzer (see PLATZER) represented the transition from the Rococo to a classicizing style in Bohemia, strongly influenced by Georg Raphael Donner. From the mid-18th century Platzer received most of the important sculptural commissions in Bohemia. The work of Peter Prachner (1747–1807), son of Richard Prachner, illustrates the turning-point, around 1780, when Josef II's reforms changed the entire life of the country and ended ecclesiastical sculpture. Prachner used traditional pattern books and later created sculptures that were both classical in style and gently

serene. In his work the female nude reappeared after two centuries.

In Moravia the development of Baroque sculpture differed from that in Bohemia. Moravia was more open to influences from Austria and Silesia. It had two cultural centres, Olomouc and Brno, and it was divided into the extensive estates of aristocratic families such as the Liechtensteins, the Dietrichsteins and the Kounic family, often of a distinctive cultural character. Until the mid-18th century Moravia actively absorbed foreign influences and only then achieved its own quiet, elegant but vigorous expression, above all in the work of Ondřej Schweigel (1735–1812). Before then, notably in the first half of the 17th century, sculptors and stuccoists were predominantly Italian; for instance, P. Conchort and Francesco Sala worked with the architect Giovanni Pietro Tencalla on the Loreto church in Mikulov, which became the example for other Loreto churches throughout Moravia and Bohemia. After the mid-17th century the Germans and Flemings arrived in Moravia, of whom Michael Zürn (fl 1679–1731) was the most important. The artists who worked in Brno from the late 17th century were predominantly of northern origin: Balthasar Frobel (d 1688) from Königsberg, Jan Kašpar Pröbstl from northern Germany and Jan Furth from Flanders.

BALDASSARE FONTANA was active in Moravia until the 1720s, and his work is of fundamental significance there. In 1700–01 GIOVANNI GIULIANI produced sculptures for the stables of the manor house at Lednice (Ger. Eisgrub) as well as for the park at Slavkov u Brna (Ger. Austerlitz; few survive). Lorenzo Mattielli (d 1748) supplied works for the park of the Louka Monastery. Another artist active in the region was Josef Winterhalder (i), who came from Bavaria. Winterhalder worked mainly for the Hradisko Monastery near Olomouc (see WINTERHALDER, (1)). Johann Georg Lehnert, whose dynamic works were probably influenced by Balthasar Permoser, was active in Opava and Silesia. Severin Tischler and Jiří Antonín Heintz were linked to the Braun circle in eastern Bohemia. Bohumír Fritsch (1714–70) and Donner's associate František Kohl (b 1711) followed up the classicism in Donner's oeuvre. In southern Moravia Josef Leonhard Weber worked in and around Znojmo, while Václav Kovanda (1719–88) and Matěj Kovanda (1714–70) were based in Jihlava. From the mid-18th century Brno became the centre of sculptural production based on the workshop of Ondřej Schweigel. The Schweigel workshop, which was active until the beginning of the 19th century, produced softly elegant figures reflecting the idea of Catholicism as a peaceful guarantee of material well-being.

4. 1780s AND AFTER. The reforms of Josef II in the 1780s and the subsequent Napoleonic wars left a gap of almost 50 years in the development of Bohemian sculpture. Sculptors were unable to get commissions, and Platzer's son Ignác Michal Platzer (1757–1826), for example, had to earn his living mainly by carving picture frames and decorating clock cases with figures. His contemporary Josef Malínský (1752–1827) showed his considerable talent in the embellishment of a few buildings with realistic genre works, but he could not find wider opportunities for his work. František Xaver Lederer (c. 1758–1811) made tombs

11. Václav Prachner: tomb of *Bishop Lev Thun-Hohenstein*, cast iron, 1830 (Prague, Košíře Cemetery)

that were a rather cold echo of the Empire style then in vogue. The most important sculptor of that period was VÁCLAV PRACHNER, who represented the third generation of a Prague family of wood-carvers. In his monumental works, such as the tomb of *Bishop Lev Thun-Hohenstein* at the Košíře cemetery (1830; see fig. 11), he anticipated late 19th-century trends. The oeuvre of the brothers Josef Max (1804–55) and Emanuel Max (*see* MAX, (1)) represented a return to the international academic style, in their monument to *Marshal Josef Radecký* (1858) or in their statues for the Charles Bridge. Bohemian gracefulness permeated works by Václav Levý (1820–70), who sculpted reliefs in sandstone. Levý's contemporary Arnošt Popp (1819–83), an excellent medallist, mostly designed small figures for a porcelain factory in Prague.

In this impoverished period, however, the greatest representative of the new era, JOSEF VÁCLAV MYSLBEK, was born. He studied with Levý and was fortunate in gaining monumental commissions from the age of 22 for the National Theatre in Prague (1871–4), for sculptural groups for the Palacký Bridge (model 1881; realization 1887–97) and for patriotic monuments in towns throughout Bohemia. He achieved a firm Italian Renaissance form that is nevertheless permeated with deep and sometimes almost lyrical feeling. His equestrian *St Wenceslas* (1900–04; erected 1913; *see* PRAGUE, fig. 10) in Wenceslas Square in Prague became the symbol of Czechoslovak national freedom.

Myslbek was the founder of modern Bohemian sculpture, yet his pupils intentionally dissociated themselves from his artistic style from about 1900. STANISLAV SUCHARDA was at first attracted to Myslbek's lyrical expression, but later, in the monument to *František Palacký* (1898–1912) in Prague, he began to move towards the spirit of French Symbolism. LADISLAV ŠALOUN was a master of brilliant Art Nouveau stylization. His work was significant in the early 20th century, as in the monument (1900–15) to *Jan Hus* in the Old Town Square, Prague, but after World War I it became repetitive. The work of the Symbolist František Bílek shared the same fate; *c.* 1900 his wood-carvings were perceived as a culmination of psychological insight, but by the 1920s they were disregarded.

Josef Mařatka, later one of the official sculptors of the new Czechoslovak Republic, made masterly variants on works by Rodin. France also influenced the early work of BOHUMIL KAFKA, but he then returned to the Myslbek style in a narrow and outdated manner. The influence of Myslbek on another of his pupils, Otakar Španiel (*b* 1881), was more organic, and Španiel went on to produce reliefs that are outstanding examples of Bohemian sculpture. JAN ŠTURSA understood Myslbek's style so thoroughly that he was able to transform it to express a wide range of subject-matter from the lyrical and erotic to the tragic, such as his *Wounded Soldier* (1920–21; Prague, N.G., Zbraslav Monastery).

Among the greatest Czech sculptors of the early 20th century was OTTO GUTFREUND, who helped to create the style known as CZECH CUBISM and, later, produced colourful realistic sculptures on social themes, such as *Industry* and *Commerce* (both 1923; Prague, N.G., Zbraslav Monastery; see fig. 12). His work influenced Bedřich Stefan

12. Otto Gutfreund: *Commerce*, plaster, 1923 (Prague, National Gallery, Zbraslav Monastery)

(1892–1982), who moved towards a further simplification of the style, roughly following the path taken by Alexander Archipenko. VINCENC MAKOVSKÝ and Hana Wichterlová, who had studied under Štursa, were, together with Stefan, members of the avant-garde between the wars. Less signigicant were those sculptors who followed Myslbek's legacy more closely: Karel Pokorný (1891–1962), Karel Dvořák (1893–1950), Jan Lauda (1898–1959), Karel Lidický and Josef Wagner. The work of Ladislav Zívr, with elements of Surrealism, and the kinetic sculpture of Zdenek Pešánek emerged as the most progressive works of that period.

After 1945 those who had studied under Myslbek and Štursa became professors at the Prague Academy of Fine Arts and Academy of Applied Arts and thus exercised a significant influence over the following generations. In 1945–7 they designed monuments that expressed the nation's gratitude for the liberation from Nazi Germany

13. Stanislav Kolíbal: *Double Perspective*, wood and iron, 1.13×0.98×1.29 m, 1987 (Prague, Museum of the City of Prague)

as well as new social ideas (e.g. *Fraternization* by Pokorný or *Partisan* by Makovský). In the post-1948 period, when the principles of Socialist Realism were imposed by the state, it became obvious that artists were being forced to use outdated, stultifying forms. Most monuments of the 1950s—of political, cultural or historical personalities—were not successful as works of art. Those sculptors (such as Zdeněk Kovář and Rudolf Svoboda) who came closer to the sphere of decorative arts, for example in the embellishment of buildings, in theatrical designs or in sculptures for fountains, were in a luckier position. The next generation built on the achievements of the inter-war avant-garde while taking into account trends in Western Europe. Important sculptors born in the period from the beginning of the 1920s to the mid-1940s are, in chronological order: Miloš Chlupáč, Zbyněk Sekal, Vladimír Janoušek, Jan Koblasa, Karel Malich, STANISLAV KOLÍBAL (see fig. 13), Adriena Šimotová, Olbram Zoubek, Zdeněk Palcr, Eva Kmentová, Vladimír Preclík, Hugo Demartini, Zdena Fibichová, Karel Nepraš, Aleš Veselý, Kurt Gebauer, Jiří Beránek and Magdalena Jetelová.

BIBLIOGRAPHY
O. J. Blažíček: *Sochařství baroku v Čechách* [Baroque sculpture in Bohemia] (Prague, 1958)
A. Kutal: *České gotické sochařství, 1350–1450* [Bohemian Gothic sculpture, 1350–1450] (Prague, 1962)
O. J. Blažíček: *Barockkunst in Böhmen* (Prague, 1967)
V. Volavka: *České malířství a sochařství 19. století* [Czech painting and sculpture of the 19th century] (Prague, 1968)
K. M. Swoboda, ed.: *Gotik in Böhmen* (Munich, 1969)
J. Neumann: *Das böhmische Barock* (Prague, 1970)
M. Stehlík: 'Nástin dějin sochařství 17. a 18. věku na Moravě' [Outline of the history of sculpture in Moravia in the 17th and 18th centuries], *Sborn. Prac. Filos. Fak. Brn. U.*, xxiv–xxv (1976), pp. 23–40
E. Bachmann: *Romantik in Böhmen* (Munich, 1977)
P. Wittlich: *České sochařství ve XX. století* [Czech sculpture in the 20th century] (Prague, 1978)
A. Merhautová and D. Třeštík: *Románské umění v Čechách a na Moravě* [Romanesque art in Bohemia and Moravia] (Prague, 1983)
F. Seibt, ed.: *Renaissance in Böhmen* (Munich, 1985)

78/1985: Přehled moderních českých výtvarníků [78/1985: Survey of modern Czech artists] (Prague, 1985)

IVO KOŘÁN

IV. Painting and graphic arts.

Painting in the Gothic style persisted in the Czech lands alongside Renaissance influences until elements of Mannerism became established in the late 16th century. The Counter-Reformation after 1620 led to the introduction of Baroque art, later under Viennese influence, which was superseded by Neo-classicism and, in the early 19th century, by the Romanticism of the national revival. Important exhibitions in Prague in the 20th century signalled the development of modern art.

1. Before 1620. 2. 1620–*c*. 1900. 3. After *c*. 1900.

1. BEFORE 1620. The earliest surviving examples of creative art from the territory of the Czech Republic are animal engravings on bone dating to the Upper Palaeolithic period. During the Neolithic period naturalism was replaced by an abstract geometrical style that prevailed until the last centuries of the pre-Christian era. The area's conversion to Christianity in the 9th century AD, during the period of the Great Moravian empire, introduced Byzantine influences, which are apparent in surviving fragments of wall paintings from churches (destr.) at Uherské Hradiště-Valy, Mikulčice and Břeclav-Pohansko.

The earliest examples of Romanesque painting in Bohemia are to be found in 11th-century manuscript illumination, including the Vyšehrad Codex (before 1085; Prague, Libs Facs & Insts Charles U., MS. XIV. A. 13), which shows abstract features as well as similarities with the Romanesque style of south German scriptoria. One of the most richly illuminated manuscripts of its period, it was probably commissioned for the coronation of Vratislav II (*reg* 1061–92; *see* PŘEMYSLID). The cycle of Romanesque wall paintings (1134) in the rotunda of the chapel of St Catherine at Znojmo is remarkable for its monumental conception and highly original iconography. The cycle is based on the chronicle of Cosmas of Prague (?1045–1125) and represents the legend of the Přemyslid dynasty (see fig. 14). Byzantine influence is evident in manuscript illumination and in wall painting throughout the 13th century, for example in the *Crucifixion* (late 13th century) in St Mary, Písek. The style was superseded by Gothic in the early 14th century.

The decorative style of French illumination was influential in the group of richly painted manuscripts (after 1315) of Queen Elizabeth Rejčka and particularly in the outstanding Passional of the Abbess Kunhuta (*c*. 1313–21; Prague, Libs Facs & Insts Charles U., MS. XIV. A. 17). In 1348 the Prague brotherhood of St Luke was founded, the earliest guild of painters in Central Europe (*see* PRAGUE, §II, 1). In the mid-14th century, Bohemian painting combined French and English realism with Italian modelling and spatial construction. This style is particularly evident in the *Virgin and Child* from Veveří in Moravia (now Prague, N.G., Convent of St George), one of the earliest surviving Bohemian panel paintings. It is from the workshop of the Master of the Vyšší Brod Altar, who produced a collection of nine panels (*c*. 1350; Prague,

14. *Calling Přemysl to the Throne* (1134), wall painting, rotunda of St Catherine, Znojmo

N.G., Convent of St George; *see* MASTERS, ANONYMOUS, AND MONOGRAMMISTS, §I: MASTER OF THE VYŠŠÍ BROD ALTAR) for the Vyšší Brod Abbey.

The magnificent scope of Bohemian painting of the period was powerfully influenced by Charles IV (*reg* 1346–78), who wanted to make a new Rome of Prague, the metropolis of the new empire (*see* LUXEMBOURG, (3)). While the *Virgin and Child* from Veveři, followed by further similar images culminating in the Glatz *Madonna* (*c.* 1350; Berlin, Gemäldegal.), provides evidence of the humanization of the image, the pathos of the religious scenes in the Vyšší Brod panels is even more pronounced and is accompanied by an increasing appeal to the senses. At this time the individual portrait became an important subject. The anonymous painter of the votive panel of Jan Očko of Vlasím (before 1371; Prague, N.G., Convent of St George) includes portraits of Očko himself and of Charles IV and his son Wenceslas. Six portraits of Charles IV survive in the wall paintings at Karlštejn (*see* KARLŠTEJN CASTLE, §2).

The main stimulus for this development probably originated in the court painting workshop, the best-known member of which was MASTER THEODORIC (*see* MASTERS, ANONYMOUS, AND MONOGRAMMISTS, §I), the first master of the Prague painters' guild. In 1365–6 he designed and supervised the decoration of the chapel of the Holy Cross at Karlštejn Castle, where there are over 120 wall-mounted panels depicting saints, prophets and angels symbolizing Christ's heavenly army (for illustration *see* GOTHIC, fig. 83). The panels reveal the influence of north Italian painting and are set against a background of hardstones and gilt pastiglia. Similarities of colour and modelling are evident in manuscript illumination. Although the Liber viaticus of the Chancellor JAN OF ŠTREDA (late 1350s; Prague, N. Mus. Lib., MS. XIII. A. 12) is conceived in the spirit of 14th-century Italian, particularly Sienese, painting, the evangeliary of JAN OF OPAVA (completed 1368; Vienna, Österreich. Nbib., Cod. 1182) is evidence of a departure from the central Italian pattern in the direction of historicism and a return to the Gothic style.

The principal representative of this return to the older Gothic tradition is the Master of Třeboň, named after the three surviving panels (*c.* 1380; Prague, N.G., Convent of St George; for illustration *see* PRAGUE, fig. 7) of the altar of the church in the Augustinian monastery at Třeboň. The visionary quality of his work, in accordance with the contemporary wave of religious feeling (*Devotio moderna*), and his use of intense colour and light had a considerable impact on his contemporaries (*see* MASTERS, ANONYMOUS, AND MONOGRAMMISTS, §I: MASTER OF TŘEBOŇ). The resulting *Schöne Stil* was a regional offshoot of the international Late Gothic style that spread throughout Europe *c.* 1400 (*see* GOTHIC, §IV, 5(xi)). Among other examples of the *Schöne Stil* are the splendidly illuminated manuscripts of Wenceslas IV (*reg* 1378–1419; *see* LUXEMBOURG, (4)).

The Hussite Wars (1420–36) put an end to this aristocratic, refined art. Prolonged civil wars, invasions by foreign armies, ideological disputes accompanied by iconoclastic tendencies and general poverty created a situation that was unfavourable to creative activity. Political and economic consolidation did not occur until the late 15th century, when Vladislav II Jagiellon (*reg* 1471–1516) endeavoured to emulate the Luxembourg era by establishing a new court art. The Master of the Litoměřice Altar combined south German and Italian influences into an individual style. His most extensive work, the decoration (*c.* 1506–9) of the chapel of St Wenceslas in St Vitus' Cathedral, Prague, expresses the spirit of the Renaissance, as does the anonymous decoration of Italian-Netherlandish origin in the Smíšek Chapel in Kutná Hora Cathedral (*see* KUTNÁ HORA, §2).

There was, however, a decline in quality in the painting of the following generation. The Late Gothic tradition persisted until elements of Mannerism became established in the late 16th century. Artistic activity was mainly confined to *sgraffito* and painted decorations of the façades and interiors of noblemen's residences, public buildings and burghers' houses, frequently in a rustic reinterpretation of major Italian creative art; the most finished examples

15. Bartholomäus Spranger: *Epitaph of Goldsmith Müller*, 1589 (Prague, National Gallery, Convent of St George)

are in the domains of the lords of Hradec and Rožmberk (Telč, Prachatice, Slavonice) and date to the second half of the 16th century. The wall paintings and *sgraffiti* were usually reproduced from graphic models, mainly of German and Netherlandish origin, as were painted funerary monuments and richly illuminated canticle books. There were few prominent panel painters, apart from Master I. W. (e.g. the panel painting in the chapel of St Wenceslas in St Vitus' Cathedral, Prague), and few outstanding portrait painters apart from the Austrian JAKOB SEISENEGGER and the Spanish artists who painted the PERNŠTEJN family's collection of portraits at Nelahozeves Castle.

This stagnation was interrupted when, at the beginning of the 1580s, Rudolf II, Holy Roman Emperor (*reg* 1576–1612), transferred his court from Vienna to Prague, thus making Prague the imperial capital for the second time (*see* HABSBURG, §I (10)). The most important court artists, BARTHOLOMÄUS SPRANGER, Hans von Aachen, Joseph Heintz (i) (*see* HEINTZ, (2)) and the sculptor Adriaen de Vries, had all lived and worked in Italy. The Antwerp artist Spranger, who introduced to Prague his version of Italian Mannerism in the 1580s, helped to establish the representational style of the period (see fig. 15). Other genres of painting also flourished at the court in Prague, particularly landscape, as in the work of PIETER STEVENS, Roelandt Savery (*see* SAVERY, (2)) and Jan Breughel I, who stayed in Prague in 1604, and manuscript illumination, for example that by JORIS HOEFNAGEL and his son Jacob Hoefnagel (1575–*c.* 1630). In 1597 the Antwerp engraver Aegidius Sadeler II settled in Prague; his graphic reproductions made Bohemian Mannerism known in cultural circles throughout Europe, while as an illustrator he also participated in contemporary book printing. After Rudolf's death in 1612, the Prague band of artists broke up. The collections were gradually transferred to Vienna, and what was left was taken to Sweden in 1648 by the armies of Queen Christina.

2. 1620–*c.* 1900. The drastic Counter-Reformation measures organized from Vienna following the Battle of the White Mountain (1620) led to the mass emigration of the Protestant intelligentsia and to the introduction of Baroque art, primarily a foreign element and an instrument of ideological re-education but gradually assimilated during the period of consolidation after the end of the Thirty Years War. Bohemian artists shared in the development of transalpine Baroque art thanks to KAREL ŠKRÉTA, who returned to Bohemia in 1638 from exile, mainly in Italy. Škréta acquainted Bohemian artists with the revolutionary art of Caravaggio, 17th-century classicism and the renewed influence of 16th-century Venetian art. Škréta produced outstanding portraits, including that of *Ignác Jetřich Vitanovský of Vlčkovice* (1669; see fig. 16) and *Dionysio Miseroni and his Family* (after 1653; Prague, N.G., Convent of St George; for illustration *see* ŠKRÉTA, KAREL). Inspired by Italian and Dutch examples, he combined sober realism with lyrical feeling and inner seriousness, thereby laying the foundation for the development not only of Bohemian Baroque painting but also of Bohemian painting as a whole.

Other artists who contributed to the culminating phase of Bohemian Baroque were MICHAEL WENZEL HALBAX

16. Karel Škréta: *Ignác Jetřich Vitanovský of Vlčkovice*, 1669 (Rychnov nad Kněžnou, Château Art Gallery)

and MICHAEL WILLMANN, whose deeply felt, dramatic compositions, sent to Bohemia from Silesia, were an educative force during the climatic period of the Counter-Reformation. Willmann's stepson and disciple Jan Kryštof Liška (*c.* 1650–1712) was also active during the period of zealous adornment of monastery churches. Liška, who worked in Prague for a number of years, gave Willmann's style a Bohemian flavour and emphasized the dynamism of colour and lyricism of execution, as in *St Francis Receiving the Stigmata* (1700–01) in the church of St Francis of the Knights of the Cross, Prague. Liška also introduced the Italian concept of illusionistic wall painting, as in the *Triumph of the Church and Faith* (*c.* 1702) in the monastery of Plasy. In 1689 the versatile painter JOHANN RUDOLF BYSS arrived in Prague, where his still-lifes inspired the work of his pupil Johann Adalbert Angermeyer (1674–*c.* 1740) and of the latter's pupil Kašpar Jan Hirschely (*c.* 1698–1743).

The greatest painter of the Bohemian Baroque period was PETR BRANDL, who was influenced by the art of Liška. The realism of Škréta, the dynamic elements in the work of Willmann and Liška and the study of Venetian and Dutch techniques in the rebuilt picture gallery at Prague Castle enabled Brandl to work out a unique synthesis of light and shade, colour and movement, as in the altar pictures (1717–19) in St Margaret's, Prague, and the *Adoration of the Magi* (1727) in the church at Smiřice. Brandl's portraits are of outstanding quality and compare well with those of his contemporary JAN KUPECKÝ, who worked abroad for much of his life.

VÁCLAV VAVŘINEC REINER, an admirer of the work of Brandl, worked within the tradition of Bohemian Baroque realism but concentrated on wall painting (in which his achievement was probably inspired by Liška) and landscapes. It was due to him that in the Baroque period Bohemian artists made up for their delay in developing landscape painting. After Reiner's death in 1743, the great period of Bohemian Baroque painting came to an end. Subsequently, the most important work was by painters trained in Vienna, such as Johann Lukas Kracker and Franz Xaver Palko (1727–67), who painted respectively the ceiling (1760–61) and the dome (1752–3) of St Nicholas in the Little Quarter, Prague. With their work, particularly that of Palko, a marked Viennese accent entered Bohemian painting. This development took place during the period of increasing centralization under Maria-Theresa and her son Joseph II (*reg* 1765–90). As an epilogue to the period, the Austrian FRANZ ANTON MAULBERTSCH painted *Allegory of the Sciences* (1794) on the ceiling of the Strahov Library, Prague. The work of Norbert Grund, the main representative of Rococo intimacy in Bohemian painting, also reveals Viennese influence as well as that of northern Italian (particularly Venetian) and French art. Grund's small, sensitive landscapes, his genre paintings and gallant and mythological scenes, aimed mainly at the burgeoning bourgeoisie, were in themselves a reflection of the changing political and intellectual climate. Grund's work was popularized in reproductions by Jan Jiří Balzer (1710–99), a pupil of the copper engraver Michal Jindřich Rentz (1701–58), who was in the service of Count Franz Anton von Sporck at Kuks.

While Viennese influences asserted themselves in Bohemian painting at the end of the Baroque period, painting in Moravia had depended on Austrian influences from the very start of the Baroque. Traditionally open to the cultural trends of the central Danube valley, particularly during the age of the Baroque, the Moravian margravate had closer contacts with Vienna than with Bohemia. Vienna was the centre of attraction for the eminent Moravian clergy and particularly for the nobles, who had closer ties with the imperial court than had the Bohemian nobility. In the period following the Battle of the White Mountain, the Baroque style was introduced into Moravia mainly by foreigners—Italians, Dutchmen and Germans—whose activities were sponsored by Vienna. The most important of these painters was the Italian Carpoforo Tencalla, who was active in Moravia in the 1670s. The first Moravian painter with a pronounced Baroque style was Martin Antonín Lublinský (1636–90), a late pupil of Škréta, who worked in Olomouc from 1664 onwards.

The wall paintings (1695) by JOHANN MICHAEL ROTTMAYR in the Hall of Ancestors at the Castle of Vranov na Dyji heralded the start of an influx by Austrian painters into Moravia. In addition to Franz Gregor Ignaz Eckstein (*d c.* 1736) and Johann Georg Etgens (1693–1757), one of the notable artists of the period was Johann Christoph Handke (1694–1774), whose works include the wall decoration and paintings in the Jesuit church of St Mary of the Snows and at the Hradisko Monastery, both in Olomouc, and at the pilgrimage church of St Mary at Svatý Kopeček, near Olomouc. The Hradisko Monastery and the church at Svatý Kopeček also contain work by the two main representatives of Viennese painting in the High Baroque period, Daniel Gran, who executed the monumental wall paintings (1734–5) in the Assembly Hall of the Moravian Diet building in Brno, and Paul Troger. Native Moravian talent flourished after 1750, when the centre of creative activity shifted to Brno. Josef Stern (1716–75), the most important Moravian painter of the 18th century, and František Vavřinec Korompay (1723–79) both worked in Brno. That city and southern Moravia were also the focus of rich creative activity by the contemporary Austrians Maulbertsch, Martin Johann Schmidt and Kracker, who lived in Moravia for several years. Maulbertsch's most important works in Moravia are the wall paintings (1759) in the feudal hall at Kroměříž Castle. The Late Baroque Viennese appeal to the senses waned in Moravia with the onset of Enlightenment Neoclassicism.

With their strict rationalism, the reforms of Joseph II had a perceptible effect on the arts. Art lost its traditional background of ideas, which had been mainly religious, and its traditional patrons. Moreover, the Czech lands were impoverished by the Napoleonic wars and by the increasingly provincial status of Prague. The role of innovator fell to ANTONÍN MACHEK, Antonín Mánes (see MÁNES, (1)) and FRANTIŠEK TKADLÍK, who combined the Neoclassicism of the French empire with a Romanticism inspired by ideals of regeneration, endeavouring to renew a Bohemian national culture that had been suppressed for two centuries by the Habsburgs. Mánes and Tkadlík worked at the Prague Academy of Fine Arts (founded in 1799), while as a portraitist Machek produced likenesses of the Bohemian patriotic intelligentsia. The urge to achieve a specifically Bohemian style in painting culminated in the work of Mánes's son Josef (see MÁNES, (2)), with his illustrations of Bohemian folk-songs and mythology and his paintings of the Bohemian landscape. Apart from his small-scale paintings, illustrations and drawings, Josef Mánes is known for his decoration of the Prague Old Town Hall clock (1865–6; original in Prague, Mus. City).

Together with his older contemporary JOSEF MATĚJ NAVRÁTIL, Josef Mánes is one of the most important painters in 19th-century Bohemia, but, while Mánes placed emphasis on national themes, Navrátil's work derived from the late Baroque heritage and revivified the colourist tradition of Bohemian painting. In the third quarter of the 19th century the realist tendencies exemplified in Navrátil's still-life studies and genre pictures and in Mánes's portraits intensified, and the depiction of objective reality became the aim. This process is evident mainly in landscape painting, which was represented by numerous specialists ranging from creators of idealized or picturesque scenes to painters of realistic landscapes. Remarkable results were achieved by Adolf Kosárek, who depicted nature from the viewpoint of its basic geological structure, as in *Czech Landscape* (1858; Prague, N.G.). After 1850 a realistic tendency appeared also in history painting, for example in the work of Jaroslav Čermák.

One consistent realist was KAREL PURKYNĚ, who sought to solve the problem of colour and its material structure in order to represent the actual substance and

17. Karel Purkyně: *Still-life with Onions and a Partridge*, 1861 (Prague, National Gallery, Convent of St Agnes)

spatial relations of objects, together with their inner significance (see fig. 17). Like Gustave Courbet, Purkyně studied the Old Masters, particularly those of the Renaissance and the Baroque, and the work of Karel Škréta among Bohemian artists. He studied in Paris, as did his contemporaries SOBĚSLAV PINKAS and Viktor Barvitius and, later, the landscape painter ANTONÍN CHITTUSSI.

The construction of the National Theatre in Prague (1868–81; rebuilt 1881–3) was an event of national significance. It brought together a whole band of artists (the so-called National Theatre Generation), who represented, in their extensive decoration of the theatre building, Czech history, people and landscape. One of the most important artists in this group was MIKOLÁŠ ALEŠ, who set out to emulate Josef Mánes and who painted the cycle *My Country* in lunettes in the foyer of the theatre. Other National Theatre artists included Václav Brožík, Julius Mařák and Vojtěch Hynais. Although a national revival was successfully achieved by the National Theatre Generation, their late Romantic style soon became a retarding factor: it had developed when Impressionism was in decline in Paris and when Post-Impressionism was already crystallizing.

3. AFTER c. 1900. Impressionism was late in reaching Bohemia and Moravia and the adjoining German-speaking countries, and Impressionism of the Monet type had only one notable representative among Bohemian painters, Mařák's pupil ANTONÍN SLAVÍČEK, and then only at one stage of his career. In most of his work Slavíček combined Impressionism with a deeper intellectual content, as in the landscapes from Kamenicky and *St Vitus' Cathedral* (1908–9; Prague, N.G.). Other painters of Slavíček's

generation, such as František Kaván (1866–1941) and the enterprising MILOŠ JIRÁNEK, who was an active organizer and publicist, came close to Impressionism, but in the work of ANTONÍN HUDEČEK, for example, the Impressionist technique is subordinated to an expressive stylization. Stylized Impressionistic colouring is evident in paintings of rural scenes by Joža Úprka (1861–1940), whose work inaugurated the integration of Moravia into the artistic development of the Czech lands after a long period of stagnation. The culturally versatile Ludvík Kuba produced a special modulation in Impressionism with his striking colouring. MAX ŠVABINSKÝ combined the sensual element of Impressionism with Symbolist content. He also produced a large and magnificent series of drawings of personalities in Bohemian public life and was the inspiration for modern Bohemian graphic art.

The decisive stimulus towards the rejection of the hegemony of the senses in favour of a philosophical approach was provided by the Edvard Munch exhibition arranged by the Mánes Union of Artists in Prague in 1905. The critic František Xaver Šalda (1867–1937) elucidated the ideas and topicality of Munch, while the first Bohemian painter to respond to Munch's example was JAN PREISLER, who had in his earlier work rejected one-sided Impressionism and created works of lyrical symbolism.

The artistic revolution that led to modern art was effected by artists who in 1906 formed the Eight (*see* EIGHT, THE (ii)), particularly EMIL FILLA, BOHUMIL KUBIŠTA, ANTONÍN PROCHÁZKA and OTOKAR KUBÍN. Some subsequently formed the GROUP OF PLASTIC ARTISTS. In 1911 the Association of the Stiff-necked (Tvrdošíjní skupina) was founded by JOSEF ČAPEK, JAN ZRZAVÝ, VÁCLAV ŠPÁLA and Rudolf Kremlička among others. Most of these artists passed through Expressionism, Fauvism and Cubism. A significant role was played not only by Šalda but also by the art critic VINCENC KRAMÁŘ, author of one of the first monographs on Cubism (1921) and collector of early works by Picasso. Owing to Kramář and the painters and theorists Filla and Kubišta, Prague became an important European centre of Cubism; moreover, the style continued to develop in the Czech lands until the 1930s in the work of, for example, Alfred Justitz (1879–1934) and Jaroslav Král (1883–1942). While Filla followed the transformations of Cubism in the work of Picasso, always with a clear individual accent, Kubišta, Procházka and Špála helped to create a variant of the Parisian trends (*see* CZECH CUBISM). Subsequently, in his luminous landscapes Špála approached Fauvism, as did Jindřich Prucha (1886–1914). FRANTIŠEK KUPKA, one of the pioneers of abstract painting in Europe, lived in Paris but maintained close contacts with his homeland, while at about the same time ALPHONSE MUCHA played an important part in the creation of Art Nouveau in Paris. Jan Zrzavý became interested in the deeper layers of the human psyche, the source of Surrealism.

Czech Surrealism derived largely from the so-called poeticism that formed part of the programme of Devětsil, founded by Karel Teige, which united the Czech avant-garde in the 1920s. The most notable Czech Surrealists were Jindřich Štyrský, TOYEN (Marie Čermínová) and František Janoušek. Several painters of imaginative vein occupied a position close to Surrealism, for example

FRANTIŠEK MUZIKA, Zdeněk Rykr (1900–40) and JOSEF ŠÍMA (see fig. 18), who lived in Paris from the 1920s and was one of the leading representatives of the group Le Grand Jeu. Czech poeticism was also the starting point of the work of the painter and graphic artist František Tichý (1896–1961). The trend towards a radically modern style also attracted František Foltýn (1891–1976), who *c.* 1930 became active in the Paris groups Cercle et Carré and Abstraction–Création. After World War I, social themes came to the forefront in the new Czechoslovak Republic as in the rest of Europe, and they are reflected in the work of Karel Holan (1893–1953), Miroslav Holý (1897–1974) and Pravoslav Kotík (1889–1970). A new mysticism of soil and homeland appeared, particularly in the work of the members of the ARTISTIC FORUM, Karel Boháček (1886–1928), VÁCLAV RABAS, Vlastimil Rada (1895–1962) and Vojtěch Sedláček (1892–1973). The remarkable Jan Trampota (1889–1942) was also close to this trend. Anti-Fascist ideas entered into the work of the Surrealists and other artists, as in Šíma's evocations of the Spanish Civil War and the paintings of Alois Wachsmann, Čapek, Filla, Král and Vladimír Sychra (1903–63).

The development of Czech graphic art, stimulated by Max Švabinský, was strengthened by the foundation of the Hollar Association (1917) and proceeded alongside the revival of Czech book illustration, in the work of Zdeňka Braunerová (1858–1934), František Kobliha (1877–1962), VOJTĚCH PREISSIG and JOSEF VÁCHAL. Several illustrators brought the heritage of Josef Mánes and Aleš up to date, including Karel Svolinský (1896–1986), Josef Lada (1887–1957), Antonín Strnadel (1910–75) and Jiří Trnka (1912–69), who as early as the 1940s set new

18. Josef Šíma: *Despair of Orpheus*, 1943 (Prague, National Gallery)

objectives, more particularly in the illustration of children's books.

A new generation of humanist, socially conscious and Surrealist artists sprang up before World War II and during the period of Nazi occupation, among them Václav Hejna, František Jiroudek, Josef Liesler, Arnošt Padrlík and Zdeněk Seydl; František Gross, František Hudeček and Kamil Lhoták (*b* 1912); and Bohdan Lacina, Václav Tikal and Josef Istler. They were associated with the Seven in October Group, the RA Group and Group 42 respectively (the latter being joined subsequently by Bohumír Matal). They continued working after 1945, although the Communist putsch of February 1948 introduced the constraints of Socialist Realism, most evident in monumental works of art and those from the studios of established artists, including Sychra's decoration of the Prague Carolinum (1951).

A turning-point was marked by the retrospective exhibition of modern Czech art held at Brno in 1957 and by the exhibition of young creative artists held by way of manifesto at Brno in 1958. The design of the Czechoslovak pavilion at the Exposition Universelle et Internationale in Brussels in 1958 signalled a return to the context of modern European art. In the following period Czech art developed on a richly expressive scale. Active representatives of the older generation, particularly landscape painters, included Bohumír Dvorský (1902–76) and Jaroslav Grus (1891–1983). Younger painters, who banded together at the end of the 1950s, were affected by the worldwide wave of non-representational art.

The Expressionist tendencies of the Eight and the Group of Plastic Artists were influential, as were the colour techniques practised in the 1940s by JAN BAUCH, which evoked the heritage of the Baroque. Many of the younger artists tended to express themselves in colourful poetic metaphors derived from the work of Zrzavý and Šíma. Other noteworthy artists include Václav Boštík (*b* 1913), JIŘÍ KOLÁŘ, Mikoláš Medek (1926–69), Jiří John, Vladimír Boudník (*d* 1968), Zdeněk Sýkora (*b* 1920) and Jiří Balcar (1929–68). Boštík produced lyrical abstract work, and Kolář was a visual poet. Medek was a representative of structural painting; John created imaginative paintings of intellectual depth; Boudník discovered so-called active and structural graphics, one of the most original phenomena of Czech abstract art; Sýkora was an adherent of geometrical abstract art; and the versatile Balcar was an early Post-modernist.

BIBLIOGRAPHY

ROMANESQUE AND GOTHIC

A. Matějček: *Česká malba gotická: Deskové malířství, 1350–1450* [Czech Gothic painting: panel painting, 1350–1450] (Prague, 1938)

J. Pešina: *Česka malba pozdní gotiky a renesance: Deskové malířství, 1450–1550* [Czech Late Gothic and Renaissance painting: panel painting, 1450–1550] (Prague, 1950; rev. 2/1958; Eng., Fr. and Ger. trans.)

J. Mašín: *Románská nástěnná malba v Čechách a na Moravě* [Romanesque wall paintings in Bohemia and Moravia] (Prague, 1954)

J. Pešina: *Gotická nástěnná malba v zemích českých, 1300–1350* [Gothic wall paintings in the Czech lands, 1300–1350] (Prague, 1958)

J. Krása: *Il gotico internazionale in Boemia* (Milan, 1960)

V. Dvořáková and others: *Gothic Mural Painting in Bohemia and Moravia, 1300–1378* (London, 1964)

De Boheemse Primitieven: Gotische Kunst in Tsjechoslowakije, 1350–1420 (exh. cat., Rotterdam, Mus. Boymans–van Beuningen, 1966)

A. Kutal: *České gotické umění* [Bohemian Gothic art] (Prague, 1972); Eng. trans. as *Gothic Art in Bohemia and Moravia* (London, 1972)

J. Pešina: *Česká gotiká desková malba* [Czech Gothic panel painting] (Prague, 1976)

J. Homolka and others: *Pozdněgotické umění v Čechách, 1471–1526* [Late Gothic art in Bohemia, 1471–1526] (Prague, 1978)

Kunst der Gotik aus Böhmen (exh. cat., Cologne, Schnütgen-Mus., 1985)

RENAISSANCE AND BAROQUE

K. Chytil: *Die Kunst in Prag zur Zeit Rudolf II* (Prague, 1904)

O. J. Blažíček: *Barockkunst in Böhmen* (Prague, 1967; Eng. trans., London, 1968)

J. Neumann: *Český barok* [The Baroque in Bohemia] (Prague, 1974)

Kunst des Barock in Böhmen (exh. cat., Essen, Villa Hügel, 1977)

P. Preiss: *Die Barockzeichnung: Meisterwerke des böhmischen Barocks* (Prague, 1979)

T. Da Costa Kaufmann: *L'Ecole de Prague: La Peinture à la cour de Rodolphe II* (Paris, 1985; rev. Eng. edn, Chicago and London, 1988)

E. Fučíková: *Die rudolphinische Zeichnung* (Prague, 1986)

P. Preiss: *Italští umělci v Praze: Renesance, manýrismus a barok* [Italian artists in Prague: Renaissance, Mannerism and Baroque] (Prague, 1986)

Prag in 1600: Kunst und Kultur am Hofe Rudolfs II, 2 vols (exh. cat., Vienna, Ksthist. Mus., 1988)

19TH AND 20TH CENTURIES

V. Kramář: *Kubismus* [Cubism] (Prague, 1921)

J. Pešina: *Česká moderní grafika* [Czech modern graphic art] (Prague, 1940)

V. Volavka: *Česká kresba 19. století* [Czech drawing in the 19th century] (Prague, 1949)

A. Matějček: *Národní divadlo a jeho výtvarníci* [The National Theatre and its artists] (Prague, 1954)

V. Novotný: *Generace Národního divadla* [The National Theatre generation] (Prague, 1954)

J. Neumann: *Czech Classic Painting of the XIXth Century* (Prague, 1955)

V. Novotný: *České malířství konce XIX a začátku XX století* [Czech painting of the late 19th century and early 20th] (Prague, 1957)

Zakladatelé moderního českého umění [Founders of modern Czech art] (exh. cat., Brno, 1957)

Moderní české malířství: Leta dvacátá [Modern Czech painting: the Twenties] (exh. cat., Brno, 1959)

L. Hlaváček: *Současná česká grafika* [Contemporary Czech graphic art] (Prague, 1964)

P. Wittlich: *Česká secese* [The Czech Secession] (Prague, 1982)

Současné české a slovenské umění [Contemporary Czech and Slovak art] (Prague and Bratislava, 1983)

T. Vlček: *Praha 1900: Studie k dějinám kultury a umění Prahy v letech, 1890–1906* [Prague 1900: studies on the history of culture and art in Prague, 1890–1906] (Prague, 1986)

IVO KRSEK

V. Interior decoration and furniture.

1. 13th-16th centuries. 2. 17th century. 3. 18th century. 4. 19th century. 5. 20th century.

1. 13TH–16TH CENTURIES. The oldest surviving pieces of furniture are chests of primitive construction consisting of iron-bound wooden planks and dating from the 13th century (e.g. Prague, St Peter). Armoires were constructed in a similar manner (e.g. Prague, Our Lady before Týn). The work of carpenters and locksmiths gradually became more sophisticated, as demonstrated by chests from Klatovy (Prague, Mus. Dec. A.). The woodworking trades benefited from the introduction of the water saw around 1322. Furniture of framed-panel construction was made, often decorated with Gothic arches (e.g. chests; Prague, Mus. Dec. A.; Brno, Morav. Gal.). Painted infill panels were sometimes used, only the frames of which were carved (e.g. Kašperk's chest from Kaněk, with floral-painted panels, 15th century; Prague, N. Mus.).

The first well-known Czech architect to supervise the design of furniture was Peter Parler. In 1386 he designed richly carved choir-stalls (destr.) for St Vitus' Cathedral,

Prague, which inspired other ecclesiastical furniture. Parler's royal workshop also carved a picture frame decorated with figures (before 1396; Prague, N.G., Convent of St George; originally intended for the St Vitus Madonna in St Vitus' Cathedral, Prague). In the 14th century much furniture was made in monastery workshops, but from the 15th century it was produced mainly by tradesmen organized in guilds. The names of craftsmen were rarely recorded, except in connection with outstanding works. In Kutná Hora, for example, Jiří Lorecký of Lkouš and Jakub Nymburský are known to have worked on the altars, armoires and choir-stalls, which are richly decorated with relief carvings (1484; Kutná Hora, Cathedral of St Barbara and Church of St James). A decorative technique characteristic of the provinces involved creating incised or engraved designs on flat softwood surfaces in a manner akin to Tyrolean work. This treatment was widely used on the fronts of chests, armoires, doors, choir-stalls and settles. Botanical motifs and scenes derived from contemporary paintings were popular (e.g. armoire, 1567; Prague, Mus. Dec. A.).

From the end of the 15th century there is evidence for the redecorating and equipping of homes by the aristocracy and wealthy middle-class citizens. Contemporary inventories reveal much about how furniture and accessories were arranged in individual rooms. Many houses had painted joist ceilings, and doors were decorated with carving or intarsia work in the same manner as the doors of churches, chapels, town halls and castles. Households apparently possessed a greater number of tables, stools and other seat furniture, often upholstered in leather. Chess-boards and games-tables were common, and such specialist furniture as the *lavabo* (a washbasin built into a cupboard), book cupboards and armoires for domestic use appeared. Chests and small trunks still abounded for general storage. The house (1564; destr. 1895) of the publisher Jiří Melantrich of Aventinum in Kunešova Street, Prague, was furnished in this manner.

From the mid-16th century the technique of intarsia inlay was widely used in Bohemia, probably brought via Germany by foreign craftsmen. Documentary sources reveal that artists from Germany, Italy and Switzerland worked alongside local masters for such aristocratic patrons as Florián Griesbeck von Griesbach, Peter Vok and others. Noblemen with a taste for luxury sometimes established their own workshops. The ROŽMBERK family, for example, employed their own specialist craftsmen in the Rožmberk Palace at Hradčany in Prague. In Bohemia furniture inlaid with architectural perspectives, often derived from the designs of Hans Vredeman de Vries (*Variae architecturae formae*, 1560), was very popular. Vredeman de Vries inspired a number of intarsia-decorated doors (1564; Nelahozeves Castle), chests (*c.* 1560; Prague, Mus. Dec. A.) and cupboards and in 1590 was appointed court artist to Rudolf II. The use of floral intarsia, featuring vases, arabesques, leafage and geometric patterns, was widespread; examples include a chest (*c.* 1560–70; Stará Boleslav, St Wenceslas), pews (1546; Prague, St Vitus' Cathedral) and numerous armoires. An exceptional, strongly architectonic cupboard (*c.* 1530; Jindřichův Hradec, Castle) belongs to the wood-carving tradition of Renaissance furniture; it has the family emblem of Adam

of Hradec and was influenced by examples from Augsburg. A highly unusual set of built-in painted library cupboards (*in situ*) was constructed at the castle at Březnice for Kateřina of Lokšany in 1588.

The high technical finish of furniture is well illustrated by several small guild treasure chests enriched with intarsia work and carved decoration (e.g. the chest of the carpenters' guild, 1594–5; Prague, Mus. City). Their fine execution is reminiscent of goldsmiths' work, and at this time Bohemian luxury furniture was sometimes set with gemstones. In 1577 Zachariáš of Hradec ordered for his castle in Telč a silver-gilt armchair and table (destr.), richly decorated with figural ornament and jewels, for which a contemporary sketch with exact instructions survives (Třeboň, State Archvs). Ladislav Velen from Žerotín also had valuable gold-mounted furniture, complemented by lavish upholstery, Turkish and Persian carpets and Italian tapestries at his castle in Moravská Třebová; from the original ensemble only the sideboard survives at the castle in Velké Losiny. Hradčany Castle in Prague contains a repertory of more routine pieces, apparently made for its domestic offices in the second half of the 16th century.

2. 17TH CENTURY. An inventory (1607–11) of the furniture amassed by Rudolf II includes details of the materials, country of origin and value of each object. The largest holdings consisted of tables and cabinets, and many pieces were made in the Prague court workshop, where masters from all over Europe were employed. These distinguished craftsmen included members of the Castrucci family from Florence, who were highly specialized as hardstone-cutters; they worked on a number of commissions for Florentine mosaic panels (*see* §IX, 2 below). Cabinets with rare intaglio decoration were ordered by many aristocrats, especially the Lobkovic and Nostic families (examples in Prague, Mus. Dec. A.). A table from the Nostic collection (Prague, Mus. Dec. A.) made of ebony embellished with ivory has a pietra dura top made in the court workshop, although a signature on the frame suggests that the support was made in Augsburg. Court officials also purchased valuable furniture; for example, Filip Lang commissioned the court artist Nicholas Pfaff (*fl* 1602–11) to make a cabinet. Luxury furniture was also available in shops; according to archives, the Prague art dealer Petr Alteršperger (*fl* after 1600) had two shops in the Vladislav Hall of Hradčany Castle, Prague, where he sold common merchandise as well as Regensburg painted chests (see fig. 19), backgammon sets, table-tops with ivory intaglios, marble table-tops, gilt chests, writing-desks of ebony etc.

The general furniture trade in the first half of the 17th century could not match the workmanship associated with the court, even though furniture-makers closely adhered to the established traditions in design, craftsmanship, decorative techniques and materials. When, after the death of Rudolf II in 1612, Emperor Matthias and his entourage moved to Vienna, the court artisans continued to make magnificent cabinets, tables and coffers for the aristocracy. Cabinets, especially those made in the second half of the 17th century, became heavier and more ostentatious. There was a marked increase in the use of such architectural features as pilasters and columns, often with chiselled

19. Carved and painted chest with intarsia decoration, walnut, maple and ash, 720×600×510 mm, Prague, 1612 (Prague, Museum of Decorative Arts)

details. Pietra dura or marble imitating ruins was used; at other times the sides were adorned with enamelled medallions (examples in Prague, Mus. Dec. A.; České Budějovice, Mus. S. Bohemia). Cabinetmakers who were members of the municipal guilds gained commissions to furnish aristocratic mansions and received orders from the Church. In working on such projects they frequently collaborated with prominent architects, sculptors and painters, who conceived the interiors in their entirety and hence were also responsible for the woodwork. For example, four types of doors, including panels and moulding, were made by Jan Pavel Schmid (fl 1667–77), a joiner in Kosmonosy, according to a design by Francesco Caratti, for the Černín Palace, Prague. The Premonstratensian monastery of Strahov, Prague, placed an order with the court joiner Kašpar Bechtler. The sculptor and woodcarver Ernst Heidelberger worked on assignments for the Wallenstein (Valdštejn) Palace, Prague, including a commission for doors with carvings of angels, lions' heads and mascarons. There was not much movable furniture here: the inventory of 1634 refers only to a large table covered with expensive carpets, long benches and seats, fourposter beds and an escritoire made of ebony inlaid with ivory. Of the original furnishings only a few pieces survive: a miniature oak chest (*in situ*), a jewellery box, a metal-plated travelling chest (*in situ*) and a pew in the chapel. The doors to the Colloredo Palace, Prague, were refurbished according to designs (1599) by the court artist Gabriel Krammer, and the joiner Samuel Kraus (fl second half of 17th century) made four doors with Auricular ornament for the Lobkovic Palace (1651–68) at Prague Castle.

During the Counter-Reformation the decoration of church interiors was considered one of the most important tasks. Commissions were shared by master woodworkers, carvers and turners in collaboration with sculptors and those who executed the ornament and gilding. The numerous carpenters named in 17th-century records are proof of the energy expended in providing new credences,

vestry furnishings, seating, pulpits, confessionals and picture frames in both large town churches and smaller chapels. Kašpar Bechtler (fl 1605–30) carved door reliefs (Prague, St Vitus' Cathedral) of historic scenes, in which he tried to create the impact of a painting. One set depicts the devastation of St Vitus' Cathedral in 1619 and the escape of Frederick II, King of Prussia, from Prague in 1620. Bechtler made another three doors (1629–30; Prague, St Vitus' Cathedral) with figures of Czech patron saints. Similar historic scenes are found in the marquetry that emerged from the workshops in Cheb during the Thirty Years War and continued in production until the mid-18th century. A typical feature of this kind of work is the relief intaglios of different, mostly native coloured woods, frequently embellished with root-wood and stained in various shades. Inlays were applied to the fronts of drawers and the doors of cabinets, backgammon sets and caskets and sometimes to wardrobes and writing-desks. The subjects were mostly copied from well-known prints by Dutch, French and German artists. The output from Cheb was so highly regarded that it found its way to the emperor's court, to aristocratic collections and sometimes also to the Church; as items were usually made to order, the ornamentation is frequently connected with a particular personality. The extensive Eck family is generally recognized as the founder of this craft. The most prominent member of the family was Adam Eck (*d* 1664), whose customers included Leopold William of Habsburg and members of the Bohemian, German and Swedish aristocracy. He signed some of his work (e.g panels, Berlin, Schloss Köpenick; music box, Vienna, Österreich. Mus. Angewandte Kst), and some wood-carvings are also attributed to him (e.g. cabinet with hunting scenes; Prague, Mus. Dec. A.).

Cabinets were popular with the aristocracy, whereas in middle-class houses cupboards were the most typical item. Cupboards with Mannerist ornament still prevailed after 1620, usually supplemented with figure-carvings. Architecturally conceived cupboards were produced at the same time, fashioned like the façades of late Renaissance houses and decorated with flat pilasters and aediculae. Only in the second half of the 17th century did they adapt to the tendencies of Baroque architecture. Spiral pilasters and columns, now set on pedestals, took on a prominent role; there were more marked contrasts between the panels and their frames. Cupboards began to look less like façades and displayed similarities to altar designs. In the middle of the century flamework mouldings were often used on cupboard panel borders, cabinets and frames. From *c.* 1650 to 1690 the Auricular style predominated (e.g. the vestry in St Thomas, Prague). From the 1670s floral festoons with veils were carved on cupboards (e.g. Prague, St Joseph) and in particular on church pews. When a huge picture frame (1696), ordered from the Dresden sculptor Johann Georg Heerman (*c.* 1650–1710) for St Wenceslas (destr.), Prague, was brought to Prague, it was received with extreme disappointment: its acanthus tendrils were considered too modern and unusual. There is evidence, however, that acanthus ornamentation was soon adopted and applied to furniture, church pews and tables (e.g. ecclesiastical throne of the Broumov Abbot Tomáš Sartorius, 1682; Prague, Mus. Dec. A.). Wood-carvers were so adept at this style that it soon became a tectonic element of furniture (e.g. console table and gilt ecclesiastical throne, late 17th century; Prague, Mus. Dec. A.). The Prague court carpenter, wood-carver and scholar MAREK NONNEN-MACHER, who established a large workshop in Prague's Little Quarter, created a synthesis of acanthus ornamentation in his late works. In 1710 he published *Der architektonische Tischler oder Pragerisches Säulenbuch*, a collection of models for furniture with acanthus decoration. Nonnenmacher ranks among the foremost woodwork craftsmen at the end of the 17th century in Bohemia and Moravia, and his work brought the early Baroque epoch to a climax.

3. 18TH CENTURY. During the Counter-Reformation woodwork of a distinctive Czech character began to flourish. Aside from workshops established by aristocratic patrons or monasteries, after 1710 there were also municipal furniture workshops that carried out simple tasks as well as undertaking complicated assignments according to sketches made by the craftsmen themselves or by an architect or sculptor. Many examples bear this out, notably the drawings of Jan Devoty (*fl c.* 1723) and Karel Antonín Devoty (1738–1817), who made a vital contribution to carpentry and wood-carving in eastern Bohemia. Apart from orders for ecclesiastical furniture, some commissions for secular furnishings (chimneys, stoves, beds, chairs, armchairs and mirrors) survive, for example for the Archbishop's Palace (1733) in Prague and from the interior of the Černín Palace, Prague, which was built according to designs of the architect František Maximilián Kaňka. From 1707 Kaňka designed the chambers, library and the door of the main hall of Wallenstein Palace in Prague. He employed prominent artists for certain assignments, such as the carving of four angels executed by the sculptor Matyáš Bernard Braun on the frame of a mirror in the palace. The luxurious furniture for the Černín Palace was valued at 27,761 guilders in 1734, but almost none of it survives.

Monasteries in particular were furnished comprehensively. The work was done in the workshops of the towns in vassalage to the Church or in the workshops actually owned by the monasteries; in the event of an unusually ambitious project the monasteries would engage a renowned artist. The Benedictine monasteries at the Břevnov, Prague, and in Broumov, north-eastern Bohemia, employed the architects Christoph Dientzenhofer and Kilian Ignaz Dientzenhofer, who were responsible both for the exteriors and the interior designs. They, in turn, were assisted by distinguished sculptors and woodworkers. Furniture made from 1709 to 1722, when Christoph Dientzenhofer was in charge, bears the hallmark of the sober forms of the early Baroque style. The Prague master craftsman Kristián Kovář (*d* 1735) and joiners from the country towns worked on the furnishings, supplying window frames and banisters, wall-panelling, cupboards, chests, chairs, tables etc for the monastery at the Břevnov, Prague. Josef Ignác Dobner (1678–1737), a member of a prominent Prague carpenter's family, collaborated with the sculptor Matyáš Václav Jäckel in creating ecclesiastical furniture (e.g. pulpit, 1719; confessional and abbot's chair, 1721; all Prague, Břevnov Monastery). These artists also

had a share in furnishing the monastery church in Broumov, which in 1721–2 was endowed with a new high altar

20. Long-case clock by Josef Winterhalder (i), carved and gilded walnut with intarsia decoration, h. 2.7 m, from Svatý Kopeček, near Olomouc, first half of 18th century (Prague, Museum of Decorative Arts)

and a vestry cupboard with sculpted ornamentation attributed to the sculptor Karl Josef Hiernle. Later work on the interiors at both Břevnov and Broumov was supervised by Kilian Ignaz Dientzenhofer; his designs expressed the culmination of the high Baroque style. He contracted most of the artisan work, in particular the woodwork and upholstery. The most demanding tasks were executed by Hiernle and Johann Anton Quittainer (1709–65), and later by Richard Prachner (*fl* 1730–60) in collaboration with the carpenter Johannes Sichtmüller (*d* 1746). Between 1741 and 1757 they worked on a new oratory, an altar and inlaid stalls for the chapter hall and choir of the church, a credence table for the second sacristy, the lectern and other carved furniture (all *in situ*).

Giovanni Santini (1677–1723) worked on commissions for the Cistercian monastery in Plasy. It was here that the small altar (Prague, Mus. Dec. A.) for Abbot Eugen Tyttl was made, a triumph of harmony between the architect's design and the carpenter's execution. Some of the furnishings at the Cistercian monastery in Vyšší Brod were probably made by the carpenter Josef Raffer (*fl* first half of 18th century); among the exceptional items are the polychrome and gilt console tables, armchairs, chairs and frames adorned with shells dating from 1755.

The Premonstratensian monasteries in Prague and Doksany and at the Svatý Kopeček, near Olomouc, possessed highly ostentatious furniture. This was the output of the monastery workshops assisted by Quittainer, František Preiss, Josef Winterhalder (i) and others, who contributed items of exceptional value (e.g. long-case clock by Winterhalder from Svatý Kopeček; Prague, Mus. Dec. A.; see fig. 20).

The Augustinian Order also had workshops, in Tábor and Brno, where furnishings were made for churches and monasteries and sometimes for the nobility (e.g. for Lnáře Castle). The Jesuits had a style of their own, produced by lay monks who had served apprenticeships to become skilled carpenters and wood-carvers. These workshops were engaged not only in furnishing churches, colleges and libraries but also in producing utilitarian items. They derived inspiration from the southern European Baroque style, creating spectacular interiors (e.g. by Ondřej Röpfel (*fl c.* 1707–24) in Bohosudov, nr Teplice, after 1704; by Martin Koller (*fl c.* 1720 at the Church of St Ignatius in Klatovy, 1720; and a pharmacy by Jan Geschwent (*fl c.* 1730–34) at the church of St Ignatius in Klatovy, which survives). Among the best-preserved monastery interiors are libraries: that of the Jesuit College in Prague (1722–7), which has hitherto been attributed to Kaňka, bears all the characteristics of the Jesuit workshop, although there is also a link with Nonnenmacher's designs of 1710. The library of the monastery of the Carthusians in Valdice, dating from the second quarter of the 18th century, with all its polychrome and gilt ornamentation is typical of Baroque extravagance, as are the library cupboards in the Plasy monastery. Library cupboards (1736–44) from the Piarist colleges in Benešov made by the Tyrolean cabinet-maker Josef Walter (*fl* 1730–40) now furnish the library of the Decorative Arts Museum in Prague. Purpose-built liturgical furniture from the 18th century indicates the technical excellence of the craftsmen and an ability to harmonize their work with a specific architectural setting.

The escritoire is among the most typical pieces of secular furniture in the 18th century. Excellent examples were made in Dobner's workshops in Prague in collaboration with Kilian Ignaz Dientzenhofer (e.g. for the monastery at Břevnov, Prague; Prague, Mus. Dec. A.). They are embellished with intaglios (*c.* 1720–40 with a band; *c.* 1740 with bars and rocaille; *c.* 1745 with combs, flames, canopies). At times the ornament was burnt into the wood and gilt carvings were often added, but sculpted ornamentation was rare. Chests-of-drawers were in common use. The fronts were usually serpentine, and they sometimes had C- and S-scroll carvings. Cupboards and wardrobes, modelled on large early Baroque German examples, became an increasingly important feature in middle-class homes. Occasionally they were designed by sculptors or architects (e.g. by Michael Ignác Platzer (1757–1826); Prague, Mus. Dec. A.; see fig. 21), or they were made in famous workshops. In some cases prominence was given to the veneered surface, or they were merely sponge-painted. Chairs in the early 18th century still had high backs and elaborately styled arms. When the early Rococo style emerged in the second quarter of the 18th century the size of the furniture was reduced, and chairs made according to French models appeared (e.g. Prague, Mus. Dec. A.).

At the beginning of the 18th century tables were of austere, rectangular design, often with turned legs and inlaid or marble tops. In the second quarter of the century tables became smaller, the legs were usually carved, and

21. Wardrobe designed by Michael Ignác Platzer, carved walnut with intarsia decoration, 2.41×1.30×0.54 m, Bohemia, *c.* 1780 (Prague, Museum of Decorative Arts)

the tops were ornamented with floral intaglio images. In the third quarter of the century furniture was frequently decorated with chess-board inlays (Prague, Mus. Dec. A.). Console tables, usually designed for the place where they would stand, were frequently decorated with wave carvings, rocailles, lattice bars etc; asymmetric designs became popular *c.* 1770. Many table-tops were made of either true or artificial marble by Jan Vilém Hennevogel (*d* 1754), who was responsible for the ornamentation of many churches in Bohemia (table-top dated 1765; Prague, Mus. Dec. A.). Among the finest items were small caskets, frames and mirrors, tables and stands, mostly gilt, which served as accessories enhancing the interiors of mansions. Besides these exceptional objects, utility furniture for everyday needs, made mostly of walnut and oak, was produced in plainer forms and shapes, with simpler carvings. This type persisted in provincial workshops until the 19th century.

The development of Neo-classicism coincided with the abolition of serfdom in 1781, which enabled a gradual movement of craftsmen from the country to Prague. Other measures taken by Emperor Joseph II (*reg* 1780–90), such as the dissolution of almost a third of the monasteries, resulted in a reduction of the large colony of carpenters in Prague. These restrictions, however, did not affect the monasteries that were involved in educational or scholarly activities; these were refurbished, and this programme provided furniture-makers with a welcome opportunity to experiment with the new Neo-classical repertory of designs. Craftsmen initially grafted such classical details as festoons and vases on to the structure of Rococo furniture. Numerous examples of this hybrid style are found in ecclesiastical furniture in Prague, Jindřichův Hradec and elsewhere. The new aesthetic ideals were more apparent in large libraries and churches (e.g. the Philosophical Hall of the Premonstratensians at the monastery of Strahov in Prague, 1782–4; the Benedictine library in Broumov, dated 1792; the palace theatre in Litomyšl, 1796–7). Later there appeared a number of Neo-classical pulpits, confessionals, pews and frames. Similar tendencies were apparent in secular furniture. Most of the furniture is anonymous; only rarely has it been possible to identify the craftsman responsible for creating a particular item, as in the case of Jan Wrschüzky (*fl* late 18th century) from Český Brod, who in 1794 carved the frame for a picture of *Joseph II*, and Anton Zelinger (*fl* late 18th century) from Kostelec nad Orlicí, who signed a writing-desk.

Mansions were more likely to be equipped with carved polychrome and gilt furniture than to be decorated in the Neo-classical taste. The wealth of colour and seductive lines of the Rococo style remained generally popular long after the doctrines of Neo-classicism had been accepted in intellectual circles. The writing-desk, which from the second half of the 18th century acquired a cylindrical lid (either a rolltop or a curved cover), a writing-board that slid out and often secret drawers with complicated mechanisms, was in great demand. The shape and ornamentation of desks were often influenced by English models. The transition from the Rococo to the Empire style is demonstrated by the achievements of the Platzer family, whose trade was in carving frames and in making cabinets

for clocks and furniture decorated with miniature sculptures. The decorative repertory seen in their detailed, almost life-size drawings of patterns for legs of armchairs and tables in the form of lions' claws and deer's legs points to the early 19th century and the onset of the Empire style.

4. 19TH CENTURY. Functional furniture in the 19th century continued to be made in the Neo-classical style. Parade furniture (couches, armchairs, tables) was, however, influenced by the Empire style, being lavishly ornamented with carved swans, figures, dolphins etc. Furniture was made predominantly from such dark polished woods as mahogany or rose-wood, enriched with gilt carving or, less frequently, with brass mounts. Typical examples of Empire furnishing schemes are found at the house of Kačina, near Kutná Hora, where the principal interiors—the reception rooms and the library (*in situ*)—are especially grand, relating more to the style of Karl Friedrich Schinkel than to Czech fashions; however, the bedrooms and guest rooms have much simpler and more functional furniture. Ecclesiastical woodwork, often designed by leading architects, also reflected the Empire style.

The Biedermeier style spanned the years from *c.* 1815 to 1840. Showy French Empire designs were rejected in favour of bourgeois culture as a source of inspiration, and native woods decorated with simple ebony inlay were favoured. Also after 1815 furniture was produced for the first time that was not commissioned for a particular setting. It could be placed either in the salons of the aristocracy or in the rented apartments of the middle class, where rooms were not differentiated according to function; living-rooms were used for sleeping and eating, and thus there was a concomitant demand for practical and solid furniture. Printed designs for furniture and interiors largely replaced the direct involvement of architects and artists and made it possible for the same furniture to be ordered for middle-class as well as for aristocratic homes. Alongside the more humble and simple pieces of Biedermeier furniture are ones richly styled to suit a customer's special requirements.

In Prague between 1834 and 1841 cabinetmakers were licensed to make quantities of furniture to be sold as stock. The most popular item was the glass display cabinet, introduced in the first decade of the 19th century. The traditional repertory of furniture was extended to include sewing- and toilet-tables, tea-tables, gaming-tables, jardinières, consoles, bedside-tables, folding tables and such small articles as decorative boxes, pipe racks, spittoons and waste-paper receptacles. Architecturally influenced furniture was also made: from the 1820s massive pieces set on plinths appeared, with columns, pilasters, cornices etc. Much furniture had an almost sculptural form: showcases were designed in the shape of a lyre, bureaux in the form of vases and sewing-tables like globes; chairs had backs in the shape of shovels, fans and lyres; and tables rested on urn-shaped supports (examples in Prague, Mus. Dec. A.). Such decorative conceits were inspired by the work of Josef Ulrich Danhauser in Vienna and by the designs of Thomas Sheraton, which were available in a German edition.

The Rococo Revival began in the late 1830s. Salons were furnished with comfortable suites of seat furniture, supplemented by tables and eliptical desks. The prominent Czech painters JOSEF NAVRÁTIL and Josef Mánes (*see* MÁNES, (2)) contributed to the design of furniture. Navrátil designed complete Rococo Revival interiors, including furniture, frames, chandeliers and stoves, for the castles in Liběchov (1838–43) and in Jirny (1843–4) and for the imperial residences in Zákupy and Ploskovice in northern Bohemia (all partly *in situ*). All were furnished with comfortable carved furniture executed by Josef Veselý (*fl c.* 1850), Prague's leading court decorator and upholsterer. It is likely that Navrátil also designed gilt furniture for the St Francis Monastery in Prague. Designs by Mánes were also influenced by the Rococo Revival: dating from the 1850s is a series of designs (Prague, N.G., Šternberk Pal.) for a screen and antler furniture, most likely intended for hunting-lodges and aristocratic country houses.

From the 1850s the Rococo Revival overlapped with the Gothic Revival, although Gothic decoration was used prior to this on country house projects (e.g. the house at Lednice, by Leistler & Son). Most of the furnishings of the grand salons were made in this style, which was favoured by Georg Gottlob Ungewitter from 1851, Joseph Nash (1808–78), Charles J. Richardson (1806–71) and others. An outstanding furniture wood-carver was Petr Bušek (1824–94), a graduate of the Prague and Vienna academies, who set up his workshop in Prague; from 1856 he worked for Kamil Rohan of Sychrov (nr Turnov) and later with his sons Dominik (1855–1934) and Konstantin (1861–1938). They followed the designs (e.g. of 1853; Litoměřice, Litoměřice Archv) of Josef Pruvot (1807–83), court builder at Sychrov, who was also inspired by the work of Joseph Nash.

Around 1870 the Renaissance Revival style appeared. Its main exponents were the architects Josef Zítek, who designed furniture in the spirit of Central European decorative traditions, and Antonín Wiehl, a champion of historic Czech styles who designed furniture with painted panels (e.g. sideboard, *c.* 1875; Prague, Mus. Dec. A.). He collaborated with the painter Mikoláš Aleš, who in 1878, while decorating the furniture of Alexander Brandejs (*fl* second half of 19th century), came by chance on the work of Walter Crane, who used similar motifs. From the 1880s marked tendencies towards vernacular traditions are noticeable (e.g. interiors and furniture by Jan Koula (1855–1919) from 1886, produced in the workshop of the Schalek firm, Prague, est. 1834; see fig. 22). This movement was strengthened by two exhibitions, the Jubilee Exhibition (1891) and the Czecho-Slavonic Folk Exhibition (1895), both held in Prague, where architects collaborated with wood-carvers and joiners. At the Jubilee Exhibition, for example, the furnishing of royal trains, the restaurant of the Hotel Pupp in Karlovy Vary and salon designs were displayed. Furniture with vernacular motifs was popular with members of the Prague intelligentsia but was used sporadically in grand interiors in the country (e.g. at Lužany, nr Plzeň, at Žinkovy, nr Klatovy, and at the castle Hrádek u Nechanic; all partly *in situ*). In the 1890s the sculptor Bohuslav Schnirch and the architects Josef Schulz and Zítek collaborated on the furnishing of Prague's most

22. Dining chair, oak with intarsia decoration, h. 1.22 m, made by Jan Koula at the workshop of the Schalek firm, Prague, 1886 (Prague, Museum of Decorative Arts)

important buildings (e.g. the National Theatre; the National Museum), equipping them with solid, refined, mostly Renaissance Revival furniture. Schnirch also designed a sideboard, made by M. V. Hiršl (*fl* second half of 19th century), decorated with brass, coloured glass and sculpture (1899; Prague, Mus. Dec. A.). During this period, when historical revivals were rampant, new trends began to appear following the Weltaustellung of 1873 in Vienna, anticipating the Czech Secessionist style.

5. 20TH CENTURY. Czech furniture and interior decoration of the 20th century can be divided into the following principal contradictory tendencies: Secessionism, geometrical modernism, Cubism and decorativism. At the beginning of the 20th century the Secessionist (Art Nouveau) style was predominant. Jan Kastner (1860–1912), professor of wood-carving at the Academy of Applied Arts in Prague, designed several interiors and furnishing accessories (frames, clocks etc) in this style as well as an exquisitely made chair (Prague, Mus. Dec. A.), exhibited in the Czech exhibition at the Exposition Universelle of 1900 in Paris. The architects Jan Koula (1855–1919) and Josef Fanta (1856–1954) exhibited Czech interiors at the same event. Koula's furniture (Prague, Mus. Dec. A.) was inspired by vernacular art; Fanta's (Prague, Mus. Dec. A.), intended for intellectuals, had a more modern concept, the decoration revealing literary inspiration. This tendency is most apparent in a cabinet decorated with motifs inspired by contemporary literature. It can also be considered a work of Czech Symbolist painting and sculpture—the interior was executed by Jan Navrátil (b 1856), the leatherwork by J. V. Spott (b 1853) and the brass plaques by the Červenka and Bendelmeyer firms in Prague, to a design by Ludvík Wurzel (1865–1913).

The architect Jan Kotěra (1871–1923) significantly influenced Czech interior design in the early 20th century. He was the first professor at the Academy of Applied Arts in Prague sympathetic to modern art, and he headed a special design studio for architecture and interior design at the Academy of Graphic Arts in Prague. Although by declaration a rationalist, he experimented with a number of styles: Secessionism, geometrical modernism and finally Constructivism. His interiors from 1900–04 show a new, simplified concept of design (e.g. Professor K. Hoffmeister's room, 1903; Prague, Mus. Dec. A.). Kotěra planned interiors by using furniture of different heights, to which he added glass, metal and mirrors. Each detail reflected his principle that 'the purpose, construction and function are the moving forces, the form, the result' (see Kotěra). The furniture he designed in 1903 uses wood of contrasting colours and has delicate floral decoration. Kotěra cooperated with such Czech sculptors as Stanislav Sucharda (1866–1916) and Jan Kastner. One of the most important of Kotěra's contributions to Czech decorative art was the design of seating, for example furnishings for tramway and railway carriages (1898), armchairs in beech and cane (1903), bentwood chairs for the Arco coffee house in Prague (1907) and chairs for the National House in Prostějov (1905–07).

The architect Dušan Jurkovič (1868–1947) was inspired by folk art. His furniture (1908–13; in situ) for the castle in Nové Město nad Metují has constructional clarity, underlined by geometrical ornament, Secessionist motifs (e.g. Winter Garden, 1910) and the unusual use of colour (e.g. Gentleman's Room). All the Prague carpentry firms, for example Navrátil, Röhrs, Strnad and Vaníček, J. Skramlík & Sons (all fl c. 1900) and František Karel Schalek, collaborated with architects. A number of furnishing firms and schools that worked from their own designs or from the designs of their in-house architects also produced Secessionist furniture: 'garniture', furniture in identically decorated sets, became the favourite idiom of the manufacturers of commercially produced furniture.

Around 1909 new styles in furniture and interior design appeared, although the Secessionist style continued to be popular. From 1904 Kotěra's work had been influenced by geometrical modernism (e.g. furniture for his own villa in Prague, 1908–09). The early work of the architect Otakar Novotný (1880–1959) was similarly orientated. He furnished the villa (1909) of the publisher J. Otto (1841–1916) at Zbraslav and the offices (1909–11) of the publisher Jan Štenc (1871–1947) in Prague with elegant black-and-white furniture. FRANTIŠEK BÍLEK designed furnishings in the Secessionist style for his own villa in Prague in 1911 (in situ) and for a number of Prague families. Bílek brought the tradition of sculptural furniture to its peak and surpassed the contemporary conventions of the Czech interior. The painter Alphonse Mucha also designed furniture, but in comparison to his contemporaries in Prague he had a more cosmopolitan attitude. Kotěra's Constructivist tendencies appeared in the armchairs and chairs (1911; in situ) for the town museum in Hradec Králové.

In the early decades of the 20th century the art schools, especially the Academy of Applied Art in Prague, produced some notable architects—Josef Gočár, Pavel Janák, Otakar Novotný, Josef Chochol and Vlastislav Hofman (1884–1964)—who successfully strove to produce a modern style of furniture design. They soon took a position diametrically opposed to Kotěra's and his ideas of function and construction. They were inspired by the work of Jože Plečnik, who led the specialized unit for architecture at the Academy of Applied Arts in Prague from 1911. He produced unusually formed furniture that he used mainly in the furnishing of Hradčany Castle, Prague. From 1910 to 1912 Cubism governed the young architects' work (see CZECH CUBISM). Furniture shapes were reduced and re-created in original ways, with the emphasis on the aesthetic rather than the functional qualities of the piece. Furniture was split into configurations of several distinguishable parts that grow into each other, as in a Cubist painting. The most progressive designs were those for seating (e.g. Janák's chair, 1914–15; Prague, Mus. Dec. A.; see fig. 23). In 1911 the architect-designers formed the GROUP OF PLASTIC ARTISTS. They were influenced by the philosophical and aesthetic opinions of the time, expressed, for example, by the philosopher Theodor Lipps (1851–1914), the aesthetician Wilhelm Worringer (1881–1965) and the sculptor Adolf von Hildebrand (1848–1921). In 1912 they established the Prague Art Workshops, orientated towards furniture production. They made sketch designs of settees, commodes and stools, mostly for the homes of Prague intellectuals. In the ensembles of 1912–13 they conceptualized furniture as abstract sculpture, cutting off the edges and lightening the furniture with sloping surfaces. The interiors they created before World War I, which synthesize these experimental beginnings, belong to the last phase of this style.

A new style was created by Janák's and Gočár's designs from 1915, inspired by contemporary abstract painting. The design of post-war furniture was also influenced by graduates from specialized schools who joined the architecture unit at the Academy of Applied Arts in Prague.

23. Chair by Pavel Janák, polished walnut, h. 950 mm, 1914–15 (Prague, Museum of Decorative Arts)

Plečnik's successor there was the architect and master carpenter Otto Rothmayer (1892–1966), who used *roksor* rods (originally used in reinforced concrete) for garden furniture, initially intended for the terraces of Prague Castle.

Adolf Loos (1870–1933) worked extensively in Bohemia. His interiors from 1907 to 1908 in Plzeň (Pilsen) show his interest in the English Arts and Crafts style. He criticized the Rondocubist 'curved' furniture (using circles, spheres, arches etc) that was made in Prague after World War I. This kind of furniture was designed by Josef Gočár for the sculptor Jan Štursa in 1917 and for the Legiobanka in Prague (1921–3; examples in Prague, Mus. Dec. A.). In 1918 Pavel Janák, inspired by Czech vernacular art, also joined the programme. He designed furnishings for a number of Prague families and the interiors of the castle in Nové Město nad Metují in the Rondocubist style (*in situ*). This style reached its zenith at the Exposition Internationale des Arts Décoratifs et Industriels Modernes of 1925 in Paris, where Czech designers were awarded many medals.

In the 1920s a generation of Functionalist architects arose. They aimed to create standardized furniture by means of mass production and a concept of interior design suitable for the widest circle of consumers. The need for rationalism, functionalism and economy was promulgated by the designer and theoretician Karel Teige. In 1921 the factories of Applied Arts were founded in Brno, where mass-produced furniture was made. The director was Jan Vaněk (1891–1960), who had created the first standardized furniture. The architects Jaroslav Grunt (1893–1988), Josef Gočár, Arnošt Wiesner (1890–1971), Jindřich Friedl and Hugo Gorge also designed furniture for mass production. Teige's opinions were shared by a number of avant-garde architects, for example Josef Havlíček (1899–1961) and Karel Honzík (1900–66), who designed a rationalist interior for a small flat. In 1927 Jaromír Krejcar designed a foldable settee, and in 1928 Antonín Heythum (1901–54) designed a collapsible armchair (1928; Prague, Mus. Dec. A.). Tubular-steel furniture, designed by the architects Jindřich Halabala (1903–78), Hana Kučerová-Záveská (1904–44), Ladislav Žák (1900–73) and Antonín Heythum (1901–56), was produced by the firms Mücke-Melder and Hynek Gottwald, among others (examples in Prague, Mus. Dec. A.). An armchair in tubular steel was created by Ludwig Mies van der Rohe for the Villa Tugendhat in Brno in 1929–30.

Functionalist architects experimented with individually designed furnishings for private houses, for example the Müller House (1930) in Střešovice, Prague, designed by Adolf Loos, and the refurbishment and decoration of flats by the architects Lubomír Šlapeta (1908–83), Jiří Kroha (1893–1974), Ladislav Sutnar (1897–1976) and Josef Havlíček, in which the old arrangements of furniture were rejected. Almost all the movable furniture disappeared from the rooms, wardrobes were built in, and function and construction became the key to all furniture design. A number of modern furnishings were produced for coffee houses, such as at the Hotel Juliš (1931–4), Prague, by Pavel Janák, research institutes and schools (e.g. furniture by Jan Gillar (1904–67) for the 'French' schools, 1932–4) and hospitals (e.g. dermatology unit (1935–6) at Bulovka by Jan Rosůlek (*b* 1900)).

At the end of the 1930s a reaction against Functionalism led to an eclecticism that looked to historical decorative tendencies. Reproduction antique furniture appeared in interiors. A number of Prague firms, led by that of Emil Gerstl, produced luxury furniture for flats, guest rooms and fashion salons. During the 1940s many firms made heavy furniture with rustic elements, often carved, and with additional metal, leather or textile decoration. The work of the younger generation of architects remained progressive: Jiří Štursa (*b* 1910), Vlasta Štursová (1912–82), Augusta Müllerová (1906–85), Jan Koula jr (1896–1975), Josef Kittrich (1901–68) and Ema Kittrichová (1909–89), for example, followed Functionalist principles but were not as dogmatic in the creation of forms.

The appearance of new materials marked the production of furniture in the 1950s, although traditional materials (metal and wood) were used, and craft skills were revived by Karel Koželka (1909–92) and others. Mass-produced furniture superseded individual pieces designed by architects for specific clients. Shelf partitions appeared, often combined with metal elements, as did multisector furniture made by V.N.P. of Brno, consisting of individual cupboards assembled at will. The Institute of Furnishing and Fashion took part in the evolution of the furniture of the 1960s, as did a number of architects and the professors and students of the Academy of Applied Arts in Prague. In 1967 the Edis group was established, inspired by classical traditions. During the 1970s and 1980s a generation of designers aimed at the standardized production of furniture of high quality, while designers of the ATIKA group (1987–92), influenced by contemporary painting, studio glass and Post-modern architecture, incorporated unconventional shapes and exaggerated decoration into their work (examples in Brno, Morav. Gal.; Prague, Mus. Dec. A.).

BIBLIOGRAPHY

GENERAL

Soupis památek historických a uměleckých v zemi české [Index of historical and artistic monuments in the Czech lands], 41 vols (Prague, 1897–1937)

Památky archeologické [Archaeological monuments], xxviii–xxxiv (Prague, 1916–25)

K. Herain: 'Z minulosti pražského nábytku' [From the past of Prague furniture], *Kniha o Praze: Pražský almanach* [Book about Prague: Prague Almanac] (Prague, 1930), pp. 130–63

P. Toman: *Nový slovník československých výtvarných umělců* [New dictionary of Czechoslovak artists] (Prague, 1947)

E. Poche and others: *Umělecké památky Čech* [Artistic monuments of Bohemia], pts I–IV (Prague, 1977–82)

V. Lorenc and K. Tříska: *Černínský palác v Praze* [Černín Palace in Prague] (Prague, 1980)

J. Lencová: 'Dveře: Umělecké vizitky domů' [Doors: artistic visiting cards of houses], *Staletá Praha* [Centuries-old Prague], xii (1982), pp. 161–70

E. Poche: *Prahou krok za krokem* [Step by step through Prague] (Prague, 1985)

BEFORE 1600

J. Pešek: 'Melantrišská pozůstalost z r.1586' [Melantrich's legacy of 1586], *Documenta pragensia I* (Prague, 1980)

J. Diviš: *Pokladny pražských cechů* [Treasuries of the Prague guilds], Prague, Mus. City cat. (Prague, 1984)

1600–1799

Z. Winter: *Přepych uměleckého průmyslu v měšťanských domech XVI. věku* [Artistic luxury in town houses of the 16th century] (Prague, 1892)

J. Morávek: *Nově objevený inventář rudolfinských sbírek na Hradě pražském* [Newly discovered inventory of the Rudolf collections at Prague Castle] (Prague, 1937)

J. Blažíček, J. Čeřovský and E. Poche: *Klášter v Břevnově* [Břevnov Monastery] (Prague, 1944)

——: *Rokoko a konec baroku v Čechách* [Rococo and the end of the Baroque in Bohemia] (Prague, 1948)

L. Lábek: 'Plzeňští truhláři od založení města do konce baroka' [Plzeň's cabinetmakers from the foundation of the town to the end of the Baroque], *Minulostí Plzně a Plzeňska* [From the past of Plzeň and its surroundings], ii (Plzeň, 1959), pp. 67–87

L. Urešová: *Obrazový rám českého baroka* [Picture frames of the Czech Baroque] (diss., Prague, Charles U., 1962)

I. Kořán: 'Umění a umělci baroka v Hradci Králové' [Baroque art and artists in Hradec Králové], *Umění*, xix (1971), pp. 35–69, 136–89

M. Lejsková-Matyášová: 'Z valdštejnského nábytku v pražském paláci' [From Wallenstein's furniture at the Prague palace], *Staletá Praha* [Centuries-old Prague], v (1971), pp. 210–16

B. Bukovinská: 'Další florentské mozaiky v Praze' [More Florentine mosaics in Prague], *Umění*, xx (1972), pp. 363–70

I. Kořán: 'Umění a umělci klasicismu v Hradci Králové' [Classicist art and artists in Hradec Králové], *Umění*, xxv (1977), p. 499

Chebská reliéfní intarzie a grafika [Cheb's relief intarsia and graphics] (exh. cat., ed. M. Mžyková; Prague, 1986)

1800–1900

Národopisná výstava českoslovanská v Praze 1895: Ilustrovaný katalog památek výtvarných a oddělení církevního [The Czecho-Slavonic ethnographic exhibition in Prague, 1895: illustrated catalogue of monuments of art and of the ecclesiastical section] (Prague, 1895)

J. Kotěra: 'O novém umění' [About new art], *Volné směry*, iv (1900), pp. 189–95

K. Chytil: *Doba klassicismu a empíru v Praze* [The period of classicism and the Empire style in Prague] (Prague, 1908)

A. Masaryková: 'Druhé rokoko v Praze' [The second Rococo in Prague], *Roč. Kruhu Pěstování Dějin Umění 1937 a 1938* (1939), pp. 13–18

H. Volavková: *Mikoláš Aleš: Kresby a návrhy* [Mikoláš Aleš: drawings and designs] (Prague, 1975)

——: *Josef Mánes: Malíř vzorků a ornamentu* [Josef Mánes: painter of patterns and ornament] (Prague, 1981)

M. Pospíšilová: *Sychrov* (Liberec, 1987)

AFTER 1900

P. Janák: 'O nábytku a jiném' [On furniture and other things], *Umělecký Měsíčník*, 2 (1912–13), pp. 21–4

——: 'Hranol a pyramida' [Prism and pyramid], *Umělecký Měsíčník*, 2 (1912–13), pp. 168–75

V. V. Štech: *Tschechische Bestrebungen um ein modernes Interieur* (Prague, 1915)

A. Loos: *Řeči do prázdna* [Talking into the void], ed. B. Markalous (Prague, 1929)

K. Teige: *Moderní architektura v Československu* [Modern architecture in Czechoslovakia] (Prague, 1930)

——: *Práce Jaromíra Krejcara* [The work of Jaromír Krejcar] (Prague, 1933)

J. E. Koula: 'Malá architektura v díle Jana Kouly, 1855–1919' [Smaller-scale creations in the work of Jan Koula, 1855–1919], *Tvar*, vii (1955), pp. 242–50

M. Benešová: *Josef Gočár* (Prague, 1957)

O. Novotný: *Jan Kotěra a jeho doba* [Jan Kotěra and his time] (Prague, 1957)

M. Benešová: *Pavel Janák* (Prague, 1959)

J. E. Koula: *Dnešní byt* [Today's flat] (Prague, 1962)

K. Honzík: *Ze života avantgardy* [From the life of the avant-garde] (Prague, 1963)

K. Teige: *Vývojové proměny v umění* [Evolutionary changes in art] (Prague, 1966)

Český kubistický interiér [The Czech Cubist interior] (exh. cat., ed. O. Herbenová and M. Lamarová; Prague, Mus. Dec. A., 1976)

Český funkcionalismus, 1920–1940 [Czech functionalism, 1920–1940] (exh. cat., ed. A. Adlerová; Prague, Mus. Dec. A.; Brno, Morav. Gal.; 1978)

Otakar Novotný, 1880–1959: Architektonické dílo [Otakar Novotný, 1880–1959: architectural work] (exh. cat., ed. V. Šlapeta; Prague, Mánes Exh. Hall; Olomouc, Reg. Gal.; 1980)

A. Adlerová: *České užité umění, 1918–38* [Czech applied art, 1918–38] (Prague, 1983)

Czechoslovakia: Cubism (exh. cat., ed. O. Herbenová; Tokyo, 1984)

OLGA HERBENOVÁ

VI. Ceramics.

1. Before *c.* 1590. 2. *c.* 1590–*c.* 1875. 3. After *c.* 1875.

1. BEFORE *c.*1590. Towards the end of the 11th century ceramic production included both utilitarian pottery—simple, unglazed kitchenware and everyday ware—and small, decorative items. From the end of the 11th century there is evidence of a fairly substantial manufacture of floor- and wall-tiles with relief motifs. These vary in shape, size and pattern and were used for decorating ecclesiastical buildings. A large quantity of tiles dating from the second half of the 12th century from the convent of St John the Baptist at Ostrov, near Davle, is in the Museum of Decorative Arts in Prague. The manufacture of tiled stoves, prompted by an increased desire for comfort, contributed to the development of ceramics. The external stove walls were decorated with moulded tiles. Typical decoration included heraldic, religious, ornamental and

genre motifs, and the style was extremely varied, ranging from simple to skilfully crafted items. The manufacture of ceramics for architectural purposes, especially of lead-glazed relief tiles, also developed. Sets of tiles from the south Bohemian castles of Zvíkov and Písek (built after 1260) symbolize the sovereignty of the Bohemian ruler Ottokar II. In addition to figural, heraldic and zoomorphic themes, such fantastic motifs as centaurs, griffins, winged dragons and sphinxes were prevalent.

Hollow ware during the Middle Ages was conservative and was made to a far lower standard. There were few marked differences in regional styles, although in some places improvements in the potter's wheel resulted in more delicately shaped vessels. The selection of everyday ware was rather limited. The cooking-pot was shaped with an open brim, sometimes with handles and a shaped lid; decoration consisted of relief, pressed or naively painted motifs. Other common kitchen utensils included bowls, pans, tripods, jugs, bottles and goblets.

Two types of Moravian ceramic goblets were significant: the so-called Brno goblets, made from the end of the 14th century, and those from Loštice, near Olomouc, which date from the second half of the 15th century. The Brno goblets were shaped into a four-lobed form at the neck, and the Loštice goblets were made of rough, reddish-brown clay; both were Gothic in form. The prevalence of Loštice goblets in neighbouring countries evinces their value as a trading commodity. In addition to producing kitchenware, pottery workshops also made small, decorative articles and ceramic toys.

From the beginning of the 16th century Kutná Hora became an important centre for the production of Renaissance-style wares. Tiles for stoves were produced, some decorated with green lead glazes and occasionally with tin glazes. The advanced figurative reliefs were often embellished with arabesques. A ceramic sign from the guild of potters and stovemakers (1530; Prague, Mus. City) was possibly inspired by contemporary trends in sculpting and is an outstanding example of Renaissance ceramics; it is decorated with an artistically sophisticated relief of *Adam and Eve* glazed in high-temperature colours. The black-glazed relief tile depicting the *Virgin and Child* in the vestry of the church in Bechyně is significant in that its hollow back indicates that it was originally a stove-tile. An outstanding vessel of the period is an earthenware jug that belonged to Šimon Nemazal from Beroun in 1577 (Prague, Mus. Dec. A.). Its colouring (brown, white and green) and the painting of a cuckoo attest to an association with folk pottery.

2. *c.* 1590–*c.* 1875. From the end of the 16th century a radical change was brought about in ceramics by faience produced by the Habáns (Anabaptists), who settled in Moravia from 1526. Habáner ware was made from *c.* 1590 to 1730. The wares were thrown or moulded, tin-glazed and painted with such high-temperature colours as yellow, blue, green and violet. The distinctive range of forms included lattice-bordered bowls, plates, jugs, washing sets, dinner-services and bottles (see fig. 24). Wares were almost always dated and decorated with botanically correct plants, initials and coats of arms. Habáner ware was influenced

24. Habáner faience bottle, white glaze with purple painted decoration, h. 200 mm, 1688 (Prague, Museum of Decorative Arts)

by Italian (especially *Bianchi di Faenza*), German, Dutch, Islamic and Iznik wares.

After 1620, strong Counter-Reformation measures caused the Habáns to move towards western Slovakia. At the end of the 1670s a Habán workshop was established at Hluboká in south Bohemia, the result of attempts by the Schwarzenberg family to attract Habán potters from Slovakia to serve on their estate. From the 17th century architectural motifs were used in the decoration—the depiction of animals and figures was not tolerated in Habán works—and a lively stream of folk-art ceramics followed in the wake of Habán faience in Moravia.

The production of earthenware developed further at the end of the 18th century. The introduction of Neo-classicism caused a fundamental stylistic change. Wares were inspired by the work of the English potter Josiah Wedgwood and by the potteries in Leeds. In 1791 a factory was established in Prague for the production of earthenware. From the beginning the products were well made and artistically accomplished; wares included lattice baskets, dinner-services and dishes, condiment sets, flowerpots, inkpots and pharmacy wares decorated with delicate relief patterns, flowers, sepia-coloured landscapes, genre motifs and figures of saints. In the early 19th century shapes were gradually simplified. By the 1820s porcelain production had begun, but pottery continued to be made until 1837.

In 1792 a pottery was established by František Josef, Count of Vrtba, in Týnec nad Sázavou, but from the beginning it was in financial difficulties owing to the high cost of importing raw materials. In 1801 the factory was granted a charter to produce earthenware, and these high-quality wares with dainty relief and floral designs competed with wares from the factory in Prague. The unfavourable location and strong competition in porcelain manufacture, however, forced the factory to close in 1866.

In 1799 a factory was established in Vranov nad Dyjí for the production of earthenware and 'Wedgwood' goods. Between 1820 and 1850 the pottery reached its pinnacle, but its unfavourable location and, later, competition from the nearby factory in Kravsko (est. 1822) and from porcelain affected the business. The early Neo-classical black, red and yellow stonewares made by the factory imitated Wedgwood jasper wares. Earthenwares, especially dinner-services, were also produced and were decorated with delicate applied and painted decoration. Wares were later produced in the more prestigious Empire style. After numerous experiments the manager, František Dürnbeck, introduced a new, high-grade material known as Wedgwood's 'light colours' in brown, blue and green. Most of this pottery, functional and elegant in form, was decorated with symmetrical, sometimes gilded lines, painted initials and coats of arms (see fig. 25). Wares were also transfer-printed: high-quality transfers included plant motifs, views of the Vranov mansion and its surroundings, Swiss and Austrian landscapes, hunting scenes and East Asian themes. In the 1840s and 1850s, during the Rococo Revival period, wares were ornately decorated.

In 1804 Jan, the Knight of Schönau, set up an earthenware factory in Dalovice. The earthenware produced was decorated with a lattice edge and delicate painted flowers and landscapes. In 1830 the factory was granted permission to produce porcelain, and production continued simultaneously until 1845.

In 1814 a pottery was established in Stará Role. In 1823 it was bought by Antonín Novotný, who expanded the factory. Wares were decorated with figures and delicate floral designs by Georg Döbler (1788–1845) and were very popular. In 1842 transfer decoration, inspired by English patterns, local prints and views of Prague, was introduced. By the 1840s porcelain production dominated output, and earthenware was discontinued.

Porcelain manufacture was concentrated in the region of Karlovy Vary, in an area rich in high-quality clay deposits. The Austro-Hungarian authorities, however, were opposed to production for fear of competition with the Viennese porcelain factories. Nevertheless, in the 1790s the manufacture of porcelain began. The first porcelain factory was established in Slavkov in 1792. After 1804, when the factory was bought by G. Lippert (1771–1843) and V. Haas (1770–1830), there was a marked improvement in the quality of the material. The Empire style prevailed during this period, especially in the design of coffee- and dinner-services; the graceful shapes were painted and gilded in high-quality designs. The paintings

25. Cream-coloured stoneware box with lid, h. 340 mm, from Vranov nad Dyjí, *c.* 1830 (Prague, Museum of Decorative Arts)

frequently consisted of landscapes, Prague vistas (based on engravings by Vincenc Morstadt), views of such spa towns as Karlovy Vary, flowers, miniatures and biblical and historical scenes.

In 1794 porcelain production began in Klášterec nad Ohří. Wares were similar to those made in Slavkov, and decoration included flower motifs, initials, hunting scenes, allegories and landscapes. The porcelain factory in Březová was established in 1803 and made favourable progress in the 1820s. Wares included coffee- and dinner-services, flower-pots, pipes and figures. From 1828 transfer-printing was also used. Decoration included views of Prague and the west Bohemian spas, landscapes, flowers, chinoiseries and figures of saints.

The porcelain factory in Loket was founded in 1816. Early wares were harmoniously shaped and decorated with hand-painted miniatures, rich colours and gilding, including the application of raised gilding. Transfer-printing was introduced in 1836. The sculptor Arnošt Popp divided his time between Loket and the Prague factory; hence the motifs used are similar on wares from both places. During the second half of the century there was a decline in artistic standards.

In the 1820s the Prague factory began producing porcelain with an emphasis on figure production. Popp designed numerous biscuit portraits of distinguished historic personalities, scientists and artists, and the factory also produced a wide variety of lively and humorous figures, including professionals, loving couples, caricatures of Prague and Viennese actors and comedians and charming personifications of flowers. Later the demand for figures was suppressed in favour of utilitarian porcelain.

The factory in Dalovice also began to produce porcelain instead of earthenware, and frequent use was made of violet, green and yellow glazes. Production, which was large-scale, was stimulated by exports to Italy, Denmark and Russia. In 1838 the factory in Stará Role was granted a charter to produce porcelain; painted decoration was limited to floral motifs, and from 1842 transfer-printing was used. During the Rococo Revival of the mid-19th century lively figures were produced.

3. AFTER *c*. 1875. The Ceramics School (est. 1874) in Teplice, northern Bohemia, exerted an influence on numerous potteries in the region. The Amfora Factory (est. 1876) in Trnovany held a prominent position in Europe. This enterprise was particularly successful between 1900 and 1910. It produced faience and porcelain wares and figures with a variety of superb glazes. The Wahlis Pottery, also in Trnovany, concentrated on similar products; in addition, however, it made artistically decorated moulds used for decorating house façades.

Secessionist (Art Nouveau) ceramics were produced between *c*. 1895 and 1910. Forms became more asymmetrical, floral motifs predominated, and the influence from Japan, via France, was apparent. At the Ceramics School (est. 1884) in Bechyně, southern Bohemia, decorative vessels and figures were produced in this style.

The influence of Cubism marked a singular stage in the development of Czech ceramics between 1910 and 1914. Wares were geometrically shaped, and there was an accent on strict, contrasting designs. The most distinguished artists working in this style were PAVEL JANÁK, Vlastislav Hofman (1884–1964), JOSEF HAVLÍČEK and the sculptor Jaroslav Horejc (1886–1983).

In the early 20th century the work of Helena Johnová (1884–1962) made a strong impact on ceramics. In 1911 she graduated from the Kunstgewerbeschule in Vienna, where she had studied under Michael Powolny. Her figures were sculptural, and her approach to the decoration of vases and jardinières was unconventional. Her ceramic portraits from the 1930s were an inspiration to her generation.

In the 1920s the sculptor OTTO GUTFREUND produced ceramics in condensed forms with civic and social features that were on show at the Exposition Internationale des Arts Décoratifs et Industriels Modernes in Paris in 1925. From 1925 functionalist tendencies were apparent in production, and there was a predominance of purely tectonic shapes, free from any decorative elements. Industrial design also became increasingly important. Indicative of this new emphasis is a globular-shaped porcelain set made in 1931 by Ladislav Sutnar (1897–1976) at the Epiag Porcelain Factory, Loket.

After World War II tuition at the secondary applied schools for ceramics at Bechyně and Karlovy Vary improved. The ceramics studio at the Academy of Applied Arts in Prague gained a significant position when headed by Otto Eckerts from 1946. The contribution made by such artists as Eckerts, already active before the war, promoted a continuity in the development of ceramics. Since the 1930s Julie Horová (1906–62) had been producing sophisticated vessels and figures. In the 1950s her output included a wide range of simply shaped vases,

jardinières and bowls, with inventive decoration inspired by natural forms.

During the 1960s there was a burgeoning of creative talent in ceramics, and, since this was more than the industry could absorb, artists turned to individual studio work. There was a general desire to go beyond traditionally accepted principles both in the selection of materials and in their treatment. This experimental approach frequently led to more free forms of art. The use of such non-traditional materials as technical earthenware, sanitary porcelain and electro-porcelain stimulated greater creativity when used for artistic purposes. Artists who experimented with these materials included Libor Těhník (1926–87), Václav Šerák (*b* 1931), Alena Kroupová, Dagmar Hendrychová and Antonín Bartoš.

During the 1970s and 1980s artists with considerable ceramic experience developed and reviewed their approach. The ceramic reliefs by Marta Taberyová (*b* 1930) represented a wide range of themes based on nature and everyday life. Jan Hausner (1922–87) expressed himself in sensitive paintings on rough, fire-clay tiles. Lubomir Šilar (*b* 1932) modelled sheets of clay to create zoomorphic sculptures. Artists working in the late 20th century included Petr Svoboda (1942–84), known for his moulded vases, inventively shaped bowls and compositions for architectural designs; Helena Samohelová (*b* 1941), who produced wall-tiles; and Jindra Viková (*b* 1946), whose work was endowed with an exceptionally high degree of fantasy. Viková worked initially in tin-glazed earthenware, but she later found porcelain more suitable.

BIBLIOGRAPHY

A. Novotný: *Helena Johnová* (Prague, 1940)
E. Poche: *Böhmisches Porzellan* (Prague, 1956)
J. Pečírka: *Pravoslav a Jindřiška Radovi* [Pravoslav Rada and Jindřiška Radová] (Prague, 1959)
J. Spurný: *Julie Horová* (Prague, 1964)
K. Hetteš: *Rada, Pravoslav: Modern Ceramics* (Prague, 1965)
D. Šindelář: *Otto Eckert* (Prague, 1979)
T. Vlček and M. Růžička: *Současná keramika* [Contemporary ceramics] (Prague, 1979)
Česká secese: Užité umění [Czech Secessionism: applied art] (exh. cat., Prague, Mus. Dec. A., 1981)
A. Adlerová: *České užité umění, 1918–1938* [Czech applied art, 1918–1938] (Prague, 1983)
P. Vlček and J. Glogarová: *Secesní keramika ze sbírek Krajského muzea v Teplicích* [Secessionist ceramics from the collections of the regional museum in Teplice] (Teplice, 1983)
Helena Johnová, Keramika [Helena Johnová, ceramics] (exh. cat., Prague, Mus. Dec. A., 1987)
Kamenina v Čechách a na Moravě [Earthenware in Bohemia and Moravia] (exh. cat., Prague, Mus. Dec. A., 1987)
Slavkovský porcelán [Porcelain of Slavkov] (exh. cat. by D. Hejdová and J. Mergl, Prague, Mus. Dec. A., 1993)
E. Poche and D. Hejdová: *Porcelán* (Prague, 1994)
D. Hejdová and others: *Dějiny uměleckého řemesla a užitého umění v Českých zemích* [A history of crafts and applied art in the Czech lands] (in preparation)

DAGMAR TUČNÁ

VII. Glass.

1. Before *c*. 1800. 2. *c*. 1800–*c*. 1900. 3. After *c*. 1900.

1. BEFORE *c*. 1800. Glass beads were manufactured in the 9th century during the Great Moravian empire, and the production of window glass and hollow-wares developed during the 13th and 14th centuries, as confirmed by

documentation found at glassworks in the Lusatian (Lužické) and Ore (Krušné) mountains and by rich findings of sherds in such towns as Prague, Plzeň, Most, Cheb and Brno. Prague was evidently the centre of the stained-glass industry, which was first mentioned in a report of 1276 when two stained-glass windows were installed in the Romanesque cathedral of SS Vitus, Wenceslas and Voitech in Prague (destr. c. 1340). In 1348 a guild of glassmakers and painters was established in Prague. Examples of their work, which is stylistically similar to panel paintings executed by artists living in the city, have been preserved: the *Crucifixion* (1360–70; chapel of St Catherine, Karlštejn Castle); the *Death of the Virgin* (c. 1370; Kolín, St Bartholomew); and *St John the Baptist* from the Cistercian monastery in Osek and the *Crucifixion and Apostles* from the church at Slivenec near Prague (both 1360; Prague, Mus. Dec. A.). In 1370–71 Charles IV commissioned from a Bohemian workshop of skilled Italian mosaicists the glass mosaic of the *Last Judgement*, which was placed on the Golden Portal of Prague's St Vitus' Cathedral (*see* PRAGUE, §IV, 2(iii)).

In the second half of the 16th century glass technology improved, particularly regarding furnace construction, melting techniques, cleaning, decolouring and colouring. The shapes and decorations were influenced by Venetian Renaissance glass and glass *à la façon de Venise* made in the Tyrol and Vienna. The most important glassmaking families of the period came from the Erzgebirge region in Saxony: the Fridrichs, who established glassworks at Kreibitz in the Lusatian Mountains; the Schürers, who started their foundry in 1530 at FALKNOV and subsequently some 20 other foundries; the Wanders, who settled at Jablonec; and the Preusslers, whose glassworks were to be found throughout Bohemia, Silesia and Bavaria. In southern Bohemia the most important glassworks were Vilémovy Hory u Dobré in the NOVÉ HRADY region, which formed part of the Rožmberk estate. The glass produced in Bohemia at this time was *Waldglas* (using a potash alkali), which was not as clear or as easy to manipulate as Venetian soda glass. Enamelling was adopted in Bohemia at the end of the 1550s, and although it was at first restricted to the wares of such important glassworks as Falknov and Kreibitz it became more widespread in the 1590s. Popular wares included the enamelled *vilkum* (a large beaker) and conical beakers used for drinking at banquets. Enamelled decoration included heraldic emblems of the nobility, symbols of the Holy Roman Empire (*see* GLASS, colour pl. VI, fig. 1) and mythological, satirical, biblical and allegorical subjects (see fig. 26). By the end of the 16th century subjects taken from work and guild signs appeared, documenting the fact that enamelled glass was being used for household and guild utensils.

Further Venetian influence is apparent in the use of diamond-point engraving and cold-painting using oil or lacquer-based pigments. From the beginning of the 17th century there are records of this method of decoration being used at the works of Vilémovy Hory u Dobré at Nové Hrady, but it was also undoubtedly used in such other glassworks as Kreibitz. Tall bowls were most frequently adorned with figures depicting the Virtues, after designs by Jost Amman, and a number of utensils have

26. Enamelled glass beaker, h. 350 mm, from Bohemia, 1584 (Prague, Museum of Decorative Arts)

survived in blue and violet glass decorated with ornamental diamond-point engraving. Both these glassworks also produced *filigrana* glass, which was used mainly for household objects.

The technique of glasscutting first appeared in Bohemia during the late Renaissance. The stimulus for the revival of this technique came from the demand at the end of the 16th century for valuable utensils incorporating rock crystal and precious stones. These were ground and carved for noble families in Munich, Madrid, Paris and Prague by such Italian stone-cutters as ANNIBALE FONTANA, the SARACCHI brothers and the MISERONI family. CASPAR LEHMANN was active in Prague from the end of the 1580s as a glasscutter in the service of Rudolf II, and in 1606–7 he worked in Dresden for the Saxon Elector Christian II. His works can be identified from the signature on a beaker (1605; Prague, Mus. Dec. A.) decorated with the allegorical figures of Power, Nobility and Liberality, after an engraving by Jan Sadeler I. A number of carved plaques survive that were intended for furniture, caskets or windows, depicting *Rudolf II* (1603; Vienna, Ksthist. Mus.), *Christian II, Elector of Saxony* (c. 1606; Prague, Mus. Dec. A.) and such members of their entourage as *Landgrave Ludwig V of Hesse-Darmstadt* (Darmstadt, Hess. Landesmus.) and

Henry Julius, Duke of Brunswick (Dresden, Grünes Gewölbe). During a stay in Dresden he decorated plaques with allegorical and mythological scenes in accordance with commissions. Among these are a plaque with *Jupiter and Juno* (Dresden, Grünes Gewölbe) and others with *Diana and Acteon* (Hamburg, Mus. Kst & Gew.) and *Diana and Perseus* (London, V&A).

After the death of Rudolf II in 1612 and during the Thirty Years War (1618–48), glass production fell into a period of decline. However, from the 1670s there was an increase in economic and cultural development, and experiments were made to improve the quality of the glass used for engraved and cut decoration. It was primarily the glassworks in southern Bohemia that spearheaded these developments. By 1683 Michael Müller (1639–1709), an employee at the Helmbach glassworks in the Vimperk region, had created a new type of potash-fluxed glass that contained a high percentage of lime. This new glass was harder, more brilliant and therefore more suitable for cutting and engraving. At first tablewares were reminiscent of Dutch glass *à la façon de Venise*, but by the end of the 1680s the style had become more simplified and geometric. The most important centres for glass engraving were the northern Bohemian districts around the Renaissance glassworks at Falknov and Kreibitz near Česká Lípa and the glassmaking region of Jablonec.

Apart from the quality, Bohemian Baroque glass rose to prominence through its cut-glass decoration, which by the last quarter of the 17th century had become highly exacting, deep-cut work with figural, mythological and allegorical scenes, the best of which must be attributed to anonymous urban carvers. From the second decade of the 18th century engraved decoration included plant tendrils and ribbon decoration with grotesque elements derived from the engravings of Jean Berain I and such German imitators as Paul Decker I (see fig. 27). This embellishment remained popular in Bohemia until the mid-18th century. Among the more unusual glass produced at the end of the 17th century was gold-ruby glass. Knowledge of the technology involved had reached Bohemia from the glassworks of Johann Kunckel (1630–1703) in Potsdam in the late 1680s. Production in Bohemia followed in 1688–9 under Johann Christophe Fiedler in the experimental glassworks of Herzog Julius Franz von Saxe-Lauenburg (*d* 1689) on the Zákupy estate. The most significant work was done by Müller at the Helmbach glassworks.

The Bohemian glass trade was concentrated in the Česká Lípa region, and production intensified after 1715 with the termination of the Franco-Austrian Wars of the Spanish Succession. Northern Bohemian traders—who were from families of glassmakers and engravers—had by the 1680s infiltrated into Transylvania, northern Germany, the Baltic states, Sweden, Russia, the Netherlands, England, France, Portugal, Spain, Italy and Turkey. During the 18th century the most important markets for Bohemian glass were Spain and Portugal, and in the second half of the century Czech traders were venturing as far as Egypt and North America. Gradually these traders built up an extensive export trade, establishing trading posts abroad. According to the requirements of the foreign market they ordered raw materials from a wide variety of Bohemian

27. Cut and engraved glass goblet with cover, h. 286 mm, from Bohemia, *c.* 1720 (Prague, Museum of Decorative Arts)

glassworks, organized refineries in northern Bohemia and marketed the products. In this way the Bohemian glass industry was second only to textiles in the field of exports and by the end of the 18th century dominated the world glass market.

In neighbouring Silesia, which until 1742 belonged to the Kingdom of Bohemia, a centre of glasscutting developed in the valley of Jelenia Góra near the glassworks of

Sklarzska Poreba. Here Friedrich Winter (*d* 1711), a hard-stone cutter and glass engraver, had a privileged position working for Graf Christoph Leopold von Schaffgotsch. The further development of 18th-century Silesian cut glass was marked by an energetic conception and combined grinding, relief-carving and engraved lettering. The wealth of subject-matter included portraits of rulers, vistas, mythological and allegorical scenes with Rococo *galantes* and views of foreign towns (e.g. goblet, 1725–30; Liberec, N. Boh. Mus.). These types of glasses were intended primarily as presentation gifts or to mark an occasion, not only for visitors at the fashionable spa at Cieplice (Warmbrunn) but also as business gifts. From the 1740s glass engravers were concentrated mainly in Cieplice: the best known was Christian Gottfried Schneider (1710–70), whose style is evident in a set of approximately 70 prints (Wrocław, Sil. Mus.). Other distinguished masters of the mid-18th century included Benjamin Maywald, Johann Gottfried May-wald and Gottfried Kahl of Voigtsdorf. The only Silesian, fully signed, cut-glass goblet (1749; Leipzig, Mus. Gesch.) was carved by Caspar Gottlieb Langer for the Lípa shopkeepers' guild. After the annexation of Silesia by Prussia in 1742, the Silesian glass industry declined.

In the second quarter of the 18th century *Zwischengold-glas* was developed. The engravings of religious, hunting or social scenes were made with a metal point on gold or silver leaf, which was protected by an outer glass casing. It would seem that they were made at small engraving workshops, which must, however, have worked in conjunction with glassworks, such as that at NOVÝ SVĚT, and an accompanying grinding plant where accurately ground glass would have been prepared for the engravers. The production of *Zwischengoldglas* may have inspired Johann Joseph Mildner (1763–1808) and G. S. Menzel to produce *Medaillonbecher*, in which an engraved foil medallion was inserted into a double-walled beaker (e.g. beaker, 1792; Hamburg, Mus. Kst & Gew.).

The decoration of glass with enamelling stagnated during the first half of the 18th century. However, an exception was the work of Ignaz Preissler (*see* PREISSLER (ii)), the only significant Czech glass and porcelain painter who decorated his wares in *Schwarzlot* (black enamel), which had been introduced by Johann Schaper (1621–70) at Nuremberg. After a lengthy period spent at Vratislav, Preissler returned *c.* 1729 to eastern Bohemia, where until his death he worked for Count František Karel Libštejn of Kolovrat. His work on mythological subjects and landscapes gradually diverged from the style of his artistic masters. Lively scenes predominate, seen for example on the large goblet (*c.* 1720; Prague, Mus. Dec. A.) decorated with the *Triumph of Bacchus* after Annibale Carracci. At the end of the 1720s Preissler decorated his wares with the popular chinoiseries accompanied by Rococo orna-mentation. After the mid-18th century the production of glass decorated with variegated enamels was revived. Rococo ornament and the example of European painted porcelain set the tone for the decorative style of tableware, which was produced largely at the Harrach glassworks in Nový Svět. These glassworks also achieved great success from the 1760s with gaily painted, opaque-white glass, which resembled porcelain (e.g. tankard, 1770; Prague, Mus. Dec. A.).   By the first quarter of the 18th century

many-branched chandeliers with cut-glass drops imitating French chandeliers with rock-crystal pendants had become an important element in the Czech glass trade and were exported to various German principalities, Spain and France. Also important was the increasing production of mirrors with 'Venetian'-style frames, the popularity of which in the second half of the 18th century was due to Count Josef Kinský. Before the Thirty Years War there were about 40 glassworks, by the first half of the 18th century approximately 50, and by the end of the century 64. In periods of economic crisis glassworkers, grinders and engravers looked abroad for work and thus spread the technology and style of Czech glass throughout Europe.

BIBLIOGRAPHY
E. Schebek: *Böhmens Glasindustrie and Glashandel* (Prague, 1878)
G. Lange: *Die Glasindustrie im Hirschberger Thal* (Leipzig, 1883)
E. von Czihak: *Schlesische Gläser* (Breslau, 1891)
F. Mareš: *České sklo* [Czech glass] (Prague, 1893)
G. E. Pazaurek: *Die Gläsersammlung des Nordböhmischen Gewerbemuseums in Reichenberg* (Leipzig, 1902)
R. Schmidt: *Die Gläser der Sammlung Mühsam* (Berlin, 1914)
——: *Die Gläser der Sammlung Mühsam, N.F.* (Berlin, 1914/rev. 1926)
——: *Das Glas* (Berlin, 1922)
K. R. Fischer: *Die Schürer von Waldheim* (Prague, 1924)
G. E. Pazaurek: *Deutsche Fayence und Porzellen Hausmaler* (Leipzig, 1925)
R. Schmidt: *Europäisches Glas* (Berlin, 1927)
F. Rademacher: *Deutsche Gläser des Mittelalters* (Berlin, 1933)
F. X. Jiřík: *České sklo* [Bohemian glass] (Prague, 1934)
J. Blau: *Glasmacher im Böhmer- und Bayerwald in Volkskunde und Kulturgeschichte*, 2 vols (Regensburg, 1954–6)
K. Hetteš: *Bohemian Glass throughout the Ages* (Prague, 1954)
——: *Glass in Czechoslovakia* (Prague, 1958)
B. Klesse: *Glassammlung Helfried Krug*, 2 vols (Munich, 1965–73)
A. von Saldern: *German Enameled Glass* (Corning, 1965)
I. Schlosser: *Das alte Glas* (Brunswick, 1965)
Bull. Journées Int. Verre, iv (Liège, 1965–6) [issue dedicated to Czech glass]
G. Weiss: *Ullstein Gläserbuch* (Berlin, 1966)
Z. Pešatová: *Böhmische Glasgravuren* (Prague, 1968)
České sklo 17. a 18. století [Bohemian glass of the 17th and 18th centuries] (exh. cat., ed. E. Poche; Prague, Mus. Dec. A., 1970)
F. C. Lipp: *Bemalte Gläser* (Munich, 1974)
F. Matouš: *Mittelalterliche Glasmalerei in der Tschechoslowakei* (Prague, 1975)
W. Spiegl: *Böhmische Gläser* (Munich, 1976)
O. J. Blažíček, P. Preiss and D. Hejdová: *Kunst des Barock in Böhmen* (Recklinghausen, 1977)
B. Klesse and A. von Saldern: *500 Jahre Glaskunst* (Zürich, 1978)
F. Frýda: *Středověké sklo v západních Čechách* [Medieval glass in western Bohemia] (Plzeň, 1979)
Czechoslovakian Glass, 1350–1980 (exh. cat., Corning, NY, Mus. Glass, 1981)
O. Drahotová: *Europäisches Glas* (Prague, 1982)
B. Klesse and H. Mayr: *European Glass, 1500–1800* (Vienna, 1987)
B. Strasser and W. Spiegl: *Dekoriertes Glas: Renaissance bis Biedermeier* (Munich, 1989)
Řezané barokní sklo, 1600–1760 [Baroque cut glass, 1600–1700] (exh. cat. by O. Drahotová, Prague, Troja Castle, 1989)
Verres de Bohême, 1400–1989 (exh. cat., ed. S. Petrová and J. L. Olivié; Paris, Mus. A. Déc., 1989)

OLGA DRAHOTOVÁ

2. *c.* 1800–*c.* 1900. Glass production was among the most important 19th-century industries in Bohemia and Moravia. The majority of glass produced in Bohemia was decorated in the northern part of the country and from there exported all over the world. The potash glass produced during the first quarter of the 19th century resembled English and Irish lead glass of that period. After 1800 Czech glass engravers also revived the use of figural

representation, which had been neglected in Bohemia at the end of the 18th century. Empire-style enamelling was perfected by Friedrich Egermann (1777–1864), an important enameller of glassware from Polevsko near Česká Lípa in northern Bohemia. He and his pupils decorated pieces with representations of ancient mythological heroes, allegories of virtues, vistas and floral motifs using translucent enamels on opaque-white or colourless glass. Sometime before 1818 Egermann discovered the technique for the production of yellow staining using silver chloride. In 1824 he improved the use of white enamel, calling it 'pearl' or 'biscuit' enamel.

In southern Bohemia Jiří, Count of Buquoy (1781–1851), discovered an opaque black glass that he called 'Hyalith'. He began to produce his glass in the Jiříkovo Údolí glassworks near NOVÉ HRADY in southern Bohemia from 1817, and from 1819 he produced a version in sealing-wax red. This glass was decorated with minute, deeply cut ornaments and often gilded with chinoiseries, which were the most popular form of decoration (e.g. jug, c. 1825; Prague, Mus. Dec. A.). The NOVÝ SVĚT glassworks in Harrach also produced black and red 'Hyalith', which successfully competed with the Buquoy 'Hyalith'. In 1828 Egermann produced his 'Lithyalin' glass (see GLASS, colour pl. VI, fig. 2), a polished opaque glass marbled to resemble hardstone, which he exhibited at the Industrial Exhibition of 1828 in Prague. To produce 'Lithyalin' Egermann applied layers of yellow and red stains on coloured glass under carefully controlled conditions. The wares were then decorated with gilding (e.g. beaker, c. 1830; Prague, Mus. Dec. A.). About 1830 the Nový Svět glassworks and the Count of Buquoy's glassworks at Nové Hrady were able to produce the simplest type of the Egermann 'Lithyalin'.

From 1831 the popularity of coloured and layered glass grew throughout Europe, and large quantities decorated with engraving, cutting and enamels were produced in Bohemia (see fig. 28). Colourless glass was stained after 1833 with ruby red. Red stained glass was used as a substitute for more precious glass that was coloured throughout with gold and copper. Coated glass was decorated by cutting, Rococo decoration, small castles, forest animals and vistas. After 1840 the production of this stained glass was introduced to France and the USA. From 1835 the Buquoy glassworks produced an opaque marbled glass called 'Agatin', which was painted with gold and enamelled. Around 1840 a uranium yellow-green glass (Annagelb) and green glass (Annagrün) were produced by the glassworks of Josef Riedel (fl 1830–48) and by glassworks at Nový Svět and in southern Bohemia. Uranium was also included in 'Isabell', an ivory-coloured glass produced by the Nový Svět glassworks. Bohemian glass of the second quarter of the 19th century was strongly influenced by the Biedermeier style and is distinguished by its complicated engraved decoration, which was subsequently copied by other European glassworks. Between 1823 and 1855 the Nový Svět glassworks produced clear crystal glass inserted with ceramic inlays (sulphides), which were bought from France. From 1839 the same glassworks also produced *filigrana* glass, most often in combinations of white, pink and light blue.

28. Cut-glass bowl, lustre-painted pink and blue, h. 275 mm, probably made at Ignác Palme & Co., Prácheň, northern Bohemia, 1835–40 (Prague, Museum of Decorative Arts)

During the 19th century engraving was the most important technique for decorating glass; popular decoration included hunting scenes, vistas, military scenes and portraits from pattern books, medals and prints. The majority of engravers worked in Kamenický Šenov, Mistrovice and Oldřichov and included Franz Anton Pelikan (?1786–1858), August Böhm (1812–90), Karl Pfohl (1826–94) and Karl Günther (1808–83). Dominik Biemann was from a family of glassworkers at the Nový Svět glassworks and was the most important Bohemian glass engraver of the 19th century; he mastered the techniques of glass engraving and made numerous portraits. In KARLOVY VARY many artists worked during the summer months at the spa, including Josef Anton Pfeiffer (1801–69), Emanuel Hoffmann (1819–78) and Johann Friedrich Hoffmann (1840–1900). František de Paula Zach (1820–81) worked in Prague and northern Bohemia and largely in Munich, where he became well known for his talents. During the second half of the 19th century Czech glassworkers made glass in response to the increasing interest in historicism throughout Europe. Painted glass was made in imitation of medieval and Renaissance glass, while excellent transparent crystal glass, engraved and cut, imitated the example of famous Bohemian glass of the 17th and 18th centuries. Outstanding glass of this period was produced at the Adolfov glassworks in the Šumava Mountains, where designs were produced by the Viennese company of J. & L. LOBMEYR. The Lobmeyr workshop in Kamenický Šenov in northern Bohemia employed a number of excellent glass engravers, including Karl Pietsch (1826–83), Peter Eisert (1828–94) and Franz Ullmann (1846–1921). Clear, engraved and cut glass decorated with garnets was designed by the architect Jan Koula (1855–1919). In the last quarter of the 19th century Czech glassworks began to produce a new type of furnace-made, iridescent-decorated glass that gained recognition especially at the World Expositions in the USA at the end of the 19th century.

BIBLIOGRAPHY

G. E. Pazaurek: *Gläser der Empire- und Biedemeierzeit* (Leipzig, 1923)
Historismus: Umělecké řemeslo [Historicism: Arts and crafts] (exh. cat. by J. Brožová, Prague, Mus. Dec. A., 1976)
České sklo, 1800–1860 [Czech glass, 1800–1860] (exh. cat. by J. Brožová, Prague, Mus. Dec. A., 1977)
České sklo 19. století [Czech glass of the 19th century] (exh. cat. by J. Brožová, Brno, Morav. Mus., 1979)
W. Spiegl: 'Glas des Historismus', *Kunst- und Gebrauchsgläser des 19. Jahrhunderts* (Brunswick, 1980)
A. Busson: *Biedermeier-Steingläser* (Vienna, 1991)

J. BROŽOVÁ

3. AFTER *c.* 1900. At the end of the 19th century the Art Nouveau style was evident in the design of Bohemian glass. At first pieces were clearly inspired by floral motifs in shape, decoration and colouring. However, after 1905 a more geometric style developed. A wide variety of techniques was used, but hot techniques and iridescence were predominant. This was due to the LÖTZ WITWE glassworks in Klostermühle (*see* GLASS, colour pl. VI, fig. 3), influenced by the work of Tiffany. The glassworks collaborated with several Bohemian artists, including Marie Kirshner (1852–1931) and Adolf Beckert (1884–1929), and later with artists from the Wiener Werkstätte, especially Josef Hoffmann. Lötz Witwe strongly influenced the style of Bohemian Art Nouveau glass. The glassworks of Ludwig Moser (1833–1916) in Karlovy Vary and the Harrach glassworks in NOVÝ SVĚT became prominent in the area of engraved glass decorated with floral motifs. The geometric style was best expressed in painted and cut decoration produced in the area of Kamenický Šenov and NOVÝ BOR, where a positive role was played by the local glass schools. Overall geometric forms and simplicity of design were exhibited by the simply cut glass designed in 1904 by the architect Jan Kotěra, professor at the Academy of Applied Arts in Prague, and by the fine arts association Artěl (founded in 1908).

The influence of the Academy of Applied Arts increased after 1918, owing to the emphasis of Professor Josef Drahoňovský (1877–1938) on engraving and cutting techniques. Drahoňovský imbued the spirit of Neo-classicism in pupils, some of whom worked in and around ŽELEZNÝ BROD. Among the glass creations produced between 1918 and 1945 were boldly designed vases by Jaroslav Horejc (1886–1983) made by J. & L. LOBMEYR in Kamenický Šenov. After 1928 such artists as Ludvika Smrčková (1903–91), Alois Metelák (1897–1980) and Ladislav Sutnar (1897–1976) designed functional glass and tableware. In the industrial sector the Moser glassworks in Karlovy Vary were prominent; they also, however, produced luxury drinking glasses and coloured cut glass.

After 1945 the structure of the Czech glass industry changed radically. The factories were nationalized and concentrated into complexes according to type of production. Near the large factories design centres were established, where graduates of the glass department of the Academy of Applied Arts in Prague were employed. They designed not only fine utilitarian glass but also art glass. The most successful pieces from this period were exhibited at the 11th Triennale in Milan in 1957 and at Expo '58 in Brussels. About 1960, as a result of increasing mechanization, glass production divided into two branches: glass design and individual studio work. Czech glass artists introduced new concepts in studio work, which had different roots from the studio glass movement in the USA. The monumental works designed first for such exhibitions as Expo '58 and later for architecture motivated this development. Among the pioneers were René Roubíček (*b* 1922), with his abstract glass sculptures shaped using hot techniques, and Jaroslava Brychtová (*b* 1924) and Stanislav Libenský (*b* 1921), who created spatial compositions working with molten glass. Another specific contribution was made by Václav Cigler (*b* 1929), whose highly polished and cut-glass blocks exploited the optical properties of glass. Libenský, who taught at the Academy of Applied Arts in Prague, and Cigler had a decisive influence on the future development of Czech glass.

In the late 20th century there were up to 60 glass artists working in the Czech lands, including Pavel Hlava (*b* 1924), František Vízner (*b* 1936), Jiří Šuhájek (*b* 1943), Oldřich Plíva (*b* 1946), Jaromír Rybák (*b* 1951) and Jiří Harcuba (*b* 1928). The most important glassworks belonged to the firm of Crystalex in Nový Bor.

BIBLIOGRAPHY

G. Pazaurek: *Moderne Gläser* (Leipzig, 1901)
——: *Kunstgläser der Gegenwart* (Leipzig, 1925)
J. Čadík: *Dílo Josefa Drahoňovského* [The work of Josef Drahoňovský] (Prague, 1933)
J. Raban: *Modern Bohemian Glass* (Prague, 1963)
A. Adlerová: *Modern Bohemian Glass* (Prague, 1979)
Czechoslovakian Glass, 1350–1980 (exh. cat., Corning, NY, Mus. Glass, 1981)
Lötz—Böhmisches Glas, 1880–1940 (exh. cat., Düsseldorf, Kstmus., 1989)
S. Petrová and J.-L. Olivié: *Bohemian Glass* (Paris, 1990)
A. Adlerová and O. Drahotová: *Böhmisches Glas* (in preparation)

ALENA ADLEROVÁ

VIII. Metalwork.

1. Gold and silver. 2. Base metals.

1. GOLD AND SILVER. The gold- and silversmiths' craft ranks among the most important trades practised in the Czech lands. There were three periods in particular when this craft attained a level of unparalleled excellence: first, during the reign of the House of Luxembourg in the 14th century; second, during the reign (1576–1612) of Emperor Rudolf II; and last, in the Baroque period of the 17th and 18th centuries. After 1800 Czech gold- and silversmiths concentrated mainly on the manufacture of domestic wares, and they began to participate in international exhibitions; many specialized schools were established.

(i) 11th–15th centuries. (ii) 16th century–early 17th. (iii) Early 17th century and after.

(i) 11th–15th centuries. The importance of gold- and silversmithing in the Czech lands is demonstrated by the fact that the earliest artist there known by name, Koyata, who lived in the 11th century, was a goldsmith. The oldest preserved objects in precious metal are the silver-gilt burial insignia (1298) of Ottokar II and the burial crown (1307) of Rudolf I (1282–1307), both in St Vitus' Cathedral,

29. Footed bowl, silver gilt and translucent enamel, with an engraved frieze of water-fowl, h. 90 mm, second half of the 14th century (Prague, Museum of Decorative Arts)

Prague. They probably originated in the workshop of the Benedictine monastery in Břevnov, Prague, which was established around the end of the 13th century by Abbot Bavor of Nečtiny. The Břevnov workshop also provided artefacts for the Benedictine convent of St George at Prague Castle (administered by Abbot Bavor), for example the reliquary of St George's arm (c. 1320; with details added in the second half of the 14th century), a bust of St Ludmilla (c. 1340; Prague, St Vitus' Cathedral, Treasury), the reliquary bust of a saint (c. 1340; Prague, N.G., Convent of St George), the reliquary bust of St Paul (c. 1340; Prague, Mus. Dec. A.) and probably also the crosier of the Abbot of Rajhrad (c. 1330; Hradec Králové, Bishop's Residence). All these works were made in the reign of John of Luxembourg (1296–1346).

From the same period records exist that underline the importance of secular work. The work of Bohemian goldsmiths was recognized throughout Europe for its technical accomplishment and advanced designs. The Prague goldsmiths were the first in the kingdom of Bohemia to form a brotherhood in 1324 and were the only craftsmen accorded recognition under Emperor Charles IV, who awarded them the mitre of their patron St Eligius (Prague, N. Mus.), which he had brought from France in 1378. Charles IV was an enthusiastic patron of goldsmiths, silversmiths and jewellers and established a court workshop before 1346 under the supervision of Peter Parler and later his son Wenzel Parler. Before 1346 a new Bohemian royal crown was made, the so-called St Wenceslas Crown (Prague, St Vitus' Cathedral, Treasury), as well as the crown of the Holy Roman Empire (Aachen Cathedral).

In addition to the new tomb of St Wenceslas (c. 1358; Prague, St Vitus' Cathedral) the court workshop produced reliquaries of various types: reliquary busts, reliquary figures, monstrance reliquaries and reliquary crosses, all emulating the style of Parler's architecture or figural compositions. Most of the reliquaries are decorated with jewels in funnel-shaped settings, imitation jewels of glass, which were highly prized in the Middle Ages, and engraved

enamels (e.g. the cross and reliquaries presented by Pope Urban V and embellished in Bohemia). These artefacts are preserved in various treasuries, including those of Aachen Cathedral and St Vitus' Cathedral, Prague; the latter, according to records of between 1354 and 1387, held the richest collection of gold and silver in 14th-century Europe. The influence of Parler's architectural style is also apparent in the tower-shaped Sedlec monstrance (Prague, N.G., Convent of St George) and the reliquary of the Blood of Christ (before 1400; Venice, Frari), while Parler's style in sculpture was imitated in the reliquary busts of St Peter and St Paul (1413; Prague, Archbishop's Pal.). Charles IV gave to Aachen Cathedral a three-towered reliquary and the bust (c. 1357) of Charlemagne, his patron, a product of the Parler school influenced by contemporary Paris statues. The tradition of the Caroline goldsmiths and jewellers flourished until the early 15th century, a fine example of their work being the crown (1381; Munich, Residenz) for Charles IV's daughter, Anne, Queen of England. Once called the Bohemian Crown, it is decorated with sapphires and pearls in typical Bohemian settings.

The imperial court workshop was rivalled by the craftsmen working for the courtiers of Charles IV. Surviving examples of their work include the reliquary of Bishop Jan Volek (1347; Baltimore, MD, Walters A.G.), two chalices from Milevsko (Prague, Strahov Abbey), with figured decoration in translucent enamel, and the Vyšší Brod ciborium (Prague, Mus. Dec. A.), inspired by the work of Nuremberg goldsmiths. Secular works from the reigns of Charles IV and his son Wenceslas IV are represented by the 387 objects that form part of the Karlštejn Treasury (Prague, Mus. Dec. A.), probably acquired by royalty in the late 14th century. This unique collection comprises vessels, including a silver-gilt bowl covered in translucent resin enamel with an engraved frieze of water-fowl (see fig. 29), and various dress ornaments.

By 1419, 71 goldsmiths were working in Prague, and others worked throughout the Czech lands. Local gold and silver mining, although extensive, failed to meet the demand, and metals had to be imported from Hungary. In the early 15th century the Hussite Wars in Bohemia disrupted the gold- and silversmiths' trade, but it revived in the second half of the 15th century. Vladislav II made efforts to promote the tradition established by Charles IV and sought to compensate for the losses suffered by the St Vitus Treasury during the Hussite period. Three silver reliquary busts (1484–7; Prague, St Vitus' Cathedral), attributed to Václav of Budějovice, survive from this period; they foreshadow the Renaissance style. Several chalices (Prague, St Vitus' Cathedral, Treasury; Prague, Loreto Treasury), Queen Eliška Rejčka's belt and a set of 24 teaspoons mounted in silver (Hradec Králové, Reg. Mus.) have also been ascribed to the reign of Vladislav II.

(ii) 16th century–early 17th. The second significant period in the development of the gold- and silversmiths' craft in the Czech lands was during the reign of Emperor Rudolf II. He inherited from his father Emperor Maximilian II a taste for luxury and for rare and unusual artworks. This interest grew into a compulsive mania that brought fame to Prague Castle, where he established his permanent seat.

Its reputation as a centre of the arts spread throughout Europe. He enlisted the services of the most celebrated gold- and silversmiths, including Anton Schweinberger (*d* 1603), Paulus van Vianen (1570–1613), Christoph Lencker (*d* 1613), Hans Petzolt, Christoph Jamnitzer (*d* 1618), Nikolaus Schmidt, Friedrich Hilebrand, Paul Hübner, Hans Schlotheim (1545–1625) and David Attemstätter (1547–1617). They made use of gemstones, particularly Bohemian crystal and garnet (which the Emperor claimed exclusively for his use), rare natural specimens, exotic gems, shells, corals, ostrich eggs, bezoars, coconuts and other types of nut. The goldsmiths derived inspiration from Italian and German patterns, predominantly from the *Libro di disegni per far vassella d'argento a d'oro . . .* (1597) written by Ottavio Strada, curator of the Emperor's collection, and from the designs of the court architect and scholar Hans Vredeman de Vries.

Rudolf II instigated a number of competitions for the design of gold and silver objects. In 1602 one such competition took place for the design of the Emperor's gold crown (Vienna, Schatzkam.). The Prague goldsmith selected was Jan Vermeyen (1559–1606), who possibly collaborated with the enameller Hans Karl (*d* 1606). Other imperial insignia, for example the sceptre and orb (Prague, St Vitus' Cathedral, Treasury), were made at the same time, probably by the same craftsmen. In the decorative use of enamel and gemstones Rudolf's regalia was a precursor of the Mannerist sceptre and orb commissioned by his brother and successor Matthias and made by the Prague goldsmith Andreas Osenbruck (*fl* 1612–22) as an addition to the imperial coronation insignia (1612–15; Vienna, Schatzkam.). Rudolf's sceptre and orb display a fine level of craftsmanship testifying to the skill of some 50 artisans in the employ of the Emperor.

There was much competition in Prague for the Emperor's commissions. Gold- and silverware, jewellery and glyptics attained fantastic ingenuity in the Mannerist style, for example the silver-gilt jug and bowl by Christoph Jamnitzer, a jug made of gold and coconut shell by Anton Schweinberger and the mechanical nef by Hans Schlotheim (Vienna, Ksthist. Mus.). The theme of the deformation of nature in these works contrasts with the classical symmetry of the gold-mounted jasper ewer (1608) and bowl of bloodstone and onyx by Paulus van Vianen (Vienna, Ksthist. Mus.). The vast majority of the objects made for Rudolf II no longer exist, but records of the names of 210 gold- and silversmiths, including those of 45 craftsmen working for the Prague court, survive. The art of the gold- and silversmiths working in Prague in the reign of Rudolf II gave the city a European prominence. The transfer of the imperial court from Prague to Vienna in 1617 under Rudolf's successor Matthias brought this to an end.

(iii) Early 17th century and after. The third significant period in the gold- and silversmith trade in the Czech lands lasted from the early 17th century until the end of the 18th. Records exist of some 600 gold- and silversmiths working in Prague during this period, producing mostly liturgical objects, for example monstrances, chalices, ciboria, reliquaries, jugs, lamps, candlesticks, censers, crosiers, cope clasps and bindings. These works are often richly jewelled decorations, the large silver figures frequently achieving monumental dimensions (examples at Prague, St Vitus' Cathedral, Treasury; Prague, Church of St Thomas in the Lesser Town; Šepekov; Church of the Holy Mount at Příbram).

The advent of a new ruling class following the defeat of the Bohemian Estate in the Battle of the White Mountain (1620) caused a revival of the production of luxury objects. The high-ranking noblemen and Catholic clergy, who regained power, displayed their wealth and status by furnishing mansions and palaces, churches, pilgrim sanctuaries, monasteries and convents with silver vessels. There was an insufficient number of gold- and silversmiths in the Czech lands to meet these new requirements. Consequently, craftsmen arrived from Austria, Germany, Silesia, Italy, Denmark and the Netherlands and settled permanently in Bohemia. Most came to Prague, which in the early 18th century was one of the centres of the Baroque style. The immigrant gold- and silversmiths trained local apprentices, who then gained experience by travelling in Europe. Gold- and silversmiths' work after *c.* 1620 initially imitated the work of the immigrant craftsmen, but gradually the native craftsmen developed their skills. From 1674, marks recording the place and date of manufacture and the goldsmiths' initials were used throughout the Czech lands (having been introduced in the Bohemian kingdom in 1562).

Distinctly Baroque features, such as undulating contours and plasticity of surfaces, were in evidence *c.* 1670 and were accentuated by embossing and engraving and by the use of filigree, frequently combined with Bohemian garnets and small enamel painted plates (see fig. 30). Filigree was also used on miniature silver chests and receptacles (examples at Prague, Loreto Treasury) and was particularly popular among the craftsmen in Jewish communities (examples at Prague, State Jew. Mus.; Prague, Mus. Dec. A.). František Kryštof Diesbach (1696–1766), Marek Hrbek (1635–1700), Jiří Zeller (*d* 1706), Jan Kryštof Haller (*d* 1696), František Václav Voitländer (1657–91), Jan Jiří Kogler (1670–1720) and Karel Taxner (1675–1745) were notable among the gold- and silversmiths of the late 17th century.

After 1700 silversmiths' work was technically improved and artistically enriched, and a wider range of themes was introduced by such artists as Jan Adam Dominik Sartorius (1668–1710), Jan Jiří Lux (1665–1724), Jakub Ebner (*fl* 1755–70; *d* 1778), Rinaldo Ranzoni (1671–1737), Philip Oberhölzer (1686–1746), Gottfried Lambrecht (1686–1736) and Anton Koher (or Karer; 1726–51). The most prominent gold- and silversmiths working in the Baroque style from the 1720s to the 1750s were those who collaborated with the architect Kilian Ignaz Dientzenhofer: Michal Josef Cocsell (*d* 1747), Jan Jiří Brullus the younger (1710–89), Leopold Lichtenschopf (1680–1774), Ferdinand Schachtel (1681–1766), Kaspar Gschwandtner (1708–65), František Josef Eberle (1690–1742), Jan Packeny (1694–1760), František Josef Seitz (1705–55) and his brother Jiří Vilém Seitz (1695–1750). This prolific generation of gold- and silversmiths also included Jan Melichar Schick (1682–1765) and František Michal Raedelmayer (1689–1749), who worked in Prague, Josef Aycher in Cheb

30. Reliquary cross by František Václav Voitländer, silver gilt with filigree work, enamel, Bohemian garnets and rock crystal, h. 440 mm, 1691 (Prague, Museum of Decorative Arts)

and Jan Michal Kaltenmacher (1763–89) in Brno. Gold- and silversmiths working in the latter half of the 18th century included František Kinda (1725–90), Adam Leidecker (1717–88), Richard Fleischmann (1741–1822), Jan Domenik Packeny (*fl* 1725–86) and Ignác Novák (1723–1803). In the 1770s and 1780s, when church property was secularized and political and economic reforms were introduced under Joseph II, the Baroque style became diluted.

The silversmiths of the 19th century in the Czech lands concentrated on the manufacture of tableware for the middle classes, while the aristocracy acquired their silver from Vienna. New hallmark regulations were introduced after 1862, and it is thus possible to trace the development of Bohemian wares. The tables of marks between 1806 and 1860 mention 506 gold- and silversmiths. Information about 19th-century Bohemian gold- and silversmiths is also provided by reports and catalogues of the first industrial exhibitions (from 1828) in Prague and, from the second half of the century, by a list of the participants at international exhibitions.

The output of Bohemian gold- and silversmiths differs from Viennese production particularly in the use of local gemstones. Filigree and granulation were often utilized in the first quarter of the 19th century. The most prominent Prague goldsmiths in the 19th century were Hynek Prokop Gindle (1753–1817) and his son Prokop Gindle, manufacturers of silver goods, the Goldschmid family, Jan Richter (1791–1855), the goldsmith Václav Kokoschka (1810–58), related to the painter Oskar Kokoschka, Matyáš Pichler (1803–85) and Ludvík Pichler (1827–71), and Jeroným Grohmann (1803–59). Some of the distinguished artists of the Christian Academy helped to establish and promote the specialized training of gold- and silversmiths, which was concentrated in vocational schools, for example the schools for gold- and silversmiths in Prague (1863–85), in Jablonec nad Nisou (founded in 1880), in Turnov (founded in 1884) and in the department of Decorative Metalwork of the Academy of Applied Arts in Prague (founded in 1885).

Secessionist (Art Nouveau) gold- and silversmiths and jewellers, including Emanuel Novák (1866–1918), Václav Němec (1845–1924) and his son Josef Ladislav Němec (1871–1943) and Franta Anýž (1876–1934) derived inspiration from floral motifs and from the Slavonic physiognomy. In the late Secessionist period and in the 1920s and 1930s original and innovative work was produced by Marie Křivánková (1883–1936) and some of the artists working for the art cooperative Artěl (founded in 1908), for example Rudolf Stockar (1886–1957) and Jaroslav Horejc (1886–1983). Owing to social turmoil the post-war era could boast of few successes until the 1960s, when graduates from the Academy of Applied Arts in Prague who had studied under professors Bedřich Stefan (1896–1982), Karel Štipl (1889–1972) and Jan Nušl (1900–86) began to participate in international competitions and exhibitions.

BIBLIOGRAPHY

L. Urešová: *Barokní zlatnictví ze sbírek Umělecko-průmyslového muzea v Praze* [Baroque goldsmith craft from the collections of the Museum of Decorative Arts in Prague] (Prague, 1974)
——: 'Stříbrný poklad z vrcholného středověku' [Silver treasures from the peak of the Middle Ages], *Acta Umělecko-Průmyslové Muz.*, xv/2 (1980), pp. 10–29
E. Poche: 'Umělecká řemesla gotické doby' [Arts and crafts of the Gothic period], *Dějiny českého výtvarného umění* [History of Czech fine arts], ed. J. Krása, I/ii (Prague, 1984–9), pp. 440–79
——: 'Pozdně gotická umělecká řemesla' [Late Gothic arts and crafts], *Dějiny českého výtvarného umění*, ed. J. Krása, I/ii (Prague, 1984–9), pp. 613–22
——: 'Barokní umělecké řemeslo v Čechách' [Baroque arts and crafts in Bohemia], *Dějiny českého výtvarného umění*, ed. J. Krása, II/i (Prague, 1984–9), pp. 136–49
——: 'Barokní umělecké řemeslo 17. století v Čechách' [17th-century Baroque arts and crafts in Bohemia], *Dějiny českého výtvarného umění*, ed. J. Krása, II/i (Prague, 1984–9), pp. 372–90
——: 'Umělecké řemeslo vrcholného baroka v Čechách' [Arts and crafts at the peak of the Baroque in Bohemia], *Dějiny českého výtvarného umění*, ed. J. Krása, II/ii (Prague, 1984–9), pp. 629–49
——: 'Umělecké řemeslo pozdního baroka a rokoka v Čechách' [Late Baroque and Rococo arts and crafts in Bohemia], *Dějiny českého výtvarného umění*, ed. J. Krása, II/ii (Prague, 1984–9), pp. 817–33
J. Hráský: 'Zlatníci pražského baroka' [Prague Baroque goldsmiths], *Acta Umělecko-Průmyslové Muz.*, xvii/5 (1987)

L. Urešová: 'Karlštejnský poklad' [The Karlštejn Treasury], *Umění*, xxxv (1987), pp. 490–97
——: 'Goldschmiedekunst', *Ksthandwke Böhmen* (1988), pp. 57–63

LIBUŠE UREŠOVÁ

2. BASE METALS.

(i) Pewter. From the beginning of the 14th century there is proof of the mining, trading and processing of tin in Czech lands. There were extensive deposits of tin in the areas of the Ore Mountains and the Slavkov forest. Tin was sold to towns outside Bohemia such as Nuremberg and Bruges, but most went to Prague. Pewtermaking became an important trade there, as it was later in other royal towns (Hradec Králové, Mladá Boleslav, Česká Lípa, České Budějovice, Brno and Plzeň) and in the mining towns (Kutná Hora, Jihlava, Cheb, Jáchymov and Slavkov). In 1387 the Brno pewterers followed the example of Prague and stipulated that goods must be marked with the emblem of the town (a simplified version of its coat of arms) and the name or initials and symbol of the pewterer, but marking remained uncommon.

The oldest preserved wrought pewter objects include numerous fonts. The characteristic shape of Bohemian fonts from the 15th to the 17th centuries was like an upside-down bell on three legs. The oldest preserved fonts date from 1406 (Hradec Králové, Church of the Holy Spirit) and 1414 (Prague, Our Lady before Týn; see fig. 31). Fonts were made in the Kutná Hora workshop of Ondřej Ptáček (*d* 1511) and his sons or were the work of the Prague master Brikcí of Cinperk (*d* 1599) and his son Bartolomej of Cinperk (*d* 1601). In 1566 the crown jewels of pewter were made by Tomáš Jaroš of Brno for the funeral of Emperor Ferdinand I.

After the defeat of the Bohemian Estate in the Battle of the White Mountain (1620) the work of pewterers, unlike that of gold- and silversmiths, was not curtailed, for they had plenty of commissions from the burghers and the guilds. The shape of guild flagons—a cylindrical form divided by bands and with engraved ornamentation—had evolved by the 15th century, with some variations. During the 16th and 17th centuries engraving was the dominant form of decoration; a special technique using an angled tool was described as 'Bohemian music'. Relief ornamentation, mainly used for applied bands on bells and fonts, was not as widely used on vessels, although this technique was popular in Jáchymov, where craftsmen modelled their work on that of Peter Flötner and others. Unusual vessels shaped to look like books, which in the 17th and 18th centuries were considered to be a Bohemian invention, were also made.

From the 1730s the main centres of pewter production were in the western Czech lands—Karlovy Vary, Slavkov (Schlagenwald) and Krásno—where mostly high-quality tableware and liturgical vessels in the Baroque and Rococo styles, imitating silverware, were produced. A tin quality mark appeared for the first time in the 18th century in the mining towns as a result of a decree issued by Empress Maria-Theresa in 1770. In the 19th century the craft stagnated as industrial techniques were introduced, and the guilds were abolished in 1859. By the first half of the 20th century there were few pewterers left; the last Prague pewterer died in 1969. After World War II craftsmen at

31. Pewter baptismal font, h. 1.02 m (without cover), 1414; cover, 1849 (Prague, Our Lady before Týn)

the Arts and Crafts Centre, Prague, began to concentrate on repairing and restoring pewter.

(ii) Iron, bronze and steel. Mineral deposits of iron ore in central Bohemia, especially in the Brdy woods, enabled the establishment of foundries, mostly royal ones, in the Middle Ages. As towns grew, the specialized processing of base metals developed—there were blacksmiths, armourers, swordmakers, knifemakers, locksmiths etc. There were six such trades in Prague in the 13th century; by the 14th century there were 34. The names of master craftsmen are known through surviving accounts. The blacksmith Václav, for example, recorded in the St Vitus' Cathedral accounts of the early 14th century, is known to have made the bars in the chapel of the Holy Cross at Karlštejn Castle, the pastophory (1372) in the St Wenceslas Chapel in St Vitus' Cathedral in Prague, and the gates to

the sanctuary and the chain around the tomb of St Wenceslas in the same cathedral. His work was influenced by that of Peter Parler, Master of the Works during the building of the cathedral. The first record of a guild of blacksmiths in Prague dates from 1418. Country guilds, mostly associations of metalworkers, were also established in the early 15th century.

Many 16th- and 17th-century works in iron and bronze survive in Kutná Hora, Jindřichův Hradec and particularly in Prague, for example the well in Little Square (c. 1560), the railings around the royal tomb of Emperor Ferdinand I, Anne of Hungary and Emperor Maximilian II by Heinrich Schmidthammer (1589; Prague, St Vitus' Cathedral) and the bars in the Strahov Monastery, Prague (1628). A treatise on casting was written by Vavřinec Křička of Bytýška (d 1568), who also collaborated with Tomáš Jaroš of Brno on the casting of the bronze Singing Fountain (1568) in the garden of the Royal Summer Palace ('Belvedere') at Hradčany Castle in Prague. In 1549 Tomáš Jaroš cast the largest bell in Bohemia, for St Vitus' Cathedral.

In the first half of the 18th century blacksmiths followed designs by architects for church railings. Notable examples include the illusory bars for the Italian Chapel in the Clementinum (1715), Prague, probably after a design by František Maximilian Kaňka, architect of the chapel, and the early Rococo railings at the entrance to Hradčany Castle. From the end of the 18th century it became fashionable to make decorative objects in cast iron, hitherto used only for casting such utilitarian objects as firebacks, tomb crosses and domestic stoves (e.g. panels depicting images from antiquity from the workshop of Ignác Michal Platzer in Prague, late 18th century; Prague, Mus. Dec. A.).

In 1785 Count Rudolf Vrbna took charge of the foundry at Hořovice near Beroun and, following the example of Berlin foundries, established a branch for artistic casting at Komárov, where he trained specialists. His son Eugen Vrbna continued this project from 1823. In the 1830s the Komárov foundry produced such small, decorative objects as paperweights, and large statues (e.g. on the tomb of Bishop Lev Thun-Hohenstein, designed by Václav Prachner, in the cemetery in Košíře, Prague) were also cast by the specialist Dominik Zafouk (1796–1879). Delicate jewellery was also made at Komárov, based on designs by the Prague goldsmith Jan Richter. Portrait medals were made at the iron foundry in the Křivoklát district of Nový Jáchymov, and at Nižbor, where the first blast furnace in Bohemia had been constructed in 1818. By the 1850s many other foundries had been established in Moravia by aristocratic entrepreneurs: the Salm foundry in Blansko, the Dietrichstein foundries in Ransko and Polička and the Liechtenstein foundry at Adamov. In the second half of the 19th century the foundries produced mostly lampposts, bars, railings and colonnades for the spa towns of Karlovy Vary and Mariánské Lázně. The last important commission carried out at the Křivoklát foundry was the so-called Count Hanavský Pavilion (now in Letná Square, Prague) for the Jubilee Exhibition (1891) in Prague.

In the 1890s, as elsewhere in Europe, there was a revival of handicrafts. In 1876 a school for artistic wrought-iron work was established in Hradec Králové. Training in this field was not repeated elsewhere until the 1950s at the Applied Arts School for Stone Masonry and Decorative Metals in Turnov (founded in 1884). From 1885 there was a prestigious department for decorative metalwork at the Academy of Applied Arts in Prague, where the teachers included A. Fanta, Emanuel Novák, Josef Ladislav Němec, Jaroslav Horejc, Bedřich Stefan and Jan Nušl. The work of Franta Anýž (1879–1934) is representative of the Secessionist period. From 1902 he had his own studio and from 1912 his own foundry, where he made bronze casts for other artists, such as the reliefs on the entrance gate of St Vitus' Cathedral, the ornamentations on the sarcophagus of Charles IV (1929) and the door to the royal crypt etc. Boxes, candlesticks and ashtrays made in non-ferrous metals were designed in the Cubist style by such architects as Vlastislav Hofman (1884–1964), Jaroslav Horejc, Rudolf Stockar and Jiří Kroha (see CZECH CUBISM) for the art cooperative Artěl (1908–34), which was modelled on the Wiener Werkstätte.

BIBLIOGRAPHY

E. Leisching: *Über Gusseisen mit besonderer Berücksichtigung des Österreichischen Kunsteisengusses* (Vienna, 1917)

F. Tischer: *Böhmisches Zinn und seine Marken* (Leipzig, 1928)

E. Poche: *Česká umělecká litina* [Bohemian artistic cast ironwork] (Prague, 1953)

Cín: Z dějin českého konvářství [Pewter: From the history of Bohemian jug-making] (exh. cat., ed. D. Stará; Prague, 1972)

Decorative Cast Ironwork (exh. cat., ed. Z. Rasl; Prague, 1980)

J. Hráský: 'Pražští cínaři 17.–19. století' [Prague pewterers of the 17th–19th centuries], *Acta UPM*, xxi/7 (1989)

HELENA KOENIGSMARKOVÁ

IX. Objects of vertu.

1. BOHEMIAN GARNETS. Deposits of garnets of the pyrope variety are found only in the south-west foothills of the Bohemian Central Mountains. From medieval times garnets were used by goldsmiths for decorating liturgical objects because of their fiery colour, which was seen to symbolize the blood of Christ. From the 16th century there are records concerning garnet deposits and mining, the oldest of which is *De natura fossilium libri* (Basle, 1546) by Georgius Agricola (1493–1555). Until the mid-17th century garnets were traded mostly in their unprocessed state from Bohemia to Nuremberg, Freiburg and Waldkirchen, where the grinding and cutting was carried out. However, a significant development in quarrying and cutting garnets took place during the reign of Rudolf II, who collected gemstones for his treasury and had facilities for the cutting and grinding of precious stones built in Prague. Goldsmiths during this period favoured the use of Bohemian garnets and mounted them on gold and silver-gilt jewelled vessels such as the Prasem Bowl (1600–06; Vienna, Ksthist. Mus.) by Jan (Hans) Vermeyen (d 1606). During the Baroque period, garnets were used for decorating liturgical vessels (see fig. 30 above), jewellery, books, boxes and cutlery handles and in embroidery. The largest garnet was set by the goldsmith Johann Frederick Dinglinger (1702–67) in 1737 (Dresden, Grünes Gewölbe).

During the 19th century the garnet industry began to thrive in Prague and Turnov. Until the 19th century garnets were cut in the same way as other hardstones and precious gems: rose cut, brilliant or cabochon. However, such special methods of cutting were introduced as the flat cut, patented in Prague in 1881 by Adolf Prevor (*d* before 1891); the star cut, adopted in the 1880s, which could be machine cut; and the wing cut, which was introduced at the School for Gold- and Silversmiths in Turnov in 1884. The faceted bead or smooth cut, brought in during the Baroque period for threaded necklaces and bracelets, was again popular for neo-Renaissance styles. Since Bohemian garnets were generally quite small, they were often mounted in gold or silver gilt, in groups or combined with a larger variety of garnet called an almandine, with diamonds or, for neo-Rococo styles, with pearls, marcasites, opals and adularia. Towards the end of the 19th century Czech artists and goldsmiths and the teachers at the academies of Applied Arts in Prague and Turnov made a concerted effort to improve the artistic quality and craftsmanship of garnet jewellery, which was highly successful at the Trade and Chamber of Commerce Fair in Prague in 1908. After World War II the production of garnet jewellery was concentrated into one cooperative of artistic production called Granát ('Garnet') in Turnov, but after 1990 many private firms were set up.

BIBLIOGRAPHY
J. Morávek: *Nově objevený inventář rudolfinských sbírek na hradě pražském* [Newly discovered inventory of the Rudolf collections at Prague Castle] (Prague, 1937)
J. Klečák and V. Holásek: *Český granát* [Czech garnet] (Ústí nad Labem, 1972)
V. Bouška and J. Kouřimský: *Drahé kameny kolem nás* [Gemstones around us] (Prague, 1976)
S. Urban: *Řezáči drahých kamenů v Čechách v 16. a 17. století* [Cutters of gemstones in Bohemia in the 16th and 17th centuries] (Prague, 1976)
Český granát [Czech garnet] (exh. cat., ed. V. Vokáčová; Prague, Mus. Dec. A., 1984)

VĚRA VOKÁČOVÁ

2. OTHER HARDSTONES. From the end of the 16th century the court workshop of Rudolf II (*see* HABSBURG, §I(10)) in Prague distinguished itself through its brilliant work in the field of hardstone carving and Florentine mosaics, an activity that lasted almost a century. Rudolf had been one of the most assiduous clients of the Milanese workshops specializing in cut vases, and in 1588 he succeeded in obtaining the permanent transfer from Milan to Prague of Ottavio Miseroni (*see* MISERONI), who was assisted at the Bohemian court by his brothers Giovanni Ambrogio and Alessandro. Ottavio's son, Dionysio (for illustration of his work *see* PRAGUE, fig. 11), and grandson, Ferdinand Eusebius, continued the workshop's activities until the latter's death in 1684. Miseroni and his followers specialized in producing hardstone vases carved in smooth forms and embellished with gold and enamel settings made by the court goldsmiths, notably Jan (Hans) Vermeyen (*see* HARDSTONES, colour pl. II, fig. 1). Miseroni

32. Hardstone panel by Cosimo Castrucci: *Landscape with a Bridge and a Chapel*, 183×245 mm, Prague, 1596 (Vienna, Kunsthistorisches Museum)

devoted special attention to the cameo and to the related genre of the small relief panel composed of various coloured hardstones, each worked separately, showing religious or mythological scenes.

Another celebrated stone-cutter working at Rudolf's court at the same time as Miseroni was CASPAR LEHMANN, who was named Court Cutter of Precious Stones in 1601. During the reign of Rudolf II improvements in the quality of Bohemian crystal permitted craftsmen to achieve effects that had previously been possible only with the more precious rock crystal, and it was Lehmann who first applied the intaglio technique used on stone to crystal (*see* §VII, 1 above).

Rudolf's enthusiasm for hardstone objects extended to the Florentine mosaic technique. In 1589 Ferdinando I de' Medici, Grand Duke of Tuscany, had sent a table inlaid with different varieties of crystal and stone to Prague. Rudolf liked it so much that he immediately commissioned a second table-top (untraced). Its execution (1589–97) was entrusted to the best craftsmen in the Grand Ducal workshop in Florence, who mostly used hardstones sent from Bohemia. Contemporary accounts describe the landscapes, military trophies, birds and flowers that surrounded the Emperor's initials, all made in inlaid stone. Rudolf's wish to establish his own Florentine mosaic workshop led to the removal from Florence to Prague of Cosimo Castrucci, documented at the Bohemian court in 1596, the year in which he signed a panel with a landscape composed of inlaid hardstones (Vienna, Ksthist. Mus.; see fig. 32). In 1598 his son Giovanni is also recorded in Prague, and he continued his father's activities, as his own son Cosimo the younger and his son-in-law Giuliano Pandolfini, who was also of Florentine origin, were to do after him.

To judge by the substantial number of panels that survive and given that the technique is by nature a slow and arduous one, the Castrucci family, whose activity in Prague continued until about 1630, must have had a large workshop. The principal characteristics of their works (which are so consistent as to make the individual personalities of the family and the chronological sequence of their works difficult to identify) are the preference for landscape subjects, often based on prints by the Flemish and mid-European artists who gravitated to Rudolf's court, and the almost exclusive use of Bohemian jaspers of predominantly green, brown and pinkish tones, often rendered more vibrant by intense speckling. Another frequently recurring decorative theme in the Bohemian panels is the representation of geometric solids, employed as symbols of Renaissance cosmology and based on engravings from a treatise on perspective published in Nuremberg in 1568.

Among the most notable works produced in the Prague workshop are an ebony cabinet with Florentine mosaic, executed perhaps by Cosimo Castrucci the younger (Vienna, Ksthist. Mus.), and a table-top made between 1620 and 1623 for Charles, Prince of Liechtenstein, decorated with fillets of gilt bronze studded with garnets (Vaduz, Samml. Liechtenstein). At about the same time a casket of ebony, gilt bronze and hardstones, probably designed by Ottavio Miseroni, was made for Prince Charles (Vaduz, Samml. Liechtenstein). The original client for whom a table-top made in Prague (Florence, Pitti) was intended is not known; it entered the Grand Ducal collection in Florence at the end of the 18th century and, like the Liechtenstein table-top, is decorated with landscapes composed of hardstones and separated by fillets of silver set with garnets.

About 1620 the overburdened Florentine workshop itself commissioned at least two works from its counterpart in Prague. Made to designs by the Florentine painter Bernardino Poccetti, they have quatrefoil panels with an allegory of *Fame* and a panel showing the *Banquet of Abraham* (both Florence, Mus. Opificio Pietre Dure). They were executed by Cosimo Castrucci the younger and Giuliano Pandolfini. The latter is documented in Florence in the 1630s, in the employ of the Grand Ducal workshop. Rudolf II's successors inherited neither his qualities as a patron nor his passion for the virtuosity of the Florentine mosaic technique, and consequently the artistic activity that he had successfully transplanted from Florence to Prague made its return to the Italian city.

BIBLIOGRAPHY

E. Neumann: 'Florentiner Mosaik aus Prag', *Jb. Ksthist. Samml. Wien*, liii (1957), pp. 75–158
B. Bukovinská: 'Další florentské mozaiky z Prahy' [More Florentine mosaics from Prague], *Umění*, iv (1972), pp. 363–70
Prag um 1600: Kunst und Kultur am Hofe Rudolfs II, 2 vols (exh. cat., Vienna, Ksthist. Mus., 1988)
Splendori di pietre dure: L'arte di corte nella Firenze dei Granduchi (exh. cat., ed. A. M. Giusti; Florence, Pitti, 1988–9)

ANNAMARIA GIUSTI

X. Textiles.

1. Woven fabrics. 2. Embroidery. 3. Lace.

1. WOVEN FABRICS. In the Middle Ages linen-weaving was the most developed branch of textiles, and towards the end of the medieval period linen-weavers' guilds were established. Until the 18th century linen was woven in both the towns and the country and was used for clothing and household textiles. As well as white and unbleached linen, from the 13th century striped linen cloth was produced and later checked patterns. The early dyes were indigo blue and Turkish red, a form of madder. This patterned cloth appears in Gothic paintings and was used in particular for bedlinen. Fine shawls and veils were also made, but production declined during the Renaissance, when the fashion for these garments changed. In the 14th and 15th centuries the manufacture of woollen cloth flourished, and drapers' guilds were set up in most towns. Rough cloth was woven and later also finer cloth, but the latter did not achieve the refined delicacy of the cloth imported from the Netherlands for the wealthy. From the 14th century expensive decorative fabrics were imported from Italy. Italian fabrics were sold in particular in the Týn courtyard in Prague's Old Town.

During the Renaissance weaving developed dramatically. From the 16th century there was an intensive increase in exports, mostly organized by foreign traders, and local linen gained a significant place on the European market. Trade in woollen cloth continued to prosper, and its quality improved to a certain degree. Gradually weavers became concentrated in particular towns. The cloth they produced was predominantly grey and sometimes black, brick-red, green, light blue or white. Late 16th-century cloth interwoven with golden threads is known, notably from Jindřichův Hradec.

The Thirty Years War and the Counter-Reformation arrested the development of textiles, especially with the banishment of non-Catholic artisans from the country. The aristocracy bought their fine textiles mostly from abroad, and the decline in linen-weaving and cloth manufacture continued until the mid-17th century, when trade recovered. In the 17th and 18th centuries the industry was concentrated in such centres as Liberec, Jindřichův Hradec, Humpolec, Jihlava, Brno and Půchov.

In the 1620s Count Albrecht von Wallenstein began to manufacture textiles on his estates in northern Bohemia, notably at Oberleutensdorf and Jičín. Originally the enterprise was stimulated by the need for military uniforms, and there were also attempts to introduce silk-weaving. In 1627 von Wallenstein ordered his staff in Jičín to plant mulberry trees and summoned silk experts from Italy. However, after his death these enterprises declined. A Jesuit textile manufactory (1684–8) was established at Soběchleby, near Teplice, producing woven cloth, woollen fabrics, stockings, veils, braids and cords. These products served ecclesiastical needs and were also sold in Prague.

In the 18th century three private silk manufacturers established themselves in Prague. In 1706 Karel Vilém Kristián Heiser began the production of woven silks using silver and golden threads, a venture that lasted probably until the 1730s. Josef Tarone, an Italian, set up a short-lived workshop in the early 1720s, producing expensive brocade and russet upholstery and draperies in imitation of French models. Jan Antonín Schmiedel's business, launched in 1723, was also short-lived. In 1725 there was a new initiative: the Supreme Czech Chancellor František Ferdinand Kinský established a silk shareholders' company in Prague and summoned Louis Jamette, a Frenchman who had initiated silk production in Moscow. The various shareholders produced brocade, russet, damask, taffeta, satin, velvet, mourning crape, handkerchiefs and ribbons. A high standard of production was achieved, probably due to Jamette's influence, but there were marketing difficulties, and the company ceased to exist c. 1738.

Maria-Theresa (reg 1743–80) devoted considerable attention to the advancement of silk production. In 1752 she issued a decree promoting the cultivation of mulberry trees: those who grew the trees, tended the silkworms and wove the silk were granted financial support. Small-scale production was dispersed in various localities, and the output in the last decade of Maria-Theresa's rule was substantial. Emperor Joseph II (reg 1765–90) continued to further his mother's projects, but silk production did not make any significant impact. Local production of luxury fabrics partly met the local needs, but imports from France predominated.

In the 18th century the production of linen reached its greatest heights. Woollen cloth-making concentrated on finer fabrics, and exports increased to such countries as Italy, Switzerland, Poland, Russia, Denmark and Turkey. The importance of cotton increased at the end of the century.

The transition to industrial textile production took place in the first half of the 19th century, later than in western Europe. After the abolition of serfdom by Joseph II in 1781, the labour force migrated from the country to the towns. Small-scale hand production gradually developed into a machine-operated industry. Machines to process cotton had been introduced at the end of the 18th century; they were subsequently used to make woollen cloth and finally came into their own in the production of linen. The first machines were used for spinning, while weaving was still done by hand until mechanical looms were introduced in the mid-19th century. Many mills were set up, but the production of handmade textiles was maintained. Industrial production continued chiefly in towns where the woollen cloth trade had traditionally flourished. The chief market for these fabrics was the countries of the Austro-Hungarian Empire.

The largest of the new mills was in Liberec, owned by Jan Liebig. In 1825 he went to England to study the latest fashions. He replaced the traditional pure woollen cloth with more crease-resistant mixtures of wool and cotton yarn (e.g. merino). In the 1840s he introduced orleans, a plain dress fabric with a cotton warp and woollen weft. In the early years he also farmed work out to domestic weavers.

A fundamental change came with the decline of linen production in favour of cotton in the first half of the 19th century. The cotton industry was concentrated in Prague and northern Bohemia. Machine spinning, and later weaving, led from hand to machine calico-printing. In the second half of the century machine printing predominated. As the production processes became more rapid, decorative patterns changed more frequently. Small-patterned, printed cottons were popular. Gradually flower and plant motifs became more geometric, and abstract shapes replaced realistic designs. The manufacture of velvet developed at the beginning of the 19th century and became the specialization of the region of Rumburk, northern Bohemia. The production of patterned velvets followed the introduction of Jacquard looms.

In the second half of the 19th century machine production prevailed in all spheres of textile manufacture. The industry was concentrated in northern Bohemia, in the towns of Brno, Jihlava and Ostrava, and in such centres as Prague, Plzeň and Humpolec. Brno and Vratislavice nad Nisou became famous for carpetmaking. The carpet factory in Vratislavice nad Nisou was founded in 1843 by Ignaz Ginzke, but from an artistic point of view it became important at the turn of the century when the traditional Oriental and historical designs were temporarily supplanted by hand-woven carpets designed by such distinguished artists as Alphonse Mucha, Felician Myrbach, Joseph Maria Olbrich and Hans Christian. The factory was among the foremost in the world and was awarded a Grand Prix at the Exposition Universelle, Paris, in 1900 and at the World's Fair, St Louis, in 1904.

The role of artistic design in textile production became increasingly pronounced. Attempts to partly reinstate traditional craft techniques followed in the wake of similar revivals in England. Folk art was a source of inspiration, especially to Marie Teinitzerová, who designed fabrics for interior decoration in the first decades of the 20th century (see fig. 33). The functionalism of the late 1920s influenced

33. Tapestry by Marie Teinitzerová and František Kysela: *Potter*, from the cycle *Crafts*, wool, 2.70×2.35 m, Jindřichův Hradec, southern Bohemia, 1925 (Prague, Museum of Decorative Arts)

her work and that of Božena Pošepná, Jaroslava Vondráčková and in particular Antonín Kybal. Functionalism was promoted by the Union of Czech Arts. The stress was on avant-garde industrial design, especially Kybal's furnishing fabrics, tablecloths and carpets. Kybal also excelled in producing exclusive designs that were made in his own workshop.

After World War II the textile industry concentrated on systematic collaboration with artists. Miniature textiles began to be made, using various techniques. Limited runs of textile prints were produced in the workshops of such organizations as the Czech Fine Arts Fund and the Arts and Crafts Centre. Leading designers from *c.* 1960 to 1990 included Ladislav Vacek, Věra Drnková-Zarecká, Květa Hamsíková, Jindřich Švec and Luba Krejčí. Further progress was made in designing hand-woven carpets for individual commissions and public institutions, especially in the tapestry workshop of the Arts and Crafts Centre in Valašské Meziříčí. From the 1960s the Vlněna enterprise in Brno produced 'Art-protis' designs by Antonín Kybal, Květa Hamsíková, Inez Tuscherová and others. The latest developments in textile technology were used in wall hangings, and in the late 20th century research continued into the use of textile wall and ceiling coverings and of room dividers in open-plan spaces.

BIBLIOGRAPHY

H. Volavková: *The Synagogue Treasures of Bohemia and Moravia* (Prague, 1949)
Umění a řemesla [Art and crafts] (Prague, 1956–)
J. Spurný: *Antonín Kybal* (Prague, 1960)
——: *Ein Meister moderner Textilkunst: Antonín Kybal* (Prague, 1960)
Dílo Marie Teinitzerové [The work of Marie Teinitzerové] (exh. cat., Prague, Mus. Dec. A., 1961)
L. Kybalová: *Emilie Paličková* (Prague, 1962)
——: *Československá gobelínová tvorba* [Czechoslovak Gobelin tapestry] (Prague, 1963)
P. Verlet and others: *Das grosse Buch der Tapisserie* (Vienna and Düsseldorf, 1965)
A. Kuenzi: *La Nouvelle Tapisserie* (Geneva, 1973)
M. Zeminová: *Barokní textilie ze sbírek Uměleckoprůmyslového muzea* [Baroque textiles in the collections of the Museum of Decorative Arts] (Prague, 1974)
Fiber Works (exh. cat., Kyoto, N. Mus. Mod. A., 1976–7)
V. Luxová and D. Tučná: *Československá tapisérie 1945–1975* [Czechoslovak tapestry, 1945–1975] (Bratislava, 1978)
B. Mráz: *Současná tapiserie* [Contemporary tapestry] (Prague, 1980)
O. Palata: 'Návrhy vratislavických secesních koberců' [Designs for Vratislavice Secessionist carpets], *Umění a řemesla*, ii (1981), pp. 21–5
Česká secese: Užité umění [The Czech Secession: applied art] (exh. cat., Prague, Mus. Dec. A., 1981)
A. Adlerová: *České užité umění 1918–1938* [Czech applied art, 1918–1938] (Prague, 1983)
Středověké umělecké řemeslo ze sbírek Uměleckoprůmyslového muzea [Medieval arts and crafts in the collections of the Museum of Decorative Arts] (exh. cat., Prague, Mus. Dec. A., 1987)
D. Hejdová and others: *Dějiny uměleckého řemesla a užitého umění v Českých zemích* [The history of crafts and applied art in the Czech lands] (Prague, in preparation)

2. EMBROIDERY. In the 14th century embroidery flourished as a branch of the fine arts. Figurative embroidery with religious themes was produced for the Church, for example the Pirna antependium (*c.* 1340; Dresden, Schloss Pillnitz), the Třeboň antependium (before 1380; Prague, N. Mus.) and the Broumov chasuble (after 1380; Prague, Mus. Dec. A.). The embroidery was worked in split stitches, using coloured silks, against a background of couched gold threads. After a period of decline following the Reformation, embroidery was revived during the Renaissance, particularly at the court of Rudolf II. Embroidery guilds were established, and in 1595 the Prague embroidery guild joined the painters' guild. Embroiderers, painters, wood-carvers, illuminators and glass craftsmen had as a common subject the Virgin and Child. The fact that figurative embroidery was still highly prized shows the conservatism of the guilds at a time when the Mannerism of Rudolf's court favoured ornament. However, freshwater pearls, a rich material, were increasingly used. Embroidery also decorated Jewish synagogue fabrics, particularly draperies and Torah covers. A remarkable collection of hangings (1590–1625; Prague, State Jew. Mus.) shows Renaissance motifs executed in appliqué.

After the Counter-Reformation, many embroidered vestments were produced. Baroque ornamental patterns predominated, often using painters' designs, carvings and patterns from books. In the 17th century three-dimensional effects were achieved by working gold threads over linen threads or across pieces of padding. The embroidery was further enriched by such additions as hardstones, pieces of glass and metal, lace and bobbinwork using gold fibres. Patterns on silk fabrics (imported from Italy in the 17th century and from France in the 18th century) influenced embroidery designs. The embroidery of synagogue fabrics developed concurrently. In the 18th century the three-dimensional technique was replaced by flat, low-relief designs, usually with cardboard as a foundation, and embroidery lost some of its ostentation.

In the countryside, women had produced domestic embroideries non-professionally since the Renaissance. Brocade remnants, metal braid and simple pieces of lace served as ornament, and a frequent motif was a crowned lion. Embroidered textiles in country synagogues had a close affinity to folk art. The types of cloth commonly in use in country households were employed as a base, and the simple embroidery drew on the animal and plant motifs used in folk art, often achieving a fresh charm (17th–19th centuries; Prague, State Jew. Mus.). In the 19th century embroidery was also used in town houses and reflected the influence of Empire and Biedermeier styles. Historical patterns and models predominated in the second half of the century. In the Secessionist period there are examples of wall hangings based on the work of such famous artists as Alphonse Mucha. In the 20th century embroidery was confined mainly to traditional folk ornament on tablecloths and clothes.

BIBLIOGRAPHY

Z. Drobná: *Les Trésors de la broderie religieuse en Tchécoslovaquie* (Prague, 1950)

M. Zeminová: 'České gotické výšivky a jejich objednatelé' [Czech Gothic embroideries and their commissioners], *Umění a řemesla* (1978), no. 2, pp. 23–9

M. Ludvíková: *Moravské lidové výšivky* [Moravian folk embroideries] (Brno, 1986)

DAGMAR TUČNÁ

3. LACE. There are references to locally made lace in the later 16th century, and by the 17th century the craft seems to have been well established in Bohemia, Slovenia and elsewhere. There were centres in the Ore Mountains and around Hostouň (in the Bohemian Forest) and the Vamperk (in the Eagle Mountains). Considerable quantities of simple white lace were made for general use, but bobbin lace also became a prominent feature of peasant dress, developing from the heavy, plaited laces of the 16th century to the tape-based laces introduced, via Hungary, from northern Italy in the late 17th century and the lighter, mesh-grounded laces of the 18th and 19th centuries. One of the most distinctive features of Czech peasant lace is its use of colour. Examples from the 19th and 20th centuries include those in which stylized floral motifs are worked in bright primary colours against a dense black mesh, while, in the most southern areas, continuous tape designs are worked in white with grounds in green, blue or yellow thread and vice versa. As in other parts of Europe, the lace industry dwindled in the late 18th and early 19th century, but in the early 1870s it was revived, largely as a means of relieving poverty in the mining areas but also as part of the international movement towards the revival of handicrafts. Bohemian lace, based mainly on French models, was shown at the Internationale Ausstellung in Vienna in 1874. The School of Decorative Arts in Prague was, like its sister school in Vienna, a vehicle for the introduction of the Secessionist style, but it also promoted designs based on the country's peasant traditions.

The development of Czech lace after World War I was largely directed by Emilie Mildeová-Paličková (1892–1973). Her work made a considerable impact at the Paris Exposition of 1925, where she showed a large, round, needle-made cloth depicting the signs of the zodiac. Many of her designs incorporated figures in peasant dress. By the late 1920s she had adopted a more stylized, geometric approach, although still using figurative motifs, and in the 1930s she turned increasingly to bobbin lace. Teachers trained by her at the School of Decorative Arts in Prague were sent to teach in lace schools throughout the country, and in 1946 she established a special lace workshop within the Prague School, where she experimented with bobbin lace in working designs of great simplicity for wall hangings and, eventually, three-dimensional sculptures. Her innovative work was continued by such artists as Vlasto Pivrncová (*b* 1919), Eva Fialová (*b* 1929), Marie Vaňková-Kuchyňková (*b* 1925), Blanka Hanušová (*b* 1930), Ludmila Kaprasová (*b* 1941), Jitka Štenclová (*b* 1952) and Marie Danielová (*b* 1953). They produced free-hanging and sculptural pieces using bobbin and needle lace techniques, both singly and in combination, and explored new forms using, for example, industrial etching techniques to create openwork cotton fabrics.

BIBLIOGRAPHY

L. Kybalová: *Emilie Paličková* (Prague, 1962)

E.-E. Pfannschmidt: *Twentieth-century Lace* (London, 1975)

L. Kybalová: *Současná krajka* [Contemporary lace] (Prague, 1981)

La Dentelle tchèque: De l'Art Déco à nos jours (exh. cat., Brussels, Musées Royaux A. Hist., 1983)

Česká krajika: Tři generace [Czech lace: Three generations] (exh. cat., Prague, Mánes Exh. Hall, 1992)

XI. Patronage.

The earliest patrons in Bohemia were members of the PŘEMYSLID dynasty (*reg* 9th century AD–1306), among them Boleslav II (*reg* 967–99), founder of the Prague bishopric and of the first monasteries in the country, and Vratislav II (*reg* 1061–92), for whose coronation the illuminated Vyšehrad Codex may have been made (Prague, Libs Facs & Insts Charles U., MS. XIV. A. 13). Building activity in the Romanesque period reached its peak under Vladislav II (*reg* 1140–73), who completed Prague Castle and the settlement around it, laid the foundation for the Judith Bridge (now the Charles Bridge) and founded great monasteries, in particular those at Strahov (see PRAGUE, §IV, 5), Doksany, Nepomuk and Plasy. By the end of the 12th century patrons included feudal lords and such church dignitaries as the Bishop of Olomouc, Jindřich Zdík, who built the basilica at Litomyšl and the Archbishop's Palace at Olomouc. The Moravian appanage prince Konrád II (*reg* 1123–8, 1134–61) commissioned the wall paintings (1134) in the rotunda of St Catherine at Znojmo (see fig. 14 above).

The Gothic style was introduced in Bohemia during the reigns of the later Přemyslids Wenceslas (Václav) I (*reg* 1230–53), founder of the convent of St Agnes in Prague, and particularly King Přemysl Ottakar II (*reg* 1253–78), who is said to have founded more than 40 towns. In addition to monumental art, the court circle encouraged the workshops that produced illuminated manuscripts, for example the Passional of Abbess Kunhuta (*c.* 1313–21; Prague, Libs Facs & Insts Charles U., MS. XIV. A. 17) and the set of manuscripts belonging to Queen Elizabeth Rejčka.

The accession of the Luxembourg dynasty to the Bohemian throne in 1310 brought about an extension of artistic contacts with western Europe, as is evident from the example of Bishop John IV of Dražice, who brought with him from his travels an architect, Vilém of Avignon, and a group of manuscript illuminators. Charles IV, Holy Roman Emperor, made Prague the capital of the Empire and was a patron of major importance not only for Bohemia but for the whole of Central Europe as well as Germany and Italy (*see* LUXEMBOURG, (3)). His patronage was also decisive in the development of Bohemian Gothic. Church dignitaries such as Jan Očko of Vlašim, JAN OF STŘEDA and Arnošt of Pardubice also played a role as patrons, although artistic patronage increasingly became restricted to court circles. This exclusive court culture culminated *c.* 1400 during the reign of Wenceslas IV, who made a unique collection of illuminated manuscripts (*see* LUXEMBOURG, (4)).

The Hussite Wars and their aftermath halted artistic activity, but the three decades after the accession in 1471 of Vladislav II Jagiellon marked a revival during which Vladislav devoted enormous energy to supporting building and artistic activity (*see* JAGIELLON, (1)). Meanwhile, royal power began to decline, while that of the magnates increased. Foremost among the latter was the ROŽMBERK family, owners of huge domains in southern Bohemia. Other powerful families included the Rožmitáls at Blatná and the Rýzemberks at Švihov Castle and Rábí. With the development of trade, royal towns began to flourish, and in their struggles for prestige they became centres of patronage, as for instance Kutná Hora, Louny, Kadaň and Most.

During the 16th century the political situation stabilized, as did the dominant role of family patrons, such as the lords of HRADEC at Telč and Jindřichův Hradec, the Rožmberks at Český Krumlov and the Barons Schlick at Jáchymov. Elsewhere, in western Bohemia, noble patrons included Jan of Lobkovice at Horšovský Týn, and among these in Moravia were Jindřich of Lipá and the lords of ŽEROTÍN. Outstanding also, through the imposing castles they erected on their estates at Litomyšl and Pardubice, were the lords of PERNŠTEJN. One of the most enterprising of these patrons was the supreme burgrave FLORIÁN GRIESBECK VON GRIESBACH, builder of castles at Kačeřov and Nelahozeves and of the family mausoleum at Kralovice. During his stay in Prague, Archduke Ferdinand II of Austria, Count of Tyrol (*reg* 1564–95), showed flair as an amateur architect by designing the Hvězda summer palace (1555–6). The wealthy patricians became progressively more active, as is apparent in the splendour of such towns of the period as Pardubice and Telč and in the large number of tombstones and epitaphs preserved in urban churches.

The reign of the Holy Roman Emperor Rudolf II (1575–1612), under whom Prague became the capital of the Empire for the second time, can be described as the peak period of artistic patronage in Bohemian history. This exceptionally cultured and generous supporter of the arts and sciences gathered around himself a broad and colourful circle of outstanding, creative personalities who spread Prague's fame widely (*see* HABSBURG, §I(10)). Several feudal lords strove to keep pace with Prague on their estates, for instance Petr Vok Rožmberk at Třeboň, Zdeněk Popel of Lobkovice, Vilém Slavata and Karel Žerotín. For a short while after Rudolf's proclamation of the Letter of Majesty (1609), the cultural role of the religious brotherhoods, the Jewish community and the wealthy patricians such as the Lord Provost of Prague, Krocín of Drahobejl, was enhanced.

After the Battle of the White Mountain in 1620, the clergy and magnates gained the upper hand at the expense of the lesser nobility and townsmen and put all their energy into the re-establishment of Catholicism and absolutism. Through munificent building and patronage the aristocracy demonstrated its desire to dazzle with its power and wealth. Some individuals, for instance Count Albrecht von Wallenstein (1583–1634) at Jičín, even eclipsed the Emperor with their ambitions in the cultural sphere. Others, such as Humprecht Jan Černín von Chudenitz (*see* ČERNÍN, (1)) and Václav Vojtěch Šternberk, succeeded in asserting the outlook and the many-sided cultural education they had acquired on their journeys through Europe. Among church dignitaries the leading supporters of the arts were Archbishop Jan Bedřich of Valdštejn, who brought Jean Baptiste Mathey to Prague in 1675, and the Olomouc bishops František of Dietrichštejn and Karel Liechtenštejn-Castelkorn, who is associated above all with the magnificent art collection at Kroměříž Castle.

The capital acquired during the economic boom of the second half of the 17th century was expended on architectural enterprise and art collections, while the great wave of patronage and church ceremonial between 1700 and 1730 was expressed in the height of the development of Baroque art. The pomp of court ritual under Charles VI and the atmosphere of permanent festivity that culminated in the canonization of St John of Nepomuk in 1729 gave rise to ostentatious competitiveness among the wealthiest members of the aristocracy, who were linked through court circles with Vienna (e.g. the Schwarzenberg, Althan and Kounic families). One of the most notable Baroque patrons was the Jansenist Count FRANZ ANTON VON SPORCK, who created the east Bohemian town of Kuks. In the early 18th century educated, energetic abbots, such as Václav Vejmluva, Abbot of Žďár (1705–38), Eugen Tyttl of Plasy and Otmar Zincke of Břevnov and Broumov, revived the past glory of their ancient communities by enlisting the aid of the best artists of the age.

In the second half of the 18th century the monopoly of the magnates and clergy as patrons was abolished by the absolutist state, which became the main patron of architecture. The new strata of patrons consisted of the commercial classes and the urban intelligentsia. The abolition of serfdom brought into being a peasant class, and the distinction between so-called official culture and mass culture became blurred. At the same time, external ostentation was replaced by emphasis on the intimacy of room interiors, and growing importance was given to arts and crafts. The foundation in 1796 of the Society of Patriotic Friends of Art was typical of the endeavours inspired by the Enlightenment, and Count František Šternberk (1763–1830) and the painter Johann Jacob Quirin Jahn (1739–1802) brought about the establishment of the Picture Gallery and Painters' Academy.

In the early 19th century the role of the state as patron of architecture continued to grow with the establishment of regional architectural directorates. The splendid work of the supreme burgrave Karel Chotek (1783–1868), the first forward-thinking urbanist, transformed Prague into a thriving modern capital. The revolutions of 1848 mobilized the historical awareness of the aristocracy, including the Rohans, Schwarzenbergs and Harrachs, who restored their palaces and reorganized their collections. An important role was also played by the newly formed associations and groups such as the Artistic Forum (Umělecká Beseda), the National Museum (1818) and the Christian Academy. Josef Hlávka (1831–1908), originally a building entrepreneur, devoted his wealth and organizational abilities to the development of a national culture and founded the Bohemian Academy of Arts and Sciences as its platform (1890). Vojtěch Lanna (1836–1909) founded the Museum of Decorative Arts (1885) in Prague.

The establishment of the Czechoslovak state in 1918 encouraged artistic development through state commissions. Conservative tastes dominated, however, and Josef Ulrych, mayor of Hradec Králové, who commissioned work from the architects Jan Kotěra and Josef Gočár, stands out as an exception among the municipal authorities. The big banks and commercial houses became patrons of the arts: at Zlín, for instance, the manufacturer Tomáš Baťa (1876–1932) financed not only a gallery and a museum but also a progressive school of art. Cooperatives were also active, such as Svaz Českého Díla, which initiated the Baba housing estate in Prague.

After World War II and the Communist putsch of 1948, patronage of art became exclusively a state affair. The positive side of this was that selected artistic and historical monuments were preserved and an extensive network of regional galleries was created. An artistic component was seen as an indivisible part of all projects (a compulsory 5% of investment costs). The content and form were strictly supervised, however, especially in the normalization period of the 1970s and 1980s. This insulated developments at home from contemporary European trends. With the overthrow of the Communist regime, however, the way was opened in the 1990s for private commissions and free trading in the arts.

BIBLIOGRAPHY
A. Wolf: *Graf Carl Chotek: Geheimer Rat und Oberstburggraf in Böhmen* (Prague, 1869)
J. Morávek and Z. Wirth: *Valdštejnův Jičín* [The Wallensteins' Jičín] (Prague, 1946)
B. Menzel: 'Ein Blick in die barocke Welt der Äbte Otmar Zinke und Benno Löbl', *Adalbert-Stift. Jb. Ver.*, viii (Munich, 1964), pp. 84–124
J. Polišenský: 'Gesellschaft und Kultur des barocken Böhmens', *Österreich. Osthft.* (1966), pp. 112–29
J. Petráň: 'Stavovské království a jeho kultura v Čechách, 1471–1526' [The estates and their culture in Bohemia, 1471–1526], *Pozdněgotické umění v Čechách* [Late Gothic art in Bohemia] (Prague, 1978)
J. Válka: 'Manýrismus a baroko v české kultuře 17. a první poloviny 18. století' [Mannerism and the Baroque in Czech culture in the 17th century and the first half of the 18th], *Stud. Comeniana & Hist.*, viii/19 (1978), pp. 155–213
P. Preiss: *Boje s dvouhlavou saní* [Struggles with the two-headed dragon] (Prague, 1981)
Umění doby posledních přemyslovců (exh. cat., ed. J. Kuthan; Roztoky u Prahy, Mus. Cent. Bohemia, 1982)
A. Merhautová and D. Třeštík: *Ideové proudy v českém umění 12. století* [Ideological trends in Bohemian art of the 12th century] (Prague, 1985)
J. Petráň: *Dějiny hmotné kultury* [History of material culture], i (Prague, 1985) pp. 11–107
A. Lodr: *Josef Hlávka* (Prague, 1988)
M. Vilímková and P. Preiss: *Ve znamení břevna a růží: Historický, kulturní a umělecký odkaz benediktinského opatství v Břevnově* (Prague, 1989)
JIŘÍ T. KOTALÍK

XII. Collecting and dealing.

In the lands of the present-day Czech Republic, there is a long tradition of acquisition of objects from abroad by the sovereign and by religious orders. In the second half of the 13th century Cistercian abbots regularly travelled to sessions of the order's chapter in France and brought back manuscripts and liturgical objects, while Bishop John IV of Dražice is said to have brought French illuminated manuscripts from Avignon in 1333. Charles IV (*reg* 1346–78) collected many works of art, mainly from Italy, including illuminated manuscripts and a diptych (*c.* 1355–60) and triptych (*c.* 1359–60) by TOMASO DA MODENA, which he had himself commissioned (both at Karlštejn Castle; *see* LUXEMBOURG, (3)). Under Wenceslas IV (*reg* 1378–1419), sculptures of the *Virgin and Child* and *Pietà* images in International Gothic style were exported throughout Europe. Wenceslas added important illuminated manuscripts to the royal library (*see* LUXEMBOURG, (4)), much of which was lost at the beginning of the Hussite Wars, although part is now in Vienna (Österreich. Nbib.). Sigismund of Luxembourg (*reg* 1419–37) took part of Charles IV's collection out of the country.

The reign (1576–1612) of Rudolf II was the golden age of collecting in Bohemia (*see* HABSBURG, §I (10)). Rudolf's outstanding *Kunstkammer* (destr. 1630s) contained works of art collected from all over Europe, including Greek and Roman statues, paintings and sculptures by artists from Germany, the Netherlands and Italy, engravings, and decorative arts (*see* PRAGUE, §II, 2). A regular art market was held in the Vladislav Hall of Prague Castle, and such noblemen as the lords of ROŽMBERK and PERNŠTEJN began their own collections.

In the 17th and 18th centuries important noble collections included those of the Lobkovic family at Roudnice on the Elbe, of the Kolovrats at Rychnov nad Kněžnou and of Humprecht Jan Čzernín von Chudenitz (*see* ČZERNÍN, (1)) in Prague. Church dignitaries set up their own collections, such as that founded by Bishop Karel Liechtenštejn-Castelkorn at Kroměříž Castle, which included works by Titian, Veronese and van Dyck. Smaller collections were held in religious foundations such as Vyšší Brod Abbey and the Strahov Monastery in Prague.

In the first half of the 19th century collections were set up by burghers and by such artists as J. Q. Jahn, František Horčička and Josef Mánes, while the French émigrés who arrived in Bohemia after the 1789 Revolution (e.g. the Rohans and Desfours) brought in paintings by such French masters as Hyacinthe Rigaud. From the early 19th century public collections (e.g. the National Museum and the gallery of the Society of Patriotic Friends of Art) competed with private collections. Vojtěch Lanna formed a large collection of paintings, prints and sculptures after the mid-19th century, while several important art collections were created in the late 19th century and early 20th. Bishop A. Podlaha's collection of paintings, sculptures and prints, most of them on religious subjects, was auctioned after his death. K. Procházka had a collection of a similar character, while collections of Italian, Netherlandish and German art of exceptional value were formed by J. V. Novák, Jindřich Waldes and R. Jahn. Vincenc Kramář's collection included several works by Picasso (Prague, N.G.).

After 1918 Russian icons and paintings were brought into the country by Russian émigrés and appeared in antique shops. In the 1918–48 period, art works were sold mostly at auction. During World War II Jewish artefacts from all over Central Europe were gathered in the State Jewish Museum in Prague, while numerous works of art were taken to Germany, and some were never returned. After 1945 the property of collaborators with the Nazi regime was confiscated by the state, and several monastic collections were destroyed after the abolition of monasteries in the 1950s. All important monuments, including those in private ownership, were declared national property.

In the late 20th century old prints, books and manuscripts were bought and sold by second-hand bookshops (Czech *antikvariát*), while paintings, sculptures and arts-and-crafts objects were sold at antiquarian shops (Czech *starožitnosti*) and at auction. Private collections of international modern art, such as that of M. Knížák, were rare at this time in the Czech Republic. Works of art were exported through state foreign trade companies, while Artia, for example, exported antiquities, old books and prints. Private export of art works still required permission from a court expert and from the National Gallery in Prague.

BIBLIOGRAPHY
Z. Kalista: *Mládí Humprechta Jana Černína z Chudenic* [Jan Humprecht Černín of Chudenice as a young man] (Prague, 1932)
K. Stejskal: *Umění na dvoře Karla IV* [Art at the court of Charles IV] (Prague, 1978)
E. Fučíková, ed.: *Prag um 1900: Kunst und Kultur am Hofe Rudolfs II.* (Freren, 1988)

JAN ROYT

XIII. Museums.

The first modern museums on the territory of the Czech lands were founded in the 19th century, continuing the tradition of collecting pursued by sovereigns, Church institutions, noblemen and burghers from the Middle Ages (*see* §XII above). Most of those collections have not survived in their original form and were of varying character and value. The immediate predecessors of the modern museums in the Czech lands were 18th-century private collections of coins, medals, paintings, sculpture, glass, prints and manuscripts that were open to the general public via scientific societies.

The theoretical principles of the first museums were formulated in 1800 by C. K. André. He emphasized the need to document the country's history, art and contemporary production as well as its character and profile, including its physical geography and natural resources. These museums aimed to prevent the export of works of art, to collect, to educate and to shape national awareness. The museums in Bohemia became cultural and educational centres with archives, departments for the preservation of monuments, and libraries.

A museum was founded at the secondary school in Troppau in Silesia (now Opava in Moravia) in 1814 (Silesian Museum, Collections of Ethnography and Art). In 1817 the Moravian Museum was founded in Brno. In 1818 the National Museum (originally the Museum of the Kingdom of Bohemia) was founded in Prague and became the centre of Bohemian cultural life, linked later to the national revival. In the second half of the 19th century numerous regional museums were founded: between 1860 and 1890 alone, 49 museums and museum associations

were founded in Bohemia, specializing in geographical documentation and education.

V. Náprstek founded an industry museum in Prague in 1862. From the beginning of the 1870s it concentrated on applied art and, eventually on the ethnography of non-European cultures (the Náprstek Museum of Asian, African and American Culture). Museums of applied or decorative art were also founded in Liberec and Brno (in 1873), České Budějovice and Ústí nad Labem (1876), Hradec Králové (1881), Prague (1885), Plzeň (1886), Chrudim (1892) and Hořice (1904). Specialized glass museums were founded at Nový Bor (1886) and Jablonec nad Nisou (1900). Their collecting policies and educational activities were energetic and progressive.

The Jubilee Exhibition and the Ethnographic Exhibition, held in Prague in 1891 and 1895 respectively, inspired the foundation of new museums and increased the emphasis on the documentation of their respective regions. Between 1891 and 1918, 97 museums and museum associations were founded in the Czech lands. The Ethnographic Exhibition provided the basis for the collection in the Museum of Ethnography in Prague. At the same time, the idea of founding an open-air museum of folk architecture (*skansen*) at Přerov on the Elbe was mooted, but it was not implemented until after 1967. The first *skansen* was in fact opened at Rožnov pod Radhoštěm in the 1920s.

After the foundation of the Czechoslovak Republic in 1918, the network of regional and specialized museums expanded rapidly: nearly 200 new museums were set up, although many were short-lived. During World War II some museums were damaged or destroyed, and they also suffered losses through confiscation. After 1945 further regional and specialized museums were founded, and the collections of existing museums were enriched. Specialized collections were established in the State Jewish Museum in Prague, the Museum of Czech Literature in the Strahov Monastery, Prague, and the Museum of Puppetry in Chrudim, among other examples. Individual museums are devoted to prominent composers, writers and artists, such as Bedřich Smetana, Karel and Josef Čapek and Antonín Dvořák.

The National Gallery, which is responsible for art collections in Prague, originated in the private gallery set up by the Society of Patriotic Friends of Art in 1796. The gallery began to build up a national collection from 1835; in 1936 the collection was transferred to state ownership, and in 1949 the National Gallery was created in its modern form. There are several branches: the Šternberk Palace (Italian, German and Dutch art of the 14th–17th centuries and French art of the 19th and 20th centuries), the convents of St George (pre-19th-century Bohemian art) and St Agnes (19th-century Bohemian art), the Municipal Library (modern Czech art), Zbraslav Castle (19th- and 20th-century Czech sculpture) and the Kinský Palace (prints and drawings). The Academy of Applied Arts has an outstanding collection of glass.

BIBLIOGRAPHY
K. Adámek: 'Muzea v království Českém' [Museums in the Kingdom of Bohemia], *Česká Rev.*, ii (1909), pp. 232–44, 262–300
J. Hanuš: *Národní muzeum a naše obrození* [The National Museum and our national revival], 2 vols (Prague, 1921–3)

V. Vlček: *K vývoji českého muzejnictví* [On the development of Czech museology] (Prague, 1970)

J. Špét: *Muzea ve vývoji společnosti a národní kultury* [Museums in the development of society and national culture] (Prague, 1979)

V. Pubal and others: *Muzea a galerie v ČSR* [Museums and galleries in the Czech Socialist Republic] (Prague, 1985)

VLADIMÍR HRUBÝ

XIV. Art libraries and photographic collections.

The first art library in Bohemia originated in the mid-18th century within the Charles University Library, in the Clementinum in Prague, and it was opened to the public in 1777. In the 19th century several art libraries were established in Bohemia and Moravia to meet the growing needs of newly founded associations and institutes such as the Moravian Industrial Society, for which the Moravian Gallery Library was established in Brno. A predecessor of the Prague National Gallery Library, the library attached to the Society of Patriotic Friends of Art, was founded in 1880. The Museum of Applied Arts Library was established in Prague in 1885 and opened to the public in 1887. It is the largest specialist library in the Czech Republic. Art school libraries include the Academy of Fine Arts Library (1830s) and the Academy of Applied Arts Library (1885).

In the 20th century the further development of art historiography led to the establishment of more specialist libraries. In 1907 an art-historical section was constituted at Charles University, later developing into the Art History Department Library. In 1918 the Library of the State Institute for the Conservation of Historical Monuments and Nature was founded. A library specializing in art theory was opened at the Art History Institute of the Czechoslovak Academy of Sciences in 1952. Photographic libraries include those at the Moravian Gallery in Brno, which specializes in the history of photography, the State Institute for Conservation, the Art History Institute and the National Technical Museum (all in Prague).

TOMÁŠ PERGLER

XV. Art education.

Until the 18th century the training of artists took place within individual guilds and specifically within workshops. The best known were in cultural centres such as Prague, Plzeň, Český Krumlov, Pardubice, Olomouc, Brno and České Budějovice. In 1709 an unsuccessful attempt was made to found an Academy of Arts in Prague. The State Engineering School was opened in 1707 and a limited number of students took courses on the building of fortifications and, later, on civic architecture.

In 1796 the Society of Patriotic Friends of Art was founded. Its interest in the education of young artists brought about the establishment of the Academy of Fine Arts in Prague in September 1799. At first the Academy taught drawing from plaster casts of Classical statuary, but in the 1830s a department of landscape painting was set up, and the study of live models was emphasized. From the 1840s history painting began to dominate, and art theory was introduced. From 1842 architecture was taught at the Academy, although the Engineering School retained its leading role in that subject. In 1805 it became the State Polytechnic Institute, where an independent department

of civil engineering was opened in 1864. This was divided into separate Czech and German sections in 1869.

After the abolition of the guilds in 1859, the first specialized technical colleges were founded in regions with traditional craft associations. These offered courses in textiles (Liberec, 1852), glassmaking (Kamenický Senov, 1856) and ceramics (Karlovy Vary, 1872) as well as design and draughtsmanship. Specialized colleges that survive include the Hořice stone masons' school (1883), the Bechyně ceramics school (1884) and the Turnov school of jewellery (1884).

The School of Applied Arts was founded in Prague in 1885 and for a while overshadowed the Academy, which then taught painting and art theory exclusively. The reform of the Academy, which came under state control at the end of the 1880s, broadened the students' artistic horizons, especially after the founding of the department of sculpture in 1896. After a long gap, the teaching of architecture at the Academy was resumed in 1910, and with the opening of the department of graphic art and medal design the Academy's teaching profile was complete. The curriculum of the College of Technology in Prague was also modernized, and a course for teachers of drawing was added.

The declaration of the independent state of Czechoslovakia in 1918 affected art education in its structure, content and the composition of teaching staff. The Academy in Prague preserved its privileged position as the only school of fine arts with university status, while many students and teachers attended both the Academy and the School of Applied Arts. In the 1920s secondary fine arts schools were reorganized territorially, and changes were made in their curricula. The basic network survived, including schools of arts and crafts in Prague and Brno, the school of glassmaking in Železný Brod and the school of graphic art in Prague. The closing of universities after the Nazi occupation of Czechoslovakia in 1938 interrupted this development, but some continuity in the war years was provided by the Prague arts and crafts secondary school. The art school at Zlín, founded by the Baťa company, played a similar role in Moravia. In 1945 the Academy of Fine Arts became the only school in the Republic to teach a course on the restoration of works of art. In 1946 the School of Applied Arts in Prague achieved university status and also became an Academy. After the Communists came to power in 1948, art education took on the characteristics of the new state, with ideological considerations impinging on the creative agendas of both teachers and students.

In the late 20th century the Academy of Performing Arts in Prague offered a course on set design, and there were courses on art education at the Teaching Faculties in Prague, Plzeň, Olomouc and Brno. Architecture was taught at colleges of technology in Prague and Brno, as well as at art schools. New secondary arts and crafts schools were founded after 1945 in Uherské Hradiště and Prague-Vinohrady, and this basic network was supplemented by several arts and crafts training institutions and people's schools of art. Study at secondary art schools took four years and six years at colleges with university status. Architectural studies at colleges of technology took five years, with the possibility of continuing in a specialized post-graduate course. In the 1990s art education was affected by radical reform, opening up to a range of trends and disciplines, and additional schools of art were established within a newly constituted regional university framework and also as independent, private institutions (in Ústí nad Labem, České Budějovice, the Faculty of Architecture, Liberec, and the Independent Faculty of Arts, Brno).

BIBLIOGRAPHY

J. Harvařík: *Vysoké školy umělecké* [Art schools with university status] (Prague, 1970)

Almanach akademie výtvarných umění v Praze [Memorial volume of the Academy of Fine Arts] (Prague, 1979)

UMPRUM–VŠUP: Sto let práce [Museum of Applied Arts–Academy of Applied Arts: one hundred years of work] (Prague, 1985)

JIŘÍ T. KOTALÍK

XVI. Historiography.

The first descriptions of Bohemian monuments, religious paintings and sculptures appeared in the 17th century in books by the Jesuit BOHUSLAV BALBÍN. In the late 18th century Bohemian artists were represented in A. Voigt's *Effigies. . .* and in writings by the painter Johann Quirin Jahn and the architect F.L. Ehemant. At the same time, the sculptors Ondřej Schweigl and P. Cerroni recorded data about Moravian artists. In 1815 JAN BOHUMÍR DLABAČ published the first encyclopedia of Bohemian artists. In the mid-19th century a Prague German, Anton Springer, adopted a more scientific approach, tentatively introducing sociology when lecturing on the history of art. J. Neuwirth, K. Chytil and AUGUST PROKOP represented positivism in this field. In the early 20th century the methodology of art history was formulated by a representative of the so-called Vienna school, MAX DVOŘÁK, whose pupil Antonín Matějček (1889–1950) became a leading art historian in the inter-war period. It had become clear that Bohemian art had two high points, the Gothic and the Baroque, and in 1938 Matějček laid the foundation for further studies by publishing a catalogue of Gothic panel paintings. Václav Vilém Štech (1885–1974), the main authority on Baroque sculpture at the time, published his works in the same period.

After 1945 Matějček's pupils emerged in the field. A. Merhautová wrote on Romanesque architecture, J. Mašín on Romanesque painting; J. Pešina produced a catalogue of Late Gothic panel painting; OLDŘICH JAKUB BLAŽÍČEK wrote on Baroque sculpture, among other works; and J. Neumann and P. Preiss each studied Baroque painting. V. Mencl and D. Líbal wrote a history of Gothic architecture, and a Brno professor, A. Kutal, published a fundamental work on Gothic sculpture. V. Kotrba dealt with Baroque historicism, while E. Poche focused on applied art and the topography of Prague. In the next generation, J. Homolka worked on Gothic sculpture, K. Stejskal and V. Dvořáková on Gothic wall paintings, J. Krása on manuscript illuminations, J. Krčálová on Renaissance architecture and V. Naňková on Baroque architecture. E. Petrová, L. Novák and E. Reitharová wrote about 19th-century art history, Petr Wittlich on the Czech Secession and Jiří T. Kotalík, F. Šmejkal and Morislav Lamač on 20th-century art.

In Moravia, Z. Kudělka worked on Baroque architecture, M. Stehlík on Baroque sculpture and I. Krsek on

Baroque painting. A catalogue of German medieval paintings in Czech collections was compiled by J. Pešina, while a similar catalogue of Dutch paintings was published by J. Vacková. A survey of Czech monuments appeared, *Umělecképamátky Čech* ('Artistic monuments of Bohemia', 4 vols, 1977–82); a similar work relating to Moravia was also published. The main periodicals in the field were *Umění* ('Art') and *Památková péče* ('Conservation of monuments').

BIBLIOGRAPHY

Dějiny českého výtvarného umění [History of Czech fine arts] (Prague, 1984–)

Kapitoly z českého dějepisu umění [Chapters from the Czech history of art], 2 vols (Prague, 1986)

IVO KOŘÁN

Czernin [Černín]. Bohemian family of patrons and collectors, active in Austria. Born into a family with medieval origins, (1) Count Humprecht Jan Czernin von Chudenitz made notable additions to its collection of paintings, for which he commissioned Francesco Caratti to build the Czernin Palace in Prague in 1666. The first phase of building began in 1669. On the death of Count Humprecht Jan in 1682, his son, Count Heřman Jakub Czernin (*b* Jan 1659; *d* Aug 1710), returned from his Grand Tour in western Europe to direct the completion of Humprecht Jan's projects for the Czernin Palace. At this time construction was supervised by Giovanni Battista Maderna (*b* 1652; last recorded 1688), who supervised the team of Italian craftsmen after Caratti's death in 1677. Heřman Jakub may also have consulted the architect Jean Baptiste Matthey (of French origin) regarding the Czernin Palace and may have commissioned a palace in Vienna from Maderna. At the end of September 1693 Domenico Egidio Rossi, recommended by his younger brother Thomas, was commissioned by Heřman Jakub to lay out the gardens and furnish the private apartments. Rossi provided designs for the stuccoists Santino de Bussi (1663–1737) and Tommaso Soldati (1665–1743), but his heavy architectural illusionistic schemes for the decoration of the Great Hall, sent from Vienna as late as 1697, were never realized. Between 1696 and 1702 plans were drawn up relating to the formal approach to the palace, in which Giovanni Battista Alliprandi, then working on the Czernin estates, may have been involved. These were, however, only partially executed at this time.

After Heřman Jakub's death in 1710, his son František Josef Czernin (*b* Oct 1697; *d* March 1733) concerned himself with the decoration and furnishing of the State Apartments and entrusted his commissions to Bohemian artists. The architect Maximilián Kaňka, who had worked at the Czernin Palace from 1708, evoked the luxurious interiors that František Josef had seen in France by creating schemes relying on coloured marbles, French and Flemish tapestries and displays of French and Meissen porcelain. The vault over the Great Stairs was raised by Kaňka and frescoed by Václav Vavřinec Reiner with scenes depicting the *Battle of the Titans* (*in situ*). The chapel was completed with a marble altar designed by Kaňka and mural decorations by Reiner. The chapel of St Matthew erected in front of the palace by Kaňka between 1727 and 1737 (destr. 1799) completed the project for the public approach. The gardens were altered (1718–22) to incorporate a marble cascade, a flight of steps, a pavilion, an orangery, pools, fountains and parterres of tulips laid out by Matěj Ledsebe.

Count Prokop Adalbert (Vojtěch) Czernin (*b* Mar 1726; *d* Jan 1777), son of Count František Josef, repaired damage done to the palace when it was occupied in 1742 by the French and Bavarian troops during the War of the Austrian Succession. He had Reiner's frescoes restored by František Kristian Ezechiel 'Siard' Nosecký (1693–1753), a priest from the neighbouring Strahov Monastery, and added a projecting main entrance (1747–9) after designs by Anselmo Martino Lurago (ii). Statues by Ignac Platzer, who had supplied a *Hercules* for the garden in 1746, were intended for the volutes and the parapet. After the damage caused by the Prussian siege of Prague in 1757, Prokop Adalbert brought in the painter Josef Kramer, the stuccoist Morazini and the sculptor Jan Antonín Quitainer to restore the ceilings in the Great Hall and Great Stairs. After Prokop Adalbert's death the Czernin Palace in Prague ceased to be occupied by the family, as his son, (2) Count Jan Rudolf Czernin, resided in Vienna after his marriage in 1781. During the early 19th century the Czernin Palace was let, and Jan Rudolf made few improvements. After 1851, when it was sold to the state, it was adapted by Achille Wolf for use by the army, with the loss of stucco decoration and the great stairs. Having fallen into disrepair, it was renovated by Pavel Janák in the 1920s and used by the Ministry of Foreign Affairs. The family collection of paintings was dispersed after 1777, and some works are located in the National Gallery in Prague and numerous other public, as well as private, collections. Jan Rudolf, however, formed a separate collection in Vienna that was acquired by the Residenzgalerie in Salzburg.

BIBLIOGRAPHY

V. Lorenc and K. Tříska: *Černínský Palác v Praze* [The Czernin Palace in Prague] (Prague, 1980) [with Eng. summary]

CLAIRE BRISBY

(1) Count **Humprecht Jan Czernin von Chudenitz** (*b* Jindřichův Hradec, Bohemia [now in the Czech Republic], 14 Feb 1628; *d* Kosmonosy, Bohemia, March 1682). He received a broad education that culminated in numerous journeys in the Netherlands, France and Italy between 1644 and 1649. Leopold I appointed him Imperial Ambassador to Venice, where his interest in Italian, and especially Venetian, painting led him to enrich the family gallery with works by the most important artists of his time. These included Pietro Liberi, Girolamo Forabosco, Carlo Saraceni (e.g. the *Nativity*, Salzburg, Residenzgal.) Giovanni Battista Langetti (e.g. *Vulcan and Jealousy*, 1663; Munich, Alte Pin.), Pietro Bellotti (1627–1700), Giuseppe Diamantini and Pietro Negri (*d* after 1679). From documents published by Kalista and from unpublished material held in the archives of the castle at Jindřichův Hradec (Ger. Neuhaus), it appears that during his Venetian sojourn (1660–63) the Count, together with his wife Maria Diana da Gazoldo and his steward Filippo Leoncelli, gave detailed specifications to artists about the content of the desired paintings. In some cases the Count commissioned several different artists to paint the same subject at the same time, as if in a competition, for example *Adam and Eve* by Johann Carl Loth, Langetti, Andrea Celesti and

Forabosco (Jindřichův Hradec, Castle), of which only that by Loth is known today.

The first inventory of the Count's collection was prepared in Venice in 1662. The most useful information concerning the original contents of the gallery, however, comes from a three-volume catalogue drafted in 1669, known as the *Imagines Galerie* (Prague, N.G. Lib.), which contains small schematic drawings by Jan van der Heyden and Caspar de Peyn of the paintings and lists more than 700 works. An inventory of 1722, however, lists only 639 works. In 1666 the Count bought the Lobkovice Palace in the Hradčany quarter of Prague. He had the old palace demolished and commissioned Francesco Caratti to build the Czernin Palace on its site to house the family collection.

UNPUBLISHED SOURCES

Prague, N.G. Lib. [*Imagines Galerie*, 1669]

BIBLIOGRAPHY

P. Bergner: 'Inventář bývalé hraběcí černínské obrazárny na Hradčanech' [Inventory of the former Count Czernin's pictures at Hradčany], *Časop. Společnosti Přátel Starožitností*, xv (1907), pp. 130–55
J. Novák: 'Dějiny bývalé hr. černínské obrazárny na Hradčanech' [History of the former Count Czernin's pictures at Hradčany], *Památky Archaeol.*, xxvii (1915), pp. 123–41
——: 'Prameny k studiu byvalé hr. černínské obrazárny na Hradčanech' [Sources for the study of the former Count Czernin's pictures at Hradčany], *Památky Archaeol.*, xxvii (1915), pp. 208–21
Z. Kalista: 'Humprecht Jan Černín jako mecenáš a podporovatel výtvarný umění v době své benátské ambasády, 1660–63' [Humprecht Jan Czernin as a patron and supporter of the plastic arts during his time at the Venetian Embassy, 1660–63], *Památky Archaeol.*, xxxv (1928–9), pp. 53–77
——: *Mládí Humprechta Jana Černína z Chudenic* [The young Humprecht Jan Czernin von Chudenitz], 2 vols (Prague, 1932)
——: 'L'ambasciata del conte Humprecht Jan Černín di Chudenice a Venezia, 1660–63', *Europa Orient.*, xxi (1941), pp. 26–7
E. A. Safarik: 'Per la pittura veneta del seicento: Girolamo Forobosco', *A. Illus.*, vi (1973), pp. 353–63

WALTER ANGELELLI

(2) Count **Jan Rudolf Czernin** (*b* Vienna, 9 June 1757; *d* Vienna, 23 April 1845). Descendant of (1) Count Humprecht Jan Czernin. After the death of his father, Count Prokop Adalbert Czernin, in 1777, he was sent to his maternal uncle and guardian, Hieronymus Colloredo, the last Prince-Bishop of Salzburg and patron of Wolfgang Amadeus Mozart. While studying law at the University of Salzburg, he developed an interest in the arts and music and undertook the customary Grand Tour through Europe. After his marriage in 1781, he resided in Vienna, where his prominence as a connoisseur of the arts brought him several official appointments. As President of the Akademie der Bildenden Künste (1823–7), he was critical of the highly regarded Nazarene school and of the prevailing sentimental historicism in painting. As Chamberlain at the Imperial Court from 1824, he was responsible for the royal collection and for the court theatre.

Jan Rudolf Czernin's discernment of quality is apparent in his own collection, which he began in 1800. He continued to add to his collection until his death, buying from Viennese dealers and auctions. Paintings from the 17th-century Italian, French, Spanish and Dutch schools formed the nucleus of the collection, and the high proportion of Dutch landscapes and genre scenes reflected prevailing taste. Purchased originally as by Pieter de Hooch, Vermeer's *Artist's Studio* (Vienna, Ksthist. Mus.) was acknowledged as by Vermeer by 1893. Jan Rudolf's appreciation of quality also led him to acquire a 14th-century north Italian altarpiece and a 15th-century panel by an artist from the circle of Rogier van der Weyden. Important 16th-century works included Titian's portrait of *Doge Gritti*, formerly in the collection of Charles I, King of England and Scotland, and a *Portrait of a Clergyman* by Albrecht Dürer (both Washington, DC, N.G.A.). The collection was housed from 1845 in a new palace on Josef Städler Glacis, today Friedrich Schmidt Platz, in Vienna, and for 100 years after Jan Rudolf's death was open to the public during the winter months. In 1954, 85 paintings from the collection were loaned to the Residenzgalerie in Salzburg. When the agreed loan period elapsed in 1974 the gallery secured 24 works, principally representing 17th-century French paintings, and has continued to acquire paintings formerly in the Czernin collection.

Jan Rudolf Czernin also extended his patronage of the arts to Bohemia, where he managed the family estates. He commissioned the sculptors Koller and Ignac Michal Platzer (1757–1826) to decorate the Czernin Palace in Prague on the occasion of the coronations as kings of Bohemia of Leopold II and Francis II. In 1796 Jan Rudolf was a founder member of a society to promote fine arts in Bohemia, which established an academy of painting and music, a polytechnic and a museum. Until 1811 he provided premises in Prague to house the art collection that forms the nucleus of the Rudolphinum, commissioned music from the Bohemian Leopold Kuželuh and sponsored the Bohemian painter František Kadalik (1786–1840) to attend the Akademie in Vienna.

BIBLIOGRAPHY
E. Blechinger, ed.: *Salzburger Landessammlungen: Residenzgalerie mit Sammlung Czernin* (Salzburg, 1980)

CLAIRE BRISBY

Czeschka, Carl Otto (*b* Vienna, 22 Oct 1878; *d* Hamburg, 30 July 1960). Austrian printmaker, painter, decorative artist and writer. He studied painting with Christian Griepenkerl (1839–1916) at the Akademie der Bildenden Künste in Vienna (1894–9). From 1899 to 1900 he renovated the Patronatskirche of Emperor Francis Joseph in Radmer an dem Hasel, decorating it with frescoes. At the same time he received his first illustration commissions from the publishers Gerlach & Wiedling in Vienna. From 1900 he was a member of the Vienna Secession (*see* SECESSION, §3). In 1902 he became an assistant tutor in draughtsmanship at the Kunstgewerbeschule (now Hochschule für Angewandte Kunst) in Vienna, and in 1905 he took over a class in painting and draughtsmanship, being one of Oskar Kokoschka's first teachers.

In Autumn 1905 Czeschka joined the WIENER WERKSTÄTTE. Under their auspices he produced jewellery, fabrics, wallpaper, enamelled pictures and furniture, and repoussé work and glass windows for the Palais Stoclet, Brussels (1905–11). A box that Czeschka made out of partly gilded, repoussé silver and ivory, which the Škoda Works at Plzeň commissioned as a gift to Emperor Francis Joseph (280×530×375 mm; Vienna, Österreich. Nbib.), was the centre of attention at the *Imperial Royal Austria* exhibition at Earl's Court, London (1906). It revealed the ornamental style that Czeschka had revitalized by the opulent emphasis he gave individual sections as an expressive encounter with architectonic form. The *Kunstschau* of 1908 in Vienna exhibited the glass display case that he made for Ludwig Wittgenstein in embossed silver, hard stones, ivory and mother-of-pearl (1.60×0.61×0.31 m; priv. col.). He filled the spandrel sections of the glass braces in the front and rear areas, which were cartridge-shaped, framed by rectangles and placed in a vertical series, and the surfaces of the half-length lateral sections with three-dimensional, exuberantly Baroque ornamental work, consisting of tendrils, foliage, grapes, birds and squirrels, emphasizing the ornamental rather than the architectonic.

In 1907 Czeschka designed Max Reinhardt's production of *King Lear* at the Deutsches Theater, Berlin. Appointed in autumn that year to the Hamburger Kunstgewerbeschule, he became a professor there in 1909. Also in 1909, Gerlachs Jugendbücherei, Vienna, published his famous illustrations to Friedrich Hebbel's *Nibelungen*, in the story by Franz Keim. In contrast to his early, naturalistically symbolic vignettes of 1902, in these works he broke through to a radically two-dimensional style and to a series of geometrical, archaically-symbolic ornamental effects in patterns of spirals, waves, rectangles and triangles, which filled the surfaces. Gold paint and unmodulated weak tones of blue and red enhanced the austere black-and-white contrast and gave the picture-sequences, which Czeschka had arranged as diptychs with geometrically constructed frame-mouldings, an exclusively artisan quality.

Czeschka's ornamental style developed under the influences of the Vienna Secession (in particular Gustav Klimt) and of the Kunstgewerbeschule, but also out of sources of folk art and the world of Nordic myth and legend. As a founder-member of the Österreichischer Werkbund he participated in the *Werkbundausstellung* in Cologne (1914) with the glass windows that he had designed for the rebuilding of the Kunstgewerbeschule in Hamburg. With the windows for the Gnadenkirche Hamburg St Pauli and the Handwerkskammer, Hamburg, which Czeschka completed in 1915, these concluded the first phase of his work.

After developing his roman typefaces, the *Czeschka-Olympia* and *Czeschka-Kursive*, Czeschka produced commercial graphic work during World War I, for example for the biscuit manufacturers Bahlsen. He also designed sets for a production of *Nibelungen* by Max Reinhardt in Berlin in 1917, as well as insignia and chains of office for the Dean of Hamburg University in 1920. His numerous commissions for the Haus Gildemeister in Hamburg during the 1920s included the tapestry *A Thousand and One Nights* (sketch, 2.26×4.00 m; Hamburg, Mus. Kst & Gew.) in an Art Deco style of international quality. He collected originals of primitive art, the exoticism of which he embodied in designs for cigar-box wrappers for Wolff, a manufacturer of smoker's requisites. The same firm also gave him commissions for poster designs, advertising graphics and shop-fittings. Although Adolf Hitler's nationalistic style took over architecture, Czeschka designed a cigar shop with the austerity of a Bauhaus workshop in *c.* 1940. All the commercial fittings he produced in the years up to *c.* 1950 revealed stylistic features of the late 1920s and have survived only in plans, perspective studies and photographs. In 1943 he retired as professor at the

Kunstgewerbeschule in Hamburg. His last major commercial graphic work was to design the title of the weekly newspaper *Die Zeit* in 1947.

WRITINGS
Die Quelle: Allerlei Gedanken in Vignettenform (Vienna, n.d.)
Kalender für das Jahr 1904 (Vienna, 1903)
Kalender für das Jahr 1906 (Vienn4a, 1905)

BIBLIOGRAPHY
ÖKL
F. Keim: *Die Nibelungen*, Gerlachs Jugendbücherei (Vienna and Leipzig, 1924)
R. Feuchtmüller and W. Mrazek: *Kunst in Österreich, 1860–1918* (Vienna, 1964), pp. 113–14, 120
Carl Otto Czeschka: Aspekte seines Lebenswerkes (exh. cat., text H. Spielmann; Hamburg, B. A. T. Haus, 1978)
W. J. Schweiger: *Wiener Werkstätte: Kunst und Handwerk, 1903–1932* (Vienna, 1982; Eng. trans., London, 1984)
G. Fliedl: *Kunst und Lehre am Beginn der Moderne: Die Wiener Kunstgewerbeschule, 1867–1918* (Vienna, 1986), pp. 314–17
K. Varnedoc: *Vienna, 1900: Art, Architecture & Design* (New York, 1986), p. 94
S. Siller: *Carl Otto Czeschka, Biographie und Gesamtwerk* (in preparation)

PETER STASNY

Częstochowa. Polish city on the Upper Warta River, *c.* 100 km north-west of Kraków in western Małopolska (Lesser Poland). It achieved city status in 1377. About 3 km to the west, on a limestone hill known as Jasna Góra, Prince Władysław of Opole founded a monastery in 1382 and brought Hungarian Paulines to live there. Since the Middle Ages it has been Poland's main pilgrimage centre, largely as a result of the cult of the Częstochowa *Madonna*. A settlement, the former village of Częstochówka, grew up around the monastery and itself achieved city status in 1712. The cities were linked in 1826 with the Avenue of the Blessed Virgin Mary, which forms the main axis of Częstochowa. The city has been greatly extended since the late 19th century.

The extensive monastery complex at Jasna Góra is enclosed within bastioned fortifications (1620–43; improved 1674–6 and 1720–45) of Italian–Dutch design. Four successive gateways form the entrance. The huge monastic church, originally a Late Gothic hall (before 1463), was redesigned, mainly by Silesian artists, as a Baroque basilica with stuccowork and paintings (1690–93) by Karl Dankwart (*d* after 1703) in the vaults. Its furnishings include a main altar (1725–8) designed by Giacopo Antonio Buzzini and made by the workshop of Johann Adam Karinger (*c.* 1690–1742) from Wrocław. The tall tower (before 1620) was heightened in 1699–1703 and rebuilt after a fire in 1900. Off the church's south aisle are characteristic annexes with cupolas: a Mannerist porch (*c.* 1620–30), the Denhoff Chapel (1644–71) and the Jabłonowski Chapel (1751–4). To the north of the church is the Chapel of Our Lady, with a Late Gothic presbytery (early 16th century) and a main hall with galleries (1641–4) containing stuccowork from this period and later (before 1682). The chapel's ebony altar (1650) is decorated with silver images and with the Częstochowa *Madonna*, based on a Byzantine *Hodegetria* ('Virgin who points the way' type (see fig.). It was probably made in Italy in the second half of the 14th century and was embellished with silver decorative plaques during restoration in 1430–34.

The other monastic buildings, which are concentrated around two cloisters, were built *c.* 1620 and renovated in

1690–1712 by Silesian builders, who built the Baroque elevation on the city side at the same time. The Knight's Hall dates to the first half of the 17th century, the refectory to *c.* 1644–70, with paintings (after 1693) by Karl Dankwart; the library dates to 1733–9. Along the west curtain wall are the old farm buildings and the arsenal (second half of the 17th century–early 18th), which houses a museum. In the south-eastern corner of the fortifications are cloisters and a chapel (1921–7; by Adolf Szyszko-Bohusz). The museum and buildings near the church contain over 150 paintings, mostly by monks, from the 17th century onwards. The treasury, sacristy and museum house an important collection of artefacts from the 15th to 19th centuries, notably goldwork, jewellery, weaving and embroidery, including gifts from ruling and noble families. In the Chapel of Our Lady there are several thousand votive offerings, mainly in silver. The library contains several illuminated manuscripts.

In the city itself there are two Pauline churches, the Baroque SS Andrew and Barbara (1637–42; enlarged second half of the 18th century) and St Zygmunt (second quarter of the 17th century; enlarged after 1783), a Baroque and Neo-classical church with a Gothic presbytery (*c.* 1350). There is also a cathedral (1901–27; by Konstanty Wojciechowsky (1841–1910)) in Gothic Revival style. Because of the pilgrim movement in the 18th and 19th centuries, Częstochowa became the largest Polish centre for the production of popular devotional images: in the mid-19th century several dozen painting workshops were in operation.

BIBLIOGRAPHY
J. Braun: *Częstochowa: Rozwój urbanistyczny i architektoniczny* [Częstochowa: urban and architectonic development] (Warsaw, 1959); rev. as *Częstochowa: Urbanistyka i architektura* [Częstochowa: urban planning and architecture] (Warsaw, 1977)
Z. Rozanow and E. Smulikowska: *Skarby kultury na Jasnej Górze* [The cultural heritage of Jasna Góra] (Warsaw, 1974, 2/1979; Eng. trans., Warsaw, 1979)
J. Pasierb, J. Samek and K. Szafraniec: *Die Kunstschätze des Klosters Jasna Góra* (Leipzig, 1977, 2/1979)
A. Kunczyńska-Iracka: *Malarstwo ludowe kręgu częstochowskiego* [Folk painting from the Częstochowa area] (Wrocław, 1978) [with Eng. summary]
Studia Claromontana, i-xi (1981–91) [period. devoted to Jasna Góra]
Jasnogórska Bogurodzica, 1382–1982 [The Madonna of Jasna Góra, 1382–1982] (Warsaw, 1982, 2/1987)

JERZY Z. ŁOZIŃSKI

Czigány [Wimmer], **Dezső** (*b* Budapest, 1 June 1883; *d* Budapest, 31 Dec 1937). Hungarian painter. He studied in Munich and Nagybánya (now Baia Mare, Romania) under Simon Hollósy, and for 18 months in Paris under Jean-Paul Laurens. Brown tones and a strong realism characterize his early pictures. On returning to Hungary, he developed close links with many leading radical intellectuals. He became a member of the radical, Fauvist-influenced group the Eight (*see* EIGHT, THE (iii)), exhibiting with them from 1909 until they disbanded in 1912. His own ideal was Cézanne.

After 1910 Czigány's style remained unchanged. He painted restrained compositions with harsh, rigid forms; his still-lifes highlight the plasticity of objects (e.g. *Still-life with Apples and Utensils*, 1910s) and his landscapes are vivid (e.g. *Lonely Tree*, 1910; Budapest, N.G.). He had an

Częstochowa *Madonna*, tempera with a chalk base on canvas and panel, 1222×822 mm, probably from Italy, second half of the 14th century, restored 1430–34 (Częstochowa, Monastery of Jasna Góra)

introvert personality with an inclination towards depression. From the 1910s to the end of his life he painted a series of portraits overwhelmingly frontal and sculptural in form (e.g. *Self-portrait*, after 1910, and *Scarlet Portrait*, 1917; both Budapest, N.G.). His most mature picture and also the best known—largely due to the dramatic economy of its composition—is *Child Burial* (*c.* 1910; Budapest, N.G.), in which he came near to the Synthetism of Gauguin's Brittany style of 1888. Between 1922 and 1927 Czigány settled in France, working mostly in Provence. On his return to Hungary in 1927 he held a one-man exhibition, but he gradually slipped into the periphery of public artistic life. In 1937, in a psychotic fit, he murdered his family and committed suicide.

BIBLIOGRAPHY

Czigány Dezső hagyatéki kiállítása [Exhibition of paintings from the estate of Dezső Czigány] (exh. cat., ed. L. Czigány; Budapest, House Creative Artists, 1944)

K. Passuth: 'Dezső Czigány', *Magyar Művészet, 1890–1919* [Hungarian art, 1890–1919], ed. L. Németh (Budapest, 1981), p. 571

For further bibliography *see* THE EIGHT (iii).

MÁRIA SZOBOR-BERNÁTH

Czóbel, Béla (*b* Budapest, 4 Sept 1883; *d* Budapest, 29 Jan 1976). Hungarian painter, also active in France. He received his first training at the Nagybánya artists' colony and at the Akademie der Bildenden Künste in Munich, before going to Paris in 1903, where he studied at the Académie Julian. He met Pablo Picasso, Maurice Asselin and André Dunoyer de Segonzac and began to adopt a more avant-garde style related to Fauvism; three of his paintings were exhibited alongside Fauvist works at the Salon d'Automne in 1905. On his return to Hungary in 1906 he was the first to introduce the new spirit of 20th-century painting to NAGYBÁNYA. His historical importance lies in his role as a link between the Ecole de Paris and Hungarian painting and in his attempts to fuse the two traditions.

Although Czóbel became a member of the Hungarian group THE EIGHT (iii) in 1909, most of his time from 1905 to 1914 was spent in Paris, where, under the influence of Paul Cézanne, he began to pay more attention to pictorial construction. During World War I he lived in the Netherlands, and from 1919 to 1925 he was in Berlin, where he was influenced to some extent by the work of Die Brücke, for example in the portrait of *Mr Meyer* (1921; Szentendre, Czóbel Mus.). From 1925 until 1939 he again lived mainly in France, returning to Hungary, to the SZENTENDRE COLONY, on the outbreak of World War II. In the post-war years he divided his time between Paris,

Szentendre and Budapest. In Budapest he was a member of the EUROPEAN SCHOOL (Hung. *Erópai Iskola*) artists' group. His characteristic paintings are still-lifes, nudes, portraits and street scenes such as *Rue Mouffetard* (1925; Szentendre, Czóbel Mus.), painted in patches of hazy colour and with sensitive brushwork.

BIBLIOGRAPHY

J. Frank: *Czóbel* (Budapest, 1983)

RONALD ALLEY

Czyżewski, Tytus (*b* Przyszów, 28 Dec 1880; *d* Kraków, 6 May 1945). Polish painter, critic and poet. In 1902–7 he studied at the Academy of Fine Arts in Kraków in the painting studios of Józef Mehoffer and Leon Wyczół-kowski. From 1908 he travelled frequently to the West, particularly to Paris, acquainting himself with the latest artistic trends. He began exhibiting in 1906, often abroad (including at the Salon des Indépendants, Paris). During his first visit to France he discovered the work of Cézanne, and he started using more vivid colours (e.g. *Salome*, 1909; Kraków, N. Mus.). He also discovered El Greco, whose work he admired until his death.

From World War I onward Czyżewski was the moving spirit behind modern art in Poland. In 1917, with the brothers Zbigniew Pronaszko and Andrzej Pronaszko (1888–1961), he organized in Kraków the first exhibition of the Polish Expressionists (later the FORMISTS) and showed multi-planar polychrome compositions (untraced). Until the break-up of the Formists in 1922 he was its main artist, theoretician and joint editor of the periodical *Formiści*. He was also co-founder of the Futurist clubs Katarynka (Barrel Organ) and Gałka Muszkatułowa (Nutmeg Apple). His best-known volumes of visual poetry (e.g. *Noc/Dzień*, 'Night/day') and dramas also stem from this period. After a brief flirtation with Surrealism (as in the illustrations to his poem 'Robespierre—Rapsod—Od romantyzmu do cynizmu', 'Robespierre—rhapsody—from romanticism to cynicism', 1927) Czyżewski produced colourist paintings until his death. His paintings were less doctrinal than those of other Polish colourists, however, containing an unusually harmonious tonal range and a poetic aura (e.g. *Still-life*; Poznań, N. Mus.). He commanded great respect as a critic, based on his practical and theoretical knowledge.

WRITINGS

Władysław Ślewiński (Warsaw, 1928)

BIBLIOGRAPHY

SAP

J. Pollakowna: *Tytus Czyżewski* (Warsaw, 1971)

WOJCIECH WŁODARCZYK

D

d'. For French and pre-19th-century Italian proper names with this preposition, *see under* the second part of the name.

da. For Portuguese proper names with this prefix *see under* the first part of the name. For pre-19th-century Italian proper names with this prefix, *see under* the first part of the name for individuals active before *c.* 1500; *see under* the second part of the name for those active *c.* 1500–*c.* 1800.

Dab'a, Tell el-. *See* AVARIS and PIRAMESSE.

Dabber. Pad made of cotton, silk or leather used to apply ink or paint. ☐

Däbeler, Michael. *See* DÖBEL, MICHAEL.

Dabhoi [anc. Dharbhavati]. Town 34 km south-east of Vadodara in Gujarat, India. Traditionally held to have been founded in the 7th century AD, the town had achieved sufficient prominence by the 11th century for a fort to be constructed. Built by King Jayasimha Siddharaja (*reg* 1093–1134) of the SOLANKI dynasty, the style of the fort's architecture and sculpture relates to contemporary monuments at Sidhpura and Jhinjuvada. Its four impressive gateways were also the work of Siddharaja; additions to them were made during the reign of Visala (*reg* 1245–61), and further changes took place after 1300. The Hira (diamond) Gate on the east is the most elaborate; those on the north, south and west walls are respectively known as the Moti, Nandod and Baroda gates. The Hira Gate with its columns and brackets resembles a temple gateway (*toraṇa*) embedded in the wall. Two temples may be ascribed to the mid-13th century: a ruined structure south of the Hira Gate and another, much restored, the Kalika Mata, set in the wall north of it. A number of tanks and accompanying shrines also date to this period. After the fall of the Solanki capital of Patan in the late 13th century (*see* PATAN (i)), most of Dabhoi's monuments were destroyed by Muslim raiders. Among the sparse Islamic remains are a minaret and a fragmentary post called the Bibi Dargah. A number of Hindu and Jaina temples were built or renovated during the 20th century. A Jaina *granth bhandar* (library) houses a large collection of manuscripts.

BIBLIOGRAPHY

H. D. Sankalia: *The Archaeology of Gujarat* (Bombay, 1941)
P. Brown: *Indian Architecture, Buddhist and Hindu Periods* (? Bombay, [1941], rev. Bombay, 1956)
S. B. Rajyagor, ed.: *Vadodara District*, Gujarat State Gazetteers (Ahmadabad, 1979)

WALTER SMITH

Dacca. *See* DHAKA.

Dachau colony. Colony of German artists formed *c.* 1807 and active until 1946. It was based in the Bavarian city situated on the River Amper, 17 km north-west of Munich. Dachau is an ancient market town that dates back to *c.* AD 800 and that was awarded its charter in 1391. Its historic buildings include a ruined 16th-century castle, built for Albert V, Duke of Bavaria, by Heinrich Schöttl and Wilhelm Egckl (completed 1570–73), and a 17th-century town hall and parish church (1624–5) designed by Hans Krumpper. The artists' colony flourished there particularly from 1890 to 1914. Over the years *c.* 1000 artists, German and international, used the colony, which did not represent any particular school, although most of the artists were Romantic, Naturalist or Impressionist landscape painters. The best-known participants were Max Liebermann and Lovis Corinth. Characteristic landscape works of the colony were *View from the Schlossberg towards the Munich Road* (*c.* 1860) by Eduard Schleich (1812–74), *Theresienwiese* (1882) by Adolf Lier (1826–86) and Corinth's *Wood near Dachau* (1893; all Dachau, Gemäldegal.). The Künstlervereinigung of Dachau was founded in 1927, but Hitler's rise to power in 1933 brought pressure on it to conform with state dictates on art. From 1933 to 1945 the town contained the notorious Nazi concentration camp, whose inmates are commemorated by a memorial and museum. After Germany's defeat in 1945 the Künstlervereinigung was dismantled, but it was re-established in 1947. In 1985 the Dachauer Gemäldegalerie reopened in celebration of the city's art-historical heritage.

BIBLIOGRAPHY

C. Thiemann: *Erinnerungen eines Dachauer Malers* (Dachau, 1966)
G. Wietek: *Deutsche Künstlerkolonien und Künstlerorte* (Munich, 1976)
H. G. Richardi: *Dachau: Führer durch die Altstadt, die Künstlerkolonie und die KZ-Gedenkstätte* (Passau, 1979)
O. Thiemann-Stoedtner: *Dachauer Maler: Der Künstlerort Dachau von 1801–1946* (Dachau, 1981)
Kunst und Künstler in Dachau und im Amperland, 1890–1930 (exh. cat., Haimhausen, near Dachau, Schloss Haimhausen, 1981)
L. J. Reitmeier, ed.: *Dachau Ansichten und Zeugnisse aus zwölf Jahrhunderten* (Dachau, 1982)
H. Heres: *Dachauer Gemäldegalerie* (Dachau, 1985)

JAMES G. TODD JR

Dacosta, António (*b* Angra do Heroísmo, Azores, 13 Jan 1914). Portuguese painter, illustrator and poet. In 1935 he moved to Lisbon where his exhibition in 1940 with António Pedro and the English sculptress Pamela Bowden was considered the first national manifestation of Surrealism. In his melancholy and menacing works of the late 1930s and early 1940s, the dream-like spaces are crowded with people and animals in attitudes of violence or alarm, for example *Antithesis of Calm* (1940; Lisbon, Mus. Gulbenkian). The Brazilian painter Cícero Dias, who was in Portugal in the early 1940s, was an important influence on him then. During the 1940s his painting became less crowded, and the overt violence gave way to gestures of greater ambiguity. In 1944 a fire in the studio he shared with António Pedro destroyed many of their paintings.

Until 1947, when he emigrated to Paris, Dacosta participated in various group shows, winning the important Amadeo de Souza-Cardoso Award in 1942. He also wrote poetry and illustrated a number of books, such as *Uma noite de chuva* ('A night of rain'), a collection of stories by Ribeiro Couto published in 1944. In 1949 he sent two works dated 1948 and verging on abstraction to the only exhibition of the Lisbon Surrealist Group in which António Pedro, Fernando Azevedo and Mário Cesariny also took part. He stopped painting in 1949, to resume again only in the late 1970s. These paintings are quiet and lyrical with large, luminous areas of colour vibrating against one another, for example *The Dream of Fernando Pessoa beneath a Trellis on a Summer's Afternoon* (1982–3; Lisbon, Mus. Gulbenkian). Although they retain the spatial ambiguity of his earlier works, they mark a departure from Surrealism in their serene portrayal of human figures, animals and plants.

BIBLIOGRAPHY
J.-A. França: 'António Pedro e António Dacosta', *Colóquio*, 32 (1965), pp. 26–32
R. M. Gonçalves: *Dacosta* (Lisbon, 1984)

RUTH ROSENGARTEN

Dacosta [da Costa], Mílton (Rodrigues) (*b* Niterói, 1915; *d* Rio de Janeiro, 1988). Brazilian painter. He entered the Escola Nacional de Belas Artes, Rio de Janeiro, in 1930 and in 1931 was one of the founders of the Núcleo Bernardelli, whose aim was to build on the initial successes of Modernism. After at first being influenced by Cézanne he painted cyclists, bathers, and children playing in compositions of carefully linked rectangles, cubes, cylinders, spheres and pyramids (*At the Swimming-Pool*, 1942; Rio de Janeiro, Roberto Marinho priv. col.). In later works he was briefly influenced by Pittura Metafisica and Surrealism, surrounding ordinary objects with a schematic architecture and mysterious *trompe l'oeil* mannequins and faces. From 1944 to 1946 he lived in the USA and Europe. In the mid-1950s, in constructions such as *On a Brown Background* (1955; U. São Paulo, Mus. A. Contemp.) and *On a Red Background* (1955; Rio de Janeiro, Mus. Manchete), he began to produce austere works close to concrete art. He established his compositions on strict mathematical principles, generally using only two or three colours and precise lines intersected at right angles. In 1963, though retaining the formal economy of his earlier work, he returned to the figure in the series *Venus, Angels and*

Pageantry, treated in a manner at once sensual and ascetic (*Venus and the Bird*, 1976; Rio de Janeiro, Gal. Acervo).

BIBLIOGRAPHY
A. Amaral, ed.: *Projeto construtivo brasileiro na arte, 1950–1962* [The Brazilian Constructivist movement in art, 1950–1962] (São Paulo, 1977), pp. 298–9
R. Pontual: *Cinco mestres brasileiros—Pintores construtivistas* (Rio de Janeiro, 1977), pp. 14–15, 23–4, 89–115
T. Spanudis: *Construtivistas brasileiros* (São Paulo, 1978)
A. Bento: *Mílton Dacosta* (São Paulo, 1980)
Mílton Dacosta (exh. cat. by A. Bento, São Paulo, Mus. A. Mod., 1981)

ROBERTO PONTUAL

Dada. Artistic and literary movement launched in Zurich in 1916 but shared by independent groups in New York, Berlin, Paris and elsewhere. The Dadaists channelled their revulsion at World War I into an indictment of the nationalist and materialist values that had brought it about. They were united not by a common style but by a rejection of conventions in art and thought, seeking through their unorthodox techniques, performances and provocations to shock society into self-awareness. The name Dada itself was typical of the movement's anti-rationalism. Various members of the Zurich group are credited with the invention of the name; according to one account it was selected by the insertion of a knife into a dictionary, and was retained for its multilingual, childish and nonsensical connotations. The Zurich group was formed around the poets HUGO BALL, Emmy Hennings, TRISTAN TZARA and RICHARD HUELSENBECK, and the painters HANS ARP, MARCEL JANCO and HANS RICHTER. The term was subsequently adopted in New York by the group that had formed around MARCEL DUCHAMP, FRANCIS PICABIA, Marius de Zayas (1880–1961) and MAN RAY. The largest of several German groups was formed in Berlin by Huelsenbeck with JOHN HEARTFIELD, RAOUL HAUSMANN, HANNAH HÖCH and GEORGE GROSZ. As well as important centres elsewhere (Barcelona, Cologne and Hannover), a prominent post-war Parisian group was promoted by Tzara, Picabia and ANDRÉ BRETON. This disintegrated acrimoniously in 1922–3, although further Dada activities continued among those unwilling to join Surrealism in 1924.

1. Early history: Zurich, 1914–18. 2. New York, 1915–21. 3. Barcelona and developments in Zurich, 1916–20. 4. Berlin Dada, 1917–22. 5. Associated developments: Merz, Constructivism and Ma, 1919–25. 6. Cologne Dada, 1919–22. 7. Final phase: Paris, 1919–24.

1. EARLY HISTORY: ZURICH, 1914–18. Zurich Dada's roots lay in the pre-war international avant-garde. Kandinsky's abstraction and theoretical writings, together with Cubism and the development of collage, liberated Dada from the dual constrictions of reality and convention. Similarly the writings of such German Expressionists as Christian Morgenstern combined with the influence of French poets, thereby allowing the Dadaists to break the direct link between words and meaning. Disgust at the war's outbreak was immediately voiced in Zurich at Walter Serner and Konrad Milo's Cabaret Pantagruel (from August 1914), and was reinforced by the arrival of intellectual refugees during 1915. Serner collaborated with the painter CHRISTIAN SCHAD on the periodical *Sirius* (1915–16), but the latter's move to Geneva restricted their

participation in the group developing around Ball and Hennings, who founded the Cabaret Voltaire (5 February 1916), establishing performance as a central Dada medium (*see also* PERFORMANCE ART, §(iii)). Inviting participants, they met Arp and the Dutch painters OTTO VAN REES and Adya van Rees-Dutilh (1876–1959), and the painter, sculptor and dancer Sophie Taeuber-Arp. They were joined by the Romanians Janco and Tzara and the Germans Huelsenbeck and Richter. Other painters contributed, including Walter Helbig (1878–1968) and Oskar Lüthy (1885–1945), as well as the Austrian Max Oppenheimer (MOPP), the Romanian Arthur Segal and the Ukrainian Marcel Slodki (1892–1943). This internationalism was reflected in the cabaret's French and Russian evenings, at which the artists exhibited. Following the example of Futurist provocations Tzara, Huelsenbeck and Janco performed *L'Amiral cherche une maison à louer*, simultaneously reading texts in three different languages. 'African' music and poetry were also performed at *soirées nègres*, emphasizing a spontaneity of expression absent from Western art. This attracted Rudolph Laban (1879–1958), who initiated African performances for which Janco made Cubist cardboard masks (e.g. 1919; Paris, Mus. A. Mod. Ville Paris).

The term 'Dada' first appeared in the periodical *Cabaret Voltaire* (June 1916), where Ball defined their activities as proving 'that there are people of independent minds—beyond war and nationalism—who live for different ideals'. The new name signalled the more combative spirit of the first Dada Soirée (Zunfthaus zur Waag, 14 July), where Ball performed astonishing *Lautegedichte* (sound poems) composed from invented words, which exposed an emotive power distinct from everyday language. Tzara read his irreverent *Manifeste de M. Antipyrine*, which acknowledged that 'Dada remains within the framework of European weaknesses, it's still shit, but from now on we want to shit in different colours'. Such shock tactics increasingly came to characterize their public position. During the summer sound poems by Huelsenbeck were published (*Phantastische Gebete*, Zurich, 1916). They were illustrated with abstract woodcuts by Arp, which showed a spontaneity centred upon chance as a governing principle. Rejecting a determining role, Arp experimented with abstract collages 'made according to the laws of chance', in which papers were glued where they fell, reflecting a reverence for forces outside rationalism (*see also* AUTOMATISM).

Despite Huelsenbeck's return to Berlin, the group's activities developed in March 1917 when the Galerie Corray became the Galerie Dada, and the cabaret was replaced by the launching of a movement. Work by Campendonk, Klee, Kandinsky and others from the Sturm-Galerie in Berlin was exhibited in the gallery and accompanied by lectures. The soirées continued, including Ball's recital of *Gadji beri bimba* while dressed in cardboard cylinders designed by Janco. Music by Hans Heusser, Stravinsky and Arnold Schoenberg accompanied a later exhibition (May) combining de Chirico, August Macke, ENRICO PRAMPOLINI, Fritz Baumann (1886–1942) and the Dadaists' works in unusual materials: Janco made plaster reliefs (e.g. *The Lock*, 1918; Tel Aviv, Mus. A.); Taeuber-Arp and Arp collaborated on geometric tapestries, for example *Pathetic Symmetry* (1916–17; Paris, Pompidou); and Arp made painted wooden reliefs, such

as *Entombment of the Birds and Butterflies (Head of Tzara)* (1916–17; Zurich, Ksthaus; see fig. 1), which introduced BIOMORPHISM into his work. At the same time Ball's withdrawal confirmed Tzara's leadership. He launched the periodical *Dada*, the first two numbers of which (July and December) reflected links with DER STURM in Berlin, Guillaume Apollinaire in Paris, Marinetti in Milan (*see* FUTURISM) and the PITTURA METAFISICA group in Ferrara. Through the latter he contributed to the Bolognese periodical *La Brigata*, inviting the editor, Francesco Meriano, to launch Italian Dada in summer 1917. However, Futurism's dominance and wider nationalism in Italy caused Tzara to break these links.

During 1917 and 1918 Serner and Schad collaborated more closely, the latter revealing a parallel concern with chance in his 'schadographs', unforeseen compositions achieved, like photograms, by laying objects on photographic paper and exposing them to light (e.g. 1918; Zurich, Ksthaus). By contrast, Richter's *Visionary Portraits* were superseded by an ordered abstraction close to that of Swedish artist VIKING EGGELING (e.g. *Composition*, *c*. 1916; Basle, Kstmus.) and resulted in a lengthy collaboration. Janco established an association of abstract artists, the NEUE LEBEN (April 1918), with Arp, Taeuber, Lüthy, Fritz Baumann, Augusto Giacometti, Otto Morach (1887–1973) and other Basle painters, while Tzara's explosive *Manifeste dada 1918* proclaimed Dada as 'the roar of contorted pains, the interweaving of contraries and of all contradictions, freaks and irrelevancies: LIFE.' By the time this appeared in *Dada 3* (December 1918), Zurich Dada was entering a more nihilistic stage resulting from contact with Picabia, who had arrived from New York, via Barcelona and Paris, earlier in the year.

1. Hans Arp: *Entombment of the Birds and Butterflies (Head of Tzara)*, painted wooden relief, 400×325×95 mm, 1916–17 (Zurich, Kunsthaus)

2. NEW YORK, 1915–21. The works made by Picabia and Duchamp in New York, which would later be acknowledged as Dada, differed from Zurich Dada by being less concerned with the war but more aggressive towards the art establishment. Picabia frequented the circle around Alfred Stieglitz's periodical *Camera Work*, including Edward J. Steichen, Marsden Hartley, Arthur Dove, Charles Sheeler and others (*see also* UNITED STATES OF AMERICA, §III, 3), and exhibited at Stieglitz's Photo-Secession gallery (*see* >291<). There he met the Mexican Marius de Zayas, who, after contributing to Apollinaire's *Les Soirées de Paris*, returned to New York to help launch the innovative periodical *291* (March 1915), named after the gallery. While Picabia collaborated on *291*, Duchamp, who had also arrived in New York in June 1915, was introduced by the collector Walter Arensberg (*see* ARENSBERG) into a literary circle including William Carlos Williams, Margaret Anderson, Wallace Stevens, Alfred Kreymborg and Elsa Freytag-Loringhoven, the painters Joseph Stella, MORTON LIVINGSTON SCHAMBERG and Man Ray. Other exiles followed, notably JEAN CROTTI, ALBERT GLEIZES and the composer Edgar Varèse; they gravitated around the Modern Gallery, which de Zayas opened in October. News of their work reached Tzara, but, although he contacted de Zayas in 1916, the parallels between them and the term Dada remained unnoticed.

In Picabia's mechanomorphic works, such as *Very Rare Picture on the Earth* (1915; Venice, Guggenheim; see fig. 2), and in Duchamp's studies on glass, images were adapted from technical diagrams. These commented upon

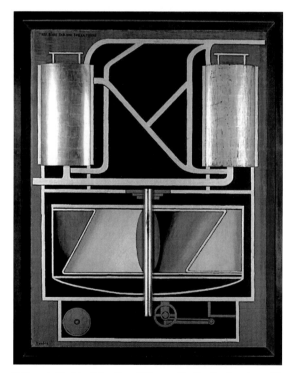

2. Francis Picabia: *Very Rare Picture on the Earth*, oil and metallic paint on paper board, and silver and gold leaf on plywood cylinders, 1257×978 mm, 1915 (Venice, Peggy Guggenheim Collection)

the human condition and even assumed erotic overtones, sometimes implied in their titles, analogies taken up by Crotti, Man Ray and Schamberg (e.g. Man Ray's *Rope Dancer Accompanies Herself with her Shadows*, 1916; New York, MOMA). However, Duchamp went further in renouncing originality when he exhibited ready-mades (*see* READY-MADE) at the Bourgeois Gallery (April 1916). These industrially produced objects constituted a deliberately anti-art gesture, raising serious questions about the accepted precepts of art. Ready-mades had been conceived in Paris, but Duchamp coined the term in New York and perfected the predetermined process of choice that removed all aesthetic judgement. While this encouraged such ironically titled objects as Schamberg and Freytag-Loringhoven's *God* (plumbing trap and mitre box, *c.* 1917; Philadelphia, PA, Mus. A.) and Man Ray's photograph of a mechanical egg-beater, *Man* (1918; Paris, Pompidou), the ready-made provoked the group's major controversy. Duchamp tested the juryless system of the Society of Independent Artists' exhibition held at Grand Central Palace, New York, in April 1917 (*see* SOCIETY OF INDEPENDENT ARTISTS) by submitting a ready-made: an upturned urinal, entitled *Fountain* and signed 'R. Mutt' (1917, untraced; editioned replica 1964; Ottawa, N.G.; for illustration *see* READY-MADE). He then publicly unmasked the fact of its concealment by the Society and defended 'Mr Mutt's' freedom of choice with a photograph of the work in *Blind Man* (no. 2, May 1917) supported by editorials written in its defence. In an additional provocation, he and Picabia (newly returned from Barcelona) invited Arthur Cravan (1887–1918), editor and sole author of the wittily insulting Parisian periodical *Maintenant* (1912–14), to lecture at the exhibition, resulting in a drunken striptease.

These events, and such periodicals as the single issue *Rongwrong* and Picabia's *391* (launched in 1916 with obvious reference to *291*, on which he had worked before), mocked establishment and avant-garde alike. They also coincided with the USA's entry into the war, which encouraged Picabia's embarkation for Europe in September 1917 and, a year later, Duchamp's move to Buenos Aires. Man Ray continued the provocation with *T. N. T.* (March 1919, edited with the anarchists Adolf Wolff and Adon Lacroix) and a replacement of artistic styles with mechanical techniques in his photographs and 'aerographs'. Meanwhile the Modern Gallery assumed de Zayas's name in 1919, and his promotion of radical art may have influenced the Estridentismo movement, launched in Mexico City in 1921. Duchamp's return to New York in 1920 brought renewed collaboration with Man Ray; they acted as advisers (and president and secretary respectively) to Katherine S. Dreier's Société Anonyme collection of international modern art founded in the same year. Man Ray and Duchamp's single issue of *New York Dada* (April 1921), which included articles by Tzara and Freytag-Loringhoven, confirmed a similarity of purpose, and both set off to participate in Paris Dada.

3. BARCELONA AND DEVELOPMENTS IN ZURICH, 1916–20. Avant-garde circles in Barcelona were aware of pre-war Parisian developments. In 1912 they had seen the

first Cubist exhibition held outside France (Galería Dalmau), and after 1914 Futurism had found echoes in the work of various artists. Parisians escaping to Barcelona from the war combined these approaches in work subsequently associated with Dada. They included Marie Laurencin, Otto van Watjen, SERGE CHARCHOUNE and Hélène Grunhof; Albert Gleizes and the Delaunays also visited the city, and Cravan was there before moving to New York. Although he was also a boxer, Cravan's bout against the World Champion, Jack Johnson, in Madrid (April 1916) was widely interpreted as a Dadaist gesture. The focus of activity was the gallery of Josep Dalmau (1867–1937), where notable shows of Charchoune, Grunhof and Gleizes were held in 1916. The group was galvanized by Picabia, who arrived in August. The gallery launched his periodical *391* in 1917, carrying contributions from others but dominated by Picabia's drawings and obscure references. It recalled activities in New York, giving them wider currency in Europe, and it went with him when he re-crossed the Atlantic in March 1917. In October his poems *Cinquante-deux miroirs* were published, and the impact of these sudden activities was extended through such periodicals as Josep Junoy's *Troços* (1916–18) and Salvat Papasseit's *Un enemic del poble* (1917–19) and *Arc-Voltaic* (1918).

Picabia established contact with Tzara while in Lucerne during 1918. He exhibited works alongside those of Arp and Janco in January 1919 (*Neue Leben*; Zurich, Ksthaus) before visiting Zurich in February. There his nihilism and inventiveness won immediate acclaim; he and Tzara wrote an 'automatic' text for *391* (no. 8, February 1919), and they collaborated on *Dada 4–5* (*Anthologie Dada*) (May 1919), which linked Zurich Dada to the New York and Barcelona groups, and orientated Tzara towards Paris. An eighth Dada Soirée (Saal zur Kaufleuten, April 1919), following Picabia's departure, included Tzara's simultanist poem for 20 voices (*Le Fièvre du mâle*) and Arp's poem *Wolkenpumpe*. At the same time the imminent post-war dispersal was counterbalanced by the formation of the Groupe des Artistes Radicaux, including Arp, Baumann, Eggeling, Janco and Richter. Arp then left for Cologne, and Janco for Bucharest. Tzara shared the editorship of *Der Zeltweg* with Serner and Otto Flake in November, but his departure in January 1920 signalled the end of Zurich Dada. The short-lived Geneva Dada, launched in December 1919 by Serner and Schad, held a final Grand Dada Ball in March 1920.

A postscript to Zurich Dada was added in summer 1920. Tzara returned to Bucharest where he was reunited with the poet Ion Vinea and with Janco, who had established the periodical *Contimporanul* (1920–30) supporting non-objective art. In Italy, Tzara also visited the Mantuan Dadaists Gino Cantarelli (1899–1950) and Aldo Fiozzi, editors of *Procellaria* (1917 and 1919) and *Bleu* (1920). They introduced him to the writer and abstract painter Julius Evola (1898–1974), who immediately became Dada's most provocative Italian agent. With encouragement from Schad, who had moved to Rome, and from Serner, Evola launched a Rome Dada season in April 1921, with an exhibition (including Cantarelli and Fiozzi) at the Galleria d'Arte Bragaglia and performances at the Grotte dell'Augusteo cabaret. His readings of his own writings and of Tzara's *Manifeste dada 1918*, and his declaration of the death of Futurism, caused uproar. However, sustained Futurist hostility and his isolation following Schad's move to realism provoked a personal crisis, and Evola suddenly abandoned Dada for philosophy.

4. BERLIN DADA, 1917–22. More so than in other cities, Berlin Dada was circumscribed by political events, as was already evident in Huelsenbeck's 'Der neue Mensch' (*Neue Jugend*, 23 May 1917), which marked his return to the collapsing city. At the artistic Alte Café des Westerns, he met political writers and artists for whom Berlin Dada constituted an extension of their opposition to the status quo; they included Franz Jung (1888–1963), Gerhard Preiss, Heartfield and his brother Wieland Hertzfelde (1896–1988), and Grosz. They were joined by Walter Mehring, Raoul Hausmann, Hannah Höch and the self-publicist Johannes Baader (1875–1955). Their disgust with the contemporary cultural situation was exposed in February 1918 in Huelsenbeck's lecture on Dada at the Galerie I. B. Neumann, which initiated the Club Dada (12 April). There he called for an art 'which in its conscious content presents the thousandfold problems of the day, the art which has been visibly shattered by the explosions of the last week, which is forever trying to collect its limbs after yesterday's crash' (*Dada Manifesto*, Berlin, 1918). While reiterating his moral concerns, he rejected the ideals of abstraction and of Expressionism, which was rapidly passing into the establishment. Hausmann, who became his close collaborator, responded with experiments across different media. Most notable were his phonetic poems (e.g. 'Selenautomobile', Dada matinée, 6 June), which, by the pronunciation of single letters, extended the Zurich sound poems. The form's abstraction was most evident in the printed 'scores', dubbed 'optophonetic poems', in which the force of each letter was indicated by its size. This was closely related to the mixed typography and overprinting of slogans that characterized Berlin Dada publications, such as *Club Dada* (1918).

The military defeat and the abdication of Emperor William II in 1918 brought the political crisis to a head and was followed by the brutal suppression of the communist-inspired Spartakist uprising (January 1919) by the Socialist Weimar government. The Dadaists responded in two publications in February: Baader's manifesto *Dadaisten gegen Weimar*, and *Jedermann sein eigner Fussball*, published by Hertzfelde's Malik Verlag. The former was simply anarchic, proclaiming Baader as President of the Earth, while the latter urged the renewal of the revolution and was immediately confiscated. Heartfield's cover of *Jedermann . . .* was one of the earliest uses of the quintessential Berlin Dada medium of PHOTOMONTAGE. The collaging of photographs from the mass media allowed the artists to dissect reality through unexpected combinations with other images or with words, without retreating into realism. Heartfield and Grosz made photomontage a satirical weapon, throwing back the images issued by the establishment media, while Höch and Hausmann added comments on everyday culture (e.g. Hausmann's *Art Critic*, 1920; London, Tate; for illustration *see* HAUSMANN,

RAOUL). Assemblages of found objects, notably Hausmann's *Mechanical Head: Spirit of our Age* (wooden hatmaker's dummy with objects, 1919; Paris, Pompidou), also employed this technique. In both works the use of immediate and ephemeral materials ensured against commercial value.

The critical nature of this work meant that few German Dada periodicals survived confiscation, the exception being Hausmann's *Der Dada* (1919–20), which included contributions from Picabia in its third number (April 1920, edited with Heartfield and Grosz). This reflected the heightened international activity of 1920. In February, Baader, Huelsenbeck and Hausmann undertook an increasingly riotous performance tour to Leipzig, Teplitz-Schönau, Prague and Karlsbad. In May, at the Erste Internationale Dada-Messe, paintings and drawings were combined with Dada posters, photomontages and assemblages, including a uniformed dummy with a pig's head, for which Grosz and Heartfield were fined for ridiculing the military. The show was accompanied by the *Dada Almanach* (Berlin, 1920), edited by Huelsenbeck, which included contributions from Zurich, Barcelona and Paris Dada. That it included Tzara is remarkable, as Huelsenbeck bitterly attacked his ambitions in *En avant Dada: Eine Geschichte des Dadaismus* (Hannover, 1920). These events marked Berlin Dada's culmination, as personal conflicts led to its fragmentation shortly after.

The celebration of VLADIMIR TATLIN in such works as *Tatlin at Home* (photomontage, 1920; Stockholm, Mod. Mus.) by Hausmann indicated the Dadaists' continuing aspiration for a revolutionary art, which developed into an exchange with international Constructivism in the 1920s. Richter and Eggeling, who arrived in 1918 but did not participate in Berlin Dada, completed the abstract film *Rhythmus 21* in 1921, the title indicating musical structures. In October Hausmann and Arp wrote 'A Call for an Elementarist Art' (*De Stijl*, iv/10, 1922) with the Suprematists Jean Pougny and László Moholy-Nagy, identifying an international art 'built up of its own elements alone'. These issues exercised the Kongress Internationaler Fortschrittlicher Künstler in Düsseldorf in May 1922, from which Richter, THEO VAN DOESBURG and El Lissitzky split to form the International Faction of Constructivists (*see* CONSTRUCTIVISM, §2). They became the nucleus for the Konstruktivisten und Dadaisten Kongress in Weimar (September), which was attended by Tzara, Arp and KURT SCHWITTERS, and which inspired Richter's periodical *G* (1923–4). In these exchanges the work of Arp, Richter, Hausmann and Schwitters maintained an unexpected balance between Dadaist chance and irony and Constructivist idealism.

5. ASSOCIATED DEVELOPMENTS: MERZ, CONSTRUCTIVISM AND MA, 1919–25. Huelsenbeck prevented Schwitters's admission to Berlin Dada because of his lack of political commitment, despite the considerable success of *An Anna Blume*, a chance poem published in *Der Sturm* in 1919. Schwitters had begun to produce such works and abstract collages (*Merzbilder*) soon after coming into contact with Hausmann and Höch in 1918. His response to Huelsenbeck's snub was to found his one-man 'movement', Merz, later in 1919, with its eponymous

periodical (1923–32). His works relied upon chance finds of everyday materials, especially waste paper, with which he established a formal harmony, for example the *Kots Picture* (1920; for illustration *see* COLLAGE). Schwitters remained close to several Dadaists, performing with Höch and Hausmann in Prague in 1921, where the latter's phonetic poem *fmsbw* inspired his own *Ursonate* (1924–5; published in *Merz*, 24, 1932). He invited Arp to collaborate on *Merz* and arranged Tzara's lecture tour on Dada (Hannover, Jena and Weimar) after the Weimar Congress (1922). He also collaborated with Van Doesburg, who, as 'I. K. Bonset', spread a mechanistic Dada through Holland via his periodical *Mécano* (1922–3) and a tour undertaken with Schwitters. This coincided with the creation of Schwitters's *Merzbau* (begun 1923; reconstructed 1980–83; Hannover, Sprengel Mus.), a haphazard construction of ephemeral material which would grow to fill his house (*see* SCHWITTERS, KURT, fig. 2).

The cross-fertilization between Dada and Constructivism was also evident in the former Austria-Hungary. Schwitters lectured in Prague throughout the 1920s, although knowledge of Cubism and Russian art meant that local interest was muted, with the exception of Hugo Dux and Artus Černik (a member of Karel Teige's Devětsil group). However, the first tours did inspire the visiting Yugoslav writers Virgil Poljanski and Dragan Aleksić, who were associated with the Zagreb periodical *Zenit* (1921–6), edited by Poljanski's brother Ljubomir Micić. Aleksić established contact with Tzara and Schwitters, organizing Dada soirées in Osijek and Subotica (1922), and Poljanski published a number of single-issue periodicals, such as *Dada-Jok* (Zagreb, 1922). Although reluctant to sacrifice *Zenit*'s independence, Micić blended Dada provocations with his admiration for Russian revolutionary culture and published the remarkable collage-paintings (known as *pafamas*, from *Papierfarbenmalerei*) of Jo Klek (pseudonym of Joseph Seissel).

A more important disseminator of Dada in Eastern Europe was the periodical *MA* (*see* MA GROUP) edited by LAJOS KASSÁK, which carried articles by Dadaists. Kassák's collages and those of Moholy-Nagy (e.g. *F dans les champs*, 1920; Bremen, Ksthandel Wolfgang Werner) reflected this sympathy, and Kassák arranged for the translation into Hungarian of such texts as Tzara's *Coeur à gaz* (1922). There were more distant echoes of Dada. In Moscow the Nichegoki ('nothingist') group formed in 1919–21 around the writers Sergey Sadikov and Suzanna Mar, Yelena Nikolayeva and the artist Boris Zemenkov; and in Tiflis (now Tbilisi, Georgia) Il'ya Zdanevich and Simon Chikovani formed the 41° and H2SO4 groups in the early 1920s. Although claiming some allegiance to Dada, they derived essentially from Russian Futurism.

6. COLOGNE DADA, 1919–22. Cologne Dada secured an autonomous and pivotal position between activities in Zurich, Berlin and Paris. MAX ERNST and JOHANNES THEODOR BAARGELD responded to the artificial calm maintained by the British occupying forces in a series of anti-authoritarian publications, beginning with *Der Ventilator* (1918), which attracted more politically motivated artists, including Franz Seiwert (1894–1933), Anton Räderscheidt, Marta Hegemann (1894–1970), Heinrich

Hoerle (1895–1935) and Angelika Hoerle (1884–1923). Rejecting Rhineland Expressionism, they were influenced by Klee's graphic style and de Chirico's sense of alienation. Ernst, Baargeld and Otto Freundlich were invited to participate in the Gesellschaft der Künst at the Kunstverein in November 1919, but the insubstantial collages and prints in their exhibition, accompanied by *Bulletin D*, provoked controversy. Arp arrived shortly after the exhibition, and with Ernst and Baargeld formed the Dada Weststupidia 3 or W/3 (named after their address), making *Fatagaga* (from 'Fabrication de tableaux garantis gazométriques'), collaborative collages whose images and titles mocked rational expectations (e.g. Ernst and Arp's photomontage *Switzerland, Birth-place of Dada or Physiomythological Flood-Picture*, 1920; Hannover, Sprengel Mus.). The Hoerles and Seiwert withdrew at the last moment, claiming that Dada was 'bourgeois art marketing', and moved towards forming the STUPID GROUP.

In April 1920 their periodical *Die Schammade* featured Arp, Huelsenbeck, Breton and Louis Aragon from Paris and was followed by the audacious exhibition *Dada Vorfrühling* (April); expelled from the Arbeitsgemeinschaft Bildender Künstler, Baargeld and Ernst rented space in the Winter brewery, access to which passed through its lavatories! An astonishing collection of exhibits, including a sculpture by Ernst that the public were invited to destroy (axe provided), brought uproar and police closure, as well as invitations to exhibit at the Berlin Dada Fair. However, Arp's departure for Berlin and Paris and the proletarian orientation of the Stupid group drained Cologne Dada of further group activity. Ernst continued to experiment with photomontages and with painting over engravings (e.g. *Perturbation, My Sister*, 1921; Berne, Kstmus.), the transformatory power of which proved astonishing when exhibited by the Paris Dadaists in May 1921. In the autumn his holiday with Arp and Tzara in the Tyrol produced the joint publication *Dada Intirol, Augrandair*. There he met Breton and subsequently began a close collaboration with Paul Eluard, supplying collages for the poet's *Répétitions* and collaborating on *Les Malheurs des immortels* (both Paris, 1922). Before moving to Paris in late 1922, Ernst also began converting his imagery of unexpected juxtapositions into oil paintings (e.g. the *Elephant Celebes, c.* 1921; *see* ERNST, MAX, fig. 2), which would be identified by Breton as one of the first Surrealist paintings.

7. FINAL PHASE: PARIS, 1919–24. Picabia was the initial focus of activity as Dada arrived in Paris by different routes. Its controversial début was marked by his blistering attack in *391* on the first post-war Salon d'Automne (1919) for concealing his mechanomorphic *Child Carburettor* (1919; New York, Guggenheim) and related works by Georges Ribemont-Dessaignes. Among his allies were the composer Erik Satie and Duchamp (who was visiting in late 1919), as well as the latter's sister Suzanne Duchamp and her husband Jean Crotti, who joined him in submitting related works to the Salon des Indépendants in January 1920. At the same time, a group of poets had formed separately around Breton, Aragon and Philippe Soupault's periodical *Littérature* (1919–24), including Eluard, editor of *Proverbe*, Théodore Fraenkel, Benjamin Péret, Jacques

Rigaut, Céline Arnauld and Paul Dermée, editor of *Z*. They drew upon the French tradition, from Rimbaud to Alfred Jarry, of a poetic revolt against all norms of contemporary art and life. This was combined with their experience of the war to form a disdainful independence, embodied by Jacques Vaché, whose ultimate gesture was to commit suicide (January 1919). They were aware of *Dada* through Tzara's contacts with Apollinaire and Pierre Albert-Birot's *SIC* and, in 1919, exchanged contributions to periodicals with him. However, *Littérature* remained predominantly literary, notable for Breton and Soupault's experiments with automatic writing, *Les Champs magnétiques* (1919).

Tzara was the catalyst for cooperation between Picabia and Breton, as they marked his arrival with the first Parisian soirée, the Premier Vendredi de Littérature (23 January 1920, Palais des Fêtes). The accompanying exhibition of works by de Chirico, Jacques Lipchitz, Léger and Gris reflected the avant-garde's confused acceptance of Dada, until their disruption brought expulsion from the Salon de la Section d'Or. Further Zurich-style soirées were publicized through *Dada 6 (Bulletin Dada)* (February), with its list of the movement's 76 presidents, *Dada 7 (Dadaphone)* (March) and *391*, no. 12, which carried Duchamp's scandalously moustachioed Mona Lisa, *L.H.O.O.Q.* (Paris, priv. col.) on the cover. The season culminated with Picabia's exhibition at Au Sans Pareil (April) and the Festival Dada (Salle Gaveau, 26 May). These events encouraged the participation of Charchoune and Vicente Huidobro, who had encountered Dada in Spain, Il'ya Zdanevich (Iliazd; 1894–1975) and the Belgian Dadaist Clement Pansaers, as well as the fashionable figures around Jean Cocteau, including Raymond Radigaet and the composers Darius Milhaud and Georges Auric.

In 1921 the group published the anti-nationalist manifesto *Dada soulève tout* (January), but their provocations no longer surprised the public. The Grande Saison Dada therefore introduced anti-cultural excursions and mock trials beginning with that of the nationalist writer Maurice Barrès (13 May) at the Salle des Sociétés Savantes. This event exposed divisions between the major participants, as Breton attempted to instil a greater sense of purpose into Dada in the face of Tzara's mockery of such authoritarianism. Ernst's exhibition of collages (Au Sans Pareil, May) provided a focus of unity, with Breton's preface praising the power of his juxtapositions, but Tzara's ambitious Salon Dada Exposition Internationale (Galerie Montaigne, June) was attacked by Picabia in *Pilhaou-Thibaou* (special issue of *391*, July). At the Salon d'Automne, Crotti and Suzanne Duchamp launched Tabu, their mystical offshoot of Dada, while Picabia again caused controversy with the submission of *Cacodylic Eye* (1921; Paris, Pompidou), a canvas simply bearing a profusion of greetings and signatures from friends. This, together with Arp's move towards sculpture and Duchamp's construction of optical machines, confirmed the divergence of all Dadaists from any uniting artistic style, an attitude that would pass into Surrealism to a certain degree. The most notable arrival was Man Ray, whose paintings and provocative objects were exhibited in December 1921 (Librairie Six), and whose photographic experiments led to cameraless rayographs (for illustration *see* MAN RAY), published as *Les Champs délicieux* (Paris, 1922), which were produced by the same chance technique as the schadographs. He took this further, by using the same technique for a film, *Retour à la raison* (1923), which was greeted with public consternation.

By the time of Ernst's arrival in 1922, Dada was disintegrating. Breton had been isolated by his project for a 'Congrès de Paris' to discuss the state of contemporary culture, as Tzara and others refused to participate. However, Picabia rallied to Breton's cause in *La Pomme de pins* (February), just as the new series of *Littérature* moved away from Dada. Although Tzara retaliated, it was evident that self-destruction would result, and his lecture in Weimar in May was called 'Conférence sur la fin de Dada'. In 1923 his *Soirée de la coeur à gaz* (Théâtre Michel, 6–7 July) included music by Satie and readings by Iliazd, René Crevel and Pierre de Massot in costumes designed by Sonia Delaunay; Breton, Aragon, Eluard and Péret stormed the stage, bringing Paris Dada to a destructive end. In launching SURREALISM in 1924 Breton claimed works made under Dada, such as *Les Champs magnétiques* and Ernst's collages; not everything passed into the new movement, however. Tzara published *Sept manifestes Dada* in 1924, while Picabia made the anarchic film *Entr'acte* (November) with Satie and René Clair. Of the major artists, Ernst, Man Ray and Arp were, at least nominally, committed to the new movement, but all continued an exploration independent of Breton's orthodoxy, while others, such as Duchamp, Picabia and Ribemont-Dessaignes, preferred to remain outside this structure. This embodied the determination to undermine established values that had characterized all contributions to Dada, both in Paris and elsewhere, and it was this that would be echoed in other art movements of the mid- to late 20th century, in particular in international Neo-Dada, Pop art and Nouveau Réalisme in the 1950s and 1960s.

WRITINGS

T. Tzara: *La Première Aventure céleste de M. Antipyrine* (Zurich, 1916)

R. Huelsenbeck: *Phantastische Gebete* (Zurich, 1916)

A. Breton and P. Soupault: *Les Champs magnétiques* (Paris, 1919; Eng. trans., London, 1985)

R. Huelsenbeck: *En avant Dada: Eine Geschichte des Dadaismus* (Hannover, 1920)

R. Huelsenbeck, ed.: *Dada Almanach* (Berlin, 1920/R New York, 1966; Fr. trans., Paris, 1980; Eng. trans., London, 1993)

P. Eluard: *Répétitions* (Paris, 1922)

——: *Les Malheurs des immortels* (Paris, 1922)

T. Tzara: *Sept manifestes Dada* (Paris, 1924); rev. as *Sept manifestes Dada, lampisteries* (Paris, 1963; Eng. trans., London, 1977)

H. Ball: *Die Flucht aus der Zeit* (Munich, 1927)

R. Hausmann: *Courier Dada* (Paris, 1958)

G. Ribemont-Dessaignes: *Déjà jadis: Ou du mouvement Dada à l'espace abstrait* (Paris, 1958)

W. Mehring: *Berlin Dada* (Zurich, 1959)

H. Richter: *Dada—Kunst und Antikunst: Der Beitrag Dadas zur Kunst des 20. Jahrhunderts* (Cologne, 1964; Eng. trans., London, 1965/R 1978)

J. Kleinschmidt, ed.: *Memoirs of a Dada Drummer* (New York, 1974/R Berkeley and Oxford, 1974, 2/1991)

See also writings in individual biographies.

BIBLIOGRAPHY

PERIODICALS
Facsimiles of Dada periodicals have been collected in *Doc. & Per. Dada*, ed. A. Schwarz (Milan, 1970) and *Dada, Zurich, Paris, 1916–22*, ed. M. Giroud (Paris, 1981)

Soirées Paris (Paris, 1912–14; facs., Geneva, 1971)

Maintenant (Paris, 1912–15; facs., Paris, 1977)

291 (New York, 1915–16; facs., New York, 1972)

Sirius (Zurich, 1915–16)

Cabaret Voltaire (Zurich, 1916) [facs. in *Dada, Zurich, Paris, 1916–22*]

Troços (Barcelona, 1916–18)

SIC (Paris, 1916–19; facs., Paris, 1980)

Blind Man (New York, 1917)

Rongwrong (New York, 1917)

Nord-Sud (Paris, 1917–18; facs., Paris, 1980)

Dada (Zurich and Paris, 1917–22)

391 (Barcelona, New York, Zurich and Paris, 1917–24; facs., Paris, 1960)

Arc-Voltaic (Barcelona, 1918)

Club Dada (Berlin, 1918)

Der Ventilator (Cologne, 1918)

Jedermann sein eigener Fussball (Berlin, 1919)

Der Dada (Berlin, 1919–20)

Littérature (Paris, 1919–24; facs., Paris, 1978)

Die Schammade (Cologne, 1920)

Contimporanul (Bucharest, 1920–30)

Proverbe (Paris, 1920–21)

New York Dada (New York, 1921)

Zenit (Zagreb, 1921–6)

Dada-Jok (Zagreb, 1922)

Mécano (Amsterdam, 1922–3)

Merz (Hannover, 1923–32)

GENERAL
R. Motherwell, ed.: *The Dada Painters and Poets: An Anthology* (Cambridge and New York, 1951/R 1981)

G. Hugnet: *L'Aventure Dada* (Paris, 1957)

W. Verkauf, ed.: *Dada: Monograph einer Bewegung* (Zurich, 1957, rev. St Gall, 2/1965; Eng. trans., London and New York, 1975)

W. Rubin: *Dada and Surrealist Art* (New York and London, 1969)

M. Sanouillet: *Dada* (Milan, 1969; Ger. trans., Munich, 1973)

L. Lippard, ed.: *Dadas on Art* (Englewood Cliffs, 1971)

D. Ades: *Dada and Surrealism* (London, 1974)

G. Hugnet: *Dictionnaire du Dadaïsme* (Paris, 1976)

A. Schwarz, ed.: *Almanacco Dada* (Milan, 1976)

L. Kundera: *Dada* (Prague, 1983)

S. Lemoine: *Dada* (Paris and London, 1987)

K. Passuth: *Les Avant-gardes de l'Europe centrale, 1907–27* (Paris, 1988)

EXHIBITION CATALOGUES
Fantastic Art, Dada, Surrealism (exh. cat. by A. Barr, New York, MOMA, 1936)

Dada, Surrealism and their Heritage (exh. cat. by W. Rubin, New York, MOMA; Los Angeles, CA, Co. Mus. A.; Chicago, IL, A. Inst.; 1968)

Vom Dadamax bis zum Grüngürtel: Köln in den zwanziger Jahren (exh. cat., ed. W. Herzogenrath; Cologne, Kstver., 1975)

Dada and Surrealism Reviewed (exh. cat. by D. Ades, London, ACGB, 1978)

Dada Photomontagen: Photographie und Photocollage (exh. cat., ed. C.-A. Haelein; Hannover, Kestner-Ges., 1979)

Dada—Constructivism: The Janus Face of the Twenties (exh. cat. by A. B. Nakov and others, London, Annely Juda F.A., 1984)

In the Mind's Eye: Dada and Surrealism (exh. cat., ed. T. A. Neff; Chicago, IL, Mus. Contemp. A., 1985)

André Breton: La Beauté convulsive (exh. cat., ed. A. Angliviel de la Beaumelle and I. Monod-Fontaine; Paris, Pompidou, 1991)

SPECIALIST STUDIES
M. Sanouillet: *Dada à Paris* (Paris, 1965)

M. Prosenc: *Die Dadaisten in Zürich* (Bonn, 1967)

E. Peterson: *Tristan Tzara: Dada and Surrealist Theorist* (New Brunswick, 1971)

Y. Poupard-Lieussor and M. Sanouillet, eds: *Documents Dada* (Geneva, 1974)

D. Tashjian: *Skyscraper Primitives: Dada and the American Avant-garde, 1910–1925* (Middletown, 1975)

S. C. Foster and R. Kuenzli, eds: *Dada Spectrum: The Dialectics of Revolt* (Iowa City, 1979)

K. Ritia, ed.: *Dada Berlin: Texte, Manifeste, Aktionen* (Stuttgart, 1979)

R. Sheppard, ed.: *Dada: Studies of a Movement* (Chalfont St Giles, 1979)

A. Melzer: *The Latest Rage, the Big Drum: Dada and Surrealist Performance* (Ann Arbor, 1980)

H. A. Watts: *Chance: A Perspective on Dada* (Ann Arbor, 1980)

R. Sheppard, ed.: *New Studies in Dada: Essays and Documents* (Driffield, 1981)

——: *Zurich: Dadaco, Dadaglobe* (Tayport, 1982)

J.-C. Gateau: *Paul Eluard et la peinture surréaliste, 1910–1939* (Geneva, 1982)

I. B. Leavens: *From 291 to Zurich: The Birth of Dada* (Ann Arbor, 1983)

H. Bolliger, G. Magnaguagno and R. Meyer: *Dada in Zürich* (Zurich, 1985)

S. C. Foster, ed.: *Dada/Dimensions* (Ann Arbor, 1985)

R. Kuenzli, ed.: *New York Dada* (New York, 1986)

G. Smid, ed.: *Dames in Dada* (Amsterdam, 1989)

F. Naumann: *New York Dada, 1915–23* (New York, 1994)

DAWN ADES, MATTHEW GALE

Dadashev, Sadykh. *See under* USEYNOV & DADASHEV.

Dadd, Richard (*b* Chatham, Kent, 1 Aug 1817; *d* Broadmoor Hospital, Berks, 8 Jan 1886). English painter. He was the fourth of nine children of Robert Dadd, an apothecary and chemist in Chatham. His mother was Mary Ann Martin. Two of his brothers and one sister were, like Dadd himself, to die insane.

Dadd began drawing when he was about 13, and it seems likely that he learnt the technique of miniature painting during his formative years. The small watercolour *Portrait of a Girl* (1832; London, BM) is a good example of his early skill in both portraiture and landscape painting, which was one of his first interests. During his childhood in Chatham, on the River Medway, he also acquired a lifelong love of shipping subjects.

In 1837 Dadd entered the Royal Academy Schools, London, where he was a contemporary and close friend of William Powell Frith, Augustus Leopold Egg and his future brother-in-law John Phillip. The painter who most clearly influenced his work from this time on was Daniel Maclise, particularly in the attention to surface detail and in some of his compositional devices, such as a framed recess like a proscenium arch to contain the main action of a painting. Dadd was regarded as one of the most promising young artists of his generation and was universally liked for his gentleness, intelligence and cheerful good nature. He began exhibiting historical and literary subjects in 1839, but his first real success came in 1841 with *Titania Sleeping* (priv. col., see 1974 exh. cat., no. 57) and its companion *Puck* (priv. col., see 1974 exh. cat., no. 58), followed in 1842 by *Come unto these Yellow Sands* (priv. col., see 1974 exh. cat., no. 68). They are small, luminous works, dramatically lit and theatrical in concept, in which the scaled-down human figures dance nude in landscapes of plants and flowers, or sea and rocks, seemingly an integral part of the natural world.

Richard Dadd: *Contradiction: Oberon and Titania*, oil on canvas, 610×750 mm, 1854–8 (Minneapolis, MN, Regis Collection: on loan to Minneapolis Institute of Arts)

In 1841 Dadd was commissioned to paint a series of panels, said to number over a hundred, for the London house of Thomas Henry Foley, 4th Baron Foley (1808–69), choosing his own subjects from Byron's *Manfred* and Tasso's *Jerusalem Delivered*. (Though now untraced, some may be still extant.) In July 1842 he left England with Sir Thomas Phillips (1801–67), a solicitor and former mayor of Newport, South Wales, accompanying him through Europe and the Middle East to make drawings. A sketchbook (London, V&A) surviving from this journey shows the quality of his draughtsmanship. Its pages are crammed with tiny, vivid and meticulously drawn images of heads, figures, boats, landscapes and architecture. Dadd returned from this journey in May 1843 showing unmistakable signs of insanity. He had become suspicious and unpredictable, occasionally bizarre and violent in his behaviour, believing that he was persecuted by devils and that he was under the power of the Egyptian god Osiris. This state of mind was to last the rest of his life. On 28 August he stabbed his father to death in Cobham Park, near Chatham, thinking him to be the devil in disguise, and escaped to France where he was caught after attempting another murder. After ten months in a French asylum he was extradited to England. In August 1844 he was certified insane and admitted to the state criminal lunatic asylum, which was then part of Bethlem Hospital, London. In 1864 he was transferred to the newly built criminal lunatic asylum at Broadmoor (nr Crowthorne, Berks), where he died of consumption.

He continued to paint throughout nearly 42 years of confinement. He appears to have had at least one of his own sketchbooks with him but otherwise relied chiefly on his imagination and a strong visual memory. In the 1850s he produced many figure compositions in watercolour, including the series of *Sketches to Illustrate the Passions* (e.g. London, V&A; BM), which combine crisp, clear drawing with finely controlled washes of low-key colour and bold strokes of shadow. His most remarkable watercolours are the small landscapes, shipping scenes and occasional fancy subjects, some smaller than a postcard, which were painted with the tip of a very fine brush using a technique that he refined and perfected over many years. Though clearly developed from the miniaturist's use of tiny hatching strokes, in Dadd's hands these become mere pinpricks of colour, building up to a tonality so delicate that the most minutely recorded details seem to be breathed lightly on to fine gauze. *General View of Part of Port Stragglin* (1861; London, BM), showing a harbour overlooked by the precipitous 'Rock and Castle of Seclusion', has all the tranquil dream-like quality of these works at their best.

Dadd is now best known for his two fairy paintings from Bethlem, the *Fairy Feller's Master-stroke* (1855–64; London, Tate) and *Contradiction: Oberon and Titania* (1854–8; Regis Col., on loan to Minneapolis, MN, Inst. A.; see fig.). They are shallow compositions, containing a proliferation of detail painted with almost microscopic exactness and intricately woven into a surface pattern resembling tapestry. In *Oberon and Titania* literally countless tiny creatures, some human, some grotesque, can be found among the flowers, leaves and other natural and unnatural objects that form a background to the main

figures. However, these pictures are unique in Dadd's output; most of his oils covered much the same ground as the watercolours, together with several portraits. The portraits of *A Young Man* (1853; priv. col., on loan to London, Tate) and *Sir Alexander Morison* (1852; Edinburgh, N.P.G.) show the subjects three-quarter-length, full-face and isolated against a landscape background. They are characterized by the trance-like stillness that is evident in most of his later paintings.

Although Dadd was virtually cut off from the art world after 1844, his work was never totally lost to his contemporaries. Six of his pictures were exhibited at the Manchester Art Treasures Exhibition of 1857, including the *Halt in the Desert* (*c.* 1845; London, BM), a spectacular example of his early watercolour style. Subsequently he always had a handful of admirers, although his qualities as an artist were not rediscovered until the 1960s, and he is still generally known through isolated pictures. The recognized fact of Dadd's insanity tends to distort public perception of his work, but it does have a strange, remote quality, which mirrors his own forced withdrawal into the private world of memory and imagination; it also contains a number of inconsequential elements, visual ambiguities and curious juxtapositions of objects, which must have seemed positive symptoms of insanity to his contemporaries, but which pass almost unnoticed in the post-Surrealist era.

UNPUBLISHED SOURCES
London, V&A [sketchbook]

BIBLIOGRAPHY
The Late Richard Dadd (exh. cat. by P. H. Allderidge, London, Tate, 1974)

PATRICIA H. ALLDERIDGE

Dadda, Francesco del. *See* FERRUCCI, (3).

Daddi [di Daddo], **Bernardo** (*fl c.* 1320–48). Italian painter. He was one of the most important Florentine painters of the first half of the 14th century. According to most critical studies Daddi was a pupil of Giotto and was certainly closely associated with Giotto's workshop, but he was also open to other influences, including the so-called miniaturist tendency, represented in Florence by the St Cecilia Master and the Master of the St George Codex, which contributed to his sweet, lyrical style. He excelled in small-scale work and made an important contribution to the development of the portable altarpiece, which subsequently became a very popular format.

1. LIFE AND WORK.

(i) Early work, before c. *1330.* According to the documents of his matriculation in the Arte dei Medici e Speziali, Daddi's career as a painter may have begun early in the 1320s. His first known work is a panel with *St Benedict* (ex-Brunelli priv. col., Milan), which is solemn in its form, rigid and sparing in line, with strong chiaroscuro modelling. These qualities characterize a stylistically homogeneous group of works, including a polyptych of the *Virgin and Child with Four Saints* (Parma, G.N.; Parma, priv. col.), a polyptych in the parish church at Lucarelli (nr Radda in Chianti), two panels from a dispersed polyptych, with the *Virgin and Child* (Rome, Pin. Vaticana) and *St Mary Magdalene* (New York, priv. col.), and the frescoes of the *Martyrdoms of SS Lawrence and Stephen* in the Pulci Beraldi

1. Bernardo Daddi: *Virgin and Child Enthroned with Saints* (central panel), the *Nativity*, *Annunciation to the Shepherds* (left wing), the *Crucifixion* (right wing) and the *Annunciation* (top left and right wings), tempera and gold leaf on panel, 875×425 mm (central panel), 1338 (London, University of London, Courtauld Institute Galleries)

Chapel in Santa Croce, Florence (Daddi's only known painting in that medium, attributed to him by Vasari). These works show a strong debt to Giotto in their firm, three-dimensional construction and in the clear modelling, achieved through a pronounced use of chiaroscuro. They also show strong connections with the work of such painters as Buffalmacco and the Master of S Martino alla Palma (*fl* 1315–40).

Daddi's art reached an expressive peak at the end of the 1320s with the signed triptych of the *Virgin and Child with SS Nicholas and Matthew* (1328; Florence, Uffizi). This painting recalls the most classical of Giotto's paintings (e.g. the frescoes in the Peruzzi Chapel, Santa Croce, Florence), and it shows that Daddi was familiar with Giotto's work but that he did not follow the style slavishly, choosing the most suitable ideas suggested by the many aspects of Giotto's painting and that of such artists in his circle as Taddeo Gaddi. Daddi's work was strongly influenced by Gaddi's severe and rigorous style, softened by Gothic effects in line and colour, especially at the time of the latter's most important work, the frescoes (begun *c.* 1328) in the Baroncelli Chapel in Santa Croce, Florence. This is evident in the *Virgin* in S Pietro, Lecore, and in such large single-panel altarpieces as that of *St Michael* in S Michele, Crespina, or in another badly damaged one in Finland (Joensuu, Mun. Mus.).

(ii) Mature work, after c. *1330.* The importance of Daddi's workshop began to emerge in the 1330s; in response to demand it specialized in panel painting, mostly on a small scale. Some monumental works were also produced, however, for example *St Paul* (1333; Washington, DC, N.G.A.) and a polyptych fragment with *SS John and Paul* (New York, priv. col.). In the latter work the figures, depicted in profile, show the wide variety of compositional and spatial solutions used by Daddi to extend the limits imposed by the wooden structure of the polyptych. He is also known to have been involved in such important public projects as the polyptych (untraced) commissioned in 1335 for the S Bernardo Chapel in the Palazzo Vecchio, Florence.

Daddi and his workshop produced innumerable small altarpieces for private devotion, most commonly with representations of the *Virgin and Child Enthroned*, the *Nativity* and the *Crucifixion*, sometimes personalized with a few thematic variations. Daddi's most individual qualities are to be found in some of these works, which include two panels from triptychs (Naples, Capodimonte, and Florence, Uffizi, 8564, respectively); a triptych (13(?33); Florence, Mus. Bigallo); a series of similar altarpieces (e.g. Washington, DC, Dumbarton Oaks; New York, Met., 32.1000.70 and 49.190.12; Prague, N.G., Šternberk Pal., O 11967–9; Altenburg, Staatl. Lindenau-Mus.); and two predellas, one with scenes from the *Life of St Cecilia* (divided between Kraków, N. Mus.; Pisa, Mus. N. S. Matteo; priv. col.), and another (divided between Berlin, Gemäldegal.; New Haven, CT, Yale U.; Paris, Mus. A. Déc.; Poznań, N. Mus.) from a Dominican triptych (untraced) painted for S Maria Novella, Florence, in 1338. Such works as the two triptychs dated 1338 (Edinburgh, N.G., and U. London, Courtauld Inst. Gals; see fig. 1) display the highest level of technical achievement and lyric inspiration. These small-scale commissions clearly provided Daddi with the format best suited to his rich narrative and illustrative skills. His fluent line and varied, brilliant colouring create precious, captivating images of an expressive character, arranged in clear and successful narrative sequences.

Daddi's workshop also owed its success to the sweet, pleasing quality of the figures of the *Virgin and Child* (e.g. Florence, I Tatti), depicted in tender attitudes similar to those in contemporary Sienese painting. Further echoes of the close contacts that existed in the 1330s between Sienese and Florentine painters, especially through Ambrogio and Pietro Lorenzetti, can be discerned in the lyrical accent and the controlled sense of drama in Daddi's *Crucifixions* (e.g. Altenburg, Staatl. Lindenau-Mus.). His rich inventiveness in coining iconographic novelties is displayed especially in predella panels, for example that with scenes from the *Legend of the Sacra Cintola* (Prato, Mus. Com.) and the predella with scenes of the *Life of St Stephen* (Rome, Pin. Vaticana).

Daddi's preference for small-scale work can be seen as part of a trend in Florentine painting, defined by Offner, which included Lippo di Benivieni, the Master of the Codex of S George and Pacino di Bonaguida, artists who according to Offner followed a 'miniaturist tendency' in contrast to Giotto's more monumental style. This trend would certainly have been influenced by the profound stylistic innovations brought to Florence by Pietro Lorenzetti with such works as the altarpiece of the *Beata Umiltà* (Florence, Uffizi), attributed to him by most scholars, or by Andrea Pisano who was then working on the first doors at Florence Baptistery.

Daddi successfully introduced these ideas into Giotto's workshop, as is shown by Taddeo Gaddi's small altarpiece (1334; Berlin, Gemäldegal., 1079–81) and the one by Maso di Banco (New York, Brooklyn Mus.), which are variations or near-replicas of Daddi's Bigallo Triptych, considered the prototype. Daddi's role in Giotto's workshop was clearly not a subordinate one. This would seem to be further confirmed by Daddi's position in relation to such a leading artist as Maso di Banco, whom Longhi regarded as the originator of many formal innovations. In fact, if the careers of Daddi and Gaddi ran in parallel, it is possible that Maso was trained in Daddi's workshop (Volpe). The altarpiece of 1336 in S Giorgio a Rubballa, near Florence, has always been attributed to Daddi's workshop and in the late 20th century to the young Orcagna (see Bellosi); if it was the work of Maso, as seems probable (Volpe, Boskovits), this would suggest that Maso learnt his trade from Daddi rather than in a more narrowly Giottesque environment.

In 1339 Daddi enrolled in the Accademia di S Luca. The works of his last period are characterized by an overall monumentality of plan, for example the complex polyptych with several registers (partly Florence, Uffizi) made for Florence Cathedral and later in S Pancrazio. Two predellas were assigned by Vasari to this work: the *Life of the Virgin* (Florence, Uffizi, see fig. 2; London, Buckingham Pal., Royal Col.) and the *Life of St Reparata* (Brussels, Mme Paul Pèchere priv. col.; Cologne, priv. col.; New York, Met.). Other late works show his concise rendering of volumes, with strongly emphasized pastiglia decoration in the haloes (e.g. *Virgin and Child*, 1346–7; Florence, Orsanmichele). These late works also include the dismembered polyptych (Florence, Uffizi, 8706–7; ex-Drury-Lowe Col., Locko Park; Milan, priv. col.; ex-Lanckoroński priv. col., Vienna) of the early 1340s from S Maria del Carmine, Florence, and Daddi's last known work, a polyptych showing the *Crucifixion with Saints* (1348; U. London, Courtauld Inst. Gals), from S Giorgio a Rubballa. The design of the latter, with pairs of saints flanking a central scene, heralds the departure from the standard, rigidly compartmentalized polyptych type, anticipating the work of Orcagna.

2. CRITICAL RECEPTION AND POSTHUMOUS REPUTATION. Bernardo Daddi is not given much attention in the early sources; he is mentioned only by Vasari, in connection with the Pulci Berardi frescoes in Santa Croce. Only through studies by Passerini and Milanesi has it been possible to associate the signature 'Bernardus de Florentia' with the Bernardo di Daddo documented in the guild records (Vitzthum). The serial character of Daddi's work has negatively influenced the critical evaluation of the vast production attributable to him and his circle. Longhi, for example, called him a 'clockwork nightingale' of painting, 'mediocre' even if 'much loved'. Offner, by contrast, restricted the catalogue of his works to the autograph paintings and those of the highest quality, praising their

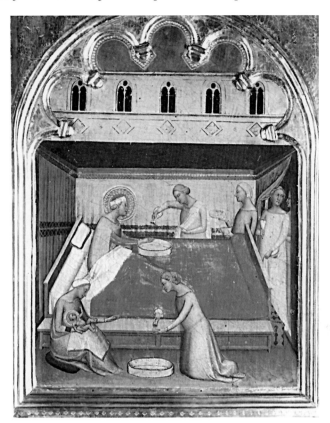

2. Bernardo Daddi: *Birth of the Virgin*, tempera on panel, 500×380 mm, *c.* 1340 (Florence, Galleria degli Uffizi); detail from the *Life of the Virgin* predella

style and the richness of their lyrical inspiration. He presented Daddi as an individual and highly refined painter, the greatest after Giotto in 14th-century Florence. In line with the reasoning of Boskovits (1984), however, it seems wiser to accept the more inclusive catalogue of the paintings of Daddi and his workshop, despite a certain repetitiveness and some instances of less-skilled execution.

Two artists have been identified as Daddi's collaborators: the 'Assistant of Daddi' (Offner), a painter with a limited sense of form but with considerable illustrative skills, to whom Offner assigned such works as a *Crucifix* (Florence, Accad., 442) and a *St Catherine* (Florence, Accad., 3457), and the Master of S Polo in Chianti (Tartuferi), a painter of very modest abilities who was also a poor imitator of Taddeo Gaddi's style. Daddi's influence on other contemporary painters was significant. One of the figures closest to him in style has been called the 'Maestro daddesco'. This artist, an illuminator of notable skill, spent his early career (*c.* 1315) working on choirbooks (Rome, Santa Croce in Gerusalemme) for the Badia a Settimo (nr Florence), together with the Master of the Codex of S George. Thus, rather than being a follower, he was first a precursor of Daddi, while later the two artists' works show a mutual influence. Another, the refined, archaizing Master of S Martino alla Palma, became a follower of Daddi only towards the end of his career.

In the middle of the 14th century, even after Daddi's death, the influence of his style had a strong resonance in

Florence. His last formal innovations in volumetric and chromatic synthesis influenced the brothers Orcagna and Nardo di Cione and were successfully adopted by such painters as Puccio di Simone and Allegretto Nuzi. During their period of collaboration these two artists adapted Daddi's late style to solutions that were even more decorative, denying any corporeal aspect. This is evident in their joint works produced in the Marches, for example *St Anthony Abbot* (Fabriano, Pin Civ. Mus. Arazzi) and a triptych of the *Virgin and Child with Saints and Angels* (1354; Washington, DC, N.G.A.), also made for a church in Fabriano.

BIBLIOGRAPHY

Colnaghi; *DBI*; Thieme–Becker

G. Vasari: *Vite* (1550, rev. 2/1568); ed. G. Milanesi (1878–85)

F. Baldinucci: *Notizie* (1681–1728); ed. F. Ranalli (1845–7)

J. A. Crowe and G. B. Cavalcaselle: *A New History of Painting in Italy from the Second to the Sixteenth Century*, 2 vols (London, 1864–6, rev. 1904–14)

L. Passerini and G. Milanesi: *Del ritratto di Dante Alighieri* (Florence, 1865), p. 16

G. Milanesi: 'Della tavola di Nostra Donna nel tabernacolo d'Or San Michele e del suo vero autore', *Nuova Antol.* (Sept 1870), pp. 116–31

C. Frey, ed.: *Il libro di Antonio Billi* (Berlin, 1872)

——: *Die Loggia dei Lanzi zu Florenz* (Berlin, 1885), p. 315

G. Milanesi: *Nuovi documenti per lo studio della storia dell'arte* (Florence, 1893)

G. G. Vitzthum: *Bernardo Daddi* (Leipzig, 1903)

W. Suida: 'Studien zur Trecentomalerei', *Repert. Kstwiss.*, xxvii (1904), pp. 385–9

A. Venturi: *Storia* (1907), v, pp. 508–23

O. Siren: *Giotto and some of his Followers*, i (Cambridge, 1917), pp. 185–7, 271–2

R. van Marle: *Italian Schools* (1924), iii, pp. 348–91

E. Sandberg-Vavalà: 'Opere inedite di Bernardo Daddi', *Cron. A.*, vi (1927), pp. 1–11

R. Offner and K. Steinweg: *Corpus* (1930–79); rev. M. Boskovits (1989–)

Pittura italiana del duecento e del trecento (exh. cat. by G. Sinibaldi and G. Brunetti, Florence, Uffizi, 1937)

R. Longhi: 'Qualità e industria in Taddeo Gaddi', *Paragone*, x (1959), no. 109, pp. 31–40; no. 111, pp. 3–12

L. Marcucci: *Gallerie nazionali di Firenze: I dipinti toscani del secolo XIV* (Rome, 1965), pp. 27–49

G. Previtali: *Giotto e la sua bottega* (Milan, 1967)

I. Hueck: 'Le matricole dei pittori fiorentini prima e dopo il 1320', *Boll. A.*, n. s. 2, lvii (1972), pp. 114–21

L. Bellosi: 'Una precisazione sulla *Madonna* di Orsanmichele', *Scritti in onore di Ugo Procacci*, i (Milan, 1977), pp. 146–51

C. Gardner von Teuffel: 'The Buttressed Altarpiece: A Forgotten Aspect of Tuscan Fourteenth Century Altarpiece Design', *Jb. Berlin. Mus.*, xxi (1979), pp. 21–65

C. Volpe: 'Il lungo percorso del "dipingere dolcissimo e tanto unito"', *Storia dell'arte italiana*, ed. F. Zeri, v (Turin, 1983), pp. 229–304

M. Boskovits: *Corpus* (1984)

R. Offner: *The Works of Bernardo Daddi* (Florence, 1989)

A. Tartuferi: 'Ipotesi su un pittore fiorentino del trecento: Il maestro di San Polo in Chianti', *Paragone*, xl (1989), no. 467, pp. 21–7

R. Offner: *Bernardo Daddi: His Shop and Following* (Florence, 1991)

A. Padoa Rizzo: 'Bernardo di Stefano Rosselli, il "Polittico Rucellai" e il "Polittico di San Pancresio" di Bernardo Daddi', *Stud. Stor. A.*, iv (1993), pp. 211–22

L. Bellosi: 'Problemi di pitture fiorentine intorno alla metà del trecento' *Atti del covegno in memorie di F. Arcangeli e C. Volpe: Bologna, 1995*

ENRICA NERI LUSANNA

Dadler, Sebastian (*b* Strasbourg, 6 March 1586; *d* Hamburg, 6 July 1657). German goldsmith and medallist. He trained as a goldsmith in France, then settled in Augsburg in 1610 and subsequently in Vienna in 1612, receiving the title of Imperial Court Goldsmith. In 1619 he was back in Augsburg; *c.* 1621 he entered the service of John-George I, Elector of Saxony, producing several very fine silver repoussé reliefs to his commission. However, Dadler demonstrated his greatest skill in the medals that he first produced after 1623, while in the Elector's service in Dresden, for example *John-George I and Magdalen Sibylla* (1630). Around 1632 he returned to Augsburg and then Hamburg, settling in Danzig (now Gdańsk) in 1634. From 1648 he was in Hamburg again, remaining there until his death. Dadler's medals, often in large format, are characterized by powerful relief, with a strong plastic effect of a kind seldom found in the work of any other German medallist of the 17th century. As well as portrait medals, among which are several of Gustav II Adolf of Sweden, such as *Riga Taken by Gustav Adolf* (1621) and the *Death of Gustav Adolf* (1632), his oeuvre comprises medals for historical events, such as the Peace of Westphalia (1650–51), and medals with religious and allegorical motifs.

BIBLIOGRAPHY

Forrer; *NDB*; Thieme–Becker

A. Więcek: 'Deux médailleurs strasbourgeois du XVIIème siècle en Pologne', *Cah. Alsac. Archéol. A. & Hist.*, iv (1960), pp. 105–28

——: *Sebastian Dadler: Medalier gdański XVII wieku* (Gdańsk, 1962)

HERMANN MAUÉ

Dado [Djuric, Miodrag] (*b* Cetinje, Montenegro, 4 Oct 1933). Montenegrin painter and printmaker, active in France. He studied at the School of Fine Arts in Herceg Novi and at the Academy of Fine Arts in Belgrade. As early as 1951 he depicted figures that departed stylistically from Social Realism and that had no links with conventional appearances. In 1956 he moved to Paris and obtained work in a lithographic studio. He was encouraged as an artist by Jean Dubuffet, Bernard Réquichot, Horst Kalinowski and the dealer Daniel Cordier, whose gallery was the venue for his first one-man show (1958). From the late 1950s he lived in the countryside outside Paris, settling in 1960 at Hérouval'Oise.

Dado's nightmarish, obsessive imagery is related to Surrealism and to the tradition of Bosch-like fantastic painting, but it is deeply rooted in a tragic, ironic vision of life influenced by his experience of growing up in Montenegro during World War II, at a time of appalling atrocities and famine. His nightmarish pictures, such as *Massacre of the Innocents* (1958–9; Paris, Pompidou; *see* MONTENEGRO, fig. 3), are populated by a variety of ferocious and grotesque monsters, weird subhuman creatures whose forms are often in a state of dismemberment and decay; yet the colours, such as lavender blue and rose, are frequently of soft delicacy and refinement. In addition to his oils, which are often of considerable size, for example *Hérouval Diptych* (oil on canvas, two panels of 2.63×1.97 m each, 1975–6; Paris, Pompidou), his work includes 12 big collage-assemblages made between 1974 and 1976 and a number of engravings beginning in 1967.

BIBLIOGRAPHY

Dado (exh. cat., Paris, Cent. N. A. Contemp., 1970)

Dado: Un Signe des temps (exh. cat., Montauban, Mus. Ingres, 1984)

RONALD ALLEY

Dadswell, Lyndon (Raymond) (*b* Stanmore, NSW, 18 Jan 1908; *d* Sydney, 7 Nov 1986). Australian sculptor and teacher. He studied at the Julian Ashton Art School (but was asked to leave), and at East Sydney Technical College. Dadswell claimed that his real training took place during his period (1929–35) as assistant to Paul Montford (1868–1938), then chief sculptor for the Shrine of Remembrance (Melbourne, south of the River Yarra). Here Dadswell undertook his first commission: 12 large relief panels depicting the activities of the Australian Imperial Forces during World War I. On the strength of this work he won a scholarship to attend the Royal Academy Schools, London (1935–6), returning to Australia in 1937 to take up an appointment as teacher of sculpture at the National Art School, Sydney.

Dadswell was wounded during war service in the Middle East (1941–2), his eyesight permanently impaired. Nevertheless, he resumed teaching in 1945, and, apart from one year spent travelling in the USA and Europe, he continued to teach in Sydney until his retirement in 1967. Modernist developments in sculpture were slow to find any echo in Australia, but when they did it was due in great part to Dadswell. His beaten aluminium sculptures for the exterior of the Commonwealth Bank (erected 1954), George Street, Sydney, were among the earliest modern sculptures in Australia. His greatest contribution to Australian art was, however, made through his teaching. He felt it his duty to make his students aware that there were many valid approaches to the making of sculpture, none of them inherently superior. Unfortunately this impartiality, while valid for him as a teacher, proved fatal to his own creative work, leaving him unable to commit himself firmly to any one course.

BIBLIOGRAPHY

J. Hetherington: 'Australian Artists in Profile', *Age* (28 April 1962), p. 18
A. McCulloch: *Encyclopedia of Australian Art*, i (Melbourne, 1968), pp. 260–61
G. Sturgeon: *The Development of Australian Sculpture, 1788–1975* (London, 1978), pp. 122–3
P. Laverty and others: 'Lyndon Dadswell', *A. Australia*, xvi (1979), pp. 239–44
K. Scarlett: *Australian Sculptors* (Melbourne, 1980), pp. 141–52

GRAEME STURGEON

Dadu. *See under* BEIJING.

Daedalus. *See* DAIDALOS, §1.

Dael, Jan van. *See* DALEM, JAN VAN.

Dael, Jean-François [Jan Frans] **van** (*b* Antwerp, 27 May 1764; *d* Paris, 20 March 1840). Flemish painter and lithographer. He first studied architecture at the Antwerp Academie from 1776, despite his early preference for painting, and in 1786 he settled in Paris as a decorator. In 1793 he acquired lodgings in the Louvre next to fellow countrymen Pierre-Joseph Redouté, Piat-Joseph Sauvage (1744–1818) and Gerard van Spaendonck; under the influence of Spaendonck he turned to flower painting, in which he specialized for the rest of his life. He was prolific in his output and successful in securing commissions from such wealthy and influential patrons as the Empresses Josephine and Marie-Louise Bonaparte (1791–1847), and both Louis XVIII and Charles X. From 1793 until 1833 he exhibited regularly at the Paris Salon and, after 1807, occasionally in the Low Countries. Van Dael remained faithful to the Flemish tradition of flower painting exemplified by Roelandt Savery, with sober composition and attention to detail (e.g. *Roses and Butterflies*, 1802; Lille,

Mus. B.-A.). But he also brought to many of his flower arrangements a French-inspired decorative monumentality. In some of his ornamental fruit and flower arrangements a landscape background is sketched in, and a few pure landscapes have survived, including *The Painter's House* (1822; Rotterdam, Boymans–van Beuningen). He painted a small number of religious and allegorical pictures; one of his most celebrated, *Julie's Tomb* (1804; Malmaison, Château N.), can be read as a reflection on life and death. He also painted occasional portraits, usually of other artists (e.g. *Robert Lefèvre*, 1804; Antwerp, Kon. Mus. S. Kst.), and made lithographs (e.g. portrait of *Jean-Baptiste Mauzaisse*, 1829).

BIBLIOGRAPHY

B. Lossky: 'Le Peintre fleuriste Jean-François van Dael et ses oeuvres au Château de Fontainebleau', *Bull. Soc. Hist. A. Fr.* (1967), pp. 123–36
De David à Delacroix: La Peinture française de 1774 à 1830 (exh. cat., ed. R. Rosenblum and A. Schnapper; Paris, Grand Pal., 1974–5), pp. 272, 635–9
1770–1830: Autour du néo-classicisme en Belgique (exh. cat. by D. Coekelberghs and others, Brussels, Mus. Ixelles, 1985–6), pp. 278–9

DOMINIQUE VAUTIER

Daffinger, Moritz Michael (*b* Vienna, 25 Jan 1790; *d* 21/22 Aug 1849). Austrian painter. His father, Johann Daffinger (*d* 1796), was a painter at the Kaiserliche Porzellanmanufaktur in Vienna and, at the age of 11, Daffinger was apprenticed there to his stepfather Philipp Krug and to Michael Weixlbaum. Daffinger studied and worked at the factory until 1812, also attending classes at the Akademie in Vienna under Hubert Maurer (1738–1818) and Heinrich Füger. Initially Daffinger worked as a painter of miniatures, for example in portraits of French officers during the occupation of Vienna in 1809. At the time of the Vienna Congress, 1814–15, he worked as a portrait painter along with celebrated artists such as Füger and Jean-Baptiste Isabey. Sir Thomas Lawrence's stay in Vienna in 1818–19 brought a new stimulus to Daffinger's work, as it did for other artists: his colours became warmer in tone and they were applied in broader strokes and more decoratively.

Daffinger swiftly became one of the most sought-after portrait painters in Vienna, reaching the peak of his fame in the 1820s and 1830s. He was a friend of many scientists, artists, writers and figures from theatrical life. He painted portraits of several of these, for example the poet *Franz Grillparzer* (miniature, 1820; Vienna, Hist. Mus.) and the dancer *Fanny Elssler* (miniature; Frankfurt am Main, Mus. Ksthandwk). In 1827 he married one of the beauties of Vienna, Marie von Smolenitz, and his paintings of her have been seen to epitomize the Biedermeier female portrait (e.g. *Marie Daffinger Seated*, 1830; Vienna, Belvedere). As the principal court painter he produced a large number of portraits of members of the royal family, including 12 of the grandson of Emperor Francis I, the Herzog von Reichstadt (e.g. *The Herzog von Reichstadt in an Armchair*, 1831; Vienna, Belvedere). From 1812 Daffinger also worked regularly for the family of Prince Metternich. In the 1830s, on a commission from Princess Melanie Metternich, he painted over 200 watercolour portraits of relations, friends and acquaintances of the family (many now Vienna, Albertina).

Daffinger had a fiery temper, but he was also a sensitive, humorous man. His portraits, mostly in miniature, or watercolour on paper, are created with a feeling for beauty and elegance. They emphasize the sitter's charm rather than analysing character. The colour in the early work is pale and reticent, but under the influence of Lawrence it becomes warm and lively, and marked by subtle colour contrasts.

Despite his achievements as a portrait painter, Daffinger abandoned the genre after the death of his daughter in 1841 and devoted himself to the portrayal of native flora. He travelled with his wife through the various districts of Austria, producing over 400 illustrations of individual plants in which he displayed a virtuoso watercolour technique, producing botanically precise and subtly coloured works (Vienna, Akad. Bild. Kst., Kupferstichkab.). Daffinger influenced a number of Viennese miniature painters such as Robert Theer (1808–63) and Emanuel Peter (1799–1873).

BIBLIOGRAPHY

ÖKL; Thieme–Becker
E. Leisching: *Die Bildnisminiatur in Österreich* (Vienna, 1907)
E. Guglia: 'Die Porträtsammlung der Fürstin Melanie Metternich', *Graph. Kst.*, xl (1917), pp. 71–112; *Mitt. Ges. für Vervielfält. Kst.* (1917), pp. 48–55
L. Grünstein: *M. M. Daffinger und sein Kreis* (Vienna and Leipzig, 1923)
E. Pirchan: *M. M. Daffinger: Miniaturenmaler des Vormärz* (Vienna and Leipzig, 1943)
Die Blumenaquarelle des Moritz Michael Daffinger (exh. cat., Vienna, Akad. Bild. Kst., 1986)
G. Kugler: *Staatskanzler Metternich und seine Gäste: Miniaturen von Daffinger, Kriehuber und anderen Meistern aus dem Gästealbum der Fürstin Melanie Metternich* (Graz, 1991)

MARIANNE FRODL-SCHNEEMANN

Dafni. Middle Byzantine monastery in Greece, 10 km west of Athens on the former Sacred Way to Eleusis. It is dedicated to the Theotokos and famous for the late 11th-century mosaics in its church. According to Pausanias (*Guide to Greece* I.xxxvii.6) a Temple of Apollo once stood at the site. The earliest remains date to the 5th or 6th century AD and include an Early Christian basilica, uncovered to the west of the present church; the side and the east and west gates of the monastery's fortified enclosure wall; a bath with hypocaust; the foundations of cells; and some sculptural pieces that are displayed in the monastery.

The first written reference to the monastery is in the Typikon (1048) of a Naupaktos religious fraternity (Confraternity of the Virgin Naupaktitissa), in which the abbot of Dafni heads the list of signatories. The monastery is also known from the seal of Abbot Paul (11th or 12th century; Athens, Numi. Mus.). The monastery was restored in the late 11th century when the present church was built and decorated, as was the refectory, of which only foundations survive. The opulence of this restoration suggests that the patrons were important people. The church has a cross-in-square plan with a central octagonal dome supported on squinches, an inner narthex and four adjoining chapels covered by groin vaults (*see* EARLY CHRISTIAN AND BYZANTINE ART, §II, 2(iii)(b)). It is modelled on the Katholikon (probably late 10th century) at HOSIOS LOUKAS, and although smaller, it is a more imposing and elegant building. In the early 12th century an outer narthex was added in the form of an open portico with an upper floor, which was probably used as the abbot's quarters or library. The walls are built of cloisonné masonry (i.e. dressed stone blocks surrounded by brick); the lower courses are interrupted by stone crosses, while the upper walls have trilobe windows, framed by dogtooth ornament in brick, with pseudo-Kufic patterns similar to those at Hosios Loukas in the lunettes above. Windows on two levels pierce the gabled portals on the north and south walls as well as the tall, three-sided main apse, which is decorated at the top with brickwork meander. The drum of the dome (rest. 1891) has 16 windows. In general, the church's external decoration is more restrained than at Hosios Loukas.

Of the church's interior decoration the marble revetment on the walls and marble floors has disappeared. What survives is some *opus sectile* in the apse, the marble skirting at the foot of the walls, the base of the marble iconostasis, champlevé plasterwork at the height of the springing of the arches and a large part of the wall mosaics (rest. late 19th century). The iconographic programme follows the order of liturgical feasts in which the *Life of the Virgin* is given special emphasis and represents the earliest example of such a cycle. The total number of scenes and portraits of monastic saints far exceeds those in the mosaics at Hosios Loukas (*c.* 1011) or at Nea Moni (1043–55). The programme is skilfully developed in relation to the plan and makes the best possible use of available surfaces. In the centre of the dome is *Christ Pantokrator* (*see* MOSAIC, fig. 7) surrounded by 16 prophets in the drum; in the apse the *Virgin and Child* are flanked by the archangels *Michael* and *Gabriel*, while the squinches and vaults are filled with the *Twelve Feasts* and the *Life of the Virgin* in a rare and learned combination of the dogmatic and the narrative. Hierarchs, deacons and healer saints occupy the lower walls of the sanctuary, with *St John the Baptist* in the *prothesis* and *St Nicholas* in the *diakonikon*; prophets and groups of holy martyrs are depicted on the nave walls. Only six scenes from the *Passion* and the *Life of the Virgin* survive in the narthex. Each composition has a single, unifying ground line and is marked by a certain uniform symmetry in which the central axis is emphasized and the human figures stand out against large expanses of gold ground and correspondingly sparse landscape and architectural backdrops (e.g. the *Annunciation* and *Crucifixion*). The classicizing figures with their modelled draperies are imbued with great charm (e.g. the *Angel* of the *Annunciation*) and restrained intensity (e.g. the *Baptism*, *Crucifixion* and *Dormition of the Virgin*). In contrast to this classicizing style, the prophets in the dome drum appear static, while the colossal *Pantokrator* shows a marked linearity of form that is also evident in *St John the Baptist* in the *prothesis*. This iconographic and compositional inventiveness is combined with delicate colouring to create an important example of early Komnenian art.

After the Frankish capture of Attica (1204), Cistercian monks settled in the monastery (*c.* 1207); they restored the outer narthex of the church, adding a Gothic arch, built a crypt for the tombs of the Frankish princes and added a cloister to the south side of the church. In 1458 Attica was occupied by the Ottoman Turks, who returned Dafni to the Orthodox church; new cells, a marble gateway and the bell tower were built, and the church was painted.

The monastery was abandoned in the early 19th century. Restoration work was undertaken in 1897, when gaps in the mosaic decoration were filled with missing scenes, and again after World War II.

BIBLIOGRAPHY

G. Millet: *Le Monastère de Dafni* (Paris, 1899)

E. Diez and O. Demus: *Byzantine Mosaics in Greece* (Cambridge, MA, 1931)

D. Mouriki: 'Stylistic Trends in Monumental Painting of Greece during the Eleventh and Twelfth Centuries', *Dumbarton Oaks Pap.*, xxxiv–xxxv (1980–81), pp. 94–8 [with bibliography]

IOANNA BITHA

Dāgaba. *See under* STUPA, §2.

Dagestan. *See under* RUSSIA, §XII, 1.

Dagly, Gerhard (*b* Spa, Belgium, 1657; *d* Bensberg, 1715). Belgian japanner, active in Berlin. He practised as a decorative artist in Spa before moving in the 1680s to Berlin, where he became famous for his painted furniture. By 1687 his proficiency in gilding and decorative painting, particularly japanning, which imitated lacquerwork from East Asia (*see* LACQUER, §I, 2 and 3), gained him the post of Kammerkünstler to Frederick William, Elector of Brandenburg. On the accession in 1688 of Frederick III, Elector of Brandenburg (after 1701, Frederick I of Prussia) he retained responsibility for interior decoration and furnishings at the court and in 1696 was appointed Intendant des Ornements. His brother Jacques Dagly (1665–1729) joined him in the management of the firm, which provided gilded, polychromed and japanned cabinets as well as such other furnishings as treen painted to imitate porcelain for the royal palaces. Their clients included harpsichord manufacturers as well as the nobility, and such was their fame that in Paris their cabinets became known as 'Berlin' cabinets. They embellished snuff-boxes, cane knobs, sword guards and tin wares and invented methods of applying silver varnish in place of gold leaf on books and leather. Dagly's researches also included methods of reviving varnish on oil paintings, which resulted in his court appointment as Kunstkammer Meister and the publication of his *Recueil des mémoires des diverses expériences fait au sujet de la conservation des tableaux* (1706). In addition he promoted methods of embalming and taxidermy, as well as treatments for preserving stone, plaster, metal and timber. He closed his workshops in 1713.

BIBLIOGRAPHY

H. Honour: *Cabinet Makers and Furniture Designers* (London, 1969), pp. 61–3

H. Huth: *Lacquer of the West* (London, 1971), pp. 65–72

J. HARDY

Dagnan-Bouveret, P(ascal-)A(dolphe-)J(ean) (*b* Paris, 7 Jan 1852; *d* Quincey, Haute-Saône, 3 July 1929). French painter. He refused to leave France when his father Bernard Dagnan moved to Brazil in 1868, and he remained with his maternal grandfather in Melun (nr Paris). Later he added the maternal surname Bouveret to his own in gratitude for his grandfather's support, which enabled him to study in Paris.

In 1869 Dagnan-Bouveret entered the Ecole des Beaux-Arts in Paris and studied in the atelier of Alexandre Cabanel. After a few months he joined the atelier of Jean-Léon Gérôme, where he trained as a draughtsman and painter. In 1875 his first works, a painting entitled *Atalante* (purchased by the State; Melun, Mus. Melun) and two drawings, were accepted at the Salon. The next year Dagnan-Bouveret received a second place in the Prix de Rome for *Priam Asking Achilles for the Body of his Son* (untraced) and a first prize for painting the human figure at the Ecole des Beaux-Arts. In 1878 he won a third-class medal at the Salon and left the Ecole des Beaux-Arts, along with his friend the genre painter Gustave Courtois (1853–1923). They went to the Franche-Comté, Courtois's native region, where Dagnan-Bouveret met and eventually married Courtois's cousin Maria Walter. The provincial life of the Franche-Comté provided numerous themes for many of Dagnan-Bouveret's landscape, still-life and genre paintings and sketches. Some of these reflected an interest in atmosphere, while others explored the effects of light and shade in a manner reminiscent of 17th-century Dutch masters. *An Accident* (exh. Salon 1880; Baltimore, MD, Walters A.G.), depicting a village doctor tending the injured hand of a peasant boy, established Dagnan-Bouveret as a naturalistic painter of great exactitude, interested in psychological character and intent on recording the customs of the region.

Like his friend Jules Bastien-Lepage, Dagnan-Bouveret painted mythological scenes and portraits of his friends and family for the Salons. The anecdotal *Wedding Party at the Photographer's Studio* (1879; Lyon, Mus. B.-A.) displayed an almost photographic realism and was an early example of the artist's interest in photography as a theme for painting.

In 1885 Dagnan-Bouveret's large naturalistic canvas *Horses at the Watering Trough* (purchased by the State; Chambéry, Mus. B.-A.; see fig.) was shown at the Salon and established him as a major figure of the Salon naturalistic school. Critics commented on the painstaking exactitude of the composition and the photographic realism of both horses and handler. For the horses, Dagnan-Bouveret had used a series of photographs (taken in the Franche-Comté). Although he never revealed this device to his public, it aided him in effectively capturing natural poses and detail.

In the same year Dagnan-Bouveret made his first visit to Brittany. *Pardon—Brittany* (1887; New York, Met.) is a naturalistic rendering of a peasant religious celebration based on scenes from Breton folklore. Again he combined preliminary sketches with photographs of models to achieve his effects. To translate the composition from one medium to another he traced photographs of his posed models, dressed in traditional Breton costume, for his colour studies.

During the 1890s Dagnan-Bouveret turned from naturalistic genre compositions to concentrate on portraiture and themes of religious mysticism. His fashionable, idealized portraits were popular with wealthy patrons and provided him with a high income, enabling him to work on religious paintings, including a *Supper at Emmaus* (1896–7; Pittsburgh, PA, Carnegie Mus. A.). The later canvases confirmed Dagnan-Bouveret's fame and importance at the Salons of the 1890s. During the rest of his life he developed numerous large-scale religious themes,

P.-A.-J. Dagnan-Bouveret: *Horses at the Watering Trough*, oil on canvas, 2.25×1.75 m, 1885 (Chambéry, Musée des Beaux-Arts)

which suggest conversion to intense Catholicism and owe much to Italian Renaissance prototypes, such as Leonardo da Vinci's *Last Supper*. Dagnan-Bouveret selected his models from the people of his local town, Vesoul; by dressing these models in appropriate historical garments and then photographing them, he was able to reconstruct an image of the past while maintaining a naturalist's inclination for exact detail within a mystical setting.

Dagnan-Bouveret received numerous awards, including nomination as Chevalier of the Légion d'honneur (1885) and as a member of the Institut de France (1900).

BIBLIOGRAPHY
J. Dampt: 'P. A. J. Dagnan-Bouveret 1852–1929', *Catalogue des oeuvres de M. Dagnan-Bouveret* (Paris, 1930), pp. 3–7
The Realist Tradition (exh. cat., ed. G. P. Weisberg; Cleveland, OH, Mus. A., 1980)
G. P. Weisberg: 'Dagnan-Bouveret, Bastien-Lepage and the Naturalist Instinct', *A. Mag.*, lvi (April 1982), pp. 70–76
——: 'Making it Natural: Dagnan-Bouveret's Constructed Compositions for the Paris Salon of the 1880s', *Scot. A. Rev.*, xv/4 (1982), pp. 7–15
——: 'P. A. J. Dagnan-Bouveret and the Illusion of Photographic Naturalism', *A. Mag.*, lvi (March 1982), pp. 100–05
——: *Beyond Impressionism: The Naturalist Impulse* (New York, 1992)
GABRIEL P. WEISBERG

Dagon. *See* RANGOON.

Daguerre, Dominique (*fl* 1772; *d* London, 27 Aug 1796). French marchand-mercier. He is known to have been trading in Paris from 14 March 1772, when he went into partnership with the marchand-mercier Simon-Philippe Poirier, who was a relative by marriage. They remained partners until 30 April 1777 when Poirier retired.

Daguerre then went into partnership with Francotay from 1777 until 1781. His third and final partner was Martin-Eloi Lignereux, from 11 May 1789 until Daguerre's death. Daguerre conducted his business from premises in the fashionable Rue St Honoré, which became famous for the high-quality furniture, clocks, porcelain and bronze items sold to the French court and to an international clientele. He and Poirier specialized in supplying furniture with plaques from the Sèvres porcelain factory for female clients including the Comtesse Du Barry and the Russian Empress Maria Fyodorovna (1759–1828). A collection of drawings of furniture and porcelain (New York, Met.) is thought to have been sent by Daguerre to the Duke Albert and Duchess Maria Christine von Saxe-Teschen. This demonstrates the way in which a Parisian merchant could communicate with foreign clients. During the 1780s Daguerre established commercial links with England; he sold goods from the ceramic factory of Josiah Wedgwood in Paris and in 1788 bought porcelain from Sèvres especially for the English market. He is known to have first visited England in 1787 and later moved there. His most important English client was the Prince Regent (later George IV), for whom he supervised the furnishing of Carlton House, London, and the Brighton Pavilion. A collection of furniture, bronze, clocks and porcelain imported into England by Daguerre was sold in 1791 (London, Christie's, 25 March 1791).

BIBLIOGRAPHY
F. J. B. Watson: 'Holland and Daguerre: French Undercurrents in English Neo-Classic Furniture Design', *Burl. Mag.*, cix (1967), pp. 282–7
G. de Bellaigue: 'George IV and French Furniture', *Connoisseur* (1977), pp. 116–25
P. Lemonnier: *Weisweiler* (Paris, 1983)
CAROLYN SARGENTSON

Daguerre, Louis(-Jacques-Mandé) (*b* Cormeilles-en-Parisis, nr Paris, 18 Nov 1787; *d* Bry-sur-Marne, Paris, 10 July 1851). French photographer, inventor, painter and stage designer. He began his artistic training *c.* 1800 as an architect's apprentice. After training as a draughtsman, he entered the studio of Ignace-Eugène-Marie Degotti (*d* 1824), stage designer at the Paris Opéra. In 1807 he became an assistant to Pierre Prévost (1764–1823) in the production of immense panorama paintings, which were popular as public entertainment spectacles. Daguerre exhibited his first independent work at the Salon of 1814, *Interior of a Chapel of the Church of the Feuillants, Paris* (Paris, Louvre). During the next twenty-six years he exhibited six works at the Salon and received the Légion d'honneur in 1824 for *Holyrood Chapel by Moonlight* (untraced; another version Liverpool, Walker A.G.; see fig.), a work combining meticulous attention to detail with a characteristic luminosity. Ten of his drawings were reproduced in the series *Voyages pittoresques et romantiques en l'ancienne France* (1820–78).

Daguerre's artistic reputation developed through his highly successful career as decorator and stage designer for Parisian theatres. In 1816 he won the contract as stage designer for the Théâtre Ambigu-Comique and immediately undertook to redesign completely the theatre's interior decorations. The *trompe l'oeil* stage curtain, which he

Louis Daguerre: *Holyrood Chapel by Moonlight*, oil on canvas, 2.11×2.56 m, ?1824 (Liverpool, Walker Art Gallery)

designed and painted, depicted architecture in deep perspective. It was a great success and led to commissions for other works at the Opéra-Comique and the Théâtre de l'Odéon. He designed stage sets for the melodramas in which these theatres specialized from 1816 to 1822; his romantic and picturesque inventions and dramatic illusionistic lighting effects greatly added to their popularity. His success was such that his designs were often considered more entertaining and artful than the plays themselves, and he was invited to become one of the chief designers at the Académie Royale de Musique, where he collaborated with other designers at the Opéra, most successfully with Pierre-Luc-Charles Ciceri (1782–1868) in the production *Aladdin and his Wonderful Lamp* (1822).

The combination of his varied artistic experience and involvement with the world of popular entertainment, along with his interest in lighting effects, led him to develop the pre-existing Diaphanorama, an illusionistic stage effect that enabled the transition from one scene to another by a change of lighting on a translucent, painted canvas.

In 1822, in partnership with the painter Charles-Marie Bouton, whom he had met in Prévost's studio, Daguerre

opened the DIORAMA in Paris. The Diorama building, designed by Daguerre in simple functional style, was built in the centre of the popular entertainment district for the sole purpose of showing the huge (as large as 13.8×22 m) painting of dramatic subjects specially painted by Daguerre and Bouton. The scenes reflect contemporary taste for the Romantic and Sublime and included alpine landscapes, chapel interiors and volcanoes. Through a combination of *trompe l'oeil* painting on thin linen (often with the addition of real props) and lighting from the front and from behind the picture, the Diorama managed to imitate changes from daylight to evening light along with the appearance and disappearance of figures. The audience, viewing from the darkened auditorium, thus saw the same scene undergoing a gradual change that could last from ten to fifteen minutes. When the transition of one scene was complete, the cylindrical auditorium was itself rotated to bring another scene into view. The novelty of such an arrangement and the success of the illusion made the Diorama one of the most popular entertainments in Paris in the 1820s and brought Daguerre international fame. In 1823 he opened the London Diorama, built on a similar scheme in Park Square East, Regent's Park, where the same scenes were displayed after their season of showing in Paris came to an end. Daguerre's assistants at the Diorama were Hippolyte-Victor-Valentin Sébron (1801–79), whose assistance was publicly acknowledged by Daguerre and whose contribution to the development of the Diorama effect was possibly substantial, and Daguerre's brother-in-law Charles Arrowsmith (*b* 1798), who also supervised the construction of the London Diorama. The Paris Diorama building, along with all the paintings kept there, was destroyed by fire in 1839. Bouton rebuilt it near by in 1842–3, but by that time Daguerre had lost interest in it.

Ever in search of novelty and greater illusionistic effect, Daguerre had begun experiments in 1824 using a lens to project an image of nature on to a surface coated with phosphorescent paint. His aim was to create a view that would glow in the dark in its natural colours. These experiments, and the desire to render exactly the views he used in constructing the Diorama paintings, led to his obsession with the notion of fixing an optically produced image by chemical means. Through the optician and lens-maker Charles Chevalier (1804–59), Daguerre heard of similar work being done by NICÉPHORE NIÉPCE, whom he contacted in 1826. This resulted in their forming a partnership to develop and exploit the promising experiments of Niépce. On Niépce's death in 1833 Daguerre was left in control of the rudiments of a practical photographic process. He continued his experiments on his own, working on principles and with materials suggested by Niépce, which eventually led to his discovery of an entirely different photographic process. In 1835 he developed a latent image with mercury vapour on an iodized silver plate, and in 1837 he discovered how to fix the image with salt solution, thus inventing one of the first practical photographic processes (*see* PHOTOGRAPHY, §I and fig. 1).

Together with Niépce's son, Isidore (1805–68), Daguerre attempted to sell his invention by subscription. However, Daguerre's reputation as a clever illusionist and the incredible nature of the discovery left the public doubtful of the achievement. He realized that he could not release details of the process without losing the opportunity to make a profit from the invention. Word of the invention soon began to circulate and other experimenters were making similar claims. Eventually, through the efforts of the prominent and influential scientist François Arago (1786–1853), the invention was purchased by the French government and its discovery was announced on 7 January 1839. This created a huge sensation and the process, named the daguerreotype, rapidly found practitioners throughout the world. The process was improved by others and remained, along with the calotype, one of the dominant forms of photography in the mid-19th century.

In 1840 Daguerre retired to Bry-sur-Marne, a suburb of Paris, on the pension granted to him by the French government in return for the rights to his invention. His remaining years were spent experimenting with different painting techniques and improvements to his photographic invention. In 1842 he painted a *trompe l'oeil* 'extension' representing the nave of a Gothic cathedral, behind the altar in the church in Bry (*in situ*).

WRITINGS

Historique et description des procédés du daguerréotype et du Diorama (Paris, 1839)

Description des nouveaux daguerréotypes perfectionnés avec instructions de Daguerre, annotées (Paris, 1841)

BIBLIOGRAPHY

P. Carpentier: *Notice sur Daguerre* (Paris, 1855)

A. Mentienne: *La Découverte de la photographie en 1839* (Paris, 1892)

J. M. Eder: *Geschichte der Photographie* (Vienna, 1905, rev. Halle, 4/1932; Eng. trans., 1945/*R* 1972)

G. Potonniée: *Histoire de la découverte de la photographie* (Paris, 1925)

——: *Daguerre, peintre et décorateur* (Paris, 1935)

A. Gernsheim and H. Gernsheim: *L. J. M. Daguerre: The History of the Diorama and Daguerreotype* (London, 1956, rev. 1968)

GRANT B. ROMER

Dahl, J(ohan) C(hristian) (Clausen) (*b* Bergen, 24 Feb 1788; *d* Dresden, 14 Oct 1857). Norwegian painter and collector, active in Germany. His paintings, imbued with Romantic and patriotic sentiments, had a strong influence on the landscape tradition both in Germany (especially Dresden) and in his native Norway.

1. EARLY CAREER AND TRAVELS, 1803–24. He was apprenticed from 1803 to 1809 to a house painter and interior decorator in Bergen and during this time took private drawing lessons. His artistic talent was soon recognized, and a group of prosperous Bergen citizens paid for him to study at the Kunstakademi (Academy of Art) in Copenhagen, where he remained from 1811 to about 1817, from 1813 teaching at the painting school of C. A. Lorentzen (1749–1828). While benefiting from the disciplined Academy course, Dahl also studied independently, copying from other works, especially those of Dutch painters, and sketching frequently from nature. He made copies partly to earn a living but also for what he could learn of both technique and the approach to the painting of architecture and, especially, of landscape. Jan Both and Claude Lorrain influenced his early 'Italianate' pictures, while he based his 'Norwegian' works on Jacob van Ruisdael, Meindert Hobbema and Allaert van Everdingen. These models also had some influence on Dahl's sketches directly from nature, which were generally made in and around Copenhagen, although occasionally during excursions further afield. While Dutch work, for example the paintings of Aert van der Neer, seems to have inspired such works as *The Castle of Frederiksborg in the Moonlight* (1817; Copenhagen, Stat. Mus. Kst), *Landscape from Praestø* (*c*. 1814; Oslo, N.G.) shows the more independent, strongly Naturalist tendency in Dahl's work at this time both in its intricate rendering of details of plants and stones and in its success in conveying the movement of clouds. Dahl's Naturalism was, however, tempered by the influence of the work of C. W. Eckersberg, whom Dahl got to know personally after the former's return from abroad in 1816. A landscape such as *From Øresund* (1818; Oslo, N.G.) suggests Eckersberg's influence in its strong, bright colours, although the lively brushwork and interest in changing atmospheric phenomena are foreign to Eckersberg's more classicizing approach.

In September 1818 Dahl left Copenhagen with the intention of making an extensive study tour of the Continent. He travelled first via Stettin (now Szczecin) and Berlin to Dresden, where he then stayed for nearly two

1. J. C. Dahl: *Seascape, Gulf of Naples*, oil on paper, pasted on cardboard, 225×360 mm, 1821 (Oslo, Nasjonalgalleri)

years until June 1820, far longer than he had originally planned. He was well received and caused a sensation with his work, especially among students and younger painters, for the striking truth to nature they saw in his approach to landscape. This reaction was evoked by paintings such as the large canvas *Norwegian Mountain Landscape* (1819; Oslo, N.G.), based on a series of observed details but evidently a confection of the studio. In Dresden, Dahl met Caspar David Friedrich, with whom he was to share a house from 1823. Dahl soon recognized that Friedrich's subjective attitude and contemplative art offered an alternative to the more matter-of-fact Danish tradition. Dahl continued his tour when invited by Prince Christian Frederik (later King Christian VIII of Denmark) to join him at the Villa Quisisana, near Castellammare di Stabia on the Gulf of Naples, where the artist stayed from August 1820 to February 1821. He made frequent excursions to Naples and the surrounding districts, sometimes accompanied by the German painter Franz Catel. Dahl subsequently spent February to June 1821 in Rome and then travelled north to Dresden, where he arrived in July and where he remained for the rest of his life, except for occasional excursions and five trips back to Norway. His Italian experience was of particular importance with regard to his oil sketching. Although he had painted oil studies in Copenhagen, such works had remained rather timid in approach and meticulous in execution; those made in Italy, however, such as the bold *Seascape, Gulf of Naples* (1821; Oslo, N.G.; see fig. 1), are much broader in handling, far more confident in technique and bolder in approach, especially in their concentration on essentials. Dahl's pen-and-wash studies show a similar change, Italian examples such as *Landscape with Rainbow* (1821; Bergen,

Billedgal.) being executed with a freedom not seen before in his work. Dahl kept notes at this time (MSS, Bergen, U. Lib.), which confirm that this change was the result of conscious endeavour.

Dahl produced far more finished oil paintings for sale when in Rome; these had both imaginary Norwegian subjects and Italian ones sketched on the spot, as in *Roman Villa* (1821; Oslo, N.G.). Dahl's Italian journey also continued to provide him with subject-matter for works executed after his return to Dresden. Exceptionally popular was the subject of *Vesuvius in Eruption*, of which he painted several versions (e.g. 1823; Frankfurt am Main, Städel. Kstinst. & Städt. Gal.). He also painted many Norwegian scenes at this time, but German views appear to have been much less in demand. Dahl continued to sketch both in and around Dresden (e.g. *Evening on the Elbe*, 1822; Oslo, N.G.) and occasionally also made sketching excursions to more distant regions such as Bohemia, Silesia and the Riesengebirge, recording both landscape and monuments, as in the pencil-and-wash sketch *The Ruined Castle of Kynest in Silesia* (1824; Oslo, N.G.).

2. DRESDEN AND LATER CAREER, FROM 1824. While he at first considered returning to Copenhagen, Dahl decided to stay in Dresden on being appointed to a post at the Akademie in 1824. He had no precise teaching responsibilities, but he tried to advise those students who approached him, urging them above all to a conscientious study of nature. His pupils included the Norwegians Thomas Fearnley and Peder Balke, while the pupil who most fully realized Dahl's intentions was the German painter Christian Friedrich Gille.

From the mid-1820s Norwegian landscape subjects began to dominate Dahl's output, as they were to do for the rest of his life. He made his first return visit to Norway in 1826, bringing to its landscape an eye now well exercised in other settings and so producing works quite distinct in their degree of truth to nature in comparison with his earlier Norwegian scenes. Interestingly, however, the rather forbidding *Winter at the Sognefjord* (1827: Oslo, N.G.) was adapted in its finished version to show the landscape under snow, perhaps in an attempt to convey something of the bleak, inhuman scale of the setting and to exploit the strange grandeur of the ancient *bauta* rock formations Dahl had sketched, as in *Bauta Rock in the Sognefjord* (1826; Bergen, Billedgal.). This divergence between sketch and finished work, though not especially typical of Dahl, prompts consideration of his view of the nature and relative importance of each. At no stage did he exhibit his sketches, and he only occasionally offered them for sale. Until about 1820 Dahl's studies were firm in appearance and rather meticulous in execution, as was his finished work from this time. Later his swiftly executed but highly articulated oil sketches from Italy, Dresden and the Elbe valley became his prime means of capturing the mood of a precise landscape. Sketches made in the more inaccessible Norwegian locations had the same aim but were largely executed in the simpler medium of pencil on paper, with ink or watercolour washes added later.

The elements Dahl added into finished works—figures, animals and such landscape features as trees—were not merely a way of meeting market demand. Studies such as those of the peasants in local costume in *Peasants from Telemark* (1830; Oslo, N.G.) reveal that these received no less attention than the landscape views themselves: they were more than mere accessories. Dahl seems to have regarded precise description and specific detail as important aspects in the rendering of landscape, for he wished to give as much information about his subject as was possible. While the goats and goatherd in *From Lyshornet* (1836; Oslo, N.G.) are certainly dwarfed by the churning sea of mountain peaks under a stormy sky, careful placing makes their presence far from negligible.

It would seem that Dahl eventually came to regard his sketches and studies as of central importance to his finished work, although several scholars have emphasized the more traditional strain in his approach to the rendering of landscape and to his own working methods in particular. This is also of relevance to the question of finish. The example of his treatment of clouds, of which he made a vast number of studies, suggests that Dahl used the degree of finish he found to be most appropriate to conveying

2. J. C. Dahl: *From Stalheim*, oil on canvas, 1.90×2.46 m, 1842 (Oslo, Nasjonalgalleri)

the appearance and nature of the subject. Sketches such as the *Study of Clouds* (1825; Berlin, Neue N.G.), with its apparently casual, abrupt cropping of the spires and roofs of Dresden along the base of the picture and its impressionistic record of the sky above, may be seen as 'finished' in their own terms.

Around 1830 Dahl was engrossed in a subject treated in several versions: *Shipwreck on the Norwegian Coast* (e.g. 1832; Oslo, N.G.). Though this reveals Dahl's advance towards a more powerfully unified treatment of landscape, sea and sky, if compared with the shipwreck scene of 1819, *Morning After a Stormy Night* (Munich, Neue Pin.), the human element is still used by Dahl to give an emotional focus within the landscape. Similarly, the semisilhouetted figures in the moonlit landscape *View from Larvik* (1839; Oslo, N.G.), in the manner of Friedrich, offer a more compelling emotional point of identification for the viewer than found in Dahl's moonlit scenes with figures from his Copenhagen years. Dahl was also associated with views that are interesting for their visual quality and evocation of atmosphere rather than for their emotional connotations, as in his many renderings of cities in moonlight, for example the oil painting *Kronborg by Moonlight* (1828; Oslo, N.G.) or the pen-and-wash sketch *Dresden by Moonlight* (1834; Bergen, Billedgal.). Atmospheric effects of greater symbolic potential, meanwhile, were essayed in the large canvas *From Stalheim* (1842; Oslo, N.G.; see fig. 2), a striking panorama of high mountains under a rainbow, and in scenes that single out motifs of drama or grandeur, such as the pen-and-wash drawing *Birch in a Storm* (1849; Bergen, Billedgal.) or the oil *Mount Stugunostet* (1851; Oslo, N.G.).

Towards the end of Dahl's life, the strong patriotic feelings implicit in many of his Norwegian landscapes were also expressed in activities such as his work for the protection of historical monuments in Norway, and for the establishment of a national gallery of Norwegian art at Christiania (now Oslo) to which he contributed his own considerable collection of drawings and paintings. In 1837 his publication on Norwegian stave churches was received with interest both in Norway and abroad. Dahl had a profound influence on the Norwegian landscape tradition. He was also important to German landscape painting, having a notable impact, for example, on Karl Blechen as well as on a host of lesser artists. The mutual influence of Friedrich and Dahl is a more complex phenomenon: one may point, for example, to Friedrich as an influence on the symbolic treatment of landscape motifs (such as the single tree) in Dahl's work; and Dahl can be seen as an important stimulus to a more carefully observed treatment of light, atmosphere and landscape features in Friedrich's work. Ultimately, however, Friedrich was too Romantic for Dahl, and Dahl too matter-of-fact for Friedrich; the extent to which Dahl's very distinct approach was already formed when the two painters met ensured his continued independence.

Dahl's son Siegwald (1827–1902) was an animal painter.

WRITINGS

Denkmale einer sehr ausgebildeten Holzbaukunst aus den frühesten Jahrhunderten in den innern Landschaften Norwegens (Dresden, 1837)

BIBLIOGRAPHY

NK; NKL

A. Aubert: *Maleren Johan Christian Dahl* [The painter Johan Christian Dahl] (Kristiania, 1920; Ger. trans., 1947)

J. C. Dahl's verk (exh. cat., ed. J. H. Langaard; Oslo, Kstnernes Hus, 1937)

S. Willoch: 'Figurmaleren J. C. Dahl', *Kst & Kult.* [Oslo], xxiv (1938), pp. 15–34

G. Zöller: *J. C. Dahl* (diss., U. Würzburg, 1945)

Johan Christian Dahl, intro. L. Østby, contributions by L. Venturi, H. Bramsen, B. Cnattingius, S. Wichmann (Oslo, 1957)

Johan Christian Dahl: Tegninger og akvareller, Bergen Billedgal. catalogue, intro. L. Østby (Oslo, 1957) [numerous pls]

S. Tschudi Madsen: 'J. C. Dahl og Avaldsnes: Motiv og fortidsminne' [J. C. Dahl and Avaldsnes: subject and historical monument], *Kst & Kult.* [Oslo], xliv (1961), pp. 97–112

M. L. Bang: 'Two Alpine Landscapes', *Burl. Mag.*, cvii (1965), pp. 571–5

L. Østby: 'Die Slindebirke: Ein romantisches Symbol in norwegischer Malerei und Dichtung', *Nordelbingen*, xxxiv (1965), pp. 222–32

——: 'En kunstner møter sitt land' [An artist meeting his country], *Höjdpunkter i norsk konst* (Stockholm, 1968), pp. 66–100

K. R. Lunde: *Johan Christian Dahl* (diss., New York, Columbia U., 1970, microfilm, Ann Arbor, 1973)

E. Wexelsen: *Skriftlige kilder vedrørende J. C. Dahl* [Manuscript sources concerning J. C. Dahl] (Bergen, 1973)

J. C. Dahl og Danmark (exh. cat., Oslo, N.G.; Copenhagen, Stat. Mus. Kst; 1973)

L. Østby: 'J. C. Dahls danske laereår' [J. C. Dahl's years as an art student in Denmark], *Kstmus. Årsskr.* (1974), pp. 3–44

H. Neidhardt: *Die Malerei der Romantik in Dresden* (Leipzig, 1976), pp. 160–72

L. Østby: 'Skipbruddet i J. C. Dahls maleri' [The shipwreck in J. C. Dahl's painting], *Kst & Kult.* [Oslo], lxiii (1980), pp. 195–218

Dahls Dresden (exh. cat., ed. M. Malmanger; Oslo, N.G., 1980)

M. Malmanger: *Norsk malerkunst: Fra klassisisme til tidlig realisme* [Norwegian painting: classicism to early realism] (Oslo, 1981), pp. 65–96

——: 'J. C. Dahls naturstudier og deres forutsetninger' [J. C. Dahl's studies from nature, their character and historical background], *Kst & Kult.* [Oslo], lxvi (1983), pp. 130–45

M. L. Bang: *Johann Christian Dahl, 1788–1857: Life and Works*, 3 vols (Oslo and Oxford, 1988) [incl. cat. rais.]

MAGNE MALMANGER

Dahl, Michael (*b* Stockholm, 29 Sept ?1659; *d* London, 20 Oct 1743). Swedish painter, active in England. He studied under Martin Hannibal (*d* 1741) and later with David Klöcker Ehrenstrahl. In 1682 he travelled to London, where he became acquainted with Godfrey Kneller and Henry Tilson, and in 1685 he left for Europe with the latter, working briefly in Paris before proceeding to Venice and Rome, where they stayed for about two years. In Rome Dahl converted to Roman Catholicism and gravitated towards the circle of Christina, former Queen of Sweden, who sat for him (Grimsthorpe Castle, Lincs). He returned to England with Tilson via Frankfurt and arrived in London in 1689; he stayed in England for the remainder of his career.

During Dahl's absence, Kneller had consolidated his supremacy in London as the fashionable portrait painter, but Dahl rapidly became Kneller's closest competitor; his clientele probably had roots in the Swedish diplomatic circles, but it expanded as a result of his ability and his agreeable personality. His prices were also appreciably lower. Dahl's art lacked Kneller's breadth and verve, but he compensated by painting carefully in short brush strokes and paying particular attention to the draperies. He favoured softer, more diffused, silvery tones and could respond to his sitters with sincerity and humanity. Politically, Kneller supported the ascendant Whigs while Dahl was a Tory, but they frequently painted the same sitters from both parties, and in spite of fundamental differences in technique and temperament, their work was sometimes similar in appearance. Dahl was prolific but rarely signed his work, and comparatively few of his portraits were engraved in mezzotint, the method adopted by Kneller to promulgate his reputation. By 1690 he had painted the aged *Duke of Schomberg* (engraved by William Faithorne) and *Prince George of Denmark* (London, Kensington Pal.). He was ignored by William III but received commissions from Princess Anne, including one for a portrait of herself (Oakly Park, Ludlow, Salop). He also painted the future Duke and Duchess of Marlborough, and his informal portrait of the Duchess (Althorp House, Northants), formerly attributed to Kneller, is perhaps the most intimate of all images of her.

Dahl's sensitive *Self-portrait* (1691; London, N.P.G.), though not a typical work, bears witness to his European experience, both in its composition and in its colour scheme of dull green and purple set against a monochrome stone background. At about the same time, he painted a number of subject pictures, including a *Holy Family* (1691; Stockholm, Nmus.) and a voluptuous *Magdalene* (York, C.A.G.). Throughout his career, he painted men of learning and letters, an early example being *John Locke* (*c.* 1696; London, N.P.G.). Also during the 1690s he secured the patronage of Charles Seymour, the 'Proud' 6th Duke of Somerset, who ordered a series of seven full-length portraits of notable contemporary beauties from Dahl (1690s; Petworth House, W. Sussex, NT). This was originally a scheme similar to Kneller's more famous 'Hampton Court Beauties', but the portraits were subsequently reduced to three-quarter-length formats. The features of the sitters are not individualized, but they possess a decorative, languorous glamour that recalls Lely rather than Kneller. Somerset gave Dahl further employment over the next 25 years.

In 1698, following the death of Klöcker Ehrenstrahl, Dahl was offered the post of court painter at Stockholm, which he apparently refused, preferring to remain in London at his studio in Leicester Fields, near the Swedish legation. In about 1700 he was joined by a young compatriot, Hans Hysing, who worked with him for many years. Dahl seems not to have married until after 1708. He had a son Michael (*d* 26 Nov 1741), also a painter, of whose work nothing is known, and two daughters.

After the accession of Queen Anne in 1701, she and Prince George sat for a number of official portraits. Dahl's limitations are exposed in his vast and dull equestrian portrait of *Prince George of Denmark* (1704; London, Kensington Pal.), in which he unwisely chose to paint the horse himself. The royal couple divided the important commission for a series of portraits of Admirals (*c.* 1702–8; London, N. Mar. Mus.) equally between Kneller and Dahl, each painter contributing seven portraits. In spite of prevailing conventions, Dahl represented his sitters sympathetically and realistically: *Sir Cloudesley Shovell* (see fig.), the most vivid of his allocated group, is one of his finest achievements.

Dahl's practice demanded versatility: he could provide the grand manner when required, as in the full-length of the *Countess of Ashburnham* (Liverpool, Walker A. G.), in

Michael Dahl: *Sir Cloudesley Shovell*, oil on canvas, 1.27×1.02 m, *c.* 1702–8 (London, National Maritime Museum)

a blue dress against an elaborate architectural backdrop, or reveal a humanity not usually associated with portraits of the period, as in the oval bust portrait of the elderly *Francis Newport, 1st Earl of Bradford* (*c.* 1705; Weston Park, Salop). His double marriage portraits, such as *Allen, 1st Earl of Bathurst, and his Wife Catherine* (*c.* 1704; Cirencester Park, Glos), tend to be decorative but vapid. In contrast, his full-scale conversation pieces can be more interesting, as with the *Three Virtuosi* (sold London, Christie's, 19 Nov 1982), in which the balance of colours and the interplay between the sitters are handled with subtle mastery.

Dahl's royal patronage ceased with Queen Anne's death, and when Dahl was asked to paint the infant Duke of Cumberland in 1722, he refused. He was suspected of Jacobite sympathies, and relations had cooled between him and the Swedish legation. However, his practice continued to prosper, and he acquired another important patron in Edward Harley, 2nd Earl of Oxford, who shared his political views and whose circle included the architect James Gibbs and the poets Matthew Prior and Alexander Pope, all of whom Dahl painted. Oxford commissioned several portraits of himself. In the earliest (1719; Welbeck Abbey, Notts), he is shown dressed informally in a cap and dressing gown, seated behind a table and holding a medal of Queen Anne. The drawing done from life for his head exists (London, BM) and shows that Dahl, like Kneller, sometimes worked from preliminary studies, although few of these have so far come to light. He used the same basic formula of a sitter behind a table for other portraits of intellectuals, such as *Joseph Addison* (1719; London, N.P.G.) and *Alexander Pope* (1727; London, N.P.G.), an unusually lively conception, where the poet lifts his quill as if at the very moment of inspiration.

The death of Kneller in 1723 left Dahl, previously overshadowed by his rival, as the doyen of London portraitists. He was still producing effective works, such as the charming pastoral portrait of Oxford's seven-year-old daughter *Margaret Harley* (*c.* 1723; Welbeck Abbey, Notts) and the ambitious equestrian portrait of *Henry Hoare II*, for which John Wootton painted the horse (1726; Stourhead, Wilts, NT). He continued to paint almost to the end of his life, but his later work became increasingly conventional and outmoded. Dahl directed in his will that his collections should be auctioned after his death, and his friend and fellow-Catholic, George Vertue, recorded that it contained 'many curious and valuable Italian paintings as well as religious and history paintings by Dahl himself'.

BIBLIOGRAPHY

H. Walpole: *Anecdotes of Painting in England* (1762–71); ed. R. N. Wornum (1849), ii, pp. 648–50
'The Note-books of George Vertue', *Walpole Soc.*, i (1911), ii (1912), iii (1913), iv (1914), v (1915); index p. 58; vi (1916), pp. 17, 19, 168
C. H. Collins Baker: *Lely and the Stuart Portrait Painters* (London, 1912), ii, pp. 96–104, 178–81
——: *Catalogue of the Petworth Collection of Pictures in the Possession of Lord Leconfield* (London, 1920), pp. 20–24
W. Nisser: *Michael Dahl and the Contemporary Swedish School of Painting in England* (Uppsala, 1927) [standard work on Dahl, incl. important transcriptions of docs, comprehensive illus.: text and check-lists out of date]
E. K. Waterhouse: *Painting in Britain 1530–1790*, Pelican Hist. A. (London, 1953, rev. 4/1978), pp. 145–7
M. Whinney and O. Millar: *English Art, 1625–1714* (Oxford, 1957), pp. 198–200
E. Croft-Murray and P. Hulton: *British Drawings: XVI and XVII Centuries*, London, BM cat., i (London, 1960), pp. 293–5
W. K. Wimsatt: *The Portraits of Alexander Pope* (New Haven, 1965), pp. 90–96
J. D. Stewart: *Sir Godfrey Kneller* (exh. cat. by J. D. Stewart, London, N.P.G., 1971), pp. 43–4
——: 'Some Portrait Drawings by Michael Dahl and Sir James Thornhill', *Master Drgs*, xi (1973), pp. 34–45
E. K. Waterhouse: *The Dictionary of British 18th Century Painters* (Woodbridge, 1981), p. 97
J. D. Stewart: *Sir Godfrey Kneller and the Baroque Portrait* (Oxford, 1983)

RICHARD JEFFREE

Dahlbergh [Jönsson], **Erik** (*b* Stockholm, 10 Oct 1625; *d* Stockholm, 16 Jan 1703). Swedish engineer, architect and draughtsman. Dahlbergh, who received this noble surname in 1660, began his military career in the final phase of the Thirty Years War (1618–48). He held the leading positions in Swedish military engineering for half a century, being appointed field marshal in 1693 and quartermaster-general in 1697. He trained as a draughtsman and topographical artist in Germany and studied in Italy and France from 1654 to 1656. As a military engineer, he planned over 50 fortified towns and fortresses, among them Karlskrona naval base (1683–7), Karlsten fortress on Marstrand and the completion (1690) of the fortifications at Göteborg with the Crown and Lion forts on elevated bastions. Throughout, he made excellent use of the local topography. In his civil architecture, Dahlbergh developed a vigorous, plastic, Baroque style based on Dutch and Roman examples, employing giant pilasters. A series of sepulchral chapels including the Soop mausoleum (after 1661) at Askersund, the Kagg mausoleum (1666) at Floda and his own mausoleum (1681) at Turinge church function as a combination of chancel and mausoleum and are self-contained, centrally planned appendages to the churches, with column or pilaster projections on both inner and outer walls. Dahlbergh's major work as a topographical artist is *Svecia antiqua et hodierna* (Stockholm, 1723; *see* STOCKHOLM, fig. 1), which depicts, in 470 drawings, the towns and architectural monuments of Sweden's 'Great Power Era'. It was engraved and printed by French and Dutch artists, including Jean Marot, Jean Le Pautre and Willem Swidde (1661–97), on the basis of the pencil and pen drawings that Dahlbergh made during many years of travel and military campaigns and the architectural drawings that he collected. Dahlbergh's swift and vivacious technique, as well as his architect's training and topographer's eye, are reflected in these volumes, which are an invaluable, if not always entirely accurate, source of knowledge about northern Europe in his time. Most of the sketches are in the collection of the Kungliga Bibliotek and in Nationalmuseets Arkiv in Stockholm; the copperplates and prints are in the Nationalmuseum.

BIBLIOGRAPHY

E. Ericsson and E. Vennberg: *Erik Dahlbergh: Hans levnad och verksamhet* [Erik Dahlberg: his life and work] (Stockholm, 1925)
G. Lindahl: *Grav och rum* [Grave and room] (Stockholm, 1969)
H. O. Andersson and F. Bedoire: *Svensk arkitektur: Ritningar, 1640–1970/Swedish Architecture: Drawings, 1640–1970* (Stockholm, 1986) [Swed. and Eng. text]

□

Dahl-Wolfe, Louise (*b* Alameda, CA, 19 Nov 1895; *d* 11 Dec 1989). American photographer. She studied painting at the San Francisco Art Institute (1914–17), where she was taught by Rudolph Schaeffer (*b* 1886), who encouraged her use of strong colour. She later studied design in New York and then architecture at Columbia University, New York (1923). A self-taught photographer, she was inspired to take it up by the nudes of Anne Brigman (1869–1950). Dahl-Wolfe worked as an interior-design assistant in San Francisco and New York. In 1927–8 she travelled with the photographer Consuelo Kanaga (1894–1978) in Europe. She abandoned interior design for photography, opening a studio first in San Francisco in 1930, and then in Gatlinburg, TN, when she married in 1932.

Dahl-Wolfe worked as a freelance advertising photographer with her own studio in New York from 1933 until 1960. Her rise to prominence coincided with a trend towards naturalism in fashion photography. During her career she photographed cultural figures and famous personalities in addition to fashion, among them *Colette*, *Cecil Beaton*, *Christopher Isherwood* and *Carole Lombard* (see Dahl-Wolfe, 1984, pp. 133, 93, 109 and 110 respectively). From 1936 until 1958 she was a staff photographer for *Harper's Bazaar* under the editor Carmel Snow; her work was characterized by richly patterned colours and arranged backgrounds, as in *The Covert Look* (for *Harper's Bazaar*, Aug 1949). After leaving *Harper's Bazaar* she worked freelance for *Vogue* and *Sports Illustrated* until 1960.

WRITINGS

Louise Dahl-Wolfe: A Photographer's Scrapbook (New York, 1984)

Dahshur, pyramidion of Ammenemes III, granite, h. 1.40 m, *c.* 1818–*c.* 1770 BC (Cairo, Egyptian Museum)

BIBLIOGRAPHY
N. Hall-Duncan: *The History of Fashion Photography* (New York, 1977)

SHERYL CONKELTON

Dahomey. *See* BENIN REPUBLIC.

Dahshur [Arab. Dahshūr]. Site of an ancient Egyptian necropolis consisting of Old and Middle Kingdom pyramids, on the west bank of the Nile, 75 km south of Cairo. The oldest pyramid is that of King Sneferu (*reg c.* 2575–*c.* 2551 BC), which is the first to have been designed from the start as a true pyramid. The angle of its sides was decreased halfway up, giving it a rhomboidal appearance, hence its name of Bent Pyramid (*see* PYRAMID, fig. 1b). Inside the pyramid is a complicated system of corridors and portcullises, and some inner chambers have high, corbelled ceilings. Reliefs in the pyramid's valley temple depict processions of female figures representing Sneferu's estates throughout the country. The pyramid is still in very good condition, retaining most of its outer casing. Sneferu's other monument, the Red Pyramid, lies 2 km north of the Bent Pyramid. The angle of its sides is the same as that of the upper part of its southern predecessor. Although the pyramid's casing was almost completely removed by later builders, its capstone has been found; this pyramidion (Cairo, Egyp. Mus.) is the oldest so far discovered and the only one surviving from the Old Kingdom.

Some 700 years later Ammenemes II (*reg c.* 1876–*c.* 1842 BC) of the 12th Dynasty built the White Pyramid about 1.2 km east of Sneferu's Red Pyramid. The building was totally plundered in later times, and not much can be ascertained about its dimensions. However, some fine examples of relief-carving have been recovered from the private tombs of Ammenemes' retainers, notably that of the vizier Siese (for illustration *see* EGYPT, ANCIENT, fig. 57). Sesostris III (*reg c.* 1837–*c.* 1818 BC) built his own tomb 1.5 km north-east of the White Pyramid. Six large wooden boats, reminiscent of the ones from Cheops' pyramid, were found near the White Pyramid. Sesostris III's pyramid complex, like that of Ammenemes II, yielded beautifully elaborate jewellery (Cairo, Egyp. Mus.; *see also* EGYPT, ANCIENT, §XIV, 3 and fig. 91), superb examples of the Middle Kingdom jeweller's art. The Black Pyramid of Ammenemes III (*reg c.* 1818–*c.* 1770 BC) —the capstone of which (see fig.) is in the Egyptian Museum, Cairo—lies about 1 km east of the Bent Pyramid. Excavations have shown that the tomb once suffered considerable damage, which explains the King's abandonment of that pyramid in favour of another at Hawara. There are other funerary complexes, of the 13th Dynasty, on the site, clustered around their 12th Dynasty predecessors.

BIBLIOGRAPHY
LÄ: 'Dahschur'
I. E. S. Edwards: *The Pyramids of Egypt* (Harmondsworth, 1947, rev. 4/1991), pp. 78–92, 211–18

R. J. LEPROHON

Dai Benxiao [Tai Pen-hsiao; *zi* Wuzhan; *hao* Ying'a] (*b* Hezhou, Anhui Province, 1621; *d* 1693). Chinese painter. His father, Dai Zhong (1602–46), a late Ming-dynasty (1368–1644) loyalist, moved his family to Nanjing in 1632. Political unrest forced them to move in 1637 and several times thereafter, always poor and often hungry. In 1645, having heard of the Manchu conquest of Nanjing, Dai Zhong helped organize resistance to the invading army but was later wounded in battle. Dai Benxiao was able to take his father back to Hezhou, but he died the following year. Thirty years later, Dai Benxiao built a commemorative shrine to his father and to Huilan, a Chan Buddhist martyr of the Southern Song period (1127–1279) whom Zhong revered.

Needing money, Dai Benxiao turned to painting. He travelled to view and paint the famous mountains Hua, Lu and Tai. Dai knew a number of contemporary artists, including Hongren, the foremost master of the ANHUI SCHOOL, whom he met in 1662. He went to Beijing in 1666 but spent much of his later life in Nanjing, where he became friendly with Daoji. Gong Xian was another acquaintance, and Dai completed one of the painter's commissions—for the playwright Kong Shangren (1648–1715)—after Gong's death in 1689.

Dai Benxiao worked initially in the dry linear manner of the Anhui school and adopted some of Hongren's motifs, such as flat-topped river banks (e.g. *Landscape after Ni Zan*; see 1970 exh. cat., pl. 41). Later he developed a distinctive style that was apparently influenced by the fantastic landscape compositions of the late Ming masters and that showed affinities with the work of his contemporaries in the NANJING SCHOOL. He shared with Daoji a fondness for extremely dry contour strokes, so that the rock edges of his landscapes appear almost to decompose into air. He experimented less than Daoji, however, and minor idiosyncracies rather than wholesale innovations characterize his painting. He shunned the monumental central mountains favoured by masters of the Orthodox school, preferring instead to portray opposing pairs of rising, twisting masses between which distant peaks can be glimpsed. He painted few large hanging scrolls; more common in his output of over 30 years were album leaves, in which he explored the theme of man in nature. The small scale of the albums allowed Dai's brushwork to assert itself: the ink, applied lightly over slightly rough paper, paradoxically gave the mountains both insubstantiality and texture, illustrating the artist's contention that in 'stripping away the bad habits of fussy detail and stiff drawing…modern artists surpass the old ones in some respects'.

BIBLIOGRAPHY
Fantastics and Eccentrics in Chinese Painting (exh. cat. by J. Cahill, New York, Asia House Gals, 1967), pp. 50–53, 114–15
Exhibition of Paintings of the Ming and Ch'ing Periods (exh. cat., Hong Kong, City Mus. & A.G., 1970), pl. 41
M. Fu and Shen Fu: *Studies in Connoisseurship: Chinese Paintings from the Arthur M. Sackler Collection in New York and Princeton* (Princeton, 1973), p. 170
M. Nishigami: 'Dai Banko ni tsuite' [Concerning Dai Benxiao], *Suzuki Kei sensei kanreki kinen Chūgoku kaigashi ronshu* [Essays on Chinese painting: Festschrift for Professor Kei Suzuki's 61st birthday] (Tokyo, 1981), pp. 291–340
H. Yoshida: 'Dai Benxiao', *Shadows of Mt. Huang: Chinese Painting and Printing of the Anhui School* (exh. cat., ed. J. F. Cahill; Berkeley, U. CA, A. Mus., 1981), pp. 115–22

VYVYAN BRUNST, with JAMES CAHILL

Daidalos [Gr.: 'cunning worker'; Lat. Daedalus] (?*fl c.* 600 BC). Legendary Greek craftsman. He is conventionally associated with Bronze Age Crete and was credited in antiquity with a variety of technical and artistic achievements.

1. LEGENDARY CAREER. The earliest reference to Daidalos is in the *Iliad*, where he is named as maker of a *choros* for Ariadne at Knossos. In the 2nd century AD Pausanias recorded seeing this *choros* as a white marble relief at Knossos (IX.xl.2), but the term used in the *Iliad* could mean equally a painting, dancing-floor or dance. In the Classical period (*c.* 480–323 BC) Daidalos was mentioned primarily as a sculptor of 'magic' statues, both in drama (e.g. Euripides: *Hecuba* 838; Aristophanes: *Daidalos* frag. 194) and in philosophy (Plato: *Menon* 97d and *Euthyphro* 11c). In Athens he was given an Athenian pedigree as the son of Palamaon or Eupalamos, son of Metion, of the line of Erechtheos, and thus related to Hephaistos (e.g. Plato: *Alkibiades* I.121). He was also reputedly the teacher or father of the early 6th-century BC Cretan artists Dipoinos and Skyllis (*see* §2 below). By the Hellenistic period (323–27 BC) he was renowned as an architect or builder as well as the inventor of statuary (e.g. Diodorus Siculus IV.76), his most famous design being the labyrinth at Knossos. Sicilian traditions also credit him with achievements in the Greek West, where according to legend he fled from Minos (Diodorus Siculus IV.77–9), including fortifications at Kamikos, baths at Selinus, a dam at Megara Hyblaia and a 'golden honeycomb' at Eryx. In Italy, poetic tradition ascribed to him the decoration of the doors of the Temple of Apollo at Cumae (Virgil: *Aeneid* VI.9–44). Hellenistic sources claim his sculptures were the first with eyes, ears and moving limbs (Diodorus Siculus IV.76), and specific works of art associated with him since the Classical period include statues of *Herakles*, *Trophonios*, *Britomartis*, *Athena* and *Aphrodite* (Pausanias V.xl.3–4). The invention of wings (e.g. Ovid: *Metamorphoses* VIII.183–235) was the achievement most often ascribed to him in Roman times and later.

BIBLIOGRAPHY
Diodorus Siculus: *Historical Library*
Pausanias: *Guide to Greece*
J. Overbeck: *Die antiken Schriftquellen zur Geschichte der bildenden Künste bei den Griechen* (Leipzig, 1868), nos 74–182
H. Brunn: *Geschichte der griechischen Künstler*, i (Stuttgart, 1889), pp. 11–19
J. E. Nyenhuis: 'Daidalos and Ikaros', *Lexicon iconographicum mythologiae classicae*, III/i (1986), pp. 313–21
N. Rudd: 'Daedalus and Icarus: (i) From Rome to the End of the Middle Ages' and '(ii) From the Renaissance to the Present Day', *Ovid Renewed*, ed. C. Martindale (Cambridge, 1988)

2. FOLLOWERS. The principal names associated with Daidalos in ancient literary sources are those of the early 6th-century BC sculptors from Crete, Dipoinos and Skyllis, active in the Peloponnese *c.* 580 BC. Described as the pupils of Daidalos or his sons by a woman of Gortyn (Pausanias II.xv.1), they were apparently the first to make important works in marble and to use Parian marble (Pliny XXXVI.9, 14). They emigrated from Crete to Sikyon, where they made statues of *Apollo*, *Artemis Mounychia* (Clement: *Protrepticus* IV.4), *Herakles*, and *Athena* (Pliny XXXVI.9). They also made an *Athena* at Kleonai (Pausanias II.xv.1), ebony statues of the *Dioskouroi* at Argos (Pausanias II.xxii.5) and a *Herakles* at Tiryns (Clement: *Protrepticus* IV.42). Their green stone statue of *Lindian*

Athena was reported by the Byzantine chronicler George Kedrenos (Cedrenus) in the palace of Lausos (destr.) at Constantinople and may be the statue sent to Kleoboulos of Rhodes by Amasis of Egypt (Herodotus: *Histories* II.182, III.47). Their pupils included: Dontas and Dorykleides from Sparta, the first sculptors of chryselephantine images, whose works were seen by Pausanias at the Sanctuary of Zeus at Olympia (V.xvii.1–2, VI.xix.12); Hegylos and his son, Theokles, also of Sparta, who made the statues of *Herakles and the Hesperides* seen by Pausanias in the Temple of Hera at Olympia (VI.xvii.2, xix.8); Klearchos of Rhegion, first to make a statue of hammered bronze parts (Pausanias III. xvii.6); Cheirisophos, sculptor of the chryselephantine *Apollo* at Tegea (Pausanias VII.liii.8); and Tektaios and Angelion, who made the *Apollo of Delos* (Pausanias II. xxxii.5).

BIBLIOGRAPHY

Pausanias: *Guide to Greece*
Pliny: *Natural History*
J. Overbeck: *Die antike Schriftquellen zur Geschichte der bildenden Künste bei den Griechen* (Leipzig, 1868), nos 321–7, 328–31
H. Brunn: *Geschichte der griechischen Künstler*, i (Stuttgart, 1889), pp. 32–8
I. B. Romano: *Early Greek Cult Images* (PhD diss., U. PA, 1980), pp. 162–89
E. D. Francis and M. Vickers: 'Green Goddess: A Gift to Lindos from Amasis of Egypt', *Amer. J. Archaeol.*, lxxxviii (1984), pp. 68–9

SARAH P. MORRIS

Daidalos of Sikyon. *See under* POLYKLEITOS, §2.

Daido Moriyama. *See* MORIYAMA, DAIDO.

Dai Jin [Tai Chin; *zi* Wenjin; *hao* Jing'an, Yuquan Shanren] (*b* Qiantang, near Hangzhou, Zhejiang Province, 1388; *d* Hangzhou, 1462). Chinese painter. An account by Lang Ying (*b* 1487) provides the most extensive early biography of Dai Jin. As a young man, probably in the 1410s, Dai travelled to the capital at Nanjing with his father, who presumably worked there in some official capacity. Dai failed to make a name for himself in the capital and returned to Qiantang to resume his study of painting, which he had probably begun with a local Zhejiang master. His reputation grew such that *c.* 1425 he was recommended to the new emperor, Xuande (*reg* 1426–35), and he went to Beijing in the hope of securing an academy appointment. His plans were thwarted, however, by the envy of established painters, in particular Xie Huan (*fl c.* 1368–1435), a favourite artist and adviser to the Emperor, who claimed to detect anti-government bias in Dai's works. Unrolling a series of Dai's landscapes representing the four seasons, Xie remarked approvingly on the spring and summer scenes but took severe exception to the autumn scene, in which the artist had depicted a fisherman wearing a red coat, attire thought suitable for gentlemen–officials but not for commoners. Yuan-period (1279–1368) artists had sometimes painted scholars dressed as fishermen, implying thereby that the educated classes deliberately avoided service under their Mongol rulers. Xie adduced as evidence another of Dai's works, *Seven Worthies Passing the Barrier* (*c.* 1425–35; untraced), which was based on an old tale (*gushi*) recounting the flight of seven men from a tumultuous and badly ruled state. The Emperor agreed with Xie, and according to

Lang Ying the eunuch responsible for recommending Dai was executed. Dai, however, escaped at night to Hangzhou.

Several versions of this episode exist. Their dramatic content aside, they represent a deeper conflict, of a nature more aesthetic than political. Xie Huan belonged to the conservative mainstream of academy painters who were especially sensitive to the moral implications of their subject-matter. Traditional legends and historical events were evaluated as much for their ideological merit and contemporary relevance as for their narrative interest or technical excellence and style (for further discussion and illustration *see* ZHE SCHOOL). By Dai Jin's time, however, there was a gradual movement away from this form of artistic protocol, as evidenced by Dai's late works, which rarely included historical subjects.

Returning to Hangzhou, Dai lived in Buddhist temples, making paintings of door guardians and votive images. He may still have been pursued by officials from the imperial court, for he soon moved to Yunnan Province where he worked for the nobleman Mu Chen (1368–1439) and came into contact with Shi Rui (*fl c.* 1426–35), also from Qiantang. Shi was a court academy painter, but he appears to have been sympathetic to Dai and even fed and housed him during this period. Following the death of the Xuande emperor, Dai Jin returned to Beijing (*c.* 1440), and this time he was well received. Two high officials, the Grand Secretary, Yang Shiqi (1365–1444), and the Minister of Personnel, Wang Ao (1384–1467), became his patrons. The imperial painting academy at this time certainly did not exist along the lines of the Song-period (960–1279) academy, when it was a fixed institution with strict entrance examinations, rigorous training and prestigious painting competitions (*see* CHINA, §V, 4(i)(c)); nevertheless, Dai's position at the capital was probably that of a respected and widely imitated court master. Towards the end of his life he returned again to Hangzhou. Claims by later biographers that he died in poverty are belied by the quality of his late works and conflict with the statement by his contemporary Du Qiong (1396–1474) that 'late in life he begged to return to Hangzhou, where his fame had increased'.

Dai Jin is commonly referred to as the founder of the Zhe school (named after Zhejiang, his home province), a controversial formulation that contrasts the tradition of professional and academy painters with that of the scholar–amateurs or literati (Chin. *wenren*) of the almost contemporary WU SCHOOL, founded by Shen Zhou. The lineage that claimed Dai as its inspiration grew to include not only academy painters but also those with similar styles and painters who neither imitated Dai nor were natives of Zhejiang. The Zhe-school label is arguably most dubious when applied to Dai Jin himself, for he drew from both professional and amateur artists of the Song and Yuan periods and rests uncomfortably in so general a category.

Most of the few dated works by the painter that survive are from the period 1439–46. Nevertheless, the 50 or more paintings that have his signature or are attributed to him exhibit a coherent stylistic development. The late dated paintings and a large group done in a consistent and obviously mature manner stand apart from Dai's earlier works, which frequently follow styles of the Southern Song (1127–1279) academy masters Ma Yuan and Xia Gui

Dai Jin: *Fishermen on the River* (detail), handscroll, ink and colours on paper, 0.46×7.40 m, first half of the 15th century (Washington, DC, Freer Gallery of Art)

(the so-called Ma–Xia manner). An early work is the *Hermit Xu You Resting by a Stream* (hanging scroll; Cleveland, OH, Mus. A.): a tired traveller sits beneath spindly pines beside a fast-running stream; behind him rise tall peaks. This painting resembles several Southern Song models but is perhaps closest to the well-known *Listening to the Wind in the Pines* (1246; Taipei, N. Pal. Mus.) by Ma Lin. In it Dai adapted two features of academy painting of that period: the diagonal composition, also known as 'one-corner composition', in which the foreground figures and landscape elements are placed in one corner of the painting in the manner of Ma Yuan; and the depiction of forms, dispensing, however, with the fine shading of Southern Song painting and relying instead on slashing, nail-like strokes and a more brusque handling of the brush. His work is less a nostalgic homage to the Southern Song academic manner than a creative reworking of it.

Other early works include two paintings with Yuan influences: *Listening to the Rain* (hanging scroll; Tokyo, Yeo Teng Young priv. col., see Cahill, pl. 13), based on similar pictures by Sheng Mou, and the curiously agitated *Five White Deer Beneath Pines* (hanging scroll; Taipei, N. Pal. Mus.), unreliably attributed to Dai in an inscription by Wen Zhengming (for a discussion of attribution see Cahill, pp. 49–50 and pl. 14).

Dai Jin's mature style can be characterized as follows. First, the scale of his figures in relation to their settings resembles Yuan paintings more than those of the Song period. Rather than being dwarfed by massive mountains, for instance, they are large enough to provide a lively visual focus. Second, his compositions are generally made up of large, equally prominent units: the viewer is more conscious of the organization of elements across the painting's surface than of receding spatial relationships. Third, Dai does not model landscape masses with texture strokes (*cun*) but relies on washes, dark ink and unpainted, 'highlighted' areas to suggest substance, recesses, shadow and light. Fourth, his landscape forms often seem unstable;

they lean and thrust forward precariously, a trait seen in Yuan painting. Finally, the brushwork itself is dynamic. Fluid outlines and swiftly executed 'split-brush' (*pobi*) strokes imbue Dai's work with movement while not detracting from its formal strength and beauty.

Foremost among Dai's later works is an undated handscroll, *Fishermen on the River* (see fig.). Although it borrows from Wu Zhen's paintings of the same subject, Dai's figures have the distinction of being real fishermen, not scholar–officials idly passing the time. Simple, cartoon-like figures line the river and its banks—conversing, drinking, bringing in nets, carrying fishing gear and poling their boats. The work exudes unparalleled ease and technical mastery. Rapidly executed in ink and muted earth tones, it evades monotony by the dynamism of the brushwork and by small touches of red and blue. The bold diagonals of the boats on the water and a constantly changing shoreline maintain the viewer's interest throughout the length of the handscroll.

Later writers varied in their opinions on Dai Jin. A century or so after his death the literary critic Wang Shizhen noted that '[in Suzhou] he was no longer considered equal to Shen Zhou...but in the eyes of real connoisseurs he will be considered the foremost of all Ming painters'. Xie Zhaozhe (*fl c.* 1600), revealing a bias in favour of the Wu school, wrote of the 'low quality' of his work, and other critics described it as more skilful than inspired.

BIBLIOGRAPHY

DMB: 'Tai Chin'

O. Sirén: *Chinese Painting: Leading Masters and Principles* (London, 1956–8), iv, pp. 128–33

K. Suzuki: *Mindai kaigashi no kenkyū: Seppa* [Research on the history of Ming-period painting: the Zhe school] (Tokyo, 1968)

E. J. Laing: *Chinese Paintings in Chinese Publications, 1956–1968* (Ann Arbor, 1969), p. 190

S. E. Lee: 'Early Ming Painting at the Imperial Court', *Bull. Cleveland Mus. A.*, lxii (Oct 1975), pp. 242–59

J. F. Cahill: *Parting at the Shore: Chinese Painting of the Early and Middle Ming Dynasty, 1368–1580* (New York, 1978), pp. 45–53

M. Loehr: *The Great Painters of China* (Oxford, 1980), pp. 266–9

Images of the Mind: Selections from the Edward L. Elliot Family and John B. Elliot Collections of Chinese Calligraphy and Painting at the Art Museum, Princeton University (exh. cat., ed. W. C. Fong; Princeton U., NJ, A. Mus., 1984), pp. 138–42

M. A. Rogers: 'Visions of Grandeur: The Life and Art of Dai Jin', *Painters of the Great Ming: The Imperial Court and the Zhe School* (exh. cat., ed. R. M. Barnhart; New York, Met.; Dallas, TX, Mus. A.; 1993), pp. 127–94

VYVYAN BRUNST, with JAMES CAHILL

Dai Mangong. *See* DOKURYŪ SHŌEKI.

Daintree, Richard (*b* Hemingford Abbots, Hunts [now Cambs], 13 Dec 1832; *d* Beckenham, Kent, 20 June 1878). Australian photographer and geologist of English birth. In 1852 he withdrew from studies at Christ's College, Cambridge (1851–2) for health reasons, joined the Australian gold-rush, and spent two unproductive years prospecting in Victoria. The experience inspired an interest in geology, and in 1854 he joined the Victorian mineralogical survey as an assistant surveyor. During six months' stay in London in 1856 and 1857 to study assaying at the Royal School of Mines, he became interested in photography. On his return to Victoria in 1858 he collaborated with Antoine Julien Fauchery (1823–61) in producing *Sun Pictures of Victoria*, a series of photographs illustrating various aspects of the life and scenery of the colony. Having rejoined the newly named Victorian Geological Survey (1859), in 1860 he began regularly using photography as a substitute for hand-drawn diagrams, and as a topographical record. With government financial support he produced photographs publicizing the colony for the International Exhibition in London of 1862.

Wearied of routine surveying, Daintree invested in a pastoral enterprise in North Queensland, resigning from the survey in 1865. In Queensland he made unofficial journeys of exploration, discovering gold and other minerals in several locations, which led to his appointment in 1868 as Geological Surveyor of North Queensland, which he combined with extensive photography of the region. Commissioned by the Queensland government to exhibit his photographs and mineral specimens in London in 1871, he was appointed as the colony's Agent-General in 1872. Throughout his four years' term he used his photographic and geological knowledge to promote Queensland's interests. Though embroiled in administrative difficulties inherited from his predecessor, he was personally vindicated, and shortly before his death was created CMG.

BIBLIOGRAPHY
G. Bolton: *Richard Daintree: A Photographic Memoir* (Brisbane, 1965)
D. Reilly and J. Carew: *Sun Pictures of Victoria: The Fauchery–Daintree Collection, 1858* (Melbourne, 1983)

ROBERT SMITH

Dainzú. ZAPOTEC site in Mexico, in the Valley of Oaxaca. Dainzú (Zapotec: 'hill of the Organ cactus') is in fact only one excavated section of the ancient city now called Macuilxóchitl. Investigations have revealed stone reliefs of ball-players in action, massive architectural terracing against a hillside and embedded reliefs of a kind unique to Mesoamerica. Associated remains suggest that construction began before *c.* 200 BC, and other evidence indicates that placement of the sculptures occurred periodically between *c.* 200 BC and *c.* AD 200. Costumes of priestly figures on four stones, like pottery fragments found near by, may date to AD 100–200. However, an adjoining ballcourt was built for the ball-game as played after *c.* AD 1000, when players did not touch the ball with their hands. From *c.* AD 1200 to 1600 Macuilxóchitl was the capital of a territory ruled by MIXTEC lords, and its rivalry with LAMBITYECO may have caused that town to be moved further away. Macuilxóchitl itself remained important until after the Spanish Conquest.

Figures of 31 ball-players, each holding a ball in his hand, are depicted in low relief on 30 stones in one wall. Their faces are protected by barred masks, most of which show an appendage resembling a jaguar's ear. Two of the four seated priests are in jaguar costumes and appear to hold jaguar heads in their outstretched hands; a third wears a jaguar mask (see fig.). A tomb door only a short distance below the reliefs has doorjambs carved to represent a jaguar's forelegs, while the lintel shows the head. The figure termed *Danzante* 41, built into 'Mound J' at MONTE ALBÁN, wears a costume similar to those of the ball-players and holds a jaguar head. Several reliefs, some probably from Dainzú, have been built into houses and public buildings at nearby Tlacochahuaya and Macuilxóchitl. Many others are carved into bedrock at the top of the Dainzú hill. These include a pair of figures possibly performing a sacrifice: a corpulent man, wearing a ballplayer's mask and holding a ball in his right hand, stands on a hill glyph, identified by an animal head inside the hill; in his left hand is what seems to be a knife, pointed at a figure shown falling at his feet; the supposed victim also wears a ball-player's mask, surmounted by a jaguar head. Dozens of detached, masked heads are carved on the surrounding rocks.

The Dainzú figures and the Monte Albán *danzantes* are alike shown in strange postures (for illustration *see* MONTE ALBÁN), one on the face of each stone slab. However, while the *danzantes*, most of which are probably several centuries earlier, are little more than outlines incised in the

Dainzú, relief depicting a priest in a jaguar mask, stone, *c.* 200 BC–AD 200

stone, at Dainzú the backgrounds of most figures are cut away, making them true reliefs.

BIBLIOGRAPHY
I. Bernal: 'The Ball Players of Dainzú', *Archaeology*, xxi (1968), pp. 246–51
——: 'The Olmec Presence in Oaxaca', *Mexico Q. Rev.*, iii (1968), pp. 5–22
——: 'Stone Reliefs in the Dainzú Area', *The Iconography of Middle American Sculpture*, New York, Met. cat. (New York, 1973), pp. 13–23
I. Bernal and A. Seuffert: 'Esculturas asociadas del Valle de Oaxaca', *Corp. Ant. Amer.*, vi (1973) [whole issue]
——: *The Ballplayers of Dainzú*, Artes Americanae, ii (Graz, 1979)
J. Marcus: 'Monte Albán II in the Macuilxóchitl Area', *The Cloud People: Divergent Evolution of the Zapotec and Mixtec Civilizations*, ed. K. V. Flannery and J. Marcus (New York, 1983), pp. 113–15

JOHN PADDOCK

Dairy. Farm building where milk is separated and butter and cheese are produced. Dairies were an important part of country-house economy and developed with the fashion for the *ferme ornée* (ornamental farm) in Britain, and to a lesser extent in France and Germany, in the late 18th century. The dairy was often the most decorative of farm buildings, and many were supervised by the lady of the house. The most famous example is Marie-Antoinette's dairy by Richard Mique at the Petit Hameau at Versailles (1782–5). As a feature of a park or garden their style varied considerably, from the chinoiserie dairy Henry Holland designed at Woburn, Beds (*c.* 1789), or the Moorish dairy at Sezincote, Glos (*c.* 1808), by Samuel Pepys Cockerell, to the Gothick at Mullearne, Perth (1824), attributed to Richard Dickson (1792–1857), and the rustic of John Nash's Blaise Hamlet, Avon (*c.* 1804).

The method of producing milk products played an important role in dairy design. Keeping the building cool and clean was a priority. Generally they were placed apart from the farmstead, in an isolated position in the park or near the house, often north-facing and even sunk a few feet into the ground (e.g. at Uppark, W. Sussex, NT, *c.* 1810–13). Thatch was a popular material for roofing (e.g. at Althorp House, Northants, 1786; by Henry Holland and the Countess Spencer). Some were surrounded by a verandah to shade the windows, which generally had ground or stained glass; sometimes they were unglazed but covered in wire-mesh to encourage air circulation. Fountains also helped to lower the temperature at Arundel, W. Sussex, Sezincote and Belvoir, Leics. Dairy windows were exempted from the 1796 window tax if they were unglazed and if the words 'Dairy' and 'Cheese Room' were painted over the door in roman letters two inches high. Generally the building had at least two rooms, sometimes with an additional scullery or scalding room, and larger ones even had accommodation for the dairymaid. Many had a separate tea-room for the ladies and their guests, for example the Strawberry Room at Hamels, Herts (by Sir John Soane, 1783). Ceilings were usually plain to prevent dust from contaminating the milk. Marble, slate or stone flags were typical washable floor coverings with marble or tiled walls. Some were lined with local minerals such as the Derbyshire alabaster used by Samuel Wyatt (1737–1807) at the Tower of the Winds (1803), Shugborough, Staffs. Delft tiles were replaced by Wedgwood Queens-ware (glazed earthenware) in the 1770s.

The dairy as part of a *ferme ornée* was popular in France in the late 18th century, for example at the Hameau at Chantilly (1773) by Jean-François Leroy (1729–91) and 'l'enclos de la laiterie' conceived by Hubert Robert and constructed in 1785–8 by Jacques-Jean Thévenin for Marie-Antoinette at Rambouillet. In Germany a notable example is Johann Gottlieb Brendel's Gothick sham-ruin dairy for Frederick William II on the Pfaueninsel, Berlin (*c.* 1795). The fashion for the decorated dairy continued until the early 20th century, when agricultural developments and the growth of the large commercial dairy signalled its decline.

BIBLIOGRAPHY
J. M. Robinson: *Georgian Model Farms* (Oxford, 1983)
G. Jellicoe and others, eds: *The Oxford Companion to Gardens* (Oxford, 1986)

VICTORIA MERRILL

Daisenberger. *See* DOSSENBERGER.

Daitō Kokushi [Shūhō Myōchō] (*b* Harima [now in Hyōgo Prefect.], 1282; *d* Kyoto, 1337). Japanese Zen abbot and calligrapher. It is to Daitō Kokushi ('national teacher Daitō') that the abbots of virtually all modern Japanese Rinzai Zen temples trace their religious heritage, and he was one of Japan's foremost monk–calligraphers. Daitō took monastic orders as a youth and at the age of about 21 became a disciple of Kōhō Kennichi (1241–1316), who had studied in Japan under the Chinese master Wuxue Zuyuan (1226–86), and who was a son of Emperor GoSaga (*reg* 1242–6). By 1305 Daitō was studying Zen under Daio Kokushi [Nanpo Jōmyō] (1235–1308), a monk who had studied for eight years in China and under whom Daitō achieved enlightenment. Daitō's early, graceful, Japanese-style calligraphy may have been the result of his training under Kōhō Kennichi. The early style is fluid, yet betrays a penetrating strength in the use of the brush tip. A fine example is his two *Enlightenment Verses* recording his experience of enlightenment (ink on paper, 410×500 mm; 1307; Kyoto, Daitokuji; Important Cultural Property). After Nanpo's death Daitō lived in a retreat or, according to legend, under the bridges of Kyoto with beggars, and eventually founded the hermitage north-west of Kyoto which, under the patronage of the emperors Hanazono (*reg* 1308–18) and GoDaigo (*reg* 1318–39), was to become the great temple Daitokuji (*see* KYOTO, §IV, 5). Daitō's religious spirit is illustrated in a famous incident, when he broke a bone in his leg, an earlier injury to which had prevented him from assuming the full lotus position, took the posture, wrote a traditional deathbed poem (*yuige*) and died.

Daitō is known for his mastery of the calligraphic style of the Northern Song-period (AD 960–1126) Chinese literatus HUANG TINGJIAN, whose wild-cursive script (Jap. *kyōsō*; Chin. *kuang cao*) combined forceful independence with restrained, rounded forms and remarkable consistency. Daitō seems to have learnt this style by studying under a number of Chinese Zen monks who were living in Japan; it is first seen in his writing in the mid-1320s. The calligraphy of his *Instructions for Zen Practice* (ink on paper, 334×1380 mm; 1330; Kyoto, Daitokuji, Daisen'in; National Treasure) inscribed for the nun Sōgo (n.d.), for example, demonstrates a thin, bony style executed with compassion and force. The most famous example of his last years, the remarkably long ceremonial announcement (untitled; 328×8359 mm; Kyoto, Daitokuji, Shinjuan; National Treasure) shows a still more mature hand overflowing with an almost overwhelming power.

BIBLIOGRAPHY

S. Furuta: 'Daitō Kokushi no bokuseki' [Daitō Kokushi's calligraphy], *Shodō zenshū* [Complete collection of calligraphy], ed. K. Shimonaka, xix (Tokyo, 1957), pp. 20–28

M. Maruoka, ed.: *Daitokuji bokuseki zenshū* [Complete collection of calligraphy from Daitokuji] (Tokyo, 1984)

H. Dumoulin: *Japan* (1990), ii of *Zen Buddhism: A History* (New York, 1990)

JOSEPH D. PARKER

Dakhla Oasis. The largest of Egypt's western oases (l. *c.* 120 km), *c.* 400 km west of Luxor. It was inhabited from earliest times, and although distant from the civilization of the Nile Valley, it was never isolated: most of the preserved monuments show a strong Egyptian influence. The absence of pressure on space and building materials, combined with a kind climate, has left a series of monuments largely complete and in a reasonable condition. Although there is a group of mud-brick mastaba tombs at Balat that dates to the late 6th Dynasty (*c.* 2325– *c.* 2150 BC), the best-preserved remains date to the Ptolemaic, Roman and Byzantine periods (304 BC–AD 641). The Tomb of Kitinos (1st century BC) at Balat is the only masonry tomb with carved relief decoration known in the southern oases. Its style is purely Egyptian, though rather provincial, and typical of the period. More important are the contemporary tombs of Petosiris and Pedubastis at Qaret el-Muzzawaqa, where the painted decoration bears an unusual juxtaposition of religious scenes rendered in the traditional Egyptian style and three excellent zodiac ceilings and several owners' portraits executed in the much freer Classical style. The nearby sandstone temple of Deir el-Haggar (1st century AD) has carved relief decoration in the sanctuary and on the façade. A Roman period room at Amhada is decorated with frescoes of mythological subjects, including the *Rescue of Andromeda by Perseus*, the *Adultery of Aphrodite and Ares* (see fig.) and the *Return of Odysseus*. The paintings, unique in Egypt, are executed in a lively style and date to *c.* AD 325, during the time of Constantine the Great. There is also a Greco-Roman Temple of Thoth at el-Qasr, a Roman town site at el-Kharab and numerous Christian monuments.

BIBLIOGRAPHY

H. E. Winlock: *ed-Dakhleh Oasis: Journal of a Camel Trip Made in 1908* (New York, 1936)

L. M. Leahy: 'The Roman Wall Paintings from Amheida', *J. Soc. Stud. Egyp. Ant.*, x (1980), pp. 331–78

J. Osing and others: *Denkmäler der Oase Dachla von dem Nachlass von Ahmed Fakhry* (Mainz, 1982)

A. J. MILLS

Dakin, James H(arrison) (*b* Hudson, NY, 24 Aug 1806; *d* Baton Rouge, LA, 10 May 1852). American architect. He spread eclectic historicism to the western states in the mid-19th century. Dakin was first trained as a carpenter but in 1829 entered the office of architects Ithiel Town and Alexander Jackson Davis in New York. Highly skilled as a draughtsman, in 1832 he became a full partner in the firm. He was responsible for the Rockaway Marine Pavilion (destr.), a large Grecian-style hotel on Long Island. Soon after starting his independent practice in 1833 he designed the Bank of Louisville (1834–6), KY, an excellent example of his adaptation of Greek elements for an American business building. The details recall similar motifs that appeared in Minard Lafever's books, for which Dakin drew some of the plates. In 1835 Dakin joined his younger brother, Charles Bingley Dakin (1811–39), and James Gallier (i) in an architectural firm they had set up in New Orleans, LA, the year before. Although Gallier withdrew a short time after, the brothers soon had a busy practice, designing large hotels, churches and public buildings in Louisiana and Alabama, most of them in the Greek Revival style. Following his brother's death, Dakin won the competition for his most important building, the Louisiana State Capitol (1847) in Baton Rouge, with an innovative castellated Gothic Revival design. He also became supervising architect of the US Custom House in New Orleans but was forced to relinquish this position due to political pressure. He was highly regarded by contemporaries and was invited by Thomas Ustick Walter in 1836 to join in forming the short-lived American Institution of Architects.

BIBLIOGRAPHY

T. F. Hamlin: *Greek Revival Architecture in America* (New York, 1944/*R* 1964)

A. Scully jr: *James Dakin, Architect: His Career in New York and the South* (Baton Rouge, 1973)

LELAND M. ROTH

dal. For pre-19th-century Italian proper names with this prefix, *see under* the first part of the name for individuals active before *c.* 1500; *see under* the second part of the name for those active *c.* 1500–*c.* 1800.

☐

Dalbono, Eduardo [Edoardo] (*b* Naples, 26 Nov 1841; *d* Naples, 23 Aug 1915). Italian painter and illustrator. His father was the literary scholar and art critic Carlo Tito Dalbono (1817–80). Around 1850 he was taught by the

Dakhla Oasis, detail of a wall painting showing the *Adultery of Aphrodite and Ares*, Amhada, *c.* AD 325

engraver Augusto Marchetti (1818–71) in Rome. He then enrolled at the Accademia in Naples, where his teachers were Giuseppe Mancinelli (1813–75) and Domenico Morelli; he also studied with Nicola Palizzi. He contributed a history painting and a *Study of a Mill* (untraced; see Dalbono, p. 39) to the last Bourbon exhibition in Naples in 1859. His interests in these years were divided between historical themes, landscapes and folklore subjects. He produced the *Excommunication of King Manfredi* (untraced, see Giordano) for a historical painting competition in 1866 and exhibited it in Naples (1868) and Parma (1870). This work clearly follows in the tradition of Saverio Altamura (1826–97) and Bernardo Celentano in that it is painted from a specially lit modello, the details of costume have been carefully researched and the architectural background showing the castle of Barletta is painted from photographs. Dalbono's *On the Terrace* (Rome, G.N.A. Mod.) takes a different approach, portraying a middle-class family in the open air with a view of the city in the background. Here more attention is paid to the effect of daytime lighting, while the sketchy painting style suggests a link with the contemporary experiments of the Tuscan MACCHIAIOLI and the painters of the SCUOLA DI RESINA.

Dalbono participated in many exhibitions held by the Naples Società Promotrice di Belle Arti, showing for example *From Frisio to Santa Lucia* (1866), the *Piazza of the Gesù Nuovo* (1867; both Naples, Capodimonte) and the *Legend of the Mermaids* (1871; Naples, Mus. N. S Martino), which became one of his best-known works. His interpretation of the myth of Parthenope as both a pleasing symbolic fable and an intensely sensual scene led to commissions for decorative works that brought him great commercial success. In 1878 he visited Paris for the first time and, through the mediation of Giuseppe De Nittis, signed a contract with the French dealer Adolphe Goupil. For Goupil, Dalbono produced a number of paintings including *Clam Fisher*, *Song of the Sea* and the *Beach at Mergellina* (all untraced). His approach in such works, which appealed to the tastes of the upper middle classes and the aristocracy, involved a somewhat superficial idealization of subject-matter, a rich and varied palette, studiedly attractive compositions (sometimes to the point of affectation) and a refined and painstaking technique.

Dalbono was a member of the Circolo Artistico founded in 1888 by Giuseppe Caravita, Prince of Sirignano (1849–1920), and he carried out various decorative cycles (now destr.), for example at Palazzo Sirignano and at Villa Rendel at Posillipo. He also painted religious works, illustrated books and such journals as *L'illustrazione italiana* and contributed designs for the theatre; for the Teatro San Carlo in Naples, for example, he painted the drop-curtain. In 1897 Dalbono became Professor of Painting at the Reale Istituto di Belle Arti and in 1905 he was made curator of the picture gallery of the Museo Nazionale, both in Naples.

BIBLIOGRAPHY
C. T. Dalbono: *Ultima mostra di belle arti in Napoli* (Naples, 1859)
V. Pica: 'Edoardo Dalbono', *Emporium*, xiv (1901), pp. 243–58
A. Margaux: 'A Painter of Naples: Edoardo Dalbono', *The Studio*, lii (1911), pp. 39–42
O. Giordano: *Edoardo Dalbono: I giorni e le opere* (Milan, 1915)
E. Giannelli: *Artisti napoletani viventi* (Naples, 1916), pp. 176–83
V. Pica: 'Edoardo Dalbono illustratore', *Emporium*, xliii (1916), pp. 323–42
E. Guardascione: *Napoli pittorica: Ricordi d'arte e di vita* (Florence, 1943), pp. 181–6
C. Siviero: *Questa era Napoli* (Naples, 1950), pp. 289–97

MARIANTONIETTA PICONE PETRUSA

Dale, Chester (*b* 3 May 1883; *d* New York, 16 Dec 1962). American financier and collector. He made his fortune in stockbroking and investment banking. In 1911 he married Maud Murphy (1873–1953), a painter and writer. He began to collect seriously in the early 1920s, later investing in the Galerie Georges Petit in Paris, and in 1934 he retired to devote more time to collecting. He initially collected work by American painters, from John Smibert to Arthur B. Davies. In the mid-1920s his wife persuaded him to concentrate on French painting of the late 18th and the 19th centuries. He bought rapidly, and by 1928, when his collection was first shown publicly, it comprised 300 paintings.

By 1940 the 700 works in the collection constituted a historical survey ranging from Edouard Manet's *The Old Musician* (1862), Vincent van Gogh's *Olive Trees* (1888) and Pablo Picasso's *Family of Saltimbanques* (1905) to Amedeo Modigliani's *Gypsy with Baby* (1919). Dale also bought the occasional Old Master painting and contemporary works by Salvador Dalí such as *Sacrament of the Last Supper*. He was a donor and trustee of a number of American museums but was most involved with the National Gallery of Art, Washington, DC, of which he became a trustee in 1943 and President in 1954. In 1941 he lent the first of many major works to this museum and in 1962 bequeathed it 250 paintings, including 150 previously on loan.

BIBLIOGRAPHY
'Chesterdale's Way', *ARTnews*, li/8 (1952), pp. 18–21, 53, 64
G. T. Hellman: 'Profiles: Custodian', *New Yorker* (25 Oct 1958), pp. 49–76
A. B. Saarinen: *The Proud Possessors* (New York, 1959), pp. 172, 375

A. DEIRDRE ROBSON

Dalem [Dale; Dalen], **Cornelis van** (*b* Antwerp, *c.* 1530; *d* Breda, 1573). Flemish painter. He was the son of a well-to-do cloth merchant living in Antwerp, but of Dutch origin. Cornelis received a humanistic education. His father, who owned land in Tholen, as a vassal to the Counts of Holland and Zeeland, was dean of the chamber of rhetorics' 'De Olijftak' (The Olive Branch) in Antwerp in 1552–3. According to van Mander, Cornelis was himself learned in poetry and history and only painted as an amateur, not for a living. Documents in the Antwerp archives invariably refer to him as a merchant, never as a painter, which no doubt accounts for the small number of known paintings by him. He learnt to paint with an otherwise unknown artist, Jan Adriaensens, who had also taught his older brother Lodewijk van Dalem (*fl* 1544–85). The latter was inscribed as a pupil in 1544–5 and became a master in the guild in 1553–4. Cornelis was himself inscribed a year after his brother, and he became a master in 1556, the same year he married Beatrix van Liedekercke, a member of an Antwerp patrician family. They lived in Antwerp until late 1565, when, apparently for religious reasons, they left for Breda, together with the artist's mother, who had become a widow in 1561. In 1571 several local witnesses testified that van Dalem, who was then living in a small castle, 'De Ypelaar', in Bavel, near Breda, was strongly suspected of being a heretic. He was never seen in church and was said, on the contrary, to have often attended Protestant services and to have publicly expressed contempt for 'Papists'.

Van Dalem limited his subject-matter to rocky landscapes and views of cities, producing paintings notable for their subtle tonal colour and their intense atmosphere. These qualities make him, along with his contemporary Pieter Bruegel the elder, important in the development of landscape painting in the Netherlands. The figures in van Dalem's paintings were often added by other artists, such as Gillis Mostaert or Jan van Wechelen (*fl* 1557). It is uncertain whether this co-operation continued after van Dalem left Antwerp in 1565. Van Dalem's paintings, the chronology of which remains to be established, were highly appreciated by 17th-century connoisseurs; Rubens owned a landscape by him, to which he added the figure of St Hubert hunting. Van Dalem's *Landscape with Primitive Men*, of which only scattered fragments survive, was in the collection of Cornelis van der Geest and was included in Willem van Haecht's imaginary depiction of his art gallery (1628; Antwerp, Rubenshuis; *see* COLLECTING, fig. 1).

BIBLIOGRAPHY

L. Burchard: 'Der Landschaftsmaler Cornelis van Dalem', *Jb. Preuss. Kstsamml.*, xlv (1924), pp. 66–71
F. Winkler: 'Nachtrag zu Cornelis van Dalem', *Jb. Preuss. Kstsamml.*, xlvi (1925), pp. 255–8
L. Demonts: 'Un Paysage de Cornelis van Dalem au Musée du Louvre', *Gaz. B.-A.*, xlii (1926), pp. 60–64
C. Sterling and O. Benesch: 'Neue Gemälde des Cornelis van Dalem', *Jb. Preuss. Kstsamml.*, liv (1933), pp. 123–30
F. Grossmann: 'Cornelis van Dalem Re-examined', *Burl. Mag.*, xcvi (1954), pp. 42–51
——: 'Notes on some Dutch and Flemish Paintings at Rotterdam', *Burl. Mag.*, xcvii (1955), pp. 335–6
C. Sterling: 'Cornelis van Dalem et Jan van Wechelen', *Studies in the History of Art Dedicated to William E. Suida* (London, 1959), pp. 277–88
E. Brochhagen: 'Zu Hans van Wechelen und Cornelis van Dalem', *Münchn. Jb. Bild. Kst*, xiv (1963), pp. 63–104
C. van de Velde: 'Archivalia over Cornelis van Dalem', *Miscellanea Jozef Duverger*, i (Ghent, 1968), pp. 237–46
T. Gerszi: 'Les Antécédents du tableau de Jan Breughel *Paysage rocheux avec Saint Antoine* et son influence', *Bull. Mus. N. Hong. B.-A.*, li (1978), pp. 107–22, 219–25

CARL VAN DE VELDE

Dalem [Dael; Dale; Dalen], **Jan van** (*fl*?Antwerp, 1646–60). Flemish painter. According to the Antwerp guild registers, he became a pupil of Daniel de Middelaer in 1632–3 and eight years later was registered as a master in the Guild of St Luke. Van Dalem's style of painting shows the influence of Anthony van Dyck and Theodoor Rombouts. Only three signed works by him are known: a *Portrait of a Family around a Harpsichord* (1646; Tournai, Mus. B.-A.), a *Bacchus* (1646; Vienna, Ksthist. Mus.) and the *Portrait of a Young Painter* (ex-Altes Schloss, Schleisheim). Among the paintings attributed to him are two other versions of *Bacchus* (Florence, Pitti, and Kortrijk, priv. col.) and a *Portrait of a Woman at a Harpsichord* (Vienna, Gemäldegal. Akad. Bild. Kst.). In Archduke Leopold William's collection there were depictions of a

Woman with Mirror and Scales and a *Bust of a Young Woman*, and Diego Duarte owned a *Bacchus* and a *Mercury with Cupid*. However, the artist cannot have been responsible for the pendants of a *Youth Holding an Egg in his Right Hand* (ex-Ksthandel M. L. de Boer, Amsterdam, 1955) and a *Young Man with a Wine Glass in his Right Hand* (ex-Brod Gal., London, 1955), which were once together in the Liechtenstein collection: each is signed and dated *J. van Dalen fec. in Roma 1631*. This early date and their Italianizing style suggest that they should be ascribed to a namesake. Two further pendants mentioned in Diego Duarte's inventory, depicting a male and a female pilgrim '. . .painted in Rome' according to their inscriptions, may have been executed by the same namesake. A *Cupid* (Vienna, Ksthist. Mus.) is signed *F. J. v. d. F*, but this monogram does not provide sufficient evidence for the work to be added to van Dalem's oeuvre.

BIBLIOGRAPHY

P. Rombouts and T. Van Lerius: *De liggeren en andere historische archieven der Antwerpsche Sint-Lucasgilde*, 2 vols (Antwerp, 1872)
H. Hymans: *Gent und Tournai* (Leipzig, 1902), pp. 113–14
G. Glück: 'Aus Rubens Zeit und Schule: Bemerkungen zu einigen Gemälden der Kaiserlichen Galerie in Wien, IV: Jan van Dalem', *Jb. Ksthist. Samml. Allhöch. Ksrhaus.*, xxiv (1903), pp. 32–5
——: *Rubens, van Dijck und ihr Kreis* (Vienna, 1933), pp. 250–55, 407
B. Nicolson: '*Youth Holding a Glass of Wine* by Jan van Dalem', *Burl. Mag.*, xciii (1955), pp. 94–6
Rubens e la pittura fiamminga del seicento nelle collezioni pubbliche fiorentine (exh. cat. by D. Bodart, Florence, Pitti, 1977), p. 104

VERONIQUE VAN PASSEL

Dalgıç Ahmet Ağa. *See* AHMED DALGIÇ.

Dalí (Domènech), Salvador (Felip Jacint) (*b* Figueres, 11 May 1904; *d* Figueres, 25 Jan 1989). Spanish Catalan painter, draughtsman, illustrator, sculptor, writer and film maker. One of the most prolific artists of the 20th century, his fantastic imagery and flamboyant personality also made him one of the best known. His most significant artistic contribution, however, was through his association with SURREALISM.

1. Childhood, training and early work. 2. Surrealism: the paranoiac–critical method. 3. The break with Surrealism: post-war painting.

1. CHILDHOOD, TRAINING AND EARLY WORK. Dalí was born into the happy, if ideologically confusing, family of a respected notary. His father was a Republican and atheist, his mother a Roman Catholic. He was named Salvador in memory of a recently dead brother. This had a profound effect: his subsequent experimentation with identity and with the projection of his own persona may have developed out of an early understanding of himself as 'a reply, a double, an absence' (Dalí, 1970, p. 92). His childhood provided him with the fertile memories, both true and false, that fill his autobiography and resound in his art. Catalonia remained important to Dalí, but for its landscape rather than its separatist politics. He painted for much of his life in a house he bought in Port Lligat, near the family holiday home in Cadaqués, but the radical political beliefs that his father had taught him were to be replaced by a self-conscious monarchism and Catholicism. Dalí's first contact with painting was through Ramon Pichot (1872–1925), a friend of his father, who was an Impressionist painter and associate of Picasso. Early

landscapes show the influence of Pichot's Impressionism, but by 1921, when he entered the Real Academia de Bellas Artes de San Fernando in Madrid, his work already exhibited a characteristically paradoxical interest in both formal innovation and aspects of the academic tradition. He was experimenting with such styles as divisionism and Futurism, but publishing (in the review *Stadium*) his admiration for Velázquez, Goya, El Greco, Dürer, Leonardo and Michelangelo.

At the Academia, Dalí met the poet Federico García Lorca and the film maker Luis Buñuel. These friendships nurtured Dalí's natural arrogance and exhibitionism, until he was suspended and eventually expelled for inciting the students to rebel and for withdrawing from an examination because he felt the teachers were not qualified to judge his work. Expulsion, however, coincided with artistic recognition, and increasing success at student shows culminated in his first one-man exhibition at the Galería Dalmau in Barcelona in 1925. The pictures were evidence of Dalí's continuing diversity: Cubist and Purist works from 1924; realism and a kind of Neo-classical Cubism from 1925; an Ingres-like purity of line in a drawing of his father and sister of 1925; mysterious still-lifes in the manner of Carlo Carrà and Giorgio de Chirico; and a clarity drawn from Neue Sachlichkeit artists displayed in the views of his sister looking out of a window (e.g. *Girl Standing at the Window*, 1925; Madrid, Mus. A. Contemp.). It is a diversity paralleled in the expanding range of outlets for Dalí's creative energy as he became involved in the Spanish avant-garde, which centred on Barcelona. From 1927 he submitted monthly contributions to the journal *L'Amic des arts*, designed scenery (1927) for Lorca's first play, *Mariana Pineda*, illustrated friends' books and, in 1928, collaborated with Lluís Montanyà and Sebastià Gasch on the Catalan anti-artistic *Manifest Groc*, which included Surrealist painters and writers in its final list of 'great painters of today'.

2. SURREALISM: THE PARANOIAC–CRITICAL METHOD. By 1928 Dalí was moving towards Surrealism. The disconnected, ambiguous forms of such paintings as *Senicitas* (1926–7; Madrid, Cent. Reina Sofía) show the influence of Yves Tanguy and especially of Giorgio de Chirico, whose work Dalí knew through the periodical *Valori Plastici*, founded to promote the ideals of Pittura Metafisica. In 1929 he made the film *Un Chien andalou* (for illustration *see* EXPERIMENTAL FILM) with Buñuel, which aimed to disorientate the viewer by simulating the conditions of the dream. It also made use of montage to achieve a transformation of objects, which was to become characteristic of Dalí's version of Surrealism, but which his paintings had not as yet achieved. The film was made and screened in Paris and brought Dalí to the attention of André Breton, the principal theorist of Surrealism. In summer 1929 the dealer Camille Goemans, René and Georgette Magritte, and Paul and Gala Eluard visited Cadaqués to look at his paintings. They found him in a state of hysteria, working on *Dismal Sport* (310×410 mm; Claude Hersaint priv. col., see 1980 exh. cat., no. iv), a tiny yet frantically detailed painting, which established both the hallucinatory realism of his mature technique and the principal elements of his private cosmogony. In the deep space of a dream world a dislocated, auto-erotic drama is played out. Dalí's characteristic symbols of grasshopper, lion and ants proliferate around the mouthless self-portrait mask that reappeared in the *Great Masturbator* (1929; priv. col., see 1980 exh. cat., no. 35) and among the soft watches of the *Persistence of Memory* (1931; New York, MOMA). This mask provides both a foretaste of the double images of the 1930s and a memory of the mutating objects of *Un Chien andalou*: its shape was inspired by a large rock on the coast at Cadaqués. There are photographs (see 1989 exh. cat., pp. 78–9) of Dalí alongside it.

With *Dismal Sport* Dalí was officially accepted into the Surrealist movement. Eluard titled it, and it was exhibited at Dalí's first one-man show in Paris at the Galerie Camille Goemans in November 1929. Breton's catalogue preface formalized Dalí's membership of the group: 'It is perhaps with Dalí that for the first time the windows of the mind are opened fully wide.' Dalí began contributing theoretical articles to Surrealist periodicals such as *Surréalisme au service de la révolution* and *Minotaure*. *Dismal Sport* also led to Dalí's association with and later marriage to Gala Eluard. She became fascinated by him over the summer and did not return home with her husband. She cured Dalí of his hysteria and of the sexual impotence expressed in the painting, and she eventually became his wife, manager and muse. She is often blamed for his alienation from his family and for his transformation into Avida Dollars, Breton's anagrammatic name for Dalí's American, ad-man persona. He painted her repeatedly throughout his career, and she became a vehicle for his visual experimentation (e.g. *Portrait of Gala: Gala's Angelus*, 1935; New York, MOMA).

Dalí's principal theoretical contribution to Surrealism was his 'paranoiac–critical method'. First expounded in his article 'L'Ane pourri' (1930), it was responsible for his famous double images and essentially required the artist to perceive and paint different images within a single collection of shapes. It depended on an understanding of paranoia as an interpretative delusion—a view shared with the psychoanalyst Jacques Lacan—and on the virtuoso technique Dalí learnt from his study of the Old Masters. The double images themselves had their roots in the painting of Giuseppe Arcimboldo. The *Endless Enigma* (1938; priv. col., see Ades, p. 129) offers six different interpretations of one set of shapes: the realistic style blurs visual fact and paranoiac fantasy.

Dalí saw the paranoiac–critical method as a means of destabilizing the world, believing everything the viewer saw was potentially something else. In this process his drawings, in pencil or pen and ink, played a vital part, allowing him to experiment freely with resemblances and associations (e.g. *Study for Suburb of the Paranoiac–critical Town*, 1935; Edward James priv. col., see 1970–71 exh. cat.). In its dependence on hidden meanings the method owed much to Sigmund Freud's understanding of the dream as an expression of unconscious desire, in which one object may signify another. Dalí's obsession with a picture by Jean-François Millet, the *Angelus* (1857–9; Paris, Mus. d'Orsay), clarifies this. He used a paranoiac resemblance between the pose of the woman and that of a post-copulatory female praying mantis about to eat her mate to trigger a re-reading of the pastorally religious image as one

1. Salvador Dalí: *Metamorphosis of Narcissus*, oil on canvas, 511×781 mm, 1937 (London, Tate Gallery)

of sexual aggression, which could be recycled into his own work. The *Atavism of Twilight* (1933; Berne, Kstmus.) is one of a number of paintings that develop the *Angelus* theme. Despite its origins in Freud's writings, the paranoiac–critical method did not allow a viewer to psychoanalyse Dalí. The ideas behind the multiple images were as self-conscious as their technical realization. Freud himself remarked to Dalí, whom he met in London in 1938: 'It is not the unconscious that I seek in your pictures but the conscious.' Dalí was in tight control of his 'delusions': 'The only difference between me and a madman is that I am not mad' (1980 exh. cat., p. 11).

Dalí showed Freud the *Metamorphosis of Narcissus* (1937; London, Tate; see fig. 1). In it he linked the Freudian implications of the paranoiac–critical method to its Surrealist application. Metamorphosis occurs as a viewer accepts an invitation to visual exchange and notices that the fossil hand-and-egg shape mirrors that of the staring Narcissus. The viewer is present at the most creative moment of simulated paranoia (the realization that one thing looks like another) and is drawn into the world of Surrealist possibility.

An attempt to communicate with a viewer the excitement of a world governed by paranoiac misunderstanding led Dalí to the development of the Surrealist object. In 1931, at Breton's request, he proposed six different types of object as potential embodiments of Surrealist principles, but it was the 'symbolically functioning object' that became the most popular. In 1936 there was an exhibition at the Galerie Charles Ratton in Paris of objects that allowed people to 'touch their dreams': Dalí made the *Lobster*

Telephone (1936; London, Tate) and the *Face of Mae West (Usable as a Surrealist Apartment)* (1936; Figueres, Teat.–Mus. Dalí), from which came the famous Mae West-lips sofa. Dalí was part of the Surrealist group throughout the 1930s. He contributed to the International Surrealist Exhibitions at the New Burlington Galleries in London in 1936 (he appeared in a diving suit) and at the Galerie Beaux-Arts in Paris in 1938, and he continued to contribute to *Minotaure*. He illustrated a key Surrealist text, the Comte de Lautréamont's *Les Chants de Maldoror* (Paris, 1934), painted a classic Surrealist dream-picture in *Sleep* (1936; priv. col., see 1980 exh. cat., no. 155) and collaborated with the fashion designer Elsa Schiaparelli (1890–1973). He also produced two paintings in response to the Spanish Civil War: *Soft Construction with Boiled Beans: Premonition of Civil War* (1936; Philadelphia, PA, Mus. A.) and *Autumn Cannibalism* (London, Tate). The apparent political commitment expressed in these two paintings—the first shows a distorted figure pulling itself apart, the second a couple eating each other—is misleading. During the 1930s Dalí's political indifference turned into a frivolity that alienated him from the other Surrealists. In 1937 he painted a series of pictures 'celebrating' Adolf Hitler (e.g. *The Enigma of Hitler*, 1937; priv. col., see 1980 exh. cat., no. 160). This was thought to be in bad taste and contributed to his expulsion from the movement.

3. THE BREAK WITH SURREALISM: POST-WAR PAINTING. Dalí spent World War II in the USA, where he became a fashionable figure, and had a retrospective (1941–2) at MOMA in New York. He painted portraits,

2. Salvador Dalí: *Christ of St John of the Cross*, oil on canvas, 2.05×1.16 m, 1951 (Glasgow, St Mungo Museum)

subjecting society women such as *Mrs Styler-Tass* (1945; Berlin, Neue N.G.) to the rigours of the paranoiac–critical method, and dressed shop windows. He created a dream sequence for Alfred Hitchcock's film *Spellbound* and planned a cartoon, *Destino*, with Walt Disney. His personal flamboyance found lucrative outlets in recycling old imagery for advertising: Avida Dollars was born and immortalized in Dalí's sensational autobiography, *The Secret Life of Salvador Dalí* (New York, 1942).

When Dalí returned to Europe in 1948, his dissociation from Surrealism was complete. He painted mainly in Spain, with a renewed eclecticism of technique and style worked out in paintings and drawings dealing with history, art history, science and religion. His output was enormous. The work seems very different from his pre-war production but essentially still turned around the contradiction between his desire on the one hand to emulate the achievements of the Old Masters and on the other to pursue visual experiments. This contradiction remained evident in the elements of optical illusionism, photographic realism, divisionism, Abstract Expressionism, Pop art, stereoscopy and holography that all appeared in his later work. There was also a continued interest in double images. The *Madonna of Port Lligat* (1949; Milwaukee, WI, Marquette U., Haggerty Mus. A.) doubles the Virgin with Gala, who becomes Christ in the *Sacrament of the Last Supper* (1955; Washington, DC, N.G.A.). Columbus carries a pennant bearing the image of Gala in the *Dream of Christopher Columbus* (1958–9; St Petersburg, FL, Dalí Found. Mus.) and is also linked with Dalí himself: 'A Catalan, Christopher Columbus, discovered America, and another Catalan, Salvador Dalí, has just rediscovered Christopher Columbus' (Dalí, 1939). Doubling is obvious in the later stereoscopic pictures such as *The Chair* (1975; priv. col., see 1980 exh. cat., no. 236), where the image itself is doubled, or in holograms that effect real transformations of objects. The *Portrait of my Dead Brother* (1963; priv. col., see 1980 exh. cat., no. 218) returns the obsession with doubles to its source. The dots that make up this image link it to Dalí's post-war excitement in scientific discovery: 'The atomic explosion of 6 August [1945] shook me seismically. Thenceforth, the atom was my favourite food for thought' (Ades, 1982, p. 174). His fascination with the atom was typically symbolic: his paintings are concerned with a general sense of the divisibility of matter. In *Exploding Raphaelesque Head* (1951; priv. col., see Ades, p. 176) Dalí doubled a Raphael Virgin with the interior of the Pantheon in Rome and shattered them both so that they reveal a structure based on the perfect logarithmic spirals of a rhinoceros horn, a post-war obsession. The same theme is taken up in many of his drawings of this period, such as the *Corpuscular Madonna* (1952; Birmingham, AL, Mus. A.).

The last major exhibition in Dalí's lifetime was at the Centre Georges Pompidou in Paris in 1979. The show drew from 60 years of work and displayed the later scientific and mystic paintings alongside the earlier masterpieces of paranoia. It included the *Anti-protonic Assumption* (1956; New York, Mrs Bruno Pagliai priv. col.), a painting that shows the influence of the Abstract Expressionists in its gestural paint application, but which is pure Dalí in subject-matter: the Virgin ascending through the power of her own anti-protons. *Christ of St John of the Cross* (1951; Glasgow, St Mungo Mus.; see fig. 2), one of the most hauntingly successful of the religious paintings, was also exhibited. Its extreme foreshortening was inspired by a visionary drawing by St John and achieved by Dalí by painting a model seen from above through a glass floor. After his death Dalí was buried in the Teatre–Museu Dalí in Figueres, which had been founded in 1974 as both a repository of his work and a theatrical monument to his ideas and personality, and where he had given drawing classes to groups of international students in his last years. Much of Dalí's work was eagerly collected in the USA. There are important examples in Britain, however, thanks largely to the interest of Surrealist associate and collector Edward James.

See also DRESS, fig. 58.

WRITINGS

'L'Ane pourri', *Surréalisme Serv. Révolution*, i (1930), pp. 9–13; Eng. trans. in *This Quarter*, v/1 (1932), pp. 49–54
La Femme visible (Paris, 1930)
'L'Interprétation paranoïaque-critique de l'image obsédante, *L'Angélus* de Millet', *Minotaure*, i (1933), pp. 65–7
La Conquête de l'irrationel (Paris, 1935; Eng. trans., New York, 1935)
Métamorphose de Narcisse (Paris, 1937; Eng. trans., 1937) [a poem to accompany the painting]
Declaration of Independence of the Imagination and the Rights of Man to his own Madness (New York, 1939)
The Secret Life of Salvador Dalí (New York, 1942)
with P. Halsman: *Dalí's Mustache: A Photographic Interview* (New York, 1954)
Le Mythe tragique de 'L'Angélus' de Millet: Interprétation paranoïaque–critique (Paris, 1963) [an account of the rereading of Millet's image that Dalí claimed to have written and lost in the 1930s]
Journal d'un génie (Paris, 1964; Eng. trans., 1965)
Dalí par Dalí de Draeger (Paris, 1970; Eng. trans., 1972)

BIBLIOGRAPHY

Salvador Dalí (exh. cat., preface by A. Breton; Paris, Gal. Goemans, 1929)
F. Cowles: *The Case of Salvador Dalí* (London, 1959)
R. Descharnes: *The World of Salvador Dalí* (New York, 1962; rev. 1972) [contains photos of Dalí's life and work, with captions by the artist]
Exposition Dalí, avec la collection de Edward F. W. James (exh. cat., Rotterdam, Mus. Boymans–van Beuningen, 1970–71)
A. Reynolds Morse: *Salvador Dalí: A Guide to his Works in Public Collections* (Cleveland, OH, 1973)
Salvador Dalí: Retrospective, 1920–1980 (exh. cat., ed. D. Abadie; Paris, Pompidou, 1979)
Salvador Dalí (exh. cat. by S. Wilson, London, Tate, 1980)
D. Ades: *Dalí*, World A. (London, 1982; rev. 1988)
Salvador Dalí: Surrealist Drawings (exh. cat. by A. Reynolds Morse, St Petersburg, FL, Dalí Found. Mus., 1988)
Salvador Dalí, 1904–1989 (exh. cat., ed. K. v. Maur; Stuttgart, Staatsgal.; Zurich, Ksthaus; 1989)
M. Etherington-Smith: *Dalí: A Biography* (London, 1992)
R. Deschasnes and G. Neret: *Salvador Dalí, 1904–1989: The Paintings*, 2 vols (Cologne, 1993)
Salvador Dalí: The Early Years (exh. cat., ed. M. Raeburn; London, Hayward Gal., 1994)

For further bibliography *see* SURREALISM.

FIONA BRADLEY

Daliwe, Jacques (*fl c.* 1380–1416). Franco-Flemish draughtsman. He signed a sketchbook (Berlin, Staatsbib., lib. pict. A 74) consisting of studies of a variety of physiognomic types, occasional drawings of animals and a few more developed scenes of a pilgrimage, an innovative *Man of Sorrows*, an *Annunciation* and a *Coronation of the Virgin*. The stylistic, thematic and compositional similarities of some of these drawings, executed in grisaille on boxwood leaves, with manuscript illumination produced for Jean, Duc de Berry, especially those for the Hours of the Holy Ghost in the Très Belles Heures de Notre Dame (Paris, Bib. N., MS. nouv. acq. lat. 3093), suggest that Daliwe was employed at the Duc de Berry's court *c.* 1380–1416. The drawings are thought to be trial sketches. They fall into four stylistic groups: one showing affinities with the style of Jacquemart de Hesdin and André Beauneveu; naturalistic studies related to the miniatures of the *Livre de chasse* (*c.* 1405–10; Paris, Bib. N., MS. fr. 616); sketches related to Burgundian art influenced by the Limbourg brothers; and drawings associated with the French court style of the 1420s. It has also been suggested that Daliwe was influenced by the Italianate art of Spain and of the court at Avignon.

BIBLIOGRAPHY
M. T. Hasselberg: *Liber pictus A 74 der preussischen Staatsbibliothek zu Berlin: Ein Beitrag zur Erforschung mittelalterlicher Skizzen- und Musterbücher* (Zeulenroda, 1936)
R. W. Scheller: *A Survey of Medieval Model Books* (Haarlem, 1963), pp. 109–11
H. Kreuter-Eggemann: *Das Skizzenbuch des 'Jacques Daliwe'* (Munich, 1964); review by M. Frinta in *A. Bull.*, lii (1970), pp. 100–02
U. Jenni and M. Winter: *Das Skizzenbuch des Jacques Daliwe* (Leipzig, 1987)
ROBERT G. CALKINS

Dall'Abacco, Antonio. *See* LABACCO, ANTONIO.

Dallaire, Jean (Philippe) (*b* Quebec, 9 June 1916; *d* Vence, 27 Nov 1965). Canadian painter. He studied painting at the Ecole Technique (1932–3) in Hull, Quebec, and then at the Central Technical School of Toronto. In 1936 he set up a studio with Dominican monks in Ottawa, receiving two mural commissions from them, one for the chapel at Ottawa and the other for the Fall River Monastery, MA. In 1938 he won a state scholarship to travel to France where he came under the influence of Surrealism, especially that of Dalí, and produced such works as *Bagatelle* (1940; Montreal, priv. col., see 1979 exh. cat., p. 7).

From 1940 to 1944 Dallaire was held prisoner by the Germans at Saint-Denis, near Paris, returning to Canada via London in 1945. His work immediately following this experience reflects his mixed feelings of bitterness and joy at being released. From 1946 to 1952 he taught at the Ecole des Beaux-Arts in Quebec and then until 1957 worked for the Office National du Film in Ottawa, producing several animated films. From 1947 to the early 1950s his work shows the influence of tapestry, especially that of Jean Lurçat, with whom he worked in 1949, as in the gouache *Nude Growing (Daphne)* (1949; Montreal, Mus. F.A.). During the 1950s he experimented with Cubism, which provided the inspiration for *Still-life with Fish* (1956–7; Montreal, Mus. A. Contemp.), with its overlapping, geometrical elements. In 1957 his paintings became abstract, sometimes resembling views of microscopic organisms, as in *Julie* (1957; Montreal, Mus. F.A.). In 1959 he moved to Paris, then to Vence and Péone in Provence. In his later works he returned to the fantastic subjects that often pervaded his work, as in *Birdy* (1961–2; Montreal, Mus. A. Contemp.).

BIBLIOGRAPHY
Jean Dallaire: Retrospective (exh. cat. by P. Dumas, Montreal, Mus. A. Contemp., 1969)
Jean Dallaire (exh. cat. by A. M. Sioui, Montreal, Mus. A. Contemp., 1979)
□

Dallas. American city in Texas, situated on the flat prairies in the north-eastern part of the state, 48 km from Fort Worth. Dallas is the second largest city in Texas (population *c.* 943,000) and was one of the fastest-growing metropolitan areas in the USA during the 1980s. It was founded on the east bank of the Trinity River by John Neely Bryan, who established a trading post there in 1841 to supply pioneers moving west. Bryan laid out a grid that established the east–west orientation of the central city streets; another grid established a few years later intersected the first at 30°, creating a grid-shift that continues to hinder traffic in downtown Dallas. Dallas rose to urban significance with the advent of the railways in the 1870s, when it became a transportation hub and commercial centre for the cotton trade, and by 1890 it had a population of *c.* 38,000. Only isolated buildings remain of its 19th-century architecture—notably the fine Richardsonian Romanesque Dallas County Courthouse (by Orlopp & Kusener, 1891–2; remodelled 1966)—but surviving steel-framed commercial buildings of the early 20th century include the Old Sanger Brothers Store (1910) by Lang and Witchell, remodelled for use by the Dallas County Community College District. The city's adjacent warehouse district, better preserved than the contemporaneous business district, was adapted as the West End Historic District in 1975.

Following electrification and the expansion of street railways in the 1890s, residential development began to extend outwards, and a number of nearby settlements were absorbed into the city. East Dallas was annexed in 1890 and Oak Cliff, on the west bank of the Trinity, in 1903; Highland Park, founded in 1907, along with neighbouring University Park, remain autonomous suburbs entirely encapsulated by the expanded municipality of Dallas. Handsome streets of stately homes, of which Swiss Avenue is the best preserved, were interspersed with enclaves of bungalows. However, the problems provoked by congestion in the city centre and unplanned residential expansion led civic leaders to commission their first formal urban plan (1911) from George Kessler (1862–1923), who was well known for his plans for Kansas City (1893) and Cincinnati (1907). Kessler's grand proposal in the City Beautiful tradition, recommending the creation of a civic centre and an extensive system of parks and boulevards, was never implemented, but Turtle Creek Parkway and White Rock Lake, two of the city's finest amenities, were developed from his proposals.

Expansion of the residential suburbs continued in the 1920s, when the Spanish Colonial Revival style became popular for both public and domestic architecture. At the same time, the tendency to concentrate commercial buildings in the city centre was reflected in a series of Art Deco skyscrapers erected in the late 1920s, including the Dallas Power and Light Building (1930) and the Lone Star Gas Building (1931), both by Lang and Witchell. In 1936 Dallas

Dallas, Hall of State, by George L. Dahl, Paul Cret and others, 1936

hosted the Texas Centennial Exposition, and the impressive complex of exhibition buildings erected in the existing State Fairgrounds forms one of the most extensive concentrations of Art Deco art and architecture in Texas. Designed by a consortium of local architects supervised by George L. Dahl (1894–1987), with Paul Cret as design consultant, the complex also contained three museums, including the Dallas Museum of Fine Art, and the Hall of State (see fig.).

After World War II urban sprawl was increasingly shaped by the construction of highways and a growing number of subcentres. Six comprehensive urban plans were commissioned between 1927 and 1980, but few restraining measures were adopted. The biggest single factor in the growth of the city in the 1970s and 1980s was the economic impact of the Dallas–Fort Worth Airport (1973) by Hellmuth, Obata & Kassabaum and Brodsky, Hopf & Adler, designed as one of the largest, most technologically advanced airports in the world. Several large corporations subsequently moved their headquarters to the city, which became the banking and financial centre of the Southwest. New commercial satellites in North Dallas and at Las Colinas were developed, and the city centre acquired several new generations of modern skyscrapers, among which the Allied Bank Plaza (1968; now First Interstate Bank Tower) by I. M. Pei and Partners, with the accompanying Fountain Place by landscape architect Dan Kiley, form a significant ensemble.

Beginning in the late 1970s, Dallas received a new generation of monumental public buildings: I. M. Pei's City Hall (1978), the new Dallas Museum of Art (1984; expanded 1992) by Edward Larrabee Barnes and the Dallas Symphony Hall (1987) by I. M. Pei. The last two form components of an arts district on the north-west corner of the central business district and join Frank Lloyd Wright's Dallas Theatre Center (1959) on Turtle Creek among the cultural facilities of Dallas. The collections of the Museum of Art, expanded with new acquisitions, notably in the decorative arts, are supplemented by the Meadows Museum and Gallery of Southern Methodist University and by numerous private galleries.

BIBLIOGRAPHY

The Prairie's Yield: Forces Shaping Dallas Architecture from 1840 to 1962 (Dallas, 1962)

W. McDonald: *Dallas Rediscovered: A Photographic Chronicle of Urban Expansion, 1870–1925* (Dallas, 1978)

D. Collier: 'Art Deco Architecture in Dallas', *Perspective*, xi/1 (1982), pp. 8–12

A. Toews: 'Spanish Colonial Revival in Dallas: The Work of Fooshee and Cheek', *Perspective*, xiii/2 (1984), pp. 9–15

D. Dillon and D. Tomlinson: *Dallas Architecture, 1936–1986* (Austin, 1986)

L. Speck and R. Payne: *Landmarks of Texas Architecture* (Austin, 1986)

J. Henry: *Architecture in Texas: 1895–1945* (Austin, 1993)

JAY C. HENRY

Dallaway, Rev. James (*b* Bristol, 20 Feb 1763; *d* Leatherhead, June 1834). English churchman and writer. He was educated at Trinity College, Oxford and subsequently entered the Church. In 1789 he was elected a fellow of the Society of Antiquaries. His first major work, *Inquiries into the Origin and Progress of the Science of Heraldry in England*, was published in London in 1792. Following a period in Turkey as chaplain to the British Ambassador, he published *Constantinople, Ancient and Modern* (London, 1779), which was translated into German in 1800. That same year Dallaway published in London the book he is best remembered for, *Anecdotes of the Arts in England, or Comparative Remarks on Architecture, Sculpture, and Painting, Chiefly Illustrated by Specimens at Oxford*, one of a number of contemporary works that sought to codify the achievements of the nascent British School. It was translated into French by Aubin-Louis Millin de Grandmaison in 1807. *Anecdotes* was followed by *Observations on English Architecture* (London, 1806). By 1811, owing to the patronage of Charles Howard, 11th Duke of Norfolk (1746–1815), Dallaway had secured a number of comfortable clerical livings. In 1816 he published *Of Statuary and Sculpture among the Antients*, again in London, an extremely valuable volume not least because two-thirds of the print-run was destroyed by fire at the publisher's warehouse. Dallaway was a fervent supporter of the aims of the British Institution, and in 1824 published a retrospective catalogue of works exhibited there since 1813. Between 1826 and 1828 Dallaway edited and republished Horace Walpole's *Anecdotes of Painting in England*, although by this time his casual amateurism looked increasingly anachronistic when set against the more polished and professional antiquarian publications of John Britton. His last published work was *A Series of Discourses upon Architecture in England* (London, 1833).

DNB   BIBLIOGRAPHY

MARTIN POSTLE

Dalmasio, Lippo di. *See* LIPPO DI DALMASIO.

Dalmasio (di Jacopo) Scannabecchi (*fl* 1342; *d* Bologna, 1373). Italian painter. He was old enough to act as a witness in 1342, which suggests that he was born before *c.* 1320. In 1350 he married the sister of Simone dei Crocefissi, to whom he entrusted his affairs during his residence in Pistoia *c.* 1365. Both Dalmasio and his son LIPPO DI DALMASIO were regularly employed in Pistoia, and the former is recorded in Bologna in 1350–56 and 1370–73.

Arcangeli attributed a *Crucifixion* triptych (1333, Paris, Louvre) to Dalmasio. Its rougher execution and more violent characterization are more typical of the Riminese-inspired phase of Bolognese painting, and the emotive faces of the Coronation figures closely resemble those of Simone dei Crocefissi. The use of bright scarlet shot with lemon-yellow reappears in a *Crucifixion* (Bologna, Pin. N.) and in the probably later *Deposition* (ex-Visconti di Modrone Col.; sold London, Sotheby's, 21 April 1982, lot 68), but in these works a wider, brighter range of pinks and greens is used.

No signed or documented works by Dalmasio Scannabecchi survive, but those attributed to him suggest that he was one of the earliest and finest of Bolognese painters. Longhi (1973) associated with him a group of Tuscan-influenced Bolognese works, including the *Crucifixion*

(Bologna, Pin. N.), frescoes of the *Life of St Francis* (*c.* 1343) in the Cappella Maggiore of S Francesco, Pistoia, and frescoes of the *Life of St Gregory the Great* (probably 1350–55) in the Bardi Chapel, S Maria Novella, Florence. These works show a particular affinity with Maso di Banco and also with the early work of Simone dei Crocefissi, supporting Longhi's hypothesis, although none shows costume features securely datable after 1342, when Dalmasio is first recorded. It has been suggested that their author worked as an assistant to Giotto on his altarpiece (Bologna, Pin. N.) for S Maria degli Angeli, Bologna. The much damaged frescoes in S Francesco, Pistoia, dated by a related inscription to 1343, are faithful copies of the *St Francis* cycle at S Francesco, Assisi. The frescoes at S Maria Novella, Florence, show elements of Dalmasio's later style, together with impressive architectural settings and a cool tonality reminiscent of the *Crucifixion* triptych for S Vitale, Bologna. The conciliar scene and the *Dictation of the Dialogues* draw on Bolognese academic imagery.

The Pistoia and S Maria Novella cycles are dated before 1340 by Bellosi and after 1356 by Skerl Del Conte following Bellosi's own early ideas: perhaps a date in the 1340s is most appropriate for the Bardi Chapel. These, and the slightly later panel paintings, a *Crucifixion* (Acton priv. col.), the *Deposition* and a dispersed predella (fragments, Dublin, N.G.) show Dalmasio to be a major influence on such artists as Jacopo Avanzi, Tomaso da Modena, Antonio Veneziano and possibly Agnolo Gaddi.

BIBLIOGRAPHY

F. Filippini and G. Zucchini: *Miniatori e pittori a Bologna: Documenti dei secoli XIII e XIV* (Florence, 1947), pp. 57–61, 153–61
G. L. Mellini: 'Commento a "Dalmasio"', *A. Ill.*, xxvii–xxix (1970), pp. 40–55
R. Longhi: *Lavori in Valpadana* (Florence, 1973)
M. Boskovits: *Pittura fiorentina alla vigilia del rinascimento* (Florence, 1975)
L. Bellosi: 'Moda e cronologia: Per la pittura di primo trecento', *Prospettiva*, 11 (1977), pp. 32–7
F. Arcangeli: *Pittura bolognese del '300* (Bologna, 1978), pp. 96–105, 228–33 [notes by M. Ferretti and P. G. Castagnoli]
M. Laclotte: *Retables italiens du XIIIe au XVe siècle*, Dossiers du Département des Peintures, xvi (Paris, 1978), pp. 14–17
R. Gibbs: 'Two Families of Painters at Bologna in the Later Fourteenth Century', *Burl. Mag.*, cxxi (1979), pp. 560–68
——: 'Cristoforo da Bologna or Dalmasio?', *Burl. Mag.*, cxxiv (1982), pp. 584–90
S. Skerl Del Conte: *Vitale e la sua bottega nella chiesa di Sant'Apollonia Mezzaratta* (Bologna, 1993), pp. 144–53

ROBERT GIBBS

Dalmata, Giovanni. *See* GIOVANNI DALMATA.

Dalmatic. *See under* VESTMENTS, ECCLESIASTICAL, §1(ii).

Dalmaticus, Georgius Matthei [Dalmatinac, Juraj Matejev]. *See* GIORGIO DA SEBENICO.

Dalmatie, Duc de. *See* SOULT, Maréchal.

Dalmatino, il. *See* BENCOVICH, FEDERICO.

Dalmau, José Ratés. *See* RATÉS DALMAU, JOSÉ.

Dalmau, Lluís (*fl* 1428–61). Spanish painter. The earliest reference to him is in 1428, when he is called 'painter of the city of Valencia' and is mentioned as being in the service of Alfonso V, King of Aragon. Dalmau remained in Alfonso's service for at least nine years, at times serving in a diplomatic capacity: he was sent to Castile in 1428, and in 1431 to the south Netherlands, although the duration and purpose of the latter visit are unknown. No works done for the King are known, and the only royal payment made to him was for some minor architectural work.

By 1438 Dalmau had moved to Barcelona, where he spent the rest of his career as a panel painter for various churches in and around the city. His most famous work was the *Virgin of the Councillors* (Barcelona, Mus. A. Catalunya; *see* BARCELONA, fig. 3). It depicts Barcelona's city council of 1443, the Virgin and Child with SS Andrew and Eulalia, and music-making angels. It echoes two works by Jan van Eyck, the Ghent Altarpiece (Ghent, St Bavo) and the *Madonna of the Canon van der Paele* (Bruges, Groeningemus.), both painted nearly a decade earlier or possibly during the period when Dalmau visited the Netherlands. The strong Eyckian motifs may have been included at the behest of the patrons. More typical of local styles and traditions is the centre panel of Dalmau's only other surviving work, the retable of *St Baudelius* (S Boi de Llobregat) of 1448. This painting may be more typical of his style, given the nature of his altarpiece commissions in Barcelona.

BIBLIOGRAPHY
J. Ainaud de Lasarte: 'Una taula documentada de Lluís Dalmau', *Cuad. Arqueol. Hist. Ciudad*, xii (Barcelona, 1968), pp. 73–84
A. Simonson Fuchs: 'The *Virgin of the Councillors* by Dalmau, 1443–1445: The Contract and its Eyckian Execution', *Gaz. B.-A.*, n. s. 5, xcix (1982), pp. 45–94
S. Alcolea Blanch and J. Gudiol Ricart: *Pintura gótica catalana* (Barcelona, 1987)

JUDITH BERG SOBRÉ

Dalou, (Aimé-)Jules (*b* Paris, 31 Dec 1838; *d* Paris, 15 April 1902). French sculptor. Dalou ranks among the greatest sculptors of the 19th century, alongside Antonio Canova, François Rude, Jean-Baptiste Carpeaux and Auguste Rodin. The son of a glovemaker, he was a modern urbanite who believed in the moral efficacy of craftsmanship and manual labour as well as the primacy of democracy and a secular social order. The imagery of his finest works bears witness to these beliefs.

After being encouraged to become a sculptor by Carpeaux, Dalou trained at the Petite Ecole (1852–4), where he learnt the fundamentals of drawing and modelling, and later studied at the Ecole des Beaux-Arts (1854–7), where he was admitted to the studio of Francisque Duret. Dalou's early ambitions were wholly conventional. He competed for the Prix de Rome four times but never won first prize. During the 1860s he exhibited four modest works at the Salon while earning his living as a decorative artist. His most impressive decorative work is in Paris at the Hôtel Menier and the Travellers' Club (formerly the Hôtel Païva). He first won critical and popular success at the Salon of 1870, when his *Embroiderer* (destr.; plaster cast from a preliminary sketch in Paris, Petit Pal.; reduction of final version, in bronze, Karlsruhe Mus.) was warmly received and purchased by the State. He was unable to execute an official commission for a marble version of this life-size genre subject because of the intervention of the Franco-Prussian War and the Commune.

Dalou's lifelong political sympathies were left-wing and republican (but not socialist, as has often been said), and he was confident of the eventual existence of a universal republic and brotherhood among mankind. With the declaration of the Commune in March 1871, he believed that this visionary era was dawning, and he became an enthusiastic participant in Gustave Courbet's Federation of Artists, assuming a curatorship of the Louvre under this branch of the Commune. After the fall of the Commune he was forced into exile, and he lived and worked in London from mid-1871 until the amnesty of 1879. While there he established his reputation with both the public and the critics with portraits and intimate subjects, for example *Mrs Gwynne* (terracotta, 1877; London, V&A) and *Woman Reading* (terracotta, 1872; Providence, RI Sch. Des., Mus. A.), which elaborated on the stylistic and narrative format first realized in his *Embroiderer*. English collectors were eager to own his works and commission portraits from him. He became a professor of sculpture at the South Kensington School of Art, where his foremost pupil was Edouard Lanteri, and was commissioned by Queen Victoria to design a memorial to her dead grandchildren for the Royal Chapel at Windsor Castle (1878). By the late 1870s, Dalou was tiring of his intimate subjects and portraits; he desired henceforth to make public sculpture of moral and social significance. The only such opportunity for him in England was the commission for a marble figure of *Charity* (1877–9) to surmount a drinking fountain behind the Royal Exchange in London (now replaced by a bronze replica).

When Dalou returned to Paris in 1879, he already held a commission from the City of Paris for the most ambitious undertaking of his career, a colossal ensemble in bronze entitled the *Triumph of the Republic* (1879–99; Paris, Place de la Nation; see fig.). This was the result of a competition that Dalou entered, but did not win, for a single figure of the Republic to serve as the focal point of the newly developed Place de la République. Dalou's Rubensian ensemble, with a lavishly decorated, lion-drawn chariot carrying the Republic, and allegorical figures of Liberty, Justice, Labour and Peace-Abundance, violated the terms stipulated by the competition but attracted enthusiastic support. Thanks to machinations of favourably disposed members of the left-wing city council of Paris, Dalou was commissioned to erect the group in the Place de la Nation, in the midst of the working-class Saint-Antoine quarter, a location with hallowed associations for the left since 1789. The monument was inaugurated twice with popular festivals meant to emulate those of the revolutionary past, once on the eve of the September elections in 1889, when a full-size patinated plaster version was inaugurated to stir up enthusiasm for candidates opposing General Boulanger's policies, and again in November 1899, when the ministry of Waldeck-Rousseau organized the inauguration of the definitive bronze as a celebration of the working classes. In both instances Dalou enthusiastically welcomed the propagandist use made of his monument.

The Salon of 1883 was dubbed 'the Salon of Dalou' by the critic Philippe Burty. Dalou re-entered the world of public exhibitions in Paris with two large and elaborate plaster reliefs, calculated to draw maximum attention to his mastery of the sculptor's art. The bronze version of

Jules Dalou: *Triumph of the Republic*, bronze, h. 11 m (excluding base), 1879–99 (Paris, Place de la Nation)

one of these reliefs, *Mirabeau Responding to Dreux-Brézé*, is in the main entrance hall of the Palais Bourbon. The other, *Fraternity*, is a secularized variant on a Baroque altarpiece type and is in the marriage chamber of the Mairie of the 10th *arrondissement* of Paris. These reliefs earned for Dalou the gold medal of that year's Salon, the Légion d'honneur, an offer of a professorship at the Ecole des Beaux-Arts (which he refused) and recognition as one of the great artists of his era.

Almost all of Dalou's public sculptures are in Paris. The superb bronze recumbent figures of Auguste Blanqui (exh. Salon 1885) and Victor Noir (exh. Salon 1890) in Père-Lachaise Cemetery are two of the most moving tomb sculptures of the 19th century. Both heroes of the left are portrayed as martyrs, and their tombs were intended as pilgrimage sites for what has been called 'the cult of revolutionary remembrance'. Three of Dalou's sculptural ensembles are in the Luxembourg Gardens: the ribald and exuberant *Triumph of Silenus* (exh. Salons 1885 and 1897), the monument to *Delacroix* (unveiled 1890), which is at once joyous and reverential, and the sober and dignified monument to *Scheurer-Kestner* (unveiled 1908), the Senator who was the first defender of Alfred Dreyfus. During the last years of his life Dalou envisaged a project that did not come to fruition, the *Monument to Workers*. For him this grandiose scheme would have been the crowning achievement of his life. His numerous preparatory clay sketches of individual workers (Paris, Petit Pal.) are among the most spontaneous and brilliant sculptures made during the 19th century. The Petit Palais in Paris houses the largest single collection of Dalou's work; outside Paris his work is known primarily through editions which were cast posthumously according to a decision made by the executors of his estate.

Lami
BIBLIOGRAPHY
P. Burty: *Salon de 1883* (Paris, 1883)
G. Geffroy: 'Dalou', *Gaz. B.-A.*, xxxiii (1900), pp. 217–28
M. Dreyfous: *Dalou: Sa vie et son oeuvre* (Paris, 1903)
H. Caillaux: *Dalou: L'Homme, l'oeuvre* (Paris, 1935)
Sculptures by Jules Dalou (exh. cat. by A. Ciechanowiecki, London, Mallett at Bourdon House Ltd, 1964)
Jules Dalou, 1838–1902 (exh. cat., Paris, Gal. Delestre, 1976)
J. Hunisak: *The Sculptor Jules Dalou: Studies in his Style and Imagery* (New York, 1977)
Dalou inédit (exh. cat., Paris, Gal. Delestre, 1978)
The Romantics to Rodin (exh. cat., ed. P. Fusco and H. W. Janson; Los Angeles, CA, Co. Mus. A., 1980), pp. 185–99
J. Hunisak: 'Rodin, Dalou, and the *Monument to Labor*', *Art the Ape of Nature: Studies in Honor of H. W. Janson*, ed. M. Baraschi, L. F. Sandler and P. Egan (New York, 1981), pp. 689–705
JOHN M. HUNISAK

Dalsgaard, Sven (*b* Randers, 1914). Danish painter and sculptor. He was self-taught and began to paint in 1928. At first he was interested in naturalistic painting, particularly the work of painters with connections with Randers, where he was living. In the early 1930s he became aware of contemporary artistic currents in Europe—particularly the work of the Bauhaus and of French artists—and for him this opened up a completely new perspective. He studied the writings of André Breton and the work of the Danish artist Vilhelm Bjerke-Petersen and became familiar with Surrealism, which had an immediate and lasting impact on his own paintings, sculptures and objects.

The content of Dalsgaard's paintings is often literary, with thin stick-figures, machine parts and other objects, as in *No-one at Home* (1953; Herning, Kstmus.), in which objects rendered with thick black outlines are displayed against a sombre monochrome background. The emotional force of his paintings, however, sometimes derives from his use of light, clear colours, as in *A Souvenir from Randers* (1964; Herning, Kstmus.). Motifs of the chair and the bird recur in his work, as does the image of the Danish flag. His sculptures tend to present an object in a great number of variations, and he often reworked the same object into a new 'reality'; this can be seen in his work *Chair with Feathers* (1968; Herning, Kstmus.), which consists of a feather-coated cafe chair suspended from the ceiling.

One of the most innovative Danish artists of the 20th century, Dalsgaard maintained that the work of art should display both creative and destructive aspects, a belief that underlies many of his sculptural works on the theme of the chair.

WRITINGS
Sven Dalsgaard (Vedelkær, 1966)
Varekatalog: Alt dette og mere til har jeg lavet 1939–1976 [Catalogue of goods: all this and more have I made, 1939–76] (Copenhagen, 1976)
Ord II [Word II] (Randers, 1983)
BIBLIOGRAPHY
Katalog: Tilrettelæggelse Sven Dalsgaard [Catalogue: Organization by Sven Dalsgaard] (exh. cat., ed. F. T. Frederiksen; Copenhagen, Charlottenborg, 1985)
K. Voss: 'Sven Dalsgaard', *Vort eget århundrede* (Copenhagen, 1975), v of *Dansk Kunsthistorie*, pp. 333–5
RIGMOR LOVRING

Dalton, Ormonde Maddock (*b* Cardiff, 3 Jan 1866; *d* Holford, Somerset, 2 Feb 1945). British Classical scholar and Byzantine archaeologist. He entered the Department of British and Mediaeval Antiquities at the British Museum under Sir A. W. Franks in 1896, and became Keeper of that department in 1921. His early interest in ethnography shifted to archaeology with the publication of his *Catalogue of Early Christian Antiquities* and his *Guide to Early Christian and Byzantine Antiquities*, which accompanied an exhibition that he organized. The Byzantine collections of the British Museum had not until then received much attention, and Dalton's scrupulous research gained him recognition as one of the leading early Byzantinists. Until his retirement in 1927 he regularly published and re-edited official guides and catalogues to the Early Christian and Byzantine antiquities in the British Museum, all of which became standard works on the subjects concerned. He also produced catalogues of the medieval collections and works of Byzantine art history. His most distinguished publication was the vast survey work *Byzantine Art and Archaeology*. In a separate volume entitled *East Christian Art: A Survey of the Monuments*, which followed his translation of Josef Strzygowski's *Origin of Christian Church Art* (1923) and pursued a similar argument, he dealt with the history of Byzantine architecture.

WRITINGS

Catalogue of Early Christian Antiquities and Objects from the Christian East in the Department of British and Mediaeval Antiquities and Ethnography of the British Museum (London, 1901)
A Guide to the Early Christian and Byzantine Antiquities in the Department of British and Mediaeval Antiquities (London, 1903, rev. 2/1903)
The Treasure of the Oxus, with Other Objects from Ancient Persia and India, Bequeathed to the Trustees of the British Museum by Sir Augustus Wollaston Franks (London, 1905)
Byzantine Plate and Jewellery from Cyprus in Mr Morgan's Collection (London, 1907)
Byzantine Art and Archaeology (Oxford, 1911)
trans. (with H. J. Braunholz): J. Strzygowski: *Ursprung der christlichen Kirchenkunst* (Leipzig, 1920) as *Origin of Christian Church Art* (Oxford, 1923)
A Guide to the Mediaeval Antiquities and Objects of Later Date in the Department of British and Mediaeval Antiquities of the British Museum (London, 1924)
East Christian Art: A Survey of the Monuments (Oxford, 1925)

BIBLIOGRAPHY

G. Hill: 'Ormonde Maddock Dalton', *Proc. Brit. Acad.*, xxxi (1945), pp. 357–73

□

Dalton, Richard (*b* ?1715; *d* London, 7 Feb 1791). English draughtsman, engraver and dealer. As agent to a number of patrons and subsequently librarian to George III, he was one of the most influential figures in the sphere of collecting in England for some four decades. He was the son of the Rev. John Dalton and younger brother of the Rev. John Dalton, poet and divine, whose connection with Algernon Seymour, Earl of Hertford (later 7th Duke of Somerset), forwarded Richard's early career in Italy. He had arrived there by 1739 and may have trained in Bologna; by 1741 he was studying under Agostino Masucci in Rome and was already active as a dealer, selling a collection of prints in that year to Henry Clinton, 9th Earl of Lincoln, and cultivating the patronage of Sir Erasmus Philipps, Bart.

In 1749 Dalton visited Calabria and Sicily and then, in his capacity as travelling draughtsman, joined the party of James Caulfeild, 1st Earl of Charlemont, on a tour of Egypt, Turkey and Greece. He was possibly the first English artist to record the ancient monuments of these places. A selection of drawings executed on this tour was engraved by Dalton and published in 1751; a definitive edition, *Antiquities and Views in Greece and Egypt . . . with Manners and Customs of the Inhabitants from Drawings Made on the Spot, A.D. 1749*, appeared in 1791.

After his return to England in 1750, Dalton was patronized by John Stuart, 3rd Earl of Bute, whose influence led to Dalton's attachment to the household of the Prince of Wales (later George III). In 1755 he was appointed librarian to the Prince. Dalton was again in Italy from 1758 to 1759, with commissions to buy drawings and medals for both the Prince and Bute and pictures for Sir Richard Grosvenor, later 1st Earl Grosvenor. Dalton became a powerful figure in the world of collecting but was much disliked by rival dealers who unfairly claimed that he was illiterate—for he was an excellent correspondent. Even after the Prince's accession to the throne in 1760, Dalton continued to act on occasion for individual collectors.

While the impetus for the King's acquisitive policy was due in part to Bute, Dalton was responsible for the details, and his concentration on the Italian schools may have been partly to complement Bute's personal interest in Dutch painting. Dalton's major coup was the completion in 1762 of the long negotiations to acquire for the King the collection of JOSEPH SMITH, British Consul in Venice. The highlight of the collection was a major series of works by Canaletto, including such paintings as *Venice: Piazza S Marco with the Basilica and Campanile* (*c.* 1730; Windsor Castle, Berks, Royal Col.). Smith's remarkable assemblage of Italian drawings was supplemented by the acquisition in 1762 of the drawings collection of Cardinal Alessandro Albani in Rome. Although the collection was purchased for the King by James Adam, it is likely that Dalton was in some way involved in the negotiations. In 1763–4 Dalton bought the major series of drawings by Guercino (now in Windsor, Royal Lib.) direct from the artist's heirs at the Casa Gennari at Bologna, having already secured a smaller selection from them in 1758. Dalton was later responsible for engaging Francesco Bartolozzi to engrave copies of the Guercino drawings in the King's possession. Bartolozzi also assisted Dalton in Italy by making drawings after pictures that Dalton was considering buying for the King.

Bute's fall from influence with George III was matched by the King's declining financial commitment to the royal collection, and from the mid-1760s Dalton's scope for acquisitions as librarian and, from 1778, as Surveyor of the King's Pictures was limited. However, his power in court circles continued to be regarded with jealousy by rival connoisseurs, and in the last year of his life he was suspected of hindering the projected acquisition by the Prince of Wales (later George IV) of pictures from the collection of Philippe II, Duke of Orléans. From 1770 to 1784 Dalton was Antiquary to the Royal Academy, having sat on the original committee for the foundation of the Academy in 1765. Dalton apparently did not hesitate to use his position to make additions to his own collection, which included paintings by Salvator Rosa, drawings by

Guercino and sculpture by Joseph Nollekens. It was sold at Christie's on 9 and 11 April 1791.

UNPUBLISHED SOURCES
Chester, Eaton Hall, Westminster MSS
Edinburgh, Register House, Rose of Kilravock MSS
Rothesay, Strathclyde, Mount Stuart, Bute MSS

BIBLIOGRAPHY
Obituary, *Gent. Mag.*, i (1791), pp. 188, 195
M. Levey: *The Later Italian Pictures in the Collection of Her Majesty the Queen* (London, 1964), pp. 28–35
F. Vivian: *Il console Smith: Mercante e collezionista* (Vicenza, 1971)
D. Sutton: 'Aspects of British Collecting, vii: From Florence to Venice', *Apollo*, cxvi (1982), pp. 390–404 (398)
W. S. Stanford and E. J. Finopoulos, eds: *The Travels of Lord Charlemont in Greece and Turkey, 1749* (London, 1984), pp. 232–3
D. Mahon and N. Turner: *Drawings by Guercino in the Collection of Her Majesty the Queen at Windsor Castle* (Cambridge, 1987)

FRANCIS RUSSELL

Dal'verzin. *See* DILBERDJIN.

Dalverzin Tepe [Dal'verzin-tepe; Dalverzine-tépé]. Site in Uzbekistan, on the Surkhan River between Denau and Shurchi. The fortified first settlement of the Greco-Bactrian period (3rd–2nd century BC) had evolved by the 1st century BC into a citadel, while a walled city (650×500 m) developed on the north side. The city is thought to have been the earliest Kushana capital, called Huzao in the Chinese *Han shu* ('History of the Han') by Ban Gu (AD 32–92). In the Great Kushana period (1st–3rd century AD) the city flourished but had declined by the 5th century, although a small 6th–7th-century settlement on top of the former citadel survived until the Arab conquest. Excavations have been carried out since 1960 by the Uzbekistan History of Art Expedition under G. A. Pugachenkova.

Within the fortifications the densely packed buildings are regularly arranged in quarters. Public utility services included an underground sewerage system with large ceramic tanks. The quarters are divided according to social class or trade. Religious buildings are found both within and outside the city. Dalverzin Tepe is typical of north Bactrian architecture of the Kushana period (*see* CENTRAL ASIA, §I, 2(i)(b)). Buildings are of mud-brick and *pisé*; roof beams are supported by walls and wooden pillars. The city and the citadel are enclosed by a moat and high fortified walls, which were greatly strengthened during the Great Kushana period. The monolithic walls have slightly projecting bastions and occasional casemates. The large private houses show variations on one basic layout: a pillared vestibule, a courtyard, a central reception room and a domestic shrine with an altar recess. The surrounding corridors lead to living and service rooms and a domestic courtyard at the rear of the building. In the general design of these houses the walls of the central room rise above those of the surrounding rooms. Religious buildings include two temples of the so-called Great Bactrian Goddess, comprising an entrance area, a sanctuary and subsidiary chambers. Two Buddhist temples, one inside and the other outside the city, contain the traditional sanctuary, stupa, chambers and courtyard for ritual circumambulation, subsidiary rooms and reception areas. Around the city are sites associated with the cult of the dead of various religions: a multi-chamber mausoleum for Zoroastrian rites and cemeteries containing burials in the earth or in terracotta sarcophagi.

An extensive potters' quarter comprised workshops and kilns. Sculpture of painted clay or clay and gypsum was found in the Temple of the Bactrian Goddess and in the Buddhist temples (*see* CENTRAL ASIA, §I, 3(ii)(a)). Small fragments of figural and ornamental wall paintings have survived in the temples and some of the houses (*see* CENTRAL ASIA, §I, 4(iii)(a)). Among a hoard of gold objects in one house were ingots with Kharoshthi inscriptions denoting weight and Kushana measures such as staters and drahms. Jewellery included bracelets, earrings, small coins, an ornate necklace, an ivory comb (see fig.), a Bactrian pectoral and a figural pendant of Scythian–Sarmatian type. Mass-produced terracotta statuettes associated with local cults included various matrix-stamped images of a Bactrian goddess and models of mounted horsemen. The process of artistic and technological development can be seen in the excavated ceramic wares. Finds from these excavations are held at the Institute of the History of Art, Tashkent.

BIBLIOGRAPHY
Ban Gu: *Han shu* [History of the Han]; Eng. trans. by A. F. P. Hulsewe as *China in Central Asia, the Early Stage, 125 BC–AD 23: An Annotated Translation of Chapters 61 and 96 of the History of the Former Han Dynasty*, intro. by M. A. N. Loewe (Leiden, 1979)
G. A. Pugachenkova: 'Kushanskaya skul'ptura iz Dal'verzin Tepe' [Kushana sculpture at Dalverzin Tepe], *Zhurnal Isk.*, i (1970), pp. 408–10
——: 'Antiochus Commagènes et le prince kushan: Du problème de la forme dans la sculpture de l'Orient hellénisé', *An. Archéol. Arabes, Syr.*, xxi (1971), pp. 113–14
G. A. Pugachenkova and B. A. Turgunov: 'Issledovaniya Dal'verzin-tepe v 1972 g.' [Investigations at Dalverzin Tepe in 1972], *Drevnyaya Baktriya* [Ancient Bactria] (Leningrad, 1974), pp. 58–74

Dalverzin Tepe, ivory comb, from edifice DT-9 (the sanctuary), 2nd–3rd centuries AD (Tashkent, Tashkent Museum of the Arts of Uzbekistan)

G. A. Pugachenkova: 'L'Art antique de la Bactriane IV s. avant–IV s. après notre ère d'après les fouilles dans la République Soviétique de l'Uzbekistan', *Acad. Inscr. & B.-Lett.: C.R. Séances* (1976), pp. 217–21

B. Ya. Stavisky: *Kushanskaya Baktriya: Problemy istorii i kul'tury* (Moscow, 1977); Fr. trans. as *La Bactriane sous les Kushans: Problèmes d'histoire et culture* (Paris, 1986), pp. 183–4, 265–7, figs 21, 34–5, pl. XXVII

G. A. Pugachenkova and others: *Dal'verzin-tepe: Kushansky gorod na yuge Uzbekistana* [Dal'verzin Tepe: a Kushana city in southern Uzbekistan] (Tashkent, 1978)

G. A. Pugachenkova: 'La Culture de la Bactriane du nord à la lumière des découvertes archéologiques dans la vallée de Soukhan-Dariya', *Colloques internationaux de C.N.R.S.*, 567 (Paris, 1978), pp. 291–6

——: *Les Trésors de Dalverzin-tépé* (Leningrad, 1978)

——: *Iskusstvo Baktrii epokhi Kushan* [The art of Bactria in the Kushana period] (Moscow, 1979)

——: 'Khram Baktriyskoy bogini na Dal'verzin-tepe' [The temple of a Bactrian goddess at Dalverzin Tepe], *Drevniy vostok i mirovaya kul'tura* [The ancient East and world culture] (Moscow, 1981), pp. 112–18

V. A. Tourgounov: 'Les Fortifications de Dalverzin-tépé: La Fortification dans l'histoire du monde grec', *Actes du colloque international: Geneva, 1986*, pp. 217–21

G. A. PUGACHENKOVA

Daly, César-Denis (*b* Verdun, 18 July 1811; *d* Wissous, 11 Jan 1894). French architect and writer. He was the son of John Daley [Daly], an Anglo-Irish naval purser held prisoner in France, and a French woman, Camille-Augustine Bernard. On the defeat of Napoleon in 1814 he was taken to England and sent to boarding school. At his father's death in 1824 his mother returned with Daly to her family property near Douai, where he entered the Collège Royal to study law. In 1829, however, he moved to Paris and entered the studio of Jacques Duban. At the outset of the Revolution of 1830 Daly went to Caen, returning to Paris in 1832, when he became involved in the Utopian Fourierist movement, contributing to the journals of *Le Glaneur* and *La Phalange*. He joined Charles Fourier's inner circle and in 1837 commenced designs for a phalanstary, or ideal community (destr.), begun at Condé-sur-Vesgre, near Chartres. By the late 1830s Daly was preparing his principal project, the publication of the first serious French monthly architectural journal, the *Revue générale de l'architecture et des travaux publics*, the prospectus for which he issued late in 1839. The first three numbers appeared on 19 March 1840. From the start his journal backed the romantic rationalism of his old *maître d'atelier* Duban and of Duban's friend Henri Labrouste, maintaining that position for the next half century (*see also* ECLECTICISM). Daly continued, however, to have other occupations. He supported the Fourierist journal *La Démocratie pacifique*. In 1844 he was appointed to restore Albi Cathedral, drawing up projects and commencing construction in 1850. He built a range of turrets above the apse, which were removed after his death as being archaeologically unjustified.

Following the Revolution of February 1848 Daly was elected in March to the Assemblée Nationale as a representative of the architectural community. Contemporaneously he campaigned among architectural and urban-planning committees and helped formulate special projects. After the coup d'état of December 1851 he became disillusioned with politics, travelled in Germany in 1854, and in 1855 left for the USA, visiting Reunion, TX, the Utopian community set up by his friend Victor Considérant, and Mexico. During these travels he reconciled himself to Napoleon III's Second Empire, and on his return to Paris in 1857 he wrote in the *Revue générale*: 'When I am asked what is the most remarkable thing I have encountered since I left, I always wish to reply that it is what I found on my return: the New Paris'. He expanded his publishing activities to include large monographs, commencing in 1864 with his own monumental *Architecture privée du XIXème siècle sous Napoléon III* in three folio volumes (completed 1872–7 with three further volumes). In 1876 Daly began the publication of a weekly periodical, *La Semaine des constructeurs*, to parallel the monthly *Revue générale*. It was edited first by Pierre Planat and later, after Planat founded the rival *Construction moderne* in 1885, by Daly's son Marcel Daly. Also during the 1870s Daly formulated a theory of the evolution of architectural form outlined in the introduction to the revised edition (1880) of his *Motifs historiques*, in pamphlets, and in a discourse at the meeting of architects coinciding with the Exposition Universelle, Paris, of 1889. In 1892 he was awarded the Gold Medal of the RIBA.

WRITINGS

Regular contributions to *Rev. Gén. Archit.* (1840–90) and *Sem. Constructeurs* (1876–94)

Architecture privée au XIXème siècle sous Napoléon III, 6 vols (Paris, 1864–77)

Théâtres de la place du Châtelet (Paris, 1865)

Motifs historiques d'architecture et de sculpture d'ornement (Paris, 1869, rev. 2/1881)

Architecture funéraire contemporaine (Paris, 1871)

BIBLIOGRAPHY

R. Becherer: *Between Science and Sentiment: César Daly and the Formulation of Modern Architectural Theory* (diss., Ithaca, NY, Cornell U., 1980)

A. L. Van Zanten: *César Daly and the Revue Générale de l'Architecture* (diss., Cambridge, MA, Harvard U., 1981)

M. Saboye: *Presse et architecture au XIXe siècle* (Paris, 1991)

DAVID VAN ZANTEN

Dalziel Brothers. *See* BROTHERS DALZIEL.

Damascene (i). Technique of decorating metalwork with an inlay of precious metal (*see* METAL, §V).

Damascene (ii). Fabric with a moiré or water pattern.

□

Damasceni, Alessandro. *See* PERETTI, (2).

Damascus [Arab. Dimashq, Dimashk, Dimishk, al-Sham; Fr. Damas]. Capital city of Syria. Built on the lower slopes of Mt Qasiyun, known in antiquity as Mons Cassius, Damascus lies on the Barada River and dominates a great oasis, the Ghuta. The situation of the city to the east of the Lebanon barred access to the Mediterranean and forced it to turn towards the caravan cities of the desert. Trade routes led from it east to the River Euphrates and thence downstream to the Gulf and the Indian Ocean, north to Aleppo, Antioch and Anatolia, and south to Palestine, Arabia and Egypt. Damascus, an important city in antiquity, became an international capital after the Muslim conquest in 635–6, the building of its Great Mosque a symbol of its status.

1. History and urban development. 2. Centre of production. 3. Great Mosque.

1. HISTORY AND URBAN DEVELOPMENT.

(i) Pre-Islamic. Settlement in the region of Damascus is of considerable antiquity. An urban centre at Tell al-Shali-hiyya, south-east of the city, dates to the 4th millennium BC. In the 11th century BC Damascus was the capital of the kingdom of Aram, mentioned in the history of Abraham (Genesis 14:15), and the mosque of Ibrahim at Berzé to the north of the city is still venerated by Muslims as Abraham's birthplace. Before 1000 BC ARAMAEANS introduced the first grid plan and canal system; their city was dominated by the temple of the storm-god Hadad (9th century BC). The city was captured by Alexander the Great in 333 BC, refounded as a Ptolemaic city and raised to a capital by the Seleucid Antiochos III later in the 3rd century BC. A new Greek colony was installed *c.* 90 BC by Demetrias III. Traces of this Hellenistic city, which grew up beside the Aramaean one, are still apparent in the streets with side arcades to the east of the Great Mosque, where the residential blocks measure 100×45 m, with the longer side orientated north–south. In 85 BC the Nabataean ruler Aretas III occupied Damascus and built a Nabataean quarter to the east of the Hellenistic city and a new canal on the slopes of Mt Qasiyun.

Syria was made a Roman province in 64 BC, but Antioch became the capital. The development of Damascus as a Roman metropolis owes much to the works of Hadrian (*reg* AD 117–38), Septimius Severus (*reg* 193–211), Caracalla (*reg* 211–17) and Severus Alexander (*reg* 222–35). The Aramaean and Hellenistic settlements were combined into a single city with regular defensive walls (1500×750 m) with seven gates and a fortress in the north-east corner. The *decumanus*, a great colonnaded street 26 m wide, ran from east to west. Corresponding to the present Suq Midhat Pasha, this road is often called the Street Called Straight, from the allusion to it in Acts of the Apostles 9:11. A second colonnaded street 300 m to its north linked the forum, a large square in the east, with the main temple, rededicated to Jupiter Damascenus, in the north-west. The temple sat within two concentric enclosures: an outer (386×305 m) and inner (157×100 m). Under Theodosios I (*reg* 379–95) the temple was transformed into the Christian church of St John the Baptist, whose head was its principal relic and is still revered by Muslims (as that of Yaḥyā b. Zakāriyyā) in the Umayyad Great Mosque (*see* §3 below), which in turn replaced the church. Although Syria remained a Byzantine province until the Muslim conquest in 635–6, the population gradually became Jacobite Monophysite and deeply resentful of their rulers. Not only was the Sasanian emperor Khusraw II (*reg* 591–628) well received on his occupation of Damascus in 612, but also the Muslim conquest was peaceful and won the active collaboration of the Christians.

BIBLIOGRAPHY
Pauly–Wissowa
C. Watzinger and K. Wulzinger: *Die antike Stadt* (1921), i of *Damaskus* (Berlin and Leipzig, 1921–4)
J. Sauvaget: 'Le Plan antique de Damas', *Syria*, xxvi (1949), pp. 314–58
J. Sourdel-Thomine: 'Les Anciens Lieux de pèlerinage damascains d'après les sources arabes', *Bull. Etud. Orient.*, xiv (1954), pp. 65–85
R. Janin: 'Damas', *Dictionnaire d'histoire et de géographie ecclésiastique*, ed. R. Aubert and E. van Cauwenbergh, xiv (1957), pp. 42–7

K. Freyberger: *Untersuchungen zur Baugeschichte des Jupiter-Heiligtums in Damaskus* (in preparation)

J. M. ROGERS

(ii) Islamic. In AD 635–6 Muslim armies conquered Damascus, and in 661 Mu'awiya, the first caliph of the Umayyad dynasty (*reg* 661–750), made this provincial centre the capital of his vast empire. Under his successors the city dominated a realm stretching from the frontiers of China to the southern borders of France, but it was never a metropolis on the scale of other medieval Islamic capitals such as Baghdad or Cairo. Only the Great Mosque (*see* §3 below), one of the masterpieces of Umayyad architecture, survives from this golden age, although many buildings, palaces and residences erected for members of the ruling family or their associates are mentioned in later texts. The city preserved its grid plan of Classical and Byzantine times, but a souk gradually encroached on the western part of the Street Called Straight and on the streets that opened on to it. Situated near the Jabya Gate, the souk symbolized the privileged position that the city always enjoyed in its commercial relations with the Hawran, the grain-producing region to its south.

With the transfer of the capital to Iraq after the 'Abbasid revolution in AD 750, Damascus became the modest capital of a region in decline. Until the 11th century the city was a pawn in the struggles among various political forces and suffered almost ceaseless disturbances. The urban fabric was slowly but definitively modified. In the absence of any stable authority capable of maintaining security, religious and social communities regrouped in well-defined sectors. The Classical grid plan was transformed into an amorphous agglomeration pierced by several major arteries serving quarters of varying sizes. Great gates blocked off these quarters, within which a network of lanes and blind alleys gave access to dwellings. In the 9th and 10th centuries Damascus was briefly occupied by the TULUNID and Ikhshidid governors from Egypt and then by FATIMID governors, who were ousted in 1076. To this interim period must date the growth of the three principal medieval Muslim cemeteries, outside Bab ('gate of') Tuma, Bab al'Faradis and Bab al-Saghir, although this last is traditionally associated with the burials of the companions of the Prophet who died in the capture of Damascus.

With the arrival of the Saljuq Turks in 1079, Damascus entered a period of political stability that continued under their successors, the ZANGID dynasty (*reg* 1154–86 in Damascus). The city expanded beyond its walls, and new quarters developed along the great axes of communication leading north to Aleppo and south to Jerusalem and Cairo. According to the local historian Ibn 'Asakir (1105–76), Christians and Jews had regrouped in the eastern part of the walled city, while the Muslims were concentrated in the west; more than 400 places of worship dotted the urban landscape. Nur al-Din (*reg* 1146–74) built a hospital (Arab. *maristān*; 1154–5; see fig. 1) and a funerary madrasa (1172), among other buildings. Both have similar plans, consisting of a central court with paired iwans, and domes and portals decorated with *muqarnas* (*see* ISLAMIC ART, §II, 5(ii)(e)). The hospital was a model for others throughout the Islamic world.

1. Damascus, hospital of Nur al-Din, portal, 1154–5

Under the Ayyubid dynasty (*reg* 1186–1260 in Damascus) the city became the seat of a princely court and experienced increased prosperity and architectural vitality. The citadel was totally reconstructed to house a palace, and male and female members of the dynasty, military officers and religious dignitaries erected many monuments in the city and in the northern suburb of Salihiyya on Mt Qasiyun, where a construction boom took place. Extant buildings include mosque-madrasas, with or without the founder's tomb attached, and free-standing mausolea. All these buildings have austere façades with high portals. They were constructed in ashlar, an uncommon (and presumably expensive) material that was replaced at the end of the period by alternating courses of basalt and limestone.

Damascus was the second capital of the Mamluk sultans of Egypt (*reg* 1250–1517). Despite unsettled periods, the city underwent significant development during the reign of Baybars (*reg* 1260–77), under the governorship of Tankiz (1312–39) for al-Nasir Muhammad (*reg* 1294–1340 with interruptions) and throughout the 14th century. A large number of mosques, madrasas and baths were erected to complete the range of facilities available in older quarters and to equip the new ones that had developed outside the walls. The Zahiriyya Madrasa (1277–81), for example, where Sultan Baybars was buried, is decorated with splendid mosaics imitating those of the Umayyad mosque. This period of growth was brutally interrupted when Timur sacked the city in 1401 and abducted its best artisans to Samarkand. In the first half of the 15th century, however, economic activity recommenced, and the city again began to expand.

Under the Ottomans (*reg* 1516–1918 in Damascus) the city was only a provincial capital, but it benefited from incorporation into a world empire. It profited from European trade, facilitated by the signing of the Capitulations, and from the intense commercial activity created by the thousands of pilgrims from the northern provinces who annually passed through the city *en route* to and from Mecca and Medina, the holy cities of Arabia. When Sultan Selim I (*reg* 1512–20) entered the city in 1516, he initiated a surge in building activity, represented by the Salimiyya hospice (Arab. *takiyya*) at Salihiyya, that continued under successive governors, particularly in the 16th and 18th centuries. Congregational mosques erected under Ottoman patronage followed Istanbul models, with slender minarets crowned with conical caps, hemispherical domes and courts enclosed with domed porticos, but they incorporated such traditional Damascene features as striped masonry of limestone and basalt. Major buildings, such as the Sulaymaniyya *takiyya* (1554–5; *see* ISLAMIC ART, fig. 67) and the mosques of Darwish Pasha (1571) and Sinan Pasha (1586), included such dependencies as schools, baths, soup-kitchens and often tombs for their founders. The commercial centre of the city remained within the walls. Souks and caravanserais, built on a standardized plan of a square central courtyard surrounded by shops and accommodations on two storeys, provided revenues for the upkeep of the congregational mosques and the salaries of their employees. The 'Azm Palace (begun 1749), the residence of the Ottoman governor, which has been made into the Musée des Arts Populaires et Traditions, is a magnificent example of a traditional urban dwelling. The city spread to the north, the west and especially the south when the large suburb of Midan with its characteristic granaries developed along the wide pilgrimage road. The different methods of construction contributed to the definitive remodelling of the urban landscape outside the walls.

In the late 19th century and early 20th, Damascus experienced a wave of modernization. Main streets were widened, and such public utilities as gas mains, water mains and a tramway were installed. A new administrative centre was built on the meadowland beside the Barada River to the west of the city. Surviving buildings include the 'Abid house, the central courtyard of which served as a light well for the surrounding storeys of rooms, and the Hijaz railway station, designed by a Spanish architect in the early 20th century as the modern departure point for the pilgrimage to Mecca.

The most important museum in the city is the Musée National de Damas, founded in 1921 and installed since 1938 in premises specially designed to house the Directorate of the Antiquities Service and the rich collection of finds from archaeological excavations throughout Syria, such as those at MARI, Ras Shamra (*see* UGARIT) and

RAQQA. It also contains reconstructions of the Iarhai Hypogeum, typical of the funerary art of Palmyra, the synagogue from Dura-Europos with its magnificent cycle of wall paintings (see DURA-EUROPOS, §3) and the façade from the Umayyad palace at QASR AL-HAYR WEST.

For further discussion and bibliography see SYRIA.

BIBLIOGRAPHY

EI/2: 'Dimashk' [Damascus]

Ibn 'Asākir (1105–76): *Ta'rīkh madīnat Dimashq* [History of the city of Damascus], i, ed. S. Munajjid (Damascus, 1951)

C. Watzinger and K. Wulzinger: *Die islamische Stadt* (1924), ii of *Damaskus* (Berlin and Leipzig, 1921–4)

J. Sauvaget: *Les Monuments historiques de Damas* (Beirut, 1932)

J. Sauvaget, M. Ecochard and J. Sourdel-Thomine: *Les Monuments ayyoubides de Damas*, 4 fasc. (Paris, 1938–50)

M. Ecochard and C. Le Coeur: *Les Bains de Damas*, 2 vols (Damascus, 1942)

N. Elisséeff: *La Description de Damas d'Ibn 'Asākir* (Beirut, 1959)

D. Duda: *Innenarchitektur syrischer Stadthäuser des 16. bis 18. Jahrhunderts* (Wiesbaden, 1971)

K. Moaz and S. Ory: *Inscriptions arabes de Damas: Les Stèles funéraires. I. Cimetière d'al'Bāb al-Saġīr* (Damascus, 1977)

D. Sack: 'Damaskus: Die Entwicklung der historischen Stadt', *Archit.: Z. Gesch. Baukst* (1983), pp. 113–35

A. Raymond: *Les Grandes Villages arabes à l'époque ottomane* (Paris, 1985)

2. CENTRE OF PRODUCTION. Damascus was famed for a variety of products in the Islamic period. Enamelled and gilded glass was produced under the Ayyubids and Mamluks, but production suffered progressively through the 14th century from the competition of the glass-houses at Murano. Typical products include beakers, covered dishes and lamps decorated with delicate friezes of arabesques and inscriptions. Many lamps were commissioned by military and civil dignitaries for use in religious monuments (see ISLAMIC ART, §VIII, 5(i) and (ii)). Damascus was also known for its metalwares. Bows and swords were made of tempered ('damascened') steel, and under the Mamluks Damascus produced fine inlaid bronzes, including candlesticks and vessels, which were chased, hammered, engraved and inlaid with silver and gold (see ISLAMIC ART, §IV, 3(iii)). Metalwares produced in the late 19th century in a revived Mamluk style have often been mistaken for their prototypes (see ISLAMIC ART, §IV, 4(ii)).

Ceramics, both everyday and luxury wares, were produced in great quantity. Thirteenth-century sources mention a potters' quarter located in the eastern sector near the city wall, and excavations uncovered a second quarter in a wide area outside the East Gate. A third quarter named Fawakhir ('the kilns') was located on the slopes of Mt Qasiyun to the north-west of the city; sherds found there indicate that the quarter was founded in the 14th century by artisans from northern Mesopotamia fleeing the Mongol invasions. The everyday pottery of Damascus was generally yellow and had incised decoration; luxury wares had a white siliceous body and underglaze decoration painted on a dark blue field. Albarelli, known in medieval inventories as 'vases de Damas', were among the city's most famous products. They were widely exported to Europe during the 14th century and imitated at Valencia during the 15th. In the 16th century underglaze-painted tiles known as *qishānī* (from Pers. *kāshānī*: '[tile] from Kashan') were used to revet domestic and monumental interiors. Introduced from Iznik in Anatolia, the technique was adopted by local workshops. A group of ceramic vessels underglaze-painted in blue, green and occasionally purple was formerly attributed to Damascus but is now known to have been produced at Iznik (see ISLAMIC ART, §V, 5(i)).

The production of turned and carved woodwork, marquetry and painted wood is attested from the 11th century and was used for ceilings and panels in the main reception rooms of Damascene houses in the Ottoman period. A particularly fine ensemble for the house of Nur al-Din (1707) has been preserved in New York (Met.). Damascus also produced fine leatherwork. The tanneries were pushed out to the north-east of the city because of their unpleasant effluvia, while saddlery was located near the horse market under the citadel. Finally, the city produced a great variety of remarkable textiles known in Europe as damask. Woven of cotton or silk and cotton and sometimes satined, these fabrics were named after the designs they bore rather than the techniques in which they were woven. At the beginning of the 16th century, a local chronicler noted the vigorous state of this craft, in which women working at home played a leading role. This industry was badly affected in the 19th century by growing competition from Europe.

JEAN-PAUL PASCUAL

3. GREAT MOSQUE. The Great Mosque of Damascus (AD 706–15), constructed by the Umayyad caliph al-Walid I (reg 705–15), is a seminal monument of Islamic architecture (see ISLAMIC ART, §II, 3). The mosque was erected in a campaign to embellish Damascus and the two other major centres of Muslim power and sanctity, Jerusalem and Medina, with major buildings. This ambitious and expensive programme made al-Walid the principal patron of the Umayyad period and, for the first time in Islamic history, made architecture an instrument of political and religious propaganda.

The central site chosen for the mosque accorded with these purposes: it was the holiest location in the city, having successively held temples to the Syrian storm-god Hadad and Jupiter Damascenus and the church of John the Baptist (see §1(i) above). Al-Walid bought the church from the Christian community and promptly demolished it, leaving only the inner perimeter walls of the Roman temple (100×157 mm), complete with corner towers and the propylaeum on the east (see fig. 2). This elaborate structure remained the principal entrance to the mosque, while the corner towers served for the call to prayer. Within the rectilinear proportions of this vast empty space, which were markedly at variance with those of earlier mosques, a new kind of religious structure was erected. The court is surrounded on three sides by covered arcades (Arab. *riwāq*) and on the fourth or qibla side by a disproportionately long prayer-hall. The hall is laid out internally on an east–west axis like a Christian basilica, and the pitched roof, carried on two-tier arcades of columns forming three long naves, runs at right-angles to the direction of prayer. A great raised gable cleaves through and above the serried ranks of pitched roofs (see ISLAMIC ART, fig. 18). This gable was the outward sign of the royal pomp and ceremony represented internally by the articulation of the area around the mihrab with a MINBAR for the preacher, a MAQSŪRA enclosure for the sovereign and

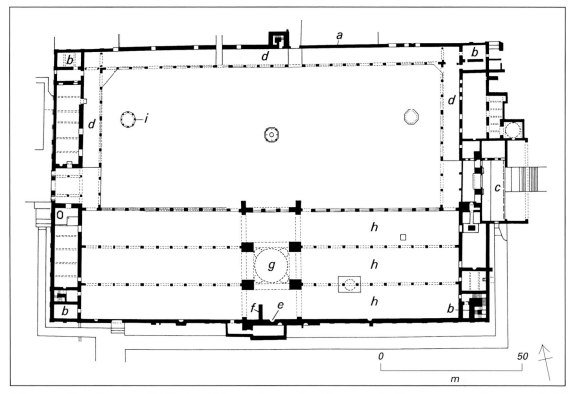

2. Damascus, Great Mosque, AD 706–15, plan: (a) inner perimeter walls of Roman temple; (b) corner towers of Roman temple; (c) propylaeum of Roman temple (Bab Jayrun); (d) covered arcade (*riwāq*); (e) mihrab; (f) minbar; (g) dome of Malikshah; (h) nave of prayer-hall; (i) treasury (*bayt al-māl*)

a dome preceding the mihrab. Externally the gable resembles the western façade of a typical Syrian church; the whole composition suggests the façade of a Late Antique palace, such as the palace of Theodoric at Ravenna (destr.), represented in a mosaic (*c.* 519) at S Apollinare Nuovo there.

The combination of aulic and ecclesiastical forms seen on the exterior may also explain the applied decoration within the mosque. The prayer-hall, the inner side of the perimeter walls and the court façades were all covered with glass mosaic above a dado of quartered marble. Byzantine workmen and materials were apparently supplied by the Byzantine emperor, and the iconographic programme was indebted to Byzantine models. An idyllic landscape panorama with a river flowing below fantastic houses and pavilions embowered in huge trees survives on the west perimeter wall (*see* ISLAMIC ART, fig. 82); most of the other mosaics have been destroyed, but textual descriptions state that the decoration featured representations of palaces and cityscapes of Mecca and Medina, and the qibla wall was ornamented with Koranic inscriptions of eschatological content. The overall theme of these mosaics is uncertain, but it has been suggested that they represented Paradise, the topography of Damascus, the new Islamic world order of peace and prosperity, or the countries and monuments of the entire world. The walls were punctuated with marble window grilles of intricate geometrical designs seen in Classical floor mosaics. In the

court, a mosaic-encrusted octagonal structure carried on an open ring of columns served as the communal treasury (Arab. *bayt al-māl*).

Before the middle of the 9th century AD a MINARET was added to one side of the north entrance to the mosque. Tall minarets were erected on the corner towers in the south-east in 1339 and the south-west in 1488. The mosque was repaired and restored after fires in 1069, 1401 and 1893. In 1082–3, under the Saljuq sultan Malikshah (*reg* 1072–92), the dome, *maqsūra*, arches and piers in front of the mihrab were rebuilt. The roofs and dome were rebuilt by Apéry in 1894, and the surviving mosaics were drastically restored in the 20th century. The mosque was an important model for later mosques, not only locally in Syria (e.g. the al-Tawba Mosque in Damascus, 1235) but also further afield in Anatolia (e.g. the congregational mosques of Diyarbekır, 1091–2, and Selçuk, 1374).

BIBLIOGRAPHY
K. A. C. Creswell: *Early Muslim Architecture*, i (Oxford, 1932; 2nd edn in 2 vols, Oxford, 1959)
O. Grabar: 'La Grande Mosquée de Damas et les origines architecturales de la mosquée', *Synthronon* (Paris, 1968), pp. 107–14
B. Finster: 'Die Mosaiken der Umayyadenmoschee', *Kst Orients*, vii (1970), pp. 83–141
V. Strika: 'La grande moschea di Damasco e l'ideologia ommiade', *An. Fac. Ling. & Lett. Stran. Ca'Foscari*, iii (1972), pp. 55–74
K. Brisch: 'Observations on the Iconography of the Mosaics in the Great Mosque of Damascus', *Content and Context of Visual Arts in the Islamic World*, ed. P. P. Soucek (University Park, PA, and London, 1988), pp. 13–24

ROBERT HILLENBRAND

Dambrowsky, Ivan. *See* GRAHAM, JOHN.

Dambulla [Jambukola; Pali: Chāta-pabbata]. A large rocky outcrop in central Sri Lanka noted for its cave shrines and paintings, which flourished from the 2nd century BC. On the upper slopes of the outcrop of gneiss 600 m long and 150 m above the surrounding plain is a series of five caves, aligned east–west and more or less contiguous, which have been occupied from the 2nd century BC and which form the nucleus of a modern Buddhist temple. At the base of the rock there are additional caves, a stupa (Sinh. *dāgaba*) and other remains of an ancient Buddhist monastery. This monastery was patronized by kings of the 2nd–1st centuries BC, as is evident from numerous inscriptions. The main Dambulla cave shrines were restored in the 12th and 18th centuries AD. The statuary belongs largely to the 12th century and consists of Buddha figures, images of *bodhisattvas*, the Hindu god Vishnu, the local god Saman and royal benefactors. While stone was used in some cases, the figures were generally modelled in clay with wooden armatures, then lightly plastered and painted. Four of the Dambulla caves have paintings on the walls and ceilings that are attributable to the 18th century.

BIBLIOGRAPHY
A. Seneviratna: *The Golden Rock Temple of Dambulla* (Colombo, 1983)
N. Katz and E. S. Goldberg: 'The Golden Rock Temples of Dambulla', *A. Asia*, xvi/4 (1986), pp. 69–76

RAJA DE SILVA

Damer, Anne Seymour (*b* Sundridge, Kent, 1748; *d* London, 28 May 1828). English sculptor. She was the daughter of Field Marshal the Hon. Henry Seymour-Conway and spent her youth in the care of her cousin Horace Walpole, who grossly over-praised her work as an artist; from him she inherited Strawberry Hill, Middx, in 1797. In 1767 she married the Hon. John Damer and turned to sculpture after his suicide in 1776. She began as a modeller in wax in the manner of Isaac Gosset and was later taught by Giuseppe Ceracchi, for whose *Muse of Sculpture* (London, BM) she sat, and John Bacon (i). Between 1785 and 1811 she was an honorary exhibitor at the Royal Academy, London. Her best-known works are the heads of the river gods *Isis* and *Thame* for the bridge at Henley-on-Thames, Oxon (stone, 1785; *in situ*), but she also produced an over life-size marble statue of *George III* (1795; Edinburgh, Register House) and numerous classicizing portrait busts, including those of *Caroline, Princess of Wales* (terracotta, 1814; London, Ranger's House) and *Horatio, Lord Nelson* (bronze, 1827; Windsor Castle, Berks, Royal Col.). She was widely praised by her contemporaries for her naturalistic and slightly sentimentalized animal sculptures, such as *Two Sleeping Dogs* (marble, 1784; Goodwood House, W. Sussex). She may have had assistance in the carving of her marble works.

Gunnis
BIBLIOGRAPHY
H. Walpole: *Anecdotes of Painting in England* (1762–71); ed. R. N. Wornum (1849), i, pp. xx–xxiii
J. Dallaway: *Anecdotes of the Arts in England* (London, 1800), pp. 408, 410–12
A. Cunningham: *The Lives of the Most Eminent British Painters, Sculptors and Architects* (London, 1829–33), iii, pp. 247–73
P. Noble: *Anne Seymour Damer: A Woman of Art and Fashion, 1748–1828* (London, 1908)
M. Whinney: *Sculpture in Britain, 1530–1830*, Pelican Hist. A. (Harmondsworth, 1964, rev. 2/1988), pp. 319–20, 465
The Treasure Houses of Britain: Five Hundred Years of Private Patronage and Art Collecting (exh. cat., ed. G. Jackson-Stops; Washington, DC, N.G.A., 1985)

KATHARINE EUSTACE

Damer, Henrik [Heinrich] (*fl* Lübeck, 1600; *d* Stockholm, 1640). German sculptor and master builder, active in Sweden. By 1629 he was in Strängnäs, Södermanland, working on the monument (marble and sandstone, completed 1633; *in situ*) to the half-brother of Gustav II Adolf, King of Sweden (*reg* 1611–32), Carl Carlsson Gyllenhielm (1574–1650), in his mortuary chapel in Strängnäs Cathedral. The monument is rather stylized and solemnly expressive and consists of a tomb surmounted by a baldacchino carried by six Ionic columns; within it are the kneeling figures of Gyllenhielm and his wife, and smaller allegorical and biblical figures and heraldic shields adorn the walls and the baldacchino. To Damer is attributed the tower-like mortuary chapel (completed 1639) of Herman Wrangel (1587–1643) at Skokloster Church, Uppland, an octagonal structure evidently influenced by Gustav II Adolf's memorial chapel (1632–3) at Riddarholm Church in Stockholm. He was also responsible (1637–9) for the sculptured gables and portals of Gyllenhielm's residences at Karlberg outside Stockholm and Sundbyholm near Strängnäs, and he contributed to the vast decorative programme (1637) of the 'Peerless' palace (destr. 1825) of the De la Gardie family in Stockholm. His ornamental work shows that he was an exponent of the German Baroque style of scrollwork.

BIBLIOGRAPHY
G. Axel-Nilsson: 'Henrik Damer', *Fornvännen*, xxviiii (1934), pp. 213–38
——: *Dekorativ stenhuggarkonst i yngre vasastil* [Decorative sculpture in the early Vasa style] (Lund, 1950)
——: *Makalös: Fultherren greve Jakob De la Gardies hus i Stockholm* [The 'Peerless' palace: the Stockholm house of the field marshal Count Jakob De la Gardie] (Stockholm, 1984)

TORBJÖRN FULTON

Damery, Chevalier de (*fl* 1760; *d* ?Paris, *c.* 1803). French collector and soldier. In the mid-18th century he acquired a renowned art collection and, according to his friend the engraver Jean-Georges Wille, associated with contemporary connoisseurs such as Jean de Jullienne and Pierre-Jean Mariette and such artists as Jean-Baptiste Greuze and Francesco Giuseppe Casanova, who painted for him. He not only owned engravings by Wille of works by Godfried Schalcken, Caspar Netscher and Gerard ter Borch but also large paintings. From 1774 financial hardship caused him to sell cheaply his remarkable collection of prints, which included many works by both northern artists (Martin Schongauer, Dürer) and Italians (Marcantonio Raimondi, Agostino Carracci, Annibale Carraci, Federico Barocci). In 1779 he sold his famous collection of curiosities. Although promoted to lieutenant–colonel of infantry, he fell into reduced circumstances. The catalogue (94 items) of the posthumous sale of his collection reflects its originality: two-thirds of the works were by French artists of the 17th and 18th centuries (e.g. François Boucher's *Mucius Scaevola Putting his Hand in the Fire*, Saint-Omer, Mus. Hôtel Sandelin), including many drawings of religious subjects. His collector's mark, a marine anchor (Lugt), 'is never on a mediocre drawing' (Goncourt, i, p. 96).

BIBLIOGRAPHY

G. Duplessis: *Mémoire et journal de J. G. Wille, graveur du roi . . .*, 2 vols (Paris, 1857)
E. de Goncourt: *La Maison d'un artiste*, 2 vols (Paris, 1881)
F. Lugt: *Marques* (1921)
Le Dessin français dans les collections du XVIIIe siècle (exh. cat., ed. A. Rubenstein; Paris, Gal. Gaz. B.-A., 1935)

ANNE LECLAIR

Damery, Walthère (*bapt* Liège, 22 Aug 1614; *d* Liège, 18 Feb 1678). Flemish painter. He studied with Antoine Durbuto (after 1580–1634) in Liège, where he quickly gained a reputation. When he was 21 he took on an apprentice. In 1639 he went to England and in 1643 he was in Rome. Returning by sea, Damery was captured by North African pirates and taken to Algiers but soon escaped or was released. In 1644 he arrived at Toulon, where he painted his masterpiece (probably as an ex-voto), the *Virgin and Child Venerated by SS Cyprian and Honorius*, for the cathedral (*in situ*). Damery then went to Paris, where he decorated the dome of St Joseph des Carmes, the first of only two domes painted in Paris in the 17th century. By July 1647 at the latest Damery had returned to Liège.

About 30 pictures are known from his second Liège period (1647–78). These are in a restrained Baroque style and influenced by Pietro da Cortona, particularly in some figure types. Unlike his rival Bertholet Flémal, whose allegiance was to Nicolas Poussin, Damery's work was more Italianate but in tune with the classicizing trend characteristic of the 17th-century Liège school. In common with his Liègeois contemporaries, most of Damery's paintings were religious commissions, particularly the mystic visions typical of the Counter-Reformation, of which Liège, together with the Spanish Netherlands, was a stronghold (e.g. the *Virgin of the Rosary*, Bilzen, vicarage of St Maurice; two versions of the *Lactation of St Bernard*, Marche-les-Dames, Notre-Dame du Vivier, and Limal, St Martin; and the *Virgin Giving the Habit of his Order to St Norbert*, Liège, Séminaire). His secular work is less well known and consists mainly of portraits (many of members of the Bocholtz family). Damery also painted eight ceiling panels, the *Four Seasons* and the *Four Elements*, for the Château Oude Biezen, Bilzen.

BIBLIOGRAPHY

P. Farcy: 'Walthère Damery', *Cah. CACEF*, cxxvii (1987), pp. 20–23
J. Hendrick: *La Peinture au pays de Liège: XVIe, XVIIe, XVIIIe siècles* (Liège, 1987)
Walthère Damery (1614–1678) (exh. cat., Bilzen, Château Oude Biezen, 1987)

PIERRE-YVES KAIRIS

Damghan [Dāmghān]. Town on the road to Mashhad in northern Iran, 344 km east of Tehran. On the southern edge of the modern town are the ruins of the prehistoric site of TEPE HISSAR. Of the numerous Parthian and Sasanian sites near Damghan, the most important is SHAHR-I QUMIS, located 32 km to the south-west. In AD 857 Qumis was hit by a violent earthquake that destroyed the town's system of underground irrigation channels (Pers. *qanāt*) and hastened its decline, to the advantage of Damghan, which received its water supply from the source of Chashma 'Ali. The walls, bazaar and main streets of Damghan were determined before the mid-12th century. The earliest remaining Islamic monument is the Tarik-khana Mosque (9th century; *see* ISLAMIC ART, fig. 23). Its elliptical arches and massive columns, resembling those of Sasanian palaces, show the adoption of pre-Islamic techniques for the construction of an Arab-type hypostyle mosque. The Imamzada Ja'far complex includes one of the earliest funerary stelae in Iran; it commemorates the martyrdom (*c.* 900) of Ja'far, the brother of al-Nasir al-Kabir, a Zaydi descendant of the third Shi'ite imam, Husayn (*see* STELE, §5). A cylindrical minaret (*c.* 1026–7), one of the earliest standing in Iran, was erected next to the Tarik-khana Mosque by the Ziyarid regent Abu Harb Bakhtyar. A similar minaret was added to the congregational mosque in the second half of the 11th century. It is crowned by an epigraphic frieze with glazed letters in relief, the first example of this technique preserved *in situ* in Iran. Three magnificent cylindrical tomb towers were built in the same period (*see* TOMB, §II). The first (1026–7), known as Pir-i 'Alamdar (h. 12.5 m; diam. 6.4 m), was ordered by Abu Harb Bakhtiyar as a mausoleum for his father. It was the inspiration for a second, known as Chihil Dukhtaran ('forty daughters'; h. 14.8 m; diam. 7.8 m), built north of the Imamzada Ja'far complex in 1054–5 by another amir, probably as a tomb for a Sufi shaykh. A third and larger tower (h. 20.8 m; diam. 10.1 m) was erected in 1097 in Mehmandust, a village 15 km east of Damghan. All of these buildings are finely decorated with bricks set in relief. The Mongol invasions in the 13th century destroyed many settlements in northern Iran, but even before this date Damghan had ceased to be a creative architectural centre.

BIBLIOGRAPHY

A. Godard: 'Le Tari Khana de Damghan', *Gaz. B.-A.*, xii (1934), pp. 226–35
C. Adle: 'Contribution à la géographie historique du Damghan', *Monde Iran. & Islam*, i (1971), pp. 69–104
C. Adle and A. S. Melikian-Chirvani: 'Les Monuments du XIe siècle du Dâmqân', *Stud. Iran.*, i (1972), pp. 229–97
C. Adle: 'Recherches archéologiques en Iran sur le Kumeš médiéval, rapport préliminaire pour 1982–1983', *Acad. Inscr. & B.-Lett.: C. R. Séances* (April–June 1984), pp. 271–99

CHAHRYAR ADLE

Damian, Horia (*b* Bucharest, 27 Feb 1922). Romanian painter and sculptor. He enrolled at the School of Architecture in Bucharest in 1941 and the same year made his début at the Salonul Oficial de Pictură at Sala Dalles in Bucharest. He had his first one-man show at the Ateneul Român in Bucharest in 1942 and was awarded the Anastase Simu Prize for painting. In 1946 he won a scholarship to Paris, where he then settled. After a few months with André Lhote he worked with Léger in 1949–50 and then studied with Auguste Herbin, also becoming acquainted with Mondrian's work through Félix del Marle (1889–1952). This encounter with abstract art led to his first really original paintings, such as *Starry Night* (1951; *see* 1976 exh. cat., p. 44), which consists of a geometric arrangement of white dots. He destroyed most of the works he produced during the second half of the 1950s, an experimental period for him. His works of the early 1960s, executed in oil on a polyester base, are in a gestural, impasto style close to Tachism, as in *Constellation* (1961; Turin, Int. Cent. Aesth.). By the later 1960s his work had become increasingly geometric and sculptural, as exemplified by the *Throne* series (begun 1967; e.g. polyurethane and polyester, 1969; Figueres, Teat.–Mus. Dalí); these are not free-standing sculptures but rather set against plane backgrounds. The first of his large-scale monuments, *Galaxy, Project for a Monument at Houston, Texas* (see 1980 exh. cat., p. 42), was designed in 1972 and constructed in 1974 at the Neue Galerie in Aachen. Several further monuments in the *Galaxy* series were constructed, others remaining as maquettes. His fascination with the monumental continued in *The Hill* (see 1976 exh. cat.), constructed for the Solomon R. Guggenheim Museum in New York from styrofoam covered with tiny paper spheres and then painted yellow. This was followed by similar monuments, such as that for San Francisco, which is illustrated in the gouache *Project for San Francisco* (1979; Marseille, Mus. Cantini; see also 1980 exh. cat.).

BIBLIOGRAPHY

Horia Damian: The Hill (exh. cat. by R. Varia, New York, Guggenheim, 1976)
Damian: Projet de San Francisco (exh. cat. by R. Varia and J.-P. Bordaz, Paris, Pompidou, 1980)

Damiani Almeyda, Giuseppe (*b* Capua, nr Naples, 13 Feb 1834; *d* Palermo, 31 Jan 1911). Italian architect, engineer, teacher and writer. He trained as an engineer and approached his many architectural projects with an emphasis on technical thoroughness and simplicity of design. He studied at the Scuola di Ponti e Strade in Naples and received instruction from two southern architects, Enrico Alvino and Antonio Cipolla, who, unlike Damiani, made their reputations in Rome and Florence. In 1859 Damiani was assigned to the province of Palermo as engineer in charge of bridges and roads; he was promoted to district engineer in 1863 and worked on restoring and improving the road system. Architecture in Palermo at this time was dominated by Francesco Di Bartolo and Giovanni Battista Basile. The latter's grandiose style found favour more than Damiani's pragmatism and as a result Basile defeated him in the competition for the Teatro Massimo in 1864 (work did not begin until 1874). Meanwhile, Damiani received a constant flow of commissions to design funerary accoutrements and tombs as well as commissions for such houses and villas as the Villa Florio (1875–8) at Favignana, Sicily. He also designed a monument (erected 1904) to the villa's owner Ignazio Florio (1839–96) in the Piazza Florio in Palermo. In 1864 Damiani took up teaching at Palermo's Istituto Tecnico Industriale (he resigned in 1880, when he was again appointed district engineer) and in 1878 he became professor of drawing at the university. He was chosen to build another theatre in Palermo, the Politeama (1864–74). By contrast with the aristocratic Teatro Massimo, the Politeama became a people's theatre and is now a cinema. The design is classical with an innovative use of metal and glass for the roof (similar to his project for the Massimo). He was later involved with the building of the Teatro Comunale (1872–97) in Syracuse. For much of his career Damiani was an isolated figure as his strictly mathematical approach did not find favour among his contemporaries.

He wrote many articles and books, which were the fruit of constant study of ancient architecture as well as his own knowledge of engineering. His writings and drawings are conserved in the Damiani archive, Palermo.

WRITINGS

Il colore, le ombre, la luce (Palermo, 1873)
Applicazioni della geometria elementare allo studio del disegno, 2 vols (Palermo, 1878)
G. Barozzi da Vignola ed il suo Libro dei cinque ordini di architettura (Palermo, 1878)
L'arte nova, ricerca dell'arte dell'avvenire e dell'arte nazionale italiana (Palermo, 1893)

BIBLIOGRAPHY

DBI
A. De Gubernatis: *Dizionario d'artisti viventi* (Florence, 1889)
Catalogo della mostra retrospettiva del Basile e del Damiani (exh. cat. by A. Pavolini and E. Calandra, Palermo, Teat. Massimo, 1939)
R. De Fusco: *L'architettura dell'ottocento* (Turin, 1980)

□

Damini [da Castelfranco], **Pietro** (*b* Castelfranco, 1592; *d* Padua, 28 July 1631). Italian painter. He came from a family of painters, which included his brother Giorgio Damini (*d* 1631) and his sister Damina Damini (*fl* first half of the 17th century). He painted religious works, historical paintings and portraits, and he worked in Padua and the surrounding area, with frequent visits to other provincial towns. Ridolfi records that Damini spent his youth in Castelfranco, where he studied Giovanni Paolo Lomazzo's theories of art and copied the prints of Dürer. He studied mathematics with the Dominican Bovio da Feltre and painting with Giovan Battista Novello (1578–1652), a follower of Palma il Giovane. He was patronized by the religious orders, who required images of the new saints of the Counter-Reformation to be executed in a style that recalled the grandeur of 16th-century art. Damini's early style was inspired by Veronese and Palma il Giovane, modified by a response to the classicism of the Carracci family. He was also indebted to the classicism of Alessandro Varotari, and to the devotional art of Giovanni Battista Bissoni (1576–1636).

In 1612 Damini moved to Padua, where a commission from the Selvatico family for a *Penitent St Jerome* for their family chapel in the cathedral suggests that he already enjoyed a high standing. Between 1617 and 1619 he painted a series of large canvases illustrating Dominican miracles for the church of S Domenico at Chioggia (*in situ*), and in 1621 a large narrative picture, the *Exchange of the Keys between the Capitani Silvestro and Massimo Valier* (Padua, Pal. Mun.). In the 1620s he visited Crema, where he painted the *Baptism of St Augustus* (Lovere, Gal. Accad. B.A. Tadini) and a *Miracle of St Anthony* (Ombriano, parish church) (see de Vierno). An *Annunciation* (Padua, S Maria in Vanzo) is a late work and reveals the influence of Caravaggio, which had reached the Veneto through Carlo Saraceni. Pietro also received many commissions from the local nobility, for whom he painted portraits of ancestors with the help of his brother. He also received commissions from the Cornaro family and from Marie de' Medici, Queen of France. A series of paintings of the *Apostles* (Castelfranco, S Liberale) is attributed to Damina Damini. Pietro and Giorgio both died of the plague on 28 July 1631.

BIBLIOGRAPHY

C. Ridolfi: *Le meraviglie dell'arte* (Venice, 1648)

P. L. Fantelli: *Tra Padova e Chioggia: Pietro Damini da Castelfranco* (Venice, 1978)

R. Pallucchini: *La pittura veneziana del seicento* (Milan, 1981)

P. L. Fantelli: *Gli affreschi della chiesetta dei Nodari del municipio del Padova* (Padua, 1985)

M. A. de Vierno: *Pietro Damini da Castelfranco* (diss., U. Turin, 1989)

Pietro Damini, 1592–1631 (exh. cat. by D. Banzato and P. L. Fantelli, Padua, Pal. Ragione, 1993)

MARC'ALVISE DE VIERNO

Damini, Vincenzo (*b* Venice, end of the 17th century; *d* L'Aquila, Abruzzo, *c.* 1749). Italian painter. He received his early training in Venice, where the artistic environment was heavily influenced by the styles of Piazzetta and Federico Bencovich. He then became a pupil of Giovanni Antonio Pellegrini, whom he accompanied to England around 1720. His first English paintings reflect that style of Venetian art that relied heavily on pathos and chiaroscuro but also demonstrate the sense of decorative ease found in the work of Pellegrini.

From his early years are the *Judgement of Midas* (*c.* 1713–16) and the *Sacrifice of Isaac* (both Kassel, Gemäldegal.) and *Edward III and the Black Prince Receiving John II of France* (ex- H. D. Molesworth priv. col.), in which Damini favoured particularly theatrical effects. A similar emphasis on the gestures, though combined with a greater decorative sense derived from Pellegrini, can be seen in the paintings of *Jacob's Dream* (Berlin, Max Friedberg priv. col.) and the *Family of Darius before Alexander* (Warsaw, N. Mus.). The frescoes (destr. 1932) in St Peter ad Arches, Lincoln, and the series in the north transept of Lincoln Cathedral (*in situ*) date from the late 1720s.

In 1730 Damini returned to Italy and, after passing through Venice and Bologna, finally settled in the Abruzzo. The works from the final 20 years of his life show clear signs of contact with Neapolitan art and in particular the painting of Solimena, from whom strong chiaroscuro effects are derived. Among the most important of his works preserved in L'Aquila are the paintings in the church of the convent of S Giuliano, depicting *St Thomas Aquinas* and *Charles II of Anjou before the Virgin and St Thomas* (both 1739; L'Aquila, Mus. N. Abruzzo). Other works are preserved in the churches of S Silvestro, S Agostino, S Antonio da Padova and S Margherita, all in L'Aquila.

BIBLIOGRAPHY

Thieme–Becker

H. Walpole: *Anecdotes of Painting in England* (1762–71); ed. R. N. Wornum (1849), ii, p. 318

E. Edwards: *Anecdotes of Painters* (London, 1808), p. 150

R. Pallucchini: *La pittura veneziana del settecento* (Venice, 1960), pp. 125–6

C. C. Cunningham: 'Vincenzo Damini—Gaius Mucius Scaevola Before Lars Porsena', *Wadsworth Atheneum Bull.*, v/17 (1964), pp. 19–21

E. Young: 'Vincenzo Damini in England', *A. Ven.*, xxxiii (1979), pp. 70–78

J. M. Lehmann: *Italienische, französische und spanische Gemälde des 16. bis 18. Jahrhunderts* (Fridingen, 1980), pp. 108–11

O. Lehmann Brockhaus: *Abruzzen und Molise* (Munich, 1983), pp. 236, 417–18

GERARDO CASALE

Damjanov, Andreja (*b* Papradište, nr Veles [now Titov Veles], ?1813; *d* Veles, 1878). Macedonian architect-builder. He was a descendant of the Renzovski family, who from the mid-18th century were the best-known Macedonian masons, painters and wood-carvers. Apprenticed in his father's workshop, by the end of the 1830s he had assumed the leadership of his family's itinerant workshop, in which his three brothers also served, mainly as painters and wood-carvers. In the 1840s, operating mostly in Macedonia, he built the church of St Panteleimon in Veles (1840) and the monastery church of St Joachim Osogovski near Kriva Palanka (1845), thus establishing his reputation. After settling in Veles *c.* 1850, he undertook commissions for ecclesiastical as well as military buildings in Serbia, Bosnia and Herzegovina. His contemporaries acclaimed his engineering skills and his convincing realization of the massive basilical structures. His approach to architectural decoration represented an aggregate of elements from medieval Byzantine masonry, as well as from Renaissance and Baroque architecture.

BIBLIOGRAPHY

K. Tomovski: *Majstor Andreja Damjanov (1813–1878)* (Skopje, 1966)

BOJAN IVANOV

Dammar. Natural resin widely used as a picture varnish and as an additive to oil paint (*see* RESIN, §1). It is obtained from several species of tree growing in South-east Asia. Dammar becomes yellow with age but is less prone to surface disfigurement than mastic, which it gradually superseded during the 19th century.

RUPERT FEATHERSTONE

Dammartin, de. French family of architects and sculptors, active from the mid-14th century to the mid-15th.

(1) **Guy** [Guillot; Guyot] **de Dammartin** (*d* 1398). He was trained in the workshop of Raymond du Temple and is first recorded in 1365 working in Paris for Charles V, King of France, on the great staircase (destr.) of the Louvre and its sculptural programme. Guy is accredited with the statue of *Philip the Bold, Duke of Burgundy* (destr.) and with the decorative vault of the staircase. By 1370 he was working for Jean, Duc de Berry (*see* VALOIS, (3)), as master of his building programmes. Guy directed the reconstruction of numerous ducal châteaux, including those of Poitiers, Bourges, Riom, Concressault (destr.) and Mehun-sur-Yèvre (ruined), beautifying them with sculptural decoration, new fenestration and such features as the sumptuous fireplace and screen of gabled Flamboyant tracery (the Belle Cheminée) in the great chamber of the ducal palace at Poitiers. One of the lavish palatine chapels that he constructed survives: that of Riom, with its advanced system of continuous prismatic mouldings and its coherent Flamboyant tracery, which may show English influence. Around 1390 he devised the plans for the repair of the west façade of Bourges Cathedral with its new west rose in the form of a great square with curved sides. Guy should be considered among the earliest named French masters working in a Flamboyant style.

(2) **Drouet** [Dreux] **de Dammartin** (*d* 1415). Brother of (1) Guy de Dammartin. He worked with Guy on many projects and seems also to have begun his professional life in the 1360s on the great staircase of the Louvre. After 1369 he worked for Jean, Duc de Berry, at Bourges and

on the Hôtel de Nesle in Paris (1377; destr.). In 1380 he visited Troyes Cathedral to inspect the defective rose window of the south transept. In 1383 he became the Maistre Général des Oeuvres for Philip the Bold, constructing the Charterhouse at Champmol (*see* DIJON, §IV, 1(i)). While in the service of the Duke, Drouet also worked on the châteaux of Rouvres (Côte d'Or) and Ecluse (Flanders) and on the portal of the Sainte-Chapelle of Dijon. He later returned to the service of the Duc de Berry (1398), working on Bourges Cathedral, the Sainte-Chapelle of Bourges (*see* BOURGES, §II, 2) and numerous other projects, including the châteaux of Mehun-sur-Yèvre, Poitiers, Lusignan, Riom and Concressault, in some cases completing work begun by Guy. Drouet's son, Jean de Dammartin (*d* 1454), was master mason at the cathedrals of Le Mans and Tours.

BIBLIOGRAPHY
A. Champeaux and P. Gauchery: *Les Travaux d'art exécutés pour Jean de France, duc de Berry, avec une étude biographique sur les artistes employés par ce prince* (Paris, 1894)
N. Canat de Chizy: 'Etude sur le service des travaux publics et spécialement sur la charge de maître des oeuvres en Bourgogne sous les ducs de la race des Valois, 1363–1417', *Bull. Mnmtl*, lxiii (1898), pp. 245–72, 341–57, 439–73
C. Monget: *La Chartreuse de Dijon d'après les documents des archives de Bourgogne*, 3 vols (Montreuil-sur-Mer, 1898–1905)
H. David: *Claus Sluter* (Paris, 1951)
R. Vaughan: *Philip the Bold* (London, 1962)
F. Lehoux: *Jean de France, duc de Berry: Sa vie, son action politique*, 4 vols (Paris, 1966–8)
P. M. de Winter: *The Patronage of Philippe le Hardi, Duke of Burgundy (1364–1404)* (diss., New York U., 1976; microfilm, Ann Arbor, 1978)
Les Fastes du Gothique: Le Siècle de Charles V (exh. cat., Paris, Grand Pal., 1981–2)
K. Morand: *Claus Sluter: Artist at the Court of Burgundy* (Austin, TX, 1991)

STEPHEN MURRAY

Damphon (*fl* earlier 2nd century BC). Greek sculptor from Messene. The only ancient author to mention him is Pausanias, who was impressed by his statues for the Peloponnesian towns of Messene, Aigion, Megalopolis and Lykosoura. Yet since Pausanias gave no dates, and the numerous inscriptions mentioning the sculptor and his family are also undated, Damophon's chronology must be inferred from the neo-classical style of his surviving works. This points to the period when the Achaian League (to which all the cities above belonged) was at the height of its prosperity and engaged in an extensive building programme.

Damophon specialized in marble cult statues, though he also produced acrolithic works, in which stone was used for heads, hands and feet, and wood for the rest. He was also chosen to restore the ivory on Pheidias' *Zeus* at Olympia. His surviving works, all in marble, include the head of *Apollo* and some other fragments from Messene (Messene Mus.) and numerous pieces from his colossal cult group of *Despoina* ('the Mistress') at Lykosoura (Lykosoura, and Athens, N. Archaeol. Mus.). In the latter, the goddess (actually Persephone) sat enthroned beside her mother, Demeter, and flanked by Artemis and the giant Anytos, who had protected her in her infancy. According to Arcadian legend, after Demeter had been raped by Poseidon she went into deep mourning and was only comforted by the intervention of Zeus. Her daughter was worshipped in elaborate and somewhat gruesome

mysteries as a powerful nature-goddess, and Damophon clearly tried to convey these details in his work. Thus, while Demeter wore black, Despoina carried a robe covered with symbols of the cult, including friezes of marine creatures (referring to Poseidon), eagles and thunderbolts (emblems of Zeus), Victories carrying incense burners, olive sprays and, as well, beasts in long gowns, dancing and playing musical instruments, which must be the sacrificial animals hacked to pieces in the mysteries. Further, Poseidon's Tritons supported the arms of the throne, while a frieze of the Kouretes on the front of the goddesses' footstool again alluded to Zeus, and a frieze of the Korybantes on its sides, flanked by lions, recalled the Great Mother, Kybele. Like Pheidias, Damophon sought to engage the spectator with his statues in a most direct way, tempering their Olympian aloofness with an array of 'revelatory' iconography that acted as a conduit between deity and worshipper. However, while Pheidias had done this with interlocking combinations of mythological scenes, Damophon included symbols from the cult itself, thereby ensuring that the statues' full meaning would be intelligible only to initiates. Consequently his group represents an extraordinary blend of primitive religious beliefs, resurgent Arcadian nationalism and Hellenistic mysticism.

BIBLIOGRAPHY
Pausanias: *Guide to Greece*, IV.xxxi.6–10, VII.xxiii.5–7, VIII.xxxi.1–5 and xxxvii.3–9
G. Dickins: 'Damophon of Messene', *Annu. Brit. Sch. Athens*, xii (1905–6), pp. 109–36
——: 'Damophon of Messene II', *Annu. Brit. Sch. Athens*, xiii (1906–7), pp. 357–404
——: 'Damophon of Messene III', *Annu. Brit. Sch. Athens*, xvii (1910–11), pp. 80–87
G. J. Despinis: 'Ein neues Werk des Damophon', *Archäol. Anz.* (1966), pp. 378–85
E. Lévy and J. Marcadé: 'Au musée de Lycosoura', *Bull. Corr. Hell.*, xcvi (1972), pp. 967–1004
A. Stewart: *Greek Sculpture: An Exploration*, i (New Haven and London, 1990), chaps 7.4, 18.3, 24.5
P. Themelis: 'O Damophon kai e drasterioteta tou sten Arkadia' [Damophon and his activities in Arcadia], *Sculpture from Arcadia and Laconia*, ed. O. Palaglia and W. Coulson (Oxford, 1993), pp. 99–109

ANDREW F. STEWART

Dampt, Jean(-Auguste) (*b* Venarcy, Côte-d'Or, 2 Jan 1854; *d* Dijon, 26 Sept 1945). French sculptor, jeweller and furniture designer. He studied at the Ecole des Beaux-Arts in Dijon and then, in 1874, under François Jouffroy and Paul Dubois (ii) at the Ecole des Beaux-Arts in Paris. He first exhibited at the Salon de la Société des Artistes Français in 1876 with his bust of an architect called *Belot* (Dijon, Mus. B.-A.) and in 1877 he came second in the Prix de Rome. In 1879 he was awarded a second-class medal for his plaster sculpture *Ismael* (Châlons-sur-Marne, Mus. Mun.) and in 1881 he won a first-class medal for the marble *St John the Baptist* (Paris, Mus. d'Orsay). He travelled in Italy from 1882 to 1883 and later visited Spain and Morocco on a travel scholarship. In 1889 he ceased exhibiting at the Salon de la Société des Artistes Français and instead exhibited at the recently established Salon de la Société Nationale des Beaux-Arts. He worked primarily in bronze but also in ivory, silver and gold, and produced some jewellery. His sculptures were mainly inspired by religious and mythological subjects executed in a highly finished academic style (e.g. *Diana Lamenting the Death* *of Actaeon*, 1887; Dijon, Mus. B.-A.), though he also made a number of portrait sculptures (e.g. *André Charles Boulle*, 1880; Paris, Hôtel de Ville). In 1900–06 he designed the decoration for the Comtesse René de Béarn's drawing-room, which included elm, ash and oak panelling, library shelves, the chimney-piece and all of the furniture (Paris, Mus. d'Orsay). In 1919 Dampt was elected to the Académie des Beaux-Arts, to which he left 600,000 francs to be used for a prize for religious sculpture.

BIBLIOGRAPHY

Bénézit; *DBF*

Damrong Rajanubhab, Prince [Prince Disvarakumarn] (*b* Bangkok, 21 June 1862; *d* Bangkok, 1 Dec 1943). Thai statesman, historian and educational administrator. The son of King Mongkut (Rama IV, *reg* 1851–68), he attained the rank of Major-General in the Military Operations Department before becoming (1890) Minister of Public Instruction, then (1892–1915) Minister of the Interior under his half-brother Chulalongkorn (Rama V, *reg* 1868–1910) and, later, Vajiravudh (Rama VI, *reg* 1910–25). In this capacity Prince Damrong restructured Thailand's provincial administration, reorganized the civil service and harnessed the kingdom's resources (notably provincial taxation, forests and mines) to the interests of the state. He was Chairman (1915–32) of the Capital (now National) Library and was appointed Founder-Chairman of the Royal Academy in 1926. The National Museum, Bangkok, came into being under his guidance. A member of the Supreme Council of State from 1926 until 1932, when Thailand changed from an absolute to a constitutional monarchy, he moved to Penang in 1933 but returned to Bangkok in 1942. His writings ranged widely over many fields of Thai studies, and in such works as *Monuments of the Buddha in Siam* he pioneered Thai archaeological and art-historical studies.

WRITINGS

'The Foundation of Ayuthia', *J. Siam Soc.*, i (1904), pp. 7–10
'Historical Sketch of Lophburi', *J. Siam Soc.*, v/3 (1908), pp. 5–6
'The Story of the Records of Siamese History', *J. Siam Soc.*, xi/2 (1914–15), pp. 1–20 [trans. by O. Frankfurter]
'Siamese History prior to the Founding of Ayuddhya', *J. Siam Soc.*, xiii/2 (1919), pp. 1–66 [trans. by J. Crosby]
'The Golden Pavilion at Wat Sai', *J. Siam Soc.*, xiv/2 (1921), pp. 1–6 [trans. by B. O. Cartwright]
'Angkor from a Siamese Point of View', *J. Siam Soc.*, xix (1925), pp. 141–52
'The Introduction of Western Culture in Siam', *J. Siam Soc.*, xx (1927), pp. 89–100
'Wat Benchamabopit and its Collection of Images of the Buddha', *J. Siam Soc.*, xxii/1 (1928), pp. 19–28
A History of Buddhist Monuments in Siam (Bangkok, 1962); rev. as *Monuments of the Buddha in Siam* (Bangkok, 1973)

M. C. SUBHADRADIS DISKUL

Dan. Mande-speaking agricultural people of north-east Liberia and the neighbouring regions of Guinea and Côte d'Ivoire. Numbering some 300,000 by the 1990s, the Dan live mainly to the east and west of the upper Cavally River. The Dan and the neighbouring Mano in Liberia share many cultural traits with Toura in Côte d'Ivoire, the We (also known as Guere, Ngere or Kran) and the Wobe, although they differ linguistically from these Kwa-speaking peoples. The most important of Dan art forms are mask and masquerade, but they are also known for figure sculpture in wood and brass, finely carved wooden spoons and pottery. Examples of Dan art are held by most museums with collections of African art. The catalogue of the *Die Kunst der Dan* exhibition (Zurich, 1976) provides comprehensive illustrations for Dan art forms and techniques.

1. Introduction. 2. Mask and masquerade. 3. Figure sculpture. 4. Spoons and ladles. 5. Other arts. 6. Artists.

1. INTRODUCTION. The Dan belong to the large 'peripheral Mande group' of slash-and-burn farmers who moved south from present-day Mali in the last few centuries, penetrating the primary forest area, where they undertook the cultivation of rice, manioc, plantains and yams, as well as hunting, fishing and rearing poultry and cattle. They also planted Cola nuts for trade, though they did not establish markets. Instead, goods were circulated through gift exchanges between equals and elaborate feasts of merit, with the display and distribution of surplus food. Politically they did not recognize any centralized power; all villages were independent political units with a network of close socio-cultural links based on such factors as family ties, war alliances, the fraternization of important elders, secret societies and jointly held circumcision rites. In the 1920s their territory was administratively divided between the French and the Americo-Liberian governments.

In the Dan view of the world a distinction is drawn between the sphere of the village, associated with women, domestic animals, order and restraint, and that of the forest, associated with wild animals, powerful spirits and the dangers experienced especially by hunters. Spirits (*dü*) are invisible powers that have no form in their forest habitat but which, when they wish to support human concerns and 'feel the urge to become active in the village', may manifest themselves in magical objects, masks or large ritual spoons. These 'helper spirits' make contact with specific men and women by revealing themselves in dreams. The possibility of establishing a relationship with the supernatural through dreams has been considered of prime importance to all Dan men and women who wish to achieve something significant and so become a *tin me*, an outstanding and famous person. Such standing may be gained by performing extraordinary deeds of physical strength, through wit and intelligence, bewitching dance performances, story-telling, soothsaying, counselling or the production of pleasing or useful implements and objects. A person 'with a good name', a man or woman of repute and praise, was protected from danger during the constant threat of war and was less likely to suffer at the hands of the village leader, who was often a tyrant. These 'chiefs' were generally strong warriors, and their accumulated wealth was used for the provision of impressive feasts for their clients, friends and visitors, offering them large quantities of rice and meat. If performed with style and decorum, the deeds of these rich men (*bou mä*) were long remembered.

2. MASK AND MASQUERADE. The most important art works of the Dan are masks. These are known as *gle* in the west and *ga* in the east and are considered to be the manifestations of forest spirits. When a spirit decides to play an active role in human society it chooses a villager

1. Dan mask of Deangle or 'smiling' type, probably carved by Tame or Uopie, wood, h. 220 mm, Nyor Diaple, Liberia, c. 1925–35 (Switzerland, private collection)

character of the performing masker. Eleven major mask types may be distinguished, relating to aspects of social control, political and judicial matters, peace-making, education, competition and entertainment.

Deangle ('smiling mask') is the most common type of Dan mask and is often very beautiful. It has a gentle face with oval outlines, narrow eye slits and a small mouth (see fig. 1). It wears a conical helmet or stiff cap and is dressed in a cotton shawl and raffia skirt. The masker moves gracefully, neither singing nor dancing. Such maskers belong to the circumcision camps of the boys and collect food for them, report the camps' news to the village and act as go-betweens, linking the initiation camps in the forest to the women's realm of the village.

Tankagle is a singing, dancing and pantomimic mask with a beautiful female face similar to that of Deangle, but generally somewhat larger. The features are carved more elaborately, and the mask may have ears, facial scarification and ornaments. Together with their musicians and companions they entertain the audience at feasts.

Gunyege ('house spirit') is a mask with large, flat, circular eyes and a very rudimentary costume. The mask is worn in races in which the fastest runner in the family owning the mask is challenged by another boy from his age group but from another household; the spirit is supposed to help its bearer.

Zakpai is a fire-extinguishing mask characterized by a wooden face covered with red cloth; its large, tubular eyes are framed with tin sheeting. The masker wears a short raffia costume and fresh leaves. During the winter it

to impersonate it, contacting him in a dream and telling him his name and the required mask-type with its special paraphernalia, as well as instructing him on the accompanying music and performance specifications. On the basis of this information the mask performer contacts a mask carver and commissions a face mask. There is much jealousy between various performers, involving fights with magical threats and even poisoning. New masks are in fact rarely 'dreamt' or 'born'; old ones, however, if successful for some time, may rise in status and take on more important roles. Thus an entertainment mask may become a Guna Gle ('village quarter spirit/mask'), representing a village faction at feasts or political meetings. After some generations the same mask may even acquire a peace-keeping or judicial role of high renown. In such cases the wooden facial form may remain but the paraphernalia change, with the addition, for example, of a moustache, white hair, brass bells and the encrustations of offerings. The mask may also be worn with a different headdress, indicating immediately to the audience the status and

2. Dan mask of Bugle or 'gun' type, possibly carved by Uopie, wood, dark-brown patination, h. 230 mm, Nyor Dan region, Liberia, c. 1900–25 (Zurich, private collection)

3. Dan war mask Gau (of Bugle or 'gun' type), accompanied by the carver Tame, Nyor Diaple, Liberia; from a photograph by Eberhard Fischer, 1960

appears in the village about noon, accompanied by youngsters, to ensure that all fires are extinguished, so avoiding the possibility of conflagration.

Bagle are grotesque masks that entertain through pantomime. They have short, tube-like eyes, a low forehead, often crowned with a band of miniature antelope horns, a moustache and a medium-sized mouth. They wear a wig made of cotton strips, a large cotton cloth and a heavy raffia skirt. These masks dance to the accompaniment of a slit-gong orchestra and recount stories and anecdotes, caricaturing the day's events or even mocking their contemporaries' misbehaviour.

Bugle ('gun') masks are associated with warriors (see figs 2 and 3). Formerly they accompanied them to battle, or at least supported them by creating, when needed, a frightening, warlike atmosphere in the village. These dark masks have tubular eyes and large, open mouths that reveal animal fangs. Their fearsome nature is depicted by big beards, feather-helmets, the encrustations of blood sacrifices, heavy raffia skirts and weapons, and they run around with their followers in a wild, frenzied manner.

Kaogle ('chimpanzee mask') has a rough wooden face with monkey-like features: a bulging forehead, triangular eye slits or tubular eyes, pyramidal cheeks and an open mouth with large teeth. Bundles of feathers are stuck behind the ears, and a wig of cotton strips usually covers

the masker's head. They jump higher and move faster than Bugle and wear a slightly lighter raffia skirt. They throw hooked sticks into the audience or whirl around and chase the youngsters through the village lanes. They are aggressive and instruct young men in the techniques of war.

Glegben is a stilt-dancer who performs acrobatic stunts and entertains the villagers at feasts. He wears a mask made of raffia wickerwork.

Gegon ('male mask') has a wooden face with beak-like features and black fur attached to its jaw. These maskers only appear in the most northern Dan region, and it is likely that they are an import from Mande neighbours.

Gle Wa ('large mask') is one of the most impressive of Dan masks. It may exhibit composite features of powerful animals with human forms or be represented by very old masks (or copies of them). Accessories that indicate a Gle Wa's important role may include a headdress with a mass of white feathers, bells suspended around its chin, red cloth, a large raffia skirt and cow-tail fly whisks. These maskers may be summoned to settle a conflict or even to end a long-lasting war. They can punish evil-doers and levy fines; if the culprit does not obey, the group associated with the mask may seek vengeance through ordeals or even poison. During the 20th century the Go ('leopard') secret society has taken over the power of many independent Gle Wa masks, thus incorporating traditional political forces into a well-knit system of social control.

The Dan also produce miniature masks of all the full-scale types except the chimpanzee mask. There are two categories of miniature masks, ranging in height from 60 to 90 mm and from 100 to 200 mm (the smaller ones tend to be owned by individuals, the larger ones by secret societies). Commonly, they depict the attractive female facial form with narrow eye slits. These masks are referred to as *ma go* ('small head'), *yi luo po* ('things that water is poured over'; a reference to offerings) or *shal buo po* ('things to which sacrifice is made'). They are used in various contexts to establish or maintain a link with the spirit of the large mask. For example a mask owner or performer may make sacrifices and address requests to the miniature when travelling, or a woman wishing to retain contact with her family's mask spirit is allowed to commission a miniature before moving to her marital home. Miniature masks are also used by members of secret societies and are displayed to initiates. Before incisions are performed in the circumcision camps, the knife is passed over a miniature mask to dispel evil influences; hence some of them have marks on the forehead and sides of the face.

3. FIGURE SCULPTURE. Figures carved in wood or cast in brass are among the possessions through which wealthy Dan men display their affluence. These figures were considered difficult to make, and only a few exceptionally gifted artists could claim the necessary skill (*see* §6 below). The ownership of such a figure or group of sculptures was therefore a matter of influence and generosity, requiring both the proper reward for the artist and the celebration of the carving's installation with a public feast. A Dan chief of the 1930s is said to have built a small house especially for his *lü me* ('wooden person') and

charged an entrance fee for viewing his exceptional treasure (Donner). These figures are not considered sacred, and they do not represent ancestors or spirits; they are prestige objects, often portraying a living person dear to the owner or intended simply to display artistic skill.

Small stelae or half-figures with mask-like, sometimes two-faced, heads were used in various secret societies to embody the powers of helpful *dü* spirits. After an often lengthy ceremony members gained access to the *dü*'s powers, which were said to enable them to perform such extraordinary deeds as transforming into powerful animals and thus gaining extra-human powers in cutting the forest or hoeing the ground, or enabling them to handle poisonous snakes without fear. The assembly of the Snake Society, the traditional association of medicine persons, was presided over by the stele known as *no le* ('mother of the society'), which was placed on a platform inside the meeting-house. Similarly, the patron spirit of the Wild Hog Society of the bush-clearers was manifested in the *kedie* figure, which was taken out to the work site in the forest and set at the furthest extremity of the area to be cleared in order to protect the labourers from injury. It became the emblem of the day's most successful worker, who carried it back to the village and danced with it to the praise songs of the community.

4. SPOONS AND LADLES. Among the Dan wooden spoons and ladles are also emblems of status, prestige and power. Small spoons used by old people to eat rice and sauce are often beautifully rendered with a shovel-shaped scoop or bowl and an elegantly shaped handle terminating in an ornament. Larger spoons, with handles mostly terminating in a 'fish-tail', are used by the principal wife of a household to divide the daily food. The carving at the end of the handle on a third, even larger, type of spoon (l. *c.* 600 mm), known as *wa ke mia* ('feast acting spoon') may represent a large female head, a pair of legs, a powerful fist, the head of a domestic animal (usually a ram or a bull), a bowl, a ring or an ornament (see fig. 4; *see also* AFRICA, figs 51 and 106). Such spoons have an oval scoop and were the personal accoutrements of the *wa ke de* or *wunkirle*, a woman who had proved herself most industrious and generous, providing surplus food and serving not only her own group but also guests and even strangers. The spoons were symbols of status: at festivals they were swung by their female owners and used to carry husked rice, which was thrown in the air to welcome guests and as a sign of prosperity. Each spoon was named individually and considered to be the embodiment of a special *dü* spirit, who helped the *wunkirle* to achieve her role, communicating with her through dreams and assisting her in her daily work. With the consent of the embodying spiritual force a spoon was handed down to a successor, usually the most efficient daughter-in-law of the aging *wunkirle*. As the manifestation of a spirit, the scoop of a spoon is thought of as a fertile womb, while the head (or legs) may often bear the likeness of the owner who originally commissioned it.

5. OTHER ARTS. Dan also devoted aesthetic attention to their houses and domestic artefacts. Until at least the 1970s, in some areas, the Dan lived in traditional circular

4. Large Dan spoon (*wa ke mia*), carved by Sra, wood, kaolin-white fibres, black patination, h. 730 mm, Belewale, Liberia, *c.* 1925–35 (Zurich, private collection)

houses with conical thatched roofs, often more than 5 m in diameter, and clay walls erected on a clay and earth platform. Each house had a single door, clay beds around the inside walls and a central hearth. The lower part of the walls was painted with dark ochre and the upper part whitewashed and sometimes decorated with stylized representations of men and animals.

Though in general Dan household equipment is simple, they have produced the finest pottery known from the region (Fischer, 1963). Female specialists, who are bound by extensive ritual rules, produce clay vessels for cooking, carrying and storing water, bowls for serving food, palm-wine containers and oil lamps. These vessels, some of which are rather heavy, are shaped with beautiful rims and decorated with skilfully incised patterns, before being fired in the open. They are not individually marked, but the potters maintain that, although unsigned, the style of each master, living or dead, can be recognized easily.

Basketry is less specialized. Men make flat mats and basket bottoms, while women produce baskets in a variety of weaves. Fine baskets are used for storing such precious goods as jewellery and for artefacts that are manifestations of spirits that do not wish to be seen in public. Simpler baskets are for storing food.

The weaving of cotton yarn on looms was known to a few men but was not a speciality. Although widely used in recent times, woven indigo and white striped cotton textile was only used in the past to a limited extent for men's loincloths and women's wrappers; the latter, together with brass jewellery and cattle, were used for gifts or barter. Wooden utensils such as mortars and pestles, large ones for husking rice and small ones for grinding snuff, are decorated with simple chip-carved patterns. Wealthier Dan also owned wooden gaming-boards, often carved on one side with the heads of women or domestic animals, and cylindrical stools carved with various geometric forms.

6. ARTISTS. Only a few men mastered the skills of wood-carving and brass-casting. They worked in secret, out of sight of young people and women, particularly when carving masks or other sacred objects. Famous carvers were much sought after and given great gifts by potential clients. Unlike the masked performers, however, they were not in contact with the spiritual world and had to be instructed by the maskers in the manifestations their mask spirits expected. Accordingly, the most famous carvers were semi-itinerant craftsmen, working only to order and usually at the client's village. Besides producing new masks, especially for the annual circumcision camps and the entertainment masquerades, they had to repair or replace old masks with copies.

A few famous Dan carvers of the 20th century have been recorded. The most eminent, who was interviewed in his village—Belewale, in the south-western Dan region—in the late 1940s, became known as Sra ('Creator', also the term for God) (Himmelheber, 1960). He was by birth a We (from the border region in Liberia), but at that time he worked mainly for Dan clients in their style, with the assistance of his Dan wife. It is difficult to identify his works stylistically, since he adapted well to local demands, but they tend to be voluminous, with large and rounded forms. He died in 1950. His two major disciples were Son of Nuopie (*d* 1985) and Dro of Tapita (*b c.* 1935). The former was a blacksmith who learned carving from Sra when the master was invited to his village to produce a monumental Bie (elephant) mask. Son incorporated many details from Sra's style, but his work tends to be more angular, particularly in the execution of chins, lips and facial outlines (Fischer, 'Künstler der Dan', 1963). Dro, who was still alive in 1990, was already active in the 1950s, producing many different sculptures for export by the missionaries at Tapita, before he found his own style (Himmelheber, 1960; Johnson, 1986).

The most prolific and sensitive sculptor in the western area during the 1930s and 1940s was Tame ('wanderer'; *d* 1972) from Nyor Diaple (see fig. 3 above). He was brought up in a household of talented craftsmen as an apprentice of Uopie (*fl* 1920–30), the elder brother of Tompieme (see below; *d* 1991), and became a versatile blacksmith, brass-caster and wood-carver. He acquired his name through being so sought after that he was constantly on the move. It is thought that Tame may have been responsible for the ideal form of the smiling female beauty represented by Deangle masks, with their soft modelling, highly arched foreheads and sharply featured lips (*see* §2 and fig. 1 above). His rendering of noses often tends to

be flat and broad. Tame taught Tompieme, whose work in the 1960s was less accomplished than that of his teacher; nonetheless he was a fair craftsman, capable of good copies. By observing the pleasing features of the local women he was able to depict individualized, portrait-like faces on masks and spoons. A third carver of the Nyor Diaple region was Si (*d* 1990), a hunter and a remarkably noble personality, who was a contemporary of Tame and also trained by Uopie. He carved large spoons with subtle faces and masks with sharp features, slightly rough in execution but with clearcut strokes (*see* AFRICA, fig. 51). Si was renowned as a splendid teacher, the leader of many circumcision camps and a good singer. Only a few sculptors from the eastern Dan of Côte d'Ivoire have become known by name. These include Yitowo (*d* before 1950) in Flanple, who was one of the more important sculptors in the 1930s and whose work is easily recognizable, although little is known about him (Vandenhoute; Gerbrands).

Apart from the work of these masters from the 1930s to the 1960s, there has been little study of other individual carvers, but the published material has made it possible to identify some of the regional iconographic and stylistic features. In the south-west, masters worked (for Mano patrons) in a more naturalistic style, depicting ears at the rims of face-masks and showing soft swellings on cheeks and foreheads. In the north-west, features are generally less detailed and more 'abstract', while in the east they show influence from the We art region, being more hypertrophic, with bulbous contours. However, since major carvers could move from one client village to another, working in remote villages and mastering various substyles, it is evident that regional substyles can give only limited guidance in the identification of individual masters and their workshops.

BIBLIOGRAPHY
E. Donner: 'Kunst und Handwerk in NO-Liberia', *Baessler-Archv*, xxiii/2–3 (1940), pp. 45–110
G. Schwab and W. Harley: *Tribes of the Liberian Hinterland*, Pap. Peabody Mus. Archaeol. & Ethnol., xxxi (Cambridge, MA, 1947)
P. J. L. Vandenhoute: *Classification stylistique du masque Dan et Guéré*, Meded. Rijksmus. Vlkenknd., iv (Leiden, 1948)
B. Holas: *Les Masques Kono* (Paris, 1952)
A. A. Gerbrands: *Art as an Element of Culture, Especially in Negro Africa*, Meded. Rijksmus. Vlkenknd., xii (Leiden, 1957)
H. Himmelheber and U. Himmelheber: *Die Dan: Ein Bauernvolk im westafrikanischen Urwald* (Stuttgart, 1958)
H. Himmelheber: *Negerkunst und Negerkünstler* (Brunswick, 1960)
E. Fischer: 'Die Töpferei bei den westlichen Dan', *Z. Ethnol.*, lxxxviii/1 (1963), pp. 100–15
——: 'Künstler der Dan', *Baessler-Archv*, x/2 (1963–4), pp. 161–262
H. Himmelheber: 'Die Geister und ihre irdischen Verkörperungen als Grundvorstellungen in der Religion der Dan', *Baessler-Archv*, n. s., xii/1 (1964–5), pp. 1–88
E. Fischer: 'Zur Technik des Gelbgusses bei den westlichen Dan', *Festschrift Alfred Bühler* (Basle, 1965), pp. 93–115
H. Himmelheber and G. W. Tahmen: 'Wunkirle: Die gastlichste Frau', *Festschrift Alfred Bühler* (Basle, 1965), pp. 171–81
E. Fischer: *Der Wandel ökonomischer Rollen bei den westlichen Dan in Liberia*, Stud. Kultknd., xxi (Wiesbaden, 1967)
H. Zemp: *Musique Dan: La Musique dans la pense et la vie sociale d'une société africaine* (Paris and The Hague, 1971)
Die Kunst der Dan (exh. cat. by E. Fischer and H. Himmelheber, Zurich, Mus. Rietberg, 1976; Eng. trans. rev., Zurich, 1984)
E. Fischer: 'Dan Forest Spirits: Masks in Dan Villages', *Afr. A.*, xi/2 (1978), pp. 16–23

——: 'Self-portraits, Portraits, and Copies among the Dan: The Creative Process of Traditional African Mask Carvers', *IA Stud. Afr. A.*, i (1984), pp. 5–28

B. C. Johnson: *Four Dan Sculptors: Continuity and Change* (San Francisco, 1986)

——: 'Ldamie: Figurative Brass Caster of the Dan', *IA Stud. Afr. A.*, ii (1987), pp. 49–64

E. Fischer and H. Himmelheber: 'Löffel der Dan (Liberia/ Elfenbeinküste)', *Löffel in der Kunst Afrikas* (exh. cat., ed. L. Homberger; Zurich, Mus. Rietberg, 1990; Eng. trans., Zurich, 1991)

EBERHARD FISCHER

Danby, Francis (*b* nr Wexford, Ireland, 16 Nov 1793; *d* Exmouth, Devon, 9 Feb 1861). English painter of Irish birth. He was a landowner's son and studied art at the Dublin Society. In 1813 he visited London, then worked in Bristol, initially on repetitious watercolours of local scenes: for example, *View of Hotwells, the Avon Gorge* (*c*. 1818; Bristol, Mus. & A.G.). Around 1819 he entered the cultivated circle of George Cumberland (1754–1849) and the Rev. John Eagles (1783–1855). Danby's discovery of the 'poetry of nature' in local scenery and insignificant incident was influenced by the theories of Eagles, published as *The Sketcher* (1856), and, less directly, by those of William Wordsworth, who had been associated with Bristol earlier in the century. Danby's distinctive work began with the small panel paintings he produced for his Bristol audience. *Boy Sailing a Little Boat* (*c*. 1822; Bristol, Mus. & A.G.) recalls the rustic scenes of William Collins and the Bristol artist Edward Villiers Rippingille, but Danby emphasized the effect of sun and shade rather than sentiment.

Danby became the best-known member of the Bristol school of painters but preferred to exhibit more ambitious paintings in London. *The Upas, or Poison-tree in the Island of Java* (London, V&A) attracted considerable attention when first shown at the British Institution in 1820, by its large scale (1.68×2.29 m) and Sublime motif: a despairing adventurer coming upon the remains of his predecessors in the moonlit poisoned valley. It has deteriorated badly, like many of his works. *Disappointed Love* (1821; London, V&A) was his first Royal Academy exhibit. It differs from his Bristol works in its narrative content and in the pathetic fallacy by which the oppressive trees and wilting weeds echo the girl's despair.

When Danby moved to London in 1824 he abandoned naturalistic landscape and contemporary genre subjects to concentrate on painting poetical landscapes in the manner of Claude Lorrain and J. M. W. Turner's *Hannibal Crossing the Alps* (1812; London, Tate), and also large biblical scenes to rival John Martin. Danby's relationship with Martin was ambiguous, but undoubtedly competitive. Danby was elected ARA following the exhibition at the Royal Academy in 1825 of the *Delivery of Israel out of Egypt (Exod. xiv)* (1824–5; Preston, Harris Mus. & A.G.). His poetic treatment of landscape seems to have inspired Martin's *Deluge* (unlocated; mezzotint pubd 1828), which was shown the following year at the British Institution. Danby himself was already contemplating painting a *Deluge* and his *An Attempt to Illustrate the Opening of the Sixth Seal (Rev. vi. 12)* (exh. RA 1828; Dublin, N.G.) in turn owed much to Martin's conception of the Sublime.

Danby quarrelled with the Royal Academy in 1829, when not elected RA (Constable won by one vote). At the

Francis Danby: *Deluge*, oil on canvas, 2.84×4.52 m, 1837–40 (London, Tate Gallery)

same time his marriage had collapsed, and he had taken a mistress; his wife left London with the Bristol artist, Paul Falconer Poole, whom she subsequently married. The ensuing scandal forced Danby to move abruptly to Paris in 1830. Between 1831 and 1836 he worked in Geneva, producing chiefly watercolours and topographical paintings. He then lived in Paris, copying Old Master paintings. He returned to London late in 1838 where *Deluge* (1837–40; London, Tate; see fig.) re-established his reputation when exhibited privately in Piccadilly, London, in May 1840. A huge rock rises in the midst of the flood, swarming with figures who struggle to gain the highest point. Their diminution implies immensity. The colour is appropriately, but uncharacteristically, sombre. Despite its success, it was his last work of this type.

Danby continued to paint poetic fantasy landscapes throughout the 1840s and 1850s (e.g. *Enchanted Castle—Sunset*, exh. RA 1841; London, V&A), although they became increasingly unfashionable. He also produced landscapes and marine paintings, which derive in colour and conception, although not in execution, from those of Turner. These found admirers, although they were too rich in colour and imprecise in detail for wide popularity. *Evening Gun* (exh. RA 1848; destr.; replica, priv. col., see Adams, 1973, no. 72), showing naval vessels in harbour, was well received at the Royal Academy in 1848 and the Paris Exposition Universelle of 1855. Danby moved to Exmouth, Devon, in 1847 where he built boats and painted. He was embittered by a life of nearly constant debt and by his failure to gain academic honours. He died a few days after Poole was elected RA. Two of his sons, James Francis Danby (1816–75) and Thomas Danby (1817–86), became painters.

BIBLIOGRAPHY

Francis Danby (exh. cat., ed. E. Adams; Bristol, Mus. & A.G., 1961)
E. Adams: *Francis Danby: Varieties of Poetic Landscape* (New Haven, CT, 1973)
The Bristol School of Artists: Francis Danby and Painting in Bristol, 1810–1840 (exh. cat., ed. F. Greenacre; Bristol, Mus. & A.G., 1973)
Francis Danby (exh. cat., ed. F. Greenacre; London, Tate, 1989)

HILARY MORGAN

Dance. English family of artists. (1) George Dance was an architect active in the city of London, whose practice was taken over upon his death by his younger son, (3) George Dance. His elder son, (2) Nathaniel Dance-Holland, was a painter.

(1) George Dance (i) (*b* London, 1695; *d* London, 10 Feb 1768). Architect. He was the son of a mason and occasional sculptor, joining him in an 'account of co-partnership' in 1717. Together they carried out extensive work at the South Sea Company's City of London premises and at the Carshalton house of the Company's governor, Sir John Fellows. Two years later George married, and by 1724 he had moved into a house in Chiswell Street, Moorfields. This was to be the family home for nearly 50 years. On 2 June 1725 he was made a freeman of the Merchant Taylors' Company. In 1727 he took the first step towards becoming an architect by collaborating with his father-in-law, the surveyor James Gould (*d* 1734), in a design for the rebuilding of St Botolph's church, Bishopsgate. This was in the Wren manner but with the tower

placed over the east end, to provide a frontispiece to the street. Dance also assisted Gould in the speculative development of a small area of land adjoining the Minories; this was completed by 1732 and named Gould Square (destr. *c.* 1880).

In 1733 Dance applied successfully for the post of Clerk of the Works to the City of London, although this was not confirmed until December 1735 because of interference by George Smith, the previous holder. At this time the post carried no salary and involved much routine maintenance, but it brought prestige and a sequence of important fee-paying architectural projects. The first of these was the Lord Mayor's Mansion House, and Dance's designs of 1735 show the influence of Colen Campbell's Wanstead House, Essex, particularly in the great hexastyle portico approached by a double flight of steps in two stages (now reduced to one). The internal arrangement around a courtyard (later filled in) included a ballroom lit by a clerestory and an 'Egyptian Hall', which took its name from a Vitruvian prototype earlier drawn upon by Richard Boyle, 3rd Earl of Burlington, in his York Assembly Rooms of 1731–2. The site chosen for the Mansion House meant clearing the old Stocks Market; to replace it, Dance designed in 1735 a long arcaded range, built on ground reclaimed from the Fleet ditch. In 1747 he built a new corn market in Mark Lane, followed by a hall for the Surgeons' Company in 1748. Two years later he was asked to design a 'Hospital for poor Lunaticks', later known as St Luke's, on a site at the end of what is now Worship Street. This emerged as a three-storey block in brick with stone dressings. It served until 1782, when a new asylum was built by Dance's son in Old Street.

Dance's design for a bridge over the Thames at Blackfriars, prompted by discussions in 1753 for general improvements in the area, did not materialize; but in 1756–60 he collaborated with (later Sir) Robert Taylor (who had carved the allegorical relief in the pediment of Dance's Mansion House) on the renovation of old London Bridge. This involved removing houses and the chapel, providing parapets and, to facilitate river traffic, replacing two central arches with a single span. Although only the Mansion House now survives of the above-mentioned works, Dance's three churches all still stand: St Leonard, Shoreditch (1735), St Botolph, Aldgate (1741), and St Matthew, Bethnal Green (1743), the last heavily restored after extensive damage in World War II. His remodelled nave and transepts of St Mary, Faversham, carried out 1754–5, are also largely intact.

A move by the City Lands Committee towards rebuilding the notorious Newgate Gaol produced an imaginative design in 1755; had it materialized, it would have enhanced Dance's reputation. His proposal was for two blocks to bestride the Newgate entrance to London, each enclosed by massive rusticated walls set with blind arcading. The design was engraved and circulated but, although discussed intermittently during the next ten years, was finally set aside.

From 1760 Dance took an active interest in the formation of the Society of Artists, at whose second exhibition of 1761 his 'Design for the Bridge at Blackfryers' was hung. The following year his perspective drawings for St

Leonard's church were displayed, and although he did not exhibit again, his name appears in the list of members dining together in 1763.

BIBLIOGRAPHY
Colvin
S. Perks: *The History of the Mansion House* (London, 1922)
George Dance the Elder and Younger (exh. cat., London, Geffrye Mus., 1972)

DOROTHY STROUD

(2) Sir **Nathaniel Dance-Holland** (*b* London, 18 May 1735; *d* Winchester, 15 Oct 1811). Painter and politician, elder son of (1) George Dance (i). He trained under Francis Hayman before travelling to Rome in 1754. As Nathaniel Dance he established himself as a portrait painter but was determined to succeed as a history painter. His picture the *Death of Virginia* (1759; untraced, but known from a sketch, London, Soane Mus.) is of documentary importance as the first dated Classical history painting by a British artist working in Rome. In 1762 Dance assisted Pompeo Girolamo Batoni, whose influence brightened his palette and introduced him to a grander clientele, including Edward Augustus, Duke of York (1739–67), who sat for both artists in 1764 (Dance's *Edward Augustus, Duke of York*, London, Buckingham Pal., Royal Col.). In the same year Dance painted a portrait of *Angelica Kauffman* (Burghley House, Cambs), with whom he was in love. He returned to London in 1765 and rapidly achieved fame as a portrait and history painter. His *Timon of Athens* (1767; London, Buckingham Pal., Royal Col.) was purchased by George III; but after the King appointed Benjamin West to be his history painter in 1772, Dance concentrated on portraits. He was among the 22 artists who successfully petitioned the King in 1768 to establish a Royal Academy, and he served for periods as a council member and visitor, until 1782. At the Academy's first exhibition (1769) Dance showed full-length portraits of *George III* and *Queen Charlotte* (Uppark, W. Sussex, NT); two years later he exhibited *David Garrick as Richard III* (Stratford-on-Avon, Town Hall). In the mid-1770s Dance became financially independent, and his output declined sharply, virtually ceasing after his marriage in 1783 to a wealthy widow. He resigned from the Academy in 1790 on his election as Member of Parliament for East Grinstead and subsequently only exhibited occasional landscapes as a 'gentleman'. In 1800 he was created a baronet and assumed the name of Dance-Holland; he died worth over £200,000.

BIBLIOGRAPHY
Waterhouse: *18th C.*
W. T. Whitley: *Artists and their Friends in England, 1700–1799* (London and Boston, 1928)
Nathaniel Dance, 1735–1811 (exh. cat. by D. Goodreau, London, Kenwood House, 1977)

DAVID RODGERS

(3) George Dance (ii) (*b* London, 1 April 1741; *d* London, 14 Jan 1825). Architect, younger son of (1) George Dance (i); and brother of (2) Nathaniel Dance-Holland. He was born in the Chiswell Street house and, after attending St Paul's School in the City, learnt the rudiments of architecture from his father before being sent to study in Italy in 1758. He was admitted to the Accademia di S Luca, Rome; there, over the next six years, he became proficient in drawing while studying Neoclassical theories of rational design, such as those found in M.-A. Laugier's *Essai sur l'architecture* of 1753. Dance also made expeditions to Naples and Parma and, on the evidence of his subsequent works, to Vicenza and Mantua. In 1763 he entered the annual competition of the Academy at Parma, where his design for a 'Public Gallery for Statues, Pictures, etc.' won the gold medal. The following year he returned to England and began work in his father's office.

In May 1765 Dance won the competition for rebuilding All Hallows, London Wall, the interior of which, in its omission of a frieze from the entablature, is the first instance of his rationalist approach to classical architecture (see fig. 1). On his father's death in February 1768, Dance succeeded as Clerk of the City's Works, and within a few days he was instructed to prepare fresh designs for the rebuilding of Newgate Gaol. The first sketches were submitted in April; as built, Dance's gaol was a monumental building reminiscent of Palladio's Palazzo Thiene at Vicenza, with walls of rusticated masonry in rising courses of diminishing size (see fig. 2). North and south of a central Governor's House, windowless walls were set with arched recesses containing pedimented frames, their massive keystones reflecting those in Giulio Romano's courtyard of the Palazzo del Te in Mantua. Behind its outward expression of retribution, emphasized by festoons of shackles above both entrances, Dance provided humane accommodation with adequate supplies of water and provision of stoves, fireplaces and privies, reflecting the contemporary movement in prison reform. Ready for occupation early in 1775, it was repaired after serious

1. George Dance (ii): interior of All Hallows, London Wall, London, begun 1765

2. George Dance (ii): Newgate Gaol, London, 1775 (destr. 1902)

damage in the Gordon Riots of June 1780 and continued to be the City's principal gaol until demolition in 1902. Less well known than Newgate is Dance's smaller but complementary block, built near by in Giltspur Street between 1787 and 1791 (destr. 1855) for the accommodation of debtors. His original idea was for the three-storey block of heavily rusticated masonry to have a form of crenellated parapet, but this was omitted in favour of a pediment.

Improvements to the Guildhall made constant demands on Dance's time, but his first important addition was a new Council Chamber in 1777 (destr. 1908) on a site hemmed in by existing buildings. He solved this difficulty with a ground-plan in which semicircular apses flanked a rectangular central space; this was lit from a glazed oculus over a shallow dome springing from four piers. In 1788 he provided a new quasi-oriental front to the Guildhall, likely to have been inspired by the recently engraved *Select Views in India* prepared by his friend William Hodges. In contrast, Dance's new block of Justice Rooms (1795; destr.) on the west side of Guildhall Yard was of sober stock-brick over a ground floor of rusticated masonry.

Dance's opportunity to display his skill in urban planning had first come in 1767 when he prepared a scheme for a small area to the west of the Minories. There he laid out the so-called Crescent, Circus and America Square (destr.) on lines comparable to developments in Bath by the John Wood family, which he had recently examined there. By 1769 he was making his first plans for the much larger City estate in Finsbury; this was to be a major preoccupation for the next 30 years, and once more a square and circus were dominant features (although the first was begun in 1777 and the latter not until after his retirement). The earliest terraces were those in Bunhill Row, City Road, and the north-east end of Chiswell Street, where Dance's own boyhood home was demolished

c. 1778 to make way for a new block. He carried out other street improvement schemes in Holborn and the West End during the 1790s, though none of these survives except in outline. Among his most imaginative but abortive schemes were those for twin bridges over the Thames to replace old London Bridge and for rebuilding the Legal Quays, a complex of docks and warehouses for the Port of London.

Towards the end of the 1780s Dance began to take a limited number of private commissions: alterations and additions to Lansdowne House, Berkeley Square (1788, destr.); alterations to Camden Place, Chislehurst (1788) and Wilderness House, near Sevenoaks (*c.* 1800); and, also in 1800, the remodelling of Stratton Park, Hants (destr. 1960). A commission in 1803 from Sir George Beaumont for a new house at Coleorton, Leics, resulted in a Gothic design by Dance of singular severity, particularly in the entrance vestibule and staircase hall. The same stark interpretation of Gothic appeared in his façade designs of 1812–13 for Ashburnham Place, Sussex (destr. 1959), but here his staircase hall and other internal additions were in the classical style. In 1807 Dance rebuilt 143, Piccadilly for his brother Nathaniel. The house was demolished in 1972, but a fragment of the original decorative iron staircase balustrading is now preserved in Sir John Soane's Museum.

As a founder-member of the Royal Academy, he followed its affairs with interest, serving as one of the auditors for several years and intermittently on the hanging committee. From about 1793 he made a large number of profile drawings of friends, particularly those who were fellow Academicians. He was appointed Professor of Architecture there in 1798 but resigned in 1806 without having given any of the customary lectures. With the exception of his pupil John Soane, who seems to have spent four years in his office from 1768 and whose subsequent work in the Bank of England Stock Offices shows the influence of his master's Council Chamber vaulting, Dance had few followers. From 1771 to 1814 he was assisted in his City office (but at his own expense) by James Peacock (?1738–1814), who relieved him of many minor and onerous duties. Dance retired from his official post in 1815 and was succeeded by William Mountague (1773–1843), who had previously acted as his clerk. Dance's remaining ten years were spent in the Gower Street house (now 91, Gower Street), to which he and his family had moved with their three sons shortly before his wife's death in 1791. In 1836 his eldest son, Charles, offered the collection of some 1300 of Dance's office drawings to Sir John Soane; he purchased these for £500, placing them in his Museum, where they remain.

BIBLIOGRAPHY

Colvin

S. Angell: 'Sketch of the Professional Life of George Dance', *Builder*, v (1847), p. 333

H. Rosenau: 'George Dance the Younger', *J. Royal Inst. Brit. Archit.*, n. s. 3, liv (1947), pp. 502–7

J. Summerson: *Architecture in Britain, 1530–1830*, Pelican Hist. A. (London, 1953, rev. 7/1983)

M. Hugo-Brunt: 'George Dance as Town-planner', *J. Soc. Archit. Hist.*, xiv (1955), pp. 13–22

D. Stroud: *George Dance, Architect: 1741–1825* (London, 1971)

George Dance the Elder and Younger (exh. cat., London, Geffrye Mus., 1972)

G. Teysott: *Città e utopia nell'illuminismo inglese: George Dance il giovane* (Rome, 1974)

DOROTHY STROUD

Dance, Suzanne (*b* Melbourne, 18 Sept 1941). Australian architect. She graduated from the University of Melbourne in 1965, and from 1970 she worked as a sole practitioner in Melbourne. She developed an active association with community groups and professional bodies, both as a founding member of a free 'store-front' service to people unable to afford the services of architects and as a member of various committees and juries of the Royal Australian Institute of Architects (RAIA). Her practice primarily involved residential and conservation schemes, including work of the Ministry of Housing, but she also designed community and commercial buildings. Work in the interstices of the inner city, carried out on a tight budget, was typical of a large part of her practice; the Elderly Citizens' Centre (1984), Fitzroy, is an example. Here the new is compressed between two existing but disparate post-war buildings; while the autonomy of the older buildings is maintained, they are physically linked through the intervention and by an overlay of exaggerated 1950s detailing distilled from the two. Dance worked closely with clients to produce finely crafted results. She was the first woman architect to receive an RAIA medal for housing (1980), awarded for her widely acclaimed North Melbourne studio (1976) for the actor Max Gillies, which was a forerunner in the urban use of the vernacular material corrugated iron. In 1981 she was invited to the conservation course at the Istituto Centrale per il Restauro in Rome. From 1980 she taught design and urban conservation part-time at the Royal Melbourne Institute of Technology.

BIBLIOGRAPHY

R. Pegrum: *Details in Australian Architecture* (Sydney, 1984), pp. 54–5

P. Davey: 'House, Melbourne: Suzanne Dance', *Archit. Rev.* [London], clxxviii/1066 (1985), pp. 78–9

J. Taylor: *Australian Architecture Since 1960* (Melbourne, 1986)

P. Goad, P. Tombesi and R. Vanuci: 'Poetry in Iron', *Spazio & Soc.*, 43 (1988), pp. 60–77

P. Reynolds, R. Irving and R. Apperley: *A Pictorial Guide to Identifying Australian Architecture* (Victoria, 1989)

L. Van Schaik: 'Suzanne Dance', *Transition* [Austral.], 31 (1990), pp. 39–47

Ardvaark II: A Selected Guide to Contemporary Melbourne Architects (Melbourne, 1992)

ANNA RUBBO

Danckerts, Hendrick (*b* The Hague, 1625; *d* Amsterdam, 1680). Dutch painter and engraver, active in Italy and England. He was the son of Johannes Danckerts the elder and the younger brother of the engraver Johannes Danckerts the younger (1615–*c*. 1681/7). From 1645 to 1653 he worked in The Hague, where he became a master in 1651. After 1653 he travelled to Italy. He was accompanied on his journey by van Steenvoorde, the student of his brother Johannes. In Rome they came into contact with those artists known as the DUTCH ITALIANATES. Their manner of depicting the Roman campagna in luminous colours and their landscape motifs recur constantly in the work of Danckerts.

In 1657 Danckerts joined his brother Johannes in England, where Dutch landscape painters were then popular. He became court painter to Charles II, who commissioned views of such royal properties as Windsor Castle, Hampton Court Palace and the Queen's House at Greenwich. The King also gave Danckerts permission to make copies of his own paintings, and Samuel Pepys and his wife took advantage of this to have their portraits painted against the background of the Queen's House. Charles also commissioned views of the harbours of England and Wales from Danckerts. His other patrons included James, Duke of York, who, when king, was reputed to have had 28 landscapes by Danckerts in his collection; there are still 16 of his paintings in the royal collection (e.g. *Classical Landscape*, *c.* 1675; London, Hampton Court, Royal Col.).

Danckerts's activities as an engraver were devoted mostly to the reproduction of paintings by Titian, Andrea del Sarto and Palma Vecchio. However, his best works in the medium are the portraits of *Charles II* after Adriaen Hanneman (e.g. Hollstein, no. 1) and the portraits of *Ewald Schrevelius* (Hollstein, no. 7) and *Christiaan Rumpf* (Hollstein, no. 5). Danckerts gave his own name as the publisher on the prints made after Italian paintings. The name of Philip, 5th Earl of Pembroke, is given on a number of prints as the owner of the painting that Danckerts had reproduced as a print. A mezzotint portraying the murder of the De Witt brothers (Hollstein, no. 10) shows that Danckerts also experimented with other printmaking techniques. He also engraved a series of 13 plates, the *Curiosities of the Beach at Walcheren* (Hollstein, nos 21–33). In 1679 the religious climate in England became strongly anti-Catholic, and Danckerts fled to Amsterdam.

BIBLIOGRAPHY

Hollstein: *Dut. & Flem.*; Thieme–Becker

H. Walpole: *Anecdotes of Painting in England* (1762–71); ed. R. N. Wornum, ii, pp. 108–9

C. Kramm: *De levens en werken van de Hollandse en Vlaamsche kunstschilders, beeldhouwers, graveurs en bouwmeesters* [The lives and works of the Dutch and Flemish painters, sculptors, engravers and architects] (Amsterdam, 1857)

H. Gerson: *Ausbreitung und Nachwirkung der holländischen Malerei des 17. Jahrhunderts* (Haarlem, 1942), p. 403
O. Millar: *The Tudor and Early Georgian Pictures in the Collection of Her Majesty the Queen* (London, 1963), pp. 153–5

JACQUELINE BURGERS

Danckerts de Rij [Danckerts]. Dutch family of architects and artists. Cornelis Danckerts (1536–95) was the city mason of Amsterdam. His son, Cornelis Danckerts de Rij (i) (*b* Amsterdam 1561; *d* 1634) possibly received from him his early training in the building trade. Judging from the addition of 'de Rij' (surveyor or clerk of works) to his name, he must have been a well-respected land surveyor or building inspector, and on his father's death he succeeded to his post. The Municipal Works Department at that time consisted of Hendrick de Keyser I (City Architect), Hendrick Jacobsz. Staets (*c.* 1588–1631; City Carpenter) and Cornelis Danckerts de Rij (i) (City Mason and Land Surveyor). Danckerts worked closely with de Keyser and probably executed his designs for the Zuiderkerk (1603), the Exchange (1608–11) and the Westerkerk (1620). The tower of the Westerkerk (h. 85 m), which was completed in 1638 and is an important feature of the city's skyline, differs markedly from de Keyser's elegant, openwork design and was probably the work of Danckerts. He continued the square stone base upwards with three progressively smaller blocklike storeys of timber clad with lead, which give the tower its majestic appearance. The angular shapes of the tower are further emphasized by diagonally placed, free-standing columns supporting ornamental urns. The tower is surmounted by the imperial crown, symbol of the city of Amsterdam.

Cornelis Danckerts de Rij (i) had three sons, Peter Danckerts de Rij (*b* Amsterdam, 1605; *d* Rudnik, 9 Aug 1661), Hendrick Danckerts de Rij (*b* The Hague, *c.* 1625; *d* after 1678) and Cornelis Danckerts de Rij (ii) (*fl* 1637–84). Peter Danckerts de Rij moved to Poland, where he became court painter to King Vladislav IV (*reg* 1633–48). He worked on the Royal Castle's Marble Room (*see* WARSAW, fig. 5) and on the Baroque chapel of St Casimir in the cathedral of St Stanislaus, Wilno (now Vilnius), which he decorated with mural paintings. Hendrick Danckerts de Rij became the City Land Surveyor of Amsterdam and designed an octagonal domed church in 1628; although never executed, the plans for this church were published in the second edition of *Architectura moderna* (1641; see below). Cornelis Danckerts de Rij (ii) also worked as the City Land Surveyor and Assistant City Mason of Amsterdam. In 1643, when the designs for Amsterdam's new town hall were already well under way, he produced a remarkable ground-plan for the building, which involved redesigning the Dam, the irregularly shaped square in the city centre on to which the town hall was to face. Danckerts tried to make the square more regular, proposing blocks of houses and triumphal arches with which to create a Renaissance-style piazza. In 1648, however, it was decided to implement Jacob van Campen's plans for the project instead.

Cornelis Danckerts I van Seevenhoven (*b c.* 1603; *d* before 10 July 1656), nephew of Cornelis Danckerts de Rij (i), worked in Amsterdam as an engraver and publisher.

He and his descendants were concerned with the publication of *Architectura moderna* (1631), a collection of designs, chiefly by de Keyser, and the first book to be published on North Netherlandish architecture. They also issued translations of works by Palladio, Jacopo Vignola and Vincenzo Scamozzi, and a book of Jacob van Campen's designs for the Amsterdam Town Hall.

BIBLIOGRAPHY
Wurzbach
J. Laurentius: *De kroniek van staets*, ed. N. de Roever (Amsterdam, 1886)
Waller-Juynboll: *Biografisch woordenboek van noord Nederlandsche graveurs* [Biographical dictionary of North Netherlandish engravers] (n.d.)
S. de Bray, ed.: *Architectura moderna of te Bouwingen van onzen tijt* (Amsterdam, 1631, *R* Soest, 1971)

PAUL H. REM

D'Ancona, Paolo (*b* Pisa, 7 Nov 1878; *d* Milan, 30 April 1964). Italian art historian. He was educated at Pisa University. From 1909 he taught art history at Milan University, where he was responsible for introducing courses in art history into the literature degree, and where he began to pursue his early interest in manuscript illumination. His first book, and one of his major works, *La miniatura fiorentina* (1914), was the result of almost a decade of documentary research and stylistic analysis—a vast corpus of material, which established the characteristics of the numerous schools and workshops. In 1925 he published *La Miniature italienne*, a work that traced the roots of Italian miniature painting in Byzantine, Carolingian, Irish and French illumination. Alongside his study of manuscript illumination D'Ancona developed an interest in other periods of art history, and published from the mid-1940s a series of monographs and works on aspects of the Italian Renaissance and of modern art. Towards the end of his life he returned to his early interests with the publication of the essay 'Contributo alla storia della miniatura del sec. XV', which was based on documents found in the archives of S Lorenzo, Florence. D'Ancona was a gifted teacher and was concerned throughout his career with the promotion of art-historical studies. He wrote a number of guides to the teaching of art history and collaborated on the three-volume work *L'arte*, which has served as a definitive manual for generations of Italian students of the subject.

WRITINGS
La miniatura fiorentina: Secoli XI–XVI, 2 vols (Florence, 1914)
L'uomo e le sue opere nelle figurazioni italiane nel medioevo (Florence, 1923)
La Miniature italienne du Xe au XVIe siècle (Paris, 1925)
with F. Wittgens: *L'antologia della moderna critica d'arte* (Milan, 1927)
with I. Cattaneo and F. Wittgens: *L'arte*, 3 vols (Florence, 1930–32)
Les Primitifs italiens du XIe au XIIIe siècle (Paris, 1935)
with E. Aeschlimann: *Dictionnaire des miniaturistes du moyen âge et de la Renaissance dans les différentes contrées de l'Europe* (Milan, 1949)
'Contributo alla storia della miniatura del sec. XV', *Scritti di storia dell'arte in onore di M. Salmi*, ii (Rome, 1962), pp. 329–37

BIBLIOGRAPHY
DBI

☐

Dandan-oilik [Dandan-uilik; Dandan-uiliq]. Site on the eastern edge of the oasis of Khotan, on the southern Silk Route, in Xinjiang Uygur Autonomous Region, China. The site, which was investigated by Aurel Stein in 1900–01, contained the ruins of six dwellings and eleven places of worship, probably built between the 7th and 9th centuries AD. Finds include two manuscripts (both London, BM)—a canonical text of Mahayana Buddhism, the *Prajñāparamitā* (Skt: 'Perfection of wisdom'), in an East Iranian language, and a *Vajracchedikā* ('diamond-knife'; sharp as a diamond) version in Sanskrit—as well as wall paintings and small wooden painted panels (?8th century; London, BM) with various motifs. One of the latter shows two riders, one above the other surrounded by a halo, the one above on a horse, the one below on a camel; each holds a dish in his right hand (Yaldiz, pl. 117). On another small wooden panel are two figures facing each other, surrounded by almond-shaped haloes: on the left a fan-bearer, on the right a figure with an animal-like head (Yaldiz, pl. 118). Stein believed this to be an illustration of the rat legend recorded by the Chinese pilgrim Xuanzang, who travelled to India between AD 629 and 645. Another small painted wooden panel has on the front an ithyphallic seated Shiva Maheshvara, holding in his four hands the sun, the moon, the trident and probably a double drum (Yaldiz, pl. 120). The back is painted with another male seated figure (Yaldiz, pl. 121). The interpretation is open to question. A composition closely related stylistically to the panels is the painting on the east wall of the small temple known as D.II (Yaldiz, pl. 119). In front of the surviving lower section directly in front of the foundation, the headless clay figure of Vaishravana (King of the North) stood on a flattened demon with a large head. The surface of the wall to the left was painted with a woman stepping out of a lake, covering her breasts coquettishly with her right hand. A small, naked, ithyphallic figure stretches its hands imploringly up to her, and three riders on piebald horses are visible to the left below. Above are two large seated figures that do not appear to belong to the scene. Interpretations of this painting differ.

BIBLIOGRAPHY

S. Beal: *Si-yu-ki: Buddhist Records from the Western World* (London, 1888/*R* San Francisco, 1976)
A. Stein: *Ancient Khotan: Detailed Report of Archaeological Exploration in Chinese Turkestan*, 2 vols (Oxford, 1907)
J. Williams: 'The Iconography of Khotanese Painting', *E. & W.*, n. s., xxiii/1–2 (1973), pp. 109–54
M. Yaldiz: *Archäologie und Kunstgeschichte Chinesisch-Zentralasiens (Xinjiang)* (1987), iii/2 of *Handbuch der Orientalistik*, ed. B. Spuler and others (Leiden, 1978–)

M. YALDIZ

Dandini. Italian family of painters. They made a significant contribution to the Florentine Baroque. The polished and elegant style of (1) Cesare Dandini was continued by his younger brother (2) Vincenzo Dandini. Their nephew (3) Pietro Dandini, was Vincenzo's pupil, and Pietro's two sons, Ottaviano (1681–1740) and Vincenzo (1686–1734), a Jesuit, worked as painters in Florence and are mentioned by Baldinucci as 'good professors of painting'. A number of paintings have been attributed to Ottaviano (Cantelli) but, as yet, none to Vincenzo. There are a large number of drawings from the Dandini studio (ex-Bishop of Truro priv. col.; see Thiem), identified by initials and often bearing biblical inscriptions in English, including some that are presumably by the younger Vincenzo (V.D.*g*), such as the pencil study of figures from a print after Charles Le Brun's *Alexander and Darius* (Williamsburg, VA, priv. col.).

(1) Cesare Dandini (*b* Florence, 1 Oct 1596; *d* Florence, 7 Feb 1657). He was a precocious artist, who trained first with Francesco Curradi, briefly with Cristofano Allori and then with Domenico Passignano (who returned to Florence in 1616). Our scant knowledge of his life comes from Baldinucci, who wrote that he was an exceptionally beautiful youth (Curradi's model for numerous Madonnas) and was offended by the scurrilous activities in Allori's studio, a reaction that accords with the sense of refinement in his art. He matriculated in 1621 in the Accademia del Disegno; of his documented paintings, the earliest known is a *Pietà* (1625; Florence, SS Annunziata, sacristy). By 1631, the year in which he painted the *Zerbino and Isabella* (Florence, Uffizi) for the musician Giovanni Battista Severi and the *Virgin and Saints* for SS Annunziata, he had acquired many patrons, notably Lorenzo de' Medici. He developed a theatrical, idealized style that was at once veristic, classicizing, harmonious in form and colour and restrained in movement and expression. His two paintings entitled *Charity* (1634; Florence, Casino Mediceo; undated, New York, Met.) illustrate this manner, which invites comparison with the work of Guido Reni in Bologna. He shared with Florentine contemporaries Jacopo Vignali and Carlo Dolci a devotion to the style initiated in the 1590s by Lodovico Cigoli, Gregorio Pagani, Jacopo da Empoli, Passignano and Curradi and refined in the 1610s and 1620s by Matteo Rosselli, Giovanni Bilivert and Allori (who was perhaps the most influential for Cesare). His production included portraits in miniature on copper (praised by Baldinucci), salon pictures of half-length religious, secular and allegorical figures, which often appear to combine portraiture with thematic conceits (e.g. *St Michael*, Florence, priv. col.; *Mithradates*, Florence, Piselli priv. col. (see 1986 exh. cat., p. 306); *Comedy*, Florence, Uffizi), and large-scale portrayals of religious and literary themes (Cantelli). *Moses Driving away the Shepherds* (1635–45; Dublin, N.G.; see fig.) is a good example of what Baldinucci characterized as his 'maniera vaga', an elegant style with figures based on the diligent study of nature but corrected with a particular grace and beauty. In his late works, such as the *Conversion of Saul* (1646–7; Vallombrosa, abbey church) and the *Death of Cleopatra* (Florence, priv. col., see 1986 exh. cat., p. 308), he introduced more rhetorical gestures and animated movement, reminiscent of Pietro da Cortona and his Florentine contemporary Baldassare Franceschini.

Cesare Dandini's drawings, the principal collection of which is held at the Galleria degli Uffizi in Florence, are in the tradition of Cigoli, Passignano and Allori. Dandini's theatrical elegance and poetic mood exerted a strong influence in Florence in the second quarter of the 17th century; among his pupils were Antonio Giusti (1624–1705), Alessandro Rosi (1627–1707), Giovanni Domenico Ferrucci and the master draughtsman and etcher Stefano della Bella.

(2) Vincenzo Dandini (*b* Florence, 17 March 1609; *bur* 22 April 1675). Brother of (1) Cesare Dandini. He first trained with his brother and then matriculated in the Accademia del Disegno in 1631. He worked in Rome *c.* 1635–6, studying ancient and modern works and also as a member of Pietro da Cortona's workshop. He then

Cesare Dandini: *Moses Driving away the Shepherds*, oil on canvas, 2.06×2.72 m, 1635–45 (Dublin, National Gallery of Ireland)

returned to Florence and collaborated over the next two decades with his elder brother. He often worked for the Medici court, particularly for Lorenzo de' Medici, for whom he painted the *Adoration of Niobe* and *Venus, Mercury and Cupid* (1637–8; Florence, Uffizi), and later for the Medici tapestry factory (1662–3). Besides working in fresco and making cartoons for tapestries, he produced numerous paintings on literary and religious themes, for example the signed and dated *SS Carlo Borromeo and Andrea Zoerandro* (1657; Arezzo, S Maria in Gradi) and *SS Bernardino of Siena and Giovanni Capestrano Adoring the Name of Jesus* (1667; Florence, Mus. Ognissanti). His drawings are clearly influenced by his brother and by Pietro da Cortona (see Thiem in 1981 exh. cat.). Those studies and copies from the Dandini studio collection inscribed V.D.*v.* are probably done by him. As with Cesare, his style became more animated and dramatic in later works. Pupils of Vincenzo included his nephew (3) Pietro Dandini and Anton Domenico Gabbiani (documented by letters of 1673–4). Briefly mentioned by Baldinucci, Vincenzo emerges (Borea and Bellesi; see 1977 and 1986 exh. cats) as a significant artistic personality, displaying at times a great truth to nature and sense of humanity, as seen in *St Anne* (Florence, priv. col.; see 1986 exh. cat., p. 405).

(3) Pietro Dandini (*b* Florence, 1646; *d* Florence, 1712). Nephew of (1) Cesare Dandini and (2) Vincenzo Dandini. During the 1650s he studied with Vincenzo, and

he produced his first paintings at the age of 18. Having studied in Venice, Lombardy, Emilia and Rome, he carried out numerous commissions in Florence for frescoes and oil paintings in a style clearly influenced by Pietro da Cortona and Giordano. Principal works are ceiling decorations in fresco in Florence (*c.* 1685; S Maria Maddalena dei Pazzi), and the *Triumph of Hercules* and the *Allegory of the World, Tyranny and War* (1695–6; Florence, Gal. Corsini; see Guicciardini Corsi Salviati). He was praised by Baldinucci, his contemporary, as a painter of incomparable vitality, and, more recently, by Cantelli, as one of the most considerable artists in late 17th-century Florence for his combination of new directions, particularly those of Giordano, with the Florentine traditions of precise design, painterly execution and ingenuity of invention.

BIBLIOGRAPHY

Thieme–Becker

F. Baldinucci: *Notizie* (1681–1728); ed. F. Ranalli (1845–7), iv, pp. 549–62 [principal source: Cesare, Vincenzo, Pietro]

F. S. Baldinucci: *Vite* (1725–30); ed. A. Matteoli (1975) [Pietro]

Series degli uomini i piu illustri, x (Florence, 1774), pp. 161–8 [Vincenzo]

G. Ewald: 'Studien zur florentiner Barockmalerei', *Pantheon*, xxiii (1965), pp. 302–18 [Cesare]

M. Gregori: 'Cesare Dandini, pittore del '600 fiorentino', *Comma*, iv (1969), pp. 7–12

The Twilight of the Medici: Late Baroque Art in Florence, 1670–1743 (exh. cat., ed. S. Rossen; Detroit, MI, Inst. A.; Florence, Pitti; 1974), pp. 210–13, nos 119–21 [Pietro]

E. Borea: 'Dipinti alla Petraia per Don Lorenzo de' Medici', *Prospettiva*, ii (1975), pp. 24–39 [Cesare]

C. Thiem: *Florentiner Zeichner des Frühbarock* (Munich, 1977), pp. 370–72, nos 153–8 [Cesare]; pp. 395–6, nos 199–200 [Vincenzo]

La quadreria di Don Lorenzo de' Medici (exh. cat., ed. E. Borea; Poggio a Caiano, Villa Medicea, 1977) [Cesare and Vincenzo]

Dessins baroques florentins du Louvre (exh. cat. by C. Monbeig Goguel, Paris, Louvre, 1981), pp. 154–5, no. 92 [Vincenzo]; pp. 206–7, nos 125–7 [Pietro]

G. Cantelli: *Repertorio della pittura fiorentina del seicento* (Fiesole, 1983), pp. 56–63 [bibliog., oeuvre, many illus.: Cesare, Vincenzo, Pietro]

Il seicento fiorentino: Arte a Firenze da Ferdinando I a Cosimo III (exh. cat., Florence, Pal. Strozzi, 1986), i, pp. 298–310, 401–5; iii, pp. 69–73, 73–6 [S. Bellesi on Cesare and Vincenzo]

Pitture fiorentine del seicento (exh. cat., ed. G. Pratesi; Florence, Pal. Ridolfi, 1987), pp. 64–7, nos 20–21 [Cesare]; p. 102, no. 35 [Pietro]

S. Bellesi: 'Una vita inedita di Vincenzo Dandini e appunti su Anton Domenico Gabbiani, Giovan Battista Marmi, Filippo Maria Galletti e altri', *Paragone*, xxxix/459–63 (1988), pp. 97–123; xxxix/465, pp. 79–96

A. Guicciardini Corsi Salviati: *Affreschi di palazzo Corsini a Firenze, 1650–1700* (Florence, 1989)

MILES L. CHAPPELL

Dandolo, Andrea, Doge of Venice (*b* Venice, 30 April 1306; *reg* 1343–54; *d* Venice, 7 Sept 1354). Italian ruler, scholar and patron. The first scholar–doge of Venetian history, he was pre-eminent among the medieval doges of Venice for the scale and co-ordination of his patronage. He was a friend of Petrarch, with whom he corresponded, and his use of art should be set against the backdrop of pre-humanist developments in Venice and Padua. His artistic campaign as doge was focused on S Marco, the state church of Venice. The Cappella di S Isidoro (1354–5) was built on to the left transept arm to house the relics of the Byzantine warrior saint, with an extensive mosaic cycle in a lively narrative, probably local, style. The Baptistery was given a complementary mosaic decoration focused on Christ and St John the Baptist, including a *Crucifixion* scene depicting Dandolo at the foot of the cross. His major initiative was the sumptuous reinstallation in 1345 of the Pala d'Oro on the high altar of S Marco (*see* VENICE, fig. 20), with Dandolo's part in the remounting recorded in an inscription. An elaborate panel (Venice, S Marco) was commissioned from Paolo Veneziano to cover the altarpiece except on ceremonial occasions. Dandolo's patronage extended to manuscripts, including an illustrated edition of the *Historia destructionis Troiae* (Madrid, Bib. N., MS. 17805), which was intended to give Venice a classical history that would put it on a footing equal to that of Rome.

WRITINGS

Chronica per extensum descripta (MS.; Modena, Bib. Estense); ed. E. Pastorello, Rerum italicarum scriptores, xii/i (Bologna, 1938–58) [includes authoritative intro. on Dandolo]

BIBLIOGRAPHY

DBI

G. Arnaldi: 'Andrea Dandolo Doge-Cronista', *La storiografia veneziana fino al secolo XVI*, ed. A. Pertusi (Florence, 1970), pp. 127–268

H. Buchthal: *Historia troiana: Studies in the History of Mediaeval Secular Illustration*, Stud. Warb. Inst., 32 (London, 1971)

M. Murano: 'Petrarca, Paolo Veneziano e la cultura artistica alla corte del doge Andrea Dandolo', *Petrarca, Venezia e il Veneto*, ed. G. Padoan (Florence, 1976), pp. 157–68

R. Katzenstein: *Three Liturgical Manuscripts from San Marco: Art and Patronage in Mid-Trecento Venice* (diss., Cambridge, MA, Harvard U., 1987)

D. Pincus: 'Andrea Dandolo (1343–1354) and Visible History: The San Marco Projects', *Art and Politics in Late Medieval and Early Renaissance Italy, 1250–1500*, Notre Dame Conferences in Medieval Studies, ii (Notre Dame, 1990), pp. 191–206

DEBRA PINCUS

Dandré-Bardon, Michel-François (*b* Aix-en-Provence, 22 May 1700; *d* Paris, 13 April 1783). French painter, draughtsman and writer. Michel-François Dandré (he later added Bardon, the name of his maternal uncle and testator) left Aix-en-Provence in 1720 for Paris, where he intended to study law. He came from an eminent Aixois legal and consular family but turned to painting, entering the studios of Jean-Baptiste van Loo and Jean-François de Troy and enrolling at the Académie Royale. In 1725 he took second place in the Prix de Rome competition and journeyed to Rome at his own expense. On the way there he stopped in Aix-en-Provence, where he decorated the audience room of the Chambre des Comptes de Provence: he completed the vast *Augustus Punishing the Extortioners* (2.40×6.28 m; Aix-en-Provence, Mus. Granet) in Rome, according to his first biographer, D'Ageville; a *Christ on the Cross* (Aix-en-Provence, St Esprit) and allegorical figures (destr. after 1791) also decorated the room.

Although Dandré-Bardon was not an official student at the Académie de France in Rome, in June 1726 he was given lodgings there, and in March 1728 he received a bursary, becoming a *pensionnaire*. He spent five years in Rome and then returned to Paris after spending six months in Venice. He was especially attracted to Venetian art, in which he would have been encouraged by Nicolas Vleughels, the liberal-minded Director of the Académie in Rome at the time.

Between 1731 and 1733 Dandré-Bardon made a series of decorations (destr. 1792) for the Hôtel de Ville at Aix-en-Provence, consisting of nine scenes from the history of the town, from Classical times until the 17th century. Some lively oil sketches survive: the *Union of Provence and the Consulate of Aix in 1523* and *Aix Rescuing Marseille from the Aragonese Siege in 1423* (both Aix-en-Provence, Mus. Granet). The largest body of Dandré-Bardon's work could be seen in Aix-en-Provence, so as a painter he would have made his greatest impression there in the 18th century. His work included religious subjects, for example *St Mark* (1732; Aix-en-Provence, Ste Marie-Madeleine). Back in Paris, he was approved (*agréé*) by the Académie on 25 August 1734 and received (*reçu*) on 30 April 1735 on presentation of *Tullia Running her Chariot over the Body of her Father* (Montpellier, Mus. Fabre).

In Paris, Dandré-Bardon pursued a respectable academic career, becoming Assistant Professor at the Académie in 1737. He spent 1741–52 in Marseille, where in 1748 he became Controller of the decoration of the royal galleys. There is an exquisitely painted and emotional *Christ on the Cross* (Marseille, Mus. B.-A.) from this period. He returned to Paris in 1752 to replace François Boucher as Professor at the Académie and was also in the same year a founder-member of the Marseille Académie, of which he became Director in 1754. He exhibited at the Paris Salon, showing two religious works each year in 1737 and 1738 and in 1742 a pair of genre scenes and a tapestry cartoon (all untraced) for the *Jason and Medea* series to be woven at Beauvais.

Dandré-Bardon is recorded as painting a number of portraits (untraced). From the evidence of a dozen preparatory drawings (e.g. U. Manchester, Whitworth A.G.) and an oil sketch (Aix-en-Provence, Mus. Arbaud), it seems that he was working on a complicated *Allegory on the Peace of 1748 at Aix-la-Chapelle* around 1748. In 1753 he sent to the Salon the precociously Neo-classical subject of the *Death of Socrates* (untraced). *The Birth* (Paris, Louvre) shows his charming and intimate ability as a genre painter, with a rich and lively impasto more readily associated with Jean-Honoré Fragonard. If Dandré-Bardon's few surviving large-scale history paintings are sometimes awkward in design, his sumptuous handling recalls his admiration for Venetian art, while his restraint and use of subtle tonalities suggest admiration for his contemporary and compatriot in Rome, Pierre Subleyras. *Adoration of the Skulls* (Washington, DC, N.G.A.; see fig.), a religious genre painting, perhaps executed in Italy, has been compared with Alessandro Magnasco for its humour and fantasy; its bold rhythms and contrasts of light and shade bring it close to his graphic work, while its rich, sketchy handling places it on the dividing line between sketch and finished work, perfectly suited to the cabinet of a connoisseur.

Dandré-Bardon became increasingly absorbed in administration and theoretical interests. From around 1750 he published a considerable number of books, brochures and papers. In 1755 he succeeded Bernard Lépicié as Professor of History and Geography at the Ecole Royale des Elèves Protégés. He published a *Traité de peinture* (1765), a liberal and eclectic summation of academic doctrines of the day. His *Vie de Carle Vanloo* (1765) is the perfect concise statement of such doctrines as applied to the best mid-18th-century practitioner of them; this admiring essay is accompanied by an impressive catalogue of Vanloo's works.

Partially paralysed in 1770, Dandré-Bardon gave up painting but continued to draw prolifically (e.g. an album dated 1780; Paris, Louvre). He was a vivid and original draughtsman, with a lively and energetic pen or chalk line, and a picturesque play of light and shade in his use of brown washes. His studio effects were sold on 23 June 1783.

WRITINGS

Anecdotes sur la mort de Bouchardon (n.p., 1764)
Traité de peinture, 2 vols (Paris, 1765)
Vie de Carle Vanloo (Paris, 1765)
Histoire universelle traitée relativement aux arts de peindre et de sculpter, 3 vols (Paris, 1769)
Costumes des anciens peuples, 6 vols (Paris, 1772–4)
Apologie des allégories de Rubens et de Le Brun, introduites dans les galeries du Luxembourg et de Versailles (Paris, 1777)

Michel-François Dandré-Bardon: *Adoration of the Skulls*, oil on canvas, 528×636 mm, mid-18th century (Washington, DC, National Gallery of Art)

BIBLIOGRAPHY
D'Ageville: *Eloge historique de M. F. d'André-Bardon* (Marseille, 1783)
J. Boyer: 'La Peinture et la gravure à Aix-en-Provence (1530–1790)', *Gaz. B.-A.*, n.s. 5, lxxviii (1971), pp. 1–188 (104–6)
P. Rosenberg: 'Dandré-Bardon as a Draughtsman: A Group of Drawings at Stuttgart', *Master Drgs*, xii (1974), pp. 137–51 [illustrates the range of his graphic work]

PHILIP CONISBEE

Dandridge, Bartholomew (*b* London, *bapt* 17 Dec 1691; *d* London, after 1754). English painter. He was the son of a house painter in London and first studied at Kneller's Academy from 1712 and later at the St Martin's Lane Academy under John Vanderbank and Louis Chéron. His patrons in the 1720s included Capt. Richard Gifford, of whom he painted a small equestrian portrait (*c.* 1725; London, N. Army Mus.). In 1731 he took over Kneller's former studio and began painting large-scale portraits. His developing French style earned him the patronage of Frederick, Prince of Wales, as evidenced by a small portrait (*c.* 1732; London, N.P.G.).

Dandridge was one of the first artists in London to paint conversation pieces. His *Price Family* (*c.* 1728; New York, Met.) is an early English example of this genre and reveals the influence of the French *fête galante*. He also used this French pastoral manner in more fanciful contexts, such as the *Lady Reading 'Belinda' beside a Fountain* (*c.* 1740–45; New Haven, CT, Yale Cent. Brit. A.). The figure groupings in his conversation pieces were determined by his use of lay figures; this practice may have been responsible for the stilted poses in such works as *The Ladies Noel* (1736–40; Manchester, C.A.G.), which otherwise shows the appealing charm with which Dandridge could construct a landscape setting. He was also praised for his ability to capture a likeness. He occasionally supplied ornamental designs for books, such as M. A. Ramsay's *Les Voyages de Cyrus* (1730) and an English edition of *Select Comedies of M. Molière* (1732). He was last recorded in 1754 in London.

BIBLIOGRAPHY
'The Note-books of George Vertue', *Walpole Soc.*, xxii (1934) [indexed in xxix (1947)]
R. Edwards: 'Portraits by Bartholomew Dandridge at Poundisford Park', *Country Life*, lxxvi (22 Dec 1934), pp. 673–4
E. Waterhouse: *Painting in Britain, 1630–1790*, Pelican Hist. A. (Harmondsworth, 1953, rev. 4/1978), pp. 184–5
Manners and Morals: Hogarth and British Painting, 1700–1760 (exh. cat. by E. Einberg, London, Tate, 1987)

SHEARER WEST

Daneel [Daniel] **de Rijcke** [Rijke; Rike; Rycke; Ryckere; Ryke] (*fl* Ghent, 1440–82). South Netherlandish painter. He is first recorded as a Master in Ghent on 11 May 1440 and was elected Dean of the Painters' Guild in 1460–61 and again from 1462 to 1464. Under his deanship an ordinance was issued in 1463 requiring manuscript illuminators to enrol in the Painters' Guild and pay a quarter of the customary dues. His earliest documented painting, however, cannot be before 1466. His oeuvre is generally considered lost, with the exception of the controversial *Calvary* triptych (Ghent, St Bavo), first ascribed in 1824 to Gerard van der Meire (*fl* 1452; *d* 1512) and tentatively attributed to de Rijcke (De Schryver). Most still favour Justus of Ghent's authorship, however, while cautious sceptics ascribe the work to the so-called Master of the Ghent Calvary Triptych. De Rijcke's lost works include those referred to in a judgement of 17 June 1466 forcing him to complete paintings, possibly wall paintings for the Bishop of Cambrai in Ghent. In the same year de Rijcke painted ornamental and heraldic scenes for the city of Ghent. From April to July 1468 he collaborated on the decorations for the marriage of Charles the Bold, Duke of Burgundy, and Margaret of York in Bruges. Of the 166 painters hired, de Rijcke, Vrancke van der Stockt of Brussels and Jacques Daret of Tournai received the highest fees. Back in Ghent, de Rijcke executed paintings to be placed at the city gates for the entry of the young Duchess. He is also documented painting a scene with figures for the wealthy Italian Odenin de Ville, originally from Chieri in Piedmont. A contract of 19 April 1469 between de Rijcke and the Augustinians in Ghent substantiates their commission of an altarpiece. Although Daneel de Rijcke is mentioned in various documents until 1482, his later whereabouts and the exact date of his death are unknown.

BIBLIOGRAPHY
BNB; Thieme–Becker
A. De Schryver: 'De Gentse schilderkunst na de Van Eycks', *Justus van Gent, Berruguete en het hof van Urbino* (exh. cat., Ghent, Mus. S. Kst., 1957), pp. 21–31
J. P. De Bruyn: 'De schilderkunst van de 15de tot de 17de eeuw', *Gent: Duizend jaar kunst en cultuur* (exh. cat., Ghent, Mus. S. Kst., 1975), i, pp. 116–20, 174–7
M. P. J. Martens: *De muurschilderkunst te Gent, 12de tot 16de eeuw* (Brussels, 1989), pp. 19–20, 186, 198–9, 203, 251, 255, cat. no. 27, doc. no. 34

HANS J. VAN MIEGROET

Danfrie. French family of medallists. Philippe Danfrie the elder (*b* 1531–5; *d* Paris, 1606) went to Paris in the 1550s and set up as an engraver of letter punches. He produced a number of books in partnership with Richard Breton in 1558–60 and later with Pierre Haman and Jean Le Royer. He also made mathematical instruments, globes and astrolabes and dies for marking bookbindings. In 1571 he cut his first dies for jettons. As Engraver-General of the French coinage from 1582, he provided the puncheons from which the dies used in every mint in France were taken. He also produced a number of medals (e.g. London, BM) commemorating the events of the first 15 years of Henry IV's reign. His son Philippe Danfrie the younger (*b* ?Paris, *c.* 1572; *d* Paris, 1604) was appointed Controller-General of effigies in 1591. On his appointment it was claimed that he had demonstrated great skill in modelling portraits in wax and engraving puncheons. His most famous and only signed medal (e.g. London, BM) is cast rather than struck and celebrates the victory of Henry IV over the Duke of Savoy in 1600.

BIBLIOGRAPHY
F. Mazerolle: *Les Médailleurs français du XVe siècle au milieu du XVIIe* (Paris, 1902–4), i, pp. lxxviii–lxxxix, 139–215; ii, nos 266–96
M. Jones: *A Catalogue of French Medals in the British Museum*, i (London, 1982), pp. 184–208

MARK JONES

Dangel, Miguel von (*b* Bayreuth, 26 Sept 1946). Venezuelan painter and sculptor of German birth. He arrived in Venezuela in 1948 and in 1963 began his studies at the Escuela de Artes Plásticas 'Cristóbal Rojas' in Caracas. His densely composed work incorporated various objects such as stuffed animals, skins, crucifixes and mirrors, which he used to develop contemplation of the contemporary, with symbolic reference to what is specifically American and to the sacred nature of art. His use of various materials, in conjunction with animal and vegetable forms, reveals the mythological landscape in which Von Dangel ultimately found expression. He represented Venezuela at the São Paulo Biennale in Brazil in 1983, and his work was included in various international touring group exhibitions. He held various one-man shows in Caracas, outstanding among which was the *Batalla de San Romano*, held at the Museo de Arte Contemporáneo in Caracas in 1990.

BIBLIOGRAPHY

Diccionario de artes visuales en Venezuela (Caracas, 1982)
Three Venezuelans in Two Dimensions: Miguel von Dangel, Ernesto León, Carlos Zerpa (exh. cat. by A. Stein, Perth, A.G. W. Australia, 1989), p. 2
La Batalla de San Romano (exh. cat. by S. Imber, Caracas, Mus. A. Contemp., 1990) [incl. texts by Miguel von Dangel]

ELIDA SALAZAR

Danhauser. Austrian family of artists. Josef David Danhauser (1753–96) was a sculptor. His son (1) Josef Ulrich Danhauser was a successful furniture manufacturer and produced a wide variety of furnishings for royal and noble patrons and middle-class homes. His son (2) Josef Franz Danhauser was a painter.

(1) Josef Ulrich Danhauser (*b* Vienna, 14 March 1780; *d* Vienna, 6 Jan 1829). Furniture manufacturer. He studied sculpture at the Akademie der Bildenden Künste in Vienna under Franz Anton Zauner. In 1804 Danhauser founded the Etablissement für alle Gegenstände des Ameublements, which manufactured all types of furniture, including gilded, silvered or bronzed ornaments made from wood-paste (a material composed of sawdust, glue and oil), which were used as a substitute for massive bronze mouldings. The factory employed no less than 130 tradesmen and was no minor workshop run by a master craftsman with journeymen trained in just one skill. As well as furniture ornaments Danhauser also manufactured small pieces of decorative sculpture and lighting fixtures. In 1814 he eventually obtained the state manufacturing warrant 'to make all types of furniture', and to distinguish his wares from those made by his competitors he signed them: K.K. PRIVILEG. LANDESFABR:ALLER GATTUNGEN MEUBL:DES JOSEPH DANHAUSER IN WIEN.

Danhauser ran the first Viennese furniture and interior decoration store, particularly promoting the BIEDERMEIER style. All items needed to equip a house—curtains, upholstered furniture, lighting fixtures and such decorative accessories as clocks and small pieces of sculpture—were manufactured and sold. Customers could select various items from the range of designs or place an order for an entire set of furnishings. After the Congress of Vienna (1815), there was an increased demand for the work of Viennese craftsmen, especially cabinetmakers and upholsterers, who achieved international recognition as a result of the elegant apartments provided for the foreign delegations. Thus Ernest I, Duke of Saxe-Coburg and Gotha (*reg* 1826–44), who had taken part in the Congress, awarded the Danhauser company a contract for providing simple furniture for the Veste Schloss in Coburg. In 1822–3 Archduke Charles (1771–1847) commissioned the firm to furnish his town house in Vienna (now the Albertina) and the Weilburg near Baden. In these interiors, known only from pictures, grand Empire pieces made of mahogany with bronze mounts predominated. Another order from the Imperial family in Vienna was for the furnishing of rooms at Laxenburg Castle near Vienna (e.g. sofa, *c.* 1820; Vienna, Bundesmobiliensamml.; *see* AUSTRIA, fig. 32). The firm furnished Archduchess Sophie's rooms, and a lady's writing-table (Vienna, Mus. Angewandte Kst) from there is still in existence.

The spectacular success of the business, which had also established a branch in Pest (now Budapest), attracted commissions from all over central Europe. The profits enabled Danhauser to acquire and install his factory in the Karoly'sches Palais in the Wieden district of Vienna in 1825. When Danhauser died, his eldest son, (2) Josef Franz Danhauser, took over the firm and directed it until it closed in 1839. Almost 3000 drawings in the Österreichisches Museum für Angewandte Kunst in Vienna illustrate the wide variety of designs and products offered by the Danhausers.

BIBLIOGRAPHY

F. Winidisch-Graetz: 'Furniture', *Vienna in the Age of Schubert* (exh. cat., London, V&A, 1979), pp. 32–49
L. Seelig: 'Wiener Biedermeier in Coburg', *Alte & Mod. Kst*, 178–9 (1981), pp. 3–10
C. Witt-Dörring: 'Beleuchtungskörper aus der k.k. privil. Landes Fabrik des Josef Danhauser in Wien', *Alte & Mod. Kst*, 178–9 (1981), pp. 50–51
E. B. Ottillinger: 'Einfachheit und Schönheit: Bemerkungen zum Wiener Biedermeiermöbel', *Die Kunst*, xcix/12 (1987), pp. 986–93
C. Witt-Dörring: 'Der differenzierte Konsum: Das Wiener Möbel, 1815–1848', *Bürgersinn und Aufbegehren: Biedermeier und Vormärz in Wien, 1815–1848* (exh. cat., Vienna, Museen Stadt, 1987–8), pp. 368–87
E. B. Ottillinger: 'Zweites Rokoko, Postmoderne im 19. Jahrhundert', *Die Kunst*, xcx/4 (1988), pp. 288–95

EVA B. OTTILLINGER

(2) Josef Franz Danhauser (*b* Vienna, 19 Aug 1805; *d* Vienna, 4 May 1845). Painter and designer, son of (1) Josef Ulrich Danhauser. He was first taught drawing by his father and then studied history painting at the Vienna Akademie (1820–26). On leaving the Akademie he took up an invitation from his patron, the Archbishop of Eger in Hungary, László Pyrker, to visit Venice; he spent five months there and paid particular attention to the work of the Old Masters. When he returned to Vienna, Danhauser was under great pressure from his family to become more involved in the running of the furniture factory, but Pyrker invited him to Eger with a commission to paint a number of portraits and to restore paintings in the gallery of the Archbishop's Palace. On his father's death in 1829, however, Danhauser returned to Vienna, where for several years he was effectively head of the factory. He returned to Erlau in 1833 when commissioned to paint the altarpiece for the new cathedral, the *Martyrdom of St John* (1834–5; *in situ*). The religious paintings that followed established his reputation: the *Expulsion of Hagar* (1836; Vienna, Belvedere), for example, was awarded a prize by the Akademie. In 1838 he accepted the post of Korrektor of history painting at the Akademie, although he was outspoken in his criticism of both the inadequate curriculum and the unimaginative approach to teaching there.

In Vienna from the late 1830s Danhauser devoted himself largely to portrait and genre painting, producing a rich stream of works that included the *Convent Supper*

(1838; Vienna, Belvedere), *A Mother's Love* (1839; Vienna, Belvedere) and *Liszt at the Piano* (1840; Berlin, Neue N.G.). The *Opening of the Will* (1839; Vienna, Belvedere) borrows directly from Sir David Wilkie's painting of the same name, bought in 1826 by Ludwig I of Bavaria and eliciting admiration from German and Austrian painters when exhibited shortly thereafter. Danhauser often deliberately blurred the line between genre and portraiture. His *Eye Specialist* (1837; Vienna, Hist. Mus.), with its emotional record of the family's joy at the success of a recent eye operation, is in fact a portrait of the Viennese eye specialist Dr Friedrich Jäger von Jaxtthal. Although contemporary critics derided Danhauser's portraits of children, these were so enthusiastically received by the public that he often produced several copies and variants to meet demand. Such pictures as the drawing of the *Violin Player* (1830s; Vienna, Albertina; see fig.) and the *Child's World* (1842; Vienna, Hist. Mus.) were as notable for their evident sympathy for the child's point of view, however self-indulgent and anarchic, as for their humour. A significant element in the appeal of Danhauser's presentation of the Viennese society of his time was his attention to details of furnishing, and this was clearly influenced by his contemporary engagement as a designer for the furniture factory. His designs for complete rooms (e.g. for a bedroom, published in the *Wiener Zeitschrift für Kunst, Literatur und Mode* in 1834) show settings similar to those seen in his paintings.

BIBLIOGRAPHY
A. Rössler: *Josef Danhauser* (Vienna, 1911, rev. 2/1946)
V. Birke: *Josef Danhauser* (Vienna, 1983)

V. BIRKE

Daniel-Dupuis, Jean-Baptiste (*b* Blois, 15 Feb 1849; *d* Paris, 14 Nov 1899). French medallist and sculptor. He was the son of a painter and became a student at the Ecole des Beaux-Arts in Paris when only 16 years old. In 1872 he won the Prix de Rome for medals. On his return from Rome he exhibited cast portrait medals of *Charles Bayet*, *Antonin Mercié* and *Luc Olivier Merson*, evincing in these his admiration for Renaissance medals. Daniel-Dupuis was a prolific medallist, who executed numerous commemorative pieces, such as those for the *Election of Jules Grévy as President* (1879); the *Municipality of Paris* (1880); the *Chamber of Deputies* (1884); the *Société des artistes français* (1885); and the *Exposition Universelle* of 1889. In a lighter vein, he also executed one of the first motoring medals (1896) for the Automobile Club of France; while his plaquettes, such as the *Source* (originally modelled in 1873, reduced, engraved and issued in 1898), the *Nest* and *Dîner de la Marmite* (both 1890), and *Madonna* and *Marriage* (both 1892) were very popular with the general public. He also produced a large number of portraits and other studies in the form of medals, plaquettes, busts and bas-reliefs. In 1897 he was appointed an Officer of the Légion d'honneur. Daniel-Dupuis's career ended prematurely in November 1899, when he was murdered by his wife as he lay asleep.

Lami
BIBLIOGRAPHY
F. Mazerolle: 'J.-B. Daniel-Dupuis', *Gaz. Numi. Fr.*, ii (1898), pp. 7–40, 167–202

MARK JONES

Daniele da Volterra [Ricciarelli, Daniele] (*b* Volterra, 1509; *d* Rome, 4 April 1566). Italian painter, stuccoist and sculptor. Much of the fascination of his career resides in the development of his style from provincial origins to a highly sophisticated manner, combining the most accomplished elements of the art of Michelangelo, Raphael and their Mannerist followers in a distinctive and highly original way. He provided an influential model for numerous later artists in Rome.

The only work to survive from Daniele's early career is a fresco, a political allegory of *Justice*, painted shortly after 1530 for the Palazzo dei Priori in Volterra (now detached, Volterra, Pin. Com.). It reflects the pervasive influence of Sodoma, with whom he is presumed to have studied in Siena. Badly damaged and overpainted, it is a generally clumsy work, demonstrating an inadequate grasp of foreshortening; it exhibits the *difficultà* of manner noted by Vasari.

It is not known exactly when Daniele travelled to Rome, but it is now generally assumed that his initial work there on the villa of Cardinal Agostino Trivulzio at Salone, outside the city, was begun after 1535. Only one portion of this work remains: a loggia decoration consisting of frescoes of gladiatorial games, landscapes and grotesques, as well as stuccowork. The style is decidedly that of the Sienese-born Baldassare Peruzzi, who designed the villa, and with whom Daniele is also thought to have trained.

Josef Franz Danhauser: *Violin Player*, pencil and white highlights on blue-grey paper, 283×215 mm, 1830s (Vienna, Graphische Sammlung Albertina)

The connection with Peruzzi may well have led to Daniele's involvement here.

Daniele's first work in Rome to show both independence of mind and maturity of style is the frieze decoration depicting scenes from the life of Fabius Maximus, in the *salone* of the Palazzo Massimo alle Colonne, Rome, which was probably started in the late 1530s. The format of the decoration still owes much to Peruzzi (here again the designer of the building) and the earliest scenes recall Daniele's Sienese background and study of works by Peruzzi, Sodoma and Domenico Beccafumi. The more ambitious scenes show the influence of Raphael's biblical frescoes, Michelangelo's muscular figures on the Sistine Chapel ceiling and Sebastiano del Piombo's work. The rhythmical complexity of the most accomplished painting suggests the influence of Perino del Vaga, at work elsewhere in the palace during the late 1530s, when this project is presumed to have begun. Daniele was characteristically a slow worker, and the development of his style towards Roman Mannerism probably reflects work over a period of several years into the early 1540s. Especially notable in this decoration is the interplay between the dynamic and suave rhythms of the surface design, and the bold spatial excavations, similar to effects in the works of Daniele's rival, Francesco Salviati. Another example of this transitional phase of Daniele's career is the austere *Holy Family with St John the Baptist* (late 1530s; Rome, Pal. Doria-Pamphili). Details of still-tentative drawing and of fracture and touch all echo Sienese precedents, but the composition is derived from Raphael's *Madonna della Rosa* (Madrid, Prado), revised in a manner emphatically reminiscent of the geometric shaping of Michelangelo's *Delphic Sibyl* on the ceiling of the Sistine Chapel.

During the 1540s Daniele's major work was the decoration of the Orsini Chapel in Trinità dei Monti, Rome, including scenes from the *Legend of the True Cross* (destr.) and his most famous work, the *Deposition* (*c.* 1545; *in situ*). Though this fresco is badly damaged, it still reveals the powerful influence of Michelangelo's sculptural style and of particular motifs derived from his drawings. It was also indebted to paintings of the same subject by Rosso Fiorentino (1521; Volterra, Pin. Com.) and Sodoma (*c.* 1500; Siena, Pin. N.). A number of drawings survive that give insight into Daniele's slow, deliberate labour and the growth of his conception towards the monumentality, grandiloquence and immediacy of his religious drama. Its influential combination of Michelangelo's *terribilità* with a Raphaelesque grace of design derived from Perino affected artists as diverse as Federico Barocci and Tintoretto and reverberated well into the next century.

During the same decade Daniele worked in the shadow of Perino on various works in Rome. He added the figures of *St Matthew* and *St Luke* to the fresco cycle in the chapel of the Crucifixion in S Marcello, which had been begun by Perino before the sack of Rome in 1527. He assisted Perino in the decoration of the Sala Regia in the Vatican for Pope Paul III and took over the project when Perino died in 1547, continuing it until the Pope's death in 1549, when work was disrupted. In the late 1540s he executed a brilliant frieze decoration in the Palazzo Farnese, illustrating scenes from the *Life of Bacchus*, adorned with highly imaginative grotesques in the manner of both Peruzzi and

Perino. Closely related to these decorations is Daniele's work in the Vatican in the Stanza della Cleopatra, begun for Pope Julius III in 1550.

The final phase of Daniele's career was dominated by his decoration of the Rovere Chapel in Trinità dei Monti. Executed largely in the early 1550s, the work may have dragged on over several years (Vasari). In the *Assumption of the Virgin* and the *Presentation of the Virgin* (see fig.), particularly, the artist employed bold and indeed stunning forms of illusionism derived from the examples of Raphael and Peruzzi. The figures are decidedly Michelangelesque, some having large, swollen volumes that betray the manner of Sebastiano del Piombo as well. Daniele was assisted on this project by a number of artists, mostly from the circle of Perino, including Pellegrino Tibaldi, Marco Pino, Gaspar Becerra, Giovanni Paolo Rossetti (*d* 1586) and Michele Alberti. This phase of his work is closely paralleled by the grand and imposing *Virgin and Child with St John and Female Saint* (*c.* 1548–50; Siena, d'Elci priv. col., see Barolsky, fig. 48).

Another important commission from Daniele's last years, executed with considerable help from assistants, was the decoration of the Ricci Chapel in S Pietro in Montorio, Rome. This was begun *c.* 1555 but not completed until 1568, two years after his death. The scheme included, on the vault, scenes from the *Life of St John the Baptist* and, flanking the altarpiece of the *Baptism*, statues of *St Peter* and *St Paul* to his design. It emulated the decoration of the del Monte Chapel opposite by the Florentines Vasari and Bartolomeo Ammanati. Daniele was similarly influenced by Florentine Mannerism in other works, for example in the paintings he made for Giovanni della Casa during the 1550s. Although these works,

Daniele da Volterra: *Presentation of the Virgin* (early 1550s), fresco, Trinità dei Monti, Rome

including the *David and Goliath* now in Fontainebleau, are generally derived from drawings by Michelangelo, their polish and finish are close to the manner of Vasari and Salviati. At the very end of his life Daniele was called on by Pope Paul IV—in the new, stricter spirit of the Counter-Reformation—to overpaint the more obviously 'shameful parts' of the nudes in Michelangelo's *Last Judgement* in the Sistine Chapel, a commission that has somewhat clouded his reputation. His finest works, however, are brilliant in invention, bold in illusionism and frequently distinguished by exquisite draughtsmanship and artificial, metallic colouring

BIBLIOGRAPHY
G. Vasari: *Vite* (1550, rev. 2/1568); ed. G. Milanesi (1878–85)
S. Levie: *Der Maler Daniele da Volterra, 1509–1566* (Cologne, 1962)
F. Sricchia Santoro: 'Daniele da Volterra', *Paragone*, ccxiii (1967), pp. 3–34
P. Barolsky: *Daniele da Volterra: A Catalogue Raisonée* (New York and London, 1979)
T. Pugliatti: *Giulio Mazzoni e la decorazione a Roma nella cerchia di Daniele da Volterra* (Rome, 1984)

PAUL BAROLSKY

Daniell. English family of painters and printmakers. Thomas Daniell (*b* Chertsey, 1749; *d* London, 19 March 1840) was apprenticed to a coach painter and in 1773 entered the Royal Academy Schools; between 1774 and 1784 he exhibited topographical views and flower pieces at the Royal Academy. Having become responsible for bringing up his orphaned nephew William Daniell (*b* 1769; *d* London, 16 Aug 1837), in 1784 he decided to travel to India with his nephew and work there as an engraver. William's brother Samuel Daniell (*b* 1775; *d* Ceylon [now Sri Lanka], Dec 1811) remained independent of his uncle and also became a topographical artist; he went to South Africa in 1801 and after his return to England published *African Scenery and Animals* (1804–5), a collection of aquatints. From 1806 he lived in Ceylon.

On arriving in Calcutta in 1786, Thomas Daniell published a proposal for engraving 12 views of the city. This seemed a promising idea, since Calcutta was rapidly expanding and its European inhabitants might be willing to buy engravings showing its latest buildings. Both he and William were inexperienced engravers and had to enlist the help of Indian craftsmen, but the set was completed in November 1788 and sold well. Thomas next began planning an ambitious tour of north India, possibly inspired by the wealth of picturesque scenery indicated in William Hodges's collection of aquatints, *Select Views in India* (1785–8). In August 1789 Thomas and William set off up-river past Murshidabad to Bhagalpur, where they stayed with Samuel Davis (?1756–1819), an employee of the East India Company and a skilled amateur artist. They continued on to Kanpur and then travelled overland to Delhi, visiting Agra, Fatehpur Sikri and Mathura on the way; the following April they made a pioneering tour to Srinagar and Garhwal in the Himalayas. On their return journey they visited Lucknow, Allahabad and Banaras (now Varanasi), made a detour to the great Mughal fort near Sasaram and to the Barabar Caves and were back in Calcutta at the end of 1791. They held a lottery of their completed work, using the proceeds to fund a tour to the south. Since the Third Mysore War was in progress, the

Daniells suspected that a market existed among the British for oil paintings and drawings of the areas in which the conflict was taking place. They duly visited various hill-forts on their way south, as well as the huge and richly carved temples at Madurai, Mamallapuram and Rameswaram. Once back in Madras they held another lottery of their work and set off on a tour to western India. On their arrival at Bombay in March 1793 they met James Wales (1747–95), then busy drawing the area's cave temples. He took them to Elephanta, Karli and Kanheri among other places.

In September 1794 the Daniells returned to England and began working up drawings into coloured aquatints, 144 of which were issued in the six-volume *Oriental Scenery* (1795–1808). They also worked up oils from their drawings for exhibitions at the British Institution and the Royal Academy, to which Thomas was elected in 1799 and William in 1822. Around 1810 Sir Charles Cockerell engaged Thomas to design a water garden for Sezincote House (*c.* 1805), a country house unique in Europe for its Mughal architectural detail; he provided several decorative features for the garden (drawings, London, RIBA), including the Temple of Surya and the Indian Bridge. Having made long tours through Britain with Thomas, William produced hand-coloured aquatints for Richard Ayton's *A Picturesque Voyage round Great Britain* (1814–25), as well as views of London. He also made aquatints from watercolours by George Dance, Samuel Davis and Robert Smith (i). Nevertheless, it was for *Oriental Scenery* that the Daniells became famous, for it took its place alongside J. Stuart and N. Revett's *Antiquities of Athens* (1762), Baron Denon's *Voyage dans la basse et la haute Egypte* (1802) and Robert Wood's *Ruins of Palmyra* (1753) and *Ruins of Balbek* (1757). It provided an entirely new vision of the Indian subcontinent that was to influence both decorative arts and British architectural design. Above all, it formed a popular vision in Britain of a romantic and picturesque India that to some extent persists.

WRITINGS
The Diary of Thomas and William Daniell, ed. M. Hardie and M. Clayton (London, 1932)

BIBLIOGRAPHY
T. Sutton: *The Daniells: Artists and Travellers* (London, 1954)
The Daniells in India, 1786–1793 (exh. cat. by M. Archer, Washington, DC, Smithsonian Inst., 1962)
M. Shellim: *India and the Daniells* (London, 1979)
M. Archer: *Early Views of India: The Picturesque Journeys of Thomas and William Daniell, 1786–1794* (London, 1980)

MILDRED ARCHER

Daniell, Edward Thomas (*b* London, 6 June 1804; *d* Adalia [now Antalya], Turkey, 24 Sept 1842). English painter and etcher. In the early 1820s he rapidly developed his skills as an etcher. Three prints, *Near Norwich*, *Whitlingham Staithe* and *Bure Bridge* (all 1827), demonstrate his developed sensitivity of line. His watercolour study for *Bure Bridge, Aylsham* (1826; Norwich, Castle Mus.) testifies to his fluid use of wash freely applied over light pencil. Daniell also began to paint in oils and received a few lessons from John Linnell in 1828, the year he graduated at Oxford. In 1829 he began the first of his continental tours, returning late 1830. His etchings developed a freedom of line that moved away from the example of his friend and teacher, Joseph Stannard of Norwich, towards that of Andrew Geddes and the Scottish etchers, whose work he probably saw while in Scotland in the summer of 1831. He exhibited once with the Norwich Society in 1832. Daniell's later etchings, c. 1831–4, excel in the use of drypoint and prefigure the work of etchers such as Whistler and Seymour Haden.

Daniell became curate of Banham, Norfolk, and was ordained priest on 3 June 1833. In 1835 he was made curate of St Mark's, North Audley Street, London. He befriended numerous artists, including Edwin Landseer and J. M. W. Turner. It was the work of David Roberts that inspired Daniell to travel to the Middle East, where he died of malaria. The surviving topographical and Romantic watercolours recording his journey, such as *Interior of Convent, Mount Sinai* (1841; Norwich, Castle Mus.), reveal a vision that emulates that of Roberts and exceeds that of Edward Lear.

BIBLIOGRAPHY
F. R. Beecheno: *E. T. Daniell: A Memoir* (Norwich, 1889)
J. Thistlethwaite: 'The Etchings of Edward Thomas Daniell 1804–1842', *Norfolk Archaeol.*, xxxvi (1974), pp. 1–22
A. W. Moore: *The Norwich School of Artists* (Norwich, 1985)
ANDREW W. MOORE

Daniëls, René (*b* Eindhoven, 23 May 1950). Dutch painter and draughtsman. He trained at the Koninklijke Academie voor Kunst en Vormgeving in 's Hertogenbosch between 1972 and 1975, where his teachers included Sipke Huismans (*b* 1938) and Edgar Fernhout. In 1976–7 he started to produce drawings in which he depicted objects by rhythmically repeating similar, usually geometric shapes. He based his paintings on his drawings. After this period a lyrical phase ensued, seen for example in *Landscape Painting* (1984; Eindhoven, Stedel. Van Abbemus.). He also incorporated the influence of Dada, in particular that of Francis Picabia, in his work.

Between 1984 and 1987 Daniëls taught at the Ateliers 63 in Haarlem. After 1985 he produced paintings of interiors and of paintings hanging in exhibitions, in which form and content were linked, for example *Painting about the Missing 'Deluge' Painting by Bosch* (1985; Amsterdam, Stedel. Mus.), which led to the questioning of a number of aspects of perception. In 1987 he began teaching at the Rijksacademie in Maastricht, but in that same year he suffered a brain haemorrhage that abruptly ended his career as a painter.

BIBLIOGRAPHY
René Daniëls (exh. cat., Eindhoven, Stedel. Van Abbemus., 1986)
René Daniëls: Kades-Kaden (exh. cat., essay U. Loock; Berne, Ksthalle, 1987)
René Daniëls (exh. cat., Amsterdam, Stedel. Mus., 1995)
JOHN STEEN

Daniil Chorny (*fl* 1408–27). Russian painter and monk. Daniil's Russian epithet of Chorny, meaning 'the Black', first appears in 17th-century sources. He is closely associated with ANDREY RUBLYOV, and they both probably came under the direct guidance of the leading spiritual and cultural figure of the time, St Sergius Radonezhsky (*d* 1392), abbot of the Trinity and St Sergius Monastery at Sergiyev Posad. His successor, Nikon (*d* 1422), later commissioned Daniil and Rublyov to decorate the monastery's cathedral. Although no individual painting can be attributed to Daniil with absolute certainty, the fact that his name always appears before Rublyov's in the sources indicates that he was probably older and partly explains why he is often credited with those compositions that are more conservative in style and execution.

Daniil's earliest known works are the wall paintings of the *Last Judgement* (1408) in the cathedral of the Dormition in Vladimir-Suzdal', which he executed together with Rublyov and other members of their workshop. Among the scenes attributed to Daniil are *Heaven*, the *Apostles Peter and Paul Leading the Righteous into Paradise*, the *Virgin with Angels* and *John the Baptist as a Child with Angels*, all of which continue in the icon tradition of the 14th century, with its strong Byzantine influence. A miniature of *Daniil and Rublyov* at work on the cathedral's wall paintings appears in the 16th-century Illustrated Chronicle (St Petersburg, Acad. Sci., Lib., MS. 31.7.30, fol. 1442). In 1425–7 Daniil, Rublyov and their circle again worked together to produce the wall paintings (destr.) and possibly the icons for the iconostasis in the Trinity Cathedral of the Trinity and St Sergius Monastery. Viktor Lazarev asserts that Daniil died shortly afterwards and was buried in the monastery, predeceasing Rublyov. Medieval sources, however, are unanimous in stating that Rublyov was the first to die, and they state that Daniil, like Rublyov, was a monk of the Andronikov Monastery (1359; now the Andrey Rublyov Mus. Anc. Rus. A.) in Moscow. This being the case, it seems probable that Daniil also participated in the decoration of that monastery.

BIBLIOGRAPHY
V. N. Lazarev: *Andrey Rublyov i ego shkola* [Andrey Rublyov and his school] (Moscow, 1966)
OXANA CLEMINSON

Dan'ko [Dan'ko-Olekseyenko], **Nataliya (Yakovlevna)** (*b* Tiflis [now Tbilisi], 1892; *d* Irbit, Sverdlovsk region, 18 March 1942). Russian sculptor. She left a highly significant mark on Russian decorative arts and sculpture of the 1920s and 1930s. By 1909, when she was working in the studio of Vasily Kuznetsov (1882–1923), after having studied at the Stroganov Institute, Moscow (1900–02) and in Vil'na (now Vilnius) (1906–8), she began to create sculptural reliefs in granite for new buildings in the main cities, for example the Azov–Don Bank in St Petersburg, and the Shcherbatov House in Moscow. In 1914, together with Kuznetsov, Dan'ko began to work at the Imperial (later the Lomonosov State) Porcelain Factory in Petrograd (now St Petersburg) and by 1919 had become head of the sculpture studio there, a position she held until 1941. Having first carried out commissions with designs by World of Art artists (in particular, Yevgeny Lansere and Konstantin Somov), immediately after the 1917 revolution Dan'ko continued to use an Art Nouveau approach, most notably in the statuettes *Sailor with a Little Flower* and *Café-chantant Singer* (both 1918; Moscow, Mus. Cer. & Kuskovo Estate). However, she quickly turned to AGITPROP themes for her designs, as in *Soldier of the Red Army* (1919) and *Reds and Whites* chess pieces (1922; both Moscow, Mus. Cer. & Kuskovo Estate). Embracing the theory of Production Art (*see* CONSTRUCTIVISM, §1),

Dan'ko's work over the next decade included statuettes, cups, candlesticks, the ink-pot *Sportswoman* (1923) and the pencil-holder *Work Inspection* (1930; both St Petersburg, Rus. Mus.). By the early 1930s, however, she began to reflect more closely utopian Soviet ideology and achievements, as in *Campaign against Illiteracy* (1932; Moscow, Mus. Cer. & Kuskovo Estate). Her more successful work included many portrait figurines, often depicting personages from the theatrical and literary worlds (e.g. *Anna Akhmatova*, 1924; Leningrad, Rus. Mus.), as well as ceramic reliefs and capitals for the Moscow metro stations Kievskaya and Teatral'naya (1936–7).

BIBLIOGRAPHY

N. Ya. Dan'ko: Skul'ptura [N. Ya. Dan'ko: sculpture] (exh. cat., essay E. Gollerbakh; St Petersburg, House Cult., 1929)

Yu. Ebin: *Nataliya Yakovlevna Dan'ko, 1892–1942* (Moscow, 1955)

Yu. Ovsyannikov: *Skul'ptor v krasnom khalate: N. Ya. Dan'ko i yeyo tvorchestvo* [The sculptor in the red smock: N. Ya. Dan'ko and her creative work] (Moscow, 1965)

JEREMY HOWARD, SERGEY KUZNETSOV

Danloux, Henri-Pierre (*b* Paris, 24 Feb 1753; *d* Paris, 3 Jan 1809). French painter and draughtsman. He was orphaned at an early age and was brought up by an uncle who was an architect and contractor. Around 1770 his uncle apprenticed him to Nicolas-Bernard Lépicié. He exhibited for the first time in 1771 at the Exposition de la Jeunesse in Paris, where he showed a *Drunkard at a Table* (untraced). About 1773 he was admitted into the studio of Joseph-Marie Vien, whom he followed to Rome in 1775 on the latter's appointment as Director of the Académie de France. Danloux's sketchbooks show that he also travelled to Naples, Palermo, Florence and Venice. He was not interested in the monuments of antiquity but concentrated instead on drawing landscapes and, in particular, portraits, among them that of *Jacques-Louis David* (untraced).

Not being a member of the Académie Royale, Danloux could not exhibit at the Paris Salon, but in 1782 he sent several paintings to the Salon de la Correspondance, including a *Hunter Sitting in a Wood and Caressing his Dog*, *Young Woman Seated on a Sofa* (engraved as the *Pleasant Surprise*), and a portrait of *Jean-Baptiste Génillion*, a pupil of Joseph Vernet (all untraced). As well as intimate genre scenes of the kind painted by Lépicié, Danloux specialized in informal small-scale portraits, both painted in oils or drawn to resemble medallions.

In 1783 Danloux left Italy and settled in Lyon, moving to Paris at the end of 1785. There he met the Baronne d'Etigny, who obtained for him many portrait commissions, including the portraits of *Pierre-François-Jean de Cluzel* (1786; Paris, Mus. Cognacq-Jay) and *Antoine-Marie de Cluzel* (1786; Tours, Mus. B.-A.). In 1787 Danloux married Antoinette de Saint-Redan, the adopted daughter of Mme d'Etigny, and afterwards returned to Rome, where his sitters belonged to the cosmopolitan aristocracy of the *ancien régime*. He posed them informally in familiar settings and paid great attention to the painting of fabrics, embroidery and accessories. He returned to Paris at the beginning of 1789 and was commissioned to execute portraits of members of the royal family, such as *Mme Elisabeth and the Dauphin* (untraced).

During the French Revolution Danloux exhibited at the 1791 Salon, but remaining loyal to the royal family he emigrated to London in 1792. His diary reveals that he cultivated French émigrés and obtained from them portrait commissions such as those for the *Abbé Saint-Far* (1792; oil sketch, Paris, Carnavalet), the actress *Mlle Duthé* (1792; see fig.) and the *Duc de Bourbon-Condé* (1795; Chantilly, Mus. Condé). He was influenced by such fashionable English portrait painters as Thomas Lawrence, John Hoppner and, in particular, George Romney, and began to excel in family group portraits and portraits of children, whom he painted in the most natural and spontaneous poses. In 1793 he exhibited the *Foster Children* (sold, London, Christie's, 26 June 1981) at the Royal Academy. This led to commissions from a number of British patrons, which took him to Portsmouth in August 1795 and to Scotland in the autumn of 1796, where he painted, among other works, the *Comte d'Artois* (Cambridge, Fitzwilliam), the sumptuous portrait of the *Family of the Duke of Buccleuch* (Duke of Buccleuch priv. col.) and *Admiral Duncan* (Dundee, Camperdown House). At this period he was using a freer technique and incorporating landscape backgrounds.

In 1801 Danloux returned to Paris. During his last years in London he had begun to work on large subject pictures, and this he continued to do. His history painting *The Flood* (Saint-Germain-en-Laye, Mus. Mun.), however, was badly received at the 1802 Salon. From that time Danloux painted only occasional portraits, among them that of the writer the *Abbé Delille* (Versailles, Château) and a few oil sketches of historical genre scenes, such as *Henry IV and Sully* (Pau, Mus. N. Château).

Henri-Pierre Danloux: *Mlle Duthé*, oil on canvas, 1792 (Karlsruhe, Staatliche Kunsthalle)

BIBLIOGRAPHY
R. Portalis: *Henri-Pierre Danloux peintre de portraits et son journal durant l'émigration (1735–1809)* (Paris, 1910)

VALÉRIE M. C. BAJOU

Dannatt, Trevor (*b* London, 15 Jan 1920). English architect, writer and teacher. He qualified at the Central London Polytechnic in 1942 and then worked from 1944 to 1948 in the office of E. Maxwell Fry and Jane Drew, after which he joined the London County Council Architects' Department. He was involved in the Festival of Britain South Bank Programme, London, designing the distinctive Tea-Bar Room (1951). The following year he established his own private practice, and in 1957 he was selected to design a Congregational church, Blackheath, London, for which he produced an innovative design. Dannatt's works are characterized by his unassertive, yet highly disciplined, dedication to progressive design. Major examples include the Leicester University Council Chamber and Library (1965) and a conference centre and hotel (1968–74) at Riyadh, Saudi Arabia. His numerous smaller projects include a highly esteemed private house (1966) at Colinsburgh, Scotland, several communal housing schemes (mostly with Colin Dollymore), and housing (1985) for the staff of the British Embassy, Riyadh. He taught (1952–4) at the Central School for Arts and Crafts, London, and in 1975 he was appointed professor of architecture at Manchester University.

WRITINGS
Regular contributions to *Architect's Y-b.* (1945–55)
ed.: *Modern Architecture in Britain* (London, 1959)
Trevor Dannatt: Buildings and Interiors, intro. by T. Crosby (London, 1972)

MICHAEL SPENS

Dannecker, Johann Heinrich (von) (*b* Stuttgart, 15 Oct 1758; *d* Stuttgart, 8 Dec 1841). German sculptor and collector. He received his initial artistic training (1771–80) at the Militärische Pflanzschule in Stuttgart, where he revealed a talent for drawing and sculpture. His most important tutors were the Belgian sculptor Pierre François Lejeune (1721–90) and the French painter Nicolas Guipal, an admirer of Mengs. Also of great importance to Dannecker were friendships with his fellow sculptor and rival Philipp Jakob Scheffauer (1756–1808), with the painter Philipp Friedrich Hetsch, and above all with the German writer Friedrich Schiller, who had a decisive influence on Dannecker's intellectual development. In 1780 Dannecker was appointed court sculptor at Stuttgart and was thus obliged to decline later offers to work in Dresden, St Petersburg and Munich. His first undertaking was to complete sculptural sketches by others, for example Lejeune. From 1783 to 1785 Dannecker visited Paris to study with Augustin Pajou and there came to know the virtuoso portrait sculpture of artists working under Louis XVI. He then went on foot to Rome, where he remained for four years. Because of his enthusiasm for antique art, he was soon known as 'il Greco'. He cultivated the acquaintance of the Swiss sculptor Alexander Trippel, the antiques restorer and dealer Capvaceppi, and, most important of all, the already well-established Italian sculptor Antonio Canova. The classical outlook favoured by Canova had a decisive effect on Dannecker's subsequent work.

After returning to Stuttgart in 1790, Dannecker became a professor at his old school, now renamed the Carlsschule. A planned journey to Rome failed to come about because of his employer's objection; and, except for a journey to Paris in 1806, Dannecker was unable to gain any more outside stimuli or impressions. Despite the provincial narrowness of Stuttgart, Dannecker was not isolated. In the early 1790s he again met Schiller, and in 1797 Goethe visited the city for a week. Later visitors were the collectors Sulpiz and Melchior Boisserée and the sculptors Bertel Thorvaldsen and David d'Angers. The house into which Dannecker moved in 1808, the 'Danneckerei' near the castle, became a focus for the city's cultural life. It accommodated not only the artist's apartment and studio but also a museum housing Dannecker's own works as well as casts from antique originals. In 1829 Dannecker suffered a grave illness; he recovered but was far less productive afterwards. In about 1835 he succumbed to insanity and this brought his career to an end.

Dannecker's earliest surviving work is a *Milon of Kroton* in plaster (Stuttgart, Staatsgal.), which, from a compositional viewpoint, draws strongly on the *Laokoon*. In 1777, Dannecker was awarded an Akademie prize for this work. Soon after arriving in Rome, Dannecker and his companion Scheffauer received a commission from Duke Charles Eugene of Württemburg to complete figures of the *Four Seasons* for the Castle of Hohenheim. Dannecker chose *Summer* and *Autumn*, which he represented as *Ceres* and *Bacchus*, completing them between 1786 and 1788 in marble (now Ludwigsburg, Schloss). Dannecker's models for these works were antique sculptures, but he was also influenced by the soft modelling of Canova's surfaces. These two figures earned approval in Italy as well as Stuttgart, for they brought Dannecker honorary membership of the academies in Milan and Bologna. Dannecker also made designs for an *Cupid and Psyche* group (never executed as a finished work) in which he kept closely to the late Hellenistic example in the Museo Capitolino in Rome.

Dannecker was principally celebrated for his numerous portrait busts, among which those of *Schiller* and of *Johann Kasper Lavater* were the most famous. He embarked on these *c.* 1790 with his robed bust of *Duke Charles Eugene*, completed in plaster (Stuttgart, Staatsgal.). His last work was the herm bust of *Prince Friedrich Wilhelm von Thurn und Taxis*, executed in marble (1832; Regensburg, priv. col.). Despite the realism of his outlook, Dannecker always represented personality in an idealized, classical manner. Characteristic features were the eschewing of contemporary costume (Lavater was the only exception) and the classically smooth rendering of the eye-ball, which conveyed an uncertainty of glance, enabling Dannecker to achieve an effect of timelessness and detachment. In 1794 Dannecker completed his first portrait of *Schiller* (plaster-casts in Weimar, Goethe-Nmus., and Marbach, Schiller-Nmus. & Dt. Litarchv; *see* GERMANY, fig. 33). Dannecker began the marble version of the figure (without a robe) in 1796 and completed the work in 1806 (Weimar, Zentbib. Dt. Klassik). Immediately after Schiller's death in 1805, Dannecker conceived the idea of an imposing monument to the poet. However, he completed only the over life-size herm bust in marble (1805–10; Stuttgart, Staatsgal.),

Johann Heinrich Dannecker: *Ariadne on a Panther*, clay model, 317×278×95 mm, 1803 (Stuttgart, Staatsgalerie)

modifying this work in 1833 (original plaster cast, Stuttgart, Staatsgal.). In 1802 Dannecker travelled to Zurich, in order to prepare a plaster model after Lavater's death mask. The work aroused admiration in the Paris Salon shortly afterwards. By 1805, Dannecker had completed the marble version (Zurich, Zentbib.). As in his colossal bust of Schiller, Dannecker achieved an ageless, idealized image, an exact and vital representation of a mature personality at the height of his powers.

Dannecker also produced works on religious themes, for example his *Christ* (1821–4; St Petersburg, Hermitage); but he concentrated on mythological subject-matter. His most popular sculpture was *Ariadne on a Panther* (1803–14; Frankfurt am Main, Liebieghaus; model, 1803; Stuttgart, Staatsgal., see fig.), representing the triumphant bride of Bacchus, and symbolizing the idea of savagery tamed by beauty. A plan to give the final, marble version of the figure a cultic aura by placing her in a temple-like rotunda was in part fulfilled by the construction, beginning in 1856, of the 'Ariadneum'.

BIBLIOGRAPHY

A. Spemann: *Dannecker* (Berlin and Stuttgart, 1909)
——: *Johann Heinrich Dannecker: Das Leben, das Werk, der Mensch* (Munich, 1958)
Ariadne auf dem Panther (exh. cat., ed. E. Kemp; Frankfurt am Main, Liebieghaus, 1979)
Johann Heinrich Dannecker: Der Bildhauer, der Zeichner, 2 vols (exh. cat., ed. C. von Holst and U. Gauss; Stuttgart, Staatsgal., 1987)

SEPP KERN

D'Annunzio, Gabriele (*b* Pescara, 12 March 1863; *d* Gardone Riviera, nr Brescia, 1 March 1938). Italian writer and collector. In his youth he was a militant critic of figurative art, especially in newspaper articles: his interest was limited to contemporary painting. All his life he was a collector of art objects, although not always of refined taste. In the early 1880s he went to Rome, where he frequented fashionable literary and journalistic circles and wrote news articles on art for periodicals such as *La tribuna*, *Il fanfulla* and the *Cronaca bizantina*, of which he was editor for a few months in 1885. His preferences as an art critic were for naturalistic painting, such as that of his great friend Francesco Paolo Michetti. He commented on Michetti's painting *The Vow* (in *Il fanfulla*, 14 January 1883), giving a symbolic interpretation of its descriptive and narrative qualities, an approach that was to pervade Italian culture a few years later.

The new aestheticism appears most prominently in the novel *Il piacere* (1889), whose protagonist, a poet and engraver, brings to mind the heroes of Oscar Wilde or Joris-Karl Huysmans. The turbid and erotic atmosphere of this work is loaded with references to the figurative arts. The cult of the Pre-Raphaelite Brotherhood had spread to Italy, and D'Annunzio took part in it together with artists and critics from the circle gathered around the art review *Il convito* in 1895, including Angelo Conti, Aristide Sartorio and Mario De Maria. In the first issue of this journal D'Annunzio reviewed a book on *Giorgione* (1894) by Angelo Conti. D'Annunzio shared Conti's faith in a creative criticism that could enrich a work rather than merely interpreting it. He also accepted his theory of a unification of all the arts, based on the model of music (derived from Arthur Schopenhauer and Walter Pater). He saw Giorgione's painting in more sensual terms than Conti, however, in accord with the concept of autumnal eroticism. This theme was triumphantly expressed in his novel *Il fuoco* (1898), which recounts the end of his love affair in Venice with the great dramatic actress Eleonora Duse.

D'Annunzio's symbolism became increasingly Classical in content, perhaps influenced by a journey to Greece in 1895, during which he wrote enthusiastic pages on Praxiteles and the sculptures of Olympus, Delphi and Athens. His poetry took on a more heroic tone; his taste in painting turned towards the work of Aristide Sartorio and A. De Carolis, exponents of the current revival of the Renaissance. In *Dante e Segantini* (1899) D'Annunzio interpreted even a solitary painter such as Giovanni Segantini in this heroic mode, which took on an increasingly nationalistic exaltation. A similar tendency can be seen in the characters of his tragedies, for example *La città morta* (1898) and *La gloria* (1899). During his years in France (1910–15), partly through his friendship with the painter Romaine Brooks, D'Annunzio became acquainted with the products of international art and taste. His life changed after his return to Italy, with his participation in World War I, his role in the seizure of Fiume (now Rijeka, Slovenia) in 1919 and the birth of Fascism. Although D'Annunzio welcomed Fascism it forced him to retreat to his villa, which he called Il Vittoriale degli Italiani, for the rest of his life. In the last phase of his work, which critics refer to as the 'nocturnal' period, after his volume of poetic prose *Il notturno* (1916), composed during a period of blindness, there is a slight reduction in the luxuriant richness of his visual references and a greater focus on inner life. He did not, however, abandon his enthusiasm for art and for collecting or his need to feel himself a part of the avant-garde. His polemical, autobiographical and lyrical prose was still permeated with references to figurative art, with a preference during this period for the heroism of Michelangelo.

WRITINGS
S. Fugazza, ed.: *Pagine sull'arte* (Milan, 1986)

BIBLIOGRAPHY
L. Bianconi: *D'Annunzio critico* (Florence, 1940)
B. Tamassia Mazzarotto: *Le arti figurative nell'arte di G. D'Annunzio* (Milan, 1949)
O. Venanzio: *G. D'Annunzio interprete delle arti figurative del suo tempo* (Milan, 1958)
Atti del convegno: L'arte di G. D'Annunzio: Milan, 1963
E. Scarano: *Dalla Cronaca bizantina al Convito* (Florence, 1970)
Atti del convegno su D'Annunzio e il Simbolismo europeo: Gardone, 1973
S. Scotoni: *D'Annunzio e l'arte contemporanea* (Florence, 1981)
'Atti del convegno su D'Annunzio, la musica e le arti figurative: Gardone, 1982', *Quad. Vittoriale*, 34–5 (1982) [whole issue]

FRANCO BERNABEI

Dantan. French family of sculptors. Antoine-Laurent Dantan (*b* Saint-Cloud, Hauts-de-Seine, 8 Dec 1798; *d* Saint-Cloud, 25 May 1878), known as Dantan the elder, and his brother Jean-Pierre Dantan (*b* Paris, 28 Dec 1800; *d* Baden Baden, 6 Sept 1869), known as Dantan the younger, both served an apprenticeship with their father, an ornamental wood-carver. Antoine-Laurent entered the Ecole des Beaux-Arts, Paris, in 1816, and Jean-Pierre in 1823. Both were the pupils of François-Joseph Bosio, who passed on to them his skill in elegant, conventional portraiture. While the elder brother was preparing his entry for the Prix de Rome, the younger worked on a variety of decorative commissions. By 1826 he had executed a statuette (Paris, Carnavalet) portraying *César Ducornet* (1805–56), an armless painter. Because of the subject's disability, this work cannot rank as the first of his caricatures or *portraits chargés*, as Jean-Pierre termed his subsequent humorous sculptures; but the interest in physical peculiarities that it displays was in accordance with the Romantics' desire to accommodate the full range of natural phenomena, even the disturbing.

Antoine-Laurent won the Prix de Rome in 1828; in the following year, the brothers travelled together to Rome. In 1831 Jean-Pierre returned to France, where he set about reproducing and marketing his statuettes caricaturing men prominent in the worlds of music, theatre, politics and the law. In Rome, his brother, following in the footsteps of François Rude and François-Joseph Duret, completed, as his farewell piece, a Neapolitan genre statue of a *Young Hunter Playing with his Dog and a Duck* (marble, 1833–5; Paris, Louvre). On his return to France, he produced a pendant to this, a *Young Neapolitan Girl* (exh. 1837 Salon; version, Halifax, W. Yorks, People's Park). He devoted himself, for the most part, to portraiture and official sculpture, displaying at times a romantic panache, as in the statue of *Abraham Duquesne* (bronze, 1844; Dieppe), which was first shown at the 1843 Salon. Jean-Pierre, despite the huge success of his caricatures, likewise produced statues for public buildings and non-humorous portraits; on one occasion he undertook a commemorative statue, that of the composer *Adrien Boieldieu*, for Rouen (bronze; 1835–7).

While the Dantan brothers' serious work hardly rose above the average of their time, Jean-Pierre's caricatures were a new departure and paved the way for Honoré Daumier's series of satirical busts of members of the Parlement. However, a comparison with Daumier makes it possible to identify the distinctive features of Jean-Pierre's approach, which is drier, more journalistic, and referential in its use of subjects' recognizable attributes. As in contemporary commemorative statuary, these references were sometimes made through reliefs on the base of the statuette or bust, an example being the portrait of *Honoré de Balzac* (plaster, 1835; Paris, Carnavalet) that depicted his jewelled cane on the base. Sometimes the subject's head was enlarged out of proportion with the body, as in the statuette of *Frédéric Lemaître* (1833; Paris, Carnavalet). In cases where the body itself was the butt of mockery, because of obesity (e.g. *Luigi Lablache*, plaster, 1831; Paris, Carnavalet) or scrawniness (e.g. *Paganini*, bronze, 1832; Paris, Carnavalet), the sculptor used a more balanced overall proportion. Jean-Pierre's preoccupation with the world of art and entertainment led him to deride the already exaggerated physical traits of 'romantic genius' in such subjects as *Victor Hugo* and *Hector Berlioz* (both 1833; Paris, Carnavalet).

Jean-Pierre Dantan visited London on several occasions between 1833 and 1841 and caricatured a number of English subjects, such as *Samuel Rogers* (plaster; London, N.P.G.). At the Great Exhibition of 1851 Jean-Pierre showed a seated figure (untraced) of *Queen Victoria*, cast in zinc. His caricatures, which made his fortune and, ironically, contributed to his subjects' celebrity, were chiefly marketed through the Paris shop of the art publishers Susse Frères. His widow donated a large collection of his works, both humorous and serious, to the Musée Carnavalet in Paris.

BIBLIOGRAPHY
Lami
H. Delloye: *Musée Dantan* (Paris, 1839)
J. Seligmann: *Figures of Fun: The Caricature Statuettes of Jean-Pierre Dantan* (London, 1957)
The Romantics to Rodin (exh. cat., ed. P. Fusco and H. Janson; Los Angeles, CA, Co. Mus. A., 1980)
A. Le Normand: *La Tradition classique et l'esprit romantique* (Rome, 1981)

PHILIP WARD-JACKSON

Dante Alighieri. *See* ALIGHIERI, DANTE.

Danti. Italian family of artists, scientists and writers. The members of the Danti family (originally the Rainaldi: the name was changed out of admiration for Dante Alighieri) are said to have pursued artistic and literary careers over several generations. Theodora Danti (*fl* early 16th century) was a painter and a pupil of Perugino (Pascoli, pp. 75–9). Like several other family members, she was also distinguished for her love of astronomy and mathematics and for making scientific instruments. Theodora's brother Giulio Danti (1500–75), an architect, goldsmith and metal-caster, was the father of (1) Vincenzio Danti, a leading Florentine Mannerist sculptor, and one of the most distinguished sculptors in 16th-century Italy. Vincenzio also wrote a celebrated treatise on proportion. His younger brother (2) Ignazio Danti, a mapmaker and mathematician, was heir to all his family's manuscripts, none of which is known to have survived. A third brother, Gerolamo Danti (1547–80), was a goldsmith and painter, who frescoed the sacristy of S Pietro in Perugia with scenes from the *Acts of the Apostles*.

(1) Vincenzio [Vincenzo] **Danti** (*b* Perugia, 1530; *d* Perugia, 26 May 1576). Sculptor, architect and writer.

1. LIFE AND WORK. Danti was probably trained by his father, Giulio Danti, and was enrolled in the Perugian guild of goldsmiths in 1548. Pascoli wrote that Danti studied grammar and rhetoric and was sent while still a youth to Rome, where he studied anatomy with Michelangelo and Daniele da Volterra. There is a certain circumstantial plausibility to this account, since Michelangelo was studying anatomy in the late 1540s with Realdo Colombo, the rival of Andreas Vesalius. Even peripheral contact with such circles, which also included Juan de Valverde, whose *Historia del cuerpo humano* (1556) is connected with Danti's later treatise, might explain the beginnings of Danti's interest in the theory and practice of anatomy.

Danti's first commission was the bronze seated statue of *Julius III* (1553–5) outside Perugia Cathedral. It is an exuberantly ornate and ambitious work and shows the impact of Guglielmo della Porta's tomb of *Paul III* in St Peter's, Rome, underway at the same time. Danti's remarkable low relief style is already fully evident in the allegorical figures encrusting the Pope's vestments.

By 1557 Danti had moved from Perugia to Florence, where he spent most of his short career. Things began auspiciously with a commission for the bronze group *Hercules and Antaeus* to complete Niccolò Tribolo's Fountain of Hercules at the Medici villa at Castello. Opportunity turned to disaster when Danti miscast the group three times. After this failure he worked at humbler projects in Giorgio Vasari's redecoration of the Palazzo Vecchio. He may also have been associated with Baccio Bandinelli during his first years in Florence, which would have given him the opportunity to learn to carve marble. Bandinelli died in 1560, during the competition for the Fountain of Neptune in the Piazza della Signoria, in which Danti was a participant. In 1561, shortly after this competition, Danti carved his group *Honour Triumphant over Falsehood* (Florence, Bargello; see fig.) for Cosimo I de' Medici's chamberlain, the fellow-Perugian Sforza Almeni. This is one of the finest works of 16th-century Italian sculpture and Danti's best work in marble. It is often used to reconstruct missing figures for Michelangelo's tomb of *Julius II*, but, beyond its psychomachic theme, the sculpture bears little relation to Michelangelo's. It is probably not far from Danti's model (untraced) for the Fountain of Neptune and records his assimilation of the styles of Bandinelli and Benvenuto Cellini, and perhaps also that of the paintings of Agnolo Bronzino.

While establishing his reputation as a sculptor in marble, Danti continued to work in bronze. The large relief of *Moses and the Brazen Serpent* (Florence, Bargello), cast in two parts, was completed in late 1559 and may have been associated with the decorations of the Palazzo Vecchio, or with a failed project to make bronze reliefs a part of Bandinelli's choir in Florence Cathedral. Whatever its original destination, the *Brazen Serpent* panel displays a freedom and variety in the treatment of relief, together with a lightness of hand and attenuation of form comparable to the best drawings of Florentine Mannerist artists. In 1560 Danti cast the safe door (Florence, Bargello) for

Vincenzio Danti: *Honour Triumphant over Falsehood*, marble, h. 1.9 m, 1561 (Florence, Museo Nazionale del Bargello)

the personal quarters of Cosimo I as part of Vasari's continuing transformation of the Palazzo Vecchio.

The *Honour* group having established his credentials, Danti began a series of marble commissions that occupied him through the next decade. Between 1562 and 1566 he worked at the monument to *Carlo de' Medici* in the cathedral at Prato. This is a stiff reprise of the composition of Michelangelo's *Madonna* in Onze Lieve Vrouw, Bruges, accompanied by two more supple putti and a delicate low relief portrait of *Carlo de' Medici* (*d* 1492). In 1564 Danti began the Medici coat of arms with allegories of *Equity* and *Rigour* and a commanding portrait of *Cosimo I* for the entrance of Vasari's Uffizi. The svelte reclining allegories are still in place, but the large seated allegorical portrait of *Cosimo I* that was to have topped the group ended up as a fountain in the Boboli Gardens. Danti's second attempt, the standing, strongly idealized portrait of *Cosimo I as Augustus* (Florence, Bargello), must have been carved in the early 1570s and was replaced about 10 years later by the present much more straightforward portrait by Giambologna.

During the late 1560s Danti also carved the standing *Virgin and Child* (Florence, Santa Croce), a group outstanding both for its Mannerist abstraction of form, line and surface and for its apparent archaism. Danti in fact seems to have specialized in imitating earlier styles: his portrait of *Carlo de' Medici* recalls 15th-century relief; in the late 1560s he completed Andrea Sansovino's *Baptism* group over the east portal of the Baptistery of Florence Cathedral, and the monument to *Giovanni da Salerno* in S Maria Novella is the most extreme of all his essays in the duplication of earlier styles.

Danti was closely connected to the Florentine Accademia del Disegno from the time of its foundation in 1563. He served as an officer in the Accademia and contributed works to its various enterprises. He was involved in the planning of the funeral of Michelangelo in 1564, for which he made an allegorical painting, *Fame Triumphant over Death and Time*, and a sculpture, *Genius Overcoming Ignorance*. Danti modelled an equestrian portrait of *Cosimo I* for the wedding decorations of Francesco I de' Medici and Joanna of Austria in 1565 and made a statue of *St Luke* for the Accademia's Cappella di S Luca in the SS Annunziata in 1571, the only one of these works to survive.

During his final years in Florence, Danti returned to bronze sculpture on a monumental scale, completing the *Beheading of St John the Baptist* group over the south portal of the Baptistery in 1571. This is one of the masterpieces of what can properly be called Mannerist sculpture and combines Danti's virtuosity and inventive mastery of modelling in wax with the restrained statement of volume of his works in marble. In the same late period, and in a similar vein, he also cast the small bronze statue *Venus Anadyomene* for the *studiolo* of Francesco I in the Palazzo Vecchio.

In 1572 Danti made an oval plan (untraced) for the church of Philip II's Escorial and was invited to Spain. Just when his career seemed to be ascending, however, he returned to Perugia, where he married. While in Florence, Danti had worked from time to time in Perugia, and on 20 July 1573 he was appointed architect of his native city. He helped establish the Perugian Accademia del Disegno, to which he donated casts of Michelangelo's statues the *Four Times of Day* in the Medici Chapel, S Lorenzo, Florence.

2. WRITINGS. Danti became a member of the literary Accademia Fiorentina in September 1565. In April 1567 he dated the dedication to Cosimo I of *Il primo libro del trattato delle perfette proporzioni* ... This was to have been the theoretical introduction to an unrealized work of 15 books, an encyclopedic presentation of the arts of design centring on human anatomy. The importance given to human anatomy itself relates Danti's scheme to the art of Michelangelo, to the authority of which he repeatedly appealed. Danti argued from a distinction between what he called portraying (*ritrarre*) and imitation (*imitare*). The first of these is the simple copying of appearances, an option rejected on the generally Neo-Platonic grounds that actual things are almost always imperfect. Therefore it is necessary to have recourse to higher knowledge, to imitate. Danti's distinction between *ritrarre* and *imitare* parallels that between history and poetry made in Aristotle's *Poetics*, just coming into the full flood of its influence after its translation in 1548. Poetry is general and philosophical, history is particular, and the arts of design, like poetry, are properly grounded in philosophical understanding. This higher understanding can be attained either by imitating works judged to be perfect or by discerning the ends nature intended to achieve in bringing imperfect individual things into existence. All things inanimate and animate are in a more or less perfect proportion to the end discernible in them. In animals the end is local movement, the evident activity of the soul. The highest form of animal movement is human movement, which is free and rational. Beautiful forms are those fully suited to their ends, and these should be imagined and imitated by the artist. Danti's 'perfect proportion' is thus continuous with the teleological explanation basic to speculation on anatomy from Aristotle and Galen through the Renaissance. Danti's deep knowledge of anatomy is certain. He claimed to have performed 83 dissections in preparation for his book, and he obtained several cadavers between 1567 and 1570. Michelangelo's art may be imitated, in short, because it displays a perfect knowledge of anatomy and therefore a grasp of the nature of things concentrated in the microcosmic human soul. The academician Danti thus avoided the anti-canonical side of Michelangelo's poetic art in favour of its philosophical and teachable side. It was perhaps during Danti's last years in Perugia that he wrote the apparently now untraced autobiography in *terza rima* and the lives of the modern sculptors attributed to him by Pascoli (pp. 143, 293).

WRITINGS

Il primo libro del trattato delle perfette proporzioni di tutte le cose che imitare e ritrarre si possano con l'arte del disegno (Florence, 1567), repr. with a critical commentary in P. Barrocchi, ed.: *Trattati d'arte del cinquecento fra Manierismo e Controriforma* (Bari, 1960), pp. 207–69

BIBLIOGRAPHY

DBI; Thieme–Becker
G. Vasari: *Vite* (1550, rev. 2/1568); ed. G. Milanesi, vii (1881), pp. 630–33
L. Pascoli: *Le vite de' pittori, scultori ed architetti perugini* (Rome, 1732), pp. 75–9, 137–43
J. Pope-Hennessy: *Italian High Renaissance and Baroque Sculpture* (1963, rev. 3/1986), iii of *Introduction to Italian Sculpture* (Oxford, 1955–63), pp. 377–80
S. Rossi: 'Il *Trattato delle perfette proporzioni* e l'incidenza della *Poetica* sulle teorie artistiche del secondo cinquecento', *Stor. A.*, xiv (1972), pp. 127–47
D. Summers: *The Sculpture of Vincenzo Danti* (New York and London, 1979)
——: *Michelangelo and the Language of Art* (Princeton, 1981)

M. Daly Davis: 'Beyond the "Primo Libro" of Vincenzo Danti's *Trattato delle perfette proporzioni*', *Mitt. Ksthist. Inst. Florenz*, xxvi/1 (1982), pp. 63–89

DAVID SUMMERS

(2) Ignazio [Egnazio] Danti (*b* Perugia, 1536; *d* Alstri, nr Rome, 1586). Mapmaker, mathematician, architect and instrument-maker, brother of (1) Vincenzio Danti. He entered the Dominican Order in 1555. In 1562 Cosimo de' Medici, to whom he had probably been presented by Vincenzio, commissioned him to paint a set of maps of the world (*see* MAP, §5) on the doors of the cabinets in the Guardaroba of the Palazzo Vecchio, Florence, and to create a large terrestrial globe (the largest now in existence, which was finished in 1567 and stands in the centre of the room). So well satisfied was Cosimo that he won permission from the Dominicans for Ignazio to live in his palace. In the early 1570s Ignazio was engaged on astronomical research and was a member of Pope Gregory XIII's commission to reform the calendar. He became increasingly interested in perspective and in 1573 published the *Prospettiva di Euclide*, together with the previously unpublished *Prospettiva di Eliodoro Larisseo*, an annotated translation that includes a description of the camera obscura and of a method of correcting images by using mirrors. Francesco I de' Medici dismissed Danti from his court, and he moved to Bologna, where he became Professor of Mathematics from 1576 to 1584. He was the architect of a chapel in S Domenico, Bologna, and painted maps in the Palazzo del Podestà. In 1577 he went to Perugia to draw a map of the city and its environs; this was published in Rome in 1580 and by order of the Pope was later extended to cover the entire Papal States. In 1578 he filled a sketchbook (Bologna, Bib. Com. Archiginnasio, Gozzadini col.; pubd 1867) with drawings of the villas, castles and churches around Bologna. Gregory XIII called him to Rome in 1580 to work on the final stages of the calendar reform and in the same year commissioned him to paint maps of the various regions of Italy, in thirty-two large panels and eight smaller ones in the Galleria delle Carte Geografiche in the Vatican. This work was finished in 1583, and in the same year Danti published Jacopo Vignola's *Le due regole della prospettiva pratica*, to which he added a long and learned commentary and a biography of Vignola; this became his best-known and most influential work and suggests the interrelationship between the interest in perspective of painters and mathematicians in this period (*see* PERSPECTIVE, §II, 2(ii)). In November 1583 he was called to Rome by Pope Sixtus V to advise on the restoration of the Porto Claudio at Fiumicino, and to work with Domenico Fontana (iii) on transferring the Vatican obelisk from the former Circus of Nero, south of St Peter's, to the centre of St Peter's Square.

BIBLIOGRAPHY

S. Mazzetti: *Repertorio di tutti i professori ecc.* (Bologna, 1847), p. 110
P. Riccardi: *Biblioteca matematica italiana* (Modena, 1870–76)
M. Fanti: *Ville, castelli e chiese bolognesi da un libro di disegni del cinquecento* (Bologna, 1967)
M. L. Bonelli: 'Danti, Egnazio (Pellegrino Rainaldi)', *Dictionary of Scientific Biography*, ed. C. C. Gillespie, iii (New York, 1971), pp. 558–9
G. Roversi: 'Il patrimonio fondiario dei Tanari a Gàggio Montano e nel Belvedere', *Strenna Stor. Bologn.*, xxiv (1974), pp. 260–62

GIORGIO TABARRONI

Danube school. Group of German and Austrian artists *c*. 1500–50, of which Albrecht Altdorfer (*see* ALTDORFER, (1)) and WOLFGANG HUBER were two of the central figures. The term came into use following an observation by Theodor von Frimmel (1853–1928) in 1892 that painting in the Danube region around Regensburg, Passau and Linz possessed certain common characteristics that entitled one to speak of a Danube style (*Donaustil*). This point was taken up by Hermann Voss in *Der Ursprung des Donaustils* (Leipzig, 1907). Once the early, Viennese works (*c*. 1500–05) of Lucas Cranach the elder (*see* CRANACH, (1)) were recognized as having provided the formative stage of this stylistic development, the name Danube school (*Donauschule*) took deeper root. The name also carried associations of the regional landscape (*Donaulandschaft*) and of the art born of that region (*Kunstlandschaft*), evoking what critics saw as its nature-orientated quality. 'Danube school' and 'Danube style' established themselves as terms of reference too convenient to be dislodged, despite the demurs of many critics. The leading artists did not form a school in the usual sense of the term, since their communality derived from neither a single workshop nor even a particular centre, and the geographical limits of the school or style are even less precise. Nevertheless, continuing discussion over the idea of a Danube school has given *de facto* acknowledgement that it does exist as a stylistic phenomenon.

1. CHARACTERISTICS. The defining characteristics of the Danube school are, on the one hand, the prominence of nature and the manner of representing it, and on the other the relationship of the human figure or human events to nature. In Altdorfer's early works, such as *St George and the Dragon* (1510; Munich, Alte Pin.), landscape dominates the scene, and in drawings such as the *Danube at Sarmingstein* (1511; Budapest, Mus. F.A.; see fig.) it was the sole subject of the work. These examples were followed by etchings and paintings of landscapes by Altdorfer from *c*. 1520 that mark the birth of landscape as an autonomous theme in European art (*see* LANDSCAPE PAINTING). No less important than the thematic emphasis on nature is the subjective portrayal of it and of human experience itself. Danube school landscapes are those not of scientific naturalists but rather of artists who were expressing the power and state of becoming in nature. There is movement in the mountainous topography, burgeoning growth in the forests and explosive radiance in the heavens. Cranach's *Crucifixion* (1503; Munich, Alte Pin.; see CRANACH, (1), fig. 1), another example of landscape in a leading expressive role rather than simply background, also shows how such handling of nature reinforces the artist's subjective presentation of the religious theme. No frontal symmetry or formal hierarchy mitigates the view of suffering and approaching storm.

In depicting the human figure, artists of the Danube school paid little heed to anatomical accuracy or skeletal structure. The treatment of both figures and landscape is emphasized in the literature as evidence for what distinguishes this art from that of Dürer or the Renaissance in Italy, although prints by Dürer and Italian engravings were important sources for Cranach, Altdorfer, Huber and other artists of the Danube school. The contorted bodies

Albrecht Altdorfer: *Danube at Sarmingstein*, pen and black ink, 148×202 mm, 1511 (Budapest, Museum of Fine Arts)

and turbulent drapery patterns, especially as seen in Cranach's early woodcuts and paintings of the *Passion*, indicate that the Danube school had roots in Late Gothic Bavarian and Austrian art, especially that of Jan Polack in Munich and the Austrian paintings of Jörg Breu (i).

2. EXTENT. The roster of artists considered part of the Danube school has grown with the literature over the past century. Ernst Buchner (1892–1962) assembled works by many of these artists in the exhibition he dedicated to Altdorfer in 1938, but for only a few of the included artists, such as Erhard Altdorfer and Michael Ostendorfer, can an association with Altdorfer and/or Regensburg be assumed certain. For most of the others, largely anonymous masters, there is no evidence of a connection with either Altdorfer or Regensburg. In his *Malerei der Donauschule* (Munich, 1964) Alfred Stange offered an anthology of works according to individual hands and renewed consideration of their common regional character. In the exhibition of 1965 in Linz and St Florian, *Die Kunst der Donauschule*, and in the related essays, *Werden und Wandlung, Studien zur Kunst der Donauschule* (Linz, 1967), the geographical scope of the Danube school was expanded to reach all of central Europe, Switzerland and parts of northern Germany. Some critics have seen this expansion of the Danube school as yet another reason to be sceptical about the validity and coherence of this term. Nevertheless,

when Erhard Altdorfer left the Danube region for Mecklenburg and Georg Lemberger moved from Landshut to Saxony, they produced woodcuts that are still easily recognized as having characteristics of the Danube school. On the other hand, when Cranach left Vienna for Wittenberg in 1504–5, those qualities of his art that had originally defined much of the Danube school rapidly diminished.

3. MEDIA. Although the art of the Danube school was essentially the work of painters, drawings and prints were the primary vehicles for pictorial ideas. The development of landscape in the graphic arts can be explained partly by the licence of prints and drawings to deal with subjects not yet considered appropriate for the thematically conservative medium of painting, but also by a special affinity between etching and the portrayal of landscape, as the nine landscape etchings by Altdorfer demonstrate (*see* ALTDORFER, (1), fig. 1). This component of the Danube school, carried into the 1540s and 1550s by Augustin Hirschvogel and Hanns Lautensack, led the way for subsequent generations of landscape etchers from Pieter Bruegel the elder to Rembrandt and beyond.

Sculpture and architecture have also figured in studies of the Danube school, especially at the time of the Linz exhibition (1965) and afterwards. Visual and historical connections between works of Hans Leinberger and Albrecht Altdorfer can clearly be seen, particularly in Leinberger's free-standing figures of the Virgin and the vigorous movement and modelling of drapery but also in his pictorial handling of reliefs. Master I.P. is the main representative of several anonymous carvers active in Passau, Salzburg and Prague who, using boxwood and fine-grained fruit woods, produced small scenes with forest settings in the manner of the Danube school (*see* MASTERS, ANONYMOUS, AND MONOGRAMMISTS, §III, MASTER I.P.). Master I.P.'s *Fall of Man* (1521; Vienna, Belvedere) defines this category of sculpture, with its engraving-like detail of foliage and other landscape motifs translated into delicate, three-dimensional forms. (*See also* AUSTRIA, §IV, 2.)

BIBLIOGRAPHY

T. von Frimmel: review of M. Friedländer: *Albrecht Altdorfer* (Leipzig, 1891), *Repert. Kstwiss.*, xv (1892), pp. 417–21

H. Voss: *Der Ursprung des Donaustils*, Kunstgeschichtliche Monographien, vii (Leipzig, 1907)

O. Benesch: 'Die Tafelmalerei des 1. Drittels des 16. Jahrhunderts in Österreich', *Bild. Kst Österreich*, iii (1938), pp. 137–48; repr. in *Collected Writings*, iii, ed. E. Benesch (London, 1972), pp. 3–11

Albrecht Altdorfer und sein Kreis (exh. cat. by E. Buchner, Munich, Neue Staatsgal., 1938), pp. 147–9

A. Stange: *Malerei der Donauschule* (Munich, 1964)

Alte & Mod. Kst, x (1965), part 80 [special edn devoted to essays on the Danube school]

Die Kunst der Donauschule, 1490–1540 (exh. cat., St Florian, Abbey; Linz, Schlossmus.; 1965)

Werden und Wandlung: Studien zur Kunst der Donauschule (Linz, 1967)

Prints and Drawings of the Danube School (exh. cat., ed. K. Holter and O. Wutzel; New Haven, CT, Yale U. A.G., 1969)

R. Janzen: *Albrecht Altdorfer: Four Centuries of Criticism*, ix of Stud. F.A.: Crit. (1980)

H. Schindler: 'Albrecht Altdorfer und die Anfänge des Donaustils', *Ostbair. Grenzmarken*, xxiii (1981), pp. 66–73

Altdorfer and Fantastic Realism in German Art (exh. cat., ed. J. Guillaud and M. Guillaud; Paris, Cent. Cult. Marais, 1984), pp. 10–47, 149–64

B. Decker: *Das Ende des mittelalterlichen Kultbildes und die Plastik Hans Leinbergers*, Bamberger Studien zur Kunstgeschichte und Denkmalpflege, iii (Bamberg, 1985), pp. 33–54

G. Goldberg: *Albrecht Altdorfer. Meister von Landschaft: Raum, Licht* (Munich, 1988)

Albrecht Altdorfer: Zeichnungen, Deckfarbenmalerei, Druckgraphik (exh. cat. by H. Mielke, W. Berlin, Kupferstichkab., 1988)

CHARLES TALBOT

Danzig. *See* GDAŃSK.

Danziger, (Max Wilhelm) Itzhak (*b* Berlin, 26 June 1916; *d* nr Ramla, Israel, 11 July 1977). Israeli sculptor of German birth. His family went to Palestine in 1923, settling in Jerusalem. After attending schools both there and in England, he studied sculpture at the Slade School of Fine Art in London (1934–7), and while there he regularly visited the British Museum to see the sculptures from Assyria, Egypt, Africa and India. After his return to Palestine in 1938, he produced his first important work, *Nimrod* (1939; Jerusalem, Israel Mus.; *see* JEWISH ART, fig. 24), which showed the influence of ancient sculpture. At the end of 1945 he travelled to Paris and until 1948 divided his time between Paris, Tel Aviv and London. During this time he worked as Ossip Zadkine's assistant in Paris and also met Brancusi there in 1946. From 1948 to 1955 he lived in London, where he became acquainted with Kenneth Armitage and Eduardo Paolozzi.

On his return to Israel in 1955 Danziger associated with the New Horizons group and began to work with welded iron. From 1956 to 1958 he worked on a large relief wall for the Givat Ram campus of the Hebrew University of Jerusalem, using symbols from the period of the Judean Kings. Through the late 1950s and early 1960s he produced a number of sculptures based on sheep, culminating in *Negev Sheep* (1964; Washington, DC, Hirshhorn). Often alternating between the figurative and abstract in his work, his sculptures of the late 1960s were mostly geometrically abstract, as in *Artillery Corps Sculpture* (1969; Jerusalem, Israel Mus.). Throughout his career he worked on a number of public commissions, such as that for the Yad Lebanim Memorial, Holon (1961–2). In the 1970s he gave up sculpture and devoted himself to ecological projects.

BIBLIOGRAPHY

Danziger (exh. cat. by M. Omer, Jerusalem, Israel Mus., 1981)

Artists of Israel: 1920–1980 (exh. cat., New York, Jew. Mus., 1981), pp. 90–91

□

Daoism. Chinese system of ethical, religious and magical beliefs traditionally ascribed to Laozi (*c.* 570–490 BC) and expounded in the *Daode jing* ('Classic of the way and virtue'). The central tenets of Daoism are concerned with the understanding and proper practice of the *Dao* ('Way').

1. INTRODUCTION. At first glance, the intellectual and artistic developments of Daoism appear to be a bewildering mixture of philosophy, alchemy and mysticism. Daoist schools have variously focused on philosophy, the pursuit of immortality, alchemy and the discovery of an earthly paradise. Although the *Daode jing* is central to much Daoist thought, it has its competitors, such as the *Liezi* (5th–4th century BC), the *Zhuangzi* (4th–3rd century BC) and the voluminous Daoist canon known as the *Daozang*.

Daoist art and thought can be separated into two distinct, though occasionally intertwined traditions: the naturalistic and the magical. Just as chemists differ from alchemists in that the former try to participate in natural processes while the latter try to transmogrify them, some Daoists, such as Wang Bi (AD 226–49), aspired to conform to the *Dao*, while others, such as Tao Hongjing (AD 456–536), attempted to influence its course. However, an enquiry into the nature of the *Dao* is the central question that unifies all Daoist art and thought. Despite the advice at the beginning of the *Daode jing* that 'the *dao* that can be told is not the eternal *Dao*', and later that 'those who know do not speak; those who speak do not know', numerous definitions of the *Dao* have been offered. According to Wang Bi, the *Dao* was noumenal, but according to Guo Xiang (*d* AD 312), it was phenomenal. In the West, the *Dao* has been translated as nature, reason, logos, truth, the undifferentiated aesthetic continuum and the Way. However, one central historical observation is possible, namely that whether one addresses naturalistic or magical Daoism, a correspondence exists between how one perceives reality and how one understands the *Dao*. From a naturalistic perspective the *Dao* is manifested in nature, reason, logos or truth, but from a magical perspective, the *Dao* is alchemical or transformative. Daoist art aspired to provide an insight into and to influence both the substance and the practice of the *Dao*. The historical development of Daoist art reveals the unfolding of the *Dao*. In China there were several distinct historical stages in the understanding of the *Dao*, each with a concomitant expression in the arts.

2. HISTORICAL DEVELOPMENT. Generally speaking, the *Dao* was first viewed as an abstract noumenal force, resulting in an aniconic approach to the arts, then as a historic personality with icons dedicated to a deified Laozi (resulting in art to a degree magical). This tendency continued during the next period, but the focus shifted from the deified Laozi to Yuanshi Tianzun, a cosmological deity. Daoist icons then represented not a historical figure but a transcendent force. The final syncretic phase occurred during the Song period (960–1279), when the *Dao* was incorporated either into the naturalistic world-view of Neo-Confucianism, where seeking the *Dao* was seen as an activity central to the pursuit of the rational and practical life, or into the intuitive proclivities of Chan (Jap. Zen) Buddhism, where it was seen as part of the realization of the intuitive and mystic life. It was at this stage that specifically Daoist art ceased to be a significant cultural force in China; consequently, Daoist art was relegated largely to the magical and popular realms.

(i) Aniconism, c. 6th century BC–3rd century BC. The *Daode jing* presents the student of Daoist thought and art with an immediate paradox. The opening lines read, 'The *dao* that can be told is not the eternal *Dao*.' For the Daoists of this period, the denial of discursive reason did not preclude cognition, but it did preclude intellectual constructs and pride. Daoism focused on intuition, resulting in the association of the intuitive with the empirical. The 3rd and 2nd centuries BC witnessed an attempt to reconcile the notion of the *Dao* as presented in the *Daode jing* with other deities and cosmologies. The *Dao* is associated with *tian* ('heaven') in the *Daode jing* (chap. 25) and possibly with *taiyi* ('supreme unity'; chap. 42). Associations were also made with *di* ('earth'), Huangdi (the Yellow Emperor) and the *yin yang wuxing* (yin-yang and the five elements) school of Zou Yan (*fl* 325 BC). The relationship between these divinities is complex, but it is merely a foretaste of the confusing pantheon of Daoist divinities that appeared during the Six Dynasties period (AD 222–589).

An aniconic orientation was central to the art of naturalistic Daoism pre-dating the Han period (206 BC–AD 220). The *Wei shu* ('History of the Wei'; 6th century AD) refers to earlier artistic practices in the following terms: 'The supreme *Dao* is without form; void and silence are its supreme characteristics. Since the Han there has been the erection of altars and shrines.' The abstract nature of naturalistic Daoism resulted in an aniconic orientation in which the visual arts were at an obvious disadvantage. This was soon overcome, however, by an intermingling of the naturalistic and the magical through the deification of Laozi.

An aspect of magical Daoism that dates from the end of the aniconic phase was the quest for the Isles of the Blessed, the paradise of immortals. Lie Zi (*fl* 5th century BC) claimed that there were five islands, with terraces and towers of gold and jade, where groves were laden with pearls and gems, and delicious fruits conferred immortality. Fantasy inspired historical fact, and according to the *Shiji* ('Records of the historian') by the Han historian Sima Qian (*fl* 145–90 BC), several expeditions were mounted to find the islands. They were depicted on Han-period bronze censers (*boshan lu*) in the shape of mountains in the

Eastern Sea (*see* CHINA, §§V, 3(iii)(a) and VI, 3(v)(b) and fig. 166). The theme persisted, and some 2000 years later it was depicted in the Qing-period (1644–1911) painting *A Picture of Fanghu* (Kansas City, MO, Nelson–Atkins Mus. A.) by Wang Yun (1652–1735).

(ii) Historicism, c. 2nd century BC–6th century AD. In his *Shiji*, Sima Qian claimed that Laozi was an obscure historical figure, but during the 2nd century AD the magical and mortal Laozi begin to merge. A votive stone dating to AD 564 depicts a seated Laozi as a deity flanked by two smaller standing attendants (see fig. 1). Beneath the figures is an incense burner shown in low relief, flanked by more deeply carved leonine animals in a frontal pose. At first glance the stone appears to be a Buddhist icon: the triadic composition, lotus-blossom daises and flanking attendants, suggestive of *bodhisattva*s, all belong to the Chinese Buddhist repertory. The appearance of a divine Laozi is open to several interpretations that affect our understanding of Daoist theology and art during this period. One interpretation places Daoism as a mere imitator of Buddhist prototypes, the other suggests an ecumenical conjoining of the two.

The earliest record of the transformation of Laozi from mortal to deity is found in an inscription, the *Laozi ming* (AD 165), which reads in part that Laozi has been active as a teacher for the sages since antiquity. This corresponds with the immortalization of Shakyamuni (the historical Buddha) in the Lotus Sutra, which was translated into Chinese in AD 286. In the Lotus Sutra Shakyamuni emphasizes that the historical Shakyamuni was but a corporeal manifestation of the eternal Buddha. These parallels are

1. Daoist votive stone depicting Laozi flanked by attendants, 470×378 mm, AD 564 (Chicago, IL, Field Museum of Natural History)

reflected in Chinese art by means of an iconographic innovation: icons depicting two figures seated side by side (*duobao xiang*, 'many-jewel image'). A Daoist icon of this type, dating to AD 515, is in the Museum of Fine Arts, Boston. The Indian Lotus Sutra is the source for such icons depicting Buddhist figures (Prabhutaratna and Shakyamuni), but there are no Indian prototypes for the *duobao xiang*, suggesting that this was inspired by the interaction of Buddhism and Daoism in China. Evidence for the complex artistic and theological interrelationship between the two faiths during this period includes a votive stone (AD 567; Washington, DC, Freer) depicting a deified Laozi flanked by attendants. Seated behind an armrest (*ji*), holding a fan in dignified repose, the central figure is presented as a Daoist philosopher, an advocate of *qingtan* ('pure discourse'). The *qingtan* ideal provided a source of imagery for both Chinese Buddhists and Daoists, as seen in an icon of the Buddha in such a pose (AD 545; Chicago, IL, Field Mus. Nat. Hist.).

(iii) Cosmology, 4th–10th century AD. During the Sui (AD 581–618) and Tang (AD 618–907) periods the deified Laozi was increasingly replaced by a less personalized cosmological deity, Yuanshi Tianzun ('Honoured celestial of the original beginning'). Yuanshi Tianzun makes his first appearance in the *Lingbao jing* ('Scriptures of the precious jewel'; 4th century AD), and this was further elaborated in the Daoist section of the *Sui shu* ('History of the Sui'). From the 6th century AD *Huayan jing* ('Flower garland scripture'; Skt *Avataṃsaka sūtra*) became prominent, establishing a concordance between Buddhist and Daoist thought. This text was the source for the Buddhist deity Vairochana. Before AD 600 most Daoist icons were dedicated to Laozi and most Buddhist icons to Shakyamuni and Maitreya. After that date these were increasingly replaced by Yuanshi Tianzun and the Buddha Vairocana. These two deities were not viewed as saviours but as the embodiment of the philosophical and creative spirit that is the ground of all existence. One fine example of a Yuanshi Tianzun icon is a votive stone (AD 726; Chicago, IL, Field Mus. Nat. Hist.; see fig. 2). In these the *Dao* is represented as a universal cosmic force that permeates an essentially naturalistic universe.

(iv) Syncretism. Both Confucianism and Buddhism enjoyed a symbiotic relationship with Daoism, but symbiosis became syncretism to a significant degree after the Tang period, when Neo-Confucianism and Chan Buddhism blossomed. From a Confucian perspective, the great Song philosopher Zhu Xi (1130–1200) summed up this syncretism in the aphorism, 'Nature is the concrete embodiment of the *Dao*.' The renderings of nature in the landscapes of painters such as LI CHENG are in fact expositions of a *Dao* that is naturalistic, rational and knowable. From a Buddhist viewpoint, the *Huayan jing* led to Chan Buddhism and was also the source of an intuitive approach to nature and art, the goal of which was sudden enlightenment: a 'vision of the *Dao*'.

For discussion of particular aspects of Daoist art *see* CHINA, §§II, 4(ii); III, 2; V, 3(iii); VI, 3(v); and GARDEN, §VI, 1(iv).

2. Daoist votive stone depicting Yuanshi Tianzun, 355×266 mm, AD 726 (Chicago, IL, Field Museum of Natural History)

BIBLIOGRAPHY

J. Needham and Wang Ling: *History of Scientific Thought* (1956), ii/8–18 of *Science and Civilization in China*, ed. J. Needham (Cambridge, 1954–)
Cheng Te-k'un: 'The Yin-yang Wu-hsing in Han Art', *Harvard J. Asiat. Stud.*, xx (1957), pp. 162–86
H. Welch: *The Parting of the Way: Lao Tzu and the Taoist Movement* (Boston, 1957)
S. Matsubara: *Chūgoku bukkyō chōkokushi kenkyū* [Research on the history of Chinese Buddhist sculpture] (Tokyo, 1966)
A. Seidel: *La Divinisation de Lao Tseu dans le taoïsme des Han* (Paris, 1969)
Wing-Tsit Chan: *The Way of Lao Tzu* (Indianapolis, 1976)
J. Fontein: 'Inscriptions on Taoist Statues', *Proceedings of the International Conference on Sinology: Taipei, 1980*, vii, pp. 95–100
A. Pontynen: 'The Deification of Laozi in Chinese History and Art', *Orient. A.*, xxvi (1980), pp. 192–202

ARTHUR PONTYNEN

Daoji [Tao-chi; *zi* Shitao, Shih-t'ao] (*b* Guilin, Guangxi Province, 1642; *d* Yangzhou, Jiangsu Province, 1707). Chinese painter and calligrapher. He was a descendant of the Ming dynasty (1368–1644) imperial Zhu family. In 1645, in the face of invading Manchu troops, a family servant fled with Daoji to nearby Quanzhou, Guangxi Province, and in 1647 they found refuge in Buddhist monastic life. A large number of the many sobriquets Daoji adopted sprang from his connection with Buddhism.

1. Paintings. 2. Theoretical writings.

1. PAINTINGS. Around 1650 Daoji and his servant left Quanzhou, travelling by boat and on foot around Hubei, Hunan, northern Jiangxi, Anhui and Zhejiang. At this time, *c*. 1655, Daoji began to paint, beginning with subjects

such as orchids. In 1664, at Mt Kun, Songjiang, Jiangsu Province, he became the disciple of a powerful Chan Buddhist priest, Lüan Benyue, who in 1665 instructed him to resume his wandering life. After a visit to Hangzhou, Zhejiang Province, Daoji visited Mt Huang, Anhui Province, in 1667 and again in 1669, when he climbed the mountain in the company of several Buddhist priests. This mountain range and the surrounding area north-west of She County, had become a favourite subject for painters working in the Anhui area (*see* ANHUI SCHOOL), as it later came to be for Daoji.

When Daoji painted *Sixteen Luohan* (1667; New York, Met.; see fig. 1), he had already fully mastered his favourite calligraphic idiom: the drawing of the veins of rocks in a pattern of concentric contour lines using brushstrokes known as the *jie suo* (Chin.: 'unravelled rope') or the *heye* ('lotus-leaf-vein'). Executed with the arm suspended and the brush held upright and with the tip of the brush hidden in the centre of the stroke, such brushstrokes follow in the tradition of the famous Song-period (960–1279) calligrapher Huang Tingjian. From 1670 Daoji led a hard and solitary life in an old temple on Mt Jingting, Anhui Province, making occasional trips to Yangzhou and Nanjing. Throughout the 1670s, as seen in extant works, for example *Watching a Waterfall from a Stone Bridge* (hanging scroll, 1672; untraced, see 1981 exh. cat., p. 133, fig. 18), Daoji mainly used a linear style. His album paintings made use of the spare, precise linear style also seen in late Ming-period woodblock-printed illustrations in the painters' manuals (*huapu*), which were produced in Anhui province (*see* CHINA, §XIII, 3 and 19(ii)).

In 1680 Daoji moved to Nanjing, where he began to sell his paintings, initially with little success. He settled at the Changgan Temple (known as the Baoen Temple in the Ming and Qing (1644–1911) periods), south of Nanjing, where he lived a secluded life for six years in a small house, which he named Yizhi ge (Pavilion of the single plum branch). While at the temple Daoji painted *Searching for Plum Blossoms* (1685; Princeton U., NJ, A. Mus.), a handscroll depicting a tangle of plum branches; on the

painting he wrote a prose introduction describing his search for the blossom, followed by nine seven-word poems. The calligraphy, executed in a uniform, small regular script (*xiao kaishu*), is fully integrated with the painting, forming a single unified composition that demonstrates the close connection between the two arts.

A calligrapher of exceptional skill, Daoji delighted in writing in a variety of script styles, ranging from the archaic squat-shaped, regular script (*kaishu*) of Zhong You (AD 151–230) and a monumental version of the archaic clerical script (*lishu*), to a mixture of the running (*xingshu*) and cursive (*caoshu*) scripts. *Sketches of Calligraphy and Paintings by Qing Xiang* (1696; Beijing, Pal. Mus.; see Fu and Fu, p. 41, fig. 4(a)), a record of his impressions of the scenery along the Grand Canal, shows, for example, Daoji's use of an archaic seal script (*zhuanshu*). The characters are well defined within a square format and are drawn by rounded, tense and unmodulated strokes. Daoji worked mainly in the album format and dealt with a wide range of themes: travel, scenic sites, bamboo, flowers and fruits, landscapes at different times of the year and illustrations to poetry, both ancient and contemporary.

Although a monk (largely as a result of his early circumstances), Daoji enjoyed his associations with the secular world and was spurred on by talent and ambition. By 1687 he had moved to Yangzhou, the thriving metropolis of commerce and art north of the River Yangzi, where he met many poets and painters, such as GONG XIAN. He also visited Beijing, where he enjoyed the company of the aristocracy and high officials. There he produced collaborative paintings with Wang Yuanqi, *Bamboo in Wind* (1691; Taipei, N. Pal. Mus.), and Wang Hui, *Bamboo, Orchid and Rock* (1691; Hong Kong, Tsi-lo-lou priv. col.; see Fu and Fu, p. 50, fig. 15). By that time, however, Daoji had become unalterably opposed to the ORTHODOX SCHOOL method of painting by imitating ancient styles, believing that many artists did not 'understand what they saw' and consequently copied only the appearance of the model and not its spirit. Finally, in late 1696, he settled down and built a retreat in Yangzhou which he called

1. Daoji: *Sixteen Luohan* (detail), handscroll, ink on paper, 470×5994 mm, 1667 (New York, Metropolitan Museum of Art)

Dadi caotang (Great cleansing thatched hall). He was tired of wandering and bored with priesthood, and, casting off his priestly robes and adopting the sobriquet Da di zi (Da di, 'great cleansing'), he decided to give up his peripatetic life and began to concentrate on his painting.

2. THEORETICAL WRITINGS. *Huayu lu* ('Remarks on painting'), which Daoji completed *c.* 1700, is regarded as the most original and systematically comprehensive theory of painting written since the Northern Song period (960–1127). A painter unschooled in the traditional scholarly sense (*see* CHINA, §XV, 1), Daoji vehemently advocated that the painter should assert selfhood (*wo*) and avoid thoughtless imitation. His emphasis on individualism echoed many of the ideas of the resurgent Neo-Confucianism of the Ming period. *Huayu lu* opens with Daoji's theory of *yihua* ('the single stroke' or 'the painting of oneness'), which Chou has also translated as 'the primordial line'. Daoji probably developed his idea from a discussion between his Chan Buddhist master, Lüan, and a master named Xiu from the Baoen Temple. Xiu reportedly said, 'Take the character one [written as a single horizontal stroke] and add no more to it' and then asked, 'What do you have?', to which Lüan answered, 'The design is complete.' For Lüan, 'one' completed the transition from nothing to everything; before 'one' nothing existed, after 'one' followed creation: a complete design. As an artist Daoji intuited this 'oneness' of creation through the act of painting. More than through the teachings of the past, his actions taught him to create a method in terms of brush and ink from 'no method'. In his painting, Daoji developed this single calligraphic line method into a broad range of complex techniques, incorporating aspects of all past methods, thereby producing his own great synthesis. By asserting selfhood and following his own mind as taught by the Neo-Confucian school of the mind, he produced the painting of 'oneness'. 'Therefore I say', he quoted Confucius (551–479 BC), 'my Dao is that of an all-embracing oneness' (*yi yi guan zhi*).

After establishing the method, Daoji expounded the need to 'understand method' (*liao fa*). He explained that method must serve rather than enslave the painter, since 'if the artist does not understand how to use it, then he will be hindered by the method', and he stressed the importance of transformation (*bianhua*), believing that the artist must adapt those ancient styles that he chose to follow. A section entitled *Zun shou* ('Respecting one's own response') states that the artist must understand his own mind, since 'painting responds to ink, ink responds to brush, brush responds to [the] wrist and [the] wrist responds to [the] mind'. The importance of combining the linear qualities of the brush with ink wash is also discussed. Daoji explained that the ability to control the movement of the brush is a skill that depends on one's mastery of transformation, a reference both to the reinterpretation of the styles of the ancient masters and to the artist's attempts to reveal the *qiyun* ('spirit resonance' or 'breath resonance') of his subject. By achieving true unity between brushstroke and ink wash, between artist and brush, the single primordial line can reveal a myriad of things. In Daoji's paintings, single brushstrokes magically change from lines to surfaces and then into dots, constantly growing and expanding as they overlap, criss-cross and interpenetrate, until they coalesce into the 'cosmic atmosphere' that represents the textures and substances of real landscape.

Daoji analysed the structure of landscape, presented his principles of organizing nature in painting, described his brushwork systems and compositional schemes and explained the interactions between nature and his art. Mountains and rivers are the forms and dynamic forces (*xing shi*) of heaven and earth, and since individual mountains and peaks are but small segments of reality, the painter must grasp larger principles and methods of transforming the reality into painting. One passage of *Huayu lu* is reminiscent of the discussion concerning the relationship between inner reality and outward appearance in landscape painting, presented by Jing Hao, the early 10th-century painter, in *Bifa ji* ('Notes on brushwork'; *see* CHINA, §V, 3(iv)(b)). Daoji recommended that the painter use principles of painting and methods of brushwork to deal respectively with the substance (*zhi*) and the ornament (*shi*) of heaven and earth. In merging himself with what he painted by means of the single brushstroke, Daoji claimed: 'I am able to embrace both the forms and the spirit of the mountains and rivers . . . they are born of me and I of them. I gather up all strange mountain peaks and make them the rough draft of my paintings.'

Daoji named 13 texture patterns including *fupi* ('axe-cut'), *pima* ('hemp-fibre') and *fantou* ('alum-head'); all 13 are necessary because mountain peaks 'vary physically . . . when a real peak becomes a texture pattern, the texture pattern grows to become the real peak . . . without the real peak, what is there to transform? Without the texture pattern, how does the peak reveal itself [in painting]?' Six compositional schemes are presented, and Daoji discussed the traditional division of the two-dimensional picture plane into three horizontal sections, one above the other, comprising the ground, the trees and the mountains. It is further divided into two main sections with scenery below and mountains above. The artist's aim must be to integrate the sections into a unity. Daoji wrote that since all elements of nature shared the same principles he could use 'mostly the same method' for drawing mountains as he did for drawing the sea. The aim in all cases was a 'raw' (*sheng*) and 'pungent' (*la*) quality in his brushwork. In sections 15 and 16, *Yuan chen* ('Away from the dust of the world') and *Tuo su* ('Escaping from the common'), Daoji dealt with the cultivation of the right state of mind while painting, stating that an artist must free his mind from the ordinariness of the world.

Daoji believed that although their methods were different, painting and calligraphy were one and the same thing, that the 'oneness' of brushstroke was a prerequisite and foundation for both. *An Ancient House under Tall Pine Trees* (*c.* 1700; Princeton U., NJ, A. Mus.; *see* fig. 2) reveals the connection between calligraphy and painting. Here the familiar motifs of trees and mountains and a remote dwelling are rendered with strong fluid calligraphic brushstrokes. The various modelling strokes that represent different rock textures are unified by a consistently moist treatment of graded ink tones. By around 1700 it seems that Daoji had abandoned the painting of actual landscapes, taking to its conclusion the injunction of Dong

2. Daoji: *An Ancient House under Tall Pine Trees*, hanging scroll, ink on paper, 1848×883 mm, *c.* 1700 (Princeton, NJ, Princeton University, Art Museum)

Qichang, founder of the Orthodox school, 'If one considers the wonders of the brush and ink, then [the real] landscape can never equal painting.' Daoji wrote in *Huayu lu*: 'While real peaks cannot change the functions of my texture strokes, my texture strokes can develop special forms and forces for the mountains.' Late works such as *An Ancient House* show that Daoji's main aim was not to reproduce the superficial appearance of nature, neither was it to develop a system of brushstrokes designed to enable him to express his personal emotions; his intention was to express the spirit of the oneness or unity of creation as experienced in the act of painting. Daoji was not a theoretical painter, his writings were an attempt late in life to rationalize an art that was almost entirely intuitive. He interpreted every subject in an intensely personal way, referring to models but transforming old styles into something unique, just as he developed unique calligraphic styles from ancient scripts. Daoji saw himself as being at the centre of a holistic universe and as such his paintings represented life itself: they were a means through which to achieve self-cultivation and they embraced all earlier methods or styles.

See also YANGZHOU SCHOOL and ANHUI SCHOOL.

BIBLIOGRAPHY

Wen Fong: 'A Letter from Shih-t'ao to Pa-ta-shan-jen and the Problem of Shih-t'ao's Chronology', *Archv Chin. A. Soc. America*, xiii (1959), pp. 22–53

Yutang Lin: *The Chinese Theory of Art: Translations from the Masters of Chinese Art* (London, 1967), pp. 137–58 [Eng. trans. of *Huayu lu*]

The Painting of Tao-chi (exh. cat., ed. R. Edwards; Ann Arbor, U. MI, Mus. A., 1967)

Ju-hsi Chou: *In Quest of the Primordial Line: The Genesis and Content of Tao-chi's 'Hua-yu-lu'* (diss., Princeton U., 1969)

M. Fu and S. Fu: *Studies in Connoisseurship: Chinese Paintings from the Arthur M. Sackler Collections in New York and Princeton* (Princeton, 1974), pp. 36–70, 168–79, 186–201 and 204–313

Shadows of Mount Huang: Chinese Painting and Printing of the Anhui School (exh. cat., ed. J. Cahill; Berkeley, U. CA, A. Mus., 1981), p. 133

Images of the Mind: Selections from the Edward L. Elliot Family and John B. Elliot Collections of Chinese Calligraphy and Painting at the Art Museum, Princeton University (exh. cat. by Wen Fong, Princeton U., A. Mus., 1984), pp. 199–209

WEN FONG

Darab. *See under* OTRAR.

Daraniyagala, Justin Pieris (*b* Colombo, 20 July 1903; *d* Colombo, 24 May 1967). Sri Lankan painter. He was best known among the painters of his generation as an enthusiastic exponent of the principles and practices of contemporary European painting (*see* SRI LANKA, §V, 2(v)). His affection for Western art was due in large measure to his artistic training at the Slade School of Fine Art, London, and Académie Julian, Paris. Daraniyagala has generally been credited with introducing POST-IMPRESSIONISM to Sri Lanka in the late 1920s. His early paintings, like those of the artists of the French school, show a marked penchant for the simplified significant form and a disregard for visual truth. Despite his obvious admiration for French artists, he was not satisfied simply to follow in their wake, but set himself the task of developing a personal idiom based on his European experience. He favoured the use of thick layers of colour set down in bold, sweeping brushstrokes and marked impasto that created a heavily textured pictorial surface. His paintings have been noted for their expressionistic spirit. Daraniyagala was indeed considered a leader among Asian expressionists. He painted with great abandon and exerted much influence on his contemporaries, who recognized the liberating effect of his style.

BIBLIOGRAPHY

N. Weeraratne: 'Daraniyagala', *Comm.*, i/4 (1955), pp. 255–7

R. Deraniyagala: 'Justin Daraniyagala, 1903–1967', *Times of Ceylon Annu.* (1968)

D. R. McClelland: 'The Paintings and Drawings of Justin Pieris Daraniyagala', *Ceylon Today*, xviii/3–4 (1969), pp. 28–30

SIRI GUNASINGHE

Dărăscu, Nicolae (*b* Giurgiu, 18 Feb 1883; *d* Bucharest, 14 Aug 1959). Romanian painter. From 1902 to 1906 he studied painting at the Academy of Fine Arts in Bucharest. His admiration for the work of Nicolae Grigorescu and Ştefan Luchian led him to take up a bursary in 1906 to study at the Académie Julian in Paris under Jean-Paul Laurens and in 1907 at the Ecole des Beaux-Arts under Luc Olivier Merson. Dărăscu's fascination with Cézanne encouraged him to travel in 1908 in the south of France. Until 1911, when he returned to Romania, he often painted at St Tropez, Ramatuelle and Grimaud. Although attracted by pointillism, his landscapes, even those painted using this technique, maintained something of Cézanne's solidity. In 1910 he exhibited a self-portrait (destr.) at the Societé des Artistes Français in Paris. Shortly after returning to Romania in 1911 he had a one-man show in December of the works painted in France, and France was to exert a continuing fascination for him until World War II. He was equally drawn to Venice, visiting it on many occasions to gain inspiration from the old walls, the effects of light on the water, and the chromatic explosions of the colourful sails of the boats, all of which he depicted with an exuberant affection (e.g. *Boats in Venice*, 1926–7; Bucharest, N. Mus. A.). Unlike many of his contemporaries, Dărăscu rarely painted interiors or still-lifes. Instead he travelled widely, searching for places that would remind him of the landscape of his youth, for example in the region of the Danube delta or on the shore of the Black Sea. He painted these in an impressionistic way, in order to catch the finest nuances of atmosphere (e.g. *Inn on the Edge of the Sea*, 1935–9; Bucharest, N. Mus. A.). During World War II his house and studio were destroyed, and he turned his concentration to an area of hills that inspired him to paint wide horizons, highly coloured but without the exuberance of his earlier work (e.g. *Bridge over the Argesh*, 1948–53; Topalu, Dinu & Sevasta Mus. A.). From 1936 to 1950 he was a professor at the Fine Arts Academy in Bucharest.

BIBLIOGRAPHY
V. Drăguţ: *Nicolae Dărăscu* (Bucharest, 1966)
Nicolae Dărăscu (exh. cat. by P. Constantinescu and H. Clonaru, Bucharest, N. Mus. A., 1966)
R. Ionescu: *Dărăscu* (Bucharest, 1987)

RADU IONESCU

Darasuram [Dārāsuram]. Temple site near Kumbakonam in southern Tamil Nadu, India. It is known for two outstanding temples, the Airavateshvara and the Deivanayaki, both of which were built by the CHOLA monarch Rajaraja II (*reg c.* 1146–72). The Airavatesvara, a fine example of the southern (Skt *drāviḍa*) temple type, was the third in a line of great Chola temples, following those at THANJAVUR and GANGAIKONDACHOLAPURAM. The square sanctum (12 m on each side) has lavishly articulated surfaces with wall icons carved in black basalt. Two large pillared halls and a vestibule precede the sanctum. The inner enclosure, containing the temple and several subsidiary shrines, is surrounded by a pillared cloister and is entered through an elegant gateway (*gopura*). The adjacent Deivanayaki temple, to the north, is one of the earliest goddess (Amman) shrines to have an independent compound and gate. Fragmentary portions of a larger gateway to the east indicate that an outer wall once enclosed both buildings.

See also INDIAN SUBCONTINENT, §§III, 6(i)(g) and IV, 7(vi)(a).

BIBLIOGRAPHY
K. R. Srinivasan: 'The Last of the Great Cola Temples', *J. Ind. Soc. Orient. A.*, xv (1948), pp. 11–33
K. A. Nilakanta Sastri: *The Cōlas* (Madras, rev. 2/1955), pp. 717–20, 751–2
C. Sivaramamurti: *The Chola Temples: Tañjāvūr, Gaṅgaikoṇḍacholapuram & Dārāsuram* (New Delhi, 1960), pp. 26–43
S. R. Balasubrahmanyam, B. Natarajan and others: *Later Chola Temples: Kulottunga I to Rajendra III (A.D. 1070–1280)* (Faridabad, 1979), pp. 221–45 [many pls and plans of temples]
K. R. Srinivasan: *Temples of South India* (New Delhi, 1979), p. 145
Encyclopedia of Indian Temple Architecture, South India: Lower Drāviḍadēśa 200 B.C.–A.D. 1324, 2 vols, ed. M. W. Meister and M. A. Dhaky (New Delhi, 1983), text vol. pp. 299–309, pls 338–55

GARY MICHAEL TARTAKOV

Darbourne & Darke. English architects and landscape planners. The partnership was formed in 1961 by John (William Charles) Darbourne (*b* London, 11 Jan 1935; *d* London, 29 Sept 1991) and Geoffrey Darke (*b* Evesham, Surrey, 1 Sept 1929). Though their work includes a football stand (for Chelsea Football Club, London, 1972–4), laboratories and offices (e.g. IBM, Hursley Park, Hants, 1979–81) and the landscaping (1976–7) of much of Heathrow Airport, London, it was in housing that Darbourne & Darke made their mark. Lillington Gardens (competition, 1961; built 1964–72), Pimlico, London, broke with the then current use of standard units in standard blocks. The required high density (543 bed spaces per ha) was achieved without high-rise, using traditional materials, an ingenious and complex section and landscaping from the ground to the upper floors. A larger scheme was later built (1966–77) on an equally difficult urban site, at Marquess Road, Islington, London. A stylistic development of the last phase of Lillington Gardens, it continued the idea of family maisonnettes with gardens at ground level and smaller flats above, fronted by wide 'roof streets' with space for planting. A linear canal-side park completed the landscaping, which was an integral part of all the firm's work.

The scheme (1970–75) for the small town of Pershore, Worcs, of red and mulberry brick with arched windows planned around a green, can be described as 'rationalized traditional', a label sometimes given to their housing work. Housing built abroad includes a courtyard scheme (1980–84) at Bolzano in northern Italy and another (1978–82) on an island on the River Leine, Hannover, Germany, where an artificial lake in the middle secures additional waterside views for the residents. The partnership was dissolved in 1987.

WRITINGS
Darbourne & Darke, Architects and Landscape Planners (1983) [office brochure]

BIBLIOGRAPHY
Architecture of Darbourne & Darke (exh. cat., ed. C. Amery and L. Wright; London, RIBA, 1977) [with list of works and bibliog.]
Obituary (John Darbourne), *The Independent* (4 Oct 1991)
D. Sudjic: 'Homing in on Public Housing', *The Guardian* (1 Oct 1991)

JILL LEVER

Darboven, Hanne (*b* Munich, 29 April 1941). German conceptual artist. She moved to New York in 1965, after studying at the Hochschule für Bildende Kunst in Hamburg, and began to produce delicate point and line drawings that gave form to sets of mathematical calculations. Although she lived in almost total solitude, her work became part of a collective effort to replace the discrete art object with CONCEPTUAL ART, grounded in ideas and actions. In the late 1960s she began to use the divisions of the calendar as the conceptual basis of her art. *One Month, One Year, One Century* (1971; Aachen, Neue Gal.) consists of 402 books, each containing series of numbers extrapolated from a single date and grouped with other volumes to represent months, years, and finally a whole century. Her books and mounted images, painstakingly handwritten, embody not only an abstract span of time but also the actual time of the artist's labour.

In the 1970s Darboven often allied her work, which she considered a form of writing, to the accomplishments of writers such as Heinrich Heine and Jean-Paul Sartre, directly transcribing portions of their texts or translating them into patterns. She further expanded her scope by including musical arrangements and photographs in her displays. In the *World View* series (exh. 1982, Venice, Biennale), she incorporated 19th-century postcards of historic sites and monuments into a vast calendar-like work that summarized her preoccupation with lived experience and passages of time.

BIBLIOGRAPHY

L. Lippard: 'Hanne Darboven: Deep in Numbers', *Artforum*, xii/2 (1973), pp. 35–9
Hanne Darboven: Ein Monat, ein Jahr, ein Jahrhundert (exh. cat., ed. J. Cladders and K. Honnef; Basle, Kstmus., 1974) [Work from 1968 to 1974]
Hanne Darboven (exh. cat., ed. J. Cladders; Venice, Biennale, 1982)

For further bibliography *see* CONCEPTUAL ART.

NANCY RING

D'Arcangelo, Allan (*b* Buffalo, NY, 16 June 1930). American painter and printmaker. He studied painting in Mexico City from 1957 to 1959 with John Golding (*b* 1929) under the terms of the G.I. Bill. His reputation as a Pop artist was established by his first New York one-man exhibition in 1963 where he showed his first acrylic paintings of the American highway and industrial landscape, such as *Highway U.S. 1 – No. 3* (1963; Richmond, VA Mus. F.A.). Such large-scale canvases visually transported the viewer through a time sequence, as if travelling along a highway, catching glimpses of trees, dividing lines, signs and route markers. In subsequent works D'Arcangelo continued to examine the American landscape both as directly experienced and in the form of generalized contemporary symbols. An essentially flat and impersonal style allowed him to suggest an illusionistic space without sacrificing the viewer's consciousness of the picture plane. This ambiguity between real and fictive space is further enforced in works such as *Guard Rail* (1964; Richmond, VA, S. and F. Lewis priv. col.) by the attachment of real objects such as rear-view mirrors or cyclone fences.

In later paintings such as *Skewed Star* (1974; Greensboro, NC, Weatherspoon A.G.) D'Arcangelo remained committed to his subject-matter, but moved away from Pop Art in favour of a stylized mechanization of the image that recalled earlier treatments of the American landscape

by Precisionists such as Charles Sheeler and Ralston Crawford.

BIBLIOGRAPHY

D'Arcangelo: Paintings of the Early Sixties (exh. cat., Purchase, SUNY, Neuberger Mus.) [with text by the artist]
Allan D'Arcangelo: Paintings, 1963–1970 (exh. cat., intro. by T. Towle; Philadelphia, U. PA, Inst. Contemp. A., 1971) [includes interview with S. Prokopoff]
Allan D'Arcangelo: Paintings, Prints, Drawings (exh. cat. by D. Ashton, Richmond, VA Mus. F.A., 1979)

FREDERICK R. BRANDT

Darcel, Alfred (*b* Rouen, 4 June 1818; *d* Paris, 26 May 1893). French museum director. He attended the Ecole Centrale, Paris, until 1841 and then managed a chemical factory in Rouen. In 1849 he turned to arts administration. As deputy inspector in the exhibitions department at the Louvre from 1852 he was responsible for travelling exhibitions held in Manchester (1858), Vienna (1860) and Rouen (1861). In 1862 he was promoted to Keeper of the Department of Medieval and Renaissance Art. From 1871 he reorganized and revitalized the Manufacture Centrale des Gobelins with his choice of patterns and the imposition of traditional techniques. He was appointed Keeper of the Musée des Thermes and the Hôtel de Cluny in 1885 and transformed Alexandre Du Sommerand's romantic collection of medieval art through the application of scientific methods. Darcel was prominent in the movement in the second half of the 19th century to promote archaeology and the industrial and decorative arts, notably what were still termed 'minor arts', and was among the founders of the Union Centrale des Arts Décoratifs, which owned the Musée des Arts Décoratifs. His writings extended beyond medieval art into the 18th century and included both learned titles, such as his collaborations on the Louvre's inventories of ceramics, enamels and goldsmiths' work, and popular books, including artistic tourist guides to Germany, Italy and England.

WRITINGS

Excursion artistique en Angleterre (Rouen, 1861)
Trésor de l'église de Conques (Paris, 1861)
Arts industriels du Moyen Age en Allemagne (Paris, 1862)
Excursion artistique en Allemagne (Rouen, 1862)
L'Art architectural en France depuis François Ier jusqu'à Louis XIV, 2 vols (Paris, 1863–6)
with H. Delange: *Recueil de faïences italiennes des XVe, XVIe et XVIIe siècles* (Paris, 1869)
with A. Basilewsky: *Collection Basilewsky: Catalogue raisonné, précédé d'un essai sur les arts industriels du Ier au XVIe siècle*, 2 vols (Paris, 1874)
Les Tapisseries décoratives du garde-meuble, mobilier national (Paris, 1878–81)
Excursion en Italie (Paris, 1879)

JEAN-MICHEL LENIAUD

D'Arco, Carlo, Conte (*b* Milan, 8 Sept 1799; *d* Mantua, 26 Jan 1872). Italian critic, historian and draughtsman. He showed a natural talent for painting at an early age and studied at the Accademia di Belle Arti in Milan, attending Carlo Botticelli's art history courses and studying painting with Agostino Comerio (1784–1829). In 1824–5 he attended Tommaso Minardi's drawing classes in Rome. In 1827 he illustrated the *Monumenti di pittura e scultura trascelti in Mantova e nel territorio*, and in 1828 the *Collezione di ritratti di celebri mantovani, disegnati dal d'Arco e incisi per la maggior parte da Lanfranco Puzzi*. He was also responsible for the drawings in his *Dipinti nuovamente* *scoperti di invenzione di Giulio Romano* (1832) and collaborated on the illustrations for Giovanni Labus's *Museo della R. Accademia di Mantova* (Mantua, 1829–37). Conscious of his artistic shortcomings, thereafter he devoted himself to art criticism and historical research. In 1838, at his own expense, he published and partly illustrated his important monograph *Istoria della vita e delle opere di Giulio Pippi Romano*. Among his other works are *Di cinque valenti incisori mantovani del secolo XVI e delle stampe da loro operate* (1840), *Delle arti e degli artefici di Mantova* (1857–9) and *Storia di Mantova: Studi intorno al municipio di Mantova* (1871–4). In December 1871, D'Arco was visited by Ferdinand Gregorovius, who found him 'in a cold and ugly room, surrounded by books and manuscripts . . . very elderly, half-blind, with a birthmark on his face, the personification of human suffering', yet still absorbed in his studies of Mantua's history.

WRITINGS

Dipinti nuovamente scoperti di invenzione di Giulio Romano, i quali servono di appendice ai monumenti mantovani (Mantua, 1832)
Istoria della vita e delle opere di Giulio Pippi Romano (Mantua, 1838/*R* 1986, rev. 2/1843)
Di cinque valenti incisori mantovani del secolo XVI e delle stampe da loro operate (Mantua, 1840)
Delle arti e degli artefici di Mantova, 2 vols (Mantua, 1857–9)
Storia di Mantova: Studi intorno al Municipio di Mantova, 7 vols (Mantua, 1871–4)

BIBLIOGRAPHY

DBI; Thieme–Becker
W. Braghirolli: 'Il conte Carlo d'Arco', *Archv Stor. It.*, iii/16 (1872), pp. 471–82
——: *Memoria biografica del conte Carlo d'Arco di Mantova* (Florence, 1873)
E. Faccioli: *Mantova: Le lettere*, iii (Mantua, 1963), pp. 290–93
G. Amadei: 'Luigi e Carlo d'Arco mantovani benemeriti', *Civiltà Mantovana*, vi/36 (1972), pp. 373–99
R. Signorini: 'Nota biografica sul conte Carlo d'Arco', *Annu. Ist. Tec. Stat. Geom. 'Carlo d'Arco'*, 1970–71 (1972), pp. 7–11
Carlo d'Arco disegnatore (exh. cat. by M. Di Giampaolo, Mantua, Casa Giulio Romano, 1972)
G. Amadei and others: *Il Palazzo d'Arco in Mantova* (Mantua, 1980), pp. 56–7
P. Carpeggiani: 'Disegni dell'ottocento (e un'eccezione) nell'album di Carlo d'Arco', *A. Lombarda*, n. s., lviii–lix (1981), pp. 67–84
F. Gregorovius: *Diari romani, 1852–1874*; ed. A. M. Arpino (Rome, 1982), p. 559

RODOLFO SIGNORINI

Dardel, Nils (*b* Bettna, 25 Oct 1888; *d* New York, 23 May 1943). Swedish painter. After a short time at the School of Art in Stockholm, which he found too conservative, he travelled for the first time to Paris in 1910. There he immediately made contact with the Scandinavian artists who were pupils of Matisse and with them made his début in Stockholm in 1912 as a member of the Man of the Year 1909 group. Under the influence of Cubism, Dardel painted a townscape of Senlis, in a style that eventually developed into the sophisticated naivety of *Funeral in Senlis* (1913; Stockholm, Mod. Mus.).

During World War I Dardel lived in Japan, remaining there until the autumn of 1918, when he travelled by train through revolutionary Russia, a journey that was later the subject of one of his most remarkable paintings, the *Trans-Siberian Railway* (1918). In 1919 he painted such bizarre subjects as *The Execution*, *The Staircase* (both Ingrid Ekwall priv. col.) and *Death's Hussars* (Caroline Lersten priv. col.), in which demons freely lay waste and in which he showed a disregard for the demands of realism. Earlier in

the year he had painted the *Dying Dandy* (Stockholm, Mod. Mus.), one of the most famous 20th-century Swedish paintings. In the same year he returned to Paris, which became his home. In the 1920s he collaborated on works with the Ballets Suédois, which had been started by Rolf de Maré in 1920. Among his best paintings in this period are *Visit to an Eccentric Lady* and *Crime of Passion* (both 1921; Stockholm, Mod. Mus.).

In the second half of the 1920s Dardel gained a growing reputation as a portrait painter, and it was this work that sustained his income during the Depression. In the 1930s his exhibitions culminated in a large retrospective in Stockholm at the Liljevalchs Konsthall, which coincided with the outbreak of World War II. That autumn Dardel travelled with the exhibition to Oslo and from there emigrated to the USA. He was not happy in New York, but he travelled widely in Central America, above all in Mexico and Guatemala. There he continued to paint watercolour portraits of racial types in a way that he had begun in North Africa and Italy. An exhibition of this material was organized at the Architectural League of New York in May 1943, shortly before Dardel's death.

BIBLIOGRAPHY

T. Dardel: *En bok om Nils Dardel* (Stockholm, 1953)
K. Asplund: *Nils Dardel*, i–ii (Stockholm, 1957–8)
I. Lindahl: *Visit hos excentrisk herre* (Stockholm, 1980)
E. Näslund: *Nils Dardel* (Stockholm, 1988)
Nils Dardel (exh. cat. by S. Fauchereau and O. Granath, Stockholm, Mod. Mus.; Paris, Mus. A. Déc.; 1988)

OLLE GRANATH

Dardel, Robert-Guillaume (*b* Paris, 1749; *d* Paris, 29 July 1821). French sculptor. He was a pupil of Augustin Pajou. He was never a member of the Académie Royale and until 1791 had no access to the official Salon, exhibiting instead at the Salon de la Correspondance, Paris, from 1781 to 1787; he was also denied access to the marble provided by the Bâtiments du Roi for royal commissions, for which only Academicians were eligible, and was forced to be principally a modeller producing works in terracotta or bronze. His chief patron was Prince Louis-Joseph de Condé, and among works commissioned by the Condé family were a bust of Louis II, the *Grand Condé* (bronze, *c.* 1780; untraced), and a statuette of the *Grand Condé at Fribourg* (exh. Salon de la Correspondance 1782), the terracotta (1780; Chantilly, Mus. Condé) and bronze (1785; Chantilly, Mus. Condé) versions of which were made were made by the great bronze-founder Pierre Philippe Thomire. Three further commemorative statuettes in bronze are at Chantilly. They represent *Henri de La Tour d'Auvergne, Vicomte de Turenne*; *Bertrand, Chevalier Du Guesclin* (both modelled 1782, cast 1785); and *Pierre du Terrail, Seigneur de Bayard* (1788), and they were cast from Dardel's models by Thomire.

Dardel was inclined by temperament to invent complex and allegorical subjects, similar to those of contemporary history painters and unusual in the context of the Salon de la Correspondance. Such works included *Descartes Piercing the Shadows of Ignorance* (terracotta, exh. 1782; London, Wallace), an ambitious group uneasily combining a real character and abstract allegory. Similarly, his numerous other portraits of famous Frenchmen shown at the Salon de la Correspondance (all terracotta; all untraced) were placed in context by means of allegory. The group *Aeneas Bearing Anchises* (terracotta, exh. 1787; Paris, Louvre) reveals Dardel's tendency to the severe Neo-classicism of Jean-François-Pierre Peyron and Jacques-Louis David.

Although Dardel was of marginal importance under the Ancien Régime, he enjoyed the protection of David during the Revolution and occupied a number of important positions. He exhibited at the 'official' Salon from 1791. He was given a number of state commissions under the Empire (1804–15), including a marble bust of *Général Elliot* (destr.; plaster version, Versailles, Château), and took part in the sculptural decoration of the Arc de Triomphe du Carrousel, Paris. Among his last exhibited works was a terracotta group entitled *Virginius Having Killed his Daughter to Save her from Dishonour Curses the Decemvir Appius* (exh. Salon 1817, see sale cat., no. 92) first presented in 1799, which in subject and style hearkens back to the austere Neo-classicism of the 1780s.

BIBLIOGRAPHY

Lami

G. Macon: *Les Arts dans la maison de Condé* (Paris, 1903), pp. 96–7, 119–20
C. Avery and A. Laing: *Finger Prints of the Artist: European Terracotta Sculpture from the Arthur M. Sackler Collections* (Washington, DC, 1981), pp. 192–5
P. Sorel: 'Trois sculptures de l'époque révolutionnaire: Propositions d'attributions', *Gaz. B.-A.* (Oct 1990), pp. 140–44

GUILHEM SCHERF

Daret, Jacques (*b* Tournai, *c.* 1400–05; *d c.* 1468). South Netherlandish painter. The son of a Tournai sculptor, by 1418 he was living in the household of ROBERT CAMPIN, 'ouvrant de son mestier', and earning his keep. Not until

Jacques Daret: *Nativity*, oil on panel, 595×530mm, 1432–5 (Madrid, Museo Thyssen-Bornemisza)

1428 was he formally registered as Campin's apprentice; after completing his four-year apprenticeship he became a master of the Tournai guild in 1432. In 1433 he himself took an apprentice, his younger half-brother Daniel Daret, who became a master in 1441 and who in 1449 was made painter and Varlet de Chambre to Philip the Good, Duke of Burgundy. In 1436 Jacques took a second apprentice, who became a master illuminator in 1438. During this period, Jacques divided his time between Tournai and Arras, where Jean du Clercq, Abbot of St Vaast, was his devoted patron. Daret seems later to have settled at Arras. His work for the Abbot and the abbey is well documented: he coloured carved altarpieces, tombs and crosses, painted wing panels for altarpieces and portraits of all the abbots and designed a tapestry and a brass candlestick. In 1454 he was the best paid of the artists summoned to Lille to provide decorations for Philip the Good's 'Feast of the Pheasant' and was accompanied by four assistants. By 1461 he was back at Tournai, where he coloured a statue for the Belfry and where in 1464 he took two apprentices. He may have left Tournai in 1466 and is last recorded in 1468, when he was at Bruges with three assistants to work on the decorations for the marriage festivities of Charles the Bold, Duke of Burgundy, and Margaret of York. He and Vrancke van der Stockt were the most highly paid of all the many artists present.

Four panels have been identified as documented works by Daret: the *Visitation* (Berlin, Gemäldegal.), the *Nativity* (Madrid, Mus. Thyssen-Bornemisza; see fig.), the *Adoration of the Magi* (Berlin, Gemäldegal.) and the *Presentation in the Temple* (Paris, Petit Pal.). They are from the exterior wing panels of a carved altarpiece made between 1432 and 1435 for Jean du Clercq for the Chapel of the Virgin at St Vaast. Described as recently finished, the altarpiece was shown on 16 July 1435 to Cardinal Albergati, who was then attending the Congress of Arras. These panels reveal Daret to have been a close follower of the MASTER OF FLÉMALLE (*see* MASTERS, ANONYMOUS, AND MONOGRAMMISTS, §I). The *Nativity* and *Adoration* are paraphrases of compositions by the Master: the *Nativity* (Dijon, Mus. B.-A.) and the lost *Adoration* known from versions at Berlin and elsewhere (Berlin, Gemäldegal.; Cambridge, Fitzwilliam; Verona, Castelvecchio). The architecture and some of the figures in the *Presentation* are adapted from the Master of Flémalle's *Marriage of the Virgin* (Madrid, Prado), and the *Visitation* may also depend on a lost painting by the same artist. Daret's four panels are carefully executed, but the draughtsmanship is faulty, the method of composition is additive and incoherent, and the figure types are idiosyncratic. Possibly by the same hand are a *Portrait of a Man* (Berlin, Gemäldegal.) and a *Portrait of a Lady* (Washington, DC, Dumbarton Oaks), to which may be related a lost picture of the *Virgin and Child with SS James and Catherine and Donors*, known from drawn copies (Paris, Louvre and Ecole N. Sup. B.-A.). Nothing is known about Daret's later style.

Daret was evidently a talented painter who enjoyed a high reputation, but his main importance is that he was certainly trained at Tournai and was Robert Campin's pupil. The close stylistic links between his work and that of the Master of Flémalle and Rogier van der Weyden provide the main argument in favour of identifying the

Master of Flémalle as Campin and Rogier as Campin's apprentice Rogelet de la Pasture.

BIBLIOGRAPHY

A. Pinchart: 'Roger de la Pasture dit van der Weyden', *Bull. Comm. Royale A. & Archéol.*, vi (1867), pp. 408–94

——: 'Quelques artistes et quelques artisans de Tournai des XIVe, XVe et XVIe siècles', *Bull. Acad. Royale Sci., Lett. & B.-A. Belgique*, n. s. 3, iv (1882), pp. 559–615

A. de la Grange and L. Cloquet: *Etudes sur l'art à Tournai et sur les anciens artistes de cette ville*, Mém. Soc. Hist. & Litt. Tournai, xx, xxi (1887–8)

M. Houtart: *Jacques Daret, peintre tournaisien du XVe siècle* (Tournai, 1907)

G. Hulin de Loo: 'An Authentic Work by Jacques Daret Painted in 1434', *Burl. Mag.*, xv (1909), pp. 202–8

——: 'Jacques Daret's *Nativity of Our Lord*', *Burl. Mag.*, xix (1911), pp. 218–25

M. Houtart: 'Quel est l'état de nos connaissances relativement à Robert Campin, Jacques Daret et Roger van der Weyden?', *An. Féd. Archéol. & Hist. Belgique, XXIIIe congrès, Gand, 1913*, pp. 88–108

E. Renders, with J. de Smet and L. Bayaert-Carlier: *La Solution du problème van der Weyden-Flémalle-Campin*, 2 vols (Bruges, 1931)

P. Rolland: 'Quelques textes relatifs à Robert Campin', *Rev. Belge Archéol. & Hist. A.*, ii (1932), pp. 335–45

——: *Les Primitifs tournaisiens, peintres et sculpteurs* (Brussels and Paris, 1932)

J. Lestocqnoy: 'Le Rôle des artistes tournaisiens à Arras au XVe siècle: Jacques Daret et Michel de Gand', *Rev. Belge Archéol. & Hist. A.*, vii (1937), pp. 211–27

P. H. Schabacker: 'Observations on the Tournai Painters' Guild with Special Reference to Rogier van der Weyden and Jacques Daret', *Acad. Anlct.: Kl. S. Kst.*, xliii/1 (1982), pp. 9–28

LORNE CAMPBELL

Daret, Jean (*b* Brussels, 1613; *d* Aix-en-Provence, 2 Sept 1668). French painter. He came from Brussels and trained there before going on the traditional journey to Italy, which not only took him to Rome but also brought him into contact with contemporary masters at Bologna. While in Italy he produced a *Self-portrait* (1636; St Petersburg, Hermitage), which alludes to both his ideal model and the necessary basis of his work: his right hand rests on a fragment of antique sculpture, while beside his palette in the foreground lie several sheets of drawings. The warm tones of the work recall Daret's Flemish training, but the lighting is Caravaggesque.

Daret was in Aix-en-Provence in 1637; his earliest work there was a strongly realistic picture of *Salvator de Horta Healing the Sick* for the church of Ste Marie-Madeleine (*in situ*). He married and settled in the city, and over the following decades he completed a series of large-scale works there. Many of these paintings were destroyed during the Revolution, but Pierre-Joseph de Haitze's book *Curiosités les plus remarquables de la ville d'Aix* (1679) has preserved an almost contemporary description of Daret's works. In 1643 Daret received a commission to decorate the newly built Oratory chapel of the Annunciation. His pictures showed scenes from the story of the Holy Family, including *Jesus Expounding the Scriptures to Mary and Joseph*. A surviving preparatory drawing (1650; Paris, Bib. Doucet) shows that Daret created a ceiling painting whose refined *trompe l'oeil* technique opened the actual space upwards and allowed the viewer to look into a higher level. Further evidence of his specialization in *quadratura* painting appears in his most important surviving work, the decorations for the Hôtel de Châteaurenard (1654) in Aix. He divided its staircase walls with Doric columns and pilasters that supported an entablature with a frieze of metopes and triglyphs, also depicted in a *trompe l'oeil* fashion. The ceiling area, dedicated to the liberal arts, is remarkable for its picturesque representation of various levels of reality; it seems to have been influenced by the murals of the Carracci in the Galleria Farnese in Rome (1597–1600). Four painted oeils-de-boeuf, behind busts of Pallas, Mercury, Apollo and Louis XIV, give on to blue sky, further extending the illusory space.

Louis XIV stayed at the Hôtel de Châteaurenard in 1660, and Daret's achievement impressed him. He took Daret back to Paris, and Daret worked on paintings (destr.) at the château of Vincennes. During his four years in Paris he also completed a portrait of *Camillo de Lilli de Camerino* (engraved by Nicolas Pitau (i), 1663) and a portrait of *Nicolas Samson* (engraved by Jean Edelinck, 1679). In 1662 Abraham Bosse made an engraved frontispiece for the *Antiqua stemmata regis christianissimi* after a sketch by Daret, but the only graphic work Daret produced himself was a series of nine drawings depicting the *Virtues*. Though Daret clearly never became rich in Paris, he acquired the title of Peintre du Roi, which he retained after his return to Aix.

Thieme–Becker   BIBLIOGRAPHY

P.-J. de Haitze: *Les Curiosités les plus remarquables de la ville d'Aix* (Aix-en-Provence, 1679)

G. Isarlo: *Caravagisme européen* (Aix-en-Provence, 1941), pp. 104–18

Le XVIIe Siècle français (exh. cat. by M. Laclotte, Paris, Petit Pal., 1958), no. 32

A. Schnapper: 'Colonna et la "quadratura" en France à l'époque de Louis XIV', *Bull. Soc. Hist. A. Fr.* (1966), pp. 65–97

J. Boyer: 'Hommage au Peintre Jean Daret', *Provence Hist.*, xviii (1968), pp. 425–49

R. Borricand: *Les Hôtels particuliers d'Aix en Provence* (Aix-en-Provence, 1971)

S. Damiron: 'Un Dessin de Jean Daret pour le plafond de la chapelle de l'oratoire d'Aix en Provence', *Archvs A. Fr.*, xxv (1978), pp. 163–6

CATHRIN KLINGSÖHR-LE-ROY

Daret, Pierre (*b* Paris, *c.* 1604; *d* Laluque, Landes, 29 March 1678). French painter, engraver and print publisher. Although it was as a painter that he was received (*reçu*) in 1663 by the Académie Royale, it is as an engraver that he is now remembered. His earliest known print is dated 1630, and he later made many plates, particularly reproductive engravings after his contemporaries Jacques Blanchard and Claude Vignon. He was one of Simon Vouet's best interpreters, and Vouet himself commissioned from him at least 11 plates after his own paintings. Daret's most important projects were the engraving of plates for and the publication of M. de Gomberville's *La Doctrine des moeurs* (Paris, 1646) and the monumental collection of over 100 portraits in the *Tableaux historiques où sont gravez les illustres français et estrangiers* (Paris, 1652). His translation of Vasari's life of Raphael, *Abrégé de la vie de Raphael Sansio d'Urbin* (Paris, 1651), is celebrated as the first monograph on an artist published in France.

BIBLIOGRAPHY

R.-A. Weigert: *Inventaire du fonds français: Graveurs du dix-septième siècle*, Paris, Bib. N., Cab. Est. cat., iii (Paris, 1954), pp. 244–316

M. Préaud and others: *Dictionnaire des éditeurs d'estampes à Paris sous l'Ancien Régime* (Paris, 1987), pp. 96–7

A. Schnapper: 'Raphaël, Vasari, Pierre Daret: A l'aube des catalogues', *'Il se rendit en Italie': Etudes offertes à André Chastel* (Paris, 1987), pp. 235–41

Vouet (exh. cat. by J. Thuillier, B. Brejon de Lavergnée and D. Lavalle, Paris, Grand Pal., 1990), pp. 73–6

Dario, Giovanni Antonio (*b c.* 1630; *d* St Florian, 8 March 1702). Italian architect, mason and sculptor, active in Austria. He is recorded as having been in Salzburg in the 1650s, when he completed the towers (1652–5) of Salzburg Cathedral, providing them with the polygonal caps that are a feature of the town's skyline. In 1659 Dario supervised the construction of the fountain at the Residenz in Salzburg, to a design by an unknown architect, and in the same year he was responsible for the plasterwork in the side chapels of the cathedral. The building of the loggias (1658–63) in front of the cathedral not only created a link between the porch of the cathedral, the Residenz and St Peter's Abbey, but also enclosed the Domplatz and lent it greater urban significance. Dario, who was in charge of the building work, is credited with being the originator of this distinguished architectural solution that displays such consistency. Dario continued to carry out work in Salzburg that he had not designed himself. In 1667 he built a fountain at the convent of Nonnberg, to designs by an unknown architect, and side chapels at the cathedral, probably to designs by Santino Solari. He also rebuilt the church (1672–9) at Seekirchen, Salzburg.

In 1671–4 Dario created his masterpiece: the pilgrimage church of Maria Plain, above Salzburg. The short nave of the church consists of two and a half bays, with a narrow apsidal choir that measures only three-eighths of the overall width. The main building has tunnel vaulting with lunettes between the reinforcing arches; above the chapel entrances there are also small galleries (*coretti*). Both internally and externally the walls are articulated with pilasters; those on the outside are really intended to be viewed from a distance, in conjunction with the powerful lines of the cornices. The architectural detail is simple and delicate in outline.

Although Dario continued to have plenty of commissions in Salzburg, in 1675 he applied for the post of official architect at the court of the archbishop. When he failed to get it he left Salzburg and entered the service of St Florian Abbey in Upper Austria. Here he appears to have worked only as a sculptor or mason. He did, however, submit plans for the architectural aspects of the altars, which he executed in the side chapels of the abbey church. In the case of the high altar, Dario was responsible only for its execution. His patrons were not always satisfied with him; records suggest that he often failed to keep to his contract, using a less valuable stone than had been specified or skimping the work to be done on the stone.

DBI

BIBLIOGRAPHY

F. Pirchmayer: *G. A. Dario: Der Erbauer des Residenzbrunnens in Salzburg* (Salzburg, 1888)
F. Hermann: *Maria Plain, Salzburg* (Salzburg, 1969)
T. Korth: *Stift St Florian* (Nuremberg, 1975)

PETER FIDLER

Dario da Pordenone. *See* DARIO DA TREVISO.

Dario (di Giovanni) da Treviso [Dario da Pordenone] (*fl* 1440; *d* before 1498). Italian painter. Described in a Paduan document of 1440 as *pictor vagabundus* (itinerant painter), he is also mentioned as being employed in the workshop of Francesco Squarcione. Still in Padua, he next moved on to work in the shop of the Milanese artist Pietro Maggi. Around 1448 he moved to Treviso, where in 1455 he married Ginevra Ziliolo, daughter of an otherwise unknown painter whose workshop he inherited. He is subsequently recorded in Treviso, Asolo, Bassano, Conegliano and Serravalle, working mainly as a fresco painter. In two of his early works, the *Crucifixion* (fresco; Treviso, Mus. Civ. Bailo) and another *Crucifixion* (fresco, 1453; Treviso, S Francesco), the influence of Squarcione and of Dario's Ferrarese background—this latter already seen in the painter's earlier *St Christopher* (panel; Venice, Ca'd'Oro)—acquires softer tones. Similar tendencies are evident in the *Madonna of Humility* (1459; Asolo, Mus. Civ.), while in the fresco cycle in S Gottardo, Asolo, painted over several years, particular characteristics emerge, as, for example, in the *St Blaise*, where clear affinities with the school of Paolo Uccello can be seen. In other parts of the decoration Late Gothic elements are evident. The Tuscan tendencies disappear in such later works as the dated *Virgin and Child* (1492; Asolo Cathedral), where the linear, decorative manner of his early education can be discerned, fixed within a figurative repertory destined to be of great influence in the Treviso area as far as Friuli and recognizable in such works as the *Virgin and Child with Saints* (fresco; Schio, S Francesco).

BIBLIOGRAPHY

G. Vasari: *Vite* (1550, rev. 2/1568); ed. G. Milanesi (1878–85), iii, p. 358
J. A. Crowe and G. B. Cavalcaselle: *A History of Painting in North Italy*, ii (London, 1871, rev. 1912), pp. 54–8
G. B. Cavalcaselle: *La pittura friulana del rinascimento* (Friuli, 1876, rev. Vicenza, 1973)
G. Gerola: 'Dario pittore', *Miscellanea di studi in onore di A. Ortis*, ii (Trieste, 1910), pp. 871–82
I. Furlan: 'Dario da Pordenone', *Noncello*, xxviii (1969), pp. 3–32
——: 'Dario da Pordenone', *Dopo Mantegna: Arte a Padova e nel territorio nei secoli XV e XVI* (exh. cat., Padua, Pal. Ragione, 1976), p. 27
M. Boskovits: 'Ricerche su Francesco Squarcione', *Paragone*, xxviii/325 (1977), pp. 40–70

UGO RUGGERI

Darius Painter. *See* VASE PAINTERS, §II.

Darjeeling. Hill town in West Bengal, India. Built on land acquired by the British from the Raja of Sikkim in 1835 and subsequently annexed by them, it was laid out by Lord Napier in 1839 and grew rapidly as a sanatorium and hot weather retreat for members of the Bengal Government. A bungalow known as 'The Shrubbery' (1877) originally served as Government House, but after an earthquake in 1934 it was rebuilt more grandly, with the addition of a dome. Near by are the Secretariat buildings, the Natural History Museum (1915) and the ornate blocks of the Eden Sanatorium, with the Lloyd Botanic Garden (1878) below. To the north of the town, near St Andrew's Church (1870), are the colonial Gothic town hall (1921) and the Darjeeling Gymkhana Club, with tennis courts, ballroom, skating rink and bijou theatre. The tea-planters had their own Darjeeling Club. Many hill-station bungalows were also built in the 19th and 20th centuries; those of the maharajas of Cooch Behar and Burdwan are the grandest. Among the schools for European children that proliferated during this period are the Loreto Convent School for girls (1847), the Anglican St Paul's School (1864) and the American Methodist Mount Herman School. The Roman Catholic St Joseph's School (1888) has a formal arcaded frontage with oriel windows, projecting wings and a mansard roof, which gives the building a rather French flavour. Darjeeling also has a large Tibetan population, and monasteries such as those at Ghoom (with its image of the Future Buddha, Maitreya), Bhutia Basti and Ging display Tibetan influence. Notable 20th-century buildings include Birch Hall (1954), home of the Himalayan Mountaineering Institute.

BIBLIOGRAPHY
E. M. A. Mitchell: *Thacker's Guide Book to Darjeeling and its Neighbourhood*, ed. G. Hutton Taylor (Calcutta, 1891, 2/1899)

J. B. HARRISON

Dark Age (i). Term referring to the period from *c.* 1050 to *c.* 750 BC in Greece, between the collapse of Mycenaean civilization (*see* HELLADIC) and the rise of the Greek city-state (*polis*). Its chief characteristics are total illiteracy, severe depopulation and loss of communication with the older civilizations of the eastern Mediterranean. The demise of the Mycenaean palaces entailed the eclipse of monumental architecture and of the fine arts associated with Mycenaean palace life, such as wall paintings, ivory-carvings, engraved gems and sophisticated gold jewellery; only the humble art of the potter displays any continuity, passing through Submycenaean, Protogeometric and Geometric stages (*see* GREECE, ANCIENT, §V, 2 and 3). At first the decoration of Dark Age pottery was almost wholly abstract, comprised of simple geometric motifs; rarely before the 8th century BC were any human and animal designs introduced. Although there was no monumental sculpture in stone, figurines in terracotta and bronze were made (*see* GREECE, ANCIENT, §§IV, 2(i)(a) and VIII, 2(i)(b)). And although the art of monumental architecture was lost, and humble dwellings were the rule (*see* GREECE, ANCIENT, §II, 2(i)), evidence from LEFKANDI on Euboea for a 10th-century building over 45 m long (possibly a heroon), along with 10th- and 9th-century graves containing objects from the Near East and Egypt, suggests that some people enjoyed a better standard of life than others.

Progress out of this Dark Age was led by the Euboeans, who maintained sporadic trading contacts with the Levantine coast from the late 10th century BC onwards. Exchanges with the Phoenicians put an end to Greek illiteracy in the 8th century BC, when the Greek alphabet developed from its western Semitic prototype. Meanwhile, a rapidly rising population encouraged progress from loose tribal organizations towards constitutional government and the central authority of the *polis*. The revival of monumental architecture reflects the need of the *polis* for a temple worthy of its patron deity.

BIBLIOGRAPHY
A. M. Snodgrass: *The Dark Age of Greece* (Edinburgh, 1971)
V. R. d'A. Desborough: *The Greek Dark Ages* (London, 1972)
J. N. Coldstream: *Geometric Greece* (London, 1977)
J. M. Hurwit: *The Art and Culture of Early Greece, 1100–480 BC* (Ithaca, NY, 1985)

NICOLAS COLDSTREAM

Dark Age (ii). Term referring to the period in Western Europe between the fall of the Roman Empire in the 5th century AD and the rise of the medieval kingdoms in the 8th. Other descriptions can be used, such as 'early Christian', 'early medieval' or 'barbarian', but none is completely satisfactory. The so-called darkness of the period is inferred through the lack of primary historical records, but archaeology has provided important evidence. Literacy is a major factor; a fully literate society can no longer be described as 'dark age', and Christianity was vital in disseminating learning.

It is only through the study of both the art and documentary evidence that the complex and sophisticated beliefs, contacts and sources of the various communities can be appreciated. In addition to the partial historical accounts, the material remains include products of great skill and beauty: gold and silver jewellery inlaid with coloured gems, stone sculpture combining deep relief with interlacing animal forms, illuminated manuscripts that echo the jeweller's craft, patterned tools and weapons, even the buckles and strap ends of everyday dress ornamented with abstract or foliate designs. The art of the period was created by the combination of Classical sources and native forms for an ultimately Christian didactic purpose; this was achieved more rapidly in some areas than others, with those furthest from Rome retaining their native styles the longest. There is, therefore, considerable variety in the development of Christian art in the different parts of Europe.

The pagan Saxon settlers in the south and east of the British Isles were gradually converted to Christianity during the 7th century and combined their jewellery techniques and designs with those of the native Celtic population (*see* CELTIC ART) to produce manuscripts, stone crosses and liturgical metalwork, which also reflected Mediterranean figural art. A sequence of interlacing animal ornament continued in Scandinavia from the 5th century to the 11th (*see* VIKING ART), virtually unaffected by the arts of Christianity until the eventual conversion of the Vikings. The Germanic tribes that occupied the territories of the Empire rapidly adopted the styles of late Roman art through direct contact with architecture, industries and figural ornament, while retaining the more abstract and animal patterns of their distinctive metalwork. The Franks in Gaul (*see* MEROVINGIAN ART), the Visigoths in Spain (*see* VISIGOTHIC ART) and the Ostrogoths in Italy (*see* OSTROGOTHIC ART) all sought to assimilate the styles of the higher civilization to which they wished to belong; their leaders initially saw themselves as Roman rulers, maintaining the forms and customs of the great empire that they had invaded.

These peoples would not have regarded themselves as living in a dark age, but in a time of advance and enlightenment. The collapse of Rome led to the foundation of medieval Europe, a series of emerging Christian states with major cities, monastic centres and royal courts. The art produced illustrates this transition through the fusion of the narrative Christian art of the Mediterranean world with the non-representational traditions of the north.

See also INSULAR ART; LOMBARD ART; MIGRATION PERIOD; PICTISH ART.

BIBLIOGRAPHY
D. Talbot Rice, ed.: *The Dark Ages* (London, 1965)
M. Backes and R. Dolling: *Art of the Dark Ages* (New York, 1969)

J. Hubert, J. Porcher and W. F. Volbach: *Europe in the Dark Ages* (London, 1969)
D. M. Wilson, ed.: *The Northern World* (London, 1980)

CAROLA HICKS

Darley, Felix Octavius Carr (*b* Philadelphia, PA, 23 June 1822; *d* Claymont, DE, 27 March 1888). American illustrator and printmaker. After being exposed early to the Neo-classical style of John Flaxman, Darley began his career as an illustrator in Philadelphia in 1842. Following a sketching trip west of the Mississippi during the summer of that year, he produced outline drawings that were adapted into lithographs appearing in *Scenes in Indian Life* (1843). His early book illustrations were published in periodicals such as *Democratic Review* and *Godey's Magazine*. Working in line drawing, lithography and wood and steel engraving, his first major success was his illustrations for John Frost's *Pictorial History of the United States* (1844).

After moving to New York in 1848, Darley dominated the field of American illustration with his illustrations of Washington Irving and James Fenimore Cooper's tales and novels. He produced about 500 illustrations for Cooper's novels and a similar number for Benson J. Lossing's *Our Country* (1875–7). He also illustrated the work of Charles Dickens, Henry Wadsworth Longfellow, Nathaniel Hawthorne, Edgar Allen Poe and William Shakespeare. His illustrations appeared in every American periodical of importance. Individual lithographs of scenes from Irving's *Rip Van Winkle*, published by the American Art Union, became highly sought after, remaining memorable images to this day.

Darley's flowing, minimally shaded drawings in the Neo-classical style have something of a romantic spirit, seeking to capture the essence of the scenes portrayed. He worked largely in pen alone, but sometimes also used sepia washes over light pencil outlines. His work exerted a strong influence on his generation of American illustrators.

BIBLIOGRAPHY

F. Weitenkampf: 'F. O. C. Darley, American Illustrator', *A. Q.* [Detroit], x (1947), pp. 100–13
T. Bolton: 'The Book Illustrations of Felix Octavius Carr Darley', *Amer. Antiqua. Soc. Proc.*, lxi (1951), pp. 136–82
W. B. Stevens jr: 'The Unpublished European Sketchbook of F. O. C. Darley', *Antiques*, xciv/11 (1968), pp. 708–11
J. C. Ewers: 'Not Quite Redmen: The Plains Indian Illustrations of Felix O. C. Darley', *Amer. A. J.*, iii (1971), pp. 88–98

DAVID M. SOKOL

Darling & Pearson. Canadian architectural partnership formed in 1895 by Frank Darling (1850–1923) and John (Andrew) Pearson (1867–1940). Frank Darling's career was founded in the Gothic Revival and conditioned by the ecclesiological inclinations of his father, the first cleric to introduce Anglican high church ritualism and fittings into Toronto. He studied for three years in London in 1870–73, in the offices of G. E. Street and Arthur Blomfield (1829–99), and in 1874 established his practice in Toronto. His most important early works were High Anglican parish churches in Toronto that drew on English Gothic Revival and then American Romanesque Revival sources, especially for the unfinished church of St Mary Magdalene in central Toronto (1886–92). The contacts made through church work led to institutional and commercial commissions, such as Trinity College, Toronto (1877–1905, destr.), and in 1880 Darling won a competition for the Legislative Buildings, Toronto (not executed), for the Province of Ontario. After 1895, when John Pearson, who had trained in England, became his partner, the firm became architects to the major institutions that were supported by Toronto's growing wealth: the University of Toronto (1901–25), Toronto General Hospital (after 1908), the Art Gallery of Toronto (after 1900) and the Royal Ontario Museum (1912–14).

In the 1880s, and especially after 1897, the landmarks of the practice were a number of large and small bank buildings for Canada's chartered banks, particularly the Bank of Commerce and the Dominion Bank. The firm completed close to a thousand bank projects which introduced monumental Edwardian Baroque Revival and, after 1905, Beaux-Arts forms into Canadian cities with a purity never seen before. These banks ranged from suburban branches to skyscrapers, including a series of prefabricated Beaux-Arts temples in wood used in western Canada. The buildings made Darling & Pearson an outstanding influence on both Canadian architecture and the form of Canadian cities.

Darling was the first Canadian to receive the RIBA Royal Gold Medal in 1915, when England was anxious to acknowledge Canadian contributions to World War I. John Pearson, a more technically orientated architect, was very much in Darling's shadow, but in 1916–24 he led the team that rebuilt the Centre Block of the Canadian Parliament Buildings in Ottawa. The firm continued after Darling's death with Barry Cleveland (1880–1934) in charge of design, until Pearson closed the office in the mid-1930s.

BIBLIOGRAPHY

W. Dendy: *Frank Darling, 1850–1923* (MA thesis, Columbia U., New York)

WILLIAM DENDY

Darly, Matthias [Mathias; Matthew] (*fl c.* 1740–early 1770s). English engraver, draughtsman and drawing-master. In 1748 his premises faced Old Slaughter's Coffee House in St Martin's Lane, London, a favourite meeting-place for adherents of the new Rococo style. His earliest known satirical print, the *Cricket Players of Europe*, is dated 1741.

In 1751 he issued *A New-book of Chinese, Gothic & Modern Chairs*, a slight publication on eight leaves. Twelve examples with bizarre backs were described as 'Hall Chairs' in a reissue of 1766, but it is more likely they were intended for gardens and summer-houses. A shell-back chair (Stratford-on-Avon, Nash's House) corresponding to one of the designs was made for the Chinese temple erected at Stratford for the Shakespeare jubilee organized by David Garrick in 1769. Five plates from a second book of chairs (*c.* 1751), of which no copy survives, were apparently reprinted in Robert Manwaring's *The Chair-maker's Guide* (1766). Described as 'Parlour Chairs', they incorporate extravagant C-scroll motifs in the backs.

Darly shared a house in Northumberland Court, London, with Thomas Chippendale (i) in 1753, and he engraved most of the plates in the first edition of Chippendale's *The Gentleman's and Cabinet-maker's Director*

(1754). In collaboration with George Edwards (1694–1773), an ornithologist, he published *A New Book of Chinese Designs* (1754), which consisted of 120 sprightly chinoiserie compositions. The 21 plates feature furniture, including beds, pagoda-like girandoles, chairs and candle stands, all invested with an Oriental or whimsically Rustic character.

The success of the *Director* led William Ince and John Mayhew (1736–1811) to employ Darly to engrave the plates for their *Universal System of Household Furniture* (1762). Another pattern book in which his engravings featured was Roger Sayer's *Houshold Furniture in Genteel Taste* (1760).

In conjunction with his wife Mary (*fl* 1756–77), Darly set up business as a publisher of caricatures (*c.* 1755–65) and was instrumental in encouraging the fashion for amateur prints, most notably with the politician George, Marquis of Townshend. An important innovation was the category of small prints mounted on paste-card that could be sent by post. From 1766 the Darlys started publishing a successful series of 'Macaroni' prints, which satirized the fops and dandies of the day.

Darly's later publications on ornament featured Neo-classical elements: tripods, vases and frames occur in *The Ornamental Architect or Young Artist's Instructor* (1770) and *A New Book of Ornaments in the Present (Antique) Taste* (1772). His last known book was *A Compleat Body of Architecture* (1773). In addition to his pattern books, Darly, who styled himself 'Professor and Teacher of Ornament', exhibited architectural designs and antique ornaments at the Royal Society of Arts in London between 1765 and 1771.

WRITINGS

A New-book of Chinese, Gothic & Modern Chairs (London, 1751, 2/1766)
with G. Edwards: *A New Book of Chinese Designs* (London, 1754)
The Ornamental Architect or Young Artist's Instructor (London, 1770)
A New Book of Ornaments in the Present (Antique) Taste (London, 1772)
A Compleat Body of Architecture (London, 1773)

BIBLIOGRAPHY

M. D. George: *Hogarth to Cruikshank* (London, 1967)
C. Gilbert: 'The Early Furniture Designs of Mathias Darly', *Furn. Hist.*, xi (1975), pp. 33–9
S. Jervis: *The Penguin Dictionary of Design and Designers* (London, 1984)

JAMES YORKE

Darmstadt. German city in Hessen, on the north-west foothills of the Odenwald, where the low-lying Upper Rhine Plain meets the 'Bergstrasse' area. It has a population of *c.* 135,000. The city, which until 1918 was the residence of the Landgravate (later Grand Duchy) of Hesse-Darmstadt, is a centre of industry and art and is dominated by the Baroque Residenzschloss. No public building survived the bombing of the city that took place in 1944 during World War II, though many were reconstructed, and most of the bourgeois villa quarters of the city have disappeared. Nevertheless, Darmstadt retains some of the character of the capital city of a principality.

1. History and urban development. 2. Artists' colony.

1. HISTORY AND URBAN DEVELOPMENT.

(i) Before 1806. The area has been continuously occupied since the late Iron Age, but the settlement was first documented at the end of the 11th century as 'darmundestat'. It belonged to the counts of Bessungen, on whose lands stood the original church of the neighbourhood, in existence as early as the year 1002. In the first quarter of the 11th century Emperor Henry II presented Bessungen to the bishopric of Würzburg, and the Bishop gave it in fief to the middle-Rhine counts of Katzenelnbogen. Emperor Ludwig IV granted Darmstadt civic rights on 23 July 1330. A moated castle was first documented in 1331, and the fortified Altstadt was clustered to the east and south of it. The cylindrical corner tower, the Weisser Turm, was reconstructed in 1953 following its near complete destruction in World War II.

The Protestant parish church also has medieval origins. In 1369 the Marienkapelle was raised to parochial status. The lower part of the five-storey west tower belongs to the 13th-century church; of the Late Gothic nave, only the outer walls were left standing in 1944 (rebuilt 1952–3, when the lantern was added to the west tower). The elongated choir is thought to have been built between 1419 and 1431: behind the high altar is the alabaster tomb with brass epitaph (1588–9) of *Landgrave George I of Hesse-Darmstadt* (*reg* 1567–96) *and his Wife, Magdalena zur Lippe* (*d* 1587) by Peter Osten. The Fürstengruft beneath the church, presumably established by George I after 1587, is richly ornamented with stuccowork post-dating 1615.

Darmstadt was bequeathed to the Landgraves of Hesse in 1479, and the impact of the Reformation reached the city in 1526. After the death of Philip the Magnanimous of Hesse (*reg* 1509–67), his son George I chose Darmstadt as his principal seat. The resultant increase in the town's importance was accompanied by an upsurge of building activity.

Between 1571 and 1579 Jakob Kesselhut (*fl* after 1568) built Kranichstein hunting lodge (now a museum of hunting) for George I. Three two-storey wings enclose a court that is open to the east, making Kranichstein a strikingly early example in Germany of a horseshoe-shaped plan. Between 1588 and 1590 the townspeople commissioned Jakob Wustmann (*fl c.* 1595) to build the Rathaus. They also built the 'Schirn' (destr.) and the hospital at the Bessungen Gate. The Rathaus is a three-storey stone building (rebuilt 1952–3); the main gables on the narrow ends, the side gables and the gable on the rectangular projecting staircase tower are in the Dutch style.

The first expansion of Darmstadt took place in 1593, when the Alte Vorstadt (now Magdalenenstrasse and the west part of Alexanderstrasse) was laid out north-east of the castle. The work, delayed by the Thirty Years War (1618–48), was not completed until *c.* 1687. Originally the houses mainly had two bays (later three), with huge Dutch gables facing on to the street and carriage entrances to the side. George I established the Herrngarten to the north of the castle in 1580, and it was enlarged in the 17th century. In 1681 Landgravine Elisabeth Dorothea (*reg* 1678–88) transformed it into a French pleasure garden, but it was converted into an English garden in 1766 and opened to the public in 1811. Building under George II (*reg* 1626–61) included the Residenzschloss (1629; destr. 1715) by Seyfried Pfannmüller (*fl* 1623–31) and the Pädagog, Hesse's first Latin grammar school.

The absolutist Landgrave Ernst Ludwig (*reg* 1688–1739)

greatly influenced the town's development. He began in 1695 by building the Neue Vorstadt to the west of the Schloss. Erich Philipp von Plönnies drew up plans that were later completed by LOUIS RÉMY DE LA FOSSE. Ernst Ludwig engaged La Fosse to build a new opera house, a project that was in 1710–11 reduced to a conversion of the Reithaus, or riding school (built 1606–7; destr.). Presumably La Fosse was responsible for designing the Prinz-Georg-Palais (*c.* 1710), a simple Baroque building that has housed the grand-ducal porcelain collection since 1907.

In 1714 La Fosse became chief architect of Darmstadt, with responsibility for both domestic architecture and fortifications. The market front of the Residenzschloss was destroyed by fire in 1715, and it was decided that a new Schloss (1716–30) for Ernst Ludwig should be built to replace it in Bessungen to La Fosse's designs. La Fosse's scheme was intended not only to replace the chancellery building but also to unify the whole castle area, in accordance with Baroque ideas. The new Schloss was on the axis of the Neue Vorstadt (begun 1695) along the Obere Rheinstrasse to the west of the town and, with the help of bridges across the moat in four directions, became the main nexus of communication for the whole area of the enlarged town. In the centre of the complex a tower with a lanterned dome was planned as a dominating landmark.

Owing to financial constraints, however, by 1726 barely a quarter of the planned project had been carried out, and the irregular grouping of the castle buildings was to a large extent retained. The appearance of the market front (south) and the west front is governed by the two Baroque wings constituting the Neuschloss. Behind this and adjoining it is the group of buildings that accumulated to form the Altschloss, with simple three-storey buildings on three inner courtyards. Between the Altschloss and the Neuschloss is the four-storey Glockenbau with its square staircase tower (1663–71). The carillon in the lantern was made by Salomon Verbeek in 1670. The Schlossmuseum is now located in the Glockenbau, its most important exhibit being the Darmstadt *Madonna* (1526; *see* HOLBEIN (ii), (3)) by Hans Holbein the younger. Also in the complex is an orangery (1719–21) by La Fosse.

The market front of the Schloss (see fig. 1) was designed as the principal façade, articulated with three pavilions of three bays and two wings of seven. The central pavilion has a banded ground floor and gigantic pilasters on the top. Above the windows relief decorations have been applied (at the sides, allegories on war and fame, in the middle the coat of arms of Hesse-Darmstadt), and four female allegories adorn the main cornice. The design is clearly influenced by French 17th-century architecture, particularly that of Louis Le Vau. Later plans by Georg Moller for the completion of the Neuschloss were never implemented. The whole complex was destroyed in 1944, and the reconstructed Schloss houses the State archives, the regional library, the town archives and the library and some departments of the college of technology.

The court at Darmstadt was curtailed by Ludwig IX (*reg* 1768–90), who lived elsewhere, but between 1777 and 1780 Friedrich Schuhknecht (1729–90) built the Kollegienhaus to Franz Ludwig Cancrin's design. The imposing

1. Darmstadt, market front of the Schloss (central building), designed by Louis Rémy de La Fosse, 1716–30

three-storey building (rebuilt 1952–4) had a flat-fronted central projection. In the reign of Ludwig X (Landgrave, 1790–1806; Grand Duke as Ludwig I, 1806–30) the territory of Darmstadt was considerably enlarged as a result of the secularization of 1803 and owing to the fact that Darmstadt became a member of the Rhine federation in 1806.

(ii) 1806 and after. As the capital of the new Grand Duchy, the city was given a Neo-classical face by GEORG MOLLER, chief architect from 1810. In keeping with Ludwig X's wishes, from 1811 Moller expanded the town westwards, developing the area west of the Schloss and linking it with the Altstadt. The streets of the Neustadt were laid out on a regular grid, with the Luisenplatz at its centre. In designing the Rheinstrasse as a *via triumphalis* Moller was guided not merely by a desire for grandeur; he was just as concerned with technical considerations relating to traffic flow and was interested in the potential for economic development.

A casino was designed by Moller in 1814–15 (destr. 1944), with an independent corner rotunda standing out from the wings. In 1818–20 he built the Hoftheater (destr. 1871; rebuilt 1875–9; destr. 1944; reconstructed and now being converted to house the State archives) with its temple-like, columned portico and triangular pediment. The Catholic Ludwigskirche (consecrated 1827; destr. 1944; rebuilt; see fig. 2), inspired by the Pantheon in Rome, was built between 1822 and 1826 to Moller's designs. In 1825–6 as an extension to Cancrin's Kollegienhaus, Moller

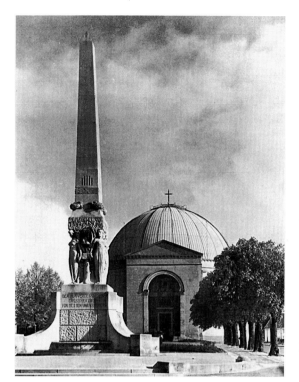

2. Darmstadt, Ludwigskirche, by Georg Moller, 1822–6; rebuilt after World War II

built a four-storey chancellery wing with a Corinthian vestibule on the ground floor. Between 1826 and 1831 he built the mausoleum for Princess Elisabeth of Darmstadt (1821–6) on the Rosenhöhe. The sarcophagus, with a statue (*c.* 1827) of the Princess by Christian Daniel Rauch, is housed in the circular domed building with its adjoining square barrel-vaulted chapel. In 1870 two wings were added as burial places for Grand Duke Ludwig I and Prince Emil. In 1844 Moller's memorial for *Grand Duke Ludwig I* was unveiled on the Luisenplatz. The 28 m-high sandstone memorial column is surmounted by a bronze statue of the Grand Duke by Ludwig von Schwanthaler (*see also* SCHOLL, JOHANN BAPTIST).

With the incorporation of Bessungen into Darmstadt in the 1880s, the industrial districts of the city expanded northwards. ERNST-LUDWIG, GRAND DUKE OF HESSE-DARMSTADT, encouraged the development of Darmstadt as a centre of industry and art. He released the Mathildenhöhe park (*see* §2 below) for building in 1898, when the Russian architect Leonty Benois constructed the Russische Kapelle as a gift from Tsar Nicholas II (*reg* 1894–1917) to his wife Alexandra (1872–1918), who was a sister of Ernst Ludwig. A year later an artists' colony was founded there. For the 1908 *Jugendstil* exhibition, and on the occasion of the Grand Duke's marriage, Josef Maria Olbrich designed the Hochzeitsturm, which has become a striking landmark in the town.

Between 1918 and 1945 Darmstadt was the capital of the free state of Hesse. In the bombing of September 1944, 80% of the town centre was destroyed. Post-war rebuilding involved the renewal of the town centre (largely completed by 1977), with considerable expansion of housing estates at the edges of the city.

BIBLIOGRAPHY

G. Haupt: *Die Bau- und Kunstdenkmäler der Stadt Darmstadt*, 2 vols (Darmstadt, 1952–4)

Darmstadt in der Zeit des Klassizismus und der Romantik (exh. cat., ed. B. Krimmel; Darmstadt, Ausstellhallen Mathildenhöhe, 1979)

Darmstadt in der Zeit des Barock und Rokoko (exh. cat., ed. B. von Götz-Mohr and J. R. Wolf; Darmstadt, Ausstellhallen Mathildenhöhe, 1980)

GUDRUN SCHMIDT

2. ARTISTS' COLONY. The Darmstadt artists' colony, which became a leading centre for *Jugendstil* (*see* ART NOUVEAU, §5) and the applied arts in Germany (*see* GERMANY, §IX, 1(iv)), was founded in 1899 by Ernst Ludwig, Grand Duke of Hesse-Darmstadt, who, inspired by Alexander Koch, wanted to raise artistic standards in local industrial products. Seven artists, including JOSEF MARIA OLBRICH and PETER BEHRENS, were summoned to the city, where Ernst Ludwig had set aside the Mathildenhöhe park as the site for the buildings for the colony. Other members included the medallist and sculptor Rudolf Bosselt, the painter and printmaker Paul Bürck (1878–1947), the painter and designer Hans Christiansen (1866–1945), the sculptor Ludwig Habich (1872–1949) and the interior decorator Patriz Huber (1878–1902). Olbrich, who led the colony until his death in 1908, designed most of the buildings and workshops; by designing the furniture and fittings as well, the colony was able to put into practice Olbrich's ideas of GESAMTKUNSTWERK, visible both in his panelled interior (1908; Darmstadt, Mus. Kstlerkolon.) from the Gluckert House and in Behrens's design for his own house (*see* GERMANY, §V, 5 and fig. 41).

Exhibitions were held in 1901, 1904, 1908 and 1914, although several of the original members left after 1901, objecting to what they saw as Olbrich's domineering attitude. They were replaced by others, notably the sculptors Heinrich Jobst (1874–1943) and BERNHARD HOETGER, and designers of furniture, glass, ceramics and metalwork, such as Albin Müller (1871–1941), Ernst Riegel (1871–1939), Jacob Julius Scharvogel (1854–1938) and Josef Emil Schneckendorf (1865–1949). All aspects of the decorative arts were covered: examples of the colony's work include Habich's elegant and romantic bronze relief of *Jacob Wrestling with the Angel* (1904), Huber's sinuous cherry-wood chair (1900–01), Müller's *Jugendstil* coffeepot (*c.* 1905; all Darmstadt, Hess. Landesmus.) and Schneckendorf's translucent lustreware glass vase (*c.* 1904; Zurich, Mus. Bellerive). For the exhibition of 1914 Hoetger created a series of sculptures (1912–14) for the grove of plane trees on the main terrace at Mathildenhöhe. The colony was closed in August 1914 at the outbreak of World War I, but Mathildenhöhe continues to be used as a venue for exhibitions.

BIBLIOGRAPHY

Darmstadt: Ein Dokument deutscher Kunst, 1901–76, 6 vols (exh. cat., ed. E. Zimmermann; Darmstadt, Ausstellhallen Mathildenhöhe; Darmstadt, Hess. Landesmus., Ksthalle; 1976) [esp. vols iv and v]

□

D'Aronco, Raimondo (*b* Gemona, Udine, 31 Aug 1857; *d* San Remo, Imperia, 3 May 1932). Italian architect. The son of a building contractor, at 14 he was working as a mason in Graz, Austria, and attending the local Baukunde where Leopold Theyer taught neo-Gothic and neo-Renaissance architectural design. He returned to Gemona in 1874 and after voluntary military service with the military engineers in Turin, where he learned the techniques of structural work in wood, he attended the Accademia di Belle Arti in Venice, studying under Giacomo Franco and graduating in 1880.

After a brief period (1881) during which he taught at the Accademia di Carrara, D'Aronco's career can be divided into three phases: in the first decade he was associated with Giuseppe Sommaruga and Ernesto Basile as one of the leading architects of the *Stile Liberty* (It.: Art Nouveau); the second, *c.* ten years either side of 1900, was when much of his work was in Turkey; and the third, after 1908, was mainly in Udine and Naples. In 1882 he won the competition for the layout of the Porta Tenaglia in Milan, in the style of Camillo Boito, and over the next five years took part in a number of others. He won a national competition for the offices of the Esposizione di Belle Arti (1887; destr.) in Venice; the building was in the neo-Greek style. He built the neo-Gothic cemetery (1889–90) at Cividale, Udine, and in 1890, in the neo-Greek style, the façade of the pavilion (destr.) of the Prima Esposizione Italiana di Architettura at Turin. His designs soon became more widely appreciated: he designed a bridge over the Neva at St Petersburg, Russia, and the Ponte Maria Teresa (1892–4) over the Po at Turin, freely inspired by Piranesi.

In 1893, with Ernesto Sambuy as intermediary, he was invited by Abdülhamid II, Sultan of Turkey, to oversee the design of the national Ottoman Exhibition in Constantinople (now Istanbul). Although this was subsequently cancelled because of the earthquake that damaged the capital, D'Aronco was commissioned to rebuild the palace at Yildiz, where an extensive programme of work over the next ten years included a layout for the park (1895–7), the archives building (1896), and on the hill the delightful ogee-domed, *Stile Liberty* library and tomb of Şeyh Zefir (1903). For most of the Turkish buildings D'Aronco abandoned European eclecticism to merge local tradition with his own intensely personal, sometimes bizarre concepts of style, particularly for the chalet houses and other more ephemeral works in timber. The remarkable, sometimes palatial chalet houses include the summer residence for the Italian ambassador at Therapia on the Bosphorus. His work in Istanbul includes the Ministry of Agriculture, the Museum of the Corps of Janissaries (1899–1900) and a number of houses, including the Botter House (1907) at Pera in the style of the Viennese Wagnerschule and the elegant bay-windowed, six-storey Santoro town house with Viennese Secession-style decoration, also in Pera.

D'Aronco also continued to work in Italy, notably on the winning competition design (1901) for the first Esposizione d'Arte Decorativa Moderna at Turin (1902). It was his best-known work (destr.; see Nicoletti, 1982, pp. 99–139) and, as well as the bizarre, colourful entrance pavilions with their echoes of the work of Joseph Maria Olbrich, included the proto-Modernist automobile pavilion with its quasi-butterfly roof. This was one of the first buildings of its kind. When political turmoil in Turkey led him to return to Udine (1908), he began work on the Palazzo Comunale (1909–29) in which he returned to the classical styles, though persisting with free interpretations in the decorative elements. He became a member of the Italian parliament in 1910 and in 1917 moved back to Naples to teach at the Politecnico and became Vice-Superintendent of the excavations at Pompeii. Although he continued to design houses in Udine (e.g. Villa Tamburlini, 1924) and Naples (e.g. Legnazzi house extensions at San Basilio dei Pisticci, 1927), his return to classical models and the coming of Fascism distanced him from the profession in these later years.

BIBLIOGRAPHY

M. Nicoletti: *Raimondo D'Aronco* (Milan, 1955)
F. R. Fratini, ed.: *Torino 1902* (Turin, 1970)
M. Nicoletti: *L'architettura Liberty in Italia* (Rome, 1978), pp. 241–54
R. D'Aronco: *Disegni di architettura* (Rome, 1980)
——: *Lettere di un architetto* (Gemona, 1982)
M. Nicoletti: *D'Aronco e l'architettura Liberty* (Rome, 1982)
D'Aronco architetto (exh. cat., ed. O. Selvafolta; Udine, Villa Manin Passariano, 1982)

VINCENZO FONTANA

Darque, Fábrica de. *See* FÁBRICA DE VIANA.

Darsan. *See* TOK-KALA.

Dartein, Fernand [Marie-Ferdinand] **de** (*b* Strasbourg, 9 Feb 1838; *d* Paris, 19 Feb 1912). French engineer, teacher and writer. He was trained as an engineer at the Ecole Polytechnique, Paris (1855–7), and at the Ecole des Ponts et Chaussées (admitted 1857). In 1860 he went to Lombardy, where he began a study of Lombard architecture that was published in 1865–82. He obtained a post with responsibilities for canals in Burgundy, but in 1866 he requested periodic leaves of absence to work as an unpaid teacher of architecture at the Ecole Polytechnique, assisting his former professor LÉONCE REYNAUD. He became a professor there in 1867. In 1869 he was also assisting Reynaud in his architecture courses at the Ecole des Ponts et Chaussées, where he became a full-time professor of architecture in 1871 and assistant director of the school in 1896. Dartein explicitly continued Reynaud's rationalist approach to architectural history in arguing that architectural forms were derived from gradual experimentation with materials and their structural capabilities, not from the forms of nature. His *Etude sur l'architecture lombarde* was dedicated to Reynaud, who had suggested the topic to him, and he eventually wrote Reynaud's biography (1885).

Dartein's best-known architectural commissions were the Public Works pavilions at the Expositions Universelles, Paris, in 1878 and 1889, of which he published illustrated folio volumes. He also produced several other books, including his courses on iron construction and historical studies of bridges. Dartein's career demonstrates the way in which architectural training was propagated in engineering institutions in France at that time, which he discussed in his *Observations* (1874).

WRITINGS

Etude sur l'architecture lombarde, 2 vols (Paris, 1865–82)
Observations sur le cours d'architecture à l'Ecole Polytechnique (Paris, 1874)
Etudes sur les ponts . . . antérieurs au XIXe siècle, 4 vols (Paris, 1907–12)

BIBLIOGRAPHY
Bénézit; *DBF*; Portoghesi; Thieme–Becker
W. Szambien: *Jean-Nicolas-Louis Durand, 1760–1834* (Paris, 1984), p. 183
D. Van Zanten: *Designing Paris* (Cambridge, MA, 1987), pp. 160–64
KAREN BOWIE

Darvish Muhammad [Darvīsh Muḥammad] (*fl* Tabriz, *c.* 1475–1500). Illustrator. Darvish Muhammad was active at the court of the Aqqoyunlu sultans Khalil (*reg* 1478) and Ya'qub (*reg* 1478–90). His name appears in a lengthy note to a fine copy (Istanbul, Topkapı Pal. Lib., H. 762, fols 316*v*–317*r*) of Nizami's *Khamsa* ('Five poems'), which was completed under the patronage of a succession of Timurid and Turkoman rulers (*see* ISLAMIC ART, §III, 4(v)(e) and fig. 124). The note recounts the complicated history of the manuscript and says that Khalil commissioned Darvish Muhammad, along with SHAYKHI, to illustrate the work. The name Darvish Muhammad also appears on three works in the two Ya'qub Beg albums (Istanbul, Topkapı Pal. Lib., H. 2153 and H. 2160). As so few works in the albums are attributed to this important painter, Robinson suggested that Darvish Muhammad be identified with Muhammad SIYAH QALAM, whose name appears on 65 works in the albums.

BIBLIOGRAPHY
B. W. Robinson: 'The Turkman School to 1503', *The Arts of the Book in Central Asia, 14th–16th Centuries*, ed. B. Gray (London and Paris, 1979), pp. 215–47
F. Çağman and Z. Tanındı: *The Topkapı Saray Museum: The Albums and Illustrated Manuscripts*, trans. and ed. J. M. Rogers (London and Boston, MA, 1986), pp. 113, 118

□

Dashwood, Sir Francis, 15th Baron Le Despenser (*b* Dec 1708; *d* West Wycombe, Bucks, 11 Dec 1781). English politician, patron and collector. He succeeded his father as 2nd Baronet in 1724 and gained the barony of Le Despenser in 1762. Between 1726 and 1741 he toured widely, visiting the Netherlands, France, Italy, Greece, Turkey and Russia. He was a founder-member of the Society of Dilettanti in 1732, in connection with which he was later portrayed by George Knapton as *St Francisco di Wycombo* (1742; London, Brooks's Club), toasting a statue of Venus. He also founded its notorious offshoot, the Hell-Fire Club. In 1762–3 he was Chancellor of the Exchequer, and he was Postmaster-General from 1766 until his death. Though he was often dismissed as a notorious rake, Dashwood's devotion to art was sincere, as is shown by his extensive alterations to the family estate West Wycombe Park, Bucks. From *c.* 1755 to 1764 John Donowell (*fl* 1753–86) was employed on making improvements to the house and constructing temples in the grounds, after which Nicholas Revett continued until 1781 as sole advisory architect; Giuseppe Borgnis and his son Giovanni were brought over from Italy by Dashwood to decorate the house interiors with frescoes. Dashwood also improved the church of St Lawrence, West Wycombe, having its tower surmounted with a hollow golden ball (supposedly for use as a drinking den) and the adjacent Mausoleum built between 1763 and 1764 by John Bastard the younger (1722–78). Dashwood's interest in painting was secondary to architecture, although he brought back a number of pictures from his Continental travels; he is reported to have paid £1500 for Adriaen van Utrecht's *Poultry Market* (West Wycombe Park, Bucks, NT) in the mistaken belief that it was by Peter Paul Rubens.

BIBLIOGRAPHY
DNB
L. H. Cust and S. Colvin: *History of the Society of Dilettanti* (London, 1898)
F. Dashwood: 'Sir Francis Dashwood and West Wycombe', *Connoisseur Yb.* (1955), pp. 3–12
——: *The Dashwoods of West Wycombe* (London, 1987), pp. 18–70, 191–232
NICHOLAS MARLOWE

Dasio, Maximilian (*b* Munich, 28 Feb 1865; *d* Oberammergau, 17 Aug 1954). German painter, medallist, designer and illustrator. He trained as a painter in the Munich Akademie from 1884, and initially won fame in this art with large decorative schemes on mythological or religious themes (e.g. *Bacchanal*, *c.* 1888; Munich, Villa Schülein) and portraits painted in a broad, realistic manner (e.g. *Elise Meier-Siel*, 1889; Munich, Schack-Gal.). He taught at the Munich Kunstgewerbeschule from 1902 to 1910. In 1905 he taught himself die-engraving and began making struck and cast medals, producing in all some 200, which combine his decorative abilities with the harsher style of his younger contemporaries (e.g. the bronze medal of *Anton von Knoezinger*, 1907; see 1985 exh. cat., no. 23). In 1907 and 1927 he produced models for coinage. Dasio also worked as a poster designer and book illustrator, as well as designing for stained glass and jewellery. The decorative symbolism of his earlier work in black and white (e.g. the cover for Jean-Philippe Rameau's ballet *Platea*, 1901; see 1985 exh. cat., no. 283) gave way in the years after World War I to a sterner approach, in which the influence of early German wood-engraving (e.g. the *St George* series of woodcuts, 1918; see 1985 exh. cat., no. 278), and on occasion the Nazarene school, is discernible. He received a number of honours before retiring in 1934 to Oberammergau.

BIBLIOGRAPHY
Forrer; *NDB*; Thieme–Becker; Vollmer
Maximilian Dasio, 1865–1954 (exh. cat. by I. S. Weber, Munich, Staatl. Münzsamml., 1985)
PHILIP ATTWOOD

Dasoku. *See under* SOGA.

Dassier. Swiss family of medallists. Jean [John] Dassier (*b* Geneva, 17 Aug 1676; *d* Geneva, 15 Nov 1763) trained under his father Domaine Dassier (1641–1719), chief engraver at the Geneva Mint, and studied in Paris under Jean Mauger and Joseph Roettier. From 1711 he was assistant engraver at the Geneva Mint and in 1720 succeeded his father as chief engraver, a post he held until his death. Around 1720 he designed and executed his first series of medals: those of French monarchs (72 medals) and religious reformers (around 24). In 1728 he visited England, where he refused the offer of a position at the Royal Mint. In 1731 he issued a series of medals dedicated to George II, depicting British sovereigns from William I to George II. This consisted of 35 medals available in gold, silver and bronze, some of which were damascened. He was joined in this project by his second son, and the medals are described in his *A Sett of Medals of all the Kings of England* (London, 1731) and *An Explanation of the*

Medals of the English Monarchs Engraved by John Dassier and Son (Birmingham, 1731). The Birmingham manufacturer Edward Thomason obtained the dies and continued to issue the series. Dassier also produced series depicting subjects from ancient Rome (silver and bronze) and remarkable men from the time of Louis XIV (silver and bronze). Many of his portraits are not authentic, but the technical skill of his die-engraving placed him among the leading European medallists and ensured for him many commissions for commemorative medals.

Of Dassier's three sons, the eldest, Jacques-Antoine Dassier (*b* Geneva, 15 Nov 1715; *d* Copenhagen, 2 Nov 1759), studied in Paris and Rome before working as assistant engraver at the Royal Mint in London from 1741 to 1745. He later worked at Geneva and from 1756 at the St Petersburg Mint. Besides many individually commissioned medals, in the 1740s he produced a series of famous Englishmen, including *Sir Hans Sloane* (bronze, 1744; see Hawkins, Franks and Grueber, ii, no. 234), and contributed to his father's Roman series. Antoine Dassier (1718–80) and Paul Dassier (1719–55) were both goldsmiths; like his elder brother, Antoine worked with his father on his medallic series and at the Geneva Mint, as chief engraver, from 1777 until his death.

BIBLIOGRAPHY

Forrer; Thieme–Becker
E. Hawkins, A. W. Franks and H. A. Grueber: *Medallic Illustrations of the History of Great Britain and Ireland*, 2 vols (London, 1885)
R. B. Waddington: 'The Iconography of Jean Dassier's Milton Medal', *Milton Q.*, xix/4 (1985), pp. 93–6

PHILIP ATTWOOD

Dassonville [Dassonneville], **Jacques** (*b* Port Saint-Ouen, nr Rouen, or Antwerp, *c*. 1619; *d c*. 1670). French or Flemish painter and etcher. He made 65 plates executed with a fine point, somewhat monotonous and greyish in tone; most of them are small-scale. They depict smoking-dens, tavern scenes and interiors with peasants and tramps, similar in inspiration to the work of David Teniers (ii) and Adriaen van Ostade. Only one of his prints is dated: *Two Tramps Split the Bill* (1656; Weigert, no. 34). He illustrated Dom Guillaume Marlot's *Histoire de l'église métropolitaine de Reims* (Lille, 1666). Dassonville signed himself sometimes DJS, sometimes *J. Dasson* or *J. Da Sonneville*, but most often *Dassonneville*. As some of his prints bear Martin van den Enden's imprint, Mariette assumed that he settled in Antwerp. None of his paintings or drawings is known.

BIBLIOGRAPHY

Mariette
A. P. F. Robert-Dumesnil: *Le Peintre-graveur français*, ii (Paris, 1836), pp. 167–91
R.-A. Weigert: *Inventaire du fonds français: Graveurs du dix-septième siècle*, Paris, Bib. N., Cab. Est. cat., iii (Paris, 1954), pp. 316–22

VÉRONIQUE MEYER

Daswanth [Dasavanta] (*fl c*. 1560; *d* 1584). Indian miniature painter. His name indicates that he was a Hindu. He was a favourite artist of the Mughal emperor Akbar (*reg* 1556–1605), who discovered his talent and sent him to the master painter 'Abd al-Samad for training. In the *Āyīn-i Akbarī*, a contemporary record of the reign, Abu al-Fazl wrote that in 'a short time he surpassed all painters and became the first master of the age' (Eng. trans.,

p. 114). He is known mainly for his highly imaginative and original compositions, where the irrational tends to dominate the realistic. Contemporary writers described him as a madman, and Abu al-Fazl acknowledged that some critics preferred the more naturalistic work of the painter Basawan.

Daswanth's earliest known works are illustrations of the *Ṭūtīnāma* ('Tales of a parrot'; *c*. 1556–61, other scholars prefer 1560–65; Cleveland, OH, Mus. A., MS. 62.279). Two paintings (fols 32*v* and 37*v*) show marginal inscriptions (partly damaged) naming Daswanth as the sole artist, while a third (fol. 32*r*) can be attributed to him. Though these are immature works, his talent is evident. The *Monkey Biting the Prince* (fol. 32*v*), for instance, is a lively painting that skilfully captures the monkey's unexpected action and also the startled responses of the prince, attendants and servants, including the astonished cook who looks up from his pots. All three paintings are characterized by refined, slightly dry brushwork. Daswanth probably contributed to the great *Ḥamzanāma* project ('Tales of Hamza'; dispersed), and it has been suggested that to some extent its original and highly imaginative qualities may be credited to him. None of the known paintings, however, has inscriptions naming artists. Daswanth's name appears in the inscription of a single illustration in the *Tīmūrnāma* ('History of Timur'; *c*. 1580; Bankipur, Patna,

Daswanth: *Holy Men*, opaque drawing on paper, 370×240 mm, *c*. 1580 (Windsor, Windsor Castle, Royal Library)

Khuda Bakhsh Lib.), where he is listed as the designer of the painting. Under contemporary procedures the colour was filled in by a second, usually lesser, artist. The work shows him heavily indebted to the style of his teacher 'Abd al-Samad.

Most of Daswanth's mature works (some 30 known paintings) are found in the great *Razmnāma* ('Book of war'; 1582–6; Jaipur, Maharaja Sawai Man Singh II Mus., MS. AG. 1638–1850), a Persian translation commissioned by Akbar of the Hindu epic the *Mahābhārata*. However, appropriately for a master painter, he is again named only as the designer of paintings completed by other hands. Nevertheless, it is clear he developed exceptional skill in the depiction of other-worldly and terrifying scenes. Figures are often weightless and proportions naturalistically inconsistent; European techniques of spatial depth, of such interest to other Mughal artists, are ignored. The effect is often fantastic. This sensitivity for the unearthly is a strong element in early Mughal painting: this is partly because in the first years of his reign Akbar was himself particularly sympathetic to narrative fantasy, but it may also have developed in response to Daswanth's particular skills. It virtually disappears as an important element in Mughal painting after Daswanth's death, at about which time the Emperor became more interested in historical themes. The one major later work known to be by Daswanth working alone is a drawing, *Holy Men* (Windsor Castle, Royal Lib.; see fig.), which shows a seated ascetic, drawn with great intensity, surrounded by six disciples.

Daswanth ended his life by suicide. According to the *Akbarnāma*, Abu al-Fazl's history of Akbar's reign: 'All at once melancholy took possession of him, and he wounded himself with a dagger. After two days he paid back the loan of life, and grief came to the hearts of connoisseurs' (Eng. trans., *R* 1972–3, iii, p. 651).

See also INDIAN SUBCONTINENT, §V, 4(i)(b).

BIBLIOGRAPHY

EWA

Abu al-Fazl: *Akbarnāma* [History of Akbar] (*c.* 1596–1602); Eng. trans. by H. Beveridge, 3 vols (Calcutta, 1907–39/*R* New Delhi, 1972–3)

——: *Āyīn-i Akbarī* [Annals of Akbar] (*c.* 1596–1602); Eng. trans. in 3 vols: i, trans. H. Blochmann, ed. S. L. Gloomer ([Calcutta], 1871/*R* Delhi, 1965); ii and iii, trans. H. S. Jarret, ed. J. Sarkar (Calcutta, 1948–9/*R* New Delhi, 1972–3)

P. Chandra: *The Tūṭi-nāma of the Cleveland Museum of Art* (Graz, 1976)

M. C. Beach: 'The Mughal Painter Daswanth', *A. Orient.*, xiii (1982), pp. 121–33

MILO CLEVELAND BEACH

Dati, Carlo (Roberto) (*b* Florence, 12 Oct 1619; *d* Florence, 11 Jan 1675). Italian scholar, antiquarian and scientist. In 1648 he became professor of classics at the Studio Fiorentino. He was an influential member of the Accademia della Crusca, an institution founded in 1582 for the study of the Tuscan language. He conceived a vast project on ancient art: a three-volume work consisting of a treatise on painting in antiquity, the lives of the most important ancient artists and a catalogue of all ancient artists whose names at least were known. Only the second part, the *Vite de' pittori antichi*, was published (1667). It contains biographies of Apelles, Zeuxis, Parrhasios and Protogenes, among others, for which Dati obtained material by systematically combing through Classical texts, but principally Pliny's *Natural History*. Dati's many contacts among the learned circles of Europe enabled him to compare almost all the available manuscripts and editions of this, so he could choose the most accurate version for his own use. Each biography takes the form of a narrative, broken up by descriptions of paintings and followed by notes quoting and discussing the references given in the margins of the text. Occasionally, to clarify points he considered obscure, Dati transcribed passages from the manuscript of his treatise on painting in antiquity. Apart from comparing available sources Dati is known to have consulted Salvator Rosa and Ciro Ferri in the course of preparing the *Vite*. His ideas on art were not original, and in the *Vite* he reiterated the main themes of 16th- and 17th-century art theory, but he was nevertheless the first writer to propose a critical reconstruction of the history of antique painting.

WRITINGS

Vite de' pittori antichi (Florence, 1667)

BIBLIOGRAPHY

DBI

G. Andreini: *'Le vite dei pittori antichi' di Carlo Roberto Dati* (Florence, 1953)

A. Minto: *'Le vite dei pittori antichi' di Carlo Roberto Dati e gli studi erudito-antiquari nel seicento* (Florence, 1953)

G. Perini: 'Carlo Malvasia's Florentine Letters: Insight into Conflicting Trends in Seventeenth-century Art Historiography', *A. Bull.*, lxx (1988), pp. 273–99 (282–4) [a negative assessment of Dati's works]

FRANCOIS QUIVIGER

Dating methods. *See* TECHNICAL EXAMINATION, §VII.

Datini, Francesco di Marco (*b* Prato, *c.* 1335; *d* Prato, 16 Aug 1410). Italian dealer and patron. He was the son of a taverner and small businessman in Prato and built up a trading company of his own dealing in works of art. This was based first in Avignon, from 1350 to 1382, where he imported and traded in Florentine panel paintings (mostly from unnamed painters, although in 1386 he purchased panels from Jacopo di Cione (i)), and afterwards in Prato, from where his business grew to cover much of Tuscany. He is important not because of the size of his enterprises but because of his voluminous surviving correspondence and the light it sheds on the commercial context of art in the 14th century. His house in Prato, planned from *c.* 1358 and still under construction after 1379, was decorated from 1391 with frescoes (some of which survive) by Agnolo Gaddi, Bartolommeo Bertozzi and Niccolò di Pietro Gerini, all three of whom were later dismissed unpaid. Gaddi's frescoes in the ground-floor office include remarkable *Forest Scenes*, and he probably also designed the lunette of *Christ* over the office door. Gerini painted a *St Christopher* in the hall and frescoes in the courtyard and loggia: a series of *Warriors* or *Kings* (perhaps including the *Nine Worthies*), the *Seven Virtues* and the *Seven Sciences*. The surviving ensemble, which includes work of *c.* 1409 by Arrigo di Niccolò, provides an unparalleled insight into private, secular, decorative iconography. The purchase for the house of several panels of sacred subjects is also documented. Datini also donated frescoes, panels (some by Gerini) and liturgical artefacts to various churches in Prato, particularly S Francesco, and stained-glass windows to many of the most important churches of Florence, including S Maria Novella and Santa Croce. After his death 16 scenes from his life were frescoed on the outside of his house.

BIBLIOGRAPHY
I. Origo: *The Merchant of Prato* (London, 1957) [extensive bibliog.]
N. Bemporad: *Palazzo Datini: Cronaca di un restauro* (Prato, 1958)
B. Cole: 'The Interior Decoration of the Palazzo Datini in Prato', *Mitt. Ksthist. Inst. Florenz*, xiii (1968), pp. 195–222
J. Larner: *Culture and Society in Italy, 1250–1400* (London, 1971)
B. Cole: *Agnolo Gaddi* (Oxford, 1977), pp. 29–30, 87

JOHN RICHARDS

Datong [Ta-t'ung]. Town in northern Shanxi Province, China. Situated between two sections of the Great Wall, on the edge of the traditional Chinese border (before the full incorporation of Inner Mongolia in 1947), Datong is the largest town in the province. It was frequently overrun by alien groups and was twice made dynastic capital, under the Tuoba or Toba Northern Wei (AD 386–534) and the Khitan (Qidan) Liao (907–1125). Most of the city wall of tamped yellow earth, dating to 1372, is still visible, and the old part of town reflects the regular layout characteristic of northern cities, with a bell-tower at the centre. Datong is famous for the nearby Buddhist cave temples at YUNGANG, begun under the Northern Wei, and for two early temples, the Huayan Temple (Huayan si), originating from the Liao, and the Shanhua Temple (Shanhua si), founded under the Tang (AD 618–907).

Under the Northern Wei, a group probably of Turkic origin, Datong was known as Pingcheng. The great task of carving out cave temples at Yungang, just west of the town, was begun by the Wei rulers, who were fervent Buddhists. The Wei continued their devotional work after the move of the capital to Luoyang in AD 493–4, by financing the cave temples at Longmen.

The Khitan, a Mongol group who had become semi-sedentary, established the Liao capital in Datong at a later period of Chinese disunity. The halls, statues and library of the Huayan Temple represent the major monuments remaining from the Liao. The original temple was destroyed by fire in 1122. The existing layout of an upper and lower temple dates from the Ming period (1368–1644), and most of the structures are Qing (1644–1911). The upper temple is unusual in that it faces east instead of south; this feature may support the suggestion that the Khitan were sun-worshippers as well as Buddhists. The upper temple's Daxiongbao dian (Mahavira or Powerful Treasure Hall), thought to date from 1140, is a rare example of 12th-century northern architecture. Set on a platform over 4 m high, it is an impressive nine-bay building. The scale of the whole is massive: the walls are well over 1 m thick, and the ridge acroteria are 4.5 m high. The ridge-end acroteria (*chiwen*) and other ridge decoration at the northern end of the roof are Jin in style and possibly original. The hall is constructed according to the 'reduced column' principle, with 12 fewer columns than might be expected, to allow for some massive Buddha figures. The five Buddhas of the Five Directions, over 5 m high and seated on elaborate high thrones, date from the Ming period. There are also 20 *bodhisattva*s and attendants, whose figures are elegantly inclined. The three central Buddhas, made in Beijing in 1427, are carved from wood and painted; the other two and the attendants are of stucco. They are all in the Sino-Tibetan style, popular for Buddhist images in the 14th and 15th centuries (*see* CHINA, §III, 1(i)). Brightly coloured wall paintings, illustrating scenes from the life of the Buddha, were executed by a local artist, Dong An, in 1875–1908. The coffered ceiling is decorated with dragons, phoenixes, flowers and Sanskrit writing. There is also a wooden tower (h. 2.5 m), made in the Qing period by Li Yangui, which is a model of one of the corner towers of the city wall.

The lower temple is south-east of the upper temple. The library (Bojia jiaocang dian or Bhagavan Hall), the second hall beyond the entrance, is a rare survivor from the Liao period, built in 1038. It is a five-bay hall four bays deep, with strong brackets supporting the eaves; the ceiling is original. Within the library stand 31 elegant Liao stucco figures. Three Buddhas (Past, Present and Future) are surrounded by attendants with flowing garments, in various poses and leaning slightly. The walls are lined with wooden bookcases made for Buddhist *sutra*s, constructed like miniature buildings: a 'suspended palace', a pavilion perched on an arch, spans the gap between the two main structures at the rear. The architectural detail is minute and precise and the design unique (*see* CHINA, §II, 4).

In the southern suburbs of Datong is the Tang-period Shanhua si (Good Transformations Temple). Founded during the Kaiyuan reign period (AD 713–42), it was largely destroyed by fire in 1122 and then restored (1128–43). The buildings lie on a north–south axis. The gateway was constructed in 1123–48 in the Song style, with 'moon-shaped' or lightly curved beams. The guardians at the gate are of stucco and date from the Ming period. The Sansheng dian (Hall of the Three Sages) was built at the same time as the gateway, but in the Liao–Jin style. It is constructed according to the 'reduced column' method. Figures of the Buddha and the *bodhisattva*s Manjushri and Samantabhadra are Jin in origin but were restored and repainted in the Qing period. The main hall, seven bays wide and five bays deep, is said to have been restored in 1123–48. It contains 30 Liao sculpted figures, including a central Buddha and a six-armed Guanyin (Skt Avalokiteshvara). Wall paintings date from the Qing period but are in Yuan style. One of the buildings to the west, a double-roofed pavilion of apparently two but actually three storeys, contains an inscription recording its construction in 1154.

The Nine Dragon Screen at Datong was built in 1392. Intended to avert evil spirits, it originally stood in front of the palace of the viceroy of Shanxi Province, the 13th son of the Hongwu emperor (*reg* 1368–98); the palace burnt down in the mid-17th century. The screen (8×45.5×20 m) is covered with glazed ceramic tiles in five colours. Just above the base are small figures of lions, tigers, elephants, *qilin* (mythical unicorn-like animals) and other animals, and above these are nine large dragons in high relief, rising from waves. The top is shaped as a roof, with tiles and ridge acroteria. The screen was moved some 10 m in 1954.

BIBLIOGRAPHY
Liu Dunzhen: *Zhongguo gudai jianzhu shi* [History of traditional Chinese architecture] (Beijing, 1980), pp. 197–9
Liang Ssu-ch'eng: *A Pictorial History of Chinese Architecture* (Cambridge, MA, 1984), pp. 58–60

FRANCES WOOD

Dat So La Lee [Keyser, Louisa] (*b* Washoe territory, CA–NV border, *c.* 1850; *d* Carson City, NV, 6 Dec 1925).

Native American Washoe basket-weaver. She worked, originally as a laundress, for Abe Cohn (1859–1934) and Amy Cohn (1861–1919), owners of the Emporium Co. clothing store in Carson City, NV. With their encouragement, she created a fine art curio style of basketwork, imitated by most Washoe weavers, and by 1897 she had developed the coiled, spheroid *degikup* basket type (see fig.), finely decorated with red (redbud) and black (bracken fern) designs in a scattered arrangement. She also created a collection of miniature baskets for Amy Cohn and made simpler twined basketwork souvenirs. She spent winters at the Emporium Co. in Carson City and summers at their outlet, The Bicose, at Tahoe City, Lake Tahoe, CA. In 1922 a short documentary film was made about her work, and in 1925 EDWARD SHERRIF CURTIS photographed her at the Emporium. Amy Cohn kept a ledger of Dat So La Lee's baskets, recording their dimensions, dates of inception and completion, along with her interpretation of the designs. The ledger is preserved in the Nevada State Museum in Carson City, which also houses over a dozen of Dat So La Lee's major works. Most of the information promulgated by Amy Cohn about Dat So La Lee was fabricated to make her appear more traditional and less innovative, including giving a birth date before the start of continued Euro-American influence in the region. In contrast to her treatment of other weavers, Amy Cohn referred to Dat So La Lee by her Washoe name, disregarding the weaver's own preference to interact with Euro-American society under her English name, Louisa Keyser.

Dat So La Lee with two of her large *degikup* baskets, finished in 1907 and 1916; from a photograph of *c.* 1916 (Reno, NV, Nevada Historical Society Museum)

Amy Cohn promoted her as an 'Indian Princess', claiming special family rights to basket shapes and designs. She also fabricated a ceremonial function and design vocabulary for Dat So La Lee's baskets and interpreted them as records of Washoe history and mythology. As Abe Cohn considered her major pieces to be works of art, he demanded high prices and in 1914 sold one (Yosemite N. Park Mus., CA) to the industrialist Gotlieb A. Steiner of Pennsylvania for £1400. Despite these efforts, three-quarters of her major works remained unsold at Abe Cohn's death in 1934, to be dispersed cheaply a decade later by his widow Margaret. Their value did not recover until the sale and dispersal of the Greene Collection in 1971.

BIBLIOGRAPHY

G. G. Gigli: *Dat So La Lee: Queen of the Washoe Basket Makers* (Carson City, 1967)

M. Cohodas: *Degikup: Washoe Fancy Basketry, 1895–1935* (Vancouver, 1979)

——: 'Dat So La Lee and the *Degikup*', *Halcyon*, iv (1982), pp. 119–40

MARVIN COHODAS

Dattaro. Italian family of architects. Francesco Dattaro (*d* ?1585) and his son Giuseppe Dattaro (*d* ?Guastalla, *c.* 1619), both of whom acquired the nickname Pizzafuoco, were from Cremona, where most of their few attributable works are situated. Francesco's career is the more prominent and more securely documented. At Cremona Cathedral he was responsible for the Chapel of the Sacrament and the Chapel of the Assumption (*c.* 1556), both elaborate sculptural works of an almost Baroque character. He also designed the more restrained and classical altar of St Michael in the cathedral. His work is more sculptural and decorative than architectural, although the Palazzo Pagliari (1566) in Cremona is usually attributed to him. It is a substantial building, the façades of which are crowded with Mannerist detail. Particularly notable are the ornate window pediments, the various forms of rustication and the small blind windows to the *piano nobile*. The interior is much simpler. Francesco was closely associated with Vincenzo Campi, who in turn collaborated with Giulio Romano on the Palazzo del Te for the Gonzaga court at Mantua. Giulio may well have been the source for much of Francesco's own Mannerist detailing. Giuseppe's style is similar to that of his father, and the monumental Palazzo Affaitai (1561; later Palazzo Ugolani Dati; now the Museo Civico Ala Ponzone) in Cremona is probably his work. It is similar in character to the Palazzo Pagliari although rather more austere and Florentine in appearance, particularly in its principal façade. In 1583 Giuseppe left Cremona to enter the service of Ferdinand II Gonzaga (*d* 1630) and went to Guastalla to work on his palace; he seems to have spent some years in the service of the Gonzaga.

BIBLIOGRAPHY

A. Haupt: *Architettura dei palazzi dell'Italia settentrionale e della Toscana dal sec. XIII al sec. XVII*, 3 vols (Milan and Rome, n.d.)

G. B. Zaist: *Notizie istoriche de' pittori, scultori ed architetti cremonesi* (Cremona, 1875)

A. Venturi: *Storia* (1901–40)

A. Perotti: *I pittori Campi da Cremona* (Milan, 1932)

M. Tafuri: *L'architettura del manierismo nel cinquecento italiano* (Rome, 1966)

A. Smart: *The Renaissance and Mannerism in Italy* (London, 1971)

Dau al Set [Cat.: 'die at seven']. Artistic and literary group based in Barcelona and active from 1948 to 1956. It was founded in September 1948 by the poet Joan Brossa, who proposed the group's name, together with philosopher Arnau Puig and the painters Modest Cuixart, Joan Ponç (*b* 1927), Antoni Tàpies and Joan-Josep Tharrats. They based their stance largely on Dada and Surrealism and related developments, notably on Max Ernst's early work and on the art of Paul Klee and Joan Miró, and directed much of their attention to the sub-conscious by way of magic and the occult. Making clear their opposition to academic and official artistic circles, they were an important force in promoting contemporary art in Catalonia after the damage to their culture effected by the Spanish Civil War (1936–9).

The group's ideas, and the work of the artists associated with it, were transmitted largely through their magazine, also titled *Dau al Set*. Their internationalism and wide-ranging interests led them to publish the magazine in Catalan, Spanish and French, and to feature poetry, music, anthropology and ethnology alongside existentialism and art. They championed the turn-of-the-century origins of modernism in Catalonia, in particular the architecture of Gaudí, and alluded to Art Nouveau metalwork even in Ponç's title lettering for the magazine. Among the critics actively involved in writing for *Dau al Set* were influential figures such as Juan Eduardo Cirlot and Alexandre Cirici Pellicer, and they counted from the beginning on the support of Joan Prats, whose editorial work from 1934 for another Barcelona-based magazine, *D'Ici i d'Allà* (Cat.: 'from here to there'), had paved the way for their own publication. Among the artists whose work became more widely known through illustrations in the magazine were Angel Ferrant, Josep Guinovart, Jorge Oteiza, Ramón Rogent, Antonio Saura and Josep Maria Subirachs, as well as the founder-members.

BIBLIOGRAPHY

Cuadernos Guadalimar, vii: *Dau al Set* (Madrid, 1978)
L. Cirlot: *El grupo 'Dau al Set'* (Madrid, 1986)
I. Julián: *Les avantguardes pictòriques a Catalunya al segle XX* (Barcelona, 1986)

INMACULADA JULIÁN

Daubigny [D'Aubigny]. French family of artists. Edmond-François Daubigny (*b* Paris, 1789; *d* Paris, 14 March 1843) was a pupil of Jean-Victor Bertin and painted historic landscapes and city scenes, such as the *Fountain of the Innocents* (1822; Paris, Carnavalet). From 1819 to 1839 he exhibited at the Salon in Paris, showing views principally of Paris and Naples. He visited Italy in 1833. His brother Pierre Daubigny (*b* Paris, 30 Oct 1793; *d* Paris, 15 July 1858) studied under Louis-François Aubry (1767–1851) and was a miniature painter, exhibiting from 1822 to 1855 at the Salon in Paris. Pierre's wife, Amélie Daubigny (*b* Paris, 1793; *d* Paris, 22 March 1861), also a miniature painter, collaborated with him on many works. She was a pupil of Louis-François Aubry and Jean-Pierre Granger (1779–1840) and showed at the Salon from 1831 to 1844. Edmond-François Daubigny's son (1) Charles-François Daubigny, an admirer of 17th-century Dutch painting, became one of the most important landscape painters in mid-19th century France. He was associated with the BARBIZON SCHOOL and was an influence on the Impressionist painters. His son (2) Karl Daubigny was a landscape painter who studied under his father and exhibited landscapes at the Salon in Paris from 1863.

(1) Charles-François Daubigny (*b* Paris, 15 Feb 1817; *d* Paris, 19 Feb 1878). Painter and printmaker. He studied under his father Edmond-François Daubigny and in 1831–2 also trained with Jacques-Raymond Brascassat. At an early age he copied works by Ruisdael and Poussin in the Louvre, while also pursuing an apprenticeship as an engraver. At this time he drew and painted mainly at Saint-Cloud and Clamart, near Paris, and in the Forest of Fontainebleau (1834–5). In 1835 he visited several Italian cities and towns, including Rome, Frascati, Tivoli, Florence, Pisa and Genoa. He returned to Paris in 1836 and worked for François-Marius Granet in the painting restoration department of the Louvre. In 1840 he spent several months drawing from life in Paul Delaroche's studio, although his early works were much more heavily influenced by 17th-century Dutch painters, whom he copied in the Louvre, than by Delaroche's work.

In 1838 Daubigny first exhibited at the Salon in Paris, with an etching, *View of Notre-Dame-de-Paris and the Ile Saint-Louis*, and he continued to exhibit regularly there until 1868. He travelled a great deal, visiting Etretat and Dieppe on the coast of Normandy in 1842. From 1843 he spent much time in the Forest of Fontainebleau, sending his first painting of a Fontainebleau scene, *The Stream at Valmondois* (1844; priv. col.), to the Salon of 1844. In 1846 he painted with Théodore Rousseau and Jules Dupré at Valmondois and L'Isle-Adam (both Val-d'Oise), two of his preferred areas. The following year he travelled through Burgundy and also visited the Morvan Mountains in central France, where he painted the *Valley of the River Cousin* (1847; Paris, Louvre). In 1849 he was in Dauphiné in south-west France and the area around Lyon, painting at Crémieu and Optevoz and meeting Auguste Ravier and Corot, and in 1850 he worked at Auvers-sur-Oise and visited the Pyrénées. Two years later he and Corot—by now his close friend—spent considerable time painting in the Dauphiné and in Switzerland. Daubigny also painted with Armand Leleux at Dardagny, near Geneva, in 1853, and on the banks of the River Oise in 1856. He spent the next year with Jules Breton at Marlotte and made his first trip on the Oise on Breton's boat *Le Botin*, which had been converted into a studio and permanent home. From this time Daubigny untiringly explored the Seine, the Marne and the Oise by boat, mooring wherever he would find a scenic spot and ascertaining the best viewpoint from which to paint his chosen motif. His method of working *en plein air* was later to be greatly significant to Monet.

From the 1850s Daubigny's financial situation improved, and he began to achieve success, eventually becoming well known. Critics praised two of his paintings submitted to the Salon of 1852—the *Harvest* (Paris, Louvre) and *View of the Banks of the Seine from Bezon* (Paris, Mus. d'Orsay)—for their luminous colours, fluid atmosphere and simple motifs, although they reproached him for what they saw as carelessness of execution. He sold several works to the French government, among them the *Pond of Gylieu near Optevoz, Isère* (1853; Cincinnati, OH, A. Mus.), *Lock in the Valley of the Optevoz*

Charles-François Daubigny: *Sunrise on the Banks of the River Oise*, oil on canvas, 1.00×1.62 m, 1865 (Lille, Musée des Beaux-Arts)

(1855; Rouen, Mus. B.-A.) and the *Valley of the Optevoz* (1857; Paris, Louvre). In 1859 he was commissioned to paint decorative scenes (the *Stags*, the *Herons*, the *Palace*, the *Garden of Tuileries*) for the entrance hall and stairway of the Salons du Ministère d'Etat in the Louvre. He also produced engravings after works by such artists as Ruisdael and Claude for the Louvre's Department of Chalcography and from 1853 executed numerous prints in the technique of *cliché-verre* (*see* CLICHÉ-VERRE, §2). In 1860 he settled in Auvers-sur-Oise but also travelled extensively in other parts of France and abroad (Brittany in 1867; London in 1865 and 1870; Spain in 1868 and 1869; the Netherlands in 1871).

Daubigny was one of the first landscape painters to take an interest in the changing and fleeting aspects of nature, depicting them with a light and rapid brushstroke; this was a highly novel technique that disconcerted such critics as Théophile Gautier, who in 1861 wrote that 'it is really a pity that this landscape artist, having so true, so apt and so natural a feeling for his subject, should content himself with an "impression" and should neglect detail to such an extent. His pictures are no more than sketches barely begun' (Gauthier, p. 119). Nevertheless, four years later Gautier was to acknowledge that 'the impression obtained by these most perfunctory means is nonetheless great and profound for all that'. In 1865 Daubigny painted *Sunrise on the Banks of the River Oise* (see fig.), which is typical of his work in both technique and subject-matter and is one of a considerable number of variations on the theme executed between 1860 and 1875 (e.g. *Evening on the Oise*, 1863; Cincinnati, OH, Taft Mus.; *Sunset on the Oise*, 1865; Paris, Louvre). These paintings are good examples of his ability to capture the essence of nature

purely in its 'sincerity' without resorting to artifice or metaphysics. His numerous pupils included Eugène Boudin and Johan Barthold Jongkind, both of whom he met in Honfleur in 1864, his son (2) Karl Daubigny, Antoine Chintreuil, Eugène La Vieille (1820–89) and Jean Charles Cazin. In 1870 he took refuge in London during the Franco-Prussian War and the following year introduced Camille Pissarro and Monet to his art dealer Paul Durand-Ruel, then in England. In 1871 Daubigny met Cézanne at Auvers. He was an important figure in the development of a naturalistic type of landscape painting, bridging the gap between Romantic feeling and the more objective work of the Impressionists.

WRITINGS

E. Moreau-Nélaton: *Daubigny raconté par lui-même* (Paris, 1950)

BIBLIOGRAPHY

T. Gauthier: *Abécédaire du Salon de 1861* (Paris, 1861), p. 119
F. Henriet: *C. Daubigny et son oeuvre gravé* (Paris, 1875)
J. Claretie: 'Daubigny', *Première série de peintres et sculpteurs contemporains: Artistes décédés de 1870 à 1880* (Paris, 1881–4), pp. 265–88
L. Delteil: *Daubigny*, xiii of *Le Peintre-graveur illustré* (Paris, 1906–26/R New York, 1969)
J. Laran: *Daubigny* (Paris, 1913)
M. Fidell-Beaufort: *The Graphic Art of Charles-François Daubigny*, 2 vols (diss., New York U., Inst. F.A., 1974)
J. Bailly-Herzberg and M. Fidell-Beaufort: *Daubigny: La Vie et l'oeuvre* (Paris, 1975)
P. Miquel: *L'Ecole de la nature*, iii of *Le Paysage au XIXe siècle, 1814–1874* (Maurs-la-Jolie, 1975), pp. 664–705

LAURENCE PAUCHET-WARLOP

(2) Karl [Charles-Pierre] **Daubigny** (*b* Paris, 9 June 1846; *d* Auvers-sur-Oise, 25 May 1886). Painter and printmaker, son of (1) Charles-François Daubigny. He studied with his father and, like him, specialized in landscape painting. He made his début at the Salon in

1863 and continued to exhibit there until the year of his death, winning medals in 1868 and 1874. His earliest works are obviously influenced by his father, but he soon came to develop a more personal and sombre style. The forest of Fontainebleau or the coastline and landscape of Brittany and Normandy provided most of his subjects (e.g. the *Return of the Fishing Fleet to Trouville*, 1872; Aix-en-Provence, Mus. Granet, and the *Banks of the Seine*, 1880; Brest, Mus. Mun.). He also produced a number of landscape etchings, including several after his father's paintings, two of which appeared in Frédéric Henriet's *C. Daubigny et son oeuvre gravé* (Paris, 1875). Despite his considerable ability, Karl's reputation has been rather eclipsed by that of his father, though he was nonetheless one of the most pleasing French landscape artists of the second half of the 19th century.

DBF

BIBLIOGRAPHY

E. Bellier and L. Auvray: *Dictionnaire général des artistes de l'école française*, 3 vols (Paris, 1868–85)

Daucher [Dauher]. German family of artists. They were among the leading artists in Augsburg during the first third of the 16th century.

(1) Bartholomäus [Bartholeme] **Dauher** [Dorer; Tawer; Thorer] (*b* ?Vienna; *fl* 1476–95; *d* ?Augsburg). Painter. He may have worked in Augsburg and was active in Ulm during the 1490s. A number of paintings have been attributed to him for this period. Of these the firmest attribution is to a portrait of *Ursula Greck* (1491/2; Ulm, Ulm. Mus.), shown in three-quarter profile facing her husband, which formed the left panel of a diptych painted in oil on pinewood; the right panel of *Bartholomäus Greck* is untraced. Documentary evidence (Ulm, Stadtarchv) states that Dauher witnessed a dispute that occurred in the Greck household in 1492. The portrait shows him to have been a confident artist, worthy to be employed by the city's patrician families. He may have been the father of (2) Adolf Daucher.

BIBLIOGRAPHY

Thieme–Becker: 'Thorer, Bartholomäus'

H. Rott: *Alt-Schwaben und die Reichsstädte* (1934), ii of *Quellen und Forschungen zur südwestdeutschen und schweizerischen Kunstgeschichte im XV. und XVI. Jahrhundert* (Stuttgart, 1933–8)

E. Treu: *Ulmer Museum: Bildhauerei und Malerei des 13. bis 16. Jahrhunderts* (Ulm, 1988)

HANNELORE HÄGELE

(2) Adolf Daucher, the elder (*b* ?Vienna, *c*. 1460; *d* Augsburg, after Oct 1523, before Oct 1524). Sculptor, possibly the son of (1) Bartholomäus Dauher. Adolf probably worked in Ulm with the sculptor Michel Erhart, whose daughter Afra he married sometime prior to 1485. Their eight children included the sculptor Adolf Daucher the younger (*b* Ulm, *c*. 1485; *d* 1557), who carved the choir-stalls (1550) and pulpit (1551) in the minster Schwäbisch-Gmünd, (3) Hans Daucher and three other sons who were artists. In 1490 Adolf and his family moved to Augsburg, where he served initially as the manager of the property owned by the Cistercian monastery at Kaisheim. On 30 July 1491 he obtained Augsburg citizenship.

The tax records of Augsburg list Adolf annually from 1492 as a 'Kistler' (joiner), and only in the census book of

1514 is his occupation given as 'Bildschnitzer' (sculptor). The often rigid, guild-enforced boundaries between different crafts bedevilled Adolf. Shortly after becoming a citizen, his right to employ both sculptors and painters in his workshop was challenged. Nevertheless, he received several important commissions for carved altarpieces, for example the *Simpertusaltar* (1493–7) and a large retable for the *Frühmessaltar* (Matins Altar; 1493–8), both for SS Ulrich and Afra, Augsburg, but destroyed in the city's iconoclastic riots. It is probably not coincidental that his brother-in-law, Gregor Erhart, one of the region's finest sculptors, moved to Augsburg in 1494 and collaborated with Adolf on several occasions. Between *c*. 1498 and 1502 these two masters, together with Hans Holbein (i), the cousin of Erhart's wife, made the high altar (destr.) for the Cistercian monastery at Kaisheim. Adolf supervised the project and constructed the frame, while Gregor executed the sculpture, and Holbein the painting. These three masters worked together again between 1503 and March 1508 on the *Frühmessaltar* (destr.) in the Moritzkirche, Augsburg. Although Adolf occasionally carved figures, he usually employed Erhart, Hans Daucher and others to make the sculptures.

In 1515 Adolf submitted a design for a wooden ceiling for the Augsburg Rathaus. He may also have made a wooden model for the Luginsland, the north-eastern corner tower of the city's fortifications (Augsburg, Maximilianmus., inv. no. 3448). Adolf's most famous creation is the high altar (*in situ*) in the Annenkirche, Annaberg, commissioned by Georg, Duke of Saxony, in 1519. The project may have been conceived the year before while Georg attended the imperial diet in Augsburg. During Lent 1520, Hans Daucher went to Annaberg to study the site of the altar and to show his father's design to Georg. Hans carved the *Tree of Jesse* figures, including 20 ancestral busts, and the angels. The stone and probably the statues were erected at great expense in 1521; an epidemic postponed the erection of the altar until 1522. The huge altar (h. 7.5 m) was unprecedented in northern Europe, incorporating ten subtly contrasting colours of marble in a Renaissance frame.

(3) Hans Daucher (*b* Ulm, *c*. 1485; *d* Stuttgart, after 11 Nov 1538). Sculptor, son of (2) Adolf Daucher. He was the finest sculptor in Augsburg during the 1520s. From October 1500 he resided with his uncle and teacher Gregor Erhart and probably travelled to Venice and northern Italy sometime prior to 1514, when he obtained Augsburg citizenship, married Susanna Spitzmacher and became a master sculptor. He is first mentioned in the city's tax records in 1516, at which time he was living in his father's house. Hans and Adolf probably shared a workshop until 1522, although Hans registered his first pupils in 1518 and 1521. During Easter week 1528, while Hans was in Vienna, the Augsburg officials raided his house and arrested Susanna and about 100 others during an Anabaptist celebration. Her subsequent fate is unknown, although approximately 100 Anabaptists left Augsburg for Strasbourg by 1529. It seems likely that she and the others were banished. That Hans chose to remain in Augsburg suggests that he did not share his wife's religious beliefs. In 1530 he moved into the house of fellow sculptor

Jacob Murmann (1467–1547), where he lived until September 1536, when he officially entered the service of Ulrich VI, Duke of Württemberg (*reg* 1504–19 and 1534–50) in Stuttgart. His daughter Susanna Daucher married a goldsmith from Regensburg in 1540, and his son Abraham Daucher (*b c.* 1525; *d* after May 1592) worked as a goldsmith in Augsburg.

As Hans Daucher was one of the few German Renaissance sculptors who frequently signed his works, a sizeable corpus of certain and attributed carvings has emerged (*see* WOOD, colour pl. II, fig. 1). His activities prior to 1518 are unclear, although a signed *Annunciation* (Vienna, Ksthist. Mus.) is often dated as early as 1510. This delicate Solnhofen limestone relief (180×150 mm) is typical of the high-quality small-scale carvings that Hans specialized in creating for patrician and noble collectors. He showed his inventiveness in setting the figures, which derive from a Dürer woodcut (B. 83), into a more elaborate Renaissance interior, with north Italian architectural motifs, constructed in a similar fashion to those by Hans Burgkmair (i).

Between 1510 and 1518 Hans collaborated with his father, with Gregor Erhart and with other artists. During this period he may also have participated in the sculptural decoration of the Fugger Chapel in the Annenkirche, the most important artistic project in Augsburg. The lack of documentation has prompted elaborate and often contradictory speculations about the roles of the Dauchers, Sebastian Loscher (*fl* 1510; *d c.* 1548) and several other Augsburg masters. Hans's angels on the Annaberg high altar suggest that he either carved or was influenced by the Fugger Chapel angels. Other critics have conjectured that Hans produced the three stone reliefs of the *Passion* on the altar at the front of the chapel and helped make the choir-stalls (fragments Berlin, Bodemus.).

The imperial diet in Augsburg in 1518 brought several commissions to the Daucher family workshop. The most significant of these was the high altar in Annaberg, which was made for Georg, Duke of Saxony. The *Lamentation* in the parish church in Saverne (Zabern), Alsace-Lorraine, was probably a gift of Wilhelm von Honstein, Bishop of Strasbourg, who had participated in the Augsburg diet. During his trip to Annaberg in 1520 Hans also travelled further north to Wittenberg to deliver some unspecified works to another participant, Frederick III, Elector of Saxony. Hans's limestone relief of the *Virgin and Child* (1518; Vienna, Ksthist. Mus.; see fig.), its signed and dated copy (1520) in Augsburg and the numerous reliefs with secular themes of 1522 were probably executed for other aristocratic patrons. In 1522, his most productive year, Hans carved limestone reliefs of the *Judgement of Paris* (Vienna, Ksthist. Mus.), the *Triumph of Charles V* (New York, Met.), *Charles V on Horseback* (Innsbruck, Tirol. Landesmus.), a portrait of *Philipp, Count Palatine* and its unsigned pendent portrait of *Ottheinrich, Count Palatine* (both Berchtesgaden, Schlossmus.). The signed but undated *Maximilian I as St George* (Vienna, Ksthist. Mus.) is approximately contemporary. Several additional unsigned reliefs, the finest of which are the profile bust portrait of *Cardinal Matthaus Lang* (*c.* 1520–25; Salzburg, Residenzgal.) and the *Meeting of Charles V and Ferdinand I* (1527

Hans Daucher: *Virgin and Child*, limestone relief, 415×305 mm, 1518 (Vienna, Kunsthistorisches Museum)

[?1530]; New York, Pierpont Morgan Lib.), are attributed to Hans.

The stone portraits of Philipp and Ottheinrich are roundels in the form of a medal. Although too large (diam. 140 mm and 144 mm) to be models for medals, these portraits raise the question of whether Hans also designed such objects. Habich ascribed 38 medals to him on the basis of the portraits. While many of these attributions are difficult to accept, he was probably responsible for a group of eight medals, cast in the 1520s by an unknown metalworker, of Philipp (*see* MEDAL, fig. 3), Ottheinrich and Ottheinrich's wife, Susanna.

During the 1520s, Hans carved several other religious reliefs and portraits such as the signed stone reliefs on the monuments to *Melchior Funk* (*d* 1521; Augsburg, Maximilianmus.) and *Konrad Adelmann, Canon of Augsburg Cathedral* (*d* 1547; Holzheim, Pfarrkirche). A series of stylistically related wooden portraits of *Frederick III, Elector of Saxony* and *Anna Dornle* (1525; both Vienna, Ksthist. Mus.), a man's head (*c.* 1530; Berlin, Dahlem, Skulpsamml.) and a male bust (*c.* 1537; Tübingen, Schloss Hohentübingen), traditionally ascribed to the 'Meister der Dosenköpfe', are now thought to be by Hans. If so, the bust would be the only sculpture that survives from the last years of Hans's career in Stuttgart. However, relatively few works that postdate 1528 have been identified.

BIBLIOGRAPHY

A. von Bartsch: *Le Peintre-graveur* (1803–21) [B.]

P. M. Halm: 'Hans Daucher', *Jb. Preuss. Kstsamml.*, xli (1920), pp. 283–343

——: *Adolf Daucher und die Fuggerkapelle bei St Anna in Augsburg*, (Munich and Leipzig, 1921)

E. F. Bange: *Die Kleinplastik der deutschen Renaissance in Holz und Stein* (Florence, 1928), pp. 15–26

G. Habich: *Die deutschen Schaumünzen des XVI. Jahrhunderts* (Munich, 1929–34), I/i, pp. 13–19; II/i, pp. lxxxv–xc

K. Feuchtmayr: 'Die Bildhauer der Fugger-Kapelle bei St Anna zu Augsburg: Stilkritische Bemerkungen zu Sebastian Loscher und Hans Daucher', *Die Fugger und die Kunst*, i, ed. N. Lieb (Munich, 1952), pp. 433–71 [the best discussion of the Fugger Chapel and its decorations]

H. Müller: 'Die Künstlerfamilie Daucher', *Lebensbilder bayerischen Schwaben*, vi (1958), pp. 131–65 [the most thorough crit. biography of Adolf and Hans, although sources for much of the documentation are not provided]

H. Reinhardt: 'Unscheinbare Kostbarkeiten aus dem Amerbach-Kabinett', *Jber. Hist. Mus. Basel* (1958), pp. 27–35

K. Oettinger: 'Hans Dauchers Relief mit dem Zweikampf Dürers', *Jb. Fränk. Landesforsch.*, xxxiv/xxxv (1975), pp. 299–307

Welt im Umbruch: Augsburg zwischen Renaissance und Barock (exh. cat., Augsburg, Städt. Kstsammlungen, 1980), ii, pp. 36, 160–65

Die Renaissance im deutschen Südwesten (exh. cat., Heidelberg, Schloss, 1986), ii, pp. 549–52

B. Bushart: *Die Fuggerkapelle bei St Anna in Augsburg* (Munich, 1994), pp. 215–30, 309–13

J. C. Smith: *German Sculpture of the Later Renaissance, c. 1520–1580: Art in an Age of Uncertainty* (Princeton, 1994), pp. 51–2, 172–4, 270–74, 338–40, 365–7

The Currency of Fame: Portrait Medals of the Renaissance (exh. cat., ed. S. Scher; New York, Frick; Washington, DC, N.G.A.; 1994)

JEFFREY CHIPPS SMITH

Daudet, Robert (*b* Lyon, 25 Oct 1737; *d* Paris, 2 June 1824). French engraver and print-seller. He belonged to a family of Lyonnais engravers that included his father, Jean-Louis Daudet (1695–1756), an engraver of illustrations and print-seller, and another Robert Daudet, probably his uncle (*fl* 1728–33). He may have attended the classes of Jean-Charles Frontier (1701–63) at the Ecole Gratuite de Dessin in Lyon (founded in 1757). In 1766 he is documented as entering the workshop of Jean-Georges Wille. There he engraved plates for Wille and for Jacques-Philippe Lebas and Pierre-François Basan. He was also active as a dealer. His correspondence with the Lyonnais artist Jean-Jacques de Boissieu reveals that he saw to the sale of the latter's drawings and prints in Paris.

Daudet's engraved work amounts to 82 pieces and consists exclusively of reproductive prints, often after a preliminary etching done by another printmaker. He specialized in reproducing the work of such fashionable 17th-century Dutch artists as Jan Asselijn, Nicolaes Berchem, Karel Dujardin and Adriaen van Ostade, as well as of contemporary painters working in a Dutch manner. He made a number of prints after works by the landscape and sea painter Joseph Vernet. His engravings contributed to the development of private collections, such as those of Jean-Denis II Lempereur and Etienne-François, Duc de Choiseul, and to the publication of the stock of the dealer Jean-Baptiste-Pierre Le Brun: *Galerie des peintres flamands, allemands et hollandais de M. Le Brun*, published by Pierre-François Basan and Etienne-Léon Poignant (1777–91). After the French Revolution Daudet engraved illustrations for travel books and archaeological publications, providing two plates for Louis-François Cassas's *Voyage pittoresque de Syrie* (1798) and several plates after Edme-François Jomard and Dutertre for the *Description de l'Egypte* (1804). He collaborated on *Le Musée français* by Simon-Célestin Croze-Magnan (1750–1818), Ennio Quirino Visconti and Toussaint-Bernard Eméric-David, engraving two plates after Giovanni Paolo Panini. He also engraved plates for the second volume of Count Alexandre-Louis-Joseph de Laborde's *Voyage d'Espagne* (1812) and finally for the *Monuments anciens et modernes de l'Indouistan* published by Louis-Mathieu Langles in 1821.

BIBLIOGRAPHY

M. Roux: *Inventaire du fonds français: Graveurs du dix-huitième siècle*, Paris, Bib. N., Dépt Est. cat., vi (Paris, 1949), pp. 47–62

M. F. Pérez: 'Quelques lettres concernant Jean-Jacques de Boissieu (1736–1810)', *Archvs A. Fr.*, xxviii (1986), pp. 115–32

MARIE-FÉLICIE PÉREZ

Daulat (*fl c.* 1596–1640). Indian miniature painter. He began his career in the imperial Mughal atelier under Akbar (*reg* 1556–1605) and became a major painter during the reign of Jahangir (*reg* 1605–27), specializing in portraiture. His early works, which appear in the *Akbarnāma* ('History of Akbar') of 1596–7 (London, BL, Or. MS. 12988 and Dublin, Chester Beatty Lib., MS. 3; alternatively dated *c.* 1604) and the *Bābarnāma* ('History of Babar') of 1597–9 (New Delhi, N. Mus.) are distinguished by clusters of narrow-shouldered, voluminous figures and a bright palette intensified by pronounced contour shading. His facial types are quite individualized, but share dark features, full cheeks and large, staring eyes, the latter frequently directed at the viewer. An unusual self-conciousness marks even Daulat's earliest works. In addition to the customary scribal ascription in the lower margin, one of his three illustrations in the *Akbarnāma* and three of his four illustrations in the *Bābarnāma* are identified by minute signatures hidden within the painting. A simple statement of authorship 'the work of Daulat' (*'amal-i Daulat*) appears on the golden girdle of a soldier in the lower left of fol. 14*v* of the *Bābarnāma*. Other signatures are embellished with formulaic expressions of humility usually employed by calligraphers. Several of these epithets, including one on a *Bābarnāma* page dated 1598–9 (fol. 228*r*), contain the phrase 'the least of the houseborn', indicating that Daulat's father was a painter in the imperial workshops. His identity is established by an inscription on a border figure on *An Imaginary Gathering of Sages* of *c.* 1640 (San Diego, CA, Mus. A., 1990.353), which reads 'Muhammad Daulat, son of La'l'. An inscription in the dispersed *Razmnāma* ('Book of war') of 1598–9, a Persian translation of the Hindu epic the *Mahābhārata*, indicates that Daulat's little-known brother Da'ud also served in the imperial atelier.

Daulat not only signed a number of works but also depicted himself several times, once in a lightly coloured drawing in the border of a *Dīvān* (collected poems) of Hafiz (1605; London, BL, Or. MS. 7573), and again in a superb double-portrait with the renowned scribe 'Abd al-Rahim added in January 1610 to the colophon page of a *Khamsa* ('Five poems') of Nizami (1593–5; London, BL, Or. MS. 12208; see fig.). Another self-portrait appears among Daulat's full-colour portraits of five important painters of the Jahangir period in the borders of a folio of the *Muraqqa'-i gulshan* (Tehran, Gulistan Pal. Lib.,

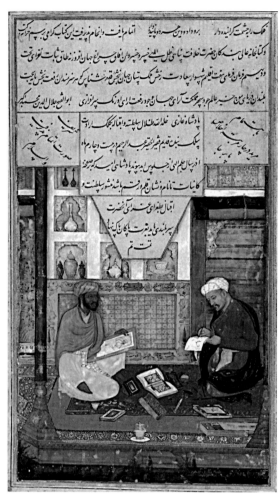

Daulat: *Self-portrait with the Scribe 'Abd al-Rahim ('Amber-pen')
Surrounded by their Professional Tools*, 200×109 mm, added in 1610 to
the colophon page of a *Khamsa* of Nizami, 1593–5 (London, British
Library, Or. MS. 12208, fol. 325v)

MS. 1663/64, p. 44). Unsurpassed in both technique and
degree of characterization, Daulat's many figures in this
album can be dated by one image of a youth inscribed
'work of the poor, the miserable Daulat Muhammad
during the month of Dhu'l-Qa'da 1018' (Jan–Feb 1610).
Daulat's skill at formal portraiture is also evident in such
works as the portrait of *'Inayat Khan* in the Kevorkian
Album (*c.* 1615; New York, Met., 55.121.10, fol. 29). His
ability to portray unique individuals beyond the court circle
is clear in the painting *A Dervish and a Musician* (*c.* 1610;
priv. col., see 1978–9 exh. cat., no. 38), inscribed in a
minute hand 'the work of the poor Daulat'.

Four signed and numerous attributed floral border
decorations in the Kevorkian Album and the Minto Album
(London, V&A, IM. 8-1925 to 28-1925, and Dublin,
Chester Beatty Lib., MS. 7) suggest that the last two
decades of Daulat's career were divided between border
illumination and the occasional portrait or illustration in

such manuscripts as the *Pādshāhnāma* ('History of the
Emperor'; Windsor Castle, Royal Lib., MS. HB. 149).

See also INDIAN SUBCONTINENT, §V, 4(i)(c).

BIBLIOGRAPHY
Y. Godard: 'Les Marges du *Murakka'* Gulshan', *Athar-e Iran*, i (1936),
    pp. 11–33
The Grand Mogul: Imperial Painting in India, 1600–1660 (exh. cat. by
    M. C. Beach, Williamstown, MA, Clark A. Inst.; Baltimore, MD, Walters
    A.G.; Boston, MA, Mus. F.A.; New York, Asia Soc. Gals; 1978–9)
J. Losty: 'The "Bute Hafiz" and the Development of Border Decoration
    in the Manuscript Studio of the Mughals', *Burl. Mag.*, cxxvii/993
    (1985), pp. 855–71
M. Randhawa: *Paintings of the Babur-Nama* (New Delhi, 1985)
S. C. Welch and others: *The Emperors' Album* (New York, 1987)
A. K. Das: 'Daulat', *Master Artists of the Imperial Mughal Court*, ed. P. Pal
    (Bombay, 1991), pp. 87–104

JOHN SEYLLER

Daulatabad [Daulatābād; anc. Devagiri, Deogiri]. Fortress site in central Maharashtra, India, a key link in the
chain of forts that once controlled the Deccan. The conical
mountain of granite, rising over 180 m, was originally a
Buddhist monastic site; some of its excavated shrines were
incorporated into the earliest defences, which were probably created in the 9th century AD by a feudatory of the
RASHTRAKUTA dynasty. In 1187, the YADAVA king Billama
V (*reg* 1185–93) made Devagiri his capital, after which a
succession of dynasties vied for its control. Devagiri first
fell in 1293 to the powerful Sultanate armies of 'Ala al-
Din Khalji (*reg* 1296–1316). The Jami' Mosque was
founded in 1318; recycled temple pillars figure in its
construction. After the TUGHLUQ dynasty took control of
the Sultanate in 1320, they continued a policy of expansion
into the Deccan. In 1328, feeling that Delhi was too far
from his military operations, Muhammad Tughluq
(*reg* 1325–51) moved the capital and all its inhabitants to
Devagiri, which he renamed Daulatabad, but this experiment was a failure, and in 1330 both court and population
returned to Delhi. As Tughluq power declined, the Governor of the Deccan, who had been left in charge of
Daulatabad, declared his independence in 1347 as Bahman
Shah and took the citadel, which was held by the BAHMANI
dynasty until 1526, when it was captured by the NIZAM
SHAHI princes. The prominent Chand Minar (Victory
Tower; h. 30.5 m) was built in 1435 under the Bahmanis.
It has four circular storeys with a fluted central section;
some of the glazed Persian-style tilework with which it
was clad is still visible. In 1636 the MUGHAL dynasty under
Shah Jahan (*reg* 1628–58) captured Daulatabad and held it
until the death of Aurangzeb (*reg* 1658–1707), when it
finally passed to the Nizams of Hyderabad.

The major military features of Daulatabad seem to date
from the Yadava period. Of the town's three (or possibly
four) concentric lines of fortification, Muslim dynasties
were responsible only for the outermost; they also
appear to have strengthened the gates in the second
circuit wall. The isolated rock of the citadel was ringed by
a moat and scarped all round to create an unscalable face.
The sole entrance to the stronghold was across a causeway
that the defenders could submerge by raising the level of
water in the moat, and along a wall-walk skirting a high
bastion. From the wall-walk, steps mount to a cavernous
L-shaped guard-chamber beyond which a narrow passage

leads to a small open court before the portal of a tunnel. The portal is embellished like the door of a Yadava-period temple. The dark, tortuous tunnel was barred by retractable stone slabs sealed with an iron trap-door; steps connect natural caves that housed additional guards and a ventilated chamber in which smoke could be produced to suffocate those attempting ascent.

See also INDIAN SUBCONTINENT, §III, 6(ii)(f) and MILITARY ARCHITECTURE AND FORTIFICATION, §V.

BIBLIOGRAPHY

L. F. Rushbrook Williams, ed.: *A Handbook for Travellers in India, Pakistan, Burma and Ceylon* (London, 21/1968), pp. 57–9

P. Davies: Penguin Guide Mnmts India, ii (London, 1989)

C. Tadgell: *The History of Architecture in India: From the Dawn of Civilisation to the End of the Raj* (London, 1990), pp. 150, 161–2, illus. p. 165

J. MARR, CHRISTOPHER TADGELL

Daullé, Jean (*b* Abbeville, 18 May 1703; *d* Paris, 23 April 1763). French printmaker and print publisher. He was a pupil of Robert Hecquet and came to specialize in engraved portraits. In 1735 he met the portrait painter Hyacinthe Rigaud and quickly became his favourite engraver, producing his best work after Rigaud's portraits. His *Comtesse de Caylus* and *Hyacinthe Rigaud* were so admired that he was approved (*agréé*) and admitted (*reçu*) by the Académie Royale on the same day, 2 June 1742. He was appointed Graveur du Roi in 1743 and *c.* 1757 became a member of the academy of Augsburg. From 1753 he engraved many paintings for the Galerie de Dresde, including *Quos Ego* and the *Artist's Children* after Rubens. Between 1748 and 1755 he gradually gave up portraits, to devote himself to mythological and genre scenes, mainly after François Boucher but also after Joseph Vernet, David Teniers the younger, Adam Frans van der Meulen and Jean-François de Troy. Around 1754 he became a publisher and made fewer prints; from 1758 he entrusted some of his work to his pupils. In 1769 his widow published a collection of 84 of his prints. Daullé produced almost 200 engravings; his work, especially in the portraits, was meticulous. Although the quality was sometimes uneven, his best work places him among the finest of the reproductive engravers of the first half of the 18th century.

BIBLIOGRAPHY

J. Delignières: *Catalogue raisonné de l'oeuvre gravé de Jean Daullé* (Abbeville, 1873)

M. Roux: *Inventaire du fonds français: Graveurs du dix-huitième siècle*, Paris, Bib. N., Cab. Est. cat., vi (Paris, 1949), pp. 62–137

P. Jean-Richard: *L'Oeuvre gravé de François Boucher dans la Collection Edmond de Rothschild* (Paris, 1978), pp. 159–71

V. Meyer: 'Jean Daullé et l'édition', *Gaz. B.-A.*, n. s. 5, cxix (1992), pp. 99–122

VÉRONIQUE MEYER

Daum. French family of glassmakers. In 1878 Jean Daum (*b* Bischwiller, 1825; *d* Nancy, 1885), from Alsace, acquired a glass factory, which he renamed Verrerie de Nancy, and there began to produce traditional tableware. His eldest son, Auguste Daum (1853–1909), joined the factory in 1879 and was followed by Antonin Daum (1864–1930), who managed the business from 1887. To save the company from financial ruin, the brothers enlarged the range of coloured glassware in the 1890s, producing etched, moulded and cameo glass with naturalistic motifs in the Art Nouveau style inspired by the work of their fellow townsman EMILE GALLÉ. Painters and decorators, chief among them being Henri Bergé, provided designs executed by numerous skilled craftsmen under the supervision of Auguste. The originality of Daum glass lies in the diversity of such decorative techniques as enamelling, etching and casing developed for large-scale production, rather than in the quality of decoration. All pieces made after 1890 bore signatures.

During the 1890s the Daum brothers collaborated with LOUIS MAJORELLE in the design and production of lamps and vases. Daum glass was exhibited regularly at international exhibitions and won a Grand Prix at the Exposition Universelle of 1900 in Paris. In 1901 Auguste and Antonin were, with Emile Gallé as president, founder-members of the Alliance Provinciale des Industries d'Art (later known as the Ecole de Nancy). In 1906 a *pâte de verre* workshop was opened and directed by Almaric Walter (1859–1942). After World War I Auguste's sons, Paul (*b* 1890, deported 1944) and Henri (1894–1966), began producing clear glass in free forms with deep, acid-etched decoration; a new range was exhibited at the Exposition des Arts Decoratifs et Industriels in Paris, 1925. After temporary closure during World War II, the firm was reopened by Antonin's son, Michel (*b* ?Nancy, 1900), who aimed at a more exclusive market with sparkling crystal glass of a high lead content. Production of *pâte de verre* was resumed after 1966, with limited editions of glass sculptures from a variety of artists, including Salvador Dalí. As president of the firm, Antonin's nephew Jacques (*b* ?Nancy, 1919; *d* 5 March 1987) was the last member of the family to have an official connection with the Compagnie Française de Cristal Daum.

BIBLIOGRAPHY

V. Arwas: *Glass: Art Nouveau to Art Deco* (London, 1977), pp. 45–51

N. Daum *Daum: Maîtres verriers* (Lausanne, 1980)

CLAIRE BRISBY

Daumet, (Pierre-Gérôme-)Honoré (*b* Paris, 23 Oct 1826; *d* Paris, 12 Dec 1911). French architect. A student of Guillaume Abel Blouet and Emile Gilbert, he won the Grand Prix in 1855. His years in Rome culminated with a pioneering study of Hadrian's Villa at Tivoli, which presaged a talent for manipulating diverse fragments into a picturesque but rational order. Following an expedition to Macedonia commissioned by Louis-Napoleon and led by the archaeologist Léon Heuzey in 1861, he began a career in public architecture and teaching in Paris. His studio produced nine Grand Prix winners and attracted numerous foreigners, including Charles McKim (1847–1909). In 1867 he was appointed to assist Louis Duc at the Palais de Justice in Paris, beginning a 44-year contribution to the epic 19th-century project of selectively restoring and greatly enlarging the ancient palace complex on the Ile de la Cité. Succeeding Duc in 1879, he revised and executed the project for the Cour d'Appel, scenographically incorporating fragments of buildings from different periods. At Grenoble he built the Palais des Facultés (completed 1879) and enlarged the French Renaissance Palais de Justice (1889–97). But his greatest work was his reconstruction of the château of Chantilly (1875–82), where he incorporated 14th-century foundations and the adjacent châtelet by Jean Bullant into a new museum for the collections of the Duc d'Aumale, son of King Louis-Philippe. It was soon donated to the Institut de France, which elected Daumet a member. He subsequently carried out extensive advisory work for Leopold II of Belgium, who ultimately entrusted his projects to Daumet's prize pupil, Charles-Louis Girault. In character, Daumet's work fused the rationalism of his teachers, the sober precision of his friend Emile Vaudremer and the scenography of Charles Garnier.

BIBLIOGRAPHY

H. d'Espouy: 'Daumet', *Architecte*, vii (1912), pp. 17–21

L. Jaussely: 'P.-J. Honoré Daumet', *Bulletin S.A.D.G.*, vii (3 Feb 1912), pp. 53–8

H. Roujon: *Notice sur la vie et les travaux de M. Honoré Daumet* (Paris, 1912)

C. Girault: *Notes sur la vie et les travaux de Honoré Daumet* (Paris, 1919)

The Architecture of the Ecole des Beaux-Arts (exh. cat., ed. A. Drexler; New York, 1975), pp. 224–5, 444–7 [pls of Grand Prix proj. and Chantilly]

KATHERINE FISCHER TAYLOR

Daumier, Honoré (*b* Marseille, 26 Feb 1808; *d* Valmondois, 10 Feb 1879). French graphic artist, painter and sculptor.

1. Training and early illustrations, before 1860. 2. Sculpture. 3. Paintings. 4. Late illustrations, 1860 and after. 5. Posthumous reputation.

1. TRAINING AND EARLY ILLUSTRATIONS, BEFORE 1860. Son of a Marseille glazier, frame-maker and occasional picture restorer, Daumier joined his father in Paris in 1816. He became a bailiff's errand boy and was then employed by a bookseller, but his real enthusiasm was reserved for drawing and politics. He studied drawing with Alexandre Lenoir and at the Académie Suisse and then worked as assistant to the lithographer Béliard. Having mastered the techniques of lithography, he published his first plate in the satirical weekly *La Silhouette* in 1829.

Daumier was 22 when the revolution of July 1830 gave the throne to Louis-Philippe as constitutional monarch and power to the French middle-class business community. On 4 November 1830 the print publisher Aubert and his son-in-law Charles Philipon launched the violently anti-monarchist weekly *La Caricature*, followed on 1 December 1832 by *Le Charivari*, the first daily paper to be illustrated with lithographs. In his association with these newspapers and in the company of Republican artists, Daumier found a favourable milieu for developing his vigorous style and progressive ideas.

Less whimsical than Grandville, less elegant than Gavarni and less brutal than Traviès, Daumier distinguished himself by a robust but controlled drawing style, with strong contrasts of volume that were nonetheless accurate in their composition, modelling and chiaroscuro, even when used in caricature. This feature of his style gained him the support of the new petit bourgeois public, who could appreciate a caricature that was neither vapid nor crude and behind the exaggerated outlines of which could be discerned traditional academic values. Balzac even compared Daumier with Michelangelo. Daumier's attacks on Louis-Philippe hit their mark so successfully that the monarch had to reintroduce censorship and condemned

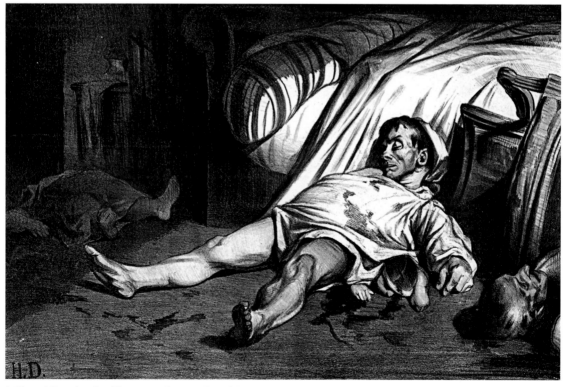

1. Honoré Daumier: *Rue Transnonain, le 15 avril 1834*, lithograph, 290×445 mm, 1834 (Paris, Bibliothèque Nationale); from *Association mensuelle* (1834)

Daumier to six months in prison (31 Aug 1832 to 14 Feb 1833) for his lithograph *Gargantua* (*see* SATIRE, fig. 2), published in *La Caricature* (15 Dec 1831). In order to pay the fines imposed on his newspapers, in 1834 Philipon launched a large-format supplement that was even more violent in tone, the *Association mensuelle*. In its pages Daumier published lithographs that have all the power of paintings and are now considered among his masterpieces: *Le Ventre législatif, Ne vous y frottez pas!, Enfoncé Lafayette* and *Rue Transnonain, le 15 avril 1834* (see fig. 1). In the last, Daumier depicted the squalid aftermath of the massacre of working-class opponents of the government. Daumier's undemonstrative title and unheroicized image of corpses sprawled among overturned bedroom furniture lent force to his denunciation of casual State violence.

On 29 August 1835 the government once more prohibited political caricature, and, in order to survive, *Le Charivari* was forced to restrict itself to subjects from everyday life, including street scenes, the theatre and portraits. It published nearly 4000 of these by Daumier. Various series of humorous scenes, all composed with great care, gave a vivid and critical panorama of France's social classes in transition: businessmen (personified by the flattering swindler Robert Macaire), the professional classes (*Les Gens de justice*, 1845–8), traders and the bourgeois in the country, at the theatre and on public transport (*Les Bons Bourgeois*, 1847–9). His work was not only the essential expression of the new taste for an art that had previously been considered trivial but also reflected developments in French society at the time of its greatest economic expansion (between 1830 and 1870). He was for this reason considered by several progressive critics—Théodore de Banville (1823–91) as early as 1852, Baudelaire in 1857 and Champfleury—as an artist worthy of comparison with Hogarth and Goya.

Besides his lithographs Daumier also made numerous drawings that were reproduced by wood-engravers as illustrations. In this way he participated in some of the great French publishing enterprises of the Romantic era: the series of *Physiologies* (1841), *Les Français peints par eux-mêmes* from the publisher Curmer (1841), *La Némésis médicale illustrée* (1841) and the most important illustrated magazines then in circulation.

2. SCULPTURE. Daumier was one of the first French artists to experiment with caricature sculpture. In 1832 he began to produce a series of small grotesque busts of parliamentarians, for instance *François-Pierre-Guillaume Guizot* and *Alexandre-Simon Pataille* (both Paris, Mus. d'Orsay), which were kept in Aubert's printshop. They were originally modelled in terracotta and were cast in bronze only after his death. Daumier succeeded in giving each of these works (generally no more than 200 mm high) individuality and considerable satiric force by gross exaggeration of his victim's most prominent features and characteristic expression. Among other important sculptures (first modelled in clay, then transferred to plaster and subsequently cast in bronze) were the bas-relief *The Emigrants* (*c.* 1848–50; plaster, Paris, Mus. d'Orsay), in which Daumier depicted a forlorn procession of unindividualized figures with grandeur and compassion, and the statuette *Ratapoil* (*c.* 1851; plaster, Buffalo, Albright–Knox

A.G.), his archetype of the swaggering and corrupt thugs who had brought Louis-Napoléon to power. The dating and priority of the numerous casts of Daumier's sculpture are difficult to establish and remain controversial. Many of Daumier's prints comment sympathetically on the difficulties of the sculptor in mid-19th-century France (e.g. *Sad Appearance of Sculpture Placed in the Midst of Painting*, 1857).

3. PAINTINGS. Although he never sought to make a career from painting and was probably self-taught, Daumier painted for his own pleasure from 1834. From 1847 these isolated attempts gave way to a solid body of work that began with copies of Millet and Rubens and interpretations in oil of details selected from the subjects he habitually treated in lithography, notably genre scenes, bathers, lawyers and so on (e.g. *Three Lawyers in Conversation*; Washington, DC, Phillips Col.). In 1848, following the creation of the Second Republic, an open competition was held among artists to represent it in allegorical form. Daumier produced an oil sketch showing two children being suckled by a muscular female embodiment of the Republic (Paris, Mus. d'Orsay), which was highly praised by Champfleury and Gautier. His design was shortlisted, and he was commissioned to produce a finished painting, but he was unable to complete it. However, he did execute some State commissions for religious paintings, *Mary Magdalene in the Desert* (priv. col., see Maison, 1968, i, pl. 171) and *We Want Barabbas!* (*c.* 1850; Essen, Mus. Flkwang), thanks to his friend Charles Blanc, who became head of the Bureau des Beaux-Arts in 1848. He exhibited at the Salon of 1849 the *Miller, his Son and the Ass* (Glasgow, A.G. & Mus.), in 1850 *Two Nymphs Pursued by Satyrs* (Montreal, Mus. F.A.) and in 1851 *Don Quixote Going to the Wedding of Gamaches* (Boston, priv. col., see Maison, 1968, i, pl. 147). Apart from one further exhibit in 1861 and the exhibition organized by his friends to help him financially in 1878, shortly before he died, Daumier's paintings were unknown to the public and remained in his studio until his death.

Daumier's paintings, more than 300 oils and numerous watercolours, gained widespread critical recognition after his death, for they reveal qualities similar to those that characterize his lithographs. The brushwork is usually rapid and vigorous, and this, together with the sense of movement and light, ranks them with the finest paintings produced under the Second Empire. He sometimes reverted to observations of daily life (e.g. *Third-class Railway Carriage*, 1864; Ottawa, N.G.; Baltimore, MD, Mus. A.; see fig. 2) but frequently drew his subject-matter from mythology (the *Drunkenness of Silenus*, 1863; Calais, Mus. B.-A.) and literature (numerous works featuring Don Quixote and Sancho Panza).

Daumier did not prime his canvases; they are often unfinished and invariably retain a sketch-like appearance. This lack of both preliminary precautions and finish gives a strong effect of spontaneity but makes the paintings fragile and difficult to conserve. Their dating is often uncertain, and when they began to become popular they were extensively 'finished' by restorers and forgers. His usual signature HD has also frequently been forged, often on unsigned genuine works.

2. Honoré Daumier: *Third-class Railway Carriage*, watercolour, 1864 (Baltimore, MD, Museum of Art)

4. LATE ILLUSTRATIONS, 1860 AND AFTER. Abandoned by *Le Charivari* in March 1860, as Philipon claimed (until December 1863) that readers had tired of him, Daumier was free to devote himself to painting, despite his lack of recognition in this field. During the authoritarian phase of the Second Empire in the 1850s satire had lost nearly all its outlets, and *Le Charivari* itself had become feeble. Nevertheless, Daumier recovered his original political and graphic energy in a dozen plates he composed for *Le Boulevard*, a newspaper founded in 1862 in opposition to the regime by his colleague Etienne Carjat. It contained such famous lithographs as *Madeleine-Bastille*, *Le Nouveau Paris* and *Nadar élevant la photographie à la hauteur de l'art*. The *Boulevard* experiment ended in 1863. However, Napoleon III's administration became more liberal, allowing and even encouraging caricature in matters of foreign policy. Daumier tended to treat these subjects with a certain loftiness, in a style that was both more sweeping and more elliptical, making great use of allegory and symbolism. Despite the technical restrictions imposed on the lithographers of *Le Charivari* during the 1870s by the use of *gillotage* (whereby the lithograph was turned into a relief plate to facilitate printing), Daumier's art so gained in luminosity and synthetic power that through the work of his late period he came to be seen as the forerunner of Impressionism, and in particular of Cézanne. Daumier's drawing style in pen and ink also became increasingly free, a mazy line no longer modelling form in any conventional sense, but taking on an expressive form of its own.

The last of Daumier's plates to appear in *Le Charivari* dates from 1875. By 1878 he was nearly blind and living in obscurity at Valmondois, to the north of Paris, in a small house bought for him by his friend Corot. His friends organized an exhibition of his work at Durand-Ruel's gallery, but despite Victor Hugo's acceptance of the honorary presidency and a visit by the eminent Republican Léon Gambetta, it was a complete failure, not even covering its costs.

5. POSTHUMOUS REPUTATION. Daumier's funeral, on 14 February 1879, coincided with the consolidation of power by the Republican party, which he had been among the first to support and whose cause he had so enthusiastically portrayed. His Republican artist friends and a number of politicians reawakened interest in his work through a further campaign of demonstrations, articles, speeches and exhibitions, and brought his body back to Père Lachaise Cemetery, Paris. At the same time critics sought to raise the status of the popular art forms of lithography, caricature and newspaper cartoons. As a result, a violent debate began on Daumier's merits as an artist, which, in France at least, has never been completely resolved: the centenary of his death in 1979 was marked by an exhibition in Marseille rather than Paris. The quality of Daumier's work has more readily been recognized and celebrated in Germany and the USA, where the main private collections are located and where several major exhibitions have been held.

BIBLIOGRAPHY

The Studio (1904) [issue ded. to Daumier and Gavarni]
L. Delteil: *Le Peintre-graveur illustré*, xx–/xxix (Paris, 1925–30/*R* New York, 1969)
E. Bouvy: *Daumier: L'Oeuvre gravé du maître* (Paris, 1933) [wood-engrs and chalk pl. prts]
J. Adhémar: *Honoré Daumier* (Paris, 1954)
Honoré Daumier und sein Kreis (exh. cat., Hamburg, Mus. Kst & Gew., 1962)
O. W. Larkin: *Daumier: Man of his Time* (Boston, 1966)
K. E. Maison: *Honoré Daumier: Catalogue Raisonné of the Paintings, Watercolours and Drawings*, 2 vols (London, 1968) [supplemented by 'Some Additions to Daumier's Oeuvre', *Burl. Mag.*, cxii (1970), pp. 623–4]
H. P. Vincent: *Daumier and his World* (Evanston, 1968)
Daumier Sculpture (exh. cat. by J. L. Wasserman, Cambridge, MA, Fogg, 1969)
A. H. Mayor: 'Daumier', *Prt Colr Newslett.* (March–April 1970), pp. 1–4
L. Barzini and G. Mandel: *Opera pittorica completa di Daumier* (Milan, 1971)
Daumier: Verlaggever van zijn tijd (exh. cat. by J. R. Kist, The Hague, Gemeentemus., 1971)
Honoré Daumier: Druckgraphik aus der Kunsthalle Bielefeld und Privatbesitz (exh. cat. by H. G. Gmelin and L. Fabricius-Josic, Bielefeld, Städt. Ksthalle, 1971)
Honoré Daumier: Gemälde, Zeichnungen, Lithographien, Skulpturen (exh. cat., ed. F. Lachenall; Ingelheim, Int. Tage, Villa Schneider, 1971)
D. Burnell: 'Honoré Daumier and the Composition of Humour', *Prt Colr Newslett.* (Nov–Dec 1973), pp. 102–5
Honoré Daumier . . . Bildwitz und Zeitkritik (exh. cat. by G. Langemeyer, Münster, Westfäl. Kstver.; Bonn, Rhein. Landesmus.; Graz, Neue Gal.; 1978–9)
R. Passeron: *Daumier: Témoin de son temps* (Paris, 1979; Eng. trans., New York, 1981)
Daumier aujourd'hui: 300 lithographies et bois gravés de la collection Louis Provost (exh. cat. by J. Rollin and B. Tabah, Saint-Denis, Mus. A. & Hist., 1979)
Daumier et ses amis républicains (exh. cat., ed. M. Latour; Marseille, Mus. Cantini, 1979)
Daumier in Retrospect, 1808–1879 (exh. cat., Los Angeles, CA, Co. Mus. A., 1979)
Honoré Daumier, 1808–1879 (exh. cat. by J. R. Kist, Washington, DC, N.G.A., 1979)
Honoré Daumier et les dessins de presse (exh. cat., Grenoble, Maison Cult., 1979)
Honoré Daumier: Kunst und Karikatur (exh. cat., ed. J. Schultze and A. Winther; Bremen, Ksthalle, 1979)
P. L. Senna: 'Daumier's Lithographic Works', *Prt Colr/Conoscitore Stampe*, 45 (1980), pp. 2–31
'Honoré Daumier: A Centenery Tribute', *Prt Rev.*, 11 (1980), pp. 5–144
Honoré Daumier, 1808–1879 (Los Angeles, 1982)
J. L. Wasserman, J. de Caso and J. Adhémar: 'Hypothèses sur les sculptures de Daumier', *Gaz. B.-A.*, n.s. 6, c (1983), pp. 57–80
Die Rückkehr der Barbaren: Europäer und 'Wilde' in der Karikatur Honoré Daumiers (exh. cat., ed. A. Stoll; Bielefield, Städt. Ksthalle; Hannover, Wilhelm-Busch-Mus.; Freiburg, Augustinum.; Mülheim an der Ruhr, Städt. Mus.; 1985–6)
M. Melot: 'Daumier and Art History: Aesthetic Judgement/Political Judgement', *Oxford A. J.*, xi/1 (1988), pp. 3–24
The Charged Image: French Lithographic Caricature, 1816–1848 (exh. cat. by B. Farwell, Santa Barbara, CA, Mus. A., 1989)
B. Laughton: *The Drawings of Daumier and Millet* (New Haven and London, 1991)
Daumier Drawings (exh. cat., ed. C. Ives, M. Stuffman and C. Sonnabend; New York, Met., 1992)

MICHEL MELOT

Dauzats, Adrien (*b* Bordeaux, 16 July 1804; *d* Paris, 18 Feb 1868). French painter, illustrator and writer. His early training was as a theatrical scene painter and a designer of lithographic illustrations. In Bordeaux he studied with Pierre Lacour (ii) (1778–1859) and worked with Thomas Olivier (1772–1839), chief scene designer at the Grand-Théâtre. He subsequently studied in Paris in the studio of the landscape and history painter Julien-Michel Gué (1789–1843) and worked for the decorators of the Théâtre Italien.

From 1827 Dauzats provided lithographic designs for Isidore-Justin-Séverin Taylor's series *Voyages pittoresques et romantiques dans l'ancienne France* (1820–78). He travelled in the French provinces, particularly Champagne, Dauphiné and Languedoc, often sketching the medieval monuments that had come into vogue during the Romantic period.

Dauzats also collaborated on lithographs for many other publications, including Taylor's *Voyage en Orient*. For this last project Dauzats travelled to Egypt, Syria, Palestine and Turkey in 1830, a trip that he described in his book *Quinze jours au Sinaï* (written with Alexandre Dumas *père*) and that ultimately inspired his best-known painting, the *Monastery of St Catherine, Mt Sinaï* (exh. Salon 1845; Paris, Louvre). Its medieval subject and dramatic setting clearly show his training as a stage designer; despite his reputation as a brilliant colourist it has a sober and restricted tonal range.

A specialist in architectural views, Dauzats travelled widely in Spain, Portugal, Germany and the Netherlands. Perhaps his most memorable journey, however, was in 1839, when he accompanied the military expedition to southern Algeria led by Ferdinand-Philippe, Duc d'Orléans. Dauzats recorded the assault on the Gates of Iron, a formidable natural fortress in the Djurdjura mountains, in his lithographic illustrations for the *Journal de l'expédition des Portes de Fer* compiled by the poet Charles Nodier in 1844. His series of watercolour studies of the Gates of Iron (Chantilly, Mus. Condé), on which he based his painting the *Gates of Iron* (1853; Lille, Mus. B.-A.), captures the sombre and forbidding atmosphere of the place.

Dauzats exhibited at the Salon from 1831 to 1867, winning numerous medals. He was awarded the Légion d'honneur as early as 1837. Though most of the views he depicted were derived from his own observations, he did accept a commission from a Bordeaux collector around 1865 for a series of four paintings from the *Thousand and One Nights*. Even in an imaginary scene such as his *Sindbad the Sailor* (1865; Bordeaux, Mus. B.-A.), however, the architecture, based on his recollections of Granada and Córdoba, completely dominates the human figure. The Orientalist architectural scenes in which Dauzats specialized, though often encountered in the work of English topographical artists such as David Roberts, were relatively rare in France.

Delacroix admired Dauzats's abilities as an architectural painter and consulted him for advice on at least one occasion: Dauzats in turn exercised his influence at court to help Delacroix win state decorative commissions. In his preference for depicting remote and inhospitable places and his taste for picturesque medieval subjects, Dauzats was fully in accord with the aesthetics of Romantic art. He had an unfailing instinct for selecting exotic and memorable views. Unlike his contemporary Prosper Marilhat, however, his need to record precisely all the details of a scene sometimes prevented him from capturing the subject in its most colourful and dramatic aspect.

WRITINGS

with A. Dumas *père*: *Quinze jours au Sinaï* (Paris, 1841)

BIBLIOGRAPHY

H. Jouin: *Adrien Dauzats: Peintre et écrivain* (Paris, 1896)

P. Guinard: *Dauzats et Blanchard: Peintres de l'Espagne romantique* (Paris, 1967)

Orientalism: The Near East in French Painting, 1800–1880 (exh. cat., U. Rochester, NY, Mem. A.G., 1982), pp. 48–9

The Orientalists: Delacroix to Matisse (exh. cat., ed. M. A. Stevens; London, RA; Washington, DC, N.G.A.; 1984), p. 123

DONALD A. ROSENTHAL

Davenport Bromley, Rev. Walter (*b* 1787; *d* 1863). English cleric and collector. The younger brother of Edward Davies Davenport of Capesthorne Hall, Cheshire, he added the name Bromley in 1822 on succeeding to the Bromley properties, which included Wootton Hall, Staffs. He first went to Italy in the same year and is thought to have begun at this time to collect Italian pictures, including *Agony in the Garden* by Giovanni Bellini (London, N.G.). From the sale of the collection of Cardinal Joseph Fesch (uncle of Napoleon Bonaparte) in Rome in 1845 he bought among other works Giotto's *Death of the Virgin* (Berlin, Gemäldegal.). Gustav Friedrich Waagen described him on a visit he made to Wootton Hall: 'Mr. Davenport Bromley is an ardent admirer of all such pictures . . . in which an unaffected and genuine feeling is expressed. I found, accordingly, in his house a number of works, chiefly altarpieces, illustrating the Italian school from their first rise in the 13th century to their highest development in the 16th, such as I have not yet met with . . . in any other gallery in England.' He owned also a house at 32 Grosvenor Street, London, where part of his collection was hung. On his death many of the pictures were sold by his son William, who inherited Capesthorne Hall and changed his name to Bromley Davenport.

BIBLIOGRAPHY

G. F. Waagen: *Treasures of Art in Great Britain*, iii (London, 1854/*R* 1970), pp. 371–80

D. Sutton: 'From Ottley to Eastlake', *Apollo*, cxxiii (1985), p. 88

Davent, Léon [L.D.] (*fl* 1540–56). French engraver. Very little is known about his life and career. Only one of his engravings, the *Apostles Contemplating Christ and the Virgin* (1546; Zerner, L.D. 55) after Giulio Romano, bears a full name, 'Lion Daven'; all the others have merely the monogram 'L.D.', under which his work is usually catalogued. Until Herbet's study, this monogram was taken to be the signature of the Fleming Léonard Thiry. Davent made engravings from 1540, turning to etching *c.* 1543–4. Herbet attributed 221 plates to him, Zerner only 98.

Davent reproduced principally the works of Francesco Primaticcio, whose style he rendered boldly and freely. Zerner considered him the finest engraver of the school of Fontainebleau. Davent was able to reproduce the elegance and grace of Primaticcio, and his best works—*Jason Slaying the Dragon* (z 16), *Rebecca and Eliezer* (z 23), *The Goddesses* and *The Muses* (z 25–36) and the medallion-shaped prints showing hunting and fishing (z 77–9), dated 1547—have a luminous poetry. He left Fontainebleau and established himself in Paris as a 'maistre eslumineur et engraveur demourant rue Sainct Jacques', illustrating *Les Quatre Premiers Livres des navigations et pérégrinations orientales* for the geographer and royal valet-de-chambre Nicolas de Nicolay. This was published in Lyon in 1548 by Guillaume Rouille the elder: Davent is assigned 61 illustrations in Herbet's catalogue (nos 95–156) but only 3 in Zerner's. The work was earlier attributed, by Baudrier and Adhémar, to a certain Louis Danet. However, Grodecki has published a contract made in 1555 between Nicolay and 'Lion Davant' for illustrations to a *Livre de la diversitée des habits du Levant*. Davent was still working in 1556, the date of the 33rd plate in the collection, *Candilesquer* (z 98), but as the publication contained only 61 plates and not the projected 80, it seems likely that he died before completing it.

BIBLIOGRAPHY

H. Baudrier and J. Baudrier: *Bibliographie lyonnaise*, 12 vols (Lyon, 1895–1921)

F. Herbet: *Les Graveurs de l'école de Fontainebleau*, i of *Catalogue de l'oeuvre de L.D.* (Fontainebleau, 1896–1901)

J. Adhémar: *Inventaire du fonds français: Graveurs du seizième siècle*, Paris, Bib. N., Cab. Est. cat., ii (Paris, 1938), pp. 284–98

H. Zerner: *Ecole de Fontainebleau: Gravures* (Paris, 1969) [z]

L'Ecole de Fontainebleau (exh. cat., Paris, Grand Pal., 1972–3)

H. Zerner: *Italian Artists of the Sixteenth Century*, 33 [XVI/ii] of *The Illustrated Bartsch*, ed. W. Strauss (New York, 1978–), pp. 307–33

C. Grodecki: *Documents du minutier central des notaires de Paris: Histoire de l'art au XVIe siècle (1540–1600)* (Paris, 1986)

MARIANNE GRIVEL

Davey, William Turner (*b* 1818; *d c.* 1890). English engraver. He was a pupil of Charles Rolls (*fl c.* 1820–55). He ultimately became known for his reproductions of such celebrated pictures as Henry Nelson O'Neil's *Eastward Ho! August 1857* (1858, priv. col.; declared for publication by Lloyd Bros & Co. in Nov 1860) and its companion *Home Again* (1859, priv. col.; declared by Moore, McQueen & Co. in Sept 1862). One of his most brilliant achievements was the large engraving in mixed mezzotint of Lady Butler's *Return from Inkerman* (Hull, Ferens A.G.), for which he received £1100. The print was commissioned by the Fine Art Society and declared for publication in April 1878. Davey exhibited 13 pieces at the Royal Academy between 1859 and 1884.

BIBLIOGRAPHY

Victorian Engravings (exh. cat. by H. Beck, London, V&A, 1973)

Great Victorian Pictures (exh. cat. by R. Treble, ACGB, 1978), pp. 62–3

R. K. Engen: *Dictionary of Victorian Engravers* (Cambridge, 1979)

ANTHONY DYSON

David I, King of Scotland (*b c.* 1085; *reg* 1124–53; *d* Carlisle, 24 May 1153). Scottish monarch and patron. He was the sixth and youngest son of Malcolm III (*reg* 1058–93) and St Margaret (1045–93) and the third of those sons to succeed to the throne of Scotland. After *c.* 1093 he was educated mainly at the English court. In 1113 his brother-in-law, Henry I of England, married him to England's richest widow, Matilda (*d* 1130–31), Countess of Northampton and Huntingdon, and he became Earl of Huntingdon. He was profoundly pious and took a close interest in the Church during a period of fervent reform.

Following the accession of his brother, Alexander I, in Scotland in 1107, David was allowed some authority over the southern parts of the kingdom and in 1113 established at Selkirk a house for the Tironensian Order, the first house in the British Isles for any of the reformed monastic orders. Both before and after he became king in 1124 David made great efforts to bring the Scottish Church into line with that of England and put much energy into founding or re-establishing the dioceses, setting up a network of properly endowed parishes and introducing several of the monastic orders. Among the many foundations with which he was involved were Benedictine houses at Dunfermline, May, Rhynd and Urquhart; Tironensian houses at Kelso and Lesmahagow; Cistercian houses at Coupar Angus, Dundrennan, Kinloss, Melrose and Newbattle; and Augustinian houses at Cambuskenneth, Holyrood, Inchcolm, Jedburgh, Loch Leven, Restenneth and St Andrews. All these foundations required buildings on a scale unprecedented in Scotland. In thus patronizing the Church David was also keenly aware of the benefits of introducing additional forms of centralized control over an unruly kingdom, but it is doubtful if so poor a nation could afford such a well-endowed Church, and his successors were rather less generous in their patronage. He was widely regarded as a saint, although James I of Scotland (*reg* 1406–37) described him ruefully as 'ane sair sanct for the croun'.

BIBLIOGRAPHY
G. Barrow: *The Kingdom of the Scots* (London, 1973), pp. 165–211
RICHARD FAWCETT

David, Claude (*fl* 1678; *d* after 1721). French sculptor, active in Italy and England. Originally from Burgundy, he is first recorded in 1678 in Rome, carving ivory crucifixes. From 1695 to 1699 he worked in Genoa, carving marble statuary for S Maria Assunta in Carignano. His *Assumption* group, originally intended for the high altar, was later finished by Bernardo Schiaffino and placed above the main door of the church. He also made, for the same church, statues of *St Peter*, *St Paul* and *St Bartholomew*. The last, in a strong, naturalistic style, was intended to complement statues of *St Sebastian* and *Bishop Alessandro Sauli* by Pierre Puget. From around 1706 David was working in London. A design by him for a fountain, to be erected in Cheapside, was apparently seen by George Vertue, who wrote that it had figures of river gods and an equestrian statue of *John Churchill, 1st Duke of Marlborough* and was surmounted by a statue of *Queen Anne*. David also made a marble statue of *Prometheus* (London, V&A), formerly at Narford Hall, Norfolk, and a series of statues now on the stables at Longleat House, Wilts. His best-known surviving English work is the marble wall monument to *Philip Carteret* (*d* 1710) in Westminster Abbey. This consists of a bust of the deceased, with a small figure of *Time* in the style of Bernini. In 1721 David tried to raise by subscription £2500 for an equestrian statue of *George I* for St James's Square, London (not executed).

BIBLIOGRAPHY
Gunnis; Thieme–Becker
'The Note-books of George Vertue', *Walpole Soc.*, xx (1932), p. 87
K. Lankheit: *Florentinische Barockplastik: Die Kunst am Hofe der letzten Medici, 1670–1743* (Munich, 1962), pp. 149, 306
M. Whinney: *Sculpture in Britain, 1530–1830*, Pelican Hist. A. (Harmondsworth, 1964, rev. 1988), p. 449, n. 15

David [Davit; Davidt], **Gerard** [Gheeraert; Gheeraedt; Gherat] (*b* Oudewater, nr Gouda, *c.* 1460; *d* Bruges, 13 Aug 1523). Netherlandish painter. He is known as the last of the 'Flemish Primitives'. Although born in the northern Netherlands, he moved to Bruges as a young man, and most of his work expresses the impassive, unmannered, microscopically realistic approach peculiar to south Netherlandish art in the time of Jan van Eyck. David was skilled at synthesizing the art of several important south Netherlandish predecessors, adapting, for instance, the compositions of van Eyck and the technique of Hugo van der Goes. He was also influenced by Hans Memling, whose example led him to refine and polish his cruder northern Netherlandish style and to adopt the popular theme of the Virgin and Child enthroned.

It is difficult to trace David's development with certainty, since all his dated works are restricted to the period 1498–1509. Moreover, there are no signed works. However, approximately 60 paintings can be ascribed to him with some authority: about half are single devotional panels, mainly Epiphanies and scenes from the Passion of Christ. There are about ten religious triptychs and one or two polyptychs, but only one secular work, the *Cambyses* diptych (Bruges, Groeningenmus.; *see* §1(ii) below), and, even more significantly, only one surviving portrait, the *Portrait of an Ecclesiastic* (?*c.* 1484–98; London, N.G.). In contrast to Memling, who had a large private clientele, David's patrons were primarily churches, monasteries, convents, societies and magistrates.

1. Life and work. 2. Working methods and technique. 3. Critical reception and posthumous reputation.

1. LIFE AND WORK.

(i) Early work, before 1484. It is usually supposed that David received his training in his native Holland. His earliest work is clearly related to that of painters from Haarlem, such as Dirk Bouts and Geertgen tot Sint Jans, and especially the work attributed to Jacob Jansz. (*fl* 1483–1509). Among the works David probably painted while still in Holland are two triptychs, one with *Christ Nailed to the Cross* (central panel, London, N.G.; wings, with soldiers and weeping women, Antwerp, Kon. Mus. S. Kst.) and the other with the *Nativity* (New York, Met.), three paintings of the *Crucifixion* (Madrid, Mus. Thyssen-Bornemisza; Norfolk, VA, Chrysler Mus.; Winterthur, Samml. Oskar Reinhart), an *Adoration of the Shepherds* (Budapest, Mus. F.A.) and the *Tree of Jesse* (Lyon, Mus. B.-A.). The works from this early period are more rustic and picturesque than his later works, the lighting clearer, the tones warmer, especially in the atmospheric landscapes. The figures are less monumental and more anecdotal, as might be expected of an artist from the northern Netherlands, and the fine and supple drapery is carefully rendered with strong tactile effects. The colouring is variegated, with striking saffron yellow and clear red accents.

(ii) Middle period, 1484–1511. David had settled in Bruges by 14 January 1484, when he became a master of the Guild of St Luke there. His early career in the city coincided with the troubled period in which Ghent and Bruges revolted against the governorship of Maximilian of Austria following the death of his wife, Mary, Duchess of Burgundy.

David was appointed second juror of the painters' guild in 1488, the same year the municipal government of Bruges was overthrown. Between 1 September 1487 and 1 March 1488 he received an advance of four pounds for an important municipal commission to make a 'costly' painting for the aldermen's room of the town hall. This picture might have been ordered by the new town government as a result of the events of 1488. Although documents relating to the commission record the subject as a *Last Judgement*, it is possible that they refer to a monumental diptych (Bruges, Groeningemus.) with the *Judgement of Cambyses* (for illustration *see* JUSTICE SCENES) and the *Flaying of Sisamnes*, which David completed in 1498 but for which he received an interim payment in 1491. The *Cambyses* panels are devoted to the theme of justice and corruption and represent scenes from a Persian story, recorded by Herodotus (*Histories* V.28), in which the corrupt judge Sisamnes is arrested and flayed alive on the orders of King Cambyses. Some of the heads are no doubt portraits, possibly of the governing magistrates.

From 1494 David lived in a house in the St Jorisstraat, near the house of Memling, who died in that year. Some time later he married Cornelia, daughter of Jacob Cnoop, a well-known goldsmith in Bruges. He later also owned a house on the Dijver (mentioned in 1522), but he probably kept his studio in the St Jorisstraat in order to take advantage of the commercial potential of the area following Memling's death. In 1495 and 1498 David was again made juror of the painters' guild. Other works probably dating from between 1484 and 1498 include the *Annunciation* (Detroit, MI, Inst. A.), the *Nativity* (Cleveland,

OH, Mus. A.), the *Adoration of the Magi* (Brussels, Mus. A. Anc.) and the *Virgin and Child* (Berlin, Gemäldegal.).

David became dean in 1501 and from this year received a series of important altarpiece commissions. David's skill in faithfully representing such everyday objects as tableware and food, which prefigures the worldly outlook of Pieter Aertsen and 17th-century still-life painting, is well demonstrated in the *Marriage at Cana* (Paris, Louvre), painted shortly after 1501 for Jan de Sedano, a member of the Spanish colony in Bruges. The donor, who became a member of the Brotherhood of the Holy Blood in the same year, is shown wearing the tabard of the Brotherhood, kneeling with his wife at the lower right. The same couple, identified by the coat of arms, appears on the wings of an earlier work by David, the Sedano Triptych of the *Virgin Enthroned with Music-making Angels* (Paris, Louvre), a devotional work that clearly reveals the influence of Memling.

Between 1500 and 1511 David painted two altarpieces for two different canons of the church of St Donatian, Bruges. Canon Bernardinus de Salviatis, the son of a Florentine merchant, commissioned an altarpiece for the altar of St John the Baptist, of which only the left panel, *Bernardinus de Salviatis and Three Saints* (*c.* 1501–2; London, N.G.) survives. The other donor, the cantor Richard de Visch van de Capelle, is portrayed kneeling in the *Virgin and Child with Female Saints* (London, N.G.); he commissioned this painting for the altar of St Catherine in the chapel of St Anthony, which he was granted permission to furnish in 1500. From the same period dates the triptych with the *Baptism* (Bruges, Groeningemus.;

1. Gerard David: triptych with the *Baptism*, oil on panel, 1320×431 mm (left wing), 1297×966 mm (central panel), 1322×422 mm (right wing), commissioned before 1502, installed 1520 (Bruges, Groeningemuseum)

2. Gerard David: *Virgo inter Virgines*, oil on panel, 1.18×2.12 m, before 1509 (Rouen, Musée des Beaux-Arts)

see fig. 1), commissioned before 1502 by Jan de Trompes, Bailiff of Ostend and Receiver-general of Flanders. He is shown on the inner wings with his first wife (*d* 1502) and children; he later had the portrait of his second wife added on the outer wings, probably *c*. 1507–8. The work was not installed until 1520 (after the donor's death), when it was placed on the magistrates' altar in the church of St Basilius, Bruges. The triptych is one of David's most remarkable works, due not only to its imposing religious gravity but also to its accurate and atmospheric rendering of nature. In fact, the important place that David accorded to the landscape and its integration within the composition were fundamental for the later development of panoramic landscape painting from Joachim Patinir onwards. According to a lost document, on 7 September 1506 David completed another altarpiece, a polyptych more than 3 m high for the abbey church of S Girolamo della Cervara in Liguria, Italy. It is unlikely, however, that he ever visited Italy himself. An 18th-century description by Don Giuseppe Spinola enabled the panels of the polyptych (now dispersed) to be identified: the central panel depicts the *Virgin and Child Enthroned*, the two lower wings *St Jerome* and *St Benedict* (all Genoa, Pal. Bianco); the two upper wings show the *Virgin* and the *Archangel Gabriel* (both New York, Met.), and the lunette above has *God the Father and Two Angels* (Paris, Louvre).

In 1507–8 David became a member of the Brotherhood of Our Lady of the Dry Tree, a religious society housed in the Minorite church, the members of which were mostly aristocrats or citizens of good standing. In 1509 he donated ('out of pity') his painting of the *Virgo inter Virgines* (*Virgin and Child Enthroned with Female Saints*; Rouen, Mus. B.-A.; see fig. 2) to the Carmelite convent of Sion aan de Vlamingdam, situated not far from his studio. The picture, more than 2 m wide, is perhaps his best work and

well illustrates the personal style he had by then developed. The figures are solidly modelled, anatomically well structured and effectively integrated into the spatial setting. The sense of depth is achieved through the fairly low viewpoint, the careful placing of the figures (often along diagonals) and the calculated diminution of scale. The drawing of figures, hands and drapery is strong and well articulated. This painting also exemplifies David's characteristic rendering of faces, usually somewhat flat, with high foreheads, almond-shaped eyes, thick eyelids, straight mouths and pronounced chins. The colouring of works of this period is generally cool and rich in contrast, with a predilection for moss green, steel blue, grey, purple and an extensive use of white. The extreme solemnity of this particular scene of quiet religious contemplation suggests close knowledge of church ritual and a liturgical, rather than mystical or devotional piety. The only foreign elements are the portraits of the artist and his wife in the upper left and right corners. There is a striking resemblance between this self-portrait and the man in the far left of the *Judgement of Cambyses*, presumably an earlier portrait of the artist.

(iii) Late period, after 1511. In 1515 a 'Meester Gheraert van Brugghe' became a member of the Guild of St Luke in Antwerp, by then a more dynamic centre than Bruges. This was almost certainly Gerard David, who, without moving house, had found a second market for his paintings. In 1519 he became involved in a legal dispute with his assistant, the Lombard painter Ambrosius Benson, who accused him of withholding two portfolios of cartoons, among which were designs belonging to Adriaen Isenbrandt and Albrecht Cornelis. A year later David was even briefly imprisoned pending judgement.

The character of David's late work is even more difficult to establish than that of his early paintings. However, it is generally assumed that works from the 1510s are characterized by a certain stiffness in the forms and a duller palette. This stiffness is usually related to the influence of Benson, who worked as David's assistant until their dispute. Typical examples of this late style are the extremely sober *Cruxifixion* (Genoa, Pal. Bianco); a multi-figured version on the same theme (Berlin, Gemäldegal.); a triptych with the *Lamentation* (Philadelphia, PA, Mus. A.); the *Deposition* (New York, Frick); panels showing *Christ Carrying the Cross* and the *Resurrection* (both New York, Met.); the monumental polyptych of *St Anne* (Washington, DC, N.G.A.); and a triptych with the *Legend of St Nicholas* (Edinburgh, N.G.). The *Legend of St Antony* (Toledo, OH, Mus. A.) and another *Lamentation* (Chicago, IL, A. Inst.) probably belong to the same group.

A final stylistic phase, between 1519 and 1523, is usually associated with the departure of Benson. Works probably painted in this period include two examples of the *Rest on the Flight into Egypt* (Madrid, Prado; Washington, DC, N.G.A.); the various versions of the well-known *Virgin with the Porridge Spoon* (e.g. Brussels, Mus. A. Anc.); and the *Adoration of the Magi* (London, N.G.). These charming pictures have an almost intimate character, with their soft, *sfumato*-like rendering of volumes and misty, subdued colouring, anticipating that of Isenbrandt.

At his death, the guild of book illuminators collected David's death duty and dedicated a mass to him, suggesting that he might also have worked as an illuminator. But although some scholars have recognized his style in a few miniatures, he was apparently a benefactor rather than an active member of that guild.

2. WORKING METHODS AND TECHNIQUE. David adopted the traditional oil painting technique of south Netherlandish masters of the second half of the 15th century. His pictures are thickly painted, the brushwork fairly free and nervous in the early works, smoother but still densely applied in the later ones. Documents prove that in his studio cartoons and sketchbooks were used to evolve the compositions. This is confirmed by the underdrawings of his paintings, which have been studied with the aid of infra-red reflectography (for illustration *see* UNDERDRAWING). The artist used various tracing techniques, including pricked cartoons and pouncing for both original works as well as workshop copies (see Comblen-Sonkes). His *Adoration of the Magi* (Munich, Alte Pin.) is thought to have been copied, using the pricked cartoon method, from a lost composition by Hugo van der Goes.

Several drawings, mostly of heads and figures, are attributed to David, among them six numbered metalpoint drawings from a sketchbook now distributed among various collections (e.g. Frankfurt am Main, Städel. Kstinst. & Städt. Gal.; Paris, Louvre). Several of the drawings can be connected with paintings. That of *Four Heads* (Ottawa, N.G.) is a copy of four heads from Hubert and Jan van Eyck's Ghent Altarpiece (Ghent, St Bavo). David's drawing style is characterized by subtle parallel diagonal hatching, which creates a picturesque effect. His strong modelling of heads and figures and his thorough knowledge of anatomy (shown, for instance, in the studies

of hands that appear with heads on the metalpoint sketchbook leaves) are remarkable for the period and produce a far more progressive proto-Renaissance impression than do any of his finished paintings.

3. CRITICAL RECEPTION AND POSTHUMOUS REPUTATION. David's fame diminished fast. In less than 50 years Guicciardini knew only of a Gerard of Bruges who was a miniature painter, a misunderstanding that doubtless arose out of David's close association with the book illuminators' guild. Van Mander recorded Pieter Pourbus's praise for a certain Gerard of Bruges. In fact, until Pourbus's arrival in Bruges c. 1538, David's influence on painting was dominant. Although he had no recorded pupils, a diluted version of his style was perpetuated by a number of artists, of whom the most important were Adriaen Isenbrandt, Albrecht Cornelis, Ambrosius Benson and the Master of the André Virgin. David's painting style was also widely imitated, sometimes slavishly, by Bruges illuminators in the first quarter of the 16th century, most notably by Simon Bening.

BIBLIOGRAPHY

Thieme–Becker

EARLY SOURCES AND DOCUMENTS

L. Guicciardini: *Descrittione di . . . tutti i Paesi Bassi* (1567)
K. van Mander: *Schilder-boeck* ([1603]–1604)
A. Sanderus: *Flandria illustrata*, ii (Cologne, 1641; Dut. trans., Leiden, Rotterdam and The Hague, 1735), p. 154
W. H. J. Weale: 'Gerard David', *Le Beffroi*, i (1863), pp. 223–34; ii (1864–5), pp. 288–97; iii (1866–70), pp. 334–46
P. Rombouts and T. Van Lerius: *De liggeren en andere historische archieven der Antwerpsche Sint Lucasgilde* (Antwerp and The Hague, 1864–76), i, p. 83
C. Vanden Haute: *La Corporation des peintres de Bruges* (Bruges, [1913]), pp. 34, 40, 47, 49, 200, 219
R. A. Parmentier: 'Bescheiden omtrent Brugsche schilders van de 16e eeuw', *Hand. Genoot. Gesch. 'Soc. Emul.' Brugge*, lxxx (1937), pp. 92–4
——: 'Bronnen voor de geschiedenis van het Brugsche schildersmilieu in de XVIe eeuw, XXI: Gerard David', *Belg. Tijdschr. Oudhdknd. & Kstgesch.*, xii (1942), pp. 5–19
H. J. Van Miegroet: 'New Documents Concerning Gerard David', *A. Bull.*, lxix (1987), pp. 33–44
D. De Vos: 'Gerard David's House', *A. Bull.*, lxix (1987)

GENERAL

M. J. Friedländer: *Die altniederländische Malerei*, vi (Berlin, 1928), pp. 71–113; Eng. trans. as *Early Netherlandish Painting*, vi/2 (Leiden, 1971; suppl., 1976)
A. Janssens de Bisthoven: *Musée communal des beaux-arts (Musée Groeninge), Bruges* (Antwerp, 1951, rev. 2/1959, rev. 3/Brussels, 1983), i of *Les Primitifs flamands, I: Corpus de la peinture des anciens Pays-Bas méridionaux au quinzième siècle*
M. Davies: *The National Gallery, London* (Antwerp, 1953), iii/1 of *Les Primitifs flamands, I: Corpus de la peinture des anciens Pays-Bas méridionaux au quinzième siècle*
E. Panofsky: *Early Netherlandish Painting: Its Origins and Character* (Cambridge, MA, 1953), pp. 350–53
H. W. von Löhneysen: *Die ältere niederländische Malerei: Künstler und Kritiker* (Eisenach and Kassel, 1956), pp. 182–6
G. Marlier: *Ambrosius Benson et la peinture à Bruges au temps de Charles-Quint* (Damme, 1957), pp. 15–19, 41–50
J. Lavalleye: *Collections d'Espagne* (Antwerp, 1958), ii of *Les Primitifs flamands, II: Répertoire des peintures flamandes des quinzième et seizième siècles*
H. Adhémar: *Le Musée national du Louvre* (Brussels, 1962), v of *Les Primitifs flamands, I: Corpus de la peinture des anciens Pays-Bas méridionaux au quinzième siècle*
C. D. Cutler: *Northern Painting from Pucelle to Bruegel* (New York, 1968), pp. 190–97
M. Comblen-Sonkes: *Bibliographic Guide for Early Netherlandish Painting* (Brussels, 1984), pp. 45–50

E. J. Mundy: *Painting in Bruges, 1470–1550: An Annotated Bibliography* (Boston, 1985), pp. 74–92

J. Snyder: *Northern Renaissance Art* (New York, 1985), pp. 186–93

The Age of Bruegel: Netherlandish Drawings in the Sixteenth Century (exh. cat. by J. O. Hand and others, Washington, DC, N.G.A.; New York, Pierpont Morgan Lib.; 1986–7), pp. 130–33

MONOGRAPHIC STUDIES

W. H. J. Weale: *Gerard David: Painter and Illuminator* (London, 1895)

E. von Bodehausen: *Gerard David und seine Schule* (Munich, 1905)

K. Boon: *Gerard David*, Palet Ser. (Amsterdam, [1946])

Gerard David (exh. cat. by M. J. Friedländer, Bruges, Stedel. Mus., 1949)

D. Graybowski Scillia: *Gerard David and Manuscript Illumination in the Lowlands* (PhD diss., Cleveland, OH, Case W. Reserve U., 1975)

E. J. Mundy: *Gerard David Studies* (PhD diss., Princeton U., 1980)

H. J. Van Miegroet: *Gerard David* (Antwerp, 1989)

SPECIALIST STUDIES

W. H. J. Weale: 'Triptyque du *Baptême du Christ*', *Le Beffroi*, i (1863), pp. 276–87

E. von Bodenhausen and W. Valentiner: 'Zum Werk Gerard Davids', *Z. Bild. Kst.*, xxii (1911), pp. 183–9

F. Winkler: 'Gerard David und die Brügger Miniaturmalerei seiner Zeit', *Mhft. Kstwiss.*, vi (1913), pp. 271–80

——: 'Das Skizzenbuch Gerard Davids', *Pantheon*, iii (1929), pp. 271–5

L. Baldass: 'Gerard David als Landschaftsmaler', *Jb. Ksthist. Samml. Wien*, x (1936), pp. 89–96

T. Van de Walle de Ghelcke: 'Le Présumé Portrait de *Jacques Cnoop le jeune*, orfèvre brugeois', *Hand. Genoot. Gesch. 'Soc. Emul.' Brugge*, lxxxvii (1950), pp. 155–62

G. V. Castelnovi: 'Il polittico di Gerard David nell'abbazia della Cervara', *Commentari*, iii (1952), pp. 22–7

F. Winkler: 'Einige Ergebnisse der van Eyckforschung', *Actes du XVIIe congrès international d'histoire de l'art: Amsterdam, 1952*, pp. 237–46

G. J. Hoogewerff: 'A proposito del politico di Gerard David nell'Abbazia della Cervara', *Commentari*, iv (1953), pp. 72–3

K. Arndt: 'Gerard David's *Anbetung der Könige* nach Hugo van der Goes: Ein Beitrag zur Kopienkritik', *Munchn. Jb. Bild. Kst.*, xii (1961), pp. 153–75

M. Comblen-Sonkes: 'A propos de la *Vierge et Enfant à la soupe au lait*: Contribution à l'étude des copies', *Mus. Royaux B.-A. Belgique: Bull.*, xxiii–xxix (1974–80), pp. 29–42

M. Wyld, A. Roy and A. Smith: 'Gerard David's *Virgin and Child with Saints and a Donor*', *N.G. Tech. Bull.*, iii (1979), pp. 51–65

E. J. Mundy: 'A Preparatory Sketch for Gerard David's *Justice of Cambyses* Panels in Bruges', *Burl. Mag.*, cxxii (1980), pp. 122–5

——: 'Gerard David's *Rest on the Flight into Egypt*: Further Additions to Grape Symbolism', *Simiolus*, xii (1981–2), pp. 211–22

D. De Vos: 'Het verzamelaarsmerk van Peter Stevens (1590–1668) en diens aantekeningen over 15de-eeuwse Brugse meesters', *Jb. Stad Brugge Stedel. Mus.* (1982), p. 258

M. Wynne Ainsworth: 'Gerard David's Working Methods: Some Preliminary Observations', *Le Dessin sous-jacent dans la peinture, Colloque V: Louvain-la-Neuve, 1983*, pp. 53–60

DIRK DE VOS

David, Giovanni (*b* Cabella Ligure, 1743; *d* Genoa, 1790). Italian painter and engraver. He moved *c.* 1770 to Rome, where he trained with Domenico Corvi, and his *Moses Giving the Law*, which is close to Corvi, won first prize at the Accademia di S Luca in 1775. In that year he moved to Venice as a protégé of the Genoese ambassador Giacomo Durazzo. There, in addition to painting and engraving, he designed scenery for the Teatro La Fenice and responded to contemporary Venetian painting. In 1775 he made a series of satirical etchings with aquatint of 12 Venetian characters (Le Blanc, 8–19). He returned to Genoa *c.* 1780, then travelled to France, England and the Netherlands.

David's main activity, however, in the 1780s was in Genoa, where he painted vast panoramic canvases, such as the *Battle of the Meloria* for the Sala del Maggior Consiglio in the Palazzo Ducale (*c.* 1783). This work contrasts sharply with the academic tradition established by Raphael Mengs, which was then dominant in Liguria. Tiepolo's influence can be seen in David's *Virgin Worshipped by the Brignoline Nuns*, painted for the church of Nostra Signora del Rifugio, Genoa, while the *Presentation of the Virgin* (*c.* 1785; Genoa, S Maria delle Vigne) sets a composition reminiscent of Giambattista Crosato against an architectural background inspired by Veronese.

David passed easily from this type of decoration to the proto-Romantic style, between Giuseppe Bernardino Bison and Felice Giani, of the watercolours depicting *Legends of Hercules* (ex-Pal. Podestà Bruzzo, Genoa; see Pesenti, 1971, figs 271–2), in which he revived a 17th-century tradition of animal painting in the manner of Giovanni Benedetto Castiglione, united with a Genoese decorative style reminiscent of Gregorio de' Ferrari. The artist's last period, devoted to the decoration (mostly destr.) of the church of S Agnese, Genoa, was characterized by a more dramatic and visionary style, also evident in drawings and engravings of those years.

BIBLIOGRAPHY

C. Le Blanc: *Manuel de l'amateur d'estampes . . .*, 4 vols (Paris, 1854–89; repr. in 2 vols, Amsterdam, 1970–71/*R* New York, 1978)

F. R. Pesenti: 'L'illuminismo e l'età neoclassica', *La pittura a Genova e in Liguria, ii : Dal seicento al primo novecento*, ed. E. Poleggi (Genoa, 1971, rev. 1987), pp. 360–61, 374

F. Sborgi: *1770–1860: Pittura neoclassica e romantica in Liguria* (Genoa, 1975)

Giovanni David (exh. cat. by G. Grasso Fravega, Tortona, 1981)

Disegni genovesi dal XVI al XVIII secolo (exh. cat. by M. Newcome Schleier, Florence, Uffizi, 1989), pp. 217–18

UGO RUGGERI

David, Jacques-Louis (*b* Paris, 30 Aug 1748; *d* Brussels, 29 Dec 1825). French painter and draughtsman. He was the most prominent and influential painter of the Neoclassical movement in France (*see* NEO-CLASSICISM). In the 1780s he created a style of austere and ethical painting that perfectly captured the moral climate of the last years of the *ancien régime*. Later, as an active revolutionary, he put his art at the service of the new French Republic and for a time was virtual dictator of the arts. He was imprisoned after the fall from power of Maximilien de Robespierre but on his release became captivated by the personality of Napoleon I and developed an Empire style in which warm Venetian colour played a major role. Following the restoration of the Bourbon monarchy in 1816, David went into exile in Brussels, where he continued to paint but was regarded as something of an anachronism. He had a huge number of pupils, and his influence was felt (both positively and negatively) by the majority of French 19th-century painters. He was a revolutionary artist in both a technical and a political sense. His compositional innovations effected a complete rupture with Rococo fantasy; he is considered the greatest single figure in European painting between the late Rococo and the Romantic era.

I. Life and work. II. Working methods and technique. III. Critical reception and posthumous reputation.

I. Life and work.

1. Training and early career, to 1789. 2. Painting and political activity during the French Revolution, 1789–95. 3. Work during the Directory and the Empire, 1795–1814. 4. Late works and exile in Brussels, 1814–25.

1. TRAINING AND EARLY CAREER, TO 1789. David was born into a well-to-do family of Parisian tradesmen. His mother's family included masons and architects, and they played an increasing role in David's education and upbringing following his father's death in a duel in 1757. At first he attempted to become a pupil of François Boucher, his grandmother's cousin. The aged Boucher, however, was disinclined to take on pupils, and instead David entered the studio of Joseph-Marie Vien. He also enrolled at the school of the Académie Royale in 1766. In 1770 he entered the Prix de Rome competition for the first time but failed to reach the final. A year later he won second prize with his Boucher-inspired *Combat of Mars and Minerva* (Paris, Louvre). Claiming that he had deserved first prize and had been downgraded at Vien's insistence, he also harboured a grudge against the first prize winner, Joseph-Benoît Suvée (whom he later described as 'ignorant and horrible'). The defeat seems to have been the start of his grievances against the Académie. In 1772 he was again earmarked for one of the two prizes, along with Pierre-Charles Jombert (1748/9–after 1777). David's suspicions concerning the conduct of the Prix were confirmed when a conspiracy caused Academicians to change votes. The first prize went not to David but to the mediocre Anicet-Charles Lemonnier (1743–1824). David also contributed

to his own downfall by painting over his first attempt— the set subject was *Apollo and Diana Killing the Children of Niobe*—before the old paint was dry. Consequently the surface blackened and deteriorated, as can be seen clearly in his picture (Paris, priv. col., see 1981 exh. cat., p. 30, fig. 3). As a result of this judgement David made a half-hearted suicide attempt but was dissuaded from it by Gabriel-François Doyen. In 1773 David was beaten again, but this time by a most accomplished rival, Pierre Peyron. David's entry, the *Death of Seneca* (Paris, Petit Pal.), attempts to depict the stoic resolve of the philosopher, but the hectic Baroque composition militates against the gravity of the subject. He finally won the Prix de Rome in 1774 with *Erasistratus Discovers the Cause of the Illness of Antiochus* (Paris, Ecole N. Sup. B.-A.), in which he adopted a friezelike grouping of the protagonists and concentrated on narrative clarity.

David left Paris for Rome in October 1775 with Vien, who had just been appointed Director of the Académie de France in Rome. He apparently felt that the eternal city had little to teach him, declaring 'the Antique will not seduce me, it lacks animation, it does not move'. In Italy David drew dutifully from the Antique, but he was not an obsessive antiquarian. Instead he studied the art of 17th-century painters, including Nicolas Poussin, Caravaggio

1. Jacques-Louis David: *Oath of the Horatii*, oil on canvas, 3.30×4.25 m, 1784 (Paris, Musée du Louvre)

and his followers, the Carracci family and Guido Reni. He then set about creating a rational synthesis of the real and the ideal that was free from the artificialities of the Rococo style. Life drawing and past masters played a crucial role in David's stylistic development. Yet such changes were accomplished only gradually. His early Roman works, such as the *Funeral of Patroclus* (*c*. 1778; Dublin, N.G.), are still crowded with figures and show little or no change from his Parisian works. However, in his first independent commission, *St Roch Interceding for the Plague-stricken* (Marseille, Mus. B.-A.), David revealed a desire for grandeur, simplicity and clarity that signalled future directions.

David left Rome in July 1780 and returned to Paris with the intention of becoming an associate member of the Académie Royale. The following year he produced as his *morceau d'agrégation* a painting of *Belisarius Receiving Alms* (Lille, Mus. B.-A.). The Belisarius story was highly topical—Jean-François Marmontel had published his historical romance *Bélisaire* in 1767, and François-André Vincent and Peyron had painted the story in 1776 (Montpellier, Mus. Fabre) and 1779 (Toulouse, Mus. Augustins) respectively. For his version David turned to a format that was striking in its directness and simplicity. A small cast of characters is set solidly against an architectural background. Clear, unequivocal gestures are made, and subdued colours are used. While David's *Belisarius* is often

hailed as the first masterpiece of Neo-classicism in France, it is perhaps more accurate to refer to neo-Poussinism, as Poussinesque references are obvious and undisguised.

At this time David started to take on pupils, remaining an influential teacher throughout his life. He operated a separate studio for teaching but also used the more able students as assistants on replicas and large-scale history paintings. The first generation of his very talented pupils included Jean-Germain Drouais, François-Xavier Fabre, Jean-François Garneray, Philippe-Auguste Hennequin and Jean-Baptiste-Joseph Wicar. In 1783 David was received (*reçu*) as a full Academician with *Andromache Mourning Hector* (exh. Salon 1783; Paris, Ecole N. Sup. B.-A., on dep. Paris, Louvre). This is David at his most severe and drab, although some contemporary critics felt that there was too little restraint in Andromache's grieving.

David's Neo-classicism found its clearest expression in 1784 with the monumental *Oath of the Horatii* (exh. Salon 1785; Paris, Louvre; see fig. 1). To undertake this work, a commission from the Direction des Bâtiments du Roi, David felt it necessary to return to Rome, where he spent October 1784 to August 1785. In the *Horatii* he arrived at an artistic solution whereby stoical content and stylistic gravity were perfectly harmonized. The Horatii theme had been suggested to him as early as 1780. In depicting the three Horatii swearing allegiance to their father (a scene not mentioned in any of the sources David would have consulted for the story, e.g. Livy, Plutarch, Corneille) he underlined the central theme of the sacrifice of the individual for the good of the state. Albert Boime (see 'David et la franc maçonnerie' in *David contre David*) has established that David was a freemason, and this possibly influenced his choice of an oath-taking ritual. David was a freemason, and the depiction of an oath might have been inspired by the rituals of the masonic lodge. A number of historians, notably Crow (1985), have identified an element of pre-Revolutionary radicalism in the painting. Although it was an overwhelming success, bringing David to a position of stylistic dominance in France that eclipsed such rivals as Vincent, Peyron and Suvée, many conservative critics were disquieted by it and wrote that it would be a bad example for young artists to follow. In its simplifications and dissonances of composition it is a profoundly anti-academic work and clear evidence of David's antagonism towards the Académie.

At the following two Salons David continued to exhibit his austere brand of Neo-classicism with the *Death of Socrates* (1787; New York, Met.) and the *Lictors Bringing Brutus the Bodies of his Sons* (1789; Paris, Louvre; *see* NEO-CLASSICISM, fig. 1). The former, although not a royal commission, nevertheless focuses on the moral rectitude of Socrates, who drinks the hemlock without ceasing the flow of his improving words. A note of hysteria is introduced by the reactions of Socrates' disciples (passion is rarely absent from David's work). *Brutus* was painted for Louis XVI and exhibited shortly after the storming of the Bastille. Due to the Republican nature of its theme—Brutus rid Rome of Tarquin, the last of the kings of Rome—the painting later acquired a political significance that David presumably did not originally intend. David invites the viewer to judge Brutus either as a hero, for his

2. Jacques-Louis David: *Antoine-Laurent de Lavoisier and his Wife Marie-Anne Pierette*, oil on canvas, 2597×1946 mm, 1788 (New York, Metropolitan Museum of Art)

devotion to Rome, or as a monster, for executing his own sons.

It would, however, be a mistake to consider David in the 1780s as simply a cold and clinical classicist. He was also interested in mythology and portraiture: his *Courtship of Paris and Helen* (1788; Paris, Louvre) is a complete contrast to the morally elevating history paintings. It has an exquisite refinement of colour, an elegant idealization of bodies and a degree of archaeological accuracy that are absent from the *Horatii*, *Socrates* and *Brutus*. In addition, portraiture played a significant, if minor, part in David's career up to and including the Revolution. Numerous early family portraits exist, for example that of his aunt *Mme Marie-Josèphe Buron* (1769; Chicago, IL, A. Inst.), an animated work reminiscent of the portraits of Joseph-Siffred Duplessis. Then in 1781 David painted the splendid equestrian portrait of the Polish nobleman *Count Stanisław Potocki* (Warsaw, N. Mus.), which reveals debts to the Baroque tradition of Peter Paul Rubens and Anthony van Dyck. David's most striking pre-Revolutionary portrait is the double full-length of *Antoine-Laurent de Lavoisier and his Wife Marie-Anne Pierette* (1788; New York, Met.; see fig. 2). This shows the eminent chemist, seated and surrounded by his experimental apparatus, with his wife leaning, muselike, on his shoulder. David could have made a handsome living painting portraits alone but sought the fame and glory that history painting brought.

2. PAINTING AND POLITICAL ACTIVITY DURING THE FRENCH REVOLUTION, 1789–95. Assessments of David as a rabid regicide who used his art as a political weapon do not take adequate account of the complexity of his political career. After 1789 he took part in the attacks against the privileges of the officers of the Académie Royale. His anti-academic feelings were also fuelled by the Académie's refusal to grant posthumous membership to Drouais, his favourite pupil, who had died in 1788. The dissidents eventually prevailed, and the Académie was abolished on 8 August 1793. It was replaced in 1795 by the Institut de France, of which David was an inaugural member (*see* PARIS, §VI, 1 and 3). He was not directly involved in politics until September 1790, when he joined the Revolutionary Jacobin Club. By this time he had been working for about six months on his first Revolutionary picture, the *Oath of the Tennis Court* (Paris, Louvre). David had originally approached the Jacobins to sponsor this project, and finance was to come from subscriptions. When this failed, the costs were taken over by the state. The event to be commemorated was that of 20 June 1789, when the Deputies of the Third Estate, meeting in the royal tennis court at the Château of Versailles, swore not to disperse until a constitution was assured. Although many drawings survive for this project (e.g. Versailles, Château), David seems not to have been present on the day and treated this as a straightforward commercial commission rather than as a patriotic duty. He planned a large canvas full of portraits of the Deputies with the President of the Constituent Assembly, Jean-Sylvain Bailly, addressing the spectator. However, political events moved too fast for David; by the winter of 1791–2 this vision of the Revolution had become outmoded, and many of the 'heroes' of 1789 had been discredited or exiled. David

painted only four Deputies' heads on the surviving canvas fragment, and a better idea of the project is gained from his highly finished drawing (both Versailles, Château). In the spring of 1792 David also received an unexpected commission to paint *Louis XVI Showing the Constitution to the Dauphin* (incomplete), a work that was intended to hang in the meeting room of the Legislative Assembly (Schnapper, Bordes). Drawings (Paris, Louvre, RF 36942) prove that he started the commission and indicate the gradual nature of his political conversion. Following these abortive projects David became increasingly involved in politics. He was elected a Deputy of the Convention in September 1792 and allied himself closely with Robespierre. In 1793 he voted for the death of Louis XVI, and in January 1794 he served a term of 13 days as President of the Convention. Part of his duties included the signing of arrest warrants—an aspect of his political career he later vehemently denied.

During the Revolution David was given the task of glorifying three martyrs of the cause: *Louis-Michel Lepelletier de Saint-Fargeau* (1793, destr.; engraving by Pierre-Alexandre Tardieu (1756–1844), Paris, Bib. N., Cab. Est.), *Joseph Bara* (1794, unfinished; Avignon, Mus. Calvet) and *Jean-Paul Marat* (1793; Brussels, Mus. A. Anc.; versions, Versailles, Château, Paris, Louvre; *see* FRANCE, fig. 25). David was called on by the Convention to paint the last-mentioned work, better known as the *Death of Marat*, the day after Marat's assassination by Charlotte Corday. The sombre greenish setting was possibly inspired by the lighting of the disaffected church of the Cordeliers, Paris, where the body lay in state; David not only exploited the emotional quality of the chill, dark void above Marat's body but leant on aspects of Christian iconography, as if transcending death to excite Revolutionary ardour. In sharp contrast to the heroic Marat is David's brutally realistic pen drawing of *Queen Marie-Antoinette on her Way to the Scaffold* (1793; Paris, Louvre).

From 1792 David also organized some of the great Revolutionary festivals and pageants. The most elaborate of these was the Festival of the Supreme Being on 20 Prairial Year II (8 June 1794), for which he evolved the overall programme and provided designs for the props and temporary architecture (destr.). Among surviving drawings for such ephemeral works is that entitled the *Triumph of the French People* (c. 1793; Paris, Louvre), designed for a theatre curtain. In addition, he continued to produce portraits, painting figures from the liberal middle and upper classes, as in the unfinished portrait of *Mme Adélaïde Pastoret* (c. 1792; Chicago, IL, A. Inst.), and representatives of foreign governments in Paris, including *Jacobus Blauw* (1795; London, N.G.; see fig. 3). One of the Batavian (Dutch) government's plenipotentiary ministers, he is depicted at work at his desk, gazing pensively out into space; David paid great attention to the still-lifes of objects on the desk and to the muted colour harmonies of Blauw's clothes. A portrait of *Bertrand Barère de Vieuzac* (1792–3; Bremen, Ksthalle), once attributed to David, is now given to his pupil Jean-Louis Laneuville.

On 9 Thermidor (27 July) 1794 Robespierre fell from power and was executed. David, who had once promised to drink the hemlock with him, was lucky to escape with his life. He underwent two periods of imprisonment,

3. Jacques-Louis David: *Jacobus Blauw*, oil on canvas, 910×720 mm, 1795 (London, National Gallery)

though under lenient conditions that allowed him to continue to work, first from 2 August to 28 December 1794 in the Hôtel des Fermes and Palais de Luxembourg and then from 29 May to 3 August 1795 in the Collège des Quatre-Nations. Suffering ill-health, he was released on parole. In prison he painted a *Self-portrait* (1794; Paris, Louvre) that shows him, palette and brush in hand, staring directly at the spectator; his swollen left cheek, concealing a huge benign tumour (the result of a youthful duelling accident), is clearly visible. In captivity David painted one or two landscapes, his only recorded excursion into this genre. However, the *View of the Luxembourg Gardens* (1794; Paris, Louvre), once attributed to him, has aroused doubts about both its subject-matter and its authorship.

3. WORK DURING THE DIRECTORY AND THE EM-PIRE, 1795–1814. During his imprisonment David also began work on an ambitious history painting, the *Intervention of the Sabine Women* (Paris, Louvre; see PERCEPTION, fig. 7), not completed until 1799. This shows the Sabine women separating the belligerent groups of Sabine and Roman men, the latter having come to reclaim their females. The painting focuses on reconciliation, a theme of some contemporary relevance, since following the Reign of Terror, French society was returning to normality under the government of the Directory. It also demonstrates a change in David's aesthetics. He said that he wanted it to be 'more Greek' and thus depicted smoother and more sculptural forms than the muscular Roman bodies of the *Horatii*. In fact, he found himself having to defend the figures' excessive nudity. The overall effect is completely different from the morally exemplary history paintings of

the 1780s. By contrast with the tense grouping of the *Oath of the Horatii*, the *Intervention of the Sabine Women* has a very large cast of characters, requiring it to be read serially, incident by incident and group by group. It shows his growing interest in 'Primitive' art, with ideas of formal purity derived from Greek sculpture and 15th-century Italian painting. Similar interests spurred some of his students to pursue these ideals even further and to form a group known as LES PRIMITIFS, led by the mysterious Pierre-Maurice Quay (*c.* 1779–1804). David's work did not adhere closely enough to the students' notion of purity; they even accused him of being too florid, with the result that he asked them to leave his studio. David painted the *Sabine Women* as a tribute to his wife, and to offset the costs of production he took the unprecedented step of exhibiting it in one of the rooms of the Louvre and charging an admission fee. This exhibition lasted from 1799 to 1804, and from the proceeds he bought a country property at Ozoeut le Voulgis in the Seine-et-Marne Valley.

Following his release from prison, David declared that he would no longer follow men, he would follow principles. This indicated a desire to steer clear of controversial subjects. However, he soon came under the spell of the brilliant young Corsican general Napoleon Bonaparte, who first posed for David early in 1798. The product of this three-hour sitting is a fragmentary canvas (Paris, Louvre) showing the figure in outline with details of the head and shoulders sketched in. David's idea was to paint Bonaparte standing full-length after the victorious battle of Castiglione, next to a horse controlled by a groom. But no more sittings followed, and the picture remained unfinished. Nevertheless, this brief meeting had a profound effect on David, who announced, 'Bonaparte is my hero'.

On 18 Brumaire (10 November) 1799, Bonaparte and the army staged a coup d'état that replaced the Directory with the Consulate and made Bonaparte First Consul. He further endeared himself to the French public in 1800 by re-conquering Italy for the second time in five years. Charles IV of Spain commissioned David to paint this event, *Napoleon Crossing the St Bernard Pass* (Malmaison, Château N.), and Bonaparte then ordered copies of the picture (Vienna, Ksthis. Mus.; Versailles, Château, 2 versions; Berlin, Schloss Charlottenburg). Napoleon refused to sit for the portrait, sending instead the uniform he had worn at the Battle of Marengo, and did not submit to David's proposed format either: David wanted to paint him sword in hand, but Napoleon replied that battles were no longer won in this way and that he wanted to be painted 'calm on a fiery steed'; David duly obliged. The magnitude of the event in David's view is indicated by the placing of Napoleon's name on a rock above those of two previous transalpine conquerors, Hannibal and Charlemagne. Like most propaganda images, the painting is economical with the truth, since Napoleon actually crossed the Alps seated on a mule. The impersonal, static quality of the work is doubtless due to the lack of any real contact between artist and sitter.

This distance between David and Napoleon contrasts sharply with the circumstances that surrounded one of his most famous portraits, that of *Mme Juliette Récamier* (Paris, Louvre), on which he worked early in 1800. The great

4. Jacques-Louis David: *Coronation of Napoleon in Notre-Dame* (detail), also known as *Le Sacre*, oil on canvas, 6.1×9.3 m, 1805–7 (Paris, Musée du Louvre)

society beauty was wilful and spoiled and obviously saw herself as something other than the vulnerable and isolated figure that David depicted. The simple and unadorned setting is redolent of tension. She reclines on a fashionable day-bed made by Georges Jacob. No rich accessories surround her, only an Antique-inspired lamp (painted by David's newest pupil, Jean-Auguste-Dominique Ingres). David finally became exasperated with Mme Récamier's late arrivals for sittings and refused to continue, leaving the picture unfinished.

David quickly enjoyed the rewards of Napoleonic patronage: in December 1803 he was made a Chevalier of the Légion d'honneur, and in December 1804, immediately after Napoleon's coronation as Emperor, he became his Premier Peintre. David's relationship with Napoleon and his ministers was, however, ambivalent, mostly due to incessant and inflated demands for remuneration. The coronation took place on 2 December, and David was charged with commemorating the event. Initially the exact subjects for the commission were not specified; not until June 1806 did David submit a detailed description of the four planned paintings. The subjects were the *Coronation of Napoleon in Notre-Dame*, the *Enthronement*, the *Distribution of the Eagle Standards* and the *Reception of the Emperor and Empress at the Hôtel de Ville*. Of these, only the *Coronation* and the *Distribution of the Eagle Standards* were completed; the *Reception at the Hôtel de Ville* got only as far as a detailed drawing (Paris, Louvre) and the *Enthronement* seems never to have been started.

The *Coronation of Napoleon in Notre-Dame*, also known as *Le Sacre* (Paris, Louvre; see fig. 4; version, 1822, Versailles, Château), occupied David from 1805 to 1807, and he was given the secularized church of Cluny, in the Place de la Sorbonne, as a studio (destr. 1833). He made exhaustive preliminary studies for all the personages to be shown and enlisted the help of Ignace-Eugène-Marie Degotti (*d* 1824), a scene painter from the Paris Opéra, for difficulties he encountered with perspective. David had the problem of which moment of the ceremony to depict: at first he proposed Napoleon crowning himself (drawing, Paris, Louvre, RF 4377), but at the suggestion of his former pupil François Gérard, this was abandoned in favour of Napoleon crowning Josephine. The open composition leads the spectator into the picture, almost as if to participate in the ceremony, a feature not lost on Napoleon. With the *Coronation* David had to find an appropriate style to celebrate the magnificence of the Empire, and to this end he turned to the opulence of Rubens, in particular his *Coronation of Marie de' Medici* (Paris, Louvre), then in the Palais du Luxembourg. Whites, reds, greens and golds dominate, and the large cast of characters is manipulated with supreme finesse and clarity. The work was a staggering success and encapsulates the splendour of the First Empire most effectively.

The *Distribution of the Eagle Standards* (1810; Versailles, Château) shows the ceremony held on the Champ de Mars, Paris, three days after the coronation. Here Napoleon, in a deliberate parallel with ancient Rome, presented flags attached to poles topped with the Imperial eagle to all the army regiments and to the National Guard. Oaths of allegiance were then sworn. David's picture is a curious amalgam of high-minded patriotism and romantic Napoleonic pageant and allegory, the end result lacking in cohesion: the group of generals swarming up the steps to the tribune has an awkward, frozen quality, and the work suffered because Napoleon insisted on changes being made. Most radical of these was the removal of the figure of Empress Josephine, whom he had recently divorced, resulting in considerable reworking of the left side of the picture. David's series of grand Napoleonic paintings ended with this work. His demands for 100,000 francs for each painting were considered excessive, and when other commissions were distributed they went to lesser (and less expensive) artists.

At this time David also began to face serious competition from his own former pupils, notably Gérard, Antoine-Jean Gros and Anne-Louis Girodet. Gros in particular was invited to execute a number of prestigious Napoleonic commissions, including the the *Plague House at Jaffa* (1804) and the *Battle of Eylau* (1808; both Paris, Louvre). In 1802 Girodet produced the wildly allegorical *Apotheosis of French Heroes who Died for the Country during the War for Liberty* (Malmaison, Château N.), a work that left David doubting Girodet's sanity. This increased competition led David to disassociate himself from many of his ex-pupils, whom he then considered as rivals. He did, however, remain on friendly terms with Gros.

Although there were no more official commissions from Napoleon, David was commissioned to paint the Emperor, surprisingly, by an Englishman, Alexander Douglas-Hamilton (later 10th Duke of Hamilton). The life-size, full-length portrait of *Napoleon in his Study* (1812; Washington, DC, N.G.A.; version, Versailles, Château) was considered an excellent likeness and depicts the Emperor as lawgiver, working on the Napoleonic code into the small hours of the morning. In the background the clock shows 4.13 and the candle on his desk is almost burnt out.

David's duties for Napoleon between 1800 and 1810 had delayed the progress on *Leonidas at Thermopylae* (Paris, Louvre), the companion piece to the *Intervention of the Sabine Women*. He also experienced difficulty in finding an image striking enough to convey what he considered to be a deep and final classical statement. Although planned in 1799, this work was not completed until 1815. The story is that of Leonidas, King of Sparta, who with his band of men defended the pass at Thermopylae against superior Persian forces in the knowledge that death awaited them. David wrote at length about his intentions for this work in the anonymously published *Explication* (1814), saying that he wanted an air of calm acceptance and contemplation to reign over the scene. This is most clearly expressed in the static and pensive figure of Leonidas, taken from a cameo illustrated in Johann Joachim Winckelmann's *Monumenti antichi inediti* (1767). Almost none of David's contemporaries liked the work; it made Napoleon feel uneasy, possibly because he construed it as a presage of defeat.

4. LATE WORKS AND EXILE IN BRUSSELS, 1814–25. In April 1814, with British, Prussian, Austrian and Russian troops on French soil, Napoleon abdicated, and the Bourbon monarchy was restored under Louis XVIII. David kept a low profile during the first year of the Restoration but returned to Napoleon's side during the Hundred Days of 1815. He also signed the 'Addendum to the Constitution of the Empire', which prohibited any attempt to restore the Bourbons. But after the final defeat of Napoleon at Waterloo in June 1815 and the re-establishment of the Bourbon monarchy, Paris became a dangerous place for David. He applied for passports for England and Switzerland and went on a brief sketching trip to the latter. In January 1816 a law was passed banishing all regicides, and although David was informed that he could be exempted from it, he decided to go into exile in Belgium. He handed his teaching studio over to Gros and departed from Paris in late January 1816. A number of David's pupils were Belgian, notably François-Joseph Navez and Joseph-Denis Odevaere, and they welcomed and assisted him in Brussels, where he settled.

Historians have paid relatively little attention to the final nine years of David's career, a common view being that in Belgium his powers declined dramatically. Yet this was not David's opinion. Undoubtedly his later pictures appear different, but this can be attributed less to an artistic decline than to a change in artistic direction. David felt his Brussels pictures to be among his best, since in them he captured 'the simple and energetic taste of ancient Greece'. In the *Anger of Achilles* (1819; Fort Worth, TX, Kimbell A. Mus.), for example, Achilles, Agamemnon, Iphigenia and Clytemnestra are shown half-length in a highly compressed space close to the picture plane. In terms of both style and content this is a departure from his Parisian work, showing a concentration on the complex emotional interactions of the protagonists. Agamemnon's gesture and gaze that stop Achilles from drawing his sword may relate to the ideas on magnetism and personal control propagated by the Austrian physician Franz-Anton Mesmer (1734–1815). The colours are hard-edged and brilliant, indicating a study of Flemish painting of the 15th and 16th centuries.

While in Brussels David built up a considerable portrait practice. He painted a whole series of former Revolutionaries and supporters of Napoleon who were fellow exiles. These include the full-length of *Gen. Etienne-Maurice Gérard* (1816; New York, Met.) and the seated three-quarter-length of *Comte Henri-Amédée de Turenne* (1816; Copenhagen, Ny Carlsberg Glyp.). He also received commissions from the Belgian upper classes and nobility, and many of these paintings remain in the possession of the families that commissioned them, such as *Vicomtesse Sophie Vilain XIIII [XIV] and her Daughter* (London, N.G.). David seems often to have enlisted the help of assistants in these portraits.

Mythological painting also occupied a good deal of David's time in Brussels. He once declared that he had no talent for such subjects, but nevertheless many of his late works deal with Anacreontic themes of pairs of lovers. The first of these was *Cupid and Psyche* (Cleveland, OH, Mus. A.), commissioned in 1813 by the distinguished Italian collector Conte Giovanni Battista Sommariva and completed in 1817. Here David's mode of mythological expression is not to idealize and create languorous rhythms. Instead his figure of Cupid is firmly rooted in realism, a rather jarring conjunction of myth and reality. There is some evidence that David was working towards this painting before he left Paris, as it shares many stylistic characteristics with *Sappho and Phaon* (1809; St Petersburg, Hermitage).

The unsettling combination of the real with the ideal is also present in David's last large-scale painting, *Mars Disarmed by Venus and the Three Graces* (1821–4; Brussels, Mus. A. Anc.). David attached great importance to this work, and he saw it as his last testament in paint. Although there is a good deal of idealization and rhythmic sophistication, a number of the figures—the three Graces especially—are in theatrical and forced poses. The element of fantasy, previously so important in mythological painting, is substituted by parody; David radically re-examined the whole framework of mythology in this and others of his late works. Hence his late activities may be seen as attempts to reinterpret mythology rather than as a regression to the Rococo style of his youth. However, these pursuits were totally out of step with contemporary Parisian developments, and French critics were dismissive of the last paintings.

During David's exile the faithful Gros had been working for his master's return to Paris. David stubbornly insisted that Brussels was to his liking. At one point in 1824 he needed only to sign a draft petition to return, but he refused to do so. In July 1825 he had a stroke and died in December of that year. He was denied burial in France, and so an impressive funeral was arranged for him by the Belgian government. Plans to return David's remains to France in 1989 were frustrated by the Belgian authorities.

II. Working methods and technique.

David had an extremely laborious working procedure, in which draughtsmanship played a major role. He used mannequins to study individual details such as drapery, and his own Roman sketchbooks (Paris, Louvre; Cambridge, MA, Fogg; Stockholm, Nmus.) or reference books (e.g. Bernard de Montfaucon's *L'Antiquité expliquée*, 1719) to ensure that antique details were accurate. He drew extensively from posed life models, and such drawings would then be squared-up and transferred to the canvas. This process can be seen particularly vividly by comparing the finished *Oath of the Horatii* with the squared drawing of the group of women on the right (Paris, Louvre, RF 4506). He sometimes went so far as to produce drawings of the skeletons of his figures. David also made numerous small oil sketches for his large canvases in order to clarify the composition and lighting. His finished history paintings show his predilection for strong local colour. His figures have a relief-like modelling with impasto highlights and thinly scumbled opaque shadows. David worked on a single passage of a picture at a time, rather than treating all areas at once. There was little underpainting, and the *ébauche* was little more than a drawing that was completely obliterated by the final paint layer. Such exhaustive preparations meant that very few pentimenti are evident. He had little time for recipes for brushwork

and handling and wrote to his former pupil Wicar on 14 June 1789, 'What does it matter if one makes strokes to the right, to the left, up and down or sideways; as long as the lights are in their places, one will always paint well' (see David, 1880, p. 56). David's occasional difficulties with perspective are evident in the incorrect orthogonals of the pavement in *Belisarius Receiving Alms*. He frequently depicted paved floors in order to facilitate the location of figures in space (e.g. the *Oath of the Horatii*, the *Death of Socrates* and the *Lictors Bringing Brutus the Bodies of his Sons*). Despite such traditional academic procedures, his compositions were often viewed as unorthodox and anti-academic. Jean-Baptiste Pierre allegedly remarked of the *Brutus*, 'You have in your *Horatii* given us three personages set in the same plane, something never seen before! Here you put your principal actor in shadow.... But where have you seen, for example, that a sensible composition can be made without using the pyramidal line?' (David, 1880, p. 57). In his portraits David strove towards a tension between the natural and the ideal and gradually evolved the use of a neutral and vibrant background, as in *Mme Adélaïde Pastoret* and *Mme Henriette Verinac* (1799; Paris, Louvre).

David's more talented pupils usually assisted on the large history paintings and occasionally with the portraits as well. Drouais is supposed to have painted the arm of the third Horatii brother and the yellow garment of Sabina in the *Oath of the Horatii*. Jean-Pierre Franque assisted with the *Intervention of the Sabine Women*, and Georges Rouget on *Le Sacre* and *Leonidas at Thermopylae*. David also engaged his best pupils to paint reductions of his most successful pictures, adding the finishing touches himself and then passing them off as autograph works. That of *Belisarius* (Paris, Louvre), painted by Fabre in 1784 for the Comte d'Angiviller, and that of the *Oath of the Horatii* (Toledo, OH, Mus. A.), painted by Girodet in 1786 for the Comte de Vaudreuil, are examples. The exact proportion of pupil–master participation is impossible to establish, however, and these reductions (particularly the *Horatii*) remain the subject of controversy. A number of artists drew or painted the interior of David's studios, notably Jean-Henri Cless (*fl* 1804–11), who drew the Louvre studio in 1804 (Paris, Carnavalet), and Léon-Matthieu Cochereau (1793–1817), who depicted the studio in the Collège des Quatre Nations (now Institut de France) in 1814 (Paris, Louvre).

III. Critical reception and posthumous reputation.

David has often been accused of opportunism, largely because he lived through a period of unparalleled social and political upheaval. Certainly, he painted successively for the *ancien régime*, the Revolution and Napoleon, but all of his conversions appear to have been genuine and not premeditated. There have been many attempts to define the nature of David's politics. Opinion is sharply divided between those who believe he displayed radical tendencies as early as the 1780s (e.g. Crow) or not until 1790 (e.g. Bordes). Perhaps his clearest characteristic is his extreme pragmatism. What is beyond doubt is that he managed to encapsulate exactly in his painting the different aspirations of successive regimes, and for long periods created his own stylistic parameters. But David's Neo-classicism was by no means static. There are significant differences in aim displayed in the *Oath of the Horatii*, the *Intervention of the Sabine Women* and *Leonidas at Thermopylae*. His diversity is also apparent in his Empire work: 'Neo-classical' would be a singularly inappropriate label for the *Coronation of Napoleon in Notre-Dame*.

Through his approach to teaching and his legions of pupils, David had an enormous influence not only on French but on European art. He himself wrote, somewhat immodestly, 'I founded a brilliant school, I painted pictures that the whole of Europe came to study' (David, 1880, p. 601). But this view is corroborated, albeit critically, by Stendhal, who wrote, 'The illustrious David has won over Europe with his manner of painting . . . only England has resisted this conquest' (*Revue Trimestrielle*, July–Oct 1828). Ironically, many of the tenets of Neo-classicism, a revolutionary art form in the 1780s and 1790s, became staples in a highly orthodox and conservative form of academicism in the 19th century. To many critics David alone was responsible for a decline in French art, whereby all vigour and expression had been reduced to sterile formulae. In addition, by encouraging an emphasis on the intellectual aspects of painting, he was accused of fostering a neglect of technical expertise in the work of young artists. These criticisms, although mostly false, coupled with his Revolutionary past, ensured that soon after his death he was quickly forgotten. Despite maverick praise, such as Charles Baudelaire's haunting evocation of the *Death of Marat* (review in *Corsaire Satan*, 21 Jan 1846, of the exhibition held in the Bazaar Bonne Nouvelle, Paris), the resurrection of David's reputation was a slow and painful process, not without bitter controversy. Only since World War II has he been returned to the centre stage of European art.

WRITINGS

There is a substantial holding of David's writings in the Bibliothèque Nationale, Paris. See also the anonymous works of 1799 and 1814 entered below. For a list of his Revolutionary speeches and reports of 1792–3 see Wildenstein (1973), p. 283. For a large part of his correspondence, see J. L. J. David (1880).

BIBLIOGRAPHY

Le Tableau des Sabines exposé publiquement au Palais national des sciences et des arts, salle de la ci-devant Académie d'architecture par le citoyen David (Paris, an VIII [1799]) [written by David]
P. Chaussard: *Le Pausanias français: Etat des arts du dessin en France à l'ouverture du XIXᵉ siècle* (Paris, 1806), pp. 145–74
Explication du tableau des Thermopyles par M. David (Paris, 1814) [written with the help of David]
Account of the Celebrated Picture of the Coronation of Napoleon by M. David, First Painter to the Emperor (London, 1821)
Notice sur la vie et les ouvrages de M. J. L. David (Brussels, 1824) [written with David's collaboration]
E. J. Delécluze: *Louis David, son école et son temps* (Paris, 1855)
J. L. J. David: *Le Peintre Louis David, 1748–1825: Souvenirs et documents inédits* (Paris, 1880)
D. L. Dowd: *Pageant-Master of the Republic: Jacques-Louis David and the French Revolution* (Lincoln, NE, 1948) [with valuable essay on sources]
L. Hautecoeur: *Louis David* (Paris, 1954)
R. Herbert: *J. L. David, Brutus* (London, 1972)
D. Wildenstein and G. Wildenstein: *Documents complémentaires au catalogue de l'oeuvre de Louis David* (Paris, 1973) [incl. extensive bibliography but with some omissions]
A. Brookner: *Jacques-Louis David* (London, 1980)
A. Schnapper: *David: Témoin de son temps* (Fribourg, 1980; Eng. trans., New York, 1982)
David e Roma (exh. cat. by R. Michel, A. Serullaz and U. van de Sandt, Rome, Acad. France, 1981) [incl. repr. of several valuable documents]
P. Bordes: *Le 'Serment du Jeu de Paume' de Jacques-Louis David: Le Peintre, son milieu et son temps de 1789 à 1792* (Paris, 1983) [amplified version of article in *Oxford A.J.*, iii/2 (1980), pp. 19–25]
T. Crow: *Painters and Public Life in Eighteenth-century Paris* (New Haven and London, 1985), pp. 212–41
M. C. Sahut and R. Michel: *David, l'art et la politique* (Paris, 1988)
W. Roberts: *Jacques-Louis David: Revolutionary Artist* (Chapel Hill and London, 1989)
David (exh. cat. by A. Schnapper and A. Sérullaz, Paris, Louvre; Versailles, Château; 1989–90)
P. Rosenblum: 'Reconstructing David', *A. America*, lxxviii (1990), pp. 188–97, 257
A. Sérullaz: *Musée du Louvre, Cabinet des dessins. Inventaire général des dessins: Ecole française, dessins de Jacques-Louis David, 1748–1825* (Paris, 1991)
D. Johnson: *Jacques-Louis David: Art in Metamorphosis* (Princeton, 1993)
'David contre David', *Proc. 1989 David Colloq.*, 2 vols (Paris, 1993)

SIMON LEE

David, Joe [Ka-ka-win-chealth: 'White Wolf Spirit'] (*b* Opitsaht, Vancouver Island, BC, 1946). Native Canadian Clayoquot painter and printmaker. His father, Hyacinth David Sr, was a renowned shaman. Joe David attended high school in Texas, 1966–7, and in 1970 turned to art as a career. He studied under Duane Pascoe and BILL HOLM, both major Northwest Coast artists and teachers. His work centres on an effort to record the art and cultural life of his people, and features marked contrasts in line, form and colour. His designs reflect traditional symbolism. He was active with pen and ink in his youth, and also experimented in sculpture and textiles. Later, he worked in oils and did some bronze-casting. He also became interested in graphics, and in 1977 turned to screenprinting as a major form of expression. In 1981 he was adopted into the Haida tribe by ROBERT DAVIDSON, one of Canada's leading artists, and honoured with a potlatch (a rank validation ceremony in which gifts are distributed and sometimes deliberately destroyed). He received a major commission in 1985 to carve the controversial *Cedar Man* figure for the front of the Parliament building in Victoria, BC (now in Vancouver, U. BC Mus. Anthropol.). A resident of Tofino, BC, near Opitsaht, David was also a shaman and an activist for environmental causes. In the late 1980s and 1990s he spearheaded an effort to preserve the natural qualities of Meares Island, a major tribal shrine.

For general discussion of 20th-century developments in Native American art *see* NATIVE NORTH AMERICAN ART §XV.

BIBLIOGRAPHY

J. C. Mills: 'The Meares Island Controversy and Joe David', *Amer. Ind. A.*, xiv/4 (1989), pp. 60–8

FREDERICK J. DOCKSTADER

Dávid, Károly (*b* Budapest, 19 March 1903; *d* Budapest, 30 Nov 1973). Hungarian architect. He entered the Faculty of Architecture at Budapest Technical University in 1922. Following his graduation in 1931 he went abroad on a study trip, during which he spent nine months with Le Corbusier's practice in Paris. On his return to Hungary in 1934 he became a member of the Hungarian affiliate of CIAM. His villa (1937–8; destr. 1944, see Máté, pp. 6–8) on Gellért Hill, Budapest, reflected Le Corbusier's influence with its ribbon windows, terrace and raised façade. Ferihegy Airport (1939), Budapest, is in a more conservative style than his previous work. A simple functional building, it features symmetrically arranged control towers, which invest the façade with a particular individuality. In 1948 he became a state-employed architect and was subsequently commissioned to design the People's Stadium (1950–53), Budapest, the largest Hungarian building project of the period. His first draft, developed in collaboration with István Janáky, suggests that he envisaged an undulating concrete foil of longitudinal sections of varied size connected by lower 'saddles'. However, the stadium (incomplete in that the top grandstand was only half-built) was eventually built in a far more conservative fashion due to a change in official attitudes to art. For some of its more functional aspects, such as the view of the playing area and the ease of spectator circulation, the stadium can be considered a model of its kind. From the late 1950s Dávid was able to design anew in the spirit of Functionalism, and an example of this style is the secondary school on the upper bank of the Tisza, Szeged (1960). Most of his work from this period is concerned with buildings for cultural purposes and he also collaborated with sculptors, providing the architectural plans for their monuments, for example the Haydn Monument, Budapest (1960; with A. Kocsis, 1905–76).

BIBLIOGRAPHY

K. Pongrácz and others: 'Ötéves tervünk nagy alkotása a Népstadion'; 'A Népstadion elhelyezési és forgalmi problémái'; 'A Népstadion tervezéstörténete'; 'A Népstadion tervezése'; 'A Népstadion'; 'A Népstadion dromosza', *Magyar Építőművészet*, ii/11–12 (1953), pp. 327–62 [six articles on the planning and building of the People's Stadium]

P. Máté: *Dávid Károly* (Budapest, 1974)

FERENC VADAS

David, Ludovico (*b* Lugano, 13 June 1648; *d* after 6 July 1709). Italian painter and theorist. He went to Milan about 1665 to study painting under Francesco Cairo. A decade later he moved to Venice, where for the Lombard chapel of S Maria dei Frari he painted *St Carlo Borromeo Distributing Alms to the Poor* (*in situ*) in the dark, dramatic, fully Baroque manner of his teacher. David's other documented works in Venice are in S Maria del Carmelo and the Palazzo Albizzi a Sant'Aponal. While in Venice he also operated a highly successful art academy, remarkably, in competition with Pietro della Vecchia, a far more successful painter. Contemporary reports indicate that 'he contradicted della Vecchia at every turn', and that he played down the importance of drawing, making it secondary to the painter's own ideas. This attitude was highly radical, given that drawing was then considered the basis of an artist's education. By May 1686 David was in Rome, where he remained for the rest of his life. His two large canvases for S Andrea al Quirinale, the *Adoration of the Magi* and the *Adoration of the Shepherds*, are generally considered his best works. Both were commissioned some time after 1691 by Cardinal Pietro Ottoboni, the nephew of Pope Alexander VIII. They are painted with rich colours and turbulent rhythms, in the manner of the much-acclaimed *Death of St Francis Xavier* by Giovanni Battista Gaulli (known as Baciccio) in the same church. David is now recognized as the first true scholar of Leonardo da Vinci. Though his essay on Leonardo is untraced, his research method (as known from his letters) was based on lengthy and painstaking examination and decipherment of the artist's original manuscripts, such as the Codex Leicester

(Holkham Hall, Norfolk, Lib.), which in the late 17th century was in Rome in the possession of the painter Giuseppe Ghezzi.

David is even better known for his treatise entitled *L'amore dell'arte*, written about 1704 and circulated in manuscript form among his friends, though never published (see Turner). The treatise, dedicated to Clement XI, is in the form of a virulent attack, somewhat in the tradition of Salvator Rosa, on the art establishment of Rome as represented by the Accademia di S Luca. The essay is divided into three parts. The most important is the first, in which David bitterly disputed the dominant position given to life drawing and drapery studies in the academy's training programme. Instead, apparently influenced by the high regard for science in the Age of Enlightenment, David recommended that pride of place should go to mathematics, and especially to Euclidian geometry, from which an overall sense of pictorial unity would be derived. The implications of this position were considerable. It challenged not only the system of art education at the Accademia and elsewhere (which, since the success of the Carracci's academy in Bologna, had given primacy to drawing from live models) but also the entire classical tradition, which held that realism, albeit an idealization of the real, was capable of expressing the most profound emotions and was thus the noblest form of art. This view reveals the growing dissatisfaction with the glorification of drawing that was part of the Disegno e colore debate. Thus to some extent the essay reflects an appreciation of the more abstract values that were prized by the Rococo age.

In the second section of *L'amore dell'arte* David assailed the Accademia di S Luca for being largely responsible for the declining importance of the Roman school of painting. This resulted partly from an increasing neglect of Raphael and partly from the proclivity of the academicians to praise foreign artists over their own. (During the latter part of the 17th century and the first part of the 18th the artistic life of Rome was increasingly dominated by the French: at one point the Accademia made Charles Le Brun its director, though he never came to Rome to receive the title; the dominance was also fostered by prominent academicians such as Pietro Bellori, who took Poussin as his ideal and dedicated his most important book to Jean Baptiste Colbert.)

The third part of David's essay, attacking the crest that Giuseppe Ghezzi had devised in 1704 for the Concorso Clementino, the annual competition of the Accademia, excited the most controversy in its day. Ghezzi's simple device, a triangle made up of a brush, a chisel and a compass, was intended to symbolize the equality of painting, sculpture and architecture, a premise intended to promote harmony within the academy. But David argued that painting was supreme over the other arts and even suggested that architecture should be dropped from the curriculum entirely. He was especially incensed at the large role that architects played in the affairs of the academy, and he went on to criticize the work of the then powerful architect Carlo Fontana. Two essays were subsequently published in defence of the crest, which continued in use for the better part of a century. Despite its querulous tone, David's treatise is important in anticipating, by more than half a century, the Romantic position of the artist, who is freed from the strictures of the establishment and thus able to follow the dictates of his own genius.

UNPUBLISHED SOURCES

Modena, Bib. Estense, Raccolta Campori Cod. 1071-γ.H.1.38 [*L'amore dell'arte*]

BIBLIOGRAPHY

Füssli; Thieme–Becker

P. A. Orlandi: *Abecedario pittorico* (Bologna, 1704), pp. 258, 293

F. S. Baldinucci: *Vite* (1725–30); ed. A. Matteoli (1975), pp. 49–51

V. da Canal: *Vita di Gregorio Lazzarini* (MS., 1732; Venice, 1809), pp. 25–6

A. M. Zanetti: *Descrizione di tutte le pubbliche pitture della città di Venezia* (Venice, 1733), p. 269

F. Titi: *Descrizione delle pitture . . . in Roma* (Rome, 1763), pp. 285, 303

G. Bottari and S. Ticozzi: *Raccolta di lettere sulla pittura . . .* (Milan, 1822), iii, pp. 361–9, and v, pp. 346–7

U. Donati: *Artisti ticinesi a Roma* (Bellinzona, 1942), pp. 607–14

F. Bassoli: 'Un pittore svizzero pioniere degli studi vinciani: Ludovico David', *Rac. Vinc.*, xvii (1954), pp. 261–314

J. Schlosser Magnino: *La letteratura artistica*, 2nd edn O. Kurz (Florence, 1956), pp. 467, 475, 599

N. Ivanoff: 'Ludovico David da Lugano e la sua Accademia veneziana', *Emporium*, cxxxvi (1957), pp. 248–53

R. Enggass: *Baciccio* (University Park, PA State U., 1964), p. 166

F. Haskell: *Patrons and Painters* (London, 1971, 2/1980), pp. 88, 220

N. Turner: 'An Attack on the Accademia di S Luca: Ludovico David's *L'amore dell'arte*', *BM Yb.*, i (1976), pp. 157–86, figs 211–15, 220–25

L. Grassi: *Teorici e storia della critica d'arte* (Rome, 1979), iii, ad indicem

R. Pallucchini: *La pittura veneziana del seicento* (Milan, 1981), i, ad indicem, ii, figs 941, 942

ROBERT ENGGASS

David, Sir Percival (*b* Bombay, 21 July 1892; *d* London 9 Oct 1964). English businessman, collector and connoisseur of Chinese art. He was educated at Elphinstone College, Bombay, and at the universities of Bombay and London. During several years in East Asia he studied the cultures and languages of China and Japan. From 1928 to 1929 he was honorary adviser to the Palace Museum, Beijing. He developed at an early date a knowledge of the imperial collections in Beijing unique in the West, and by the early 1930s he had formed an extremely important collection of Chinese ceramics, with a high number of dated and inscribed pieces, many of which are of historical value. From 1933 to 1938, and again from 1953 onwards, he was active as a member of the Council of the Oriental Ceramic Society in London, of which he became Honorary Vice-President in 1961. In 1935 he served as Director of the International Exhibition of Chinese Art held in London (1935–6). His collection constituted the largest individual contribution to this exhibition, exceeded only by that of the Chinese government. He continued to make further additions to his collection in later years, until in 1951 he offered it as a gift to the University of London. The Percival David Foundation of Chinese Art of the School of Oriental and African Studies (*see* CHINA, §§VII, 7 and XIX) was opened to the public in 1952. His collected ceramics date largely from the 10th to the 18th century and comprise about 1400 items (*see* CHINA, fig. 208 for an illustration of the 'David vases').

David's approach to collecting was intellectual, based on imperial precedent, and influenced by two important Chinese literary works: the *Gegu yaolun* ('Essential criteria of antiquities'; 1387), a handbook on antiquities by Cao Zhao, which David later translated and edited, and Zhu Yan's *Taoshuo* (1774), translated in 1910 by Stephen Bushell as *Description of Chinese Pottery and Porcelain*. David's studies of Chinese and Japanese art were more broadly based than the scope of his collection. Among his small number of publications, 'A Commentary on Ju Ware' was important for establishing the identity of the rare Song porcelains.

WRITINGS

'A Commentary on Ju Ware', *Trans. Orient. Cer. Soc.* xiv (1936–7), pp. 18–69

trans.: Cao Zhao: *Gegu yaolun* (Nanjing, 1387) as *Chinese Connoisseurship: The Ko ku yao lun, the Essential Criteria of Antiquities* (London, 1971)

BIBLIOGRAPHY

R. L. Hobson: *A Catalogue of Chinese Pottery and Porcelain in the Collection of Sir Percival David* (London, 1934)

S. David: *Percival David Foundation of Chinese Art: Illustrated Guide to the Collection* (London, 1956)

H. M. Garner: Obituary, *Trans. Orient. Cer. Soc.*, xxxv (1963–4), pp. xxi–xxii

M. Medley: *Percival David Foundation of Chinese Art: Illustrated Guide to the Collection* (London, 1974)

R. E. Scott: *Percival David Foundation of Chinese Art: A Guide to the Collection* (London, 1989)

For further bibliography on the Percival David collection *see* CHINA, §VII, 3(vi) and (vii).

S. J. VERNOIT

David d'Angers [David, Pierre-Jean] (*b* Angers, 12 March 1788; *d* Paris, 6 Jan 1856). French sculptor. A remarkably comprehensive view of this most prolific of 19th-century sculptors is provided by the collection of his work in the Musée des Beaux-Arts et Galerie David d'Angers in Angers. Begun in 1839 from models for the sculptor's public statues that he had consistently sent to his home town, the collection was enriched after his death by numerous donations; in 1983 it was rehoused in the 13th-century abbey of Toussaints adjacent to the Musée des Beaux-Arts. Unless otherwise stated, plaster or marble versions of specific works mentioned in this article can be found in this collection.

1. Training and travels abroad, to 1816. 2. 1816–41. 3. 1842 and after.

1. TRAINING AND TRAVELS ABROAD, TO 1816. Son of the ornamental wood-carver Jean-Louis David (1760–1821), who enrolled in 1793 in the Republican force that opposed the anti-revolutionary uprising, Pierre-Jean worked with his father and was further encouraged in his artistic ambitions by Jacques Delusse (1757–1833), painter and curator of the Musée des Beaux-Arts in Angers. In 1807 he went to Paris and found employment as a decorative sculptor on the Arc de Triomphe du Carrousel. Living at this time in dire poverty, he entered the studio of Philippe-Laurent Roland in 1809. A first effort at the Prix de Rome in 1810, *Othryades Dying*, brought him a second prize and attracted the attention of the painter Jacques-Louis David. A grant from the municipal council of Angers in 1811 allowed him to continue his studies. These were rewarded with success in the same year, when his relief of the *Death of Epaminondas* won the Prix de Rome. While in Rome (1811–15), David d'Angers experimented with a linear mannerism, akin to that of Ingres or Girodet, in the relief *Nereid Bringing Back the Helmet of Achilles*. In the *Young Shepherd* he adopted an introverted Greek Revival mode close to Bertel Thorvaldsen's. Later he claimed to have resisted the 'antique sensualism' of Canova, preferring to devote himself to an art celebrating

heroes and men of genius. In Rome his imagination was deeply marked by a doomed liaison with a girl of patrician family, Cecilia Odescalchi. Her death, after their forced separation, caused him to retain a poeticized romantic image of her which frequently recurs in his work. In 1816 David travelled to London on Canova's recommendation, to see the Parthenon marbles (which had been transferred to the British Museum that year at the instigation of Thomas Bruce, 7th Earl of Elgin) and also to visit John Flaxman. The latter, confusing him with the painter David, turned him away.

2. 1816–41. Back in France, David d'Angers suppressed his Republican principles and compromised with the restored Bourbons, participating in official decorative schemes such as the adornment of the Cour Carrée (1824) of the Louvre, and the modification of the Arc de Triomphe du Carrousel (1827). The first of such state commissions was passed down to him in 1816, following the death of his master Roland. It was for a colossal marble statue of the *Grand Condé* (destr.), destined for the Pont Louis XVI (now Pont de la Concorde). The figure can best be judged from the surviving half-size, but still over life-size, plaster model. It harks back to the series of statues of great men commissioned for the state in the 1770s and 1780s by the Comte d'Angiviller. David d'Angers added emphatic drama and simplified the costumed pageantry of the earlier historical figures, producing an image in strong contrast to the preponderantly Neo-classical sculpture exhibited at the Salon of 1817.

For other statues executed during the following decade, David d'Angers preferred to retain elements of the timeless convention of Neo-classical sculpture. His monument to *Jean Racine* (marble, 1819–33) for La-Ferté-Milon combines 17th-century hairstyle with a loosely draped nude figure. In the monument to *Gen. Bonchamps* (marble, 1816–25) at Saint-Florent-le-Vieil, the nature of the event commemorated (a last act of clemency by the dying royalist general towards Republican prisoners of the Vendée War, including David's own father) validates the general's draped nude figure. His dramatically raised hand and commanding expression bring back to life, in its original location, an historical event of which David had a personal recollection. A compromise is reached in the monument to *Gen. Foy* (marble, 1827–31) in Père Lachaise Cemetery, Paris. Here the portrait statue of the soldier–legislator, framed by Léon Vaudoyer's miniature Doric temple, is rendered in antique guise, while the biographical reliefs around the upper podium are formalized interpretations of modern scenes. Following his appointment in 1826 as professor at the Ecole des Beaux-Arts in Paris, David had begun to pursue more personal preoccupations. He undertook at his own expense, having been frustrated in his requests for state sponsorship, a monument to *Marco Botzaris*, one of the martyrs of the Greek War of Independence, to be erected at Missolonghi in Greece (marble, Athens, Hist. Mus.). The statue of the *Young Greek Girl* seated on the tomb of Botzaris and spelling out his epitaph with her finger, was exhibited at the Paris Salon of 1827. This very original rendering of the pre-pubescent female figure was a work for which David retained an almost paternal affection.

Around the same time, David's project began to take shape for a portrait pantheon in the form of a series of medallions and busts of all the outstanding men and women of his time. These, along with the commemorative statues that David executed for towns throughout France, formed the core of that morally uplifting national art for which David found the model in the republics of the ancient world. The medallion series, which he began to think of as a comprehensive survey in 1828 (though a number of significant examples had been executed before this), took David to England and to Germany, in pursuit of persons prominent in the national life. In the medallions, and even more so in his busts, David was influenced by the phrenological theory of Franz Josef Gall to emphasize those physiognomic developments that were supposed to designate specific propensities—sensual, intellectual or emotional—in the subject. Of the more than 500 that he executed, most are large, measuring between 130 and 180 mm, and are profile portraits, with assertively modelled features and tousled hair predominating over elegance of composition. Several others, including *Théodore Gericault* and *Alfred de Musset*, are three-quarter views. Only one, of David's American patron, *Uriah Phillips Levy* (1792–1862), shows its subject full face, while *Mme Récamier* is seen from the back with head turned to present a slightly obscured profile.

1. David d'Angers: *Niccolò Paganini*, bronze, h. 600 mm, 1830–33 (Angers, Galerie David d'Angers)

Having until then been mainly concerned with marble statuary, the medallion series alerted David to the expressive potential of sculpture modelled for casting in bronze. This coincided with his acceptance into the emergent Romantic *cenacles*, particularly that of Victor Hugo, and, after 1830, a new search for colouristic effects in bronze was shared by David with a number of other Romantic sculptors such as Antoine-Louis Barye, Auguste Préault and Antonin-Marie Moine. David can be seen responding with maximum intensity to the medium in the bust of *Niccolò Paganini* (1830–33; Angers, Gal. David d'Angers, see fig. 1) and the statue of *Thomas Jefferson* (1832–4), donated by Levy to the US Capitol in Washington, DC. Both were cast by Honoré Gonon, using the lost-wax method, and reveal a restless pursuit of rugged surface effects. The *Paganini* departs from David's more usual tendency towards the static and monumental in portrait busts. In those of *Chateaubriand* (marble, 1829; Combourg, Château) and *Goethe* (marble, 1831; Weimar, Goethe-Nmus.), Romantic hyperbole is contained within an abruptly truncated symmetrical format.

The statue of *Jefferson* was the first of a series of bronze commemorative statues, with the subjects seen in the costume of their own time, which David produced thereafter at regular intervals until the end of his life. More than any other artist, David was responsible for promoting the 19th-century cult of the commemorative statue. His seated or standing figures are usually accompanied by distinguishing attributes: *Johann Gutenberg* (bronze, 1839–40) for Strasbourg, standing with his printing press; *Bernardin de Saint Pierre* (bronze, 1851) for Le Havre, seated with the infants Paul and Virginie sleeping amid tropical foliage at his side. On other occasions costume and attitude suffice, as in the *Pierre Corneille* (bronze, 1834) at Rouen, or the *Gerbert* (bronze, 1850) at Aurillac. In many cases narrative reliefs decorate the statue's base. These are in a crowded and purposefully naive style reminiscent of popular imagery, indicating David's intention to make these monuments an elevating text accessible to all. David sculpted two statues of *King René of Anjou*, the first of which had been a marble for Aix-en-Provence commissioned as far back as 1819. (In the second, inaugurated at Angers in 1846, the sculptor surrounded the base of his statue with 12 free-standing bronze statuettes representing figures from medieval and earlier French history.)

The stylistic peculiarities that feature in the narrative reliefs are also to be found in the two major commissions David received from the newly formed government of the July Monarchy. These were the marble pediment relief for the Panthéon, with the subject *To Great Men the Fatherland is Grateful* (commissioned 1830; see fig. 2), and the marble decoration of the Porte d'Aix at Marseille (1831–5), with subjects relating to Napoleon's campaigns, the latter commission shared with the sculptor Etienne-Jules Ramey. The Panthéon pediment departs radically from the standard iconography of apotheosis, in bringing together both famous figures and men of the people distinguished for learning or heroism, and also in its emphasis on secular and Republican achievement. Here, as on the Porte d'Aix, Napoleon is celebrated as a soldier and not as emperor. As the complexion of the July Monarchy grew increasingly authoritarian, David was called on to defend his choices.

2. David d'Angers: *To Great Men the Fatherland is Grateful*, detail of the marble pediment of the Panthéon, Paris, commissioned 1830

He remained adamant, and his work was surreptitiously unveiled in September 1837. The populist theme is repeated in the huge relief on the west interior face of the Marseille arch. The subject, like that of François Rude's better-known relief on the Arc de Triomphe de l'Etoile, is the *Departure of the Volunteers*, but, whereas Rude's Frenchmen are depicted as ancient Gauls, David's allegorical Patrie distributes arms to vigorously portrayed representatives of the revolutionary era wearing the costumes of their time. In David's relief the modes are mixed (just as they had been in Delacroix's *Liberty Leading the People* of 1830), whereas history and allegory are firmly segregated on the outer faces of the Marseille arch.

3. 1842 AND AFTER. Although ill health obliged David to relinquish his courses at the Ecole in 1842, his productivity as a commemorative sculptor continued unabated. His contribution of funerary monuments to Père Lachaise Cemetery reached its climax with the heroic pathos of the monument to *Gen. Gobert* (1847), in which the young general slips dying from his horse as it tramples his Spanish adversary. In the Salon of 1845, David showed a more intimate piece, an allegorical nude statue of his son Robert, entitled *Child with a Bunch of Grapes* (plaster, Angers, Mus. B.-A.; marble, modified from the original model, Paris, Louvre). The homely philosophizing characteristic of David's voluminous private journals (see Bruel) finds an outlet in this work, though its moral message was overlooked by Baudelaire, who, in his review of the Salon, complained only of its excessive naturalism.

During the shortlived Republic of 1848, David was appointed mayor of the 11th arrondissement of Paris and was elected deputy for Anjou to the Constituent Assembly. He was not re-elected to the assembly the following year but had been sufficiently outspoken during his period in office to provoke arrest and exile after the Bonapartist *coup d'état* of 1851. He had always been insistent in his refusal to celebrate the imperial legend. A sympathetic interest in the fate of Queen Hortense, mother of Louis-Napoléon, had allowed him to submit a project for a monument to her, after her death in 1837. However, when the commission for the monument went instead to Lorenzo Bartolini and then to Jean-Auguste Barre, David was relieved that his sympathy had not led him in the end to compromise his Republicanism.

In exile David travelled to Belgium, then to Greece, where he was distressed to find that his monument to *Botzaris* had been vandalized. The poet Béranger interceded on his behalf in 1852, and he was permitted to return to France. In 1855, the year before his death, he visited the museum at Angers that had been enshrining his works since 1839, having at last overcome his scruples at such a pre-posthumous celebration.

WRITINGS
A. Bruel, ed.: *Les Carnets de David d'Angers* (Paris, 1958)

BIBLIOGRAPHY
R. David and E. About: *Les Médaillons de David d'Angers* (Paris, 1867)
H. Jouin: *David d'Angers: Sa Vie, son oeuvre, ses écrits, ses contemporains*, 2 vols (Paris, 1878)
G. Chesneau and C. Metzger: *Les Oeuvres de David d'Angers*, Angers, Mus. B.-A. cat. (Angers, 1934)
The Romantics to Rodin (exh. cat., ed. H. W. Janson and P. Fusco; Los Angeles, CA, Co. Mus. A., 1980) [esp. contributions by J. Holderbaum on portrait sculpture and on David d'Angers]
N. McWilliam: 'David d'Angers and the Panthéon Commission: Politics and Public Works under the July Monarchy', *A. Hist.*, v/4 (1982), pp. 426–46
J. de Caso: *David d'Angers: L'Avenir de la mémoire: Etude sur l'art signalétique à l'époque romantique* (Paris, 1988)
S. G. Lindsay: *David d'Angers' Monument to Bonchamps: A Tomb Project in Context* (Ann Arbor, 1992)

PHILIP WARD-JACKSON

David Garedzhi. Complex of cave monasteries in the Garedzhi Desert, 60–70 km south-east of Tbilisi, Republic of Georgia. In the early 6th century the monk David, one of the 13 'Syrian fathers' who preached Christianity in Georgia, and his pupil Lukian inhabited the caves, thus forming the basis of the Lavra of David. During the following centuries 11 further monasteries were founded in the cave complex, including Tsamebuli, Natlismtsemeli (John the Baptist), Chichkhituri, Dodos-Rka, Bertubani and Sabereyebi. They are spread over a wide area and include hundreds of cells, churches, chapels, refectories and living-quarters hollowed out of the rock face.

Despite the harsh environment, David Garedzhi remained an important centre of religious and cultural activity for many centuries; at certain periods the monasteries owned extensive agricultural lands and many villages. King David III the Builder (*reg* 1089–1125) made David Garedzhi a royal property. Its main period of development was in the late 12th century and the early 13th, with the construction and decoration in fresco of numerous cave churches and refectories. These structures are much larger than the earlier ones and are decorated with exceptionally beautiful murals, displaying a distinctive school of Georgian monumental painting. Among the portraits of historical figures are those of *Queen Tamar* (*reg* 1179–1212) and her son *Lasha Georgy IV* (*reg* 1212–23; both Tbilisi, Mus. A. Georgia) from the church of Bertubani Monastery and

David Garedzhi, Bertubani Monastery, refectory, wall painting of the *Eucharist*, early 13th century

that of *King Dimitry II* (*reg* 1273–89) in the church of the Annunciation in Udabno Monastery (*in situ*). The refectory of Udabno Monastery is painted with scenes from the *Life of St David of Garedzhi* (11th–12th century), based on the text of the ancient Georgian Apocrypha, while at Bertubani the refectory's wall paintings (early 13th century) include the *Eucharist* (see fig.) and such related scenes as the *Last Supper*, the *Marriage at Cana*, the *Miracle of the Loaves and Fishes* and *Christ and the Samaritan Woman*.

David Garedzhi was attacked by Timur (*reg* 1370–1405) in the late 14th century, by Iranian troops in 1616–17 and by the Lezgin tribe from Dagestan in the 18th century. As a result, separate defensive buildings and residential towers were built in the 16th to 18th centuries, enabling the monasteries to function until the late 19th century. They continue to house many valuable manuscripts.

BIBLIOGRAPHY

G. Chubinashvili: *Peshchernyye monastyri David-Garedzhi* [The cave monasteries of David Garedzhi] (Tbilisi, 1948)

A. Vol'skaya: *Rospisi srednevekovykh trapeznykh Gruzii* [Wall paintings in medieval Georgian refectories] (Tbilisi, 1974)

V. Beridze and others: *The Treasures of Georgia* (London, 1984)

V. BERIDZE

Davidson, Bruce (*b* Chicago, IL, 1933). American photographer. While still at school he took photography lessons using a Rolleiflex. He studied photography at Rochester Institute of Technology, NY (1951–4), then philosophy, painting, photography and (under Josef Albers) graphic design at Yale University, New Haven, CT (1955). While serving in the US Army (1955–7), he was stationed in Paris where he met Henri Cartier-Bresson and photographed Montmartre, Les Halles and other areas, in the style of Alfred Stieglitz. In 1958 he joined Magnum Photos, working as a fashion photographer and becoming a prominent photojournalist. He covered the race riots in the American South during the 1960s, and his work appeared in many leading international magazines. He is best known for numerous photographic essays on people living on the fringe of society (e.g. *Clown*, 1958; Rochester, NY, Int. Mus. Phot.), recorded with sensitivity and a visual richness, which were hallmarks of his style.

PHOTOGRAPHIC PUBLICATIONS

East 100th Street, intro. by J. Szarkowski (Cambridge, MA, 1970)

Bruce Davidson Photographs, intro. by H. Geldzahler (New York and London, 1979)

BIBLIOGRAPHY

J. Szarkowski, ed.: *Mirrors and Windows: American Photography since 1960* (New York, 1978), p. 36

□

Davidson, J(ulius) R(alph) (*b* Berlin, 7 Feb 1889; *d* Ojai, CA, 2 May 1977). American architect of German birth. He grew up in northern Germany and acquired his architectural education by apprenticeship, working in 1908–9 in the Berlin office of the Hungarian architect Moritz Hirschler and in 1910–12 in London with Frank Stuart Murray. It was in Murray's office that he first confronted the world of industrial design, through this firm's work on the interiors of ocean liners. He then worked briefly in Paris before doing military service in Germany during World War I. After a short period of private practice in Berlin (1919–23), he moved to the USA. He established himself in Los Angeles, working in 1923–

4 in the office of the Beaux-Arts architect Robert D. Farquhar (1872–1967) and then as a set designer for a number of the Hollywood films of Cecil B. De Mille. In the later 1920s he increasingly turned his attention to commercial design. In 1926 he replanned the famous Cocoanut Grove Restaurant in Hollywood, and this was followed by such widely published designs as the Satyr Bookshop and the High Hat Restaurant, both in Los Angeles (1929). In the early years of the Depression he moved his office to Chicago, where he was engaged in the remodelling of a number of large hotels from 1932 to 1935. After his return to Los Angeles in 1936, most of his commissions were domestic, either the extensive remodelling of existing houses or the design of new dwellings. Two of his most widely published Modernist designs of the pre-World War II years were the Stothart house, 2501 La Mesa Drive, Santa Monica, CA (1937), and the Thomas Mann house, 1550 San Remo Drive, Pacific Palisades, CA (1941). In 1946 Davidson was one of the first architects selected by the magazine *Arts and Architecture* to design a Case Study House. This was a small single-floor dwelling whose open plan and sliding glass walls fully united the garden with the interior of the house. This house was followed by a number of single and multiple family houses, all of which seemed akin to finely designed pieces of furniture. He continued to practise architecture until his retirement in 1972.

WRITINGS

'Herbert Stothart House, Santa Monica', *A. & Archit.*, lvii/5 (1940), pp. 26–7

'House for Thomas Mann', *A. & Archit.*, lix/12 (1942), pp. 36–7

'Case Study House No. 11', *A. & Archit.*, lxv/5 (1948), pp. 26–7

BIBLIOGRAPHY

E. McCoy: *Modern California Houses: Case Study Houses, 1945–1962* (New York, 1962), pp. 12–19

——: *The Second Generation* (Salt Lake City, 1984), pp. 2–35

DAVID GEBHARD

Davidson, Robert (*b* Masset, Queen Charlotte Islands, BC, 4 Nov 1946). Native American Haida sculptor, metalworker, printmaker and blanket-maker. He was the grandson of the Haida blanket- and basket-maker Florence Davidson (1895–1993), and great-grandson of the Haida wood-carver CHARLES EDENSHAW. He began carving argillite as a teenager in Masset, and in 1966 he met BILL REID, who offered him workshop space in Vancouver. There Davidson developed new carving skills and learnt the fundamentals of the two-dimensional ('formline') designs used by the Haida and other tribes of the northern Northwest Coast (*see* NATIVE NORTH AMERICAN ART, §III, 2). In 1969 he returned to Masset to carve a 12.2 m-high totem pole, the first heraldic column to be raised on the Queen Charlotte Islands since the end of the 19th century. In 1987 Davidson and his crew produced a set of three totem poles entitled *Three Variations on Killer Whale Myths* for the Pepsicola Sculptural Garden in Purchase, NY. In these totem poles Davidson worked within the strict conventions of the Haida style, refining it by introducing subtle variations in design but preserving a degree of conservative austerity in which movement and individual expression are sacrificed to overall unity of form. In his early work in silver Davidson used flat patterns influenced by Edenshaw, and he went on to develop these into an innovative style of his own in screenprints, silver and bronze. Davidson's younger brother, Reg Davidson (*b* 1954), is an argillite carver in the Haida tradition.

BIBLIOGRAPHY

H. Stewart: *Robert Davidson: Haida Printmaker* (Seattle, 1979)
The Legacy: Continuing Traditions of Canadian Northwest Coast Indian Art (exh. cat. by P. L. Macnair, A. L. Hoover and K. Neary, Victoria, BC, Prov. Mus., 1980)

MARTINE REID

Davíðsson, Kristján (*b* Reykjavík, 28 July 1917). Icelandic painter. He studied with the painters Finnur Jónsson and Jóhann Briem in Reykjavík (1932–3 and 1935–6) and at the Barnes Foundation and the University of Pennsylvania in Philadelphia (1945–7). He was in Paris and London in 1949. A fine draughtsman and a sensitive colourist, Davíðsson was Iceland's most important exponent of ART INFORMEL. His first models were the early modernists that he encountered at the Barnes Foundation, Merion Station, PA, in 1945. In 1949 Davíðsson met the critic Michel Tapié in Paris, who in turn introduced him to the work of Jean Fautrier and Wols as well as the *art brut* of Jean Dubuffet. Dubuffet exerted a strong influence on Davíðsson well into the 1950s, as can be seen in his startling series of portraits of Icelandic writers and intellectuals (e.g. *Halldór Laxness*, 1950; Reykjavík, N.G.), some of which were shown at the ground-breaking September exhibitions in Reykjavík in the early 1950s, where they came in for a good deal of abuse.

During the 1960s, Davíðsson showed a lyrical impulse in large abstract works inspired by nature, which combine the vigorous brushstrokes of American action painting with the more delicate brushwork of the French Art informel painters. Davíðsson's later paintings hover between abstraction and figuration. They are richly atmospheric, endlessly suggestive, and teem with organic shapes and the particular reds, blues and greens of the Icelandic landscape; e.g. his *Water and Land* series (1989, Reykjavík, priv. cols).

BIBLIOGRAPHY

B. Ásgeirsson: 'Painter with Bold Use of Colours', *Iceland Rev.* (1970), 1, pp. 17–27
Eimreiðin (1974), 4 [interview with the artist]
A. Ingólfsson: 'Master of the Spontaneous Gesture—A Profile of Painter Kristján Davíðsson', *Iceland Rev.* (1989), 3, pp. 41–6
——: *Kristján Davíðsson* (Reykjavík, 1992) [Icelandic and Eng. texts]

AÐALSTEINN INGÓLFSSON

David-Weill, David (*b* San Francisco, 30 Aug 1871; *d* Neuilly, 7 Feb 1952). French banker, philanthropist and collector. Born David Weill, the son of Alexandre Weill, he was a partner in the Banque Lazard Frères, founded by his father and uncles. David-Weill and his wife, Flora Raphael, began collecting in 1900, buying at auction and from dealers; at his death he was one of the major patrons of art and education in France. President of the Council of National Museums, Vice-president of the Friends of the Louvre and holder of other influential posts, David-Weill helped direct the course of French museums for 50 years. In addition to donating numerous works from his collection, he advised on, and discreetly contributed to, the acquisition of many objects by the museums and libraries of France. His family has continued his service to the arts.

David-Weill's eclectic collection, displayed within his home and office, included French 18th-century art and important examples of early Chinese bronzes, Mesopotamian and Neolithic Japanese pottery and Syrian glassware, as well as goldsmiths' designs, French silver and Chinese and Japanese lacquer. In 1936 he sold half of his collection of enamels and miniatures to Wildenstein and Co., New York (acquired by Sir Charles Clore), later donating the remaining 396 examples to the Louvre. Wildenstein also acquired most of his collection of French 18th-century paintings, sculptures and drawings, which it displayed in three exhibitions in New York. Among the paintings was François Boucher's portrait of his wife, *Mme Boucher* (New York, Frick). David-Weill's collection was pillaged during World War II but largely reassembled. In 1971, following the death of Mme David-Weill, over 500 pieces were sold from the collection; further sales followed in 1972, 1976, 1977 and 1987. His collection of Chinese bronzes is now in the Musée Guimet and his collection of Chinese cloisonné at the Musée des Arts Décoratifs, both in Paris.

WRITINGS

Collection David Weill, 3 vols (Paris, 1926–8)
Miniatures and Enamels from the D. David-Weill Collection (Paris, 1957)

BIBLIOGRAPHY

C. Morice: 'Collection David Weill', *A. & Artistes*, v (1907), pp. 227–35
E. Dacier: 'La Collection David Weill', *Soc. Repr. Dessins Maîtres*, v (1913), pp. 7–11
H. d'Ardenne de Tizac: 'L'Art chinois dans la collection David Weill', *Amour A.*, v (1925), pp. 25–9
G. Henriot: 'La Collection David Weill', *Amour A.*, v (1925), pp. 1–24
'David-Weill Pictures Come to New York', *A. Digest*, xiii/3 (1937), p. 13
H. Comstock: 'The Connoisseur in America: The David Weill Exhibition', *Connoisseur*, ci (1938), pp. 34–5
'These Artists Distilled the Gallic Spirit', *A. Digest*, xiii/4 (1938), p. 7
French XVIIIth Century Sculpture: Formerly of the David-Weill Collection (exh. cat., New York, Wildenstein's, 1940)
Donations de D. David-Weill aux musées français (exh. cat., Paris, Mus. Orangerie, 1953)
Donation de D. David-Weill au Musée du Louvre: Miniatures et émaux (exh. cat., intro. J. Bouchot-Saupique; Paris, Louvre, Cab. Dessins, 1956–7)
P. Amiet: 'Les Antiquités orientales de la collection David-Weill', *Rev. Louvre*, xxii (1972), pp. 425–34
M. David: 'Musée Guimet: Bronzes chinois de la donation David-Weill', *Rev. Louvre*, xxii (1972), pp. 217–20
P. Amiet: *Les Antiquités du Luristan: Collection David-Weill* (Paris, 1976)

AMY L. WALSH

Davie, Alan (*b* Grangemouth, Scotland, 28 Sept 1920). Scottish painter and printmaker. He trained as a painter at Edinburgh College of Art from 1938 to 1940, initially favouring poetic imagery and coming into contact with modernism at exhibitions held in London of works by Picasso (1945; V&A) and Paul Klee (1945; Tate). He explored a diverse range of activities, however, before returning to painting: from 1949 to 1953 he earned his living by making jewellery and in 1947 he worked as a jazz musician, an activity he continued in later life. He wrote poetry during the early 1940s.

From 1947 to 1949 Davie travelled extensively in Europe; in Italy he studied pre-Renaissance art and saw a wide range of modern art, including the Peggy Guggenheim collection in Venice, to which he later continued to have access. Among the works owned by Guggenheim were paintings of the early 1940s by Jackson Pollock, which led Davie to adopt mythic imagery and forceful painterly gestures. He also adopted from later Pollock a procedure of painting rapidly with his canvases on the floor. From this time his pictures concentrated on themes of organic generation and sinister ritual, fluctuating between turbulent paintwork, animate presences and more geometric forms, sometimes in the same work, as in *Golden Seam* (1952; London, Brit. Council).

From 1953 to 1956 Davie taught in London at the Central School of Arts and Crafts, where he became interested in African and Pacific art. Encouraged by his critical and commercial success from the mid-1950s and by the large studio space made available to him during his Gregory Fellowship at Leeds University (1956–9), Davie increased his scale in works such as the *Creation of Man, or Marriage Feast* (2.13×3.66m, 1957; London, priv. col., see 1958 exh. cat., pl. VIII). With its teeming animal, human and pictographic forms, this triptych exemplifies Davie's search for a proliferation of painted signs and images, which bore more of an affinity to artists of the Cobra group such as Asger Jorn than to American Abstract Expressionism. Influenced by his reading of Eugene Herrigel's *Zen in the Art of Archery* (1953) in 1955, Davie became interested in Zen Buddhism and concluded that conscious decision-making was incompatible with a spiritual quest; as a result he rejected the emphasis on existential choice and immediate emotionalism central to Harold Rosenberg's definition of action painting.

As early as 1958 Davie emphasized the importance in his work of intuition, as expressed in the form of enigmatic signs. During the 1960s, both in paintings and in coloured lithographs, he represented such images with increasing clarity at the expense of gestural handling. From 1967 to 1971 he worked intermittently on a Berlin school mural involving an angled wall; he later introduced more representations of room-like spaces with zigzagging walls into his paintings. In 1971 he made his first visit to the island of St Lucia, where he began to spend half of each year and which brought Caribbean influences to bear on his suggestive imagery, as in *Bird Gong No. 10, Opus 730* (1973; London, Brit. Council). Taking on the role of a disinherited shaman, Davie created a synthesis of mythologies from a variety of cultures for a modern civilization devoid of its own village myths.

BIBLIOGRAPHY

Alan Davie (exh. cat., ed. B. Robertson; London, Whitechapel A.G., 1958)
M. Horowitz: *Alan Davie* (London, 1963)
A. Bowness: *Alan Davie* (London, 1967)
Alan Davie (exh. cat., intro. W. Januszczak; London, Gimpel Fils, 1983)
D. Hall, ed.: *Alan Davie* (London, 1991)
M. Tucker, ed.: *Alan Davie: The Quest for the Miraculous* (London, 1994)
ADRIAN LEWIS

Davies. English painters, copyists, writers and epigraphers. Norman de Garis Davies (*b* Glasgow, 14 Sept 1865; *d* Oxford, 5 Nov 1941) and his wife, Nina [née Cummins] Davies (*b* Thessaloníki, 6 Jan 1881; *d* Hinskey Hill, Berks, 21 April 1965), recorded the tomb paintings of dynastic Egypt. Their scrupulous work was of unparalleled importance, both in preserving a vanishing archaeological record and in shaping 20th-century perceptions of ancient Egyptian funerary art.

Norman had no formal artistic training and became interested in Egyptian archaeology while working as a Nonconformist minister in Australia. In 1898 he joined Flinders Petrie's excavations at Deshasheh as a copyist and epigrapher, later working at Deir el-Gebrawi, Sheikh Said, Saqqara and Amarna for the Egypt Exploration Society. Nina studied at the Slade (1900–02) and later at the Royal College of Art under Walter Crane. They met and married in Alexandria in 1907 and in the same year copied their first Theban tomb, that of Nakht (TT 52). For over 30 years they worked in the Theban necropolis as part of a project sponsored partly by the Metropolitan Museum of Art, New York, to record the principal painted tombs of Thebes through watercolour copies, line drawings and photographs.

Nina and Norman Davies operated as a team, and it is often difficult to distinguish their individual work. At all times they tried to avoid the imposition of their own interpretations of the tomb scenes, and they evolved a technique of reproducing the original impasto and colours of the paintings through a painstaking use of natural pigments, thus achieving remarkably accurate facsimiles. Initially they used watercolour as a copying medium but in 1921 changed to egg tempera, the composition of tempera approximating more closely to that of Egyptian paints and its opacity giving a better reproduction of the original. Nina exhibited some of her tempera copies at the Victoria and Albert Museum, London, in 1923. This exhibition, with the couple's various tomb publications, formed the core of her book *Ancient Egyptian Paintings*, which had an incalculable effect on disseminating knowledge of ancient Egyptian art.

Besides Thebes, the couple also copied at Beni Hassan and Amarna. They left Egypt in 1939 to live in Oxford. After Norman's death, Nina continued her Egyptological work, producing a selection of representative New Kingdom hieroglyphs for the world's first standardized hieroglyphic print font. The last decade of her life was unproductive due to crippling arthritis. On her death, her original copies were bequeathed to the Ashmolean Museum, Oxford, and the British Museum, London.

WRITINGS

The Mastaba of Ptahhetep and Akhethetep at Saqqara, 2 vols (London, 1900–01)
The Rock Tombs of Sheikh Said (London, 1902)
The Rock Tombs of Deir el Gebrawi, 2 vols (London, 1902) [Norman Davies]
The Rock Tombs of Amarna, 6 vols (New York, 1903–8) [Norman Davies]
The Tomb of Nakht at Thebes (London, 1907)
Five Theban Tombs, Being those of Mentuher Khepeshef, User, Daga, Nehemawy and Tati (New York, 1913)
The Tomb of Antefoker, Vizier of Sesostris, and of his Wife, Senet, no. 60 (New York, 1920)
The Tomb of Puyemre at Thebes, 2 vols (New York, 1922–3) [Norman Davies]
The Tomb of Two Sculptors at Thebes (New York, 1925)
Two Ramesside Tombs at Thebes (New York, 1927)
with H. R. Hopgood: *The Tomb of Ken-Amun at Thebes*, 2 vols (London, 1930)
The Tomb of Nefer-Hotep (New York, 1933)
Ancient Egyptian Paintings, 3 vols (Chicago, 1936) [Nina Davies]
Picture Writing in Ancient Egypt, 3 vols (Chicago, 1936) [Nina Davies]
Paintings from the Tomb of Rekhmire at Thebes, 2 vols (New York, 1943) [Norman Davies]

BIBLIOGRAPHY
Obituary of Norman Davies, *J. Egyp. Archaeol.*, 28 (1942), pp. 59–60
W. R. Dawson: *Who Was Who in Egyptology* (London, 1951), 2nd edn ed. E. P. Uphill (London, 1972)
Obituary of Nina Davies, *J. Egyp. Archaeol.*, 51 (1965), pp. 196–9

Davies, Arthur B(owen) (*b* Utica, NY, 26 Sept 1862; *d* Florence, 24 Oct 1928). American painter and illustrator. He first trained as an architectural draughtsman at the Academy of Design, Chicago (1878). After studying briefly at the Art Institute of Chicago, he went to New York, where he attended the Gotham School and the Art Students League (1886–8). By 1887 he was working as an illustrator for *Century* magazine. A realist landscape painter in the 19th-century academic tradition, he was influenced by the painters of the Hudson River school and particularly by the luminescent, dream-like landscapes of George Inness.

Around 1900 Davies's paintings became Symbolist in style, with the introduction of mystical nude figures in the landscape, as in *Meeting in the Forest* (1900; Montclair, NJ, A. Mus.). Themes combining classical figures and landscape, which evolved in a mythical classicist style reminiscent of the work of Puvis de Chavannes, typified Davies's work throughout his career. Increasingly drawn to ancient art and Greco-Roman civilization, he eventually identified the archaic with modernism, for example in *A Double Realm* (*c.* 1905; Worcester, MA, A. Mus.), as a way of projecting eternal truths. He became one of New York's most influential artists, and, despite his obvious stylistic antithesis to the social realism of the Ashcan school, he was included in the exhibition by The Eight (i), led by Robert Henri, at the Macbeth Galleries in 1908. Nevertheless, he was an avid proponent of European modernism, also acting as an adviser to his friend and patron LILLIE P. BLISS on the purchase of modern art. As president of the Association of American Painters and Sculptors (1911–13), he was the galvanizing force behind the exhibition of 1913 known as the Armory Show (*see* NEW YORK, fig. 7), the first major introduction of progressive European art trends to the USA.

In his own work Davies was interested in the visual depiction of movement, but rather than pursue an abstract Synchromist style he adopted a narrative realist format inspired at one point by the dancer Isadora Duncan, for example *Rhythms* (*c.* 1910; Milwaukee, WI, A. Mus.). He took up yoga and developed a theory of inhalation as part of his interest in eurhythmics, which at the end of his life became crucial to his ideas of 'continuous composition', as realized in works such as *Falling Figures* (*c.* 1922; New York, James Graham & Sons).

BIBLIOGRAPHY
J. M. Frank jr: 'The Art of Arthur B. Davies', *Arthur B. Davies: Essays on the Man and his Art* (New York, 1924)
R. Cortissoz: *Arthur B. Davies* (New York, 1931)
M. Brown: *The Story of the Armory Show* (New York, 1963)
S. Reich: 'The Paradoxes of Arthur B. Davies', *Apollo*, xcii/105 (1970), pp. 366–71
Arthur B. Davies: A Chronological Retrospective (exh. cat. by D. Wigmore, New York, Knoedler's, 1975)
R. Pincus-Witten: 'On Target: Symbolist Roots of American Abstraction', *A. Mag.*, 1/8 (1976), pp. 84–91
CHARLOTTE MOSER

Davies, David (*b* Ballarat, 21 May 1864; *d* Looe, Cornwall, 26 March 1939). Australian painter. He trained at the Ballarat School of Design, the National Gallery School, Melbourne, and the Académie Julien, Paris. He was associated with the Heidelberg school in the 1890s, when he specialized in poetic evocations of evening, for example *Moonrise* (1894; Melbourne, N.G. Victoria). In 1897 he moved permanently to Europe, working in St Ives, Cornwall, England; the Conway Valley, Wales; and Dieppe, France, for 25 years and finally settling in Looe, Cornwall. He produced oils and watercolours of all these localities, as well as, portraits and flowerpieces. Among his more important European work in oil was *St Ives Bay, Cornwall* (1904; Adelaide, A.G. S. Australia) and *A Normandy Village* (1919; priv. col., see 1984 exh. cat., p. 53).

Although uninterested in theory and independent of contemporary artistic movements, Davies admired Monet and may have been influenced by Jean-Charles Cazin and Achille-Théodore Cesbron. His style was essentially simple, picking out a few details within a broader atmospheric effect. In his early work he favoured sombre earth colours, which brightened when he moved to Europe, particularly when he worked in watercolour although he retained a penchant for the muted tones of dusk and grey weather.

BIBLIOGRAPHY
David Davies (exh. cat. by C. Sparks, Ballarat, F.A. Gal., 1984)
CAMERON SPARKS

Davies, Sir Martin (*b* London, 22 March 1908; *d* 7 March 1975). English art historian. He was educated at Rugby School, Warwicks, and King's College, Cambridge (1926–30), where he studied modern languages. In 1930 he became an attaché of the National Gallery, London, joining its permanent staff as Assistant Keeper in 1932. In 1937 he instituted a scholarly revision of the National Gallery's published catalogues of the picture collections, a task interrupted by the outbreak of World War II. He was in charge of the wartime storage in Wales of the gallery's holdings, an operation involving some 6,000 pictures, carried by train in 3 consignments during the final 10 days before war broke out. He had the complete works removed again to safer accommodation in the underground caverns of Manod Quarry, near Ffestiniog, in 1941, staying with the collection for the duration of the war. He was made Deputy Keeper in 1947 and Keeper in 1960. The first of his catalogues for the National Gallery was *The Early Netherlandish School* (London, 1945–7, rev. 3/1968), for which period he had particular sympathy, followed by catalogues for *The French School* (London, 1946, rev. 2/1957) and *The British School* (London, 1946, rev. 2/1959). In 1951 he published a major catalogue, *The Earlier Italian Schools* (London, 1951, 2/1961/*R* 1986), confirming his gift for lucid, critical appraisal. He returned to Netherlandish painting with his three-volume *Les Primitifs flamands: Corpus de la peinture des anciens Pays-Bas* (London, 1953–70). In 1968 he succeeded Sir Philip Hendy (1900–80) as Director of the National Gallery and during his tenure made several notable acquisitions, including the *Death of Actaeon* by Titian (mid-1560s) and ? *St Ivo* (*c.* 1450) by Rogier van der Weyden (on whom he published a monograph in 1972). He also contributed to the gallery's 'Themes and Painters' series, with studies on

Carlo Crivelli (1972) and *Rembrandt* (1973). He retired in 1973. As a lifelong bachelor, respected for his modesty and erudition, Davies spent his entire career in service to the National Gallery, its history and picture collection, bequeathing the bulk of his fortune to the institution upon his death.

BIBLIOGRAPHY
M. Levey: Obituary, *Burl. Mag.*, cxvii (1975), pp. 729–31

Davies, Thomas (*b* ?Shooter's Hill, London, *c.* 1737; *d* Blackheath, London, 16 March 1812). English soldier and painter, active in North America. He entered the Royal Military Academy, Woolwich, in 1755 and, like other officers of his day, studied topographical drawing there. Subsequently he took part in many expeditions to North America, making maps, plans and surveys. In 1757 he produced his first dated work, a watercolour of Halifax, NS, and five years later a view of Montreal from St Helen's Island (both Ottawa, N.G.) that is a fine example of his characteristically picturesque style. Returning to England in 1763, he must have met Paul Sandby, who was chief drawing-master at Woolwich from 1768 and whose water-colour style was widely influential. An extensive series of watercolours of American waterfalls, made in 1766 and engraved *c.* 1768 (e.g. *View of Casconchiagon or Great Seneca Falls*; Toronto, Royal Ont. Mus.), marks the beginning of Davies's personal style, characterized by vigorous composition and glowing colours. The following year he exhibited at the Royal Academy in London. Davies gradually achieved recognition for his nature studies, in particular his drawings of exotic birds, and in 1781 he was elected a Fellow of the Royal Society in London. He returned to America in 1786, and during his peacetime posting to Quebec he made his most beautiful and technically accomplished watercolours, of the city and the surrounding region (e.g. *View of the Bridge on the River La Puce*; Ottawa, N.G.). Most of these pictures are set in autumn and are distinguished by their brilliant colour and lively, rhythmic line. His last and most successful work, perhaps painted after he had returned to Britain, is a magnificent view of Montreal from the mountain (dated 1812; Ottawa, N.G.).

DCB

BIBLIOGRAPHY
Thomas Davies, c. 1737–1812/Thomas Davies, vers 1737–1812 (exh. cat. by R. H. Hubbard and C. P. Stacey, Ottawa, N.G., 1972) [bilingual text]
MARIO BÉLAND

Davila, Juan (*b* Santiago, 6 Oct 1946). Australian painter and performance artist of Chilean birth. He studied law and fine arts at the University of Chile. Following the coup of 1973, he arrived in Melbourne as a tourist after meeting an Australian in Buenos Aires, and later took up residence. He exhibited widely in Australia, Europe and South America, returning frequently to Chile, which, thematically and politically, remained a focus for his art. He worked primarily with the quotation of minor cultural material (e.g. newspaper photographs, advertisements, etc). Origi-nally noted for his adaptations of Pop art in an effort to rewrite the international history of painting from a provin-cial or Third World perspective, he increasingly developed a hybrid pictorial language that refused the strict confines

of modernism or post-modernism, seen, for example, in *Fable of Australian Painting* (1982–3; U. Sydney, Power Gal. Contemp. A.). His art deals with fragments, attempt-ing to present a utopia of narrative from another place and time. In canvases such as *Echo* (2.74×8.22 m, 1987; Perth, A.G.W. Australia), he dealt with a 'bastard aesthetic' of Latin-American kitsch. He also achieved some notoriety through film and video performances, and as an editor, writer and curator. He is chiefly known for his attempts to address the problem of the portrayal of a homosexual language.

WRITINGS
with P. Foss: *The Mutilated Pietà* (Melbourne, 1986)
BIBLIOGRAPHY
P. Taylor: 'Juan Davila at the Adelaide Festival', *Studio Int.*, cxcvii/1006 (1984), pp. 20–21
P. Taylor, ed.: *Juan Davila, Hysterical Tears* (Melbourne, 1985)
A. & Text, 21 (1986), pp. 94–9 [special issue on art in Chile after 1973]
F. Zegers, ed.: *El fulgor de lo obsceno* (Santiago, 1988)
PAUL FOSS

Davioud, Gabriel(-Jean-Antoine) (*b* Paris, 30 Oct 1824; *d* Paris, 6 April 1881). French architect. He attended the free school of drawing, mathematics and ornamental sculpture run by Jean-Hilaire Belloc (1786–1866) before enrolling (1841) at the Ecole des Beaux-Arts, Paris, studying in the ateliers of Adolphe-Marie-François Jay (1789–1871) and Léon Vaudoyer. Winning only second prize in the competition for the Prix de Rome (1849) and hampered by his financial situation, he was unable to study in Italy. In 1851, however, he won the Grande Médaille d'Emulation and in that same year gained his first com-mission, for the theatre at Etampes, designed in the Neo-classical style. In 1854 he was appointed inspector with the Service des Promenades et Plantations, Paris, under the supervision of Adolphe Alphand, in which capacity he designed the layout and ornaments of the new green spaces with which Paris was endowed by Georges-Eugène Haussmann, prefect of Paris from 1853 until 1870. Dav-ioud was responsible (1855–67) for the lodges, chalets, cafés, kiosks, wrought-iron grilles and fountains in the Bois de Boulogne, the Bois de Vincennes and the parks of Montsouris, Monceau and the Buttes-Chaumont, as well as numerous squares. In 1858 he was selected, controversially, to design the buildings around the Place St Michel and its central fountain. The critics were shocked, believing that Davioud was not distinguished enough and that the scheme should have been open to competition. Davioud's design harked back to the First Empire, with a triumphal arch inspired directly by the Arc de Triomphe du Carrousel (1806–7) by Charles Percier and Pierre-François-Léonard Fontaine. Haussmann also commis-sioned him to design the new square in front of the Hôtel de Ville, with two new theatres, the Théâtre du Cirque Impérial (now Théâtre du Châtelet) and the Théâtre Lyrique (both 1860–61).

In 1864, as part of Haussmann's scheme to provide the poorer districts of Paris with shopping and entertainment facilities matching those around the new Opéra, Davioud designed the Orphéon, a popular opera house with 10,000 seats (second project 1867; unexecuted) and the Magasins Réunis (1867) on what is now the Place de la République. The inner courtyard of this department store was originally laid out as a garden, in imitation of the Palais-Royal. Davioud devoted the last years of the Second Empire to completing the parks of Buttes-Chaumont and Mont-souris, and to the monument (1868–70) to *Peter IV, King of Portugal* (*reg* 1826) in Lisbon, which he designed with Elias Robert (1821–74). In 1870 he visited Italy, returning to supervise the works of fortification of Paris during the Franco-Prussian War (1870–71). At the end of hostilities he was appointed Inspecteur-Général des Travaux d'Architecture de la Ville de Paris, competing unsuccessfully in the competition (1873) to design a new Hôtel de Ville. The old one had been destroyed by fire (1871), together with the Théâtre Lyrique, which Davioud was asked to rebuild. Other unsuccessful competition entries included those for the Sacré-Coeur (1874), Paris, and the Palais de Justice (1875), Charleroi, although that same year he won first prize for a theatre and museum design at Cannes.

During the early years of the Third Republic Davioud produced his most famous work, the Palais du Trocadéro (1877–8), Paris, opposite the Champ-de-Mars, for the Exposition Universelle of 1878. It was built in collaboration with Jules Bourdais (*b* 1835), the architect and engineer with whom he also built the annexe (1876–8) of the Mairie of the 19th arrondissement. The Trocadéro (centre destr. and wings recased 1936 by Jacques Carlu; now the Palais de Chaillot) was closely related to a third project (1876; unexecuted) by Davioud for the Orphéon. Its façade combined vaguely Oriental motifs with a deliberately modern style, and the finished building, completed in only 18 months, attracted the admiration of such contemporaries as Eugène-Emmanuel Viollet-le-Duc, although the acoustics of the great central concert hall were never satisfactory. Davioud's career would not have been so successful without the huge building and municipal service schemes undertaken by Haussmann, and he cannot be considered the equal of such architects of the previous generation as Louis Duc and Léon Vaudoyer, whose work he so respected.

WRITINGS

L'Art et l'industrie (Paris, 1873)

BIBLIOGRAPHY

Gabriel Davioud, architecte (exh. cat., Paris, 1981–2)

THOMAS VON JOEST

Davis, Alexander Jackson (*b* New York, 24 July 1803; *d* Orange, NJ, 14 Jan 1892). American architect. From the 1830s to the 1850s he was one of the most influential architects in the USA. His work ranges from major government and institutional buildings to ornamental garden structures; his main contribution to American architecture was his introduction of the European picturesque in his designs for Italianate and Gothic Revival country houses and cottages. With his partner, Ithiel Town, he also refined and popularized the American Greek Revival. He revolutionized American architectural drawing through rendering buildings in romantic landscapes rather than in the analytical, Neo-classical style that preceded him. In 1836 he helped form the American Institution of Architects and advanced professionalism in American architecture through his scrupulous office practices, being, for example, the first American architect to use printed, standardized specifications.

1. Training and the Town & Davis partnership. 2. Independent works.

1. TRAINING AND THE TOWN & DAVIS PARTNERSHIP. At the age of 16 Davis left school in New York to work as a type compositor in Alexandria, VA. During this time, probably influenced by reading contemporary Gothic novels, he made drawings of prison and castle interiors akin to Piranesi's engravings of imaginary prisons. In 1823 he returned to New York and entered the Antique School (later the National Academy of Design), where he studied drawing and perspective. In 1826 he worked as a draughtsman with the New York architect and builder Josiah Brady (*c.* 1760–1832), gaining practical knowledge in building construction. In the same year he opened his own office and executed high-quality perspective views of existing buildings for New York lithographers. On the strength of these, the National Academy of Design elected him a member in 1827. That year he went to Boston to draw perspectives of buildings, again for lithographic reproduction, and (with help from local patrons) studied at the Boston Atheneum.

In 1829 Davis returned to New York, where the architect and engineer ITHIEL TOWN made him a full partner; the partnership of Town & Davis lasted until 1835 and was briefly resumed in 1842–3. Town's structural knowledge and connections, combined with Davis's drawing and compositional abilities, quickly made the firm among the most influential in the USA. Although Davis never visited Europe, Town's European travels (1829–30) and library gave the partners an enormous advantage over most American architects. In the 1830s they introduced ideas that, for the first time since Benjamin Henry Latrobe's death in 1820, made American architecture current with European developments. During this period Davis formed the aesthetic theories that he held for the rest of his life. He recorded his reliance on classical works, including those of Palladio, Claude Perrault, Jacques-François Blondel, Etienne-Louis Boullée, Claude-Nicolas Ledoux, Jean-Nicolas-Louis Durand and William Chambers; his picturesque theory was developed from the study of British writers, including Edmund Burke, Uvedale Price, Richard Payne Knight and Humphry Repton. The range of Davis's sources in the 1830s and 1840s is suggested by his diary entries and drawings: he designed theatres after Vitruvius and Palladio; from Pliny the younger's letters he made reconstructions of the Laurentine Villa; and he followed Marc-Antoine Laugier's *Essai sur l'architecture* (1753) to design log-cabins with the appearance of rustic temples.

Town & Davis produced designs for three state capitols: those of Connecticut at New Haven (1827–31; destr.), Indiana at Indianapolis (1831–5; destr.) and North Carolina at Raleigh (1833–42). Davis later submitted a competition entry for the Ohio Statehouse (1839) at Columbus, which influenced its final form. The partners designed the US Customs House (1833–42), New York City, and did highly influential drawings for the US Patent Office (1834) in Washington, DC. In many cases, competitions were poorly conducted, and clients and contractors often altered their designs, causing Davis to complain bitterly against government commissions and building committees. Town & Davis's monumental public buildings have a Grecian character but always include creative infusions of Roman structural forms. These Neo-classical public edifices often follow the formula of a Greek, amphiprostyle temple (having porticos at either end but no columns at the side), occasionally topped by a Roman dome. Along the temple flanks are files of huge square piers or antae. Between the piers windows rise through two or three storeys; floor levels are indicated on the exterior only by shallow, wooden panels, flush with the planes of the glass. Davis called these piers 'pilastrades' and the windows 'Davisean'. Although these designs, which transformed Greek temples into modern, functional, public buildings, resemble the works of Karl Friedrich Schinkel in Berlin, evidence suggests that neither Davis nor Town knew Schinkel's buildings.

Town & Davis also designed many Grecian suburban and country villas, typically consisting of central temple units often with lower, flanking wings and cruciform plans, possibly modelled on villas by John Nash (i) and Decimus Burton in Regent's Park, London. Three fine, early villas were the Hillhouse (1828; destr.) and Skinner Villas (1830), New Haven, CT, and the Russell Villa (1829), Middletown, CT. Later Grecian villas by Davis, such as the Stevens Mansion (1845, destr.; see fig. 1), New York, tended to be giant, cubic masses articulated with pilasters and lush, Corinthian porticos.

The partnership took on several pupils and draughtsmen, usually trained by Davis, such as James Gallier (i) and John Stirewalt (1811–71). Davis's most brilliant pupil was James Harrison Dakin, who was a partner in the firm in 1832–4 and assisted in the design of New York University (1833–4 and 1835–8; destr. 1894), the finest collegiate Gothic building of its time in the USA. The central unit of this five-part composition was adapted from King's College Chapel, Cambridge. Dakin also executed designs for the architect Minard Lafever, who published them in his *The Modern Builder's Guide* (1833) and *The Beauties of Modern Architecture* (1835), influential books that caused Town, Davis, & Dakin's Grecian domestic formulae to spread throughout the USA.

2. INDEPENDENT WORKS. After the dissolution of the Town & Davis partnership, Davis turned to Italianate and Gothic Revival designs. He did not forsake his earlier Greco-Roman forms entirely but adapted them with Tuscan elements. Responding to the increasing size and complexity of American institutions, Davis abandoned the self-contained units of the Greek temple, substituting for them Etruscan–Roman temples that became the centrepieces of expanded systems of interconnected wings and pavilions. The three finest of his large institutional complexes are the Lunatic Asylum (begun 1834; one octagon extant) on Blackwell's Island, New York, the North Carolina State Hospital for the Insane (1850–56; partly destr.) at Raleigh, NC, and Davidson College (1856–60), Davidson, NC. Each of these edifices had centre pavilions

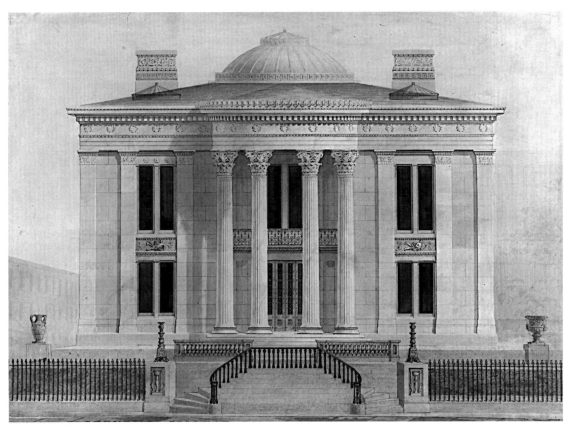

1. Alexander Jackson Davis: Stevens Mansion, New York, 1845 (New York, New-York Historical Society)

from which stretched lateral wings lit by vertical, multi-storey Davisean windows. Davis planned the wings, some measuring up to 244 m in length, to enclose three or four sides of vast, central courtyards. These flexible schemes were planned for completion in stages as the institutions grew or as public funds became available. Davis also designed numerous Italianate villas ranging from diminutive wooden examples to immense country houses, such as Grace Hill (1854–7), for Edwin C. Litchfield in Brooklyn, New York, which is composed asymmetrically on a cruciform plan with radiating octagonal rooms.

Davis designed a few Gothic Revival churches but remained basically outside the mainstream of ecclesiastical theory and practice of his day. He designed impressive (but unexecuted) Gothic collegiate complexes for Bristol College, PA (1835), and for the University of Michigan at Ann Arbor (1838), both similar to the earlier designs for New York University. In 1848 Davis designed the Virginia Military Institute at Lexington, a symmetrical, castellated Gothic composition with bold, octagonal towers and four wings wrapped around a central courtyard.

Davis is best remembered for his large Gothic Revival country houses, for which he sometimes designed furniture as well as interiors. Some 19th-century critics objected to the use of this style in the USA, maintaining that it was inappropriate for republican institutions, and serious Gothic Revival church architects such as Richard Upjohn eschewed it because of the objections raised in England by A. W. N. Pugin and the Ecclesiological Movement. Davis ignored these criticisms and designed over a dozen castellated villas. His clients were mostly wealthy, élitist Episcopalians of British descent. Davis's first castellated villa, and the earliest in the USA, was Glen Ellen (destr.), near Baltimore, MD, designed with Town in 1832. The client, Robert Gilmor, had visited Sir Walter Scott at Abbotsford and had spent time at Horace Walpole's Strawberry Hill, which he admired. The design of the American villa owed much to the 18th-century English Gothick castle style. For the Gothic details of his later villas, Davis relied heavily on the beautiful plates published in Augustus Charles Pugin's books. Davis, surprisingly, developed his Gothic villa ground-plans using the rational, geometric design processes recommended in Durand's *Précis du leçons d'architecture* (1802–5). Davis's combination of English picturesque Gothic elevations with French rationalist plans resulted in villas with handsome, asymmetrical exteriors and interpenetrating interior volumes, instead of the static, self-contained spatial units of earlier Neo-classical houses.

The best-preserved of Davis's large Gothic villas is Lyndhurst (originally 'Knoll'; 1838; see fig. 2), at Tarrytown, NY, built for General William Paulding and for which Davis made 50 furniture designs in the Gothic style. The villa was later extended by Davis (1864–7) for George Merritt. At Lyndhurst, Davis deftly fused castellated, monastic and cottage Gothic forms and responded with great sensitivity to the Hudson River site. The plan is an elongated cruciform, its longest axis parallel to the twin lines of the public road in front and the river behind; opposite façades of striking asymmetry face both road and river. Davis effectively connected the villa with its landscape by a one-storey verandah encircling three of the

2. Alexander Jackson Davis: Lyndhurst, Tarrytown, New York, 1838, enlarged 1864–7

outer walls, thus affording dramatic views of the Hudson River Valley. Davis designed several Gothic 'river villas' from the late 1830s to the early 1850s, mostly for sites along the Hudson River and Long Island Sound but also as far afield as the James River in Virginia, for example the Cocke Villa (1845–8), Belmead. In 1849 Davis read Ruskin's newly published *The Seven Lamps of Architecture* and radically altered his approach to the castellated Gothic villa. Responding to Ruskin's lamps of Truth and Power, he abandoned the delicate details of his ashlar or stucco-surfaced villas for bold, fortress-style castles with heavy, round towers and rock-faced masonry walls. Examples of this style are Ericstan (1855–8; destr.), the Herrick castle at Tarrytown, NY, and Castlewood (1857–60), the Howard villa at Llewellyn Park, NJ.

Davis published a few early villa designs in his book *Rural Residences* (1837–8); further volumes were planned but did not materialize. In the 1840s, however, the landscape gardener A. J. Downing published dozens of Davis's designs for smaller Italianate and Gothic villas, farmhouses and cottages in his influential journal *The Horticulturist* and in his phenomenally popular architectural patternbooks *Cottage Residences* (1842) and *The Architecture of Country Houses* (1850). These books greatly expanded Davis's practice and resulted in his designs influencing the work of local architects and builders throughout the USA.

After the Civil War (1861–5) Davis's creative force in American architecture declined as a result of several factors: the rising numbers of immigrant European architects, the increased training of American architects abroad and the introduction of formal architectural education in American universities. His aesthetic theories of the late 18th century and early 19th and the rural character of his architectural practice hindered his understanding of the synthetic complexities of urban buildings of the 1860s and 1870s, predominantly in the High Victorian Gothic and French Second Empire styles that elicited vitriolic responses from Davis. His last significant project was to collaborate with the developer Llewellyn S. Haskell on the Llewellyn Park project (1853–70) at Orange Mountain, NJ, the finest picturesquely planned residential enclave in the USA, for which Davis designed many of the villas and ornamental structures. In the 1870s Davis retired to Wildmont, his own villa in Llewellyn Park, where, despite losses from a fire, he spent the rest of his life organizing and annotating his immense collection of drawings, letters and diaries.

UNPUBLISHED SOURCES

New York: Columbia U., Avery Archit. Lib.; NY Hist. Soc.; Met.; Pub. Lib. [primary col. of drgs, diaries and doc.]

WRITINGS

Rural Residences, etc., Consisting of Designs, Original and Selected, for Cottages, Farmhouses, Villas and Village Churches (New York, 1837 [1838]/*R* 1980)

BIBLIOGRAPHY

Macmillan Enc. Architects

W. Dunlap: *History of the Rise and Progress of the Arts of Design in the United States*, iii (New York, 1834), pp. 210–13

Obituary, *Amer. Architect & Bldg News*, xxxv (1892), p. 24

E. Donnell: 'A. J. Davis and the Gothic Revival', *Met. Mus. Stud.*, v (1936), pp. 183–233

R. H. Newton: *Town & Davis, Architects: Pioneers in American Revivalist Architecture, 1812–1870* (New York, 1942)

W. Andrews: 'Alexander Jackson Davis', *Archit. Rev.* [London], cix (1951), pp. 307–12

M. Card: 'A. J. Davis and the Printed Specification', *Coll. A. J.*, xii (1952), pp. 354–9

J. B. Davies: 'The Wadsworth Atheneum's Original Building: Ithiel Town and A. J. Davis Architects', *Wadsworth Atheneum Bull.*, 5th ser. (1959), pp. 7–18

——: 'A. J. Davis' Projects for a Patent Office Building', *J. Soc. Archit. Hist.*, xxiv (1965), pp. 229–51

——: 'Alexander J. Davis: Architect of Lyndhurst', *Hist. Preserv.*, xvii/2 (1965), pp. 54–9

'Alexander Jackson Davis Material in the Metropolitan Museum of Art', *Bull. Met.*, xxv (1967), p. 216

C. M. McClinton: 'Furniture and Interiors Designed by A. J. Davis', *Connoisseur*, clxx (1969), pp. 54–61

C. E. Brownell: *In the American Style of Italian: The E. C. Litchfield Villa* (MA thesis, Newark, U. DE, 1970)

J. B. Davies: 'Blandwood and the Italian Villa Style in America', *19th C.* [New York], i (1975), pp. 11–14

——: 'Llewellyn Park in West Orange, New Jersey', *Antiques*, cvii (1975), pp. 142–58

——: 'Gothic Revival Furniture Designs of Alexander J. Davis', *Antiques*, cxi (1977), pp. 1014–27

J. Donoghue: *Alexander Jackson Davis: Romantic Architect, 1830–1892* (diss., New York U., 1977)

W. H. Pierson jr: 'Alexander Jackson Davis and the Picturesque', *American Buildings and their Architects: Technology and the Picturesque, the Corporate and Early Gothic Styles* (New York, 1978), pp. 270–384

R. G. Wilson: 'Idealism and the Origin of the First American Suburb: Llewellyn Park, New Jersey', *Amer. A. J.*, xi (1979), pp. 79–90

M. Lane: 'A. J. Davis in North Carolina', *Architecture of the Old South: North Carolina* (Savannah, GA, 1985), pp. 234–57

——: 'A. J. Davis in Virginia', *Architecture of the Old South: Virginia* (Savannah, GA, 1987), pp. 230–51

P. A. Snadon: *A. J. Davis and the Gothic Revival Castle in America* (diss., Ithaca, NY, Cornell U., 1988)

J. B. Davies: 'Davis and Downing: Collaborators in the Picturesque', *Prophet with Honor: The Career of Andrew Jackson Downing, 1815–1852*, ed. G. B. Tatum and E. B. MacDougall (Washington, DC, 1989), pp. 81–123

P. A. Snadon: 'Loudoun: Two New York Architects and a Gothic Revival Villa in Ante Bellum, Kentucky', *KY Rev.*, xi/3 (1989), pp. 41–82

PATRICK A. SNADON

Davis, Arthur Joseph. *See under* MEWÈS & DAVIS.

Davis [Davies], John Scarlett (*b* Leominster, Hereford & Worcs, 1 Sept 1804; *d* London, 29 Sept 1845). English painter. The son of a watchmaker, he was sent in 1818 to London, where he studied at De La Pierre's Academy in Hackney; two years later he entered the Royal Academy Schools. In London he quickly won a reputation as a portrait painter. In 1824–5 he was commissioned to draw copies of the paintings hanging in the royal palaces, and he was also engaged by Sir Thomas Lawrence to make pencil versions of the latter's portraits. From 1825 to 1828 he worked in Yorkshire, exhibiting 31 works at the Northern Society, Leeds. To the principal annual exhibitions in London he contributed only 27 works (mostly oils); the great majority of his pictures were commissioned by private patrons, above all the merchant John Hinxman, who at his death in 1846 owned 489 works by Davis.

From 1830 until 1842 he travelled widely in France, the Low Countries, Italy and Germany. His continental scenes have often been confused with those of Richard Parkes Bonington, Thomas Shotter Boys, James Holland (a companion on some of these trips) and William Callow. To a greater extent than these artists, however, Davis specialized (from the late 1820s) in delicately detailed interiors, in both oils and watercolour; his views of churches and picture galleries often contain small-scale representations of paintings that are clearly identifiable. A typical example is an *Exhibition in the British Institution* (1829; Birmingham, Mus. & A.G.). He also produced architectural, topographical and marine scenes, and 15 etched *Views of Florence and Other Parts of Italy* (begun 1833).

BIBLIOGRAPHY

G. Watkin Williams: 'The Life and Works of John Scarlett Davis (1804–1845)', *Old Wtrcol. Soc. Club*, xlv (1970), pp. 8–28

PATRICK CONNER

Davis, Owen William (*b* 1838; *d* ?London, 1913). English architect and designer. He studied under the architect James Kellaway Colling (*c.* 1815–1905), an expert on Gothic architecture, and spent several years as assistant to Matthew Digby Wyatt, who at the time was working on the then India Office (1867–8), Whitehall, London. Davis was a designer of architectural ornament, furniture, wallpaper, textiles, ironwork and ceramics, and in 1870 some of his designs were published in *Building News*. For James Shoolbred & Co., London (*fl* 1870–1900s), he designed furniture in the medieval, Jacobean, Stuart, Louis XVI and Japanese styles and in the style of Robert Adam and James Adam, illustrated in the company's catalogue *Designs of Furniture . . . and Interior Decoration* (1876). A selection of furniture designed by Davis and manufactured by Shoolbred was shown at the Centennial Exhibition in Philadelphia in 1876. In 1885 he published *Art and Work*, which contains 85 lithographic plates of ornament for marble, stone and terracotta and designs for furniture, ceramics, metalwork and textiles, accompanied by notes on the design sources; among the plates are several after drawings, previously unpublished, by the Adam brothers. In his wallpaper designs of the 1880s and 1890s for Jeffrey & Co. and Woollams & Co., Davis added Arts and Crafts to his range of styles. His 'Rydal' wallpaper (1886) for Woollams, with its crisp, vigorously scrolled plant forms, was among several patterns that resemble those of William Morris. In 'King's College', his best-known design, he adapted 17th-century strapwork and motifs in an elaborate wallpaper featuring deep borders. Davis is noted for his ability to work in a plurality of styles, executed in a rich yet disciplined manner.

WRITINGS

Art and Work (London, 1885)

BIBLIOGRAPHY

A. V. Sugden and J. L. Edmondson: *A History of English Wallpaper, 1509–1914* (London, 1925)
S. Durant: *Ornament: A Survey of Decoration since 1830* (London, 1986)

Davis, Ron(ald) (*b* Santa Monica, CA, 29 June 1937). American painter. He studied engineering at the University of Wyoming, Laramie (1955–6). After this he took a number of short-term jobs before starting to paint in 1959. He then studied at the San Francisco Art Institute from 1960 to 1964, while also spending a period in 1962 studying with Philip Guston at the University Summer School of Music and Art, Norfolk, CT. He had his first one-man show in 1965 at the Nicholas Wilder Gallery in Los Angeles. From 1966 to 1972 he made his paintings from coloured polyester resin on a fibreglass support, the resin being applied to a waxed surface in many layers from the front backwards. In this way he produced abstract works of geometrical solids employing an illusionistic two-point perspective, reflecting his admiration for Renaissance painters, particularly Uccello. In these works the framing edge is the same as the edge of the solid depicted, as in the polygonal *Zodiac* (1969; artist's col., see 1970 exh. cat., p. 10), and the colour is often splashed in places in allusion to the drip paintings of Jackson Pollock. Like most of these works the geometrical shape in *Zodiac* is presented as if seen from above, whereas the paintings are invariably hung at eye level, so puzzling the viewer.

In 1972 Davis gave up the polyester resin process for aesthetic and health reasons, and used instead the more traditional medium of acrylic on canvas. Geometry and perspectival illusionism continued to be his main concern, but he now painted tent-like geometrical constructions within a network of incompatible perspective lines, as in *Archway* (1977; San Francisco, CA, John Berggruen Gal.; see 1978 exh. cat., p. 9). This interest in geometrical images continued in his later work also.

BIBLIOGRAPHY

Los Angeles 6 (exh. cat. by J. Coplans and others, Vancouver, A.G., 1968), pp. 15–19
Colour: Ron Davis, Ellsworth Kelly, Morris Louis, Kenneth Noland, Jules Olitski, Frank Stella (exh. cat. by C. Kessler and others, Los Angeles, UCLA, 1970), pp. 5–10
Four Contemporary Painters: Arakawa, Bruce Boice, Ronald Davis, Agnes Martin (exh. cat. by J. E. Hinson, Cleveland, Mus. A., OH, 1978), pp. 8–9

Davis, Stuart (*b* Philadelphia, 7 Dec 1894; *d* New York, 24 June 1964). American painter and printmaker. He was born into an artistic family: his parents studied with Thomas Anshutz at the Pennsylvania Academy of Fine Arts, and his father was the art editor at the *Philadelphia Press*, a newspaper that included among its employees the Robert Henri circle of artist–reporters. Davis studied art under Henri in New York between 1909 and 1912. His earliest works, which chronicle urban life in the streets, saloons and theatres, are painted with the dark palette and thickly applied brushstrokes typical of the ASHCAN SCHOOL style inspired by Henri. Davis also published illustrations in the left-wing magazine *The Masses* between 1913 and 1916, and in *The Liberator*, which succeeded it in the 1920s.

With his contribution of five watercolours Davis was one of the youngest exhibitors at the ARMORY SHOW, the international exhibition of modern art that opened in New York in 1913 and introduced European avant-garde art to the USA. In the following years Davis abandoned his Ashcan realist style and experimented with a variety of modern European styles, including Post-Impressionism and Cubism. From 1915 he began to spend his summers in Gloucester, a seaside town and artists' resort north of Boston, where he painted panoramic landscapes with an artistic vocabulary derived from Cézanne, Gauguin, Matisse and van Gogh. He travelled and painted in Havana in 1918, and in New Mexico in 1923.

In the 1920s Davis began to develop the themes and artistic style that characterize his mature work. He painted images of American commercial products in a style loosely derived from Synthetic Cubism. In 1921 he began a series based on cigarette packaging in which the large, flat, overlapping shapes reveal the influence of Cubist collage. A work such as *Odol* (1924; priv. col., see 1965 exh. cat., no. 24, p. 58), depicting a popular mouthwash bottle, uses strong simplified forms and vibrant colours and shows an interest in surface brushstrokes. The title of *Itlksez* (1921; Leominster, MA, Lane Found.)—a shortening of the phrase 'it looks easy'—reveals a further debt to Cubism in the form of Picasso's word play. From the 1920s Davis's works share certain characteristics with the paintings of Precisionist artists (*see* PRECISIONISM) such as Charles Demuth, whose sharply defined forms and visual puns were also inspired by European avant-garde styles including Cubism and Dada.

Davis grew increasingly dissatisfied with his work towards the end of the decade, because he felt it lacked the structure of European art, and he started working on compositions freely abstracted from a still-life consisting of an egg-beater, electric fan and rubber glove. The resulting four paintings, known collectively as the *Egg-beater* series (1927–8; priv. col., see 1978 exh. cat., pp. 44, 80, 103, 141), play with the tension between plane and space, allowing the eye to recede along suggested orthogonals, then leading it back to the surface again with the interposition of flat coloured planes. In 1928 his predilection for realism briefly re-emerged when he spent a year in Paris painting scenes of French cafés and aging buildings.

On his return to a Depression-ridden America, Davis tried, throughout the 1930s, to balance his dedication to painting with his commitment to politics. During the period of the Popular Front Davis joined various organizations designed to protect artists' cultural freedom and economic security. In 1934 he became a member of the Artists' Union and was elected its President; between January and November 1936 he served as the editor of the Union's journal, *Art Front*. In 1936 he became National Secretary of the American Artists' Congress and its National Chairman in 1938. His personal journals, which include sketches, reveal his concern to reconcile abstract art with Marxism and modern industrial society. His pen-and-ink drawings from this period work out

Stuart Davis: *Untitled*, oil on canvas, 2.13×3.35 m, mural from Studio B, WNYC Municipal Broadcasting Company, New York, 1939 (City of New York: on loan to New York, Metropolitan Museum of Art)

spatial relationships with lines and planes and serve as studies for his oils, in which the element of colour adds to the abstract sense of space.

Davis's works of the late 1930s, which continue to celebrate the urban and technological environment, are increasingly complex and frequently recall Léger's brightly coloured geometric forms. They also reveal the strong influence of jazz, which Davis considered to be the musical counterpart to abstract art. Some of his earliest works depict saloons and ragtime musicians; both the titles and images of his works of the late 1930s, however, reflect the syncopations and unusual rhythms of jazz, particularly Swing. Among his murals for the WPA Federal Arts Project are *Swing Landscape* (1938; Bloomington, IN U. A. Mus.) for the Williamsburg Housing Project in Brooklyn and an untitled work (1939; New York, Met.; see fig.) for Studio B, WNYC Municipal Broadcasting Company, a radio station in New York, both of which are filled with references to jazz.

In 1942–3 Davis produced several paintings abstracted from nature, but after World War II he returned for inspiration to the urban environment, maintaining a continuity with the imagery and witty calligraphy of works of the 1930s. His post-war paintings also have affinities with Abstract Expressionism through their abstract 'all-over' composition, surface texture and shallow illusionistic space, for instance the paintings from the *Mellow Pad* series (1945–51; examples in 1978 exh. cat., pp. 63, 148, 149, and Honolulu, HI, Acad. A.), which also contain single words taken from jazz or slang. *Owh! In San Pao*

(1951; New York, Whitney), based on a work from 1927 entitled *Percolator* (New York, Met.), demonstrates the artist's tendency to rework motifs from earlier paintings in a new idiom. This working method epitomizes the continuity of pictorial themes and painting techniques that Davis maintained throughout his career.

UNPUBLISHED SOURCES
Cambridge, MA, Harvard U., Houghton Lib. [priv. journals]

BIBLIOGRAPHY
E. C. Goossen: *Stuart Davis* (New York, 1959)
R. Blesh: *Stuart Davis* (New York, 1960)
Stuart Davis Memorial Exhibition, 1894–1964 (exh. cat., intro. H. H. Arnason; Washington, DC, N. Col. F.A., 1965)
D. Kelder, ed.: *Stuart Davis* (New York, 1971)
R. Smith: 'Stuart Davis: Picture Builder', *A. America*, lxiv (1976), pp. 80–87
Stuart Davis (exh. cat., ed. B. Urdang; Paris, Gal. Zabriskie, 1976)
J. Lane: 'Stuart Davis and the Issue of Content in New York School Painting', *A. Mag.*, lii (1978), pp. 154–7
Stuart Davis: Art and Art Theory (exh. cat., ed. J. Lane; New York, Brooklyn Mus., 1978)
Stuart Davis (exh. cat., New York, Whitney, 1980)
J. Myers: 'A Reality Parallel to Nature: Stuart Davis's Lithographs, 1929–31', *Tamarind Pap.* (Autumn 1986), pp. 46–51
J. Myers, ed.: *Stuart Davis: Graphic Work and Related Paintings with a Catalogue Raisonné of the Prints* (Fort Worth, 1986)
K. Wilkin: *Stuart Davis* (New York, 1987)
C. Whiting: *Antifascism in American Art* (New Haven, 1989)
W. C. Agee, ed.: *Stuart Davis: A Catalogue Raisonné* (New Haven, 1991)
CÉCILE WHITING

Davis, William (*b* Dublin, 1812; *d* London, 22 April 1873). Irish painter. He was trained in Dublin and exhibited portraits at the Royal Hibernian Academy from 1833 to 1835. He was in Sheffield in 1837 and by 1846 was in Liverpool, probably drawn there by the flourishing Liverpool Academy. He exhibited at the Academy from 1842 to 1844, became a Member in 1853 and Professor of drawing from 1856 to 1859. He also exhibited at the Royal Academy in London (1851–72) and at the Liverpool Autumn Exhibition (1871–3). He turned from figure and still-life subjects of game to landscape painting *c*. 1853, probably persuaded by his chief patron, John Miller, and influenced by the Liverpool landscape painter Robert Tonge (1823–56) and later by the Pre-Raphaelites. During the late 1850s Davis was a member of the Hogarth Club in London.

Dante Gabriel Rossetti admired Davis's first landscape exhibited at the Royal Academy in 1855 (untraced) and alerted Ruskin, who judged it merely as 'good Pre-Raphaelite work', and found Davis's subjects, which were never obvious views, without interest. The paintings were usually small and recorded the north-west of England, and occasionally Ireland, (e.g. Liverpool, Walker A.G.) either in wide-sweeping depth or by close-up confrontation of duck-pond, windmill or cornfield, and effective use was made of a high horizon. Davis's fluid technique tightened under the influence of the Pre-Raphaelites (sometimes becoming over-spotty), and his colour brightened.

Davis was a highly productive artist, although the quality of his work was uneven. At his best, as in *A Field of Green Corn* (*c*. 1860; priv. col., see Staley, pl. 76a) and *At Hale, Lancashire* (*c*. 1860; Liverpool, Walker A.G.), he expressed a gentle awareness of the dappled shimmer of light through verdure. He was chiefly supported by Miller and by George Rae of Birkenhead, but nevertheless remained unsuccessful despite his association with the Pre-Raphaelites and his move to London in *c*. 1870, where he embarked on a broader style and larger canvases. A memorial exhibition in Liverpool, 1890, was organized chiefly by Ford Madox Brown. Davis's sons, Valentine (1854–1930), Lucien (*b* 1860) and William Paul (*fl* 1883–1917), were also artists.

BIBLIOGRAPHY

F. G. Stephens: 'William Davis: Landscape Painter, of Liverpool', *A. J.* [London] (1884), pp. 325–8

H. C. Marillier: *The Liverpool School of Painters* (London, 1904), pp. 99–113

A. Staley: *The Pre-Raphaelite Landscape* (Oxford, 1973), pp. 139–44 [major reassessment]

M. Bennett: *Merseyside Painters, People and Places: Catalogue of Oils in the Walker Art Gallery, Liverpool* (Liverpool, 1978), i, pp. 84–9; ii, reproductions

The Pre-Raphaelites (exh. cat., ed. L. Parris; London, Tate, 1984) [section on Davis by R. Hamlyn]

P. McEvansoneya: 'William Davis: The Irish Pre-Raphaelite?', *Irish A. Rev.* (in preparation)

MARY BENNETT

Davison, George (*b* Lowestoft, Suffolk, 1854; *d* Antibes, Alpes-Maritimes, 1930). English photographer. He was born into a working-class family and became an audit clerk in the Exchequer in London. He took up photography in 1885, when he joined the newly formed Camera Club in London. He soon became club secretary, a post he carried out with great distinction. This, and his growing reputation as a Pictorial photographer, led George Eastman to appoint him assistant manager of the Eastman Photographic Materials Company set up in 1889 in London. He became Managing Director of the re-formed Company, Kodak Ltd, a post he held until 1908. Davison was intensely interested in photography as a medium of artistic expression, and became a disciple of P. H. Emerson, whose theories of 'naturalistic photography', which proposed that photography should imitate natural vision by using soft focus for peripheral detail, Davison eagerly applied. Davison extended this into the development of a style of photographic Impressionism, in which the aim of the photographer was to convey the impression of, or emotional reaction to, a subject by the suppression of detail. In order to produce soft focus images Davison used pinhole, instead of lens, cameras and printing methods such as gum bichromate. Images such as the *Onion Field* (1890; see Newhall p. 144) played a central role in the debates concerning photography as a fine art. His photograph *An Old Farmstead* (1890) won the gold medal at the Photographic Society of Great Britain exhibition of 1890. Davison broke with the latter, however, and became a founder-member of the LINKED RING, a brotherhood of photographers committed to excellence in all styles of photography. Through his writings in English, French, American and other journals, Davison became a leading figure in PICTORIAL PHOTOGRAPHY. From 1911 Davison no longer took photographs.

BIBLIOGRAPHY

Pictorial Photography in Great Britain, 1900–1920 (exh. cat., intro. J. Taylor; ACGB, 1978)

B. Newhall: *The History of Photography* (London, 1982/*R* 1986), pp. 142, 144–6

B. Coe: 'George Davison: Impressionist and Anarchist', *British Photography in the Nineteenth Century: The Fine Art Tradition*, ed. M. Weaver (Cambridge, 1989), pp. 215–41

BRIAN COE

Davud Ağa (*d* Istanbul, Sept 1598). Ottoman architect. He followed the standard career pattern for architects at the Ottoman court: recruited as a janissary, he studied architecture under Sinan (*see* SINAN (ii)) in the imperial palace in Istanbul, rose to the rank of superintendent of the water supply, the second ranking official in the corps of imperial architects, in 1576 and finally replaced his teacher as chief court architect in 1588. He also participated, presumably as a military engineer, in the campaign against Iran in 1583. He worked on various projects under Sinan's direction, including the Selimiye Mosque (1569–75) in EDIRNE, the mosque (and probably the tomb) of Mehmed Ağa (1585) in the Çarşamba district of Istanbul and a hall and bath for the Yeni Saray. Davud Ağa's own works in Istanbul include the Incili Kiosk (1589), the Septeciler Kiosk (1591), the complex of Sinan Pasha (1593), the mosque of Cerrah Mehmed Pasha (1594), the tomb, fountain and madrasa of Gazanfer Ağa (completed 1599) and the tomb of Murad III (*reg* 1574–95), which may also have been incomplete at the architect's death. His last years were devoted to the construction of the Yeni Valide Mosque at Eminönü in Istanbul, which he began in 1594 for the queen mother, Safiye Sultan. His conservatism is evident in its plan, which is a modified version of the Şehzade Mosque, designed by Sinan at the start of his career.

BIBLIOGRAPHY

A. Refik: 'Mimar Davut', *Darülfünun Edibiyat Fak. Mecmuası*, vii (1932), pp. 1–16

——: *Türk mimarları* [Turkish architects] (Istanbul, 1936), pp. 26–33

M. Erdoğan: 'Mimar Davut Ağa'nın hayatı ve eserleri' [The life and works of the architect Davud Ağa], *Türkiyat Mecmuası*, xii (1955), pp. 178–204

L. A. Mayer: *Islamic Architects and their Works* (Geneva, 1956), pp. 58–9

G. Goodwin: *A History of Ottoman Architecture* (Baltimore and London, 1971), pp. 338–42

A. Kuran: *Sinan: The Grand Old Master of Ottoman Architecture* (Washington, DC, 1987)

HOWARD CRANE

Dawber, Sir (Edward) Guy (*b* King's Lynn, Norfolk, 1861; *d* London, 24 April 1938). English architect. He was articled to William Adams (1806–85) in King's Lynn and then worked in the Dublin office of Sir Thomas Deane until 1882, when he went to London to work for George & Peto. In 1887 he had trouble with his eyes and was sent as clerk of works to George's Batsford Park House, Glos. He became an expert in the vernacular buildings of the Cotswolds and in 1890 started his own practice in Bourton-on-the-Hill, returning to London in 1891. The majority of his early works before 1900 are in Gloucestershire and Worcestershire, examples being Millbrook, Broadwell, Glos (1890), the post office, Broadway, Hereford & Worcs, and the White House, Moreton-in-Marsh, Glos (1898). After 1900 his practice increased, and he became a leading exponent of the traditional English domestic house, alternating between stone classical houses and Tudor and vernacular building styles. Dawber stated that his aim was 'to try to carry on that fine tradition of quiet building which has stamped our countryside with an indefinable charm' (*RIBA J.*, 1928). Typical examples are Nether Swell Manor, Stow-on-the-Wold (1909–13), and Burdocks, Fairford (1911), both in Gloucestershire. Two isolated examples of buildings in an urban setting are the London and Lancashire Fire Insurance Co., 59–60 Pall Mall, London (1906; destr. World War II, rebuilt to a modified design by his practice), and the Foord Alms-houses, Rochester, Kent (1926).

Dawber was President of RIBA from 1925 to 1927 and in 1928 received the Royal Gold Medal, the first award of this distinction to an architect for domestic work. With David Alexander Edward, 27th Earl of Crawford and 10th Earl of Balcarres (1871–1940), Dawber was a founder-member of the Council for the Protection of Rural England (1926), of which he was Vice-President and Chairman.

WRITINGS

with W. Galsworthy Davie: *Old Cottages and Farmhouses in Kent and Sussex* (London, 1900)

——: *Old Cottages, Farmhouses and Other Stone Buildings in the Cotswold District* (London, 1905)

'The Preservation of Rural England', *RIBA J.* (14 July 1928), pp. 580–85

BIBLIOGRAPHY

'The Royal Gold Medal: Presentation to Mr E. Guy Dawber, A.R.A.', *RIBA J.* (23 June 1928), pp. 543–54

C. H. Reilly: *Representative British Architects of the Present Day* (London, 1931), pp. 80–87

A. R. Fox: Obituary, *Builder* (29 April 1938), pp. 824, 827

'Obituary and List of Works', *RIBA J.* (9 May 1938), pp. 631, 633, 666

A. Stuart Gray: *Edwardian Architecture: A Biographical Dictionary* (London, 1985), pp. 160–63

MARGARET RICHARDSON

Dawe, George (*b* London, 8 Feb 1781; *d* London, 15 Oct 1829). English painter and writer. He was the son of the mezzotint engraver Philip Dawe who taught him engraving. He continued to concentrate on engraving when he entered the Royal Academy Schools, London, in 1796, producing portraits until 1802, when he turned to history painting. In 1803 he won a gold medal and the following year made his début at the Royal Academy, where he exhibited until 1818, often showing such anecdotal and literary works as *Imogen Found in the Cave of Belarius* (exh. RA 1809; London, Tate). He was elected an ARA in 1809 and an RA in 1814 and soon afterwards returned to portrait painting. In 1816 he painted a number of portraits of George IV's daughter Princess Charlotte (e.g. London, N.P.G.), several of which were engraved. In 1817 he went to Brussels and was present at the review of the allied troops by Arthur Wellesley, 1st Duke of Wellington in Cambrai. Soon afterwards he was invited by Tsar Alexander I of Russia to paint the portraits of all the senior officers who had taken part in the Napoleonic Wars. He travelled to St Petersburg in 1819 where, over the next nine years, he painted nearly 400 portraits. These were placed in a specially built gallery (destr.) in the Winter Palace in St Petersburg. He returned briefly to England in 1828 before travelling to Berlin, where he painted the portraits of *Ernest Augustus, Duke of Cumberland* (1828; London, N.P.G.) and *Frederick William III, King of Prussia* (1828; untraced). From Berlin he moved to St Petersburg and then to Warsaw before being forced by illness to return to England, where he died shortly afterwards. His book *The Life of George Morland with Remarks on his Works* (1807) is both a lively account of his godfather's dissipated lifestyle and a fairly critical appreciation of his work.

WRITINGS

The Life of George Morland with Remarks on his Works (London, 1807)

BIBLIOGRAPHY

DNB

S. Redgrave: *A Dictionary of Artists of the English School* (London, 1878)

A. Graves: *The Royal Academy of Arts: A Complete Dictionary of Contributors and their Works from its Foundation in 1769 to 1904*, ii (London, 1905–6)   □

Dawenkou [Ta-wen-k'ou]. Chinese Neolithic site in Taian, Shandong Province. It gives its name to a Neolithic culture that stretched across Shandong, western Henan, northern Anhui and Jiangsu provinces *c.* 4300–*c.* 2400 BC. In the core area, Shandong, the Dawenkou culture developed from the Beixin culture and was succeeded by the LONGSHAN culture.

The beginnings of many of the characteristic features of Longshan pottery may be seen in the ceramics of the Dawenkou culture: the use of the potter's wheel, elaborate ritual vessels and polished blackwares and whitewares. There is evidence in the pottery produced from *c.* 3500 BC that on some vessels the rim was retouched on a slow potter's wheel. Smaller vessels that seem to have been turned on a fast wheel also appeared at the same time. The amount of wheelmade pottery increased towards the end of the period. Although most Dawenkou pottery was undecorated, styles of surface treatment changed significantly on those vessels that were decorated. Early Dawenkou (*c.* 4300–*c.* 3500 BC) decorated ceramics were dominated by painted vessels, the designs painted in red, black and white on a red or orange slip. Some of the designs are reminiscent of the floral and curvilinear triangle designs of the Miaodigou I culture, while others were geometric. The geometric designs continued into the Middle Dawenkou (*c.* 3500–*c.* 2900 BC), but the painted pottery tradition gave way in the Late Dawenkou (*c.* 2900–*c.* 2400 BC) to surface treatments such as basket and cord impressions. The Dawenkou ceramic shapes are primarily upright forms such as tripods and pedestalled vessels.

Other characteristic artefacts of Dawenkou culture include the deer-tooth hook, ivory combs and carved ivory tubes, the use of pig mandibles in burials and the construction of *ercengtai* (ledges between the inside edge of the grave pit and the actual burial chamber). Many of the larger Dawenkou graves also show evidence of log chambers or coffins built over the principal tomb occupant(s) (*see also* CHINA, §II, 6(i)(a)). Dawenkou cemeteries of all phases contain extremely wealthy graves alongside much more modest ones. The wealthiest graves contain over 100 artefacts each, including such high-status objects as carved ivory, stone and jade beads, jade axes and spades. Good selections of Dawenkou artefacts are on display in the Historical Museum, Beijing, the Jiangsu Provincial Museum, Nanjing, and the Shandong Provincial Museum, Jinan, Shandong Province.

See also CHINA, §VII, 3(i)(c).

BIBLIOGRAPHY
K. C. Chang: *The Archaeology of Ancient China* (New Haven, 1963, rev. New Haven and London, 4/1986)
'Jiangsu Pi xian Sihu zhen Dadunzi yizhi tan jue baogao' [Trial diggings at Dadunzi in Sihu zhen, Pi xian, Jiangsu Province], *Kaogu Xuebao* (1964), 2, pp. 9–56 [Eng. abstract pp. 55–6]
Dawenkou: Xinshiqi shidai muzang fajue bao [Dawenkou: an excavation report of a Neolithic cemetery] (Beijing, 1974)
'1987 nian Jiangsu Xinyi Huating yizhi de fajue' [Excavation of the Huating site at Xinyi, Jiangsu Province], *Wenwu* (1990), 2, pp. 1–26

CHRISTOPHER FUNG

Dawkins, James (*b* 1722; *d* Jamaica, Dec 1757). English traveller and antiquarian. He was educated at Oxford University, spent several years as a young man travelling in Italy and was elected as a member of the Society of Dilettanti in 1755. He was referred to in James Boswell's *Life of Johnson* as 'Jamaica Dawkins', as his family had extensive sugar plantations in Jamaica. He travelled with ROBERT WOOD and JOHN BOUVERIE to Baalbek and Palmyra in 1750. For this journey they chartered a boat from London and joined it in Naples; it was well equipped with a library of Greek histories and poems, volumes of antiquities and travel books. They visited many of the Greek islands and part of the Greek mainland, the Bosporus and the coast of Turkey, before travelling overland to Baalbek and Palmyra, where Bouverie died. Together with Wood, Dawkins later published *The Ruins of Palmyra* and *The Ruins of Balbec*, to which he contributed the measured drawings (and all of the costs). He and Wood gained a great reputation by these splendid publications of antiquities, though most of the credit for them has gone to Wood.

WRITINGS
with R. Wood: *The Ruins of Palmyra, otherwise Tedmor, in the Desert* (London, 1753)
——: *The Ruins of Balbec, otherwise Heliopolis, in Coelosyria* (London, 1757)

BIBLIOGRAPHY
T. Spencer: *Fair Greece Sad Relic* (London, 1954), pp. 162–3

MARGARET LYTTELTON

Dawlat al-Bahrayn. *See* BAHRAIN.

Dawson, Neil (*b* Christchurch, NZ, 6 Nov 1948). New Zealand sculptor. After graduating from the University of Canterbury School of Fine Arts in 1973, Dawson taught drawing systems at Christchurch Polytechnic. In 1978 an exhibition titled *House Alterations* at the Brooke Gifford Art Gallery in Christchurch established him as a sculptor. It introduced a number of characteristics that continued to be significant in his work: the sculptures were constructed from mesh, wire and wood, they were hung on the wall and they played with aspects of perception as mediated by systems of drawing. In 1984, now a full-time sculptor, he was commissioned to produce a large, permanent outdoor work, *The Rock*, for the Bank of New Zealand in Wellington; it was one of a series of permanent or temporary site-specific projects.

Dawson was included in the exhibition *Magiciens de la terre* held at the Centre Georges Pompidou in Paris in 1989. For the exhibition he constructed *Globe*, a hollow, fibreglass representation of the earth as photographed from outer space. It was suspended above the plaza outside the museum. The translation of photographic sources into sculpture, which he explored for *Globe*, provided a strong direction for later work. To enable him to produce such large installations he built up his own extensive studio workshop in Christchurch.

BIBLIOGRAPHY
Peter Leech: 'Elusive Objects: Recent Work by Neil Dawson', *A. NZ*, 25 (1982), pp. 24–9
Neil Dawson: Site Works, 1981–1989 (exh. cat. by J. Barr and M. Barr, Canberra, N.G., 1989)

JIM BARR, MARY BARR

Dax [Lat. Aquae Tarbellicae]. French spa town on the left bank of the River Adour in the Landes département. The site has been inhabited since the early Bronze Age. The walls of the Roman town, which were built after AD 276, survived largely intact until the 19th century; fragments remain along the river-bank. The present cathedral, the fourth on the site, was begun in 1647 but completed only in the late 19th century. It replaced a Gothic building (begun 13th century), the west façade of which was finally demolished in 1894. A portal (probably third quarter of the 13th century) is preserved inside the north transept. Its *Last Judgment* tympanum was probably reassembled wrongly: the intercessors originally flanking Christ now flank the Archangel Michael, once represented in the level above. The resurrected emerge from coffins and urns on the lintel and proceed to their fates across the lowest range of voussoirs. The archivolts bear angels, female saints with books, deacon and bishop saints, including *St Lawrence* with his attribute, a gridiron, and other male and female figures. The trumeau figure of *Christ* is flanked by six jamb figures on either side, representing the Apostles, standing on low mounds that resemble those on the central portal (late 1230s) of the west front of Amiens Cathedral (*see* AMIENS, §1(ii)). The proportions of the figures, with the length of the torso and head almost exceeding that from the waist downwards, are found on other provincial reflections of Amiens, such as St Eliphe, Rampillon (Seine-et-Marne), but the Dax sculptors imitated both the severe stereometry of the drapery and the spatial projection of the Amiens figures. The draperies crossing the figures, however, stand away from the bodies so as to destroy the columnar effect and disguise their articulation. A detail peculiar to Dax is the crowding of the delicate features in the centre of the broad faces. The drapery of the archivolt figures is derived from Amiens, while the jamb figures show signs of the influence of Reims Cathedral in the motif of an arm wrapped in a mantle, in St John's smile and in the large columns behind the figures.

BIBLIOGRAPHY

F. Salet: 'Dax', *Congr. Archéol. France*, cii (1939), pp. 380–90
W. Sauerländer: *Gotische Skulptur in Frankreich, 1140–1270* (Munich, 1970; Eng. trans., London and New York, 1972), pp. 511–12

GEORGIA WRIGHT

Daxi [Ta-hsi]. Chinese Neolithic culture of the middle Yangzi River basin, dating from *c.* 4400 BC to *c.* 3300 BC; it is named after the type-site at Daxi Wushan, Sichuan Province. Other important sites exhibiting this culture include Guanmiaoshan Zhijiang, in Hubei Province, Honghuatao, Yidu, in Hubei Province and Sanyuangong, Li xian, in Hunan Province.

The Daxi culture is characterized primarily from burials, although square, clay-plastered house floors have been discovered at a handful of sites. Burials were generally single. Many graves contained few or no grave goods, a smaller number contained as many as 30; several were accompanied by dog sacrifices. The most distinctive artefacts are the ceramics, which are predominantly hand-built red wares. Small numbers of red-ware vessels have grey or black interiors, and some grey and black wares have also been found. Daxi ceramics are generally plain, although some have a red slip. The most common surface treatments are painting, stamping, incising, cord impressions, appliqué and openwork. Painted designs were executed primarily in black on red. Decorative elements include chevrons, intertwined curvilinear designs, flower-petal designs and curvilinear triangular designs. The most important vessel forms are upright vessels such as deep-bowled *dou* and ring-footed bowls, plates and cups (for illustrations of this and other forms, *see* CHINA, figs 138 and 178). Other distinctive forms include cups with a crooked profile, conical or cylindrical vessel-stands, necked *guan*, flaring vases and flat-bottomed, high-necked *hu* and bottles (see Ren Wunan, fig. 41).

Non-ceramic artefacts from Daxi sites include tools made of stone and ornaments such as rings, beads, necklaces and arm-rings made of jade, stone, bone and shell.

See also CHINA, §VII, 3(i)(a).

BIBLIOGRAPHY

K. C. Chang: *The Archaeology of Ancient China* (New Haven, 1963, rev. New Haven and London, 4/1986)
Ren Wunan: 'Changjiang zhongyou he Hanshui liuyu de Xinshiqi shidai wenhua' [Neolithic cultures of the middle reaches of the Yangtze and the Han river valleys], *Xin Zhongguo de kaogu faxian he yanjiu* [Archaeological excavation and researches in New China] (Beijing, 1984), pp. 125–37

CHRISTOPHER FUNG

Day, Alexander (*b* Somerset, *c.* 1753; *d* London, 12 Jan 1841). English art dealer, painter and medallist. He spent much of his early life in Italy and in 1774 was in Rome, where he was detained by the French during their war with Naples. While in Italy he studied and made copies of paintings, and he also made portrait medallions showing only the head of the sitter. On his return to London in 1800 he worked as a picture dealer, achieving brief public prominence in 1816 when he was called to give evidence before the Parliamentary Committee set up to investigate the merits of the Elgin Marbles. Of the many paintings he bought from abroad several were for the National Gallery, London, including Gaspard Dughet's *Landscape with Abraham and Isaac Approaching the Place of Sacrifice*, Raphael's *St Catherine of Alexandria* (*c.* 1507), Correggio's *Ecce homo* (late 1520s), Anthony van Dyck's *Emperor Theodosius Forbidden by St Ambrose to Enter Milan Cathedral* (*c.* 1620) and a *Venus and Adonis* from the studio of Titian.

BIBLIOGRAPHY

DNB
Art-Union, iii (1841), p. 87
Gent. Mag. (July 1841), pp. 101–2

Day, F(red) Holland (*b* Norwood, MA, 8 July 1864; *d* Norwood, 2 Nov 1933). American photographer. He was an eccentric who sought to express his ideas on life and art through Pictorial photography, which he took up in 1887, frequently by interpretations of two opposites—the sacred and the profane. He regarded Classical Greece as the ideal and he pursued an intensive study of the human form, attempting to represent physical perfection in his photographs. These were in medium or large format, with mainly platinum prints.

Day was a cultivated and sensitive man of independent means. As well as studying painting, he was an admirer of Keats, owning a fine collection of the poet's manuscripts, letters and early editions. He published books as a hobby (1893–9), co-founding the Boston publishing house of Copeland and Day and importing the then scandalous works of Aubrey Beardsley and Oscar Wilde.

In January 1896 he was elected a member of the LINKED RING brotherhood, which aimed to promote photography as a visual art, and became obsessed with photography. In 1899, with Coburn and his mother, he went to England, renting a studio and darkroom in London in an alley north of Mortimer Street, W1. During the summer of 1899 Day worked on a series of photographs devoted to sacred subjects. Some 250 negatives were made, including studies of the *Crucifixion*, the *Descent from the Cross*, the *Entombment* and the *Resurrection* and others showing incidents connected with the Stations of the Cross. He regarded 25 of these as having been fairly successful and a dozen as really successful. He himself posed as Jesus Christ, having fasted until his features and body were emaciated; he grew his hair and beard for over a year in preparation for the photographs. Several of the studies required groups of people, and Day said that the posing of them was a long and arduous task. The models were his friends and professional actors, who wore specially imported antique costumes. Exhibitions of Day's Sacred Art photographs in 1899–1900 brought interesting reactions. Some art critics were prepared to accept photography as a medium for portraying such subjects, while photographers in the main were strongly opposed to it.

In 1900 Day was responsible for arranging and displaying a major exhibition: *The New School of American Photography*. Alfred Stieglitz, of whom Day was by now considered a peer, refused to support the exhibition, although it included work by the leading American pictorialists. Both were aiming to establish photography as a pictorial art, and this may explain why Day, although regarded as a distinguished member of the Linked Ring, never joined the PHOTO-SECESSION, founded by Stieglitz in 1902.

Some of Day's most imaginative photographs are in a series illustrating the legend of Orpheus, in which the exotic models included his protégé, Khalil Gibran, one of many immigrant boys he protected. His cousin, the photographer Alvin Langdon Coburn, said: 'To be in the company of this intellectual and artistic man was an education in itself . . . In his house, on elegant Beacon Hill (Boston), Day used to exhibit his photographs in an incense-laden atmosphere to the élite of Boston society.' A disastrous fire about 1914 destroyed Day's collection of photographs, with the exception of those which he had given to friends or donated to other collections. From 1917 he maintained a self-imposed isolation from society.

WRITINGS
'The New School of American Photography', *Brit. J. Phot.* (20 Nov 1900)
'Opening Address' [to the Royal Photographic Society], *Phot. J.* (21 Oct 1900)
'Photography as a Fine Art', *Photo-Era* (March 1900)

BIBLIOGRAPHY
R. C. Hazell: 'A Visit to Mr. F. Holland Day', *Amat. Photographer* (27 Oct 1899)
E. F. Clattenburg: *The Photographic Work of F. Holland Day* (Wellesley, 1975)
M. Harker: *The Linked Ring: The Secession in Photography, 1892–1910* (London, 1979)
J. W. Kraus: *Messrs. Copeland and Day* (Philadelphia, 1979)
E. Jussim: *Slave to Beauty* (Boston, 1981)

MARGARET HARKER

Day, Lewis Foreman (*b* Peckham Rye, London, 29 Jan 1845; *d* London, 18 April 1910). English designer and writer. He was educated in France and Germany, but his interest in design was provided by visits to the South Kensington Museum, London (now the Victoria & Albert Museum). In 1865 he entered the office of Lavers & Barraud, glass painters and designers. Some time later he became keeper of cartoons at Clayton & Bell and by 1870 had joined Heaton, Butler & Bayne, for whom he worked on the decoration of Eaton Hall, Ches. In late 1880 Day started his own business designing textiles, wallpapers, stained glass, embroidery, carpets, tiles, pottery, furniture, silver, jewellery and book covers. He designed tiles for Maw & Co. and Pilkington's Tile and Pottery Co., stained glass and wallpaper for W. B. Simpson & Co., wallpapers for Jeffrey & Co. and textiles for Turnbull & Stockdale where he was made Art Director in 1881.

Day was a founder-member and Secretary of the Fifteen, a group of artists interested in design who came together in 1882 to discuss the role of art and design in daily life. Day helped form the Art Worker's Guild in 1884. In 1888 he led several members of this group to form the Arts and Crafts Exhibition Society. Possibly Day's greatest contributions were in the field of design education. He advocated originality of design based on natural forms and high standards of craftsmanship. He wrote numerous books on pattern-making, ornament and design and was a regular contributor to the *Art Journal* and the *Magazine of Art*. He was a lecturer at the School of Design, London (later the Royal College of Art), and at the Glasgow College of Art and Handicraft.

WRITINGS
The Anatomy of Pattern (London, 1887)
The Planning of Ornament (London, 1887)
The Application of Ornament (London, 1888)
Nature in Ornament (London, 1892)
Pattern Design (London, 1903)

BIBLIOGRAPHY
D. M. Ross: *Lewis Foreman Day: Designer and Writer on Stained Glass* (Cambridge, 1929)

JOELLEN SECONDO

Day, Robin (*b* High Wycombe, Bucks, 25 May 1915). English designer. He studied at High Wycombe Art School and worked for a local furniture manufacturer for a year, winning a scholarship to the Royal College of Art, London, in 1935. In 1948 he and his wife Lucienne Day (*b* 1917), a textile and wallpaper designer (*see* WALLPAPER, colour pl. V, fig. 3), opened a London office where he practised as a graphic, exhibition and industrial designer. That year he and Clive Latimer (*b c.* 1916) won first prize in the International Low-cost Furniture Competition, held at MOMA in New York, for their storage furniture design. Such storage units became standard elements in 1950s British homes, contributing to contemporary ideas of flexibility in interiors. The prize brought him to the attention of Hille International, a British manufacturer looking to produce modern, contract furniture in a post-war market and to whom he became a design consultant with the opportunity to explore new materials and techniques in the production of low-cost furniture. In 1950 he designed the 'Hillestak' stacking chair (*see* ENGLAND, fig. 57), made of plywood, using newly available plastic glues and with inverted V-shaped splayed legs, characteristic of the period. His most successful chair for Hille, the 'Polyprop', of injection-moulded polypropylene on a slim metal tube base, developed the principle of different materials for base and seat established in the mid-1950s by the American designer Charles Eames. The 'Mark II' shell of 1963 continued to be produced in the late 20th century (*see* MASS PRODUCTION, fig. 2). Day designed seating for the Festival Hall (1951), for the Barbican Arts Centre (from 1968), both in London, and furniture for Gatwick Airport, W. Sussex (1958).

BIBLIOGRAPHY
M. Gray: 'Designer: Robin Day ARCA FSIA', *A. & Indust.*, 52 (May 1952), pp. 154–9
R. Carr: 'Design Analysis: Polypropylene Chair', *Design*, 194 (Feb 1965), pp. 33–9
Modern Chairs, 1918–1970 (exh. cat., London, Whitechapel A.G., 1970)
J. Cooper: 'Problems of a Packed House', *Design*, 337 (Jan 1977), pp. 36–40
S. Lyall: *Hille: 75 Years of British Furniture* (London, 1981)

MARGARET WAGSTAFF

Daybul. *See under* BANBHORE.

Dayes, Edward (*b* London, 6 Aug 1763; *d* London, May 1804). English painter, draughtsman and printmaker. He is chiefly remembered for his topographical watercolours. He was versatile in technique and subject-matter and often undertook drawing and oil painting (including both large-scale history subjects and miniatures), etching and aquatint. After studying printmaking under William Pether, he enrolled at the Royal Academy Schools, London, in 1780 and began to exhibit at the Academy in 1786. In the 1790s he was active in supplying drawings for topographical publications and working up sketches by amateur artists, notably the antiquary James Moore (1762–99). Some of his architectural views, for example *Greenwich Hospital* (1788; London, V&A), are highly finished and peopled with elegant figures, tinted over an assured pen-and-ink outline. Dayes's sketches have often been confused with early works by J. M. W. Turner and Thomas Girtin. The latter was a pupil of Dayes's from 1789, but the two men quarrelled: according to popular legend (unsubstantiated by contemporary sources) Dayes resented his pupil's success and had him imprisoned as a refractory apprentice.

In the late 1790s Dayes embarked on a series of large biblical and classical subjects in oils, such as the *Fall of the Angels* (1798; London, Tate), but here as elsewhere his ambitions were not matched by recognition or reward. A meticulous draughtsman, he saw himself as an upholder of traditional standards in the face of the 'new and more dashing style'. His angular personality and mastery of faint praise are clearly illustrated in his *Professional Sketches of Modern Artists*, published with his didactic essays on painting and drawing and with a picturesque tour to Yorkshire and Derbyshire, a year after the embittered Dayes had committed suicide.

WRITINGS

The Works of the Late Edward Dayes, ed. E. W. Brayley (London, 1805/*R* 1971) [repr. incl. biog. intro. by R. W. Lightbown, Dayes's diary for 1798, his lib. cat. and other docs]

PATRICK CONNER

Dazaincourt. *See* AZINCOURT, BARTHÉLÉMY-AUGUSTIN BLONDEL D'.

D'Azeglio, Massimo (Taparelli), Marchese (*b* Turin, 24 Oct 1798; *d* Turin, 15 Jan 1866). Italian painter, writer and statesman. After visiting Rome in 1814, he lived there intermittently between 1818 and 1828. Until 1820 he trained under Martin Verstappen (1773–1853) and then spent extended periods in the Roman Campagna, sketching and painting numerous landscapes, such as *Wood and Glade, Alban Hills* (Turin, Gal. Civ. A. Mod.), which display a lingering 18th-century vocabulary and a northern European taste for detail. In an effort to reconcile his interests as artist, writer and patriot, D'Azeglio began to adapt landscape motifs to heroic scenes from romantic literature and history (especially battles). In the *Death of Montmorency* (1825; Turin, Gal. Civ. A. Mod.), a subject taken from a romantic novel by Sophie Cottin (1770–1807), he set out to innovate traditional Netherlandish landscape by substituting knights and paladins for rustic figures. He made a fundamental contribution to the development of history painting in Italy by using his subjects to evoke patriotic sentiment. The *Duel of Barletta* (1831; Milan, Contessa Angela Porro Schiaffinati priv.

col., see 1973–4 exh. cat., no. 52) depicts in a conventional manner an episode of 1503 of Italian romantic heroism, which D'Azeglio used again in a celebrated novel of 1833. His reputation rests primarily on his small landscape pictures—endowed with a new intensity in later years—for they prepared the way for the naturalistic expressions of Romantic landscape painting in Piedmont.

In 1831 D'Azeglio moved to Milan and worked there intensely for ten years. Although the demands of his political career caused him to stop painting while he was Prime Minister of Savoy–Sardinia (1849–52), D'Azeglio was a committed artist, who exhibited and sold regularly and received many commissions. In 1855 he succeeded his brother Roberto Taparelli, Marchese D'Azeglio (1790–1862), as Director of the Reale Galleria (later the Regia Pinacoteca, now Galleria Sabaudia) in Turin.

WRITINGS

I miei ricordi (Turin, 1867)

BIBLIOGRAPHY

Massimo D'Azeglio (exh. cat., ed. A. Dragone; Turin, Gal. Civ. A. Mod., 1966)
Romanticismo storico (exh. cat., ed. S. Pinto; Florence, Pitti, 1973–4)
Il primo '800 italiano (exh. cat., ed. R. Barilli; Milan, Pal. Reale, 1992)

EFREM GISELLA CALINGAERT

de. For Dutch, French, early Netherlandish, Portuguese, Spanish, Swiss and pre-19th-century Flemish and Italian proper names with this prefix or preposition, *see under* the first part of the name for individuals active before *c.* 1500; *see under* the second part of the name for those active after *c.* 1500. For tripartite Portuguese and Spanish surnames, *see under* the first part of the surname.

de'. For pre-19th-century Italian proper names with this preposition, *see under* the second part of the name.

De 8. *See* ARCHITECTENGROEP DE 8.

Deacon, Richard (*b* Bangor, 15 Aug 1949). Welsh sculptor. In 1980 he began making a series of sheet metal and laminated wood sculptures in simple organic shapes, their surfaces congruent with their structure. Deacon considered himself a fabricator rather than a constructor and used unformed basic material to make sculptures that explored, by the use of metaphor, ideas that defined human experience through language and the senses. Although the forms devised by Deacon were fundamentally abstract in appearance, this metaphorical reference to the body and its methods of gathering information was alluded to in idiomatic titles such as *The Eye Has It* (1984; London, ACGB; *see* ENGLAND, fig. 34). As Deacon widened both his vocabulary and his range of materials, incorporating, for instance, vinyl and plywood into *Boys and Girls* (1982; London, British Council), so he increased the depth and complexity of metaphor into a highly flexible personal idiom.

BIBLIOGRAPHY

Richard Deacon: Sculpture, 1980–84 (exh. cat. by M. Newman, Edinburgh, Fruitmarket Gal., 1984)
M. J. Jacob: 'Richard Deacon: The Skin of Sculpture', *A Quiet Revolution: British Sculpture since 1965*, ed. T. A. Neff (London, 1987), pp. 72–91
Richard Deacon: Recent Sculpture, 1985–1987 (exh. cat. by C. Harrison, Maastricht, Bonnefantenmus., 1987)

LYNNE COOKE

Dead colouring [laying in]. Term used in oil painting to describe the first application of paint or underpainting in monochrome or reduced colour on top of the ground and underdrawing. This fixes the tonal relationships and composition, before further layers of paint are applied to give colour and details of texture. This traditional painting method, which developed from egg tempera painting practice, is in direct contrast with *alla prima* methods of painting, in which a single application of paint creates the effect.

RUPERT FEATHERSTONE

Deák-Ébner, Lajos [Ebner, Louis] (*b* Pest, 18 July 1850; *d* Budapest, 20 Jan 1934). Hungarian painter. He studied in Munich from 1868 to 1873. He was inspired by French painting at the Weltausstellung in Vienna in 1873, and he decided to move to Paris where, apart from short summer vacations in Hungary, he lived until 1887. In Barbizon he made friends with László Paál and Mihály Munkácsy. His painting was considerably influenced by the latter but also, among French artists, by Jules Bastien-Lepage and Jean-François Millet. Deák-Ébner spent his summers in Szolnok, in the Hungarian Great Plains, where he created his most significant work (*see* SZOLNOK COLONY). His pictures were, for the most part, naturalist genre paintings with several figures, informal and skilful depictions of everyday life (e.g. *Market-square in Szolnok*, 1878, *Home-bound Harvesters*, 1881 and *Evening on the Tisza*, 1887; all Budapest, N.G.). Deák-Ébner dealt less with *plein-air* problems. He frequently used gypsies as models.

In 1887 Deák-Ébner was offered the position of Director of the Women Painters' School in Budapest. In 1889–90 he collaborated with Károly Lotz and Bertalan Székely on frescoes at the abbey of Tihany in Hungary and in 1895–9 at the Art Hall, Budapest. His contributions tended to be large-scale allegorical drawings with a certain degree of pathos. Following these commissions his paintings became rather more decorative, and they began to take on the character of drawings. He never regained his former expressive tone, although he later painted genre scenes at Szolnok. He had an exhibition at the Ernst Museum, Budapest, in 1918, and he also exhibited at the Szolnok colony.

BIBLIOGRAPHY
I. Möbius: *Deák-Ébner Lajos* (Budapest, 1940)

For further bibliography *see* SZOLNOK COLONY.

MÁRIA SZOBOR-BERNÁTH

De Albertis, Sebastiano (*b* Milan, 14 Jan 1828; *d* Milan 28 Nov 1897). Italian painter. In 1848 he abandoned his studies at the Accademia di Belle Arti di Brera, Milan, to participate in the Milanese uprising against Austrian domination. He also joined Garibaldi on his 1859, 1860 and 1866 campaigns. This period marked a transformation in De Albertis's style and subject-matter. While under the influence of Francesco Hayez and Domenico Induno at the academy, he produced a series of history paintings, the most notable of which was the *Death of Ferruccio and Gavinana* (1852; untraced) for Conte Giulio Litta. Under the influence of Risorgimento ideals his subjects became increasingly concerned with themes relating to the new

Italy (e.g. *Garibaldi at Digione*, 1877; Milan, Mus. Risorgimento), or, as in the work of Giovanni Fattori, Michele Cammarano and the Induno brothers, based on his military experiences, for example *Charge of the Carabinieri at Pastrengo* (exh. Turin 1880; Rome, Mus. Carabinieri). Simultaneously, De Albertis's palette became more clearly influenced by the changes brought about by the Scapigliati artists, and his use of colour and light grew more open and atmospheric.

For his paintings and watercolours of military life, De Albertis made many studies of horses. Horses also appeared in his scenes of Milanese life, such as *Carriages on the Bastions of Porta Venezia* (1887; Milan, Mus. Milano). De Albertis was a well-known caricaturist, especially during his formative period *c.* 1850–60, and worked mainly for the newspaper *Spirito Folletto*.

BIBLIOGRAPHY
Comanducci; Luciani
L. Caramel and C. Pirovano: *Opere dell'ottocento*, Milan, Gal. A. Mod. cat., i (Milan, 1975), pp. 47–8
1886–1986: La Permanente: Un secolo d'arte a Milano (exh. cat., Milan, Pal. Permanente, 1986)
Soldati e pittori nel Risorgimento italiano (exh. cat., Turin, Cir. Ufficiale, 1987)

CLARE HILLS-NOVA

De Andrea, John (Louis) (*b* Denver, CO, 24 Nov 1941). American sculptor. He studied at the University of Colorado, Boulder (1961–5), and in 1966–8 was an art assistant at the University of New Mexico, Albuquerque. He had his first one-man show at the O. K. Harris Gallery in New York in 1970. He rapidly developed a style of casting and then painting fibre-glass or polyvinyl acetate sculptures of figures from life. The extreme verism of his work links it to PHOTOREALISM, although it lacks the strong cultural identity evident in much Photorealist sculpture and painting. The sculptures are usually of one or two young, elegant and casually posed nude figures, as in *Dorothy* (1969–70; Aachen, Neue Gal.). The mechanical technique and lack of expression distance the viewer, while the glossy realism sours any beauty the sculptures might otherwise have. Some sculptures were inspired by the works of other artists, while others reflect the artistic process, as in *Untitled (Studio Scene)* (1977; Cologne, Mus. Ludwig), which shows the artist and his model.

BIBLIOGRAPHY
Contemp. Artists
John De Andrea: Sculptures, 1978–81 (exh. cat. by P. Yenawine, Aspen, CO, Cent. Visual A., 1982)

□

Deane, Thomas (*b* Cork, 4 June 1792; *d* Dublin, 2 Sept 1871). Irish architect. He was the founding partner of the firm of DEANE & WOODWARD, the most significant exponent in the 1850s of the architectural precepts of John Ruskin. Deane, whose family had been in the building trade in Cork since the middle of the 18th century, began his architectural career as a builder and contractor in Cork in 1806, when he took over the family business with his mother following his father's death. While the firm's later work was Gothic Revival, Deane's early work was classical. In 1811 he won his first major commission for the Cork Commercial Buildings (1811–13) in a competition against William Wilkins. In the 1820s and 1830s Deane became one of the principal architects and builders in the county. In partnership with his brothers, Alexander Sharpe Deane (*c.* 1800–47) and Kearns Deane (1804–47), he executed a number of banks and other civic structures in Cork, including the Old Savings Bank (1824, destr. 1902), the portico of the County Court House (1835), the Bank of Ireland (1838–40) and the New Savings Bank (1840–42). Elegant if conventional Neo-classical works, they are characterized by restrained monumentality, strong three-dimensionality and an academically correct use of antique forms. The sound functional planning, solid construction and keen sense of economy and utility exhibited by these buildings give evidence of Deane's skill in dealing with the more pragmatic aspects of design. These qualities, as well as the bold but finely detailed architectural ornament and evident sensitivity to materials, continued to characterize the firm's later buildings.

Deane's one Gothic Revival work of this period, Dromore Castle (1831–6), Kenmare, Co. Kerry, was a rambling castellated structure with mock battlements and sham vaults and archways. It lacks the scholarship and originality of Deane & Woodward's Gothic Revival work of the 1840s and 1850s. In 1845 Benjamin Woodward (1816–61) entered Deane's office and was largely responsible for the design of the firm's principal commissions of the 1840s; for Queen's College (1846–9), Cork, and the Killarney Lunatic Asylum (1847–50). In 1851 Woodward and Sir Thomas's son, Thomas Newenham Deane (1828–99), were made partners and Sir Thomas soon ceased to play a central role in the firm.

Active in local politics, Deane was twice elected High Sheriff, or Mayor, of Cork, in 1815 and 1830, and was knighted for his public service. In 1861 he moved from Cork to Dublin, where he lived until his death. In the last decade of his life Deane became increasingly involved in the corporate activities of the Royal Hibernian Academy and the newly organized Royal Institute of the Architects of Ireland, serving as president of both institutions during the 1860s.

BIBLIOGRAPHY

'Sir Thomas Deane, Architect', *Builder*, xxix (1871), p. 804

J. Coleman: 'Sir Thomas Deane, P.R.H.A.', *Cork Hist. & Archaeol. Soc. J.*, xxi (1915), pp. 180–86

T. F. McNamara: 'The Architecture of Cork, 1700–1900', *Royal Inst. Architects Ireland Yb.* (1960), pp. 15–39

M. Bence-Jones: 'Old Towns Revisited: Cork II—Two Pairs of Architect Brothers', *Country Life*, cxlii (10 Aug 1967), pp. 306–9

E. M. Blau: 'The Earliest Work of Deane and Woodward', *Archit.: Z. Gesch. Archit.*, ix (1979), pp. 170–92

E. Blau: *Ruskinian Gothic: The Architecture of Deane and Woodward, 1845–1861* (Princeton, 1982)

Deane & Woodward. Irish architectural partnership. It was formed in 1851 by THOMAS DEANE, Benjamin Woodward (*b* Tullamore, Co. Offaly, 16 Nov 1816; *d* Lyon, France, 15 May 1861) and Thomas Deane's son, Thomas Newenham Deane (*b* Cork, 15 June 1828; *d* Dublin, 8 Nov 1899). The first significant exponent of the architectural principles of John Ruskin, Deane & Woodward created a Ruskinian Gothic style in the 1850s that was distinct in form and theoretical basis from the High Victorian Gothic that was evolving at the same time.

The firm was founded in Cork by Sir Thomas Deane. Benjamin Woodward, the leading personality and designer of the firm's work in the late 1840s and 1850s, had trained as a civil engineer, but a love of medieval art led him to become an architect. After a possible brief association with William Morrison, Woodward entered Deane's office in 1845 to assist with the designs for Queen's College (1846–9), Cork, and the Killarney Lunatic Asylum (1847–50). The firm's first large-scale Gothic Revival works, they show Woodward's thorough knowledge of Irish medieval architecture as well as the work of contemporary Gothic Revivalists, in particular the Irish conventual buildings and published writings of A. W. N. Pugin.

Thomas Newenham Deane was educated at Trinity College, Dublin, and joined his father's practice in 1850. He and Woodward were made partners in 1851 and the firm's name was changed to Deane, Son & Woodward. Shortly afterwards, Sir Thomas Deane ceased to play an active role in the partnership, and the firm's name was gradually shortened to Deane & Woodward.

Trinity College Museum Building (1852–7) (*see* IRELAND, fig. 5), Dublin, the first major building of the new partnership, secured Deane & Woodward's reputation in Ireland and England and established the character of the firm's Ruskinian work. The Italian Gothic forms, classicizing containment of volume and mass, rich sculptural decoration, surface texture and colour of the building were very different from the firm's Gothic Revival work of the 1840s. Trinity College Museum Building was praised by Ruskin, who acknowledged it as the first significant realization of his architectural principles lately put forward in the *Seven Lamps of Architecture* (1849) and *The Stones of Venice* (1851–3).

At Trinity, Deane & Woodward also first implemented one of Ruskin's most important precepts regarding the role of the craftsman. The stone-carvers responsible for the naturalistic and richly associational carving on the building were allowed to design the details of the ornament themselves and even to a certain extent to determine their subjects. Deane & Woodward continued this practice in their subsequent work, employing the Irish stone-carvers, James and John O'Shea and later Charles Harrison.

The University Museum (1855–61), Parks Road, Oxford, Deane & Woodward's most influential building, was the first large-scale civic building in the Gothic Revival style in England since the Houses of Parliament. The large interior courtyard has steep glass roofs supported by arched iron braces which have delicate tracery. There is much elaborate decoration in stone, marble and wrought iron. Ruskin was directly involved and played an active role in the planning and design of the decorative scheme for the building. A friend of the Pre-Raphaelites, Woodward collaborated with members of the Brotherhood and their associates on other projects in Oxford, most notably the Oxford Union (1857), with murals of scenes from Malory's *Morte Darthur* [*sic*].

The firm also made significant contributions in commercial, civic and domestic architecture. Their Crown Life Assurance Company Office (1855–7), New Bridge Street, London, and Government Offices competition design (1857, not executed) were both well publicized and extended Ruskin's influence beyond the universities to the city, creating a Ruskinian urban mode characterized by regular classicizing plans, broad simplified forms and Italian Gothic detail with an emphasis on structural polychromy and rich sculptural ornament. Deane & Woodward's Irish houses of the late 1850s, including Brownsbarn (1858), Co. Kilkenny, Clontra (1858) and Glandore (1858–9) in Co. Dublin, St Austin's Abbey (1858–61), Co. Carlow, and the Kildare Street Club (1858–61) in Dublin, constitute a Ruskinian domestic mode in their contained masses, emphasis on craft and materials and corresponding richness of detail.

The partnership ended in 1861 with Woodward's death. Thomas Newenham Deane continued to practise until his death. Most of his work in the 1860s and 1870s was in Dublin and Oxford, where the firm still had strong ties, though some domestic work was executed elsewhere in Ireland. These buildings show a considerable dependence on Woodward's designs of the 1850s. In 1878 he formed a partnership with his son, Thomas Manly Deane (1850–1933), who took over the practice.

BIBLIOGRAPHY

H. Acland and J. Ruskin: *The Oxford Museum* (London, 1859)
C. P. Curan: 'Benjamin Woodward, Ruskin, and the O'Sheas', *Stud.: Irish Q. Rev. Lett., Philos. & Sci.*, xxix (1940), pp. 255–68
H. R. Hitchcock: 'Ruskin or Butterfield: Victorian Gothic at Mid-century', *Early Victorian Architecture in Britain*, 2 vols (New Haven and London, 1954/*R* New York, 1972)
P. Ferriday: 'The Oxford Museum', *Archit. Rev.* [London], cxxxii (1962), pp. 409–16
D. Richardson: *Gothic Revival Architecture in Ireland* (New York, 1978)
E. M. Blau: 'The Earliest Work of Deane and Woodward', *Archit.: Z. Gesch. Archit.*, ix (1979), pp. 170–92
E. Blau: *Ruskinian Gothic: The Architecture of Deane and Woodward, 1845–1861* (Princeton, 1982)
M. W. Brooks: *John Ruskin and Victorian Architecture* (New Brunswick and London, 1987)

EVE BLAU

Deare, John (*b* Liverpool, 26 Oct 1759; *d* Rome, 17 Aug 1798). English sculptor. He was born into a family of jewellers and as a child showed prodigious carving skills before serving his apprenticeship in the workshop of Thomas Carter (*d* 1795) from 1776. The following year he enrolled at the Royal Academy Schools, where his fine draughtsmanship is said to have prompted Joseph Nollekens (then Visitor) to abandon sketching altogether. In 1780 Deare became the youngest artist to win the Academy's gold medal, with a model representing *Adam and Eve from Milton's 'Paradise Lost'* (probably terracotta; untraced). After a further three years with Carter he set up his own workshop in 1783, modelling figures for John Bacon (i), John Cheere and others, and exhibiting that year at the first exhibition of the Society for Promoting Painting and Design in Liverpool. Like John Gibson (i) later, he was encouraged by William Roscoe, the Society's Vice-President. The four exhibited works represented *Adam and Eve* (a bas-relief; presumably the gold medal winner), a terracotta Crucifix, *Bellerophon* and *Virginius and his Daughter*, a plaster cast (all untraced). Deare's first independent commission was for a painted plaster pediment for Whitton Place, Middx, representing the *Destruction of the Titans by Jupiter* (house destr. *c.* 1847).

A year later, Deare successfully applied for the Academy's stipend to study in Rome for three years, and in 1785 he travelled to Italy, where he lived until his death. He resisted the traditional temptation of financial gain from 'restoring' antique marbles in Rome, instead executing a large number of chimney-pieces, busts, copies of antique statues and bas-reliefs, mostly for British travellers. His precise drawings after the Antique and studies of historical subjects (London, V&A; Preston, Harris Mus. & A.G.; Liverpool, Walker A.G.) reflect both the influence of Fuseli and Neo-classical tastes shared with John Flaxman, his contemporary in Rome. Deare's plaster relief of *Edward I and Eleanor of Castile* (1786; Liverpool, Walker A.G.) is a subject from English medieval history transposed into the Neo-classical style; the finished marble

John Deare: *Judgement of Jupiter*, marble, 1.48×2.98 m, 1786 (Los Angeles, CA, County Museum of Art)

(priv. col.) was the only work Deare exhibited at the Royal Academy, where it appeared in 1788. His *Judgement of Jupiter* (Los Angeles, CA, Co. Mus. A.; see fig.) is one of the great works of Neo-classical sculpture. A marble relief, containing 23 figures, it was begun in 1786 for the Academy exhibition of the following year, but probably did not reach England, since it was rediscovered in France two centuries later. The extreme range of depth in the carving and the variety of expression and compression of narrative sequence into a single image reveal Deare's intention to rival rather than imitate the Antique.

In 1791 Deare exhibited a marble bas-relief *Liberality Supported by Justice and Fortitude* (untraced) at the Society of Artists. Other examples of his work include *Venus* (marble, 1787; Parham House, W. Sussex), the *Landing of Julius Caesar* (marble, 1793; Stoke Park, Stoke Poges, Bucks) and his marble bust of John Penn (1793; Eton, Berks, Coll. Lib.). In 1797 Deare was considered a likely candidate for the series of public monuments in St Paul's Cathedral, London, but he died the following year, supposedly as a result of sleeping on a block of marble in the hope of finding inspiration in his dreams. Deare succeeded, where his fellow countrymen (such as Thomas Banks and John Flaxman) largely failed, in attracting patrons for sculptures on historical and ideal subjects. That he achieved less prominence is probably due only to his early death.

Deare's nephew, Joseph Deare (1803–35), also a sculptor, won the Academy's gold medal in 1825 and exhibited there from 1826 until 1832 when he moved to Liverpool. He too died young, from a fall suffered while climbing a wall to reach his studio.

BIBLIOGRAPHY

Gunnis
J. T. Smith: *Nollekens and his Times* (London, 1828), pp. 302–32
'Three Decades of Collecting: Gifts of Anna Bing Arnold', *Bull. LA Co. Mus. A.*, xxvi (1980), pp. 34–5

JULIUS BRYANT

De arte illuminandi. Medieval treatise and the most important source on the techniques of manuscript illumination (*see* MANUAL, MANUSCRIPT). The manuscript (Naples, Bib. N., MS. XII.E.27) has no title or signature and was entitled *De arte illuminandi* by its first editor, Demetrio Salazaro. Containing recipes for the making, preparation and mixing of pigments and colorants, it is a simple and well-organized manual, clearly composed for teaching the illuminator's craft. It describes consecutively the colours, gold, the temperas and various applications. Unlike most other medieval technical sources, *De arte illuminandi* is not a compilation of earlier treatises. The manuscript was probably written in southern Italy and dates from the end of the 14th century. No other copies of this text are known.

BIBLIOGRAPHY

D. Salazaro: *L'arte de la miniatura nel secolo XIV* (Naples, 1877)
A. Lecoy de la Marche: *L'Art d'enluminer* (Paris, 1890)
D. V. Thompson and G. H. Hamilton: *An Anonymous Fourteenth-century Treatise, 'De arte illuminandi': The Technique of Manuscript Illumination* (New Haven, 1933)
F. Brunello: *'De arte illuminandi' e altri trattati sulla tecnica della miniatura medievale* (Vicenza, 1975)

A. WALLERT

Deas, Charles (*b* Philadelphia, PA, 22 Dec 1818; *d* New York, 23 March 1867). American painter. After an unsuccessful attempt to obtain an appointment at West Point Military Academy, he turned to an artistic career. He quickly earned recognition at the annual exhibitions of the National Academy of Design, New York, to which he was elected an associate member in 1839, with subjects taken from James Fenimore Cooper, such as the *Turkey Shoot* (*c.* 1836; Richmond, VA Mus. F.A.), and from Washington Irving, *The Devil and Tom Walker* (1838; Richard P. W. Williams priv. col.).

In 1840, apparently anxious for adventure and perhaps in emulation of George Catlin's travels, Deas journeyed west and there discovered the subjects that established his reputation over the next eight years as a painter of Native American Indian and trapper life. During his first year in Wisconsin Territory he observed the trappers, travellers and Native American Indians who gathered at Forts Crawford and Snelling and persuaded the Indians to sit for their portraits (none extant). He also frequently travelled beyond the safety of the forts, especially to observe the Winnebago tribe, who that year were enduring another resettlement further west.

By late 1841 Deas had settled in St Louis, MO, but continued to venture beyond the city to see Indians, notably with Major Clifton Wharton's expedition to the Pawnee in 1844. Typical of his widely exhibited and much praised work are *Winnebagos Playing Checkers* (1842; Madrid, Mus. Thyssen-Bornemisza), *A Group of Sioux* (1845; Fort Worth, TX, Amon Carter Mus.) and *Long Jakes* (1844; priv. col.).

Most of Deas's paintings, whether taken from a literary source, from his own experience, or inspired by the compositions of 18th- and 19th-century European precedents, express psychological tension, perceived danger, alarm and flight. The most famous is the *Death Struggle* (1845; Shelburne, VT, Mus.), which depicts a trapper and Indian locked together as they fall to their death from a cliff. Such frenzied subjects may have been symptomatic of his impending illness, for in 1848 the apparently deranged Deas was hospitalized in New York. Although he exhibited a few bizarre pictures in the later 1840s, his career of less than a dozen years had ended.

BIBLIOGRAPHY

H. Tuckerman: *Book of the Artists* (New York, 1867), pp. 424–9
J. McDermott: 'Charles Deas: Painter of the Frontier', *A. Q.*, xiii (1950), pp. 293–311
C. Clark: 'Charles Deas', *American Frontier Life* (exh. cat., Fort Worth, TX, Amon Carter Mus., 1987), pp. 51–77

CAROL CLARK

Debabov, Dmitry (Georgiyevich) (*b* Koncheyevo, Moscow district, 24 Oct 1899; *d* Moscow, 11 Sept 1949). Russian photographer. He worked as a lathe operator's mate in a factory and then as a burlesque actor, taking up photography in the mid-1920s. He was stills photographer for Sergey Eisenstein's film *The General Line* (1929), and took a series of portraits of Eisenstein during shooting (1926). His first published photograph, in the magazine *Sovetskoye foto*, was *Going to Work* (1929). He became a photographic correspondent for *Izvestiya* and executed a series of distinctive photographs on industrial themes. His early work is characterized by the symbolic depth of the frame, as in *Hooter* (1930), which was used as a vignette in the first issue of the magazine *USSR in Construction*, for which Debabov later worked. He was a pioneer of expedition photography and in the mid-1930s made numerous journeys with Polar expeditions. Debabov's pictures, among them *Polar Night* (1935) and *All Hands on Deck on the Icebreaker 'Krasin'* (1936), were shown at many exhibitions, including the *Masters of Soviet Photographic Art* exhibition (Moscow, Un. Artists, 1935). Debabov published a book *Sledopyty dal'nego severa* ('Trackers of the far north') in collaboration with the writer El' Registan, with whom he made many journeys to northern areas of the USSR. His photographs are distinguished by the profound handling of tone and by the intense and authentic quality of the moment captured.

WRITINGS

with El' Registan: *Sledopyty dal'nego severa* [Trackers of the far north] (Moscow and Leningrad, 1937)
——: *Stal'noy kogot* [The steel claw] (Moscow and Leningrad, 1940)

BIBLIOGRAPHY

G. Shudakov: *Pioneers of Soviet Photography* (London and New York, 1983)
S. Morozov and V. Lloyd, eds: *Soviet Photography, 1917–1940: The New Photojournalism* (London, 1984)
S. Morozov: *Tvorcheskaya fotografiya* [Creative photography] (Moscow, 1986)

A. N. LAVRENTIEV

Debal. *See under* BANBHORE.

Debat-Ponsan [Ponsan-Debat], **Edouard-Bernard** (*b* Toulouse, 25 April 1847; *d* Paris, 29 Jan 1913). French painter. He trained in Toulouse and later at the Ecole des Beaux-Arts in Paris under Alexandre Cabanel. In 1873 he won second place in the Prix de Rome and in 1874 the Prix Troyon of the Institut. From the Institut he received a bursary that enabled him to visit Italy. In 1870 he made his début at the Salon under the name Ponsan-Debat and afterwards exhibited there such genre and history paintings as *Jephthah's Daughter* (1876; Carcassonne, Mus. B.-A.). He also executed religious works, some of which were for churches and cathedrals: he painted *St Paul before the Areopagus* (1877) for the church at Courbevoie and the *Pity of St Louis for the Dead* (1879) for the cathedral at La Rochelle. From 1880 Debat-Ponsan was the name under which he exhibited. *The Massage* (1883; Toulouse, Mus. Augustins) shows a white female nude massaged by a negress, and the subject attracted comment from contemporary critics. He also painted a number of landscapes, including *Corner of the Vineyard* (1888; Nantes, Mus. B.-A.). These were painted in a style similar to that of Jules Bastien-Lepage and, when they included figures, were often sentimental. His reputation depended, however, on his portraits, which are distinguished by their vigorous colour and precision, as seen in the portrait of *Pouyer-Quertier* (*c*. 1885; Rouen, Mus. B.-A.). Most notable was his portrait of *General Boulanger* (1887; untraced), which was shown at the Salon of 1887 and was accepted in 1889 for the Exposition Universelle in Paris. Amid scandal, Debat-Ponsan withdrew it soon after the opening because he thought that the Exposition was badly organized and his painting was not shown to advantage. He refused the bronze medal awarded it by the jury. In later years, while producing such paintings as *Christ on the Mountain* (1889; Toulouse, Mus. Augustins), he increasingly responded to

contemporary events in his work. During the Dreyfus affair he sided with Emile Zola and those calling for Dreyfus's retrial, and his allegorical work *Nec mergitur* (Amboise, Mus. Mun.), depicting Truth stepping out of a well restrained by a soldier and a priest, was exhibited at the Salon of 1898.

BIBLIOGRAPHY

Bénézit; *DBF*; Thieme–Becker
G. Vapereau: *Dictionnaire des contemporains*, 2 vols (Paris, 1893)
J. Martin: *Nos peintres et sculpteurs* (Paris, 1897), p. 130

Debat-Ponsan, Jacques (*b* Copenhagen, 1882; *d* Paris, 1942). French architect. He was a student of Victor Laloux at the Ecole des Beaux-Arts, Paris, where he was awarded the Premier Grand Prix de Rome in 1912. He produced several buildings for the postal administration in France as well as an educational complex, Groupe Scolaire J.-B. Clément (1932) in Boulogne-Billancourt, which relies on a straightforward expression of the reinforced-concrete frame and the use of large expanses of windows. Together with Tony Garnier, whom he assisted in the construction of the Hôtel de Ville (1931–4) at Boulogne-Billancourt, and François Le Coeur, Debat-Ponsan was one of the best proponents of a style stressing functionalism as opposed to historicism in public commissions, which stemmed from progressive circles at the Ecole des Beaux-Arts at the turn of the century.

BIBLIOGRAPHY

Travaux d'architecture: Jacques Debat-Ponsan (Strasbourg, *c.* 1936)

ISABELLE GOURNAY

Debias-Aubry, François (*d* Paris, June 1755). French architect. He specialized in designing residential architecture in Paris; his only known public commission is the hospital (1719) at Chaumes-en-Brie. His private clients essentially comprised financiers and tax collectors (*fermiers généraux*), including the banker Hogguer, who commissioned him to build a town house at 78, Rue de Varenne (1720; now the Ministère de l'Agriculture) for his mistress, the actress Mlle Desmares, and Barthélémy Thoynard de Vougy, for whom he designed a house (now the Caisse d'Epargne) on the Rue Coq-Héron, Paris. He was appointed architect to Président Duret, a magistrate and speculator, for whom he designed the Hôtel de La Vrillière at 14, Rue Saint-Dominique (1724; now the Hôtel de Brienne); it was originally intended for the Marquise de Prie but was bought by the Marquise de La Vrillière. The three-bay, pedimented central pavilion is articulated by Tuscan pilasters below and Ionic above. Debias-Aubry also designed several blocks of flats, notably the Maison Cotelle (1739; Rue St André-des-Arts). He was commissioned by the Bouillon family, members of the French aristocracy, to design the Grand and Petit Hôtel de Bouillon at 17, Quai Malaquai (1740–45; now part of the Ecole des Beaux-Arts) and stables (1749–50; destr.) at the château de Navarre in the Eure. Debias-Aubry's architecture is characterized by the use of oval courtyards and rooms, the latter expressed externally by semi-oval projecting bays. All his town houses were richly decorated.

BIBLIOGRAPHY

J.-F. Blondel: *L'Architecture françoise*, 8 vols (Paris, 1752–6/*R* 1904–5)
Hébert: *Dictionnaire pittoresque et historique*, ii (Paris, 1766), p. 21

M. Gallet: *Paris Domestic Architecture* (London, 1972), p. 154
La Rue de Varenne (exh. cat., Paris, Mus. Rodin, 1981), p. 61
La Rue Saint-Dominique (exh. cat., Paris, Mus. Rodin, 1984), p. 190

BRUNO PONS

De Biasi, Mario (*b* Belluno, 2 June 1923). Italian photographer. He began taking photographs in Milan in 1946, working with the Circolo Fotografico Milanese. He turned professional in 1953 and worked as a photojournalist for the magazine *Epoca*, of which he later became editor. His spectacular photoreportages from all over the world came to characterize not only his own magazine but the whole field of Italian photojournalism for almost 20 years. One of his most memorable series was that covering the Hungarian revolt of 1956. As well as news items and travel reports, De Biasi was also a photographer of nature and urban landscapes, and he published numerous books of photographs.

PHOTOGRAPHIC PUBLICATIONS
Il terzo occhio sulla natura (Milan, 1979)

BIBLIOGRAPHY
A. Colombo and A. Piovani: *Lettera di un fotografo* (Milan, 1982)
A. Piovani: *Mario De Biasi* (Milan, 1983)
C. Sgorlon and B. Munari: *Il romanzo del legno* (Udine, 1989)

ITALO ZANNIER

Dębno Church. Church dedicated to St Michael at Dębno in the province of Nowy Sącz, southern Poland. The 15th-century wooden church at Dębno has interested art historians since the middle of the 19th century; the stencilled paintings that decorate the interior were then regarded as an expression of 'Slavonic taste'; soon afterwards the monument was defined as 'a work in the pointed arch style'. In the 1920s it was included in the 'Tatra Highlands group of wooden churches' and regarded as

Dębno Church, interior, second half of the 15th century

the most characteristic and earliest example of a medieval wooden church in Poland.

A church was first mentioned on the site in 1335. Most of the present church is now dated to the second half of the 15th century: the curtain arch surmounting the south door is typical of Saxon architecture of the period, and the paintings are independently dated *c.* 1500. The nave and the chancel are both rectangular with a narrow sacristy north of the chancel. The spacing of the roof rafters with collar-beams corresponds to the width of the chancel, creating 'plank-boxes' on the sides of the wider nave, a structural solution typical of wooden Gothic church architecture in Little Poland. The lap joints and dowels survive, with the incised carpenter's marks. Also original are the beam-framed ceiling, the same height in the nave and chancel; the ornate rood-screen; the western choir gallery; the west door and the door leading to the sacristy, both with pointed arches, and the south door; and a window with a curtain arch in the east wall of the chancel.

The wall construction is full-timbered, resting on stone foundations; the corners are curb-plated with tenon joints. The walls are now planked but were originally exposed, as indicated by their outer surface, which is divided into three progressively narrowing sections, of which the plinth and part of the middle section have chamfered edges. The pitched roof has one ridge running the length of the church.

In 1601 or 1607 the west tower was built, incorporating an upper chamber and a helm. The original helm, which resembled that of the upper part of the south tower of Tyn Church, Prague, is known from a drawing on the south jamb of the west door. In the 18th and 19th centuries some additions were made: a small bell-tower; low arcades round the outside of the church, the planking of which is 19th-century; and a south porch. The window in the south wall of the chancel was also enlarged. Before the present arcades were built the church was surrounded by higher and wider ones, while the west entrance was shielded by a tower, porch or arcades.

The church is now seen as part of a group of Late Gothic churches in Little Poland of an uncommon type (the more usual plan comprises two square elements, the nave and the smaller chancel being enclosed on three sides). The closest analogies to Dębno are the nearby churches of Grywald, Harklowa, Łopuszna and Nowy Targ (St Anne's), all of which were probably built in the second half of the 15th century, possibly by the same workshop.

Dębno is no longer regarded as pre-eminent in the history of wooden architecture in Poland, because it has now been established that there are earlier examples, such as the churches in Haczow (last quarter of the 14th century), Humniska (*c.* 1410), Zborowek (1459) and Mogila (1466). It is, however, noteworthy for its stencilled paintings, which cover in a carpetlike fashion the beamed ceiling, nave and chancel walls, the rood-beam, choir gallery and certain fittings (e.g. the pulpit and collation seat; see fig.). There are 77 motifs combined in various patterns and colours, with blacks, greens, light blues and reds prevailing. There is plant and flower ornament, rosettes, geometric patterns and tracery, and next to them, deer, dragons, birds, hunting-scenes, St George and the heraldic emblem of the eagle, all in a Late Gothic–early Renaissance style. The paintings at Dębno and Harklowa were by the same workshop, using the same stencil. This painted, decorative stencilling occurs *c.* 1500 in several wooden churches in Little Poland (e.g. Binarowa, Lipnica Murowana, Łopuszna, Podole and Skrzyszów) and in wooden and stone churches in Silesia (e.g. Pniów, Syrynia, Gać, Małujowice, Zielęcice). The origins of this unusual and rich decoration seem to lie in combining woodcut techniques with graphic art and cloth; there are some analogies with earlier painted secular interiors, for example the 14th-century ceiling of the Palazzo Chiaramonte in Palermo, Sicily.

The church was restored and conservation work carried out between 1958 and 1962.

BIBLIOGRAPHY

J. Łepkowski and J. Jerzmanowski: 'Ułamek z podróży archeologicznej po Galicji, odbytej w r. 1849' [An episode from an archaeological excursion to Galicia undertaken in 1849], *Bib. Warszaw.*, xxxix (1850), pp. 416–54

N. Eljasz: 'Kościół w Dębnie' [The church at Dębno], *Józefa Czecha Kalendarz Krakowski* (1889), pp. 53–6

W. Łuszczkiewicz: 'Polichromia kościółka drewnianego w Dębnie' [The wall paintings of the wooden church in Dębno], *Sprawozdania Komisji Hist. Sztuki*, v (1896), pp. 186–92

T. Szydłowski: 'Odkrycie starodawnej polichromii kościółka w Harklowej na Podhalu' [The discovery of the ancient wall paintings of the church in Harklowa in Podhale], *Kurier Literackonaukowy*, 29 (1932), pp. ii–iii

W. Krassowski: 'Notatka o konstrukcji i podziałach architektonicznych ścian kościoła w Dębnie, pow. Nowy Targ' [A note on the construction and architectural divisions of the walls of the church at Dębno, district of Nowy Targ], *Ochrona Zabytków*, xv/2 (1962), pp. 14–18

Z. Medwecka: 'Inwentaryzacja malowideł ściennych w kościele w Dębnie Podhalańskim' [Inventory of the wall paintings in the church at Dębno Podhalanskie], *Ochrona Zabytków*, xv/2 (1962), pp. 19–24

H. Pieńkowska: 'Badania warunków otoczenia, stanu technicznego, polichromii oraz możliwości zachowania drewnianego kościoła w Dębnie Podhalańskim' [Investigations of the environmental conditions, the technical state of the wall paintings and the possibilities of preserving the wooden church in Dębno Podhalanskie], *Ochrona Zabytków*, xv/2 (1962), pp. 11–13

R. Brykowski: *Drewniana architektura kościelna w Małopolsce XV wieku* [Wooden church architecture in Little Poland in the 15th century] (Wrocław, 1981)

R. Brykowski and M. Kornecki: *Drewniane kościoły w Małopolsce Południowej* [Wooden churches in southern Little Poland] (Wrocław, 1984)

M. Kornecki: *Gotyckie kościoły drewniane na Podhalu* [Wooden churches in Podhale] (Kraków, 1987)

RYSZARD BRYKOWSKI

De Braekeleer. Belgian family of painters. (1) Ferdinand the elder was an immensely successful painter of humorous genre scenes of contemporary life. He also depicted episodes from the lives of the great 17th-century Flemish and Dutch painters. Two of his 13 children were painters, Ferdinand the younger (1828–57) and (2) Henri, who was one of the first Belgian Realist painters.

(1) Ferdinand De Braekeleer, the elder (*b* Antwerp, 12 Feb 1792; *d* Antwerp, 16 May 1883). The son of poor parents, he was first accepted by Mathieu Van Brée's art school for orphans and later by the Antwerp Academie. He gained several prizes there in 1809 and 1811, and he distinguished himself in the Paris Salon of 1813 with *Aeneas Carrying Anchises* (untraced). De Braekeleer's avowed aim on becoming a painter was to find the most lucrative field, and in his early years he tried his hand at most genres, including history painting, religious pictures (*St Sebastian*, 1818; Wynegen, Church of Notre-Dame)

Ferdinand De Braekeleer the elder: *Visit of Adriaen Brouwer to Joos van Craesbeeck*, oil on canvas, 0.87×1.05 m, 1824 (Brussels, Musée d'Art Moderne)

and popular scenes. It was not until 1819 (an earlier award having been withdrawn) that he was able to go to Italy after winning the Antwerp Prix de Rome with *Tobias Restoring his Father's Sight* (untraced). Van Brée joined him in Rome, where he furthered his training, and together they visited Naples, Ancona, Florence, Bologna and Venice. Captivated by Rome and the surrounding countryside, De Braekeleer filled a sketchbook (Brussels, Bib. Royale Albert 1er, Cab. Est.) with landscapes and picturesque views of the city, drawn with considerable virtuosity in black chalk. He also produced paintings such as *Peasant Woman from Frascati* (1822) and *Neptune's Grotto in Tivoli* (1822; both untraced).

In April 1823 De Braekeleer returned to Antwerp. Having realized that the public was more interested in national than imported subjects, he began to produce small anecdotal pictures. These sold well, unlike his history paintings, although he continued to work in this genre, successfully submitting *Defeat of the People of Antwerp by the Duc d'Alençon* (untraced) to the Salon of 1828. After this, however, the substantial reputation he made for himself was based on his genre paintings. He specialized in subjects taken from the lives of Flemish painters, painted in the style of Teniers, for example the *Visit of Adriaen Brouwer to Joos van Craesbeeck* (1824; Brussels, Mus. A. Mod.; see fig.) and *Frans van Mieris, Jan Lievens and Brekelenkamp in Front of Jan Steen's Tavern* (1827).

In 1830 De Braekeleer returned to grander themes, such as the *Inauguration of King Leopold I* (Brussels, Mus. A. Mod.) and the *Death of Frédéric de Mérode* (Antwerp, Kon. Mus. S. Kst.). The bombardment of Antwerp in 1832, the siege and surrender of the citadel and the fire at the city warehouse were the subjects of many paintings (examples in museums in Brussels, Antwerp and Amsterdam). During this period De Braekeleer opened his studio to take in pupils, of whom the most famous was his brother-in-law, Henri Leys. The disappointing reception given to *Spanish Fury* (exh. Paris Salon 1836; Antwerp.

Kon. Mus. S. Kst.) led him to abandon history painting definitively in favour of less ambitious, more popular and cheerful subjects. These genre scenes were increasingly sought after by his many admirers, who were willing to pay extremely high prices for his work. *Saying Grace*, the *Happy Marriage* and *Coming Back from Market* (untraced) are typical of the familiar scenes from daily life he treated with humour and disconcerting facility.

The success of the *Golden Wedding Anniversary* and the *Celebration of the Third Thursday in Lent* (Brussels, Mus. A. Mod.) at the 1839 Paris Salon crowned his professional career. He received the cross of Knight of the Order of Leopold and was given a variety of official appointments. When Van Brée died in 1839, De Braekeleer's admirers hoped that he would succeed him as director of the Antwerp Academie, but Gustaf Wappers was chosen instead. In 1836 he headed the committee responsible for erecting in Antwerp a statue of Rubens, whose life had inspired many of his paintings. He also supervised the restoration of Rubens's *Raising of the Cross* and *Deposition* (both Antwerp Cathedral).

Besides his merits as colourist and draughtsman, De Braekeleer was noted for the caustic wit, verve and rousing cheerfulness of his pictures, which are full of realism. The spirit of the 17th-century Dutch and Flemish paintings of Jan Steen, van Ostade and Teniers was never far away. Although there is a facile quality to much of his work, De Braekeleer was among the most accomplished 19th-century genre painters.

BIBLIOGRAPHY

H. Hymans: *Ferdinand De Braekeleer: Notice biographique* (Brussels, 1884); repr. in *Annu. Acad. Royale Sci., Lett. & B.A. Belgique*, li (1885)

D. Coekelberghs: *Les Peintres belges à Rome de 1700 à 1830* (Brussels, 1976)

1770–1830: Autour du néo-classicisme (exh. cat., Brussels, Mus. Ixelles, 1985), pp. 312, 380–82

(2) Henri(-Jean-Augustin) De Braekeleer (*b* Antwerp, 11 June 1840; *d* Antwerp, 20 July 1888). Son of (1) Ferdinand De Braekeleer.

He was the nephew of Henri Leys. Having already been taught drawing by his father and uncle, he entered the Antwerp Academie in 1854. He learnt figure drawing and drawing from the Antique from Jan Verschaeren (1803–63) and landscape from Jacob Jacobs (1812–79). He remained a pupil there until 1861, becoming friendly with fellow-student Jan Stobbaerts, who shared his scorn for the Romantic conventions inculcated by the Academie.

In 1858 De Braekeleer exhibited for the first time in the triennial Salon in Antwerp, showing *Reaper* and *Washerwoman* (untraced), themes he was to treat throughout his career. Although the unvarnished realism of *Laundry* (Tournai, Mus. B.-A.) was not well received when the picture was shown at the 1861 Salon, he continued to work in this vein, depicting humble trades (for the most part solitary occupations) with affection and nostalgia. His choice of subject-matter reflected his withdrawn personality and his lack of interest in any form of public life. He never belonged to the Société Libre des Beaux-Arts, and the person to whom he was undoubtedly closest was his uncle, Henri Leys, whose love of the Old Masters and slow, meticulous and precise technique he shared. They often worked together, and De Braekeleer was involved in several of his uncle's commissions. In 1863 he went to Germany to paint for Leys *Luther's Room in Wittenberg* (Liège, priv. col.), in which his interest in the effects of light is more clearly discernible; this interest took on increasing importance during the rest of his career. At the end of 1864 he went to the Netherlands, where he was able to familiarize himself with the Dutch masters, and in particular with Vermeer, who had a decisive influence on his painting. The contribution of the lesser Dutch masters such as Terborch and Metsu is apparent even in his early works.

After the death of Leys in 1869, De Braekeleer began to find his own direction. He was then 29 and had just signed a contract with the banker Gustave Coûteaux; this connection continued until 1876 and inaugurated a period of intensive production. He always worked very slowly, sometimes spending three months on a single canvas. His most famous paintings were created at this time: *Antwerp Cathedral*, *The Catechism*, the *Painter's Studio*, the *Man at the Window*, *View of Antwerp* and the *Pilots' House*. In his famous *The Geographer* (1871, Brussels, Mus. A. Mod.) the single figure (seen from behind) is less important than his white shirt, the stool covered with Utrecht velvet on which he is seated and the old atlas he consults. From the early 1870s De Braekeleer gave to all his works an astonishing unity achieved by means of light effects, in which objects acquired a new density. In many paintings the window is the principal focus, flooding the sad and melancholy interiors with air and light. Sometimes the window is merely suggested by a stream of light that makes a wide range of effects possible. He manipulated reds, ochres and oranges with great subtlety and picked out carafes, bottles and copper pots with sparkling highlights. His canvases present a complete contrast to those of his father, which were crowded with noisy, gesticulating figures. Henri De Braekeleer was often satisfied with a single figure, usually inactive, sunk in reverie or in a book, in a room upholstered in Córdoba leather and furnished with a Flemish Renaissance cabinet.

De Braekeleer's last years were clouded by mental illness; he abandoned painting altogether between 1879 and 1881. When he started to work again he found a new direction, in such pictures as his two versions of *Interior of the Pumping Station* (1883 and 1886), which reveal his undiminished fascination with recording light effects—here in an almost Impressionist manner. The energetic brushwork of his last landscapes was particularly admired by van Gogh. De Braekeleer died poor and almost unknown.

BIBLIOGRAPHY

C. Lemonnier: *Henri De Braekeleer: Peintre de la lumière* (Brussels, 1905)

L. Delteil: *Henri Leys, Henri de Braekeleer, James Ensor* (1925), xix of *Le Peintre-graveur illustré* (Paris, 1906–26/*R* New York, 1969)

C. Conrardy: *Henri de Braekeleer* (Brussels, 1957)

F. Leytens: 'Justice pour De Braekeleer, graveur', *Livre & Est.*, 63–4 (1970), pp. 203–13

Hendrik De Braekeleer te Brugge (Antwerp, 1975)

DOMINIQUE VAUTIER

Debret, François (*b* Paris, 27 June 1777; *d* Saint-Cloud, 19 Feb 1850). French architect. He studied with Charles Percier *c.* 1793, and in 1813 he succeeded Jacques Cellerier as the architect responsible for restoring the royal abbey church of Saint-Denis, near Paris. Debret's restorations revealed his ignorance of Gothic architecture and included a structurally dangerous trimming of stone from the church's buttresses, the removal of authentic ornament and such ill-conceived additions as the historically implausible Gallery of Kings on the west façade. Already under attack by medievalists, Debret then rebuilt the spire of the façade's north tower (which had been struck by lightning in 1837) with materials that proved too heavy and threatened the façade with collapse. He was dismissed for incompetence in 1846 and replaced by Viollet-le-Duc, who dismantled the tower in 1847.

In 1818–19 he was commissioned to convert the former Augustinian convent in Paris into the Ecole des Beaux-Arts as a result of the school's official organization in 1816. Work progressed slowly, and Debret had built only the utilitarian Bâtiment des Loges (1822–8) and the foundations and south wing of the Italianate Palais des Etudes (begun 1820) before he was replaced in 1832 by his brother-in-law and former student, Félix-Jacques Duban, who redesigned the project.

Debret was more adept as a theatre architect. After restoring Samson-Nicolas Lenoir's opera house (1781) on the Boulevard Saint-Martin in 1818 and Victor Louis's Salle Louvois (Théâtre des Arts, 1791–3) in 1819, he was commissioned in 1820 to replace the Salle Louvois with a new Parisian opera house, the Salle Lepelletier. This was intended to be a temporary structure and was eventually replaced by Charles Garnier's Opéra (1860–75), although it remained in use until its destruction by fire in 1873. Behind a new façade, whose two-storey loggia was modelled after Palladio's Basilica (begun 1548; see PALLADIO, ANDREA, fig. 3) in Vicenza, Debret rebuilt the acoustically popular auditorium of the Salle Louvois. His modifications, which included the substitution of Corinthian capitals for the original Ionic capitals that supported the ceiling in order to increase the height of the auditorium, proved so successful that Debret's auditorium was adopted as the official model for the Nouvel Opéra in the competition of 1861. Debret was elected to the Académie des Beaux-Arts in 1825 and appointed an inspector-general to the Conseil Général des Bâtiments Civils in 1841. In 1846 he was replaced as the architect of the Opéra by Charles-Rohault de Fleury and in 1848, following the February revolution, he lost his position as inspector-general. Although little of his work survived the 19th century, Debret was one of a group of architects that dominated French academic architecture in the 1820s and 1830s and promulgated the doctrines of Percier and Fontaine.

BIBLIOGRAPHY
Bellier de La Chavignerie–Auvray; *DBF*
A. Lance: *Dictionnaire des architectes français*, 2 vols (Paris, 1872)
V. Baltard: *L'Ecole de Percier* (Paris, 1873)
A. Soubies: *Les Membres de l'Académie des Beaux-Arts, 1816–1852*, 2nd ser. (Paris, 1906)
L. Hautecoeur: *Architecture classique* (1943–1957)
P. Léon: *La Vie des monuments français* (Paris, 1951)
C. Mead: *Charles Garnier's Paris Opera: Architectural Empathy and the Renaissance of French Classicism* (New York, 1991)
CHRISTOPHER MEAD

Debret, Jean-Baptiste (*b* Paris, 18 April 1768; *d* Paris, 28 June 1848). French painter and draughtsman, active in Brazil. When very young he accompanied his cousin, Jacques-Louis David, on a trip to Italy from which he returned in 1785. He then enrolled in the Académie Royale de Peinture et de Sculpture in Paris, initially following parallel studies in civil engineering, but soon devoting himself to painting. Between 1798 and 1814 he entered several of the annual Paris Salons with historical or allegorical paintings, Neo-classical in both spirit and form, for instance *Napoleon Decorating a Russian Soldier at Tilsit* (1808; Versailles, Château). He also collaborated at this time with the architects Charles Percier and Pierre-François Fontaine on decorative works. With the fall of Emperor Napoleon Bonaparte I, whom he greatly admired, he agreed to take part in the French artistic mission which left for Brazil in 1816. He stayed there longer than the rest of the group, returning to France only in 1831. During those years spent in Rio de Janeiro and in neighbouring provinces, he was in the vanguard of local artistic life, still in its infancy. He founded and encouraged the Academia Imperial das Belas Artes, of which he became professor of history painting. He painted many historical works such as the *Acclamation of Peter I* (1822; Rio de Janeiro, Mus. N. B.A.). He and two other members of the French mission, the architect Auguste-Henri Grandjean de Montigny and the sculptor Auguste-Marie Taunay (1768–1824), were responsible for preparing the decorations in Rio de Janeiro for the celebrations in 1818 acclaiming John VI as King.

Debret's most important works are the impressive number of drawings and paintings in which documentary exactitude is combined with a certain exoticism to record the most varied aspects of everyday Brazilian life: historic events, ethnic types, scenes, costumes and landscapes. This rich iconographic collection was transposed onto lithographs from which he selected 150 plates, augmented with his own writings, published in three volumes as *Voyage pittoresque et historique au Brésil* (Paris, 1834–9). The Fundaçao Raymundo Castro Maya in Rio de Janeiro has nearly 350 of his paintings and drawings.

Pontual
BIBLIOGRAPHY
A. Taunay: *A missão artistica de 1816* (Rio de Janeiro, 1912)
A. Morales de los Rios Filho: *O ensino artístico: Subsídio para a sua história* (Rio de Janeiro, 1942)
Art of Latin America since Independence (exh. cat. by S. L. Catlin and T. Grieder, New Haven, CT, Yale U. A.G.; Austin, U. TX, A. Mus.; San Francisco, CA, Mus. A.; La Jolla, CA, A. Cent.; 1966)
ROBERTO PONTUAL

De Broe, Pierre-Jean (*b* Ghent, 1761; *d* Ghent, 1852). Flemish architect. He was the son of a master carpenter and originally worked as a cabinetmaker before training as an architect at the Académie Royale in Ghent, where he won first prize for architecture in 1788. He was appointed chief draughtsman and inspector of public works in the province of East Flanders, and his earliest commissions included the temporary theatres, set up on the Marché du Vendredi, Ghent, for the reception (1791) of Emperor Leopold II (*reg* 1790–92) as Count of Flanders and for that of the French invaders (1792) following the annexation to France of the Austrian Netherlands (1792–1814). In 1810 he was appointed city architect, a position he held until 1841. His work was generally in a Neo-classical style with Italian influences, and his many official building projects included various guardhouses at the city gates, public pumps at Zandberg (1810) and the Groentenmarkt (1812), a great many wharves and swing-bridges, a fire station in Hoogpoort, a cavalry barracks in Brusselse-poortstraat, the orangery and conservatories for the botanic garden, the layout of a museum within the Académie Royale and a new entrance stairway for the Renaissance section of the Hôtel de Ville. He also made designs for rood lofts and organ cases, notably for the churches of St Nicholas and St Sauveur, the main façade of which he rebuilt (1810–12). Other works included the gateway (1819) of the Petit Béguinage on the Lange-Violettenstraat and a small number of houses. He was one of the founders of the Société Royale des Beaux-Arts et de Littérature de Gand and was appointed vice-president of the section concerned with architecture.

UNPUBLISHED SOURCES
Ghent U., MS. G 6058[1-3] [P. J. Goetghebuer: *Notes sur sculpteurs et architectes des Pays-Bas, recueillis pendant les années 1831–51*]

BIBLIOGRAPHY
Provincie Oost-Vlaanderen: Stad Gent, De Kuip van Gent, Bouwen door de eeuwen heen: Inventaris van het cultuurbezit in Vlaanderen. Architectuur (Liège, 1976)
Provincie Oost-Vlaanderen: Stad Gent, De 16de-eeuwse stadsuitbreiding, noordelijk deel [Province of East Flanders: the city of Ghent, the 16th-century expansion of the city, northern part] and *Provincie Oost-Vlaanderen: Stad Gent, De 16de-eeuwse stadsuitbreiding, zuidelijk en westelijk deel* [Province of East Flanders: the city of Ghent, the 16th-century expansion of the city, southern and western parts], Bouwen door de eeuwen heen: Inventaris van het cultuurbezit in Vlaanderen. Architectuur (Liège, 1976)

FRIEDA VAN TYGHEM

Debschitz, Wilhelm von (*b* Görlitz, 21 Feb 1871; *d* Lüneburg, 10 March 1948). German designer, painter, teacher and theorist. A self-taught artist, he made several study trips to Italy and the Tyrol. In painting he found inspiration in late German Romanticism, before turning to the English Arts and Crafts Movement. His designs were exhibited in 1899 at the exhibition of the Bayerische Kunstgewerbeverein (Munich, Glaspal.) and in 1901 at the first *Ausstellung für Kunst im Handwerk* in Munich. In 1902 he founded the Lehr- und Versuch-Atelier für Angewandte und Freie Kunst with the Swiss artist HERMANN OBRIST, developing a modern co-educational teaching system based on reformist pedagogy and popular psychology. In preliminary courses, classes and workshops, a broad practical training was offered primarily in arts and crafts. This precursor of the Bauhaus encouraged contact with dealers and collectors and was widely accoladed. When Obrist resigned from the school in 1904, Debschitz founded the Ateliers und Werkstätten für Angewandte Kunst and the Keramischen Werkstätten production centres attached to the school. In July 1914 he was made director of the Städtische Handwerker- und Kunstgewerbeschule in Hannover, a post he held until April 1921. He published essays on art theory in a number of periodicals, including *Dekorative Kunst*. In later years he lived at Bernau in the Black Forest, mainly producing textile designs.

WRITINGS
'Eine Methode des Kunstunterrichts', *Dek. Kst*, vii (March 1904), pp. 207–27

BIBLIOGRAPHY
Thieme-Becker
H. Eisenwerth [Schmoll]: *Kunstschule Debschitz München: Kunstschulreform, 1900–1933* (Berlin, 1977), pp. 66–82

A. ZIFFER

Debucourt, Philibert-Louis (*b* Paris, 13 Feb 1755; *d* Paris, 22 Sept 1832). French painter and printmaker. He was a protégé of Gabriel-Christophe Allegrain and was taught by Joseph-Marie Vien. His own preference was for genre painting in the Flemish style. In 1781 he was approved (*agréé*) as a member of the Académie Royale, Paris, on the basis of several works to be exhibited at that year's Salon; among these, the *Charitable Gentleman* (Paris, Gal. Cailleux) is a moralistic scene clearly inspired by Jean-Baptiste Greuze but using the technique of Isaack van Ostade. The pictures Debucourt exhibited at the Salons of 1783 and 1785 continued to draw their inspiration from Flemish art, then very popular in Paris, while remaining faithful to the realities of French peasant life. One of these works, *The King's Act of Charity and Humanity* (untraced; engraved in 1787 by Laurent Guyot), was accepted for exhibition in 1785 only after Debucourt had, by royal command, changed the title and made Louis XVI less easy to recognize.

Debucourt was principally known, however, as an engraver. In 1782, he reproduced in etching and dry point one of his own paintings of 1781, *The Judge or the Broken Pitcher* (Fenaille, nos 1 and 2). Shortly afterwards he took up colour printing; trained by his friend Guyot, by 1785 he was able to publish his first prints, the *Lovers Revealed* (F4) and its pendant, the *Lovers Pursued* (F5), both printed from four plates but in rather coarse colours. By 1786 he had perfected the technique in the *Bride's Minuet* (F8), engraved on five plates and forming a pendant to the *Village Wedding*, engraved by Charles-Melchior Descourtis after Nicolas-Antoine Taunay.

The following year Debucourt published one of his most famous prints, *Walk in the Gallery of the Palais-Royal* (F11), inspired by Thomas Rowlandson's *Vauxhall Gardens*. Here Debucourt caricatured in a comic vein the crowd in one of the busiest places in Paris. He returned to the same subject in 1792 in his engraving and aquatint *Public Promenade* (F33; for illustration *see* GOUACHE MANNER). These two large colour prints were apparently his greatest successes.

From 1785 to 1800 Debucourt created 64 engraved works, all after his own paintings in oil, gouache and watercolour: they include several portraits, such as those of *Louis XVI* (1789; F19) and *Marie-Joseph, Marquis de La Fayette* (1790; F23), as well as several small patriotic scenes, such as *Almanach National* (1791; F26). Most numerous were genre scenes; some, such as the *Happy Family* (1796; F61), are in a tender vein, but most are on themes of gallantry, such as the *Rose in Danger* (1791; F27). He experimented widely with colour-printing techniques, including intaglio engraving, mezzotint, soft-ground etching and aquatint. For the most part the colour was printed using several plates, but in a few cases a single plate was coloured à la poupée. He later took up crayon manner and lithography. This many-sided production, the quality of which was uneven, became even more intensive after 1800; by the end of his life Debucourt had engraved

494 plates, chiefly reproductions of other artists' work. He made prints after the paintings of Carle Vernet, Louis-Léopold Boilly, Jean-Baptiste Isabey, Nicolas-Toussaint Charles and Martin Drolling. When engraving his own works, he exploited in particular his caricature style, as in *The Visits* (1800; F65) and its pendant, *The Orange, or a Modern Judgement of Paris* (F66). At about the same time Debucourt began to paint again, exhibiting his works, chiefly peasant scenes, at the Salons of 1810, 1814, 1817 and 1824. He died poor, however, as the dependant of his nephew and pupil Jean-Pierre-Marie Jazet, who left interesting accounts of the artist.

BIBLIOGRAPHY
F. Fayot: 'Jazet et Debucourt', *L'Artiste*, n. s. 1, viii (1841), pp. 138–9
E. and J. de Goncourt: 'Debucourt', *L'Art du XVIIIème siècle* (Paris, 1875, rev. 1914), iii, pp. 161–210
M. Fenaille: *L'Oeuvre gravé de P.-L. Debucourt (1755–1832)* (Paris, 1899) [F] [cat. rais.]
Debucourt (exh. cat., Paris, Mus. A. Déc., 1920)
M. Roux: *Inventaire du fonds français: Dix-huitième siècle*, Paris, Bib. N., Cab. Est. cat., vi (Paris, 1949), pp. 162–91
J. Adhémar: *Inventaire du fonds français: Dix-neuvième siècle*, Paris, Bib. N., Cab. Est. cat., vi (Paris, 1953), pp. 66–79

CHRISTIAN MICHEL

Decadence and decline. The word decadence has been used in the Western world to mark an evident decline in society, culture and art from some perceived 'higher' or better state of being or form. The German historian Oswald Spengler (1880–1936) explained decadence phenomenologically as the final stage of a historical cycle, when the pursuit of material comfort exhausts the creative forces of society; Freud found a prime source of human suffering in 'the disposition to decay of our bodies', and others have put forward the concept of decadence to oppose the idea of continuous progress in civilization. The term also indicates the wilful rejection of contemporary social and artistic norms by rebellious individuals or groups seeking to bring attention to themselves or to their causes. Such rejection can be retrogressive; the Arts and Crafts Movement sought to reverse the apparent decline in the arts caused by the Industrial Revolution by going back to the 'purer' work of the individual artisan. Decadence can, however, have a positive connotation, pointing to the breakup of an old society or style out of which something new emerges, or to the rejection of a society in order to regenerate it with fresh spiritual values and creative vigour. In its typical application to society, literature and the fine arts, decadence is usually pejorative, implying a negative moral judgement. Such usage marks the hostile response to change, to uncertainty, to the loss of ideals and ultimately to death. This article examines three notable and distinct patterns in art culture that exemplify this emotional response to decay.

1. Fleshly decadence: medieval and early Renaissance. 2. Historical decadence: the image of Rome. 3. Cultural decadence in the 19th century.

1. FLESHLY DECADENCE: MEDIEVAL AND EARLY RENAISSANCE. Medieval Christian preoccupation with the Fall of Man, buttressed by Aristotelian theories about the cycle of generation and corruption in the natural world, was heightened by the experience of the Black Death. Signs of the body's physical decay preoccupied the secular and sacred imagery of sculpture and painting in the late 14th century and the 15th and led to representations of the decayed figures of the worldly great on their tombs (*see* TOMB, §VI, 2; see also Cohen, 1973) and to the morbid realism of the ANDACHTSBILD image of devotion. Man humbled himself before death, aware that even great power and wealth could not shield him from the corruption of the flesh; the passage from life to death to decay was swift, brutal and inevitable.

Imagery pursuing this theme in early Renaissance German art dwelt less on the overt signs of physical degeneration than on the interactive companionship of life and death in the lifetime of the individual. Dürer, Altdorfer, Hans Baldung, Hans Holbein the younger, Lucas Cranach and others represented the transitoriness of the human condition more indirectly, through symbols and portents and the figure of Death. For the young, the beautiful, the brave, the recently married, and even for Erasmus, that most secure of Catholic humanists, these artists suggested the imminent end of life's joys and wholeness. A passage from Job (14:1–2), comparing human life to a flower, inspired much of the VANITAS imagery in Netherlandish painting of the late 16th century and the 17th. Still-lifes with wilted flowers and over-ripe fruits, genre scenes replete with indications of decay and damage, and portraits with skulls hidden among the finery reveal an ambivalent attitude about material things and the sufficiency of their possession. The bloom is soon off the flower, the peach, the cheek, but the desire for them remains fixed in these paintings.

2. HISTORICAL DECADENCE: THE IMAGE OF ROME. 15th-century Italian Renaissance painting, representing the advent of the Magi or the martyrdom of saints, especially St Sebastian, often features elements of ancient, ruined Roman architecture. In this context Roman ruins suggested both the decay of the pagan empire and, as St Augustine had earlier and Hegel would later insist, the environment necessary for the generation of a new spiritual order, Christianity, in the West. Such a view of Rome's fall was prospective, but no less significant was the retrospective view of Rome's passage from greatness to decline developed by Robert de Montesquieu and Edward Gibbon in the 18th century. They both saw a change in the moral climate of Roman society, the destructive effects of which became evident in a late phase of its history.

This location of decline in the late or autumnal phase of the Roman Empire confirmed the tripartite biological and temporal metaphor of beginning, middle and end. Thus, lateness in style or period, however determined, could be considered decadent, so late Roman art was deemed 'decadent' by definition, culminating in Bernard Berenson's diatribe (1954) on the Arch of Constantine as a monumental degeneration of idealized, Classical forms. For Alois Riegl, however, late Roman art had begun to realize its latent potential, developing new forms that led eventually to the formation of the early medieval art of the West. Therefore, he considered late Roman art more positively as the early creative stage of a new style, a position now generally supported. Riegl developed his views in *fin-de-siècle*, 'decadent' Vienna, where he found his justification in a close analysis of late Roman crafts, ignoble arts set firmly against an élitist conception of stylistic change and against the traditional devaluation of the 'minor arts'. Even the idea of 'lateness' itself is now open to challenge and with it the hierarchical conception of periodicity (*see* PERIODIZATION), except among those archaeologists who rely on pottery sequences in their excavations.

3. CULTURAL DECADENCE IN THE 19TH CENTURY. Decadence had its own allure as a challenge to conventional bourgeois attitudes in 19th-century France. For Désiré Nisard (1806–88) and CHARLES BAUDELAIRE, decadent late Latin literature was estimable because it was so elegant, so artificial, so expressive of dissatisfaction with contemporary life and so personal. A decadent aesthetic of rejection, retreat and subjectivity took form in French literature and art, especially after the period of unrest in the 1870s, and manifested itself in works that were sensational in content, composition and reception and generally pessimistic in tone.

Thomas Couture's *Romans of the Decadence* (1847; Paris, Mus. d'Orsay) had previously offered to a bedazzled public a bravura gesture on the theme of Roman decadence, a gloss on Roman sexual depravity and *vanitas*, a sublimated commentary on contemporary life and a sensation. Despite its blatant imagery this painting lacked the strong anti-establishment ethos characteristic of the later *décadence*, which emphasized rebellious themes and human types on the margins of society and was fully represented by Joris-Karl Huysmans's novel *A Rebours* (1884).

The dandy, or *flâneur*, ultimately derived from the English dandy Beau Brummell, was the prominent figure in the urban environment of decadence and in the paintings of Manet and Constantin Guys. In and out of society the dandy wore black as a mark of separation, as a sign of his elegance, but it soon became a more general symbol of apartness. Baudelaire always wore black, and black entered the palette of French painters, especially Manet and Degas, for its own sake and in opposition to current academic painting.

Elegance, a self-conscious feature of decadence, hovered on the edge of the precious, itself a route to a fantastic world in which private escape, however disturbing, was possible. The *éminence grise* of this movement was Edgar Allan Poe, especially as transmitted by Baudelaire and STÉPHANE MALLARMÉ. Fantasy was exploited by Flaubert in *Salammbô* (1862), and its sensational, titillating and troubling forms enriched the paintings of Gustave Moreau in the 1870s and 1880s and the work of Odilon Redon. Indeed, in *A Rebours* Huysmans found in Moreau's paintings the complete realization of the decadent, modern sensibility, while both artists shared the 'unhealthy dreams' of their febrile imaginations. In the later 19th century escapist fantasies often focused on the world of the circus, its magicians, clowns, acrobats and jugglers being pregnant themes in the art of Seurat, Signac and later Picasso.

Moreau and Redon were more than fantasts. Their images were disquieting and often morbid, creating an atmosphere of unease reminiscent of Baudelaire's *Les Fleurs du Mal* (1857). The contemporary French psychologist Pierre Bourget characterized this disquiet as a peculiarly creative sensibility of great value, perhaps first used

in this fashion by the Danish philosopher Søren Kierkegaard (1813–55). The conversion of mental and emotional disturbance into art enriched the work of writers as diverse as Flaubert and Oscar Wilde and reached fruition in the central erotic theme of decadence, the *femme fatale*. Salomé was her most frightening embodiment for Moreau and other artists of the time, although the unfaithful wife and the courtesan were her partners. Mallarmé's poem *Hérodiade* (begun 1864) and Manet's painting *Olympia* (1863; Paris, Mus. d'Orsay) suggest the disturbing nature of these images of sexuality, whose force would be perverted by Felicien Rops in Belgium, Aubrey Beardsley in England and Gustav Klimt in Austria. The demimonde of prostitutes, courtesans and cabaret entertainers thus entered the repertory of Impressionism and Post-Impressionism, reaching a terrifying climax in Picasso's *Demoiselles d'Avignon* (1907; New York, MOMA), while a more hedonistic view of women, or of their bodies, shaped the work of Degas, Matisse and Derain.

Spreading through Europe, the wilful, self-conscious aestheticism of decadence in the last third of the 19th century helped advance the claim of *l'art pour l'art*, thereby energizing the avant-garde and supporting its own sense of significant creativity. This was manifest particularly in various movements of the time, some of which also affected the USA (*see* AESTHETIC MOVEMENT, ART FOR ART'S SAKE, ARTS AND CRAFTS MOVEMENT and SYMBOLISM). Mallarmé's eclogue *L'Après-midi d'un faune* (1876) participated equally in the art of decadence, in Impressionism and in the stirrings of the Symbolist movement, but above all it revealed the subjective intensity of the artist and the liberation of his language from sterile convention. In the 1880s Paul Verlaine began to develop a new, less affected language of poetry, just as his painter contemporaries, especially Cézanne, were similarly ridding themselves of old pictorial conventions. Walter Pater (*Marius, the Epicurean*, 1885) and Arthur Symons (1865–1945) were creating a disruptive counter-poetics that would soon liberate English prose and poetry, if not painting; Valery Bryusov would attempt a similar poetics of liberation in early 20th-century Russia, Gabriele D'Annunzio in Italy, and the writers Ibsen and Strindberg and the painter Edvard Munch in Scandinavia. Decadence may be chiefly historically important as a literary movement, but it helped open the doors to modernism in all the arts.

Fin-de-siècle mentality of the late 19th century formed the most pessimistic phase of decadence. Following the Franco-Prussian War, the rise of European militarism and nationalism, increasing social and labour unrest and new studies of criminality and neuroses, a strongly pessimistic view of life came to the fore, championed by FRIEDRICH NIETZSCHE. He had come to see nihilism as the problem of the age, a consequence of decadence and the collapse of traditional values, but for him decadence or corruption gave greater energy to the individual and stimulated the demand for freedom from imposed values.

Max Nordau (1849–1923) in *Entartung* (1893) offered Germans an aggressive aestheticism as a means of artistic liberation, an appeal answered by Klimt in Vienna, and the writings of Frank Wedekind (1864–1918), Heinrich Mann (1871–1950), Hugo von Hofmannsthal (1874–1929), Rainer Maria Rilke and Thomas Mann (1875–1955) in the 1890s and 1900s conveyed the sense of something 'old' coming to an end. The Austrian artist Alfred Kubin pictured the nightmare of this end phase of civilization in his writing and prints, anticipating the horrors of World War I and its aftermath so graphically depicted by George Grosz, Otto Dix and the German Expressionists. Yet these artists had responded to this disruptive end phase by creating great works of art such as Mann's *Magic Mountain* (1924) and Max Beckmann's great triptychs. These works, and the artists who created them, were rejected by the Nazis as '*dekadent*', and with them the avant-garde was exiled from Germany (*see* ENTARTETE KUNST).

BIBLIOGRAPHY

R. Montesquieu: *Considérations sur les causes de la grandeur des Romains et de leur décadence* (Amsterdam, 1734)
E. Gibbon: *The History of the Decline and Fall of the Roman Empire*, 6 vols (London, 1776–88)
D. Nisard: *Etudes de moeurs et de critique sur les poètes latins de la décadence* (Paris, 1834)
P. Bourget: *La Vie inquiète* (Paris, 1875)
J.-K. Huysmans: *A rebours* (Paris, 1884); Eng. trans. intro. H. Ellis (New York, 1922)
A. Baju: *L'Ecole décadente* (Paris, 1887)
A. Riegl: *Die spätrömische Kunstindustrie* (Vienna, 1901)
O. Spengler: *The Decline of the West*, 2 vols (London, 1926–8)
S. Freud: *Civilization and its Discontents* (New York, 1930)
H. Rudolph: 'Vanitas: Die Bedeutung mittelalterlicher und humanistischer Bildinhalte in der niederländischen Malerei des 17. Jahrhunderts', *Festschrift Wilhelm Pinder zum sechzigsten Geburtstage* (Leipzig, 1938), pp. 405–33
B. Berenson: *The Arch of Constantine or the Decline of Form* (London, 1954)
H. Lehmann-Haupt: *Art under a Dictatorship* (Oxford, 1954)
S. Sandström: *L'Oeuvre imaginaire d'Odilon Redon* (Lund, 1955)
Odilon Redon, Gustave Moreau, Rodolphe Bresdin (exh. cat. by J. Rewald, D. Ashton and H. Joachim, New York, MOMA; Chicago, IL, A. Inst.; 1961–2)
H. P. L'Orange: *Art Forms and Civic Life in the Late Roman Empire* (Princeton, 1965)
F. Bächtiger: *Vanitas–Schicksalsdeutung in der deutschen Renaissance-graphik* (diss., U. Munich, 1969)
K. Cohen: *Metamorphosis of a Death Symbol: The Transi Tomb in the Late Middle Ages and the Renaissance* (Berkeley, 1973)
H.-I. Marrou: *Décadence romaine ou antiquité tardive?* (Paris, 1973)
M. Warnke, ed.: *Bildersturm: Die Zerstörung des Kunstwerks* (Munich, 1973)
P.-L. Mathieu: *Gustave Moreau* (Boston, MA, 1976)
J. Pierrot: *L'Imaginaire décadent (1880–1900)* (Paris, 1977)
R. Gilman: *Decadence: The Strange Life of an Epithet* (New York, 1979)
A. Boime: *Thomas Couture and the Eclectic Vision* (New Haven, 1980), pp. 131–88
B. Hinz: *Art in the Third Reich* (New York, 1980)
C. E. Schorske: *Fin-de-siècle Vienna: Politics and Culture* (New York, 1980)
P. Ariès: *Images of Man and Death* (Cambridge, MA, 1985)
J. D. Grossman: *Valery Bryusov and the Riddle of Russian Decadence* (Berkeley, 1985)
L. Dowling: *Language and Decadence in the Victorian Fin de Siècle* (Princeton, 1986)
D. Kuspit: 'Diagnostic Malpractice: The Nazis on Modern Art', *Artforum* (Nov 1986), pp. 90–98
W. Rasch: *Die literarische Décadence um 1900* (Munich, 1986)
D. Scott: *Pictorialist Poetics: Poetry and the Visual Arts in 19th Century France* (Cambridge, 1988)

RICHARD BRILLIANT

Decalcomania (i). Decoration made by using cut up sheets of paper printed with lithographic designs stuck down and varnished on to a surface (*see also* DÉCOLLAGE).

Decalcomania (ii). Technique for generating images used, for example, by the Surrealist artist Oscar Domínguez: paint is applied to a piece of paper that is then either folded, creating a mirrored pattern, or pressed against another sheet (for illustration *see* DOMÍNGUEZ, OSCAR). The resulting image can then be elaborated, as in a blot drawing. It is a popular technique with young school children (*see also* AUTOMATISM).

☐

De Cambray-Digny, Luigi (*b* Florence, 14 Feb 1778; *d* Florence, 22 Feb 1843). Italian architect, landscape designer and teacher. He studied architecture at the Accademia di Belle Arti in Florence under Gasparo Maria Paoletti, the leader of the Tuscan Neo-classical school, and won prizes for his projects in 1797; in 1801 he became a professor of architecture there and presented a project for a Pantheon of famous men to the Accademia. In 1803 he began to work for the Tuscan state, making important contacts in the Napoleonic period at a time when he is known to have become a freemason. His first important commission, received from the Accademia di Belle Arti, was the remodelling of the famous Cappella di S Luca (1810–13) in SS Annunziata, Florence, as part of a project to transform the convent into the new seat of the French bishop. Following the restoration in 1814 of the House of Lorraine to the Grand Duchy of Tuscany, he played a prime role in the reconstruction of the Scrittoio delle Reali Fabbriche, first as Secretary, then Director (1820–35). This important department controlled all public building within the Grand Duchy. De Cambray-Digny was a prolific architect; he undertook many works of restoration and adaptation of public and private buildings in Florence and Prato as well as projects for the building of the port, the dockyard and the area to the north of the Via Grande (1817) in Livorno; he also built the Filigare Customs House (1818) at the Passo Appeninico della Raticosa, the churches of S Maria Assunta (1822–7; destr.), Montecatini, and SS Pietro e Paolo (1829–35), Livorno, and a number of important theatres, including the Teatro Metastasio (1827–30) in Prato. His early Neo-classical style is particularly evident in the hunting lodge of Montili (1818), which stands above the park of the former Villa Medici in Pratolino, and the Loggia Reale (1819–27), Via del Prato, Florence. Garden design was an important aspect of his career; three of his best-known gardens, for the Orti Oricellari (1813), the Marchese Pietro Torrigiani (1813–14), both in Florence, and the Puccini di Scornio (1821–8) at Pistoia, were transformed into romantic parks, with architectural additions following the philosophical and symbolic tendency, particularly masonic, in Tuscan architecture that was invented and championed by Giuseppe Manetti (1762–1817). Many drawings for unexecuted official projects survive in Florentine archives; they combine a grandiose urban vision typical of the Napoleonic years with Vitruvian Classical motifs.

BIBLIOGRAPHY

DBI; Thieme–Becker
G. Gargiolli: 'Elogio del Conte Luigi De Cambray-Digny', *Atti Imp. & Reale Accad. Georgofili*, xxi (1843), pp. 250–56
P. Contrucci: *Monumenti del Giardino Puccini* (Pistoia, 1845)
L. Ginori Lisci: *I palazzi di Firenze* (Florence, 1972), pp. 93, 305, 791

C. Cresti and L. Zangheri: *Architetti e ingegneri nella Toscana dell'ottocento* (Florence, 1978), pp. 74–5

L. Zangheri: *Pratolino: Il giardino delle meraviglie* (Florence, 1979), pp. 69ff and 138

M. Dezzi Bardeschi: 'Le macchine desideranti', *Atti: Il giardino romantico: Firenze, 1984*, pp. 41–5

MARIO BENCIVENNI

De Camp, Joseph Rodefer (*b* Cincinnati, OH, 5 Nov 1858; *d* Boca Grande, FL, 11 Feb 1923). American painter. He first studied in Cincinnati, at the McMicken School of Design, and in 1875 travelled to Munich, where he attended the Kunstakademie with Frank Duveneck, whom he later accompanied on a trip to Italy. De Camp returned to America in 1883 and settled in Boston, where he embarked on a highly successful career. He exhibited regularly with many arts organizations in Boston and New York and held several influential teaching posts, including instructor of antique drawing at the Boston Museum School. In 1897, with John H. Twachtman and others, he became a founder-member of the group of American Impressionists known as the Ten American Painters.

Like his Boston colleagues Edmund Tarbell and Frank Weston Benson, De Camp is best known for his portraits of elegant, fashionable women, in which he paid great attention to bodily structure and the precise delineation of facial contours. He was less vulnerable than some of his contemporaries to criticisms of studied prettiness and excessive gentility; he often eschewed elaborate interiors and decorative furnishings in favour of flat, dark backdrops, as in the introspective portrait of his daughter *Sally* (1908; Worcester, MA, A. Mus.). When he did paint accompanying domestic objects, their sparseness and deliberate placement within the composition generally contribute to a cooler tone. De Camp's portraits of men are less well known and include a full-length study of *Theodore Roosevelt*, commissioned by the President's former classmates at Harvard (1908; Cambridge, MA, Harvard U., Portrait Col.). His landscapes, painted with a freer hand than his figural work, exhibit the traditional Impressionist concerns with reflected light and the dissolution of form, as seen in the *Little Hotel* (1903; Philadelphia, PA Acad. F.A.).

BIBLIOGRAPHY

W. H. Downes: 'Joseph De Camp and his Work', *A. & Prog.*, i (1913), pp. 918–25

W. H. Gerdts: *American Impressionism* (Seattle, 1980)

The Bostonians: Painters of an Elegant Era, 1870–1930 (exh. cat. by T. J. Fairbrother, Boston, MA, Mus. F.A., 1986)

ROSS C. ANDERSON

Decamps, Alexandre-Gabriel (*b* Paris, 3 May 1803; *d* Fontainebleau, 23 Aug 1860). French painter, draughtsman and printmaker. With his brother Maurice-Alexandre (1804–52), the art critic and essayist, he spent some years of his youth at Orsay, in Picardy, 'in order to learn to rise early and know the hard life of the fields'. The artwork of the peasants stimulated an interest in drawing. He entered the atelier of Etienne Bouhot (1780–1862) in 1816. Towards the end of 1818 he left Bouhot to study under Alexandre-Denis Abel de Pujol, quitting his studio in 1819–20 in order to embark upon a career as an independent professional artist. He had been an inattentive student, who thought that 'the formula of instruction of the

academic doctrine reduced the least examination almost to the proportions of silliness'. Memories of Orsay remained his point of departure throughout his working life, and in this sense he was a self-trained artist. Nevertheless, he admired, and learnt from, the art of such diverse artists as Raphael, Titian, Giovanni da Bologna, Poussin, Rembrandt, Géricault and Léopold Robert.

Decamps made his début at the Salon of 1827/8 with *Hunting in a Swamp* (untraced) and *The Janissary* (London, Wallace), simple compositions where recession is effected by the overlapping of edges, with fresh local colour and a finesse of touch. In 1828 he travelled throughout Asia Minor and eastern North Africa, becoming the first major European artist to travel extensively in the Near East. On his return he began a vogue for Oriental themes with such works as *Turkish Patrol* (*c*. 1830–31; London, Wallace) and *Route of Smyrna* (1833; Chantilly, Mus. Condé). At the same time he painted his memories of Orsay in *Chasse au miroir* (1830; Williamstown, MA, Clark A. Inst.), developed a long-lasting interest in rendering animals, evinced in the *Monkey Painter* (*c*. 1833; Paris, Louvre; see fig.), and painted numerous genre scenes, such as *The Mendicants* (*c*. 1833; Algiers, Mus. N. B.-A.). The size of these works ranges from 1.15×1.79 m to 0.35×0.28 m.

Decamps sent his most famous work, *Defeat of the Cimbrians* (1833; Paris, Louvre), to the Salon of 1834; it is a large painting, consistent in style with other works but demonstrating a fully developed understanding of atmospheric perspective. It is painted in his characteristic *cuisine*, a golden, brittle, dry-brushed texture. He spent the rest of his career trying to reconcile his two strengths: a desire to create high-minded art and an interest in rendering his immediate surroundings.

During the late 1830s, after travelling to Italy in 1835, Decamps completed numerous canvases with biblical themes, such as *Joseph Sold by his Brothers* (1838; London, Wallace). Characteristic of such works is an emphasis on horizontal recession into space, with the principal action taking place in a valley, and a fusion of classical elements with naturalistic description. The result was a completely new approach to religious subjects. Through such devices as small architectural structures in the background and barren landscapes, Decamps created a believable image of the Orient, both historically and geographically, whereas previous artists had unconvincingly located scenes in Egypt and other Near Eastern countries merely by inserting pyramids or tropical growths. His work of the 1840s continued in the same stylistic vein, although he placed a greater emphasis on the figures and strong contour lines. The *History of Samson* series (Salon 1845; Paris, priv. col.) is characteristic of the period; these nine drawings also show that Decamps's drawing style paralleled that of his paintings and of his printmaking. His oeuvre includes over 2000 paintings, drawings and prints, though he was not highly active during the last decade of his life. However, his style took on a new interest in light, while colour began to play a minor role. *Job and his Friends* (1853; Minneapolis, MN, Inst. A.) and the *Truffle Searcher* (*c*. 1858; Amsterdam, Stedel. Mus.) are characteristic works of this period.

Decamps received most of the major awards and recognitions bestowed on contemporary artists and enjoyed economic success: Eugène Leroux (1807–63) made

Alexandre-Gabriel Decamps: *Monkey Painter*, oil on canvas, 320×405 mm, *c.* 1833 (Paris, Musée du Louvre)

lithographs after many of his works, and Decamps's patrons included such important 19th-century collectors as Marquis Maison (1771–1840), the 4th Marquess of Hertford, Henry, Lord Seymour (1805–59), the Barons Rothschild and the Duc d'Orléans. The *Job* was commissioned by the French government in 1849. Perhaps the crowning point of his career was the Paris Exposition Universelle of 1855, where he was given a retrospective exhibition, as were Ingres and Delacroix: all three were awarded the Grand Medal of Honour. Decamps was an avid sportsman and champion of artists' rights. The esteem in which he was held is illustrated by Albert-Ernest Carrier-Belleuse's *Monument to Decamps*, erected in 1862 in the Place Decamps, Fontainebleau.

BIBLIOGRAPHY

Dr Véron: *Mémoires d'un bourgeois de Paris* (Paris, 1854)
P. Mantz: 'Decamps', *Gaz. B.-A.*, 1st ser., xii (1862), pp. 97–128
A. Moreau: *Decamps et son oeuvre* (Paris, 1869)
G. Hédiard: *Les Maîtres de la lithographie: Decamps* (Le Mans, 1893)
D. F. Mosby: 'The Mature Years of Alexandre-Gabriel Decamps', *Minneapolis Inst. A. Bull.*, lxiii (1976–7), pp. 97–109
——: *Alexandre-Gabriel Decamps, 1803–1860*, Outstanding Diss. F.A., 2 vols (New York, 1977)
——: 'Decamps dessinateur', *Rev. Louvre*, i (1980), pp. 148–52
——: 'Decamps' *History of Samson* Series in Context', *Art the Ape of Nature: Studies in Honor of H. W. Janson* (New York, 1981), pp. 569–84

DEWEY F. MOSBY

Dečani Monastery. Monastic church dedicated to Christ Pantokrator in the Serbian Republic of Yugoslavia, situated 15 km south of Peć. It was founded by King Stephen Uroš III Dečanski (*reg* 1321–31) and his son, Stephen Uroš IV Dušan (*reg* as king 1331–46; emperor 1346–55). A sturdy wall surrounds the complex, which is entered by a fortified gate. Few of the conventual buildings remain. Archbishop Danilo II (1324–37) participated in the founding of the main church, which was built between 1327 and 1335 by Fra Vita, a Franciscan from Kotor (*see* SERBIA, fig. 3). It is a five-aisled basilica modelled on Romanesque architecture with bands of grey, white and pink marble, a tripartite gabled façade and richly carved portals, windows, ribbed vaults and columns. These features are combined with a dome rising from a square base supported by four piers, three eastern semicircular apses and a narthex divided into three bays. The two lateral bays for the singers place the church within the so-called Raskian school of architecture.

The interior is entirely covered in frescoes, which were completed between 1335 and 1348.

Among the church's elegant carvings, again in Romanesque style, is a relief showing *Christ Enthroned between Two Angels* in the tympanum of the west central portal. Above it is a mullioned window with carved surrounds depicting *St George Rescuing the Princess*. Dragons, griffins, centaurs and lions appear around the window of the eastern central apse and on the archivolts of doors as reminders of the ever-present threat of evil and sin. The building's corbels are adorned with anthropomorphic and zoomorphic heads, as well as floral motifs symbolizing the created world. The tympanum of the south door has a relief of the *Baptism of Christ* and an inscription by the architect in Cyrillic letters; a cross occupies the tympanum of the north portal. The marble parapet slabs that separate the central aisle from the side aisles and the sarcophagi, which include that of King Dečanski, are carved with familiar Byzantine motifs.

The narthex contains wall paintings depicting an ecclesiastical calendar, the *Ecumenical Councils*, the *Legends of St George*, portraits of *Emperor Stephen Uroš IV Dušan*, his wife *Jelena* and their son *Uroš*, and the *Nemanjić Family Tree* with a portrait of every member of the dynasty. The placing of the baptismal font in front of the latter stresses the connection between kingship and baptism. Above the narthex's central portal leading into the nave is a bust of *Christ Pantokrator*; below him to the left and right are portraits of the two founders and beside them are figures of David and Solomon as saintly models of these Serbian kings. In the nave the lowest level is occupied by figures of saints and portraits of some members of the Nemanjić royal family, while above are cycles representing the *Life of Christ*, the *Acts of the Apostles* and the *Twelve Great Feasts*. Cycles illustrating *St John the Baptist Preaching*, the *Book of Daniel*, the *Last Judgement* and the *Dormition of the Virgin* cover the walls of the western bays. Here also is represented the *Tree of Jesse*, which parallels the *Nemanjić Family Tree* on the other side of the wall in the narthex. The *Akathistos of the Virgin* starts in the south bay of the nave and continues in the south aisle, while the *Genesis* covers the upper parts of walls and vaults in the north aisle. The south and north aisles are decorated also with the *Life of St Nicholas* and the *Life of St Demetrius* respectively. Cycles illustrating the *Liturgy* are in the sanctuary. The late Palaiologan style of the paintings in the nave is characterized by the three-dimensional and classicizing proportions of the figures, who move within shallow spaces and whose emotions are conveyed by gesture rather than facial expression. In the calendar, however, the despair of the martyrs can be seen in their distorted faces.

The iconostasis preserves its original mid-14th-century icons painted in a classicizing style; several other icons are on display in the mid-14th-century refectory, together with collections of 15th- to 16th-century liturgical objects and vestments and 150 illuminated manuscripts dating from the 13th to the 19th century.

BIBLIOGRAPHY

V. R. Petković and Dj. Bošković: *Manastir Dečani* [Dečani Monastery], 2 vols (Belgrade, 1941) [with Fr. summary of vol. 1 and Ger. summary of vol. 2]

A. Grabar: 'Les Images de la Vierge de Tendresse: Type iconographique et thème: A propos de deux icônes à Dečani, *Zograf*, vi (1975), pp. 25–30

M. Šakota: *Dečanska riznica* [The treasury of Dečani] (Belgrade, 1984) [with Fr. summary]

Dečani i vizantijska umetnost sredine XIV veka: Medjunarodni naučni skup povodom 650 godina manastira Dečani: Belgrade and Dečani, 1985 [Dečani and Byzantine art of the 14th century: papers celebrating the 650th anniversary of the monastery]

GORDANA BABIĆ

De Carlo, Giancarlo (*b* Genoa, 12 Dec 1919). Italian architect and urban planner. He graduated in engineering at the Polytechnic in Milan in 1942, took an active part in the wartime resistance movement and subsequently studied at the Istituto Universitario di Architettura in Venice (Dip.Arch., 1949), where, on the invitation of Giuseppe Samonà, he became Professor of Urban Design in 1955. He took part in the debate on Rationalism led by the Movimento di Studi per l'Architettura and collaborated with Piero Bottoni and others on designs for the experimental area Quartiere T.8 (QT8) at the VIII Triennale in Milan (1946–7). He set up his practice in Milan in 1950. These experiences helped form his idea of architecture as part of a complex system of interrelationships that develop for social reasons, and through politico-economic means, and expand to encompass both urban and country planning.

Dissatisfied with a formalist vocabulary derived in a reductive way from the theories of the Modern Movement, De Carlo used the Spontaneous Architecture display at the IX Triennale (1950) to experiment with new combinations, which he then implemented in the INA-Casa buildings at Baveno, Novara, and at Stresa (both 1951) and in the block of flats and shops in the Spine Bianche district of Matera (1945–57). These schemes were presented at the last meeting of CIAM at Otterlo (1959), and when the work of the Italian members was criticized for 'deviationism', he strongly defended the anti-formal qualities of his own work. He then distanced himself politically from the editorial line of *Casabella* and became an adherent of the new cultural directions proposed by Team X. Also at this time he was able to focus an early interest in planning by a period of intense activity at the Istituto Lombardo di Scienze Economiche e Sociali and the Istituto Nazionale di Urbanistica rethinking planning methods. He had collaborated with Franco Albini on a master plan for Reggio Emilio as early as 1947. From the Triennale of 1954, where the planning exhibition was intended to involve the public, De Carlo's populist ideology led him to a major interest in the process of planning and design with continuous client- and user-participation, and this became a vital factor in all his projects.

De Carlo found an ideal centre for developing his planning ideas in Urbino, beginning with the staff quarters for the Free University in 1955. This extended his relationship with the city, for which he drew up a master plan (1958–64), and with the university over several decades. In a process of continuous development he designed the University Colleges (1962–66, 1973–81) and the Faculties of Jurisprudence and Education (1968–76): from the modified New Brutalism of the residential accommodation for the colleges, to the sympathetic restoration and integration of Jurisprudence with existing 15th-century convent buildings, and the great semicircular sweep of the roof-light of the Education lecture halls (see fig.), the sensitive compositions protect and bind together the historic fabric of the site. Other work in Urbino included the Istituto Statale d'Arte (1970–82) and the reconstruction of the Teatro Sanzio (1970–79).

The full fruition of De Carlo's participatory planning methods is best seen in the steelworkers' village of Matteoti at Terni (1969–74), where, despite a somewhat unyielding Brutalist aesthetic, the variety of provisions, gardens and interlinking passageways suggests success for the method even though operational and political conflicts prevented its completion. The approach was used successfully in other applications: the unexecuted University of Dublin project (1964), development plans for the University of Pavia (1970–75), the centre of Rimini (1968–72), the San Miniato district of Siena (1977–79) and, for solutions to the new problems of the post-industrial period, in proposals for the Breda district of Pistoia (1983–5), for a new Pirelli-Biccoca development in Milan (1986), and in the plan for the Mazzorbo district of Venice (from 1979), in which his earlier interest in a language of urban morphology began to re-emerge. His work was supported by research and teaching and by his writings.

Giancarlo De Carlo: Faculty of Education, University of Urbino, 1968–74

WRITINGS

Questioni di architettura e urbanistica (Urbino, 1964/R 1965)
Urbino (Padua, 1970)
An Architecture of Participation (Melbourne, 1972); It. trans. in *L'architettura degli anni '70* (Milan, 1973)
'Corpo, memoria, e fiasco', *Spazio & Soc.*, 4 (1978), pp. 3–16

BIBLIOGRAPHY

C. Columbo: *Giancarlo De Carlo* (Milan, 1964)
Forum, xxiii/1 (1972) [issue on De Carlo]
F. Brunetti and F. Gesi: *Giancarlo De Carlo* (Florence, 1981)

MERCEDES DAGUERRE

De Carolis, Adolfo (*b* Montefiore Dell'Aso, nr Ascoli Piceno, 6 Jan 1874; *d* Rome, 7 Feb 1928). Italian painter, illustrator and wood-engraver. He studied at the Accademia di Belle Arti in Bologna (1888–92) and at the Scuola di Decorazione Pittorica at the Museo Artistica Industriale in Rome (1892–5). De Carolis began painting *en plein-air* in the Roman Campagna under the influence of Nino Costa's group, *In Arte Libertas*, with whom he exhibited in 1897. At the Venice Biennale of 1899 he exhibited allegorical paintings inspired by the Pre-Raphaelites. De Carolis became a distinguished wood-engraver and illustrator, working with such writers as Giovanni Pascoli and Gabriele D'Annunzio (for whom he also created stage designs). He himself wrote essays on art for various periodicals, including *Hermes* and *Rinascimento*. His greatest achievements, however, were in decorative painting. While creating mythological frescoes at the Salone del Consiglio Provinciale at Ascoli Piceno (1907–9), De Carolis, together with the architect Alfredo Brizzi, won the competition (1908) for the decoration of the Salone del Palazzo del Podestà di Bologna. In 1911 he began a Renaissance-inspired scheme depicting aspects of the history of civilization, with a particular emphasis on Bologna's past; the project was completed by assistants after his death. The wall paintings are *in situ*, but for safety reasons the ceiling paintings were detached in 1972–3, and some were ruined in the process. During the rest of his career De Carolis executed numerous frescoes and wood-engravings.

WRITINGS

'L'arte decorativa moderna', *Hermes* (1904)

BIBLIOGRAPHY

Il Liberty a Bologna e nell'Emilia Romagna: Retrospettiva di Roberto Franzoni, Adolfo de Carolis e Leonardo Bistolfi (exh. cat., Bologna, Gal. Com. A. Mod., 1977)
F. Solmi, ed.: *Adolfo de Carolis: La sintesi immaginaria: Gli affreschi del Salone del Podestà di Bologna* (Bologna, 1979)

CHRISTOPHER MASTERS

Decastyle. Term applied to a building with a portico of ten columns.   □

Decembrio, Angelo (*b* Milan, ?1413–22; *d* after 1466). Italian humanist and writer. Son and younger brother of well-known humanists, he received his early education in Milan, transferring to Ferrara, probably after 1431, where he studied medicine and literature. He later joined the courtly circle of Lionello d'Este, after whose death he moved to Naples and then Spain, returning to Ferrara in 1465.

Decembrio's major work is a dialogue, *De politia litteraria* (1462), which purportedly records conversations between Lionello, his (and Decembrio's) teacher Guarino da Verona and various members of the Ferrarese court on scholarly, literary and artistic topics, such as the proper content and decoration of libraries. Part LXVIII is an extensive discussion of art, cast in the form of a monologue by Lionello, whose ideas reflect the influence of Leon Battista Alberti's *De pictura*. Lionello focuses on the importance of the artist achieving a true representation of nature through the accurate depiction of nude figures. He discusses ancient statues and engraved gems as well as contemporary tapestries and portraits of himself by Pisanello (Bergamo, Gal. Accad. Carrara) and Jacopo Bellini, possibly the *Virgin and Child with Lionello d'Este* (Paris, Louvre). Drawing on the popular comparison between poetry and painting, he attributes a far greater descriptive power to literature than to art.

WRITINGS
De politia litteraria (MS. 1462, Augsburg, 1540; Basle, 2/1562)

BIBLIOGRAPHY
M. Baxandall: 'A Dialogue on Art from the Court of Leonello d'Este: Angelo Decembrio's *De politia litteraria* pars LXVIII', *J. Warb. & Court. Inst.*, xxvi (1963), pp. 304–26 [with Eng. trans.]

P. Scarcia Piacentini: 'Angelo Decembrio e la sua scrittura', *Scritt. & Civiltà*, iv (1980), pp. 247–77

A. Biondi: 'Angelo Decembrio e la cultura del principe', *La corte e lo spazio: Ferrara estense*, ed. G. Papagno and A. Quondam, ii (Rome, 1982), pp. 637–57

JILL KRAYE

De Chirico, Andrea. *See* SAVINIO, ALBERTO.

De Chirico, Giorgio (*b* Vólos, Greece, 10 July 1888; *d* Rome, 20 Nov 1978). Italian painter, writer, theatre designer, sculptor and printmaker. De Chirico was one of the originators of PITTURA METAFISICA. His paintings are characterized by a visionary, poetic use of imagery, in which themes such as nostalgia, enigma and myth are explored. He was an important source of inspiration for artists throughout Europe in the inter-war years and again for a new generation of painters in the 1980s. His abrupt stylistic changes, however, have obscured the continuity of his approach, which was rooted in the philosophy of Friedrich Nietzsche, and this has often led to controversy.

1. Life and work. 2. Working methods and technique.

1. LIFE AND WORK.

(i) Vólos and Athens, 1888–1905. His parents came from the Italian diaspora within the Ottoman empire. He was very close to his brother, Andrea (who later adopted the pseudonym ALBERTO SAVINIO). As children they identified themselves with the heavenly twins, Castor and Pollux, while their closest associates became the Argonauts (a reference to Giorgio's birthplace, Vólos, from which, in Greek legend, the Argonauts departed to retrieve the Golden Fleece). The brothers' inherited Greek culture was a consistently rich source of inspiration. Their father, Evaristo de Chirico, was an engineer engaged in supervising the construction of the railway in Thessaly. He encouraged his sons' artistic talents, engaging drawing tutors for Giorgio and sending him to study with the Swiss painter Emile Gilleron (*b* 1851). From *c.* 1903 to 1905, at the Higher School of Fine Arts in Athens, de Chirico studied drawing under Georges Roilos (1867–1928) and Constantinos Bolonakis (1837–1907) and painting under the Munich-trained Georges Jacobidis (1852–1932). His failure in the final exams was probably due to the shock of his father's death in May 1905. De Chirico's mother, Gemma, remained a driving force behind her sons, pouring her ambition into their success.

(ii) Munich and Florence, 1906–11. In the autumn of 1906 the family left Greece, visiting Florence before moving to Munich. There de Chirico enrolled at the Akademie der Bildenden Künste and became interested in the bizarre narratives of Max Klinger's prints. His early work, however, owed most to the mythological and symbolic paintings of Arnold Böcklin. It seems likely that de Chirico found in the world depicted by Böcklin parallels with his own childhood memories. In the 1920s he published an appreciation of both artists. Other painters whose work attracted his attention included Hans Thoma and, later, Alfred Kubin. De Chirico's departure from the academy before graduation was perhaps as a result of his growing interest in the Munich avant-garde. By March 1910, when he left Munich to rejoin his mother and brother in Milan, his work was already less dependent on Böcklin.

It was probably in Florence in 1910, rather than in Munich as he later suggested, that de Chirico began to study Schopenhauer and Nietzsche through the writings of Giovanni Papini. In the same year he painted his first important work, *Enigma of an Autumn Afternoon* (priv. col., see 1982 exh. cat., p. 134, pl. 4). The painting shows a small pedimented building with curtained openings set into a wall, beyond which the sail of a ship is visible; two figures stand near the base of a tall statue in the foreground, and there is a feeling of anticipation. It was de Chirico's first attempt to capture the notion of the enigma and to penetrate to the reality concealed behind the everyday, where the commonplace becomes unfamiliar and reveals its true essence. The revelation of this parallel reality, inspired by the philosophy of Nietzsche, was a central concern of metaphysical painting.

(iii) Paris, 1911–15. De Chirico moved to Paris with his mother in July 1911 to join his brother. They stopped in Turin on the way for de Chirico to experience at first hand the city where Nietzsche, in embracing a beaten horse in 1888, first showed signs of madness. De Chirico associated this event symbolically with his own date of birth. In Paris, illness initially prevented him from painting, so his exhibition of three works at the Salon d'Automne in 1912 included the *Enigma of an Autumn Afternoon*, which he had brought from Italy. By the end of 1912 his paintings of Italianate town squares, inhabited by statues or lurking figures, began to be occupied instead by the mythological figure of Ariadne; her assistance to Theseus in the escape from the Minotaur's labyrinth was a symbol of revelation. In order to enhance the feeling of disjuncture in these works, de Chirico undertook a radical reordering of perspective, creating deep, dislocated spaces closed off by rapidly receding arcades and high brick walls.

In 1913 de Chirico sold his first painting at the Salon d'Automne, and this seems to have inspired a new commitment to his work. At this time he attended the Saturday evening gatherings of Guillaume Apollinaire, finding in him an encouraging critic and an inspiring friend. Apollinaire was the first to apply the term 'metaphysical' to de Chirico's art (in an article of 30 October 1913 published in *L'Intransigeant*), and through him the de Chirico brothers met Picasso, André Derain, Brancusi and Ardengo Soffici. Giorgio was less gregarious than Andrea (by then known as Alberto Savinio) and remained more aloof, maintaining his artistic isolation. Stylistically, his work was closer to the work of Henri Rousseau than to the formal concerns of the Cubists at this time.

1. Giorgio de Chirico: *Soothsayer's Recompense*, oil on canvas, 1.36×1.81 m, 1913 (Philadelphia, PA, Museum of Art)

Apollinaire was nonetheless attracted by the mysterious and enigmatic qualities of de Chirico's paintings (see fig. 1) and gave him his imaginative support, a factor that undoubtedly reinforced de Chirico's reputation.

De Chirico's paintings with fruit, such as the *Transformed Dream* (1913; St Louis, MO, A. Mus.), were followed by a series of arcade paintings, in which the growing subtlety of his handling of oppressive spaces is most evident. In *Mystery and Melancholy of a Street* (1914; priv. col., see 1982 exh. cat., p. 154, pl. 31) the shadow of an invisible statue creeps across the centre of the canvas towards a darkened portico, while from the other direction a girl with a hoop runs across the open space.

The highpoint of de Chirico's Pittura Metafisica was 1914. Series were replaced by works that were thematically linked but increasingly independent, culminating in such masterpieces as the *Child's Brain* (1914; Stockholm, Mod. Mus.) and the portrait of *Guillaume Apollinaire* (1914; Paris, Pompidou; see fig. 2). In the latter de Chirico's characteristic device of filling the foreground is exaggerated by the steep perspective and the vertical white slab with fish and shell moulds. Colour is restricted almost to monochrome, and the composition as a whole is almost abstract but for the classical bust, which acts as a partner to the silhouette of the poet above. Apollinaire encouraged

the suggestion that the portrait likened him to the mythical poet Orpheus, an interpretation that appealed to the de Chiricos since Orpheus too was an Argonaut. The portrait is the product of an intimate and exclusive circle of friends, which included the de Chirico brothers, Apollinaire, Pierre Roy (who made a woodcut from the portrait) and Paul Guillaume. At Apollinaire's suggestion, Guillaume became de Chirico's first dealer in 1914. This productive association came to a premature end at the outbreak of World War I. The art world dispersed, and Apollinaire volunteered for the French Army. While Italy remained unaligned, de Chirico continued to work in Paris, producing works filled with brightly coloured toys, such as the *Evil Genius of a King* (1914–15; New York, MOMA). As the war progressed, however, life became more difficult, and his output diminished.

(iv) Ferrara, 1915–18. In May 1915 the brothers were called up as Italy prepared to enter the war, and they returned to Florence. De Chirico, hoping that hostilities would soon be over, left behind his unfinished canvases. He was not to return for nine years. In June 1915 the brothers were sent to join their regiment in Ferrara. De Chirico found Ferrara strange and beautiful, and despite the demands of military life he continued to paint, producing works that are imbued with the peculiar spirit of

2. Giorgio de Chirico: *Guillaume Apollinaire*, oil on canvas, 815×650 mm, 1914 (Paris, Pompidou, Musée National d'Art Moderne)

the city: his paintings are filled with brightly coloured mathematical instruments and with cakes and biscuits seen in shop windows. Others include maps and views of buildings and factories, often illusionistically rendered. Ferrara also provided an ideal setting for the mannequin, a symbolic construction that de Chirico had begun to use in Paris, which was inspired by a character in Savinio's dramatic poem *Les Chants de la mi-mort*. He painted a series of works featuring composite figures, part-statue, part-mannequin. In the *Disquieting Muses* (1917; Milan, priv. col., see 1982 exh. cat., p. 182, pl. 71) three mannequins are placed on a steeply receding wooden platform before the red-brick Castello Estense in Ferrara. They seem expectant, and the deep shadows capture the feeling of tension suggested in the title.

During the war de Chirico managed to keep in touch with Apollinaire and Guillaume (to whom he continued to send paintings), and he made contact with Tristan Tzara about contributing to his *Dada* journal. In Ferrara a small group formed that included the poets Corrado Govoni (1884–1965) and Filippo de Pisis (later a painter). De Chirico, suffering from a nervous condition, was admitted to the military hospital, where in 1917 he was joined by Carlo Carrà. While there he produced a number of claustrophobic metaphysical interiors. Carrà rapidly assimilated de Chirico's style with the results of his own researches and in turn undoubtedly stimulated him, particularly in the creation of mannequin paintings. Out of this exchange grew Pittura Metafisica, but the friendship was soured when Carrà left for Milan at the end of the year to exhibit his new works alone. De Chirico remained isolated

in Ferrara, Savinio having been sent to the Macedonian front. In their correspondence with each other the brothers voiced hopes of forming a new, specifically Italian art movement, which would include Carrà, Soffici and Papini. While they had long expressed an interest in the de Chirico brothers' work, all three remained uncommitted to such a project.

(v) Rome, 1918–24. De Chirico first exhibited in Italy with Carrà in Rome in May 1918. Nine months later he held his first one-man show, at the Galleria Bragaglia, also in Rome. During this time he began to contribute theoretical articles to periodicals, most importantly to VALORI PLASTICI, which, with its international contributions and distribution, became the mouthpiece for Pittura Metafisica, publishing work by de Chirico, Savinio, Soffici, Giorgio Morandi and Arturo Martini. Mario Broglio (1891–1948) became de Chirico's dealer in Italy and produced the first monograph on the artist, as well as organizing the group exhibition that toured Germany in 1921. Pittura Metafisica's theoretical basis was formulated through the pages of *Valori Plastici* in a series of articles stressing the importance of time and memory as generators of the new art, which sought renewal through the use rather than the rejection of history. In this respect, Pittura Metafisica came close in spirit to the contemporary *rappel à l'ordre* in Paris.

In June 1919 de Chirico experienced a revelation before a painting by Titian in the Galleria Borghese in Rome. Consequently he began to reconsider the human figure and to make copies after Old Masters. This research brought about stylistic confusion in a series of Roman villas and Böcklin-inspired knights-errant. However, he

3. Giorgio de Chirico: *Painter's Family*, oil on canvas, 1.46×1.15 m, 1928 (London, Tate Gallery)

produced a series of portraits that expressed his continued commitment to the metaphysical ideal. These works were quite independent of his other work of this time and were increasingly populated by statuary or by second sitters. In Florence de Chirico often stayed with the critic Giorgio Castelfranco, while in Rome in the early 1920s he frequented the theatrical circle around the composer Alfredo Casella and the writers Luigi Pirandello and Massimo Bontempelli whose *Siepe a nord ovest* he illustrated in 1924. Both de Chirico and Savinio were involved in theatrical projects, and through this connection de Chirico met Raissa Gurievich Krohl, whom he married.

(vi) Paris, 1924–31. In November 1924 de Chirico returned to Paris to work on designs for *La Giara*, a ballet commissioned by the Ballets Suédois, based on a short story by Pirandello and with music by Casella. After disappointment with the state of Italian art, this project allowed de Chirico to gauge the situation in Paris, much changed since Apollinaire's death in 1918, and to make contact with the Surrealists. Their admiration for Apollinaire had led the group (centred around the poets André Breton, Louis Aragon and Paul Eluard) to de Chirico's painting, and in the war years they had been the principal buyers when Guillaume sold off the contents of the artist's studio. Breton's enthusiastic review of the *Valori Plastici* monograph had been used as a preface for the catalogue of the important one-man show of 1922 mounted by Guillaume, and a correspondence between them had begun. The Surrealists were familiar with de Chirico's works of 1914 and 1917 and had interpreted them in the

light of their interest in the subconscious, derived from Freudian analysis. De Chirico probably had no knowledge of Freud's theories until the 1920s and was unaware of the Surrealists' interpretation of his work, formulated during his absence from Paris.

In 1923 Eluard and his wife Gala had visited de Chirico in Rome. They became the subject of one of his finest double portraits (ex-Penrose priv. col., see Fagiolo dell'Arco, 1981, p. 1) showing the poet inspired by his muse. The Surrealists were, however, unprepared for the stylistic change in de Chirico's work, which became fully apparent to them in 1924 when he returned to Paris. For a time, though, de Chirico complied with their hopes that he would paint metaphysical works, and he published an account of a dream in the first number of their periodical, *La Révolution surréaliste.* By Christmas 1924 de Chirico was back in Rome, encouraged by his reception in Paris; only in 1926 did the gulf between his philosophy and the Surrealists' interpretation of it become unbridgeable.

In late 1925 the de Chiricos moved to Paris. There Raissa de Chirico studied archaeology, and her studies provided inspiration for his painting. Old contacts were reinforced, and new ones were established. In May 1925 de Chirico had a one-man show at Léonce Rosenberg's Galerie de l'Effort Moderne, heralding a period of prosperity. He also maintained his association with Guillaume in whose gallery he held a one-man show in 1926. Elsewhere in Europe, thanks to the activities of Broglio and Castelfranco, his reputation was extremely high. Even

4. Giorgio de Chirico: *Combat*, oil on canvas, 1.6×2.4 m, 1928–9 (Milan, Galleria d'Arte Moderna)

the Surrealists' criticisms did not have an immediate effect on this; indeed they may have been beneficial since they provoked Jean Cocteau and the critic Waldemar George into taking up his cause. His new style was most clearly embodied in another series of mannequin paintings, for example the *Painter's Family* (1928; London, Tate; see fig. 3): these seated figures retain the blank heads of their metaphysical ancestors but now have muscular limbs and elongated torsos, composed of geometrical instruments or architectural elements and suggesting the exposure of inner experience, memory and myth.

De Chirico's main inspiration in this period was memory transformed and sublimated to become mythology. This is most effectively evoked in his only novel *Hebdomeros* (1929), which is rich in imagery and in its use of non-sequitur to convey the broken line of memories. The novel was hailed even by the artist's detractors as a masterpiece and was intimately bound to his paintings of the period, such as the gladiator series commissioned by Rosenberg for the decoration of his Parisian home. In *Combat* (1928–9); Milan, Gal. A. Mod.; see fig. 4) tightly knit groups of battling but static figures are piled in the centre of a room. The complexity and size of the paintings show that de Chirico had reached a new peak of confidence. In 1929 he also made a series of lithographs for the republication of Apollinaire's *Calligrammes*. Crisp crescent moons and suns that cast spidery shadows enter through the windows of rooms in a series of simple but extraordinary transpositions. They were regarded by de Chirico not as illustrations but as parallel visions, inspired by his reading and personal memory of the poet.

(vii) Milan and New York, 1932–8. De Chirico's marriage to Raissa ended, and in 1931 he met Isabella Pakszwer Far, who, as his second wife, exerted as great an influence on his work as had his first. In 1930 and 1932 he exhibited with the 'Italiani di Parigi' at the Venice Biennale. His return to Italy was marked by shows in Milan and Florence in 1932, where his female nudes showed the influence of Renoir. In 1933 he carried out two public commissions: a large mural for the fifth Milan Triennale and sets and costumes for Vincenzo Bellini's opera *I puritani* in Florence. For Cocteau's *Mythologie* of 1934, de Chirico made a number of prints entitled *Mysterious Bathers*, depicting pools through which nude men are wading and on which bathing cabins are supported by platforms on stilts. The cabins, accessible by ladders and with portholed doors, and the empty spaces beneath them create a strangely disquieting atmosphere.

Aften a brief stay in Paris de Chirico left for New York in August 1935, prompted by the success of his earlier exhibitions there. New York brought him renewed prosperity. At five exhibitions, works were bought by public collections and by his American patron Alfred Barnes. These were primarily *Horses by the Sea* paintings, executed in his new classical style but retaining the theme of the heavenly twins. Despite the success of these shows de Chirico had returned to Italy by January 1938. After his mother's death (July 1936), he and his brother Savinio slowly drifted apart.

(viii) Milan, Florence and Rome, 1938–47. In the months leading up to World War II, after the anti-Semitic laws had been passed in Italy, de Chirico made extended trips to Paris with his wife, who was Jewish. His work was nevertheless exhibited regularly in Italy, even during the 1940s, and he continued to receive public commissions from the Fascist hierarchy. His more conservative subject-matter, which consisted predominantly of horsemen in landscapes and official portrtaits (he painted Mussolini's daughter in 1942), perhaps reflected the political pressures of the time. However, he also accepted new challenges, in 1941 illustrating *The Apocalypse* with remarkable, tight-lined lithographs of the visionary scenes. After a period in Florence in 1942, the couple settled in Rome in 1944. The uncertainties of wartime were matched by growing critical doubt about de Chirico's work. The argument centred on his reuse of earlier styles, which was felt to be deceptive chronologically and hence in terms of value. De Chirico fired a broadside at his critics in his *Memorie*, published in 1946. Old scores were settled with former critics (the Surrealists) and old friends (Carrà) alike. The tone of defiance is tinged with paranoia, however, and conspiracy theories abound. This is counterbalanced by the fine early passages about his childhood in Greece, revealing the inspiration for *Hebdomeros* and describing the sharp loss of innocence at the death of his father.

(ix) Rome, 1947–78. While controversies continued, the contents of an exhibition of metaphysical works in Paris in 1946 were all declared fakes by the artist. He made similar assertions about other exhibitions. Some of the rejected works have been reinstated by recent research, and others confirmed as fakes produced by Oscar Domínguez and others. It became clear that along with reusing old styles, de Chirico had been painting copies of his famous works. He produced 20 versions of the *Disquieting Muses*, and there is little doubt that he sold some of them as the original. His defence was that both the concept and the work were his and the date of execution immaterial. This argument was intensified by de Chirico's campaign throughout the 1950s against the Venice Biennale and modernism in general. His own reputation had become so fraught with difficulties, however, that his reaction against the commercialism of the post-war art scene was not taken very seriously. De Chirico proposed a painterly alternative in his neo-Baroque works, executed with a richness of brushwork reminiscent of Rubens, such as the *Self-portrait in Black Costume* (1948; Rome, G.N.A. Mod.). The culmination of this sumptuous painting style came in the large *Still-life with Silverware* (1962; priv. col., see 1985 exh. cat., p. 44). His continuing concern with the unity of the past and future is restated in this depiction of the *Apollo Belvedere*, accompanied by gleaming silverware and ripe fruit.

De Chirico continued to be active in a variety of media well into his old age. He worked on a large number of theatrical designs and illustrations and experimented with colour lithographs as well as sculpture. Around 1968 he began to produce small bronze sculptures of figures taken from his paintings: mannequins from the Ferrara years and horses from the 1920s, handled with somewhat less confidence than their painted counterparts. The *Grand Metaphysician* (c. 1969; Ferrara, Gal. Civ. A. Mod.) was scaled up from 0.52 m to over 3 m and is an extraordinary work, isolated and monumental, with a visionary aura. The same confidence and effectiveness are found in his paintings from the mid-1960s, when he dispensed with the neo-Baroque in favour of the neo-metaphysical, a style that occupied him until his death. In this phase, de Chirico began to treat his own work as part of history. Again, the subjects are mannequins from Ferrara and the 1920s, metaphysical compositions and calligrams, still-lifes and 'mysterious bathers'. If proof were needed that his stylistic changes disguised a unity of intent, he provided it in these works by his use of a bright translucent style that paradoxically recalls its neo-Baroque predecessor. The neo-metaphysical was not just a reworking of old ideas; through it de Chirico produced some of his most perplexing images. Tumbling pedimented buildings form the unexpected head of his *Mysterious Animal* (1975; priv. col., see 1985 exh. cat., p. 31), almost certainly to be identified with Nietzsche's horse. In the *Return of Ulysses* (1973; Rome, Fond. Giorgio & Isa de Chirico, on loan to Rome, G.N.A. Mod.) a man tries to rise from a boat crossing the sea in the centre of a room: the hero, like the artist, is caught in the wheel of time. This uniting of his career under one style was an act of defiance directed at all those who might dismiss the years between Pittura Metafisica and the neo-metaphysical. De Chirico always wished his work to be approached as a unified whole, and he finally forced his public to accept an interpretation of his work that corrected the imbalance produced originally by the Surrealists.

2. WORKING METHODS AND TECHNIQUE. De Chirico's early paintings show a sparing use of paint, reflecting perhaps in part his financial situation, although it was also a characteristic of the avant-garde works of the time: his use of dry, flat colours relates to works of Analytical Cubism, while the exposed areas of canvas recall the Fauves. Despite having studied in two academies, his early figure painting, inspired by Böcklin, still betrayed deficiencies of anatomical knowledge. It was not until his years in Rome from 1919 to 1924 that he began to take an interest in technique. Since he believed that the popularity of 17th-century painting during the early 1920s was due to the ease with which oil paintings could be faked, he concentrated instead of tempera. His research led him to make copies from the Old Masters, and in this he was encouraged by the restorer Nicolai Locoff and the painter Enrico Betterini. The resulting paintings have the dry, bright, detailed appearance typical of tempera.

About 1925, de Chirico became interested in the rich brushwork of Gustave Courbet, and on his return from Paris in 1931 he studied Velázquez and Rubens. In 1928 he published a treatise on painting technique. The fruit of his inquiry was the development of emulsions, which allowed the overlaying of translucent brushstrokes without those underneath losing their consistency. De Chirico may have derived this technique from his work in pastels during the 1920s. This allowed him to increase the density of the paint layers and to achieve effects of great richness in the neo-Baroque period from 1947 to 1965. Paradoxically, many of his paintings from these years show extensive cracking, suggesting that he was over-hasty in the preparation and working of the canvas. Stranger still, after a lifetime of experimentation, are the thin washes of paint

found in works of the neo-metaphysical period from 1965 to 1978. De Chirico's research led him finally to simplicity.

WRITINGS

Piccolo trattato di tecnica pittorica (Milan, 1928, rev. 2/1945; Eng. trans. in *Memoirs*, 1971)
Hebdomeros (Paris, 1929, rev. 2/1964; Eng. trans., 1968)
with I. Far: *Commedia dell'arte moderna* (Rome, 1945) [sel. articles, 1918–45]
Memorie della mia vita (Rome, 1947, rev. 2/1965); Eng. trans. as *Memoirs* (1971)
M. Carrà, ed.: *Metafisica* (Milan, 1968); rev. and Eng. trans., ed. M. Carrà, P. Waldberg and M. Rathke as *Metaphysical Art* (New York and London, 1971) [sel. articles, 1918–21]
M. Fagiolo dell'Arco, ed.: *Il meccanismo del pensiero: Critica, polemica, autobiografia 1911–1943* (Turin, 1985)
L. Cavallo, ed.: *Penso alla pittura, solo scopo della vita mia: 51 lettere e cartoline ad Ardengo Soffici 1914–1942* (Milan, 1987)

BIBLIOGRAPHY

12 opere di Giorgio de Chirico, precedute a giudici critici (Rome, 1919) [*Valori plastici* monograph]
R. Vitrac: *Georges de Chirico et son oeuvre* (Paris, 1927)
W. George: *Chirico: Avec des fragments littéraires de l'artiste* (Paris, 1928)
J. T. Soby: *The Early Chirico* (New York, 1941, rev. 2/1955); *R* as *Giorgio de Chirico* (New York, 1966)
J. Sloane: 'Giorgio de Chirico and Italian Art', *A. Q.* [Detroit], xxi (1958), pp. 3–22
A. Cirana: *Giorgio de Chirico: Catalogo delle opere grafiche (incisioni e litografie), 1921–69* (Milan, 1969)
Giorgio de Chirico (exh. cat., ed. W. Schmied; Milan, Pal. Reale, 1970)
C. Bruni Sakraischik, ed.: *Catalogo generale dell'opera di Giorgio de Chirico*, 8 vols (Milan, 1971–8)
I. Far and D. Porzio: *Conoscere di Chirico* (Milan, 1979)
P. L. Senna: 'L'opera grafica di de Chirico—De Chirico's graphic works', *Prt Colr/Conoscitore Stampe*, 45 (1980), pp. 2–31
M. Fagiolo dell'Arco: *Et quid amabo nisi quod aenigma est?*, 3 vols (Rome, 1981; abridged Eng. trans. of 3rd vol. in 1982 exh. cat.)
Giorgio de Chirico, 2 vols (exh. cat. ed. P. Vivarelli; Rome, G.N.A. Mod., 1981) [good bibliog.]
De Chirico (exh. cat., ed. W. Rubin; New York, MOMA; rev. Paris, Pompidou, 1982)
P. Baldacci and M. Fagiolo dell'Arco: *Giorgio de Chirico, Parigi, 1924–29* (Milan, 1982)
M. Fagiolo dell'Arco: *L'opera completa di Giorgio de Chirico* (Milan, 1982)
Late de Chirico, 1940–76 (exh. cat., ed. R. Martin; Bristol, Arnolfini Gal., 1985)
Giorgio de Chirico: L'Atelier (exh. cat., Ferrara, Gal. Civ. A. Mod., 1985)

MATTHEW GALE

Deck, Joseph-Théodore (*b* Guebwiller, Alsace, 1823; *d* ?Paris, 1891). French potter. He followed his father into the silk-dyeing trade, where no doubt he acquired his predilection for colour. About 1842 he was apprenticed at a Strasbourg stove factory and from 1844 travelled and worked in France, Germany and Austria. In 1856 he established his own workshop in Paris, where he experimented with glazes, eventually creating his much-admired *bleu de Deck* (1861). He produced lustre and polychrome painted, tin-enamelled wares based on Isnik and Persian ceramics and Italian maiolica. He also made 'inlaid' pottery in the style of 16th-century wares from Saint-Porchaire; a selection of these was shown at the Exposition Internationale des Arts et Industries of 1861 in Paris. His reputation as the first 'modern' studio potter rests on the range and quality of his technical innovations and his successful use of historical methods. Many early pieces from his workshop (e.g. dish painted by Eléonore Escallier, *c.* 1867; Paris, Mus. A. Déc.) were painted by such other artists as Albert Anker, Félix Bracquemond and Eléonore Escallier (1827–88). During the 1870s he became a pioneer of Japonisme and began experimenting with reduced copper glazes on porcelain, developing flambé glazes similar to Chinese glazes used during the period of the Qianlong emperor (*reg* 1736–96). Deck was appointed administrator (1887–91) at the porcelain factory of Sèvres, where he introduced a new type of glassy, soft-paste porcelain suitable for making reproductions of the factory's 18th-century styles. Under his direction Sèvres extended its production to include porcelain with rich, monochrome glazes (e.g. faceted urn vase, 1883; Paris, Mus. A. Déc.).

WRITINGS
La Faïence (Paris, 1887)

BIBLIOGRAPHY
S. Kuthy: *Albert Anker Fayencen in Zusammenarbeit mit Théodore Deck* (Zurich, 1985)
P. Dupont: *Porcelaines françaises aux XVIIIe et XIXe siècles* (Paris, 1987), pp. 169

Decker, Francis. *See* DUVENECK, FRANK.

Decker, Joseph (*b* Württemberg, 1853; *d* Brooklyn, NY, 1 April 1924). American painter of German birth. He moved with his family to the United States in 1867 and lived most of his life in Brooklyn, NY. While earning his living as a sign-painter, he studied for three years in the evening classes of the National Academy of Design in New York and is first recorded as a portrait and landscape painter in exhibitions in the late 1870s in Brooklyn and New York. In 1879 he returned to Germany where he studied for a year at the Akademie in Munich with the history painter Wilhelm von Lindenschmidt (1829–95). After his return to the USA, he exhibited regularly throughout the 1880s at the National Academy of Design, the Brooklyn Art Association and the Society of American Artists.

Decker's reputation rests on his still-lifes of the 1880s: sharply focused close-up depictions of pears, apples, nuts and the like, whose cropped compositions suggest the influence of advertisements (e.g. *Russet Apples on a Bough*, probably 1884; Washington, DC, priv. col.). Rendered in firm, visible brushstrokes, these images convey a sense of disquiet and ambiguity, provoked by the contradiction between a three-dimensional object rendered with intense realism and a two-dimensional surface pattern that denies any sense of real space. He also painted genre scenes.

About 1886, Decker attracted the attention of the prominent collector of American art, Thomas B. Clarke, who bought eight of his paintings. However, Decker sold few paintings to others and was not able to support himself through his art alone. In the 1890s, perhaps in reaction to negative reviews (critics called his earlier style 'harsh'), he began to paint in a more tonal, painterly style (e.g. *Twelve Plums*, 1896; New Haven, CT, Yale U., A.G.). His still-lifes of this period suggest the influence of Jean-Baptiste Siméon Chardin, while his landscapes are close to the late style of George Inness, whom he admired. Decker received more favourable notice during the 1890s, but after 1900 his work weakened. He died in obscurity.

BIBLIOGRAPHY
A. Frankenstein: *After the Hunt: William Harnett and Other American Still Life Painters, 1870–1900* (Berkeley, 1953)
H. A. Cooper: 'The Rediscovery of Joseph Decker', *Amer. A. J.*, x/1 (1978), pp. 55–71
W. H. Gerdts: *Painters of the Humble Truth: Masterpieces of American Still Life, 1801–1939* (Columbia, MO, 1981)

HELEN A. COOPER

Deckle edge. Ragged rough edge on untrimmed hand-made paper, sometimes imitated on machine-made paper (*see* PAPER, §I, 1(iv)).

De Cock, César (*b* Ghent, 23 July 1823; *d* Ghent, 16 July 1904). Belgian painter and etcher. He initially studied music at the Ghent Conservatory. Then, under the influence of his elder brother, the landscape painter Xavier De Cock (1818–96), he took courses in painting at the Art Academy in Ghent with Félix De Vigne (1806–62). In 1855 he went to Paris where he worked as a musician, but deafness forced him to devote himself instead to painting. He became friends with Jean-Baptiste-Camille Corot and, like his brother, stayed in Barbizon with Narcisse Diaz, Charles-François Daubigny, Théodore Rousseau and Constant Troyon. He also visited Gasny, Normandy, where he painted *Evening in Normandy*, *Surroundings of Saint-Christophe* and *Surroundings of Gasny* (all Ghent, Mus. S. Kst.). From 1857 he exhibited regularly at the Paris Salon and won medals there in 1867 and 1869. After several brief stays in Paris, he settled definitively in Ghent in 1880.

A prolific artist, De Cock often collaborated with his brother. His output consisted of poetic landscapes with a delicate touch, which tended towards rather sombre tonality in the Barbizon style. He had a preference for spring landscapes simply rendered: for example *Haymaking* (Ghent, Mus. S. Kst.) and *Surroundings of Saint-Germain-en-Laye* (1879; Antwerp, Kon. Mus. S. Kst.). His style, though conventional, was new in the 1860s in Belgium; although he painted with members of the more avant-garde Laethem-Saint-Martin school, he cannot be considered part of that movement.

BIBLIOGRAPHY
J. Van Hoorde: *Xavier et César De Cock* (Ghent, 1897)
De School van Barbizon (exh. cat., ed. J. Sillevis and H. Kraan; The Hague, Gemeentemus., 1985), pp. 120–21

ALAIN JACOBS

Décollage. Process of unsticking and ripping through successive layers of glued paper. The term first appeared in print in the *Dictionnaire abrégé du surréalisme* accompanying the catalogue of the *Exposition internationale du surréalisme* held at the Galerie Beaux-Arts in Paris in 1938. The technique developed through the use of posters torn from street walls to expose underlying images as interpenetrating forms within an overall surface. The altered posters revealed the fragmentary, confusing and alienating character of representation. *Décollage* represents a socially engaged practice. Unlike the constructive and atemporal unification of disparate materials in collage, from which it is derived, *décollage* is deconstructive and historical, an archaeological process unmasking the sequential, continuous relation of apparently dissociated images and events. In 1949 Raymond Hains began to collect, and perform the *décollage* technique on, commercial and political posters to exhibit them as aesthetic objects and sociological documents. Throughout the 1950s he and other artists associated with Nouveau Réalisme, notably Jacques de La

Villeglé (*b* 1926), François Dufrêne (*b* 1930) and Mimmo Rotella, applied the technique consistently to printed posters; they are sometimes referred to as *affichistes* and their pictures as *affiches lacérées*.

Wolf Vostell, who was not a Nouveau Réaliste, also developed the process, having noticed the word in *Le Figaro* on 6 September 1954, where it was used to describe the simultaneous take-off and crash of an aeroplane. He appropriated the term to signify an aesthetic philosophy, applied also to the creation of live performances, by which the destructive, violent and erotic events of contemporary life were assembled and juxtaposed. Emphasizing the syllabic division, *dé-coll/age,* he underscored the dialectical meaning of the term applied to both the creative and destructive processes in natural and biological systems and in cultural and social structures. In 1962 Vostell founded and edited *Dé-coll/age: Bulletin aktueller Ideen,* a magazine devoted to the theoretical writings and manifestos of artists involved in Happenings, Fluxus, Nouveau Réalisme and Pop art. It ceased publication in 1969.

BIBLIOGRAPHY

P. Restony: *Les Nouveaux Réalistes* (Paris, 1968); rev. as *Le Nouveau Réalisme* (Paris, 1978)

J. de la Villeglé: 'L'Affiche lacérée: Ses successives immixtions dans les arts', *Leonardo*, 2 (1969)

For further bibliography *see* NOUVEAU RÉALISME, ROTELLA, MIMMO and VOSTELL, WOLF.

KRISTINE STILES

De coloribus et artibus Romanorum. One of the few surviving, early medieval, Latin technical treatises. Its attribution, localization and dating rest largely on internal evidence variously interpreted and inconclusive. The treatise now comprises three books: it is generally agreed that Books I and II, written in verse by one hand at some time between the 7th and 12th centuries, constitute the original text; Book III, written in prose, was added piecemeal during the 12th and 13th centuries. The treatise is commonly attributed to (H)Eraclius, who is cited as the author in Books I and III but probably wrote only Books I and II. It is not known whether he was a native of Italy or a northerner promoting his knowledge of Roman techniques, and accordingly *De coloribus* has been located to either Italy or northern Europe.

Relatively complete versions of the text survive in two manuscripts, both accompanied by Theophilus's treatise *De diversis artibus* (extracts of the text within compilations of technical material are more common): the first (ex-Trinity Coll., Cambridge, MS. R. 15 5; London, BL, Egerton MS. 840 A) is German and dated 1250–1300; the second (Paris, Bib. N., MS. lat. 6741) is French and was compiled in 1431. The prologue of Book I bemoans the loss of appreciation for and practice of the pre-eminent arts of the Romans. Thirteen titled chapters follow, which include advice on pigment preparation, the decorative use of glass, the cutting and polishing of precious stones and crystal and the gilding of ivory. Book II contains seven chapters providing further pigment recipes and instructions for glazing earthenware and giving copper the appearance of gold. There is little mention of the arts of the Romans in Book III, but there are several instances of repetition of information provided in earlier chapters. In the London manuscript, Book III comprises 25 chapters

arranged by medium: it includes instructions for glazing pottery; cutting glass, precious gems and crystal; gilding metals; shaping ivory; and painting on wood, stone and parchment. Certain elements are drawn from the writings of Isidore of Seville and Vitruvius. Book III in the Paris manuscript is in a different order with a further 33 chapters appended dealing with pigment preparation, the incompatibility of certain pigments and methods for mixing colours for shadows and highlights.

De coloribus is a general compilation of information concerning the materials and techniques of medieval artists and the theories and practices of their craft. Amid occasional apocryphal advice, it provides one of the earliest references to what some have interpreted as the use of oil as a tempering medium for paint (Raspe and Eastlake). Roosen-Runge demonstrated the correlation between much of its content and the practice of manuscript painting in western Europe between the 10th and 13th centuries. In addition, *De coloribus* confirms that early medieval craftsmen had wide-ranging skills. Although it has received scant attention since it was first published (Raspe), *De coloribus* should be considered alongside such other medieval treatises as the *Mappae clavicula* and Theophilus's *De diversis artibus*; Theophilus was certainly familiar with it and used various elements from Books I–III in his own treatise.

BIBLIOGRAPHY

R. E. Raspe: *Critical Essay on Oil-Painting, Proving that the Art of Painting in Oil Was Known before the Pretended Discovery of John Hubert Van Eyck* (London, 1781)

C. L. Eastlake: *Materials for a History of Oil Painting* (London, 1847)

M. P. Merrifield: *Original Treatises Dating from the XIIth to the XVIIIth Centuries on the Arts of Painting in Oil, Miniature, Mosaic, and on Glass; of Gilding, Dyeing and the Preparation of Colours and Artificial Gems,* i (London, 1849), pp. 166–257

A. Giry: 'Notice sur un traité du moyen âge intitulé De coloribus et artibus Romanorum', *Bib. Ecole Hautes Etud.,* xxxv (1878), pp. 209–37

J. C. Richards: 'A New Manuscript of Heraclius', *Speculum,* xv (1940), pp. 255–71

H. Roosen-Runge: *Farbgebung und Technik frühmittelalterlicher Buchmalerei: Studien zu den Traktaten 'Mappae Clavicula' und 'Heraclius',* 2 vols (Berlin, 1967)

SALLY E. DORMER

Deconstruction. Philosophical movement associated with JACQUES DERRIDA, which began to flourish in the 1970s. It rejects the traditional distinction between the literary style of a text and its content, and also that between non-poetic writing, which offers arguments, and literature, which does not. Derrida suggested that such distinctions, together with the general activity of paraphrasing a writer's claims in order to question their truth, fail to do justice to the rhetorical aspects found in all writing. Like POST-STRUCTURALISM, also associated with Derrida, deconstruction is concerned mostly with an analysis of texts but can also be applied to the visual arts. The deconstructionist denies that there is a single, intrinsic meaning to be found in a text. It is, on the contrary, asserted that texts are both more open and interlinked than is normally assumed. This approach can be incorporated into art history and so extended to apply to works of art. Given these premises, it becomes hard to evaluate Derrida's own arguments, which are inevitably expressed through texts. It is perhaps therefore best to think of deconstruction as not so much a doctrine whose rules can be stated but more as an activity whose aim is to find the conflicts and possibilities in a text or work of art.

Derrida's own texts move from one subject to another and involve word play, suggesting that any attempt to explain their content without taking account of their literary style must be inadequate. In *Marges de la philosophie* (1972) he discussed the neologism *'différance'* and its multiple meanings. When spoken it cannot be distinguished from *différence*, and its meaning cannot be known until explained. For Derrida *différance* refers to delaying and to movements in both time and space. He used *différance* to indicate the problems that are always important in interpretation and to raise the issue of whether it is ever possible to know what such a word means if various meanings are always in play. In *L'Ecriture et la différence* (1967) he questioned the common practice of using spatial metaphors when analysing a text, for example, to make a distinction between the meaning 'in' a text and that 'outside' it. Furthermore, to speak of the writer's ideas when examining a text presupposes that the meaning of the text is only that which the author intended. Derrida, in contrast, maintained that the meaning was more open because of the relationships between different texts. For example, in *Glas* (1974) he presented parallel-column commentaries on the work of two very different thinkers, Jean Genet (1910–86) and Hegel, therefore implying that their ideas are somehow related, though he left the identification of such a relationship to the reader. He was more explicit in *Eperons: Les Styles de Nietzsche* (1978) in which he connected the many expressions of misogyny in Nietzsche's writings to a seemingly anomalous sentence in his unpublished manuscripts about a lost umbrella. He then used this connection to question the usual accounts of the German philosopher's theory of truth.

Derrida's most fully developed account of visual art is *La Vérité en peinture* (1978) in which he applied the same techniques to painting as he had to written texts. The book includes a study of an argument between the art historian Meyer Schapiro (*b* 1904) and the philosopher Martin Heidegger about an interpretation of van Gogh's painting *Old Shoes with Laces* (Amsterdam, Rijksmus. van Gogh). Derrida argued that we can never be sure whose shoes are depicted in the work (a problem familiar to iconographers). He linked the shoes to psychoanalytic accounts of fetishism, Heidegger's aesthetic theory and politics, other paintings showing shoes, and the ear that van Gogh cut off. Such a potentially open-ended commentary therefore makes it hard to ascribe a fixed meaning to the painting.

In addition to its effect on art history, deconstruction has been influential in the field of architecture (*see* POST-MODERNISM). Such architects as BERNARD TSCHUMI and PETER EISENMAN have adopted a deconstructionist approach to design. Rather than aiming for a unified form in their buildings, these architects used elements from other traditions, such as modernism, and incorporated them into constructions that altered their usual function or meaning. They attempted a deconstruction of the components of architecture that was analogous to Derrida's approach to texts. They thus treated actual buildings as if they were texts. For the deconstructive architect, *Glas* provides a model for thinking about the places inhabited in everyday life. Just as Derrida played with words, so such

architects played with three-dimensional structures. However, what would seem, judged by traditional standards of harmony, to be merely a kind of architectural eclecticism, could be identified, rather, as a novel, post-modern spatial order.

BIBLIOGRAPHY

J. Derrida: *L'Ecriture et la différence* (Paris, 1967; Eng. trans., Chicago and London, 1978)
M. Baxandall: *Giotto and the Orators* (Oxford, 1971)
J. Derrida: *Marges de la philosophie* (Paris, 1972; Eng. trans., Chicago, 1972)
——: *Glas* (Paris, 1974; Eng. trans., Lincoln, NE, 1986)
——: *Eperons: Les Styles de Nietzsche* (Paris, 1978; Eng. trans., Chicago, 1979)
——: *La Vérité en peinture* (Paris, 1978; Eng. trans., Chicago, 1987)
R. Rorty: 'Philosophy as a Kind of Writing: An Essay on Derrida', *New Lit. Hist.*, x (1978–9), pp. 141–60
D. Carrier: 'Derrida as Philosopher', *Metaphilosophy*, xvi (1985), pp. 221–34
S. Melville: *Philosophy Beside Itself: On Deconstruction and Modernism* (Minneapolis, 1986)
A. Danto: 'Philosophy as/and/of Literature', *Language and the Question of Philosophy* (Baltimore, 1987), pp. 1–23
P. Johnson and M. Wigley: *Deconstructivist Architecture* (New York, 1988)
P. Barolsky: *Why Mona Lisa Smiles and Other Tales by Vasari* (University Park, PA, 1991)
G. Broadbent: *Deconstruction: A Student Guide* (London, 1991)

DAVID CARRIER

Decorated style. Term referring to the styles of architecture and decoration in Britain from *c.* 1250 to *c.* 1360. It was coined in 1817 by Thomas Rickman, who divided English medieval architecture into four stylistic phases: Norman, Early English, Decorated and Perpendicular. These divisions have, with modifications, persisted, despite being criticized by such mid-19th-century writers as Sharpe in 1849 and condemned as inadequate by Prior in 1900. They have been confirmed in popular use by their adoption as convenient style labels in Pevsner's Buildings of England series.

Following a contemporary preoccupation with definition and classification, 19th-century scholars identified Decorated by its component details, above all by window tracery (*see* TRACERY). The term Decorated does not define any new structural ideas, which, although they did occur in, for example, the nave of York Minster (begun 1291), were evidently less important to contemporaries than the new ways of embellishing buildings. Decorated is seen as beginning with the introduction of window tracery at Westminster Abbey, gradually giving way a century later to the Perpendicular style defined by rectilinear forms. Decorated itself underwent a change when the ogee, or reversed, curve appeared on a monumental scale *c.* 1290, and it is convenient to divide the style into two phases, the earlier often called Geometric and the later Curvilinear, although many characteristics of the later phase were already present in the earlier.

Later 13th-century buildings, such as the Angel choir of Lincoln Cathedral (*see* LINCOLN, §2), Old St Paul's Cathedral, London (destr.), Tintern Abbey, Gwent, and York Minster (*see* YORK, §III, 1(i)), have large windows with tracery patterns based on such geometric forms as cusped circles, quatrefoils and trefoils. As at Westminster, interiors could be sculptural in quality, with emphasis on arch and pier mouldings, surface ornament, foliage and figure sculpture and on the use of marbles in contrasting colours. By the end of the century such architectural motifs as arches, gables and pinnacles were used decoratively on a reduced scale. This type of ornament was particularly suited to the walls of smaller ecclesiastical buildings, such as private chapels (St Etheldreda's, London, 1284–6; St Stephen's Chapel, Palace of Westminster, founded 1292), and tombs, screens and other monumental pieces of church furniture. The same motifs appeared in designs for metalwork, ivories, embroidery and manuscript illuminations, so that more than ever before all the arts drew on a common repertory of ornament.

This so-called micro-architecture was the basis of Decorated in its later phase. The introduction of the ogee curve in the 1290s, on the royal tombs at Westminster Abbey and St Stephen's Chapel and on the Eleanor crosses (*see* CROSS, §II, 3), encouraged the emergence of more yielding, sculptural effects in details that could strictly be classed as architectural, such as mouldings (the wave moulding) and window tracery (curvilinear flowing tracery, as in the south transept of Lincoln Cathedral, *c.* 1330, and the west window of York Minster, *c.* 1335). While load-bearing arches could not be ogival, ogees defined the heads of niches, either flush with the wall or 'nodding' forward into space (e.g. the north porch of St Mary Redcliffe, Bristol, *c.* 1325). Polygonal ground-plans, such as the Octagon of Ely Cathedral (1322–8; *see* ELY, §1(i)(d)) and the Lady Chapel of Wells Cathedral (first quarter of the 14th century; see fig. and *see* WELLS, §1), were a large-scale manifestation of this desire to blur the clear lines of architectural space. While, in the earlier phase of Decorated, vaults had been composed of multiple ribs springing from the same level, in the later phase the lierne, a short

connecting rib, was used to create net or carpet patterns over the whole surface of the vault (e.g. Bristol Cathedral choir, *c.* 1320s; Ottery St Mary, Devon, *c.* 1340). Seaweed foliage and diaper ornament spread across plain walls, and figure sculpture, both miniature and monumental, was deployed copiously: angels in the choir vault of Gloucester Cathedral (1337–50; *see* GLOUCESTER, §1), as well as slightly earlier in the door to the choir from the south transept; secular figures in the choir triforium and aisle parapets of Selby Abbey, N. Yorks (*c.* 1340); and ecclesiastics in the upper walls (destr.) and dado of Ely Cathedral Lady Chapel (*c.* 1330s).

Although the sources of the most popular Decorated motifs were French, from the Geometric tracery of the earlier phase to the later micro-architectural ornament, there was a specifically English contribution in the sculptural interior, lierne vaults and flowing tracery. The French sources remained unidentified until Hastings (1955) argued that the Westminster works of the 1290s formed a 'Court' school, independent of the Decorated style, which was inspired by French Rayonnant (*see* RAYONNANT STYLE) designs and led directly to the development of the Perpendicular style. Decorated, on the other hand, was seen as an English style that occurred only in the provinces. In the ensuing argument, which lasted for a generation and was concerned with the origins of the Perpendicular style, Decorated, regarded as a stylistic dead end, was pushed to the margins, and 'Court' art continued to be opposed to 'provincial' art. It was not until 1979 that Bony and Wilson reinstated the Westminster works as crucial to Decorated, pointing out that their designs contained some elements essential to the Decorated style, while others contributed to the development of Perpendicular. In this reading the Westminster works were the source of artistic ideas outside London. Later scholars, pursuing the idea that Decorated is more than the sum of architectural parts, have concentrated on questions of symbolism and iconography.

The influence of Decorated on European Late Gothic has been much debated, with Bony (1979) arguing that it was the basis of many developments in the late 14th century and the 15th. Although English influence is detectable in the earliest examples of the French FLAMBOYANT STYLE, such as the Ste-Chapelle, Riom (1380s), it is less clear in later buildings. The extent of English inspiration in the work of Peter Parler (*see* PARLER, (3)) and his associates in Bohemia and southern Germany has been questioned. Many Decorated motifs, the tracery in particular, became extremely popular in the Gothic Revival of the 19th century, and it was to ensure that architects used 'correct' designs that such scholars as Sharpe and Freeman wrote their books.

BIBLIOGRAPHY

T. Rickman: *An Attempt to Discriminate the Styles of English Architecture, from the Conquest to the Reformation* (London, 1817)

E. Sharpe: *Decorated Windows* (London, 1849)

E. A. Freeman: *Window Tracery* (London, 1851)

E. S. Prior: *A History of Gothic Art in England* (London, 1900/ *R* 1974)

N. Pevsner and others: *Bldgs England* (Harmondsworth, 1951–)

J. M. Hastings: *St Stephen's Chapel* (Cambridge, 1955)

J. Harvey: 'The Origin of the Perpendicular Style', *Studies in Building History Presented to B. St. J. O'Neill*, ed. E. M. Jope (London, 1961), pp. 134–65

Decorated style: Wells Cathedral, Lady Chapel and retrochoir, first quarter of the 14th century

H. Bock: *Der Decorated Style: Untersuchungen zur englischen Kathedral— Architektur der ersten Hälfte des 14. Jahrhunderts*, Heidelberg. Kstgesch. Abh., n. s., vi (Heidelberg, 1962)

P. Crossley: 'Wells, the West Country and Central European Late Gothic', *British Archaeological Association Conference Transactions*, iv: *Medieval Art and Architecture at Wells and Glastonbury: Wells, 1978*

J. Bony: *The English Decorated Style* (London, 1979)

C. Wilson: *The Origins of the Perpendicular Style and its Development to c. 1360* (diss., U. London, 1979)

N. Coldstream: 'The Lady Chapel at Ely: Its Place in the English Decorated Style', *Reading Med. Stud.*, xi (1985), pp. 1–30

P. Binski: *The Painted Chamber at Westminster*, Soc. Antiqua. London Occas. Pap., n. s., ix (London, 1986)

P. Lindley: 'The Imagery of the Octagon at Ely', *J. Brit. Archaeol. Assoc.*, n. s. 2, cxxxix (1986), pp. 75–99

Age of Chivalry (exh. cat., ed. J. Alexander and P. Binski; London, RA, 1987)

N. Coldstream: *The Decorated Style: Architecture and Ornament, 1240–1360* (London, 1994)

NICOLA COLDSTREAM

Decorum. Principle of appropriateness, controlling composition, representation and location in the visual arts. Decorum may determine that a pictorial or sculptural subject is suitable for an architectural setting, such as Vulcan's forge over a fireplace, or that kinds of buildings are fitting in urban or rural contexts or appropriate for persons of certain status. Liturgical functions influenced by decorum dictate the placement of paintings, mosaics and sculpture in religious buildings. In narrative painting, graphic art and sculpture, decorum affects how the protagonists dress, gesture and move, the intensity of their emotional expression, their facial or physical types and skin colour, the identifying attributes given the figures, their numbers, scale and proximity to sacred personages if they are the artist or patron and the historicity of the landscape or architectural settings.

Changing devotional and theological considerations also regulated these details. Compare, for example, the suppression of physical suffering in depictions of Christ's Passion in Early Christian art and its accentuation in brutal martyrdoms painted for Catholic patrons in Counter-Reformation Italy. The display of the Christ child's genitals in Italian Renaissance painting was sanctioned by Incarnation theology, but Michelangelo's depiction of nudes in his *Last Judgement* (1536–41; Rome, Vatican, Sistine Chapel; *see* MICHELANGELO, §I, 2) was condemned by Lodovico Dolce as 'unworthy' of the papal chapel: the religious justification of the nudes did not compensate for their lack of decency (*honestà*).

While decorum in art relates to fluctuating notions of social decency, it is mediated and legitimized by artists, critics and historians. Society in 19th-century England espoused ideals of modesty, but many artists painted historical pictures that exploited erotic nudity. During the 1970s practitioners of PERFORMANCE ART enacted events that might have occasioned arrest for obscenity outside the studio or art museum. Some historians and critics tacitly use decorum to justify appraisals of past and present art or to maintain pejorative judgements of period styles, such as Italian Mannerism.

In the ancient world, decorum was an important element of Egyptian religious and funerary art (*see* EGYPT, ANCIENT, §IV, 1). In Greece, Plato introduced ancient discussion of artistic decorum in his debate in *Hippias Major* as to whether the appropriate is identical with the beautiful, using handcrafted objects as examples. Aristotle prescribed that the style of a rhetorical discourse should be harmonious with the subject-matter and suitable to the age, sex or country of the characters. Such Roman writers as Cicero and Quintilian compared theory and practice in rhetoric and the visual arts to illustrate correct procedure in oratory. Horace extended this comparative method to poetry. The dispute over the limits of architectural decorum between St Bernard of Clairvaux and Abbot Suger of Saint-Denis in the 12th century offers valuable insights into medieval attitudes. Artists' workshops clearly had established traditions of self-regulation, but these were sensitive to changing devotional ideas, such as the responsiveness of artists to the Cistercian and mendicant orders. Liturgical propriety, observing fitness for ritual purpose, was a dominant concern in medieval art criticism. Cicero's ideas on decorum, now adapted to Christian exigencies, were circulated widely. In the 1430s, Alberti emphasized the kinship of art theory and rhetoric. He proposed that every figure in a narrative picture (*see* ISTORIA) be given characteristics appropriate to its form and behaviour in literary tradition. Expression, including gesture, was to be moderate and dignified. Leonardo made these constraints more specific but related them to contemporary social decorum. In the 1580s Giovanni Paolo Lomazzo offered very detailed instructions for painters seeking to depict the appropriate passions and movements of religious or Classical figures. This approach found variant developments in writings of French theorists of the 17th and 18th centuries such as Le Brun, de Piles, Henri Testelin and Dandré-Bardon. The revival of Aristotle's notions on rhetoric and of Horace's maxim UT PICTURA POESIS in the Renaissance underpinned this theory. Many recent art movements have sought to separate painting from literature, but a new theory of decorum has not emerged. The 20th-century preoccupation with art as language, linguistically based theories of criticism and iconographic research have reinforced a 'literary' comprehension of decorum among critics and art historians.

After Alberti, the idea of the 'learned' artist came to entail an ever more sophisticated understanding of decorum. Critics and artists colluded to demand a poetic, historical and philosophical sensibility in the artist. It was also a presupposition of this tradition that the artist's personal morality and social deportment came within the critic's purview and influenced the decorum of the work. Italian Renaissance artists prepared the ground, while such Counter-Reformation theorists as Johannes Molanus and Gabriele Paleotti, urging decency and didactic simplicity in the arts in the service of Church policy, presumed the moral probity of the artist. Bellori liked the fact that Reni painted in a mantle, at least when observed by others. Shaftesbury noted that Poussin and Rosa were 'honest moral men' (*Second Characters; Or the Language of Forms*, ed. B. Rand (London, 1914), p. 15). This professional decorum could sustain ideas of the artist as courtier, such as Vasari or Rubens, or as gentleman scholar, as with Poussin or Reynolds. Artists who reacted against such an ideal risked losing aristocratic patrons. Some 19th- and 20th-century artists directly challenged conventional morality in their lives and works, persuading historians of the avant-garde that subverting conventional deportment was one of its aims. Roger Fry stated that in art there is no 'moral responsibility' (*Vision and Design* (London, 1920, rev. 1923), p. 21). When George Orwell wrote that Dalí lacked 'bedrock human decency', he was stigmatizing his art as well as his want of decorum (*Critical Essays* (London, 1946), p. 123); alternatively, Clement Greenberg argued that Camille Pissarro's 'decency' rendered his art monotonous (*The Collected Essays and Criticism*, ed. J. O'Brien, i (Chicago, 1986), p. 215). Harold Rosenberg announced in 1972 that 'taste has ceased to exist' (*The De-definition of Art . . .* (New York, 1972), pp. 17, 26, 57). In this climate decorum almost vanished as a critical device, but it lived on more subtly in the rhetoric of criticism, in art history and in the etiquette of the commercial art gallery.

Ecclesiastical and lay proponents of scriptural verism in painting in Counter-Reformation Italy and Spain stressed moral decency, the dignity befitting sacred figures and clarity of meaning in narrative. Most were bitterly opposed to the assumptions of PAOLO VERONESE when in 1573 he faced the Inquisition over his *Last Supper*. For him decorum meant painting the rich setting of a grand dining hall with appropriate servants and entourage. Claiming the freedom that poets and madmen enjoyed, he was forced to rename the painting *Feast in the House of Levi* (Venice, Accad. Pitt. & Scul.). In 1602 CARAVAGGIO had to repaint his first altarpiece of *St Matthew* for the church of S Luigi dei Francesi, Rome, as the clergy were unhappy with the figure, which did not have 'the decorum or appearance of the Saint' (G. P. Bellori: *Vite* (1672); ed. E. Borea (1976), p. 219). Reynolds in turn praised Raphael's *Cartoons* (London, V&A) for the 'great nobleness' given the Apostles: 'yet we are expressly told in scripture they had no such respectable appearance' (*Discourses on Art* (London, 1769–91); ed. R. Wark (San Marino, CA, 1959, rev. New Haven and London, 1975), pp. 59–60). This he called the 'poetical' aspect of history painting. Poussin applied his theory of 'modal' painting, using the analogy of musical modes to determine pictorial style through measure, proportion, colour range and balance as well as through emotional tone. These are versions of what Gombrich called 'doctrines of mutual reinforcement of various sense modalities and scales'. Diderot, in the footsteps of Vasari, Félibien and Le Brun, proposed a 'law' of 'unity of action' (and also of place and time) common to dramatic poetry and painting. He presupposed the artist's deep knowledge of nature and history, imaginative genius and fitting taste (*goût convenable*). 'Unity of action' was applied by Ruskin as a criterion for establishing a canon of artists who satisfied the demands of decorum.

The relations between beauty and fitness-for-purpose were investigated by Edmund Burke, profoundly influencing Diderot and Lessing, among others. Burke had noted David Hume's argument that most works of art 'are esteem'd beautiful, in proportion to their fitness for the use of man' (*A Treatise of Human Nature* (London, 1739–40), ed. L. A. Selby-Bigge, 2/1928, pp. 577, 612). Hume made decorum depend upon 'experience'. He was followed by Uvedale Price, who separated decorum from 'that more refined, and delicate sense of judgement, called taste'; meanwhile the landscape gardener Humphry Repton disagreed: 'propriety and convenience are not less objects of good taste, than picturesque effect' (both

U. Price, *Essays on the Picturesque*, iii (London, 1810), pp. 6, 49). Goethe noted sceptically that the appropriate could easily be mistaken for the commonplace (*Goethe on Art*, ed. J. Gage (London, 1980), p. 18).

Decorum in Western architectural theory derives from the treatises of Vitruvius (*On Architecture*) and Alberti (*De re aedificatoria*, 1485). In Vitruvius, appropriateness (*decor*) binds form to function, so that the siting of a building, its approaches, aspect and choice of order are determined by its purpose. Alberti amplifies Vitruvius's concern with fitting dignity (*dignitas*), introduces the term *concinnitas* (from which the dignity derives) and makes the architect's judgement of decorum so decisive that it determines even placement of the altar in churches. Of later theorists, Nicolas Le Camus de Mezières is important for the idea of appropriate architectural 'character' (*caractère*), as is A. W. N. Pugin and his 'Ecclesiological' followers, who justified a Gothic Revival style on grounds of fitness-for-purpose. This concept of decorum formed a theoretical basis for the ARTS AND CRAFTS MOVEMENT in Great Britain and France initially, then elsewhere. Indeed, the theory of FUNCTIONALISM both in architecture and in 'craft' is tied to fitness-for-purpose and therefore to decorum.

BIBLIOGRAPHY

A. T. Edwards: *Good and Bad Manners in Architecture* (London, 1924)

K. Clark: *The Gothic Revival: An Essay in the History of Taste* (London, 1928)

A. Blunt: *Artistic Theory in Italy, 1450–1600* (Oxford, 1940, rev. 4/1962), pp. 1–22

R. W. Lee: '*Ut pictura poesis*: The Humanistic Theory of Painting', *A. Bull.*, xxii (1940), pp. 197–296

E. de Bruyne: *Etudes d'esthétique médiévale*, 3 vols (Bruges, 1946)

R. Wittkower: *Architectural Principles in the Age of Humanism* (London, 1949, rev. 3/1962)

P. Barocchi, ed.: *Trattati d'arte del cinquecento*, 2 vols (Bari, 1961)

P. Fehl: 'Veronese and the Inquisition: A Study of the Subject-matter of the So-called *Feast in the House of Levi*', *Gaz. B.-A.*, n. s. 5, lviii (1961), pp. 325–54

M. Wittkower and R. Wittkower: *Born under Saturn: The Character and Conduct of Artists . . .* (London, 1963, rev. 2/1969)

R. Krautheimer: 'Alberti and Vitruvius', *Studies in Early Christian, Medieval and Renaissance Art* (New York, 1969), pp. 323–32

P. Barocchi, ed.: *Scritti d'arte del cinquecento*, 2 vols (Milan, 1971–3)

M. Baxandall: *Giotto and the Orators: Humanist Observers of Painting in Italy and the Discovery of Pictorial Composition, 1350–1450* (Oxford, 1971)

D. Freedberg: 'Johannes Molanus on Provocative Painting', *J. Warb. & Court. Insts*, xxxiv (1971), pp. 229–45

E. H. Gombrich: *Symbolic Images*, Studies in the Art of the Renaissance, ii (London, 1972, rev. 3/1985), pp. 1–25

W. Messerer: 'Die *Modi* im Werk von Poussin', *Festschrift Luitpold Dussler* (Berlin, 1972), pp. 335–56

J. Dobai: *Die Kunstliteratur des Klassizismus und der Romantik in England*, 4 vols (Berne, 1974–84)

J. J. Pollitt: *The Ancient View of Art: Criticism, History and Terminology* (New Haven, 1974)

R. de Maio: *Michelangelo e la Controriforma* (Rome, 1978)

M. Cali: *Da Michelangelo all'Escorial: Momenti del dibattito religioso nell'arte del cinquecento* (Turin, 1980)

P. Fehl: 'Veronese's Decorum: Notes on the *Marriage at Cana*', *Art the Ape of Nature: Studies in Honor of H. W. Janson* (New York, 1981), pp. 341–65

M. Donker and G. M. Muldrow: 'Decorum', *Dictionary of Literary-rhetorical Conventions of the English Renaissance* (Westport, 1982), pp. 64–7

M. Eaves: *William Blake's Theory of Art* (Princeton, 1982)

D. R. Smith: *Masks of Wedlock: Seventeenth-century Dutch Marriage Portraiture* (Ann Arbor, 1982)

L. Steinberg: *The Sexuality of Christ in Renaissance Art and in Modern Oblivion* (New York, 1983)

R. Haussherr: 'Convenevolezza: Historische Angemessenheit in der Darstellung von Kostüm und Schauplatz seit der Spätantike bis ins 16. Jahrhundert', *Abhandlungen der Akademie der Wissenschaften und der Literatur in Mainz: Geistes- und Socialwissenschaftliche Klasse*, 4 (1984)

G. Wihl: *Ruskin and the Rhetoric of Infallibility* (New Haven and London, 1985)

J. Onians: *Bearers of Meaning: The Classical Orders in Antiquity, the Middle Ages, and the Renaissance* (Princeton, 1988)

D. Freedberg: *The Power of Images: Studies in the History and Theory of Response* (Chicago, 1989)

Decorum in Renaissance Narrative Art: Papers Delivered at the Annual Conference of the Association of Art Historians: London, 1991

ROBERT W. GASTON

Découpage. *See* DÉCOLLAGE.

Decretal. Essentially a papal letter concerning a matter of canonical discipline. Throughout the Middle Ages numerous collections of decretals were compiled, which served as the basis of ecclesiastical administration and canon law; in the 12th century they began to be extensively illustrated.

Decretal, illuminated folio from Gratian: *Decretum*, Italian, 14th century (Rome, Vatican, Biblioteca Apostolica, MS. lat. 1366, fol. 1*r*)

Between the 12th and 15th centuries illustrated canon law manuscripts, primarily comprising decretals, were made and used throughout western Europe, with major centres of production located in such university cities as Paris and Bologna. These books, along with civil law manuscripts, are numerically the most important type of non-liturgical manuscript illustrated in the medieval period, and a wide range of stylistic developments is represented in the hundreds of extant examples.

The earliest illustrations in decretal manuscripts are Trees of Consanguinity and Affinity. These full-page schemata depict degrees of familial relationships in order to demonstrate the legal implications of marriage bonds. The Tree of Consanguinity shows a man standing with outstretched arms before a tree containing the Table of Consanguinity; the affinities were similarly depicted but also included a woman. These illustrations first appeared in manuscripts of the *Collectio canonum* of Burchard of Worms, *c.* 1015, a text that was otherwise undecorated. The first compilation of canon law to be illuminated extensively was the *Decretum*, or *Concordantia discordantium canonum*, written in Bologna *c.* 1140 by a Camaldolese monk named Gratian. This was the first systematic and encyclopedic discussion of Church law, bringing together, in a scholastic fashion, papal, episcopal and conciliar rulings from throughout the history of the Church in an attempt to reconcile seemingly contradictory canons. By the late 12th century, in contrast to Gratian's historical survey, the dominant type of canon law collections were compilations of contemporary decretals. Although there were a number of these, all of which had the potential to be fully illustrated, the most important were the *Decretales* (1234) of Gregory IX, the *Liber sextus* (1298) of Boniface VIII, the *Clementinae* (1325) and the *Extravagantes Ioannis XXII* (1325). These four collections, along with the *Decretum*, were used as university texts as well as reference works in ecclesiastical courts.

A typical page of a canon law manuscript has two central columns of the main text, surrounded on all four margins by a running commentary. Most of the extant copies of these manuscripts are also profusely illustrated. Fully decorated examples appeared in Bologna shortly after Gratian's text first appeared. Thereafter such manuscripts were illuminated throughout western Europe until the end of the 15th century, the most intense period of production occurring in the 14th century. In general, all canon law manuscripts were illuminated in a similar fashion, with illustrations introducing the various divisions within the texts. For example, the *Decretum* is composed of the *Distinctiones*, 36 *Causae* and the *De consecratione*. In a fully illustrated manuscript each of these sections is introduced by various combinations of full-page miniatures, historiated panels or initials, decorative initials, intercolumnar decorations or marginalia (see fig.). The books and titles that comprise the textual divisions of the decretal collections are similarly prefaced by illustrations. The subject-matter of the illustrations is generally innovative, didactic and faithful to the text. As there was no earlier tradition of illuminated legal manuscripts new iconographic programmes and designs had to be created, and although some scenes were derived from contemporary Bibles, most of the illustrations in legal manuscripts are unique. The types of theme represented range from abstract concepts involving the nature and origin of law to concrete images used to illustrate particular canons. The desire to depict individual cases resulted in the frequent appearance of such genre scenes as people arguing cases in court, committing various crimes or performing services to the Church.

UNPUBLISHED SOURCES

Columbus, OH State U. [iconographic index of juridical MSS]

BIBLIOGRAPHY

A. Melnikas: *The Corpus of the Miniatures in the Manuscripts of the Decretum Gratiani*, Studia Gratiana, xvi–xviii (Rome, 1975); review by C. Nordenfalk in *Z. Kstgesch.*, xliii (1980), pp. 318–37

G. von Schmidt: 'Materialen zur französischen Buchmalerei der Hochgotik (kanonistische Handschriften)', *Wien. Jb. Kstgesch.*, xxviii (1975), pp. 159–70

F. Hospital: 'Illustration des livres de droit: Les Manuscrits des décrets de Gratien décorés d'enluminures', *Doss. Archéol.*, xvi/3 (1976), pp. 8–14

H. Schadt: *Die Darstellung der Arbores Consanguinitatis und der Arbores Affinitatis: Bildschemata in juristischen Handschriften* (Tübingen, 1982)

A. von Euw and J. M. Plotzek: *Die Handschriften der Sammlung Ludwig*, iv (Cologne, 1985)

M. HEINLEN

Decumanus. Term for a transverse street in an ancient Roman city. The *decumanus maximus* was the main street running east–west (*see* ROME, ANCIENT, §III, 2).

□

De Curte, Louis (*b* Ghent, 12 March 1817; *d* Brussels, 7 Aug 1891). Belgian architect. He received his architectural training in Paris at the Ecole des Beaux-Arts and then worked in France as a restoration architect under Eugène-Emmanuel Viollet-le-Duc. After returning to Belgium *c.* 1856 he executed several important works of monumental character in Brussels. Chief among these was the flamboyant Gothic Revival monument to *King Leopold I* (completed 1881), erected opposite the Palais Royal in the district of Laeken; its design owes much to the Albert Memorial (completed 1876; London, Kensington Gardens) by George Gilbert I Scott (ii) and perhaps even more to the Scott Memorial (1840–46; Edinburgh, Princes Street) by George M. Kemp. De Curte's rather dry, archaeological manner as a Gothic Revivalist is also seen in the north porch (1881–6), which he added to Brussels Cathedral, already heavily restored and improved. Such works and several restoration projects with which he was involved in Ghent, Tongeren, Halle, Laeken and elsewhere as a member of the Commission Royale des Monuments linked De Curte's name firmly with the Gothic Revival in Belgium. Yet his work was eclectic and unaffiliated with the mainstream Belgian Gothic Revival movement. His Hôtel des Postes (1885–93), Brussels, was a classical building of Second Empire style and strong Parisian flavour. De Curte's nearby façade of the Passage des Postes, which received a prize in the municipal façade competition of 1879, was similarly French in feeling, but with accentuated Baroque overtones carried through in the pierced balconies, rich cornices, caryatids and a broken pediment overflowing with figural sculpture.

BIBLIOGRAPHY

'Sterfgeval', *Vl. Kstbode*, xxi (1891), p. 392

Poelaert et son temps (exh. cat., ed. R. Vandendaele; Brussels, Crédit Com. Belg., 1980), pp. 192–7

ALFRED WILLIS

Dedan. *See under* ARABIA, PRE-ISLAMIC, §§I; II, 2(iv); III, 1.

Dedeke, Wilm [Master of the Halepagen Altar] (*b* Lübeck, *c.* 1460; *d* Hamburg, 1528). German painter. His Lübeck origins are demonstrated stylistically in his contribution to the altar of the Lübeck Corpus Christi Brotherhood (1496; Lübeck, St Annenmus.). In 1499 he probably married a woman previously married, in succession, to Hans Bornemann, Hinrik Funhof and Absalon Stumme (*fl c.* 1486–98): this enabled him to become established in Hamburg as a workshop proprietor. Both Stumme and his wife's son Hinrik Borneman died that year. Dedeke's first task was therefore to complete their work on the wings of the *St Luke* altar for the Jakobikirche in Hamburg. He was accepted into the painters' guild in 1500: in 1502 he became master of the Brotherhood of St Thomas. After his second surviving altarpiece in Hamburg, for the Company of Fishers (1508; Jakobikirche), he probably remained the leading artist of Hamburg until his death.

Dedeke's style remained basically unchanged from the Corpus Christi altar. Of this now incomplete double-winged altarpiece, with a carved shrine by Henning von der Heide, the most interesting scene is the *Banquet of King Ahasuerus*. The figures of this courtly scene, painted in cool, light colours, show an unusual contraction of the faces characteristic of Dedeke: one side is fully frontal, the other reduced to a minimum. An altar (?before 1508) at the Petrikirche, Buxtehude, donated by the magistrate Halepagen, has scenes on the outside showing St Peter with the donor and St Jerome with the portrait head of Hermann Langenbeck, the Hamburg burgomaster, who had the altarpiece completed. (Hasse identified the 'Master of the Halepagen Altar' with Dedeke.) The scenes of *St Peter* in the Fishers' altar of 1508 show a relapse into an archaic rigidity; the deep, spacious landscapes are replaced by set-pieces. Langenbeck's spiritual face appears, unusually, a second time, in a portrait (*c.* 1513; Lübeck, St Annen-Mus., cut down). Dedeke's talent as a portrait painter is also demonstrated by the diptych panels of *A Married Couple* (Bremen, Roseliushaus) and a *Virgin* (Lübeck, St Annen-Mus.).

BIBLIOGRAPHY

M. Hasse: 'Lübecker Maler und Bildschnitzer um 1500', *Niederdt. Beitr. Kstgesch.*, iii (1964), pp. 307–12

HANS GEORG GMELIN

De Domenicis, Gino (*b* Ancona, 1947). Italian conceptual and performance artist. At 17 he mounted his own exhibition (1964; Ancona, Gal. D.D.), before moving to Rome where he was influenced by Arte Povera. His one-man show (1969; Rome, Gal. Attico), for which he published an obituary announcing his death, included traces of 'invisible objects': a square outlined on the floor constituted *Invisible Pyramid*. Such dematerialization was associated with mortality, with which de Domenicis was primarily concerned, investigated through autobiography and self-portraiture, as well as through juxtapositions of Urvasi, the Hindu goddess of beauty, and the partially divine Ghilgamesh, who sought immortality in vain. Invisibility became a paradoxical and primary conceptual means: *D'io* ('of me'/'God', 1971) filled the Galleria

L'Attico with a recording of laughter. Having included live animals in his *Zodiac* exhibition (1970; Rome, Gal. Attico), de Domenicis increasingly used people to embody such concepts as ageing (e.g. the opposition of a young and an old man at Incontri Internazionale d'Arte, Rome, 1971). However, the appearance of a Downs Syndrome boy alongside the 'invisible objects' in *The Second Possibility for Immortality (The Universe is Immobile)* at the Venice Biennale of 1972 caused outcry and his exhibition's closure. He continued to address immortality and the Sumerian myth in the 1980s in an extended series of paintings but avoided disclosing biographical details or participating in monographic exhibitions or publications.

BIBLIOGRAPHY
G. Celant: 'Art to the Power N', *Artforum*, xxv/4 (1986), pp. 100–06
I. Tomassoni: 'Il caso Gino de Domenicis', *Flash A.*, 144 (June 1988), pp. 38–41

MATTHEW GALE

Dedreux, Alfred (*b* Paris, 23 May 1810; *d* Paris, March 1860). French painter and draughtsman. His father was the architect Pierre-Anne Dedreux (1788–1849); Alfred's sister, Louise-Marie Becq de Fouquières (1825–92), was also an artist. His uncle, Pierre-Joseph Dedreux-Dorcy (1789–1874), a painter and intimate friend of Gericault, took Dedreux frequently to the atelier of Gericault whose choice of subjects, especially horses, had a lasting influence on him. During the 1820s he studied with Léon Cogniet, although his early style was more influenced by the work of Stubbs, Morland, Constable and Landseer, exposure to which probably came through Gericault and the painter Eugène Lami who lived in London in the mid-1820s.

Dedreux's stylistic development can be traced from 1830 with the *White Stallion* (exh. Salon 1831; sold London, Sotheby's, 31 March 1965, lot 87), which recalls both the work of Gericault and Stubbs's *Horse Attacked by a Lion* (1770; New Haven, CT, Yale U. A.G.). This style remained unchanged in the *Battle of Baugé* (1838; Narbonne, Mus. A. & Hist.). Although Dedreux did not usually paint history subjects, his penchant for painting horses led him to depict historical cavalry scenes, ranging in size from 1.65×2.30 m (*Baugé*) to 980×810 mm (*White Stallion*). Dedreux's most famous work of the period, *La Fuite* (1840; whereabouts unknown), depicts medieval lovers on horseback and is dominated by his preferred colours at this stage, deep greens, blues and reds, bathed in the brooding light of Romanticism.

Dedreux's mature style dates from *c.* 1848. Although his subjects remained the same, they were characterized by less rugged landscape settings, by luminous colour and crisp light, as in *L'Amazone: Portrait of Marguerite Mosselman Riding in the Champs-de-Mars* (Detroit, MI, Inst. A.). He received medals from the Salons of 1834, 1844 and 1848, the Cross of the Légion d'honneur in 1857, and commissions from the Duc d'Orléans, Queen Victoria and Napoleon III. Archille Giroux (1820–54) and Eugène Ciceri made lithographs after his works. He was killed in a duel provoked by an argument over the price of a painting.

BIBLIOGRAPHY
C. Blanc: *Histoire*, iii (Paris, 1861–76)
J. Doin: 'Alfred Dedreux, 1810–1860', *Gaz. B.-A.*, iv (1921), pp. 237–51

D. F. Mosby: 'Notes on Two Portraits of Alfred Dedreux by Géricault', *A. Mag.*, lviii (1983), pp. 84–5

DEWEY F. MOSBY

Deepadih. Village and temple site on the Rajpur–Shankargarh–Kusmi road on a plateau close to the confluence of the rivers Kanhar, Galphulla and Surya in Madhya Pradesh, India. It flourished between the 7th century AD and the 10th. The temple ruins fall into three groups. One group, in the Oraontola area of the village, consists of a ruined Shiva temple with remains of a sanctum (Skt *garbhagrha*) and hall (*maṇḍapa*) and remnants of pillars and foundations of a few other temples. The largest of these temples yielded a damaged 17-line inscription (in two fragments; *c.* 9th century). A second group, known as Samatsarna, is near the rivers and consists of a large Shiva temple, a five-shrined (*pañcāyatana*) temple with Devi and Chamunda images, a double Shiva temple with three sanctums, a double row of small Shiva temples, a stepwell and the remains and foundations of other shrines. The third group of remains is scattered in the vast area between Samatsarna and Oraontola. It includes a five-shrined Vishnu temple near Samatsarna, four ruined Shiva temples close to an ancient tank with stone embankments known as Ranipokhra (Queen's Tank) near Oraontola and two monastic residences. The temples are mostly in stone, while brick is used in the flooring of the monastic residences. They are generally built on a square or rectangular plan, but two temples are made on the stellate plan popular in South Kosala (*see* INDIAN SUBCONTINENT, §III, 5(i)(f)).

BIBLIOGRAPHY
D. M. Stadtner: 'Ancient Kośala and the Stellate Plan', *Kalādarśana*, ed. J. G. Williams (New Delhi, 1981), pp. 137–45

KALYAN KUMAR CHAKRAVARTY

De Fabris, Emilio (*b* Florence, 28 Oct 1807; *d* Florence, 28 June 1883). Italian architect. He studied at the Accademia di Belle Arti in Florence, where he held a scholarship (1836–8), and then went to Rome, where he studied ancient monuments and collaborated with the archaeologist Antonio Nibby. After that he spent three years in Venice, where he met and became friendly with the critic and art historian Pietro Estense Selvatico. In 1845 he joined the staff of the Accademia in Florence, teaching perspective and later also geometry and architecture; in 1850 he became professor of architecture, a post he retained until 1874, when he was appointed director of the Accademia. From 1870 to 1889 he was a member of various conservation committees in Florence. De Fabris began his own architectural work in 1858, as a consultant for Maiolfi's Camera di Commercio, Florence. In the 1870s he was engaged in various projects, including the restoration of the Palazzo Giugni (1871), Florence, the plans for Leopoldo Galeotti's country villa in Montevettolini (1874), the monumental cemetery of Città di Castello (1878; with Luigi Del Moro) and the plans for the enlargement of the villa of the Demidov princes in Pratolino (1880; unexecuted). His fame is based on the tribune that houses Michelangelo's *David* in the Gallery of the Accademia (begun in 1882), Florence, and above all the new façade of Florence Cathedral. His first plan for the façade dates from 1843, but it was not until 1867, after three competitions for its design, that he emerged as the winner. Because of the long controversy that followed, regarding the choice between a tricuspidal or basilical design, he did not live to see the façade completed; it was finished in May 1887, under Del Moro's direction.

UNPUBLISHED SOURCES

Florence, Archv Stato [papers relating to De Fabris's role in conservation in Florence]

WRITINGS

Del sisteme tricuspidale per il coronamento della facciata di S Maria del Fiore (Florence, 1864)

La facciata di S Maria del Fiore: Appendice artistica (Florence, 1875)

Dell'insegnamento nel Reale Istituto delle Arti del Disegno in Firenze: Rapporto (Florence, 1876)

BIBLIOGRAPHY

M. Tabarrini: *La vita e le opere dell'Arch. Emilio De Fabris* (Florence, 1887)

M. Ferrara: 'Aggiunte a De Fabris', *Architettura in Toscana dal periodo napoleonico allo stato unitario* (Florence, 1978), pp. 47–58

C. Cerretelli: 'Emilio De Fabris: 40 anni di facciate (1843–1883)', *Due granduchi, tre re e una facciata* (Florence, 1987), pp. 203–68

C. Cresti, M. Cozzi and G. Carapelli: *Il Duomo di Firenze, 1822–1887: L'avventura della facciata* (Florence, 1987), pp. 126–8, 153–6, 161–293

MARIO BENCIVENNI

Defernex, Jean-Baptiste (*b* ?Paris, *c.* 1729; *d* ?Paris, 1783). French sculptor. He stood outside the official academic establishment of French art in the 18th century, beginning his career as a modeller at the Vincennes-Sèvres porcelain manufactory, where he worked between 1754 and 1757, prior to the appointment of Etienne-Maurice Falconet as head of the sculpture studio. His task was to translate designs by François Boucher into clay models from which porcelain figures were made. Among his works for Sèvres are the *Milkmaid* and the *Butter Churner* (both Sèvres, Mus. N. Cér.), reduced versions of the stone statuettes designed by Boucher for Mme de Pompadour's dairy at the Château de Crécy, near Abbeville. In 1760 Defernex became a member of the Académie de St-Luc and in 1762 exhibited at its Salon two talc statuettes in a similar charming manner, the *Stone-cutter* and its pendant, the *Girl Shelling Oysters* (both untraced).

Defernex's principal activity was as a portrait sculptor. His earliest known bust, that of *Jacques-François-Léonor de Goyon Matignon, Duc de Valentinois* (bronze, 1750; Paris, Bib. Mazarine), is a sound work but gives no hint of the virtuoso execution and lively grace of his busts of such well-known beauties as the actress *Marie-Justine Duronceray, Mme Favart* (terracotta, 1757; Paris, Louvre) and *Louise-Marie Bailly de Saint-Mars, Mme de Fondville* (terracotta, 1759; Le Mans, Mus. Tessé). His male portraits, such as those of *Prince Nicholas Repnine in the Guise of Hercules* (plaster, 1762; marble, 1764, Paris, Mus. Jacquemart-André) and of *Gabriel de Sartine* (marble, 1774; Versailles, Château), are colder and more formal than his female portraits.

Excluded from royal commissions because he was not a member of the Académie Royale, Defernex obtained the patronage of the Orléans family; about 1763, under the direction of the architect Pierre Contant d'Ivry, he was involved in the decoration of the Palais Royale, Paris, providing stone trophies (*in situ*) for the façade and two gilt-lead lampstands in the form of groups of children (*in situ*) for the great staircase. In 1765 he was appointed assistant professor at the Académie de St-Luc and opened a private school of sculpture and drawing in Paris.

BIBLIOGRAPHY

L. Réau: 'Jean-Baptiste Defernex, sculpteur du duc d'Orléans', *Gaz. B.-A.*, n. s. 6, v (1931), pp. 350–65

Deferrari, Defendente. *See* FERRARI, DEFENDENTE.

De Finetti, Giuseppe (*b* Milan, 5 March 1892; *d* Milan, 19 Jan 1952). Italian architect. He left Milan in 1912 and went first to Berlin and then to Vienna where he studied under Adolf Loos (1913–15). Returning to Italy in 1920, he graduated from the Istituto di Belle Arti in Bologna (1920) and then settled permanently in Milan (1921) where all his executed works are located. Initially his interest centred on the design of hotels, and in 1923 he edited the building sections of the *Manuale dell'industria alberghiera*. In the same year he designed and built the Hotel Touring, Via Parini, in a style that favoured the burgeoning Novecento Italiano, and by 1926 he was participating in the competition for Milan's urban development with some of its members. The Casa della Meridiana (1924–5), Via Marchiondi, a six-storey, stucco-faced building housing five flats, is possibly his best-known work. He combined elements of the modern architecture of Loos—simple volumes, smooth undecorated surfaces and flat roofs—with an elegant and restrained use of classical motifs such as a lightly modelled frieze that defines a two-storey base (also with flat brick quoins) to the whole composition of set-back masses (originally designed to avoid a tree that no longer exists), string courses and pilasters. The house by De Finetti on Via S Calimero (1930) attempts the same stylistic conciliations, and his commitment to tasteful restraint is expressed even more brilliantly in his interior designs for the Bottega di Poesia (1923), Via Montenapoleone, and Negozio Moda (1927), Piazza Duomo (both destr.), and above all in the Villa Crespi (1938) at Ronchi di Vigevano, near Milan. In 1931 political conscience obliged him to resign from the Sindicato d'Architetti, and from this date his interventions took the form of articles on aspects of town-planning development in Milan: the Arena-Parco Sempione district (1933), Piazza S Babila (1937) and Piazza Diaz (1937). This activity was intensified in the period between 1944 and 1950, when war damage made the problem of reconstruction particularly urgent. In 1946–7 he founded and financed a periodical called *La città*, the contents of which were brought together in a book published in 1963.

WRITINGS

Stadi: Esempi, tendenze, progetti (Milan, 1934)

G. Cislaghi, M. De Benedetti and P. Marabelli, eds: *Giuseppe De Finetti: Milano costruzione di una città* (Milan, 1969)

BIBLIOGRAPHY

G. Minucci: 'La casa della Meridiana in Milano dell' arch. Giuseppe De Finetti', *Archit. & A. Dec.*, ii (1926–7), pp. 373–9

F. Reggiori: 'In memoria di Giuseppe De Finetti', *Urbanistica*, 9 (1952)

G. Cislaghi, M. De Benedetti and P. Marabelli, eds: *Giuseppe De Finetti: Progetti, 1920–1951* (Milan, 1981)

GUIDO ZUCCONI

Deforge, Armand-Auguste (*b* Saint-Germain-en-Laye, Yvelines, 1802; *d* Paris, 10 May 1886). French dealer. He was listed in a commercial directory for 1840 as a dealer in artists' materials in Paris, although in 1839 he had exhibited a painting by Narcisse Diaz that had been refused at the Salon and in the same year moved from Rue St Martin to 8 Boulevard Montmartre. There he began to deal more in pictures and showed Thomas Couture's *Young Venetians after an Orgy* (Montrouge, priv. col., see Boime, p. 85), recently hung at the Salon and praised by Théophile Gautier for its elegant composition and light, brilliant colour. During the 1840s Deforge's gallery supported more painters than any other and was considered by several critics, including Champfleury and Baudelaire, as having created a school of painting, known as the 'Ecole Deforge', based on the 18th-century revival of the period. In 1846 Baudelaire named Couture as the leader of this school and discussed some of its adherents, all of whom were supported by Deforge. These included Diaz, Celestin Nanteuil (1813–73), Charles-Louis Muller (1815–92), Henri Baron, Faustin Besson, François Claudius Compte-Calix and Jean-François Millet. The decorative, painterly style of Millet's early work was entirely consistent with the taste associated with the Galerie Deforge. In October 1856 Deforge joined in partnership with Marie Charles Edouard Carpentier and in March of the following year held an important sale of his collection. Several of the 24 lots were works by Constant Troyon, and five were by Couture, including *The Falconer* (1844–5; Toledo, OH, Mus. A.). In 1858 the gallery became known as Deforge et Carpentier. By this time it was no longer buying works of art but rather renting pictures, a common practice of the period. Deforge seems to have gradually withdrawn from artistic concerns and later invested his capital in property, although the gallery, managed by Carpentier, was still in existence as late as 1871.

BIBLIOGRAPHY

A. Boime: *Thomas Couture and the Eclectic Vision* (New Haven, 1980)

A. I. Davenport: *Thomas Couture: The Leader of the 'Ecole de fantaisie' at the Galerie Deforge* (PhD diss., Philadelphia, U. PA, 1981)

N. Davenport: 'Armand-Auguste Deforge: An Art Dealer in Nineteenth-century Paris and "la peinture de fantaisie"', *Gaz. B.-A.*, n. s. 5, ci (1983), pp. 81–8

LINDA WHITELEY

Defrance, Léonard (*b* Liège, 5 Nov 1735; *d* Liège, 25 Feb 1805). Franco-Flemish painter and draughtsman. He was apprenticed in 1745 to Jean-Baptiste Coclers (1698–1772). In 1755 he travelled to Italy to study painting and worked at the Académie de France, Rome, under Laurent Péchéux for a year, assisting Péchéux with his studies from the Antique for Robert Adam. An interest in philosophy led to difficulties with the Inquisition, and in 1760 he left Rome and settled in Montpellier until 1763, exhibiting paintings at the Académie Royale de Peinture in Toulouse each year. Although many of his patrons were from the clergy, Defrance's interests continued to be philosophical and scientific; his portrait of the Toulouse astronomer *Antoine Darquier* (priv. col., see *Mémoires*, p. 56) dates from this period. Defrance found the persecution of Protestants in Toulouse antipathetic to his liberal beliefs and in 1763 returned to Liège. In 1773 he visited the northern Netherlands with Nicolas Fassin and copied the genre paintings of such artists as David Teniers (i) and

Philips Wouwerman. These copies and his own low-life and domestic genre paintings (e.g. *Card Game*, Liège, Mus. A. Wallon) sold well. In the same year Defrance and Fassin opened an academy of which Defrance was director from 1775 to 1784. In 1784 the new Prince-Bishop of Liège, Constantin François de Haensbroech (1724–92), instituted a severely repressive regime, and Defrance went into exile on several occasions. In 1786 and 1787 he exhibited in the Paris Salon de la Correspondance, and in 1791 and 1793 in the Salon Révolutionnaire. After the Revolution of 1789 Defrance became a member of the Assemblée Liégeoise from 1792 to 1794 and of the Conseil Municipal in 1800.

Defrance's best works are those celebrating technological progress and showing men and machinery at work; for example the *Visit to the Tobacco Factory* (*c*. 1787–9; Liège, Mus. A. Wallon). He also painted political and allegorical subjects, such as the *Abolition of Servitude in the Domains of the King of France* (after 1779; priv. col., see 1985–6 exh. cat., p. 355), and made sketches and drawings (e.g. *Blacksmiths Casting Iron*; Liège, Cab. Est. & Dessins).

WRITINGS

Réflexions sur le dessin (Liège, 1772)

Mémoire sur la nature et l'emploi des couleurs (Liège, 1782)

Mémoires (MS.; ?1804); ed. F. Dehousse and M. Pauchen (Liège, 1980)

BIBLIOGRAPHY

T. Vissol: 'Léonard Defrance', *1770–1830: Autour du Néo-classicisme en Belgique* (exh. cat., Brussels, Mus. Ixelles, 1985–6), pp. 353–65, 396

BERNADETTE THOMAS

Defregger, Franz von (*b* Stronach, Tyrol, 30 April 1835; *d* Munich, 2 Jan 1921). Austrian painter. He was first trained in wood-carving by the Innsbruck sculptor Michael Stolz (1820–90), who recognized his talent for oil painting and in 1860 introduced him to Karl Theodor von Piloty in Munich. On Piloty's recommendation, he studied for a year under Hermann Dyck (1842–74) at the private school of the Kunstgewerbeverein, then under Hermann Anschütz (1802–80) at the Munich Akademie. In 1863–4 he was in Paris, but he seems to have been little influenced by developments in contemporary French painting. He returned to Munich, via the Tyrol, in 1864 and entered Piloty's studio, where he remained until 1870, working alongside Hans Makart and Gabriel von Max.

With such pictures as the *Wounded Hunter* (1868; untraced, see Hammer, p. 279), the first in a series of rather sentimental narrative paintings of Tyrolean and Bavarian life, he won immediate public acclaim and established a reputation for peasant genre scenes. In addition to portraits and interiors (e.g. *The Chess Game*, 1880s; priv. col., see Hammer, p. 129), he produced many history paintings: he specialized in portraying episodes from Tyrolean history, particularly scenes from the war of 1809 against the French, for example the various versions of the theme the *Final Call to Arms* (e.g. 1874; Vienna, Belvedere). Technically, Defregger's pictures owe much to his training under Piloty, but they are far less severe in conception than Piloty's own work. In 1878, after successful exhibitions in Vienna (1869 and 1873) and Munich (1870), Defregger was appointed Professor of Painting at the Munich Akademie. He was ennobled in 1883.

For illustration *see* MUNICH, fig. 4.

BIBLIOGRAPHY
H. Hammer: *Franz von Defregger* (Innsbruck, 1940)
H. P. Defregger: *Defregger (1835–1921)* (Rosenheim, 1983)

COLIN J. BAILEY

Degas, (Hilaire Germain) Edgar (*b* Paris, 19 July 1834; *d* Paris, 27 Sept 1917). French painter, draughtsman, printmaker, sculptor, pastellist, photographer and collector. He was a founder-member of the Impressionist group and the leader within it of the Realist tendency. He organized several of the group's exhibitions, but after 1886 he showed his works very rarely and largely withdrew from the Parisian art world. As he was sufficiently wealthy, he was not constricted by the need to sell his work, and even his late pieces retain a vigour and a power to shock that is lacking in the contemporary productions of his Impressionist colleagues.

I. Life and work. II. Working methods and technique. III. Critical reception and posthumous reputation.

I. Life and work.

1. Early years, to 1860. 2. France and New Orleans, 1861–73. 3. Impressionism and Realism, 1874–81. 4. Independence and security, 1882–9. 5. The late works, 1890–1912.

1. EARLY YEARS, TO 1860. The eldest son of a Parisian banking family, he originally intended to study law, registering briefly at the Sorbonne's Faculté de Droit in 1853. He began copying the 15th- and 16th-century Italian works in the Musée du Louvre and in 1854 he entered the studio of Louis Lamothe (1822–69). The training that Lamothe, who had been a pupil of Ingres, transmitted to Degas was very much in the classical tradition; reinforced by the Ecole des Beaux-Arts, which he attended in 1855–6, Degas developed a rigorous drawing style and a conviction of the importance of line that remained with him for the whole of his career. One of his enduring aims was to be a classical painter of modern life: 'My art has nothing spontaneous about it, it is all reflection'.

In 1856 Degas arrived in Italy where he had an extensive family network. His father's sister, Laura Bellelli, was closest to the young painter, and he spent lengthy periods with her and her family in Naples and Florence over the three-year period that he spent in Italy. He also paid several long visits to Rome, where he worked at the Villa Medici with other young French artists and executed a large number of copies after Old Masters. In July 1858 he left Rome for Florence, stopping at Viterbo, Orvieto, Perugia,

1. Edgar Degas: *Bellelli Family*, oil on canvas, 2.0×2.5 m, 1858–67 (Paris, Musée d'Orsay)

2. Edgar Degas: *Gentlemen's Race: Before the Start*, oil on canvas, 485×615 mm, 1862 (Paris, Musée d'Orsay)

Assisi, Spello and Arezzo; during the journey, he made numerous sketches in his notebooks, including drawings of the frescoes by Signorelli at Orvieto. In Florence Degas stayed with the Bellellis until March 1859; during this period he produced dozens of preparatory drawings for a projected family portrait, which he finished in 1867 (the *Bellelli Family*, 1858–67; Paris, Mus. d'Orsay; see fig. 1). The sketches range from rough compositional notations to formal portraits, among them some showing the artist's first use of pastel (*Laura Bellelli*, 1858–9; Paris, Mus. d'Orsay). The final painting, which shows Baron Bellelli seated with his back to the viewer, combines classical serenity with psychological tension; the unconventional composition gives the work an unsettling atmosphere, which is one of the most characteristic aspects of Degas's later portraits.

This formative period spent studying and copying the Italian masters laid the foundations of Degas's later career; study after study reveals the influences that were to have a profound effect on most of Degas's oeuvre. A trip to Siena and Pisa with Gustave Moreau in March 1859 was especially important; together they copied the frescoes of Benozzo Gozzoli in the Campo Santo, Pisa. Moreau broadened Degas's interests, encouraging him to experiment with texture and to develop an appreciation of Delacroix. In April 1859 Degas returned to settle in Paris

with his father, who encouraged him to study further. In 1860 he visited Naples and Florence again.

2. FRANCE AND NEW ORLEANS, 1861–73. In 1861 Degas stayed in Normandy with his friend Paul Valpinçon; together they visited the Haras du Pin stud-farm, which undoubtedly inspired Degas's first racehorse scenes. *Gentlemen's Race: Before the Start* (1862; Paris, Mus. d'Orsay; see fig. 2) is the earliest of his works to have a resolutely contemporary subject. At the Louvre in 1862, while copying Velázquez's *Infanta Maria Margarita*, Degas met Edouard Manet for the first time and through him made contact with the young Impressionists who met at the Café Guérbois.

Until 1865, when Degas exhibited the *Misfortunes of the City of Orléans* (Paris, Mus. d'Orsay) at the Salon, he continued to work on such history paintings as *Semiramis Building Babylon* (1861; Paris, Mus. d'Orsay) and *Young Spartans Exercising* (1860–62; London, N.G.); after that date he concentrated on portraits (*Woman with Chrysanthemums*, 1865; New York, Met.) and racing scenes. In the summer of 1869 Degas returned to the Normandy coast, where he executed a number of pastels before going to meet Manet at Boulogne-sur-Mer. Mostly seashore scenes (e.g. *Cliffs at the Edge of the Sea*, 1869; Paris, Mus. d'Orsay), they are unusual subjects for an artist who normally avoided unpopulated landscapes.

In the 1860s, Degas expanded his subject-matter into the themes of urban leisure typical of Impressionist painting. Towards 1869 he began to make wax sculptures of horses, possibly to help in conceiving and composing such paintings as *The Steeplechase* (1866, reworked 1880–81; Upperville, VA, Paul Mellon priv. col.), and around 1870 he began to take an interest in dance and opera. In 1870, during the Franco-Prussian War, Degas enlisted in the National Guard; in 1871, after the war, he travelled to London. In 1872 he left for New Orleans, where his uncle and two of his brothers were engaged in the cotton trade. While there he painted the *Cotton Market at New Orleans* (1873; Pau, Mus. B.-A.; smaller version (600×730 mm), Cambridge, MA, Fogg). The picture includes several family portraits; carefully chosen as a modern and 'commercial' subject, the Pau version was the first of his works to be bought by a public collection (1878). Other major canvases from this period include the *Orchestra of the Opéra* (c. 1870; Paris, Mus. d'Orsay), *Orchestra Musicians* (1870–71, reworked c. 1874–6; Frankfurt am Main, Städel. Kstinst. & Städt. Gal.) and *Dance Class* (1871; New York, Met.). In 1873 Paul Durand-Ruel bought several of Degas's paintings, including *Dance Class at the Opéra* (1872; Paris, Mus. d'Orsay).

3. IMPRESSIONISM AND REALISM, 1874–81. This was an important period during which Degas considerably broadened his scope and extended his exploration of Realist subject-matter. On 27 December 1873 Degas, Claude Monet, Camille Pissarro, Alfred Sisley, Berthe Morisot, Paul Cézanne and other artists had joined together to form the Société Anonyme Coopérative à Capital Variable des Artistes, Peintres, Sculpteurs, Graveurs etc with the aim of organizing independent exhibitions without juries, selling the works exhibited and publishing a journal. On 15 April 1874 the first exhibition opened at 35 Boulevard des Capucines; Degas exhibited ten works, among them *Carriage at the Races* (c. 1872; Boston, MA, Mus. F.A.). On 15 May, however, the company was dissolved following hostile criticism in the press and lack of buyers. Over the next 22 years, a further seven group exhibitions were held; Degas participated in six, despite a lack of sympathy with some tendencies exhibited by the Impressionists. He shared the group's taste for clear, light painting and for the technique of juxtaposing strokes of paint or pastel, but he rarely painted *en plein air* and seldom directly before the motif, preferring to work up his pictures from memory and from sketches. This emphasis on the role of the imagination distinguished him from Renoir, Monet and Sisley; among the Impressionists he was closest to Pissarro and at one stage to Manet, while in later years he was intermittently intimate with Gauguin.

Degas saw himself as a 'Realist' or 'Naturalist' painter and disliked the term 'Impressionist'; his preference for urban subjects, artificial light and concentration on drawing became increasingly pronounced after the first group exhibition. As a keen observer of everyday scenes, he attempted to capture natural positions and break down movement, grasping its underlying rhythms; this was an essential part of his work, as was made clear in his repetitions and variations on a few themes (e.g. there are over 600 versions of ballerinas). Fascinated by new inventions, he experimented ceaselessly, making technical discoveries in engravings, photography and monotypes. He had a predilection for developing pioneering mixtures of materials and for using a wide variety of techniques, both in his works on paper and canvas and in his sculptures. He viewed his sculptures as stages in the progress of his research into the nature of movement, similar in their way to the photographs of Eadweard Muybridge, which he admired and was influenced by.

At the Second Impressionist Exhibition in 1876 Degas exhibited 24 works including the *Cotton Market at New Orleans*. In 1877 he showed 25 works at the Third Impressionist Exhibition, including his first monotypes. His difference from the other Impressionists was increasingly apparent, and he wanted the fourth exhibition title to be expanded to 'Groupe d'Artistes Indépendants, Réalistes et Impressionnistes'. In 1878 his *Ballet Rehearsal* (1876–7; Kansas City, MO, Nelson–Atkins Mus. A.) was lent by Louisine Havemeyer to a New York exhibition: this was the first time that his work had been shown there. At the Fourth Impressionist Exhibition in 1879 he exhibited 20 paintings and pastels and 5 fans; at the fifth (1880) he exhibited 12 works. A crisis in the Degas family finances in the mid-1870s made it important to him to sell his work; part of the attraction of the monotypes that he started to produce during this period was the rapidity with which they could be executed. Although his prints and pastels were inexpensive, their subjects—brothel scenes and low-life—were not calculated to please the general public. This became particularly clear in 1881, when he showed the *Little Fourteen-year-old Dancer* (wax original; Upperville, VA, Paul Mellon priv. col.) at the Sixth Impressionist Exhibition. A polychrome wax figure fixed on a wooden base, wearing a real tulle tutu, a satin ribbon and a wig, the sculpture created an uproar. The most controversial work at the exhibition, it was seen as the apotheosis of scientific Naturalism: 'The terrible realism of this statuette creates a distinct unease; all ideas about sculpture, about cold, lifeless whiteness . . . are demolished . . . at once refined and barbaric . . . [it is] the only truly modern attempt that I know of in sculpture.' (Huysmans, 1883, pp. 226–7). Reviewers suggested that it should be placed in a museum of zoology or anthropology; it was seen as a social 'type', an ethnological specimen, rather than a work of art. Degas had deliberately encouraged this view of the sculpture by including two portraits of teenage males (untraced; see Lemoisne, 1946–9, nos 638–9) in the exhibition under the title *Criminal Physiognomies*; taken from courtroom sketches of prisoners in the dock, they were presented as part of a semi-scientific examination of contemporary society—a theme that can also be seen in such other works of this period as the *Absinthe Drinker* (1875–6; Paris, Mus. d'Orsay), *Dancer Bowing with Bouquet* (c. 1877; Paris, Mus. d'Orsay) and the *Dancing Lesson* (1881; Philadelphia, PA, Mus. A.).

4. INDEPENDENCE AND SECURITY, 1882–9. By the start of the 1880s Degas was well-established as a major figure in the Parisian art world. His financial troubles were largely over, and by the end of the decade he was able to

be highly selective about selling his work. During this period he became increasingly interested in a variety of women workers: dancers, milliners, café-concert singers and laundresses. The human figure acquired even greater importance in a series of pastels of women washing themselves, including *After the Bath* (1885; Pasadena, CA, Norton Simon Mus.) and *Woman in a Tub* (1885–6; London, Tate; *see* NUDE, fig. 5). In these works the figures dominate the picture, filling a shallow space, and are shown in intimate surroundings with a naturalism that Degas had sought since the beginning of his career; typically, a low point of view brings the viewer right into the scene. In these works Degas studied the gestures and movements of his subjects in a process of research that was described by Félix Fénéon (Fénéon, p. 30):

> It is an art of Realism which however does not stem from a direct vision; as soon as a person knows they are being observed, they lose their naive spontaneity of behaviour. Degas therefore does not copy from life but accumulates a large number of sketches on a single subject from which he derives the indisputable veracity with which he endows his work. Never have paintings evoked so little the painful image of the 'model' who 'poses'.

After the last Impressionist exhibition, in 1886, Degas stopped presenting works at group shows and instead sold his works to a small number of dealers including Durand-Ruel, Boussod & Valadon, Bernheim-Jeune, Hector Brame and Ambroise Vollard. He also made a considerable number of purchases for his own collection of ancient and modern art, including works by Manet (*The Ham*; Glasgow, A.G. & Mus.), El Greco (*St Ildefonso*; Washington, DC, N.G.A.) and Gauguin (the *Moon and the Earth*; New York, MOMA). In 1889 he travelled to Madrid with Giovanni Boldini and then to Tangiers, returning to France by way of Cádiz and Granada. The major works of this period are mainly pastels, variations on the themes of milliners, ironers and women at their toilette, including *At the Milliner's* (1882; New York, Met.), *Ironer* (*c.* 1884–6; Paris, Mus. d'Orsay) and *Bather Lying on the Ground* (1886–8; Paris, Mus. d'Orsay).

5. THE LATE WORKS, 1890–1912. During the last years of Degas's career, his work moved away from Naturalism; his use of colour grew more strident and brilliant and his line more expressive and independent. At this time the artist was close to Gauguin, and such works as the *Return of the Herd* (*c.* 1898; Leicester, Mus. & A.G.) are almost Fauvist in their colouring. Paradoxically, as his work became increasingly non-naturalistic, he launched into a series of landscapes in colour monotype inspired by a journey through Burgundy by horse-drawn caravan with the family of his friend the artist Pierre-Georges Jeanniot (1848–1934). Imaginative re-creations done from memory,

3. Edgar Degas: *Combing the Hair* (*La Coiffure*), oil on canvas, 1.14×1.46 m, *c.* 1896 (London, National Gallery)

they were exhibited by Durand-Ruel in 1892 (*Landscape*, 1890–92; New York, Met.). Towards the end of the 1890s new and still more intense colours appeared in his work in such paintings as *Combing the Hair* (*c.* 1896; London, N.G.; see fig. 3), in a range of flaming reds and oranges, and in the pastel series of *Russian Dancers* (e.g. of 1899; Houston, TX, Mus. F.A.), in electric blues, pinks and purples. His modelling became cursory and the figures more angular and distorted (e.g. *Fallen Jockey*, *c.* 1896–8; Basle, Kstmus.). After 1900 he began to use tracing paper as a support, treating familiar subjects with a strong black outline and searing colours (*After the Bath*, 1896–1907; Paris, Mus. A. Déc.). Other important works from this period include the *Morning Bath* (*c.* 1895; Chicago, IL, A. Inst.), *After the Bath* (*c.* 1896; Philadelphia, PA, Mus. A.) and *Two Bathers on the Grass* (*c.* 1896; Paris, Mus. d'Orsay). Depressed by failing eyesight and poor health and distressed by an enforced move from his lodgings of 20 years, he produced no more works after 1912.

II. Working methods and technique.

1. Drawing. 2. Printmaking. 3. Sculpture. 4. Pastel.

1. DRAWING. Degas never forgot the emphasis on the importance of line that he had received during his early training. His use of a clear, hard outline distinguished his works from those of the other Impressionists. A consummate draughtsman, he worked with both energy and delicacy. While he sometimes indicated a desire to follow a specific working method (see Guérin, p. 219), in reality he allowed himself to be carried away by a spontaneous ardour, which can be seen in all his drawings. During the earlier part of his career he drew large numbers of preparatory studies for all his historical paintings. Starting with disparate elements of varied origins (Assyrian, Egyptian, Greek and Italian), he integrated them into his composition to achieve a genuine synthesis. While working on a piece, Degas would frequently recall an image he had seen previously and copy it; he would then go on to reinterpret it, often preserving the original movement or position but stylizing the details. This method, based on the progressive assembly of accumulated elements, conformed to the 19th-century academic tradition of Ingres and Moreau. In the drawings executed in his youth Degas showed a need to relate his work to that of his great predecessors and in addition revealed one of his most impressive abilities, the capacity for observation that enabled him to capture an image, a gesture or a movement, so evident in his later work. An attentive observer of the most diverse scenes, he took a passionate interest in everyday gestures. He would often draw a figure from several angles and execute various studies of the same subject on a single page (*Four Studies of a Dancer*, 1878–9; Paris, Mus. d'Orsay). The juxtaposition of these studies within the space of a single sheet, oriented in different directions, suggests movement. Degas invented many ways of breaking up his forms, isolating a detail in order to intensify perception and multiplying the facets of a figure the better to explore it. He always preferred pencils and pastels to such water-based media as watercolour, as opaque techniques allowed more spontaneity in working and were easier to change. In 1897 a series of 20 of his early drawings, *Degas: Vingt dessins, 1861–1869*, was published in Paris.

2. PRINTMAKING. Degas worked extensively in black and white (*see* ETCHING, §V) and in colour, producing etchings (e.g. *Aux Ambassadeurs*, 1875; Paris, Bib. N.; *see* PRINTS, fig. 5), lithographs and, most importantly, monotypes (the application of black or coloured paint or ink with a high oil content to a zinc or copper metal-plate; *see* MONOTYPE, fig. 2). He had been introduced to the monotype method by Ludovic Lepic in 1876; the *Ballet Master* (1876; Washington, DC, N.G.A.) carries the signature of both artists. Degas worked on the plate in a variety of intaglio techniques before applying a damp sheet of paper and placing the ensemble in a press. Normally only the first impression produced by this method is considered adequate; Degas, however, generally did not restrict himself to a single print but used the same plate until every trace of colour had been used up. He then used the last residual impressions as the basis of new compositions, which he picked out in pastel. Between 1876 and 1881 more than two-thirds of his works in colour were pastelized monotypes (e.g. *Women on the Terrace (A Café on the Boulevard Montmartre)*, 1877; Paris, Mus. d'Orsay; *see* URBAN LIFE, fig. 2). In the 1890s he executed a series of landscapes in this way; with a very distinctive, hazy texture, they have uneven patches made by the marks of the brushes, rag, inking pad and the artist's fingers when he applied the ink by hand (e.g. *Landscape*, 1892; Geneva, Gal. Jan Krugier).

Degas was fired by the effects of the contrast between the basic image on the plate—reconstructed in the form of the inverted print—and the variations made possible by the use of pastels, which he applied directly to pick out the forms, creating a play between the image laid down indirectly on the plate and the line drawn directly on the paper. Sometimes he would wet the pastel embellishments copiously in order to obtain smooth areas and runs. Each colour was applied to the plate in a different manner, using a fine brush, a dry brush or a brushtip to suggest a clump of trees, or vertical lines to represent a mass of trees. These textural effects served to differentiate the elements. Degas's research was essentially into tactical perception, and he viewed these works as scientific experiments. His unremitting fascination with variations on a single theme led to the development of such monotype series as *Leaving the Bath*, which has 22 states (e.g. 14th state, 1879–80; Williamstown, MA, Clark A. Inst.).

3. SCULPTURE. From the late 1860s Degas produced numerous small sculptures in wax. He concentrated on the subjects that feature in his two-dimensional works—horses, dancers and women washing. The combination of soft wax and frail armatures (often cork) meant that the sculptures were highly perishable: many crumbled during the artist's lifetime, and he often reworked them. His interest in sculpture increased from the mid-1880s and is often attributed to his failing eyesight.

Although these works were largely private and intended almost as sketches, some were quite elaborate: *The Tub* of

1889 (bronze version; Edinburgh, N.G.) originally included a real sponge in the bather's hand and a cloth frill around the bathtub. The only sculpture he decided to exhibit was the *Little Fourteen-year-old Dancer*, which he included in the Impressionist exhibition of 1881. He had thought of having his wax pieces cast in bronze, but in fact casts were only made in 1919, after his death. The caster Adrien Hébrard used the lost-wax method to produce 22 or more copies of each sculpture.

4. PASTEL. Pastel opened up several possibilities for Degas: contours could be defined by lines or by hatching, which could then be covered by layers of paint, concealing the strokes and blurring the forms. He used various techniques on a single sheet of paper, executing some elements sharply and leaving others blurred. His virtuosity in this medium appears in *The Star* (or *Dancer on Stage*, *c.* 1878; Paris, Louvre; see fig. 4): the dancer's body is lit from below by a spotlight, which marks her neck and chin with a flash of white. The composition is vertiginous and slants diagonally; Degas left a large empty space in the lower left-hand part of the picture, indicating the space occupied by the stage. Dazzling colours—red, ochre, green and turquoise—radiate across the picture in a series of brusque, informal and highly visible lines. In this work, the use of pastels made it possible to represent the swiftness and immediacy of the subject seized in midmovement. Intense colours co-exist with sharply contrasting brown or black tones standing out against them, for

4. Edgar Degas: *The Star* (or *Dancer on Stage*), pastel, 600×440 mm, *c.* 1878 (Paris, Musée du Louvre)

example in the silhouette of the man in evening dress halfhidden behind the stage set, brushed in with a few brief strokes. This kind of framing became increasingly important in Degas's work from the 1870s onwards; he often accentuated the oddity of his compositions by framing them in such a way as to allow the viewer to see only part of a silhouette or a figure, a common Impressionist device that he used especially drastically to give an unsettling feeling to familiar scenes (*At the Café des Ambassadeurs*, 1885; Paris, Mus. d'Orsay). He also regularly used close-ups of faces lit from below, as if by footlights, in scenes connected with the stage—ballet, opera and café-concerts.

As with his oils, prints and sculptures, Degas tended to produce series of pastels on a single subject. In 1869 he began a series of women ironing; often blended with charcoal and white chalk, these works may have influenced Picasso's Blue Period. Around 1876 dancers became his major theme; he used pastels to capture moments of fleeting equilibrium with a rare dynamic intensity (*see* IMPRESSIONISM, colour pl. VI, fig. 1, and PASTEL, colour pl. III). In the 1880s more vigorous lines began to enclose the contours of the figures, and the forms were more clearly marked out against the surrounding space. Towards 1885 Degas obtained some innovative mixtures by superimposing layers of pastels; a linear structure delimited each different, densely textured area of colour, while stratifications, stripes, streaks and hatching created shades and hues of colour that were difficult to define. Most of the pastels executed during this period have daring layouts and show both skilful organization of line and accentuated schematization (e.g. *Dancers on the Stage*, *c.* 1882–4; Dallas, TX, Mus. F.A.). By *c.* 1886 Degas's pastels were more briefly sketched out than previously; they were worked in stripes and zigzags, displaying a more violent style of execution in a more acid range of colours (*Reclining Bather*, 1886–8; Paris, Mus. d'Orsay). Around 1895 Degas used the medium in a new manner. He was growing old, and his sight was deteriorating, but he succeeded in imbuing his works with a new power. His line was less precise; he reworked the outlines time after time, allowing layers of different colours to overlap; he varied his methods, using parallel lines, intersecting hatching, stripes, short and broken lines and white chalk highlights. The combination of different layers of colour, with their unexpected tonal interrelations, created unusual harmonies. Forms and colours melted into one another in these pastels, and Degas's figures were more fully integrated into backgrounds whose purely descriptive elements seemed as if absorbed into his colour and light, although he was still using the same subjects (*After the Bath*, *c.* 1896; Philadelphia, PA, Mus. A.).

Degas continued to work in pastels during the last period of his life as he pursued the theme of dancers resting. He made this the object of extensive research; every gesture of an arm or a leg was used in the play of curve and counter-curve. Around 1910 he began to work with increasing freedom, emphasizing colour with splashes and patches of luminous pastel powder, as in *Two Dancers Resting* (*c.* 1910; Paris, Mus. d'Orsay).

III. Critical reception and posthumous reputation.

Largely free from the financial pressures of his Impressionist colleagues, Degas was able to view public criticism of his works with a degree of detachment. Up to the New Orleans period, he produced few works for public exhibition, apart from the history paintings destined for the Salon, and spent most of his time working on portraits of his family and friends. Once he had begun to show in the Impressionist group exhibitions, he never returned to the Salon; unlike Monet and Renoir, who continued to hope for fashionable portrait commissions and positive reviews from establishment journals, he always maintained a certain independence. Within the group, Degas's works were usually singled out as substantially different in feeling from the other pictures on show. Charges of sloppy paintwork, incompetent drawing and lack of finish, which were the staple complaints about Impressionism, were not generally levied at Degas—Emile Zola indeed criticized the *Cotton Market at New Orleans* for excessive clarity and detail. Instead, it was the subject-matter of Degas's work that aroused critical ire; the ugliness of his models was a constant theme, and his fascination with Parisian low-life was either approved of or disliked according to the viewer's position on Realism. From the 1874 show onwards Degas was cited by the more discerning critics as the head of the Realist or Naturalist faction within the Impressionist group; the Realist novelist Edmond de Goncourt described him as 'the one who has been able to capture the soul of modern life'. Louis-Edmond Duranty, a close friend and eloquent advocate of the artist, singled out Degas and Gustave Caillebotte as representing the most vital tendency within the Parisian avant-garde in *La Nouvelle Peinture* (Paris, 1876), the first substantial publication devoted to the Impressionists. By the late 1880s Degas enjoyed a privileged position: he was able to choose his dealers, to exhibit only when he wished to and to lead a rather reclusive existence, secure in the knowledge that discerning buyers and respectful reviews were guaranteed. As he moved away from Realism to a style closer to Symbolism, he won the admiration of a new generation of painters, among them Gauguin and Odilon Redon, who recorded his view of Degas in a journal entry of 1889: 'Respect here, absolute respect' (*A Soi-même: Journal*, Paris, 1922, p. 93).

By 1917 Degas had become almost a public monument; after his death, his reputation mounted steadily. Many of his works entered public collections in Europe, the USA and Japan; most major museums of modern art have acquired at least one Degas. Since the publication (1946–9) of a catalogue raisonné by Lemoisne, there has been a constant stream of research and exhibitions devoted to Degas; a major retrospective (1988–9) in Paris, Ottawa and New York produced an authoritative catalogue and a spate of critical discussion, much of it focused on the issue of Degas's representations of women, which have been variously interpreted as misogynistic and as proto-feminist.

WRITINGS

M. Guérin, ed.: *Lettres de Degas* (Paris, 1931, rev. 1945; Eng. trans., rev., Oxford, 1947)
T. Reff, ed.: *The Notebooks of Edgar Degas*, 2 vols (London, 1976, rev. New York, 1986)

BIBLIOGRAPHY

GENERAL

L. E. Duranty: *La Nouvelle Peinture* (Paris, 1876)
J.-K. Huysmans: *L'Art moderne* (Paris, 1883)

L. Delteil: 'Degas', *Le Peintre-graveur illustré*, ix (Paris, 1906–26; New York, 1969)
L. W. Havemeyer: *Sixteen to Sixty: Memoirs of a Collector* (New York, 1961)
F. Fénéon: *Oeuvres plus que complètes*, ed. J. U. Halperin (Geneva, 1970) [incl. his reviews of the Impressionist exhibitions]
J. Rewald: 'Theo van Gogh, Goupil and the Impressionists', *Gaz. B.-A.*, 6th ser., lxxxi (1973), pp. 1–108
R. Huyghe: *La Relève du réel: Impressionnisme, symbolisme* (Paris, 1974)
Centenaire de l'impressionnisme (exh. cat. by A. Dayez and others; Paris, Grand Pal.; New York, Met.; 1974–5)
The Painterly Print: Monotype from the Seventeenth to the Twentieth Century (exh. cat. by B. S. Shapiro; New York, Met.; Boston, MA, Mus. F.A.; 1980–81)
The New Painting: Impressionism, 1874–1886 (exh. cat., ed. C. Moffett; Washington, DC, N.G.A.; San Francisco, F.A. Museums; 1986)
La Sculpture française au XIXe siècle (exh. cat., Paris, Grand Pal., 1986)

MONOGRAPHS AND COLLECTIONS OF ESSAYS

P.-A. Lemoisne: *Degas* (Paris, 1912)
J. Meier-Graefe: *Degas* (Munich, 1920/R 1924; Eng. trans., London, 1923)
P. Jamot: *Degas* (Paris, 1924)
A. Vollard: *Degas* (Paris, 1924)
P. Valéry: *Degas, danse, dessin* (Paris, 1934/R 1965)
J. Lassaigne: *Edgar Degas* (Paris, 1945)
J. Fèvre: *Mon oncle Degas* (Geneva, 1949)
D. C. Rich: *Degas* (New York, 1951)
P. Cabanne: *Edgar Degas* (Paris, 1957)
T. Reff: *Degas: The Artist's Mind* (New York, 1976)
I. Dunlop: *Degas* (New York, 1979; Fr. trans., Neuchâtel, 1979)
M. Sérullaz: *L'Univers de Degas* (Paris, 1979)
A. Terrasse: *Edgar Degas* (Frankfurt am Main, Berlin and Vienna, 1981)
R. McMullen: *Degas: His Life, Times and Work* (Boston, 1984)
R. Kendall, ed.: *Degas, 1834–1984* (Manchester, 1985)
D. Sutton: *Edgar Degas: Life and Work* (New York, 1986)
Burl. Mag., cxxx/1020 (1988) [issue ded. to Degas]

CATALOGUES RAISONNÉS AND EXHIBITION CATALOGUES

J. Rewald: *Degas: Works in Sculpture: A Complete Catalogue* (New York and London, 1944)
P.-A. Lemoisne: *Degas et son oeuvre*, 4 vols (Paris, 1946–9/R with suppl. by P. Brame and T. Reff, New York and London, 1984)
Edgar Degas: His Family and Friends in New Orleans (exh. cat., New Orleans, LA, Delgado Mus., 1965)
Drawings by Degas (exh. cat. by J. S. Boggs; St Louis, MO, A. Mus.; Philadelphia, PA, Mus. A.; Minneapolis, MN, Soc. F.A.; 1967)
Degas Monotypes (exh. cat. by E. P. Janis, Cambridge, MA, Fogg, 1968)
Degas: Oeuvres du Musée du Louvre (exh. cat., Paris, Mus. Orangerie, 1969)
J. Adhémar and F. Cachin: *Edgar Degas: Gravures et monotypes* (Paris, 1973; Eng. trans., New York, 1974)
The Degas Bronzes (exh. cat. by C. Millard, Dallas, TX, Mus. F.A., 1974)
Edgar Degas: The Reluctant Impressionist (exh. cat. by B. S. Shapiro, Boston, MA, Mus. F.A., 1974)
The Complete Sculptures of Degas (exh. cat., intro. J. Rewald; London, Lefevre Gal., 1976)
Degas (exh. cat. by F. Daulte; Tokyo, Seibu Mus. A.; Kyoto, City A. Mus.; Fukuoka, Cult. Cent.; 1976–7)
Degas in the Metropolitan (exh. cat., New York, Met., 1977) [the Charles S. Moffett col.]
Degas and the Dance (exh. cat. by L. D. Muehlig; Northampton, MA, Smith Coll. Mus. A., 1979)
Degas, 1879 (exh. cat. by R. Pickvance, Edinburgh, N.G., 1979)
Degas: La Famille Bellelli (exh. cat., intro. Y. Brayer; Paris, Mus. Marmottan, 1980)
Degas et la famille Bellelli (exh. cat. by H. Finsen, Copenhagen, Ordrupgaardsaml., 1983)
Degas in the Art Institute of Chicago (exh. cat. by R. R. Brettall and S. Folds McCullagh, Chicago, IL, A. Inst., 1984)
Edgar Degas: Pastelle, Ölskizzen, Zeichnungen (exh. cat. by G. Adriani, Tübingen, Ksthalle, 1984)
Degas: The Dancers (exh. cat. by G. Shackelford, Washington, DC, N.G.A., 1984–5)
Degas e l'Italia (exh. cat. by H. Loyrette, Rome, Villa Medici, 1984–5)
Degas: Le Modelé et l'espace (exh. cat., Paris, Cent. Cult. Marais, 1984–5)

Edgar Degas: The Painter as Printmaker (exh. cat. by S. W. Reed and B. S. Shapiro; Boston, MA, Mus. F.A.; Philadelphia, PA, Mus. A.; London, Hayward Gal.; 1984–5)

Degas Monotypes (exh. cat. by A. Griffiths, London, Hayward Gal., 1985)

Degas scultore (exh. cat.; Florence, Pal. Strozzi; Verona, Pal. Forti; 1986)

R. Fernandez and A. R. Murphy: *Degas in the Clark Collection* (Williamstown, MA, Clark A. Inst. cat., 1987)

The Private Degas (exh. cat. by R. Thomson; U. Manchester, Whitworth A.G.; Cambridge, Fitzwilliam; 1987)

Degas (exh. cat.; Paris, Grand Pal.; Ottawa, N.G.; New York, Met.; 1988–9) [extensive bibliog.]

Degas: Images of Women (exh. cat. by R. Kendall, Liverpool, Tate, 1989)

Degas (exh. cat. by R. Pickvance, Martigny, Fond. Pierre Gianadda, 1993)

SPECIALIST STUDIES

G. Moore: 'Degas: The Painter of Modern Life', *Mag. A.*, xiii (1890), pp. 416–25

——: 'Memories of Degas', *Burl. Mag.*, xxxii (1918), pp. 22–9, 63–5

L. Burroughs: 'Degas in the Havemeyer Collection', *Bull. Met.*, xxvii (1932), pp. 141–6

D. Rouart: *Degas à la recherche de sa technique* (Paris, 1945)

——: *Degas monotypes* (Paris, 1948)

L. Browse: *Degas Dancers* (London, [1949])

D. Cooper: *Pastels by Edgar Degas* (Basle, 1952/*R* New York, 1953)

J. S. Boggs: 'Degas Notebooks at the Bibliothèque Nationale', *Burl. Mag.*, c (1958), pp. 163–71, 196–205, 240–46

——: *Portraits by Degas* (Berkeley, 1962)

——: 'Edgar Degas and Naples', *Burl. Mag.*, cv (1963), pp. 273–6

R. Pickvance: 'Degas's Dancers, 1872–1876', *Burl. Mag.*, cv (1963), pp. 256–66

T. Reff: 'Degas's Copies of Older Art', *Burl. Mag.*, cv (1963), pp. 241–51

——: 'The Chronology of Degas's Notebooks', *Burl. Mag.*, cvii (1965), pp. 606–16

R. Pickvance: 'Some Aspects of Degas's Nudes', *Apollo*, lxxxiii (1966), pp. 17–23

E. P. Janis: 'The Role of the Monotype in the Working Method of Degas', *Burl. Mag.*, cix (1967), pp. 20–27, 71–81

G. Monnier: 'Les Dessins de Degas du Musée du Louvre: Historique de la collection', *Rev. Louvre*, 6 (1969), pp. 359–68

C. W. Millard: *The Sculpture of Edgar Degas* (Princeton, 1976)

G. Monnier: 'La Genèse d'une oeuvre de Degas: *Sémiramis construisant une ville*', *Rev. Louvre*, 5–6 (1978), pp. 407–26

R. Thomson: 'Degas in Edinburgh', *Burl. Mag.*, cxxi (1979), pp. 674–7

M. E. Shapiro: 'Three Late Works by Edgar Degas', *Bull. Mus. F.A., Houston* (Spring 1982), pp. 9–22

A. Terrasse: *Degas et la photographie* (Paris, 1983)

E. Lipton: *Looking into Degas: Uneasy Images of Women and Modern Life* (Berkeley and Los Angeles, 1986)

R. Thomson: 'Degas's Nudes at the 1886 Impressionist Exhibition', *Gaz. B.-A.*, 6th ser., cviii (1986), pp. 187–90

R. Kendall: *Degas Landscapes* (New Haven, 1993)

GENEVIÈVE MONNIER

Degenerate art. *See* ENTARTETE KUNST.

Deglane, Henri-Adolphe-Auguste (*b* Paris, 10 Dec 1855; *d* Laussel, Dordogne, 13 May 1931). French architect and teacher. He entered the Ecole des Beaux-Arts, Paris, in 1874 as a pupil of Louis-Jules André and won the Prix de Rome in 1881. His student *envois* from Rome attracted considerable attention, in particular his restoration of the imperial palaces on the Palatine hill. After some success in public competitions, notably for monuments, including the Carnot monument (1881) at Nolay (Côte d'Or), Deglane obtained a number of official posts in Paris, first in the Conseil des Bâtiments Civils (1885), then as Inspecteur des Travaux for the Exposition Universelle (1889) and for the Louvre and Tuileries (1890); he finally became chief architect in the Conseil (1894). His highly original competition project for the rebuilding of the Opéra-Comique (1893) was unsuccessful, but his career as a designer began in earnest in 1896 when he won second

prize (with René Binet) in the competition for the Grand-Palais on the Champs-Elysées, intended for the Exposition Universelle of 1900. Commissioned to design the main façade and central exhibition space, Deglane combined a grand stone façade in the French Baroque style, enhanced with polychromy, with a soaring iron-framed structure behind, which utilized the latest structural technology. A series of free-standing sculpted figures completes the palatial character of the building. Deglane's government work included construction of the government house at Dakar (1904), Senegal, and the French West Africa Pavilion at the Colonial Exhibition (1906), Marseille. Of his private commissions, two of his Parisian blocks of flats, both in the 7e arrondissement, were awarded prizes in the façade competitions held by the City of Paris: at 90 Rue de Grenelle (1906) and at 12 bis Avenue Elisée-Reclus (1910), where a stork motif recurs on the façade in brick, stone and ceramic tiles and in the wrought-iron balconies. Deglane was a professor at the Ecole des Beaux-Arts for 40 years and was elected to the Institut in 1918.

BIBLIOGRAPHY

Thieme–Becker

Obituary, *Suppl. Bull. Mens. Soc. Cent. Architectes*, 5 (1931)

VINCENT BOUVET

Degler, Hans (*b* ?Munich, 1564; *d* Weilheim, *c.* 1635). German sculptor. He was one of the leading sculptors active in Weilheim. During the late 16th and early 17th centuries this small Bavarian town produced a disproportionate number of major sculptors, including Adam and Hans Krumpper, Bartholomäus Steinle (*c.* 1580–1628/9), Hans Spindler (*c.* 1597–*c.* 1660), Christoph Angermair, Philipp Dirr (*fl* 1617–25), Melchior Pendl (*fl* 1617–31) and Georg Petel. Degler probably trained with Adam Krumpper between *c.* 1576 and 1582, and he worked with him in the Hofkapelle of the Munich Residenz in 1590 and on other projects for Duke William V in 1593 and 1595. He settled in Weilheim, where in 1590 he acquired citizenship and married Krumpper's daughter Helene. From 1607 to 1628 Degler served on councils in Weilheim. His final years were beset with financial problems, and he sold his house in 1626 to settle debts. Although he had a difficult personality, Degler enjoyed great success as a teacher. Besides his sons David (1600/05–82) and Andreas, he had at least eight pupils, including Spindler, Angermair and Hans Jakob Zürn (*fl* 1617–*c.* 1635).

From 1600 to 1630 Degler's career is fairly clear. At least 25 projects are either signed or documented and another 13 are attributed to him; unfortunately, only about half of these survive. His most famous and earliest creations are the high altar (1604; see fig.), two side altars (1607) and pulpit (*c.* 1608) in SS Ulrich und Afra, Augsburg. The three lime-wood altars are monumental, measuring between 21 m and 23 m high, each having around 50 figures, often life-size. They form a coherent ensemble reminiscent of a massive triptych, their unity heightened by their nearly identical designs. The large central scenes of the *Adoration of the Shepherds* (high altar), the *Pentecost* (St Afra altar) and the *Resurrection* (St Ulrich altar) are each placed in a large arch flanked by single standing saints in the smaller arches, to form an ornate triumphal arch. Each has five horizontal zones, from the large predella

Hans Degler: *Adoration of the Shepherds*, detail from the high altar, lime-wood, h. *c.* 22 m, 1604 (Augsburg, SS Ulrich und Afra)

Gothic features, such as the rich polychromy and complex designs, were intentionally revived.

Besides carving numerous smaller altarpieces for Bavarian and Austrian churches (untraced), Degler specialized in richly painted life-size statues of the Virgin and Child such as that of *c.* 1615 in the Franciscan monastery in Ingolstadt. Mary is regally dressed and crowned as the Queen of Heaven or she is posed as Virgin of the Apocalypse, either standing or seated on a cloud with her feet on a crescent moon.

Degler continued to receive commissions for altarpieces and religious statues until at least 1630. Between 1629 and 1631 he completed the high altar begun by his close friend Bartholomäus Steinle in the Stiftskirche, Polling.

BIBLIOGRAPHY
K. Feuchtmayr: 'Hans Degler: Leben und Schaffen eines Weilheimer Bildschnitzers', *Das Bayerland*, l (1939), pp. 539–48
W. Zohner: 'Hans Degler (1564–1634/35): Ein Beitrag zur Erforschung seines Wirkens', *Lech-Isar-Land* (1977), pp. 76–89
K. Kosel: 'Ein neuentdecktes Hauptwerk Hans Deglers: Seine religiösen und künstlerischen Voraussetzungen', *Jb. Ver. Augsburg. Bistumsgesch.*, xvi (1982), pp. 268–92
R. Laun: *Studien zur Altarbaukunst in Süddeutschland, 1560–1650* (Munich, 1982), pp. 116–31
I. Igler: 'Die Schicksale der Hofheimer Degler-Madonna', *Lech-Isar-Land* (1985), pp. 162–6
H. J. Savermost: *Die Weilheimer* (Munich, 1988), pp. 79–92
I. Igler: 'Hans Deglers Werke zwischen München und Ingolstadt', *Lech-Isar-Land* (1990), pp. 162–9

JEFFREY CHIPPS SMITH

degli' [degli]. For pre-19th-century Italian proper names with this preposition, *see under* the second part of the name.

Degottex, Jean (*b* Sathonay, nr Lyon, 25 Feb 1918; *d* Paris, 6 Dec 1988). French painter, draughtsman and sculptor. From the early 1950s he showed an interest in mark-making and in the rendering of calligraphic shapes engaging both the surface and the space of the paper or canvas (e.g. *Sea Spears*, 1954; Paris, Gal. Fournier), an approach similar to the Surrealist method of automatic writing and drawing. In 1955 he held an exhibition at the Galerie l'Etoile Scellée in Paris. André Breton co-wrote the preface to the catalogue and pointed out Degottex's strong affinity to Zen philosophy and to the drawings of 12th-century Oriental calligraphers. Shortly after, directed in part by Breton, Degottex began a comprehensive study of the history of Oriental calligraphy and read histories of Zen painting from the 8th century to the 12th. His works from the late 1950s to the mid-1960s are an attempt to express the soul of the artist through the spirit of Zen thought. Several quickly executed strokes of paint or India ink are placed against a thinly painted contrasting monochromatic background suggesting the 'void' often referred to in Eastern philosophies (e.g. *Untitled 4*, 1957; Dunkirk, Mus. A. Contemp.). He was concerned at this time with the purity and pre-eminence of a line and the energy it exuded, and he attached great significance to the physical gesture that created the 'sign'.

By the mid-1960s Degottex was increasingly using the more placid, self-contained motif of a circle. Although he focused more on the material properties of paint, canvas and paper, his works still retained a transcendent quality.

beneath to the angel holding a laurel crown at the apex. Some critics credit Hans Krumpper, Degler's brother-in-law, with the overall design, on the evidence of Krumpper's other altar sketches and the documented collaboration between the two masters on other projects such as the *SS Philip and James* (1610; Altötting, Pfarrkirche, untraced). This is plausible but does not diminish Degler's sculptural contribution.

Degler's style is best seen in the high altar, a brilliant realization of the Counter-Reformation *theatrum sacrum*. The adoring Mary, Joseph and shepherds are fully carved limewood figures set on a spacious stage. Their bold, even overstated, gestures are both theatrically effective and needed to be clearly legible to the worshippers in the nave. The multitude of angels praying and singing above the infant Jesus heightens the festive mood. The ensemble, especially the humanity of Mary and Joseph and the unbridled responses of the shepherds, consciously evokes comparison with popular Bavarian nativity plays. Degler exploited the strong light from the three large windows, creating contrast through deep undercutting, fractured drapery surfaces and the figures' placement within the deep stage. The Weilheim painter Elias Greither I's brilliant, almost garish, polychromy strengthens the play of light and the theatrical impact. Degler's Augsburg altars, like Jörg Zürn's high altar in the Nikolauskirche, Überlingen, testify to the renewed interest in monumental wooden altarpieces in southern Germany *c.* 1600. Many Late

Burnt, torn and folded papers often overlapped in the manner of a collage. The support for *Paper Bag 5* (1966; artist's estate), for example, is a torn and creased bag for cement. From the early 1970s he generally abandoned a figure–ground relationship. Such works as those comprising the *Media* series (1972–3) deal instead with large fields of acrylic paint and areas of India ink; a thin horizontal strip of light paper or unprimed canvas often bisects the compositions. Many works of the mid-1980s have expanses of white cotton canvas ground with parallel and widely spaced corrugated strokes of acrylic paint, often set slightly off the perpendicular (e.g. *Traces oblicollor (III) 22–5*, 1984; artist's estate). Degottex usually worked in series, insisting that his compositions be displayed sequentially and with the actual space between each painting being given as much importance as the painted space. In his last years he also expressed the primacy of simple shape and texture in a series of wood sculptures.

BIBLIOGRAPHY
Jean Degottex (exh. cat. by R. Beslon, Paris, Gal. Kleber, 1958)
Degottex (exh. cat., intro. M. C. Beaud; Grenoble, Mus. Peint. & Sculpt.; Saint-Etienne, Mus. A. & Indust.; 1978), pp. 9–46
Ecritures dans la peinture (exh. cat. by G.-G. Lemaire, Nice, Villa Arson, 1983)
J. Frémon: *Degottex* (Paris, 1986) [bilingual text]
E. Daniel: 'Jean Degottex: "Entre deux vides, tout est dans l'intention"', *Artstudio*, 9 (1988), pp. 104–11
Croisement de signes (exh. cat., ed. M. Métalsi; Paris, Inst. Monde Arab., 1989) [bilingual text]
KIRK MARLOW

Degouve de Nuncques, William (*b* Monthermé, France, 28 Feb 1867; *d* Stavelot, 1 March 1935). Belgian painter of French birth. After the Franco-Prussian war (1870–71), his parents settled in Belgium. Although self-taught, he was advised by Jan Toorop, with whom he shared a studio, and later lived with Henry de Groux. In 1894 he married Juliette Massin, a painter and Emile Verhaeren's sister-in-law, who introduced him to the circle of Symbolist poets. His art, which bears the influence of poetry, transfigures reality in the sense that it affords a view of the invisible. Degouve de Nuncques belonged to the avant-garde group Les XX and later exhibited at the Libre Esthétique. He travelled widely and painted views of Italy, Austria and France, often of parks at night. He excelled in the use of pastel. Two works, in particular, demonstrate the magical quality of his work: *Pink House* (1892; Otterlo, Kröller-Müller) and *Peacocks* (1896; Brussels, Mus. A. Mod.).

From 1900 to 1902 Degouve de Nuncques lived with his wife in the Balearic Islands; he painted the rugged coastline and the orange groves. After suffering a religious crisis *c.* 1910, he painted pictures that revealed his tormented state of mind, and during World War I, while living as a refugee in the Netherlands, he produced only minor works. In 1919 he was overwhelmed by the death of his wife and lost the use of one hand. In 1930 he married the woman who had helped him through this crisis. They settled in Stavelot, where he devoted himself to painting snow-covered landscapes.

BIBLIOGRAPHY
A. H. De Meester Obreen: 'William Degouve de Nuncques', *Elsevier's Geïllus. Mdschr.* (Feb 1920)
A. De Ridder: *William Degouve de Nuncques* (Antwerp, 1957)
William Degouve de Nuncques (exh. cat. by J. Parisse, Stavelot, Mus. Anc. Abbaye, 1979)

Belgian Art, 1880–1914 (exh. cat., foreword M. Botwinick; New York, Brooklyn Mus., 1980)
FRANCINE-CLAIRE LEGRAND

De Groux. Belgian family of artists.

(1) Charles(-Auguste-Corneille) De Groux (*b* Comines, 4 Aug 1825; *d* Brussels, 30 March 1870). Painter, printmaker and designer. In 1833 he settled in Brussels, where he was a pupil of François-Joseph Navez in 1843 and was advised by J. B. Van Eycken (1809–53), winning the Prix de Rome at the Brussels Academy in 1850. At that time he was painting historical compositions set mainly in the Middle Ages, which had absorbed the flavour of Parisian Romanticism. His copies of the live model and the Antique were unsuccessful, and he distinguished himself only in competitions for good composition.

In 1851 De Groux went to Düsseldorf, which encouraged him to adopt realist subjects and anti-classical ideas. During a particularly fertile period, which began around 1853, he produced pictures in predominantly grey and brown tones showing the grim existence of society's poorest classes: for example *The Drunkard* (1853) and *Grace* (1861; both Brussels, Mus. A. Mod.). He also portrayed the life of the soldier (*Departure of the Conscript*; Brussels, A. Mod.), as well as painting several religious scenes such as *Pilgrimage to Saint-Guidon* (1857; Brussels, Mus. A. Mod.), which earned him a gold medal.

De Groux's melancholy and biting wit was expressed in a series of inscriptions engraved beneath his lithographs for the paper *Ulyenspiegel*. He also did a series of etchings and illustrated a number of literary works, such as Charles de Coster's *Les Légendes flamandes*. He designed cartoons for stained-glass windows in a Neo-Gothic style, which owed much to German art, and was working on the decoration of Ypres town hall at the time of his death. He was wrongly seen as a socialist painter, when in fact he was happy to be merely an interested observer of the human condition.

BIBLIOGRAPHY
E. Leclercq: *Charles De Groux* (Brussels, 1871)
C. Lemonnier: *L'Ecole belge de peinture, 1830–1905* (Brussels, 1906), pp. 72–8
M. E. Traulbaut: *Vincent van Gogh en Charles De Groux* (Antwerp, 1953)
BERNADETTE THOMAS

(2) Henry [Henri] **(-Jules-Charles) De Groux** [Degroux] (*b* St-Josse-ten-Noode, nr Brussels, 16 Nov 1866; *d* Marseille, 12 Jan 1930). Painter, pastellist and lithographer, son of (1) Charles De Groux. He studied under Jean-François Portaels from the age of 11 and at the Académie de Bruxelles (1882–3). Until 1890 he participated in exhibitions organized by the avant-garde circles La Chrysalide, L'Essor and Les XX, of which he was a member. He was a close friend of William Degouve de Nuncques, in whose studio he executed the frieze *Procession of Archers* (pastel, 2.5×14.0 m, *c.* 1886–90; Belgium, priv. col.), first exhibited at Les XX in 1887 and 1889, and the *Mocking of Christ* (1889; Avignon, Pal. Roure), to which he gave his friend's features. Masses of tangled bodies with crazed expressions haunt his considerable oeuvre, marked by literary symbolism and by a tendency towards depicting such renowned figures as Christ, Napoleon and Wagner.

De Groux's highly personal style moved and disturbed as much by its force and ardour as by its 'unfinished' look and awkwardness. These characteristics were already evident in the *Mocking of Christ*, whose presentation at the Salon Triennal of 1890 in Brussels and two years later in Paris, first privately and then at the Salon des Arts Liberaux, aroused the admiration of artistic and fashionable circles. Despite this success and his influential friends, who included Léon Bloy and the art critic and writer Camille Lemonnier (1844–1913), he rejected a life of comfort and respect, spurred by a vital need to express his own physical and moral sufferings, his permanent destitution, his wanderings and fantasies; he remained a painter of the imagination, of the apocalypse and of movement. He continued to paint and draw dramatic and Symbolist subjects until the end of his life, for example the *Death of Andronicus* (c. 1925; Brussels, Mus. A. Mod.). De Groux was also active as an illustrator (e.g. for *Le Fantôme* by Remy de Gourmont; Paris, 1893) and lithographer (e.g. the *Eagle's Nest*, Brussels, Bib. Royale Albert 1er, Cab. Est.).

WRITINGS
Léon Bloy et Henry de Groux, correspondance, preface by M. Vaussard (Paris, 1947)

BIBLIOGRAPHY
'Henry de Groux et son oeuvre', *La Plume* (Paris, 1899) [special issue]
E. Baumann: *La Vie terrible d'Henry de Groux* (Paris, 1936)
D. Derrey-Capon: 'Henry de Groux', *Académie des Beaux Arts de Bruxelles: 275 ans d'enseignement* (exh. cat., Brussels, Musées Royaux B.-A., 1987)

DANIELLE DERREY-CAPON

Dehio, Georg Gottfried (*b* Reval [now Tallinn, Estonia], 22 Nov 1850; *d* Tübingen, 19 March 1932). German art historian. He originally studied history at the University of Göttingen, but while working on his thesis in Munich during the late 1870s he began to concentrate increasingly on the history of art and architecture. In 1883 he was appointed professor of art history at Königsberg (now Kaliningrad, Russia) and later taught at the universities of Strasbourg (1892–1918) and Tübingen. Dehio published numerous books and articles on the history of art, particularly architecture. From his time in Munich, he collaborated with Gustav von Bezold (1848–1928) on a monumental work on the ecclesiastical architecture of the Middle Ages, *Die kirchliche Baukunst des Abendlandes* (1884–1901), which contains comprehensive research and detailed drawings; it quickly became a prime source on the subject. His *Handbuch der deutschen Kunstdenkmäler* (1905–12) was based on the official inventories of the German states and became the standard guide to the architecture of Germany. He was a prominent member of the German conservation movement. During the controversies concerning the proposed restorations of the Friedrichsbau of Heidelberg Castle (1895–1903) and Meissen Cathedral (from 1903), he opposed the overzealous projects for conjectural restorations by Carl Schäfer and advocated 'conservation, not restoration'.

WRITINGS
with G. von Bezold: *Die kirchliche Baukunst des Abendlandes: Historisch und systematisch dargestellt*, 7 vols (Stuttgart, 1884–1901)
Handbuch der deutschen Kunstdenkmäler, 5 vols (Berlin, 1905–12, rev. 3/1925–38)
Kunsthistorische Aufsätze (Munich and Berlin, 1914)
Geschichte der deutschen Kunst, 4 vols (Berlin and Leipzig, 1919–26, rev. 1930–34)
Das Strassburger Münster (Munich, 1922)
Der Bamberger Dom (Munich, 1924)
ed.: *Aus Skizzenbüchern und Briefen* (Hameln, 1947)

BIBLIOGRAPHY
NDB; Wasmuth

Dehne, Christoph (*b* Magdeburg, *c.* 1578; *d* after 1640). German sculptor. He was the last important Magdeburg sculptor before the city's destruction in 1631. He trained there under Sebastian Ertle (*c.* 1570–*c.* 1612) and later married his master's widow. It has been suggested (Stauch, 1936) that Dehne travelled to Konstanz to work with Hans Morinck and then continued to Italy, but there is no documentary evidence to support this. Dehne may have learnt of Morinck's Mannerist work through Ertle, who grew up in Überlingen on Lake Constance. In 1605–10 Dehne assisted Ertle on the sandstone *Kannenberg* monument (1605–6) in Halberstadt Cathedral and several others in Magdeburg Cathedral. From March to September 1607 he worked with the Wolff brothers at the Schloss, Bückeburg. He established his own workshop in Magdeburg between 1610 and 1612.

Dehne produced numerous large wall monuments between 1610 and 1630. In his monument to *Heimo von Brösicke* (sandstone and alabaster, 1612–14) in Ketzür, Ertle's influence is evident: caryatid figures support a platform, on which kneel the deceased and his family. Behind these free-standing stone figures are elaborate reliefs and statuettes set in a large architectural frame with Dehne's characteristic intricate scrollwork. The curving foliate patterns, volutes and strong contrasts of the consoles on his monuments to *Cuno von Lochow* (bronze, 1623) and *Christian von Hopkorff* (sandstone and alabaster, 1625; both Magdeburg Cathedral) anticipate Rococo decoration.

Dehne's carvings can also be found in the churches of Nennhausen, Sydow and Kletzke and in Halle and Brandenburg cathedrals. On some monuments and pulpits, Dehne may have been assisted by his talented son-in-law Lulef Bartels (*fl* 1619–31). Little is known about Dehne's career after 1631. Schubert believed that he died in 1631 during the Catholic bombardment of Magdeburg, but Stauch (1936) claimed that he lived there until 1640, when he left the city.

BIBLIOGRAPHY
G. Deneke: 'Magdeburger Renaissance-Bildhauer', *Mhft Kstwiss.*, vi (1913), pp. 205–12
L. Stauch: *Christoph Dehne, ein Magdeburger Bildhauer um 1600* (Berlin, 1936)
——: 'Dehne, Christoph', *Neue deutsche Biographie*, iii (Berlin, 1956), p. 567
E. Schubert: *Der Magdeburger Dom* (Berlin, 1974, rev. Leipzig, 1984), pp. 218–19

JEFFREY CHIPPS SMITH

Dehodencq, (Edmé-Alexis-)Alfred (*b* Paris, 23 April 1822; *d* Paris, 2 Jan 1882). French painter. He studied at the Collège Bourbon, where he met the poet Théodore de Banville. In 1839 he entered the atelier of Léon Cogniet, and he made his Salon début in 1844 with two figure paintings and a biblical subject, *St Cecilia in Adoration* (untraced). Wounded in the arm during the Revolution in 1848, he left Paris in June 1849 to convalesce at Barèges in the Pyrenees and from there travelled via Pau to Madrid. Apart from a brief visit to Paris in 1855, Dehodencq spent the next 15 years in Spain. In 1850 he entered the atelier of the Madrazo family and with their encouragement exhibited his *Fight of the Novillos* (1850; Pau, Mus. B.-A.) in Madrid, where it attracted the favourable attention of Manet. His robust style was popular with the Spanish authorities and with the international community in Madrid from whom he received several portrait commissions between 1850 and 1855; for example *Prince Piscinelli* (Bordeaux, Mus. B.-A.).

Dehodencq's image of Spanish and Arab life was coloured by his youthful obsession with the romantic writings of Byron and Chateaubriand. His oeuvre is dominated by dramatic scenes of violence, despotism and fanaticism (*Execution of the Jewess*, 1862; untraced, see Séailles, no. 113), although he also painted more tranquil scenes of Spanish peasantry and gypsies (*Andalusian Peasants*, 1862; Condom, Mus. Armagnac). Works painted after his return to Paris in 1863 show a pronounced debt to Delacroix (*Jewish Festival at Tangiers*, 1870; Poitiers, Mus. B.-A.). A feeble draughtsman, Dehodencq preferred colour as a means of expression. His palette is rich, often gaudy, and his handling robust and sketchlike. He received medals at the Salons of 1846, 1853 and 1865. In 1870 he was made Chevalier of the Légion d'honneur.

BIBLIOGRAPHY

G. Séailles: *Alfred Dehodencq: L'Homme et l'artiste* (Paris, 1910)
V. Plat: *Alfred Dehodencq, 1822–1882* (diss., Paris, Ecole Louvre, 1977)

JANE MUNRO

Dehoy, Charles (*b* Brussels, 14 April 1872; *d* Brussels, 11 Sept 1940). Belgian painter. Orphaned at the age of 14, he worked successively as a house painter, cobbler and picture framer before devoting himself to painting. He was completely self-taught, and like Louis Thévenet he was supported by Auguste Oleffe, who took him in and advised him generously. As with many other Belgian painters the Midi had an enormous influence on his work. Some time before World War I he made several journeys there and so came into contact with French avant-garde painting.

Dehoy exhibited from 1901, particularly at the Antwerp Salon, showing paintings that were light in touch and with a luminosity that owed much to Impressionism. He met Ferdinand Schirren and began to develop his mature style in the context of BRABANT FAUVISM. During World War I his work was marked by the influence of Cézanne and Rik Wouters, as in the *Tea Table* (1918; Brussels, Mus. A. Mod.). Although his style developed gradually, his paintings were always delicate in execution. After 1920 his colours grew somewhat darker, his forms more closed and his volumes more dense, enveloped in a warm atmosphere. He sought his subjects in his immediate surroundings and treated figures, landscapes and still-lifes as overlapping volumes of vivid colour.

Although wary of contractual commitments with commercial galleries, he regularly took part in the triennial exhibitions held in Liège and Antwerp as well as in the Salons held by L'Art Contemporain. A retrospective of his work was shown in 1923 at the Galerie Georges Giroux in Brussels, in the context of a group exhibition of contemporary French painters that included Charles Dufresne, Raoul Dufy and Derain. As a Post-Impressionist colourist Dehoy is worthy of comparison with James Ensor and Wouters.

BIBLIOGRAPHY

R. de Bendère: 'Le Peintre Charles Dehoy', *Clarté* (March 1930)
L. Haesaerts and P. Haesaerts: *Flandre: Essai sur l'art flamand depuis 1880* (Paris, 1931)
Charles Dehoy (exh. cat., intro. P. Fierens; Brussels, Gal. Apollo, 1941–2)
S. Goyens de Heusch: *L'Impressionnisme et le fauvisme en Belgique* (Tielt, 1988)

GISÈLE OLLINGER-ZINQUE

dei. For pre-19th-century Italian proper names with this prefix, *see under* the first part of the name for individuals active before *c.* 1500; *see under* the second part of the name for those active after *c.* 1500.

dei'. For pre-19th-century Italian proper names with this preposition, *see under* the second part of the name.

Dei, Benedetto (*b* Florence, 4 March 1418; *d* Florence, 28 Aug 1492). Italian historian. He was the son of a goldsmith, Domenico di Deo, and in 1440 was enrolled in the Florentine Arte della Seta (silk workers' guild) to which his father and brothers belonged. In 1442 he enrolled in the Arte della Lana (wool workers' guild). A political agent of the Medici, he travelled on commercial and diplomatic missions around Europe, Africa and the Middle East between 1459 and 1467. In 1472 he wrote *La cronica*, a chronicle of Florentine history from 1400 containing a laudatory description of the city of Florence as it was in the time of Lorenzo de' Medici and including detailed lists of the important families, palaces and piazzas of the city that he called 'un' altra Roma novella'. After 1480 he left Florence and entered the service of a number of North Italian noble families, notably the Sforza and the d'Este. He cultivated a wide network of correspondents with whom he exchanged political information. Dei is reputedly among the onlookers portrayed by Domenico Ghirlandaio in the fresco (1486–90) of the *Angel Appearing to Zachariah* in the chapel of the Tornabuoni family, S Maria Novella, Florence. The identification is based on a list supposedly dictated in 1561 by Benedetto di Luca Landucci, then aged 89 years.

WRITINGS

La cronica dall'anno 1400 all'anno 1500 [MS.]; ed. R. Barducci (Florence, 1985)

BIBLIOGRAPHY

G. Vasari: *Vite* (1550, rev. 2/1568); ed. G. Milanesi (1878–85), iii, p. 266, n. 1
G. Davies: *Ghirlandaio* (London, 1909)
M. Pisani: *Un avventuriero del quattrocento: La vita e le opere di Benedetto Dei* (Genoa, 1923)
G. C. Romby: *Descrizioni e rappresentazioni della città di Firenze nel XV secolo* (Florence, 1976)

JEREMY MUSSON

Dei, Pietro di Antonio. *See* BARTOLOMEO DELLA GATTA.

Deibel [Deibler], Jan Zygmunt. *See* DEYBEL, JAN ZYGMUNT.

Deighton, Robert. *See* DIGHTON.

Deilmann, Harald (*b* Gladbeck, 30 Aug 1920). German architect, teacher and writer. After serving in the German army, he studied architecture (1946–8) at the Technische Hochschule, Stuttgart, under Richard Döcker and Rolf Gutbrod (*b* 1910), remaining there as a lecturer until 1951. In that year he formed a partnership with Heinrich Bartmann (Bartmann & Deilmann) in Münster, but it was his second partnership (1953–5) with Architektenteam, a group of architects in Münster including Max Clemens von Hausen (*b* 1919), Ortwin Rave (*b* 1921) and Werner Ruhnau, that brought him professional recognition. In 1954 the group won the competition for the new Stadttheater (1954–6), Münster, whose asymmetrical, informal planning and setting embody a deliberate move away from the formal architecture of the Third Reich. Built of glass and concrete, the front façade demonstrates the idea of exposing the theatre-goer to the street, with auditorium and stage both clearly expressed on the exterior elevations. Part of the old theatre wall was incorporated into the foyer of the new building as a memorial, a characteristic device of post-World War II German architecture, the most prominent example being Egon Eiermann's Kaiser-Wilhelm-Gedächtniskirche (1957–63), Berlin.

The uncompromisingly Modernist design of the theatre in Münster is typical of the architecture Deilmann adhered to throughout his career. After setting up his own private practice in Münster (1955), he won a very great number of competitions for a variety of buildings. Notable works include the Volkswohlbund Building (1967), Münster, with steep gables and strong vertical emphasis in its concrete window mullions, both features reworking elements of the surrounding traditional architecture in a Modernist idiom; the almost Brutalist Clemens-Sels-Museum (1972), Neuss, which, unconstrained by any adjoining buildings, has a boldly exposed concrete framework against a plain, red-brick surface; and the Neues Rathaus (1974–8), Minden, where he again sensitively adapts Modernist forms to a prevailing historic environment, in this case the market and Romanesque cathedral. Deilmann was an extremely prolific architect, also designing hospitals, cultural buildings and many office blocks. In its variety and modern design approach, his work is typical of much German architecture since World War II. His practice opened further offices in Stuttgart (1963) and Düsseldorf (1973). Later in his career he became increasingly involved in urban planning and interior and furniture design.

Parallel to his career as a practising architect, Deilmann continued his teaching role. He became professor at the Technische Hochschule, Stuttgart (1963), and subsequently founded and headed the Institute of Building Studies at the University of Stuttgart until 1969, when he became a professor at the University of Dortmund. He also taught at the universities of Berlin and Hannover, published a number of books on planning and design issues and exhibited widely. He continued to participate in architectural and planning competitions and frequently won prizes; examples include his projects for the finance office (1979; unexecuted), Bochum, and the Karstadt development (1981–91), Tempelhof, Berlin. A highly respected member of the architectural profession, he received many awards including the prize of the Bund Deutscher Architekten (1980).

WRITINGS

Bauten des Gesundheitswesen: Planungsgrundlagen für allgemeine Krankenhäuser (Gütersloh, 1972)
Bau und Wohnforschung (Bonn, 1974)

BIBLIOGRAPHY

'Harald Deilmann: Bauten und Projekte, 1955–1965', *Dt. Bauztg*, xcix/8 (1965), pp. 627–42
J. Joedicke: 'Zur Charakteristik des Architekten Harald Deilmann', *Dt. Bauztg*, xcix/8 (1965), pp. 663–6
J. Burchard: *The Voice of the Phoenix: Post-war Architecture in Germany* (Cambridge, MA, 1966)
H. W. Theil: *Das Haus in dem wir wohnen* (Stuttgart, 1978)
P. Schweger, W. Schneider and W. Meyer: *Architekturkonzepte der Gegenwart* (Stuttgart, 1983), pp. 63–7

CLAUDIA BÖLLING

Deinos. *See* DINOS.

Deira, Ernesto (*b* Buenos Aires, 1928; *d* Buenos Aires, 1 July 1986). Argentine painter. He studied with the artists Leopoldo Torres Agüero (*b* 1924) and Leopoldo Presas (*b* 1915), and from the early 1960s he had recourse to elements of *art informel*, applying the paint with violent gestures and allowing it to drip down the canvas, as in *Grandmother's Stories* (1964; see Glusberg, p. 269). While fervently defending the importance of the human figure, he subjected images of the body to a distortion and Expressionist treatment that almost destroyed their legibility. From the mid-1970s Deira moved towards a more coherent and lyrical but mannered treatment of the figure, as in *Don't Cry for Us Argentina* (1982; see Glusberg, p. 271).

BIBLIOGRAPHY

J. Glusberg: *Del Pop-art a la Nueva Imagen* (Buenos Aires, 1985), pp. 269–72

JORGE GLUSBERG

Dejoux, Claude (*b* Vadans, Jura, 23 Jan 1732; *d* Paris, 18 Oct 1816). French sculptor. He worked as a carver and joiner in his native village before studying at the Académie de Peinture et Sculpture in Marseille, where he won second place in the sculpture competition of 1763. He then entered the studio in Paris of Guillaume Coustou (ii). In 1768 he accompanied his fellow student Pierre Julien to Rome at his own expense. He remained in Rome until 1774. On his return to Paris, he was received (*reçu*) as a member of the Académie Royale in 1779. His *morceau de réception*, a very traditional statue of *St Sebastian* (h. 1.08 m; Paris, Louvre), was carved from a block of marble given to him by the Académie because he was too poor to buy his own. In the same year he executed busts of *Aesculapius* and *Hygeia* (bronze versions, Arbois, Hôp.). He was later awarded a commission by the Comte d'Angiviller, Directeur des Bâtiments du Roi, for a statue in the patriotic series of *Illustrious Frenchmen*, producing the standing marble statue of *Nicolas, Maréchal de Catinat* (exh. Salon 1783; Versailles, Château). The bulk of his work has, however, disappeared: his statue of a *Doctor of the Greek Church* for St Geneviève, Paris, was destroyed in 1791, and a colossal statue of *Fame* designed for the same church during its transformation into the Panthéon never got beyond the stage of a model (untraced). His monument to *Gen. Louis Desaix de Veygoux* (bronze, 1808) in the Place des Victoires, Paris, was demolished after the Restoration of the Bourbon monarchy in 1814, and his sculpture for the façade of the Pavillon de Flore at the Louvre, Paris, was destroyed during the reconstructions of the Second Empire (1851–70). Nevertheless, the surviving low-relief of *Charity* (marble, 1788), which serves as a monument to the *Curé Dubuisson* in the church at Magny-en-Vexin, Val-d'Oise, and the terracotta bust of *Marie-Christine de Brignole, Princesse de Monaco* (h. 570 mm, 1783; Paris, Louvre) show Dejoux as a competent portrait sculptor and a modeller of sensibility.

BIBLIOGRAPHY

J. Gauthier: *Dictionnaire des artistes Franc-Comtois antérieurs au XIXe siècle* (Besançon, 1892), p. 8

M. Beaulieu: 'Deux Bustes de la fin du XVIIIe siècle', *Rev. Louvre*, 3 (1978), pp. 197–8

Diderot et l'art de Boucher à David (exh. cat., Paris, Admin. Monnaies & Médailles, 1984), no. 129

De Keyser, Nicaise (*b* Zandvliet, 26 Aug 1813; *d* Antwerp, 26 Aug 1887). Belgian painter. He trained at the Academie in Antwerp with Mathieu Ignace Van Brée and achieved his first success with altarpieces influenced by Rubens, which he exhibited at the Salons of 1834 and 1835. In 1836 he made a name for himself as one of the leading figures of historical Romanticism, a genre then flourishing in Antwerp, with the enormous *Battle of the Gold Spurs* (destr. World War II). Numerous commissions from royal courts and prominent families in Belgium and abroad followed. He travelled to England and Scotland (1835), Italy (1840), Germany (1865, 1868, 1869 and 1871) and Spain (1878, 1880). In 1848 he became a member of the Koninklijke Academie in Brussels and from 1855 to 1879 he was director of the Academie in Antwerp. Between 1862 and 1872 he painted a series of scenes for the Koninklijk Museum voor Schone Kunsten in Antwerp illustrating the history and nature of the Antwerp School and the effect and influence it had abroad (Antwerp, Kon. Mus. S. Kst.). Both his large history paintings and the genre pieces that he produced alongside them are Romantic in subject-matter, inspiration and in the Baroque character of composition. They remain, however, academic in their cold execution with taut lines and sharply drawn details. De Keyser was also a painter of elegantly refined portraits. He enjoyed great fame during his lifetime but soon passed into oblivion after his death.

BIBLIOGRAPHY

Les Peintures du grand vestibule du Musée d'Anvers (Antwerp, 1873)

H. Hymans: *Notice sur la vie et les travaux de N. De Keyser* (Antwerp, 1889)

D. Cardyn: 'Enkele altaarstukken van N. De Keyser' [Some altarpieces by N. De Keyser], *Jb.: Kon. Mus. S. Kst.* (1985), pp. 309–33

N. De Keyser: Antwerps Portret (exh. cat., Antwerp, Kon. Acad. S. Kst., 1987)

D. CARDYN-OOMEN

Dekkers, Ad(riaan) (*b* Nieuwpoort, 21 March 1938; *d* Gorcum, 27 Feb 1974). Dutch draughtsman and sculptor. He trained at the Academie voor Beeldende Kunsten (1954–8) in Rotterdam. In 1961 he had his first group exhibition in Gorcum with Jan van Munster (*b* 1939) and Henk Visser (*b* 1940), in which he showed polychrome wood reliefs influenced by Piet Mondrian, Ben Nicholson and Hans Arp. From 1962, apart from wall reliefs, he produced sculptures. In addition to using his two-colour method he sometimes worked in monochrome, black or white. From 1964 until 1966 he made reliefs with compilations and displacements of the same geometric shape. His work began to show a certain affinity with that of Jan van Schoonhoven; both artists shared a partiality for white. From 1965 he produced mainly monochrome work in which he experimented with contrasts of light and shadow. His sources of inspiration included freemasonry. Between 1965 and 1970 he used polyester in wall reliefs. In 1965, during a trip to New York, he got to know the work of Frank Stella and Elsworth Kelly, and in 1966 his first retrospective exhibition was held at the Stedelijk Museum, Schiedam. Around this time he also suffered a mental crisis, which developed again in subsequent years. In his last four years he produced more than half of his total oeuvre. From 1970 he made transparent drawings and wood reliefs with sawn grooves. In 1971 he designed a relief for the two long corridor walls of the Kröller-Müller Museum, Otterlo.

BIBLIOGRAPHY

R. H. Fuchs: 'Ad Dekkers, 1961–1971', *Museumjournaal*, iv/3 (1975), pp. 137–46

Ad Dekkers: tekeningen, 1971–1974 [Ad Dekkers: drawings, 1971–1974] (exh. cat., Otterlo, Kröller-Müller, 1977)

C. Blotkamp: *Ad Dekkers* (The Hague, 1981)

JOHN STEEN

De Knyff, Alfred (Edouard Hyacinthe) (*b* Antwerp, 20 March 1819; *d* Paris, 22 March 1885). Belgian painter. Born into an aristocratic Brussels family, he studied at the Antwerp Academie at an extremely young age. He made many study trips, including one to Sicily, and thereafter settled in Paris where he was taught by the Swiss painter and lithographer Alexandre Calame. He was also friendly with Joseph Stevens and especially his brother Alfred Stevens. From the late 1850s de Knyff worked regularly in the area around Fontainebleau, where he came into contact with Jean-Baptiste-Camille Corot, Jean-François Millet (ii) and Constant Troyon; Théodore Rousseau often advised him as well. De Knyff set up a studio in Fontainebleau shortly after 1860. Under the direct influence of the painters of the Barbizon school he developed from a fairly conventional landscape painter to a realist who attempted to depict nature and *plein-air* effects as faithfully as possible. Although he was based in Paris until his death, de Knyff stayed in contact with Belgium, where he regularly exhibited and worked. He acquired an important collection of Barbizon paintings, and many younger Belgian artists, the generation of the Société Libre des Beaux-Arts and the magazine *L'Art libre*, received their first exposure to modern French landscape painting through him. He also exhibited frequently at the Paris Salons.

De Knyff's calm landscapes in subtle greys and greens, which often have cows as staffage, are simple in structure and rather reminiscent of the work of Corot (e.g. *Landscape with Cattle in a Field*, Liège, Mus. A. Mod.). Some of his wooded views, such as another *Landscape with Cattle in a Field* (Antwerp, Kon. Mus. S. Kst.), clearly show the influence of Rousseau. One of the strengths of de Knyff's modest talent lay in his handling of light (which was noted by such contemporary critics as Théophile Thoré-Bürger, who praised the grandiose and poetic quality of his work);

The Village of Chaslepont (exh. 1882; Antwerp, Kon. Mus. S. Kst.) is a fine example.

BIBLIOGRAPHY

T. Thoré-Bürger: *Les Salons: Etudes de critique et d'esthétique*, i (Brussels, 1893), p. 63

J. du Jardin: *L'Art flamand* (Brussels, 1896–1900), iv, pp. 141–3

Het landschap in de Belgische kunst, 1830–1914 (exh. cat. by R. Hoozee and M. Tahon-Vanroose, Ghent, Mus. S. Kst., 1980), pp. 97–9

SASKIA DE BODT

De Koninck, Louis Herman (*b* Brussels, 31 March 1896; *d* Brussels, 21 Oct 1984). Belgian architect and designer. He completed his architectural studies at the Académie Royale des Beaux-Arts, Brussels, in 1916. Disappointed by what he considered an old-fashioned syllabus, he decided to continue his education at the Ecole Industrielle, Brussels, enrolling for the course on reinforced concrete. The thorough scientific knowledge that he acquired on this material became the basis for his researches into industrial standardization and into prefabrication. At the same time he worked for the architect Gabriel Charle (*d* 1919) and then for Albert Callewaert (1888–1957) under whom he drew up lists of war-damaged farms in the Brabant region of Belgium, an apprenticeship that familiarized him with the patterns and principles of traditional rural architecture.

From 1917 De Koninck was responsible for running the research department, workshops and construction sites of the firm De Smaele, an experience that acquainted him with the techniques involved in casting and surfacing concrete. After a brief collaboration with the architects Jean-Baptiste Dewin (1873–1948) in 1919 and Léon Bochoms (*b* 1875) and Fernand Petit (1885–1955) in 1920, De Koninck worked on some projects on his own, including the remodelling in 1922 of the A Campo house on the Val-Duchesse estate, Brussels, inspired by the Viennese Secession. The simplicity of this work shows De Koninck's wish to create a balance between solid and void by excluding the intervention of any applied ornament. Between 1922 and 1937 he built numerous pavilions and exhibition stands, in particular for the prefabricated concrete company Geba; this work enabled him to experiment with forms and concepts that were too daring to be given permanent expression in lasting works.

In 1924 De Koninck built his own house at 103 Avenue Fond'Roy, of cubic form on a square plan, whose structural supports were four exterior walls and two central pillars. This was an early example of a *plan libre* in Belgium and allowed the rooms to be arranged to suit an air-gravity heating system. In 1926 he built a house and studio for a painter, Lenglet, at 105 Avenue Fond'Roy; its more complex appearance marked the beginning of his more mature and well-known manner, an individual and intensely detailed version of the International style. In 1928 he introduced to Belgium the use of thin layers of reinforced concrete; this construction method was henceforth central in his designs, which concentrated on achieving a severity of form stemming from the logic of construction itself, as well as economy and spatial effect. The Dotremont house, 3 Avenue de l'Echevinage (1931), the Canneel villa, Avenue I. Gerard (1931), and the Berteaux house, 59 Avenue du Fort Jaco (1937), all built

on the outskirts of Brussels, are among the executed projects that best embody these aims; the Berteaux house is one of the most characteristic with its vertical ribbon windows, rounded exterior corners and three circular portholes.

As a member of the Belgian section of the Congrès Internationaux d'Architecture Moderne (CIAM), De Koninck presented his own house to the CIAM II in Frankfurt am Main (1929) as a model for minimalist housing. At the CIAM III in Brussels (1930) he exhibited the Cubex kitchen, one of the earliest standardized furniture systems that could be juxtaposed and superposed. Marketed by the Van de Ven company until 1950, the Cubex kitchens were extremely successful in Belgium and were used in many high-rise flats. From 1942 to 1973 he taught architecture and later construction at the Ecole Nationale Supérieure d'Architecture et des Arts Décoratifs de la Cambre in Brussels. De Koninck's central concern was with a precise architectural entity: the individual house and the design of interior elements such as furniture (*see* BELGIUM, fig. 34), carpets and windows. The depth of his involvement in small-scale problems enabled him to attain a pure and accomplished style.

BIBLIOGRAPHY

P. Puttemans: 'L.-H. De Koninck', *Rev. Archit.*, 58 (1964) [special issue]

L.-H. De Koninck (exh. cat. by M. Culot and R.-L. Delevoy, Brussels, Ecole N. Sup. A. Visuels, 1970)

L.-H. De Koninck: Architect (exh. cat. by M. Culot and R.-L. Delevoy, London, Archit. Assoc., 1973); rev. as *L.-H. De Koninck*, ed. R.-L. Delevoy (Brussels, 1980)

M. Culot, C. Mierop and A. van Loo, eds: *Louis Herman de Koninck: Architecte des années modernes* (Brussels, 1989)

ANNE VAN LOO

De Kooning. American artists. (1) Willem de Kooning met (2) Elaine de Kooning *c*. 1938, and they married five years later. They were both influential on each other's work. In 1957 they amicably separated but reunited in 1975.

(1) Willem de Kooning (*b* Rotterdam, 24 April 1904; *d* East Hampton, NY, 19 March 1997). Painter and sculptor of Dutch birth. He was a leading figure of ABSTRACT EXPRESSIONISM whose painterly gesturalism transcended the conventional definitions of figuration and abstraction and substantially influenced art after World War II.

1. Early work, to *c*. 1945. 2. Mature work, *c*. 1945 and after. 3. Influence.

1. EARLY WORK, TO *c*. 1945. De Kooning's artistic talent was recognized at an early stage, and from 1916 to 1924 he attended the Academie van Beeldende Kunsten in Rotterdam while working at a commercial art and decorating firm. His earliest-known works, of which few survive, reflect his academic training and the influence of Old Masters, for example *Still-life: Bowl, Pitcher and Jug* (*c*. 1921; New York, Met.). In 1926 he emigrated to the USA, moving in 1927 to New York, where he continued to make a living as a commercial artist. Soon he became involved with the New York avant-garde, in particular with John Graham, Arshile Gorky and Stuart Davis. Their influence and that of Miró, Arp, Picasso and Mondrian is apparent in de Kooning's abstract still-lifes of the 1930s and early 1940s, compositions of biomorphic and geometric shapes and lines in high-key colours, integrated

into an architectonic structure. He employed similar techniques while working in 1935–6 for the Federal Art Project of the Works Progress Administration on various mural projects, none of which was executed. The increasingly simple and flat poetic abstractions exercised the metamorphosis of perceived reality into ambiguous abstract images, an elemental technique employed throughout his career.

De Kooning's work is characterized by an inherent stylelessness, resulting from the constant parallel exploration of divergent themes and techniques. In the 1930s he worked simultaneously on abstractions and on a series of male figures. The generally unfinished paintings combine classically inspired anatomy (influenced particularly by Ingres's work) with the formal fragmentation of Cubism, as in *Seated Figure (Classic Male)* (*c.* 1940; U. Houston, TX, Sarah Campbell Blaffer Gal.). The silent appeal of the solitary figures, positioned in vague and indefinite surroundings, reflected the uncertainty and isolation of the Depression era, for example in *Working Man* (drawing, *c.* 1938; Max Margulis priv. col., see Hess, 1972).

In 1938, after meeting his future wife, the American painter Elaine Fried, de Kooning began his first series of *Women*, the central theme in his work. The images of women of the late 1930s and early 1940s, in increasingly bright colours and violent contrasts, possess a powerful and erotic immediacy, as in *Seated Woman* (*c.* 1940; Philadelphia, PA, Mus. A.). The figures are progressively

1. Willem de Kooning: *Woman I*, oil on canvas, 1.93×1.47 m, 1950–52 (New York, Museum of Modern Art)

fragmented into irregular planar shapes and contrasted with geometric backgrounds. De Kooning named the anonymous and indefinite backgrounds 'no-environments', leaving the possibility for a multiplicity of places and situations. *Pink Angels* (*c.* 1945; Los Angeles, CA, Frederick Weisman Co.) is the climax of the first *Women* series, transgressing the static frontality of the earlier figure paintings and indulging in a dynamic frenzy, barely controlled by the receding geometric structure of the background. De Kooning's attempt to overcome the restrictions of rational control, inspired by Surrealist automatism, is reflected in their strong graphic quality and unfinished state.

2. MATURE WORK, *c.* 1945 AND AFTER. The reduction of de Kooning's palette and the close-textured composition of irregular shapes in the *Black-and-white Abstractions* (1945–50) balanced the figure–ground relationship and created a dense, shallow space, as previously suggested in *Pink Angels*. Random fragments of memory are evoked by letters and figures in some of the *Black-and-white Abstractions*, evidence of de Kooning's early training as a sign-painter (e.g. *Zurich*, 1947; Joseph H. Hirshhorn estate, see 1983 exh. cat., New York, pl. 161). *Excavation* (2.03×2.54 m, 1950; Chicago, IL, A. Inst.) is the violent and shocking climax of the *Black-and-white* paintings and de Kooning's largest painting up to that time. The primarily white canvas with black contours and glimpses of red, yellow and blue bursts with a complex network of superimposed and interlocked shapes, reminiscent of human limbs. The composition moves around an obvious focal point, despite its all-over fragmentation, consuming everything in an apocalyptic vortex. *Excavation* highlights de Kooning's continuous balancing act between representation and abstraction, hardly ever succumbing to complete non-objectivity. 'Even abstract shapes must have a likeness', as de Kooning stated (see 1968 exh. cat., p. 47).

From 1950 to 1955 de Kooning worked on a second series of *Women*, rejecting the then dominant stylistic canon of abstraction: 'It's really absurd to make an image, like a human image. . . But then all of a sudden it becomes even more absurd not to do it' (see Sylvester, p. 57). He had, however, never completely abandoned figurative work, and his suite of fragmented *Women* between 1947 and 1949, such as *Woman* (1948; Washington, DC, Hirshhorn), forecasted the challenge to established notions of femininity. For two years he worked on the momentous *Woman I* (1950–52; New York, MOMA; see fig. 1), 'an image which has become a totem and icon of the times' (see 1968 exh. cat., p. 12). The genesis of *Woman I* is documented in Rudolph Burckhardt's celebrated photographs, illustrating the innumerable revisions and cinematographic process of creation in the quest for a true, yet subconscious image (see Waldman, pp. 88–9). De Kooning perpetually referred to drawings, attaching many of them to the canvas and subsequently overpainting them. Drawing was always an important and integral part in the evolution of his pictorial solutions. In the place of her mouth he fixed a cut-out of a female smile from a magazine advertisement, as a point of orientation and as epigrammatic reference to the ubiquitous American idols of femininity. De Kooning was always a very eclectic artist, and the *Women* were also inspired by classical formulations by Rubens, Rembrandt, Matisse and Picasso. Gradually the woman's clearly defined surrounding was transformed into his typical 'no-environment', with its implications of vagueness and insecurity, emphasizing the blank stare, the frozen grin and the overwhelming presence of the monstrous figure with its large breasts. When *Woman I* was exhibited in 1953 in New York at the Sidney Janis Gallery with five other *Women* paintings, it shocked the public and critics. Images of the bulky women, with their frontal immediacy and destructive fragmentation into gestural brushstrokes, were attacked as violent, ferocious and sexist. De Kooning's detractors failed to recognize that the amalgam of stereotypes was an ironic comment on the obsession with the banal and artificial world of film, television and advertising. It is this iconoclastic quality and diversity of references condensed into a single image that makes *Woman I* such a controversial and successful painting.

De Kooning liberated himself from the power of the *Women* through their gradual transformation into landscapes, as in *Woman as Landscape* (1955; Janet and Robert Kardon priv. col., see Waldman, p. 103), which led to the *Abstract Urban Landscapes*, (1955–8) and *Abstract Parkway Landscapes* (1957–61). From 1955 the female figure was slowly absorbed by its environment, creating hybrid images that defy conventional genre categorizations, as de Kooning intimated in his remark, 'The landscape is in the Woman and there is Woman in the landscape' (see 1968 exh. cat., p. 100). The messy and elaborate all-over surfaces of the *Abstract Urban Landscapes*, such as *Gotham News* (*c.* 1955; Buffalo, NY, Albright–Knox A.G.), record the chaos of New York, the cacophony of its events, sounds, smells and visual impressions. A more poetic mood emanates from the broad and dramatic brushstrokes of the *Abstract Parkway Landscapes*, extending over the whole width of the canvas and conveying 'sensations of the feeling of going to the city or coming from it' (see Sylvester, p. 57). A sweeping painterliness is achieved in the *Abstract Pastoral Landscapes* (1960–63) with lush and sensual splashes of white, pink and yellow paint capturing the atmosphere at Long Island, NY, of brilliant light, sea and nature, as in *Door to the River* (1960; New York, Whitney). Like Franz Kline's bold calligraphic paintings, de Kooning's *Abstract Landscapes* seem to represent only an enlarged detail of a larger scene, thereby avoiding traditionally composed European images. He achieved a virtuosity of touch, quickness and security of execution that was unusual in artists of his generation but akin to the technique of Old Masters.

The thematic centrality of the *Women* and the *Abstract Landscapes* continued throughout the 1960s, as de Kooning produced ever more novel formulations of his basic themes, contradicting premature proclamations of the decline of his creative powers. Though his brushwork and colours softened, the *Women* of the 1960s are more vivid, physical and erotic than ever. *Woman, Sag Harbour* (1964; Washington, DC, Hirshhorn) appears frontally in sensuous fleshlike colours, her extremities spread out in a provocative and overtly sexual pose. The late 1960s and early 1970s witnessed a revival of the 'Woman in Landscape' theme, celebrating the idyllic harmony of human figure

2. Willem de Kooning: *Untitled V*, oil on canvas, 2.02×1.76 m, 1977 (Buffalo, NY, Albright–Knox Art Gallery)

and nature in such works as *Woman in Landscape III* (1968; priv. col., see 1983 exh. cat., New York, pl. 229).

De Kooning's versatility was exemplified by his venture into sculpture, a medium completely new to him (1969–74). In his sculptures he translated the physicality of the painted figure into three dimensions without compromising their vitality and energy. The twisted and distorted figures reveal the traces of their creation, products of the direct contact with the hands of the sculptor, as in *Seated Woman on a Bench* (1972; Amsterdam, Stedel. Mus.). As with his paintings and drawings the closed form is destroyed and the sculptures reach out and respond to their environment, extending a process initiated by Auguste Rodin, Matisse and Alberto Giacometti. Aesthetic autonomy is manifest in de Kooning's constant oscillation between abstraction and representation, figurative and landscape painting, that continued in the 1970s with a smooth transition from the 'Women in Landscape' to a series of *Untitled* works (1975–9). The atmosphere of his environment in East Hampton, NY, is reflected in an impasto of short and hectic brushstrokes with enigmatic appearances of the human figure, as in *Untitled V* (1977; Buffalo, NY, Albright–Knox A.G.; see fig. 2). An increasingly lyrical quality began to infuse his work in the early 1980s. In 1982 he reduced broad shapes to an intricate web of arabesque lines on a transparent white ground. The intense luminosity of colours and weightlessness of floating curves correspond to the calm movement of the sea and its interplay of water and light, in works such as *Untitled XVII* (1982; New York, Xavier Fourcade).

The central issue in de Kooning's art was his creative use of ambiguity, achieved through disorientation and fragmentation, manipulation of perspective, mutilation, dissolution and a reassemblage of figures and objects. For de Kooning the process of painting and drawing was a way of experiencing, recording and appropriating reality, ideas and subjects emerging in the process of creation through free association. The variety and constant transformation of basic themes reflected his view of the world as a sum of indefinite and ever-changing possibilities. The ambiguity that reigns in the formal structure of the paintings continues on a semantic level, evoking a multiplicity of meanings and moods: joy, lust and effusiveness to some; brutality, drama and violence to others. De Kooning maintained deliberate stylistic contradictions and a strong element of uncertainty, open for developments in any direction.

3. INFLUENCE. From the 1950s de Kooning's fame and success spread, making him one of the most influential artists of the period. While a number of serious followers, such as the American painters Michael Goldberg (*b* 1924), Alfred Leslie (*b* 1927), Grace Hartigan and Joan Mitchell, developed de Kooning's example into an individual pictorial mode, many others were deceived by his seemingly easy-to-imitate style. The attempt to liberate themselves from the powerful example of de Kooning, the archetypal gestural painter, led to an ironical appropriation by Jasper Johns, Robert Rauschenberg and Pop artists. A revival of interest in his work came with the renaissance of figurative and Neo-expressive painting in the early 1980s.

BIBLIOGRAPHY

T. B. Hess: 'De Kooning Paints a Picture', *ARTnews*, lii (March 1953), pp. 30–33, 64–7
——: *Willem de Kooning* (New York, 1959)
H. Janis and R. Blesh: *De Kooning* (New York, 1960)
Willem de Kooning (exh. cat. by D. Ashton, Northampton, MA, Smith Coll. Mus. A., 1965)
D. Sylvester: 'De Kooning's Women', *Sunday Times Mag.* (8 Dec 1968), pp. 44–57
Willem de Kooning (exh. cat. by T. B. Hess, New York, MOMA, 1968)
T. B. Hess: *De Kooning: Drawings* (New York, 1972)
H. Rosenberg: 'Interview with Willem de Kooning', *ARTnews*, lxxi/5 (1972), pp. 54–9 [repr. in 1979 exh. cat.]
——: *Willem de Kooning* (New York, 1974)
De Kooning: Drawings/Sculptures (exh. cat. by P. Larson and P. Schjeldahl, W. Palm Beach, FL, Norton Gal. & Sch. A., 1975)
The Sculpture of de Kooning with Related Paintings, Drawings and Lithographs (exh. cat. by A. Forge, Edinburgh, Fruitmarket Gal., 1977)
De Kooning: 1969–78 (exh. cat. by J. Cowart and S. S. Shaman, Cedar Falls, U. N. IA, Gal. A., 1978)
Willem de Kooning in East Hampton (exh. cat. by D. Waldman, New York, Guggenheim, 1978)
Willem de Kooning (exh. cat. by L. Arkus, Pittsburgh, PA, Carnegie Mus. A., 1979)
H. F. Gaugh: *Willem de Kooning* (New York, 1983)
Willem de Kooning: Drawings, Paintings, Sculptures (exh. cat. by P. Cummings, J. Merkert and C. Stoulling, New York, Whitney, 1983)
Willem de Kooning: Het noordatlantisch licht (exh. cat., essays E. de Wilde and C. Ratcliff; Amsterdam, Stedel. Mus.; Humlebæk, Louisiana Mus.; Stockholm, Mod. Mus.; 1983) [in Dut. and Eng.]
S. E. Yard: *Willem de Kooning: The First Twenty-six Years in New York, 1927–1952* (New York and London, 1986)
D. Waldman: *Willem de Kooning* (New York, 1988)
B. Berkson and R. Downes, eds: 'Willem de Kooning, on his Eighty-fifth Birthday', *A. J.* [New York], iii (Autumn 1989) [special issue]
L. Graham: *The Prints of Willem de Kooning: Catalogue raisonné, 1957–71* (Paris, 1991)

CHRISTOPH GRUNENBERG

(2) Elaine de Kooning [née Fried] (*b* Brooklyn, PA, 12 March 1920; *d* Southampton, NY, 1 Feb 1989). Painter, sculptor, draughtsman, printmaker and writer, wife of (1) Willem de Kooning. She studied art at the Leonardo da Vinci Art School under Conrad Marca-Relli. There she met de Kooning, Arshile Gorky and Milton Resnick (*b* 1917). She later transferred to the American Artists School, where her teachers included Benjamin Wilson. In her early work de Kooning concentrated primarily on formal, pictorial problems, such as the placement of objects in an environment and the spatial relationships between them, for example *Still-life (with Scissors)* (oil on masonite, *c.* 1939; artist's estate). She was always interested in both figurative and abstract art, and from the 1940s her work included portraits and gestural abstraction. She acknowledged the influence of her husband and of the Abstract Expressionists of the New York School, with whom she associated.

In 1948 de Kooning became Editorial Associate for *Art News* and wrote some of the first reviews and articles on Franz Kline, David Smith, Josef Albers, Gorky and others. Other works for which she became known are the portraits of basketball and baseball players, based on magazine and newspaper photographs. Later she travelled with the New York Yankees and the Baltimore Orioles and recorded the sport in a series of paintings (1953–4). Her first one-person show was at the Stable Gallery, New York, in 1954. The subjects of her portraits were almost always friends or close associates and include *Leo Castelli* (1954; priv. col.), *Merce Cunningham* (1962; New York, Found. Contemp. Perf. A., Inc.) and President *John F. Kennedy* (1962; Independence, MO, Harry S. Truman Lib.), for which she made scores of drawings in pencil or charcoal and oil sketches (artist's estate). Throughout her life she taught at numerous colleges in the USA.

WRITINGS

Elaine de Kooning: The Spirit of Abstract Expressionism, preface, M. Luyckx (New York, 1994) [also incl. essay by R. Slivka]

BIBLIOGRAPHY

A. *America* (Jan–Feb 1975), pp. 35–6 [interview and statements by de Kooning]
Obituary, *East Hampton Star* (2 Feb 1989)
Elaine de Kooning (exh. cat., intro. J. K. Beldsoe, essays by L. Campbell, H. A. Harrison and R. Slivka; Athens, U. GA Mus. A.; Santa Barbara, CA, Mus. A.; Baltimore, MD Inst., Decker Gal.; Little Rock, AR A. Cent., and elsewhere; 1992)

☐

del. For Spanish and pre-19th-century Italian proper names with this prefix or preposition, *see under* the first part of the name for individuals active before *c.* 1500; *see under* the second part of the name for those active after *c.* 1500. For tripartite Portuguese and Spanish surnames, *see under* the first part of the surname.

de la. For French, Swiss and pre-19th-century Flemish proper names with this prefix *see under* 'La'. For Spanish and pre-19th-century Italian names *see under* the first part of the name for individuals active before *c.* 1500; *see under* the second part of the name for those active after *c.* 1500. For tripartite Portuguese and Spanish surnames, *see under* the first part of the surname.

Delaborde, Henri (*b* Rennes, 2 May 1811; *d* Paris, 24 May 1899). French painter and critic. He trained from 1829 with Paul Delaroche, with whom he made his first trip to Italy in 1834. A second visit to Italy in 1839 and then a three-year stay (1842–5) resulted in a large number of drawings and watercolours, including a series of copies after the masters of the Italian Renaissance, some of which were published as prints in *Les Maîtres florentins du quinzième siècle* (Paris, 1878). Delaborde exhibited at the Salon between 1836 and 1850, showing such works as *Hagar in the Desert* (1836) and *Offering to Hygeia* (1842; both Dijon, Mus. B.-A.). The inspiration for some of his subjects is Romantic, but their conception is classical in the manner of the school of Ingres, whom Delaborde admired all his life.

The State bought a number of Delaborde's paintings, including *Dante at La Verna* for the château of Saint-Cloud (untraced, possibly destr. 1871). He was commissioned to produce some history paintings for the Musée d'Histoire de Versailles, including the *Capture of Damietta* and the *Knights of St John of Jerusalem* (both 1839; Versailles, Mus. Hist.). He also produced large wall paintings for chapels of Ste-Clotilde in Paris.

During the 1850s Delaborde's state of health obliged him to give up painting, and he became curator of the Cabinet des Estampes at the Bibliothèque Nationale in Paris from 1855 to 1885 and art critic for the *Revue des deux mondes* and the *Gazette des beaux-arts*. He published articles on Italian art, for example *Marc-Antonio Raimondi* (Paris, 1888), on engraving and on his contemporaries, of which the most important are *Lettres et pensées d'Hippolyte Flandrin* (Paris, 1865), accompanied by a catalogue of his work, and *Ingres: Sa Vie, ses travaux, sa doctrine* (Paris, 1870). Delaborde was elected to the Académie des Beaux-Arts in 1868, and he became its permanent secretary in 1874. The collection of the library of the Ecole des Beaux-Arts, Paris, contains many of his drawings and watercolours.

BIBLIOGRAPHY
E. Michel: 'Le Comte Henri Delaborde', *Gaz. B.-A.*, ii (1899), pp. 71–81
G. Larroumet: *Derniers portraits . . . Le Comte Henri Delaborde* (Paris, 1904)
M. Sandoz: 'Le Vicomte Henri Delaborde, peintre d'histoire, 1811–1899', *Bull. Soc. Hist. A. Fr.* (1968), pp. 135–48

HÉLÈNE GUICHARNAUD

Dela Censerie [Delacenserie], **Louis** (*b* Bruges, 27 Sept 1838; *d* Bruges, 2 Sept 1909). Belgian architect. He trained at the Municipal Academy of Fine Arts, Bruges, under Jean-Baptiste Rudd (1792–1870). In 1870 he was appointed City Architect in Bruges and Professor of the Academy, becoming Director in 1889. In 1879 he became a member of the Provincial Committee of the Royal Commission of Monuments. He was involved in the restoration of most of the major historical monuments in Bruges: the Chapel of the Holy Blood (1870 and 1877), the Registry (1873–83), the Toll House (1879), the Gruuthuse Palace (1883–95), the Town Hall (1894–5 and 1903–4), St John's Hospital (1905–9) and the west façade of Notre-Dame (1907–8). In addition he restored several houses in the historic town centre. His approach to restoration was drastic, consisting in the completion of a project according to the intentions of the original master builder or architect and the removal of later additions that destroyed the stylistic unity.

For his new buildings Dela Censerie used the Late Gothic brick architecture of Bruges as a model. This traditional local style lasted until *c.* 1750 and was known as the 'Brugse trant' or Bruges manner. Good examples of Dela Censerie's approach are the large complexes of the State Teacher Training School (1878–83) and the Minnewater Hospital (1881–92), both in Bruges. The monumental east façade of the Grote Markt of Bruges comprises, besides the Gothic Revival residence of the Provincial Governor (1920–21) by Jules Coomans (1871–1937), Dela Censerie's Post Office (1887–90) in the 'Brugse trant' and his Provincial Court, built in the same period but inspired by the 15th-century High Gothic town halls of Brabant. His later work includes the highly eclectic Central Station (1895–8), Antwerp, and the Gothic Revival church of SS Peter and Paul (1901–5), Ostend, closely based on the ideal 13th-century Gothic cathedral published by Eugène-Emmanuel Viollet-le-Duc in his *Dictionnaire de l'architecture française du XIe au XVIe siècle* (1854–68).

BIBLIOGRAPHY
NBW: 'Censerie, Louis dela'
H. Lobelle: 'Enkele neogotische realisaties van arch. L. Delacenserie te Brugge' [Some neo-Gothic realizations of the architect Delacenserie at Bruges], *Vlaanderen*, clxxiv (1980), pp. 32–4
L. Constandt, ed.: *Stenen herleven: 111 jaar 'kunstige herstellingen' in Brugge, 1877–1988* [Stone revivals: 111 years of 'artistic restoration' in Bruges, 1877–1988] (Bruges, 1988)

LUC VERPOEST

Delacroix, (Ferdinand-)Eugène(-Victor) (*b* Charenton-Saint-Maurice, nr Paris, 26 April 1798; *d* Paris, 13 Aug 1863). French painter, draughtsman and lithographer. He was one of the greatest painters of the first half of the 19th century, the last history painter in Europe (*see* HISTORY PAINTING, §II) and the embodiment of ROMANTICISM in the visual arts. At the heart of Delacroix's career is the paradox between the revolutionary and the conventional: as the arch-enemy of JEAN-AUGUSTE-DOMINIQUE INGRES and as the leading figure of the French Romantic movement, he was celebrated for undermining the tradition of painting established by JACQUES-LOUIS DAVID, yet he nevertheless enjoyed official patronage from the beginning of the Restoration (1814–30) until the Second Empire (1852–70).

Delacroix disliked the 19th century, hated progress, was conservative in his tastes and manners, but—for Baudelaire, at least—was the most modern of artists, resembling the great painters of the First Republic (1792–1804) and the First Empire (1804–14) in his wish to rival the written word. His subjects, like those of David, were serious and historical, but he replaced the Stoic ideal with one equally grand and dramatic, yet lacking any kind of moral or political certainty. Nevertheless, he was the last representative of the GRAND MANNER. He lived long past the years of the Romantic movement, although a Romantic interest in suffering, insanity, death and violence is always present in his art, which is essentially literary and personal.

I. Life and work. II. Working methods and technique. III. Character and personality. IV. Critical reception and posthumous reputation.

I. Life and work.

1. Early years, to 1821. 2. Public recognition, 1822–31. 3. North Africa and Spain, 1832. 4. Literary and historical subjects and mural decorations, 1833–*c.* 1850. 5. Later years, *c.* 1850–1863.

1. EARLY YEARS, TO 1821. Eugène Delacroix's father, Charles Delacroix (*d* 1805), was briefly Ministre des Affaires Etrangères during the Directory (1795–9) and was later Préfet de la Gironde. At the time of Delacroix's birth, he was Ministre Plénipotentiaire at The Hague. Théophile Silvestre was the first to suggest, in his *Histoire des artistes vivants* (Paris, 1856), that the French statesman Charles-Maurice de Talleyrand was Delacroix's father, a persistent rumour for which there is no documentary evidence. The cultivated milieu in which Delacroix grew up, and where Talleyrand was a frequent visitor, was that of his mother, Victoire Oeben (*d* 1815), daughter of the cabinetmaker Jean-François Oeben. Delacroix's step-grandfather was the well-known cabinetmaker Jean-Henri Riesener, and his mother's half-brother was the painter Henri-François Riesener (1767–1828), who was a pupil of David, and who later took a warm interest in Delacroix's education. Delacroix was always conscious of his French origins but was one of the first artists of his generation to respond to the writings of Goethe and Schiller and to Shakespeare, Sir Walter Scott and Lord Byron; he first read Byron's *Childe Harold* (begun 1809) with the help of his aunt, Henri-François Riesener's wife. It is probable that during his youth he absorbed from this clever and cosmopolitan background a breadth of interest uncommon during the long isolation of French culture under successive Napoleonic regimes. He was not only one of the first 'Shakespeareans', as the writer Etienne-Jean Delécluze called the young Romantics, but was also devoted to the writings of Voltaire and was passionately fond of Mozart's opera *The Marriage of Figaro*. Nevertheless, Delacroix's work is as inconceivable without the Romantic movement as Antoine-Jean Gros's would have been without Napoleon's battles and campaigns.

Between 1806 and 1815 Delacroix attended the Lycée Imperial (now Lycée Louis-le-Grand) in Paris, which was noted for its teaching of Classics. He won prizes in Classics and drawing and acquired a love of French literature that he retained the rest of his life. While still at school, he met Pierre Guérin, a friend of his uncle Henri-François Riesener, and, having decided to study painting, he entered Guérin's popular studio in October 1815. The studio came to be seen as a nursery of Romanticism: Gericault, seven years older than Delacroix, was one of his fellow students, as were Ary Scheffer and Léon Cogniet. Delécluze, commenting on Guérin's teaching methods, related that, like David, he was a liberal master. In 1816 Delacroix entered the Ecole des Beaux-Arts and from an early age he frequently visited the Musée du Louvre, where he was particularly attracted to the paintings of Raphael, Titian, Veronese and Rubens. During this time he met and admired the young English artist Richard Parkes Bonington, who was also making copies after Flemish paintings in the Louvre.

Delacroix's first commission, a *Virgin and Child* (1819; Orcemont, parish church), was painted in the tender and sentimental vein of early Romanticism. His notes for it contain studies after Leonardo, Raphael and Domenichino, although in appearance the painting is very nearly a pastiche of Raphael. In 1821 he executed a second religious painting, a *Madonna of the Sacred Heart* (Ajaccio Cathedral), originally commissioned from Gericault. It appears to have been based on Gericault's style: sweetness has been abandoned for a monumental strength, and, although rather clumsy in handling, it is impressive in its uncompromising solidity. Several drawings (Paris, Louvre) he made for it were starting-points for later compositions, and, in spite of its awkwardness, there is already some hint of the power, relief and eloquence of gesture that were later to characterize his art. During these years his interests—copying Old Masters in the Louvre, experimenting in lithography and drawings from coins, medals and Persian miniatures—found expression in a variety of ways. He dabbled in literature, played the harpsichord and violin and in 1821 painted four panels representing *The Seasons* (Paris, Mme F. Jouët-Pastré priv. col., see Johnson, 1981–9, nos 94–7) in Pompeian Revival style for the dining-room of the actor François-Joseph Talma.

2. PUBLIC RECOGNITION, 1822–31. In 1822 Delacroix made his début at the Salon with *Dante and Virgil* (or the *Barque of Dante*; Paris, Louvre; see fig. 1), which caused a sensation and immediately heralded him as a major figure of the French school. The theme of a fragile craft on a stormy sea was derived from Gericault's *Raft of the Medusa* (1819; Paris, Louvre; *see* GERICAULT, THÉODORE, fig. 3), and the curious composition combined elements from the works of Michelangelo, Rubens and John Flaxman with swaying upright figures and with the horizontal naked bodies of the damned who cling to the boat. The pose of Dante in the painting was already part of Delacroix's invented repertory of pathetic gesture. The literary subject distinguishes it from the works of Gericault and Gros, its immediate models, while the palette, though sombre, is rich in hue, unlike the livid tones of Gericault's work. Moreover, as one critic remarked, Delacroix may have been constitutionally incapable of painting his own times, which were, in any case, so different from those of the Napoleonic era. Guérin had tried to discourage Delacroix from exhibiting the picture, but Gros admired it, and it was bought by the State and exhibited at the Musée du Luxembourg.

For the Salon of 1824 Delacroix painted the *Massacres at Chios* (Paris, Louvre), a huge canvas inspired by contemporary life in the Near East. Oriental subjects had interested him since his youth: before having painted *Dante and Virgil* he had been considering a scene from the Greek War of Independence (1821–32), which was at that time attracting much interest in France. After his success at the Salon of 1822, he returned to the idea and in 1823 decided on the subject of Turkish massacres of the Greek population on the island of Chios, in which all but 900 of the 90,000 inhabitants were killed or abducted. Although this was a subject from contemporary life, Delacroix knew nothing about Greeks or Turks and based his scene on newspaper reports and eye-witness accounts,

1. Eugène Delacroix: *Dante and Virgil* (or the *Barque of Dante*), oil on canvas, 1.89×2.46 m, 1822 (Paris, Musée du Louvre)

supplemented by a study of costumes and accessories in the collection of his friend, the amateur painter M. Auguste. The immediate pictorial source was probably Gros's *Bonaparte Visiting the Victims of the Plague at Jaffa, 11 March 1799* (1804; Paris, Louvre; *see* GROS, ANTOINE-JEAN, fig. 1). As Delacroix worked on the painting, he returned to his reading of Dante, and notes in his *Journal* reveal a morbid and literary response: 'O smile of the dying . . . embraces of despair'. The most pathetic motif, that of the child trying to feed from the breast of its murdered mother, occurred in Colonel Olivier Voutier's account, *Mémoires sur la guerre actuelle des Grecs* (1823), but was also used as a motif in earlier subjects dealing with plagues. The wicked Turk on his rearing horse appears to belong to the group of Oriental subjects in Byron's writings; at this time Delacroix was reading Byron's *Giaour* (pubd 1813), which he illustrated in 1826. The *Combat of the Giaour and Hassan* (oil on canvas; Chicago, IL, A. Inst.) shows the Giaour as a heroic figure, but the ambiguity of the triumphant Turkish horseman in the painting is characteristic of Delacroix. The richly sombre coloration, very different from the contrasting hues of *Dante and Virgil*, probably owes something to Delacroix's study of Spanish art; the assistance of his friends, the watercolourists Charles Soulier (*fl* after 1774) and Thales Fielding, combined with the example of Constable, whose

work he had known for some time, gave the surface of the picture an unfamiliar brilliance of effect, causing Delécluze to make the startling comparison with Watteau's *Pilgrimage to the Isle of Cythera* (1717; Paris, Louvre; *see* WATTEAU, (1), fig. 3).

The State's purchase of the *Massacres at Chios* enabled Delacroix to visit England, where he stayed from May to August 1825. His first impressions were unfavourable: he found London immense and 'lacking in all that we call architecture', and the people seemed savage and ill-bred. He was received by the painters David Wilkie, whose sketches he admired; William Etty, whose Rubensian nudes were rather like his own; and Sir Thomas Lawrence, 'the flower of politeness', who showed him his incomparable collection of Old Master drawings. With Bonington, Delacroix visited the collection of armour (most London, Wallace) belonging to Dr (later Sir) Samuel Rush Meyrick and sketched various pieces. He was also able to improve his knowledge of contemporary British literature, notably Byron and Scott, and earlier literature, especially Shakespeare. He attended the theatre and saw Edmund Kean's performances in Shakespeare's *Richard III*, *Othello* and *The Merchant of Venice* and was struck by a musical version of Goethe's *Faust* at the Theatre Royal, Drury Lane, which he recalled many years later. The painting most obviously influenced by his stay in England was the portrait of *Louis-*

Auguste Schwiter (1826; London, N.G.), rejected at the Salon of 1827. It is a bravura exercise in the manner of Lawrence, whose work inspired the pose, elegance and handling. In the same year Delacroix painted a subject taken from Byron, the *Execution of the Doge Marino Faliero* (London, Wallace), on which Bonington's Anglo-Venetian manner has left its mark. Byron's poems, which Delacroix probably read in Amédée Pichot's French translation, were to provide him with exactly the kind of subject to which he was drawn. *Greece on the Ruins of Missolonghi* (1826; Bordeaux, Mus. B.-A.), Delacroix's second subject from the Greek Wars, is perhaps in part a tribute to Byron, who had died at Missolonghi in April 1824. Indeed, Byron, Greece and the exhibition in aid of the Greek cause held in 1826 at the Galerie Lebrun in Paris (to which Delacroix sent *Marino Faliero*) all absorbed his attention at this time.

The *Death of Sardanapalus* (1827; Paris, Louvre; *see* ROMANTICISM, fig. 1) was shown at the Salon of 1827 (though after the opening, from Feb 1828) and became as important a manifesto for Romantic painting as Victor Hugo's *Préface de Cromwell* of the same year was for Romantic literature. It provoked more general hostility than any other painting by Delacroix, and Sosthène de la Rochefoucauld, the Surintendant des Beaux-Arts, warned the artist that, unless he changed his style, he could no longer expect to receive State commissions. Delacroix instantly became the leader of the Romantic school. In fact, the painting bears a slight resemblance to Horace Vernet's *Massacre of Mamelukes* (1812; Amiens, Mus. Picardie) and rather incongruously combines Byronic exoticism and melancholy with the cheerful sensuousness of Rubens, for which Delacroix's own copy of a *Nereid* (*c.* 1822; Basle, Kstmus.) from the Flemish artist's *Landing of Marie de' Medici at Marseille* (1622–5; Paris, Louvre) may have provided a model. The subject is ostensibly based on Byron's *Sardanapalus* (1821), although, unlike Delacroix's painting, Byron's play ends with the Assyrian king alone on a pyre set alight by Myrrha. The tangle of bodies and the friezelike foreground countering the extravagant recession make this a difficult picture. Delacroix remained attached to the painting, which stayed in his studio until 1846.

In 1828, in the course of a somewhat short-lived friendship with Victor Hugo, Delacroix made costume designs for the latter's play *Amy Robsart* (1828), based on Scott's novel *Kenilworth* (1821) and produced at the Théâtre de l'Odéon in Paris that year. In February of the same year, a set of 17 lithographs illustrating Goethe's *Faust* (see fig. 2) was published to accompany a new French translation by Albert Stapfer. As Delacroix later remembered, these were full of the grotesque and a 'sense of the mysterious'. The plate of *Faust and Mephistopheles on Walpurgisnacht* inspired at least one early imitation, Scheffer's *The Dead Go Quickly* (1829; Lille, Mus. B.-A.). In 1828, Delacroix received a government commission to depict the *Battle of Nancy* (Nancy, Mus. B.-A.), and the following year the Duchesse de Berry commissioned him to paint the *Battle of Poitiers* (Paris, Louvre). Both owe much to Gros's work but also to Delacroix's recognition of the picturesque possibilities inherent in medieval subjects, presented as moments of dramatic conflict. This is also the theme of the *Murder of the Bishop of Liège* (1829;

De temps en temps j'aime à voir le vieux Père,
Et je me garde bien de lui rompre en Visière.

2. Eugène Delacroix: *Mephistopheles in Flight*, lithograph, 270×230 mm, 1828 (New York, Metropolitan Museum of Art)

Paris, Louvre), based on Scott's novel *Quentin Durward* (1823) and bought by Ferdinand-Philippe, Duc d'Orléans. These paintings show that Delacroix's palette darkened in these years, possibly owing to his use of bitumen, a pigment also favoured by English artists, but also, probably, to his dawning interest in Rembrandt, shared by such friends as Bonington and Hippolyte Poterlet (1803–35).

Delacroix's next important painting, *Liberty Leading the People* (1830; Paris, Louvre; *see* ALLEGORY, fig. 10), shows the obvious influence of Gericault, which had been evident even in his early works. Like the *Raft of the Medusa*, *Liberty* combines fact with allegory and represents a scene witnessed by Delacroix near the Pont d'Arcole in Paris during the early, troubled days of the July Monarchy as a heroic emblem of the struggle for freedom from oppression. Despite the difficulties inherent in representing an ideal in the form of a realistic portrait of a young working-class woman, the painting was generally well received by both critics and the public, was bought by the State (though exhibited for only a few months) and earned Delacroix the Légion d'honneur.

3. NORTH AFRICA AND SPAIN, 1832. During the late 1820s and early 1830s Delacroix had maintained his interest in the East and in the last years of the Restoration painted a number of Oriental genre scenes. Between January and July 1832, he accompanied the Comte de Mornay, Louis-Philippe's ambassador to the Sultan of Morocco, to Spain, Morocco and Algeria. The notes and

sketches he made on this journey provided him with material for the rest of his life (for further discussion *see* ORIENTALISM). The most important result of the journey was the discovery, as he saw it, of a living antiquity in the nobility of bearing and gesture that he saw around him. As he wrote to a friend, 'Imagine what it is to see, lying in the sun, walking in the streets, or mending shoes, men of consular type, each one a Cato or a Brutus'. The pages of his sketchbook from this journey are filled with written descriptions of a richly pictorial kind and finely composed vignettes drawn from life (see fig. 3; *see also* WATERCOL-OUR, colour pl. VII, fig. 2). From Meknes he wrote, 'At every step there are ready-made pictures', expressing an enthusiasm for the external reality of objects that was matched only by his interest in painting flowers during the 1840s. His visit to Spain, though brief, was equally intense, and in addition to admiring paintings by Murillo, he was reminded, by the bustle of life in the streets, of those of Goya. The Dominican monastery at Cádiz later provided the setting for *Christopher Columbus at the Monastery of La Rabida* (1838; Washington, DC, N.G.A.). In Algeria he was able to visit a harem, where he admired the tranquil domestic occupations of its inhabitants. While there he made notes that formed the basis for his first large painting based on his recollections, the *Women of Algiers in their Apartment* (1834; Paris, Louvre; *see* COLOUR, colour pl. II, fig. 2). Although this work seemed to herald a new mood of realism combined with a scientific use of colour, it is not, however, the fragment of observed life it appears. The pose of the figure on the left (of which there is a watercolour of 1832; Paris, Louvre) is close to one in a Persian miniature that Delacroix copied in 1817, and the tall figure seen from the back adopts the curious twisting pose of Ariadne in Titian's *Bacchus and Ariadne* (1522–3; London, N.G.; *see* TITIAN, fig. 4). The colour, like the forms, is calculated and is a blend of observation and invention. The harmonious lines, the flatly drawn and decorative character of many of the elements and the occasionally exaggerated brilliance of the colours—particularly the reds, pinks and blues—later appealed to Matisse. A similarly artful use of colour intensified for decorative effect, while giving an appearance of documentary realism, is found in the painting of the *Comte de Mornay's Apartment* (1832–3; Paris, Louvre).

4. LITERARY AND HISTORICAL SUBJECTS AND MU-RAL DECORATIONS, 1833–*c*. 1850. Although Arab subjects were to recur in the years following Delacroix's journey to North Africa, the general tenor of his work became increasingly literary. The death of his young nephew, Charles de Verninac, in New York in 1834 was a source of profound grief and almost certainly played a part in the increasingly sad character of his subject-matter during the 1830s. The *Prisoner of Chillon* (Paris, Louvre), painted for the Duc d'Orléans in 1834, depicts François Bonivard (*c*. 1496–1570) in prison for opposing the increasing power of Emanuel-Philibert, 10th Duke of Savoy, and watching helplessly as his two younger brothers die. It is at least possible that the tragic mood of the picture was intensified by the death of the young Verninac.

In 1834, while staying with his cousin Alexandre Bataille at the abbey of Valmont, Delacroix painted three subjects

3. Eugène Delacroix: *Two Seated Arab Women; One Called Zera Bun Sultane*, watercolour and pencil, 107×138 mm, 1832 (Paris, Musée du Louvre, Cabinet des Dessins)

in fresco (*Anacreon and a Girl*, *Leda and the Swan* and *Bacchus and a Tiger*; *in situ*) as overdoors in a corridor of the abbey. All mythological, they are Delacroix's only known work in fresco, a technique that, unlike Ingres's pupils, he did not use for his decorative schemes. However, this experiment marks an increasing interest in the technical problems of mural painting. The subjects, in a light-hearted antique idiom, as well as the decorations for the Salon du Roi at the Palais-Bourbon in Paris that were already in hand (see below), developed the classicism he had discovered in Morocco, which he then characteristically applied to literary subjects. At the same time, he moved closer to Titian and to Rubens, two artists whom he considered closest to the true spirit of antiquity. *St Sebastian Tended by the Holy Women* (1836; Nantua, St Michel) recalled Titian for some critics; others mentioned Pietro da Cortona and Carlo Maratti. The painting also contains references to the work of Michelangelo and, in the saint's pose, to Rubens's *Descent from the Cross* (1612–14; Antwerp Cathedral). While preparing drawings for this subject, Delacroix began to plan one of his most striking pictures, *Medea* (exh. Salon 1838; Lille, Mus. B.-A.; see fig. 4). Indeed, this can be seen as the culmination of the various currents of the 1830s, combining the exoticism of the *Women of Algiers in their Apartment* and the frenzy of the *Fanatics of Tangiers* (1838; Minneapolis, MN, Inst. A.; see fig. 5) with references to the Old Masters, specifically Leonardo's *Virgin of the Rocks* (1482–3), Raphael's *La Belle Jardinière* (1507) and especially Andrea del Sarto's *Charity* (1518; all Paris, Louvre; *see* SARTO, ANDREA DEL, fig. 3). The result is a highly original example of Delacroix's own statuesque, allegorical figures.

During the 1830s Delacroix received two commissions for pictures to hang in Louis-Philippe's Musée de l'Histoire de France at the château of Versailles: in 1834 the *Battle of Taillebourg* for the Galerie des Batailles (1837; *in situ*) and in 1838 the *Entry of the Crusaders into Constantinople* (1840; Paris, Louvre) to be placed in the Salles des

4. Eugène Delacroix: *Medea*, oil on canvas, 1.22×0.84 m, 1838 (Lille, Musée des Beaux-Arts)

Croisades. The subject of the earlier painting was Louis IX's victory over the English in 1242 as they guarded the bridge over the River Charente at Taillebourg. Delacroix, who attended the opening of the gallery on 10 June 1837 before the *Battle of Taillebourg* was actually installed, found the galleries anything but historic and felt that the painting had no place there. Clearly indebted to Rubens, it also contains several archaizing elements that almost recall Uccello's panels of the *Rout of San Romano* (Florence, Uffizi; London, N.G.; Paris, Louvre; see UCCELLO, PA-OLO, fig. 3): a restricted field of vision, an enlarged scale for the foreground figures and a central white horse of wooden solidity, in spite of its tossing head. The same imaginative fancy is brought to bear on the second commission, depicting the arrival in Constantinople of one of the leaders of the Fourth Crusade (1202–4), Baldwin VI of Flanders, who in 1204 became the first Latin emperor of Constantinople, together with a Venetian, Tommaso Massini, who became Patriarch, and Doge Dandolo, who thus added part of the eastern empire to his own possessions. Delacroix called the picture his 'third massacre', but it shows the invaders' procession through the streets rather than the actual assault on the city. The painting is a magnificent summation of Delacroix's mature style: Count

Baldwin reins in his horse with a gesture appropriate to an Arab chief; the central group, enlarged, as in the *Battle of Taillebourg*, but without loss of reality, is united in a complex mass. A dreary sadness fills the picture, conveyed by a half-light that Delacroix found in Veronese's paintings (*see* §II below). As the new barbarians, the Christians arrive in the city, their pennons and winged helmets fluttering against the smoking sky, while the infidel, imploring at their feet, have all the beauty and pathos of the Greeks in the foreground of the *Massacres at Chios*. The *Entry of the Crusaders* was Delacroix's last medieval subject on a large scale.

The work of Delacroix's mature years was largely dominated by mural decoration. Through his friend Adolphe Thiers, who had become Ministre du Commerce et Travaux Publics, he received a commission in 1833 to decorate the Salon du Roi in the Palais-Bourbon (now Assemblée Nationale), Paris, and the library of the Chambre des Députés (begun 1838) in the same building. In 1840 he decorated the cupola and half-dome in the library of the Senate in the Palais du Luxembourg. Further commissions came in rapid succession: the paintings for the chapel of Saints-Anges in St Sulpice (1849; *see* §5 below), the ceiling of the Galerie d'Apollon in the Musée du Louvre (1850) and the Salon de la Paix in the Hôtel de Ville (1851; destr. 1871), all in Paris.

As the Salon du Roi in the Palais-Bourbon was a dark room with many doors and windows, Delacroix realized that his paintings there would have to have a strong effect of relief. His decoration represents the components of the State—Industry, Agriculture, Justice and War—above friezes depicting related subjects. On the piers dividing the room he painted allegories of the rivers of France. For the five small cupolas of the library in the Chambre des Députés, painted in 1845–7, he chose subjects traditional for the divisions of a library: Philosophy, Natural History, Theology, Literature and Poetry. In the half-domes, his depiction of the dawning of civilization and its collapse—*Orpheus Bringing the Art of Peace to Primitive Greece* (*see* ICONOGRAPHIC PROGRAMMES, fig. 2) and *Attila and his Hordes Overrunning Italy and the Arts*—epitomizes the sense of a precarious balance between civilization and barbarism, which was so often the subject of his work and which reached its apotheosis in the ceiling of the Galerie d'Apollon in the Louvre. In this case, it has been suggested that the scheme may be indebted to a cyclical concept of history held by Delacroix's friend the painter Paul Chen-avard, which was an elaboration of a view first proposed by Giambattista Vico, whose *Scienza nuova* (Naples, 1725) had been translated from the Italian in 1827 by Jules Michelet.

The mural commission for the library of the Senate comprised paintings for a cupola, pendentives and a half-dome, prepared, as was Delacroix's habit, on canvas in the studio. The cupola decoration is loosely based on Canto 4 of Dante's *Inferno* and depicts great figures of antiquity, forming four groups symbolizing the achievements of the human spirit and all represented in a continuous landscape: Dante and Virgil; Orpheus; Socrates, Aspasia and Alcibiades; and a group of distinguished Romans that includes Marcus Aurelius, Portia, Trajan and Julius Caesar.

5. Eugène Delacroix: *Fanatics of Tangiers*, oil on canvas, 0.98×1.31 m, 1838 (Minneapolis, MN, Minneapolis Institute of Arts)

Delacroix's painting in the Galerie d'Apollon was part of the restoration of the room that had been begun just after the Revolution of 1848. After a fire in 1661, the gallery had been redecorated under the supervision of Charles Le Brun using the sun symbolism often chosen as a compliment to Louis XIV. The decorative scheme had never been completed, and the central panel of the ceiling remained empty. Delacroix, whose sympathies for Le Brun were limited, nonetheless chose to adopt the original scheme, a combat between Apollo and the serpent Python, after which Victory descends to crown Apollo, and Iris unfurls her scarf as a symbol of the triumph of Light over Darkness.

During the 1840s an increasing preoccupation with his health led Delacroix to nurse his strength and to spend more time in the country. He rented a house at Champrosay, near Fontainebleau, and also spent part of several summers at Nohant, Indres, with the composer Chopin and the writer George Sand. In 1843 his set of lithographs illustrating Shakespeare's *Hamlet* appeared, and he completed the series from Goethe's play *Goetz von Berlichingen* (1771). Around this time he also painted several pathetic subjects from literature, including the familiar theme of the *Shipwreck of Don Juan* (1840; Paris, Louvre) from Byron's poem *Don Juan* (begun 1818) and several subjects from Shakespeare's *Romeo and Juliet* (*Romeo Bids Juliet Farewell*; priv. col.), *Macbeth* (*Macbeth and the Witches*, 1825; London, Wildenstein's; *Lady Macbeth Sleepwalking*,

1850; on dep. Ottawa, N.G.) and *Othello* (*Othello and Desdemona*, 1849; Ottawa, N.G.). In 1844 he depicted Marcus Aurelius, one of his moral heroes, in *Marcus Aurelius on his Deathbed* (Lyon, Mus. B.-A.). This gives a prominent place to his son Commodus, already a very unpromising young man, and sounds the ever-present note of pessimism as the spectator ponders the reign of tyranny that is to follow. Delacroix was not altogether pleased with the picture, a feeling apparently shared by the jury of the 1845 Salon. When the government wished to acquire it for the Musée des Augustins in Toulouse, Delacroix requested that the *Sultan of Morocco and his Retinue* (1845; Toulouse, Mus. Augustins) be sent in its place.

The stoic resignation of Marcus Aurelius and the spiritual isolation of the poet Torquato Tasso in *Tasso Imprisoned in the Madhouse at Ferrara*, the latter a subject painted by Delacroix in 1824 (Zurich, Stift. Samml. Bührle) and in 1839 (Winterthur, Samml. Oskar Reinhart), were qualities that he also found in certain religious subjects. For example, his first commission for a church mural, the *Pietà* (1844) in St-Denis-du-St-Sacrement, Paris, is a continuation of his own distinctive vein of pathos combined with formal qualities derived from Rosso Fiorentino. Throughout his later career he returned to religious themes of suffering and isolation, though not always in response to a commission.

5. LATER YEARS, *c.* 1850–1863. From his early years Delacroix, like Gericault, was attracted by the savagery of wild animals; a note made in Morocco mentions a scene of fighting horses. Among the precedents for this kind of imagery was the antique group of a *Lion Attacking a Horse* (Rome, Mus. Conserv.), said to have been particularly admired by Michelangelo and copied in stone (1740; Rousham Park, Oxon) by Peter Scheemakers (ii). George Stubbs used the theme in a naturalistic setting in several paintings (e.g. *Horse Attacked by a Lion*, 1770; London, Tate; *see* STUBBS, GEORGE, fig. 1) of which Gericault made at least one copy (1820/21; Paris, Louvre). In Delacroix's versions of the subject, he was able to synthesize the classical with the exotic, with his studies of ECORCHÉ (Fr. flayed bodies), with the example of English art and with the work of Rubens, of whose paintings of hunts he owned engravings by Pieter Claesz Soutman. On 25 January 1847 he described two of them in detail, making clear how important to him were the formal values of movement, variety and unity. Of his three great lion hunts, there remain a fragment (1855; Bordeaux, Mus. B.-A.) and two complete paintings (1858; Boston, MA, Mus. F.A.; 1861; Chicago, IL, A. Inst.; *see* ANIMAL SUBJECTS, fig. 3). The one in Chicago is the most spacious and free in handling, and its circular, dancelike movement suggests a perpetual struggle, one of the underlying themes in which, however, form and content are inseparable.

After Delacroix's brief interest in the events of 1848—Théophile Thoré, in his review of the Salon of 1848, implied that Delacroix had begun to paint a pendant to *Liberty Leading the People*, and he became joint president of the new Assemblée Générale des Artistes—he soon retreated to Champrosay, where he began his great series of flower paintings, of which two finally appeared at the Salon of 1849: *Basket of Fruit in a Flowergarden* (Philadelphia, PA, Mus. A.) and *Basket of Flowers Overturned in a Park* (New York, Met.). In 1850 he began work on sketches for his great commission to decorate the chapel of Saints-Anges in St Sulpice, Paris, which was to occupy him until 1861. The subjects for the walls were *Heliodorus Driven from the Temple* and *Jacob Wrestling with the Angel* and, for the ceiling, *St Michael Defeating the Devil. Heliodorus* derives, in theme and treatment, from the work of Raphael, a constant inspiration; *Jacob Wrestling* combines, as do the best of Delacroix's pictures, references to all that he had learnt from his study of nature and the Old Masters, resulting in a work that was to remain a touchstone for succeeding generations of artists.

II. Working methods and technique.

Although his critics were chiefly concerned by Delacroix's apparent indifference to technique, very much more than by the nature of his subject-matter, Delacroix himself was more consistently exercised by problems of technique than almost any other artist of the 19th century. An early *Nude Study* (*c.* 1820; priv. col., see Johnson, 1981–9, no. 4), for example, reveals a correctness in the handling of the transparent glazes, similar to that in David's paintings, with a revealing preference for softly dramatic effects of chiaroscuro. However, from an early age he preferred the works of Gros and Pierre-Paul Prud'hon to those of Guérin and Anne-Louis Girodet. While *Dante and Virgil* (see fig. 1 above), his earliest Salon painting, is Neoclassical in the sculptural quality of the figures and their parallel relationship to the picture-plane, the handling is strikingly bold when compared with the refined finish of a painting by David or Ingres. Delacroix admired the emphatic handling of paint in the works of Gericault and Gros, in which shadows are so loaded that they become dense and dark. The drops of water on some of the foreground figures in *Dante and Virgil* appear to be pure pigment. It has been suggested, following Delacroix's pupil Pierre Andrieu (1821–92), that these originated from a study of prismatic colour and particularly from a study of the nereids in Rubens's *Landing of Marie de' Medici at Marseille*, one of which Delacroix had copied (*see* §I, 2 above). In the *Massacres at Chios* (1824), he seemed concerned to depart from the sculptural relief of the figures in *Dante and Virgil* and, according to his *Journal*, to be pursuing something like a synthesis of the techniques of Michelangelo and Velázquez. He even mentioned Ingres as a painter whose soft and melting impasto had some of the qualities he was seeking; these qualities he also found in the paintings of Raphael, whose contour was always a model for him. The influence of Delacroix's friends Charles Soulier (who had first taught him the techniques of watercolour) and Thales Fielding, his new knowledge of Constable's work and the example of Bonington combined to lead him in the direction of lighter tonality and liveliness of surface. A group of pastel studies (Paris, Louvre, Cab. Dessins) for the *Death of Sardanapalus* reveals the extent to which he was seeking a pale tonality combined with a startling variety of hue, to be achieved by a literal translation of the pastel technique into the handling of oil paint, something that was later practised by Jean-François Millet, Degas and van Gogh. In Delacroix's work this approach can be seen in the application of graphic techniques of coloration, most memorably in the still-life of hat and staff in the foreground of *Jacob Wrestling with the Angel* in St Sulpice, Paris. Bonington's brilliant work in watercolour and gouache seems to have had the effect of brightening Delacroix's palette, particularly for his smaller pictures: the use of bright impasto in the *Execution of the Doge Marino Faliero* is a good example. Many years later, when working on the decorations in the library of the Palais-Bourbon, Paris, Delacroix thought about the effect of white ground in watercolour, in which the transparency of the medium allows maximum luminosity. He attempted to achieve a similar luminosity (rather like the Pre-Raphaelites in Britain) by using a white oil ground, a practice that became commonplace with the Impressionists. In the course of his mural decorations he experimented, as did Ingres's pupils, with a number of mixtures, most commonly using a combination of oil and wax. The only time he used the fresco technique was at Valmont, yet the resulting pale luminous quality was one he valued and was able to achieve in other works by the increasing use of pale grounds and translucent pigment. Related to his work in pastel is the technique of *flochetage*, which implies a visible interweaving of brushstrokes. This is particularly associated with his later work; it is found in some landscapes of the 1850s (e.g. *Ovid among the Scythians*, 1859; London, N.G.) and is most noticeable in the murals in St Sulpice. Delacroix had used it earlier in his *Pietà* for St Denis-du-St-Sacrement, Paris, and in the *Entry of the Crusaders into Constantinople* (1840), in which the comparatively blond tonality was achieved, as at St Sulpice, by a mixture of wax and turpentine as well as by a thoughtful application of principles learnt from Veronese.

Repeatedly in his *Journal* Delacroix insisted on the necessity of applying scientific principles to the resolution of technical problems. For this reason, there is little doubt that he was aware of, if not influenced by, the theory of colour proposed by MICHEL-EUGÈNE CHEVREUL. For the practising artist, the most significant of Chevreul's ideas was that a colour seen alone will appear to be surrounded by a faint ring of its complementary colour. One of Delacroix's North African sketchbooks contains a note on colour that may be derived from Chevreul (see Joubin), indicating that a half-tone should be made not by adding black but rather the complementary of the colour. Delacroix seems to have applied this principle while working on the *Entry of the Crusaders*, as a sheet of preparatory studies (Paris, Louvre, Cab. Dessins) shows a colour circle bearing notes on primary colours and their complementaries. However, a new clarity of light and atmosphere in the painting was due primarily to the influence of Veronese, who, as Delacroix noted in his *Journal*, was able to paint brightly without violent contrasts of value (Johnson, 1963). In fact, as Delacroix worked on his large decorative schemes, Veronese was often in his thoughts, precisely because the Venetian artist's work was a splendid example of luminosity and also because his mastery of large, simple forms was a way of achieving an essential clarity of composition in work intended to be seen from a great distance. Delacroix developed a range of brushstrokes partly, presumably, as a result of his interest in the technique of pastel and partly because of his general interest in Venetian art. Critics sometimes suggested the influence of Tintoretto, whose free brushwork and handling of highlights and folds are all comparable with Delacroix's own.

The chief sources of information about Delacroix's technique are the reminiscences of his assistants, Gustave Lassalle-Bordes (1814–68), Louis de Planet (1814–75) and Pierre Andrieu. He had few pupils in any conventional sense, although after receiving his first decorative commission in 1833 he opened a studio for assistants, whom he regarded as employees. His practice cannot be compared with a Renaissance workshop; although Planet's *St Theresa* (untraced) was warmly praised by Baudelaire at the Salon of 1846, none of the artists appears to have absorbed any influence from Delacroix's own practices, nor did they show any marked success in pursuing a career. However, Planet, in his memoirs, indicated that Delacroix was conscientious in teaching the preparatory techniques of mural decoration. Planet recorded in detail the transfer of drawing to canvas, the preparation in grisaille and the supervision of the work. Occasionally he assisted Delacroix in the preparation of such easel paintings as *Marcus Aurelius on his Deathbed*. The memoirs contain a detailed discussion of Delacroix's technique of drawing, one by which he sought to assert the masses first of all. Delacroix drew continually, copying engravings

daily, almost as a musician practises scales. His working drawings, in pencil, black chalk or pen and ink, are generally loose, animated and exploratory. He constantly pursued 'relief', as he called it, which he found above all in Rubens's work, and thought this could best be obtained in drawing by using oval shapes he called *boules*. This was a long-established technique found in Leonardo's work, for example, or some of the pen-and-ink drawings of Raphael, and later used by Gros and Gericault. Delacroix's preoccupation with mass also extended to paint, and Planet explained how the drawing technique could also be applied to the grisaille preparation. Delacroix taught his pupils to attend to these and to use pure tones placed beside one another in a certain order. He stressed the importance of reflections and taught the composition and arrangement of colours on a palette and how to arrange them on the canvas. The order was carefully prescribed: Planet's notes on his master's advice for painting flesh tones are based on observations from nature and are similar to the notes Delacroix occasionally made for himself.

In 1850 Lassalle-Bordes returned to his home in the south of France, and Planet, from Toulouse, a little later. Delacroix's principal assistant on later commissions was Andrieu, who also left an account of their working practices. He described, for example, the 'van Dyck palette' used during the decoration of the library in the Senate of the Palais du Luxembourg, a limited and traditional arrangement to which Delacroix added ultramarine and viridian green. Delacroix generally used a prepared palette on which the colours were in a fixed order, though they could be modified according to the requirements of the picture. It is evident from his work that he increasingly moved towards the use of bright, pure colour of a pale tonal range and in which, as in the work of the Impressionists, the contrasts are of hue rather than of tone. His use of a contour slightly separated from the coloured area it encloses is derived from the work of the Venetians, especially Veronese; this particular use of outline, not usually associated with Delacroix, was also found in the work of Millet and Degas. As the range of Delacroix's style and brushwork reveals, the technical experimentation was unceasing. However, it was his use of colour at the service of his imagination, rather than in pursuit of a documentary and scientific realism, that provided resources for artists of a younger generation, Odilon Redon and Gauguin being the keenest followers of his example. For an illustration of Delacroix's studio *see* STUDIO, fig. 4.

III. Character and personality.

Delacroix's work had much to do with his character; this is the essence of his romanticism that, as Baudelaire argued, lay neither in subject-matter nor in style but in a way of feeling. Delacroix's first wish had been to write, and several short pieces survive from 1817: a novella set in the time of William the Conqueror and a sombre drama entitled *Victoria*. They perhaps owed their initial inspiration to the ruins at Valmont Abbey, where he first felt the lure of the past. His parents died when he was young, and all that he inherited was a lawsuit. Poor, proud and dispossessed, he nevertheless contrived, in a Parisian way, to live a rather grand social life. He was a frequent guest at François Gérard's salon, and there are numerous descriptions in his *Journal* of dinner parties, concerts and visits to the opera. He was deeply pessimistic; the range of his subjects makes clear his predilection for pathos, if not tragedy, and there are few exceptions to this in his work. He therefore found Shakespeare a particularly rich source of inspiration, especially subjects taken from *Hamlet*, with whose principal character he probably felt some affinity; an early *Self-portrait* (1829; Paris, Louvre; see fig. 6) is sometimes thought to represent him as this character. His active social life was often a source of ironic and contemptuous comment, and as he grew older, he felt an increasing need for periods of solitude or to be in the company of his closest friends. One of the most valued was Chopin, 'a man of rare distinction, the truest artist I have ever met'. The two enjoyed discussing the principles of musical composition, and on one occasion Chopin explained the use of counterpoint in music. In spite of his acknowledged role as leader of the Romantic movement in painting, Delacroix maintained that even in that domain he was a pure 'classique', valuing balance, order and clarity above all. His tastes in music were largely for works by 18th-century composers, while in literature he liked Voltaire and admired Jean Racine but could spend days happily reading Alexandre Dumas *père*. His early interest in writing found expression in the consistently literary character of his work, but he also began to publish some of his writings on aspects of art, the first appearing in 1829. He published articles on Poussin, Gros, Raphael, Michelangelo and Prud'hon but, like Joshua Reynolds, excluded some of his

favourite artists from his essays. His thoughts on art, although occasionally theoretical—as in his consideration of the PARAGONE (the question of the relative qualities of the different arts)—were always discussed with some particular painterly problem in mind. He even began work on a dictionary of art, but this project was never completed.

In a mood of high spirits accompanying the favourable reception of *Dante and Virgil* and its purchase by the State, Delacroix began to keep a journal in 1822. His diaries break off in 1824, and when he resumed them in 1847, 23 years later, the tone is far more serious, with extended passages discussing such aesthetic issues as the relative qualities of Beethoven and Mozart, both of whom he found 'modern'. Nor was he afraid to describe his moods of melancholy. The journal, which conveys something of the range and spaciousness of his art, is written with transparent honesty and good sense.

In spite of his official success and his social position, he admitted to having a wish for *gloire*. He was, not surprisingly, sensitive to criticism, and it must have been painful to his dignity to have made so many fruitless visits to the Académie des Beaux-Arts when seeking election to its ranks; he was eventually successful, on the eighth attempt, in 1857. His election, which allowed him to teach at the Ecole des Beaux-Arts, marked the point at which he began systematically to arrange his thoughts on the art and artists of the past. He frequently changed his choice of favourite artists, but his interests generally reflected problems of composition. The 'darkness' he found in Spanish art attracted him when he was working on the *Massacres at Chios*, while Veronese's 'splendid afternoon light' delighted him as he painted the *Entry of the Crusaders into Constantinople*.

In the course of painting the *Massacres at Chios*, Delacroix reflected on the 'Romantic' label that had been attached to his name: 'If by romanticism they mean the free manifestation of my personal impressions, my effort to get away from the types eternally copied in the schools, my dislike of academic recipes, then I admit that not only am I romantic but also that I have been one since I was fifteen.'

IV. Critical reception and posthumous reputation.

From the outset, the critics at the Salons found Delacroix's works challenging. His restless pursuit of forms and techniques appropriate to an art tied to his own imaginative response to literature could not fail, at times, to appear unorthodox. *Dante and Virgil*, in many ways a conventional painting, struck Delécluze, a former pupil of David, as 'a daub', when it was shown at the Salon of 1822, though he acknowledged its energy of form and colour. He felt that Delacroix and his friends were 'Shakespeareans', borrowing English techniques and dealing in extravagant and exotic subject-matter. Though he never denied Delacroix's gifts, he did not find them much to his taste, though he tried to judge them on their own terms. He was offended by what seemed a deliberate pursuit of ugliness in the *Massacres at Chios*: the cadaverous hues, so satisfactory to Delacroix, were unpleasing, and the suffering depicted seemed to exceed the limits of artistic propriety. Nonetheless, he conceded that the artist had vigour and a

6. Eugène Delacroix: *Self-portrait*, oil on canvas, 640×510 mm, 1829 (Paris, Musée du Louvre)

true sense of colour. Charles Paul Landon, who, like Delécluze, had received a traditional training, found that the *Massacres* turned ugliness into a system. Stendhal, who would have liked to have admired Delacroix, found that he could not, though he praised a sense of movement in which he thought he discerned the influence of Tintoretto. In short, an older generation of critics, who judged Delacroix's work by the standard of moderation, and of Nicolas Boileau's *L'Art poétique* (Paris, 1674), were affronted by what they saw as a cult of misery and ugliness. For Auguste Jal and Adolphe Thiers, on the other hand, occasional faults of execution did not conceal the evidence of a rich imagination, and both were touched by the beauty of the conception. Delacroix, not averse to having publicity surrounding his work, had deliberately chosen the subject of a massacre for its ability to arouse considerable interest. The scale and dramatic incident of his treatment, combined with such a subject, made public notice inevitable. It is clear from contemporary comments, and not only those that were hostile, that Delacroix was perceived as setting out to subvert Neo-classical practice. The artist Arnold Scheffer (1795–1858), not unsympathetic to the painting, wrote that it was, more than any other work, in opposition to tradition and that Delacroix was taking as much trouble not to arrange his picture as David's pupils took to arrange theirs. Delacroix's position as an *enfant terrible* was established. The critics most sympathetic to Delacroix's work in the 1820s were Jal, a former naval officer, and Thiers, who later became a government minister in the July Monarchy. Thiers (sometimes thought to have been prompted by his friend Gérard) wrote in particularly glowing terms about *Dante and Virgil*, in which he recognized spiritual affinities with Michelangelo and Rubens, and he announced to his readers that Delacroix had 'received genius'.

Although neither the *Execution of the Doge Marino Faliero* nor the *Agony in the Garden* (1824–7; Paris, St-Paul-St-Louis) could be thought to have anything of the disturbing character of the *Massacres*, they both attracted strongly worded criticism. Writing for *Le Globe*, Louis Vitet, although a strong sympathizer with the Greek cause, seems to have had no particular sympathy for the new school and took Delacroix to task for an excessively literary treatment in *Marino Faliero*. In fact, as was often the case, the chief burden of his criticism fell on what he felt were faults of drawing and colour. Delécluze, too, complained of the treatment of the subject, the drawing and particularly the prominent position of the dazzling white staircase, finally dismissing the work as a 'brilliant sketch'. Once again Jal took for a virtue what Vitet had seen to be a fault; the design that Vitet found too mannered was for Jal charming in that it recalled medieval wood-engravings. Jal, with some prescience, added that Delacroix would not always retain the small-scale and mannered appearance of *Marino Faliero*, of which he had so many imitators. As for the *Agony in the Garden*, Jal found the figure of Christ too human, while Delécluze disliked Christ's stoic resignation. Almost all critics, however, found the angels appealing, Delécluze remarking that they looked like pretty English schoolgirls.

On the other hand, the *Death of Sardanapalus* stirred up a roar of indignation that, however, did not include

Stendhal or Victor Hugo. On this occasion, Jal shared Delécluze's view that the picture lacked unity. However, he subsequently wrote of Delacroix's gifts in terms that anticipated Baudelaire, expressing his view that his execution was almost savage, that Dante would have understood him and that his palette was rich and terrible. *Liberty Leading the People*, shown at the Salon of 1831, was probably the most discussed of Delacroix's submissions. Delécluze and Landon were doubtful of its merits, the former admiring the concept but finding it exaggerated, the latter appreciating the composition but intensely disliking the figure of Liberty. The greatest enthusiasm was expressed by the young poet Heinrich Heine, who found in it 'the real appearance of the July days' (*Französische Maler: Gemäldeausstellung in Paris, 1831*; Hamburg, 1834). Victor Schoelcher, writing for the newly founded journal *L'Artiste*, whose editor Achille Ricourt was a friend of Delacroix's, mentioned the painter's 'transformation through the brush of the ugly into an object of beauty'. The young Gustave Planche objected to the alliance of fact and allegory but within two years was writing with approval about the painting for that very reason.

During the July Monarchy, reviews of Delacroix's work continued to be mixed, and Planche's sympathies moved away from Delacroix as he looked for a less purely Romantic artist. Jal and Thiers ceased to publish art criticism. However, Delacroix's cause was taken up by several young critics: Maurice-Alexandre Decamps (1804–52), brother of the painter, Alexandre-Gabriel Decamps; Théophile Thoré; Théophile Gautier; and Charles Baudelaire, the critic whose name, more than any other, is linked with Delacroix's. In his poem *Les Phares*, Baudelaire characterized the artist as 'a lake of blood haunted by wicked angels', an extreme example of his tendency to stress the molochism, as he termed it, of Delacroix's imagination. On 30 May 1856 Delacroix admitted in his *Journal* that Baudelaire was right to claim that he found enjoyment in the terrible but he was anxious to disclaim any affinity with Edgar Allan Poe, whose incoherence and obscurity of expression were not at all to his taste. The 35 canvases Delacroix exhibited in 1855 at the Exposition Universelle in Paris created a favourable impression. The Salon of 1859, on the other hand, was somewhat unsatisfactory, and Philippe Burty referred to it as the painter's Waterloo. Maxime Du Camp's criticism was particularly wounding and Delacroix never again showed at the Salon.

Delacroix's posthumous reputation began almost immediately after his death in 1863. The studio sale organized by Burty six months after his death brought in 360,000 francs against an estimate of 100,000. In the following year Théophile Silvestre published *Eugène Delacroix: Documents nouveaux*, Burty began to prepare an edition of Delacroix's letters and Alfred Robaut had already embarked on his catalogue raisonné. During the 1860s the dealers Hector Brame and Paul Durand-Ruel bought a series of Delacroix's major works and sold them at great profit. For new generations of artists, he was the great liberator. Henri Fantin-Latour's group portrait, *Homage to Delacroix* (1864; Paris, Mus. d'Orsay), was a summation of the debt owed to Delacroix by such young artists as

Manet, Puvis de Chavannes, Théodore Chassériau and Paul Signac. By 1880 his status was unassailable with artists, collectors and the general public. In that year, Henry James wrote that 'he belongs to the family of the great masters of the past—he had the same large liberal way of understanding his business'. In the 20th century, substantial scholarship, both in England and France, has greatly increased the knowledge of his work, and the great retrospective held at the Louvre in 1963 on the centenary of his death confirmed his position as the only truly universal artist of the French school after Poussin.

WRITINGS

P. Burty, ed.: *Lettres d'Eugène Delacroix* (Paris, 1878, rev., 2 vols, 1880)
E. Faure, ed.: *Eugène Delacroix: Oeuvres littéraires*, 2 vols (Paris, 1923)
A. Joubin, ed.: *Journal d'Eugène Delacroix*, 3 vols (Paris, 1932/*R* 1981; Eng. trans., ed. W. Pach, London, 1938)
——: *Correspondance générale d'Eugène Delacroix*, 5 vols (Paris, 1935–8) [essentially supersedes Burty's edn]
A. Dupont, ed.: *Lettres intimes: Correspondance inédite* (Paris, 1954)
L. Johnson, ed.: *Eugène Delacroix: Further Correspondence, 1817–1863* (Oxford, 1991)

BIBLIOGRAPHY

EARLY SOURCES

T. Silvestre: *Eugène Delacroix: Documents nouveaux* (Paris, 1864)
A. Moreau: *E. Delacroix et son oeuvre* (Paris, 1873)
A. Robaut: *L'Oeuvre complet de Eugène Delacroix: Peintures, dessins, gravures, lithographies* (Paris, 1885/*R* New York, 1969) [cat. rais.]
M. Tourneux: *Eugène Delacroix devant ses contemporains: Ses écrits, ses biographies, ses critiques* (Paris, 1886)
P. Signac: *D'Eugène Delacroix au néo-impressionnisme* (Paris, 1899/*R* 1964)
L. Delteil: *Ingres et Delacroix* (1908), iii of *Le Peintre-graveur illustré (XIXe et XXe siècles)* (Paris, 1906–26/*R* New York, 1969)
L. de Planet: *Souvenirs de travaux de peinture avec M. Eugène Delacroix*, ed. A. Joubin (Paris, 1929)

GENERAL

T. Silvestre: *Histoire des artistes vivants: Etudes d'après nature* (Paris, 1856); expanded edns, 1878, 1926 as *Les Artistes français*
P. Andrieu: *Musée de Montpellier: La Galerie Bruyas* (Paris, 1876)
N. M. Athanassoglou-Kallymer: *French Images from the Greek War of Independence, 1821–1830* (New Haven and London, 1989)

MONOGRAPHS AND EXHIBITION CATALOGUES

E. Moreau-Nélaton: *Delacroix raconté par lui-même*, 2 vols (Paris, 1916)
R. Escholier: *Delacroix, peintre, graveur, écrivain*, 3 vols (Paris, 1926–9)
L. Johnson: *Delacroix* (London, 1963) [best short account; fundamental for colour theory]
Mémorial de l'exposition Eugène Delacroix organisée au Musée du Louvre à l'occasion du centenaire de la mort de l'artiste (exh. cat., ed. M. Sérullaz; Paris, Louvre, 1963)
R. Huyghe: *Delacroix ou le combat solitaire* (Paris, 1964; Eng. trans., London, 1963)
F. A. Trapp: *The Attainment of Delacroix* (Baltimore and London, 1971)
L. Rossi Bortolatto: *L'opera pittorica completa di Delacroix* (Milan, 1972) [summary cat. of paintings]
De David à Delacroix: La Peinture française de 1774 à 1830 (exh. cat., ed. F. J. Cummings, R. Rosenblum and A. Schnapper; Paris, Grand Pal., 1974–5); Eng. edn as *David to Delacroix: French Painting, 1774–1830: The Age of Revolution* (Detroit, MI, Inst. A.; New York, Met., 1975), pp. 377–84 [important for context]
L. Johnson: *The Paintings of Eugène Delacroix: A Critical Catalogue*, 6 vols (Oxford, 1981–9) [supersedes all previous accounts; vols 5 and 6 deal with public decorations]
Eugène Delacroix, 1798–1863: Paintings, Drawings and Prints from North American Collections (exh. cat. by L. Johnson and others, New York, Met., 1991)
T. Wilson-Smith: *Delacroix: A Life* (London, 1992)
Copies créés de Turner à Picasso: 300 oeuvres inspirées par les maîtres du Louvre (exh. cat., ed. J.-P. Cuzin and M.-A. Dupuy; Paris, Louvre, 1993), pp. 234–71

SPECIALIST STUDIES

L. Rudrauf: *Eugène Delacroix et le problème du romantisme artistique* (Paris, 1942)
L. Horner: *Baudelaire, critique de Delacroix* (Geneva, 1956)
L. Johnson: 'The Formal Sources of Delacroix's *Barque de Danté*', *Burl. Mag.*, c (1958), pp. 228–32
M. Sérullaz: *Les Peintures murales de Delacroix* (Paris, 1963) [excellent plates, especially of details]
G. P. Mras: *Eugène Delacroix's Theory of Art* (Princeton, 1966)
J. J. Spector: *The Murals of Eugène Delacroix at Saint-Sulpice* (New York, 1967)
H. Bessis: 'L'Inventaire après décès d'Eugène Delacroix', *Bull. Soc. Hist. A. Fr.* (1969), pp. 199–222
J. J. Spector: *Delacroix: The Death of Sardanapalus* (London, 1974)
G. Doy: 'Delacroix et Faust', *Nouv. Est.*, 21 (May–June 1975), pp. 18–23
H. Toussaint: *La Liberté guidant le peuple de Delacroix*, Les Dossiers du département des peintures (Paris, 1982)
F. Haskell: 'Chios, the Massacres and Delacroix', *Chios: A Conference at the Homereion in Chios, 1984*, pp. 335–58
M. Sérullaz: *Dessins d'Eugène Delacroix*, 2 vols, Paris, Louvre, Cab. Dessins cat. (Paris, 1984)
N. M. Athanassoglou-Kallymer: *Eugène Delacroix: Prints, Politics and Satire, 1814–1822* (New Haven and London, 1991)
T. Wilson-Smith: *Delacroix: A Life* (London, 1992)
E. Davies: *Portrait of Delacroix* (Edinburgh, 1994)

COLIN HARRISON

Delacroix, Henri-Edmond-Joseph. *See* CROSS, HENRI EDMOND.

Delafontaine, Pierre-Maximilien (*b* Paris, *c.* 1774; *d* Paris, *bur* 3 Dec 1860). French painter, bronze-founder and collector. He was born into a family of bronze-founders. He studied in Jacques-Louis David's atelier and on David's arrest in 1794 accompanied him on his way to prison and with 16 of his fellow students signed an address to the National Convention calling for his master's release. He exhibited for the first time at the Salon of 1798 both the full-length *Portrait of a Man Skating*, or the portrait of *Bertrand Andrieu* (Paris, Hôtel de la Monnaie), a rather stiff and awkward treatment of the subject in comparison with, for instance, Gilbert Stuart's *Skater* (1782; Washington, DC, N.G.A.), and the *Deluge* (Gray, Mus. Martin), inspired by the poems of Salomon Gessner (1730–88) (the episode in which Phanor carries the fainting Semira). Delafontaine considered this painting to be his masterpiece. At the Salon of 1799 he showed the portrait of *Alexandre Lenoir*, a somewhat gauche, full-length depiction of the creator of the Musée des Monuments Français (Paris, Louvre). The portrait of *Bichat* (*c.* 1800; Versailles, Château) dates from the same period.

He exhibited again in the Salons of 1801 and 1802, but his career as a painter was interrupted in 1804: on the reverse of a drawing, the *Death of General Marceau* (Chartres, Mus. B.-A.), he explained 'sketch of a painting I was to execute for the Government until I was forced by circumstances to give up painting after a long illness and to succeed my father in the manufacture of bronzes in 1804'. He resumed the direction of his father's foundry until 1840, when it passed into the hands of his son Augustin-Maximilien. Delafontaine became one of the most skilful bronze-chasers in Paris (e.g. sconces in gilded bronze in the tabernacle of the chapel of the Holy Trinity, château of Fontainebleau, and bronzes in the chapel of Dreux). He regularly worked with François-Honoré-Georges Jacob (1770–1841), a cabinetmaker, and played an important role in furniture and the decorative arts during the Empire and the Restoration. He also cast two statues by François Rude, *Aristaeus* and *Eurydice* (both Dijon, Mus. B.-A.).

Delafontaine collected paintings and drawings by contemporary artists (e.g. Merry Joseph Blondel, who married Delafontaine's daughter in 1832, David, François Granet, Pierre Révoil, Lancelot Turpin de Crissé), which were sold in Paris on 6 February 1861. Several items were bought back by the family and bequeathed in 1932 to the Musée Baron Martin in Gray and to the Musée des Arts Décoratifs in Paris (including the famous *Raphael's Casino in Rome* by Jean-Auguste-Dominique Ingres). He left his manuscript reminiscences to the Bibliothèque de l'Institut de France; they constitute an important source for David and his circle.

UNPUBLISHED SOURCES
Paris, Bib. Inst. France, MS. 782–4 [autobiographical fragments]

BIBLIOGRAPHY
A.-P. de Mirimonde: 'Pierre-Maximilien Delafontaine: Elève de David', *Gaz. B.-A.*, n.s. 5, xlviii (Oct 1956), pp. 31–8
De David à Delacroix: La Peinture française de 1774 à 1830 (exh. cat., ed. F. J. Cummings, R. Rosenblum and A. Schnapper; Paris, Grand Pal., 1974–5); Eng. edn as *David to Delacroix: French Painting, 1774–1830: The Age of Revolution* (Detroit, MI, Inst. A.; New York, Met.; 1975), pp. 382–3
P. Durey: 'XIXe siècle: Peintures et dessins de 1800 à 1870', *Rev. Louvre*, 5–6 (1980), pp. 299–300

MARIE-CLAUDE CHAUDONNERET

Delafosse, Jean-Charles (*b* Paris, 1734; *d* Paris, 11 Oct 1789). French decorative designer, engraver and architect. In 1747 he was apprenticed to the sculptor Jean-Baptiste Poullet (*d* 1775), but he seems not to have completed his apprenticeship. By 1767 he styled himself 'architecte et professeur pour le dessin'. In 1768 he published the first volume of his most important work, the *Nouvelle iconologie historique*. It contains 110 plates, nearly all engraved by Delafosse himself, with designs for furniture, decorative objects and architectural ornament in the heavy, classicizing, Louis XVI style. In addition, each design bears a particular, usually complex, symbolic or iconological meaning, pertaining to an almost encyclopedic range of subject-matter. In some of his designs he manipulated abstract shapes in new ways, using such forms as truncated columns, cones, pyramids, spheres, discs and rectangles, sometimes carefully shaded to appear simultaneously three-dimensional and flat. His compositional methods were characteristic of the most revolutionary architectural designs of the period, such as those of Étienne-Louis Boullée and Claude-Nicolas Ledoux. In these images he used discrepancies of size, employing Piranesi's device of juxtaposing tiny human figures with immense architectural elements, sometimes heavily rusticated to emphasize the contrast further; reversals of weight and balance; and spatial ambiguities, playing off three-dimensional objects against two-dimensional shapes. He divorced familiar architectural elements—the base of a column, a pediment, a single Ionic volute—from their usual functions and placed them in new and witty contexts.

Delafosse was responsible for two houses (1776–83) in the Rue du Faubourg-Poissonière, Paris: the Hôtel Titon and the Hôtel Goix. They show little structural innovation, but their ornamentation reveals characteristic touches: at the Hôtel Titon there are lions' heads decorating the main entrance, laurel branches above the doors, friezes of classical arabesques between the floor levels in the inner courtyard and two large classical urns in niches in the

vestibule. In 1780 Delafosse was in Bordeaux, where in 1781 he became a member of the Académie de Peinture. In 1789 he joined the Garde National, Paris, and he is known to have played an active role in the Revolution.

UNPUBLISHED SOURCES
London, RIBA [drgs]
Paris, Mus. A. Déc. [drgs]

WRITINGS
Nouvelle iconologie historique, 2 vols (Paris, 1768, 2/1771)

BIBLIOGRAPHY
G. Levallet: 'L'Ornemaniste Jean-Charles Delafosse', *Gaz. B.-A.*, i (1929), pp. 158–69
E. Kaufmann: *Architecture in the Age of Reason* (Cambridge, MA, 1955, New York, 2/1968), pp. 151, 154–6
M. Gallet: 'Jean-Charles Delafosse, architecte', *Gaz. B.-A.*, 6th ser., lxi (1963), pp. 157–64
——: *Demeures parisiennes, l'époque de Louis XVI* (Paris, 1964), pp. 66–7
A. Braham: *The Architecture of the French Enlightenment* (London, 1980, 2/1989)
D. Wiebenson and C. Baines: 'Oeuvres de J. Ch. Delafosse', *French Books: Sixteenth through Nineteenth Centuries* (1993), i of *Nouvelle Iconologie historique*; *The Mark J. Millard Architectural Collection* (Washington, DC, and New York, 1993–), pp. 130–35, nos. 58–9

CLAIRE BAINES

De la Gardie, Magnus Gabriel (*b* Reval [now Tallinn], Estonia, 15 Oct 1622; *d* Vänngarn, Uppland, 26 April 1686). Swedish statesman and patron. He was one of the most influential noblemen of the era when Sweden was a great power. His wife was a cousin of Queen Christina (*reg* 1632–54) and sister of her successor, Karl X Gustav (*reg* 1654–60). He was Chancellor from 1660 to 1680 and also held some of the kingdom's other highest offices. He was the country's greatest landowner and builder, as well as its foremost cultural patron. As *riksmarskalk* (state marshal), his building projects included castles, churches, hospitals, schools and even whole planned cities. He invited to Sweden such artists as Pierre Signac (*d* 1684) and Hendrik Munnichoeven. He commissioned Signac's masterpiece, a portrait miniature of *Queen Christina as Diana* (1646), painted on the lid of a tankard (Stockholm, Kun. Husgerådskam.), while Munnichoeven executed a double portrait of *De la Gardie and his Wife, Maria Euphrosyne* (1652; Mariefred, Gripsholm Slott).

In his many residences De la Gardie gathered together significant art collections, now dispersed or destroyed. His library and collection of engravings provided models for many artists and craftsmen. He also made a lasting contribution to the new field of antiquarian research. At his own cost he restored and rebuilt ancient monuments. He was also one of the initiators behind the creation of the Antikvitetskollegium (now the Riksantikvarieämbetet och Statens Historika Museer [Central Board of National Antiquities and National Historical Museums]), and the medieval collections that are the foundation of the Statens Historiska Museum. Among the valuable manuscripts that he donated to the Uppsala Universitet, the renowned Gothic *Codex argenteus* is notable.

De la Gardie employed various painters, sculptors and stuccoists in the decoration of his residences. The formidable castle at Läckö, the small elegant castle at Mariedal, and Karlberg Castle in Stockholm constitute the few surviving magnificent Baroque interiors that he created. Among the buildings that have been lost is the palace in

Stockholm, known as 'Peerless', built between 1635 and 1642 by Hans Jakob Kristler (1592–1645) for De la Gardie's father. This was one of the most magnificent Swedish residences of the period, whose interior De la Gardie remodelled (1655–67), but which burnt down in 1825. He employed the most prominent architects, such as Jean De la Vallée and Nicodemus Tessin (ii), and was himself extraordinarily actively involved in planning his buildings. Owing to inventories, as well as his own letters, instructions, sketches and plans (now Stockholm, Riksarkivet and Lund Ubib., De la Gardie Arkv), it is possible to understand in detail his projects and ideas.

BIBLIOGRAPHY

P. Wieselgren, ed.: *DelaGardieska Archifet* [The De la Gardie archive], 20 vols (Lund, 1833–40), pp. 4–9, 11–13

A. Hahr: *Konst och konstnärer vid Magnus De la Gardies hof* [Art and artists at the court of Magnus Gabriel De la Gardie] (Uppsala, 1905)

G. Lindahl: *Magnus Gabriel De la Gardie: Hans gods och hans folk* [Magnus Gabriel De la Gardie: his possessions and his people] (Stockholm, 1968)

Magnus Gabriel De la Gardie (exh. cat., Stockholm, Nmus., 1980), no. 434

PONTUS GRATE

Delaissé, L(eon) M. J. (*b* Herseaux [Flem. Herzeeuw], 7 Sept 1914; *d* Oxford, 4 Jan 1972). Belgian art historian. He studied the philology of Romance languages at the Catholic University of Leuven and in 1940, after the outbreak of World War II, took part in the 18-day campaign and thereafter joined the Resistance. He was seriously injured in the Normandy landings of 1944. In 1946 he joined the Bibliothèque Royale Albert 1er in Brussels, working first in the department of Belgian bibliography and later in the department of manuscripts. He was appointed librarian in 1948 and assistant curator in 1956. From 1959 to 1963 he taught in several American universities (Princeton, Berkeley and Harvard); he resigned from the Bibliothèque Royale in 1963 and became a fellow of All Souls College, Oxford, where he worked until his death.

As a codicologist, Delaissé contributed to the knowledge of manuscripts of the late Middle Ages, particularly by his study of the original manuscript of Thomas à Kempis (Brussels, Bib. Royale Albert 1er, MSS. 5855–61), the subject of his doctoral thesis, later published as *Le Manuscrit autographe de Thomas à Kempis et 'L'Imitation de Jésus Christ'* (Brussels, 1956). He had already published articles on codicology in *Scriptorium* and then, following his teacher, Professor Frédéric Lyna (1888–1970), he concentrated on the study of illuminated manuscripts, publishing articles mainly devoted to manuscript illumination in the northern and southern Netherlands. Through long and numerous study trips, Delaissé collected a large amount of material about the art of manuscript illumination in the southern Netherlands, much of which is to be found in his exhibition catalogue of 1959. The emphasis in this important work is on the collection of Philip the Good, Duke of Burgundy, indisputably one of the most important bibliophiles of his time, and it discusses 275 manuscripts from European and American collections.

WRITINGS

La Miniature flamande: Le Mécénat de Philippe le Bon. Exposition organisée à l'occasion du 400e anniversaire de la fondation de la Bibliothèque Royale de Philippe II, le 12 avril 1559 (exh. cat., Brussels, Bib. Royale Albert 1er, 1959)

A Century of Dutch Manuscript Illumination (Berkeley, CA, 1968)

Regular contributions to *Scriptorium* (1946–69)

BIBLIOGRAPHY

NBW

F. Remy: *Le Personnel scientifique de la Bibliothèque Royale de Belgique, 1837–1962: Répertoire bio-bibliographique* (Brussels, 1962), p. 48

L. Gilissen: 'In Memoriam L. M. J. Delaissé: 1914–1972', *Quaerendo*, ii (1972), pp. 83–6

G. Dogaer and E. König: 'A Bibliography of L. M. J. Delaissé and a Note on the Delaissé Papers Deposited in the Bodleian Library, Oxford', *Quaerendo*, vi (1976), pp. 352–9

GEORGES DOGAER

Delaistre, François-Nicolas (*b* Paris, 9 March 1746; *d* Paris, 23 April 1832). French sculptor. He was a pupil of Félix Lecomte and of Louis-Claude Vassé. He won the Prix de Rome in 1772 and, after a year at the Ecole Royale des Elèves Protégés, completed his training at the Académie de France in Rome between 1773 and 1777. It was there that he probably first met the architect Pierre-Adrien Pâris, for whom he later worked and who owned several of his terracotta models (Besançon, Mus. B.-A. & Archéol.). His best-known work, the group *Cupid and Psyche*, was originally executed in Rome (later marble version; Paris, Louvre); it is a graceful, rather precious treatment of a theme popular with Neo-classical sculptors, made for the collector Pierre-Marie Gaspard Grimod, Comte d'Orsay.

Delaistre was approved (*agréé*) by the Académie Royale in 1785. Under the *ancien régime* he was especially active as a religious sculptor. He exhibited in 1787 a group of the *Virgin and Child* for St Nicolas-des-Champs, Paris (plaster; destr.), and later executed a statue of *St Teresa* for the church at Meung (Loiret) and four *Evangelists* and eight *Angels* (1789–90), based on drawings by Pâris, for Orléans Cathedral.

The Revolution put an end to Delaistre's career as a religious sculptor and, although he exhibited regularly at the Salon between 1785 and 1824, he received relatively few commissions. Most notable were a low relief of *Astronomy* (stone, 1792–3; untraced) for the Panthéon, Paris, a statue of *Phocion* (marble, 1804 Salon; untraced) for the chamber of the Sénat in the Palais du Luxembourg, Paris, a bust of *Veronese* (marble, 1804–6; Paris, Louvre) and a statue of *Joseph Bonaparte* (marble, 1805–8; Versailles, Château). His models (1808; untraced) for the reliefs of the Colonne de la Grande Armée, Place Vendôme, Paris, were rejected. Throughout his career he was an accomplished portrait sculptor with works ranging in date from the bust of *Jacques–Philibert Varenne de Fenille* (1782; Bourg-en-Bresse, Mus. Ain.) to that of *Empress Marie-Louise* (1813; Fontainebleau, Château).

BIBLIOGRAPHY

Lami

PHILIPPE DUREY

De Lalaing, Jacques, Comte (*b* London, 4 Nov 1858; *d* Brussels, 10 Oct 1917). Belgian painter and sculptor. He was born into a noble family: his father was a diplomat and his mother an English aristocrat. In England he received a rigid Protestant education that may explain the unemotional quality of much of his work. After serving in the British Navy between 1872 and 1874, he decided to become an artist, joining the studio of Jean-François Portaels in Brussels. He was also in contact with Louis

Gallait, Alfred Jean André Cluysenaer (1837–1902) and Edouard Agneesens.

De Lalaing made his début in 1882 at the Salon de L'Essor in Brussels. *The Intercepted Courier* (Lille, Mus. B.-A.), a large canvas inspired by the Franco-Prussian War, dates from this period. It is sober in style and of a tragic simplicity, qualities that recur in his *Equestrian Portrait* (1883; Ghent, Mus. S. Kst.). The figure of the lancer is sculptural in its simplicity and grandeur. When the portrait of the *Father of the Sculptor Thomas Vinçotte* (1884; priv. col.) was shown, De Lalaing was unanimously recognized by the critics as a great portrait painter. In his many society portraits a strong concern with psychology and plastic form is apparent. He was not, however, interested in colour.

Around 1884 De Lalaing was encouraged by his friends Vinçotte and Jef Lambeaux to take up sculpture. He produced several remarkable groups as well as a number of portrait busts. He delighted in the representation of physical strength, especially in depictions of wild animals (e.g. *Tigers Fighting over their Prey*; bronze, Ghent, Mus. S. Kst.). Among other important sculptures are *Fighting on Horseback* (bronze, 1908; Brussels, Bois de la Cambre) and *To the English Soldiers who Fell at Waterloo* (1890; Evere, Brussels cemetery). Even in his most energetic works a certain dryness is discernible. In this respect De Lalaing differs from Lambeaux, for whom he nevertheless had a deep admiration. He also executed an *Equestrian Statue of Leopold I* (1901–4; Ostend) and a series of allegorical bronzes for the Square Ambiorix in Brussels depicting *L'Elément barbare*, *La Société organisée*, and *La Société ornée* (all 1899; see Meirsschaut, pp. 182–3).

De Lalaing continued to paint while working as a sculptor. In 1885 he produced the austere, huge canvas *The Primitive Hunter* (Brussels, Mus. A. Anc.). In 1893 he executed the decoration of the Escalier d'Honneur in the Hôtel de Ville in Brussels (*in situ*); it illustrates allegorically the opposition between democratic freedom and feudal power in a style that exploits historicism and symbolism to the full. He also decorated the Salle des Séances in the Senate, Brussels, with paintings (*in situ*) depicting memorable events in Belgian history. The colours of the murals have faded to such an extent that they resemble monochrome bas-reliefs. Despite these official commissions De Lalaing became increasingly disenchanted with his own work and the criticism it received. He remained outside, and scarcely aware of, the artistic developments of his times.

BIBLIOGRAPHY

P. Meirsschaut: *Les Sculptures de plein air en Bruxelles* (Brussels, 1900)
P. Lambotte: *Le Comte Jacques de Lalaing* (Nijmegen, 1918)
J. Delville: 'Notice sur le comte Jacques de Lalaing', *Annu. Acad. Royale Sci., Lett. & B.-A. Belgique* (1927), pp. 159–72
Cent Cinquante Ans de vie artistique (exh. cat., Brussels, Pal. Acad., 1980), pp. 59–60
R. Kerremans: 'Jacques de Lalaing', *La Sculpture belge au XIX siècle* (exh. cat., Brussels, Générale de Banque, 1990), pp. 342-3
H. Lettens and others: *Jacques de Lalaing (1858–1917): Le Mat électrique* (Brussels, 1993)

RICHARD KERREMANS

Delamair [de Lamair], **Pierre-Alexis** (*b* Paris, *c.* 1676; *d* Châtenay-Malabry, nr Paris, 1745). French architect. He was the son of Antoine Delamair, architect and contractor

to the Royal Works. He was involved with the embellishment of the city of Paris, and in 1699 he submitted designs for a pedestal for the statue (destr.) of King Louis XIV in the Place Vendôme, Paris. In 1704 he began to build a town house at 142, Rue de Grenelle, Paris, for the Abbé de Pompadour; this was a single-storey building in which the articulation of the façade and sculptural decoration prefigured his later work. At the age of 28 Delamair was brought to prominence by Cardinal de Rohan, Chief Almoner of France, who recommended him to his parents, the Prince and Princess of Soubise, for the most important architectural project of the time: the design of the Hôtel du Soubise in the Marais district of Paris (now the Archives Nationales). The former Hôtel de Guise was to be transformed into a princely residence, and the stroke of genius was Delamair's use of the old riding school as the *cour d'honneur*, surrounded on three sides by a colonnade of coupled composite columns that sweeps round in a curve behind the screen wall to the street, while at the other end of the court the motif of coupled columns is carried across the façade of the house, thereby achieving a closely interrelated composition. At the same time, Cardinal de Rohan commissioned Delamair to design a new town house at the end of the garden that extended in front of the main façade of the Hôtel du Soubise. Beginning in 1705, Delamair erected a vast building of 13 bays, with a central columned frontispiece. On the side of the Rue Vieille-du-Temple this was linked to service wings, which bounded a *cour d'honneur* that ended in a semicircle. Delamair also produced designs for the interior layouts of the two hôtels, for the staircases and for the decoration of the *appartements*. Cardinal de Rohan continued to favour him for his own residence, but the Rohan-Soubise family considered his scheme, involving *pièces en enfilade* with doors on a central axis, to be old-fashioned and soon transferred its patronage to Germain Boffrand. Anxious to stake his claim to the work, Delamair specified in his accounts of the sums due to him that the purpose of the document was to 'provide definite evidence for posterity that the works mentioned...were the results of his designs'.

In his writings, Delamair provided a list of other buildings for which he was responsible, including houses and hôtels in Paris and châteaux in various regions of France, but it is difficult to determine to what extent these were actually completed. He is known, however, to have rebuilt the Hôtel de Duras (destr.) in the Faubourg Saint-Honoré, Paris, and was very proud of some of his solutions for the arrangement of the *appartements en enfilade* and for the construction of French-style stoves. Among the memoirs and statements that were intended to protect the authorship of his architectural and technical achievements are an album of his *Oeuvres d'architecture*, which he dedicated to the Elector of Bavaria, whose patronage he was seeking, and *La Pure Vérité*. A major work on town planning, *Le Songe et le réveil d'Alexis Delamair* (1731), which he dedicated to King Louis XV, was lost in the fire at the Royal Library in 1871. Delamair's work was characteristic of the style at the end of Louis XIV's reign, displaying a love of monumental architecture articulated with columns and pediments and adorned with numerous sculptural figures; he skilfully introduced frontispieces and designed staircases of magnificent grandeur. However, the heavy influence of the style of Versailles in the layout of his *appartements* lost him the favour of the Soubise family and reveals his inability to adapt to changing tastes.

UNPUBLISHED SOURCES

Munich, Bayer. Staatsbib. [MS. of P.-A. Delamair: *Oeuvres d'architecture* (1714)]

Paris, Bib. Arsenal [MS. of P.-A. Delamair: *La Pure Vérité* (1737)]

BIBLIOGRAPHY

C. V. Langlois: *Les Anciens Hôtels de Clisson, de Guise et de Rohan-Soubise au Marais* (Paris, 1922)

L. Hautecoeur: *Histoire de l'architecture classique en France*, iii (Paris, 1950)

J.-P. Babelon: *Les Archives nationales: Histoire et description des bâtiments*, i of *Catalogue du Musée de l'Histoire en France* (Paris, 1958, 2/1969), pp. 26, 49, 87

——: 'Les Façades des palais Rohan-Soubise sur le jardin', *Rev. A.* [Paris], 4 (1969), pp. 66–73

M. Gallet: *Paris Domestic Architecture of the 18th Century* (London, 1972)

JEAN-PIERRE BABELON

Delamayne, John. See MAIANO, DA, (3).

Delamere Station. See LIGHTNING BROTHERS.

Delamotte [De La Motte]. English family of artists. (1) William Delamotte was a painter in watercolours and oils, mostly topographical scenes. His brother George O. Delamotte was a landscape painter. William Alfred Delamotte (*fl* 1825–55), perhaps a son of William and brother of (2) P. H. Delamotte, executed topographical watercolours (many of them engraved) in a style that is broader and more sharply delineated than that of William, with whom he is often confused; a volume of lithographs of Oxford colleges, drawn and lithographed by William Alfred, was published in 1841.

(1) William (Alfred) Delamotte (*b* Weymouth, Dorset, 2 Aug 1775; *d* Oxford, 2 Feb 1863). Painter. As a boy in Weymouth, Delamotte was encouraged in his drawing by the attention of George III, a frequent visitor to the town. In 1794 he went to London to study under Benjamin West at the Royal Academy. Soon afterwards he moved to Oxford; many of his drawings of university architecture survive, such as *Christ Church from Hinksey Meadows* (n.d.; London, V&A). In 1803 he was appointed Drawing-master at the Royal Military College, Great Marlow, Bucks, and he continued to teach there for 40 years. He produced muted but carefully drawn watercolours and a smaller number of oils. He visited Paris during the Peace of Amiens (1802) and travelled widely on the Continent in the aftermath of the Napoleonic Wars. Delamotte exhibited at the Royal Academy from 1793 to 1850 and at the Society of Painters in Water-Colours from 1806 to 1808; most of his exhibits were topographical views. His *Thirty Etchings of Rural Subjects* was published in 1816.

PATRICK CONNER

(2) P(hilip) H(enry) Delamotte (*b* Sandhurst, Kent, 1820; *d* Bromley, Kent, 24 Feb 1889). Photographer and illustrator, son of (1) William Delamotte. By the late 1840s he had established himself as an illustrator. He made watercolours for Matthew Digby Wyatt's *Industrial Arts of the XIX Century at the Great Exhibition* (London, 1851–3) and drawings for *Choice Examples of Art Workmanship* (London, 1851). Delamotte is best known for his *Photographic Views of the Progress of the Crystal Palace, Sydenham*. He began to record its reconstruction in 1852; and his work was published by the Photographic Institution (London, 1855). Delamotte took out a calotype portrait licence from William Henry Fox Talbot and offered his services to artists, sculptors, architects and engineers. He produced and sold topographical photographs and advertised his services as a calotype printer and teacher of photography. Queen Victoria and Prince Albert were his most prestigious pupils.

In 1853 Delamotte organized the first commercial photographic exhibition at the Photographic Institution in New Bond Street; 352 photographs were catalogued for sale. His photographs were published in the *Photographic Album* (London, 1853–4), and he collaborated with Joseph Cundall on a *Photographic Tour among the Abbeys of Yorkshire* (London, 1856). He became Drawing-master at King's College, London, in January 1855. After this date his photographic activities began to diminish, although he continued to take and publish photographs, for example *Views in Oxford* (London, 1857) and his photographs of the Manchester exhibition in 1857, *Recollections of the Art Treasures Exhibition* (Manchester, 1857; *see* MANCHESTER, fig. 2). The same year he became the editor of *The Sunbeam: A Photographic Magazine* and photographed a private collection of Old Master drawings, the *Henry Reveley Collection of Drawings* (London, 1858).

During the 1860s Delamotte continued to teach at Kings College, worked as an illustrator and a decorative arts consultant and wrote *A Progressive Drawing Book for Beginners* (London, 1869) and *The Art of Sketching from Nature* (London, 1871). The final evidence of Delamotte's continued interest in photography is Princess Mary Liechtenstein's book *Holland House* (London, 1874), which was illustrated with engravings taken from his photographs.

BIBLIOGRAPHY

S. C. Mallett Kilgore: *Philip Henry Delamotte: Photographic Views of the Crystal Palace at Sydenham* (MA thesis, Austin, U. Texas, 1981)

A Vision Exchanged: Amateurs and Photography in Mid-Victorian England (exh. cat. by C. Bloore and G. Seiberling, London, V&A, 1985)

G. Seiberling and C. Bloore: *Amateurs, Photography and the Mid-Victorian Imagination* (Chicago, 1986)

CAROLYN BLOORE

Delano & Aldrich. American architectural partnership formed in 1903 by William A(dams) Delano (*b* New York, 21 Jan 1874; *d* New York, 12 Jan 1960) and Chester H. Aldrich (*b* Providence, RI, 4 June 1871; *d* Rome, 26 Dec 1940). Aldrich graduated from Columbia University, New York, in 1893. After a year with the New York architects Carrère & Hastings he attended the Ecole des Beaux-Arts, Paris (diploma 1900). He returned to Carrère & Hastings until he formed the partnership with Delano. The latter also studied architecture at Columbia University and the Ecole des Beaux-Arts (diploma 1902). After about a year with Carrère & Hastings working as a draughtsman, he became Aldrich's partner. Their initial commissions were private residences in the stately neo-classical styles fashionable in the early 20th century, for example the John D. Rockefeller House (1906–8), Pocantico Hills, New York, and 925 Park Avenue (1909), New York. Their first major commission was the Walters Art Gallery (1910),

Baltimore, MD. The severely classical façade is relieved only by a series of Corinthian pilasters and a decorative frieze on the uppermost of four horizontal levels. Equally restrained in decoration, but less severe in surface treatment, are the residences and private clubs executed between 1915 and 1935, for which the firm is best known. The Knickerbocker Club (1915) on Fifth Avenue and 62nd Street, New York, for example, has a limestone and brick exterior and uses a variety of classical elements on both the interior and exterior. The firm also executed buildings on the campuses of Smith College (Music School, 1926), Northampton, MA, and Yale University (Harkness Hall, 1928), New Haven, CT. Other public buildings include the Japanese Embassy (1931) on Massachusetts Avenue, Washington, DC, and the American Embassy (1933), Place de la Concorde, Paris. The firm's mature style is marked, overall, by an adherence to 18th- and 19th-century British and American styles (rather than French Beaux-Arts), although the clarity and simplicity of their plans strongly reflect the architects' French training. Aldrich's association with the firm ended in 1935, when he became resident director of the American Academy in Rome, but Delano continued his practice, major works being the North Beach Airport (1939–40; now La Guardia), which uses elements of the 'style moderne', and additions to the US Military Academy (1944), West Point, NY.

WRITINGS
Delano & Aldrich: *Portraits of Ten Country Houses* (New York, 1924)
W. A. Delano: 'My Architectural Creed', *Pencil Points*, xiii/3 (1932), p. 154

DAB [Aldrich]
BIBLIOGRAPHY
W. L. Bottomly: 'A Selection from the Works of Delano & Aldrich', *Archit. Rec.*, liv/1 (1923), pp. 2–71
B. Gill: 'William Adams Delano—Gentleman Architect', *Archit. Dig.*, xlvii (1990), pp. 88–96

Delaplanche, Eugène (*b* Paris, 28 Feb 1836; *d* Paris, 10 Jan 1891). French sculptor. Son of a poor wine merchant and a dressmaker, he studied under Louis Auguste Déligand (1815–74) and then at the Ecole des Beaux Arts, Paris, under François-Joseph Duret. He won the Prix de Rome in 1864, by which time he had already exhibited twice at the Salon and executed an elaborate marble fireplace with figures of *Music* and *Harmony* for the mansion of the Marquise de Païva in the Champs-Elysées (1864; *in situ*). The two statues of youths produced during his years in Rome, *Boy Riding on a Tortoise* (1866) and *Shepherd Boy* (1868) (both bronze; Marseille, Mus. B.-A.), belong to the tradition of Italian genre sculpture initiated by François Rude and Duret. However, another work begun in Rome, *Eve after the Fall* (marble, 1869; Paris, Mus. d'Orsay), points the way to Delaplanche's future identification with sensuous renderings of the female body. One of the most acclaimed of these was the rapturous allegorical statue of *Music* for the Paris Opéra (marble, exh. Salon 1878). Even before he won the Prix de Rome, Delaplanche had been connected with the group known as Les Florentins, which included Marius-Jean-Antonin Mercié, Alexandre Falguière and Paul Dubois. His allegiance to this group is especially conspicuous in his *Maternal Education* (plaster, exh. Salon 1873; marble, exh.

Salon 1875; now Paris, Place Samuel Rousseau), a modern genre piece interpreted in a Quattrocento manner.

BIBLIOGRAPHY
Lami

PHILIP WARD-JACKSON

Delaroche. French family of artists, dealers, collectors and arts administrators. (1) Gregoire-Hippolyte Delaroche was one of the most prominent dealers and art experts in Paris at the end of the 18th century and the beginning of the 19th. His brother-in-law Adrien-Jacques Joly (1795–1849) was curator of the Cabinet des Estampes at the Bibliothèque Nationale in Paris. Gregoire-Hippolyte had two sons who were active as artists. Jules-Hippolyte Delaroche (*b* Paris, 7 April 1795; *d* Versailles, 1849) trained under David but eventually turned from painting to arts administration. (2) Paul Delaroche became one of the most important and renowned history painters in France in the first half of the 19th century.

(1) Gregoire-Hippolyte Delaroche (*b* ?Paris, *c*. 1750; *d* Paris, *c*. 1824). Dealer and collector. He specialized in the sale of Old Master paintings but on at least one occasion (1798) he launched a scheme, together with Alexandre-Joseph Paillet, to set up a permanent exhibition and to hold regular auctions of paintings; this probably included contemporary art and was based on the methods of the painter–dealer JEAN-BAPTISTE-PIERRE LE BRUN. Paillet was also Delaroche's partner in many of the sales of collections that Delaroche directed. When the Mont de Piété, a pawnbroking scheme set up by the State, was re-established in 1797, Delaroche and Paillet held official positions in connection with the sale of what presumably were unredeemed collections. Their premises were at 24–25, Rue Vivienne. Among important sales of collections they conducted were those of Robit and Tolozan (both 1801) and Choiseul-Praslin (1808). As a rule, the sales with which they were involved contained a high proportion of works by Flemish artists and others from northern Europe, and this presumably was the main area of their expertise. However, they also compiled a scholarly catalogue—unrelated to a sale—of the collection of Prince Giustiniani, which required considerable knowledge of Italian art. In 1812 Delaroche brought out a second edition without Paillet's collaboration. His own private collection was sold at auction in 1824 (24–6 April).

LINDA WHITELEY

(2) Paul (Hippolyte) Delaroche (*b* Paris, 17 July 1797; *d* Paris, 4 Nov 1856). Painter and sculptor, son of (1) Gregoire-Hippolyte Delaroche. Though he was offered a post in the Bibliothèque Nationale by his uncle, Adrien-Jacques Joly, he was determined to become an artist. As his brother Jules-Hippolyte was then studying history painting with David, his father decided that Paul should take up landscape painting, and in 1816 he entered the Ecole des Beaux-Arts to study under Louis-Etienne Watelet (1780–1866). Having competed unsuccessfully for the Prix de Rome for landscape painting, he left Watelet's studio in 1817 and worked for a time with Constant-Joseph Desbordes (1761–1827). In 1818 he entered the studio of Antoine-Jean Gros, where his fellow pupils included Richard Parkes Bonington, Eugène Lami and Camille Roqueplan.

Delaroche made his début at the Salon in 1822 with *Christ Descended from the Cross* (1822; Paris, Pal. Royale, Chapelle) and *Jehosheba Saving Joash* (1822; Troyes, Mus. B.-A. & Archéol.). The latter work clearly showed the influence of Gros, and it was greatly praised by Géricault. At the same Salon, Delacroix exhibited *Dante and Virgil in Hell* (1822; Paris, Louvre; *see* DELACROIX, EUGÈNE, fig. 1), a highly influential painting, which could be said to mark the arrival of Romanticism in Paris, challenging the dominance of Neo-classicism. Delaroche's response to this conflict of influences was to steer a course between the two currents, unwilling to opt for full-blooded Romanticism for fear of jeopardizing his public standing. Such a compromise can be seen in one of his entries for the Salon of 1824, *Joan of Arc in Prison* (1824; Rouen, Mus. B.-A.; sketch and reduced replica, London, Wallace), and it was the distinguishing feature of his subsequent works. In 1828 he exhibited the *Death of Queen Elizabeth* (see fig.), the first of a series of paintings from English history that traded on the growing French interest in English culture; it established the artist's reputation. Centred upon the very masculine figure of the dying Queen, the picture's obsessive attention to details, such as the rendering of different rich materials, creates a grotesque contrast between the shrivelled, haggard monarch and her resplendent surroundings.

In 1830 Delaroche was commissioned to paint the *Storming of the Bastille,* a large and important work for the Hôtel de Ville (destroyed when the Hôtel was burnt down during the Commune in 1871). He had great success at

Paul Delaroche: *Death of Queen Elizabeth,* oil on canvas, 4.22×3.43 m, 1828 (Paris, Musée du Louvre)

the 1831 Salon exhibiting, among other works, the *Children of Edward: Edward V, King of England, and Richard, Duke of York, in the Tower of London* (1831; Paris, Louvre) and *Cromwell Opening the Coffin of Charles I* (1831; Nîmes, Mus. B.-A.). These and other works exhibited that year, such as *Cardinal Richelieu Dragging Cinq-Mars and de Thou in the Wake of his Barge* (1829; London, Wallace), greatly impressed contemporary artists; Delaroche was hailed as the leader of the contemporary French school of history painting. Combining scrupulous accuracy in historical detail with a glossy finish, his highly theatrical compositions often resemble waxworks or stage tableaux; for many he made wax or plaster models to help him achieve the best arrangement of the figures. Sometimes he took bronze casts from successful models, such as the head of Charles I from *Cromwell Opening the Coffin of Charles I.* His sculptures were sufficiently accomplished for him to be invited to produce a work for the Champs-Elysées, but the Revolution of 1830 prevented this scheme from being realized.

In 1832 Delaroche was elected a member of the Académie des Beaux-Arts, and the following year he became a professor at the Ecole des Beaux-Arts, where his pupils included Thomas Couture and Jean-Léon Gérôme. In 1833 he received his first commission for a religious work when he was asked to decorate the central nave of the Madeleine in Paris. Having never produced any paintings of this kind, and aware of his lack of knowledge of the great religious works of the past, he travelled to Italy from 1834 to 1835 to study early frescoes in Tuscany and elsewhere. When he returned to France he was told that he was expected to collaborate with Jules-Claude Ziegler; he felt that any such arrangement would ruin his proposed scheme and withdrew from the commission altogether. At the Salon of 1834 he had exhibited one of his most acclaimed pictures, the *Execution of Lady Jane Grey* (1834; London, N.G.). His first major religious work was a Salon entry of 1837, *St Cecilia* (1836; London, V&A). This change of subject and the painting's austere manner were ill received, and after 1837 Delaroche ceased exhibiting altogether. Much of his time over the next few years was taken up by his most famous work, *The Hemicycle* (also known as the *Artists of all Ages*), for the Ecole des Beaux-Arts. This monumental work, a 27 m encaustic panorama, included over 70 painters, sculptors and architects, an international group ranging from antiquity up to the 18th century; among them are Pheidias, Raphael, Leonardo and Inigo Jones. Assisted by four students, Delaroche worked on the project from 1837 to 1841; the final result proclaims its origins in Raphael's *School of Athens* (1508–11; Rome, Vatican, Stanza della Segnatura; *see* ITALY, fig. 32) and Ingres's *Apotheosis of Homer* (1827; Paris, Louvre). In 1855 the work was severely damaged by fire; Delaroche started the restoration himself and it was completed after his death by Robert-Fleury. A second huge project for the Palais de Justice was never carried out.

Delaroche spent 1843 to 1844 in Italy, developing an interest in early Italian painting, which encouraged him to attempt a series of religious works (*Virgin and Child,* 1844; London, Wallace); religious themes dominated his later works. He also turned from English to French history, both distant (*Charlemagne Crossing the Alps*, 1847; Versailles, Château) and more recent (*Napoleon Abdicating at the Palace of Fontainebleau*, 1845; Leipzig, Mus. Bild. Kst.). Throughout his career Delaroche had occasionally painted portraits, such as *Marquis de Pastoret* (*c.* 1829; Boston, MA, Mus. F.A.). From 1840 these became an increasingly important part of his output; among his sitters were such august figures as *Pope Gregory XVI* (1844; Paris, Louvre). At the time of his death Delaroche was working on a series of four scenes from the Life of the Virgin; only the *Virgin Contemplating the Crown of Thorns* (1856; see Delaborde, pl. 84) was finished. Having ceased to exhibit in 1837, the last of his paintings to be seen in public was *The Hemicycle*.

BIBLIOGRAPHY

E. de Mirecourt: *Les Contemporains No. 72: Paul Delaroche* (Paris, 1856)
H. Delaborde: *Oeuvre de Paul Delaroche, reproduit en photographie par Bingham, accompagné d'une notice sur la vie et les ouvrages de Paul Delaroche, par Henri Delaborde; et du catalogue raisonné de l'oeuvre, par Jules Goddé* (Paris, 1858)
E. de Mirecourt: *Les Contemporains No. 119: Delaroche, Decamps* (Paris, 1871)
J. R. Rees: *Horace Vernet, Paul Delaroche* (London, 1880), pp. 54–88
Historical Illustrations by Paul Delaroche, with a Brief Memoir of the Artist and Historical Descriptions from Holinshed, Carlyle, Froude, Merle d'Aubigné and other writers (London, 1883) [incl. memoir by Delaborde]
E. de Lalaing: *Les Vernet, Joseph, Carle et Horace: Géricault et Delaroche* (Lille and Paris, 1888), pp. 215–38
N. D. Ziff: *Paul Delaroche: A Study in French Nineteenth Century History Painting* (New York, 1977)
J. Ingamells: *The Wallace Collection: Catalogue of Pictures II, French Nineteenth Century* (London, 1986), pp. 98–116

☐

Delarue. *See* LA RUE, DE.

Delatour, Maurice-Quentin. *See* LA TOUR, MAURICE-QUENTIN DE.

Delâtre, Auguste (*b* Paris, 1822; *d* Paris, 26 July 1907). French printmaker. From the age of 12 he worked for the same jobbing printer, but *c.* 1840–41 he was employed by two well-known printmakers, Charles Jacque and Louis Marvy (1815–50), to handle their presses. Jacque and Marvy taught him how to paint and draw, and his experience with them turned him into an artist's printer. He then set up his own studio. In 1848 he completed his first series of etchings, mainly landscape scenes. Although Delâtre was versatile in the various forms of etching, he is best known for the excellence and sensitivity of his work as a printer. He developed the 'mobile etching' technique, a way of painting ink on to the plate so that up to 40 unique impressions could be made from the same plate, rather than a uniformly wiped edition. This skill served the Impressionists and influenced the practice of monotype in such artists as Ludovic Lepic and Degas. It also inspired fierce debate on the question of printer intrusion. He quickly established a considerable reputation and soon became the only printer to whom the majority of talented etchers would entrust their work. His print shop became a meeting place for such etchers as Charles-François Daubigny and James McNeill Whistler. The cult of Japonisme is said to have begun there through the *Hokusai manga* ('Sketches by Hokusai', 1814–34) he owned.

In 1862 Delâtre helped found the Société des Aquafortistes in Paris, and in 1864, largely at the instigation of Whistler and Seymour Haden, he was invited to England to advise on the setting up of an etching class at the National Art Training Schools, part of the South Kensington Museum (now the Victoria and Albert Museum). He also began painting in oils: *Autumn Evening*, a fine landscape, was shown in the Paris Salon of 1868. In the siege of Paris in 1870 his studio was destroyed, together with all his works and most of his equipment. He took refuge in London, working with other expatriate French artists, such as James Tissot and Jules Dalou. He returned to Paris in 1876 and set up a new studio in Montmartre.

BIBLIOGRAPHY

Bénézit
H. Béraldi: *Les Graveurs du XIXe siècle* (Paris, 1884–92), pp. 168–74
J. Bailly-Herzberg: *L'Eau-forte de peintre au dix-neuvième siècle: La Société des Aquafortistes, 1862–1867*, 2 vols (Paris, 1972)
E. P. Jauis: 'Setting the Tone: The Revival of Etching, the Importance of Ink', *The Painterly Print: Monotypes from the 17th–20th Centuries* (exh. cat., New York, Met., 1980), pp. 9–28

ETRENNE LYMBERY

Delaunay (i). *See* LAUNAY, DE.

Delaunay (ii). Painters and printmakers. (1) Robert Delaunay's critical role in establishing a fully abstract idiom immediately before World War I continues to assure for him an important place in 20th-century art, however much his reputation remains overshadowed by that of his contemporaries, such as Picasso, Braque and Matisse. His wife, (2) Sonia Delaunay, was equally committed to the promotion of abstract art.

BIBLIOGRAPHY

M. Hoog: *Robert et Sonia Delaunay* (Paris, 1967)
Sonia & Robert Delaunay (exh. cat., Paris, Bib. N., 1977)
A. A. Cohen, ed.: *The New Art of Colour: The Writings of Robert and Sonia Delaunay* (New York, 1978)
Le Centenaire Robert & Sonia Delaunay (exh. cat., intro. C. Delaunay and others; Paris, Mus. A. Mod. Ville Paris, 1985)

(1) Robert Delaunay (*b* Paris, 12 April 1885; *d* Montpellier, 25 Oct 1941). French painter, printmaker and writer. Taking Cubism as one of his points of departure, he first developed a vocabulary of colour planes only distantly dependent on observed motifs, and by the 1930s he had arrived at a purely self-sufficient language of geometric forms. He remained active as a theoretician until the end of his life, leaving a legacy of influential writings on the development of abstract art.

1. Early work, to 1912. 2. 'Constructive' phase, 1912–14. 3. Representational paintings, 1914–29. 4. Return to abstraction: late works, 1930–41.

1. EARLY WORK, TO 1912. Delaunay was apprenticed from 1902 to 1904 to the Ronsin stage-painting studios in Paris, but he was fundamentally self-taught as a painter from 1904. His early paintings are indebted to Post-Impressionism, especially to Gauguin, as in *Still-life: Vases and Objects* (1907; Paris, Pompidou). His rapid absorption of avant-garde tendencies is revealed in a sequence of early self-portraits. The first (1905–6; Paris, Pompidou) is a literal representation of his appearance against an almost abstract background, with violent, Fauve-influenced colour contrasts of greens and violets and their complementaries red and yellow. On the reverse of the canvas is *Landscape with Discs* (1906–7), which is painted in a

pointillist technique adapted from the work of Henri-Edmond Cross and Paul Signac rather than from Georges Seurat's paintings of the 1880s. Two characteristics of Delaunay's later work are already evident in this early painting: a new pictorial language based on colour contrast (derived from Neo-Impressionism and from Delaunay's study of the theories of Eugène Chevreul) and the use of circles as formal elements and cosmic symbols. A subsequent *Self-portrait* (1909; Paris, Pompidou) employs a faceting of planes of colour, which is derived from Cézanne and from Cubism.

Delaunay's first significant series of paintings, depicting the ambulatory of the Gothic church of St Séverin in the Quartier Latin, Paris, uses an architectural subject to investigate Cubist devices for suggesting the movement of the spectator through space and for representing the pictorial dissolution of solid objects by light. His systematic and increasingly stylized treatment of the motif was to prove typical of the single-mindedness with which he pursued formal problems. He also gradually abandoned the virtually naturalistic colour scheme dominated by greys in *St Séverin No. 3* (1909; New York, Guggenheim) in favour of bold contrasts of heightened colour that emulate the effect of coloured light streaming in through stained-glass windows, as in *St Séverin No. 5: The Rainbow* (1909–10; Stockholm, Mod. Mus.). In this series Delaunay introduced themes that formed the basis of his later work: light, colour and the pictorial expression of the process of vision as a conscious activity. The sensation created by the distorted rendering of piers and transverse vaults is akin to the changing perspectives that would be experienced when walking through the building. This series established Delaunay's reputation, especially with the Blaue Reiter in Germany: at the invitation of Kandinsky, Delaunay took part with great success in the group's first exhibition at the Galerie Thannhauser, Munich, in 1911.

Delaunay freed himself still further from earlier conventions of painting in a series of 30 pictures of the Eiffel Tower instigated in 1909. The inscriptions on the earliest of these, *Tower: First Study* (1909; Paris, C. Delaunay priv. col.), suggest that it was conceived as a celebration of Eiffel's structure as a technical miracle and symbol of modernity at the Exposition Universelle of 1889. The study was followed by eight large compositions from 1909 to 1911, such as *Red Tower* (1911; New York, Guggenheim), and by a further group of paintings and drawings between 1922 and 1928, such as *Eiffel Tower* (1926; Paris, Mus. A. Mod. Ville Paris), in which the motif is treated as a flat pattern of interlocking shapes of colour.

One of the largest of the first *Eiffel Tower* series (1910–11; Basle, Kstmus.) is typical of what Delaunay termed his 'destructive' phase in the apparent disintegration of a solid structure by the action of light. The tower and surrounding buildings are represented by means of fragmented and interpenetrating planes, as in Cubism, while sunlight seems to acquire physical substance as conglomerations of whitish discs. In a number of works from a related and exactly contemporaneous series, *The City* (1910–11), Delaunay again represented the Eiffel Tower, this time as a distant presence on the horizon in a dense, urban view that includes the roofs of Paris, a giant Ferris

wheel temporarily erected on the Champ-de-Mars, aeroplanes and the sun. Taking his imagery from postcards of Paris, Delaunay subjected the city view to a process of increasing abstraction. In *City: First Study* (1909; London, Tate) he largely adhered to the naturalistic conventions of perspective and tonal modelling, but in *City No. 2* (1910; Paris, Pompidou) he emphasized the picture plane as an almost abstract entity by treating the buildings as a rhythmic succession of interlocking light and dark shapes and by superimposing a regular pattern of large dots, which can be taken to represent the reflections of light on a window. In the third (1911–12) and fourth (1911) paintings of the series (both New York, Guggenheim), Delaunay wove together still further the veil of dots with the underlying architectural motifs, anticipating his 'constructive' phase. It was not until the related *Window* series of 1912 that Delaunay completed his transformation of the Renaissance concept of space as if viewed through a window into a 20th-century sense of that space as a flat pattern on the surface of a window.

In January 1912, accompanied by his wife, (2) Sonia Delaunay, and the landscape painter Robert Lotiron (1886–1966), Delaunay travelled to Laon, where he had completed his military service in 1905. There he painted a number of oil studies culminating in *Towers of Laon* (1912; Paris, Pompidou), in which he synthesized his previous interest in Cubist dissolution with abstract relationships of complementary colours and a transparency and faceting of planes derived from a study of the late watercolours of Cézanne.

Delaunay returned to Paris in February 1912 to prepare for his first one-man exhibition at the Galerie Barbazanges. He quickly completed a large painting for the Salon des Indépendants, *City of Paris* (12.67×4.06 m, 1910–12; Paris, Pompidou), in which he restated some of his favourite recent themes and images. The central motif of the Three Graces, based on a postcard reproduction and used here to symbolize the grace of Paris, is surrounded by the Eiffel Tower and the cities of Delaunay's 'destructive' phase; the bridge and ship constitute a homage to Henri Rousseau, whom Delaunay admired.

2. 'CONSTRUCTIVE' PHASE, 1912–14. In April 1912 Delaunay inaugurated his 'constructive' phase with a series of window paintings, for example *Simultaneous Windows on the City* (1912; Hamburg, Ksthalle; see ABSTRACT ART, fig. 1). Although fragments of buildings or of the Eiffel Tower are still recognizable, they are blended almost imperceptibly into the overall pattern of coloured shapes. The subject of the painting is not observed reality, to which it makes only minimal reference, but the self-contained relationships, tensions and harmonies of pure colour. This style was christened Orphism by Delaunay's friend GUILLAUME APOLLINAIRE, after the cycle of poems *Le Cortège d'Orphée*, on which Apollinaire was then working. The concept of Orphism embraced associated ideas on colour, light, music and poetry. Finding this designation too poetic, Delaunay preferred the term 'pure painting', which emphasized the conceptual character of his art. Delaunay regarded the *Window* series as a new type of painting based entirely on colour contrasts, as equivalents to the interaction of light, space and movement. He

used the term 'simultaneity', also favoured by the Futurists, not only to describe the technique of simultaneous contrasts of colour but also as a model of the forces at work in the universe at large. Delaunay's philosophy of painting is contained in his manifesto on light, written in 1912 and first published in a translation by Paul Klee as 'Über das Licht' (1913). The influence of the *Window* series, especially on German painters such as Klee, Lyonel Feininger, Franz Marc, August Macke, Johannes Itten and Georg Muche, cannot be overestimated.

Delaunay continued with another virtually abstract series, *Circular Forms*, in which he explored further his notion of pure painting. The circle was used by other contemporary artists such as František Kupka, Albert Gleizes and Vasily Kandinsky as a compositional element, but in such works as *Circular Forms: Sun and Moon* (1912–13; Amsterdam, Stedel. Mus.) Delaunay derived such forms from observing the natural light of the sun and the moon. The 'suns' and the 'moons' form two distinct groups. The 'suns' contain more complementary and dissonant contrasts and light–dark effects, which, in Delaunay's opinion, were essential for the creation of the optical sensation of movement. For the 'moon' pictures, Delaunay favoured graduated passages of cold colours and more harmonious transitions of colour and tone. His observation of the different optical oscillations created by colour contrasts became the guiding principle for all his subsequent work. In the circular form he found the elemental basis of his painting. Unlike the largely symbolic allusions to motion in Futurist paintings, in Delaunay's pictures effects of movement appear as immediate optical phenomena created by the interplay of coloured forms. Delaunay also used circular forms in large, semi-representational compositions containing figures and objects, for example *Homage to Blériot* (*c.* 1914; see fig.). Among the abstract circular forms can be recognized the Eiffel Tower with a biplane flying overhead, a reference to Louis Blériot, the first man to cross the English Channel by air. A more symbolic representation of an aeroplane appears at the top left, and in the lower left corner are the clearly rendered propeller and wheels of a machine at rest. Everything is unified in a colour-intensive vision, a hymn to light, colour and modern life.

3. REPRESENTATIONAL PAINTINGS, 1914–29. An extended stay in Spain and Portugal from 1914 to 1921 enabled the Delaunays to withdraw from the turbulence of World War I. There Delaunay created pictures using the folk motifs of his adopted countries, influenced also by the brilliant sunshine that challenged his own sense of colour. From this period date Delaunay's only nudes, for example *Female Nude Reading* (1915; Paris, Mus. A. Mod. Ville Paris). Delaunay later regarded this return to representational, pictorial themes as regressive, despite always having pointed out the possibility of extending the technique of simultaneous contrasts to all areas of human life, which was a view shared by Sonia, who, especially after her husband's death, concerned herself with the transformation of the visual world into colourful plays of contrasts.

In complete opposition to his own theories, Delaunay clung to representational themes once back in Paris, strengthening the conventional character of the themes by

Robert Delaunay: *Homage to Blériot*, oil on canvas, 2.5×2.5 m, *c.* 1914 (Basle, Kunstmuseum)

returning to drawing. At the Delaunays' soirées and in subsequent sittings, he produced a number of portraits of their literary friends, including *Tristan Tzara* (1922; Paris, C. Delaunay priv. col., see 1985 exh. cat., pl. 44) and *Philippe Soupault* (1922; Washington, DC, Hirshhorn); André Breton, Louis Aragon, Ivan Goll, Joseph Delteil, Walter Mehring and Il'ya Zdanevitch (Illiazd) also sat for him. Contact with newly formed Surrealist and Dadaist circles gave the Delaunays the opportunity to work in other artistic areas, for example designing scenery for such Dadaist plays as Tzara's *Le Coeur à gaz* (1923) and for Le Somptier's film *Le P'tit Parigot* (1926).

4. RETURN TO ABSTRACTION: LATE WORKS, 1930–41. In 1930 Delaunay returned to a fully abstract painting of colour, perhaps in response to Gleizes's lectures, in which Delaunay's historical role was noted. In addition, the advocates of geometric abstraction in Paris had formed such groups as Cercle et Carré (1930) and Abstraction-Création (1931), which organized lectures, exhibitions and discussions, and to which Delaunay was invited. Delaunay's new large-format pictures, entitled *Rhythm: Joy of Life* (e.g. 1930; Paris, Pompidou), attest to a renewed flourishing of pure colour. These pictures are in the same tradition as *Circular Forms* but carry on a completely abstract play of pure colours, supplemented for the first time with black and white.

Delaunay began his last major series, *Rhythms Without End*, in 1933, from which *Rhythm Without End* (1934; Paris, Pompidou) is a typical example. Each painting is organized around an axis aligned either strictly vertically or, more often than not, diagonally. Along these axes, discs are painted in an alternating sequence of large and small rings, using either contrasting colours or black and white, as if indefinitely extendable. Most of these pictures are very tall, as though yielding to a tendency towards the infinite. With their smooth, thin application of colour, clean contours and zones of saturated, non-graduated colours, these works come the closest to geometric abstraction. Delaunay must be counted among the most important precursors of this movement.

In 1935 Delaunay was commissioned to paint the interiors of the aviation and railroad pavilions (both destr.) for the *Exposition internationale des arts et techniques dans la vie moderne* (Paris, 1937; *see* INTERNATIONAL EXHIBITION, fig. 2). A quarter of a century after *Homage to Blériot* he was once again able to create a hymn to the modern world, to technological progress and to the spirit of invention. For the aviation pavilion Delaunay and a team of painters, which included his wife, painted a large composition of which only a sketch, *Propeller and Rhythm* (*c.* 1937; Paris, Pompidou), survives. It shows a construction of interwoven rings, rhythms and propellers. With the interpenetration of the various elements and themes, Delaunay succeeded in creating a light, airy and spacious composition well suited to the theme of aviation.

Delaunay's graphic work is modest, while his sculpture consists of only a few colourfully painted wooden objects. He limited himself to the techniques of painting until 1930, when he became occupied with technical experiments and plans for murals and reliefs, for which he invented, or had made, new materials. Besides the sketches for the *Exposition internationale des arts et techniques dans la vie moderne* in 1937, there remains a series of reliefs (e.g. *Bronze Relief No. 1*, plaster on canvas, 1936–7; Paris, Pompidou). Here also Delaunay showed himself to be a visionary, a forerunner in coloured wall design.

Delaunay's last works, produced in 1938 when he was already seriously ill, were designs for the sculpture hall in the Salon des Tuileries, Paris. After preparatory gouache sketches, Delaunay made three medium-sized paintings (Paris, C. Delaunay priv. col.) on which the murals were to be based, once again proving himself a master of colour composition. The colours are harmoniously balanced; complementary contrasts are found at compositionally important points and mark the culmination of the colour rhythms. The interlacing and interpenetration of rhythms of circles, rings and colour planes are painted confidently and with much more freedom than had earlier been the case. Delaunay's visual language of pure colours, as seen in these final works, continued to exert an important influence after his death.

WRITINGS
'Über das Licht', *Der Sturm*, 144–5 (Jan 1913), pp. 255–6 [written 1912; trans. P. Klee]
P. Francastel, ed.: *Du Cubisme à l'art abstrait* (Paris, 1957) [with cat. rais. by G. Habsque]
H. Düchting, ed.: *Zur Malerei der reinen Farbe: Schriften, 1912–40* (Munich, 1983)

BIBLIOGRAPHY
G. Vriesen and M. Imdahl: *Robert Delaunay* (Cologne, 1967)
H.-J. Albrecht: *Farbe als Sprache: Robert Delaunay—Josef Albers—Richard Paul Lohse* (Cologne, 1974)
J. Loyer and C. Pérussaux: 'Catalogue de l'oeuvre lithographique de Robert Delaunay', *Nouv. Est.* (May–June 1974), pp. 3–9
B. Dorival: *Robert Delaunay, 1885–1941* (Paris, 1975)
M. Hoog: *Robert Delaunay* (Paris, 1976)
R. Rosenblum: *Cubism and 20th-century Art* (New York, 1976)
Robert Delaunay (exh. cat., preface J. Cassou, intro. M. Hoog; Paris, Mus. Orangerie; Baden-Baden, Staatl. Ksthalle; 1976)
W. Hofmann: 'Zu einem Bild R. Delaunays', *Bruchlinien: Aufsätze zur Kunst des 19. Jahrhunderts* (Munich, 1979)
V. Spate: *Orphism: The Evolution of Non-figurative Painting in Paris, 1910–14* (Oxford, 1979)
Abstraction: Towards a New Art (exh. cat., London, Tate, 1980), pp. 26–8, 32
M. Imdahl: *Bildautonomie und Wirklichkeit: Zur theoretischen Begründung moderner Malerei* (Mittenwald, 1981)
H. Düchting: *Robert Delaunay's 'Fenêtres': Peinture pure et simultanée. Paradigma einer modernen Wahrnehmungsform* (diss., Munich, Ludwig-Maximilians-U., 1982)
Robert Delaunay (exh. cat., intro. C. Delaunay and B. Dorival; Cologne, Gal. Gmurzynska, 1983)
Delaunay und Deutschland (exh. cat., ed. P.-K. Schuster; Munich, Haus Kst, 1985–6)

HAJO DÜCHTING

(2) Sonia [Sophie] **Delaunay** [née Stern; Terk; Delaunay-Terk] (*b* Gradizhsk, Ukraine, 14 Nov 1885; *d* Paris, 5 Dec 1979). Russian painter, designer and printmaker of Ukrainian birth, active in France, wife of (1) Robert Delaunay. She was the youngest of three children and in 1890 was adopted by her maternal uncle, Henri Terk, a lawyer in St Petersburg, where she spent her youth. She had early contacts with Germany, visiting the artist Max Liebermann in Berlin (1899) and studying drawing with Ludwig Schmidt-Reutter (1863–1909) in Karlsruhe from 1903 to 1905. In 1905 she moved to Paris to study at the Académie de la Palette. There she met Amédée Ozenfant, André Dunoyer de Segonzac and Jean-Louis Boussingault. She learnt printmaking from Rudolf Grossmann (1882–1941). Her early painting was figurative, with frequent references to van Gogh, Gauguin and the Fauves. The links with Germany continued after her move to France: she exhibited at the Erster Deutscher Herbstsalon at the Galerie Der Sturm, Berlin, in 1913 and again at the Galerie Der Sturm in 1920 and 1921.

In order to remain in Paris she contracted a marriage of convenience in 1908 with Wilhelm Uhde, a German art critic and dealer. Her first solo exhibition was held that year at Uhde's Galerie Notre Dame des Champs, and through him she met many painters, including Picasso, Braque, Maurice de Vlaminck and Robert Delaunay. In 1910 she and Uhde were amicably divorced, and she married Delaunay; she used the name Sonia Delaunay-Terk until the mid-1920s.

Together the Delaunays pursued the study of colour, influenced by the theories of Michel-Eugène Chevreul. They adopted the stylistic label 'simultaneity' in order to distinguish their work, and in 1912 Sonia began her series of non-figurative *Contrastes simultanés* (e.g. 1912; Paris, Pompidou; see fig.). She was already active as a designer of embroideries and bookbindings: her best-known book collaboration was with Blaise Cendrars, for whose *La Prose du Transsibérien et de la petite Jehanne de France* (published in October 1913 in the form of a vertical scroll almost 2 m long) she designed a cover and pochoir illustrations.

After the loss of her private income in 1917 as a result of the Russian Revolution, Sonia expanded her design practice, first with the Casa Sonia in Madrid (where the Delaunays spent part of World War I) and then with her Atelier Simultané in Paris, producing textiles, clothing and interior design. Her Boutique Simultanée, run in conjunction with the couturier Jacques Heim, at the Exposition

Internationale des Arts Décoratifs et Industriels Modernes (Paris, 1925), established her reputation as a designer of 'modern' fashions. Her work was also commissioned for the stage and cinema, the latter including Le Somptier's *Le P'tit Parigot* and Marcel l'Herbier's *Vertige* (both 1926).

During the 1930s she and Robert Delaunay became preoccupied with public art and with projects for neon advertising. Both artists painted large-scale murals for the Exposition Universelle (Paris, 1937), where Sonia worked in the pavilions of air and rail transport. The Delaunays were energetic promoters of abstract art: they joined the Abstraction–Création group in 1931 and were founder-members of Réalités Nouvelles (1939).

After her husband's death in 1941, Sonia Delaunay remained active in her support for abstract art, as well as promoting Robert's reputation by securing numerous exhibitions of his work and making bequests of their work to public institutions. In 1964 her gift of works to the Louvre was exhibited as the *Donation Delaunay*, and she was thus the first woman to receive an exhibition in the Louvre. Her continuing practice as an artist, designer and printmaker received wide recognition in France and internationally. She exhibited extensively and was awarded the Légion d'Honneur in 1975. From 1977 many of her designs were reissued in limited editions.

WRITINGS

Tissus et tapis (Paris, 1929)
Compositions, couleurs, idées (Paris, 1930)
Nous irons jusqu'au soleil (Paris, 1978) [autobiography]

BIBLIOGRAPHY

A. Lhote, ed.: *Sonia Delaunay: Ses peintures, ses objets, ses tissus simultanés, ses modes* (Paris, 1925)
Sonia Delaunay (exh. cat., Bielefeld, Städt. Ksthalle, 1958)
J. Damase: *Sonia Delaunay: Rhythms and Colours* (London, 1972)
A. A. Cohen: *Sonia Delaunay* (New York, 1975)
Sonia Delaunay: A Retrospective (exh. cat., Buffalo, NY, Albright–Knox A.G., 1980)

TAG GRONBERG

Delaunay, (Jules-)Elie (*b* Nantes, 13 June 1828; *d* Paris, 5 Sept 1891). French painter. He entered the Ecole des Beaux-Arts in Paris on 7 April 1848, where he was a pupil of Joachim Sotta (1810–77), Hippolyte Flandrin and Louis Lamothe (1822–69). He became a disciple of Flandrin, and, though making his début in the Salon in 1853 with the *Saltworkers of Guérande* (Nantes, Mus. B.-A.), he soon concentrated on history painting. In 1856 he won the Prix de Rome with the *Return of the Young Tobias* (Paris, Ecole N. Sup. B.-A.) and left Paris to study at the Académie de France in Rome. His work is imbued with a deep religious sentiment cast in the restrained, controlled style and formal repertoire of Neo-classicism. From early in his career he produced many easel and wall paintings on religious subjects, such as *Jesus Healing the Lepers* (1850; Le Croisic, Hôp.). In 1854 he received a commission to produce four fresco decorations for the church of the monastery of the Visitation-Ste-Marie in Nantes, which he completed the following year. In 1865 he returned to the monastery to decorate the chapel of St-François de Sales with scenes from that saint's life. He also contributed to the decoration of at least two Parisian churches, the Trinité (*Assumption of the Virgin* and *Isaiah and Ezekiel*) and St-François-Xavier (*Four Prophets*).

Sonia Delaunay: *Contrastes simultanés*, 1912 (Paris, Pompidou, Musée National d'Art Moderne)

In addition to these religious works, Delaunay painted classical subjects, as in the *Oath of Brutus* (Tours, Mus. B.-A.) and the *Death of the Nymph Hesperia* (Copenhagen, Ny Carlsberg Glyp.), both of which were much admired at the Salon of 1863. Perhaps the painting that best encapsulates Delaunay's iconographic and stylistic concerns is the *Plague at Rome* (1869; Paris, Mus. d'Orsay; *see* FRANCE, fig. 28), a subject he had first treated in a sketch made during his stay in Rome. He took up the theme again in Paris, turning it into this finished painting, which celebrates the superior healing powers of the Christian over the pagan faith. The scene combines Delaunay's favourite Christian and classical motifs. It also shows his capacity to construct a dramatic narrative and to render a variety of emotions, as is evident in the figures of the plague sufferers and the exterminating angel.

From around 1870 onwards Delaunay concentrated on painting portraits, which are intensely characterized, vivid and colourful. The sitters stand out as if they were carved in low relief, as shown in the portrait of *Mme Georges Bizet* (1878; Paris, Mus. d'Orsay). Delaunay also produced some watercolour drawings for an illustrated edition of La Fontaine's *Fables* (Paris, 1860). In this later period he produced his best fresco decorations, for the Panthéon in Paris, for which he was commissioned in 1874. There he executed scenes from the life of the patron saint of Paris, St Geneviève, the most admired of which is *Attila and St Geneviève*. He died before completing this commission, which was then passed on to Henri Courselles-Dumont (*b* 1856). Also in Paris, Delaunay decorated the staircase of the Hôtel de Ville and worked with Paul Baudry on the decorations of Charles Garnier's new Opéra. His *Parnassus* is considered superior to all Baudry's contributions. In 1879 he was elected a member of the Académie des Beaux-Arts and in 1889 was appointed head of an atelier at the Ecole des Beaux-Arts in Paris.

BIBLIOGRAPHY

Bellier de La Chavignerie-Auvray; Bénézit; DBF; Thieme–Becker
E. Maillard: *L'Art à Nantes* (Paris, 1889)

P. Leroi: 'Elie Delaunay', *L'Art*, ii (1891), pp. 105, 226, 271
G. Lafenestre: *La Tradition dans la peinture française* (Paris, 1898), pp. 227–92

ATHENA S. E. LEOUSSI

Delaune, Etienne (*b* ?Paris, *c.* 1519; *d* Paris, 1583). French goldsmith, medallist, draughtsman and engraver. He was recorded as a journeyman goldsmith in Paris in 1546 and was appointed to the royal mint in January 1552. He was, however, removed in June that year. A number of medals, including one of *Henry II* (Paris, Bib. N., Cab. Médailles), are attributed to him. He did not become an engraver until about 1557; his first dated prints, a series of 12 plates illustrating the Old Testament (Linzeler and Adhémar, nos 3–14) and two designs for hand mirrors (L & A 308–9), were made in 1561. He found his models in the work of such Italian artists of the FONTAINEBLEAU SCHOOL as Rosso Fiorentino, Nicolò dell'Abate and especially Luca Penni, rather than in that of Francesco Primaticcio. The year 1569 seems to have marked the peak of Delaune's Fontainebleau production, with about ten prints inspired by the Italian masters. As a Calvinist he left Paris at the time of the St Bartholomew's Eve massacre on 24 August 1572 and took refuge in Strasbourg, a free city of the Holy Roman Empire. He stayed there for four months, then obtained commissions to make 'portraits' elsewhere, probably in Augsburg, where in 1576 he made two engravings depicting a goldsmith's workshop (L & A 265–6). He was in Strasbourg again the following year and was still there in 1580, the date of his suite of 20 engravings of moral allegories (L & A 216–35) based on drawings by his son Jean Delaune (*fl c.* 1580). His last dated engraving, a portrait of *Ambroise Paré* (L & A 307), dates from 1582.

Delaune was a skilled practitioner of the Italianate style favoured at the Valois court. His engravings of mythological and allegorical subjects, and especially his ornamental designs for jewellery and goldsmiths' work, of great precision despite their small dimensions, contributed to the spread of the Fontainebleau style among a wide variety of artists and craftsmen in France and abroad. There are collections of his drawings in Paris (Louvre and Ecole N. Sup. B.-A.) and the British Royal Collection (Windsor Castle, Berks).

BIBLIOGRAPHY
A. Linzeler and J. Adhémar: *Inventaire du fonds français: Graveurs du seizième siècle*, Paris, Bib. N., Cab. Est. cat. (Paris, 1932–8), i, pp. 218–301; ii, p. 299 [L & A]
C. Eisler: 'Etienne Delaune et les graveurs de son entourage', *L'Oeil*, 132 (1965), pp. 10–19, 78
Y. Hackenbroch: 'New Knowledge on Jewels and Designs after Etienne Delaune', *Connoisseur*, clxii (1966), pp. 83–9
L'Ecole de Fontainebleau (exh. cat., Paris, Grand Pal., 1972), pp. 73–7, 253–4
J. Jacquiot: 'Hommage à Etienne Delaune, célèbre graveur et médailleur français, 1519–1583', *Bull. Club Fr. Médaille*, 80 (1983), pp. 56–73, 77
C. Grodecki: *Documents du Minutier central des notaires de Paris: Histoire de l'art au XVIe siècle (1540–1600)*, ii (Paris, 1986)
The French Renaissance in Prints from the Bibliothèque Nationale de France (exh. cat., New York, Met., 1995)

MARIANNE GRIVEL

Delauney, Pierre-François (*b* Bayeux, 21 Sept 1759; *d* Bayeux, 26 Aug 1789). French painter. His recorded oeuvre includes landscapes, portraits and genre paintings, but examples of only the last two are known; these include two self-portraits (1781 and 1789) and a small painting entitled *The Sulkers* (all Bayeux, Mus. Gérard). His portraits are all half-length, unornamented and somewhat shaky in their facial modelling. His most notable surviving genre painting, the *Offering to St Nicholas* (Munich, priv. col., see Wrigley), exhibited in Paris in 1788 at the Exposition de la Jeunesse (in the Place Dauphine), was engraved by Jean Mathieu (1749–1815). It illustrates a local custom subscribed to by spinsters invoking St Nicholas's assistance in procuring dowries and so husbands. The engraving exists in a second state, transformed some time after 1792 into an *Offering to Liberty* (see Wrigley). The painting was also altered to include a figure of Liberty in place of St Nicholas: given Delauney's death in 1789 (when he was a member of the National Volunteers in Bayeux) and the development of revolutionary iconography, the alterations were probably made during the early 1790s. This work exemplifies a late, provincial but adept topographical form of *fête champêtre* ultimately inspired by Watteau, which constitutes the most distinctive aspect of Delauney's oeuvre.

BIBLIOGRAPHY
E. Bellier de La Chavignerie: 'Notes pour servir à l'histoire de l'Exposition de la Jeunesse', *Rev. Univl. A.*, xiv (1864), p. 47
R. de Gomiecourt: *Recherches sur les artistes originaires de Bayeux et de sa région du XVème au XVIIIème siècle* (Bayeux, 1901), pp. 35–8
R. Wrigley: 'Pierre-François Delauney, Liberty and Saint Nicholas', *Burl. Mag.*, cxxiii (1981), pp. 745–7

RICHARD WRIGLEY

De la Vallée. Swedish family of architects of French origin. They came from a Parisian family of builders and architects. (1) Simon De la Vallée was a Calvinist who left France to serve William II, Prince of Orange. His son, (2) Jean De la Vallée, is regarded as one of the leading representatives of the early Swedish Baroque, a style largely derived from French and Italian models.

(1) Simon De la Vallée (*b* ?Paris, *c.* 1590; *d* Stockholm, 21 Nov 1642). He entered the service of the Swedish court in 1637. During his five years in Sweden, until he was killed in a duel, he obtained several important commissions, foremost among them the House of the Nobility in Stockholm, for which he designed a grand project (1641) on the lines of Solomon de Brosse's Luxembourg Palace in Paris. This project was continued (on a smaller scale) by others: the giant order of pilasters was added by the Dutch architect Justus Vingboons, and its grand staircase and curved two-tier roof by (2) Jean De la Vallée. The building is a splendid example of Dutch Baroque classicism.

See also SWEDEN, §II, 2.

(2) Jean De la Vallée (*b* ?Paris, 1620; *d* Stockholm, 9 March 1696). Son of (1) Simon De la Vallée. His early training was with his father; he was later sent to France and Italy for further studies. He was appointed Royal Architect by Queen Christina in 1651 and was responsible for the rebuilding of the Royal Castle in Stockholm as well as for town-planning projects for Stockholm, Eskilstuna and elsewhere. In 1671 he became building magistrate in Stockholm, and from 1680 to 1686 he was City Architect in succession to Nicodemus Tessin (i).

De la Vallée designed several palaces and mansions, some of which were completed by Nicodemus Tessin (ii) and others. The executed wing of the project for the Oxenstierna House in Stockholm (1653) is in the style of a Mannerist Roman palazzo, but he preferred French pavilion architecture with prominent curved roofs, as at Karlberg and Runsa, outside Stockholm. His major works are two churches in Stockholm, Hedvig Eleonora (*c.* 1660) and the Katarinakyrka (1656). Both are centrally planned and domed, the former an octagon with a circular central space, the latter cruciform. The Katarinakyrka is interesting for its unconventional Reformist layout. De la Vallée placed the altar and pulpit in the centre, under a domical vault with a lantern opening. The scheme was altered as building progressed, and a normal chancel was created in the eastern arm of the cross. The original cupola and turrets were destroyed by fire in 1723, but the interior survives, as do the lower parts of the exterior with a giant order of pilasters and four corner chapels with low cupolas.

BIBLIOGRAPHY

P.-M. Hamberg: *Tempelbygge för protestanter* [Protestant church-building] (Uppsala, 1955)

T. O. Nordberg: *De la Vallée: En arkitektfamilj i Frankrike, Holland och Sverige/Les De la Vallée: Vie d'une famille d'architectes en France, Hollande et Suède* (Stockholm, 1970)

H. O. Andersson and F. Bedoire: *Swedish Architecture: Drawings, 1640–1970* (Stockholm, 1986)

☐

Delcour [del Cour], **Jean** (*b* Hamoir, 13 Aug 1631; *d* Liège, 4 April 1707). Flemish sculptor. He was the son of a cabinetmaker and brother of the painter Jean Gilles Delcour (1632–95), and was a pupil of Robert Arnold Henrard. He left Liège in 1648 and travelled to Rome. His later works indicate his admiration for Bernini, with whom he may have studied, probable contact with Ercole Ferrata and an inclination for the classicism of Alessandro Algardi and François Du Quesnoy. He returned to Belgium via France in 1657 and settled in Liège *c.* 1660–63. He travelled briefly to Paris in 1665, where he may have renewed his acquaintance with Bernini. Delcour worked largely for Liège patrons. Commissions for bronze work from the city of Liège included the fountain of the *Perron* in the Place du Marché, the fountain of the *Virgin* (1695–6) at Vinave d'Ile, the monumental well (1667) in the Rue Hors Château, with its figure of *St John the Baptist*, and the magnificent bronze *Christ* (1663; Liège, St Paul) for the Pont des Arches. His polychrome wooden figures (*c.* 1691) of *St James the Less*, *St Hubert*, *St Benedict*, *St Scholastica* and *St Rock*, all originally in the Benedictine monastery (Liège, St Jacques) are executed in a mannered, somewhat nervous, dramatic style reminiscent of Bernini. The marble *Entombment* (Liège, St Paul), signed and dated 1696 and perhaps his best work, and his silver figure of *St Adalbertus* (*c.* 1700; Liège, St Jean) reveal his technical skill. His work for the chapel of the Holy Sacrament in St Martin, Liège, in 1704 included a marble relief of the sacrament of *Unction* (terracotta; Liège, Mus. B.-A.). He executed the marble high altar for the abbey church at Herkenrode (1680; Hasselt, Onze-Lieve-Vrouw) and the impressive marble wall tomb of *Eugène d'Allamont, 9th Bishop of Ghent* (1667–72; Ghent, St Bavo; *see* BELGIUM, fig. 24).

He had no workshop and only one student, Jean Hans (1670–1742), has been associated with him; nevertheless,

Delcour's influence on sculptors in Liège at the end of the 17th century was pervasive.

BIBLIOGRAPHY

R. Le Suisse: *Le Sculpteur Jean del Cour, sa vie, ses oeuvres, son évolution, son style, son influence: Etude historique, esthétique et critique* (Nivelles, 1953)

——: 'Jean del Cour d'après ses archives', *Bull. Soc. A. & Hist. Dioc. Liège*, xliv (1964), pp. 1–50

B. L'Hoist-Coelman: 'Jean del Cour dans les archives liégeoises', *Bull. Soc. A. & Hist. Dioc. Liège*, xlviii (1968), pp. 23–40

M. Robbeyns: 'Les Oeuvres monumentales de Jean del Cour conservées à Liège', *Vie Liége.*, v (1971), pp. 3–13

P. Colman: 'Jean del Cour,' *De beeldhouwkunst in de eeuw van Rubens* [Sculpture in the century of Rubens] (Brussels, 1977), pp. 47–60

CYNTHIA LAWRENCE

Delécluze, Etienne-Jean (*b* Paris, 26 Feb 1781; *d* Versailles, 12 July 1863). French writer and painter. The son of the architect Jean-Baptiste Delécluze, in 1796 he entered the studio of Charles Moreau (1762–1810), who introduced him to Jacques-Louis David. He tried to make a career as a painter between 1808 and 1814, exhibiting pictures, such as *The Rape of Europa* (exh. Salon 1808) and *Augustus and Cinna* (exh. Salon 1814; both untraced), that show his loyalty to the Neo-classical school. He also produced three watercolours depicting the events of 1814 (Versailles, Château).

In 1815 Delécluze abandoned painting in favour of writing art criticism. After travelling in Italy and England, he wrote his first article, published in the *Lycée français*, and he subsequently wrote an account of the Salon of 1822 in the *Moniteur universel*. In November 1822 he wrote an obituary of Antonio Canova for the *Journal des débats* and continued to contribute to that newspaper until his death. He wrote for several other journals, including *L'Artiste* (1831–40), the *Revue des deux mondes*, the *Revue française*, the *Revue de Paris* and the *Gazette des beaux-arts* (from 1859). He wrote books on the history of the arts in Italy and France, and on David. At his death he left unfinished the vast *Histoire des arts et des lettres au moyen-âge*.

Delécluze's theory of aesthetics allied him to the Neo-classical school of David. He argued for an idealist, Platonic conception of beauty, inspired by the ideas of Antoine Quatremère de Quincy, Toussaint-Bernard Emeric-David and Victor Cousin. Delécluze believed that the art of antiquity had left an unparalleled model; that architecture and sculpture were of secondary importance to painting; and that art must have a social and a moral dimension. Works of art intended to add to the moral, intellectual and civic learning of the French people should no longer clutter up museums; their purpose should be to decorate palaces, churches and public buildings. He particularly championed Jean-Auguste-Dominique Ingres as the most distinguished living exponent of his classical ideal of beauty. He attacked Eugène Delacroix for the sketchy quality of such works as the *Massacres at Chios* (1824; Paris, Louvre) and for depicting the gratuitously ugly; at the same time, however, he acknowledged Delacroix's imaginative power. Delécluze resolutely opposed the Gothic tradition, medieval architecture in general and the Gothic Revival in particular (although his nephew was the Gothic Revival architect Eugène-Emmanuel Viollet-le-Duc). Delécluze was an unashamedly conservative critic, but he won widespread respect, even in avant-garde circles, for the honesty and erudition with which he put forward his well-considered beliefs.

WRITINGS

Précis d'un traité de peinture (Paris, 1828)
Précis historique sur les beaux-arts en France (Paris, 1836)
Florence et ses vicissitudes (Paris, 1837)
L'Italie littéraire et artistique (Paris, 1850)
Louis David: Son école et son temps (Paris, 1855, rev. 1863)
Les Beaux-arts dans les deux mondes (Paris, 1856)
Souvenirs de soixante années (Paris, 1862)
R. Baschet, ed.: *Journal, 1824–1828* (Paris, 1948)

DBF

BIBLIOGRAPHY

R. Baschet: *E.-J. Delécluze: Témoin de son temps* (Paris, 1942)
A. Boime: *The Academy and French Painting in the Nineteenth Century* (London, 1971), pp. 89–91

PAUL GERBOD

Delemer, Jean (*fl c.* 1428–59). South Netherlandish sculptor. He was paid in 1428 for carving a life-size stone *Annunciation* group, painted by ROBERT CAMPIN for St Pierre, Tournai (Tournai, Mus. B.-A., on dep. from Ste Marie-Madeleine; heads and colour restored). This group is the earliest example of the Late Gothic style that was to dominate the sculpture of the Netherlands and most of Europe for the following century. The dramatization of the theme in terms of organic movement and abrupt discontinuity of angular drapery rhythms has a direct parallel in contemporary paintings. No other works by the sculptor have survived in Tournai, but a number of later Tournaisian sculptures appear to reflect lost works by Delemer. Among these are several wood sculptures, including a *Trinity* group (*c.* 1430–35; Lille, Mus. Dioc. A. Relig.), a *St Michael* in the church of Ellezelles (Hainaut) and a brass statuette of *St Catherine* on the lectern of Saint-Ghislain (Brussels, Mus. Royaux A. & Hist.) cast by the founder Guillaume Lefèvre in 1446.

In 1440 Delemer's name appeared among the governing members of the Brussels stoneworkers' corporation. Only one commission is documented from his period in Brussels: his collaboration with the bronze-founder Jacques de Gérines and the painter Rogier van der Weyden on the tomb of *Joan of Brabant* (*d* 1406) and her great-nephew William (*d* 1410), ordered by Philip the Good, Duke of Burgundy, for the Carmelite church in Brussels (completed 1458–9; destr.). It appears likely that the same team was responsible for the earlier, virtually identical tomb of *Count Louis of Mâle* (*d* 1384), his wife Margaret of Brabant and their daughter, commissioned for St Pierre in Lille by the same patron (1453–5; destr.). The sculptural conception of these monuments, which besides the principal effigies included free-standing statuettes of ancestor weepers, may be ascribed to Delemer, who undoubtedly supplied wooden models. Both monuments are known from prints and drawings as well as through a later, slightly modified copy, the bronze tomb of *Isabella of Bourbon* (*d* 1465; effigy in Antwerp Cathedral, weepers in Amsterdam, Rijksmus.) created in or soon after 1477.

Other works that may plausibly be associated with Delemer's Brussels period include a dismembered wooden altarpiece (*c.* 1440; Laredo (Spain), church of Our Lady) and the *Calvary* group on the brass paschal candlestick in St Leonardus, Zoutleeuw (Brabant), cast in 1482–3 by Renier van Tienen (*fl* 1465–94) but probably based on models carved by Delemer before 1450.

It is uncertain whether Jean Delemer can be identified with a namesake listed in the accounts of Molenbeek (Brussels) from 1445 until 1471 (Destrée, p. 326) or with a 'Jan van der Meeren' inscribed in the Brussels stoneworkers' corporation list of 1471.

BIBLIOGRAPHY

A. Pinchart: 'Jacques de Gérines, batteur de cuivre du XVe siècle, et ses oeuvres', *Bull. Comm. Royales A. & Archéol.*, v (1866), pp. 114–36
J. Destrée: 'Etude sur la sculpture brabançonne au moyen âge', *An. Soc. Royale Archéol. Bruxelles*, xiii (1899), pp. 315, 326–9
P. Rolland: 'Une Sculpture encore existante polychromée par Robert Campin', *Rev. Belge Archéol. & Hist. A.*, ii (1932), pp. 335–45
J. Duverger: *De Brusselsche steenbickeleren (beeldhouwers, bouwmeesters-metselaars, enz.) der XIVe en XVe eeuw* (Ghent, 1933), p. 55
J. Leeuwenberg: 'De tien bronzen "ploranen" in het Rijksmuseum te Amsterdam, hum herkomst en de voorbeelden waaraan zij zijn ontleend', *Gent. Bijdr. Kstgesch. & Oudhdknd.*, xiii (1951), pp. 13–57
R. Didier: 'Sculptures des années 1400–1450 en Hainaut', *Recueil d'études d'histoire hainuyère offertes à Maurice A. Arnould* (Mons, 1983), pp. 361–400

J. STEYAERT

De Lempicka [née Gorska], **Tamara** (*b* Warsaw, 1898; *d* Texas, 18 March 1980). American painter of Polish birth. She lived among the wealthy aristocracy in St Petersburg and fled with her husband from the Russian Revolution of 1917. In 1918 she arrived in Paris, where she studied briefly at the Académie de la Grande Chaumière in Montparnasse, before studying under Maurice Denis at the Académie Ranson, and then under André Lhote. Lhote's theories of composition, his insistence on careful figure studies and the precise application of paint, often using pure colour, provided the groundwork for her own style of freely interpreted Synthetic Cubism. This rapidly became identified with Art Deco and with modernity of style and subject-matter. All her paintings were carefully composed. She made little attempt to create three-dimensional effects, but using hard, angular lines and shapes contrasted against rounded, soft forms she created a highly stylized view of the world, in particular of the sophisticated society of Paris. Her subject-matter was generally exotic, whether in the celebratory feminine 'glamour' of *Young Girl in Green* (*c.* 1928; Paris, Pompidou) or in the suave, elegantly dressed, fashionable figures in the quasi-religious *Adam and Eve* (1932; Geneva, Petit Pal.). Occasionally scenes of naked women in intertwined compositions recall those of Ingres. Her stylish and mannered portraits sought to convey the wealth of her aristocratic sitters. Her reputation went into eclipse after her move to the USA in 1939, although a retrospective exhibition in Paris in 1972 heralded a renewed interest in the paintings of her youth.

BIBLIOGRAPHY

Tamara de Lempicka de 1925 à 1935 (exh. cat., Paris, Pal. Luxembourg, 1972)
G. Marmori: *The Major Works of Tamara de Lempicka, 1925–1935* (London, 1978)
K. Foxhall and C. Phillips: *Passion by Design; The Art and Times of Tamara de Lempicka* (Oxford, 1987)

EMMANUEL COOPER

Delen, Dirck (Christiaensz.) van (*b* Heusden, nr 's Hertogenbosch, 1604–5; *d* Arnemuiden, 16 May 1671). Dutch painter. When he married in 1625 he was a citizen of Middelburg, but he settled in nearby Arnemuiden, where he became master of the toll-house. From 1628 until his death he was almost continually a member of the town council, mostly as burgomaster. He was widowed three times and had at least one son, though no children survived him. The inventory of his estate testifies that he was well-to-do.

Van Delen devoted his painting entirely to architectural subjects. His earliest works, particularly the views of palaces, borrow heavily from the graphic work of Hans Vredeman de Vries and Paul Vredeman de Vries. The architecture is Renaissance but not governed by classical rules. The buildings look more heavily constructed than the Vredeman de Vries prototypes and are decorated in a more modern manner, based on that found in such Italian prints as Bernadino Radi's sepulchre designs and Michelangelo's porch of the Campidoglio reproduced in the Vignola editions. He also painted church interiors, for the earliest of which (e.g. 1627; St Petersburg, Hermitage) he used the print by Johannes van Londerseel after a painting by Hendrick Aertsn (*d* Gdańsk, 1603) as a point of departure. Other sources for his gothicizing church architecture may have been the work of Antwerp architectural painters, although he did not adopt their rigid tunnel perspective. His style seems closer to that of church interiors by his contemporary Bartholomeus van Bassen. Certainly some of van Bassen's works served as models for the interior views that van Delen produced from 1628. The architecture in these is massive, more suited to the exterior of a building, with rooms covered by heavy coffered ceilings. The use of colour, too, is heavy, with many dull brownish tints. The figures, traditionally thought to have been painted by others, are almost all by van Delen and until *c.* 1630 were often inspired by or copied from Dirck Hals, as in *Interior with Ladies and Cavaliers* (1629; Dublin, N.G.).

After 1630 van Delen's style became more exuberant, and his output was dominated by palace exteriors. In making his courtyard scenes more spacious he was influenced by the work of Hendrick van Steenwijck II, whose *Courtyard of a Renaissance Palace* (1609; London, N.G.) he copied, adding his own staffage (*c.* 1632; St Petersburg, Hermitage, falsely signed *HvSteenw 1623*). Van Delen's palette became lighter and brighter, the paint surface glossier. In the architecture, predominant features are pink, black and white marble and an excess of sculpture, in which he was influenced by the Antwerp Baroque style. The figures, often copied from prints by Abraham Bosse, Marcantonio Raimondi, Gian Jacopo Caraglio, Annibale Carracci and others, are rich and fashionable.

Around 1640 van Delen produced his most ambitious works, after which his output rapidly declined. These compositions become more sober, the colours softer and yellowish. In the foreground of his larger compositions there is usually a palace, receding diagonally from the left or right, as in *Architectural View with the Return of the Prodigal Son* (1649; Cologne, Wallraf-Richartz- Mus.). A similar composition, *Exterior of a Palace* (after 1660; Lille, Mus. B.-A.), was formerly attributed to Willem van Ehrenberg (1630–76), who is likely to have been van Delen's pupil. Known pupils were Daniël de Blieck (*fl* 1648–73) and Hans Jurriaensz. van Baden (1604–63). Van Delen

was the most important inspirational force to succeeding architectural painters in Antwerp.

See also ARCHITECTURAL PICTURES, §2.

BIBLIOGRAPHY
H. Jantzen: *Das niederländische Architekturbild* (Leipzig, 1910/R Brunswick, 1979)
W. A. Liedtke: 'From Vredeman de Vries to Dirck van Delen: Sources of Imaginary Architectural Painting', *RI Des. Bull.* (Winter 1970), pp. 15–25
T. Trent Blade: *The Paintings of Dirck van Delen* (diss., U. MN, 1976; microfilm, Ann Arbor, 1980)

BERNARD VERMET

Delen, Jan van (*b* Brussels or Mechelen; *d* Brussels, 10 March 1703). Flemish sculptor. Van Delen was the pupil of and later collaborated with Lucas Faydherbe, whose daughter he married in 1666. Through Faydherbe he inherited the stylistic tendencies of Rubens, a tradition passed on to his only recorded pupil, Jan Michaels (*fl* 1688–*c.* 1720). The only work in Mechelen attributed to van Delen is a stone *Salvator Mundi* in Onze-Lieve-Vrouw-over-de-Dyle. Van Delen was probably still in Faydherbe's workshop when he carved two marble figures for the monument to the *Thurn und Taxis Family* (Brussels, Notre-Dame-du-Sablon) in 1653. He became a master of the Brussels sculptors' guild in 1664 and sculptor to Charles II, King of Spain, in 1675. Between 1659 and 1662 he completed five monumental oak confessionals, commissioned for the church of St Michiel by the city of Brussels; pairs of slender, elongated angels with sharply pleated drapery flank the central portals of the confessionals. Van Delen's marble monument to the Brussels magistrate *Carolus Hovyne* (1672; Brussels, Notre-Dame-de-la-Chapelle) includes a figure of Death flanked by allegorical figures and crowned by a portrait bust, and his wall monument to *Jacques and Philippe d'Ennetières* (marble and gilded wood, *c.* 1690; Brussels, St Michiel) is similar. Among his late works are decorations carved for the façade of the headquarters of the Mercers' Company in 1698.

BIBLIOGRAPHY
S. Zajadacz-Hastenrath: *Das Beichtgestühl der Antwerpener St.-Pauluskirche und der Barockbeichtstuhl in den südlichen Niederlanden* (Brussels, 1970), pp. 125, 184, no. 39
G. Derveaux-Van Ussel: 'VI: Beeldhouwkunst en meubilair' [VI: Sculpture and furniture], *Sint-Michielskathedraal: Kunst en geschedenis* [Cathedral of St Michiel: art and history] (exh. cat., Brussels, 1975), pp. 176–8, 197–8
——: 'Jan van Delen', *De beeldhouwkunst in de eeuw van Rubens* [Sculpture in the century of Rubens] (Brussels, 1977), pp. 209–12

CYNTHIA LAWRENCE

Delessert. French family of bankers and collectors. (Gabriel-)Etienne Delessert (*b* Lyon, 30 April 1735; *d* Paris, 18 June 1816) was the son of Benjamin Delessert (*b* 1692), who had founded a silk factory at Lyon in 1725; he moved to Paris *c.* 1775 and began lending money to sellers of luxury goods. From this he became a banker, being one of the founders of the Caisse d'Escompte, and later founded one of France's first insurance companies. After the French Revolution he re-established and extended his financial and industrial interests. His eldest son (Jules-Paul-)Benjamin Delessert (*b* Lyon, 14 Feb 1773; *d* Paris, 2 March 1847) took lessons in botany from his father's friend Jean-Jacques Rousseau, but after service in the army, he joined his father in business. In 1802 he was appointed Régent of the Banque de France and in 1812 was ennobled as Baron Delessert. Under the Bourbon Restoration he combined his function as *député* (intermittently between 1817 and 1842) with business interests, his most notable achievement being the creation of the Caisse d'épargne in 1818. As a result of his scientific interests he amassed a celebrated collection of plants and some 150,000 specimens of shells; in 1816 he was elected a member of the Académie des Sciences. His considerable wealth enabled him to collect paintings, a field in which he showed individuality and distinction. His most spectacular purchase was made at the sale in 1843 of the collection of Alejandro Maria Aguado, Marqués de Las Marismas de Guadalquivir, when he spent 27,250 francs on Raphael's Orléans *Madonna* (Chantilly, Mus. Condé). Among other Old Master paintings, he owned a strong group of Dutch cabinet pictures, such as Pieter de Hooch's *Merry Company* (*c.* 1657; New York, Met.), and 18th-century French paintings, including Greuze's portrait of the engraver *Jean-Georges Wille* (1763; Paris, Mus. Jacquemart-André). One of the most distinctive features of Benjamin's collection was the consistency with which he bought contemporary art at the Salon. Among works acquired in this way were Alexandre-Jean-Baptiste Hesse's *Funeral Honours Rendered to Titian* (Salon 1833; untraced, sketch Philadelphia, PA, Mus. A.); Ernest Meissonier's *Amateurs of Painting* (1843 Salon) and Alexandre Decamps's series of nine drawings illustrating the *History of Samson* (Salon 1845; dispersed; variants Paris, Louvre).

Benjamin's younger brother François-Marie Delessert (*b* Paris, 2 April 1780; *d* Passy, 5 Oct 1868) was notably successful as a businessman and banker and was a *député* between 1831 and 1848. He, too, collected paintings, although as the 1844 catalogue shows, his collection was less impressive than his brother's. Both Delessert collections were united on Benjamin's death; they became one of the best-known cabinets in Paris, being dispersed in 1869.

François-Marie's son Benjamin Delessert (*b* Paris, 15 Nov 1817; *d* Passy, 25 Jan 1868) was also a collector, of prints and drawings rather than paintings. Although he worked in the family bank and spent a brief period between 1849 and 1851 as a *député*, he succeeded in acquiring the almost complete oeuvre of Marcantonio Raimondi, which formed the basis of his *Notice sur la vie et l'oeuvre de Marc-Antoine Raimondi, graveur* (Paris, 1852–3). Most of his prints were sold between 29 March and 3 April 1852.

DBF

BIBLIOGRAPHY

Notice sur la collection de tableaux de MM. Delessert (Paris, 1844, rev. 1846)
C. Blanc: 'La Galerie Delessert', *Gaz. B.-A.*, n.s. i, i (1869), pp. 105–27, 201–22
A. Boime: 'Entrepreneurial Patronage in Nineteenth-century France', *Enterprise and Entrepreneurs in 19th- and 20th-century France*, ed. E. C. Carter and R. Forster (Baltimore and London, 1976), pp. 137–207 (147–8)
R. Marshall: *Etienne Delessert* (New York, 1992)

□

Delf, Coppin [Copin] (*fl* 1456–88). Painter, probably of south Netherlandish or French origin. He served as a cleric in Saint-Flour, near Tours. A highly esteemed decorator and artist, he became known to King René I of Anjou, probably through the King's second wife, Jeanne de Laval, who in 1456 had paid Delf for a panel destined for the 'belle mere [sic] de Laval'. In letters exchanged between René and his Treasury at Angers in 1459, Delf is named as the artist to be commissioned for a *Genealogy of Anjou* on parchment (the King later withdrew the commission owing to lack of funds).

In 1460 René finalized his plans for the Angevin tomb in Angers Cathedral. They provided for recumbent figures of himself and his first wife, Isabelle de Lorraine, a panoply of escutcheons and a representation, designated the *Roi mort*, on the wall behind the effigies. The sculpture was entrusted to Pons (*fl* 1452–60), son of Jean Poncet, and the polychrome work and decoration to Delf, particularly for the 'reliquaire'. There is no documentary evidence to confirm a hypothesis that Delf was responsible for executing the *Roi mort* itself. The terms of René's last will in 1474 exhorting his heirs and assigns to complete the family monument imply that it was still unfinished by that date. A letter dated 1477 from René to his Treasurer suggests that Delf be given the task of completing the colouring of a *Domine quo vadis* in St Pierre, Saumur. In 1482 Coppin decorated for the Dauphin a chapel in St Martin, Tours (destr.); he is named in 1488 as a collaborator of Jean Michel, author of a mystery play, in the festivities for King Charles VIII's solemn entry into Tours. None of Delf's works is known to survive, but Schaefer suggested that miniatures in a *Cité de Dieu* manuscript, attributed to the Master of Jouvenel des Ursins, could have originated in Coppin Delf's workshop.

BIBLIOGRAPHY

A. Lecoy de la Marche: *Extraits des comptes et mémoriaux du Roi René* (Paris, 1873), pp. 60–61, 170–71
C. Schaefer: 'Le Maître de Jouvenel des Ursins (Coppin Delf?), illustrateur du *Speculum historiale* de Vincent de Beauvais (MS. 126 de la Biblioteca Nacional à Lisbonne)', *Arquivs Cent. Cult. Port.*, viii (1974), pp. 81–114 (106–9)
E. König: *Französische Buchmalerei um 1450* (Berlin, 1982), pp. 15–16, 75, 245
F. Robin: *La Cour d'Anjou-Provence: La Vie artistique sous le règne de René* (Paris, 1985)
C. de Mérindol: *Le Roi René et la seconde Maison d'Anjou* (Paris, 1987), pp. 72–4

PETER ROLFE MONKS

Delff [Delft], **Willem Jacobsz.** (*b* Delft, 15 Sept 1580; *d* Delft, 11 April 1638). Dutch engraver. He was the son of the Delft portrait painter Jacob Willemsz. Delff the elder (*c.* 1550–1601), from whom he presumably received his earliest artistic instruction. Because his earliest known work, an engraved portrait of *Christianus Goesius* ('Bailiff in Delft'; 1600; Hollstein, no. 29), was made after a drawing by the Antwerp engraver Johan Wierix, it has sometimes been assumed that Delff studied engraving under this Flemish artist. This, however, is unlikely since the original drawing had been made over 20 years earlier. It is far more probable that Delff was taught engraving by a Dutch artist, possibly Hendrick Goltzius. In the first part of his career Delff devoted himself primarily to producing book illustrations. He also produced portrait prints after the work of such painters as Michiel Jansz. van Mierevelt and Jan Anthonisz. van Ravesteyn.

As far as is known Delff worked exclusively as a reproductive engraver; there are no known prints made after his own designs. His excellent technique produced portrait prints that are among the best of their type ever made in Holland; they are worthy replicas of paintings by prominent portrait painters of the first half of the 17th century.

Delff's career as a successful portrait engraver began only after his marriage in 1618 to Geertruid van Mierevelt, daughter of the well-known Delft portrait painter Michiel van Mierevelt. After his marriage, Delff became the exclusive engraver of the portraits painted by his father-in-law. In the next 20 years about 50 engraved likenesses were made by Delff after examples by van Mierevelt, some of them portraits of Delft burghers, others portraits of prominent figures from Holland and abroad. During the same period Delff also made a number of portrait prints after other artists, including Adriaen van de Venne, David Bailly and Daniel Mijtens the elder.

Delff's portrait prints of rulers and high-ranking nobles are generally in a large format, *c.* 420×300 mm. The majority are busts. The painter obtained an eight-year licence from the Dutch government for his portraits of famous people, protecting him against copies by others. His best-known prints include the various engraved portraits of the Dutch stadholders: *William the Silent of Nassau* (1623; Hollstein, no. 55, and 1624; Hollstein, no. 56), *Maurice* (Hollstein, no. 59) and *Frederick Henry, Prince of Orange Nassau* (1624; Hollstein, no. 61)—the portraits of William after van de Venne and Cornelis Visscher, the others after van Mierevelt. He engraved portraits of *Charles I of England* (1628; Hollstein, no. 2) and his consort *Henrietta Maria* (1630; Hollstein, no. 3) after paintings by Daniel Mijtens the elder, while paintings by van Mierevelt served as the model for the prints of *Frederick V of Bohemia* (1622 and 1623; Hollstein, nos 8 and 10), his consort, *Elizabeth Stuart* (1623 and 1630; Hollstein, nos 9 and 11), and their sons, *Frederick Henry* (1629; Hollstein, no. 12) and *Charles Louis* (1634; Hollstein, no. 67). Other internationally famous persons of whom Delff made portrait prints after paintings by van Mierevelt were *George Villiers, 1st Duke of Buckingham* (1626; Hollstein, no. 13), *Sir Dudley Carlton* (1620; Hollstein, no. 26), *Hugo Grotius* (1632; Hollstein, no. 30), *Ernest, Count of Mansfeld* (1624; Hollstein, no. 43), *Axel, Count Oxenstierna* (1636; Hollstein, no. 66) and *Gustav II Adolf of Sweden* (1633; Hollstein, no. 87).

In addition to portraits, Willem Delff also produced illustrations for books after 1618, including those for the famous edition of *L'Académie de l'espée* by Gérard Thibault (1628), for which he provided three engravings (Hollstein, nos 102–4).

Delff's work was highly successful, and he was awarded the title of engraver to the King of England. Records also indicate that he was a prosperous man. In 1638, the year that he died, his portrait was painted by his father-in-law (Schwerin, Staatl. Mus.). His son Jacob Willemsz. Delff the younger (1619–61) was trained as a portrait painter in the workshop of his grandfather, continuing van Mierevelt's work after he died in 1641.

BIBLIOGRAPHY

Hollstein: *Dut. & Flem.*; Thieme–Becker; Wurzbach

D. Franken: *L'Oeuvre de Willem Jacobsz. Delff* (Amsterdam, 1872) [with cat. rais.]

H. Havard: *Michiel van Mierevelt et son gendre* (Paris, 1894)

RUDOLF E. O. EKKART

Delft. Dutch town in the province of Zuid-Holland, with a population of *c.* 86,000.

1. History and urban development. 2. Art life and organization. 3. Centre of ceramics production.

1. HISTORY AND URBAN DEVELOPMENT. The origins of Delft can be traced to the 10th century, when a community started to develop around some farmsteads in the fertile delta region between the Rhine and Meuse rivers. Former sea inlets, which over time had hardened with sand and clay, were an ideal building ground in otherwise soft fenlands. While peat was dug for fuel, the remaining saliferous soil was good for meadows and the cultivation of barley and oats. These local characteristics led to Delft's particular dependence on canals for the drainage of the surface waters and to its production of dairy goods and beer. The man-made waterways also facilitated the transport of goods. The oldest canal, known as the Oude Delft (*delf* meaning to dig), gave the settlement its name and became the spine for the later urban development. Most traces of early buildings are found between this canal, the Voldersgracht and the Burgwal, in an area where the market-place was located, and where the counts of Holland built one of their strongholds in the course of the 11th century. A fortified tower, dating slightly later, but belonging to the same structure, is preserved as the centre of the 17th-century town hall. Near by, 13th-century remains of the earliest parish church exist under the present Oude Kerk.

After the community received its charter in 1246, a period of economic and material growth transformed Delft into an important commercial centre, with a prosperous cloth industry. Once fortifications were built in the mid-14th century Delft's economy flourished and a direct link with the Meuse was dug in 1389, providing access to the sea. Several wealthy members of the Devotio Moderna movement founded communities in specially donated town houses. The three most important were the convents of St Agatha, St Barbara and St Ursula. At least four more female and four male convents were founded, but most have been destroyed since the Reformation and only the buildings of the St Agatha (now Stedel. Mus. Prinsenhof) and St Barbara convents survive. About 1400, aisles and a choir were added to the Oude Kerk, while its nave was raised in 1430. Around the same time an apparition of the Virgin in the market-place inspired the building of the Nieuwe Kerk, dedicated to St Ursula. The lower part of the tower and the transept date from the last years of the 14th century, while the nave and the choir were erected during the 15th (for illustration see WITTE, EMANUEL DE). In the early 16th century Anthonis Keldermans I designed a Lady Chapel (partially executed) in the north transept, and another Lady Chapel in the north transept of the Oude Kerk (see also NETHERLANDS, THE, §IV, 2).

Both churches contain significant monuments. In the Oude Kerk the most notable are the tombs of 17th-century admirals, including *Piet Hein* (*c.* 1636) and *Maarten Harpersz. Tromp* (1658) on which the sculptors Pieter and Willem de Keyser and Rombout Verhulst worked. The Nieuwe Kerk houses the monument to *William the Silent, Prince of Orange*, commissioned by the States of Holland in 1614 from the Amsterdam city architect and sculptor

Hendrick de Keyser I (for illustration *see* KEYSER, DE, (1)). Four years later Hendrick de Keyser I was employed by the burgomasters of Delft to build their new Stadhuis (see fig. 1), after a fire had destroyed the old one in 1618. His classically conceived and ornamented building was constructed on a square plan, around the medieval tower of its predecessor, and was in use by 1620. In 1645, when beer production had almost ceased, the splendid early 16th-century town house—built for Jan de Huyter, collector of taxes on hops—was turned into the office of the dyke reeve. Trade and industry changed dramatically during the 17th century. Although Delft acquired a chamber of both the Dutch East and West India Companies, involvement with these overseas enterprises was never very significant, and trade became concentrated on the new luxury industries of pottery and tapestry-weaving. Delft took on another new role during the Eighty Years War, when the town was considered an ideal location for the storage of armaments and ammunition for the States of Holland and the States General. The oldest part of the Armamentarium at the south end of the Oude Delft was begun in 1602 and displays an image of *Pallas Athene*, while the last wing of this impressive complex was finished only in 1692 and decorated with a relief sculpture of *Mars*. The explosion in 1654 of a gunpowder magazine in the north-east end of the town destroyed a large area, creating a new urban space which became the horsemarket. As a result two new ammunition stores were constructed. The most splendid was the Kruitmagazin built for the States General by Pieter Post and located safely outside the city walls.

In the 18th century Delft's economy declined, but the construction of the railway in the mid-19th century brought growth and new industries. The enlightened director of one of the most important of these—the Distillery and Yeast Factory—was responsible for the development in 1884 of one of the first purpose-built model towns. Workers' cottages were situated close to the directors' villas in a picturesque woodland park, with a recreation hall, education centre and several shops near by. Post-war development, some of it associated with the expansion of the Technical University, has included several new institutional buildings constructed along the road leading south from the old centre of Delft.

BIBLIOGRAPHY

D. E. van Bleyswyck: *Beschryvinge der stadt Delft* (Delft, 1667)
J. Schopp: *Delphorum urbis amoenitates* (Delft, 1699)
R. Boitet: *Beschryving der stadt Delft* (Delft, 1729)
H. S. Veldman: *Catalogus van de topografische atlas van Delft en Delftland* (Delft, 1898)
C. M. A. Gips: 'Oude Gebouwen in Delft', *Bull. Kon. Ned. Oudhdknd. Bond*, 2nd ser., xi (1918), pp. 135–87
C. Visser: *De Technische Hoogeschool te Delft van 1905–1930* (Delft, 1930)
R. F. P. de Beaufort: *Het Mausoleum der Oranjes te Delft* (Delft, 1931)
P. Beydals: *Kroniek der stad Delft* (The Hague, 1936)
L. H. H. van der Kloot Meijburg: *De Nieuwe Kerk te Delft* (Rotterdam, 1941)
M. Kossman: 'Het woonhuis van Jan de Ruyter te Delft en de herbergen der Graven van Holland', *Bull. Kon. Ned. Oudhdknd. Bond*, 6th ser., xiii (1960), cols 81–98
C. L. Temminck Groll: 'Een sleutel tot de Geschiedenis van de Oude Kerk te Delft', *Bull. Kon. Ned. Oudhdknd. Bond*, 6th ser., xiv (1961), cols 77–92
A. Berendsen: *Verborgenheden uit het oude Delft* (Zeist, 1962)
B. van 't Hoff: *De oude plategronden van de stad Delft* (Rotterdam, 1963)
R. Meiscke and others: *Delftse studien, Delft* (Delft, 1964)
D. P. Oosterban: *De Oude Kerk te Delft gedurende de Middeleeuwen* (The Hague, 1973)
I. V. T. Spaander and R.-A. Leeuw, eds: *De Stad Delft: Cultur en maatschappij*, 3 vols (Delft, 1979–82)

ELISABETH DE BIÈVRE

2. ART LIFE AND ORGANIZATION. Delft's position in the 15th century as an important town and religious centre is still apparent from its numerous richly furnished late medieval churches and monasteries. A number of the monasteries specialized in the illumination of manuscripts; a few examples bear a date and place of origin, thereby allowing an entire series of manuscripts to be ascribed to Delft. In 1477 the first book to be printed in Dutch, the so-called Delft Bible, was produced in the town.

The best-known painters from the late 15th century and the early 16th were the Master of the Virgo inter Virgines and the Master of Delft. In contrast to other Dutch cities, no indigenous school of painting was established at this time in Delft. Artistic activity was given a new impetus in the mid-16th century, when a number of works were commissioned from artists outside the city, including Jan van Scorel (high altarpiece, Nieuwe Kerk), Pieter Aertsen and Maarten van Heemskerck (*Lamentation* altarpiece, 1566; Delft, Stedel. Mus. Prinsenhof).

Delft was an important centre for the production of metalwork and the town's many gold- and silversmiths belonged to the guild of St Eligius. The membership lists from 1591 onwards give the names and marks of all the masters of the guild. High-quality display tankards and nautilus cups survive from the late 16th century and early 17th and show the influence of the numerous refugees

1. Delft, Stadhuis by Hendrick de Keyser I, 1618–20

arriving from the southern Netherlands. The Guild of St Luke represented both painters and glassmakers as well as tilemakers, tapestry-weavers, embroiderers, printers and booksellers. The records also include the names of south Netherlandish members. Such famous Antwerp tapestry-weavers as Frans Spiering (*c.* 1550–1630) and his designer Karel van Mander II (1579–1623) laid the foundations for the Delft tapestry industry, which flourished in the 17th century (*see* NETHERLANDS, THE, §XI, 1).

By contrast, the southern Netherlanders had a relatively minor influence on local painting. Not until 1613–48 was there a significant increase in the number of painters, but many of them departed for Amsterdam in the 1650s. The most important masters in the first half of the century were the portrait painter MICHIEL VAN MIEREVELT and the history painter LEONARD BRAMER (*see* NETHERLANDS, THE, §III, 4). Between 1645 and 1660, local painting attained an international reputation through the work of such artists as JOHANNES VERMEER (see fig. 2), PIETER DE HOOCH, Carel Fabritius, Paulus Potter, Gerard Houck-geest, and Emanuel de Witte, who shared a new interest in the handling of interiors, perspective, light and the sky (*see* DELFT SCHOOL (i)). Vermeer was the only one to

spend his entire life in Delft; all the others came from other towns and left Delft after some time. Genre and interior painting were the areas of greatest innovation. Cornelis de Man (1621–1706) and Jan Verkolje I were among the most important of the later artists working in the tradition of the Delft School. The greatest period of Delft painting coincided with the rise of the Delft ceramics industry (*see* §3 below); in the last quarter of the 17th century art in Delft once again declined to a provincial level, and did not regain its international reputation until well into the 20th.

By the 18th century the role of the guilds had diminished and they were abolished following the French occupation of the Netherlands in 1795. This had far-reaching conse-quences particularly for the Delft gold- and silversmiths, who were prevented from using their own hallmark during the French occupation (1795–1813); a national system was imposed in 1813.

For most of the 19th century the arts and crafts were in decline, until the foundation of the Technical University in 1864. In 1876 Adolf de Comte (1850–1921), of the university's art department, worked with Joost Thooft to revive the only remaining ceramics factory, the Porceleyne

2. Johannes Vermeer: *View of Delft*, oil on canvas, 985×1175 mm, *c.* 1661 (The Hague, Mauritshuis)

Fles. From 1955 to 1977 there was an experimental department for young ceramicists at the factory.

Modern art received a fresh impulse in the 1950s. In 1958 the first exhibition of the Informele Groep was held at the Technical University; the participants were either natives of Delft (Jan Schoonhoven, Jan Henderikse (*b* 1937), Bram Bogart), or in some way related to the city (Henk Peeters (*b* 1925), Armando, Kees van Bohemen). They sought a spontaneous, unplanned style of painting, related to the Abstract Expressionism of the USA. In 1960, Schoonhoven, Hendrikse, Peeters, and Armando founded Nul, a group akin to the German Zero, with the artists avoiding all subjective emotion. Schoonhoven remained interested in structural organization for his entire life. His influence can be seen in the work of many younger Delft artists, including Jaap van den Ende and Aart Houtman.

BIBLIOGRAPHY

Kunst van nu: Encyclopedisch overzicht vanaf 1960 (Amsterdam, 1971)

J. M. Montias: *Artists and Artisans in Delft: A Socio-economic Study of the Seventeenth Century* (Princeton, 1982)

Informele kunst in België en Nederland, 1955–1960 (exh. cat., The Hague, Gemeentemus., 1983)

G. Imanse, ed.: *De Nederlandse identiteit in de kunst na 1945* (Amsterdam, 1984)

T. F. Wijsenbeek-Olthuis: *Achter de gevels van Delft: Bezit en bestaan van rijk en arm in een periode van achteruitgang, 1700–1800* (Hilversum, 1987)

INEKE SPAANDER

3. CENTRE OF CERAMICS PRODUCTION. Maiolica wares (those with a tin-glazed front and lead-glazed back) and tiles were made in Delft from *c*. 1580 following the trend set by such other Dutch towns as Haarlem, Amsterdam and Rotterdam (*see* TILE, §II, 2). In reaction to the importation of Chinese porcelain by the Dutch East India Company, two potteries—the Porceleyne Schotel (est. 1616) and the Porceleyne Lampetkan (est. 1627)—were established in Delft for the production of faience (Delftware), which at that time was known as *Hollands Porceleyn*. From *c*. 1645 the importation of Chinese porcelain virtually ceased due to a series of domestic wars; this gave rise to an increasing number of new factories in Delft producing blue-and-white faience in the style of porcelain made in China during the Wan li period (1573–1620) and in the Transitional style (1620–44). Delft became the most famous centre for the production of faience in the Netherlands (*see* NETHERLANDS, THE, §VII). About 1670 production was complemented by the manufacture of blue-and-manganese wares decorated with chinoiserie (see fig. 3). About 1680 experiments were carried out with colours influenced by imported Japanese Kakiemon porcelain made in the kilns of Arita, Hizen Province (now Saga and Nagasaki Prefectures): blue, yellow, green, red, purple and sometimes gilding. A new direction in production was introduced by the Hoppesteyn family, owners of the faience factory Het Jonge Moriaenshoofd, who manufactured redwares decorated with gilding; red stoneware teapots, imitative of Chinese Yixing wares, were a particular speciality of the potter Ary de Milde. The influence of Delft is apparent in the number of factories that were either set up by or run by Dutch workers for the manufacture of blue-and-white faience and/or porcelain: Hanau (1661), Frankfurt am Main (1666), Saint-Cloud

3. Delftware, blue-and-white tulip vase, h. 1.02 m, *c*. 1700 (Delft, Stedelijk Museum Het Prinsenhof)

(1667/8), Lambeth, London (1671), and Berlin (1678). Between *c*. 1690 and 1695 decoration in white and yellow on a coloured (blue, brown, olive-green) ground was introduced. After 1700 a greater range of high-fired colours was used on a black ground. About 1705 wares decorated with both high-fired and enamel decoration were introduced, first imitating Japanese Imari porcelain and later Kakiemon porcelain, Chinese porcelain decorated with both the *famille verte* and *famille rose* palettes and Meissen porcelain.

In the early 1720s the factories entered a period of decline due to the economic depression in Europe, the increased competition from other faience and porcelain factories and the subsequent deterioration in standard and quality. In order to minimize the effects, a number of factory owners took action in 1724 by drawing up price agreements and limiting production. In the 1740s, however, some factories were forced to close. After the Seven Years War (1756–63) there was a short period of revival;

production included figures and objects modelled as animals and fruit after Meissen porcelain and Strasbourg faience. The period of revival was, however, brief and the increased production of the hugely popular English cream-ware (cream-coloured earthenware) in the mid-1760s effectively marked the end of the Delftware industry. By 1800 there were only about eight factories left in Delft and from 1850 only one factory, the Porceleyne Fles, continued production.

For further illustration *see* NETHERLANDS, THE, figs 47 and 48.

BIBLIOGRAPHY
F. W. Hudig: *Delfter Fayence* (Berlin, 1929)
C. H. Jonge: *Oud-Nederlandsche maiolica en Delftsch aardewerk* [Old Netherlandish maiolica and Delft earthenware] (Amsterdam, 1947)
D. Korf: *Nederlandse majolica* (Bussum, 1981)
J. D. van Dam: *Gedateerd Delfts aardwerk* [Dated Dutch earthenware] (Amsterdam and Zwolle, 1991)

J. D. VAN DAM

Delft school (i). Name given to the Dutch painters active in Delft in the second half of the 17th century who specialized in either realistic architectural paintings or genre scenes. Before *c.* 1650 there was no coherent group of painters in Delft; each artist specialized in his own genre. However, in the late 17th century, the city became the centre of a remarkable artistic flowering that included both these genres, each of which attained special distinction. Gerrit Houckgeest, Hendrick van Vliet and Emanuel de Witte concentrated from 1650 onwards on the depiction of the interiors of Delft churches, frequently taking the mausoleum of William of Orange, in the Nieuwe Kerk, or the grave of Piet Heyn in the Oude Kerk as their subjects. In most of these works the vanishing-point is no longer located on the central axis, but instead to one side, thereby creating a more natural viewing angle. There is a more illusionistic character to these paintings than is found in those of Pieter Saenredam, who had first introduced the genre. De Witte, in particular, excelled in his control of chiaroscuro effects.

Carel Fabritius, who settled in Delft *c.* 1650, after a period of study with Rembrandt, was also expert in the use of perspective, with a sensitivity to atmosphere and light effects. Although he was killed in the great gunpowder explosion of 1654 at Delft, his work can be considered as the basis for the Delft school genre painters, who are exemplified in the work of Pieter de Hooch and Johannes Vermeer. De Hooch came to Delft in 1653 and worked there until 1661; during this period he produced the best and most characteristic work of his career. His work centres around scenes of daily life: burghers in and around their houses against a carefully composed background of views reaching through to the distant background. Like Fabritius, de Hooch strove for a subtle use of well-observed, natural light, combined with the expert use of perspective. Johannes Vermeer came to Delft in 1632, probably after studying with the Utrecht Caravaggisti. Although he began by producing narrative pieces, from 1656 until his death in 1675 he specialized primarily in interiors containing only one or two figures, in which the interior itself is an important element of the composition. A typical feature of the Delft school is the use of a camera obscura in order to create the most realistic scene possible.

BIBLIOGRAPHY
I. Manke: *Emanuel de Witte, 1617–1692* (Amsterdam, 1963)
A. K. Wheelock: 'Gerard Houckgeest and Emanuel de Witte: Architectural Painting in Delft around 1650', *Simiolus*, viii (1975–6), pp. 168–85
——: *Perspective, Optics and Delft Artists around 1650* (New York and London, 1977)
P. C. Sutton: *Pieter de Hooch* (New York and Oxford, 1979)
C. Brown: *Carel Fabritius* (Oxford, 1981)
W. A. Liedtke: *Architectural Painting in Delft: Gerard Houckgeest, Hendrick van Vliet, Emanuel de Witte* (Doornspijk, 1982)
J. M. Montias: *Artists and Artisans in Delft: A Socio-economic Study of the Seventeenth Century* (Princeton, 1982)
B. Haak: *Dutch Painters of the Golden Age* (Amsterdam and New York, 1984), pp. 438–53
A. Blankert, J. M. Montias and G. Millard: *Johannes Vermeer* (Amsterdam, 1987)
J. M. Montias: *Vermeer and his Milieu: A Web of Social History* (Princeton, 1989)
Perspectives: Saenredam and the Architectural Painters of the 17th Century (exh. cat., Rotterdam, Boymans-van Beuningen, 1991)

ILJA M. VELDMAN

Delft school (ii). Term applied to conservative Dutch architects associated with the Technische Hogeschool, Delft, in the 1920s and 1930s, and by extension to anti-progressive architecture in Holland in the 1940s and 1950s. It was probably first used in 1946 in an article entitled 'De dictatuur van de Delftse school' by the critic J. J. Vriend (1896–1975) in the journal *De Groene Amsterdammer*. Vriend, an adherent of *Nieuwe Zakelijkheid* (*see* NEUE SACHLICHKEIT), opposed the traditionalist tendency that dominated post-war reconstruction in the Netherlands outside Rotterdam. He traced its origins to the group of architects led by the architect and urban planner MARINUS JAN GRANPRÉ MOLIÈRE and their followers. Granpré Molière, a charismatic personality and able teacher, became professor of architecture at the Technische Hogeschool, Delft, in 1924. Unhappy with the 'unprincipled' architecture of the time, he sought clear values and norms for the art of building. In contrast to the Functionalism that was increasingly prominent in the 1920s and which took its norms and values from industrial processes and forms, Granpré Molière found his convictions in medieval scholastic philosophy. He was strongly influenced by the ideas of Thomas Aquinas, as interpreted by the French neo-Thomist Jacques Maritain, and particularly the Thomist notions of 'perfection, proportion and radiance'. Architecture was conceived as a hierarchical entity, in which age-old values, symbolism and the building's location were important. In construction preference was given to natural materials and traditional techniques, but the past also had symbolic value in a visual sense, and consequently modern technology and the architecture associated with it were avoided.

The architecture actually created under the influence of these ideas is less elaborate than its theoretical basis might indicate. Use of the sloping roof and simplicity and sobriety in conception and details are notable characteristics, while in church construction the influences of Early Christian and Romanesque architecture are apparent. Examples of Delft school work include the Muzenhof housing block (1938; see fig.) by Johannes F. Berghoef; the Raadhuis (1930), Naaldwijk, and the church of St Anthony (1935–6) at Groesbeek, both by Granpré Molière; competition designs for the Stadhuis (1937–9; unexecuted), Amsterdam, by Johannes F. Berghoef and J. J. Vegter (1906–82);

Johannes F. Berghoef: Muzenhof housing block, Stadionsweg, Amsterdam, 1938

the Provincial Registry (1948–60), Middelburg, by J. F. Berghoef and H. de Lussanet de la Sablonière (*b* 1907), and the church of Our Beloved Lady On the Hill (1953) in Breda by Granpré Molière.

Between the 1930s and 1950s the ideas of the Delft school and of *Nieuwe Zakelijkheid* were in sharp opposition. Although both groups rejected 19th-century eclecticism and emphasized architecture's social and moral role, their ideological foundations were incompatible. At a debate in Doorn in 1941, unsuccessful attempts were made to reconcile the two sides. During the 1940s Delft school plans were favoured, for example at Middelburg, but the enlarged scale of development in the early 1950s demanded industrialization of the building trades, making Delft school ideas impractical. Granpré Molière retired in 1953, and the newly appointed lecturers at Delft, including Cor van Eesteren, J. H. van den Broek and J. Bakema (*see* VAN DEN BROEK & BAKEMA), were committed to modernist architecture. In the 1950s the adherents of the Delft school generally adopted the prevailing International Style.

BIBLIOGRAPHY
Plan, 6 (1972) [complete issue devoted to Granpré Molière]
J. de Heer: 'De Delftsche school en de katholieke architectuur tussen 1945 en 1955', *Eltheto*, 64 (1981), p. 21
A. Kuyper: *Visueel en dynamisch: De stedebouw van Granpré Molière en verhagen* (Delft, 1991)
OTAKAR MÁČEL

Delgado, Gaspar Núñez. *See* NÚÑEZ DELGADO, GASPAR.

Delhi [anc. Ḍhillikā, Ḍhillī; Arab., Pers., Urdu: Dihlī]. Capital of the Republic of India, situated on the west bank of the River Yamuna. Delhi has grown and prospered due mainly to its location on the river, its proximity to the 'granaries' of north India (the fertile lands between the Rivers Ganga and Yamuna as well as those of Haryana and Punjab) and its strategic position in the corridor leading from the mountain passes of Afghanistan to the Gangetic plain. Delhi's role as a capital during the period of Muslim rule (*c.* 1200–1857) made it the premier centre of Islamic architecture in India. A majority of the city's 1300 listed monuments date to this period. New Delhi was inaugurated as the capital of British India in 1931.

I. History and urban development. II. Art life and organization. III. Buildings.

I. History and urban development.

Archaeological excavations indicate that Delhi (see fig. 1) was settled as early as 1000 BC. At the Purana Qil'a (Urdu: 'Old Fort'; 1a) archaeologists uncovered shards of Painted Grey ware (a fine grey earthenware often with designs in black) datable to about the 10th century BC. The presence of Painted Grey ware, uncovered at HASTINAPURA and other sites associated with the *Mahābhārata* epic, tends to confirm the theory that the mound on which the Purana Qil'a stands conceals the ancient city of Indraprastha, the capital of the Pandava heroes in the epic. The area was known as Inderpat until recent times. The Painted Grey

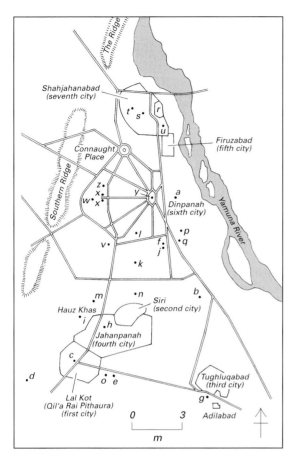

1. Delhi, plan showing the 'seven cities' and main buildings: (a) Purana Qil'a, Qil'a-i Kuhna Mosque, Sher Mandal; (b) Ashoka rock edict; (c) Quwwat al-Islam Mosque complex, Qutb Minar, Iron Pillar, tomb of Iltutmish, 'Alai Darvaza; (d) Sultan Ghari; (e) 'Balban's tomb'; (f) Nizam al-Din shrine complex; Jama'at Khana Mosque; (g) tomb of Ghiyath al-Din Tughluq; (h) Begumpuri Mosque; (i) tomb of Firuz Shah Tughluq; (j) tomb of Khan-i Jahan Maqbul Telingani; (k) tomb of Mu'izz al-Din Mubarak Shah Sayyid, nearby Kale Khan ka Gumbaz, Chhote Khan ka Gumbaz, Bare Khan ka Gumbaz; (l) Lodi Gardens, tomb of Muhammad Shah Sayyid, tomb of Sikandar Lodi, Shish Gumbaz, Bara Gumbaz, Bara Gumbaz Mosque; (m) Moth ki Mosque; (n) Bagh-i 'Alam ka Gumbaz; (o) Jamali Mosque and tomb; (p) tomb of Humayun; (q) tomb of 'Abd al-Rahim Khan-i Khanan; (r) Lal Qil'a; (s) Jami' or congregational mosque; (t) Fatehpur Mosque; (u) Zinat al-Masjid; (v) tomb of Safdar Jang; (w) Rashtrapati Bhavan ('Viceroy's residence'; formerly Viceroy's House); (x) Secretariats; (y) India Gate; (z) Parliament House

ware at the Purana Qil'a was, however, mixed with later deposits, and the excavations showed continuous habitation only from about the 4th century BC. A rock edict (1b) of the Mauryan emperor Ashoka (*reg c.* 269–*c.* 232 BC), on an outcrop overlooking the Yamuna south of the Purana Qil'a, confirms the importance of Delhi in the 3rd century BC, perhaps as a link in ancient trade routes along the river.

The city's political history becomes clear only in the 10th century AD, when a clan of Tomara Rajputs established themselves in the Delhi region. Inscriptions from

as early as the 12th century refer to the city as Dhillī or Dhillikā. From the 10th to the 17th centuries the city centre and fortified palaces were moved at least seven times over an area stretching 25 km along the river and 10 km west of it. Delhi's history is thus often told as a tale of seven cities (fig. 1). The 'new' cities were centres for the élite founded by the state; the fortified palaces were planned, and sometimes also the main residential areas. Perhaps the most important motivation for building was the urge of each dynasty to seek and establish legitimacy through architecture. Other reasons included a steady growth in population due to arrivals from other parts of India and politically disturbed areas in Iran and Central Asia. Delhi offered security, the comforts of urban life and prospects through state patronage. The growth of the empire ruled from Delhi, and the consequent administrative expansion also created a need for new buildings.

Although anxiety about internal security was not a major reason for building new centres, each city was enclosed by walls. These sometimes overlapped with previous constructions. Each city had its own gates, which were customarily closed at night. Although the Yamuna was navigable and used for trade and transport, only the last three cities were built on or near its banks. Older cities were not immediately deserted when a new city was founded, but the desire to be at the heart of urban life tended to attract people to the new centre. Some old cities gradually lost their glory and crumbled, others were absorbed in new cities, and several were sacked. Something survives, however, from each of Delhi's seven cities.

1. The first city. 2. Siri, the second city. 3. Tughluqabad, the third city. 4. Jahanpanah, the fourth city. 5. Firuzabad, the fifth city. 6. Dinpanah, the sixth city. 7. Shahjahanabad, the seventh city. 8. Delhi in the British period.

1. THE FIRST CITY. The Rajput ruler Anangapala Tomara is credited with founding the first city of Delhi in the 10th century in what is now known as Mehrauli (some 12 km south of the present city centre). It is said that he built his citadel, called Lal Kot, near an already ancient temple site. The Tomaras were defeated by Vigraharaja IV (*reg c.* 1153–64) of the Chahamana (Chauhan) Rajput clan. Accepting Chahamana suzerainty, the Tomaras retained Delhi. The fort was enlarged and came to be known as Qil'a Rai Pithaura ('Fort of King Prithviraja', popularly known as Prithviraj Chauhan). Only ruins survive. An inscription on the eastern gate of the Quwwat al-Islam Mosque (*see* §III, 1 below) hints at the lost splendour of ancient Delhi when it states that 27 temples were destroyed and their stone reused to build the mosque complex. To judge from the pillars in the Quwwat al-Islam Mosque, most of these temples dated from the 10th and 11th centuries, but some were as early as the 7th century.

Delhi was captured in 1192 by Qutb al-Din Aybak, a former slave promoted to general by the GHURID ruler Mu'izz al-Din Muhammad ibn Sam (known in India as Muhammad of Ghur), whose kingdom comprised Afghanistan and parts of Iran and Central Asia. In 1206, on the death of Muhammad of Ghur, Qutb al-Din established an independent dynasty (termed Mamluk or Slave), the first of five consecutive dynasties of the Delhi sultanate (*see* INDIAN SUBCONTINENT, §III, 6(ii)(b)). The dates of their rule are: Mamluk (*see* MAMLUK, §I), 1206–90;

KHALJI, 1290–1320; TUGHLUQ, 1320–1413; SAYYID, 1414–51; and LODI, 1451–1526.

The Mamluks kept Qil'a Rai Pithaura and its surrounding city as their capital. Their most impressive architectural contributions were the Quwwat al-Islam Mosque (1198; 1c) and the adjacent tower known as the Qutb Minar (see fig. 2), both begun by Qutb al-Din Aybak. The Mamluks extended and reinforced the fort, building ramparts 5–6 m thick and 18 m high. The fort is said to have had 13 gateways, the largest known as the Ghaznin Gate. Outside the walls was a wide moat. Two Mamluk palaces (no longer extant) are known from contemporary chronicles: the Qasr-i Safid (probably a white-plastered palace) and the Kushk-i Lal (probably a red sandstone pavilion). Iltutmish (*reg* 1211–36) improved the water supply of the city by building a large reservoir, the Hauz-i Shamsi. Stepwells (Urdu/Hindi: *bā'olī*) were dug to supplement the water supply. Delhi's first monumental Islamic tomb (1231–2), now known as Sultan Ghari (1d), was built by Iltutmish and used as the burial place for his eldest son, Nasir al-Din Mahmud. It was renovated in the time of Firuz Shah Tughluq (*reg* 1351–88). Iltutmish's own tomb is within the Quwwat al-Islam complex (*see* §III, 1 below). His daughter Raziyya (*reg* 1236–40) was the only woman to rule Delhi in the Muslim period. She was killed by rebels at Kaithal, some 8 km from Delhi, and may be buried there, although Delhi folklore maintains that she is buried in an unroofed grave preserved in the later city of Shahjahanabad.

A tomb not far from the Quwwat (1e) is known as that of Sultan Balban (*reg* 1266–87), but the identification is uncertain. Balban is said to have built a palace, but it is no longer extant. His successor, Kayqubadh (*reg* 1287–90), is credited with laying out a new city, Shahr-i Nav, on the banks of the Yamuna at Kilokari (also called Kilagarhi or Kilokri). Chroniclers extolled its beautiful gardens, palaces and gateways, and the poet Amir Khusrau (1253–1325) wrote eulogies on it. Jalal al-Din Firuz (*reg* 1290–96),

founder of the KHALJI dynasty, is said to have completed its unfinished buildings. However, as nothing substantial remains, Kilokari is not counted among Delhi's seven cities.

2. SIRI, THE SECOND CITY. Siri was founded *c.* 1303 by the sultan 'Ala al-Din Khalji (*reg* 1296–1316), the Khalji dynasty's foremost patron of architecture. It was built on the site of a village of the same name, about 4 km northeast of Qil'a Rai Pithaura. The city walls are ovoid in plan and are said to have had seven gateways. The city was sacked in the 16th century, and little survives except the ruins of several mosques and tombs. 'Ala al-Din also built a reservoir, the Hauz-i 'Alai, which had a catchment area of several kilometres and contained water all year round. The continuing importance of the Quwwat al-Islam Mosque is shown by 'Ala al-Din's building projects there. He extended the mosque and planned to add four gateways; the magnificent 'Alai Darvaza on the south (*see* §III, 1 below) is the only one to survive and was probably the only one completed. A square, domed structure of red sandstone with decoration in white marble, it influenced many later buildings at Delhi.

During the Khalji period an important suburb emerged around the *dargāh* or shrine (1f) of the Sufi saint of the Chisti Order, Nizam al-Din Auliya (1236–1325), who was greatly revered by the court. The Jama'at Khana Mosque, apparently built by Khidr Khan, the son of 'Ala al-Din Khalji, is the oldest building in the area (although much of it may have been rebuilt in the Lodi or early Mughal period). Nizam al-Din has been steadily venerated since his death and his shrine renovated through the centuries. The general area around the tomb became a popular necropolis.

3. TUGHLUQABAD, THE THIRD CITY. The first three sultans of the Tughluq dynasty were major patrons of architecture, each founding a new city. Ghiyath al-Din (*reg* 1320–25) founded Tughluqabad in 1321, choosing a site on a rocky outcrop some 8 km east of Qil'a Rai Pithaura. Its massive walls, large stretches of which are still standing, were roughly octagonal in plan with a perimeter of about 6 km. Made of local quartzite stone, they are 10–15 m high with an inward batter and are said to have had 56 bastions and 52 gates. The vast walled area was divided into two main parts. On one side was the fort, separated and secured by walls and bastions. Part of it was demarcated for palaces, including the no longer extant Jahannuma, praised in contemporary chronicles. The city stretched to the north, and the ruins of its houses are still visible. Streets, connecting the gateways, followed a grid pattern. Underground passages and drains are discernible. A vast reservoir stretched to the south of the city.

The Tughluqs were particularly skilled at using water for the security and enhancement of an architectural setting. Ghiyath al-Din Tughluq built himself a fortified tomb (1g; *see* §III, 2 below) once surrounded by water and connected to the fort by a raised causeway. While the rest of Tughluqabad is in ruins, the tomb is well preserved. Muhammad Tughluq (*reg* 1325–51) built a smaller citadel of his own called 'Adilabad ('City of Justice'). It was situated about 1 km to the south on an island in a lake

2. Delhi, Mehrauli, Qutb Minar, *c.* 1198–1215

formed by rain-water and was once connected to Tugh-luqabad by a causeway. Little remains within its walls, although a Hazar Sutun ('Thousand Pillared') white marble palace is said to have been built there.

4. JAHANPANAH, THE FOURTH CITY. Muhammad Tughluq also built Jahanpanah ('Refuge of the World'), the fourth city of Delhi. Its walls connected with those of Siri and Qil'a Rai Pithaura to create one large urban area. Written accounts mention 30 gates in all, 13 in Jahanpanah, 7 in Siri and 10 in Qil'a Rai Pithaura. Some led from one city to another, creating a complex, interconnecting net-work. The Begumpuri Mosque (c. 1343; alternatively dated c. 1370; 1h) was probably the city's congregational mosque. Several palaces are now in ruins. A dam known as Satpul ('Seven Bridges') formed part of the city's enclosure wall. It had a bridge above and sluices below, which were used to regulate the flow of water into an artificial lake, beautifying the city and providing water for irrigation and other purposes.

Delhi's development came to an abrupt standstill in 1328 when Muhammad Tughluq moved the capital to DAULATABAD in the Deccan, a distance of nearly 1000 km. The residents of Delhi were ordered to move, and the city is described in contemporary accounts as deserted (al-though recent evidence suggests it was not totally aban-doned). When disturbances in Bengal and elsewhere emerged, Muhammad Tughluq came back to Delhi, and the population was allowed to return.

5. FIRUZABAD, THE FIFTH CITY. Firuz Shah Tughluq (reg 1351–88) was an enthusiastic patron of architecture and attempted to raise the prestige of the Sultanate through his building projects. He not only built Delhi's fifth city, Firuzabad, but also repaired and expanded earlier struc-tures and carried out building projects outside the capital. His autobiography records that he built 30 towns, 100 dams, 50 canals, 20 hospices for Sufis (Pers. khānagāh), 100 palaces, 200 inns, 5 hospitals, 100 tombs, 10 baths and 10 minarets, and that he laid out 1200 gardens. Nobles of the court also patronized architecture, building a number of impressive mosques and tombs in Delhi.

Most of the extant buildings in Delhi from the Tughluq period are constructed of rubble covered with thick layers of plaster. Having little or no decoration, they appear sombre, but weathering may have removed the colourful decorative effects of paint and tilework. In some cases cut plaster decoration has survived. Changes in building materials and style (surviving earlier buildings are typically faced with carved sandstone ashlar) may be related to the move to the Deccan and the consequent dispersal of craftsmen and funds. Moreover, building ambitions were running high, while the territory and revenues of the Sultanate were smaller than before. On the other hand, many pre-Tughluq palaces (which have disappeared) may have been rubble-built.

Firuz Shah built his city of Firuzabad on the bank of the Yamuna canal in close proximity to the river. It is said to have absorbed 18 villages, the entire area being sur-rounded by battlemented ramparts with regular gateways. The citadel was built with the palace enclosure facing directly on to the river. The main gate was on the west

side. Firuz Shah brought two monolithic pillars of the MAURYA (3rd century BC) to Delhi, one from near Ambala in Haryana and the other from Meerut in Uttar Pradesh. One of the pillars was placed on top of the remarkable three-storey structure beside the congregational mosque in the sultan's citadel. It was designated the 'golden minaret' (Pers. minār-i zarrīn). The other Mauryan pillar was placed near a hunting palace that Firuz Shah had built on the high ground outside Delhi known as 'the ridge'. The sultan's other projects included repairs to the Qutb Minar and the restoration of the Hauz-i 'Ala i reservoir. He built his own tomb (1i) and a madrasa along its shores (see INDIAN SUBCONTINENT, fig. 88).

One of the most important non-royal patrons of the period was Firuz Shah's vizier or minister Khan-i Jahan Junan Shah. He built the Kalan Mosque outside the sultan's citadel in 1387. The mosque has two storeys and is approached by a long staircase that leads to a monumental gateway. The courtyard is surrounded by arcades with domed bays resting on large stone piers. The prayer-hall is divided into fifteen domed bays and has five mihrabs. The building was apparently modelled on the mosque (now ruined) built by Firuz Shah within the citadel. Junan Shah built another mosque at the shrine of Nizam al-Din in 1370–71 (AH 772). Also known as the Kalan or Kali Mosque, it appears to have been modelled on the Khirki Mosque in Jahanpanah (c. 1352–4).

Khan-i Jahan Junan Shah also seems to have built the tomb of his father (1j), Khan-i Jahan Maqbul Telingani (although it may have been begun by the father and completed by the son). Maqbul Telingani was a convert to Islam who became Firuz Shah's minister and was granted the title 'Khan-i Jahan', which he passed on to his son. Maqbul Telingani died in 1368, and his tomb was raised near the shrine of Nizam al-Din. The tomb is an octagonal domed structure surrounded by a vaulted am-bulatory, itself an open verandah with arched openings on each side; the arcade is protected by a prominent stone projection (Urdu/Hindi chajjā) resting on brackets. While not the first octagonal mausoleum in Delhi (the tomb of Zafar Khan in Tughluqabad dates from c. 1323–5), Maqbul Telingani's tomb nonetheless had a significant impact on the later tombs of the Sayyid and Lodi dynasties.

A decade of political instability followed the death of Firuz Shah in 1388. Delhi was left vulnerable to the armies of the Central Asian conqueror Timur, who occupied the city in 1398 and plundered it. Many inhabitants were killed, but, according to Timur's own records, builders and stone masons were spared so that they could be taken to his capital, SAMARKAND, to build a congregational mosque. After Timur's retreat Delhi was impoverished and dispir-ited. Sultans of the Sayyid and Lodi dynasties built few monuments. Mu'izz al-Din Mubarak Shah Sayyid (reg 1421–34) is said to have founded a new city called Mubarakabad, but little remains. It was probably located near his tomb (1k), which stands in the area now known as Mubarkpur, about halfway between the shrine of Nizam al-Din and Siri, the second city. Such tombs are the most conspicuous memorials of the Sayyid and Lodi periods, and form a significant part of the urban landscape. For the most part, the Sayyid and Lodi tombs are clustered around the park known as the Lodi Gardens (1l), which seems to have been the favoured necropolis during the 15th century. The tombs are of two distinct types: square and octagonal. The three royal octagonal tombs are those of Mubarak Shah Sayyid (*c.* 1435), Muhammad Shah Sayyid (*c.* 1444; see fig. 3) and Sikandar Lodi (*c.* 1517). On the two Sayyid tombs, octagonal *chatrī*s (small domed pavilions) around the base of the dome replace the eight small cupolas used on Khan-i Jahan Maqbul Telingani's tomb. Another new feature appearing in these buildings is the stone buttress at each angle of the octagon. The tomb of Mubarak Shah Sayyid appears somewhat squat; the proportions were improved in Muhammad Sayyid's tomb by raising the drum to give additional height to the dome and the elevated *chatrī*s. Although the tomb of Sikandar Lodi no longer has any *chatrī*s, traces of them survived until the early 20th century. The interiors of the tombs were embellished with stuccowork and painted decoration.

The square tombs of the Lodi period are known by local designations often containing the word *gumbaz* (Ind.-Pers.: 'dome'; from Pers. *gunbad*) because the names of most of those they commemorate have been lost. Those instances in which the names are preserved demonstrate that the square plan was usually for non-royal usage. They include the Kale Khan ka Gumbaz (Mubarak Khan Lohani, 1481), Chhote Khan ka Gumbaz (*c.* 1490) and Bare Khan ka Gumbaz (*c.* 1510), all in Mubarakpur. The Shish Gumbaz (*c.* 1489) and Bara Gumbaz (*c.* 1489) are in the Lodi Gardens, while the Bagh-i 'Alam ka Gumbaz (tomb of Taj Khan, *c.* 1501; 1n; see also fig. 4) is outside Hauz Khas. In each case the façade is broken into two or three registers (often by string courses), creating the impression of two or three storeys. The hall is generally closed on the west side to mark the qibla, and roofed by a single high dome. *Chatrī*s flank the corners in some instances. The prototype for the group seems to have

4. Delhi, Bagh-i 'Alam ka Gumbaz, tomb of Taj Khan, *c.* 1501

been the 'Alai Darvaza. The central entrance portal, rising nearly the full height of the façade, was set in a prominent frame that projected slightly forwards. The door proper, usually of the post-and-bracket type, often had a small window or balcony (Ind.-Pers. *jharokā*) above. Construction was usually in ashlar, which was originally plastered (some traces remain). Occasional glazed tiles decorated the exterior; the interiors had stucco and painted decoration, mainly arabesques and calligraphic designs.

Two small mosques survive from the Lodi period; one is in the Lodi Gardens at the Bara Gumbaz complex (1494), and the other is the Moth ki Mosque (*c.* 1505; 1m) near Mubarakpur. The Moth ki Mosque was probably built by Miyan Bhuwa, a minister of Sikandar Lodi (*reg* 1489–1517). In both cases the prayer-hall has three domes and the façade five main arches, the central one rising nearly the full height of the structure. On the outer corners of the prayer-hall are tapering towers. These mosques had some impact on later designs, notably the Jamali Mosque (*c.* 1536) and the Qil'a-i Kuhna Mosque (16th century) in the Purana Qil'a (*see* §III, 3 below).

6. DINPANAH, THE SIXTH CITY. Sikandar Lodi spent much of his reign at Agra, constructing several buildings there and initiating that city's ascent to a position rivalling that of Delhi. After Babur (*reg* 1526–30), founder of the MUGHAL dynasty, defeated Ibrahim Lodi (*reg* 1517–26), he also resided mainly at Agra. The only known Delhi building dating to Babur's time is a mosque at Palam constructed, according to its inscription, in 1528–9 (AH 935) by a non-royal patron, one Ghazanfar. The Jamali Mosque (1o) and tomb of the poet–saint Fazl Allah 'Jamali' (*d* 1536) were probably begun in Babur's reign but may not have been completed until after Fazl Allah's death.

3. Delhi, Lodi Gardens, tomb of Muhammad Shah Sayyid, *c.* 1444

Humayun (*reg* 1530–40; 1555–6) returned the capital to Delhi and founded the sixth city, which he named Din-panah ('Refuge of Religion'). It was located along the Yamuna between Firuzabad and the shrine of Nizam al-Din. However, Humayun was driven into exile in 1540 by Sher Shah Sur (*reg* 1540–45), and the Sur dynasty (*see* SUR (ii)) briefly ruled at Delhi. For this reason it is unclear what was built by Humayun and what by Sher Shah. The 16th-century structures consist of the impressive fort known as the Purana Qil'a (*see* §III, 3 below), and inside it the Sher Mandal pavilion and the Qil'a-i Kuhna Mosque (see fig. 5 below). A variety of views have been expressed about the patronage of these buildings, and on the available evidence no completely final conclusions can be made (*see* INDIAN SUBCONTINENT, §III, 7(i)(a)). In any case, Humayun died shortly after returning to Delhi. His tomb (1p; *see* §III, 4 and fig. 6 below) was built to the south of the Purana Qil'a not far from the shrine of Nizam al-Din. It is a magnificent structure and served as the prototype for a series of Mughal garden tombs.

Emperors Akbar (*reg* 1556–1605) and Jahangir (*reg* 1605–27) favoured AGRA, FATEHPUR SIKRI and LAHORE. However, a few buildings were constructed in Delhi during Akbar's reign by non-royal patrons. These include the tomb of one of Akbar's generals, Adham Khan (1562), built at Mehrauli on the model of earlier octagonal tombs, and the tomb of Akbar's minister, Ataga Khan (1566), at Nizam al-Din. The Khayr al-Manazil Mosque (1561–2), opposite the Purana Qil'a, was built by Adham Khan's mother and Akbar's wet-nurse, Maham Anga. Buildings in Delhi from Jahangir's reign include the tomb of 'Abd al-Rahim Khan-i Khanan (1q), a general, high-ranking courtier and patron of the arts. This large, fine structure, modelled on Humayun's tomb, was stripped of its white marble and fawn sandstone in the 18th century; these were reused for the tomb (1753–4) of Safdar Jang.

7. SHAHJAHANABAD, THE SEVENTH CITY. The fifth Mughal emperor, Shah Jahan (*reg* 1628–58), was a prodigious builder (*see* INDIAN SUBCONTINENT, §III, 7(i)(a)). In 1639, just before the Taj Mahal in Agra was complete, the Emperor founded the city of Shahjahanabad, re-establishing Delhi as the premier Mughal city. He chose a site on high ground along the Yamuna River. The city was laid out in an irregular semicircle, the 'straight' side paralleling the river. Much of 14th-century Firuzabad was absorbed in it. The city was walled and had 13 gates; among the few that survive are the Delhi Gate (originally known as the Akbarabad Gate as it led to the Agra road) on the south-east, the Turkman Gate on the south and the Ajmeri Gate on the south-west.

The city's fortified palace, the Lal Qil'a ('Red Fort'; 1r; *see* §III, 5 below), was built on the riverbank. Its luxurious white marble palaces and gardens were protected by a high red sandstone wall and moat on all but the river side. On a rocky outcrop outside the fort a great congregational mosque (1s; *see* §III, 6 below) was begun in 1650. Also outside the Lal Qil'a was the city's main commercial area, consisting of two broad thoroughfares intersecting at right angles. Chandni Chauk extended east–west from the fort's Lahore Gate to the Fatehpur Mosque (1t), built in 1650 by one of Shah Jahan's wives, Fatehpuri Begum. It was

intersected by the shopping area later known as Faiz Bazaar, running north–south. A masonry-lined water-channel was laid down the middle of each thoroughfare; on each side were pavements and tree-lined avenues. 'Ali Mardan Khan was put in charge of organizing Shah Jahan's water projects. To supply water for them, he extended the old canal of Firuz Khalji, previously extended by Firuz Shah Tughluq and repaired during Akbar's reign. Water entered the city through the Kabuli Gate, flowed through Chandni Chauk and Faiz Bazaar and was released in the moat of the Lal Qil'a. Some studies indicate that the same water was pumped into the palace for fountains and water channels, but polluted water from the city would have been unsuitable for the Mughal emperor. A separate system supplied fresh water to the Lal Qil'a. Shahjahanabad's unique canals supplied pure water to the citizens and beautified the urban environment. A number of gardens were laid out on the north and north-west side of the city, where the canal water was readily available for irrigation. Nobles erected large family residences (Ind.-Pers. *haveli*), usually built around one or several courtyards.

Aurangzeb (*reg* 1658–1707) added little to Delhi. His daughter Zinat al-Nisa Begum built the mosque popularly known as the Zinat al-Masjid (1u), near the Lal Qil'a in Shahjahanabad. It was modelled on the congregational mosque. The Lal Qil'a remained the residence of the later Mughal emperors and Delhi the capital of the disintegrating empire until its dissolution by the British following the rebellion of 1857. A notable 18th-century addition to Delhi was the Jantar Mantar, an astronomical observatory built by Maharaja Sawai Jai Singh II of Jaipur (*reg* 1700–43) during the reign of the Mughal emperor Muhammad Shah (*reg* 1719–48). Its large-scale stone instruments were designed to measure the movement of the sun and planets precisely, to tell local time accurately and to forecast the occurrence of eclipses. The observatory, much admired in modern times for its stunning abstract forms, documents the spirit of empiricism in 18th-century India.

Delhi's last outstanding Mughal monument is the tomb (1753–4; 1v) of Safdar Jang, governor of Avadh and vizier of Muhammad Shah. Built of fawn sandstone and white marble, the tomb is square in plan, set on a high plinth and situated in a walled garden. A bulbous dome roofs the central chamber; double-storey octagonal towers at the four corners are topped by *chatris*. An impressive structure, it has been judged by critics as lacking the fine proportions and balance of earlier Mughal buildings.

8. DELHI IN THE BRITISH PERIOD. Delhi was officially brought under British control in 1803; Calcutta was at that time the capital of British India. Due to its historical importance, however, Delhi was chosen for the durbar of 1877 at which Queen Victoria was proclaimed Empress of India; for the durbar of 1903 held to mark the accession of Edward VII; and for the durbar of 1911 marking the coronation of George V. It was on this last occasion that George V proclaimed the decision to transfer the capital from Calcutta to Delhi and to build a new city at Delhi 'worthy of its predecessors'. EDWIN LUTYENS was given the commission; HERBERT BAKER was later named his associate. A site south of Shahjahanabad was selected, stretching from Raisina Hill on the west to the Purana

Qil'a on the east. Lutyens worked out the overall plan; he and Baker shared in designing the government complex (*see* LUTYENS, EDWIN, fig. 3), which both agreed should be built to a unified conception expressing the order and unity of British India and the grandeur and prestige of the empire. Lutyens designed the focal point, the Viceroy's House (1w), the residence of the Viceroy of India (now Rashtrapati Bhavan or President's House). Built on a grand scale, it has a modified H-shaped plan, with a long central section (152.4 m in length) flanked by two projecting wings. A colonnade dominates the east front, facing the Viceroy's Court (now Great Court), a vast expanse graced by the Jaipur Column, also designed by Lutyens. The building is crowned by a great dome rising 51.8 m from the courtyard. Lutyens designed a 'Mughal' garden extending from the west front (*see* GARDEN, §IV, 3 and fig. 12).

Baker was responsible for the Secretariats (1x), two buildings (now known as the north and south blocks) designed to frame the Viceroy's House. They were to accommodate the Indian Civil Service. The approach to the complex, laid out by Lutyens, was a broad avenue named Kings Way (now Raj Path) with green spaces and canals on either side stretching some 3 km to the site of the All India War Memorial Arch (now India Gate; 1y). Baker also designed the Legislative Assembly (now Samsad Bhavan or Parliament House; 1z), a great circular building (diam. 114 m) resembling an amphitheatre.

The complex is built mainly of buff and red sandstone, the materials of many of Delhi's earlier buildings. British architectural designs were skilfully blended with Indian elements such as stone screens (*jālīs*), balconies (*jharokās*), overhanging stone projections (*chajjās*) and domed pavilions (*chatrīs*). The style is quite grand, liberal and homogeneous.

Lutyens's contributions to the capital also include a memorial for *George V*, located east of the All India War Memorial Arch (the statue of *George V* was later removed). Lutyens also designed palaces in Delhi for two Indian princes, the Nizam of Hyderabad and Gaekwar of Baroda. As architectural adviser to the capital, Lutyens was able to ensure that other structures suited his overall conception of the city.

Although New Delhi, the 'eighth city', was formally inaugurated in 1931, several important additions were completed slightly later. Robert Tor Russell, the chief architect of the government of India, laid out the main shopping and commercial centre, Connaught Place, with double-storey colonnades around an inner and outer circle. The complex was completed in 1934. His successor, Henry Medd, designed both the Anglican church of the Redemption (based on Lutyens's sketches, completed 1935) and the Roman Catholic church of the Sacred Heart (completed 1934). Both were later made cathedrals.

R. NATH

II. Art life and organization.

The evolution of the visual arts in Delhi is closely linked with the history and political fortunes of the city. Excavations beneath the Purana Qil'a have revealed archaeological evidence identifying this site with a part of the ancient city of Indraprasthar, central to the *Mahābhārata* (1st millennium BC). The Tomara Rajputs established themselves south of Delhi in the 10th century AD and their successors, the Chahamana (Chauhan) Rajputs, did the same: Prithviraj Chauhan (*reg* 1178–92) built several temples in the Delhi region (*see* §I, 1 above). Subsequent Muslim dynasties also undertook building projects (*see* §I, 2–6 above).

Although Akbar (*reg* 1556–1605) was a perceptive patron of the arts, Delhi did not attain any aesthetic autonomy or identity during his reign, since he ruled from Agra and Fatehpur Sikri. Similarly, his son Jahangir (*reg* 1605–27)—an itinerant monarch—spent little time in Delhi. However, when Shah Jahan (*reg* 1628–58) assumed the Mughal throne he focused more time and attention on Delhi, building the Lal Qil'a (*see* §III, 5 below), which he occupied in 1648. Artists followed the royal court as it moved from one locale to another and with Shah Jahan, the city of Shahjahanabad—which exists today as Old Delhi—blossomed (*see* §I, 7 above). Itinerant craftsmen carried their style to the ruler for whom they worked, and it is methodologically inaccurate to assign dynastic names to particular styles. However, in some cases the aesthetic tastes of a ruler were strong enough to be identified not only with his city but also with the area over which he ruled. Consequently, under the exacting patronage of Shah Jahan art life was invigorated, and for the first time a distinctive Delhi style was developed (*see* INDIAN SUBCONTINENT, §V, 4(i)(d)).

When Shah Jahan's comparatively puritanical son Aurangzeb (*reg* 1658–1707) seized the throne, the arts declined. Shorn of patronage, artists left the city for other courts and markets. In this way the central Dehli style (Kalam) surfaced elsewhere, transformed into regional styles with specific identities of their own—among them the Kangra and Basohli schools of the Punjab hills. This parent Kalam evolved with a specific regional flavour and aesthetic identity. One result was that art life and activity in Delhi itself remained static. By the 19th century, what emerged was a mixture of the indigenous idiom and the prevailing Western style. This hybrid became famous as the East India Company style, also known as the 'Company' style (*see* INDIAN SUBCONTINENT, §V, 4(ix)(g)). Mildred Archer notes that the indigenous tradition was stronger in Delhi than in any other city occupied by the British.

With the gradual disappearance of the traditional patron, several administrators and educationists in positions of responsibility felt the urgent need to resurrect the old crafts. To this end the tented township created for the durbar of 1903 by Lord Curzon, the British Viceroy (1899–1905) was sumptuously embellished with the finest examples of both the fine arts and crafts—notable inclusions being traditional Indian textiles and metalwork. This special project was the creation of Lord Curzon, who had an abiding interest in Indian art and archaeology, in which he shared the thoughts and attitudes of Ernest Binfield Havell and Rabindranath Tagore. Although Lahore remained the artistic hub of northern India, the political significance accorded to Delhi permanently transformed its art life with the decision at the coronation durbar of

1911 to shift the capital of British India from Calcutta to Delhi and to create New Delhi (see §I, 8, above); by this time state patronage of the arts was resurrected.

In 1925, Sarada Ukil, an exponent of the neo-Indian art movement, which began in Calcutta, shifted his studio to New Delhi and founded the Sarada Ukil School of Art, which became for a time the most influential art centre in northern India. In 1928, the All India Fine Arts and Crafts Society (AIFACS) was formally launched; its journal, *Roopa-Lekha*, is the oldest Delhi art publication.

The partition of India and Pakistan that followed independence from British rule in 1947 brought an influx of established artists and art teachers from Lahore. Prominent among these were Bhabesh Chandra Sanyal (*b* 1902), who was associated with the Mayo School of Art and the School of Fine Arts in Lahore, SATISH GUJRAL and Pran Nath Mago. Art institutions proliferated in Delhi: the present College of Art began as a polytechnic college in 1942, attaining fully fledged art college status in 1964. The state-run Lalit Kala Akademi (National Academy of Fine Arts) and the National Gallery of Modern Art were established in 1954, realizing the vision of several senior artists and theorists and including the active support of the prime minister, Jawarhalal Nehru.

Over the decades, Delhi grew into an important centre of Asian art. The AIFACS had already begun the practice of holding international exhibitions, and the first international art exhibition, held in 1946, was followed by an inter-Asian exhibition in 1948 and the All India Art Conference in 1953. The Lalit Kala Akademi opened regional chapters and holds an annual national art exhibition and, since 1968, an international triennale (see also INDIA, Republic of, §IX). More institutional support for the arts led to the establishment of other art centres. Under state patronage the Delhi Sahitya Kala Parishad and the Crafts Museum were founded. Enlightened private patronage included the establishment of the Triveni Kala Sangam by Sundari Shridarani and the Sanskriti Pratishthan by Om Prakash Jain. In 1949, a splinter group of the AIFACS formed the Delhi Silpi Chakra. Commercial galleries also played their part in nurturing art activity; Dhoomimal is one of the oldest galleries in the city. Influential art critics and commentators have included Charles Fabri, a Hungarian resident of Delhi, and Krishna Chaitanya.

By the end of the 20th century, the city was vibrant in terms of artistic activity; the presence of the National Gallery of Modern Art and Delhi's status as the national capital also added to the level of its art life. Many of India's better-known artists were first noticed in Delhi, and resident artists have included Sailoz Mookherjea (1908–60), Maqbool Fida Husain, Satish Gujral, Krishen Khanna, Ram Kumar, Gaitonde, Anjolie Menon, Arpita Singh, Manjit Bawa, Rameshwar Broota, Anupam Sud and Devraj Dakoji. By the 1990s New Delhi was home to over 35 public and private galleries, and the art market was very active; sales of contemporary Indian art were held by such major auction houses as Christie's and Sotheby's.

C. UDAY BHASKAR

III. Buildings.

1. Quwwat al-Islam Mosque complex. 2. Tomb of Ghiyath al-Din Tughluq. 3. Purana Qil'a. 4. Tomb of Emperor Humayun. 5. Lal Qil'a. 6. Jami' Mosque.

1. QUWWAT AL-ISLAM MOSQUE COMPLEX. Built as Delhi's first congregational mosque (Jami' Masjid), the mosque now known as the Quwwat al-Islam ('Might of Islam'; see INDIAN SUBCONTINENT, fig. 87) is the central structure of a large partially ruined complex (see fig. 1c above), including the Qutb Minar (see fig. 2 above), the tomb of Sultan Iltutmish (reg 1211–36) and the 'Ala'i Darvaza. The mosque was founded in 1192 with the conquest of north India by Qutb al-Din Aybak, commander of the armies of the GHURID ruler Muhammad ibn Sam. Temple spolia were used in the construction; following the preferred hypostyle plan for mosques, pillars and lintels form a colonnade around a central courtyard (43×32 m). Figurative sculptures were defaced, but other carved decorations, such as the overflowing pot motif, were retained. Corbelled ceilings from temples were also employed and probably reset by indigenous craftsmen. A screen of five lofty arches (15 m high) was added across the façade of the qibla colonnade in 1198. These ogee arches, of unusual grace and impressiveness, were skilfully corbelled to create the arch shape without the use of voussoirs. The screen was constructed of red and grey sandstone, quartzite and black slate. The ornamentation included graceful wave patterns and lotus scrollwork drawn directly from temple decoration. These elements were combined with calligraphy. As the craftsmen were undoubtedly Indian and ignorant of Arabic, the calligraphy was probably prepared on a cartoon.

In front of the façade in the mosque's courtyard is the Iron Pillar (c. 400), a relic of the GUPTA period cast in a pure, non-corrosive iron. The tapering column (7.21 m) was a victory standard (Skt *dhvaja*), as its inscription states; it was probably crowned by a *garuda* figure, which no longer survives. Qutb al-Din Aybak probably placed (or retained) the standard as a victory symbol.

The Quwwat al-Islam Mosque was extended by the sultans Iltutmish and 'Ala al-Din Khalji (reg 1296–1316). The portions built in the time of Iltutmish, dated 1229–30 (AH 627), decisively turn away from the decorative repertory of temple architecture and reproduce in stone the geometric ornaments used in Iran. 'Ala al-Din, the greatest builder of the KHALJI dynasty, continued the expansion of the mosque by adding a façade-screen to the north and building a colonnade that embraced all the earlier structures. This colonnade may have had a number of gateways, of which the 'Ala'i Darvaza ('Lofty Gate'; a play on the ruler's name) on the south is the only preserved example. Dated 1311, the structure is square in plan (16.76 m to a side) and crowned by a shallow dome, the whole rising to a height of 18.29 m. Red sandstone is the main building material with contrasting bands of white marble. The effectiveness of this combination led to its use in many later buildings. The façades of the gateway are similar, each with a pointed horseshoe arch (*īwān*) rising nearly the full height of the building. The arch is edged on the intrados with a spearhead fringe and is supported by nook-shafts. On either side of the central arch, the façade is divided into two registers creating the impression of a two-storey structure. The upper register has a pair of rectangular panels on each side, outlined with white marble and inset with miniature niches. The lower register has large arched niches (one screened and the other blind) that echo the design of the main portal. The sumptuous carved decoration of the exterior includes calligraphic, floral and geometric motifs. The interior has graceful squinches supporting the dome. It has been suggested that Seljuk builders (possibly migrants fleeing the Mongol invasion) had a hand in the 'Ala'i Darvaza. However, it is the extensions of Iltutmish that can properly claim west Asian pedigree; the 'Ala'i Darvaza is an authentic Indian creation, integral to the evolution of Indo-Islamic architecture.

The Qutb Minar (see fig. 2 above) stands at the southeast corner of Qutb al-Din Aybak's original mosque. Inscriptions indicate it was begun by Qutb al-Din c. 1198 and completed by his successor Iltutmish in 1215. Rising in five storeys (probably four originally), it is 72.54 m in height and 14.73 m in diameter at the base. Most of the tower is faced in red sandstone; local grey quartzite was also used in the construction. The top part of the fourth storey and all of the fifth storey, faced in white marble, probably date to the reign of Firuz Shah Tughluq (reg 1351–88), during whose time repairs were undertaken. Four balconies supported by stalactite brackets separate the storeys. Each level takes a different form and has 23 projecting ribs; in the lowest level they are alternately pointed and round, on the second level all are round and on the third all are pointed. The fourth and fifth levels are plain. In the lower three storeys a stunning effect was achieved by contrasting the fluted masonry with broad carved bands in which calligraphy has been interwoven with graceful floral motifs. The minaret has an internal spiral stairway of 360 gradually diminishing stairs. Sculptures found in the Qutb (apparently temple spolia used to build up the fabric) have prompted the theory that the tower was a pre-Islamic structure converted to a minaret after the conquest of Delhi. Though the symbolism of the kīrti stambha (Skt 'pillar of glory') was similar, the Qutb Minar is clearly based on victory towers in Afghanistan, surviving, for example, at GHAZNA and Jam (see also MINARET). The builders of the Qutb Minar seem to have used as their prototype the minaret of Khwaja Siyah-Push (c. 1150) in southern Afghanistan, which also employs alternating round and pointed ribs. The Qutb celebrates the victory of Islam in northern India.

North of the Qutb Minar is the unfinished stump (24.5 m high) of a second minaret begun by 'Ala' al-Din Khalji. Intended to be twice the height of the Qutb Minar, this project of unprecedented scale was left incomplete. 'Ala al-Din also built his tomb and a madrasa (Islamic college) immediately west of the Quwwat al-Islam Mosque; these structures are mostly ruined.

The tomb of Sultan Iltutmish (c. 1235) is situated northwest of the Quwwat al-Islam Mosque. A square structure (12.5 m on each side) faced with red sandstone, it has arched entrances on three sides. The qibla side is closed, with three mihrabs on the interior. Surviving squinches indicate that the tomb was originally domed, though this has fallen. The exterior is relatively plain, but the interior is extensively embellished with carved decoration.

2. TOMB OF GHIYATH AL-DIN TUGHLUQ. Built in c. 1325 by Ghiyath al-Din Tughluq, this 'fortified' tomb (see fig. 1g above) was situated on an outcrop within a reservoir (now dry) and connected with Tughluqabad Fort by a raised causeway. Its high wall, an irregular pentagon in plan, has rounded bastions at four of its angles. Constructed of red sandstone with white marble trim, the tomb adopts some of its decorative scheme from the 'Ala'i Darvaza, but its proportions differ, and it has a number of distinctive features. The pronounced batter of the walls, which characterize Tughluq-period buildings from this time onwards, was probably derived from the sloping walls of brick structures, such as those in MULTAN, where Ghiyath al-Din originally served as governor.

The tomb is square in plan (about 8 m on each side) and has high recessed archways on the north, south and east; the qibla wall is closed and marked by a mihrab on the interior. The entrance portals have a spearhead fringe on the intrados and are outlined with a band of white marble. This band is carried down into a bold string course of white marble running round the middle of the entire structure. Above the string course in the upper register are small ornamental niches with rectangular white marble surrounds. The tomb's white marble dome is set on an octagonal drum and crowned with a sandstone finial typical of Indian temple architecture. It consists of a grooved disc (Skt āmalasārika) and pot (kalaśa). On the interior the dome is supported by squinches like those on the 'Ala'i Darvaza. There are three graves inside the tomb. The central one belongs to Ghiyath al-Din Tughluq and the others are probably those of his wife and his son and successor, Muhammad Tughluq (reg 1325–51).

3. PURANA QIL'A. The Purana Qil'a ('Old Fort'; see fig. 1a above) was built in the 16th century on an ancient mound along the River Yamuna (which has since changed course). It is a massive irregular oblong, with bastioned grey walls and three towering red sandstone gates: the Bara Darvaza ('Great Gate') on the west designed as the main entrance, the Talaqi Darvaza ('Forbidden Gate') on the north and the Humayun Darvaza ('Humayun Gate') on the south. With decoration of white marble and blue glaze, they are forceful yet elegant structures. Only two original buildings survive within the fort: the Qil'a-i Kuhna Mosque ('Mosque of the Old Fort') and the Sher Mandal, an octagonal pavilion.

The Qil'a-i Kuhna Mosque (see fig. 5) is a magnificently conceived and finished building. It consists of a prayer-hall (51.2×14.9 m) facing an open courtyard with a well for ablutions. The customary colonnades surrounding the court have been omitted. The prayer-hall has five bays, each with an arched entrance. The entrances in turn are recessed in higher arches with rectangular frames. The central portal is the most prominent; its frame is outlined with panels carved with Koranic verses and set off with fluted turrets on the corners. The intrados of the central arch is lined with a fringe of lotus buds, a 16th-century transformation of the earlier spearhead motif. Above the entrance is a small balcony (Ind.-Pers. jharokhā) supported by carved brackets. The walls around this balcony are decorated with inlay work in white marble and red sandstone. Black slate provides a third tone in other inlaid patterns. This type of work is a standard feature of early Mughal architecture. The other arched entrances to the prayer-hall are protected by a wide *chajjā* (stone projection), above which runs a battlemented parapet. Three-storey towers are attached to the corners of the qibla wall, and *jharokhās* relieve the sides of the building. A projection in the centre of the qibla carries two tapering turrets. The mosque has a single dome set on a 16-sided drum amid 16 short pinnacles, one at each of the drum's angles. (Early paintings show two smaller domes flanking the central dome.) The finial consists of a lotus flower surmounted by a grooved disc (*āmalasārika*). On the inside, the dome over the central bay is supported by squinches. The halls flanking the central bay are covered with ingenious and evidently experimental vaulting systems: the spaces flanking the dome have ornamental stalactite pendentives, while the end bays have cross-ribs supporting semi-vaults. The middle three bays are square and built of red sandstone, while the end bays are oblong and in grey quartzite. The qibla wall of the interior has a series of five exquisite marble mihrabs (the central one being the most elaborate). The mihrabs have recessed arches, echoing the portals of the façade. The arches are lined with lotus buds and supported by double shafts set in nooks. The decoration of the mihrabs includes Koranic verses and inlaid black slate contrasting with white marble. As a whole, the Qil'a-i Kuhna Mosque is important in marking the genesis of the Mughal style of architecture.

The octagonal red sandstone structure known as Sher Mandal, located a short distance from the mosque, has been variously identified as Sher Shah's pleasure pavilion or Humayun's library and observatory. It has two storeys and is crowned by an octagonal *chatrī*. The exterior has decoration in white marble and the interior was embellished with glazed tiles and cut and painted plasterwork, now badly damaged.

There is disagreement as to whether the Purana Qil'a and its buildings were constructed by Humayun (*reg* 1530–40, 1555–6) or by Sher Shah Sur (*reg c.* 1540–45), who forced Humayun into exile and briefly ruled at Delhi (*see* INDIAN SUBCONTINENT, §III, 7(i)(a)). The stylistic features of the Qil'a-i Kuhna Mosque do not rule out the possibility that the building was completed early in the reign of Akbar (*reg* 1556–1605).

4. TOMB OF EMPEROR HUMAYUN. The first monumental mausoleum of the Mughal dynasty, the tomb of Humayun (see figs 6 and 1p), was situated on the Yamuna south of the Purana Qil'a. (The course of the river has shifted slightly since the 16th century.) It was completed in 1571 under the supervision of Mirak Mirza Ghiyath. It has often been said that it owes much to the patronage of Haji Begum, Humayun's widow. There is no evidence to support this, however, and it is more likely that the project benefited from the interest of Humayun's son Akbar.

The tomb is situated in the centre of a series of four-plot gardens (Ind.-Pers. *chār-bāgh*), with shallow water channels, pools and paved pathways laid out symmetrically on all sides. Garden settings with channels of water were

5. Delhi, Purana Qil'a, Qil'a-i Kuhna Mosque, 16th century

6. Delhi, tomb of Emperor Humayun, *c.* 1558–71

employed by Babur (*reg* 1526–30), but in Humayun's tomb such a scheme is used for the first time with a mausoleum. The garden complex is enclosed by high walls with large gateways. The tomb is constructed of red sandstone and faced with coloured slate. The lavish use of white marble to outline panels and arches was an important precedent for subsequent Mughal architecture. The tomb building stands on a high double plinth (base level 1.5 m high, upper level 6.1 m high); the upper plinth is lined with arched alcoves on all sides. The tomb itself (47.54 m sq) consists of four octagonal structures clustered around the central domed chamber, a scheme already used in Iranian secular architecture of the 15th century. All the façades are essentially alike. They are dominated by a high central portal and the lofty marble-faced dome. The octagonal wings flanking the portals are two-storey and have small arched portals and alcoves. These portions of the building are crowned by *chatrīs*. The entrance is located in the south portal; the other sides are closed by stone screens. The cenotaph of Emperor Humayun is in the central chamber. Above the cenotaph is the double dome; this construction technique allowed for impressive proportions externally with relatively little weight, while the interior remained appropriate in proportion to the space covered. The dome rests on a drum with decorative inlay. The rooms surrounding the central domed chamber contain cenotaphs of the royal family as well as those of several late Mughal emperors. Passages connect these rooms to each other and to the central chamber. In the second storey is another series of interconnected rooms, some of which overlook the main space under the dome.

5. LAL QIL'A. The Lal Qil'a ('Red Fort'; see fig. 1r above), takes its name from the red sandstone of its outer walls. Built by the emperor Shah Jahan (*reg* 1628–58) between 1639 and 1648, the Lal Qil'a was the citadel of his new city Shahjahanabad. The ramparts are provided with a battlemented parapet, machicolations and embrasures. The ornamental cusps of the parapet's merlons are a typical Shah Jahan-period feature. The fort was laid out on the western bank of the Yamuna, while a moat protected the city side. Its two main entrances are the Lahore Gate on the west (the principal entrance) and that known as the Delhi Gate on the south. The emperor Aurangzeb (*reg* 1658–1707) added barbicans in front of both gates. Most of the palace buildings inside date from Shah Jahan's reign, but a few were added in later times. Some structures, mainly those damaged in the rebellion of 1857, have been demolished.

The fort's more public areas are on the city side, while its private palaces are in an enclosure along the river. The Lahore Gate leads to a broad, vaulted passage lined with arcades. This opens into a courtyard facing the Naubat Khana ('Drum House'), from which the royal drums were sounded and in which music was played. The Naubat Khana leads to the courtyard of the Divan-i 'Am ('Hall of Public Audience'), a pillared pavilion (57×21 m) of red sandstone probably once covered with polished white plaster. The façade has nine cusped arches (a typical Shah Jahan-period feature) supported on double pillars. The interior is composed of three aisles formed by cusped arches, creating a pleasing vista of elegant receding curves. The emperor's throne was placed at the rear of the hall, elevated on a white marble platform carved with delicate floral patterns. Above it is a curved marble canopy with a prominent cornice. The form was used in many buildings of the Shah Jahan period and became a standard feature of later Mughal and regional architecture. The wall behind the throne is decorated with inlaid panels of black marble,

some apparently of Florentine origin (one depicts *Orpheus Playing his Lyre*; see Koch, 1988). They were acquired as royal gifts or through trade. In this pavilion the emperor received petitions and requests from the public.

The private palaces are arranged in a line on a high terrace, facing the river on the east and a *chār-bāgh* garden on the west. The buildings, from south to north, are presently known as the Mumtaz Mahal (now a museum), the Rang Mahal ('Painted Palace'), the Khwabgah ('Sleeping Chamber'), the Divan-i Khas ('Hall of Private Audience'; *see* INDIAN SUBCONTINENT, fig. 100), the Hamman ('bath') and the Shah Burj ('King's Tower'). Most are flat-roofed, single-storey pavilions built either of marble or brick masonry covered with fine polished white plaster. The façades usually have a line of cusped arches of equal size supported by piers or pillars and protected by a broad *chajjā*. Most have four *chatrīs* at the corners of the roof. The interiors consist of intersecting arcades dividing the space into square or rectangular bays. The most elaborately decorated are the Rang Mahal and Divan-i Khas, which are embellished with painted decoration, gilt, inlaid floral patterns and sumptuously carved marble. The cusped arches are outlined in inlaid stone, emphasizing their graceful shapes. The effect is luxurious, yet restrained and elegant.

Both the palaces and the garden make use of water. It appears that water was raised from the river to the Shah Burj in the north-east corner of the fort and then flowed into the Nahar-i Bihisht ('Stream of Paradise'), a channel passing through the line of palaces. One of the most stunning uses of water is in the Rang Mahal (originally known as the Imtiaz Mahal), where the entire middle bay is taken up by a lotus pool. The carved marble petals appear to undulate as the water ripples over their surface. The pool is framed with inlay decoration. As the palace gardens are situated 1.52 m below the terrace on which the palace buildings stand, the water could be diverted into them through various cascade and waterfall devices. Niches for candles were sometimes made behind the waterfalls to enhance the sparkle of the water at night. A broad, shallow canal with fountains and cross bridges ran through the garden. Flowered areas and pathways were placed on either side of the canal.

The Moti ('Pearl') Mosque was added near the line of palaces probably during the reign of Aurangzeb (though it has also been attributed to Shah Jahan). Built of white marble with three bulbous domes (originally plated with copper), it is a magnificent specimen of mature Mughal architecture. Later palaces in the Lal Qil'a include the Moti Mahal, built by Shah Bahadur II (*reg* 1837–58). Apparently a second identical pavilion was destroyed in the rebellion of 1857. Shah Bahadur also added a red sandstone pavilion known as the Zafar Mahal, so called because the Emperor's pen-name was Zafar. It is situated in a large pool in the garden and was originally reached by a causeway.

6. JAMI' MOSQUE. Built by Shah Jahan in six years (1650–56), the Jami' or congregational mosque (see fig. 1s above) is one of the largest mosques in India. Erected on an outcrop and set on a high plinth, it towers above its surroundings. It is built of red sandstone with white marble used extensively for decoration.

Flights of steps on the north, south and east lead to monumental gateways. Beyond these is the mosque's vast courtyard (100 m each side) edged by an arcade with a prominent *chajjā*. The prayer-hall (27.4×60.96 m) has a large central portal set in a rectangular frame with turrets attached to the outer corners. The flanking wings of the prayer-hall have cusped entrance arches with panels above carrying inlaid inscriptions in Persian praising the building and Shah Jahan. The façade is topped by a merloned parapet and terminated on each side by three-storey minarets. These lofty towers are of red sandstone with vertical stripes of white marble. The three domes over the prayer hall are faced in white marble and have vertical stripes in black. This emphasis on line and colour, as opposed to mass and volume, is typical of later Mughal architecture.

See also INDIAN SUBCONTINENT, §III, 6(ii)(b) and 7(i)(a).

BIBLIOGRAPHY

Sayyid Ahmed Khan: *Āthār al-Ṣanādīd* [Great heritage] (Delhi, 1847); Eng. trans. by R. Nath as *Monuments of Delhi: A Historical Study* (New Delhi, 1979)
A. Cunningham: *Archaeol. Surv. India Annual Rep.* (1871), pp. 132–3; (1874), pp. 1–91; (1885), pp. 142–61
R. Byron: 'New Delhi', *Archit. Rev.* [London], lxix/410 (1931), pp. 1–30
P. Brown: *Indian Architecture, Islamic Period* (Bombay, 1942, rev. Bombay, 1956) [rev. edn with add. photographs]
P. Spear: *Twilight of the Mughals: Studies in Late Mughal Delhi* (Cambridge, 1951)
Y. D. Sharma: *Delhi and its Neighbours* (New Delhi, 1964, rev. 1974)
G. Hambly: *Cities of Mughal India: Delhi, Agra and Fatehpur Sikri* (London, 1968)
Y. Yamamoto, M. Ara and T. Tsukinowa: *Delhi: Architectural Remains of the Delhi Sultanate Period*, 3 vols (Tokyo, 1968–70)
Marg, xxvi (Dec. 1972) [issue on Mughal gardens]
S. Crowe, S. Hayward, S. Jellicoe and G. Patterson: *The Gardens of Mughal India* (London, 1972)
R. Nath: 'The Moti Masjid of the Red Fort Delhi', *Some Aspects of Mughal Architecture* (New Delhi, 1976)
E. Moynihan: *Paradise as a Garden in Persia and Mughal India* (London, 1979)
W. E. Begley: 'The Symbolic Role of Calligraphy on Three Imperial Mosques of Shah Jahan', *Kaladarsana*, ed. J. Williams (New Delhi, 1981), pp. 7–18
R. G. Irving: *Indian Summer—Lutyens, Baker and Imperial Delhi* (New Haven, CT, 1981)
R. Nath: *History of Mughal Architecture*, i (New Delhi, 1982)
A. Welch and H. Crane: 'The Tughluqs: Master Builders of the Delhi Sultanate', *Muqarnas*, i (1983), pp. 123–66
R. E. Frykenberg, ed.: *Delhi through the Ages* (New Delhi, 1986)
E. Koch: *Shah Jahan and Orpheus* (Graz, 1988)
S. Blake: *Shahjahanabad: The Sovereign City in Mughal India, 1639–1739* (Cambridge, 1991)

R. NATH

De Ligne, Jean (*b* Brussels, 17 Dec 1890; *d* Brussels, 24 June 1985). Belgian architect, urban planner, writer and teacher. He studied at the Académie Royale des Beaux-Arts in Brussels and then built several houses (1912–13) in the Rue Marcel Liétard, Brussels, including his own, that were inspired by English domestic architecture. During World War I he was a prisoner in Germany, where he built a commemorative monument in the prison camp at Munsterlager and wrote a book on the formation and reconstruction of Ypres (1918). De Ligne became an important architect of the modern movement in Belgium and was one of the few Modernists to write on the history of towns and study their development. From 1919 to 1921 he built the garden city of Zaventem and several private houses, as well as garden city suburbs at Auderghem and Woluwe-Saint-Pierre, Brussels. Other major works included a prize-winning entry (1927; with J. Hendricks) to the international competition for the Palace of the League of Nations, Geneva; a dispensary (1933) for the Ligue Belge contre la Tuberculose in the Marolles district of Brussels, for which he designed the first curtain-wall structure in Belgium; and a factory (1930) at Wygmael for Usines Rémy, for whom he also designed a pavilion at the Exposition Universelle et Internationale in Brussels (1935) that had a remarkable glass-walled rotunda. From 1939 to 1968 De Ligne taught architecture and urban history at the Institut Supérieur des Arts Décoratifs in Brussels; he also published other books on urban planning, including one on the reconstruction of Tournai, in which he participated. He became Director of Fine Art at the Académie Royale de Belgique.

WRITINGS
La Formation et la reconstruction d'Ypres (Lausanne, 1918)
Le Mécanisme urbain (Brussels, 1939)
La Reconstruction de Tournai (Brussels, 1945)

BIBLIOGRAPHY
Musée des Archives d'Architecture Moderne: Collections, Brussels, Mus. Archvs Archit. Mod. cat. (Brussels, 1986)

ANNE VAN LOO

Delisle, Léopold(-Victor) (*b* Valognes, Normandy, 24 Dec 1826; *d* Chantilly, 22 July 1910). French art historian. He obtained the diploma of Archiviste-paléographe from the Ecole des Chartes in 1849 and in 1851 was awarded the first Prix Gobert by the Académie des Inscriptions et Belles-Lettres for his essay *Etudes sur la condition de la classe agricole et l'état de l'agriculture en Normandie au Moyen Age*. In 1852 he joined the staff of the department of manuscripts of the Bibliothèque Nationale in Paris and remained there until his retirement in 1905, being promoted to curator of his department in 1871 and general administrator in 1874.

A man of immense energy, Delisle was both a fine scholar and a great administrator, and the catalogues and inventories compiled by him and under his direction were models of their kind. From 1868 to 1881 he published a four-volume study of the history of the manuscript collections (*Le Cabinet des manuscrits de la Bibliothèque Impériale*) and it was due to him that in 1897 the first volume of the general catalogue of printed books was published, to be followed by 20 more before his retirement. His own scholarly output continued unabated until the year before his death. Lacombe's bibliography of his publications and its supplement record over 2000 titles.

WRITINGS
Chronique de Robert de Torigni (Rouen, 1872–3)
ed.: *Catalogue général des livres imprimés de la Bibliothèque Nationale* (Paris, 1897–)
Recherches sur la librairie de Charles V (Paris, 1907)
Rouleau mortuaire du B. Vital, Abbé de Savigni (Paris, 1909)
Regular contributions to the *Bibliothèque de l'Ecole des Chartes* and the *Journal des Savants*

BIBLIOGRAPHY
DBF
P. Lacombe: *Bibliographie des travaux de M. Léopold Delisle, 1847–1902* (Paris, 1902); *Supplément, 1902–10* (Paris, 1911)
X. Delisle, ed.: *Lettres de Léopold Delisle*, 5 vols (Saint-Lô, 1911–13)
Léopold Delisle: Exposition organisée pour le cinquantenaire de sa mort (exh. cat., Paris, Bib. N., 1960)

ANDREW G. WATSON

Delitio, Andrea (*fl* Abruzzo, *c.* 1440–80). Italian painter. His career has been reconstructed on the basis of his one surviving signed and dated work, a gigantic image of *St Christopher* (1473) on the façade of S Maria Maggiore in Guardiagrele. He is known to have painted frescoes in 1450 for S Francesco in Sulmona and two panels for S Maria Maggiore in 1463 and 1467 (all untraced). On the basis of the *St Christopher* he has been credited with a cycle of frescoes on the *Life of the Virgin* (*c.* 1480; Atri Cathedral), two frescoes of the *Virgin and Child* (L'Aquila, S Amico; Sulmona, Pal. Sanità), a diptych of the *Crucifixion* and *Virgin and Child with a Saint* (L'Aquila, Mus. N. Abruzzo) and a triptych of the *Virgin and Saints* (Baltimore, MD, Mus. A.). In these works Delitio appears as a Late Gothic provincial master, rather backward by comparison with painters working in the large cities, his style characterized by linear, swirling folds of drapery and landscape backgrounds of stylized mountains crowned with castles. More modern Renaissance elements are evident in the plasticity of his figures and in some experimentation with fragile perspective structures. The latter feature led some scholars to conjecture that he may have been in Florence *c.* 1440–50, in contact with such first-generation Renaissance painters as Fra Filippo Lippi and Paolo Uccello. In those years the last of the painters who developed in the Late Gothic period were still active, for example Masolino da Panicale, who was once thought to have painted the *Annunciation* from the Lehman collection (New York, Met.) that is now attributed to Delitio.

BIBLIOGRAPHY

E. Carli: 'Per la pittura del '400 in Abruzzo', *Riv. Ist. N. Archeol. & Stor. A.*, ix/1–3 (1942), pp. 164–211

F. Bologna: 'Andrea Delitio', *Paragone*, i/5 (1950), pp. 44–50

G. Romano: 'A. Delitio', *Petit Larousse de la peinture*, i (Paris, 1979), pp. 450–51

MINA BACCI

Dell. German family of sculptors. Peter Dell (i) (*b* Würzburg, *c.* 1490; *d* Würzburg, 1552) was the leading sculptor in Würzburg during the second quarter of the 16th century and was documented as a pupil of Tilmann Riemenschneider sometime between 1505 and 1510. His style owes more, however, to the powerful monumentality of Hans Leinberger, who probably employed him as an apprentice in Landshut around 1515. Before returning to Würzburg in 1534, Dell probably worked in Regensburg (*c.* 1520–21), the Lower Main River area (1520s) and Freiberg, Saxony (1528–33). While in Freiberg, he carved at least four limewood reliefs, of the *Crucifixion, Resurrection* and *Holy Teaching* (all Dresden, Grünes Gewölbe) and the *Fall of the Rebel Angels* (untraced), for Henry, Duke of Saxony. Other religious reliefs by Dell are in Berlin, Nuremberg and Stuttgart. Dell was also an important portrait sculptor; his small wooden portrait reliefs include *Wolfhart von Werensdorff* (1528; priv. col.), the allegorical two-sided plaquette of *Jakob Woler* (1529; Munich) and the pearwood portrait of *Georg Knauerr* (1537; art market). In contrast to these, he also carved many large stone funerary monuments, armorials and free-standing Crucifixions. His monuments, for example those to *Paul Fuchs* (*d* 1540) and *Bishop Konrad von Bibra* (*d* 1544) in Würzburg Cathedral, tend to be simple in design with a deeply carved central relief of the donor kneeling before the crucified Christ, a clear display of armorials and inscriptions, and a Renaissance frame. The formula was inspired in part by the monument to *Konrad von Thungen, Bishop of Würzburg* (*d* 1540) by the Eichstätt sculptor Loy Hering. Peter Dell (ii) (*b* ?Würzburg; *d* ?Würzburg, 1600), the son of Peter Dell (i), became a master sculptor in 1551 and ran the family's shop until his death. Over 40 monuments are attributed to him. His finest, for example that to *Bishop Melchior Zobel* (1558) in Würzburg Cathedral, are close in style to those by his father but have more richly ornamented frames. Like his father, Peter Dell (ii) frequently signed his work with the monogram PD.

NDB

BIBLIOGRAPHY

G. Habich: 'Porträtstücke von Peter Dell', *Jb. Preuss. Kstsamml.*, xxxix (1918), pp. 135–44

L. Bruhns: *Würzburger Bildhauer der Renaissance und des werenden Barock, 1540–1650* (Munich, 1923), pp. 38–67

G. Lill: 'Aus der Frühzeit des Würzburger Bildhauers Peter Dell des Älteren', *Mainfränk. Jb. Gesch. & Kst*, 3 (1951), pp. 139–59

E. Vetter: 'Das allegorische Relief Peter Dells d. Ä. im Germanischen Nationalmuseum', *Festschrift für Heinz Ladendorf* (Cologne, 1970), pp. 76–88

J. C. Smith: *German Sculpture of the Later Renaissance, c. 1520–1580: Art in an Age of Uncertainty* (Princeton, 1994), pp. 51–2, 61–8, 127–9, 310–11, 345–6, 367–8, 434–5

JEFFREY CHIPPS SMITH

della. For pre-19th-century Italian proper names with this prefix, *see under* the first part of the name for individuals active before *c.* 1500; *see under* the second part of the name for those active *c.* 1500–*c.* 1800.

Della Paolera, Carlos Maria (*b* Buenos Aires, 7 Sept 1890; *d* Buenos Aires, 15 Sept 1960). Argentine urban planner. He was the first South American graduate of the Institut d'Urbanisme, Université de Paris, where he studied from 1921 to 1928 under Marcel Poëte. After World War II Della Paolera founded the Instituto Superior de Urbanismo, Universidad de Buenos Aires (1949). He was an advocate of a beaux-arts 'geometrical' approach to urban planning. One of his particular interests was the provision of open spaces in metropolitan areas, and he became an early advocate of the concept of appropriate environment. His main planning studies were for Buenos Aires, but he also worked on development policy proposals for a number of other Argentine cities, including La Plata, Rosario (Santa Fé), Concepción del Uruguay and Tafí (Tucumán).

WRITINGS

'El símbolo y el día del urbanismo, 1934–1949', *Rev. Arquit.* [Arg.] (1949), no. 347, pp. 326–9

Buenos Aires y sus problemas urbanos, intro. P. Randle (Buenos Aires, 1977)

LUDOVICO C. KOPPMANN

Dellaurana, Luciano. *See* LAURANA, LUCIANO.

Della Valle, Angel (*b* Buenos Aires, 10 Oct 1852; *d* Buenos Aires, 10 July 1903). Argentine painter. He travelled to Europe, studying for several years in Florence under Antonio Ciseri and undergoing the influence of large-scale evocations of historical scenes. In 1883 he returned to Buenos Aires, where he devoted himself to painting and to teaching at the Escuela Estímulo de Bellas

Artes. He was a gifted technician and in his early pictures relied on thinly painted surfaces and muted colours, preferring the impact to arise from the subject-matter. Country scenes, Indians, Indian raids, gaucho musicians and the breaking-in of horses were among his favourite themes, which he depicted in subdued tones or full sunlight, for example *Gauchos on Horseback* (Buenos Aires, Mus. N. B.A.) and *Horse-breaking* (Buenos Aires, Mus. A. Blanco). He painted the gaucho and the Indian without resorting to superficial picturesqueness, and his preference for country subjects made him a painter of animals as well as landscapes. He gave a true picture of the limitless Argentinian plains.

Over the years Della Valle's style became more modern, especially in his portraits, for which he began to use a richer palette and looser brushwork; he subsequently incorporated these qualities into his landscapes, which became more luminous and colourful. His work betrays a romantic temperament more evident in his choice of subject than in his technique, which had closer links to Italian realist and academic art of the period, as in his splendid painting *The Return of the Indian Raiding-party* (1892; Buenos Aires, Mus. N. B.A.).

BIBLIOGRAPHY

J. L. Pagano: *El arte de los argentinos*, i (Buenos Aires, 1937), pp. 339–48
C. Córdova Iturburu: *La pintura argentina del siglo veinte* (Buenos Aires, 1958), p. 25

NELLY PERAZZO

Delleani, Lorenzo (*b* Pollone, Vercelli, 17 Jan 1840; *d* Turin, 13 Nov 1908). Italian painter. He attended the Accademia Albertina in Turin, and he first exhibited work at the Società Promotrice delle Belle Arti in Turin at the age of 15. Having already made his name as a history painter, from 1860 he painted from nature, dedicating himself primarily to landscapes with figures, for example the famous *Processions*, a genre in which he is today considered as one of the most important artists of his time. Delleani worked on such paintings, all of the same format, daily and dated each precisely. His earliest landscapes were small-scale views of Venice and its lagoon, dating from 1873. In 1878 he completed some smaller works on panel, such as *The Orchard*, the *Seine at Paris* and the *Market Place at Berne*.

With the first of several large-scale landscapes, shown in Turin in 1880, Delleani began to take part in official exhibitions, both in Italy and abroad. In 1907 the Venice Biennale paid tribute to him with a one-man exhibition of 35 paintings: these had been produced during periods spent in the region of Bielle, on the Ligurian coast, and also in Rome, in Venice, at Morozzo and abroad. In 1883 Delleani was in the Netherlands, where he painted views of Leiden, The Hague, Scheveningen and Rotterdam, and in 1892 in Switzerland, where he visited Basle and Lucerne. Delleani was a lively and original colourist, with an eye for both detail and overall effect. His paintings have a strong sense of depth and mass, and were carried out with decisive and often heavily loaded brushstrokes.

BIBLIOGRAPHY

A. Dragone: *Lorenzo Delleani: La vita, l'opera e il suo tempo*, 2 vols (Turin, 1973–4) [cat. rais.]
P. M. Prosio: '"Fonti" figurative e influssi pittorici nella poesia di C. Camerana: Fontanesi, Delleani, Böcklin', *Stud. Piemont.*, viii/2 (1979), pp. 304–18
A. Dragone: 'Le arti visive', *Torino città viva: Da capitale a metropoli 1880–1980* (Turin, 1980), pp. 541–733

ANGELO DRAGONE

Delli, Dello (di Niccolò) (*b* Florence, *c.* 1404; *d* Spain). Italian painter and sculptor. Nothing is known of his training in painting and sculpture. Vasari attributed to him the terracotta *Coronation of the Virgin* in the tympanum of a portal at S Maria Nuova, Florence; in 1424 Bicci di Lorenzo was paid for painting the figures. Stylistically it is related to Ghiberti's figural forms. Vasari also indicated that Dello was responsible for paintings on furniture, although no attributable examples survive. In 1424 Dello moved to Siena with his father Niccolò, who had been exiled from Florence for having failed in his role of civil guardian of the Rocca di Montecerro by surrendering it to Filippo Maria Visconti, Duke of Milan. In 1425 Dello was commissioned to make a figure of a man in bronze to strike the bell in the Torre del Mangia of the Palazzo Pubblico of Siena, but he seems to have left the city before carrying out the work.

In 1427 Dello moved with his father and his brother Sansone to Venice, where he stayed until 1433. This has led to the suggestion that he may have worked in Uccello's workshop both in the Veneto and also later in Florence in the Chiostro Verde, S Maria Novella. In 1433 he enrolled in the Arte dei Medici e degli Speziali in Florence, which would suggest that he was active as a painter in Florence; however, in the same year he left for Spain with his brother Sansone. His career as a painter in Spain was apparently enormously successful, and by 1446 he was negotiating to be knighted. He returned to his native city in 1447, was knighted in 1448 and seems to have left again for Spain. No documented works survive from Dello's career in Spain although a long painted rotulus, or scroll, is recorded depicting the Battle of Higuezuela in 1431; this painting was reportedly signed *Dello eques florentinus*, which would place it after 1448. Paintings attributed to Dello in Salamanca Cathedral are actually by his brother Niccolò. The date of Dello's death is unknown.

BIBLIOGRAPHY

F. Quilliet: *Le arti italiane in Ispagna* (Rome, 1825)
G. Milanesi: *Documenti per la storia dell'arte senese*, ii (Siena, 1854), p. 290, no. 204n
M. Gómez Moreno: 'Maestre Nicolao Florentino y sus obras en Salamanca', *Archv Esp. A. & Arqueol.*, iv (1928), pp. 1–24
G. Fiocco: 'Dello Delli, scultore', *Riv. A.*, xi (1929), pp. 25–42
M. Salmi: 'Un'opera giovanile di Dello Delli', *Riv. A.*, i (1929), pp. 104–10
G. Gronau: 'Il primo soggiorno di Dello Delli in Spagna', *Riv. A.*, xiv (1932), pp. 385–6
G. Pudelko: 'The Minor Masters of the Chiostro Verde', *A. Bull.*, xvii (1935), pp. 71–89
U. Middeldorf: 'Dello Delli and *The Man of Sorrows* in the Victoria and Albert Museum', *Burl. Mag.*, lxxviii (1941), pp. 71–8
J. Rubio: 'Alfons El Magnanim, Rei de Napols, I Daniel Florentino, Leonardo da Bisuccio I Donatello', *Misc. Puig & Cadafalch*, i (1947), pp. 25–35
G. Fiocco: 'Il mito di Dello Delli', *Arte in Europa: Scritti di storia dell'arte in onore di Edoardo Arslan* (Milan, 1966), pp. 341–9
A. Condorelli: 'Precisazioni su Dello Delli e su Nicola Fiorentino', *Commentari*, xix (1968), pp. 197–211
M. Lisner: 'Intorno al Crocifisso di Donatello in Santa Croce', *Donatello e il suo tempo* (Florence, 1968), pp. 122–5

A. Parronchi: 'Probabili aggiunte a Dello Delli scultore', *Cron. Archeol. & Stor. A.*, viii (1969), 103–10

J. Beck: 'Masaccio's Early Career as a Sculptor', *A. Bull.*, xii (1971), pp. 177–95

E. Casalini: 'Un *Calvario* a fresco per la *Pietà* di Dello Delli', *La SS Annunziata di Firenze* (Florence, 1971), pp. 11–24

R. Lunardi: *Arte e storia in Santa Maria Novella* (Florence, 1983)

B. Borngässer: 'Die Apsisdekoration der alten Kathedrale zu Salamanca und die Gebrüder Delli aus Florenz', *Mitt. Ksthist. Inst. Florenz*, xxxi (1987), pp. 237–90

JOHN T. PAOLETTI

Dellit, (Cedric) Bruce (*b* 1900; *d* 1942). Australian architect. His major work began in 1929 when he won the competition for the Anzac War Memorial in Hyde Park, Sydney, with a design for a monumental, blocky and sculptural building to commemorate World War I. The Memorial, completed by 1934, incorporates sculpture by RAYNER HOFF and emotive architectural imagery to contrive a building closely allied to the popular sentiment of the period. Dellit was one of the first Australian architects to embrace modern architectural forms, and he became an outspoken critic of the use of historic motifs in contemporary city buildings. His highly personalized architecture used the decorative motifs and forms of the Art Deco style. His commercial work in Sydney included the Liberty Cinema (1934; destr.), with a striking, stepped Art Deco façade; Kinsela Funeral Chapel (1933), now remodelled as a nightclub, designed in Art Deco-inspired 'gothic'; and the office blocks Kyle House (1931) and Delfin House (1940), formerly the Bank of New South Wales. The latter exemplifies Dellit's sophisticated use of Art Deco devices. It is designed as a small skyscraper, with a stepped summit, vertically emphasized façade and glossy granite base pierced by an oversize arch; within the arch are bronze doors decorated with an allegorical low relief of modern life, industry and prosperity.

BIBLIOGRAPHY

The Book of the Anzac Memorial, NSW (Sydney, 1934)

H. Tanner: *Architects of Australia* (Melbourne, 1981), p. 119

D. Ellsmore: 'Sydney's Anzac Memorial: More than a Shrine?', *Hist. Envmt*, v/3 (1986), pp. 35–41

M. STAPLETON

Delorme, Adrien Faizelot (*b* Paris, *c.* 1715–20; *d* after 1783). French cabinetmaker and dealer. He was the most famous member of a family of cabinetmakers; his father, François Faizelot Delorme (1691–1768), and his brothers Jean-Louis Faizelot Delorme and Alexis Faizelot Delorme were all *maîtres-ébénistes*. Adrien became a *maître-ébéniste* on 22 June 1748 and was a juror of his guild from 1768 to 1770. He stamped his work DELORME. He made and sold luxury furniture in the Louis XV style, decorated with japanning either in imitation of Chinese lacquer (e.g. Amsterdam, Rijksmus.) or with European decoration (e.g. Waddesdon Manor, Bucks, NT). He also carried out sumptuous floral marquetry (e.g. Paris, Petit Pal.). His most distinguished work consisted of small pieces of furniture (e.g. Paris, Louvre; London, V&A; Washington, DC, Hillwood Mus.) embellished with floral marquetry or inlays of scrolls and foliation executed in end-grain wood on a dark-veined, light-wood ground forming a chevron pattern (e.g. Lyon, Mus. B.-A.). His work in the Neoclassical style, however, failed to impress connoisseurs.

BIBLIOGRAPHY

F. de Salverte: *Les Ébénistes du XVIIIème siècle, leurs oeuvres et leurs marques* (Paris, 1923, rev. 5/1962)

JEAN-DOMINIQUE AUGARDE, JEAN NÉRÉE RONFORT

Delorme, Philibert. *See* L'ORME, PHILIBERT DE.

Delorme [de Lorme], Pierre (*b* Rouen; *fl* 1501/2–1515). French mason and sculptor. During 1501–2 Delorme worked on the churches of St Nicolas and St Michel in Rouen. His name appears in a document of 1502 as Pierres de Lourme. He was employed in 1502–3 by Cardinal Georges I d'Amboise, Archbishop of Rouen, to carry out work on the episcopal palace, where he led a team of 22 masons and carried out work on 'la grande galerie et du préau du jardin'. Together with Pierre Fain (*fl* 1501/2–22), Delorme was again employed by the Cardinal on the second phase (1506–11) of the building campaign of the château of Gaillon (Seine-Maritime), during which period Italianate decorative motifs were introduced. Delorme's name occurs ten times in the detailed accounts for the building project, but none of the parts of Gaillon associated with him has survived. He modified the large square tower of the north wing and created a passage leading from the great courtyard to the gardens. The tower (1508) is known variously as the Portail Neuf, Portail du Jardin, Portail du Chastel or Pavillon Pierre Delorme. The two-storey southwest wing of the great central courtyard was remodelled (1506–8) by Delorme and is referred to in contemporary accounts as the Maison Pierre Delorme. He was no doubt an inventive and original mason involved in various aspects of the construction. In his capacity as a sculptor, Delorme was in 1509 called upon to produce frames for a series of medallions made by a certain Paguenin on the façade of the Cour d'Honneur; Delorme was required to blend *all'antica* motifs with the indigenous French style. He also made a stone carving of the Cardinal's coat of arms. Around 1508, with Toussaint Delorme, he produced sculptural decoration for the Gallery on the first floor of the Grand Maison (rebuilt 1988). Simultaneously with this work, Delorme and Fain collaborated on the extension of the residence of St Ouen Abbey, Rouen; it was largely complete in 1507, but payments were still being made to them both in 1509. Delorme is last recorded in 1515, when he is described as 'maistre des ouvrages en la ville et banlieu de Rouen'.

BIBLIOGRAPHY

A. Deville: *Comptes de dépenses de la construction du château de Gaillon*, Documents Inédits de l'Histoire de France (Paris, 1850), pp. xcix–cii

C. de Beaurepaire: 'Les Architectes de Rouen dans la première moitié du XVIe siècle', *Bull. Soc. Amis Mnmts Rouen.* (1904), pp. 119–31, 141–2

E. Chirol: *Un Premier Foyer de la Renaissance en France: Le Château de Gaillon* (Rouen and Paris, 1952), pp. 49–51, 69

☐

de los. For Spanish names with this preposition, *see under* the second part of the name.

Delos. Small Greek island (5 sq. km) in the Cyclades. It was inhabited at least as early as the 3rd millennium BC and throughout antiquity was one of the most important religious and trading centres of the Aegean. It was sacred to the ancient Greeks as the birthplace of the deities

Apollo and Artemis, and numerous sanctuaries established from the 7th century BC onwards have been excavated. In the early 3rd century BC Delos was at the height of its prosperity. Around 250 BC Roman merchants began to settle there and soon came to dominate its cosmopolitan mercantile community. In 88 BC, during the First Mithridatic War, Delos was sacked, and, although partly rebuilt, it had become virtually uninhabited by the 2nd century AD. Abandoned in the 6th or 7th century AD, it was subsequently exploited as a marble quarry. Excavations were begun in 1873 by the French School at Athens and are still in progress. During the first excavations most of the Imperial Roman and Early Christian buildings were destroyed, often without being studied, and almost the only remains still *in situ* are those of a Roman peristyle house built above the Hypostyle Hall and one of the four or five churches known to have existed.

1. Architecture. 2. Sculpture. 3. Mosaics.

1. ARCHITECTURE. The earliest architectural remains are those of a late 3rd-millennium BC dwelling at the top of Mt Kynthos and of a Mycenaean dwelling beneath the Sanctuary of Apollo. The remains of many buildings have been found, dating from the Archaic period (*c.* 700–*c.* 480 BC) to Roman times and situated mainly on the west coast of Delos near the modern Little Harbour. The ancient sacred area was to the north of this, the town to the south. These buildings fall into three categories: religious, civic and domestic (*see* §(i)–(iii) below). They were built of marble, which came from Delos itself and from other Cycladic islands, or local stones such as granite and gneiss. The local stones are difficult to work, a fact that explains the irregular finish of most of the walls on Delos. To disguise the roughness of the finish, they were typically coated with stucco. This was applied in several layers, the fine top layer being mixed with marble dust to make it a brilliant white. There are also magnificent examples of marble walls with oblique joints, for example in the Hypostyle Hall and the theatre. Other characteristic features common to all types of Delian architecture include the relatively frequent use of lanterns; taste for superimposed colonnades, sometimes only weakly bonded, since Delos was supposed to be immune from earthquakes; and the use of curved elements, including both true arches made up of blocks of stone and false arches cut in the soffits of monolithic lintels, six of which occur in the gymnasium alone.

(i) Religious. (ii) Civic. (iii) Domestic.

(i) *Religious.* Delos has several temples, some of which date to the Archaic period. The Temple of Hera is a distyle *in antis* Doric building, constructed in the late 6th century BC on the site of a 7th-century BC shrine. The Temple of Leto dates from the mid-6th century BC and is unusual in having a side door and a honeycomb pattern sculpted on its exterior walls. This type of decoration also occurs in the contemporary Hexagon Monument. The Oikos ('house') of the Naxians (*c.* 650 BC; see fig. 1) may also be a sacred structure and is sometimes identified as the first Temple of Apollo. It had a central colonnade and was rebuilt and altered in the century following its construction, first by the insertion of a doorway in the west side and

1. Delos, Oikos of the Naxians, view from the west, Archaic, *c.* 650 BC

later by the addition of a prostyle porch to the east façade. Three temples of Apollo stand next to each other a little to the north-east: unusually, all face west. They are the Archaic Porinos Naos, the Doric Temple of the Athenians, built by Athens *c.* 425–420 BC and also known as the Temple of the Seven after the seven statues originally set at the end of the cella on a horseshoe-shaped base, and the large Doric temple (begun 5th century BC, completed 3rd century BC), which is the only peripteral temple on Delos.

Although most Delian temples are of normal Greek types, some other religious buildings have unusual plans to suit particular cult practices. Examples of this include the Apsidal Building (5th and 4th centuries BC), which may simply have been a base or enclosure, and Monument GD 42, which the Athenians set up in the 4th century BC. This had an almost square cella with three naves and was illuminated by a lantern. One of these buildings probably held the Altar of Horns, believed to have been the work of Apollo himself. (The identification of the buildings is in fact far from certain, and there are many contradictory hypotheses: for example, if Monument GD 42 is not the 'Keraton', it could be the 'Pythion', which is known from the accounts of the sanctuary administrators but has not yet come to light.)

Some Delian sanctuaries formed elaborate architectural complexes. The Sanctuary of Artemis was partly bounded by an L-shaped stoa, and the Sanctuary of Asklepios comprised a temple, a propylon, an *oikos* and two peristyle buildings, probably used for the rite of incubation. The sanctuary of Apollo was particularly elaborate, with stoas giving access or functioning as boundaries, such as the South Stoa (mid-3rd century BC), the Stoa of Philip V (*c.* 210 BC) and the Stoa of Antigonos Gonatas, which had two projecting wings (*paraskenia*) and an unusual Doric frieze with alternate triglyphs decorated with bull's-head protomes (see fig. 2). The Sanctuary of Apollo also contained several treasuries and banqueting rooms (*hestiatoria*)

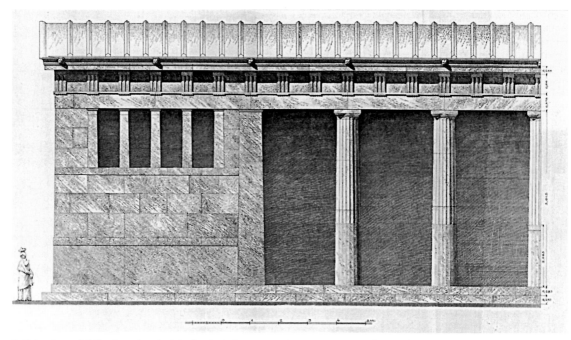

2. Delos, Stoa of Philip V, south end of the façade, Hellenistic, *c.* 210 BC; reconstruction drawing from R. Vallois: *Le Portique de Philippe*, Exploration archéologique de Délos (Paris, 1923), pl. 5

and the famous Monument of the Bulls, a long marble gallery with roof-beams supported by bull's-head brackets. This appears to have housed an ex-voto offering of a ship. The identity of the monument's dedicator is still unknown: the evidence of two ancient texts at first pointed to the Macedonian King Antigonos Gonatas II (*reg c.* 320–239 BC), but the building is too early, dating back at least to the end of the 4th century BC.

Delos is unusual in having about 20 sanctuaries of non-Greek gods. Most are due to its cosmopolitan religious and commercial character during the 2nd and 1st centuries BC. Of the three sanctuaries to Egyptian gods, the two most notable are the Serapeion A, a private foundation of the later 3rd century BC, consisting of a meeting hall and a courtyard within which stood a temple with an underground vault, and the Serapeion C, the official sanctuary, containing a paved avenue, flanked by two rows of small sphinxes, leading up to the temple, and several votive chapels, of which the best preserved is the Temple of Isis donated by the Athenians *c.* 130 BC and built as a distyle *in antis* Greek temple. The Sanctuary of the Syrian Gods (before 166 BC) was originally just a courtyard surrounded by shrines, but a later extension added a long terrace with a sacred theatre. The remaining 'oriental sanctuaries', some still unidentified, were dedicated to Semitic gods and often contained banqueting halls. Finally, Delos also had a synagogue, dating back to at least the 1st century BC and perhaps still in use in the 2nd century AD. It was open on the seaward side and included a meeting hall with three doors, a familiar feature in synagogues of this period. This hall contained a bench and a throne. An open-air cistern was no doubt used for ritual ablutions.

(ii) Civic. Most of the usual ancient Greek building types have been found on Delos. These include the assembly building (*ekklesiasterion*), altered several times between the 5th century BC and Roman Imperial times, the prytaneion (4th century BC) and a nearby Archaic building, which may have been the bouleuterion. A public water supply was provided by the Minoe Fountain (6th century BC) and the Reservoir of the Inopos (4th or 3rd century BC), a vast basin built partly of marble, which collected the waters of the largest river on Delos. The addition of stoas to one agora in the 4th and 3rd centuries BC made this civic area progressively more imposing, and a large theatre with a capacity of over 5000 was built gradually during the 3rd century BC. The latter had an unusual ellipsoidal *theatron* and a unique stage building with a portico around the three sides not occupied by the *proskenion*. There were also two palaestras and a gymnasium. The function of the great Hypostyle Hall (3rd century BC) is uncertain. Of its 44 internal columns, 40 were arranged in two concentric rectangles, while the rest formed a short central line. The outermost were Doric, the others Ionic, and the eight columns nearest the middle of the building supported a square lantern.

Certain foreign communities who settled on Delos after 166 BC also erected buildings connected with the civic life of the island. The Institution of the Poseidoniasts of Berytos (now Beirut), begun before 152 BC, contained not only dwellings and shops but also shrines—to the 'ancestral gods', Poseidon and no doubt Astarte, and to the goddess Roma. The Agora of the Italians was a large open space surrounded by a two-storey stoa with openings in its back walls for exedrae and niches for honorific statues. It has been suggested, though without a convincing argument, that this was the slave market of Delos.

Since it was forbidden, for religious reasons, to die on Delos, the Delian cemetery is on the neighbouring island of Rheneia. Apart from many sculpted stelai, some more elaborate funerary monuments have been found there, including a communal tomb with rows of niches and two enclosures with funerary vaults and a small marble shrine (*naïskos*).

(iii) Domestic. Delian houses, some of which are famous for their mosaics and paintings (e.g. the House of Dionysos, House of the Trident, House of the Dolphins etc), constitute the island's most exceptional architectural remains. In their surviving state they represent the urban development of the 2nd and 1st centuries BC, stimulated by the influx of foreign merchants. They conform to a characteristic ancient Greek house plan with a central courtyard surrounded by various rooms (*see also* GREECE, ANCIENT, §II, 1(i)(c) and fig. 12). The external walls, mostly built of gneiss, covered with stucco, were almost blank, being interrupted only by one or more doorways: at least, this was the case on the ground-floor, for, though fragments of upper-storey windows survive, ground-floor windows are extremely rare. Only in a few streets of shops or workshops do the plain façades give way to a row of separate rooms, accessible from outside. Within this general scheme, however, there are many variations.

In the most opulent houses the central courtyard contains a peristyle, which provided a covered walkway between the courtyard itself and the rooms (see fig. 3). The number of columns varies greatly: they are almost always Doric but have facets instead of flutes on the lower part. The arrangement of the peristyle also varies: instead of surrounding all four sides of the courtyard, it may take up only two or three sides. The House of the Masks and the House of the Trident provide examples of the type of peristyle that Vitruvius termed 'Rhodian' (*On Architecture* VI.vii.3). In this, one of the four sides is higher than the others, and the corner columns have consoles, placed at the same height as the column capitals of the other three sides, which supported the ends of two side architraves. In the House of the Tritons, a row of pillars on a parapet ran along two sides of the courtyard. The houses normally had at least one upper storey. The three types of evidence for this are: fragments of collapsed floors; staircases, where these were made of stone and have survived, as in the House of Hermes; and fragments of an upper order in marble. In fact, most peristyles did not have an upper order, but there are some spectacular exceptions. These include the House of Hermes, built against the theatre hill, which is also unusual in having three storeys partly preserved above the ground-floor, and the House of the Comedians and the House of the Tritons, which, together with the House of the Pediments, make up the most unusual housing block on Delos, with a tower adorned by two pediments at its north-west corner. The presence of raised columns in front of the façades of some houses suggests that the upper storey may have jutted out over the street.

The arrangement of the rooms also varied considerably, and sometimes lack of space meant that there were none

3. Delos, aerial view of private houses in the theatre quarter, Hellenistic, mainly 2nd and 1st centuries BC

at all on one side of the courtyard. It is thus often difficult to determine their functions, though some particularly spacious examples, richly decorated with paintings or mosaics, were presumably used as reception rooms (*see also* §3 below). These rooms often occupy the north side of the house: as they opened on to the courtyard they faced south, ensuring they benefited from sunlight in winter but remained cool in the summer. Latrines, which many houses did not have, are easy to identify: they took the form of a channel built along two or three sides of a small room and were probably covered by wooden benches with several holes. A sloping trench led to the drain in the street, and, to avoid passing a sewer through the house, latrines were usually sited at the entrance.

Dirty water was removed through a communal system involving a network of drains leading down to the sea. These ran beneath both paved and unpaved streets. In contrast, the provision of fresh water was the responsibility of each household, and both wells and, more frequently, cisterns were employed. The presence of underground water on Delos made it very easy to sink wells, some of which have been located, though the water from them is often brackish. The Delians preferred to use rainwater, and most houses had vast cisterns. These consisted of a large cavity, usually coated with a pinkish waterproof cement, with a covering of paving slabs or mosaic supported by pillars of wood or stone or by parallel arches built of stone blocks. The rainwater flowed from the roof to the cistern along a lead pipe, of which traces sometimes remain. The cisterns are in almost every case beneath the central courtyard, where there was no pressure on the cover from architectural members. An opening, in most cases with a marble lip, enabled the water to be drawn up easily. The deepest cistern found on Delos has a capacity of 270 cubic metres: indeed, each household's reserve had to supply dozens of people throughout a summer dry period of several months. Little is known so far of Delian rural architecture, since the farms on Delos and Rheneia, referred to in the accounts of the sanctuary administrators, are only just beginning to be excavated.

BIBLIOGRAPHY

G. Leroux: *La Salle hypostyle*, Explor. Archéol. Délos (Paris, 1909)

R. Vallois and G. Poulsen: *Nouvelles recherches sur la Salle hypostyle*, Explor. Archéol. Délos (Paris, 1914)

C. Picard: *L'Etablissement des Poséidoniastes de Berytos*, Explor. Archéol. Délos (Paris, 1921)

J. Chamonard: *Le Quartier du théâtre*, 2 vols, Explor. Archéol. Délos (Paris, 1922–4)

R. Vallois: *Le Portique de Philippe*, Explor. Archéol. Délos (Paris, 1923)

F. Courby: *Les Temples d'Apollon*, Explor. Archéol. Délos (Paris, 1931)

E. Lapalus: *L'Agora des Italiens*, Explor. Archéol. Délos (Paris, 1939)

R. Vallois: *Les Monuments* (1944), i of *L'Architecture hellénique et hellénistique à Délos* (Paris, 1944–78)

F. Robert: *Trois Sanctuaires sur le rivage occidental*, Explor. Archéol. Délos (Paris, 1952)

P. Bruneau and J. Ducat: *Guide de Délos* (Paris, 1965, rev. 3/1983)

R. Vallois: *Grammaire historique de l'architecture délienne*, 2 vols (1966–78), ii of *L'Architecture hellénique et hellénistique à Délos*, (Paris, 1944–78)

P. Bruneau and others: *L'Ilot de la maison des comédiens*, Explor. Archéol. Délos (Paris, 1970)

P. Courbin: *L'Oikos des Naxiens*, Explor. Archéol. Délos (Paris, 1980)

E. Will: *Le Sanctuaire de la déesse syrienne*, Explor. Archéol. Délos (Paris, 1985)

PHILIPPE BRUNEAU

2. SCULPTURE. The sculpture from Delos essentially consists of works in marble. Hardly any bronze effigies survive, though according to Pliny bronze was highly prized as a material on Delos. Sculptures in wood and precious metal, which would have included most of the cult statues, have disappeared. Some idea can be formed of the most venerated of these, the Archaic *Apollo* by Tektaios and Angelion (made of wood with applications of beaten gold), which is referred to in literary texts, inscriptions and later iconography. Funerary sculpture from Delos is almost non-existent, as a result of the prohibition on dying on the island. Even so, the finds from Delos hold an important place in the history of Greek sculpture, especially for the Archaic and Hellenistic periods.

(i) Archaic (*c.* 700–*c.* 500/480 BC). (ii) Classical (*c.* 500/480–323 BC). (iii) Hellenistic (323–27 BC).

(i) Archaic (c. 700–c. 500/480 BC). The Nikandre Kore (Naxian marble, h. 1.74 m; Athens, N. Archaeol. Mus.; *see* KORE, fig. 1) is the oldest known large-scale female effigy from ancient Greece. It is flat in profile, with a triangular face framed by the foremost strands of a wig, and the figure wears a cloak over a straight dress belted at the waist. These characteristics of 'Daidalic' style, combined with its scale and material, justify its dating as mid-7th century BC. A verse inscription on the side of the left leg states that it was dedicated to Artemis by Nikandre of Naxos. Also from the nearby island of Naxos are the *Crouching Lions* from the famous terrace opposite the Sacred Lake, flanking the approach to the Temple of Leto (late 7th–early 6th century BC; *in situ*). Another Archaic Naxian work, the *Colossos* (*c.* 590 BC; fragment, London, BM), was four times life size. Its torso and pelvis emerging from ruins are depicted in 17th-century drawings. Its enormous base, against the long north wall of the Oikos

of the Naxians (*in situ*), bears on its east side part of the original inscription celebrating the technical achievement of its construction and on its west side the 4th-century BC renewal of the dedication by the Naxians to Apollo.

The predominance of Naxian works in the early sculpture of Delos is evident, but from about 580 BC the influence of the island of Paros and its marble is noticeable, becoming increasingly marked in the course of the 6th century BC. In male statuary the form of the early kouros figures was altered: the sculpted or inlaid belt disappeared; flat torsos and curved hips gave way to more deliberately modelled anatomies with an exaggerated slant in the groin. In female statuary the single long dress of earlier korai was replaced by the combined *chiton* and *himation*, which gave sculptors a pretext for effects of modelling that denoted folds of material, fluted pleats and the curves of the body these revealed. Hair and jewellery were also vividly handled. From eastern Ionia came small figures of enthroned goddesses or draped kouroi, and Attic works began to occur. At the end of the 6th century BC and beginning of the 5th, divine effigies identifiable by their attributes

4. Delos, *Nike* (?Artemis) of Delos, marble, h. 900 mm, Archaic, *c.* 550 BC (Athens, National Archaeological Museum)

appeared in the area to the south-west of the Temple of Leto, among them *Athena Bearing the Aegis* (Delos, Archaeol. Mus.).

An interesting feature of Archaic sculpture from Delos is its diversity of legendary and animal subjects. An inscription from the mid-6th century BC naming ARCHERMOS OF CHIOS, son of Mikkiades of Chios, as sculptor probably belongs to the winged female figure of a *nike* (victory). The *Nike* (?Artemis) of Delos (Athens, N. Archaeol. Mus.; see fig. 4) has its knees bent in a running posture, a tiara on its head and delicately worked hair. Figures of sphinxes occurred at least twice surmounting votive Ionic columns (mid-6th century BC; Delos, Archaeol. Mus.). Lions and lionesses were further represented several times in the 6th century BC and at the beginning of the 5th (Delos, Archaeol. Mus.), and there may well have been specific associations of wild beasts with Apollo and other, female deities worshipped on Delos: for example two aquatic birds supported a throne (? of Leto) and large marble doves were appropriate to Aphrodite (all Delos, Archaeol. Mus.). There were also statues of horses and equestrian statues (*c.* 525 BC; Delos, Archaeol. Mus.)—favourite subjects of ancient Greek art throughout its history.

(ii) Classical (c. 500/480–323 BC). Early Classical sculpture is represented by four torsos of athletes (Parian marble, *c.* 490–470 BC; Delos, Archaeol. Mus.), which are remarkable for their sense of strength and movement. In 478 BC Delos fell under the power of Athens, and thereafter it received few important sculptures. It was not until the construction *c.* 425–420 BC of the Temple of the Athenians, with its acroteria in Pentelic marble, that high-quality decorative work again occurred. At the top of the temple pediments were two narrative groups representing abduction stories (both in Delos, Archaeol. Mus.): above the west pediment the *Abduction of Kephalos by Eos*; on the east, the *Abduction of Orithyia by Boreas* (see fig. 5). At the angles of the roof were fleeing figures of female spectators. During this period the most important offering must have been the bronze palm tree dedicated *c.* 417 BC by Nikias of Athens, though only its round base in the corner formed by the Stoa of the Naxians now remains. According to Plutarch (*Nikias* iii.6), the palm tree, blown over in high winds, knocked down the Archaic *Colossos*.

Sculpture from the 4th century BC includes the badly damaged remains of a frieze depicting the *Exploits of Theseus* (mid-4th century BC; Delos, Archaeol. Mus.). These scenes decorated Monument GD 42 (the 'Athenian Building') adjoining the Temple of Artemis but are now almost indecipherable. The *Bearded Hermes* (Delos, Archaeol. Mus.) erected in 341–340 BC in front of the propylaia to the south of the Sanctuary of Apollo by the Amphictions (Athenian administrators of the sanctuary) recalls, perhaps intentionally, Alkamenes' *Hermes* from the Athenian Acropolis and is notable as a precisely dated archaizing work.

(iii) Hellenistic (323–27 BC). A fragmentary marine *thiasos* (troop of worshippers) in high relief depicting sea animals and spirits (*in situ*) adorned the central gallery of the Monument of the Bulls. Also from this monument are scenes from a *Land Battle*, featured in the lantern of the

5. Delos, acroterion depicting the *Abduction of Orithyia by Boreas*, marble, h. 1.7 m, from the Temple of the Athenians, Classical, *c.* 425–420 BC (Delos, Archaeological Museum)

north chamber (Delos, Archaeol. Mus.), and a *nike* acroterion in the south façade. These works must commemorate a specific land-and-sea victory, but the exact occasion remains uncertain. Though the exact date of the monument is uncertain, these works are clearly Hellenistic.

Having become independent from Athens in 314 BC, Delos benefited from the benefactions of Hellenistic rulers with an interest in displaying their political prestige in the Aegean. Of the princely monuments in bronze that once adorned the Sanctuary of Apollo and its surroundings, only the pedestals survive. Religious activity intensified, with a proliferation of shrines to different Greek gods, sometimes with interesting ex-votos. To the north-east of the Sanctuary of Apollo the base of the choregic monument erected *c.* 300 BC by a Delian named Karystios bears Dionysiac reliefs on its sides, each depicting three figures, including Dionysos, maenads and, in front, a cockerel, whose head and neck are replaced by a phallus, resembling the huge figure carried around Delos at the yearly festival of Dionysos. A bronze plaque (3rd century BC; Delos, Archaeol. Mus.), found in the Minoe Fountain, depicts *Artemis Offering Sacrifice*. The goddess is shown standing

6. Delos, relief depicting *Artemis Offering Sacrifice*, bronze, Hellenistic, 3rd century BC (Delos, Archaeological Museum)

a more humanized conception of deities can be seen in picturesque evocations and in the introduction of lesser supernatural beings. Examples include such subjects as *Apollo Crushing Galatian Shields with his Feet*, *Artemis Killing the Doe* (both second half of the 2nd century BC; Delos, Archaeol. Mus.), and *Aphrodite Defending herself with her Sandal against the Amorous Advances of Pan* (the 'Slipper-slapper' Group; Athens, N. Archaeol. Mus., 3335). Muses and nymphs were given a poetic air; figures of Priapus and Hermaphrodite flaunt their monstrousness, and Eros or Harpokrates were represented as playful or comical little children. In particular the companions of Dionysos (satyrs, silenes and papposilenes) were often depicted, in sculpture and in other media, during the second half of the 2nd century BC. Such subjects, competently executed in marble, belong to the category of sculpture for domestic interior decoration, though it is not easy to distinguish between purely decorative and votive functions.

Social, professional and political groups erected sculptures in honour not only of their divine patrons but also of their human protectors. The influence of the Italian colony on Delos is particularly evident in the proportions of the Agora of the Italians (late 2nd century BC), which was edged with niches and exedrae containing works explicitly evoking the military power of Rome. A series of statues of Gauls, from which came the *Wounded Gaul* in Athens (?late 2nd century BC; N. Archaeol. Mus., 247), alluded to the heritage of the kingdom of Pergamon, bequeathed to Rome in 133 BC in the will of its last king, Attalos III. Figures in armour, full-length or on horseback, and heroic statues, such as that of *C. Ofellius Ferus* (*c.* 100 BC; Delos, Archaeol. Mus.), also decorate the Agora of the Italians. Towards 100 BC the Monument to Mithridates, erected in the Sanctuary of the Samothracian Gods, was decorated with medallions depicting his officers and allies in military dress, and statues of figures in armour have been found near by in the excavation of the reservoir of the Inopos. It is clear that with the onset in the first half of the 1st century BC of the wars that were to ruin Delos, the number of warrior effigies considerably increased.

Near Eastern contacts and the presence of Athenian and Italian communities on Delos in late Hellenistic times also resulted in a rich variety of portrait sculpture. Not all portraits are conventional representations of officials or officers, priests and magistrates, or patrons being thanked for their actions or their generosity. In wealthy homes the master of the house was sometimes portrayed either by a full-length sculpture, or, more rarely, by a bust. The most famous example is that of the Athenian couple *Diskourides and Kleopatra* (*c.* 135 BC; Delos, Archaeol. Mus.) in the House of Kleopatra. The heads are missing, but delightful effects of transparency in the drapery of the female statue are remarkable. Several statues with clearly individualized faces or marked ethnic features have been preserved, including a bronze head of a *Levantine* (Athens, N. Archaeol. Mus., 14612). The melancholy expression, with its suggestion of an inner life, is rendered in the best Greek tradition. Other works show the emphasis on such external characteristics as the marks of old age and the colder objectivity that denote Roman taste. A combination

between two young satyrs with a torch in each hand in front of her own image (see fig. 6).

The fashion for foreign deities was confirmed above all by the establishment of sanctuaries to Egyptian gods; first in the area around the River Inopos, then on the slopes of Mt Kynthos. The proliferation of Oriental, Syrian, Phoenician, Arabian and other cults followed, in conjunction with the growing commercial importance of the island and the development of the port. The Romans made Delos a free port and in 166 BC placed it again under Athenian control. The sculptural repertory, however, remained essentially Hellenic. The statue of *Isis* in the Doric Temple of Isis in the Serapeion C (*c.* 130 BC; *in situ*) and the torso of the goddess *Roma* in the Foundation of the Poseidoniasts of Berytos (*c.* 150 BC; *in situ*) are good examples. Moreover, it was not only run-of-the-mill votive marble figurines, including innumerable representations of Aphrodite, that kept to the traditional Greek iconography; more important sculptures also testify to the taste of some patrons for the Classical works of the past. Examples include copies of the 5th-century BC *Diadoumenos* of Polykleitos and of the 'Small Woman of Herculaneum' type (Athens, N. Archaeol. Mus., 1826, 1827), the latter based on a 4th-century BC original; a statue by Praxiteles was once in the House of Hermes on Delos. This fashion also favoured the spread on the island of the archaizing and neo-Attic styles, as evidenced by several bearded herms and a relief from the House of the Lake (end of 2nd century BC; all Delos, Archaeol. Mus.).

Specifically Hellenistic characteristics were no less in evidence. Leaving aside the extraordinary range of herms, of an idealizing tendency in the treatment of anatomy and in choice of posture, with a determined realism in the appearance of the head, seems particularly to have characterized those portraits on Delos that were commissioned from Athenian artists by Romans: a fine example is the bald 'Pseudo-athlete' from the House of the Diadoumenos (late 2nd or early 1st century BC; Athens, N. Archaeol. Mus., 1828). Despite an often mediocre mass production of sculpture (though this in itself provides important evidence of copying techniques; *see* GREECE, ANCIENT, §IV, 1(iv)(d)) and the repeated devastations of the 1st century BC, the evolution of the Hellenistic sculpture of Delos reveals some interesting and important aspects of the early stages of the transition from Greek to Roman art in the eastern Mediterranean.

BIBLIOGRAPHY
A. Hermary: *Catalogue des sculptures classiques de Délos*, Explor. Archeol. Délos (Paris, 1984)

JEAN MARCADÉ

3. MOSAICS. Approximately 350 mosaic floorings of various kinds, including fragments, have been found on Delos, all from houses of Hellenistic date (late 2nd–early 1st century BC). This is a considerable quantity in comparison with other ancient sites, but in relation to the area of the town now excavated on Delos the figure is small. The walls of houses were regularly stuccoed, but mosaic (rather than earthen or paved) floors apparently remained a luxury.

As with mosaics elsewhere (*see* GREECE, ANCIENT, §VII), those on Delos were both ornamental and practical. Since they rendered the floor-surface impervious to water and easy to wash, they are found in the parts of houses where water is normally used: latrines, kitchens, bathrooms and dining-rooms, and the central courtyards into which the rainwater fell. Effective mosaic flooring could be made of cheap materials, such as fragments of tiles or amphorae and marble chips, though in reception rooms this practical function, which did not necessitate the use of multicoloured pictorial effects, was often combined with more decorative elements.

The decorative principle followed in Delian mosaics is also found elsewhere throughout the Hellenistic period: the flooring is laid so as to create the illusion of a carpet (e.g. from House III N; see fig. 7). Several concentric bands, either plain or decorated with such motifs as meanders, guilloches, triangles, saw-teeth and, most often, wave-crests, define a square or rectangular area that is always centrally placed and smaller than the total floor surface. The central area (emblema) of the mosaic may be left as a plain white surface (the least expensive method) or it may contain one, two or even three decorative panels bearing geometric or floral motifs, or figural scenes rendered in *opus tessellatum* or in *opus vermiculatum*. In the latter technique the tesserae are minuscule (*c.* 1–4 mm or smaller) and vary considerably in shape, sometimes being set in a cement of the same colour as the surrounding tesserae, giving an overall effect close to that of painting (e.g. *Winged Dionysos with a Tiger*, from the House of Dionysos; *in situ*).

Though Delian mosaics do not often have figural scenes, certain subjects recur in several versions: there are four examples of dolphins with anchors; three mosaics with theatrical masks (e.g. in the House of the Masks); Dionysos

7. Delos, House III N in the theatre quarter, tessera mosaic with floral emblema surrounded by plain bands and wave-crests, Hellenistic, *c.* 100 BC (*in situ*)

riding a wild beast (e.g. in the House of Dionysos and House of the Masks); three amphorae or hydriai with victors' palms (e.g. in the House of the Trident and House of the Masks). This repetition must be attributable equally to the customers' preferences and to the working habits of the mosaicists, who were trained in a limited repertory. Most of their subjects derive from marine creatures (e.g. dolphins, a tritoness in the House of the Tritons), from games and the theatre, or from mythology. One mosaic represents the earliest known version of a subject that the mosaicists of the Imperial Roman period later treated several times, the legend of *Lykourgos Offending Dionysos by Attacking the Nymph Ambrosia*. Another, also possibly the oldest extant version of its subject, has a panel showing *Doves Perched on a Gilt Bronze Basin* (Delos, Archaeol. Mus.). It is a copy of the only ancient mosaic mentioned in ancient literature, Sosos' 'Unswept Floor' from Pergamon (Pliny: *Natural History* XXXVI.lx.184).

Decorative mosaics on Delos are sometimes simply in two tones, with a black motif on a white ground. In the case of figural subjects, however, the use of colour may be as highly developed as in wall decoration. Yet nowhere does it seem that the entire decoration of a room was conceived as a harmonious whole involving the motifs and colours of both the mosaics and the stuccos. Only two Delian mosaics are signed, one by Antaios, son of Aischrion, and one by ASKLEPIADES.

BIBLIOGRAPHY
P. Bruneau: *Les Mosaïques*, Explor. Archéol. Délos (Paris, 1972)

PHILIPPE BRUNEAU

Delphi. Site in Phokis in central Greece, *c.* 165 km northwest of Athens, which flourished from the 8th century BC to the 2nd century AD. It was one of the most important sacred sites of ancient Greece, the home of the Delphic Oracle and reputed to be the centre of the world. High in the foothills of Mt Parnassos, Delphi lies between the twin cliffs of the Phaidriades ('shining rocks'), overlooking the valley of the River Pleistos and the plain of Kirrha (now Itea) on the shores of the Gulf of Corinth.

Delphi is widely regarded as the most strikingly beautiful ancient site in Greece. The Oracle was formally abolished by the emperor Theodosios I *c*. AD 385, and thereafter Delphi was almost entirely neglected until the site was rediscovered in 1676. Excavations started in the mid-19th century, and in 1892 a systematic survey was begun by the French School at Athens. Work on the site was intensive until 1903 and has continued since, with the results published in a series of excavation reports and in *Fouilles de Delphes* (Paris, 1902–).

1. Architecture. 2. Sculpture.

1. ARCHITECTURE. Delphi comprises five main areas of architectural interest: the Sanctuary of Athena Pronaia at the Marmaria; the gymnasium (for illustration *see* GYMNASIUM); the Kastalian Spring; the Sanctuary of Apollo (see figs 1 and 2); and the Hellenistic stadium. These rise in sequence from east to west up a steep slope on a series of terraces supported by strong retaining walls, blending into the mountain setting. Despite Delphi's remoteness, its architecture shows that it was the most panhellenic of all Greek sanctuaries. In contrast to the Dorian sanctuary at Olympia, for example, where all but one of the pre-Hellenistic sacred buildings were built by Dorian cities in the Doric order using Peloponnesian limestone, Delphi contains buildings erected by Greek cities from throughout the Mediterranean region, using three different orders and various types of stone, including limestone, both Attic and island marbles, and breccia. Every type of sanctuary building is represented—temples, tholoi, treasuries, stoas, a gymnasium, a theatre, a stadium, fountains, a 'club-house' (*lesche*), heroa, altars and monumental bases for votive offerings—so that the full evolution of ancient Greek architecture can be traced at Delphi on a single site. Furthermore, some of the buildings are of a quality rivalled only by those on the Acropolis at Athens.

The earliest, meagre, remains are those of village houses and a few cist tombs of Mycenaean date (*c*. 1600–*c*. 1050 BC); the first large-scale buildings were the late 7th-century BC Temple of Apollo and Temple of Athena. Both were built in the Doric order of Corinthian poros limestone, though only a few blocks survive, including column drums and flat, spreading capitals decorated with

1. Delphi, Sanctuary of Apollo, view from the Phaidriades cliffs

blue paint. The temple roofs were hipped and thus did not have the pediments characteristic of later Greek temples.

In the 6th century BC architectural sculpture flourished at Delphi. Around 560 BC the Naxians erected a monument in the form of a marble Ionic column 9.9 m high (see fig. 2a). It had 44 flutes and a superb capital supporting a *Crouching Sphinx* (*see* §2(i) and fig. 4 below). It is the only monumental Ionic column of this period to have survived, and it is thus of great architectural importance in estimating the proportions of the fragmentary Ionic columns of the huge Archaic temples at Ephesos and Samos. At around the same time the Sikyonians dedicated two small but equally unusual Doric poros monuments. One was a simple rectangular monopteral shelter (4×5 columns; 4.29×5.57 m) for an offering or altar. It had slender columns with wide capitals and fine metopes depicting various mythological scenes. The other is the only surviving pre-4th-century BC peripteral tholos (diam. 6.32 m), and it is more severe. Interestingly, its 20 triglyphs and 20 blank metopes did not correspond to its 13 columns and intercolumniations, thus emphasizing that they had lost the structural function of their prototypes in early, wooden entablatures.

In 548 BC the Archaic Temple of Apollo was destroyed by fire, and the Amphiktyonic League, which administered the sanctuary, reorganized it completely, doubling its area and demolishing any monuments, including the two Sikyonian buildings, that obstructed the new plan. The League then constructed a new Temple of Apollo (*c*. 510 BC; 2b) on a terrace retained on its south side by an impressive wall of curvilinear polygonal masonry. The temple was Doric and made largely of poros, though its east façade was built of Parian marble at the expense of exiled Athenian aristocrats, the Alkmaionids. One of the largest temples of its period (59.5×23.8 m), it had an elongated plan (6 by 15 columns) to incorporate the altar of Hestia (*thymele*), 'the common hearth for all Hellas' (Plutarch: *Aristides* XX.iv), and the adyton with the pit from which the oracular vapour (*pneuma*) emanated, beneath the tripod and beside the Pythian laurel tree. At the same date a new Doric temple entirely of limestone was dedicated to Athena at the Marmaria.

Four sumptuous Ionic marble treasuries, dating from *c*. 530 to *c*. 520 BC, attest to the prosperity of the Greek world at this time and the inventive vitality of its architects. Their distyle *in antis* plans are unremarkable, but the supports themselves have innovative forms: columns with palm-leaf capitals of a type later adopted by the architects of Pergamon were used in the Massaliot Treasury at the Marmaria and in that of an unknown Aiolian city; pillars (*parastades*) of a type popular with later Athenian architects were used in the Knidian Treasury (2c), and caryatids, two *in antis*, wearing Ionic dress and standing on pedestals, replaced the usual columns. The caryatids in the Siphnian Treasury (2d; *see* GREECE, ANCIENT, fig. 22) prefigure the famous examples from the Erechtheion at Athens. Only the Siphnian Treasury retained its sculptural decoration relatively intact. This includes numerous carved mouldings, but its most notable element is the continuous frieze that extends over all four sides of the building. These

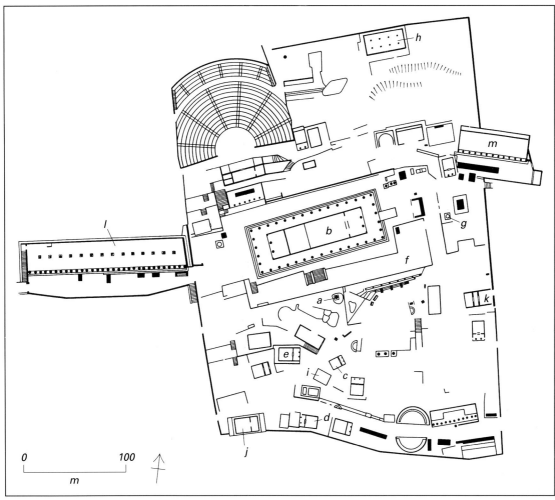

2. Delphi, Sanctuary of Apollo, 6th–3rd century BC, plan: (a) Naxian column; (b) Temple of Apollo; (c) Knidian Treasury; (d) Siphnian Treasury; (e) Athenian Treasury; (f) Stoa of the Athenians; (g) site of tripod of the Crotonians, supposed site of tripod of Plataia; (h) *Lesche* of the Knidians; (i) Treasury of the Syracusans; (j) Treasury of the Thebans; (k) Treasury of Cyrene; (l) West Stoa; (m) Stoa of Attalos

make the Siphnian Treasury the finest extant example of Aegean architecture and sculpture of its period.

Less building took place during the 5th century BC at Delphi; nevertheless some important works were produced. After their victory at Marathon (490 BC) the Athenians built a Doric treasury (2e) in Parian marble in the Sanctuary of Apollo. It has been completely reconstructed (for illustration *see* TREASURY) and rivals the temples on the Acropolis at Athens in quality. The style of the metope relief sculpture is transitional and combines the freshness of Archaic art with the severity of Early Classical. After the Battle of Salamis (480 BC) the Athenians also built a small Ionic stoa against the polygonal wall (2f). Its marble columns prefigure those of the Temple of Athena Nike at Athens, and it probably housed the great flax cables that had secured the Persian king Xerxes' bridge of boats across the Hellespont during his invasion of Greece. Similarly, after the Battle of Plataia (479 BC) all the Greek states contributed to the making of a monument in the shape of a golden tripod on a bronze column

formed by three entwined serpents; now situated at Meidan Square, Istanbul). The base on which it was long believed to have stood (2g) has been identified instead as the base of a monumental tripod consecrated to Apollo by the Crotonians after their victory over the city of Sybaris at the end of the 6th century BC (see Jacquemin and Laroche). The tripod of Plataia probably stood in the temple square (see Laroche). Around 470–460 BC the Knidians commemorated their liberation from the Persians by building a *lesche* (2h) in which the inhabitants of Delphi and visiting pilgrims could relax. It was decorated with wall paintings by the greatest painter of the period, POLYGNOTOS OF THASOS. In addition to these monuments celebrating the Persian Wars, others commemorated disputes between the Greeks themselves, for example the Doric Treasury of Brasidas and the Acanthians (424 BC) and the Treasury of the Syracusans (414 BC; 2i), both built after victories over the Athenians.

One monument at Delphi had a particular influence on the architecture of the 4th century BC. This was the Doric

3. Delphi, Sanctuary of Athena Pronaia, Tholos, *c.* 390 BC

Tholos (*c.* 390 BC; see fig. 3), built at the Marmaria, of Pentelic marble, by Theodoros of Phokaia. This was the only peripteral tholos of its time and the most ornate sacred building since the Parthenon. It had 80 sculpted metopes (40 over the 20-column peristyle and 40 over the cella wall), acroteria on top of the marble roof and 9 chryselephantine statues between 10 internal Corinthian columns. The latter helped to popularize the Corinthian order, while the peristyle hastened the development of more slender Doric columns, and the lavish double gutter created a fashion for gutters decorated with lions' heads between acanthus scrolls (especially at Epidauros). The Tholos as a whole stimulated the construction of great circular buildings at Epidauros, Olympia and Samothrace (*see also* THOLOS). Theodoros' treatise about it was later known to Vitruvius, and its influence on Roman architecture is readily apparent, for example in buildings depicted in Pompeian wall paintings.

The third Temple of Athena, built *c.* 370 BC next to the Tholos, was non-peripteral and more severe. Together with the Doric Treasury of the Thebans (2j) and the Ionic peristyle in the gymnasium, it is among the first buildings to be made of the fine St Elias limestone from Mt Parnassos. Behind the six Doric columns of its façade the cella was closed only by three screens between two Ionic half-columns *in antis*. The latter's half-capitals were of a new type, with volutes on all three sides, as in the Temple of Apollo at Bassai. The cella's open, well-ventilated entrance and elongated plan suggest that it contained an altar, perhaps similar to that in the Hieron at Samothrace. In the Sanctuary of Apollo, the marble Treasury of Cyrene (2k) provides an example of the softer Doric forms of the 4th century BC, with its half-columns added to antae, and mouldings on the abaci of its capitals and on its blank metopes. Its design involved the solution of complex mathematical problems being studied at the time by the famous mathematics school at Cyrene: the squaring of the circle, the trisection of any angle and the 'Delian' problem, the duplication of the cube.

The largest construction project at Delphi in the 4th century BC was the rebuilding of the second Temple of Apollo (*see* GREECE, ANCIENT, fig. 19), destroyed in 373 BC. This took until the end of the century. The new building was similar to the old one and shared its foundations. It was designed by the Corinthian architect Spintharos, and the ramp at its front is a typical Peloponnesian feature. Though largely of limestone, the temple had pediments of marble. Most of the inscribed building accounts survive, and they provide valuable information on the financing, organization and administration of a large 4th-century BC building project of this kind.

In the second half of the 4th century BC the gymnasium complex was built on two terraces, one above the other, between the Marmaria and Kastalia (for plan *see* GYMNASIUM). The higher level was largely in the open air, with trees, space for ball games and a running track (*paradromis*) roughly as long as the stadium area itself, though this included a further, covered track (*xystos*) enclosed by a Doric colonnade. Below it was the gymnasium proper, with rooms around an Ionic peristyle courtyard and a washing area (*loutron*) with basins fed by 11 spouts and a pool for the athletes to bathe in. This is the oldest extant Greek gymnasium, but its plan is nevertheless typical. The Kastalian Spring to the north-west of the gymnasium is of Roman or Hellenistic date.

Like other sanctuaries and cities, Delphi was embellished with large stoas and theatral buildings in the 3rd and 2nd centuries BC. The one-storey (?Doric) West Stoa (l. 74.2 m; 2l) was probably erected by the Aitolians around 278 BC. At about the same time the stadium was moved from the plain of Kirrha to the highest part of the sanctuary. In about 230 BC the King of Pergamon, Attalos I, built a Doric stoa (l. 32.14 m; 2m) on an artificial terrace to the east of the sanctuary. This had large paintings on wooden panels on its walls; the east end of the terrace was closed by a small cult building (5.10×7.25 m), perhaps dedicated to Dionysos. A huge base (27.0×3.5 m) with colossal statues commemorated Attalos' victories. In the basement was an exedra, where pilgrims could rest, roofed with a rectangular-section barrel vault, the first extant example in Western architecture. Attalos' successors later completed the theatre in Pergamene style. In the 2nd century AD Herodes Atticus provided the stadium with tiers of stone seats and a triumphal arch. The Corinthian funerary chapel, built in blue marble above a vaulted limestone crypt in the West Necropolis, is from the same period. Finally, some Early Christian monuments were also built on the site after the Oracle of Apollo was abolished.

BIBLIOGRAPHY
R. Demangel and G. Daux: *Les Temples de tuf: Les Deux Trésors*, Fouilles de Delphes (Paris, 1923)
J. Charbonneaux: *La Tholos*, Fouilles de Delphes (Paris, 1925)
R. Demangel: *Topographie du sanctuaire*, Fouilles de Delphes (Paris, 1926)
F. Courby: *La Terrasse du temple*, Fouilles de Delphes (Paris, 1927)
J. Audiat: *Le Trésor des Athéniens*, Fouilles de Delphes (Paris, 1933)
P. Amandry: *La Colonne des Naxiens et le portique des Athéniens*, Fouilles de Delphes (Paris, 1953)
J. Jannoray: *Le Gymnase*, Fouilles de Delphes (Paris, 1953)
J. Pouilloux: *Le Région nord du sanctuaire*, Fouilles de Delphes (Paris, 1960)
G. Roux: *Delphes: Son oracle et ses dieux* (Paris, 1976)
J. P. Michaud: *Le Temple en calcaire*, Fouilles de Delphes (Paris, 1977)

G. Daux and E. Hansen: *Le Trésor de Siphnos*, Fouilles de Delphes (Paris, 1987)

G. Roux: *La Terrasse d'Attale I*, Fouilles de Delphes (Paris, 1987)

——: 'La Tholos d'Athéna Pronaia à Delphes', *Comptes rendus de l'Académie des Inscriptions et Belles-Lettres* (Paris, 1988), pp. 290–309, 835–9

D. Laroche: 'Nouvelles Observations sur l'offrande de Platées', *Bull. Corr. Hell.*, cxiii (1989), pp. 183–98

A. Jacquemin and D. Laroche: 'Une Offrande monumentale à Delphes: Le Trépied des Crotoniades', *Bull. Corr. Hell.*, cxiv (1990), pp. 299–323

——: 'La Tholos de Sicyone à Delphes et l'origine de la frise dorique', *Delphes, colloque P. Perdrizet: Strasbourg, 1991; Brill, Leyde, 1992*, pp. 151–66

J. F. Bommelaer: 'Guide de Delphes, 1. Le Site', *École Française d'Athènes, sites et monuments*, vii (Paris, 1991) [contains extensive bibliog.]

GEORGES ROUX

2. SCULPTURE. During antiquity Delphi received many important works of sculpture, but these were often plundered or destroyed, as when costly metal dedications were melted down to finance wars: Nero, for example, took about 500 statues to Rome, and others were later carried off to Constantinople. Even so, excavations have uncovered several works of great interest, and though few bronzes survive among these compared with the number listed by Pausanias in the 2nd century AD (*Guide to Greece* X.viii.4–xxxii.1), some sculptures provide examples of unusual techniques. All the works discussed below are now in the Archaeological Museum, Delphi.

(i) Archaic. (ii) Classical. (iii) Hellenistic and Roman.

(i) Archaic. The earliest surviving large-scale sculptures at Delphi are two colossal marble kouroi, thought to represent the Argive heroes *Kleobis* and *Biton* (h. 2.16 m; *c.* 580 BC; see Herodotus: *Histories* I.xxxi) and indeed signed by a certain [?Poly]medes of Argos. A word in the dedicatory inscription suggests, however, that they could represent the Dioscuri. Their rugged, thick-set bodies and wide faces, flexed arms and faintly outlined boots are all unparalleled by other works in marble of the period. Another colossal work of slightly later date is the *Crouching Sphinx* (*c.* 560 BC; see fig. 4), placed by the Naxians on top of their tall Ionic votive column. Its decorative, linear treatment contrasts with the powerfully built Argive kouroi, and it represents the Aegean island version of the Ionic style. The mid-6th-century BC fragments of chryselephantine figures found in front of the Stoa of the Athenians were also East Greek, while the ?late 6th-century BC life-size bronze *Bull*, which has a hide of partly gilded silver plates, recalls the precious offerings made by the Lydian king Croesus (Herodotus: *Histories* I.l).

The most numerous Archaic female figures at Delphi are the caryatids of the Ionic treasuries (*see also* CARYATID). The earliest are traditionally attributed to the Knidian Treasury (mid-6th century BC), while the most securely dated are from the Siphnian Treasury (*c.* 525 BC). The upper part of one of the latter survives, and the modelling of the round, plump, solid face suggests Cycladic workmanship. The head of another caryatid with a similar, though better preserved, cylindrical headdress (*kalathos*) may come from the same building, though it is perhaps by a Chian sculptor. Its hair, however, is differently styled, and it may be earlier.

Archaic relief sculpture consists mainly of Doric metopes and Ionic friezes. The metopes discovered in the

4. Delphi, *Crouching Sphinx*, marble, h. 2.3 m, *c.* 560 BC (Delphi, Archaeological Museum)

foundations of the Sikyonian Treasury date from *c.* 560 BC and originally adorned all four sides of a monopteral shelter. They depict several subjects and were carved in a pale poros limestone, enhanced by the use of paint. They recall the refined figural decoration of Proto-Corinthian miniature vases. The best-preserved Ionic frieze comes from the Siphnian Treasury (*c.* 525 BC) and is of Parian marble. It is possible to discern two distinct styles. The slabs from the west and south sides are in low relief with flat surfaces and sharp contours, probably carved by north Ionian sculptors. By contrast, those from the north and east sides are in high relief with rounded, finely detailed forms, suiting their complex narrative scenes, and are attributed to Chian or Parian sculptors. Four subjects are represented: on the west side, the *Judgement of Paris*; on the south side, an unidentified procession of horsemen with an abduction scene (possibly of the Leukippidai by the Dioscuri or of Hippodameia by Pelops); on the east side, *Achilles and Memnon Fighting over the Dead Antilochos*, which shows their mothers, respectively Thetis and Eos, each begging Zeus for her son's victory; and, on the long north side, a skilfully animated *Gigantomachy* containing many vivid details (*see* GREECE, ANCIENT, fig. 53). Combat scenes also adorned the pediments of the 'Alkmaionid' Temple of Apollo (*c*. 510 BC) and the second Temple of Athena Pronaia (end of the 6th century BC). The former's west pediment bore a *Gigantomachy* with figures of stuccoed and painted limestone, and the central group in the Parian marble east pediment represented Apollo in his chariot bringing law to mankind to replace the savagery symbolized by the wild beasts fighting in the corners. The style suggests that they may be the work of ANTENOR.

The Athenian Treasury (*c*. 490 BC) was entirely of Parian marble. The metopes on its prominent south side depict the *Exploits of Theseus*, the Athenian national hero, thus raising him to the status of the panhellenic hero Herakles. The *Labours of Herakles* adorn the north and west sides, while the *Amazonomachy* on the east side apparently alludes to the Battle of Marathon (490 BC). The sculptural technique and the compositions mark the transition between the Archaic and the Early Classical styles (for general discussion *see* GREECE, ANCIENT, §IV, 2(ii)(c) and (iii)(a)).

(ii) Classical. During the 5th century BC Delphi received several monuments commemorating the Persian Wars and reflecting Athenian power and prosperity, including groups of statues by the greatest sculptors of the period. Thereafter, cities throughout the Greek world vied with each other in the splendour of their dedications, making Delphi itself a monument to the vicissitudes of Greek history. However, almost all the numerous large-scale bronzes have disappeared, and only literary accounts, dedicatory inscriptions and sculptors' signatures remain. One exception is the almost intact *Charioteer* (*c*. 478–474 BC; see fig. 5), dedicated by the Sicilian prince Polyzalos after his victory in a chariot race in 478 or 474 BC as part of a bronze chariot group. The figure wears a long charioteer's tunic secured by a high belt and by a cord crossed over at the back. The hair is encircled by a fillet with a meander pattern inlaid in silver. Many features combine to make this a masterpiece of Greek art: the fine, dense folds of the drapery; the ascending rhythm that turns the head almost imperceptibly to the right; the detailed rendering of the feet and the arm holding the reins; and above all the intense expression on the face, with its rather heavy features and lifelike coloured eyes.

Works from the 5th century BC, even in marble, are rare, but 4th-century BC works survive in greater numbers. The Tholos in the Marmaria (*c*. 390 BC) had sculpted metopes above its external colonnade and around the top of its cella wall, as well as several figural acroteria. The 80 metopes depicted duels from an *Amazonomachy* and a *Centauromachy*, as well as heroic exploits watched by the gods. Though only fragments survive, the virtuosity of the high relief work, the boldness of the intense, vivid action and of the positioning of figures in space and the subtle reworkings of 5th-century BC compositional schemes are

5. Delphi, *Charioteer*, bronze, h. 1.8 m, *c*. 478–474 BC (Delphi, Archaeological Museum)

remarkable. At the same time, the one remaining female acroterion, an exquisitely sensual figure, recalls those from the Temple of Asklepios at Epidauros.

According to Pausanias (*Guide to Greece* X.xix.4), the pedimental sculptures of the 4th-century BC Temple of Apollo represented *Apollo with Artemis and Leto* and *Dionysos with Thyiades*, the *Muses* and the *Setting Sun*. The fragmentary remains include a seated god with his upper body naked (?*Apollo*) and a standing figure wearing a long robe. The fillet across the latter's forehead suggests Dionysos, but the socket below the figure's left shoulder probably secured a cithara. Some female torsos wrapped in animal skins may belong to figures of Thyiades (a kind of maenad), while other fragments apparently come from figures of nymphs or Muses.

An unusual monument in Pentelic marble, probably dedicated by the Athenians (*c*. 330 BC) and variously known as the Thyiades column, the Dancers column or the Acanthus column, consists of a plantlike stalk with intricately carved outcurved acanthus leaves surmounted by three graceful female standing figures in identical dress and pose. Their short dresses, pressed against their stomachs and thighs as if by the wind, and their crowns of long, pointed leaves suggest that they represent dancers;

above them once rose a bronze tripod with its feet on the uppermost acanthus leaves. The monument dedicated by Daochos of Pharsalos, the representative of Thessaly on the Amphiktyonic Council between 336 and 332 BC, depicted his most famous ancestors and was apparently a copy of a bronze group by LYSIPPOS in Pharsalos itself. The one remaining figure, that of the great athlete *Agias*, is of exceptional quality (*see* GREECE, ANCIENT, fig. 64). In the portrayal of a fleeting moment of rest from exertion, the sculptor combined an elegant and vigorous frame with an expression of spiritual energy.

6. Delphi, *Philosopher*, marble, h. 1.73 m, probably 3rd century BC (Delphi, Archaeological Museum)

(iii) Hellenistic and Roman. During the 3rd and 2nd centuries BC many cities and rulers erected monuments at Delphi, though the bronze statues that were part of them have now disappeared. All that remains of an allegorical effigy of *Aitolia* is the base with its sculpted trophy. The battle frieze from the Pillar of Aemilius Paulus commemorating the Romans' victory over Perseus of Macedonia at Pydna is significant mainly for its secure date of 168 BC. Several large marble statues come from the exedrae on the terrace overlooking the Temple of Apollo, but most are headless. An exception is the *Philosopher*, a portrait of an elderly man with a beard and balding head (probably 3rd century BC; see fig. 6). The folds of its drapery are skilfully rendered, and the face effectively conveys a sense of the subject's inner life and stern character. Half-life-size figures of a young boy struggling with a goose (3rd century BC) and a young girl with an enigmatic smile (early 3rd century BC) also reflect the Hellenistic fondness for depicting childhood and old age. The finest pieces are often difficult to date. A portrait head in Parian marble with distinguished features and a rather mournful expression may depict Titus Quinctius Flamininus, who defeated Philip V of Macedon at Kynoskephalai in 197 BC, but this is uncertain. Similarly, the date of the relief on the round altar from the Sanctuary of Athena in the Marmaria, depicting elegantly draped young women attaching fillets to a garland of foliage, is disputed.

The numerous adaptations and copies of traditional representations of gods and heroes produced under the Roman Empire varied considerably in quality. The friezes of the *Labours of Herakles*, added to the *proskenion* of the theatre in the 1st century AD, bear no comparison with the statues looted from elsewhere by Nero. However, those representing episodes from the *Legend of Meleager*, on a large sarcophagus in the shape of a funeral couch (2nd century AD), are more successful. Similarly, the classicizing statue of Hadrian's favourite, Antinous, lacks the conviction of the pensive bust of an anonymous philosopher (2nd or 3rd century AD).

BIBLIOGRAPHY
P. de La Coste-Messelière: *Delphes* (Paris, 1943)
B. C. Petrakos: *Delphi* (Athens, 1971)
P. G. Themelis: *The Delphi Museum* (Athens, 1981)
P. Amandry: *Delphes et son histoire* (Athens, 1984)
J. Marcadé and others: 'Guide de Delphes: Le Musée', *Ecole Française d'Athènes, sites et monuments*, vi (Athens and Paris, 1991)
                                                    JEAN MARCADÉ

Del Prete, Juan (*b* Vasto, Chietti, 5 Oct 1897; *d* Buenos Aires, 14 Feb 1987). Argentine painter and sculptor of Italian birth. He lived in Argentina from 1909, becoming an Argentinian citizen in 1929. In 1925 he began submitting work to national and provincial salons and in 1926 his first one-man exhibition was held at the Asociación Amigos del Arte in Buenos Aires; the latter also awarded him a scholarship to study in Paris, where he remained until his return to Argentina in 1933.

Del Prete, who exhibited with Abstraction–Création in Paris in 1933 and was in productive contact with Hans Arp, Massimo Campigli, Georges Vantongerloo, Joaquín Torres García and Jean Hélion, is generally considered an important precursor of abstract art in Argentina. He was self-taught, intuitive, rebellious and independent and had demonstrated a receptiveness to contemporary artistic developments even before travelling to Europe. On his return to Argentina he exhibited a series of abstract plaster carvings as well as works made of wire, maquettes for stage sets and masks.

Convinced that one type of work should not rule out other options, Del Prete produced both abstract and figurative works that registered the impact of the new pictorial languages. Although his pictures of 1944–7 fused Cubist structure and Futurist dynamism, his best works of the 1940s, such as *Bottle of Chianti* (Buenos Aires, Mus. N. B.A.), with their sketchy brushstrokes, testify to his impetuous, lively spirit. Although many of his works are balanced compositions composed of geometrical forms, the evident pleasure in the handling of paint revealed in other paintings (through rough textures, directional brushstrokes or thick impasto) distinguished his art from the rational severity that characterized that of other abstract painters in Argentina. *Tropical Abstraction* (1957; Buenos Aires, Mus. Mun. A. Plást. Sívori) is a clear instance of this more sensual aspect of his art, which in turn led him to investigate the expressive potential of *Art informel* in paintings and in collages of great fantasy made from paper, fabrics and other materials.

BIBLIOGRAPHY

E. C. Yente: *Obras destruídas de Del Prete* (Buenos Aires, 1971)
J. Merli: *Del Prete* (Buenos Aires, 1976)

NELLY PERAZZO

Delteil, Loys-Henri (*b* Paris, 7 May 1869; *d* Paris, 9 Nov 1927). French collector, writer and etcher. He began to collect prints at the age of 13 and rapidly established a reputation as a connoisseur and expert, particularly in the field of modern prints. His principal work is the 31-volume series *Le Peintre-graveur illustré* (Paris, 1906–30); his other publications include works on 19th- and 20th-century prints and *c.* 500 auction-room catalogues. His own etchings were exhibited at the Salons of 1888 and 1897, and he was an officer of the Société des Peintres-graveurs Français and the Société pour l'Etude de la Gravure Française. His first print collection was sold at auction in 1890, the second in Paris, 13–15 June 1928, comprising 404 lots of modern prints.

WRITINGS

with N. A. Hazard: *Catalogue raisonné de l'oeuvre lithographié de H. Daumier* (Paris, 1904)
Le Peintre-graveur illustré, 31 vols (Paris, 1906–30)
Manuel de l'amateur d'estampes du XVIII siècle (Paris, 1910)
Manuel de l'amateur d'estampes des XIX et XX siècles, 2 vols (Paris, 1925)
Maîtres de l'art contemporain: Meryon (Paris, 1927; Eng. trans. by F. Lugt, London, 1928)

BIBLIOGRAPHY

F. Lugt: *Marques* (1921), p. 138
——: *Marques*, suppl. (1956), p. 111

LAURA SUFFIELD

Delton, Louis-Jean (*b* before 1820; *d* after 1896). French photographer. Best known for his equestrian photography, he was an early member of the Jockey Club in Paris. He photographed racehorses, jockeys and women riders and by 1865 his work was very well known throughout Europe. He had a studio in Paris from 1861, and he produced albums of horse-racing photographs from 1866. From 1889 to 1894 he published *La Photographie hippique*, a journal that used many of his photographs. His interest in photographing movement is also shown by his device for attaching a camera to a bicycle, and by his photographs of human movement that were used for advertising purposes. Other subjects were a series of photographs of clowns and acrobats (e.g. *The Clowns Georges and Samuel*, 1863; see Berger and Levrault, pl. 52) and series of members of the European royal families.

PHOTOGRAPHIC PUBLICATIONS

Album hippique (Paris, 1866–7)
Chevaux et équipages à Paris (Paris, 1878)

BIBLIOGRAPHY

Regards sur la photographie en France au XIXe siècle, Berger–Levrault (Paris, 1980)

PATRICIA STRATHERN

Delvaux, Laurent (*b* Ghent, 17 Jan 1696; *d* Nivelles, 24 Feb 1778). South Netherlandish sculptor, active also in England. After training in the studio of Pieter-Denis Plumier in Antwerp, he left in 1717 for London, where he formed an association with his compatriot Peter Scheemakers the younger. They were joined shortly afterwards by Plumier and collaborated on a number of marble funerary monuments, including that in Westminster Abbey to *John Sheffield, 1st Duke of Buckingham* (*d* 1721). After Plumier's death in 1721 it is assumed that Delvaux and Scheemakers collaborated with Francis Bird on the marble monument to *John Holles, Duke of Newcastle* (*d* 1711), also in Westminster Abbey. Vertue relates that the following year Delvaux made a life-size marble statue of *Hercules* (Waddesdon Manor, Bucks, NT) for Richard Tylney (1680–1750), Viscount Castlemaine. Among the last collaborative works made by Delvaux with Scheemakers are the marble funerary monuments to *Lewis Watson-Wentworth, 1st Earl of Rockingham, and his Wife* (*c.* 1725; St Leonard, Rockingham, Northants) and to *Sir Samuel Ongley* (1726; St Leonard, Old Warden, Beds).

In addition to these monumental works, Delvaux also made mythological sculptures of smaller scale, such as the marble group *Vertumnus and Pomona* (London, V&A). During their time together in London Delvaux and Scheemakers assembled a collection of drawings and prints by and after Flemish, Italian and French artists of the 16th and 17th centuries, as well as sculptures by François Du Quesnoy and copies of antique pieces. These works, which served as an indispensable reference tool for the two sculptors, were sold at an auction at Covent Garden in 1726, together with a group of terracotta models by them and by Plumier. It is possible that this was done in order to raise money for the journey to Italy that Delvaux and Scheemakers undertook in 1728, Delvaux remaining in Rome until 1732. It would seem that it was before they left that they received a commission for a marble monument to *Dr Hugo Chamberlen* (*d* 1728; for illustration *see* SCHEEMAKERS, (2)), for which Delvaux made a number of models: the finished marble monument was erected in Westminster Abbey in 1731, before his return from Italy.

While in Rome, Delvaux made the acquaintance of influential patrons, including Cardinal Melchior de Polignac and Cardinal Lorenzo Corsini (later Pope Clement XII). He studied the work of his fellow Flemings Giambologna and Du Quesnoy, as well as Italian sculpture of the 17th century and that of his contemporaries. He displayed the greatest interest in the sculpture of Classical antiquity and had the opportunity both to see and to copy such pieces as the newly discovered group of *Biblis and Caunus* (untraced) from Hadrian's villa at Tivoli. John Russell (1710–71), 4th Duke of Bedford, ordered from him a number of works inspired by antique examples, most notably *Biblis and Caunus* (also known as *Hermaphrodite and Salmacis*); a *Hermaphrodite*; a bust of *Caracalla* and a *Venus with a Shell* (all Woburn Abbey, Beds).

On his return to the Netherlands, Delvaux was in 1733 appointed a court sculptor in Brussels. The following year he settled in Nivelles, where he established a busy workshop and trained many pupils, including Pierre-François Leroy, Gilles-Lambert Godecharle and Adrien-Joseph Anrion. Among his commissions, most of which came from religious foundations, was the group of the *Conversion of St Paul* (oak, 1736), now in the Collegiate Church of Ste Gertrude at Nivelles, for which he also sculpted a series of statues of the *Apostles* (oak, 1743–4; *in situ*); and the monumental pulpit (1741–5) at the Cathedral of St Bavo, Ghent, from a design by Henricus-Franciscus Verbrugghen. The funerary monument of the *Van der Noot Family* (marble, 1746–8; Amsterdam, Rijksmus.) for the Carmelite Church in Brussels is one of Delvaux's most successful compositions.

With the arrival in Brussels in 1750 of Charles of Lorraine (1712–80) as Governor, Delvaux found himself occupied with decorative works at this prince's various residences in Brussels, at Tervuren, near Brussels, and at Mariemont in Hainaut. For the palace in the capital—the only one to survive, albeit partially—he undertook the allegorical reliefs for the façade and the staircase and freestanding statues, including the masterly marble *Hercules* (1768–70) at the foot of the stairs. The last decade of Delvaux's life was less productive, as little by little he allowed his pupils to take over from him. Besides his monumental works Delvaux, a transitional figure between the Baroque and Neo-classicism, left innumerable models in terracotta, often of outstanding quality.

BIBLIOGRAPHY
Gunnis
G. Willame: *Laurent Delvaux, 1696–1778* (Brussels and Paris, 1914)
M. Devigne: 'De la parenté d'inspiration des artistes du XVIIe et du XVIIIe siècle: Laurent Delvaux et ses élèves', *Mém. Acad. Royale Belgique: Cl. B.-A.*, n. s. 1, ii (1928), pp. 7–12
'The Note-books of George Vertue', *Walpole Soc.*, xxii (1934), p. 36, 44–5, 53, 66, 145–6
M. D. Whinney: *Sculpture in Britain, 1530–1830*, Pelican Hist. A. (Harmondsworth, 1964, rev. J. Physick, 1988), pp. 157–9, 182–6
Laurent Delvaux: Les Terres cuites dans les collections publiques belges (exh. cat., Nivelles, 1975)
W. Halsema-Kubes: 'Laurent Delvaux' grafmonument voor Leonard Mathias van der Noot en Helena Catharina de Jonghe', *Bull. Rijksmus.*, xxiv/3 (1976), pp. 123–39
R. van Peteghem: 'Généalogie du sculpteur Laurent Delvaux', *Rif Tout Dju*, 217 (April 1978), pp. 13–17
Laurent Delvaux, 1696–1778 (exh. cat., ed. J. L. Delattre and R. Laurent; Nivelles, Collégiale Ste Gertrude, 1978)
C. Avery: 'Laurent Delvaux's Sculpture in England', *NT Stud.*, ii (1980), pp. 150–70
——: 'Laurent Delvaux's Sculpture at Woburn Abbey', *Apollo*, cxviii (1983), pp. 312–21
1770–1830: Autour du Néo-classicisme en Belgique (exh. cat., Brussels, Mus. Ixelles, 1985), pp. 44–8
J.-J. Hoebanx: 'Laurent Delvaux et les Carmes de Nivelles (14 novembre 1774)', *An. Hist. A. & Archéol.*, iii (1986), pp. 75–81
E. Duyckhaerts: *Le Sculpteur Laurent Delvaux (1698–1778)*, Musées vivants de Wallonie et de Bruxelles, 15 (Liège, 1987), pp. 2–16
M. Lecomte: 'Oeuvres inconnues de Laurent Delvaux à Bornival ?', *Rif Tout Dju*, 301 (Sept 1987), pp. 11–13
C. Theuerkauff: 'Laurent Delvaux' *Biblis und Caunus* nach der Antike: Neuerwerbung für die Skulpturengalerie', *Jb. Preuss. Kultbes.*, xxvi (1989), pp. 247–57

HELENA BUSSERS

Delvaux, Paul (*b* Antheit, nr Huy, 23 Sept 1897; *d* Veurne, 20 July 1994). Belgian painter and printmaker. He was, with René Magritte, one of the major exponents of SURREALISM in Belgium. He began his training in 1920 at the Académie des Beaux-Arts in Brussels, initially as an architect, but he soon changed to decorative painting, and he completed his studies in 1924. In his earliest works, such as *Seascape* (1923; Ostend, Mus. S. Kst.) and *The Couple* (1929; Brussels, Mus. A. Mod.), he was strongly influenced by the Flemish Expressionism of painters such as Constant Permeke and Gustav De Smet. In the mid-1930s, however, he turned decisively to Surrealism, not as an orthodox member of the movement but to a large extent under the influence of Giorgio De Chirico's *Pittura Metafisica*, which he had first seen *c.* 1926. Among his first characteristic works in this vein are *Pink Bows* (1937; Antwerp, Kon. Mus. S. Kst.; see fig.) and *Phases of the Moon* (1939; New York, MOMA), in both of which he incorporated the somnambulant figures that were to become his trademark.

Delvaux's dream-like vision eschewed the shocking and disconcerting juxtapositions sought by other Surrealists. He chose familiar scenes that he activated with figures placed in odd or unexpected situations, as in the *Iron Age* (1951; Ostend, Mus. S. Kst.), in which a reclining female nude is incongruously set against the interior of a 19th-century railway station. The hallucinatory quality of the imagery was emphasized by precise draughtsmanship and a strict adherence to local colour, with memories often relayed, as in this case, through a concentration on an austere and cold architectural setting. Delvaux's preference was for nocturnal scenes because of their mysteriousness and their associations with childhood fears.

The female figures that feature prominently in many of Delvaux's paintings are sometimes dressed in an old-fashioned way, as if recalling a lost past, for example in the *Public Voice* (1948; Brussels, Mus. A. Mod.). More often, however, they are presented as placid and almost innocent nudes totally lacking in sensuality. As impassive and static as sculptural monuments, such figures, sometimes scantily draped, are of an almost unvarying type: blonde, with large dark eyes, rather heavy breasts and black pubic hair. Often they are presented in groups, as in *Awakening in the Forest* (1939; priv. col., see Butor and others, p. 184), in which a large number of nudes luxuriate in a woodland setting.

Delvaux's work is striking in its unity; apart from in the very early works before he had found his way, he was one of those rare artists who found his style almost at the outset and remained faithful to it throughout his career. His paintings and even the prints made late in his life, such as *The Balcony* (engraving with watercolour, 1978–9; see 1987 exh. cat., p. 121), demonstrate virtually no stylistic

Paul Delvaux: *Pink Bows*, oil on canvas, 1.15×1.65 m, 1937 (Antwerp, Koninklijk Museum voor Schone Kunsten)

evolution. Indeed the emphasis on a dream-like atmosphere conveyed with utter conviction ruled out any variations in paint handling, line or colour, since any such reminders of the image's material identity as a painting would serve only to break its spell over the spectator and thus shatter the illusion. In spite of Delvaux's essentially conservative pictorial language, his originality as an artist lay paradoxically in this ability to distract attention from his painting procedures, for it was through such means that he subverted traditional ways of looking at art.

Delvaux worked generally on canvas, sometimes on a large scale, but he also produced some important mural paintings, for example for the Casino at Ostend (1952), the Palais des Congrès in Brussels (*Earthly Paradise*, 4.13×41.3 m, 1959), the Institut Zoologique at Liège University (*Genesis*, 1960) and the Casino de Chaudfontaine (*Mythical Voyage*, 1974). A collection of his work was opened in 1982 as the Musée Paul Delvaux at Saint-Idesbald, a small town on the North Sea coast, two years before the creation of the Fondation Paul Delvaux, Koksijde.

BIBLIOGRAPHY
C. Spaak: *Paul Delvaux* (Antwerp, 1948)
E. Langui: *Paul Delvaux* (Venice, 1949)
P. A. De Bock: *Paul Delvaux: Der Mensch, der Maler* (Hamburg, 1965)
M. Nadeau: *Les Dessins de Paul Delvaux* (Paris, 1967)
M. Butor, J. Clair and S. Hubart-Wilkin: *Paul Delvaux: Catalogue de l'oeuvre peint* (Brussels, 1975)
M. Jacob: *Paul Delvaux, oeuvre gravé* (Paris, 1976)
B. Emerson: *Delvaux* (Antwerp, 1985)
P. *Delvaux* (exh. cat. by M. van Jole and J. Meuris, interview by L. Gianadda, Martigny, Fond. Pierre-Gianadda, 1987)
M. Rombaut: *Paul Delvaux* (London, 1991)

VIDEO RECORDINGS
A. Maben: *Le Somnambule de St Idesbald* [film]

ROGER AVERMAETE

Delville, Jean (*b* Leuven, 19 Jan 1867; *d* Brussels, 19 Jan 1953). Belgian painter, decorative artist and writer. He studied at the Académie Royale des Beaux-Arts, Brussels, with Jean-François Portaels and the Belgian painter Joseph Stallaert (1825–1903). Among his fellow students were Eugène Laermans, Victor Rousseau and Victor Horta. From 1887 he exhibited at L'Essor, where in 1888 *Mother* (untraced), which depicts a woman writhing in labour, caused a scandal. Although his drawings of the metallurgists working in the Cockerill factories near Charleroi were naturalistic, from 1887 he veered towards Symbolism: the drawing of *Tristan and Isolde* (1887; Brussels, Musées Royaux B.-A.), in its lyrical fusion of the two bodies, reveals the influence of Richard Wagner. *Circle of the Passions* (1889), inspired by Dante Alighieri's *Divina* *commedia*, was burnt *c*. 1914; only drawings remain (Brussels, Musées Royaux B.-A.). Jef Lambeaux copied it for his relief *Human Passions* (1890–1900; Brussels, Parc Cinquantenaire). Delville became associated with Joséphin Péladan, went to live in Paris and exhibited at the Salons de la Rose+Croix, created there by Péladan (1892–5). A devoted disciple of Péladan, he had his tragedies performed in Brussels and in 1895 painted his portrait (untraced). He exhibited *Dead Orpheus* (1893; Brussels, Gillion-Crowet priv. col.), an idealized head, floating on his lyre towards reincarnation, and *Angel of Splendour* (1894; Brussels, Gillion-Crowet priv. col.), a painting of great subtlety.

Distanced from Les XX, Delville was an active polemicist for modern art. In 1892 he broke with L'Essor and created Pour l'Art, regrouping the Idealists to which Emile Fabry belonged (1892–5). In his preface to the first catalogue (Brussels, 1892), Delville declared that no work could truly be called art if it did not combine three absolutes: spiritual beauty, plastic beauty and technical beauty. These qualities are apparent in his most famous portrait, *Mme Stuart Merrill* (1892; California, priv. col.), a medium with a halo of red hair, and averted eyes, whose white face is laid on a book stamped with a triangle. In 1894 he founded the Coopérative Artistique and organized a pension fund for it and the building of artists' housing. In 1894 he won the Prix de Rome. He founded the Salon d'Art Idéaliste (1896–8) and showed there the *Treasures of Satan* (1895; Brussels, Mus. A. Mod.) and *Plato's Academy* (1898; Paris, Mus. d'Orsay), his masterpiece, where, in an ideal landscape, languorous androgynes are grouped around Plato to form a very rhythmical composition. Its ambiguity aroused some reservations, but the overall impression was of serene beauty.

Delville taught at Glasgow School of Art from 1900 to 1905/6, briefly became its director and then assumed the same post at the Académie Royale des Beaux-Arts, Brussels, until 1937. In 1900 he published *La Mission de l'art*, in which he defended a messianic ideal and the redemptive quality of idealist art. *Spiritual Love* (1900; Brussels, Mus. Ixelles), a nude couple rising in unison into Art Nouveau scrolls, and *Man–God* (1903; Bruges, Groeningemus.) accord with his theories. Over a period of many years he worked on a decorative scheme for the Palais de Justice in Brussels: *Justice down the Ages*, commissioned in 1911, destroyed in 1944, and replaced by large sketches, then *The Troops* (1924) and the *Spirit of Conquest*. In 1914 his family went into voluntary exile in England. Delville founded the League of Patriots there and published *Belgian Art in Exile*; he created a masonic lodge, spoke at Hyde Park Corner and waged a polemic against the avant-garde. He became an ardent proselyte of Krishnamurti and painted portraits of English personalities such as the educationalist John Russell (Delville family priv. col.). Back in Brussels, he created the Groupe d'Art Monumental, which in 1924 executed the mosaics for the Arcade du Cinquantenaire there.

WRITINGS

Dialogue entre nous (Bruges, 1895)
La Mission de l'art (Brussels, 1900)
Belgian Art in Exile (London, 1916)

BIBLIOGRAPHY

A. Ciamberlani: 'Notice sur Jean Delville', *Annu. Acad. Royale Sci., Lett. & B.-A. Belgique*, cxx (1954), p. 181
C. Piérard: 'Jean Delville, peintre, poète, esthéticien', *Mem. Soc. Sci. & Lett. Hainaut*, lxxxiv (1971–3), pp. 209–47
M. L. Frongia: *Il simbolismo di Jean Delville* (Bologna, 1978)
O. Delville and F.-C. Legrand: *Jean Delville, peintre, 1867–1953* (Brussels, 1984)

FRANCINE-CLAIRE LEGRAND

Demachy, Robert (*b* St Germain-en-Laye, 7 July 1859; *d* Hennequeville, Normandy, 29 Dec 1936). French photographer, writer and theorist. He was from a banking family and was financially secure, which enabled him to devote all his time to photography from 1880 to 1914. He was especially interested in the gum bichromate printing process, which could be easily hand tinted, and in which he achieved remarkably subtle effects. He tackled all the genres: oriental scenes, nudes, dancers (e.g. *Behind the Scenes*, 1900; New York, Met.), portraits (e.g. of *Mlle D.*, pubd in *Camera Work*, 16 Oct 1906), landscapes and scenes from everyday life. In subject-matter his works oscillate between naturalism, as in *Académie* (1900; New York, Met.), and symbolism as in *Struggle*. His works were frequently exhibited (Paris, London, Vienna, New York) and were an instant success. In 1904 Alfred Stieglitz devoted a portfolio to Demachy in his review *Camera Work*.

Demachy was also a theorist of 'art' photography, giving numerous lectures, and writing articles for the *Bulletin du Photo-Club de Paris* and the *Revue de Photographie*, as well as aesthetic and technical works. The processes used and the treatment of the images (contrasts of light, opacity, soft focus, granulation, monograms, layout), partly inspired by Impressionism, made him the leader of French PICTORIAL PHOTOGRAPHY. He was closely linked to the main representatives of this movement and corresponded with Stieglitz, Edward Steichen and Heinrich Kuehn.

WRITINGS

with C. Puyo: *Les Procédés d'art en photographie* (1906)
Sur la photographie en tant qu'art (1910)
B. Jay: *Robert Demachy: Photographs and Essays* (London, 1974)

BIBLIOGRAPHY

R. Martinez: *Robert Demachy* (Paris, 1976)
Robert Demachy (exh. cat., Chalon-sur-Saône, Mus. Nicéphore Niépce, 1977)
The Collection of Alfred Stieglitz: Fifty Pioneers of Modern Photography (exh. cat., text W. Naef; New-York, Met., 1978)

HÉLÈNE BOCARD

De Maria, Mario [Marius Pictor] (*b* Bologna, 8 Sept 1852; *d* Venice, 18 March 1924). Italian painter, photographer, architect and illustrator. He trained initially as a musician and only later became a painter, studying (1872–8) at the Accademia di Belle Arti in Bologna under the history and portrait painter Antonio Puccinelli (1822–97). He made several short trips to Paris and London before moving to Rome where he became friends with Vincenzo Cabianca (1827–1902), a *plein-air* painter, and joined the group founded by Nino Costa, In Arte Libertas (*see* ROME, §III, 7). He made his name in 1885 when he exhibited 18 paintings at the group's first exhibition. In the 1880s he experimented with photography, and in certain cases photographs acted as preliminary stages for his paintings. In 1892 he settled definitively in Venice and two years later adopted the pseudonym 'Marius Pictor'. His work expressed the romantic and literary climate of the *fin-de-siècle*, and his painting is linked with the work of such writers as Charles Baudelaire and Edgar Allan Poe. De Maria's work derives from flower painting and from the painting of Alexandre-Gabriel Decamps; brushstrokes are carefully built up, and rough, chalky colour is thickly applied. He was extremely skilful in his manipulation of colour and light to express the richness of his imagination. He liked to create evocative images and to represent the most fantastic and unusual aspects of nature, as in the famous painting the *Moon on the Tables of a Tavern* (1884; Rome, G.N.A. Mod.). He was also an architect: for example, he prepared the first design (Venice, Archv Stor. A. Contemp.) for the Italian Pavilion at the Venice Biennale of 1895 (altered in execution, and replaced in 1914; see 1983 exh. cat., p. 42); he also designed and built his own house and studio, the Casa dei Tre Oci, on the Giudecca in Venice in 1912, in an individualized Venetian Gothic style. He also illustrated books, for example *Isotta Gattadauro* by Gabriele D'Annunzio (Rome, 1886). In 1926 the Venice Biennale dedicated a one-man show to him, exhibiting 31 paintings and 18 drawings.

BIBLIOGRAPHY

Bolaffi

U. Ojetti: *Ritratti di artisti italiani* (Milan, 1923)

Presentazione della mostra personale di Marius Pictor (exh. cat. by A. Conti, Venice, Biennale, 1926)

M. Falzone del Barbarò and C. Tempesta: *Marius Pictor, fotografo; L'album fotografico di Mario de Maria, 1882–1887* (Milan, 1979)

Mario de Maria: Nell'atelier del pittore delle lune (exh. cat. by F. Scotton, Venice, Casa Tre Oci, 1983)

SILVIA LUCCHESI

De Maria, Nicola (*b* Foglianise, nr Benevento, 6 Dec 1954). Italian painter. When he was 12 his family moved to Turin, where he was to remain, although he frequently returned to Foglianise. He had his first group exhibition in 1973 (Turin, Gal. Punto) and in 1975 his first one-man shows (Naples, Villa Volpicelli, and Genoa, Galforma). In the 1980s he was associated with the group known as the Transavanguardia, which also included Francesco Clemente, Mimmo Paladino, Enzo Cucchi and Sandro Chia. De Maria's paintings are on canvas, paper or even velvet, and are extremely colourful and lyrical, incorporating symbolic writing that enhances their poetic effect. Some are highly abstracted (e.g. *Song of the Heavenly Sea*, 1990; see 1992 exh. cat., p. 29), while others are more obviously representative but imbued with a strong metaphorical significance (e.g. the *Slaughter-house of Poetry*, 1980–81; see Bonito Oliva, p. 97). Although much of his work is small-scale, he was also asked to decorate whole rooms at the Kaiser Wilhelm Museum (1983), Krefeld, and the Castello Rivoli (1985), Turin, in which some of his paintings were hung.

BIBLIOGRAPHY

A. Bonito Oliva: *Transavantgarde International* (Milan, 1982)

Nicola de Maria: Libertà segreta segreta (exh. cat., intro. J.-C. Ammann; Basle, Ksthalle, 1983)

Nicola de Maria: Musica del mare (exh. cat., intro. G. Raillard; Paris, Gal. Lelong, 1992)

CHRISTOPHER MASTERS

De Maria, Walter (*b* Albany, CA, 1 Oct 1935). American sculptor. He studied history at the University of California,

Berkeley (1953–7), and then art, under David Park (MA, 1959). In 1960 he moved to New York where he associated with other Californians including the sculptor and painter Robert Morris, the dancer Yvonne Rainer (*b* 1934) and the composer La Monte Young (*b* 1935). His sculpture of the early 1960s reveals a debt to Dada and other 20th-century avant-garde movements then under revision by young artists. His simple, often cryptically inscribed works owe much of their oblique spirit and deadpan execution to Marcel Duchamp's ready-mades, yet they explore the appeal of pure, usually serialized forms, which become characteristic of Minimalism.

De Maria's first exhibitions consisted of machine-turned objects in highly finished wood, metals and other industrial materials. At the same time he began to experiment with alternative exhibition spaces such as the desert of the south-western USA. In early projects like *Mile Long Drawing* (1968; Mojave Desert, CA), comprising two parallel chalk lines extending over that distance, he showed an interest in austerity and economy of expressive terms, although always retaining monumentality.

During the mid-1960s De Maria engaged in numerous other activities, including the composition of two musical recordings (*Cricket Music*, 1964; *Ocean Music*, 1968) and the production of two films (*Three Circles and Two Lines in the Desert*; *Hard Core*, both 1969), and for a brief period he was the drummer for the New York pop group Velvet Underground (1965).

From 1969 De Maria's work was divided between pieces developed specifically for conventional exhibition spaces and land art proposals (*see* LAND ART). For *New York Earth Room* (1977; New York, Dia Art Found.) he brought 190 cubic m of soil into a 334 sq m. gallery space to create an environment where he attempted to close the schism between the civilized and the natural. In his later exhibition rooms he dealt with the polarities of science and the occult, mathematical progression and chaos and other opposing themes. He is perhaps most widely known for his vast, permanent work in the New Mexico wilderness, *Lightning Field* (1977), a rectangular plot pierced by 400 steel poles of even height in a region known for its frequent and sudden thunderstorms. The plainly artificial environment is subtly delimited by both its remote location and by the requirement of the visitors to remain at the site for 24 hours, thereby ensuring that the spectator invest in time and travel to view the work. This juxtaposition of nature and culture, artifice and entropy, serves as an index of his art. The delicate, if systematic, manipulation of isolated spaces is consistent throughout his work, and it is this persistence that allows him to claim that he feels 'proud to have started minimal art and Land art'.

BIBLIOGRAPHY

D. Bourdon: 'Walter De Maria: The Singular Experience', *A. Int.*, xii/10 (1968), pp. 39–43

G. Muller: *The New Avant-garde: Issues for the Art of the Seventies* (New York, 1972), pp. 150–57

Walter De Maria: Skulpturen (exh. cat., Basle, Kstmus., 1972)

Walter De Maria (exh. cat., ed. W. Beeren; Rotterdam, Boymans-van Beuningen, 1984)

DERRICK R. CARTWRIGHT

Demarne, Jean-Louis (*b* Brussels, ?1752; *d* Batignolles, Paris, 24 Jan 1829). French painter. He went to Paris at the age of 12 after the death of his father, who had been in Brussels as an officer in the service of the Emperor of Austria. Having spent eight years studying history painting with Gabriel Briard (1729–77), he entered the Prix de Rome in 1772 and 1774 but failed to win. Thereafter he concentrated on landscape and genre painting, in which he was greatly influenced by such 17th-century Dutch masters as Aelbert Cuyp, the van Ostade brothers, Adriaen van de Velde and Karel Dujardin, all artists enjoying a tremendous vogue and high prices in Paris at that time. Demarne was made an associate (*agréé*) of the Académie Royale in 1783 but did not become a full member. He seems to have cared little for official honours and later, in 1815, was unwilling to seek membership of the Institut de France. He was, however, awarded the Légion d'honneur at the Salon of 1828.

Demarne was a very commercially minded artist and in the 1780s not only exhibited at the official Salon but also sent work to the Exposition de la Jeunesse and the Salon de la Correspondance. His output was considerable, and the difficulty of dating and identifying specific paintings is compounded by their repetitious nature (especially after 1815) and their imprecise titles. He was particularly fond of painting village and town fairs and road scenes. His first depiction of a fair appeared at the Salon of 1785, and dozens of similar works followed; the *Village Fair* (1814; Paris, Louvre) and the *Parish Feast* (Brussels, Mus. A. Anc.) are scenes of animated activity with numerous subordinate anecdotal incidents. His road scenes appeared from 1799 and were at times rectilinear and rigid, as in *Road with a Stagecoach* (Paris, Louvre). Occasionally he diversified into historical scenes, for example the *Return of Cincinnatus* (1795; untraced), and Troubadour-style pictures that have fanciful monuments inserted into them.

Largely apolitical, Demarne did not participate in the French Revolution and was only marginally involved in Napoleon's patronage of the arts. He painted the figures for the *Meeting of Napoleon and Pius VII at Fontainebleau* (Versailles, Château), for which Alexandre-Hyacinthe Dunouy (1757–1841) produced the landscape. Demarne also sometimes contributed figures to the landscapes of Lancelot-Théodore Turpin de Crissé, César van Loo, Georges Michel and Louis-Léopold Boilly. He had a devoted array of admirers, and his work was eagerly collected. In 1817 the Comte de Nape held 13 of his works and the Empress Josephine four. He was also very popular in Russia, and many of his best works were bought by Russian aristocrats, much to the regret of French collectors.

BIBLIOGRAPHY
Comte de Nape: 'Jean-Louis Demarne: Notice sur la vie et sur quelques-uns de ses ouvrages', *Rev. Univl. A.*, xxi (1865), pp. 269–99
J. Watelin: *Le Peintre J. L. Demarne, 1752–1829* (Paris, 1962)
French Painting, 1774–1830: The Age of Revolution (exh. cat., ed. P. Rosenberg; Paris, Grand Pal.; Detroit, MI, Inst. A.; New York, Met.; 1974–5), pp. 392–6
SIMON LEE

Demarteau, Gilles (*b* Liège, 19 Jan 1722; *d* Paris, 31 July 1776). French engraver and print publisher. He was descended from a family of gunsmiths. In 1739 he went to Paris to join a brother who had established himself there as a goldsmith. Beginning as an engraver and chaser,

in 1746 he obtained the rank of master. As early as 1757 he began to specialize in crayon manner (*see* CRAYON MANNER, §2) using a roulette, a process that brought him success; Jean-Charles François contributed in developing this process, but Demarteau, because of his superior skill, outstripped his rival. At a time when drawing was greatly in vogue, he offered the public faithful reproductions, first of red chalk drawings and then of drawings intended for decoration or teaching, in two or three colours, by contemporary artists. His oeuvre comprises 560 numbered plates, half of them after specially provided drawings by François Boucher (for illustration *see* CRAYON MANNER) or after drawings owned by collectors such as Blondel d'Azincourt. Demarteau also engraved some 40 drawing manuals, consisting of collections of plates after Edme Bouchardon, Jean-Pierre-Louis-Laurent Houël and Jean-Baptiste Huet I (*see* HUET, (2)). He was a protégé of Charles-Nicolas Cochin (II) and was praised by Denis Diderot; in 1769 he was admitted (*reçu*) to the Académie Royale with his engraving after Cochin of *Lycurgus Wounded* (exh. 1769 Salon; Roux, no. 142 bis). In 1770 he succeeded François as Graveur des Dessins du Cabinet du Roi.

Demarteau's nephew Gilles-Antoine Demarteau (*c.* 1750–1802), who was his pupil and collaborator, succeeded him in his business in the Rue de la Pelleterie. He mostly continued to publish prints from existing plates, though he also made a few engravings of genre scenes, such as *Autumn* (1786; R 47) after Huet, printed in colour with careful registration. In 1788 Gilles-Antoine Demarteau published a *Catalogue des estampes gravées au crayon d'après différents maîtres* of the Demarteau collection; this catalogue included both his and his uncle's plates in the same numbering system.

BIBLIOGRAPHY
A. Wittert: *Gilles Demarteau, graveur du Roi* (Brussels, 1883)
L. de Leymarie: *L'Oeuvre de Gilles Demarteau l'aîné, graveur du roi* (Paris, 1896)
H. Bouchot: 'Les Graveurs Gilles et Gilles-Antoine Demarteau, d'après des documents inédits', *Rev. A. Anc. & Mod.*, xviii (1905), pp. 95–112
M. Roux: *Inventaire du fonds français: Graveurs du dix-huitième siècle*, Paris, Bib. N., Cab. Est. cat., vi (Paris, 1949), pp. 327–501 [R]
MADELEINE BARBIN

Demayanns [Demyans], **John.** *See* MAIANO, DA, (3).

Demereto, Lorenzo. *See* SENES, LORENZO.

Dēmētriadēs, Kostas (*b* Stanimaka, Eastern Rumelia [now Asenovgrad, Bulgaria], 1881; *d* Athens, 28 Oct 1943). Greek sculptor. He studied at the School of Fine Arts in Athens and from 1904 at the Ecole des Beaux-Arts in Paris; he lived in Paris until 1930, before returning to Athens to become director of the School of Fine Arts. In France he underwent the influence of Auguste Rodin both in his choice of psychologically expressive themes and in his presentation of the human body in fragmentary form. He also made portraits and treated the body in action, as in *Diskobolos* (exh. 1924; New York, Central Park).

BIBLIOGRAPHY
F. Giofillis: *Istoria tēs neoellēnikēs tekhnēs, 1821–1941* [History of modern Greek art, 1821–1941], ii (Athens, 1963), pp. 471–4

S. Lidakis: *Oi Ellēnes gluptes: Ē neoellēnikē gluptikē* [The Greek sculptors: modern Greek sculpture] (Athens, 1981), p. 314

ATHENA S. E. LEOUSSI

Demetrios of Alexandria (*fl* mid-2nd century BC). Greek painter. He was the son of Seleukos and, although he was from Alexandria, worked in Rome; none of his work survives. He illustrates the shift of artistic patronage from the great Hellenistic cities to Rome in the 2nd century BC. Demetrios is the earliest recorded landscape painter (*topographos*: Diodorus Siculus: *History* XXXI.xviii.2). Alexandrian artists began to depict Nilotic scenes in mosaics and paintings from the 2nd century BC, and Demetrios stands at the head of that genre (*see* ALEXANDRIA, §2(v)). A story is told that he gave shelter at Rome to Ptolemy VI Philometor (*reg c.* 181–145 BC) when that king was driven from Egypt by his younger brother in 164 BC.

BIBLIOGRAPHY

J. Overbeck: *Die antiken Schriftquellen zur Geschichte der bildenden Künste bei den Griechen* (Leipzig, 1868/*R* Hildesheim, 1959), nos 2141–2

C. HOBEY-HAMSHER

Demetrios of Alopeke (*fl* Athens, ?*c.* 400–*c.* 360 BC). Greek sculptor. Although none of his works (mainly bronze portraits) survive, the signatures of Demetrios on bases of statues that he made suggest a date in the early 4th century BC (*Inscr. Gr./2*, ii, 3828, 4321, 4322 and 4895). He was celebrated for the uncompromising realism of his portrayals. Quintilian (*Principles of Oratory* XII.i.9–10) stated that he was 'criticized because he was too realistic and was hence more fond of verisimilitude than of beauty', and Lucian of Samosata (*Philopseudes* xviii) described his portrait of the Corinthian general *Pellichos* as showing the sitter 'with a pot belly, a bald head, half exposed by the hang of his garment, with some of the hairs of his beard blown by the wind and with his veins showing clearly'. Even though the statue may be an invention of Lucian for comic effect, the description of a brutally realistic portrait must have been plausible to his readers.

Pliny (*Natural History* XXXIV.76) listed among his works a statue of *Lysimache*, priestess of Athena for 64 years, an *Athena* and a portrait of *Simon*, who wrote the first treatise on horsemanship. An inscribed base found on the Acropolis may belong to the *Lysimache*, and a good argument has been made for a torso (Basle, Antikenmus.) and two heads (London, BM, and Rome, Mus. N. Romano) to be Roman copies of the statue: the stooped posture and lined and sunken face would have been a harsh representation of old age typical of Demetrios. The statue of *Simon* perhaps celebrated the bronze horse that the horseman dedicated in the Eleusinion at Athens, with his own exploits represented on the base (Xenophon: *On Horsemanship* I.i).

BIBLIOGRAPHY

V. Zinserling: 'Zur Datierung des Demetrios von Alopeke', *Festschrift G. von Lücken* (Rostock, 1968), pp. 829–31

M. Robertson: *A History of Greek Art*, i (Cambridge, 1975), pp. 504–6

A. Stewart: *Greek Sculpture: An Exploration*, i (New Haven and London, 1990)

□

Demidov [Demidoff]. Russian family of industrialists, patrons and collectors. The earlier members of the family belonged to the leading industrial house in 18th-century Russia, having made their immense fortune in the development of the mining industry and iron works in Siberia. Nikita (Grigor'yevich) (*b* Tula, 5 April 1656; *d* Tula, 28 Nov 1725), originally a blacksmith, became an armourer during the reign of Peter the Great and was the chief supplier for the Russian forces during the war with Sweden (1700–21). When he was awarded the title of Tsar's Commissar, his surname was changed to Demidov. Over the next 50 years the family's holdings in the Urals, apart from iron deposits, included such metals and minerals as copper, silver, porphyry and malachite. Five years before his death, Demidov was raised to hereditary nobility. His son Akinfy Demidov (*b* Tula, 1678; *d* Yatskoye Ust'ye, nr Izhevsk, 16 Aug 1745) continued the mining operations, and by the mid-18th century the family had established 33 factories. Nikita (Akinfiyevich) Demidov (1724–1789) took over his father's industrial enterprises and expanded them. He was also a dilettante scientist and the first family member to become active as a patron of the arts and sciences.

Nikita's son Count Nikolay (Nikitich) Demidov (or Nicolas Demidoff; *b* Chirkovitsy, nr St Petersburg, 20 Nov 1773; *d* Florence, 22 April 1828), served in the Imperial Guard and fought in the first Russo–Turkish War (1787–92). During the reign of Catherine the Great he became a Gentleman of the Chamber at her Court, and after squandering his financial resources he married into the Stroganov family, which placed him in the ranks of the highest Russian nobility and restored his financial stability. Because of poor health he left Russia in 1815, taking up a position in Florence as the Russian Envoy and spending his remaining years at the Villa di S Donato (formerly Villa Pratolino) near Florence and his hôtel in Paris. While still managing his Russian industries, he founded new factories in Italy.

At Nikolay's Italian villa he set up a theatre for performances of the latest Parisian vaudevilles and comic operas, established an academy for foreign teachers to study languages, mathematics and physics, and formed an art collection (known as the Galleria S Donato) and library that became famous throughout Europe. In addition to its private quarters, containing priceless furnishings, the villa had 14 salons built expressly for the display of oil paintings and watercolours, drawings, sculpture, furniture, porcelain, glass, tapestries and *objets d'art* of all types; it also had an extensive library of rare books. It is not always possible to ascertain which works were acquired by him and which were acquisitions made by his son (1) Anatoly Demidov. An early sale in Paris listed by Lugt (15370) as 'the collection of Nicolay Nikitich Demidov' (8–13 April 1839) appears to be Anatoly's elimination of the less desirable works inherited from his father and consisted of works by artists of no standing or by the 'school of' or in the 'manner of' a well-known artist. Nikolay's preference was for 18th-century French art, especially the paintings of Greuze and Jean-Louis Demarne. He also collected Dutch, Flemish and Italian Old Master paintings and decorative art, and it was probably he who built up the spectacular collection of armoury. The collection of the Galleria S Donato also contained ethnographic curiosities, costumes, antique fabrics and precious stones and minerals.

At Nikolay's death, his estate was divided between his two sons Anatoly and Pavel (Nikolayevich) Demidov (or Paul Demidoff; *b* Moscow, 17 Aug 1798; *d* Mainz, 6 April 1840). Pavel returned to Russia to take up a military career. He became an enlightened patron of arts and letters and a philanthropist, founding several charitable institutions. His son Pavel or Paul (Pavlovich) Demidov (*b* Weimar, 21 Oct 1839; *d* Pratolino, 29 Jan 1925) received the title of Principe di San Donato in 1872 and had a distinguished career in the Russian diplomatic and civil service. He also became the mayor of Kiev and founded the first Bessemer steel plant in Russia. Although he collected art, this was not as important an activity for him as it was for his uncle, Anatoly Demidov, and his grandfather Nikolay.

BIBLIOGRAPHY

Michaud
E. Galichon: 'La Galerie de San Donato', *Gaz. B.-A.*, xxiv (1868), pp. 404–8
P. Burty: 'Collection de San Donato: Les Curiosités', *Gaz. B.-A.*, n. s. 1, iii (1870), pp. 261–8
E. Galichon: 'La Galerie San Donato', *Gaz. B.-A.*, n. s. 1, iii (1870), pp. 5–13
C. Blanc: 'Une Visite à San Donato', *Gaz. B.-A.*, n. s. 1, xvi (1877), pp. 5–14
F. Lugt: *Marques* (1921), pp. 395–6
——: *Ventes* (1938–64)
T. Esper: 'Demidov Family in the Nineteenth Century', *The Modern Encyclopedia of Russian and Soviet History*, ed. J. L. Wieczynski (1976–), ix, pp. 51–4
H. D. Hudson jr: 'Demidov Family in the Eighteenth Century', *The Modern Encyclopedia of Russian and Soviet History*, ed. J. L. Wieczynski (1976–), ix, pp. 46–51

(1) Prince Anatoly Demidov [Anatole Demidoff] (*b* ?Florence, 1812; *d* Paris, 29 April 1870). He was educated in Paris and entered the Russian diplomatic service, briefly serving at embassies in Paris, Rome and Venice. In 1840, for his efforts in founding a silk manufactory in Tuscany, he received the title of Principe di San Donato from Leopold II, Grand Duke of Tuscany (*reg* 1824–59). In 1841 he married Princess Mathilde, daughter of Jérôme Bonaparte, former King of Westphalia. There were no children from the marriage, and the couple separated in 1846. Often shunned by society for his scandalous personal reputation, his failed marriage and the lack of recognition of his title by the Russian Court, Demidov attempted to secure social acceptance through his philanthropic deeds and by building a large art collection. He created numerous charitable institutions, hospitals, orphanages and schools, and his most ambitious humanitarian effort was to organize an international committee devoted to the relief of prisoners of the Crimean War (1853–6). On a scientific expedition (1837–8) to southern Russia and the Crimea that he organized, he met the artist Auguste Raffet, with whom he began a lasting friendship. Demidov published the results of the expedition in *Voyage dans la Russie méridionale et la Crimée. . .* (1857), which contained 100 original lithographs by Raffet. He sent Alexandre Durand to Russia to record landscape views, published in 1839 as *Voyage pittoresque et archéologique en Russie*. In a series of articles for the *Journal des débats*, later published in *Lettres sur l'empire de Russie* (1840), he addressed French misconceptions of Russian society. In 1847 he went with Raffet to Spain and later recorded the trip in *Etapes maritimes sur les côtes d'Espagne. . .* (1858).

Anatoly Demidov was the most important art collector of the family, upgrading the status of the family's collection of Old Master paintings and indulging a personal preference for the works of contemporary French artists. He had begun collecting in the 1830s, purchasing the choicest works from the collections of Etienne-François, Duc de Choiseul, Charles Maurice de Talleyrand-Périgord, Prince de Bénévent (1754–1838) and Charles Ferdinand, Duc de Berry (1778–1820). Paul Delaroche's the *Execution of Lady Jane Grey* (1834; London, N.G.) was bought in 1834, directly from the Salon in Paris. In 1853 he obtained such French paintings as Ingres's *Antiochus and Stratonice* (1840; Chantilly, Mus. Condé), Alexandre-Gabriel Decamps's *Samson Fighting the Philistines* (1839; priv. col.) and Ary Scheffer's *Francesca da Rimini* (exh. Salon 1835; London, Wallace) from the sale of Helen, Duchesse d'Orléans and Grand Duchess of Mecklenburg-Schwerin (1814–58), as well as watercolours and wash drawings by Richard Parkes Bonington, Jacques-Raymond Brascassat, Decamps, Delacroix, Delaroche, Gericault and Scheffer. Between 1836 and 1840 he commissioned from Eugène Lami a series of 61 elegant watercolours on bourgeois scenes, entitled *Histoire de mon temps*. Demidov's large collection of Dutch and Flemish paintings included such pieces as Aelbert Cuyp's *Avenue in Meerdervoort* (early 1650s; London, Wallace) and the *Peace of Munster* (1648; London, N.G.) by Gerard ter Borch (ii), and he owned two important paintings by Ribera, the violent *Martyrdom of St Bartholomew* (1639; Madrid, Prado) and the *Martyrdom of St Lawrence* (1618–20; Kansas City, MO, Nelson–Atkins Mus. A.). His collection of Italian art included portraits by Titian, Bronzino and Sebastiano del Piombo. He was also interested in sculpture, owning such marbles as Canova's *Young Girl with a Greyhound*, James Pradier's *Satyr and Bacchante* (exh. Salon, 1834; Paris, Louvre) and the silver *Surtout de table* by Antoine-Louis Barye. He spent the last decade of his life as a semi-invalid, although he still continued to collect. He began to disperse his collection, selling the works at auction in Paris in 1863 (13–16 Jan and 13–16 April) and 1868 (18 April). The major portion of the collection was sold in Paris in ten lots in 1870 (21–22, 26 Feb; 3–4, 8–10 March; 22 March–28 April), just before he died. The remaining contents of the Villa di S Donato, including the library, were auctioned on site in 1880 (15 March–13 May) by his nephew Pavel.

WRITINGS
Voyage pittoresque et archéologique en Russie (Paris, 1839)
Lettres sur l'empire de Russie (Paris, 1840)
Voyage dans la Russie méridionale et la Crimée par la Hongrie, la Valachie et la Moldavie, 4 vols (Paris, 1857)
Etapes maritimes sur les côtes d'Espagne de la Catalogne à l'Andalousie, 2 vols (Florence, 1858)
Regular contributions to *J. Débats*

BIBLIOGRAPHY
Anatole Demidoff, Prince of San Donato (1812–70) (exh. cat. by F. Haskell, London, Wallace, 1994)

PATRICIA CONDON

Demikovsky, Jules. *See* OLITSKI, JULES.

Demio [de Mio; Fratina; Fratini; Fratino; Visentin], **Giovanni** (*b* Schio, *c.* 1510; *d* ?Cosenza, *c.* 1570). Italian painter and mosaicist. He is first recorded in 1537 collaborating with Vincenzo Bianchini (1517–63) on mosaic work in S Marco, Venice, and he also worked as a mosaicist in 1538 and 1539 in the Camposanto, Pisa. In the *Martyrdom of St Lawrence* (Torrebelvicino, Vicenza, parish church), possibly an early work, his style reflects not only the Tuscan Mannerism of Giorgio Vasari and Francesco Salviati, both of whom Demio had probably met in Venice in 1542, when he was still working at S Marco, but also the Tusco–Roman manifestation of the style as seen in the work of Salviati, Jacopino del Conte (1510–98), Pirro Ligorio and Battista Franco in the oratory of S Giovanni Decollato, Rome.

Demio was called to Milan by the Marchese del Vasto, and there he executed some frescoes (formerly attributed to Simone Peterzano) and an altarpiece depicting the *Crucifixion* in the Sauli Chapel, S Maria delle Grazie. These works are closely modelled on the style of Giulio Romano, both directly and as interpreted by Maarten van Heemskerck, and seem also to reflect the influence of Paris Bordone. Demio next travelled to Naples, perhaps at the request of Vasari, whose *Presentation in the Temple* (Naples, S Anna dei Lombardi) he copied, with certain variations, for the parish church at Maiori. Around 1550 he executed some frescoes for the Villa Thiene, Quinto Vicentino, commissioned by Palladio, who regarded him as a 'man of very fine talent'. In 1556 he painted three allegorical tondi in the Libreria Marciana, Venice, which again show strong links with Romano and also with Giulio Clovio. His patrons, the Grimani family, recommended him to the authorities of Orvieto Cathedral for the task of restoring the mosaics on the façade, but he soon returned to the Veneto, where in 1558 he executed two altarpieces for S Maria in Vanzo, Padua. Demio subsequently travelled to central Italy, where he probably worked on the *Last Judgement* (Farfa Abbey, near Rieti) that was signed in 1561 by Hendrik van den Broeck, with whom he later collaborated in Rome. In 1570 he was working at Cosenza. Even in his late works Demio adhered to the Mannerist tradition, albeit interpreted in a highly personal way and within the context of the Netherlandish influences then prevailing in Rome (*see* ROMANISM).

BIBLIOGRAPHY

G. Guglielmi: 'Profilo di Giovanni Demio', *A. Ven.*, xx (1966), pp. 98–111
G. Bora: 'Giovanni Demio', *Kalòs*, ii (1971), pp. 17–23
——: 'La cultura figurativa a Milano, 1535–1565', *Omaggio a Tiziano: La cultura artistica milanese nell'età di Carlo V* (exh. cat., Milan, Pal. Reale, 1977), pp. 45–54
P. L. De' Vecchi: 'Nota su alcuni dipinti di artisti veneti per committenti milanesi', ibid., pp. 55–58
G. Previtali: *La pittura del cinquecento a Napoli e nel vicereame* (Turin, 1978)
V. Scarbi: 'Aspetti della maniera nel Veneto', *Paragone*, xxxi/369 (1980), pp. 65–80
——: *Palladio e la maniera: I pittori vicentini del cinquecento e i collaboratori del Palladio* (Venice, 1980)
——: 'Giovanni Demio', *Da Tiziano a El Greco: Per la storia del manierismo a Venezia, 1540–1590* (exh. cat., Venice, Doge's Pal., 1981), pp. 123–9

UGO RUGGERI

Demmler, Georg Adolph (*b* Berlin, 22 Dec 1804; *d* Schwerin, 2 Jan 1886). German architect. He studied at the Bauakademie in Berlin from 1819 and in 1823 became Feldmesser in Potsdam. A year later he joined the civil service in Mecklenburg and worked on the façade of the Kollegienhaus (1825–34; now Verwaltungsgebäude) at Schwerin. Demmler became Baumeister (1832) and ultimately Hofbaurat (1841). His first independent building was the theatre in Schwerin (1831–6; destr. 1882), influenced by the theatre at Schloss Charlottenburg, Berlin, by Carl Gotthard Langhans. Many of his buildings in Schwerin survive, including his refronting in the Tudor style (1834–5) of the old Rathaus, and the Marstall (1838–43; now Mehrzweckhalle). His many buildings outside Schwerin include spa establishments (1837–8; destr.) and the Logierhaus Glückauf (*c*. 1850), at Bad Doberan; and the Appellationsgericht (1840–41; now Zoologisches Institut), the Neues Museum (1845) and several city gateways (1841–4), at Rostock. He also restored and enlarged medieval buildings. His most important work was undertaken at the Schwerin Schloss, where he produced designs for a new building (1840) on the Alter Garten. Construction began in 1842, but on the death of Grand Duke Paul-Frederick (*reg* 1837–42) it was abandoned; it was later completed as a museum (1876–82) by Hermann Willebrand (1816–99). Demmler was then commissioned to rebuild the old schloss, involving extensive demolition and new work in the style of Windsor Castle, England. His plans were initially rejected by Grand Duke Frederick-Franz II (*reg* 1842–83), but after proposals had been made by Gottfried Semper (1843) and Friedrich August Stüler, Demmler was finally engaged, on condition that his designs were in Renaissance Revival style. The result tends towards the style of the Loire châteaux, particularly Chambord. In 1845 reconstruction work began, but Demmler's social democratic views and political activities (1848–50) led to his dismissal in 1851 from his court and government offices. The rest of his life was largely devoted to politics, and although he entered competitions, little was built to his designs, apart from an extension (1870) to the Hoftheater at Schwerin.

WRITINGS

Der Erweiterungs- und Verschönerungsplan der Residenzstadt Schwerin in seiner Entstehung und geschichtlichen aktenmässigen Entwicklung von 1862 bis Ende August des Jahres 1866 (Schwerin, 1866)
Neues und Altes, eine Verteidigungsschrift (Schwerin, 1874)

BIBLIOGRAPHY

A. Stüler, E. Posch and H. Willebrand: *Das Schloss zu Schwerin*, i (Berlin, 1869)
K. E. O. Fritsch: 'Die Konkurrenz für Entwürfe zum Haus des deutschen Reichstages', *Dt. Bauztg*, vi (1872), pp. 227–9
K. Milde: *Neorenaissance in der deutschen Architektur des 19. Jahrhunderts* (Dresden, 1981)
M. Krempien: *G. A. Demmler, Schweriner Schlossbaumeister, 1804–1886* (Schwerin, 1991)

MICHAEL BOLLÉ

De Morgan. English family of artists.

(1) William (Frend) De Morgan (*b* London, 16 Nov 1839; *d* London, 15 Jan 1917). Designer, potter and novelist. One of the most original artist–craftsmen associated with the ARTS AND CRAFTS MOVEMENT, he was interested in both the artistic and technical aspects of ceramic decoration. His artistic training began with evening classes at F. S. Cary's art school in Bloomsbury, London, and in 1859 he entered the Royal Academy Schools. After completing half of the eight-year programme, he left to work for the firm of Morris, Marshall, Faulkner & Co. as a designer of stained glass and a painter of panels for furniture. De Morgan's interest in the iridescence caused by the firing of the silver paint used to outline designs on stained glass led him to experiment with reproducing the effect on tiles. Initially he worked from his home, but in 1873 he opened a separate studio and showroom (known as Orange House) in Chelsea, London, and hired employees. The main production was tiles with floral and foliate patterns in the style of William Morris and animal and bird designs, often grotesque or whimsical, painted in lustre glazes (examples in London, William Morris Gal.). In the early years of the Chelsea studio tile blanks were used, but by the late 1870s the factory was making its own tiles; in 1879 De Morgan produced tiles after Frederic Leighton's collection of Islamic tiles to complete the scheme (*in situ*) for the Arab Hall at Leighton House, London. Large ready-made dishes in the form of Chinese rice dishes were also decorated.

In 1882 expansion necessitated a move to a larger workshop at Merton Abbey, Surrey, close to William Morris's textile workshop. Orange House was kept as a showroom until 1886 when a new shop was opened at 45 Great Marlborough Street, London. At Merton Abbey De Morgan concentrated on producing hollow-ware and had pots thrown to his specifications. In addition to experimenting further with lustre glazes De Morgan developed his 'Persian' style of decoration, based on Middle Eastern ornament and executed in turquoise, blues and greens.

De Morgan's marriage to the painter (2) Evelyn Pickering in 1887 and his declining health prompted a move back to London. The architect Halsey Ricardo became De Morgan's partner in 1888 in the new pottery at Sands End, Fulham, London. Here De Morgan developed his 'Moonlight' and 'Sunlight' series, which consist of wares with double and triple lustre effects (e.g. vase, *c.* 1890; London, V&A). Also in 1888, De Morgan was a founder-member of the Arts and Crafts Exhibition Society. In 1892 De Morgan began spending winters in Florence, where he employed decorators at the Cantagalli pottery to paint his new designs, which were then sent to Sands End. The partnership with Ricardo was dissolved in 1898 due to financial difficulties and another was formed with his longtime employees, kilnmaster Frank Iles (*fl* 1872–1911) and tile painters Charles Passenger and Fred Passenger. Leaving his partners to carry on the pottery, De Morgan retired in 1907 and pursued a successful career as a novelist.

BIBLIOGRAPHY
R. Pinkham: *Catalogue of Pottery by William De Morgan* (London, 1973)
J. Catleugh: *William De Morgan Tiles* (London and New York, 1983)
M. Greenwood: *The Designs of William De Morgan* (Shepton Beauchamp, 1989)
JOELLEN SECONDO

(2) Evelyn De Morgan [née Pickering] (*b* London, 1850 or 1855; *d* London, 2 May 1919). Painter, wife of (1) William De Morgan. She was a pupil of her uncle, the painter Roddam Spencer Stanhope. In 1873–5 she attended the Slade School of Art, London. While there, she was awarded a Slade scholarship entitling her to financial assistance for three years. The scholarship required that she draw in charcoal from the nude, but she eventually declined it because she did not wish to continue working in this technique, although she excelled in it. She was influenced by the work of the Pre-Raphaelite artists (*see*

PRE-RAPHAELITISM) and became a follower of Burne-Jones. In 1877 she first exhibited at the Grosvenor Gallery, London, and continued to show there thereafter. From 1875 she spent several winters in Florence working and studying; some of her work is reminiscent of Botticelli, possibly because of her visits to Florence. She often depicted women in unfamiliar ways though in a manner more in tune with a female perspective. For example, in *Medea* (1889; Birkenhead, Williamson A.G. & Mus.), the heroine is portrayed as a woman skilled in sorcery, rather than as a murderer of her own children. In 1887 she married William De Morgan (*see* §1 above) and was involved in his pottery enterprises, assisting him financially and contributing ideas for ceramic designs.

BIBLIOGRAPHY
C. E. Clement Waters: *Women in the Fine Arts* (Boston and New York, 1904, Cambridge, MA, 2/1905)
G. Greer: *The Obstacle Race* (London, 1979)
C. Petteys, H. Gustow and V. Ritchie: *Dictionary of Women Artists* (Boston, 1985)
W. Chadwick: *Women, Art and Society* (London and New York, 1990)

Demotte, Georges (J.) (*b* 17 June 1877; *d* Chaumont-sur-Tharonne, 3 Sept 1923). French dealer of Belgian origin. Originally a diamond merchant, in 1899 Demotte married Semha Stora, whose family was prominent as antique dealers, and by 1900 he had established a reputation as an art restorer and a dealer in medieval European antiquities. His business was centred in Paris. He soon began to deal also in Islamic and Ancient Near Eastern art, and the object most closely associated with his name is the Demotte *Shāhnāma* ('Book of kings'; *c.* 1335; *see* ISLAMIC ART, §III, 4(v)(b)). Demotte apparently acquired this Persian manuscript *c.* 1910, but was unable to sell the book intact and hence dismembered it, selling individual folios to major collectors and museums in Europe and North America. In 1921 Demotte opened a second gallery in New York. Many major works passed through his hands, but he was involved in several law suits (including one with Sir JOSEPH DUVEEN) over questions of authenticity. Demotte reportedly died in a hunting accident; his son Lucien inherited the New York business which passed, upon his suicide in 1934, to NASLI M. HEERAMANECK.

BIBLIOGRAPHY
O. Grabar and S. Blair: *Epic Images and Contemporary History: The Illustrations of the Great Mongol Shah-nama* (Chicago and London, 1980)
MILO CLEVELAND BEACH

Dempster, Thomas (*b* Aberdeenshire, ?1579; *d* Bologna, 6 Sept 1625). Scottish scholar and writer. Educated mainly in France and Belgium, he was appointed Professor of Civil Law at Pisa by Cosimo II de' Medici, Grand Duke of Tuscany, who invited him to write a history of ancient Etruria. This commission was evidently intended to substantiate the politically desirable myth that the contemporary rulers of Tuscany were descended from Etruscan kings. Written in 1616–19, Dempster's *De Etruria regali* combined flattery of the Medici, including an attempted Etruscan derivation of their name, with a diligent synthesis of references to the Etruscans in Classical and later literature. Despite its exaggerated claims, for example that the Etruscans invented music and agriculture, it was the first comprehensive account of Etruscan origins, customs, history, cities, art and language and correctly treated these as aspects of an indigenous civilization. Publication was impeded by court intrigue and by Dempster's characteristically irascible reaction to it. He moved to the prestigious Chair of Humanities at Bologna, where the posthumous publication of his eccentric *Historia ecclesiastica gentis Scotorum* (1627) irreversibly damaged his reputation. *De Etruria regali* itself was eventually published in 1723 in Florence at the instigation of Thomas Coke, with additions by Filippo Buonarroti. It was highly regarded in the 18th century by the local exponents of Etruscheria in their uncritical attempts to retrieve the Etruscan past (for further discussion *see* ETRUSCAN, §VIII).

WRITINGS

De Etruria regali libri vii nunc primum editi curante T. Coke, 2 vols (Florence, 1723–4)

BIBLIOGRAPHY

D. Irving: *Lives of the Scottish Writers*, i (Edinburgh, 1839), pp. 347–70
R. Leighton and C. Castelino: 'Thomas Dempster and Ancient Etruria', *Pap. Brit. Sch. Rome*, 58 (1990 [1992]), pp. 337–52

DAVID RIDGWAY

Demre. *See under* MYRA.

Demus, Otto (*b* nr St Pölten, 1902; *d* Vienna, 1990). Austrian art historian. A highly influential scholar of Byzantine art, he was also concerned with western medieval painting, particularly Romanesque, and with the restoration of Austrian monuments. He studied art history under Josef Strzygowski at the University of Vienna (1921–8). From 1930 to 1936 he worked for the Austrian monuments service as keeper of monuments in Carinthia. In 1939 he emigrated to England where he worked as librarian of the Warburg Institute in London and taught at the Courtauld Institute. In 1946 he returned to Austria as president of the reconstituted monuments service, and from 1963 to 1973 held the chair of art history in the University of Vienna, where he taught medieval and Byzantine art.

Although he often demonstrated an unerring ability to set a medieval monument in the context of its artistic tradition, he appears sometimes to have been inattentive to detail and to historical textual issues. Yet, even in his earliest work (*Byzantine Mosaics*, 1931; *Die Mosaiken*, 1935), his articulate descriptions in German and English of style and his recognition of stylistic trends across periods remain unsurpassed.

In seeking to uncover the underlying system of Byzantine monumental decoration (*Byzantine Mosaic*, 1948), he may perhaps have been pursuing a chimera; similarly his artificial identification of abstract stylistic currents may hinder the understanding of broader cultural issues. It may be, however, that the reductivism his thinking encouraged has intruded more into the work of his imitators. His views on Byzantium and the West (*Byzantine Art*, 1970), in which the initial superiority of the Byzantine empire inevitably dissolved when its role as catalyst in the western revival of Classical forms was fulfilled, are distinctively teleological and weighted in favour of the aesthetics of Classical and Renaissance art over the innovations of medieval Christian art. He was the acknowledged authority on the Byzantinizing monuments of Sicily and Venice, where in the 1970s he began a campaign to clean the mosaics in S Marco (*The Mosaics*, 1984). In the 1980s he returned to his study of Late Gothic wooden carved and painted altarpieces of Carinthia.

WRITINGS

with E. Diez: *Byzantine Mosaics in Greece: Hosios Lucas and Daphni* (Boston, 1931)
Die Mosaiken von San Marco in Venedig, 1100–1300 (Baden bei Wien, 1935)
Byzantine Mosaic Decoration (London, 1948)
The Mosaics of Norman Sicily (London, 1950)
The Church of San Marco in Venice: History, Architecture, Sculpture (Washington, DC, 1960)
Romanesque Mural Painting (London, 1970)
Byzantine Art and the West (London, 1970)
The Mosaics of San Marco in Venice (Chicago, 1984)

BIBLIOGRAPHY

H. Belting: Obituary, *Dumbarton Oaks Pap.*, xlv (1991), pp. vii–xi

ROBIN CORMACK

Demuth, Charles (Henry Buckius) (*b* Lancaster, PA, 8 Nov 1883; *d* Lancaster, 23 Oct 1935). American painter and illustrator. He was deeply attached to Lancaster, where his family had run a tobacco shop since 1770. Although not a Regionalist, Demuth maintained a strongly localized sense of place, and Lancaster provided him with much of the characteristic subject-matter of both his early and later work. He trained in Philadelphia at the Drexel Institute of Art, Science and Industry (1901–5) and at the Pennsylvania Academy of the Fine Arts (1905–11), where his teachers included Thomas Anshutz, Henry McCarter (1864–1942), Hugh Breckenridge (1870–1937) and William Merritt Chase. While still a student, he participated in a show at the Academy (1907), exhibiting his work publicly for the first time.

Demuth was one of the first American artists to be receptive to modernism, to which he was exposed during several extensive and significant trips to Europe in 1907–8, 1912–14 and 1921. While abroad, he painted little but became involved with Gertrude and Leo Stein, Jo Davidson and Ezra Pound in Paris. Further contact with avant-garde styles and ideas came through the frequent trips he made from Lancaster to New York, where his close associates included Alfred Stieglitz, Georgia O'Keeffe, Marsden Hartley and Marcel Duchamp. He was also close to literary and artistic circles in Provincetown, MA, which he first visited in 1914.

Demuth's first one-man exhibition was mounted in 1914 at the Daniel Gallery, New York, run by Charles Daniel, who presented the work of many significant early American modernists. Still later, he exhibited regularly at Stieglitz's gallery, An American Place. Such critics as Henry McBride, Paul Rosenfeld and Carl Van Vechten were early admirers of his work, and his paintings were purchased by perceptive collectors including Albert Barnes, A. E. Gallatin, Louise and Walter Arensberg and Ferdinand Howald. He maintained a close homosexual relationship from around 1909 with Robert Evans Locher (1888–1956), an Art Deco interior decorator and stage designer who was also from Lancaster.

By *c.* 1915 Demuth had achieved his characteristic style and imagery. His first serious exploration of Cubism was a series of landscapes and architectural views painted during the winter of 1916–17 while he was in Bermuda with Marsden Hartley, for example *Trees and Barns, Bermuda* (1917; Williamstown, MA, Williams Coll. Mus. A.). He continued to experiment with these formal ideas after a trip to Gloucester, MA, in the summer of 1917. At the same time he painted a series of watercolours inspired by vaudeville themes (1917–19). Not only was Demuth a regular visitor to night-clubs and cafés in New York, but Lancaster was an important stop for vaudeville performers and several local theatres regularly presented such entertainments. Demuth took considerable anatomical liberties with his figures. In their bright colours, deft lines and fluid movements, these watercolours recall the spirit of Henri de Toulouse-Lautrec, Edgar Degas, Auguste Rodin and Henri Matisse, for example *In Vaudeville: Dancer with Chorus* (1918; Philadelphia, PA, Mus. A.). Chronologically and stylistically related to his vaudeville works is a series of watercolour illustrations produced between 1915 and 1919 inspired by the works of Emile Zola, Franz Wedekind and Henry James. Demuth's illustrations were unpublished, but examples include *Flora and the Governess* (1918; Philadelphia, PA, Mus. A.) for James's *The Turn of the Screw*, and *Lulu and Alva Schoen* (1918; Merion Station, PA, Barnes Found.) for Wedekind's *Pandora's Box*. Also at this time, he began to paint still-lifes of flowers, fruit and vegetables, which were to remain favourite subjects. These and his vaudeville works were the most popular among critics and collectors.

In 1919 Demuth began a series of paintings depicting themes inspired (with the exception of two views of nearby Coatesville) by the architecture of Lancaster. Executed in oil and tempera, the series marks a shift from his previously favoured watercolour medium. Larger in scale than any of his other works, these paintings maintain a striking balance between abstraction and realism. The industrial images he used are strongly formalized, structured in simplified Cubist planes and Futurist lines of force, but remain specific. Although Demuth produced relatively few of these industrial landscapes, they established him as an important Precisionist artist (*see* PRECISIONISM). His most famous work, *My Egypt* (1927; New York, Whitney; see fig.), was from this series. Like the accompanying works, it records an identifiable site in the city, not far from the artist's home on East King Street. Demuth's last work on this theme was painted in 1933.

From the mid- to the late 1920s, Demuth produced a series of symbolic 'poster portraits' of several of his friends, the most famous of which is *I Saw the Figure Five in Gold (Homage to William Carlos Williams)* (1928; New York, Met.). He also painted tributes to John Marin, Georgia O'Keeffe, Arthur Dove, Gertrude Stein and others. The highly personal iconography and less accessible style of these portraits, combined with their unusual titles, made them difficult for most viewers to appreciate when they were first exhibited. These works, as well as those of Lancaster's architecture, were not well received by critics.

Demuth's last works, a series of luminous studies made while on holiday in Provincetown in the summer of 1934, reveal a renewed interest in the human figure. By 1920 the effects of diabetes became debilitating; the disease increasingly drained his artistic energies and led to his death.

Charles Demuth: *My Egypt*, oil on composition board, 908×762 mm, 1927 (New York, Whitney Museum of American Art)

BIBLIOGRAPHY

E. E. Farnham: *Charles Demuth: Behind a Laughing Mask* (Norman, OK, 1971) [with bibliog.]
Charles Demuth: The Mechanical Encrusted on the Living (exh. cat. by D. Gebhard and P. Plous, Santa Barbara, U. CA, A. Gals, 1971) [with bibliog.]
A. Davidson: 'Demuth's Poster Portraits', *Artforum*, xvii (1978), pp. 54–7
K. A. Marling: '*My Egypt*: The Irony of the American Dream', *Winterthur Port.*, xv (1980), pp. 25–39
B. Fahlman: *Pennsylvania Modern: Charles Demuth of Lancaster* (exh. cat., Philadelphia, PA, Mus. A., 1983) [with bibliog.]
T. A. Burgard: 'Charles Demuth's *Longhi on Broadway: Homage to Eugene O'Neill*', *A. Mag.*, lvi (1984), pp. 110–13
B. Fahlman: 'Modern as Metal and Mirror: The Work of Robert Evans Locher', *A. Mag.*, lix (1985), pp. 108–13
——: 'Charles Demuth's Paintings of Lancaster Architecture: New Discoveries and Observations', *A. Mag.*, lxi (1987), pp. 24–9
Charles Demuth (exh. cat. by B. Haskell, New York, Whitney, 1988) [with bibliog.]
J. Weinberg: *Speaking for Vice: Homosexuality in the Art of Charles Demuth, Marsden Hartley and the First American Avant-Garde* (New Haven, 1993)

BETSY FAHLMAN

Demut-Malinovsky, Vasily (Ivanovich) (*b* St Petersburg, 13 March 1779; *d* St Petersburg, 28 July 1846). Russian sculptor. He was the son of a carver and studied at the Academy of Arts from 1785 to 1800, where he very soon distinguished himself. In 1800 he produced the bronze low-relief *Battle at Gangut* for the base of Bartolommeo Carlo Rastrelli's monument to *Peter I*, placed in front of the Mikhaylovsky Castle in St Petersburg (*in situ*). In 1802–3 he executed the tombstone for *Mikhail Ivanovich Kozlovsky* (marble; St Petersburg, Mus. Sculp.). Between 1803 and 1806 he worked in Rome under Antonio Canova.

On his return to St Petersburg, Demut-Malinovsky played an active role in the decoration of the buildings then being erected in the capital. He was responsible for the statue of *Andrey Pervozvanny* (bronze, 1808–11; Kazan' Cathedral), the sculptural group *Pluto and Proserpine* (Pudozh stone, 1809–11; St Petersburg, Plekhanov Mining Inst.) and also a number of statues for the Admiralty (untraced). His statue *The Russian Scaevola* (bronze, 1813; St Petersburg, Rus. Mus.), one of the most accomplished works of Russian Neo-classicism, was produced in response to the Russian achievement in the struggle against Napoleon in 1812. Later Demut-Malinovsky worked with the architect Karl Ivanovitch Rossi, providing Neo-classical reliefs and figures for the Yelagin Palace, the Mikhaylovsky Palace, the Aleksandrovsky Theatre and the Senate and Synod building (all *in situ*). Demut-Malinovsky's most significant work was the triumphal chariot (copper sheeting, 1827–9; *in situ*) for the Arch of the General Staff, produced together with Stepan Pimenov. Later the two artists, with the architect Vasily Petrovich Stasov, worked on the statues (copper, 1830–34; *in situ*) for the Narva triumphal gate in St Petersburg.

Demut-Malinovsky is notable for his portrait busts, where a classical style is balanced by an expressive treatment of the subject, as in *Aleksandr Vasil'yevich Suvorov* (bronze, 1814; St Petersburg, Mus. Sculp.), and *Mikhail Vasil'yevich Lomonosov* (marble, 1821; St Petersburg, Lit. Mus. Inst. Rus. Lit.). Demut-Malinovsky also executed a series of tombstones that are varied in appearance, for example for the vice-president of the Academy of Arts, *Piotr Petrovich Chekalevsky* (bronze, *c.* 1817; St Petersburg, Mus. Sculp.), and for *Vladimir Dmit Novosil'tsev* (bronze,

1820s; Moscow, Donskoy Monastery). Demut-Malinovsky's late works reflect the uncertainty in Neo-classicism that heralded its decline: for example in the unsuccessful monument to *Ivan Susanin* in Kostroma, in which the folk hero is depicted kneeling before the bust of Tsar Michael (bronze, 1836–43).

BIBLIOGRAPHY

I. M. Shmidt: *Vasily Ivanovich Demut-Malinovsky* (Moscow, 1960)
Istoriya russkogo iskusstva [The history of Russian art], viii/1 (Moscow, 1963), p. 331
L. B. Aleksandrova: *Vasily Ivanovich Demut-Malinovsky, 1779–1846* (St Petersburg, 1980)

SERGEY ANDROSSOV

Demyans, John. *See* MAIANO, DA, (3).

Denafū. *See* OKADA, (2).

Denbigh, 2nd Earl of. *See* FEILDING, BASIL.

Den Bosch. *See* 'S HERTOGENBOSCH.

Dendara [anc. Egyp. Iunet; Gr. Tentyris]. Egyptian site on the west bank of the Nile *c.* 65 km north of Luxor. It was an important provincial centre throughout Egyptian history; its chief artistic monuments are successive temples of the goddess Hathor from the 6th Dynasty (*c.* 2325–*c.* 2150 BC) to the 2nd century AD (see fig. 1a). The site stands to the south of the Nile, about 1 km away at the edge of the low desert. The temples stand within a high mud-brick enclosure wall and occupy the north-west part of the sacred space. The site was cleared by Auguste Mariette in the mid-19th century, and work continued sporadically until about 1960.

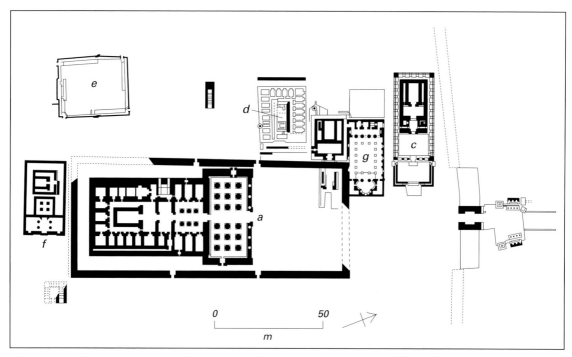

1. Dendara, central area of temple compound, 4th century BC–5th century AD, plan: (a) Temple of Hathor; (b) *mammisi* of Nectanebo I; (c) Roman *mammisi*; (d) sanatorium; (e) sacred lake; (f) Temple of Isis; (g) Christian basilica

2. Dendara, Temple of Hathor, façade, Greco-Roman period, 1st century BC–1st century AD

Activity of Pepy I (*reg c.* 2289–*c.* 2256 BC) is referred to in the Greco-Roman temple and attested by a fine statue. The 11th-Dynasty king Mentuhotpe II (*reg c.* 2008–*c.* 1957 BC) built a chapel to Hathor and her son Harsomtus which also celebrated his own status (Cairo, Egyp. Mus.). This chapel still stood in the time of Merneptah (*reg c.* 1213–*c.* 1204 BC), but its basically provincial style had no lasting influence. Its reliefs, the composition of which is iconographically very interesting, include an image of Horus and Seth tying together the heraldic plants of Upper and Lower Egypt, vividly commemorating the King's reunification of the country.

The oldest building in the main temple complex, and the oldest such structure still standing, is the *mammisi* (birth house) of Nectanebo I (*reg* 380–362 BC; 1b). Redecorated early in the Ptolemaic period (304–30 BC), it was replaced by a larger birth house decorated in the early 2nd century AD under Trajan and Hadrian (1c; *see also* EGYPT, ANCIENT, fig. 69). Other subsidiary buildings include a mud-brick sanatorium (1d) and a sacred lake (1e), both to the west of the temple.

The Greco-Roman Temple of Hathor is the grandest and most richly decorated of its period (see fig. 2). The earliest dated inscriptions refer to Ptolemy XII (*reg* 80–58 BC; 55–51 BC); its outer hypostyle hall was dedicated in November AD 34. It was built of sandstone on the conventional Egyptian plan, but only the inner apartments were completed. These comprise the outer hypostyle hall with twenty-four columns, an inner hypostyle hall with six columns, two vestibules and the usual suite of service rooms and cult chambers surrounding a free-standing sanctuary. A remarkable feature is the use of the emblem of Hathor, the Hathor head, which also forms part of the naos-shaped sistrum, a musical instrument used in her worship. The capitals of the outer hypostyle hall are in the form of naos sistra, their four Hathor heads facing the cardinal points, and the head motif also occurs in the friezes above the main entrance, throughout the temple interior and on the exterior rear wall. This last, colossal head was gilded and covered by a canopy. Since the east–west axis of a temple is the path of the sun through the sky, the gilded Hathor head reflected and embodied the sun's presence on earth and represented the goddess's epithet of 'gold'. The same associations are present in a delicate kiosk in the south-west corner of the roof, where the union of Hathor with the solar disc was celebrated. This solar emphasis contrasts with the temple's actual north–south orientation, which was determined by the direction of the Nile nearby; despite the gloom within, it focuses on sun and light. Three levels of crypts were constructed; unusually, they are decorated with reliefs, many of which show and describe cult objects. The reliefs record a vast range of sculptural types, few of which are otherwise preserved; they also give details of their materials and dimensions. The roof of the temple contains two suites of rooms dedicated to Osiris. The ceiling of one was decorated with a carved zodiac (Paris, Louvre, D 38); its composition contrasts with others known from Egypt in being roughly circular, and is one of the rare cases of Classical influence in native Egyptian temples.

Behind the Temple of Hathor is a temple commemorating the birth of Isis (1f); its preserved parts, incorporating reused Ptolemaic blocks, date from the time of Augustus (*reg* 27 BC–AD 14). Its dual orientation is almost unique: the hypostyle halls (destr.) faced the eastern gateway of the enclosure, while the sanctuary faces north towards the Temple of Hathor; the east wall of the inner part has a false door linking the two areas symbolically. The temple is compact, and the rooms flanking the sanctuary are scarcely more than corridors, but they are fully decorated. The sanctuary focuses on a unique scene of the birth of Isis, partly carved in high relief, which fills two registers; it was severely damaged in Early Christian times. It was not the cult image, however, which would have been a statue kept in a shrine. Its style recalls rock-cut sculpture in Nubian temples of the New Kingdom (*c.* 1540–*c.* 1075 BC), but differs in being integrated into the reliefs on a wall.

Also set among the temple buildings is a basilica (5th century AD; 1g), which represents one of the earliest surviving Christian churches in Egypt.

BIBLIOGRAPHY

A. Mariette: *Dendérah*, 4 vols (Paris, 1870–73)
E. Chassinat with F. Daumas: *Le Temple de Dendara*, 8 vols (Cairo, 1934–78)
F. Daumas: 'La Valeur de l'or dans la pensée égyptienne', *Rev. Hist. Relig.*, cxlix (1956), pp. 1–17
——: *Les Mammisis de Dendara* (Cairo, 1959)
Labib Habachi: 'King Nebhepetre Mentuhotp: His Monuments, Place in History, Deification and Unusual Representations in the Form of Gods', *Mitt. Dt. Archäol. Inst.: Abt. Kairo*, xix (1963), pp. 16–52
F. Daumas: *Dendara et le temple de Hathor: Notice sommaire* (Cairo, 1969)
P. Derchain: *Hathor Quadrifrons* (Istanbul, 1972)
F. Daumas: 'Derechef Pepi Ier à Dendara', *Rev. Égypt.*, xxv (1973), pp. 7–20
J. Baines: *Fecundity Figures: Egyptian Personification and the Iconology of a Genre* (Warminster, 1985), pp. 229–34
C. Traunecker: 'Cryptes décorées et anépigraphes', *Hommages à François Daumas*, ii (Montpellier, 1986), pp. 571–7

JOHN BAINES

Dendra [Dhendrá]. Site in the north-eastern Peloponnese in southern Greece, on the eastern fringe of the Argive plain 10 km north-north-east of Navplion. To the settlement, which flourished *c.* 1350–*c.* 1200 BC, belong a necropolis near the village of Dendra and the acropolis of Midea east-south-east of the village. In Greek legend Midea was the home of Alkmene, the mother of Herakles. The necropolis was excavated by a Swedish expedition in 1926, 1927, 1937 and 1939, both the tombs and the acropolis by Greek and Swedish archaeologists between 1960 and 1995 (in progress).

In the necropolis a Mycenaean tholos tomb was excavated, as were 16 rock-cut chamber tombs, mostly with long dromoi, one (No. 12) with a vertical entrance shaft. The chambers are rectangular, sometimes with side-chambers. Several of the tombs were unusually rich in metal objects (rings, vessels, weapons and armour). The citadel of Midea was inhabited from the Early Helladic period (*c.* 3600/3000–*c.* 2050 BC) onwards. In the 13th century BC it was fortified with a huge wall in Cyclopean masonry. Two main gates are preserved, in the east and in the south-west; some fresco fragments are reported from the latter. The fortification seems to have been destroyed by an earthquake *c.* 1200 BC. The objects found at the site are divided between the National Archaeological Museum at Athens (metal items from early excavations, including the gold Octopus Cup from the tholos tomb, dated *c.* 1400 BC) and the Archaeological Museum at Navplion (pottery; bronze panoply from Chamber Tomb 12, dated *c.* 1400 BC).

BIBLIOGRAPHY

A. W. Persson: *The Royal Tombs at Dendra near Midea* (Lund, 1931)
——: *New Tombs at Dendra near Midea* (Lund, 1942)
P. Åström and others: *The Cuirass Tomb and Other Finds at Dendra*, 2 vols (Gothenburg, 1977–83)
P. Åström, K. Demakopoulou and others: 'Excavations in Midea, 1989–90', *Opuscula Athen.*, xix (1992), pp. 12–22

ROBIN HÄGG

Denecker, Jost de. *See* NEGKER, JOST DE.

Denes, Agnes (*b* Budapest, 1931). American conceptual and environmental artist of Hungarian birth. She was educated in Sweden and the USA. In much of her work she presented analytical propositions in visual form, seeking to re-evaluate existing knowledge, and her work came to be seen as a process of investigation, incorporating both philosophy and science but also using elements of myth. In her book *Map Projections* she relinquished accepted forms of knowledge of the planet earth and sought new possibilities, presenting them in the form of drawings. Thus, for example, 'longitude and latitude lines were unravelled, points of intersection cut, continents allowed to drift, gravity tampered with [and] earth mass altered.' The element of game-playing in this was important, as was the belief in the possibility of changing our understanding of the world. Denes felt it was important to 'accept the possibility that there may be no language to describe ultimate reality, beyond the language of visions' (e.g. *Matrix of Knowledge*, monoprint, 1970; New York, MOMA, and *Pascal's Triangle II*, India ink on orange graph paper, 1973; Joyce Kozloff priv. col.). Other works were inspired by ecological concerns and included the planting of a cornfield (1987) on a site in Manhattan destined for development, planting a rice field and burying a canister filled with philosophical questions to be unearthed at some future date.

WRITINGS
Isometric Systems in Isotropic Space: Map Projections, Study of Distortions (Rochester, NY, 1979)

BIBLIOGRAPHY
Sculptures of the Mind: Agnes Denes (exh. cat., U. Akron, OH, Emily H. David A.G., 1976)
Agnes Denes (exh. cat., Ithaca, NY, Cornell U., Johnson Mus. A., 1992)

□

Dénes, Valéria. *See* GALIMBERTI, (1).

Deneuville, Alphonse. *See* NEUVILLE, ALPHONSE DE.

Dengfeng [Teng-feng]. County in Henan Province, China, east of the city of Luoyang. The presence of Mt Song (also called Mt Xiaoshi, Mt Songyue or Mt Songgao) means that the county is primarily known as a centre of Buddhism. Mt Song was a Buddhist sanctuary as early as the Three Kingdoms period (AD 220–80). When Emperor Xiaowendi (*reg* AD 471–99) of the Northern Wei (386–534) moved the dynastic capital from Datong in north-western Shanxi Province to Luoyang, the mountain was selected as an ideal place to establish Buddhist temples.

The Fawang Temple (Fawang si) is the oldest Buddhist sanctuary on Mt Song, supposedly dating to AD 234. It features a large, square, brick pagoda of the mid-8th century AD, 15 storeys and 40 m high, built in the same style as the Xiaoyan ta (Small Wild Goose Pagoda) in Xi'an. Other buildings in the Fawang Temple, including the Precious Hall of the Great Hero (the main hall), the Hall of the Four Heavenly Kings and the Ksitigarbha Hall, date from the Qing period (1644–1911).

The Songyue Temple (Songyue si), at the foot of Mt Taishi in the Mt Song region, was founded under the Northern Wei. Originally an imperial residence, it was converted to a Buddhist temple in the 520s. It has one of the oldest brick pagodas in China, dating to the Zhengguang reign period (AD 519–25). The pagoda (see CHINA, fig. 17) is 12-sided and multi-storey; the main upper storey has windows on each side with lotus arches. The ornamental brickwork is unusual and thought to be influenced by the contemporary architectural style of Gupta India (4th–5th centuries AD). The other remaining buildings in the temple are of later date.

The famous Shaolin Temple (Shaolin si), built in AD 496 on the order of Emperor Xiaowendi, is located on the northern slope of Mt Song at the foot of Mt Hou (also known as Wuru Peak). Since the Tang period (AD 618–907) the temple has been connected with the First Patriarch of the Chan (Jap. Zen) school, the Indian monk Bodhidharma (d c. AD 530). Some buildings in the temple date to the 16th century, but most are of later date, rebuilt after several fires. The layout of the temple follows the late Ming (1368–1644) pattern found in most rebuilt Chinese temples. The most important structures are the Vairochana Hall, the Avalokiteshvara Hall, the Ksitigarbha Hall, the Monks' Hall, the Dharma Hall, the Buddha Hall and the Patriarch's Hall; this last contains an image of Bodhidharma. The temple contains several stelae (bei) that date to the Tang and Yuan (1279–1368) periods, including the famous Taizong stele of AD 728. West of the temple is the Ta lin (Stupa Forest), where stupas contain the remains of deceased abbots. Behind the main compound is the memorial hall for the Second Patriarch, Huike (c. AD 485–555), and in the hills behind the temple is a cave in which Bodhidharma is said to have meditated. In later times the temple has been associated with the practice of martial arts, said to have been introduced by Bodhidharma, though this is largely based on legend.

At the foot of Jicui Peak is the Huishan Temple, the largest Buddhist temple on Mt Song after the Shaolin Temple, said to have been originally the summer residence of Emperor Xiaowendi. During the Tang period the temple housed a well-known ordination platform (lütan). A number of brick tomb-pagodas date from the 8th century AD. Among these is that of the two Chan monks Daoan (or Huian, c. AD 581–708) and Jingcang (AD 675–746) in the form of a small octagonal tower with a vaulted entrance and false doors and windows. Two other brick pagodas date to AD 970 and 1185. The buildings in the temple compound date to the Ming period.

The Yongtai Temple was originally founded in the Northern Wei, but during the Buddhist persecution under Emperor Wudi (reg AD 561–77) of the Northern Zhou (557–81) it was completely destroyed. Rebuilt under the emperor Wendi (581–604) of the Sui dynasty (581–618), it was later abandoned. According to tradition, the temple was reopened at the behest of the princess Yongtai at the beginning of the 8th century. It features several stelae with religious and historical inscriptions, including one from AD 752 with an inscription by the monk Jingzhang; two square, brick pagodas are located behind the compound. The Wanfo (Ten Thousand Buddhas) Hall is made of large, square bricks, on each of which is depicted the image of a Buddha.

Beilu Temple is a small temple dating from the mid-6th century AD. Located east of Dengfeng City, the county seat, it has a large stele with carvings of Buddhist images and dragons.

BIBLIOGRAPHY
Tokiwa Daijo and Sekino Tadasu: Shina bukkyō shiseki [Buddhist monuments in China], ii (Tokyo, 1930), pp. 111–42
L. Sickman and A. Soper: The Art and Architecture of China (Harmondsworth, 1956, rev. 3/1971), pp. 391–2, 407–8
Gu Tiefu: 'Tang Fandan Chanshi ta' [The stupa of the Chan master Fandan of the Tang period], Wenwu (1963), no. 3, pp. 50–52
Chūgoku bukkyō no ryo [A tour of Chinese Buddhism], iii (Kyoto, 1980), pp. 77–93
Sosan haito shiryō [Bowing at the stupas at the patriarchs' mountain] (Kyoto, 1981), pp. 26–41
Luoyang (Luoyang, 1990), pp. 88–93
Tonami Mamoru: The Shaolin Monastery Stele on Mount Song, Italian School of East Asian Studies, epigraphical ser., i (Kyoto, 1990)

HENRIK H. SØRENSEN

Deng Shiru [Teng Shih-ju; zi Wanbai] (b Huaining, Anhui Province, 1743; d 1805). Chinese calligrapher and seal-carver. He is generally recognized as the founder of the stele studies (beixue) movement, which sought inspiration from the stelae of the Northern Wei period (AD 386–534; see CHINA, §IV, 2(vii)(a)). He is also considered the founder of the so-called Deng school of seal-carving. Deng spent most of his adult life as the guest of wealthy patrons, and supported himself at other times by selling his calligraphy and seals. His earliest and longest sojourn was with Mei Liu (zi Shijun) and lasted for eight years. Mei had an extensive collection of original bronze and stone objects and rubbings of stelae from the Qin to the Three Kingdoms period (221 BC–AD 280). Deng familiarized himself with these through painstaking imitation: he is said to have devoted six months to copying the earliest dictionary, the Dictionary of Words and Phrases (Shuowen jiezi; AD 120), 20 times before he was satisfied. His assiduous copying of scores of early stelae models produced one of the most distinctive hands in the history of Chinese calligraphy.

Deng's interest in early inscriptions is evident in his Four Styles Album (Siti tie; Tokyo, N. Mus.; see CHINA, fig. 104). His decision to base his calligraphy on early styles ran counter to the practice of the time, which was to look to more recent models, such as the works of Dong Qichang. The significance of early writing had been recognized since the early Qing period (1644–1912) and used in etymology and to reinterpret the classics. Deng was influenced by the freedom of character formation in the early stelae, in which scripts had not yet become codified. After centuries of separate and standardized scripts, he took brush movements that had been restricted to one script and applied them to others. Despite this revolutionary approach, he still sought to express traditional concepts of restraint and beauty in his calligraphy: the subtle, off-balance placement of his strokes displays a profound fluidity and power.

Deng was not acknowledged by the leading circle of calligraphers around Weng Fanggang (1733–1818) in Beijing. He became famous only after he was discovered by the art historian and calligrapher Bao Shichen in 1803, only two years before Deng's death. Bao praised Deng as the greatest seal-script (zhuanshu) calligrapher of the period in his famous treatise, Oars of the Boat of Art (Yizhou shuangji; preface 1829). Deng was skilled in all the scripts, but was particularly talented in seal script and clerical script (*lishu*); these became the popular scripts of the 19th century, supplanting cursive script (*caoshu*) and running script (*xingshu*). His incorporation of brush-strokes from one script into others led to the deliberate awkwardness of ZHAO ZHIQIAN in the late Qing (1644–1911) and culminated in modern minimalist calligraphy.

BIBLIOGRAPHY

Shimonaka K., ed.: *Shodō zenshū* [Complete collection of calligraphy], xxiv (Tokyo, 2/1961), pp. 146–7, 170, pls 16–21

Traces of the Brush: Studies in Chinese Calligraphy (exh. cat. by Shen Fu and others, New Haven, CT, Yale U. A.G.; Berkeley, U. CA, A. Mus.; 1977)

Yu Jianhua: *Zhongguo meishujia renming cidian* [Dictionary of Chinese artists] (Shanghai, 1981), p. 181

ELIZABETH F. BENNETT

Denia, Marqués de. *See* SANDOVAL Y ROJAS, (1).

Denis, Maurice (*b* Granville, 25 Nov 1870; *d* Paris, 13 Nov 1943). French painter, designer, printmaker and theorist. Although born in Normandy, Denis lived throughout his life in Saint-Germain-en-Laye, just west of Paris. He attended the Lycée Condorcet, Paris, where he met many of his future artistic contemporaries, then studied art simultaneously at the Ecole des Beaux-Arts and at the Académie Julian (1888–90). Through fellow student Paul Sérusier, in 1888 he learnt of the innovative stylistic discoveries made that summer in Pont-Aven by Paul Gauguin and Emile Bernard. With Sérusier and a number of like-minded contemporaries at the Académie Julian—Pierre Bonnard, Paul Ranson, Henri-Gabriel Ibels and others—Denis found himself fundamentally opposed to the naturalism recommended by his academic teachers. They formed the NABIS, a secret artistic brotherhood dedicated to a form of pictorial Symbolism based loosely on the synthetic innovations of Gauguin and Bernard. Denis's first article, 'Définition du néo-traditionnisme', published in *Art et critique* in 1890 (and republished in *Théories*), served almost as a group manifesto and gave a theoretical justification for the practical and technical innovations of the Pont-Aven school. With its opening statement, 'It is well to remember that a picture, before being a battle horse, a nude woman, or some anecdote, is essentially a flat surface covered with colours assembled in a certain order' (frequently quoted out of context), Denis contributed to the development of a formalist, modernist aesthetic in the 20th century. The bold experiments in flat paint application and anti-naturalistic colour that characterized his early Nabi work seemed to prefigure later abstract initiatives. Both as an artist and as a theorist, however, Denis retreated from the radical position he had adopted as a student in 1890. He had never denied the

Maurice Denis: *Homage to Cézanne*, oil on canvas, 1.80×2.40 m, 1900 (Paris, Musée d'Orsay)

importance of subject-matter, and in his later painting he devoted himself to the revival of religious imagery.

Denis's career as a painter was industrious and prolific. Exhibiting regularly with the Symbolists and Neo-Impressionists throughout the 1890s, notably at the gallery of Louis Le Barc de Boutteville, he was quick to gain a reputation and following, at first among a restricted artistic and literary élite but later in wider Roman Catholic, official and international circles. Coming from modest circumstances and eventually having a sizeable family of his own to support—eight children resulting from two marriages—Denis depended upon artistic success to earn his living, unlike wealthier friends such as Bonnard or Sérusier. He mainly drew his subject-matter from his immediate surroundings, making frequent use of members of his family as models for his figure compositions, many of which have a Catholic theme. Apart from regular summer visits to Perros-Guirec in Brittany (he bought a villa, Le Silencio, there in 1908), Denis travelled to Italy, in particular to Florence, where he made a special study of the work of Fra Angelico.

Denis's early works were especially admired by the generation of Symbolist critics who came to the fore at the end of the 1880s. His modern-day annunciation, *Catholic Mystery* (1889; Switzerland, Mme M. Poncet priv. col.), was so well liked that he subsequently painted a number of variants, experimenting with the Divisionist technique (1891; Otterlo, Kröller-Müller). Such works offered a new mystic interpretation of traditional Catholic subject-matter, using pastel colour harmonies and flattened, simplified forms inspired by Puvis de Chavannes and Italian 15th-century frescoes. His successes brought him in touch with a cultured literary circle. Between 1892 and 1893 he was commissioned to produce lithograph illustrations for the vocal score of Claude Debussy's *La Damoiselle élue* and for André Gide's Symbolist tale *Le Voyage d'Urien.*

Denis's experiments with small-scale, flat and Synthetic work in the early 1890s, often in oil on cardboard, gave way to more traditional working methods. He prepared himself carefully, with figure drawings, oil sketches and cartoons, for the more complex decorative projects he undertook from *c.* 1900 onwards. Cultivating the dry, matt surface of fresco and generally favouring a muted Symbolist palette of pastel blues, pinks, greys and mauves, Denis never lost his youthful love of the decorative arabesque. His best-known easel painting, *Homage to Cézanne* (1900; Paris, Mus. d'Orsay; see fig.), reminiscent of Fantin-Latour's group portrait manifestos of the 1860s and 1870s, represents a shift in his artistic admirations, a turning away from the more spectacular, subjective Symbolism of Gauguin and van Gogh towards what he saw as the reassertion of classical values in Cézanne. In 1898 a visit to Rome with Gide had awakened his interest in classicism. In articles such as 'Cézanne' in 1907 and 'De Gauguin et de Van Gogh au classicisme' in 1909 (both reprinted in *Théories*) Denis disseminated the view that classicism was the essence of the French cultural tradition, a view that had considerable influence on a younger generation of artists in France and elsewhere.

In the wake of his first important private decorative commission in 1897 for the Paris hôtel of Baron Denys

Cochin, the *Legend of St Hubert* (Paris, Denys Cochin priv. col.), Denis was kept busy by a succession of decorative projects for religious and secular settings, notable among them being the enormous decorative scheme on the theme of the *History of Music* for the Théâtre des Champs-Elysées (1912–13; *in situ*) and the *History of the French Arts* for the cupola of the Petit Palais (1924–5; *in situ*).

In the 20th century Denis exhibited regularly both at the Salon de la Société Nationale and at the Salon des Indépendants. His friendships and occasional working collaborations with other Nabis sustained the group's life well after it had ceased to meet formally, and although his commitments to the revival of religious art and to such reactionary and nationalistic movements as *L'Action française* set him apart from them, his intelligence as a critic and theorist made him the effective and respected spokesman of his artistic generation. In 1919 he established the Ateliers d'Art Sacré with the artist Georges-Olivier Desvallières, a venture dedicated to the sound formation of young artists in the variety of methods and media required for modern religious decoration. His restoration of the 17th-century priory in Saint-Germain-en-Laye, which he was able to buy in 1914, involved him in the full range of decorative work implied within the original scope of the Nabi movement, studies for fresco and stained glass as well as designs for church furniture and ornaments. In 1980 the priory was established as the Musée Départemental du Prieuré, devoted to the works of Maurice Denis and the Nabis.

WRITINGS

L. Rouart and J. Watelin, eds: *Théories (1890–1910): Du symbolisme et de Gauguin vers un nouvel ordre classique* (Paris, 1912) [incl. 'Définition du néo-traditionnisme', pp. 1–13; 'Cézanne', pp. 245–61; 'De Gauguin et de Van Gogh au classicisme', pp. 262–78]
——: *Nouvelles théories, sur l'art moderne, sur l'art sacré (1914–21)* (Paris, 1922)
Journal (1884–1943), 3 vols (Paris, 1957–9)
O. Revault d'Alonnes, ed.: *Du symbolisme au classicisme: Théories* (Paris, 1964)

BIBLIOGRAPHY

S. Barazetti-Demoulin: *Maurice Denis* (Paris, 1945)
P. Cailler: *Catalogue raisonné de l'oeuvre gravé et lithographié de Maurice Denis* (Geneva, 1968)
Maurice Denis (exh. cat., Paris, Mus. Orangerie, 1970)
Maurice Denis: Gemälde, Handzeichnungen, Druckgraphik (exh. cat., ed. G. Gerkens, J. Schultze and A. Winther; Bremen, Ksthalle, 1971)
Maurice Denis et la Bretagne (exh. cat., Morlaix, Mus., 1985)
D. M. Denis and others: *Maurice Denis: Catalogue raisonné de l'oeuvre peint* (Saint-Germain-en-Laye, Mus. Dépt Prieuré, in preparation)

BELINDA THOMSON

De Nittis, Giuseppe (*b* Barletta, Puglia, 25 Feb 1846; *d* Saint-Germain-en-Laye, nr Paris, 21 Aug 1884). Italian painter, pastellist and printmaker. Throughout his career he was committed to a *plein-air* aesthetic and was particularly interested in rendering varying light effects, a concern that brought him into contact with the Impressionists. He was also acquainted with the members of the Macchiaioli, for whom his work was influential. In addition to oils, he experimented with printmaking and made innovative use of pastels. Practising a restrained, and therefore 'acceptable', form of Impressionism, he achieved great success in his lifetime, both nationally and internationally.

1. Before 1873. 2. 1873–84.

1. BEFORE 1873. The grandchild of an architect, he received his earliest training in Barletta from Giovanni Battista Calò (?1832/3–1895), an artist known for his drawing ability. In 1860 De Nittis moved with his brother, Vincenzo De Nittis, to Naples, where he may have studied briefly with Vincenzo Dattoli (1831–99) in 1861. He attended the Istituto di Belle Arti di Napoli (Jan 1862 to June 1863), where he was rapidly advanced from the basic drawing class under Giuseppe Mancinelli (1813–75) to the Scuola di Paesaggio under Gabriele Smargiassi (1798–1882) and Teodoro Duclere (1815–69), but was expelled because of his rebelliousness against academic discipline and methods. He also attended Mancinelli's evening life classes.

De Nittis's early desire to approach nature directly attracted him to Marco De Gregorio (1829–76) and Federico Rossano (1835–1912), with whom he formed the Scuola di Resina. The group was greatly influenced by the Florentine Adriano Cecioni, a promoter of the Macchiaioli, with whom De Nittis formed a close friendship. During this time (1863–7) De Nittis spent long periods in the countryside around Naples and his native Barletta, developing a novel approach to landscape painting. *Rendezvous in the Woods of Portici* (1864; Viareggio, G. Matteucci priv. col., see 1990 exh. cat., p. 65), for example, is an original attempt to render the effect of sunlight filtering through trees in a manner that recalls certain works by Corot, whom De Nittis greatly admired. Its diagonal perspectival construction prefigures that found in De Nittis's later compositions.

Throughout his career De Nittis was fascinated by cloud effects, and this led to a number of studies (from at least 1864) in which he recorded the changing sky in a restricted palette of light and dark tonalities (e.g. *Approaching Storm*, 1868; Valdagno, G. Marzotto priv. col., see 1990 exh. cat., p. 72). In 1866 he received critical recognition at the Società Promotrice di Belle Arti 'Salvator Rosa' in Naples with *Farmhouse on the Outskirts of Naples* (1866, Naples, Capodimonte), which was bought by King Victor Emmanuel II. Organized in planes, this composition has its immediate precedents among the works of the Scuola di Posillipo and also shows a debt to the landscapes of Filippo Palizzi and Nicola Palizzi.

By the age of 21 De Nittis was an acclaimed painter not only in Naples but also nationally. In 1867 he went to Rome, Paris and Florence. In Paris he met Jean-Léon Gérôme and Jean-Louis-Ernest Meissonier, admiring the latter's work. De Nittis's sojourn in Florence was important for the Macchiaioli: *Crossing of the Appenines* (1867; Naples, Capodimonte; see fig. 1) was exhibited that season in both Florence and Naples (and was also purchased by King Victor Emmanuel II for the Pinacoteca di Capodimonte). It had an enormous effect on the group, especially on Telemaco Signorini, who became a close friend of De Nittis. Depicting a sombre village road in turbulent winter weather, it achieves its emotive impact by the tonal structuring of the composition in greys and browns that are veiled with subtle yellow–rose tones. Throughout his career De Nittis showed a great predilection for the motif of the road, whether it be the rustic roads of southern Italy, or railways or the bustling, elegant streets and squares of Paris and London.

In 1868 De Nittis settled permanently in Paris, having signed a contract with the dealer Reitingler, though he continued to spend time in Italy. For a brief period (1869–70) he executed genre scenes in 17th- and 18th-century Rococo dress in the manner of Meissonier and Mariano José Bernardo Fortuny y Marsal (e.g. *Visit to the Antique*

1. Giuseppe De Nittis: *Crossing of the Appenines*, oil on canvas, 410×760 mm, 1867 (Naples, Museo e Gallerie Nazionali di Capodimonte)

Dealer, exh. Salon 1869; Philadelphia, PA, J. G. Johnson priv. col., see Dini and Marini, ii, fig. 263), in order to meet the demands of the market. He also continued to paint landscapes and contemporary subjects, such as *Passing Train* (?1869; Barletta, Mus.-Pin. Com.), a strikingly modern work that uses misty atmospheric effects.

With the outbreak of the Franco–Prussian War in 1870, De Nittis went to Naples and Barletta, where he remained for most of the period until 1873. In these locations he painted wonderfully atmospheric seascapes and landscapes that established his reputation in Paris. The *Road between Brindisi and Barletta* (1871, New York, ex-Andersen priv. col., see 1990 exh. cat., p. 15), for example, is an image of a dusty road flooded with sunlight, and it received great acclaim at the Salon in Paris in 1872. Its blue–violet shadow presages certain elements of Impressionism. Though seemingly spontaneous, such landscapes were often based on numerous studies that were assembled and finished in the studio. From 1872 to 1874 he painted under an exclusive contract with the dealer Adolphe Goupil, and he was in Naples at the time of the eruption of Vesuvius. To meet the pressing demands of his dealer, he executed a number of picturesque views (e.g. *Rain of Ashes*, 1872; Florence, Pitti) that conformed to the more typical iconography of the *vedutisti*. Far more interesting and numerous (perhaps over 100) are the quickly-brushed little panels of unprimed wood, mostly entitled *Impressions of Vesuvius* (1872; Milan, Gal. A. Mod.) or *On the Slopes of Vesuvius*. Using broadly simplified geometric shapes and intense local colouring, they evocatively convey a sense of the primordial and monumental.

In 1873, probably inspired by Marcellin Desboutin and perhaps also by Degas, De Nittis experimented with printmaking, producing etchings, drypoints and a few lithographs. He used fine, short lines and tonal effects, so emphasizing the whiteness of the paper. In *Liliale* (etching; Rome, Gal. Stampe), for example, the white figure is defined by the grey tones of the delicately cross-hatched background and accentuated by the heavy, dark lines of the ribbon around her neck.

2. 1873–84. Having begun to adapt the motif of the road to the local urban setting in 1871, in 1873–4 De Nittis painted many views of Paris. In these he captured the spectacle of a modern city, often indulging in images of elegant women walking or riding or promenading children and dogs. Adopting a Naturalistic approach, he used complex and bold compositional structures, as in *How Cold it Is!* (1874; Milan, Eredi Jucker priv. col., see 1990 exh. cat., p. 101). The vivid sense of movement created by the figures in this work reflects De Nittis's habit of sketching and painting them in motion; here they are modelled, as usual, by his wife, Leontine Gruvelle. *How Cold it Is!* was enthusiastically received at the Salon of 1874, and the same year De Nittis participated in the First Impressionist Exhibition on the invitation of Degas. He exhibited five works (unidentified) but went to London before the opening. De Nittis had established good friendships with Degas, Manet, Caillebotte and Desboutin but was not welcomed by other Impressionists, particularly Renoir, who resented his success. His works were not hung until some days after the opening, a fact that may

explain his absence from all the other Impressionist exhibitions. One of his most highly impressionistic works of this period, *In the Fields around London* (*c.* 1874–9; Milan, priv. col., see 1990 exh. cat., p. 159), depicts women and children in a sunbathed poppy field, an image that parallels contemporary works by Monet and Renoir. De Nittis's thematic choices and concern with the expressive power of natural light reveal an affinity with the Impressionists, though he found their style somewhat unvaried and lacking in form. His own style reflects his great enthusiasm for the work of Manet and Degas.

Until 1882 De Nittis worked for several months of most years in London for an enthusiastic clientele, particularly the art dealer A. M. Marsden and the banker Kaye Knowles. His major patron, Knowles, commissioned him to paint ten views of London and two portraits. These included such scenes as *Piccadilly* (1875; Valdagno, G. Marzotto priv. col., see 1990 exh. cat., p. 111), an image of an animated street bustling with crowds of all classes, and they were greatly admired and made available in many versions. De Nittis established contacts with several artists in London, in particular with James Tissot, with whom he shared a great admiration for Whistler.

By the mid-1870s De Nittis enjoyed a wide international reputation. Under the influence of his socially ambitious wife, a writer, from 1876 his house became famous for its lively Saturday soirées, which were attended by artists, writers, critics and other prominent personalities. The last ten years of his life were intensely active, and he worked primarily *en plein air*. He had an awareness of photography and a growing interest in Japanese art, which is evident in his creation of unconventional compositions. In *Effects of Snow* (?1875; Barletta, Mus.-Pin. Com.), for example, he achieved a new type of pictorial effect by the use of a high viewpoint and bold contrasts between the off-centred, silhouetted figure and the vast greyish-white ground.

In 1875 De Nittis began to use pastel, because it permitted him to work quickly and boldly. Originally introduced to the medium by his first teacher, Calò, and perhaps inspired by the large exhibition and sale of Jean-François Millet's pastels (1875), De Nittis played a major role in reviving interest in this medium. He concentrated on exploring its expressive potential and raising it to the level of oil, for example in such large-scale portraits as the informal image of *Edmond de Goncourt* (1880–81; Paris, Acad. Goncourt) and other ambitious compositions. For these large pastels he used specially treated canvases and applied a fixative to the finished work. De Nittis also turned to watercolour painting in this period, an interest that was probably inspired by the popularity of the medium in England. Around 1876–7 he executed such jewel-like works as *Boulevard Haussmann* (exh. Salon 1877; Milan, C. Giussani priv. col., see 1990 exh. cat., p. 128), in which he created effects of light and movement using brilliant blotches of colour.

The Exposition Universelle in Paris in 1878 was a real triumph for De Nittis, who exhibited 12 paintings there. He was awarded a gold medal and soon after received the Légion d'honneur. Among the paintings shown was *Westminster* (1878; Valdagno, G. Marzotto priv. col., see 1990 exh. cat., p. 141), one of his largest and most accomplished images of London. The Whistler-like, indistinct river and

2. Giuseppe De Nittis: *La Place du Carrousel: Ruins of the Tuileries in 1882*, 1882 (Paris, Musée d'Orsay)

horizontal row of buildings across the background are dramatically contrasted with the bold, diagonal thrust of the bridge with its clearly defined figures. This painting led to figureless and more abstract versions.

It was in his pastels that De Nittis's pictorial expression became more audacious and that he worked in larger dimensions than his oils. A major exhibition of 18 large-scale pastels at the Cercle des Mirlitons in Paris in 1881 included a monumental triptych entitled *Races at Auteuil* (1881; Rome, G.N.A. Mod.). In this De Nittis elevated a theme of contemporary bourgeois entertainment into an altarpiece format using a modern, asymmetrical structure derived from photography and Japanese prints. In such other pastels as *Yard* (Barletta, Mus.-Pin. Com.) he transformed an industrial scene into an evocative study of the harmony of luminescent tones, and its abstract, almost gestural, quality testifies to its startling modernity.

The greater expressive freedom that De Nittis achieved in his pastels resulted in the broader impressionistic manner that characterizes the oils of his last years. Typical of these is the exquisite *On the Lake of the Four Cantons* (1881; Montecatini Terme, Piero Dini priv. col., see 1990 exh. cat., p. 109), depicting his wife on a boat during their trip to Switzerland. Bearing a stylistic affinity with Manet's work, this poetic scene is a beautifully harmonized study of the subtle contrasts between interior and exterior illumination. About 1882–3 De Nittis also explored the

effects of artificial illumination in a number of interior scenes.

In 1882, with gallery owner Georges Petit and the painters Raimundo Madrazo y Garreta and Alfred Stevens (i), De Nittis founded and organized the Exposition Internationale de Peinture to assist and promote foreign artists in Paris. In 1883 the French government purchased *La Place du Carrousel: Ruins of the Tuileries in 1882* (1882; see fig. 2) for the Musée du Luxembourg, the first time a contemporary Italian painting had been bought for a Parisian museum.

De Nittis's last works were exhibited at the Salon a few months before his death and included broadly impressionistic interpretations of his road-and-sky motif and *Luncheon in the Garden* (1884; Barletta, Mus.-Pin. Com.). Like the two other unfinished variants, this latter image portrays his wife and son in the garden. De Nittis recorded the colour effects of subtle, reflected light and bright sunlight on white using a light palette of luminous greens and rich nuances of whites. In the light-drenched zone the forms are dissolved into patterns of colour, the whole creating a striking last statement.

A *plein-air* painter of light and atmosphere, De Nittis was viewed by contemporary critics and public as an Impressionist, but as an 'acceptable' one. His attitude and style, though novel and modern, were never quite as extreme as those of other avant-garde contemporaries. In different ways he influenced many painters, including his compatriots Signorini and Lorenzo Delleani and the Englishman Atkinson Grimshaw as well as his friend Caillebotte and the Americans Childe Hassam and William Merritt Chase. After his death his wife donated his library, papers and the 234 works (paintings, studies, prints, drawings and photographs) left in his studio to the city of Barletta, where they are now held in the Museo-Pinacoteca Comunale.

WRITINGS

Notes et souvenirs du peintre Joseph [sic] de Nittis [ed. L. Gruvelle] (Paris, 1895)
Notes et souvenirs: Diario, 1870–1884, ed. E. Cecchi (Fasano di Puglia, 1990)

BIBLIOGRAPHY

DBI
J. Claretie: 'J. de Nittis', *L'Art et les artistes français contemporains* (Paris, 1876), pp. 397–416
D. Martelli: 'Giuseppe De Nittis' (1884), in *Scritti d'arte di Diego Martelli*, ed. A. Boschetto (Florence, 1952), pp. 124–30
V. Pica: *Giuseppe De Nittis: L'uomo e l'artista* (Milan, 1914)
L. Benedite: *De Nittis* (Paris, 1926)
A. Petrucci: 'Incisioni di G. De Nittis', *Emporium*, lxxix (May 1934), pp. 280–85
M. Pittaluga and E. Piceni: *De Nittis* (Milan, 1963)
E. Piceni and M. Monteverdi: *I De Nittis di Barletta* (Barletta, 1971)
R. Causa: *Giuseppe De Nittis* (Bari, 1975)
E. Piceni: *De Nittis: L'uomo e l'opera* (Busto Arsizio, 1979)
——: *De Nittis* (Busto Arsizio, 1982)
A. Paolillo: *La galleria De Nittis di Barletta* (Brindisi, 1984)
Three Italian Friends of the Impressionists: Boldini, De Nittis, Zandomeneghi (exh. cat. by E. Piceni, New York, Stair Sainty Matthiesen, 1984)
Il secondo '800 italiano: Le poetiche del vero (exh. cat., ed. R. Barilli; Milan, Pal. Reale, 1988)
P. Dini and G. L. Marini: *Giuseppe De Nittis: La vita, i documenti, le opere dipinte*, 2 vols (Turin, 1990)
G. Lamacchia: *Giuseppe De Nittis capolista degli impressionisti* (Florence, 1990)
Giuseppe De Nittis: Dipinti, 1864–1884 (exh. cat. by R. Monti and others, Milan, Pal. Permanente; Bari, Pin. Prov.; 1990)
R. Mascolo: *I De Nittis di Barletta* (Turin, 1992)

EFREM GISELLA CALINGAERT

Denmark, Kingdom of [Danmark]. Country in northern Europe. Lying between the North Sea on the west and the Baltic Sea on the east, it is separated from Norway in the north by the Skagerrak Strait and from Sweden in the east by the Kattegat Strait and the Øresund. The country consists of the western peninsula of Jutland, which borders Germany to the south and constitutes *c.* 70% of the land mass, and *c.* 450 islands, of which the largest are Fyn (Funen) and Zealand (Sjaelland). The capital, Copenhagen, lies on the east coast of the latter (see fig. 1). The land is mostly flat or undulating and highly cultivated. Of the population of over 5 million, *c.* 84% live in the urban centres. Denmark constitutes a connecting link between the European mainland and northern Scandinavia. This has had a marked effect on the country's culture, which has been influenced from many sides, often through maritime contacts. As Denmark ruled over much of Scandinavia after the 9th century, a common Nordic culture developed. This article covers the art produced in Denmark from the establishment of a kingdom covering the present-day area. For a discussion of the art produced by the peoples of Scandinavia during the 9th to 11th centuries *see* VIKING ART. Although under Danish protection, the FAROE ISLANDS and GREENLAND are self-governing units and are treated separately in this dictionary.

I. Introduction. II. Architecture. III. Painting and graphic arts. IV. Sculpture. V. Interior decoration. VI. Furniture. VII. Ceramics. VIII. Glass. IX. Metalwork. X. Objects of vertu. XI. Textiles. XII. Vernacular arts. XIII. Patronage. XIV. Collecting and dealing. XV. Museums. XVI. Art education. XVII. Art libraries and photographic collections. XVIII. Historiography.

I. Introduction.

Remains from the prehistoric period have been found in Denmark, and items dating from the beginning of the 1st century AD show that Roman culture came to Denmark via mercenaries and trade, but *c.* AD 400 Germanic influence was dominant. When the Viking expeditions began in 800, Denmark became powerful in the territories of the North and Baltic Seas, with political, economic and cultural consequences. A lengthy period of expansion began, the Danelaw in England was surrendered, and southern Sweden became part of the realm. Ansgar introduced Christian missionary activity in Denmark in 826–9, and the Greater Jelling Stone, liberally embellished with Irish and other Celtic decorations, has a runic inscription stating that Denmark was Christianized *c.* 960 under Harald I Bluetooth (*reg c.* 950–85). The idioms of the Catholic Church were introduced, and despite decreases in the national wealth, both in the 12th century due to wars and in the 14th century due to famine and plague, the majority of Danish churches were erected in the Middle Ages, the oldest stone churches dating from 1050 to 1125; bricks made of fired clay became the predominant building material from the time of the Valdemar kings (1157–1241). Church building and interior decoration provided the basis for artistic activity and patronage.

Under the rule of Margaret I (*reg* 1387–1412), Denmark was united with Norway (including the Faroes, Iceland and Greenland) and Sweden (with Finland) in the Kalmar Union in 1397. The joint realm with Sweden lasted until 1523, with Norway until 1814 and with Iceland until 1943. The Reformation took place in 1536, and an economic boom brought in its wake abundant secular building activity and decoration, drawing inspiration from the Renaissance, particularly in the Netherlands, and culminating in the royal castles of Kronborg and Frederiksborg. Political rivalry between Denmark and Sweden led to wars, and during the period 1600–1800 Denmark lost its position of power. After the Karl X Gustav wars (1657–60), southern Sweden was relinquished, and booty, including works of art, was removed to Sweden.

In 1660 an absolute monarchy was established, and only then did southern European ideals prevail, with Baroque architecture and visual arts in their different phases: Italian Baroque under Frederick IV (*reg* 1699–1730); and German Baroque and French Rococo, gravitating towards Neo-classicism after the middle of the 18th century, under Christian VI (*reg* 1730–46). The Napoleonic Wars led to impoverishment in Denmark due to the French alliance, and the State became bankrupt in 1813; Norway was relinquished to Sweden in 1814. During the 19th century, however, important Danish artists and architects such as C. F. Hansen and Bertel Thorvaldsen rose to prominence.

The demand for a 'national art' became more acute

1. Map of Denmark; those sites with separate entries in this dictionary are distinguished by Cross-reference type.

after the Schleswig wars of the mid-19th century with the loss of southern Jutland, and in 1849 the absolute monarchy was undramatically abolished. A change of the system of governments, following the acknowledgement of Cabinet responsibility, took place in 1901, which created a climate for architectural and other innovations. Denmark remained neutral during World War I, following which North Schleswig was regained from Germany. Numerous social reforms were introduced, leading to a comprehensive welfare state and again fostering artistic innovations. During World War II Denmark was occupied by Germany. Although still part of Scandinavia, Denmark strengthened its links with the rest of Europe by joining the European Community in 1973.

BIBLIOGRAPHY

L. Bobe, ed.: *Rom og Danmark gennem tiderne* [Rome and Denmark through the ages], 3 vols (Copenhagen, 1935–42)

F. von Jessen, ed.: *Danske i Paris gennem tiderne* [Danes in Paris through the ages], I–II, 1 (Copenhagen, 1936–8)

P. Lauring: *A History of the Kingdom of Denmark* (Copenhagen, 1960, rev. London, 3/1968)

——: *Geschichte Dänemarks* (Neumünster, 1964)

A. Andersson and P. Anker: *L'Art scandinave*, 2 vols (Paris, 1968; Eng. trans., London, 1970)

J. Danstrup and H. Koch, eds: *Danmarks historie*, 5 vols (Copenhagen, 1969–72)

W. G. Jones: *Denmark* (London, 1970)

S. Oakley: *The Story of Denmark* (London, 1972)

GRETHE KUSK

II. Architecture.

1. Before 1540. 2. 1540–1840. 3. After 1840.

1. BEFORE 1540.

(i) Viking era. With the exception of prehistoric tombs, the beginnings of a more monumental architecture were closely connected with the unification of the realm and the introduction of Christianity during the reign of Harald I Bluetooth (*reg c.* 950–85). The most interesting buildings from the late Viking age are four ring-camps, which have all been excavated: Aggersborg, Fyrkat (Jutland), Nonnebakken (Fyn) and Trelleborg (Sjaelland). The dimensions of the camps vary, but the ground-plans are identical: a circular rampart with four gates positioned to the north, south, east and west and connected to a grid street plan, with accommodation barracks built around quadrangles. The largest camp was Aggersborg, with an inner diameter of 240 m and 48 houses in 12 barrack blocks. Dendrochronological dating of the timber and earth buildings to *c.* 980 strengthens the theory that the fortresses formed part of Harald I's unification programme.

Archaeological investigations and a few partly preserved monuments have shown that the period's architecture is primarily represented by the construction of churches. Those that resulted from Ansgar's mission (826–9) were confined to the southern part of Jutland, but church building was boosted by Harald's baptism in Jelling (*c.* 960). By 1060 the country was divided into eight new dioceses. Scania (now Skåne, Sweden) had 300 churches, Zealand 150 and Fyn 100; the number was presumably higher in Jutland. The oldest churches (11th century), of which none remains, were built of timber. From excavations a picture emerges of single-aisle churches comprising chancel and nave with wattle-and-daub walls and a roof structure supported by freestanding poles. In cases where several wooden churches replaced one another on the same site (e.g. in Jelling three churches preceded the preserved stone church of *c.* 1100), gradual technical improvements occurred including the replacement of earth-clad timber with stone foundations. Parts of the timber churches (e.g. lintels) were often reused in stone churches. One famous such relic is the plank (dated 1066) from Hørning (Copenhagen, Nmus.).

In the 12th century a great increase in the use of stone occurred, although often in stages, which explains the appearance of timber and stone together in some churches. Stone churches represented a technical revolution and also linked Denmark to mainstream European architecture, with the initiative being taken by the Crown and the Church. It is believed that Harald I Bluetooth's wooden memorial church in Roskilde (a predecessor of the cathedral; *see* ROSKILDE, §1) was replaced in 1026 by a stone building, although the remains of this have not been established with certainty. Little remains of those stone churches that can be dated accurately to the 11th century. Major parts remain of the walls of Helligkorskirken in Dalby, Scania (begun 1060–70 as a cathedral), and of Bishop Svend Normand's Vor Frue, Roskilde; the latter was built of calcareous tufa, which, together with Scanian quarrystone, appears to have been used consistently for the oldest stone churches.

Stone buildings varied greatly in type: there were both single-aisle churches and basilicas, occasionally enriched with a crypt (e.g. Århus), apses, transept and towers. The new buildings must for some time have been designed by foreign experts, and stylistically they show a dependence on Germany. Details in Dalby point directly to St Michael's, Hildesheim and the tower of Roskilde Cathedral. Elsewhere English influence reflects the North Sea empire of Knut IV (*reg* 1080–86): English details (e.g. roll-billets, columns with spiral thongs) adorn the Benedictine abbey church in Venge (early 12th century). This single-aisle church with apses, two-storey annexes and west tower is the best-preserved early medieval monastery in Europe. For further discussion of Viking architecture *see* VIKING ART, §III.

(ii) Romanesque. In the 12th century and the early 13th, there was a general European boom, characterized by increased ties with France. In monumental building programmes, the transition from timber to stone was probably completed during the 12th century. Apart from the Swedish provinces the country was mostly poor in stone suitable for building; calcareous tufa deposits were soon depleted, and underground chalk was found only in a few locations. But the Ice Age had left abundant boulders; on Zealand these were supplemented with softer stone types and used for heterogeneous masonry covered with stucco. Elsewhere, particularly in Jutland, boulders for use on façades were fashioned into rectangular ashlars and were sometimes used for decorative sculpture around portals, doors and windows. Although in some areas such as Ribe volcanic tufa and sandstone were imported from the Rhine region, in general materials were a problem for large building projects. The introduction of bricks by Valdemar the Great (*reg* 1157–82) in his modernization of the southern border's defence wall, the Dannevirke, provided a solution. Brick architecture may have been introduced with assistance from Lombardy, effected via the monastic orders' international contacts. Architecturally the new building method was influenced by contact with France.

In church construction, brick building gained prominence in the latter part of the 12th century; by the end of the century it was dominant in major building projects. The most prestigious building projects were cathedrals, the renovation of which was to span several generations. Asser, the primate of the new ecclesiastical province in Lund, decided to replace the cathedral with a basilica (completed *c.* 1160; *see* LUND, §1(i)) of sandstone with twin-tower façade and hall crypt. Its closest parallels are

2. Tømmerby Church, Thy, Jutland, 12th century; porch and tower *c.* 1500

in the upper Rhineland, where north Italian masons also left their mark on sculptural decoration.

The renovation of Jutland's cathedrals from 1150 was predominantly German-inspired, especially at Ribe Cathedral (*c.* 1150–1250; *see* RIBE, §1), which has its roots in the Rhine-Meuse area both architecturally (e.g. the centralized choir and west façade with tower) and decoratively (in the division of pilaster strips and capital shapes). The chief monument among granite churches, Viborg Cathedral, is similarly inspired, while the later cathedrals in Børglum and Århus show their dependence on the building programme of the orders. The early replacement (*c.* 1175) of Bishop Normand's cathedral in Roskilde with a brick structure reflects the detailed knowledge of northern French cathedral plans (e.g. Tournai) on the part of masons and patrons and is an isolated attempt at appropriating the newest European ideals.

The period was also characterized by tremendous growth in the monastic orders, encouraged by Archbishop Eskil, but the destruction brought by the Reformation (1536) makes it difficult to assess the importance of the architecture of the monastic orders as a gateway for new ideas and techniques. Especially lamentable was the loss of a series of large abbeys complete with conventual buildings. Excavations of the ruins of Cistercian abbeys at Esrom (Zealand), Vitskøl and Øm (both Jutland) indicate the importance of these building complexes. Three abbey churches on Zealand have been preserved (Ringsted, Sorø

and Skovkloster, now Herlufsholm School, near Næstved). Ringsted and Sorø were begun in the latter part of the 12th century and were brick-built.

The strongest evidence of the Valdemar period's hectic building activity and the popular appropriation of aesthetic ideals from the Romanesque period is in the parish churches. More than 1500 churches from this period have been preserved. Only a handful are dated precisely (e.g. Gjellerup Church, Jutland, 1140). Most are modest single-aisle churches comprising chancel and nave and distinguished from their early Romanesque predecessors only by the wall treatment and occasional sculptural decoration. The chancel sometimes has an apse, and occasionally a tower has been added, the shape of which varies considerably from broad westworks (e.g. Notmark, Als) to small, elegant twin towers above the tribune of the west end (e.g. Tveje Merløse, Zealand). The main spaces were, with a few exceptions, covered with flat timber roofs and lit by small round-arched windows. Tømmerby Church (12th century; see fig. 2) in Thy, built of granite ashlars, comprised an apse, chancel and nave; a porch and tower were added later (*c.* 1500).

Among parish churches, few are centralized buildings. The four round churches on the island of Bornholm have circular, vaulted naves, providing one or two upper storeys that could be organized for defence. Similar churches are found on Øland and the coastal areas around Kalmar; most were converted during the 13th century to cope with the strife and piracy in this area of the Baltic. Centralized church buildings of a different kind are found in, among other places, Bjernede, Zealand (begun before 1186). The circular nave is in two storeys divided by four columns that support vaults in the lower storey, while the four pillars in the attic-like upper storey support a small tower. This type was fairly widespread on Zealand (e.g. Hørve) and also occurs in Scania, Fyn and Jutland. The patron was the king or a prominent nobleman, and these churches should therefore be considered more as a local variation on manor churches of central European inspiration (e.g. St Michael's, Helsingborg), combined with notions of sacred tomb churches (e.g. St Michael's, Schleswig) and the German variant of the two-storey church. The most remarkable centralized church is Vor Frue, Kalundborg, a five-tower building on a cross-plan (see ROMANESQUE, fig. 21), traditionally dated to 1170–90 but more likely erected c. 1225.

Secular buildings of this period have been either demolished or radically rebuilt, and new information is therefore primarily obtained through excavation. The majority of dwellings (presumably of earth and timber) have disappeared; only those in positions of power were built in stone. The castle did not gain a foothold until the 12th century, when it was fully developed in Europe. Examples include the ruin of a huge mid-12th-century tower in calcareous tufa in Bastrup, north Zealand, and Archbishop Eskil's slightly later brick castle on an islet in Søborg Lake. This ring-wall construction comprised a tower, accommodation and a chapel, all modelled on a German imperial palace. Valdemar the Great's strategically positioned castles of Vordingborg, at the assembly point of the fleet, and Helsingborg (both destr.), by the Øresund crossing, were ring-wall constructions with chapels. There were also private castles, financed by the King's noble allies and by his foster brothers Absalon and Esbern Snare, who built castles respectively at Havn (Copenhagen) and Kalundborg. Relics from both castles, including the ring-wall around Havn from 1167, were unearthed under Christiansborg Palace (1732). Parts of a brick-walled residence, whose trifoliate windows repeat the pattern from the cathedral, have been preserved from the Roskilde bishop's castle, Dragsholm.

(iii) Gothic. The century following the death of Valdemar II (*reg* 1202–41) was marked by unrest and decline. The receptiveness to European trends gradually gave way to a more distinct provincialism, emanating from the brick architecture of the prosperous Hanseatic cities of northern Germany and the Baltic coast. The most important building areas were the new market towns, although ecclesiastical patronage continued. Gothic styles now began to be more generally acceptable in church architecture, which is seen in the renovation (c. 1250) of the great Romanesque cathedrals and abbey churches (Ribe, Lund, Ringsted and Sorø) with pointed arches and groin vaults. The new style's emphasis on light and the dissolution of wall masses into an organic system of supporting and supported elements is best seen in the late 13th-century conversion of St Canute (Knud), Odense, started under Bishop Gisico (1285–1301). Important examples of the influence of north German brick architecture and its adaptation of the Gothic

cathedral plan (ambulatory with radiating chapels, flying buttresses and pseudo transept) are the sister churches St Peter, Malmø, and Vor Frue, Copenhagen; both were begun in the 1310s and symbolize the prosperity of cities along the Øresund, which attracted merchants from all over Europe. Such examples were, however, relatively isolated.

The churches built by the mendicant friars were for ideological reasons stylistically quite different. They were erected as simple naves, at times only vaulted in the chancel. Both the Franciscans and the Dominicans came to Denmark in the 1210s, and their oldest preserved churches date from the mid-13th century. Renovations and extensions took place during the 14th and 15th centuries, and extant examples include the former Franciscan church in Ystad, Scania, and the Dominican St Catherine, Ribe.

The hall church and the pseudo-basilica were also common types. The hall church, with three aisles of equal height, appears in the conversion of Haderslev (1260s). In the 15th century the plan was used by the Nordic conventual order, the Bridgetines, whose church (the present cathedral) in Maribo influenced the hall chancel in the conversion (late 15th century) of the Romanesque brick cathedral in Århus. Its 12 tall windows effectively illustrate the Gothic principle of light. The pseudo-basilica plan, with its slightly raised nave and no clerestory, appeared in the 13th century and was used in 14th-century conversions in Zealand market towns (e.g. St Peter's, Næstved), where the windowless nave is an effective contrast to the light-filled polygonal chancels. This Germanic trend characterized several minor 15th-century market town churches (e.g. Middelfart). In some cases a hall church approached the basilica type through the insertion of modest windows in the nave (e.g. St Olai, Helsingør), while the well-preserved Carmelite abbey church in Helsingør (from c. 1450) varied the plan by having all three aisles under one roof.

Extensions, such as porches, sacristies, towers and chapels, were also common. Roskilde Cathedral was surrounded by a ring of extensions that include fine examples of exterior brick architecture, with gable recesses and pinnacles. New towers became status symbols and landmarks for market towns. The big tower beside Ribe Cathedral was exceptional for belonging partly to the town, despite its position; a brick colossus, it was erected between 1283 and 1333 as a counterpart to a Flemish bell-tower. Conversion and extension were also the fate of the many Romanesque village churches, particularly in eastern Denmark; vaults replaced wooden ceilings, and both chancel and nave were often extended. A ring of extensions around the central core testified to the ability of local masons to vary the recess architecture of Gothic brick building; gradual alteration during the Middle Ages led to the archetypal Danish village church. In rare cases the original church was altered to the hall church plan (e.g. Helsinge, west Zealand); late Middle Age pilgrimages occasionally resulted in conversions into cruciform churches or pseudo-basilicas.

During this period castles were built with unprecedented zeal. Although most private fortifications have disappeared, there remain ruins of several important stone

3. Gjorslev Castle, Stevns, Zealand, c. 1400; from a drawing c. 1700 (Brunswick, Herzog Anton Ulrich-Museum) (much less survives)

castles. The archbishop's castle, Hammershus, on the northern tip of Bornholm, was extended to become one of northern Europe's largest strongholds during the Middle Ages. Its core is a ring-wall castle, the big donjon of which also housed the residence in the manner of older European castles. Kalundborg, by then in royal hands, was refortified, among other things with a large ring-wall castle. The new castle (destr. 1660) included a large tower that housed the national archives. Gurre Castle, from the same period, was built by Valdemar near Helsingør. An earlier tower was surrounded by a square ring wall with corner towers. Across the Øresund, Helsingborg was extended with a vast central tower.

A number of residences built for the bishopric and nobility in the 14th and 15th centuries have been preserved. Most noteworthy is Gjorslev Castle (see fig. 3), built in Stevns c. 1400 for the Bishop of Roskilde, Peder Jensen Lodehat. The cruciform building with ground floor vaulting supported by columns has at its core a big tower; the east side of the south wing was originally extended with a private chapel. Certain details point to Belgian and northern French manor architecture, but genuine parallels have not been established. Spøttrup Castle was erected by the Viborg bishop Jørgen Friis, probably during the 1520s. The firearms of modern warfare were taken into account: ramparts reaching the outer cornice of the house were built all around the moat castle, itself built around a quadrangle. More typical of a lord's residence is the Tjele manor house near Viborg. This stone house placed the residence above the storerooms, all of which had their own outside access.

BIBLIOGRAPHY

V. Lorenzen: *De danske klostres bygningshistorie* [The architectural history of Danish monasteries], 9 vols (Copenhagen, 1912–41)
Danmarks kirker [Denmark's churches] (Copenhagen, 1933–)
H. Langberg: *Danmarks bygningskultur* [Denmark's building tradition], 2 vols (Copenhagen, 1955)
Trap Danmark, 31 vols (Copenhagen, 1958–72)
H. Lund and K. Millech, eds: *Danmarks bygningskunst* [Denmark's architecture] (Copenhagen, 1963) [Eng. summary]
H. Krins: *Die frühen Steinkirchen Dänemarks* (diss., Hamburg, Hans. U., 1968)
V. La Cour: *Danske borganlæg til midten af det trettende århundrede* [Danish castles until the mid-13th century], 2 vols (Copenhagen, 1972)
H. Lund, ed.: *Danmarks arkitektur*, 6 vols (Viborg, 1979–81)
Frühe Holzkirchen im nordlichen Europa (exh. cat. by C. Ahrens, Hamburg, Helms-Mus., 1981), pp. 571–6
E. Roesdahl: 'The Building Activities of King Harald Bluetooth', *Château Gaillard*, ix–x (1982), pp. 543–5
J. Hertz: 'Kalundborg: A Danish Medieval Fortified Town and Castle', *Château Gaillard*, xii (1985)
——: 'Some Early 16th Century Fortifications in Denmark', *Château Gaillard*, xii (1985), pp. 49–63
R. A. Olsen: *Borge i Danmark* [Castles in Denmark] (Herning, 1986)
'Middelalderlige stenhuse i danske og skaanske købstæder' [Medieval stone houses in Danish and Scanian market towns], *Hikuin*, 13 (1987) [Eng. summary; 11 articles]
H. Johannsen: 'Om vore tidlige teglstenskirkers oprindelse' [On the origins of our early brick churches], *Festskrift til Olaf Olsen* (Copenhagen, 1988), pp. 247–63 [Eng. summary]

2. 1540–1840. The Lutheran reformation of 1536 was decisive for architecture, with the monarchy and nobility replacing the clergy as the leading patrons. Churches and monastery buildings were either demolished (which provided materials for castle building) or converted into manor houses (e.g. Bjørnholm in Jutland). Active programmes thus continued after 1540 for building castles and manor houses, including single or double houses with corner and staircase towers (e.g. Borreby, near Skelskør, 1556).

Under Frederik II (*reg* 1559–88) there was prolific building activity. In the prestigious large-scale construction of Frederiksborg Castle (1560; *see* HILLERØD, FREDERIKSBORG CASTLE) the three-wing main castle was still made up of independent houses, with external galleries and staircase towers. The latter, where they occurred on castles, manor houses, town halls and churches, were usually decorated in a non-Italianate style, with spires divided into storeys; they constituted the chief prestige symbol of the Nordic Renaissance. Churches (e.g. Odense Cathedral, 1558) also acquired magnificent spires. The building style was marked overwhelmingly by contact with the Netherlands. Frederick II's Kronborg Castle at Helsingør (1574–85; see HELSINGØR, §2) attracted many building experts, including Hans van Steenwinckel. Although half-timbering was preferred in market towns, most monumental buildings of the era were of red brick, with painted sandstone details in the form of level mouldings, door- and window-frames and decorated ornamental gables. Particular attention was paid to the portal casings and gables, which were often decorated systematically. Cultivation of the orders, or Vitruvianism, was introduced, together with other elements inspired by antiquity, such as triumphal arches, frontons, volutes and more abundant ornamentation (e.g. grotesques and roll-moulding). These were inspired by various treatises and source-books by, among others, Serlio, Palladio, Gualtherus Rivius, Vignola and Hans Vredeman de Vries, which, together with the dissemination of printed illustrations, played a significant role in the constant interaction with and opposition to local traditions.

Many of the master builders of the age were apprenticed in fortification building. In the spirit of the Renaissance, geometric forms were cultivated; this can be seen in Kronborg and in the Netherlandish interpretations of Renaissance style in the fortifications of, among others, Varberg (from 1589), Halland. In house building only rarely, as in Tycho Brahe's home Uranienborg (started 1576), were the plan and elevation truly linked to the demand for symmetry and geometry, which at Uranienborg was additionally extended to the gardens.

The period up to the Thirty Years War (1618–48) was the heyday of manor house construction. Single houses on an E-shaped plan, related to the 'manor castles' of the previous era, were still built, such as Lystrup (1579), Zealand. Rosenholm (between Århus and Randers) occupied a unique position: it was begun in 1558 as a single house, with a pilaster-decorated loggia, and was gradually enlarged to a four-wing moated castle on a trapezoid plan, with a (well-preserved) summerhouse, Pirkentavl, in the grounds. The rectangular single house with four square corner towers was introduced by Hercules van Oberberg (d 1602), for example at Grøngård (1570), and was used in Engelsholm (near Vejle), built in 1591–2 for Tycho Brahe's brother Knud. A much imitated design of a manor house, inspired by Jacques Androuet Du Cerceau's publication Les Plus Excellents Bastiments de France (Paris, 1576), was the three-wing construction opened up by a separate gatehouse. Nørlund (1581–92) in Himmerland, with a gallery on the main façade, is a typical example. The towns were also planned with a strictly regulated street system in accordance with the geometric aesthetic. The activity in this field shows the limitations of the Renaissance ideals. The centralized city plans, such as Johann Semp's first draft for Christianshavn (1617), gave way to more traditional and workable grids.

After the Swedish wars military installations were extended. In Copenhagen, which alone had resisted attack, Christian IV's fortifications were modernized and extended. The Citadel was already being built in the 1660s under the direction of the Dutch architect Hendrik Rüse (1624–79). The monarchy was made absolute under Frederick III (reg 1648–70) in 1660, and Copenhagen gained the status of capital city. The need for a suitable residence to replace Copenhagen Castle was pressing. Various projects included a four-wing castle inside the Citadel, which resulted only in the construction of a pleasure castle (destr. 1689) with gardens facing the harbour, for Queen Sophie Amalie. From 1665 to 1673 the King enriched the old castle with the Kunstkammer and library building (now rebuilt and part of the state archives). The library hall, with its columned gallery (partially re-erected in Copenhagen, Nmus.), was inspired by the library of the Palais Mazarin (1646), Paris, by Pierre Le Muet.

Christian V (reg 1670–99) was an absolute monarch from his accession, and this fact contributed to increased artistic and architectural activities. In 1671 Lambert van Haven (see HAVEN, VAN, (3)) was appointed as general master builder and 'inspector of painting and sculpture'. The position was conceived as a parallel to Charles Le Brun's work for Louis XIV of France. Several noble palaces were built around Kongens Nytorv, a monumental square between medieval Copenhagen and Sophie Amalienborg, beginning in 1671 with Charlottenborg, designed by the immigrant Dutchman Ewert Janssen (?1665–c. 1692). In 1685–92 a rampart was erected against the Øresund, running from Christianshavn to the northern harbour mouth opposite the Citadel, and the capital was secured as one of Europe's strongest fortifications.

In the 1680s van Haven designed a new royal residence (unexecuted), a four-wing castle with extensive grounds, all subordinated to a main axis in line with the Arsenal, the Kunstkammer building and the new district of Frederiksholm. After the burning of Sophie Amalienborg in 1689, the Swede Nicodemus Tessin the younger was commissioned to build a new residential castle; this Roman-French-inspired project (never executed) overshadowed van Haven's, whose chief achievements were the cross-shaped Vor Frelser (1682–96; see fig. 4) in Christianshavn and the redecoration of the audience chamber and the secret passage in Frederiksborg Castle. His essentially European sources of inspiration were gathered on a study trip supported by the King, which included a stay in Rome. His purchases of copperplate engravings and architectural books, and his own surveys and sketches (Copenhagen, Stat. Mus. Kst), were used in an original body of work, inspired by modern Roman Baroque but adapted to the native, Dutch-influenced tradition. Dutch Palladianism was the model for a great number of manor houses and palaces built by the new nobility. Among surviving examples are Nysø near Præstø (1671–3) and the naval hero Niels Juel's palace (1683–6; now the French Embassy) on Kongens Nytorv. Old-fashioned exterior communications (staircase towers, galleries) were replaced by internal staircases and corridor systems. Enfilade doors became symptomatic of the modern formalism and the ceremonial needs of an architecture of power (e.g. Chancellor Claus Reventlow's

4. Lambert van Haven: Vor Frelser, Christianshavn, 1682–96; corkscrew spire added by Laurids De Thurah, 1749–50

Clausholm, near Randers, 1693–9, built by Ernst Brandenburger).

Wilhelm Friederich von Platen was responsible for, among others, the building of Staldmestergården (1703–6; now the Ministry of Education) and the new summer castle, Frederiksberg (1703, rebuilt 1707–9), for Frederick IV (reg 1699–1730). In contrast to the red brick of the Dutch pilaster style, smoothly finished walls are common to these buildings, as are, moreover, details from Roman models. The view of Frederiksberg, with its low Italianate roof, standing on a hill overlooking the elaborate gardens, must have been inspired by the Aldobrandini villa in Frascati, which the King had visited. Von Platen was succeeded in 1716 as master builder by Johann Conrad Ernst (1666–1750), who built the Opera House (1701–3; now the Eastern High Court) in Copenhagen.

Frederik IV, who was an indefatigable planner of gardens, gained exceptional professional support from Johan Cornelius Krieger, whose architectural masterpiece is the summer residence FREDENSBORG (1719–22), North Zealand. The main room of this Italianate villa, the cupola room, contains stuccowork by Carlo Enrico Brenno (1688–1745). A solution to the problem of a residence in

Copenhagen was first reached under Christian VI (reg 1730–46), who demolished Copenhagen Castle regardless of his father's earlier modernizations. Christiansborg Palace, erected from 1732 on the castle island, was a masterpiece in Danish architecture, although all but the grounds were destroyed by fire in 1794. The construction was led by the new general master builder, Elias David Häusser (1687–1745), but the design of the four-wing, towered main castle bears a pronounced south German-Austrian stamp and was presumably commissioned. The castle's construction stretched into the second half of the century and attracted a great number of experts, among them NIELS EIGTVED and NICHOLAS-HENRI JARDIN.

From the 1730s a new, sophisticated architecture flourished, centred around the court, the nobility and the affluent Copenhagen middle classes. The leading architects were Eigtved and Lauritz Lauridsen de Thurah (1706–59). The former's French-influenced, delicate façade treatments attest to his apprenticeship in Saxony, while the latter is the exponent of a more powerful, southern Germanic Baroque (see also fig. 4). This modern Danish architecture combined with a nostalgia for Renaissance and medieval ideas. Other competent architects worked around Thurah, including P. de Lange (c. 1704–66), who generally carried out large-scale contract work in Copenhagen during the new merchants' boom.

Under Frederik V (reg 1746–66) the development that had begun under his father continued and intensified. The training of architects was given a proper framework in 1754 by the foundation of the Kongelige Danske Kunstakademi in Copenhagen. The capital increased its status as the leading site for architecture. The most prestigious project of the period was the foundation of the new city district Frederiksstad (started 1749), in the Sophie Amalienborg area, after designs by Eigtved. The nucleus was formed by an octagonal main square (Amalienborg Slotsplads) with four palaces and a large cupola-topped church, the Frederikskirke. The district was to contain housing, the elevation of which was governed by city regulations. With Eigtved's death and reorganization of the Kunstakademi in 1754 a closer connection with the latest trends in French architecture began, represented by Nicolas-Henri Jardin, who was to continue work on Eigtved's Frederikskirke. Approved in 1756, the church project illustrates the shift from Eigtved's Rococo style to Jardin's solemn and rigorous Neo-classicism. In 1770 Christian VII (reg 1766–1808) halted the church's construction (later completed 1876–94, in a changed form, by Ferdinand Meldahl), and Jardin left the country.

From 1771 the leading buildings were executed by architects trained at the Kunstakademi. The first main figure was Caspar Friedrich Harsdorff, who also studied in France and Rome and whose French-influenced classicism influenced, among other things, the rebuilding programme that followed the Copenhagen fire of 1795. One of Harsdorff's most important pupils, C. F. HANSEN, who studied in Rome c. 1780, was responsible for a number of important buildings after the fires of 1794, 1795 and 1808, including the town hall and gaol complex (completed 1814) and Vor Frue (1811–29), which later became the cathedral. For more than 25 years Hansen was the dominant figure in Danish architecture and art life, as chief buildings inspector in 1808 and Director of the Kunstakademi from 1811 to 1833. The German-born G. F. Hetsch helped him (1815–c. 1832) design a number of the interiors in the new Christiansborg Palace. Peter Meyn (1749–1808) and the Norwegian-born J. H. Rawert (1751–1823) were chiefly involved in rebuilding the capital and created a late classical residential style that is still evident. In north Zealand the prosperous middle class continued the tradition of elegant country houses, on which Hansen worked, as did the French architect Joseph Ramée between 1801 and 1806 (e.g. Sophienholm, nr Copenhagen).

The rediscovery of Greek architecture through the Paestum temples and works such as James Stuart's and Nicholas Revett's *Antiquities of Athens* (London, 1762–1816) was noted in Harsdorff's Amalienborg colonnade (1795); Harsdorff had shown in his renovation of older buildings an exceptional understanding of the Middle Ages and the domestic Gothic renaissance. The main building of the University (started 1829), after designs by Peder Malling (1781–1865), is, with its mixture of medieval and classical elements, typical of this new direction. Hetsch, inspired by Karl Friedrich Schinkel, also worked with historical styles other than the Classical (e.g. the synagogue, 1830–33). The Roman Catholic Church, ushering in a changed attitude in its use of red, unpolished brick, gathered inspiration from Early Christian and north Italian medieval churches. Gottlieb Bindesbøll's Thorvaldsens Museum (1839–47; for illustration *see* BINDESBØLL, (1)), Copenhagen, demonstrated his interpretation of antique polychrome architecture.

BIBLIOGRAPHY

C. Elling and V. Sten Møller: *Holmens bygningshistorie, 1680–1930* [The building history of Holmen, 1680–1930] (Copenhagen, 1932) [Fr. summary]
V. Lorenzen: *Lambert v. Haven* (Copenhagen, 1936)
O. Norn: *Christian III.s borge* [The castles of Christian III] (Copenhagen, 1949) [Eng. summary]
C. Elling and K. Fisker, eds: *Monumenta architecturae danicae: Danish Architectural Drawings, 1660–1920* (Copenhagen, 1961) [dual lang. text]
K. Voss: *Bygningsadministrationen i Danmark under enevælden* [Building administration in Denmark under the absolute monarchy] (Copenhagen, 1966) [Ger. summary]
E. Unnerbäck: *Welsche Giebel: Ein italienisches Renaissancemotiv und seine Verbreitung in Mittel- und Nordeuropa* (Stockholm, 1971)
P. Hirschfeld: *Herrenhäuser und Schlösser in Schleswig-Holstein* (Berlin and Munich, 1974)
T. Roepstorff: *Frederik IV.s generalbygmestre* [General master builders of Frederik IV] (Copenhagen, 1975)
H. R. Hitchcock: *Netherlandish Scrolled Gables of the Sixteenth and Early Seventeenth Centuries* (New York, 1978)
H. E. Nørregård-Nielsen: 'Omkring Evert Janssen: Af Charlottenborgs bygningshistorie' [About Evert Janssen: from the building history of Charlottenborg], *Architectura: Arkithist. Aarsskr.*, 6 (1984), pp. 140–60
K. von Folsach: *Fra nyklassicisme til historicisme: Arkitekten G. F. Hetsch* [From Neo-classicism to historicism: the architect G. F. Hetsch] (Copenhagen, 1988) [Eng. summary]
Forblommet antik: Klassicismer i dansk arkitektur og havekunst—Studier tilegnede Hakon Lund [Covert antiquity: classicism in Danish architecture and garden landscaping—studies dedicated to Hakon Lund] (Copenhagen, 1988)
M. Smed: 'Vor Frelsers kirke på Christianshavn: Til ære for Gud og Christian den femte' [Vor Frelsers church in Christianshavn: for the honour of God and Christian V], *Synligt og usynligt: Studier tilegnede Otto Norn* [Visible and invisible: studies dedicated to Otto Norn] (Copenhagen, 1990), pp. 201–15 [Eng. summary]

HUGO JOHANNSEN

3. AFTER 1840. The transition from the classical revival to free historicism (or National Romanticism) had begun before 1840 in Denmark and was continued by Bindesbøll, Hetsch, Hansen (*see* §2 above), J. D. Herholdt (1818–1902; e.g. the library, 1855–61, of Copenhagen University, in which he combined impressions of northern Italian Gothic with the use of cast iron, and numerous Italianate villas, subsequently of decisive importance for later Danish residential villa building) and Henning Wolff (1828–80). A more international architecture was created by such architects as Vilhelm Dahlerup (1836–1907) and Ferdinand Meldahl. In Copenhagen Dahlerup built the Renaissance Revival style Kongelige Teater (1872–4), the oldest part of the Ny Carlsberg Glyptotek (1890–91), inspired by Venetian architecture, and the colourful Chinese Pantomimeteater (1874) in Tivoli. Meldahl, who was equally widely travelled, was also inspired by Venice, as seen particularly in his use of segment-shaped gables, for example in the Institute for the Blind (1857–8) in Copenhagen. Meldahl established a National Romantic historicist style, the 'Christian IV style', with his rebuilding in Hillerød of Frederiksborg Castle, which had burnt down in 1859. His sense of the monumental showed itself in his design of Frederikskirke and its surroundings (1876–94) in Copenhagen. Through his position of power at the Kongelige Danske Kunstakademi over many years, Meldahl played a decisive role in architectural development during the last quarter of the century.

Meldahl's interest in earlier Danish architecture led such architects as H. B. Storck (1839–1922), Martin Nyrop and Ulrik Plesner (1861–1933) to incorporate characteristic elements of Danish Baroque, including red brick, as seen in the Abel Catrine Foundation (1885–6) by Storck in Copenhagen. The Town Hall (1892–1905; *see* COPENHAGEN, fig. 2) in Copenhagen by Nyrop constitutes the culmination of the National Romantic period. In it he introduced anecdotal elements, and several of his buildings show an affinity with popular culture. Taking inspiration from the Danish brick building tradition and referring to Italian medieval brickwork, it presents simplified faces to the streets on three sides, rises to medieval battlements with pinnacled corner turrets above a pitched roof and has an asymmetrically placed clock-tower of Gothic and Romanesque extraction. Although Art Nouveau did not play a prominent role in Danish architecture, it can be seen in stylistic details, for example in the decorations of Plesner's buildings by Thorvald Bindesbøll. Anton Rosen and P. V. Jensen-Klint each designed buildings closely affiliated to Art Nouveau: the Palace Hotel (1907–10) by Rosen and the Tramway Waiting-room (1904–7) by Jensen-Klint at Trianglen, both in Copenhagen. Around this time urban planning began in Denmark with competitions for such schemes as the Fælledpark (1905) in Copenhagen, won by Svend Koch (1867–1943) and Ole Nobel (1867–1916), and continued through to the world-renowned work of Steen Eiler Rasmussen, from Hirtshals in 1919 to his advocacy and promotion of the urban-planning acts of 1925 and 1938.

In 1910 a passionate discussion about the positioning of a Baroque spire on top of C. F. Hansen's Vor Frue, Copenhagen, gave rise to a renewed interest in classicism, supported in particular by Carl Petersen. His major work

5. Kay Fisker and C. F. Møller: Vestersøhus, Copenhagen, 1930s

is the Museum for Fynsk Malerkunst (1912–15) in Fåborg, which expresses his interest in material and colouristic effects, aspects that interested him also at a theoretical level. His importance for Nordic classicism lay particularly in his teachings and writings. One of the most outstanding monumental classicist works is the Police Headquarters (completed 1924) in Copenhagen by Hack Kampmann and Aage Rafn, the architecture of which is marked by its strongly Mannerist features (*see* RAFN, AAGE).

Classicist tendencies dominated in the 1920s in such works as Edvard Thomsen's Øregaard Grammar School (1923–4) in north Zealand and *c.* 1930 in villas by Arne Jacobsen and others, echoing the most famous classicist artist's residence, Nicolai Abraham Abildgaard's villa, Spurveskjul (Sparrow Hideaway), of 1805. P. V. Jensen-Klint stood somewhat apart from the mainstream although he had the same connections as Nyrop with the popular movements. His major work is the Grundtvig Church (1921–40) in Copenhagen (completed by his son, Kaare Klint), in which he monumentalized the Danish village-church type into the form of a cathedral. The monumentality is emphasized by the surrounding low-level residential housing, which he also designed. Klint was to have great importance for the raising of the standard of humble housing developments brought about by the association Bedre Byggeskik (Better Building Practice).

International Functionalism took a long time to infiltrate Denmark. Early signs were visible in the house (1925) that Edvard Heiberg (1897–1958) built for himself north of Copenhagen, which joined the ranks of the experimental houses of the Bauhaus, where Heiberg had taught briefly. The Stockholm Exhibition (1930) of Swedish architect Gunnar Asplund provided the impetus for Functionalism's breakthrough in Denmark. Notable experiments were the one-family houses in reinforced concrete (1931) by Frits Schlegel (1898–1965) and the many houses in the northern districts of Copenhagen by Arne Jacobsen and Mogens Lassen (1901–87). Of the major Functionalist buildings in Copenhagen the Vesterport office building (1930–32) by Ole Falkentorp (1886–1948) and Povl Baumann, and the Meat Market (1931–4) by Poul Holdsøe (1883–1966) should be mentioned. The Functionalist tradition in Denmark in the 1930s to 1950s is characterized by an amalgamation of the modern with traditional elements. The most important representatives of Danish Functionalism include Kay Fisker, C. F. Møller and Palle Suneson (1904–87). In Copenhagen, Fisker and Møller's blocks of flats at No. 2 Vodroffsvej (1930s) and their Vestersøhus (1930s; see fig. 5) are typical examples using the characteristic Danish feature of facing in red bricks. The widespread use of tiled roofs and bricks in the 1930s and during World War II distinguishes Danish functionalist architecture from the German. Århus University (begun in 1932) by Fisker, Møller, Povl Stegmann and Carl Theodor Sørensen is the most monumental expression of this movement.

After the war the building industry was rationalized. The Statens Byggeforskningsinstitut (National Building Research Institute) and the Ministry for Housing were established in 1947 and the Byggecentrum (Building Centre) in 1956. These new institutions prompted the development of industrialized building methods, which developed out of functionalism. The state supported non-traditional building activity and, as a link in a larger development plan, the first high-rise residential housing project, Bellahøj (begun in 1950) in Copenhagen, was erected with the help of a number of architects, using prefabricated building materials. However, the majority of building projects continued to be traditionally built, including many one-family houses, financed by government loans after the housing support bills of 1946. Such developments as Arne Jacobsen's terraced houses (1950–52) in Søholm, north of Copenhagen, created international interest as original and innovative building types. Jørn Utzon's own house at Hellebæk (1951) shows the influence of American and Japanese models on Danish architecture of the period.

Jacobsen in particular (who was well acquainted with American architecture) represented the International Style and Modernism in Denmark with such works as the Town Hall (1957) in Rødovre, perhaps the purest of all glass curtain wall buildings. Modernism was closely connected to the economic boom in the 1950s, which brought about the construction of numerous public buildings and museums, including the first phase of the Louisiana Museum (1957–8) at Humlebæk by Jørgen Bo (*b* 1919) and Vilhelm Wohlert (*b* 1920). The first satellite town, Albertslund, west of Copenhagen, designed by a number of architects, was built in the 1960s, one of the most productive periods of Danish architecture. Numerous public buildings were developed, including Odense University (from 1967), a model of system building by Knud Holscher. In the early 1970s large joint developments, such as Midtpunkt (1970–74), Farum, by Jorn Ole Sørensen (*b* 1923), Viggo Møller Jensen (*b* 1907) and Tyge Arnfred (*b* 1919), which is an original low-rise development of terraces with internal streets, represented the culmination of technological and economic developments and further advances in prefabrication. New trends and a reaction against unimaginative industrialized building resulted in low-rise developments with more varied and interesting architecture, for example Tinggården (1978) near Køge designed by the Vandkunsten community architecture specialists' practice in Copenhagen. Bagsværd Church (1974–6), by Jørn Utzon, is notable among the public buildings of the 1970s. Postmodernist practice in Danish architecture can be seen in the use of traditional and historicist elements. The first time Neo-rationalism appeared was in the competition for Høje Taastrup Station and City Centre (1978), west of Copenhagen, which was won by Jacob Blegvad (*b* 1921). Several Danish architects attracted international attention in the 1980s, including Hans Dissing (*b* 1926), Otto Weitling (*b* 1930) and Henning Larsen, especially for work outside Denmark. Notable buildings erected in Denmark in the 1980s include Larsen's Gentofte Library (1985) and Utzon's Paustian Mobilhus (1987), Copenhagen. In housing, the exhibition town (1988) at Blangstedgård, Odense, was memorable, especially the Post-modern housing by Poul Ingemann (*b* 1952).

BIBLIOGRAPHY

S. E. Rasmussen: *Nordische Baukunst* (Berlin, 1940)
H. Finsen: *Ung dansk arkitektur, 1930–1945* [Young Danish architecture, 1930–1945] (Copenhagen, 1947)
K. Millech and K. Fisker: *Danske arkitekturstrømninger, 1890–1950: En arkitekturhistorisk undersøgelse* [Trends in Danish architecture, 1850–1950: an architectural historical investigation] (Copenhagen, 1951)
E. Hiort: *Housing in Denmark since 1930* (Copenhagen, 1952)
H. Lund and K. Millech, eds: *Danmarks bygningskunst* (Copenhagen, 1963)
T. Faber: *New Danish Architecture* (London and Stuttgart, 1968)
'Dansk arkitektur/Danish Architecture/Dänische Architektur, 1879–1979', *Arkitektur DK*, xxiii/7–8 (1979) [whole issue]
H. Lund, ed.: *Danmarks arkitektur*, 6 vols (Copenhagen, 1979–87)
Nordisk klassicism/Nordic Classicism, 1910–1930 (exh. cat., ed. S. Paavilainen; Helsinki, Mus. Fin. Archit., 1982)

GRETHE KUSK

III. Painting and graphic arts.

1. Before *c.* 1540. 2. *c.* 1540–1840. 3. After 1840.

1. BEFORE *c.* 1540. Prior to the introduction of Christianity, the consolidation of the Roman Catholic Church and the establishment of a kingdom of Denmark, painting seems mainly to have been used as a decorative colouring on wood- and stone-carvings. However, the smooth reverse side of the Hørning Plank, a roof beam from an 11th-century wooden church in Hørning, near Randers, Jutland (now in Copenhagen, Nmus.), displays a painted vine surrounded by ogees, which suggests the use of painted ornament in the interiors of wooden churches erected between the mid-9th century and the early 11th, before stone churches became common. There is no indication, however, of painted representations before the late 11th century.

The majority of extant rural churches in Denmark were built between the early 11th century and the mid-13th. Despite many later alterations, such as Gothic stone vaults being built into the churches replacing the original wooden ceilings, windows being enlarged and thereby destroying parts of the original paintings, or later medieval paintings being painted over the originals, numerous examples of early Romanesque paintings from the period *c.* 1080–1175 are *in situ*. Considering the many fragments found on walls above Gothic vaults or discovered, though not uncovered, beneath later paintings, it seems likely that all the early Romanesque churches once had their entire interiors covered by paintings. A tradition was established in the early centuries of Danish Christendom and lasted throughout the Middle Ages, dying out gradually after the Reformation of 1536. From the late 12th century the paintings were renewed, additions to the churches such as towers and porches were decorated, and the interiors of new churches were painted. Even in the late medieval, Gothic cathedrals and abbey churches, painted vaults, walls and columns played an important part in interior decoration, as the Gothic brick architecture of northern Europe did not have those vast windows typical of Gothic architecture elsewhere.

The amount of preserved wall painting from the late 12th century until the Reformation surpasses by far the early medieval examples. The good state of preservation of works of this period results from the smooth transition from Roman Catholicism to Lutheranism, as well as the whitewashing of church interiors during the puritan period in the 17th century, thereby preserving the paintings until interest in medieval art and conservation arose in the 19th century. However, with a few late exceptions such as

Morten the Painter's work of 1409 in Gimlinge Church on Zealand and that of Ebbe Olesen and Simon Petersen of 1496 in Bellinge Church on Fyn, virtually none of the paintings is signed or dated. There is an almost complete lack of written sources for research on medieval Danish painting, and so works are largely attributed to masters and workshops named after the most prominent work within each group.

The introduction of wall painting in Denmark shows an 'internationalization' in Danish art: no traces of earlier Nordic art exist in these paintings. The style and iconographical details are Byzantine or Italo-Byzantine in wall paintings of *c.* 1080 to *c.* 1175, followed in the latter part of the Romanesque period by a gradual incorporation of influences from French, German and English art. The wall paintings of the 11th century were executed in an innovative combination of fresco and secco on a layer of fine-grained plaster, with the occasional use of gilded stucco for haloes and details on dress. They are of a high general European standard, and they were probably executed by skilled, immigrant craftsmen. Church walls were completely covered with colour. The east end would carry a depiction of *Christ in Majesty* (see fig. 6), and the walls of the body of the church would contain two friezes with the *Life of Christ* or *Legends of Saints*. In a number of churches in Jutland the lower band is taken up by mounted knights in combat, as seen in paintings dated *c.* 1200 in the churches in Ål, Hornslet, Højen and Skibet. The two friezes were divided by ornamented borders, and each picture divided

by similar borders or by fragments of architecture. The triumphal arch displayed ornament with medallion-portraits of saints or full-length figures of saints or Old Testament figures. The lower part of the walls was often decorated with painted curtains, the window openings with ornament.

While only a small number of paintings from the period 1200–1375 are known, it is clear that this period marks the transition from the Romanesque to the Gothic style. Wall paintings of *c.* 1350–75 display a marked deterioration of quality if compared with paintings from the preceding centuries, most probably due to the early 14th-century climatic, agricultural and economic crises and to the Black Death, which was particularly marked in Denmark. By the end of the century wall painting was revitalized. A number of supposed indigenous workshops began to establish themselves with competence, although the execution of wall paintings in the Gothic period (*c.* 1375–1536) was a swift and inexpensive matter in comparison to the Romanesque period. The preparation of wall surfaces was less careful, the range of colour reduced, and expensive imported colours, such as those made from lapis lazuli and azurite, were rarely used.

While Gothic wall painting in Denmark contains a higher degree of individuality than in Romanesque paintings, the sources of inspiration and the models for style and iconography were French, German and English art: paintings and enamels, as well as illuminated books; and, during the 15th century, graphic work of German or Netherlandish origin. Backgrounds were mostly white with painted ornament in a pattern specific to the individual workshop. Ribs were often painted with bricklike ornaments and crockets, or with ornamental foliage. Vaults were decorated with such narratives as the Passion or the Childhood of Christ, with one scene in each section. The story sometimes continued on the walls or was supplemented by saintly legends or depictions of saints. To this might be added grotesque figures and masques or moralities showing scenes from everyday life. During the first decades of the 16th century the late medieval idea of transforming the church interior into a bower, by covering walls and vaults with garlands of leaves and flowers, appears in a number of churches throughout Denmark, for example in two chapels painted in 1511 in Roskilde Cathedral, Zealand, and in the choir painted *c.* 1520 in Løjt Church, North Schleswig.

Paintings on wood are preserved from the early 14th century. The oldest examples (both *c.* 1325) are the painted altar front with scenes from the *Life of the Virgin* (Copenhagen, Nmus.) and the painted wings on a reliquary cabinet for the Cistercian church in Løgumkloster, North Schleswig (*in situ*). Although style and iconography place these works in a general European context, they are believed to be the product of a workshop active in northern Germany or Schleswig-Holstein. The majority of paintings on wood in Denmark before 1540 were on the wings of wooden altarpieces with carved central panels, which were common in the 15th century and the early 16th. To what extent these altarpieces were produced in Denmark cannot be determined definitively, but most of them are considered to be imported works from northern Germany, especially Lübeck, with the addition after 1500 of works

6. *Christ in Majesty*, *c.* 1125, wall painting, Sønder Jernløse Church, Zealand

7. Ebbe Olesen and Simon Petersen: *Last Supper* (1496), wall painting, Bellinge Church, Fyn

from Antwerp in Belgium. The only recorded workshops in Denmark producing such altarpieces were run by artists of German origin, one example being the workshop of Bernt Notke, which made the altarpiece (1479) for Århus Cathedral. This altarpiece is the sole documented work in Denmark by a master otherwise active in Lübeck and Reval (now Tallinn). The other workshop was that of Claus Berg (*c.* 1470–*c.* 1532), active on Fyn during the early decades of the 16th century (*see also* §IV, 1 below). Portrait painting developed late in Denmark, the only portrait of before 1540 being that of *Christian II* (1514; Copenhagen, Stat. Mus. Kst), painted during a brief visit to Denmark by the Estonian painter Michel Sittow.

The existence of graphic works in Denmark from the late 15th century is documented indirectly by the fact that many paintings of that period show a marked resemblance to either single-leaf woodcuts or book illustrations, all, however, of foreign, mainly German or Netherlandish, origin. Among the most popular models for the church painters were the editions of the *Biblia pauperum* printed in the mid-15th century, as illustrated by the wall paintings (1496) in Bellinge Church, Fyn, by Ebbe Olesen and Simon Petersen (see fig. 7), by works by the workshop of the so-called Isefjordmaster (*fl c.* 1460–80 in northern Zealand) or in the paintings of 1498 by Andreas Johannis in Linderöd Church in Scania (now Skåne, Sweden). Sophisticated graphic models, such as prints by Albrecht Dürer, Lucas Cranach the elder and Martin Schongauer,

were used in the workshop of Claus Berg. These imported graphic works did not encourage local production, which started late, and which did not manifest itself properly until the end of the 16th century. The earliest-known Danish prints are two crude woodcuts, one depicting the king of Denmark, the other the national coat of arms, among the illustrations in *Den danske rimkrønike* ('The Danish chronicle') published in Copenhagen in 1495 by a resident Dutch printer, Gotfred of Ghemen (*d c.* 1510). The earliest engraving produced in Denmark is a portrait of *Christian, Duke of Schleswig-Holstein* (later Christian III), dated 1535 and attributed to the German painter Jakob Binck, then active in Denmark (for illustration *see* Binck, Jacob). With these exceptions, Danish prints during most of the 16th century, which were mainly woodcuts for books, were copies after illustrations in foreign books, and they were printed with imported blocks or with casts of print-blocks used abroad.

BIBLIOGRAPHY

E. Zahle, ed.: *Danmarks malerkunst fra middelalder til nutid* [Denmark's painting from the Middle Ages to the present] (Copenhagen, 1937, rev. 4/1956)

P. Nørlund and E. Lind: *Danmarks romanske kalkmalerier* [Denmark's Romanesque wall paintings] (Copenhagen, 1944) [Fr. summary]

E. Moltke: *Bernt Notkes altertavle i Århus domkirke og Tallinntavlen* [Bernt Notke's retables in Århus Cathedral and Tallinn] (Copenhagen, 1970) [Ger. summary]

E. K. Sass: *Studier i Christian II.s ikonografi* (Copenhagen, 1970)

ICO: Den iconographische post [Review of iconography] (Copenhagen, 1970–78; Stockholm, 1979–) [quarterly period. with articles on med. art in Denmark; incl. Eng. summaries from 1979]

V. Poulsen, E. Lassen and J. Danielsen: *Dansk kunsthistorie: Billedkunst og skulptur* [Danish art history: painting and sculpture], i (Copenhagen, 1972)

V. E. Clausen: *Populäre Druckgraphic Europas: Skandinavien: Vom 15. bis zum 20. Jahrhundert* (Munich, 1973)

U. Haastrup: 'Die Maler der Werkstatt Claus Berg und Cranachs Holzschnitte', *Bild och betydelse* [Picture and meaning], ed. L. Lillie and M. Thøgersen (Kvarnträsk, 1974), pp. 91–107

A Catalogue of Wall-paintings in the Churches of Medieval Denmark: Scania—Halland—Blekinge, 4 vols (Copenhagen, 1976–82)

Medieval Iconography and Narrative: A Symposium Held at Odense University: Odense, 1979 [contains articles by K. Banning, U. Haastrup and S. Kaspersen on the wall ptgs at Bellinge]

U. Haastrup: 'Byzantine Elements in Frescoes in Zealand from the Middle of the 12th century', *Acta U. Upsaliensis: Figura*, xix (1981), pp. 315–31

——: 'Brugen af forlæg i Claus Bergs værksted i Odense i 1. fjerdedel af 1500-tallet' [The use of models in Claus Berg's workshop in Odense in the first quarter of the 16th century], *Imagines Medievales: Studier i medeltida ikonografi, arkitektur, skulptur, måleri och konsthandverk* [Imagines Medievales: studies in medieval iconography, architecture, sculpture, painting and craft] (Uppsala, 1983), pp. 113–30 [Ger. summary]

P. Svensson, ed.: *Løjttavlen* [The Løjt retable] (Frøslev, 1983) [Eng. and Ger. summaries]

——: *Løgumskabet* [The Løgum cabinet] (Frøslev, 1985) [Eng. and Ger. summaries]

U. Haastrup and R. Egevang, eds: *Danske kalkmalerier* [Danish wall paintings], 3 vols (Copenhagen, 1985–7) [covers Romanesque, 1080–1275, and Gothic, 1275–1475]

N. M. Saxtorp: *Danmarks kalkmalerier* [Denmark's wall paintings] (Copenhagen, 1986)

P. Svensson, ed.: *Mariatavlen fra Løgum* [The Maria altar front from Løgum] (Frøslev, 1986)

U. Haastrup, ed.: *Danske kalkmalerier* [Danish wall paintings] (Copenhagen, 1989–92), 3 vols [covers Early and Late Gothic, 1275–1375 and 1475–1536]

E. L. Lillie: *Efter Reformationen, 1536–1700* (Copenhagen, 1992)

ELISABETH KOFOD-HANSEN

2. *c.* **1540–1840.** During the first decades after the Lutheran reform of 1536, there was a reluctance to produce pictorial art for churches. Decorative ornamentation or decorations with biblical inscriptions often compensated for figurative painting on fittings (e.g. catechism-altarpieces). Frescoes and book illustrations, however, continued to be produced as important pedagogical tools for the reformers. During the second half of the 16th century sepulchral art gained a new impetus. A group of circular memorial tablets (*c.* 1535) for the Rosenkrantz family (Frederiksborg Castle, Rosenholm and Magleby) are precursors of the painted portrait epitaphs with religious motifs that came to be preferred by the middle classes and the clergy from the second half of the 16th century.

Secular portraiture developed gradually during the 16th century. Jakob Binck, who was attached to the court of Christian III (*reg* 1533–59), was of particular importance. His graphic works (*see* §1 above) reveal the influence of south German miniature masters, while the painted portraits (today known mostly through copies or attrib.) reflect the possible influence of Barthel Bruyn, as well as of Lucas Cranach the elder and his followers. Melchior Lorck, who was patronized by both Christian III and Frederik II (*reg* 1559–88), was, like Binck, versatile in a number of skills and educated in Germany, the Netherlands and Italy. Mainly active outside Denmark, he produced as his most important contribution an extensive body of drawings with views, folk scenes and studies after antique monuments collected during his travels in Turkey

(1555–9), later reworked in woodcut. His large engraving of *Frederick II* (1582; see fig. 8) was produced during a short stay in Denmark.

Frederick II's rebuilding of Kronborg Castle (1574–85), Helsingør, attracted numerous Netherlandish artists and craftsmen: the painter Hans Knieper (*d* 1587) was summoned from Antwerp in 1577 to work on the castle's decoration. In a newly established tapestry workshop in Helsingør he produced, among other things, 40 tapestries featuring the Danish kings for the castle's banqueting hall, of which 14 survive (Helsingør, Kronborg Slot; Copenhagen, Nmus.) as well as an allegorical canopy (Stockholm, Nmus.; *see* §XI, 1 below). Knieper's full-length portrait of *Frederick II* (1581; Hillerød, Frederiksborg Slot) introduced the courtly style of the Habsburgs. Contemporary portraits of the nobility, however, were characterized by their conservatism.

The improved economic conditions in the late 16th century and the early 17th are reflected in an increase in demand for paintings, at court as well as among the nobility, the middle classes and the Church. Christian IV (*reg* 1588–1648) made use of painting and architecture to an even greater degree than his father in order to strengthen the prestige of the Crown. During the period *c.* 1600–40 a series of great decorative schemes were set in motion, most importantly at Frederiksborg Castle (Hillerød), Rosenborg Castle (Copenhagen) and Kronborg Castle (Helsingør). To this end painters were attached to the court as royal painters, several of them foreign (predominantly

8. Melchior Lorck: *Frederick II*, engraving, 45×32 mm, 1582 (Copenhagen, Kongelige Kobberstiksamling, Statens Museum for Kunst)

Dutch or German), and only a few Danish: Søren Kjaer (*fl* 1609–30), Morten Steenwinckel (1595–1646), Reinhold Timm (*fl* 1618–39), Johan Timm (1615–74) and, presumably, Remmert Piettersz. (Pettersen) (*d* 1649). They were not bound by compulsory guild membership but took on work outside the court in competition with the local painters, who were organized in guilds (see below). Christian IV also made acquisitions in the Netherlands and Germany and commissioned directly from foreign painters, especially for Rosenborg, Frederiksborg and Kronborg (*see* HELSINGØR, §2; HILLERØD, FREDERIKSBORG CASTLE; and COPENHAGEN, §1).

Portraiture flourished under Christian IV. The most important portrait painter in the early part of his reign was the German-born Jacob van Doort, who continued an international court style in the manner of Antonis van Moor. The major work of the Amsterdam-trained Pieter Isaacsz. was the portrait of *Christian IV* (*c.* 1612; Hillerød, Frederiksborg Slot), portraying the King as victor of the Kalmar War, with lively, variegated colour handling and a virtuoso rendering of fabric. During the King's later years Karel van Mander III and Abraham Wuchters were great innovators who reinterpreted Baroque Dutch and Flemish court art. Several full-length portraits of the King were executed during the 1640s as well as portraits of his family and the high nobility. After the change of government in 1648 van Mander maintained his position at court and among the aristocracy, but he also portrayed members of Copenhagen's merchant and professional classes in more informal, intimate portraits. Abraham Wuchters's earliest work for the court of Christian IV was an unusual full-length portrait of the King (1638; Hillerød, Frederiksborg Slot) standing in a dramatic, stormy landscape. During the last years of Christian IV's reign he still received court commissions, including full-length portraits of members of the royal family. Under Frederick III (*reg* 1648–70) Wuchters concentrated more on teaching at the Royal Academy in Sorø and private commissions. He made drawings for engravings in close cooperation with Albert Haelwegh (including a projected series of portraits of the Royal Council members between 1655 and 1658). After the accession of Christian V (*reg* 1670–99), he regained his position as royal portrait painter in 1671 and created a very widely used portrait-type of Christian V.

During the 17th century there was a considerable impetus behind the graphic arts, which were used partly in the propaganda campaign for the monarchy, partly in ever-growing book production, in funeral sermons and in various kinds of printed matter. In 1622 a permanent post was created for an engraver to the University of Copenhagen and it was held by such prominent artists as Simon de Pas (*c.* 1595–1647) and Albert Haelwegh, both also royal engravers.

The reorganization of religious life after 1600 towards a more orthodox Lutheran form may help to explain the marked increase in the production of church fittings rich in figurative art (e.g. altarpieces, pulpits, pews, galleries). There was also a steady stream of epitaphs. The King's own painters likewise produced religious works, for example the altarpiece (1655–6) in Sorø Church by Abraham Wuchters. The majority of commissions, however, went to local masters who carried out painting for private

individuals as well. In general numerous works are anonymous and only a few names are known. However, the situation in a small provincial town such as Ribe, a centre for trade with Northern Germany and the Netherlands, is well documented. Around six painters were active in Ribe before the 1660s, including a Dutch emigrant, Jakob Adriansz. van Meulengracht (*d* 1664). The paintings on the cathedral's altarpiece (1597) are attributed to Lauritz Andersen Riber (*d* 1637), who also worked in Tønder, Kolding, Randers and Århus. Hans Olufsen Schütte (1635–75) also had numerous clients on Fyn and Zealand and in Jutland. It was normal practice among such painters to use engraved prototypes, sometimes more than 50 years old.

After the introduction of the absolute monarchy in 1660 and the appointment of Lambert van Haven as chief master builder and inspector of pictures and sculptures, the foundation was laid for a more deliberate, central control of the arts in the service of the monarchy. Van Haven directed a number of important decorative schemes, including the embellishment of the audience room at Frederiksborg (1681–9) with allegorical ceiling paintings by Peder Andersen Nordmand (*d* 1694), portraits of kings by Jacques d'Agar and paintings van Haven had bought in Italy; and of the Banqueting Hall at Rosenborg with tapestries (1684–93) woven by Berent van der Eichen (*d* 1700) from Brabant, depicting Christian V's victories in the Scanian War of 1675–9.

Jacques d'Agar became the first Chief Royal Portrait Painter in the early 1680s. His portrait of *Christian V* (*c.* 1686; Hillerød, Frederiksborg Slot) depicts the monarch as a Roman emperor. Portraits of members of the royal family, particularly the women, reveal a penchant for the court style represented in France by Pierre Mignard and in England by Peter Lely. Court commissions under Frederick IV (*reg* 1699–1730) were largely connected with the decoration of numerous new or rebuilt palaces (e.g. Frederiksberg Castle, Fredensborg Palace, Rosenborg Castle and Copenhagen Castle) public buildings and churches in and around the capital. Two history and portrait painters, Benoît Le Coffre and Hendrik Krock (1671–1738), were prominent in several royal decorative schemes. Both artists were educated abroad (Germany, Italy and France). An attempt to establish a society of artists in Copenhagen in 1701 failed, and a regular academy of art was not established in Copenhagen until 1738 (reorganized in 1754) (*see* §XVI below).

Both Christian VI (*reg* 1730–46) and Frederick V (*reg* 1746–66) took an active interest in art and had energetic advisers. In addition to the academy's students, who did not play a prominent role until the middle of the century, a stream of talented painters and graphic artists were summoned to Denmark: the French tapestry-weaver François Léger (*d* 1744), the Venetian painter Hieronymus Miani (*fl* 1739–45) and, from Nuremberg, the painter and architect Marcus Tuscher as well as the copperplate engraver Johann Martin Preissler (1715–94), who both became teachers at the academy along with the Swedish portrait painter Carl Gustaf Pilo. After 1740 French paintings and tapestries, including works by François Boucher and Nicolas Lancret were imported for the royal apartments in the newly built Christiansborg Palace and the mansions of the nobility in Frederiksstadden, laid out after 1749. The transition from the reign of Christian VI to Frederick V was reflected in a change of attitude from a prevailing German dominance to an increasing orientation towards France. In portraiture Johan Salomon Wahl and his circle represented a more conservative, pro-German direction, which gradually gave way to a brighter, lighter handling of colour and a freer and more informal perception of the sitter that is characteristic of French Rococo. The most important exponent of this style was Pilo, whose later portraits, however, show a restrained handling of colour, dramatic treatment of light and more serious characterization (possibly under the influence of Louis Tocqué in Denmark in 1758–9), and reflect a renewed study of the works of Rembrandt. The reaction against the Rococo and the interest in Neo-classicism also showed itself in the preference for Peder Als, who on his return from Italy introduced the new impulses from Winckelmann and Anton Raphael Mengs, along with the Swedish-born history painter Johan Edvard Mandelberg (1730–86).

Christian VII's accession in 1766 and even more so the regency (1770–72) of the court doctor and Royal adviser J. F. Struense, left a crucial mark on artistic life. In efforts to reform the country's economy, such larger projects as the Royal Frederick's Church (Frederikskirke) were cancelled and foreign artists were dismissed. The attempt to encourage indigenous Danish art was in the short term instrumental in favouring such young talents as Nicolai Abraham Abildgaard and Jens Juel, but at the same time it carried the risk of provincialism and the cultivation of mediocrity. In the late 18th century Abildgaard was the most important representative of Neo-classical history painting. His period in Rome (1772–8) fostered in him a more dramatic, emotive interpretation of the Antique. He worked on a series of paintings (1778–91) on national historical themes for the Banqueting Hall at Christiansborg Palace (destr. by fire in 1794). Later commissions included decorative works (e.g. the interior of the palace of the heir, Copenhagen), architectural designs, furniture (see fig. 16 below), monuments and sarcophagi. His more private works reflect his personal taste for humorous, lyrical and also erotic aspects of classical literature. The early portraits of Juel already show an exquisite sense of colour and virtuosity in rendering textures; these qualities and an amiable characterization of his models soon led to his being favoured by the court and by Copenhagen's bourgeosie. During eight years in Germany, Switzerland, Italy and France, he developed an interest in *plein-air* portraits, and after his return in 1780 he was the country's most employed portrait painter, along with the internationally celebrated miniature painter Cornelius Høyer. The copperplate engraver Johan Frederik Clemens made a series of book illustrations after Abildgaard and portrait engravings after Juel.

The deaths of Juel, Abildgaard and the sculptor Johannes Wiedeweldt in the first decade of the 19th century left a vacuum. In the 1820s, however, a new generation of highly talented painters grouped around the professors C. W. Eckersberg and J. L. Lund (1777–1867) came to prominence, principally in portraiture but also in genre and landscape painting, producing work characterized by an insistent realism. This fertile period in Danish art (and literature), which reached its zenith *c.* 1820–50, has been called the 'Golden Age'. Although the motifs often concentrated on national historical themes, the Danish, nature and everday life, the art of the Golden Age was not truly Danish in character but centred exclusively on Copenhagen. This period coincided with an economic and political recession, and large commissions from king and nobility receded in favour of purchases by the middle class. The academy retained its position of power, although it gradually became more conservative and far from just in the distribution of bursaries and prizes. From the 1820s Eckersberg and Lund held painting lessons as part of the educational course, and Eckersberg introduced private classes in *plein-air* painting. Lund was responsible for important contacts with Munich and Düsseldorf.

Before 1820 Eckersberg had established a portrait style with simple, quiet compositions, clear local colour, restrained pictorial space and sober characterization of the sitter. A more painterly treatment and livelier rendering can be seen in the predominantly small-scale portraits of the slightly younger Christian Albrecht Jensen and Christen Købke. During the 1830s, however, younger painters emphasized more monumental dimensions and greater detail. Family portraits and paintings of the artist in the studio were popular, as was genre painting, though some Italian folk scenes became exaggeratedly idyllic and sentimental in the work of some painters (e.g. Ernst Meyer). Before 1800 there had been only a few indigenous exponents of landscape painting (Juel, Lund and Erik Pauelsen), but Eckersberg's *plein-air* views of Paris and

9. Martinus Rørbye: *View from the Artist's Window, c.* 1825 (Copenhagen, Statens Museum for Kunst)

Rome (1810–16), with their carefully constructed linear perspective, were a decisive influence on the compositional drawing and the use of colour of the younger generation of painters. The landscape paintings of the Norwegian J. C. Dahl (in Denmark in 1811–18), characterized by a scientific study of light and atmospheric effects and by a romantic, evocative choice of motif, were equally important.

The art historian N. L. Høyen was instrumental in focusing interest on Danish nature and historical monuments as subjects. Young painters chose typical Danish landscape motifs: Johan Thomas Lundbye and the open landscape of Zealand; P. C. Skovgaard and the Danish beech forest; Dankvart Dreyer and the landscapes of Jutland and Fyn. Similarly, some (Christen Købke, Jørgen Roed, Constantin Hansen) depicted such national monuments as the cathedrals in Århus, Ringsted, Ribe and Roskilde, as well as Kronborg and Frederiksborg castles. Familiar surroundings were also used as suitable motifs, as in the *View from the Artist's Window* (*c.* 1825; Copenhagen, Stat. Mus. Kst; see fig. 9) by Martinus Rørbye. Although emphasized by the academy, history painting was of minor importance during this period. The new religious attitudes of the time are evident in a markedly increased production of altarpieces. The influence of the Nazarenes is particularly noticeable in works by Lund, Albert Kuchler and Adam Muller.

BIBLIOGRAPHY

M. Krohn: *Frankrig og Danmarks kunstneriske forbindelse i det 18. aarhundrede* [France and Denmark's artistic links in the 18th century] (Copenhagen, 1922)

F. Beckett: *Renæssancens portrætmaleri* (Copenhagen, 1932)

C. Elling: *Rokokoens portrætmaleri* (Copenhagen, 1935)

H. Bramsen: *Landskabsmaleriet i Danmark, 1750–1875* (Copenhagen, 1935)

E. Zahle, ed.: *Danmarks malerkunst fra middelalder til nutid* [Denmark's painting from the Middle Ages to the present] (Copenhagen, 1937, rev. 4/1956)

J. Sthyr: *Dansk grafik, 1500–1800* (Copenhagen, 1943, R 2/1970)

K. Fabricius, L. L. Hammerich and V. Lorenzen, eds: *Holland—Danmark: Forbindelserne mellem de to lande gennem tiderne* [Holland—Denmark: the links between the two countries through the ages], ii (Copenhagen, 1945)

Danske tegninger fra Melchior Lorck til Fyenboerne [Danish drawings from Melchior Lorck to the Fyn painters], 3 vols (Copenhagen, 1945)

M. Mackeprang and S. F. Christiansen: *Kronborgtapeterne* [The Kronborg tapestries] (Copenhagen, 1950)

C. Elling: *Paraden: Kunst i enevældens Danmark* [The parade: art in the Denmark of absolute monarchy] (Copenhagen, 1958)

E. Fischer: *Melchior Lorck: Drawings from the Evelyn Collection and from the Department of Prints of the Royal Museum of Fine Arts* (Copenhagen, 1962)

K. Voss: *Guldaldermalerens malerkunst: Dansk arkitekturmaleri, 1800–1850* (Copenhagen, 1968)

P. Eller: *Kongelige portrætmalere i Danmark, 1630–82* (Copenhagen, 1971)

T. la Brie Sloane: *Neoclassical and Romantic Painting in Denmark, 1754–1848* (Ann Arbor, 1972)

V. Poulsen, E. Lassen and J. Danielsen: *Dansk kunsthistorie: Billedkunst og skulptur*, ii (Copenhagen, 1972–5)

S. Theimann: *Hinrich Krock, 1671–1738: Der Hofmaler im absolutistischen Dänemark* (Copenhagen, 1980)

Danish Painting: The Golden Age (exh. cat., ed. H. Bramsen, A. Smith and K. Monrad; London, N.G., 1984)

S. Heiberg: 'Art and Politics: Christian IV's Dutch and Flemish Painters', *Leids Ksthist. Jb.* (1984), pp. 7ff

M. Stein: *Christian den Fjerdes billedverden* [The pictorial world of Christian IV] (Copenhagen, 1987)

Christian IV and Europe (exh. cat., 19th Council of Europe exh.; Copenhagen, 1988)

T. Gunnarson: *Frilufts måleri före friluftsmåleriet: Oljestudien i nordiskt landskapsmåleri, 1800–1850* [Painting *en plein air* before *plein-air* painting: the oil sketch in Nordic landscape painting, 1800–1850] (Stockholm, 1989) [Eng. summary]

H. Honnens de Lichtenberg: *Tro, håb og forfængelighed: Kunstneriske udtryksformer i 1500-tallets Danmark* [Faith, hope and vanity: artistic means of expression in 16th-century Denmark] (Copenhagen, 1989)

K. Monrad: *Hverdagsbilleder: Dansk guldalder—kunstnere og deres vilkår* [The everyday picture: the Danish Golden Age—artists and their roles] (Copenhagen, 1989)

E. Nyborg: 'Malerne Hans og Sten af Ribe: Om Ribes malermiljø og det "marked" i 1600rnes Vestjylland' [The painters Hans and Sten of Ribe: Ribe's circle of painters and its 'market' in West Jutland in the 1600s], *Synligt og usynligt: Studier tilegnede Otto Norn* [Visible and invisible: studies dedicated to Otto Norn], ed. H. Johannsen (Copenhagen, 1990), pp. 143–71

T. Holck Colding: *Miniature-og Emaillemaleriet i Danmark, 1606–1850* [Miniature and enamel painting, 1606–1850], 2 vols (Copenhagen, 1990)

E. L. Lillie, ed.: *Danske kalkmalerier* [Danish wall paintings] (Copenhagen, 1992), vii [covers 1536–1700]

B. Bøggild Johannsen and H. Johannsen: *Kongens Kunst* [Royal art], Ny dansk kunsthistorie, ii (Copenhagen, 1993)

H. Bramsen: *Fra rokoko til guldalder* [From Rococo to the Golden Age], Ny dansk kunsthistorie, iii (Copenhagen, 1994)

For further bibliography *see* OLDENBURG, (1) and (2) and individual biographies of artists.

BIRGITTE BØGGILD JOHANNSEN

3. AFTER 1840. From the mid-19th century to the late 1870s the Golden Age of Danish painting was drawing to a close, and the period is without great innovations. Christen Dalsgaard (1824–1907), Frederik Vermehren and Johan Julius Exner (1825–1910) painted mostly rural genre scenes in a National Romantic spirit and with a tendency towards the nostalgic; and Carl Bloch drew attention to the Düsseldorf school in his historical and religious paintings. Following contact with contemporary French art, however, *plein-air* painting came to the fore, especially in the work of P. S. Krøyer and Theodor Philipsen. The latter was the only Danish artist to be heavily influenced by Impressionism. The Skagen painters, centered around Anna Ancher and Michael Ancher, painted the life of the fishermen and the artists at Skagen, concentrating on the strong local light and its reflection in the ocean.

At this time, the brothers Joakim Skovgaard and Niels Skovgaard represented an alternative to naturalism with biblical themes, and Kristian Zahrtmann still favoured the Grand Manner and Renaissance art. Zahrtmann exerted most influence as a teacher: among his first generation of pupils were the Fyn painters (*Fynboerne*), Johannes Larsen (1867–1961), Fritz Syberg and Peter Marius Hansen. Towards the end of the century, along with Laurits Andersen Ring, they introduced a new, realistic view of rural life and landscape. At the same time Symbolism was adopted by Jens Ferdinand Willumsen, whose highly experimental graphic work brought Danish graphic art out of its chiefly reproductive role and changed it to an independent mode of expression in the 1890s. Vilhelm Hammershøi stands out, at this time, as a transitional figure, whose quiet, grey-tone interiors unite the close intimacy of the Golden Age with the independence of the medium, characteristic of the new century.

From 1905 to 1914 a large group of young Danish artists travelled to Paris, where they were highly impressed by French art. Cézanne in particular was of lasting importance for such artists as Karl Isakson, Harald Giersing,

10. Edvard Weie: *Standing Model*, oil on canvas, 1210×975 mm, 1923 (Copenhagen, Statens Museum for Kunst)

Edvard Weie (see fig. 10) and Olaf Rude (1886–1957). The same artists participated in the breakthrough of modernism during World War I, with Vilhelm Lundstrøm, William Scharff and Jais Nielsen (1885–1961), who were all influenced by Cubism. However, in the post-war period modernism lost its momentum, although in the 1920s Vilhelm Lundstrøm represented the continuation of the French connection with his Purist models and still-life arrangements. Expressionist-influenced landscapes were produced by Jens Søndergaard and Oluf Høst (1884–1966). Franciska Clausen (1899–1986), who participated in the Cercle et Carré exhibition in Paris in 1930, was one of the few Danish artists active in inter-war Constructivism. These years were characterized by the work of lyrical naturalists including Erik Hoppe (1897–1968) and Niels Lergaard.

In the 20th century graphic art developed largely independently of painting. In the early years Oluf Hartmann (1879–1910) worked with condensed figure compositions in a technique inspired by Goya. In 1920 a department of graphic art was established in the Kunstakademi with Axel Jørgensen (1883–1957) as head for many years. Experiments in a variety of printmaking techniques were carried out, in particular etching, woodcut and linocut. In these works artists showed more interest in human and socially committed themes than in contemporary painting.

In painting Surrealism was introduced in the 1930s by Vilhelm Bjerke-Petersen, Ejler Bille and Richard Mortensen. In 1934 they were the driving force behind the exhibition and the periodical *Linien* ('The line'), which promoted abstract Surrealism as inspired by Miró; and in

1935 a group of artists centred around Bjerke-Petersen and Wilhelm Freddie formed a figurative Surrealist group that was in contact with the international Surrealist movement. Towards 1940 the abstract Surrealist group, joined by Egill Jacobsen, Carl-Henning Pedersen, Else Alfelt (1910–75) and Asger Jorn, developed an abstract expressionism, which became the Danish contribution to the post-war group Cobra, in which Asger Jorn was a leading figure.

In the years after World War II there was also a breakthrough for Concrete art as a reaction to Cobra's fantastic imagery and predilection for popular forms of expression. Richard Mortensen and a group of younger artists who exhibited under the name Linien II belonged to this movement. They included Gunnar Aagaard Andersen, Paul Gadegaard (b 1920), Ib Geertsen (b 1919) and Albert Mertz (b 1920). Svend Wiig Hansen, who from the 1950s used man as the central motif in his fiercely dramatic compositions, was one of the leading figures of post-war art, as was Arne Haugen Sørensen (b 1932), who combined abstract expressionist elements with the surrealistic.

In the 1960s traditional concepts of art were questioned. The innovations of the decade were created in and around a number of circles. Arthur Köpcke (1928–77) was of crucial importance, partly as an intermediary between the Danish and foreign avant-garde in Gallery Köpcke (1958–63), partly as an active member of Fluxus. The Eksperimenterende Kunstskole was another important centre of creativity, which experimented with fundamental pictorial structures. Poul Gernes (b 1925) worked with anonymous, standardized primary forms; Per Kirkeby introduced Pop art and during the 1980s took up the pictorial thread of Edvard Weie and Asger Jorn.

In graphic art in the 1960s, besides the currents represented by Askel Jørgensen's pupils, research into the various expressive means of the medium was carried out at the Eksperimenterende Kunstskole under Jørgen Rømer (b 1923) and Richard Winther (b 1926), while at the same time Ole Sporring (b 1941) introduced a fantastic and socially critical figurative art. From the end of the 1960s the offset lithograph occupied an increasingly prominent position.

In the 1970s Neo-Constructivism featured prominently in the work of the group Ny Abstraktion, which included such artists as Merete Barker (b 1944), a pioneer in computer art, and Viera Collaro (b 1946), whose media include neon. At this time a politically targeted graphic art appeared, mostly linocut, dominated by the commune known as Røde Mor (Red Mother) with Dea Trier Mørch (b 1941) among its members. Fantastic, decorative screenprints were produced by Bent Karl Jacobsen (b 1934) and Karl Aage Riget (b 1933).

During the 1970s and 1980s artists with feminist sympathies, such as the former pupil of Joseph Beuys, Ursula Reuter Christiansen (b 1943), and Lene Adler Petersen (b 1944), were working within a powerful figurative idiom nurtured by myths and fairy tales. They paved the way for a new figurative art for such artists as Inge Ellegaard (b 1953), Claus Carstensen (b 1957), Dorthe Dahlin (b 1955), Nina Sten Knudsen (b 1957) and Peter Bonde (b 1958), who aligned themselves with the German

Neue Wilden, although their works were less vehement and more grounded in Minimalism.

BIBLIOGRAPHY

E. Zahle, ed.: *Danmarks malerkunst fra middelalder til nutid* [Denmark's painting from the Middle Ages to the present] (Copenhagen, 1937, rev. 4/1956)
Danske tegninger fra Melchior Lorck til Fyenboerne [Danish drawings from Melchior Lorck to the Fyn painters], 3 vols (Copenhagen, 1945)
J. Zibrandtsen: *Moderne dansk maleri* [Modern Danish painting] (Copenhagen, 1948, rev. with Eng. summary, 1967)
J. Styhr: *Dansk grafik, 1800–1910* (Copenhagen, 1949)
E. Fischer: *Moderne dansk grafik, 1940–1956* (Copenhagen, 1957)
G. Jespersen: *De abstrakte: Linien, Helhesten, Høstudstillingen, Cobra* (Copenhagen, 1967)
V. Poulsen, E. Lassen and J. Danielsen, eds: *Dansk kunsthistorie: Billedkunst og skulptur* [Danish art history: painting and sculpture], 5 vols (Copenhagen, 1972–5)
B. Irve: *Dansk grafik gennem 25 år* [Danish graphic art over 25 years] (Copenhagen, 1985)
1880-erne i nordisk maleri [The 1880s in Nordic painting] (exh. cat., Copenhagen, Stat. Mus. Kst, 1986)
Im Lichte des Nordens: Skandinavische Malerei um die Jahrhundertwende (exh. cat., text by R. Andree and M. Kreutzer; Düsseldorf, Kstmus., 1986)
Surrealismen i Danmark, 1930–1950 (exh. cat., text by B. Irve and others; Copenhagen, Stat. Mus. Kst, 1986)
J. J. Thorsen: *Modernisme i dansk malerkunst* [Modernism in Danish painting] (Copenhagen, 1987)
K. Varnedoe: *Northern Light: Nordic Art at the Turn of the Century* (New Haven and London, 1988)
Linien II (exh. cat. by C. Sabroe and M. Barbusse, Copenhagen, Stat. Mus. Kst, 1988)
Modernismens genombrott: Nordiskt måleri, 1910–1920 [The emergence of modernism: Nordic painting, 1910–1920] (exh. cat., Göteborg, Kstmus., 1989)
P. M. Hornung: *Realismen*, Ny Dansk Kunsthistorie, iv (Copenhagen, 1993)
H. Wivel: *Symbolisme og impressionisme*, Ny Dansk Kunsthistorie, v (Copenhagen, 1994)
H. Abildgaard: *Tidlig modernisme*, Ny Dansk Kunsthistorie, v (in preparation)

HANNE ABILDGAARD

IV. Sculpture.

1. Before *c.* 1540. 2. *c.* 1540–1840. 3. After 1840.

1. BEFORE *c.* 1540. Though poor in easily worked stone, Denmark is extraordinarily rich in medieval sculpture. The sculpture of the Romanesque and Early Gothic periods was the most internationally oriented and most independent in its expression, before the Hansa towns made Scandinavia to a wide extent an economic and cultural province of north Germany. Some pieces, such as the Crucifixion figure in Herlufsholm (see below), are masterpieces of medieval art. Others are also of interest as representatives of forms (such as early retables) that no longer survive in the European heartlands. Most of the domestic works are craftsmanlike, not to say provincial, but constitute in their numbers an unrivalled source for the study of workshops and of the spread and decline of artistic trends.

The oldest examples of sculptural work are a series of engraved stylized Germanic animal motifs, mythological scenes, symbols and crosses on runic monuments from the missionary period of the 10th and 11th centuries. A low-relief work can be seen on the large Christianization stone (*c.* 960) of King Harald I Bluetooth (*reg c.* 950–85) at Jelling, where older motifs are imbued with a Christian influence from Britain or elsewhere in the empire (*see* VIKING ART, fig. 7).

Romanesque stone sculpture on portals, fonts and funerary monuments was widespread, but appears chiefly in Jutland and in Scania (now Skåne, Sweden). In the Jutland peninsula granite blocks were used for building and for sculpture, which flourished *c.* 1125–*c.* 1250. The most important masons' schools sprang from the cathedral building sites in Slesvig (now Schleswig, Germany), Ribe and Viborg, where Lombard sculptural traditions of the Rhine area were modified and adapted to indigenous materials. The hardness and the coarse grain of the granite compelled the masons to concentrate on the main forms of the motifs. In the most successful works this produces an effect of monumental plastic strength, supported by the powerful positions of the figures. A masterpiece is the lion-bearing, four-pillared portal with a huge tympanum relief of the *Deposition* at Ribe Cathedral (for illustration *see* RIBE). The same masons obviously worked in Slesvig and on a series of parish churches, such as Østre Starup, where the corners of the building have almost free-standing man-eating lions, while a dragon-slaying St Michael guards the entrance. The lion motif was especially popular on portals and baptismal fonts, often in the form of double-bodied lions with one head. In the northern part of Jutland Anglo-Norman influences also made themselves felt, most clearly in Vor Frue, Ålborg, where the portal (see fig. 11) is decorated with deeply carved billets, chevrons and zigzags as well as low reliefs of *Majestas Domini* and motifs from the childhood of Christ. From the decades around 1200, granite was supplemented in Jutland with imported finished Namur and Bentheim fonts, as well as an easily worked German sandstone and

11. Portal of Vor Frue, Ålborg, 12th century

limestone, which made possible the progression, in Ribe, to elegant Early Gothic in the console figures of the vault (*c.* 1225–50). Their closest parallels seem to be in the Matthiaskapelle, Kobern, near Koblenz.

In the other main area of Romanesque stone sculpture, the eastern Danish province of Scania, the building workshop at Lund Cathedral became the gateway for a somewhat different Lombard sculptural tradition, inspired by the upper Rhine area and Alsace. The good Scanian sandstone here allowed a direct implantation of the classicizing, Lombard-Byzantine repertory, with deep, lion-bearing canopied portals, sharply cut vines, acanthus leaves, braided ribbons etc, which, in a more or less coarsened form, also spread to the neighbouring provinces. From the later part of the 12th century several of the best Scanian sculptors moved to the Swedish island of Gotland, where the excellent limestone made it the main centre for stone sculpture in the Baltic.

With the decline in Danish church building in the second half of the 13th century, the domestic stone-carving traditions died out. The almost universal, flat gravestones were brought in unfinished from Gotland (Danish from 1361 to 1645) and carved by ordinary masons in Denmark. More demanding commissions, for instance all the royal funerary monuments up to the beginning of the 16th century, were imported. Christopher I (*d* 1259) and Erik VI (*d* 1319) were laid to rest under Flanders brasses with alabaster inlay (in Ribe and Ringsted). The cast-bronze grave figures, reliefs and other parts survive from the monument of Christopher II (*d* 1332) in Sorø (of Lübeck workmanship), while Valdemar III (*d* 1375) and Margaret I (*d* 1412) had tombs of black Belgian marble with effigies and reliefs in alabaster (Sorø and Roskilde).

Like stone sculpture, Danish wood sculpture (and, in part, related metalwork) flourished in the high Middle Ages. A number of roods survive from the Romanesque period, six of them with a then common (but now exceedingly rare) metal cladding of gilded copper (all Copenhagen, Nmus.). The same technique was used on ten chased and gilded altar table fronts (frontals) from the period 1150 to 1250, the 'golden altars' (of which six are in Copenhagen, Nmus., one in Nuremberg, Ger. Nmus., and the rest *in situ* in the parish churches of Sahl, Stadil and Lyngajö). Three of these frontals, from Lisbjerg, Odder and Sahl churches, have characteristic arched retables, which are among the earliest retables in Western art. These seem chiefly to be a matter of domestic work after partly English, later prevailingly Rhine-Westphalian inspiration.

A classicizing, Early Gothic style appeared *c.* 1220 in a group of exquisite carvings (in wood and ivory), which became formative for the rich wood sculpture of the 13th century in Denmark. Both historical and art-historical evidence shows that the new impulses—represented by, among others, the Crucifixion figure in Herlufsholm (*see* Gothic, fig. 96)—came directly from northern France to an artistic environment around the powerful king Valdemar II (*reg* 1202–41) and his principally French-oriented bishops. Among the chief pieces is a Crucifixion group in Roskilde Cathedral (pieces survive) and an exceptional rood (h. 5.56 m) in Sorø, which is not fully rounded but carved in relief (possibly because of the order's ban on sculpture). The amount of parish church wood sculpture from the 13th century is almost overwhelming, consisting of more than 300 roods and Crucifixion groups, statuary, carved gallery fronts of rood-lofts etc.

The Danish image-carving workshops degenerated from the later part of the 13th century and had to give way in competition with the fast-expanding Hansa towns. In general, very few works from the 14th century are known, while from the period from *c.* 1425 to the Reformation in 1536 hundreds of crucifixes and richly carved altar retables survive. The style is thoroughly north German even in the relatively large number of domestic works, and where quality products were concerned, the Danish market was almost completely conquered by the workshops in the north German Hansa towns. The choir-stalls of Lund Cathedral are an exception to this, having been executed in an international, middle European style during the time of Valdemar III (*reg* 1340–75), and they belong among the richest of the Middle Ages. Several decades later a skilful north German workshop carved the choir-stalls in Roskilde Cathedral (1420) and in Ringsted Monastery Church, while the country's other large churches generally have choir-stalls (or parts thereof) from the decades towards 1500. Among the German masters represented in Denmark, Bernt Notke of Lübeck should be mentioned: his unusually well-preserved high altarpiece in Århus Cathedral (1479) is among the most monumental in northern Europe.

Towards the end of the Middle Ages English alabaster retables (from Nottingham) and some Netherlandish altarpieces (all those known are from Antwerp) were also imported. In the 16th century it became more usual for foreign sculptors to work and settle in the country. Thus Danish art regained a higher quality and greater versatility, with, among other things, a revival of stone sculpture. Notable is the architect and mason Adam van Düren, probably from the Rhineland, who worked *c.* 1500–30 in eastern Denmark, chiefly at Lund Cathedral, Helsingør (Carmelite convent), on Glimminghus Castle and Copenhagen Castle. Claus Berg from Lübeck was of greater significance: after years of training in southern Germany, he settled with a large workshop in Odense *c.* 1508–10. From here an extensive series of works in both stone and wood was produced up to 1532. The most important work is connected to the tombs in Odense for King John and his family, who are shown kneeling on Berg's masterpiece, the cathedral's mighty altarpiece (*c.* 1521). The forms and decoration of the early Renaissance broke through earliest in the rich, newly discovered limestone façade (*c.* 1530) of Gottorp Castle, Schleswig, for Frederick I (*reg* 1523–34), and, presumably from the same period, at Copenhagen Castle, where the architect and sculptor Martin Bussaert worked. The gravestone (1536; Sorø Church) for Archbishop Absalon (*d* 1201), attributed to Bussaert, is Denmark's earliest Renaissance funerary monument.

BIBLIOGRAPHY

F. Beckett: *Danmarks kunst* [Denmark's art], 2 vols (Copenhagen, 1926)
P. Nørlund: *Gyldne altre: Jydsk metal kunst fra Valdemarstiden* [Golden altars: Jutland metalwork from the Romanesque period] (Copenhagen, 1928) [Eng. summary]
Danmarks kirker [Denmark's churches] (Copenhagen, 1933–) [inv. pubd since 1933; Eng. summaries]

M. Rydbeck: *Skånes stenmästare före 1200* [Scanian masons before 1200] (Lund, 1936) [Ger. summary]

M. Mackeprang: *Danmarks middelalderlige døbefonte* [Denmark's medieval baptismal fonts] (Copenhagen, 1940) [Eng. summary]

P. Nørlund: 'Lübeck und die dänische Plastik im 13.–14. Jahrhundert', *Acta Archaeol.* [Copenhagen], xi/1–2 (1940), pp. 132–9

M. Mackeprang: *Jyske granitportaler* [Jutland granite portals] (Copenhagen, 1948) [Eng. summary]

V. Thorlacius-Ussing, ed.: *Danmarks billedhuggerkunst* [Denmark's sculptural art] (Copenhagen, 1950)

C. A. Jensen: *Danske adelige gravsten fra sengotikens og renæssancens tid: Studier over værksteder og kunstnere* [Tombstones of the Danish nobility from the Late Gothic and Renaissance: studies on workshops and artists], 5 vols (Copenhagen, 1951–3) [Eng. summary]

O. Norn: 'Rhinlandsk stil på Sjælland' [Rhineland style in Zealand], *Nordisk medeltid: Konsthistoriska studier tilägnade Armin Tuulse* [Nordic Middle Ages: art historical studies for Armin Tuulse] (Uppsala, 1967), pp. 99–113 [Ger. summary]

W. Slomann: *Bicorporates: Studies in Revivals and Migrations of Art Motifs*, 3 vols (Copenhagen, 1967)

O. Norn: *Jysk granit* [Jutland granite] (Copenhagen, 1968) [Eng. summary]

A. Andersson: 'The Holy Rood of Skokloster and the Scandinavian Early Gothic', *Burl. Mag.*, cxii (1970), pp. 132–40

E. Moltke: *Bernt Notkes altertavle i Århus domkirke og Tallinntavlen* [Bernt Notke's retables in Århus cathedral and Tallinn] (Copenhagen, 1970) [Ger. summary]

H. Thümmler: 'Die Soest-Erwitter romanische Bildhauer-Werkstatt und ihre Ausstrahlung nach Schonen', *Ksthist. Tidskr.*, xl/3–4 (1971), pp. 65–88

E. Bøggild Johannsen: 'Studier i Christoffer II.s gravmæle' [Studies on Christopher II's tomb], *En bog om kunst til Else Kai Sass* [A book on art for Else Kai Sass] (Copenhagen, 1978), pp. 27–52

T. Hinrichsen: *Corpus der 'romanischen' Grabsteine Dänemarks* (diss., U. Hamburg, 1978)

J. Vellev, ed.: *Romanske stenarbejder* [Romanesque stone works], 4 vols (Højbjerg, 1981–9)

H. Langberg: *Gunhildskorset: Gunhild's Cross and Medieval Court Art in Denmark* (Copenhagen, 1982) [parallel Dan. and Eng. texts]

N.-K. Liebgott: *Elfenben* [Ivory] (Copenhagen, 1985)

E. Moltke: *Runes and their Origin: Denmark and Elsewhere* (Copenhagen, 1985)

J. Barfod: *Holzskulptur des 13. Jahrhunderts im Herzogtum Schleswig* (Husum, 1986)

L. Gotfredsen and H. J. Frederiksen: *Troens billeder: Romansk kunst i Danmark* [Pictures of the faith: Romanesque art in Denmark] (Herning, 1987)

E. Nyborg: 'Korbue, krucifiks og bueretabel: Om de ældste vestjyske triumfkrucifikser, deres udformning og anbringelse' [Chancel arch, rood and arched retable: on early roods in West Jutland, their forms and positions], *Hikuin*, 14 (1988), pp. 133–52 [Eng. summary]

——: 'Det gamle Sorø-Krucifiks: Et forsøg på at indkredse cistercensiske traditioner for udformningen af monumentale krucifikser' [The elder Sorø crucifix: an attempt to define Cistercian traditions for the elaboration of monumental crucifixes], *Ksthist. Tidskr.*, lix/1–2 (1990), pp. 88–113

O. Norn and S. Skovgaard Jensen: *The House of Wisdom / Visdommen i vestjylland* (Copenhagen, 1990) [Eng. and Dan. text]

Kunstschätze Jütlands, Fünens und Schleswigs aus der Zeit Waldemar des Siegers (exh. cat., Viborg Stiftsmus., 1991) [Dan. and Ger. edn]

E. Nyborg: 'The Holy Rood Crucifixion Group of Roskilde Cathedral and the Scandinavian Early Gothic', *Hafnia* (1993)

EBBE NYBORG

2. *c.* 1540–1840. The new Lutheran church service introduced after the Reformation of 1536 gradually brought changes to church interiors. Fixtures such as pulpits and pews became indispensable, and there was an increasing need to renew such items as altarpieces, baptismal fonts and galleries. Masons, joiners and carvers also found ample work in the production of tombstones and epitaphs, where Renaissance architectural forms and ornamentation soon took effect. A major disseminator of Renaissance motifs was the Netherlandish sculptor Cornelis Floris of Antwerp, who principally produced sepulchral monuments for the royal family and the nobility (e.g. the canopied tomb of *Christian III*, Roskilde Cathedral, 1569–76). A number of Netherlandish artists produced works or established themselves in Denmark after 1574, attracted especially by the activities at Kronborg Castle, Helsingør though only a few can be linked to particular works with certainty. One sculptor of international reputation was Johan Gregor van der Schardt (*c.* 1530–81), who created portrait busts (1577–9) of Frederick II and his queen. A magnificent bronze Neptune Fountain (*c.* 1576) in Kronborg courtyard was executed by Georg Labenwolf from Nuremberg.

Numerous sculptural commissions were linked to the building projects of Christian IV (*reg* 1588–1648), culminating in Frederiksborg Castle, Hillerød. The Neptune Fountain (1615–17) and the marble gallery (1619–21) were contributed by Netherlandish masters: Adrian de Vries and Geraert Lambertz. from the workshop of Hendrik de Keyser I respectively. A number of Germans were also represented, including Statius Otto. Special treasures such as the church's altar (1606, by Jacob Mores the younger) and the altar of the royal pew (*c.* 1615, by Matthias Wallbaum) were imported. An equestrian statue of the king was begun (1643–4) by the Flemish sculptor François Dieussart (*c.* 1600–61), who also produced a portrait bust of the king *all'antica* (Copenhagen, Rosenborg Slot).

Cabinetmakers and wood-carvers continued to work on church fixtures and fittings in the 17th century, and cabinetmakers' guilds were set up in several major provincial towns. The most important commissions, altarpieces and pulpits, were still characterized *c.* 1600 by a rigid, architectonic structure but gradually the figurative links grew and the ornamentation became more sumptuous in the Auricular style. A principal figure in East Jutland was Peder Jensen Kolding (before 1646–1675), who executed the pulpit (1670) for Klosterkirken (since 1794 Vor Frelser), Horsens (see fig. 12).

The most prestigious sculptural commission of the new absolute monarchy of Christian V (*reg* 1670–99) was the equestrian statue of the King erected in 1688 on the newly laid out Kongens Nytorv by Abraham-César Lamoureux from Metz. Christian Nerger (before 1671–1708), from Saxony, left his mark on many major decorative schemes with stuccowork (e.g. the gallery and audience chamber, Frederiksborg Castle, 1680s) and wood-carving (e.g. the organ front in Vor Frelser, Christianshavn, 1697–8). The dramatically structured altarpiece in the same church was designed after a draft (1694–5) by the Swedish architect Nicodemus Tessin the younger, who was a significant channel of influence from Bernini and Roman Baroque. Away from the Court, the Flemish sculptor Thomas Quellinus created a series of grandiose funerary monuments (e.g. Vor Frue, Copenhagen), which synthesized elements of Roman Baroque with direct inspiration from the Netherlands. The most stately funerary monuments, the sarcophagi (1716–19) of *Christian V* and *Queen Charlotte Amalie*, Roskilde Cathedral, are attributed to Johan Christopher Sturmberger (*d* 1722) from Vienna and Andreas Gercken (*d* 1717) and Didrik Gercken (1692–1748), possibly after designs by the architect Wilhelm

12. Peder Jensen Kolding: carved oak, mahogany, ivory and palisander pulpit, Klosterkirken (since 1794 Vor Frelser), Horsens, 1670

Friedrich von Platen. Didrik Gercken also executed the sarcophagi (1736–42) for *Frederick IV* and *Queen Louise*, also in Roskilde Cathedral, after a design by Lauritz de Thurah (1706–59). Magnus Berg (1666–1739), born in Norway, won contemporary European recognition with his skilfully executed ivory carvings. The Copenhagen fire of 1728 resulted in more commissions for furnishings for Copenhagen's four gutted churches. In his pulpits in Copenhagen as well as in the chapels of Fredensborg Palace (1726) and Vallø Castle (1728–32), Friedrich Ehbisch (c. 1672–1748) introduced new iconographic themes influenced by contemporary biblical exegesis and devotional literature. The newly built Christiansborg Palace, Copenhagen, drew several foreign artists to Denmark, including the French sculptor Louis-Augustin Leclerc (c. 1688–1771), who introduced the French Rococo style in the gilt dining-room (begun 1738) at Christiansborg Palace and in the banqueting hall at Amalienborg Palace, Copenhagen (1752–4); Leclerc also became a professor at the Kongelige Danske Kunstakademi, Copenhagen.

The summoning in 1753 of the French sculptor Jacques-Francois-Joseph Saly (1717–76) was of great importance for the increasing orientation towards France and the dawning Neo-classicism. Saly executed the bronze equestrian statue of *Frederick V* (completed 1771; Copenhagen,

Amalienborg Square) and became Director (1754–71) of the reorganized Akademi. The first recipient of the Akademi's travel bursary was the Danish-born Johannes Wiedeweldt, who in 1754–8 stayed in Rome, where his friendship with Johann Joachim Winckelmann was of crucial importance, inspiring him to campaign for Neo-classicism. Wiedeweldt returned to Denmark in 1758, and for the next 40 years was given many public commissions, including sculptures for the Christiansborg banqueting hall (1765; destr. 1794), as well as interior and garden designs, decorations for festive occasions, portraits and designs for decorative arts. In the production of funerary monuments and sarcophagi he exploited his insight into antique emblems. His dominant role over more than a generation overshadowed such younger artists as Carl Frederick Stanley (i).

The golden age for sculpture centred around the work of Bertel Thorvaldsen, a major figure in international Neo-classicism, who practised in Rome for more than 40 years before returning to Denmark in 1838. His students Hermann Ernst Freund and Hermann Wilhelm Bissen developed individual styles: Freund's *Ragnarok* frieze, commissioned in 1827 for Christiansborg, represented a new departure in its use of dramatic expression and Nordic mythological theme, as did his introduction of Pompeiian style interiors in his Copenhagen home (*see* §V, 2 and fig. 15 below). He and Bissen, with great realism, represented in their portrait busts the character and physiognomy of the subject, breaking with Thorvaldsen's idealizing style.

BIBLIOGRAPHY

C. A. Jensen: *Danmarks snedkere og billedsnidere i tiden 1536–1660* [Denmark's cabinetmakers and wood-carvers during the period 1536–1660] (Copenhagen, 1911)

H. Friis: *Rytterstatuens historie i Europa fra oldtiden indtil Thorvaldsen* [The history of the equestrian statue in Europe from antiquity to Thorvaldsen] (Copenhagen, 1933)

C. A. Jensen: *Danske adelige gravsten fra sengotikens og renæssancens tid* [Tombstones of the Danish nobility from the Late Gothic and Renaissance periods], 2 vols (Copenhagen, 1951–3) [Eng. summary]

L. O. Larsson: 'Bemerkungen zur Bildhauerkunst am dänischen Hofe im 16. und 17. Jahrhundert', *Münch. Jb. Bild. Kst*, xxxvi (1975), p. 177ff

Fyrste og hest: Rytterstatuen på Amalienborg [Prince and horse: the equestrian statue at Amalienborg] (exh. cat., ed. E. Salling and J. Erichsen; Copenhagen, Bymus., 1976)

K. Kryger: *Allegori og borgerdyd: Studier i det nyklassicistiske gravmæle i Danmark, 1760–1820* [Allegory and bourgeois virtue: studies in the Neo-classical tomb monument in Denmark, 1760–1820] (Copenhagen, 1985)

H. Jonsson: *Gud til Aere kiercken til zirat: Peder Jenssøn Koldings praedikestol i Vor Frelsers kirke i Horsens, 1670* [Honour be to God; the Church as Ornament: Peder Jenssøn Kolding's pulpit in Vor Frelser, Horsens, 1670] (Horsens, 1987)

A. D. Ketelsen-Volkhardt: *Schleswig-Holsteinische Epitaphien des 16. und 17. Jahrhundert*, Stud. der Schleswig-Holsteinischen Kstgesch., 15 (Neumunster, 1989)

A. Paulsen: *Magnus Berg (1666–1739): En kunstner ved kongens hoff* [Magnus Berg (1666–1739): an artist at the king's court] (Oslo, 1989)

V. Michelsen: 'Snedkere og billedskærere i Horsens snedkerlav, 1603–1745' [Cabinetmakers and wood-carvers in Horsens Cabinetmakers' Guild, 1603–1745], *Synligt og usynligt: Studier tilegnede Otto Norn* [Visible and invisible: studies dedicated to Otto Norn] (Copenhagen, 1990), pp. 127–42 [Eng. summaries]

L. H. Honneus de Lichtenberg: *Johan Gregor van der Schardt: Bildhauer bei Kaiser Maximilian II, aus dänischem Hof und bei Tycho Brahe* (Copenhagen, 1991)

B. Bøggild Johannsen and H. Johannsen: *Kongens kunst* [Royal art], Ny dansk kunsthistorie, ii (Copenhagen, 1993)

H. Bramsen: *Fra rokoko til guldalder* [From Rococo to the Golden Age], Ny dansk kunsthistorie, iii (Copenhagen, 1994)

B. L. Grandjean: *Stukarbejder i Danmark 1660–1800* [Stucco works in Denmark, 1660–1800] (Herning, 1994)

BIRGITTE BØGGILD JOHANNSEN

3. AFTER 1840. When Bertel Thorvaldsen, the leading representative of Neo-classicism in Denmark, died in 1844, he left a legacy that influenced several generations of Danish sculptors, first and foremost Hermann Wilhelm Bissen, who completed a number of Thorvaldsen's pieces. Bissen, in turn, ensured that the Thorvaldsen tradition continued until the 20th century through his many pupils. After 1850, however, Bissen represented a move in a more Romantic direction. Jens Adolf Jerichau (i) was also rooted in classicism, but his work marked the beginnings of opposition to it. With his preoccupation with psychological aspects, he paved the way for Naturalism, which made a true breakthrough just before the 1880s in the work of such artists as Vilhelm Bissen (1836–1913) and August Saabye (1823–1916), the latter with a predilection for human drama. At the end of the 19th century there was a break with Naturalism in favour of Symbolism and fantasy in the work of two artists: Jens Ferdinand Willumsen, influenced by French art, produced philosophically oriented, Symbolist reliefs and sculptures; Niels Hansen Jacobsen (1861–1941) produced sculptures featuring death and devils.

The early 20th century was characterized by opposition to all that was academic and classicist, and contemporary French sculpture, especially that of Auguste Rodin, had a clear influence on Danish sculptors who emerged at this time. For Kai Nielsen his contact with Rodin's work became an important stimulus to revolt against the legacy of Thorvaldsen. Uplifted by vitalist ideas and a predilection for the erotic, Nielsen's work concentrated on mythological presentations of the childhood of man (see fig. 13). Gerhard Henning (1880–1967) also strove to give sculptural form to the erotic, especially in a number of female figures. He was, however, gradually influenced by a new wave of classicism, which was very much in evidence in the work of Johannes C. Bjerg (1886–1955), Einar Utzon-Frank (1888–1955) and Adam Fischer (1888–1968). All of them had been highly influenced by French modernism in Paris before World War I, and they contributed to the breakthrough of modernism in Denmark a few years later with work dominated by formal stylization.

In the inter-war years naturalistic sculpture experienced a new revival in conjunction with a pronounced reaction to modernism. Mogens Bøggild (1901–87) made a thorough study of nature the basis for his work, in which animals generally played the leading role. Knud Nellemose (*b* 1908) worked with unheroic depictions of ordinary people and with sports motifs. Although sculpture did not play a leading role in the breakthrough of Surrealism in the 1930s, Ejler Bille, Henry Heerup and Sonja Ferlov Mancoba all made sculptures linked with the ideas and idioms of Surrealism, Heerup often using debris. They all created sculptures that combine abstraction with organic forms. The abstractions of the human figure by Erik Thommesen (*b* 1916) and Sonja Ferlov Mancoba's later, supple figures based on the mask form appeared as a continuation of this trend. As Concrete art began to flourish in the years following World War II, Robert

13. Kai Nielsen: *Leda and the Swan*, sandstone, h. 1.10 m, 1918 (Copenhagen, Statens Museum for Kunst)

Jacobsen started to work with a stringent, open, non-figurative style. Taking this as his point of departure, Willy Ørskov (1920–90) revived the ideas and forms of early Constructivism and helped make way for the new trends of the 1960s.

The 1960s were characterized by a broadly based revolt against both the older, academically influenced tradition of monumental sculpture and modernism. Closed, autonomous sculptures were abandoned in favour of works incorporating space. A large group of sculptors responsible for the Sommerudstillingen (summer exhibitions), held in Den Frie Udstillings Bygning, Copenhagen, 1961–7, worked on a structuralist basis with sculptural syntax. For Stig Brøgger (*b* 1941) and Hein Heinsen (*b* 1935), this led to increasingly Minimalist work in the late 1960s, while Kasper Heiberg (1928–84) melded form and colour in commissions that entered into a dialogue with the sites for which they were created. Egon Fischer (*b* 1935) began to work with a more organic style, rich in its associations and at times humorous. Jørgen Haugen Sørensen combined the destructive with the beautiful in his work in marble. Contemporary with the Sommerudstillingen, the Eksperimenterende Kunstskole endeavoured to start from scratch. Paul Gernes (*b* 1925), Per Kirkeby and Bjørn Nørgaard (*b* 1947) were the leading figures in experimental work to test the elementary characteristics of materials and forms in a number of Happenings or sculptural demonstrations. Around the mid-1970s this group produced sculptural tableaux that often commented on the cultural heritage. Richard Winther (*b* 1926) made an important contribution to this phase, and with Nørgaard and Kirkeby he laid the foundation for the 'recycled classicism' of the 1980s that was seen in a number of gigantic monuments. In the late 1970s the group Ny Abstraktion formed around a revival of Constructivist geometric and architectural sculpture in urban spaces, combined with the use of contemporary materials and colours, in work by, for example, Margrethe Sørensen (*b* 1949) and Torben Ebbesen (*b* 1945).

A new generation in sculpture appeared in the 1980s. Its typical representatives were the Leifsgade Collective, which worked with artistic intervention in deserted and dilapidated rooms, often playing on the relationship between nature and culture. Outside this circle, Christian Lemmerz (*b* 1959) produced sculpture that, with references to Joseph Beuys, challenges the viewer with unusual, association-rich materials, endeavouring to embrace cultural criticism and function as an energy field in space.

BIBLIOGRAPHY

S. Schultz: *Nyere dansk billedhuggerkunst fra Niels Skovgaard til Jais Nielsen* [Modern Danish sculpture from Niels Skovgaard to Jais Nielsen] (Copenhagen, 1929)

V. Thorlacius-Ussing, ed.: *Danmarks billedhuggerkunst fra oldtid til nutid* [Denmark's sculpture from Antiquity to the present] (Copenhagen, 1950)

V. Poulsen, E. Lassen and J. Danielsen, eds: *Dansk kunsthistorie: Billedkunst og skulptur*, 5 vols (Copenhagen, 1972–5)

L. Krogh: *Kunst i rummet: Monumental udsmykning i Danmark, 1964–1988* [Art in space: monumental commissions in Denmark, 1964–1988] (Copenhagen, 1989)

HANNE ABILDGAARD

V. Interior decoration.

1. Before *c*. 1750. 2. *c*. 1750 and after.

1. BEFORE *c*. 1750. Before the Renaissance, interior decoration consisted of rather simple wall paintings with secular motifs (e.g. at Hesselagergaard House, Fyn, *c*. 1550) or walls hung with tapestries. Surviving inventories bear witness to the continued use of these during the Renaissance, and, as in the rest of Europe, panelled rooms became popular. Christian IV's winter room in Rosenborg Castle, Copenhagen, for example, has an extensive collection of Netherlandish landscape paintings set into panelling from floor to ceiling. Carved and gilt ornamentation of Netherlandish origin, executed by the wood-carver Gregor Greus (*d* 1616) in 1614–15, embellishes the wood and complements the paintings. The ceiling was originally stucco but was later replaced with a contemporaneous ceiling, with inset paintings, from another room in the palace. The floor is painted with *trompe l'oeil* marble slabs, and an enormous chimney-piece crowned by the king's monogram occupies the space between the windows. The furnishing may have consisted of highly ornate cabinets imported from Germany. Velvet or gilt-leather covered chairs may have been placed around a monumental table.

The main rooms of Frederiksborg Castle at Hillerød (*see* HILLERØD, FREDERIKSBORG CASTLE), also commissioned by Christian IV, must have looked similar. Most of the interiors were destroyed by fire in 1859, but in some rooms it was possible to reconstruct the carved and painted wooden or stucco ceilings. The king's private oratory (1615–20) in the Chapel had Dutch paintings with biblical motifs painted on copper, set into richly ornamented ebony panelling. Inlays of vineleaves in exotic dark woods on a lighter background in differently shaped panels are characteristic of the Christian IV period. On the ceiling there were geometrically shaped wooden panels embellished with turned and carved ebony rosettes. In the Banqueting Hall there is a lavish stucco ceiling with an animal frieze, the stags of which carry real antlers, and the walls are clad with gilt leather. The Ålborg Room (Copenhagen, Nmus.) shows that the taste for panelled rooms spread from the court and nobility to the middle class. Beams in the ceiling, which had previously been left untreated or were painted, were now enclosed and embellished, and ornamented pilasters divided the walls; the sparse but often lavishly carved wall-fixtures add to the harmony of the room.

During the early Baroque, German influence continued to dominate, although artists from the rest of Europe began to receive commissions. The audience chamber and matching antechamber in the extension (1680s) to Frederiksborg Castle are probably the most dignified—and unchanged—interiors from the Baroque. The architect was Lambert van Haven, and French, Italian and Dutch artists were commissioned for the interior decoration. Paintings depicting Christian V's deeds were set above the marbled knee-high skirtings, and the room's coffered dome arches from a huge cornice. The windows are embellished with ornate wood and stucco decorations of garlands and putti.

One of the earliest examples of chinoiserie in European interiors is Christian IV's bedroom at Rosenborg Castle, for which the Dutch painter Francis de Bray executed Chinese motifs (ships, landscapes and genre scenes), based on engravings, in gold on a dark green lacquered background (1667–70). Frederick IV (*reg* 1699–1730) had a chinoiserie cabinet (1709–11) in Frederiksborg Castle, presumably carried out by the court lacquerers Christian van Bracht (*c*. 1637–1720) and Johan van Bracht (1684–1710); the walls are clad with panelling in blue, red and white, representing Chinese porcelain. Blue and white was also used in a room in Clausholm Castle (1731–43). In 1732 work began on Christiansborg Palace in Copenhagen to replace the medieval castle. The chief architect was Elias David Häusser (1687–1745), while the two court architects NIELS EIGTVED and Laurids Lauridsen De Thurah were responsible for the interiors; they provided the designs, which were executed by the sculptor Louis-Auguste Leclerc. A delicate Rococo, inspired by François de Cuvilliés I, characterized the decoration, which was destroyed when the palace burnt down in 1794. Similar work by Eigtved can be seen, however, in the small château of Frederiksdal, at Lake Fure (nr Copenhagen), built for the Foreign Minister J. S. Schulin in 1745. The principles for the interior decoration were taken from the work of Jacques-François Blondel, which resulted in a more restrained Rococo than that used in Germany. The elegant white stucco decoration in the room opening on to the garden was carried out to Eigtved's design by the Italian stuccoists Carlo Enrico Brenno (1688–1745) and Joan Battista Fossati (*d* 1756).

About seven years later Eigtved designed a far more sumptuous interior, the Great Hall of Moltke House at

Amalienborg Palace, in which the gilt Rococo ornamentation is more plastic: the former coolness was replaced by lavish Rococo decoration, with illusionistic leaves and garlands. The structure of the room is clear, and the individual elements are subordinated to the collective idea. Allegories of art and science painted by François Boucher crown the five double doors, and portraits of *Frederick V* and *Julia-Maria* by Louis Tocqué were inserted in two of the panels on the back wall. The other two walls, as well as the two pilasters on the window wall and the wall above the two chimney-pieces, are taken up by large mirrors. Leclerc took part in the decoration of the walls and designed the mirror-frames and console tables.

2. *c.* 1750 AND AFTER. In 1757 the dining-room of Moltke Mansion (see fig. 14) was decorated in the Neoclassical style by Nicolas-Henri Jardin; the resulting interior, early even in an international context, is an original and solid masterpiece. By means of linked columns the room was divided in three, and in front of either end wall a sideboard was built up with a huge fountain. On them classical vases crowned with leaves were surrounded with rushes and reed maces, and on either side were candelabra decorated with putti in rushes. This juxtaposition of classical elements with a naturalistic rendering of flora, characteristic of early Neo-classicism, became a continuous feature of subsequent Danish decorative arts. Opulent trophies were placed on the trumeaux on the longitudinal

walls, and the naturalistic, gilt garlands of leaves and flowers recur in the gently curved ceiling cornice, where they frame oval panels with allegorical motifs. The cabinetmaking was carried out by Christian Frederik Lehmann, and 36 lacquer and gilt dining-chairs with cane seats and backs were imported from France.

Caspar Frederik Harsdorff replaced Jardin's Rococo Classicism with a purer Classicism, which, despite foreign inspiration in terms of choice of materials and colours as well as its principles, is perceived as characteristically Danish. Blondel's guidelines were maintained, but the expression of style was radically changed, notably through reduced ornamentation: the ceiling is undecorated, and the doors and panels have inlaid profilings but are otherwise undecorated. The decoration is focused instead on console mirrors and chimney-pieces. The walls are either hung with oil or easel paintings or decorated with 'antique' paintings, as in the Queen's Apartment in Fredensborg Palace with vases with putti in niches painted in *trompe l'oeil* on a green background (1776), or in the Countess's Dressing-room in Moltke Mansion painted with tendrils in grisaille (before 1778), both painted by Johan Mandelberg (1730–86). These simply decorated wall sections, inspired by antique frescoes, signify the beginning of a Danish tradition that was to last into the 20th century.

The court decorator Joseph Christian Lillie (1760–1827) was influenced to a certain extent by the style of the Adam

14. Dining-room of Moltke Mansion, Amalienborg Palace, Copenhagen, decorated by Nicolas-Henri Jardin, 1757

15. Panelling from the apartment of Hermann Ernst Freund, Copenhagen, c. 1830 (Copenhagen, Danish Museum of Decorative Art)

brothers, but he also looked to such sources as engravings of the Baths of Titus, Raphael's Loggias and Piranesi for inspiration for the painted grotesques that frame the wide, middle sections of the wall in the interiors at Marienlyst in Helsingør (1791) and Jomfruens Egede (1798), near Prastó. In the central sections he placed a framed antique motif in grisaille. Lillie's colours are more delicate and the interiors even simpler than those by Harsdorff. Both architects designed their own furniture, the fine, often gilt, classical ornamentation of which added a warm accent to the simplicity of the rooms. In 1792 Lillie designed the interiors of the small Château Liselund on the island of Møn in a rustic style, in which the grotesque decoration of the so-called 'Monkey Room' is combined with chinoiserie in pale colours. Some of Lillie's English-inspired furniture for Liselund survives *in situ*.

The Pompeian Revival interiors in the Erichsen Mansion (later the Københavns Handelsbank) in Copenhagen, created in 1801 by Joseph Ramée with Pierre Etienne Le Sueur (*d* 1802) as chief painter, are tightly decorated in a quite different manner. Models for the motifs, taken from contemporary engravings, were freely juxtaposed to create a classicizing effect. Floral motifs, relief-like sections and grotesques vie with one another. The interior has no parallel in Denmark, although from the beginning of the 19th century the Pompeian Revival style became widespread. The new Christiansborg Palace, erected after fire destroyed the first in 1794, suffered the same fate and burnt down in 1884. However, a number of drawings and some furniture by the architect C. F. Hansen and his son-in-law, G. F. Hetsch, have been preserved (Copenhagen, Kstindustmus. and Kon. Dan. Kstakd.) and show that, along with the Empire style inspired by Karl Friedrich Schinkel, they continued to use Harsdorff's saturated Pompeian colours. In the king's large dining-room (1832),

for example, the principles for the arrangement of the room remain the same as before: decorated mirrors and panels alternate, and the simple doors are crowned by painted sections. In the wide sections the base colour is Pompeian red with a dancing nymph motif in the centre, framed by fine tendrils. In the narrow sections there are grotesques, and the sections are divided by pilasters.

In the 1830s the sculptor Hermann Ernst Freund began to redecorate his professorial residence under the Kunstakademi, Copenhagen. He based his plans on the direct study of domestic interiors from the Roman Republic, particularly the simpler homes in the ancient towns around Naples. At the lowest level of each room there were black knee-high panels on which simple tendrils and animal motifs were painted. Above this, the main wall sections were divided by narrow, black sections with thyrses. The basic colour in the main sections was either Pompeian red or a warm yellow, and small antique motifs were painted in the central sections by the best of the Kunstakademi's pupils (see fig. 15). The plain wooden floor was painted to look like a mosaic, and light rhombic decorations embellished the ceilings. The reception rooms were furnished with copies of Greek and early Roman pieces (*see* §VI below). Everything in Freund's home was stamped by antiquity, by the dream of Italy. Even the garden was laid out in an Italian fashion, and the manner of the residents' dress as well as the soft furnishings were inspired by Johann Joachim Winckelmann's phrase *edle Einfalt, stille Grösse*.

A whole generation of artists and intellectuals of Copenhagen became fascinated with this pure, simple home. This style—or rather lifestyle—which is without any real parallel in Europe, was to have a lasting importance for the Danish interior. Gottlieb Bindesbøll adopted the style in his sophisticated decorative scheme for the Thorvaldsens Museum (1839–47), Copenhagen, in which intense colouristic features contrast with the cool white sculptures. The dark, vibrant green and the saturated Pompeian red and yellow have virtually become standard colours in Danish museum interiors. These colours were also used in domestic interiors into the 20th century as a background for the display of Golden Age paintings.

The Renaissance Revival was given a strong bias towards the Christian IV style following the fire at Frederiksborg Castle in 1859. The manor house Frijsenborg (1860s), near Hammel, is one of the main examples of the monumental historicist decorative style of the period. Art Nouveau had only limited impact in Denmark, its influence is mainly seen in a preference for foliage decoration. The contemporaneous Arts and Crafts movement, however, sought inspiration for rustic forms from earlier periods. Martin Nyrop's Town Hall (1892–1905) in Copenhagen contains a number of colourful national-romantic interiors with gilt-leather or tapestry-clad walls, carved wooden panels and stucco and tiles for decoration, with motifs from Danish history.

From 1910 to 1930 simplified versions of the Danish Pompeian and Neo-classical styles appeared, as well as the Empire style for domestic interiors. With the advent of Functionalism, developments in domestic interiors receded somewhat while elegant examples of late 20th-century interior decoration can be found in many public buildings by, among others, ARNE JACOBSEN.

BIBLIOGRAPHY
T. Clemmensen: *Møbler af N. H. Jardin, C. F. Harsdorff og J. C. Lillie og eksempler på deres interiørdekorationer* [Furniture by N. H. Jardin, C. F. Harsdorff and J. C. Lillie and examples of their interior decoration schemes] (Copenhagen, 1973) [with Eng. summary]
M. Gelfer-Jørgensen: *Dansk kunsthåndvaerk fra 1730 til vor tid* [Danish crafts from 1730 to our time], 2 vols (Copenhagen, 1973–82)
T. Clemmensen: *Skæbner og interiører: Danske tegninger fra barok til klunketid* [Fates and interiors: Danish drawings from the Baroque to the Victorian period] (Copenhagen, 1984)
I. M. Antonsen: *Prinsens Palais*, 2 vols (Copenhagen, 1992)

VI. Furniture.

1. Before 1790. 2. 1790–1900. 3. After 1900.

1. BEFORE 1790. Until the 19th century furniture-making in Denmark followed the rest of Europe. Renaissance pieces were inspired by the Netherlands and Germany; during the 17th century and the first half of the 18th German influence persisted, but from the middle of the century first French and then English traditions made an impact on the style of Danish furniture. While many excellent examples survive, a group of furniture that stands apart from the prevailing fashions is the pieces designed by C. F. Harsdorff. During the 1750s he visited Italy and Paris, where he must have seen Louis-Joseph Le Lorrain's furniture in the Greek Revival style, made for Ange-Laurent de La Live de Jully, and become acquainted with François de Neufforge's engravings. As well as a number of fine, gilded pieces of furniture with simple yet powerful ornamentation, Harsdorff designed a repertory of mahogany furniture in a clear, pure style. The embellishment consists of simple, gilded, classical ornaments, borders in the Greek Revival style, rosettes, fluting, well-cut mouldings and narrow inlaid bands around the drawers, all

subordinate to the simplicity of form (examples in Copenhagen, Kstindustmus.).

2. 1790–1900. Similar characteristics recur in early 19th-century domestic Danish Empire style furniture. Although some grand pieces conforming to official Danish Empire designs influenced by Charles Percier, Pierre-François Fontaine and Karl Friedrich Schinkel were made, many more examples of ordinary household furniture have been preserved, dating from approximately 1800 to 1840 with later offshoots. This range of furniture was made from mahogany with decorations in pale or black woods. It is mostly anonymous, designed and made in urban and rural workshops. Its consistency was promoted by the uniformity of the cabinetmakers' training. The background for this style was in part laid by Harsdorff and his contemporaries, but it was also inspired by the work of Joseph Christian Lillie (1760–1827), which betrayed the influence of Robert Adam (i). These design attitudes were spread through the teaching of craftsmen at the Kunstakademi, Copenhagen, and by the example of English furniture. This style is sometimes mistakenly called Danish Biedermeier during its last phase because of certain stylistic features that are in fact merely traditional Neo-classical designs. However, the extravagant geometric Biedermeier styling is non-existent, and such architectural elements as pediments, bases and strongly profiled cornices are the exception rather than the rule. Smooth, simple forms that display the figure of the mahogany are emphasized only by thin, light bands. Some furniture is decorated with pictorial motifs (dancing nymphs, antique genre scenes, sphinxes etc) and vine leaves in the Classical taste, inlaid with light wood. Many pieces are without any decoration.

Side by side with quantities of this furniture there is a distinctive, more exclusive group of élite furniture created by a coterie of painters, sculptors and architects. Its sources are found in the furniture of antiquity: in contrast with Neo-classical furniture, which derived its decoration from ancient architecture, these artists aimed to revive the furniture that was depicted in engravings of Greek and Roman frescoes, vases, cameos and sculpture. These Neo-antique artists had studied antique art in Italy and had become fascinated with some of the simpler domestic interiors of Pompeii as opposed to the Imperial style so favoured by adherents of the Danish Empire style. The main group of Neo-antique furniture dates from between 1830 and c. 1870, although the first Danish artist who went directly to the furniture of antiquity was the painter Nicolai Abraham Abildgaard. From 1790 to 1809 he produced a highly original range of furniture, which is closer in proportions, form and details to antique furniture than any earlier examples, even if his furniture also has such contemporary features as upholstery and includes other elements for which no antique model exists. Only the Klismos chair had contemporary parallels, but nobody reproduced the prototype so exactly as Abildgaard did (c. 1800; Copenhagen, Kstindustmus.; see fig. 16). The most distinctive feature of this furniture is the legs. Besides the strongly curved legs of the Klismos chair, there were twisted legs with beads, based on the bronze furniture of antiquity. The antique Greek throne with its rectangular, incised legs (c. 1795; Copenhagen, Nmus.) is another type,

16. Gilt Klismos chair by Nicolai Abraham Abildgaard, 765×580×690 mm, *c.* 1800 (Copenhagen, Danske Kunstindustrimuseum)

while others were tapered downwards in stages. The Greek *diphros*, or stool with bell-shaped joints, was also copied. Some of the furniture was made for Abildgaard's own home, and other pieces were commissioned by the royal family, who employed him as their architect (Hillerød, Frederiksborg Slot).

When the sculptor Hermann Ernst Freund returned in 1828 from a lengthy visit to Italy, he wished to create a 'Danish Herculaneum' in his official residence belonging to the Kunstakademi (*see* §V, 2 above). As far as furniture was concerned, he continued the traditions begun by Abildgaard and supplemented the various types of furniture with, among other things, a high-backed mahogany sofa, the legs of which were copied from antique sarcophagi benches, and the armrests and back of which were copied from the Greek throne or armchair with its sphinx arm supports, known from grave stelae. Such furniture as a piano or a crib, which never existed in antiquity, were designed by Freund with antique legs, and he had them decorated with motifs and colours from ancient vases (Hillerød, Frederiksborg Slot).

The architect Gottlieb Bindesbøll continued this tradition. The beautifully inlaid bronze seat in the Museo Nazionale di S Martino in Naples became the model for a set of gilt chairs and stools (Copenhagen, Stat. Mus. Kst) and for a library table in the Thorvaldsens Museum, Copenhagen, which was furthermore furnished with simple and elegant display cases; these laid the foundation for the high standard of fittings and furnishings in Danish museums. The showcases in the Antique Collections room were decorated with restrained, inlaid lines copied from Pompeian ornamentation. Bindesbøll was fascinated by the principles of construction of antiquity rather than the decoration, and his ideas on furniture-making were of decisive importance for future developments in the Danish cabinet trade. The painters Constantin Hansen, Jørgen Roed and G. C. Hilker (1807–75) designed furniture for their own and their friends' homes from the same antique prototypes between the 1840s and the 1860s. For each of them it was the simple Greek or early Republican furniture rather than the more pompous Roman imperial furniture that provided models.

The fascination with the Neo-antique was vigorous, even at the time of the national-romantic movement, among the group of artists and intellectuals who were supporters of a united North. Research has established that patrons who commissioned Neo-antique furniture belonged to the national-liberal circle, which laid the foundation for the abolition of the absolute monarchy and the introduction of a constitution in the 1840s. Denmark lacked an indigenous furniture style, and a potent reason for this revival of the Neo-antique style was its association with democratic Greece. Neo-antique furniture retained its popularity into the 20th century and formed the basis of modern Danish furniture.

3. AFTER 1900. Through the historicist movement and the Arts and Crafts period at the turn of the century (at which point Denmark did not adopt the Art Nouveau style), the Neo-antique style persisted. It served KAARE KLINT, who in 1924 became the first associate professor in furniture-art at the Kunstakademi, as a starting-point and influenced his furniture designs before 1920. He created a series of variations on simple furniture types based on a system of classical proportions. As well as being inspired by the Neo-antique, he was influenced by 18th-century English furniture in his insistence on obvious but solid construction. His own love of fine wood and carefully studied profiles was passed on to his students. Only rarely was steel used in Danish Functionalism. Foremost among Klint's successors was Mogens Koch (*b* 1898), whose shelving system (1928) and folding chair (1933) continue to be produced and are widely used in Danish homes and offices. BORGE MOGENSEN, who was trained as a cabinetmaker, added new expressions to the Klint tradition; his style was more powerful and more dependent on such Danish woods as oak and pine. The latter was used by Mogensen in a range of furniture he began designing in 1942: simple, cheap furniture for small apartments, in which the individual elements could be put together as required. Ole Wanscher (1903–85), professor of furniture-art, carried on Klint's classical Functionalism in a series of well-designed pieces. Poul Kjærholm (1929–80), who succeeded Wanscher as professor, designed frame chairs that evoke the notion of the Neo-antique. Kjærholm also worked in a restrictive idiom in which simple themes are constantly varied. He supplemented wood with steel and can be seen as a Danish exponent of Ludwig Mies van der Rohe's Minimalism, which eventually reached Denmark after World War II.

ARNE JACOBSEN was an exponent of international Functionalism in his architecture but not in his furniture. The largest group he designed, manufactured by the Fritz Hansen's Eftf., has steel legs and is moulded and laminated in organic forms, such as the chairs the 'Egg', the 'Swan' and the 'Ant'. Together with Jacobsen's floral curtains and

17. Armchair by Hans J. Wegner, cherry-wood with leather cushion, made by Fritz Hansens Eft., 1944 (Copenhagen, Danske Kunstindustrimuseum)

wallpapers, these pieces brought to Functionalism a distinctly Nordic flavour. Finn Juhl (1912–89) also worked with free forms inspired by the international art of the 1950s. The backs and seats of his chairs are mounted on a frame—always executed in handsome wood—the individual components sometimes being modelled in soft forms; this tradition was continued by Jørn Utzon. Hans J. Wegner (b 1914) incorporated elements from both schools in his comprehensive output (see fig. 17). His range of frame chairs continued the tradition but with a cross-current from Chinese furniture. At the end of the 1940s Wegner designed a series of innovative shell chairs, in wood; they were widely disseminated, as was much of Mogensen's factory-produced furniture. Wegner created a series of new concepts within the Danish tradition of furniture-making.

The interaction between architect and cabinetmaker or manufacturer was to be of decisive importance for the development of Danish furniture. In 1927 leading cabinetmakers entered the cheap mass furniture market. Together with architects, they arranged exhibitions, and the Snedkermestrenes Møbeludstilling (Cabinetmakers' Furniture Exhibition) became a forum for the best of the craft until the 1950s. The idea was resurrected by two groups of architects and cabinetmakers, the Møbelgruppen of 1983 and the Snedkernes Efterårsudstilling (Cabinetmakers' Autumn Exhibition).

BIBLIOGRAPHY

T. Clemmensen: *Møbler af N. H. Jardin, C. F. Harsdorff og J. C. Lillie og eksempler på deres interiørdekorationer* [Furniture by N. H. Jardin, C. F. Harsdorff and J. C. Lillie and examples of their interior decoration schemes] (Copenhagen, 1973) [Eng. summary]

G. Jalk: *40 Years of Danish Furniture Design*, 4 vols (Copenhagen, 1987)

M. Gelfer-Jørgensen, ed.: *Herculanum på Sjælland* [Herculaneum on Zealand] (Copenhagen, 1988) [Eng. summary]

A. Steensberg and G. Lerche: *Danish Peasant Furniture*, 2 vols (Copenhagen, 1989)

A. Karlsen: *Dansk møbelkunst i det 20. århundrede*, 2 vols (Copenhagen, 1990–91)

MIRJAM GELFER-JØRGENSEN

VII. Ceramics.

About the time of the first Christian missions in AD 826, the potter's wheel, the kiln and lead glazing were introduced in Denmark. Tilemaking began c. 1150, and the oldest thrown, lead-glazed pots were made from the beginning of the 13th century. From the Middle Ages black, unglazed earthenwares were made in the Fyn and Jutland regions. These hand-moulded pots were made by women and were an important cottage industry until the late 19th century. During the late Middle Ages tiled stoves were much in demand. During the Renaissance, polychromed wares were produced in potteries in country towns.

The first Danish faience factory, Store Kongensgade (1722–69), in Copenhagen, was given a monopoly on blue-decorated wares, and there was a simultaneous ban on the import of Dutch faience, which it hoped to replace. The factory's best period was between 1727 and 1749, under the artistic management of Johan Ernst Pfau (c. 1685–1752), when the blue-and-white wares produced were similar to those made in Delft (see fig. 18). In 1750 Christian Gierløf (1706–86) took over the concern and

18. Hexagonal plate with leaf decoration, made at the Store Kongensgade faience factory, Copenhagen, and signed with the monogram JP, diam. 260 mm, c. 1740 (Copenhagen, Davids Samling)

attempted to modernize forms and motifs into the exuberant Rococo style. Characteristic forms included the mitre-shaped 'Bishop' bowls and tea-trays for the tops of tables. In the 1750s the factory began to decline after other faience factories were established, some of which attempted to contravene Store Kongensgade's monopoly of blue-decorated wares, while other factories manufactured faience with polychrome decoration. The factory of Blåtårn (1738–54) in Copenhagen manufactured stovetops and tiles and consoles for the royal palaces as well as more everyday utilitarian wares. The factory at Kastrup (1754–94), on the island of Amager, took over the Blåtårn moulds and produced gaily coloured wares, which were in keeping with contemporary demands and imitative of the wares of the Strasbourg faience factories. Kastrup specialized in artichoke- and duck-shaped tureens and dishes shaped like cabbage leaves. They also produced whiteglazed busts and sculptural groups after well-known sculptors' works, such as Jacques-François-Joseph Saly's bust of *Frederick V*, *Pluto and Proserpina* by Gianlorenzo Bernini and *Leda and the Swan* by Corneille van Clève. From 1780 to 1781 the factory was taken over for the manufacture of Neo-classical-style stone wares, which had pierced decoration. The Østerbrofabrikken (1764–9) in Copenhagen manufactured blue-decorated faience despite the privilege of Store Kongensgade.

After 1750 a number of factories were established outside Copenhagen, most of which were set up by landowners and produced only mediocre goods. Factories in the Duchies of Schleswig and Holstein were established in order to compete with Store Kongensgade's monopoly and produced more fashionable wares in the popular and complex Rococo style. Peripatetic artists gave production a common character. The factory in Schleswig (1755–1814) had strong links with the Kingdom, which was its main market, and was well-known for its predilection for Rococo-style wares and centrepieces. The factory of Criseby (1759–65) was established by Johann Nicolaus Otte (1714–80). Around 1765 the concern was moved to the nearby factory of Eckernförde (1765–80), which attempted to produce wares that would rival the standard of those from German and French porcelain factories. The factory at Kiel (1758–87), Holstein, specialized in stately pot-pourri vases painted in enamel colours, one example of which (1770; London, V&A) is decorated with a scene from Molière's play *L'Amour médecin* painted by Abraham Leihamer (*c*. 1745–74). The factory of Stockelsdorff (1771/2–86) near Lübeck specialized in the manufacture of polychrome Rococo-style stoves: other wares included plates with pierced rims, pot-pourri vases, jardinières and helmet-shaped jugs. In Kellinghusen, Holstein, there were as many as six competing faience factories from 1763 to 1860, producing similar wares that had a distinctly peasant character with freely painted yellow-and-purple flower decoration.

During the 1770s the production of faience declined after the establishment of the Kongelige Porcelainsfabrik in Copenhagen in 1775, which, until the founding of the factory of Bing & Grøndahl in 1853, was Denmark's only porcelain factory (*see* COPENHAGEN, §3 and fig. 4). In order to keep up with changing tastes, several faience factories began producing stoneware. Such factories as

Rendsborg (1765–1813) in Holstein were completely reorganized, and two stoneware factories in Rønne, on the island of Bornholm, were established to produce relief-decorated stone wares. However, these factories were to suffer after the Napoleonic wars when trade opened up, and such popular foreign goods as Staffordshire cream wares were imported once again.

The production of simple utilitarian wares continued in the 19th century at the factory of HERMAN AUGUST KÄHLER (est. 1839) in Næstved and at the terracotta factory of LAURITZ ADOLPH HJORTH (est. 1859) in Rønne. In 1863 the Aluminia Fajancefabrik was established in Copenhagen to compete with the foreign markets. Early production consisted exclusively of cheap, transfer-printed, utilitarian wares.

The first important Danish concern to produce decorative objects was P. Ipsen's Widow, Royal Court Terracotta Factory (1843–1955) in Copengagen. Small reproductions of well-known sculptures and copies of antique Greek vases were produced there to a high technical standard. Ipsen's Widow took part in the world exhibitions with increasing success, culminating in 1877 in Amsterdam, which enhanced its international reputation.

During the 1880s a small circle of artists who were interested in the wares being imported from Japan and China began to experiment with pottery as a medium for artistic expression, and the factory of Johan Wallman in Utterslev and the Københavns Lervarefabrik, Valby, allowed artist-potters to use their studios and materials. Thorvald Bindesbøll (*see* BINDESBØLL, (2)) worked at the Københavns Lervarefabrik producing wares with abstract decoration (e.g. enamelled and sgraffito-decorated plate, 1901; Paris, Mus. A. Déc.). The work of Bindesbøll and his circle anticipated the abstract art pottery of the later 20th century. At the Kongelige Porcelainsfabrik ARNOLD KROG introduced naturalistic underglaze painting of Danish landscapes, flora and fauna. In 1882 the Kongelige Porcelainsfabrik was bought by Aluminia. After 1900 the painters Christian Joachim (1870–1943) and Harald Slott-Møller were employed at the new factory, where they promoted the production of art pottery, decorated in strong colours with simplified, naturalistic motifs.

About 1900 the production of stoneware was revived, pioneered by JENS FERDINAND WILLUMSEN, who was artistic director at Bing & Grøndahl, and Niels Hansen Jacobsen (1861–1941), who was especially interested in glazed effects. The Kongelige Porcelainsfabrik also began experimenting with crystalline, liquid and crackled glazes and with stone wares (*c*. 1904). The Swedish potter Patrick Nordström (1870–1929) was the technical manager of the stoneware department at the Kongelige Porcelainsfabrik and produced flambé, aubergine and ox-blood glazes. Sculptural works by Axel Salto were also produced in stoneware by the factory. From 1911 to 1912 the architect Carl Petersen was the artistic consultant at Bing & Grøndahl, where he revived the tradition of horn-painting (slip-trailing using a cow's horn through which liquid clay is applied). Stoneware continued to be made by such potters as Cathinca Olsen (1868–1947) and Knud Kyhn (1880–1969), who specialized in glaze effects; Jais Nielsen (1885–1961), who produced such works as 'Pontius Pilate' with dark ox-blood glazes; Jean Gauguin (1881–1961), son of the painter Paul Gauguin, who produced unglazed stoneware; and Mogens Bøggild (1901–87) and Gertrud Vasegaard (b 1913). Bing & Grøndahl had their first stoneware exhibition in 1914 and concentrated on production by individual artists.

Stone wares produced by Nathalie Krebs (1895–1978) and Eva Staehr-Nielsen (1911–76) at the factory of SAXBO (1929–68), in Herlev, were to have considerable influence through their simplified forms and figured glazes. Bjørn Wiinblad (b 1918), whose works reflect his interest in Nordic folklore, produced a large number of decorative works for the Nymølle Fajancefabrik (1936–) in Kongens Lyngby. He also designed such tablewares as the 'Midsummer Night's Dream' service (1954; London, V&A) for the Fuurstrøm Fajancefabrik. Although stoneware was a more popular medium than porcelain during the early 20th century, the artist Erik Reiff (b 1923) successfully created a purely ornamental underglazed blue-and-white porcelain for Bing & Grøndahl. Dinner services continued to be developed by such potters as Grethe Meyer (b 1918), who designed the 'Blue Line' earthenware service for the Kongelige Porcelainsfabrik. In the 1960s and 1970s primitive-style rustic wares were popular, and Gutte Eriksen (b 1918) experimented with hard-fired earthenwares that resembled stoneware. In 1987 the Kongelige Porcelainsfabrik and Bing & Grøndhal merged to become Royal Copenhagen.

BIBLIOGRAPHY

J. Andersen and V. Sten Møller, eds: *Keramik, keramisk teknik, keramisk kunst* (Copenhagen, 1946)

E. Hiort: *Modern Danish Ceramics* (Copenhagen, 1955)

B. L. Grandjean, ed.: 'Dansk keramik', *Porslin*, 5–6 (1960) [special issue]

B. L. Grandjean: *Kongelig dansk porcelain, 1775–1884* [Royal Danish porcelain, 1775–1884] (Copenhagen, 1962)

L. Ehlers: *Dansk lertøj* [Danish pottery] (Copenhagen, 1967)

K. Uldall: *Gammel dansk fajence fra fabriker i kongeriget og hertugdømmerne* [Old Danish faience from factories in the kingdom and the duchies] (Copenhagen, 1967)

J. Ahlefeldt-Laurvig and K. Uldall: *Fajencer fra fabriken i St Kongensgade* [Faiences from the factory in Store Kongensgade] (Copenhagen, 1970)

F. Lynggaard: *Jydepotter og ildgrave* [Pieces of Jutland pottery and fire pits] (Copenhagen, 1972)

B. L. Grandjean, D. Helsted and M. Bodelsen: *Den Kongelige porcelainsfabrik, 1775–1975* [The Royal Porcelain Factory, 1775–1975] (Copenhagen, 1975)

J. Ahlefeldt-Laurvig and A.-M. Steimle: *Fajencer og stengods fra fabriken i Kastrup* [Faiences and stoneware from the factory in Kastrup] (Copenhagen, 1977)

E. Lassen: *En københavnsk porcelainsfabriks historie: Bing & Grøndahl, 1853–1978* [The history of a Copenhagen porcelain factory: Bing & Grøndahl, 1853–1978] (Copenhagen, 1978)

B. L. Grandjean: *Aluminia fajancer gennem hundrede år* [Alumina faiences through one hundred years] (Copenhagen, 1981)

W. Hull: *Danish Ceramic Design* (Pennsylvania, 1982)

B. L. Grandjean: *Kongelig dansk porcelain, 1884–1980* [Royal Danish porcelain, 1884–1980] (Odense, 1983)

H. V. F. Winstone: *Royal Copenhagen* (London, 1984)

B. Holst: *P. Ipsens Enke: En keramisk fabrik gennem 100 år* [P. Ipsen's widow: a ceramics factory during 100 years] (Copenhagen, 1990)

E. Winge Flensborg: *Hundrede år med Aluminia* [A hundred years with Aluminia] (Copenhagen, 1990)

LENE OLESEN

VIII. Glass.

The manufacture of glass in Denmark began after 1550 during the Danish Renaissance. Frederick II, subsequent kings and the nobility employed German glassblowers at the furnaces in the woods of eastern Jutland to produce glass, in particular panes and drinking glasses, for the newly built castles and manor houses. After about a hundred years production ceased because of the lack of fuel; Denmark's woods were too small to cope with the demand, and there was no indigenous supply of coal. Glass was not produced again in Denmark until 1825 when the Holmegaards Glasværker was built beside the Holmegaard moor, on Zealand, in order that peat could be used for fuel. The factory was founded by Countess Henriette Danneskiold-Samsøe (1776–1843) and began producing green beer bottles made by Norwegian glassblowers. In 1835 the factory began manufacturing handmade glass as wine glasses and other tableware. Glassblowers from Bohemia and Germany were employed, and the German glass tradition characterized Danish glass during this period. Denmark's second glass factory was the Conradsminde Glasværker (1835–57) near Ålborg, Jutland. Its period of manufacture was short; production included colourless and blue-tinted glass. These wares were also modelled on glass from northern Germany and Holstein, and the tradition of the German glassblowers employed again characterized the output. In 1847 the Kastrup Glasværker in Kastrup, near Copenhagen, was founded as a branch of Holmegaards Glasværker for the manufacture of bottles. In 1852 another factory, Glasværket i Aalborg, was established in Ålborg for the production of bottle glass. In 1867 Kastrup acquired a furnace for the production of handmade glass and manufactured a large range of traditional tableware. In 1873 Kastrup was sold to an independent company and soon dominated bottle production. In the 1880s Kastrup was the first Danish factory to produce pressed glass and had a special line in etched glass. In 1874 the Fyns Glasværker was built in Odense, on the island of Fyn. It specialized in the production of lighting accessories in opalescent glass, which was also used for tableware and often decorated with transfer-printing or painted motifs. Denmark's first glass designer, the artist H. A. BRENDEKILDE, worked at the Fyns Glasværker for a brief period (1901–4) designing lamps, vases and biscuit containers in typical Art Nouveau styles.

In 1924 a cooperative programme between Holmegaard and the Kongelige Porcelainsfabrik (see COPENHAGEN, §3) gave rise to a more artistic production of wine glasses to accompany the porcelain dinner services. The first result of this contract was the 'Lace' line of glasses designed by the porcelain painter Oluf Jensen (1871–1934). The design work was continued by Orla Juul Nielsen (1899–1985), who designed several sets of wine glasses for the Kongelige Porcelainsfabrik from 1925 to 1928. Following Nielsen's departure Holmegaard appointed Jacob Bang (1899–1965) as chief designer. He had trained as an architect and was a follower of Functionalism with a distinct feeling for elegant detail. He was the only Danish glass artist in the 1930s, and his first works were two large series—'Violets' (1928) and 'Primula' (1930)—both of which consisted of almost a hundred pieces. His works show an awareness of the stylistic developments of the period and are sometimes embellished with wheel-cut or trailed decoration. Later Bang designed sturdier glasses, which nevertheless retained a fine sense of line.

In 1942 Bang was succeeded as chief designer by Per Lütken (*b* 1916). During the 1950s Lütken forged his own distinctly individual style using thick, soft, colourless glass in simple shapes (see fig. 19). Later he added colour and produced more rustic shapes; 'Lava' (1970) was a strongly blistered and coloured glass, blown in wet, clay moulds, and 'Africa's Rose' was inspired by the flower of the South African shrub *Protea*. From the late 1950s a number of other such notable artists as the Swede Christer Holmgren (*b* 1933), the architect Sidse Werner (1931–89), Bang's son, Michael Bang (*b* 1944), and Torben Jørgensen (*b* 1945) were employed by Holmegaards Glasværker. Werner and Jørgensen have been particularly concerned with the modern centrifugal technique, developed during the 1950s in Sweden and Finland. This production technique, which has to some extent replaced the old pressware methods, involves turning at centrifugal force a lump of hot glass in an iron mould that is usually bowl shaped. The glass is then flung out into shape in the mould, its thickness depending on the initial quantity of glass used.

In 1965 the factories of Holmegaard, Fyn and Kastrup were merged, and Kastrup's production of tableware was discontinued. About 1970 Michael Bang designed the large 'Palette' series of opalescent, white tableware flashed with multicolours. Both Bang and Werner designed lamp bases and pendants using the technique devised at the Fyns Glasværk, which employs a triple layer of glass: a clear parison, covered by an opaline layer cased in a clear or coloured layer. In the late 20th century Holmegaard is the only glass factory in Denmark. It has two separate sections: one producing designer glass and fine tableware, the other manufacturing glass packaging material. All the other glassworks have been closed down.

BIBLIOGRAPHY

C. Nyrop: 'Danmarks glasindustri indtil 1750: Med nogle bemærkinger om ruder, drikkekar o. lign. gjenstande, før glasset trængte igjennem' [Denmark's glass industry until 1750: with some observations on window panes, drinking vessels and similar objects before glass prevailed], *Hist. Tidsskr.*, i (1879), pp. 434–523

G. Boesen: *Gamle glas* [Old glass] (Copenhagen, 1961)

P. Lütken and P. Riismøller: *Glasset* [The glass] (Copenhagen, 1962)

A. Larsen, P. Riismøller and M. Schlüter: *Dansk glas, 1825–1925* (Copenhagen, 1963)

T. Jexlev, P. Riismøller and M. Schlüter: *Dansk glas i Renæssancetid, 1550–1650* (Copenhagen, 1970)

M. Schlüter: *Glashåndværk i Danmark* [Glass craft in Denmark] (Copenhagen, 1973)

Danish Glass, 1814–1914: The Peter F. Heering Collection (exh. cat. by B. Wolsrup, London, V&A, 1974)

G. Buchwald and M. Schlüter, eds: *Kastrup and Holmegaard's Glassworks, Denmark, 1825–1975* (Copenhagen, 1975)

E. Lassen and M. Schlüter: *Dansk glas, 1925–1975* (Copenhagen, 1975)

P. Lütken: *Glass is Life* (Copenhagen, 1986)

Scandinavia: Ceramics and Glass in the Twentieth Century (exh. cat. by J. Hawkins Opie, London, V&A, 1989)

MOGENS SCHLÜTER

IX. Metalwork.

Although there has been a concentration of metalworkers in Copenhagen, provincial craftsmen have also produced high-quality products. Until 1857, when the Freedom of Trade Act was introduced, the guilds regulated the production of metalwork. The forms and style of Danish metalwork were particularly influenced by developments in Germany, England, France and the Netherlands until the 1920s, when Scandinavian craftsmen created their own distinctive functional style. The artist-craftsman often has his or her own workshop as well as being employed as a designer in a large organization. Since the beginning of the 20th century craftsmen or workshops often work in several different metals.

1. GOLD AND SILVER. The goldsmiths' guild received its privileges in 1429 and is thus one of the oldest in Denmark. In 1491 the first provision for hallmarking was established: the silver was not to be less than 14 weight (1 *quintin*; pure silver was 16 weight): in the 20th century silver hallmarked in Copenhagen is 13.5 weight. Since 1685 Copenhagen silver has been stamped with a maker's mark, town mark, assayer's mark and mark of the month. Provincial silver has a maker's mark and often also a town mark. Silver products made after 1900 throughout the country are marked with S 830 or S 925 to indicate the sterling value and a maker's mark.

Ecclesiastical silver and gold have been produced in Denmark since the 12th and 13th centuries, and from *c.* 1500 many types of tableware and items for personal use appeared. Large and often richly ornamented silver tankards in chased work, often supported on three orbs or fruits, were produced from *c.* 1550–*c.* 1730 (e.g. of 1680; London, V&A). There were also many other types

19. Smoked glass 'Duckling' vases, made by Per Lütken at the Holmegaards Glasværker, h. 415 mm and 215 mm, 1952 (Fensmark, Holmegaards Glasværker)

20. Silver fish platter and cover designed by Henning Koppel, 170×680×320 mm, Copenhagen, 1954 (Copenhagen, Danske Kunstindustrimuseum)

of drinking cups and goblets, vessels with flat, lobed handles and covered dishes. Spoons have a round bowl and a short round handle that often ends in a bud or a bunch of grapes. Around 1700 gadrooning appeared on bowls, dishes and the bases of candlesticks. During the early 18th century plain silverware without engraving or chased work, influenced by the Queen Anne style in England, was made. When coffee, tea and chocolate were introduced in the 18th century, new forms of tableware appeared. Danish silversmiths became particularly renowned for their hollow ware with swirling fluted decoration from the mid-18th century. The ornament—rocaille shapes, cast flowers and leaves—grew out of the forms. The Icelander Sivert Thorsteinsson (1714–99) was well known; he was also the royal goldsmith. Silver tableware was imported from France for the court and supplemented by indigenous copies. Cutlery with threaded edges, inspired by French examples, appeared in the 1740s in connection with the interior decoration of the Christiansborg Palace in Copenhagen (*see* §V above), and it has been produced in Denmark ever since. Egg-shaped pomanders, châtelaines and snuff-boxes (*see* §X below) were the height of fashion and were produced in great numbers in the tortuous forms characteristic of the Rococo style.

Andreas Holm (1735–1812) is well known for the simple objects and engravings in the Neo-classical style that he produced at the end of the 18th century. From this period there is some delicate silverware in openwork lined with blue glass, for example salt and sugar bowls. Delicate threadwork and filigree work also appeared. Between 1820 and 1840 silverware was characterized by the austere Neo-classical style promoted by the architect G. F. Hetsch at the Kunstakademi in Copenhagen. Hollow ware produced in this style is either barrel- or vase-shaped and embellished with chased vine-leaf decoration and cast ornament. From the mid-19th century industrially manufactured, pressed hollow ware elements and ornaments that were soldered together were incorporated into silverware. Vilhelm Christesen (1822–99), a jeweller and silverware manufacturer, was one of the first to introduce the use of machines in his workshop, including apparatus for electroplating and electrotyping. Like the goldsmith Jørgen Balthasar Dalhoff (1800–90), purveyor of silverware to the court, he was inspired by the styles of earlier periods, but they both also created goods with few embellishments.

From *c*. 1900 Danish gold- and silverware has been produced by both individual workshops and a number of fairly large companies, including those of Anton Michelsen (est. 1841), GEORG JENSEN (est. 1904) and Just Andersen (est. 1914) in Copenhagen, and Hans Hansen (est. 1906) in Kolding, Jutland. These companies established links with independent craftsmen and have thus been able to adapt to changing styles. From the 1920s and 1930s Danish applied and industrial arts have become renowned for their pure lines and forms. Modern silverware designs synthesize function with material, for example the sculptural hollow ware designed from 1945 by the sculptor Henning Koppel (1918–81) for Georg Jensen Sølvsmedie (e.g. silver fish platter and cover, 1954; Copenhagen, Kstindustmus.; see fig. 20). The craftsman and artist Kay Bojesen (1886–1958) produced an entirely plain set of silver cutlery in 1938 (e.g. Copenhagen, Kstindustmus.) that won the Grand Prix at the Triennale in Milan in 1951. This cutlery has since been produced in stainless steel.

2. BASE METALS. From the end of the 16th century until well into the 18th domestic utensils and tableware were usually made of pewter until ceramics and new alloys came into general use from the mid-19th century. The tight lines, rounded forms and engraved decoration of 16th- and 17th-century styles suited the material, and pewterware in these designs was produced well into the 19th century. From the first half of the 18th century covered tureens in the plain fluted style were produced. Until about 1850 pewterware was produced by specialist craftsmen of whom only those in Copenhagen formed their own guild. Pewter was marked according to three different qualities: 'English pewter', with a ratio of tin to lead of 15:1, 'Krontin' (6:1) and 'Mangods' (4:1).

Copper and brass have been widely used for kitchen and scullery utensils, warming-pans, braziers or chafing dishes and tea urns, often in simple, functional forms. These items were originally produced by coppersmiths, but from the 17th century they faced competition from six copper and brass factories: Hellebæk Værk (est. 1597), Flensborg Kobbermøller (1612), Nymølle Kobbermølle, Ørholms (1649), Brede Værk (1668), Rådvad Værk (1767), and Frederiksvoerk (1800). From 1746 copper and brass goods were marked. The coppersmiths used marks with the local town arms, their initials and the year for trade licence. The factories marked products with the reigning monarch's signature, often with a crown above it. The independent brass moulders mainly produced smaller items, for example candlesticks, chandeliers, irons, taps and lanterns (see fig. 21). These types of objects were also produced by bronze-founders who were usually involved in the casting of such larger items as bells, gratings and statues.

From about 1850 new alloys and industrial methods of production were introduced. Metalware manufacturers and iron foundries replaced the independent workshops. Carl M. Cohr, who set up a silverware factory in 1860 in Fredericia, Jutland, also specialized in inexpensive kitchen- and tableware in various base metals. Sheet iron, later covered with enamel, replaced pewter and copper in the kitchen. German (nickel) silver, Britannia metal (see PEWTER, §1) and stainless steel replaced or supplemented silver tableware. Danish iron foundries produced kitchenware in simple designs intended for woodburning kitchen ranges, whereas decorative items and tiled stoves were designed and decorated in accordance with the styles of the period.

In the 20th century kitchen- and tableware is produced in simple designs in cast-iron—with or without a coating of enamel—aluminium, stainless steel and copper. Pewterware has experienced a renaissance in the 20th century, partly through the work of MOGENS BALLIN and the firm of Just Andersen, whose tableware is characterized by simple, smooth forms with few decorative details. Danish silverware companies, for example Georg Jensen Sølvsmedie, produce high-quality everyday items—cutlery, tableware and tea and coffee sets—in stainless steel and other base metals, as well as in silver (e.g. the 'Cylinda' line of stainless steel tableware designed in 1967 by the architect Arne Jacobsen).

BIBLIOGRAPHY

G. Boesen and C. A. Bøje: *Old Danish Silver* (Copenhagen, 1949)
E. Lassen: *Dansk sølv* [Danish silver] (Copenhagen, 1964)
V. S. Møller: *Dansk kunstindustri* [Danish applied art], 2 vols (Copenhagen, 1969–70) [with short Eng. epilogue]
C. A. Bøje: *Danske guld og sølvmærker* [Danish gold and silver hallmarks], 3 vols (Copenhagen, 1979–80)
M. Thygesen: *Dansk kobbertøj, 1750–1850* [Danish copperware, 1750–1850] (Copenhagen, 1980)
Georg Jensen, 77 Artists, 75 Years (exh. cat., Washington, DC, Renwick Gal., 1980)
E. Johannsen: *Danske antiviteter af støbejern* [Danish cast-iron antiques] (Copenhagen, 1982)
J. E. R. Moller: *Georg Jensen: The Danish Silversmith* (Copenhagen, 1985)
H. Rasmussen: *Gammelt tin* [Old pewter] (Copenhagen, 1987)
M. Bencard: *Silver Furniture* (Copenhagen, 1992)

KIRSTEN RYKIND-ERIKSEN

X. Objects of vertu.

Danish objects of vertu include jewellery, ivory carving, hardstone carving and gold boxes. An early object of vertu is the sword (1551; Copenhagen, Rosenborg Slot) of Christian III (*reg* 1534–59) made in Copenhagen by the Fleming Johan Siebe (1542–64) and decorated with grotesques and scrollwork in the style of Frans Floris of Antwerp. The open crown (1596; Copenhagen, Rosenborg Slot) by Dirich Fyring (1580–1603) is a masterly interpretation of the *schweifwerk* (openwork) of Daniel Mignot. From 1580 turned and carved ivory, narwhal tusk and amber from the Baltic was produced. The Norwegian Jacob Jensen Normand (*c.* 1614–95) made models of ships in ivory and goblets in narwhal tusk. The throne of Frederick III (1662–71; Copenhagen, Rosenborg Slot) was made from narwhal tusk by the German Bendix Grodtschilling I (1662–90). From 1670 JOACHIM HENNE and from 1690 Gottfried Wolffram carved tankards, busts, plaques and portrait medallions. Absolutism, introduced in 1660, fostered splendour: the three life-size silver lions (Copenhagen, Rosenborg Slot) by Ferdinand Küblich (1664–87) that guard the throne of Frederick III epitomize the Baroque style; however, the crown (1671; Copenhagen, Rosenborg Slot) of Christian V (*reg* 1670–99) by Paul Kurtz (1655–76) is classical in style. The Huguenots Paul Prieur (1663–81) and Iosias Barbette (1694–1731) enamelled miniature portraits and boxes. A few vases and boxes of porphyry and rock crystal from Norway and obsidian from Iceland were made for the court from *c.* 1690 to 1730 (Copenhagen, Rosenborg Slot), but no real production ensued. Gold boxes were standard court gifts in the 18th century, but few have survived, for example the enamelled Rococo box (1758) by Jacob Henriksen-Moinichen (1754–88) and an oval Louis XVI-style box by Frederik Fabritius II (1740–1829), both in Rosenborg

21. Sheet-brass folding hand-lantern with crowned monogram of Christian VII, h. 250 mm, diam. 172 mm, late 18th century (London, Victoria and Albert Museum)

Castle. From *c.* 1707 the Norwegian Magnus Berg (1666–1739) carved extremely fine, biblical ivory bas–reliefs, which exploited the milky-blue, transparent ground. From *c.* 1750 to 1770 the Swiss ivory-turner LORENZ SPENGLER and the Swedish carver Iohan Ephraim Bauert (1726–99) made such items as statues, goblets and nécessaires in a Franco-Saxonian Rococo style.

The Fabritius dynasty, which included Frederik Fabritius I (1688–1755), who made the crown for Queen Magdalen (1700–70) in 1731, spanned four generations of court jewellers (*c.* 1680–1820) who made high-quality goods in contemporary designs. The diamond-studded watchcase (1767; Copenhagen, Rosenborg Slot) made for Queen Caroline Mathilda by Jean-François Fistaine (1719–92) is an example of the rise of Neo-classicism in Denmark; it is also a late example of royal patronage, which was largely replaced in the 19th century by bourgeois patronage. However, Julius Diderichsen (1823–96) received such important commissions from Frederick VII (*reg* 1848–63) as a Neo-Baroque diamond-and-pearl necklace (British Royal Col.) that was presented to Princess Alexandra (1844–1925) on her marriage in 1863 to the Prince of Wales (later Edward VII, *reg* 1901–10). Some fine, revivalist jewellery was produced during the later 19th century, including pieces in the Old Norse style by Emil Ferdinand Dahl (1849–79). From 1904 a Danish version of Art Nouveau jewellery was executed in silver and amber by the silversmith GEORG JENSEN (see fig. 22). In the 1920s this type of work was replaced by that of Johan Rohde, whose Naturalist style was tempered with classicism. From the 1930s there was a growth in mass production of simple and abstract jewellery, which evolved from Functionalism into a distinctive post-war Scandinavian style in the hands of such designers as Nanna Ditzel (*b* 1923), Torben Hardenberg (*b* 1945) and Arje Griegst (*b* 1938) whose work showed revivalist tendencies. Bent Knudsen (*b* 1924) and Arje Griegst design jewellery with simple, graceful forms, using different types of stones and enamel inlay.

BIBLIOGRAPHY

B. Bramsen: *Nordiske snusdåser* [Nordic snuff-boxes] (Copenhagen, 1965) [Eng. summary]
J. Rasmussen: 'Joachim Henne: Ein höfischer Kleinmeister des Barock', *Jb. Hamburg. Kstsamml.*, xxiii (1978), pp. 25–64
H. Steen Møller: *Arje Griegst: En verden i guld* [Arje Griegst: a world in gold] (Copenhagen, 1982)
G. Boesen: *Danmarks riges regalier* [Regalia of the Danish Kingdom] (Copenhagen, 1986) [Eng. summary]
M. Bencard: 'Märchenhafte Steine aus dem Meer: Der Bernsteinsammlung der Kunstkammer in Schloss Rosenborg', *Kst & Ant.*, vi (1987), pp. 22–34
J. Hein: 'Christian IV and the Goldsmiths', *Apollo*, cxxviii (1988), pp. 93–8
——: 'Goldemail des Manierismus und Frühbarock', *Kst & Ant.*, ii (1988), pp. 26–38
Å. Paulsen: *Magnus Berg* (Oslo, 1989) [Eng. summary]
P. Mellbye-Hansen: *De danske kronjuveler* [The Danish crown jewels] (Copenhagen, 1990)
A. K. Snowman: *Eighteenth Century Gold Boxes of Europe* (London, 1990)
J. Thage: *Danish Jewelry* (Copenhagen, 1990)
T. H. Colding: *Miniature- og email-maleri i Danmark, 1606-1850* [Miniature- and enamel-painting in Denmark, 1606-1850] (Copenhagen, 1991) [Eng. summary]
J. Hein: 'Ivories by Gottfried Wolffram, 1683–1716', *Scand. J. Des. Hist.*, i (1991), pp. 7–34

22. Necklace, silver and amber, l. 450mm, designed by Georg Jensen and made by Georg Jensen Sølvsmedie, Copenhagen, 1908 (Copenhagen, Danske Kunstindustrimuseum)

——: 'Splendour in Defeat: Danish Court Jewellery by Paul Kurtz and his Workshop', *Scand. J. Des. Hist.*, iv (1994), pp. 58–80

JØRGEN HEIN

XI. Textiles.

The history of Danish textiles dates back to the Bronze Age. The remains of garments made of woollen cloth, sprang and *masketing* (single-needle knitting) have been found in Bronze Age, Iron Age and Viking burials. A rare example of embroidery on a Bronze Age blouse excavated in Jutland in 1935 shows that this technique was also known from an early period. These textile crafts, including sprang and single-needle knitting, continued to be practised well into the 19th century, mainly in response to local needs. It was only intermittently that more important commercial industries were established, usually as a result of royal patronage.

BIBLIOGRAPHY

E. Andersenn and E. Budde Lund: *Folkelig vævning i Danmark* [Danish folkweaving] (Copenhagen, 1941)
G. Garde: *Dansk billedvævning, c. 1500–1800* [Danish pictureweaving, *c.* 1500–1800] (Copenhagen, 1949)
M. Hald: *Olddanske tekstiler* [Old Danish textiles] (Copenhagen, 1950)
Danish Arts and Crafts, Danish Arts and Crafts Association (Rønne, 1977)
A. Geijer: *A History of Textile Art* (Stockholm, 1979)
C. S. Talley: *Contemporary Textile Art: Scandanavia* (Uppsala, 1982)
N. Hertoft, ed.: *Textilkunst, 1987* (Copenhagen, 1987)

1. Tapestry. 2. Silk and embroidery. 3. Lace. 4. Other.

1. TAPESTRY. The earliest surviving examples of tapestry in Denmark are a group of hangings and cushion covers with primitive renderings of biblical motifs (Hamburg, Mus. Kst & Gew., and Copenhagen, Nmus.), dating from the mid-16th century and the early 17th, probably produced by weavers from the Netherlands who had set up workshops in Schleswig-Holstein. The first important Danish workshop was established in 1577 at Kronborg Castle, Helsingør, where the medieval castle was being extended and redecorated by Frederick II. It was managed by the Flemish painter and tapestry-weaver Hans Knieper and the tapestry-weaver Antonius da Corte (d 1578). Their major work was a series of 43 tapestries in wool and silk (1581–5; 15 preserved, Copenhagen, Nmus. and Helsingør, Kronborg Slot) ordered for the castle's vast ballroom. The series depicted 100 Danish kings, from the legendary King Dan to Frederick himself. Full-length portraits of one or two monarchs appeared on each tapestry, set in landscapes stylistically related to those produced by the Brussels tapestry workshops. Each king's biography in German verse appeared in an inscription panel above his portrait, with his crest in another narrower panel at the bottom, and both panels had ornamental surrounds. The surviving pieces show a wealth of detail, including flowers, animals and people hunting. The ornamentation, with festoons of flowers and fruit, is based on the Flemish version of Italian Renaissance decoration, known through the engravings of such artists as Cornelis Floris. Also belonging to this series of tapestries is a magnificent seat canopy for Frederick II (1585–6; Stockholm, Nmus.; see fig. 23) worked in wool, silk and gold and silver thread. It is embellished with the royal crests and shows three large female figures representing Justice, Temperance and Fortitude, surrounded by grotesque ornamentation partly inspired by Hans Vredeman de Vries. After Knieper's death in 1587 the workshop in Helsingør closed.

In the 17th century tapestries were much in demand to furnish the castles of Christian IV, but many of them were imported, especially from the Netherlands. Tapestries were commissioned from workshops in Delft: Karel van Mander II (1579–1623) supplied Frederiksborg Castle with 26 tapestries after his own designs (1617–19; destr. 1859) depicting the King's coronation and his military victories over the Swedes. Meanwhile Christian IV fostered a modest Danish production of tapestries by establishing a workshop (c. 1600–20) at the Hellig Gejstes Tugthus (Holy Ghost Gaol) in Copenhagen.

Tapestry weaving in Denmark revived under Christian V (reg 1670–99). In 1684, needing tapestries to decorate the Banqueting Hall at Rosenborg Castle, he summoned Berent van der Eichen (d 1700) from Brabant. Taking as his model the large tapestry schemes created for Louis XIV by Charles Le Brun at the Gobelins, Christian V commissioned a series of tapestries to illustrate his military achievements. Between 1684 and 1693 van der Eichen wove 12 tapestries in Copenhagen for the Banqueting Hall at Rosenborg, in addition to tapestries for other castles.

After van der Eichen's death Danish tapestry production declined, and tapestries were once again mostly

23. Seat canopy by Hans Knieper, tapestry, wool, silk and gold and silver thread, 3.56×2.70 m, 1585–6 (Stockholm, Nationalmuseum)

imported. The court became more French-oriented, and it wanted tapestries from the Gobelins and Beauvais. In 1736 a French weaver, François Leger (d 1744), probably trained at the Gobelins, was summoned to decorate Christiansborg Palace, Copenhagen, and Hirschholm, the summer palace. Three more weavers from the Gobelins joined him in 1740. Surviving examples of their work include two allegorical compositions (c. 1737–7; Copenhagen, Christiansborg Slot and Hillerød, Frederiksborg Slot) after cartoons by the Danish painter Hendrik Krock (1671–1738) and a series (1746–7) of seven garden and architectural scenes for the manor house at Ledreborg, Zealand, after a series (1738–40; destr.) commissioned for Christiansborg.

After Leger's death, the workshop continued until 1747, when it ceased production. Tapestries in interior decoration went out of fashion at the end of the 18th century, and there were no major tapestry workshops in Denmark until the beginning of the 20th century when an initiative to re-weave Karel van Mander II's great series of tapestries for Frederiksborg Castle (destr. by fire in 1859) revived interest in traditional techniques and patriotic themes. Three new workshops were established in Copenhagen, managed by the daughters of artists and with a female workforce. At the first of these workshops the Frederiksborg tapestries were woven to designs by Heinrich Hansen (1821–90) and F. C. Lund (1826–1901) between 1901 and 1928, when the workshop closed. The second workshop was set up in 1902 in the newly built Copenhagen Town Hall under the management of painter and weaver Dagmar Olrik (1860–1932) and produced a series of tapestries after cartoons by Lorenz Frølich to decorate the building. The third workshop was established at the time of the rebuilding of Christiansborg Palace, destroyed by fire in 1884. Between 1920 and 1927 it produced a series of seven tapestries with folk-song motifs after cartoons by the Danish artist Joakim Skovgaard, and these are still in their original position in the Queen's Apartment.

In the 20th century the large central workshops of earlier centuries were replaced by individual weavers in their own workshops. Inspired by the renaissance of French tapestry after World War II, several Danish artists, such as William Scharff (b 1886), Mogens Andersen (b 1916) and Ole Schwalbe, had their designs woven in traditional tapestry technique by small workshops where they could work in close cooperation with the weavers. Other artists, such as Richard Mortensen (1910–92) and Naja Salto (b 1945), collaborated with tapestry workshops at Aubusson. In 1990, as a gift to Queen Margrethe II on her 50th birthday, a series of 11 tapestries depicting subjects from Danish history, after cartoons by the artist Bjørn Nørgaard (b 1947), was commissioned from Les Gobelins, Paris, to decorate the great ballroom at Christiansborg Palace, Copenhagen.

BIBLIOGRAPHY

A. L. Sidenius: 'Un Tapissier français à la cour de Danemark', *Bull. Soc. Hist. A. Fr.*, i (1928), pp. 16–36
O. Andrup: 'Bidrag til Karel van Manders biografi' [Contributions to the biography of Karel van Mander], *Kstmus. Årsskr.*, xix (1932), pp. 104–40
G. Boesen: *Christian den femtes Rosenborgtapeter fra den skaanske krig* [Christian V's Rosenborg tapestries from the Scanian War] (Copenhagen, 1949) [with Eng. summary]
G. Garde: *Dansk billedvævning* [Danish pictorial weaving] (Copenhagen, 1949)
M. Mackeprang and S. F. Christiansen: *Kronborgtapeterne* [The Kronborg tapestries] (Copenhagen, 1950) [Fr. summary]
C. Portman: 'Gobelin Weaving at the Turn of the Century', *Danish Handicrafts Guild*, 3 (1976–7), pp. 4–9
M. Bligaard: 'Frederiksborgmuseets gobelinvæveri' [Frederiksborg Museum's tapestry workshop], *Carlsbergfond., Frederiksborgmus., Ny Carlsbergfond., Årsskr.* (1980), pp. 96–103
A. Graae and others: *Textilkunst i Danmark, 1960–1987* (Copenhagen, 1987)
P. M. Hornung, ed.: *Dronning Margrethe II's gobeliner* [Queen Margrethe II's tapestries] (Copenhagen, 1990)

VIBEKE WOLDBYE

2. SILK AND EMBROIDERY. The first silk-weaving industry in Denmark was established by Christian IV in the early 17th century. As well as the Hellig Gejstes Tugthus tapestry workshop (*see* §1 above), he set up a silk factory in Copenhagen, using imported weavers; but its success was short-lived (*c.* 1619–26). Christian V (*reg* 1670–99) established a second silk factory in 1680, which also failed within a decade. Only the third royal workshop, set up in 1735 under Christian VI (*reg* 1730–46), prospered after being taken over by a consortium of merchants. In 1763 there were over 900 people employed in the silk factories, but the number fell sharply as patterned silks went out of fashion towards the end of the 18th century.

The court of Christian IV also supported a number of professional embroidery workshops in Copenhagen. In addition to fine silk and whitework embroideries, they produced pieces that were lavishly embellished with seed pearls and raised metal-thread embroidery in an international style. This kind of work was used on such ceremonial objects as the seat canopy for Frederick II (1585–6; Stockholm, Nmus.; see fig. 23) and the horse trappings embroidered with gold thread, jewels and pearls (Copenhagen, Rosenborg Slot) made by Gert Osserijn (1609–*c.* 1640) for the wedding of Crown Prince Christian in 1634. Embroidery was also done in well-to-do households. Finely embroidered bed-linen worked with linen thread in flat satin and stem stitches, and embellished with cutwork and needle lace stitches, survives from the late 16th century and the 17th. Table-covers and bed-hangings were embroidered with polychrome silks and metal threads on linen, silk and wool grounds. The designs, which include coats of arms, curving floral sprigs and sometimes figures, show the influence of German and Italian pattern books, although the embroideries are distinctively Danish.

In the later 17th century and during the 18th, embroidered canvas furnishings were popular. Queen Charlotte (1650–1714) and her ladies worked the covers for six armchairs and 12 chairs in a mixture of floral and pictorial chinoiserie motifs (*c.* 1700; Copenhagen, Rosenborg Slot). Quilting and fine muslin embroidery in the style of Dresden work were also fashionable. During the 18th century and into the 19th, the embroidery produced by certain peasant communities developed distinctive styles, notably on the island of Amager and in the district of Heden, to the west of Copenhagen. Three forms of embroidery were made on Amager. In one, heavy linen panels were decorated with wool, silk or cotton in cross-stitch, featuring isolated motifs ultimately derived from 16th- and 17th-century pattern books. Several of these panels bear dates between the 1770s and the 1850s. In a second form of linen work, vertical lines of long-armed cross-stitch were worked in black silk. The finished pieces were then dyed dark blue and heavily starched, before being made into christening bibs and caps. In the third form of embroidery, in the early 19th century, imported scarves of patterned silk were embroidered with brightly coloured silks in floral patterns. Heden was renowned for its whitework embroidery (known as Hedebo), which in the 18th century was mostly worked with surface stitches together with a little cutwork and drawn thread work. During the first half of the 19th century the amount of cutwork increased, and the patterns became based on those of Italian reticella laces. In the late 19th century more elaborate filling stitches were introduced, and the surface stitching virtually vanished.

In the mid- and late 19th century Danish embroidery was affected by the universal popularity of Berlin woolwork. Large floral patterns with naturalistic shading were dominant, although in the 1860s and 1870s designs based on the work of the sculptor Bertel Thorvaldsen achieved widespread popularity. Embroidered with white beads or in grisaille wools, they were in marked contrast to the more typical, gaudy Berlin woolwork pieces. Danish followers of the Arts and Crafts Movement looked to peasant crafts for inspiration, and Hedebo work was one form of peasant embroidery revived at this time that was adopted worldwide. This revival led to the founding (1928) of the

Danish Handicrafts Guild, which played a major role in training teachers and encouraging quality textile work. In the early years of the 20th century Art Nouveau embroideries were designed by such artists as Kristian Møhl Hansen (1876–1962).

BIBLIOGRAPHY

R. Krarup: *Historien om en silkebroderet lærredsdug* [History of a silk-embroidered linen cloth] (Copenhagen, 1889)

F. J. Meyer: 'Nogle faa efterretninger om danske perlestikkere' [Danish bead embroidery], *Tidsskrift for Kunstindustri*, ed. C. Nyrop (Copenhagen, 1889), pp. 37–52

G. Garde: *Danske silkebroderede lærredsduge fra det 16. og 17. århundrede* [Danish silk-embroidered linen from the 16th and 17th centuries] (Copenhagen, 1961)

H. F. Dalgaard: *Hedebo* (Copenhagen, 1979)

Alverdens broderier [Embroidery from around the world] (exh. cat. by C. Paludan, Copenhagen, Kstindustmus., 1983)

KATIA JOHANSEN

3. LACE. Danish lace is usually known as Tønder lace, after the principal town in southern Jutland that was the centre of the lace industry. When the industry was at its height in the 18th century and the beginning of the 19th it stretched across the whole of southern Jutland and the northern part of the province of Schleswig (hence the early alternative name of Schleswig lace), providing employment for thousands of lacemakers. The craft was probably introduced by German or Dutch lacemakers before 1600, but domestic lacemaking was practised in convent schools in Jutland from the 1550s, if not earlier. Lace was also produced at the Børnehuset (Children's House) in Copenhagen, founded in 1605. No distinction between this and the lace made in the Tønder area is recognized, but early Danish lace is often distinguished by a design of roundels. Generally European fashion lace provided the model for Danish lacemakers.

In 1688 in Tønder there were 29 known lace dealers, who imported patterns and thread from the Netherlands and employed lacemakers in the surrounding area. Throughout the 18th century Tønder lace was exported to Germany and the Baltic states, among other places, as well as being produced for the Kingdom of Denmark and Norway. It was frequently sold, falsely, as 'Brabantine goods', which often makes identification difficult but shows that the lace was of equally high quality. From about 1775 there was a yarn factory in Tønder, using flax imported from Westphalia. At this date the export of lace was worth 33,000 rix dollars annually, while the value of lace sold on the domestic market amounted to 25,000 rix dollars.

The prototypes for Danish lace were the early Italian plaited laces, followed by the softer Netherlandish clothwork lace. From the end of the 17th century, patterns were taken from the Flemish centres of Valenciennes, Binche, Mechelen and Brussels, and from the end of the 18th century also from England. By the 1800s French Lille lace had come to the fore as a fashion lace, and it was to leave its mark on the Tønder production for the first two-thirds of the 19th century. Using Lille lace as a model, Tønder lace finally developed as a distinct type. Once an exclusive product reserved for the upper classes, it became widely available, and the thousands of pieces of Tønder lace that the peasant women procured for their headdresses have become collectors' items (examples in Copenhagen,

Kstindustmus.; Tønder, Sonderjyllands Kstmus.; Flensburg, Städt. Mus.). The rather heavy designs show prolific variation; stylized flower motifs are popular, also Rococo motifs, crowns, medallion patterns etc. In the late 19th century Cluny and guipure lace, which had been introduced as fashion laces in several European centres, appeared in distinct Tønder forms.

In 1864, after the Danish–German war, most of the Tønder area became part of Germany. The production of Tønder lace was transferred to Berlin, and the local industry destroyed. In the 20th century, especially after the reunion of North Schleswig with Denmark in 1920, efforts were made to revive the craft while the old lacemakers were still alive to pass it on, but with limited success.

BIBLIOGRAPHY

E. Hannover: *Tønderske kniplinger* [Tønder lace] (Copenhagen, 1911/R 1974 with Eng. summary)

E. Busch: *Monstertegning til knipling* [Pattern designing for lace] (Copenhagen, 1980)

C. Paludan and S. Schoubye: *Tønderske kniplinger* [Tønder lace] (Tønder, 1989) [Ger. summary]

Pragt & poesi: Knipling gennem 400 år [Pomp & poetry: 400 years of lace] (exh. cat., Copenhagen, Kstindustmus., 1991) [Eng. and Dan. text]

S. M. Levey and P. Wardle: *The Finishing Touch: Lace in Portraits at Frederiksborg* (Hillprød, 1994)

CHARLOTTE PALUDAN

4. OTHER. In the 1930s plain or simply patterned textiles, often in blue and white, were woven and printed by such artists as Kaare Klint and Marie Gudme Leth. After World War II their work was developed by the Textile Printers' and Weavers' Guild (founded 1964, Copenhagen). During the 1950s Danish design was internationally admired and copied, and the textile industry was stimulated to hire trained designers to create industrially produced yardage for interior decoration. In the late 20th century most hand-weavers produced rugs and hangings in traditional techniques, honed to a perfection of well-composed design. Weavers in the terse Danish style included Vibeke Klint (*b* 1927; e.g. textiles for Copenhagen Cathedral, 1979), Kim Naver (*b* 1940), Annette Juel (e.g. in Copenhagen, Kstindustmus.) and Jette Nevers (*b* 1943; e.g. in Copenhagen, Kstindustmus.); Berit Hjelholt (*b* 1920; e.g. *Homesick*, 1978; Copenhagen, Kstindusmus.) and Nanna Hertoft (*b* 1936) produced more organic work. At the end of the 20th century textile printing was increasingly important as an art form and in industrial design.

KATIA JOHANSEN

XII. Vernacular arts.

The Danish vernacular-art tradition is not as old as those in Sweden and especially Norway, where there is more evidence for Viking and medieval influences. This has been attributed to Denmark's relative population density and small size, and to its rapid social upheavals in the 19th century, when many products of the old rural order disappeared (Uldall). Nor have Danish folk models been translated into modern domestic, textile and industrial design to the same extent. The decoration of Danish furniture and fittings from the last few centuries reveals a balance between wider European influences and an underlying stratum of older traditions apparent elsewhere in

Scandinavia, although Denmark was closer to the style-creating European centres. In this way Denmark became a conduit for traditional styles in relation to its twin, Norway. After 1800, however, vernacular art in Norway developed various local styles (*see* NORWAY, §XII), and Denmark's was influenced by the larger, unified stylistic areas of the western North Sea and, further east, the Baltic.

Vernacular decorative traditions developed especially from the late 16th century until the mid-19th. One of the richest areas was south Jutland and Schleswig, where a fruitful interplay between Danish and north German culture developed from the Renaissance, while Frisian influences can be detected throughout Jutland. Oak was an important material for houses and their furnishings in the North Sea lands, and Danish interiors from the 16th century and the early 17th often consisted of oak panelling and furniture. The late medieval chests of dressed-log construction, decorated with Gothic reliefs and geometric cut profiles, must to some extent comprise a professional production that continued up to the 18th century. From *c.* 1550 numerous Renaissance chests were produced around Ribe and Tønder, and many richly carved bridal chests can be attributed to the workshops of named craftsmen. The same is true of the well-proportioned oak wall cupboards (late 16th century-early 17th; e.g. Copenhagen, Nmus.), wonderfully decorated with Renaissance rosettes and symmetrical, shallow-carved vines, seen in work associated with or following the so-called Ribe school.

Guild regulations restricted finer work to the market-towns, but certain specialities developed in rural areas. There was a gradual shift to painted interiors *c.* 1650 and, in the 18th century, painted furniture. Cupboards and chests decorated with flower vases, roses, tulips and cartouches, often on a blue ground, can be found in similar forms along the North Sea, from Friesland and north Germany to Jutland and west Norway, which had trade links by sea in the 17th and 18th centuries. Ceramic wall tiles, mostly Dutch, were also found in domestic interiors along the North Sea from the Netherlands to north Germany and Jutland, replacing the older, wood-panelled walls of west Schleswig and the west coast of Jutland. Their wide-ranging decorative motifs included ships, sea monsters, proverbs, childrens' games, animals, flowers and, above all, a multitude of biblical themes to form a ceramic *Biblia pauperum.*

Another decorative tradition anchored in vernacular culture can be found in the Danish–German border areas of Schleswig–Holstein, Saxony and Friesland. This was associated with linen damask, an important manufacture. The cloth was decorated with biblical stories, town prospects and (especially in the 17th century) hunting scenes. Coverlets have strong geometric patterns or, more closely resembling silk-weaving, graceful botanical motifs and animal figures, including the rhinoceros, deer (a symbol of baptism), lion (Christ) and pelican. Christ on the Cross, the Cardinal Virtues, and Faith, Hope and Charity, represented as three women, are encountered in many contexts, including the samplers or 'name-cloths' embroidered by young girls around 1800 to practise their skills (Poulsen; *see also* §XI, 2 above).

Many pictorial motifs were taken from popular prints, penny prints and *kistebrev* ('chest-letters'), a widely distributed 18th-century type that originated in medieval block-books. Biblical scenes, portraits of kings and nobles, military officers on horseback and sensational current events circulated widely and often had strong moral undertones (Clausen). They were produced in large numbers from the late 16th century to the 19th, first as woodcuts and later as lithographs.

The many surviving linen-presses, lovers' gifts before a marriage, are decorated to evoke good marriage and household duties and boast symbolic and more directly magical prophylactic motifs that are also found on many other types of household goods in the North Sea lands and Scandinavia (e.g. Copenhagen, Nmus.). Some simple geometric motifs, such as the six-part circle or six-petalled rose go far back in European, and Asian, history. The six-petalled rose indeed has a protective symbolic content, which can be interpreted as representing both eternity and the seasons. The simple wheel, sun-cross on scroll-rosette has been interpreted as solar symbols, clearly connected with prehistoric art. Another ancient symbol with protective functions is the wall-knot, formed like a quadrat with four corner loops. In Denmark this term is also used to denominate the motif of three interwoven rope rings; a figure that in Norwegian tradition is called 'Olavsrose'. The wall-knot with corner loops is known from gold bracteates and amulets (e.g. 6th century AD; Schleswig, Schleswig–Holstein, Landesmus.), Viking textiles, for example from Oseberg (9th century, Oslo, U. Oldsaksaml.), medieval church furnishings and an enormous variety of later popular art forms: single and double knots, combined with the cross, or inscribed in the six-petalled rose. It has been conjectured that this was a sacred motif in the Iron Age, and it certainly appears in combination with other symbolic motifs. In more recent folk culture the symbolic meaning is derived from the idea that a knot is difficult to loosen (i.e. something that binds and involves a secret). In Danish tradition the wall-knot is associated with the *bindebrev* ('binding letter') sent on someone's name-day, usually with a riddle, and tied with a knotted thread (Uldall). Since the late Middle Ages flower vases with roses and tulips, one of the most prized decorative motifs, have probably been emblematic of the Virgin and Christ. The symbolic content of vernacular art and the transformations undergone in its decoration have been little studied.

BIBLIOGRAPHY

A. Steensberg: *Danske bondemøbler* [Danish peasant furniture] (Copenhagen, 1949, rev. 1964)

H. Poulsen: 'Dansk folkekunst på land og i by' [Danish vernacular art in country and town], *Dagligliv i Danmark, 1790–1870* [Daily life in Denmark, 1790–1870], ed. A. Steensberg (Copenhagen, 1963), pp. 138–52

K. Uldall: *Dansk folkekunst* [Danish folk art] (Copenhagen, 1963)

V. E. Clausen: *Folkelig grafik i Skandinavien* [Scandinavian popular prints] (Copenhagen, 1973)

W. Brückner: *Populäre Druckgraphik Europas* (Munich, 1975)

A. Steensberg and G. Larche: *Danish Peasant Furniture*, 2 vols (Copenhagen, 1989)

NILS GEORG BREKKE

XIII. Patronage.

Patrons and artists from the introduction of Christianity until the Reformation (1536) remain largely anonymous.

Private patrons had stones and crosses erected (e.g. the Jelling Stone, *c.* 965, for Harald I Bluetooth, and the Gunhild Cross, Copenhagen, Nmus.). Chronicles and other evidence show royal patronage of large burial churches, as at Ringsted and Roskilde, and ecclesiastical patronage (e.g. of the seat of the archbishop in Lund); other patrons included local landowners and noblemen such as Asser Rig (*d c.* 1148) of the Hvide family, who built the church at Fjenneslev on Zealand. With the rise of portraiture in the late 15th century the individual features of the patron were depicted. The altarscreen (1477–9) from Århus Cathedral by Bernt Notke portrays Bishop Jens Iversen Lange of Århus. Christian II (*reg* 1513–23) briefly employed foreign portrait painters such as Michel Sittow and Jan Gossart.

After the Reformation the pattern of patronage changed with the increase in individual commissions, and artists were attracted to the court. Melchior Lorck (*c.* 1527–after 1583) was under royal patronage to travel for four years and was a court painter (1580–83) to Frederick II (*reg* 1559–88). The King started important projects at Kronborg Castle in Helsingør and at Frederiksborg Castle in Hillerød; he also ordered the production of tapestries (Helsingør, Kronborg Castle; Copenhagen, Nmus.) depicting the Danish kings, after cartoons by Hans Knieper. Frederick's successor, Christian IV (*reg* 1588–1648), asserted his position through the visual arts, using Classical mythology and presenting an image of Denmark as a strong Christian nation. The unprecedented levels of artistic activity involved artists predominantly from the Netherlands or local artists trained by foreigners (*see* §III, 2 above).

Through the court and the power of the monarchy new French trends reached the country, and although there were a number of Danish court artists such as Lambert van Haven, the majority were foreigners, engaged by royalty and the nobility. The traders Asiatisk Kompagni sponsored one of Danish art's most expensive projects, the statue of *Frederick V* (completed 1771; Copenhagen, Amalienborg) by the French sculptor Jacques-François-Joseph Saly. In 1754 Frederick V (*reg* 1746–66) founded the Kongelige Danske Kunstakademi, Copenhagen. In addition to educational provision, the academy sponsored a competition for a gold medal, the winner of which was able to travel abroad; many Danish artists could therefore go to Rome. Another form of state patronage was the foundation Ad Usus Publicus, which gave direct financial support to a number of artists from the late 18th century and well into the 19th.

Artistic production in the first half of the 19th century was oriented towards private buyers. In 1825 the Kunstforening (Art Society) was founded to buy and exhibit art, and supported the Eckersberg School. The most significant patron in the late 19th century was the brewer CARL JACOBSEN, who sponsored art and architectural projects that made art accessible to a larger public. From 1910 the Ny Carlsbergfond, also established by Jacobsen, became the major private patron in Danish art. Other contemporary collectors and patrons included HEINRICH HIRSCHSPRUNG, who sponsored Peder Krøyer on his travels to Italy; and Mads Rasmussen (1856–1916) in Fåborg, who bought from contemporary painters in Fyn. Both patrons

turned their collections into museums. Knud W. Jensen (*b* 1921) continued Carl Jacobsen's style of patronage by involving architects and artists in his Louisiana Museum of Art in Humlebæk (founded 1958); in Herning Aage Damgaard (1917–91) commissioned Carl-Henning Pedersen and Poul Gadegaard (*b* 1920) to decorate his factory, which was later turned into a museum. From 1964 the state again became a significant patron through the Statens Kunstfond, which is responsible for large public art schemes, gives lifelong economic support to artists and provides aid to museums and galleries. A large number of art societies also represent a form of decentralized patronage in Danish art.

BIBLIOGRAPHY

A. Rasch: *Staten og kunstnerne: Bevillinger og meninger under enevælde og folkestyre* [The state and artists: appropriation and opinion during absolutism and democracy] (Århus, 1968)

E. Salling: *Kunstakademiets guldmedalje, 1755–1857* [The gold medal at the Kunstakademi, 1755–1857] (Copenhagen, 1975)

D. Zanker von Meyer: *Die Bauten von J. C. und Carl Jacobsen* (Berlin, 1982)

Christian IV and Europe (Copenhagen, 1988)

JULIE HARBOE

XIV. Collecting and dealing.

In the first inventory of the Kongelige Danske Kunstkammer (1673) approximately 200 paintings are listed, including paintings by Rubens, Jordaens and Honthorst. By 1690 the collection had grown to about 300. In the 1660s auctions had been established in Copenhagen; Karel van Mander III's collection was sold in 1672 and that of the painter Anton van Steenwinkel in 1688. The locksmith Ulrik Grob's collection was auctioned in 1689 and that of the wine merchant Frederik Gamborg in 1692.

In the 18th century several private collections emerged among the nobility, including that of the Lord High Steward ADAM GOTTLOB MOLTKE, mainly of Netherlandish and Flemish paintings (open to the public from 1804 and sold at auction 1932). Grev Otto Thott (1703–85) left approximately 1000 paintings and 2000 artefacts, which were sold at auction after his death. Both of these collectors, as well as Frederick V (*reg* 1746–66), who had increased the royal collections considerably during the 1750s and 1760s, used the Kunstkammer agent Gerhard Morell (*c.* 1710–71). Grev J. H. E. VON BERNSTORFF (1712–72) acquired French art through Deputy J. Wasserschlebe (1709–87), who had close connections with Parisian art life in the mid-1700s. Grev Ove Høegh-Guldberg (1731–1808) collected Egyptian and Roman antiquities. The Consul Hans West (1758–1811) exhibited his Dutch and Flemish collection publicly (1805–9), after which it was sold to the king.

In the early 19th century several collectors in Copenhagen bought from contemporary Danish artists on a limited scale. In contrast Bertel Thorvaldsen amassed a large collection of ancient Roman and contemporary art (now Copenhagen, Thorvaldsens Mus.). Towards the end of the century various large private collections were formed. The tobacco manufacturer HEINRICH HIRSCHSPRUNG collected 19th-century Danish art (now Copenhagen, Hirschsprungske Saml.); the landowner Johannes Hage (1842–1923) collected Netherlandish art (now Nivå,

Nivaagaards Malsaml.); and the bank director Emil Gluck-stadt (1875–1923) collected antique, Danish and foreign art. Most important of all was the brewer CARL JACOBSEN, who collected antique art, which from 1882 formed part of the foundation of the Ny Carlsberg Glyptotek, Copenhagen. (His son, Helge Jacobsen (1882–1946), added the large collection of French Impressionists.) The Copenhagen dealer Valdemar Kreis (1845–1918) played a prominent role for rebel artists from the 1880s. Towards the end of the 19th century several auction houses were established, including Winkel Magnussen (1898–1953), which began as a gallery in 1884.

Around 1910–20 four private Danish collections, primarily of French Impressionism and Cubism, and of international value, were formed: by the merchant CHRISTIAN TETZEN-LUND, sold abroad in 1923–5 and 1934; by Hermann Heilbuth (1861–1945); by the insurance company director Vilhelm Hansen (1868–1936), partly sold in 1923 and partly used later to form the Ordrupgaardsamlingen, Charlottenlund; and by the engineer JOHANNES RUMP, donated to the Statens Museum for Kunst, Copenhagen, in 1928. During the inter-war years, two considerable collections of older Danish art were sold, that of the dealer Martin Grosell, which also contained German Romantic paintings, and that of the Consul General Johannes Hansen (open to the public 1917–32). Elise Johansen (1884–1970), whose collection is now partly in the Statens Museum for Kunst, Copenhagen, and Elna Fonnesbech-Sandberg (b 1892), whose collection is now partly in the Nordjyllands Kunstmuseum, Ålborg, were closely associated with Danish abstract artists and the Cobra group. The collection of Erik C. Mengel (1908–83) was incorporated in the Lolland-Falster Kunstmuseum, Maribo, in 1984, and the painter Asger Jorn's collection was bequeathed to Silkeborg Kunstmuseum. From the end of the 1950s John Hunov (b 1936) collected contemporary works, from the Fluxus artists, through the Eks school to De Vilde ('The wild ones') of the 1980s. Among the other important 20th-century dealers are Ole Haslund, Børge Birch (1960–87) and Galleri Asbæk (from 1975), Copenhagen. Kunsthallens Kunstauktioner began in 1926, and in 1948 Arne Bruun Rasmussen founded his auction house. Late 20th-century interest in earlier Nordic art resulted in the opening of branches by Sotheby's, Christie's and Bukowski in Copenhagen.

BIBLIOGRAPHY
A. Leth: *Lidt om auktioner* [Briefly about auctions] (Copenhagen, 1943)
V. Poulsen, E. Lassen and J. Danielsen, eds: *Dansk kunsthistorie: Billedkunst og skulptur* [Danish art history: painting and sculpture], 5 vols (Copenhagen, 1972–5) [esp. vols ii & iii]
'Kunstsamlerne og museerne' [The art collectors and the museums], *Kst & Mus.*, xix (1984) [whole issue]

XV. Museums.

The Danish museum system is rooted in the royal collections. After his accession to the throne (1648), Frederick III gathered together the varied collections at Copenhagen Castle, and in 1655 a special extension to the castle was built to house the royal library and Kunstkammer, the latter containing curiosities and works of art. Between 1759 and 1764 a picture gallery was constructed at Christiansborg Palace, Copenhagen, and at the same time

Frederick V (*reg* 1746–66) made considerable acquisitions in the Netherlands and Germany through the Kunstkammer agent Gerhard Morell (*c.* 1710–71).

In the early 1800s the Kunstkammer was dissolved into a number of separate museums, including the Oldnordisk Museum (1807), Etnografisk Museum (1841) and Danske Samlinger (1855). These merged in 1892 to form the Nationalmuseet. The Kongelige Billedgalleri was founded in 1825 and opened to the public in 1827, and the Kongelige Kobberstik Samling in 1835; in 1896 they merged into the Statens Museum for Kunst, which houses the national collection of Danish art beginning in the 1700s, older European collections, Scandinavian art from the turn of the century and modern French art. During the reign of Frederick VI (*reg* 1808–39) a portrait gallery was established in Frederiksborg Castle (1812), Hillerød, and when rebuilt after the fire in 1859 the castle was made the Nationalhistorisk Museum. It houses portrait collections (beginning in the 1500s), history paintings, furniture and applied arts. Over the years the Kongelige Danske Kunstakademi (founded 1754) amassed a fine collection of art. It also contains the Collection of Architectural Drawings (Samlingen af Arkitekturtegninger). In 1833 the Chronological Collections of the Danish Kings (Danske Kongers Kronologiske Samlinger) were established at Rosenborg Castle, containing interiors, the crown jewels, royal costumes and personal relics.

Bertel Thorvaldsen was the first Danish private citizen to donate his collections to the public in 1837. Thorvaldsens Museum, which houses his own sculptures, antique works, later European paintings and drawings, was completed in 1847 and opened in 1848 in a building with polychrome exterior decoration designed by Gottlieb Bindesbøll (for illustration *see* BINDESBØLL, (1)). The Ny Carlsberg Glyptotek was founded in 1882 by the brewer Carl Jacobsen and his wife. It houses very important collections of Egyptian, Greek, Etruscan and Roman sculpture, plus fine collections of 19th-century French art and 19th- and 20th-century Danish art, particularly sculpture. In 1902 the tobacco manufacturer Heinrich Hirschsprung and his wife Pauline Hirschsprung donated their collection of 19th-century Danish art to the nation. The Hirschsprungske Samling opened in 1911. In 1908 the Nivaagaards Malerisamling, Nivå, was founded by the landowner Johannes Hage (1842–1923), who had collected primarily Netherlandish and Italian art. The Davids Samling, Copenhagen, was founded in 1945 by the barrister C. L. David as a museum for interiors, with an emphasis on European and especially Islamic applied arts. The businessman Vilhelm Hansen (1868–1936) bequeathed his collection of French Impressionist paintings and older Danish art to the state in 1952, forming the Ordrupgaardsamlingen, Charlottenlund. The Louisiana Museum in Humlebæk, which was based on the Director Knud W. Jensen's collection, opened in 1958 and became the most important Danish museum of modern international art.

Many Danish art galleries were established by popular initiative through art associations, museum associations or local authorities, for example the Kunstmuseum in Århus (founded 1854), which, together with Randers Kunstmuseum (1887), the Nordjyllands Kunstmuseum (1877),

Ålborg, and Fyns Kunstmuseum (1885), Odense, is among the older provincial museums. The art galleries in Herning, Holstebro, Silkeborg, Esbjerg, Tønder, Kolding (Trapholt) and Sorø, among other towns, contain wide and rather varied collections of mostly modern Danish art, although several galleries also have international collections (including Århus, Randers, Ålborg, Herning and Silkeborg). Two art galleries with particular local affinities are Skagens Museum (founded 1908), with works by the artists who settled there from the 1870s, and the Museum for Fynsk Malerkunst (founded 1910) in Fåborg, dedicated to the Fyn painters of around the turn of the century.

Museums devoted mainly to one artist include the J. F. Willumsens Museum in Frederikssund (founded 1957), which houses Willumsen's works and European Old Master drawings. Between 1958 and 1973 the Kunstmuseum in Silkeborg received Asger Jorn's collections, containing Jorn's works and others from the 1700s to the present. The main museum for furniture and decorative art is the Danske Kunstindustrimuseum (founded 1890), Copenhagen, which houses European works from the Middle Ages to the present. In addition there are collections of Chinese and Japanese art and other applied arts. In 1987 the Museum for Fotokunst was founded in Odense.

From 1890 Danish museums were eligible for government subsidies, which are partly responsible for the great spread of public art galleries. With its donations and contributions to acquisitions, the Ny Carlsbergfond was important for public art galleries from 1902. In 1964 the government subsidy became statutory law, and in 1979 legislation was passed in order to provide grants on a percentage basis in relation to local contributions, administered by the Statens Museumsnævn, which comes under the Ministry of Culture, as well as by the County Museum Councils. In 1990 there were 40 public and government grant-aided art galleries in Denmark, organized by Foreningen af Danske Kunstmuseer, a nationwide organization from 1979.

BIBLIOGRAPHY

H. C. Bering Liisberg: *Kunstkammeret: Dets stiftelse og ældste historie* [The Royal Museum: its foundation and earliest history] (Copenhagen, 1897)
P. Hertz: 'Den kongelige malerisamlings tilblivelse' [The making of the royal collection of paintings], *Kstmus. Årsskr.* (1921–3)
G. Boesen: *Danish Museums* (Copenhagen, 1966)
Danske museer gennem 200 år., 1648–1848 [Danish museums over 200 years, 1648–1848] (exh. cat., Copenhagen, Thorvaldsens Mus., 1974)
Alle danske museer [All Danish museums], intro. P. Lauring (Copenhagen, 1976)
P. Svendsen: *Museer og seværdigheder i Danmark* [Museums and sights in Denmark], 2 vols (Copenhagen, 1989)
'Danish Art Museums over 150 Years', *Arkitektur DK*, iv (1989) [whole issue; Dan., Eng. & Ger. text]

XVI. Art education.

Although Danish workshops had been established from the Middle Ages, large numbers of artists came from abroad and many Danish artists trained abroad. Christian VI (*reg* 1730–46) was the first king to recognize the need for an art education that would provide the court with Danish artists in order to avoid the dependence on foreigners. In 1738 he initiated the establishment of an art school in Copenhagen, which opened in 1740 with a modest number of students. In 1751 the Kongelige Danske

Kunstakademi was reorganized by the architect Niels Eigtved, and in 1754 it moved to Charlottenborg Palace, where it is still housed. Also in that year Frederick V (*reg* 1746–66) gave the academy its first charter, and 1754 has traditionally been regarded as the foundation year. With the appointment of the French sculptor Jacques-François-Joseph Saly (1754) as director of the academy, the institution was further developed through new charters and regulations. Taking the Académie Royale de Peinture et de Sculpture in Paris as its model, academic training progressed through freehand drawing classes via the life class, competitions and medals, to six-year travel bursaries, followed by the award of an academic title and membership of the Academy Council, the uppermost authority on aesthetic issues and other matters. From 1755 annual exhibitions were held. During the 1750s and 1760s the driving force in the Kongelige Danske Kunstakademi was the Lord High Steward Adam Gottlob Moltke, whose aim was to strengthen and further art and thus lend lustre to the absolute monarchy. In 1764 the school had 216 students. As well as painters and sculptors, the academy trained architects and engravers and admitted craftsmen to the classes at the lowest level of training.

The strong French influence and the high level of ambition came to an abrupt end in 1771 when the rationalist reform policies of the Minister of the Privy Council, J. F. Struense, limited the Kunstakademi's financial resources and replaced foreign professors with Danish ones. The first generation of students were by this stage ready to take over the management. Despite reduced circumstances, the academy's basic principles were maintained, and under Johannes Wiedewelt and Nicolai Abraham Abildgaard it retained its good reputation. Around 1800 a number of important North German artists applied for admission. The painter C. W. Eckersberg was appointed professor in 1818, and his teaching was influential on the Golden Age of Danish art. From 1822 he offered students the novel opportunity of painting from female models. Furthermore, he taught perspective privately from the end of the 1820s and practised painting *en plein air* with his students. In 1826 the art historian N. L. Høyen, later the leading theorist of National Romanticism, was appointed lecturer; his appointment was followed by that of the art historian Julius Henrik Lange in 1871.

In protest against the conservative attitudes of the Kunstakademi, the Kunstnernes Frie Studieskole was set up in 1883 as a rejuvenating alternative to traditional academic teaching. Both the *Fynboerne* (Fyn painters) and the leading artists were trained in a modern approach at Zahrtmanns Skole. In 1888 the Kvindelige Kunstskole (Women's Art School) was set up at the Kunstakademi, which in 1908 experienced a series of structural changes as a result of the directorship of the architect Ferdinand Meldahl. The tense relationship between traditional teaching and modernist artists characterized the beginning of the 20th century. Among the teachers who were highly influential were the architectural historian Wilhelm Wanscher (at the Kunstakademi, 1915–41), the sculptor E. Utzon-Frank (professor, 1918–55) and the painter Aksel Jørgensen (professor, 1920–53), who on his appointment set up the Grafiske Skole. Steen Eiler Rasmussen (professor, 1938–68) started teaching urban planning in

1924, and in the same year the Skole for Møbelkunst (School of Furniture) was established with Kaare Klint (professor, 1944–54) as teacher. In 1951 the Skole for Industriens Kunst opened.

In 1920, after leaving a teaching post at the Kunstakademi, the painter Peter Rostrup Bøyesen (1882–1952) set up a private school of draughtsmanship that enjoyed wide patronage. In 1961 a society of artists with the characteristics of an art school was established as the 'Eksperimentalskole' or 'Eksskole'. Among its members were Per Kirkeby, Poul Gernes (b 1925) and Bjørn Nørgaard (b 1947). The decentralization of the Danish educational system led to the establishment in 1964 of the Jyske Kunstakademi in Århus and in 1972 the Fynske Kunstakademi in Odense.

BIBLIOGRAPHY

F. Meldahl and P. Johansen: *Det Kongelige Akademi for de Skønne Kunster, 1700–1904* (Copenhagen, 1904)

A. Marcus, ed.: *Det Kongelige Akademi for de Skønne Kunster, 1904–1954* (Copenhagen, 1954)

M. Saabye: 'Wiedewelt—Kunstakademi og kunstpolitik', *Johannes Wiedewelt* (exh. cat., ed. S. Brøgger; Copenhagen, Sophienholm, 1985), pp. 67–72

E. Salling: 'Tanker om akademiet og teorien, 1754–71' [Thoughts about the academy and the theory, 1754–71], *Forblommet antik: Studier tilegnet Hakon Lund* [Covert antiquity: studies dedicated to Hakon Lund] (Copenhagen, 1988), pp. 77–95

'Academies of Art between Renaissance and Romanticism', *Leids Ksthist. Jb.*, v–vi (1989) [articles on Kongelige Danske Kunstakademi, pp. 511–58]

MARIANNE SAABYE

XVII. Art libraries and photographic collections.

The Kunstakademiets Bibliotek was founded in 1758 in association with the Kongelige Danske Kunstakademi. It has a photographic collection of European painting, sculpture and architecture and a large slide collection. The print and photographic collection at the Kunstakademiets Bibliotek is the central collection for documentary, historical and art photography. The Byggeriets Studiearkiv, the national centre for building documentation, is a specialized architecture library. The library of the department of prints and drawings and the library of the department of paintings, both at the Statens Museum for Kunst, Copenhagen, contain literature specifically related to the collections and act as reference libraries to the public. The latter holds a collection of catalogues for all exhibitions held in Denmark as well as for Danish exhibitions held outside the country. The library of the Thorvaldsens Museum, Copenhagen, holds the artist's book collection and works on Neoclassicism and Romanticism. The library of the Kunstindustrimuseet, Copenhagen, is the principal Danish library for decorative arts, design and Asian and oriental art; it also has a collection of Danish and foreign posters. A collection of art photographs is held by the Museum for Fotokunst in Odense. In Århus the library of the Arkitektskolen and the Statsbiblioteket hold collections on architecture and fine arts.

BIBLIOGRAPHY

A. Marcus: 'Akademiets Bibliotek', *Det Kongelige Akademi for de Skønne Kunster, 1904–1954* (Copenhagen, 1954), pp. 495–505

JULIE HARBOE

XVIII. Historiography.

N. L. HOYEN was the first person in Denmark to pursue the study of art history and (from 1829) to promote it as a branch of scholarship. Posthumous publication (1871–6) of his collective writings showed an understanding of his pioneering work. In particular Høyen's critical and methodical research, based on a historico-archaeological approach, has been of lasting value, just as his works on Danish architecture have had practical importance for the preservation, restoration and reconstruction of Danish buildings. Høyen's influence was decisive for much of Danish pictorial art, such as the demand for a national art. Another pioneer, Carl Friedrich Ludwig Felix Rumohr (1785–1843), with his three-volume *Italienische Forschungen* (Berlin and Stettin, 1826–31), formulated a systematic method that influenced both Høyen and Bertel Thorvaldsen's biographer, Just Mathias Thiele (1795–1874). Høyen's architectural studies were continued by Jacob Helms (1824–1906), author of *Ribe Domkirke* (Copenhagen, 1870), Frederik Weilbach (1863–1937), author of *Dansk bygningskunst i det 18. aarh.* (Danish architecture in the 18th century; Copenhagen, 1930) and Harald Skerin Langberg (b 1919), author of the two-volume *Danmarks bygningskultur* (Denmark's building culture; Copenhagen, 1955). Vilhelm Birkedal Lorentzen (1877–1961), Knud Millech (1890–1980), Jan Steenberg (1901–71), Otto Norn (b 1915), Hakon Lund (b 1928) and Knud Voss (b 1929) were also important.

JULIUS HENRIK LANGE broke new ground from 1870 with an approach based on the history of ideas. A humanist, he was predisposed towards a universally broad view on a wide, classical basis and he concentrated on the perception and representation of the human form in art, from Antiquity to the present. His major work, the three-volume *Billedkunstens fremstilling af menneskeskikkelsen* (Representation of the human form in the pictorial arts; Copenhagen, 1892–8), demonstrating the law of frontality, made him famous in the European art world. One of Høyen's pupils, Philip Weilbach (1834–1900), edited the first edition of *Dansk konstnerlexikon* (Copenhagen, 1877–8), which was followed later by the important reference work by Merete Bodelsen (1907–86) and Aage Marcus (b 1888), *Dansk kunsthistorisk bibliografi* (Danish art-historical bibliography; Copenhagen, 1935).

The transition to the 20th century was marked by the opening of large public collections, and henceforward the importance to the subject of such museums increased. Two of the leading art historians of the period, Karl Madsen (1855–1938) and Emil Hannover (1864–1923), were self-taught museum employees. Madsen introduced a new form of objectively substantiated art criticism, using new terminology. His *Hollandsk malerkunst* (Dutch painting; Copenhagen, 1891) was the first work on art sociology in the history of Danish art. Madsen and Hannover wrote enthusiastically about modern art currents and were the authors of the first monographs on Danish *guldalderkunst*, the art of the Danish Golden Age.

Vilhelm Wanscher (1875–1961), professor at the Kunstakademi, became another creative power who exerted his influence on younger art historians and artists. In *Den aestetiske opfattelse af kunst* (The aesthetic perception of art; Copenhagen, 1906) he reacted against Lange's humanism. Wanscher himself had far-reaching and singular opinions (for instance on the mathematical solution to the problem of line and space), and in his major work, the three-volume *Arkitekturens historie* (History of architecture; Copenhagen, 1927–31), he covered the whole of world art. Other contributions to European art history were made by Martha Drachmann Bentzon (1866–1912) in *Michelangelo* (Copenhagen, 1908); Ernst Goldschmidt (1879–1959), Leo Swane (1887–1968) and Haavard Rostrup (*b* 1907), with their work on French art; T. Holck Colding (*b* 1918), author of *Aspects of Miniature Painting* (Copenhagen, 1953); Christian Elling (1901–74), with *Rom* (Copenhagen, 1956); and Merete Bodelsen, who wrote about Gauguin. Danish art history was the province of Francis Beckett (1868–1943), author of *Altertavler i Danmark fra den senere Middelalder* (Altarpieces in Denmark from the late Middle Ages; Copenhagen, 1895). Carl Mouritz Cold Mackeprang (1869–1959) and Sigrid Flamand Christensen (*b* 1904) wrote *Kronborgtapeterne* (The Kronborg tapestries; Copenhagen, 1950). The 19th century was dealt with by Sigurd Schultz (1894–1980) and Henrick Bramsen (*b* 1908), and portrait iconography by Otto Andrup (1883–1953) and Poul Eller (1925–89). More recently there have been Else Kai Sass (*b* 1912), with the three-volume *Thorvaldsens portrætbuster* (Thorvaldsen's portrait busts; Copenhagen, 1963–5); Meir Stein (*b* 1921), with *Christian den Fjerdes billedverden* (Christian IV's world of images; Copenhagen, 1987); and, among others, Poul Vad (*b* 1927) and Troels Andersen (*b* 1940), authors of works on modern art.

BIBLIOGRAPHY

C. Elling: 'Kunsthistorie', *Danmarks kultur ved aar 1940*, vii (Copenhagen, 1943), pp. 204–9
M. Stein: 'Art History', *Denmark: An Official Handbook* (Copenhagen, 1974), pp. 600–605
E. Kai Sass: *Kunsthistorie: Københavns Universitet, 1479–1979*, xi (Copenhagen, 1979)

GRETHE KUSK

Denner, Balthasar (*b* Hamburg, 15 Nov 1685; *d* Rostock, 14 April 1749). German painter. His first teacher was the Dutch painter Franz von Amama; he studied in Danzig (now Gdańsk) from 1698 to 1700 and from 1707 at the Akademie der Künste in Berlin. He began his career as a painter of miniature portraits, although he subsequently painted mostly half-length and head-and-shoulders portraits and a few group portraits of families in interiors. In 1717 he worked in Copenhagen, then from 1721 to 1728 in London, where his miniatures were already highly regarded. He then worked for Christian-Ludwig II, Duke of Mecklenburg-Schwerin, painting a series of portraits of the ducal family and of court officials (Schwerin, Staatl. Mus.). He worked in Amsterdam from 1736 to 1739, finally returning to Hamburg in 1740. He portrayed his subjects in a serious and austere style, similar to Dutch painting, as in *The Painter's Family* (Copenhagen, Stat. Mus. Kst), the *Portrait of Burgomaster Wiese* and the *Portrait of Councillor Brocke's Children* (both Hamburg, Ksthalle).

Denner's genre figures and character heads depicting wrinkled old women and men were particularly popular and were admired for their detailed execution and meticulous accuracy. They ensured the artist international success and attracted especially high fees: Emperor Charles VI of Austria is believed to have sent 600 ducats from Vienna in payment for a typical head of a woman, an extraordinary sum at that time.

BIBLIOGRAPHY

Thieme–Becker
C. L. von Hagedorn: *Lettre à un amateur de la peinture* (Dresden, 1755)
Zwei Hamburger Maler: Balthasar Denner und Franz Werner Tamm (exh. cat., Hamburg, Ksthalle, 1969)

KLÁRA GARAS

Dennis, George (*b* London, 21 July 1814; *d* London, 15 Nov 1898). British consul and antiquarian. He was first employed at the Excise Office in London. His early tours of the ancient sites of Etruria led to the monumental achievement of *The Cities and Cemeteries of Etruria* in 1848. This Victorian masterpiece was written for the benefit of 'those swarms of our countrymen who annually traverse that classic region in their migrations between Florence and Rome'. Eminently readable, it is also a major contribution to scholarship; its wealth of accurately observed topographical detail, some of it now lost, is still of use to all serious fieldworkers in the area it covers. A thoroughly revised edition (1878) was dedicated to Sir Austen Henry Layard 'of Nineveh', whom Dennis much admired. From 1849 until 1863 Dennis combined a Colonial Service post in British Guiana with an interest in ancient and modern Sicily; consular appointments followed, in Benghazi, Crete, Sicily and, finally, Smyrna (1879–88). He was one of a number of scholarly consuls who held a watching brief on matters of interest to the British Museum throughout the Mediterranean. His own excavations in Sicily and North Africa and at Sardis were far from spectacular; his enduring reputation rests on *The Cities and Cemeteries of Etruria*.

WRITINGS

The Cities and Cemeteries of Etruria (London, 1848; rev. 2/1878/*R* 1883)

BIBLIOGRAPHY

D. E. Rhodes: *Dennis of Etruria* (London, 1973)

DAVID RIDGWAY

Dennistoun, James (*b* Dumbartonshire, 17 Mar 1803; *d* Edinburgh, 13 Feb 1855). Scottish antiquarian, writer and collector. He was born into the noble Scots family of the Lords of Danzielstoun, which traced its ancestry to the reign of Alexander III (*reg* 1249–86). He was educated at the universities of Edinburgh and Glasgow, studying law but inclining towards history and literature. He qualified as an advocate in 1824 but never practised; instead he involved himself in researching the history of Scotland, particularly where it pertained to art and literature. He was a member of the Bannatyne and Maitland Clubs, for which he edited several cultural publications. He also contributed regular articles on art to the leading periodicals of the day, including the *Edinburgh Review* and the *Quarterly Review*. In 1825 and 1826 he travelled in Italy, a country that was to be his chief interest in his middle years. On the death of his father, James Dennistoun, in 1834, he sold the family estates, retaining Dennistoun Mains, Strathclyde, the centre of the original possessions. In 1836 he settled for a period in Rome, spending the summers travelling in

Italy and devoting himself to Italian studies and the collecting of Italian art; he also visited Germany.

In 1847 Dennistoun settled permanently in Edinburgh, where he displayed his small but important collection of religious paintings by such early Italian masters as Taddeo Gaddi and Giorgio Schiavone, together with medieval carved ivories, crucifixes and embroideries, as well as silver, niello and bronze items. He later added examples of German, Flemish, French, British and Spanish painting, including works by Diego Velázquez and Bartolomé Esteban Murillo, as well as paintings by the Italians Agnolo Bronzino and Giovanni Santi and Titian's *Portrait of a Man (?Ariosto)* (*c.* 1506; London, N.G.). The fruit of his sojourn in Italy was his three-volume *Memoirs of the Dukes of Urbino: Illustrating the Arms, Arts and Literature of Italy, from 1440 to 1630* (1851), an illuminating, discursive study that remained the standard work on the illustrious Italian houses of Montefeltro and Della Rovere for many years. Dennistoun continued to produce learned essays and memoirs until his death. In 1853 he gave evidence before the committee of the House of Commons on the National Gallery, London. His collection was dispersed by auction at Christie & Manson, London, on 14 June 1855.

WRITINGS

Memoirs of the Dukes of Urbino: Illustrating the Arms, Arts and Literature of Italy, from 1440 to 1630, 3 vols (London, 1851, rev. New York and London, 2/1908)

BIBLIOGRAPHY

J. W. Dennistoun: *Some Account of the Family of Dennistoun of Dennistoun and Colgrain* (Glasgow, 1906)

Denon, Baron **(Dominique-)Vivant** (*b* Givry, nr Chalon-sur-Saône, 4 Jan 1747; *d* Paris, 28 April 1825). French museum director, writer, graphic artist, collector, archaeologist and diplomat. He was the son of a provincial aristocrat. He went to Paris to further his law studies *c.* 1765 but entered the studio of Noël Hallé. He became Gentleman-in-Ordinary to Louis XV and was appointed keeper of the collection of engraved gems and medals that Mme de Pompadour had left to the King. In 1772 he entered the diplomatic service as attaché to the French embassy at St Petersburg, he was subsequently posted to Stockholm, Geneva (where his disrespectful engraving *Repast at Ferney*, of 4 July 1775, angered Voltaire) and, from spring 1776, Naples. There he became acquainted with Sir William Hamilton, the British ambassador, and made many drawings of his future wife Emma. Denon began to acquire a diverse collection of paintings and engravings as well as antiquities from excavations at Nola, Catania, Agrigento, Pompeii and Herculaneum. He purchased the painting of the *Resurrection of Lazarus* (Paris, Louvre) by Guercino for Louis XVI, an etching after which was his reception piece at the Accademia in Florence. He collected 520 Etruscan vases, which were later acquired by Louis XVI and deposited at Sèvres to be copied. Denon advised the Abbé Richard de Saint-Non in the preparation of the travel book *Voyage pittoresque dans les royaumes de Naples et de Sicile* (1781–6), supervising artists and composing a descriptive journal of the expedition. He was appointed chargé-d'affaires in Naples in 1782. Following a disagreement with Saint-Non, Denon

made his journal available to Henry Swinburne (1752–1803) for his *Travels in the Two Sicilies, in the Years 1777, 1779 and 1780*. Denon's own *Voyage en Sicile* was published in 1788.

Denon was dismissed from Naples in 1785 and spent two years in Rome, where he became a member of the circle of Cardinal de Bernis and engraved plates after the Carracci, Anthony van Dyck and Rembrandt. After his return to France in 1787, he published a review of the Salon and submitted to the Académie Royale an engraving after Luca Giordano's *Adoration of the Shepherds*, the only etching recorded as a *morceau de réception* during the 18th century. He was elected to the Académie on 31 March 1787 and registered as an 'engraver and artist of diverse talents'.

In June 1788 Denon settled in Venice, where he remained during the French Revolution. He moved in high social circles, giving lessons in engraving, and drew and engraved portraits of members of Venetian society, including those of *Countess Albrizzi* and the exiled court painter *Elisabeth Vigée-Lebrun* (both untraced). Denon was forced to leave in August 1792 when the city expelled all French nationals. Learning that his name had been placed on the list of émigrés and his French property confiscated, he courageously returned to France. He sought the protection of Jacques-Louis David, then a deputy of the National Convention. David had Denon's name removed from the émigré list and commissioned him to engrave his unfinished painting of the *Tennis Court Oath*. Denon attended meetings of the Revolutionary Tribunal and sketched its members including Georges-Jacques Danton, Antoine Quentin Fouquier-Tinville and Jean-Baptiste Carrier (New York, Met.; Paris, Bib. N.). In 1793 Denon published *L'Oeuvre priapique*, a group of engravings supposedly inspired by the sexual practices of the ancient Pompeians.

In 1798 Denon joined the scholars who accompanied the French army under Napoleon on its Egyptian campaign. He went with General Desaix along the Nile Valley and made over 150 sketches (London, BM), some of which were included in his *Voyage dans la Basse et la Haute Egypte . . .* of 1802, the first serious description of the antiquities discovered in Egypt (for illustrations *see* ARMANT and HERMOPOLIS MAGNA); Denon's text and engravings were largely responsible for promoting the Egyptian Revival style in France. In November 1802 Denon was appointed director-general of the Imperial Museums, a role which gave him control of the Musée Central des Arts (shortly to become the Musée Napoléon), the Musée des Monuments Français and the Musée de l'Ecole Française at Versailles. He presided over the French museums during the years when artistic booty brought from all over Europe made Napoleon's Paris the artistic capital of the world. In 1803 he became director of the Monnaie des Médailles, where he designed most of the medals commemorating contemporary events. In the same year he was elected a member of the Institut, where he gave a *Discours sur les monuments de l'antiquité arrivés d'Italie*. He was also artistic adviser to the Manufacture Impériale de Sèvres and the Gobelins Tapestry Factory. Denon organized and distributed imperial commissions not only to such artists as David, Antoine-Jean Gros and

Vivant Denon: *Denon Drawing Some Friends*, lithograph, 136×212mm, 1823 (Paris, Bibliothèque Nationale, Cabinet des Estampes)

BIBLIOGRAPHY

L. J. J. Dubois: *Description des objets d'art qui composaient l'une des parties du cabinet du feu M. le Baron V. Denon. . .monuments, antiques historiques* (Paris, 1826)
J. Duchesne: *Catalogue des livres et ouvrages à figures du cabinet de feu M. le Baron V. Denon* (Paris, 1826)
A. N. Perignon: *Description des objets d'art qui composent le cabinet de feu M. le Baron V. Denon . . . tableaux, dessins et miniatures* (Paris, 1826)
Brunet-Denon: *Monuments des arts du dessin chez les peuples tant anciens que modernes recueillis par le Baron Vivant Denon* (Paris, 1829)
P. Lelièvre: *Vivant Denon, directeur des beaux-arts de Napoléon* (Paris, 1942)
L. Armand-Calliat: *Vivant Denon* (Chalon-sur-Saône, 1964)
J. Chatelain: *Dominique Vivant Denon et le Louvre de Napoléon* (Paris, 1973)
P. Wescher: *Kunstraub unter Napoleon* (Berlin, 1976)
P. ten-Doesschate Chu: *French Masters of the Nineteenth Century, Dominique Vivant Denon*, 121–1 of *The Illustrated Bartsch*, ed. W. Strauss (New York, 1985)

JOANNA BARNES

De Noter, Pierre-François (*b* Waelhem, 23 Feb 1779; *d* Ghent, 22 Nov 1843). Belgian painter, designer and printmaker. The son of the painter and architect, Pierre-François De Noter the elder (1747–1830), and brother of Jean-Baptiste De Noter (1786–1855), a painter of architectural views, he had an early grounding in the arts. He was taught by Guillaume-Jacques Herreyns at the Mechelen Academie and attended Jan Frans Van Geel's sculpture class until 1793, when the French invasion prevented further study. One of his earliest commissions, shared with his father and Herreyns, was the decoration (begun shortly after 1793) of the SS Pieter en Pauwelkerk in Mechelen. This project had a determining influence on his career. The French had transformed the church into a Temple of Reason, and it seems likely that the damage done by them to the suppressed religious institutions of the Low Countries awakened the interest of Pierre-François De Noter and his brother in the architectural heritage of the Flemish towns. Pierre-François worked as a designer for a printed fabric manufacturer and as a printer before devoting himself to painting. He settled in Ghent in 1810 and subsequently was a frequent exhibitor at the Salons of Belgium and northern France, where he won numerous prizes.

De Noter's townscape paintings are notable for their documentary value as well as their artistic merit. Architecture predominates, although there is almost always some human interest, as in the *View of St Bavon du Reep Cathedral* (1831; Ghent, Mus. S. Kst.). In his watercolours and drawings he concentrated on documenting Flemish towns, such as Antwerp, Ghent, Bruges and Mechelen, and dispensed with the human figure. They are particularly noteworthy for their compositional quality and their meticulous transcription of all the complexities of the urban environment. A collection of 126 of his drawings are preserved at the Steinmetzkabinet in Bruges. Work of secondary importance includes his Dutch-inspired winter landscapes and market scenes: for example, *Fish Market* (1838; Brussels, Pal. Royal). Under his brother's influence, he occasionally tackled a historical reconstruction with figures in period costume, such as *The Van Eyck Brothers' 'Adoration of the Lamb' in the Veydt Chapel at Ghent* (1829; Amsterdam, Rijksmus.). In 1821 he visited Switzerland; he also travelled to the Netherlands and France. Appointed professor in 1822, he continued teaching to

François Gérard, but also to lesser-known artists, and he recognized the talent of such sculptors as Guillaume Boichot and François Rude. He accompanied Napoleon as artistic adviser on his campaigns in Austria, Spain, Italy and Poland. In 1811 he visited Italy to examine the works of art to be requisitioned from suppressed churches and convents, making a selection of early Italian paintings for the Louvre. On 5 August 1812 he was created Baron of the Empire. After the battle of Waterloo in 1815 and the final defeat of Napoleon, he refused to relinquish the works of art in his care until the Grenadier Guards forced him to submit. He resigned as director of the Musée Napoléon on 5 October 1815 on the pretext of failing health and went into retirement on the Quai Voltaire, Paris, where he housed his own collection. The last decade of his life was spent engraving and working on a general history of the arts (published posthumously by his nephews in 1829), a project that had been a preoccupation for some years. The catalogues of his possessions compiled after his death list 200 paintings, among them *Gilles* (Paris, Louvre) by Antoine Watteau and a *Deposition* (ex-Louvre) by Raphael, 750 drawings (many from the Zanetti collection in Venice), 600 prints and a wide variety of gems, medals, bronzes, maiolica, enamels, engravings and relics. The collection was dispersed in posthumous sales in 1826 and 1827. Among the numerous portraits of Denon are those by Pierre-Paul Prud'hon (Paris, Louvre), Jean-Baptiste Greuze (Cherbourg, Mus. B.-A.), a bust by Antoine-Denis Chaudet (Dijon, Mus. B.-A.), his bronze funerary monument by Pierre Cartellier (Paris, Père-Lachaise Cemetery) and a self-portrait, *Denon Drawing Some Friends* (1823; Paris, Bib. N., Cab. Est.; see fig.).

WRITINGS

Voyage en Sicile (Paris, 1788)
Voyage dans la Basse et la Haute Egypte pendant les campagnes du général Bonaparte, 2 vols (Paris, 1802)
Description de l'Egypte, 24 vols (Paris, 1809–22) [contains engravings after 150 drawings by Denon]

the end of his life. Frans Vervloet, A. C. M. Engel (1801–33) and A. E. Moerman (1808–56) were among his pupils. He also published the *Recueil de gravures à l'eau forte dont plusieurs d'après Hobbema* (Ghent, 1831).

BIBLIOGRAPHY
1770–1830: Autour du Néo-classicisme en Belgique (exh. cat., Brussels, Mus. d'Ixelles, 1985), pp. 322–4, 375

DOMINIQUE VAUTIER

De Noyette, Modeste (*b* Ledeberg, 22 Feb 1847; *d* Ledeberg, 22 Dec 1923). Belgian architect. Registered as a carpenter at the academy in Ghent, he studied there under the direction of Adolphe Pauli, in whose studio he continued to work. At the beginning of his career, he collaborated with his brother, Ferdinand De Noyette (*d* 1869), an architect who built the parish hall (1866) of St Anne's in Ghent in a remarkable High Victorian style. After his brother's early death, Modeste De Noyette took over his work on the churches at Gentbrugge (1868–72) and Haaltert (1869–72) and was soon in demand as an architect of churches and convents. He built churches mostly in a 13th-century style at Welle (1871), Eeklo (1878), Ronse (1892) and Balgerhoeke (1903), finished those of St Joseph at Alost (1868–91) and St Martin at Arlon (1910) and transformed or restored many others, such as Ghent-Ekkergem (1901), Asper and Deurle.

De Noyette was in sympathy with the flourishing Gothic Revival movement, and his ecclesiastical works were mostly conceived in a unified style, as *Gesamtkunstwerk* realized under the supervision of the architect. There was also much emphasis on craftsmanship, with many specialists in different crafts being employed. In his other work, comprising presbyteries (Ronse, 1894; Sint Amandsberg, 1901; Ghent-Ekkergem, 1902), houses (Ghent, Sint Amandsberg) and town halls (Sint Amandsberg, 1883; Gentbrugge, 1892), he sometimes abandoned strict Gothic Revival vocabulary to experiment with the Renaissance Revival and Baroque Revival. His Caserne Leopold of 1902 in Ghent is a remarkable example of *fin-de-siècle* eclecticism: Gothic details and Second-Empire roofs combine with an Art Nouveau sense of materials and texture.

BIBLIOGRAPHY
J. C.: Obituary, *L'Emulation*, xliv (1924), p. 15
J. van Cleven: 'De dekanale Sint-Vincentiuskerk te Eeklo', *Vlaanderen*, xxix/174 (Jan–Feb 1980), pp. 29–31
F. van Tyghem: 'Het stadhuis van Sint-Niklaas en het gemeentehuis van Sint-Amandsberg', *Vlaanderen*, xxix/174 (Jan–Feb 1980), pp. 28–9
M. Pattin: *De neogotische kerken van architect Modeste de Noyette (1847–1923)* (diss., Ghent U., 1984)
J. van Cleven: '19th Century: Architecture', *Flemish Art*, ed. H. Liebaers (Antwerp, 1985), p. 509

JEAN VAN CLEVEN

Dente [da Ravenna], **Marco** (*b* Ravenna; *d* Rome, 1527). Italian engraver. He was active in Rome during the early 16th century. Some early writers confused him with Silvestro da Ravenna, and his family name was unknown until its rediscovery by Zani. He studied with Marcantonio Raimondi and was strongly influenced by the latter's style. He often collaborated with Agostino Veneziano, another Marcantonio student who also had some influence on Dente's work. Dente was evidently born in Ravenna, although his birth date is undocumented. His earliest signed and dated print is inscribed 1515, suggesting that he was active from *c.* 1510 and was probably born in the late 15th century. He was killed in the Sack of Rome in 1527. He produced over 60 reproductive engravings, primarily after works by Raphael and his circle and after the Antique. Occasionally he made engravings after other artists, such as the *Massacre of the Innocents* (1520–21; B. 21) after Baccio Bandinelli. He engraved several copies after Marcantonio prints that were based on Raphael designs. Two examples of this, the *Massacre of the Innocents* (B. 20) and *Judgement of Paris* (B. 246), were considered by Bartsch to be among Dente's best works. Other engravings may derive directly from Raphael drawings, such as the *Venus Wounded by the Rose's Thorn* (B. 321). Dente's only print to include an inscription with his full name (MARCVS RAVENAS), rather than a monogram, is his engraving after the *Laokoon* (B. 353), which shows the antique statue before its restoration.

BIBLIOGRAPHY
G. Vasari: *Vite* (1550, rev. 2/1568); ed. G. Milanesi (1878–85)
G. Gori Gandellini: *Notizie istoriche degl'intagliatori*, iii (Siena, 1771), pp. 144–5; xii (Siena, 1818), pp. 233–42
K. H. Heinecken: *Dictionnaire des artistes dont nous avons des estampes avec une notice detaillée de leurs ouvrages gravés* (Leipzig, 1778–90), i, pp. 642ff
P. Zani: *Enciclopedia metodica critico-ragionata delle belle arti* (Parma, 1820), ii, part 5, p. 327
G. K. Nagler: *Neues allgemeines Kunstler-Lexikon oder Nachrichten von dem Leben und den Werken der Maler, Bildhauer, Baumeister* (Munich, 1835–52), xiv, pp. 6–27
———: *Die Monogrammisten* (Munich and Leipzig, 1858–1920), ii, no. 2373; iv, no. 3468; v, no. 265
K. Oberhuber: *Die Kunst der Graphik II: Renaissance in Italien 16. Jahrhundert* (Vienna, 1966), pp. 107–9
S. Ferrara and G. Gaeta Bertelà: *Incisori bolognesi ed emiliani del sec. XVI* (Bologna, 1975), nos 175–226
K. Oberhuber, ed.: *The Works of Marcantonio Raimondi and of his School (1978)*, 26 [XIV/i] and 27 [XIV/ii] of *The Illustrated Bartsch* (New York, 1978–) [B.]

BABETTE BOHN

Denti, Girolamo (*b* ?Venice, *c.* 1510; *d* ?Venice *c.* 1572). Italian painter. He was in Titian's workshop, probably from about 1520, and became his most prominent assistant, signing himself *di Tiziano*. His fame is based mainly on two paintings traditionally ascribed to him: the *Four Seasons* (Paris, priv. col.) and the *Holy Family with Donors* (Dresden, Gemäldegal. Alte Meister), both executed between 1540 and 1550. In the early 1530s he painted a *Virgin and Child Enthroned with Saints* for Cesena Cathedral, and about ten years later he sent another altarpiece of that subject (Monópoli, Vescovado) to Apulia. A portrait of the *Two Pesaro Brothers* (1540s; United Kingdom, priv. col., see 1983 exh. cat., no. 120), once assigned to Titian, belongs to the same period, as does *SS Andrew, Sebastian and Roch* (Mel, nr Belluno, Parrocchiale) and *SS Mark, Leonard and Francis* (Ancona, Pin. Com.). In 1557 Denti received the commission for the official portrait of *Doge Lorenzo Priuli* (sold London, Sotheby's, 28 April 1971) and for the huge *Annunciation* (1557–61; Venice, Accad., on dep. Mason Vicentino) in the Scuola della Carità in Venice, the companion piece to Titian's *Presentation of the Virgin* (Venice, Accad.). The *Annunciation* is a theatrical work, recalling perhaps his documented activity as a scene painter, and reveals various influences, from Andrea Palladio to Raphael and Lorenzo Lotto. Denti's sensitivity to the works of Paris Bordone is seen in the

Virgin and Child with Saints (1559; Venice, Accad.), once in Belluno. Between 1560 and 1570 Denti reached the height of his career, narrowly missing a commission from Philip II, King of Spain, to paint a copy of Titian's *Martyrdom of St Lawrence* (Madrid, Escorial). He is last mentioned in 1566, when he may have been the main executant, with Marco Vecellio and Emanuele d'Augusta, of the frescoes (destr.) after Titian's cartoons in the archdiaconal church of Pieve di Cadore.

BIBLIOGRAPHY

G. Vasari: *Vite* (1550, rev. 2/1568); ed. G. Milanesi (1878–85), vii, p. 468

M. R. Fisher: *Titian's Assistants during the Later Years* (New York, 1977), pp. 31–42

F. Heinemann: 'La bottega di Tiziano', *Tiziano e Venezia*, ed. N. Pozza (Vicenza, 1980), pp. 434–5

D. Rosand: *Painting in Cinquecento Venice: Titian, Veronese, Tintoretto* (New Haven and London, 1982)

The Genius of Venice, 1500–1600 (exh. cat., ed. J. Martineau and C. Hope; London, RA, 1983)

S. Claut: 'All'ombra di Tiziano', *Ant. Viva*, 5–6 (1986), pp. 16–29

SERGIO CLAUT

Dentil. Term for an ornamental band of small, square, toothlike blocks in the bed-mould of a cornice (*see* GREECE, ANCIENT, §II, 1(i)(a), and ORDERS, ARCHITECTURAL, fig. 1xxv; *see also* POLYCHROMY, colour pl. I, fig. 1). In ancient Greek architecture the dentils probably represent the ends of wooden joists that originally supported the roof.

□

Dentone. *See* CURTI, GIROLAMO.

Dentone, il. *See* RUBINO, GIOVANNI.

Denucé, Jan (Baptist Ferdinand) (*b* Antwerp, 13 Feb 1878; *d* Antwerp, 11 Feb 1944). Belgian historian, museum curator and archivist. He studied history at the Rijksuniversiteit, Ghent, in 1900 and wrote his doctoral thesis in 1904 on Magellan and the 16th-century voyages of discovery. In the same year he became a professor of history at the Vrije Universiteit in Brussels. Denucé took the post of assistant curator of the Museum Plantin-Moretus in Antwerp and in 1914 succeeded Max Rooses as principal curator. Four years later he was discharged for political activism and became an antiquarian book dealer. In 1925 he was appointed city archivist, a post which from 1930 he combined with that of the curatorship of the Antwerp Oudheidkundige Musea (Antiquarian museums). He retired in 1943. Denucé accomplished an enormous amount of work in cataloguing the holdings of the Stadsarchief, including the inventory he drew up of the department of insolvent estates, which contained the archives of bankrupt merchants and firms. He published several books of source material drawn from the archives on the history of art dealers and collectors in Antwerp.

WRITINGS

Kunstuitvoer te Antwerpen in de 17e eeuw: De firma Forchoudt [Art experts in Antwerp in the 17th century: The firm of Forchoudt] (Antwerp, 1931)

De Antwerpsche konstkamers: Inventarissen van kunstverzamelingen in de 16e–17e eeuw [The Antwerp *kunstkammern*: Inventories of 16th- and 17th-century collectors] (Antwerp, 1932)

Brieven en documenten betreffende Jan Breugel I en II (Antwerp, 1934)

Antwerpsche tapijtkunst en -handel [Antwerp tapestries and tapestry merchants] (Antwerp, 1935)

Na Peter Pauwel Rubens: Documenten uit de kunsthandel Mattijs Musson te Antwerpen in de 17e eeuw [On Peter Paul Rubens. Documents from the art dealer Mattijs Musson in 17th-century Antwerp] (Antwerp, 1949)

JAN VAN ROEY

Den'yer, Andrey (Genrikh Ivanovich) (*b* ?St Petersburg, 1820; *d* ?St Petersburg, 1892). Russian photographer. He studied at the Academy of Arts in St Petersburg, probably intending to become a painter. He graduated in 1849 and in 1851 opened a daguerreotype portrait studio in St Petersburg. Den'yer was very much a part of the St Petersburg artistic milieu and represents an important early link between photography and the academic tradition. He attempted to bring to his portraits the knowledge and experience he had gained at the Academy, as can be seen in his portrait of the poet *Fyodor Ivanovich Tyutchev* (1864; Muranov, Tyutchev Estate–Mus., see Morozov, 1977, fig. 3), with its strong pose and effective use of vignetting. He also set high standards in retouching, using professional artists, notably Ivan Kramskoy. His contacts with the Academy (especially his photographic portraits of its professors) were important in gaining recognition for photography as a fine art. He was one of the first in Russia to make photographic reproductions of artists' pictures, and his own photographic portraits were in turn used by painters (especially Kramskoy, who made use of Den'yer's portrait of Tyutchev in 1883). In 1865 Den'yer published an album of well-known faces of Russia, designed as a carte-de-visite album.

Den'yer soon moved on from the daguerreotype to the wet collodion process (*see* PHOTOGRAPHY, §I). He also extended his subject-matter to include portraits of ethnic types, for example *Nenets People* (1860s; see Morozov, 1977, fig. 11). Advised by Sergey Zaryanko to attempt to soften the edges of his portraits and thereby lessen the need for retouching, Den'yer devised a method of printing using two negatives of different thicknesses at the same time, which he patented in 1873 and which became known as the Den'yer method.

BIBLIOGRAPHY

G. Boltyansky: *Ocherki po istorii fotografii v SSSR* [Studies in the history of photography in the USSR] (Moscow, 1939), pp. 21–2

S. Morozov: 'Early Photography in Eastern Europe: Russia', *Hist. Phot.*, i/4 (1977), pp. 327–47

——: *Tvorcheskaya fotografiya* [Creative photography] (Moscow, 1986)

KEVIN HALLIWELL

Denzler, Juraj (*b* Zagreb, 12 April 1896; *d* Zagreb, 27 Sept 1981). Croatian architect. He studied at the Technische Hochschule, Vienna (1918–19), and the High Technical School, Zagreb, and then worked in the studios of Hugo Ehrlich and Edo Šen, both in Zagreb. He later collaborated with Mladen Kauzlarić. His earlier buildings were influenced by Viktor Kovačić and show the decorative touches of the Viennese tradition combined with pure volumes, notably in the residential building (1926) at Zvonarnička Street, Zagreb, and the National Health Building (1927), Zvijezda, Zagreb. Denzler later turned his attention to pure forms and spaces of clear functional expression, for example the City Services Building (1935), Kavurić Street, Zagreb. He was a master of formal organization, particularly in the use of materials to emphasize the relationship of different elements, such as doors and windows, to the whole composition. Of his considerable output, other important buildings are a chapel on Mount Sljeme (1931), Zagreb; the church of the Holy Ghost (1932), Zagreb; the Jesuit Church (1933), Belgrade; and private villas. In his work as a professor of the history of architecture at the University of Zagreb (from 1939), he emphasized the importance of classical forms.

BIBLIOGRAPHY

S. Planić: *Problemi savremene arhitekture* [Problems of contemporary architecture] (Zagreb, 1932)
S. Sekulic-Gvozdanovic: 'Juraj Denzler, 1896–1981', *Covjek i Prostor*, xxx/368 (1983), pp. 30, 31

PAUL TVRTKOVIĆ

Deodato (di) Orlandi [Deodata; Deodatus] (*fl* Lucca, *c.* 1280; *d* before 1331). Italian painter. He was an eclectic and apparently prolific artist whose works record the transition from Italo-Byzantine painting of the 13th century to the Giottesque milieu of the 14th. They also indicate the importance of Florentine styles for Lucchese painting in his time. The earliest work attributed to him is a Crucifix with a living Christ (*c.* 1280; Pisa, Mus. N. & Civ. S Matteo), and if this attribution is correct it suggests that his early development was influenced by Berlinghiero Berlinghieri. Deodato was probably the 'Datuccius Orlandi' documented in 1284, and in 1288 he signed a richly ornamented Crucifix for S Cerbone, Lucca (Lucca, Villa Guinigi; see fig.). This was evidently strongly influenced by Cimabue, for example in the way the hair spills from the (rather larger) head on to Christ's shoulder, although

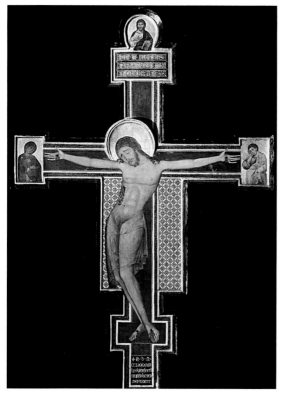

Deodato Orlandi: Crucifix, tempera on panel, 2.72×1.89 m, 1288 (Lucca, Museo Nazionale di Villa Guinigi)

the figure of the dead Christ has none of Cimabue's monumentality. The style is linear, largely devoid of chiaroscuro though not without grace, and the modelling is barely structural. Some attempt has been made to reproduce the translucent drapery of the Christ of Cimabue's later Crucifix (Florence, Santa Croce), but the swaying body keeps closer to the axis of the apron than is the case with Cimabue's versions. The terminal figures of St John and the Virgin are seen in three-quarter length.

Deodato worked for a time in Pisa, where he was paid by the Operario del Duomo in 1298 as 'Datus Pictor'. In 1301 he assisted Francesco da Pisa with a mosaic for the cathedral apse and in the same year signed a low gabled dossal of the *Virgin and Child Enthroned with Saints and Angels* (Pisa, Mus. N. & Civ. S Matteo) and another Crucifix (San Miniato al Tedesco, S Chiara), which shows him reacting to the example of the Crucifix attributed to Giotto in S Maria Novella, Florence. Here Deodato simply adapted the traditional form of cross to the new, three-nail format while ignoring most of the accompanying naturalistic innovations, with the result that the jutting-out of the body to the right looks merely awkward, and the design of the torso is markedly less satisfactory in this context than that of the S Cerbone Crucifix. Deodato's attempt to reproduce the tilt of the head seen in the S Maria Novella Crucifix is both structurally illogical and lacking the pathos of his source. An extensive fresco scheme in S Piero in Grado near Pisa has also been attributed to Deodato and dated *c.* 1300. It comprises scenes from the *Lives of SS Peter and Paul* above a continuous series of busts of popes set within an ambitious fictive architectural setting. If the lively narratives are accepted as his, they should be considered his most impressive surviving work. In 1308 he signed a mosaic in Lucca Cathedral (destr.) and a lively *Virgin and Child* (ex-Hurd priv. col., New York), part of a dismembered dossal. Documents show that he was still alive in 1315 but dead by 1331.

BIBLIOGRAPHY

R. Van Marle: *Italian Schools*, i (1924)
E. B. Garrison: *Italian Romanesque Panel Painting* (Florence, 1949), pp. 16–17
——: 'Towards a New History of Lucchese Painting', *A. Bull.*, xxxiii (1951), pp. 11–31
B. Berenson: *Central and North Italian Schools*, i (1968), p. 107
J. T. Wolleson: *Die Fresken von San Piero a Grado bei Pisa* (Bad Oeynhausen, 1977)
E. Sandberg-Vavalà: *La croce dipinta italiana* (Rome, 1980), pp. 564–7, 797–800, 898–9
E. Castelnuovo, ed.: *La pittura in Italia: Le origini* (Milan, 1982, 2/1986), p. 646

JOHN RICHARDS

Deodatus. *See under* COSMATUS.

Deogarh [Deogaṛh, Devagaḍh; anc. Luacchagira, Kīrtidurga]. Site of Vaishnava and Jaina temples ranging from the 5th to 11th centuries in Lalitpur District, Uttar Pradesh, India. It appears that the ancient name Luacchagira, known from inscriptions, was changed to Kirtidurga after the CHANDELLA conquest of the 11th century under Kirtivarman.

The earliest extant building at Deogarh (*c.* AD 475), sometimes called the Dashavatara temple, is sacred to Vishnu, and its images of this god are the finest *in situ* examples of Gupta-period sculpture in India. The temple, square in plan (about 5 m on each side), stands on a square plinth (Skt *jagatī*) with remains of shrines at each corner, following a five-shrine (*pañcāyatana*) scheme. An elaborately carved doorway faces west. The temple has a simple moulding around its base. The plinth also carries mouldings and was once topped with reliefs depicting scenes from the life of Krishna and Rama (e.g. New Delhi, N. Mus.). The temple's iconographic scheme focuses on various manifestations of Vishnu. The wall sections (*jaṅghā*) have large niches (*rathikā*) flanked by sumptuously carved pillars and jambs (*see* INDIAN SUBCONTINENT, fig. 29). The niches contain relief panels of *Vishnu Reclining on the Serpent Ananta* (south), the *Sages Nara and Narayana*, generally considered among the 22 minor incarnations of Vishnu (east; see fig.) and *Vishnu Liberating Indra's Elephant* (north). These may be assigned to *c.* 475 on the basis of their formal similarity to the Buddhas from Sarnath of the same date. The niches were originally sheltered by stone awnings (*chādya*). The temple's superstructure, now badly damaged, was probably composed of receding tiers of cornices adorned with arch-shaped motifs (*candraśālā*) and free-standing finials on the corners of each storey.

Around the temple are a large number of small ruined shrines, probably ranging in date from the 5th to 10th

Deogarh, *Sage Narayana*, detail from a red sandstone relief panel, east side of the Vishnu Temple, *c.* 475 AD

century. Numerous sculpted pieces and architectural fragments have been removed from the grounds (some are in the Archaeological Survey of India storage building, and others have been set up in a pilgrims' centre at the site). Assorted fragments have been used as building material in the houses of the nearby village. On the village outskirts is a brick mound with 5th-century sculpture fragments.

A ruined fort and extensive Jaina temple complex are located on a rocky hill a short distance from the 5th-century temple. The largest of the Jaina temples, dedicated to Shantinatha, was built before AD 862, the date on a pillar in front of the structure. The temple's damaged and partly rebuilt superstructure is of the curvilinear northern type (*latina* or *nāgara*). The large pillared hall (*maṇḍapa*) in front of the temple is a subsequent addition. Hundreds of sculptures, mainly 8th–10th century, have been cemented into a modern wall enclosing the temple. Some 30 other temples in the Jaina complex date between the 9th and 11th centuries. Most are relatively humble shrines and have been substantially rebuilt.

To the south-west of the Jaina complex is a ruined temple dedicated to Vishnu's incarnation as Varaha, the cosmic boar. The main image dates from the late 7th century. Other sculptures from the temple (now in the Archaeological Survey of India storage building) were probably produced around the 11th century.

To the south of the Varaha temple, stepped walkways lined with rock-cut sculptures lead to the Betwa River. Sculptures include a panel of mother-goddess figures (*mātṛkā*) attended by Ganesha, with a dedicatory inscription from around the late 6th century; an image of Vishnu, stylistically a local parallel to the Buddha from Mathura dated 599–600 (Lucknow, State Mus.); a second panel of seated mother-goddess figures, probably early 7th century; and a well-preserved relief of *Durga Slaying the Buffalo Demon* (Mahiṣāsuramardinī), a close parallel to sculpture of the large Shiva temple at Mahua and thus probably late 7th century.

See also INDIAN SUBCONTINENT, §§III, 4(i) and IV, 5(i)(b).

BIBLIOGRAPHY

P. C. Mukherjee: *Report on the Antiquities in the District of Lalitpur, N. W. Provinces, India* (Roorkee, 1899)

H. D. Sankalia: 'Jain Monuments from Deogarh', *J. Ind. Soc. Orient. A.*, ix (1941), pp. 97–104

M. S. Vats: *The Gupta Temples at Deogarh*, Mem. Archeol. Surv. India, lxx (Delhi, 1952)

K. Bruhn: *The Jina-Images of Deogarh* (Leiden, 1969)

O. Viennot: 'The Mahiṣāsurmardinī from Siddhi-ki-Gupha at Deogarh', *J. Ind. Soc. Orient. A.*, n. s., iv (1971–2), pp. 66–7

J. Harle: *Gupta Sculpture* (Oxford, 1973)

A. Ghosh, ed.: *Jaina Art and Architecture*, 3 vols (New Delhi, 1974)

M. Meister: 'Jaina Temples in Central India', *Aspects of Jaina Art and Architecture*, ed. U. P. Shah and M. A. Dhaky (Ahmadabad, 1975), pp. 223–41

J. Williams: *The Art of Gupta India: Empire and Province* (Princeton, 1982)

MICHAEL D. WILLIS

De Opbouw. *See* OPBOUW, DE.

Deori Kalan [Deorī Kālān; Marhia; Maṛhiā Kālān]. Site of ruined 5th-century temple in Madhya Pradesh, India. The temple appears to be the oldest extant example in India dedicated to Vishnu in the form of Vamana, the dwarf incarnation. A broken image of Vamana, still set in its spouted plinth, lies outside. The temple faces west and sits on a low platform (Skt *jagatī*). The building itself is constructed of large blocks of ashlar and is approximately 3.8 m on each side. The base is dominated by a single half-torus moulding (*kumbha*). The walls (*jaṅghā*) are completely plain, but the entrance door on the west side has a wide jamb (*śākhā*) with undulating lotus scrolls. The scrollwork is almost identical to the richly carved jambs from BHUMARA, now in the Allahabad Museum. Door-guardians (*dvārapāla*) in high relief flank the entrance. A row of dentils, carved with lion heads, tops the entrance. The interior is devoid of decoration.

A complex entablature (*varaṇḍikā*) rests on top of the wall section, consisting of a cornice (*kapota*) crowned by a row of panels carved with musicians, dancers and *kīrtimukha* (beastlike faces). The central relief panels (where they have survived) are larger than the rest and carry depictions of Vishnu as Hayagriva and Narasimha. Above this is a second cornice and upper row of decorative panels, alternating between squat figures in small niches and blind windows of key-hole shape. The blind windows represent a radically compressed clerestory derived from vanished prototypes in wood and brick. Roof slabs, some with rainwater spouts, mark the top of the structure.

The Vamana temple can be grouped with a number of 5th-century shrines in the region, such as the Kankali Devi temple at Tigowa and Temple 17 at SANCHI. All show a dependence on wood and brick prototypes but differ in configuration and specific details. Sculptural style suggests a date of *c*. AD 475.

See also INDIAN SUBCONTINENT, §§III, 4(i) and IV, 6(iv)(b).

BIBLIOGRAPHY
P. Chandra: 'A Vāmana Temple at Maṛhiā and Some Reflections on Gupta Architecture', *Artibus Asiae*, xxxii (1970), pp. 125–45
M. Meister: 'A Note on the Superstructure of the Maṛhiā Temple'; *Artibus Asiae*, xxxvi (1974), pp. 81–8
J. Williams: *The Art of Gupta India: Empire and Province* (Princeton, 1982)

MICHAEL D. WILLIS

Department store. Large retail establishment. It developed primarily in Paris in the second half of the 19th century, selling a variety of merchandise, but examples can be now found throughout the world. It is typically housed in an impressive, multi-storey building with prominent display windows on the ground floor and is located near a city centre.

During the Middle Ages, European itinerant merchants sold their wares in markets and street fairs. From the 17th century, French merchants began to rent street-level quarters in residential buildings. After 1750 retailing changed dramatically in Europe; guilds lost their traditional privileges, marketing and production became separate activities, and in the wake of the French Revolution (1789–99) restrictions on selling more than one kind of ware were lifted. Favourable economic conditions under Napoleon also contributed to competition between shop owners and spurred the development of *magasins de nouveautés* (dry goods stores), which were larger institutions selling a variety of goods. Small speciality shops clustered together to compete, often in glazed arcades.

The Bon Marché in Paris began as a small haberdashery shop in the 1820s. By the 1850s its proprietor, Aristide Boucicaut, had introduced the trade policies that now define the department store: a wide range of merchandise, low prices, rapid turnover, *entrée libre* (customers were not expected to pay for their entrance with a purchase), liberal arrangements for the return of goods and free delivery services. At the same time the development of low-cost mass-produced goods and improvements in transport systems in the 1830s facilitated both the transfer of goods and the travel of customers in the quantities required by big stores.

In 1867 Boucicaut commissioned the first building designed specifically as a department store (see fig.). It was designed in the then fashionable Beaux-Arts style by the architect Jean-Alexandre Laplanche (1839–1910), with Louis-Auguste Boileau. It was finally completed in 1887 by Boileau's son Louis-Charles, with the help of Gustave

Bon Marché department store, Rue de Sèvres, Paris, by Jean-Alexandre Laplanche, Louis-Auguste Boileau and Louis-Charles Boileau, 1867–87

Eiffel. The iron-framed, five-storey structure provided ample space to display and sell goods. Its remarkably large windows, arranged in regular grids on the façades, allowed both wares and customers to be lit to advantage. Eye-catching corner rotundas and monumental entrances on the exuberantly classical stone façades were complemented inside by spacious and light glazed courts.

The Bon Marché department store proved immensely successful. Throughout the world subsequent department stores adhered to the Bon Marché type, with variations in each country according to economic conditions and architectural traditions. The department store proliferated rapidly: Printemps (Paul Sédille (i), 1881–5), Samaritaine (Frantz Jourdain, 1905–10; addition by Jourdain and Henri Sauvage, 1926–9) and Galeries Lafayette (Georges-Paul Chedanne, 1907) in Paris; Wertheim (Alfred Messel, 1896–7) and Hermann Tietz (Sehring & Lachmann, 1898) in Berlin; Harrods (Stevens & Hunt, 1905) and Selfridges (Daniel Burnham and Frank Atkinson, 1906) in London; Wanamakers (1877; remodelled by Daniel Burnham, 1903–11) in Philadelphia; Marshall Fields (D. H. Burnham & Co., 1902) and Carson Pirie Scott (Louis Sullivan, 1898–1904; see SULLIVAN, LOUIS, fig. 2) in Chicago; and Macy's (DeLemos & Cordes, 1902) in New York.

Well-designed, lavishly decorated façades and interiors were necessary to attract customers and to create an ambience conducive to shopping. Changes in architectural styles led to frequent updating of façades and remodelling of interiors. The Schocken Store (1926), Stuttgart, by Erich Mendelsohn preserved the basic type but was a non-historicizing, unornamented, steel-framed structure with a continuous display-window at street level; alternating bands of glazing and brick and travertine spandrels reinforced its dynamic, curved horizontality. Several years later, W. M. Dudok designed the Bijenkorf department store, Rotterdam (1929–30; destr.), with long horizontal glazed volumes locked into place by solid vertical masses.

Changes in technology also affected store design. The development of fluorescent lighting after the 1930s led to widespread reliance on artificial lighting and to the windowless façade, such as that of Nieman-Marcus (1962–5), Dallas, by Kevin Roche. More fundamentally, new transport patterns affected the design and location of department stores. The proliferation of private transport prompted the rise of the branch store and the suburban shopping mall. Despite this competitive threat, the department store held its own and remained an important modern building type.

BIBLIOGRAPHY
G. d'Avenel: 'Les Grands Magasins', *Rev. Deux Mondes*, cxxiv (1894), pp. 329–69
K. Welch: 'Department Stores', *Forms and Functions of 20th Century Architecture*, ed. T. Hamlin (New York, 1952), pp. 36–81
H. Pasdermadjian: *The Department Store: Its Origins, Evolution, and Economics* (London, 1954/R New York, 1976)
M. L. Clausen: 'The Department Store', *Frantz Jourdain and the Samaritaine: Art Nouveau Theory and Criticism* (Leiden, 1987), pp. 191–215
MEREDITH L. CLAUSEN

Depaulis, Alexis-Joseph (*b* Paris, 30 Aug 1792; *d* Paris, 15 Sept 1867). French medallist. He entered the Ecole des Beaux-Arts, Paris, in 1813 and trained there under Bertrand Andrieu, for medal making, and Pierre Cartellier, for sculpture. Early in his career he contributed to the medallic history of Napoleon I's reign (*Conquest of Illyria*; *French Academy at Rome*; *Orphanage of the Legion of Honour*) and to James Mudie's *National Medals* (*George III*; *Return of Napoleon*; *British Army in the Netherlands*; *Charge of the British at Waterloo*). He was responsible for a number of the portraits in the *Galerie métallique des grands hommes français*, including those of *Antoine Arnaud* (1817), *Pierre Jolyot de Crébillon, Jacques Amyot* (1819), *Abbé Suger* and *Bayard* (1822), also for *Martin Luther* (1821), among others, in the *Series numismatica universalis virorum illustrium* by Amédée Pierre Durand (1789–1873). Depaulis's later work became increasingly ambitious in scale and in relief. His monumental commemorative medals for the *Bombardment of the Fort of St Jean d'Ulloa* (1838), the *Battle of Isly* (1844) and the *Capture of Sebastopol* (1855) were much admired by contemporaries. In these medals, as in his later piece celebrating the *Suez Canal* (1864), he re-established the technical supremacy enjoyed by French engravers at the Paris Mint.

BIBLIOGRAPHY
Bellier de La Chavignerie-Auvray; Forrer
C. Gabet: *Dictionnaire des artistes de l'école française au XIXe siècle* (Paris, 1834), pp. 200–201
MARK JONES

Depay [Depey]**, Johann.** *See* PAY, JOHANN DE.

Depero, Fortunato (*b* Fondo, Val di Non, Trentino, 30 March 1892; *d* Rovereto, 29 Nov 1960). Italian painter, stage designer, illustrator, decorative artist and writer. After difficult years of study, during which he made his first artistic experiments, he travelled to Turin in 1910 and worked as an apprentice decorator at the Esposizione Internazionale. In spite of spending a year as apprentice to a marble-worker, on his return to Rovereto, he decided to become a painter, choosing subjects associated with Symbolism and social realism. Shortly after publishing *Spezzature–Impressioni: Segni e ritmi* (Rovereto, 1913), a collection of poetry, prose and illustrations, he moved to Rome, where he met Filippo Tommaso Marinetti at the Galleria Permanente Futurista, run by Giuseppe Sprovieri; through Marinetti he met the Futurists, with whom he exhibited at the same gallery in the spring of 1914 (*see* FUTURISM, §1). This was followed by a one-man show at Trento in July 1914, which closed after a few days because of the outbreak of World War I. He succeeded in returning to Rome, where he was officially welcomed into the Futurist group. Before volunteering for the front, he was co-signatory with Giacomo Balla of the manifesto *Ricostruzione futurista dell'universo* (Rome, 11 March 1915). The two artists affirmed the need to create dynamic 'plastic complexes' with which to enliven the world, using materials of every kind.

Depero's pictorial expression was now characterized by an abstract synthesis of dynamic, coloured shapes with curvilinear outlines, enlivened by an intuitive and joyous imagination. Discharged from the army because of poor physical health, he threw himself into his work, developing an eclecticism that led him to experiment with new techniques and also to compose poetry. The formal synthesis achieved in the preceding years acquired, from 1916, a mechanical character, which Depero also applied to his contemporaneous experiments with stage designs; his backdrops and costumes in 1916 for Igor Stravinsky's *Le Rossignol*, commissioned from him by Serge Diaghilev for the Ballets Russes, were particularly inventive, but the project was suspended when almost complete and never staged. Nevertheless this first theatrical commission led to others.

In 1917, after being invited to Capri by the Swiss poet and Egyptologist Gilbert Clavel (1883–1927) to illustrate his book *Un istituto per suicidi* (Rome, 1918), he worked with Clavel on the choreography of his Teatro Plastico, involving synthetic theatrical actions without actors. This came to life in the *Balli plastici*, staged in 1918 at the Teatro dei Piccoli in Rome, for which he designed the marionettes. In Rovereto in 1919 he founded the Casa d'Arte Depero, also known as the Casa d'Arte Futurista, where he and his wife Rosetta Depero undertook the design and production of household objects, tapestries and advertising posters, an enterprise to which they devoted the rest of their lives. In the 1920s Depero turned his attention to the decoration and furnishing of commercial premises and pavilions, including the Cabaret del Diavolo (1921–2) in Rome, with its complex symbolism of psychological journeys; the Padiglione della Venezia Tridentina at the Milan Trade Fair in 1923–4; and the Padiglione del Libro, Bestetti, Tumminelli e Treves for the second Biennale Internazionale d'Arte Decorativa at Monza in 1927.

These activities, whose powers of suggestion Depero enhanced through the magic of his imagination, were to occupy him during his stay in America between 1928 and 1930, which was preceded by a brief visit to France. He became increasingly involved in graphic art and advertising, fields in which he had worked from *c.* 1910: in addition to designing covers for magazines such as *Emporium* and *Vogue*, he was also in charge of publicity for the Campari company. His work as a designer culminated in a theoretical text, 'Manifesto dell' arte pubblicitaria futurista' (1932). At the same time he threw himself into the creation of typographic designs in the *parole in libertà* form devised by Marinetti; a collection of these was published as a 'bolted' book, *Depero futurista* (1927).

In 1929 Depero signed the *Manifesto dell'Aeropittura*, together with Balla, Benedetta (Marinetti's wife, the painter and writer Benedetta Cappa, 1897–1977), Gerardo Dottori, Fillia, Marinetti, Enrico Prampolini, the painter and sculptor Mino Somenzi (1899–1948) and the painter Tato (pseud. of Guglielmo Sansoni, 1896–1974). Through his association with AEROPITTURA his painting began to crystallize into a colourism with repetitive subject-matter, losing its joyfulness and inventive freshness. In Rovereto in 1933 he founded the magazine *Dinamo futurista*, which he edited himself, and during the 1930s he became active as an art critic. In 1941 he created a mosaic for the exterior of the Museo Nazionale delle Arti e delle Tradizioni Popolari in Rome, part of the ambitious but unrealized plans for an Esposizione Universale di Roma in 1942. After a short stay in New York in 1948–9 he returned to Italy, settling permanently in Rovereto, where he pursued his decorative commissions and exhibition activities. In 1957, three years before his death, the municipality of Rovereto decided to establish the Galleria Museo Depero

as a repository for his works; this opened to the public in 1959.

WRITINGS

Spezzature–Impressioni: Segni e ritmi (Rovereto, 1913)
Depero futurista (Milan, 1927)
'Manifesto dell'arte pubblicitaria futurista', *Futurismo*, i/2 (1932)
So I Think so I Paint (Trento, 1947)
Revues de Depero (Paris, 1979) [facs. of *Numero unico futurista Campari* (1931), *Futurismo* (1932) and *Dinamo futurista* (1933), with intro. by G. Lista]

BIBLIOGRAPHY

B. Passamani, ed.: *Depero e la scena da 'Colori' alla scena mobile, 1916–1930* (Turin, 1970)
B. Passamani: *Fortunato Depero* (Trento, 1981)
Fortunato Depero (exh. cat., ed. B. Passamani; Rovereto, Gal. Mus. Depero, 1981)
E. Crispolti: 'Depero, Fortunato', *Futurismo & Futurismi* (exh. cat., ed. P. Hultén; Venice, Pal. Grassi, 1986), pp. 465–7
Depero futurista+New York (exh. cat., ed. M. Scudiero and D. Lieber; Rovereto, Gal. Mus. Depero, 1986)
Depero motorumorista futurista mimismagico astrattista formidabile architetto e poeta (Milan, 1986)
M. Scudiero: *Fortunato Depero: Opere* (Trento, 1987)

For further writings and bibliography *see* AEROPITTURA and FUTURISM, §1.

ESTER COEN

Deperthes, Jean-Baptiste (*b* Reims, 25 Oct 1761; *d* Paris, 25 Oct 1833). French writer and painter. He trained with the landscape painter Pierre-Henri de Valenciennes and between 1793 and 1800 exhibited at the Salon such works as *Moonlight on the Seashore* (1793) and *Landscape with Houses* (1795). Personal circumstances forced him to abandon painting for government service, but he retained a wide range of cultural interests. His *Théorie du paysage* and *Histoire de l'art du paysage* are among a number of early 19th-century treatises that reflected and influenced a change towards a more naturalistic depiction of landscape. The *Théorie* follows Valenciennes's seminal *Eléments de perspective pratique* (Paris, 1799–1800) in insisting on the necessity of studying from nature, although it pays lip-service to the traditional academic hierarchy of genres by preserving the primacy of historical landscape, where the figures, often heroes of Classical antiquity, are more important than the landscape background. Boime suggests that knowledge of a manuscript of Deperthes's work influenced the Académie des Beaux-Arts towards instituting a Prix de Rome for historical landscape in 1816. Deperthes's second book is remarkable for dignifying landscape painting by charting its history, and it further reinforces the need to follow nature by praising the output of the 17th-century Dutch school. The emotional description of natural phenomena and works of art indicates an attitude close to that of the ostensibly naturalistic but romantically inclined artists who emerged in the 1830s (e.g. Théodore Rousseau).

WRITINGS

Théorie du paysage (Paris, 1818)
Histoire de l'art du paysage (Paris, 1822)

BIBLIOGRAPHY

Biographie universelle ancienne et moderne, x (Paris, 1852), pp. 442–3
A. Boime: *The Academy and French Painting in the Nineteenth Century* (London, 1971/R New Haven, 1986), pp. 139–41, 143–4, 151, 163, 168
C. R. Wenzel: *The Transformation of French Landscape Painting from Valenciennes to Corot* (diss., Philadelphia, U. PA, 1979; microfilm, Ann Arbor, 1981), pp. 110–16

E. D. LILLEY

De Pisis, (Luigi) Filippo (Tibertelli) (*b* Ferrara, 8 May 1896; *d* Milan, 2 April 1956). Italian painter, poet and writer. He was born into the nobility, and he particularly identified with a 12th-century ancestor, Filippo, a condottiere. De Pisis shared his romantic view of his ancestry with his sister, Ernesta Tibertelli (1895–?1973), who was a distinguished illustrator with libertarian views, and who probably introduced De Pisis to mystical writings and possibly collaborated with him on poems and paintings. De Pisis spent his childhood studying literature, drawing, collecting butterflies and wild flowers and preparing herbaria (now U. Padua). He enrolled at the University of Bologna, where he studied literature and philosophy, in 1914. The following year he met the poet Corrado Govoni and the literary scholars Salvator Gotta and Giuseppe De Robertis. De Pisis maintained an interest in Futurism through the periodicals *Lacerba* and *La voce*.

In 1916 in Ferrara, De Pisis met Giorgio De Chirico and his brother Alberto Savinio, as well as Carlo Carrà. Through the De Chiricos, De Pisis came into contact with the French avant-garde; he began corresponding with Guillaume Apollinaire and Tristan Tzara. His literary works of the period reflect philosophic and esoteric interests. In his first artistic project, the 'museum' in his studio he filled with his botanical and antiquarian objects, he experimented with collage, a contribution to Pittura Metafisica that anticipates later heterogeneous compositions. Between 1920 and 1924 De Pisis was in Rome, where he worked as a schoolteacher, frequented the *Valori plastici* circle and wrote in support of Pittura Metafisica. He began to paint seriously, developing a form of still-life that combined loose handling with curious juxtapositions. He held his first one-man shows in the Galleria Bragaglia (1920) and the foyer of the Teatro Nazionale (1924). In March 1925 De Pisis left Rome to live in Paris. There, technically influenced by the Impressionism of Sisley and Pissarro, he turned to cityscapes. His control of colour shows the influence of Matisse, whom he met; in his more private work he began to explore his own sexuality through the ideal figure of the hermaphrodite. In 1926 he held a one-man show at the Galerie au Sacre du Printemps, for which De Chirico wrote a presentation. In the same year he exhibited in Milan, with a presentation by Carrà.

De Pisis was soon established as one of the most interesting figures of the loose association, the Italiani di Parigi. His relationship with Italy, which had been somewhat distanced, returned to normal after 1931, when he exhibited in Rome at the Quadriennale and the Galleria di Roma. In 1936 he submitted 15 paintings to the Quadriennale. During this period De Pisis established himself as an artistic figure of European standing; his fresh and sensual painting style enlivened a subject-matter full of esoteric and intellectual references. A distinct style is shared by his male nudes, cityscapes and extraordinary still-lifes, in their liberal juxtaposition of disparate objects and the free ordering of space, the whole suspended in delicate patterns of light and patches of colour (e.g. the *Piazza Cavalli in Piacenza*, 1937; Rome, Vatican, Col. A. Relig. Mod.). The favourite and unsettling device of merging the surface supporting the objects with the seascape beyond survived the transition from the early broken brushwork to the broader washes of later works (e.g. *Large Still-life*, 1944; Milan, Padiglione A. Contemp.). Only after 1935, just as the structural fabric of his compositions seemed on the point of disintegration, did De Pisis begin to adopt a perspective system in the construction of his paintings.

In the years that followed De Pisis was intensively active in the literary and artistic fields, and he travelled and exhibited widely in Europe. At the outbreak of World War II he returned to Italy, finally settling in Venice in 1944. His niece, the painter Bona De Pisis, joined him as a companion. He continued to explore cityscapes, but his overriding concern remained his still-lifes, which seem symbolic of his declining health in their focus on ephemeral details, while echoing the botanical enthusiasms of his youth. In 1948 he was admitted to a neurological clinic in Bologna; his long illness drastically reduced his output. From 1949 until his death he spent almost all his time in the Brugherio clinic near Milan, where he painted his last works, dramatic and often profound pieces.

WRITINGS
La città dalle 100 meraviglie (Rome, 1920); rev. as *La città dalle 100 meraviglie ed altri scritti*, ed. B. De Pisis (Florence, 1965)
Prose e articoli (Milan, 1947)
B. De Pisis and S. Zanotto, eds: *Il marchesino pittore* (Milan, 1970)

BIBLIOGRAPHY
W. George: *Filippo de Pisis* (Paris, 1928)
G. Raimondi: *Filippo De Pisis* (Florence, 1952)
P. Tibertelli De Pisis and D. Bonuglia: *De Pisis, mio fratello; Ricordi romani* (Milan, 1957)
G. Ballo: *Filippo De Pisis* (Turin, 1968)
L'opera pittorica e grafica di Filippo de Pisis (exh. cat., eds L. Magagnato, M. Malabotta and S. Zanotto; Verona, Gran Guardia, 1969)
Filippo De Pisis (exh. cat., eds G. Marchiori and S. Zanotto; Ferrara, Pin. N., 1973)
100 opere di Filippo De Pisis (exh. cat., eds G. Marchiori and S. Zanotto; Prato, Gal. A. Mod. Farsetti, 1973)

MATTHEW GALE, VALERIO RIVOSECCHI

Dequevauviller. French family of engravers. (Nicolas-Barthélemy-)François Dequevauviller (*b* Abbeville, 1745; *d* ?Paris, *c.* 1807) trained under Jean Daullé and is considered to have been one of his best pupils. He was a particularly good interpreter—second only to Nicolas de Launay—of Niclas Lafrensen, or Nicolas Lavreince (1737–1807). Two of his finest works are engravings after this artist: *Gathering in a Salon* (1783–4; *see* HÔTEL PARTICULIER, fig. 2) and *Gathering at a Concert* (Paris, Bib. N. cat. no. 63), both of which represent extremely detailed interiors. His other genre scenes after Lafrensen, *Awakening of the Dressmakers*, *Retiring of the Dressmakers*, the *Dancing School* and *Le Contretemps* (Paris, Bib. N. cat. nos 64, 66, 65 and 67 repectively), all date to 1784–6. Dequevauviller was also an engraver of illustrations for some of the best-known publications of the time, including the *Tableaux. . .de la Suisse* (1780–86; Paris, Bib. N. cat. nos 15–34) of Jean-Benjamin de La Borde, the *Voyage. . .de Naples et de Sicile* (1781–86; Paris, Bib. N. cat. nos 36–50) of Saint-Non and the *Voyage pittoresque de la Grèce* (1782; Paris, Bib. N. cat. nos 51–5) of the Comte de Choiseul-Gouffier. He also contributed to a number of albums of collections of Old Master paintings, such as Jacques Couché's *Galerie du Palais Royal* (1786–1808; Paris, Bib. N. cat. nos 69–79) and Jean-Baptiste Wicar's *La Galerie de Florence* (1789–1807; Paris, Bib. N. cat. nos 87–92).

Dequevauviller married a member of an illustrious family of engravers, Marguerite-Angélique-Scolastique DE POILLY, and their son François Jacques Dequevauviller (*b* Paris, 1783; *d* Paris, *c.* 1848) also became an engraver. François studied first with his father and then with Auguste-Gaspard-Louis Boucher-Desnoyers (1779–1857). His engraved portraits include that of *Charles Ferdinand d'Artois, Duc de Berry*, after Bourdon (*c.* 1820; Paris, Bib. N. cat. no. 12), and he provided numerous plates for, among other works, the *Voyage pittoresque et historique de l'Espagne* (1806–20; Paris, Bib. N. cat. nos 1–4). He engraved for several albums of museum collections, including S.-C. Croze-Magnan's *Musée français* (1803–9; Paris, Bib. N. cat. no. 14), to which his father had also contributed.

BIBLIOGRAPHY

E. Dacier: *La Gravure en France au XVIIIe siècle: La Gravure de genre et de moeurs* (Paris, 1925), p. 105

Inventaire du fonds français: Graveurs du dix-huitième siècle, Paris, Bib. N., Cab. Est. cat., vii (Paris, 1951), pp. 34–60; vi (Paris, 1953), pp. 261–6

M.-E. HELLYER

Derain, André (*b* Chatou, nr Paris, 17 June 1880; *d* Garches, 8 Sept 1954). French painter, sculptor, illustrator, stage designer and collector. He was a leading exponent of FAUVISM. In early 1908 he destroyed most of his work to concentrate on tightly constructed landscape paintings, which were a subtle investigation of the work of Cézanne. After World War I his work became more classical, influenced by the work of such artists as Camille Corot. In his sculpture he drew upon his knowledge and collection of non-Western art.

1. EARLY PERIOD, FAUVIST WORKS AND HISTORICISM. Derain abandoned his engineering studies in 1898 to become a painter and attended the Académie Carrière. He also sketched in the Musée du Louvre and painted on the banks of the Seine. On a visit to the Louvre in 1899 he met the painter Georges Florentin Linaret (1878–1905), who had been his companion at school, and who was copying Uccello in an extraordinary manner; he was studying under Gustave Moreau and later introduced Derain to a fellow pupil, Henri Matisse. Derain's painting was already influenced by the work of Cézanne, and in 1901, like many painters of his generation, he was deeply moved by the exhibition of van Gogh's work at Bernheim-Jeune, Paris. At the exhibition Derain introduced Matisse to Maurice de Vlaminck, with whom he had shared a studio in Chatou in 1900–01. During the following three years' military service, Derain painted only on his periods of leave. He read widely, notably Friedrich Nietzsche and other modern German philosophers. His letters to Vlaminck in this period reflect his serious intentions as a painter and the beginning of the rich philosophical speculation that was to delight his friends in Montmartre and Montparnasse, and in the early 1920s to inform his treatise on painting.

On leaving the army in September 1904, Derain grew closer to Matisse and Matisse's interest in Gauguin and Cézanne. The Gauguin exhibition at the Salon d'Automne in 1906 was largely due to the enthusiasm of Matisse and to Gauguin's friend Georges-Daniel de Monfried. The subsequent influence of Gauguin is most striking in

1. André Derain: *Crouching Man*, sandstone, h. 330 mm, 1907 (Vienna, Museum des 20. Jahrhunderts)

Derain's wood-carvings, his decorated furniture, the painting *Dance* (1906; Lausanne, priv. col.), and the wood block prints made for Guillaume Apollinaire's *L'Enchanteur pourrissant* (1909). In 1905 Derain sold the contents of his studio to Ambroise Vollard and painted in London and in the south of France with Matisse. *Big Ben* (1905; Troyes, Mus. A. Mod.) and *Collioure, Le Faubourg* (1905; Paris, Pompidou) show the loosely divisionist structure of bold blocks of colour that Derain shared with Matisse. Matisse encouraged Derain to enter the Salons. He exhibited in the 1905 Salon des Indépendants and in September Derain exhibited at the Salon d'Automne, at which the critic Louis Vauxcelles described him, Vlaminck, Matisse and others as the *fauves* (wild beasts), a label that quickly gained currency. The Fauvists were involved with late Symbolist poetics. By 1906 Derain had formed close friendships with Max Jacob, André Salmon and Guillaume Apollinaire, and with Georges Braque they frequented the artistic and poetic society of Montmartre.

In 1907 Derain moved from Chatou to the Rue Tourlaque, and he and Braque became close friends of Picasso. They all shared an interest in Cézanne, a passion for exotic arts, particularly African sculpture, and an interest in the mystic and esoteric studies of their friends. Derain's *Bathers* (1907; New York, MOMA), painted around the same time as Picasso's *Demoiselles d'Avignon* (New York, MOMA), is one of his rare surviving works of this period. He continued to sculpt, but direct carving into stone replaced his earlier Gauguin-influenced wood-carving (e.g. *Crouching Man*, sandstone, 1907; Vienna, Mus. 20. Jhts; see fig. 1). The totemic quality of the earlier work survives, however, in the stone sculpture, the inspiration for which was drawn particularly from his sketching trips to the Musée du Louvre, and from the Indian erotic sculpture admired by the Montmartre circle. Derain continued to exhibit at Berthe Weill, and until 1909 at the Salons. In 1907 he had begun to sell to Daniel-Henry Kahnweiler, who was also acquiring the work of Braque and Picasso. By 1910 Kahnweiler was buying Derain's entire production, and in December 1912 signed him to an exclusive contract. Kahnweiler sold Derain's work abroad, particularly to Germany and Russia, and in 1913 sent three of his paintings to the Armory Show in the USA. From 1908 to 1910 Derain, Picasso and Braque were inseparable companions. The *Old Bridge at Cagnes* (1910; Washington, DC, N.G.A.), however, demonstrates their increasingly divergent interests. In this work Derain sought to apply the legacy of Cézanne to a conception of painting based on the work of Poussin and of 16th-century Venetian painters. It was this direct historicism in painting that set Derain apart from the Cubists, with whom he nevertheless maintained friendly contact. In 1911 he concentrated on still-life painting. In place of the fine scaffolding of Cubism, however, his still-lifes increasingly adopted the tenebrism of 17th-century painting. Its *vanitas* symbolism of chance and fatality was similar to that, based on such motifs as playing cards and written words, in the work of his Cubist friends.

In 1911 and 1912 Derain spent very little time in Paris, instead extending his usual summer painting session from April to December. The *Bagpiper* (1910–11; Minneapolis, MN, Inst. A.) with its echoes of primitive and early Renaissance painting is closer in spirit to the contemporary poets of the Ecole Romane than to the work of Picasso

2. André Derain: *Harlequin and Pierrot*, oil on canvas, 1.75×1.75 m, *c*. 1924 (Paris, Musée de l'Orangerie)

and Braque. At Vers in 1912 Derain painted several still-lifes with a calvary cross, an overtly religious symbolism that may reflect the eucharistic poetry of Paul Claudel. In 1913 he returned to painting figurative subjects. The Italian sisters who modelled for him are painted with a restraint and poignancy that reveals a tragic anxiety or a pathetic resignation. His *Saturday* (1914; Moscow, Pushkin Mus. F.A.) summarized many of Derain's preoccupations of the preceding years. This large-scale composition of figures and still-lifes in an interior takes as its theme the profound and complex liturgy of Holy Saturday, signifying universal death and resurrection. By World War I Derain had confirmed both his metaphysical interests and his devotion to the traditional virtues of figurative painting and its powerful language of gesture, tenebrism and compositional metaphor. He added to this his own self-conscious historicism, which allowed him to call upon a complex of ideas by situating his work in the style of another period. Apollinaire recognized this in his introduction to the catalogue of Derain's exhibition of 1916 at the Galerie Paul Guillaume. The catalogue includes poems by Pierre Reverdy, Blaise Cendrars, Max Jacob and Fernand Divoire.

2. Work after World War I. Upon demobilization, following four years at the Front, Derain found himself celebrated among the dealers in Paris and seriously promoted by the writings of such friends as André Salmon. The portrait of *Mme Carco* (*c.* 1920; Basle, Kstmus.), with its reference to the mummy portraiture found at such sites as Faiyum, indicates the persistence of Derain's pre-war ideas, as do such still-lifes as *Kitchen Table* (1923–4; Paris, Mus. Orangerie). In this period the work of Corot also became influential on his landscape painting, as seen in *Landscape of the Midi* (Paris, Mus. Orangerie) and other works painted at Eygalières.

Derain had lived in the Rue Bonaparte in the Latin Quarter from 1912, and he now became an influence upon dozens of young Montparnasse painters and the object of admiration of a new generation of poet critics, including André Breton. During the 1920s Derain attempted to write a treatise on painting, *De picturae rerum*, which, although unpublished, survives in manuscript. Characteristic of the ideas that attracted young poets and painters to Derain, it is essentially a mystical exposition on painting that assumes a world equally spiritual and material, which proposes that the function of painting is to integrate the two to offer to human understanding a reality that otherwise escapes the senses; light and line are essential to this task, and colour auxiliary or incidental. The large-scale *Harlequin and Pierrot* (*c.* 1924; Paris, Mus. Orangerie; see fig. 2) surpasses the pre-war work in the poignancy of its expression. The heavy liturgical dance of the apparently silent musicians, strumming stringless instruments alone in a barren landscape, extends the profound sadness on their faces to the whole composition. These pathetic *commedia dell'arte* figures incline their heads and direct their gaze in the manner of accompanying saints in a Renaissance Lamentation. The simple and controlled range of colour, the arid and merciless light, and the powerful and lucid line exact a clear reading from the spectator and a growing awareness of the fatal significance of the dance.

In 1928 Derain moved to another new studio, which he had built in the Rue Douanier (now Rue Braque). Braque's studio was in the same building, and they were in close contact during the late 1920s and 1930s. Derain had arrived at an understanding with the dealer Paul Guillaume in 1923, who, until his death in 1934, assured the artist's comfort and tranquillity. With Guillaume, Derain was in greater contact with Parisian society, and he took a great interest in the performing arts. He had many musician friends and he was close to the composer Georges Auric. Derain's first ballet design was for *Boutique fantasque* (1919) for Serge Diaghilev, and he continued to design for the ballet thereafter. Guillaume sold his work widely, notably in the USA, enabling Derain to add to his personal collection of exotic and African treasures, many excellent Greek, Roman and Renaissance sculptures, East Asian art, paintings (including works by Corot), rare books and curios of all kinds.

In the 1930s Derain painted several large-scale nudes and still-lifes, for example *The Glade* (1.38×2.5 m, 1938; Geneva, Petit Pal.), based on numerous studies in the form of paintings, drawings, lithographs and etchings. A sombre religious sensibility continued to mark his many still-lifes, for example *Still-life with Hare* (1938; Paris, Pompidou). Classical mythology occupied Derain a great deal throughout the 1930s and 1940s: his notes show a long consideration of Bacchus as a part of the Osiris–Christ myth of the sacrificed and resurrected god. The *Golden Age* (Paris, Pompidou), a large canvas later used as a design for a tapestry, depicts the defence of the young Bacchus by wild beasts. Narrative is avoided in order to create a universal image as powerful as that in *Saturday* and *Harlequin and Pierrot*. In 1935 Derain bought a country home at Chambourcy, and on the eve of World War II he began his last monumental works, among them the *Return of Ulysses* (Paris, Pompidou), a Last Supper composition, subtly developed into an image of the Homeric banquet. Also shortly before the war, Derain began to create small clay sculptures using earth from his garden at Chambourcy or from his landscape sites. These many coloured clay sculptures, both masks and figures (e.g. Paris, Mus. A. Mod. Ville Paris), were not discovered until after his death, when Pierre Cailler commissioned their bronze-casting. The masterpiece of his wartime period was not a painting but a series of nearly 400 colour woodcuts with which Derain illustrated Skira's 1943 edition of Rabelais's *Pantagruel*. Although Derain had illustrated many books throughout his career, including works by Jacob, Apollinaire, Antonin Artaud, Breton and Vincent Muselli, as well as Petronius and Ovid, this was the largest and most elaborate. Derain had made masks from shells and shrapnel during World War I, and just before his death he began again to build sculptures in sheets of metal; several unfinished works of this type are still in his former studio at Chambourcy.

UNPUBLISHED SOURCES
Paris, Bib. Doucet [MS., *De picturae rerum*]

WRITINGS
Lettres à Vlaminck (Paris, 1955)

BIBLIOGRAPHY
Derain, peintre-graveur (exh. cat. by J. Adhémar, Paris, Bib. N., 1955)
D. Sutton: *Derain* (London, 1959)
Collection Jean Walther–Paul Guillaume, Musée de l'Orangerie (Paris, 1966)
Derain (exh. cat., ed. J. Leymarie; ACGB, 1967)
M. Kalitina: *A. Derain* (Leningrad, 1976) [cat. of the major works by Derain in Russian mus.]
Derain (exh. cat., ed. J. Leymarie; Paris, Grand Pal., 1977)
G. Salomon: 'Les Notes d'André Derain', *Cah. Mus. N. A. Mod.*, v (1980), pp. 343–62
Derain (exh. cat., ed. J. de Mons; Tokyo, Takashimaya Gal., 1981)
P. Chabert: *La Collection Pierre et Denise Levy, Musée d'art moderne, Troyes*, 2 vols (Troyes, 1982)
André Derain in North American Collections (exh. cat., ed. M. Parke-Taylor; U. Regina, Mackenzie A.G.; Berkeley, U. CA, A. Mus.; 1983)
J. Lee: *Derain* (Oxford, 1990) [pubd on occasion of exh. at MOMA, Oxford]
Derain (exh. cat., Paris, Mus. A. Mod. Ville Paris, 1994)

JANE LEE

Derand, Père François (*b* Vic-sur-Seille, Moselle, 1588 or 1591; *d* Agde, Hérault, 29 Oct 1644). French Jesuit priest and architect. Entering the novitiate of the Society of Jesus in 1611, he studied in Rouen and La Flèche, was ordained a priest in 1621 and studied theology in Paris (1621–2). He had also taught grammar at Rennes (1615–18) and mathematics at La Flèche (1618–21). He worked first as an architect at the Jesuit college in Rouen, where from 1622 to 1629 he was *praefectus fabricae*; then as *architectus* at the college in Rennes, where he supervised the building works; at the college of Orléans, for which he provided plans in 1632; and, above all, at the Jesuit church in Paris, St Louis (now St Paul–St Louis). In plans for the latter he found himself in competition with Etienne Martellange. Both sets of plans were submitted to Rome; those by Martellange were preferred, and he began work on the church in 1627. Two years later, however, the Father Provincial brought in Derand, who found the building erected to a height of two metres. He finished it in 1641, including the vaults and the great façade on the Rue Saint-Antoine, the first stone of which was laid in 1634.

Derand's style is very different from the architectural propriety sought by Martellange: it is Baroque in its expressiveness, its use of strong chiaroscuro and its abundance of sculptural decoration. The façade of St Paul–St Louis, visibly inspired by that of St Gervais by Salomon de Brosse (1616), is a great stone screen, scarcely pierced by openings, in which attention is focused on its articulation of columns and niches. Derand was a theoretician of stereotomy and in 1643 published a treatise on it, which was much used. An album of drawings of designs for doors, windows and chimneypieces (Paris, Louvre), called the 'Album Derand' on the strength of an inscription *Der* or *Dev*, has been attributed to him, though probably erroneously.

WRITINGS
L'Architecture des voûtes; Ou l'art des traits et coupes des voûtes (Paris, 1643)

BIBLIOGRAPHY
M. P. Morey: *Notice sur la vie et les oeuvres du R. P. François Derand, architecte lorrain* (Nancy, 1868)
L. Hautecoeur: *Histoire de l'architecture classique en France*, i (Paris, 1943, rev. 1966), p. 252
P. Moisy: *Les Eglises des Jésuites de l'ancienne Assistance de France* (Rome, 1958)
J. Vallery-Radot: *Le Recueil des plans d'edifices de la Compagnie de Jésus conservé a la Bibliothèque Nationale de Paris* (Rome, 1960)

JEAN-PIERRE BABELON

Derbais, Jérôme (*b* Paris, ?*c.* 1645; *d* Paris, 5 Oct 1712). French marble mason and sculptor. He was the most prominent marble mason of the reign of Louis XIV and, together with lesser suppliers such as Misson, Legrue, Lisqui, Dezaigre and Tarlé, provided much of the splendid marble panelling, flooring, fountain basins etc for the châteaux of Versailles and the Trianon and for Marly, Yvelines, as well as for Paris churches such as the Invalides, Notre-Dame and St Germain-des-Prés. He also supplied blocks of marble to sculptors, including those for Antoine Coyzevox's famous equestrian groups *Mercury* and *Fame* (Paris, Louvre). In addition, his workshops were able to supply portrait busts such as those of *Henri de La Tour d'Auvergne, Maréchal de Turenne* and *Louis II de Condé* (*Le Grand Condé*) (both marble; Chantilly, Mus. Condé), which were sold to Henri-Jules de Bourbon, Prince de Condé, and the bronze cast of Gianlorenzo Bernini's *Louis XIV*, which was supplied to the city of Quebec in 1686. Derbais became a member of the Académie de St Luc in 1676, and his business activities made him a wealthy man.

Lami

BIBLIOGRAPHY

J. Guiffrey: *Comptes des Bâtiments du Roi sous le règne de Louis XIV*, 5 vols (Paris, 1881–1901)

FRANÇOISE DE LA MOUREYRE

Derby. English centre of ceramic production. A factory producing soft-paste porcelain was in operation in Derby, Derbys, by *c.* 1750, possibly started by Thomas Briand of the Chelsea porcelain factory. Early output included white cream jugs and some figures that have biscuit visible at the base and are therefore known as dry-edge figures. The main Derby factory was established *c.* 1756 by William Duesbury, who joined with John Heath, a banker who also had an interest in the Cockpit Hill Pottery (1751–79), Derby, and the Frenchman André Planché. Early wares included tea and coffee services. About 1764 Richard Holdship of the Worcester factory had an agreement with Duesbury to improve the paste and to introduce transfer printing to the factory. Blue-and-white wares were also produced until 1770 but thereafter only for special commissions. Figures produced during the early years show the influences of the Chelsea and Meissen porcelain factories, and specifically the modelling of Johann Joachim Kändler. This was later intensified by the modeller Nicolas-François Gauron (*fl* 1753–88), who had previously worked at Mennecy, Vincennes and Tournai before moving to Derby in 1773.

In 1769, with financial assistance from John Heath, Duesbury bought the Chelsea factory and in 1775 acquired the Bow factory. The years 1769–84 are known as the Chelsea–Derby period; the Sèvres porcelain factory provided the main source of inspiration for the wares, and the production of biscuit figures also began. The best painters of the period were specialists, for example Zachariah Boreman (1736–1810) for landscapes, William Pegg (1775–1851) for flowers, Richard Dodson for exotic birds and William Billingsley for cabbage roses. In 1784 Duesbury closed the Chelsea factory and moved the men and equipment to Derby.

In 1786 Duesbury was succeeded by his son William Duesbury II (*d* 1797); he took Michael Kean as his partner from 1795 to 1797, when Kean took over until 1811.

Many of the original wares continued to be made, as well as Neo-classical wares and figures. One of the best modellers during the 1790s was Johann Jakob Wilhelm Spengler, who had previously worked in Zurich. In 1811 William Duesbury III took over, but in 1815 he leased the factory to Robert Bloor, and there was a deterioration in the quality of the wares. Bloor's brother Joseph Bloor managed the factory until it closed in 1848.

During the 19th century several porcelain factories were set up in Derby, often making imitations of 18th-century products. The most significant was the Derby Crown Porcelain Co., which was founded in 1876 to make high-quality porcelain. The name was changed to the Royal Crown Derby Porcelain Co. following a visit by Queen Victoria in 1890. The factory continued to produce tablewares decorated with rich gilding and Japanese patterns in the late 20th century.

BIBLIOGRAPHY

F. B. Gillhespy: *Derby Porcelain* (London, 1961)

A. L. Thorpe and F. A. Barrett: *Derby Porcelain, 1750–1848* (London, 1971)

J. Twitchett: *Derby Porcelain* (London, 1980)

G. Bradley and others: *Derby Porcelain, 1750–1798* (London, 1990)

K. SOMERVELL

Dereağzı. Settlement in a remote mountain area of southwest Turkey, situated *c.* 20 km north-west of Demre (anc. Myra). Pottery and coins suggest that the site may have been inhabited continually from as early as the late 9th century BC. The earliest monumental remains include a large hilltop fort of the Lycian period (7th–4th centuries BC), which guarded access to the site and the Kasaba Valley. The fort, which is similar to others in the region, is arranged in three consecutive circuits around the summit of the hill and built mostly of large coursed, well-cut polygonal stones; it may have been the stronghold of a landed nobleman. The remains, partly *in situ*, of a stone relief representing a sacrifice, suggest that it was built in the first half of the 4th century BC. Inside the fort and around the hill are 11 rock-cut tombs of a non-Hellenized type often found in Lycia (*see* LYCIA, §2), including one with an inscription, and two rock-cut sarcophagi; all probably date to the late 5th century BC or the first half of the 4th.

Coins and pottery indicate that from the 2nd century BC there was a substantial settlement at the site, which was connected by a paved Roman road with the interior and with Myra. Many fragments of early Byzantine architectural sculpture also point to a Christian presence by the 5th or 6th century AD. Between the first half of the 9th century and the early 10th the fort was extended to a length of nearly 190 m and reinforced with bastions, an abutment and a long spur wall terminated by a tower. The combination of reinforcements, all of which were built of mortared-rubble masonry faced with stone, is comparable to those of the forts at Ancyra (now Ankara, Turkey; *see* EARLY CHRISTIAN AND BYZANTINE ART, §II, 3(i)(a)) and the monastery of St John at PATMOS.

At about the same time an important church complex was constructed 2 km to the north-east on the valley floor. The large, ruined church, which is a cross-domed basilica (*c.* 21×38 m; see fig.) with inscribed aisles and galleries, recalls Ayia Irini in Constantinople (as remodelled after 740; *see* ISTANBUL, §III, 5). The five-apsed east end, which includes quatrefoil pastophories and two domed octagons of uncertain function and the gallery chapels, are similar to those of the church of Constantine Lips (907; now Fenarı Isa Camii, Istanbul). The buttressed exterior, faced with alternating bands of coursed brick and stone, and the recessed doors and windows are comparable with those of the Lips church and the church of the Myrelaion (*c.* 920; now Bodrum Camii, Istanbul).

Fragments of mosaics and painting are all that remain of the once rich interior wall decoration. Among the mosaics that can be identified are part of a narrative cycle on the nave vaults, standing bishops in the north octagon and a *Vision of Christ in Majesty* in the diakonikon. The latter can be compared iconographically with similar representations from Lmbat (Armenia) and Dodo and stylistically with work in Ayia Sophia in Constantinople, as can the bishops in the north octagon. The complex was also decorated with architectural sculpture comparable with some from the church of the Panagia at SKRIPOU (873–4) and St Gregory (872) at Thebes in Greece, the Lips church and Agrai (now Atabey, Turkey). It is not clear whether the church functioned as a cathedral, perhaps related to a reorganization of the eparchy of Lycia in the late 9th century or early 10th, or as a monastic or pilgrimage church. Its close relationship to Byzantine monuments in Constantinople and the appearance of imported materials from the same region may suggest direct patronage from the capital.

BIBLIOGRAPHY
H. Rott: *Kleinasiatische Denkmäler aus Pisidien, Pamphylien, Kappadokien und Lykien* (Leipzig, 1908), pp. 299–314
J. Morganstern: *The Byzantine Church at Dereağzı and its Decoration* (Tübingen, 1983)
J. Morganstern and others: *The Fort at Dereağzı and Other Material Remains in its Vicinity: From Antiquity to the Middle Ages* (Tübingen, 1993)

JAMES MORGANSTERN

Dereham, Elias of. *See* ELIAS OF DEREHAM.

De Rivera, José (*b* West Baton Rouge, LA, 18 Sept 1904; *d* New York, 19 March 1985). American sculptor. He grew up on a sugar plantation and refinery in Louisiana, where his father was an engineer. The experience he gained as a blacksmith and in the maintenance of machinery proved useful when he later began constructing sculpture in metal. In 1924 he settled in Chicago, IL, and attended night classes at the Studio School of Art. John Norton (1877–1934), his instructor in life classes, recognized the sculptural quality in De Rivera's drawings and encouraged him to experiment with three-dimensional work. In 1930 De Rivera produced his first sculptures. These figurative pieces, including the female *Bust* (1930; artist's estate, see 1972 exh. cat., p. 1), carved from a single brass rod, are related to the streamlined, elegant designs of Art Deco. His works of the early 1930s are also indebted to the Cubist-inspired polished torsos of Alexander Archipenko, whose work was exhibited in Chicago during the 1920s, and to Brancusi's *Golden Bird* (1919), which was in the collection of the Arts Club of Chicago by 1927.

In 1931 De Rivera visited Spain, North Africa, Greece, Italy and France. On returning to the USA in 1932, he

Dereağzı, cross-domed basilica church, 9th–10th century

moved to New York where he met other young American artists who were exploring avant-garde concepts. During the 1930s he experimented with various sculptural methods and made some stone carvings, including some biomorphic sculptures that resembled the 'concretions' of Jean Arp (e.g. *Life*, 1939; see 1961 exh. cat., p. 24). From 1937 to 1938 he was employed by the sculpture division of the Works Progress Administration's Federal Art Project and produced *Flight* (1938; Newark, NJ, Mus.), one of his finest early works, for Newark airport, NJ. It is an abstract form of a bird in flight carved from solid aluminium rods and mounted on a high base to encourage the suggestion of dynamic forms soaring upwards in space. Its sleek metal surfaces, fusing modern technology with stylized natural forms, allude to aircraft and reveal his admiration for Brancusi's polished bronze *Bird in Space* (1924; Philadelphia, PA, Mus. A.). Most of De Rivera's sculpture during and after the 1930s could be described as Constructivist. In openwork constructions made of hammered sheet metal and wire he explored a sculpture of spaces rather than of static masses. He was led in this direction by the concepts of space and time developed by the Russian-born German mathematician Herman Minkowski (1864–1909), which involved an interchange between static and dynamic elements. *Black and Red (Double Element)* (1938; New York, Guggenheim) characterizes De Rivera's analysis of space, form, and material. Pieces cut from flat sheets of aluminium and hammered into curved shapes were smoothly finished and painted in primary colours. Placed on a flat wooden base the two elements were positioned so that the curves partially enclosed spatial volumes.

After military service in the 1940s, De Rivera developed his signature works: linear, tubular constructions that curve through and define space, such as *Construction #1: Homage to the World of Minkowski*, made of chrome, nickel and stainless steel (1955; New York, Met.). The active interrelationship of interior and exterior space is visible when the construction is in motion, each revolution creating a multitude of forms by the play of light on the surface. In later years he continued to make constructions that were variations on his 'linear' forms, such as the stainless steel *Construction* (1958; Chicago, IL, A. Inst.) originally made for the Brussels Exposition Universelle et Internationale of 1958. At times he attached a motor to the constructions so that the metal contours slowly rotated. Some examples were made of copper, others had the polished surfaces of industrial metals; all were fashioned by hand.

BIBLIOGRAPHY

José de Rivera (exh. cat. by J. Gordon, New York, Amer. Fed. A., 1961)

José de Rivera: Retrospective Exhibition, 1930–1971 (exh. cat., ed. T. Tibbs; La Jolla, CA, Mus. Contemp. A., 1972) [incl. cat. rais.]

J. Marter: *José de Rivera Constructions* (Madrid, 1980)

JOAN MARTER

Derizet, Antoine (*b* Lyon, 18 Nov 1685; *d* Rome, 6 Oct 1768). French architect and teacher, active in Italy. He won first prize at the Académie Royale d'Architecture in Paris in 1720, which allowed him to study at the Académie de France in Rome. He left for Rome in 1723 and remained there for the rest of his life. In 1728 he became a professor at the Accademia di S Luca, teaching geometry and perspective; his reputation was greater as a teacher than as a designer. He was acclaimed an authority on the theory of musical proportion in architecture by his contemporary Benedetto Galiani, but this interest was not manifest in his built works. He enjoyed great prestige in Rome, maintaining close contacts with both the Académie de France and the Curia. He was a judge in the competition (1732) for the façade of the Lateran Basilica, forcefully defending the severely classical design by Alessandro Galilei that subsequently won. Derizet's practical work was meagre. His first commission was for the rebuilding of the church of S Claudio dei Borgognoni (1728–31). The church of SS Nome di Maria in Trajan's Forum (1736–8; consecrated 1741) was his most important work. Cardinal Lodovico Pico della Mirandola greatly favoured Derizet's project and imposed it on the Confraternity. Although initial drawings (Berlin, Kstbib.) show a determinedly Rococo design, with a two-storey, pedimented, curved façade, the final building was a conscious imitation of the adjacent S Maria di Loreto (begun early 16th century), with a drum over an octagonal base. The plan was a transverse ellipse, perhaps derived from Jacopo Vignola's S Anna dei Palafrenieri, Rome (1565–76). Derizet's last work (1756) was the restoration of the 16th-century church of S Luigi dei Francesi, Rome, which was redecorated with eclectic ornamentation.

BIBLIOGRAPHY

A. Martini and M. L. Casanova: *SS Nome di Maria*, Chiese Roma Illus., lxx (Rome, 1962), pp. 21–36

W. Oechslin: 'Contributo alla conoscenza di Antonio Deriset, architetto e teorico dell'architettura', *Quad. Ist. Stor. Archit.*, xvi (1969), pp. 47–66

P. Portoghesi: *Roma Barocca: The History of an Architectonic Culture* (Cambridge, MA, 1970)

C. Cozzolino: 'Due chiese romane di Antonio Derizet', *Palladio*, ii/4 (1989), pp. 77–90

Derkinderen, Antoon [Antonius] (**Johannes**) (*b* 's Hertogenbosch, 20 Dec 1859; *d* Amsterdam, 2 Nov 1925). Dutch painter, designer, printmaker and writer. He trained at the Koninklijke School voor Nuttige en Beeldende Kunsten in 's Hertogenbosch (1878–80) and at the Rijksakademie in Amsterdam (1880–84) under the direction of August Allebé. In 1882–3, on the advice of Allebé, he spent a year studying at the Académie Royale, Brussels. He received his first important commission in 1884 for a mural painting for the Begijnhof church in Amsterdam. The *Procession of the Miraculous Holy Sacrament*, which was painted on canvas and not directly on to the wall, was rejected by his patrons after its completion in 1889 because of its unusual, innovative character. Only in 1929, four years after Derkinderen's death, was the enormous canvas (2×11 m) placed in the Begijnhof church (*in situ*). Inspired by the work of Giotto and that of Pierre Puvis de Chavannes, whom he had met during a journey to Italy and France in 1887, and under the influence of Walter Crane and other theorists of the English Arts and Crafts Movement, Derkinderen became one of the first in the Netherlands to subscribe to the notion that a mural painting must be subservient to its architectural setting and must not have a strong naturalistic or illusionistic character. The pale tonality and severe figure style of the Begijnhof mural are particularly indebted to Puvis de Chavannes.

During Derkinderen's next major project, the mural paintings for the Stadhuis of 's Hertogenbosch, which include symbolical representations of the foundation and early history of his native town (*First Bosch Wall*, 1889–91), he carried this principle further. In a brochure on these paintings, his friend Jan Pieter Veth used for the first time the term *Gemeenschapskunst* ('communal art') to characterize a monumental art intended for the entire community. Derkinderen was the most important exponent of *Gemeenschapskunst*, a specifically Dutch branch of Symbolism that sought to integrate art more directly into society. In spite of some harsh criticism, in 1893 he was commissioned to paint a second mural for the Stadhuis (*Second Bosch Wall*, 1893–6; both *in situ*). He then painted murals for the Amsterdam office of the insurance company Algemeene Maatschappij van Levensverzeering en Lÿfrente (1896–1900; destr. 1963, see e.g. 1980–81 exh. cat.) containing symbolical representations of such appropriate themes as *Abundance, Want, Health, Illness*, the *Ladder of Life* and the *Wheel of Fortune*.

In 1898 Derkinderen was commissioned to design murals and a stained-glass window for H. P. Berlage's new Koopmansbeurs (1896–1903) in Amsterdam. The stained-glass window, installed in 1903 in the south wall of the hall in front of the Chamber of Commerce, consists of 21 scenes relevant to trade and shipping. His designs for the murals (primarily depicting events from Amsterdam's history), however, were rejected in 1901 by Berlage, who felt Derkinderen had not taken the total decorative programme of the building sufficiently into account and had concentrated excessively on the Middle Ages at the expense of modern references. Despite this setback he was considered one of the most important and influential monumental artists in the Netherlands at the beginning of the 20th century.

Derkinderen's oeuvre also includes easel paintings, mainly portraits, some etchings and lithographs (he helped to found the Dutch Etching Club in 1885). He was involved in the production of a number of books, notably the *Gijsbreght van Aemstel* portfolio, published in serial form between 1893 and 1901, for which he executed most of the illustrations as well as designing the typography. This work is considered an innovative milestone in late 19th-century Dutch book design. He also designed postage stamps and a banknote. When Allebé retired as director of the Rijksakademie in 1907, Derkinderen was chosen as successor. He fulfilled few important commissions after this date, but he had ample opportunity through teaching and writing to disseminate his ideas on mural paintings and their relationship to architecture and, in a wider sense, the relationship between art and society as a whole.

WRITINGS

Langs den ouden weg in nieuwe landen [Along old roads in new lands] (n.p., 1918)

Over de geschiedenis der Academie van Beeldende Kunsten te Amsterdam en hare beteekenis voor onzen tijd [On the history of the Academy of Art in Amsterdam and its significance for our time] (Amsterdam, 1918)

De jeugd van Antoon Derkinderen door hemzelf beschreven anno 1892 [The youth of Antoon Derkinderen described by himself in the year 1892] (Bussum, 1927)

BIBLIOGRAPHY

A. M. Hammacher: *De levenstijd van Antoon Derkinderen* [The life of Antoon Derkinderen] (Amsterdam, 1932) [extensive bibliog.]

W. Arondeus: *Figuren en problemen der monumentale schilderkunst in Nederland* [Practitioners and problems of monumental painting in the Netherlands] (Amsterdam, 1941), pp. 28–57

B. Polak: *Het fin-de-siècle in de Nederlandse schilderkunst: De symbolistische beweging, 1890–1900* [The fin-de-siècle in Dutch painting: the Symbolist movement, 1890–1900] (The Hague, 1955), pp. 187–229, 401–7

E. Braches: *Het boek als nieuwe kunst: Een studie in Art Nouveau* (Utrecht, 1973)

Antoon Derkinderen, 1859–1925 (exh. cat. by R. Verheyen and others, 's Hertogenbosch, Noordbrabants Mus.; Amsterdam, Hist. Mus.; Assen, Prov. Mus. Drenthe; 1980–81)

The Age of Van Gogh: Dutch Painting, 1880–1895 (exh. cat., Glasgow, Burrell Col.; Amsterdam, Rijksmus. van Gogh; 1990–91)

JAN JAAP HEIJ

Derkovits, Gyula (*b* Szombathely, 13 April 1894; *d* Budapest, 18 June 1934). Hungarian painter, printmaker and draughtsman. He was trained, like his father, as a carpenter, but not wanting to pursue this vocation he volunteered for the army during World War I. He was subsequently gravely wounded and also contracted tuberculosis. In 1916, as a war casualty, he moved to Budapest, where he worked as a joiner and studied drawing and painting. From 1918 he trained at the free school set up by Károly Kernstok. In 1923 he settled in Vienna for three years, where his exhibition in 1925 met with considerable success. He exhibited 40 pictures in Budapest in 1927, and he was immediately ranked among the best Hungarian painters. He became a member of the Hungarian Communist Party in 1918. Although he later lost active contact with the Communist movement, he remained committed to its ideals. This is reflected in the iconography of his work; even his early works, most of which are untraced, show a conspicuous social concern. The sentimentality of this early painting was soon superseded by a mixture of Cubist composition and Expressionist concern. His copperplate engraving, *Self-portrait with Bishop's Mitre* (1921;

Budapest, N.G.), shows a hammer and sickle in a five-pointed star on the mitre. In his *Last Supper* (1922; Budapest, N.G.) the faces are all self-portraits. During this period he also painted mock-classical idylls (e.g. *Concert*, 1921–2; *Under a Big Tree*, 1922; both Budapest, N.G.).

During Derkovits's years in Vienna the influence of the German Expressionists became stronger, and the elements of his pictures became more sharply defined. The principal works of this period are the etching and the painting entitled *Mourning of the Dead* (1924; Budapest, N.G.), in which the proportion of the positive–negative masses suggests an acquaintance with Käthe Kollwitz's commemorative print, the *Memorial to Karl Liebknecht* (1919–20). A light-coloured sheet covers the purple-brown patch of the young male corpse, while the face and hands of the mourners are dark brown; this is Derkovits's darkest picture. A desperate tension shows through the etchings and paintings of the *Flight* series (1926; Budapest, N.G.), and he used a similar, unsettling transverse composition in works produced after his return to Hungary, such as *Street* (1927; Budapest, N.G.). However, with his wash drawing *Timber Carriers* (1926; Szombathely Gal.) he also started to compose by combining more sharply defined and larger forms. *Organ Grinders (Fire-eating Itinerant Acrobats)* (1927; Budapest, N.G.) points to the compositional technique of his next period: the complicated spatial arrangement is packed into the tight yard of a workers' tenement; the colours are a combination of cold and warm.

Between 1927 and 1930 Derkovits moved from street to domestic scenes. His etchings *We Two* and *Self-portrait (Myself and my Wife)* (1927; Budapest, N.G.) express his aspirations for personal security. The *Grape Eater* (1929; priv. col., see 1979 exh. cat., no. 58) articulates this same yearning but is a more mature composition of the same mode: on the left, the figure of the artist has his back to the viewer and his face in the mirror opposite, while in the third plane behind the table is the figure of his wife eating grapes. Several versions of *Still-life with Fish* were prepared between 1928 and 1930; this Cubist work shows workers seen from above. In the gouache *Self-portrait* of 1929 (Budapest, N.G.) dense rows of strikers can be seen through the window behind the head facing the viewer.

Around 1930 the anguish of Derkovits's previous work developed into tragedy. In their entirety the 12 woodcuts of the *Dózsa* series (a commission from the Communist Party, originally entitled *1514*; see Körner, 1968) refer to the fate of the 1514 peasant rebellion, yet individually they have contemporary relevance. The *Marchers* and the *Hammerers at the Gate* show organized workers moving in unison; among the victims of the *Stakes* and the *Defeat* is the artist himself. The series was continued in 1930 with six etchings of *Dózsa*. From this time the content of Derkovits's work reflected daily events more immediately. In *Order* (1930; Budapest, N.G.) the painter, standing at an open window, is reading the papers, his wife behind him; in front of him on the window-sill lies an eviction order under a piece of bread. In the background the shadow of a cat can be seen on the partition wall. The *Winter Window* (Budapest, N. Mus., Dept Mod. Hist.), painted at the same time, depicts, in warm colours, a piece of bread lying on a newspaper on the window-sill. Sickle-feathered hats and bayonets of gendarmes can be glimpsed through the frosty window. *For Bread (Terror)* (Budapest, N.G.) is an expression of his reaction to the bloody suppression of a workers' demonstration in 1930. In this picture cold and warm colours have specific meanings; in later works, Derkovits emphasized this colour symbolism by the use of silver and gold powder paints.

In his satirical works Derkovits caricatured the bourgeoisie and merchants. *Auction* (1930; priv. col., see 1979 exh. cat., no. 67) shows one quarter of a picture to be auctioned; only the gilded frame of the painting is visible, while the figures of the brokers are reflected in the glass. *Hungry Ones in Winter* (1930; priv. col., see Körner, 1968, no. 292) shows a crowd in front of a picture-shop window, while a pair of policemen stride past from behind a glass door. In the *Fish Merchant* (Budapest, N.G.), which complements the latter, the merchant's knife glints menacingly as he measures his fish in his shop.

From 1932 the internal tensions in Derkovits's work eased somewhat. In the small-scale *Execution* (472× 622 mm, priv. col., see 1979 exh. cat., no. 90), a strange sort of calm emanates from the figure standing with his back to the viewer. In *Along the Railway* (Budapest, N.G.), the train wheels are silvery cold; yet behind them, a shivering pair of workers, painted in warm colours, stroll peacefully past. The complicated space in the *Bridge Builders* (Budapest, N.G.) is dominated by the cold silvery metallic elements that frame the warm-coloured workers who are stripped to the waist. *Three Generations* (or *Generations*; Budapest, N.G., see fig.) concentrates present,

Gyula Derkovits: *Three Generations*, lead, oil and silver paint, 1030×778 mm, 1932 (Budapest, Hungarian National Gallery)

past and future in a single perspective. The head reading a red book, a self-portrait, represents the present, a portrait of Marx reflected in the mirror behind him, the past, and the mother and child, the future. In this manner Derkovits transformed sociohistorical concepts into simple symbols. At the same time he made many versions of the dense compositions *Builders* and *Hodman* (1932; Budapest, N.G.).

Between 1932 and 1934 Derkovits concentrated on the female figure, particularly the shivering woman and the mother. These drawings and paintings are as dense in composition as the *Hodman*, and the everyday life of workers is portrayed as bleak rather than tragic. The last of these works, *Mother* (1934; Budapest, N.G.), painted in oil and silver paint, depicts a diagonally placed, over life-size face, covered on the left by the arm and profile of the infant. The mellow composition is particularly characteristic of the last two years of Derkovits's short career. The new direction in his work can be best seen in *Bridge in Winter* (1933; Budapest, N.G.), where the role of cold and warm colours in shaping the content and underlining the meaning of the motifs is the same, but the numerous objects are held together by a more dispersed, at places almost pointillist, application of paint. The work of his last year is characterized by a drive towards monumentality. In the *Shipbuilder* (Budapest, N.G.) the monumental aspect is heightened by impasto colours matured on a distemper base. This monument to the worker, this ideal, reappears more strongly in the *Sand Transporters of the Danube* (Budapest, N.G.). Its light colours and airiness are typical of these monumentalizing works.

Derkovits's symbolic system is based on real objects and their physical relations to each other. A closed or open window, for example, becomes a real and an abstract separation, and the internal and external aspects of the self are similarly juxtaposed. The newspaper, or any written or printed material, represents the hostile exterior world; bread and fish symbolize hunger; winter, snow and ice symbolize the threats of everyday life. From the multitude of disguised self-portraits it emerges that the artist considered himself a victim, but there are also drawings in which, montage-like, he appears both as the imprisoned convict and as his own prosecutor announcing his condemnation. His identification with the proletariat and their daily struggle explains why Derkovits chose to continue the artistic legacy of the Group of Socialist Artists founded in Budapest in 1934. His primary motif was the reading worker, with which he extended the ideas presented in *Three Generations*. His importance as a painter was recognized by his colleagues and contemporaries, but this did little to alleviate his difficult circumstances. In 1948 he was awarded a posthumous Kossuth Prize and from the end of the 1950s his pictures and exhibitions moved frequently around Europe. He left over 700 paintings, drawings and prints. Most of his works are in the Hungarian National Gallery, Budapest, and some are in the Gyula Derkovits and Dési Huber Memorial Museum in Szombathely.

BIBLIOGRAPHY

I. Hevesy: 'Derkovits Gyula linóleummetszetei' [Linocuts of Gyula Derkovits], *Magyar Irás* [Hungarian writing], i/9 (1921)

Julius Derkovits: Kollektiv-Ausstellung (exh. cat., intro. H. Menkes; Vienna, Weihburg Gal., 1925)

I. Artinger: *Derkovits Gyula* (Budapest, 1934)

Derkovits Gyula: '1514', foreword G. Bálint and E. Kállai (Budapest, 1936)

Derkovits Gyula emlékkiállítás [Memorial exhibition of Gyula Derkovits] (exh. cat., foreword Z. Székely; Budapest, Mus. F.A., 1954)

Gyuláné Derkovits: *Mi ketten: Emlékezés Derkovits Gyulára* [We two: remembering Gyula Derkovits] (Budapest, 1954) [by the artist's wife]

M. Szabolcsi: 'Attila József, Gyula Derkovits, Béla Bartók', *Magyar Tudományos Akad. Nyelv & Irodalmi Tudományok Osztályának Közleményei* [Publications of the Section for Linguistic and Literary Sciences of the Hungarian Academy of Sciences], xiv/1–4 (1959), pp. 35–63

L. Németh: 'Das Gemälde von Gyula Derkovits *Drei Generationen*', *Acta Hist. A. Acad. Sci. Hung.*, vii/1–2 (1960), pp. 103–14

Derkovits (exh. cat., foreword Ö. G. Pogány; Amsterdam, Stedel. Mus., 1960)

G. Ö. Pogány: *Derkovits* (Budapest, 1960) [in Eng. and Ger.]

Derkovits (exh. cat., foreword D. Micacchi; Rome, Nuo. Paese, 1961)

G. Ö. Pogány: 'Gyula Derkovits', *New Hung. Q.*, ii/1 (1961), pp. 109–17

Expositia de pictura si grafica Gyula Derkovits (exh. cat., foreword A. Oelmacher; Bucharest, Gal. A. Dalles, 1963)

J. Szabó: 'Die Holzschnittfolge *1514* von Gyula Derkovits' [*1514*, a woodcut series by Gyula Derkovits], *Acta Hist. A. Acad. Sci. Hung.*, x/1–2 (1964), pp. 171–210

Derkovits Gyula emlékkiállítása [Gyula Derkovits retrospective] (exh. cat., foreword G. Ö. Pogány; Budapest, N.G., 1965)

J. Szabó: 'Derkovits Gyula önarcképei' [Self-portraits of Gyula Derkovits], *Magyar Nemzeti Gal. Közleményei* [Bulletin of the Hungarian National Gallery] (1965), no. 5, pp. 5–20

——: 'Derkovits és a magyar mükritika a két viláháború között' [Derkovits in the light of Hungarian art criticism between the two World Wars], *Müvészettörténeti Értesítö* [Art Historian Reporter], xv/1 (1966), pp. 40–51

N. Aradi: *Daumier, Derkovits és utódaik* [Daumier, Derkovits and their successors] (Budapest, 1968)

É. Körner: *Gyula Derkovits* (Budapest, 1968) [contains list of works]

N. Aradi: 'Bildnis und Selbstbildnis als Mittel der Widerspiegelung des Klassenkampfes in der Malerei und Grafik von Gyula Derkovits', *Wiss. Z. Friedrich-Schiller-U. Jena* (1969), no. 1, pp. 11–16

É. Körner: *Gyula Derkovits* (Leipzig, 1969)

Derkovits, Gyula: Emlékkiállítása [Gyula Derkovits retrospective] (exh. cat. by G. Ö. Pogány, Budapest, N.G., 1979)

NÓRA ARADI

Derkzen van Angeren, Antoon [Anthonius Philippus] (*b* Delft, 21 April 1878; *d* Bedford, Quebec, on or before 14 June 1961). Dutch printmaker, draughtsman and painter. After training as a delftware artist Derkzen van Angeren worked at a pottery factory in Delft until *c.* 1901. As a self-taught printmaker he also made his first etchings at this time. Between 1911 and 1952 he lived mostly in Rotterdam, where he worked as a teacher at the Academy of Visual Arts (1911–43). The subjects of Derkzen van Angeren's paintings and drawings vary from townscapes to figure studies, portraits (for example *Self-portrait*, 1907; Rotterdam, Boymans–van Beuningen), gardens, still-lifes and landscapes. From around 1905 he concentrated increasingly on printmaking: his etchings, engravings and lithographs are remarkable for the clarity with which, in particular, the vastness of the Dutch polder and river landscape is captured, as in his series of 18 etchings of river landscapes along the Merwede, Waal and Rhine (1924).

BIBLIOGRAPHY

Antoon Philippus Derkzen van Angeren (exh. cat., Rotterdam, Boymans–van Beuningen, 1961)

A. J. Vervoorn: *Nederlandse Prentkunst, 1840–1940* (Lochum, 1983), pp. 25–6, 107

CHRISTIAAN SCHUCKMAN

Dermyans, John. *See* MAIANO, DA, (3).

De Rossi, Giovanni Battista (*b* Rome, 22 Feb 1822; *d* Castelgandolfo, 20 Sept 1894). Italian archaeologist. Educated at the Collegio Romano and the university of Rome, he was the founder of the scientific archaeology of early Christianity. Using his extensive knowledge of ancient topography, literary sources and the researches of the humanists (especially those of ANTONIO BOSIO), he illuminated contemporary understanding of Early Christian life and art in Rome. His earliest excavations were carried out between 1847 and 1850 at the ancient Christian Catacomb of Praetextatus. His researches revealed the extent of the underground galleries at the site as well as the richness of the material remains. He was a formidable epigrapher and in 1861 published the first volume of *Inscriptiones christianae urbis Romae septimo saeculo antiquiores*, in which he collected, discussed and often depicted the earliest Christian inscriptions from the city of Rome. In 1863 De Rossi founded the *Bullettino di archeologia cristiana*, which aimed to publish and discuss all aspects of Christian art, archaeology and history. The following year he produced the first volume of his magisterial *Roma sotteranea*, a comprehensive study of the life and organization of the Christian community at Rome with particular reference to the Catacomb of St Calixtus on the Via Appia. The subsequent volumes broadened the scope of his reconstruction to include the Catacomb of St Generosa on the Via Portuense as well as an exploration of the relationship between the cemeteries of suburban Rome and the layout of the churches inside the walls. He enjoyed strong papal backing and was appointed to senior posts connected with the Holy See. He organized the Lateran Museum and also classified the codices of the Vatican Library, and in 1890 he published, in the *Bullettino*, a 16th-century collection of inscriptions pertaining to Roman artists. He was much honoured during his lifetime and was President of the Pontifical Academy of Roman Archaeology, Secretary for the Pontifical Commission for Sacred Archaeology and Prefect of the Museum of the Vatican Library.

WRITINGS

Inscriptiones cristianae urbis Romae, 3 vols (Rome, 1857–85, 2/1915)

La Roma sotteranea cristiana, 3 vols (Rome, 1864–77); Eng. trans., abridged by J. Spencer Northcote and W. R. Brownlow as *The Roman Catacombs* (London, 1872)

Musaici cristiani e saggi di pavimenti delle chiese di Roma anteriori al sec. XV (Rome, 1872–96)

Piante iconografiche e prospettiche di Roma anteriori al secolo decimosesto (Rome, 1879)

BIBLIOGRAPHY

P. M. Baumgarten: *Giovanni Battista De Rossi: Eine biographische Skizze* (Cologne, 1892)

'De Rossi, Giovanni Battista', *Enciclopedia cattolica* (Florence, 1948–54)

JOHN CURRAN

Derpt. *See* TARTU.

Derrick. *See under* CONSTRUCTION MACHINERY.

Derrida, Jacques (*b* El-biar, Algiers, 15 July 1930). French philosopher. In 1967 he published *De la grammatologie* and *L'Ecriture et la différence*. Subsequently he became identified with DECONSTRUCTION, a process of critical analysis whose effects have been widespread in the English-speaking world (*see also* POST-STRUCTURALISM). Although 'deconstructionist' criticism has been largely confined to literary studies, Derrida's contribution to the analysis and understanding of the visual arts is potentially almost as great. The strength of his approach derives from a decision to examine the historical and philosophical origins of the distinctions that are customarily made between different types of sign: between linguistic and visual signs, and between the messages of speech and writing. For Derrida, the dialogues of PLATO display an explicit hierarchisation of spoken and written language: as in the myth of the origins of writing recounted in Plato's *Phaedrus*. Written language is regarded as a mere secondary substitute for the presence and plenitude of the human voice, and Socrates described writing as a 'dead word', implying that it has no status except as an inadequate representation of a prior act of speech. Derrida, by contrast, has insisted on the condition of written language, as a 'trace' or network of traces recorded in the act of writing, rather than as a record of a prior event. It is easy to see the relevance of this notion to the theory and practice of painting. On the one hand, he has implied a unity between the process of painting and the process of writing, such as obtains in the Chinese practice of calligraphy. On the other hand, he has loosened somewhat the bond between painting and the traditional requirement of 'imitation' (the Platonic *mimesis*); in so far as his argument gives primacy to the 'trace', it can be used as the basis for a new evaluation of the course that Western painting has taken, applicable equally to Cézanne and to American Abstract Expressionism.

Derrida brought together a number of essays dealing directly with the visual arts in his collection *La Vérité en peinture* (1978). Ranging from a searching enquiry into the bases of Immanuel Kant's aesthetics to discussions of the work of such contemporary European artists as Valerio Adami, this volume of essays illustrates Derrida's virtuosity in visual matters. His discussion in dialogue form of one of van Gogh's *Boots* paintings, which contrasts Martin Heidegger's assertion that they are the boots of a peasant with the art historian Meyer Schapiro's view that they are the artist's own, is a powerful analysis of the difficulties of specifying the referent in a work of representation.

WRITINGS

De la grammatologie (Paris, 1967; Eng. trans., Baltimore, 1976)
L'Ecriture et la différence (Paris, 1967; Eng. trans., Chicago and London, 1978)
La Dissémination (Paris, 1972; Eng. trans., Chicago and London, 1981)
La Vérité en peinture (Paris, 1978; Eng. trans., Chicago, 1987)

BIBLIOGRAPHY

M. Phillipson: *Painting, Language and Modernity* (London, 1985)

STEPHEN BANN

Derrynaflan Treasure. Treasure hoard found in 1980 within the boundary of the ancient monastic site of Doire na bhFlann near Cashel, Co. Tipperary. The hoard (Dublin, N. Mus.), dating from the 8th–9th centuries AD, comprises a silver chalice, a paten, a silver hoop, which was almost certainly the foot-ring of the paten, and a large bronze strainer-ladle, all clearly liturgical. They were concealed in a pit under a bronze basin of fairly common insular form, c. 450 mm wide and c. 190 mm deep. They may have been deposited in the later 9th or 10th century during the most intense period of Viking disturbance.

The paten is a large hammered and lathe-polished silver dish (350×30 mm) attached to an elaborate rim. Its construction is very complex, with more than 300 separate components. Twelve cast gilt-bronze double frames on the upper surface of the edge display twenty-four elaborate gold filigree panels depicting beasts, a bird, interlaced snakes, mannikins and abstract designs. The frames carry ornamental enamel studs at their centres and are held in place by twelve pins, each of which is capped by a further complex stud. Twelve die-stamped gold foils with interlace and curvilinear designs decorate the side of the paten: between each pair is an elaborate rectangular inlaid enamel set in a cast bronze mount. Decorative mouldings of knitted silver and copper wire lapped around metallic forms border the edges of the decorative zones. Under the filigree panels, engraved on the surface of the silver, is an assembly code of carefully engraved letters suggesting that a literate person was concerned in its design. The stand clearly imitates the design of the side of the paten, being a hoop of tinned bronze to the front of which are attached eight die-stamped panels of interlace and Ultimate La Tène motifs. Its workmanship is less accomplished than that of the paten, and it may have been added as a secondary feature. The paten's stylistic similarities to the Ardagh Chalice (see ARDAGH TREASURE) suggest that it and the stand date from the 8th century AD. The paten may be regarded as a rendering in Irish taste and techniques of a large late Roman dish with repoussé rim decoration. Its form relates it to elaborate, footed patens of semi-precious stone preserved in the treasury of S Marco (see VENICE, §IV, 1(iv)). Large but plainer patens are a feature of Syrian silver finds of the 6th century AD.

The chalice (see fig.), one of four known surviving Irish early medieval chalices, is closely comparable to the Ardagh Chalice. It is a *calix ministerialis*, measuring 192×210 mm. It has two opposed strap handles springing from large escutcheons, a large bowl with an everted rim, a complex

Derrynaflan Treasure, silver chalice, h. 192 mm, 8th–9th centuries AD (Dublin, National Museum of Ireland)

gilt copper-alloy stem cast in three parts and a large sub-conical foot with a broad, flat foot-ring. A band of filigree panels and amber settings girdles the bowl, which, where it passes through the handles, bears two cast copper-alloy ornaments in the so-called *kerbschnitt* technique. Filigree panels and amber studs decorate the handles, escutcheons, stem and foot. Cast panels of interlace and animal ornament occur on the stem and foot-ring. The upper and lower rings of the stem are riveted to the bowl and foot respectively, which are united, as on the Ardagh Chalice, by a large copper-alloy pin passing through the stem. On the underside of the foot, where the pin emerges, there is a cast gilt copper-alloy decorative plate with amber studs. The bowl and foot were raised by hammering and then lathe-polished. The animal style of the filigree is simpler than that of the paten, consisting of single beasts sketched in outline, executed in a coarse and less complex filigree that sometimes embodies the *disjecta membra* of Early Christian iconographical themes. The chalice is stylistically related to 9th-century AD silver pseudo-penannular brooches, and it may well date to the earlier part of that century.

The strainer is 380 mm long and has a deep ladle-bowl (diam. 115 mm; divided in line with the handle by a perforated plate) and a long handle terminating in a round pommel, on the reverse of which is a suspension loop. The pommel bears a polished crystal in a ring of gem-set enamels. The rim of the bowl bears applied stamped silver panels held with domed rivets and thin bronze mouldings. Along the upper edge of the strainer-plate are two applied silver strips and three enamel studs, one with *millefiori* inlay. The object represents the adaptation of a common insular ladle form to liturgical use.

Although much has been made of the apparently oriental aspect of Irish liturgical vessels, the Derrynaflan Treasure shows that they were essentially insular adaptations of local vessel forms and techniques. Contemporary Irish liturgical documents suggest that they were intended for use in a mass that was largely Roman in character.

See also INSULAR ART, §2.

BIBLIOGRAPHY
A. B. O Ríordáin: 'The Derrynaflan Hoard', *Antiquity*, liv (1980), pp. 216–17
M. Ryan: 'An Early Christian Hoard from Derrynaflan, Co. Tipperary', *N. Munster Antiqua. J.*, xxii (1980), pp. 9–26
M. Ryan, ed.: *The Derrynaflan Hoard* (Dublin, 1983–)
M. Ryan: 'The Derrynaflan and Other Irish Eucharistic Chalices', *Ireland and Europe: The Early Church*, ed. M. Richter and P. Ní Chatháin (Stuttgart, 1984), pp. 135–48
——: *Early Irish Communion Vessels: Church Treasures of the Golden Age* (Dublin, 1986)

MICHAEL RYAN

Déruet, Claude (*b* Nancy, *c.* 1588; *bur* Nancy, 20 Oct 1660). French painter, engraver and draughtsman. After a period of training in Rome he returned to his native Lorraine in 1619 to succeed Jacques Bellange as the most important painter in the duchy. For more than 40 years he ran a large and successful workshop in Nancy that provided mural decorations, portraits, devotional pictures and secular easel paintings for the court, the nobility and bourgeoisie; Claude Lorrain worked in his studio in 1625–6. Déruet continued to work in a Mannerist style long after this had become old-fashioned in Italy and in Paris. The

scale of production in his workshop can be judged from an inventory drawn up two years after his death and published by Jacquot in 1894. Many of his works survive, but they have yet to be studied in depth as a corpus. Déruet's son Charles Déruet (1635–66) was also a painter.

1. NANCY AND ROME, TO 1619. Déruet came from a family of clockmakers originating in Champagne. His father entered the service of Charles III, Duke of Lorraine (*reg* 1559–1608), before 1585. On 19 April 1605 Claude was apprenticed for four years to Bellange, the predominant painter in the duchy. In 1613 he was in Italy working for Agostino Tassi, who was then engaged on the decoration of Cardinal Montalto's Casino (now the Villa Lante) at Bagnaia, near Viterbo. He is also recorded in Rome in the studio of the Cavaliere d'Arpino and worked for the French engraver Philippe Thomassin and for Antonio Tempesta. His earliest known works are three engravings of the *Resurrection*, the *Descent of the Holy Ghost* and the *Assumption of the Virgin* for a missal (e.g. Nancy, Mus. Hist. Lorrain) published in Rome in 1615. In 1617 Thomassin engraved and published a print after Déruet entitled *Jesus Condemned* or the *Council of the Jews*; another version of this composition, engraved in the reverse sense to Thomassin's, was cut in Paris after 1617 (for a discussion of the problems raised by these versions see 1982 exh. cat., no. 11). Around 1618 Déruet painted an *Assumption of the Virgin* in the chapel of the Villa Borghese, Rome, the only one of his many mural decorations to survive, apart from fragments in a chapel in St Joseph-des-Carmes, Paris, probably executed after 1625. In 1619 Déruet was appointed a Knight of the Papal Order of Portugal and returned to Lorraine.

2. NANCY, AFTER 1619. In Nancy, Déruet rapidly became the foremost painter (Bellange had died in 1616) and enjoyed the favour of Duke Henry II (*reg* 1608–24). He decorated various rooms (destr.) in the ducal palace and in 1620 signed a contract to decorate the Carmelite church in Nancy (completed 1626; destr. 1790s). In 1621 he was granted letters patent of nobility and bought a large property in Nancy, the first of many, where he established his workshop; he married in 1623. An *Assumption of the Virgin* (1621; Mirecourt, Vosges, Notre-Dame) is based on Déruet's 1615 engraving of the same subject, showing a lack of inventiveness characteristic of some of his output. A set of four landscapes of *Amazons on Horseback* (Strasbourg, Mus. B.-A.) probably dates from the 1620s. The influence of Tempesta's hunting scenes is clear both in the subject and in details such as the plump, twisting horses. Such scenes of battle and hunting set in landscape recur in Déruet's easel paintings. Some survive (e.g. New York, Met., and La Fère, Mus. Jeanne d'Aboville), and many more are listed in the studio inventory. The influence of Bellange is apparent in a *St Roch* of 1625 (Nancy, Mus. Hist. Lorrain).

Déruet continued to enjoy the favour of Henry II's successor, Charles IV (*reg* 1624–75), and his career prospered even during the French occupation of Lorraine, which began with the siege and capture of Nancy in 1633. He sought commissions from Louis XIII, who made a

Claude Déruet: *Rape of the Sabine Women*, oil on canvas, 1.15×1.86 m, 1650 (Munich, Alte Pinakothek)

pastel portrait of the artist (Nancy, Mus. Hist. Lorrain) in 1634, and from Cardinal Richelieu, for whom around 1640 he painted a set of fantastic scenes representing the *Four Elements* (Orléans, Mus. B.-A.). These four paintings are his best-known works and among the most inventive. He was rewarded some time before 1645 with the title of Knight of the Order of St Michel. He continued to be active as an engraver in this period, examples being the *Battle of Northlingen* (after 1634; e.g. Paris, Bib. N.) and the *Ducal Palace at Nancy* (*c.* 1640; e.g. Paris, Bib. N.), both of which present archaisms in the handling of perspective. A similar archaism is apparent in Déruet's portrait of *Mme de Saint-Baslemont* (Nancy, Mus. Hist. Lorrain) of 1643, in which the equestrian figure is set parallel to the picture plane and several incidents distinct in time and place are incorporated into the landscape background.

Nevertheless, some of Déruet's paintings show great virtuosity in the handling of colour and of their multi-figure compositions in elaborate architectural settings, as is the case with the Richelieu *Elements* and the *Rape of the Sabine Women* (Munich, Alte Pin.; see fig.), which was bought from him in 1650 by the town of Nancy as a gift for the French governor of Lorraine, Henri, Maréchal de La Ferté-Sénectère (1600–80). They are pervaded by Mannerism, though this is more apparent in the forms than in the subject-matter: eroticism is largely absent, and, although some of the subjects are enigmatic, there are probably no arcane meanings to be sought. Much of the production of Déruet's studio was designed to satisfy a delicate and refined court taste; this was also often true of his religious paintings, in which hardship and death seem to have no place.

BIBLIOGRAPHY

E. Meaume: 'Recherches sur la vie et les ouvrages de Claude Déruet, peintre et graveur lorrain (1588–1660)', *Bull. Soc. Archéol. Lorraine*, iv (1853), pp. 135–250

A. Jacquot: 'Note sur Claude Déruet, peintre et graveur lorrain (1588–1660)', *Réun. Soc. B.-A. Dépt.*, xviii (1894), pp. 763–945

F. G. Pariset: 'Les Débuts de Claude Déruet', *Bull. Soc. Hist. A. Fr.* (1947–8), pp. 117–22

M. Fessenden: *The Life and Works of Claude Déruet—Court Painter, 1588–1660* (New York, 1952) [numerous illus.]

R. A. Weigert: *Inventaire du fonds français: Graveurs du dix-septième siècle*, Paris, Bib. N., Cab. Est. cat., iii (Paris, 1954), pp. 408–10

F. G. Pariset: 'Les Amazones de Claude Déruet', *Pays Lorrain*, xxxvii/4 (1956), pp. 97–114

Claude Lorrain e i pittori lorenesi in Italia nel XVII secolo (exh. cat. by J. Thuillier, Rome, Acad. France; Nancy, Mus. Hist. Lorrain; 1982), pp. 103–33

H. Tanaka: 'Le Portrait du samouraï Hasekura Tsunenaga par Claude Déruet', *Pays Lorrain*, lxx/3 (1989), pp. 160–64

L'Art en Lorraine au temps de Jacques Callot (exh. cat. by C. Pétry and J. Thuillier, Nancy, Mus. B.-A., 1992) [incl. writings by J.-C. Boy, pp. 210–17, 337–49, and M. Sylvestre, pp. 394–8]

MICHEL SYLVESTRE

Deruta. Italian centre of maiolica production. It was the main centre of pottery production in Umbria during the Renaissance. A document of 1358 records the sale of ceramic wares to the convent of S Francesco in nearby Assisi, although potteries probably existed in Deruta even earlier. Between *c.* 1490 and 1550 production increased in quantity and quality, and plain and decorated wares were supplied to a wide market (*see* ITALY, fig. 83). By the early 16th century 30 to 40 kilns were in operation, of which

only three or four used the metallic gold and red lustres for which Deruta and Gubbio are renowned. As in Gubbio, lustres were applied to local wares and to those brought from such other centres of production as Urbino for this specialized finish. In addition to lustred ceramics, quantities of polychrome maiolica were produced, the predominant colours of which are yellow, orange and blue. In the 17th and 18th centuries the quality of ceramic production declined and was characterized by the manufacture of votive plaques that were placed in churches and homes. 16th-century tin-glazed earthenware from Deruta was noted for a conservatism and consistency, both in style and shape, which was probably engendered by its geographical isolation. The large, deep dishes, known as *piatti da pompa*, painted with idealized portraits of women or men set within formalized floral and geometric borders (e.g. of *c.* 1500–40; London, BM), were particularly popular. Other common subjects for these dishes were images of SS Francis, Jerome and Rocco, the Virgin, angels, equestrian figures or scenes based on local fables, allegories or proverbs. Products from Deruta of this period also include polychrome drug jars decorated with complex floral and grotesque designs, moulded plates with relief patterns and *istoriato* wares with religious, historical, literary or mythological subjects. Giacomo Mancini (*fl c.* 1540–60; known as 'El Frate') was the most notable Deruta *istoriato* painter and one of the few who signed his works. His dated pieces were made between 1541, when he came to Deruta from Urbino, and 1545, although it is likely that he was responsible for some important tile-pavements of the 1560s. His work, typified by a signed plate with the subject of *Alexander and Roxanne* (*c.* 1540–50; Paris, Petit Pal.), is characterized by a stylized linearity and somewhat awkward spatial conception.

BIBLIOGRAPHY

L. De-Mauri: *Le maioliche di Deruta* (Milan, 1924)

C. Fiocco and G. Gherardi: 'Contributo allo studio della ceramica derutese', *Faenza*, lxix (1983), pp. 90–93

Ceramiche umbre dal medioevo allo storicismo, i (Faenza, 1988)

WENDY M. WATSON

Derwent Wood, Francis. *See* WOOD, FRANCIS DERWENT.

De Saedeleer, Valerius (*b* Aalst, 4 Aug 1876; *d* Leupegem, 26 Sept 1946). Belgian painter. He learnt the art of weaving from his father and studied at academies in Aalst and Ghent and in the studio of Franz Courtens. After a turbulent period in Ghent, where he was active in anarchist circles, in 1898 he settled in LAETHEM-SAINT-MARTIN. There he had close ties with like-minded artists and was converted to Catholicism. He painted panoramic views of the flat landscape of the Leie in late autumn, winter and early spring, for example *Stormy Day* (1900; Ghent, Mus. S. Kst.). Small houses, hedges and finely-drawn branches stand out against the extensive landscape and vast skies. The contrast between sharply-drawn detail and panoramic views resembled the landscape vision of Pieter Bruegel I, whose work he saw at an exhibition of work by the Flemish 'Primitives' in Bruges in 1902. De Saedeleer considered *Calm Evening by the River* (1904; priv. col., see Walravens, pl. 2) to be the first of his Symbolist landscapes. These images of tranquillity and grandeur are a reflection of his own inner calm, absorption in nature and sense of eternity.

He achieved a timeless, unreal atmosphere by applying thin, smooth brushstrokes of colour with a dominance of white, green or grey.

In 1908 De Saedeleer settled in Tiegem, where he painted snowy landscapes, entirely devoid of people or animals, such as *Winter Plain* (1911; priv. col., for detail see Haesaerts, p. 142). He spent the period of World War I with his family in Wales. There he painted weaker landscapes, tending towards the decorative and sentimental, with a very thin, almost transparent layer of paint. On his return to Belgium in 1921 he settled in Etikhove. Here he recaptured in an increasingly sober manner the panoramic views of the undulating hilly landscape of Southern Flanders. He also set up a studio for weaving for his daughters (now the Centrum voor Kunst en Kunstambachten Valerius De Saedeleer). After a short stay in Oudenaarde, he settled in Leupegem. His landscapes influenced Gustave Van de Woestyne, Albert Servaes and Constant Permeke.

BIBLIOGRAPHY
A. De Ridder: *Laethem-Saint-Martin, colonie d'artistes* (Brussels and Paris, 1945)
J. Walravens: *Valerius De Saedeleer* (Antwerp, 1949)
P. Haesaerts: *Laethem-Saint-Martin: Le Village élu de l'art flamand* (Brussels, 1963, 5/1970)
Valerius De Saedeleer (exh. cat., Aalst, Stedel. Mus., 1967)

D. CARDYN-OOMEN

De Sanctis, Guglielmo (*b* Rome, 8 March 1829; *d* Rome, 6 March 1911). Italian painter, writer and teacher. He was one of the youngest pupils of Tommaso Minardi and was one of his most devoted, learning from him the principles of PURISMO. He began his career as a painter of religious subjects, executing such frescoes as *St Paul Preaching in Damascus* and the *Flight of St Paul* (both *c.* 1855; Rome, S Paolo fuori le Muri) and various altarpieces, including *St Vincent de Paul* (*c.* 1860; Rome, Apostolico Collegio Leoniano, Cappella della Regina Apostolorum) and *St Severus Preaching* (*c.* 1860; Porto Maurizio church). After the 1860s he began to paint historical scenes that appealed to the general taste for romanticized portrayals of Italy's past (e.g. *Michelangelo and Ferrucio*; Turin, Gal. Civ. A. Mod.). However, the only works that distinguish him from the most minor of his contemporaries are his portraits of royalty and society, including those of *King Umberto I* and *Queen Margherita* (both Rome, Pal. Senato) and of *Adele Castellani* (1891; Rome, G.N.A. Mod.). He achieved considerable recognition in his day, was President of the Società Amatori e Cultori delle Belle Arti and was responsible for organizing the Italian section of the Exposition Universelle in Antwerp in 1885. In 1900 he published *Tommaso Minardi e il suo tempo*, a biography of his teacher; he also wrote short biographies of such contemporaries as the composer Giaocchino Rossini and the novelist Alessandro Manzoni that appeared in *Memorie studi dal vero* (1901). These writings are evidence of De Sanctis's wide acquaintanceship with and role—albeit peripheral—in the culture of the Risorgimento. He had several pupils, including Onorato Carlandi (1848–1939) and Pietro Gabrini (1856–1926).

WRITINGS
Tommaso Minardi e il suo tempo (Rome, 1900)
Memorie studi dal vero (Rome, 1901)

Luciani
BIBLIOGRAPHY
L. Callari: *Storia dell'arte contemporanea italiana* (Rome, 1909), pp. 197, 199, 274, 280
Galleria Comunale d'Arte Moderna: Prima mostra di una selezione di opere, intro. by A. di Segni, cat. (Rome, 1963), p. 16
L. Mallé: *Galleria Civica d'Arte Moderna*, cat. (Turin, 1968), p. 132

Desanges, Louis William (*b* Bexley, Kent, 1822; *d c.* 1887). British painter of French descent. From an aristocratic émigré family, he went to school in Kent and studied painting in France and Italy before settling in London in 1842. He was unsuccessful in the competition held in 1843 for the decoration of the new Houses of Parliament, and the Royal Academy rejected such ambitious works as the *Excommunication of Robert, King of France, and his Queen, Berthe* (untraced). He subsequently abandoned history painting for the more lucrative business of painting portraits of society ladies. His first work at the Academy, *Portrait of an English Lady* (1846; untraced), owed much to Ingres in its modelling and treatment of texture. Desanges was a member of the Association for the Free Exhibition of Modern Art in the late 1840s. He exhibited at the Royal Academy until 1877, though he did not receive any honours from that institution. In the late 1850s he embarked on a series of portraits of soldiers and sailors who had been awarded the recently instituted Victoria Cross for their actions during the Crimean War and Indian Mutiny. The series was begun under the aegis of the Prince of Wales, later Edward VII, but was financed by the artist, who was presumably inspired by patriotic sentiments and a desire for recognition as a painter of important national subjects. The paintings were on display at the Crystal Palace by 1862. Numerous moves to acquire the collection for the nation failed. It was given to Wantage Town Council and later dispersed; among the works from the series now held at the National Army Museum, London, is *Private Sims Winning the Victoria Cross*, an idealized representation of a soldier saving the life of a superior officer.

BIBLIOGRAPHY
H. Blackburn: *Academy Notes* (London, 1877–8), p. 26
J. Hichberger: 'Democratising Glory: The Victoria Cross Series of Louis Desanges', *Oxford A. J.*, vii/2 (1985), pp. 45–51

JOAN HICHBERGER

Desargues, Gérard [Girard] (*b* Lyon, 2 March 1591; *d* ?Paris, before 8 Oct 1661). French mathematician, engineer and theorist. He settled at an early age in Paris, where he associated with such intellectuals as Marin Mersenne and Etienne Pascal; the latter's son, Blaise Pascal, claimed to be Desargues's disciple and was interested in his geometry of conic sections. Desargues was particularly interested in building techniques that involved the application of scientific knowledge, for example for the draught of chimneys, on which he corresponded with Mersenne and René Descartes, and lifting pumps, the subject of a proposal approved by the city of Paris in 1626, in which a series of fountains to clean the streets was planned. In 1636 he published a treatise on perspective, but he subsequently concentrated on architecture, including a design proposal for the Hôtel de Ville, Lyon. He also became interested in stonecutting (stereotomy), publishing a treatise on the subject in 1640. He used this specialized knowledge when building staircases, which were greatly admired by his contemporaries. Examples (all destr.) include the stairs of the north wing in the courtyard of the château of Vizille, Isère (1653), interior staircases at the Palais Cardinal, the Hôtel de Turenne and the Hôtel de L'Hôpital (all Paris), and the staircases in the house he built on the Rue de Cléry for a M. Roland and in another on the Rue des Bernardins. Two of these staircases are recorded in plan in François Blondel's *Cours d'architecture* (1675–98). The skill of these designs derived from Desargues's mastery of perspective effects. In the Rue de Cléry house, for example, he sited the staircase in a square stairwell, which the first flight traversed diagonally to reach a landing located in the corner opposite that of the entrance, the ascent then continuing to the right or left, following the walls of the stairwell.

WRITINGS

Méthode universelle de mettre en perspective les objets donnés...sans employer aucun point qui soit hors du champs de l'ouvrage (Paris, 1636)
Traité des coniques: Brouillon project d'une attente aux événemens des rencontres d'une cone avec un plan (Paris, 1639)
La Pratique du trait à preuves pour la coupe des pierres en l'architecture (Paris, 1640)

BIBLIOGRAPHY

M. Poudra, ed.: *Oeuvres de Desargues*, 2 vols (Paris, 1864) [i, all treatises by Desargues; ii, corr. and miscellanea]
L. Hautecoeur: *Architecture classique* (1943–57)
A. Machabey: 'Gérard Desargues, géomètre et musicien', *Rev. Soc. Etud. XVIIe Siècle*, xxi–xxii (1954), pp. 396–402
R. Taton: 'Documents nouveaux concernant Desargues', *Archvs Int. Hist. Sci.*, xvi (1958), pp. 620–30
——: *L'Oeuvre mathématique de Desargues* (Paris, 1961)

JEAN-PIERRE BABELON

Desbois, Jules (*b* Parcay-les-Pins, Maine-et-Loire, 20 Dec 1851; *d* Autheuil, Paris, 2 Oct 1935). French sculptor. He studied at the Ecole des Beaux-Arts under Pierre-Jules Cavelier, and made his Salon début with a head of *Orpheus* in 1875. His exhibit of 1877, *Othryades* (untraced), was bought by the state. Around this time he met Rodin in the studio of Eugène Legrain (1837–1915), where both Desbois and Rodin were assisting with the ornamental sculpture for the Palais du Trocadéro. After spending two years in the United States in the studio of John Quincy Adams Ward, Desbois returned to France. He collaborated with Rodin on several major works including the *Burghers of Calais*, and, at certain points, there is close correspondence between their works. *Misery* (wood, 1894; Nancy, Mus. B.-A.), an aged, emaciated female figure, may be compared with Rodin's *La Vieille Heaulmière*. More typical of Desbois's production is the massive sensualism of his *Leda* (1891; marble version, Luxembourg, Mus. Etat; bronze version, Stockholm, Nmus.). From the mid-1890s he aligned himself with the group of decorative sculptors whose works were sold through Siegfried Bing's shop, La Maison de l'Art Nouveau. His 'art pewters' were exhibited at the Salon of the Champ de Mars in 1896, and at the exhibition of the Société des Six in 1899. His vigorous monumentalism is in evidence in the two allegorical figures that he executed for the façade of the Hôtel de Ville, Calais (1911–18). From 1924 to 1929 Desbois was the Vice-president of the Société Nationale des Beaux-Arts.

BIBLIOGRAPHY

J. Mercier: *Jules Desbois: Illustre, statuaire, angevin* (Longué, 1978)
De Carpeaux à Matisse (exh. cat., ed. D. Vieville; Calais, Mus. B.-A.; Boulogne, Mus. Mun.; Paris, Mus. Rodin; 1982–3)
La Sculpture française au XIXe siècle (exh. cat., ed. A. Pingeot; Paris, Grand Pal., 1986)

PHILIP WARD-JACKSON

Desboutin, Marcellin(-Gilbert) (*b* Cérilly, nr Moulins, 26 Aug 1823; *d* Nice, 18 Feb 1902). French painter, printmaker, collector and writer. Born into a wealthy, aristocratic family, he showed an early talent for drawing but initially trained and registered as a lawyer, though he never practised. In 1845 he entered the Ecole des Beaux-Arts in Paris, studying first under the sculptor Louis-Jules Etex (1810–89) and from 1847–8 under Thomas Couture. From 1849 to 1854 he travelled—to England, Belgium, the Netherlands and finally to Italy, where in 1854 he bought the historic Villa dell'Ombrellino in Bellosguardo outside Florence. He lived there until his return to Paris in 1872, building up an art collection and making engravings. The content of his purportedly large collection has not been established, though he is known to have had a particular love for early Italian Renaissance works and also paintings from the Spanish school. While in Italy he wrote several plays, of which one, *Maurice de Saxe*, was performed at the Comédie Française, Paris, in 1870. Having exhausted his inherited fortune, he returned to Paris in August 1872, now forced to work as a printmaker for a living. He soon became involved with the group of young Impressionists who met at the Café Guerbois and later at the Café de la Nouvelle Athènes in Paris. Degas included him in his painting the *Absinthe Drinker* (1876; Paris, Mus. d'Orsay) together with the actress Ellen Andrée. Desboutin produced several engraved portraits of his Impressionist friends, particularly in drypoint, as in *Renoir* (1877; see Clément-Janin, p. 216). He also painted such works as *The Musician* (1874; Moulins, Mus. Moulins). From 1880 to 1888 he lived in Nice, returning to Paris in 1890, when he was a founder-member of the Société Nationale des Beaux-Arts. His painted portrait of *Josephin Péladan* (1891; Angers, Mus. B.-A.) was included in the Salon de la Rose + Croix of 1893. He returned to Nice in 1896 and remained there until his death.

BIBLIOGRAPHY

N. Clément-Janin: *La Curieuse Vie de Marcellin Desboutin, peintre, graveur, poète* (Paris, 1922)
The Realist Tradition: French Painting and Drawing, 1830–1900 (exh. cat. by G. P. Weisberg, Cleveland, Mus. A.; New York, Brooklyn Mus.; St Louis, A. Mus.; Glasgow A.G. & Mus.; 1980–81), pp. 190, 256–7, 286–7

□

Descamps, Jean-Baptiste (*b* Dunkirk, 14 June 1715; *d* Rouen, 14 July 1791). French painter, writer and dealer. He began his artistic training in Dunkirk, continuing it in Antwerp. In Paris, Descamps frequented the studios of Nicolas Lancret and Nicolas de Largillierre and drew at the Académie Royale. He later settled in Rouen and gathered around him a circle of pupils to whom he taught drawing. By 1749 teaching had become formalized on the model of the Académie Royale in Paris and Descamps's institution was granted the title of Ecole Royale, Gratuite et Académique de Dessin, de Peinture, de Sculpture et d'Architecture. It became the model for other provincial academies.

In April 1764 Descamps was made a member of the Académie Royale in Paris on submission of the painting *Peasant Girl in her Kitchen* (Paris, Ecole N. Sup. B.-A.). He was admitted to the Académie as a 'peintre dans le genre des sujets populaires'. His paintings, which typically depict scenes of daily life, were influenced by the work of Chardin and Greuze. He exhibited several genre paintings at the Salon of 1765. The main body of his work is now in the Musée des Beaux-Arts, Dunkirk (six *Allegories*), and the Musée des Beaux-Arts, Rouen (two *Self-portraits*). He is known to have dealt in Old Master paintings, particularly of the Dutch and Flemish schools. His most important writings on art are *La Vie des peintres flamands, allemands et hollandais* (1753–63) and the *Voyage pittoresque de la Flandre et du Brabant* (1759). Although they contain many inaccuracies they were very successful in their day. In 1767 Descamps produced a work on the importance of drawing schools in art education, for which he was awarded a prize by the Académie Royale.

WRITINGS

La Vie des peintres flamands, allemands et hollandais, 4 vols (Paris, 1753–63)

Voyage pittoresque de la Flandre et du Brabant (Paris, 1759)

Sur l'utilité des établissements d'écoles gratuites de dessin (Paris, 1767)

BIBLIOGRAPHY

J.-B.-M.-A. Descamps: *Notice historique sur J.-B. Descamps par un de ses élèves* (Rouen, 1807)

E. Chesneau: *La Peinture au 19e siècle* (Paris, 1883)

A. Rostand: *J.-B. Descamps* (Caen, 1936)

Diderot et l'art de Boucher à David. Les Salons: 1759–81 (exh. cat., ed. M.-C. Sahut and N. Volle; Paris, Grand Pal., 1984–5), p. 170

AMAL ASFOUR

Descartes, René (*b* La Haye, Indre-et-Loire, 31 March 1596; *d* Stockholm, 11 Feb 1650). French philosopher. He studied at the Jesuit college of La Flèche and served in the army in the Netherlands, Bavaria and elsewhere in Europe. He began his scientific and philosophical investigations during this period. He settled in the Netherlands in 1629. Apart from his early *Compendium musicae* (composed 1618; pubd 1650), Descartes hardly referred to beauty or the arts. Nevertheless, the treatise entitled *Les Passions de l'âme* (1649) profoundly affected the art of portraying the passions; and the philosophical method defended and exemplified in the *Discours de la méthode* (1637) and the posthumously published *Regulae ad directionem ingenii* (1701) exercised a powerful influence on the aesthetics of the Academy, despite Descartes's concession that poetry 'is a gift of the mind rather than the fruit of study' (*Discours*, pt 1). A Renaissance creation, the Academy was initially an informal setting for philosophical and literary debate, but in the 17th century it became the institutional framework for the promotion of classicism, in theory and in practice. The Cartesian model of science as a deductive system, constructed out of long and intricate chains of pellucid reasoning, and ultimately founded on the fixed and unassailable certainty of a single principle—the existence of the self—was echoed in particular by the requirement that history painting should display a rational unity controlled by the central dramatic idea, and in general

underwrote the analytical and legislative zeal of the academicians.

Perhaps the most significant contribution of French academicism to art theory was the supreme importance it accorded to the portrayal of emotion. This is already attested in Poussin's letters and conversations and to some extent may be seen as a corollary of the pre-eminence of history painting. However, it was CHARLES LE BRUN, co-founder of the French Académie Royale de Peinture et de Sculpture in 1648, who, in his lectures and published works (especially the posthumous *Méthode pour apprendre à dessiner les passions*, 1698), provided a fantastically detailed physiognomic catalogue of the passions, which represented the culmination of the Académie Royale's attempt to formalize the art of painting. Le Brun's catalogue was based directly on his study of Descartes's *Les Passions de l'âme*.

Les Passions de l'âme was the outcome of Descartes's correspondence with Princess Elizabeth of Bohemia and her dissatisfaction with his explanation of the interaction between mind and body. In *Les Passions de l'âme*, Descartes maintained that, although it is 'united to all the parts of the body conjointly . . . ., the soul has its principal seat in the small gland located in the middle of the brain. From there it radiates through the rest of the body by means of the animal spirits, the nerves, and even the blood' (ss 30, 34). The *passions de l'âme*, 'joy, anger and the like', are those impressions made on the soul that, although they are caused by 'the objects that stimulate our nerves' (s. 25), seem to us to be independent of anything beyond the soul. These feelings and emotions are aroused in the soul when the spirits 'produce in the gland a particular movement that is ordained by nature to make the soul feel this passion' (s. 36), and the physical symptoms of emotion—physiological, physiognomic and behavioural—are simultaneously caused by the effects of the spirits on the nerves and venous system.

While the first part of *Les Passions de l'âme* is devoted principally to the relation between mind and body, the second and third propound an elaborate taxonomy of the emotions and describe in detail the physical processes that cause both the emotions themselves and their physical symptoms. Wonder, love, hatred, desire, joy and sadness are designated as primitive passions, 'the genera of which all the others are the species' (s. 149). Le Brun's theory of expression, which incorporates Descartes's distinction between primitive and composite emotions, was explicitly founded on Descartes's mechanistic physiology. The human body, and above all the human face, examined in the uncomfortable but unequivocal light of reason, are revealed as a supremely intricate and finely tuned register of the effects of emotional stimuli, mechanically connected with the soul, but scarcely animated by it.

WRITINGS

Discours de la méthode (Leiden, 1637)

Les Passions de l'âme (Amsterdam and Paris, 1649)

Compendium musicae (Utrecht, 1650)

Regulae ad directionem ingenii (Amsterdam, 1701)

C. Adam and P. Tannery, eds: *Oeuvres de Descartes*, 12 vols (Paris, 1897–1913, rev. 1964–76)

The Philosophical Writings of Descartes, trans. J. Cottingham, R. Stoothoff and D. Murdoch, 2 vols (Cambridge, 1985)

BIBLIOGRAPHY
E. Krantz: *Essai sur l'esthétique de Descartes* (Paris, 1882)
A. Fontaine: *Les Doctrines d'art en France* (Paris, 1909)
E. Cassirer: *Die Philosophie der Aufklärung* (Tübingen, 1932; Eng. trans., Princeton, 1951)
R. W. Lee: 'Ut pictura poesis: The Humanistic Theory of Painting', *A. Bull.*, xxii (1940), pp. 197–269
G. Sebba: *Bibliographia Cartesiana: A Critical Guide to the Descartes Literature, 1800–1960* (The Hague, 1964)

JOHN HYMAN

Deschamps [des Champs]. French family of architects. The name Deschamps has been attached to seven major late 13th-century and early 14th-century cathedrals in the French Midi, either directly by documentation or indirectly by stylistic comparison. According to a lost copy of an inscription on his tomb slab (destr.), Jean Deschamps began Clermont-Ferrand Cathedral in 1248. He was named first master at Narbonne Cathedral by a contract dated 1286; finally, *magister Johannes de Campis* appeared among witnesses to oaths sworn to the chapter of Clermont-Ferrand in 1287. Pierre Deschamps was called *magistri edificii Claromontensis* in a Clermont dispute of 1357, and a will made in Rodez in 1345 mentions a wife of Pierre Deschamps, son of Master Pierre Deschamps of Clermont. The Clermont Pierre has been assumed to be the son and successor of Jean Deschamps at Clermont. Bertrandus de Campus is established at Bordeaux Cathedral in 1320 by a document of 1579, in which he is called *magister operum ecclesiarum Burdigale.*

From these references historians have constructed the career of 'Jean Deschamps' and the existence of a Deschamps family. Limoges Cathedral has been attributed to Jean Deschamps by comparison with Clermont-Ferrand; the cathedrals of Toulouse and Rodez by comparison with Narbonne; and Agen by comparison with Toulouse. Similarities in plan, elevation and structure justify grouping these buildings, but differences in the form and character of detailing argue against a single architect. Rather, they may be divided into two groups: Clermont and Limoges, then Narbonne, Rodez and Toulouse. The attribution of Agen to Jean Deschamps is tenuous. Further, 38 years separate the references to Jean Deschamps at Clermont and Narbonne. This and the different character of the two buildings suggest that, at most, Clermont's Jean Deschamps may have been the father of Narbonne's Jean Deschamps. Nor is it certain, despite the contract of 1286, that Jean Deschamps was the original architect of Narbonne; the cathedral was begun in 1272, and a document of 1271 implies that 'masters' of the cathedral were to be consulted about the selected construction site, which suggests that they were already present. Foundations mentioned in a document of 1284 may be variously interpreted, and the real question is whether the contract of 1286 refers to the original or to a subsequent master. In fact, the progress of construction, changes in detail and drawings engraved in the floor of the axial chapel suggest that Jean Deschamps was the second architect of Narbonne Cathedral, a visiting architect who was simultaneously supervising construction at Rodez Cathedral and who may have been involved with Toulouse. As for Pierre, the reference *magistri edificii Claromontensis* might indicate that he was master of the works, but it does not necessarily

make him either Jean's son or his successor. Bertrand was master at Bordeaux Cathedral; he is linked to the other Deschamps primarily by his name, and similarities between the upper choir at Bordeaux and that at Rodez, a building for which the original scheme (by comparison with Narbonne) may be attributed to the younger Jean Deschamps. There were, therefore, probably four Deschamps: Jean the father, Jean the son, Pierre and Bertrand. The two Jeans and Bertrand were definitely architects, masters of at least four major buildings. Pierre may have been an architect. If, as seems likely, they were related, they represent an architectural family with great significance for the development of southern French and Late Gothic architecture.

The 'Deschamps buildings', combining as they do a northern French cathedral type and Rayonnant linearity with southern French austerity and emphasis on plane, introduced a new interpretation of Gothic into the French Midi. Austerity and control, dying mouldings, sharp, crisp line, interpenetrating planes and angularity, curve and countercurve, and a willingness to minimize divisions, thus emphasizing the architectural space, provided an alternative to the indigenous southern Gothic style and anticipated many characteristics of Late Gothic.

BIBLIOGRAPHY
Thieme–Becker: 'Deschamps, Jean'
D. Dourif: 'Le Tombeau de Jean Deschamps', *Mém. Acad. Sci., B.-Lett. & A. Clermont-Ferrand*, xxv (1883), pp. 96–100
G. Rouchon: 'Notes sur les architectes de la cathédrale de Clermont', *Mémoires publiés par la Faculté des Lettres de Clermont à l'occasion du centenaire de sa fondation* (1910), pp. 319–28
H. du Ranquet: 'Les Architectes de la cathédrale de Clermont-Ferrand', *Bull. Mnmtl.*, lxxvi (1912), pp. 70–124
L. Sigal: 'Contribution à l'histoire de la cathédrale de Saint-Just de Narbonne', *Bull. Comm. Archéol. Narbonne*, xiv (1921), pp. 12–153
E. Mâle: 'L'Architecture gothique du Midi de la France', *Rev. Deux Mondes*, n.s. 9, xxxi (1926), pp. 826–57
E. Lambert: 'L'Ancienne Cathédrale Saint-Etienne d'Agen', *Abbayes et cathédrales du Sud-Ouest* (Toulouse, 1958), pp. 127–47
J. Gardelles: *La Cathédrale Saint-André de Bordeaux* (Bordeaux, 1963)
J. Bousquet: 'La Construction de la cathédrale gothique (1277–1400): Les Premiers Changements de parti et le problème du pilier rond', *VIIe centenaire de la cathédrale de Rodez. Communications présentées à la séance de la Société des Lettres, Sciences et Arts de l'Aveyron: Aveyron, 1977*, pp. 19–65
M. T. Davis: *The Cathedral of Clermont-Ferrand: History of its Construction, 1248–1512* (diss., U. Michigan, 1979)
——: 'The Choir of the Cathedral of Clermont-Ferrand: The Beginning of Construction and the Work of Jean Deschamps', *J. Soc. Archit. Hist.*, xl/3 (1981), pp. 181–202

VIVIAN PAUL

Deschamps, Léon(-Julien) (*b* Paris, 26 May 1860; *d* after 1913). French medallist and sculptor. He studied under the French sculptors Augustin-Alexandre Dumont, Emile Thomas (1817–82), Hippolyte Moreau and Léon Delhomme (1841–95). He started exhibiting at the Salon Champs-Elysées in 1887 and was made a Sociétaire des Artistes Français in 1896. At the turn of the century be became a professor at the Ecole Supérieure Professionelle Estienne in Paris. Deschamps's output consists mainly of relief plaques and medals depicting allegorical subjects and portraits, such as the relief plaque of a young girl *Renée* (1891; see Forrer, i, p. 567), showing the influence of flowing Art Nouveau forms, and *Old Age* (1897; see Forrer, i, p. 568).

BIBLIOGRAPHY
Bénézit; Forrer; Thieme–Becker

Deschler, Joachim (*b c.* 1500; *d* ?Vienna, after Oct 1571). German sculptor and medallist. He is known to have married in Nuremberg in 1532 and to have become a citizen in 1537. He was recorded in 1547 as having made a two-year study journey that took him to Venice and Rome, from which he brought back numerous drawings and works of art; he was also said to be skilled in working marble. Except for this journey, Deschler mostly remained in Nuremberg; only the Imperial Diets were to him worth a journey, in order to obtain commissions, mainly for portrait medals. In 1534 he received a commission from Archduke Maximilian (later Emperor Maximilian II), and in 1548 from King Ferdinand of Bohemia and Hungary (later Emperor Ferdinand I); it was probably he who ordered the costly artefact that Deschler's son delivered to Prague in 1553: the price paid was 1000 taler.

From the end of the 1550s Deschler lived in Vienna, where, as Maximilian's court sculptor, he received a fixed salary until his death, the last payment being made in October 1571. Deschler's achievements in the field of medal art were remarkable: 115 pieces, produced between 1533 and 1570 (e.g. London, V&A; Nuremberg, Ger. Nmus.), are ascribed to him, and several stone models (e.g. London, BM; Paris, Louvre) also survive. The earliest medals portray Nuremberg citizens and members of the Franconian nobility; the later ones, members of the Habsburg family and Viennese citizens. An entry of 1659 in the inventory of Archduke Leopold William suggests that he also produced richly decorated ornamental pieces. The 'settings' mentioned there are thought to be frames that Deschler had decorated with costly images. Habich also ascribes to him the fine alabaster bust of the corpulent Elector Palatine *Ottheinrich*, with two medallions set in the pedestal (Paris, Louvre).

BIBLIOGRAPHY
Forrer; *NDB*; *ÖKL*; Thieme–Becker
G. W. K. Lochner: *Des Johann Neudörfer Nachrichten von Künstlern und Werkleuten aus dem Jahre 1547* (Vienna, 1875), p. 116
G. Habich: 'Joachim Deschler: Der Meister der Otto-Heinrich-Büste im Louvre', *Münchn. Jb. Bild. Kst*, ix (1914–15), pp. 67–86
G. Probszt: 'Zwei unbekannte Medaillen Joachim Deschlers', *Archv Medaillen- & Plakettenknd.*, iv (1923–4), p. 142
V. Katz: 'Die Signaturen Joachim Deschlers', *Berliner Münzblätter*, 317 (1929), pp. 454–6
G. Habich: *Die deutschen Schaumünzen des 16. Jahrhunderts*, i (Munich, 1931), pp. 221–35
M. Bernhart: 'Kunst und Künstler der Nürnberger Schaumünze des 16. Jahrhunderts', *Mitt. Bayer. Numi. Ges.*, liv (1936), pp. 1–64, 20–21
HERMANN MAUÉ

Descho da parto. Tray used in medieval Italy for carrying gifts to a woman who had given birth. Both *deschi da parto* and the related maiolica accouchement services (*vasi puerperali*), which were offered to women in confinement, were usually painted with suitable subjects.

Deschwanden, Melchior Paul von (*b* Stans, 10 Jan 1811; *d* Stans, 25 Feb 1881). Swiss painter. He first studied in Stans with the amateur artist Louis Viktor von Deschwanden (*fl* 1820s), the husband of his cousin, and, after 1825, in Zug, where he was a pupil of Johann Kaspar Moos (1774–1835). Between 1827 and 1830 he studied with the Protestant Romantic circle in Zurich, although himself a Catholic, working first with Daniel Albert Freudweiler (1793–1827), and then with Johann Kaspar Schinz (1797–1832). In 1830 he studied at the Akademie in Munich under Peter Joseph Cornelius, Heinrich Maria von Hess, Clemens Zimmerman (1788–1869) and Julius Schnorr von Carolsfeld.

After a period of recurrent pulmonary illness, Deschwanden spent the years 1838 to 1840 in Italy: this proved a decisive experience for him. In 1838 he attended the Accademia in Florence, where his work was highly praised. His formal and rather cerebral painting, *Elysium*, brought him his first major success. In December 1839 he went to Rome, where he became a member of the circle of young artists around Friedrich Overbeck. Deschwanden's admiration for Raphael soon led him to study the masters of the Quattrocento, above all Fra Angelico, in whom he found purity, simplicity and innocence. A written recommendation from Ludwig Vogel enabled Deschwanden to study with Overbeck, and he soon established himself as the ablest draughtsman among Overbeck's pupils. Under Overbeck's guidance, he began to plan the composition of his first important commission, the altarpiece for the Peterskapelle in Lucerne.

During the 1840s, after his return to Stans, Deschwanden did much work as a portrait painter. In his portraits he tended to idealize the sitter but never lost his characteristic sense of detail. Deschwanden's real gifts lay in drawing, however, and painterly qualities are generally lacking in his work. After 1850, influenced by the strong religious beliefs of Overbeck, he turned away from portrait painting in favour of other genres. He had a marked sense of religious mission, and his eagerness to meet the demand for inexpensive devotional pictures led to a certain carelessness in execution. Over 2000 paintings by Deschwanden are known, and those from his middle and later years are very uneven in quality. His work is most successful where it is combined with contemporary, classicizing architecture, as in his earlier paintings and many of his altarpieces. This is especially the case at the Peterskapelle in Lucerne. Like Overbeck and his circle, Deschwanden also undertook commissions for large-scale mural decoration: notable among these is his *Day of Judgement* in the choir vault of the Gothic church of St Oswald in Zug (1865). From 1846 Deschwanden maintained a large studio in Stans where his pupils included his cousin, Theodor von Deschwanden (1826–61), Joseph A. Balmer (1828–74) and Karl Georg Kaiser (1843–1916).

BIBLIOGRAPHY
A. Kuhn: *Melchior Paul von Deschwanden: Ein Leben im Dienste der Kunst und der Religion* (Einsiedeln, 1882)
O. Pestalozzi: 'Die Unterwaldner Maler Paul und Theodor von Deschwanden', *Neujbhl. Kstges. Zurich* (1883)
B. M. Lierheimer: 'Melchior Paul von Deschwanden's künstlerische Entwicklung', *Jber. Kant. Lehranstalt Sarnen* (1894–5)
Zur religiösen Schweizer Malerei im 19. Jahrhundert (exh. cat., Lucerne, Kstmus., 1985)
MATTHIAS FREHNER

Descourtis, Charles-Melchior (*b* Paris, 1753; *d* Paris, 1820). French printmaker. He was a pupil of Jean-François

Janinet and, like him, specialized in the production of colour prints using aquatint and wash-manner. Among his earliest known works is a series of four engravings of views of Paris and Rome after paintings by Pierre Antoine de Machy, which appeared in 1784. He collaborated with Janinet on the illustrations for *Vues remarquables des montagnes de la Suisse* (1785; see Roux and Pognon, no. 7), which were engraved after several artists. He is best known, however, for his four colour prints after the genre scenes of Nicolas-Antoine Taunay, notably the *Village Wedding* (1785; RP 8) and its pendant, the *Village Fair* (1788; RP 10). The subtle green tones of the landscape setting, complementing the white and red of the small figures, successfully convey the gentle mood of Taunay's rural scenes. The second pair, the *Tambourine* (RP 12) and the *Brawl* (RP 13), both animated, slightly grotesque compositions, are less finely executed. Such prints of genre scenes were avidly collected by contemporaries. Descourtis also produced a number of portrait engravings, including *Princess Wilhelmina of Prussia* (1791; see 1985 exh. cat., no. 128). From the later 1790s he engraved numerous works after Jean-Frédéric Schall, notably the *Lover Surprised* (RP 16) and the *Peeping Toms* (RP 17), as well as a series of illustrations to Bernardin de Saint-Pierre's novel *Paul et Virginie* (1788).

BIBLIOGRAPHY
M. Roux and R. Pognon: *Inventaire du fonds français, XVIIIe siècle*, Paris, Bib. N., Cab. Est. cat., vii (Paris, 1951), pp. 61–6 [RP]
Graveurs français de la seconde moitié du XVIIIe siècle (exh. cat., ed. R. Bacou; Paris, Louvre, 1985), pp. 98–101

EMMA BARKER

Deseine [De Seine]. French family of artists. The brothers (1) Claude-André Deseine and (2) Louis-Pierre Deseine, both sculptors, came from a family of carpenters. Their younger brother, Louis-Etienne Deseine (*b* 1756), became an architect, and their sister, Madeleine-Anne Deseine (1758–1839), was a painter and draughtsman as well as a sculptor; among her works is a bust of *Louis-Pierre Deseine* (terracotta, 1807; Paris, Carnavalet).

(1) Claude-André Deseine (*b* Paris, 6 April 1740; *d* Petit Gentilly, Val-de-Marne, 30 Dec 1823). Sculptor. Although deaf and mute, he studied from 1775 at the Académie Royale, Paris. He subsequently pursued a moderately successful career as a portrait sculptor, working in a style that combined Neo-classical sobriety with a personal ability to capture an expressive likeness. Among his earlier works, his bust of *Pierre Victor Besenval de Bronstatt* (plaster; Paris, priv. col.) and a statuette of *Jean-Jacques Rousseau* (untraced) were exhibited at the Salon de la Correspondance of 1782. During the French Revolution he made a number of busts of Republican leaders, including *Honoré Gabriel Riqueti, Comte de Mirabeau* (plaster, 1791; Rennes, Mus. B.-A. & Archéol.), *Le Peletier de Saint-Fargeau* (marble, 1793; Bourges, Mus. Berry), *Jean-Paul Marat* (1793; untraced) and *Maximilien Robespierre* (terracotta, 1793; Visille, Mus. Révolution Fr.). In 1797 he executed a bust of *Napoleon Bonaparte* (untraced), but he seems to have retired from artistic life *c.* 1801.

BIBLIOGRAPHY
G. Le Châtelier: 'Deseine le sourd muet', *Rev. Gen. Ens. Sourds Muets*, iii (1903)
F. Le Châtelier: *Louis Le Châtelier et Elizabeth Durand, leurs ascendants, leurs descendants* (Nancy, 1972)
P. Bordes: 'Le *Mirabeau* de Claude-André Deseine', *Rev. Louvre*, ii (1976), pp. 61–6

(2) Louis-Pierre Deseine (*b* Paris, 30 July 1749; *d* Paris, 11 Oct 1822). Sculptor, brother of (1) Claude-André Deseine. Like his brother, he studied at the Académie Royale, where he was a pupil of Louis-Philippe Mouchy and Augustin Pajou. In 1780 he won the Prix de Rome, and from 1781 to 1784 he was in Rome at the Académie de France, where he absorbed the principles of Neo-classicism and showed an interest in sketching scenes from popular life (sketchbook in Paris, Louvre). Both these tendencies, the idealizing and the realistic, were to remain a feature of his work, finding resolution in his fine portrait sculptures.

Following his return to Paris, in 1789 Deseine became Premier Sculpteur to Louis-Joseph de Bourbon, Prince de Condé, having earlier executed for him marble statues of *Bacchus* and *Hebe* (Chantilly, Mus. Condé). In 1791 he was received (*reçu*) as one of the last members of the Académie Royale, presenting the marble statuette *Mucius Scaevola Enduring Pain* (Paris, Louvre). He maintained an active practice as a portrait sculptor, producing busts of *Louis XVI* (plaster; Paris, Carnavalet) and the *Dauphin* (later Louis XVII; marble, 1790; Versailles, Château) and of contemporary political figures such as *Jean-Sylvain Bailly* (plaster, 1789), the lawyer *J.-A. Thouret* (plaster, 1791; both Paris, Carnavalet) and *François-Armand Saige* (marble, 1789; Bordeaux, Mus. A. Déc.). He also provided posthumous portraits, such as those for the Musée des Monuments Français, Paris, of *Michel Eyquem de Montaigne* (marble, 1819; Bordeaux, Mus. A. Déc.) and *Johann Joachim Winckelmann* (terracotta, 1800, Versailles, Orangerie; marble, 1819, Toulouse, Mus. Augustins). He also produced monumental works for many of the major sculptural projects of the Directory and the Empire, including statues of *Prudence* for the Senate (1803–5; untraced), *Michel de l'Hospital* for the Palais Bourbon (stone, 1807–11; *in situ*) and *Jean Portalis* for the Conseil d'Etat (marble, 1808–12; Versailles, Château). He was less successful as a sculptor of funerary monuments; in his tombs for *Jean-Baptiste de Belloy* (marble, 1808; Paris, Notre-Dame) and *Louis-Antoine-Henri de Bourbon, Prince de Condé and Duc d'Enghien* (marble, 1816–22; château of Vincennes, Queen's Chapel), for instance, he concentrated on the elaboration of the individual figures to the detriment of the compositional design. His religious works include five plaster reliefs illustrating the *Passion of Christ* (1801–5) and a plaster *Entombment* (1807) for St Roch, Paris, which show the influence of Italian Renaissance prototypes.

An ardent polemicist, Deseine defended the Académie Royale when it was on the point of being dissolved in 1790–91, and he strongly supported its re-establishment in 1816. During the Revolution, on finding himself excluded from the Panthéon building project by Antoine Quatremère de Quincy, he conducted a polemical campaign against him, and he was also one of those falsely considered to have been responsible for the downfall of Alexandre Lenoir, because of his attacks in 1802–3 on the Musée des Petits Augustins.

BIBLIOGRAPHY

G. Le Châtelier: *Louis-Pierre Deseine statuaire* (Paris, 1906)

J. Thirion: 'Le Monument funéraire du Cardinal de Belloy à Notre-Dame de Paris', *Bull. Archéol. Cté Trav. Hist. & Sci.*, iii (1967), pp. 227–52

A.-M. de Lapparent: *Louis-Pierre Deseine, statuaire, 1749–1822: La Vie, son oeuvre* (diss., Paris, Ecole Louvre, 1985)

ANNE-MARIE DE LAPPARENT

Desenfans, Noel Joseph (*b* Avesnes-sur-Helpe, near St Quentin, Dec 1744; *d* London, 8 July 1807). French dealer and collector, active in London. He was educated at the universities of Douai and Paris and published a number of works in the 1760s, including an essay on education and a stage comedy. In 1769 he moved to London as a private tutor and in 1776 married Margaret Morris (1731–1813), a woman older than himself and with private means. From this period Desenfans became active as a picture dealer, holding a number of important sales at Christie's and privately. In 1784 he moved into a large house at the north end of Charlotte (now Hallam) Street, which he used for the display of his personal collection. He was assisted in his activities by Francis Bourgeois, a younger man whom he had adopted as a child, and who shared his enthusiasm for collecting. He also had close links with Paris, collaborating with J. B. P. Le Brun over a number of purchases.

In 1790 Desenfans was invited by the King of Poland, Stanislav Augustus, to make a collection of paintings suitable for a national gallery in Warsaw and was awarded the title of Polish Consul General in London. Over the next five years Desenfans and Bourgeois assembled an important group of pictures, buying at major London sales of French aristocratic collections such as that of Charles-Antoine de Calonne. In 1795, however, Poland was partitioned for the third and final time between Austria, Prussia and Russia, and Stanislav ceased to be a reigning monarch. Desenfans found himself left with some 150 pictures, for which he had not been paid.

Energetic efforts were made to dispose of this collection, including appeals to the Tsar of Russia, an invitation to the British Government to use it as the basis for a national gallery in London, and an auction in 1802. Many of the works were disposed of, but Desenfans retained a collection of his own. In his last years he was persuaded by Bourgeois of the desirability of keeping the remaining paintings together as a group and of adding to them to form a collection that would represent all the artists most admired at the time. These included Poussin's *Triumph of David* and Rubens's *Venus, Mars and Cupid* (both *c.* 1630; London, Dulwich Pict. Gal.). This group was to be left to an institution that would preserve and exhibit them to the public. In this object Desenfans was characteristic of his age, the foundation of such a collection being the subject of much discussion and propaganda in the early 19th century. His house in Charlotte Street had the character of a museum-habitation, of the kind seen at Sir John Soane's house in Lincoln's Inn Fields (later the Sir John Soane Museum).

On Desenfans's death he left his property jointly to his wife and to Bourgeois, with instructions that the latter should select an institution that would preserve and exhibit the paintings. The institution eventually chosen was Dulwich College. Though many of Desenfans's attributions have been revised, the collection is a rare and important survival of a period that witnessed intense activity in the acquisition of pictures in England.

Desenfans was well known for his role as an art politician and for his social aspirations, the latter being a prime motive in his collecting. His ambitions are to some extent realized by the mausoleum, an annexe to the Dulwich Gallery, where his remains lie.

WRITINGS

A Plan, Preceded by a Short Review of the Arts (London, 1799)

A Descriptive Catalogue of Some of the Pictures Purchased for His Majesty the Late King of Poland (London, 1802)

BIBLIOGRAPHY

J. Taylor: *Memoir of Noel Desenfans* (London, 1810)

P. Murray: *The Dulwich Picture Gallery: A Catalogue* (London, 1980)

G. Waterfield: *Collection for a King* (London, 1985)

GILES WATERFIELD

Désert de Retz. See RETZ, DÉSERT DE.

Déserteur, le. See BRUN, CHARLES-FRÉDÉRIC.

Desfossé & Karth. French wallpaper manufacturing company. It was founded in Paris in 1864 by Jules Desfossé (*d* 1889), who had been trained in the wallpaper business in Paris and in 1851 took over the Mader Frères factory in the Faubourg Saint-Antoine. In 1864 he took on his brother-in-law, Hippolyte Karth, as a partner and bought out the Clerc & Margeridon factory about 1866. The business continued to operate until it became part of the Isidore Leroy factory in 1947.

The Desfossé factory was known for high-quality work using both plates and machine-printing (examples in Paris, Mus. A. Déc). Its considerable reputation rested on its 'panoramic' wallpapers, based on images of nature, presented at the Exposition Universelle in Paris in 1855 and the International Exhibition in 1862 in London, for which the company had taken the innovative step of commissioning designs from such well-known artists as Thomas Couture and Auguste Clésinger on the theme of the Vices and the Virtues. The factory also printed a great number of other, highly elaborate designs. The Desfossé collection is part of the Leroy collection in the Musée des Arts Décoratifs, Paris.

BIBLIOGRAPHY

H. Clouzot and C. Follot: *Histoire du papier peint en France* (Paris, 1935), pp. 219–20

Le Mirage du luxe: Les Décors de papier peint (exh. cat., Rixheim, Mus. Pap. Peint, 1988)

O. Nouvel-Kammerer, ed.: *Papiers peints panoramiques* (Paris, 1990), p. 320

BERNARD JACQUÉ

Desfriches, Aignan-Thomas (*b* Orléans, 7 March 1715; *d* Orléans, 25 Dec 1800). French collector and painter. He briefly studied painting in Orléans under Jacques Dominé (1676–1752). In 1733 he moved to Paris, where his masters were Nicolas Bertin and Charles-Joseph Natoire. Having become director of the drawing school of Louis, Duc de Rohan-Chabot (1710–91), he met distinguished artists and collectors, including Joseph Vernet, Jean-Baptiste Descamps, Joseph-Marie Vien, Hubert Robert and Claude-Henri Watelet. Towards the end of the 1730s Desfriches returned to Orléans to direct his family's import business. He painted seven panels with views of the river Loiret for the dining-room of his country house, La Cartaudière, and made numerous topographical drawings, including a vast panorama of Orléans (Orléans, Mus. B.-A.). His early drawings were in lead or black chalk with highlights of coloured crayon and sepia or bistre washes. Later, working on *papier-tablette*, a grey-blue, coated drawing-paper he had invented, which permitted great delicacy of execution, he produced less finished drawings, many of which he mounted on wooden snuff-boxes and presented to friends.

Desfriches's work was influenced by Dutch landscapes: he travelled to the Netherlands in 1753 and by 1755 was in regular communication with dealers in Amsterdam. He purchased the bulk of his collection of Dutch paintings and drawings in Amsterdam in 1766 and acquired the rest through exchange with other collectors. The paintings he particularly admired (none of which can be easily identified) were landscapes by Jan van Goyen, Jacob van Ruisdael, Jan Wijnants and Esaias van de Velde. He was the friend and patron of Jean-Baptiste Perronneau and Jean-Siméon Chardin; of the latter's paintings he owned, among others, *Still-life with Dead Pheasant and Game Bag* (Berlin, Gemäldegal.) and *Dead Hare with Stocks and Onions* (Detroit, MI, Inst. A.). His 1778 inventory listed 114 paintings and sculptures and 300–400 drawings; many of the contemporary French works of art it included were gifts from the artists (e.g. the sculpture of *The Philosopher* by Jean-Baptiste Pigalle). In 1824 Desfriches's daughter, Mme de Limay, donated most of the contemporary works to the Musée des Beaux-Arts in Orléans; among them was a portrait of *Jacques Dominé* (*c.* 1720) by Alexis Grimou. Following Mme de Limay's death in 1834, most of the rest of the collection was sold by auction (Paris, Paillet, 6–7 May).

BIBLIOGRAPHY
P. Ratouis de Limay: *Un Amateur orléanais au XVIIe siècle: Aignan-Thomas Desfriches (1715–1800): Sa vie, son oeuvre, ses collections, sa correspondance* (Paris, 1907)
—: 'Un Inventaire de la collection de l'amateur orléanais Aignan-Thomas Desfriches', *Archvs A. Fr.*, viii (1916), pp. 261–70
A.-T. Desfriches (1715–1800) (exh. cat., Orléans, Mus. B.-A., 1965–6)
B. Scott: 'Aignan-Thomas Desfriches: Artist and Collector from Orleans', *Apollo*, xcvii (1973), pp. 36–41

Desgodets [Desgodetz], **Antoine** (*b* Nov 1653; *d* Paris, May 1728). French architect and theorist. He figures as a draughtsman of plans in the *Comptes des Bâtiments du Roi* from the age of 16. He may have taken part in the competition to invent a French order of architecture in 1672, before being sent to Rome on a royal bursary. He spent his two-year stay there recording ancient architecture. On his return, at the request of Jean-Baptiste Colbert, he published *Les Edifices antiques de Rome dessinés et mesurés très exactement* (1682). For this work he was formally congratulated by the Académie and rewarded with the sum of 2,000 livres. Claude Perrault used the variations noted by Desgodets in the proportions of the Classical orders as a basis for his theory that the canons of the orders were subject to free interpretation.

The *Edifices antiques* was reprinted in 1779, and Desgodets's work is today regarded as the beginning of modern scientific archaeology. In 1680 the architect is mentioned as 'Contrôleur des Bâtiments du Roi'; he is thought to have worked on the construction of the dome of Les Invalides in Paris. In 1700 the Académie requested Desgodets to prepare drawings of the different orders of architecture, intended as the basis for large-scale models. This task (which was not completed) prompted him to compose a *Traité des ordres d'architecture*, completed in 1711 (Paris, Bib. Inst. France), which remained in manuscript. In 1718 he attained the First Class of the Académie and the following year became Professor of Architecture there. Three manuscripts of his volumes of lectures survive (Paris, Bib. N.; Paris, Bib. Arsenal; London, RIBA), more or less identical. The first volume contains a *Treatise on the Orders*, which follows the 1711 text, with an additional chapter on 'the manner of regularly placing columns and pilasters on buildings'. In it, he proposes a great portico on two levels, surmounted by statues; the columns, which are sometimes paired, support a continuous architrave prefiguring the manner of Ange-Jacques Gabriel.

The second volume of the lectures is entitled *Traité de la commodité de l'architecture concernant la distribution et les proportions des édifices*. The first section is devoted to religious buildings, and, after describing basilicas of ancient Rome, Desgodets proposed a sample plan for each type of religious architecture. It is the first instance of such an interest, particularly remarkable at a time when opportunities to build new churches were very rare. The project for a cathedral uses a plan with a double transept and an axial chapel inspired by the great cathedrals of the Middle Ages; the interior elevation with columns supporting an architrave is reminiscent of the original Roman basilicas. The project for a parish church is based on the design (1706) for St Roch in Paris by Jules Hardouin Mansart, and that for a convent chapel is modelled on the convent of the Visitation in the Rue St-Jacques by Robert de Cotte (1710; destr.); finally, the monastery chapel follows closely the chapel of the Jacobins (now the church of Saint-Thomas-d'Aquin) by Pierre Bullet. Drawings of these church projects are preserved at Stockholm (Nmus., Col. Tessin-Hårlemann, MSS 934, 8146 and 8183). The second section of the *Traité de la commodité* remained unfinished and contains only a plan for a hospital—a panopticon on a square plan with a central chapel—and another for a town hall, a large, multi-purpose building.

Desgodets composed two works for teaching purposes: one, the *Traité du toisé*, remained in manuscript form (Paris, Bib. Arsenal; Paris, Bib. N.; New York, Columbia U., Avery Archit. Mem. Lib.); the other, his juridical treatise, *Loix des bâtiments*, was printed 20 years after his death and retained its authority until the Revolution. Jacques-François Blondel copied whole passages from the lecture series (the chapter on taste) in his *L'Architecture française* (1752–6), testifying to Desgodets' enduring influence.

UNPUBLISHED SOURCES
London, RIBA, MS. 72 [lectures]
New York, Columbia U., Avery Archit. Mem. Lib., MS. AA 1050 D 45 [*Traité du toisé*]
Paris, Bib. Arsenal, MS. 2530 [*Traité du toisé*]; MS. 2545 [lectures]
Paris, Bib. Inst. France, MS. 1031 [*Traité des ordres d'architecture*, finished 1711]
Paris, Bib. N., MS. anc. Fr. 14843 [*Traité du toisé*]; Est. Ha 23 & 23A [lectures]

WRITINGS

Les Edifices antiques de Rome dessinés et mesurés très exactement (Paris, 1682)
Les loix des bâtiments suivant la coûtume de Paris (Paris, 1748)

BIBLIOGRAPHY

W. Herrmann: 'Antoine Desgodets and the Académie royale d'architecture', *A. Bull*, ix (1958), pp. 23–53
F. Hamon: 'Les Eglises parisiennes du XVIIIème siècle', *Rev. A.* [Paris], xxxii (1976), pp. 6–14

FRANÇOISE HAMON

Desgoffe, Blaise(-Alexandre) (*b* Paris, 17 Jan 1830; *d* Paris, 2 May 1901). French painter. His uncle, the landscape painter Alexandre Desgoffe (1805–82), had studied under Ingres; this perhaps accounts for Blaise's decision to train under Ingres's pupil Hippolyte Flandrin. He entered the Ecole des Beaux-Arts on 7 October 1852, apparently intending to study history painting. At his first Salon in 1854 he exhibited a genre painting, *A Game of Cup and Ball in the Studio*, a portrait and two studies of agate cups (all untraced). He is not otherwise known as a painter of genre subjects or portraits but regularly exhibited still-life compositions of precious objects painted on smooth panels with a heightened *trompe l'oeil* realism that was widely compared by critics with 17th-century Dutch still-life painting. He varied the pattern little. Most of his work in the 1860s seems to have been based on 16th-century objects in the Louvre. In the 1870s he added Chinese, Japanese and Greek items, probably on demand. The *Vase of Rock Crystal and Other Objects* (exh. Salon, 1874; New York, Met.) was commissioned from Desgoffe by Catharine Wolfe, who herself selected the items to be depicted from the Louvre. His sense of composition was rudimentary, but his virtuosity was much admired. Two paintings were bought for the Musée du Luxembourg in 1859 and in 1863 (now in Arras, Mus. B.-A., and Angoulême, Mus. Mun.), but by the mid-1870s his meticulous style was going out of fashion. He won a bronze medal at the Exposition Universelle of 1889 and continued to exhibit at the Société des Artistes Français until his death.

BIBLIOGRAPHY

C. Sterling and M. M. Salinger: *French Paintings: A Catalogue of the Collection of the Metropolitan Museum of Art*, ii: *XIX Century* (New York, 1966), pp. 184–5
Le Musée du Luxembourg en 1874 (exh. cat. by G. Lacambre and J. de Rohan-Chabot, Paris, Grand Pal., 1974)

JON WHITELEY

Desgots [Desgotz]. French family of garden designers. They were related by marriage to ANDRÉ LE NÔTRE and, together with the Mollet family, formed a loose grouping of designers and horticulturists that undertook the execution of Le Nôtre's plans for the most important French formal gardens of the mid- and late 17th century. In 1614 Jean Desgots was responsible for the upkeep of the Tuileries gardens in Paris; in 1624 he was replaced by his brother Pierre, a celebrated draughtsman who in 1616 had married Elizabeth, Le Nôtre's sister. Pierre Desgots and Le Nôtre collaborated on a number of garden designs, with Pierre often drawing up finished plans based on Le Nôtre's sketches. He probably served as clerk of works at Chantilly, where, after 1644, Le Nôtre was working for Louis II, Prince de Condé; in 1673 Pierre made two detailed plans of the Chantilly gardens.

Pierre's son Claude Desgots was sent on a bursary to the Académie de France in Rome in 1675. He collaborated with his father and Le Nôtre at Chantilly (from *c.* 1679) and during his career was involved in plans and improvements for numerous gardens, including those at the Palais du Luxembourg and the Palais Royal in Paris. He was also responsible to a large degree for the exportation of the French formal style of garden design. His *Abrégé de la vie d'André Le Nostre* (*c.* 1700) was published at a time when he was developing Le Nôtre's plans for gardens at Windsor Castle, Berks, and Greenwich Palace, London, during visits to England in 1698 and 1700. Although these were not fully realized, as a result of this work Claude was appointed to modernize the gardens at Het Loo and Apeldoorn, Gelderland (not executed). Around 1704 he laid out formal gardens for the Elector Maximilian II Emanuel at Schloss Schleissheim. He continued his connections with patrons in England, sending plans in 1713 to George Hamilton, 1st Earl of Orkney, for his gardens at Cliveden, Bucks. Other commissions included the grand staircase at Anet, Eure-et-Loire, for Louis-Joseph, Duc de Vendôme, and reconstruction of the château at Perrigny (*c.* 1720). Claude Desgots was admitted to the Académie d'Architecture in 1718.

BIBLIOGRAPHY

DBF; Thieme–Becker
J. Guiffrey: 'Testament et inventaire après décès de André Le Nostre', *Bull. Soc. Hist. A. Fr.* (1911), pp. 217–82
L. Hautecoeur: *Architecture classique*, iii (1950), pp. 114–16
R. Strandberg: 'André Le Nôtre et son école: Dessins inédits ou peu connus dans la collection Tessin-Hårleman, au Musée national de Stockholm', *Bull. Soc. Hist. A. Fr.* (1960), pp. 109–28 (117–20)
——: 'Het ontwerp van Claude Desgots voor het park van Het Loo', *Bull. Kon. Ned. Oudhdknd. Bond*, lxxii (1973)
——: 'The French Formal Garden after Le Nostre', *The French Formal Garden*, ed. E. B. MacDougall (Washington, DC, 1974), pp. 43–67
G. Jackson-Stops: 'Formal Garden Designs for Cliveden: The Work of Claude Desgots and others for the 1st Earl of Orkney', *NT Yb.* (London, 1977–8), pp. 100–17
F. H. Hazlehurst: *Gardens of Illusion: The Genius of André Le Nostre* (Nashville, 1980), pp. 1–15, 187–95, 303–26

SUSAN B. TAYLOR

Deshays [Deshayes], **Jean-Baptiste(-Henri)** [Deshays de Colleville] (*b* Colleville, nr Rouen, 26 May 1729; *d* Paris, 10 Feb 1765). French painter. He first trained with his father, Jean-Dominique Deshays (*b* ?1700), an obscure painter in Rouen. After a brief period at Jean-Baptiste Descamps's Ecole Gratuite de Dessin, he entered the studio in Paris of Hyacinthe Collin de Vermont *c.* 1740. There he acquired the foundations of the mastery of drawing for which he later became celebrated. In late 1749 he moved to the studio of Jean Restout II, who was, like Collin de Vermont, a pupil of Jean Jouvenet, and whose work continued the grand tradition of French history painting. It was from Restout that Deshays learnt the importance of dramatic composition and strong colouring in large religious paintings. While he was in Restout's studio, Deshays entered the Prix de Rome competition, winning second prize in 1750 with *Laban Giving his Daughter in Marriage to Jacob*, and the first prize in 1751 with *Job on the Dung-hill* (both untraced). Before going to Rome, Deshays spent the obligatory three years at the Ecole des Elèves Protégés; from its director Carle Vanloo he learnt a more fashionable facility and tempered the severity inherited from Jouvenet with a more appealing manner. During this period he undertook a number of commissions for religious paintings (all untraced), including two vast canvases, a *Visitation* and an *Annunciation*, for the monastery of the Visitation at Rouen. He completed his artistic education with four years at the Académie de France in Rome under its director, Charles-Joseph Natoire. During this time he made a great many copies of works by Raphael and the Bolognese masters Domenichino, Guercino and the Carracci.

Deshays's years of study bore immediate fruit on his return to Paris in 1758, when he was approved (*agréé*) by the Académie Royale. In the same year he married Jeanne-Elisabeth-Victoire Boucher, the elder daughter of François Boucher. In 1759 Deshays was received (*reçu*) into the Académie, and his *morceau de réception*, *Hector, Slain by Achilles, Laid on the Banks of the Scamander* (Montpellier, Mus. Fabre), was shown at the Salon, where it excited little enthusiasm. Nevertheless, the 1759 Salon marked the beginning of his success. It was as a religious painter that he attracted most attention: his *St Andrew Refusing to Worship Idols* (Rouen, Mus. B.-A.; see fig.) was considered to be among the most important works of 1759, despite its awkwardly tall and narrow format. It was one of three paintings commissioned, perhaps as early as 1753, for the church of St André at Rouen; the first, the *Entombment of St Andrew*, was probably completed in 1758. In its crude realism, *St Andrew Refusing to Worship Idols* marked a turning-point in French painting, and Diderot's description of it as a 'horrible butchery' indicates the extent to which it shocked contemporary standards of decorum.

Such was the success of *St Andrew Refusing to Worship Idols* that at the Salon of 1761 Deshays, still only Adjoint au professeur in the Académie, was hailed by Diderot as the most important painter in France, continuing in the great lineage of Charles Le Brun and Eustache Le Sueur. At this Salon his *Scourging of St Andrew*, the last of the cycle, was universally acclaimed, and the three paintings were well received when they reached Rouen in December 1761. In these works are reminiscences of Italian and French masters of the 17th century, such as Domenichino, Reni and Poussin, but more remarkable is the absolute conviction with which Deshays treated these conventional subjects. The other large-scale religious work of 1761 was the *Last Communion of St Benedict* (Orléans, Mus. B.-A.), one of a cycle of paintings commissioned from various celebrated Paris artists, including Jean Restout II and Joseph-Marie Vien, by the Benedictine community of Bonne Nouvelle at Orléans. The painting's mood of quiet reflection shows Deshays's versatility and mastery of sentiment. Another, much smaller religious work of 1761 was *St Anne Teaching the Virgin to Read* (1761 Salon; Angers, Mus. B.-A.), in which great intimacy and tenderness of feeling are not allowed to lapse into the sentimental.

Deshays's sympathies were not confined to Christian subjects, and his mythologies were distinctive and successful. The most important were the cartoons (destr.) he made, possibly through Boucher's intervention, for a suite of tapestries (Madrid, Pal. Real) illustrating six scenes from Homer's *Iliad*. Although they betray the influence of Boucher in certain details, such as the female heads,

Jean-Baptiste Deshays: *St Andrew Refusing to Worship Idols*, oil on canvas, 4.45×2.14 m, 1759 (Rouen, Musée des Beaux-Arts)

Deshays's grand mythological compositions have a muscular toughness and monumentality that Boucher never sought.

In addition to history painting, Deshays also practised the relatively undemanding genres of decorative painting and portraiture. The *Caravanes* (untraced), large, decorative paintings of biblical journeys in the manner of Giovanni Benedetto Castiglione, which he exhibited at all his Salons, were clearly inspired by Boucher, to Diderot's despair. Most of Deshays's portraits, including those of *Louis XV* and *Madame de Pompadour*, have disappeared. Two surviving portraits of unknown women (both 1761; both priv. col., see Sandoz, 1977, figs 31–2) are frank rather than subtle or flattering.

In 1764 Deshays contracted the illness, probably tuberculosis, that caused his early death. He exhibited posthumously at the Salon of 1765, but even Diderot, his most ardent champion, could not deny the decline in his powers. Although his period of maturity lasted only six years, Deshays was the most important history painter in mid-18th-century France; it was not until 1781, when Jacques-Louis David exhibited his *Belisarius Receiving Alms* (Lille, Mus. B.-A.), that this position was usurped.

BIBLIOGRAPHY

M. Sandoz: 'Études et esquisses peintes ou dessinées de Jean-Baptiste Deshays (1721–1765)', *Gaz. B.-A.*, n. s. 5, xxxviii (1951), pp. 129–46
——: 'Jean-Baptiste Deshays: Peintre d'histoire (1721–1765)', *Bull. Soc. Hist. A. Fr.* (1958), pp. 7–21
——: *Jean-Baptiste Deshays (1729–1765)* (Paris, 1977) [with detailed cat.]
Diderot et l'art de Boucher à David (exh. cat., ed. M.-C. Sahut and N. Volle; Paris, Hôtel de la Monnaie, 1984), pp. 172–8 [quotes Diderot's remarks on Deshays]

☐

Desiderii, Gian Domenico (*b* Rome, *c.* 1620; *d* Rome, after 1664). Italian painter and draughtsman. He was the pupil of Claude Lorrain, whose household in Via Margutta, Rome, he joined in 1633 as a servant, aged 13. He remained with Claude until 1656, and his existence is recorded for the last time in 1664, though at a different address. His personal relationship with Claude, but not his work, is described by Filippo Baldinucci in his life of the French artist. Two drawings from nature in the State Hermitage Museum, St Petersburg, bear Desiderii's name, and others in the same museum are broadly similar. They show the influence of Claude's nature drawings of *c.* 1640, but also resemble some of a large miscellaneous group of drawings of trees traditionally attributed to Nicolas Poussin, now in various locations. Because of this, Desiderii has sometimes been thought of as the author of several of those drawings. In addition, references exist in 17th-century sources to a handful of paintings by Desiderii, though none of them can be identified today. Two pictures in an English private collection painted in close imitation of Claude have been tentatively but not implausibly ascribed to Desiderii on *a priori* grounds by Roethlisberger (1983), and it may be possible to attribute other paintings to him.

BIBLIOGRAPHY

M. Dobroklonsky: 'Drawings by Claude's Pupil, Giovanni Domenico Desiderii', *Burl. Mag.*, lvii (1930), pp. 111–12
M. Roethlisberger: *Claude Lorrain: The Drawings*, 2 vols (Berkeley and Los Angeles, 1968), pp. 443–4, nos 1227–8
Im Licht von Claude Lorrain (exh. cat. by M. Roethlisberger, Munich, Haus Kst, 1983), pp. 155–7, nos 90–91

MICHAEL KITSON

Desiderio, Monsù. *See* BARRA, DIDIER and NOMÉ, FRANÇOIS DE.

Desiderio da Firenze (*b* Florence; *fl* 1532–45). Italian sculptor and bronze-founder. He probably trained in Padua and Florence, and he worked extensively in Padua until at least 1545. He was noted for his bronze sculptures, and his workshop produced such decorative objects as inkwells and candlesticks. It is difficult to establish the attributions of these small bronze pieces, but it is certain that Desiderio created the bronze voting urn (1532–3; Padua, Mus. Civ.; see fig.) commissioned by the Maggior Consiglio of the Comune of Padua. Payments to him are

Desiderio da Firenze: *voting urn*, bronze, partly gilt, h. 510 mm, 1532–3 (Padua, Museo Civico)

documented in 1532–3. The style of the tripartite bronze urn, which combines Florentine clarity with hints of Venetian models, seems more indebted to Andrea Verrocchio than, as has been suggested, to Andrea Riccio. On the three-faced base there are putti bearing the Comune's coat of arms; the upper sections display an intricate arrangement of motifs, including lions of St Mark, dolphins, *grotteschi* and garlands. The urn is considered to be one of the best poured bronzes of 16th-century Padua. In 1537 Pietro Bembo recommended Desiderio for the commission to execute the cover for the baptismal font in S Marco in Venice (*in situ*), for which the contract was signed in 1545. He collaborated with the Paduan sculptor Tiziano Minio (*c.* 1511–52), but their specific roles are not known, and Desiderio may have functioned solely as the founder. According to Planiscig, although Desiderio distinguished himself as a bronze-founder, he became sufficiently original as a sculptor to move beyond the essentially 15th-century style of Riccio. Stylistic analysis of his work is complicated by problems of attribution. Venetian influence came from both Riccio and Jacopo Sansovino, but his Tuscan links remained strong, and the influence of Verrocchio should not be discounted.

BIBLIOGRAPHY

L. Planiscig: 'Desiderio da Firenze: Dokumente und Hypothesen', *Z. Bild. Kst*, lxiv (1930–31), pp. 70–78

W. Wixom: *Renaissance Bronzes from Ohio Collections* (exh. cat., Cleveland, OH, Mus. A., 1975)

A. Radcliffe: 'Desiderio da Firenze', *The Genius of Venice, 1500–1600* (exh. cat., ed. J. Martineau and C. Hope; London, RA, 1983)

J. Carrington: 'A New Look at Desiderio da Firenze and the Paduan Voting Urn', *Boll. Mus. Civ. Padova* lxxiii (1984), pp. 105–45

D. Banzato and F. Pellegrini: *Bronzi e placchete dei Musei Civici di Padova*, (Padua, 1989)

□

Desiderio da Settignano (*b* Settignano, nr Florence, 1429–32; *d* Florence, *bur* 16 Jan 1464). Italian sculptor. His career lasted only about 12 years, but during that time he produced some of the most delicate and intimate sculptural works of mid-15th-century Florence. There are problems of dating and attribution even with his partially documented works, and records survive of several unidentifiable commissions; consequently, it is difficult to chart the course of his stylistic development, and the reliefs and portrait busts attributed to him are grouped around two works: the tomb of *Carlo Marsuppini* (Florence, Santa Croce) and the sacrament tabernacle (Florence, S Lorenzo).

1. Life and work. 2. Workshop.

1. LIFE AND WORK. He was the son of Bartolommeo di Francesco, described after 1451 as a stone-carver. His two elder brothers, Francesco (*b* 1413) and Geri (*b* 1424), were stone masons, in whose guild, the Arte dei Maestri di Pietro e Legname, Francesco matriculated in 1447 and Geri in 1451. At that date Desiderio was too young to join the guild independently. He finally matriculated in 1453 and in the same year, with Antonio Rossellino, assessed Buggiano's pulpit in S Maria Novella, Florence. His initial training was probably with members of his family, but it is possible that he was associated with Donatello at an early stage of his career, since Vasari stated that the frieze of terracotta putti heads on the façade of the Pazzi Chapel, Santa Croce, was the joint work of Donatello and Desiderio. There is also a constant reflection in Desiderio's oeuvre of Donatello's sculpture, particularly in technique. It has been proposed that he was an assistant in Bernardo Rossellino's shop (Markham, 1963), but Desiderio's exuberant decorative detail on, for example, the *Marsuppini* tomb, is closer in spirit to Donatello than the drier, more severe handling of Bernardo Rossellino. According to Vasari, Desiderio made a marble base (untraced) decorated with harpies and bronze swags for Donatello's bronze *David* (Florence, Bargello); however, an attempt to identify the base, which presumably would have been commissioned in the 1450s, with the lavabo in the sacristy of S Lorenzo (Passavant, 1981) is not convincing. In November 1453 Desiderio was ordered to make 12 'heads' for Giovanni de' Medici's study, for which he was paid in 1455. These have been associated with reliefs of the *Heads of the Roman Caesars* such as, for instance, *Julius Caesar* (Paris, Louvre) and with several profile heads of emperors in marble copied after Desiderio (Middeldorf, 1979). In 1455 Desiderio was also paid for a Madonna, in 1456 for two basins and a mantelpiece and in 1458 for 'heads'; none of these works has been identified.

1. Desiderio da Settignano: marble tomb of *Carlo Marsuppini*, originally partly gilt and painted, *c.* 1453–60 (Florence, Santa Croce)

The tomb of *Carlo Marsuppini* (see fig. 1), Desiderio's only monumental work, is described by Vasari in Desiderio's *Vita*. Marsuppini (*d* 1453) had been State Chancellor of Florence, and presumably his tomb was begun soon after his death, but, assuming Desiderio was accepting other commissions during its execution, it may not have been finished until 1460. It is placed in the nave of Santa Croce, across from Bernardo Rossellino's tomb of *Leonardo Bruni* (*d* 1444). Bruni was Marsuppini's predecessor as Chancellor and both men were noted humanists. Desiderio's tomb deliberately echoes that of Rossellino in both design and ornament. Both tombs are framed by an arch and have the effigy of the dead man placed on an elaborate bier over an inscribed sarcophagus, both have a relief of the *Virgin and Child* in a lunette above the effigy and youthful angels carrying garlands above the gable. The effigy of Marsuppini is more steeply tilted on the bier, making the portrait more visible, and the free-standing, shield-bearing putti who flank the base of the arch are not present in the *Bruni* tomb; they act as intermediaries between the observers' space and that of the monument, as do the youths with their striding poses on the entablature, whose garlands fall outside the confines of the architectural framework. Similarly, in the tondo of the *Virgin and Child*, the haloes and drapery break beyond the carved frame. Desiderio used softer forms in the sphinxes at the base and in the acanthus leaf that serves as a keystone of the arch. Compared with the *Bruni* tomb, decoration takes precedence over architectural structure. Filarete praised Desiderio's skill in decorative carving. Desiderio had a facility for finishing surfaces and creating an effect of palpable life in his faces; this verisimilitude would have been enhanced by the colour with which the

2. Desiderio da Settignano (attrib.): *Youthful St John the Baptist*, marble relief, 500×240 mm (Florence, Museo Nazionale del Bargello)

monument was originally decorated; traces of gilding, green paint on the drapery and porphyry red on the panelling remain. Although the participation of assistants is evident in several details, and early sources claimed that Verrocchio was involved in the execution, the high quality of the carving suggests that Desiderio was responsible for much of it. The tomb slab of Carlo Marsuppini's father, Gregorio, placed directly before his son's monument, may be the work of Desiderio's shop (Pines).

Several works have been attributed to Desiderio on the grounds of their similarity to the *Marsuppini* tomb. The marble relief of the *Virgin and Child*, known as the Foulc *Madonna* (c. 1455–60; Philadelphia, PA, Mus. A.), originally from the hospital of S Maria Nuova, Florence, is close to the tondo of the *Virgin and Child* on the tomb. The low relief is, in terms of composition and expressive power, one of Desiderio's best works. The relief of the *Virgin and Child* (Turin, Gal. Sabauda) is accepted as an autograph early work; another relief of the same subject known as the Pantiatichi *Madonna* (c. 1461–4; Florence, Bargello) is also universally accepted. Other reliefs of the same subject that have not been so accepted include the Dudley *Madonna* (London, V&A; see Pope-Hennessy, 1964, Strom, 1984) and the Beauregard *Madonna* (Malibu, CA, Getty Mus.). The latter appears to be closer to the work of either Domenico Rossellino or Francesco di Simone Ferrucci, both skilled imitators of Desiderio.

Even more contentious is the attribution of a group of female portrait busts to Desiderio, none of which has been universally accepted as his work. Vasari mentioned a portrait bust by him of Marietta Strozzi in the Palazzo Strozzi, and a marble head was listed in a Medici inventory, but neither has been positively identified. The *Portrait of a Lady*, sometimes called *Marietta Strozzi* (Berlin, Skulpgal.), has been attributed by Pope-Hennessy (1958) to Antonio Rossellino; a presumed portrait of *Simonetta Vespucci* (Washington, DC, N.G.A.) has been tentatively connected with Verrocchio (Middeldorf). Another female bust (Florence, Bargello) seems to have the strongest stylistic relationship with Desiderio's extant work (Pope-Hennessy, 1985), although it has been rejected by Markham (1963).

Other problematic works attributed to Desiderio include the group of small heads that may represent the Christ Child or the Infant St John, or may possibly be portraits of children. Of the three most frequently discussed—the Mellon *Christ Child*, the Kress bust (both Washington, DC, N.G.A.) and the *Laughing Boy* (Vienna, Ksthist. Mus.)—the Vienna bust seems most likely to be autograph. The attribution of another infant's head (Florence, priv. col., see Negri-Arnoldi, 1967) is not convincing. Three marble reliefs in this genre seem likely to be autograph: the *Youthful St John the Baptist* (Florence, Bargello; see fig. 2) with an unusual three-quarter view of the profile, presumed to be an early work; the *Youthful Hero* (Paris, Mus. Jacquemart-André), which resembles the Bargello relief in the treatment of the hair and the facial expression and features but is probably slightly later; and the tondo of the *Infant Christ and the Infant St John*, known as the Arconati–Visconti Tondo (Paris, Louvre), which, although sometimes dated c. 1453–5 (see 1985 exh. cat.), may be dated in the 1460s, given the similarity of the children's faces to those in the sacrament tabernacle of S Lorenzo.

The tabernacle is the central work of Desiderio's later career. A document refers to its installation in 1461, but a letter written to Francesco Sforza, Duke of Milan, in February 1462 explains that the sculptor was 'occupied and will be for a long time on a certain work in San Lorenzo', which implies that it was not finished. It is conceivable that the letter refers to some other work for the church; alternatively it might suggest that not all the elements of the tabernacle were installed simultaneously. The tabernacle's original location and configuration are unknown: it has been moved at least three times since its initial installation and its present arrangement is unlikely to be as it was originally. It has been suggested that it first formed part of the high altar (Beck) and that the supporting members only were installed at first (Spencer), although this last hypothesis seems unlikely; more probably the tabernacle and its architectonic surround were positioned first and the free-standing elements were added later. The attribution to Desiderio of some of the sculptural elements has been questioned. Albertini (1510) said that the *Blessing Christ Child* that crowns the altar was replaced by a copy by Baccio da Montelupo before 1500. Attempts have been made to identify Desiderio's original figure with a *Christ Child* (Cleveland, OH, Mus. A.), and the figure *in situ* has been given to Baccio (Verdier, 1983). A more likely suggestion is that a faithful copy of the S Lorenzo *Christ Child* (Paris, Louvre) is Baccio's version (Gaborit, 1987), and that the *Christ Child* in S Lorenzo is Desiderio's work. The central relief has been attributed to an anonymous assistant of Brunelleschi working from his master's design (Parronchi, 1980), but the central relief with its steep perspectival rendering of a vaulted interior and its delicacy and decorative elaboration is compatible with Desiderio's certain works and with a date in the second half of the 15th century. The half-length relief of the *Lamentation over Christ* forming the lower half of the tabernacle, with the outlines of the figures deeply undercut, is stylistically distinct from the sculptor's other late work and has led to the suggestion that it is not by Desiderio at all (Cardellini, 1962), although iconographically it is appropriate for an altar dedicated to the sacrament. Finally, it is unclear if all the elements were intended to form part of a wall tabernacle or were part of a free-standing altar. A wall tabernacle was probably intended: not only was it a common solution at this date, but the perspective of the central relief would work best in this context. A group of late 15th-century drawings (London, V&A; Florence, Uffizi) with various solutions for the arrangement of a wall tabernacle have been associated with Desiderio (Kurz).

In Desiderio's later reliefs he employed an increasingly sophisticated *relievo schiacciato* technique. *St Jerome in the Wilderness* (Washington, DC, N.G.A.), exhibiting the influence of Donatello both in technique and in the dramatic presentation of the subject, is his only extant narrative composition (an untraced narrative relief by Desiderio with 'fauns and other figures' was listed in the Medici inventory in 1492). Only three large-scale, free-standing figures can be connected with the sculptor. The Martelli *Youthful St John the Baptist* (Florence, Bargello),

notable for the extreme shallowness of its carving and delicacy of expression, was once attributed to Donatello, but it can be given to Desiderio on stylistic grounds and on the strength of a documented connection between Desiderio and the Martelli family (Beck). The polychromed wooden statue of *St Mary Magdalene* (Florence, Santa Trinita) was, according to Vasari, started by Desiderio and finished by Benedetto da Maiano; it also shows the influence of Donatello, as does a wooden crucifix from the convent at Bosco ai Frati, also formerly given to Donatello but now attributed to Desiderio (Lisner, 1970). These works have been dated to Desiderio's early period, but instead seem to be the products of his last years, that is during the 1460s, when both he and Donatello were working on different projects in S Lorenzo. In 1461 Desiderio submitted a design (untraced) in competition for the chapel of the Madonna della Tavola in Orvieto Cathedral, and in 1463 he was paid for a death mask made in connection with the tomb of the *Cardinal of Portugal* executed by the Rossellino brothers in S Miniato al Monte, Florence. He was buried in S Pier Maggiore, Florence.

2. WORKSHOP. It is assumed that Desiderio's brothers, Francesco and Geri, were active in Desiderio's workshop. Geri shared a house and shop with Desiderio from 1456 until 1461, at which point Desiderio gained control of the shop, though both brothers probably continued to work there. Although it has been suggested that Geri's contribution to works produced by the shop can be identified, it may be that he strove to imitate his more famous brother's style and never developed one of his own. Contemporary sources say that Verrocchio worked on the *Marsuppini* tomb, and his hand has been identified in elements of the S Lorenzo tabernacle (Seymour, 1966), but if he did work in Desiderio's shop, it was probably only for a few years at the end of the work for Santa Croce. Vasari claimed that Desiderio was Mino da Fiesole's master, but this is patently impossible in terms of date. The work of Francesco di Simone Ferrucci shares some qualities with that of Desiderio, but he was also influenced by other sculptors. It is possible that the majority of regular assistants in the shop came from Settignano, Desiderio's place of birth.

There are numerous contemporary versions in stucco and terracotta of Desiderio's reliefs of the Virgin and Child. Francesco Sforza, Duke of Milan, attempted to obtain such a work in 1462, which suggests that they were renowned. Neri di Bicci, in his *Ricordanze*, refers to colouring works by Desiderio made of stucco and marble (Middeldorf, 1978), and this practice may have continued after Desiderio's death. Marble replicas of devotional reliefs seem to have been produced in the workshop both during his lifetime and, probably, later. This would explain the many small-scale works in marble tentatively attributed to Desiderio.

BIBLIOGRAPHY

EARLY SOURCES AND DOCUMENTS

Filarete: *Trattato di architettura* (MS., *c.* 1460–64); trans. J. Spencer (New Haven, 1965), pp. 170, 258, 284, 391

Neri di Bicci: *Le ricordanze* (MS., 1453–75); ed. B. Santi (Pisa, 1976)

F. Albertini: *Memoriale di molte statue e pitture della città di Firenze* (Florence, 1510); ed. L. Mussini (Florence, 1863), p. 11

G. Vasari: *Vite* (1550, rev. 2/1568); ed. G. Milanesi (1878–85), ii, p. 483; iii, pp. 107–12

G. Richa: *Notizie istorische delle chiese fiorentine divise nei suoi quartieri* (Florence, 1754–62), i, p. 90; v, p. 28

C. Kennedy: 'Documenti inediti su Desiderio da Settignano e la sua famiglia', *Riv. A.*, 2nd ser., ii (1930), pp. 243–91

R. Mather: 'Documents, Mostly New, Relating to Florentine Painters and Sculptors of the Fifteenth Century', *A. Bull.*, xxx (1948), pp. 20–66

G. Corti and F. Hartt: 'New Documents Concerning Donatello, Luca and Andrea della Robbia, Desiderio, Mino, Uccello, Pollaiuolo, Filippo Lippi, Baldovinetti and others', *A. Bull.*, xliv (1962), pp. 155–67

I. Cardellini: 'Desiderio e i documenti', *Crit. A.*, ix/53–4 (1962), pp. 110–12

J. R. Spencer: 'Francesco Sforza and Desiderio da Settignano: Two New Documents', *A. Lombarda*, xiii/1 (1968), pp. 131–3

J. Beck: 'Desiderio da Settignano (and Antonio del Pollaiuolo): Problems', *Mitt. Ksthist. Inst. Florenz*, xxviii (1984), pp. 203–24

GENERAL

Thieme–Becker

A. Venturi: *Storia* (1901–40), vi, pp. 410–28

F. Burger: *Geschichte des florentinischen Grabmals von der ältesten Zeiten bis Michelangelo* (Strasbourg, 1904)

J. Pope-Hennessy: *Italian Renaissance Sculpture* (London, 1958, rev. Oxford, 3/1986), pp. 29–30, 37–8, 49–50, 283–7, 355–6

C. Seymour jr: *Sculpture in Italy, 1400–1500*, Pelican Hist. A. (Harmondsworth, 1966), pp. 139–43, 149

M. Lisner: *Holzkruzifixe in Florenz und in der Toskana von der Zeit um 1300 bis zum frühen Cinquecento* (Munich, 1970), pp. 73–4

J. Schuyler: *Florentine Busts: Sculptured Portraiture in the Fifteenth Century* (diss., New York, Columbia U., 1976)

Italian Renaissance Sculpture in the Time of Donatello (exh. cat., ed. A. Darr and G. Bonsanti; Detroit, MI, Inst. A., 1985); also as *Donatello e i suoi: Scultura fiorentina del primo rinascimento* (Florence, Forte Belvedere, 1986)

La Maddalena tra sacro e profano (exh. cat., ed. M. Mosco, Florence, Pitti, 1986)

MONOGRAPHS

C. da Prato: *Desiderio da Settignano e diverse opere sue* (Florence, 1890)

L. Planiscig: *Desiderio da Settignano* (Vienna, 1942)

M. Cardellini: *Desiderio da Settignano* (Milan, 1962); rev. by A. Markham in *A. Bull.*, xlv (1963), pp. 35–45, and by F. Negri-Arnoldi in *Paragone*, xv/171 (1964), pp. 69–73

SPECIALIST STUDIES

P. Giordani: 'La rappresentazione del "Genietto" in Desiderio da Settignano', *Rass. A.*, viii (1908), pp. 151–4

C. Kennedy: *The Tomb of Carlo Marsuppini by Desiderio da Settignano and Assistants* (Northampton, MA, 1928)

——: *The Tabernacle of the Sacrament by Desiderio* (Northampton, MA, 1929)

——: *Magdalen and Sculptures in Relief by Desiderio da Settignano and Associates* (Northampton, MA, 1929)

L. Becherucci: 'Un angelo di Desiderio da Settignano', *L'Arte*, xxxv (1932), pp. 153–60

W. R. Valentiner: 'Leonardo and Desiderio', *Burl. Mag.*, lxi (1932), pp. 53–61

W. Paatz: 'Vergessene Nachrichten über einige Hauptwerke der Florentiner Quattrocento-Skulptur', *Mitt. Ksthist. Inst. Florenz*, ix/2–3 (1932–4), pp. 140–41

L. Planiscig: 'Di alcune opere falsamente attribuite a Donatello', *Phoebus*, ii (1948–9), pp. 55–9

——: 'Santa Maria Maddalena di Desiderio da Settignano', *A. Medit.*, iii (1949), pp. 5–11

O. Kurz: 'A Group of Florentine Drawings for an Altar', *J. Warb. & Court. Inst.*, xviii (1955), pp. 35–53

M. Lisner: 'Die Büste des Heiligen Laurentius in der alten Sakristei von S Lorenzo: Ein Beitrag zu Desiderio da Settignano', *Z. Kstgesch.*, xii (1958), pp. 51–70

G. Laschi, P. Roselli and P. Rossi: 'Indagini sulla Cappella dei Pazzi', *Commentari*, xiii/1 (1962), pp. 24–41

A. Markham: 'Desiderio da Settignano and the Workshop of Bernardo Rossellino', *A. Bull.*, xlv (1963), pp. 35–45

F. Negri-Arnoldi: 'Un Desiderio da Settignano vero (e uno falso)', *Paragone*, xv/175 (1964), pp. 69–73

J. Pope-Hennessy: *Catalogue of Italian Sculpture in the Victoria and Albert Museum* (London, 1964)

A. Parronchi: 'Sulla collocazione originaria del Tabernacolo di Desiderio da Settignano', *Cron. Archeol. & Stor. A.*, iv (1965), pp. 130–40

F. Negri-Arnoldi: 'Un marmo autentico di Desiderio all'origine di un falso Antonio Rossellino', *Paragone*, xviii/209 (1967), pp. 23–6

U. Schlegel: 'Zu Donatello und Desiderio da Settignano: Beobachtungen zur physiognomischen Gestaltung im Quattrocento', *Jb. Berlin. Mus.*, ix (1967), pp. 135–55

R. Wittkower: 'Desiderio da Settignano's *St. Jerome in the Desert*', *Stud. Hist. A.*, iv (1971–2), pp. 7–37

C. Avery: 'The Beauregard Madonna: A Forgotten Masterpiece by Desiderio da Settignano', *Connoisseur*, cxciii/777 (1976), pp. 186–95

A. Parronchi: 'Tabernacolo brunelleschiano', *Prospettiva*, ix (1977), pp. 55–6

U. Middeldorf: 'Some Florentine Painted Madonna Reliefs', *Collaboration in Italian Renaissance Art*, ed. W. S. Sheard and J. Paoletti (New Haven, 1978), pp. 77–90

——: 'Die Zwölf Caesaren von Desiderio da Settignano', *Mitt. Ksthist. Inst. Florenz*, xxiii (1979), pp. 297–312

A. Parronchi: 'Un tabernacolo brunelleschiano', *Filippo Brunelleschi: La sua opera e il suo tempo* (Florence, 1980), pp. 239–55

G. Passavant: 'Beobachtungen am Lavabo von San Lorenzo in Florenz', *Pantheon*, xxxix (1981), pp. 33–50

G. C. Vines: *Desiderio da Settignano* (diss., Charlottesville, U. VA, 1981)

M. Godby: 'The "Boni Chimney-piece" in the Victoria and Albert Museum: A Fifteenth-century Domestic Cenotaph', *A. & Libris*, xxvii (1982), pp. 4–17

V. Herzner: 'David Florentinus', *Jb. Berlin. Mus.*, xxiv (1982), pp. 107–25

D. Strom: 'Desiderio and the Madonna Relief in Quattrocento Florence', *Pantheon*, xl (1982), pp. 130–35

P. Verdier: 'Il putto ignoto: A Marble Statue of Christ in Quest of a Father', *Bull. Cleveland Mus. A.*, lxx/7 (1983), pp. 303–11

D. Strom: 'A New Look at the Mellon Christ Child in the National Gallery of Art', *Ant. Viva*, xxii/3 (1983), pp. 9–12

——: 'A New Identity for the Dudley Madonna and Child in the Victoria and Albert Museum', *Ant. Viva*, xxiii/4–5 (1984), pp. 37–41

D. S. Pines: *The Tomb Slabs of Santa Croce: A New 'Sepoltuario'* (diss., New York, Columbia U., 1985)

J. R. Gaborit: 'Desiderio da Settignano, Baccio da Montelupo et le "Bambino" de San Lorenzo', *Hommage à Hubert Landais* (Paris, 1987), pp. 97–103

SHELLEY E. ZURAW

Desiderius [Victor III] (*b* Benevento, 1027; elected pope 1086; *d* Montecassino, 16 Sept 1087). Italian pope, Abbot of Montecassino and patron. He was born, with the name Dauferius, to an aristocratic Lombard family. After a brief monastic career at La Cava, near Salerno, and at S Sophia in Benevento, where he assumed the name Desiderius, he joined the community at the great monastery of MONTECASSINO in 1055, becoming abbot in 1058. During his abbacy Montecassino attained its greatest prestige. The monastery was closely involved with the principles of contemporary church reform. He was much involved in the political intricacies of his time, and maintained especially friendly relations with, and received benefits from, the Norman rulers of southern Italy. He supported many literary and scholarly activities, such as the poetry of Alberic of Montecassino (*b c.* 1030), the medical books of Constantius Africanus (*d c.* 1087), and the historical writings of Amatus of Montecassino (*b c.* 1010) and Leo of Ostia (*d* 1115). He composed a book, *Dialogi de miraculi S Benedicti*, on the monastery's founder. His short and turbulent period as pope, however, scarcely allowed for any cultural patronage.

Desiderius's encouragement of art and architecture is recorded in several contemporary descriptions, the most valuable being that by Leo of Ostia, the librarian of Montecassino, in the *Chronicle of Montecassino*. He planned to rebuild the monastery in a splendid form, beginning with the construction of a library building, an abbot's lodging, monks' dormitories and a chapter house. In 1066 he started work on a new basilica. For the decoration of the buildings he acquired artists skilled in mosaic and other techniques from Constantinople, both to work on the project and to teach local artists. He also ordered works of art from Constantinople, including bronze doors and a golden altar frontal. The basilica was dedicated in 1071 by Pope Alexander II in a grandiose ceremony attended by leading Italian ecclesiastics and lay noblemen. Desiderius continued to develop his monastery with new dormitories, a revised chapter house, novices' quarters, a hospice for visitors, an infirmary and so on (*see* MONTECASSINO, fig. 1).

Most of Desiderius's Montecassino buildings and their decoration were destroyed by an earthquake in 1349. The basilica, based on the pattern of Old St Peter's in Rome, on a much reduced scale, was a conservative design, in keeping with his artistic policy of recalling the Early Christian monuments of Rome, an aspect of his devotion to the reform movement. The lost Montecassino mosaics are perhaps reflected in the fragmentary late 11th-century mosaics in Salerno Cathedral. They show strong Byzantine influence and were possibly made by Italian artists trained by Byzantines according to Desiderius's programme of art education.

Byzantine stylistic influence is also present, but far less dominant, in the late 11th-century frescoes in the church of SANT'ANGELO IN FORMIS, near Capua, the sole surviving work of monumental art commissioned by Desiderius. The impressive quality of the Sant' Angelo paintings owes much, however, to a vivid, native Italian Romanesque manner; it is impossible to gauge to what extent they may have resembled any of the mural art at Montecassino.

The sumptuous example of the Desiderian buildings may, however, have given an impetus to art in central Italy. The use of mosaic at Montecassino did much to stimulate the revival of an art that had been largely forgotten in Italy for more than 200 years but was to flourish in Rome and its vicinity throughout the 12th century. Similarly, the complex inlaid stone decorations of Montecassino were primary works in a technique that formed a major tradition in subsequent Italian art.

Several examples of another form of art fostered by Desiderius—the decoration of manuscripts—have survived. The most extensively illustrated manuscript contains the lives of SS Benedict, Maurus and Scholastica (Rome, Vatican, Bib. Apostolica, MS. Vat. lat. 1202; *see* MONTECASSINO, fig. 2), with hagiographic scenes and a prefatory miniature of Desiderius offering the book to St Benedict. Two manuscripts of HOMILIES (Montecassino Abbey, Lib., MSS 98–9) are illustrated with full-page line drawings. Of a few illustrated 11th-century Exultet rolls from Montecassino, at least one (London, BL, Add. MS. 30337) may be assigned to the period of Desiderius. Byzantine influence, detectable in all these works, is most apparent in the homily illustrations. The miniatures in the Vatican manuscript have a certain angularity that may reflect knowledge of Ottonian book painting: many elaborately decorated initials in the Desiderian manuscripts were evidently derived from Ottonian initials.

WRITINGS

Dialogi de miraculi S Benedicti, Mnmt Ger. Hist., Scriptores, xxx/2, pp. 1111–51

BIBLIOGRAPHY

Leo of Ostia: 'The Chronicle of Montecassino', *A Documentary History of Art*, ed. E. G. Holt (New York, 1957), i, pp. 8–17 [selections] [early 12th century]

C. R. Dodwell: *Painting in Europe, 800–1200*, Pelican Hist. A. (Harmondsworth, 1971), pp. 128–38

E. Kitzinger: 'The Gregorian Reform and the Visual Arts: A Problem of Method', *Trans. Royal Hist. Soc.*, n.s. 4, xxii (1972), pp. 87–102

Leo of Ostia: *Chronica monasterii Casinensis* (MS.; late 11th century); ed. H. Hoffmann, Mnmt Ger. Hist., Scriptores, xxxiv/3 (1980), pp. 358–457

H. Bloch: *Monte Cassino in the Middle Ages* (Cambridge, MA, 1986), i, pp. 40–112

DON DENNY

Design. Term derived from the Italian *disegno* and the French *dessin*, both meaning 'a drawing'; from the 20th century, it has been used in a wider sense to describe the aesthetic and functional characteristics of an object. It has become increasingly identified with product design for industry (*see* INDUSTRIAL DESIGN) and MASS PRODUCTION and is seen as an essential part of the process of making, marketing and selling mass-produced goods. This article covers the history and concept of design in Western Europe and the USA since 1800.

1. 19th century. 2. 20th century.

1. 19TH CENTURY. Design in its contemporary sense emerged from the social, economic, technological and ideological conditions that transformed Western society at the time of the Industrial Revolution, i.e. the late 18th century and early 19th in Britain, and a little later in the rest of Europe and the USA. The move from craft to mass production through the reorganization of labour and the use of machines resulted in a breakdown of the traditional process of the manufacture of goods: the design process became separated from the making stage. This fundamental separation, which meant that a product had to be planned in its entirety before it could be made, gave birth to the modern meaning of design and, subsequently, to the profession of designer.

The task of the early designers—who were initially described as draughtsmen, engineers or by a number of other titles that related to specific product areas—was to conceive a product, to define its function, materials, means of assembly, cost etc, and to communicate these to the people who would be involved in the process of manufacture. However, in the early consumer goods industries—ceramics, textiles, furniture—copying rather than the creation of new models and forms was often the norm, and much design was simply a question of adapting pattern book decorations to the surfaces of objects in order to render them stylish and fashionable (*see* ORNAMENT AND PATTERN, §II, 3; PATTERN BOOK, §I, 2(i); and INDUSTRIAL DESIGN, fig. 1). This type of design was primarily a two-dimensional activity that gave little thought to the forms of the objects being embellished, the latter being created by workmen on the factory floor.

In the early 19th century, design continued to be associated with surface decoration and the use of historical styles. The schools of design that were established in

London (1837) and subsequently in Manchester, Birmingham, Glasgow and other industrial towns in Britain were intended to train students to draw so that they would be able to apply their talents in the context of manufacture. The first British museum dedicated to design, the South Kensington Museum, London (now the Victoria and Albert Museum), was established in 1837 as a repository of decorative art objects that would serve as inspiration and stimulation for students of design.

At this time design was seen as the answer to Britain's need to compete with France in the area of trade by raising the aesthetic level of British goods. The government and the Society of Arts (founded in 1754 by William Shipley) were behind the formation of both the schools and the museum, and in 1851 the Great Exhibition at Crystal Palace, London (see INTERNATIONAL EXHIBITION), attracted visitors from all over the world to see British goods alongside those from many other countries. The Great Exhibition was a testimony to the progress made by British industry over the previous century and a mark of the importance of style and decoration in the goods it produced. It was also a turning-point for British design, as it stimulated the development of the design reform movement. John Ruskin, WILLIAM MORRIS and the later followers of what came to be called the ARTS AND CRAFTS MOVEMENT saw what they considered the stylistic excesses of the Great Exhibition as a symptom of the overt materialism and conspicuous consumption of Victorian society. The aesthetic principles that they outlined as a reaction to it—epitomized by such tenets as 'fitness to purpose' and 'truth to materials'—were to underpin the good design movement that was predominant in the first six decades of the 20th century. They transformed design from a pragmatic concept into an ethical and aesthetic ideal, giving it a new level of meaning that it still retains.

2. 20TH CENTURY. The ideas and ideals of the Arts and Crafts Movement had a profound effect on 20th-century European design: the apparent democratization of design seemed to express the spirit of the new century (see MODERNITY). Many artists and architects, particularly in Austria and Germany, turned to product design, for example JOSEF HOFFMANN and KOLO MOSER, members of the Vienna Secession, who both designed bentwood furniture that was mass-produced by the firm of Gebrüder Thonet in Vienna (see INDUSTRIAL DESIGN, fig. 3). In 1903 Hoffmann and Moser founded the WIENER WERKSTÄTTE, which was modelled on C. R. ASHBEE's Guild of Handicrafts and was dedicated to the production of handmade goods that would combine function with aesthetically pleasing forms. Designers and craftsmen collaborated to produce goods that, in the early years, were characterized by simplicity and geometrical austerity (e.g. brass vase designed by Moser, 1903–4; for illustration see WIENER WERKSTÄTTE). Meanwhile PETER BEHRENS, RICHARD RIEMERSCHMID and Henry Van de Velde had been designing well-made objects for commercial production (e.g. porcelain plate from a dinner service designed by Van de Velde for Meissen, c. 1905; Darmstadt, Hess. Landesmus.), and in 1907 the DEUTSCHER WERKBUND was formed, an association of designers, architects and industrialists whose aim was to improve the quality of hand- and machine-made goods through cooperation between designers and manufacturers. In his role of design consultant to the German electrical company AEG, Peter Behrens recognized that the new generation of electrical consumer goods, which had no craft precedent, required consistency of quality, new materials, new machines and new technologies. His range of electrical kettles (see INDUSTRIAL DESIGN, fig. 4) brought Morris's tenets of 'truth to materials' and 'sound workmanship' into line with industrial production. The seventh Deutscher Werkbund exhibition in Cologne in 1914 inspired the setting up of the Design and Industries Association (DIA) in Britain in 1915.

European designers were looking for new ways of expression that were appropriate to life in the 20th century; the trend was towards a new functional purism (see FUNCTIONALISM) and away from the self-representation and display associated with the previous century. While in Europe the emphasis was primarily on the mass manufacture of the products of the traditional decorative art industries, in the USA it was on goods that had a more technological bias: guns, sewing machines, bicycles etc. By the turn of the century the American system of mass production had been perfected, and the Ford Motor Company's 'Model T' (see MASS PRODUCTION, fig. 1), launched in 1913, was the symbol of the standardized product that the system inevitably encouraged. Henry Ford's famous statement that his automobile could be bought in any colour 'so long as it was black' epitomized that stage in industrial design where aesthetics had been overtaken by engineering principles and the desire to keep the cost of the product as low as possible.

The rigorous methods embraced by Ford led to a crisis in the 1920s because his idea of continuous, standardized manufacture failed to take into account the psychological needs of the consumers who, in more prosperous times, wanted novelty and style. The industrial designer emerged as a response to these needs that went beyond the requirements of function and price. Ford's chief competitor in the 1920s was the General Motors Co., which allowed for product variation in its output and employed an in-house designer to give its automobiles 'consumer appeal'. This awareness of the consumer's psychological relationship with products, enhanced by advertising, was crucial to the role of design in manufacture in the 20th century: that of ensuring that goods meet not only the demands of mass manufacture but, perhaps even more importantly, those of mass consumption.

The first American industrial designers were recruited from advertising and theatre design. WALTER DORWIN TEAGUE, NORMAN BEL GEDDES, RAYMOND LOEWY and Henry Dreyfuss (1904–72), among others, combined the skills of a businessman with those of a fine artist and played a vital role in ensuring that many large American corporations survived the Depression of the 1930s. Later recruits, such as Charles Eames and Ray EAMES, often combined product design (see INDUSTRIAL DESIGN, fig. 6) with architectural design. By the end of the decade industrial design was seen as the 'saviour of the day', and in 1939 the World's Fair in New York gave further evidence of its success in fulfilling the desires and aspirations of the American nation.

While the Americans were involved with the programme of industrial design and mass production, designers in Europe during the inter-war years continued to be more interested in the metaphorical and aesthetic implications of contemporary life and in evolving objects that were appropriate to it. Designers in such countries as Germany, the Netherlands, France, Austria, Russia and elsewhere had, by the end of World War I, all developed an avant-garde approach set within a framework of fine art and architectural modern ideals. This was especially evident in the work of the De Stijl artists and such designers as GERRIT RIETVELD in the Netherlands, the Constructivists in Russia, LE CORBUSIER and the Purists in France and the artists, architects and designers associated with the BAUHAUS design school in Germany. The Bauhaus set out to encourage young designers to create form out of abstract principles that were in tune with the modern age of technology and mass production.

Inevitably, the high idealism of what came to be called the MODERN MOVEMENT in design prevented its widespread commercial application, but it was an important ideological and educational influence worldwide in the mid-20th century. Although the objects it produced (e.g. Bauhaus ashtray by Marianne Brandt, 1924; see BAUHAUS, fig. 2) were few in number, it nonetheless set a tone that dominated the philosophy of design until the late 1960s. Its attraction as a design theory lay in its rigour and the uncompromising nature of its rules. During the 1930s, however, many of the Modern Movement protagonists—among them WALTER GROPIUS, MARCEL BREUER and LUDWIG MIES VAN DER ROHE—left Europe when the Bauhaus was forced to close by the Nazi authorities. They eventually settled in the USA, where they disseminated Bauhaus design and teaching methods in such institutions as the Graduate School of Design at Harvard University, MA, BLACK MOUNTAIN COLLEGE, NC, and the New Bauhaus in Chicago.

In the early post-war years there was a resurgence of the Modern Movement, although it was defined more in terms of national identity; in Italy and Scandinavia, for example, national variants of Modernism were developed as part of the expanded programme of trade. In Italy design was seen as a fundamental element of the programme of economic and cultural reconstruction that was undertaken from 1945. The focus was on the role of the artist-designer and his part in creating 'added value' in industrial products. Such designers as Marcello Nizzoli, Carlo Mollino and ETTORE SOTTSASS collaborated with the new furniture and product manufacturers who aimed their goods at a sophisticated international audience (e.g. 'Lettera de Luxe' portable typewriter and case, designed by Sottsass for Olivetti, 1965; see INDUSTRIAL DESIGN, fig. 8). Italian glass design became more colourful, inventive and freer in form under the influence of Paolo Venini (1905–59), who employed such designers as Carlo Scarpa at Venini & Co., experimenting with patchwork glass techniques and a range of shapes (see VENICE, fig. 13). A concept of Italian design emerged that was characterized by sculptural forms, the use of new materials—especially plastics—and a commitment to quality.

1. Stacking stools designed by Alvar Aalto, laminated bent birch, 450×350 mm, 1930–33 (Helsinki, Museum of Applied Arts)

By contrast, the Scandinavian modern design movement, which came to the forefront in the 1950s, emphasized the role of traditional craft skills and materials. The turning-point for Swedish design had been the Hemutställningen (Home Exhibition) held in 1917 in Stockholm. It had been organized by the Svenska Slöjdsforeningen (Swedish Society of Industrial Design; now Svensk Form), which, inspired by the activities of the Deutscher Werkbund, sought to encourage collaboration between designers and manufacturers to produce good design at affordable prices. Among the most successful collaborations were those between Wilhelm Kåge (1889–1960) and the Gustavsberg Ceramic Factory (e.g. 'Grey Bands' dinner service, 1944; London, V&A) and between the Orrefors Glasbruk and such designers as Simon Gate (1883–1945) and Edward Hald (1883–1980; see SWEDEN, §§VII, 1 and VIII, 2). In the 1930s the Finnish architect ALVAR AALTO successfully combined simplicity, the use of readily available natural materials, human scale and comfort in his designs for mass-produced furniture (e.g. stacking stools, 1930–33; see fig. 1). Similar concerns are reflected in the glassware designs by his wife, Aino Marsio-Aalto (1894–1949), for the Karhula Glassworks (e.g. pressed glass pitcher and glasses, 1932; Helsinki, Mus. Applied A.). This emphasis on beautiful utility was fundamental to Finnish Functionalism and to the Scandinavian style of design that was pre-eminent in the 1950s. The latter is exemplified in the designs for cutlery and chairs by the Danish designer ARNE JACOBSEN, the furniture designed by BØRGE MOGENSEN and the glassware and furniture designs by the Finnish designer Tapio Wirkkala (see FINLAND, fig. 14).

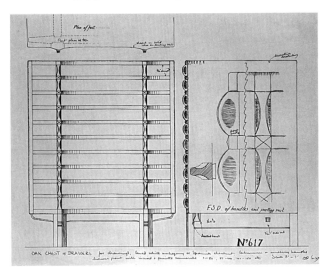

2. Design for an oak chest-of-drawers by Gordon Russell, pen and ink on tracing paper, 336×415 mm, 1927 (London, Victoria and Albert Museum)

By the 1950s design had helped industry to define the way in which it presented its goods to the marketplace. The philosophy of the 'good design' movement became institutionalized through design education bodies world-wide (e.g. the German Bauhaus), through museum collections (e.g. the design collection of MOMA, New York, formed in the early 1930s) and through the growing number of specialist design magazines that flourished during the 1950s (e.g. *Design*, first pubd 1949). Government bodies were formed to encourage high standards of design and thus help boost trade figures. In Britain, the Council of Industrial Design was formed in 1944, and in 1947 GORDON RUSSELL became its director. He had trained as a furniture-maker and designer (see fig. 2) and had been an influential figure in the development of the Utility furniture scheme of the 1940s, which he had seen as an opportunity to re-educate public taste and make people more critical of poor design. He was also on the committee of the Festival of Britain which, in 1951, a century after the Great Exhibition, acted as a showcase for British design, including the work of ERNEST RACE and ROBIN DAY. In 1956 the Design Centre was set up in the Haymarket, London. Design had become an international concept, recognized by industry, the retail sector and, to an increasing extent, by the general public as well. It became the primary means by which the concept of modernity penetrated everyday life in prosperous societies. In 1964, for example, TERENCE CONRAN opened the first Habitat store in London, making good, reasonably priced design for all a reality and not only transforming the middle-class British domestic interior but raising the profile of design in everyday life by re-establishing Morris's tenet of the aesthetic of the everyday object.

The greater spread of mass consumption, however, meant that the clash between pragmatism and idealism in design reached its peak in the 1960s. The idea of good design was threatened in a number of countries by alternative models of design that embraced the values of mass culture and subcultures: this represented part of the larger effort to overthrow what were seen as 'Establishment' values, in which good design inevitably played a part, and to democratize culture. POST-MODERNISM succeeded Modernism as a dominant cultural force, and design, along with other cultural forms, entered a period of self-criticism and revision. This was most obvious in Britain and Italy: in the former, the influence of Pop art, with its brash colours and ephemeral forms (e.g. a 'paper' chair, designed by Peter Murdoch, 1964; 'Jigsaw' furniture, designed by Max Clendenning, mid-1960s), challenged all the rules of good design; in the latter the 'anti-design' movement allied itself with the more general cultural revolutions of the day.

The shifts in the aesthetic and meaning of design in the 1960s were a sign of the high level of penetration by design into society and culture as a whole. The fact that it could respond to changes in dominant cultural values was a sign that it had become fully integrated into the processes of production and consumption; at the same time, however, it stood outside these processes, which were in essence the mechanism of the capitalist economy, and retained something of its earlier idealism through such designers as Le Corbusier, Walter Gropius, Marcel Breuer, Dieter Rams and Ettore Sottsass, who saw themselves as the initiators rather than merely the agents of change.

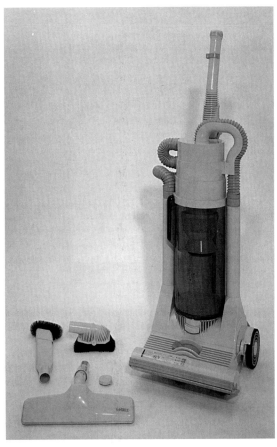

3. G-force 'Cyclone' vacuum cleaner designed by James Dyson, pink plastic, 1983 (London, Victoria and Albert Museum)

By the 1980s design had become part of daily life. It was described and discussed in mass publication magazines, and its new high profile was visible in such exhibition spaces as the Boilerhouse in the Victoria and Albert Museum, London, and the Design Museum, established in London's Docklands in 1989 and sponsored by the Conran Foundation. Design had also become part of popular language: such phenomena as 'designer' jeans, 'designer' vacuum cleaners (see fig. 3) and even 'designer' lemon squeezers (e.g. squeezer for Alessi designed by PHILIPPE STARCK, 1988) acknowledged that the most potent meaning of the word was that of 'added value' in the form of style—an indefinable quality that made things not only useful but also more desirable, albeit in a somewhat intangible way. Idealism and pragmatism had finally come together in a synthetic definition that had mass appeal. In the inevitable pendulum swing that followed in the 1990s, however, a neo-Ruskinian response to the conspicuous consumption of the 1980s and the role that design played within it suggested that a new approach was needed to redefine design as a tool for the improvement of society, albeit in an environmental rather than an aesthetic way.

BIBLIOGRAPHY

C. Hobhouse: *1851 and the Crystal Palace* (London, 1937)
A. Boe: *From Gothic Revival to Functional Form* (Cambridge, 1957)
G. Naylor: *The Arts and Crafts Movement* (London, 1971)
F. Klingender: *Art and the Industrial Revolution* (London, 1972)
V. Papanek: *Design for the Real World: Making to Measure* (London, 1972)
F. MacCarthy: *A History of British Design, 1830–1970* (London, 1979)
J. Meikle: *Twentieth-century Limited: Industrial Design in America, 1925–1939* (Philadelphia, 1979)
J. Heskett: *Industrial Design* (London, 1980)
P. Sparke: *Consultant Design: The History of the Designer for Industry* (London, 1981)
D. McFadden, ed.: *Scandinavian Modern Design, 1880–1980* (New York, 1982)
J. M. Woodham: *The Industrial Designer and the Public* (London, 1983)
Pattern and Design: Designs for the Decorative Arts, 1480–1980 (exh. cat., ed. S. Lambert; London, V&A, 1983)
A. Branzi: *The Hot House: Italian New Wave Design* (London, 1984)
D. Hounshell: *From the American System to Mass Production* (Baltimore, 1985)
G. Naylor: *The Bauhaus Reassessed: Sources and Design Theory* (London, 1985)
A. Forty: *Objects of Desire* (London, 1986)
J. Heskett: *German Design, 1870–1918* (London and New York, 1986)
P. Sparke: *Italian Design 1870 to the Present* (London, 1986)
M. Collins: *Towards Post-modernism: Design since 1851* (London, 1987)
H. Conway, ed.: *Design History: A Student Handbook* (London and Boston, 1987)
J. Thackara: *Design after Modernism: Beyond the Object* (London, 1989)
R. Craig Miller: *Modern Design, 1890–1990* (New York, 1990)
P. Greenhalgh, ed.: *Modernism in Design* (London, 1990)
P. Sparke: *An Introduction to Design and Culture in the Twentieth Century* (London, 1992)
Design of the Times: One Hundred Years of the Royal College of Art (exh. cat., ed. C. Frayling and C. Catterall; London, Royal Coll. A., 1996)

PENNY SPARKE

Dési Huber, István (*b* Nagyenyed [now Aiud, Romania], 6 Feb 1895; *d* Budapest, 22 Feb 1944). Hungarian painter, printmaker and writer. After a difficult childhood and military service during World War I, he learnt silversmithing and drawing in Dés (now Dej, Romania). From 1921 he worked in a factory in Budapest. He studied drawing in the evenings at the School of Applied Arts, then at the Free School of Artur Podolni-Volkmann (1891–1943), Budapest. Between 1924 and 1927 he worked in Milan, where he visited the museums and learnt etching, later exhibiting in Florence. As a socialist he considered art to be part of the ideological struggle. His first committed work, *Fourth Order*, is a series of linocuts produced soon after his return home and showing the impact of Frans Masereel. In 1928 Dési Huber held a small exhibition, and he subsequently joined the left-wing artists' group, KÚT (Képzőművészek Új Társasága: New Society of Fine Artists), which was active from 1924 to 1949. He perfected his techniques and studied art theory, but he never gave up his money-earning activity as a factory hand.

Dési Huber's first period was marked by his enthusiasm for Cubism. The social themes appear through simplified forms bounded by planes in a rigorously organized static space. But he soon abandoned the rational conceptions of synthetic Cubism and from the 1930s created a more expressive style that depicts humans more concretely, still retaining structural emphases (e.g. *Noon Siesta*, 1933–4; Budapest, N.G., see fig.). His first real success came at the KÚT exhibition of 1934, and at his first one-man exhibition at the Ernst Museum, Budapest, in 1938, which received much attention. Dési Huber's worsening lung condition, the problems of subsistence and the growth of Hungarian Fascism deeply worried him and led to a preponderance of passionate compositions.

From 1936 Dési Huber's earlier subdued earth colours were exchanged for richer, more contrasting colours, which, with the use of lines of a broken rhythm and sporadic dashes, produced a dramatic effect. *Storm Birds* (1938; Budapest, Min. Cult.) shows the artist's intention to signal his love of and solidarity with the land and the people. During this period his expression is determined by his moral viewpoint, but it is still reminiscent of van Gogh, and the dynamism is checked by structural discipline. Between 1938 and 1943 Dési Huber travelled a lot in Hungary and Transylvania, producing a large number of landscape paintings, including a favourite subject of his early years, the *Church of Dés* (1942–3; Budapest, N.G.). In 1943 he won the landscape award of the Pál Szinyei Merse Society. By that time his draughtsmanship had mellowed, his contours had become softer and sometimes the constructive skeleton of the picture fades in the dissolving colour (e.g. *Twisted Trees on the Bank of the Szamos*, 1943; Budapest, N.G.). His last period can be seen as a link between the two major tendencies in modern Hungarian painting, the Expressionism of Gyula Derkovits and the expressive realism of Great Plains painting.

WRITINGS

A művészetről [On art] (Budapest, 1959)
A. Timár, ed.: *Művészeti írások* [Essays on art] (Budapest, 1975)
A. Huber, ed.: *Levelek a szülőföldre* [Letters to the fatherland] (Budapest, 1982)

BIBLIOGRAPHY

E. Kállai: 'Dési Huber István festményei' [Paintings of István Dési Huber], *Magyar Művészet* (1938), no. 10, pp. 326–34
Istvánné Dési Huber: *Dési Huber István* (Budapest, 1964) [Memoirs of the artist's wife]
István Dési Huber (exh. cat., ed. O. Manga-Heil; Budapest, N.G., 1964) [retro.]
O. Manga-Heil: 'Contribution à l'étude de l'art d'István Dési Huber', *Bull. Gal. N. Hong.*, 5 (1965), pp.41–51
O. Mezei: *Dési Huber István* (Budapest, 1972)
G. Horváth: *Dési Huber István* (Budapest, 1976)

István Dési Huber: *Noon Siesta*, tempera on cardboard, 0.80×1.00 m, 1933–4 (Budapest, Hungarian National Gallery)

O. Manga-Heil: *Dési Huber István* (Budapest, 1982) [with Eng., Fr. and Ger. summary]

ANNA SZINYEI MERSE

De Simone, Alfredo (*b* Latarico, Cosenza, Italy, 29 Oct 1898; *d* Montevideo, 27 Jan 1950). Uruguayan painter of Italian birth. He studied (1917–1920) under the Uruguayan Guillermo Laborde (1886–1940) at the Círculo de Bellas Artes in Montevideo and in 1927 participated in an exhibition at Amigos del Arte in Buenos Aires presented by Teseo, a group of Uruguayan artists. While his paintings of the 1920s were affected to some extent by the romantic currents then dominant in Uruguay, his work soon changed direction because of his passion for the neighbourhoods and streets of the southern zone of Montevideo, its tenement houses and local scenes. In small oil paintings such as *Suburb* (1941), *Street in the Rain* (*c.* 1940) and *City* (*c.* 1940) (all Montevideo, Mus. N. A. Plást.), he rejected all concessions to conventional ideas of beauty and culture, rendering large forms in a heavy impasto applied with a palette knife. Noteworthy among the many exhibitions in which he participated were the *Exposición pro víctimas de la guerra civil española*, held in 1938 at the Ateneo of Montevideo, the fifth Salón Nacional (1941), at which he obtained the Banco de la República prize, and *20 pintores uruguayos* at the Salón Kraft in Buenos Aires in 1949.

BIBLIOGRAPHY
J. P. Argul: *Las artes plásticas del Uruguay* (Montevideo, 1966); rev. as *Proceso de las artes plásticas del Uruguay* (Montevideo, 1975)
G. Peluffo: *Historia de la pintura uruguaya* (Montevideo, 1988–9)

ANGEL KALENBERG

De Simone, Antonio (*b* Naples, 1759; *d* Naples, 1822). Italian architect. He served as royal architect during the French rule in Naples (1806–15) and the subsequent Bourbon restoration, becoming a member of the ten-strong Consiglio degli Edifici Civili on the accession of Joseph Bonaparte as King of Naples in 1806. In 1807 he succeeded Carlo Vanvitelli (1740–1821) as designer of the interiors of the Palazzo Reale, Caserta; here he was responsible for the splendid Empire-style Sala di Marte and Sala di Astrea.

It is difficult to make a judgement on De Simone's achievements since in general he worked as part of a group or alongside more creative figures such as Antonio Niccolini, with whom he worked on the repair and restoration of the Teatro S Carlo following a fire (1816). At the royal palace in Naples he refurbished the state apartments, including the Sala del Trono, and remodelled the royal chapel. Recent documentary finds (Naples, Archv Stato) show that at that time he was also active at the royal properties of Astroni and Capodimonte, where he was assisted by Tommaso Giordano. Accounts for work still in progress at his death were drawn up by the architect Pietro Bianchi (ii), who was then engaged on the construction of the church of S Francesco di Paola in front of the royal palace.

BIBLIOGRAPHY
A. Venditti: *Architettura neoclassica a Napoli* (Naples, 1961)
C. Garzya: *Interni neoclassici a Napoli* (Naples, 1978)
A. Buccaro: *Istituzioni e trasformazioni urbane nella Napoli dell'ottocento* (Ercolano, 1985)

De Simone, Francesco (*b* Lecce, 1859; *d* Naples, 1932). Italian urban planner and architect. He was brought up in Trani, a town in the Puglie, and graduated at the Scuola d'Applicazione degli Ingegneri in Naples, the city where he was most active. He was primarily an urban planner but also designed public and private buildings. A thorough theoretical and practical knowledge underpinned his schemes, which were concerned particularly with problems associated with road networks, functional planning and economy. In 1889 he made a plan (unexecuted) for the transformation of the area surrounding the Museo Archeologico in Naples. The project was drawn up for a competition for the improvement, enlargement and beautification of the city and it was intended to resolve the road arrangement at this pivotal urban point, replacing the smaller buildings on the site. Other unexecuted schemes include those commissioned by the Comune di Trani for the Palazzo di Giustizia (1900) and the area around the port (1901–14). For the law courts he considered a number of possible locations and in his designs applied eclectic forms to an essentially classical framework; the rectangular, symmetrical building has an arcade running transversely through it. In 1906 he produced designs for the Villa Velardi that are considered to have introduced the Art Nouveau style to Naples (see De Fusco).

De Simone is best known, however, for his urban plan for the city of Naples, first exhibited in 1914, which is regarded as a work of fundamental importance. The plan's reputation is due not only to the quality of its content but also to the completeness and clarity with which it is expressed. Its originality lies essentially in the division of the city into zones or areas. De Simone assigned one of five different functions to each of these urban areas: dwellings, industry, public buildings, commerce and the university and hospitals. The plan shows how he adopted and developed the urban-planning innovations of Art Nouveau (see De Fusco). The same kind of flexibility is apparent in a partially realized plan for the Rione Carelli at Posillipo. Here, a series of villas is distributed beside a winding road. This scheme, like his earlier project for the Museo Archeologico, is integrated within the general plan for Naples. De Simone felt that a plan of this kind was an urgent necessity for Naples because he realized that its development was out of step with other European cities and he considered the well-being of a city to reside in the certainty of its future.

De Simone's last years were devoted to the study of the inter-urban infrastructure. His project for a motorway between Rome and Naples dates from 1923 and in this he was once again ahead of his time. In 1928 he recommended new legislation to form the basis of the new building regulations for Naples passed in 1935. De Simone's writings, designs and works show that he was a thorough and systematic professional, knowledgeable and well-informed about contemporary developments in Europe.

WRITINGS
Progetto di un palazzo di giustizia e municipio di Trani (Trani, 1900)
'Piano regolatore della città di Napoli', *Atti Coll. Architetti & Ingeg.* (1917)

BIBLIOGRAPHY
R. De Fusco: *Il floreale a Napoli* (Naples, 1959)
S. Pastore, G. Carbone and M. Schiralli: *L'architettura napoletana del primo novecento a Trani: Francesco de Simone* (Molfetta, 1984)

ISABELLA DI RESTA

Desjardins [van den Bogaert], **Martin** (*b* Breda, *bapt* 11 Nov 1637; *d* Paris, 2 May 1694). French sculptor and stuccoist of Dutch birth. He trained in Antwerp with Peeter Verbrugghen (i) and at some time in the 1650s went to Paris. There he worked with the sculptors Gérard van Opstal and the brothers Gaspard and Balthazar Marsy, who had also trained in the southern Netherlands. He worked (*c.* 1659–60) for van Opstal on the portal of the château of Vincennes (destr.) and with the Marsy brothers *c.* 1658 on stucco decorations at the Hôtel d'Aubert de Fontenay (now Hôtel Salé), Paris. By *c.* 1660, when he executed the stucco decoration of the staircase of the Hôtel de Beauvais, he was working independently. These early works show his Antwerp schooling. In 1661 he became a member of the Académie de St Luc under his adopted name of Desjardins. Throughout the 1660s he concentrated on church decorations and funerary monuments. This phase ended in 1671 with his marble monument to *Antoine d'Aubray, Comte d'Offemont* for the chapel of the Paris Oratory. This work, which is known through a plaster cast (Versailles, Château), consisted of a reclining female figure of *Justice* holding a portrait medallion of the deceased. It is typical of Desjardin's ornamental use at this time of draped figures composed from a single, frontal viewpoint. In the same year he was received (*reçu*) as a member of the Académie Royale on presentation of his subtly executed marble relief *Hercules Crowned by Glory* (Paris, Louvre). Henceforth he began to receive important commissions from the crown, undertaking work (1676–9) for the Hôtel des Invalides and its church of St Louis, Paris, for the château of Clagny (1675–82; destr.), near Versailles, as well as for the façades, interiors and gardens of the château of Versailles.

Among Desjardins's works for the park at Versailles is the well-known marble statue of *Diana* (or *Evening*), executed after a design by the Premier Peintre du Roi Charles Le Brun; begun in 1675 and completed in 1681, the *Diana* is not indebted to antique examples for its composition, which is remarkably dynamic and designed to be seen from a multiplicity of viewpoints. His monumental stone relief of the *Capture of Besançon* (1675–6; *in situ*) on the Porte St Martin, Paris, was a commission from the city of Paris, and during the same period (1670–77) he also carried out a considerable part of the sculptural decoration of the capital's Collège des Quatre-Nations (now the Palais de l'Institut). Characteristic of Desjardins's work of this decade is conciseness of composition and an increasing confidence in the use of multi-viewpoint, as in his marble bust of the painter *Pierre Mignard* (*c.* 1675; Paris, Louvre). The latter, his most important private commission undertaken at this time, was later used as a model for the bust on Mignard's tomb (Paris, St Roch) and shows the artist's head turned at an expressive angle. It is among the earliest French busts of an artist in which the subject's character and profession are conveyed through intensity of expression and informality of drapery.

In 1679 François d'Aubusson, Duc de La Feuillade, commissioned from Desjardins a marble statue of *Louis XIV* as a Roman emperor (Versailles, Château), intended for his château of Oiron, Deux-Sèvres. Two years later La Feuillade decided to have this statue set up in Paris, with four bronze statues of slaves (now Paris, Louvre) round its pedestal, who between them symbolized the Holy Roman Empire, Spain, Brandenburg and the Netherlands. Four bronze reliefs (now Paris, Louvre), also for the pedestal, referred to France's continued advances as Europe's leading power. In 1682 La Feuillade resolved to replace the marble statue of the monarch by a bronze group (h. 5 m) of *Louis XIV Crowned as the Gallic Hercules by Victory*; beneath the King, who was depicted wearing his coronation robes, was Cerberus, symbolizing the powers of the Triple Alliance—probably Britain, Sweden and the Netherlands—ranged against France. The following year La Feuillade determined to have a new square laid out in the capital as a setting for this monument; the result was the Place des Victoires designed by the architect Jules Hardouin Mansart. Work began on four lamps intended to illuminate the square in 1685; their supporting columns were to be decorated with relief pendants in the form of bronze medallions, and of the 24 planned at least 11 were completed (e.g. Paris, Louvre). The *Louis XIV* group and its pedestal—the largest standing figure of a French monarch hitherto made and the most important monument to Louis XIV to have been privately commissioned—was destroyed in 1792, although it is known from engravings (see, e.g., Souchal, fig. 45). In the imperialist assertions of its subject-matter the *Louis XIV* group represents a culminating point in French monumental iconography. Desjardins had cast it in his own workshop, thereby demonstrating his expertise in large-scale bronze-casting. As a result, in 1687–8 he was commissioned to produce two huge equestrian statues of *Louis XIV*. One, destined for Aix-en-Provence, was to portray the King on a rearing horse; the other, for Lyon, had the monarch on a walking horse. The Aix statue was never executed, but a bronze statuette (priv. col., see Souchal, fig. 46b) provides a record of Desjardins's design. He did cast the bronze statue intended for the Place Bellecour, Lyon, shortly before his death, though it was not installed until 1715. Destroyed in 1792, its appearance can be gauged from numerous surviving bronze statuettes (e.g. Copenhagen, Stat. Mus. Kst; New York, Met.; London, Wallace). Because his time was so taken up with statues of the King, from *c.* 1680 Desjardins more or less ceased to get involved in major sculptural commissions from the crown; one exception was the design in terracotta (*c.* 1680; priv. col.) for a statue of *Charlemagne* for the Dôme des Invalides.

Desjardins's late style, from *c.* 1685, is notable for its loosened linear structure and increased emphasis on

Martin Desjardins: *Edouard Colbert de Villacerf*, marble, 1.05×0.78 m, 1693 (Paris, Musée du Louvre)

plasticity: flowing drapery is sculpted in detail to convey the sense of movement. On two occasions he collaborated with François Girardon: *c.* 1690 on the posthumously carved marble bust of *Queen Marie-Thérèse* (Troyes, Mus. B.-A. & Archéol.), and in 1693 when they began the tomb of *François Michel Le Tellier, Marquis de Louvois and his Wife* (Tonnerre, Hôp.). In the last decade of his life Desjardins also independently executed two large marbles: a *Virgin* (1681–6; untraced) for the church of the Sorbonne, Paris, and the official portrait bust of *Edouard Colbert de Villacerf* (1693; Paris, Louvre; see fig.). Desjardins's works, especially the monuments and busts, occupy an important place in 17th-century French sculpture, introducing a powerful yet refined Netherlandish quality to French classicism.

BIBLIOGRAPHY

Souchal

L. Seelig: *Studien zu Martin van den Bogaert (1637–1694)* (diss., U. Munich, 1973)

M. Martin: *Les Monuments équestres de Louis XIV* (Paris, 1986), pp. 138–56, 178–88

L. Seelig: 'Eine Reiterstatuette Kurfürst Max Emanuels von Bayern aus dem Jahr 1699', *Anz. Ger. Nmus.* (1986), pp. 61–74

G. Bresc-Bautier: *Musée du Louvre: Nouvelles Acquisitions du département des sculptures* (Paris, 1992), pp. 58–61

LORENZ SEELIG

Desk. *See under* BUREAU.

Deskey, Donald (*b* Blue Earth, MN, 23 Nov 1894; *d* 1989). American interior and industrial designer. He gained a degree in architecture and studied painting before working in advertising. From 1922 to 1924 he was head of the art department at Juniata College, Huntingdon, PA.

In 1921 and 1925 he made trips to Paris, where he attended the Ecole de la Grande Chaumière and the Académie Colarossi, returning to New York in 1926 as a champion of modern art and design. In 1926–7 he created the city's first modern window displays for the Franklin Simon and Saks Fifth Avenue department stores. In 1927 he was joined by the designer Philip Vollmer, and the partnership became Deskey–Vollmer, Inc. (to c. 1929). Deskey expanded into designing interiors, furniture, lamps and textiles, becoming a pioneer of the *Style moderne* (as Art Deco was known in America). His earliest model for the interior of an apartment was shown at the American Designers' Gallery, New York, in 1929. With its cork-lined walls, copper ceiling, movable walls, pigskin-covered furniture and linoleum floor, it demonstrated his novel approach. He was one of the first American designers to use Bakelite, Formica, Fabrikoid, brushed aluminium and chromium-plated brass, which he would combine with more exotic materials (e.g. desk, macassar ebony, mixed woods and brass, 1929; New Haven, CT, Yale U. A.G.). In 1931, for the showman Samuel L. Rothafel and the Rockefeller family, he created the interiors of Radio City Music Hall, Rockefeller Center, New York, introducing aluminium foil wallpaper in the men's smoking lounge. His Radio City interiors, together with a luxury apartment he designed for Rothafel in the same building (c. 1931–2), survive as his masterpieces.

BIBLIOGRAPHY

A. J. Pulos: *American Design Ethic: A History of Industrial Design* (Cambridge, MA, 1983/R 1986)

A. Duncan: *American Art Deco* (London, 1986)

D. A. Hanks with J. Toher: *Donald Deskey: Decorative Designs and Interiors* (New York, 1987)

☐

Desmarées, Georges (*b* Gimo, Sweden, 29 Oct 1697; *d* Munich, 3 Oct 1776). Swedish painter, active in Germany. His father was descended from French émigrés to Sweden, his mother from the Mijtens family of Netherlandish artists. Desmarées was a pupil at the painting school of his uncle, Martin van Mytens II, in Stockholm from 1710. His early portraits, painted while he was still in Sweden, reveal the influence of van Mytens and his French models, Hyacinthe Rigaud and Nicolas de Largillierre. Desmarées left Sweden in 1724 and after a short stay in Amsterdam went to Nuremberg to continue his training with Johann Daniel Preissler at the Akademie der Bildenden Künste. A year later he went to Venice to study with Giovanni Battista Piazzetta, whose art made a considerable impression on him. Desmarées returned to Bavaria in 1728 and was summoned to Munich in 1730 for appointment as court painter to Elector Charles. He was initially involved in the furnishing and decoration of the Ahnengalerie at the Residenz in Munich. From 1745 to 1749 and from 1753 to 1754 he worked in Bonn for Prince–Bishop Clemens August of Cologne, and in 1752 he worked for Landgrave William VIII of Hesse- Kassel. The influence of French Rococo painting was becoming increasingly prominent during this period, and the Venetian chiaroscuro of his painting gradually gave way to brighter, more emphatic colouring. Such portraits as those of *Countess Holstein* (1754; Munich, Lenbachhaus), *Elector Maximilian III Joseph and his Director Graf Seeau* (1755; Munich,

Residenzmus.) and *Princess Portia* (Stuttgart, Staatsgal.) assured Desmarées' place among the most important representatives of Rococo court painting in Germany. In later years his portraits were marked by a more measured and objective style. Besides large formal portraits of noble patrons, Desmarées also undertook commissions for middle class patrons and church paintings.

BIBLIOGRAPHY

C. Hernmarck: *George Desmarées: Studien über die Rokokomalerei in Schweden und Deutschland* (Uppsala, 1935)

W. Holzhausen: *Kurkölnische Hofmaler des 18. Jahrhunderts* (Cologne, 1957)

L. Seelig: 'Die Ahnengalerie der Münchener Residenz: Untersuchungen zur malerischen Ausstattung', *Quellen und Studien zur Kunstpolitik der Wittelsbacher vom 16. bis zum 18. Jahrhundert*, ed. L. Seelig (Munich, 1980), pp. 253–327

L. Koch: *George Desmarées* (diss., U.Würzburg, in preparation)

JOSEF STRASSER

Desmarquet(s), Pauline. *See* AUZOU, PAULINE.

De Smet, Gustave [Gust; Gustaaf] (*b* Ghent, 21 Jan 1877; *d* Deurle, 8 Oct 1943). Belgian painter and printmaker. He studied from 1889 to 1896 at the Académie Royale des Beaux-Arts in Ghent, and together with his younger brother Léon De Smet (1881–1966), also a painter, he helped his father Jules De Smet with the decoration of inns, stores and fairground buildings. From c. 1902 Gustave de Smet spent time in Deurle and with Frits Van den Berghe at Laethem-Saint-Martin near Ghent, where he was part of the second generation of artists who sought out the rural surroundings of the river Leie to live and paint. From 1911 he once again lived in Ghent. When World War I broke out he fled with his wife and son to the Netherlands and worked there in close contact with Van den Berghe, who had also left Belgium. He stayed in Amsterdam and in the villages of Laren and Blaricum.

During the years up to World War I, De Smet painted mostly cityscapes and landscapes in an impressionistic style, derived from the example of Emile Claus and Albert Baertsoen, for example *Spring* or *The Red Chairs* (1913; Brussels, Georges Remi priv. col., see Haesaerts, p. 281). In this period, however, there were also a few canvases with symbolic elements. The change came in the Netherlands through contact with modern Dutch painters such as Jan Sluyters and the émigré Frenchman Henri Le Fauconnier, but especially through exposure to exhibitions and periodicals concerned with modern German and French art. From 1916 outside influences, primarily those of Cubism and German Expressionism, can be seen in his work. De Smet painted landscapes, village- and cityscapes, and figures in an interior or against a village background. These paintings are remarkable for their warm palette, heavy impasto and angular distortions that sometimes produce highly dynamic compositions. He also made linocuts of some of his compositions. Around 1920 he evolved away from this experimental phase towards a moderately expressionistic style, characterized by synthetic design, formal order, a warm palette and a rich texture.

From 1920 De Smet again lived in Belgium in the Leie region, taking part in village life and continuing to work with Van den Berghe. Some of his most important paintings were produced in this period. He was supported by the Brussels galleries Sélection and Le Centaure, which promoted him in their eponymous periodicals as the practitioner of a classical, pastoral expressionism. His work dealt with the human figure, fairs and village life, for example *Sunday* (1921; Antwerp Kon. Mus. S. Kst., see Haesaerts, p. 385). The dissonant elements from his Dutch period disappeared in favour of harmoniously composed canvases, dominated by the orchestration of purely painterly qualities. He produced a formally refined art, in harmony with a general European tendency towards classicism; from 1926 his work even acquired a decorative, constructivist quality, while the palette became clear and bright (e.g. *Blue Nude*; Lierre, Joseph Janssen priv. col, see Haesaerts, p. 305).

After this phase De Smet returned to the use of warmer earth tones and developed a more painterly manner and a freer compositional technique. His themes remained unchanged, although the intimate quality became more important in still-lifes, interiors, nudes and portraits of couples. This intimate, realistic character became a constant in his work from the 1930s. During this period the artist continued to work near Laethem-Saint-Martin, and in 1943 he built himself a house in Deurle, subsequently converted to a small museum named after him. De Smet remained attached to his rural setting but frequently participated in exhibitions in various Belgian cities. Exhibitions were organized by the galleries Le Centaure and Sélection, and while the painter was still alive, the Palais des Beaux-Arts in Brussels devoted three retrospectives to his work: in 1936, 1940 and 1942.

BIBLIOGRAPHY

F. Huebner: *Gustaaf De Smet*, Nieuwe Kunst, 2 (Amsterdam, 1921)
A. De Ridder: *Laethem-Saint-Martin, colonie d'artistes* (Brussels and Paris, 1945)
E. Langui: *Gust De Smet, de mensch en zijn werk* (Brussels, 1945)
Gustave De Smet (exh. cat., Antwerp, Kon. Mus. S. Kst., 1961)
P. Haesaerts: *Laethem-Saint-Martin, le village élu de l'art flamand* (Brussels, 1963, 5/1970)
E. Langui: *L'Expressionnisme en Belgique* (Brussels, 1970)
P. Boyens: *Gust De Smet: Kroniek – Kunsthistorische analyse* (Antwerp, 1989)

ROBERT HOOZEE

Desmoulins, Jean-Baptiste. *See* MAILLOU, JEAN-BAPTISTE.

Desneux de la Noue. *See* LA NOUE, Abbé de.

Desnoyer, François (*b* Montauban, 30 Sept 1894; *d* Perpignan, 21 July 1972). French painter, printmaker, stage designer, illustrator and tapestry designer. He was encouraged to study art by Emile-Antoine Bourdelle, to whom he showed his drawings at the age of 16, and was taught by him at the Ecole de Dessin à la Manufacture des Gobelins. From 1912 to 1914 he attended the Ecole des Arts Décoratifs in Montauban, and after serving in the infantry during World War I he moved to Paris, where he showed his work regularly at such exhibitions as the Salon des Indépendants and the Salon d'Automne.

Desnoyer lived and worked among the Cubists, but like the Fauves he favoured bright primary colours, marrying colour and line in landscapes, still-lifes and portraits. His debt to both movements is visible in paintings such as *La Foire du Trône* (1927; Paris, Pompidou). He also produced an illustrated edition of La Fontaine's *Dies Irae* (Editions Mortier, 1947) and stage designs for the Opéra Comique in Paris, for example for Henri Barrand's *Maître Pathelin* in 1948, for which he based his design directly on his painting *Chatenay with Black Roofs* (1944; Paris, Mus. A. Mod. Ville Paris). He taught at the Ecole Nationale des Arts Décoratifs in Paris and received various awards, including the Grand Prix Blumenthal in 1923, the Gold Medal of the International Exhibition in 1937 and the Grand Prix de la Peinture Contemporaine in 1950. Following the custom in Paris for artists to exchange paintings and due to his popularity, Desnoyer accumulated an impressive art collection with his wife Souza. The Fondation François-et-Souza-Desnoyer was established at Saint-Cyprien to administer the collection, which passed to the state on his death.

BIBLIOGRAPHY

G. Besson: *François Desnoyer* (Paris, 1947)
François Desnoyer (exh. cat. by N. Wallis and B. Dorival, London, Marlborough New London Gal., 1955)
S. Desnoyer: *Desnoyer: Sa vie, son oeuvre, ses amis, ses voyages* (Montfermeil, 1977)
Donation François et Souza Desnoyer (exh. cat., Saint-Cyprien, Mus.–Fond. Desnoyer, 1981)

ALBERTO CERNUSCHI

De Soissons, Louis (Emmanuel Jean Guy de Savoie-Carignan), Viscount d'Ostel, Baron Longroy (*b* Montreal, 31 July 1890; *d* London, 23 Sept 1962). English architect. His earliest architectural training was at the Ecole des Beaux-Arts, Paris, and then with J. H. Eastwood (1843–1913). By winning the Henry Jarvis Studentship (1913), De Soissons was entitled to two years at the British School at Rome, but this was interrupted by World War I, and he resumed in 1919. He was briefly in partnership with his fellow Rome scholar, Philip Hepworth (1890–1963), and for a longer period with Grey Wornum, during which time the partnership designed Larkhall Flats (1929), Wandsworth Road, London, and Haig Homes at Liverpool (1929) and Morden, Surrey (1931), all distinguished examples of neo-Georgian style.

The major work of De Soissons' career was Welwyn Garden City, for which he was appointed planner and company architect in 1920. The plan, which was influenced by S. D. Adshead's work in the Duchy of Cornwall Estate (from 1911), has a formal centre, becoming informal in domestic zones. He designed all the main buildings, civic, residential and educational, creating a unified effect of style, mostly in red brick neo-Georgian, sited to keep existing trees and hedges. De Soissons lived in the town he created, and had great loyalty to it, continuing to add to it until his death, although other architects made important contributions, notably A. W. Kenyon (1885–1969) and H. Clapham Lander (1869–1955). His design for the Shredded Wheat Factory (1925) has impressive concrete silos, using the Kahn system of reinforced concrete.

De Soissons became architect to the Duchy of Cornwall Estate in Kennington, designing Newquay House (1934), Sancroft Street, London. He was also employed by the Dartington Hall Trust to build rural workers' housing at Dartington, Devon, and speculative detached houses of superior quality for Staverton Builders Ltd (1933) in the St James's Park Estate, Exeter, and elsewhere in Devon in the 1930s. Following World War II he became architect to the Imperial War Graves Commission in Greece and Italy. Much of his English work was concerned with restorations, for example of Carlton House Terrace and many of the Nash terraces surrounding Regent's Park, London, to which De Soissons added new buildings on the mews sites. He also designed the Royal College of Obstetricians (1958), Park Road, Regent's Park. De Soissons was elected RA in 1953.

BIBLIOGRAPHY

F. J. Osborn: *The Genesis of Welwyn Garden City* (London, 1970, rev. 1973)
R. Filler: *Welwyn Garden City* (Chichester, 1986)
M. de Soissons: *Welwyn Garden City* (Cambridge, 1988)

ALAN POWERS

Despenser, 15th Baron **Le.** *See* DASHWOOD, FRANCIS.

Despiau, Charles (*b* Mont-de-Marsan, 4 Nov 1874; *d* Paris, 28 Oct 1946). French sculptor and illustrator. In 1891 he entered the Ecole des Arts Décoratifs in Paris, where he studied under the French sculptor Hector Lemaire (1846–1933). Two years later he went to the Ecole des Beaux-Arts in Paris, where for three years he studied under Louis-Ernest Barrias. He also frequented the Louvre and the Musée des Monuments Français, learning as much there as at the fine art schools. He first exhibited in 1898 at the Salon des Artistes Français in Paris with a bust of *Joseph Biays* and continued to exhibit there until 1900. In 1901 he exhibited his bust of *Marc Worms* (1901; Paris, Mme Cl. Michel priv. col., see 1974 exh. cat., pl. 4) at the Salon de la Société Nationale des Beaux-Arts in Paris. He exhibited there until 1923.

Despiau's first success at the Salon came with his bust *Little Girl from Landes* (1904; Paris, Pompidou), a bronze version of which was commissioned by the French government. Later he exhibited his bust entitled *Paulette* (1907; Paris, Pompidou), which persuaded Auguste Rodin to invite Despiau to join his studio as an assistant. Despiau remained there until 1914, executing under Rodin's direction two marble busts, of *Mme Barbre Elisseief* (1909; St Petersburg, Hermitage) and of the bacteriologist *Gabritchevsky* (Moscow, Pushkin Mus. F.A.). He also produced the unfinished work *The Genius of Eternal Repose* (1914; Paris, Mus. Rodin), designed by Rodin as a monument to honour Pierre Puvis de Chavannes in the Panthéon. Rodin had a beneficent influence on Despiau, equipping him with a greater technical facility without imposing his own artistic style. Despiau in fact rebelled against Rodin's romanticism in his own work, adopting a more static, classical style.

After World War I Despiau was commissioned to produce a war memorial for his native town of Mont-de-Marsan, which he worked on from 1920 to 1922. In 1923 he began exhibiting in Paris at the Salon d'Automne and the Salon des Tuileries, of which he was a co-founder, and two years later received a commission from the French government for his *Female Faun* (1925; Paris, Pompidou). In 1927 he was appointed professor of sculpture at the Académie Scandinave in Paris, and in 1930 he was vice-president of the Salon des Tuileries. Also in 1930 he began work on the monument in honour of the Luxembourg

industrialist *Emile Mayrisch* in the park at Colpach (plaster version, 1930; Paris, Pompidou).

An edition of Charles Baudelaire's *Les Fleurs du mal* was published in 1933 with 50 illustrations by Despiau, and he also illustrated Henri de Montherlant's *Les Olympiques* (1943). In 1934 he began using his cousin Odette Dupeyron as a model, which he continued to do for the rest of his life. From 1937 to 1946 he worked on the monumental statue *Apollo* for the terrace of the Musée d'Art Moderne de la Ville de Paris. Most of Despiau's output consisted of portrait busts, such as *Dunoyer de Segonzac* (1942; Paris, Pompidou). He worked painstakingly on these, often requiring 60 sittings in an attempt to capture the intimate character of his model. In all his sculpture the style is similar to the sober classicism of Aristide Maillol.

BIBLIOGRAPHY

C. Roger-Marx: *Charles Despiau* (Paris, 1922)
L. Deshairs: *Charles Despiau* (Paris, 1930)
Sculpture by Despiau (exh. cat. by R. Cogniat, London, Wildenstein's, 1938)
W. George: *Despiau* (Paris, 1947)
——: *Despiau* (Amsterdam, 1958)
Charles Despiau: Sculptures et dessins (exh. cat. by C. Roger-Marx, Paris, Mus. Rodin, 1974)   □

Desportes. French family of painters and a writer. (1) François Desportes was the most eminent painter of animals and still-lifes in late 17th- and early 18th-century France. His son (2) Claude-François Desportes assisted him in his numerous commissions and gained a reputation for his lectures delivered to the Académie Royale.

(1) (Alexandre-)François Desportes (*b* Champigneule, Marne, 24 Feb 1661; *d* Paris, 20 April 1743). Painter. He was an artist of the late Baroque who trained in the Flemish tradition of animal painting. After a slow start and a brief trip to Poland, where he painted royal portraits, he became in 1700 the official painter of hunting scenes and animals to Louis XIV. He continued in this role under Louis XV. He also painted a variety of still-lifes and tapestry cartoons for the Gobelins, and he is noted for his landscape studies made directly from nature. He is credited with helping to popularize Flemish art, one of the essential ingredients of the Rococo style in France.

1. Early Career, 1661–99. 2. Royal Patronage, 1700–43.

1. EARLY CAREER, 1661–99. Desportes's father, a prosperous agricultural labourer, sent him at the age of 12 to live with an uncle in Paris. Shortly after his arrival he became ill, and to amuse him during his recovery his uncle gave him an engraving to copy, thus revealing his talent. Soon after this he became a student in Paris of the Flemish painter Nicasius Bernaerts (1620–78), who had trained with Frans Snyders and had enjoyed a considerable success as a painter of animals at the Gobelins. Bernaerts encouraged Desportes to draw directly from nature and to make copies after Flemish prints and paintings of animal scenes and still-lifes. These rudimentary lessons undoubtedly instilled in Desportes what was to become a lifelong fascination with animal subjects and Flemish realism. He was, however, far from satisfied with his master's lessons: Bernaerts, old and infirm from alcohol, was unable to

offer any practical advice or assistance. When he died Desportes vowed never again to follow any master except nature and his own intelligence.

After Bernaerts's death Desportes studied at the Académie Royale, making traditional academic drawings as well as continuing to draw directly from nature. To support himself he designed stage sets, painted portraits and assisted other artists in painting decorations in Paris hôtels. In the late 1680s and early 1690s he assisted Claude Audran III at the château of Anet for the Duc de Vendôme, at Clichy for the Grand Prieur Philippe de Vendôme, at the Hôtel de Bouillon in Paris, and at the Ménagerie at Versailles for Louis XIV. All these paintings are untraced but were described by contemporaries as lively animal scenes. Desportes's sole consolation during this difficult period was his marriage in 1692 to Eléonore-Angélique Baudet, a linen- and lacemaker, who continued her trade to relieve financial burdens and free her husband's time for further studies.

Financial and military disasters in France in the early 1690s reduced funds for artistic projects and left many unestablished artists such as Desportes without work. Lacking commissions of consequence, he accepted an invitation in 1695 from the French ambassador to Poland to paint royal portraits at the Polish court. The Polish king John III Sobieski, his French wife Marie-Casimire and several court officials were among his subjects. His portrayals were highly esteemed, but his stay ended late in 1696 when the king died and Louis XIV recalled him to France. Desportes had established himself as a credible portrait painter abroad, but with stiff competition at home

1. François Desportes: *Still-life with Dead Game in a Marble Niche*, oil on canvas, 1.04×0.97 m, 1706 (Le Havre, Musée des Beaux-Arts)

from François de Troy, Nicolas de Largillierre and Hyacinthe Rigaud he again focused his energies on animal painting. On 1 August 1699, at the age of 38, Desportes was received (*reçu*) into the Académie Royale as an animal painter. His *morceau de réception, Self-portrait as a Hunter* (Paris, Louvre, on dep. Paris Mus. Chasse & Nat.), shows the artist seated in a landscape with two hunting dogs and an impressive display of dead game. In a single, highly acclaimed piece, he had demonstrated his diverse abilities, indicated by the array of animals the future direction of his art and appealed to the tastes of the nobility, who considered hunting one of the last marks of class distinction. One month later he enjoyed another success with the exhibition of two still-lifes at the Salon.

2. ROYAL PATRONAGE, 1700–43. In 1700 Desportes received the first of many royal commissions that spanned nearly half a century. Louis XIV ordered five pictures depicting diverse animals and facets of the hunt for the Ménagerie at the château of Versailles, which he was having decorated for the Duchesse de Bourgogne. Four of the paintings have survived: *Deer Kill, Wolf Hunt, Boar Hunt* and *Hounds Guarding a Dead Deer* (Paris, Mus. Chasse & Nat.). Such subjects were unprecedented in French art, and Desportes relied heavily in his compositions on the successful formulae of the Flemings Frans Snyders and Paul de Vos. Two years later Louis XIV requested six portraits of his favourite huntings dogs for the anteroom of the château of Marly. *Bonne, Nonne and Ponne* and *Diane and Blonde* (1702; Paris, Mus. Chasse & Nat.), which show the dogs flushing pheasants and partridges in a natural setting, are two examples of this work. To depict the animals and their settings accurately Desportes took up hunting and even accompanied Louis XIV on his campaigns in the forests around Versailles, Fontainebleau and Meudon. The King reportedly found the paintings so realistic that he could identify the dogs by name and the exact location of the hunt. Other royal commissions included painting the rare and exotic animals of the Ménagerie and, in 1714, updating the portraits of the royal kennel. Desportes also provided Louis de Bourbon, the Grand Dauphin, with three sets of hunting scenes (e.g. *Dogs Guarding Wild Game*, Paris, Louvre) for the château of Meudon between 1704 and 1709. In a very short time Desportes had become the premier animal painter in France and had popularized this typically Flemish genre among the upper echelons of French society. His works, moreover, provided important prototypes for younger painters such as Jean-Baptiste Oudry and Carle Vernet.

While executing hunting scenes in the service of the King, Desportes also helped to pave the way for a renaissance of still-life painting in the 18th century. Around 1700–02, taking his cue from Flemish and Dutch sources, he started to paint trophies of the hunt and dead game arranged with flowers, fruits and vegetables on tabletops or in landscape settings. A superb example is his *Still-life with Dead Game in a Marble Niche* (1706; see fig. 1), in which a hare and partridges, suspended statue-like in an empty marble niche, are accompanied on a marble plinth by ripe fruit and a Delft bowl. (Marble appears frequently in Desportes's still-lifes in the form of niches, balustrades and columns and is considered one of his trademarks.) Flemish influences are evident in the subject, microscopic realism and brilliant colours. Nevertheless, Desportes's still-lifes are distinctively French in their limited range of objects, idealization of dead game and fruits and compositional reserve. Like many French artists of his generation, he combined classical and colourist principles in his works and thereby provided an important transition to the early Rococo.

Desportes's paintings brought him recognition and prosperity. In 1702 Louis XIV awarded him a pension and lodgings in the Louvre, in 1704 the Académie appointed him a councillor, and in the same year he exhibited 15 paintings at the Salon. His name appeared regularly thereafter in the Salon *livrets*, and annually between 1737 and 1742. By the early 1710s his reputation had spread beyond France's borders with commissions from members of the English nobility. He even visited England for six months in 1712 to deliver four still-lifes to James, 1st Earl Stanhope (1673–1721), and to secure further work. Desportes's prices had by this time tripled from their level only 10 years earlier, and in 1712 he was so prosperous that he could afford to buy a house for 23,200 livres.

After the death of Louis XIV in 1715, Desportes maintained favour with Philippe, Duc d'Orléans, the Regent of France during the minority of Louis XV, and continued to provide paintings for the royal houses. He executed hunting scenes for the residences of the Duc d'Antin at the Tuileries and Petit-Bourg and for Louis-Henri de Bourbon, Prince de Condé (1692–1740) at Chantilly. However, his commissions during the Regency were increasingly for larger and more opulent varieties of still-lifes, as in his *Musical Instruments with a Pheasant* (Grenoble, Mus. Grenoble) and the *Fountain with Exotic Birds* (Lyon, Mus. B.-A.). Desportes executed these in 1717 for the Duc d'Orléans, as decorations for the château of La Muette, the elegant residence of his daughter, the Duchesse de Berry. Appropriate to the tastes of the patron, these are sumptuous arrangements in park settings, accented by a sculpted balustrade or fountain. Trophies of the hunt and domestic fruits have been replaced by fragments of contemporary aristocratic life, such as musical instruments, velvet draperies, exotic birds and monkeys, and Japanese porcelain. By the late 1720s, nearly every prince and princess of the blood and many important private collectors had acquired works by Desportes.

During the reign of Louis XV, Desportes's still-lifes grew even richer in variety and seem to reflect the epicurean interests that created the first great age of French cuisine. His work at this time included, for example, food ready for cooking, as in the *Kitchen Table* (1734; Paris, priv. col., see Faré, 1976, p. 84). These are simple, ungarnished groupings of raw foods, the kind for which Jean-Siméon Chardin was to become famous. Desportes

2. François Desportes: *Silver Platters with Peaches*, oil on canvas, c. 1740 (Stockholm, Nationalmuseum)

also produced during this period a type of painting called a 'buffet', which has as its subject displays of costly silver and gold plate. His *Silver Platters with Peaches* (*c.* 1740, see fig. 2) is famous for its arrangement of Thomas Germain silver and its glinting reflections of peaches and brown velvet drapery. Once again the antecedents of both types lie in Netherlandish art.

Louis XV's commissions for Desportes were much like those of his great-grandfather Louis XIV. He had the artist furnish hunting scenes for the Petits Appartements at Versailles, as well as portraits of the royal kennel and pictures of the rare and exotic animals from the Ménagerie. In 1735 Desportes also undertook a series of tapestry cartoons representing the tropical plants and animals of the West Indies, which he exhibited at the Salon between 1737 and 1741. The series was so popular that the Gobelins produced 12 sets before the Revolution. Desportes last exhibited at the Salon in 1742, at the age of 81.

Desportes is estimated to have produced more than 2,000 paintings in his career, and behind these lay numerous pencil drawings and oil sketches made directly from nature. More than 600 of these have survived, most dating between 1690 and 1706. They were eventually inherited by his nephew, Nicolas Desportes (1718–87), who in 1784 sold the studies and sketches as a collection to the Comte d'Angiviller, Directeur des Bâtiments du Roi under Louis XVI, for student use at the ceramic factory of Sèvres. The collection has since remained intact and demonstrates by its diversity how meticulously Desportes studied every object in his paintings: wild game, dogs, fruits and vegetables, silver platters and ewers, and landscapes. The most remarkable of these, however, are a series of oil sketches of landscapes made as preparations for the backgrounds of his hunting scenes. Armed with only a makeshift easel and a charged palette, he recorded these open-air scenes in the neighbourhood of Paris and the Seine Valley with results that are extraordinarily direct, fresh in colour and uncomposed by classical standards of landscape (e.g. *Landscape with a View of a Distant Village, c.* 1700; Sèvres, Mus. N. Cér.). In spirit and method these oil sketches are closer to the Barbizon school or the English watercolourists of the 19th century than to anything of the late 17th century.

Desportes's contemporaries frequently expressed surprise at his prodigious activity even in old age, and at how its rigours had not affected the quality of his work. At the age of 82, in the midst of preparing new projects, he contracted pneumonia and died five days later. He was buried in the Paris church of St Germain-l'Auxerrois.

(2) **Claude-François Desportes** (*b* Paris, 1695; *d* Paris, 31 May 1774). Painter and writer, son of (1) François Desportes. He worked under the direction of his more celebrated father as a painter of animals and still-lifes. He was received (*reçu*) into the Académie Royale on 25 September 1723. His *morceau de réception* was a *Still-life of Dead Game, Fruits, a Cat and a Parrot on a Marble Console* (Paris, Louvre). He was a competent painter, but he was never able to develop an artistic persona independent of that of his father. Even in later works, he employed François Desportes's formula of grouping varieties of dead game in the foreground of a park setting (e.g. *Dead*

Game Guarded by Dogs, 1766; Troyes, Mus. B.-A. & Archéol.). His paintings, moreover, lack his father's mastery of organization and often degenerate into cluttered accumulations of artefacts. His forms are also flatter and the brushwork drier. Despite his mediocre talent he did achieve some success and exhibited paintings at the Salons of 1725, 1737, 1739 and 1758.

The younger Desportes made his deepest mark as a literary figure and intellectual at the Académie Royale, where he delivered a number of lectures. On 4 May 1748 he read *Discours sur les avantages des conférences académiques*, which promoted increased regulation in the education of young artists and public taste. This was followed on 3 August by his most famous lecture, on the subject of his father's life and career. This is one of the best primary sources on the elder Desportes. Another lecture addressed the priority of colour over line. The manuscripts of his lectures are preserved in the library of the Ecole Nationale Supérieure des Beaux-Arts, Paris.

WRITINGS

'La Vie de M. Desportes (3 août 1748)', *Mémoires inédits*, ed. L. Dussieux and others, ii (Paris, 1854), pp. 98–113
'Conférence sur le coloris', *Conférences inédites de l'Académie Royale*, ed. A. Fontaine (Paris, 1910), pp. 53–68 [as by François Desportes]

BIBLIOGRAPHY

A.-J. Dézallier d'Argenville: *Abrégé de la vie des plus fameux peintres* (1745–52, rev. 2/1762), iv, pp. 332–9
C. Blanc: *Histoire*, ii (Paris, 1865), pp. 1–8
F. Engerand: *Inventaire des tableaux commandés et achetés par la direction des Bâtiments du Roi* (Paris, 1900), pp. 151–6
E. Dumonthier: 'Les Tapisseries des Gobelins d'après François Desportes', *Ren. A. Fr. & Indust. Luxe*, ix (1920), pp. 359–64
L. Hourticq: 'L'Atelier de François Desportes', *Gaz. B.-A.*, n. s. 4, ii (1920), pp. 117–36
J. Lechevallier-Chevignard: 'Les Collections de la Manufacture de Sèvres, l'atelier de François Desportes', *Rev. A. Anc. & Mod.*, xxxviii (1920), pp. 164–74
H. Quignon: 'La Révélation de l'atelier de François Desportes (1661–1743)', *Ren. A. Fr. & Indust. Luxe*, ix (1920), pp. 353–8
M. Florisoone: *La Peinture française du XVIIIe siècle* (Paris, 1948), pp. 20–23
A. Blunt: *Art and Architecture in France, 1500–1700*, Pelican Hist. A. (Harmondsworth, 1953, 4/1980, rev. 1982), pp. 403–4
G. de Lastic Saint-Jal: 'Un Peintre de Louis XIV et de Louis XV: François Desportes', *Conn. A.*, cvii (1961), pp. 56–65
M. Faré: *La Nature morte en France: Son histoire et son évolution du XVIIe au XXe siècle*, i (Geneva, 1962), pp. 155–60
M. Faré and F. Faré: *La Vie silencieuse en France: La Nature morte au XVIIIe siècle* (Fribourg, 1976), pp. 62–98 [excellent plates]
French Landscape Drawings and Sketches of the Eighteenth Century (exh. cat. by R. Bacou, London, BM, 1977), nos 6–17
L'Atelier de Desportes à la Manufacture de Sèvres (exh. cat. by R. Bacou and others, Paris, Louvre, Cab. Est., 1982–3)
D. Wakefield: *French Eighteenth-century Painting* (London, 1984), pp. 117–19
G. de Lastic: 'Une Nature morte de Desportes venant du Muséum Central des Arts', *Rev. Louvre*, xxxix (1989), pp. 233–5

LAURIE G. WINTERS

Despotikon. *See under* ANTIPAROS.

Despotopoulos, Ioannis [Despo, Jan] (*b* Chios, 7 Jan 1903; *d* 1 Oct 1992). Greek architect, teacher and writer. He studied under Hannes Meyer at the Bauhaus, Weimar (1924–5), and at the Königliche Technische Hochschule, Hannover (1928), and worked for Erich Mendelsohn in Berlin. In the 1930s he was a major figure in Greek architecture, being the only architect to relate Modernism to socio-economic structures and to socialist views. In 1932 he was co-founder of the Greek group of CIAM. His pre-war buildings include three sanatoria: Sotiria (1934) in Holargos, Attica, one (1936–40) in Tripolis, Peloponnese, and one (1937–40) in Asvestochori, near Thessaloniki; these were the first buildings of this type in Greece to show the influence of Modernism. From 1942 to 1946 and 1961 to 1966 he was Professor of Architectural Composition at the National Technical University, Athens, the intervening years being spent in Sweden, where he taught at various universities. In 1959 he was awarded first prize in the urban-planning competition for the Cultural Centre of Athens. The Athens School of Music (1969–85), the only part realized, is a balanced Neo-Rationalist composition, considered the most interesting post-war major public building in Athens.

WRITINGS
'Das neuzeitliche Kulturzentrum, die Agora', *Bauen & Wohnen*, xvii/2 (1963), pp. 331–40
Die ideologische Struktur der Städte, Schriftenreihe der Akademie der Künste, iv (Berlin, 1973)

BIBLIOGRAPHY
F. Loyer: *Architecture de la Grèce contemporaine* (diss., U. Paris III, 1966)
ALEXANDER KOUTAMANIS

Desprez, Louis-Jean (*b* Auxerre, *bapt* 28 May 1743; *d* Stockholm, 19 March 1804). French painter, stage designer and architect. After studies at Jacques-François Blondel's private school, Desprez continued his architectural training at the Académie Royale d'Architecture, Paris, in the 1760s and, after several attempts, won the Prix de Rome in 1776. Soon after his arrival in Rome (1777) he was asked by the Abbé de Saint-Non to prepare illustrations for his famous *Voyage pittoresque, ou description des royaumes de Naples et de Sicile* (Paris, 1781–6; drawings in London, BM, and Besançon Mus. B.-A. & Archéol.). With the permission of the Académie, he joined Saint-Non's team, and during their pioneering tour of southern Italy Desprez produced innumerable topographical drawings and watercolours that are remarkable for their vitality and accuracy. Back in Rome (1779), he completed the 135 illustrations selected for the engravings and resumed his architectural studies.

By the time Desprez sent a design for a public bath to the Académie in Paris in 1782, however, he had in fact abandoned his architectural career and was working as a painter and stage designer. On a visit to Rome in 1783–4, King Gustav III of Sweden asked Desprez to produce stage designs for the Royal Opera, Stockholm. He left Rome in July 1784, and his debut in Sweden with a performance of *Queen Christina* (1785; drawings in Stockholm, Nmus.) was an immediate success. His designs for *Gustav Wasa* (1786; drawings in Stockholm, Nmus.) were an even greater victory and the King renewed his contract for twelve more years. Desprez's individualistic style was characterized by dramatic effects of colour and light, and he freely combined impressions from southern Italy with Classical or Egyptian motifs. This romantic approach informed both his historical settings, such as that for *Frigga* (1787; drawings in St Petersburg, Hermitage), and sublime scenes of darkness and horror, such as those designed for *Elektra* (1787; drawings in Stockholm,

Drottningholm Slottsteat. & Teatmus.). He even tried to evoke volcanic eruptions (*Cora and Alonzo*, 1788; drawings in Stockholm, Drottningholm Slottsteat & Teatmus.) and atmospheric phenomena (*Aeneas in Carthage*, 1799; Stockholm, Nmus.). The paintings Desprez produced at Gustav's request never had quite the same dramatic play of light and colour as those he had produced during his years in Italy. However, the strong attraction he felt for the dynamic composition of the Baroque is still found, for example, in *Battle of the Sybarites and the Crotoniates* (Stockholm, Nmus.).

In Sweden Desprez resumed his architectural activities. He first designed a 'Turkish tent' (1785) for Haga Park, then in 1787 he took over responsibility from Olof Tempelman for the royal palace there, a scheme based on Andrea Palladio's Rotunda at Vincenza, which Desprez ultimately developed into a circular, self-contained building (not completed). This recourse to elementary solids shows him to have been a 'revolutionary' architect of the school of Etienne-Louis Boullée and Claude-Nicolas Ledoux. In his grandiose scheme for the stables at Drottningholm (1788)—where he also designed a Gothic tower (1792; drawings in Stockholm, Kun. Bib.)—he placed an oblong central block through the middle of a horizontal range that contrasts with it in texture, size and shape. In another scheme, for a 'Royal Theatre' (1789), possibly intended for London, the auditorium appears as a huge semi-cylinder extruded from an oblong block that was intended to house the sumptuous staircases. To unify discrepant masses in his schemes, Desprez made use of recurrent motifs, such as arched openings, or, less directly, of features in one part recalling those in others, such as triangular pediments echoing a conical roof. To preserve the purity of his simple geometrical forms, he often eschewed all external decoration, even omitting architraves round the windows. This was the case, for example, with the Botany Department (completed 1807) at Uppsala University, where a heavy Doric portico is attached to an unadorned façade (drawings in Uppsala Ubib.; *see* SWEDEN, §II, 2 and fig. 5).

The death of Gustav III in 1792 was a devastating blow for Desprez, whose contract was not renewed after its expiry in 1798; six years later he died in poverty. He remains well known, however, as one of the great pioneers in the art of stage design.

BIBLIOGRAPHY
N.-G. Wollin: *Desprez en Italie* (Malmö, 1935)
——: *Desprez en Suède* (Stockholm, 1939)
Piranèse et les Français, 1740–1790 (exh. cat., ed. B. K. de Rola; Rome, Acad. France, 1976)
M. Olausson: *Den Engelska parken i Sverige under gustaviansk tid* [The English landscape garden in Sweden during the Gustavian era] (diss., Uppsala, 1993)
——: 'Desprez et Piranèse fils: De l'original à la reproduction', *La Chimère de Monsieur Desprez* (exh. cat., Paris, Louvre, 1994), pp. 47–50
MAGNUS OLAUSSON

Dessau. German town situated on the River Mulde, just above the confluence with the River Elbe. The former capital of the duchy of Anhalt, it has a population of *c.* 104,000 (1989). Finds dating from the Late Bronze Age Lausitz culture (*c.* 1200–*c.* 1000 BC) have been made within the area of the town. Dessau did not develop as a town until the 11th–12th centuries and was first documented in 1213; within the area of the modern town, however, Kühnau and Stene were mentioned as early as 945, while the suburbs of Mildensee, Mosigkau and Törten have Romanesque churches. The castle (1341; most destr.) of the Ascanian princes of Anhalt served as their official residence (Residenzschloss) from 1474. The Late Gothic Marienkirche (1506–12; ruined 1945), which belonged to the complex, was vaulted in 1541 by Ludwig Binder and had rich decoration (destr.) by Binder and the Cranach studio. In 1530–31 the west wing (Johannbau) of the Residenzschloss was rebuilt in central German early Renaissance style, with an important *Wendelstein* by Binder. The complex was unified to form a citadel by Prince Joachim Ernst (*reg* 1536–86) in 1549, and a new building (1577–83) with an imposing High Renaissance four-wing layout was executed by Rochus Quirinus Lynar and Peter Niuron (*fl* 1570–1607).

Dessau was a brilliant intellectual centre during the Reformation. Typical town houses, such as those (destr. 1945) in the Grosser Markt, had twin Renaissance gables. In the late 17th century Dutch influence was dominant; Princess Henrietta Catharina (1637–1708), the daughter of Frederick Henry, Prince of Orange, brought to Dessau the 'Orange legacy', an important collection of paintings (now in Dessau, Staatl. Gal., Staatl. Mus. Schloss Mosigkau and Wörlitz, Schloss). She attracted painters and architects to the principality. Cornelis Ryckwaert (*d* 1693) built the market hall. Gabriel Baguereth (*fl* 1694–1700) built the Hofkammer. The Cavalierstrasse was laid out in 1713 as a grand north–south main thoroughfare by Prince Leopold I (1676–1747), whose daughter, Anna Wilhelmine (1715–80), built the Rococo Schloss Mosigkau in 1752. After the north wing of the Residenzschloss was demolished in 1709, Georg Wenceslaus von Knobelsdorff's plans (1747–53) to remodel the remaining three wings in Rococo style were partially implemented in the east and south wings.

Dessau's cultural life reached its peak under Francis, Prince of Anhalt-Dessau, who encouraged the so-called Dessau-Wörlitz cultural circle. Owing to the presence of FRIEDRICH WILHELM ERDMANNSDORFF, the area became the source of continental Neo-classicism, based on English and antique Italian models. A Schloss and park (1764–*c*. 1805) were laid out at WÖRLITZ, and a 25 km stretch of meadows along the Elbe was landscaped to create a series of parks and gardens known collectively as the Dessau-Wörlitzer Gartenreich. Educational reform was introduced by Johann Bernhard Basedow (1724–90) through the Philanthropinum. Erdmannsdorff's theatre (1795–8; destr. 1855) was extended by Carlo Ignazio Pozzi (1766–1842) in 1820–22 to form one of the most perfect German Neo-classical buildings. The Johannbau of the Residenzschloss was simplified in 1812 by the removal of its Renaissance gables. The Georg Palais (1822–4) successfully combines Neo-classical and Biedermeier elements.

Many important artists were linked to Dessau later in the 19th century, including Carl Wilhelm Kolbe (i) (*see* KOLBE, (1)), the brothers Heinrich, Ferdinand and Friedrich Olivier, Franz Krüger and Hans Reinhard von Marées. Franz Schwechten built the Mausoleum (*c*. 1900), and Alfred Messel built the Palais Cohn-Oppenheim (destr.

1959–60). From *c*. 1925 to 1932 Dessau was home to the BAUHAUS, which was led by WALTER GROPIUS, who designed the Bauhaus buildings (1925–6). Teachers included Gropius, Lyonel Feininger, Paul Klee, Vasily Kandinsky, László Moholy-Nagy, Josef Albers, Oskar Schlemmer, Ludwig Mies van der Rohe and Hannes Meyer. Staff housing, offices and a residential development for working people in the suburb of Törten were also designed by the Bauhaus. Inspiration spread all over the world from Dessau through the Bauhaus's many important pupils. The city was badly damaged in 1945 and subsequently reconstructed.

BIBLIOGRAPHY

A. Rode: *Wegweiser durch die Sehens Würdigkeiten in und um Dessau*, 3 vols (Wörlitz, 1795–8/*R* Berlin, 1988)
E. Hirsch: 'Bildung und Erziehung zu bürgerlicher Kultur: Eine Deutung der Dessau-Wörlitzer Gärten als Kulturpropaganda', *Wiss. Z. Martin-Luther-U. Halle-Wittenberg*, xxvii (1978), pp. 51–73
R. Alex: *Schlösser und Gärten um Dessau* (Leipzig, 1988)
Ansichten: Das Schöne mit dem Nützlichen (exh. cat. by D. Hempel and others, Wörlitz, Schloss, 1988)
E. Hirsch, ed.: *Bibliographie zur Erforschung und Pflege des Dessau-Wörlitzer Kulturkreises* (Halle, 1989)
U. Jablonowski and H. Günther: *Werte der Heimat* (1990)

For further bibliography *see* WÖRLITZ and BAUHAUS.

ERHARD HIRSCH

Dessin héliographique [*sur verre bichromaté*]. *See* CLICHÉ-VERRE.

Destailleur. French family of architects. François-Hippolyte Destailleur (*b* Paris, 22 March 1787; *d* Paris, 15 Feb 1852) studied under Charles Percier and later became architect to the Ministère de la Justice (1819), the Ministère des Finances (which he rebuilt, 1822–4; destr. 1871) and the Hôtel de la Monnaie (1833). He also built up an extensive private practice among the new aristocracy and in business circles, designing numerous Palladian-style country houses around Paris for this group of customers, for example at Dieuville, Aube (1819), and several town houses, such as that of Baron Delmas (1835) in the Rue Marigny in Paris.

Hippolyte(-Alexandre-Gabriel-Walter) Destailleur (*b* Paris, 27 Sept 1822; *d* Paris, 17 Nov 1893) was an architect and collector, son of François-Hippolyte Destailleur. He was a pupil of François-René Leclère at the Ecole des Beaux-Arts (1842–6) and later worked with his father and with Etienne-Hippolyte Godde. From 1853 he ran the family practice and succeeded his father as architect to the Ministère de la Justice. He was, however, chiefly a fashionable architect to rich and titled clients. His numerous buildings both in France and abroad are distinguished by his use of French models of the 16th to 18th centuries, in contrast to the more common contemporary use of medieval, Italian Renaissance or antique examples. Among his works are the Rococo Revival interiors of the Hôtel de Pourtalès (1865), Paris, the town house of Graf Hans Heinric von Pless (1874–6), Berlin, and the town house of Baron Albert de Rothschild (1876–82), Vienna. He was also involved in the restoration of a number of important historic buildings, including the château of Vaux-le-Vicomte (1877–80), Seine et Marne, and the château of Courances (1873–6 and 1881–4), Essonne. His two major projects were the château of Franconville (1876–85), Oise,

Paris, for the Duc de Massa and Waddesdon Manor (1874–85), Bucks. The former building is modelled on the château of Maisons, one of the masterpieces of French classical architecture of the 17th century, built by François Mansart from 1642. The latter, built for Baron Ferdinand de Rothschild, is an eclectic structure based on French Renaissance prototypes and designed to accommodate de Rothschild's opulent art collection in interiors fitted up with panelling and other decorative features from important demolished Parisian houses.

Hippolyte Destailleur was a passionate collector of books, prints and drawings and owned numerous works by French artists of the 18th and 19th centuries. His concern to promote a national architectural style led him to write and to assemble an important collection of works illustrating the history of French architecture, decoration and ornament, some of which he published in facsimile. Much of his collection is now in the Cabinet des Estampes of the Bibliothèque Nationale, Paris. His son Walter-André Destailleur (*b* Thais, Seine, 12 June 1867; *d* March 1940) built the château of Trévarez (1893–1907), Finistère, where he achieved a happy synthesis of French Renaissance motifs from the Loire Valley châteaux, anticipating the American buildings of George B. Post and Richard Morris Hunt on New York's Fifth Avenue.

WRITINGS

H.-A.-G.-W. Destailleur: *Recueil d'estampes relatives à l'ornementation des appartements au XVIe, XVIIe et XVIIIe siècle*, 2 vols (Paris, 1863 and 1871)

——: *Jacques Androuet du Cerceau: Les Plus Excellents Bastiments de France* (Paris, 1868)

——, ed.: *Mathurin Jousse: La Fidelle Ouverture de l'art du serrurier* (Paris, 1874)

BIBLIOGRAPHY

G. Duplessis: 'Notice sur Mr. Hippolyte Destailleurs, architecte', *Catalogue de livres et d'estampes relatifs aux beaux-arts provenant de la bibliothèque de feu Mr. Destailleur* (Paris, 1895), pp. i–xvii

F. Lugt: *Marques* (1921)

E. Berckenhagen: 'Hippolyte Destailleur', *Fünf Architekten aus fünf Jahrhunderten* (Berlin, 1976), pp. 115–54

Le Parisien chez lui au XIXe siècle: 1814–1914 (exh. cat., Paris, Archvs N., 1976)

JEAN-PAUL MIDANT

De stijl. *See* STIJL, DE.

Destorrents. Catalan family of artists.

(1) Ramón Destorrents (*b* 1351; *d* 1391). Painter. He was the foremost painter of his time in Barcelona; his son (2) Rafael Destorrents was equally renowned as an illuminator of manuscripts. One of the earliest records of Ramón, a payment for the illumination of a Psalter (untraced) for King Pedro IV (1351), shows that the Destorrents's workshop already enjoyed royal patronage. Additional royal commissions followed, and in 1353 Ramón was paid when he began work on retables for the royal chapel in Valencia and for the chapel of the royal palace (the Almudayna) in Palma de Mallorca. The latter had been started by Ferrer Bassa in 1343, and it was completed by Ramón *c.* 1358, when he received payment for it. He was also paid for retables for the chapel in the royal castle at Lleida (Sp. Lérida) in 1356 and for the Aljaferia, Saragossa, in 1358. He collaborated with sculptor Pere Morágues on a sphere for the astrologer Dalmau ces

Planes in 1362. He was a witness in 1385, and he is last mentioned in 1391, when he made his will.

Ramón Destorrents's style can be seen in the panels of *St Anne* (Lisbon, Mus. Cidade) and *Calvary* (Palma de Mallorca, Soc. Arqueol. Lul-Liana), part of the retable of *St Anne* completed *c.* 1358 for the Almudayna, Palma de Mallorca. They are his only surviving documented works. The panels are painted in a style that recalls the work of Duccio, Simone Martini and Giotto. Ramón's compositions are marked by a monumental calm and populated by figures that interact in a controlled and dignified manner. Soft pastel colours are punctuated by occasional touches of brilliant, saturated hues balanced by the use of strong earth tones.

(2) Rafael Destorrents (*b* 1375; *d c.* 1425). Illuminator, son of (1) Ramón Destorrents. He evidently had a successful career since by 1403 he was engaged in the illumination of the Missal of S Eulália (Barcelona, Anxiv Capitolare S Església Catedral), one of the principal works of Spanish 14th-century manuscript illumination. The often celebrated *Last Judgement* (fol. 1*r*) of this Missal reveals the work of an accomplished illuminator working in a delicate Gothic style (seen in the depiction of *Heaven*). Rafael was, however, also fully conversant with the more realistic, if fantastic, manner used for the representation of the damned souls. As in Ramón's work, traces of Sienese influence are apparent in the choice of colour. By 1408, Rafael had been ordained a priest and was also known as *Gregori, presbiter Barchinone*. Most of his works are now lost, including a Missal illuminated in 1410 for the Councillors of Barcelona. In 1425 he was working on a retable (untraced).

BIBLIOGRAPHY

F. P. Verries: 'Una obra documentada de Ramón Destorrents', *A.B. Museo de Arte*, Barcelona, vi (1948), pp. 321–40

J. M. Madurell: 'El iluminador de libres Rafael Destorrents, artifice del Misál de Santa Eulália', *Scrinium* (1949), pp. 1–8

——: 'Rafael Destorrents, sacerdote y miniaturista', *Scrinium* (1954–5), pp. 1–5

M. Durliat and G. Maillet: 'Ramón Destorrents et le retable d'Iravals', *Tramontane* (1958), pp. 45–57

M. Durliat: 'Notre-Dame de l'Aurore à Manresa', *Congr. Archéol. France*, cxvii (1959), pp. 199–207

J. Ainaud de Lasarte : 'En Katalansk handskrift i Stockholm', *Arsb. f. Svensk. Statens Konstsamlungen*, viii (1960), pp. 37–50

M. Gallotti-Minola: 'Il Museo diocesano di Barcelona', *Emporium*, cxxxii (1960), pp. 219–21

J. Camón Aznar: 'Pintura español medieval', *Goya*, 54 (1963), pp. 344–54

P. Bohigas y Balaguer: *La decoración i la ilustración del Misál de Santa Eulália* (Madrid, 1977)

A. Fabrega Gran and P. Bohigas Balaguer: *El Misál de Santa Eulália* (Madrid, 1977)

LYNETTE BOSCH

Destre, Vincenzo dalle [Vincenzo da Treviso] (*b* ?Treviso, *fl* from 1488; *d* before 1543). Italian painter. He was a pupil of Girolamo da Treviso the elder and in 1495 collaborated with Giovanni Bellini in the Sala del Maggior Consiglio of the Doge's Palace, Venice. In the same city he was connected with the Scuola di S Giovanni Evangelista and the Scuola di S Maria della Misericordia and enrolled as a member of the painters' guild (*fraglia*). Two of his paintings, both signed (Padua, Mus. Civ.; Venice, Correr), are based on Bellini's *Presentation in the Temple*. The two versions differ from each other only in the figure of the woman on the left. In the version in Venice she is derived, as is the figure of St Joseph, from Bellini's grisaille depicting the *Lamentation* (Florence, Uffizi). In the painting in Padua, on the other hand, she appears to be based on a type of Virgin that was first introduced by Bellini and also used early in his career by Rocco Marconi. Two altarpieces have been assigned to Vincenzo: the *Virgin and Child Enthroned with SS Andrew and Liberalis* (Treviso, Mus. Civ.) and *St Erasmus Enthroned between SS John the Baptist and Sebastian* (1503; Treviso, S Leonardo; figures of Virgin and Child added later in 16th century) and he may also have executed the *Virgin and Child* (on sale Munich, J. Böhler, 1 and 2 June 1937, lot 1653) that derives from a prototype by Bellini (two versions; Frankfurt am Main, Städel. Kstinst.; Urbino, Pal. Ducale), in which the Virgin is flanked by SS John the Baptist and Elizabeth.

BIBLIOGRAPHY
Thieme–Becker

G. Mariacher: *Il Museo Correr di Venezia: Dipinti dal XIV al XVI secolo* (Venice, 1957), pp. 229–30

F. Heinemann: *Giovanni Bellini e i Belliniani*, 2 vols (Venice, 1962)

L. Gargan: 'Lorenzo Lotto e gli ambienti umanistici trevigiani fra quattro e cinquecento', *Lorenzo Lotto a Treviso: Ricerche e restauri* (exh. cat., Treviso, S Nicolo, 1980), pp. 1–10

D. Banzato: *La quadreria Emo Capodilista* (exh. cat., Padua, 1988), pp. 51, n.12

ANCHISE TEMPESTINI

Destrez, Abbé **Jean** (*b* Paris, 23 Oct 1889; *d* Dec 1950). French historian. He entered the Dominican Order in 1910 and studied at Paris, Rome and Fribourg. Extreme deafness resulting from service in World War I forced him to leave the Order in 1925 and he became a priest in the diocese of Versailles. He was the editor of *Bulletin Thomiste* 1924–8, and his early studies were on the works of Thomas Aquinas. In the manuscripts of Aquinas he frequently found marginal notes, which he realized related to provisions on the production of texts found in medieval university statutes (*see* MANUSCRIPT, §I). These covered the official examination and approval of exemplars of texts needed for study, which were to be hired out for copying by the university stationers. These official exemplars were divided into small gatherings of *peciae* ('pieces'; generally of four leaves), which could be hired out one at a time to professional scribes or students, thus facilitating the multiplication of the texts, since several people could be copying different parts of an exemplar at the same time. Destrez realized that the notes that he had found were made by scribes indicating in their copies the beginning or end of the *peciae* that they had borrowed. He decided to search for the notes in 13th- and 14th-century university manuscripts in the hope of discovering how the system worked in practice, what texts were involved and how their transmission was affected by the system. He devoted himself single-mindedly to this task for the rest of his life. By the end of his life he had examined some 15,000 manuscripts in France and the rest of Europe, finding *pecia* notes in 300 different texts. By 1935, when he published his brilliant preliminary study, *La Pecia*, he had found notes in over 1000 manuscripts, mostly attributable to Paris, Bologna, Oxford or Naples. He had also found by then about 30 of the original exemplars (he later found over 50 more). The system appeared to have been in use

at the universities, especially Paris and Bologna, by the second quarter of the 13th century and to have died out in the 15th (it now seems that it was very little used after the mid-14th century). Unfortunately, Destrez never completed the publication of his findings. Later studies have refined his conclusions, but his basic outline stands. His unpublished notes and descriptions may be consulted at the Dominican convent of Le Saulchoir in Paris.

WRITINGS
La Pecia dans les manuscrits universitaires du XIIIe et du XIVe siècles (Paris, 1935)

with M. D. Chenu: 'Exemplaria universitaires des XIIIe et XIVe siècles', *Scriptorium*, vii (1953), pp. 68–80

BIBLIOGRAPHY
G. Fink-Errera: 'Jean Destrez et son oeuvre', *Scriptorium*, xi (1957), pp. 264–80

L. J. Bataillon, B. G. Guyot and R. H. Rouse, eds: *La Production du livre universitaire au moyen âge: Exemplar et pecia* (Paris, 1988)

A. C. DE LA MARE

Desvallières, Georges-Olivier (*b* Paris, 14 March 1861; *d* Paris, 5 Oct 1950). French painter. Initially a pupil of Elie Delaunay, he studied for a while at l'Académie Julian, where he befriended René Ménard and Lucien Simon. However, the meeting that most influenced his personality and determined his stylistic and iconographic development for several years was with Gustave Moreau in about 1880. Moreau's influence is most clearly seen in Desvallières's taste for gem colours, famous episodes from biblical history and from Greek mythology and the masters of the Quattrocento. In 1884 he spent several months in Italy, where he made copies in the style of Bernardino Pinturicchio at l'Ara Coeli. His works continued to show a debt to Moreau, but he also produced vast decorative compositions such as *The Archers* (1895; Paris, Mus. d'Orsay).

By the time of a stay in London in 1903 Desvallières had abandoned the grand mythological episodes inspired by Moreau in favour of paintings reflecting his observation of daily life: nocturnal scenes, café and theatre interiors, as in *At the Empire, London* (1903; Kurashiki, Ōhara Mus. A.), and society portraits, such as his *Portrait of Madame Pascal Blanchard* (1903; Paris, Petit Pal.). After 1905 he devoted his time to religious subject-matter, such as *Le Sacré-Coeur* (1905; untraced), which showed his style becoming brutal and expressive. He was involved with Maurice Denis in 1919 in the creation of the Ateliers d'art sacré, which contributed to the renaissance of Christian art in France. He undertook important projects of church decoration, notably at the church in the industrial town of Wittenheim, Haut-Rhin (1929).

BIBLIOGRAPHY
R. Vallery-Radot: 'Desvallières', *A. & Artistes*, 100 (Oct 1929), pp. 1–32

A. Garreau: *George Desvallières* (1942)

THALIE GOETZ

Desvergnes, Charles-Jean-Cléophas (*b* Bellegarde, Loiret, 19 Aug 1860; *d* 1928). French sculptor. He studied at the Ecole des Beaux-Arts in Paris under François Jouffroy, Henri-Michel-Antoine Chapu and the French sculptor Emile Thomas (1817–82) and made his début at the Salon des Artistes Français in 1880 with a plaster bust. He won the Prix de Rome in 1889 and received a silver medal at the Exposition Universelle of 1900 in Paris. He specialized in busts and relief sculpture, producing such works as *Thomy Thierry* (Paris, Louvre), the relief portrait *Gaston Thys* (Angers, Mus. B.-A.), *Ste Jeanne de Valois* (Bourges, Mus. Berry), the bust *Lazare Carnot* (Versailles, Officer Sch.) and the group *History and Archaeology* for the Petit Palais in Paris. He also produced a number of memorial monuments in the French provinces and the monument to *Jehan de Meung* in Meung-sur-Loire.

DBF   BIBLIOGRAPHY

De Syllas, Leo. *See under* ARCHITECTS' CO-PARTNERSHIP.

Detaille, (Jean-Baptiste-)Edouard (*b* Paris, 5 Oct 1848; *d* Paris, 23 Dec 1912). French painter. He was born into a prosperous family from Picardy with a military background, his grandfather having served as an arms supplier to Napoleon. Detaille's early interest in art was encouraged by his father, an amateur artist and friend of collectors and painters, including the battle-painter Horace Vernet. At 17 he approached Ernest Meissonier for an introduction to Alexandre Cabanel, but Meissonier preferred to take on Detaille as a pupil himself and was an enormously important influence on his artistic development. From Meissonier he learnt finesse of execution and an appreciation for precise observation. He was soon encouraged to set up on his own and at the Salon of 1869 won approval for his canvas *A Rest During the Manoeuvre, Camp St Maur* (untraced). In the spring of 1870 he and three other young artists, E. P. Berne-Bellecour (1838–1910), L. Leloir (1843–84) and J. G. Vibert (1840–1902), undertook a sketching trip to Algeria. At the outbreak of the Franco-Prussian War (1870), Detaille obtained a staff position with General Appert, which enabled him to observe the hostilities first hand; this experience provided the mainstay of his subsequent artistic output.

Detaille submitted two Franco-Prussian War subjects, *The Victors* and *A German Convoy* to the Salon of 1872 (both untraced), but he was forced to withdraw them by a French regime still anxious about offending German opinion. Other treatments of the War were nonetheless submitted to later Salons: for example the *Charge of the Ninth Regiment of Cuirassiers into the Village of Morsbronn* (exh. Salon 1874; untraced) and the *Salute to the Wounded!* (exh. Salon 1877; untraced). Visits to Austria, England and Russia acquainted him with the uniforms and customs of the armies of those nations, but the history of the French Army remained his abiding interest. In 1883 his two lavishly illustrated volumes treating the uniforms and classifications of the army from 1789 to 1870 were issued in collaboration with Jules Richard. The 346 figures and 60 coloured plates in *Types et uniformes de l'armée française* comprise an encyclopedia of their subject. Many of these illustrations were studied from the artist's own extensive collection of uniforms and other military artefacts.

Detaille's devotion to accuracy was also to be seen in his two masterpieces, vast panoramas depicting episodes from the Franco-Prussian War, which were subsequently dispersed: the panorama of *Champigny* (exh. Paris, 1882; central section, Versailles, Château) and the panorama of *Rezonville*. The first was based on his 1879 canvas, the

Defence of Champigny (New York, Met.), and was undertaken in collaboration with Alphonse de Neuville. It shows the desperate French defence against assault by divisions from Saxony and Württemberg on the second day of the battle. The second panorama was done without the aid of de Neuville. For the Salle du Budget of the Hôtel de Ville, Paris, Detaille painted a dramatic allegory *Victory Leading the Armies of the Republic* (Dunkirk, Mus. B.-A.) and two elaborate scenes of leave-taking and return (completed 1905), which emphasize the place of Paris in the military history of the Revolution and the First Empire, and the links between these two eras.

Detaille was the doyen of French military painters of the 'Belle Epoque'. As compared with de Neuville's debonair military personages, Detaille's combatants are rather more credible in their dangerous roles of defending the national honour. He treated the illusion of victory with all the signs of pain and suffering it occasioned.

BIBLIOGRAPHY
G. Duplesis: 'Detaille', *Gaz. B.-A.*, n. s. 2, i (1874), pp. 419–33
M. Vachon: *Detaille* (Paris, 1898)
J. Humbert: *Edouard Detaille: L'Héroïsme d'un siècle* (Paris, 1979)
F. Robichon: 'Les Panoramas de Champigny et Rezonville, par Edouard Detaille et Alphonse Deneuville', *Bull. Soc. Hist. A. Fr.* (1979), pp. 259–77
Le Triomphe des mairies (exh. cat., Paris, Petit Pal., 1986), pp. 439–43
                                        FRANK TRAPP

De Thurah, Laurids [Lauritz] **(Lauridsen)** (*b* Århus, 4 March 1706; *d* Copenhagen, 5 Sept 1759). Danish architect and architectural historian. He trained as a military engineer and served in the Engineers' Corps from 1725. With the financial support of King Frederick IV, he departed in 1729 on a tour to Germany, Italy, France, Holland and England in order to study civil architecture. He returned to Denmark in 1731 and began work on the Royal Palace in Roskilde, demonstrating his familiarity with south German and Austrian Baroque architecture. In 1733 he became a court architect and in 1735 was entrusted with the royal building on Zealand and Lolland-Falster. His most important projects of this period were the repeated rebuilding of and extensions (1733–44) to the Hirschholm Castle (destr.), north of Copenhagen. He appears here to have used ideas gathered in France and Germany, without giving the impression of eclecticism.

In 1736, when the interiors of Christiansborg Castle in Copenhagen (begun in 1731 under the supervision of E. D. Häusser) were to be completed, De Thurah was given the task of planning the arrangement of half the rooms on each of the two most important floors: the queen's apartment on the king's floor, and the corresponding rooms on the crown prince's floor. None of these is preserved, but it is possible to obtain an impression of De Thurah's interior style from the small hunting-lodge (the Eremitage; 1734–6) in the Deer Park north of Copenhagen, where both the exteriors and interiors show the influence of Johann Lukas von Hildebrandt's late Baroque style. This was considered old-fashioned by King Christian VI, and De Thurah was made to surrender responsibility for several of the rooms at Christiansborg to the sculptor Louis-Auguste Leclerc (1688–1771). Furthermore, when Häusser resigned as Chief Court Architect in 1742, Niels Eigtved was assigned responsibility for the most important regions, including Copenhagen, while De Thurah had responsibility for only the more remote provinces. He did, however, build two of Copenhagen's church steeples, those of the church of Our Lady (1742–4), inspired by James Gibbs, and the spirally coiled steeple of the church of Our Saviour (1749–52; for illustration see DENMARK, fig. 4), which is a festive, elongated version of Borromini's lantern on S Ivo della Sapienza in Rome.

From 1746 De Thurah worked on completing the *cour d'honneur* of Ledreborg manor house, with the construction of two sweeping wings to house the library and orangery and the erection of six obelisks. This is one of the most successful examples of Danish Baroque architecture. After Eigtved's death in 1754 De Thurah was promoted to Chief Court Architect and thus to the supervision of all crown building activities. He continued the laying-out of Frederiksstaden, Copenhagen's new district, and erected four large buildings to flank the Frederiks Hospital. He also built a house for himself at Amaliegade 25. Although these buildings were in conformity with Eigtved's principles for Frederiksstaden, De Thurah's interpretation was markedly more Baroque, and throughout his career he made no concessions to changing taste.

De Thurah is also acknowledged as the founder of Danish architectural history: his two-volume *Den danske Vitruvius* is not theoretical, but it provides a thorough survey of the most important buildings in Denmark and Schleswig-Holstein. The text lacks details such as dates and the names of patrons and architects, which are now greatly missed, but the 281 engravings of plans, sections and façades from all periods provide the best information available about many of the buildings. At the time of his death the manuscript of a third volume had been prepared: this contains descriptions of buildings completed during 1749–59, as well as copies of older views of Copenhagen and drawings of a number of sepulchral monuments in Copenhagen churches.

WRITINGS
Den danske Vitruvius, 2 vols (Copenhagen, 1746–9/R 1966–7)

BIBLIOGRAPHY
F. Weilbach: *Arkitekten Lauritz Thurah* (Copenhagen, 1924)
C. Elling: 'Lauritz de Thurah und die Frederikskirche in Kopenhagen', *Artes: Mnmts & Mém.*, vii (1939), pp. 57–94
——: *Christiansborg-interiører* (Copenhagen, 1944)
H. Lund: 'Frederiks Hospital og Frederiks Stad', *Kunstindustrimuseet* (Copenhagen, 1969), pp. 15–50
——: 'Det første Christiansborg Slot', i (Copenhagen, 1975) [Eng. summary]

HAKON LUND

Detrimont, Alexis-Eugène (*b* 1825). French dealer, restorer and framer. He began his career managing a modest framing business in Rue Notre-Dame-des-Champs, Paris. The dealer Alexis Febvre (1810–81) became aware of him, provided encouragement and helped him to set up premises in the Rue Laffitte, which in the early years of the Second Empire (1852–70) was rapidly becoming the centre of the art trade. By 1857 Detrimont was buying paintings from Charles-François Daubigny, and in the next few years he gained a reputation as a dealer in contemporary paintings, with a particular interest in landscapes. For a time he was Courbet's dealer and supervised the stretching and varnishing of his paintings for the Salon of 1861; one of these was *Stags Fighting* (1861; Paris, Mus. d'Orsay), a picture to which Courbet attached particular importance. It was perhaps through Courbet that Detrimont also dealt with the reclusive painter Amand Gautier, who had briefly enjoyed some success at the Salon of 1859. In 1866 Monet wrote to Gautier, asking for a letter of introduction to Detrimont, whom he hoped to use as an outlet. Detrimont, who was described as more of an art-lover than a businessman, seems to have had a particular liking for a slightly older generation of landscape artists, particularly Théodore Rousseau, at whose sale in 1861 he was the only dealer among the buyers, and although many of the paintings were unsold, he was the largest purchaser. In 1864 he organized an exhibition of contemporary paintings at the Cercle de l'Union Artistique in the Rue de Choiseul; this was one of several attempts at this time to hold independent exhibitions. Occasionally he collaborated with Francis Petit, who was associated with several successful exhibitions of this kind.

BIBLIOGRAPHY
A. Distel: *Les Collectionneurs des Impressionnistes: Amateurs et marchands* (Dudingen, 1989)

LINDA WHITELEY

Detroit. American city in Michigan, located on the north shore of the Detroit River between lakes St Clair and Erie. One of the oldest cities in the Midwest, it has a population of *c.* 1.2 million and is known particularly for its motor industry. It was founded as Fort Pontchartrain-du-Détroit (1701) as a fort and fur-trading post by Antoine Laumet de La Mothe Cadillac (1658–1730), on behalf of Louis XIV, King of France (1661–1711). The city was captured in 1760 by the British, who renamed it Detroit; in 1794 it passed to the USA, becoming capital of the state of Michigan in 1805, when it was virtually destroyed by fire. Detroit was rebuilt to a grid plan, with one- or two-storey clapboard dwellings of simple colonial type, with low-gabled roof-lines, shallow mouldings, small sash windows and pilaster-framed doorways. The establishment of a steamboat route between Buffalo and Detroit led to the development of industries. In 1847 Lansing took over as the state capital.

An era of European-influenced architecture began with the adoption of Jeffersonian-type classical structure and details, while the Jesuit cathedral of SS Peter and Paul (1849) was designed as a triple-aisled basilica. From the 1850s the Gothic Revival style was also popular. In the period of considerable industrial expansion following the Civil War (1861–5), architecture in the city was dominated by Queen Anne Revival and Georgian Revival styles, although public buildings were in French Renaissance and Romanesque Revival or Neo-classical styles, the latter surviving well into the 20th century (e.g. Public Library, 1917–21; by Cass Gilbert).

Among the various immigrant European artists and craftsmen attracted to Detroit were the German sculptor Julius Theodore Melchers (1829–1909), who arrived in 1855 and executed various works in stone, including the statue of *Cadillac* (Detroit, MI, Inst. A.); his workshop thrived between 1870 and 1890. His son Gari Melchers became a successful painter. In 1885 a group of affluent

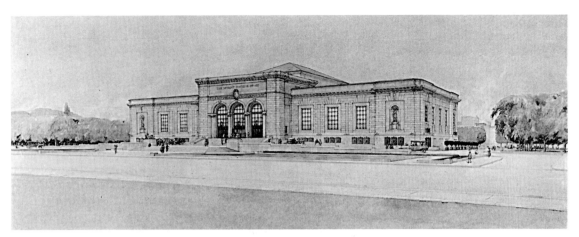

Detroit Institute of Arts, by Paul Cret, 1919–27

collectors established the Museum of Art (later Institute of Arts), although the city's most important annual exhibition was held at the Hopkin Club, run by Scottish painter Robert Hopkin (1837–1900). The Pewabic Pottery was founded *c.* 1900 by Mary Chase Stratton (1867–1961) with Horace J. Caulkin; Chase's artistry and unique iridescent glazes brought the pottery wide renown.

Detroit was transformed in the early 20th century by the motor industry. The first precision-engineered, hand-finished Model A Cadillac (named after the city's founder) was made by Martyn Leland (1843–1932) in 1903. From the 1920s car design virtually became an art form (*see* INDUSTRIAL DESIGN). ALBERT KHAN designed many of Detroit's factory and office buildings (e.g. Fisher Building, 1927). The new Institute of Arts building by Paul Cret was completed in 1927 (see fig.); in 1932–3 Diego Rivera executed the fresco series *Detroit Industry* (1932–3) for its garden courtyard (*see* RIVERA, DIEGO, fig. 1). A number of skyscrapers dating from the 1900s to the 1960s grace Griswold Street, including the Ford Building (1909) and Dime Building (1910) by Daniel H. Burnham and several by Smith, Hinchman & Grylls (Buhl Building, 1925; City National Bank, formerly Penobscot Building, 1928; Guardian Building, 1929). Notable post-World War II architecture includes the International Style McGregor Memorial Conference Center (1958) and the Reynolds Metal Company Building (1959), both by Minoru Yamasaki; the Lafayette Park development (1956–63) by LUDWIG MIES VAN DER ROHE; the concrete, columnar Center for Creative Studies (1974–5) by William Kessler; and the glass and steel Renaissance Center (1973–7) by John Portman. In the late 20th century the city's art life was enhanced by the presence of a number of museums, including the Pewabic Pottery Museum and the Detroit Historical Museum, the latter containing artefacts relating to architectural and urban history, among other areas.

BIBLIOGRAPHY
The Machine Age in America 1918–1941, exh. cat. by R. G. Wilson, D. H. Pilgrim and D. Tashjian (New York, Brooklyn Mus., 1968–9)
The Legacy of Albert Kahn (exh. cat. by W. H. Ferry, Detroit, MI, Inst. A., 1970)
H. D. Brown and others: *Cadillac and the Founding of Detroit* (Detroit, 1976)
W. H. Peck: *The Detroit Institute of Arts: A Brief History* (Detroit, 1991)
☐

Dettmann, Ludwig (*b* Adelbye, nr Flensburg, 25 July 1865; *d* Berlin, 15 Nov 1944). German painter. After training at the Gewerbe- und Kunstschule in Hamburg (1884–9), he attended the Königlich-akademische Hochschule für Bildende Künste in Berlin. His work on the Berliner Dioramen in the late 1880s helped him to further his knowledge of depicting illusionistic states of colour and light. In the 1890s, at first in response to the influence of Fritz von Uhdes's socio-religious themes, Dettmann initially joined the Secession movement. His exploration of purely pictorial objectives became more important to him. He endeavoured to combine subject-matter, the immediacy of his visual impressions and atmosphere into a unified whole. A result of this phase is *Princess and Swineherd* (1896; Kiel, Christian Albrechts-U., Ksthalle), the subject taken from a fairy tale by Hans Christian Andersen. More importance was given to the woodland scene drenched in sunlight than to the two protagonists in the painting. From 1900 Dettmann concentrated on paintings that identified with the Fatherland. *Tomorrow Is a Holiday* (1900; Kiel, Christian Albrechts-U., Ksthalle) shows his attempts to fulfil a thematic objective by applying his own pictorial principles. His identification with the Fatherland led him to espouse the racist theory of culture that was developing in Germany at that time, which restricted his vision for artistic development.

WRITINGS
'Lebenserinnerungen', *Nordelbingen*, xlii (1973), pp. 23–69, 79–106

BIBLIOGRAPHY
F. Fuglsang: 'Ludwig Dettmann: Rede anlässlich der Eröffnung einer Gedächtnisausstellung im Flensburger Museum', *Nordelbingen*, xix (1950), pp. 50–60
Ludwig Dettmann (exh. cat., Flensburg, Städt. Mus., 1965)
BARBARA LANGE

Deubler, Jan Zygmunt. *See* DEYBEL, JAN ZYGMUNT.

De Unga. *See* YOUNG ONES.

Deutsch [Alleman; Manuel]. Swiss family of artists, writers and politicians. (1) Niklaus Manuel Deutsch I was the son of the apothecary Emanuel Alleman, whose family came from Chieri in Piedmont, and Margaretha Fricker, natural daughter of Dr Thüring Fricker, town clerk of

Berne. Niklaus had six children by his wife Katharina Frisching, of whom (2) Hans Rudolf Manuel Deutsch and Niklaus Manuel Deutsch II (1528–88) became artists. Niklaus I adopted the surname Manuel, but 'Alleman' lingered in the translation 'Deutsch'; for example, Niklaus Manuel I usually signed his works with the monogram NMD, for Deutsch.

(1) Niklaus Manuel Deutsch I (*b* Berne, ?1484; *d* Berne, 28 April 1530). Painter, draughtsman, designer, writer and politician. Some early designs in pen and wash—for example one of *c*. 1508 featuring the Manuel arms (Paris, Louvre)—suggest that he may have trained in a glass-painter's workshop. The design's motif, composition and technique correspond closely with the contemporary glass panels in the church of Kirchberg, near Burgdorf, two of which bear his monogram. It is assumed that he was self-taught as a painter, although the wings of a *St Anne* altarpiece (Berne, Dominikanerkirche) reflect knowledge of the work of Hans Fries and of Dürer's *Life of the Virgin* woodcuts. The style, technique and subject-matter of Manuel's early drawings show an awareness also of Hans Burgkmair, Hans Baldung and Urs Graf. Probably he and Graf met personally while both were participating in the Italian campaigns as mercenaries. Their vivid, unorthodox renditions of soldiers, women and death in various graphic media are quite similar around 1513, although Manuel's interpretations, such as *Allegory on Man's Mortality*, are more allegorical (see fig. 1).

The documents name Manuel as a member of the Great Council of Berne from 1510 onwards. Two years later he was admitted to the local guild and in 1514 purchased a house. He joined the mercenaries fighting for the French in Lombardy in 1516 and again in 1522. Wounded near Novara, he was present when the French army was defeated at Bicocca. Intensely busy in the second decade of the century, Manuel produced autonomous drawings, panel and canvas paintings, as well as designs for stained glass, metalwork, woodcuts and even sculpture (the rood screen of Berne Cathedral, *c*. 1510); he painted banners, decorative frescoes (choir vault of the cathedral, *c*. 1517) and monumental wall paintings (*Solomon's Idolatry* on the house of Anthoni Noll, 1518; destr. 1758).

Manuel's *c*. 90 extant drawings range in date from 1507 to 1529, with most coming from 1510 to 1516. Most are undated, but changes of signature style help establish a chronology. A sheet with *Five Female Nudes* (*c*. 1510; Basle, Kstms.) is typical of his early drawings. Executed in pen and ink against a neutral background, the slender bodies still adhere to the Late Gothic ideal of physical beauty. Their veils stand for lost virginity, the pomegranate belongs to Venus, the distaff to witches' paraphernalia. Thus these nudes allegorize the power of women, a recurrent theme in Manuel's oeuvre. *Two Girls* with hearts impaled on spears and *Gentleman Talking with Girl* (both *c*. 1510; Basle, Kstms.) reflect knowledge of Dürer prints. Abbreviated mottoes suggest the erotic nature of these images. The popular subject of *Unequal Lovers* (*c*. 1510; Basle, Kstms.) resembles an engraving of 1507 by Baldung, under whose influence Manuel probably developed his chiaroscuro technique from 1510 (e.g. in *Four Women*, after 1510; Karlsruhe). A few years later he expressed

1. Niklaus Manuel Deutsch I: *Allegory on Man's Mortality*, pen and ink, heightened with white, on yellow-brown tinted paper, 264×167 mm, *c*. 1513 (Basle, Kupferstichkabinett)

personal concern with women and death in a fine chiaroscuro drawing of a *Witch* aloft, hourglass in one hand, in the other a skull with the artist's initials. Outstanding among Manuel's shieldbearer drawings is a *Female Supporter* (1513–14; Basle), evidently seen as a camp follower, coyly looking at the escutcheon with its leashed ram. Such drawings are works of art in their own right, free of their former subservient function. Also among his finest drawings are five studies of *Foolish Virgins* (1513–14; Basle, Kstms.), examples of his vibrant later charcoal-work, and a monumental, voluptuous *Female Nude Playing a Flute* in a landscape (1514–18; Basle, Kstms.). Two chalk and pen drawings of a *Confederate* and a *Lansquenet* (1529; Basle, Kstms.) are the last in his oeuvre. Of special interest is the *Schreibbüchlein*, a model-book of minute but brilliantly spirited drawings (*c*. 1517; Basle, Kstms.). It consists of thin, grounded leaves of wood on which Manuel drew in silverpoint saints, mythical and allegorical figures, army life, drapery studies and ornaments. A set of woodcuts of *Wise and Foolish Virgins* (1518) are his only known signed prints. They are loosely based on the earlier drawings, but extensive landscape settings have been added.

All Niklaus Manuel's known paintings come from the period 1513 to 1520. The patently early canvas of *Pyramus and Thisbe* (1513–14; see fig. 2), with its stiff, ill-integrated figures, is a night landscape that relates to the Danube school. The unsigned *St Anne, Virgin and Child* (Basle, Kstmus.) is very close in style and figure types. The wings of the *St Anne* altarpiece for the Dominikanerkirche (1518–20) are Manuel's first major artistically independent work. Spaces are still inelegantly rendered, but with Italianizing architectural detail and rather monumental figures in contemporary Swiss dress. Soon after, Niklaus provided the painted wings (Berne, Kstmus.) of an altarpiece for the Franciscan church at Grandson, where a weekly mass was read in honour of the Swiss confederates slaughtered by Burgundian troops in 1476. The *Martyrdom of the Ten Thousand* on the outsides allegorically refers to this. Alongside these works Manuel had begun his central work, a life-size *Dance of Death* in 41 pairs, accompanied by his own verses, on the outer wall of the Franziskanerkirche in Berne. The paintings (destr. 1660) showed, according to gouache copies by Albrecht Kauw (1649; Berne, Kstmus.), members of contemporary society as Death's victims—Death even grabbing the artist's mahlstick. Deutsch's monumental figures, placed against wide arcades, were conceived in a true Renaissance spirit. The same theme appears in a Basle panel of 1517, in chiaroscuro on brown ground, representing *Death Embracing a Young Woman*. Manuel is close to Baldung with these forcefully rendered images of great immediacy. He used the same rare technique again in a grisaille-framed, richly adorned *Lucretia* (1517; Basle, Kstmus.). The only other Classical subject in Manuel's oeuvre is a *Judgement of Paris* (1517–18; Basle, Kstmus.). Painted on canvas in brilliant colours, it shows reminiscences of Dürer in the figures of Venus and Minerva and of Cranach in the overall composition. The *Beheading of St John*, with its dramatic, exaggerated action heightened by an expressive night landscape, is close to the *Judgement*. Manuel's last extant religious paintings, the wings (1520) of a carved altarpiece for the Berne hospital church of the Antonites, show similarities with Grünewald's Isenheim altarpiece; Manuel may have been asked to study it, bringing back to his own work a subtlety of colour and luxuriant landscape if not Grünewald's expressive depth. Also from 1520 are a *Self-portrait* and a portrait of a *Knight of the Holy Sepulchre* (both on parchment; Berne, Kstmus.).

The diminution of Manuel's artistic activity in the early 1520s relates to his rising career as a statesman and indirectly to his growing involvement with the Protestant Reformation. He was governor of Erlach from 1523 to 1528, from which time only five drawings are known. In 1522 he wrote two anti-clerical carnival plays, *Vom Papst und seiner Priesterschaft* and *Von Papsts und Christi Gegensatz*, promulgating reform ideas in the city. A third piece, *Der Ablasskrämer*, castigated the indulgence trade. Manuel's handwritten copy with a fresh, pen-drawn title-page is still extant (1525; Berne, Burgerbib.). Further writings criticized monasticism and the mass: Manuel played a major role in bringing the Reformation to Berne (2 Feb 1528) and was subsequently voted into the Small Council, or governing body.

(2) Hans Rudolf Manuel Deutsch (*b* Erlach, 1525; *d* Morges, 23 April 1571). Painter, designer and poet, son

2. Niklaus Manuel Deutsch I: *Pyramus and Thisbe*, tempera on canvas, 1.51×1.61 m, 1513–14 (Basle, Kunstmuseum)

of (1) Niklaus Manuel Deutsch I. Probably apprenticed with Maximilian Wischack in Basle in the early 1540s, he often designed for publishers in that city, although he lived in Berne. Less than a dozen known independent pen drawings and stained-glass designs bear dates (1540–50) and the monogram RMD with dagger and ribbon. With their themes of mercenary life, they imitate works by his father and Urs Graf. His first dated and initialled woodcut is a *Standard Bearer* with camp follower (1546). In the following year Hans Rudolf copied Niklaus Manuel's *Confederate* and *Lansquenet* drawings for woodcuts and added a verse dialogue to them. By 1548 he had written a carnival play, *Das Weinspiel*. He also designed greatly acclaimed topographical views of cities for Sebastian Münster's *Cosmographey*. Many of these woodcuts are signed and dated, 1548 and 1549. A *Battle of Sempach* (1551), printed from six woodblocks, is characteristic of his meticulous but dry and eclectic work. His one extant oil painting represents his brother *Niklaus Manuel the Younger* (1553; Berne, Hist. Mus.) in full figure as mercenary against a landscape background. A pen contour design for stained glass of a *Female Shieldbearer with a Judgement of Paris* (1550s; Berne, Hist. Mus.) belongs with a group of drawings in this technique. Hans Rudolf also contributed seven signed woodcuts to the first modern book on mining, George Agricola's *De re metallica* (Basle, 1556). They are the freshest among his designs. The artist was married twice (1558 and 1561) and called to the Great Council in 1560. From 1562 he was governor of Morges in the canton of Waadt.

BIBLIOGRAPHY
Thieme–Becker
C. Grüneisen: *Niklaus Manuel: Leben und Werke eines Malers und Dichters, Kriegers, Staatsmannes und Reformators im sechzehnten Jahrhundert* (Stuttgart, 1837)
J. Baechtold: *Niklaus Manuel* (Frauenfeld, 1878)
L. Stumm: *Niklaus Manuel Deutsch von Bern als bildender Künstler* (Berne, 1925)

H. Koegler: *Beschreibendes Verzeichnis der Basler Handzeichnungen des Niklaus Manuel Deutsch* (Basle, 1930)

C. von Mandach: 'Die Antonius-Tafeln von Niklaus Manuel im Berner Kunstmuseum', *Z. Schweiz. Archäol. & Kstgesch.*, iv (1942), pp. 225–9

C. A. Beerli: *Le Peintre poète Nicolas Manuel et l'évolution sociale de son temps* (Geneva, 1953)

P. Zinsli, ed.: *Niklaus Manuel, der Ablasskrämer* (Berne, 1960)

——: *Der Berner Totentanz des Niklaus Manuel (ca. 1484–1530) in den Nachbildungen von Albrecht Kauw (1649)* (Berne, rev. 1979)

Niklaus Manuel Deutsch: Maler, Dichter, Staatsmann (exh. cat., Berne, Kstmus., 1979)

ROSEMARIE BERGMANN

Deutsch, Julije. *See under* HÖNIGSBERG & DEUTSCH.

Deutsche Gartenstadtgesellschaft. German association of architects, urban planners and writers. Founded in 1902 and active until the 1930s, it was modelled on the English Garden Cities Association. In contrast to the English precursor, however, which was grounded on Ebenezer Howard's practical theories of economic decentralization, the Deutsche Gartenstadtgesellschaft had literary roots. Its direct predecessors were the communes established by literati seeking to re-establish contact with the land, which flourished in the countryside around Berlin at the turn of the century. Among its founder-members were the writers Heinrich Hart (1855–1906) and Julius Hart (1859–1930), Bruno Wille (1860–1928) and Wilhelm Bölsche (1861–1939), and the literary tendencies of the group were clearly stated in the founding manifesto: 'The Deutsche Gartenstadtgesellschaft is a propaganda society. It sees the winning over of the public to the garden city cause as its principal aim' (quoted from *Founding Statutes of Deutsche Gartenstadtgesellschaft*, article 1, in Hartmann, p. 161). Practical skills were brought to the group by the cousins Bernhard (*b* 1867) and Hans (*b* 1876) Kampffmeyer, who had both trained as landscape architects and were active in literary and socialist circles in both Berlin and Paris.

The Deutsche Gartenstadtgesellschaft's first practical venture, a garden suburb in Karlsruhe, was begun in 1906 but remained incomplete for many years. A more successful project was the Gartenstadt Hellerau, near Dresden, on which building began in June 1909. The overall plan and a series of standard house designs were by Richard Riemerschmid, with further housing designs by Hermann Muthesius and Heinrich Tessenow. Like the 19th-century developments of Port Sunlight and Bournville in England, and the Krupp estates in Essen, the Hellerau estate was linked to a manufacturing firm, the Deutsche Werkstätten, which used industrial techniques to produce well-designed, standardized furniture. Riemerschmid's factory complex (1909) was given low profiles and high-pitched roofs to create the impression of a large group of farm buildings. This attempt to create a rural idyll dedicated to machine fabrication reflected the ideals of Karl Schmidt (*b* 1873), the owner of the Deutsche Werkstätten, who founded Hellerau as a model community in which artistic production, labour, leisure and education were to be fused into a harmonious entity. His idealistic vision was symbolized by the Bildungsanstalt (1910–12), built to the design of Heinrich Tessenow, a school for music and eurhythmic dance directed by the music educationalist Emile Jaques-Dalcroze and intended as the social focus of the community.

In 1912 Bruno Taut was appointed advisory architect to the Deutsche Gartenstadtgesellschaft and provided designs for two successful garden suburbs, the Gartenstadt Falkenberg near Berlin (1913–14), notable for its coloured façades, and the Gartenstadt Reform near Magdeburg (1913–14 and 1921). At the same time Jakobus Göttel, Taut's assistant, produced schemes for garden suburbs at Bonn and Bergisch-Gladbach that were only partially realized. Further model suburbs were built in the period up to 1914 at Ratshof, outside Königsberg, at Wandsbeck near Hamburg, and at Strasbourg, Mannheim and Nuremberg. By 1914 some 5600 houses had been built in model estates and suburbs throughout Germany, none of which were on the scale of Letchworth, the first English garden city. After 1918 the initiative in housing reform was seized by the newly constituted city councils, and the great housing schemes built in Berlin and Frankfurt during the 1920s implemented many of the ideas put forward in the pre-war years by the Deutsche Gartenstadtgesellschaft. Under the guidance of the Kampffmeyers the society remained active throughout the 1920s as a forum for debate on housing policy; it is significant that both Ernst May and Bruno Taut, who were responsible for large estates in Frankfurt and Berlin respectively, were on the committee of the Deutsche Gartenstadtgesellschaft in 1931. By this time, however, the association was moribund, and the last issue of its journal *Gartenstadt* appeared in November 1931. The 1937 supplement to *Wasmuths Lexikon der Baukunst* confirmed that the Deutsche Gartenstadtgesellschaft was no longer active.

BIBLIOGRAPHY

E. Howard: *Garden Cities of Tomorrow* (London, 1902); Ger. trans. as *Gartenstädte in Sicht*, intro. F. Oppenheimer (Jena, 1907)

H. Kampffmeyer: *Die Gartenstadtbewegung* (Leipzig, 1909)

——: *Die deutsche Gartenstadtbewegung* (Berlin, 1911)

K. Hartmann: *Deutsche Gartenstadtbewegung: Kulturpolitik und Gesellschaftsreform* (Munich, 1976)

F. Bollerey, G. Fehl, K. Hartmann, eds: *Im Grünen wohnen—im Blauen planen: Ein Lesebuch zur Gartenstadt mit Beiträgen und Zeitdokumenten* (Hamburg, 1990)

A. Schollmeier: *Gartenstädte in Deutschland: Ihre Geschichte, städtebauliche Entwicklung und Architektur zu Beginn des 20. Jahrhunderts* (Münster, 1990)

Deutscher Werkbund. German association of architects, designers and industrialists. It was active from 1907 to 1934 and then from 1950. It was founded in Munich, prompted by the artistic success of the third Deutsche Kunstgewerbeausstellung, held in Dresden in 1906, and by the then current, very acrimonious debate about the goals of applied art in Germany. Its founder-members included Hermann Muthesius, Peter Behrens, Heinrich Tessenow, Fritz Schumacher and Theodor Fischer, who served as its first president.

1. History and growth, until 1919. 2. Functionalism and Neue Sachlichkeit, 1920–30. 3. Dissolution and re-formation, after 1930.

1. HISTORY AND GROWTH, UNTIL 1919. In the spring of 1907 Muthesius gave a lecture at the Handelshochschule, Berlin, in which he condemned eclecticism and applauded the new directness and simplicity of design that

had dominated at the Dresden exhibition. This was against current trends, for, as Muthesius noted, 'domestic furnishing and decoration in present-day Germany are based on social pretensions, and an industry working with imitations and surrogates provides the material for this'. Such sentiments predictably upset the various interest groups involved with industrial design and led to demands for Muthesius's resignation from his official positions in the Prussian Handelsministerium and in the Berliner Kunstgewerbeverein. A series of stormy meetings in the Interessenverband des Kunstgewerbes revealed that further collaboration between the established interest groups and the progressive designers would be impossible; this conviction, coupled with the desire to build on the success of the Dresden exhibition, led to the foundation of the new association.

As the founding statutes explained, the function of the Werkbund was 'the ennobling of commerce through the collaboration of art, industry and craftsmanship, through education, propaganda, and a united position on relevant questions'. The nationalistic basis of the group was also made clear from the outset, with the collaboration of the best artistic and commercial minds seen as the sole guarantee of German culture. This nationalistic stance was strongly influenced by the political theorist Friedrich Naumann (1860–1919), the mentor of the first three secretaries of the Werkbund: Wolf Dohrn (1878–1914), Alfons Paquet (1881–1944) and Ernst Jäckh (1875–1959).

Between 1908 and 1915 the Werkbund published the deliberations of its annual conference, originally in pamphlet form, later in handsomely illustrated and highly influential yearbooks. Among the important contributions published in these volumes were essays by Muthesius (1912; an account of the particularly German ability to achieve universally valid design solutions); Walter Gropius (1913; illustrated with the American grain silos that were to become canonical images of architectural Modernism in the 1920s); and Behrens (1914; on time, space and modern form).

Although the architects were influential in defining the early goals of the Werkbund, architecture and urban planning played a less important role in the pre-1914 Werkbund than they were to do later. The membership expanded rapidly, from 491 in 1908 to 1972 in 1915, and reflected a wide spectrum of artistic credos, embracing Modernism and traditionalism, luxury and austerity. The commercial interests were also diverse, and they extended from craft workshops such as the WIENER WERKSTÄTTE to industrial giants such as the Allgemeine Elektricitäts-Gesellschaft (AEG), Krupp, Mannesmann and Daimler. Thus there could be no single Werkbund style or design philosophy, and this diversity of interests provoked a bitter debate at the Werkbund conference of 1914 in Cologne. In the principal speech Muthesius proposed that standard designs should be developed for objects intended for industrial production. Although he admitted that universally acceptable archetypes had traditionally evolved over long periods, he felt that in the industrial age these might be arrived at more rapidly through a more conscious design process, *Typisierung* (standardization). This suggestion, although entirely in accord with Behrens's practice as artistic adviser to AEG, was badly formulated, and in

the ensuing discussion Behrens himself declared that he was unsure of the meaning of Muthesius's key term, *Typisierung*. Other members of the artists' group, which included Henry Van de Velde, August Endell, Hermann Obrist, Gropius and Bruno Taut, were equally unclear and condemned Muthesius's proposals as an attack on artistic freedom. This open conflict within the Werkbund between the Nietzsche-inspired élitism of the artists, who felt that they alone were the custodians of beauty, and the more pragmatic interests of the industrialists and exporters was, however, terminated by the outbreak of World War I.

Although the standardization arguments were rehearsed again at the conference of 1916, held in Bamberg, the Werkbund was preoccupied with other matters during the war years: propaganda exhibitions in Basle, Winterthur, Berne and Copenhagen; a competition for the design of a German House of Friendship in Constantinople (now Istanbul); and morbid deliberations on the design of military graves. The defeat in 1918 and the reduction of Germany's industrial base following the Treaty of Versailles swept away the conditions on which the nationalist and export-orientated premises of the pre-war years were based, and the Werkbund reassembled in Stuttgart in September 1919 to discuss the future. While the opening lecture by the President, Peter Bruckmann (*b* 1865), reiterated the pre-war views of the importance of the Werkbund for nationalist *Kulturpolitik*, the radicals struck back in a speech by the architect Hans Poelzig which, in accord with the anti-industrialist and anti-capitalist sentiment of the immediate post-war years, supported hand-craftsmanship and condemned industrial fabrication. Poelzig was elected President at this meeting and was joined on the executive committee by supporters of the radical, 'Expressionist' position—Gropius, César Klein, Karl Ernst Osthaus, Bernhard Pankok and Bruno Taut. At this time the Werkbund was lobbying successfully for a 'Reichskunstwart', and Edwin Redslob (1884–1973), formerly the Werkbund representative in Thuringia, was appointed to the position in October 1919.

2. FUNCTIONALISM AND NEUE SACHLICHKEIT, 1920–30. Between 1920 and 1923 escalating inflation precluded any meaningful activity, and the Werkbund publications became sporadic. The Stuttgart compromise also collapsed, and Poelzig gave way to the more conservative Richard Riemerschmid as President in May 1921. Following the demise of the Expressionist hopes of regeneration through craftsmanship, the Werkbund's identification with the *Handwerk* lobby appeared to commit it to a regressive ideology, quite inconsistent with the founding ambitions. This conflict was resolved in 1923, when the association regained a positive new direction. Three important factors in this process were the location of the annual conference at Weimar, coinciding with the first major exhibition there by the Bauhaus; Gropius's speech at this meeting, hailing the new unity of art and technology; and the Werkbund's withdrawal from the Arbeitsgemeinschaft für Handwerkskultur in November 1923, which signalled the group's formal dissociation from the handcraft lobby. The highpoint of the Werkbund's fortunes was from 1924 to 1929. For the only time in its history it was strongly linked to one style—to Functionalism and

Weissenhofsiedlung, Stuttgart, 1927; view from the north

Neue Sachlichkeit—and concerned pre-eminently with architecture and urban design. This focusing of interest was reflected in the membership of the executive. In 1924 the architects Ludwig Mies van der Rohe and Hans Scharoun joined the committee, and Mies van der Rohe became First Vice-President in 1926, a position that gave him ultimate control, since Bruckmann, the President, exercised only a nominal authority at the time.

Mies van der Rohe's regime was marked by a virtual takeover of the executive by the progressive architects of Der Ring: Hugo Häring and Adolf Rading joined in 1926, Ludwig Hilberseimer in 1927. These disciples of architectural Modernism spread their gospel in the Werkbund journal, *Die Form*, which, after a short run in 1922, achieved great influence between 1925 and 1930 and survived until 1934. A second major propaganda forum was the Weissenhofsiedlung in Stuttgart, built in 1927 (see fig.). Conceived as a direct rebuff to the traditionalism of Paul Bonatz, Paul Schmitthenner and the Stuttgart school, and as a model for future Functionalist housing, the estate was laid out following Mies van der Rohe's site-plan, with 60 housing units in 21 buildings, designed by 16 architects: Mies van der Rohe, Gropius, Scharoun, Richard Döcker, Behrens, Poelzig, Hilberseimer, Adolf Schneck (*b* 1883), Adolf Rading, Bruno Taut and Max Taut from Germany; J. J. P. Oud and Mart Stam from the Netherlands; Josef Frank from Austria; Le Corbusier from France; and Victor Bourgeois from Belgium. This foretaste of the brave new world of concrete, steel and glass attracted half a million visitors and the antagonism both of the local traditionalists and of the extreme left, who regarded the whole enterprise as an aesthetes' indulgence. In organizing the next building exhibition, *Wohnung und Werkraum*, held in Breslau in 1929, the Werkbund countered some of the Stuttgart critics by employing only Silesian architects and artists.

3. DISSOLUTION AND RE-FORMATION, AFTER 1930. At this point the membership of the Werkbund reached its peak at just under 3000, and the association enjoyed pre-eminence not only in Germany but throughout Europe as the most important pressure group for Neues Bauen. Yet its achievements in architecture and industrial design were those of an élite for an élite and had little practical impact as models for mass housing or industrial mass production, the association being unable to reconcile its intellectual and artistic goals with the demands of a mass culture. Squeezed between Communist demands for a proletarian culture and Nazi exhortations to return to the *Volk* and the soil, the Werkbund in 1930 had little to offer but aesthetic precepts. The facile identification of technology and artistic Modernism was already being questioned from within, however, and at the conference of 1930 in Vienna, Frank posed the important question, 'Was ist modern?'. This crisis of Modernism was exacerbated by the world economic collapse and the Depression, widely seen as a failure of capitalism. An ambitious exhibition planned for Cologne in 1932, entitled *Neue Zeit*, would have given the Werkbund an opportunity to answer its critics, with the construction of a new university, housing estates and schools, extensive coverage of the applied and performing arts, and a series of scientific and philosophical congresses. None of this came to fruition, however, due to the Depression, and by the end of 1932 the Werkbund was effectively dead. *Gleichschaltung*, the process of assimilation into the new Nazi power structure, followed in June 1933, and in December 1934 the Werkbund finally lost its identity when it was incorporated into the Reichskammer der Bildenden Künste.

In March 1947 a group of former members, including Otto Bartning, Willi Baumeister, Egon Eiermann, Gerhard Marcks, Max Pechstein, Lilly Reich, Schumacher, Rudolf Schwarz, Max Taut, Döcker and Tessenow, signed a manifesto calling for the regeneration of the war-damaged cities and towns of Germany through simple, modern design rather than historical reconstruction. The aim, they said, should be 'das Einfache und das Gültige'. Local and regional initiatives followed, such as the founding of the Werkkunstschule in Krefeld in 1947 and of the celebrated Hochschule für Gestaltung in Ulm in 1950. A national Werkbund was re-established in September 1950 with Hans Schwippert (*b* 1899) as Chairman. From 1951 to 1961 the Werkbund collaborated with the Rat für Formgebung in the publication of *Deutsche Warenkunde*, and a monthly Werkbund journal, *Werk und Zeit*, first appeared in March 1952.

Towards the end of the 1950s the reconstituted Werkbund developed ambitions that went beyond the promotion of good industrial design. More directly political positions were adopted, concerned with the future form of both city and country. In the urban context, the *Interbau* exhibition of 1957 in Berlin gave several Werkbund architects the opportunity to build modern mass housing in a park landscape, and at Marl in 1959 the Werkbund discussed the destruction of the West German landscape through ill-conceived housing, roads and water-regulation projects. Anticipating the ecology lobby of the 1970s, the Werkbund incorporated countryside conservation into its programme in 1960. The optimistic belief in a rationally planned future found expression in the 1960s in a series of public discussions organized by the Werkbund, most notably the conference 'Bildung durch Gestalt' held in Berlin in 1965, with contributions from Ernst Bloch (1885–1987) and Theodor W. Adorno (1903–69). In common with most institutions in West Germany, the Werkbund was subjected to the critical scrutiny of the New Left in the late 1960s, particularly at the Berlin conference of 1968, held under the title 'Die Generationen und ihre Verantwortung für unsere Umwelt'. Although it survived the anti-authoritarian assault, the Werkbund in the 1970s and 1980s took on a resigned, introspective character, and its principal achievements were concerned with documenting its own history: the Werkbund-Archiv was established in Berlin in 1972, and an exhibition on the history of the Werkbund was held in Munich in 1975.

For further discussion, *see* MODERN MOVEMENT, §§2 and 4 and figs 1 and 3.

WRITINGS
Die Durchgeistigung der deutschen Arbeit (Jena, 1912) [incl. 'Wo stehen wir?' by Muthesius]
Die Kunst in Industrie und Handel (Jena, 1913) [incl. 'Die Entwicklung moderner Industriebaukunst' by Gropius]
Der Verkehr (Jena, 1914) [incl. 'Einfluss von Zeit- und Raumausnutzung auf moderne Formentwicklung' by Behrens]
Deutsche Form im Kriegsjahr (Munich, 1915)
Kriegergräber im Felde und daheim (Munich, 1916–17)
Handwerkliche Kunst in alter und neuer Zeit (Berlin, 1920)

BIBLIOGRAPHY
H. Eckstein: *50 Jahre Deutscher Werkbund* (Frankfurt, 1958)
J. Posener: *Anfänge des Funktionalismus: Vom Arts and Crafts zum Deutschen Werkbund* (Berlin, 1964)
U. Conrads and others, eds: *'Die Form': Stimme des Deutschen Werkbundes, 1925–1934* (Gütersloh, 1969)
S. Müller: *Kunst und Industrie: Ideologie und Organisation des Funktionalismus in der Architektur* (Munich, 1974)
J. Campbell: *The German Werkbund: The Politics of Reform in the Applied Arts* (Princeton, 1978) [extensive bibliog.]
K. Junghanns: *Der Deutscher Werkbund: Sein erstes Jahrzehnt* (Berlin, 1982)
'75 Jahre Deutscher Werkbund', *Werk & Zeit*, 3 (1982) [special issue]
K. Kirsch: *Die Weissenhofsiedlung* (Stuttgart, 1987)

IAIN BOYD WHYTE

Devagadh. *See* DEOGARH.

Devagiri. *See* DAULATABAD.

Devenish, John (*b* Sydney, 13 Dec 1944; *d* Melbourne, 17 Aug 1990). Australian architect and urban planner. He studied architecture at the University of New South Wales, Sydney, graduating in 1967; he later completed a Master's degree in town and country planning there (1977). From 1967 to 1972 he worked for the Commonwealth Department of Works in Sydney, where he had been a cadet (1963–6). After travelling in the UK, Europe and Asia, he was invited in 1975 to establish and direct a multi-disciplinary team to plan the Woolloomooloo Redevelopment Project (1975–81) for the Housing Commission of New South Wales. This project, involving the rehabilitation and redevelopment of a large historic inner city precinct between the centre of Sydney and Kings Cross, predominantly with public housing, received local and international acclaim as a demonstration of effective community consultation and urban regeneration. Following this success, Devenish joined the Ministry of Housing in Victoria and from 1981 to 1983 was instrumental in implementing several innovative and award-winning infill housing schemes in Melbourne; he was also responsible for major public housing schemes involving external consultants, openly encouraging innovative domestic design. In 1987 he became Director General of Victoria's Public Works Department and in 1988 he was appointed Director, Design and Development, of the new Ministry of Housing and Construction in Victoria. He became the leading government architect in the state, establishing a reputation for design excellence in public building.

WRITINGS
'Woolloomooloo Townscape: An Exercise in Controlled Diversity', *Archit. Australia*, lxx/4 (1981), pp. 54–63
'Filling in the Gaps', *Medium Density Housing in Australia*, eds B. Judd and J. Dean (Canberra, 1983), pp. 51–60

BIBLIOGRAPHY
Obituary, *Archit. Australia*, lxxx/1 (1991), pp. 22–3

PHILIP GOAD

Deverell, Walter Howell (*b* Charlottesville, VA, 1 Oct 1827; *d* London, 2 Feb 1854). English painter. Although not a member of the Pre-Raphaelite Brotherhood (PRB), he was a close friend of the Pre-Raphaelites and during his short career was greatly influenced by their artistic principles and practices. His father placed him in a solicitor's office in Westminster, London, but he was permitted to give up studying law in favour of painting in 1844. He first trained at Henry Sass's Academy, where he met Dante Gabriel Rossetti, who became his mentor and friend. In 1846 he entered the Royal Academy Schools, where his fellow students included John Everett Millais and William Holman Hunt. Deverell was reputedly very popular: William Michael Rossetti recalled that 'If there was one man who, more than others, could be called the "pet" of the whole circle, it was Deverell'.

In 1848 Deverell was appointed Assistant Master of the Government School of Design at Somerset House, where his father was Secretary. The same year he joined Millais, Rossetti, Hunt and others in forming the Cyclographic Society, whose members produced drawings for mutual criticism at weekly meetings. Although he had exhibited at the Royal Academy in 1847 and 1848, it was not until 1850 that he attracted critical attention, when he exhibited *Twelfth Night* (London, Forbes Mag. Col.). Painted in the style of the Pre-Raphaelites, it prominently features the love-sick Duke Orsino from the play. Rather than use professional models, Deverell portrayed himself as the Duke and used Dante Gabriel Rossetti as the model for Feste. Elizabeth Siddal posed as Viola, thus making her first appearance in a Pre-Raphaelite painting. Painted with flat, angular forms, the painting provoked cautious praise and was described in the *Art Journal* as being 'as a whole...successful in its imitation of the post-Giottesque epoch'. In the same year Deverell contributed to *The Germ*, the literary magazine of the PRB.

During the early 1850s Deverell lived in the family house in Kew, near London. His mother had died in 1850 and his father three years later, leaving him to support his younger brothers and sisters. In 1853 the collector Francis McCracken expressed an interest in purchasing *Twelfth Night*, but Deverell found his terms, a form of part-exchange, unacceptable. Meanwhile he was working on his next picture, *A Pet* (London, Tate), which he exhibited that autumn at the Liverpool Academy. Painted from the garden of his house at Kew and showing a young woman standing in the doorway of a conservatory, it was executed in a naturalistic style typical of Pre-Raphaelitism with bright, clear colours and a detailed finish.

Deverell fell ill during 1853 and by the autumn was obliged to give up teaching. In an act of friendship and generosity, Millais and Hunt bought *A Pet*, and the poet William Allingham (1824–89) commissioned a drawing for his forthcoming *Day and Night Songs*. In his last months Deverell turned to painting modern-life subjects. In the unfinished *Irish Vagrants* (Johannesburg, A.G.), inspired by Thomas Carlyle and Charles Kingsley, he depicted unemployed Irish labourers with their destitute families begging by the roadside, a clear departure from the literary and domestic themes he had treated earlier.

BIBLIOGRAPHY

V. Hunt: *The Wife of Rossetti* (London, 1932)
M. Lutyens: 'Walter Howell Deverell', *Pre-Raphaelite Papers*, ed. L. Parris (London, 1984), pp. 76–96 [based on an unpub. memoir by F. Deverell (sister-in-law) with preface and annotations by W. M. Rossetti (added 1899); San Marino, CA, Huntington Lib.]

For a full bibliography up to 1965 see W. E. Fredeman: *Pre-Raphaelite Brotherhood* (Cambridge, MA, 1965), pp. 138–44, 289–95. For general works *see* PRE-RAPHAELITISM.

JENNY ELKAN

Devereux, Robert, 2nd Earl of Essex (*b* Netherwood, Herts, 19 Nov 1566; *d* London, 25 Feb 1601). English military leader and patron. He was introduced at court by his stepfather Robert Dudley, 1st Earl of Leicester, and became the favourite of Elizabeth I in her last years. He fought against the Spanish and in Ireland, a country over which he was appointed Governor-General in 1599. His frequent absences abroad and at sea may explain the fact that he seems not to have built a great country house, though he lived expensively when in London, at Essex House (destr.) on the Strand, formerly the London residence of the Bishops of Exeter. He was executed following a plot in which he had attempted to raise the citizens of London. Essex is chiefly important in the visual arts for the imagery to be found in portraits made of him; these can be interpreted in ways that encompass the late Elizabethan ideal of the courtier as both warrior and suitor. The full-length miniature by Nicholas Hilliard of a *Young Man Leaning against a Tree among Roses* (*c.* 1596; London, V&A) has been suggested as a portrait of Essex. He can be more positively identified in a series of military images: the portrait by William Segar, depicting Essex as he appeared in the Accession Day tilt of 1590 (Dublin, N.G.); Hilliard's miniature of the *Queen's Knight* (*c.* 1593–5; priv. col.; see Strong, p. 67, pl. 42); and, in what may have been a shift of patronage towards a newer, more realistic mode, the great full-length by Marcus Gheerhaerts (ii) (*c.* 1596; Woburn Abbey, Beds), which shows him by the seashore in a full landscape setting. There is also a miniature by Isaac Oliver (*c.* 1596; London, N.P.G.).

BIBLIOGRAPHY

R. Strong: *Tudor and Jacobean Portraits*, 2 vols (London, 1969)
R. Lacey: *Robert, Earl of Essex: An Elizabethan Icarus* (London, 1970)
R. Strong: *The Cult of Elizabeth* (London, 1977)
M. Edmond: *Hilliard and Oliver* (London, 1983)

MAURICE HOWARD

Devéria. French family of artists.

(1) Achille(-Jacques-Jean-Marie) Devéria (*b* Paris, 6 Feb 1800; *d* Paris, 23 Dec 1857). Painter, lithographer and stained-glass designer. He was a pupil of Louis Lafitte (1770–1828) and, like him, specialized in illustration, which formed the greater part of his output until 1830 (e.g. his illustrations to Goethe's *Faust*, 1828). His experience in the art of the vignette influenced his numerous lithographs (over 3000), most of which were issued by his father-in-law, Charles-Etienne Motte (1785–1836). Devéria was an excellent portrait artist, and his lithographs included portraits of Victor Hugo, Alexandre Dumas (père), Prosper Mérimée, Franz Liszt and numerous other artists and writers whom he entertained in his Paris studio in the Rue de l'Ouest.

Devéria chronicled the taste and manners of the Romantic era in a series of brilliantly coloured lithographs entitled *The Times of the Day* (*c.* 1829), which depicted the day of an elegant Parisienne in 18 detailed scenes, for example *Five o'Clock in the Morning, Annette Boulanger* (Paris, Carnavalet; see fig.). Baudelaire believed that the series showed all 'the morals and aesthetics of the age'. In 1831–9 Devéria portrayed his friends wearing elaborate fancy dress in another series of coloured lithographs, *Historical Costumes* (125 plates). Most of his lithographs consisted of pseudo-historical, pious, sentimental or erotic scenes, and these images, disseminated in vast numbers by the new medium of lithography, fed the dreams and fantasies of a generation. Béraldi (1886) felt that such commercial output was devoid of artistic merit, but Farwell (1977) demonstrated how several of Devéria's erotic prints foreshadowed similar paintings by Courbet and Manet by 20 to 30 years, for example a suite of lithographs *Six Female Nudes Studied from Life* (1829).

Achille Devéria: *Five o'Clock in the Morning, Annette Boulanger*, colour lithograph, 290×235 mm, *c.* 1829 (Paris, Musée Carnavalet)

Devéria was a regular contributor of religious paintings to the Salon. The monumental *Apotheosis of St Clotilda* (1851; Paris, St-Roch) is one of his few surviving works of this type. He also participated in the French 19th-century revival of stained glass. He designed a large number of windows depicting saints for the Sèvres factory and the figures of monarchs for the Henry II staircase in the Louvre, Paris (1840–41). He also designed glass for the church at Sèvres (1839–47) and the chapels of the royal residences at Dreux (1841), Eu (1841–2) and Notre-Dame-d'Auray in Carheil (1847).

Foucart (1987) described Devéria's painting as 'colourful, happy and animated'. The sense of movement is particularly well expressed in the lively gestures of the ascending saint in *Apotheosis of St Clotilda*. A passion for colour is a feature in his work, not only in the lithographs but also in his stained glass for Versailles, the magnificent colour of which accords perfectly with the richness of the architecture. In his choice of subject-matter Devéria was less Romantic than Géricault and Delacroix and rarely depicted grave or tragic themes. Devéria ended his career as curator of the Cabinet des Estampes in the Bibliothèque Nationale, Paris, which has examples of most of his work and an important collection of documents left at his bequest.

(2) Eugène(-François-Marie-Joseph) Devéria (*b* Paris, 22 April 1805; *d* Pau, 3 Feb 1865). Painter, brother of (1) Achille Devéria. He was a pupil of Anne-Louis Girodet and Guillaume Lethière but was greatly influenced by his brother. Despite differences of taste and temperament—Eugène had an official career and painted on a grand scale—the brothers remained close until Eugène went to Avignon in 1838. He first exhibited at the Salon of 1824 and had his first success with the *Birth of Henry IV* (1827; Paris, Louvre). He approached this well-worn subject (made fashionable by the Restoration and usually portrayed in engravings or small-scale works) with unusual panache. The ambitious scale, the crowds of people painstakingly depicted in period costume and the rich colours revealed his desire to raise the subject to the rank of history painting. With Delacroix and Louis Boulanger, Devéria was hailed as a champion of the Romantic movement and the successor to Veronese and Rubens.

The success of the *Birth of Henry IV* brought Devéria numerous official commissions. He was asked by the Direction des Musées Royaux to decorate the Salle d'Amasis in the Louvre with the mural *Puget Presenting Louis XIV with his 'Milos of Croton' in the Gardens of Versailles* (1832) and was one of several artists called by Louis-Philippe to decorate the Musée de l'Histoire de France at Versailles. In the *Oath of King Louis-Philippe before the Chamber of Deputies* (1836) he depicted the new alliance between the sovereign and his subjects, and with this history painting joined the tradition of David and Baron François Gérard.

Devéria was one of the few Romantic painters (apart from Delacroix and Théodore Chassériau) to produce religious works, for example his five canvases of the *Life of Christ* (a sixth by Achille) for the church at Fougères, Brittany (1835), and two paintings of the *Life of St Genevieve*

for Notre-Dame-de-Lorette, Paris (1835). His most important decorative work was for Notre-Dame-des-Doms, Avignon (1838–40), for which he devised an elaborate programme, though only part was realized. The chapels of the Virgin and St Charlemagne were decorated in encaustic painting and fresco and completed by four large oil paintings depicting scenes from the *Litanies of the Virgin* (1851–6).

Devéria's Romantic style was a synthesis of various elements, combining the influence of Rubens and Veronese with that of his contemporaries. His work is distinguished by vivid colours, robustly modelled forms (which recall the work of Ingres) and a painstaking attention to detail in the depiction of costume and landscape, characteristic of nascent Orientalism. He was also a skilled portrait painter. His best works are of his family and friends; the intimate charm and engaging character of these works rely on his evident sympathy for his models, for example the portraits of his sister-in-law *Céleste Devéria* (1837; Pau, Mus. B.-A.) and *Eugène and Achille Devéria* (1836; Versailles, Château).

In 1841 Devéria settled in Pau, in the Pyrenees, where he painted village scenes and portraits of local worthies. His conversion to Protestantism in 1843 led to a break with his brother. In his last paintings he remained faithful to the historical vein that had brought him success in 1827. He sent to the Salon the *Death of Jane Seymour* (1847; Valence, Mus. B.-A. & Hist. Nat.), *Cardinal Wolsey and Catherine of Aragon* (1859; Le Havre, Mus. B.-A.) and *Christopher Columbus Being Received by Ferdinand and Isabella* (1861; Pau, Mus. B.-A.).

BIBLIOGRAPHY
H. Béraldi: *Les Gravures du XIXe siècle*, v (Paris, 1886)
M. Gauthier: *Achille et Eugène Devéria* (Paris, 1925)
P. Gusman: 'Achille Devéria, illustrateur et lithographe romantique (1800–1857)', *Byblis*, vi (1927), pp. 34–40
J. Lethève and J. Adhémar: *Inventaire du fonds français après 1800*, vi (Paris, 1953)
The Cult of Images: Baudelaire and the Nineteenth-century Media Explosion (exh. cat., ed. B. Farwell; Santa Barbara, U. CA, A. Mus., 1977)
P. Comte: 'La *Naissance d'Henri IV* de Devéria', *Rev. Louvre* (1981), pp. 137–41
R. Rapetti: 'Eugène Devéria et le décor de la chapelle de la Vierge à la cathédrale d'Avignon', *Bull. Soc. Hist. A. Fr.* (1984), pp. 207–27
Achille Devéria: Témoin du romantisme parisien (exh. cat., ed. D. Morel; Paris, Mus. Renan-Scheffer, 1985)
B. Foucart: *Le Renouveau de la peinture religieuse en France (1800–1860)* (Paris, 1987)
The Charged Image: French Lithographic Caricature, 1816–1848 (exh. cat. by B. Farwell, Santa Barbara, CA, Mus. A., 1989)
Autour de Delacroix: La Peinture religieuse en Bretagne au 19ème siècle (exh. cat., essay P. Bonnet, Vannes, Mus. B.-A., 1993)

DOMINIQUE MOREL

Devĕtsil. Czech avant-garde group of architects, painters, sculptors, collagists, photographers, film makers, designers and writers, active 1920–31. Its name is a composite of the words 'nine' and 'forces'. The group's leader, KAREL TEIGE, advocated a reconciliation between utilitarianism and lyrical subjectivity: 'Constructivism and Poetism'. Devĕtsil's architects, including JAROMÍR KREJCAR and KAREL HONZÍK, invested the geometry of architecture with an element of poetry, while painters and photographers such as TOYEN and JINDRICH ŠTYRSKÝ moved towards Surrealism, and when the group dissolved many of its members, including Teige, joined the Czech Surrealist group.

See also PERIODICAL, §IV, 5(iii).

BIBLIOGRAPHY
Czech Art of the Twenties and Thirties, 2 vols (exh. cat. by J. Kotalík and Bernd Kimmel, Darmstadt, Ausstellhallen Mathildenhöhe, 1988)
Czech Modernism, 1900–1945 (exh. cat., Boston, MA, Mus. F.A., 1990)
Devětsil: Czech Avant-garde Art, Architecture and Design of the 1920s and 1930s (exh. cat., ed. R. Svacha; Oxford, MOMA; London, Des. Mus.; 1990)

NICHOLAS WEGNER

Devey, George (*b* London, 23 Feb 1820; *d* Hastings, E. Sussex, 4 Nov 1886). English architect. Chiefly known as the designer of large country houses and estate buildings, he was the first architect to apply vernacular building methods, particularly those of the Weald and east Kent, in the design of his smaller and medium-sized houses and to use 17th-century buildings in the Dutch style as models for his larger mansions.

The son of a solicitor, Devey was educated at King's College School, London, where he was taught watercolour painting by John Sell Cotman, and he also took lessons from J. D. Harding. His ambition to become a painter was opposed by his father, and by way of compromise at the age of 17 he became a pupil of the architect and surveyor Thomas Little (1802–59). In 1841 Devey exhibited a design for a cottage at the Royal Academy, and in 1846 he set out with his fellow pupil Coutts Stone (*d* 1902) on a tour of Germany, Italy and Greece. He probably set up in practice soon after his return and had great difficulty establishing himself, but the friendship of his father with the curate of Penshurst, Kent, secured introductions to Philip Sydney, 2nd Lord de l'Isle, and Henry, 1st Viscount Hardinge, who employed Devey on alterations to Penshurst Place and its gardens and on small houses in Penshurst and Fordcombe. Here in the Weald of Kent he became familiar with and began to use such local vernacular details as half-timbering, tile-hanging and ragstone—the last as a foundation for brick walls and rough cast in a highly picturesque manner derived from Cotman's watercolours—features that came to characterize his work. His best early buildings are the cottages in Leicester Square

George Devey: Leicester Square cottages, Penshurst, Kent, 1848–51

(1848–51; see fig.) and South Park Farm, Penshurst, and the Chafford Arms, Fordcombe (1850–51).

Devey continued to work on nothing larger than cottages and lodges until in 1856 he was commissioned to make an addition to Betteshanger House, Kent. Here, for the first time, he used red brick and Dutch gables borrowed from buildings such as Fairfax Court in Putney, Kew Palace and several examples in east Kent, notably Broome Park and farmhouses at Sarre. He later returned to Betteshanger to make further additions, notably the James Tower, which, built of brick and flint on ragstone footings, was intended to resemble a medieval stone building that had been first ruined and then patched up in Tudor times. This use of stonework merging into brickwork became a favoured motif. He found himself almost entirely confined to designing small estate buildings at Cliveden, Mentmore and elsewhere until the mid-1860s, when at last he began to receive commissions for large country houses, including Brantingham Thorpe (1868–74), Humberside; Akeley Wood (1867–8), Bucks; Calverley Grange (1867–70), near Tunbridge Wells; and Coombe Warren, Surrey. This last house he began in 1868 in his Wealden style, but since it was burnt down soon after completion, Devey rebuilt it immediately in the Dutch style (destr.). Coombe Warren was built for the banker B. W. Currie, and Devey made useful connections among bankers; the Rothschilds, Smiths, Glyns and Barings were among his clients. He also established a link with the Liberal Party through Granville George Leveson-Gower, 2nd Earl Granville, for whom he carried out repairs and alterations at Walmer Castle (1872–86), which led to work from other members of Gladstone's cabinets such as G. J. Shaw Lefevre, for whom he remodelled Oldbury Place (1878–81), Kent.

In the 1870s Devey embarked upon a series of large country mansions: Gaunt's House (1870–86), Dorset; Goldings (1871–7), Herts; Hall Place (1871–4; partly destr.), Leigh, Kent; St Alban's Court (1875–8), Kent; Ashfold (1875–8; destr.), Sussex; Adderley (1877–81; destr.), Salop; Killarney (1877–83; destr.), Co. Kerry; Membland (1877–80; destr.), Devon; and Longwood (1881–3; destr.), Hants. These houses are ingeniously planned, and most employ the device of diminishing the impact of large service wings (usually the height of the house) by setting them back at an angle, allowing such recessions to reduce their apparent size. In these houses Devey used a mixture of his Wealden and Dutch styles but with increasing insensitivity, seemingly unable to apply on a grand scale what began as small-scale architectural features. They were best employed on his smaller country houses: Broomford Manor (1871–3), Devon; Lynwood (1871–7), Hants; and Blakesware (1876–9), Herts. In addition to this extensive business in new country houses, Devey was frequently called upon to enlarge, adapt and restore old mansions, which he did with considerable tact and success, notably at Smithills Hall (1874–86), Lancs; Pitchford Hall (1883–4), Salop; and at Melbury (1885–6), Dorset, where he also added a new tower.

By the 1880s Devey had become involved in building new houses in central London, beginning with 36 Grosvenor Square (1883–6) for Henry Wilson, and then designing houses in Lennox Gardens, both for private clients and for speculative builders, for example S. J. Wyand. He also designed a block of four houses in Cadogan Square for Messrs Trollop in 1886. His church work, however, was limited to a few minor restorations.

Devey became a Fellow of the RIBA in 1856 but took no part in its activities. He never married (an engagement to the daughter of the vicar of Chiddingstone in Kent was broken off because of his unusual religious views); subsequently he became a member of the Rev. Charles Voysey's Theistic Church, and it was for this reason that C. F. A. Voysey spent some time in his office. Devey died after contracting pneumonia on a visit to Ireland, after which his partner of some years, James Williams, and his principal draughtsman Arthur Castings divided the office work in progress between them and completed the outstanding commissions.

Devey's contribution to English domestic architecture up to and even beyond World War I cannot be overemphasized. He discovered, chiefly through his artistic training, the charm of small farmhouses and rejected the normal 19th-century alternatives of classicism and the Gothic Revival ten years before those who are usually credited for that major innovation in style, Philip Webb, R. N. Shaw and W. E. Nesfield. There is no doubt that Shaw and Nesfield saw his work at Penshurst, and for them it must have been an object lesson in what might be achieved by a return to vernacular domestic architecture. It was to lead them to adopt the Old English and Queen Anne styles and ultimately to the architecture of the Arts and Crafts Movement.

BIBLIOGRAPHY

P. G. Stone: 'The Late George Devey', *Bldg News* (12 Nov 1886), p. 721
W. H. Godfrey: 'George Devey, FRIBA: A Biographical Essay', *RIBA J.*, n. s. 3, xii (1906), pp. 502–25
——: 'The Work of George Devey', *Archit. Rev.*, xxi (1907), pp. 23–30, 83–8, 293–306
J. Williams: 'George Devey and his Work', *Archit. Assoc. J.*, xxiv (1909), pp. 95–103
M. Girouard: *The Victorian Country House* (London, 1979)
J. Franklin: *The Gentleman's Country House and its Plan, 1835–1914* (London, 1981)
J. Allibone: *George Devey, Architect, 1820–1886* (Cambridge, 1991)

JILL ALLIBONE

De Vigne. Belgian family of artists. The sons of the Ghent decorative artist Ignace De Vigne (1767–after 1849) included two painters, Félix (1806–62) and Edouard (1808–66); a sculptor, (1) Pierre De Vigne; and a musician, Alexandre. Ignace's granddaughters Louise (1844–1911), Malvina (who died at the age of 28) and Emma (1850–98) were flower painters; Louise married the sculptor Gérard van der Linden (1830–1911). Ignace's grandson Edmond (1842–1918) was an architect, and his grandson (2) Paul De Vigne, a sculptor, was the most celebrated artist of the family.

(1) Pierre De Vigne (*b* Ghent, 29 July 1812; *d* Ghent, 7 Feb 1877). Sculptor. He studied in Bruges under Jan-Robert Calloigne (1775–1830), of whom he later made a bust (Brussels, Mus. A. Mod.). After success in competitions in both Ghent (1831) and Rome (1832), he lived in Paris and in Rome between 1837 and 1840, settling in Ghent in 1841. He became a teacher at the Academie voor Schone Kunsten in Ghent in 1850. He executed several monuments for the town of Ghent, including the statue of *Jacques van Artevelde* (1863; Vrijdagmarkt) and that of

the manufacturer *Livin Bauwens* (1885; François Laurent-plein). He also designed two allegorical works for the railway station (destr.) at Ghent, *Commerce* and *Industry*.

(2) Paul De Vigne (*b* Ghent, 26 April 1849; *d* Brussels, 13 Feb 1901). Sculptor, son of (1) Pierre De Vigne. Between 1856 and 1862 he studied at the Academie voor Schone Kunsten in Ghent, where his teachers included his uncle Félix, his father Pierre and the painter Thomas Canneel (1817–92); between 1864 and 1866 he studied at the Academie voor Beeldende Kunsten in Antwerp, where he was taught by the painter Lodewijk Jan De Taeye (1822–90), his uncle Gérard van der Linden and the sculptor Joseph Geefs (1808–85), brother of Guillaume Geefs. He also studied at the Academie in Leuven (*c.* 1866–70). In June 1870 he went to Italy at his own expense, after two unsuccessful applications for the Prix de Rome. He first visited Florence, where he studied the masters of the early Renaissance, particularly Donatello and Luca della Robbia. He then went to Rome where, among other works, he executed a bust of a young girl, *Beatrice* (1872; Ghent, Mus. S. Kst), strongly influenced by Florentine Renaissance sculpture. He made a second trip to Italy in 1873. A serious illness prevented him from working until 1874, when he made a bust of his friend the sculptor *Gaston Marchant* (Brussels, Mus. A. Mod.), who had died in 1873.

Between 1873 and 1887 De Vigne lived in Brussels, where he sculpted busts and caryatids for the façade of the new Conservatoire de Musique. During the same period he executed several refined and delicate works influenced by his Florentine studies and by the Antique, including *Poverella*, a sleeping adolescent street singer (1876; Brussels, Mus. A. Mod.). From 1878 to 1882 he lived in Paris, where his exhibited works included the bust of *Psyche* (exh. Salon 1878; Ghent, Mus. S. Kst). He also created *Immortality* (1881; Brussels, Mus. A. Mod.) in honour of the recently deceased Lievin Winne; it is a restrained and sensitive allegorical figure of a young girl.

On his return to Brussels De Vigne started work on the *Triumph of Art*, a group for the façade of the Musée des Beaux-Arts in Brussels, which had been commissioned while he was in Paris. It was completed in 1885 and was generally well received, although in the eyes of some members of the supervisory committee its realistic nudes were excessively daring. In 1884 he won first prize at the Salon for his monument to *J. Breidel and P. De Coninck* in Bruges, which he completed in 1887. Recalling a famous incident in 14th-century Flemish history, the struggle between the Lelliaerts and the Klauwaerts, this work symbolizes the triumph of communal power over the feudal system and of national prerogatives over the alien ascendancy of France. De Vigne's *Marnix de Sainte-Aldegonde* (1881–9; Brussels, Square du Petit Sablon), a legendary figure from the struggles of the Netherlands against the Spanish occupying forces, was made in a similar historicist and nationalist vein. In addition to his political commissions he executed several funerary monuments, including those of the *Gevaert Family* (1892, Bruges) and of *Hippolyte Metdepenningen* (1893, Ghent). In 1895 the sculptor's health declined, and he had to abandon his work on the monument to *Jules Anspach*, which had been commissioned by the Conseil Communal of Brussels.

BIBLIOGRAPHY

H. Hymans: *L'Art au XVIIe et au XIXe siècle dans les Pays-Bas* (Brussels, 1921), pp. 321–2

M. Devigne: *La Sculpture belge, 1830–1930* (Brussels, 1930)

M. Fransolet: 'Le Sculpteur Paul De Vigne', *Mém. Acad. Royale Belgique: Cl. B.-A.*, xi/4 (1960) [whole issue]

J. van Lennep: 'De Vigne, Paul', *La Sculpture belge au 19ème siècle* (exh. cat., Brussels, Gén. de Banque, 1990), pp. 353–7

RICHARD KERREMANS

Devillers and Perot. French architectural practice established in 1977 in Paris by Marina Devillers (*b* Bucharest, 15 Sept 1947) and her sister Lena Perot (*b* Bucharest, 3 Aug 1945). Devillers received a Master of Architecture degree from the University of Pennsylvania, Philadelphia, in 1972. Perot received a graduate diploma in urban studies at the Institut d'Etudes Politiques de Paris in 1976. They began working together in Paris in 1972 and during the 1970s and 1980s entered several architectural competitions, winning numerous awards. Their principal client was the State, and they specialized in social housing (e.g. in Reims, Cergy-Pontoise and Chambéry) and public buildings. Their renovation and extension (1988) of the town hall at Aubervillers employed a stark, geometrically orientated modernism. A four-storey building, it has an overall surface that is flat and planar, relieved on the first floor by the punctuating element of vertical rectangular windows. Some relief is given, however, by the upper and lower storeys, the windows being deeply recessed within the planar wall. The exterior design of their housing complex (1987) at Pierrefitte, with 143 flats, is more relaxed and inventive. Expanses of wall are not flat but concave, with cylindrical, skylit stairwells placed within this curved space. Their training as urban planners was also brought to bear on their designs for housing complexes; at Pierrefitte, for example, they were concerned to create systems of streets, courts, alleys and buildings that could make a transition between surrounding high-rise buildings of the 1960s and the old town. Devillers and Perot found their relationship as sisters advantageous in many ways, their innate closeness allowing agreement on many design issues. It also helped them solve a problem faced by many women in such a demanding profession as architecture: integrating work with the logistical and emotional demands of child-rearing.

WRITINGS

L. Perot, with M. G. Gangneus and J. Darrai: 'Le Collège Paul Eluard, Nanterre', *Un Bâtiment, un architect* (May, 1984)

BIBLIOGRAPHY

C. Lorenz: *Women in Architecture: A Contemporary Perspective* (New York, 1990), pp. 26–7

WALTER SMITH

Devis. English family of painters. (1) Arthur Devis specialized in painting fashionable 18th-century conversation pieces, while his half-brother (2) Anthony Devis concentrated on topographical painting. Among the former's pupils were his sons (3) Thomas Anthony Devis, his first son to survive infancy, and (4) Arthur William Devis, his 19th child.

(1) Arthur Devis (*b* Preston, Lancs, 12 Feb 1712; *d* Brighton, 25 July 1787). By 1728 he had left Preston, and the following year he was working in London for the Flemish topographical and sporting painter Peter Tillemans. There he specialized in landscape painting and copying various works in Tillemans's studio after Marco Ricci, Giovanni Paolo Panini and Jan van Bloemen. Devis's earliest known commission, *Hoghton Towers from Duxon Hill, Lancashire* (1735; priv. col., see 1983 exh. cat., no. 3), painted for Sir Henry Hoghton during a trip to Preston in 1734–5, shows Tillemans's influence in its attention to detail and the use of thin, transparent paint. *Thomas Lister with his Family* (*c.* 1738; Chicago, IL, A. Inst.) demonstrates a similar interest in landscape, featuring the family group in Gisburn Park, Lancs. Devis had returned to London by 1742 and established himself as a painter of conversation pieces, with a studio in Great Queen Street. *Roger Hesketh with his Family* (*c.* 1742–3; priv. col., see 1983 exh. cat., fig. 11) is typical of his work at this time; it shows how Devis transformed the intimacy of a Dutch 17th-century genre scene into an elegant interior with the group of sitters connected by formal, schematic gestures. Roger Hesketh stands apart, in a tastefully contrived pose, his legs crossed and right arm thrust inside his waistcoat. His son, Fleetwood, stands with his hand resting on a dog next to his wife, who is seated with an infant on her lap. The adjacent telescope, globe and marine paintings are intended to advertise Hesketh's interest in astronomy and travel.

After *c.* 1748 Devis preferred to place his sitters out of doors and he moved away from his earlier dependence on lay figures, although the stiff postures of the children in *Family Group in a Garden* (1749; priv. col.; *see* CONVERSATION PIECE, fig. 2), despite the air of Rococo elegance, suggest that on occasion he still relied on such props. This was clearly the case in *Mr and Mrs Van Harthals and their Son* (1749; Upton House, Warwicks, NT; see fig.), where an intricate series of formal gestures made by the Van Harthals couple over the head of their young son implies their intimacy, while a telescope placed near to Mr Van Harthals and a river indicates his involvement in foreign trade. By *c.* 1755 Devis had moved away from his reliance on pose and accessories and was beginning to invest each of his sitters with individual personality. *John Orde with his Wife Anne and Son William* (*c.* 1754–6; New Haven, CT, Yale Cent. Brit. A.) and *Edward Gordon with Mr and Mrs Milnes* (1756; Leicester, Mus. & A. G.) depict more sophisticated formal relations between his sitters; there is also a greater use of modelling and an increase in the importance of the landscape setting.

Devis exhibited at the Free Society between 1761 and 1775 and in 1780, and he became its president in 1768. By this time, however, his popularity was waning, perhaps because of his unwillingness to join the contemporary reaction against Rococo art; he nevertheless contrived to produce such adept portraits as those of *Francis Vincent with his Wife Mercy and Daughter Ann* and *Nicholas Fazackerly* (both 1763; Preston, Harris Mus. & A.G.). He had several students, including George Senhouse, Robert Marris (1750–1827) and his own sons. Towards the end of his life Devis was forced to supplement his income by repairing paintings for Sir Roger Newdigate (from 1762)

Arthur Devis: *Mr and Mrs Van Harthals and their Son*, oil on canvas, 884×1190 mm, 1749 (Upton House, Warwickshire, NT)

and by cleaning and repairing the Painted Hall at Greenwich Hospital, London, in 1777. He also painted several works on glass, for example *Margaret Ainge* (London V&A). After a studio auction on 10 and 11 April 1783 he retired to Brighton.

See also ENGLAND, fig. 40.

(2) **Anthony (Thomas) Devis** (*b* Preston, Lancs, 18 March 1729; *d* Albury, Surrey, 26 April 1816). Half-brother of (1) Arthur Devis. He was working in London from 1742 as a specialist in topographical paintings, which he produced in both oils and watercolours. He exhibited at the Free Society (1761 and 1763) and at the Royal Academy (1772 and 1781). In 1780 he moved to Surrey, where he was later to paint a view in oils of his home, *Albury House, Surrey* (1792; Preston, Harris Mus. & A. G.). He travelled throughout Britain in search of suitable subjects and commissions, both landscapes and country houses, such as the view of the lake, temple and house painted for the owners of *Upton House, Warwicks* (1803; *in situ*).

(3) **Thomas Anthony Devis** (*b* London, 15 Sept 1757; *d* 28 Sept 1810). Son of (1) Arthur Devis. He entered the Royal Academy Schools in 1773. From 1775 to 1779 he exhibited at the Free Society, in 1777 at the Society of Artists and between 1782 and 1788 at the Royal Academy. His few known works are portraits, for example *Thomas*

Henry Bund and William Bund (sold London, Christie's, 29 March 1935, lot 67, see Waterhouse, *18th-C.*, p. 110); these show that while he maintained the directness of his father's work, he never managed to achieve his sophistication. The lists of his exhibited works include landscapes and copies from Old Masters (untraced).

(4) **Arthur William Devis** (*b* London, 10 Aug 1762; *d* London, 11 Feb 1822). Son of (1) Arthur Devis. He entered the Royal Academy Schools in 1774 and soon attracted the attention of Sir Joshua Reynolds. He exhibited various drawings at the Free Society between 1775 and 1780 and at the Royal Academy in 1781–2. In 1782 he joined an expedition to the East Indies as a draughtsman. When the ship foundered he seized the opportunity to live and work in Canton for a year. In November 1784 he sailed to India, where he painted a portrait of *Warren Hastings* (New Delhi, Rashtrapati Bhavan). Works such as *Colin Shakespear* (*c*. 1785; see Waterhouse, *18th-C.*, p. 109) suggest the influence of Johan Zoffany, who was in India at the same time. The relaxed pose of the youthful Shakespear, depicted against a landscape background, differs dramatically from the stiff sitters of Devis's father, but the attention to detail and treatment of drapery shows parental influence.

In 1792 Devis began a series of 30 paintings for engravings, intended to depict the 'arts, manufactures and agriculture of Bengal' (Oxford, Ashmolean). When the scheme was abandoned in 1804 only a few prints had been published. Around 1793 Devis visited Madras and embarked on a large history painting, *Lord Cornwallis Receiving the Sons of Tipu Sultan as Hostages* (completed 1805; priv. col., see Archer, pl. 187). In 1795 he brought the half-finished canvas back to England, hoping that exhibiting it would lead to further commissions. Devis was declared bankrupt in 1800, however, although John Biddulph of Ledbury purchased the Indian paintings, commissioned portraits of his family and encouraged Devis to paint other history pieces, such as the *Death of Nelson* (exh. 1809; London, N. Mar. Mus.).

BIBLIOGRAPHY

Waterhouse: *18th-C.*
S. H. Pavière: *The Devis Family of Painters* (Leigh on Sea, 1950)
E. Waterhouse: *Painting in Britain, 1530 to 1790*, Pelican Hist. A. (Harmondsworth, 1953, rev. 4/1978), pp. 192–5
M. Archer: *India and British Portraiture, 1770–1825* (London and New York, 1979)
The Conversation Piece: Arthur Devis and his Contemporaries (exh. cat., ed. E. G. D'Oench; New Haven, CT, Yale Cent. Brit. A., 1980)
Polite Society by Arthur Devis (exh. cat., ed. S. Sartin; Preston, Harris Mus. & A. G.; London, N.P.G.; 1983)

HUGH BELSEY

Devlin, Stuart (*b* Geelong, Victoria, 9 Oct 1931; *d* 1986). Australian silversmith, jeweller and designer, active in England. He trained at the Royal Melbourne Institute of Technology, Melbourne, the Royal College of Art, London, and Columbia University, New York, between 1950 and 1962. Based in London from 1965, he specialized in the production of elaborately decorated wares distinguished by the extensive use of textured surfaces, filigree and gilding, frequently incorporating figurative and floral motifs. His range of products, which includes flatware, hollow-ware and jewellery, extends from large sculptural presentation pieces to such luxury novelty items as surprise eggs. He also designed the first Australian decimal coins (1965), commemorative medallions and insignia, as well as interiors and furniture. Devlin was made a freeman of the Goldsmiths' Company by special grant in 1966 and elected a liveryman in 1972. In 1980 he was made a Companion of the Order of St Michael and St George 'for services to the art of design' and in 1982 was granted the Royal Warrant of Appointment as Goldsmith and Jeweller to Queen Elizabeth II.

BIBLIOGRAPHY

25 Years of Stuart Devlin in London by the Worshipful Company of Goldsmiths (exh. cat., London, The Worshipful Company of Goldsmiths, 1983)
C. Blair, ed.: *The History of Silver* (London, 1987), pp. 205–6, 219, 221
20th Century Silver (exh. cat. by H. Clifford and others; London, Crafts Council Gal., 1993), p. 46

JUDITH O'CALLAGHAN

Devonshire, Dukes of. *See* CAVENDISH.

De Voorst. Dutch country house near Zutphen, in the province of Gelderland. It was built in 1695–7 by Arnold Joost van Keppel (1669–1718; Earl of Albemarle, 1697), an intimate of the Stadholder William, Prince of Orange, who financed the construction of the building. As in the original design (1684) for Het Loo, two quadrant Ionic colonnades link the square main building with its curved pavilion roof to two smaller pavilions, which flank the courtyard. The reception rooms and van Keppel's apartments were on the ground-floor, and the entire first floor was reserved as an apartment for William. The design, in brick, was probably the result of a collaboration between the architect Jacob Roman and the decorative designer Daniel Marot I. William Talman has also been suggested as the possible architect because of the English-style chimneys on the roof of the wooden model (destr. 1943). The building was gutted by fire in 1943, but it has been restored, except for the luxurious interior, executed according to the designs of Marot. The gardens are known from contemporary prints, also by Marot. *Parterres de broderie* extended along a square plan; two basins were located along the central axis. The statuary may have been the work of Rombout Verhulst. A bank planted with trees surrounded the property. Among other elements, the semicircular boundary of the main path suggests the influence of Marot and a similarity with the garden at Het Loo.

BIBLIOGRAPHY

C. A. Baart de la Faille: 'De geschiedenis de restauratie van het Huis de Voorst', *Bull. Kon. Ned. Oudhdknd. Bond* (1963), pp. 167–92
H. W. M. van der Wyck: 'De Voorst', *Bull. Kon. Ned. Oudhdknd. Bond* (1963), pp. 149–66
J. Harenberg: *De Voorst* (Alphen aan den Rijn, 1981)
The Anglo-Dutch Garden in the Age of William and Mary (exh. cat., ed. J. D. Hunt and E. de Jong; Apeldoorn, Pal. Het Loo; London, Christie's; 1988), pp. 192–3 [special issue of *J. Gdn Hist.*, vii/2–3, 1988]
H. W. M. der Wyck: *De nederlandse buidenplaats: Aspecten von ontwikkeling, bescherming en horstel* (Alphen aan den Rijn)

K. A. OTTENHEYM

Devosges [Devosge], **(Claude-)François, III** (*b* Gray, Haute-Saône, 25 Jan 1732; *d* Dijon, 22 Dec 1811). French painter, draughtsman and teacher. He was descended from a dynasty of sculptors. At the age of 14 he was painting for the Carmelite convent and the church at Gray; he then moved to Paris, where for some years he studied sculpture with Guillaume Coustou (ii). Having lost the sight of one eye in a cataract operation, Devosges was obliged to give up sculpture, but he continued with his painting, living at the home of Jean-Baptiste-Henri Deshays, Boucher's son-in-law. During this period Devosges refused an invitation to go to Russia to teach drawing to the future Tsar Paul I. In 1760 he moved to Burgundy, where he painted and also illustrated the writings on law by Claude-Philibert Fyot de La Marche, by then many years premier président of the Parlement of Bourgogne.

Around 1764 Devosges became tutor to a society of artists who used to hire a life model. He founded in Dijon in 1765 a free school of drawing that was open to everyone, and with assistance he obtained a subsidy for it from the States of Burgundy, which in 1775 established a Rome scholarship, awarded every four years. During the French Revolution, Devosges managed to keep the school running; he tried to keep safe the region's works of art and from 1792 kept an inventory of those that had been seized. He was particularly noted for his qualities as a teacher: among his pupils were Pierre-Paul Prud'hon and François Rude, both of whom benefited from his teaching and his example.

The few paintings by Devosges that have survived include the *Assumption of the Virgin* (Dijon, Mus. Magnin) and a portrait (Langres, Mus. Du Breuil St-Germain) of the sculptor *Edmé Gaulle* (1762–1841). Devosges is, however, best known as an artist from his drawings, many of which have been preserved, the majority at the Musée Magnin, Dijon, to which they were bequeathed by Anatole Devosges (1770–1850), his son and successor as director of the school. François Devosges favoured the serious-minded, classicizing trends in subject-matter, composition and facture that were apparent in France towards the middle of the 18th century. Some of his biblical scenes take their inspiration from Raphael, Poussin and Eustache Le Sueur. His mythological and pastoral scenes, on the other hand, are in a modified version of Boucher's idiom, although with an atmosphere of sensibility rather than of voluptuous pleasure. Some of his figures, such as *Zephyrus and Flora*, possess the frozen grace of the art of Pompeii. Devosges's improvised works display the 'passion, the sensual ardour' (Quarré; see 1961 exh. cat.) of his contemporary Jean-Honoré Fragonard.

BIBLIOGRAPHY
Thieme–Becker
L. Fremiet-Monnier: *Eloge de M. Devosges, fondateur et professeur de l'Ecole de dessin, peinture et sculpture de Dijon* (Dijon, 1813)
A. Bougot: 'François Devosges', *Rev. Bourguignonne Ens. Sup.*, ii (1892), pp. 297–378
M. Imperiali: 'François Devosges: Créateur de l'Ecole de dessin et du Musée de Dijon', *La Révolution en Côte-d'Or*, 3 (Dijon, 1927) [whole issue]
P. Quarré: 'Remarques sur les dessins de François Devosge', *An. Bourgogne*, xiii (1941), pp. 114–24
Une Ecole provinciale de dessin au XVIIIe siècle: L'Académie de peinture et sculpture de Dijon (exh. cat., Dijon, Mus. B.-A., 1961) [introduction by P. Quarré]
S. Laveissière: *Dictionnaire des artistes et ouvriers d'art de Bourgogne* (1980), i of *Dictionnaire des artistes et ouvriers d'art de la France par provinces* (Paris, 1980–), pp. 168–74

CELIA ALEGRET

Devotional objects and popular images. Objects and images used for protection, intercession and as votive offerings. They were believed to guard against evil, the hostility of enemies, bad health, the plague, the temptation to sin and the wrath of God, and were often given to a church, cult image or shrine as a thank-offering for preservation from such adversities. Much of this type of imagery is of low artistic quality, but its value is to be found in the understanding of its function and its iconography. This article is concerned with the Western Christian tradition; for other traditions see under the relevant geographical and cultural headings.

Some types of popular imagery were clearly inspired by superstition and magic, for example the erotic symbols that often occur in ecclesiastical art, above all in Romanesque sculpture. Popular themes such as phallic motifs, the display of the anus or genitals, particularly the female genitals, were undoubtedly rooted in some primitive tradition of the apotropaic power of such images. Other symbols in the sculpture of corbels, bosses, capitals, bench-ends and choir-stalls, some of which persist in Gothic art, may not be erotic but may have an origin in folklore and pagan beliefs. Cult statues and icons of the Virgin and the saints are also essentially 'popular' images and may in some cases have perpetuated pagan and folklore imagery. Images of the 'Black Virgin', often considered indicative of some primitive devotion, can probably be explained in terms of

the respect for an old image that could not be touched. Cleaning or restoration of the faces of such images was not allowed because many of them were supposed to have originated miraculously.

Amulets, rings and talismans were common throughout the Middle Ages and the Renaissance and often had pagan and erotic imagery. Amulets and talismans were usually either worn on the person or placed in the house, often over a door, as a symbol of protection. Rings could serve similar functions, although some, such as the bishop's ring or the marriage ring, have other symbolism. From earlier pagan traditions, some dating back to the times of ancient Egypt and Mesopotamia, certain engraved stones and gems fulfilled a protective function and were often worn in finger-rings, which were in their turn also inscribed; brooches could also have such inscriptions. Amulets, talismans and rings were often made of precious stones or material such as coral, which were thought to have symbolic properties of value to the wearer. Horns, teeth and hair of certain animals were believed to have protective powers; for example, pieces of what was supposed to be a unicorn's horn (in fact usually that of a narwhal) were set in mounts of precious metal as amulets. Such objects continued to be used after the decline of paganism, often retaining pagan forms and motifs although these were gradually replaced by specifically Christian ones, for example the IHS monogram of Christ, the M for Mary and the Tau, the sign made at the Passover on the houses of the Israelites to preserve them from the plague of the destruction of the first-born in Egypt. The foremost symbolic form adopted by Christians is the cross, which from the earliest years was worn on a chain around the neck or carried on the person.

Another type of devotional image was associated with pilgrimages. A pilgrim visiting a shrine could purchase souvenirs of the visit in the form of ampoules or pilgrim badges of lead or of silver and painted or woodcut images on single sheets of the saint or relic (*see* PILGRIM BADGE and DEVOTIONAL PRINTS). The badges were worn on the cap or clothes, and the sheets were pinned up in houses or pasted into prayerbooks and Books of Hours, both forms serving a dual protective and devotional function. The smaller lead badges were sometimes also sewn into Books of Hours. In 15th-century Netherlandish Books of Hours, pilgrim badges were often painted in the borders, possibly in some cases designating the shrines visited by the patron.

Popular images were also produced expressly for the purpose of intercession, protection and instruction. In particular the Virgin, Christ and the saints were depicted, for they were considered to be advocates before God and agents of protection against evil. The Old Testament provided the Church with many images of the wrath of God directed against sinful people: God brandishing arrows signified punishment by famine, plague and war, for example, and was sometimes so represented in the late Middle Ages. Some of these paintings show the Virgin as the Madonna of Mercy, sheltering people under her cloak and protecting them from the arrows. This image was a favourite subject for banners of guilds and confraternities dedicated to the Virgin and for images, particularly in woodcuts, invoking protection against plague. In some cases, as in the 15th-century wall paintings at S Procolo, Naturns, the *Madonna of Mercy* is accompanied by the *Man of Sorrows*, who also shelters people under his cloak. These wall paintings also show the protective figures of the Virgin and Christ as intercessors, she showing her breast and he pointing to the wound in his side. A fine example of the arrows of God bringing plague, famine and war, together with the intercession of the Virgin, in this case accompanied by St John the Baptist, is in the wall painting of 1485 by Thomas Artula von Villach at Graz Cathedral.

The Wounds and Heart of Christ, particularly the side wound, came to be represented in isolation as emblems in the 14th and 15th centuries. In popular devotion these images seem to have been considered to have a protective function and occur on amulets and rings as well as in Books of Hours and single sheet woodcuts. The ANDACHTSBILD of the Man of Sorrows was used in another context of popular imagery, that of moralizing images. The idea of man wounding Christ through his sins was shown in powerfully physical images. The breaking of the obligation to attend mass on Sundays and feast days by continuing work was shown by the standing Man of Sorrows surrounded and wounded by the implements of trade and farm work. This image, the Feast Day Christ (*Feiertagschristus*), occurs mainly in small rural churches surviving mostly in England and Switzerland, but is also occasionally seen in grander buildings, such as in the south nave aisle of S Miniato al Monte in Florence in an early 15th-century fresco of the Florentine school. Another moralizing image that seems unique to England shows the Pietà with the dismembered limbs of Christ held by men who are designated as sinners and blasphemers, as at Broughton Church (Bucks). The intercession of the Virgin at the Last Judgement is represented in a variety of ways in popular imagery: for example, she shows her breast to Christ in the Last Judgement as a reminder of how she suckled him as a child, or she places her prayer beads on the scales as St Michael weighs the souls. The image of the weighing of the souls to assess the relative balance of an individual's sins and merits incorporates various popular themes in which devils attempt to interfere with the weighing.

Popular imagery related to the Last Judgement includes the representation of the means by which hell, purgatory and heaven could be reached. Images of bridges, ladders, hell mouths, demons carrying souls in carts, and the birds, insects and animals that inhabit such places often incorporate folklore and pagan traditions. The release of the souls from purgatory after their purification, a rare subject in art, may also incorporate popular religious beliefs. The Virgin and the angels in a fresco (Paganico, S Michele) by Bartolo di Fredi lift up the miniature naked souls in their arms from the edge of purgatory. The release of souls from purgatory combined with the intercession of Christ and the Virgin is depicted in the late 15th-century Bavarian painted Altar of the Souls in the Historischen Verein für Oberpfalz und Regensburg in Regensburg. A related theme involves the depiction of devils, reflecting the primitive belief in the struggle between the powers of good and evil. In one moralizing variant, often found in sculpture and stained glass, the devil is shown recording

Tutivillus and the Gossips, nave arcade corbel, 1325–40, St Denys, Sleaford, Lincolnshire

sinful conversation. This could serve as a warning against gossip, as in the image of the devil Tutivillus sitting on women's shoulders and writing down their words (see fig.).

The EX-VOTO offered for release from adversity could be just a wax, wood or metal image of, for example, a leg that had been healed as a result of the intercession of the saint. This was its most popular form for much of the Middle Ages, but from the 14th century it was also customary to give small sculpted or painted images of the saint as a thank-offering. Since the second half of the 15th century there has been a tradition of small painted images that illustrate the healed limb or portray the disaster or illness with the saint intervening. Such ex-votos are usually of very poor artistic quality, but collective expressions of gratitude often took the form of major works of art in public places, for example paintings of doges of Venice and their military leaders shown kneeling in thanks before the Virgin, Christ and saints (e.g. Venice, Doge's Palace).

BIBLIOGRAPHY

EWA: 'Devotional Objects and Images, Popular'; *LCI*: 'Intermessio, Mariae und Christi vor Gottvater', 'Pest, Pestbilder', 'Schutzmantelschaft', 'Votive, Votivbilder'; *RDK*: 'Armeseelen', 'Feiertagschristus'

E. Kitzinger: 'The Cult of Images in the Age before Iconoclasm', *Dumbarton Oaks Pap.*, viii (1954), pp. 83–150

R. Wildhaber: 'Der "Feiertagschristus" als ikonographisches Ausdruck der Sonntagsheiligung', *Z. Schweiz. Archäol. Kstgesch.*, xvi (1956), pp. 1–34

L. Kretzenbacher: *Die Seelenwaage* (Klagenfurt, 1958)

P. Halm: 'Der schreibende Teufel', *Cristianesimo e ragion di stato: L'umanesimo e il demoniaco nell'arte. Atti del III congresso internazionale di studi umanistici: Milan, 1962*, pp. 235–49

K. Köster: 'Religiöse Medaillen und Wallfahrts-Devotionalien in der flämischen Buchmalerei des 15 und frühen 16 Jahrhunderts', *Festschrift Gustav Hofmann* (Wiesbaden, 1965), pp. 459–504

F. Wormald: 'Some Popular Miniatures and their Rich Relations', *Miscellanea pro Arte; Hermann Schnitzler zur Vollendung des 60 Lebensjahres* (Düsseldorf, 1965), pp. 279–85

L. Hansmann and L. Kriss-Rettenbeck: *Amulett und Talisman* (Munich, 1966)

A. Grabar: *Les Ampoules de la Terre Sainte* (Paris, 1968)

L. Kriss-Rettenbeck: *Bilder und Zeichen religiösen Volksglaubens* (Munich, 1971)

I. H. Forsyth: *The Throne of Wisdom: Wood Sculptures of the Madonna in Romanesque France* (Princeton, 1972)

L. Kriss-Rettenbeck: *Ex Voto: Zeichen, Bild und Abbild im christlichen Votivbrauchtum* (Zurich, 1972)

C. Oman: *British Rings, 800–1914* (London, 1974)

C. Belting-Ihm: '*Sub matris tutela*': *Untersuchungen zur Vorgeschichte der Schutzmantelmadonna* (Heidelberg, 1976)

B. Plongeron: *La Religion populaire dans l'occident chrétien* (Paris, 1976)

J. Andersen: *The Witch on the Wall: Medieval Erotic Sculpture in the British Isles* (Copenhagen, 1977)

G. Taylor and D. Scarisbrick: *Finger Rings from Ancient Egypt to the Present Day* (Oxford, 1978)

G. Vikan: *Byzantine Pilgrimage Art* (Washington, 1982)

P. A. Sigal: 'L'Ex-voto au moyen âge dans les régions du nord-ouest de la Mediterrannée', *Provence Hist.*, xxxiii (1983), pp. 13–31

C. Gaignebet and J. D. Lajoux: *Art profane et religion populaire au moyen âge* (Paris, 1985)

P. Dinzelbacher: 'Die tötende Gottheit. Pestbild und Todesikonographie als Ausdruck der Mentalität des Spätmittelalters und der Renaissance', *Anlct. Cartus.*, cxvii/2 (1986), pp. 5–137

——:'The Way to the Other World in Medieval Literature and Art', *Folk-Lore*, xcvii (1986), pp. 70–87

J. B. Friedman: ' "He Hath a Thousand Slayn this Pestilence": The Iconography of the Plague in the Late Middle Ages', *Social Unrest in the Late Middle Ages*, ed. F. X. Newman (Binghamton, 1986), pp. 75–112

M. Lauwers: '"Religion populaire", culture folklorique, mentalités: Notes pour une anthropologie culturelle du moyen âge', *Rev. Hist. Ecclés.*, lxxxii (1987), pp. 221–58

L. Kötzsche: 'Zwei Jerusalemer Pilgerampullen aus der Kreuzfahrerzeit', *Z. Kstgesch.*, li (1988), pp. 13–32

NIGEL J. MORGAN

Devotional prints. Works in various graphic media used principally for the veneration of religious figures or events.

1. EARLY 15TH CENTURY. The use of prints for devotional purposes dates as far back as the history of printmaking in the West. The oldest extant woodcuts (early 15th century; *see* WOODCUT, §II, 2) commonly portray popular saints as well as Christ and the Virgin. Sold and possibly also manufactured by monks at pilgrimage shrines, these simple depictions of venerated holy figures provided relatively inexpensive, portable devotional objects for the faithful. Not treasured for their intrinsic artistic value, the few known works have survived by accident, having been pasted into manuscript or book covers or on to box lids. Many lost woodcuts decorated home shrines or modest chapels; others were pasted over fireplaces or on to walls and doors. Prints depicting guardian saints also functioned as amulets to ward off disease and death; many were sewn into articles of clothing.

The appearance of these mass-produced devotional images *c.* 1400 testifies to the major shift in religious practice that had taken place during the Gothic period: personal, private, often meditative devotions came to occupy an important place alongside communal, public worship. The new woodcut process allowed those of lesser means to possess their own visual aids to devotion. The subjects and compositions of the early devotional prints are characteristically simple and direct; they usually consist of large figures with minimal attributes and indications of setting used for identification. Although most of the surviving prints from 1400–50 come from Germany

(particularly the Upper Rhine and Bavaria), equally vital centres of production may already have existed in other areas of Germany, as well as France, the Netherlands and Italy.

During the 15th century various factors contributed to an expanding range and use of devotional prints. Although rates of production are difficult to establish, devotional prints now survive from this larger geographic area, and artists both elaborated on earlier subject-matter and increased the complexity of their compositions. An additional step in this direction was taken with the development of new graphic techniques—engraving, drypoint and etching—which inspired the creation of more detailed prints. Monastic pilgrimage shrines continued as important centres for the sale of devotional prints, but production and distribution increasingly also spread to individual municipalities.

The broadening variety of subjects appearing in devotional prints include episodes from Christ's infancy and Passion, the Life of the Virgin and the Lives of saints. Common themes include the Crucifixion, the Virgin and Child and SS Sebastian, Christopher, Dorothy, Barbara, Francis and Gregory. From the 1440s prints were also issued in series; especially popular were series of Christ's Passion. Other prints depict iconic, allegorical or symbolic

1. Devotional print of the *Virgin of the Rosary*, hand-coloured woodcut, from Germany, 1485 (Washington, DC, National Gallery of Art)

2. Devotional print by Albrecht Dürer: *Crucifixion*, engraving, 134×980 mm, 1508 (Coburg, Kupferstichkabinett der Kunstammlungen der Veste)

subjects, such as the Path to Salvation, the Sacred Heart, the Salvator Mundi and the Man of Sorrows.

Devotional prints could aid private worship in many ways. Some contained texts of prayers for divine assistance; others served to stimulate affective meditations, making concretely apprehensible familiar stories of sacred lives; others fulfilled a more didactic function, explaining doctrine or illustrating events for sequential veneration. One example of the latter is a German woodcut depicting the *Virgin of the Rosary* (1485; Washington, DC, N.G.A.; see fig. 1), inspired by the recently founded Confraternity of the Rosary; it portrays the Virgin and Child amid ten medallions illustrating the Joyful and Sorrowful Mysteries; an unusually lengthy text provides instructions on the use of the rosary by reciting prayers in honour of each of the portrayed events.

2. LATE 15TH CENTURY AND AFTER. The identification of devotional prints becomes less clear during the late 15th century and the 16th, when major artists turned to print media and included a range of religious subjects in their oeuvres. Artists such as Martin Schongauer, Albrecht Dürer, Lucas Cranach (i), Lucas van Leyden and Andrea Mantegna expanded the pictorial possibilities of graphic media and produced work of high aesthetic value. While these religious prints tend to be restricted in subject-matter

to familiar themes, the frequently large, elaborate formats, fine workmanship and more complex iconographic programmes have led scholars to conclude that many of these works were created as collector's items rather than devotional objects. Nevertheless, works of this period display some of the most innovative and sensitive treatments of devotional subjects. Dürer's engraved *Crucifixion* (1508; Coburg, Veste Coburg; see fig. 2) focuses on the anguished grief of the attendant mourners, enhancing the dramatic impact of the event. Indeed, the asymmetrical placement of the crucified Christ deliberately engages the viewer by suggesting an accidental encounter with the scene and inclusion among the group of mourners. Graphic media proved ideal for the creation of such intimate treatment.

Despite the difficulties in determining the balance between the devotional and aesthetic functions of these more accomplished works, they mark the high point in the production of devotional prints. Although artists such as the KLAUBER family continued to create devotional prints until the 20th century, they rarely achieved the high graphic quality of the late 15th- and 16th-century masters. By the 18th century production had moved to commercial centres, followed by the expansion of media to include more recent techniques, such as steel engraving and lithography. On the whole, these prints were designed by lesser artists, resulting in conservative, repetitive compositions. Works connected with and sold at pilgrimage shrines occupy a pre-eminent place in this later history, thus continuing the tradition dating back to the earliest devotional prints.

BIBLIOGRAPHY

W. L. Schreiber: *Handbuch der Holz- und Metalschnitte des XV. Jahrhunderts*, 8 vols (Leipzig, 1926–30/*R* Stuttgart, 1969–76, 8 vols and suppl. atlas)

A. Spamer: *Das kleine Andachtsbild vom XIV. bis zum XX. Jahrhundert* (Munich, 1930)

A. M. Hind: *An Introduction to a History of Woodcut: With a Detailed Survey of Work Done in the Fifteenth Century*, 2 vols (London, 1935/*R* New York, 1963)

R. S. Field: *Fifteenth-century Woodcuts and Metalcuts: From the National Gallery of Art, Washington, D.C.* (Washington, DC, 1965)

A. H. Mayor: *Prints and People: A Social History of Printed Pictures* (New York, 1971)

CAROL M. SCHULER

Dewasne, Jean (*b* Lille, 21 May 1921). French painter, writer and sculptor. He began painting at the age of 12 and was producing pointillist works at the age of 18. He studied architecture for two years at the Ecole des Beaux-Arts in Paris as a preparation for his painting. In about 1943 he began painting abstract works, and he remained an abstract painter for the rest of his career. He was associated with the group of abstract artists who exhibited at the Galerie Denise René in Paris, including Hans Hartung, Nicolas de Stäel and Serge Poliakoff, and he himself exhibited there from 1945 to 1956. Together with Sonia Delaunay, Hans Arp, Antoine Pevsner and others he was a co-founder of the Salon des Réalités Nouvelles in Paris in 1945. In the following year he was awarded the first Kandinsky prize.

Dewasne's painting *The Great She-bear* (1958; Paris, Pompidou), with its violently contrasting colours, is characteristic of his mature abstract style. In response to the criticism that his style consisted of technique alone, he founded the Atelier d'Art Abstrait in 1950 with the French painter Edgar Pillet (*b* 1912); it was designed to teach an abstract aesthetic. The first of Dewasne's 'antisculptures' appeared in 1951. These were made from free-standing car parts on to which Dewasne painted abstract designs, as in *The Tomb of Anton Webern* (1952; Paris, Pompidou). Having painted murals from 1948, in 1968 he was commissioned to produce a vast mural for the Stade de Glace in Grenoble for the Winter Olympics. The following year he painted a vast 90 m mural, entitled *The Long March*, for the University of Lille.

BIBLIOGRAPHY
P. Descargues: *Jean Dewasne* (Paris, 1952)
Dewasne (exh. cat. by D. Cordier, New York, Lefebre Gal., 1972)

Dewey, John (*b* Burlington, VT, 20 Oct 1859; *d* New York, 1 June 1952). American philosopher and writer. He wrote major works on metaphysics, ethics, logic, social philosophy and particularly the philosophy and theory of education. He was one of the group of American philosophers, including Charles Sanders Peirce, William James and George Herbert Mead, who developed the philosophical view known as American Pragmatism. Dewey's major work in aesthetics, *Art as Experience* (1934), summarizes important features of his general philosophy as well as being one of the most influential works of 20th-century Anglo-American aesthetics.

The central notion in Dewey's thought is that of 'experience'. For Dewey experiencing the world is an interaction between the whole organism and the environment, rather than a relation between a subject and a distinct object. Much of human experience is incoherent and meaningless, but sometimes we have an 'experience' that stands out from the surrounding flux. Every experience allows us to achieve self-knowledge and to guard against alienation, and it has a distinctively aesthetic quality. An experience is an individualized, self-sufficient whole, pervaded by a single emotional quality and characterized by a certain rhythm of tension and relaxation (difficulty and solution of difficulty). It is also a unity in which the completion of the experience has a meaning or significance that sums up and in a sense contains all the previous phases of the experience. This description can apply to hoeing the garden, testing a scientific theory, or merely having a conversation. For Dewey a meaningful life should include many such experiences. However, an experience that is predominantly aesthetic—rather than intellectual or practical—is one in which the peculiar features of the experience as he defined them are clarified and intensified: an aesthetic experience is one in which we are predominantly aware of the experience's tension and relaxation, its unity, its pervasive quality and the cumulative nature of its meaning. The best examples of aesthetic experience are our experiences of (interactions with) objects of fine art.

A work of art for Dewey is not an art object *per se* but our experience of it, whether as producer or audience, just as the meaning of a work of art is not some intrinsic property of the art object but the quality of the experience it causes in its audience. Creating an art object is an act of expression, which exemplifies in the highest degree what it is to have an experience. Expression is not mere emotional discharge—which would involve getting rid of the emotion—but the meaningful embodiment of an emotion in a resisting medium such as paint, wood, sound etc. In expression there is development carried to completion, the interaction of past experience with present, a series of phases of resistance and overcoming of resistance, and an end result that embodies the cumulative meaning of these phases. In contemplating a work of art, the audience is said to re-create the experience of the artist. This is a problem for Dewey's view, since communication of this sort between artist and audience is impossible to guarantee.

One of Dewey's chief aims as a philosopher was to break down what he saw as unhelpful dualisms: for example art versus life, fine arts versus useful arts, science versus art, art object versus spectator or artist, the mental expression of a feeling versus the physical expressive object, form versus content. Life and art differ primarily in their degree of expressive unity. The fine arts differ from the useful arts, and art as a whole differs from science, primarily in their media. The work of art is an experienced interaction between art objects and persons. The expression of something mental is brought about through the artist working upon a physical medium, and there is no coherent way of distinguishing the content of the resultant work from its form. Throughout his work Dewey stressed the importance of meaningful integration in all aspects of life; in works of art we see this possibility realized at its clearest.

WRITINGS
Experience and Nature (Chicago, 1925)
with others: *Art and Education* (Merion, PA, 1929)
Art as Experience (New York, 1934)

BIBLIOGRAPHY
S. Hook: *John Dewey: An Intellectual Portrait* (New York, 1939)
P. Zeltner: *John Dewey's Aesthetic Philosophy* (Amsterdam, 1975)
T. Alexander: *John Dewey's Theory of Art, Experience and Nature: The Horizons of Feeling* (Albany, NY, 1987)
J. E. Tiles: *Dewey* (London, 1988)

JENEFER ROBINSON

Dewez, Laurent Benoît (*bapt* Petit Rechain, 14 April 1731; *d* Groot-Bijgaarden, 1 Nov 1812). Flemish architect. He probably received his early training in Liège, where he obtained a bursary from the Fondation Lambert Darchis in 1754 to continue his studies in Rome. In 1755 he began working in Rome as a draughtsman for Robert Adam (i), alongside Agostino Brunias and Charles-Louis Clérisseau, Adam's drawing teacher. Between 1755 and 1757 Dewez also worked on the proposed revision (unpublished) of *Les Edifices antiques de Rome* (Paris, 1682) by Antoine Desgodets, surveyed Hadrian's Villa at Tivoli and studied the buildings of Onorio Longhi, Jacopo Vignola, Francesco Borromini, Carlo Rainaldi and Pirro Ligorio.

In 1757 Dewez, Brunias and Adam left Rome together, and after an intensive archaeological survey of Diocletian's Palace at Spalato (now Split) and a brief stay in Vicenza, they all settled in London in 1758. There the brothers Robert and James Adam opened an architectural office, in which Dewez briefly worked. At the end of 1758 Dewez moved to Brussels, probably to undertake a commission to plan a new Cistercian abbey at Orval, a building that evoked considerable approval in monastic circles. He was, in effect, introducing a style influenced by the Palladianism he had seen in England, which was to herald the end of the Baroque in Belgium and prepare the way for Neo-classicism. English Palladianism is also reflected in Dewez's next religious commission, Gembloux Abbey (1761), which features a tetrastyle portico articulating the centre of a restrained and well-proportioned two-storey façade with regular fenestration. Many similar commissions followed, a later example being the abbey church of Bonne Espérance (1770) at Hainault, where unfluted Corinthian columns are used to carry a straight entablature.

The government's close supervision of the monasteries and other religious institutions contributed to Dewez's reputation in Brussels and helped to secure him the commission from Maria-Theresa, Empress of Austria, to design the church of St Begga (1763) at Andenne. His appointment as Director of Royal Works in 1766, immediately after the death of Jean Faulte, was predictable. The following year he was appointed architect to Charles Alexander of Lorraine, Governor-General of the southern Netherlands, in which capacity he undertook works at Mariemont Castle (substantially destr.) and the construction of 'Château Charles' (destr.) at Tervuren. His contact with government circles in Brussels led to a variety of other commissions (1766–80). He worked on the building for the Privy Council and Council of Finance (1770) and renovated the gable top of the house of the Counts of Brabant (1768) on the Grand'Place, Brussels. At Leuven University he designed the large auditorium of the arts faculty (1766), extended the library and rebuilt the glass-house (both 1769) in the botanical gardens. He built a hospital (1768) at Bouillon, the Town Hall (1771) at Binche and a lighthouse (1772) at Ostend in the shape of a Tuscan column.

Dewez also obtained a series of important private commissions, starting in 1763–8 with a château for Julien G. Depestre on his estate in Seneffe. The *corps de logis* had a slightly projecting centre and end pavilions, articulated by Corinthian pilasters. The forecourt is flanked on each side by Ionic colonnades, curving in to the house at the ends. He subsequently built country houses at Wasseiges (1767), Brugelette and Vilvoorde (both 1776) and worked on a number of town houses in Brussels, the interiors of which were decorated in the Neo-classical style. This exceptional success seems to have been his undoing, however, and criticisms were raised from 1774 about the technical quality of his buildings: Claude-Antoine Fisco criticized his reconstruction of the church of St Pierre (1774) in the Uccle district of Brussels; the intervention of the architect Barnabé Guimard prevented Dewez from being involved with the major replanning of the Upper Town and the administrative centre of Brussels; and the influential Jesuit François Xavier de Feller dubbed his architecture 'bizarre'. Difficulties with the construction of the prison at Vilvoorde caused the States of Brabant to set up a legal inquiry in 1777, and budget excesses and lack of supervision of the construction of a hermitage at 'Château Charles' led to his dismissal from the project in 1780. Dewez returned to his property at Elewijt and tried to redeem his fortune by selling off land. At his own expense in 1779 he built a large hall in Brussels, later called the Concert Noble, for concerts and balls, which he let to the Société de l'Académie de Musique. He also built a few

town houses (1783) near the Parc de Bruxelles for Affligem Abbey and other private clients.

When the Austrian Netherlands were invaded by French troops in 1795 Dewez moved to Prague, where he built a large town house (1795) for Graf Adalbert von Czernin. He returned to the Netherlands some years later. The detailed inscription on his gravestone in the south wall of St Egide, Brussels, is noteworthy in many respects, including its statements that he became Court Architect to King Joseph of Portugal (*reg* 1750–77) and that he studied under Luigi Vanvitelli in Rome and Naples, while saying nothing about his time spent with Robert Adam in Rome and London. Dewez's architectural oeuvre certainly possesses all the characteristics of 'ideal' architecture, which also defines Vanvitelli's greatest works. Dewez's vocabulary, however, was strongly influenced by French interior decoration and English Palladian designs.

BIBLIOGRAPHY

G. De Dijn: 'L'influenza di Luigi Vanvitelli sull'architetto belga L. B. Dewez, 1731–1812: Prime considerazioni', *Atti di celebrazioni vanvitellane MCMLXXIII. Luigi Vanvitelli e il '700 europeo. Congresso internazionale di studi: Naples, 1973*, i, pp. 117–34

X. Duquenne: 'L'Abbaye d'Orval construite au XVIIIe siècle', *Aureavallis-Mélanges historiques réunis à l'occasion du neuvième centenaire de l'abbaye d'Orval* (Liège, 1975), pp. 247–70

——: *Le Château de Seneffe* (Brussels, 1978)

CLEMENS GUIDO DE DIJN

DeWilde, John. *See under* COXE-DEWILDE POTTERY.

De Wilde, Samuel (*bapt* London, 28 July 1751; *d* London, 19 Jan 1832). English painter and etcher of Dutch descent. He was the son of a Dutch joiner who had settled in London by 1748. On 19 November 1765 he was apprenticed for seven years to his godfather, Samuel Haworth, a joiner in London. However, he left after five years and enrolled as a student at the Royal Academy Schools in 1769. He exhibited small portraits at the Society of Artists (1776–8) and at the Royal Academy (from 1778), where he also showed fancy pictures of banditti in the style of Philippe Jacques de Loutherbourg. But the genre that he made very much his own was theatrical portraiture: he exhibited theatrical portraits at the Royal Academy almost every year from 1792 to 1821.

De Wilde's first connection with this genre was his work for John Bell's second collection of miscellaneous plays, published serially as *The British Theatre* (1791–7). As in the first collection (1776–81)—which had been illustrated principally by James Roberts—each play had an engraved frontispiece showing an actor or actress in a role from that play. The engravings, executed by various hands, were based on small, full-length oil paintings depicting a costumed actor standing in a vaguely theatrical setting. This format was inspired by Zoffany's single-figure theatrical portraits of the 1760s. De Wilde's oil portrait of *Thomas Blanchard as Ralph in 'The Maid of the Mill'* (engraving published 1791; London, Garrick Club) reveals his special skill with comic figures, and the precise moment of the action is identifiable through clues of gesture, setting and prop. De Wilde contributed 36 character plates to Bell's *The British Theatre* in 1791 and 33 in 1792, eventually providing 93 portraits. He continued with the project when George Cawthorne took it over in 1795, and he was still working for Cawthorne on other publications as late as 1815.

De Wilde's early theatrical work is technically disappointing, with its curious anatomy, expressionless faces and thin and tenuous use of paint, but by the early 1790s he had gained confidence and ability. Theatrical scenes such as *Maria Bland, Ursula Booth and John Bannister in 'The Children in the Wood'* (1794; London, Royal N. Theat.) compare favourably with those of Zoffany. In these works his figures became more elegant and expressive and his application of paint thicker and creamier, with a startling use of colour that may reflect the bright garments worn on the stage.

De Wilde continued to produce portraits for theatrical publications such as the *Monthly Mirror* (1795–1811) and William Oxberry's *New English Drama* (1818–21). From his studio in Tavistock Row, Covent Garden, he ran a production line of small full-length watercolour portraits of actors coming to pose in costume from the nearby Drury Lane and Covent Garden theatres. His diary for 1810–11 and a letter dated 28 June 1815 (both London, Garrick Club) indicate that he charged £6 for a small full-length in oil and £3 for a watercolour. His popular watercolours invariably show the figure in front of a plain background and include *Sarah Harlowe as Beatrice in 'The Anatomist'* (1805; Brit. Royal Col.). He also painted replicas and produced soft-ground etchings of some of his portraits. De Wilde's theatrical portrait formula was adopted by Thomas Charles Wageman (1787–1863) and George Clint, who developed a tighter and more linear style during the 1820s.

BIBLIOGRAPHY

The De Wildes (exh. cat. by I. Mayes, Northampton, Cent. Mus. & A.G., 1971)

I. Mayes: 'John Bell, *The British Theatre* and Samuel De Wilde', *Apollo*, cxiii (1981), pp. 100–03

GEOFFREY ASHTON

Dewing, Thomas Wilmer (*b* Boston, 4 May 1851; *d* New York, 1938). American painter. Apprenticed at an early age in a lithography shop, he went to Paris in 1876 to study under Jules Lefèbvre and Gustave Boulanger at the Académie Julian. There he learnt an academic technique; the careful delineation of volumetric form and meticulous but subtle evocation of texture were to be constant features of his work. Paintings done after his return to the USA in 1878, such as *Morning* (1879; Wilmington, DE, A. Mus.), in which two enigmatic figures in Renaissance costume blow delicate, elongated horns before a pair of attentive whippets, have a symbolic quality closer to the work of the Pre-Raphaelites than to contemporary French painting. In addition they have an aesthetic languor and preciousness reminiscent of James Abbott McNeill Whistler. In the considerably more vigorous *The Days* (1887; Hartford, CT, Wadsworth Atheneum), the shallow frieze-like arrangement of robust, rhythmically interacting women in classical drapery strongly recalls the art of Albert Moore and Lawrence Alma-Tadema.

Dewing's predominant theme emerged in the 1890s with elegant, aristocratic women lost in reverie within sparse but tastefully furnished interiors, or wandering idly in lush but barely indicated landscapes, as can be seen in *After Sunset* (1892; Washington, DC, Freer). Dewing referred to works of this type as 'decorations'; they are usually large in scale and were occasionally applied to folding screens in the Japanese manner. Such works also show the influence of Tonalism in Dewing's use of a single predominating colour and diffuse, gentle lighting.

Dewing's studies of interiors are smaller and more detailed works, although they also exhibit a narrow tonal range and evoke the same understated melancholy. The women are dignified rather than beautiful and often appear with a book or musical instrument, as in *A Reading* (1897; Washington, DC, N. Mus. American A.). Devoid of anecdotal drama, yet imbued with an aura of quietude and internal tension, these works recall those of Johannes Vermeer, who was much admired at this time. Dewing also became adept with pastel and the demanding medium of silverpoint, producing figure studies and nudes of extraordinary beauty.

In 1881 Dewing began teaching at the Art Students League in New York; in the same year he married Maria Oakey (1845–1927), a flower painter, who provided the landscapes in several of Dewing's paintings. In 1898 he was a founder-member of the TEN AMERICAN PAINTERS, after becoming dissatisfied with the aesthetic aims and exhibition policies of the Academies.

Dewing enjoyed considerable success in his career. Stanford White was an influential supporter, who designed frames for many of his paintings and introduced him to two influential collectors, John Gellatly and Charles Lang Freer. In his later years Dewing often expressed bewilderment and dismay over the array of modernist styles that gained credibility in American art following the Armory show of 1913. After 1920 he painted very little and spent his last years in relative isolation at his home in Cornish, NH.

BIBLIOGRAPHY

The Color of Mood: American Tonalism, 1880–1910 (exh. cat. by W. M. Corn, San Francisco, CA, de Young Mem. Mus., 1972)

S. Hobbs: 'Thomas Wilmer Dewing: The Early Years, 1851–1885', *Amer. A. J.*, xiii/2 (1981), pp. 4–35

ROSS C. ANDERSON

De Winne, Liévin (*b* Ghent, 24 Jan 1821; *d* Brussels, 13 May 1880). Belgian painter. A pupil of Félix De Vigne (1806–62) and Hendrik Van der Haert (1790–1846) at the Ghent Art Academy, he began his career as a history painter but made a living by producing a large number of small-scale genre scenes. In 1850 he obtained a grant from the Belgian government that enabled him to go to Paris, where from 1852 to 1855 he shared a studio with his friend and biographer, Jules Breton.

In 1861 De Winne settled permanently in Brussels and rapidly made his mark there as a portrait painter to the court and high society. His talent for strongly characterizing his sitters with great clarity and accuracy of feeling attracted many leading Belgian figures of the time: for example *Capt. Van de Woestyne* (Antwerp, Kon. Mus. S. Kst.), *Jean Cardon, Mme Cardon, M. Wymand-Janssens* (all Brussels, Mus. A. Mod.), *Felix De Vigne, Mme De Vigne, Frère Orban* and *The Duchess of Arenberg* (all Ghent, Mus. S. Kst.). De Winne rejected the romantic type of portrait for a more direct and realistic style, painted in a robust and lively manner that marks him out as one of the liberalizing forces in Belgian art in the 1870s. His portrait of *Leopold I* (1860; Brussels, Mus. A. Mod.) is considered a masterpiece of 19th-century Belgian painting.

BIBLIOGRAPHY
J. Breton: *Liévin De Winne* (Ghent, 1880)
O. Roelandts: *Liévin De Winne* (Ghent, 1930)

ALAIN JACOBS

De Wint, Peter (*b* Hanley, Staffs, 21 Jan 1784; *d* London, 30 June 1849). English painter. Drawing lessons from a local Stafford landscape painter named Rogers led the young De Wint to abandon plans for a medical career, and in 1802 he was apprenticed for seven years to John Raphael Smith. A fellow apprentice was William Hilton, who became a lifelong friend and whose sister De Wint married in 1810. From the first De Wint's taste seems to have been for landscape, and his progress in that line is indicated by his arrangement with Smith in 1806 to be released from the remaining years of his indenture in exchange for 18 landscape paintings in oils. In November 1806 De Wint and Hilton moved into lodgings in Broad Street, Golden Square, London, where they were neighbours of John Varley. Acquaintance with Varley and involvement with the circle of Dr Thomas Monro must have determined De Wint's adoption of watercolour and introduced him to the drawings of Thomas Girtin, which later influenced his own work in the medium. He enrolled as a student in the Royal Academy Schools in 1809 and was admitted to the Life School in 1811.

De Wint became an associate of the newly formed Associated Artists in Water-colours in 1808, becoming a full member in the following year. Among his exhibits there was *Westminster* (1808; London, V&A). However, in 1809 he left to become an associate of the more prestigious Society of Painters in Water-colours and was elected a full member of the Society in 1811. On its reconstitution at the end of 1812 as the Society of Painters in Oil and Water-colours, De Wint did not rejoin. Although he continued to exhibit with the Society, he did not become a full member again until 1825. Although his contemporary reputation was based on his watercolours, De Wint continued to produce oil paintings, exhibiting them at the Royal Academy and the British Institution between 1807 and 1824. His oils were generally less appealing, lacking brightness, and few of them sold; after his death a considerable cache was discovered in the attic of his London home.

De Wint regularly spent his summers in Lincoln, the childhood home of his wife and brother-in-law. He made frequent sketching excursions through Yorkshire, Cumberland, Westmorland, Gloucestershire and Norfolk and along the valleys of the Trent and the Thames. In 1824 he visited South Wales, and in 1829 or 1830 he made the first of several visits to North Wales. His only trip outside Britain was a short tour of Normandy in 1828, which resulted in a handful of French subjects among his exhibited watercolours in 1829 and 1830. A severe case of bronchitis contracted during a sketching expedition in Hampshire in 1843 initiated a six-year-long decline in health leading to his death.

De Wint's watercolour style changed relatively little, and he frequently left his works unsigned and undated, making a chronological assessment of his work difficult.

Peter De Wint: *Cornfield, Windsor*, watercolour, 291×460 mm, 1841 (Cambridge, Fitzwilliam Museum)

However, some drawings have been remounted, revealing dates on the works. His early watercolours are characterized by a broad, simplified approach to form and a warm, deep-toned colour. Later watercolours, such as *Cornfield, Windsor* (1841; Cambridge, Fitzwilliam; see fig.), are more elaborately finished exhibition pieces, as well as fluid sketches, which he also regarded as worthy of exhibition. Naturalistic landscape formed the subject of most of his work, but in several instances he produced historical landscapes, such as *Elijah* (exh. 1829, untraced, two pen-and-ink compositional studies, New Haven, CT, Yale Cent. Brit. A.), as well as a few still-lifes. He provided topographical illustrations for a number of publications, including W. B. Cooke's *Picturesque Views on the Southern Coast of England* (1849), Charles Heath's *Views of London* (1825) and the *Oxford Almanack* (1839, 1841).

UNPUBLISHED SOURCES
Lincoln, Usher Gal. [Harriet De Wint's press-cuttings book]
BIBLIOGRAPHY
W. Armstrong: *Memoir of Peter De Wint* (London, 1888)
H. De Wint: *A Short Memoir of Peter De Wint and William Hilton R.A.* (privately pubd [1912])
P. Shakeshaft: *Peter De Wint* (diss., U. Cambridge, 1972)
Drawings and Watercolours by Peter De Wint (exh. cat. by D. Scrase, Cambridge, Fitzwilliam, 1979)
H. Smith: *Peter De Wint, 1784–1849* (London, 1982)
SCOTT WILCOX

Dexter, George Minot (*b* Boston, MA, 1802; *d* Brookline, MA, 26 Nov 1872). American architect and engineer. After leaving Harvard University in 1821, he travelled in England, France and Germany during the following decade. He was impressed by the evidence of Romanticism that he saw in England and by the work of Karl Friedrich Schinkel in Germany, where he studied engineering. In Paris he bought architectural books for the Boston Athenaeum and the library of the architect and civil engineer Alexander Parris. In the 1830s Dexter trained as an engineer in Boston. His engineering studies enabled him to undertake major commissions with advanced engineering requirements, but his technical competence was combined with a romantic sensibility. He designed the houses in Pemberton Square (1836; destr.), Boston, which resembled Charles Bulfinch's Tontine Crescent in plan. He designed two important railway stations (the Haymarket and the Fitchburg, 1844 and 1848 respectively; both destr.) in Boston, which solved the transport problems of the Boston peninsula. He won the competition of 1844 to design the Boston Athenaeum and provided engineering and design expertise to E. C. Cabot (1818–1901), who was credited in 1847 as architect.

Dexter introduced picturesque planning and the Gothic style to the Boston area with two stone mansions, namely Oberland (1845), Manchester-by-the-Sea, MA, for F. G. Dexter, and Cottage Farm (1850), Brookline, MA, for Amos Lawrence. Red Cross Cottage (1843), Newport, RI, built for David Sears in the Gothic Revival style, was a modular, prefabricated design, shipped by water to Newport.

UNPUBLISHED SOURCES
Boston, MA, Athenaeum [over 1200 archit. drgs]
BIBLIOGRAPHY
W. Lawrence: *The Life of Amos Lawrence* (Boston, 1888)
'Founding Fathers', *J. Boston Soc. Civil Engineers*, xxiii (1936)

W. Kilham: *Boston after Bulfinch* (Cambridge, MA, 1946)
B. Bunting: *Houses of Boston's Back Bay* (Cambridge, MA, 1967)
A. Wardwell: 'Longwood and Cottage Farm in Brookline', *Victorian Boston Today*, ed. P. C. Harrell and M. S. Smith (Boston, 1975)
'Changing Images of the Boston Athenaeum', *Change and Continuity* (exh. cat. by J. S. Knowles, Boston, MA, Athenaeum, 1976)
M. J. Lamb: *Homes of America* (New York, 1979)
J. N. Pearlman: 'The Red Cross Cottage and Designs for a Villa in Newport', *Buildings on Paper* (exh. cat., ed. W. F. Jordy and C. Monkhouse; Providence, RI, 1982)
MARGARET HENDERSON FLOYD

Deybel [Deibel; Deibler; Deubler; Teubel; Teubler; Teybell], **Jan Zygmunt** [Johann Siegmund] (*b* ?Hammerau, nr Salzburg, *c.* 1685–90; *d* Warsaw, 1752). German architect, active in Poland. He arrived in Warsaw at the beginning of the 18th century and in 1712 was registered in the Royal Office of Works there as an architectural assistant with the rank of second lieutenant. Initially he worked under the supervision of Johann Christoph von Naumann (*d* 1742), and later with Joachim Daniel Jauch, drawing up plans (unrealized) for the reconstruction of several buildings in Warsaw: Vjazdów Castle (*c.* 1725), the Saski Palace (1725–30) and the Kazimierzowski Palace (1728). In 1726 he worked with Karl Friedrich Pöppelmann (*d* 1750) on the construction of the Blue Palace (Pałac Błękitny). The barracks in Wielopole, of which one pavilion survives, were built to Deybel's plans in 1731–2. Between 1730 and 1733 the extension of the southern wing of the palace at Wilanów, near Warsaw (then the summer residence of Augustus II, King of Poland), was completed according to his plans. It features a great hall articulated with clusters of fluted pilasters.

During the late 1720s Deybel had come to the notice of several members of the Polish nobility; Elżbieta Sieniawska of the Lubomirski family became his patron. When she died, her daughter Maria Zofia Denhoff continued to employ him. He rebuilt the palace in Puławy for her between 1730 and 1736. The elevation towards the River Vistula is articulated with Doric pilasters above a battered base. There is a Rococo pillared entrance hall. From 1728 he had established contact with the great crown hetman Jan Klemens Branicki, for whom he rebuilt the palace in Białystok (1728–56), extending it and adding upper storeys. In 1731 he began building his most important work, the palace of Chancellor Jan Fryderyk Sapieha at 6, Zakroczymska Street (destr. by fire 1944; rebuilt 1951–5). The main range is capped by a pediment enclosing a trophy; flanking pavilions have chamfered corners in banded masonry. From 1739 to 1741 he built the palace in Warsaw (destr. *c.* 1850) for Stanisław Poniatowski, Governor of Kraków. During the same period he built a palace at 6, Miodowa Street in Warsaw (1740–43; destr. 1939–44; rebuilt 1947–53). Deybel was the most outstanding architect working in Poland during the second quarter of the 18th century. He made an appreciable fortune from his career and owned several properties in the Warsaw area. His mature style incorporates the architectural elements and decorative motifs that he had adopted during his work for the Royal Building Office, although his personal architectural concepts originated from his direct contact with Polish artistic tradition and with ideas of French origin acquired mainly from the work of Jean Mariette. Deybel's drawings are kept in the collections of the Sächsische Landesbibliothek, Dresden, and in the Drawing Collections at the Warsaw University Library and Warsaw National Museum.

BIBLIOGRAPHY

W. Hentschel: *Die sächsische Baukunst des 18. Jahrhunderts in Polen* (Berlin, 1967)
I. Malinowska: 'Twórczość Jana Zygmunta Deybla w świetle badań W. Hentschla' [The creative output of Jan Zygmunt Deybel in the light of the research by W. Hentschel], *Biul. Hist. Sztuki*, xxxii/3–4 (1970), pp. 376–7

ANDRZEJ ROTTERMUND

Deyck, Barthélemy. *See* EYCK, BARTHÉLEMY D'.

Deyneka, Aleksandr (Aleksandrovich) (*b* Kursk, 21 May 1899; *d* Moscow, 5 June 1969). Russian painter, graphic artist and designer. He studied at the Khar'kov Art School (1915–17), breaking off his studies to join the Red Army. By 1919 he had returned to Kursk, where he was designing the stencilled propaganda ROSTA posters that spread throughout the Russian Socialist Federal Soviet Republic following Mayakovsky's original examples (*see* AGITPROP). In 1921 he moved to Moscow and studied under Vladimir Favorsky at Vkhutemas (the Higher Artistic and Technical Workshops) until 1925. While still a student he worked on illustrations and designs for a number of new magazines such as *Bezbozhnik* ('The Atheist') or *Prozhektor* ('Searchlight').

In the mid-1920s Deyneka started to make easel paintings and became a leading member of the SOCIETY OF EASEL PAINTERS (OST), which reflected advanced tendencies in representational painting rather than the literalism of the Wanderers. His major paintings of the period are *The Defence of Petrograd* (1927; Moscow, Tret'yakov Gal.) and *Textile Workers* (1927; St Petersburg, Rus. Mus.), which in their stark composition and lack of detail reflect Deyneka's background as a graphic artist. During the Cultural Revolution (1928–32) Deyneka's work became more monumental and more painterly. His subject-matter optimistically embraced the new communal life, the ideals of the new Soviet man, woman and child and the advances of industrialization and collectivization under the first Five-Year Plan. Yet the paintings themselves have an invention and formal vitality that prevents them from becoming merely illustrative. Deyneka received international recognition for this work when in 1932 his painting *On the Balcony* (1931) won first prize at the Pittsburgh, PA, International Art Exhibition. In 1935 Deyneka's favoured position under Stalin was shown by his being granted permission to travel to France, Italy and the United States. While there he made a number of paintings that revealed a softer, more French-influenced style and an ambition to become part of the mainstream of European Realist art, for example *Street in Rome* (1935; Moscow, Tret'yakov Gal.).

From the late 1930s until World War II Deyneka's paintings became larger, more theatrical and propagandist, in response to A. A. Zhdanov's demand for 'revolutionary romanticism', which was at the head of the newly formulated state doctrine of Socialist Realism. *Future Pilots* (1937; Moscow, Tret'yakov Gal.) and *Defence of Sebastapol*

(1942; St Petersburg, Rus. Mus.) both fall within this category. The best works of this period are probably his decorative schemes: the ceiling mosaics for the newly built Mayakovsky (1938) and Novokuznetskaya (1943) metro stations in Moscow are among the most impressive examples. After the War, Deyneka was unable to recapture the freshness of his earlier work and with few exceptions lapsed into decorative and vacuous formulae. Acclaim in the former USSR, however, was matched by international recognition, and during these years he was awarded a number of honours.

BIBLIOGRAPHY

N. Barabanova: *Deyneka: Obraz i tsvet* [Deyneka: Form and colour] (Moscow, 1981)
Alexander Deineka: Malerei, Graphik, Plakat (exh. cat., Düsseldorf, Städt. Ksthalle, 1982)
A. Tsegodayev: *Aleksandr Deyneka* (Leningrad, 1983)
I. Kharitonova, ed.: *Monumental Works by Aleksandr Deyneka* (Leningrad, 1985)
V. P. Sysoyev: *Aleksandr Deyneka*, 2 vols (Moscow, 1989)

DAVID ELLIOTT

Deyrolle, Jean (*b* Nogent-sur-Marne, 20 Aug 1911; *d* Toulon, 30 Aug 1967). French painter, draughtsman and printmaker. He grew up in Brittany, moving to Paris to study art and advertising from 1928 to 1931. Having decided to become a painter, he worked alone until World War II at Concarneau (1930–33 and 1938–41) and Rabat, Morocco, painting landscapes and still-lifes and documenting these places and their inhabitants in a number of undated and largely untitled lithographs and linocuts (Paris, Bib. N., see Richar 1976, nos. 1–23). He lived briefly in Brittany during the war, where he studied the work and theories of Paul Sérusier after being introduced to his widow. Deyrolle, however, dated his birth as an artist to 1944, when he first exhibited abstract works at the Salon d'Automne. In Paris, where he had settled in 1942, he met other abstract painters such as Jean Dewasne and Hans Hartung through his association with the Galerie Denise René. He continued to draw on Paul Sérusier's work, particularly in terms of figure/ground relationships, but used black outlines, not to detach figures from the background, as with Sérusier, but to create contradictory sensations of space with flat shapes in muted earth colours. In later works such spatial concerns were conveyed by rhythmic patterns of visible brushstrokes, as in *Alpinien* (1956; Paris, Mus. A. Mod. Ville Paris). After 1950 he also painted in tempera and continued working as a printmaker, notably for *Séjour* (Paris, 1970), a limited edition book produced in collaboration with the writer Samuel Beckett.

BIBLIOGRAPHY

L. Degand and G. Richar: *Jean Deyrolle* (Paris, 1974)
Proposition pour une rétrospective: Deyrolle, 72 peintures de 1944 à 1967 (exh. cat., Paris, Mus. A. Mod. Ville Paris, 1975)
G. Richar: *Deyrolle, l'oeuvre gravé* (Paris, 1976)
Jean Deyrolle: Oeuvres sur papier (exh. cat., essay by G. Richar, Rennes, Mus. B.-A. & Archéo.; 1984)

VANINA COSTA

Dezallier d'Argenville. French family of writers, one of them also an engraver and collector.

(1) Antoine-Joseph Dezallier d'Argenville (*b* Paris, 2 July 1680; *d* Paris, 29 Nov 1765). Writer, collector and engraver. He was the son of Antoine Dezallier, a bookseller in Paris who had acquired the estate of d'Argenville; his maternal uncle was Pierre Mariette *le fils*. He was educated at the Collège du Plessis and studied drawing and engraving with Bernard Picart, Roger de Piles and Jean Leblond (ii). His first researches were into natural history, with particular reference to gardening, and his earliest publication was *La Théorie et la pratique du jardinage* (1709). This was the most important codification of the formal French garden, and its successive editions traced the development of the art of gardening through the first half of the 18th century. He also published papers on shells and fossils that reveal a collector's instinct for classification and identification. These interests brought him the membership of a number of learned societies, and he was asked by D'Alembert and Diderot to write articles about hydraulics and the art of gardening for their *Encyclopédie*. In 1714 he set out on a prolonged tour of Italy, where he made engravings of landscapes and copied various Old Master paintings. On his return in 1716 he obtained social standing by purchasing various administrative posts, including that of Secrétaire du Roi and subsequently, in 1733, Maître des Comptes, finally becoming a Conseiller du Roi.

Dezallier d'Argenville established numerous contacts with the most notable collectors of the period and acquired a highly regarded collection of paintings in the course of visits to the Netherlands, Germany and England. Having become something of an expert in art techniques and styles, in 1723 he published *Le Traité des vernis*, a translation of a work by Buonanni. His first original art-historical work is the 'Lettre sur le choix et l'arrangement d'un cabinet curieux' (1727), which shows that his interest in collecting works of art arose directly from his study of natural history. This long 'letter' dealt with collections not only of *objets d'art* but also of 'curiosities', exceptional or unusual natural objects, the criterion for inclusion in a collection being the object's strangeness and rarity. Dezallier d'Argenville contrived systems of classification that permitted the identification of similarities between such objects; this attempt at classification was firmly rooted in the thinking of the Enlightenment and, as such, was opposed to the *Wunderkammer* type of collection. His aim was also to help enthusiasts and collectors to choose and identify paintings they intended to acquire.

Between 1745 and 1752 Dezallier d'Argenville published his most important art-historical work, *Abrégé de la vie des plus fameux peintres*, intended to help collectors to recognize styles and periods of art, as well as the work of individual artists. He wished to teach enthusiasts to evaluate the quality of Old Masters, to identify the school they belonged to and, last and most important, to distinguish originals from copies. His descriptions of artists were concise, and his perspective was essentially biographical. He classified artists by school but did not explore or define the notion of a school, most often making it a matter of geography: thus an artist's removal to another city or country was perceived as the source of a new style. Another principle of classification that he emphasized was by studio: in order to characterize the great masters, he thought it essential to understand which of their qualities caused less significant artists to gravitate around them. His taste was eclectic and did not respect the traditional hierarchy of genres; he was particularly critical of history

painting. He devoted considerable attention to analysing painters' technical skills, and he was more concerned with describing their styles than the subject-matter of the paintings, characterizing the latter as '*écriture pittoresque*'. He believed that attribution was possible on the basis of purely stylistic criteria. Although he protested his impartiality, he did attempt to redress the balance away from the Italian schools towards the Northern ones, especially the French.

The *Abrégé* also contains precise technical details of drawings, based directly on the works in Dezallier d'Argenville's own extensive collection—he claimed to possess about 6000 drawings. The drawing's spontaneity seemed to him to convey most directly an artist's style. He assembled a large cabinet of paintings, gouaches, pastels, drawings and etchings, as well as objects of scientific interest, such as minerals and shells. The catalogues of the two posthumous sales of his collections give precise information about their contents. At the first sale (Paris, Didot l'aîné, 3 March 1766), 70 paintings and 9 gouaches and pastels were offered, as well as a large collection of prints. Twelve of the canvases were of the Italian school and included works by Andrea del Sarto, Veronese, Bassano and Federico Barocci; 33, among which were works by Rubens, Jan Breughel I and Bartholomeus Breenbergh, were of the Northern school, and the rest were French and included works by Poussin, Claude and Eustache Le Sueur. Among the artists responsible for the gouaches and pastels were Johann Wilhelm Baur, Noël Coypel, Rosalba Carriera and François Boucher. At the second sale (Paris, Didot l'aîné, 18 Jan 1779), which took place following the death of Dezallier d'Argenville's widow, the few remaining prints and some 3350 drawings in 555 lots were sold. A large number were purchased by Charles Paul Jean-Baptiste Saint-Morys. Dezallier d'Argenville had given to each item a number, followed by his paraph. It has been established (Labbé and Bicart-Sée) that this corresponds to Lugt 2951 and Lugt 2952 (F. Lugt: *Marques*, 1921). He numbered his drawings in a sequence that corresponded closely to the system advocated in the *Abrégé*.

WRITINGS

La Théorie et la pratique du jardinage (Paris, 1709/*R* Geneva, 1972)
'Lettre sur le choix et l'arrangement d'un cabinet curieux', *Mercure de France* (June 1727), pp. 1294–330
Abrégé de la vie des plus fameux peintres, 3 vols (Paris, 1745–52; rev. as 4 vols, 1762/*R* Geneva, 1972)

BIBLIOGRAPHY

DBF
C. Blanc: *Le Trésor de la curiosité*, i (Paris, 1857), pp. 441–3
M. Roux: *Inventaire du fonds français: Graveurs du dix-huitième siècle*, Paris, Bib. N., Dept Est. cat., vii (Paris, 1951), pp. 274–5
R. Vallet: *L'Histoire de l'art vue par un amateur du XVIIIème siècle: Dezallier d'Argenville et son 'Abrégé de la vie des peintres' (1745–52)* (diss., U. Clermont-Ferrand, 1967)
J. Labbé and L. Bicart-Sée: 'Antoine-Joseph Dezallier d'Argenville as a Collector of Drawings', *Master Drgs*, xxv (1987), pp. 276–81

LISE BICART-SÉE, PASCAL GRIENER,
JACQUELINE LABBÉ

(2) A(ntoine-)N(icolas) Dezallier d'Argenville (*b* Paris, 27 Aug 1723; *d* Paris, 26 Sept 1796). Writer, son of (1) Antoine-Joseph Dezallier d'Argenville. He lived, like his father, in a highly cultured environment and inherited from him a taste for nature and art. He married the sister of the Abbé Mercier de Saint-Léger, a renowned scholar and bibliographer, particularly distinguished for setting up the Bibliothèque Sainte-Geneviève in Paris. In 1746 he was appointed Maître des Comptes and later became a Conseiller du Roi. He wrote several books on gardening: most notably the *Manuel du jardinier* (1772) and a *Dictionnaire du jardinage* (1777). He is better known for his work in the field of art: still of great use is the *Voyage pittoresque de Paris*, first published in 1749. It is a valuable guide that divides Paris into 20 areas and enumerates and describes with great care and precision the main objects of architectural and artistic interest, including private collections. Dezallier d'Argenville's next work, the *Voyage pittoresque des environs de Paris* (1755), performs a similar task for the region surrounding the capital. In 1781 he published a *Description sommaire des ouvrages de peinture, sculpture et gravure exposés dans les salles de l'Académie Royale*, which includes in its preface a history of architecture. Finally, he completed, but with less flair, the work begun by his father on painters, draughtsmen and engravers; it appeared in 1787 in two volumes as *Vies des fameux architectes et vies des fameux sculpteurs depuis la Renaissance des arts*: he claimed that this work had taken him 40 years to produce.

WRITINGS

Voyage pittoresque de Paris ou indication de tout ce qu'il y a de plus beau dans cette grande ville en peinture, sculpture et architecture (Paris, 1749/R Geneva, 1972) [numerous subsequent editions]
Voyage pittoresque des environs de Paris ou description des maisons royales, châteaux et autres lieux de plaisance à quinze lieues aux environs de cette ville (Paris, 1755, rev. 4/1779)
Manuel du jardinier ou journal de son travail distribué par mois (Paris, 1772, rev. 3/1801)
Dictionnaire du jardinage (Paris, 1777)
Description sommaire des ouvrages de peinture, sculpture et gravure exposés dans les salles de l'Académie Royale (Paris, 1781)
Vies des fameux architectes et vies des fameux sculpteurs depuis la Renaissance des arts, 2 vols (Paris, 1787)

BIBLIOGRAPHY

DBF (1939)
LISE BICART-SÉE, JACQUELINE LABBÉ

dga 'ldan. *See* GANDEN.

D'Haese, Roel (*b* Geraardsbergen, nr Ronse, 26 Oct 1921). Belgian sculptor. He studied drawing and modelling at the Academy in Alost between 1932 and 1935. After this he was apprenticed to a blacksmith and then to a sculptor of religious images in wood. Between 1938 and 1942 he was a pupil of Oscar Jespers at the Ecole Nationale Supérieure d'Architecture et des Arts Décoratifs La Cambre in Brussels. After this he lived near Brussels, carving stone and forging, riveting and welding iron and copper. During this period he met Asger Jorn, Pierre Alechinsky and Enrico Baj.

In 1954 D'Haese won the Prix de la Jeune Sculpture Belge and began working in bronze, using a sandcasting technique in his own studio. By 1957 he had come to prefer the lost-wax technique, and in 1959 he took up argon welding in order to assemble the bronze elements of more monumental works such as the *Song of Evil* (1964; Antwerp, Kon. Mus. S. Kst.). This emphatically marked his return to figuration and was the beginning of a long series of sculptures, such as *The Lieutenant* (1966; Brussels, Mus. A. Mod.), born of a highly personal vision. By 1964 he had moved to Nieuport, where he continued executing sculptures without the assistance of technicians, displaying a frame of mind that was in turn mocking, interrogative and denunciatory.

BIBLIOGRAPHY

J. Meuris: *Roel D'Haese* (Brussels, 1964)
Roel D'Haese (exh. cat., Brussels, Pal. B.-A., 1978)
Roel D'Haese: Sculptures et dessins (Paris, Gal. Claude Bernard, 1987)
PIERRE BAUDSON

Dhaka [Dacca]. Capital of Bangladesh, located about 160 km above the mouths of the Ganga on the northern bank of the Buriganga River (known to Muslim historians as the Dulai River). The city gained ascendancy in the 17th century as a provincial capital of the Mughal empire.

1. HISTORY. Dhaka was part of the ancient region of Vanga. Its earliest history is unclear, but terracotta plaques with seated Buddha images as well as post-Gupta-period gold coins (Dhaka, N. Mus. Bangladesh) of the 7th–8th centuries AD discovered at Savar, 25 km to the north of Dhaka, indicate the antiquity of local settlements. The area was brought under the sultans of Delhi in the 13th century; these rulers were then replaced by the independent sultans of Bengal in the 14th century. The settlement of Muslims in Dhaka is attested by two stone inscriptions, one recording the building of Binat Bibi's mosque in 1457 (AH 861) and the other of a gate in 1459 (AH 863). The earliest known mention of the name 'Dhaka' is in an Arabic inscription dated 1460 (AH 864) from Birbhum in West Bengal, India, which records the construction of a mosque by Ulugh Ajelka Khan, son of the Chief Controller of Dhaka. Other references to Dhaka are found in Mughal histories of Delhi and Bengal, for example 'Abu'l Fazl's *Akbarnāma* and Mirza Nathan's *Bahāristān-i Ghaibī*, as well as early European travellers' accounts.

Though Akbar conquered Bengal in 1576, local zamindars (landholders) continued to defy Mughal authority. In 1608 Musa Khan, the zamindar of the Dhaka region, was defeated by the Mughal governor Islam Khan, who subsequently moved the provincial capital from Rajmahal in Bihar to Dhaka, renaming it Jahangirnagar after the reigning Delhi monarch. From 1639 to 1659 the capital was temporarily re-established at Rajmahal. At the close of the century Dhaka was a major commercial and administrative centre, particularly well known for its fine cotton muslin. In 1717 the capital was moved to Murshidabad by the nawabs of Bengal, and the population of Dhaka dwindled. As the fortunes of the nawabs declined, the East India Company became a new power. In 1858 Queen Victoria's Proclamation brought all the territories held by the Company (including Dhaka) under the administration of the British government. After the partition of the subcontinent and the independence of India and Pakistan in 1947, Dhaka became the capital of Pakistan's eastern wing. In 1971 East Pakistan formed the independent nation of Bangladesh, and Dhaka became the new nation's capital.

2. MONUMENTS. The earliest dated monument in Dhaka is Binat Bibi's mosque (1457). Though rebuilt, enlarged and plastered over, the mosque retains, on one side, the curved cornice and parapet that are typical of pre-Mughal architecture (*see* INDIAN SUBCONTINENT, §III,

6(ii)(d)). There are numerous architectural remains from the Mughal period in and around Dhaka. The mosques are generally square, single-domed structures or have a single aisle broken into three domed bays. They are built of brick, their external surfaces plastered and articulated with rectangular panels. The straight cornices are generally decorated with merlons; domes are raised on drums. The Mughal mosques that retain their original appearance include the Lalbagh Fort mosque (begun 1649, restorations 1780), the mosque and tomb of Haji Khwaja Shahbaz (1679), the Satgumbad mosque (mid- to late 17th century) and the mosque of Khan Muhammad Mridha (1679).

Fortifications include the river forts of Hajiganj and Sonakanda in Narayanganj, used as outposts for the defence of the city, as well as Lalbagh Fort. According to tradition, this fort was founded when Prince A'zam Khan was governor (1678–9) and later embellished by Shayista Khan, Mughal governor in 1679–88. Never completed, it consists of a group of structures built on a single axis. A tomb, traditionally known as that of Bibi Pari, daughter of Shayista Khan, is almost identical to one erected earlier at Gaur for Shah Ni'matallah. The nine-chambered interior is a plan derived from Mughal mausoleums.

Two caravanserais survive in a dilapidated state: the Bara Katra (1644), built by Diwan Mir Abu'l-Qasim, and the Chota Katra (1663), built by Shayista Khan. These consist of an open quadrangle enclosed on four sides, with entrances on the north and south and arcaded rooms and shops all around. The shops were meant as an endowment for the building and the maintenance of poor travellers. The Bara Katra had a magnificent river frontage with an elaborate multi-storey gateway. Mir Abu'l-Qasim also built an *'idgah*, a large enclosed platform intended for 'Id prayers. Only the qibla wall remains.

Other notable buildings include the Dhakeswari temple, dedicated to the presiding Hindu deity of Dhaka. It is not dated, but the three-bayed temple and vaulted verandah closely resemble the plans of Mughal-period mosques. Buildings of the colonial period are a blend of Indian and European styles in the eclectic tradition of British building elsewhere in the subcontinent. The Assembly Building was commissioned to the American architect Louis Kahn in 1962 and completed in 1984. It is the most monumental architectural complex in the city. Rising from an aquatic setting, it exhibits an interplay of open courts and volumes that reveal the architect's understanding of Mughal architecture, although the stereotypical vocabulary associated with that tradition is not employed. Dhaka's museums include the National Museum, which has a fine sculpture collection. The Lalbagh Fort Museum, set up by the Department of Archaeology, has Mughal arms, miniatures, calligraphy and *farman*s (royal orders). Folk art and crafts are preserved in the Folk Art Museum in Sonargaon. Artists receive training at the Institute of Art of Dhaka University, and exhibitions of contemporary art are held in its gallery as well as in the National Art Gallery of the Bangladesh Shilpakala Academy.

BIBLIOGRAPHY
S. A. Hasan: *Notes on the Antiquities of Dacca* (Calcutta, 1904)
S. Ahmed: *Inscriptions of Bengal*, iv (Rajshahi, 1960)
A. H. Dani: *Muslim Architecture of Bengal* (Dhaka, 1961)
——: *Dacca* (Dhaka, 1962)
A. Karim: *Dacca: The Mughal Capital* (Dhaka, 1964)
S. M. Ashfaque: *Lalbagh Fort: Monuments and Museum* (Karachi, 1970)
G. Michell, ed.: *The Islamic Heritage of Bengal* (Paris, 1984)
S. U. Ahmed: *Dacca: A Study in Urban History and Development* (London, 1986)

PERWEEN HASAN

Dhannu [Dhanu] (*fl c.* 1580–*c.* 1600). Indian miniature painter. A Hindu, he was established in the studio of the Mughal emperor Akbar (*reg* 1556–1605) by the early 1580s and thus would have worked on the *Hamzanama* ('Tales of Hamza'; *c.* 1567–82; alternatively dated 1562–77). His five compositions in the *Darabnama* ('Story of Darab'; *c.* 1580–85; London, BL, Or. 4615, fols 38*r*, 41*r*, 41*v*, 75*r* and 104*v*) are imaginative, with some attempt at naturalism in drawing and palette. His single contribution to the *Razmnama* ('Book of wars'; 1582–6; Jaipur, Maharaja Sawai Man Singh II Mus., MS. AG. 1683–1850, fol. 12) was as the colourist of a design by Basawan, although in the *Timurnama* ('History of Timur'; 1584; Bankipur, Patna, Khuda Bakhsh Lib., 269) he was the sole artist of two illustrations (fols 178*v* and 269*r*) and worked as a colourist on designs by Basawan (fol. 53*v*) and Lal (fol. 87*r*). He also worked on Nizami's *Khamsa* ('Five poems', Yazd, 1502–1506; miniatures *c.* 1585; Pontresina, Keir Col., fols 218*v* and 214*r*) as designer/painter and also as designer, although not on any other literary manuscripts with the exception of one folio in the *'Iyar-i Danish* ('Book of fables'; *c.* 1590–95; Dublin, Chester Beatty Lib., Ind. MS. 4, fol. 89). His finest work is *Babar Laying out the Garden of Bagh-i-vafa in Adinapur* in the second *Babarnama* ('History of Babar'; *c.* 1591; London, BL, Or. 3714, fols 173*v*, 386*r*, 389*v* and 393*v*). This illustrates his facility for natural history subjects and his rich, controlled palette, a striking contrast to the pale tones used to colour designs by Lal, Basawan and Miskin in the *Jami' al-tavarikh* ('History of the world', known as Chinghiznama; 1596; Tehran, Gulistan Pal. Lib., fols 57*v*, 263*v*, 266*r* and, as sole artist, fol. 288*v*). His late work consists of eight folios in the imperial *Razmnama* ('Book of wars'; 1598; London, BL, Or. 12076, fols 87*v*, 110*v* and dispersed), the fourth *Babarnama* (1598; New Delhi, N. Mus., MS. 50.326) and the later *Akbarnama* ('History of Akbar'; begun *c.* 1597; alternatively dated *c.* 1602–5; Dublin, Chester Beatty Lib., Ind. MS. 3).

BIBLIOGRAPHY
H. Suleiman: *Miniatures of Babur-nama* (Tashkent, 1970)
The Imperial Image: Paintings for the Mughal Court (exh. cat. by M. C. Beach, Washington, DC, Freer, 1981)

PHILIPPA VAUGHAN

Dharbhavati. *See* DABHOI.

Dharm Das [Dharamdas] (*fl* 1580s–*c.* 1609). Indian miniature painter. Although he was not included in Abu'l Fazl's list of 17 leading painters of the workshop of the Mughal emperor Akbar (*reg* 1556–1605), starting as a colourist in the 1580s he matured into a top-class painter, producing many superb miniatures in the last decade of the 16th century. He worked as a colourist to Kesav Das in a miniature of the *Harivamsa* volume of the *Razmnama* ('Book of wars'; *c.* 1586; Jaipur, Maharaja Sawai Man Singh II Mus.). In the companion volume of the *Ramayana*

(1589), also in Jaipur, he assisted Basawan in two miniatures and Lal in one. The painting illustrating the abduction of Sita in the *Rāmāyana* composed by Basawan and completed by Dharm Das is one of the finest of this period. Basawan took him as assistant for Nizami's *Khamsa* (Pontresina, Kier priv. col.), the *Akbarnāma* (London, V&A) and the dispersed copy of the *Bābarnāma* believed to be the imperial copy. In the first he was associated with Farrukh Beg and in the second with Kesav Das. He was given the charge of illustrating as many as seven miniatures for the *Dārābnāma* ('Story of Darab'; London, BL) and the *Tīmūrnāma* ('History of Timur'; Bankipur, Patna, Khuda Bakhsh Lib.) completed in the same decade.

During the next few years, when the imperial studio opted for elegantly calligraphed, tastefully decorated and handsomely bound volumes of Persian classics, fables and historical works with miniatures of the highest quality by individual painters, Dharm Das was given major responsibility. Some of his finest creations are to be found in the *Khamsa* ('Five poems') of Nizami (London, BL, and Baltimore, MD, Walters A.G.), the *Khamsa* of Amir Khusrau Dihlavi (Baltimore, MD, Walters A.G. and New York, Met.), the *Anvār-i Suhaylī* ('Lights of Canopus'; Varanasi, Banaras Hindu U., Bharat Kala Bhavan), the *Gulistān* ('Rose garden') of Sa'di (Cincinnati, OH, A. Mus.) and the *Chinghiznāma* ('History of Genghis'; mainly Tehran, Gulistan Pal. Lib.). In the last named he even retouched the faces of important people. The individual works of his mature phase display his perfect sense of composition, absorption of European perspective techniques in rendering distant landscape or architectural details, use of a wide range of colour tones and depiction of people with liveliness and individual character.

He continued to paint at a vigorous pace in the next few years, as revealed by his works in the *Bābarnāma* (New Delhi, N. Mus.), *Akbarnāma* (London, BL, and Dublin, Chester Beatty Lib.), *Layla and Majnun* (Oxford, Bodleian Lib.), *Kullīyāt* ('Complete works') of Sa'di (Geneva, Prince Sadruddin Aga Khan priv. col.) and *Anvār-i Suhaylī* (London, BL). In the last-named manuscript, started in the studio of Prince Salim (the later Emperor Jahangir, *reg* 1605–27) in 1604 and completed five years later, his name is associated with another painter in one painting, perhaps indicating his inability to complete it. This is the last mention of him.

BIBLIOGRAPHY

The Imperial Image: Paintings for the Mughal Court (exh. cat. by M. C. Beach, Washington, DC, Freer, 1981), pp. 105–7

A. K. Das: 'An Introductory Note on the Emperor Akbar's *Ramayana* and its Miniatures', *Facets of Indian Art*, ed. R. Skelton and others (London, 1986), pp. 94–104

ASOK KUMAR DAS

Dhauli [Dhauligiri]. Hill about 8 km south of Bhubaneshwar, Orissa, India. The emperor Ashoka (*reg c.* 269–*c.* 232 BC) left a rock-inscription at the site containing several edicts, including two bearing conciliatory messages to the newly conquered people of Kalinga. Also attributed to Ashoka's time is an image of the front part of an elephant, appearing to emerge from the rock out of which it is carved. Naturalistically rendered, it lacks the typical 'Mauryan polish' of sculptures of this period. An inscription of the 7th century AD found within a small rock-cut

chamber records the building of a monastery (*matha*) during the reign of the Bhauma–Kara king Shantikara. The badly ruined Vahirangeshvara Temple, datable to the 8th century, contains images of the Shaiva deities Ganesha and Karttikeya. At the foot of the hill are several ruined temples of *c.* 11th-century date, a few of which have been reconstructed. The hilltop bears two recent structures: the Dhabaleshvara Temple, built in 1972 on the ruins of an old temple, and the Kalinga Peace Pagoda, a monumental stupa with Bharhut-style reliefs, completed in the same year. The latter project was initiated by the Japan Buddha Sangha, and a board of management, the Kalinga Nippon Buddha Sangha, was created to supervise construction.

BIBLIOGRAPHY

K. C. Panigrahi: *Archaeological Remains at Bhubaneswar* (Bombay, 1961)

N. Nenapati, ed.: *Puri*, Orissa District Gazetteers (Bhubaneswar, 1977)

D. Mitra: *Bhubaneswar* (New Delhi, 1978)

T. E. Donaldson: *Hindu Temple Art of Orissa*, i (Leiden, 1985)

WALTER SMITH

Dhendrá. *See* DENDRA.

Dhimíni. *See* DIMINI.

Dholka [anc. Dhavalakkaka]. Town about 30 km southwest of Ahmadabad, Gujarat, India. Its earliest known monument is an artificial lake built by Queen Mainaladevi in the late 11th century. Al-Idrisi (*c.* 1100–*c.* 1165), Court Geographer of Roger II of Sicily, mentioned the town (as Dhulaka) as an important centre of trade. Inscriptions and manuscripts refer to the building of Hindu and Jaina temples by wealthy merchants and by the brothers Vastupala and Tejapala, ministers of King Viradhavala (*reg* 1243–61), who established his capital in Dholka, but none of these structures survives.

During the 14th century Dholka was the seat of the semi-independent governors of the Delhi Sultanate (*see* INDIAN SUBCONTINENT, §I, 2(iv)). The mosques of this period adhere to indigenous forms, using the structural and decorative vocabulary of the Gujarati tradition; the Hilal Khan Qadi mosque (1333), for example, is set within a walled courtyard and has five bays, each covered with a conical corbelled dome supported by columns salvaged from Hindu or Jaina temples. Its ceiling panels are elaborately carved, and the central niche, or mihrab, is decorated with 'Hindu' window motifs (Skt *gavākṣa*s) and miniature temple forms. The marble pulpit (minbar) is carved with a variety of intricate perforated designs and crowned with a canopy resembling a Hindu arched gateway (*toraṇa*). The entry at the eastern end of the courtyard is a domed and stepped pavilion reminiscent of the entrance to a Hindu or Jaina temple. The Taka, or Tanka, Masjid, datable by inscription to 1361, was built as a congregational mosque (Jami' Masjid). It comprises two open courts flanking a pillared hall containing the mihrab; the whole is enclosed by colonnades of columns taken from demolished temples (all human figuration has been cut away). Panels with low cusped domes decorate the ceiling. The brick mosque of Alif Khan Bhukai, a companion of Sultan Mahmud Bigara (*reg* 1448–1511) dates to *c.* 1460. The prayer-hall is flanked by two square towers and has three bays, each capped by an arcuate dome. Most of the stucco surface decoration has fallen away, but some is preserved on the northern and western exterior walls. Several windows carved with perforated stone tracery also survive. A new Jami' Masjid was built *c.* 1480, a date based on comparisons of its architecture with that of the Shah Alam and Miyan Khan Chisti mosques in Ahmadabad. Set within a walled courtyard, the prayer-hall has a façade with three large arches; the central arch is flanked by two towers, each three (originally five) storeys high. Their decoration resembles sections of a temple façade, with vertically arranged angular projections divided by horizontal mouldings and a projecting eave supported by brackets at the top of each storey.

BIBLIOGRAPHY
J. Burgess: *On the Muhammedan Architecture of Bharoch, Cambay, Dholka, Champanir, and Mahmudabad in Gujarat* (London, 1896)
K. F. Sompura: *The Structural Temples of Gujarat* (Ahmadabad, 1968)
S. B. Rajyagar, ed.: *Ahmadabad District Gazetteer*, Gujarat State Gazetteers (Ahmadabad, 1984)
G. Michell and S. Shah, eds: *Ahmadabad* (Bombay, 1988)

WALTER SMITH

Dhrami, Muntaz (*b* Gjirokastër, 10 Nov 1936). Albanian sculptor. He studied at the Jordan Misja Arts Lyceum in Tiranë (1952–6), the Academy of Arts, Leningrad (now St Petersburg; 1957–61) and the Higher Institute of Art in Tiranë (1962), where he later taught monumental sculpture. He became established as a Socialist Realist artist with his earliest works, for example *Keep the Revolutionary Spirit Strong* (bronze, 3.1 m, 1966; Tiranë). Attempting to create dynamic works, Dhrami introduced new means of plastic expression into Albanian sculpture, combining fractured surfaces with soft and gentle forms conveying a sense of optimism. His work became more lyrical, for example the bust of the popular hero *Liri Gero* (bronze, 1974; Tiranë, A.G.). He produced monumental sculptures for architectural contexts, for example the sculptural group *Drashovicë 1920–1943* (bronze, 1980; Vlorë). Dhrami also wrote critical articles on art.

WRITINGS
'Jeta e zjarreve partizane' [Life in partisan fires], *Drita* (2 Oct 1983), p. 5

BIBLIOGRAPHY
Përmendore të Heroizmit Shqiptar [Monuments of Albanian heroism: catalogue of Albanian sculpture] (Tiranë, 1973), pls 30, 39, 46, 59, 62, 127, 128, 131, 133
A. Kuqali: 'Monumente të gjalla në vizatimet dhe bocetet e një skulptori' [Vivid monuments in the drawings and sketches of a sculptor], *Drita* (16 May 1982), p. 5

ANDON KUQALI

Dhumvarahi [Dhum-Vārāhī, a corruption of Skt Dhumra Varāha]. Site 4 km north-east of Kathmandu, not far from the Bagmati River, important for an early statue of Varaha, Vishnu's boar incarnation. The magnificent image (h. 1.14 m), carved in a light-coloured stone, appears to have been consecrated by the Lichchhavi ruler Bhaumagupta (*reg c.* AD 567–90), though it is alternatively dated to the 7th century. As the saviour of the Earth Goddess (Bhūdevī or Pṛthvī), Varaha is shown surging from the watery abyss, symbolized by the cosmic serpent. The goddess is perched in an attitude of adoration on his upraised elbow, in an image type that has been emulated in Newar art up to the present. In the course of time, under the influence of Tantric (or Sahajiya) Vaishnavism,

the image came to be understood as an emanation of the Sow Goddess (Dhumvārāhī).

See also NEPAL, §IV, 1 and 2.

BIBLIOGRAPHY
P. Pal: *Vaiṣṇava Iconology in Nepal, a Study of Art and Religion* (Calcutta, 1970)
——: *The Arts of Nepal*, i: *Sculpture* (Leiden, 1974)
M. S. Slusser: *Nepal Mandala: A Cultural Study of the Kathmandu Valley*, 2 vols (Princeton, 1982)

ERBERTO F. LO BUE

di. For Portuguese proper names with this prefix *see under* the first part of the name. For pre-19th-century Italian proper names with this prefix, *see under* the first part of the name for individuals active before *c.* 1500; *see under* the second part of the name for those active *c.* 1500– *c.* 1800.

Diaghilev, Serge (de) [Dyagilev, Sergey (Pavlovich)] (*b* Grusino estate, Novgorod Province, ?19 March 1872; *d* Venice, 19 Aug 1929). Russian collector, patron and impresario. He is best known as the director of the BALLETS RUSSES. He arrived in St Petersburg in 1890 to study law, at the same time taking music lessons from Nikolay Rimsky-Korsakov; he became involved with the Nevsky Pickwickians, a circle of young musicians, writers and artists including Alexandre Benois, Léon Bakst, Konstantin Somov and Yevgeny Lansere, who later became known under the name WORLD OF ART (Mir Iskusstva). Diaghilev edited the group's periodical *Mir Iskusstva* from its first edition in November (October) 1898 (dated January 1899) to its last, in December 1904.

Diaghilev organized eleven exhibitions between 1897 and 1906, six under the auspices of the World of Art; these introduced western European artists to Russia (e.g. Monet, Renoir, Gustave Moreau, Puvis de Chavannes, Whistler and Frank Brangwyn). He wrote a monograph on Dmitry Levitsky and began one on Vladimir Borovikovsky, tracking down many works subsequently lost in the Revolution of 1917; the research served as a basis for his grandiose exhibition of historic Russian portraits in the Tauride Palace in St Petersburg, 1905.

From 1899 Diaghilev was special assistant to Prince Sergey Volkonsky, director of the Imperial Theatres. He edited a lavish issue of the *Yearbook of the Imperial Theatres* (Ezhegodnik Imperatorskikh Teatrov) in 1901 but he was dismissed in that same year, aborting plans for a production of the ballet *Sylvia* to have been designed by the World of Art associates. He organized an installation (designed by Bakst) of Russian art at the Salon d'Automne in Paris in 1906 and accompanying concerts of Russian music. He also presented a season of Russian music at the Paris Opéra in 1907. In 1908, with assistance from the Imperial Theatres, he brought a production of Musorgsky's *Boris Godunov* to the Opéra; designed by Aleksandr Golovin, Ivan Bilibin and Benois, and starring Feodor Chaliapin (Shalyapin), the production anticipated the unity of spectacle and visual richness that later became a hallmark of the Ballets Russes.

Diaghilev's first season of Russian ballet and opera, with dancers and singers from the Imperial Theatres, opened in Paris on 19 May 1909 (*répétition génerale* 18

May) at the Théâtre du Châtelet, and from 1911 he managed his own touring company, its fusion of visual art, music and choreography guided by the aesthetic of the World of Art. At first Diaghilev employed his World of Art colleagues Benois, Bakst (for illustration *see* WORLD OF ART) and Roerich, but in 1914 he commissioned sets and costumes for *Le Coq d'or* from Natal'ya Goncharova (for illustration *see* BALLETS RUSSES). He never returned to Russia after 1914 and began to move away from the more exotic richness and splendour of his earlier productions towards a western European orientation, employing artists such as Picasso (e.g. *Parade*, 1917), Gris (e.g. *Les Tentations de la bergère*, 1924), Braque (*Les Fâcheux*, 1924; *Zéphyr et Flore*, 1925), Ernst and Miró (*Romeo and Juliet*, 1926), and the Russian sculptors Naum Gabo and Antoine Pevsner (*La Chatte*, 1927) and Georgy Yakulov (*Le Pas d'acier*, 1927).

Diaghilev's virtues as an impresario included an inquisitiveness about contemporary artistic movements and an ability to spot and nurture talent, especially choreographers and musicians; most of his designers, however, came to him as mature artists. He knew how to forge successful collaborations over which he presided as lighting designer: the 1924 production of *Le Train bleu* employed Darius Milhaud as composer, Jean Cocteau as librettist, the Cubist sculptor Henri Laurens as designer, with costumes by Coco Chanel (1883–1971) and a drop curtain by Picasso (London, Theat. Mus.), with the choreographer Bronislava Nijinska and the dancers Anton Dolin and Lydia Sokolova.

Diaghilev bought paintings for himself while a young man and established collections of sketches and paintings by the Ballets Russes designers for his young male protégés. In the last few years of his life he developed an increasing passion for rare books. His schemes encompassed far more than he was able to realize: in the mid-1920s he contemplated presenting art exhibitions, experimental dance and theatre and traditional operas at the winter base in Monte Carlo, although these never materialized, and he continued to plan future seasons up to his death in 1929.

As an impresario Diaghilev contributed to the acceptance of avant-garde modernity as a chic, fashionable commodity. Daniel-Henry Kahnweiler assessed Diaghilev's interventive patronage in his monograph on Juan Gris: 'Diaghilew was quite capable of permitting several little novelties (even so he rejected a great number) which seemed to him interesting eccentricities, so long as they remained on the surface and did not fundamentally alter his conception of the stage.'

WRITINGS
Regular contributions to *Mir Iskusstva*, 1899–1904
D. E. Levitsky, 1735–1822 (St Petersburg, 1901)

BIBLIOGRAPHY
A. Haskell: *Diaghileff* (London, 1935)
S. Lifar: *Serge Diaghilev: His Life, his Work, his Legend* (New York, 1940)
B. Kochno: *Diaghilev and the Ballets Russes* (New York, 1970)
R. Buckle: *Diaghilev* (London, 1979)
L. Garafola: *Diaghilev's Ballets Russes* (Oxford, New York, Toronto, 1989)
MELISSA MCQUILLAN

Diamante (di Feo), Fra (*b* Terranuova, Val d'Arno, *c.* 1430; *d* after 1492). Italian painter. He was brought up in the Carmelite convent in Prato and first worked as *garzone* for the Carmelite painter Fra Filippo Lippi. On 17 July 1447 he was paid for gilding a temporary predella for Lippi's *Coronation of the Virgin* (Florence, Uffizi). At Prato he assisted Lippi on his fresco cycle in the choir of the parish church (now the cathedral) between 1452 and 1466. In July 1460 Diamante received payment on Lippi's behalf for the latter's completion of Pesellino's *Trinity with Saints* (London, N.G.), and in the same month he is recorded as a Vallombrosan monk. At this time he probably executed the frescoes of *St John Gualbertus* and *St Albert of Trapani* beside the window of the choir of Prato Cathedral. In 1463 Diamante was imprisoned in Florence for an undisclosed crime. His absence from Prato coincided with a halt on Lippi's fresco project, and in January 1464 the *comune* of Prato implored the Archbishop of Florence to grant Fra Diamante's release. Work on Lippi's frescoes recommenced in March, apparently without Diamante, and the next mention of him there is in October 1465. But on 18 November he received 15 florins for his work on the final scene in Lippi's cycle, either the *Celebration of the Relics of St Stephen* or the *Feast of Herod*.

Diamante was appointed to Lippi's former post as chaplain of the Augustinian convent of S Margherita, Prato, in 1466. By the spring of 1467 he had probably joined Fra Filippo at Spoleto to assist him with the fresco decoration of the cathedral choir. On Lippi's death in October 1469, Diamante was appointed guardian of his son, Filippino Lippi, and commissioned to complete the frescoes in Spoleto Cathedral. His final payment was made in February 1470. Of a total payment of 697 ducats for the cycle, Diamante received 137, almost a fifth. His share in the work was thus considerable. The *Coronation of the Virgin*, probably the first scene to be painted, and finished at least by the end of 1468, is largely by Lippi, while the other scenes—the *Annunciation*, *Death of the Virgin* and *Nativity*—increasingly show the presence of assistants working from Lippi's designs. The *Nativity* was certainly not executed by Lippi. It was painted by the same hand responsible for another *Nativity* panel (Paris, Louvre; inv. no. 1343). Since the latter came from S Margherita in Prato, where Fra Diamante was chaplain from 1466 onwards, it is tempting to attribute this work and the execution of the *Nativity* fresco at Spoleto to Diamante, as Oertel and other critics have done.

In May 1468 and the spring of 1469, Diamante made two short trips to Rome, where he painted a work whose location, date and subject are unknown. Whatever it was, the method of its payment caused him frequent legal problems. By May 1470 he returned to Prato, where he painted a fresco portrait of the *podestà* (destr.). In 1472 he was a member of the Compagnia di S Luca, the artists' confraternity in Florence, and lived in the Vallombrosan convent of San Pancrazio. In 1483 he was prior of S Pietro di Gello, near Volterra, and in 1489, at the command of the Vallombrosan abbot of S Salvi, Florence, he was again imprisoned in that city. Fra Diamante is last mentioned in 1492. Although he was Fra Filippo Lippi's assistant and, later, collaborator for 22 years, no surviving painting can be firmly attributed to him. The problem of his oeuvre involves the question of Lippi's workshop in Prato, still a highly complex issue.

DBI

BIBLIOGRAPHY

M. Pittaluga: 'Fra Diamante collaboratore di Fra Filippo Lippi', *Riv. A.*, xxiii (1941), pp. 19–71

——: 'Note sulla bottega di Filippo Lippi', *Arte*, xliv (1941), pp. 20–37, 67–81

R. Oertel: *Fra Filippo Lippi* (Vienna, 1942), p. 51

M. Pittaluga: *Filippo Lippi* (Florence, 1949), p. 184

B. Berenson: *Florentine School* (1963), pp. 58–9

E. Borsook: 'Fra Filippo Lippi and the Murals for Prato Cathedral', *Mitt. Ksthist. Inst. Florenz*, xix (1975), pp. 1–148

G. Marchini: *Filippo Lippi* (Milan, 1975), pp. 168–9, 215

E. Borsook: 'Cults and Imagery at Sant'Ambrogio in Florence', *Mitt. Ksthist. Inst. Florenz*, xxv (1981), pp. 147–202

Additional information was supplied by Eve Borsook.

ELIOT W. ROWLANDS

Diamantini, Giuseppe (*b* Fossombrone, 1621; *d* Fossombrone, 11 Nov 1705). Italian painter and printmaker. It seems likely that as a young man he visited Bologna and came into contact with such artists as Guercino and Simone Cantarini. He then went to Venice, probably *c.* 1650, and is documented there as a painter (Sansovino/Martinioni). His earliest surviving work is a design for the title page of an opera libretto (*L'inganno riconosciuto* by Camillo Contarini) dating from 1666. At about the same time he decorated the ceiling of the choir of S Giovanni Grisostomo, Venice, with frescoes on the theme of *God the Father*; here he combined Bolognese classicism with a Venetian sense of colour derived from Pietro Liberi. Liberi and Federigo Cervelli (1625–before 1700) were the two main stylistic influences on his most important works, which date from the 1670s and 1680s: an altarpiece of the *Adoration of the Magi* (Venice, S Moïse) and paintings depicting *Mercury and Argus, Juno, Jupiter and Io* and *Venus*, made for the hall of the Palazzo Badoer, Venice (*in situ*). These three canvases are all that has been identified of Diamantini's apparently sizeable production of paintings of profane subjects for private patrons, unless the *Acis and Galatea* in the Palazzo Koch in Rome is indeed by him, as has been suggested. He also produced a series of about 60 prints, mainly on mythological subjects, some of which bear inscriptions suggesting that they were made on commission. These are variously reminiscent of the refined eclecticism of Liberi, the brilliant freedom of Sebastiano Mazzoni and the delicate Venetian classicism of Giulio Carpioni. In 1698 Diamantini returned to Fossombrone, where he remained for his last years.

BIBLIOGRAPHY

Thieme–Becker

F. Sansovino: *Venetia città nobilissima et singolare descritta in XIV libri* (Venice, 1581); rev. G. Martinioni (Venice, 1663/*R* Farnborough, 1968)

A. Calabi: 'Le acqueforti di Giuseppe Diamantini', *Graph. Kst*, n. s. 1, i (1963), pp. 25–40

P. Mattioli: 'Giuseppe Diamantini incisore', *A. Ven.*, xxiv (1970), pp. 151–60

C. Thiem: *Italienische Handzeichnungen, 1400–1800* (Stuttgart, 1977), pp. 139–48

P. Bellini: *Italian Masters of the Seventeenth Century* (1983), 47 [XXI/ii] of *The Illustrated Bartsch*, ed. W. Strauss (New York, 1978–), pp. 385–424

B. Aikema: 'Diamantini e Molinari in Palazzo Gritti-Badoer a Venezia', *A. Ven.*, xxxix (1985), pp. 165–7

BERNARD AIKEMA

Diamantis, Adamantios (*b* Nicosia, 23 Jan 1900; *d* Nicosia, 28 April 1994). Cypriot painter and teacher. From 1921 to 1923 he studied painting at the Royal College of Art in London, and in 1926 he returned to Cyprus, where he combined his painting with extensive art teaching at numerous schools. His earlier works show a certain amount of experimentation with modernist styles, particularly Cubism, but he was also concerned with the rendering of the human form as he observed it in the villages of Cyprus. *At the Festival of Our Lady of Araka* (1942; Nicosia, Gr. Embassy) shows his characteristic monumental and schematized female forms constructed of broad unified surfaces of colour with a similarly schematized but atmospheric landscape in the background. From the 1940s Diamantis depicted many of his subjects in a rather more realistic and individual manner. The four seated figures in *Coachmen of Asmaalti* (1943; Nicosia, State A.G.) have the vitality and character typical of many of his male subjects; generalized architectural forms also begin to appear, their broad surfaces intensifying the monumentality of the figures they frame. From the 1960s his works became more expressive, with a higher degree of generalization and use of abstract forms. His best-known work is the *World of Cyprus* (l. 17.5 m, 1967–72; Aristotelian U. Thessaloniki), a series of 11 acrylic panels. In it he depicts the architecture and colour of Cyprus, as well as its people and their relationships, presented to the viewer in the form of a great pageant, in which the individuality of particular characters and of Cyprus itself is set against the generalization of the human form and spirit. Diamantis had a major influence on succeeding generations of Cypriot artists.

WRITINGS

'O kosmos tis Kyprou': *Aphiyisi* ['The world of Cyprus': an account] (Nicosia, 1975)

DBI

BIBLIOGRAPHY

A. Diamantis: *A Retrospective Exhibition of Paintings and Drawings, 1922–1978* (exh. cat., London, Mall Gals, 1979)

C. Christou: *Sindomi istoria tis neoteris kai synchronis kypriakis technis* [A brief history of modern and contemporary Cypriot art] (Nicosia, 1983)

Adamantios Diamantis (exh. cat., ed. E. S. Nikita; Nicosia, State A.G., 1994)

MICHAEL GIVEN

Diamantopoulos, Diamantis (*b* Magnisia, 1914). Greek painter and stage designer. After the defeat of the Greeks in the Asia Minor campaign, his family settled in Athens in 1922. He started painting during his school years and had his first exhibition of works in tempera in 1931 (at the Shelter of Art, Athens). These, as well as the illustrations he contributed to various Greek magazines in 1929 to 1930, such as *Still-life* (1928–30; priv. col., see Papastamos, p. 162), show him experimenting in a post-Cubist style that was then totally unknown in Greece. The works shown at the exhibition of 1931, as well as other works reflecting the influence of Surrealism and Pittura Metafisica, were received with hostility from the Establishment. Between 1931 and 1936 Diamantopoulos studied at the Higher School of Fine Arts in Athens under Konstantinos Parthenis. While there he discovered Greek folk art and also became involved with the movement for the re-evaluation of Greekness that prevailed in Greek intellectual circles in the early 1930s. His interest in folk art is manifested in drawings, costumes and sets he designed for the theatre during this period. After fighting in the Albanian campaign early in World War II he spent the rest of the war years in Athens, taking part in the group exhibitions of contemporary Greek artists at the National Archaeological Museum (1942–3). In 1946 he participated in the exhibition *Six Greek Artists* organized by the British Council in London, and also in the exhibition of Greek art at the Royal Academy, London. In 1947 and again in 1949 he had one-man shows at the Gallery Romvos, Athens, but from 1950 onwards he disappeared from the Greek artistic scene. His wartime activity with the resistance made him unacceptable in the period of right-wing political oppression in Greece, and he worked as a teacher, painting in isolation in his spare time. He reappeared in 1975 with a one-man show at the Gallery Ora, Athens. In 1977 he participated in the *Exposition internationale des arts plastiques* in Belgrade and in the Balkan exhibition in Bucharest. In 1978 he had a retrospective exhibition at the National Picture Gallery, Athens, which was highly acclaimed by the critics. Diamantopoulos's early subjects were still-lifes; later he became exclusively interested in the human figure, especially workers and masons, developing a style that fused elements and themes from Greek everyday life with a geometric monumentality reminiscent of Léger's later work.

BIBLIOGRAPHY

B. Spiliadi: 'D. Diamantopoulos and C. Koulentianos', *Arti visive '82: Catalogo generale* (exh. cat., ed. C. Pirovano; Venice, Biennale, 1982) [Greek section]

D. Papastamos: *Painting, 1930–40: The Artistic and Aesthetic Vision of the Decade* (Athens, 1986), pp. 161–79

FANI-MARIA TSIGAKOU

Diamond, Hugh Welch (*b* Kent, 23 Oct 1808; *d* Twickenham, Middx, 21 June 1886). English photographer. The son of a surgeon with the East India Company, he was educated at Norwich Grammar School, the Royal College of Surgeons and Bethlem Hospital. During the early 1850s Diamond photographed many mentally ill women patients at the Surrey County Asylum, Wandsworth, where he was superintendent. He claimed that these photographs were used both as medical records and for self-discussion in the treatment of some patients. Throughout the 1850s his portraits of the mentally ill dominated reviews of exhibitions of photographs. His paper 'On the Application of Photography to the Physiognomy and Mental Phenomena of Insanity' was read before the Royal Society on 22 May 1856. A number of his photographs, translated into engravings and accompanied by case studies, were published in the *Medical Times and Gazette*. Diamond was one of the earliest photographic experimenters: in April 1839 he had made photogenic drawings (photograms) of feathers and lace. He was a close friend and the doctor of Frederick Scott Archer (1813–57), the inventor of the wet collodion process (*see* PHOTOGRAPHY, §I), which Diamond was one of the first to use in 1850. Diamond did not confine his use of photography to professional purposes. He photographed works of art and objects and places of archaeological and antiquarian interest. In his capacity as Honorary Photographer to the Society of Antiquaries he donated photographs of antiquities to the society. During the 1850s Diamond established himself as a disseminator of photographic information. He welcomed discussion of problems

and improvements with both experienced and aspiring photographers. One of the latter, Henry Peach Robinson, recalled Diamond as a father figure of early photography.

WRITINGS

Notes and Queries (1852–9) [series of articles]

BIBLIOGRAPHY

Hugh Welch Diamond: Doctor, Antiquarian, Photographer (exh. cat. by C. Bloore, London, Orleans House Gal., 1980)

A Vision Exchanged: Amateurs and Photography in mid-Victorian England (exh. cat. by C. Bloore and G. Seiberling, London, V&A, 1985)

G. Seiberling and C. Bloore: *Amateurs, Photography and the mid-Victorian Imagination* (Chicago, 1986)

CAROLYN BLOORE

Dian. Ancient kingdom, listed by early chroniclers as one of several small tribal states in south-west China; it occupied the area around Lake Dian and Lake Er, south-west of modern Kunming in Yunnan Province. In 109 BC the Han (206 BC–AD 220) conquered Dian, reducing it to a vassal state of the empire. It is chiefly known for its extraordinary bronzes, many of them quite unlike the contemporary bronze-castings of the Zhou (*c.* 1050–256 BC) and Han periods (*see* CHINA, §VI, 3(iii)–(vi)) from other parts of China. Characteristic Dian forms include drums, wind musical instruments, cowrie containers and daggers. These are often decorated with elaborate animal and human motifs, either in relief or free-standing, modelled with great realism and skill.

1. Introduction. 2. Characteristic artefacts. 3. Stylistic influences.

1. INTRODUCTION. Based on archaeological evidence, bronzes of Dian style did not appear before the 7th century BC, after which they evolved rapidly, reaching a zenith shortly before the Han conquest. Motifs and forms such as spearheads and axes cast with simple geometric designs current in other parts of China were present in the Dian bronze-casters' repertory from the beginning but played only a minor role until just before the Han conquest, when Chinese influence became very strong. The art of Dian as a recognizable cultural entity disappeared completely by the 1st century AD.

The existence of an independent bronze tradition focused on the kingdom of Dian was unknown before the mid-1950s. The only early record of Dian in relation to metalwork appears in the writings of the historian Sima Qian, who noted in his *Records of the Historian* (*Shiji, juan* cxvi, completed *c.* 90 BC) that a golden seal bearing the inscription 'King of Dian' was bestowed on the tribal chief by the Han emperor Wudi in 109 BC, after the Han conquest. One such seal was found in 1957 at a burial site excavated at SHIZHAISHAN on the south-eastern shore of Lake Dian. Strictly speaking, only objects recovered at Shizhaishan should be considered as belonging properly to the Dian kingdom. However, archaeological investigations since the 1960s have shown that a coherent bronze culture extended well beyond the immediate vicinity of Lake Dian. A number of ancient cemeteries, including Dabona in Xiangyun, Wanjiabei in Chuxiong, Lijiashan in Jiangchuan and Taijishan in Anning, have yielded bronze and other artefacts that seem to be an integral part of the Dian culture.

Perhaps because of the richness of local deposits of copper and tin, Dian craftsmen used bronze in impressive, and by northern standards wasteful, quantities. Not only were ritual objects such as drums and funeral headrests made of bronze, but also weapons, musical instruments, personal ornaments and even utilitarian articles such as cups and cooking pots. At Lijiashan, over 1000 bronze artefacts were recovered from only 27 tombs. At Dabona, a superbly cast bronze coffin covered with a peaked, house-like roof and decorated on the sides with geometric patterns combined with vivid scenes of animals and birds on the end panels (5th–4th century BC; Kunming, Yunnan Prov. Mus.), was part of a single burial furnished with 103 bronzes and only 5 pottery vessels. Indeed, bronze seems to have been the chief metal used by the Dian people, although they were also competent workers in iron. Their frequent and skilful use of the lost-wax process (*see* CHINA, §VI, 2(iii)(b)), which permitted decorative elements and the main body of vessels to be cast in one pour of molten metal or allowed figures to be cast, then soldered in place, distinguishes Dian bronze-casting from contemporary metropolitan traditions in China.

2. CHARACTERISTIC ARTEFACTS. Bronze drums are the best known of Dian artefacts. The large, single-headed drums made entirely of bronze are not, however, unique to Dian or to Yunnan Province. Many have been found at archaeological sites in Sichuan, Guangxi and Guangdong provinces in China, as well as in neighbouring countries of South-east Asia. In terms of the classification imposed by the Austrian ethnologist Franz Heger at the beginning of the 20th century, Dian drums all belong to the early type known as Heger I. The typical Dian drum, in use throughout the period of Dian culture, has a flat top, a bulging neck curving into a waisted cylindrical body equipped with two to four handles, and a wide base. The earliest examples have little decoration other than simple geometric patterns in relief. Those of the 3rd and 2nd centuries BC, by contrast, exhibit a complex series of stylized motifs, most of them two-dimensional, including birds, boats, cows, men with feathered headdresses and spiral zigzag designs (see *The Chinese Bronzes of Yunnan*, pls 27, 48, 109; Rawson, pl. 145). All these motifs are arranged in bands, either concentrically on the head or horizontally on the body. Drums from both early and late periods are also ornamented with an eight-to-twelve-rayed sun in the centre of the drumhead.

In burials the bronze drums of Dian were often employed as containers for cowrie-shell money. Most were furnished with removable drumhead covers (some may have been permanently affixed) in the form of thin bronze discs bearing elaborate three-dimensional scenes. These depict gatherings, sacrifices or battles with numerous cast-bronze figures in lifelike poses: seated women weaving and cooking, kneeling and marching figures bearing tribute or offerings, cavalry and infantry in battle, dignitaries in litters, dancers and figures performing human sacrifices. Some compositions tell a story by moving through a series of small scenes; others present a main character, often gilded, surrounded by subsidiary players. An example from Shizhaishan (2nd century BC–the early 1st; see fig. 1) depicts a group of women at work around a gilded female figure who is receiving offerings (Kunming, Yunnan Prov. Mus.). Animals are also shown: standing cattle, running

1. Dian bronze drum containing cowrie shells, h. 270 mm, from Shizhaishan Tomb 1, 2nd century BC–the early 1st (Kunming, Yunnan Provincial Museum)

dogs and horses and snakes twined around what appear to be totem poles. Other elements are houses built on piles and even miniature drums (see *The Chinese Bronzes of Yunnan*, pls 1–8). Drum sides were also decorated. Drums with scenes on top could not have been used to produce sound and thus must have filled a largely ritual role. At least one drum found at Dabona had a more humble function: added handles and a carbon-encrusted exterior show that it was converted into a cooking pot. Gourd-pipes are rare at Dian sites, for only eight have been excavated. Their shapes were clearly inspired by natural gourds: the pipes are either curved or straight, emerging from a gourd shape at the lower end, and have free-standing animals such as cattle and tigers killing prey in Dian style soldered on to the mouthpiece (see *The Chinese Bronzes of Yunnan*, pls 110–13). Holes at the top were apparently intended to accommodate a number of wood or bamboo pipes. Scenes on other Dian bronzes show musicians playing similar gourd-pipes along with cymbals and drums.

Of bronze vessels, one type seems to have been used mainly for keeping cowrie shells. This vessel was always made in two parts: a flat lid and a cylindrical body with three legs, either animal or human in shape. The lid may be covered with sets of miniature figures similar to those found on the heads of drums or, more frequently, figures of long-horned cattle. The lid of a vessel from Shizhaishan, dated to the middle of the Western Han period (206 BC– AD 9), shows four oxen surrounding a gilt figure on horseback (see *The Chinese Bronzes of Yunnan*, pls 82–5). The cylindrical body characteristic of this type has an everted rim and curves smoothly downward to form a restricted waist, flaring outward again above a flat bottom.

2. Dian bronze plaque depicting three animals attacking a buffalo, 80×124 mm, from Shizhaishan Tomb 13, 2nd century BC–the early 1st (Kunming, Yunnan Provincial Museum)

Typical of this vessel type are two handles in the form of tiger-like animals crawling upward along the sides.

Flat plaques intended to be fastened on leather or cloth are also characteristic of the Dian culture. Some, in rounded shapes, are inlaid with jade or cornelian against a background of tiny, closely packed discs of malachite. Others, of bronze alone, are cast as openwork scenes that depict hunting, dancing or animals in combat. The composition of these wholly bronze plaques invariably includes a snake in the lower section, surmounted by combinations of two or more intertwined figures, including tigers, boars, horses, buffalo, deer, monkeys, swallows, parrots, cranes, peacocks, frogs and human hunters. One such plaque (see fig. 2) depicts three animals attacking a buffalo. Not only is the treatment outstandingly naturalistic in these plaques, but the artists have also achieved a powerful three-dimensional effect. In contrast to the decorative repertory of the artists of central China, mythical animals are absent as subject-matter in Dian bronzes.

3. STYLISTIC INFLUENCES. The bronze objects of the Dian kingdom are distinct both from the restrained and formal styles of metropolitan China and from other southern and northern styles. Unlike their northern and central Chinese contemporaries, Dian bronze-casters fully exploited the stylistic freedom inherent in lost-wax casting.

Chinese influence is discernible to varying degrees in the shape and decorative design of Dian bronzes. Three groups can be distinguished: Dian, 'Sino-Dian' and Sinicized. The objects in the Dian style are the most prominent and include, besides drums, gourd-pipes, decorative plaques and cowrie-shell containers, tall headrests shaped like or decorated with cattle, canopies, shoe-shaped axes and cooking pots made from converted drums. None of these forms is known from northern or central China. They are without exception highly ornamented with free-standing and two-dimensional animal and human effigies often arranged in scenes. Although a few decorative details, such as chevrons and opposed spirals used as background and a fondness for animals in combat, might be related to

central Chinese or ORDOS styles, the overall effect is distinctively Dian.

Objects in the 'Sino-Dian' style usually share shapes common elsewhere in China, such as hoes, swords and bells, but are ornamented with unmistakable Dian motifs. Animal and human effigies often form integral parts of the original casting but may also be hooked or soldered on to separately cast implements. Two examples of spearheads from Shizhaishan, although typical in form of those from central China, have a pair of human figures—apparently captives, with their heads drooping and their hands bound behind their backs—hanging on chains from the base of the blade (see *The Chinese Bronzes of Yunnan*, pl. 142).

The Sinicized style marks those objects that seem to be more or less faithful copies of objects used elsewhere in China at that time: agricultural implements, such as ploughshares, sickles and heart-shaped hoes, and household goods, including *hu* (tall-necked jars; *see* CHINA, fig. 138x) and large *fu* (rectangular food vessels; *see* CHINA, fig. 138xxi). These artefacts are thought to have been local products rather than actual imports. They were often roughly made in shapes subtly different from those preferred elsewhere in China. The stylistic connection between Dian and central Chinese regions grew stronger in the years before the Han conquest. More and more tools such as hoes, picks and sickles appeared that were very similar to tools used outside Yunnan Province, while imported Chinese objects—round *wuzhu* coins, discoid bronze mirrors with knobbed backs and precisely machined crossbow locks—came into common use. Two types of archaic Chinese weapons, socketed and tanged *ge* halberds, survived in the Dian area long after they had disappeared from China proper.

Certain elements of the Dian style can be related to cultures beyond central Yunnan Province. Bronze drums, widely distributed in southern China and South-east Asia, together with shoe-shaped axes and spiral zigzag decorative details, have been regarded as distinguishing features of the Dong Son culture (3rd century–111 BC; *see* VIETNAM, §VI, 4 and 6; and BRONZE, §II, 3), centred on the Red River Valley near Hanoi. Dian bronzes fit into the general Dong Son pattern but have a markedly individual character and a more diversified inventory. The lively scenes of gatherings in relief or in the round that are almost invariably present on Dian bronze objects are absent from Dong Son artefacts, as is the tradition of intricate animal art. The animal-hunting and combat themes of Dian have frequently been compared with (and were probably influenced by) the ORDOS animal art of north-western China. The Dian animal style, however, is characterized by a greater degree of realism, both in the representations of the individual animals and in the pictorial composition. The forms are more naturally rounded, the surfaces are textured rather than smoothly polished and the compositions are rarely confined within frames as they are in the animal art of the Ordos. Northern tribal influence perhaps can also be seen in the weapons of Dian. Daggers with W-shaped guards were common in areas right up to Gansu Province in the north, though such northern traits do not seem to have reached as far south as Dong Son itself.

BIBLIOGRAPHY

Yunnan Jinning Shizhaishan gumuqun fajue baogao [Excavation report on the ancient cemetery at Shizhaishan at Jinning, Yunnan] (Beijing, 1959)

Yunnan sheng bowuguan tonggu tulu [Bronze drums at the Yunnan Provincial Museum] (Yunnan, 1959)

'Yunnan Anning Taijishan gumuzang qingli baogao' [A report on the ancient cemetery at Taijishan of Anning, Yunnan], *Kaogu*, ix (1965), pp. 451–8

W. Watson: *Cultural Frontiers in Ancient East Asia* (Edinburgh, 1971), pp. 149–52

The Genius of China (exh. cat. by W. Watson, London, RA, 1973), pp. 113–16

M. Pirazzoli-t'Serstevens: *La Civilisation du royaume de Dian à l'époque Han, d'après le matériel exhumé à Shizhai Shan (Yunnan)* (Paris, 1974)

'Yunnan Jiangchuan Lijiashan gumuqun fajue baogao' [An excavation report on the ancient cemetery at Lijiashan of Jiangchuan, Yunnan], *Kaogu Xuebao*, ii (1975), pp. 97–156

'Yunnan sheng Chuxiong Wanjiabei gumuqun fajue jianbao' [A brief report on the Wanjiabei ancient cemetery excavated at Chuxiong, Yunnan], *Wenwu*, x (1978), pp. 1–18

M. von Dewall: 'Local Workshop Centres of the Late Bronze Age in Highland South East Asia', *Early South East Asia: Essays in Archaeology, History, and Historical Geography*, ed. R. Smith and W. Watson (New York, 1979), pp. 137–66

J. Rawson: *Ancient China: Art and Archaeology* (London, 1980), pp. 170–72

Wang Ningsheng: 'Shilun Zhongguo gudai tonggu' [On ancient Chinese bronze drums], *Yunnan qingtongqi luncong* [A collection of papers on Yunnan bronzes] (Beijing, 1981), pp. 108–43 [useful diagrams and line drgs]

The Chinese Bronzes of Yunnan, foreword by J. Rawson (London, 1983) [excellent pls]

HO CHUIMEI

Diana [Rusconi], **Benedetto** (*b c.* 1460; *d* Venice, 9 Feb 1525). Italian painter. In 1482 he was listed as a painter on the rolls of the Scuola della Carità in Venice; in 1485 his wife and his mother made a joint will. On this basis, his birth is usually placed *c.* 1460 but may be somewhat earlier. He is thought to have been a pupil of Lazzaro Bastiani. In 1485–6 he completed a fresco of *The Flood* begun by Bartolomeo Montagna for the Scuola Grande di S Marco in Venice. The influence of Montagna, Bastiani and Giovanni Bellini is evident in Diana's first surviving painting, a *Virgin and Child Enthroned between Two Saints and Donors* (Venice, Ca' d'Oro), commissioned in 1487 for the Venetian Mint by its magistrates. Its colour is characteristic of his work: a pale, luminous tonality achieved by the subtle gradation and relation of unsaturated cool hues. In terms of light and volume it is radically sophisticated: space is conceived as no less a presence than the forms it separates; and there is a calculated play of geometrically conceived forms: squat against slim, dense against ethereal. The background shows an astonishing mastery of the optical effects of a summer landscape seen through haze and of buildings reduced to geometry by light and shadow.

In the absence of other dated works, the chronology of Diana's work is conjectural. Paintings that show a close study of Antonello da Messina's work probably date from the 1490s. The half-length *Christ Blessing* (London, N.G.) revises Antonello's painting of the same subject (1465; London, N.G.) with reference to Alvise Vivarini and Cima, retaining Antonello's solid-geometric abstraction of forms but intensifying their lighting. A small *Standing Christ* (Modena, Gal. & Mus. Estense) has a deep landscape, reminiscent of van Eyck, which achieves a standard of execution hardly below Antonello's own. A polyptych of the *Virgin and Child Enthroned with Saints* (Cremona, Mus. Civ. Ponzone) must also date from the 1490s. At first glance it seems Bellinesque, but the figures are so abstracted as to be geometric integers; those of the main register are marooned on a vast sunlit terrace, which continues across the three panels, while far behind them flows a beautiful and subtly integrated landscape, its details realized mostly in values of colour and light. Colour is low-key and carefully calibrated as in the Ca' d'Oro picture, but warmer.

Shortly after 1500 Diana, Gentile Bellini and Carpaccio each painted a large narrative canvas for the Scuola Grande di S Giovanni Evangelista's series of *Miracles of the True Cross* (Venice, Accad.). Diana's painting of the *Miraculous Cure of the Son of Ser Alvise Finetti* illustrates for the first time the weightier figures and idiosyncratic faces of his later style. These recur in, for instance, a group of singular predella paintings (ex-Longhi Col., Florence; Washington, DC, N.G.A.) and a series of *sacre conversazioni* (e.g. Coral Gables, FL, U. Miami, Lowe A. Mus.; three in Venice, Accad.), in which massive figures are set before or within spacious, geometrically simplified landscapes and all things are linked by the play of silvery light and shadow. They attain a 16th-century monumentality, despite the quirkiness of detail that allies them with such artists as Jacopo de' Barbari and Lorenzo Lotto.

In 1505 Diana and Bastiani were commissioned to paint three giant standards for S Marco 'according to Diana's design' and in 1507 Diana won a competition to paint the standard (*gonfalone*) of the Scuola della Carità in Venice, beating Carpaccio. In 1512 he became president of the painters' guild.

In the paintings of his last ten or fifteen years Diana attempted to keep pace with younger artists such as Cariani and Pordenone, while retaining his formidable individuality. A monumental *Assumption* (Crema, S Maria della Croce) seems to adapt architectural elements from Pordenone and to take on some of his eccentric dynamism, but its spectacular colour and its figure style are Diana's own. Still more extraordinary is the large *Madonna Enthroned with Saints* from the church of S Maria dei Servi in Venice (Venice, Accad.): facial types recall Pordenone, but Diana alone is responsible for the sleek geometry of the architecture, the subtle perfection of lighting, and the beauty and refinement of the silvery colour.

Diana, admired by 16th- and 17th-century writers, has since sometimes been grouped mistakenly with Giovanni Bellini's followers. Like Bastiani, but on a higher level of quality, Diana represented a 'third force' in late 15th-century Venetian painting, independent both of the Bellini and Vivarini workshops. As such he was important for other individualists at the turn of the century, notably Pier Maria Pennacchi, Marco Basaiti, and Lotto. His greatest contribution, however, lies in the originality, sophistication and perfection of his own paintings as formal entities.

BIBLIOGRAPHY

Thieme–Becker

M. Michiel: *Notizie d'opere di disegno* (MS. 16th century); ed. J. Morelli (Bassano, 1800, rev. Bologna, 1884); Eng. trans. of 2nd edn, ed. G. Williamson (London, 1903/*R* New York, 1969), pp. 24, 87

G. Vasari: *Vite* (1550, rev. 2/1568); ed. G. Milanesi (1878–85), iii, pp. 628, 650

C. Ridolfi: *Meraviglie* (1648); ed. D. von Hadeln (1914–24/*R* 1965), pp. 41–2

M. Boschini: *Le ricche miniere della pittura veneziana* (Venice, 1674)

A. Zanetti: *Della pittura veneziana* (Venice, 1771), pp. 70–71

G. Ludwig: 'Archivalische Beiträge zur Geschichte der venezianischen Malerei', *Jb. Kön.-Preuss. Kstsamml.*, xxvi (1905), suppl., pp. 56–61 [essential docs]

R. van Marle: *Italian Schools* (1923–38), xviii, pp. 406–18 [unperceptive but useful]

B. Berenson: *Venetian School* (1957), i, pp. 73–4, pl. 376–83

A. Paolucci: 'Benedetto Diana', *Paragone*, cxcix (1966), pp. 3–20 [excellent article]

FRANCIS L. RICHARDSON

Diana [Diano], **Giacinto** (*b* Pozzuoli, 1731; *d* Naples, 1804). Italian painter. He is first recorded in 1752 working with Francesco de Mura (1696–1782). Diana's early commissions, for example the ceiling decoration (1755) in the Seminary, Pozzuoli, or the paintings (1758–9) in the apse and vault of S Pietro Martire, Naples, depicting, respectively, *St Catherine of Siena Predicting the Return of the Holy See to Rome*, the *Triumph of the Doctrine of St Thomas Aquinas* and the *Miraculous Image of St Dominic at Soriano*, show de Mura's strong influence on Diana's compositions and use of colour. In 1763, 1768 and 1776 Diana worked in S Agostino della Zecca in Naples (*Dedication of the Temple at Jerusalem* and a *Deposition*). Further Neapolitan commissions included the Ospedale di S Maria della Pace (1764) and some rooms in the Palazzo Serra di Cassano. The influence of Roman painters, in particular Pompeo Batoni and Luigi Vanvitelli (whose portrait by Diana is in the Palazzo Reale, Caserta), is evident in the more direct approach to composition and greater poise of the figures in these works. Diana probably absorbed these influences during a sojourn in Rome *c*. 1760. His style, however, remains essentially a Neapolitan interpretation of Roman classicism, with its rich use of colour and grand, but not pompous, compositions. He became professor at the Accademia del Disegno in 1773 but nonetheless maintained his prolific output. Later commissions included work at the Santa Trinità dei Pellegrini, Naples (1778), Lanciano Cathedral (1785–90), the Palazzo Cellamare, Naples (1780s), the Congrega dei Bianchi, San Potito (1791), and the Palazzo Martinelli Bianchi, Chieti (1796).

BIBLIOGRAPHY
L. Mortari: 'Pittori settecenteschi napoletani nel Molise e a Chieti', *Napoli Nob.*, n. s. 2, xv/2 (1978–9), pp. 50–56

N. Spinosa: 'Neapolitan Painting under Charles and Ferdinand Bourbon: Continuity and Crisis within a Tradition' and 'Giacinto Diana', *The Golden Age of Naples: Art and Civilisation under the Bourbons, 1734–1805* (exh. cat. by R. Causa and others, Detroit, MI, Inst. A.; Chicago, IL, A. Inst.; 1981–2), i, pp. 55–71, 94–6

ALEXANDER KADER

Diane de Poitiers, Duchesse de Valentinois (*b* Poitiers, 1499; *d* Anet, Eure-et-Loir, 1566). French noblewoman and patron. She was the daughter of Jean de Poitiers, Comte de Saint-Vallier, and married Louis de Brézé, Grand Seneschal of Normandy (*d* 1531), subsequently becoming a Lady in Waiting. In 1536 she became the mistress of the Dauphin (the future Henry II), and they, together with the Constable of France, Anne de Montmorency, became for a time the centre of opposition to Francis I; this was the cause of Diane's temporary disgrace (1541–3). On the death of Francis I in 1547 she was the central figure in the reorganization of the royal household. In 1548 she was created Duchesse de Valentinois and was regarded as one of Henry II's counsellors. Although the King, who had married Catherine de' Medici in 1533, was 20 years Diane's junior, he remained her lover until his death in 1559, wearing her colours of black and white and including her initials in the royal monogram. When the widowed Queen Catherine became Regent, she exiled Diane from the court and took the château of Chenonceaux away from her; Diane then retired to her Château of ANET.

Diane de Poitiers was a great patron of the arts. She entrusted the architect Philibert de L'Orme with the construction of Anet (1547–52). Today only the entrance and chapel remain, the central façade having been reconstructed at the Ecole des Beaux-Arts in Paris. De L'Orme became Surintendant des Bâtiments for Henry II and was responsible in particular for the modifications to Fontainebleau and the bridge at the château of CHENONCEAUX.

Diane de Poitiers was her age's symbol of femininity. Her legendary beauty was celebrated by the most renowned poets, among them Joachim du Bellay and Pierre de Ronsard. In the realm of the plastic arts she inspired the renewed iconographic development of the subject of the goddess Diana, starting with the decoration of Anet. There were sculptures by Benvenuto Cellini on the gateway (1543; plaster casts, Paris, Louvre) and a fountain statue of *Diana* by Germain Pilon (1558; Paris, Louvre). Inside there were tapestries of *Diana the Huntress* after cartoons by Luca Penni and a picture gallery, now destroyed but known to have contained landscapes and portraits of Diana both old and young, nude in the Antique manner, or richly dressed. The only surviving work appears to be a portrait by François Clouet, *Lady at her Toilet*, called 'Diane de Poitiers' (Washington, DC, N.G.A.). Clouet's *Diana Bathing* (Rouen, Mus. B.-A.), known in various versions, also seems to depend on a lost original from Anet.

BIBLIOGRAPHY
P. Erlanger: *Diane de Poitiers* (Paris, 1955)

F. Bardon: *Diane de Poitiers et le mythe de Diane* (Paris, 1963)

A. Chastel: 'Diane de Poitiers: L'Eros de la beauté froide', *Figures, fables et formes*, i (Paris, 1966, rev. 1980), pp. 263–72

L'Ecole de Fontainebleau (exh. cat., ed. Sylvie Béguin; Paris, Grand Pal., 1972)

SOPHIE BIASS-FABIANI

Diaper. All-over decoration of repeated geometric patterns such as squares or lozenges, which sometimes contain foliate ornament. Diaper can be found on metalwork, sculpture, painting and textiles as well as architecture. An early architectural example is seen in such Roman masonry patterns as *opus reticulatum*, which was often imitated in Romanesque architecture, for example on the choir gallery tympana of Peterborough Cathedral (*c*. 1107). In the Gothic period architectural diaper took the form of low-relief carving as at St Nicaise (*c*. 1231), Reims, and at Westminster Abbey (begun *c*. 1245; see fig.). Other buildings, such as the Sainte-Chapelle in Paris (completed 1248; *see* PARIS, §V, 2(i)) were painted or drawn from other media, particularly such metal reliquaries as the Three Kings' shrine in Cologne Cathedral (*c*. 1198; *see* NICHOLAS OF VERDUN).

Diapering was commonly used as background in both Romanesque and Gothic painting. Early examples, such as the *Ascension* page (*c.* 1100) from the Sacramentary of Limoges Cathedral (Paris, Bib. N., MS. lat. 9438, fol. 84*v*) also seem to be influenced by metalwork. Later diaper in such Gothic manuscripts as the *Battle of David and Goliath* miniature from the Breviary of Philip the Fair (Paris, Bib. N., MS. lat. 1023, fol. 7*v*) of *c.* 1296 by MASTER HONORÉ may be drawn from either metalwork or architectural interiors. Other examples, such as the Rucellai *Madonna* (*c.* 1285; Florence, Uffizi) by DUCCIO, illustrate how the motif was used in textiles. As wall hangings these may be the source for the use of diaper in painting. The use of this background pattern in painting is a reminder of the extensive decoration and rich colour that have been lost from medieval interiors.

BIBLIOGRAPHY
R. Branner: *Saint Louis and the Court Style in Gothic Architecture* (London, 1965)
R. Martin: *Textiles in Daily Life in the Middle Ages* (Cleveland, OH, 1985)
C. Wilson and others: *Westminster Abbey* (London, 1986)

LISA A. REILLY

Diaphanorama. Illusionistic stage show in which the transition from one scene to the next was effected by a change in lighting on translucent panoramas painted on canvas. The art form was developed *c.* 1821 by Louis Daguerre from the *Diaphanorama* by Franz Niklaus König, a series of pictures painted in oil on paper mounted on wooden screens. Daguerre's Diaphanorama was the precursor of the DIORAMA, which he invented in 1822 with the painter Charles-Marie Bouton.

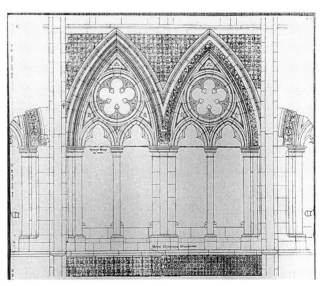

Diaper decoration in the choir triforium, Westminster Abbey, London, begun *c.* 1245; detail from a drawing by Sydney Vacher, 1876

Dias, Antonio (*b* Campina Grande, 22 Feb 1944). Brazilian painter. In 1958 he moved to Rio de Janeiro where he soon began to produce works influenced by the symbolic Constructivism of Joaquín Torres García. From 1964 he moved away from flat surfaces towards a greater use of space in emotionally charged montages that make aggressive use of images and materials. After winning a prize at the Paris Biennale of 1965 he went to Europe and from 1968 lived in Milan. There he adopted a conceptual approach in paintings, videos, films, records and artist's books, using each medium to question the meaning of art. After a visit to Nepal in 1977 and under the influence of Jung, a reassessment of his work led to the incorporation of a symbolic dimension, in pictures often drawn on handmade Nepalese paper (*Song of the Axe*, ferrous oxide, shellac, graphite, metallic pigment, 1982; São Paulo, Robert Blocker priv. col.).

WRITINGS
Some Artists Do, Some Not (Brescia, 1974)

BIBLIOGRAPHY
P. Duarte: *Antonio Dias* (Rio de Janeiro, 1979)
S. Sproccati: *Antonio Dias* (Milan, 1983)
R. Brito: *Antonio Dias* (Rio de Janeiro, 1985)

ROBERTO PONTUAL

Dias, B.H. *See under* POUND, EZRA.

Dias, Cícero (*b* Recife, 5 May 1907). Brazilian painter. In 1925 he moved to Rio de Janeiro, where for a short time he studied architecture at the Escola Nacional de Belas Artes. There he came into contact with artists and intellectuals of the modernist movement, including Mário de Andrade, and had his first show in 1927. His preferred medium until the beginning of the 1930s was watercolour; several of his watercolours painted between 1927 and 1930 are in the Instituto de Estudos Brasileiros at the University of São Paulo. At the 1931 National Salon of Fine Arts (Rio de Janeiro)—called the 'revolutionary salon' because of its preponderance of avant-garde artists—he exhibited *I Saw the World: It Began in Recife* (watercolour, 2×12 m; Rio de Janeiro, Mus. N. B.A.), a work that already displayed a lyrical, slightly erotic Surrealism that sought to recapture the memory of his childhood in the north-east of Brazil. He became acquainted with Surrealism at first hand only after settling in Paris in 1937. On his return to Paris at the end of World War II after two years spent in Lisbon, he developed a vividly coloured geometric abstraction, joining the Groupe Espace and taking part in exhibitions at the Galerie Denise René. In 1948 he painted an abstract mural in the Ministry of Finance in Recife. By the time of his 1965 São Paulo Biennial retrospective he had returned to figurative art, to imaginary landscapes and portraits in a vehemently regional tropical style. Later figurative works include a series of paintings on the life of *Brother Caneca* (1983–5; Recife, Casa Cult.).

BIBLIOGRAPHY
G. Freyre: 'Dois modernos pintores do Brasil: Cícero Dias e Francisco Brennand', *Humboldt*, 14 (1966)
P. M. Bardi: *Profile of the New Brazilian Art* (Rio de Janeiro, 1970)
M. R. Batista and Y. S. de Lima: *Coleção Mário de Andrade: Artes plásticas* (São Paulo, 1984)
Un Art autre, un autre art (exh. cat. by D. Abadie, Paris, Artcurial, 1984)
R. Pontual: *Entre dois séculos: Arte brasileira do século XX na Coleção Gilberto Chateaubriand* (Rio de Janeiro, 1987)

ROBERTO PONTUAL

Dias, Gaspar (*b* Lisbon, *fl* 1566–90). Portuguese painter. He was an important exponent of Portuguese Mannerism during its consolidatory 'Italianate' phase. He was sent to

Rome with António Campelo on a bursary and in his studies there was strongly influenced by Parmigianino. He returned to Lisbon *c.* 1560; that year he was Examiner of Painters with Diogo de Contreiras, a post he occupied again in 1566. Having also been a page of the royal household, in 1574 he was appointed Painter to the Trading House and House of Mina and India.

Around 1584 Dias was commissioned to paint the altarpiece for the chapel of S Roque in the church of the same name in Lisbon. He produced a large panel of the *Angel Appearing to St Roch* and *St Roch in Prison* on the predella. His finest work, it recalls Parmigianino in the serpentine poses of the saint and the angel, in the agitation and tension of the composition and in his sensitivity in rendering the background with finely drawn architectural settings containing figures. A bistre wash drawing of *SS Peter and Paul* (Lisbon, Mus. N.A. Ant.), in strong chiaroscuro, also shows his knowledge of Parmigianino's work. Many of Dias's paintings that were praised by 19th-century authors are untraced (e.g. *Circumcision*, Celorico da Beira; *Descent from the Cross*, Castanheira, Convento de S António). He spent his late years painting the altarpiece for the church of S Catarina do Monte Sinai (untraced) with scenes from the *Life of St Catherine* (1590); he did not complete it, as he refused to make changes to the figures demanded by the Brotherhood. The commission was transferred to António da Costa.

BIBLIOGRAPHY

F. da Costa: *Antiguidade da arte da pintura* [The antiquity of the art of painting] (MS.; 1696); ed. G. Kubler (New Haven and London, 1967), p. 265

R. dos Santos: 'A pintura da segunda metade do século XVI ao final do século XVII' [Painting from the mid-16th century to the late 17th], *Arte portuguesa*, ed. J. Barreira (Lisbon, 1951), pp. 259–60

V. Serrão: *A pintura maneirista em Portugal* [Mannerist painting in Portugal] (Lisbon, 1982), pp. 59–62

VITOR SERRÃO

Dias, Manuel (*b* ?Lisbon; *d* 1754). Portuguese sculptor. He was a pupil of Manuel Gomes de Andrade. His nickname, 'Pai dos Cristos' (Father of Christs), refers to the many Crucifixes carved in his workshop in the Calçada de Santo André, Lisbon. He became a member of the Irmandade de S Lucas (Fraternity of St Luke) in 1713. He was a capable modeller, but his work tends to lack personality. He produced terracotta *presépio* (Christmas crèche) figures, but he is better known for his carvings in wood. He made two monumental *Crucifixions*, one in the Palace of Mafra and another in Évora Cathedral (both 1736) after the design by Francisco Vieira Lusitano. A third (untraced) was presented by John V to the Tertiaries at the Convent of Mafra, for which Dias also made 14 pedestal figures (now in poor condition), a type in which he specialized. At Mafra he is recorded as having carved two *Praying Angels* (untraced) and *St Francis* and *St Louis of France* (*in situ*).

BIBLIOGRAPHY

A. Raczynski: *Dictionnaire historico-artistique du Portugal* (Paris, 1847)

A. de Carvalho: *A escultura em Mafra* (Mafra, 1950), pp. 24–5

F. de Pamplona: *Dicionário de pintores e escultores*, ii (Lisbon, 1954), p. 203–4

ANTÓNIO FILIPE PIMENTEL

Díaz, Diego Valentín (*b* Valladolid, 1586; *d* Valladolid, Dec 1660). Spanish painter and collector. He was the son and pupil of the painter Pedro Díaz Minaya (*c.* 1555–1624), who worked in Valladolid, the location of Philip III's court from 1600 to 1606. For more than 50 years, Diego Valentín Díaz was Valladolid's most important painter, producing a great number of religious works and portraits containing colourful imagery; many of these are widely dispersed in collections and churches throughout Spain. Although his early works were executed in a style of late Mannerism, he gradually introduced more naturalistic elements, resulting in paintings with precise drawing, a varied but rather dull colouring, an emphasis on decorative details and a sweet expression on the faces of his religious figures. His earliest surviving works are the altarpiece (1608) of the convent of S Catalina, Valladolid, and the *Martyrdom of St Sebastian* and the *Penitent St Peter* (both 1610; Zamora, Hosp. Encarnación). In 1612, with his father and his brothers Francisco Díaz and Marcelo Martínez Díaz, he formed a family workshop. The *Holy Family* (*c.* 1621; Valladolid, Mus. Pasión) is reminiscent of the work of Rubens, while the paintings (e.g. of *Martino de San Lorenzo*) for the altarpiece of S María de la Corte, Oviedo, use strong chiaroscuro and a naturalistic style. In 1647, by then a well-established artist in Valladolid, he acquired the patronage of Niñas Huerfanas (*d* 1653) and helped in the promotion of the fraternity of S Lucas, obtaining commissions to paint their altarpieces. As a portrait painter, he worked for the nobility of Valladolid and painted some of the bishops of the city (e.g. *Don Juan Vigil de Quiñones*, *c.* 1632; Valladolid Cathedral). He also kept himself well informed about events in Seville and Madrid through his correspondence with Velázquez and Francisco Pacheco and was involved in other preoccupations such as collecting; his collection included engravings by Raphael. His last painting (the *Immaculate Conception*, *c.* 1660) was the altarpiece of the Palacio de Campos, Palencia. It was executed mostly by his pupil Bartolomé Santos (*fl* 1661), as Díaz died in 1660, the year the contract was drawn up.

BIBLIOGRAPHY

E. Valdivieso González: *La pintura en Valladolid en el siglo XVII* (Valladolid, 1971)

J. Urrea and J. C. Brasas: 'Epistolario del pintor Diego Valentín Díaz', *Bol. Semin. Estud. A. & Arqueol.*, xlvi (1980), pp. 435–49

ISMAEL GUTIÉRREZ PASTOR

Díaz, Luis (*b* Guatemala City, 5 Dec 1939). Guatemalan painter, sculptor, printmaker and architect. Although he studied architecture at the Universidad de San Carlos in Guatemala (1959–61), as an artist he was essentially self-taught. One of the most important abstract artists in Guatemala, he worked in a variety of media, favouring new materials and bold geometric forms. As an architect he co-designed two important public buildings in Guatemala City: a library at the Universidad de San Carlos known as the Edificio de Recursos Educativos (1969; with Augusto de León Fajardo), and the Instituto de Fomento Municipal (1973). He produced a number of murals in Guatemala City: *Genesis* (clay, 5 sq. m) in the residence of the architect Max Holzheu; *Genesis* (1972; Banco Inmobiliario Col.); *Nest of Quetzals* (acrylic, 1974; Inst. Fomento Mun.); *Fissure* (concrete, 9 sq. m, 1975; Casa Salem); *Untitled* (concrete and mirror, 160 sq. m, 1980) at the Cámara Guatemalteca de la Construcción; and *Quetzal* (aluminium, 1.35×7.2 m, 1984; Banco del Quetzal Col.). He exhibited widely as a printmaker, painter and sculptor and established the Galería DS in Guatemala City, one of the first commercial galleries in Guatemala to promote modern art. Examples of his work can be found in the Museo Nacional de Arte Moderno in Guatemala City.

BIBLIOGRAPHY

L. Méndez Dávila: *Arte vanguardia Guatemala* (Guatemala City, 1969)
Luis Díaz (Guatemala City, 1989)

JORGE LUJÁN-MUÑOZ

Diaz (de la Peña), (Virgilio) Narcisse [Narcisso] (*b* Bordeaux, 21 Aug 1807; *d* Menton, 18 Nov 1876). French painter. After the death of his Spanish parents he was taken in by a pastor living in Bellevue (nr Paris). In 1825 he started work as an apprentice colourist in Arsène Gillet's porcelain factory, where he became friendly with Gillet's nephew Jules Dupré and made the acquaintance of Auguste Raffet, Louis Cabat and Constant Troyon. At this time he executed his first oil paintings of flowers, still-lifes and landscapes. Around 1827 Diaz is thought to have taken lessons from the Lille artist François Souchon (1787–1857); perhaps more importantly, he copied works by Pierre-Paul Prud'hon and Correggio in the Louvre, Paris, and used their figures and subjects in such later paintings as *Venus and Adonis* and the *Sleeping Nymph* (both Paris, Mus. d'Orsay). He soon became the friend of Honoré Daumier, Théodore Rousseau and Paul Huet. Diaz's pictures exhibited at the Salon from 1831 to 1844 derive from numerous sources, including mythology, as in *Venus Disarming Cupid* (exh. Salon 1837; Paris, Mus. d'Orsay), and literature, as in *Subject Taken from Lewis's 'The Monk'* (exh. Salon 1834; possibly the picture in the Musée Fabre, Montpellier, entitled *Claude Frollo and Esmerelda*). His other themes include a fantastical Orientalism inspired by his admiration for Alexandre-Gabriel Decamps and Eugène Delacroix, as in *Eastern Children* (Cincinnati, OH, Taft Mus.) and such genre scenes as *In a Turkish Garden* (Boston, MA, Mus. F.A.); these are all the more theatrical in that Diaz never travelled in the East. Nevertheless, they display his skill as a colourist and his ability to render light.

From 1835 Diaz regularly stayed in the Forest of Fontainebleau. Although Decamps's influence persisted,

Narcisse Diaz: *Heights of Le Jean de Paris*, oil on canvas, 0.86×1.06 m, 1867 (Paris, Musée d'Orsay)

Diaz sought greater precision in his composition and executed numerous studies of tree trunks inspired by Théodore Rousseau. In *Ferry Crossing with the Effect of the Setting Sun* (exh. Salon 1837; Amiens, Mus. Picardie) he used the sombre tones of Dutch 17th-century landscapes but alleviated them with chiaroscuro and an effect of transparency. According to Silvestre, Diaz presented his first Fontainebleau subject, *View of the Gorges of Apremont* (untraced), at the Salon of 1837. From 1844 the brilliance of Diaz's flecked colours intensified. The lyricism of his unfinished technique can be appreciated in the numerous landscapes that he executed in the Forest of Fontainebleau, such as the *Pack in the Forest of Fontainebleau* (exh. Salon 1848; Copenhagen, Ordrupgaardsaml.) and the *Forest of Fontainebleau* (1859; U. Rochester, NY, Mem. A.G.). His minutely detailed studies, which recall Dutch painting (e.g. *Study of a Silver Birch*; Paris, Mus. d'Orsay), were executed on the spot and then used to compose finished pictures in the studio. Diaz turned increasingly to gypsy subject-matter, as in *The Gypsies* (exh. Salon 1850–51; Paris, Mus. d'Orsay), using the Forest of Fontainebleau and its foliage, bathed in a shimmering light, as a background for picturesque and imaginary scenes.

In an attempt to satisfy the 19th-century vogue for the *fête galante*, Diaz produced numerous genre scenes and pictures featuring fantastical characters and allegorical nudes. Although such works as *The Clown* (Phoenix, AZ, A. Mus.), after Antoine Watteau's *Gilles* (1720–21; Paris, Louvre), represent Diaz's interpretation of 18th-century painting, the quality of his mythological groups (e.g. *Venus with Cupid on her Knee*, 1851; Moscow, Pushkin Mus. F.A.) suffered from his overabundant production. Diaz's poetical style and technique inspired a number of epithets among Salon critics, from Théophile Thoré's 'heaps of precious stones' to Charles Baudelaire's 'nauseating sweeties and sugary stuff' on the subject of the *Lamentations of Jephthah's Daughter* (exh. Salon 1846; St Petersburg, Hermitage). In response to these criticisms, Diaz executed a picture 4 m in height in 1855; the *Last Tears* (priv. col.) is in a drier style, with heavy contours. It symbolizes souls departing from earth and shedding their last tears before attaining eternal bliss. The last pictures that Diaz sent to the Salon, such as *Don't Enter* (exh. Salon 1859; Paris, Mus. d'Orsay), marked a return to the laboured qualities of his earlier work.

Diaz often reused the same compositions, with the centre of the foreground occupied by a clearing, a pond or a path, framed by rows of trees that disappear into the distance and direct the eye from the centre of the picture towards secondary gleams of light, as in the *Pond under the Oaks* (Paris, Mus. d'Orsay). Diaz's late landscapes express a tormented aspect of nature and a realism that, by way of Rousseau, recalls Salomon van Ruysdael. The light came to have a more tragic quality, as in the leaden sky of the *Heights of Le Jean de Paris* (1867; Paris, Mus. d'Orsay; see fig.), and the composition became more grandiose in the series of landscapes executed towards the end of his life (e.g. the *Threatening Storm*, 1870; Pasadena, CA, Norton Simon Mus.). These works have nothing of the anecdotal about them, with their almost total disregard for the human figure and for civilization, as in *Undergrowth* (1874; Reims, Mus. St-Denis). In 1863 Diaz had met

Claude Monet, Auguste Renoir, Alfred Sisley and Frédéric Bazille, who admired his brilliant colours, and his late landscapes may have influenced the Impressionists.

BIBLIOGRAPHY

T. Silvestre: *Histoire des artistes vivants français et étrangers* (Paris, 1861), pp. 163–78
J. Claretie: 'Notice biographique', *Exposition des oeuvres de N. Diaz* (exh. cat., Paris, Ecole N. Sup. B.-A., 1877)
——: *Peintres et sculpteurs contemporains*, i (Paris, 1882)
Narcisse Diaz de la Peña, 1807–1876 (exh. cat., Paris, Pav. A., 1968)
P. Miquel: *Le Paysage au XIXe siècle*, ii: *L'Ecole de la nature* (Maurs-la-Jolie, 1975), pp. 282–319

VALÉRIE M. C. BAJOU

Díaz Bencomo, Mario (*b* Pinar del Río, 26 July 1953). Cuban painter, active in the USA. He left Cuba at the age of 14 as a political exile, going first to Spain and then in 1968 to Miami, where he settled. There he became a leading figure in the Cuban–American generation of artists that emerged in Miami during the 1970s (*see* LATIN-AMERICAN ARTISTS OF THE USA, §4). Working in acrylic, he was concerned with the strength of colour and texture; thematically topography and distance are the key elements of his flat, Expressionist abstraction. The influences of Peruvian painter Fernando de Szyszlo and of the Catalan Antoni Tàpies, as well as of the New York School, are visible in his work. His *Wind Paintings* (e.g. 1986; Miami, FL, Barbara Gilman) address motion and change, themes latent in his work after 1980.

BIBLIOGRAPHY

P. Plagens: 'Report from Florida: Miami Slice', *A. America*, lxxiv/11 (1986), pp. 27–39
Outside Cuba (exh. cat. by I. Fuentes Pérez and others, New Brunswick, NJ, Rutgers U., Zimmerli A. Mus.; New York, Mus. Contemp. Hisp. A.; Oxford, OH, Miami U., A. Mus.; Ponce, Mus. A.; and elsewhere; 1987–9), pp. 254–7

RICARDO PAU-LLOSA

Díaz Caneja, Juan Manuel. *See* CANEJA, JUAN MANUEL.

Díaz [Díez] del Valle, Lázaro (*b* Leon, 3 April 1606; *d* Madrid, 27 Feb 1669). Spanish writer. He was a court servant, a singer in the Capilla Real and Chaplain to Charles II of Spain. He was a friend of Velázquez, whom he revered, as well as the painters Sebastián de Herrera Barnuevo, Pedro de la Torre and Juan Escalante. He wrote various works that are in manuscript form, most notably the three-volume *Noticia histórica del principio de la Inquisición y la historia y nobleza del Reino de León y Principado de Asturias* (vol. 1 destr. 1939; vol. 2 untraced; vol. 3, London, BL). His writings on art were collected in *Varones ilustres* (1656 and 1659; Madrid, Consejo Sup. Invest. Cient.), an unsystematic accumulation of notes taken from Italian and Spanish theoretical treatises. Its main function is to show the nobility and ingenuousness of painting and it continues the approach of Gaspar Gutiérrez de los Ríos and Juan Alonso de Butrón. This work was later a source for the writers Acisclo Antonio Palomino y Velasco and Juan Agustín Ceán Bermúdez. Díaz del Valle also wrote some useful short biographies of Madrid painters such as Antonio de Pereda, Alonso Cano, Francisco Camilo and Antonio Arias Fernández. These follow the model of Vasari's *Vite*.

BIBLIOGRAPHY
J. L. Castrillon : 'D. Lazaro Díaz del Valle y de la Puerta', *Bol. Acad. Hist.*, xii (1888), pp. 471–9
F. J. Sánchez Cantón: *Siglo XVII*, ii of *Fuentes literarias para la historia del arte español* (Madrid, 1933)
Varia Velazqueña : Homenaje a Velásquez en el III centenario de su muerte, ii (Madrid, 1960), pp. 59–62
J. A. Gaya Nuño: *Historia de la crítica de arte en España* (Madrid, 1975)
F. Calvo Serraller: *La teoría de la pintura en el siglo de oro* (Madrid, 1981)
A. BUSTAMANTE GARCÍA

Díaz de Oviedo, Pedro (*fl* 1487–1510). Spanish painter. He worked in Navarre and Aragon. His paintings, in oil on panel, show the influence of northern European Gothic acquired through his contact with Castilian and Aragonese painters, although German engravings, such as those by Martin Schongauer, were also a source of inspiration. He painted highly expressive and dramatic religious scenes, using brilliant colour and gold applied over stucco in relief as decoration for the haloes and clothing of the sacred figures.

Pedro Díaz de Oviedo executed the high altar retable of the Colegiata, Tudela, with Diego del Aguila. Completed in 1494, it depicts scenes from the *Life of St Mary*, the patron saint of the church. Also in Navarre is the altarpiece of *St Mark* in the church of the Virgen del Romero, Cascante, finished in 1510, which shows signs of artistic decline. His works in Aragon, for example the altarpieces of *St James the Greater* (1497) and *St Andrew* for Tarazona Cathedral (Saragossa), must be dated between these paintings. He also painted the high altar retable for S Lorenzo, Huesca (1495–1500), of which four panels survive (Huesca, Mus. Arqueol. Prov., and Huesca, Banco Bilbao/Vizcaya) and display his best style. All his works show that he was a faithful interpreter of the naturalistic style that originated in the Netherlands.

BIBLIOGRAPHY
M. Sanz Artibucilla: 'Pedro de Oviedo, pintor de retablos', *Rev. Ecles.*, iii (1931), pp. 68–73
J. R. Castro: 'Pedro Díaz de Oviedo y el retablo mayor de la catedral de Tudela', *Príncipe Viana*, 7 (1942), pp. 121–37
M. C. Lacarra Ducay: 'Pintores aragoneses en Navarra durante el siglo XV', *Príncipe Viana*, 154–5 (1979), pp. 81–6
——: 'Pedro Díaz de Oviedo', *Aragon y la pintura del Renacimiento* (exh. cat., Saragossa, Inst. Mus. Camón Aznar, 1980), pp. 45–52
——: 'Influencia de Martin Schongauer en los primitivos aragoneses', *Bol. Inst. Mus. Camón Aznar*, xvii (1984), pp. 15–39 (24–5)
M. C. LACARRA DUCAY

Díaz de Vivar y de Mendoza, Rodrigo. *See under* MENDOZA.

Diaz Morales, Ignacio (*b* Guadalajara, 16 Nov 1905). Mexican architect, teacher and urban planner. He studied civil engineering and architecture at the Escuela Libre de Ingenieros, Guadalajara, between 1921 and 1928. From 1927 he was responsible for redesigning and completing the vaults of the Expiatory Temple, Guadalajara, a Gothic Revival building begun in 1897 by Adamo Boari Dandini. In 1936 Diaz Morales began independently to plan the Cruz de Plazas, a group of four open spaces around Guadalajara Cathedral. The plan, which included large fountains, was accepted around 1947 and completed in 1957. In November 1948 Diaz Morales founded the Escuela de Arquitectura of the Universidad de Guadalajara, and in 1950 he travelled to Europe and recruited a group of teachers of architecture and art, including the sculptor Mathias Goeritz. From 1949 he also presided over the technical committee responsible for preserving and restoring the frescoes of José Clemente Orozco in Guadalajara, and in 1959 he was made responsible for the restoration of the Teatro Degollado, Guadalajara. He was Director of the Escuela de Arquitectura until 1960 and taught there until 1963.

BIBLIOGRAPHY
L. Gómez and M. A. Quevedo: 'Testimonios vivos: 20 arquitectos', *Cuad. Arquit. & Conserv. Patrm. A.*, 15–16 (1981), pp. 111–14
ALBERTO GONZÁLEZ POZO

Diaz Morante, Pedro (*b* Alcázar de San Juan, *c.* 1565; *d* Madrid, 1636). Spanish calligrapher and woodcutter. He lived in Toledo from 1591 and settled in Madrid in 1612. Renowned as a calligrapher, he devised a new system for teaching writing, the *Arte nueva de escribir*. In collaboration with Adrian Boon (*fl* 1602–18) he produced a series of plates for this work, showing ornate examples of calligraphy. These were realized using a woodcut technique, usually in negative, as a white image on a black background. Interspersed with human figures, animals, birds, fish and ornamental lettering, they are the last Spanish examples of didactic woodcuts, a technique that was to become relegated to portraying popular subjects. A copper-plate engraving of the *Sea of Love*, signed *Morante* and dated 1636, may be by a son of the same name.

WRITINGS
Arte nueva de escribir, 5 vols (Madrid, 1616–31)

BIBLIOGRAPHY
Ceán Bermúdez
E. Cotarelo y Mori: *Diccionario de calígrafos españoles* (Madrid, 1914–16)
J. Ainaud de Lasarte: *Grabado*, A. Hisp., xviii (Madrid, 1962), p. 279
A. Gallego: *Historia del grabado en España* (Madrid, 1979), p. 142
E. Páez Rios: *Repertorio* (1981–3)
BLANCA GARCÍA VEGA

Diba, Kamran (Tabatabai) (*b* Tehran, 5 March 1937). Iranian architect, urban planner and painter. He studied architecture at Howard University, Washington, DC, graduating in 1964 and then adding a year of post-graduate studies in sociology. He returned to Tehran in 1966 and a year later became President and Senior Designer of DAZ Consulting Architects, Planners and Engineers. DAZ undertook numerous and diverse projects in Iran and grew rapidly; it had a staff of 150 in 1977. Diba worked entirely in the public sector in Iran and was interested in both vernacular traditions and the demands of modern urban society, especially for human interaction. The partially completed Shushtar New Town (1974–80) in Khuzestan, where he was both architect and planner, owes much of its success to the traditional construction patterns and building types used by Diba in place of the Western-style planning favoured by the authorities. The town, planned for a population of 30,000, was designed along a central communications spine with crossroads and public squares around which small neighbourhoods were established, with gardens and bazaars to encourage community life. The poetic brick-clad buildings produce a unified architecture that is elegant, and the sequencing of the urban spaces is highly refined. Other significant works in Iran include several buildings at Jondi Shapour University (1968–76) at Ahvaz, and what is perhaps his best-known work, the Museum of Contemporary Art (1976), Tehran, which is lit by half-vaults in the roof reminiscent of the traditional wind catchers of the Middle East. He was also the museum's founder and first Director (1976–8). In addition he designed a number of small mosques. Diba served as urban planning consultant to Iran's Ministry of Housing and Urban Development and his firm developed master plans for a number of cities including Khorramshahr, an important port in the Persian Gulf, where he collaborated with the Greek planner Constantinos A. Doxiades. In 1977 he left Iran to live in Paris and Washington, DC, working in private practice. His projects included speculative housing schemes in Virginia and hotel developments in Spain. In 1977 he was Visiting Critic at Cornell University, Ithaca, NY. As a painter, Diba had several one-man shows in Iran; he was also a collector of and a dealer in contemporary Western paintings.

WRITINGS

Kamran Diba: Buildings and Projects (Stuttgart, 1981)

BIBLIOGRAPHY

J. M. Dixon: 'Cultural Hybrid—Tehran Museum of Contemporary Art', *Prog. Archit.*, lix/5 (1978), pp. 68–71

Y. Pontoizeau: 'Architectures iraniennes', *Archit. Aujourd'hui*, cxcv (1978), pp. 5–16

'Garden of Niavaran', *Mimar*, viii (1983), pp. 42–7

'Shustar New Town', *Space for Freedom: The Search for Architectural Excellence in Muslim Societies*, ed. I. Serageldin (London, 1989), pp. 156–65

HASAN-UDDIN KHAN

Dibbets, Jan [Gerardus Johannes Maria] (*b* Weert, 9 May 1941). Dutch photographer and conceptual artist. From 1959 to 1963 he trained as an art teacher at the Akademie Bouwkunst in Tilburg, while at the same time taking painting lessons with Jan Gregoor in Eindhoven from 1961 to 1963. He had his first one-man show in 1965 at Galerie 845 in Amsterdam. He then taught in Enschede until 1967 when he studied at the St Martin's School of Art in London on a British Council scholarship. Until then he had produced monochrome, Minimalist paintings and was influenced by Mondrian, Vermeer and Pieter Saenredam, but after the period in London he worked primarily with photography. He began with a series called *Perspective Corrections* (1967–9), characterized by optical effects. In *Perspective Correction—My Studio II, I: Square on Floor* (1969; Amsterdam, Stedel. Mus.), for example, he placed a white trapezium on the floor of his studio. He then photographed it from an angle that made it appear square and consequently detached from its surroundings.

Dibbets then moved on to works consisting of numerous photographs, often sequential. In the mid-1970s he concentrated on *Structure Pieces*, derived from the surface of materials like water and leaves. *Waterstudy of Structures* (1975; Canberra, N.G.), for example, presents a series of photographs of rippled water. By their arrangement they form a unified surface, though each image is slightly different to emphasize the constructive nature of perception. He also produced sequential photographs of architectural features, often set on monochrome backgrounds, as in *Octagon I* (1982; New York, Guggenheim). After 1984 he was a professor at the Staatliche Kunstakademie in Düsseldorf.

BIBLIOGRAPHY

Jan Dibbets (exh. cat. by R. H. Fuchs, Eindhoven, Stedel. Van Abbemus., 1980)

Jan Dibbets (exh. cat. by R. H. Fuchs and others, Minneapolis, Walker A. Cent., 1987)

□

Dibra, Jakup (Isuf) (*b* Shkodër, 6 June 1878; *d* Shkodër, 15 July 1952). Albanian metalworker and gunsmith. At the age of 15 he was sent as an apprentice to one of the many small workshops in the 'Rus i vogël' (Little Rus) district. After graduating from the School of Arts and Crafts in Shkodër, he devoted his skills to the production and decoration of pistols, muskets, sabres, cartouches, grease-boxes and other weapons. Using such techniques as hammering, casting, etching, filigree work and silver-plating, he became renowned for his fine decorative works that incorporated traditional motifs. About 1909 he opened a small private workshop that handled special commissions. The fire-arms that he made are noted for both their technical precision and their decorative designs. In 1917 he was one of the first craftsmen in Shkodër to obtain a lathe and a modern grindstone, and consequently he was able to produce innovative designs. Some of his finest and most unusual weapons include the *arma bastun* ('walking-stick' rifle) of 1931 (sporting gun, calibre 5.6 mm, composed of 42 pieces assembled without a single screw) with Neo-classical style ornament, geometric patterns and organic motifs, the *arma pipë* ('tobacco-pipe' rifle) of 1937 (calibre 6.35 mm) and the *arma skrivani* ('writing-table' gun) of 1938, which has an intricate and complex design, consisting of five cartridges (calibre 7.62 mm). To fire the gun the user has to depress a trigger shaped like an inkpot. The gun is richly decorated with a central motif of stylized versions of the national flag. The *arma stilograf* ('fountain-pen' gun) of 1949 (calibre 6.35 mm) is also ornamented with national emblems. In 1946 Dibra was a founder-member of the '29 November' Cooperative of Handicraft Works in Shkodër. He is regarded in Albania as one of the outstanding artists of the National Renaissance period.

BIBLIOGRAPHY

Z. Shkodra: *Esnafet shqiptarë* [Albanian corporations] (Tiranë, 1973)

R. Drishti: *Armët dhe armëtarët shqiptarë* [Albanian weapons and gunsmiths] (Tiranë, 1976), pp. 150–53

Z. Shkodra: *Qyteti shqiptar gjatë Rilindjes Kombëtare* [The Albanian town during the National Renaissance] (Tiranë, 1984), pp. 139–57

GJERGJ FRASHËRI

Dick, Alexander (*b* ?Edinburgh, 1791–1800; *d* Sydney, 15 Feb 1843). Australian silversmith of Scottish origin. He probably trained as a silversmith in Edinburgh before emigrating to Australia in 1824. After his arrival in Sydney, he was employed in the workshop of James Robertson (*b* 1781), a watchmaker who also traded in silver. By 1826 Dick was advertising as a gold and silver plate manufacturer, brass-founder and plater. Within two years his workshop staff included two jewellers and two silversmiths, all assigned convicts. In 1829 he was convicted on a charge of receiving stolen spoons and transported to Norfolk Island. Pardoned in 1833, he returned to Sydney where within a few years his expanded workshop offered services in watchmaking, jewellery, gilding and engraving as well as the manufacture of silver plate. Among his commissions was a gold cup (destr.)—possibly the first executed in the colony—made for the Sydney Races in 1834. Dick retired *c.* 1842. His widow, Charlotte Dick (*d* 1875), continued the business until *c.* 1846. From the number and quality of surviving works—predominantly flatware—Dick is considered to be the most accomplished and prolific of the early colonial silversmiths in Australia.

BIBLIOGRAPHY

K. Fahy: 'Alexander Dick—Silversmith', *Descent*, vi/2 (June 1973), pp. 49–57

J. B. Hawkins: *Nineteenth Century Australian Silver*, i (Woodbridge, 1990)

JUDITH O'CALLAGHAN

Dickens, Charles (John Huffam) (*b* Portsmouth, 7 Feb 1812; *d* Gads Hill, Kent, 8 June 1870). English writer. His early experience of the fine arts was restricted. He admired Hans Holbein the younger's *Dance of Death* woodcuts (1538) and the work of William Hogarth and was an occasional visitor to the Dulwich Picture Gallery. In 1844–5 he spent 11 months abroad. *Pictures from Italy* (London, 1846) is vigorously inconoclastic about the Old Masters, castigating hypocrites who profess to admire damaged or incompetent paintings. Dickens's response to Rome was largely hostile, and he greatly preferred Venice, where he delighted in Titian's Assumption of the Virgin altarpiece (1518; S Maria dei Frari) and in Domenico Tintoretto's *Paradise* (1588; Venice, Doge's Pal.), a surprising choice at a time when few rated Tintoretto's work highly. A second visit to Venice in 1853, reflected in *Little Dorrit* (London, 1857), confirmed the impression.

Dickens's friendships with such artists as David Wilkie, Daniel Maclise, Clarkson Stanfield and Augustus Egg influenced his taste in contemporary painting. He occasionally expressed weariness with English genre painting, particularly at the Exposition Universelle of 1855 in Paris, where he preferred the French works, but he never faced the implications of his own disillusionment. In 1850 he violently attacked John Everett Millais's *Christ in the Carpenter's Shop* (1849–50; London, Tate), finding blasphemous realism in the artist's treatment of a religious subject. Dickens worked closely with the illustrators of his own novels, among whom were George Cruikshank, George Cattermole, John Leech, Daniel Maclise, Marcus Stone, Sir Luke Fildes and his son-in-law Charles Allston Collins. His closest association, with HABLOT KNIGHT BROWNE ('Phiz'), began with *The Pickwick Papers* (London, 1837) and continued until 1859.

WRITINGS

'The Spirit of Chivalry', *Shilling Mag.* (1845); repr. in *Miscellaneous Papers*, i (London, 1908), pp. 20–25

Pictures from Italy (London, 1846)

'The Ghost of Art', *Household Words*, i (1850), pp. 385–7

'New Lamps for Old Ones', *Household Words*, i (1850), pp. 265–7

BIBLIOGRAPHY

K. Perugini: 'Charles Dickens as a Lover of Art and Artists', *Mag. A.* (1903), pp. 125–30, 164–9

J. R. Harvey: *Victorian Novelists and their Illustrators* (London, 1970)

G. Reynolds: 'Charles Dickens and the World of Art', *Apollo*, xci (1970), 422–9

J. D. Hunt: 'Dickens and the Traditions of Graphic Satire', *Encounter*, ed. J. D. Hunt (London, 1971), pp. 124–55

M. Hollington: 'Dickens and the Dance of Death', *The Dickensian*, lxxiv (1978), pp. 65–75

M. Steig: *Dickens and Phiz* (Bloomington, 1978)

J. R. Cohen: *Dickens and his Original Illustrators* (Columbus, 1980)

L. Ormond: 'Dickens and Painting: The Old Masters', *The Dickensian*, lxxix (1983), pp. 131–51

——: 'Dickens and Painting: Contemporary Art', *The Dickensian*, lxxx (1984), pp. 2–25

LEONÉE ORMOND

Dickinson, Edwin (Walter) (*b* Seneca Falls, NY, 11 Oct 1891; *d* Cape Cod, MA, 2 Dec 1978). American painter and draughtsman. After moving to New York he studied at the Pratt Institute (1910–11) and then at the Art Students League under William Merritt Chase (1911–13). He lived in Provincetown, MA, during the summers of 1912–14 and then all year round from 1913 to 1917 while working with Charles Hawthorne (1872–1930). After World War I he spent a year in France and Spain before returning to Cape Cod to live (1920–44). One of his early works, *The Anniversary* (1921; Buffalo, NY, Albright–Knox A.G.), shows Dickinson's admiration for the Mannerism in El Greco's *Burial of Count Orgaz* (1586; Toledo, S Tomé), which he had seen in Spain, and his interest in odd, composite spatial relationships and enigmatic combinations of humans and objects.

From 1937 to 1938 Dickinson was in France. His atmospheric landscapes and small pencil drawings were more abstract, the latter often depicting ambiguous figures or unusual angles of vision. In 1944 he moved to New York, where he taught at Cooper Union (1945–9), the Art Students League (from 1945) and the Brooklyn Museum School (1950–58). He also taught later at the Skowhegan summer school (1956–8), ME. In his paintings he became more involved with science in the form of both archaeological subject-matter and perspective drawing. In *Ruin at Daphnae* (1943–53; New York, Met.) he depicted an architectural fantasy that combined archaeological elements with a constantly moving viewpoint. This mixture of real parts, paradoxical viewing position, sensuous, haunting atmosphere and overriding sense of design also characterize his finest drawings after 1950. In 1959 he spent a year in Greece, returning there for the summer during the following years, and made fine pencil drawings of ancient ruins.

BIBLIOGRAPHY

J. I. H. Baur, ed.: *New Art in America: Fifty Painters of the 20th Century* (New York, 1957)

L. Goodrich: *The Drawings of Edwin Dickinson* (New Haven and London, 1963)

——: *Edwin Dickinson* (New York, 1965)

JUDITH A. BARTER

Dickinson, William (*b* London, 1747; *d* Paris, 1823). English engraver and print publisher. He worked first for the painter Robert Edge Pine, exhibiting mezzotints of Pine's pictures at the Society of Artists between 1769 and 1773. He then began publishing some of his own mezzotints independently: his portrait of *Joseph Banks* (Chaloner Smith, no. 4), made in 1774, was the first of 22 excellent mezzotints made after Sir Joshua Reynolds, 12 of which appeared during the 1770s. His 100 or so portrait mezzotints were well drawn and finely scraped; their brilliance was often enhanced by the use of warm brown inks. From 1776 to 1781 Dickinson published prints with Thomas Watson from New Bond Street, London; they engraved and published stipples as well as mezzotints and became the principal publishers of humorous stipples after the amateur artist Henry William Bunbury. In the decade after 1783 Dickinson engraved only two mezzotint portraits, while publishing plates by other engravers, such as his pupil George Keating (1762–1842) and Charles Knight. He bought or commissioned some 30 plates by Francesco Bartolozzi, including the well-known *Resurrection of a Pious Family* (1790), after one of a pair of pictures by the Rev. Matthew William Peters, which Dickinson had purchased and exhibited in 1788; he was one of the first to publish prints after the rustic genre scenes of George Morland. Dickinson eventually overreached himself and was declared bankrupt on 13 April 1793; his stock, including some 400 plates, was auctioned (London, Christie's, 14–20 Feb 1794). He subsequently engraved a few mezzotints, but it was not until he moved to Paris sometime after 1800 that his talents as an engraver found further expression. During his career there he produced some accomplished plates, including the full-length *Mme Talleyrand* (Le Blanc, no. 42) after François Gérard and *Malvina* after Elisabeth Harvey (*fl* 1802–12).

DNB   BIBLIOGRAPHY

C. Le Blanc: *Manuel de l'amateur d'estampes*, ii (Paris, 1856), pp. 125–6
J. Chaloner Smith: *British Mezzotinto Portraits*, i (London, 1878), pp. 171–203
W. G. Menzies: 'William Dickinson and his Work', *Connoisseur*, xxi (1908), pp. 107–110

                              DAVID ALEXANDER

Dicksee, Sir Frank [Francis] **(Bernard)** (*b* London, 27 Nov 1853; *d* London, 17 Oct 1928). English painter and illustrator. He studied in the studio of his father, Thomas Francis Dicksee (1819–95), who painted portraits and historical genre scenes; he then entered the Royal Academy Schools, London, where he was granted a studentship in 1871. He won a silver medal for drawing from the Antique in 1872 and a gold medal in 1875 for his painting *Elijah confronting Ahab and Jezebel in Naboth's Vineyard* (untraced), with which he made his début at the Royal Academy in 1876. He also began to work as an illustrator during the 1870s, contributing to *Cassell's Magazine*, *Cornhill Magazine*, *The Graphic* and other periodicals. During the 1880s he was commissioned by Cassell & Co. to illustrate their editions of Longfellow's *Evangeline* (1882), Shakespeare's *Othello* (1890) and *Romeo and Juliet* (1884).

Dicksee's paintings are executed with textural fluidity and rich orchestrations of colour. They reveal a curious blend of influences, in particular the classicism of Frederic Leighton and the abstracted idealism of G. F. Watts. His predilection for the decorative aspects of painting grew out of his studies with Henry Holiday, a designer of stained glass. He passionately championed the Victorian ideals of High Art and publicly condemned the artistic trends that emerged towards the end of his life. His work covers a wide range of subject-matter and genres, including biblical and allegorical paintings; among those derived from literary sources are *Chivalry* (1885; priv. col., see *The Royal Academy Revisited*, exh. cat. by C. Forbes, New York, Met., 1975, p. 38). He also painted society portraits and social dramas, such as *The Confession* (1896; priv. col., see *Great Victorian Pictures*, exh. cat. by R. Treble, ACGB, 1978, p. 30).

Dicksee was elected ARA in 1881, RA in 1891 and PRA in 1924. He was knighted in 1925 and made KCVO in 1927. His sister Margaret Isabel (1858–1903) and brother Herbert Thomas (1862–1942) were also painters, as was his uncle John Robert Dicksee (1817–1905).

BIBLIOGRAPHY

S. Hodges: 'Mr. Frank Dicksee', *Mag. A.*, x (1887), pp. 217–22
E. R. Dibdin: 'The Art of Frank Dicksee', *A. Annu.* (1905), pp. 1–32 [Christmas issue]
A. Kavanagh: 'Sir Frank Dicksee', *Country Life*, clxxvii (31 Jan 1985), pp. 240–42

                              AMANDA KAVANAGH

Diday, François (*b* Geneva, 12 Feb 1802; *d* Geneva, 28 Nov 1877). Swiss painter and engraver. He trained at the Ecole de Dessin des Beaux-Arts in Geneva, then spent 18 months in Italy before studying with Antoine-Jean Gros in Paris in 1830. Neither France nor Italy made a great impression on him: from his first trip to the Bernese Oberland in 1827 he was certain that he wished to paint Swiss landscapes. His mountain and lake scenes of Geneva, Interlaken and Brienz quickly established his reputation in Geneva as well as abroad. Diday was admired for his breadth of vision and the storm-laden atmosphere of his painting, which was coupled with great topographical accuracy, as in *The Oak and the Reed* (1843; Geneva, Mus. A. & Hist.). He won official recognition in 1840, when his painting *Evening in the Valley* (1848, destr.) was bought by Louis-Philippe; two years later *Bathers* (Basle, Kstmus.) earned him the Légion d'honneur.

Diday's works were particularly popular with aristocratic tourists who wanted souvenir pictures of the best-known beauty spots in Switzerland. His most popular subjects were therefore often repeated several times, and although he did not employ assistants these works are somewhat lacklustre. From the late 1860s he began to be criticized in the press, especially for his use of colour, which was said to be dull and unrealistic. Diday produced engravings after several of his own compositions, collected in *Croquis par Diday* (Geneva, 1843). Among his dozens of pupils was Alexandre Calame; together they dominated the Romantic school of Geneva. On his death he left the majority of his fortune to the city of Geneva to establish the Fondation Diday. The funds were intended for the promotion of young Swiss artists and for the acquisition of their work by the Musée d'Art et d'Histoire of Geneva.

BIBLIOGRAPHY

A. Schreiber-Favre: *François Diday, 1802–77: Fondateur de l'école suisse de paysage* (Geneva, 1942)
M. Huggler: *Der Brienzersee in der Malerei* (Berne, 1980)
Maximilien de Meuron et les peintres de la Suisse romantique (exh. cat., Neuchâtel, Mus. A. & Hist., 1984)

                              PAUL LANG

Diderot, Denis (*b* Langres, Haute-Marne, 5 Oct 1713; *d* Paris, 31 July 1784). French writer, philosopher and critic. He was a man of the most wide-ranging talents: novelist, dramatist, philosopher and writer on science, mathematics and music. In his lifetime he was probably best known as editor of the *Encyclopédie* (1751–65)—an encyclopedic dictionary of the arts, sciences and trades—and came comparatively late to art criticism. Characteristically determined to express a personal view on art and to attempt to justify his judgements, he had his only noteworthy precursor in Etienne La Font de Saint-Yenne; periodical journalism devoted to the arts in 18th-century France yielded no commentator to match Diderot in vigour and independence of mind. He was early acquainted with the writings of Leonardo da Vinci, Roland Fréart, Jean Cousin (i), Roger de Piles and Charles Le Brun, and the theory of drama he published in 1757, the *Entretiens sur 'Le Fils naturel'*, reveals a keen interest in the relations between the visual arts and the theatre. Diderot was convinced that taste is the product of experience and observation, a notion he developed in his *Pensées détachées sur la peinture* (1776–7); his physiological studies for the *Lettre sur les aveugles* (1749) and the *Eléments de physiologie* (1774) persuaded him that the human eye has to be educated to see. He profited from his acquaintance with artists to learn about the technicalities of painting.

The original impetus to Diderot's writing on art came from his friend MELCHIOR GRIMM, who employed him to write on the biennial Salons organized by the Académie Royale de Peinture et de Sculpture in Paris for the *Correspondance littéraire*, from 1759 to 1781. This was a period of transition for French painting in both style and subject-matter, from the 'frivolity' of Rococo to the seriousness of Neo-classicism (*see* FRANCE, §III, 4). The *Correspondance littéraire* was an informal bi-monthly newsletter, privately circulated to subscribers, who included Catherine the Great of Russia and Frederick the Great of Prussia. Its sale was prohibited within Paris, which meant that the *Salons* articles were subject neither to royal censorship nor to the jealous attentions of the Académie Royale and those it protected; Diderot could thus speak his mind freely without fear of reprisal.

Despite his expressed conviction that foreign travel should be undertaken only between the ages of 18 and 21, and although he never went to Italy, Diderot was able to extend his knowledge of European art by visiting Holland, Germany and Russia in the 1770s; additionally, he was familiar with the cabinets of Parisian collectors and had access to the Italian paintings of the Palais Royal and the Rubens gallery of the Palais du Luxembourg. The expertise thus obtained is intermittently evident in the *Salons*, in the comparisons drawn between contemporary painters and such predecessors as Raphael, Nicolas Poussin and the Dutch masters. Yet for all the advantages he derived from his extraordinary pictorial memory—the *Eléments de physiologie* remarks on his ability to conjure up mentally every picture seen in a gallery 20 years previously—Diderot was conscious that his technical competence as a critic lagged far behind his ability to talk enlighteningly about composition, the expression of passion and what he termed the 'idea' behind a work. His friend the sculptor Etienne-Maurice Falconet, with whom he conducted a lively correspondence, despaired at Diderot's propensity to pass value judgements on the basis of the content of art rather than its execution, a tendency particularly apparent in the 1761 *Salon*'s famous commentary on Jean-Baptiste Greuze's *Marriage Contract* (Paris, Louvre). However, this proclivity may partly have resulted from Diderot's reluctance to mystify his intended readers, only a few of whom would have been acquainted with the language of art.

Frequent targets for Diderot's attacks were artists whose canvases flouted the laws of common sense (a deficiency of 'idea') or betrayed a lack of moral purpose. It is on the latter grounds that he repeatedly berated François Boucher and, while conceding that the 'vice' he discerned in the painter's work was an 'amiable' one, called his influence on other artists reprehensible. Thus Jean-Honoré Fragonard, whose historical painting *Coresus and Callirhoë* (Paris, Louvre) of 1765 inspired Diderot to flights of eloquence, was found wanting in the Rococo offering the *Swarm of Cupids* (Paris, Louvre) of 1767, which Diderot described as nothing more than an 'omelette'. Diderot's rage when Boucher was appointed Premier Peintre du Roi in 1765 is of a piece with his conviction that art should be serious in theme and austere of outline, a purity of conception he associated with the Neo-classical current in painting, epitomized in its earlier phase by Joseph-Marie Vien's *The Cupid Seller* (1763; Fontainebleau, Château).

Yet the ambivalence of Diderot's attitude is as clear as the ambiguity of his response to Boucher, for Vien's painting also displays both Rococo prettiness and a certain suggestiveness. Furthermore, if Diderot had, indeed, seen his fill of breasts and buttocks, as he declared in the *Pensées détachées sur la peinture*, it is inconsistent of him to express such lyrical enthusiasm over the works of Greuze (*see* GREUZE, JEAN-BAPTISTE, §§I, 3 and 4, and III), regarding him as a sincere preacher of bourgeois morality, for they frequently included depictions of women in a state of semi-undress or an attitude of sexual provocativeness. But such inconsistency is perhaps best regarded as an aspect of Diderot's celebrated flexibility, the easy acknowledgement of which prevented him from claiming absolute rightness for any judgement he passed in the *Salons* and enabled him to countenance Grimm's arbitrary alterations of whatever he had written. Diderot's perception of Greuze's erotic preoccupations may sometimes appear mistaken—none of his contemporaries saw in the *Girl Weeping over her Dead Bird* (Edinburgh, N.G.) the parable of lost virginity that Diderot detected in it—but it is generally well-founded.

Jean-Siméon Chardin's paintings elicited a more purely aesthetic appreciation from Diderot, frustrating that urge to be practically engaged by art that Friedrich Schiller deplored in him. Just as the subjects Chardin chose necessarily diverted attention from the 'little infamies' of Boucher and his son-in-law Pierre-Antoine Baudouin to a realm of detached contemplativeness, so his technique embraced the world of nature standing apart from the manneredness of academic history painters who painted from memory and training rather than observation. While Chardin was less preoccupied with natural appearance than Diderot contends (a fact betrayed by Diderot's recurrent appeal to the 'magic' pervading his work), his devotion to the real stood out triumphantly against the vapid imaginings of the Rococo style.

The *Salons* reveal, however, both the complexity and the uncertainty of Diderot's attitude to the representation of reality; his occasionally mystified response to Chardin highlighted a state of some aesthetic confusion. In part, the requirement to paint truthfully was seen by him as dependent on the type of painting being executed: still-life, portraiture and genre scenes were subordinate to a rule of representational accuracy, which Diderot relaxed in the case of historical canvases; Greuze's rejected effort at a historical subject, *Septimus Severus Reproaching Caracalla* (Paris, Louvre), was described in the 1769 *Salon* as being deficient in the 'exaggeration' requisite to the mode. However, the ontological question of what a given reality actually is clearly troubled Diderot the philosopher as deeply as it did Diderot the critic. In portraiture, for example, the 'truth' of a visage was seen as ever-shifting, as Diderot remarked in the 1767 *Salon* apropos his own portrait by Louis-Michel van Loo (Paris, Louvre, see fig.); consequently, the artist's goal was to interpret rather than copy, a right Diderot seemed in the *Salon* of 1767 to concede even to the 'marvellous machinist' Maurice-Quentin de La Tour, the author of remarkably faithful portraits. While Diderot's dislike of allegory, shared with the Abbé Jean-Baptiste Dubos of the *Réflexions critiques sur la poésie et sur la peinture* (1719), is explicable in terms of his taste for realism, he is also conscious of the merits of imagination, even in the genre practised by Chardin, and of the necessary incursion of painterly invention into the depiction of certain subjects. He remarks that the passions shown in Deshays's *St Victor* (1761, untraced) have no equivalent in the phenomenal world, and the painter's portrayal of them is therefore mysterious. The requirement for truth, in other words, may ultimately yield to aesthetic values.

The same acknowledgement is made where the mimetic task faced by the artist presents him with certain technical difficulties: rather than paint a tricky light effect, the painter will veil the sun or moon with cloud, so making the most harmonious canvas into a tissue of lies. Diderot allows a degree of deviation from actuality, on the grounds that the painter's sun is not the sun of the universe and that the mark of true greatness in the artist is to reconcile invention with truth. It is for this reason too that he paradoxically permits their own style to those artists whom he adjudges most faithful in the imitation of nature. Artistic depiction is both subjective and conditional on the resources that the medium makes available; even a Chardin can render the world only in pigment. The critic's task is even harder, for he must conjure up in (conventional) language a visual object; that is, imitate at a further remove. Like others of his time, Diderot frequently reflected on the connections between *pictura* and *poesis* but was as often driven in his criticism to declare the impossibility of translating verbally the aspect and essence of a painting or sculpture. Although desiring to be 'grand and voluptuous with Deshays, simple and true with Chardin, delicate with Vien, pathetic with Greuze', he chafed at the problems he faced—and gratefully adopted the expedient of recomposing canvases in order to make them tell a story. Words, he notes in the *Pensées détachées sur la peinture*, are almost never sufficient to convey what one feels, and pictures, he writes in a discussion of Joseph Vernet, should be seen rather than described.

It is perhaps Diderot's discouragement at the difficulty of his critical task, as well as a frustrated awareness that private criticism such as his own could not change the course of painting, that explain the brevity and baldness of his last *Salons*. Yet his best work exploits the expressive possibilities of language to full effect, mingling dialogue, drama and soliloquy and interleaving lyricism with argot, the sublime register with the language of the atelier. If his judgements often strike the reader as primarily literary— as when he praises Greuze for linking together in a single picture a sequence of events about which a novel could have been written—Diderot was strongly persuaded of his own acutely visual imagination. The writing of *La Religieuse* (1760–82) reportedly led him to exclaim 'Son' pittor anch'io!', and the 1767 *Salon* mentions that his artist friends praised his ability, unusual in a man of letters, to conceive of pictorial topics for them to treat. His imagination, he affirmed, had long been subjected to the rules of art by his determined scrutiny of pictures. Diderot was proud of his *Salons*: he wrote to his mistress Sophie Volland that the 1765 commentary was the best thing he had ever written. Although he regarded his criticisms as the testing-ground for ideas that might be false as often as they were true, he also assumed that his reader would in some way learn from them. He had no coherent doctrine of art to offer, acknowledging in his opinions the same mutability that characterizes Vertumnus, the god of change who is the presiding genius of Diderot's celebrated dialogue *Le Neveu de Rameau* (*c.* 1760): moral fervour mingles with sensuality, a taste for control and decorum with a penchant for horror, melodrama and high sentimentality. But in their blending of verve and seriousness, unashamed subjectivity and attention to plastic fact, and in their sustained effort to discover the principles and laws of artistic creation, Diderot's *Salons* deserve to be seen as the pioneering work of modern art criticism.

Denis Diderot by Louis-Michel van Loo, oil on canvas, 810×650 mm, 1767 (Paris, Musée du Louvre)

Diderot's contribution to the spread of information about contemporary art in France had also a practical side: he was responsible for the sale to Catherine the Great of the Gaignat (1769), Crozat de Thiers (1771) and Choiseul (1772) collections.

For portrait bust of Diderot *see* PARIS, fig. 19.

WRITINGS
J. Adhémar and J. Seznec, eds: *Salons* (1759–81), 4 vols (Oxford, 1957–67, rev. 1983)
H. Dieckmann and J. Varloot, eds: *Oeuvres complètes*, xiv (Paris, 1984) [*Salon* of 1765]; xvi (Paris, 1990) [*Salons* of 1767 and 1769]
P. Vernière, ed.: *Oeuvres esthétiques de Diderot* (Paris, 1959) [incl. *Essais sur la peinture* (Paris, 1795) and *Pensées détachées sur la peinture* (Paris, 1798)]

BIBLIOGRAPHY
A. Fontaine: *Les Doctrines d'art en France de Poussin à Diderot* (Paris, 1909)
A. Langen: 'Die Technik der Bildbeschreibung in Diderots *Salons*', *Romanische Forsch.*, lxi (1948), pp. 324–87
J. Proust: 'L'Initiation artistique de Diderot', *Gaz. B.-A.*, n. s. 5., lv (1960), pp. 225–32
M. T. Cartwright: 'Diderot critique d'art et le problème de l'expression', *Diderot Stud.*, xiii (1969)
S. Jüttner: 'Die Kunstkritik Diderots (1759–1781)', *Beitr. Theorie Kst. 19. Jht*, i (1971), pp. 13–29
J. Chouillet: *La Formation des idées esthétiques de Diderot* (Paris, 1973)
E. M. Bukdahl: *Diderot, critique d'art*, i (Copenhagen, 1980)
H. Žmijewska: *La Critique des Salons en France du temps de Diderot (1759–1781)* (Warsaw, 1980)
Diderot et la critique de Salon, 1759–1781 (exh. cat., Langres, Mus. Du Breuil de Saint-Germain, 1984)
Diderot et l'art de Boucher à David (exh. cat., Paris, Hôtel de la Monnaie, 1984)
Diderot et Greuze: Actes du colloque de Clermont-Ferrand: Clermont-Ferrand, 1986
La France et la Russie au siècle des lumières (exh. cat., Paris, Grand Pal., 1986)
M. Delon and W. Drost, eds: *Le Regard et l'objet: Diderot critique d'art* (Heidelberg, 1989)
P. N. Furbank: *Diderot: A Critical Biography* (London, 1992)
ANGELICA GOODDEN

Didot. French family of typographers, printers, publishers and collectors. The first to settle in Paris was Denis Didot (2nd half of 17th century), whose son François Didot (1689–1759) founded in 1713 the family publishing business. His sons François-Ambroise Didot (1730–1804) and Pierre-François Didot (1731–93) developed the business, adding a type foundry and a paper-mill. The elegance of their publications brought them the patronage of the brothers of Louis XVI: Monsieur (later Louis XVIII) and the Comte d'Artois (later Charles X). The sons of François-Ambroise included (1) Pierre Didot, a publisher, among whose illustrators were some of the most distinguished artists of the day, and Firmin Didot (1764–1836), who designed the Didot typeface for his brother's use. Firmin Didot's son (2) Ambroise Firmin-Didot was a notable collector of prints. The cadet branch of the family, Didot Jeune, the descendants of Pierre-François Didot, included (3) Saint Marc Didot, who assembled a fine collection of paintings.

(1) Pierre Didot (*b* Paris, 25 Jan 1761; *d* Paris, 31 Dec 1853). Typographer, printer and publisher. He was the son of François-Ambroise Didot, whom he succeeded in 1789 in the family publishing business. He hoped to surpass Giambattista Bodoni (1740–1813) as typographer; he was later to buy the Baskerville founts from the dramatist Pierre-Augustin-Caron de Beaumarchais. He is best remembered for producing fine illustrated books, directly inspired by John Boydell's Shakespeare Gallery, for which, with his friend Jacques-Louis David as artistic director, he drew on the services of some of the best contemporary artists. Between 1798 and 1801 he brought out a series of five large folios, known as the Louvre editions, because in 1797 he had been given the privilege of premises there, formerly occupied by the Imprimerie Royale.

The first publication was a two-volume edition of Virgil, for which illustrations were commissioned from David but delegated to François Gérard and Anne-Louis Girodet. The second, an edition of Horace (1799), was illustrated by Charles Percier. In 1801–5 eight artists contributed to a famous three-volume edition of Racine's plays: Pierre-Paul Prud'hon (the frontispiece); Jean-Guillaume Moitte (*La Thébaïde*); Antoine-Denis Chaudet (*Britannicus, Esther* and *Athalie*); Girodet (*Andromaque, Phèdre*); Gérard (*Alexandre le Grand, Bajazet, Iphigénie*); Pierre Peyron (*Mithridate*); Gioacchino Giuseppe Serangeli (1768–1852) (*Bérénice*); and Nicolas-Antoine Taunay (*Les Plaideurs*). Most of the designs were, however, by Gérard, Girodet and Chaudet. Didot's funding probably came from printing *assignats* (banknotes current during the French Revolution), in collaboration with David; a promised government subsidy failed, and the Racine did not prove profitable. Years later many of the 250 copies of each volume were still unsold. Most of the original drawings were bought by Schroth after the Firmin-Didot sale of 1814 and subsequently dispersed (examples Paris, Louvre; Paris, Ecole N. Sup. B.-A.; Angers, Mus. B.-A.; Lille, Mus. B.-A.; Pontoise, Mus. Pissarro; Nantes, Mus. B.-A.). Didot's later productions included Vivant Denon's *Voyage en Egypte* (1808–17), and the *Voyage pittoresque et romantique dans l'ancienne France* by Charles Nodier, I. Taylor and A. de Cailleux (from 1820) included contributions by Gericault, Richard Parkes Bonington and Louis Daguerre and was, for a post-classical generation, an eloquent pictorial expression of the new literary sensibilities of its day.

(2) Ambroise Firmin-Didot (*b* Paris, 20 Dec 1790; *d* Paris, 22 Feb 1876). Publisher and collector, nephew of (1) Pierre Didot. The eldest son of Firmin Didot, he inherited his family's scholarly and bibliophile tastes. He began to collect paintings, books and particularly prints; beginning with early German woodcuts, he expanded into the field of Old Master prints and later to those of the French 18th century. In 1829, two years after succeeding his father in the family business, he purchased all Giovanni Battista Piranesi's plates. One set of the edition he published from these was presented to the British Museum, London, in 1865. Firmin-Didot sold the plates in 1839 to Pope Gregory XVI for 20,000 francs and a choice of prints from the Vatican collection of plates, the Calcografia Camerale, to which the Piranesi plates were transferred. After Firmin-Didot's death, his print collection was sold at auction in Paris (16 April to 12 May 1877); G. Pawlowski published a catalogue raisonné of this collection in seven volumes.

(3) Saint Marc Didot [Didot de Saint Marc] (*d* Paris, 1835). Publisher, art historian and collector, cousin of (1) Pierre Didot. He was the son of Pierre-François Didot and thus belonged to the junior branch of the family. One of his sisters married Jacques-Henri Bernardin de Saint-Pierre (1737–1814), whose novel *Paul et Virginie*, illustrated by Prud'hon, was published by Didot in 1806. Under the guidance of Jean-Baptiste-Pierre Le Brun, Didot became a connoisseur, collector and art historian: he began to collect in 1795. His tastes were conventional for the period: 17th-century Dutch artists and contemporary French figures who followed in their footsteps, such as Jean-Louis Demarne, Jean-Baptiste Mallet and Louis-Léopold Boilly; *The Fountain* by Chardin (priv. col.); and some minor works more particularly in the Didot taste, by Anne-Louis Girodet, Jacques-Louis David, Prud'hon and Jean-Auguste-Dominique Ingres.

BIBLIOGRAPHY

P. L. Jacob: *Collection des cinquante-sept estampes pour les oeuvres de Racine: Edition du Louvre par les premiers artistes de la République française avec une notice historique* (Paris, 1877)
Le Néo-classicisme français: Dessins des musées de province (exh. cat., ed. Jean Lacambre; Paris, Grand Pal., 1974)
C. M. Osborne: *Pierre Didot the Elder and French Book Illustration, 1759–1822* (New York, 1985)
O. Speciale: 'Dai Firmin Didot alla Calcografia: Vicende dei rami di Piranesi dai documenti dell'archivio di stato di Roma', *Piranesi tra Venezia e l'Europa*, ed. A. Bettagno (Florence, 1988)

LINDA WHITELEY

Didron, Adolphe-Napoléon (*b* Hautvilliers, nr Reims, 13 March 1806; *d* Paris, 13 Nov 1886). French archaeologist and journalist. After studying at the seminaries at Meaux and Reims, he moved to Paris in 1826 to learn Greek and Latin, and taught history to support himself. In 1831 he was encouraged by his mentor and friend Victor Hugo (1805–85) to undertake his first archaeological field trip to Normandy. He went on to become one of the founders in France of the science of medieval archaeology, and as Secretary of the Historical Commission of Arts and Buildings he published the results of its work from 1835 to 1852 in the *Bulletin Archéologique*: in 1844 he founded the *Annales Archéologiques*, and he remained its editor-in-chief until his death. His research was based on the study of iconography and topographical data; his accurate use of a specialized vocabulary, attention to the evidence of his finds and its careful illustration established him as one of the most original medievalists of his time.

Alongside his scientific activities Didron undertook several enormous publishing projects, as well as establishing a bookshop in 1845, a factory specializing in stained glass (1849) and another producing religious ornaments in bronze (1858). He became a great advocate of the Gothic Revival style, which he presented, whenever its inspiration could be traced to 13th-century exemplars, as the ultimate in Christian art.

Didron's objective was not only to breathe new life into contemporary architecture and the decorative arts through the work of the archaeologists: it was also to arouse an awareness of the medieval heritage, and so prevent the unnecessary demolition or excessive restoration of the monuments and the erection of aggressively modernist architecture. It must, however, be admitted that religious art remained impervious to his influence. The medievalist ideals he championed so vigorously produced not a single major work in the field of French decorative art, and the mainstream of 19th-century religious painting continued on its course without him.

WRITINGS
Monographie de Notre Dame de Brou (Lyon, 1842)
Iconographie chrétienne: Histoire de Dieu (Paris, 1844; Eng. trans., 2 vols, London, 1851–86)
Statistique du département de la Marne (Paris, 1847)

BIBLIOGRAPHY
F. F. de Guilhermy: 'Didron', *An. Archéol.*, xxv (1865), pp. 378–95
C. Brisac and J. M. Leniaud: 'Adolphe-Napoléon Didron, ou les médias au service de l'art chrétien', *Rev. A.* [Paris], lxxvii (1987), pp. 33–42

JEAN-MICHEL LENIAUD

Didyma [Branchidai; now Didim]. Ancient Greek oracular sanctuary on the west coast of Asia Minor (now Turkey), which flourished from the 7th century BC to the 2nd century AD. The site is on an exposed peninsula 75 m above sea level, *c.* 20 km south of Miletos.

Didyma was originally a spring sanctuary of the indigenous Carians (Herodotus: I.clvii.3), antedating the Ionian colonization of the coast in the 11th–10th century BC (Pausanias: VII.ii.6). The mythological founder of the oracle was the shepherd Branchos, who received the gift of prophecy from Apollo (Konon: xxxiii; Strabo: IX.iii.9). Dedications were made by the Egyptian pharaoh Necho II in 608 BC (Herodotus: II.clix.3) and by the Lydian king Croesus in the earlier 6th century BC (Herodotus: I.xcii.2); during the 6th century BC, under the 'Branchidai' dynasty of priests, Didyma became the most important oracular sanctuary in East Greece, and was linked to Miletos by a Sacred Way 6 m wide and *c.* 24 km long. The earliest monument in the sanctuary was the Archaic Temple of Apollo Didymaios, though there is also evidence of an early cult of Leto, Artemis and Hekate. The sanctuary was destroyed either by the Persian king Darius (494 BC; Herodotus: VI.xix.3) or by Xerxes (479 BC; Strabo: XIV.i.5, and Pausanias: VIII.xlvi.3). In 334 BC Alexander the Great liberated Miletos from Persian domination, and at least from the time of its endowment by Seleukos Nikator (*c.* 300 BC) Didyma was under Milesian control. Inscriptions record a further building programme in the 2nd century BC involving a market, an office for recording oracles, assembly halls and a sanctuary of Aphrodite. In the 1st century BC the sanctuary was plundered by pirates (Plutarch: *Pompey* xxiv.5), the Sacred Way became a covered street and the earliest settlement was established (Strabo: XIV.i.5). Around AD 100–01 the Sacred Way within the sanctuary was paved by Trajan, and in the 2nd century AD a market and a basilica were constructed. Around AD 250 the peristyle of the Temple of Apollo was walled in, presumably to counter attacks by the Goths, turning it into a fortress. In the 4th century AD the sanctuary of Artemis and the buildings along the Sacred Way were destroyed, perhaps by an earthquake; the earliest reports of Christian worship also belong to this time. In the 5th–6th century AD a basilica was built in the courtyard of the fortress and rebuilding undertaken on the Sacred Way; the fortress was enlarged by an outer castle in the 10th century AD, and architectural sculpture attests the existence of other 9th–12th-century buildings. Earth-quakes in the 13th century and in 1493 effectively destroyed the site.

The earliest remains in the courtyard of the Hellenistic Sanctuary of Apollo are from Temple I (*c.* 700 to mid-6th century BC) and consist of foundations of a courtyard (10.4×*c.* 21 m) enclosing a rocky ridge running north-west to south-east, which probably determined the sanctuary's orientation. Near by are the remains of the fountain house of the oracular spring, while 25 m to the south are a stone socle and orthostates belonging to the south stoa (*c.* 600 BC). In the north-east of the sanctuary are the remains of a circular building with two towers, perhaps the circular altar supposedly built by the Theban Herakles from the blood of sacrificed animals (Pausanias: V.xiii.11). Other remains belong to the terrace for votive offerings and two 6th-century BC stoas.

The Archaic Temple II (mid-6th century BC to early 5th) consisted of a courtyard measuring 19.5 m by at least 34.5 m, which incorporated the courtyard of Temple I and was apparently surrounded by a double marble peristyle; the overall dimensions were *c.* 42×75 m (87 m according to Gruben). It had walls with pilasters on their inner side and an undercut Ionic cyma; these walls bore the earliest egg-and-tongue moulding in Asia Minor. No traces of the peristyle remain *in situ*, but the columns were Ionic with relief sculptures of korai (Berlin, Antikenmus.) and ornamental bases, while the architrave bore figured reliefs of gorgons at the corners flanked by lions (Berlin, Antikenmus.; Istanbul, Archaeol. Mus.). The sculpture dates to 540–520 BC. The cult statue from the temple represented *Apollo Philesios Seizing a Deer* (destr.) and appears to have been related to early Anatolian work. It was taken to Persia after the unsuccessful Ionian Revolt at the beginning of the 5th century BC, but according to tradition was recovered at the end of the 4th century BC and set up again in the Temple of Apollo. Inside the courtyard are scanty remains of Naiskos I (*c.* 574–*c.* 550 BC), a fountain-house built in the form of a distyle *in antis* shrine.

Temple III (*c.* 300 BC to Roman times) was among the most colossal of ancient Greek temples (*c.* 118×60 m; see fig. 1 and GREECE, ANCIENT, fig. 29). It was designed by the architects Paionios of Ephesos and Daphnis of Miletos (Vitruvius: VII.Pref.16). Early building work was carried out by the Milesians and sponsored by funds donated by Seleukos Nikator *c.* 300 and 288/7 BC. The courtyard was surrounded by walls (h. over 25 m) lined with pilasters set on a high socle. At its western end are the remains of the tetrastyle prostyle Naiskos II, probably the oracle's Hellenistic fountain-house. This small marble building can be reconstructed almost completely; estimates of its date vary, earlier scholars favouring early Hellenistic times, later writers suggesting *c.* 250 BC or later. The east wall of the courtyard has a monumental façade with two Corinthian half columns *in antis* on a podium incorporating a wide flight of steps. Three doorways in the façade lead to an antechamber 20 m high with two free-standing Corinthian columns on its long axis: two narrow flights of stairs at each end ascend to the terrace roof that probably covered the eastern part of the building. The antechamber's east wall contains a doorway over 14 m high, opening into the lower-lying pronaos with its 12 Ionic columns. The door

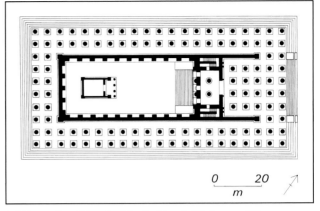

1. Didyma, plan of Temple of Apollo (Temple III), begun *c.* 300 BC

was strictly ornamental, since its threshold is *c.* 1.4 m high, and two sloping barrel-vaulted passages linked the pronaos directly to the sunken courtyard. Only half of the 108 Ionic columns planned for the double peristyle were ever erected, and according to Strabo (XIV.i.5), 'the temple remained roofless because of its size'. Even the temple's seven-stepped base was never completed, though it served as seating for the stadium that ran along the building's south side. Building plans were scratched on parts of the ashlar masonry, especially the socle inside the courtyard, and these combine with the remains themselves to provide valuable insights into ancient architectural practice (*see* GREECE, ANCIENT, §II, 3(ii)).

Excavations in the north-west of the site since 1975 have uncovered various buildings belonging to a sanctuary of Artemis bordering the south-west side of the Sacred Way. As in the Sanctuary of Apollo, the presence of springs near a rock outcrop seems to have determined the sanctuary's location, since the earliest architectural remains (7th–6th century BC) include parts of a fountain-house and the footing for the surrounding wall of a spring precinct, as well as a stone frame (perhaps a depository for ashes) and the foundations of the old sanctuary wall. A later wall (6th century BC) extended Sanctuary I as far as the Sacred Way, and during the construction of Sanctuary II in the 3rd–2nd century BC the Sacred Way was actually moved to the north-east. Two courtyards, the Slope Building and the North Building, were constructed in the 2nd–1st century BC, though linked by an earlier gateway; in the 2nd century BC the area between the rock outcrop and the road was enclosed in a peribolus hall with a north-west wing leading to the West Building.

The Sacred Way leading to the Temple of Apollo was lined on both sides with votive sculpture. The extant sculpture is of marble and dates from the Archaic period, when the shrine was at the height of its fame; it was removed to the British Museum, London, by Charles Newton in the 19th century. The sculpture comprises recumbent lions and seated figures, both male and female. The seated figures wear a *chiton* (light, baggy-sleeved linen tunic) and a *himation* (short, pleated and buttoned mantle): the sculptors appear to have been more interested in the decorative texture of the garments than in the forms of

2. Didyma, marble statue of *Chares*, h. 1.49 m, *c.* 560 BC (London, British Museum)

W. Voigtländer: 'Quellhaus und Naiskos im Didymaion nach der Perserkriegen', *Istanbul. Mitt.*, xxii (1972), pp. 93–112

K. Tuchelt: *Vorarbeiten zu einer Topographie von Didyma* (Tübingen, 1973)

W. Voigtländer: *Der jüngste Apollontempel von Didyma* (Tübingen, 1975)

L. Haselberger: 'Werkzeichnungen am jüngeren Didymaion', *Istanbul. Mitt.*, xxx (1980), pp. 191–215

——: 'Die Werkzeichnung des Naiskos im Apollontempel von Didyma', *Bauplanung und Bautheorie der Antike: Diskussionen zur archäologischen Bauforschung*, iv (Berlin, 1984), pp. 111–19

K. Tuchelt: 'Fragen zum Naiskos von Didyma', *Archäol. Anz.* (1986), pp. 33–50

P. Schneider: 'Zur Topographie der Heiligen Strasse von Milet nach Didyma', *Archäol. Anz.* (1987), pp. 101–29

PETER SCHNEIDER

Die (i). Dado of a pedestal.

Die (ii). Intaglio stamp used for impressing a design when striking coins or embossing paper.

Die (iii). Hollow mould in metal-casting.

Diebenkorn, Richard (Clifford), jr (*b* Portland, OR, 22 April 1922; *d* Berkeley, CA, 30 March 1993). American painter and printmaker. He was most widely recognized for his large-scale, luminous abstractions known as the *Ocean Park* paintings. His abstract and figurative work alike is devoted to the delicate balance between surface modulation and illusionistic depth, between the establishment of structure and its dissolution in light and space.

Diebenkorn was brought up in San Francisco. His first interest was in the American illustrators Howard Pyle (1853–1911) and N. C. Wyeth (1882–1945). He studied at Stanford University from 1940 to 1943 and received his first formal art training with Daniel Mendelowitz (*b* 1905), who introduced him to the work of Edward Hopper, and to paintings by the artists of the Ecole de Paris. Diebenkorn's study was interrupted by service in the Marine Corps during World War II, but while stationed at Quantico, VA, he often visited the Phillips Collection in Washington, DC. There, Henri Matisse's *Studio, Quai Saint-Michel* (1916) inspired him. Matisse's technique of exposing the painting process, marrying indoor and outdoor space and aligning the planes of the composition with the edges of the canvas itself raised formal issues that Diebenkorn did not forget.

In 1946 Diebenkorn returned to California to continue his education at the California School of Fine Arts (CSFA) from 1946 to 1947 with David Park, whom he met in the first week and who would become his most important teacher and friend. Park encouraged him to look at the work of Joan Miró and Picasso. During the mid-1940s he also became aware of the work of Robert Motherwell and William Baziotes. However, it was not until 1948 that he first saw paintings by Willem de Kooning in magazine reproductions. In 1947 Diebenkorn was offered a position on the faculty of the CSFA, which at the time included Park, Elmer Bischoff (*b* 1916), Clyfford Still and, during the summer of 1947 and of 1948, Mark Rothko. His teaching career lasted more than two decades with few breaks. He enrolled at the University of New Mexico in Albuquerque in 1950 (MFA, 1951). His abstract paintings of this period, such as *Albuquerque No. 4* (1951; St Louis,

the body beneath, which is typical of East Greek work in the Archaic period. The seated figures are slightly over life-size; one of them represents *Chares*, the tyrant of nearby Teichioussa (see fig. 2). One of the recumbent lions has an inscription saying that it was dedicated to Apollo by the sons of Orion, a magistrate (London, BM, B281).

BIBLIOGRAPHY

Herodotus: *Histories*

Vitruvius: *On Architecture*

Konon: *Narratives* (see F. Jacoby: *Fragmente der griechischen Historiker*, i (Berlin, 1923), no. 26)

Strabo: *Geography*

Pausanias: *Guide to Greece*

R. Chandler, N. Revett and W. Pars: *Ionian Antiquities* (London, 1769)

C. T. Newton: *A History of the Discoveries at Halicarnassus, Cnidus, and Branchidae*, 2 vols (London, 1862–3)

H. Knackfuss: *Die Baubeschreibung*, 3 vols (1941), i of *Didyma*, ed. T. Weigand (Berlin, 1941–58)

A. von Gerkan: 'Der Naiskos im Tempel von Didyma', *Jb. Dt. Archäol. Inst.*, lvii (1942), pp. 183–98

A. Rehm: *Die Inschriften* (1958), ii of *Didyma*, ed. T. Weigand (Berlin, 1941–58)

G. Gruben: 'Das archaische Didymaion', *Jb. Dt. Archäol. Inst.*, lxxviii (1963), pp. 78–177

W. Hahland: 'Didyma im 5. Jahrhundert v. Chr.', *Jb. Dt. Archäol. Inst.*, lxxix (1964), pp. 142–240

K. Tuchelt: 'Die archaischen Skulpturen von Didyma', *Istanbul. Forsch.*, xxvii (Berlin, 1970)

W. Günther: *Das Orakel von Didyma in hellenistischer Zeit* (Tübingen, 1971)

MO, A. Mus.), were stylistically rooted in the New York school; they were characterized by linear planes, which gave the impression of aerial landscape views, and by a fluid line that defined a type of biomorphic abstraction. His palette resembled that of de Kooning but, in fact, the pinks and earth colours were derived from the New Mexico landscape.

The travelling Matisse retrospective exhibition that Diebenkorn saw on a trip to Los Angeles in 1952 influenced paintings such as *Urbana No. 4* (1953; Colorado Springs, CO, F.A. Cent., see 1976 exh. cat., p. 20), which he made while teaching at the University of Illinois. At the end of the school year in 1953 he briefly considered moving to New York but instead returned to Berkeley where he established a studio. The *Berkeley* paintings of 1953 to 1955, such as *Berkeley No. 23* (1955; San Francisco, CA, Mus. Mod. A.), are evidence of his personal response to Abstract Expressionism, in particular to the gestural force of de Kooning and the colour veils of Rothko. The sense of landscape predominates in these dense, calligraphic canvases, and in 1954 *Life* magazine appropriately used the term 'abstract landscape' (cited in 1976 exh. cat., p. 23) in association with his work.

On his return to the Bay Area, Diebenkorn renewed his friendships with Park and Bischoff, both of whom had recently given up abstraction for figuration. Toward the end of 1955, feeling that the highly expressionist *Berkeley* paintings offered no room for the contemplative aspect of the painting process, Diebenkorn too began to make more direct reference to observed subjects. The small studio still-lifes of 1955–6, such as *Still-life with Orange Peel* (1955; San Francisco, priv. col.), signalled a new era.

The period of Diebenkorn's figurative work corresponds (with the exception of the last of the *Berkeley* abstractions in 1955) to his remaining years as a teacher in the Bay Area. With Park, Bischoff and other artists such as Nathan Oliveira (*b* 1928), William Theo Brown (*b* 1919) and Paul Wonner (*b* 1920), Diebenkorn became known as one of the founders of the Bay Area figurative school. He always resisted the notion of a 'school' in any formal sense, noting that the artists involved simply enjoyed a close association, but he led the way in developing a unique northern Californian realism. Paintings such as *Figure on Porch* (1959; Oakland, CA, Mus.) continued the fluid, horizontal landscape references of the *Berkeley* series, while they introduced a skeletal grid with elements, such as a solitary figure anchoring shallow space at a central point. The new colours—intense sunlit blues, greens and yellows—were those of the California landscape. After visiting the former Soviet Union in 1964, where he saw paintings by Matisse previously in the Shchukin Collection (now Moscow, Pushkin Mus. F.A.), he paid further homage to him in his use of arabesques and fusions of exterior and interior spaces.

The titles of Diebenkorn's paintings often alluded to the places that inspired them. His move to the Los Angeles area in 1966 to teach at the University of California at Los Angeles (UCLA) led to a dramatic change in his work. One of his last figurative paintings, *Window* (1967; Stanford, CA, U. A.G. & Mus.), was made after he settled in Santa Monica. It recalls Matisse in the forms of the balcony door, restates the familiar empty chair motif and introduces

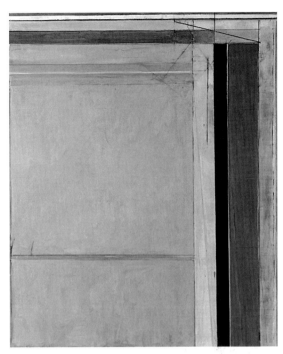

Richard Diebenkorn: *Ocean Park No. 83*, oil on canvas, 2.54×2.06 m, 1975 (Washington, DC, Corcoran Gallery of Art)

the broad, open expanses of colour suggested by the view from his new Ocean Park studio.

From that time, in a series of more than 140 paintings entitled *Ocean Park*, Diebenkorn gave priority to formal concerns in his monumental abstract compositions. Eliminating the figure but retaining allusions to the landscape, he created paintings distinguished by geometric scaffolding visibly aligned and re-aligned, overlaid with glazes of luminescent colour. *Ocean Park No. 83* (1975; Washington, DC, Corcoran Gal. A.; see fig.) typifies his continuous struggle to balance structural elements, proportion, spatial illusion, the weight of his sensuous lines (the 'bones' of the composition) and the mutations of atmospheric colour. Characteristically, the works are broadly brushed yet animated by small passages of detail. Although he made no studies for the *Ocean Park* paintings, preferring to work directly on the canvas, his prints and drawings, such as *Untitled* (1980; New York, Whitney; see Newlin, p. 155), provide the most intimate access to his highly personal search for order and the means to express it. In 1988 he left Santa Monica to return to the Bay Area, where he built a studio in Healdsburg, in the vineyards north of San Francisco. After a heart attack in 1989, followed by a series of operations and illnesses, he gave up working on his characteristically large canvases to concentrate on a series of gouache drawings and two beautifully refined etchings made at Crown Point Press, San Francisco, in 1991 and 1992.

BIBLIOGRAPHY
Richard Diebenkorn: Paintings and Drawings, 1943–1976 (exh. cat. by R. Buck and others, Buffalo, NY, Albright--Knox A.G., 1976)
M. Stevens: *Richard Diebenkorn: Etchings and Drypoints, 1949–1980* (Houston, 1981) [cat. rais., 1949–80 and extensive technical inf.]

D. Ashton: *Richard Diebenkorn: Small Paintings from Ocean Park* (Houston, 1985)
R. Newlin: *Richard Diebenkorn: Works on Paper* (Houston, 1987)
G. Nordland: *Richard Diebenkorn* (New York, 1987)
Richard Diebenkorn (exh. cat., ed. P. Bonaventura and C. Lampert; London, Whitechapel A.G., 1991)
A. Gopnik: 'The Art World, Diebenkorn Redux', *New Yorker* (24 May 1993), pp. 97–100
T. Hilton: 'Some Divine Inkling . . .', *The Guardian* (1 April 1993)
Obituary, *The Times* (1 April 1993)

CONSTANCE W. GLENN

Diego de la Cruz (*fl c.* 1475–1500). Spanish painter. He trained in the Netherlands and made a significant contribution to Hispano-Flemish painting in Castile. From 1482 his name appears in chronicles together with that of the sculptor Gil de Siloé (*see* SILOÉ, (1)) in connection with carved altarpieces in Burgos Cathedral, in the charterhouse of Miraflores near Burgos and in the Colegio de S Gregorio, Valladolid. He was formerly believed to have been a sculptor in Siloé's workshop, but in fact he was responsible only for the painting of the carvings. He was also thought to have collaborated on the altarpiece of the Catholic Kings (dismantled; 1496–7; the *Marriage at Cana*, Washington, DC, N.G.; *Annunciation* and *Nativity*, San Francisco, CA, Mus. A.; *Presentation in the Temple*, Cambridge, MA, Fogg) formerly in Valladolid. In 1966 Diego's *Man of Sorrows with the Virgin and St John* (*c.* 1475–80; Barcelona, Col. Bonova; see fig.), signed *Diego de la +*, was discovered, and it is known from the publication (1946) of the records of S Esteban in Burgos that between 1487 and 1489 he was paid for a panel depicting the *Stigmatization of St Francis* (Burgos, S Esteban). These findings have allowed historians to trace Diego's artistic character, to assess his presence in Burgos in the last quarter of the 15th century and to attribute to him a corpus of works,

including a *Mass of St Gregory* (*c.* 1475–80; Barcelona, Col. Torello), a *Man of Sorrows with Angels* (*c.* 1480–85; Covarrubias, SS Cosme y Damián), a *St John the Baptist with a Donor* (*c.* 1480–85; Madrid, Prado) and an *Adoration of the Magi* (*c.* 1495; Burgos Cathedral).

Diego's style is characterized by elongated figures with absent expressions that suggest an inner piety, by the use of devices that emphasize three-dimensional values and by the combination of reds and blues with yellows, greens, browns and violets, contrasted with the figures' pale skin. It has been difficult to establish Diego's origins, owing to his bright palette that lacks the bronze tonalities of Hispanic works, his command of oil painting and his style in general. His use of Netherlandish prototypes shows a direct contact with northern workshops: his work reflects elements of Rogier van der Weyden's language as interpreted by Hans Memling, and the work of Hugo van der Goes in its intense realism; his style also coincides with the temperament of Dieric Bouts in the expressiveness of the figures. Studies have revealed, however, that the underlying elaborate and fully finished drawing does not tally with contemporary northern practice. Diego's style was to be influenced later by Hispanic trends, and in his late works decorative elements tend to predominate to the detriment of narrative and expressive features.

BIBLIOGRAPHY
C. R. Post: 'Diego de la Cruz', *Gaz. B.-A.*, liii (1959), pp. 21–6
J. Camón Aznar: *Pintura medieval española* (Madrid, 1966)
J. Gudiol: 'El pintor Diego de la Cruz', *Goya*, 70 (1966), p. 208
M. P. Silva Maroto: *Pintura hispanoflamenca castellana*, 3 vols (Valladolid, 1990)
Reyes y mecenas (exh. cat., Toledo, Mus. Santa Cruz, 1992)

A. M. MENCHACA

Diehl, (Michel-)Charles (*b* Strasbourg, 4 July 1859; *d* Paris, 1 Nov 1944). French Byzantinist. After studying at the Ecole Normale Superieure (1878–81) he became a member of the French School in Rome, and in 1883 was elected to the French School in Athens. He taught Greek history and archaeology at the University of Nancy from 1885 to 1889, when he became Professor of Byzantine History at the Sorbonne and a member of the Institut de France: he was the foremost authority of his time on the Byzantine empire. His early interests included studies of the Byzantine administration of Ravenna and the history of Africa up to the Arab conquest of AD 697; he also had an admirable grasp of the interlocking themes of political, social and economic life in the age of Emperor Justinian I. Diehl travelled extensively in Italy, where he studied the art of eremitical dwellings of the Byzantine period, and later more widely, becoming an expert on all aspects of Byzantine art. His *Manuel d'art byzantine* which appeared in 1910 at once became the standard work on the subject. In it he analysed the origins of Byzantine art and traced major developments in the monumental, sculptural and figurative spheres through to the mid-16th century. To the end of his life he retained an interest in Byzantine architecture, studying the major monuments of Greek and Italian cities, especially Thessaloniki, Syracuse and Palermo.

WRITINGS
Afrique byzantine: Histoire de la domination byzantine en Afrique de 533 à 709 (Paris, 1896)

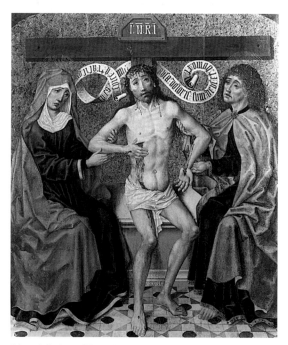

Diego de la Cruz: *Man of Sorrows with the Virgin and St John, c.* 1475–80 (Barcelona, Bonova Collection)

Figures byzantines, 2 vols (Paris, 1906–8)
Manuel d'art byzantin (Paris, 1910, rev. 2/1925)
Dans l'Orient byzantin (Paris, 1917)
Byzance: Grandeur et décadence (Paris, 1919)
Salonique (Paris, 1923)
Choses et gens de Byzance (Paris, 1926)
Mélanges Charles Diehl: Etudes sur l'histoire et sur l'art de Byzance, 2 vols (Paris, 1930)

BIBLIOGRAPHY
M. A. A. Vasiliev and others: 'A la mémoire de Charles Diehl', *Byzantion*, xvii (1944–5), pp. 414–23
R. Guilland: 'Hommage à Charles Diehl', *Etud. Byz.*, iii (1945), pp. 5–18
JOHN CURRAN

Dienecker, Jost de. *See* NEGKER, JOST DE.

Dieng Plateau. Hindu temple site, 1800 m above sea-level in Central Java. Volcanic activity in the area led to the creation there from the 8th century AD of temples for the worship of the ancestors, who were deified and identified with the Hindu god Shiva. The site's name is derived from Old Javanese *di-hyang*, 'the abode of the gods'. The Dieng temples are spread over a pear-shaped valley and its bordering elevations. Many, however, have been destroyed, and the few that remain standing cannot be ascribed to any one period. Even the temples that belong to the 'Arjuna group' show at least two styles: the squat *candi* (ancient religious monuments built of stone) Arjuna, Semar, Srikandi and Gatokaca, which are strongly influenced by south Indian architecture, and the slender Candi Puntadewa with its two-tier foundation and its high protruding niches. Quite different is Candi Bima, 1.6 km south of the Arjuna compound (*see* INDONESIA, fig. 5). Its upper structure is obviously a north Indian shikhara, but the ornamental elements reveal south Indian influence. Remains of monasteries indicate that the plateau was a lively pilgrimage resort, possibly for many centuries, as is suggested by a date equivalent to AD 1210 painted on a rock-face.

See also INDONESIA, §II, 1(i).

BIBLIOGRAPHY
N. J. Krom: *Inleiding tot de Hindoe-Javaansche kunst*, i (The Hague, 1923)
A. J. Bernet Kempers: *Ancient Indonesian Art* (Amsterdam, 1959)
R. Soekmono: 'Notes on the Monuments of Ancient Indonesia', *Ancient Indonesian Art of the Central and Eastern Javanese Periods* (New York, 1971), pp. 13–17
——: 'The Archaeology of Central Java from before 800 A.D.', *Early Southeast Asia* (London, 1979), pp. 457–72
J. Dumarçay: *The Temples of Java* (Oxford, 1986)
R. SOEKMONO

Dientzenhofer. German family of architects. Active in central Europe in the late 17th century and first half of the 18th, they played a decisive role in the development of late Baroque architecture in the region. There were five brothers: Georg Dientzenhofer (1643–89), Wolfgang Dientzenhofer (1648–1706), (1) Christoph Dientzenhofer, Leonhard Dientzenhofer (1660–1707) and (2) Johann Dientzenhofer. The style of their works suggests that they kept in contact, and their buildings demonstrate common aims. Of particular importance is a general interest in the organization of dynamic groups and sequence of spaces. The most talented of the brothers, Georg, Christoph and

Johann, introduced a method of composing with interdependent spatial elements, which was later developed by Christoph's son, (3) Kilian Ignaz Dientzenhofer.

(1) Christoph Dientzenhofer (*b* Rosenheim, Upper Bavaria, 1655; *d* Prague, 20 June 1722). He was originally trained as a mason and in 1676 moved with his brothers to Prague, where work was plentiful. They were accompanied by their sister Anna, who in 1678 married the influential architect Abraham Leuthner von Grund, a connection that undoubtedly boosted the brothers' careers. In 1682 Christoph was in Waldsassen, on the border between Franconia and Bohemia, where he and Leonhard were assisting Georg on Leuthner's project for the rebuilding of the Cistercian abbey church. A few years later Christoph was responsible for completing the pilgrimage church of the Holy Trinity (1684–9; see fig. 1) near Waldsassen, designed by Georg but unfinished at his death. This church, generally known as the Kappel, is an important building in the history of Baroque architecture because of its original plan and articulate form. It consists of three apses joined by a triangular vault and surrounded by an outer ambulatory. The plan obviously resulted from a conscious wish to symbolize the Holy Trinity. Beyond this meaning, however, it represents a first attempt at composing with interdependent spatial cells within an enveloping wall, an approach that was systematically sought by the Dientzenhofers.

The development of these ideas was strongly influenced by the work of Guarino Guarini, which became widely known after the publication of his projects in 1686. In 1690 Christoph Dientzenhofer travelled to Marseille, and on the way he probably visited Turin, thus gaining direct

1. Christoph Dientzenhofer and Georg Dientzenhofer: pilgrimage church of the Holy Trinity, near Waldsassen, 1684–9

knowledge of Guarini's buildings. Christoph is generally recognized as the designer of a remarkable group of churches built in Bohemia in the early years of the 18th century: the church (1699–1712) in Obořiště; the chapel (1700–13) of Smiřice Castle; St Nicholas (1703–11) in the Little Quarter, Prague; St Clare (1707–11), Cheb; and St Margaret (1709–15) at Břevnov, near Prague. All these buildings present spatial and formal analogies, and they also represent a certain architectural development. The church in Obořiště has a bi-axial plan that is directly derived from Guarini's church of the Immacolata Concezione (begun 1673) in Turin, and his plan for S Lorenzo (from 1668), Turin, reappears in the chapel at Smiřice. At about the same time Guarini's ideas were also introduced in Bohemia by Johann Lukas von Hildebrandt, who in 1699 began construction of the church of St Lawrence in Gabel, north of Prague. Travelling to Gabel, Hildebrandt must have passed through Prague, and it is likely that he met Christoph Dientzenhofer, who later sent his son Kilian Ignaz to study with Hildebrandt in Vienna. In order to make a composition with spatial cells effective, it is essential that the primary structure be defined as a skeleton; that is, the walls should not constitute the spaces but rather play the role of a secondary 'skin'. Such a system comes close to the structure of Gothic architecture. In Guarini's works the skeletal character is quite pronounced, although he usually maintained a continuous horizontal entablature. In the early Baroque architecture of central Europe, however, attempts were made to transform the wall into a true skeleton by using the local wall-pillar construction. The WALL-PILLAR CHURCH structure was introduced into Baroque architecture by Hans Alberthal and was later developed by the Vorarlberg builders, who created a type of Baroque wall-pillar church. The Vorarlberg masons were not, however, familiar with Guarini's spatial ideas, and their rather conventional longitudinal halls do not show any interdependence of the spatial units. Because of his knowledge of Guarini's works, Christoph Dientzenhofer was more creative in his use of wall-pillar construction, and his achievement may in general be understood as an ingenious combination of this type of structure with the compositional method using interdependent spatial cells.

The chapel at Smiřice was the first full-grown expression of Christoph's intentions. It consists of an elongated octagon with internally convex sides. Secondary oval spaces are added on the longitudinal axis, whereas the transverse axis is closed by neutral walls filled in between the slightly projecting wall-pillars. The diagonals are extended by lens-shaped recesses. The space was thus treated as an open system, where cells may be added at will. At Smiřice this possibility was used to create a highly original synthesis of centralized and longitudinal space. The exterior presents itself as an integrated organism enveloped in a continuous, undulating surface. The potential openness of the main axes, however, is indicated by large segmented pediments. A convincing complementary relationship between interior and exterior is thus realized.

At St Nicholas in the Little Quarter, Prague, Christoph built a much more complex organism, although the longitudinal plan may be understood as a more systematized version of the Obořiště church. Deep wall-pillars

2. Christoph Dientzenhofer: interior of St Nicholas, Little Quarter, Prague, 1703–11

were introduced at St Nicholas, between which chapels and galleries were inserted (see fig. 2). The chapels are treated as centralized baldacchinos with neutral panels filled in towards the outside. Towards the nave, the wall-pillars are faced by obliquely placed pilasters from which double-curved arches spring to cross the vault (the arches were later removed to make room for a large painting). The system has an ambiguous character; it may be understood as a series of interpenetrating ovals defined by the pilasters and the arches, as well as a normal bay system. The ovals, however, open where the bays meet, and the bays open where the ovals touch each other. Two contradicting spatial definitions are thus realized, creating an effect that has been called 'spatial syncopation' or 'syncopated interpenetration'. The principle represents an original and important invention by Christoph, and it was later taken up by Balthasar Neumann. Because of the new principle, St Nicholas has a spatial organization that is simultaneously articulated and integrated. Its impact is extraordinary, and it must be counted among the greatest achievements of the Czech Baroque (for illustration of façade see CZECH REPUBLIC, fig. 5).

St Clare in Cheb and St Margaret at Břevnov both show a desire for simplification without losing the spatial richness of the earlier works. At Břevnov, Christoph employed the syncopated interpenetration explored in St Nicholas, so that the vault contracts where the space below expands and vice versa. The nave is, however, reduced to two transverse ovals with smaller ovals added at both ends.

The bi-axial organism introduced at Obořiště has thus become fully integrated. The interior walls at Břevnov appear as a succession of high wall-pillars filled in by secondary neutral surfaces, thus achieving an effect of strength and clarity. The exterior is similarly powerful, being held together by a single giant order of Ionic pilasters. In contrast to Smiřice, however, the outer envelope is split at the entrance to make the spatial system of the interior visible.

(2) Johann Dientzenhofer (*b* 1663; *d* Bamberg, 20 July 1726). Brother of (1) Christoph Dientzenhofer. He was the only one of the brothers who received a formal education in architecture. He probably had an early training at Christoph's workshop in Prague, but before 1700 he moved to Bamberg to assist Leonhard Dientzenhofer with the rebuilding of the church of St Martin (1696) at the Michelsberg in Bamberg, and with the new Residenz (1697–1703) in the same city. He also visited Italy in 1699 to study Roman Baroque architecture. After his return, he was commissioned to rebuild Fulda Cathedral (1704–12; *see* FULDA, §1), a fact that testifies to the professional status of the Dientzenhofers. After a somewhat hesitant start in Fulda, Johann came to maturity with the splendid Benedictine abbey church (1710–13) of Banz in Franconia. The plan is based on Christoph's Obořiště scheme: two transverse ovals are connected by a narrow intermediate section. The latter is defined as a wide wall-pillar, a solution that had already been used by Christoph in St Clare, Cheb. Similar sections are added at the extremes of the nave, creating a rhythmical succession of narrow and wide intervals. This rhythm, however, forms a counterpoint to the spaces defined by the double-curved transverse arches, which expand over the narrow intervals and contract over the wide ones, the spatial units simultaneously contracting and expanding. The church at Banz thus exploits all the spatial possibilities developed by Christoph and may be considered the most mature work of the entire group of buildings built by the Dientzenhofer brothers.

After Banz, Johann was mainly occupied with the planning and construction of the great Palace at POMMERSFELDEN (1711–18; *see* BAROQUE, fig. 3) for the Archbishop and Elector of Mainz and Bishop of Bamberg, Lothar Franz von Schönborn. The basic disposition shows a U-shape with a *cour d'honneur* and corner pavilions. A most impressive novel feature is the dominant central unit, which incorporates a great symmetrical staircase (by Hildebrandt; *see* PALACE, fig. 2), a *sala terrena* based on interdependent spatial units, and the Kaisersaal (by Hildebrandt) above. The idea of creating an unusually large and monumental staircase (*Treppenhaus*) is supposed to have originated with Lothar Franz himself, but the truly splendid solution was the product of a collaboration between Johann and Hildebrandt. The decoration is mainly the work of Hildebrandt, whereas the other principal rooms and the exterior clearly show Johann's style. The monumental staircase introduced an element that was to play a prime role in Neumann's palaces, first of all in the Würzburg Residenz (begun 1720; *see* WÜRZBURG, §2), where Johann acted as a consultant at the outset of the planning.

(3) Kilian Ignaz Dientzenhofer (*b* Prague, 1 Sept 1689; *d* Prague, 18 Dec 1751). Son of (1) Christoph Dientzenhofer. He was a contemporary of Dominikus Zimmermann, Balthasar Neumann, Johann Michael Fischer and Johann Conrad Schlaun, and was thus one of the last great generation of central European Baroque architects. Whereas the others concentrated their attention on particular aspects of the Borromini-Guarini tradition, Kilian Ignaz developed its systematic potential. In doing this, he brought the ideas of his father Christoph and his uncle Johann to their logical conclusion. In addition, he enriched the vocabulary of Bohemian Baroque architecture by means of sensitive detailing and plastic articulation, mostly derivative of Hildebrandt.

In contrast to the older members of the Dientzenhofer family, Kilian Ignaz received a thorough education, and he was well prepared in Latin, philosophy and theology. He studied and worked in Vienna from 1707 to 1717 and returned there for another visit in 1725, possibly in connection with a trip to Italy. He inherited from his father a considerable fortune, and as early as 1725 he could afford to build for himself a beautiful mansion (now Villa Portheim) on the outskirts of Prague. His professional career started in 1717 with the construction of a small summer residence for Count Michna, the garden palace Villa Amerika in the New Town of Prague. The layout consists of three pavilions, which form an open *cour d'honneur*. The central one is an exceptionally fine essay in Hildebrandtian articulation, combined with a characteristic Bohemian plasticity.

In 1719, Kilian Ignaz received his first ecclesiastical commissions, designing St John Nepomuk on the Hradčany in Prague and the pilgrimage church of the Nativity of the Virgin at Nicov in western Bohemia (both built 1720–28). Based on similar plans, they both clearly manifest the basic intentions of their architect. Around a dominant, central dome, secondary spaces are added as

1. Kilian Ignaz Dientzenhofer: St Adalbert, Počaply, 1724–6

canopies resting on a skeleton of piers. The most significant fact about their designs is the way in which Kilian Ignaz attempted to compose a complex organism by means of open canopies, which are freely placed within a continuous, extended space. He then built a series of churches in which the spaces were made interdependent by means of alternating concave and convex sides. St Hedwig (1723–31) at Wahlstatt, Silesia (now Legnickie Pole, Poland) is an important example, but several of his smaller buildings in Bohemia were also influential. They include a group of village churches in the Broumov area, St Bartholomew (1726–31) in Prague and, above all, St Adalbert (1724–6; see fig. 1) in Počaply near Limoměřice. At St Adalbert he based the whole plan on an octagon with longer, internally convex sides on the main axes. A longitudinal direction is created through the addition of transverse ovals on two opposite sides. But the two other sides are also curved in the same way; other ovals could have been added, and the organism must be characterized as a reduced or elongated central church. The Počaply church also shows a more conscious treatment of the exterior plastic articulation, which was thereafter mainly used to express the spatial organization. The transverse axis is thus characterized as open through an interruption of the architrave and frieze, and a gable marks the 'portal' thereby created. The neutral, provisory character of the wall that closes the opening is expressed by a large chasuble-shaped window, which naturally has an analogous function when seen from the inside.

2. Kilian Ignaz Dientzenhofer: St Nicholas, Old Town Square, Prague, 1732–6

Kilian Ignaz Dientzenhofer's exploration of interdependent spaces culminated with three masterpieces: St John of Nepomuk on the Rock (1730–39; partly rest.) in Prague, St Clement (1732–5) in Odolená Voda, north of Prague, and St Mary Magdalene (1732–7) in Karlovy Vary. St John of Nepomuk on the Rock is probably the best known of Kilian's works, and it is often considered the most exemplary Bohemian Baroque church. In no other buildings is the plastic dynamism and dramatic quality so dear to the country expressed with more ability and conviction. The position of the church on a rock accentuates the effect and the staircase in front enhances the vertical movement of the façade. The solution is, however, based on almost rigorous composition. The plan repeats the general layout of Počaply, but the greater importance of the later building is emphasized by the addition of a twin-tower front and a circular apse. The central octagon is here slightly elongated, but a series of similar arches over the entablature contribute to the creation of a domed space. Both the centralization and the longitudinal movement are thus strengthened. Due to the arches penetrating the vaults and the windows placed within them, it seems as if the canopies are immersed in a much higher, luminous space. The plastic articulation of the exterior corresponds to the interior organization. St John of Nepomuk on the Rock constitutes an unsurpassable example of complementary correspondence between inside and outside. Even the diagonally placed bell-towers are integrated in the spatial disposition. The architect's series of elongated centralized churches culminated with St Mary Magdalene in Karlovy Vary. Here, the main space is transformed into an oval with an outspoken domed effect. Simultaneously, however, the longitudinal axis is emphasized by the introduction of internally convex zones of transition towards the secondary ovals (narthex and presbytery). The open character of the system is thereby maintained, and the organizing principle is, as usual, spatial interdependence. The exterior is related to St John of Nepomuk on the Rock, but, as a logical consequence of the plan, the bell-towers are frontally disposed. In general, this church may be ranked as Kilian Ignaz's most important achievement.

These churches may all be characterized as elongated, centralized buildings. In some cases, Kilian Ignaz also tackled the problem of the centralized, longitudinal plan. The most important is the Jesuit church of St Francis Xavier (1732–5) in Opařany, which represents the same stage of consummate mastery as the church in Karlsbad. In 1734 he repeated the disposition of Opařany in monumentalized form in his first design (unexecuted) for the great church of the Ursuline convent in Kutná Hora. The final version (unexecuted), however, shows his growing interest in the development of a dominant central rotunda. The development of his work thus moved from the open system of interdependent cells, towards the vision of a unitary, seemingly infinitely extended space, in which a large baldacchino is immersed. If built, the church in Kutná Hora would have been the crowning achievement of his career. Kilian Ignaz did, however, build another centralized structure that shows similar intentions. St Nicholas on the Old Town Square (1732–6) in Prague has a dominant octagonal dome, which forms a counterpoint to a strongly emphasized, longitudinal axis. The exterior is a triumph of plastic articulation (see fig. 2). The basic theme is a gradual liberation of the forms in the vertical direction, a solution characteristic of Prague in general and the works of Kilian in particular. The tripartite façade is united by a continuous, rusticated basement, while the main storey is split apart and the bell-towers rise freely towards the sky. The characteristic Baroque increase in plasticity towards the middle of the façade contrasts with the linear treatment of the dome, which appears light and distant. As a result, St Nicholas is the most intensely expressive of Kilian's buildings. He also added (1737–51) a great dome and bell-tower to his father's church of St Nicholas in the Little Quarter of Prague. The strong and picturesque pair of vertical forms not only represents a great architectural creation but is also one of the city's major landmarks (see PRAGUE, fig. 2)

Kilian Ignaz was professionally active until the end of his life, and his late works show a characteristic wish for simplification. Examples include the small centralized church of St Florian (1746–8) in Kladno and the longitudinal village church (1747–51) in Paštiky near Blatná, southern Bohemia. In these two works his basic themes reappear, but the character is less dramatic. In general, Kilian's works show an original synthesis of Bohemian and Austrian traits. Whereas his father concentrated on a few locally rooted types, mainly the wall-pillar church, Kilian studied all possible combinations of centralized and longitudinal plans. His art was a true expression of its time, and it became immensely popular. Together with the works of his father and his uncles, his buildings repesent a most significant interpretation of the aims of the Catholic Counter-Reformation. In the baldacchino spaces of the Dientzenhofers, Heaven comes down to earth, at the same time as the lateral openness of the spatial systems expresses a symbolic interaction with the surrounding everday world.

BIBLIOGRAPHY

H. Schmerber: *Beiträge zur Geschichte der Dientzenhofer* (Prague, 1900)
H. G. Franz: *Die Kirchenbauten des Christoph Dientzenhofer* (Munich and Vienna, 1942)
H. Kreisel: *Das Schloss zu Pommersfelden* (Munich, 1953)
H. G. Franz: *Bauten und Baumeister der Barockzeit in Böhmen* (Leipzig, 1962)
R. Kömstedt: *Von Bauten und Baumeistern des fränkischen Barocks* (Berlin, 1963)
K. M. Swoboda: *Barock in Böhmen* (Munich, 1964)
C. Norberg-Schulz: *Kilian Ignaz Dientzenhofer e il barocco boemo* (Rome, 1968)
J. Neumann: *Český barok* (Prague, 1969)
C. Norberg-Schulz: *Late Baroque and Rococo Architecture* (New York, 1974)
H. Zimmer: *Die Dientzenhofer* (Rosenheim, 1976)
H. G. Franz: *Dientzenhofer und 'Hausstätter'* (Munich and Zurich, 1985)

CHRISTIAN NORBERG-SCHULZ

Diepenbeeck, Abraham (Jansz.) van (*b* 's Hertogenbosch, *bapt* 9 May 1596; *d* Antwerp, 31 Dec 1675). Flemish glass-painter, draughtsman, painter and tapestry designer. His reputation rests primarily on his drawings and oil sketches, of which several hundred survive, intended mainly as designs for stained-glass windows and prints. He was strongly influenced by the work of other important Flemish artists of the late 16th century and early 17th, notably Rubens, whose motifs and stylistic elements he frequently reworked in his own compositions.

1. LIFE AND WORK. He was the son of the glass painter Jan (Roelofsz.) van Diepenbeeck (*d* 1619) and first acquired the skills of his trade in his father's workshop in 's Hertogenbosch. In 1622–3 he became a master glass painter in the Guild of St Luke in Antwerp; it is possible that his move from 's Hertogenbosch in 1621 was related to the war negotiations that were underway that year, which particularly threatened the northern border provinces of the southern Netherlands, where 's Hertogenbosch was located.

Abraham van Diepenbeeck's earliest activity apparently consisted mostly of designing and glazing stained-glass windows for various churches and monasteries in Antwerp. Among the most important of these commissions were the episodes from the *Life of the Virgin* (1622–5; destr.) made for the cloister of the Discalced Carmelites, the scenes from the *Life of St Francis of Paola* (*c.* 1630) for the Minims and the cycle of episodes from the *Life of St Paul* (*c.* 1630–36; destr.) for the Dominicans (see §2 below). Painting commissions are also extant from the 1630s onwards, notably those for the Norbertine Order, which was apparently among van Diepenbeeck's most important clients for such work. Chrysostomus van der Sterre (*d* 1652), Abbot of the Norbertine abbey of St Michael between 1629 and 1652, commissioned many works from van Diepenbeeck in Antwerp, including the series of *Norbertine Saints* that decorated the sanctuary of Kortenbos, near St Truiden. Van Diepenbeeck also worked in Paris in the early 1630s. It appears, however, that although he joined the painters' Guild of St Luke in 1638, genuine monumental painting accounted for only a minor part of his activities. Far more important was his role as a designer for stained glass and prints. Hundreds of prints were originally conceived, drawn and sketched by van Diepenbeeck, among them illustrations and title-pages for books published by the leading Antwerp publishers, van Meurs and Moretus, as well as separate sheets published by van Diepenbeeck himself, including some devotional prints. The best known of his cycles of illustrations are the prints designed in the late 1630s for the *Temple des muses* (before 1638; published Paris, 1655), the engravings for the *Méthode nouvelle. . .de dresser les chevaux* (Antwerp, 1658) by William Cavendish and the numerous scenes of Roman Catholic martyrs in the *Kerckelijke historie* (1667) by Cornelius Hazart. Mythological themes, fashionable especially in aristocratic circles, and the religious ideals of the Counter-Reformation are both adequately expressed in these book illustrations and print cycles. In his later years van Diepenbeeck also made many designs for tapestry cartoons, his known works including a number of cycles from the Bible and ancient history, notably scenes from the lives of Moses, Marcus Aurelius and Semiramis, and the Acts of the Apostles.

A particularly distinctive aspect of van Diepenbeeck's role as a designer was the part he played in commissions for the decoration of palaces of the House of Orange in Holland, whose members such as Prince Frederik-Hendrik and his wife Amalia, through the agencies of Constantijn Huygens (i), were well acquainted with the Flemish narrative painters. In 1648 van Diepenbeeck was commissioned to make sketches for a series of large-scale paintings of the *Story of Psyche* (destr.) to be executed by other

Antwerp masters, including Gonzales Coques, to decorate the castle of Honselaarsdijk. Two years later van Diepenbeeck visited Paris again.

2. STYLE AND SOURCES. Van Diepenbeeck was a highly eclectic artist with a remarkable talent for adapting motifs and other stylistic elements from the work of his illustrious predecessors and reworking them in different compositions. The high level of productivity that he must have maintained, to judge at least from his many hundreds of compositions, may well have driven him to seek more economical working methods. His adaptation of elements from the work of other artists was sometimes fairly blatant: in 1648, for example, Huygens established that van Diepenbeeck's sketches for the series depicting the *Story of Psyche* were taken all too literally from Raphael's famous fresco cycle of the same subject in the Farnesina in Rome.

It was Rubens, however, who exerted the greatest influence on van Diepenbeeck's early work, that carried out before 1640. Indeed, several times van Diepenbeeck executed work initially conceived by Rubens. In 1627, following Rubens's instructions, he drew the design for the *Vitae patrum* by Heribertus Rosweyde; in 1636 he realized Rubens's ideas for a print of *Neptune and Minerva*. Rubens knew how to exploit the drawing talents of the young van Diepenbeeck for other purposes as well. Recently it has been shown that, probably in 1632, van Diepenbeeck made drawings after famous Mannerist paintings of Primaticcio and Niccolo dell'Abbate in Paris and Fontainebleau on behalf of Rubens. Rubens must have considered van Diepenbeeck capable of assimilating his design concepts. It is not surprising, therefore, that certain of van Diepenbeeck's stylistic features unmistakably recall Rubens's relatively late work of the mid-1620s. Elements of motion, motifs of dramatic expression and, in particular, the predilection for foreshortened faces most clearly betray van Diepenbeeck's acquaintance with Rubens's formal vocabulary. Rubens's influence on van Diepenbeeck's earlier work can be seen most directly in a number of the prints of mythological scenes for the *Temple des muses*.

Rubens's influence is less obvious in other early works by van Diepenbeeck. The design for the *Presentation in the Temple* (1622–5; ex-J. S. Held priv. col.; now Washington, DC, N.G.A.) is probably van Diepenbeeck's earliest datable work. It is a preliminary study for one of the 12 stained-glass windows depicting episodes from the *Life of the Virgin*, which must have been commissioned soon after van Diepenbeeck settled in Antwerp. The figures' somewhat elongated body type and their long, sharply pointed fingers indicate a preference for Mannerist forms. Van Diepenbeeck's earliest known painting depicts *St Francis of Paola before the Holy Sacrament* (c. 1630; Brussels, Mus. A. Anc.), a work in which these Mannerist features are accompanied by a powerfully realistic depiction of facial types, unthinkable without the influence of Rubens. The whole of van Diepenbeeck's oeuvre from this period onwards is remarkable for its vigorous articulation of musculature, pictorially suggested by a studied use of chiaroscuro. This pronounced sense of volume can also be found in the few surviving modelli (c. 1630–36) for the stained-glass windows depicting episodes from the *Life of*

St Paul, for example an oil sketch of the *Conversion of St Paul* (c. 1633–6; Munich, Alte Pin.; see fig. 1). Van Diepenbeeck's style is also characterized by a heavy, broad outline, which clearly sets off his figures. Another example of van Diepenbeeck's early and strongly modelled work is the painting of *St Norbert* (1634; Antwerp Cathedral), commissioned by Abbot van der Sterre.

After Rubens's death, his work remained crucially important to van Diepenbeeck's artistic activity. As early as 1642, van Diepenbeeck had the engraver Hendrik Snyers print a number of Rubens's compositions that he had copied. Van Diepenbeeck's later work remains indebted to Rubens's style and range of motifs. His paintings, including the *Blessed Waltmann Crowned Abbot of the Abbey of St Michael in Antwerp* (c. 1640–50; Deurne-Antwerp, St Fredeganduskerk; oil sketch, c. 1640, Strasbourg, Mus. B.-A.; see fig. 2) and many oil sketches, are distinctive for their more contrived character and their richer and more varied motifs and compositions. At the same time a striving for greater elegance became apparent, particularly in the poses of the figures and the treatment of light. This occasionally led to a forced quality in the anatomical structure of the figures: their limbs are powerfully muscular but seem to be anatomically imperfect.

1. Abraham van Diepenbeeck: *Conversion of St Paul*, oil sketch on panel, 4.75×2.85 m, c. 1633–6 (Munich, Alte Pinakothek)

Van Diepenbeeck's later work is also characterized by a greater intensity of gesture and expression. The influence of van Dyck, of considerable importance to many Flemish narrative painters in the second half of the 17th century, undoubtedly played a part in this development. Van Dyck's influence is also apparent in the few portraits known to have been produced by van Diepenbeeck, for example the elegant *Family Portrait* (*c.* 1662–3), for which only a drawing survives (Paris, Fond. Custodia, Inst. Néer).

BIBLIOGRAPHY

Thieme–Becker

E. Duverger: 'Abraham Van Diepenbeeck en Gonzáles Coques aan het werk voor de stadhouder Frederik-Hendrik, prins van Oranje', *Jb.: Kon. Mus. S. Kst.* (1972), pp. 181–237

——: 'De moeilijkheden van Abraham van Diepenbeeck met de Antwerpse Sint-Lukasgilde', *Jb.: Kon. Mus. S. Kst.* (1972), pp. 239–62

M. L. Hairs: *Dans le sillage de Rubens: Les Peintres anversois au XVIIe siècle* (Liège, 1977), pp. 151–81

D. Steadman: *Abraham van Diepenbeeck: Seventeenth-century Flemish Painter* (Ann Arbor, 1982); rev. by D. B. Hensbroek-van der Poel in *Oud-Holland, c* (1986), pp. 206–8

J. Wood: 'Padre Resta's Flemish Drawings: Van Diepenbeeck, Van Thulden, Rubens and the School of Fontainebleau', *Master Drgs*, xxviii (1990), pp. 3–53

The Age of Rubens (exh. cat., ed. P. C. Sutton; Boston, MA, Mus. F.A.; Toledo, OH, Mus. A.; 1993–4), pp. 367–70

H. Vlieghe: '"Des peintures très exquises": Abraham van Diepenbeeck's scholderwerk te Parijs', *Wallraf-Richartz-Jb.*, lv (1994)

HANS VLIEGHE

Dieste, Eladio (*b* Artigas, Uruguay, 1 Dec 1917). Uruguayan engineer. He is the only Uruguayan engineer to have made an impact on the international architectural scene, and he achieved this although he was trained as a civil engineer; he graduated in 1943 from the University of Montevideo. He is associated with the substance known as reinforced ceramic, a material produced by combining brick, Portland cement and iron rods. With Dieste's inventiveness and rigorous application of scientific analysis, this material was used to create frameworks of surprising slenderness and to roof large areas using few supports. As Dieste himself explained, the striking results that can be obtained depend less on calculation than on the creation of an appropriate form capable of combining the material with the physical laws of equilibrium and a wider consciousness of the universe. By using bent surfaces or singly or doubly curved vaulting, Dieste achieved significant results in terms of cost reduction and structural efficiency. His deep religious feelings convinced him that there was a basic coincidence between what is moral and what is economic. It is perhaps because of this belief that a method initially devised to resolve problems arising from the construction of such utilitarian buildings as shopping centres (e.g. in Montevideo, 1983–4), storehouses, silos, aerials and industrial buildings was also used with striking aesthetic effect, for example in the wave-walls of the parish church at Atlántida (from 1957) and the restoration (1967–71) of S Pedro in Durazno. In these works Dieste achieved a sensitive handling of space and an interesting use of lighting at a low height to enhance the plasticity of shape and the texture and chromatic quality of brick, which he used not only as a durable material but also as an expressive element.

2. Abraham van Diepenbeeck: *Blessed Waltmann Crowned Abbot of the Abbey of St Michael in Antwerp*, oil sketch on panel, 530×480 mm, *c.* 1640 (Strasbourg, Musée des Beaux-Arts)

BIBLIOGRAPHY

J. P. Bonta: *Eladio Dieste* (Buenos Aires, 1963)

F. Bullrich: *New Directions in Latin American Architecture* (London, 1969), pp. 54–5, 93

D. Bayón and P. Gasparini: *Panorámica de la arquitectura latinoamericana* (Barcelona, 1977), pp. 176–97

J. F. Liernur, ed.: *America latina: Architettura gli ultimi vent'anni* (Milan, 1990)

Arquitectura en Uruguay, 1980–90 (Montevideo, 1992)

MARIANO ARANA

Diet, Arthur-Stanislas (*b* Amboise, 5 April 1827; *d* Paris, 18 Jan or 17 April 1890). French architect. He entered the Ecole des Beaux-Arts, Paris, in 1846 as a student of Félix-Jacques Duban and Guillaume-Abel Blouet, and in 1853 he won the Prix de Rome with a project for a capitol; its scheme of wings connecting mansard-roofed pavilions decorated with engaged orders and caryatids evoked Louis-Tullius-Joachim Visconti's design (1852) for the new Louvre in Paris. In 1854 Diet forfeited his fellowship at the Académie de France in Rome by marrying the daughter of Emile Gilbert, whose practice in Paris he joined. Simultaneously he entered the state architectural bureaucracy. He served on the Conseil Général des Bâtiments Civils in 1854–8 and 1878–9, and in 1881 he became one of its three inspectors-general. Concurrently Diet completed the Musée Napoléon (1859–64; now Musée de Picardie), Amiens, and enlarged the Ecole Nationale Vétérinaire (from 1864) at Alfort, Seine. In 1864 he became architect to the Asile des Aliénés, Charenton, built by Gilbert; he also worked with Gilbert on the Préfecture de Police (1862–76), Paris, and took over its construction in 1869. Between 1865 and 1876 Diet erected and modified

Gilbert's design (1864) for the Hôtel Dieu in Paris (*see* GILBERT, EMILE), to which Diet contributed an Italianate chapel on a Greek-cross plan at the end of the central court. In 1871 Diet succeeded Gilbert as one of the four chief architects of Paris and he was elected to the Académie des Beaux-Arts in 1884. A bureaucratically efficient architect, Diet is remembered chiefly for his collaboration with Gilbert.

BIBLIOGRAPHY

Bellier de La Chavignerie—Auvray; *DBF*
H. Daumet: 'Arthur Diet, architecte: Notice sur sa vie et ses oeuvres', *L'Architecture*, iii (1890), pp. 294–5
A. Normand: 'Notice sur la vie et les travaux de M. Diet', *Institut de France: Académie des beaux-arts* (Paris, 1892)
L. Hautecoeur: *Architecture classique*, vii (1957)
J. Foucart-Borville: 'Quelques constructions publiques à Amiens', *Mnmts Hist.*, cii (1979), pp. 46–51
R. Middleton and D. Watkin: *Neoclassical and 19th century architecture* (New York, 1980)

CHRISTOPHER MEAD

Dietrich [Dietricy], **Christian Wilhelm Ernst** (*b* Weimar, 30 Oct 1712; *d* Dresden, 24 April 1774). German painter and etcher. He received his first training from his father, Johann Georg Dietrich (1684–1752), a court painter at Weimar, and was sent to Dresden at the age of 13 to study under the landscape painter Johann Alexander Thiele (1685–1752). In 1728 they travelled to Arnstadt to paint landscapes for stage sets. In 1730 Thiele presented his pupil to Frederick-Augustus I, Elector of Saxony, as a prodigy; Frederick-Augustus appointed him court painter and entrusted him to his minister Heinrich, Graf von Brühl, for whom he worked on some decorative paintings. From 1732 he used the name 'Dietricy' to sign his paintings. He travelled in Germany from 1734 and may have visited the Netherlands, the source of his artistic inspiration. He returned from his travels in 1741 and was appointed court painter to Frederick-Augustus II, Elector of Saxony, who sent him to Italy in 1743 to study. He visited Venice and Rome but returned to Dresden in 1744. In 1748 he was appointed Inspector of the Gemäldegalerie in Dresden, which had recently become more influential because of important purchases from Italy. The following period saw Dietrich at the height of his success, and his works were in demand all over Europe.

Dietrich was an eclectic painter, mastering the styles of all the 17th- and 18th-century schools, although his preference was for Dutch Italianate painters and the Dutch Little Masters. He was also considerably influenced by Rembrandt, Rubens and Jordaens, and by Watteau (e.g. in his *Gathering in the Park*; Karlsruhe, Staatl. Ksthalle), Titian, Sebastiano Ricci and Rosa. His success lay in his ability to reproduce the painting style of his models with subtlety, while retaining his own stylistic individuality. His landscapes and paintings after Rembrandt were particularly admired. Dietrich's work is frequently dismissed as lacking creativity, but his eclecticism can be understood in response to 18th-century art theorists' requirements concerning selection and imitation.

Dietrich spent the Seven Years War (1756–63) in Freiberg and Meissen. In 1763 he was appointed professor of landscape painting at the newly founded Akademie der Bildenden Künste in Dresden, and in the same year he became Director of the Kunstschule at the porcelain manufactory in Meissen, a post he held until 1770. He was a prolific painter—his oeuvre consists of *c.* 2000 paintings—and a skilled etcher. He had two sisters, Maria Dorothea Dietrich (1719–92), a landscape painter, and Rahel Rosina Dietrich (1720–70), who painted porcelain in Meissen and Berlin.

BIBLIOGRAPHY

Bénézit; Thieme–Becker
W. Becker: *Paris und die deutsche Malerei, 1750–1840* (Munich, 1971)
Neuerwerbungen deutscher Malerei (exh. cat. by H. Marx, Dresden, 1974)
I. M. Keller: *Studien zu den deutschen Rembrandtnachahmungen des 18. Jahrhunderts* (Berlin, 1981)
P. Michel: *C. W. E. Dietrich und die Problematik des Eklektizismus* (Munich, 1984)
Kopie, Nachahmung und Aneignung in den graphischen Künsten des 18. Jahrhunderts (exh. cat., Bremen, Ksthalle, 1986–7)
E. Bagnol: *Christ. W. E. Dietrich: Etat des travaux et recensement de l'oeuvre* (diss., Montpellier, U. Paul Valéry, 1988)
Königliches Dresden (exh. cat. by H. Marx, Munich, 1990)
Katalog der ausgestellten Werke, Dresden, Gemäldegal. Alte Meister cat. (Leipzig, 1992), pp. 172–5

PETRA SCHNIEWIND-MICHEL

Dietrich, (Johann) Joachim (*b* Wernfels-Theilenhofen, near Spalt, 1690; *d* Munich, 24 March 1753). German sculptor. He was the son of a cabinetmaker. In 1712–13 he began his travels as a journeyman from Eichstätt, where he probably trained under the sculptor Christian Handschuher (*fl c.* 1699–1701). He visited Prague, where he met Matyás Václav Jäckel, and Italy. Around 1720 Dietrich settled near Munich and worked as an independent sculptor in turn for the court sculptor Anton Faistenberger and in the court joinery of Johann Adam Pichler (*fl* 1717–61). His first independent works that can be exactly dated—and the only signed ones—are two picture retable altars (1726–7) in the church at Schloss Urfarn near Reisach. The altar of the *Fathers of the Church* (*c.* 1739) at Diessen is one of the finest examples of Rococo sculpture in South Germany. Other notable works by Dietrich are the decoration of the frame altars and a Crucifix (1732) in the Hofmarkskirche at Schönbrunn; a reliquary altar (1739–42) in the chapel of Nymphenburg Palace; a life-size statue of St John of Nepomuk (1750; Berlin, Gemäldegal.); and the choir-stalls (donated 1750) in St Peter, Munich, his last major religious work.

Dietrich's artistic quality is also well displayed in his secular work, such as his ornamental filigree carving. As a collaborator with François de Cuvilliés I, he received many commissions for the decoration of rooms for the court at Munich and for noblemen's houses; they included decorative woodwork for Amalienburg, Nymphenburg (1734–9), and the Residenztheater (1750–53), Munich. Taking into account the difficult carving technique, his ornamental and scenic reliefs are among the finest examples of interior decoration in the Bavarian Rococo style. His formal and technical mastery shows signs of Bohemian and South German influence and, not least, the influence of the Roman Baroque. His elaborate sculptures have a monumental effect; the individual physiognomies present a calm expression, full of spirituality and far removed from Baroque emotionalism. Dietrich ranks alongside Johann Baptist Straub as one of the leading wood-carvers in Munich in the second quarter of the 18th century and is a worthy member of a notable generation of South German and Austrian sculptors in wood.

BIBLIOGRAPHY

H. Keller, ed.: *Die Kunst des 18. Jahrhunderts*, Propyläen-Kstgesch. (Berlin, 1971), pp. 300–01 [entry by P. Volk]
H. von Poser: *Johann Joachim Dietrich und der Hochaltar zu Diessen* (diss., Munich, Ludwig-Maximilians-U., 1975)
P. Volk: *Rokokoplastik in Altbayern, Bayrisch-Schwaben und im Allgau* (Munich, 1981)
Bayerische Rokokoplastik: Vom Entwurf zur Ausführung (exh. cat., ed. P. Volk; Munich, Bayer. Nmus., 1985)

BARBARA DAENTLER

Dietrich, Wendel (*b* Augsburg, *c.* 1535; *d* Augsburg, Nov 1621–April 1622). German cabinetmaker and architect. His name first appears on the tax registers for Augsburg in 1557 and continues to appear regularly until 1621. He married *c.* 1558 and bought a house in 1561, by which time he probably already had his master's certificate. Although there is little mention of his work in the 1560s, his reputation was such that he was employed by Hans Fugger (*see* FUGGER, (3)) in 1569 to work on the new state apartments in the Fuggerhaus on the Weinmarkt in Augsburg. Here he came into contact with such artists as Friedrich Sustris, Alessandro Paduano and Carlo Pallago, whose Grotesque style clearly influenced his later work. By 1573 he had provided tables, chairs, wood panelling and vaults for Fugger's house. Other commissions from the Fugger family followed: there is documentary evidence of a sizeable commission for Marx Fugger, probably for his burial chapel (the Andreaskapelle) in the abbey of SS Ulrich and Afra at Augsburg. Its decoration and furnishings made between 1578 and 1584 included a large carved altar (1580) and choir-stalls (1581), which are generally attributed to Dietrich. The design for the marble screen enclosing the Fugger chapel may also have been by Dietrich. The figures of the apostles on the screen can be ascribed to Hubert Gerhard and Pallago, with whom Dietrich again collaborated from 1582 at Hans Fugger's country house at Kirchheim an der Mindel. In 1582 he was commissioned to make the wooden ceiling and doorways of the Banqueting Hall and the adjoining rooms. The coffered ceiling (see fig.) covers an area of 375 sq. m, using different woods to produce a subtle range of colours. With its rich ornamentation of mouldings, cartouches, garlands of flowers and masks, it is a remarkable example of the German late Renaissance style.

From 1582 or 1583 Dietrich also worked on the new Jesuit church of St Michael in Munich, founded by William V, Duke of Bavaria, and Roeck suggests that he may have been involved in the design of the building as well as its construction. The design and model for the new college buildings (1584) for St Michael have been attributed to Dietrich (Dischinger, 1980). Possibly in collaboration with his son, Jakob Dietrich (*b* 1559–60, *d* after 1636), Dietrich made the high altar (1586–9) and choir-stalls for St Michael.

In 1587 Dietrich became technical and administrative supervisor at the architects' office in the court of William V in Munich; his son Jakob continued to run the cabinet-making workshop in Augsburg. Dietrich kept his position until William abdicated in 1597, after which he continued to work privately for William on such projects as the

Wendel Dietrich: detail of the ceiling of the Banqueting Hall in Schloss der Fugger, Kircheim an der Mindel, begun 1582

rebuilding of the Marienberg fortress at Würzburg in 1600 and possibly on his country estate at Schleissheim, near Munich, which had seven wooden chapels.

Thieme–Becker

BIBLIOGRAPHY

A. Buff: 'Wendel Dietrich', *Z. Hist. Ver. Schwaben & Neuburg*, xv (1888), pp. 89–147
L. Gmelin: *Die St Michaelskirche in München* (Bamberg, 1890)
G. Lill: *Hans Fugger (1531–1598) und die Kunst* (Leipzig, 1908), pp. 97–113
M. von Freeden: *Schloss Marienberg unter Fürstbischof Julius Echter von Mespelbrunn, 1573–1617* (Würzburg, 1951)
G. Dischinger: 'Die Jesuitenkirche St Michael in München: Zur frühen Planungs- und Baugeschichte', *Um Glauben und Reich: Kurfürst Maximilian I* ii/1 of *Wittelsbach und Bayern* (exh. cat., ed. H. Glaser; Munich, Residenz, 1980), pp. 152–66
B. Roeck: 'Matthias Kager und die süddeutsche Architektur des frühen 17. Jahrhunderts', *Oberbayer. Archv*, cxi (1986), p. 58

DOROTHEA DIEMER

Dietterlin, Wendel [Grapp, Wendling] (*b* Pfullendorf, nr Konstanz, 1550–51; *d* Strasbourg, 1599). German painter, draughtsman and engraver. He was the son of a Protestant pastor and spent his childhood in Lissenheim before moving to Strasbourg with his widowed mother. On 12 November 1570 he married Catherina Sprewer, and in 1571 he obtained Strasbourg citizenship. In 1575 he painted frescoes on the façade of the Brüderhof (destr. 1769). He was at Hagenau in 1583 and at Oberkirch in 1589. Also in 1589, he worked on the decoration of the Neu Bau (now Chambre de Commerce) in Strasbourg; the frescoes, known from engravings of the building (e.g. by Jean-Martin Weiss) and from descriptions, combined mythological and biblical scenes in an interesting iconographical relationship and emphasized the architectural structure of the façade. Dieterlin's only authenticated easel painting is the signed and dated *Raising of Lazarus* (?1582 or ?1587; Karlsruhe, Staatl. Ksthalle; see fig.), which has the characteristics of northern Mannerism: the centre of the composition, towards which the figures look, is deliberately brought out of symmetry to the right; the scene is viewed from below, and the ample gestures of the figures cause them to mingle and intertwine, creating arbitrary rhythmic connections. The intensity of these deliberately complicated movements and tensions is not accentuated by contrasted effects of light. The painting as a whole shows the influence of the Netherlands, while the bright colours are typically German, although some of the figures reveal an Italian influence, probably mediated through German art; others are taken directly from earlier German paintings or inspired by Tobias Stimmer. The only figure looking at the viewer may be a self-portrait (see Martin).

Two engravings by Matthäus Greuter (*c.* 1566–1638) reproduce untraced works by Dieterlin, both probably ceiling paintings: the *Fall of Phaeton* (1588) and the *Ascension of Elijah* (1589). The latter was his best-known work, according to Sandrart; it accentuates the view from below with exaggerated foreshortening and intensifies the forward flight of the chariot of fire. Another work, *Truth*

Wendel Dieterlin: *Raising of Lazarus*, oil on panel, 838×105 mm, ?1582 or ?1587 (Karlsruhe, Staatliche Kunsthalle)

Triumphant, known through an engraving by his grandson Bartholomaus Dieterlin (*b c.* 1590), is reminiscent of works Dieterlin produced in Stuttgart after 1590, when he was at the court of Württemberg to paint the ceiling of the upper room of the Lusthaus. These frescoes (lost) are known through an engraving by Brentel (1619) and a description in the Stuttgart chronicle in 1622. The detailed iconographic programme was determined by Gadner, Privy Councillor to Duke Ludwig VI of Württemberg, and by the court preacher, Lucas Osiander: *Christ in Majesty with the Lamb* was in the centre, between the *Creation and Original Sin* and the *Last Judgement*. Two drawings are possibly connected to the Lusthaus ceiling: a *Vision of the Apocalypse* (Hamburg, Ksthalle) and a *Last Judgement* (Stuttgart, Staatsgal.). Their overall organization in a visionary celestial space is the same, but the juxtaposition of deeply cut-away or empty planes deprives the compositions of spatial unity. However, two later drawings, the *Story of Abraham* and the *Story of Jacob and Joseph* (both *c.* 1595; Basle, Kstmus.), possess a more coherent treatment of space.

As a Mannerist painter, Dieterlin was influenced by Stimmer, Christoph Murer and the Haarlem School, and he was one of the precursors of the German Baroque. He is, however, now best known for his book *Architectura*. The definitive version was published in Nuremberg in 1598; its 203 engravings are divided into 5 parts, corresponding to the 5 orders—Tuscan, Doric, Ionic, Corinthian and Composite—modelled on Vitruvius' *On Architecture*. Like Vitruvius, Dieterlin attributed a particular quality to each order: the two 'masculine' orders, Tuscan and Doric, are represented by a peasant and a soldier, and the two 'feminine' orders, Ionic and Corinthian, by a young and a mature woman respectively. Dieterlin deals only briefly with the construction of columns on the first plate of each order (the only plates accompanied by text) before giving free rein to his imagination, suggesting various ways of using the five orders for doors, windows, chimney-pieces, tombstones and fountains. He was not particularly interested in pure architectural theory or in specifying measurements and proportions, though his treatise did influence later architects and cabinetmakers. In his role as painter rather than architectural theorist (he put his name to the book as a 'painter of Strasbourg') he was more concerned with the meaning of the principle of each order and the free transformation of architecture by ornament; in the plates he included figures and animals, juxtaposing Classical mythology and biblical scenes and combining masks, grotesques and volutes with Late Gothic motifs, giving a new dimension to the orders in a language that was both naturalistic and fantastic.

PRINTS
Architectura und Ausstheilung der V. Seulen: Das erst Buch (Stuttgart, 1593)
Architectur von Portalen und Thürgerichten mancherley arten: Das ander Buch (Strasbourg, 1594)
Architectura von Aussheilung Symetria und Proportion der fünf Seulen und aller darauss volgender Kunst Arbeit von Fenstern, Caminen, Thürgerichten, Portalen, Bronnen und Epitaphien, 2 vols (Nuremberg, 1598) [rev. edn of the 1593 and 1594 vols]

BIBLIOGRAPHY
Thieme–Becker
J. von Sandrart: *Teutsche Academie* (1675–9); ed. A. R. Pelzer (1925)
K. Ohnesorge: *Wendel Dieterlin: Maler von Strassburg* (Leipzig, 1893)

M. Pirr: *Die Architectura des Wendel Dietterlin* (Stuttgart, 1940)

K. Martin: 'Der Maler Wendel Dietterlin', *Festschrift für Karl Lohmeyer* (Saarbrücken, 1954), pp. 14–29

E. Forsmann: *Säule und Ornament: Studien zum Problem des Manierismus in den nordischen Säulenbüchern und Vorlageblättern des 16. und 17. Jahrhunderts* (Stockholm, 1956), pp. 159–73

W. Pfeiffer: 'Zur eine Deckenvisierung des Wendel Dietterlin', *Jb. Hamburg. Kstsamml.*, vi (1961), pp. 54–71

A. K. Placzek: *The Fantastic Engravings of Wendel Dietterlin: The 203 Plates and Text of his 'Architectura'* (New York, 1968)

Die Renaissance im deutschen Südwesten zwischen Reformation und Dreissigjährigem Krieg (exh. cat. by H. Appuhn and others, Heidelberg, Schloss; Karlsruhe, Bad. Landesmus.; 1986)

MICHÈLE-CAROLINE HECK

Dietz, Feodor [Theodor] (*b* Neustetten, Baden, 29 May 1813; *d* Arc le Gray, France, 18 Dec 1870). German painter. In 1831 he entered the Munich Akademie der Bildenden Künste, where his abilities were so remarkable that he was employed as assistant to Philipp von Foltz on the encaustic wall paintings for the Queen's apartment in the Residenz. In 1835 his *Death of Piccolomini* (1835; Karlsruhe, Staatl. Ksthalle), a dramatically charged scene from the Thirty Years War inspired by Schiller's drama *Wallenstein*, received considerable acclaim; it is a characteristic example of his work. In 1837 he moved to Paris, where he spent three years studying, principally under Horace Vernet. In 1839 he won a Gold Medal at the Salon with the *Death of Piccolomini*. In 1840 he was appointed court painter at Baden, and in 1841 he took up residence in Munich, entering the intellectual circle around the king, Ludwig I. In his new position he embarked on a series of national and military subjects; *Military Display at Night* (1853) was well received in Paris and was acquired by the emperor, Napoleon III.

Dietz played a formative if conservative role in the German art establishment. In 1864 he was appointed professor at the Karlsruhe Akademie der Bildenden Künste, and in 1867 he represented his country at the Exposition Universelle in Paris, as president of the German Kunstverein. In 1870 he volunteered as a medical auxiliary during the Franco-Prussian war, dying of an apoplectic fit during the campaign.

BIBLIOGRAPHY

ADB; Seubert; Thieme–Becker

G. K. Nagler: *Monogrammisten* (1858–1920)

Dietz, (Adam) Ferdinand. *See* TIETZ, FERDINAND.

Dieu, Antoine (*b* Paris, 1662; *d* Paris, 12 April 1727). French painter, dealer, draughtsman and designer. He was a pupil of Charles Le Brun and in 1686 won the Prix de Rome with his painting *Entry of Noah, his Family and the Animals into the Ark* (untraced). He evidently earned his living from both painting and picture-dealing; the picture-dealing establishment that he founded in 1699 and left in 1714 was subsequently taken over by Edmé-François Gersaint.

Around 1700 Dieu contributed to the decoration of the Ménagerie at the château of Versailles, producing *Young Girls Playing at Knuckle Bones* (untraced; two copies exist, one at Versailles, Château). In 1708–9, in collaboration with Christophe and Nicolas Bertin, he provided drawings (untraced) for the stained-glass windows of the chapel at Versailles (*in situ*). The following year he was commissioned to paint the *Birth of the Duke of Burgundy* and then the *Marriage of the Duke of Burgundy* (both Versailles, Château), two rather static and artificially posed works. He also painted a number of allegorical portraits of Louis XIV; the only extant record of these is Jean Arnold's engraving after Dieu's *Louis XIV Enthroned* (Paris, Bib. N.).

In 1722 Dieu was received (*reçu*) as a member of the Académie Royale on presenting *Hannibal's Battle at Lake Trasimene* (Paris, Louvre), a work strongly reminiscent of Le Brun's battle scenes, as was *Horatius Cocles Defending the Bridge* (untraced; drawing, Florence, Uffizi), Dieu's unsuccessful entry in the special 1727 history painting competition for Academicians.

Although few of Dieu's paintings survive, many of his drawings are known. They display a wide range of styles and media but share certain basic characteristics: his figures tend to be elongated, with small heads. At his best he was an elegant and inventive draughtsman, producing graceful allegories such as his *Allegorical Homage to Louis-Auguste de Bourbon, Duc du Maine, Grand-Maître de l'Artillerie* (1697 or before; New York, Met.; see fig.), as well as scenes from ancient history and the Bible and refined decorative designs full of serpentine curves and scrolls. The latter, for instance the *Frontispiece with Allegory of Faith* (Moscow, Pushkin Mus. F.A.), are early examples of the Rococo style. His brother Jean Dieu (1658–1714) was an engraver.

Antoine Dieu: *Allegorical Homage to Louis-Auguste de Bourbon, Duc du Maine, Grand-Maître de l'Artillerie*, pen and black ink and grey wash over traces of red chalk, 209×156 mm, 1697 or before (New York, Metropolitan Museum of Art)

BIBLIOGRAPHY

P.-J. Mariette: 'Abecedario', *Archvs A. Fr.*, ii (1851–3), p. 112

P. Rosenberg: 'Le Concours de peinture en 1727', *Rev. A.* [Paris], xxxvii (1977), pp. 29–42

——: 'Dieu as a Draughtsman', *Master Drgs*, xvii, no. 17 (1979), pp. 161–9

SIMON LEE

Dieu Soult, Jean de. *See* SOULT, Maréchal.

Dieussart [Dusart; Dysart], **François** (*b* Arquinghem, nr Armentières, *c.* 1600; *d* London, 1661). Flemish Walloon sculptor. He was probably already a fully-fledged sculptor at the time of his arrival in Rome, recorded in 1622 in the register of the Brotherhood of S Giuliano dei Fiamminghi, a charitable foundation run by and for the Flemish colony in the city; by 1630 Dieussart had become its *proviseur*. While in Rome he called himself Francesco Vallone (i.e. Walloon), to emphasize that he came from French Flanders. A Crucifix and an ivory statuette of the *Woman of Samaria*, as well as a plaster statue to Bernini's design for the catafalque of *Cardinal Carlo Barberini* (all untraced), are the only works recorded from his prolonged stay in Rome.

Between 1636 and 1641 Dieussart was employed in London by Queen Henrietta Maria and Thomas Howard, 2nd Earl of Arundel. In 1636 he made a monumental monstrance (destr.) in the Baroque style for the Queen's Roman Catholic chapel in Somerset House (then Denmark House), London. In connection with Arundel's diplomatic efforts in 1636 to restore the Palatinate to Charles Louis (*d* 1680), the exiled Elector Palatine and nephew of Charles I, Dieussart carved four superb portrait busts, portraying *Charles I* (1636) and *Prince Charles Louis* (1637; both Arundel Castle, W. Sussex); *Prince Rupert of the Rhine*, Charles Louis's younger brother (1637) and the *Earl of Arundel* himself (1637–8; both Oxford, Ashmolean). The bust of *Charles I* was executed in the same year as van Dyck's portrait of him in three positions (Windsor Castle, Berks, Royal Col.), painted to be used by Bernini in Rome as a model for a bust. Dieussart likewise modelled the head of his bust on that portrait, but he clothed the shoulders in armour decorated only with a pendant of St George from the Order of the Garter. In contrast, the bust of *Charles Louis* wears armour carved all over with figures in relief, representing a fashionable repoussé steel coat; the breastplate depicts Vulcan making Weapons for Mars, watched by Venus and Cupid. The bust of *Prince Rupert* has a plain cuirass with a generous sword-sash running diagonally across it, knotted on the right shoulder, as in Bernini's bust of *Charles I* (destr.), which arrived in London in July 1637. Dieussart was thus responsible for spreading through England the very latest stylistic developments of Baroque Rome.

At the start of the Civil War in England Dieussart moved to The Hague, where in 1641 he carved busts of the deceased Elector Palatine *Frederick V* and of his widow, *Elizabeth Stuart*—the exiled 'Winter King' and 'Winter Queen' of Bohemia (both Marienburg, Ernst August Prinz von Hannover; version of the Queen's bust, London, V&A). In the same year Dieussart also carved a bust of the Stadtholder of the Netherlands, *Frederick Henry of Orange Nassau* (ex-Wörlitz, Schloss, Gotische Haus) and one (untraced) of his new daughter-in-law, *Princess Mary Stuart* (1631–60). Frederick Henry is shown in armour and wearing a Berninesque sword-sash knotted on his shoulder, both arms cradling his commander's baton. The half-length format proves that Dieussart was familiar with developments in Rome. He also carved rather stolid busts of *Pieter Spieringh van Silfvercrona* (*d* 1652) and of his wife *Joanna* (Amsterdam, Rijksmus.). Dieussart next moved to Denmark, where in 1644 he carved a marble bust of *Christian IV* (1577–1648) and cast a still more sumptuous one in bronze (both Copenhagen, Rosenborg Slot); the stout warrior monarch is shown in Roman armour and wreathed with laurel, a military cloak draped round his shoulders to give an impression of movement. Dieussart also planned an equestrian statue of the King, which was never completed; he carved a marble portrait of the *Crown Prince Christian* (untraced) and modelled a bust of the King's actual successor, the future *Frederick III* (*reg* 1648–70), which was cast in bronze only in 1661–4 (Copenhagen, Kastellet).

From *c.* 1644 Dieussart returned to the Netherlands, executing a wall tomb (The Hague, Grote Kerk) for *Charles Morgan*, Governor of Bergen op Zoom (*d* 1642), with portrait statues of his widowed daughter and two of her children gathered in a niche behind the effigy. He subsequently received from the Dutch court numerous commissions, including a bust of *Prince Maurice of Orange Nassau* (1645; ex-Sonnenburg in Neumark, Johanniterkirche) and a series of statues of the four successive Princes of Orange Nassau (1646–7; destr. 1945) for the vestibule of the Huis ten Bosch in The Hague. These grandly conceived figures, clad in contemporary full-length armour that recalls statues by Giuliano Finelli in Naples (e.g. *Carlo Maria Carraciolo*, *c.* 1641; San Giovanni a Carbonara) and Hubert Le Sueur's *Earl of Pembroke* in the quadrangle of the Old Schools, Oxford, were the documented core of his oeuvre. Dieussart further executed a half-length bust (*c.* 1647–50; ex-Wörlitz, Schloss, Gotische Haus) of *Prince William II of Orange Nassau* (1626–50) and another of his brother-in-law, *Frederick William, Elector of Brandenburg* (Berlin, Bodemus.), as well as portrait medallions in marble of the *Elector* and his new bride, *Princess Louise Henrietta of Orange* (1647; Doorn, Huis Doorn). None of these works is very vivacious by Italian standards, though this may be an accurate reflection of the personalities of Dieussart's sitters rather than a shortcoming of his powers of portraiture. It was probably through the dynastic link with Brandenburg that Dieussart next went to work in Berlin (1650–55), carving yet more images of members of the houses of Orange Nassau and Brandenburg, as well as some statues and fountain figures (destr.) for the Elector's new garden.

The last phase of Dieussart's career was in his native Flanders, where in 1656 he carved his last works: an imposing bust of the Regent of the southern Netherlands, *Leopold William* (Vienna, Ksthist. Mus.), and two of *Charles II* of England, then living in exile in Bruges (1656–8; Bruges, Gruuthusemus. and Kon. Hoofgilde St Sebastian). Dieussart probably accompanied Charles II to London at the Stuart Restoration in the very real hope of having his appointment as Court Sculptor renewed—but he was foiled by death.

Dieussart played an important role as a portrait sculptor throughout the Protestant courts of northern Europe by spreading examples of the Baroque style, which he must have learnt under Bernini's aegis in Rome. Several of his busts are memorable; he bridged the gap between the late Mannerist images that were current *c.* 1600–30 and the great flowering of Flemish and Dutch Baroque portraiture, in the hands of Artus Quellinus (i) and of Rombout Verhulst, in the second half of the 17th century.

BIBLIOGRAPHY
M. D. Whinney and O. Millar: *English Art, 1625–1714* (Oxford, 1957), pp. 122–4
M. Whinney: *Sculpture in Britain: 1530 to 1830*, Pelican Hist. A. (Harmondsworth, 1964, rev. 1988), pp. 91–2
M. Vickers: 'A New Portrait by Dieussart and Bernini's Charles I', *Apollo*, cvii (1978), pp. 161–9
C. Avery: *Studies in European Sculpture*, i (London, 1981), pp. 205–35
D. Howarth: *Lord Arundel and his Circle* (New Haven and London, 1985), pp. 161–4
A. MacGregor, ed.: *The Late King's Goods* (London and Oxford, 1989), pp. 97–8
N. Penny: *Catalogue of European Sculpture in the Ashmolean Museum: 1540 to the Present Day*, iii: *British* (Oxford, 1992), pp. 37–41
CHARLES AVERY

Diez, Ernst (*b* Lölling, 27 July 1878; *d* Vienna, 8 July 1961). Austrian historian of Byzantine, Islamic and Indian art. He studied art history and archaeology at the universities of Vienna and Graz and in 1902 completed his doctorate at Graz under Josef Strzygowski and Wilhelm Gurlitt, a study of the paintings in a manuscript of Dioskurides' *De materia medica* (Vienna, Österreich. Nbib., Cod. med. gr. 1) copied for the Byzantine princess Juliana Anicia before AD 512. After military service (1902–3), Diez pursued further research in Rome and Istanbul and worked in Vienna as a volunteer (1905–7) at the Österreichisches Museum für Kunst und Industrie. From 1908 to 1911 he worked in Berlin at the Kaiser-Friedrich Museum with MAX JACOB FRIEDLÄNDER, WILHELM BODE and FRIEDRICH SARRE. He was then appointed lecturer at the University of Vienna. From 1912 to 1914 he made trips to Iran, India, Egypt and Anatolia, which led to articles on Islamic art and architecture and *Die Kunst der islamischen Völker*. After World War I he continued at the University of Vienna, where he was appointed professor in 1924. He wrote about Buddhist and Islamic art in India and Afghanistan, publishing *Die Kunst des Islam* in 1925. From 1926 he taught at Bryn Mawr College in Pennsylvania and travelled to China, Japan, India and Java (1930–31). In the 1930s he wrote about Byzantine mosaics in Greece and contributed articles on Islamic art to the *Encyclopaedia of Islam* and the *Survey of Persian Art*. At the outbreak of World War II he resumed work at the University of Vienna, publishing *Entschliertes Asien* and *Iranische Kunst*. From 1943 to 1948 he taught art history at the University of Istanbul, where he researched Ottoman and Byzantine art. He returned to Vienna for the remainder of his life.

WRITINGS
Die Kunst der islamischen Völker (Berlin, 1915)
with H. Glück: *Die Kunst des Islam* (Berlin, 1925)
Entschliertes Asien: Alte Kulturen vom Zweistromland bis zum gelben Fluss (Berlin, 1940; Vienna, 1954); Eng. trans. as *The Ancient Worlds of Asia* (London, 1961)
Iranische Kunst (Vienna, 1944)

BIBLIOGRAPHY
O. Aslanapa, ed.: *Beiträge zur Kunstgeschichte Asiens: In Memoriam Ernst Diez* (Istanbul, 1963)
S. J. VERNOIT

Diez, Julius (*b* Nuremberg, 18 Sept 1870; *d* 1954). German painter and designer. From 1888 to 1892 he studied in Munich under the German painters Ferdinand Barth (1842–92) and Rudolf Seitz (1842–1910) at the Akademie der Bildenden Künste. He worked on the newspaper *Jugend*, producing historical scenes reminiscent of those of the Jugendstil in Munich, as well as bookplates, posters and the pelican motif for the art suppliers Gunther & Wagner in 1898. He also designed furniture, ceramics for the firm Villeroy & Boch, windows for the town halls in Essen, Duisburg and Leipzig and engraved glass for the factory of Ferdinand von Poschinger. In 1907 he became a professor at the Kunstgewerbeschule in Munich, and in the following year made wall paintings for the exhibition *München 1908*. The success of these led to commissions for frescoes and mosaics at the Kurhaus in Wiesbaden, the Bahnhof in Nuremberg, the Rathaus in Hannover and the Ehrenhalle at the Ludwig-Maximilians-Universität in Munich. In these he used Classical mythological motifs in a modern style, influenced to some extent by Franz von Stuck. He also followed in von Stuck's footsteps as president of the Munich Secession and from about 1925 as a professor at the Akademie der Bildenden Künste in Munich.

BIBLIOGRAPHY
P. Westheim: 'Diez', *Kst & Handwk*, lx (1909–10), pp. 361–72
G. P. Woeckel: 'Glasfenster-Entwürfe des Münchner Jugendstilmalers Julius Diez (1870–1954)', *Die Weltkunst*, lvii/15 (1987), pp. 2025–9
J. A. SCHMOLL gen. EISENWERTH

Diez de Armendariz, Lorenzo María Muntaner y. *See* MUNTANER.

Díez del Valle, Lázaro. *See* DÍAZ DEL VALLE, LÁZARO.

Díez Navarro, Luis (*b* Málaga, *c.* 1700; *d* Guatemala, *c.* 1780). Spanish military engineer, active in Mexico and Guatemala. In 1731–2 he arrived in New Spain with a royal commission. By 1733 he was director of works for the new Real Casa de la Moneda (Royal Mint; 1731–4) in Mexico City. He was involved with the fortifications (1731, 1733, 1738) at Veracruz and worked at the Sanctuary of the Villa de Guadalupe (1737–8), outside Mexico City. Díez Navarro also collaborated on the largest engineering project in New Spain, the draining of the Valle de México (1736–41). In 1740 he designed the church of S Brígida (destr.) in Mexico City, one of the only churches in Spanish America with an oval plan. In Mexico City in 1739 he became Maestro Mayor at the Palácio de los Virreyes and at the Reales Alcázares as well as in the Cathedral. In 1741 he became Ingeniero Ordinario and shortly after was assigned to the Kingdom of Guatemala. One of his first tasks was to inspect the Caribbean coast, paying particular attention to its defences. He continued to be involved with coastal defences and made the first designs (1743–4) for the fort at Omoa. From 1751 he carried out major modifications to the Real Palacio, Santiago de Guatemala (now Antigua). The two-storey stone arcading along the main square (1760s) is similar to that previously built for the Ayuntamiento in the same square. He also designed the building for the royal Renta de Tabacos (1766–8) and the Casa de Chamorro (1762) in the same city, and probably also made the designs (1765; Seville, Archv Gen. Indias) for the unbuilt Hospicio de S Vicente, El Salvador, which feature an oval chapel similar to that of S Brígida, Mexico City. Following the Guatemala earthquake of 1773, he played a major role in assessing damage and made the first plans for Guatemala City (1776). Despite his age and lack of mobility, he continued to supervise all royal works until 1777.

BIBLIOGRAPHY

D. Angulo Iñiguez: *Planos de monumentos arquitectónicos de América y Filipinas en el Archivo de Indias* (Seville, 1939)
H. Berlin: 'El ingeniero Luis Díez Navarro en México', *An. Soc. Geog. & Hist. Guatemala*, xx (1974), pp. 89–95

JORGE LUJÁN-MUÑOZ

Diffusion. *See under* DISSEMINATION.

Dighton. English family of graphic artists and painters. John Dighton was a print-seller; his son Robert Dighton (i) (*b* ?London, ?1752; *d* London, 1814) exhibited drawings annually from the age of 17 (at first calling himself Deighton) at the Society of Artists and the Free Society. Robert entered the Royal Academy Schools in 1772 and contributed to the Academy exhibitions. He eventually settled at 4 Spring Gardens, Charing Cross, where he owned a print shop and gave drawing lessons, calling himself a drawing-master. By the 1790s he had produced many watercolours and coloured engravings, including *A Book of Heads*, and had become well known as an actor–singer at Sadler's Wells Theatre.

Robert was often in financial difficulties and as a remedy stole prints from the British Museum, including a Rembrandt landscape that he competently copied and sold to a dealer. When the theft was traced to Dighton in 1806, he agreed to return the prints he had, but the scandal forced him to flee London. He went to live in Oxford, Cambridge, Bath, Cheltenham and Brighton, where he produced slightly satirical full-length portraits of leading personalities. He returned, acclaimed and apparently forgiven, to London in 1810 to manage his own printing-press with his sons until his death.

Compared with those of his contemporaries James Gillray and George Cruikshank, Robert Dighton's caricatures were fairly mild, poking fun—with attractively coloured and humorously titled portrait etchings—at royal, noble, military, university, sport, political, law, church and stage personalities; the British Museum and the Victoria & Albert Museum in London have substantial collections of these. In 1953 a volume of 128 watercolours was sold at Sotheby's, and in 1978 a quantity of them were bought for the Yale Center for British Art, New Haven, CT. It was then discovered that many of these were related to a group of hitherto unattributed mezzotints that evidently date from Dighton's early period. Dighton's work progressed from clumsy beginnings to a more precise attention to detail and colour; his caricatures provide a valuable record of contemporary social habits and Georgian pageantry, pastimes and wit.

Robert Dighton (ii) (*b* 1786; *d* 1865), the son of Robert (i), but like his brothers probably illegitimate, followed an army career and drew many full-length portraits of soldiers, with meticulous attention to the uniforms and customs of the regiments. Most were signed *Dighton Jun* or *R. Dighton Jun*. A large collection of his work is at Windsor Castle. Denis Dighton (*b* London, 1792; *d* St Servan, Brittany, 8 Aug 1827) was also the son of Robert (i) and obtained an army commission from George, Prince of Wales, but resigned a year later. He produced some full-length portraits before exhibiting battle scenes at the Royal Academy and in 1815 was appointed 'battle painter and military draughtsman' to the Prince of Wales. *Nelson Falling Mortally Wounded at Trafalgar* (1805; London, Nat. Mar. Mus.) is characteristic of his historical work. He died in France of mental derangement. His wife, also an artist, became 'fruit and flower painter' to Queen Adelaide, exhibiting at the Royal Academy between 1824 and 1854.

Richard Dighton (i) (*b* 1795; *d* Hammersmith, 1880), another son of Robert (i), at first made prints of a caricature type, but after 1828 he produced a few silhouettes and rather stiff watercolours and engravings, usually full-length, of City and West End characters and prominent stage personalities. He also lived in Worcester and Cheltenham. One of his sons, Richard Dighton (ii) (*b* 1823; *d c.* 1900), was an artist and so possibly was another son, Joshua Dighton (*b* 1831; *d* 1908), whose work consisted of proficient watercolour profiles of sporting personalities and landed gentry. The existence of a fourth son of Robert Dighton (i), also called Joshua, has been conjectured, and Joshua's work attributed to him.

BIBLIOGRAPHY

D. C. Calthorp: 'Robert and Richard Dighton', *Connoisseur*, xiv (1906), pp. 231–6
Bickerstaffe: 'The Dightons', *The Field*, 12 (1926)
H. M. Hake: 'Dighton Caricatures', *Print Colr Q.*, xiii/2 (1926), pp. 137–55, xiii/3 (1926), pp. 237–47
R. Edwards: 'The Watercolours of Robert Dighton', *Apollo*, xiv (1931), pp. 98–102
A. P. Oppé: *English Drawings of the Stuart and Georgian Periods in the Collection of His Majesty the King at Windsor Castle* (London, 1950)
A. E. Haswell Miller and N. P. Dawnay: *Military Drawings and Paintings in the Collection of Her Majesty the Queen at Windsor Castle* (London, 1966)
M. D. George: *Hogarth to Cruickshank: Social Change in Graphic Satire* (London, 1967)
A. Bury: 'Unknown Drawings by Robert Dighton', *Connoisseur*, clxvi/670 (1967), pp. 237–41
D. Rose: *Life, Times and Recorded Works of Robert Dighton (1752–1814) and Three of his Artist Sons* (London, 1981)
D. Patten: 'Richard and Joshua Dighton Discovered', *Ant. Colr*, liv/3 (1983), pp. 86–9
English Caricature, 1620 to the Present (exh. cat., ed. R. Godfrey; London, V&A, 1984)

DENNIS ROSE

Digneffe, Bartholomé [Barthélémy] (*b* Liège, 6 Oct 1724; *d* Liège, 14 June 1784). Flemish architect. His early works in Liège included enlarging the abbey of St Laurent (1750–58; now a hospital) and completing the Premonstratensian church (1762; now the chapel of the Palais des Princes-Evêques); the adjoining buildings, also to Digneffe's designs, were finished posthumously in 1793. He also designed a theatre (1766–7; destr. 1805) in Liège and was involved in a project to improve the urban planning of the town, a scheme that was later partly executed (1810–11). Around 1780 he began major rebuilding works on the château of Amstenrade, 20 km north-east of Maastricht.

The style he used, which was typical of the region at the end of the 18th century, borrowed heavily from the contemporary French Neo-classical idiom. Broad bands of natural stone decorate the full length of the building, which is crowned by a giant pediment. During the same period Digneffe worked on the Hôtel de Hayme de Bomal (now the Musée d'Armes), Liège; he closely followed the Louis XVI style for this building, exemplified by its rusticated ground-floor, its giant rusticated pilasters, crowned with rosettes and knots, spanning the second and third storeys, and its mansard roof. Digneffe designed numerous private houses in Liège throughout his career. He was a friend of the French architect Jacques-Germain Soufflot. Like Laurent Benoît Dewez and others in the southern Netherlands, he worked in a strict Neo-classical style, his close adherence to which may have inhibited his own powers of invention.

BIBLIOGRAPHY

Thieme–Becker

J. van Ackere: *Baroque and Classic Art in Belgium: 1600–1789* (Brussels, 1972)

Le Patrimoine monumental de la Belgique, iii, Ministère de la Culture Française (Liège, 1974)

RENÉE VAN DER VLOODT

Dijck [Dyck], **Abraham van** (*b* Amsterdam, 1635–6; *bur* Amsterdam, 26 Feb 1672). Dutch painter and draughtsman. He is thought to have been a pupil of Rembrandt in Amsterdam *c*. 1650. There is no documentary evidence for this, but his earliest dated painting, the *Presentation in the Temple* (1655; ex-priv. col. Sidney van den Bergh, Wassenaar, see Sumowski, 1983, no. 357), shows that he had certainly seen examples of Rembrandt's work. He was an eclectic artist, given to following several models simultaneously. This is evident from two versions of *Elijah and the Widow of Zarephath*; one (1655–60; Copenhagen, Stat. Mus. Kst) is painted in horizontal format in the style of Barent Fabritius, while the other (1655–60; Milwaukee, WI, A. Bader priv. col., see Sumowski, 1983, no. 362) features large half-length figures in the manner of Nicolaes Maes. In another biblical scene, *Benjamin and Judah* (1655–60; Chicago, IL, A. Inst.), he followed the example of Rembrandt. His best works, such as *Saying Grace* (1655–60; Hannover, Niedersächs. Landesmus.) and the *Old Prophetess* (1655–60; Leipzig, Mus. Bild. Kst), show old women either praying or sleeping and confirm that Maes was his main source of inspiration. Similar subjects are represented in the drawings attributed to him (e.g. *Old Woman Seated, Holding a Book*; New York, Pierpont Morgan Lib.). In the late 1650s van Dijck also seems to have been influenced by the genre paintings of Gabriël Metsu and above all by Quiringh van Brekelenkam, as in *Hermit Praying in a Cave* (late 1650s; St Petersburg, Hermitage) and *Family Saying Grace* (late 1650s; Stockholm, Nmus.).

BIBLIOGRAPHY

W. Sumowski: *Drawings of the Rembrandt School* (New York, 1980), iii, pp. 1247–1309

——: *Gemälde der Rembrandt-Schüler* (Landau/Pfalz, 1983), i, pp. 666–711; review by J. Bruyn in *Oud-Holland*, xcviii (1984), pp. 146–62

B. P. J. BROOS

Dijck, Floris van. *See* DYCK, FLORIS VAN.

Dijk [Dyk]**, Philip van** (*b* Amsterdam, 10 Jan 1680; *d* The Hague, 2 Feb 1753). Dutch painter and art dealer. After his apprenticeship with Arnold Boonen, which began in 1696, he worked for some time in Amsterdam, settling in Middelburg, capital of Zeeland, after his marriage and becoming a member of the painters' guild in 1708. In Middelburg he was highly successful as a portrait painter and produced numerous paintings of prominent Zeelanders, done in the style of Boonen and of Boonen's predecessors, Nicolaes Maes and Caspar Netscher. In view of this conservatism, van Dijk, whose personal style is typified by a smooth finish and the elegant but often rather strained poses of his models, can be seen as an epigon of 17th-century Dutch painting. His portraits are sometimes life-sized, but more often in smaller format.

Besides painting, van Dijk also worked as an art dealer in Middelburg, an occupation that made him many contacts in The Hague, where he settled after a ten-year residence in Middelburg. In 1719 he joined Pictura, the painters' society of The Hague. Continuing to work as both painter and art dealer, he served several clients in both capacities: Cornelis van Schuylenburch, for instance, for whose house on the Lange Vijverberg (now the German Embassy) in The Hague he provided decorative paintings and a family portrait, and for whose art collection he provided paintings by other masters. The future Landgrave William VIII of Hesse-Kassel, who had been in service to the Netherlands since 1699 and assembled an art collection (Kassel, Schloss Wilhelmshöhe), was another important patron for whom van Dijk also worked in a double capacity. Through William, van Dijk came into contact with the Kassel court of William's father, Landgrave Charles of Hesse, and also with the Leeuwarden court of William's sister, Mary Louise, widow of Prince John William Friso of Orange Nassau and mother of the future Dutch Stadholder Prince William IV, of whom van Dijk painted several portraits (e.g. Apeldoorn, Pal. Het Loo). In 1725, Philip van Dijk and his student Louis de Moni (1698–1771) travelled to Kassel, where van Dijk received the title of court painter and was awarded numerous commissions, including one for the group portrait of *Landgrave Charles of Hesse with his Family* (Kassel, Schloss Wilhelmshöhe). The painting, in fairly small format, contains no fewer than 22 figures, including the painter himself. Although van Dijk returned to The Hague in 1726, his relationship with the court in Kassel continued, and he spent time there again in 1736. In the meantime, he had continued his work as painter and art dealer in The Hague, producing portraits of numerous government officials. He also continued to paint many portraits of important Zeelanders, suggesting that he still returned to Zeeland regularly. Characteristic examples of his work, such as the portrait of *Isaac Parker* and his wife, *Justina Johanna Ramskrammer* (1734), and the group portrait of the same couple with their young son (1742), can be found in the Rijksmuseum in Amsterdam. The Rijksmuseum also holds one of van Dijk's genre paintings, the *Bird's Nest*, done in a style similar to that of the Leiden 'fine' painters.

Unceasing industry as a painter and art dealer brought van Dijk great prosperity, and he continued to receive commissions into his old age, despite always adhering to the style of his youth, which came to seem more and more old-fashioned. In addition to Louis de Moni, his students included Hendrik Pothoven and van Dijk's own nephew, Philip van der Linden van Dijk, who may have worked for many years as his uncle's assistant.

BIBLIOGRAPHY

Thieme–Becker

J. van Gool: *De Nieuwe Schouburg der Nederlandtsche kunstschilders en schilderessen*, i (The Hague, 1750), pp. 440–48

J. W. Niemeijer: 'Zelfportretten van Philips van Dijk', *Oud-Holland*, lxxiv (1959), pp. 245–7

Dutch Masterpieces from the Eighteenth Century: Paintings and Drawings, 1700–1800 (exh. cat. by E. R. Mandle, Minneapolis, MN, Inst. A.; Toledo, OH, Mus. A.; Philadelphia, PA, Mus. A.; 1971–2)

RUDOLF E. O. EKKART

Dijon. French city in Burgundy, at the confluence of the rivers Ouche and Suzon and the Canal de Bourgogne. It flourished particularly as the seat of the Valois dukes of Burgundy from 1363 to 1477, when its situation between Flanders and Italy and general political circumstances contributed to the rich artistic life of the city.

I. History and urban development. II. Art life and organization. III. Centre of furniture production. IV. Buildings.

I. History and urban development.

A Roman city may have existed close to a legionary camp near the road from Lyon to Trier before the 3rd century AD, when a *castrum* was built (see fig 1a), the enclosure walls of which contained reused sculpted blocks, mostly from funerary monuments. The *castrum* (perimeter 1.2 km) was well fortified with walls 10 m high and 33 towers. In the 5th century the bishop of Langres was forced to abandon his city, and he installed himself at Dijon. The cathedral of St Etienne (1b), the church of Ste Marie and the baptistery of St Vincent were built as an episcopal complex within the *castrum*. Outside the walls a tomb in the western cemetery was identified as that of St

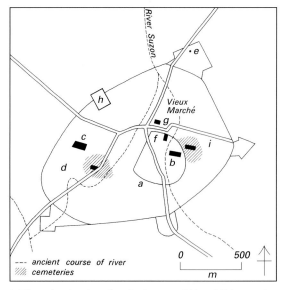

1. Dijon, plan showing urban development, 14th and 15th centuries: (a) castrum; (b) St Bénigne; (c) St Bénigne; (d) St Jean; (e) St Nicolas; (f) ducal palace; (g) Notre-Dame; (h) castle of Louis XI; (i) St Michel

Benignus, who was believed to have evangelized the region in the 2nd century. A basilica was built there *c.* AD 535, and a monastic community was established in the second half of the 6th century (*see* §IV, 2(i) below). St Bénigne was briefly secularized in the first half of the 8th century and, after 990, reformed on the Cluniac pattern and rebuilt by Abbot William of Volpiano (1c). The neighbouring basilica of St Jean (1d) was the burial church of the bishops. Although the bishops returned to Langres, possibly in the 9th century, St Etienne retained the privileges of a cathedral chapter until the canons adopted the Rule of St Augustine *c.* 1125.

The *castrum* itself remained a citadel. A dispute at the end of the 10th century between the king of France and the bishop of Langres was resolved in 1016 when the *castrum* became the property of Henry, son of King Robert II (*reg* 996–1031), the first Capetian Duke of Burgundy, and then became the capital of the duchy. Dijon began to expand in the 11th century. St Etienne was rebuilt by the provost, Garnier de Mailly, who broke through the enclosure wall of the *castrum* to build the choir. Ste Marie was rededicated to St Medard and achieved parochial status. Between the *castrum* and St Bénigne a settlement known as the Bourg developed along the small River Suzon, with St Jean as its parish church. North of the *castrum* a market was established, with a quarter called la Ville. The churches had to be rebuilt after fire ravaged the whole city in 1137. Before 1153 and despite the opposition of the bishop, Duke Odo II (*reg* 1143–62) completed an enclosure wall around both new quarters, other settlements and some fields. The bishop lost his last rights over Dijon, and between 1170 and 1178 the city was divided into seven parishes, of which St Nicolas had its church outside the walls (1e). Duke Hugh III (*reg* 1162–92) added a collegiate church, the Chapelle-le-Duc (1172), to his palace in the *castrum* (1f).

In 1183–7 Hugh III granted free status to the inhabitants. The Gothic parish church of Notre-Dame (1220–50), with a deep narthex, a façade with superimposed galleries and a lantern-tower, became the centre of municipal life (1g); the city clock was installed there in 1386 (Dijon had no town hall before 1500). The Franciscans and Dominicans appeared respectively *c.* 1230 and 1248. The main employment of Dijon was centred on the market, which attracted a vast rural clientele. The city was surrounded by vines, producing a prized wine. The wool market was frequented by the Milanese.

In the middle of the 14th century the dukes of Burgundy installed themselves in the somewhat neglected palace. Philip the Bold had it altered and built a house for his Chamber of Accounts (1386). Before 1455 Philip the Good reconstructed the kitchens, the banqueting hall and the high tower dominating the palace. The Chapelle-le-Duc, called from then on the Sainte-Chapelle, became the seat of the Order of the Golden Fleece. From 1386 Philip the Bold had built the Charterhouse of Champmol (*see* §IV, 1 below) as a dynastic burial church. St Jean was rebuilt, and the Romanesque church of St Philibert received a Flamboyant porch and spire.

In 1356, under the threat of war, repairs to the walls had destroyed part of the suburbs, the inhabitants of which were moved to zones as yet unsettled. The *castrum* lost its

2. Dijon, Place Royale, before 1780; engraving by Jean-Baptiste Lallemand (Dijon, Bibliothèque Municipale)

moat and ceased to function as the citadel. After 1477 Burgundy became a frontier province facing the Franche-Comté, and the wall was reinforced with bastions and earthworks. The suburbs, including St Nicolas, were razed entirely in 1513. To hold the city in submission Louis XI built a castle astride the walls (1h), which was reinforced by Louis XII.

The wealth of Dijon's middle classes, retail tradesmen to the duke, lawyers and financiers, was spent on fine houses, such as the Hôtel Chambellan, and to the construction of St Michel (1i), where Abbot Richard Chambellan replaced a small Carolingian church with a vast Flamboyant edifice. It was built and vaulted between 1499 and 1513, and it was provided in 1537–41 with a Renaissance façade with a magnificent *Last Judgement* carved on the tympanum by Nicolas de la Cour (1550). The streets began to be paved in 1386, and the city was adorned with public fountains, which were to be destroyed in the 17th century for fear of spreading the plague.

In 1477 the people of Dijon had opened their gates to Louis XI, and in recompense he recognized the Parliament of Burgundy, which was established in Dijon. The Palais de Justice was built for it from 1512. The Parliament was to dominate the life of the city. Its strength increased considerably, councillors and presidents accumulating great fortunes and building comfortably and, in time, sumptuously. From the 16th century the Rue des Forges was lined with ornate classicizing town houses in the style of HUGUES SAMBIN, which incorporated elements of fantasy into motifs drawn from Fontainebleau. Many houses, however, had stone ground storeys, with half-timbering above. Seventeenth-century mansions followed the general evolution of taste, with great architects collaborating on them. Among the finest examples are the Hôtel Bouhier de Chevigny (c. 1615) and the Palladian Hôtel Bouhier de Lantenay (now the Préfecture), with the folly of Montmusard in its gardens.

Pursuing a deliberate planning policy, the mayoralty of Dijon straightened and widened the streets; in front of the old ducal palace, which was provided with a classical façade by Jules Hardouin Mansart, it created a Place Royale (1683; see fig. 2), further opened by the perspective views offered by the new streets. A promenade was cut towards the Parc de la Colombière, which had been given to the mayoralty by the Prince de Condé. The old fortified gates were replaced by triumphal arches. The engineer Pierre-Joseph Antoine (1730–1814) even projected building a new city of semicircular plan, facing the Canal de Bourgogne, upon which work had started. The States of Burgundy built two wings flanking the palace, one of which, the Salle des Etats (1700), was the starting point of a Palais des Etats designed by Jacques Gabriel V. Chapels intended for the newly established Carmelite, Jesuit and Bernardine congregations conformed to comtemporary styles of sacred art.

The French Revolution interrupted this development. François Devosges III saved a number of monuments, but the Sainte-Chapelle, St Bénigne, Champmol and Montmusard were destroyed or badly damaged, and the tympanum of the west portal of Notre-Dame was smashed. The city lost its rich inhabitants and its role as a provincial capital. After Dijon became a railway junction in 1854 a period of industrial development began, but without a single dominant industry; agriculture remained important. The population increased tenfold between 1800 and 1970, but Dijon remained essentially a non-industrial town.

During the 19th century the fortifications and castle were demolished in a partially realized town-planning scheme, and at the end of the 19th century and the beginning of the 20th there appeared some official buildings following Parisian models, such as the Post Office (by Perreau) and the Faculté des Lettres. Art Nouveau inspired some private builders, but the outlying districts were built up with no overall plan, although some effort was made to construct monumental buildings (e.g. Sacré-Coeur, *c.* 1930, by Barbier). The medieval churches were restored by Charles Suisse (1846–1906), a follower of Viollet-le-Duc.

After World War II, in which Dijon largely escaped destruction, properly planned suburbs, such as La Fontaine d'Ouche on an artificial lake, were built round the old centre, which had preserved its historic identity. Within the circle of the former city walls, Dijon remains rich in Baroque and classical buildings.

BIBLIOGRAPHY

H. Chabeuf: *Dijon: Monuments et souvenirs* (Dijon, 1894/*R* 1977)
——: *Dijon à travers les âges: Histoire et description* (Dijon, 1897/*R* 1982)
G. Roupnel: *La Ville et la campagne: Etude sur les populations du pays dijonnais* (Paris, 1922, 2/1955)
E. Fyot: *Dijon: Son passé évoqué par ses rues* (Dijon, 1928, rev. 1979)
M. Oursel-Quarré: *Les Origines de la commune de Dijon* (Dijon, 1944)
Site et plans de l'agglomération de Dijon des origines à nos jours, Centre regional de documentation pédagogique de Dijon (Dijon, 1969, rev. 1985)
P. Gras, ed.: *Histoire de Dijon* (Toulouse, 1981, rev. 1987)
Y. Beauvalot: *La Construction du palais des Etats de Bourgogne et de la Place Royale à Dijon, 1674–1725* (Dijon, 1985)

JEAN RICHARD

II. Art life and organization.

Surviving Gallo-Roman sculptures (Dijon, Mus. Archéol.), worn, but of a clearly individualized style, are evidence of the existence of a local workshop in that period. The art history of the settlement remains obscure, however, until the reconstruction of St Bénigne from 1002 (*see* §IV, 2(i) below). Although there was much building in the city during the high Middle Ages (*see* §I above), artists came in great numbers only with the rule of the Valois dukes from 1363. Philip the Bold's marriage to Margaret of Flanders (1350–1405) encouraged the arrival of artists from the north, and their activities were concentrated mainly on the ducal palace and the burial church, the Charterhouse of Champmol (*see* §IV, 1 below). The sculpture workshops were directed by Jean de Marville and, after his death in 1389, by CLAUS SLUTER, who continued Marville's work at the Charterhouse and was succeeded in 1406 by his nephew Claus de Werve. In 1443 Juan de la Huerta began the tomb of *John the Fearless and Margaret of Bavaria* (Dijon, Mus. B.-A.), which was completed in the 1460s by Antoine Le Moiturier. The painters, who were mainly Flemish, were directed from 1376 by JEAN DE BEAUMETZ, by Jean Malouel from 1397

to 1415, and then by Henri Bellechose. Illuminators and stained-glass painters were also employed at Champmol.

Northern traditions survived the absorption of Burgundy into France in 1477, but Italian styles slowly infiltrated the art of Dijon. In 1522 Antoine Gailley installed a coffered ceiling in the Law Courts. The Gothic church of St Michel was decorated in Renaissance style. In his designs of, for example, the Hôtel Milsand, Hugues Sambin incorporated elements of fantasy into motifs derived from Fontainebleau, and Nicolas de Hoey from Leiden (*d c.* 1612), in Dijon in 1564, drew inspiration from Marten de Vos (see Guillaume, figs 464, 466, 472–3). In direct contrast to the latter's elaborate style are the solid, rustic figures by Philippe Quantin (e.g. Dijon, Mus. B.-A.). Jean Tassel produced appropriate paintings for the newly established religious orders in the city, including for the chapel of the Ursuline convent the *Coronation of the Virgin with St Angela and Other Saints* (Dijon, Mus. B.-A.). In the modernization of the Palais des Etats, classicism was generally preferred to Baroque, although the latter was influential in the sculptures of Jean Dubois, for instance his monumental stone mantelpieces. Rocaille also appeared in the Palais but was otherwise generally avoided in Dijon.

In 1776 François Devosges III established the Ecole de Dessin, which was one of the most important academies outside Paris. An annual prize was set up in 1768, and from 1775 the Assembly of Bourgogne, under the Governor, Louis Joseph, Prince de Condé (1736–1818), inaugurated a Prix de Rome to be awarded every four years. The first winner for painting was BÉNIGNE GAGNERAUX in 1776, and the third, in 1784, PIERRE-PAUL PRUD'HON

3. Pierre-Paul Prud'hon: *Georges Anthony*, oil on canvas, 990×820 mm, 1796 (Dijon, Musée des Beaux-Arts)

(see fig. 3). In 1781 special premises for the school were fitted out in a new building attached to the Palais, with two rooms to exhibit paintings, and casts and marble reproductions of sculpture, sent over by the Rome prize-winners. This became the Musée des Beaux-Arts; distinguished pupils included CLAUDE HOIN, who became director of the Musée des Beaux-Arts in 1811, and FRANÇOIS RUDE.

Dijon is also the birthplace of the sculptor Jean Bouchard (1875–1960) and the painters Colson, Félix Trutat (1824–48), Alphonse Legros and Jean Bertholle (*b* 1909). The collections formerly put together by the Parliamentarians, together with the art treasures from the Charterhouse of Champmol and the manuscripts from Cîteaux Abbey, formed the basis of the collections of the Bibliothèque Municipale and the Musée des Beaux-Arts. In 1938 the Musée Magnin, exhibiting works bequeathed to the state by the collector Maurice Magnin (1861–1939), was opened to the public. In 1982, to encourage artistic creativity, the national and regional governments together set up a fund for contemporary art.

BIBLIOGRAPHY
L'Académie de Peinture et de Sculpture de Dijon: Une Ecole provinciale de dessin au XVIIIème siècle (exh. cat., Dijon, Mus. B.-A., 1961)
Y. Beauvalot: *Dijon: Palais des Etats* (Lyon, 1965)
S. Laveissière: *Dictionnaire des artistes et ouvriers d'art de Bourgogne*, Dictionnaire des Artistes et Ouvriers d'Art de la France par Provinces (Paris, 1980–)
M. Guillaume: 'Un Flamand italianisant en Bourgogne: Nicolas de Hoey', *Scritti di storia dell'arte in onore di Federico Zeri* (Milan, 1984)
Claus Sluter en Bourgogne: Mythe et représentations (exh. cat., Dijon, Mus. B.-A., 1990)
MARGUERITE GUILLAUME

III. Centre of furniture production.

No 14th- or 15th-century woodworkers in Dijon are recorded by name, although a workshop of *huchiers* (coffermakers) operating at the beginning of the 14th century is mentioned, and the distinction between the trades of carpenter and cabinetmaker is emphasized. HUGUES SAMBIN was the first notable wood-carver working in Dijon, achieving great fame with his illustrated treatise, *L'Oeuvre de la diversité des termes dont on use en architecture* (Lyon, 1572), which he signed 'Architecteur en la ville de Dijon'. The bold, inventive terms and caryatids illustrated in this work reveal the influence of Italian Mannerism as adopted by the Fontainebleau school. Sambin's treatise was extremely influential among other wood-carvers in Burgundy: many pieces feature the fantastical terms (e.g. *armoire à deux corps*; Philadelphia, PA, Mus. A.), although none can be attributed to Sambin.

In the 18th century the Demoulin family were the most important family of *ébénistes* in Dijon. Jean Demoulin (1715–98), *ébéniste* to the Prince de Condé, was recorded in Paris in 1745 and active in Dijon until 1788 (e.g. japanned commode in the Rococo style; Tours, Mus. B.-A.). His sons Jean-Baptiste Demoulin and Bertrand Demoulin carried on the business under the trade name Les Frères Demoulin, using local and foreign walnut, flame and bird's-eye mahogany and exotic woods.

BIBLIOGRAPHY
H. Sambin: *L'Oeuvre de la diversité des termes dont on use en architecture* (Lyon, 1572)

A. Castan: 'L'Architecteur: Hugues Sambin', *Disours, procès-verbaux et rapports: Réunion des Sociétés des Beaux-Arts des Départements du 27 au 31 Mai 1890* (Paris, 1890), pp. 217–40
B. Prost: 'Une Nouvelle Source de documents sur les artistes dijonnais du XVe siècle', *Gaz. B.-A.*, 3rd ser., iv (1890), pp. 347–60; vi (1891), pp. 161–76
——: 'Hugues Sambin: Sculpteur sur bois et architecte', *Gaz. B.-A.*, 3rd ser., vii (1892), pp. 123–35
F. de Salverte: *Les Ebénistes du XVIIIe siècle* (Paris, 1962)
MONIQUE RICCARDI-CUBITT

IV. Buildings.

1. Charterhouse. 2. St Bénigne.

1. CHARTERHOUSE. The former Carthusian monastery is situated north-west of Dijon on a site known as Champmol, bordering the River Ouche. Founded by Philip the Bold in 1385 to house his tomb and those of his heirs (*see* BURGUNDY, (1)), the Charterhouse was among the most famous monasteries of late medieval Europe. The size of the complex and the wealth of its sculptural and painted decoration were greater than any other French 14th-century monastery. It influenced later sister houses such as the Certosa di Pavia, Italy.

(i) *Architecture*. Building began after 20 August 1383, when the corner-stone was laid, and was essentially complete by 24 May 1388, when the church was dedicated. Philip the Bold signed the foundation charter on 15 March 1385. Drouet de Dammartin, Charles V's architect, established the plan, but the building was supervised by the master mason Jacques de Neuilly (*fl* after 1353; *d* 1398), who was in ducal service from 1367. Most of the limestone was quarried at nearby Is-sur-Tille. While following the traditional plan of Carthusian monasteries, Champmol was specifically influenced by the royal Charterhouse of Paris (1270–1325; destr.). A large cloister (102.5 m square) was surrounded by 24 monastic cells that were independent two-storey structures, each with an enclosed yard. To the north-east lay the church, composed of a single vessel without transepts (57×11 m), a trapezoidal eastern apse and a richly sculpted west portal. The tomb of *Philip the Bold* (for illustration *see* WEEPER) was laid in the nave, to be joined *c.* 1470 by that of *John the Fearless and Margaret of Bavaria* (both Dijon, Mus. B.-A.). On the north side were projecting chapels, each roofed by two sets of quadripartite vaults; nearest to the portal was the chapel of St Agnes, the second was dedicated to St Andrew, and that near the apse was the two-storey ducal chapel 'of the Angels'. Diagonally across the latter was an entrance to the sacristy, above which the treasury was housed, its roof reaching the height of the sanctuary and thus suggesting, when seen in conjunction with the two-storey ducal chapel, the presence of a transept. Extending south from the sacristy and enclosing a small cloister was the chapter house and, at right angles to it, the refectory, kitchen and other amenities. Four dependencies housed the guest-quarters, stables, barns and wine-press. The grounds included vegetable gardens, orchards, vineyards and a large fish pond, replenished by the Ouche.

In 1664 two external chapels were added to the apse. The complex was razed in 1792 with the exception of the church portal, the remains of the Well of Moses (*see* SLUTER, CLAUS, §2) in the main cloister and the turret encasing the spiral staircase leading to the upper storey of the ducal chapel. Arcades from the small cloister, now in the Jardin de l'Arquebuse, Dijon, had already been removed in 1774. The grounds of Champmol became the site of a villa and since 1833 have harboured psychiatric wards. The best records of Philip the Bold's foundation are the elevation drawing (1686) by Aimée Piron (1640–1727) and the ground-plan established by G. Ruellet in 1760 (both Dijon, Archv Ville).

BIBLIOGRAPHY
C. Monget: *La Chartreuse de Dijon d'après les documents des archives de Dijon*, 3 vols (Montreuil-sur-Mer, 1898–1905)
M. Aubert: 'La Chartreuse de Champmol', *Congr. Archéol. France*, xci (1929), pp. 110–20
La Chartreuse de Champmol: Foyer d'art au temps des ducs Valois (exh. cat., ed. P. Quarré; Dijon, Mus. B.-A., 1960)

PATRICK M. DE WINTER

(ii) Sculpture. The sculptural decoration of the Charterhouse is bold and innovative and includes the finest surviving work of Claus Sluter. The Duke appointed Jean de Marville to direct work in 1384, but his exact role in designing the monuments has been obscured by the alterations made by Sluter, who succeeded him in 1390. The programme consisted primarily of three projects: the sculptures of the entrance portal to the church, the large group sculpture of the Well of Moses and the tomb of *Philip the Bold* (Dijon, Mus. B.-A.; for further discussion *see* SLUTER, CLAUS).

The function of the medieval church portal as the dividing line between the secular and sacred realms and,

4. Dijon, Charterhouse of Champmol, church portal, begun *c.* 1384; sculptures by Claus Sluter: (left) *St John the Baptist* and *Philip the Bold, Duke of Burgundy*; (centre) the *Virgin and Child*; (right) *Margaret of Flanders, Duchess of Burgundy* and *St Catherine of Alexandria*

in the case of mausolea, between the worlds of the living and the dead, is apparent in the iconography and design of Sluter's portal, which shows SS John the Baptist and Catherine of Alexandria commending their charges, Philip and his wife, Margaret of Flanders, to the Virgin and Child on the trumeau (see fig. 4). Sluter's adaptation of a donor scene and the inclusion of mortals in a monumental portal was new. Moreover, he broke the traditional subordination of sculptural decoration to its architectural setting, the latter now serving as a stage for the human drama occurring before it. The figures communicate across the intervening space and, with their boldly flowing drapery and intense expressions, appear ready to break out of the bonds of their setting.

Whereas the portal sculpture focused on the Duke's personal request for salvation, the Well of Moses in the Great Cloister had a complex iconographic programme combining themes of salvation through Christ's sacrifice, the cleansing of sin through Baptism, the meaning of the Eucharist and the image of the Fountain of Life (*see* FRANCE, fig. 33). The large monument is now fragmented; all that remains are the corpus of *Christ* (Dijon, Mus. Archéol.; *see* SLUTER, CLAUS, fig. 1) and the pedestal decorated with full-length sculptures of six Old Testament prophets and attendant angels. These figures, like those on the portal, are marked by a new sense of bodily substance and individual expression. With their original polychrome they must have appeared almost alive, and they have been compared to actors in contemporary mystery plays.

BIBLIOGRAPHY
A. Leibreich: *Claus Sluter* (Brussels, 1936)
H. David: *Claus Sluter* (Paris, 1951)
T. Müller: *Sculpture in the Netherlands, Germany, France and Spain, 1400–1500*, Pelican Hist. A. (Harmondsworth, 1966)
P. Quarré: *La Sculpture en Bourgogne à la fin du moyen âge* (Fribourg, 1978) [Fr., Eng. and Ger. texts]
K. Morand: *Claus Sluter: Artist at the Court of Burgundy* (Austin and London, 1991); review by D. Goodgal-Salem in *Burl. Mag.*, cxxxiv (1992), pp. 37–40

JANE NASH MALLER

(iii) Painting. The Charterhouse became a repository of painting and the source of a distinctive style that blended Sienese forms with the idealized Parisian manner, fusing into this gentle realism an interest in volume and decorative splendour. Jean de Beaumetz was active at Champmol until 1396. He decorated the sanctuary, coloured statues (destr.) by Jean de Marville and Claus Sluter and produced two triptychs (untraced). Two panels painted by Jean de Beaumetz for the monks' cells have survived, both depicting the *Crucifixion with a Carthusian* (Cleveland, OH, Mus. A.; Paris, Louvre). One of Jacques de Baerze's carved altarpieces, depicting the *Passion of Christ* (Dijon, Mus. B.-A.), commissioned for the Charterhouse in 1390 and set up in 1399, includes *Infancy of Christ* scenes painted by MELCHIOR BROEDERLAM. Other imports before Philip the Bold's death were panels of the *Life of Christ* (the 'Antwerp' or 'Orsini' polyptych; Antwerp, Kon. Mus. S. Kst.; Berlin, Gemäldegal.; Paris, Louvre) by Simone Martini, a triptych with the *Trinity and the Evangelists* (Berlin, Gemäldegal.), probably from Utrecht, and two polyptychs from the Maastricht region (Antwerp, Mus. Mayer van den Bergh; Baltimore, MD, Walters A.G.).

Jean Malouel, court painter from 1396 until his death in 1415, provided five panels and one triptych for the sanctuary (all untraced) and perhaps a *Virgin and Child* on linen (Berlin, Gemäldegal.). In 1400–04 he supervised the colouring of statuary by Claus Sluter and Claus de Werve, including the Well of Moses, and in 1410 he coloured the tomb of *Philip the Bold*. Malouel's successor Henri Bellechose completed the large *Martyrdom of St Denis* (Paris, Louvre) in 1416, as well as coloured statues. It is thought that Robert Campin's *Nativity* (*c.* 1425; Dijon, Mus. B.-A.) was once at Champmol. In 1436 Jean de Maisoncelles painted a portrait of *Philip the Good* (untraced; possible copy, 16th century; Cincinnati, OH, A. Mus.), to be added to representations of earlier Valois dukes. At the same time the anonymous altarpiece of *St George* (Dijon, Mus. B.-A.), an eclectic pendant to Bellechose's, was produced. The foundation also acquired two compositions by Jan van Eyck, a triptych, of which the *Annunciation* survives (Washington, DC, N.G.A.), and an untraced panel (fragment in Paris, Mus. A. Déc.). Isabella of Portugal, Duchess of Burgundy (1397–1472), probably commissioned the anonymous *Calvary with a Carthusian* (*c.* 1440; Dijon, Mus. B.-A.). In the 17th century and especially in the 1770s, the sanctuary was refurbished and earlier paintings were replaced with works (some now Dijon, Mus. B.-A.) by Richard Tassel, Carle Vanloo and others.

For bibliography *see* §(i) above.

PATRICK M. DE WINTER

2. ST BÉNIGNE. Established in the first half of the 6th century AD, from the early 9th century St Bénigne was the personal monastery of the bishops of Langres (*see* §I above). The Benedictine Rule was introduced in 869. From 871 Bishop Isaac reconstructed the church, which was consecrated in 882. The lower walls of the surviving easternmost chapel (*see* §(i) below) and some reused fragments carved with interlace and foliate motifs may belong to this building. The present church, however, is principally the work of campaigns from the early 11th century to the 14th, modified by minor changes in the 16th and 17th centuries, radical destruction in 1792 and over-zealous restoration between 1858 and 1888. The original appearance can be deduced from early descriptions, from pre-1792 plans and views and from excavations.

(i) The basilica and rotunda. In 989 the reform of St Bénigne was entrusted to Abbot Mayeul of Cluny (although the abbey remained independent), and William of Volpiano (962–1031) became abbot in 990. His new church (l. *c.* 90 m) was built from 1002 in two parts, a basilica and an eastern rotunda. The basilica, raised over a columnar hall crypt extending beneath much of the nave and non-projecting transept, terminated at the east in an apse echelon. There was a short crossing tower and a west apse. It is uncertain if the main elevation had galleries and/or a wall passage. Only the apsidal chapels and the colonnade round the saint's tomb in the crypt just west of the rotunda survive, all heavily restored, together with some carved capitals. Although the hall crypt is an Italian feature, the hypothesis that the basilica was crucial in the

dissemination in France of architectural ideas from north Italy, William's birthplace, cannot be substantiated on present evidence. The west apse was in the Carolingian liturgical tradition, and while the apse echelon may have derived from Abbot Mayeul's second church at Cluny (*see* CLUNIAC ORDER, §III, 1(i)), the plan of the latter is too little clarified for certainty.

Of the three-storey eastern rotunda, dedicated to the Virgin, only the crypt survives, much rebuilt. Views and plans from before 1792 show that it was entered directly from the transept at crypt and ground-floor levels. Access between floors within the rotunda was provided by big, circular stair-turrets to north and south, and each storey opened into the rectangular eastern chapel that housed the main altar. The central 'well' of the rotunda rose the full height of the building, surrounded on the two lower floors by a double ring of massive columns supporting barrel and groin vaults. The top storey had one ring of columns supporting a small central lantern which, with the stair-turrets and a square tower on the eastern chapel, created a cluster of four towers. As the exterior corbel table of the rotunda was added in the 12th century, and the *opus reticulatum* and two animal reliefs on the eastern chapel may date from *c.* 1100, it is clear that the building underwent refurbishment, and the arrangement as reconstructed may not represent its original state.

The rotunda was evidently linked by association to S Maria ad Martyres, the medieval church within the Pantheon in Rome; although there were Carolingian rotundas in Burgundy, such as at St Germain, Auxerre, Flavigny Abbey, Geneva Cathedral and St Pierre-le-Vif, Sens, this was much bigger, and its interior was richly decorated. Vestiges of floor mosaics include a fragment with affronted lions, which may date from the early 11th century. Many columns were antique spolia. The capital sculpture was varied, precocious and significant (although some of the smaller capitals may be of the later 11th century). The large capitals include massive blocks carved with orant figures, a recurring motif of Early Christian sarcophagi, here already deployed to show the capital as a forceful architectural element. Two capitals on the columns round the saint's tomb have a series of men, beasts and birds, deeply cut and composed to respect the shape of the block; the motifs seem to derive from Frankish jewellery, particularly Franco-Burgundian fibulae. Although this sculpture has been attributed to Italian sculptors, no convincing antecedents survive in Italy.

About 1150 a west porch was added to the nave (*see* §(ii) below), and in 1271 the basilica was largely destroyed when the crossing tower collapsed. The hall crypt was mostly filled in, and by 1287 the present east end had been built; work on the nave continued into the 14th century, when two towers were added to the west porch. The 13th-century church, with a minimal adoption of Rayonnant features and conservative use of wall passages, is a good representative of later Gothic architecture in Burgundy.

BIBLIOGRAPHY
U. Plancher: *Histoire générale et particulière de la Bourgogne*, i (Dijon, 1739), pp. 476–523 [engravings]
L. Chomton: *Histoire de l'église Saint-Bénigne de Dijon* (Dijon, 1900)
R. Branner: *Burgundian Gothic Architecture* (London, 1960)

L. Grodecki: 'Guillaume de Volpiano et l'expansion clunisienne', *Cent. Int. Etud. Romanes, Bull. Trimest.* (1961), no. 2, pp. 21–31; also in *Le Moyen Age retrouvé* (Paris, 1986), pp. 199–210

A. Martindale: 'The Romanesque Church of Saint-Bénigne at Dijon and MS. 591 in the Bibliothèque Municipale', *J. Brit. Archaeol. Assoc.*, xxv (1962), pp. 21–55

H. Stern: *Province de Belgique* (1963), i/3 of *Recueil général des mosaïques de la Gaule* (Paris, 1957–75), pp. 152–3

N. Bulst: *Untersuchungen zu den Klosterreformen Wilhelms von Dijon, 962–1031* (Bonn, 1973)

C. Heitz: 'Lumières anciennes et nouvelles sur Saint-Bénigne de Dijon', *Du VIIIe au XIe siècle: Edifices monastiques et culte en Lorraine et en Bourgogne*, ed. C. Heitz and F. Héber-Suffrin (Paris, 1977), pp. 63–106 [early texts on the church]

W. Schlink: *Saint-Bénigne in Dijon: Untersuchungen zur Abteikirche Wilhelms von Volpiano, 962–1031* (Berlin, 1978)

C. M. Malone: 'Les Fouilles de Saint-Bénigne de Dijon (1976–1978) et le problème de l'église de l'an mil', *Bull. Mnml*, cxxxviii (1980), pp. 253–84

C. Sapin: *La Bourgogne préromane: Construction, décor et fonction des édifices religieux* (Paris, 1986)

——: 'Saint-Bénigne de Dijon, Saint-Pierre de Flavigny et les ateliers de sculpture de la première moitié du XIe siècle', *Mém. Comm. Ant. Dépt Côte-d'Or*, xxxv (1993), pp. 215–42

NEIL STRATFORD

(ii) 12th-century sculpture. The sculpture of the central portal of the west façade of St Bénigne, probably built in the 1150s and destroyed in 1792, is known from an engraving published by Dom Plancher in 1739 and a few fragments now in the Musée Archéologique, Dijon. Although reused in the 13th-century construction, this portal was clearly related to the Early Gothic portals of the Ile-de-France (e.g. Chartres Cathedral). The tympanum, archivolts and upper lintel were dedicated to the *Apocalyptic Vision* and the *Infancy of Christ*. Among the eight column statues, *Moses* is identifiable, as is the *Queen of Sheba*, who is represented with webbed feet, as on several other Early Gothic portals (e.g. Notre-Dame, Nesle-la-Reposte; destr.), and *SS Peter and Paul. St Benignus* was represented on the trumeau.

Dom Plancher illustrated two other tympana from St Bénigne. One, built into the wall of the porch until it was destroyed in 1803, depicted the *Martyrdom of St Benignus*. The other, situated above the refectory doorway, represented the *Last Supper*. This relief is now in the Musée Archéologique with yet another tympanum from St Bénigne, which was discovered only in 1833. Carved with *Christ in Majesty* flanked by four angels and the *Evangelist Symbols*, it reflects the iconography of the lost Romanesque tympanum of Cluny Abbey. The original positions of these three tympana are not known with certainty. Those showing the *Martyrdom* and *Last Supper* may have belonged to the lateral portals of the façade, while the *Christ in Majesty* tympanum probably surmounted a door leading from the cloister into the abbey church. All three are stylistically related to the Early Gothic sculpture of the Ile-de-France rather than to the Romanesque sculpture of Burgundy, and they probably all date from the 1150s.

BIBLIOGRAPHY
Dom U. Plancher: *Histoire générale et particulière de Bourgogne* (Dijon, 1739)

P. Quarré: 'La Sculpture des anciens portails de Saint-Bénigne de Dijon', *Gaz. B.-A.*, n. s. 5, 1 (1957), pp. 177–94

A. Lapeyre: *Des Façades occidentales de Saint-Denis et de Chartres aux portails de Laon* (Paris, 1960), pp. 101–8

W. Sauerländer: *Gotische Skulptur in Frankreich, 1140–1270* (Munich, 1970; Eng. trans., London, 1972), pp. 389–91

KATHRYN MORRISON

Dijsselhof, Gerrit Willem (*b* Zwollerkerspel, nr Zwolle, 8 Feb 1866; *d* Bloemendaal, nr Haarlem, 14 June 1924). Dutch painter and designer. He studied at the Academie voor Beeldende Kunsten in The Hague, and at the Rijkskunstnijverheidsschool and Rijksnormaalschool in Amsterdam. In 1889–1890 he travelled with T. W. Nieuwenhuis to Berlin, Vienna and Paris. His woodcut design for a diploma for the Vereeniging van Boekhandels (Society of Bookshops; 1892) and his decorations for the book *Kunst en Samenleving* ('Art and society'), the Dutch edition of Walter Crane's *Claims of Decorative Art* (London, 1892), are some of the earliest examples of Nieuwe Kunst. Dijsselhof is thus considered to be one of the most important innovators of this movement. He also designed furniture (*see* NETHERLANDS, THE, fig. 43), wallpaper, embroidery patterns and batik wall hangings. An example of his luxurious, meticulously detailed interiors can be seen in the room he designed for Dr van Hoorn in 1895, the Dijsselhofroom (The Hague, Gemeentemus.). After 1900 he occupied himself mainly with painting, usually depicting underwater scenes of fish and plants.

BIBLIOGRAPHY
L. Gans: *Nieuwe Kunst: De Nederlandse bijdrage tot de Art Nouveau: Dekoratieve kunst, kunstnijverheid en architektuur omstreeks 1900* [Nieuwe Kunst: the Dutch contribution to Art Nouveau: decorative art, applied arts and architecture *c.* 1900] (Utrecht, 1966), pp. 50–54

M. W. F. SIMON THOMAS

Dikaios, Charilaos (*b* Nicosia, 5 Oct 1912). Cypriot architect and painter. He graduated from the Pancyprian Gymnasium in Nicosia in 1931 and until 1936 designed houses under the supervision of Odysseus Tsangarides (1907–74), Municipal Architect of Nicosia. Dikaios studied architecture and fine art at the Ecole des Beaux-Arts in Paris (1937–40) and Lyon (1942–6), graduating from the Ecole des Beaux-Arts, Lyon, in 1946. He was a protégé of Tony Garnier, working with him in his studio, on the *Cité industrielle* project, and this experience influenced his design aesthetic. His characteristic use of reinforced concrete was derived from exposure to the works of Auguste Perret. Dikaios returned to Cyprus in 1947 and simultaneously began painting and practising architecture. In the 1950s he primarily designed small private houses, some of which were avant-garde for Cyprus and reflected the form and character of structures in Garnier's *Cité industrielle*; others catered to the aesthetic interests of expatriate British clients, through their stylistic references to Byzantine and medieval antecedents in Cyprus. Among the large buildings he designed are the Cooperative Central Bank (1960) and a Maronite church and business complex (1961; both Nicosia). Each expresses its reinforced concrete structure, but in a contrasting manner: the Central Bank has a crisp rectangularity, recalling buildings of the *Cité industrielle*, while the Maronite church has towering, yet delicate, filigree tracery as seen in Perret's Notre-Dame-du-Raincy (1922–3), near Paris. Dikaios's paintings are mainly impressionistic landscapes in watercolours or oils, reflecting the brilliant light of Cyprus. In 1969 the French government honoured Charilaos Dikaios as a 'Chevalier de l'ordre des arts et des lettres'.

BIBLIOGRAPHY

P. Georghiades: 'Akinita Maronitikes kinotetos' [Premises of the Maronite community], *Architektoniki*, 55 (Athens, 1966), p. 58

——: 'Synergatiki trapeza' [Cooperative Central Bank], *Architektoniki*, 55 (Athens, 1966), p. 59

A. Pavlides: 'Dikaios, Charilaos', *Megali kypriaki enkyklopaideia* [Great Cypriot encyclopedia], iv (Nicosia, 1986), p. 268

KENNETH W. SCHAAR

Dilberdjin [Dal'verzin; Dil'berdžin]. Site in northern Afghanistan, 40 km north-west of Balkh, which flourished from the Achaemenid period (*c.* 6th century BC) to the Hephthalite invasion (*c.* 5th century AD). It was excavated by a Soviet-Afghan team in 1970–77; all finds are in the Kabul Museum.

The fortified town (383×393 m) is enclosed by mud-brick walls with rectangular bastions. There was a circular citadel in the centre, and at the north-east corner of the town a 2nd-century BC temple, perhaps to the Dioscuri, was excavated, which shows several phases of rebuilding. Only a fragment of a wall painting from the earliest period is extant, depicting two nude youths painted red leading white horses by the bridle. Above this are the fragmentary red legs of athletes. To the latest period belongs a polychrome wall painting depicting Shiva and Parvarti on a bull, flanked by two men with four worshippers below. In the main part of the temple a throne ornamented with sculpture was found.

A new shrine was built against the north defensive wall in the late 1st century AD to early 2nd. The walls of three chambers bear fragments of wall painting. Three distinct layers of work have been found: the bottom layer employs green paint and gilding, while the middle layer contains representations of helmeted goddesses and standing or recumbent men, the latter with lotus wreaths. The top layer is apparently associated with the Hephthalites or Hyons. It depicts an enthroned figure, a deity seated on a bird, gift-bearers and a scene of ritual libation. In their detail the paintings are analogous to those of PENDZHIKENT and Balalyk Tepe.

In one of the multi-chambered buildings to the west of the citadel a shrine of the Kushano-Sasanian period (3rd–4th century AD) contained three enthroned clay figures. A clay figure of Herakles and a number of primitive statuettes were found in a shrine beside the southern wall of the town. Outside the south-east corner of the defensive wall was a Buddhist temple with a circular stupa, clay statues of the Buddha and wall paintings.

See also AFGHANISTAN, §II, 1(iii) and fig. 10.

BIBLIOGRAPHY

I. T. Kruglikova: *Dil'berdzhin*, i, iii (Moscow, 1974–86)

I. T. Kruglikova, ed.: *Drevnyaya Baktriya* [Ancient Bactria], 3 vols (Moscow, 1976–84)

I. Kruglikova: 'Les Fouilles de la mission archéologique soviéto-afghane sur le site gréco-kushan de Dilberdjin en Bactriane (Afghanistan)', *Acad. Inscr. & B.-Lett.: C. R. Séances* (1977), pp. 407–27

I. T. Kruglikova and G. A. Pugachenkova: *Dil'berdzhin*, ii (Moscow, 1977)

B. Ya. Stavisky: *Kushanskaya Baktriya: Problemy istorii i kul'tury* (Moscow, 1977); Fr. trans. as *La Bactriane sous les Kushans: Problèmes d'histoire et culture* (Paris, 1986), pp. 268–72, figs 36–7

P. Bernard and H.-P. Francfort: 'Nouvelles découvertes dans la Bactriane afghane', *Annali: AION*, n. s., xxxix (1979), pp. 117–48 [synopsis of *Drevnyaya Baktriya*, i (Moscow, 1976)]

V. I. Gulíaev: 'Dilberdjin Kushanskiy gorod', *Arkheologiya starogo i novogo sveta* [Archaeology of the old and new world] (Moscow, 1982), figs 7–9

I. KRUGLIKOVA

Dilettanti, Society of. *See* SOCIETY OF DILETTANTI.

Dilich [Scheffer]. German family of architects, draughtsmen and engravers. Wilhelm Dilich (*b* Wabern, 1571–2; *d* Dresden, April 1655) studied in Wittenberg and Marburg and entered the service of the Landgrave Moritz of Hesse-Kassel in 1592, touring Hesse as a topographer and historiographer. In 1596 he also visited Hamburg and Bremen, producing drawings and engravings of views of towns that were later copied by Matthäus Merian I. On a journey to Holland he studied the art of building fortifications, which enabled him to work as a building engineer from 1607. Later he fell out of the Landgrave's favour, and he was imprisoned in 1621. On his escape in 1625 he went to Dresden, where he was employed as an architect, cartographer and military engineer at the electoral court. His first commission was to place vaulting over the Riesensaal in the Residenzschloss (destr. 1701) and to design its painting, completed by Kilian Fabritius (*d* 1633) and Christian Schiebling (1603–63) in 1650. In 1626–9 he documented the Saxon towns in 140 drawings, and in 1632 he modernized the fortifications in Altendresden (Dresden-Neustadt). He also wrote textbooks on fortification, *Peribologia* (Frankfurt am Main, 1640) and *Kurtzer Underricht Bollwercke anzulegen* (1645), and revised his *Kriegsbuch* (1607).

Johann Wilhelm Dilich (*b* Kassel, 1600; *d* Frankfurt am Main, 1660) was Wilhelm's son and pupil and accompanied him to Dresden in 1625. From 1627 he built new fortifications at Frankfurt am Main that he and his father had designed together. He made copperplate engravings to accompany his father's texts. Of Wilhelm's fourteen children, two other sons—Johann Dilich (*b* Kassel, 1597; *d* Dresden, 1667) and Crato Dilich (*b* Kassel, 1611; *d* Wittenberg, 1639)—also built fortifications.

BIBLIOGRAPHY

NDB; Thieme–Becker

P. E. Richter and C. Krollmann, eds: *W. Dilich: Federzeichnungen kursächsischer und meissnischer Ortschaften aus den Jahren 1626–1629*, 3 vols (Dresden, 1907)

F. Löffler: *Das alte Dresden* (Dresden, 1955, rev. Leipzig, 6/1981), pp. 37, 63

W. Schade: *Dresdener Zeichnungen, 1550–1650* (Dresden, 1969), pp. 14, 23, 32

GERALD HERES

Dilke, Lady [née Strong, Emilia Francis, later Mrs Mark Pattison] (*b* Ilfracombe, Devon, 2 Sept 1840; *d* Woking, Surrey, 24 Oct 1904). English art historian and social reformer. She was a bank manager's daughter, brought up in Oxford. On the recommendation of John Ruskin, she entered the South Kensington School of Art in London in 1859, leaving in 1861 on her marriage to Mark Pattison, Rector of Lincoln College, Oxford. In 1872 she began her researches into French art, starting with the Renaissance; her thorough and painstaking method resulted in the publication in 1879 of *The Renaissance of Art in France*. Her monograph on Claude, which remains the fullest narrative account of his life and art, appeared in 1884. In the same year, her husband died; in 1885 she married the Radical politician Sir Charles Dilke. She continued her researches and between 1899 and 1902 published her series of monumental books on 18th-century French art. Although they lacked the idiosyncratic brilliance of the Goncourt brothers' *L'Art du XVIIIe siècle* (12 vols; Paris, 1859–75), they did much to foster interest in the period and were especially valuable for their coverage of the applied arts and furniture. Lady Dilke's research was firmly based on documents and objects.

WRITINGS
The Renaissance of Art in France, 2 vols (London, 1879)
Claude Lorrain: Sa vie et ses oeuvres d'après des documents inédits (Paris, 1884)
French Painters of the XVIIIth Century (London, 1889)
French Architects and Sculptors of the XVIIIth Century (London, 1900)
French Furniture and Decoration of the XVIIIth Century (London, 1901)
French Engravers and Draughtsmen of the XVIIIth Century (London, 1902)

BIBLIOGRAPHY
DNB
B. Askwith: *Lady Dilke: A Biography* (London, 1969)

Dillens. Belgian family of artists. Henrik Dillens (1812–72), like his brother (1) Adolphe-Alexandre Dillens, was active as a painter and etcher. He had two sons, the painter Albert (*b* 1844), who produced fishing scenes, portraits and a few religious works, and the sculptor (2) Julien Dillens.

(1) Adolphe-Alexandre Dillens (*b* Ghent, 2 Jan 1821; *d* Brussels, 1 Jan 1877). Painter and etcher. He studied at the academy in Ghent. The source of most of his genre subjects was Zealand, and he represented scenes of that region's daily life (e.g. *Skaters in Zealand*, exh. 1860; Brussels, Musées Royaux B.-A.). He also produced a few portraits and a number of etchings. At the end of his life Dillens turned to painting historical and military scenes from Flemish life, such as *Enlistment in the Austrian Netherlands* (Brussels, Musées Royaux B.-A.). He was a prolific and successful artist, who worked with facility and did not hesitate to repeat himself in order to satisfy collectors. Although his pictures lack originality, they are notable for their precise draughtsmanship, clear composition and rich colouring.

BIBLIOGRAPHY
Bénézit; Thieme–Becker
G. Flippo: *Lexicon of the Belgian Romantic Painters* (Antwerp, 1981)

BERNADETTE THOMAS

(2) Julien Dillens (*b* Antwerp, 8 June 1849; *d* Brussels, 24 Dec 1904). Sculptor and medallist, nephew of (1) Adolphe-Alexandre Dillens. Influenced by the sculptor Léopold Harzé (1831–93), he studied at the Brussels Académie between 1861 and 1874. While working under the direction of Albert-Ernest Carrier-Belleuse on the sculptural decoration (1870–73) of the Brussels Bourse, he met Auguste Rodin, who employed him in his Brussels studio until 1877. At the Antwerp Salon of 1875 he exhibited *Enigma* (Ghent, Mus. S. Kst.), a seated female nude whose informal pose and lack of allegorical disguise were considered subversive. The following year he founded the group L'Essor in Brussels. In 1877 he won the Prix de Rome and went to Italy after visiting London and Paris. In Florence he made the acquaintance of Léon Frederic and executed *Justice between Clemency and Law* (1880; Brussels, Pal. Justice), a Mosaic old man seated between standing female figures. After visits to Vienna and Berlin he returned to Brussels in 1881. Among his most impressive monuments are those to the advocate *Hippolyte Metdepenningen* (1886; Ghent, Koophandel-plein) and to the 14th-century alderman *Everard 't Serclaes* (1902; Brussels, Grand Place), a free variation on an early Renaissance wall tomb. In his statuette of *Allegretto* (Brussels, Musées Royaux B.-A.) he was one of the first European artists to make use of the rich supply of ivory from the Belgian Congo (now Zaire). He also produced portrait busts (e.g. *Léon Frederic*, before 1888; Brussels, Musées Royaux B.-A.) and medals (e.g. *Ernest Slingeneyer*, 1890). From 1898 until his death, he taught at the Brussels Académie, and in 1903 he was made a member of the Académie Royale de Belgique.

BIBLIOGRAPHY
S. Pierron: *Portraits d'artistes: Julien Dillens* (Brussels, 1905)
J. Potvin: *Julien Dillens, statuaire* (Brussels, 1913)
A. Goffin: *Julien Dillens* (Turnhout, 1919)
G. M. Matthijs: *Julien Dillens sculpteur* (Brussels, 1955)
J. van Lennep: 'Dillens, Julien', *Académie royale des beaux-arts de Bruxelles* (exh. cat., Brussels, Musées Royaux B.-A., 1987), pp. 292–3, 321–4

JACQUES VAN LENNEP

Diller, Burgoyne (*b* New York, 13 Jan 1906; *d* New York, 30 Jan 1965). American painter and sculptor. He grew up in Michigan and moved to New York in 1928. The following year he enrolled in classes at the Art Students' League where, during the subsequent five years, he was most influenced by the teachers Jan Matulka and Hans Hofmann. In the early 1930s he showed an interest in Kazimir Malevich and Russian Constructivist painters, whose work he first encountered in *Modern Russian Art* (New York, 1925) by Louis Lozowick (1892–1973). At about the same time he became aware of the work of the De Stijl artists.

Diller's use from the mid-1930s of horizontal and vertical forms and primary colours, plus black, white and grey, in such paintings as *Second Theme* (1937–8; New York, MOMA) and *Third Theme* (1946–8; New York, Whitney) demonstrates his debt to Theo van Doesburg's and Mondrian's Neo-plastic paintings, while his exploration of three-dimensional spatial relationships in a series of coloured relief constructions, for example *Construction* (1938; New York, MOMA) and *Construction* (1940; New Haven, CT, Yale U., A.G.), owes something to El Lissitzky and other Constructivist artists.

Due to the Depression and his commitment to an austere abstract style, Diller found it impossible to sell his work, and therefore in 1935 he accepted the position of co-director of the mural division of the Works Progress Administration Federal Art Project in New York. In that capacity he was instrumental in securing jobs or commissions for numerous modern artists, many of whom were fellow members of American Abstract Artists, a group that Diller helped to found in 1936. In 1940 he was appointed Assistant Technical Director of the Art Project in New York and later directed the War Service Art Section there.

Although Diller became Associate Professor of Art at Brooklyn College in 1945, his artistic output over the next 15 years was relatively small, primarily as a result of his alcoholism. During the 1960s, however, he was encouraged by the support of Arthur and Madeleine Lejwa—who gave him a series of one-man shows in their Galerie Chalette in New York—to work on a relatively large, even monumental scale with rectangular forms in primary colours that appear to be suspended in space and are in most cases seen against a grey or black background, for example *First Theme* (1963–4; New York, Whitney). Unlike the many overlapping elements and more agitated compositions that characterized much of his earlier work, in these symmetrically composed canvases Diller came close to the austere simplicity of Ad Reinhardt and Josef Albers while nonetheless adhering to the fundamental tenets of Neo-plasticism. Related to these late paintings are the sculptures that he began in 1963. Constructed of plywood covered with Formica in the same range of colours found in the paintings, these works, such as *Project for Granite No. 5* (1963; Trenton, NJ State Mus.), made literal the spatial relationships adumbrated on canvas.

Looking back on his career in 1961, Diller explained in a notebook that his work had not developed in a regular progression of discrete stages but involved a tangential development of three visual themes. Each of these was an exploration of a different relationship between the basic plane of the flat canvas and the movement generated by either lines or planes or smaller geometrical elements.

UNPUBLISHED SOURCES

Washington, DC, Archvs Amer. A., Smithsonian Inst. [transcript of interviews with B. Diller, 3 and 21 March 1964]

BIBLIOGRAPHY

E. de Kooning: 'Diller Paints a Picture', *ARTnews*, li/9 (1953), pp. 26–9, 55–7

Burgoyne Diller, 1906–1965 (exh. cat., Trenton, NJ State Mus., 1966) [incl. essay by L. Campbell from *ARTnews*, lx/3 (1961), pp. 34–5, 56–9]

L. Campbell: 'Diller: The Ruling Passion', *ARTnews*, lxviii/6 (1968), pp. 36–7, 59–61

Burgoyne Diller: Paintings, Sculptures, Drawings (exh. cat., essay P. Larsen; Minneapolis, MN, Walker A. Cent., 1971–2)

Burgoyne Diller (exh. cat., essay H. Rand; New York, Meredith Long Contemp. A., 1980)

NANCY J. TROY

Dillis. German family of artists.

(1) (Maximilian) Johann Georg von Dillis (*b* Grüngiebing, Wasserburg, 26 Dec 1759; *d* Munich, 28 Sept 1841). Draughtsman, painter, engraver, museum director and teacher. He was the eldest son of the Elector's head forester, Wolfgang Dillis, and godson of Maximilian III Joseph, Electoral Prince of Bavaria, who paid for him to attend the Gymnasium in Munich. In 1782, after studying theology in Ingolstadt, Dillis became a pupil of Ignaz Oefele (1721–97) and Johann Jakob Dorner the elder at the Munich Zeichnungsakademie, supporting himself by giving drawing lessons to the children of noble families. His earliest surviving drawings from the 1770s (Munich, Stadtarchv and Stadtmus.) show villages around Munich.

This evident gift for landscape was encouraged by Benjamin Thompson, Count Rumford (1753–1814), an American who worked for the Bavarian Elector and created the Englischer Garten in Munich. He commissioned Dillis to make drawings of the most interesting areas in the Bavarian mountains (almost all Munich, Staatl. Graph. Samml. and Schloss Nymphenburg). Through Rumford, Dillis was able to accompany Henry Temple, 2nd Viscount Palmerston, and his family to Salzburg in 1794. Following this, Dillis made the first of many journeys to Italy (1794–5). In addition to his contact with English culture through Rumford, Dillis widened his knowledge of art on journeys to Prague, Dresden and Vienna (1792), Rome (1805) and Paris (1806).

In the service of Maximilian I Joseph (*reg* 1806–25) and then Ludwig I, Dillis came to occupy an influential position in the artistic life of Munich. From 1790 he was supervisor of the Gemäldegalerie and from 1822 its director. The gallery had inherited several important Wittelsbach family collections and established collections of items from deconsecrated churches and monasteries. Dillis played an important role in recording, reorganizing and enlarging the collection. The Alte Pinakothek was opened in 1836, and Dillis compiled its first catalogue. In 1808 his services were rewarded with the Bavarian Royal Order of Merit and elevation to the nobility. In addition to his wide-ranging work for the Gemäldegalerie and his advisory role to King Ludwig I on all matters relating to art, he was also a professor of landscape painting at the Munich Akademie (1808–14). He resigned in 1814, disillusioned with academic methods of training artists.

A secure existence as a court official allowed Dillis to work relatively independently of public taste but left him little time for artistic endeavour. The extent of his output is thus all the more remarkable. His landscape etchings date from the early part of his career (1783–1800), consisting of nearly 60 works (almost all Munich, Staatl. Graph. Samml.). The drawings (most important collections Munich, Staatl. Graph. Samml., Stadtarchv, Stadtmus. and Lenbachhaus) play an important part in his work as a whole. Most are landscape drawings in a variety of techniques: pencil, pen, red chalk, black chalk, white chalk, crayon, sepia and watercolour; subject-matter was provided by his European travels. One separate group is formed by idealized landscapes after the work of Claude Lorrain and Gaspard Dughet. The large group of swiftly executed sketches of clouds drawn on blue paper with white chalk (*c.* 1810–20; Munich, Stadtarchv) are among the earliest studies of such motifs. There are also important portrait drawings (1785–1800) documenting Dillis's interest in the physiognomy of such social outsiders as peasants, herdsmen, beggars, paupers, old people, Jews and lunatics.

From 1808 Dillis produced oil portraits of relations and friends. His portraits of *Clemens Neumayr* and his wife, *Therese Neumayr* (both 1809; Munich, Neue Pin.), are outstanding examples of unconventional portraiture, executed swiftly and spontaneously in glowing colours. His landscape sketches in oil also appear advanced in relation to German painting of the time. Dillis's sketch of the *Triva House* (1797; Munich, Neue Pin.) anticipates Impressionism with its sense of light and spontaneous application of colour, while his three views of Rome from the Villa Malta

Johann Georg von Dillis: *View of St Peter's, Rome*, oil on paper, 293×434 mm, 1818 (Munich, Schack-Galerie)

(1818; Munich, Schack-Gal.; see fig.), in the tradition of Pierre Henri de Valencienne's Roman oil sketches of the 1780s, were long attributed to the much younger Carl Rottmann largely because of their advanced treatment of light as the dominant factor in each scene. In 1818 Dillis travelled as companion and artist in the suite of Crown Prince Ludwig of Bavaria and produced 39 large-scale drawings, *Views of Rome, Naples and Sicily* (Munich, Staatl. Graph. Samml.). Although contemporaries saw these merely as mementos of places visited, they have since been regarded as perfect examples of representative yet evocative watercolour painting. During Dillis's lifetime, Ludwig I never acquired a sketch in oils or a painting by him, although Dillis did paint a few 'official' landscapes (e.g. the *Old Tower at Marino*, 1821; see Hardtwig, 1987, p. 419) that conformed to the public's expectations of a finished painting. These are similar in style to Dutch 17th-century painting (Jacob van Ruisdael or Jan Wijnants, for example) or to works by Claude and Dughet. The spontaneity and skill of Dillis's oil sketches are lacking in these works, which were derived from a long preparatory process involving numerous sketches from nature and composition studies. In his more characteristic, freer landscape style, however, Dillis may be seen as a link between the tradition of classical landscape painting and the new realism. In Germany he pointed the way for the work of Karl Blechen and Adolph Friedrich Erdmann Menzel.

(2) Ignaz Dillis (*b* Grüngiebing, Wasserburg, 1772; *d* Munich, 1808). Engraver and painter, brother of (1) Johann Georg von Dillis. From 1789 he worked under the guidance of his elder brother. Pencil drawings made by the two while on a walking expedition to the Chiemsee in 1792 (Munich, Stadtarchv) reveal the less practised hand of the younger brother. Watercolours survive from their journey together to Lake Constance in 1794 (Munich, Stadtarchv). Ignaz Dillis's work is typified by strong colours and skilfully achieved contrasts juxtaposing storm clouds, falling rain and a rainbow or reddish sunset. For some time watercolours of this kind were usually attributed to Johann Georg von Dillis. In 1805 Ignaz abandoned his artistic career to become royal head forester.

(3) (Johann) Cantius Dillis (*b* Grüngiebing, Wasserburg, 1779; *d* Munich, 12 Sept 1854). Engraver and painter, brother of (1) Johann Georg von Dillis and (2) Ignaz Dillis. He lived in Munich from 1789 and studied under his brother Johann Georg, at whose instigation he was appointed court copperplate engraver in 1801 and court painter in 1807. In 1796 Cantius accompanied Johann Georg to Linz, where paintings from the gallery were taken for safe keeping during the advance of French forces under Napoleon. In 1805 the two men went to Rome, and in 1815 to Paris to bring back paintings that had been removed by the French. The earliest of the six known etchings by Cantius Dillis dates from 1790 (Munich, Stadtmus.). His first known painting, the landscape *Grottaferrata* (1806; Munich, Neue Pin.), shows the influence of Johann Georg's teaching but also reveals a certain independence. He helped Johann Georg with larger commissions, such as the eight wall paintings for the Schilcher Forestry Commission at Dietramszell (*c.* 1808–9); these are idealized landscapes in the style of Gaspard Dughet, mainly executed by Cantius from Johann Georg's sketches (Munich, Neue Pin.). His brother was certainly instrumental in procuring Cantius the commission for the painting *Waterfall near Golling* (1813; *in situ*) for Maximilian I Joseph to decorate a wall at Schloss Nymphenburg; this accompanies five pictures of Bavarian lakes and waterfalls by other artists. The drawings and oil sketches of Cantius (Munich, Stadtmus. and Staatl. Graph. Samml.) often resemble those of Johann Georg, but his style usually lags behind in development. When unsigned, such works have easily been confused with the work of his eldest brother.

WRITINGS
R. Messerer, ed.: *Briefwechsel zwischen Ludwig I von Bayern und Georg von Dillis, 1807–1841* (Munich, 1966)

BIBLIOGRAPHY
Thieme–Becker
E. Hanfstaengl: 'Die drei römischen Ansichten in der Münchner Schack-Galerie', *Z. Bild. Kst*, n. s., lviii (1924), pp. 51–3
W. Lessing: *J. G. von Dillis als Künstler und Museumsmann* (Munich, 1951)
J. G. von Dillis (exh. cat., ed. D. Schmidt; Munich, Staatl. Graph. Samml., 1959)
R. Messerer: *J. G. von Dillis: Leben und Werk* (Munich, 1961)
B. Hardtwig: 'J. G. von Dillis, Wilhelm von Kobell und die Anfange der Münchner Schule', *Münchner Landschaftsmalerei von 1800–1850* (exh. cat., Munich, Lenbachhaus, 1979), pp. 58–69
Von Dillis bis Piloty (exh. cat., ed. G. Scheffler and B. Hardtwig; Munich, Staatl. Graph. Samml., 1979)
C. Heilmann: 'Eine frühe Berührung Münchens mit englischer Land-schaftsmalerei', *Sind Britten hier? Relations between British and Continental Art, 1680–1880* (Munich, 1981), pp. 147–60
B. Hardtwig: 'J. G. Dillis und das Porträt um 1800: "Armeleutekunst" und Individualität', *Münch. Jb. Bild. Kst*, xxv (1984), pp. 157–88
——: 'Claudes Glut und Poussins Grösse: Von Dillis erreicht? *Der alte Turm bei Marino* zwischen Naturstudie und offiziellem Landschaftsbild', *Festschrift Norbert Lieb zum 80. Geburtstag* (Munich, 1987), pp. 278–89
BARBARA HARDTWIG

Dillwyn Llewelyn, John. *See* LLEWELYN, JOHN DILLWYN.

Dilmun. *See* BAHRAIN.

Dilthey, Wilhelm (*b* Biebrich, Hesse, 19 Nov 1831; *d* Seis, Tyrol [now Bolzano, Italy], 1911). German philosopher. He had a profound influence on philosophy in the 20th century, particularly on Martin Heidegger in Germany and José Ortega y Gasset in Spain. He revived the discipline of HERMENEUTICS, in which it is held that parts of a complex whole can be understood only in terms of that whole. He argued that this was the correct form of investigation of the human world, which he believed to be characterized by just such complex part–whole relationships. One consequence of hermeneutics is that there are no self-evident starting-points or certainties on which to base investigation. In the context of the visual arts, Dilthey believed there to be no timeless aesthetic principles with which to judge technique or content. He held that art was one among many forms of human expression that had to be appreciated in the light of its historical context, although he did suggest that human nature provides a repertory of universal principles that govern aesthetic appreciation. He believed certain colours and lines, and certain relations of symmetry and rhythm to be intrinsically pleasing.

Dilthey's practical concern was to develop an aesthetic applicable to the nascent modernist movement, whose tendency to express subjective experience rendered classical aesthetics inadequate because of the latter's being designed to deal with objective representations. Dilthey's solution was to suggest that great art is that which points both to the artist's life and to the general historical conditions in which it was created, and which aspires to form an expressive, transcendent unity of the two. For Dilthey, the degree to which an artist successfully distils a moment of the subjective–objective relationship and is able to unify the two dictates the quality of a work of art.

WRITINGS
'Beiträge zum Studium der Individualität', *Gesammelte Schriften*, v (Stuttgart, 1957)
'Poetik', *Gesammelte Schriften*, vi (Stuttgart, 1958)

BIBLIOGRAPHY
M. Philipson: 'Dilthey on Art', *J. Aesth. & A. Crit.*, xvii (1958), pp. 72–6
U. Hermann: *Bibliographie Wilhelm Dilthey* (Weinheim, 1969)
F. Rodi: *Morphologie und Hermeneutik: Zur Methode von Diltheys Ästhetik* (Stuttgart, 1969)
R. A. Makkreel: *Dilthey: Philosopher of the Human Studies* (Princeton, 1975)
H. P. Rickman, ed.: *Wilhelm Dilthey: Selected Writings* (Cambridge, 1976)
ANDREW DOBSON

Diluent. SOLVENT used to dilute or thin a solution such as turpentine for oil paint.

Dimand, Maurice S(ven) (*b* 1892; *d* 1986). American curator. He studied under JOSEF STRZYGOWSKI at the University of Vienna, where he earned a PhD in 1916, writing a thesis on Coptic tapestries, particularly those in the museum of the University of Lund, Sweden. In 1923 he joined the staff of the Metropolitan Museum of Art in New York City as a research assistant in the Egyptian department, charged with cataloguing Coptic textiles. In 1925 he was put in charge of the new subdepartment for Islamic art in the Department of Decorative Arts, and in 1932 he became Associate Curator of Near Eastern Art. He became the first full Curator of Near Eastern Art in 1933, a position he held until retirement in 1959. Dimand developed a special interest in Islamic textiles, particularly carpets, and he catalogued the important James F. Ballard collection of carpets in St Louis, as well as negotiating gifts of carpets to the museum by such collectors as J. V. McMullan, J. Pierpont Morgan and John D. Rockefeller. Dimand wrote many articles on rugs and textiles, particularly those acquired by the museum. His handbook of Islamic decorative arts and paintings, based on the collections in the Metropolitan, went into three editions and was translated into Arabic, Persian and Urdu. He also organized six major exhibitions, including one on the 'Polonaise' carpets (1930) and another on Oriental carpets (1935).

WRITINGS
Die Ornamentik der koptischen Wollwirkereien (Leipzig, 1921)
A Handbook of Mohammedan Decorative Arts (New York, 1930); rev. as *A Handbook of Muhammadan Art* (New York, 1944, 3/1958)
Loan Exhibition of Persian Rugs of the So-Called Polish Type (exh. cat., New York, Met., 1930)
Loan Exhibition of Ceramic Art of the Near East (exh. cat., New York, Met., 1931)
'An Early Cut-pile Rug from Egypt', *Met. Mus. Stud.*, iv (1932–3), pp. 151–62
A Guide to an Exhibition of Islamic Miniature Painting and Book Illumination (exh. cat., New York, Met., 1933)

A Guide to an Exhibition of Oriental Rugs and Textiles (exh. cat., New York, Met., 1935)

The Ballard Collection of Oriental Rugs in the City Museum of St Louis (St Louis, 1935)

'Studies in Islamic Ornament, I: Some Aspects of Omaiyad and Early Abbasid Ornaments', *A. Islam.*, iv (1937), pp. 293–337

'Studies in Islamic Ornament, II', *Archaeologica Orientalia in Memoriam Ernst Herzfeld* (Locust Valley, NY, 1952), pp. 62–8

'An Exhibition of Islamic and Indian Paintings', *Bull. Met.*, n. s. xiv (1955), pp. 85–102

with J. Mailey: *Oriental Rugs in the Metropolitan Museum* (New York, 1973)

☐

Dimashq. *See* DAMASCUS.

Dimchev, Emil, I (*b* Varna, 5 Feb 1926). Bulgarian architect. He studied architecture at the Polytechnic Institute in Sofia (graduated 1950) under Dimiter Tsolov (1896–1970), one of the last major Bulgarian architects of 1920s and 1930s classicism. Dimchev began his career at the time when architecture in Bulgaria began to be dominated by the so-called Stalinist style, which remained a major trend until the beginning of 1960s. Even in this period, however, Dimchev was inspired by Bulgarian nationalist principles of the 18th and 19th centuries and achieved some elements of synthesis between public and private architecture. His best-known works are the hotels (1956) at the Black Sea resorts Druzba and Varna and the Hotel Yantra (1956–9) in Veliko Türnovo. The latter was influenced by the organic architecture of Frank Lloyd Wright. In 1960 Dimchev reconstructed the Telegraph-capia at the medieval fortress by the River Danube in Vidin in collaboration with the architect Kolandjiev and the artist P. Dobrinovich. He also reconstructed the club of the Union of the Bulgarian Writers (1970) in Sofia with the sculptors G. Malkchiev and S. Boiadjieva. Dimchev created several restaurants and bars as tourist attractions, for example Fisherman's Hut (1970) and the tourist complex Leventtabiya (1968–71) with the artist M. Nanev, both outside the city of Russe. At the same time he worked on exhibition halls and pavilions. The projects that followed were mainly interiors and decorative schemes for government and public buildings, for example the State Council (1971), Sofia; the Ministry Council (1972–3), Sofia; and the museum exposition (1977) of Bulgaria at the Auschwitz concentration camp in Poland.

BIBLIOGRAPHY
P. Gulabova: 'The Road of an Artist', *Nash Dom*, 3 (1974)
Encyclopedia of the Fine Arts in Bulgaria, i (Sofia, 1980)

JULIANA NEDEVA-WEGENER

Dimech, Vincenzo (*b* 3 March 1768; *d* 19 Feb 1831). Maltese sculptor. He was the leading architectural sculptor of the early 19th century in Malta and was for some time Professor of Architecture and Sculpture in the School of Design at the University of Malta, in Msida. His most important public monument is the memorial to *Judge Zammit* at the Upper Barracca in Valletta, where he was assisted by his cousin, Ferdinando Dimech. His other works include the sculptures for the English Doric Revival temple at the Lower Barracca in Valletta, commemorating Sir Alexander Ball, the first British Civil Commissioner in Malta. He was also responsible for the complete sculptural decoration of the Royal Palace at Corfu. Sir George

Whitmore, who was in charge of the project, might have been referring to Dimech when he complained about a 'Malta mastermason who could not understand working drawings'. He was also in popular demand for devotional wooden polychrome sculptures. His most successful work in this genre is the processional statue of *St Publius* in the parish church of Floriana.

BIBLIOGRAPHY
'Vincenzo Dimech', *Heritage: Enc. Malt. Cult. & Civiliz.*, 63 (1986)

MARIO BUHAGIAR

Dimier, Louis (*b* Paris, 11 Feb 1865; *d* Saint-Paul, Haute-Savoie, 21 Nov 1943). French art historian. His principal works date from the years 1895–1904; their chief purpose is to attack a nationalist view of art history and to demonstrate that until the 17th century French painting had been subject to foreign influences and the influx of foreign artists, so that it lacked the distinct and homogeneous character that would allow one to talk of a 'French School'. This stance reveals an exceptional independence of mind in a man who co-founded the extreme right-wing Action Française in 1898 and helped promote it until his break with Charles Maurras in 1920. His doctoral thesis on Francesco Primaticcio (Paris, 1900), still considered a standard work, served as a basis for studies of the Fontainebleau school: in it Dimier emphasized foreign contributions to French painting. His *French Painting in the 16th Century* (1904) opposed the nationalist viewpoint of the famous exhibition of French Primitives held in Paris in 1904. This proposed the 15th-century painter Jean Fouquet as the initiator of the French school: Dimier stressed the part played by the 16th-century Italian Primaticcio, by Toussaint Dubreuil at Fontainebleau later in the century and by Simon Vouet, who brought the experience of classicizing Italian painting from Rome to Paris in the 1620s. His book, *Histoire de la peinture de portrait en France au XVIème siècle* (1924–5), includes a catalogue of all the early portraits then known. Dimier's ambitious project on French 18th-century painting, *Les Peintres du XVIIIème siècle*, which he served both as editor and as contributor, was concluded after only two volumes. He also turned his attention to the 19th century in his *Histoire de la peinture française au XIXème siècle, 1793–1903* (1914).

WRITINGS
Le Primatice, peintre, sculpteur et architecte des rois de France (Paris, 1900)
French Painting in the 16th Century (London, 1904)
Histoire de la peinture française au XIXème siècle, 1793–1903 (Paris, 1914)
Histoire de la peinture de portrait en France au XVIème siècle, 2 vols (Paris, 1924–5)
Les Peintres du XVIIIème siècle, 2 vols (Paris, 1928–30)
H. Zerner, ed.: *L'Art français* (Paris, 1965)

DBF

BIBLIOGRAPHY

SOPHIE BIASS-FABIANI

Dimini [Dhimíni]. Site in the coastal plain of Thessaly near modern Volos in central Greece. This Late Neolithic settlement on a low hill was occupied from *c.* 4200 to *c.* 3600/3000 BC. Like nearby SESKLO, it was first explored by Christos Tsountas. In 1903 he discovered the concentric rings of walls with three entrances, which suggested a strongly fortified village occupying an area of *c.* 100×90 m. Recent excavation by Hourmouziades has shown that the primary function of each ring of walls was structural, to support terraces on the sides of the mound where small stone-built houses stood. In the centre of the mound there was an open courtyard with a single large building with a porch and main room thought to be the chief's house (megaron). In the Late Bronze Age (*c.* 1300 BC) the mound was chosen for the construction of a fine tholos tomb as a result of the spread of Mycenaean civilization into northern Greece.

Dimini has given its name to the most striking pottery produced in Neolithic Greece. Angular pottery bowls and jars are decorated with bichrome or polychrome geometric patterns. The 'Classic' Dimini style uses curvilinear meanders painted with a chocolate-coloured slip on a cream ground. Finds of this pottery outside Thessaly (e.g. in Albania) are a sign of the increasing contact between communities in different parts of south-east Europe in the Late Neolithic period.

BIBLIOGRAPHY

C. Tsountas: *Oi proistorikoi akropoleis Dhiminiou kai Sesklo* [The prehistoric acropoleis of Dimini and Sesklo] (Athens, 1908)
D. R. Theokharis: *Neolithic Greece* (Athens, 1973), pp. 101–2
G. Hourmouziades: *To neolithiko Dhimini: Prospatheia gia mia nea proseggisi tou neolithikou ulikou* [Neolithic Dhimini: an attempt at a new approach to neolithic material] (Volos, 1979)

K. A. WARDLE

Dimitrijević, Braco (*b* Sarajevo, 18 June 1948). Bosnian artist. He graduated from the Zagreb Academy in 1971, continuing at St Martin's School of Art, London. He lived in London and Paris. His work was conceptual, and until the mid-1970s he focused on the problem of non-information in contemporary civilization. The starting-point of his exhibitions and projects was the confrontation of public figures with anonymous people. In executing large busts or monuments to unknown persons in busy urban centres, parks and exhibition halls, the artist wished to draw attention to the importance of the context in creating public opinion.

Indicative of the underlying concept of the works Dimitrijević produced after the mid-1970s was a statement he made in 1973: 'Just as a piano is not music, a painting is not art'. A series entitled *Triptychos post historicos* dates from that period. *Repeated Secret* (1978–83; Liverpool, Tate) was a typical example of a painting in which he commented on well-known works of art, confronting them with the most commonplace everyday things.

BIBLIOGRAPHY

Braco Dimitrijević (exh. cat. by E. Weiss, Cologne, Mus. Ludwig, 1984)
Braco Dimitrijević (exh. cat. by D. Brown, London, Tate, 1985)
Braco Dimitrijević (exh. cat. by B. Holeczek, L. von Mendgen and R. Gassen, Ludwigshafen, Hack-Mus. & Städt. Kstsamml., 1987)

JURE MIKUŽ

Dimitrov, Zakhary. *See* ZOGRAPH, ZAKHARY.

Dimitrov-Maistora, Vladimir [Dimitroff, Vladimir; Maistora] (*b* Frolosh, nr Kyustendil, 1 Feb 1882; *d* Sofia, 29 Sept 1960). Bulgarian painter, draughtsman and teacher. He is considered one of the leading Bulgarian artists of the 20th century. From a poor family, he left school at an early age and worked at various jobs before becoming a clerk (1898–1903) at the Kyustendil District Court, where he drew portraits of its employees. In 1903 he entered the School of Drawing in Sofia and, while there, began to be called 'Maistora' ('Master'), a respectful title in acknowledgement of his talent. He served as a painter for the Bulgarian army during the Balkan Wars (1912–13) and World War I, executing landscapes and genre paintings such as *A Rest from the March* (1917; Sofia, N. Mus. Mil. Hist.). He later taught and travelled, visiting Rome in 1922, where he met the American collector John Crane who bought his entire stock of paintings and signed a four-year contract with him for production of his work. Maistora returned to Bulgaria and for more than 20 years lived in the village of Shishkovci, near Kyustendil, from there sending all of his paintings to the Ministry of Education. He drew and painted exclusively portraits and self-portraits, employing pencil, oil, India ink or watercolour (e.g. *Portrait of N. Checklarov*, 1910; *Self-portrait*, 1913; both Sofia, N.A.G.). His work is a combination of the traditions of Bulgarian folk art and Post-Impressionism; from the latter he developed the use of clean colours, an expressive deformation of nature and a contrast of warm and cool tones in the modelling. His models, agricultural workers and pretty village women, are usually placed in static and frontal poses close to the picture plane and are framed behind by decorative friezes of fruit and flowers (e.g. *Bulgarian Madonna*, *c.* 1932; *Women Reapers from Shishkovci*, *c.* 1935; both Sofia, N.A.G.). In 1982 UNESCO celebrated the 100th anniversary of his birth. There is a Dimitrov-Maistora Museum in Kyustendil.

WRITINGS

A. Pavlova-Stavreva, ed.: *Vladimir Dimitrov-Maistora: Conversations, Letters, Memories* (Sofia, 1972)

BIBLIOGRAPHY

M. Tzoncheva: *Vladimir Dimitrov-Maistora* (Sofia, 1981)
D. Avramov: *Vladimir Dimitrov-Maistora* (Sofia, 1983)

MARIANA KATZAROVA

Dimsdale, Thomas (*b* 1756; *d* 1825). English banker and collector. He was the son of the eminent physician Thomas Dimsdale (1712–1800), who inoculated Catherine II, Empress of Russia, against smallpox. Some of the finest works in Dimsdale's collection (e.g. Raphael's drawing of *St Cecilia* (1514; Paris, Petit Pal.)), many of which had been owned by Paignon-Dijonval, had been provided by the dealer SAMUEL WOODBURN. In 1823 Woodburn acquired the collection of Jean-Baptiste Wicar, and Dimsdale, although very ill at the time, bought the drawings by Michelangelo and Raphael from this collection. He died shortly afterwards and Woodburn sold the best works of the Italian Masters from the collection to Sir Thomas Lawrence, a rival of Dimsdale's who had unsuccessfully attempted to buy the collection before Dimsdale's death. Dimsdale's library was sold in 1824 (London, Sotheby's, 18 June); his collection of coins and medals was sold later the same year.

BIBLIOGRAPHY

F. Lugt: *Marques* (1921)   □

Dinan Castle. Castle in Brittany, France. It was built from 1382 by John IV of Montfort, Duke of Brittany (*reg* 1341–99), after his return from exile in England (1379). The site was particularly important to him: it was from Dinan, a strongly fortified city and commercial centre, that John organized resistance by the nobility to the threatened annexation of the Duchy by France. The castle, adjoining the city but independent of it, could both provide defence and compel submission in case of revolt: it was a substantial political symbol.

The castle, attached to the city ramparts, was enlarged in 1595–8 by the Duc de Mercoeur through the annexation of the fortified 13th-century Porte du Guichet and the artillery Tour de Coëtquen (built 1474), both of which were part of the city walls; this ensemble forms the existing castle. The building was altered between 1693 and 1711 by the military engineer Garanjeau (in particular, the roof was suppressed and replaced by a terrace) and then by the Monuments Historiques and the city of Dinan, which are now responsible for its preservation.

The main part of John of Montfort's castle, built by Etienne le Tur and in use by 1384, comprises a massive donjon, 34 m high. Its intricate plan is composed of two great round towers joined by a slightly projecting fore-building, to which the principal entrance, defended by a drawbridge, opens on the ground floor (see fig.). The donjon has five storeys, crowned by a parapet walk with machicolation decorated with trefoils and supported on long, elegant corbels; a sixth storey, covered with slate, formerly made up the upper part of the structure. On the

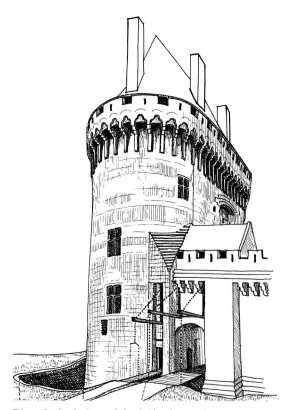

Dinan Castle, donjon and drawbridge, begun 1382; reconstruction drawing by Robert-Henri Martin

opposite side to the projecting entrance block the donjon dominated a very small courtyard, which was provided with a postern and drawbridge leading to the outside and a well that controlled a complex system of water supply.

While the exterior of the castle has a fortified appearance, the interior is primarily residential. The floors are linked by a continuous spiral staircase. There is a kitchen on the ground floor, and the first to fourth storeys have the usual late medieval layout of hall and chamber, supplemented by garderobes and latrines etc. The rooms have huge fireplaces and are generously lit by large casement windows with mullions and transoms. A chapel provided with a heated stall on the second floor completes this seigneurial residence.

The donjon of Dinan is important in the history of Breton civil and military medieval architecture. It was the outcome of a long series of experiments carried out by ducal architects: the first ducal donjon, Pirmil (1365) at Nantes, was nothing more than a strong, gloomy cylinder; the Tour Solidor (before 1371) at Saint-Servan was the first attempt to unite round towers in order to form a donjon of complex plan, but the living arrangements were crude. Dinan perfectly combines military considerations with efficient residential accommodation; and its skilful and subtle proportions enhance this achievement.

BIBLIOGRAPHY

R. Cornon: 'Dinan', *Congr. Archéol. France*, cvii (1949), pp. 172–86
R. Richelot: 'Les Remparts et le château de Dinan en 1693 d'après un mémoire inédit de l'ingénieur Garanjeau', *Nouv. Rev. Bretagne*, vii (1953), pp. 191–202
M. E. Monier: *Dinan: Mille ans d'histoire* (Dinan, 1968)
V. Burnod-Saudreau: *Château de Dinan* (Dinan, 1985) [contains documentary sources and full bibliography]
M. Deceneux: *Il était autrefois Dinan* (Dinan, 1985)

MARC DECENEUX

Dinant, Herri de. *See* BLES, HERRI MET DE.

Dine, Jim (*b* Cincinnati, OH, 6 June 1935). American painter, sculptor, printmaker, illustrator, performance artist, stage designer and poet. He studied art at the Cincinnati Arts Academy (1951–3) and later at the Boston Museum School and Ohio University (1954–7). In 1957 he married Nancy Minto and the following year they moved to New York. Dine's first involvement with the art world was in his Happenings of 1959–60. These historic theatrical events, for example *The Smiling Workman* (performed at the Judson Gallery, New York, 1959), took place in chaotic, makeshift environments built by the artist–performer. During the same period he created his first assemblages, which incorporated found materials. Simultaneously he developed the method by which he produced his best known work—paintings, drawings, prints and sculptures that depict and expressively interpret common images and objects.

Clothing and domestic objects featured prominently in Dine's paintings of the 1960s, with a range of favoured motifs including ties, shoes and bathroom items such as basins, showers and toothbrushes (e.g. *Child's Blue Wall*, 1962; Buffalo, NY, Albright-Knox A.G.). He was equally preoccupied with the elements of his own profession, for example palettes, paint-boxes and brushes, as well as with a variety of tools, which he regarded as extensions of the hand (e.g. *Five Feet of Colorful Tools*, 1962, New York, MOMA; see fig.). As early as 1964 he used an image of a man's dressing-gown, borrowed from a newspaper advertisement, as the basis for a recurring self-portrait, for example *Self-portrait next to a Colored Window* (1964; Dallas, TX, Mus. A.). These were followed by portraits of Nancy Dine and by a series of still-lifes, and by other images such as a heart, Venus de Milo, a gnarled tree and a wrought-iron gate, reintroduced in so many guises as to become personal trademarks.

Dine's method involved repeating his theme again and again, often in several mediums. Through a process of exploration and reinvention the common image lost its place in the public domain and was stamped exclusively with the artist's signature, becoming his vehicle for communicating a range of emotional and aesthetic intentions. This commitment to a personally invested, image-dictated content and a continuing interest in the technical and expressive potential of every medium has characterized Dine's work as a whole. Thus, Dine has often been out-of-step with the major movements of the post-World War II period and must be considered a modern individualist. While he was part of a group during the time of the Happenings and was linked with the Pop art movement through his use of subjects from everyday life, he was at odds with Pop's deadpan style and then with pure abstraction, Minimalism and conceptual art. In the late 1970s and 1980s, however, he was viewed as a forerunner of the figurative and Neo-Expressionist trends.

While Dine has remained devoted to the depiction and incorporation of common objects, elevated to an almost iconic stature, his changing expressive intentions and his experimental approach towards technique have yielded different stylistic results. Although Dine's stylistic shifts

Jim Dine: *Five Feet of Colorful Tools*, oil on canvas surmounted by board on which 32 tools hang from hooks, 1.36×1.53×0.11 m, 1962 (New York, Museum of Modern Art)

do not follow a clear, linear path, it can generally be stated that his work of the early 1960s is characterized by the aggressive, haphazard energy of his Happenings and the heritage of the Abstract Expressionist gesture. At times his line appears a random scrawl and the image-making brutal. Real objects are often incorporated into the compositions. Later in the 1960s and in the 1970s Dine consciously refined his draughtsmanship and painterly techniques, taking greater care and control to achieve a quieter, more romantic and sensual effect. In the 1980s he found increased confidence with greater emphasis on the grand gesture, yet a more sombre tone.

Dine is an unusually prolific artist, producing large numbers of paintings, drawings, prints and sculptures of diverse scale, as well as illustrated books and stage design. His peripatetic lifestyle has been designed to maximize productivity, as he moves from place to place to take advantage of the numerous opportunities offered an artist of his reputation and to refuel himself through living in different environments. He has always maintained a home base of operation with a studio (1958–68 in New York; 1967–71 in London; 1971–85 in Putney, VT; from 1986 in New York and Washington, CT). He often visits printshops and foundries and has set up dozens of temporary studios in cities all over the USA and Europe in order to focus on special projects or to prepare exhibitions.

BIBLIOGRAPHY
Jim Dine Designs for 'A Midsummer Night's Dream' (New York, 1968)
J. Gordon: *Jim Dine* (New York, 1970)
Jim Dine: Complete Graphics (exh. cat., W. Berlin, Gal. Mikro, 1970) [cat. rai. from 1960 to 1970]
Jim Dine: Prints, 1970–1977 (exh. cat., Williamstown, MA, Williams Coll. Mus. A., 1977) [cat. rai.]
C. W. Glenn: *Jim Dine: Figure Drawings, 1975–1979* (New York, 1979) [excellent illustrations]
N. Smilansky: 'An interview with Jim Dine', *Prt Rev.*, xii (1980), pp. 56–61
D. Shapiro: *Jim Dine* (New York, 1981)
C. Ackley: *Etchings by Jim Dine: Nancy Outside in July* (New York, 1983)
G. W. J. Beal: *Jim Dine: Five Themes* (New York, 1984) [excellent colour pls]
C. W. Glenn: *Jim Dine: Drawings* (New York, 1985) [excellent pls]
E. G. D'Oench and J. E. Feinberg: *Jim Dine: Prints, 1977–1985* (New York, 1986) [fully illus. cat. rai.]

JEAN E. FEINBERG

Dinglinger, Johann Melchior (*b* Biberbach, 26 Dec 1664; *d* Dresden, 6 March 1731). German goldsmith and jeweller. He was one of the most famous goldsmiths of his time, and almost all his works are in the Grünes Gewölbe, Dresden. After his training in Ulm he travelled as a journeyman to Augsburg, Nuremberg and Vienna. He is first recorded in Dresden in 1692. His two brothers, the enameller Georg Friedrich Dinglinger (1666–1720) and the jeweller Georg Christoph Dinglinger (1668–1728), are documented as active there in 1693; they remained his closest collaborators, particularly Georg Friedrich.

From the beginning of his career, Johann Melchior Dinglinger worked for Frederick-Augustus I of Saxony, even before the latter became Elector in 1694. The jewellery produced for Frederick-Augustus's coronation as King Augustus II of Poland (also known as Augustus the Strong) in 1697 was Dinglinger's first important commission. In 1698 he was appointed Court Jeweller,

and all his projects were personally supervised by the King. In the late 17th century and early 18th Dinglinger probably produced most of the jewellery for the court: almost all the orders of chivalry and military decorations came from his workshop, including those in emeralds and diamonds for the revived Polish Order of the Knights of the White Eagle. Various designs for banquets for the King are also kept in the Grünes Gewölbe.

The large number of treasury pieces that Dinglinger supplied to the King, usually at his own expense, includes a gilt coffee-set of 1701. The fashion of coffee drinking gave rise to coffee-sets on trays, but Dinglinger's work was an exaggeration of this type. He arranged a coffeepot, cups, rinsing bowls, scent bottles, figurines and garlands of gold, silver, enamel, gems, ivory and wood, one on top of the other, in the manner of a Baroque display buffet but in the form of a free-standing pyramid. The painted enamels by Georg Friedrich Dinglinger simulate porcelain.

This was followed in 1704 by *Diana Bathing*, an agate bowl on a foot. Diana, an ivory figure carved by Balthasar Permoser, sits on the rim of the bowl with her weapons and garments of gold and enamel scattered about her. In 1707, after six years' work, Dinglinger, his brothers and other collaborators completed the *Court of Aurangzeb*. It depicts the homage paid to the Mughal emperor on his birthday, with 165 enamelled gold figures on a silver-gilt stage. A written explanation of the scene was attached. The idea for this piece was conceived by the King and anticipated the later cult of Orientalism. The work was probably also inspired by travellers' descriptions of East Asia and India and by the court festivities in Dresden, which included processions in exotic costumes. This apotheosis of worldly power was long regarded as the most important piece in the Grünes Gewölbe. At the same time Dinglinger produced a number of sumptuous bowls and new mounts for earlier pieces in the *Kunstkammer* of Frederick-Augustus.

Dinglinger's work became widely renowned, and kings, including Peter I, Tsar and Emperor of Russia, and the nobility sought commissions from him. The death of his brother Georg Friedrich, however, together with the King's increasing interest in antiquity, resulted in a change of style in Dinglinger's late work. The *Obeliscus Augusteus*, conceived for the Grünes Gewölbe and erected there in 1722, is a type of monument to the King: portraits of ancient rulers are set in a symbolic relationship to the enamel profile portrait of *Augustus II the Strong, King of Poland*, which imitates a cameo (for illustration *see* WETTIN, (7)). In the centrepieces depicting the *Three Ages of Man* (1727–8) Dinglinger's growing interest in allegorical themes is evident. The structure, similar to that of a monstrance, rises from a stone pedestal with two figures to an immense sardonyx cameo framed by goldwork and gems. His last important work is the *Apis Altar* (1731), conceived with the aid of the scholar Rüger and following engraved designs. The overall form is derived from the Baroque high altar. An immense cameo also forms the centre. Dinglinger's work gave rise to a school of goldsmithing in Dresden that remained active until the end of the 18th century and even influenced Fabergé in the 19th.

BIBLIOGRAPHY

E. von Watzdorf: *Johann Melchior Dinglinger: Der Goldschmied des deutschen Barock* (Berlin, 1962)

FABIAN STEIN

Ding Yunpeng [Ting Yün-p'eng; *zi* Nanyu; *hao* Shenghua Jushi] (*b* Xiuning, Anhui Province, 1547; *d* after 1625). Chinese painter. The son of a physician with modest artistic aspirations, he inherited his father's love for art but was left with no financial means and was obliged to paint for a living. Ding became known primarily for his Buddhist figure painting, though he also painted landscapes and designed woodblock book illustrations. Ding was the most conservative of the major late Ming-period (1368–1644) figure painters with whom he is often grouped, but although he did not develop a distinctive or inventive personal style, he was a versatile artist of eclectic tastes, displaying a wide range in subject-matter and style.

In the late 1570s Ding left Xiuning for the influential artistic centre of Huating in Jiangsu Province (modern Songjiang, Shanghai Municipality). He lived occasionally in Buddhist monasteries as a lay practitioner and made religious pictures for various temples. His earliest surviving dated work, an album depicting *luohan* (Skt *arhat*s; enlightened beings), was painted in 1577–8 (Taipei, N. Pal. Mus.). The placing of finely drawn archaistic figures against a landscape setting of the WU SCHOOL type was a pictorial scheme that he repeated throughout his career. Another fine example is the handscroll *Five Forms of Guanyin* (*c*. 1579; Kansas City, MO, Nelson–Atkins Mus. A.), which emulates figure styles of both the Five Dynasties (AD 907–79) and Song (960–1279) periods. At the same time, Ding became interested in the amateur Huating landscape-painting tradition, through his association with Huating literati, among them the prominent artist and theoretician Dong Qichang. The landscape hanging scroll *Parting at the End of the Year* (1585; see Cahill, 1981, p. 27, fig. 1), with its spare, linear style, is firmly in the Huating mode.

Ding's penchant for untextured, fine-line drawing may reflect his involvement with woodblock design as well. In the 1580s he returned to Anhui, which had become the centre of late Ming printing, and where he designed most of the woodblock illustrations for two collectanea of ink-cake designs, the *Fangshi mopu* ('Mr Fang's ink collection'; 1588) and the *Chengshi moyuan* ('Mr Cheng's ink collection'; 1604).

In 1594, Ding collaborated with the Suzhou painter SHENG MAOYE on a series of *luohan* hanging scrolls (Kyoto, priv. col.; see Cahill, 1971, no. 78), which represent the latest extant dated paintings in his mature style. Their lively compositions, refined drawing and naturalistic portraiture were replaced in Ding's late work by patternized flatness and harsh angularity, a style that was more successfully applied to landscape themes, such as *Morning Sun over the Heavenly Citadel* (hanging scroll; 1614; Cleveland, OH, Mus. A.). Although Ding began to explore certain expressive possibilities in his painting, he is best regarded as a precursor to more powerfully imaginative painters such as CHEN HONGSHOU.

BIBLIOGRAPHY

Huizhou fuzhi [Huizhou gazetteer], xiv (1827/*R* Taipei, 1975), pt 2, p. 6

Dantu xianzhi [Dantu gazetteer], xxii (1880), p. 16

J. Cahill, ed.: *The Restless Landscape: Chinese Painting of the Late Ming Period* (Berkeley, 1971)

S. Oertling: 'Ting Yün-p'eng: A Chinese Artist of the Late Ming Dynasty' (Ph.D. diss., Ann Arbor, U. MI, 1980)

J. Cahill, ed.: *Shadows of Mt. Huang: Chinese Painting and Printing of the Anhui School* (Berkeley, 1981)

——: *The Distant Mountains: Chinese Painting of the Late Ming Dynasty, 1570–1644* (New York and Tokyo, 1982)

DAWN HO DELBANCO

Dinkeloo, John. *See under* ROCHE, KEVIN.

Dinkelsbühl. Town in Bavaria, Germany. A Hohenstaufen possession, it was a free imperial city by the 13th century, and in the 1370s the walls were expanded to their present extent. The parish church of St Georg, one of the most famous Late Gothic, south German hall churches, dominates the town at the main crossroads; its south side, facing the old Town Hall and cemetery, was originally the show side. Civic pride is evident in the building, symbols of the bakers' and coopers' guilds in the east window demonstrating the importance of the guilds, which shared power with the patrician families from the late 14th century.

The earliest known church on the site of St Georg was built in the 12th century. The existing west tower was added *c.* 1220–30, and in the second half of the 14th century the church was expanded to include a six-bay nave of nearly the same dimensions as the present one and a single-aisled choir terminating in a five-sided apse. The present church, slightly off the axis of its predecessor, was founded in 1448. Documented in Dinkelsbühl in 1456, Niclas Eseler the elder was probably its designing mason from the beginning. Contrary to the common 15th-century occurrence of a succession of masters, Dinkelsbühl clearly manifests Eseler's style. His son Niclas Eseler the younger took charge in 1471, although the elder Eseler did not die until 1482.

Inscriptions record the masters and the building history: the laying of the foundation stone on 5 March 1448 is recorded on the eastern axial buttress; above, a 'portrait bust' of Eseler supports a statue of *St Bartholomew*, patron of the previous church. The west gable carries the date 1469. The church was consecrated on 17 October 1488, but an inscription in the west wall cites the setting of the last stone only in 1499. The ambulatory vault bears the date of 1492 over the names of the Eselers, but vaulting elsewhere is documented as still under construction in 1495. The belfry in the west tower was built in the 1540s, the two-storey octagon in 1550. The unfinished north tower was terminated at second-storey height in 1535; deep foundations suggest that it would have been 65–70 m high. Contemporaneous with the building are several furnishings: the font and pulpit, the west tribune with a *Man of Sorrows* and the *Twelve Apostles*, the sacrament-house and the music gallery of the north tower. In the mid-16th century, two chapels were inserted between the north buttresses of the ambulatory, two others to the east and south in 1728. Restoration work in 1856–98 removed tombs and later furnishings, replacing the latter in neo-Gothic style.

Typical of hall churches, Dinkelsbühl has a compact, three-aisled, transept-less plan, with an ambulatory but originally without chapels. The smooth exterior silhouette, broken only by buttresses, is dominated by the mass of its huge roof (h. 19 m) and west tower (h. *c.* 58 m). Inside (see fig.), the sequence of tall, multi-shafted piers and the net vaults across ten bays leads not to the usual east window but, as if through a shift in axis, to the axial vaulting shaft. The spacious aisles are lit by 26 four-light windows that occupy nearly the whole height of the wall and are filled with different animated patterns of mouchette tracery. Unlike such hall churches as St Georg, Nördlingen, in which reduced architectural elements underscore open space, at Dinkelsbühl the nave and axiality were emphasized, and cathedral architecture was rivalled through rich articulation of piers, tracery, vaults and the ambulatory plan.

Several elements enhance the Late Gothic dynamic treatment of forms: sliding diagonals of the octagonal piers, curvilinear jambs, piers without capitals so that mouldings die into the shafts directly, and ribs suddenly breaking off beyond their point of intersection. The vaults, their surfaces flattened for a wider drawing surface, were a special field for virtuoso display. The net vaulting patterns of centre and side aisles change in relation to the liturgical division between nave and choir, which corresponds to the break in construction at the seventh bay from the west. A further alteration in the vault design of the two western bays (east of the tribune) is less easily explained. The square-turned-within-a-square pattern hovers over pulpit and font, and at their centres bosses display the church's two patron saints, George and Bartholomew. Visually

these vaults provide the slowest rhythm, which becomes progressively faster as the eye moves east.

A particular vaulting technique, characteristic of the Eselers, increases spaciousness by avoiding a low descent of the vault. Since the flattened surface of the segmental barrel (built in brick) would otherwise abut the arcade almost at a right angle, a thin section of wall mediates the joint. This device appears in Eseler's other work at St Georg, Nördlingen, and St Jakob, Rothenburg-ob-der-Tauber, as well as at Basle Minster and St Katherine's, Oppenheim, which are not documented as being connected with Eseler. Using a fine-grained, greyish local sandstone, the Eselers maintained regular construction, including a modular layout. The piers of both nave and hemicycle use the same elements. The arcade arch has the same diameter as the pier shaft below. On the exterior the buttresses and windows extend to the same height. All the bays have nearly the same length, so that the nave and choir are continuous and the side aisles continue evenly into the ambulatory, creating a radial layout unusual in 15th-century choirs.

Dinkelsbühl belongs to the architectural milieu of the Parler workshop in south Germany and central Europe (*see* KUTNÁ HORA, §1; PRAGUE, §I, 2; SCHWÄBISCH GMÜND, CATHEDRAL OF THE HOLY CROSS, §1). The hall-church type with ambulatory and regular intercolumniation between choir and hemicycle follows the church of the Holy Cross at Schwäbisch Gmünd. The eastern axial element is seen in the Parler churches at Kutná Hora and Kolín. The Dinkelsbühl nave vault patterns are an enriched version of the high vault of Prague Cathedral, whereas the western bays play on the pattern of the St Wenceslas Chapel there.

The transmission from Prague to Dinkelsbühl may have come with the feature of the architect's bust via the work of HANS VON BURGHAUSEN in Landshut, which is closely related to Dinkelsbühl. St Martin (from *c.* 1385) shows similar vaulting and pier design, whereas the Spitalkirche (1407) has a very similar plan and copious inscriptions. Additional similarities to the choir of St Sebaldus (1361) in Nuremberg and other Parler-influenced churches indicate a widespread architectural environment with a large shared repertory of motifs that knowledgeable Late Gothic masters called on in varying combinations to create their dynamic art.

BIBLIOGRAPHY

K. Gerstenberg: *Deutsche Sondergotik* (Munich, 1913)

W. Bogenberger: 'Fundberichte, Dinkelsbühl, Grabung in St. Georg', *Hist. Ver. 'Alt Dinkelsbühl' Jb.* (1977–9), pp. 8–17

T. Breuer and others: *Bayern, i: Franken*, Dehio-Handbuch (Munich, 1979), pp. 221–4

W. Helmberger: *Architektur und Baugeschichte der St. Georgskirche zu Dinkelsbühl, 1448–1499* (Bamberg, 1984)

N. Nussbaum: *Deutsche Kirchenbaukunst der Gotik: Entwicklung und Bauformen* (Cologne, 1985)

VIRGINIA JANSEN

Dinkelsbühl, St Georg, 1448–99; interior looking east

Dinos [deinos]. Ancient form of vessel, used as a mixing bowl (*see* GREECE, ANCIENT, figs 96 and 98).

☐

Dinsmoor, William Bell (*b* Wyndham, NH, 29 July 1886; *d* Athens, 2 July 1973). American architect and Classical archaeologist. He studied architecture at Harvard University, graduating in 1906, and worked for three years in architectural practice. Architectural history claimed him, however, and he devoted his life to the study of Greek architecture, becoming one of the leaders in this field. He divided his time between teaching at Columbia University, where he received a PhD in 1929, and conducting field research, mainly in Greece. He wrote four books and numerous articles between 1908 and 1968, mostly on Athenian architecture. Dinsmoor was associated throughout his life with the American School of Classical Studies at Athens, serving as Fellow in Architecture, Architect of the School and Professor of Architecture. He served as president of the Archaeological Institute of America between 1936 and 1945 and was later (1969) awarded the gold medal of the Institute for his archaeological achievements. At the end of World War II Dinsmoor was a member of the American Commission for the Protection and Salvage of Artistic and Historic Monuments in War Areas.

WRITINGS
Observations on the Hephaisteion (Princeton, 1941)
The Architecture of Ancient Greece (London, 1950)

BIBLIOGRAPHY
'Bibliography of William Bell Dinsmoor', *Hesperia*, xxxv (1966), pp. 87–92

ANASTASIA N. DINSMOOR

Dinteville. French family of diplomats, collectors and patrons. The family had a tradition of service to the medieval dukes of Burgundy and kings of France. François Dinteville, Bishop of Auxerre (*b* Troyes, 26 July 1498; *d* Château de Régennes, Polisy, 27 Sept 1554), was a connoisseur of the decorative and fine arts, filling his residence with costly furnishings and works of art and his private chapel with elaborate religious artefacts; his favourite painter was Felix Crétien. As French ambassador to the Vatican, he campaigned for the divorce of Henry VIII, King of England, also advocated by his brother, Jean de Dinteville, Seigneur de Polisy (*b* Thennelière [Aube], 21 Sept 1504; *d* Polisy, 23 March 1555), ambassador to the English court. During this period Hans Holbein the younger portrayed Jean de Dinteville with Georges de Selve, Bishop of Lavaur, in a full-length portrait of *The Ambassadors* (1533; London, N.G.; *see* HOLBEIN, (3) and fig. 2). In 1537 Jean and François fled to Italy to escape charges of high treason, and François's property was confiscated and sold; however, the brothers were eventually restored to the French court's highest favour. After *c.* 1542 Jean, who suffered complete paralysis, abandoned public life, retiring to Polisy. Francesco Primaticcio and Domenico Fiorentino were his guests there in 1544, when he began to build his new Château de Régennes. They probably decorated the inner façade overlooking the court (destr.) of the Italian-style château. Jean de Dinteville himself decorated the château with paintings by his own hand.

UNPUBLISHED SOURCES
Paris, Bib. N. [letters and chronicles]

BIBLIOGRAPHY
M. F. S. Hervey: *Holbein's 'Ambassadors': The Picture and the Men* (London, 1900)

A. Vidier and P. Pernier: *Catalogue général des MSS français*, Paris, Bib. N. cat. (Paris, 1933), p. 318

Diocaesarea. *See* OLBA.

Diocletian [Gaius Aurelius Valerius Diocletianus] (*b* Dalmatia, 22 Dec AD ?244; *reg* AD 284–305; *d* ?3 Dec AD 311). Roman emperor and patron. In order to strengthen Imperial control at a time of extreme danger to the Roman world, Diocletian created the Tetrarchy in AD 293, a four-man system under which two Caesars were appointed: one served under Diocletian, the Augustus in the East, the other under Maximian, the Augustus in the West. The whole was held together only by the personality and authority of Diocletian himself, so that by the time of his death the Empire was once again beset by civil wars; his division of the Empire, however, and many of his administrative reforms lasted for much longer. The impersonal cult image of the emperors, in which one Augustus is indistinguishable from the other (*see*, for example, ROME, ANCIENT, fig. 82), symbolized the solidarity of Tetrarchic rule and laid the foundation for the Imperial style of the 4th century AD. The Tetrarchy also encouraged a revival of provincial art through the creation of several new capitals; the remains at Trier and Thessaloniki are particularly impressive. Diocletian himself set up his court at Nicomedia in Bithynia, embellished Antioch in Syria and retired to his palace at Split on the Dalmatian coast, a fortified villa that exhibits an amalgam of influences from East and West (*see* SPLIT, §1). Although Diocletian only visited Rome once, in AD 303, he instituted a great renewal of public buildings there too—the last before Constantine transferred the seat of government to Constantinople. The buildings restored or erected include the curia and the great baths north-east of the Viminal Hill, the culmination of the Imperial bath buildings (*see* ROME, ANCIENT, §II, 2(i)(g) and fig. 9). In AD 301 Diocletian issued the famous *Edict on Prices*, reconstituted from Greek and Latin inscriptional fragments, which set a ceiling on prices of over 1000 items. As these included craftsmen's wages, the document provides important evidence for the social and economic status of artists in the Roman world.

BIBLIOGRAPHY
J. B. Ward-Perkins: *Roman Imperial Architecture*, Pelican Hist. A. (Harmondsworth, 1981)

KIM RICHARDSON

Diogg [Diog], **Felix Maria** (*b* Andermatt, 1 July 1762; *d* Rapperswil, Schwyz, 19 Feb 1834). Swiss painter. From 1782 he was a pupil of Johann Melchior Wyrsch in Besançon, under whom he developed the essential aspects of his portrait style. He also studied further in Rome and Naples from 1786 to 1788. He was capable of executing bright, incisive portraits in the manner of Angelica Kauffman, as in *Portrait of an Artist* (*c.* 1784; Stanford, CA, U. A. G. & Mus.), or psychological studies, best seen in *Ulysses von Salis-Marschlins* (1794; Chur, Rätisches Mus.). Several of his group portraits, such as the *Esslinger Family* (1793; priv. col., see Hugelshofer, pl. 7), show the influence of Italian and British painting, with which he seemed to be familiar. He was a friend of Johann Kaspar Lavater, discoursed with Goethe and enjoyed the company of the Swiss historian Johannes von Müller (1752–1809), whose portrait (1797; Schaffhausen, Mus. Allerheiligen) he painted. His portraits are generally bust-length types set against a solid, dark background. This format was favoured by his Swiss clientele and is seen in *Burgomaster Heinrich Krauer* (1799; Lucerne, Kstmus.), which also reveals the dignified wooden pose frequently selected by his models. His direct, fashionable treatment of the sitter attracted a wide range of clients from all levels of society. He seemed to be as much at ease painting the Empress of Russia, *Yelisaveta Alekseyevna* (1814; Karlsruhe, Staatl. Ksthalle) as he was portraying the bourgeoisie of central Switzerland. Diogg represents one of the few examples of a painter who came from a then primitive region of Switzerland that had virtually no artistic tradition, but who was nevertheless able to establish an international reputation.

BIBLIOGRAPHY

W. Hugelshofer: *Felix Maria Diogg: Ein schweizer Bildnismaler, 1762–1834* (Zurich and Leipzig, 1938)
W. Dolf: 'Ulysses von Salis-Marschlins, 1728–1800', *Bedeutende Bündner aus fünf Jahrhunderten*, i (Chur, 1970), pp. 303–16
L. Dosch: 'Herr Felix Maria Diogg, ein Portraitmaler', *Bündner Jb.*, xxvi (1984), pp. 151–2
O. Bätschmann: 'La Peinture de l'époque moderne', *A. Helvet.*, vi (1989), p. 124
Emblèmes de la liberté (exh. cat., Berne, Kstmus., 1991), p. 473

WILLIAM HAUPTMAN

Diomede, Miguel (*b* Buenos Aires, 20 July 1902; *d* Buenos Aires, 15 Oct 1974). Argentine painter. He was self-taught and began painting in 1929, first exhibiting in 1941 and elaborating a personal language in the tradition of Cézanne and Bonnard. In small intimate paintings he restricted himself to the world of objects, using light to suggest form and to give vibrancy to the rich colouring, and sketchy brushstrokes to insinuate the presence of objects within a solid geometric structure. Although he maintained perceptible outlines in his early works, these later disappeared, allowing the forms to dissolve in a space that becomes the main protagonist, for example in *Oranges* (Buenos Aires, Mus. N. B.A.). Reality becomes transformed into something light and airy, revealing the emptiness within which objects exist, with colour defining imaginary layers of space interwoven into a single atmosphere, as in *Grapes, Fig and Peach* (1945; Buenos Aires, Mus. N. B.A.). As a painter of everyday themes Diomede inquired into the spirit of things. In 1958 he received a bronze medal at the Exposition Universelle in Brussels.

BIBLIOGRAPHY

E. Poggi: *Miguel Diomede* (Buenos Aires, 1953)
M. L. San Martín: *Pintura argentina contemporánea* (Buenos Aires, 1961), p. 104

NELLY PERAZZO

Dion. Canadian family of potters. The St Charles River valley, Quebec, where the family had settled as early as 1671, had been the scene of some of the first pottery-making in New France; the tradition handed down was French provincial. It was in this style that the Dions began working in Ancienne Lorette, Quebec, producing simple, utilitarian wares of local, red-burning clay. Although Jean-Baptiste Dion (1827–1901) began the pottery *c.* 1854, it was his brother Antoine Dion (1825–1902) who expanded operations on the family land in the 1860s, winning recognition for Dion wares in crockery shops in Quebec City and at provincial exhibitions. Antoine Dion never used imported clay; he used plaster moulds for some wares (possibly taken from imported English earthenware) but for others devised the patterns himself. His sons joined him in the business, and in 1881 the pottery had an estimated capital of £2000–5000, which ranked it with other successful Canadian potteries of the day. Large tobacco jars with moulded figures probably belong to this period (*see* CANADA, fig. 13). Antoine Dion jr (1846–1915) was in charge from 1889; but coarse earthenware, such as teapots, jugs and dishes, was becoming less popular even when covered with colour-spattered glazes. Antoine Dion jr's son Joseph Dion sold the pottery *c.* 1916, and by 1918 it was no longer in operation.

BIBLIOGRAPHY

E. Collard: *Nineteenth-century Pottery and Porcelain in Canada* (Montreal, 1967, rev. 2/1984)
H. H. Lambart: *The Rivers of the Potters* (Ottawa, 1970)
J. Dion and J.-P. Dion: *La Poterie des Dions* (St Lambert, Qué., 1984)

ELIZABETH COLLARD

Dionisio Fiammingo. *See* CALVAERT, DENYS.

Dionisy [Dionisii; Dionissi; Dionysius] (*b c.* 1440; *d* after 1502–3). Russian painter. He worked in Moscow and the surrounding towns and in several northern monasteries, including those of Iosifo-Volokolamsky, Ferapontov and St Paul at Obnorsk (founded 1414; see below). Paintings attributed to him represent the apogee of the classicizing style in Russian religious art, although by the end of his life much of his work was apparently done with the help of assistants. Various sources refer to Dionisy, but he is first mentioned in the *Life of Pafnuty of Borovsk*, which records that he decorated the cathedral of the Nativity of the Virgin (Rozhdestvo bogoroditsy) in the Pafnut'ev Monastery in Borovsk with wall paintings (*c.* 1467; destr.), together with the older icon painter, Mitrofan, and their assistants. According to a chronicle source, in 1481 Dionisy, Timofey, Yarets and Konya painted a *Deësis* with festivals and prophets (destr.) for the cathedral of the Dormition (Uspensky) in the Moscow Kremlin and decorated two of the cathedral's chapels with wall paintings. In 1482 Dionisy restored the Greek icon of the *Virgin Hodegetria* in the monastery of the Ascension (Voznesensky) in the Moscow Kremlin after it was damaged by fire. Between 1484 and 1500 the workshop of Dionisy painted an extensive series of icons for the cathedral in the Iosifo-Volokolamsky Monastery. An inventory of 1545 compiled by a contemporary of Dionisy records that of these works 87 were by Dionisy, 37 by his sons Vladimir and Feodosy and 20 by their colleague Paisy.

Dionisy apparently worked with more than one workshop and was extremely prolific, with the result that numerous icons and wall paintings attributed to him have survived. His vigilance in ensuring the stylistic unity of products from his workshop, however, makes it almost impossible to distinguish the hand of Dionisy himself. The earliest surviving works are the wall paintings and the individual icons executed for the cathedral of the Dormition in the Moscow Kremlin. The masonry arches of the altar screen are decorated with half-figures of the founders of monasticism. These finely drawn, brightly coloured paintings have an overall delicacy similar to that of the later wall paintings in the Ferapontov Monastery. Dionisy's style seems to have been established *c.* 1480 and underwent little change in the succeeding years. This stylistic evenness makes the dating of his work difficult, hence the controversy concerning the dating of the icon of the Moscow *Metropolitan Pyotr* that hangs above his tomb in the cathedral of the Dormition and that of *Metropolitan Aleksey* (Moscow, Tret'yakov Gal.; see fig.), originally from the same cathedral. Suggested dates vary between 1481 and 1519, the last putting these works outside the oeuvre of Dionisy. On the basis of style, at least two icons from the Iosifo-Volokolamsky Monastery can be attributed to Dionisy or his workshop: the *Martyr St Barbara* (Sergiyev Posad, Mus. Hist. & A.) and the *Dormition of the Virgin* (Moscow, Andrey Rublyov Mus. Anc. Rus. A.).

Among later works that can be more firmly attributed to Dionisy and his sons are surviving icons from the iconostasis of the monastery of St Paul, including a *Crucifixion* and a *Christ in Majesty* (both Moscow, Tret'yakov Gal.); on the back of the latter is a carved inscription: 'in the year 1500 this Deësis and festivals and prophets were painted by Denisy'. His most important works are the wall paintings (1502) in the cathedral of the FERAPONTOV MONASTERY. The overall iconographic programme is a Marian cycle that is well preserved and thus provides a good example of the development of Russian monumental painting between the late 15th century and the early 16th. His single figures and compositions are rhythmically arranged on the arches, walls and vaults, imparting a sense of tranquillity to the whole ensemble. The paintings are imbued with a decorative quality that is to some extent achieved at the expense of their psychological expressiveness: Dionisy's saints and holy men have no impulsiveness or passion and are depicted in a contemplative state as if in slow motion. The sense of harmony is emphasized by the pastel colour scheme, in which the paints have been blended to produce a variety of soft hues dominated by light blue, grass-green, golden-yellow and reddish-brown tones. The same decorative aims guided the work of Dionisy and his assistants in the creation of the icons for the cathedral's iconostasis (Moscow, Tret'yakov Gal.; St Petersburg, Rus. Mus.; Kirillov, Kirillo-Belozersky Monastery). The icon with scenes from the *Life of the Venerable Dmitry of Prilutsk* (*c.* 1503; Vologda, Local Mus.) was probably one of Dionisy's last works. Although the image of the saint surrounded by scenes from his life is derived from Byzantine models, Dionisy has taken particular care to create a balanced painting so that the proportions and colouring of the main image and accompanying scenes correspond.

BIBLIOGRAPHY

V. T. Georgiyevsky: *Freski Ferapontova monastyrya* [The frescoes of the Ferapontov Monastery] (St Petersburg, 1911)

B. V. Mikhaylovsky and B. I. Purishev: *Ocherki istorii drevnerusskoy monumental'noy zhivopisi so vtoroy poloviny XIV v. do nachala XVIII v.* [Studies in the history of Old Russian monumental painting from the second half of the 14th century to the early 18th] (Moscow, 1941)

V. N. Lazarev: 'Dionisy i yego shkola' [Dionisy and his school], *Istoriya russkogo iskusstva* [The history of Russian art], iii (Moscow, 1955)

N. K. Goleyzovsky: 'Zhivopisets Dionisy i yego shkola' [The painter Dionisy and his school], *Voprosy Istor.*, iii (1968), pp. 214–17

I. Ye. Danilova: *The Frescoes of the Ferapontov Monastery* (Moscow, 1970)

Dionisy: *Metropolitan Aleksey*, icon from the cathedral of the Dormition in the Moscow Kremlin, tempera on panel, 1.97×1.52 m, ?1480s (Moscow, Tret'yakov Gallery)

——: *Dionissi* (Vienna, Munich, Dresden, 1970)

N. K. Goleyzovsky: 'Zametki o Dionisii' [Notes on Dionisy], *Vizant. Vremennik*, xxxi (1971), pp. 175–87

G. Chugunov: *Dionisy* (Leningrad, 1979)

Dionisy i iskusstvo Moskvy XV–XVI stoletiy [Dionisy and the art of Moscow in the 15th to 16th century] (exh. cat., ed. T. B. Vilinbakhova, V. K. Laurina and G. D. Petrova; Leningrad, Rus. Mus. 1981)

Ferapontovskiy sbornik [Ferapontov anthology], 3 vols (Moscow, 1985–91)

T. V. Popov, ed.: *Drevnerusskoye iskusstvo.: Khudozhestvennyye pamyatniki russkogo severa* [Ancient Russian art: Artistic monuments of the Russian north] (Moscow, 1989)

G. I. VZDORNOV

Dionysios (*fl* ?later 2nd century BC). Greek sculptor. He was the son of TIMARCHIDES and a member of a family of Athenian sculptors that included POLYKLES and TIMOKLES. Dionysios signed (together with Timarchides, son of Polykles) a portrait of *C. Ofellius Ferus* on Delos (*c.* 100 BC; Delos, Archaeol. Mus.), its Classicizing style recalling works of the 4th century BC associated with Praxiteles. Dionysios' signature is first in this inscription, and it is believed that the Timarchides with whom he collaborated was Timarchides the younger, probably his nephew, rather than Timarchides the elder, Dionysios' father. Dionysios also worked at Rome with Polykles (possibly his brother; Pliny (*Natural History* XXXVI.

iv.35) attributed to them the possible cult statue of *Jupiter Stator* in Metellus Macedonicus' temple, built *c.* 146 BC in the Campus Martius. The same two sculptors were also responsible for one or more statues of *Juno* in the adjacent Temple of Juno Regina (ded. 179 BC), but Pliny's wording here is open to various readings. These works in Rome were in marble and are assumed to have been Classicizing in style.

BIBLIOGRAPHY

G. Becatti: 'Attikà: Saggio sulla scultura attica dell'ellenismo', *Riv. Reale Ist. Archeol. & Stor. A.*, vii (1940), pp. 7–116
J. Marcadé: *Recueil des signatures de sculpteurs grecs*, ii (Paris, 1957), pp. 41–2
A. Stewart: *Attika: Studies in Athenian Sculpture of the Hellenistic Age* (London, 1979), pp. 42–6

MARK D. FULLERTON

Dionysios of Furna (*b* Furna, *c.* 1670; *d* after 1744). Greek painter, writer and monk. Son of the village priest at Furna in the district of Agrafa, central Greece, Dionysios went to Constantinople at the age of 12, probably for further education; four years later he moved to Mt Athos. Wall paintings and icons (1701 or 1711; rest. 1731) by Dionysios are known at Karyes, in the kellion (cell) and parekklesion dedicated to St John the Baptist. In 1721 he painted the chapel of St Demetrios at Vatopedi and the west wall of the katholikon at Docheiariou on Mt Athos. There are six icons (1724–8) by him in the church of the Transfiguration at Furna; the wall paintings, which may have been his, were destroyed in 1821. He returned to Furna in 1734 and in 1740/41 obtained the patronage of the patriarch of Constantinople for the construction of a school in Agrafa; his letter to the patriarch Neophytos in 1744 is the last known trace of him.

His surviving literary work consists of four letters, eighteen epigrams, two liturgical works and the most complete version of the 'Mt Athos Painters' Guide' (St Petersburg, Saltykov-Shchedrin Pub. Lib., cod. gr. 708), the work for which he is best known. Also known as 'The Book of the Painter's Art' and 'The Painter's Manual', it was probably written between 1730 and 1734. The first part of the guide deals with materials and techniques, including recipes for mixing colours and for making glue and gesso, and ways of establishing the proportions of the human figure, and partly derives from the 12th-century *De diversis artibus* of THEOPHILUS. The second and longest section contains extensive iconographical directions for depicting the principal events of the Old and New Testaments, the standard groups of prophets and saints and all the feasts and saints' days of the church calendar, as well as other major subjects such as the Second Coming, all seven Ecumenical Councils, the 24 stanzas of the Akathist Hymn and episodes in the lives of a number of major saints. The only known prototypes for parts of this section are: for the Apocalypse scenes, a set of 22 woodcuts by Hans Holbein the younger in a New Testament (Basle, 1523); and for the portraits of Byzantine hymnographers, the title-page of a Triodion (Venice, 1600) edited by Bishop Maximos of Cythera (Michael Margounios). The third section establishes the appropriate location within a Byzantine monastery of each of the portraits or scenes. There were many other versions of the guide; more than 25 manuscripts, written in either Greek or Romanian, survive; their texts differ radically and none is illustrated.

WRITINGS

Ermenia tis zographikis technis kai ai kyriai autis anekdotoi pigai ekdidomeni meta prologou nyn to proton pliris kata to prototypon autis keimenon [An explanation of the painter's art and the main unpublished sources concerning it, now published with an introduction and first complete edition of the original text] (St Petersburg, Rus. N. Lib., cod. gr. 708, *c.* 1730–34); ed. A. Papadopoulos-Kerameus (St Petersburg, 1909)

BIBLIOGRAPHY

V. Grecu: 'Cărti de pictură bisericească bizantina: Introducere si editie critică a versiunilor românesti atât după redactiunea lui Dionisie din Furna tradusă la 1805 de Arhimandritul Macarie cât si dupa alte redactiuni mai vechi traduceri anonime cu 6 plane afară din text' [Books on Byzantine church illustrations: introduction and critical edition of the Romanian versions after the edition of Dionysios of Furna translated in 1805 by Archimandrite Makarios, with material from other earlier anonymous translations and 6 plates hors texte], *Candela*, xliii-xlvi (1932–5)
P. Hetherington: *The 'Painter's Manual' of Dionysius of Fourna: An English Translation, with Commentary, of Cod. gr. 708 in the Saltykov-Shchedrin State Public Library, St Petersburg* (London, 1974) [incl. bibliog. on the 'Painters' Guide' and handlist of MSS]

J. VAN GINKEL, PAUL HETHERINGTON,
A. N. PALMER

Diorama [Gk: 'through view']. Large-scale, illusionistic form of transparency painting, developed in 1821–2 as a public entertainment by the French scenic artist and pioneer of photography LOUIS DAGUERRE, in association with the architectural painter Charles-Marie Bouton (1781–1853); also the special building in which it was shown. Like the earlier PANORAMA, the diorama was a late step in the history of attempts to recreate the appearance of nature by means of painting and the mechanical regulation of light. Daguerre's subsequent progression from the diorama to photography marks the vital change of medium by which this aim was eventually achieved in the form of cinematography. Daguerre's device consisted of a fine cloth painted with landscape subjects such as mountains and evocative ruins, in a manner exploiting popular taste for the Sublime and the picturesque. The solid features of the paintings were executed in opaque colour, but transparent tints were used for the effects of atmosphere, weather and time of day. The audience sat in near-darkness: the pictures were shown by means of daylight admitted through windows concealed both above the spectators and behind the intervening cloth and regulated by a system of shutters and coloured filtering screens. Light reflected off the front of the cloth was modified by light transmitted through it to produce effects ranging from sunshine to thick fog. Daguerre's oil painting *Ruins of Holyrood Chapel* (Liverpool, Walker A.G.) is a near-replica of one of his early subjects and well evokes the diorama's atmospheric style.

Daguerre's inspiration for both the diorama and its name almost certainly derived from the 'diaphanorama' of the Swiss artist Niklaus König; this was shown in Paris in 1820–21 and produced similar effects from watercolour on sheets of treated paper that measured up to 0.85×1.18 m. By contrast, Daguerre and Bouton's images measured *c.* 14×22 m. They were first seen by an astonished public at the Paris 'Diorama' that Daguerre and Bouton had built on the corner of the Rue Sansom and the Place du Château d'Eau (now Place de la République), and which opened on 11 July 1822. On 29 September 1823 the partners opened a second Diorama, of similar construction, in Regent's Park, London (see fig.). The façade formed the centre of the new development of Park Square East by John Nash (i); the remainder was designed by his associate A. C. Pugin and the civil engineer James Morgan (*fl c.* 1806–34), who was responsible for the machinery. Until 1830 this Diorama showed the views previously seen in Paris; Bouton then took sole management, and the programmes diverged. The pictures were also sent on tour elsewhere in Britain and in America. There were temporary or permanent diorama buildings in Edinburgh, Manchester, Liverpool, Bristol and Dublin, and Philadelphia and New York. Other dioramas were built in Stockholm, Breslau, Cologne and Berlin, the last partly designed and with paintings by Schinkel.

By 1834 Daguerre's painting method developed into a full double-effect process by which daytime scenes could be changed to night, buildings reduced to ruins by fire or mountain villages engulfed by avalanche. His principal collaborator in this advance was his pupil Hippolyte-Victor-Valentin Sébron (1801–79), and its main element was a means of painting before-and-after versions of the scene on the front and rear of the cloth. Until he published it in 1839, Daguerre kept his painting method secret. In England he protected the mechanics of his system by a patent, taken out in 1824 in the name of John Arrowsmith, a brother of his Anglo-French wife and a key but otherwise ill-defined figure in the matter. The most remarkable feature of the London and Paris dioramas was the way in which the audience was manoeuvred to view the pictures. In London there were two pictures in each programme, in Paris sometimes three, set on radially adjacent stages. The spectators, 200 in London and 350 in Paris, sat in a circular auditorium with a proscenium lined up on the first stage. The picture was 13 m from the front row, framed by tunnel-like masking that enhanced the illusion by persuading viewers that the image was at an indefinably greater distance. The first picture was put through its effects for about 10 to 15 minutes, then the whole drum of the auditorium was rotated on a central pivot through about 73°, to bring the second stage and picture into view.

The Paris Diorama burnt down in 1839, ending Daguerre's already decreasing involvement in it; the London Diorama closed in 1851. The building still exists, though much altered internally: since 1989 it has been an arts centre. Of the diorama houses built or adapted elsewhere, none survives. Daguerre's diorama spawned much imitation and plagiarism, in similar exhibitions and in toy form. Most significantly, the word 'diorama' was rapidly adopted in the theatre, and to some extent elsewhere, to describe moving panoramas with transparency and multiple-plane scenic effects. These were generally travelogue spectacles in Christmas pantomimes of the period 1823–*c.* 1840, but they sometimes featured, both then and later, in more serious drama. The first example, capitalizing directly on Daguerre's London opening, was a 'Moving Diorama of Plymouth Breakwater' at the Theatre Royal Drury Lane, 26 December 1823; its originator, CLARKSON STANFIELD, became the most celebrated theatrical exponent of this form. In the 20th century, 'diorama' has come to denote various forms and sizes of model or tableau used in film

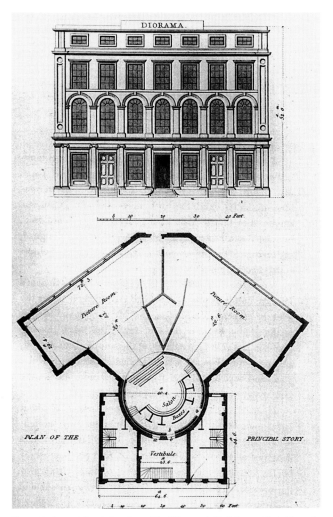

Ground-plan and front elevation of the Diorama in Park Square East, Regent's Park, London; engraving from John Britton and A. C. Pugin: *Illustrations of the Public Buildings of London* (London, 1825–8), pl. 18

and television work and in museum displays. Even where these models employ transparency techniques, such as glass painting, they are remote from Daguerre's device.

BIBLIOGRAPHY

H. Gernsheim and A. Gernsheim: *L.-J. M. Daguerre: The History of the Diorama and the Daguerrotype* (New York, 1968)

R. D. Altick: *The Shows of London* (Cambridge, MA, 1978)

R. Hyde and P. van der Merwe: 'The Queen's Bazaar', *Theatrephile*, ii (1985), pp. 10–14

Panoramania! (exh. cat. by R. Hyde, London, Barbican A.G., 1988)

R. D. Wood: 'The Diorama in Great Britain in the 1820's', *Hist. Phot.*, xvii/3 (1993), pp. 284–95

PIETER VAN DER MERWE

Diospolis Parva [Egyp. Hut-sekhem; now Hiw]. Site in Egypt about 50 km west of modern Qena, occupied continuously from prehistoric to Roman times. A large variety of Predynastic tombs and associated artefacts (including amulets, beads and slate and ivory statuettes of animals) have survived, indicating that Diospolis flourished during this phase. The earliest finds date from the

Tasian–Badarian period (*c.* 4000 BC). The site was first excavated by Flinders Petrie in 1899, providing some of the information for his 'sequence dating' system of pottery styles, which led directly to the establishment of a Predynastic chronology. Renewed excavation at the site in the 1980s allowed this ceramic material to be re-examined, producing greater refinement and broad corroboration of Petrie's system.

The excavations have also revealed about 40 burials of the 4th or 5th dynasties (*c.* 2575–*c.* 2325 BC), as well as a number of shallow pit graves dating to the 6th–11th dynasties (*c.* 2325–*c.* 1938 BC), mainly along the desert edge. The bodies, accompanied by amulets, necklaces, axes, bone figurines and beads, and ceramic and alabaster vessels containing scarabs, were placed in wooden coffins. Each tomb consisted of a rectangular pit with an open chamber at one end. There are several surviving Pangrave tombs dating to the Second Intermediate Period (*c.* 1630–*c.* 1540 BC), which indicate the presence of Nubian mercenaries in Egypt. Although some New Kingdom (*c.* 1540–*c.* 1075 BC) material has been found, it has tended to be mixed with earlier finds and is therefore difficult to interpret. The Ptolemaic- and Roman-period (304 BC–AD 395) remains consist of tombs and a temple enclosure of Egyptian construction.

BIBLIOGRAPHY

W. M. F. Petrie: *Diospolis Parva* (London, 1901)

ELIZABETH L. MEYERS

Diotisalvi (*fl* Pisa, 1152). Italian architect. The name appears in three inscriptions: one on a pilaster in the baptistery at Pisa ('DEOTISALVI MAGISTER HUIUS OPERIS'), one on the campanile of S Sepolcro, Pisa, and one on the inside north wall of S Cristoforo, Lucca. The last is generally attributed to a different craftsman of the same name.

At the Pisa Baptistery (*see* PISA, figs 3 and 6), begun in 1152, Diotisalvi presumably worked on the planning, on the execution of the lower storey of the exterior and, inside, on the erection of the monumental granite columns from Elba and Sardinia and of the piers (excluding the capitals). The centralized design is based on the rotunda of the Holy Sepulchre in Jerusalem, which may suggest that Diotisalvi's original scheme included the arcaded gallery and truncated conical roof. The signed inscription on the campanile of the Pisan church of S Sepolcro probably refers to the whole church. This is characterized by a similar centralized plan with a cupola, but it is smaller than the baptistery. The original octagonal structure—with eight tall pilasters, pointed arches and a dome raised on a drum—has, however, been much altered and restored.

BIBLIOGRAPHY

P. Bacci: *Per la istoria del battistero di Pisa* (Pisa, 1919)
C. Smith: *The Baptistery of Pisa* (New York and London, 1978)

ROSSELLA CARUSO

Diotti, Giuseppe (*b* Casalmaggiore, Cremona, 21 March 1779; *d* Bergamo, 30 Jan 1846). Italian painter. He studied at the Accademia di Belle Arti under the history painter Gaetano Callani (1736–1809). Despite initial support from the financier Gian Vincenzo Ponzoni, by the late 1790s he was having to earn money through small decorating jobs and sign-painting. However, Diotti had learnt from the luminosity and sense of colour of Emilian fresco painting as practised by Andrea Appiani, who became his friend and supporter after 1800 when Diotti arrived in Milan. In 1804 he won a four-year scholarship to Rome with *Hercules Stabbing Nessus* (untraced). Here he studied under Vincenzo Camuccini, who had recently completed his Poussinesque frescoes at the Villa Borghese.

Diotti continued to send works back to Milan for exhibition, achieving enough success to ensure a steady flow of minor ecclesiastical and secular commissions after his return to Lombardy in 1810. The most representative of his religious paintings are the four frescoes in Cremona Cathedral, the *Ascension*, *Incredulity of Thomas*, *Christ Blessing the Little Children* and *Christ Giving the Keys to St Peter* (1830–34). The stilted compositions are enlivened by a cheerful use of colour, characteristic of his oil paintings. In 1811, probably due to Appiani's advocacy, Diotti was appointed director of the Accademia Carrara di Belle Arti at Bergamo. His teaching commitments, which continued until 1844, did not impede the prolific production of religious, mythological and history paintings and also portraits. *Count Ugolino* (1832; Brescia, Pin. Civ. Tosio-Martinengo) was considered by contemporaries to be his masterpiece. The betrayed Count is shown in prison surrounded by his grandsons; the models were all Diotti's pupils. While the composition is strictly academic, with the figures grouped in a neat pyramid, the painting's exaggerated pathos is entirely Romantic. *Pontida's Conspiracy* (1837; Milan, Gal. A. Mod.), commissioned by Luigi Chiozzi, an admirer of patriotic and historical subjects, was equally well received. The figures to the right of the picture recall, in a simplistic fashion, David's *Oath of the Horatii* (1784; Paris, Louvre).

Diotti's teaching in Bergamo influenced several local artists, the most notable being Giovanni Carnevali. Although Diotti was an adherent of the Neo-classical theories of Johann Joachim Winckelmann and Anton Raphael Mengs, his paintings have a strong Romantic streak that stretches conventional Lombard Neo-classical painting to its limits.

BIBLIOGRAPHY

G. Rovani: 'Diotti e la sua scuola', *Tre arti in Italia nel secolo XIX*, i (Milan, 1874)
A. G. Comanducci: *Dizionario illustrato dei pittori. . .*, 5 vols (Milan, 1934, rev. 4, 1970–74)
A. Ottino della Chiesa: *Il Neoclassicismo nella pittura Italiana* (Milan, 1968)

Illustration Acknowledgements

We are grateful to those listed below for permission to reproduce copyright illustrative material and to those contributors who supplied photographs or helped us to obtain them. The word 'Photo:' precedes the names of large commercial or archival sources who have provided us with photographs, as well as the names of individual photographers (where known). It has generally not been used before the names of owners of works of art, such as museums and civic bodies. Every effort has been made to contact copyright holders and to credit them appropriately; we apologize to anyone who may have been omitted from the acknowledgements or cited incorrectly. Any error brought to our attention will be corrected in subsequent editions. Where illustrations have been taken from books, publication details are provided in the acknowledgements below.

Line drawings, maps, plans, chronological tables and family trees commissioned by the *Dictionary of Art* are not included in the list below. All of the maps in the dictionary were produced by Oxford Illustrators Ltd, who were also responsible for some of the line drawings. Most of the line drawings and plans, however, were drawn by the following artists: Diane Fortenberry, Lorraine Hodghton, Chris Miners, Amanda Patton, Mike Pringle, Jo Richards, Miranda Schofield, John Tiernan, John Wilson and Philip Winton. The chronological tables and family trees were prepared initially by Kate Boatfield and finalized by John Johnson.

Cossiers, Jan Pierpont Morgan Library, New York

Costa: (1) Lorenzo Costa (i) Gabinetto Fotografico, Soprintendenza per i Beni Artistici e Storici, Bologna

Costa, Giovanni Photo: Archivi Alinari, Florence

Costanzi: (1) Placido Costanzi J. Paul Getty Museum, Malibu, CA

Costa Rica *2* Art Museum of the Americas (OAS), Washington, DC

Cosway: (1) Richard Cosway Collection of Grimsthorpe and Drummond Castle Trust

Côte d'Ivoire Musée National de la Côte d'Ivoire, Abidjan

Coter, Colijn de Photo: © ACL Brussels

Cotes, Francis York City Art Gallery, New York

Cotman, John Sell *1–2* Norfolk Museums Service (Norwich Castle Museum), Norwich

Cottage orné Photo: RCHME/© Crown Copyright

Cotte, Robert de *1* Bibliothèque Nationale de France, Paris; *2* Photo: Ute Schendel

Cotton *1–4* Board of Trustees of the Victoria and Albert Museum, London

Coucy-le-Château Photo: Arch. Phot. Paris/© DACS, 1996

Counterproof Royal Collection, Windsor Castle/© Her Majesty Queen Elizabeth II

Country house *1–2* Photo: RCHME/© Crown Copyright; *3* Photo: Country Life Picture Library, London; *4* Country Life Picture Library, London/Photo: Henson; *5* Photo: Macmillan Publishers Ltd, London

Courbet, Gustave *1, 3* Photo: © RMN, Paris; *2, 4* Photo: Giraudon, Paris; *5* Musées de la Ville de Paris/© DACS, 1996; *6* Glasgow Museums (Burrell Collection)

Courtyard Photo: Ampliaciones y Reproducciones MAS, Barcelona

Cousin: (1) Jean Cousin (i) *1–2* Photo: © RMN, Paris

Coustou: (1) Nicolas Coustou Yale University Press Photo Library, London/Photo: Roland Bonnefay

Coustou: (2) Guillaume Coustou (i) Photo: Zodiaque, St-Léger-Vauban

Coutances Cathedral Photo: Conway Library, Courtauld Institute of Art, London

Couture, Thomas Musée Départemental de l'Oise, Beauvais

Covarrubias, Alonso de *1–2* Photo: Ampliaciones y Reproducciones MAS, Barcelona

Cox, David Trustees of the British Museum, London

Coxcie, Michiel Bildarchiv, Österreichische Nationalbibliothek, Vienna

Coypel: (2) Antoine Coypel Photo: © RMN, Paris

Coyzevox, Antoine Photo: Arch. Phot. Paris/© DACS, 1996

Cozens: (1) Alexander Cozens Trustees of the British Museum, London

Cozens: (2) John Robert Cozens *1* Leeds City Art Galleries; *2* Board of Trustees of the Victoria and Albert Museum, London

Cozza, Francesco Statens Museum for Kunst, Copenhagen

Cozzarelli: (2) Giacomo Cozzarelli Photo: Archivi Alinari, Florence

Crabeth: (1) Dirck Crabeth Stichting Fonds Goudse Glazen, Gouda

Crabeth: (3) Wouter Crabeth (ii) Rijksmuseum, Amsterdam

Cradle (i) Museum of London

Craesbeeck, Joos van Bayerische Staatsbibliothek, Munich

Cram, Ralph Adams Cathedral Church of St John the Divine, New York

Cranach: (1) Lucas Cranach I *1, 4* Bayerische Staatsgemäldesammlungen, Munich; *2* Overseas Agenzia Fotografica, Milan/Photo: Oscar Savio, Rome; *3* Hamburger Kunsthalle, Hamburg

Crane, Walter Tate Gallery, London

Crayer, Gaspar de *1* Photo: Bildarchiv Foto Marburg; *2* Bayerische Staatsbibliothek, Munich

Crayon manner Bibliothèque Nationale de France, Paris

Cremona Photo: Archivi Alinari, Florence

Cremona, Tranquillo *1* Photo: Archivi Alinari, Florence; *2* Galleria d'Arte Moderna, Milan

Crespi (ii): (1) Giuseppe Maria Crespi *1* Kunsthistorisches Museum, Vienna; *2* Photo: Archivi Alinari, Florence; *3* Photo: © RMN, Paris; *4* Staatsgalerie, Stuttgart

Crespi, Daniele *1* Photo: Archivi Alinari, Florence; *2* Soprintendenza ai Beni Artistici e Storici, Milan

Crete Photo: Koulatsoglou Monterna Photographia, Thessalia

Creti, Donato *1* National Gallery of Art, Washington, DC (Samuel H. Kress Collection); *2* Yale University Press Photo Library, London/Photo: A. Villani and Figli s.r.l., Bologna

Critz, de Photo: A.C. Cooper Ltd, London

Crivelli: (1) Carlo Crivelli *1* Photo: Archivi Alinari, Florence; *2* Courtauld Institute of Art, London; *3* Trustees of the National Gallery, London; *4* Photo: Scala, Florence

Crivelli, Taddeo Bodleian Library, Oxford (MS. Holkham Misc. 49, fol. 5r)

Croatia *2* Photo: Paul Tvrtkovíc; *3* Photo: Zelimir Koscević; *4* Moderna Galerija, Zagreb

Croce, Baldassarre Photo: Gabinetto Fotografico Nazionale, Istituto Centrale per il Catalogo e la Documentazione, Rome

Crocket Photo: Conway Library, Courtauld Institute of Art, London

Crome, John Norfolk Museums Service (Norwich Castle Museum), Norwich

Cronaca Photo: Archivi Alinari, Florence

Cropsey, Jasper F. National Gallery of Art, Washington, DC

Crosato, Giovanni Battista Photo: Osvaldo Böhm, Venice

Crosier Photo: Archivi Alinari, Florence

Cross *1* Commissioners of Public Works in Ireland; *2* Photo: RCHME/© Crown Copyright; *3* Photo: Scala, Florence; *4–5* Photo: Bildarchiv Foto Marburg; *6* National Museum of Ireland, Dublin; *7* Charterhouse School, Godalming, Surrey; *8* Board of Trustees of the Victoria and Albert Museum, London

Crucifix *1* Photo: Bardazzi Fotografia, Florence; *2, 5* Photo: Archivi Alinari, Florence; *3* Photo: Rheinische Bildarchiv, Cologne; *4* Photo: Bildarchiv Foto Marburg

Crypt *2* Photo: Bildarchiv Foto Marburg

Csontváry, Tivadar Csontváry Museum, Pēcs

Cuba *2–3* Photo: Gerardo Mosquera; *4* Photo: Paolo Gasparini; *5* Colección Museo Nacional, Havana/© DACS, 1996; *6, 8* Photo: Rebeca Gutiérrez; *7* Museo de Artes Decorativas, Havana

Cubism *1* Photo: RMN, Paris/© DACS, 1996; *2* Musée National d'Art Moderne, Paris

Cubo-Expressionism National Gallery, Prague/Photo: Zdeněk Matyasko

Cuenca Photo: Ampliaciones y Reproducciones MAS, Barcelona

Cult of carts Photoo: Arch. Phot. Paris/© DACS, 1996

Cult statue Historical Museum of Crete, Heraklion (Archaeological Receipts Fund)

Cupboard Germanisches Nationalmuseum, Nuremberg

Cupisnique Peabody Museum, Harvard University, Cambridge, MA/ Photo: Hillel Burger (neg. no. 30203)

Curradi: (2) Francesco Curradi Staatsgalerie, Stuttgart

Currier & Ives Library of Congress, Washington, DC

Curtain wall (i) Photo: British Architectural Library, RIBA, London

Curtain wall (ii) Photo: British Architectural Library, RIBA, London

Cutlery *1–3* Photo: Simon Moore

Cuvilliés, François de, I *1* Bayerische Verwaltung der Staatlichen Schlösser, Gärten und Seen, Munich; *2* Photo: Bildarchiv Foto Marburg

Cuyp: (2) Benjamin Cuyp Gemäldegalerie der Akademie der Bildenden Künste, Vienna

Cuyp: (3) Aelbert Cuyp *1, 4* Trustees of the National Gallery, London; *2* Metropolitan Museum of Art, New York (Bequest of Michael Friesdam, 1931; Friesdam Collection, no. 32.100.29); *3* National Gallery of Art, Washington, DC (Andrew W. Mellon Collection)

Cuypers: (1) P. J. H. Cuypers Rijksdienst voor de Monumentenzorg, Zeist

Cycladic *2, 10–13, 15* National Archaeological Museum, Athens (Archaeological Receipts Fund); *4* Photo: Christos G. Doumas; *8* Nicholas P. Goulandris Foundation; *14* Ashmolean Museum, Oxford

Cyprus *2, 5, 8–10, 12, 14, 16–18, 20–21, 24* Department of Antiquities, Nicosia, Cyprus; *4* Lemba Archaeological Project; *11* Board of Trustees of the National Museums and Galleries on Merseyside, Liverpool; *19* Trustees of the British Museum, London; *22* Polish Archaeological Mission, Cairo; *25* Dumbarton Oaks, Washington, DC/Photo: Byzantine Visual Resources/© 1996; *26* Photo: Michael D. Willis

Cyrene *1–2* Fototeca Unione, American Academy at Rome

Cyriac of Ancona Staatliche Museen zu Berlin, Preussischer Kulturbesitz

Czech Republic *2, 4–5* Photo: Bildarchiv Foto Marburg; *3* Photo: Pamatkovy Ustav, Pardubice; *6* Photo: Conway Library, Courtauld Institute of Art, London; *7* Museum of the City of Prague; *8, 10, 12* Photo: Ivo Kořán; *9, 11, 15, 17–18* National Gallery, Prague; *13* Galerie Hlavniho Mest, Prague; *14* Photo: Paul Prokop; *16* Czech Academy of Sciences, Prague/Photo: Paul Prokop; *19, 23–8* Museum of Decorative Arts, Prague; *20, 22, 33* Museum of Decorative Arts, Prague/Photo: Antonín Halaš; *29–30* Museum of Decorative Arts, Prague/Photo: Gabriel Urbánek; *31* Photo: Pavel Štecha; *32* Kunsthistorisches Museum, Vienna

Częstochowa Institute of Art PAN, Warsaw

Dada *1* Kunsthaus Zurich/© ADAGP, Paris, and DACS, London, 1996; *2* Peggy Guggenheim Collection, Venice/© ADAGP, Paris, and DACS, London, 1996

Dadd, Richard Regis Collection, Minneapolis, MN/Photo: Private collection, UK

Daddi, Bernardo *1* Courtauld Institute Galleries, London; *2* Photo: Overseas Agenzia Fotografica, Milan

Dagnan-Bouveret, P.-A.-J. Photo: Studio Fontana-Thomasset, Chambéry

Daguerre, Louis Board of Trustees of the National Museums and Galleries on Merseyside, Liverpool

Dahl, J. C. *1–2* Nasjonalgalleriet, Oslo

Dahl, Michael National Maritime Museum, London

Dahshur Egyptian Museum, Cairo

Dai Jin Freer Gallery of Art, Smithsonian Institution, Washington, DC (no. 30.80-1)

Dainzú Akademische Druck- und Verlagsanstalt, Graz

Dakhla Oasis Royal Ontario Museum, Toronto

Dalí, Salvador *1* Photo: © Demart Pro Arte BV/DACS, 1996; *2* Glasgow Museums (St Mungo Museum of Religious Life and Art)

Dallas Dallas Historical Society, Dallas, TX

Dalou, Jules Photo: Conway Library, Courtauld Institute of Art, London

Dalverzin Tepe Museum of Fine Arts of Uzbekistan, Tashkent

Damascus *1* Photo: Grabar

Dan *1–4* Museum Rietberg, Zurich/Photo: Eberhard Fischer

Danby, Francis Tate Gallery, London

Dance: (3) George Dance (ii) *1* Photo: RCHME/© Crown Copyright; *2* Photo: RCHME/© Crown Copyright/B.T. Batsford Ltd, London

Dandini: (1) Cesare Dandini National Gallery of Ireland, Dublin

Dandré-Bardon, Michel-François National Gallery of Art, Washington, DC (Gift of Lewis Einstein)

Danhauser: (2) Josef Franz Danhauser Graphische Sammlung Albertina, Vienna

Daniele da Volterra Photo: Gabinetto Fotografico Nazionale, Istituto Centrale per il Catalogo e la Documentazione, Rome

Danloux, Henri-Pierre Staatliche Kunsthalle, Karlsruhe

Dannecker, Johann Heinrich Staatsgalerie, Stuttgart

Danti: (i) Vincenzio Danti Photo: Archivi Alinari, Florence

Danube school Szépművészeti Múzeum, Budapest

Daoism *1* Field Museum of Natural History, Chicago, IL (neg. no: 39215); *2* Field Museum of Natural History, Chicago, IL (neg. no: A98237)

Daoji *1* Metropolitan Museum of Art, New York (Gift of Douglas Dillon, 1985; no. 1985.227.1); *2* Art Museum, Princeton University, Princeton, NJ (Gift of John B. Elliott)

Daret, Jacques Museo Thyssen-Bornemisza, Madrid

Darmstadt *1* Photo: Bildarchiv Foto Marburg; *2* Photo: Ingeborg Limmer, Bamberg

Daswanth Royal Collection, Windsor Castle/© Her Majesty Queen Elizabeth II

Dat So La Lee Nevada Historical Society, Reno, NV

Daubigny: (1) Charles-François Daubigny Photo: Arch. Phot. Paris/ © DACS, 1996

Daucher: (3) Hans Daucher Kunsthistorisches Museum, Vienna

Daulat British Library, London (MS. Or. 12208, fol. 325)

Daumier, Honoré *1* Bibliothèque Nationale de France, Paris; *2* Walters Art Gallery, Baltimore, MD

David, Gerard *1* Groeningemuseum, Bruges/Photo: Bridgeman Art Library, London; *2* Photo: Giraudon, Paris

David, Jacques-Louis *1* Photo: © RMN, Paris; *2* Metropolitan Museum of Art, New York (Purchase, Mr and Mrs Charles Wrightsman; Gift in honour of Everett Fahy, 1977; no. 1977.10); *3* Trustees of the National Gallery, London; *4* Photo: Bridgeman Art Library, London

David d'Angers *1–2* Photo: Conway Library, Courtauld Institute of Art, London

David Garedzhi Photo: VAAP, Moscow

Davis, Alexander Jackson *1* New-York Historical Society, New York; *2* Lyndhurst (property of the National Trust for Historic Preservation)

Davis, Stuart Collection of the City of New York (Art Commission of the City of New York)/© Estate of Stuart Davis/DACS, London/ VAGA, New York, 1996

Deare, John Los Angeles County Museum of Art, CA (Gift of Anna Bing Arnold)

Dębno Church Union of Polish Art Photographers/Photo: Zbigniew Kamykowski

De Braekeleer: (1) Ferdinand De Braekeleer Photo: © ACL Brussels

Decamps, Alexandre-Gabriel Photo: © RMN, Paris

De Carlo, Giancarlo © Angelo Mioni, Architect's Studio, Milan

De Chirico, Giorgio *1* Philadelphia Museum of Art, Philadelphia, PA (Louise and Walter Arensberg Collection)/© DACS, 1996; *2* Musée National d'Art Moderne, Paris/© DACS, 1996; *3* © DACS, 1996; *4* Museo d'Arte Antica, Castello Sforzesco, Milan/Civica Galleria d'Arte Moderna, Milan/Civico Museo d'Arte Contemporanea, Palazzo Reale, Milan/© DACS, 1996

Decorated style Photo: Conway Library, Courtauld Institute of Art, London

Decretal Biblioteca Apostolica Vaticana, Rome

Degas, Edgar *1–2, 4* Photo: © RMN, Paris; *3* Trustees of the National Gallery, London

Degler, Hans Photo: Bildarchiv Foto Marburg

De Kooning: (1) Willem De Kooning *1* Museum of Modern Art, New York (Purchase); *2* Albright–Knox Art Gallery, Buffalo, NY (Gift of Seymour H. Knox, 1977)/© Willem de Kooning, ARS, New York, and DACS, London, 1996

Delacroix, Eugène *1* Photo: Giraudon, Paris; *2* Metropolitan Museum of Art, New York (Rogers Fund, 1917; no. 17.12); *3, 6* Photo: Arch. Phot. Paris/© DACS, 1996; *4* Photo: Bridgeman Art Library, London; *5* Minneapolis Institute of Arts, Minneapolis, MN

Delaroche: (2) Paul Delaroche Photo: © RMN, Paris

Delaunay (ii): (1) Robert Delaunay Öffentliche Kunstsammlung, Kunstmuseum Basel, Basle/© ADAGP, Paris, and DACS, London, 1996

Delaunay (ii): (2) Sonia Delaunay Musée National d'Art Moderne, Paris/© ADAGP, Paris, and DACS, London, 1996

Delft *1* Rijksdienst voor de Monumentenzorg, Zeist; *2* Mauritshuis, The Hague; *3* Gemeente Musea, Delft (Stedelijk Museum Het Prinsenhof)

Delft school (ii) Photo: Jan Derwig, Architectuur Fotografie, Amsterdam

Delhi *2–6* Photo: R. Nath

Delos *1, 3, 6–7* Ecole Française d'Archéologie, Athens; *2* British Library, London (no. Ac. 5206. b/2); *4* National Archaeological Museum, Athens (Archaeological Receipts Fund); *5* Deutsches Archäologisches Institut, Athens

Delphi *1, 3* Photo: James Austin, Cambridge; *4–6* Delphi Archaeological Museum (Archaeological Receipts Fund)

Delvaux, Paul Koninklijk Museum voor Schone Kunsten, Antwerp/ Photo: ACL Brussels/© Fondation P. Delvaux, St Idesbald/DACS, 1996

Demuth, Charles Whitney Museum of American Art, New York

Dendara *2* Photo: John R. Baines, Oxford

Denis, Maurice Photo: © RMN, Paris

De Nittis, Giuseppe *1* Photo: Scala, Florence; *2* Photo: Bridgeman Art Library, London

Denmark *2, 4, 6–7, 12* National Museum of Denmark, Copenhagen; *3* Herzog Anton Ulrich-Museum, Brunswick; *5* Royal Academy of Fine Arts Library, London (Art Documentation); *8–10, 13* Statens Museum for Kunst, Copenhagen; *11* Ålborg Historiske Museum/Photo: Jan Slot-Carlsen; *14–15, 20* Museum of Decorative Art, Copenhagen/ Photo: Ole Woldbye, Copenhagen; *16* Museum of Decorative Art, Copenhagen; *17, 22* Photo: Ole Woldbye, Copenhagen; *18* David Collection, Copenhagen/Photo: Ole Woldbye, Copenhagen; *19* Holmegaards Glasvaerker, Fensmaek; *21* Board of Trustees of the Victoria and Albert Museum, London; *23* Statens Konstmuseer, Stockholm

Denon, Vivant Bibliothèque Nationale de France, Paris

Deodato Orlandi Photo: Archivi Alinari, Florence

Department store Bibliothèque Nationale de France, Paris

Derain, André *1* Photo: © ADAGP, Paris, and DACS, London, 1996; *2* Photo: © RMN, Paris/© ADAGP, Paris, and DACS, London, 1996

Dereağzı Photo: James Morganstern

Derkovits, Gyula Hungarian National Gallery, Budapest/Photo: Mester Tibor, Budapest

Derrynaflan Treasure National Museum of Ireland, Dublin

Déruet, Claude Bayerische Staatsgemäldesammlungen, Munich

Deshays, Jean-Baptiste Musée des Beaux-Arts, Rouen

Desiderio da Firenze Photo: Archivi Alinari, Florence

Desiderio da Settignano *1–2* Photo: Archivi Alinari, Florence

Design *1* Museum of Applied Arts, Helsinki; *2–3* Board of Trustees of the Victoria and Albert Museum, London

Dési Huber, István Hungarian National Gallery, Budapest/Photo: Mester Tibor, Budapest

Desjardins, Martin Photo: © RMN, Paris

Desportes: (1) François Desportes *1* Musée des Beaux Arts, Le Havre; *2* Statens Konstmuseer, Stockholm

Detroit Detroit Institute of Arts, Detroit, MI (Founders Society Purchase; Miscellaneous Memorials Fund)

Deutsch: (1) Niklaus Manuel Deutsch I *1–2* Öffentliche Kunstsammlung Basel, Kunstmuseum, Basle

Deutscher Werkbund City of Stuttgart

Devéria: (1) Achille Devéria Musée Carnavalet, Paris/© DACS, 1996

Devey, George Photo: Jill Allibone

Devis: (1) Arthur Devis National Trust Photo Library, London/Photo: Angelo Hornak

Devotional objects and popular images Photo: Douglas C. Hoare

Devotional prints *1* National Gallery of Art, Washington, DC (Rosenwald Collection); *2* Kunstsammlungen der Veste Coburg

De Wint, Peter Syndics of the Fitzwilliam Museum, Cambridge

Dian *1–2* Yunnan Provincial Museum, Kunming

Diaper Photo: Conway Library, Courtauld Institute of Art, London

Diaz, Narcisse Photo: © RMN, Paris

Diderot, Denis Photo: Giraudon, Paris

Didyma *2* Trustees of the British Museum, London

Diebenkorn, Richard Corcoran Gallery of Art, Washington, DC (Museum Purchase, with aid of funds from the National Endowment for the Arts, William A. Clark Fund and Mary M. Hitchcock)

Diego de la Cruz Photo: Ampliaciones y Reproducciones MAS, Barcelona

Dientzenhofer: (1) Christoph Dientzenhofer *1* Photo: Anthony Kersting, London; *2* Photo: Christian Norberg-Schulz

Dientzenhofer: (3) Kilian Ignaz Dientzenhofer *1* Yale University Press Photo Library, London/Photo: Fr. Illek a Alex Paul, Prague; *2* Photo: Tim Benton, Cambridge

Diepenbeeck, Abraham van *1* Bayerische Staatsgemäldesammlungen, Munich; *2* Musée de la Ville de Strasbourg

Dietrich, Wendel Zentralinstitut für Kunstgeschichte, Munich

Dietterlin, Wendel Staatliche Kunsthalle, Karlsruhe

Dieu, Antoine Metropolitan Museum of Art, New York (Rogers Fund, 1964; no. 64.193.2)

Dijon *2* Bibliothèque Municipale, Dijon; *3* Musée des Beaux-Arts, Dijon; *4* Photo: Conway Library, Courtauld Institute of Art, London

Dillis: (1) Johann Georg von Dillis Bayerische Staatsgemäldesammlungen, Munich

Dine, Jim Museum of Modern Art, New York (Sidney and Harriet Janis Collection)

Dinkelsbühl Photo: Bildarchiv Foto Marburg

Dionisy Photo: VAAP, Moscow

Diorama Guildhall Library, Corporation of London